THE GUINNESS BOOK OF

2nd Edition

THE HISTORY OF THE GAME IN OVER 150 COUNTRIES

GUY OLIVER

GUINNESS PUBLISHING

To my parents, true internationalists: readers have them to thank for this book

This edition first published 1995
Reprint 10 9 8 7 6 5 4 3 2 1 0
First edition 1992

Published in Great Britain by Guinness Publishing Limited, 33 London Road, Enfield, Middlesex

Cover design by Ad Vantage

Text design and layout by Sallie Collins

Printed in Great Britain by The Bath Press, Bath, Avon

A catalogue record for this book is available from the British Library

ISBN 0-85112-654-5

CONTENTS

WORLD

EUROPE

SOUTH AMERICA

AFRICA

CONTENTS Continued

INTRODUCTION

Es entonces cuando se detecta el primer signo futbolistico: "Un juego que en la ribera practican marineros ingleses que corren tras una pelota." Poco a poco, y extendiéndose a lugares muy abiertos de Flores y Palermo, el juego fue ganando entusiasta apoyo de los jóvenes criollos, y aquellos ingleses locos no parecieron tanto.

Buenos Aires a fines de siglo

It was then that football first made its appearance: "A game that by the riverside many English sailors play running after a ball." Little by little, and extending to the more open areas of Flores and Palermo, the game began winning the enthusiastic support of the local youths, and those crazy English did not seem so crazy after all.

Buenos Aires at the end of the century

Most people who saw the first edition of The Guinness Record of World Soccer looked at me with a mixture of puzzlement and sympathy. "How long did it take you to write that?" they asked. El loco ingles, indeed. When I first had the idea to write the book in 1987, there was little on the market to guide the football supporter through the maze of football clubs and countries. Now there are a number, as football writing has flourished. And true to the origins of the game, much of this has come out of England. I am proud to be a part of a small but growing tradition that looks beyond the shores of this island.

Having written the first edition I thought most of the hard work had been done, but with political instability, especially in Europe, this second edition has had to reflect a changing geography. To cope with this, Europe remains the largest section of the book, with every new country represented. For both Europe and South America, I have also filled in gaps where information was missing from the first edition. This has meant restrictions on space, despite the increase in the number of pages. The planned expansion of both the African and Asian sections has had to be put on hold but will be included in the next edition.

I have been gratified by the response to the first edition, especially where people have pointed out where I have gone wrong or given me extra information. Any advice is always appreciated, especially in relation to Africa or Asia. If anyone has interesting anecdotes with regard to the history of football in those two continents, or indeed on anything, please write to me at Guinness Publishing.

Inevitably, the biggest source I have drawn on is the large number of books that are now on the market on world football. These range from desktop publications, to books like Mike Hammond's European Yearbook which is unparalleled in its season-by-season coverage of Europe. Also of note are the number of books on off-beat subjects emanating from Serge Van Hoof's Heart Books, especially the North and Latin American Yearbook. I have drawn heavily on these sources for the second edition and can recommend them to others who wish to go into greater depth on certain topics than I can hope to do in this one volume. Other publications which have proved invaluable are Salvatore Lo Presti's Annuario del Calcio Mondiale, Italy's answer to Rothmans though with a wider coverage of world events, and the number of publications by Andrzej Gowarzewski in Poland. There are also a number of outstanding new magazines available. For its Pan-African coverage, African Soccer is superb, whilst the Asian Football Confederation News does likewise for Asia.

Many people have helped me over the years, but with particular reference to this edition, I would like to thank Francesco Mascalchi for his generous advice, and Ahmed Laidi and Brynjar Selseth, both of whose efforts are greatly appreciated. Thanks also go to Tito Ticeran Guerra, Emmanuel Maradas and Mark Gleeson for their comments on Africa, and to Scott Gleba of CONCACAF. Thank you to those who have given me advice whilst on my travels filming for Futbol Mundial, and to everyone on Futbol Mundial: it's a great show to work on! To Felix, Mike, David and Mauricio, many thanks. Once again I would like to thank the numerous football associations which have provided information, and thanks are also due to Andreas Herren and his colleagues at FIFA.

On a personal note, apologies to my family and friends. Travelling with my job and then spending all my spare time in front of my computer has meant that I have become something of a stranger to them, a situation I hope to rectify. Once again thanks to Tom for sometimes putting up with a rather irritable flatmate! The biggest thanks go to Sharyn. Others might have given up on me a long time ago. Many thanks and all my love.

Guy Oliver
July 1995

KEY TO THE CHAMPIONSHIP LISTINGS

For each European country's national championship, the listings include a code showing what format the championship was played under each year. For example, England's league goes under the code y from 1920 (42 games, 2 pts for a win), becomes y1 in 1982 (3 pts for a win), x1 in 1988 (40 games, still 3 pts for a win), v1 in 1989 (38 games) and reverts to y1 in 1992. The full list of codes:

code	*games*	*teams*	*max pts*	*pts*
aa	2	2	4	2,1,0
aj	2	3	4	2,1,0
ab	3	4	6	2,1,0
ac	5	6	10	2,1,0
ao	5	4	10	2,1,0
	(1 team withdrew at 1/2 way)			
ad	7	8	14	2,1,0
am	7	8	21	3,2,1
ae	9	10	18	2,1,0
ak	9	4	18	2,1,0
	(3 rounds of play-off group)			
af	11	12	22	2,1,0
ap	11	7	22	2,1,0
	(1 team withdrew at 1/2 way)			
ag	13	14	26	2,1,0
al	13	8	26	2,1,0
an	13	10	26	2,1,0
	(9 games in 1st stage, 4 in 2nd)			
ah	15	16	30	2,1,0
a	4	3	8	2,1,0
a1	4	5	8	2,1,0
a2	4	3	12	3,2,1
a3	4	6	8	2,1,0
	(2 groups of 3. Pts include play-offs)			
a4	4	2	8	2,1,0
b	6	4	12	2,1,0
b1	6	7	12	2,1,0
b2	6	4	12	2,1,0
	(4 teams in play-off group)			
b3	6	7	18	3,2,1
c	8	5	16	2,1,0
c1	8	9	16	2,1,0
d	10	6	20	2,1,0
d1	10	6	30	3,2,1
e	12	7	24	2,1,0
e1	12	13	24	2,1,0
f1	14	8	42	3,2,1
f2	14	16	28	2,1,0
	(2 groups of 8. 1&2, 3&4 etc play-off. Bonus for next season - 1/2 - 8, 3/4 - 7, etc)			
f3	14	8	28	2,1,0
	(1st round 2 groups of 10, each playing 18 games with top 4 qualifying for 2nd round.)			
f4	14	8	46	2,1,0
	(18 games in 10-team 1st round. Top 8 play-off taking half their 1st round pts)			

code	*games*	*teams*	*max pts*	*pts*
fg	15	15	30	2,1,0
g	16	9	32	2,1,0
g1	16	12	32	2,1,0
	(11 games in first stage, 5 in play-off)			
g2	16	9	48	3,2,1
g3	16	17	48	3,1,0
h	18	10	36	2,1,0
h1	18	10	54	3,2,1
h2	18	10	54	3,1,0
i	20	11	40	2,1,0
i1	20	11	60	3,2,1
j	21	12	42	2,1,0
	(1 team dropped out after 11 games)			
k	22	12	44	2,1,0
k1	22	12	66	3,2,1
k2	22	12	66	3,2,1,0
k3	22	12	66	3,1,0
k4	22	12	44	2,1,0
	(Top 4 play-off for the title)			
k5	22	12	66	3,1,0
	(As for k4)			
l	24	13	48	2,1,0
m	25	26	50	2,1,0
m1	25	13	50	2,1,0
n	26	14	52	2,1,0
n1	26	14	78	3,1,0
o	27	10	54	2,1,0
	(3 rounds)			
o1	27	15	54	2,1,0
	(1 team dropped out after 14 games)			
o2	27	14	54	2,1,0
	(1st round of 13 games, top 8 play 14 more)			
p	28	15	56	2,1,0
p1	29	12	58	2,1,0
	(22 games in first stage, 7 in play-off)			
p2	29	12	36	2,1,0
	(As for p1 but with only half points taken forward to the play-offs)			
p3	28	12	34	2,1,0
	(As for p2 but with only 6 play-off games)			
p4	28	10	38	2,1,0
	(18 games in first stage, 10 in play-off with half pts taken to play-off)			
p5	28	15	84	3,1,0
p6	29	12	87	3,1,0
	(As for P1)			
q	30	16	60	2,1,0
q1	30	16	90	3,2,1
q2	30	16	90	3,2,1,0
q3	30	16	90	3,1,0
q4	30	10	60	2,1,0
q5	30	16	90	3,2,1,0,-1
q6	30	16	105	4,3,2,1,0
r	32	17	64	2,1,0
r1	32	12	64	2,1,0
	(22 games in first stage, 10 in play-off)			

code	*games*	*teams*	*max pts*	*pts*
r2	32	12	42	2,1,0
	(As in r1 but with half pts taken to play-offs)			
r3	32	12	96	3,1,0
	(As in r1)			
r4	32	12	64	2,1,0
	(1st round of 22 games, top 6 play off)			
r5	32	12	96	3,1,0
	(1st round of 22 games, top 6 play off)			
s	33	12	66	2,1,0
	(3 rounds)			
s1	33	12	99	3,1,0
s2	33	18	66	2,1,0,0
	(One team withdrew at half way)			
t	34	18	68	2,1,0
t1	34	18	102	3,2,1
t2	34	18	102	3,1,0
t3	34	18	68	2,1,0,0
u	36	19	72	2,1,0
u1	36	14	72	2,1,0
	(26 games in first stage, 10 in play-off)			
u2	36	10	72	2,1,0
	(4 rounds)			
u3	36	12	72	2,1,0
	(22 games in first stage, 14 in play-off)			
u4	36	12	50	2,1,0
	(As for u3 but with only half points taken forward to the play-offs)			
u5	36	14	46	2,1,0
	(As in u1 but with half pts taken for ward to play-offs)			
u6	36	19	108	3,1,0
u7	36	19	72	2,1,0,0
u8	36	25	72	2,1,0
	(Top 12 play-off for title)			
u9	18	20	36	2,1,0
	(Two groups of 10 teams. 18 games - top 2 in each play knock-out for title)			
u10	19	20	57	3,1,0
u11	36	10	108	3,1,0
u12	36	20	79	2,1,0
	(Two 1st round groups of 10, bonus pts awarded, top 10 play off for title			
v	38	20	76	2,1,0
v1	38	20	114	3,1,0
w	39	14	78	2,1,0
	(3 rounds)			
x	40	21	80	2,1,0
x1	40	21	120	3,1,0
y	42	22	84	2,1,0
y1	42	22	126	3,1,0
z	44	12	88	2,1,0
	(4 rounds)			
z1	44	18	88	2,1,0
	(2 rounds then play-off for top 6)			

4 figures – win, win on pens, loss on pen, lost
q5 – 3 pts for win by three goals or more. 1 pt deducted for defeat by a similar margin
q6 – 4 pts away win, 3 pts home win, 2 pts away draw, 1 pt home draw

LIST OF ABBREVIATIONS

Official FIFA abbreviations

Afghanistan .... AFG
Albania .... ALB
Algeria .... ALG
Angola .... AGO
Antigua and Barbuda .... ATG
Argentina .... ARG
Armenia .... ARM
Aruba .... ARU
Australia .... AUS
Austria .... AUT
Azerbaijan .... AZE

Bahamas .... BHM
Bahrain .... BHR
Bangladesh .... BGD
Barbados .... BRB
Belgium .... BEL
Belize .... BLZ
Belorussia .... BLR
Benin .... BEN
Bermuda .... BER
Bolivia .... BOL
Botswana .... BWA
Brazil .... BRA
Brunei-Darussalam .... BRU
Bulgaria .... BGR
Burkina Faso .... BFA
Burundi .... BDI

Cameroon .... CMR
Canada .... CAN
Cape Verde Islands .... CPV
Cayman Islands .... CYM
Central African Republic .... CTA
Chad .... CHD
Chile .... CHI
China .... CHN
Chinese Taipei (Taiwan) .... TPE
Colombia .... COL
Congo .... COG
Cook Islands .... COK
Costa Rica .... CRC
Côte d'Ivoire CIV
Croatia .... HRV
Cuba .... CUB
Cyprus .... CYP
Czech Republic .... CZE

Denmark .... DEN
Djibouti .... DJI
Dominica .... DMA
Dominican Republic .... DOM

Ecuador .... ECU
Egypt .... EGY
El Salvador .... SLV
England .... ENG
Equatorial Guinea .... EQG
Estonia .... EST
Ethiopia .... ETH

Faeroe Islands .... FRO
Fiji .... FIJ
Finland .... FIN
France .... FRA

Gabon .... GAB
Gambia .... GMB
Georgia .... GEO
Germany .... GER
Ghana .... GHA
Greece .... GRE
Grenada .... GRD
Guatemala .... GUA
Guinea .... GUI
Guinea-Bissau .... GNB
Guyana .... GUY

Haiti .... HTI
Honduras .... HND
Hong Kong .... HKG
Hungary .... HUN

Iceland .... ISL
India .... IND
Indonesia .... IDN
Iran .... IRN
Iraq .... IRQ
Israel .... ISR
Italy .... ITA

Jamaica .... JAM
Japan .... JPN
Jordan .... JOR

Kampuchea (Cambodia) .... KHM
Kazakhstan .... KAZ
Kenya .... KEN
North Korea .... PRK
South Korea .... KOR
Kuwait .... KUW
Kyrgyzstan .... KGZ

Laos .... LAO
Latvia .... LVA
Lebanon .... LIB
Lesotho .... LSO
Liberia .... LBR
Libya .... LBY
Liechtenstein .... LIE
Lithuania .... LTU
Luxembourg .... LUX

Macao .... MAC
FYR Macedonia .... MKD
Madagascar .... MDG
Malawi .... MWI
Malaysia .... MYS
Maldives .... MDV
Mali .... MLI
Malta .... MLT
Mauritania .... MTN
Mauritius .... MUS
Mexico .... MEX
Moldova .... MOL
Morocco .... MOR
Mozambique .... MOZ
Myanmar .... MMR

Namibia .... NAM
Nepal .... NPL
Netherlands .... HOL
Netherlands Antilles .... ANT
New Zealand .... NZL
Nicaragua .... NIC
Niger .... NIG
Nigeria .... NGA
Northern Ireland .... NIR
Norway .... NOR

Oman .... OMN

Pakistan .... PAK
Panama .... PAN
Papua New Guinea .... PNG
Paraguay .... PAR
Peru .... PER
Philippines .... PHI
Poland .... POL
Portugal .... POR
Puerto Rico .... PUR

Qatar .... QAT

Republic of Ireland .... IRL
Romania .... ROM
Russia .... RUS
Rwanda .... RWA

Saint Kitts and Nevis .... KNA
Saint Lucia .... LUC
Saint Vincent and the Grenadines .... VCT
San Marino .... SMR
Sao Tomé e Principe .... STP
Saudi Arabia .... KSA
Scotland .... SCO
Senegal .... SEN
Seychelles .... SYC
Sierra Leone .... SLE
Singapore .... SIN
Slovakia .... SVK
Slovenia .... SVN
Solomon Islands .... SOL
Somalia .... SOM
South Africa .... RSA
Spain .... ESP
Sri Lanka .... SRI
Sudan .... SDN
Surinam .... SUR
Swaziland .... SWZ
Sweden .... SWE
Switzerland .... SUI
Syria .... SYR

Tahiti .... TAH
Tajikistan .... TJK
Tanzania .... TAN
Thailand .... THA
Togo .... TGO
Tonga .... TON
Trinidad and Tobago .... TTO
Tunisia .... TUN
Turkey .... TUR
Turkmenistan .... TKM

Uganda .... UGA
Ukraine .... UKR
United Arab Emirates .... UAE
United States of America .... USA
Uruguay .... URU
Uzbekistan .... UZB

Vanuatu .... VAN
Venezuela .... VEN
Vietnam .... VNM

Wales .... WAL

LIST OF ABBREVIATIONS Continued

Western Samoa....................................WSM

Yemen ....YEM
Yugoslavia..YUG

Zaire ....ZAI
Zambia ....ZAM
Zimbabwe ....ZIM

Competitions

WCq World Cup qualifying game
WCr1 World Cup Final Tournament - first round
WCr2 World Cup Final ......Tournament - ....second round
WCqf World Cup Final Tournament - quarter-final
WCsf World Cup Final Tournament - semi-final
WC3p World Cup Fina Tournament - .. Third place play-off
WCf World Cup Final Tournament - final

The same system applies to the Olympic Games, European Championship, South American Championship and CONCACAF Gold Cup

OGq Olympic Games qualifying game
OGr1 Olympic Games Final Tournament first round etc
ECq European Championship qualifying game
ECr1 European Championship Final Tournament - first round etc
SC South American Championship - 1910-67
SCr1 South American Championship post 1967 - First round etc
CC CONCACAF Championship pre 1991
CCr1 CONCACAF Gold Cup - First round etc

Other worldwide tournaments tournaments include

AFT Artemo Franchi Cup
Clr1 Copa Independencia do Brasil - round 1 etc
CN Copa de las Naciones
ICC Intercontinental Championship
JNC Nehru Cup
KC Kirin Cup
ML Copa d'Oro (Mundialito)

Intra European tournaments include

BC Balkan / Baltic Cup
BCE Balkan and Central European Championship
DGC Dr Gerö Cup
HC British International Championship

Intra American tournaments include

AC Artigas Cup
BG Bolivar Games
CA Atlantic Cup
CDC Carlos Dittborn Cup
CG Central American and Caribbean Games
HGC Hector Gomez Cup
JMC Juan Mignaburu Cup
LC Lipton Cup
MC Montevideo Cup
MEA Argentine Ministry of Education Trophy
MEU Uruguayan Ministry of Education Trophy
NAC North American Championship
NC Newton Cup
OCC Osvaldo Cruz Cup
OHC O'Higgins Cup
PAC Pan American Championship
PC Pacific Cup
PDC Pinto Duran Cup (CHI/ARG)
PDC Paz del Chaco Cup (BOL/PAR)
RC Roca Cup
RBC Rio Branco Cup
RCB Rosa Chevallier Boutell Cup
RCC Ramon Castilla Cup
RGP Roque Gomez Pena Cup
SPC Saenz Peña Cup

And last but certainly not least, the most common of them all

Fr A friendly match

A match marked with an * is of disputed status.

WORLD

The origin of the football we play today can be traced to a series of five meetings between 26 October and 8 December 1863. The first of these, the historic occasion at the Freemason's Tavern in London's Great Queen Street, was where the Football Association was formed and the initial set of laws drawn up. The split with rugby occurred in the last of the meetings as supporters of that code, led by the Blackheath club, withdrew, leaving the way free for the adoption of the first laws of Association Football.

The ancient origins of the game are more difficult to define, however, for kicking an object such as a stone on the ground is a natural thing to do. Exactly when this simple action of kicking was turned into a game involving more than one person has been the source of much study, and various ancient civilisations can lay claim to a game that resembles football.

The Ancient Chinese had a game called Tsu Chu, Tsu referring to the action of kicking, Chu to a stuffed ball of animal skin. Kemari was a Japanese game played at roughly the same time as Tsu Chu, nearly 3000 years ago. Its resemblance to modern-day football is strong – in pictures drawn of the game there are two bamboo posts which the players seem to be trying to kick the ball between.

The Romans and the Greeks also played ball games, the former playing a sport called Harpastum, the latter a sport called Episkyros. It has to be assumed that wherever the Greeks or Romans went they took the game with them and there is an argument that Harpastum is the origin of football in the British Isles.

Football of a kind was being played all around the world by the Middle Ages. William Fitzstephen in 1175 gives us the first account of 'the famous game of ball' on a Shrove Tuesday in London, a tradition that remains to this day in some parts of England. These games were often violent, lasted a whole day and involved hundreds of people chasing a ball across the countryside.

Elsewhere, in Brittany there was a game called *la soule*, in Italy *giuoco del calcio fiorentino*, in Chile *pilimatun*, in Patagonia *tchoekah*, whilst the eskimos are known to have played a game called *aqsaqtuk*.

It was in Britain, however, that these often chaotic games were transformed into a pastime more resembling the modern-day version, and this happened in the public schools of Victorian England. These aristocratic and very exclusive schools, there to educate the children of the English gentry, developed the game as a form of exercise.

Each school tended to have their own rules, and as pupils went on to university they found that they did not have any common rules to play by. In 1848 students at Cambridge, perplexed by all the different codes, drew up their own code and it is this that the rules of 1863 are loosely based on.

Football is now the most popular sport in the world due to a combination of events. The Football Association in London helped spread the new game around Britain at a time when the country was in the midst of an industrial revolution. The rural population was moving into the cities and they needed a form of entertainment. Football was, to borrow one of its own clichés, in the right place at the right time.

Even more crucial, however, was the fact that Britain was an imperial power and was spreading its influence around the world. The tradesmen and workers who had learnt the game in the cities were in high demand around the world for their skills as other countries sought to industrialise. Thus the railway workers, engineers, clerks and business owners were responsible for the spread of the game to Europe, South America and elsewhere.

Perhaps most important was the fact that football is in essence a simple game and, unlike rugby or cricket, easy to learn. Only in the countries which the British colonised such as India, Australia, New Zealand and parts of Africa, especially South Africa, did they take to rugby or cricket because the British presence was much more imposing. Football remained a sport much more associated with the British merchant class than its ruling class.

The formation in 1904 of the Fédération Internationale de Football Association, or FIFA as it is more commonly known, was a recognition of the inroads the game had made around the world. FIFA is now one of the largest international bodies, having as it does, more members than the United Nations. Some even claim that it has done a better job than the United Nations in bringing the world closer together. In football terms, it has been instrumental in making the game the world's favourite pastime, not just through staging events like the World Cup but also through its coaching courses which are taken to every corner of the globe.

As football spread out of Great Britain at the turn of the century, the French in particular were quick to recognise the need for a controlling organisation in order that all countries played to the same rules, and so on 21 May 1904, representatives from Belgium, France, Holland, Denmark, Spain, Sweden and Switzerland met in Paris and founded FIFA. None of the four British Associations were present, being somewhat sceptical of the level of football in these countries compared to that at home.

At the outset, FIFA's tasks were somewhat limited. In particular, it did not control the law-making process, and technically it still does not. This is left to the International Football Association Board, a strange body made up of 20 seats, 16 of which are reserved permanently for the four British Associations. The four remaining seats are filled by election for a fixed term from amongst other FIFA members.

As FIFA's membership has grown, so have its responsibilities. From being an organisation representing a small corner of Europe, with responsibilities amounting to the organisation of the Olympic Games football tournament, it is now a worldwide body with many different powers. These range from the control of the movement of players and administering referees to the organisation of various tournaments at both senior and youth level, as well as administering a range of Standing Committees that look into topics as diverse as sports medicine and proposed changes in the laws of the game.

By the beginning of the Second World War, membership had grown to over 50 countries, the bulk of whom were from either Europe or South America. After 1945 however, as the shackles of colonialism were thrown off by the countries of Africa and Asia, membership began to rise dramatically and by 1966 it had reached 130.

The leadership of FIFA mirrored this shifting trend. Stanley Rous, president from 1961 to 1974, had come to represent the old world, and although a very capable administrator and a man who devoted his life to spreading the game worldwide, he was eventually undone by those forces he helped unleash. In 1974, Joao Havelange was elected under the banner of change, with the backing of the African and Asian countries. FIFA is now a more overtly commercial organisation, and the 'New World' has become an integral part of the organisation, where once it was marginalised.

In the early 1950s, FIFA sanctioned the formation of continental football confederations for countries within defined geographical zones, and these have also helped increase the profile of the less well-established nations of the world, as well as providing a vehicle through which FIFA's policies can be implemented.

The 'parliament' of FIFA is its biennial congress, held at the venue of either the World Cup or Olympic Games. Issues are decided here on a one vote per country basis, irrespective of size or population. A three-fourths majority must be obtained in each vote. It is FIFA's intention to remain politically neutral, and given the turmoil of the 20th century, it has coped admirably.

The major problems for FIFA have been Israel and China. The Asian Football Confederation has been the most overtly political of the regional confederations. In 1976 both Israel and Taiwan were expelled 'with regret', as they were felt to be holding up progress. Israel's presence was causing a rift with the Arab nations who were starting to join the AFC in the 1970s, whilst Taiwan's membership meant the exclusion of China.

South Africa and the former Rhodesia proved to be another thorn in FIFA's side; both were eventually expelled in the early 1970s for contravening FIFA's anti-discrimination code.

FIFA is best known for the World Cup, the final tournament of which is held every four years in a designated country. It is open to every member of FIFA to participate, but despite this, not every country does enter. Many of the smaller nations prefer to take part in the Olympic Games or in FIFA's two junior tournaments. Part of the problem might be that African, Asian and Central American nations had only seven places in the final tournament of the World Cup until 1994, despite these continents having 112 members between them. The qualifying competition has therefore been a long process with, for many, very little prospect of reward at the end of it.

The unequal distribution of places does not occur in the Under-17 championship. Europe is restricted to just three entries, as are Africa, Asia and Central America, and it is worth noting that given equal opportunity, Africa has won two tournaments to Europe's one. The two junior championships and the World Cup for Women are indicative of the attempt since the 1970s to spread football to parts of the world where the game is less established. Tournaments have been staged in locations as diverse as China and Saudi Arabia, and in 2002 the senior World Cup will be held in Asia, breaking the traditional Europe-Americas stranglehold for the first time.

THE WORLD GOVERNING BODY

Fédération Internationale de Football Association
FIFA House
PO Box 85
Hitzigweg 11
CH-8030 Zürich
Switzerland
Tel: + 41 1 3849595
Fax: + 41 1 3849696

Year of formation: 1904

Presidents of FIFA - 7

Robert Guérin	France	1904-06
Daniel Woolfall	England	1906-18
Jules Rimet	France	1921-54
Rodolphe Seeldrayers	Belgium	1954-55
Arthur Drewry	England	1956-61
Sir Stanley Rous	England	1961-74
João Havelange	Brazil	1974-

MEMBER COUNTRIES OF FIFA - 191

Afghanistan – Albania – Algeria – Angola – Antigua and Barbuda – Argentina – Armenia – Aruba – Australia – Austria – Azerbaijan – Bahamas – Bahrain – Bangladesh – Barbados – Belgium – Belize – Belorussia – Benin – Bermuda – Bolivia – Botswana – Brazil – Brunei – Bulgaria – Burkina Faso – Burundi – Cameroon – Canada – Cape Verde Islands – Cayman Islands – Central African Republic – Chad – Chile – China – Chinese Taipei – Colombia – Congo – Cook Islands – Costa Rica – Côte d'Ivoire – Croatia – Cuba – Cyprus – Czech Republic – Denmark – Djibouti – Dominica – Dominican Republic – Ecuador – Egypt – El Salvador – England – Equatorial Guinea – Estonia – Ethiopia – Faeroe Islands – Fiji – Finland – France – French Polynesia 'Tahiti' – Gabon – Gambia – Georgia – Germany – Ghana – Greece – Grenada – Guatemala – Guinea – Guinea-Bissau – Guyana – Haiti – Honduras – Hong Kong – Hungary – Iceland – India – Indonesia – Iran – Iraq – Northern Ireland – Republic of Ireland – Israel – Italy – Jamaica – Japan – Jordan – Kampuchea – Kazakhstan – Kenya – North Korea – South Korea – Kuwait – Kyrgyzstan – Laos – Latvia – Lebanon – Lesotho – Liberia – Libya – Liechtenstein – Lithuania – Luxembourg – Macao – FYR Macedonia – Madagascar – Malawi – Malaysia – Maldives – Mali –

Malta – Mauritania – Mauritius – Mexico – Moldova – Morocco – Mozambique – Myanmar – Namibia – Nepal – Netherlands – Netherlands Antilles – New Zealand – Nicaragua – Niger – Nigeria – Norway – Oman – Pakistan – Panama – Papua New Guinea – Paraguay – Peru – Philippines – Poland – Portugal – Puerto Rico – Qatar – Romania – Russia – Rwanda – Saint Kitts and Nevis – Saint Lucia – Saint Vincent and the Grenadines – San Marino – Sao Tomé e Principe – Saudi Arabia – Scotland – Senegal – Seychelles – Sierra Leone – Singapore – Slovakia – Slovenia – Solomon Islands – Somalia – South Africa – Spain – Sri Lanka – Sudan – Surinam – Swaziland – Sweden – Switzerland – Syria – Tajikistan – Tanzania – Thailand – Togo – Tonga – Trinidad and Tobago – Tunisia – Turkey – Turkmenistan – Uganda – Ukraine – United Arab Emirates – United States of America – Uruguay – Uzbekistan – Vanuatu – Venezuela – Vietnam – Wales – Western Samoa – Yemen – Yugoslavia – Zaire – Zambia – Zimbabwe

NON MEMBERS - 46

Åland – Alderney – American Samoa – Andorra – Anguilla – Bhutan – Bosnia – British Virgin Islands – Christmas Island – Cocos Islands – Comoros – Eritrea – Falkland Islands – French Guiana – Gibraltar – Greenland – Guadeloupe – Guam – Guernsey – Isle of Man – Jersey – Kiribati – Marshall Islands – Martinique – Mayotte – Micronesia – Monaco – Mongolia – Montserrat – Nauru – New Caledonia – Niue – Norfolk Island – Northern Marianas – Palau – Palestine – Pitcairn Island – Réunion – Saint Helena – Saint Pierre and Miquelon – Tokelau – Turks and Caicos Islands – Tuvalu – Vatican – Virgin Islands of the U.S. – Wallis and Fotuna

FIFA WORLD PLAYER OF THE YEAR

Voted by the coaches of the national teams of each country in the world.

1991

1	Lothar Matthäus	Germany	128
2	Jean-Pierre Papin	France	113
3	Gary Lineker	England	40
4	Robert Prosinecki	Yugoslavia	38
5	Marco Van Basten	Holland	23
6	Franco Baresi	Italy	12
7	Ivan Zamorano	Chile	10
8	Andreas Brehme	Germany	9
9	Gianluca Vialli	Italy	8
10	Enzo Scifo	Belgium	7

1992

1	Marco Van Basten	Holland	151
2	Hristo Stoichkov	Bulgaria	88
3	Thomas Hässler	Germany	61
4	Jean-Pierre Papin	France	46
5	Brian Laudrup	Denmark	44
	Peter Schmeichel	Denmark	44
7	Dennis Bergkamp	Holland	29
8	Frank Rijkaard	Holland	23
9	Abedi Pelé	Ghana	10
	Franco Baresi	Italy	10
	Jurgen Klinsmann	Germany	10

1993

1	Roberto Baggio	Italy	152
2	Romario	Brazil	84
3	Dennis Bergkamp	Holland	58
4	Peter Schmeichel	Denmark	29
5	Hristo Stoichkov	Bulgaria	22
6	Faustino Asprilla	Colombia	21
7	Bebeto	Brazil	16
8	Ronald Koeman	Holland	15
9	Anthony Yeboah	Ghana	13
10	Rai	Brazil	12

1994

1	Romario	Brazil	346
2	Hristo Stoichkov	Bulgaria	100
3	Roberto Baggio	Italy	80
4	Georghe Hagi	Romania	50
5	Paolo Maldini	Italy	40
6	Bebeto	Brazil	16
7	Dennis Bergkamp	Holland	11
8	Dunga	Brazil	9
9	Franco Baresi	Italy	7
	Tomas Brolin	Sweden	7
	Jurgen Klinsmann	Germany	7
	Mauro Silva	Brazil	7

WORLD FOOTBALLER OF THE YEAR

Voted by readers of *World Soccer* magazine

1982

				%
1	Paolo Rossi	Juventus	ITA	23
2	Karl-Heinz Rummenigge	Bayern München	FRG	14
3	Falcao	Roma	BRA	12
4	Zico	Flamengo	BRA	10
5	Socrates	Corinthians	BRA	9
6	Dino Zoff	Juventus	ITA	6
7	Bruno Conti	Roma	ITA	4
8	Johan Cruyff	Ajax	HOL	3
9	Gaetano Scirea	Juventus	ITA	3
10	Zbigniew Boniek	Juventus	POL	2

1983

				%
1	Zico	Udinese	BRA	28
2	Michel Platini	Juventus	FRA	24
3	Falcao	Roma	BRA	18
4	Diego Maradona	Barcelona	ARG	6
5	Karl-Heinz Rummenigge	Bayern München	FRG	4
6	Kenny Dalglish	Liverpool	SCO	3
7	Felix Magath	Hamburger SV	FRG	3
8	Bryan Robson	Manchester United	ENG	3
9	Charlie Nicholas	Arsenal	SCO	2
10	Erwin Vandenbergh	RSC Anderlecht	BEL	2

1984

				%
1	Michel Platini	Juventus	FRA	54
2	Ian Rush	Liverpool	WAL	9
3	Zico	Udinese	BRA	7
4	Fernando Chalana	Bordeaux	POR	5
5	Jean Tigana	Bordeaux	FRA	2
6	Morten Olsen	RSC Anderlecht	DEN	2
7	Renato	Gremio	BRA	1
8	Paolo Rossi	Juventus	ITA	1
9	Graeme Souness	Sampdoria	SCO	1
10	Bryan Robson	Manchester United	ENG	1

1985

	Player	Club	Country	%
1	Michel Platini	Juventus	FRA	20
2	Preben Elkjaer-Larsen	Verona	DEN	11
3	Diego Maradona	Napoli	ARG	7
4	Peter Reid	Everton	ENG	6
5	Bernd Schuster	Barcelona	FRG	5
6	Rudi Völler	Werder Bremen	FRG	4
7	Neville Southall	Everton	WAL	3
8	Hans-Peter Briegel	Verona	FRG	3
9	Karl-Heinz Rummenigge	Internazionale	FRG	3
10	Andy Gray	Everton	SCO	2

1986

	Player	Club	Country	%
1	Diego Maradona	Napoli	ARG	35
2	Igor Belanov	Dynamo Kiev	URS	6
3	Gary Lineker	Barcelona	ENG	5
4	Emilio Butragueño	Real Madrid	ESP	4
5	Jan Ceulemans	Club Brugge	BEL	4
6	Michael Laudrup	Juventus	DEN	4
7	Preben Elkjaer-Larsen	Verona	DEN	3
8	Careca	Sao Paulo FC	BRA	3
9	Jean-Marie Pfaff	Bayern München	BEL	3
10	Jorge Burruchaga	Nantes	ARG	3

1987

	Player	Club	Country	%
1	Ruud Gullit	Milan	HOL	38
2	Diego Maradona	Napoli	ARG	13
3	Marco Van Basten	Milan	HOL	8
4	Emilio Butragueño	Real Madrid	ESP	6
5	Paulo Futre	Atlético Madrid	POR	5
6	Ian Rush	Juventus	WAL	3
7	Gary Lineker	Barcelona	ENG	3
8	Hugo Sanchez	Real Madrid	MEX	2
9	Michel Platini	Juventus	FRA	1
10	Rabah Madjer	FC Porto	ALG	1

1988

	Player	Club	Country	%
1	Marco Van Basten	Milan	HOL	43
2	Ruud Gullit	Milan	HOL	21
3	Frank Rijkaard	Milan	HOL	7
4	Ronald Koeman	PSV Eindhoven	HOL	6
5	Alexei Mikhailichenko	Dynamo Kiev	URS	5
6	Diego Maradona	Napoli	ARG	2
7	Gianluca Vialli	Sampdoria	ITA	2
8	Alexander Zavarov	Juventus	URS	2
9	John Barnes	Liverpool	ENG	2
10	Romario	PSV Eindhoven	BRA	1

1989

	Player	Club	Country	%
1	Ruud Gullit	Milan	HOL	24
2	Marco Van Basten	Milan	HOL	18
3	Bebeto	Flamengo	BRA	10
4	Diego Maradona	Napoli	ARG	7
5	Franco Baresi	Milan	ITA	6
6	Peter Shilton	Derby County	ENG	6
7	Romario	PSV Eindhoven	ITA	5
8	Michael Laudrup	Barcelona	DEN	4
9	Lothar Matthäus	Internazionale	FRG	3
10	Ruben Sosa	Lazio	URU	2

1990

	Player	Club	Country	%
1	Lothar Matthäus	Internazionale	FRG	21
2	Salvatore Schillaci	Juventus	ITA	12
3	Diego Maradona	Napoli	ARG	6
4	Jurgen Klinsmann	Internazionale	FRG	6
5	Paul Gascoigne	Tottenham Hotspur	ENG	5
6	Roberto Baggio	Juventus	ITA	5
7	Andreas Brehme	Internazionale	FRG	5
8	Roger Milla	Saint-Denis (Reunion)	CMR	4
9	Franco Baresi	Milan	ITA	4
10	John Barnes	Liverpool	ENG	4

1991

	Player	Club	Country	%
1	Jean-Pierre Papin	Olympique Marseille	FRA	25
2	Robert Prosinecki	Real Madrid	YUG	15
3	Darko Pancev	Crvena Zvezda Beograd	YUG	13
4	Mark Hughes	Manchester United	WAL	8
5	Lothar Matthäus	Internazionale	GER	6
6	Gianluca Vialli	Sampdoria	ITA	5
7	Gabriel Batistuta	Boca Juniors	ARG	4
8	Sergio Goycochea	Brest	ARG	4
9	Stuart Pearce	Nottingham Forest	ENG	3
10	Gary Lineker	Tottenham Hotspur	ENG	3

1992

	Player	Club	Country	%
1	Marco Van Basten	Milan	HOL	18
2	Dennis Bergkamp	Ajax	HOL	13
3	Peter Schmeichel	Manchester United	DEN	11
4	Thomas Hässler	Roma	GER	7
5	Brian Laudrup	Fiorentina	DEN	7
6	Ronald Koeman	Barcelona	HOL	4
7	Ally McCoist	Rangers	SCO	3
8	Frank Rijkaard	Milan	HOL	3
9	Rai	Sao Paulo	BRA	3
10	Tomas Brolin	Parma	SWE	2

1993

	Player	Club	Country	%
1	Roberto Baggio	Juventus	ITA	13
2	Dennis Bergkamp	Internazionale	HOL	11
3	Ruud Gullit	Sampdoria	HOL	9
4	Romario	Barcelona	BRA	7
5	Faustino Asprilla	Parma	COL	7
6	Ryan Giggs	Manchester United	WAL	6
7	Eric Cantona	Manchester United	FRA	6
8	Frank Rijkaard	Ajax	HOL	5
9	Michael Laudrup	Barcelona	DEN	5
10	Rai	Paris Saint-Germain	BRA	5

1994

	Player	Club	Country	%
1	Paolo Maldini	Milan	ITA	27
2	Roberto Baggio	Juventus	ITA	23
3	Romario	Barcelona	BRA	14
4	Georghe Hagi	Barcelona	ROM	7
5	Hristo Stoichkov	Barcelona	BUL	4
6	Franco Baresi	Milan	ITA	2
7	Eric Cantona	Manchester United	FRA	2
	Jurgen Klinsmann	Tottenham Hotspur	GER	2
9	Tomas Brolin	Parma	SWE	2
10	Gabriel Batistuta	Fiorentina	ARG	1

THE WORLD CUP

The World Cup is the pre-eminent tournament not only in football but perhaps in all sports. Only the Olympic Games can rival it for prestige and spectator interest. The final of each tournament reaches a worldwide audience, through television, of hundreds of millions and is seen in every corner of the globe.

The idea of a World Cup, mooted as early as 1904 when FIFA was formed, was 26 years in the making. With amateurism dominant in all but a select few countries, the football tournament of the Olympic Games was in most people's eyes the world championship of football, and this held true right up until the first World Cup was played.

The winners of the Olympic Tournament were regarded as World Champions, and with the possible exception of Belgium in 1920, the winners deserved that honour. Without doubt England were the pre-eminent world power prior to 1914, and they duly won the 1908 & 1912 Olympic titles. In the 1920s Uruguay twice won the Olympic title, and as if to prove a point, they won the very first World Cup, thus confirming their superiority.

After 1918, amateurism as the dominant concept in football was increasingly under threat. Countries such as Czechoslovakia in 1925 and Austria and Hungary in 1926, all major football powers at the time, introduced professionalism and therefore could no longer send their full international sides to the Olympics. There were also doubts as to the true amateur nature of the South American entrants. The issue of 'shamateurism' did much to damage the credibility of the tournament.

By the time of the 1928 FIFA congress in Amsterdam, Jules Rimet, the president of FIFA, knew that more countries would soon follow the example of Czechoslovakia, Austria and Hungary, and so along with Henri Delaunay, the general-secretary of the French Football Federation, he moved a motion that FIFA should organise a quadrennial championship, open to anyone, and this was passed by 25 votes to 5. Hugo Meisl along with Delaunay, Bonnet and Linnemann drew up the regulations and set about organising the first tournament. The French sculptor, Albert Lafleur, was commissioned to design a trophy, and the venue of the first tournament was decided upon at the 1929 FIFA congress in Barcelona.

Year	Winner	Score	Runner-up
1930	Uruguay	4-2	Argentina
1934	Italy	2-1	Czechoslovakia
1938	Italy	4-2	Hungary
1950	Uruguay	2-1	Brazil
1954	West Germany	3-2	Hungary
1958	Brazil	5-2	Sweden
1962	Brazil	3-1	Czechoslovakia
1966	England	4-2	West Germany
1970	Brazil	4-1	Italy
1974	West Germany	2-1	Holland
1978	Argentina	3-1	Holland
1982	Italy	3-1	West Germany
1986	Argentina	3-2	West Germany
1990	West Germany	1-0	Argentina
1994	Brazil	0-0 3-2p	Italy

ORDER OF MERIT

	Country	G	S	B	Finals	S-Finals
1	Brazil	4	1	2	5	5
2	Germany	3	3	2	6	8
3	Italy	3	2	1	5	6
4	Argentina	2	2	-	4	3
5	Uruguay	2	-	-	2	3
6	England	1	-	-	1	2
7	Czechoslovakia	-	2	-	2	2
	Holland	-	2	-	2	-
	Hungary	-	2	-	2	2
10	Sweden	-	1	2	1	3
11	France	-	-	2	-	3
12	Poland	-	-	2	-	1
13	Austria	-	-	1	-	2
	Yugoslavia	-	-	1	-	2
15	Chile	-	-	1	-	1
	Portugal	-	-	1	-	1
	USA	-	-	1	-	1
18	Belgium	-	-	-	-	1
	Bulgaria	-	-	-	-	1
	Soviet Union	-	-	-	-	1

1930

THE 1ST WORLD CUP
HELD IN URUGUAY, 13TH - 30TH JULY 1930

Italy, Spain, Holland and Sweden all applied for the right to stage the tournament. Uruguay, however, were chosen ahead of the European quartet - they offered to pay everyone's travel and accommodation expenses, they were the current Olympic champions, and 1930, the date set for the tournament, would mark Uruguay's centenary as an independent nation.

In retrospect, the decision seems to have been a mistake. One by one the European nations withdrew citing domestic commitments and the long journey time as their reasons. When the tournament opened only four remained, and they were not considered to be amongst the strongest on the continent. None of the powerful central Europeans were represented, nor were the British.

Only France, Yugoslavia, Belgium and Romania made the journey, and they were joined by nine countries from the Americas. Of the South American contingent Uruguay, the hosts, were overwhelming favourites to reach the final along with Argentina. Brazil had not yet developed into the powerhouse that it would later become, whilst the other South Americans, Paraguay and Chile apart, had played little competitive football.

Uruguay had struggled to build a brand new stadium for the championships, and as the tournament got underway, the 93,000 capacity Centenary Stadium was not completely finished. The first match, however, was not scheduled to be played there, but in Penarol's Pocitos stadium, where on 13 July 1930 a crowd of 1,000 turned up to see France defeat Mexico 4-1.

The 13 nations were divided into four groups, and the four winners of each of these would advance to the semi-finals. This combination of a league and cup format was decided upon when it was realised that due to the withdrawals, a wholly knock-out system was not possible. A precedent had been set that was to shape the pattern of future World Cups.

In the event the semi-final line-up was a surprising one. Despite their opening win, the French did not make it past the first round, due mainly to a problem that would plague the entire history of the World Cup: bad refereeing decisions. After falling behind to an 81st minute goal in their next match, against Argentina, they seemed certain to score through Langiller only for the Brazilian referee to blow for full time some six minutes early! Realising his mistake, he restarted the game, but by then it was too late for the French. A defeat by Chile in their next game in a near-empty Centenary Stadium saw them sail for home unrewarded.

Argentina, after their good fortune against France, qualified with some ease for the last four. Playing a blend of rugged and skilful football, they cruised past the Mexicans, winning 6-3 having been 5-1 up, and beat Chile 3-1 in the crucial last game of the group. Before only 1000 supporters in the Centenary Stadium, Guillermo Stabile, the goalscoring sensation of the tournament, scored twice in the first 14 minutes to effectively seal the match.

The attendances were no better in Group 2. Only 800 turned up at Central Park, home of Nacional, to see Yugoslavia beat the Bolivians who were clearly out of their depth. Yugoslavia qualified after winning 2-1 against the Brazilians in the first game of the group. Both were relatively inexperienced sides, but Brazil were the seeded side in the group and had been expected to win.

Group 3 did not produce any surprises. By 18 July the Centenary Stadium was ready for use and 70,000 turned up for its inauguration on Independence day to witness a difficult 1-0 victory for the Uruguayans over Peru, who had already lost to Romania. The deciding game of the group was played four days later before a crowd of 80,000 and by half-time, playing what was to be regarded as the best football of the whole tournament, the Uruguayans had swept the Romanians aside scoring four goals without reply.

The semi-final line-up was completed by the real surprise of the tournament, the United States. In perhaps the first case of a World Cup side containing foreign nationals to boost its chances, the United States team seemed almost to be a 'Scottish XI' as the names of players like McGhee, Gallacher and Auld will testify. Belgium were easily disposed of in their first game, as were Paraguay in the second. The semi-finals were both well-attended and one-sided affairs, and the results meant that the final would be a repeat of the 1928 Olympic Games. Argentina defeated the Americans 6-1 in the first of the games, but their tactics were not to everybody's liking: Raphael Tracy, the American centre-half, had his leg broken after 10 minutes. Only 1-0 down at half-time, the United States collapsed in the second half in the face of some scintillating football from the Argentines.

Uruguay, on the other hand, had a much tougher game against Yugoslavia who scored first, were unlucky to have a goal disallowed when 2-1 down, and conceded their third after the ball had seemingly gone out of play. Like the Americans however, they collapsed in the second half. It was to become a familiar sight: the Yugoslavs so close to winning a tournament but falling just short of the finishing post.

The final could have gone either way. The two teams were very familiar with each other, playing as they had more times against each other than even England and Scotland had managed. Uruguay were the Olympic champions, but Argentina were the current South American champions. Home advantage in the end swayed the tie. Boats had been hired by large numbers of Argentines to take them the short trip across the River Plate from Buenos Aires to Montevideo, but the majority of fans in the Centenary Stadium were Uruguayans.

Despite the encouragement given to the home team, Argentina had the better of the first half and they led 2-1 at half time, though Stabile's goal after 37 minutes should have been disallowed for offside. The second half was a different story. Playing the type of football that had made them famous in Europe, Uruguay broke down the Argentine defence three times to steal a victory and Jose Nasazzi became the first captain to lift sport's most coveted trophy.

FIRST ROUND

Group 1

Pocitos, Montevideo, 13-07-1930, 1,000

France 4 (Laurent 19, Langiller 40, Maschinot 42, 86)
Mexico 1 (Carreño 68)

Central Park, Montevideo, 15-07-1930, 3,000

Argentina 1 (Monti 81)
France 0

Central Park, Montevideo, 16-07-1930, 500

Chile 3 (Subiabre 12 50, Vidal 64)
Mexico 0

Centenario, Montevideo, 19-07-1930, 2,000

Chile 1 (Subiabre 64)
France 0

Centenario, Montevideo, 19-07-1930, 5,000

Argentina 6 (Stábile 8 17 80, Zumelzù 22, Varallo 52 61)
Mexico 3 (Rosas.M 38, Rosas.F 65, López 75)

Centenario, Montevideo, 22-07-1930, 1,000
Argentina 3 (Stábile 12 14, Evaristo.M 51)
Chile 1 (Subiabre 16)

	Ar	Ch	Fr	Me	Pl	W	D	L	F	A	Pts
ARGENTINA	-	3-1	1-0	6-3	3	3	0	0	10	4	6
CHILE	-	-	1-0	3-0	3	2	0	1	5	3	4
FRANCE	-	-	-	4-1	3	1	0	2	4	3	2
MEXICO	-	-	-	-	3	0	0	3	4	13	0

Group 2
Central Park, Montevideo, 14-07-1930, 5,000
Yugoslavia 2 (Tirnanic 21, Bek 31)
Brazil 1 (Preguinho 62)

Central Park, Montevideo, 17-07-1930, 800
Yugoslavia 4 (Bek 60 67, Marjanovic 65, Vujadinovic 85)
Bolivia 0

Centenario, Montevideo, 20-07-1930, 1,200
Brazil 4 (Carvalho Leite 37, Preguinho 57 73 75)
Bolivia 0

	Yu	Br	Bo	Pl	W	D	L	F	A	Pts
YUGOSLAVIA	-	2-1	4-0	2	2	0	0	6	1	4
BRAZIL	-	-	4-0	2	1	0	1	5	2	2
BOLIVIA	-	-	-	2	0	0	2	0	8	0

Group 3
Pocitos, Montevideo, 14-07-1930, 300
Romania 3 (Desu 1, Stanciu 77, Kovacs 85)
Peru 1 (Souza 63)

Centenario, Montevideo, 18-07-1930, 70,000
Uruguay 1 (Castro 60)
Peru 0

Centenario, Montevideo, 22-07-1930, 80,000
Uruguay 4 (Dorado 7, Scarone.H 24, Anselmo 30, Cea 35)
Romania 0

	Ur	Ro	Pe	Pl	W	D	L	F	A	Pts
URUGUAY	-	4-0	1-0	2	2	0	0	5	0	4
ROMANIA	-	-	3-1	2	1	0	1	3	5	2
PERU	-	-	-	2	0	0	2	1	4	0

Group 4
Central Park, Montevideo, 13-07-1930, 10,000
United States 3 (McGhee 23 38, Patenaude 68)
Belgium 0

Central Park, Montevideo, 17-07-1930, 800
United States 3 (Patenaude 10 50, OG 15)
Paraguay 0

Centenario, Montevideo, 20-07-1930, 900
Paraguay 1 (Peña 40)
Belgium 0

	US	Pa	Be	Pl	W	D	L	F	A	Pts
UNITED STATES	-	3-0	3-0	2	2	0	0	6	0	4
PARAGUAY	-	-	1-0	2	1	0	1	1	3	2
BELGIUM	-	-	-	2	0	0	2	0	4	0

SEMI-FINALS
Centenario, Montevideo, 27-07-1930, 93,000
Uruguay 6 (Cea 18 67 72, Anselmo 20 31, Iriarte 60)
Yugoslavia 1 (Sekulic 4)

Centenario, Montevideo, 26-07-1930, 80,000
Argentina 6 (Monti 20, Scopelli 56, Stábile 69 87, Peucelle 80 85)
United States 1 (Brown 88)

FINAL
Centenario, Montevideo, 30-07-1930, 93,000. Referee: Lanegus, Belgium
URUGUAY 4 (Dorado 12, Cea 58, Iriarte 68, Castro 89)
ARGENTINA 2 (Peucelle 20, Stábile 37)
Uruguay - Ballesteros - Nasazzi, Mascheroni - Andrade.J, Fernández, Gestido - Dorado, Scarone, Castro, Cea, Iriarte. Tr: Supicci
Argentina - Botasso - Della Torre, Paternóster - Evaristo.J, Monti, Suárez - Peucelle, Varallo, Stábile, Ferreira, Evaristo.M. Tr: Olazar

Top Scorers: Guillermo Stábile, Argentina 8
Pedro Cea, Uruguay 5
Guillermo Subiabre, Chile 4
Preguinho, Brazil 4
Total goals scored: 70
Average per game: 3.9

1934
THE 2ND WORLD CUP
11TH JUNE 1933 - 10TH JUNE 1934

Italy was chosen as host for the 1934 competition. Again it was a strange choice of venue. If Montevideo had been too far away for most of the European nations, Italy posed another problem. Like all dictators, Mussolini was always on the lookout for a propaganda opportunity, and the World Cup provided him with the perfect vehicle.

FIFA's insistence that the World Cup was too big for one city alone swung the balance in favour of Italy. The Italian government offered to foot what promised to be a hefty bill. The political motives of the Italian government seemed to be a small price to pay for a tournament. Mussolini was not to be disappointed either. Fortunately for him Italy were at the height of their powers: between June 1930 and May 1948 they lost only one match played on home soil, and during the 1930s only seven altogether. It seemed predestined that Italy would win, and they did. Home advantage was not Italy's sole advantage.

Uruguay, still upset that so few Europeans had bothered to come to her tournament, refused to take part thus robbing the tournament of the defending champions. The losing finalists in 1930, Argentina, weakened the line-up further by sending a virtual 'C' team, in response to the Italians poaching three of their best players, Monti, Orsi and Guaita. Monti had even played in the 1930 final for Argentina. This time he would go one better and win in the final for Italy. Vittorio Pozzo, Italy's trainer, justified their inclusion on the grounds that they were of Italian ancestry, but Argentina were quite naturally unimpressed. They did not want to risk losing their best players to the Italian game so they simply were not sent.

The British were again not present. It is possible that either England or Scotland would have won the tournament, but both had suffered losses against Continental sides. Two weeks before the World Cup began England lost to both Hungary and Czechoslovakia in Budapest and Prague respectively, whilst Scotland, on their last trip to the continent in 1931, had lost 5-0 to the Austrians and 3-0 to the Italians.

Stockholm saw the first World Cup game played on European soil. On 11 June 1933 Sweden kicked off the World Cup qualifiers with a convincing 6-2 win over Estonia. Because the number of entrants was 31, qualifying rounds were needed to reduce the number of teams to 16 for the final tournament which was to be played on a purely knock-out basis. There were few surprises in the qualifying rounds except Yugoslavia's elimination at the hands of Switzerland and Romania.

This meant that two of the 1930 semi-finalists were not represented in Italy. March 16th 1934 was also an historic date as Egypt met Palestine in the first World Cup match to be played on African soil, whilst the return in Tel Aviv three weeks later saw the first on Asian soil. On 27 May 1934 the final tournament got underway, and all of the first round games were completed. After one day of competition there were no American representatives left. Argentina, Brazil and the USA all left for home, the first two having played just one match in the whole competition, their opponents in their qualifying groups having withdrawn.

The USA had at least played two games in Italy. Apart from their defeat by the hosts in the first round, they had played a qualifying game against Mexico in Rome three days before the tournament started. Mexico had therefore made the trip across the Atlantic only to be denied the opportunity to play in the competition proper.

The quarter-finals were played three days after the first round, and the hosts were lucky to qualify for the semi-finals. Having gone a goal behind to Spain, their equaliser seemed to have an element of foul play about it, as did most of the Italian play. In the replay the following day, Spain were forced to make seven changes due to injury and unsurprisingly lost 1-0, their cause again not being helped by a referee who seemed to favour the Italians.

The most intriguing tie of the round was that between Austria and Hungary. Both teams would have graced the final, but it was the Austrian 'Wunderteam' who stole the honours. In the previous three years, they had lost only to England and Czechoslovakia and were many people's favourites to win the title. The best game of the round, however, was Czechoslovakia's 3-2 win over Switzerland, the result of which was in doubt right until the final whistle.

The semi-finals pitted Italy against Austria and Czechoslovakia against Germany. The Italians had their Argentine forward Guaita to thank for their victory over the Austrians. Despite heavy pressure, Austria could not level his 19th minute goal. Italy were playing their third game in four days and were not expected to win, but win they did in front of a delighted Mussolini.

At the same time in Rome before a small crowd, Czechoslovakia were having little trouble in disposing of the Germans who could not match their skill or the goalscoring prowess of Oldrich Nejedly who scored a hat-trick. The final between Italy and Czechoslovakia was not played until a week later, but in the meantime that most dubious of fixtures, the third place play-off was used for the first time in a tournament. The Austrians did not have the heart for the game, a feature that has blighted so many of them since. Certainly the public of Naples could see little point in the game as only 7,000 bothered to turn up to see the Germans win 3-2.

For the final, Italy, with the crowd behind them and the great tactical awareness of Pozzo binding together some talented individuals, were slight favourites. In the event they almost lost. The Czechs had played and beaten the Italians often enough before not to be intimidated, and when they took the lead 20 minutes from time it looked all over for the Italians. Both Svoboda and Sobotka could have sealed the match shortly after, the latter hitting the post, but after 82 minutes Italy were again saved by an Argentinian. Orsi scored a freakish goal with a shot that he tried to repeat the following day for photographers but couldn't.

The match turned against the Czechs and in extra time Schiavio scored the winner. Stamina had in the end been the telling factor. The Italian captain, their goalkeeper Giampiero Combi, gratefully received the cup from an admiring Mussolini. All was well with Fascism it seemed. Two years later this myth would be further reinforced when it was Hitler's turn to host a propaganda event, the 1936 Berlin Olympics. Privately most wondered how good the Italians really were and if they would have won the tournament anywhere else and without their Argentine imports who had played so crucial a role.

QUALIFYING TOURNAMENT

Group 1

Round 1

Haiti .... 1-3 0-6 1-1 .... Cuba

Round 2

Mexico .... 3-2 5-0 4-1 .... Cuba

Round 3

United States .... 4-2 .... Mexico

Group 2

BRAZIL qualified as Peru withdrew

Group 3

ARGENTINA qualified as Chile withdrew

Group 4

EGYPT .... 7-1 4-1 .... Palestine

Group 5

	Sd	Li	Es	Pl	W	D	L	F	A	Pts
SWEDEN	-	-	6-2	2	2	0	0	8	2	4
LITHUANIA	0-2	-	-	1	0	0	1	0	2	0
ESTONIA	-	-	-	1	0	0	1	2	6	0

Group 6

SPAIN ....9-0 2-1 ....Portugal

Group 7

ITALY ....4-0 ....Greece

Group 8

	Hu	Au	Bu	Pl	W	D	L	F	A	Pts
HUNGARY	-	-	4-1	2	2	0	0	8	2	4
AUSTRIA	-	-	6-1	1	1	0	0	6	1	2
BULGARIA	1-4	-	-	3	0	0	3	3	14	0

Group 9

Poland ....1-2 0-2 ....**CZECHOSLOVAKIA**

Group 10

	Sz	Ro	Yu	Pl	W	D	L	F	A	Pts
SWITZERLAND	-	2-0*	-	2	1	1	0	4	2	3
ROMANIA	-	-	2-1	2	1	0	1	2	3	2
YUGOSLAVIA	2-2	-	-	2	0	1	1	3	4	1

* Awarded to Switzerland 2-0, after the game had ended 2-2

Group 11

	Ho	Be	RI	Pl	W	D	L	F	A	Pts
HOLLAND	-	-	5-2	2	2	0	0	9	4	4
BELGIUM	2-4	-	-	2	0	1	1	6	8	1
REP. IRELAND	-	4-4	-	2	0	1	1	6	9	1

Group 12

	Ge	Fr	Lu	Pl	W	D	L	F	A	Pts
GERMANY	-	-	-	1	1	0	0	9	1	2
FRANCE	-	-	-	1	1	0	0	6	1	2
LUXEMBOURG	1-9	1-6	-	2	0	0	2	2	15	0

FINAL TOURNAMENT,
HELD IN ITALY, 27TH MAY - 10TH JUNE 1934

FIRST ROUND

PNF, Rome, 27-05-1934, 30,000

Italy 7 (Schiavio 18 29 64, Orsi 20 69, Ferrari 63, Meazza 89)
United States 1 (Donelli 57)

Luigi Ferraris, Genoa, 27-05-1934

Spain 3 (Iraragorri 16, Langara 27 77)
Brazil 1 (Leónidas 56)

Ascarelli, Naples, 27-05-1934

Hungary 4 (Teleki 7, Toldi 18 57, Vincze 59)
Egypt 2 (Fawzi 26 67)

Mussolini, Turin, 27-05-1934

Austria 3 (Sindelar 34, Schall 100, Bican 112)
France 2 (Nicolas 19, Verriest 117)

Giovanni Berta, Florence, 27-05-1934, 8,000

Germany 5 (Kobierski 18, Conen 72 77 87, Siffling 56)
Belgium 2 (Voorhoof 24 35)

Littoriale, Bologna, 27-05-1934

Sweden 3 (Jonasson 33 67, Kroon 80)
Argentina 2 (Belis 16, Galateo 47)

San Siro, Milan, 27-05-1934

Switzerland 3 (Kielholz 10 36, Abegglen.A 57)
Holland 2 (Smit 22, Vente 80)

Littorio, Trieste, 27-05-1934

Czechoslovakia 2 (Puc 61, Nejedly 73)
Romania 1 (Dobai 37)

QUARTER-FINALS

Giovanni Berta, Florence, 31-05-1934, 35,000

Italy 1 (Ferrari 47)
Spain 1 (Regueiro 31)

Replay. Giovanni Berta, Florence, 1-06-1934, 43,000

Italy 1 (Meazza 12)
Spain 0

Littoriale, Bologna, 31-05-1934

Austria 2 (Horvath 5, Zischek 53)
Hungary 1 (Sárosi 67)

San Siro, Milan, 31-05-1934, 3,000

Germany 2 (Hohmann 60 63)
Sweden 1 (Dunker 83)

Mussolini, Turin, 31-05-1934

Czechoslovakia 3 (Svoboda 24, Sobotka 49, Nejedly 83)
Switzerland 2 (Kielholz 18, Abegglen.A 71)

SEMI-FINALS

San Siro, Milan, 3-06-1934, 60,000

Italy 1 (Guaita 19)
Austria 0

PNF, Rome, 3-06-1934, 10,000

Czechoslovakia 3 (Nejedly 21 60 81)
Germany 1 (Noack 50)

3RD PLACE

Ascarelli, Naples, 7-06-1934, 7,000

Germany 3 (Lehner 1 42, Conen 29)
Austria 2 (Horvath 30, Sesta 55)

FINAL

PNF, Rome, 10-06-1934, 55,000. Referee: Eklind, Sweden

ITALY 2 (Orsi 81, Schiavio 95)
CZECHOSLOVAKIA 1 (Puc 71)

Italy - Combi - Monzeglio, Allemandi - Ferraris IV, Monti, Bertolini - Guaita, Meazza, Schiavio, Ferrari, Orsi. Tr: Pozzo

Czechoslovakia - Plánicka - Zenisek, Ctyroky - Kostálek, Cambal, Krcil - Junek, Svoboda, Sobotka, Nejedly, Puc. Tr: Petru

Top scorers: Oldrich Nejedly, Czechoslovakia....................5
Angelo Schiavio, Italy....................4
Edmund Conen, Germany....................4

Total goals scored: 70
Average per game: 4.1

1938

THE 3RD WORLD CUP
16TH JUNE 1937 - 19TH JUNE 1938

The practice of alternating the World Cup between South America and Europe was broken at the 1936 FIFA congress in Berlin. Both Argentina and France had applied to host the next event. The Argentines were upset that the French were chosen and it would be another 20 years before they entered a team. With some justification they felt that Europe had let them down again. If nothing else, however, awarding the World Cup to France was a tacit recognition of their services to the competition.

The tournament was not, however, trouble free, held as it was under the shadow of war. The Spanish Civil War was at its height, Italy had invaded Abyssinia, whilst the Germans had marched into and taken the Rhineland and Austria. Austria had even qualified for the final tournament but was now no longer a separate country. They were withdrawn and as a result Sweden received a bye in the first round. The tournament also proved to be the most unrepresentative of all the World Cups ever held. Only three non-European countries entered. Two of them, Cuba and the Dutch East Indies, had no football heritage whatsoever. Only Brazil were serious contenders. Missing again were the 1930 champions Uruguay, as well as the British quartet who despite pleas from FIFA still would not enter.

Sweden once more got the qualifying tournament underway in Stockholm, this time beating the Finns 4-0. Again, the only surprise of the qualifiers was the elimination of the Yugoslavs, at the hands of Poland. Not surprisingly, no qualifying games were needed outside Europe and so after the shortest qualifying tournament in the history of the World Cup, the 16 teams gathered in France in June 1938.

The Fascist states were confident of victory, through either Germany or Italy. The Germans were involved in the opening game on 4 June but were outplayed by the Swiss who were unlucky not to win at the first attempt. Despite the presence in the German team of the best Austrians, Germany put in their worst World Cup performance to date in the replay, where they were beaten 4-2. In a round full of shocks and surprises, Cuba's 2-1 victory over Romania after a 3-3 draw was perhaps the biggest.

The defending champions Italy nearly fell at the first hurdle, but a goal in extra time by Silvio Piola saved their blushes against the plucky Norwegians, who had almost knocked them out in the semi-finals of the Olympic Games two years previously. The Italian team had only three survivors from the 1934 winning side, Monzeglio, Ferrari and Meazza, and it was undoubtedly a much better one, as they would prove in the latter rounds. The most sensational game of the tournament, perhaps even in the entire history of the competition, was the first round clash between Brazil and Poland. Two players scored four goals: Leonidas, Brazil's 'Black Diamond', scored a hat-trick before half-time, then Ernst Willimowski undid all of Leonidas' good work by himself scoring a hat-trick, his third after 88 minutes making the score 4-4. Both scored again in extra-time, but Romeo snatched the winner for Brazil.

The quarter-finals were less full of surprises though no less exciting than the previous round. The giant-killers of Switzerland and Cuba were both knocked out, Switzerland by the stylish Hungarians, the Cubans 8-0 by Sweden, thereby putting Romania's first round performance into perspective. At Colombes in Paris, before the largest crowd of the tournament, the holders knocked out the hosts. France were not a very strong side at the time and not even home advantage could give them the edge over Italy for whom Piola scored twice in the second half.

One game did stand out, however: the first of the two matches between Czechoslovakia and Brazil, a game which has become known as the 'Battle of Bordeaux'. Zeze Precopio of Brazil had been sent off early in the first half and the match never recovered. Both Machado of Brazil and Riha of Czechoslovakia were sent off just before half-time; Nejedly, Czechoslovakia's star forward, had his leg broken, whilst Planicka played in goal for the Czechs with a broken arm. Both were missing from the replay and this told as Brazil ran out 2-1 winners in a much milder game.

In the semi-finals Brazil were drawn against the Italians and so confident of victory were they that they rested Leonidas. This proved to be their downfall because without him they lacked any punch in front of goal. The Italians could hardly believe their luck and went on to win 2-1 with Meazza inspirational at the heart of the team, Brazil's only goal coming three minutes before the end. Not for the last time would Brazil suffer through over-confidence.

As Czechoslovakia had done in 1934, Hungary represented the finer side of football in the 1938 tournament. Zsengeller, Sarosi and Tikos were among the best pre-war footballers on the continent and all three scored in their impressive 5-1 victory in the other semi-final over the Swedes, who were simply outclassed as had Switzerland and the Dutch East Indies been in the previous rounds.

Hopes were high that the Hungarians could inflict on Italy their first World Cup defeat. They were certainly the more skilful side, but were often accused of lacking the killer punch, and so it proved in the final. Italy had put the game out of Hungary's reach by half-time, Colaussi's two goals and one from the star of the tournament, Piola, giving them a 3-1 lead. Though Sarosi reduced the Italian lead midway through the second half, the Hungarians could not break down a stout Italian defence again.

In a foretaste of the way they would play later on in the century, the Italians had simply 'shut up shop'. Forced to attack, the Hungarians gave away a fourth goal eight minutes from time, Piola's second of the game and fifth of the tournament. Pozzo's tactical genius had triumphed again as Meazza became the third different man to collect the famous trophy. Italy had now won the last three major championships they had entered. Two World Cups and the intervening Olympic Games had proved their worth as the top continental side, if not necessarily the best in the world.

QUALIFYING TOURNAMENT

Group 1

	Ge	Sd	Es	Fi	Pl	W	D	L	F	A	Pts
GERMANY	-	5-0	4-1	-	3	3	0	0	11	1	6
SWEDEN	-	-	7-2	4-0	3	2	0	1	11	7	4
ESTONIA	-	-	-	-	3	1	0	2	4	11	2
FINLAND	0-2	-	0-1	-	3	0	0	3	0	7	0

Group 2
NORWAY..............3-2 3-3..............Rep. Ireland
POLAND..............4-0 0-1..............Yugoslavia

Group 3
ROMANIA qualified as Egypt withdrew

Group 4
SWITZERLAND..............2-1..............Portugal

Group 5
FIRST ROUND
Palestine..............1-3 0-1..............**Greece**

SECOND ROUND
HUNGARY..............11-1..............Greece

Group 6
Bulgaria..............1-1 0-6..............**CZECHOSLOVAKIA**

Group 7
FIRST ROUND
Latvia..............4-2 5-1..............Lithuania

SECOND ROUND
AUSTRIA..............2-1..............Latvia

Group 8

	Ho	Be	Lu	Pl	W	D	L	F	A	Pts
HOLLAND	-	-	4-0	2	1	1	0	5	1	3
BELGIUM	1-1	-	-	2	1	1	0	4	3	3
Luxembourg	-	2-3	-	2	0	0	2	2	7	0

Group 9
BRAZIL and **CUBA** qualified

Group 10
DUTCH EAST INDIES qualified as Japan withdrew

Group 11
ITALY qualified as holders

Group 12
FRANCE qualified as hosts

FINAL TOURNAMENT, HELD IN FRANCE 4TH - 19TH JUNE 1938

FIRST ROUND

Vélodrome, Marseilles, 5-06-1938
Italy 2 (Ferraris 2, Piola 94)
Norway 1 (Brustad 83)

Colombes, Paris, 5-06-1938
France 3 (Veinante 1, Nicolas 12 69)
Belgium 1 (Isemborghs 38)

Cavée Verte, Le Havre, 5-06-1938
Czechoslovakia 3 (Kostalek 92, Nejedly 111, Zeman 115)
Holland 0

Meinau, Strasbourg, 5-06-1938
Brazil 6 (Leónidas 18 25 44 93, Peracio 72, Romeo 102)
Poland 5 (Willimowski 22 59 88 107, Piontek 50)

Sweden -
Austria -
Austria withdrew

Chapou, Toulouse, 5-06-1938, 6,000
Cuba 3 (Socorro 40 103, Maquina 69)
Romania 3 (Bindea 30, Baratki 59, Dobai 105)

Replay. Chapou, Toulouse, 9-06-1938, 5,000
Cuba 2 (Socorro 50, Maquina 80)
Romania 1 (Dobai 9)

Parc des Princes, Paris, 4-06-1938, 30,000
Switzerland 1 (Abegglen.A 43)
Germany 1 (Gauchel 23)

Parc des Princes, Paris, 9-06-1938, 22,000
Switzerland 4 (Walaschek 41, Bickel 64, Abegglen.A 75 78)
Germany 2 (Hahnemann 8, OG 22)

Vélodrome, Reims, 5-06-1938
Hungary 6 (Kohut 18, Toldi 22, Sárosi.G 28 77, Zsengellér 38 53)
Dutch East Indies 0

QUARTER-FINALS

Colombes, Paris, 12-06-1938, 58,000
Italy 3 (Colaussi 9, Piola 52 72)
France 1 (Heisserer 10)

Parc de Lescure, Bordeaux, 12-06-1938, 25,000
Brazil 1 (Leónidas 30)
Czechoslovakia 1 (Nejedly 64)

Replay. Parc de Lescure, Bordeaux, 14-06-1938
Brazil 2 (Leónidas 57, Roberto 89)
Czechoslovakia 1 (Kopecky 30)

Fort Carré, Antibes, 12-06-1938
Sweden 8 (Andersson 15, Jonasson 32, Wetterström 38 41 53 89, Keller 55, Nyberg 60)
Cuba 0

Victor Boucquey, Lille, 12-06-1938
Hungary 2 (Zsengellér 42 68)
Switzerland 0

SEMI-FINALS

Vélodrome, Marseilles, 16-06-1938, 35,000
Italy 2 (Colaussi 55, Meazza 60)
Brazil 1 (Romeo 87)

Parc de Princes, Paris, 16-06-1938, 17,000
Hungary 5 (Zsengellér 18 38 86, Titkos 26, Sárosi.G 61)
Sweden 1 (Nyberg 1)

3RD PLACE

Parc de Lescure, Bordeaux, 19-06-1938
Brazil 4 (Romeo 43, Leónidas 63 73, Peracio 80)
Sweden 2 (Jonasson 18, Nyberg 38)

FINAL

Colombes, Paris, 19-06-1938, 55,000. Referee: Capdeville, France

ITALY 4 (Colaussi 5 35, Piola 16 82)
HUNGARY 2 (Titkos 7, Sárosi.G 70)

Italy - Olivieri - Foni, Rava - Serantoni, Andreolo, Locatelli - Biavati, Meazza, Piola, Ferrari, Colaussi. Tr: Pozzo

Hungary - Szabó - Polgar, Bíró - Szalay, Szücs, Lázár - Sas, Vincze, Sárosi.G, Zsengellér, Titkos. Tr: Dietz

Top scorers: Leónidas da Silva, Brazil 8
Gyula Zsengeller, Hungary 7
Silvio Piola, Italy 4

Total goals scored: 84
Average per game: 4.7

1950

THE 4TH WORLD CUP
2ND JUNE 1949 - 16TH JULY 1950

The Second World War put paid to the World Cup for 12 years. Brazil, Argentina and Germany had all made a bid for the 1942 tournament at FIFA's 1938 congress in Paris, but no decision was taken. At the next congress in Luxembourg in 1946, FIFA decided to hold the next tournament in 1949. They also decided to change the name of the tournament from the World Cup to the World Championship. The trophy was given the name of the Jules Rimet Cup in honour of its instigator. Legend has it that during the war, Rimet kept the trophy under his bed to hide it from the Germans.

As Brazil were the only applicants they were given the task of organising the 1949 tournament. Unlike Europe, football had carried on unabated in South America during the war years. Indeed, between the 1938 and 1950 World Cups, seven South American Championships had been played, the last of which, held in Brazil in May 1949, occupied the time originally intended for the World Cup but instead acted as a dress rehearsal for the tournament which had been put back a year.

The qualifying competition was the most disorganised ever and was plagued by withdrawals. Originally there were 32 entries, but Argentina, Ecuador and Peru pulled out before a ball had been kicked, as did Belgium and Austria. Turkey withdrew after they had qualified, as did Scotland. The Scots had come second in the British Home Championship, which acted as a qualifying group, but decided that as they had not finished top they would not enter. This would be the last World Cup where the British could afford to be so disdainful.

Uruguay returned, 20 years after their previous appearance, and for the first time the British quartet entered. For the first time also, the Far East was represented, though both Burma and India later withdrew. For the third World Cup running, Stockholm saw the first encounter of the competition, the Swedes this time playing host to the Republic of Ireland. Notable for their absence were the Communist countries of Europe, especially Hungary and Czechoslovakia. Germany, the defeated power in the European war, was also absent – they were not invited to take part.

Because of the withdrawals, FIFA invited France and Portugal, both of whom had been eliminated, to play in the final tournament. France accepted and were grouped with Uruguay and Bolivia but pulled out once they had seen their itinerary and the amount of travel it involved. The Brazilian organisers were roundly criticised, and the complaints were largely justified. Yugoslavia in particular were unhappy about their programme. Their first match against Switzerland was in Belo Horizonte, their second four days later in Porto Alegre and their third, the all-important game against Brazil, two days after that in Rio.

The other groups were not much better, Italy being the only team who did not have to change cities. The withdrawals had also left the ridiculous situation where one group had only two teams, despite the fact that two other groups both had four teams. Apart from these problems, the atmosphere of the tournament was good. The huge Maracana stadium had been specially built, though like the Centenary stadium in Uruguay 20 years before, it was not finished in time for the opening match between Brazil and Mexico.

A crowd of 81,000 were in a carnival mood as they welcomed Brazil, the overwhelming favourites to win the tournament, onto the pitch. There, a 21-gun salute awaited them as well as a firework display. In the game itself, the hosts had no trouble in sweeping aside the Mexicans, the hero of the side, Ademir, scoring two of their four goals. Switzerland and Mexico were no match for either Brazil or Yugoslavia, although the Swiss did hold the hosts to a draw in Sao Paulo. That result meant that Brazil had to beat the Yugoslavs to qualify for the next round. In Yugoslavia's previous appearance in a World Cup finals, in Montevideo in 1930, they had beaten Brazil to qualify for the semi-finals. The biggest crowd that had ever gathered for a World Cup game, 147,000, packed into the Maracana. This time the Brazilians were triumphant. Ademir after three minutes and Zizinho on the hour ensured their progression to the next round.

Group 2 produced one of the biggest upsets ever in the World Cup. England, regarded by many as the World's number one, had started the tournament well, beating Chile 2-0. In their next game they faced the United States, who in their first game had almost defeated Spain but conceded three goals in the last ten minutes to lose 3-1. In Belo Horizonte a small crowd of 10,000 gathered to see the 'inevitable' English victory. Instead they witnessed a result that was so unlikely that on receiving the news, some British newspapers thought there had been a printing mistake and listed the score as 10-1! Larry Gaetjens scored the only goal, and unlike their 1930s semi-final team, the American team in Brazil was almost entirely composed of American-born players. Haitian-born Gaetjens was a notable exception. Going into the last game both England and America still had a chance to qualify for the next round, but the Americans lost heavily to Chile whilst England went down to a Zarra goal in the game against Spain.

The other two groups comprised only four games in total, out of which Sweden and Uruguay qualified for the final pool. Sweden, relying on only three of their superb Olympic Games winning side of two years previously, inflicted a first World Cup defeat on the reigning champions Italy, whose squad had been decimated the previous year by the Superga air crash. It was the decisive game as Paraguay, who drew with the Swedes in the second match of the group, lost to Italy in the last. Uruguay had the easiest first round any team has ever had or is likely to have. Their record against Bolivia consisted of five wins out of six with a goal difference of 27 for and 5 against. The game in Belo Horizonte saw the Uruguayans add another eight to that total in convincing fashion.

Unlike any other World Cup, the 1950 tournament did not have a knock-out element and as a result did not actually have a final. Instead, the second round consisted of another group where the four 'semi-finalists' played each other once. It is fortunate therefore that the final game in the group also proved to be the decisive game and so is treated as the final.

Brazil were positively spellbinding in their first two games in the group. Sweden and Spain were swept aside with such arrogant ease that everyone was certain they would lift the Jules Rimet Trophy. Ademir, Zizinho, Jair, Chico and Friaca were in stunning form in front of goal. Uruguay, perceived to be their greatest threat, started off badly, drawing with Spain and only just beating Sweden.

Sweden beat Spain in a meaningless match in Sao Paulo to finish third in the tournament, whilst on the same day, a world record crowd of 199000 gathered in the Maracana expecting to see Brazil lift the cup in a game they did not even have to win. A draw, and therefore five points, would have been enough to see them through. After two minutes of the second half it looked as if they were home and dry. A pass from Ademir put Friaca through to open the scoring, but the dreaded over-confidence crept into the Brazilian game, a fact the Uruguayans exploited splendidly. The Brazilians could have fallen back into defence but they continued to attack. Obdulio Varela, the Uruguayan captain, and Victor Andrade, nephew of Jose Andrade of the 1930 winning team, were inspirational, as was Maspoli in goal. Uruguay equalised when Schiaffino converted a pass from Ghiggia who was having an excellent game on the wing.

Technically Brazil were still winning, but 11 minutes from the end the unimaginable happened. Running in from the touchline Ghiggia scored a lovely individual goal to seal the match for the Uruguayans. Uruguay had only entered the World Cup twice, but had won both times. Brazil had entered all four but were still without a title to their name. Nobody inside Brazil, or Montevideo for that matter, could quite believe it.

QUALIFYING TOURNAMENT

Group 1

	En	Sc	Wa	NI	Pl	W	D	L	F	A	Pts
ENGLAND	-	-	-	9-2	3	3	0	0	14	3	6
SCOTLAND	0-1	-	2-0	-	3	2	0	1	10	3	4
WALES	1-4	-	-	0-0	3	0	1	2	1	6	1
NTH. IRELAND	-	2-8	-	-	3	0	1	2	4	17	1

Scotland withdrew

Group 2

TURKEY..............7-0 ....Syria

Both Turkey and Austria withdrew

Group 3

First round

Yugoslavia..............6-0 5-2 ....Israel

Second round

Yugoslavia..............1-1 1-1..............France

Play-off in Florence

YUGOSLAVIA..............3-2..............France

Group 4

SWITZERLAND..............5-2 3-2 ....Luxembourg

Belgium withdrew

Group 5

	Sd	RI	Fi	Pl	W	D	L	F	A	Pts
SWEDEN	-	3-1	-	2	2	0	0	6	2	4
REP. IRELAND	1-3	-	3-0	4	1	1	2	6	7	3
FINLAND	-	1-1	-	2	0	1	1	1	4	1

Group 6

SPAIN..............5-1 2-2 ....Portugal

Group 7

BOLIVIA and **CHILE** qualified as Argentina withdrew

Group 8

URUGUAY and **PARAGUAY** qualified as Ecuador and Peru withdrew

Group 9

	Me	US	Cu	Pl	W	D	L	F	A	Pts
MEXICO	-	6-0	2-0	4	4	0	0	17	2	8
UNITED STATES	2-6	-	1-1	4	1	1	2	8	15	3
CUBA	0-3	2-5	-	4	0	1	3	3	11	1

Group 10

Both India and Burma withdrew

Group 11

BRAZIL qualified as hosts

Group 12

ITALY qualified as holders

FINAL TOURNAMENT, HELD IN BRAZIL 24TH JUNE - 16TH JULY 1950

FIRST ROUND

Group 1

Maracana, Rio, 24-06-1950, 81,000

Brazil	4	(Ademir Menezes 32 81, Jair R.Pinto 66, Baltazar 72)
Mexico	0	

Sete de Setembro, Belo Horizonte, 25-06-1950, 7,000

Yugoslavia	3	(Tomasevic 58 64, Ognjanov 82)
Switzerland	0	

Pacaembu, Sao Paulo, 28-06-1950, 42,000
Brazil 2 (Alfredo 2, Baltazar 31)
Switzerland 2 (Fatton 16 88)

Beira-Rio, Porto Alegre, 29-06-1950, 11,000
Yugoslavia 4 (Bobek 19, Ciakowski.Ze 22 52, Tomasevic 81)
Mexico 1 (Casarin 88)

Maracana, Rio, 1-07-1950, 142,000
Brazil 2 (Ademir Menezes 3, Zizinho 69)
Yugoslavia 0

Beira-Rio, Porto Alegre, 2-07-1950, 3,000
Switzerland 2 (Bader 12, Antenen 45)
Mexico 1 (Casarin 88)

	Br	Yu	Sz	Me	Pl	W	D	L	F	A	Pts
BRAZIL	-	2-0	2-2	4-0	3	2	1	0	8	2	5
Yugoslavia	-	-	3-0	4-1	3	2	0	1	7	3	4
Switzerland	-	-	-	2-1	3	1	1	1	4	6	3
Mexico	-	-	-	-	3	0	0	3	2	10	0

Group 2
Maracana, Rio, 25-06-1950, 29,000
England 2 (Mortensen 37, Mannion 52)
Chile 0

Brito, Curitiba, 25-06-1950, 9,000
Spain 3 (Basora 80 82, Zarra 85)
United States 1 (Souza.J 18)

Maracana, Rio, 29-06-1950, 19,000
Spain 2 (Basora 19, Zarra 35)
Chile 0

Mineiro, Belo Horizonte, 29-06-1950, 10,000
United States 1 (Gaetjens 39)
England 0

Maracana, Rio, 2-07-1950, 74,000
Spain 1 (Zarra 49)
England 0

Ilha de Retiro, Recife, 2-07-1950, 8,000
Chile 5 (Robledo.G 20, Cremaschi 32 54 89, Prieto 60)
United States 2 (Pariani 46, Souza.E 49)

	Sp	En	Ch	US	Pl	W	D	L	F	A	Pts
SPAIN	-	1-0	2-0	3-1	3	3	0	0	6	1	6
England	-	-	2-0	0-1	3	1	0	2	2	2	2
Chile	-	-	-	5-2	3	1	0	2	5	6	2
United States	-	-	-	-	3	1	0	2	4	8	2

Group 3
Pacaembu, Sao Paulo, 25-06-1950, 56,000
Sweden 3 (Jeppson 25 68, Andersson 33)
Italy 2 (Carapellese 7, Muccinelli 75)

Brito, Curitiba, 29-06-1950, 7,000
Sweden 2 (Sundqvist 23, Palmer 25)
Paraguay 2 (Lopez 35, Lopez Fretes 80)

Pacaembu, Sao Paulo, 2-07-1950, 25,000
Italy 2 (Carapellese 12, Pandolfini 62)
Paraguay 0

	Sd	It	Pa	Pl	W	D	L	F	A	Pts
SWEDEN	-	3-2	2-2	2	1	1	0	5	4	3
Italy	-	-	2-0	2	1	0	1	4	3	2
Paraguay	-	-	-	2	0	1	1	2	4	1

Group 4
Mineiro, Belo Horizonte, 2-07-1950, 5,000
Uruguay 8 (Schiaffino 10 18 56 73, Miguez 23 83, Ghiggia 45, Vidal 59)
Bolivia 0

	Ur	Bo	Pl	W	D	L	F	A	Pts
URUGUAY	-	8-0	1	1	0	0	8	0	2
Bolivia	-	-	1	0	0	1	0	8	0

FINAL ROUND

	Ur	Br	Sd	Sp	Pl	W	D	L	F	A	Pts
URUGUAY	-	2-1	3-2	2-2	3	2	1	0	7	5	5
Brazil	-	-	7-1	6-1	3	2	0	1	14	4	4
Sweden	-	-	-	3-1	3	1	0	2	6	11	2
Spain	-	-	-	-	3	0	1	2	4	11	1

Maracana, Rio de Janeiro, 3-07-1950, 138,000
Brazil 7 (Ademir Menezes 17 36 52 54, Chico 39 88, Maneca 85)
Sweden 1 (Andersson 67)

Pacaembu, Sao Paulo, 9-07-1950, 44,000
Spain 2 (Basora 38 40)
Uruguay 2 (Ghiggia 30, Varela 73)

Maracana, Rio de Janeiro, 13-07-1950, 152,000
Brazil 6 (Ademir Menezes 15 71, Jair R.Pinto 21, Chico 30 55, Zizinho 67)
Spain 1 (Igoa 57)

Pacaembu, Sao Paulo, 13-07-1950, 7,000
Uruguay 3 (Ghiggia 39, Míguez 77 85)
Sweden 2 (Palmer 5, Sundqvist 40)

Pacaembu, Sao Paulo, 16-07-1950, 11,000
Sweden 3 (Sundqvist 15, Mellberg 33, Palmer 80)
Spain 1 (Zarra 82)

Though not technically a final tie, the last game in the group, between Brazil and Uruguay, decided the outcome of the tournament and is regarded as the final.

FINAL

Maracana, Rio de Janeiro, 16-07-1950, 199,000. Referee: Reader, England
URUGUAY 2 (Schiaffino 66, Ghiggia 79)
BRAZIL 1 (Friaça 48)
Uruguay - Máspoli - Gonzáles, Tejera - Gambetta, Varela.O, Andrade.V - Ghiggia, Peréz, Míguez, Schiaffino, Morán
Brazil - Barbosa - Augusto, Juvenal - Bauer, Danilo Alvim, Bigode - Friaça, Zizinho, Ademir Menezes, Jair R.Pinto, Chico. Tr: Flavio Costa

Top scorers: Ademir Menezes, Brazil 9
Juan Schiaffino, Uruguay 5
Estanislao Basora, Spain 5
Total goals scored: 88
Average per game: 4

1954

THE 5TH WORLD CUP

9TH MAY 1953 - 4TH JULY 1954

Switzerland was chosen to host the 1954 tournament at the same time that Brazil was awarded the 1950 tournament, at the 1946 FIFA congress in Luxembourg. Given the state of Europe at the time, Switzerland, which had remained neutral during the war, was the only candidate. Zurich was also the headquarters of FIFA, and 1954 marked their 50th anniversary. More teams entered than in 1950, but representation was still low outside Europe. West Germany returned as did the Eastern European bloc with the exception of the Soviet Union and Poland, but amongst the American nations the entries were few and far between. All but Venezuela had taken part in recent South American Championships, but only four could see fit to enter the World Cup. Argentina were again noticeable by their absence, their continued persecution complex denying the world the opportunity to see some of that continent's best footballers.

In Asia, both South Korea and Japan entered, but it is strange that more did not enter given that a month before their appearance in the World Cup, the Koreans starred in the 1954 Asian Games football tournament in Manila where 11 other countries were represented as well. If so many teams could make the trip to Manila, why did more not enter the world's premier tournament?

Asia's reluctance to join in may be mysterious, but Africa's was wholly understandable. Egypt was the only independent country that had organised football. Other countries tended to be part of either the French or British football associations, given their colonial status, and therefore were not entitled to enter. Furthermore, in an extraordinary episode, FIFA refused the entries of India, Peru, Vietnam, Cuba, Iceland, Bolivia and Costa Rica because their entries were either received too late or on the wrong forms!

Belgrade saw the first match of a qualifying tournament that saw several surprises, the most notable of which was the elimination of Spain by Turkey. The two countries were all square after three matches and for the first time lots were used to decide a tie. Spain were just beginning to dominate European club football, but as far as their national side was concerned, the 1950s was not to be their most successful era. Sweden were the other surprise elimination, losing both home and away to Belgium. This meant that both the third and fourth placed sides from the 1950 World Cup would not be present in Switzerland. Perhaps the third surprise was that although Scotland came second in their qualifying group behind England, this time they eagerly sent a team.

The formula adopted at the finals reverted to that of the 1930 tournament with two differences. Instead of just the group winners qualifying for the next round, they were joined by the runners-up. With eight teams left, a knockout competition would then begin. This system would also be used for the next four World Cups. Curiously though, in Switzerland each team played only two first round matches. Each group had two seeds both of whose matches would be against the non-seeds in the group.

Not surprisingly, with each team playing only two first round games, play-offs were needed in two of the four groups. In Group 2, Hungary easily qualified for the quarter-finals having resoundingly thrashed both the South Koreans and the Germans. The Germans were accused of not playing to the spirit of the game by fielding a weakened team against the Hungarians, a match in which, crucially as it turned out, Puskas the Hungarian captain was injured. The Germans gambled that after losing to Hungary they could beat the Turks, who they had beaten in their first match, in a play-off. By doing this they would almost certainly avoid playing the fancied Brazilians, and this turned out to be the case.

Group 4 was a little less controversial, and for the second successive World Cup, Italy flopped. The Swiss surprisingly beat them 2-1 in an ill-tempered game; not for the first or last time, with luck not having gone their way, the Italians resorted to intimidatory tactics. Victory over Belgium and England's victory over Switzerland meant a play-off between the Italians and the Swiss, and once again the hosts surprised everyone. Tactically more advanced, they outplayed the Italians, and their 4-1 victory was far more convincing and deserved than their triumph of the previous week.

The other two groups were far more straightforward. Uruguay and Austria simply outplayed their opponents, Czechoslovakia and Scotland. Scotland's 7-0 defeat at the hands of the champions Uruguay was a particularly salutary experience for them, brushing away the last vestiges of their 'Ivory Tower' attitude.

In Group 1, the French never recovered from losing the opening game of the tournament to the talented Yugoslavs, whose team consisted almost entirely of the one that had reached the final of the Helsinki Olympic Games two years previously. Brazil easily defeated Mexico in their opening game, which meant that a draw between the Yugoslavs and the Brazilians when they met in the next game would be sufficient to see them both through. Surprise surprise, the result? A draw.

The quarter-finals continued the high scoring pattern of the tournament. The most extraordinary game of them all was Austria's 7-5 victory over the hosts. Losing 3-0 after 23 minutes, the Austrians must have thought it was all over, but ten minutes later they were winning 5-3! All 12 goals came in the space of an hour. The Austrian team, considered too young to enter the previous World Cup, were putting on a splendid performance in Switzerland. Yugoslavia, faced for the first time in a World Cup by their jinx team, West Germany, dominated the game but could not break down a solid German defence. The Germans scored right at the beginning and the end of a match they really did not deserve to win. The other two quarter-finals pitted Europe against South America.

In the first encounter Uruguay, playing better football than they had done in winning the 1950 tournament, beat an English side handicapped by poor goalkeeping 4-2 in an entertaining game. The following day in Berne, Hungary beat Brazil by the same score but in a game marked by some disgraceful scenes. Commonly called the 'Battle of Berne', the game was plagued by vicious tackling from both sides, three sending-offs and a dressing-room brawl afterwards. Much of the blame was pinned on the Brazilians, fearful and finally distressed at their exit from the World Cup, but the Hungarians were not blameless.

The semi-finals thankfully were much calmer affairs, though no less intriguing. Germany reached the final and no one could understand quite how. Their 6-1 victory over Austria was very convincing but totally unexpected. The Austrians, marshalled by the excellent Ernst Ocwirk, one of the finest players in Europe, fell apart at the seams and the Germans swept up the pieces. Much of the blame has been laid at the feet of their goalkeeper Zeman who had previously been dropped because of lost confidence, but the Germans played some excellent football in the second half to totally demoralise the Austrians who had no answer.

The semi-final between Uruguay and Hungary has been called the finest game of football ever played by many of those present. Indeed it saw the Hungarians at their staggering best, and in the sort of form that had seen them undefeated since May 1950. Without doubt the Hungarian team was the finest to have played in the first five editions of the World Cup. The four goals scored against the Uruguayans took their total to 27 for the tournament in only four games played. Kocsis, Czibor and Hidegkuti were in devastating form and all three contributed to the goals.

Against anyone else, the Uruguayans would surely have qualified for the final. Schiaffino in particular had an excellent game, but there was nothing he or his teammates could do about Hungary's extra-time victory. With the score at 2-2 after 90 minutes and the South Americans visibly tiring, Hungary stole a victory. Nine minutes from the end, with Andrade receiving treatment for cramp, Kocsis put the Hungarians into the lead and he sealed it five minutes later with his second. Uruguay had lost for the first time in a World Cup match. They lost for the second time three days later in the dreaded third place play-off against Austria.

There have probably never been greater favourites to win the World Cup than Hungary in 1954, and yet amazingly they failed to do so. From 1950 to 1956 Hungary lost only one match and that was the most important of them all, the World Cup Final, against the apparent no-hopers from West Germany. After eight minutes of the game, even the Germans must have wondered why they had turned up. They were trailing 2-0 and on the precipice of a thrashing, but eight minutes later they were level.

Puskas, who had insisted on playing in the final despite injury, seemed to justify his inclusion at the expense of Budai when he put Hungary into the lead after six minutes, latching on to a Kocsis shot that had rebounded off a defender. Hungary's second goal two minutes later was the result of a dreadful mix-up between the German goalkeeper Turek and his defender Kohlmeyer who had tried to pass back to him. Czibor dispossessed them both and scored from close range.

Three minutes later Morlock was on the lucky end of a deflection by Bozsik. Schafer crossed from the left wing, Bozsik went for the ball but only succeeded in pushing it into Morlock's path and the German forward had no trouble in scoring. After 16 minutes, Rahn, the hero of the day, scored from a corner after Grosics in the Hungarian goal had misjudged the flight of the ball. Germany were level. For the rest of the game, played in pouring rain, Hungary attacked the German goal. Turek was in fine form making save after save. The post saved the Germans on two occasions, as did Kohlmeyer who cleared a Toth shot off the line. Five minutes before the end, Schafer broke away down the left wing. His cross was cleared but the ball fell to Rahn, who with four defenders in front of him made for goal.

Before he could be tackled he drove the ball perfectly into the corner of the goal. Grosics even at full stretch could not reach it. Totally against the run of play the West Germans had gone into the lead. Two minutes later Puskas was sure he had scored, but controversially it was ruled out for offside.

West Germany were the new world champions. For the second successive tournament the overwhelming favourites had been beaten in the final.

QUALIFYING TOURNAMENT

Group 1

	WG	Sa	No	Pl	W	D	L	F	A	Pts
WEST GERMANY	-	3-0	5-1	4	3	1	0	12	3	7
SAAR	1-3	-	0-0	4	1	1	2	4	8	3
NORWAY	1-1	2-3	-	4	0	2	2	4	9	2

Group 2

	Be	Sd	Fi	Pl	W	D	L	F	A	Pts
BELGIUM	-	2-0	2-2	4	3	1	0	11	6	7
SWEDEN	2-3	-	4-0	4	1	1	2	9	8	3
FINLAND	2-4	3-3	-	4	0	2	2	7	13	2

Group 3

	En	Sc	NI	Wa	Pl	W	D	L	F	A	Pts
ENGLAND	-	-	3-1	-	3	3	0	0	11	4	6
SCOTLAND	2-4	-	-	3-3	3	1	1	1	8	8	3
NTH. IRELAND	-	1-3	-	-	3	1	0	2	4	7	2
WALES	1-4	-	1-2	-	3	0	1	2	5	9	1

Group 4

	Fr	RI	Lu	Pl	W	D	L	F	A	Pts
FRANCE	-	1-0	8-0	4	4	0	0	20	4	8
REP. IRELAND	3-5	-	4-0	4	2	0	2	8	6	4
LUXEMBOURG	1-6	0-1	-	4	0	0	4	1	19	0

Group 5
AUSTRIA 9-1 0-0 Portugal

Group 6
Spain 4-1 0-1 Turkey

Play-off in Rome
TURKEY 2-2 * Spain
* Turkey won on lots

Group 7
HUNGARY qualified as Poland withdrew

Group 8

	Cz	Ro	Bu	Pl	W	D	L	F	A	Pts
CZECHOSLOVAKIA	-	2-0	0-0	4	3	1	0	5	1	7
Romania	0-1	-	3-1	4	2	0	2	5	5	4
Bulgaria	1-2	1-2	-	4	0	1	3	3	7	1

Group 9
Egypt 1-2 1-5 **ITALY**

Group 10

	Yu	Gr	Is	Pl	W	D	L	F	A	Pts
YUGOSLAVIA	-	1-0	1-0	4	4	0	0	4	0	8
Greece	0-1	-	1-0	4	2	0	2	3	2	4
Israel	0-1	0-2	-	4	0	0	4	0	5	0

Group 11

	Me	US	Ha	Pl	W	D	L	F	A	Pts
MEXICO	-	3-1	8-0	4	4	0	0	19	1	8
United States	0-4	-	3-0	4	2	0	2	7	9	4
Haiti	0-4	2-3	-	4	0	0	4	2	18	0

Group 12

	Br	Pa	Ch	Pl	W	D	L	F	A	Pts
BRAZIL	-	4-1	1-0	4	4	0	0	8	1	8
Paraguay	0-1	-	4-0	4	2	0	2	8	6	4
Chile	0-2	1-3	-	4	0	0	4	1	10	0

Group 13
Japan 1-5 2-2 **SOUTH KOREA**
Both games played in Tokyo
China withdrew

Group 14
SWITZERLAND qualified as hosts

Group 15
URUGUAY qualified as holders

FINAL TOURNAMENT
HELD IN SWITZERLAND 16 JUNE - 4 JULY 1954

FIRST ROUND
Group 1
La Pontaise, Lausanne, 16-06-1954, 16,000
Yugoslavia 1 (Milutinovic 15)
France 0

Les Charmilles, Geneva, 16-06-1954, 12,000
Brazil 5 (Baltazar 23, Didi 30, Pinga 34 43, Julinho 69)
Mexico 0

La Pontaise, Lausanne, 19-06-1954, 21,000
Brazil 1 (Didi 69)
Yugoslavia 1 (Zebec 48)

Les Charmilles, Geneva, 19-06-1954, 19,000
France 3 (Vincent 19, OG 39, Kopa 88)
Mexico 2 (Naranjo 54, Balcazar 85)

	Br	Yu	Fr	Me	Pl	W	D	L	F	A	Pts
BRAZIL	-	1-1	-	5-0	2	1	1	0	6	1	3
YUGOSLAVIA	-	-	1-0	-	2	1	1	0	2	1	3
France	-	-	-	3-2	2	1	0	1	3	3	2
Mexico	-	-	-	-	2	0	0	2	2	8	0

Group 2
Hardturm, Zürich, 17-06-1954, 13,000
Hungary 9 (Puskas 12 89, Lantos 18, Kocsis 24 36 50, Czibor 59, Palotas 75 83)
South Korea 0

Wankdorf, Berne, 17-06-1954, 28,000
West Germany 4 (Schäfer 14, Klodt 52, Walter.O 60, Morlock 81)
Turkey 1 (Suat 2)

St. Jakob, Basle, 20-06-1954, 56,000
Hungary 8 (Kocsis 3 21 67 78, Puskas 17, Hidegkuti 50 54, Toth 73)
West Germany 3 (Pfaff 25, Rahn 77, Herrmann 81)

Les Charmilles, Geneva, 20-06-1954, 4,000
Turkey 7 (Suat 10 30, Lefter 24, Burhan 37 64, 70, Erol 76)
South Korea 0

Play-off. Hardturm, Zürich, 23-06-1954, 17,000
West Germany 7 (Walter.O 7, Schäfer 12 79, Morlock 30 60 77, Walter.F 62)
Turkey 2 (Mustafa 21, Lefter 82)

	Hu	Tu	WG	SK	Pl	W	D	L	F	A	Pts
HUNGARY	-	-	8-3	9-0	2	2	0	0	17	3	4
Turkey	-	-	1-4	7-0	2	1	0	1	8	4	2
WEST GERMANY	-	-	-	-	2	1	0	1	7	9	2
South Korea	-	-	-	-	2	0	0	2	0	16	0

Group 3
Hardturm, Zürich, 16-06-1954, 25,000
Austria 1 (Probst 78)
Scotland 0

Wankdorf, Berne, 16-06-1954, 20,000
Uruguay 2 (Miguez 24, Schiaffino 82)
Czechoslovakia 0

Hardturm, Zürich, 19-06-1954, 21,000
Austria 5 (Stojaspal 3 24, Probst 4 21 51)
Czechoslovakia 0

St. Jakob, Basle, 19-06-1954, 34,000
Uruguay 7 (Borges 17 47 83, Miguez 30 57, Abbadie 54 85)
Scotland 0

	Ur	Au	Cz	Sc	Pl	W	D	L	F	A	Pts
URUGUAY	-	-	2-0	7-0	2	2	0	0	9	0	4
AUSTRIA	-	-	5-0	1-0	2	2	0	0	6	0	4
Czechoslovakia	-	-	-	-	2	0	0	2	0	7	0
Scotland	-	-	-	-	2	0	0	2	0	8	0

Group 4
St. Jakob, Basle, 17-06-1954, 14,000
England 4 (Broadis 26 63, Lofthouse 36 91)
Belgium 4 (Anoul 5 71, Coppens 78, OG 94)

La Pontaise, Lausanne, 17-06-1954, 40,000
Switzerland 2 (Ballaman 17, Hügi 78)
Italy 1 (Boniperti44)

Wankdorf, Berne, 20-06-1954, 43,000
England 2 (Mullen 43, Wilshaw 69)
Switzerland 0

Cornaredo, Lugano, 20-06-1954, 24,000
Italy 4 (Pandolfini 40, Galli 48, Frignani 58, Lorenzi 78)
Belgium 1 (Anoul 81)

Play-off. St. Jakob, Basle, 23-06-1954, 29,000
Switzerland 4 (Hügi 14 85, Ballaman 48, Fatton 90)
Italy 1 (Nesti 67)

	En	It	Sz	Be	Pl	W	D	L	F	A	Pts
ENGLAND	-	-	2-0	4-4	2	1	1	0	6	4	3
ITALY	-	-	1-2	4-1	2	1	0	1	5	3	2
SWITZERLAND	-	-	-	-	2	1	0	1	2	3	2
BELGIUM	-	-	-	-	2	0	1	1	5	8	1

QUARTER-FINALS

Les Charmilles, Geneva, 27-06-1954, 17,000
West Germany 2 (OG 9, Rahn 85)
Yugoslavia 0

La Pontaise, Lausanne, 26-06-1954, 31,000
Austria 7 (Wagner 27 29 52, Körner 28 34, Ocwirk 32, Probst 76)
Switzerland 5 (Ballaman 16 41, Hügi 17 23 58)

St. Jakob, Basle, 26-06-1954, 50,000
Uruguay 4 (Borges 5, Varela 43, Schiaffino 47, Ambrois 78)
England 2 (Lofthouse 16, Finney 67)

Wankdorf, Berne, 27-06-1954, 40,000
Hungary 4 (Hidegkuti 4, Kocsis 7 89, Lantos 54)
Brazil 2 (Santos.D 18, Julinho 66)

SEMI-FINALS

St Jakob, Basle, 30-06-1954, 58,000
West Germany 6 (Schäfer 30, Morlock 49, Walter.F 54 65, Walter.O 60 89)
Austria 1 (Probst 51)

La Pontaise, Lausanne, 30-06-1954, 37,000
Hungary 4 (Czibor 13, Hidegkuti 47, Kocsis 111 116)
Uruguay 2 (Hohberg 75 86)

3RD PLACE

Hardturm, Zurich, 3-07-1954, 31,000
Austria 3 (Stojaspal 16, OG 59, Ocwirk 79)
Uruguay 1 (Hohberg 21)

FINAL

Wankdorf, Berne, 4-07-1954, 60,000. Referee: Ling, England
WEST GERMANY 3 (Morlock 11, Rahn 16 83)
HUNGARY 2 (Puskás 6, Czibor 8)

West Germany - Turek - Posipal, Liebrich, Kohlmeyer - Eckel, Mai - Rahn, Morlock, Walter.O, Walter.F, Schäfer. Tr: Herberger

Hungary - Grosics - Buzánszky, Lóránt, Lantos - Bozsik, Zakariás - Czibor, Kocsis, Hidegkuti, Puskás, Tóth. Tr: Sebes

Top scorers: Sandor Kocsis, Hungary 11
Maximilian Morlock, West Germany 6
Josef Hügi, Switzerland 6

Total goals scored: 140
Average per game: 5.4

THE 6TH WORLD CUP
30TH SEPTEMBER 1956 - 29TH JUNE 1958

Sweden was chosen to host the 1958 World Cup and so once again the Europe-South America pattern had been broken. Indeed, out of the first six tournaments only two were held in South America. The entry was the biggest yet, but still represented under half of FIFA's total membership. Forty-eight countries played in the tournament as opposed to 36 four years previously. The qualifying rounds were once more full of shocks and this time political turmoil. Both Italy and Uruguay, who between them had won four of the five competitions played, failed to qualify. Portugal and ultimately Northern Ireland put paid to Italy's hopes, whilst Paraguay and Colombia between them saw that the Uruguayans did not make the trip to Sweden. Paraguay's 5-0 victory over Uruguay in Asuncion marked one of their best international performances ever.

The Uruguayans must have rued the return of the Argentines after a 24-year absence. Had their traditional enemies not returned, their passage to the finals would have been more likely because Paraguay would have been seeded into a different group. Argentina's return was generally welcomed, especially by those who had admired their victory in the 1957 South American Championship. That side, however, was disgracefully torn to pieces by the vulture-like Italian clubs and federation as yet again they ate up the best Argentina had to offer. Sivori, Angelillo, Maschio and Grillo all left their native land, and inexcusably the first three were picked to play for Italy. The loss of Sivori hurt Argentina most and they only just managed to qualify, having lost to Bolivia in the process.

Spain were the third of the big names not to qualify. With Di Stefano, another star Argentina had lost to Europe, and half of the all-conquering Real Madrid team in the side, they came second in their group behind Scotland. It was ironic that FIFA, having been put under pressure to change the system whereby the British Home Championship was used as a qualifying group because it guaranteed at least two places for British teams, sanctioned a change that ultimately led to all four of the British nations qualifying, a feat never since repeated.

Wales were the luckiest of the quartet. They had finished second in their group and been eliminated but political troubles in the Asia-Africa group soon gave them a second chance. South Korea and Ethiopia had both tried to enter the tournament but FIFA refused on the grounds that they had not applied properly. Now trouble involving Israel provided Wales with a second bite at the cherry.

In 1954, Israel had taken part in the European qualifying rounds. This time they did not and it turned out to be a mistake the organising committee should have avoided. One by one their opponents pulled out. Turkey, Indonesia, Egypt and Sudan, all Muslim countries, refused to play them. Only a year previously Egypt and Israel had been at war with each other!

Israel had therefore qualified for the finals without playing a game. This had happened to Hungary in the previous World Cup, and to others before that, but a new rule disallowed this. Lots were drawn among the European group runners-up to meet Israel in a play-off and Wales were the lucky winners.

The dominant forces in the European qualifying rounds had been the British and Eastern European sides, both of whom had four qualifiers each. A novel system was therefore used to construct the four groups for the final tournament. Each group would have one British, one Eastern European, one Western European and one South American team as there were four of each. This slightly arbitrary system produced groups of varying strengths.

The strongest without doubt was Group 4 which contained Brazil, the Soviet Union, England and Austria, all in good form although England had suffered a cruel blow losing vital players in the Munich air crash only four months previously. The weakest group contained the hosts, Wales, Mexico and a Hungary side depleted by mass defections after the 1956 uprising.

As the tournament got underway no-one was really quite prepared for the emergence of the team who were to steal most of the limelight. Brazil, adopting a tactical awareness not previously evident in their game, had moulded together a side of outstanding ball artists. One player however caught the headlines, further promoting the mystique of the Brazilian side. Pele, at the age of 17 then the youngest player to appear in the World Cup finals, became the first of football's worldwide superstars. Helped by the fact that television was covering the event for the first time, he was soon a household name around the world.

Winning their first game easily against the Austrians with two goals from another star in the making, Altafini, who would play for Italy in the next World Cup, they drew their next against England against whom they could not score - the first match, incidentally, ever to finish 0-0 in the World Cup finals.

For their final game, against the Soviets who had drawn with England and beaten Austria, the Brazilians brought in Pele, Garrincha and Zito for the first time. Before the highest attendance of the tournament, 51,000 in Gothenburg's Ullevi Stadium, Brazil made everyone sit up and take notice of them. Didi, the main creator of a team playing to a new 4-2-4 formation, led Brazil to a convincing victory, Vava scoring both of the goals.

Brazil's revolutionary new tactics took the Europeans in the group, who were still stuck on the old 2-3-5 system or variations of it, by surprise. Though they lost to Brazil, the Soviets qualified for the second round after a play-off victory over England.

Groups 1 and 3 also needed play-offs to see who would join the group winners in the quarter-finals, and in both ties British teams qualified at the expense of Eastern European sides. Wales beat Hungary, whilst Northern Ireland defeated Czechoslovakia. Britain was therefore represented by two teams, but not the two that everyone would have predicted. Scotland had a second successive disastrous tournament, finishing bottom of their group. Argentina, whose disappointments continued, also finished bottom of their group, obviously missing the players languishing in Italy.

Yugoslavia and France, though, qualified for the quarter-finals in style. Both were playing excellent football and were tipped to at least reach the semi-finals. This France did, destroying the Irish in a convincing performance in Norrköping. Fontaine, having scored six goals in the first round, added two more to his tally. Danny Blanchflower, the Irish captain, could do nothing to hold the rampant French at bay.

Yugoslavia, facing West Germany in the quarter-finals again, lost again. As in 1954 they were the better side, but the holders refused to give up their title without a struggle. An early Rahn goal meant that the Germans sat back and protected their lead for most of the match, but they were lucky to survive a penalty appeal for a foul on Milutinovic nine minutes before the end.

The Welsh, inspired by their goalkeeper Kelsey, and without the injured John Charles, put up the bravest fight of the round, holding the Brazilian attack for most of the match but eventually losing to a Pele goal 13 minutes from time. Sweden completed the semi-final line-up. They beat a weary Soviet side in the half-full Rasunda Stadium in Stockholm. One would have expected the Swedish public to be fully behind their team, but crowds in the tournament had generally been poor with the exception of Gothenburg.

Fortunately for Sweden that was where they played their semi-final against the Germans. Had the game been in Stockholm, they might never have recovered from Schafer's 21st minute goal, but the crowd, egged on by cheerleaders, got behind the team, which sufficiently intimidated the Germans. Skogland equalised after half an hour, but the turning point came when Juskowiak was sent off after 58 minutes. Sweden began to exploit the defensive gaps this created and the crowd, sensing a victory, urged them on. They had to wait until nine minutes from time, but two quick goals saw them through.

In the other semi-final, Brazil and France, the two most entertaining teams of the tournament, served up an excellent game. An injury to Jonquet, their centre-half, did not help the French cause, but the Brazilians were playing sensational football, and a 20-minute second-half hat-trick from the magnificent Pele sealed the game for Brazil.

The final therefore matched the hosts with the favourites. It seemed certain that the Brazilians would be the first team to win the prize outside of their own continent. Sweden, however, were starting to impress. The decision to let professional footballers playing abroad represent Sweden was paying dividends. Players like Nils Liedholm, Gunnar Gren, Kurt Hamrin, Nacka Skoglund, Gunnar Nordahl and Julli Gustavsson who had made the exodus to Italy after the 1948 Olympics and 1950 World Cup and had not been selected since were invited back to play in the team, once again under the control of the Englishman George Raynor. Without them, despite the presence of new talents like Agne Simonsson, they almost certainly would not have reached the final.

Brazil in the event were much too good for them once they got there, though they did fall behind to a fourth minute Liedholm goal. Worried that the Swedish crowd would be as intimidatory as in the semi-final, the Brazilians were pleasantly surprised by the quiet, friendly atmosphere in Stockholm and they took advantage of it. Five minutes after Sweden's goal, they equalised through Vava after Garrincha had crossed well. After half an hour Brazil scored an almost identical goal involving the same players to go into half-time leading 2-1.

As he had done in the semi-final against France, Pele stole the show in the second half. After 56 minutes, collecting the ball on his chest in the penalty area, he flicked the ball over the head of a Swedish defender, rounded the man and, the ball only having bounced once, shot Brazil into a 3-1 lead. Zagalo, destined to be Brazil's manager in the 1970 tournament, scored the fourth goal, running in from the left and beating two defenders in the process, but Pele was to have the last word. Zagalo, having provided the pass for Pele's first goal, did the same for his second, but not until he had first received the ball from the 17-year old courtesy of an arrogant backheel. This time Pele looped it into the net with his head. Sweden had put together a final rally before Pele scored during which Simonsson had reduced the deficit, but it was too little too late.

Brazil had won playing football to a standard rarely witnessed before. They won the admiration of all the Swedes in the stadium and as a gesture paraded a huge Swedish flag around the stadium at the end. They and France, who the previous day had beaten West Germany 6-3 to finish third, had both lit up what was by and large a lacklustre tournament played before relatively small crowds.

QUALIFYING TOURNAMENT

EUROPE

Group 1

	En	RI	De	Pl	W	D	L	F	A	Pts
ENGLAND	-	5-1	5-2	4	3	1	0	15	5	7
Rep. Ireland	1-1	-	2-1	4	2	1	1	6	7	5
Denmark	1-4	0-2	-	4	0	0	4	4	13	0

Group 2

	Fr	Be	Ic	Pl	W	D	L	F	A	Pts
FRANCE	-	6-3	8-0	4	3	1	0	19	4	7
Belgium	0-0	-	8-3	4	2	1	1	16	11	5
Iceland	1-5	2-5	-	4	0	0	4	6	26	0

Group 3

	Hu	Bu	No	Pl	W	D	L	F	A	Pts
HUNGARY	-	4-1	5-0	4	3	0	1	12	4	6
Bulgaria	1-2	-	7-0	4	2	0	2	11	7	4
Norway	2-1	1-2	-	4	1	0	3	3	15	2

Group 4

	Cz	Wa	EG	Pl	W	D	L	F	A	Pts
CZECHOSLOVAKIA	-	2-0	3-1	4	3	0	1	9	3	6
Wales	1-0	-	4-1	4	2	0	2	6	5	4
East Germany	1-4	2-1	-	4	1	0	3	5	12	2

Wales qualified to meet Israel in play-off

Group 5

	Au	Ho	Lu	Pl	W	D	L	F	A	Pts
AUSTRIA	-	3-2	7-0	4	3	1	0	14	3	7
Holland	1-1	-	4-1	4	2	1	1	12	7	5
Luxembourg	0-3	2-5	-	4	0	0	4	3	19	0

Group 6

	SU	Pd	Fi	Pl	W	D	L	F	A	Pts
SOVIET UNION	-	3-0	2-1	4	3	0	1	16	3	6
Poland	2-1	-	4-0	4	3	0	1	9	5	6
Finland	0-10	1-3	-	4	0	0	4	2	19	0

Play-off in Leipzig
Soviet Union .... 2-0 .... Poland

Group 7

	Yu	Ro	Gr	Pl	W	D	L	F	A	Pts
YUGOSLAVIA	-	2-0	4-1	4	2	2	0	7	2	6
Romania	1-1	-	3-0	4	2	1	1	6	4	5
Greece	0-0	1-2	-	4	0	1	3	2	9	1

Group 8

	NI	It	Pt	Pl	W	D	L	F	A	Pts
NTH. IRELAND	-	2-1	3-0	4	2	1	1	6	3	5
Italy	1-0	-	3-0	4	2	0	2	5	5	4
Portugal	1-1	3-0	-	4	1	1	2	4	7	3

Group 9

	Sc	Sp	Sz	Pl	W	D	L	F	A	Pts
SCOTLAND	-	4-2	3-2	4	3	0	1	10	9	6
Spain	4-1	-	2-2	4	2	1	1	12	8	5
Switzerland	1-2	1-4	-	4	0	1	3	6	11	1

SOUTH AMERICA

Group 1

Peru .... 1-1 0-1 .... **BRAZIL**

Group 2

	Ar	Bo	Ch	Pl	W	D	L	F	A	Pts
ARGENTINA	-	4-0	4-0	4	3	0	1	10	2	6
Bolivia	2-0	-	3-0	4	2	0	2	6	6	4
Chile	0-2	2-1	-	4	1	0	3	2	10	2

Group 3

	Pa	Ur	Co	Pl	W	D	L	F	A	Pts
PARAGUAY	-	5-0	3-0	4	3	0	1	11	4	6
Uruguay	2-0	-	1-0	4	2	1	1	4	6	5
Colombia	2-3	1-1	-	4	0	1	3	3	8	1

CENTRAL AND NORTH AMERICA

FIRST ROUND

Group 1

	CR	Cu	Gu	Pl	W	D	L	F	A	Pts
Costa Rica	-	4-0	3-1	4	4	0	0	15	4	8
Curacao	1-2	-	-	4	1	0	2	4	7	2
Guatemala	2-6	1-3	-	4	0	0	3	4	12	0

Group 2

	Me	Ca	US	Pl	W	D	L	F	A	Pts
Mexico	-	2-0	6-0	4	4	0	0	18	2	8
Canada	0-3	-	5-1	4	2	0	2	8	8	4
United States	2-7	2-3	-	4	0	0	4	5	21	0

SECOND ROUND

MEXICO .... 2-0 1-1 .... Costa Rica

ASIA-AFRICA

FIRST ROUND

Group 1

Indonesia .... 2-0 3-4 .... Taiwan

Play-off in Rangoon

Indonesia .... * 0-0 .... Taiwan

* Indonesia qualified for the next round on goal average

Group 2

Israel qualified for the next round as Turkey withdrew

Group 3

Egypt qualified for the next round as Cyprus withdrew

Group 4

Sudan .... 1-0 1-1 .... Syria

SECOND ROUND

Sudan and **Israel** qualified for the next round as Indonesia and Egypt withdrew

THIRD ROUND

Israel qualified as Sudan withdrew. However, a FIFA ruling that no team could qualify without playing a match meant that Israel had to meet Wales in a play-off

Israel .... 0-2 0-2 .... **WALES**

SWEDEN qualified as hosts

WEST GERMANY qualified as holders

FINAL TOURNAMENT, HELD IN SWEDEN 8TH - 29TH JUNE 1958

FIRST ROUND

Group 1

Örjans Vall, Halmstad, 8-06-1958, 10,000
Northern Ireland 1 (Cush 16)
Czechoslovakia 0

Malmö Stadium, Malmö, 8-06-1958, 31,000
West Germany 3 (Rahn 32 79, Seeler 40)
Argentina 1 (Corbatta 2)

Örjans Vall, Halmstad, 11-06-1958, 14,000
Argentina 3 (Corbatta 38, Menendez 55, Avio 59)
Northern Ireland 1 (McParland 3)

Olympia, Helsingborg, 11-06-1958, 25,000
Czechoslovakia 2 (Dvorak 24, Zikan 43)
West Germany 2 (Schäfer 59, Rahn 70)

Malmö Stadium, Malmö, 15-06-1958, 21,000
Northern Ireland 2 (McParland 17 58)
West Germany 2 (Rahn 20, Seeler 79)

Olympia, Helsingborg, 15-06-1958, 16,000
Czechoslovakia 6 (Dvorak 8, Zikan 17 40, Feureisl 69, Hovorka 82 89)
Argentina 1 (Corbatta 65)

Play-off. Malmö Stadium, Malmö, 17-06-1958, 6,000
Northern Ireland 2 (McParland 44 54)
Czechoslovakia 1 (Zikan 19)

	WG	Cz	NI	Ar	Pl	W	D	L	F	A	Pts
WEST GERMANY	-	2-2	2-2	3-1	3	1	2	0	7	5	4
Czechoslovakia	-	-	0-1	6-1	3	1	1	1	8	4	3
NTH. IRELAND	-	-	-	1-3	3	1	1	1	4	5	3
Argentina	-	-	-	-	3	1	0	2	5	10	2

Group 2

Arosvallen, Västerås, 8-06-1958, 9,000
Scotland 1 (Murray 49)
Yugoslavia 1 (Petakovic 6)

Idrottspark, Norrköping, 8-06-1958, 16,000
France 7 (Fontaine 24 30 67, Piantoni 52, Wisnieski 61, Kopa 68, Vincent 83)
Paraguay 3 (Amarilla 20 44, Romero 50)

Idrottspark, Norrköping, 11-06-1958, 11,000
Paraguay 3 (Aguero 4, Re 45, Parodi 71)
Scotland 2 (Mudie 24, Collins 72)

Arosvallen, Västerås, 11-06-1958, 12,000
Yugoslavia 3 (Petakovic 16, Veselinovic 61 88)
France 2 (Fontaine 4 85)

Eyravallen, Örebro, 15-06-1958, 13,000
France 2 (Kopa 21, Fontaine 45)
Scotland 1 (Baird 58)

Tunavallen, Eskilstuna, 15-06-1958, 13,000
Paraguay 3 (Parodi 20, Aguero 52, Romero 80)
Yugoslavia 3 (Ognjanovic 12, Veselinovic 28, Rajkov 73)

	Fr	Yu	Pa	Sc	Pl	W	D	L	F	A	Pts
FRANCE	-	2-3	7-3	2-1	3	2	0	1	11	7	4
YUGOSLAVIA	-	-	3-3	1-1	3	1	2	0	7	6	4
Paraguay	-	-	-	3-2	3	1	1	1	9	12	3
Scotland	-	-	-	-	3	0	1	2	4	6	1

Group 3

Råsunda, Stockholm, 8-06-1958, 34,000
Sweden 3 (Simonsson 17 64, Liedholm 67)
Mexico 0

Jernvallen, Sandviken, 8-06-1958 15,000
Hungary 1 (Bozsik 5)
Wales 1 (Charles 27)

Råsunda, Stockholm, 11-06-1958, 15,000
Wales 1 (Allchurch 32)
Mexico 1 (Belmonte 89)

Råsunda, Stockholm, 12-06-1958, 38,000
Sweden 2 (Hamrin 34 55)
Hungary 1 (Tichy 77)

Råsunda, Stockholm, 15-06-1958, 29,000
Sweden 0
Wales 0

Jernvallen, Sandviken, 15-06-1958, 13,000
Hungary 4 (Tichy 19 46, Sandor 54, OG 69)
Mexico 0

Play-off. Råsunda, Stockholm, 17-06-1958, 2,000
Wales 2 (Allchurch 55, Medwin 76)
Hungary 1 (Tichy 33)

	Sd	Hu	Wa	Me	Pl	W	D	L	F	A	Pts
SWEDEN	-	2-1	0-0	3-0	3	2	1	0	5	1	5
HUNGARY	-	-	1-1	4-0	3	1	1	1	6	3	3
WALES	-	-	-	1-1	3	0	3	0	2	2	3
MEXICO	-	-	-	-	3	0	1	2	1	8	1

Group 4
Rimnersvallen, Uddevalla, 8-06-1958, 21,000
Brazil 3 (Altafini 38 89, Nilton Santos 49)
Austria 0

Nya Ullevi, Gothenburg, 8-06-1958, 49,000
England 2 (Kevan 66, Finney 85)
Soviet Union 2 (Simonian 13, Ivanov.A 55)

Ryavallen, Borås, 11-06-1958, 21,000
Soviet Union 2 (Ilyin 15, Ivanov.V 62)
Austria 0

Nya Ullevi, Gothenburg, 11-06-1958, 40,000
Brazil 0
England 0

Ryavallen, Borås, 15-06-1958, 16,000
England 2 (Haynes 56, Kevan 78)
Austria 2 (Koller 16, Körner 70)

Nya Ullevi, Gothenburg, 15-06-1958, 50,000
Brazil 2 (Vavá 35 78)
Soviet Union 0

Play-off. Nya Ullevi, Gothenburg, 17-06-1958, 23,000
Soviet Union 1 (Ilyin 78)
England 0

	Br	SU	En	Au	Pl	W	D	L	F	A	Pts
BRAZIL	-	2-0	0-0	3-0	3	2	1	0	5	0	5
SOVIET UNION	-	-	2-2	2-0	3	1	1	1	4	4	3
ENGLAND	-	-	-	2-2	3	0	3	0	4	4	3
AUSTRIA	-	-	-	-	3	0	1	2	2	7	1

QUARTER-FINALS
Nya Ullevi, Gothenburg, 19-06-1958, 25,000
Brazil 1 (Pelé 73)
Wales 0

Idrottspark, Norrköping, 19-06-1958, 11,000
France 4 (Wisnieski 44, Fontaine 56 64, Piantoni 68)
Nth. Ireland 0

Malmö Stadium, Malmö, 19-06-1958, 20,000
West Germany 1 (Rahn 12)
Yugoslavia 0

Råsunda, Stockholm, 19-06-1958, 31,000
Sweden 2 (Hamrin 49, Simonsson 88)
Soviet Union 0

SEMI-FINALS
Råsunda, Stockholm, 24-06-1958, 27,000
Brazil 5 (Vavá 2, Didi 38, Pelé 53 64 76)
France 2 (Fontaine 8, Piantoni 83)

Nya Ullevi, Gothenburg, 24-06-1958, 49,000
Sweden 3 (Skogland 30, Gren 81, Hamrin 88)
West Germany 1 (Schäfer 21)

3RD PLACE
Nya Ullevi, Gothenburg, 28-06-1958, 32,000
France 6 (Fontaine 16 36 78 89, Kopa 27, Douis 50)
West Germany 3 (Cieslarczyk 18, Rahn 52, Schäfer 83)

FINAL
Råsunda, Stockholm, 29-06-1958, 49,000. Referee: Guigue, France
BRAZIL 5 (Vavá 10 32, Pelé 56 89, Zagalo 68)
SWEDEN 2 (Liedholm 4, Simonsson 80)
Brazil - Gilmar - Djalma Santos, Bellini, Orlando Peçanha, Nilton Santos - Zito, Didi - Garrincha, Vavá, Pelé, Zagalo. Tr: Feola
Sweden - Svensson - Bergmark, Gustavsson, Axbom - Börjesson, Parling - Hamrin, Gren.G, Simonsson, Liedholm, Skoglund. Tr: Raynor

Top scorers: Juste Fontaine, France 13
Pelé, Brazil 6
Helmut Rahn, West Germany 6
Total goals scored: 126
Average per game: 3.6

1962

THE 7TH WORLD CUP
21ST AUGUST 1960 - 17TH JUNE 1962

Chile was awarded the 1962 World Cup at the 1956 FIFA congress in Lisbon in preference to both Argentina and Germany. It was a surprising choice. Both Uruguay and Brazil had hosted the tournament, and as the other member of the continent's 'big three', Argentina was confident of success. It had the stadia, Chile did not; it had an eager football public, Chile did not; and most important of all, it had a proud footballing heritage and Chile did not.

Not even a serious earthquake in May 1960, during which the damage and loss of life was widespread, could put the Chileans off their task. Carlos Dittborn, the president of the Chilean Football Federation, claimed, 'We have nothing, that is why we must have the World Cup,' when FIFA thought it might be a good idea to relocate the tournament, a phrase that has been immortalised in World Cup folklore. Unfortunately for Dittborn, he died a month before the tournament he had done so much to organise got off the ground. In his memory they named the stadium in Arica after him.

For the first time a non-European city saw the opening qualifying game, Costa Rica beating their traditional rivals Guatemala in San José, but again Mexico qualified from the Central American group. In one of a series of intercontinental play-offs, the Mexicans had to beat Paraguay to qualify for Chile and this they did.

The idea of playing qualification matches on an intercontinental basis has long been argued as being fairer and in the 1990s where standards have equalled out to a great degree this is probably true. In the 1962 tournament however, it left Africa and Asia without a representative. Spain defeated Morocco, Italy beat Israel and Yugoslavia knocked out the South Koreans. Yet again the World Cup finals did not have a representative from two continents that contained the majority of the world's population. With Chile as hosts and Brazil as holders only six qualifying games were needed in South America to whittle six countries down to three. Argentina and Uruguay had little trouble in disposing of Ecuador and Bolivia respectively, whilst Colombia, thanks to a 1-0 win in Bogota, knocked out Peru to qualify for the first time.

The European section did see a couple of shocks as the teams who had finished second and third in 1958 both failed to qualify. Sweden were knocked out after a play-off with Switzerland, despite having a better goal difference, whilst France lost to the fast emerging Bulgarians who forced a play-off after scoring a last minute goal in their last group match against the French. Otherwise those who were expected to qualify did. Britain was represented only by England this time, Scotland losing in a play-off with Czechoslovakia and Wales to Spain, whilst Northern Ireland finished second in their group behind West Germany. Of the eight quarter-finalists in Sweden, four failed to qualify for Chile. The only change in the format of the final tournament was the abolition of play-offs for teams that finished equal on points in second and third places. Instead goal difference would be used.

Group 1 was the most entertaining, played in far away Arica. The Soviet Union, the European champions, topped the standings followed by Yugoslavia, the team they had beaten to win the European title two years previously. Both were scoring freely, though the Soviets did have a scare in their second match against Colombia. Racing into a 3-0 lead after 11 minutes and leading 4-1 just into the second half, they then conceded three goals in the last 25 minutes and were lucky not to lose the game.

Group 2 was interesting, not for entertaining games but for the bad atmosphere amongst the teams, which sparked off the 'Battle of Santiago'. At the centre of the controversy were the Italians. Due to the constant poaching of players from the South American continent, the Italians were not the most popular team in Chile. Scouts from Italian clubs constantly plagued the training camps of other teams, while most controversially two Italian journalists covering the tournament sent home articles that were scathing about life in Chile.

Italy had begun the tournament against West Germany with a stale 0-0 draw before a large hostile crowd in Santiago. Three of their team were South Americans. Altafini had played for Brazil in 1958, whilst Sivori and Maschio were members of the famous 1957 Argentine side which had won the South American Championship.

In their next game the Italians faced the hosts before 66,000 extremely hostile fans in the Estadio Nacional. The game dissolved into absolute chaos which even the experienced referee, Ken Aston, could do little to control. He sent off the Italian Ferrini after eight minutes for retaliation but for 10 minutes Ferrini refused to leave the field, until FIFA officials and the police removed him. This was just the start of the trouble. A violent tackle by Maschio on Sanchez resulted in the Chilean forward breaking Maschio's nose with a punch seen on television around the world, but amazingly he stayed on the pitch as Aston had not seen it.

The tackling and histrionics were so bad that at one point Aston nearly abandoned the game. David, the Italian full back, was sent off in the second half for a head tackle on Sanchez, but it was not until 15 minutes from time that Chile could exploit their numerical advantage. Much to the crowd's delight Ramirez and Toro both scored to give the hosts a victory which ensured their qualification for the next round. Despite victory over Switzerland in their last game, the Battle of Santiago proved decisive for the Italians and they left for home. The World Cup was not proving a happy hunting ground for them in the post-war period.

Perhaps the most picturesque stadium the World Cup has ever seen is the Sausalito Stadium in Viña del Mar. Surrounded by woods on two sides and by the Pacific Ocean on the other two, the stadium played host to the group which contained both the eventual finalists as well as Spain and Mexico. Spain, like Italy, contained non-Spaniards in the team. Alfredo di Stefano finally had the chance to appear on the world stage that his talents so richly deserved. Alongside him was Puskas, the captain of the Hungary team eight years before. In the event an injury kept Di Stefano out of all three of Spain's games. Despite having a team of household names due to Real Madrid's exploits in the European Cup, Spain failed to perform and finished bottom of the group.

Brazil, with an almost unchanged team from Sweden, ran out easy winners despite losing Pele in their second match, against Czechoslovakia, with a torn muscle. The star of 1958 missed the rest of the tournament, though as Brazil proved, they had many replacements up their sleeve. Attendances were low in all of the groups with the exception of Group 2 in Santiago. The lowest of them all occurred in Rancagua at the stadium of the Braden Copper Company, where the average crowd was 7,000, as opposed to 8,000 in Arica and 13,000 at Viña del Mar. Hungary, regaining some of their pre-1956 strength, easily won the group.

The tie that decided the other qualifier from the group was England's 3-1 victory over Argentina. The Eastern Europeans were having a particularly fine tournament.

Four of the quarter-finalists hailed from behind the Iron Curtain, whilst only two came from each of Western Europe and South America. Both of the Western European sides lost. For the third tournament running Yugoslavia faced West Germany in the quarter-finals, only on this occasion they won. It was a close run thing but a Radakovic goal three minutes from time saw the Slavs through, much to their relief.

As this match was progressing the large crowd in the Estadio Nacional were all paying more attention via radios to Chile's match against the Soviet Union being played at the same time in Arica. Lev Yashin, the Soviet goalkeeper, played another bad game to follow that against Colombia in the first round. He was blamed for both of the goals that Chile scored, both of which were long range shots from Sanchez and Rojas respectively. Though it may have appeared a shock result, Reira, the trainer of Chile, had prepared the side for five years for the tournament, and although they had been inconsistent in their build-up, victories over West Germany and Hungary had hinted at the success that lay ahead in the finals.

Had Yashin played as well for the Soviets as Schroiff did for Czechoslovakia, the Soviets might well have progressed to the semi-finals, for Schroiff, generally regarded as an able but not brilliant goalkeeper, kept Hungary at bay for the whole match, which they should easily have won. Having taken an early lead, the Czechs were under pressure for the rest of the game. Hungary seemed to have equalised after 78 minutes, but Tichy's goal was surprisingly disallowed for offside.

The fourth quarter-final, between Brazil and England at Viña del Mar, was lit up by a dazzling display from Garrincha, no longer playing in the shadow of Pele. He was responsible for all three of Brazil's goals, scoring the first and third and creating the second. Hitchens equalised Garrincha's first-half goal to send the teams in level at half-time, but in the second half England were no match for the Brazilians who were beginning to sense that the World Cup would be theirs again, and that this game would represent their toughest test.

Brazil's game in the semi-final, in contrast to their quarter-final, was a one-sided affair. The hosts were no match for the champions, despite the largest crowd of the tournament willing them on. After half an hour Brazil were 2-0 up, both goals coming from Garrincha, and although Toro pulled a goal back just before half-time, Vava put the issue beyond doubt just after the break. A Sanchez penalty on the hour gave the Chilean fans a brief moment of hope but Vava soon ended that with his second goal. Brazil had Garrincha sent off near the end for retaliation and for a while it seemed as though he might miss the final.

The other semi-final was inexplicably played before the second lowest crowd of the tournament. Only 5890 people turned out in Viña del Mar to watch Czechoslovakia double the amount of goals they had scored in the tournament. Again their defence was solid and Schroiff inspired. After a goalless first half, Kadraba put the Czechs into the lead just after the restart. When Jerkovic levelled the scores for Yugoslavia they seemed set to win, but Schroiff kept them at bay as he had done with the Hungarians in the quarter-finals. Two goals in the last ten minutes by Scherer, the second a penalty, took the Yugoslavs by surprise. Having scored with ease in the first round group, the Yugoslavs' old disease of dominating a match but never finishing the opposition off returned.

Undoubtedly Czechoslovakia were surprising finalists. Unlike their counterparts who had lost the 1934 final to Italy, they were not the most entertaining team in the tournament. Instead their strength was based on defence. Novak, Pluskal, Popluhar, Pospichal, Scherer and Masopust were all fine players but they were not a great attacking side. Brazil were, and with Garrincha reprieved after his sending-off, no-one gave the Czechs much hope. As they had done in Stockholm, Brazil conceded the first goal of the game: Masopust scored after 15 minutes, receiving a lovely defence-splitting pass from Scherer; but the Czech lead lasted only two minutes.

The hero of the previous two rounds, Schroiff, turned villain in the final. Amarildo scored Brazil's first goal from the edge of the penalty area and at the most acute of angles. Schroiff, expecting a cross, did not react fast enough. He was also out of position for Brazil's second goal which came midway through the second half. Up until then the Czechs had just about matched the Brazilians, but Zito's goal spelled their downfall. Amarildo was again involved. It was his lobbed cross from inside the penalty area which gave Zito a free header to score. The goal for which the Czechoslovakian keeper had to take most blame, however, was the third. Djalma Santos, out on the right wing, crossed the ball hopefully and high into the penalty area. Schroiff was there to collect it but he let it fall out of his hands straight to the feet of Vava who touched it into an empty net, and Brazil had won.

Four years previously Bellini had collected the trophy as captain. This time it was Mauro who had the honour.

QUALIFYING TOURNAMENT

EUROPE

Group 1

	Sz	Sd	Be	Pl	W	D	L	F	A	Pts
SWITZERLAND	-	3-2	2-1	4	3	0	1	9	9	6
SWEDEN	4-0	-	2-0	4	3	0	1	10	3	6
BELGIUM	2-4	0-2	-	4	0	0	4	3	10	0

Play-off in Berlin

Switzerland .... 2-1 .... Sweden

Group 2

	Bu	Fr	Fi	Pl	W	D	L	F	A	Pts
BULGARIA	-	1-0	3-1	4	3	0	1	6	4	6
FRANCE	3-0	-	5-1	4	3	0	1	10	3	6
FINLAND	0-2	1-2	-	4	0	0	4	3	12	0

Play-off in Milan
Bulgaria .... 1-0 .... France

Group 3

	WG	NI	Gr	Pl	W	D	L	F	A	Pts
WEST GERMANY	-	2-1	2-1	4	4	0	0	11	5	8
Nth. Ireland	3-4	-	2-0	4	1	0	3	7	8	2
Greece	0-3	2-1	-	4	1	0	3	3	8	2

Group 4

	Hu	Ho	EG	Pl	W	D	L	F	A	Pts
HUNGARY	-	3-3	2-0	4	3	1	0	11	5	7
Holland	0-3	-	-	3	0	2	1	4	7	2
East Germany	2-3	1-1	-	3	0	1	2	3	6	2

Group 5

	SU	Tu	No	Pl	W	D	L	F	A	Pts
SOVIET UNION	-	1-0	5-2	4	4	0	0	11	3	8
Turkey	1-2	-	2-1	4	2	0	2	4	4	4
Norway	0-3	0-1	-	4	0	0	4	3	11	0

Group 6

	En	Pt	Lu	Pl	W	D	L	F	A	Pts
ENGLAND	-	2-0	4-1	4	3	1	0	16	2	7
Portugal	1-1	-	6-0	4	1	1	2	9	7	3
Luxembourg	0-9	4-2	-	4	1	0	3	5	21	2

Group 7
FIRST ROUND
Cyprus .... 1-1 1-6 .... Israel

SECOND ROUND
Israel .... 1-0 3-2 .... Ethiopia

THIRD ROUND
Israel received a bye as Romania withdrew

FOURTH ROUND
Israel .... 2-4 0-6 .... **ITALY**

Group 8

	Cz	Sc	RI	Pl	W	D	L	F	A	Pts
CZECHOSLOVAKIA	-	4-0	7-1	4	3	0	1	16	5	6
Scotland	3-2	-	4-1	4	3	0	1	10	7	6
Rep. Ireland	1-3	0-3	-	4	0	0	4	3	17	0

Play-off in Brussels
Czechoslovakia .... 4-2 .... Scotland

Group 9
FIRST ROUND
Morocco .... 2-1 1-2 .... Tunisia
Ghana .... 4-1 2-2 .... Nigeria
Play-off in Palermo
Morocco .... 1-1 * .... Tunisia
* Morocco qualified on lots

SECOND ROUND
Ghana .... 0-0 0-1 .... Morocco
Wales .... 1-2 1-1 .... Spain

THIRD ROUND
Morocco .... 0-1 2-3 .... **SPAIN**

Group 10
FIRST ROUND
South Korea .... 2-1 2-0 .... Japan
Yugoslavia .... 2-1 1-1 .... Poland

SECOND ROUND
YUGOSLAVIA .... 5-1 3-1 .... South Korea

SOUTH AMERICA

Group 1
Ecuador .... 3-6 0-5 .... **ARGENTINA**

Group 2
Bolivia .... 1-1 1-2 .... **URUGUAY**

Group 3
COLOMBIA .... 1-0 1-1 .... Peru

CENTRAL AND NORTH AMERICA

FIRST ROUND
Group 1
United States .... 3-3 0-3 .... Mexico

Group 2

	CR	Ho	Gu	Pl	W	D	L	F	A	Pts
Costa Rica	-	5-0	3-2	4	2	1	1	13	8	5
Honduras	2-1	-	1-1	3	1	1	1	3	7	5
Guatemala	4-4*	-		3	0	2	1	7	8	2

* Match abandoned with Honduras leading 2-0. Honduras awarded both Points

Play-off in Guatemala City
Costa Rica .... 1-0 .... Honduras

Group 3
Surinam .... 1-2 0-0 .... Netherlands Antilles

SECOND ROUND

	Me	CR	NA	Pl	W	D	L	F	A	Pts
Mexico	-	4-1	7-0	4	2	1	1	11	2	5
Costa Rica	1-0	-	6-0	4	2	0	2	8	6	4
Neth. Antilles	0-0	2-0	-	4	1	1	2	2	12	3

THIRD ROUND
MEXICO .... 1-0 0-0 .... Paraguay

CHILE qualified as hosts

BRAZIL qualified as holders

FINAL TOURNAMENT,
HELD IN CHILE 30TH MAY - 17TH JUNE 1962

FIRST ROUND
Group 1

Carlos Dittborn, Arica, 30-05-1962, 7,000
Uruguay 2 (Sacia 57, Cubilla 73)
Colombia 1 (Zuluaga 19)

Carlos Dittborn, Arica, 31-05-1962, 9,000
Soviet Union 2 (Ivanov.V 53, Ponedelnik 85)
Yugoslavia 0

Carlos Dittborn, Arica, 2-06-1962, 8,000
Yugoslavia 3 (Skoblar 27, Galic 38, Jerkovic 47)
Uruguay 1 (Cabrera 18)

Carlos Dittborn, Arica, 3-06-1962, 8,000
Soviet Union 4 (Ivanov.V 9 14, Chislenko 11, Ponedelnik 51)
Colombia 4 (Aceros 20, Coll 67, Rada 71, Klinger 77)

Carlos Dittborn, Arica, 6-06-1962, 9,000
Soviet Union 2 (Mamikin 37, Ivanov.V 89)
Uruguay 1 (Sacia 53)

Carlos Dittborn, Arica, 7-06-1962, 7,000
Yugoslavia 5 (Galic 20 52, Jerkovic 25 87, Melic 73)
Colombia 0

	SU	Yu	Ur	Co	Pl	W	D	L	F	A	Pts
SOVIET UNION	-	2-0	2-1	4-4	3	2	1	0	8	5	5
YUGOSLAVIA	-	-	3-1	5-0	3	2	0	1	8	3	4
URUGUAY	-	-	-	2-1	3	1	0	2	4	6	2
COLOMBIA	-	-	-	-	3	0	1	2	5	11	1

Group 2
Estadio Nacional, Santiago, 30-05-1962, 65,000
Chile 3 (Sanchez.L 43 56, Ramirez 51)
Switzerland 1 (Wuthrich 8)

Estadio Nacional, Santiago, 31-05-1962, 65,000
West Germany 0
Italy 0

Estadio Nacional, Santiago, 2-06-1962, 66,000
Chile 2 (Ramirez 74, Toro 87)
Italy 0

Estadio Nacional, Santiago, 3-06-1962, 64,000
West Germany 2 (Brülls 44, Seeler 61)
Switzerland 1 (Antenen 75)

Estadio Nacional, Santiago, 6-06-1962, 67,000
West Germany 2 (Szymaniak 22, Seeler 82)
Chile 0

Estadio Nacional, Santiago, 7-06-1962, 59,000
Italy 3 (Mora 3, Bulgarelli 65 68)
Switzerland 0

	WG	Ch	It	Sz	Pl	W	D	L	F	A	Pts
WEST GERMANY	-	2-0	0-0	2-1	3	2	1	0	4	1	5
CHILE	-	-	2-0	3-1	3	2	0	1	5	3	4
ITALY	-	-	-	3-0	3	1	1	1	3	2	3
SWITZERLAND	-	-	-	-	3	0	0	3	2	8	0

Group 3
Sausalito, Viña del Mar, 30-05-1962, 10,000
Brazil 2 (Zagalo 56, Pelé 72)
Mexico 0

Sausalito, Viña del Mar, 31-05-1962, 12,000
Czechoslovakia 1 (Stibranyi 78)
Spain 0

Sausalito, Viña del Mar, 2-06-1962, 14,000
Brazil 0
Czechoslovakia 0

Sausalito, Viña del Mar, 3-06-1962, 11,000
Spain 1 (Peiro 88)
Mexico 0

Sausalito, Viña del Mar, 6-06-1962, 18,000
Brazil 2 (Amarildo 71 89)
Spain 1 (Adelardo 34)

Sausalito, Viña del Mar, 7-06-1962, 10,000
Mexico 3 (Diaz 10, Del Aguila 29, Hernandez.H 89)
Czechoslovakia 1 (Masek 1)

	Br	Cz	Me	Sp	Pl	W	D	L	F	A	Pts
BRAZIL	-	0-0	2-0	2-1	3	2	1	0	4	1	5
CZECHOSLOVAKIA	-	-	1-3	1-0	3	1	1	1	2	3	3
MEXICO	-	-	-	0-1	3	1	0	2	3	4	2
SPAIN	-	-	-	-	3	1	0	2	2	3	2

Group 4
Braden, Rancagua, 30-05-1962, 7,000
Argentina 1 (Facundo 4)
Bulgaria 0

Braden, Rancagua, 31-05-1962, 7,000
Hungary 2 (Tichy 15, Albert 75)
England 1 (Flowers 60)

Braden, Rancagua, 2-06-1962, 9,000
England 3 (Flowers 14, Charlton.R 42, Greaves 57)
Argentina 1 (Sanfilippo 83)

Braden, Rancagua, 3-06-1962, 7,000
Hungary 6 (Albert 1 6 53, Tichy 8 70, Solymosi 12)
Bulgaria 1 (Sokolov 64)

Braden, Rancagua, 6-06-1962, 7,000
Hungary 0
Argentina 0

Braden, Rancagua, 7-06-1962, 5,000
England 0
Bulgaria 0

	Hu	En	Ar	Bu	Pl	W	D	L	F	A	Pts
HUNGARY	-	2-1	0-0	6-1	3	2	1	0	8	2	5
ENGLAND	-	-	3-1	0-0	3	1	1	1	4	3	3
ARGENTINA	-	-	-	1-0	3	1	1	1	2	3	3
BULGARIA	-	-	-	-	3	0	1	2	1	7	1

QUARTER-FINALS
Sausalito, Viña del Mar, 10-06-1962, 17,000
Brazil 3 (Garrincha 31 59, Vavá 53)
England 1 (Hitchens 38)

Carlos Dittborn, Arica, 10-06-1962, 17,000
Chile 2 (Sánchez 11, Rojas 27)
Soviet Union 1 (Chislenko 26)

Estadio Nacional, Santiago, 10-06-1962, 63,000
Yugoslavia 1 (Radakovic 87)
West Germany 0

Braden, Rancagua, 10-06-1962, 11,000
Czechoslovakia 1 (Scherer 12)
Hungary 0

SEMI-FINALS
Estadio Nacional, Santiago, 13-06-1962, 76,000
Brazil 4 (Garrincha 9 31, Vavá 49 77)
Chile 2 (Toro 41, Sánchez 61)

Sausalito, Viña del Mar, 13-06-1962, 5,000
Czechoslovakia 3 (Kadraba 49, Scherer 80 86)
Yugoslavia 1 (Jerkovic 69)

3RD PLACE
Estadio Nacional, Santiago, 16-06-1962, 66,000
Chile 1 (Rojas 89)
Yugoslavia 0

FINAL
Estadio Nacional, Santiago, 17-06-1962, 68,000. Referee: Latichev, Soviet Union

BRAZIL 3 (Amarildo 18, Zito 69, Vavá 77)
CZECHOSLOVAKIA 1 (Masopust 16)
Brazil - Gilmar - Djalma Santos, Mauro R.Oliveira, Zózimo, Nilton Santos - Zito, Didi - Garrincha, Vavá, Amarildo, Zagalo. Tr: Moreira
Czechoslovakia - Schrojf - Tichy, Pluskal, Popluhár, Novák - Kvasnák, Masopust - Pospíchal, Scherer, Kadraba, Jelínek. Tr: Vytlacil

Top scorers: Florian Albert, Hungary 4
Garrincha, Brazil 4
Valentin Ivanov, Soviet Union 4
Drazen Jerkovic, Yugoslavia 4
Leonel Sánchez, Chile 4
Vavá, Brazil 4
Total goals scored: 89
Average per game: 2.8

1966

THE 8TH WORLD CUP
24TH MAY 1964 - 30TH JULY 1966

For the first time post-war, the major Western European football nations put in serious bids to stage the World Cup. England emerged as the favourites over both Spain and West Germany, and at FIFA's 1960 congress in Rome they were chosen in a close vote over the Germans, the Spanish having withdrawn their bid at the last moment. The year 1963 marked the centenary of the founding of modern association football in London, so in a way England was being honoured for her part in the development of the game.

The number of entries totalled seventy, 21 more than for Chile. At last it seemed the world outside Europe and the Americas was beginning to take an interest in the competition. Alas, it was a false dawn. Out of the whole of Asia and Africa just North Korea and Australia ended up playing a game. The point of conflict was the allocation of just one finals place to cover the two continents. Justified in their anger to the extent that as a World Cup, the competition should represent the world and not just Europe and South America, the representatives of the two continents withdrew en masse. It is interesting to note, however, that only four teams from Asia had entered in the first place. One of these, North Korea, were the eventual qualifiers.

Holland kicked off the qualifying tournament with a match against Albania in Rotterdam. The Dutch had not qualified since 1938 and their luck was not about to change. The Swiss, one of Europe's weaker nations, qualified from this group. It would have been interesting to see how an African nation like Ghana or Nigeria would have fared in Switzerland's place, given their poor performance in the final tournament. Not that this group was the only weak-looking European group. To lose in the final of the World Cup seemed to be a bad omen for the next competition as Czechoslovakia, like Sweden before them, failed to qualify for England. Losing semi-finalists Yugoslavia, who seemed to blow either hot or cold, blew cold in this tournament, and they too failed to qualify. The rest of the groups went much to plan in Europe as they did in South America, where there were no surprises. No surprises either in Central America where Mexico once again qualified at the expense of her smaller neighbours.

Four months before the final tournament started, the Jules Rimet trophy was stolen whilst on display in Westminster. For a week it could not be located, but a dog called Pickles found it hidden under a bush in a London suburb. Who had stolen it and why they had hidden it under a bush will never be known, but Pickles became an overnight hero. It was a shame that when the same trophy was stolen again in 1984 from the offices of the Brazilian Football Federation, Pickles was not still alive! Instead, the thief, who was later caught, admitted that he had melted it down.

In the finals, the greatest talking point of the first round again involved Italy, and again they failed to qualify for the quarter-finals. Their conquerors this time were the North Koreans. The country that liked to think itself at the top of the football tree was humbled by a group of players who had no experience of competitive football in Asia, let alone at world level. The crowds in the North-East of England, where the Koreans were based, warmed to their guests, even though it looked certain after the first round of games in Group 4 that the Soviet Union and Italy would qualify. The Korean victory over Italy, courtesy of a goal by Pak Doo-ik, was possibly the greatest upset the World Cup has seen, and on their return to Italy, the Italian team were pelted with all manner of objects by disgusted fans.

The other groups produced only one surprise, the elimination of the champions Brazil. England was not a happy tournament for the Brazilians. Regarded as favourites, they never adapted to the conditions in the North-West or the tackling of the Bulgarian and Portuguese defenders. Although they defeated Bulgaria, Pele was injured and missed the next match against the Hungarians, a game in which the Magyars outplayed their South American opponents. Indeed the Hungarians had recovered from the traumas of ten years previously and were amongst the best teams in Europe. Portugal, making their World Cup debut, were also an outstanding side. Eusebio, a naturalised Mozambican, emerged as the star and top scorer of the tournament. He was instrumental in Portugal's victory over Brazil, a game in which Pele was again on the receiving end of some disgraceful tackles. After the game he threatened never to play again in the World Cup. Thankfully he was back four years later.

Group 2 did not manage the excitement of Brazil's group, but it contained three very highly-rated teams. Spain were the unlucky ones not to qualify, defeats by the two qualifiers, West Germany and Argentina, sealing their fate. Like Italy, the Spaniards were learning that success at club level could be a positive hindrance at national level, a fact England would learn in the 1970s.

England looked comfortable enough in qualifying from Group 1, probably the weakest of the four. None of their opponents were tipped to proceed far and after a sterile opening game with Uruguay, both France and Mexico were defeated with ease by the hosts in front of full houses at Wembley. In the quarter-finals they played Argentina who were confident of victory, but in a show of temper they spoiled what was potentially an excellent game. Their captain Rattín, in particular, behaved deplorably and when sent off he refused to go. Playing against ten men, all of whom seemed intent on avenging Rattín's dismissal, England deservedly won the game when Hurst headed home a cross from Martin Peters 12 minutes from time. That an Argentinian team containing players of the quality of Artime, Rattín, Onega, Albrecht and Mas should resort to intimidatory tactics was a shame, but it was to be a familiar sight over the next few years, particularly at club level.

South American cries of conspiracy against them were heightened further after the match between West Germany and Uruguay during which two Uruguayans were sent off. It was a match Uruguay could have won, but they reacted badly to German provocation, and with only nine men for most of the second half, they conceded three goals to add to the one the Germans had scored in the first. All manner of rumour circulated in South America following these two games. A German referee in the England-Argentina game had sent off an Argentinian, and an English referee in the West Germany-Uruguay game had sent off two Uruguayans. Not surprisingly, two and two was put together and the South American press came up with five.

Two of the strongest teams met at Roker Park, Sunderland, where two defensive errors by the Hungarians let the Soviets in to win. The Soviet Union defended well and Yashin in particular made up for the errors he had made four years previously with a fine performance to deny the Hungarians, who had most of the play.

Goodison Park in Liverpool witnessed an extraordinary game. After 22 minutes North Korea led Portugal 3-0, and had victory in their grasp. Had they had more international experience they might well have won, but instead of concentrating more on defence they went out for more goals. Marshalled by the brilliant Eusebio, Portugal regrouped and exploited the gaps in the Korean defence. After an hour the Portuguese led 4-3, all of the goals scored by Eusebio. The 5-3 victory was comfortable enough in the end, but if ever a match sealed two reputations, that of the Koreans and of Eusebio, this was it.

The semi-finals starkly contrasted each other. The Goodison Park spectators had witnessed two excellent matches, between Hungary and Brazil and North Korea and Portugal, but the semi-final encounter between the Soviet Union and West Germany was not in the same class. Haller scored for the Germans just before half-time and Beckenbauer made it 2-0 halfway through the second half, and although Porkujan scored just before the end, the game was never exciting.

Not so the game at Wembley between England and Portugal, which was an open encounter and one of the best games of the tournament. Bobby Charlton, the scorer of both England's goals, was in superb form. His second goal even merited handshakes from a couple of the Portuguese players. The final ten minutes were especially tense, after Bobby's brother Jackie handled the ball on the line and Eusebio scored from the penalty spot. Try as they might, Portugal could not equalise, and the sight of Eusebio leaving the field in tears after the game is one of the most poignant pictures in World Cup history.

West Germany were back for their first final in 12 years. For England it was their first in 54 years. Not since the 1912 Olympic Games had they progressed so far. Home advantage was being made to tell: Italy in 1934 had been the last host nation to win the tournament and England were to become the third, in somewhat controversial style. After Haller had put the Germans ahead on 12 minutes following a poor clearance from Wilson, England applied the pressure and six minutes later they were on level terms after a quickly taken free-kick by Bobby Moore was headed home by Geoff Hurst. It was not until 12 minutes from time that the English pressure told when Peters scored, following a shot from Hurst.

It looked as though the game was beyond West Germany and they left it very late to equalise. From a free-kick blasted into the penalty area by Emmerich, Weber prodded the ball home seconds before the final whistle was blown. In extra-time the match was effectively decided by one of the most talked about goals in the history of the World Cup. From a cross by Ball, Hurst, with his back to the goal, controlled the ball, turned and shot. The ball hit the underside of the bar and came down. Hunt, who was following in, turned away in celebration. Dienst, the Swiss referee, after consulting his Soviet linesman Bakhramov, blew his whistle for a goal. The Germans hotly disputed the decision and still do to this day. They point to the fact that Bakhramov was not really in a position to give a proper verdict.

The issue was put beyond doubt seconds before the end of extra time when Hurst ran on to a long clearance and scored with a lovely left-footed shot. England had deservedly won the World Cup in what had proved to be a very exciting game, and brought the highest honour the game has back to the country that gave the world the game in the first place.

QUALIFYING TOURNAMENT

EUROPE

Group 1

	Be	Bu	Is	Pl	W	D	L	F	A	Pts
Belgium	-	5-0	1-0	4	3	0	1	11	3	6
BULGARIA	3-0	-	4-0	4	3	0	1	9	6	6
Israel	0-5	1-2	-	4	0	0	4	1	12	0

Play-off in Florence

Bulgaria .... 2-1 .... Belgium

Group 2

	WG	Sd	Cy	Pl	W	D	L	F	A	Pts
WEST GERMANY	-	1-1	5-0	4	3	1	0	14	2	7
Sweden	1-2	-	3-0	4	2	1	1	10	3	5
Cyprus	0-6	0-5	-	4	0	0	4	0	19	0

Group 3

	Fr	No	Yu	Lu	Pl	W	D	L	F	A	Pts
FRANCE	-	1-0	1-0	4-1	6	5	0	1	9	2	10
Norway	0-1	-	3-0	4-2	6	3	1	2	10	5	7
Yugoslavia	1-0	1-1	-	3-1	6	3	1	2	10	8	7
Luxembourg	0-2	0-2	2-5	-	6	0	0	6	6	20	0

Group 4

	Pt	Cz	Ro	Tu	Pl	W	D	L	F	A	Pts
PORTUGAL	-	0-0	2-1	5-1	6	4	1	1	9	4	9
Czechoslovakia	0-1	-	3-1	3-1	6	3	1	2	12	4	7
Romania	2-0	1-0	-	3-0	6	3	0	3	9	7	6
Turkey	0-1	0-6	2-1	-	6	1	0	5	4	19	2

Group 5

	Sz	NI	Ho	Al	Pl	W	D	L	F	A	Pts
SWITZERLAND	-	2-1	2-1	1-0	6	4	1	1	7	3	9
Nth. Ireland	1-0	-	2-1	4-1	6	3	2	1	9	5	8
Holland	0-0	0-0	-	2-0	6	2	2	2	6	4	6
Albania	0-2	1-1	0-2	-	6	0	1	5	2	12	1

Group 6

	Hu	EG	Au	Pl	W	D	L	F	A	Pts
HUNGARY	-	3-2	3-0	4	3	1	0	8	5	7
East Germany	1-1	-	1-0	4	1	2	1	5	5	4
Austria	0-1	1-1	-	4	0	1	3	3	6	1

Group 7

	SU	Wa	Gr	De	Pl	W	D	L	F	A	Pts
SOVIET UNION	-	2-1	3-1	6-0	6	5	0	1	19	6	10
Wales	2-1	-	4-1	4-2	6	3	0	3	11	9	6
Greece	1-4	2-0	-	4-2	6	2	1	3	10	14	5
Denmark	1-3	1-0	1-1	-	6	1	1	4	7	18	3

Group 8

	It	Sc	Pd	Fi	Pl	W	D	L	F	A	Pts
ITALY	-	3-0	6-1	6-1	6	4	1	1	17	3	9
Scotland	1-0	-	1-2	3-1	6	3	1	2	8	8	7
Poland	0-0	1-1	-	7-0	6	2	2	2	11	10	6
Finland	0-2	1-2	2-0	-	6	1	0	5	5	20	2

Group 9

Rep. Ireland ....1-0 1-4 ....Spain

Syria withdrew

Play-off in Paris

SPAIN............................1-0 ....Rep Ireland

SOUTH AMERICA

Group 1

	Ur	Pe	Ve	Pl	W	D	L	F	A	Pts
URUGUAY	-	2-1	5-0	4	4	0	0	11	2	8
Peru	0-1	-	1-0	4	2	0	2	8	6	4
Venezuela	1-3	3-6	-	4	0	0	4	4	15	0

Group 2

	Ch	Ec	Co	Pl	W	D	L	F	A	Pts
CHILE	-	3-1	7-2	4	2	1	1	12	7	5
Ecuador	2-2	-	2-0	4	2	1	1	6	5	5
Colombia	2-0	0-1	-	4	1	0	3	4	10	2

Play-off in Lima

Chile............................2-1 ....Ecuador

Group 3

	Ar	Pa	Bo	Pl	W	D	L	F	A	Pts
ARGENTINA	-	3-0	4-1	4	3	1	0	9	2	7
Paraguay	0-0	-	2-0	4	1	1	2	3	5	3
Bolivia	1-2	2-1	-	4	1	0	3	4	9	2

CENTRAL AND NORTH AMERICA

FIRST ROUND

Group 1

	Ja	NA	Cu	Pl	W	D	L	F	A	Pts
Jamaica	-	2-0	2-0	4	2	1	1	5	2	5
Neth. Antilles	0-0	-	1-0	4	1	2	1	2	3	4
Cuba	2-1	1-1	-	4	1	1	2	3	5	3

Group 2

	CR	Su	Tr	Pl	W	D	L	F	A	Pts
Costa Rica	-	1-0	4-0	4	4	0	0	9	1	8
Surinam	1-3	-	6-1	4	1	0	3	8	9	2
Trinidad	0-1	4-1	-	4	1	0	3	5	12	2

Group 3

	Me	US	Ho	Pl	W	D	L	F	A	Pts
Mexico	-	2-0	3-0	4	3	1	0	8	2	7
United States	2-2	-	1-1	4	1	2	1	4	5	4
Honduras	0-1	0-1	-	4	0	1	3	1	6	1

SECOND ROUND

	Me	CR	Ja	Pl	W	D	L	F	A	Pts
MEXICO	-	1-0	8-0	4	3	1	0	12	2	7
Costa Rica	0-0	-	7-0	4	1	2	1	8	2	4
Jamaica	2-3	1-1	-	4	0	1	3	3	19	1

AFRICA-ASIA-OCEANIA

NORTH KOREA....................6-1 3-1 ....Australia

All of the African entries and all bar North Korea of the Asian entries withdrew over the allocation of just one place for them in the final tournament

ENGLAND qualified as hosts

BRAZIL qualified as holders

FINAL TOURNAMENT,
HELD IN ENGLAND 11TH - 30TH JULY 1966

FIRST ROUND

Group 1

Wembley, London, 11-07-1966, 87,000
England 0
Uruguay 0

Wembley, London, 13-07-1966, 69,000
France 1 (Hausser 52)
Mexico 1 (Borja 48)

White City, London, 15-07-1966, 45,000
Uruguay 2 (Rocha 27, Cortes 32)
France 1 (De Bourgoing 15)

Wembley, London, 16-07-1966, 92,000
England 2 (Charlton.R 37, Hurst 75)
Mexico 0

Wembley, London, 19-07-1966, 61,000
Uruguay 0
Mexico 0

Wembley, London, 20-07-1966, 98,000
England 2 (Hunt 38 75)
France 0

	En	Ur	Me	Fr	Pl	W	D	L	F	A	Pts
ENGLAND	-	0-0	2-0	2-0	3	2	1	0	4	0	5
URUGUAY	-	-	0-0	2-1	3	1	2	0	2	1	4
MEXICO	-	-	-	1-1	3	0	2	1	1	3	2
FRANCE	-	-	-	-	3	0	1	2	2	5	1

Group 2
Hillsborough, Sheffield, 12-07-1966, 36,000
West Germany 5 (Held 15, Haller 21 77, Beckenbauer 40 52)
Switzerland 0

Villa Park, Birmingham, 13-07-1966, 47,000
Argentina 2 (Artime 64 80)
Spain 1 (Pirri 72)

Hillsborough, Sheffield, 15-07-1966, 32,000
Spain 2 (Sanchis 57, Amancio 75)
Switzerland 1 (Quentin 29)

Villa Park, Birmingham, 16-07-1966, 51,000
Argentina 0
West Germany 0

Hillsborough, Sheffield, 19-07-1966, 31,000
Argentina 2 (Artime 52 80)
Switzerland 0

Villa Park, Birmingham, 20-07-1966, 51,000
West Germany 2 (Emmerich 38, Seeler 89)
Spain 1 (Fuste 22)

	WG	Ar	Sp	Sz	Pl	W	D	L	F	A	Pts
WEST GERMANY	-	0-0	2-1	5-0	3	2	1	0	7	1	5
ARGENTINA	-	-	2-1	2-0	3	2	1	0	4	1	5
SPAIN	-	-	-	2-1	3	1	0	2	4	5	2
SWITZERLAND	-	-	-	-	3	0	0	3	1	9	0

Group 3
Goodison Park, Liverpool, 12-07-1966, 52,000
Brazil 2 (Pelé 15, Garrincha 63)
Bulgaria 0

Old Trafford, Manchester, 13-07-1966, 37,000
Portugal 3 (Augusto 1 67, Torres 90)
Hungary 1 (Bene 60)

Goodison Park, Liverpool, 15-07-1966, 57,000
Hungary 3 (Bene 2, Farkas 64, Meszoly 73)
Brazil 1 (Tostao 14)

Old Trafford, Manchester, 16-06-1966, 33,000
Portugal 3 (OG 5, Eusébio 36, Torres 75)
Bulgaria 0

Goodison Park, Liverpool, 19-07-1966, 62,000
Portugal 3 (Simoes 15, Eusébio 26 85)
Brazil 1 (Rildo 73)

Old Trafford, Manchester, 20-07-1966, 20,000
Hungary 3 (OG 43, Meszoly 47, Bene 54)
Bulgaria 1 (Asparukov 15)

	Pt	Hu	Br	Bu	Pl	W	D	L	F	A	Pts
PORTUGAL	-	3-1	3-1	3-0	3	3	0	0	9	2	6
HUNGARY	-	-	3-1	3-1	3	2	0	1	7	5	4
BRAZIL	-	-	-	2-0	3	1	0	2	4	6	2
BULGARIA	-	-	-	-	3	0	0	3	1	8	0

Group 4
Ayresome Park, Middlesbrough, 12-07-1966, 22,000
Soviet Union 3 (Malafeev 32 88, Banichevski 33)
North Korea 0

Roker Park, Sunderland, 13-07-1966, 30,000
Italy 2 (Mazzola 10, Barison 80)
Chile 0

Ayresome Park, Middlesbrough, 15-07-1966, 15,000
North Korea 1 (Seung-zin 88)
Chile 1 (Marcos 20)

Roker Park, Sunderland, 16-07-1966, 31,000
Soviet Union 1 (Chislenko 58)
Italy 0

Ayresome Park, Middlesbrough, 19-07-1966, 18,000
North Korea 1 (Doo-ik 41)
Italy 0

Roker Park, Sunderland, 20-07-1966, 22,000
Soviet Union 2 (Porkujan 28 85)
Chile 1 (Marcos 32)

	SU	NK	It	Ch	Pl	W	D	L	F	A	Pts
SOVIET UNION	-	3-0	1-0	2-1	3	3	0	0	6	1	6
NORTH KOREA	-	-	1-0	1-1	3	1	1	1	2	4	3
ITALY	-	-	-	2-0	3	1	0	2	2	2	2
CHILE	-	-	-	-	3	0	1	2	2	5	1

QUARTER-FINALS
Wembley, London, 23-07-1966, 90,000
England 1 (Hurst 78)
Argentina 0

Goodison Park, Liverpool, 23-07-1966, 51,000
Portugal 5 (Eusébio 27 42 56 59, Augusto 78)
North Korea 3 (Seung-zin 1, Dong-woon 21, Seung-kook 22)

Roker Park, Sunderland, 23-07-1966, 26,000
Soviet Union 2 (Chislenko 5, Porkujan 48)
Hungary 1 (Bene 50)

Hillsborough, Sheffield, 23-07-1966, 33,000
West Germany 4 (Held 11, Beckenbauer 65, Seeler 76, Haller 83)
Uruguay 0

SEMI-FINALS
Wembley, London, 26-07-1966, 94,000
England 2 (Charlton.R 30 79)
Portugal 1 (Eusébio 82)

Goodison Park, Liverpool, 25-07-1966, 43,000
West Germany 2 (Haller 44, Beckenbauer 68)
Soviet Union 1 (Porkujan 88)

3RD PLACE
Wembley, London, 28-07-1966, 87,000
Portugal 2 (Eusébio 12, Torres 88)
Soviet Union 1 (Metreveli 43)

FINAL
Wembley, London, 30-07-1966, 96,000. Referee: Dienst, Switzerland
ENGLAND 4 (Hurst 19 100 119, Peters 77)

WEST GERMANY 2 (Haller 13, Weber 89)

England - Banks - Cohen, Charlton.J, Moore, Wilson - Stiles, Charlton.R - Ball, Hunt, Hurst, Peters. Tr: Ramsey

West Germany - Tilkowski - Höttges, Schulz, Weber, Schnellinger - Haller, Beckenbauer - Seeler, Held, Overath, Emmerich. Tr: Schön

Top scorers:		
	Eusébio, Portugal	9
	Helmut Haller, West Germany	5
	Franz Beckenbauer, West Germany	4
	Ferenc Bene, Hungary	4
	Geoff Hurst, England	4
	Valeri Porkujan, Soviet Union	4

Total goals scored: 89
Average per game: 2.8

1970

THE 9TH WORLD CUP
19TH MAY 1968 - 21ST JUNE 1970

At the FIFA congress in Tokyo in 1964, FIFA surprisingly gave the 1970 World Cup to Mexico. Once again Argentina was overlooked and their delegation was furious. The conditions in Mexico were thought by many to be unsuitable, both in terms of the heat and altitude, but the persistent lobbying by the Mexican delegation won the day.

As it turned out, the 1970 Mexican World Cup will be remembered as perhaps the best tournament ever to be staged. For those who were not there, it was the first chance to see the tournament not only live on the television but also in colour, definitely a contributing factor to the mystique which has surrounded the tournament since.

After failing to secure the staging of the tournament, Argentina failed even to qualify. This perhaps was a blessing in disguise. The three previous World Club Championships between European and Argentinian sides had been marred by brutal behaviour on the pitch, mainly by the Argentines, though not exclusively. Mexico was spared such confrontations. Instead, South America was represented by three supremely gifted teams in Brazil, Uruguay and Peru. Peru in particular were a welcome sight. Managed by Didi, the former Brazilian midfielder, they were responsible for Argentina's demise thanks to a 1-0 victory in Lima and a 2-2 draw in Buenos Aires.

Peru's presence in the final tournament was threatened by an earthquake just before the tournament began, but that was nothing compared to the traumas of the CONCACAF qualifying tournament, where full-scale war was declared as a result of three matches between El Salvador and Honduras. Relations had been tense for many months between the two countries. Border disputes and the problems of Salvadoran migrant workers in Honduras just needed a spark to start the fire. That spark was provided when the two countries were drawn to play each other in the semi-finals of the qualifying group. After all three games that were played, rioting and border skirmishes ensued and finally all-out war, though remarkably there was little trouble during the games themselves. Known as the Fútbol War, over 2,000 lives were lost in the fighting.

There were disputes elsewhere in the qualifying competition, but thankfully not on the same scale. The North Koreans, hoping to repeat their 1966 success in Mexico, were forced to withdraw after refusing to play Israel, the eventual qualifiers from Asia. The Asian entry was again rather low, considering the fact that the Asian Games, Asian Cup and Asian Club Championship were regularly attracting a high number of entries. Only Japan and South Korea from the AFC bothered to enter.

For the first time since 1934, Africa was represented at the final tournament, this time by Morocco, who won a close run play-off against Nigeria and Sudan. Ghana, without question the best team on the continent, having appeared in the four previous Cup of Nations final ties, did not live up to their billing as favourites, Nigeria defeating them 2-1 in a crucial game in Ibadan.

Europe was full of surprises too. Eusebio could do no more than inspire Portugal to finish bottom of their qualifying group behind Romania. Also out were Hungary, the fourth of the quarter-finalists in 1966 who did not qualify for Mexico. They lost to Czechoslovakia, 4-1 in a play-off in Marseille. Spain once again failed to live up to her clubs' reputation, finishing third in a group which Yugoslavia, runners-up two years previously in the European Championships, were expected to win. Belgium surprised both countries by qualifying with some ease.

The final tournament was played at the hottest time of the year in Mexico, and quite inexcusably, due to television commitments, many of the games kicked off at midday. That the tournament produced any good football at all is a wonder, but it did: the standard was of the highest quality. Group 3 in particular served up a feast of games, the best of which was the game between the holders and Brazil in Guadalajara. England had a team that was regarded as better than their 1966 side, and the predictions were that the first round game with the Brazilians would be a rehearsal for the final. They were unlucky to lose to a goal by Jairzinho, but Banks had earlier kept a Pele header out by producing one of the best saves ever witnessed. Both teams qualified for the quarter-finals by beating both the Czechs and Romanians, who were no match.

Group 4 produced lots of goals and some excellent football. Morocco put up excellent displays against West Germany and Bulgaria, whilst Peru with Chumpitaz and Cubillas in excellent form saw off both the Moroccans and the Bulgarians. Bulgaria, often criticised as one of the most negative teams in Europe, even played their part, though they could not match the skill shown by the Germans for whom Gerd Müller was in devastating form. His seven goals in three games included hat-tricks against both Bulgaria and Peru.

Group 1, played in the most imposing football stadium in

the world, the newly constructed Azteca, got off to a poor start with a tedious 0-0 draw between the hosts and the Soviet Union in the opening game. El Salvador and Belgium, the other two teams in the group, were no match for the Soviets or the Mexicans. Mexico, for years the whipping boys at each World Cup, were enjoying home advantage and were determined to make the most of it.

Group 2 was the poorest. Both Uruguay and Italy were expected to qualify, and this they did without much trouble. Italy, after beating Sweden 1-0, simply shut up shop and played out two 0-0 draws. The Italians were determined that there would be no repeat of the fiascos of the previous five World Cups. Uruguay were very tight defensively and although they lost against the Swedes in the last game, the Scandinavians needed to win by two goals to qualify. The one goal they did score came in the last minute.

The quarter-finals threw up a repeat of the 1966 final, and this time the West Germans gained a measure of revenge. England, missing Banks in goal through food poisoning, led 2-0 with 22 minutes remaining, but the Germans fought back magnificently and eventually won with a goal from Müller in the second period of extra-time. Ramsey, the England manager, has been blamed for substituting Bobby Charlton instead of Cooper, as has Peter Bonetti, Banks' replacement in goal, for a poor display, but West Germany, forced into attack, never lost the initiative once they had scored.

In Guadalajara, Brazil continued to delight the public there with another inspired display against Peru. Pele, in his fourth World Cup, was proving why he was regarded as the best footballer ever to play the game, but he was not the only star in the side. Rivelino, Tostao, Jairzinho and Gerson with Pele represented an attacking unit that has rarely, if ever, been equalled. Peru might well have qualified against any other of the quarter-finalists, and against Brazil, Cubillas scored a stunning goal after an excellent run by Sotil, but they could not match the overall quality of the Brazilians.

Uruguay, Brazil's opponents in the semi-finals, beat the Soviet Union in the quarter-finals with a hotly disputed goal three minutes from the end of extra-time. The Soviets were adamant that the ball went out of play before Esparrago put it in the net to win a game in which the Soviets were frustrated by the excellent Uruguayan defence. The game was played in a half-full Azteca stadium, and it would have made more sense to have moved the game to Toluca were Mexico and Italy played their quarter-final. Had the Mexicans played in the Azteca, not only would it have been a sell-out, but their chances of winning would have been improved. Instead, in front of only 24,000 in Toluca they floundered and lost badly, despite taking an early lead, to an Italian side that showed it could attack as well as it could defend. Rivera and Riva were in particularly fine form.

In the semi-final against West Germany three days later, the Italians continued in this vein, scoring four more goals. That they also let in three was astonishing given that Italian football was dominated by catenaccio at the time. Every tournament seems to throw up a real thriller of a game, and in Mexico this was it. The Italians scored after seven minutes and went on the defensive for the rest of the game, only for Schnellinger to score right at the death for the Germans. In extra-time the game came alive. Müller, the tournament's top scorer, put West Germany ahead only for Burgnich to equalise. Just before the end of the first period Riva put the Italians ahead again only for Müller to equalise. When Rivera scored to put Italy into the lead for the third time, West Germany had nothing left to give.

Brazil, still playing in Guadalajara in front of a crowd that were fiercely behind them, won the other semi-final in some style. Uruguay had played Brazil often enough not to be intimidated, and they took the lead through Cubilla after 19 minutes, a lead they kept right up to half-time. Just before the interval, however, the inevitable happened and Clodoaldo equalised. It was not until the last quarter of an hour that the Brazilian pressure paid off. Brazil were on a roll and there was nothing the Uruguayans could do to stop them. First Jairzinho and then Rivelino scored the goals that won the match for them.

The final, before a full house in the Azteca, was a match that showed football at its best. At stake was the permanent possession of the Jules Rimet trophy, both sides having won it twice before. Pele opened the scoring, thus matching Vava, the only other man who had scored in two World Cup Finals, when he headed home from Rivelino's cross. Italy pulled level just before half-time after careless play in the Brazilian defence let in Boninsegna to score, but Italian optimism that they could win the game proved a false hope.

Again Brazil left it to the last quarter of the match to convert their supremacy into goals. A brilliant left-footed shot by Gerson from outside the area put the Brazilians ahead. Gerson was again involved in the third goal as his high cross was headed down by Pele for Jairzinho to score a goal that made him the only player ever to have scored in every round of the World Cup. In fact he scored in every game Brazil played in Mexico. Brazil's last goal, just before the end, remains one of the best goals ever scored. Working the ball cleverly out from defence, a long ball found Jairzinho on the wing. He passed to Pele who with arrogant ease slipped the ball into the path of Carlos Alberto the captain. The first Albertosi in the Italian goal saw of the ball was when he retrieved it from the net.

A remarkable goal finished off a remarkable tournament for Brazil. They had conceded seven goals, but worked to the philosophy that as long as you scored more than you conceded you would win. The World Cup in Mexico should have been the spur to break the defensive mentality that was becoming prevalent in the game. Instead, systems were devised by coaches all over the world to stop the threat of a team playing like Brazil had done. Indeed Brazil themselves, four years later in an attempt to keep their crown played a defensive game designed to snuff out their opponents. The World Cup in Mexico therefore will be remembered as an oasis of attacking football in a time when the 0-0 draw was an ever more familiar scoreline.

QUALIFYING TOURNAMENT

EUROPE

Group 1

	Ro	Gr	Sz	Pt	Pl	W	D	L	F	A	Pts
ROMANIA	-	1-1	2-0	1-0	6	3	2	1	7	6	8
Greece	2-2	-	4-1	4-2	6	2	3	1	13	9	7
Switzerland	0-1	1-0	-	1-1	6	2	1	3	5	8	5
Portugal	3-0	2-2	0-2	-	6	1	2	3	8	10	4

Group 2

	Cz	Hu	De	RI	Pl	W	D	L	F	A	Pts
CZECHOSLOVAKIA	-	3-3	1-0	3-0	6	4	1	1	12	6	9
Hungary	2-0	-	3-0	4-0	6	4	1	1	16	7	9
Denmark	0-3	3-2	-	2-0	6	2	1	3	6	10	5
Rep. Ireland	1-2	1-2	1-1	-	6	0	1	5	3	14	1

Play-off in Marseille
Czechoslovakia..............................4-1 ....Hungary

Group 3

	It	EG	Wa	Pl	W	D	L	F	A	Pts
ITALY	-	3-0	4-1	4	3	1	0	10	3	7
East Germany	2-2	-	2-1	4	2	1	1	7	7	5
Wales	0-1	1-3	-	4	0	0	4	3	10	0

Group 4

	SU	NI	Tu	Pl	W	D	L	F	A	Pts
SOVIET UNION	-	2-0	3-0	4	3	1	0	8	1	7
Nth. Ireland	0-0	-	4-1	4	2	1	1	7	3	5
Turkey	1-3	0-3	-	4	0	0	4	2	13	0

Group 5

	Sd	Fr	No	Pl	W	D	L	F	A	Pts
SWEDEN	-	2-0	5-0	4	3	0	1	12	5	6
France	3-0	-	0-1	4	2	0	2	6	4	4
Norway	2-5	1-3	-	4	1	0	3	4	13	2

Group 6

	Be	Yu	Sp	Fi	Pl	W	D	L	F	A	Pts
BELGIUM	-	3-0	2-1	6-1	6	4	1	1	14	8	9
Yugoslavia	4-0	-	0-0	9-1	6	3	1	2	19	7	7
Spain	1-1	2-1	-	6-0	6	2	2	2	10	6	6
Finland	1-2	1-5	2-0	-	6	1	0	5	6	28	2

Group 7

	WG	Sc	Au	Cy	Pl	W	D	L	F	A	Pts
WEST GERMANY	-	3-2	1-0	12-0	6	5	1	0	20	3	11
Scotland	1-1	-	2-1	8-0	6	3	1	2	18	7	7
Austria	0-2	2-0	-	7-1	6	3	0	3	12	7	6
Cyprus	0-1	0-5	1-2	-	6	0	0	6	2	35	0

Group 8

	Bu	Pd	Ho	Lu	Pl	W	D	L	F	A	Pts
BULGARIA	-	4-1	2-0	2-1	6	4	1	1	12	7	9
Poland	3-0	-	2-1	8-1	6	4	0	2	19	8	8
Holland	1-1	1-0	-	4-0	6	3	1	2	9	5	7
Luxembourg	1-3	1-5	0-2	-	6	0	0	6	4	24	0

SOUTH AMERICA

Group 1

	Pe	Bo	Ar	Pl	W	D	L	F	A	Pts
PERU	-	3-0	1-0	4	2	1	1	7	4	5
Bolivia	2-1	-	3-1	4	2	0	2	5	6	4
Argentina	2-2	1-0	-	4	1	1	2	4	6	3

Group 2

	Br	Pa	Co	Ve	Pl	W	D	L	F	A	Pts
BRAZIL	-	1-0	6-2	6-0	6	6	0	0	23	2	12
Paraguay	0-3	-	2-1	1-0	6	4	0	2	6	5	8
Colombia	0-2	0-1	-	3-0	6	1	1	4	7	12	3
Venezuela	0-5	0-2	1-1	-	6	0	1	5	1	18	1

Group 3

	Ur	Ch	Ec	Pl	W	D	L	F	A	Pts
URUGUAY	-	2-0	1-0	4	3	1	0	5	0	7
Chile	0-0	-	4-1	4	1	2	1	5	4	4
Ecuador	0-2	1-1	-	4	0	1	3	2	8	1

CENTRAL AND NORTH AMERICA

FIRST ROUND

Group 1

	Ho	CR	Ja	Pl	W	D	L	F	A	Pts
Honduras	-	1-0	3-1	4	3	1	0	7	2	7
Costa Rica	1-1	-	3-0	4	2	1	1	7	3	5
Jamaica	0-2	1-3	-	4	0	0	4	2	11	0

Group 2

	Ha	Gu	Tr	Pl	W	D	L	F	A	Pts
Haiti	-	2-0	2-4	4	2	1	1	8	4	5
Guatemala	1-1	-	4-0	4	1	2	1	5	3	4
Trinidad	0-4	0-0	-	4	1	1	2	4	10	3

Group 3

	ES	Su	NA	Pl	W	D	L	F	A	Pts
El Salvador	-	6-0	1-0	4	3	0	1	10	5	6
Surinam	4-1	-	6-0	4	2	0	2	10	9	4
Neth. Antilles	1-2	2-0	-	4	1	0	3	3	9	2

Group 4

	US	Ca	Be	Pl	W	D	L	F	A	Pts
United States	-	1-0	6-2	4	3	0	1	11	6	6
Canada	4-2	-	4-0	4	2	0	2	8	3	5
Bermuda	0-2	0-0	-	4	0	1	3	2	12	1

SECOND ROUND

Haiti...2-0 1-0 ....United States
Honduras ....1-0 0-3 ....El Salvador

Play-off in Mexico City
El Salvador ....3-2.......................................Honduras

THIRD ROUND

Haiti...1-2 3-0..................................El Salvador

Play-off in Kingston, Jamaica
EL SALVADOR ....1-0 ....Haiti

ASIA-OCEANIA

FIRST ROUND

Group 1

First round

	Au	SK	Ja	Pl	W	D	L	F	A	Pts
Australia	-	2-1	1-1	4	2	2	0	7	4	6
South Korea	1-1	-	2-2	4	1	2	1	6	5	4
Japan	1-3	0-2	-	4	0	2	2	4	8	2

SECOND ROUND

Australia	1-1 0-0 3-1	Rhodesia

All three matches played in Lourenço Marques, Mozambique

Group 2

Israel	4-0 2-0	New Zealand

North Korea withdrew

SECOND ROUND

ISRAEL	1-0 1-1	Australia

AFRICA

FIRST ROUND

Algeria	1-2 0-0	Tunisia
Morocco	1-0 1-2 2-0*	Senegal
Libya	2-0 1-5	Ethiopia
Zambia	4-2 2-4**	Sudan
Nigeria	1-1 3-2	Cameroon
Ghana	Bye	

* Play-off in Las Palmas, Spain
**Sudan qualified by scoring more goals in the second game

SECOND ROUND

Tunisia	0-0 0-0 2-2*	Morocco
Ethiopia	1-1 1-3	Sudan
Nigeria	2-1 1-1	Ghana

* Morocco qualified on the toss of a coin after a play-off in Marseille

THIRD ROUND

	Mo	Ni	Su	Pl	W	D	L	F	A	Pts
MOROCCO	-	2-1	3-0	4	2	1	1	5	3	5
NIGERIA	2-0	-	2-2	4	1	2	1	8	7	4
SUDAN	0-0	3-3	-	4	0	3	1	5	8	3

MEXICO qualified as hosts
ENGLAND qualified as holders

FINAL TOURNAMENT,
HELD IN MEXICO 31ST MAY - 21ST JUNE 1970

FIRST ROUND

Group 1

Azteca, Mexico City, 31-05-1970, 107,000
Mexico 0
Soviet Union 0

Azteca, Mexico City, 3-06-1970, 92,000
Belgium 3 (Van Moer 12 54, Lambert 76)
El Salvador 0

Azteca, Mexico City, 6-06-1970, 59,000
Soviet Union 4 (Bishovets 15 63, Asatiani 56, Khmelnitski 76)
Belgium 1 (Lambert 86)

Azteca, Mexico City, 7-06-1970, 103,000
Mexico 4 (Valdivia 45 46, Fragoso 54, Basaguren 83)
El Salvador 0

Azteca, Mexico City, 10-06-1970, 89,000
Soviet Union 2 (Bishovets 51 74)
El Salvador 0

Azteca, Mexico City, 11-06-1970, 105,000
Mexico 1 (Peña 15)
Belgium 0

	SU	Me	Be	ES	Pl	W	D	L	F	A	Pts
SOVIET UNION	-	0-0	4-1	2-0	3	2	1	0	6	1	5
MEXICO	-	-	1-0	4-0	3	2	1	0	5	0	5
BELGIUM	-	-	-	3-0	3	1	0	2	4	5	2
EL SALVADOR	-	-	-	-	3	0	0	3	0	9	0

Group 2

Cuauhtemoc, Puebla, 2-06-1970, 20,000
Uruguay 2 (Maneiro 23, Mujica 50)
Israel 0

Luis Dosal, Toluca, 3-06-1970, 14,000
Italy 1 (Domenghini 10)
Sweden 0

Cuauhtemoc, Puebla, 6-06-1970, 30,000
Uruguay 0
Italy 0

Luis Dosal, Toluca, 7-06-1970, 9,000
Israel 1 (Spiegler 56)
Sweden 1 (Turesson 54)

Cuauhtemoc, Puebla, 10-06-1970, 18,000
Sweden 1 (Grahn 90)
Uruguay 0

Luis Dosal, Toluca, 11-06-1970, 9,000
Italy 0
Israel 0

	It	Ur	Sd	Is	Pl	W	D	L	F	A	Pts
ITALY	-	0-0	1-0	0-0	3	1	2	0	1	0	4
URUGUAY	-	-	0-1	2-0	3	1	1	1	2	1	3
SWEDEN	-	-	-	1-1	3	1	1	1	2	2	3
ISRAEL	-	-	-	-	3	0	2	1	1	3	2

Group 3

Jalisco, Guadalajara, 2-06-1970, 50,000
England 1 (Hurst 65)
Romania 0

Jalisco, Guadalajara, 3-06-1970, 52,000
Brazil 4 (Rivelino 24, Pelé 59, Jairzinho 61 81)
Czechoslovakia 1 (Petras 11)

Jalisco, Guadalajara, 6-06-1970, 56,000
Romania 2 (Neagu 52, Dumitrache 75)
Czechoslovakia 1 (Petras 5)

Jalisco, Guadalajara, 7-06-1970, 66,000
Brazil 1 (Jairzinho 59)
England 0

Jalisco, Guadalajara, 10-06-1970, 50,000
Brazil 3 (Pelé 19 67, Jairzinho 22)
Romania 2 (Dumitrache 34, Dembrovski 84)

Jalisco, Guadalajara, 11-06-1970, 49,000
England 1 (Clarke 50)
Czechoslovakia 0

	Br	En	Ro	Cz	Pl	W	D	L	F	A	Pts
BRAZIL	-	1-0	3-2	4-1	3	3	0	0	8	3	6
ENGLAND	-	-	1-0	1-0	3	2	0	1	2	1	4
ROMANIA	-	-	-	2-1	3	1	0	2	4	5	2
CZECHOSLOVAKIA	-	-	-	-	3	0	0	3	2	7	0

Group 4

Guanajuato, León, 2-06-1970, 14,000
Peru 3 (Gallardo 50, Chumpitaz 55, Cubillas 73)
Bulgaria 2 (Dermendjiev 13, Bonev 49)

Guanajuato, León, 3-06-1970, 9,000
West Germany 2 (Seeler 56, Müller 78)
Morocco 1 (Houmane Jarir 21)

Guanajuato, León, 6-06-1970, 13,000
Peru 3 (Cubillas 65 75, Challe 67)
Morocco 0

Guanajuato, León, 7-06-1970, 12,000
West Germany 5 (Libuda 20, Müller 27 52 88, Seeler 69)
Bulgaria 2 (Nikodimov 12, Kolev.T 89)

Guanajuato, León, 10-06-1970, 18,000
West Germany 3 (Müller 19 23 39)
Peru 1 (Cubillas 44)

Guanajuato, León, 11-06-1970, 12,000
Bulgaria 1 (Jechev 40)
Morocco 1 (Ghazouani 61)

	WG	Pe	Bu	Mo	Pl	W	D	L	F	A	Pts
WEST GERMANY	-	3-1	5-2	2-1	3	3	0	0	10	4	6
PERU	-	-	3-2	3-0	3	2	0	1	7	5	4
BULGARIA	-	-	-	1-1	3	0	1	2	5	9	1
MOROCCO	-	-	-	-	3	0	1	2	2	6	1

QUARTER-FINALS

Jalisco, Guadalajara, 14-06-1970, 54,000
Brazil 4 (Rivelino 11, Tostao 15 52, Jairzinho 77)
Peru 2 (Gallardo 27, Cubillas 64)

Azteca, Mexico City, 14-06-1970, 45,000
Uruguay 1 (Esparrago 117)
Soviet Union 0

Guanajuato, León, 14-06-1970, 24,000
West Germany 3 (Beckenbauer 68, Seeler 81, Müller 108)
England 2 (Mullery 31, Peters 49)

Luis Dosal, Toluca, 14-06-1970, 24,000
Italy 4 (Domenghini 25, Riva 64 75, Rivera 69)
Mexico 1 (González 13)

SEMI-FINALS

Jalisco, Guadalajara, 17-06-1970, 51,000
Brazil 3 (Clodoaldo 45, Jairzinho 76, Rivelino 88)
Uruguay 1 (Cubilla 19)

Azteca, Mexico City, 17-06-1970, 80,000
Italy 4 (Boninsegna 7, Burgnich 99, Riva 104, Rivera 111)
West Germany 3 (Schnellinger 90, Müller 95 110)

3RD PLACE

Azteca, Mexico City, 20-06-1970, 104,000
West Germany 1 (Overath 26)
Uruguay 0

FINAL

Azteca, Mexico City, 21-06-1970, 107,000. Referee: Glöckner, East Germany
BRAZIL 4 (Pelé 18, Gérson 66, Jairzinho 71, Carlos Alberto 86)
ITALY 1 (Boninsegna 37)

Brazil - Félix - Carlos Alberto, Brito, Piazza, Everaldo - Clodoaldo, Gérson - Jairzinho, Tostao, Pelé, Rivelino. Tr: Zagalo
Italy - Albertosi - Burgnich, Cera, Rosato, Facchetti - Bertini (Juliano), Mazzola, De Sisti - Domenghini, Boninsegna (Rivera), Riva. Tr: Valcareggi

Top scorers: Gerd Müller, West Germany 10
Jairzinho, Brazil........7
Teófilo Cubillas, Peru 5
Total goals scored: 95
Average per game: 3

1974

THE 10TH WORLD CUP
14TH NOVEMBER 1971 - 7TH JULY 1974

As it was the turn of Europe to stage the 1974 World Cup, West Germany were the clear favourites and they were awarded the tournament at FIFA's 1968 congress in Mexico City. As with Mexico in 1968 and 1970, Germany had the honour of staging both the Olympic Games and then the World Cup within two years of each other. The space-age Olympic stadium in Munich was designated to stage the final, so there were no worries about the final venue being ready on time. The main worry was that of terrorism. During the Olympic Games in 1972, eleven Israeli athletes had been murdered by Palestinian terrorists, and consequently, even though Israel was not represented at the World Cup, security throughout the tournament was on a level never witnessed before.

A new trophy was also necessary, Brazil having been given permanent possession of the Jules Rimet Trophy. Football therefore lost, as did the Brazilians, literally, six years later, a beautiful, simple trophy and gained an ugly replacement, an 18-carat gold globe on an 18-carat gold pedestal.

Many famous names were not in Germany to fight for the new trophy, the most famous of which was England. Grouped with the Olympic champions Poland, England could do no more than draw with them at home, in a game marked by some fine goalkeeping by Tomaszewski in the Polish goal. Spain were also absent once again. Having finished level on points with Yugoslavia in their group they lost a play-off 1-0 in Frankfurt.

Hungary, Czechoslovakia, Austria, France and Portugal, all semi-finalists in previous tournaments, failed to qualify along with the Soviet Union, though the latter's exit from the competition was controversial. Forced to play-off against Chile, they drew the first leg in Moscow 0-0. The return leg, however, was due to be staged in the National Stadium in Santiago, and with some justification the Soviets refused to play there.

Earlier in the year, during the coup which saw the Marxist President Allende ousted by the right-wing General Pinochet, thousands of people had been herded into the stadium and never seen again. Many, though not all, were communists, and the Soviets did not feel happy about playing a game of football in such surroundings. Despite pleas to play the game elsewhere, the Chileans refused, and on the appointed day took to the field in the National Stadium. In one of the most bizarre sights the World Cup has ever seen, Chile kicked off the game and scored in the empty net. As the Soviets were not there to restart the game, it was abandoned and awarded to Chile.

There were not many other surprises in the qualifying tournament, except perhaps the elimination of Mexico by Haiti in the CONCACAF group. Bolstered by countries from the Arab world, the number of entrants in Asia rose dramatically, though ultimately they were all disappointed as Australia won through the qualifying tournament after being given a hard fight by Iran, the Asian champions, and South Korea, who took the more robust Australians to a play-off in Hong Kong in the final round before losing to a solitary goal.

The number of entries in Africa rose dramatically as well, as sub-Saharan Africa joined in for the first time in numbers. The Arab countries of North Africa had always been the part of Africa most taken note of by the rest of the world – given its proximity to Europe – but with the qualification of Zaire the focus shifted further south. The Zaireans won a final group against Morocco and Zambia, and they were considered to be among the best on the continent. Three months before the final tournament in West Germany began, they were crowned African champions after beating Zambia in the final of the African Cup of Nations in Cairo.

The format of the final tournament was changed in an attempt to increase revenue. Instead of eight games from the second round onwards there would now be fourteen. Gone were the quarter-finals and semi-finals which were replaced by two groups of four, the winners of which would qualify for the final, with the runners-up contesting the third place play-off. The system was heavily criticised as there would only be one knock-out game, the final. Also changed, three days before the finals began, was the presidency of FIFA. Out went Sir Stanley Rous and in came Joao Havelange who had the support of the majority of members from Africa and Asia.

The first round threw up a very interesting pairing in Group 1. East Germany, appearing in the finals for the first time, were drawn in the same group as West Germany. Since the division of Germany after the war, the two had never met in an international. Surprisingly, the men from the East won the day through a Jurgen Sparwasser goal, though both sides had already qualified for the second round at the expense of the weak Australians and Chileans. It was the only time the two countries ever played each other in 45 years of separate existence.

The defending champions Brazil were not the same team as they had been four years previously. Gone were Pele, Gerson and Tostao, and gone also was the free-flowing football and spirit of 1970. Brazil did not go out to win the tournament, instead they tried to prevent the opposition from taking a title they thought was rightfully theirs. Goalless draws against both Yugoslavia and Scotland set the tone and although they qualified with Yugoslavia at the expense of Scotland it was only on goal difference, and one goal at that. Zaire performed creditably against both Brazil and Scotland, but unfortunately will always be remembered for their drubbing at the hands of Yugoslavia, who although they scored nine could easily have taken the total well into double figures.

If the 1974 World Cup is remembered for one aspect in particular, it is for the introduction into the vocabulary of the phrase 'Total Football'. The masters at playing it were Holland, who had qualified for the World Cup for the first time since 1938. It was not a form of tactics as such, but a system whereby players would not be stuck to one position on the pitch. To make it work, players had to be very versatile and Holland had such men. They were by general consent the most talented team in the tournament and they qualified for the second round with ease, along with Sweden. Uruguay failed to qualify as they, like Brazil, seemed intent on playing hard, defensive football.

Not so Argentina, South America's third representatives, who played attractive, open football in their group matches. They qualified along with Poland, the real surprise package of the tournament, in what was an exciting group. Haiti in particular nearly caused an upset when they raced into an early second-half lead against Italy, but the thought of North Korea no doubt spurred the Italians on and they eventually ran out winners. They did not qualify for the next round, however. In their third game they had to beat the Poles, who were much too good for them. If any solace for England was to be found, this was it.

The second round separated the two arch-exponents of total football, Holland and West Germany. Holland now had to get past the challenge of Brazil, who were considered their greatest threat. Argentina, though full of promise, had not matured into a world-beating side just yet, and they lost to both Holland and Brazil in their first two matches. East Germany did likewise, which meant that although technically there was no semi-final, the final tie of the group between Brazil and Holland was just that, though a superior goal difference meant that Holland only had to draw to qualify for the final.

Holland were not to be denied by the champions. Goals by Neeskens and Cruyff in the second half of a game that saw some over-the-top tackling from both sides, gave Holland their place in the final, a place they richly deserved. Krol, Neeskens, Van Hanegem, Rep, Haan and Cruyff were all masters of their trade, but they needed the dominating figure of Rinus Michels, the manager, to make them function as a unit. Without him they might not have even reached the finals. Larger than life egos among the players had threatened to destroy the very basis of the team, that of combining together.

The other second round group saw a similar 'semi-final' situation develop. Both Poland and West Germany won their first two matches, leaving the game between the two of them as the decider. Like Holland, however, the Germans knew they could rely on a draw, and this gave them the advantage. Poland, who had been considered fortunate to beat both the Swedes and Yugoslavia, were this time unfortunate to lose to the Germans. The game was played on a rain-soaked Frankfurt pitch and only some excellent goalkeeping by Maier kept Lato at bay. Twelve minutes from time, however, Müller, who had not played as well as he had in Mexico, scored the killer goal that saw the hosts through.

The final therefore matched two perfectly balanced teams and was built up as a contest between Cruyff and Beckenbauer, both of whom vied to inherit the title of the world's greatest footballer, a position Pele had held for what seemed like an eternity. Beckenbauer was building a fearsome reputation as a libero, a sweeper who unlike the Italian model was not confined to defensive duties. Instead Beckenbauer was used as a springboard for attacking moves as well as clearing up in defence. Cruyff was regarded as the more skilful of the two, a player who could either make or score goals.

Beckenbauer was the one who emerged triumphant on this occasion, though not before Cruyff had given the game a start that would not be forgotten. Holland kicked off and before a German player had touched the ball they were a goal up. A superb run by Cruyff from outside the penalty area ended up with him being upended by Hoeness in it. Neeskens scored from the penalty spot with barely a minute gone.

For the first quarter of the game West Germany simply were not in it, and had the Dutch bothered to press home their advantage, Germany would have been out of the game completely. After 25 minutes, however, they were back in it when Breitner scored from the second penalty of the game after Holzenbein had been tripped by Jansen. Two minutes before half-time West Germany took the lead. Müller, receiving the ball from Bonhof, showed lightning reactions in first stopping the pass and then retrieving the ball when it looked as though it had gone behind him.

Before any of the Dutch defenders had a chance to clear, the ball was in the back of the net. Try as they might in the second half, the Dutch could not score. Again Maier showed why he was considered to be the best goalkeeper in the world, saving well from Neeskens, but Holland had lost the momentum they had built up in the first half, and for the second time the World Cup was West Germany's. Beckenbauer became the first captain to lift the new FIFA trophy.

QUALIFYING TOURNAMENT

EUROPE

Group 1

	Sd	Au	Hu	Ma	Pl	W	D	L	F	A	Pts
SWEDEN	-	3-2	0-0	7-0	6	3	2	1	14	7	8
Austria	2-0	-	2-2	4-0	6	3	2	1	15	8	8
Hungary	3-3	2-2	-	3-0	6	2	4	0	12	7	8
Malta	1-2	0-2	0-2	-	6	0	0	6	1	20	0

Play-off in Gelsenkirchen

Sweden .... 2-1 .... Austria

Group 2

	It	Tu	Sz	Lu	Pl	W	D	L	F	A	Pts
ITALY	-	0-0	2-0	5-0	6	4	2	0	12	0	10
Turkey	0-1	-	2-0	3-0	6	2	2	2	5	3	6
Switzerland	0-0	0-0	-	1-0	6	2	2	2	2	4	6
Luxembourg	0-4	2-0	0-1	-	6	1	0	5	2	14	2

Group 3

	Ho	Be	No	Ic	Pl	W	D	L	F	A	Pts
HOLLAND	-	0-0	9-0	8-1	6	4	2	0	24	2	10
Belgium	0-0	-	2-0	4-0	6	4	2	0	12	0	10
Norway	1-2	0-2	-	4-1	6	2	0	4	9	16	4
Iceland	0-5	0-4	0-4	-	6	0	0	6	2	29	0

Group 4

	EG	Ro	Fi	Al	Pl	W	D	L	F	A	Pts
EAST GERMANY	-	2-0	5-0	2-0	6	5	0	1	18	3	10
Romania	1-0	-	9-0	2-0	6	4	1	1	17	4	9
Finland	1-5	1-1	-	1-0	6	1	1	4	3	21	3
Albania	1-4	1-4	1-0	-	6	1	0	5	3	13	2

Group 5

	Pd	En	Wa	Pl	W	D	L	F	A	Pts
POLAND	-	2-0	3-0	4	2	1	1	6	3	5
England	1-1	-	1-1	4	1	2	1	3	4	4
Wales	2-0	0-1	-	4	1	1	2	3	5	3

Group 6

	Bu	Pt	NI	Cy	Pl	W	D	L	F	A	Pts
BULGARIA	-	2-1	3-0	2-0	6	4	2	0	13	3	10
Portugal	2-2	-	1-1	4-0	6	2	3	1	10	6	7
Nth. Ireland	0-0	1-1	-	3-0	6	1	3	2	5	6	5
Cyprus	0-4	0-1	1-0	-	6	1	0	5	1	14	2

Group 7

	Yu	Sp	Gr	Pl	W	D	L	F	A	Pts
YUGOSLAVIA	-	0-0	1-0	4	2	2	0	7	4	6
Spain	2-2	-	3-1	4	2	2	0	8	5	6
Greece	2-4	2-3	-	4	0	0	4	5	11	0

Play-off in Frankfurt

Yugoslavia .... 1-0 .... Spain

Group 8

	Sc	Cz	De	Pl	W	D	L	F	A	Pts
SCOTLAND	-	2-1	2-0	4	3	0	1	8	3	6
Czechoslovakia	1-0	-	6-0	4	2	1	1	9	3	5
Denmark	1-4	1-1	-	4	0	1	3	2	13	1

Group 9

	SU	RI	Fr	Pl	W	D	L	F	A	Pts
Soviet Union	-	1-0	2-0	4	3	0	1	5	2	6
Rep. Ireland	1-2	-	2-1	4	1	1	2	4	5	3
France	1-0	1-1	-	4	1	1	2	3	5	3

Soviet Union qualified for play-off against South American Group 3 winners Chile

SOUTH AMERICA

Group 1

	Ur	Co	Ec	Pl	W	D	L	F	A	Pts
URUGUAY	-	0-1	4-0	4	2	1	1	6	2	5
Colombia	0-0	-	1-1	4	1	3	0	3	2	5
Ecuador	1-2	1-1	-	4	0	2	2	3	8	2

Group 2

	Ar	Pa	Bo	Pl	W	D	L	F	A	Pts
ARGENTINA	-	3-1	4-0	4	3	1	0	9	2	7
Paraguay	1-1	-	4-0	4	2	1	1	8	5	5
Bolivia	0-1	1-2	-	4	0	0	4	1	11	0

Group 3

Peru ....2-0 0-2 ....Chile

Play-off in Montevideo

Chile....................2-1 ....Peru

Chile qualified for a play-off with Europe Group 9 winners Soviet Union

Soviet Union....................0-0 * ....**CHILE**

* Soviet Union refused to play the second leg and were disqualified

CENTRAL AND NORTH AMERICA

FIRST ROUND

Group 1

	Me	Ca	US	Pl	W	D	L	F	A	Pts
Mexico	-	2-1	3-1	4	4	0	0	8	3	8
Canada	0-1	-	3-2	4	1	1	2	6	7	3
United States	1-2	2-2	-	4	0	1	3	6	10	1

Group 2

Guatemala....................1-0 1-0 ....El Salvador

Group 3

Honduras ....2-1 3-3 ....Costa Rica

Group 4

Netherlands Antilles received a bye as Jamaica withdrew

Group 5

Haiti....................7-0 5-0....................Puerto Rico

Group 6

	Tr	Su	An	Pl	W	D	L	F	A	Pts
Trinidad	-	1-1	11-	14	3	1	0	16	4	7
Surinam	1-2	-	3-1	4	2	1	1	11	4	5
Antigua	1-2	0-6	-	4	0	0	4	3	22	0

SECOND ROUND

Tournament held in Haiti

	Ha	Tr	Me	Ho	Gu	NA	Pl	W	D	L	F	A	Pts
HAITI	-	2-1	0-1	1-0	2-1	3-0	5	4	0	1	8	3	8
Trinidad	-	-	4-0	1-2	1-0	4-0	5	3	0	2	11	4	6
Mexico	-	-	-	1-1	0-0	8-0	5	2	2	1	10	5	6
Honduras	-	-	-	-	1-1	2-2	5	1	3	1	6	6	5
Guatemala	-	-	-	-	-	2-2	5	0	3	2	4	6	3
Neth. Antilles	-	-	-	-	-	-	5	0	2	3	4	19	2

AFRICA

FIRST ROUND

Morocco....................0-0 2-1 ....Senegal
Algeria....................1-0 1-5 ....**Guinea**
Egypt ....2-1 0-2....................**Tunisia**
Sierra Leone....................0-1 0-2....................**Côte d'Ivoire**
Kenya....................2-0 0-1....................Sudan
Mauritius ....W-O ....Madagascar
Ethiopia....................1-1 0-0 3-0*....................Tanzania
Lesotho ....0-0 1-6....................**Zambia**
Nigeria....................2-1 1-1....................Congo
Dahomey....................0-5 1-5....................**Ghana**
Togo....................0-0 0-4 ....**Zaire**
Cameroon....................W-O....................Gabon

* Play-off in Addis Ababa

SECOND ROUND

Kenya....................3-1 2-2 ....Mauritius
Guinea ....1-1 0-2....................**Morocco**
Tunisia ....1-1 1-2 ....**Côte d'Ivoire**
Nigeria ....0-2 1-1 ** ....**Ghana**
Cameroon....................0-1 1-0 0-2* ....**Zaire**
Ethiopia....................0-0 2-4....................**Zambia**

* Play-off in Kinshasa

** First match abandoned with Ghana leading 3-2. Ghana awarded the game 2-0

THIRD ROUND

Côte d'Ivoire....................1-1 1-4....................**Morocco**
Zambia ....2-0 2-2 ....Kenya
Ghana....................1-0 1-4 ....**Zaire**

FOURTH ROUND

	Zr	Zm	Mo	Pl	W	D	L	F	A	Pts
ZAIRE	-	2-1	3-0	4	4	0	0	9	1	8
Zambia	0-2	-	4-0	4	1	0	3	5	6	2
Morocco	0-2*	2-0	-	4	1	0	3	2	9	2

* Morocco against Zaire was not played. Tie awarded to Zaire 2-0

ASIA

FIRST ROUND

Group A

Preliminary round (To determine group placements)

South Vietnam....................1-0 ....Thailand
Israel ....2-1 ....Japan
Hong Kong....................1-0 ....Malaysia

FIRST ROUND

Sub Group 1

	HK	Ja	SV	Pl	W	D	L	F	A	Pts
Hong Kong	-	1-0	1-0	2	2	0	0	2	0	4
Japan	-	-	4-0	2	1	0	1	4	1	2
South Vietnam	-	-	-	2	0	0	2	0	5	0

Sub Group 2

	Is	SK	Ma	Th	Pl	W	D	L	F	A	Pts
Israel	-	0-0	3-0	6-0	3	2	1	0	9	0	5
South Korea	-	-	0-0	4-0	3	1	2	0	4	0	4
Malaysia	-	-	-	2-0	3	1	1	1	2	3	3
Thailand	-	-	-	-	3	0	0	3	0	12	0

SEMI-FINALS

Israel ....1-0 ....Japan
South Korea ....3-1 ....Hong Kong

FINAL

South Korea ....1-0 ....Israel

Group B

FIRST ROUND

Sub Group 1

	Au	Ir	Id	NZ	Pl	W	D	L	F	A	Pts
Australia	-	3-1	2-1	3-3	6	3	3	0	15	6	9
Iraq	0-0	-	1-1	2-0	6	3	2	1	11	6	8
Indonesia	0-6	2-3	-	1-1	6	1	2	3	6	13	4
New Zealand	1-1	0-4	0-1	-	6	0	3	3	5	12	3

Sub Group 2

	Ir	Sy	NK	Ku	Pl	W	D	L	F	A	Pts
IRAN	-	1-0	0-0	2-1	6	4	1	1	7	3	9
SYRIA	1-0	-	1-1	2-1	6	3	1	2	6	6	7
NORTH KOREA	1-2	3-0	-	0-0	6	1	3	2	5	5	5
KUWAIT	0-2	0-2	2-0	-	6	1	1	4	4	8	3

FINAL

Australia ....3-0 0-2 ....Iran

SECOND ROUND

Australia ....0-0 2-2 ....South Korea

Play-off in Hong Kong
AUSTRALIA ....1-0 ....South Korea

WEST GERMANY qualified as hosts
BRAZIL qualified as holders

FINAL TOURNAMENT
HELD IN WEST GERMANY 13 JUNE - 7 JULY 1974

FIRST ROUND

Group 1

Olympiastadion, Berlin, 14-06-1974, 83,000
West Germany 1 (Breitner 16)
Chile 0

Volksparkstadion, Hamburg, 14-06-1974, 17,000
East Germany 2 (OG 57, Streich 69)
Australia 0

Volksparkstadion, Hamburg, 18-06-1974, 53,000
West Germany 3 (Overath 12, Cullmann 34, Müller 53)
Australia 0

Olympiastadion, Berlin, 18-06-1974, 27,000
Chile 1 (Ahumada 69)
East Germany 1 (Hoffmann 55)

Olympiastadion, Berlin, 22-06-1974, 14,000
Australia 0
Chile 0

Volksparkstadion, Hamburg, 22-06-1974, 60,000
East Germany 1 (Sparwasser 77)
West Germany 0

	EG	WG	Ch	Au	Pl	W	D	L	F	A	Pts
EAST GERMANY	-	1-0	1-1	2-0	3	2	1	0	4	1	5
WEST GERMANY	-	-	1-0	3-0	3	2	0	1	4	1	4
CHILE	-	-	-	0-0	3	0	2	1	1	2	2
AUSTRALIA	-	-	-	-	3	0	1	2	0	5	1

Group 2

Waldstadion, Frankfurt, 13-06-1974, 62,000
Brazil 0
Yugoslavia 0

Westfalenstadion, Dortmund, 14-06-1974, 27,000
Scotland 2 (Lorimer 26, Jordan 33)
Zaire 0

Waldstadion, Frankfurt, 18-06-1974, 62,000
Brazil 0
Scotland 0

Parkstadion, Gelsenkirchen, 18-06-1974, 31,000
Yugoslavia 9 (Bajevic 7 29 70, Dzajic 13, Surjak 18, Katalinski 21, Bogicevic 34, Oblak 60, Petkovic 62)
Zaire 0

Waldstadion, Frankfurt, 22-06-1974, 56,000
Yugoslavia 1 (Karasi 81)
Scotland 1 (Jordan 89)

Parkstadion, Gelsenkirchen, 22-06-1974, 36,000
Brazil 3 (Jairzinho 13, Rivelino 67, Valdomiro 79)
Zaire 0

	Yu	Br	Sc	Zr	Pl	W	D	L	F	A	Pts
YUGOSLAVIA	-	0-0	1-1	9-0	3	1	2	0	10	1	4
BRAZIL	-	-	0-0	3-0	3	1	2	0	3	0	4
SCOTLAND	-	-	-	2-0	3	1	2	0	3	1	4
ZAIRE	-	-	-	-	3	0	0	3	0	14	0

Group 3

Niedersachsenstadion, Hanover, 15-06-1974, 55,000
Holland 2 (Rep 7 87)
Uruguay 0

Rheinstadion, Düsseldorf, 15-06-1974, 23,000
Bulgaria 0
Sweden 0

Westfalenstadion, Dortmund, 19-06-1974, 53,000
Holland 0
Sweden 0

Niedersachsenstadion, Hanover, 19-06-1974, 13,000
Bulgaria 1 (Bonev 75)
Uruguay 1 (Pavoni 87)

Westfalenstadion, Dortmund, 23-06-1974, 53,000
Holland 4 (Neeskens 6 45, Rep 71, De Jong 86)
Bulgaria 1 (OG 78)

Rheinstadion, Düsseldorf, 23-06-1974, 28,000
Sweden 3 (Edström 46 78, Sandberg 74)
Uruguay 0

	Ho	Sd	Bu	Ur	Pl	W	D	L	F	A	Pts
HOLLAND	-	0-0	4-1	2-0	3	2	1	0	6	1	5
SWEDEN	-	-	0-0	3-0	3	1	2	0	3	0	4
BULGARIA	-	-	-	1-1	3	0	2	1	2	5	2
URUGUAY	-	-	-	-	3	0	1	2	1	6	1

Group 4

Olympiastadion, Munich, 15-06-1974, 53,000
Italy 3 (Rivera 52, OG 66, Anastasi 79)
Haiti 1 (Sanon 46)

Neckarstadion, Stuttgart, 15-06-1974, 32,000
Poland 3 (Lato 6 62, Szarmach 8)
Argentina 2 (Heredia 61, Babington 66)

Neckarstadion, Stuttgart, 19-06-1974, 70,000
Argentina 1 (Houseman 19)
Italy 1 (OG 35)

Olympiastadion, Munich, 19-06-1974, 25,000
Poland 7 (Lato 17 87, Deyna 19, Szarmach 30 34 51, Gorgon 32)
Haiti 0

Olympiastadion, Munich, 23-06-1974, 25,000
Argentina 4 (Yazalde 15 67, Houseman 18, Ayala 56)
Haiti 1 (Sanon 63)

Neckarstadion, Stuttgart, 23-06-1974, 70,000
Poland 2 (Szarmach 38, Deyna 44)
Italy 1 (Capello 86)

	Pd	Ar	It	Ha	Pl	W	D	L	F	A	Pts
POLAND	-	3-2	2-1	7-0	3	3	0	0	12	3	6
ARGENTINA	-	-	1-1	4-1	3	1	1	1	7	5	3
ITALY	-	-	-	3-1	3	1	1	1	5	4	3
HAITI	-	-	-	-	3	0	0	3	2	14	0

SECOND ROUND

Group A

Niedersachsenstadion, Hanover, 26-06-1974, 59,000
Brazil 1 (Rivelino 60)
East Germany 0

Parkstadion, Gelsenkirchen, 26-06-1974, 55,000
Holland 4 (Cruyff 11 89, Krol 25, Rep 72)
Argentina 0

Parkstadion, Gelsenkirchen, 30-06-1974, 69,000
Holland 2 (Neeskens 8, Rensenbrink 61)
East Germany 0

Niedersachsenstadion, Hanover, 30-06-1974, 39,000
Brazil 2 (Rivelino 31, Jairzinho 48)
Argentina 1 (Brindisi 34)

Parkstadion, Gelsenkirchen, 3-07-1974, 54,000
East Germany 1 (Streich 14)
Argentina 1 (Housemann 20)

Westfalenstadion, Dortmund, 3-07-1974, 53,000
Holland 2 (Neeskens 50, Cruyff 65)
Brazil 0

	Ho	Br	EG	Ar	Pl	W	D	L	F	A	Pts
HOLLAND	-	2-0	2-0	4-0	3	3	0	0	8	0	6
BRAZIL	-	-	1-0	2-1	3	2	0	1	3	3	4
EAST GERMANY	-	-	-	1-1	3	0	1	2	1	4	1
ARGENTINA	-	-	-	-	3	0	1	2	2	7	1

Group B

Neckarstadion, Stuttgart, 26-06-1974, 45,000
Poland 1 (Lato 43)
Sweden 0

Rheinstadion, Düsseldorf, 26-06-1974, 67,000
West Germany 2 (Breitner 39, Müller 77)
Yugoslavia 0

Waldstadion, Frankfurt, 30-06-1974, 53,000
Poland 2 (Deyna 25, Lato 62)
Yugoslavia 1 (Karasi 43)

Rheinstadion, Düsseldorf, 30-06-1974, 67,000
West Germany 4 (Overath 50, Bonhof 51, Grabowski 88, Hoeness 89)
Sweden 2 (Edström 26, Sandberg 53)

Rheinstadion, Düsseldorf, 3-07-1974, 37,000
Sweden 2 (Edström 30, Torstensson 86)
Yugoslavia 1 (Surjak 27)

Waldstadion, Frankfurt, 3-07-1974, 62,000
West Germany 1 (Müller 76)
Poland 0

	WG	Pd	Sw	Yu	Pl	W	D	L	F	A	Pts
WEST GERMANY	-	1-0	4-2	2-0	3	3	0	0	7	2	6
POLAND	-	-	1-0	2-1	3	2	0	1	3	2	4
SWEDEN	-	-	-	2-1	3	1	0	2	4	6	2
YUGOSLAVIA	-	-	-	-	3	0	0	3	2	6	0

3RD PLACE

Olympiastadion, Munich, 6-07-1974, 79,000
Poland 1 (Lato 76)
Brazil 0

FINAL

Olympiastadion, Munich, 7-07-1974, 77,000. Referee: Taylor, England
WEST GERMANY 2 (Breitner 25, Muller 43)
HOLLAND 1 (Neeskens 1)

West Germany - Maier - Vogts, Schwarzenbeck, Beckenbauer, Breitner - Bonhof, Hoeness, Overath - Grabowski, Müller, Hölzenbein. Tr: Schön

Holland - Jongbloed - Suurbier, Rijsbergen (De Jong), Haan, Krol - Jansen, Neeskens, Van Hanegem - Rep, Cruyff, Rensenbrink (Van de Kerkhof.R). Tr: Michels

Top scorers: Grzegorz Lato, Poland 7
Andrzej Szarmach, Poland 5
Johan Neeskens, Holland 5
Total goals scored: 97
Average per game: 2.6

1978

THE 11TH WORLD CUP
7TH MARCH 1976 - 25TH JUNE 1978

In 1978 the World Cup finally came to the home of South American football, Argentina. They had been awarded the tournament 12 years previously when no-one could foresee the problems that were to face the country in 1978. A brutal right-wing dictatorship under General Videla was busy terrorising its own people, many of whom simply 'disappeared' and were never seen again. Left-wing guerillas were in turn fighting back, and the country seemed to be on the verge of collapse. At one stage it seemed likely that the tournament would be relocated to Holland and Belgium as the threat of withdrawals became evident.

Despite these political problems, and concern that some of the stadia might not be ready on time, in the event the tournament passed off without incident off the field, helped by a truce tacitly agreed between the government and guerillas.

Both Uruguay and England failed to qualify. The former lost out to Bolivia in one of the biggest shocks in South American football history, the latter to Italy in a group that was decided on goal difference. Questions were asked about a system that allowed two former world champions to be grouped together in one group whilst another could contain Sweden, Switzerland and Norway, none of whom were relatively strong at the time. The Soviet Union were another established nation to miss out for the second time in a row, Hungary returning to the fold at their expense after a 12-year absence. The European champions Czechoslovakia were another surprise failure, and apart from West Germany, Holland and Italy, the European representation in Argentina did not look to be that strong.

Brazil were forced to play in the qualifying competition for only the second time in 20 years and along with Peru, qualified with relative ease. Despite knocking out the Uruguayans, who were ruing the missed chance to play so close to home, Bolivia could not beat off the challenge of Hungary in the intercontinental play-off; indeed they were trounced 6-0 in Budapest.

In Central America, Mexico made no mistake in qualifying, winning a tournament held in Mexico. To reach the finals, the Mexicans had to play nine games. Tunisia, who qualified from Africa, had to play ten, whilst Iran, Asia's representatives, had to play 12, double, and in some cases three times, the number required by most European nations. As the number of entries rose, it was evident that the number of places afforded Africa and Asia would have to rise in the future, and the 1978 World Cup was the last to be played to the 16-team formula.

Iran and Tunisia, especially, both strengthened the case for increased representation by playing well once in Argentina. Tunisia comfortably beat Mexico, narrowly lost against Poland and held the world champions West Germany to a goalless draw in a match that the North Africans needed to win to qualify for the second round. Instead it was the Poles and West Germans who qualified, but no longer would European teams play African sides and expect scores similar to Yugoslavia's 9-0 win four years previously.

Iran were expected to do better than Tunisia, dominating Asian football as they had for over ten years, but unfortunately for them they were grouped with Holland, who although they were without Cruyff who had temporarily retired, were still the favourites, along with the hosts, to win the tournament. Two penalties in a Rensenbrink hat-trick saw the Dutch beat Iran in the opening game of Group 4, but in their next game against Scotland, Iran, but for an extraordinary own goal, would have won. The much-fancied Peru made up the teams in Group 4 and they made sure the Iranians did not progress further.

Group 4 was in the event the most dramatic of the first round. Scotland needed to beat the Dutch by three clear goals in the final group game to qualify at their expense, and at one stage in the match, leading 3-1, they looked set to do it. After having played badly in the first two games, the Scots were turning on the style. The third goal in particular, a mazy dribble and shot by Gemmill, was possibly the best of the tournament. But a Rep goal 20 minutes from time put paid to any hopes they may have had.

Group 3 was the most dour, but was enlivened by an extraordinary refereeing decision in the match between Sweden and Brazil. With the scores at 1-1, Zico headed home a corner to seemingly win the match, but as the ball was sailing into the net, Clive Thomas the referee blew the whistle for full time. The Brazilians were furious but the result stood.

Playing in the same style that they had done in West Germany, Brazil drew their next game 0-0 with Spain, who once again did not have a happy tournament. The Austrians proved to be the surprise package, and although beaten by Brazil in the final game, they were already assured of their qualification. Argentina, based in the refurbished River Plate stadium, beat both Hungary and France, as did the Italians, based further down the coast in Mar del Plata. France however were no push-overs and with a young Platini in the side, showed promise that would stand them in good stead for the following World Cup. Argentina were spurred on by a partisan crowd, though in the final game against Italy, with nothing to play for, they lost 1-0 in an ill-tempered game, a result that left them in what looked like a marginally easier group for the second round, though the Argentine fans in the River Plate stadium had hoped for a win to keep their team in Buenos Aires.

Following the same system as four years previously, the second round was played in two groups of four, the winners of which would contest the final. The groups were divided almost exactly on continental lines. Along with Argentina were grouped Brazil and Peru as well as one European team, Poland, whilst Group A was a totally European affair.

Neither West Germany or Poland were of the same strength that had taken them to first and third places in 1974 and both flopped badly. Holland roundly disposed of the Austrians in their opening game whilst the Italians played out a 0-0 draw with the Germans, and although the Germans still had a mathematical chance of reaching the final going into the last game, courtesy of a draw against the Dutch, Austria saw to it that they would not. The game between Italy and Holland was therefore in effect a semi-final. Italy needed to win, whereas Holland could rely on a draw, and after 19 minutes a Brandts own goal put the Italians in the driving seat. The same player made amends early in the second half with a long range shot, an effort that Haan bettered after 75 minutes from even further out.

Group B was full of controversy as both Brazil and Argentina finished level on five points. Both had beaten Peru and Poland respectively in the opening games of the group, and they met in Rosario in the second set of games. No goals were scored in a highly charged game, which meant that if, as expected, Brazil beat Poland and Argentina beat Peru, goal difference would be needed to decide the finalists. In a piece of crass organisation, the Brazil-Poland game kicked off before the Argentina-Peru game which meant that the Argentinians knew exactly the result they needed.

The Brazilians cried cheat and they were largely justified. The organisers put the case that if Argentina played at the same time, no-one would go to the Brazil-Poland match, and they had a point; but the fact remained that the hosts derived a clear advantage. Knowing that they needed to win 4-1 at the very least, Argentina went even further than that, winning 6-0. To the accusations of bad organisation those of foul play were added, though Brazilian claims that the Peruvians had been bribed were totally unfounded. The final therefore was between the hosts and the runners-up of four years previously. Unfortunately for the Dutch, they joined both Czechoslovakia and Hungary as nations who had reached two finals and lost them both. Holland's misfortune was that on both occasions they lost to the hosts.

Had either of the finals been staged on neutral ground, they might well have won them. Ernst Happel was their manager in Argentina, and despite the absence of Cruyff, Van Hanegem, Van Beveren and Geels, he fashioned a side that looked capable of beating the Argentines, despite their home advantage. Argentina meanwhile, managed by the chain-smoking Menotti, had suffered the usual Argentine disease, players leaving Argentina for Europe. Of the exiles, only Kempes was recalled. Menotti decided to rely on home-based players, and the ploy worked.

Argentina won the final before a passionate crowd in the River Plate stadium in Buenos Aires. So much light blue and white confetti had been used to celebrate the home team's arrival on the pitch that at both ends it looked as if it had been snowing. Mario Kempes, leading the Argentine attack, played one of the best games of his life, and he opened the scoring in the 38th minute, cleverly touching home a pass from Luque. The Dutch, annoyed by Argentina's late arrival on the pitch at the beginning of the game, and by a protest about a bandage Rene Van de Kerkhof was wearing, did not approach the game with the right attitude.

The match was plagued by fouls and the referee seemed to have lost control, but Argentina hung onto their lead. In the last ten minutes, however, the Dutch nearly stole the match. Rene Van de Kerkhof beat the offside trap after an excellent through ball by Haan. He crossed and the substitute Nanninga was there to head home the equaliser. In the very last seconds of the game, Rensenbrink hit the post from close range after receiving a perfectly weighted long ball from Krol, and Holland's chance was gone. In extra time, with the crowd roaring them on, Argentina regrouped and went into the lead again. Kempes it was who scored, this time after a dazzling run from outside the penalty area during which he took on and beat three players, including the goalkeeper. Kempes was involved in Argentina's third goal as well. Setting off on another run he flicked the ball to Bertoni, Bertoni knocked it back, and it fortuitously came back off Kempes' chest for Bertoni to sweep it home.

Argentina had won a colourful and sometimes controversial tournament and deservedly so. None of the threatened problems had materialised. Having contributed so much to the game over the years, they finally had some tangible reward.

QUALIFYING TOURNAMENT

EUROPE

Group 1

	Pd	Pt	De	Cy	Pl	W	D	L	F	A	Pts
POLAND	-	1-1	4-1	5-0	6	5	1	0	17	4	11
Portugal	0-2	-	1-0	4-0	6	4	1	1	12	6	9
Denmark	1-2	2-4	-	5-0	6	2	0	4	14	12	4
Cyprus	1-3	1-2	1-5	-	6	0	0	6	3	24	0

Group 2

	It	En	Fi	Lu	Pl	W	D	L	F	A	Pts
ITALY	-	2-0	6-1	3-0	6	5	0	1	18	4	10
England	2-0	-	2-1	5-0	6	5	0	1	15	4	10
Finland	0-3	1-4	-	7-1	6	2	0	4	11	16	4
Luxembourg	1-4	0-2	0-1	-	6	0	0	6	2	22	0

Group 3

	Au	EG	Tu	Ma	Pl	W	D	L	F	A	Pts
AUSTRIA	-	1-1	1-0	9-0	6	4	2	0	14	2	10
East Germany	1-1	-	1-1	9-0	6	3	3	0	15	4	9
Turkey	0-1	1-2	-	4-0	6	2	1	3	9	5	5
Malta	0-1	0-1	0-3	-	6	0	0	6	0	27	0

Group 4

	Ho	Be	NI	Ic	Pl	W	D	L	F	A	Pts
HOLLAND	-	1-0	2-2	4-1	6	5	1	0	11	3	11
Belgium	0-2	-	2-0	4-0	6	3	0	3	7	6	6
Nth. Ireland	0-1	3-0	-	2-0	6	2	1	3	7	6	5
Iceland	0-1	0-1	1-0	-	6	1	0	5	2	12	2

Group 5

	Fr	Bu	RI	Pl	W	D	L	F	A	Pts
FRANCE	-	3-1	2-0	4	2	1	1	7	4	5
Bulgaria	2-2	-	2-1	4	1	2	1	5	6	4
Rep. Ireland	1-0	0-0	-	4	1	1	2	2	4	3

Group 6

	Sd	No	Sz	Pl	W	D	L	F	A	Pts
SWEDEN	-	2-0	2-1	4	3	0	1	7	4	6
Norway	2-1	-	1-0	4	2	0	2	3	4	4
Switzerland	1-2	1-0	-	4	1	0	3	3	5	2

Group 7

	Sc	Cz	Wa	Pl	W	D	L	F	A	Pts
SCOTLAND	-	3-1	1-0	4	3	0	1	6	3	6
Czechoslovakia	2-0	-	1-0	4	2	0	2	4	6	4
Wales	0-2	3-0	-	4	1	0	3	3	4	2

Group 8

	Sp	Ro	Yu	Pl	W	D	L	F	A	Pts
SPAIN	-	2-0	1-0	4	3	0	1	4	1	6
Romania	1-0	-	4-6	4	2	0	2	7	8	4
Yugoslavia	0-1	0-2	-	4	1	0	3	6	8	2

Group 9

	Hu	SU	Gr	Pl	W	D	L	F	A	Pts
Hungary	-	2-1	3-0	4	2	1	1	6	4	5
Soviet Union	2-0	-	2-0	4	2	0	2	5	3	4
Greece	1-1	1-0	-	4	1	1	2	2	6	3

Hungary qualify to meet the 3rd placed team in the South American group final, Bolivia

SOUTH AMERICA

FIRST ROUND

Group 1

	Br	Pa	Co	Pl	W	D	L	F	A	Pts
Brazil	-	1-1	6-0	4	2	2	0	8	1	6
Paraguay	0-1	-	1-1	4	1	2	1	3	3	4
Colombia	0-0	0-1	-	4	0	2	2	1	8	2

Group 2

	Bo	Ur	Ve	Pl	W	D	L	F	A	Pts
Bolivia	-	1-0	2-0	4	3	1	0	8	3	7
Uruguay	2-2	-	2-0	4	1	2	1	5	4	4
Venezuela	1-3	1-1	-	4	0	1	3	2	8	1

Group 3

	Pe	Ch	Ec	Pl	W	D	L	F	A	Pts
Peru	-	2-0	4-0	4	2	2	0	8	2	6
Chile	1-1	-	3-0	4	2	1	1	5	3	5
Ecuador	1-1	0-1	-	4	0	1	3	1	9	1

SECOND ROUND

Tournament in Cali, Colombia

	Br	Pe	Bo	Pl	W	D	L	F	A	Pts
BRAZIL	-	1-0	8-0	4	2	0	0	9	0	4
PERU	-	-	5-0	4	1	0	1	5	1	2
Bolivia	-	-	-	4	0	0	2	0	13	0

Bolivia qualified to meet the winners of Europe Group 9, Hungary

HUNGARY .... 6-0 3-2 .... Bolivia

CENTRAL AND NORTH AMERICA

FIRST ROUND

Group 1

	Me	US	Ca	Pl	W	D	L	F	A	Pts
Mexico	-	3-0	0-0	4	1	2	1	3	1	4
United States	0-0	-	2-0	4	1	2	1	3	4	4
Canada	1-0	1-1	-	4	1	2	1	2	3	4

Play-off in Port-au-Prince

Canada .... 3-0 .... United States

Group 2

	Gu	ES	CR	Pa	Pl	W	D	L	F	A	Pts
Guatemala	-	3-1	1-1	7-0	6	3	2	1	15	6	8
El Salvador	2-0	-	1-1	4-1	6	2	3	1	10	7	7
Costa Rica	0-0	1-1	-	3-0	6	1	4	1	8	6	6
Panama	2-4	1-1	3-2	-	6	1	1	4	7	21	3

Group 3

First round

Dominican Rep. .... 0-3 0-3 .... Haiti

SECOND ROUND

Guyana .... 2-0 0-3 .... Surinam
Neth. Antilles .... 1-2 0-7 .... Haiti
Jamaica .... 1-3 0-2 .... Cuba
Barbados .... 2-1 0-1 1-3* .... Trinidad

* Play-off in Port of Spain, Trinidad

THIRD ROUND

Surinam .... 1-1 2-2 3-2* .... Trinidad
Cuba .... 1-1 1-1 0-2** .... Haiti

* Play-off in Cayenne, Surinam
** Play-off in Panama City

SECOND ROUND

Tournament in Mexico City and Monterrey

	Me	Ha	Ca	ES	Gu	Su	Pl	W	D	L	F	A	Pts
MEXICO	-	4-1	3-1	3-1	2-1	8-1	5	5	0	0	20	5	10
Haiti	-	-	1-1	1-0	2-1	1-0	5	3	1	1	6	6	7
Canada	-	-	-	1-2	2-1	2-1	5	2	1	2	7	8	5
El Salvador	-	-	-	-	2-2	3-2	5	2	1	2	8	9	5
Guatemala	-	-	-	-	-	3-2	5	1	1	3	8	10	3
Surinam	-	-	-	-	-	-	5	0	0	5	6	17	0

AFRICA

PRELIMINARY ROUND

Sierra Leone .... 5-1 1-2 .... Niger
Upper Volta .... 1-1 2-0 .... Mauritania

FIRST ROUND

Algeria .... 1-0 0-0 .... Libya
Zambia .... 4-1 1-0 .... Malawi
Upper Volta .... 1-1 0-2 .... **Côte d'Ivoire**
Sierra Leone .... 0-0 2-6 .... **Nigeria**
Togo .... 1-0 1-1 .... Senegal
Congo .... 2-2 2-1 .... Cameroon
Egypt .... 3-0 2-1 .... Ethiopia
Morocco .... 1-1 1-1 2-4p .... **Tunisia**
Ghana .... 2-1 1-2 0-2* .... **Guinea**
Zaire .... W-O .... Cent. African Rep.
Kenya .... W-O .... Sudan
Uganda .... W-O .... Tanzania

* Play-off in Lome, Togo

SECOND ROUND

Tunisia .... 2-0 1-1 .... Algeria
Togo .... 0-2 1-2 .... **Guinea**
Côte d'Ivoire .... 3-2 3-1 .... Congo
Kenya .... 0-0 0-1 .... **Egypt**
Uganda .... 1-0 2-4 .... **Zambia**
Nigeria .... W-O .... Zaire

THIRD ROUND

Guinea .... 1-0 1-3 .... **Tunisia**
Nigeria .... 4-0 2-2 .... Côte d'Ivoire
Egypt .... 2-0 0-0 .... Zambia

FOURTH ROUND

	Tu	Eg	Ni	Pl	W	D	L	F	A	Pts
TUNISIA	-	4-1	0-0	4	2	1	1	7	4	5
Egypt	3-2	-	3-1	4	2	0	2	7	11	4
Nigeria	0-1	4-0	-	4	1	1	2	5	4	3

ASIA-OCEANIA

FIRST ROUND

Oceania

	Au	Nz	Ta	Pl	W	D	L	F	A	Pts
Australia	-	3-1	3-0	4	3	1	0	9	3	7
New Zealand	1-1	-	6-0	4	2	1	1	14	4	5
Taiwan	1-2	0-6	-	4	0	0	4	1	17	0

Both Australia, Taiwan matches played in Suva, Fiji

Both New Zealand, Taiwan matches played in Wellington, New Zealand

Asia

Group 1

Tournament in Singapore

	HK	Si	Ma	Id	Th	Pl	W	D	L	F	A	Pts
Hong Kong	-	2-2	1-1	4-1	2-1	4	2	2	0	9	5	6
Singapore	-	-	1-0	0-4	2-0	4	2	1	1	5	6	5
Malaysia	-	-	-	0-0	6-4	4	1	2	1	7	6	4
Indonesia	-	-	-	-	2-3	4	1	1	2	7	7	3
Thailand	-	-	-	-	-	4	1	0	3	8	12	2

FINAL

Singapore .... 0-1 .... Hong Kong

Group 2

	SK	Is	Ja	Pl	W	D	L	F	A	Pts
South Korea	-	3-1	1-0	4	2	2	0	4	1	6

				Pl	W	D	L	F	A	Pts
ISRAEL	0-0	-	2-0	4	2	1	1	5	3	5
JAPAN	0-0	0-2*	-	4	0	1	3	0	5	1

* Played in Tel Aviv, Israel

Group 3

	Ir	SA	Sy	Pl	W	D	L	F	A	Pts
IRAN	-	2-0	2-0*	4	4	0	0	8	0	8
SAUDI ARABIA	0-3	-	2-0	4	1	0	3	3	7	2
SYRIA	0-1	2-1	-	4	1	0	3	2	6	2

* Game awarded to Iran 2-0

Group 4

Tournament in Doha, Qatar

	Ku	Ba	Qa	Pl	W	D	L	F	A	Pts
KUWAIT	-	2-0	2-0	4	4	0	0	10	2	8
BAHRAIN	1-2	-	0-2	4	1	0	3	4	6	2
QATAR	1-4	0-3	-	4	1	0	3	3	9	2

SECOND ROUND

	Ir	SK	Ku	Au	HK	Pl	W	D	L	F	A	Pts
IRAN	-	2-2	1-0	1-0	3-0	8	6	2	0	12	3	14
SOUTH KOREA	0-0	-	1-0	0-0	5-2	8	3	4	1	12	8	10
KUWAIT	1-2	2-2	-	1-0	4-0	8	4	1	3	13	8	9
AUSTRALIA	0-1	2-1	1-2	-	3-0	8	3	1	4	11	8	7
HONG KONG	0-2	0-1	1-3	2-5	-	8	0	0	8	5	26	0

ARGENTINA qualified as hosts
WEST GERMANY qualified as holders

FINAL TOURNAMENT
HELD IN ARGENTINA 1ST - 25TH JUNE 1978

FIRST ROUND

Group 1

Estadio Mar del Plata, Mar del Plata, 2-06-1978, 42,000
Italy 2 (Rossi 29, Zaccarelli 52)
France 1 (Lacombe 1)

Monumental, Buenos Aires, 2-06-1978, 77,000
Argentina 2 (Luque 15, Bertoni 83)
Hungary 1 (Csapó 10)

Estadio Mar del Plata, Mar del Plata, 6-06-1978, 32,000
Italy 3 (Rossi 34, Bettega 36, Benetti 61)
Hungary 1 (Tóth.A 81)

Monumental, Buenos Aires, 6-06-1978, 77,000
Argentina 2 (Passarella 45, Luque 72)
France 1 (Platini 61)

Monumental, Buenos Aires, 10-06-1978, 77,000
Italy 1 (Bettega 67)
Argentina 0

Estadio Mar del Plata, Mar del Plata, 10-06-1978, 28,000
France 3 (Lopez 22, Berdoll 37, Rocheteau 42)
Hungary 1 (Zombori 41)

	It	Ar	Fr	Hu	Pl	W	D	L	F	A	Pts
ITALY	-	1-0	2-1	3-1	3	3	0	0	6	2	6
ARGENTINA	-	-	2-1	2-1	3	2	0	1	4	3	4
FRANCE	-	-	-	3-1	3	1	0	2	5	5	2
HUNGARY	-	-	-	-	3	0	0	3	3	8	0

Group 2

Monumental, Buenos Aires, 1-06-1978, 77,000
Poland 0
West Germany 0

Rosario Central, Rosario, 2-06-1978, 25,000
Tunisia 3 (Kaabi 53, Ghommidh 80, Dhouieb 87)
Mexico 1 (Ayala 45)

Rosario Central, Rosario, 6-06-1978, 15,000
Poland 1 (Lato 42)
Tunisia 0

Estadio Córdoba, Córdoba, 6-06-1978, 46,000
West Germany 6 (Müller.D 14, Müller.H 29, Rummenigge 37 71 , Flohe 43 73)
Mexico 0

Estadio Córdoba, Córdoba, 10-06-1978, 35,000
West Germany 0
Tunisia 0

Rosario Central, Rosario, 10-06-1978, 25,000
Poland 3 (Boniek 43 78, Deyna 56)
Mexico 1 (Rangel 52)

	Pd	WG	Tu	Me	Pl	W	D	L	F	A	Pts
POLAND	-	0-0	1-0	3-1	3	2	1	0	4	1	5
WEST GERMANY	-	-	0-0	6-0	3	1	2	0	6	0	4
TUNISIA	-	-	-	3-1	3	1	1	1	3	2	3
MEXICO	-	-	-	-	3	0	0	3	2	12	0

Group 3

Estadio Mar del Plata, Mar del Plata, 3-06-1978, 38,000
Brazil 1 (Reinaldo 45)
Sweden 1 (Sjöberg 37)

José Amalfitani, Buenos Aires, 3-06-1978, 49,000
Austria 2 (Schachner 10, Krankl 78)
Spain 1 (Dani 21)

José Amalfitani, Buenos Aires, 7-06-1978, 46,000
Austria 1 (Krankl 43)
Sweden 0

Estadio Mar del Plata, Mar del Plata, 7-06-1978, 40,000
Brazil 0
Spain 0

Estadio Mar del Plata, Mar del Plata, 11-06-1978, 40,000
Brazil 1 (Roberto Dinamite 40)
Austria 0

José Amalfitani, Buenos Aires, 11-06-1978, 48,000
Spain 1 (Asensi 75)
Sweden 0

	Au	Br	Sp	Sd	Pl	W	D	L	F	A	Pts
AUSTRIA	-	0-1	2-1	1-0	3	2	0	1	3	2	4
BRAZIL	-	-	0-0	1-1	3	1	2	0	2	1	4
SPAIN	-	-	-	1-0	3	1	1	1	2	2	3
SWEDEN	-	-	-	-	3	0	1	2	1	3	1

Group 4

San Martin, Mendoza, 3-06-1978, 42,000
Holland 3 (Rensenbrink 38 62 77)
Iran 0

Estadio Córdoba, Córdoba, 3-06-1978, 45,000
Peru 3 (Cueto 42, Cubillas 70 76)
Scotland 1 (Jordan 15)

San Martin, Mendoza, 7-06-1978, 30,000
Holland 0
Peru 0

Estadio Córdoba, Córdoba, 7-06-1978, 8,000
Scotland 1 (OG 43)
Iran 1 (Danaifar 77)

San Martin, Mendoza, 11-06-1978, 40,000
Scotland 3 (Dalglish 43, Gemmill 52 68)
Holland 2 (Rensenbrink 34, Rep 71)

Estadio Córdoba, Córdoba, 11-06-1978, 25,000
Peru 4 (Velasquez 2, Cubillas 36 39 78)
Iran 1 (Rowshan 40)

	Pe	Ho	Sc	Ir	Pl	W	D	L	F	A	Pts
PERU	-	0-0	3-1	4-1	3	2	1	0	7	2	5
HOLLAND	-	-	2-3	3-0	3	1	1	1	5	3	3
SCOTLAND	-	-	-	1-1	3	1	1	1	5	6	3
IRAN	-	-	-	-	3	0	1	2	2	8	1

SECOND ROUND

Group A

Monumental, Buenos Aires, 14-06-1978, 60,000
Italy 0
West Germany 0

Estadio Córdoba, Córdoba, 14-06-1978, 15,000
Holland 5 (Brandts 6, Rensenbrink 35, Rep 36 53, Van de Kerkof.W 83)
Austria 1 (Obermayer 80)

Estadio Córdoba, Córdoba, 18-06-1978, 46,000
Holland 2 (Haan 26, Van de Kerkof.R 83)
West Germany 2 (Abramczik 3, Müller.D 70)

Monumental, Buenos Aires, 18-06-1978, 50,000
Italy 1 (Rossi 13)
Austria 0

Estadio Córdoba, Córdoba, 21-06-1978, 20,000
Austria 3 (OG 60, Krankl 67 88)
West Germany 2 (Rummenigge 19, Hölzenbein 72)

Monumental, Buenos Aires, 21-06-1978, 70,000
Holland 2 (Brandts 51, Haan 75)
Italy 1 (OG 19)

	Ho	It	WG	Au	Pl	W	D	L	F	A	Pts
HOLLAND	-	2-1	2-2	5-1	3	2	1	0	9	4	5
ITALY	-	-	0-0	1-0	3	1	1	1	2	2	3
WEST GERMANY	-	-	-	2-3	3	0	2	1	4	5	2
AUSTRIA	-	-	-	-	3	1	0	2	4	8	2

Group B

San Martin, Mendoza, 14-06-1978, 40,000
Brazil 3 (Dirceu 14 27, Zico 70)
Peru 0

Rosario Central, Rosario, 14-06-1978, 40,000
Argentina 2 (Kempes 15, 70)
Poland 0

San Martin, Mendoza, 18-06-1978, 35,000
Poland 1 (Szarmach 64)
Peru 0

Rosario Central, Rosario, 18-06-1978, 46,000
Argentina 0
Brazil 0

San Martin, Mendoza, 21-06-1978, 44,000
Brazil 3 (Nelinho 12, Roberto 57 62)
Poland 1 (Lato 44)

Rosario Central, Rosario, 21-06-1978, 40,000
Argentina 6 (Kempes 20 48, Tarantini 43, Luque 49 72, Housemann 66)
Peru 0

	Ar	Br	Pd	Pe	Pl	W	D	L	F	A	Pts
ARGENTINA	-	0-0	2-0	6-0	3	2	1	0	8	0	5
BRAZIL	-	-	3-1	3-0	3	2	1	0	6	1	5
POLAND	-	-	-	1-0	3	1	0	2	2	5	2
PERU	-	-	-	-	3	0	0	3	0	10	0

3RD PLACE

Monumental, Buenos Aires, 24-06-1978, 76,000
Brazil 2 (Nelinho 64, Dirceu 71)
Italy 1 (Causio 38)

FINAL

Monumental, Buenos Aires, 25-06-1978, 77,000. Referee: Gonella, Italy
ARGENTINA 3 (Kempes 37 104, Bertoni 114)
HOLLAND 1 (Nanninga 81)

Argentina - Fillol - Olguín, Galván, Passarella, Tarantini - Ardiles (Larrosa), Gallego, Kempes - Bertoni, Luque, Ortíz (Houseman). Tr: Menotti

Holland - Jongbloed - Krol, Poortvliet, Brandts, Jansen (Suurbier) - Van de Kerkhof.W, Neeskens, Haan - Rep (Nanninga), Rensenbrink, Van de Kerkhof.R. Tr: Happel

Top scorers: Mario Kempes, Argentina 6
Teófilo Cubillas, Peru 5
Rob Rensenbrink, Holland 5

Total goals scored: 102
Average per game: 2.7

1982

THE 12TH WORLD CUP
26TH MARCH 1980 - 11TH JULY 1982

As the hosts had won three of the previous four World Cups, Spain were regarded as among the favourites for the 1982 tournament. The Spanish league was among the best in the world, and although their track record in the tournament was not good, many felt that this could be the year when the Spanish national team finally made their mark, and that the run of home victories would continue. Joao Havelange kept his promise to increase the number of competitors in the final tournament, made at the time of his election. From 16 teams in most of the previous tournaments, the total rose to 24, a highly questionable number in that although it gave more representation to the developing world, the final tournament became protracted and unwieldy. Two rounds of league groups would be used to thin the number of competitors down to four semi-finalists, and then two finalists, all over the period of a month.

Africa and Asia might have each gained another place in the finals, but the real beneficiary of the increased size of the tournament was Europe which gained an extra four places to take its total to 13. As two teams instead of one now qualified from each group, the scope for surprises was drastically reduced. There was one, though: Holland's failure to make it to the finals. Suffering a downward turn in their fortunes after the successes of the 1970s, they missed out by a point to France and Belgium, though the Republic of Ireland were even more unlucky. They failed to qualify for their first finals on goal difference behind the French.

England and the Soviet Union both made welcome returns after missing West Germany and Argentina, and for the first time since 1958 more than one country from the British Isles was represented. Scotland and Northern Ireland came first and second respectively in their group and so only Wales were missing.

From South America, Uruguay were again absent despite the continent having four places in the finals, whilst from CONCACAF, Mexico were surprisingly eliminated by Honduras and El Salvador.

Both Africa and Asia had their representation doubled – to two each! Of the four who qualified, the Asian pair looked the weaker and so it proved. Kuwait were the current Asian champions. Oil money had seen a succession of European and South American coaches visit the rich city state and this had made the difference in turning them from an ordinary side into a good one, but one which was slightly out of its depth in Spain. New Zealand had qualified after defeating China in a play-off, but like the Kuwaitis, the All-Whites, as the New Zealand footballers were known, were clearly outclassed.

Not so Algeria or Cameroon. Neither qualified for the second round in the finals, but both deserved to. Cameroon, playing in Group 1 in the north-western towns of Vigo and La Coruña, were grouped with Italy, Poland and Peru. Poland were enjoying something of a revival. Zmuda, Lato and Boniek were still instrumental in the team and courtesy of a heavy win over a weak Peru, for whom Cubillas was still the most influential player, they won the group. All the other games finished as draws, but because Italy had been involved in two 1-1 draws as opposed to Cameroon's one, they qualified at the Africans' expense. That Cameroon should lose out to the eventual champions only on goal difference served as a warning that Africa had arrived.

Events in Group 2 provided further proof, if any were needed. Algeria were denied a place in the second round courtesy of inexcusably inept organisation on FIFA's behalf and a blatant piece of cheating by the West Germans and the Austrians. Algeria beat the Germans in the opening game of the group in Gijón, a result likened to North Korea's victory over Italy and America's victory over England in previous World Cups. In their second game the Algerians faltered, losing to Austria who thus effectively qualified having beaten the hapless Chileans in their first game. West Germany's victory over Chile left them with two points from their first two games, like Algeria.

FIFA obviously had not learnt the lessons of the Argentina-Peru match four years previously, because Algeria played against Chile the day before the Germans and the Austrians met. Chile were beaten in an exciting game, once again marked by the quality of the Algerian players. Missing Belloumi, the star of the game against Germany, they were now inspired by Madjer and raced into a 3-0 half-time lead. Had the result stayed that way, all of the controversy of the following day would have been avoided, but the Algerians conceded two second-half goals.

The following day therefore, West Germany knew that a 1-0 win would put them through whilst the same score would also see the Austrians through. What has become known as the 'Great Gijón Swindle' or 'Anschluss' saw the game finish with just that result. After the Germans had taken an early lead, both teams might just as well have left the field, so little football was played. The Algerians were outraged. They immediately appealed to FIFA, who limply did nothing, knowing full well that ultimately it was they who were the culprits, for not insisting that the final games in each group were played simultaneously. Mindful of their mistake they implemented just such a policy four years later in Mexico.

In Group 3, the champions Argentina were beaten in the opening game of the tournament by Belgium, but both these two qualified at the expense of Hungary who, despite a 10-1 victory over El Salvador and a draw with Belgium, could not find a passage to the next round. In Group 4 both England and France qualified. Kuwait, having drawn against Czechoslovakia, lost heavily to the French, who for the only time in the first round showed the form that would take them to the semi-finals. The game was marred when Prince Fahed, the president of the Kuwaiti FA, who years later was killed defending his country against the invasion by Iraq, came onto the pitch to protest about a French goal. The referee then extraordinarily reversed his decision! Fahed not only had the money to hire the best coaches in the world but also, it seems, was a very persuasive man!

The hosts struggled to qualify for the next round from Group 5. Only a dubious penalty saved them from defeat at the hands of Honduras with whom they drew 1-1. Honduras were unlucky not to qualify. They also drew with Northern Ireland, and although they lost to Yugoslavia, it was only courtesy of a goal three minutes from time. Northern Ireland went into the last game needing a victory or a high-scoring draw against the Spaniards, who had beaten Yugoslavia 2-1 with the help of another penalty. Again the hosts looked overwhelmed by the pressure and their defeat at the hands of the Irish meant that they qualified for the second round but went into a much harder group containing both England and West Germany. The defeat also dispelled any notions the Spanish public might have had that their team could win the Cup.

Group 6 was the best of the first round. Brazil were back on song, playing lovely open football. After 12 years of living in the shadow of Pele, they had found their self-belief again. Based in the southern city of Seville, Socrates, Junior, Falcao, Eder, Zico and co put on a marvellous show, scoring 10 goals in their three games, and became the favourites for the title. Scotland, for the third tournament running, missed out on qualification on goal difference, but if their performance in Argentina had been inept, they could salvage some pride this time from their excellent contribution to a fascinating group.

The second round was left with four groups of unequal strength. Group C was especially strong, containing as it did the holders, the favourites and the ultimate winners. Both Brazil and Italy beat Argentina, who despite having Maradona in their side could not match the achievements of four years before. This left a decider between Brazil and Italy in the final game of the group. The match was a classic, and it saw the re-emergence of the man who was to win Italy the Cup, Paolo Rossi. Reprieved from a ban imposed after a match-fixing and bribery scandal, he suddenly burst into life in the game, scoring a hat-trick.

Brazil would rue the fact that, needing only a draw to qualify, they went out to win the game with the scores level at 2-2. Had they played more defensively after they levelled the scores they might not have let Rossi in for the winner 15 minutes from time. Out they went, but despite not winning the tournament they certainly made the biggest impression.

The other strong group on paper contained West Germany, the hosts and England. Spain bowed out after their defeat by Germany who had already drawn a sterile game with the English. England therefore had to beat Spain by two clear goals in the Bernabeu, but Spain, with the pressure off, were determined not to be humiliated and they defended admirably. England, who had come close on a number of occasions, went out. They had conceded just one goal and remained unbeaten, a record the West Germans could not match, but it was they who were in the semi-finals.

In Group D France began to play to the best of their ability. With a powerhouse midfield of Platini, Ghengini, Giresse and Tigana they outplayed both Austria and the Northern Irish to set up a semi-final meeting with West Germany.

The first semi-final saw Italy meet Poland. The latter had qualified due to the fact that they had beaten Belgium by more goals than the Soviets, but they were without Boniek for the semi-finals and it told. Playing before a half-full Nou Camp in Barcelona, Paolo Rossi was again the difference, scoring both the goals that saw Italy through to their second final in twelve years.

The France-West Germany match, held before a full house in Seville, was a much better game altogether, and vindicated the return to the use of semi-finals instead of group winners meeting in the final. The game saw the French at their very best, and the Germans at their most tenacious. The French, playing the fluent, outstanding football that made them European Champions two years later, quickly equalised a first-half Littbarski goal, and for the rest of normal time the score did not change. A crucial incident occurred in the second half which was ultimately to turn the game. Minutes after coming on as a substitute, Patrick Battiston, the French defender, was wickedly felled by Schumacher in the German goal. The Frenchman was carried off unconscious. West Germany were awarded a goal kick.

After scoring two goals early in extra time, France looked set for their first major final appearance, but in a show of Gallic extravagance they went forward in search of more goals. Had Battiston been on the field to shore up a weary defence this might not have mattered, but the Germans brought on Karl-Heinz Rummenigge and at his instigation they pulled level. For the first time in the World Cup, penalties were used to decide a game, a most unsatisfactory way of deciding the finalists for a competition of such importance. Unfortunately for France, after five kicks each and with the scores at 4-4, Schumacher saved from Bossis and Hrubesch scored the winner.

West Germany were without doubt the most unpopular finalists ever. They had lost to Algeria, been accused of a flagrant act of gamesmanship, and had now beaten the team most neutrals wanted to win, on penalties. Before the final Poland and France were involved in that most rare of events, an entertaining third place play-off. The French gave the rest of their squad an outing and lost 3-2 in the process, but for Poland third place capped a remarkable ten-year spell in world football which had seen them crowned Olympic Champions in 1972 and runners-up in 1976, achieve third place in the 1974 World Cup and reach the second round in 1978.

There are few better sights in football than a full Bernabeu stadium lit up against the night sky, and as Italy lifted the World Cup at the end of the final they knew they had graced the grand setting with some equally lovely football. The Germans were simply outclassed, although when Antonio Cabrini missed a first-half penalty many Italians must have thought it was not to be their day. After all, West Germany had progressed thus far against all the odds.

Once again it was Paolo Rossi who turned Italian domination into a goal, diving to head home a Gentile cross ten minutes into the second half. Tardelli had been quick to see Gentile free on the wing at a free kick and given him the ball before the Germans had time to react. Unusually for the Germans, their heads sank and Italy took over. Tardelli scored their second ten minutes later, after Rossi and Scirea had played a one-two in the area, and substitute Altobelli made sure of victory nine minutes from the end, Conti having run almost the full length of the pitch to cross it to him.

Breitner scored a consolation goal for West Germany right at the death, thus becoming only the third man after

Vava and Pele to score in two finals. Italy, having played some dreadfully dour football in the first round, had suddenly sprung to life in the second and played attractive and entertaining football. For once they forgot about defence and concentrated on attack, and it won them the World Cup.

QUALIFYING TOURNAMENT

EUROPE

Group 1

	WG	Au	Bu	Al	Fi	Pl	W	D	L	F	A	Pts
WEST GERMANY	-	2-0	4-0	8-0	7-1	8	8	0	0	33	3	16
AUSTRIA	1-3	-	2-0	5-0	5-1	8	5	1	2	16	6	11
Bulgaria	1-3	0-0	-	2-1	4-0	8	4	1	3	11	10	9
Albania	0-2	0-1	0-2	-	2-0	8	1	0	7	4	22	2
Finland	0-4	0-2	0-2	2-1	-	8	1	0	7	4	27	2

Group 2

	Be	Fr	RI	Ho	Cy	Pl	W	D	L	F	A	Pts
BELGIUM	-	2-0	1-0	1-0	3-2	8	5	1	2	12	9	11
FRANCE	3-2	-	2-0	2-0	4-0	8	5	0	3	20	8	10
Rep. Ireland	1-1	3-2	-	2-1	6-0	8	4	2	2	17	11	10
Holland	3-0	1-0	2-2	-	3-0	8	4	1	3	11	7	9
Cyprus	0-2	0-7	2-3	0-1	-	8	0	0	8	4	29	0

Group 3

	SU	Cz	Wa	Ic	Tu	Pl	W	D	L	F	A	Pts
SOVIET UNION	-	2-0	3-0	5-0	4-0	8	6	2	0	20	2	14
CZECHO-SLOVAKIA	1-1	-	2-0	6-1	2-0	8	4	2	2	15	6	10
Wales	0-0	1-0	-	2-2	4-0	8	4	2	2	12	7	10
Iceland	1-2	1-1	0-4	-	2-0	8	2	2	4	10	21	6
Turkey	0-3	0-3	0-1	1-3	-	8	0	0	8	1	22	0

Group 4

	Hu	En	Ro	Sz	No	Pl	W	D	L	F	A	Pts
HUNGARY	-	1-3	1-0	3-0	4-1	8	4	2	2	13	8	10
ENGLAND	1-0	-	0-0	2-1	4-0	8	4	1	3	13	8	9
Romania	0-0	2-1	-	1-2	1-0	8	2	4	2	5	5	8
Switzerland	2-2	2-1	0-0	-	1-2	8	2	3	3	9	12	7
Norway	1-2	2-1	1-1	1-1	-	8	2	2	4	8	15	6

Group 5

	Yu	It	De	Gr	Lu	Pl	W	D	L	F	A	Pts
YUGOSLAVIA	-	1-1	2-1	5-1	5-0	8	6	1	1	22	7	13
ITALY	2-0	-	2-0	1-1	1-0	8	5	2	1	12	5	12
Denmark	1-2	3-1	-	0-1	4-0	8	4	0	4	14	11	8
Greece	1-2	0-2	2-3	-	2-0	8	3	1	4	10	13	7
Luxembourg	0-5	0-2	1-2	0-2	-	8	0	0	8	1	23	0

Group 6

	Sc	NI	Sd	Pt	Is	Pl	W	D	L	F	A	Pts
SCOTLAND	-	1-1	2-0	0-0	3-1	8	4	3	1	9	4	11
NTH. IRELAND	0-0	-	3-0	1-0	1-0	8	3	3	2	6	3	9
Sweden	0-1	1-0	-	3-0	1-1	8	3	2	3	7	8	8
Portugal	2-1	1-0	1-2	-	3-0	8	3	1	4	8	11	7
Israel	0-1	0-0	0-0	4-1	-	8	1	3	4	6	10	5

Group 7

	Pd	EG	Ma	Pl	W	D	L	F	A	Pts
POLAND	-	1-0	6-0	4	4	0	0	12	2	8
East Germany	2-3	-	5-1	4	2	0	2	9	6	4
Malta	0-2	1-2	-	4	0	0	4	2	15	0

SOUTH AMERICA

Group 1

	Br	Bo	Ve	Pl	W	D	L	F	A	Pts
BRAZIL	-	3-1	5-0	4	4	0	0	11	2	8
Bolivia	1-2	-	3-0	4	1	0	3	5	6	2
Venezuela	0-1	1-0	-	4	1	0	3	1	9	2

Group 2

	Pe	Ur	Co	Pl	W	D	L	F	A	Pts
PERU	-	0-0	2-0	4	2	2	0	5	2	6
Uruguay	1-2	-	3-2	4	1	2	1	5	5	4
Colombia	1-1	1-1	-	4	0	2	2	4	7	2

Group 3

	Ch	Ec	Pa	Pl	W	D	L	F	A	Pts
CHILE	-	2-0	3-0	4	3	1	0	6	0	7
Ecuador	0-0	-	1-0	4	1	1	2	2	5	3
Paraguay	0-1	3-1	-	4	1	0	3	3	6	2

AFRICA

FIRST ROUND

Ethiopia	0-0 0-4	**Zambia**
Sierra Leone	2-2 1-3	**Algeria**
Libya	2-1 0-0	Gambia
Guinea	3-1 1-1	Lesotho
Senegal	0-1 0-0	**Morocco**
Tunisia	2-0 0-2 3-4p	**Nigeria**
Kenya	3-1 0-5	**Tanzania**
Cameroon	3-0 1-1	Malawi
Zaire	5-2 2-1	Mozambique
Niger	0-0 1-1*	Somalia
Egypt	W-O	Ghana
Madagascar	W-O	Uganda
Zimbabwe	Bye	
Sudan	Bye	
Liberia	Bye	
Togo	Bye	

* Niger won on away goals

SECOND ROUND

Cameroon	2-0 0-1	Zimbabwe
Morocco	2-0 0-2 5-4p	Zambia
Nigeria	1-1 2-0	Tanzania
Madagascar	1-1 2-3	**Zaire**
Liberia	0-0 0-1	**Guinea**
Algeria	2-0 1-1	Sudan
Niger	0-1 2-1	Togo
Egypt	W-O	Libya

THIRD ROUND

Guinea	1-1 0-1	**Nigeria**
Zaire	1-0 1-6	**Cameroon**
Morocco	1-0 0-0	Egypt
Algeria	4-0 0-1	Niger

FOURTH ROUND

Nigeria	0-2 1-2	**ALGERIA**
Morocco	0-2 1-2	**CAMEROON**

CENTRAL AND NORTH AMERICA

FIRST ROUND

Group 1

	Ca	Me	US	Pl	W	D	L	F	A	Pts
Canada	-	1-1	2-1	4	1	3	0	4	3	5
Mexico	1-1	-	5-1	4	1	2	1	8	5	4
United States	0-0	2-1	-	4	1	1	2	4	8	3

Group 2

	Ho	ES	Gu	CR	Pa	Pl	W	D	L	F	A	Pts
Honduras	-	2-0	0-0	1-1	5-0	8	5	2	1	15	5	12
El Salvador	2-1	-	1-0	2-0*	4-1	8	5	2	1	12	5	12
Guatemala	0-1	0-0	-	0-0	5-0	8	3	3	2	10	2	9
Costa Rica	2-3	0-0	0-3	-	2-0	8	1	4	3	6	10	6
Panama	0-2	1-3	0-2	1-1	-	8	0	1	7	3	24	1

* El Salvador awarded match 2-0

Group 3

Preliminary round

Guyana..............5-2 3-2..............Grenada

Group A

	Cu	Su	Gu	Pl	W	D	L	F	A	Pts
Cuba	-	3-0	1-0	4	3	1	0	7	0	7
Surinam	0-0	-	4-0	4	2	1	1	5	3	5
Guyana	0-3	0-1	-	4	0	0	4	0	9	0

Group B

	Ha	Tr	NA	Pl	W	D	L	F	A	Pts
Haiti	-	2-0	1-0	4	2	1	1	4	2	5
Trinidad	1-0	-	0-0	4	1	2	1	1	2	4
Neth. Antilles	1-1	0-0	-	4	0	3	1	1	2	3

SECOND ROUND

Tournament in Tegucigalpa, Honduras

	Ho	ES	Me	Ca	Cu	Ha	Pl	W	D	L	F	A	Pts
HONDURAS	-	0-0	0-0	2-1	2-0	4-0	5	3	2	0	8	1	8
EL SALVADOR	-	-	1-0	0-1	0-0	1-0	5	2	2	1	2	1	6
Mexico	-	-	-	1-1	4-0	1-1	5	1	3	1	6	3	5
Canada	-	-	-	-	2-2	1-1	5	1	3	1	6	6	5
Cuba	-	-	-	-	-	2-0	5	1	2	2	4	8	4
Haiti	-	-	-	-	-	-	5	0	2	3	2	9	2

ASIA-OCEANIA

FIRST ROUND

Group 1

	NZ	Au	Id	Ta	Fi	Pl	W	D	L	F	A	Pts
New Zealand	-	3-3	5-0	2-0	13-0	8	6	2	0	31	3	14
Australia	0-2	-	2-0	3-2	10-0	8	4	2	2	22	9	10
Indonesia	0-2	1-0	-	1-0	3-3	8	2	2	4	5	14	6
Taiwan	0-0	0-0	2-0	-	0-0	8	1	3	4	5	8	5
Fiji	0-4	1-4	0-0	2-1	-	8	1	3	4	6	35	5

Group 2

Tournament in Riyadh, Saudi Arabia

	SA	Iq	Qa	Ba	Sy	Pl	W	D	L	F	A	Pts
Saudi Arabia	-	1-0	1-0	1-0	2-0	4	4	0	0	5	0	8
Iraq	-	-	1-0	2-0	2-1	4	3	0	1	5	2	6
Qatar	-	-	-	3-0	2-1	4	2	0	2	5	3	4
Bahrain	-	-	-	-	1-0	4	1	0	3	1	6	2
Syria	-	-	-	-	-	4	0	0	4	2	7	0

Group 3

Tournament in Kuwait City

	Ku	SK	Ma	Th	Pl	W	D	L	F	A	Pts
Kuwait	-	2-0	4-0	6-0	3	3	0	0	12	0	6
South Korea	-	-	2-1	5-1	3	2	0	1	7	4	4
Malaysia	-	-	-	2-2	3	0	1	2	3	8	1
Thailand	-	-	-	-	3	0	1	2	3	13	1

Group 4

Tournament in Hong Kong

Preliminary round to determine group placements

Hong Kong..............0-1..............China

North Korea..............3-0..............Macao

Singapore..............0-1..............Japan

First round

Group A

	Ch	Ja	Mc	Pl	W	D	L	F	A	Pts
China	-	1-0	3-0	2	2	0	0	4	0	4
Japan	-	-	3-0	2	1	0	1	3	1	2
Macao	-	-	-	2	0	0	2	0	6	0

Group B

	NK	HK	Si	Pl	W	D	L	F	A	Pts
North Korea	-	2-2	1-0	2	1	1	0	3	2	3
Hong Kong	-	-	1-1	2	0	2	0	3	3	2
Singapore	-	-	-	2	0	1	1	1	2	1

Semi-finals

North Korea..............1-0..............Japan

China..............0-0 5-4p..............Hong Kong

Final

China..............4-2..............North Korea

SECOND ROUND

	Ku	NZ	Ch	SA	Pl	W	D	L	F	A	Pts
KUWAIT	-	2-2	1-0	2-0	6	4	1	1	8	6	9
NEW ZEALAND	1-2	-	1-0	2-2	6	2	3	1	11	6	7
China	3-0	0-0	-	2-0*	6	3	1	2	9	4	7
Saudi Arabia	0-1	0-5	2-4*	-	6	0	1	5	4	16	1

* Played in Kuala Lumpur, Malaysia

Play-off in Singapore

New Zealand..............2-1..............China

SPAIN qualified as hosts

ARGENTINA qualified as holders

FINAL TOURNAMENT, HELD IN SPAIN
13TH JUNE - 11TH JULY 1982

FIRST ROUND

Group 1

Balaidos, Vigo, 14-06-1982, 33,000

Italy 0

Poland 0

Riazor, La Coruña, 15-06-1982, 11,000

Peru 0

Cameroon 0

Balaidos, Vigo, 18-06-1982, 25,000

Italy 1 (Conti 19)

Peru 1 (OG 84)

Riazor, La Coruña, 19-06-1982, 19,000

Cameroon 0

Poland 0

Riazor, La Coruña, 22-06-1982, 25,000

Poland 5 (Smolarek 55, Lato 58, Boniek 61, Buncol 68, Ciolek 76)

Peru 1 (La Rosa 83)

Balaidos, Vigo, 23-06-1982, 20,000

Italy 1 (Graziani 60)

Cameroon 1 (M'Bida 61)

	Pd	It	Ca	Pe	Pl	W	D	L	F	A	Pts
POLAND	-	0-0	0-0	5-1	3	1	2	0	5	1	4
ITALY	-	-	1-1	1-1	3	0	3	0	2	2	3

CAMEROON	-	-	-	0-0	3	0	3	0	1	1	3
PERU	-	-	-	-	3	0	2	1	2	6	2

Group 2

El Molinón, Gijón, 16-06-1982, 42,000
Algeria 2 (Madjer 54, Belloumi 70)
West Germany 1 (Rummenigge 69)

Carlos Tartiere, Oviedo, 17-06-1982
Austria 1 (Schachner 21)
Chile 0

El Molinón, Gijón, 20-06-1982, 42,000
West Germany 4 (Rummenigge 9 56 66, Reinders 81)
Chile 1 (Moscoso 90)

Carlos Tartiere, Oviedo, 21-06-1982, 22,000
Austria 2 (Schachner 56, Krankl 67)
Algeria 0

Carlos Tartiere, Oviedo, 24-06-1982, 16,000
Algeria 3 (Assad 8 31, Bensaoula 35)
Chile 2 (Neira 60, Letelier 74)

El Molinón, Gijón, 25-06-1982, 41,000
West Germany 1 (Hrubesch 10)
Austria 0

	WG	Au	Al	Ch	Pl	W	D	L	F	A	Pts
WEST GERMANY	-	1-0	1-2	4-1	3	2	0	1	6	3	4
AUSTRIA	-	-	2-0	1-0	3	2	0	1	3	1	4
ALGERIA	-	-	-	3-2	3	2	0	1	5	5	4
CHILE	-	-	-	-	3	0	0	3	3	8	0

Group 3

Nou Camp, Barcelona, 13-06-1982, 95,000
Belgium 1 (Vandenbergh 63)
Argentina 0

Manuel Martínez Valero, Elche, 15-06-1982, 23,000
Hungary 10 (Nyilasi 3 83, Pölöskei 10, Fazekas 23 54, Toth 51, Kiss 70 73 78, Szentes 71)
El Salvador 1 (Ramírez Zapata 54)

José Rico Perez, Alicante, 18-06-1982, 32,000
Argentina 4 (Bertoni 26, Maradona 28 56, Ardiles 60)
Hungary 1 (Pölöskei 76)

Manuel Martínez Valero, Elche, 19-06-1982, 15,000
Belgium 1 (Coeck 18)
El Salvador 0

Manuel Martínez Valero, Elche, 22-06-1982, 37,000
Belgium 1 (Czerniatynski 76)
Hungary 1 (Varga 28)

José Rico Perez, Alicante, 23-06-1982, 32,000
Argentina 2 (Passarella 22, Bertoni 52)
El Salvador 0

	Be	Ar	Hu	ES	Pl	W	D	L	F	A	Pts
BELGIUM	-	1-0	1-1	1-0	3	2	1	0	3	1	5
ARGENTINA	-	-	4-1	2-0	3	2	0	1	6	2	4
HUNGARY	-	-	-	10-1	3	1	1	1	12	6	3
EL SALVADOR	-	-	-	-	3	0	0	3	1	13	0

Group 4

San Mamés, Bilbao, 16-06-1982, 44,000
England 3 (Robson 1 66, Mariner 82)
France 1 (Soler 25)

José Zorrilla, Valladolid, 17-06-1982, 25,000
Czecheslovakia 1 (Panenka 21)
Kuwait 1 (Al Dakhil 58)

San Mamés, Bilbao, 20-06-1982, 41,000
England 2 (Francis 63, OG 66)
Czechoslovakia 0

José Zorrilla, Valladolid, 21-06-1982, 30,000
France 4 (Genghini 30, Platini 42, Six 48, Bossis 90)
Kuwait 1 (Al Buloushi 75)

José Zorrilla, Valladolid, 24-06-1982, 29,000
France 1 (Six 66)
Czechoslovakia 1 (Panenka 84)

San Mamés, Bilbao, 25-06-1982, 39,000
England 1 (Francis 27)
Kuwait 0

	En	Fr	Cz	Ku	Pl	W	D	L	F	A	Pts
ENGLAND	-	3-1	2-0	1-0	3	3	0	0	6	1	6
FRANCE	-	-	1-1	4-1	3	1	1	1	6	5	3
CZECHOSLOVAKIA	-	-	-	1-1	3	0	2	1	2	4	2
KUWAIT	-	-	-	-	3	0	1	2	2	6	1

Group 5

Luis Casanova, Valencia, 16-06-1982, 49,000
Spain 1 (López Ufarte 65)
Honduras 1 (Zelaya 7)

La Romereda, Zaragoza, 17-06-1982, 25,000)
Northern Ireland 0
Yugoslavia 0

Luis Casanova, Valencia, 20-06-1982, 48,000)
Spain 2 (Juanito 14, Saura 77)
Yugoslavia 1 (Gudelj 10)

La Romereda, Zaragoza, 21-06-1982, 15,000
Northern Ireland 1 (Armstrong 10)
Honduras 1 (Laing 60)

La Romereda, Zaragoza, 24-06-1982, 25,000)
Yugoslavia 1 (Petrovic 87)
Honduras 0

Luis Casanova, Valencia, 25-06-1982, 49,000
Northern Ireland 1 (Armstrong 48)
Spain 0

	NI	Sp	Yu	Ho	Pl	W	D	L	F	A	Pts
NTH. IRELAND	-	1-0	0-0	1-1	3	1	2	0	2	1	4
SPAIN	-	-	2-1	1-1	3	1	1	1	3	3	3
YUGOSLAVIA	-	-	-	1-0	3	1	1	1	2	2	3
HONDURAS	-	-	-	-	3	0	2	1	2	3	2

Group 6

Sánchez Pizjuán, Seville, 14-06-1982, 68,000
Brazil 2 (Sócrates 75, Éder 88)
Soviet Union 1 (Bal 33)

La Rosaleda, Málaga, 15-06-1982, 36,000
Scotland 5 (Dalglish 18, Wark 30 34, Robertson 73, Archibald 80)
New Zealand 2 (Sumner 55, Wooddin 65)

Benito Villamarín, Seville, 18-06-1982, 47,000
Brazil 4 (Zico 33, Oscar 48, Éder 64, Falcão 86)
Scotland 1 (Narey 18)

La Rosaleda, Málaga, 19-06-1982, 19,000
Soviet Union 3 (Gavrilov 24, Blokhin 48, Baltacha 69)
New Zealand 0

La Rosaleda, Málaga, 22-06-1982, 45,000
Soviet Union 2 (Chivadze 59, Shengelia 84)
Scotland 2 (Jordan 15, Souness 87)

Benito Villamarín, Seville, 23-06-1982, 43,000
Brazil 4 (Zico 29 31, Falcão 55, Serginho 70)
New Zealand 0

	Br	SU	Sc	NZ	Pl	W	D	L	F	A	Pts
BRAZIL	-	2-1	4-1	4-0	3	3	0	0	10	2	6
SOVIET UNION	-	-	2-2	3-0	3	1	1	1	6	4	3
SCOTLAND	-	-	-	5-2	3	1	1	1	8	8	3
NEW ZEALAND	-	-	-	-	3	0	0	3	2	12	0

SECOND ROUND

Group A

Nou Camp, Barcelona, 28-06-1982, 65,000
Poland 3 (Boniek 4 26 53)
Belgium 0

Nou Camp, Barcelona, 1-07-1982, 45,000
Soviet Union 1 (Oganesian 50)
Belgium 0

Nou Camp, Barcelona, 4-07-1982, 65,000
Poland 0
Soviet Union 0

	Pd	SU	Be	Pl	W	D	L	F	A	Pts
POLAND	-	0-0	3-0	2	1	1	0	3	0	3
SOVIET UNION	-	-	1-0	2	1	1	0	1	0	3
BELGIUM	-	-	-	2	0	0	2	0	4	0

Group B

Bernabeu, Madrid, 29-06-1982, 75,000
West Germany 0
England 0

Bernabeu, Madrid, 2-07-1982, 90,000
West Germany 2 (Littbarski 51, Fischer 75)
Spain 1 (Zamora 81)

Bernabeu, Madrid, 5-07-1982, 75,000
England 0
Spain 0

	WG	En	Sp	Pl	W	D	L	F	A	Pts
WEST GERMANY	-	0-0	2-1	2	1	1	0	2	1	3
ENGLAND	-	-	0-0	2	0	2	0	0	0	2
SPAIN	-	-	-	2	0	1	1	1	2	1

Group C

Sarriá, Barcelona, 29-06-1982, 43,000
Italy 2 (Tardelli 57, Cabrini 67)
Argentina 1 (Passarella 83)

Sarriá, Barcelona, 2-07-1982, 44,000
Brazil 3 (Zico 12, Serginho 67, Junior 72)
Argentina 1 (Díaz 89)

Sarriá, Barcelona, 5-07-1982, 44,000
Italy 3 (Rossi 5 25 74)
Brazil 2 (Sócrates 12, Falcao 68)

	It	Br	Ar	Pl	W	D	L	F	A	Pts
ITALY	-	3-2	2-1	2	2	0	0	5	3	4
BRAZIL	-	-	3-1	2	1	0	1	5	4	2
ARGENTINA	-	-	-	2	0	0	2	2	5	0

Group D

Vicente Calderón, Madrid, 28-06-1982, 37,000
France 1 (Genghini 39)
Austria 0

Vicente Calderón, Madrid, 1-07-1982, 20,000
Austria 2 (Pezzey 51, Hintermaier 67)
Nth. Ireland 2 (Hamilton 27 74)

Vicente Calderón, Madrid, 4-07-1982, 37,000
France 4 (Giresse 33 80, Rocheteau 48 63)
Nth. Ireland 1 (Armstrong 75)

	Fr	Au	NI	Pl	W	D	L	F	A	Pts
FRANCE	-	1-0	4-1	2	2	0	0	5	1	4
AUSTRIA	-	-	2-2	2	0	1	1	2	3	1
NTH. IRELAND	-	-	-	2	0	1	1	3	6	1

SEMI-FINALS

Nou Camp, Barcelona, 8-07-1982, 50,000
Italy 2 (Rossi 22 73)
Poland 0

Sánchez Pizjuán, Seville, 8-07-1982, 63,000
West Germany 3 (Littbarski 18, Rummenigge 102, Fischer 107)
France 3 (Platini 27, Trésor 93, Giresse 97)
West Germany won 5-4 on penalties

3RD PLACE

José Rico Perez, Alicante, 10-07-1982, 28,000
Poland 3 (Szarmach 41, Majewski 44, Kupcewicz 47)
France 2 (Girard 14, Couriol 75)

FINAL

Bernabeu, Madrid, 11-07-1982, 90,000. Referee: Coelho, Brazil
ITALY 3 (Rossi 56, Tardelli 69, Altobelli 80)
WEST GERMANY 1 (Breitner 82)

Italy - Zoff - Cabrini, Scirea, Gentile, Collovati - Oriali, Bergomi, Tardelli - Conti, Rossi, Graziani (Altobelli) (Causio). Tr: Bearzot

West Germany - Schumacher - Kaltz, Stielike, Förster.K-H, Förster.B - Breitner, Breigel, Dremmler (Hrubesch) - Rummenigge (Müller.H), Littbarski, Fischer. Tr: Derwall

Top scorers: Paolo Rossi, Italy 6
Karl-Heinz Rummenigge, West Germany 5
Zbigniew Boniek, Poland 4
Zico, Brazil 4

Total goals scored: 146
Average per game: 2.8

1986

THE 13TH WORLD CUP

2ND MAY 1984 - 29TH JUNE 1986

The common pattern for the World Cup had been to alternate it between Europe and South America, and the 1986 tournament looked set to follow that pattern when Colombia were chosen as hosts. But in 1982, four years before the event, a combination of events forced them to withdraw, not least the fact that when they were awarded the tournament it was to comprise only 16 teams. Even with that number, a poor economic situation, as well as the violence associated with the drug trade, meant that it was not possible for them to go ahead and stage the event.

Brazil, the United States and Mexico all applied for the right to stage the tournament, and somewhat surprisingly Mexico emerged as the victors, becoming the first country to stage the tournament twice. A terrible earthquake in Mexico City a year before the finals nearly caused a second relocation but the tournament went ahead as planned. The problems with heat, altitude and an ever-worsening pollution problem, especially in the large sprawling capital, did not make conditions ideal, but like the 1970 tournament the 1986 World Cup was a success, despite these problems.

A record 121 countries entered initially, although after withdrawals only 113 nations set out on a qualification road that contained relatively few surprises. In Europe, Portugal qualified for only the second time and made a piece of history into the bargain when they inflicted on West Germany their first and only defeat to date in the World Cup qualifying tournament, with a 1-0 victory in Stuttgart.

All of the other major European powers qualified, although Holland, who would be crowned European Champions two years later, saw their revival cut short by Belgium in a play-off. There were few surprises in South America either as the 'big three' all made it to the finals for the first time since 1974. They were joined by Paraguay who made their first appearance since 1958.

North Africa provided both of the representatives for that continent as both Algeria and Morocco qualified. Such was the supremacy of that part of Africa that all five nations north of the Sahara made it to the quarter-finals of the qualifying competition and only Egypt missed out on the semi-finals.

The Asian qualifying group was divided into East and West which ensured that both the Middle East with Iraq and the Far East with South Korea were represented in Mexico. As by far and away the most powerful nation in the region, South Korea finally qualified for the first time since 1954 after so many near misses. Iraq's qualification was all the more remarkable in that all of their matches were played away from home due to the war with Iran.

CONCACAF were only given one berth in the finals due to the fact that Mexico as hosts qualified automatically, and it was to general surprise that the previously unknown Canadians won through at the expense of the supposedly superior Costa Rica and Honduras. With the demise of the North American Soccer League in the early 1980s, it had seemed as though football in that part of the world was on the decline.

The final tournament opened with a game between Italy and Bulgaria in the magnificent Azteca Stadium in Mexico City, the scene of the 1970 final. From the outset, the finals were regarded as the most open since they were last held in Mexico. There were no clear favourites. Mexico were not expected to win, despite a fanatical home following. West Germany, France, England, Italy and the Soviet Union were seen as potential winners from Europe whilst Brazil and Argentina were tipped from South America. If there were favourites, it was Argentina who took the fancy, largely due to the presence of Maradona who was at the peak of his career and playing football unrivalled since Pele had graced the World Cup 16 years previously.

Argentina duly won Group A, drawing 1-1 with the Italians in the big game of the group. The Italians, however, were at times given the run-around by South Korea in their final match. Fearful of another defeat by a Korean team, remembering their 1966 humiliation at the hands of the North, they eventually won 3-2. The new format of playing knock-out games from the second round meant that four of the third-placed teams with the best records in the six groups would qualify to make the numbers up to a workable 16. Italy's win over South Korea meant that the extremely dour Bulgarians qualified from Group A instead of the entertaining if somewhat cynical Koreans.

The effect of this format change was double-edged. Few doubted that knock-out games were potentially more exciting than group matches, but to achieve 16 second round qualifiers meant playing 36 first round games to eliminate just eight teams. The increase in the number of knock-out games also increased the spectre of the penalty shoot-out, as teams played for a draw in the hope of winning on spot-kicks.

Group B also saw three teams qualifying for the second round as Asia's other representatives, Iraq, were knocked out after playing some very sterile football. Mexico, playing to capacity crowds in the Azteca, were good value for their first place in the group. Inspired by their Real Madrid striker Hugo Sanchez, they beat ultimate semi-finalists Belgium 2-1 in their opening match after which qualification was virtually assured.

Group C saw the Soviet Union and France both finishing on five points, but having beaten Hungary 6-0 in their opening game the Soviets had a much better goal difference. Despite beating the weak Canadians 2-0, Hungary were disappointing after having initially been seen as a possible dark horse, and they were one of the two third-placed sides who failed to qualify. They deserve some credit, however. In their six games in the 1982 and 1986 finals, 29 goals had been scored in total. In an era when goals were beginning to dry up drastically, this was an achievement of sorts.

The third-placed team in Group D also failed to qualify for the second round as both Northern Ireland and Algeria were outclassed by Spain and Brazil in the most uneven first round group. Four years is a long time in football, and neither could live up to the reputations built in Spain in 1982. Northern Ireland's defeat by Brazil did have one event of note, however. Pat Jennings, the Irish goalkeeper, won his 119th and last cap, making him then the most capped player in history.

Called the 'group of death' by journalists, Group E was the hardest of the first round. All four teams were capable of qualifying and it was Scotland who were the unlucky team when for the fourth time running they failed to reached the second round. Denmark were in devastating form, winning all three of their games including a 6-1 annihilation of Uruguay, after which they were widely tipped as potential winners.

The last of the groups was by contrast called the 'group of sleep'. Based in the faraway and low-lying Monterrey, the first four games produced just two goals. Despite beating England in their opening game, Portugal were surprisingly eliminated when the group suddenly sprang into life with the final two fixtures. England recovered from a torpid start to the tournament when Gary Lineker scored three first-half goals in Monterrey against the mesmerised Poles to ensure England progressed to the second round when it had seemed likely that they would be returning home in disgrace. Even greater events were unfolding in Guadalajara where Morocco made sure of finishing top of the group with a stunning 3-1 victory over the hapless Portuguese. Thus for the first time an African nation had qualified for the second round. Nobody could now deny the growing strength of that continent.

The second round got underway in the Azteca when Mexico took on the Bulgarians. Looking for their first win in 16 games in the finals, Bulgaria were never in danger of breaking that most dubious of records, and they feebly succumbed to a spectacular overhead kick by Negrete and a header from Servin.

Later that afternoon the public of León were treated to an absolute thriller in what was undoubtedly the game of the tournament. With the score at 2-2 after full time, Belgium eventually beat the Soviet Union 4-3 after extra-time having twice been behind. Igor Belanov, later to be voted European Footballer of the Year, scored a hat-trick for the Soviets, but it was not enough and one of the best and most entertaining sides in the tournament bowed out of the competition.

The following day it was the turn of the South Americans to hold centre stage, and after having been thrashed by England, Poland were on the receiving end of another big score. Try as he might, Boniek could not inspire his team-mates to the same form which had seen them finish third in Spain. Instead, Brazil with Alemao, Junior, Zico and the irrepressible Socrates in midfield and the excellent Muller and Careca in attack, easily swept aside the Polish challenge to win 4-0.

If Brazil were beginning to look like champions, Argentina increased the prospect of an all-South American final by overcoming a potentially difficult tie against their neighbours and fierce rivals Uruguay, in a repeat of the 1930 final. This was also the first time the two teams had met in the World Cup since then, and in difficult conditions Argentina gained some semblance of revenge for the defeat in 1930 when Pasculli scored the winner for them just before half-time.

World Champions Italy faced European Champions France in the Olympic Stadium in the next match of the tournament. For Italy, gone was Rossi and much of their inspiration, and they meekly lost to the French, for whom Platini was still the driving force in a team with which it was hard to find much fault. Giresse, Tigana and Fernandez were brilliant alongside Platini in midfield, whilst Battiston, Amoros and Bossis were firm in defence. If there was a weakness it was in attack, where Jean-Pierre Papin was still a rising star and unable to command a regular place.

France would ultimately lose again in the semi-finals to West Germany, who scraped through the second round against Morocco courtesy of a last-minute winner from a Matthäus free-kick. The Germans were looking as unconvincing as they had done in 1982 yet they seemed to get the results. Morocco returned home to a heroes' welcome, and had they not been a little too much in awe of the Germans they might well have progressed further.

The last day of the second round saw England take on Paraguay and Spain play Belgium. In a near-capacity Azteca, England carried on where they had left off against Poland. Lineker, this time with two goals, was the star of the show as the English staked their claim to be seen as serious title contenders. Both Hoddle and Beardsley were in fine form and the latter scored the other England goal to take their total to six in two games after having failed to score in their first two.

The real surprise of the round was Denmark's defeat at the hands of Spain in Queretaro. Defeat in itself was not so surprising - the Spanish had, after all, beaten the Danes in the semi-finals of the European Championships two years previously - but the manner in which Denmark fell apart after having taken the lead after half an hour was extraordinary. Emilio Butragueño scored four goals in the space of 46 minutes as Spain walked away with the match 5-1 before the bewildered Danes.

The unsatisfactory side of the knock-out tournament reared its ugly head in the quarter-finals when three of the four ties were settled on penalties, whilst the fourth was settled by an incident that will forever live in World Cup folklore.

In a good game between France and Brazil in Guadalajara, where as in 1970 Brazil were based, France reached their second successive semi-final. The game was not without incident. Muller had given the South Americans an early lead but Platini equalised just before half-time. In the second half, Zico, the hero of Brazilian football, temporarily became a villain when he missed a penalty after having just come on as a substitute and Brazil's chance had gone.

Carlos, their goalkeeper, was lucky to stay on the field after a wild challenge outside the area on Bellone just before the finish. The French striker had managed to stay on his feet but was off balance and could not make the advantage the referee had played count. French nerves at the prospect of losing a second penalty shoot-out were calmed after Socrates missed from Brazil's first effort and they eventually won 4-3.

West Germany and Mexico played out a sterile draw in the match later on in the day. After 120 minutes of no goals, it may have been something of a relief for the crowd to see the ball hit the back of the net even if it was from penalties. In 1970, Mexico had lost at home to Italy in the quarter-finals. They were to go no further this time either. Playing in Monterrey and not in the Azteca, the Mexicans' game suffered and even in the penalty shoot-out they could only score once. The Germans could hardly believe their luck. Once again they were in the semi-finals and no one could quite understand how.

The third quarter-final, played the following day, was potentially the most explosive, involving as it did England and Argentina. Four years previously the two countries had fought a war over the Falkland Islands and emotions were still running high. In the event it will be remembered as one of the most controversial matches in World Cup history. The football rivalry between the two countries had always been intense, no more so than in the 1966 World Cup when controversy surrounded England's victory in the quarter-final of that tournament. In that match, the sending-off of Rattin, the Argentine captain, had been a crucial factor. Maradona, the captain in 1986, was also to be a key figure.

His first goal early in the second half has become known as 'The Hand of God' goal, which is how Maradona described it after the match. As he went for a high ball in the area with Peter Shilton, the England goalkeeper, Maradona cleared fisted the ball into the net, but despite vehement protests from Shilton, the Tunisian referee would not change his mind and the goal stood. Four minutes later the English, still smarting at the goal, were two down. This time it was Maradona at his most brilliant. Collecting the ball in his own half he simply strode through a mesmerised English defence to score one of the best goals football, let alone the World Cup, has ever seen. Lineker scored a consolation for England to make him the top scorer in the tournament, but the Argentines won through and the English somewhat unluckily bowed out of a tournament they could have won.

The last quarter-final saw Belgium reach the semi-finals for the first time in their history as once again the World Cup jinx hit Spain. The Spaniards came closer to reaching their first semi-final than they had ever done before but were denied 5-4 on penalties. Butragueño and Michel were the stars of the side but they had to thank Señor for equalising a first-half Begium goal just five minutes from time. Not so fortunate was Eloy, whose miss proved vital in the shoot-out.

The France-West Germany semi-final was a repeat of 1982 and again the Germans triumphed, although this time they did not need penalties to reach the final. It also failed to live up to the pedigree of the 1982 match as France performed strangely below par, never recovering from conceding an eighth-minute Brehme free-kick. Only in the final stages of the game did the French really threaten the German goal, and it was not surprising that with a minute left Völler scored a vital second goal on the breakaway.

In the other semi-final, Maradona was again turning on the magic, but this time without any of the controversy. As in the quarter-final with England, he scored his two goals early in the second half, the second of which was almost as good as his outstanding effort against the English. The Belgians, no doubt delighted to have proceeded so far, knew they had been beaten by a far superior team. Argentina, meanwhile, knew that they were overwhelming favourites to win their second world title, and win it they did.

Having lost the third place play-off in Spain, France made no mistake this time, beating Belgium 4-2 in Puebla, but once again the value of the fixture was brought into question as the French used it to give a run out to those players who had not featured heavily in the other matches.

Throughout the tournament, Franz Beckenbauer, the West German coach, had been saying his team was not good enough to win it. They had reached the final thanks largely to the 'tournament mentality' so prevalent in German sportsmen. They also undoubtedly had some fine players. Karl-Heinz Rummenigge was again the inspiration, but alongside him were players of the calibre of Lothar Matthäus and Felix Magath in midfield, Andreas Brehme, Thomas Berthold and Karl-Heinz Förster in defence, and Klaus Allofs and Rudi Völler in attack.

Argentina were obviously reliant on Maradona for much of their inspiration, but they were by no means a one-man team. In midfield, Sergio Batista, Ricardo Giusti, Hector Enrique and Jorge Burruchaga were all in excellent form, whilst Oscar Ruggeri was proving to be one of the best defenders Argentina had ever had. Alongside Maradona in attack, Jorge Valdano was also at the top of his game.

In a packed Azteca with the majority of the crowd behind Argentina, a slightly nervous performance by both sides in the first half saw Brown, the Argentine defender, give his side the lead after 22 minutes with a header from a Burruchaga free-kick. Ten minutes into the second half, Argentina were 2-0 up when Valdano, put clean through by Enrique, coolly slotted the ball past Schumacher. The Argentines were coasting to victory, but the Germans rose to the occasion and gave them a nasty shock.

With 17 minutes left the Germans pulled a goal back from a corner when Rummenigge prodded the ball home after it had been headed down by Völler, and from an almost identical situation eight minutes later it was Völler himself who sensationally levelled the scores, heading home after Berthold had played on a Brehme corner. It was anybody's game, but Maradona was not going to let his hour of glory slip away. With an exquisite pass he found Burruchaga in acres of space, and the Argentine midfielder had no trouble in finishing off a glorious move to seal the title for the South Americans.

Though he had not managed to score in the final, there was no doubt who the man of the tournament had been, and as he went up to collect the trophy, Maradona knew he had inherited Pele's title of the world's best footballer. Argentina had played the most consistent football throughout the tournament and had won all but one of their matches. Their manager Carlos Bilardo had built a side that complemented Maradona well and they fully deserved their victory. If there had been some lingering doubts about their victory eight years previously on home soil, few begrudged them their triumph in Mexico.

QUALIFYING TOURNAMENT

EUROPE

Group 1

	Pd	Be	Al	Gr	Pl	W	D	L	F	A	Pts
POLAND	-	0-0	2-2	3-1	6	3	2	1	10	6	8
BELGIUM	2-0	-	3-1	2-0	6	3	2	1	7	3	8
Albania	0-1	2-0	-	1-1	6	1	2	3	6	9	4
Greece	1-4	0-0	2-0	-	6	1	2	3	5	10	4

Belgium qualified to meet the runners-up of European group 5, Holland, in a play-off

Group 2

	WG	Pt	Sd	Cz	Ma	Pl	W	D	L	F	A	Pts
WEST GERMANY	-	0-1	2-0	2-2	6-0	8	5	2	1	22	9	12
PORTUGAL	1-2	-	1-3	2-1	3-2	8	5	0	3	12	10	10
Sweden	2-2	0-1	-	2-0	4-0	8	4	1	3	14	9	9
Czechoslovakia	1-5	1-0	2-1	-	4-0	8	3	2	3	11	12	8
Malta	2-3	1-3	1-2	0-0	-	8	0	1	7	6	25	1

Group 3

	En	NI	Ro	Fi	Tu	Pl	W	D	L	F	A	Pts
ENGLAND	-	0-0	1-1	5-0	5-0	8	4	4	0	21	2	12
NTH. IRELAND	0-1	-	3-2	2-1	2-0	8	4	2	2	8	5	10
Romania	0-0	0-1	-	2-0	3-0	8	3	3	2	12	7	9
Finland	1-1	1-0	1-1	-	1-0	8	3	2	3	7	12	8
Turkey	0-8	0-0	1-3	1-2	-	8	0	1	7	2	24	1

Group 4

	Fr	Bu	EG	Yu	Lu	Pl	W	D	L	F	A	Pts
FRANCE	-	1-0	2-0	2-0	6-0	8	5	1	2	15	4	11
BULGARIA	2-0	-	1-0	2-1	4-0	8	5	1	2	13	5	11
East Germany	2-0	2-1	-	2-3	3-1	8	5	0	3	19	9	10
Yugoslavia	0-0	0-0	1-2	-	1-0	8	3	2	3	7	8	8
Luxembourg	0-4	1-3	0-5	0-1	-	8	0	0	8	2	27	0

Group 5

	Hu	Ho	Au	Cy	Pl	W	D	L	F	A	Pts
HUNGARY	-	0-1	3-1	2-0	6	5	0	1	12	4	10
Holland	1-2	-	1-1	7-1	6	3	1	2	11	5	7
Austria	0-3	1-0	-	4-0	6	3	1	2	9	8	7
Cyprus	1-2	0-1	1-2	-	6	0	0	6	3	18	0

Holland qualified to meet the runners-up of European group 1, Belgium, in a play-off

BELGIUM .... 1-0 1-2 * .... Holland

* Belgium won on away goals

Group 6

	De	SU	Sz	RI	No	Pl	W	D	L	F	A	Pts
DENMARK	-	4-2	0-0	3-0	1-0	8	5	1	2	17	6	11
SOVIET UNION	1-0	-	4-0	2-0	1-0	8	4	2	2	13	8	10
Switzerland	1-0	2-2	-	0-0	1-1	8	2	4	2	5	10	8
Rep. Ireland	1-4	1-0	3-0	-	0-0	8	2	2	4	5	10	6
Norway	1-5	1-1	0-1	1-0	-	8	1	3	4	4	10	5

Group 7

	Sp	Sc	Wa	Ic	Pl	W	D	L	F	A	Pts
SPAIN	-	1-0	3-0	2-1	6	4	0	2	9	8	8
SCOTLAND	3-1	-	0-1	3-0	6	3	1	2	8	4	7
Wales	3-0	1-1	-	2-1	6	3	1	2	7	6	7
Iceland	1-2	0-1	1-0	-	6	1	0	5	4	10	2

Scotland qualified to meet the winners of the Oceania group, Australia, in a play-off

SOUTH AMERICA

Group 1

	Ar	Pe	Co	Ve	Pl	W	D	L	F	A	Pts
ARGENTINA	-	2-2	1-0	3-0	6	4	1	1	12	6	9
Peru	1-0	-	0-0	4-1	6	3	2	1	8	4	8
Colombia	1-3	1-0	-	2-0	6	2	2	2	6	6	6
Venezuela	2-3	0-1	2-2	-	6	0	1	5	5	15	1

Peru and Colombia qualified for South American play-offs

Group 2

	Ur	Ch	Ec	Pl	W	D	L	F	A	Pts
URUGUAY	-	2-1	2-1	4	3	0	1	6	4	6
Chile	2-0	-	6-2	4	2	1	1	10	5	5
Ecuador	0-2	1-1	-	4	0	1	3	4	11	1

Chile qualified for South American play-offs

Group 3

	Br	Pa	Bo	Pl	W	D	L	F	A	Pts
BRAZIL	-	1-1	1-1	4	2	2	0	6	2	6
Paraguay	0-2	-	3-0	4	1	2	1	5	4	4
Bolivia	0-2	1-1	-	4	0	2	2	2	7	2

Paraguay qualified for South American play-offs

Play-offs

FIRST ROUND

Paraguay .... 3-0 1-2 .... Colombia

Chile .... 4-2 1-0 .... Peru

FINAL

PARAGUAY .... 3-0 2-2 .... Chile

CENTRAL AND NORTH AMERICA

FIRST ROUND

El Salvador .... 5-0 3-0 .... Puerto Rico

Neth Antilles .... 0-0 0-4 .... **United States**

Canada .... W-O .... Jamaica

Panama .... 0-3 0-1 .... **Honduras**

Costa Rica .... W-O .... Barbados

Guatemala .... Bye

Trinidad	W-O	Grenada
Haiti	4-0 1-2 *	Antigua
Surinam	1-0 1-1	Guyana

* Both legs played in Haiti

SECOND ROUND

Group 1

	Ho	Es	Su	Pl	W	D	L	F	A	Pts
Honduras	-	0-0	2-1	4	2	2	0	5	3	6
El Salvador	1-2	-	3-0	4	2	1	1	7	2	5
Surinam*	1-1	0-3	-	4	0	1	3	2	9	1

* Surinam played all her games away from home

Group 2

	Ca	Gu	Ha	Pl	W	D	L	F	A	Pts
Canada	-	2-1	2-0	4	3	1	0	7	2	7
Guatemala	1-1	-	4-0	4	2	1	1	7	3	5
Haiti	0-2	0-1	-	4	0	0	4	0	9	0

Group 3

	CR	US	Tr	Pl	W	D	L	F	A	Pts
Costa Rica	-	1-1	1-1	4	2	2	0	6	2	6
United States	0-1	-	1-0	4	2	1	1	4	3	5
Trinidad *	0-3	1-2	-	4	0	1	3	2	7	1

* Trinidad played all her games away from home

THIRD ROUND

	Ca	Ho	CR	Pl	W	D	L	F	A	Pts
CANADA	-	2-1	1-1	4	2	2	0	4	2	6
Honduras	0-1	-	3-1	4	1	1	2	6	6	3
Costa Rica	0-0	2-2	-	4	0	3	1	4	6	3

AFRICA

FIRST ROUND

Egypt	1-0 1-1	Zimbabwe
Kenya	2-1 3-3	Ethiopia
Mauritius	0-1 0-4	**Malawi**
Zambia	3-0 0-1	Uganda
Madagascar	W-O	Lesotho
Tanzania	1-1 0-0 *	**Sudan**
Sierra Leone	0-1 0-4	**Morocco**
Libya	W-O	Niger
Benin	0-2 0-4	**Tunisia**
Guinea	W-O	Togo
Côte d'Ivoire	4-0 2-3	Gambia
Nigeria	3-0 1-0	Liberia
Angola	1-0 0-1 4-3p	Senegal
Algeria	Bye	
Cameroon	Bye	
Ghana	Bye	

* Sudan won on away goals

SECOND ROUND

Zambia	4-1 1-1	Cameroon
Morocco	2-0 0-0	Malawi
Angola	0-0 2-3	**Algeria**
Kenya	0-3 1-3	**Nigeria**
Egypt	1-0 0-1 4-2p	Madagascar
Guinea	1-0 0-2	**Tunisia**
Sudan	0-0 0-4	**Libya**
Côte d'Ivoire	0-0 0-2	**Ghana**

THIRD ROUND

Algeria	2-0 1-0	Zambia
Ghana	0-0 0-2	**Libya**
Nigeria	1-0 0-2	**Tunisia**
Egypt	0-0 0-2	**Morocco**

FOURTH ROUND

Tunisia	1-4 0-3	**ALGERIA**
MOROCCO	3-0 0-1	Libya

ASIA

FIRST ROUND

Group 1

Saudi Arabia	0-0 0-1	United Arab Emirates

Group 2

	Iq	Qa	Jo	Pl	W	D	L	F	A	Pts
Iraq	-	2-1	2-0	4	3	0	1	7	6	6
Qatar	3-0	-	2-0	4	2	0	2	6	3	4
Jordan	2-3	1-0	-	4	1	0	3	3	7	2

Iraq played Jordan in Kuwait City, and Qatar in Calcutta, India

Group 3

	Sy	Ku	NY	Pl	W	D	L	F	A	Pts
Syria	-	1-0	3-0	4	3	1	0	5	0	7
Kuwait	0-0	-	5-0	4	2	1	1	8	2	5
North Yemen	0-1	1-3	-	4	0	0	4	1	12	0

Group 4

South Yemen	1-4 3-3	Bahrain

Group 5

	SK	Ma	Ne	Pl	W	D	L	F	A	Pts
South Korea	-	2-0	4-0	4	3	0	1	8	1	6
Malaysia	1-0	-	5-0	4	2	1	1	6	2	5
Nepal	0-2	0-0	-	4	0	1	3	0	11	1

Group 6

	Id	In	Th	Ba	Pl	W	D	L	F	A	Pts
Indonesia	-	2-1	1-0	2-0	6	4	1	1	8	4	9
India	1-1	-	1-1	2-1	6	2	3	1	7	6	7
Thailand	0-1	0-0	-	3-0	6	1	2	3	4	4	4
Bangladesh	2-1	1-2	1-0	-	6	2	0	4	5	10	4

Group 7

	HK	Ch	Mc	Br	Pl	W	D	L	F	A	Pts
Hong Kong	-	0-0	2-0	8-0	6	5	1	0	19	2	11
China	1-2	-	6-0	8-0**	6	4	1	1	23	2	9
Macao	0-2	0-4	-	2-0	6	2	0	4	4	15	4
Brunei	1-5	0-4*	1-2	-	6	0	0	6	2	29	0

* Played in Hong Kong
** Played in Macao

Group 8

	Ja	NK	Si	Pl	W	D	L	F	A	Pts
Japan	-	1-0	5-0	4	3	1	0	9	1	7
North Korea	0-0	-	2-0	4	1	2	1	3	2	4
Singapore	1-3	1-1	-	4	0	1	3	2	11	1

SECOND ROUND

United Arab Emirates	2-3 2-1 *	**Iraq**
Bahrain	1-1 0-1	**Syria**
South Korea	2-0 4-1	Indonesia
Japan	3-0 2-1	Hong Kong

* Second leg played in Ta'if, Saudi Arabia

THIRD ROUND

Syria .... 0-0 1-3 * .... **IRAQ**
Japan .... 1-2 0-1 .... **SOUTH KOREA**

* Second leg played in Ta'if, Saudi Arabia

OCEANIA

	Au	Is	NZ	Ta	Pl	W	D	L	F	A	Pts
Australia	-	1-1	2-0	7-0	6	4	2	0	20	2	10
Israel	1-2	-	3-0	6-0	6	3	1	2	17	6	7
New Zealand	0-0	3-1	-	5-1	6	3	1	2	13	7	7
Taiwan *	0-8	0-5	0-5	-	6	0	0	6	1	36	0

* Taiwan played all her matches away from home
Australia qualified to meet the runners-up of European group 7, Scotland in a play-off

Play-off
SCOTLAND .... 2-0 0-0 .... Australia

FINAL TOURNAMENT, HELD IN MEXICO 31ST MAY - 29TH JUNE 1986

FIRST ROUND

Group 1

Azteca, Mexico City, 31-05-1986, 95,000
Italy 1 (Altobelli 43)
Bulgaria 1 (Sirakov 85)

Olimpico, Mexico City, 2-06-1986, 60,000
Argentina 3 (Valdano 5 46, Ruggeri 17)
South Korea 1 (Park Chang-sun 75)

Cuauhtemoc, Puebla, 5-06-1986, 32,000
Argentina 1 (Maradona 34)
Italy 1 (Altobelli 6)

Olimpico, Mexico City, 5-06-1986, 45,000
South Korea 1 (Kim Jong-boo 68)
Bulgaria 1 (Getov 11)

Olimpico, Mexico City, 10-06-1986, 65,000
Argentina 2 (Valdano 3, Burruchaga 78)
Bulgaria 0

Cuauhtemoc, Puebla, 10-06-1986, 20,000
Italy 3 (Altobelli 18 73, OG 82)
South Korea 2 (Choi Soon-ho 62, Hoh Jung-moo 89)

	Ar	It	Bu	SK	Pl	W	D	L	F	A	Pts
ARGENTINA	-	1-1	2-0	3-1	3	2	1	0	6	2	5
ITALY	-	-	1-1	3-2	3	1	2	0	5	4	4
BULGARIA	-	-	-	1-1	3	0	2	1	2	4	2
South Korea	-	-	-	-	3	0	1	2	4	7	1

Group 2

Azteca, Mexico City, 3-06-1986, 110,000
Mexico 2 (Quirarte 22, Sanchez 37)
Belgium 1 (Vandenbergh 44)

Bombonera, Toluca, 4-06-1986, 24,000
Paraguay 1 (Romero 35)
Iraq 0

Azteca, Mexico City, 7-06-1986, 114,000
Mexico 1 (Flores 2)
Paraguay 1 (Romero 84)

Bombonera, Toluca, 8-06-1986, 20,000
Belgium 2 (Scifo 15, Claesen 21)
Iraq 1 (Rhadi 57)

Bombonera, Toluca, 11-06-1986, 16,000
Belgium 2 (Vercauteren 32, Veyt 60)
Paraguay 2 (Cabañas 50 76)

Azteca, Mexico City, 7-06-1986, 114,000
Mexico 1 (Quirarte 54)
Iraq 0

	Me	Pa	Be	Iq	Pl	W	D	L	F	A	Pts
MEXICO	-	1-1	2-1	1-0	3	2	1	0	4	2	5
PARAGUAY	-	-	2-2	1-0	3	1	2	0	4	3	4
BELGIUM	-	-	-	2-1	3	1	1	1	5	5	3
Iraq	-	-	-	-	3	0	0	3	1	4	0

Group 3

Nou Camp, León, 1-06-1986, 65,000
France 1 (Papin 78)
Canada 0

Estadio Irapuato, Iraputo, 2-06-1986, 16,000
Soviet Union 6 (Yakovenko 2, Aleinikov 4, Belanov 23, Yaremchuk 66 74, Rodionov 79)
Hungary 0

Nou Camp, León, 5-06-1986, 36,000
France 1 (Fernández 61)
Soviet Union 1 (Rats 53)

Estadio Irapuato, Iraputo, 6-06-1986, 13,000
Hungary 2 (Esterhazy 2, Détári 75)
Canada 0

Nou Camp, León, 9-06-1986, 31,000
France 3 (Stopyra 30, Tigana 62, Rocheteau 84)
Hungary 0

Estadio Irapuato, Iraputo, 9-06-1986, 14,000
Soviet Union 2 (Blokhin 58, Zavarov 75)
Canada 0

	SU	Fr	Hu	Ca	Pl	W	D	L	F	A	Pts
SOVIET UNION	-	1-1	6-0	2-0	3	2	1	0	9	1	5
FRANCE	-	-	3-0	1-0	3	2	1	0	5	1	5
Hungary	-	-	-	2-0	3	1	0	2	2	9	2
Canada	-	-	-	-	3	0	0	3	0	5	0

Group 4

Jalisco, Guadalajara, 1-06-1986, 35,000
Brazil 1 (Sócrates 63)
Spain 0

Trez de Marzo, Guadelajara, 2-06-1986, 22,000
Algeria 1 (Zidane 58)
Northern Ireland 1 (Whiteside 5)

Jalisco, Guadalajara, 6-06-1986, 48,000
Brazil 1 (Careca 66)
Algeria 0

Trez de Marzo, Guadelajara, 7-06-1986, 28,000
Spain 2 (Butragueño 1, Salinas 18)
Northern Ireland 1 (Clarke 47)

Jalisco, Guadalajara, 12-06-1986, 51,000
Brazil 3 (Careca 15 87, Josimar 41)
Northern Ireland 0

Tecnológico, Monterrey, 12-06-1986, 23,000
Spain 3 (Calderé 16 68, Eloy 71)
Algeria 0

	Br	Sp	NI	Al	Pl	W	D	L	F	A	Pts
BRAZIL	-	1-0	3-0	1-0	3	3	0	0	5	0	6
SPAIN	-	-	2-1	3-0	3	2	0	1	5	2	4
NTH. IRELAND	-	-	-	1-1	3	0	1	2	2	6	1
ALGERIA	-	-	-	-	3	0	1	2	1	5	1

Group 5

La Corregidora, Querétaro, 4-06-1986, 30,000
West Germany 1 (Allofs 84)
Uruguay 1 (Alzamendi 4)

Nezahualcoyotl, Toluca, 4-06-1986, 18,000
Denmark 1 (Elkjaer-Larsen 58)
Scotland 0

La Corregidora, Querétaro, 8-06-1986, 30,000
West Germany 2 (Völler, 21,Allofs 51)
Scotland 1 (Strachan 17)

Nezahualcoyotl, Toluca, 8-06-1986, 26,000
Denmark 6 (Elkjaer-Larsen 10 69 70, Lerby 41, Laudrup.M 52, Olsen.J 87)
Uruguay 1 (Francescoli 45)

La Corregidora, Querétaro, 13-06-1986, 36,000
Denmark 2 (Olsen.J 42, Eriksen 63))
West Germany 0

Nezahualcoyotl, Toluca, 13-06-1986, 20,000
Uruguay 0
Scotland 0

	De	WG	Ur	Sc	Pl	W	D	L	F	A	Pts
DENMARK	-	2-0	6-1	1-0	3	3	0	0	9	1	6
WEST GERMANY	-	-	1-1	2-1	3	1	1	1	3	4	3
URUGUAY	-	-	-	0-0	3	0	2	1	2	7	2
SCOTLAND	-	-	-	-	3	0	1	2	1	3	1

Group 6

Universitario, Monterrey, 2-06-1986, 19,000
Morocco 0
Poland 0

Tecnológico, Monterrey, 3-06-1986, 23,000
Portugal 1 (Carlos Manuel 75)
England 0

Tecnológico, Monterrey, 6-06-1986, 20,000
Morocco 0
England 0

Universitario, Monterrey, 7-06-1986, 19,000
Poland 1 (Smolarek 68)
Portugal 0

Universitario, Monterrey, 11-06-1986, 22,000
England 3 (Lineker 7 13 36)
Poland 0

Jalisco, Guadalajara, 11-06-1986, 28,000
Morocco 3 (Khairi 18 28, Krimau 63)
Portugal 1 (Diamantino 80)

	Mo	En	Pd	Pt	Pl	W	D	L	F	A	Pts
MOROCCO	-	0-0	0-0	3-1	3	1	2	0	3	1	4
ENGLAND	-	-	3-0	0-1	3	1	1	1	3	1	3
POLAND	-	-	-	1-0	3	1	1	1	1	3	3
PORTUGAL	-	-	-	-	3	1	0	2	2	4	2

SECOND ROUND

Cuauhtemoc, Puebla, 16-06-1986, 26,000
Argentina 1 (Pasculli 41)
Uruguay 0

Azteca, Mexico City, 18-06-1986, 98,000
England 3 (Lineker 31 72, Beardsley 55)
Paraguay 0

La Corregidora, Querétaro, 18-06-1986, 38,000
Spain 5 (Butragueño 43 57 79 88, Goicoechea 68)
Denmark 1 (Olsen.J 32)

Nou Camp, León, 15-06-1986, 32,000
Belgium 4 (Scifo 54, Ceulemans 75, Demol 102, Claesen 108)
Soviet Union 3 (Belanov 27 69 111)

Olimpico, Mexico City, 17-06-1986, 70,000
France 2 (Platini 13, Stopyra 56)
Italy 0

Jalisco, Guadalajara, 16-06-1986, 45,000
Brazil 4 (Sócrates 29, Josimar 56, Edinho 78, Careca 82)
Poland 0

Azteca, Mexico City, 15-06-1986, 114,000
Mexico 2 (Negrete 34, Servin 60)
Bulgaria 0

Universitario, Monterrey, 17-06-1986, 19,000
West Germany 1 (Matthäus 89)
Morocco 0

QUARTER-FINALS

Azteca, Mexico City, 22-06-1986, 114,000
Argentina 2 (Maradona 51 55)
England 1 (Lineker 81)

Cuauhtemoc, Puebla, 22-06-1986, 45,000
Belgium 1 (Ceulemans 34)
Spain 1 (Señor 85)
Belgium won 5-4 on penalties

Jalisco, Guadalajara, 21-06-1986, 65,000
France 1 (Platini 41)
Brazil 1 (Careca 18)
France won 4-3 on penalties

Universitario, Monterrey, 21-06-1986, 44,000
West Germany 0
Mexico 0
West Germany won 4-1 on penalties

SEMI-FINALS

Azteca, Mexico City, 25-06-1986, 110,000
Argentina 2 (Maradona 51 62)
Belgium 0

Jalisco, Guadalajara, 25-06-1990, 45,000
West Germany 2 (Brehme 9, Völler 90)
France 0

3RD PLACE

Cuauhtemoc, Puebla, 28-06-1986, 21,000
France 4 (Ferreri 27, Papin 42, Genghini 103, Amoros 108)
Belgium 2 (Ceulemans 10, Claesen 73)

FINAL

Azteca, Mexico City, 29-07-1986, 114,000. Referee: Arppi Filho, Brazil

ARGENTINA 3 (Brown 22, Valdano 56, Burruchaga 84)

WEST GERMANY 2 (Rummenigge 73, Völler 82)

Argentina - Pumpido - Cuciuffo, Brown, Ruggeri, Olarticoechea - Batista, Giusti, Enrique, Burruchaga (Trobbiani) - Maradona, Valdano. Tr: Bilardo

West Germany - Schumacher - Jakobs, Förster.K-H, Breigel, Brehme - Eder, Berthold, Matthäus, Magath (Hoeness.D) - Rummenigge, Allofs (Völler). Tr: Beckenbauer

Top scorers: Gary Lineker, England 6
Emilio Butragueño, Spain 5
Careca, Brazil 5
Diego Maradona, Argentina 5

Total goals scored: 132
Average per game: 2.5

1990

THE 14TH WORLD CUP
17TH APRIL 1988 - 8TH JULY 1990

For the first time since 1950, the number of countries taking part in the World Cup fell, perhaps in anticipation of the poor tournament that was to result at the end of the qualifying matches. Italia '90 will be remembered for dull, defensive football, and ultimately proved a test not of footballing prowess but of penalty-taking technique. Italy were awarded the tournament in 1984 during the FIFA congress at the Los Angeles Olympic Games. Their only competition was from the Soviet Union whose case was shot to pieces by their boycott of those very Games.

Italy therefore became the second nation to be awarded the tournament twice. They promised a host of new facilities, and although it looked like a close call at times, with a number of building workers being killed in the process, the tournament started as planned with 10 refurbished stadiums and two totally new ones, in Bari and Turin.

The qualifying tournament produced a couple of surprises, the major one being the elimination of France. Coached by the star of their three previous World Cup campaigns, Michel Platini, they were busy restructuring their team and came third in their group behind Yugoslavia and Scotland. The rest of the European zone went much to form. Of the countries who finished in second place in the three groups containing four sides, Denmark were the unfortunate ones to miss out on Italy as only the two with the best records, England and West Germany, qualified. Like France the Danes were a team in transition but the finals would have undoubtedly benefited from their flair.

Making their first appearance in the finals were the Republic of Ireland. Following on from their success in qualifying for the European Championships two years previously, they inherited the mantle left by their neighbours in the North whom they eliminated. They also made sure Hungary were not present for the first time since 1974, and also missing were Portugal and Bulgaria both of whom had been finalists four years previously.

South America saw no surprises, but a huge scandal instead. In one of the most outrageous pieces of cheating ever seen, Chile left the field in the final and crucial group match with Brazil when they were losing 1-0 and on their way out of the competition. The reason for their departure was a flare thrown from the crowd at Rojas, their goalkeeper, and they claimed to fear for their safety. At first sight it looked as though he was badly injured as his team-mates carried him off, but it soon transpired that the flare had not hit him and that the bleeding conveniently visible to the television cameras was self-inflicted.

For their rather ridiculous efforts, the perpetrators of this pre-arranged plan were given lengthy bans and Chile were barred from the 1994 tournament. Banned from the 1990 tournament were Mexico, for cheating in the World Youth Cup by fielding over-age players. This left the CONCACAF field wide open and for the first time ever Costa Rica made it to the finals. Traditionally the second power in the region behind Mexico, it was surprising that it had taken them so long to qualify, but they did so with ease. That was not the case with the United States, who accompanied them to Italy. A 1-0 victory in Port of Spain meant that they and not the colourful Trinidadians qualified, much to the relief of FIFA who had just awarded America the staging of the 1994 tournament.

Asia was once again represented by South Korea, who won a tournament staged in Singapore for the six first round group winners. They were expected to be joined by either China or Saudi Arabia, two growing continental powers. Instead it was the tiny oil-rich United Arab Emirates who joined the Koreans in Italy. It seems remarkable that a country with a population of under two million could humble a country like China with over 500 times the population, but the Emirates showed the benefits that good organisation and a few petro-dollars can bring.

The number of teams taking part from Africa was at its lowest level since 1970. Undoubtedly the difficult economic situation on the continent affected the entry, but there was also continued resentment at the allocation of just two places, and some of the smaller nations, with little chance of qualifying, decided not to enter or pulled out at a later date. Having generally been run on a knock-out basis, the competition now saw group matches used in the first round, from which four teams emerged.

Once again North Africa was strongly represented, with three of the four teams. Egypt qualified for the first time since 1934 at the expense of Algeria who were attempting to make it three final tournaments in a row, but it was the other qualifiers, Cameroon, who were to make all the headlines in Italy. By beating Tunisia 3-0 on aggregate, they made their second appearance in the finals and once there, were minutes away from becoming the first African nation to reach the semi-finals. Their performance in Italy had one major benefit for the rest of African football in that FIFA found it hard to resist the African demands for an extra finals place which they were duly awarded for the 1994 tournament.

The build up for the finals in Italy promised much more than the tournament delivered. The Italian league had the majority of the top players in the world playing there and the shackles of catenaccio were slowly but surely being thrown off. The hosts were capable of playing some excellent football and with home advantage they were overwhelming favourites to win the tournament.

The 1986 champions, Argentina, were also regarded as likely challengers before the tournament started, but after the opening game, staged in the beautifully revamped Giuseppe Meazza Stadium in Milan, they were regarded in an entirely different light. The champions were humbled by Cameroon, despite the Africans having two men sent off. Francois Oman Biyik scored the only goal of the game five minutes after his brother, Kana Biyik, had been sent off. Roared on by the crowd, Cameroon held on to their lead and scored one of the most sensational victories the World Cup had ever seen.

Cameroon followed up this victory with another one in their second game, against Romania. The hero of that performance was the 38-year-old Roger Milla who came on as a substitute with 15 minutes remaining and scored two goals to qualify his side for the next round. The surprise failures of Group B were the Soviet Union who were strongly fancied at the start of the tournament. They showed their potential by beating Cameroon 4-0 in a final game that ultimately had no bearing on the outcome of the group. Romania finished second and Argentina qualified as one of the four best third-placed teams.

Group A was very clear cut. Italy won all three of their games in fine style and were joined by Czechoslovakia in the next round. Both Austria and the United States had miserable World Cups. Austria were expected to do much better; the same could not be said about the United States. Alarmingly for FIFA, interest in the tournament back home in America was limited to the numerous ethnic communities who usually followed the fortunes of other teams, most notably the Irish. The one consolation for the Americans was a fine goal scored by Caligiuri against Czechoslovakia which many rated as one of the best of the tournament.

Brazil were easy winners of Group C even if their coach Lazaroni did come in for much criticism for adopting too 'European' an approach. What was surprising in the group was that Costa Rica finished second and eliminated both Scotland and Sweden, both of whom they defeated in some style. With much of the attention focused on Cameroon, the achievements of Costa Rica have largely been forgotten. Scotland were eliminated in the first round for the fifth consecutive tournament.

Three teams qualified from Group D which was won by West Germany, who looked in very good form. Having demolished both Yugoslavia and the United Arab Emirates, they let their form slip against the Colombians, whose presence in the tournament had provoked a huge operation by America's Drug Enforcement Agency. At times it seemed as though they ought not to look any further than the Colombian goalkeeper, Rene Higuita, so strange were some of his antics. The majority of the crowds loved him for his cavalier attitude, though he did have his critics.

This was not Asia's tournament. The Emirates were obviously outclassed in Group D, whilst in Group E, South Korea could not rekindle the spirit that had seen them perform well four years previously in Mexico. The group was won by Spain who were hoping to win on Italian soil just as the Italians had won on Spanish soil in 1982. The side had matured well since reaching the quarter-finals in Mexico and they had little trouble in beating both Belgium and the Koreans and drawing with Uruguay, who won through to the next round in third place courtesy of a last-minute winner against South Korea.

The most closely fought group in the first round was Group F containing England, Holland, the Republic of Ireland and Egypt, the outcome of which was in doubt right to the very end. Five of the six games were drawn, the only exception being England's victory over Egypt in the final match. This result meant that England won the group and Egypt were eliminated. Lots had to be drawn to decide the placings of Holland and Ireland and it was kind to the Irish who were pitted against Romania in the next round instead of West Germany.

Much of the football in the first round had been predictable, and if not exactly boring, it had lacked the passion to bring the tournament to life. In every match apart from Costa Rica's 2-1 win over Sweden, the side who scored first either went on to win or at least draw the game. Much more criticism was to follow in the rest of the tournament, particularly in relation to the use of penalties to decide drawn games.

It looked as if the opening game of the second round would be decided in just that way when after 90 minutes and one period of extra-time, both Colombia and Cameroon had failed to muster a goal. Just as in the game against Romania in the first round, however, it was to be Roger Milla's day as again he scored two goals after having come on as a substitute. The second of these goals was in no small part down to Higuita who was robbed of the ball way outside of his penalty area. Although Redin scored for the Colombians just before the end, the Cameroons went one further than Morocco in 1986 and became the first African nation to reach the quarter-finals.

Later the same night another side from the Americas was dumped out of the tournament when the Czechs beat Costa Rica 4-1 in Bari. The Costa Ricans were not disgraced. Trailing 2-1 with 15 minutes to go they let Czechoslovakia in twice as they pushed forward for an equaliser.

The South American agony continued the following day in Turin and it was the turn of Brazil to exit the tournament at the hands of their fierce rivals Argentina. Despite dominating most of the match and coming close on several occasions, they were beaten by a Caniggia goal after a clever through pass by Maradona, his only really noteworthy contribution to the tournament. Once again the Brazilians had failed, and the result only served to enhance the perception that the Brazilians were a fading world power. They might have won the tournament on three occasions, but with each successive World Cup it seemed these victories were being consigned further into the annals of soccer history.

The best match of the second round was between Holland and West Germany in Milan. The Germans faced potentially their biggest threat in the form of the European Champions. Six of the players on the pitch plied their trade in that very stadium in Milan: Brehme, Klinsmann and Matthäus of West Germany with Inter, the Dutch trio of Gullit, Rijkaard and Van Basten for Milan.

The Dutch had been rather subdued in the first round, but the game burst into life after 20 minutes when both Rijkaard and Völler were sent off after a bad-tempered exchange. The incident gave the match a cutting edge that most of the other games in the tournament lacked, and in a pulsating second half Klinsmann and Brehme scored to give the Germans victory. Ronald Koeman's reply for Holland came too late.

There was no such excitement the following day in Genoa, except for the penalty shoot-out in which the Irish knocked out Romania. Neither side managed to score in 120 minutes of open play but were remarkably efficient at the spot kicks. Only Timofte failed to convert his, but that was enough to see Ireland through to the quarter-finals, even though in the four games they had played they had failed to win at all and had only scored two goals in the process.

Italy's progress to the quarter-finals had been far more confident and assured and against Uruguay in the Stadio Olimpico in Rome they chalked up another comfortable win. Their new hero, Salvatore Schillaci, scored their first midway through the second half and Serena made sure of the game just before the end. The Italians were the only quarter-finalists to have won all of their games and they had not conceded a goal either. In the quarter-finals they were pitted against the Irish whose record could not have been more different.

The final day of the second round saw Yugoslavia take on Spain in Verona and England play Belgium in Bologna. Spain yet again failed to live up to their promise and were beaten by the ever-improving Yugoslavs, thanks in no small part to some excellent finishing by Dragan Stojkovic. His two goals were the decisive factor in a close-fought tie that went to extra-time.

Extra-time was also needed in Bologna and it was not until the very last minute, when David Platt coolly finished off a Paul Gascoigne free-kick, that the two sides could be separated. Belgium, inspired by the brilliant Enzo Scifo and the ageless Ceulemans and Gerets, came close on a couple of occasions, but they were not to repeat their success of four year previously and England qualified to meet the Cameroons in the next round.

The first three quarter-finals produced just two goals between them. In one of the worst games of the tournament, Argentina and Yugoslavia played out a tedious 0-0 draw in Florence which was only enlivened by the penalty-kicks at the end. Sergio Goycochea, who was Pumpido's replacement in goal after the first-choice keeper had broken his leg in the match against the Soviet Union, was Argentina's hero as they triumphed 3-2 after both sides had at one point been ahead.

Argentina were to come in for great criticism on their route to the final. They rarely offered any positive football and seemed content to take their chances on post-match penalties. In 1986, though Maradona played a crucial role, he was only one of a very good team. In Italy, the Argentinians seemed to abdicate all responsibility to him, and as he was not one hundred per cent fit the team suffered as a result.

Italy took on the Republic of Ireland later on in the day in Rome and again Schillaci was the telling factor, although the Irish put up their best performance in defeat. Italy's victory was hardly surprising. They looked threatening whenever they attacked and should have scored more goals. It was the end of the road for the Irish whose fans had made the most of their first World Cup appearance and certainly added much colour to the occasion.

The following day in Milan, the West Germans moved relentlessly into the semi-finals even if it did take a somewhat dubious penalty for them to do so. Despite their fine football some of the Germans' antics were beginning to raise questions about their excessive will to win. A disturbing feature of the tournament had been the number of times referees were prompted into giving decisions that resulted from play-acting by the players, and unfortunately the Germans were more guilty than most. The Czechs, who had played good football throughout the tournament, could have won the game had they made their early pressure count, but in the end, with two goal-line clearances by Hasek and Bilek, they were fortunate to lose only 1-0.

The last quarter-final between England and Cameroon in Naples was by far the best game of the tournament. Cameroon came within ten minutes of a semi-final place and only lack of experience told against them. The match was unique in Italia '90 in that it was the only time that the lead in a game changed hands twice. England went ahead through a David Platt header midway through the first half, only for Cameroon to equalise after fifteen minutes of the second half with a Kunde penalty after Roger Milla was felled in the area.

Both sides were playing fluent, open football and it was no surprise when Milla and Ekeke combined well for the latter to put the Africans ahead four minutes later, but the drama was not over yet. Cameroon appeared to be coping well with containing England in the last 25 minutes, but nine minutes from the end they gave away a silly penalty which Gary Lineker converted. England had been given a considerable fright coming so close to elimination, but they made sure of qualifying for their first semi-final since 1966 when Lineker was again brought down in the area and converted his second penalty in extra-time. Cameroon had without question been one of the highlights of the tournament and in Roger Milla certainly had the star of the show.

The semi-finals were surrounded with controversy as both finalists were decided on penalty kicks. In Naples, Argentina knocked the hosts and favourites out after a 1-1 draw. Italy went into the lead after 17 minutes when Schillaci scored his fifth goal of the series. It seemed as though they would cruise through the game, but Argentina were forced to take the game to the Italians who inexcusably tried to sit back on their lead.

Had they attacked with more enterprise they might well have won with ease but instead Walter Zenga in the Italian goal was forced to pick the ball out of his own net for the first time in the tournament when midway through the second half Caniggia headed home an Olarticoechea cross. Neither side thereafter seemed to have enough imagination to win the game in open play and the Argentinians, thanks once more to the skill of Goycochea in goal, won the ensuing shoot-out. It was a desperately unsatisfactory end to Italy's campaign.

Turin was the location for the second of the semi-finals the following day. England and West Germany took to the field in the new Stadio Delle Alpi and served up an excellent game. Like the previous evening, however, it ended 1-1, and the Germans qualified for their third successive final, the second time they had done so courtesy of penalty kicks. Like the England-Cameroon match, the game was open and flowing and full of incident. England were much on top, but against the run of play the Germans took the lead on the hour when a Brehme free-kick was deflected over Shilton by Parker's attempted block.

Again England left it late and with only ten minutes remaining, Lineker, who had had a quiet first round in the tournament, was again on hand to rescue his side with a well-taken goal from a Parker cross. Both sides hit the post in extra-time but no further goals were scored. In the penalties that followed, West Germany scored all four of theirs with clinical precision, but first Stuart Pearce and then England's best player in the tournament, Chris Waddle, missed their kicks and England were out.

To have both semi-finals decided on penalties was totally unsatisfactory in such an important tournament, and since then the whole concept of penalties has been brought into question. Many regard them as responsible for dull and tedious football, as weaker teams pack their defences in the knowledge that even if they don't score, as long as the other side does not either they still have a fighting chance of winning the match. It is perhaps no coincidence that in the earlier years of the World Cup, draws were less frequent in the knock-out stages because there was no such escape clause. In 40 later-stage games between 1954 and 1970, not one single match was drawn!

If the final had been decided on a penalty shoot-out, it would not have been inappropriate. Instead it was decided by a penalty in normal time, and the Germans won the world's highest honour having scored just one goal from open play in their final three games, and that came from a set piece. The final itself was a disgrace and both sides were equally responsible. Argentina clearly played for penalties whilst the Germans indulged in gamesmanship that saw two of their opponents sent off.

It was also the first final that saw less than three goals scored. Without fail, finals in the past had always lived up to their billing as the showpiece of world football. The best teams had not necessarily always reached the final nor won, but they had all been entertaining affairs. The third-place match between Italy and England might well have produced a much better final. Certainly, in the later stages, the matches those teams had been involved in were amongst the best in the tournament, and the third-place match itself was a most engaging game, even if the pressure was off.

West Germany were expected to win with ease. Lothar Matthäus was at the peak of his game, whilst Maradona was a mere shadow of his former self. Only seven players remained from when the two teams had met in the final four years previously but both coaches were the same. Beckenbauer was out to become the first man to captain and coach a winning side whilst Carlos Bilardo was determined to follow in the footsteps of Vittorio Pozzo and become only the second coach to retain the title.

Few expected it to be a good game and sure enough the world had to witness 90 minutes of the most uninspiring football imaginable. The only goal came five minutes from the end, much to the relief of the crowd who were spared another 30 minutes' tedium. Völler was brought down in the penalty area and Brehme's kick won the game for Germany. Ten minutes previously, however, Calderon had been brought down in the German area in a not dissimilar incident, but Argentine appeals went unnoticed by the Mexican referee.

If Argentina thought they had been hard done by in that incident, their feelings towards the referee weren't improved by the two sendings-off which reduced them to nine men by the end. After 68 minutes, Klinsmann's over-exaggerated dive when tackled by Monzon got the

Argentine sent off for his troubles, whilst with three minutes to go Dezotti was dismissed after trying to retrieve the ball from Köhler, who refused to let go. On their performance throughout the tournament, a West Germany win was far more preferable than an Argentinian one, but the 1990 final left a bad taste in the mouth.

QUALIFYING TOURNAMENT

EUROPE

Group 1

	Ro	De	Gr	Bu	Pl	W	D	L	F	A	Pts
ROMANIA	-	3-1	3-0	1-0	6	4	1	1	10	5	9
Denmark	3-0	-	7-1	1-1	6	3	2	1	15	6	8
Greece	0-0	1-1	-	1-0	6	1	2	3	3	15	4
Bulgaria	1-3	0-2	4-0	-	6	1	1	4	6	8	3

Group 2

	Sd	En	Pd	Al	Pl	W	D	L	F	A	Pts
SWEDEN	-	0-0	2-1	3-1	6	4	2	0	9	3	10
ENGLAND	0-0	-	3-0	5-0	6	3	3	0	10	0	9
Poland	0-2	0-0	-	1-0	6	2	1	3	4	8	5
Albania	1-2	0-2	1-2	-	6	0	0	6	3	15	0

Group 3

	SU	Au	Tu	EG	Ic	Pl	W	D	L	F	A	Pts
SOVIET UNION	-	2-0	2-0	3-0	1-1	8	4	3	1	11	4	11
AUSTRIA	0-0	-	3-2	3-0	2-1	8	3	3	2	9	9	9
Turkey	0-1	3-0	-	3-1	1-1	8	3	1	4	12	10	7
East Germany	2-1	1-1	0-2	-	2-0	8	3	1	4	9	13	7
Iceland	1-1	0-0	2-1	0-3	-	8	1	4	3	6	11	6

Group 4

	Ho	WG	Fi	Wa	Pl	W	D	L	F	A	Pts
HOLLAND	-	1-1	3-0	1-0	6	4	2	0	8	2	10
WEST GERMANY	0-0	-	6-1	2-1	6	3	3	0	13	3	9
Finland	0-1	0-4	-	1-0	6	1	1	4	4	16	3
Wales	1-2	0-0	2-2	-	6	0	2	4	4	8	2

Group 5

	Yu	Sc	Fr	No	Cy	Pl	W	D	L	F	A	Pts
YUGOSLAVIA	-	3-1	3-2	1-0	4-0	8	6	2	0	16	6	14
SCOTLAND	1-1	-	2-0	1-1	2-1	8	4	2	2	12	12	10
France	0-0	3-0	-	1-0	2-0	8	3	3	2	10	7	9
Norway	1-2	1-2	1-1	-	3-1	8	2	2	4	10	9	6
Cyprus	1-2	2-3	1-1	0-3	-	8	0	1	7	6	20	1

Group 6

	Sp	RI	Hu	NI	Ma	Pl	W	D	L	F	A	Pts
SPAIN	-	2-0	4-0	4-0	4-0	8	6	1	1	20	3	13
REP. IRELAND	1-0	-	2-0	3-0	2-0	8	5	2	1	10	2	12
Hungary	2-2	0-0	-	1-0	1-1	8	2	4	2	8	12	8
Nth. Ireland	0-2	0-0	1-2	-	3-0	8	2	1	5	6	12	5
Malta	0-2	0-2	2-2	0-2	-	8	0	2	6	3	18	2

Group 7

	Be	Cz	Pt	Sz	Lu	Pl	W	D	L	F	A	Pts
BELGIUM	-	2-1	3-0	1-0	1-1	8	4	4	0	15	5	12
CZECH.	0-0	-	2-1	3-0	4-0	8	5	2	1	13	3	12
Portugal	1-1	0-0	-	3-1	1-0	8	4	2	2	11	8	10
Switzerland	2-2	0-1	1-2	-	2-1	8	2	1	5	10	14	5
Luxembourg	0-5	0-2	0-3	1-4	-	8	0	1	7	3	22	1

SOUTH AMERICA

Group 1

	Ur	Bo	Pe	Pl	W	D	L	F	A	Pts
URUGUAY	-	2-0	2-0	4	3	0	1	7	2	6
Bolivia	2-1	-	2-1	4	3	0	1	6	5	6
Peru	0-2	1-2	-	4	0	0	4	2	8	0

Group 2

	Co	Pa	Ec	Pl	W	D	L	F	A	Pts
Colombia	-	2-1	2-0	4	2	1	1	5	3	5
Paraguay	2-1	-	2-1	4	2	0	2	6	7	4
Ecuador	0-0	3-1	-	4	1	1	2	4	5	3

Colombia qualified to meet the winners of the Oceania group, Israel, in a play-off

Group 3

	Br	Ch	Ve	Pl	W	D	L	F	A	Pts
BRAZIL	-	2-0*	6-0	4	3	1	0	13	1	7
Chile	1-1	-	5-0**	4	2	1	1	9	4	5
Venezuela	0-4	1-3	-	4	0	0	4	1	18	0

* Match abandoned after 65 minutes with Brazil leading 1-0. Brazil awarded game 2-0

** Played in Mendoza, Argentina

OCEANIA

FIRST ROUND

Taiwan	0-4 1-4	New Zealand
Fiji	1-0 1-5	Australia
Israel	Bye	

SECOND ROUND

	Is	Au	NZ	Pl	W	D	L	F	A	Pts
Israel	-	1-1	1-0	4	1	3	0	5	4	5
Australia	1-1	-	4-1	4	1	2	1	6	5	4
New Zealand	2-2	2-0	-	4	1	1	2	5	7	3

Israel qualified to meet winners of South America group 2, Colombia, in a play-off

COLOMBIA	1-0 0-0	Israel

CENTRAL AND NORTH AMERICA

FIRST ROUND

Guyana	0-4 0-1	**Trinidad**
Cuba	0-1 1-1	**Guatemala**
Jamaica	1-0 2-1	Puerto Rico
Antigua	0-1 1-3	**Neth. Antilles**
Costa Rica	1-1 2-0	Panama
Mexico	Bye	
United States	Bye	
Canada	Bye	
El Salvador	Bye	
Honduras	Bye	

SECOND ROUND

Jamaica	0-0 1-5	**United States**
Guatemala	1-0 2-3 *	Canada
Neth. Antilles	0-1 0-5	**El Salvador**
Trinidad	0-0 1-1 *	Honduras
Costa Rica	W-O	Mexico

*Won on away goals

THIRD ROUND

	CR	US	Tr	Gu	ES	Pl	W	D	L	F	A	Pts
COSTA RICA	-	1-0	1-0	2-1	1-0	8	5	1	2	10	6	11
UNITED STATES	1-0	-	1-1	2-1	0-0	8	4	3	1	6	3	11
Trinidad	1-1	0-1	-	2-1	2-0	8	3	3	2	7	5	9
Guatemala	1-0	0-0	0-1	-	-	6	1	1	4	4	7	3
El Salvador	2-4	0-1	0-0	-	-	6	0	2	4	2	8	2

AFRICA

FIRST ROUND

Uganda	1-0 1-3	**Malawi**
Angola	0-0 2-1	Sudan
Zimbabwe	W-O	Lesotho
Zambia	W-O	Rwanda
Libya	3-0 0-2	Burkina Faso
Ghana	0-0 0-2	**Liberia**
Tunisia	5-0 0-3	Guinea
Gabon	W-O	Togo
Algeria	Bye	
Côte d'Ivoire	Bye	
Egypt	Bye	
Kenya	Bye	
Cameroon	Bye	
Nigeria	Bye	
Zaire	Bye	
Morocco	Bye	

SECOND ROUND

Group A

	Al	Cl	Zi	Pl	W	D	L	F	A	Pts
Algeria	-	1-0	3-0	4	3	1	0	6	1	7
Côte d'Ivoire	0-0	-	5-0	4	1	2	1	5	1	4
Zimbabwe	1-2	0-0	-	4	0	1	3	1	10	1

Libya played one match and then withdrew

Group B

	Eg	Li	Ma	Ke	Pl	W	D	L	F	A	Pts
Egypt	-	2-0	1-0	2-0	6	3	2	1	6	2	8
Liberia	1-0	-	1-0	0-0	6	2	2	2	2	3	6
Malawi	1-1	0-0	-	1-0	6	1	3	2	3	4	5
Kenya	0-0	1-0	1-1	-	6	1	3	2	2	4	5

Group C

	Cm	Ni	An	Ga	Pl	W	D	L	F	A	Pts
Cameroon	-	1-0	1-1	2-1	6	4	1	1	9	6	9
Nigeria	2-0	-	1-0	1-0	6	3	1	2	7	5	7
Angola	1-2	2-2	-	2-0	6	1	2	3	6	7	4
Gabon	1-3	2-1	1-0	-	6	2	0	4	5	9	4

Group D

	Tu	Zm	Zr	Mo	Pl	W	D	L	F	A	Pts
Tunisia	-	1-0	1-0	2-1	6	3	1	2	5	5	7
Zambia	1-0	-	4-2	2-1	6	3	0	3	7	6	6
Zaire	3-1	1-0	-	0-0	6	2	2	2	7	7	6
Morocco	0-0	1-0	1-1	-	6	1	3	2	4	5	5

THIRD ROUND

Algeria	0-0 0-1	**EGYPT**
CAMEROON	2-0 1-0	Tunisia

ASIA

FIRST ROUND

Group 1

	Qa	Iq	Jo	Om	Pl	W	D	L	F	A	Pts
Qatar	-	1-0	1-0	3-0	6	3	3	0	8	3	9
Iraq	2-2	-	4-0	3-1	6	3	2	1	11	5	8
Jordan	1-1	0-1	-	2-0	6	2	1	3	5	7	5
Oman	0-0	1-1	0-2	-	6	0	2	4	2	11	2

Group 2

	SA	Sy	NY	Pl	W	D	L	F	A	Pts
Saudi Arabia	-	5-4	1-0	4	3	1	0	7	4	7
Syria	0-0	-	2-0	4	2	1	1	7	5	5
North Yemen	0-1	0-1	-	4	0	0	4	0	5	0

Group 3

	Em	Ku	Pa	Pl	W	D	L	F	A	Pts
United Arab Emirates	-	1-0	5-0	4	3	0	1	12	4	6
Kuwait	3-2	-	2-0	4	3	0	1	6	3	6
Pakistan	1-4	0-1	-	4	0	0	4	1	12	0

Group 4

Tournaments held in Seoul and Singapore

	SK	Ma	Si	Ne	Pl	W	D	L	F	A	Pts
South Korea	-	3-0	3-0	9-0	6	6	0	0	25	0	12
Malaysia	0-3	-	1-0	2-0	6	3	1	2	8	8	7
Singapore	0-3	2-2	-	7-0	6	2	1	3	12	9	5
Nepal	0-4	0-3	0-3	-	6	0	0	6	0	28	0

Group 5

	Ch	Ir	Ba	Th	Pl	W	D	L	F	A	Pts
China	-	2-0	2-0	2-0	6	5	0	1	13	3	10
Iran	3-2	-	1-0	3-0	6	5	0	1	12	5	10
Bangladesh	0-2	1-2	-	3-1	6	1	0	5	4	9	2
Thailand	0-3	0-3	1-0	-	6	1	0	5	2	14	2

Group 6

	NK	Ja	Id	HK	Pl	W	D	L	F	A	Pts
North Korea	-	2-0	2-1	4-1	6	4	1	1	11	5	9
Japan	2-1	-	5-0	0-0	6	2	3	1	7	3	7
Indonesia	0-0	0-0	-	3-2	6	1	3	2	5	10	5
Hong Kong	1-2	0-0	1-1	-	6	0	3	3	5	10	3

SECOND ROUND

Tournament in Singapore

	SK	Em	Qa	Ch	SA	NK	Pl	W	D	L	F	A	Pts
SOUTH KOREA	-	1-1	0-0	1-0	2-0	1-0	5	3	2	0	5	1	8
ARAB EMIRATES	-	-	1-1	2-1	0-0	0-0	5	1	4	0	4	3	6
Qatar	-	-	-	2-1	1-1	0-2	5	1	3	1	4	5	5
China	-	-	-	-	2-1	1-0	5	2	0	3	5	6	4
Saudi Arabia	-	-	-	-	-	2-0	5	1	2	2	4	5	4
North Korea	-	-	-	-	-	-	5	1	1	3	2	4	3

FINAL TOURNAMENT,
HELD IN ITALY 8TH JUNE - 8TH JULY 1990

FIRST ROUND

Group A

Olimpico, Rome, 9-06-1990, 72,000
Italy 1 (Schillaci 77)
Austria 0

Comunale, Florence, 10-06-1990, 33,000
Czechoslovakia 5 (Skuhravy 25 79, Bilek 38, Hasek 51, Luhovy 90)
United States 1 (Caligiuri 60)

Olimpico, Rome, 14-06-1990, 73,000
Italy 1 (Giannini 11)
United States 0

Comunale, Florence, 15-06-1990, 38,000
Czechoslovakia 1 (Bilek 29)
Austria 0

Comunale, Florence, 19-06-1990, 34,000
Austria 2 (Ogris 49, Rodax 63)
United States 1 (Murray 83)

Olimpico, Rome, 19-06-1990, 73,000
Italy 2 (Schillaci 9, Baggio.R 77)
Czechoslovakia 0

	It	Cz	Au	US	Pl	W	D	L	F	A	Pts
ITALY	-	2-0	1-0	1-0	3	3	0	0	4	0	6
CZECHOSLOVAKIA	-	-	1-0	5-1	3	2	0	1	6	3	4
Austria	-	-	-	2-1	3	1	0	2	2	3	2
United States	-	-	-	-	3	0	0	3	2	8	0

Group B

Giuseppe Meazza, Milan, 8-06-1990, 73,000
Cameroon 1 (Omam Biyik 67)
Argentina 0

Sant Nicola, Bari, 9-06-1990, 42,000
Romania 2 (Lacatus 40 54)
Soviet Union 0

San Paolo, Naples, 13-06-1990, 55,000
Argentina 2 (Toglio 27, Burruchaga 78)
Soviet Union 0

Sant Nicola, Bari, 14-06-1990, 38,000
Cameroon 2 (Milla 78 87)
Romania 1 (Balint 88)

Sant Nicola, Bari, 18-06-1990, 37,000
Soviet Union 4 (Protasov 20, Zygmantovich 29, Zavarov 52, Dobrovolski 64)
Cameroon 0

San Paolo, Naples, 18-06-1990, 52,000
Argentina 1 (Monzon 61)
Romania 1 (Balint 67)

	Ca	Ro	Ar	SU	Pl	W	D	L	F	A	Pts
CAMEROON	-	2-1	1-0	0-4	3	2	0	1	3	5	4
ROMANIA	-	-	1-1	2-0	3	1	1	1	4	3	3
ARGENTINA	-	-	-	2-0	3	1	1	1	3	2	3
Soviet Union	-	-	-	-	3	1	0	2	4	4	2

Group C

Delle Alpi, Turin, 10-06-1990, 62,000
Brazil 2 (Careca 40 62)
Sweden 1 (Brolin 78)

Luigi Ferraris, Genoa, 11-06-1990, 30,000
Costa Rica 1 (Cayasso 49)
Scotland 0

Delle Alpi, Turin, 16-06-1990, 58,000
Brazil 1 (Müller 33)
Costa Rica 0

Luigi Ferraris, Genoa, 16-06-1990, 31,000
Scotland 2 (McCall 10, Johnston 81)
Sweden 1 (Strömberg 85)

Luigi Ferraris, Genoa, 20-06-1990, 30,000
Costa Rica 2 (Flores 75, Medford 88)
Sweden 1 (Ekström 31)

Delle Alpi, Turin, 20-06-1990, 62,000
Brazil 1 (Müller 81)
Scotland 0

	Br	CR	Sc	Sd	Pl	W	D	L	F	A	Pts
BRAZIL	-	1-0	1-0	2-1	3	3	0	0	4	1	6
COSTA RICA	-	-	1-0	2-1	3	2	0	1	3	2	4
Scotland	-	-	-	2-1	3	1	0	2	2	3	2
Sweden	-	-	-	-	3	0	0	3	3	6	0

Group D

Dall'Ara, Bologna, 9-06-1990, 30,000
Colombia 2 (Redin 50, Valderrama 85)
United Arab Emirates 0

Giuseppe Meazza, Milan, 10-06-1990, 74,000
West Germany 4 (Matthäus 28 63, Klinsmann 39, Völler 70)
Yugoslavia 1 (Jozic 54)

Dall'Ara, Bologna, 14-06-1990, 32,000
Yugoslavia 1 (Jozic 73)
Colombia 0

Giuseppe Meazza, Milan, 15-06-1990, 71,000
West Germany 5 (Völler 35 75, Klinsmann 36, Matthäus 46, Bein 58)
United Arab Emirates 1 (Khalid Mubarak 45)

Dall'Ara, Bologna, 19-06-1990, 27,000
Yugoslavia 4 (Susic 4, Pancev 8 46, Prosinecki 90)
United Arab Emirates 1 (Jumaa 21)

West Germany 1 (Littbarski 88)
Colombia 1 (Rincón 90)

	WG	Yu	Co	AE	Pl	W	D	L	F	A	Pts
WEST GERMANY	-	4-1	1-1	5-1	3	2	1	0	10	3	5
YUGOSLAVIA	-	-	1-0	4-1	3	2	0	1	6	5	4
COLOMBIA	-	-	-	2-0	3	1	1	1	3	2	3
UAE	-	-	-	-	3	0	0	3	2	11	0

Group E

Bentegodi, Verona, 12-06-1990, 32,000
Belgium 2 (Degryse 51, De Wolf 62)
South Korea 0

Friuli, Udine, 13-06-1990, 35,000
Spain 0
Uruguay 0

Friuli, Udine, 17-06-1990, 32,000
Spain 3 (Michel 23 60 80)
South Korea 1 (Bo-kwan 43)

Bentegodi, Verona, 17-06-1990, 33,000
Belgium 3 (Clijsters 14, Scifo 21, Ceulemans 46)
Uruguay 1 (Bengoechea 71)

Friuli, Udine, 21-06-1990, 29,000
Uruguay 1 (Fonseca 90)
South Korea 0

Bentegodi, Verona, 21-06-1990, 35,000
Spain 2 (Michel 26, Gorriz 38)
Belgium 1 (Vervoort 29)

	Sp	Be	Ur	SK	Pl	W	D	L	F	A	Pts
SPAIN	-	2-1	0-0	3-1	3	2	1	0	5	2	5
BELGIUM	-	-	3-1	2-0	3	2	0	1	6	3	4
URUGUAY	-	-	-	1-0	3	1	0	2	2	3	2
South Korea	-	-	-	-	3	0	0	3	1	6	0

Group F

Sant'Elia, Cagliari, 11-06-1990, 35,000
England 1 (Lineker 8)
Rep. Ireland 1 (Sheedy 73)

Della Favorita, Palermo, 12-06-1990
Holland 1 (Kieft 58)
Egypt 1 (Abedelghani 82)

Sant'Elia, Cagliari, 16-06-1990, 35,000
England 0
Holland 0

Della Favorita, Palermo, 17-06-1990, 33,000
Rep. Ireland 0
Egypt 0

Della Favorita, Palermo, 21-06-1990, 33,000
Rep. Ireland 1 (Quinn 71)
Holland 1 (Gullit 10)

Sant'Elia, Cagliari, 21-06-1990, 34,000
England 1 (Wright.M 58)
Egypt 0

	En	RI	Ho	Eg	Pl	W	D	L	F	A	Pts
ENGLAND	-	1-1	0-0	1-0	3	1	2	0	2	1	4
REP. IRELAND	-	-	1-1	0-0	3	0	3	0	2	2	3
HOLLAND	-	-	-	1-1	3	0	3	0	2	2	3
EGYPT	-	-	-	-	3	0	2	1	1	2	2

SECOND ROUND

Giuseppe Meazza, Milan, 24-06-1990, 74,000
West Germany 2 (Klinsmann 50, Brehme 84)
Holland 1 (Koeman.R 88)

Sant Nicola, Bari, 23-06-1990, 47,000
Czechoslovakia 4 (Skuhravy 11 62 82, Kubik 77)
Costa Rica 1 (Gonzalez 56)

San Paolo, Naples, 23-06-1990, 50,000
Cameroon 2 (Milla 106 108)
Colombia 1 (Redin 116)

Dall'Ara, Bologna, 26-06-1990, 34,000
England 1 (Platt 119)
Belgium 0

Olimpico, Rome, 25-06-1990, 73,000
Italy 2 (Schillaci 65, Serena 82)
Uruguay 0

Luigi Ferraris, Genoa, 25-06-1990, 31,000
Rep. Ireland 0
Romania 0
Rep. Ireland won 5-4 on penalties

Bentegodi, Verona, 26-06-1990, 35,000
Yugoslavia 2 (Stojkovic 77 92)
Spain 1 (Salinas 83)

Delle Alpi, Turin, 24-06-1990, 61,000
Argentina 1 (Caniggia 82)
Brazil 0

QUARTER-FINALS

Giuseppe Meazza, Milan, 1-07-1990, 73,000
West Germany 1 (Matthäus 24)
Czechoslovakia 0

San Paolo, Naples, 1-07-1990, 55,000
England 3 (Platt 25, Lineker 82 105)
Cameroon 2 (Kunde 61, Ekeke 64)

Olimpico, Rome, 30-06-1990, 73,000
Italy 1 (Schillaci 37)
Rep. Ireland 0

Comunale, Florence, 30-06-1990, 38,000
Argentina 0
Yugoslavia 0
Argentina won 3-2 on penalties

SEMI-FINALS

Delle Alpi, Turin, 4-07-1990, 62,000
West Germany 1 (Brehme 59)
England 1 (Lineker 80)
West Germany won 4-3 on penalties

San Paolo, Naples, 3-07-1990, 59,000
Argentina 1 (Caniggia 67)
Italy 1 (Schillaci 17)
Argentina won 4-3 on penalties

3RD PLACE

Sant Nicola, Bari, 7-07-1990, 51,000
Italy 2 (Baggio.R 71, Schillaci 84)
England 1 (Platt 80)

FINAL

Olimpico, Rome, 8-07-1990, 73,000. Referee: Codesal, Mexico
WEST GERMANY 1 (Brehme 85)
ARGENTINA 0
West Germany - Illgner - Berthold (Reuter), Kohler, Augenthaler, Buchwald, Brehme - Hässler, Matthäus, Littbarski - Völler, Klinsmann. Tr: Beckenbauer
Argentina - Goycochea - Ruggeri (Monzon), Simón, Serrizuela - Sensini, Basualdo, Burruchaga (Calderon), Troglio, Lorenzo - Maradona, Dezotti. Tr: Bilardo

Top scorers: Salvatore Schillaci, Italy 6
Tomás Skuhravy, Czechoslovakia....5
Gary Lineker, England....4
Lothar Matthäus, West Germany 4
Michel, Spain....4
Roger Milla, Cameroon 4
Total goals scored: 115
Average per game: 2.2

1994

THE 15TH WORLD CUP
21ST MARCH 1992 - 17TH JULY 1994

The fifteenth World Cup had it all. From very unpromising beginnings, with the award of the tournament to the United States, through an eventful qualifying competition which saw the elimination of some big names, to a final tournament full of excitement, USA '94 ranks among the very best.

The football played showed a renaissance of the ideals which had made Mexico in 1970 such an historic tournament. Fear of defeat was on the whole replaced by a desire to play creative football. No-one, perhaps, reached the heights of the 1970 Brazilians, but overall, in a far more technical game, skill and the enjoyment of playing flourished, where it had been subdued in Italy four years previously.

It was fitting, therefore, that it should be Brazil again who ultimately emerged victorious. They may have lacked the flair of their famous predecessors but coach Carlos

Alberto Parreira, not to be confused with the captain of the 1970 side, knew exactly what he wanted from his team and there can be little doubt that not only did they contribute hugely to the excitement of the tournament, but that they were the best side present.

For years FIFA had been anxious to see football take off in America, the potential for fuelling their ever-increasing coffers not lost on the men from Zürich. The United States it was, therefore, who got the vote ahead of Morocco at the FIFA congress in Berne in 1988, the date of the announcement strategically switched to 4th July to coincide with American Independence Day. There were many dissenting voices. Morocco were furious that their bid had been turned down, claiming, justifiably, that decisions were being made according to financial and not sporting criteria, and that the award of the tournament to an African country would help the growth of the game there. But FIFA were unmoved.

If the final tournament turned out to be a classic, the qualifying tournament was no less full of incident. It kicked off in Santo Domingo in March 1992 with a match between the Dominican Republic and Puerto Rico, but was soon marred by one of the greatest tragedies ever to befall the World Cup.

On the night of 27 April 1993, a Zambian military plane crashed off the coast of Gabon. On board were eighteen members of the Zambian national side on their way to a match in Senegal. All of them were killed. Battling on with a side of inexperienced players led by Kalusha Bwalya, who was not on the plane, Zambia came within one point of qualifying for America. Needing only a draw in their final match away to Morocco, they lost, alas, 1-0.

Morocco's victory ensured their third appearance in the finals, and they were joined by the heroes of Italia '90, Cameroon, who qualified despite a strong push from Zambia's neighbours Zimbabwe. Another nation from the south of the continent made an emotional return to the world football, after an absence of twenty-eight years, following their suspension and eventual expulsion from FIFA. South Africa had the misfortune, however, to be grouped in the first round with Nigeria, and in their first ever World Cup match, in Lagos in October 1992, they lost 4-0. Nigeria, after years of being on the verge of qualifying, finally did so, beating Algeria and the Côte d'Ivoire in the second round to make up the trio of African nations at USA '94.

Without the presence of the United States, who qualified automatically as hosts, CONCACAF were given only one automatic berth in the finals. Mexico, having been banned from Italia '90, had little trouble in claiming it. A second spot was up for grabs in a three continent play-off and so the CONCACAF runners-up, Canada, faced Australia, who had won the Oceania tournament. The Australians won this tie on penalties and with it the right to play the runners-up in South America's group 1 for a place in the finals.

This turned out to be Argentina, but only after an extraordinary South American qualifying tournament which saw a number of upsets. The Argentinians suffered one of the most humiliating experiences in their 93-year international history when they lost their final match 5-0 at home to Colombia, their worst defeat ever. The Colombians won the group easily, but Argentina came perilously close to not qualifying at all. Had Paraguay managed to beat Peru, the worst of all the South American nations in the qualifiers, in their final game, they and not Argentina would have faced Australia over two legs for a place in the finals. As it was, Argentina made heavy weather of the play-off, a single goal in Buenos Aires sending them through.

In group two, there was sensation also. On 25 July 1993, Brazil suffered their first ever defeat in a World Cup qualifier when they went down 2-0 to Bolivia in La Paz. A 6-0 victory in the return ensured that Brazil would not be missing out on the finals for the first time, but it was Bolivia who accompanied them at the expense of Uruguay. A 3-1 victory, again in La Paz, proved to be the difference.

Asia was no less interesting, and at one stage threatened alarming possibilities for the American organisers. After an initial first round which featured one of the worst performances in World Cup history – Macao lost all six games, conceding an amazing 46 goals – there remained a final group of six teams which included Iran, Iraq and North Korea, none of whom were on the best of terms politically with the United States. To the relief of all at USA '94 headquarters it was the much more compatible Saudi Arabia and South Korea who qualified.

In the end the challenge to the eventual qualifiers came not from the United States' three *bêtes noires* but from Japan. Indeed, the Japanese were within seconds of qualifying, but in the final seconds of the last match of the group they conceded a goal to Iraq which gifted their place in the finals to South Korea.

With the award of an extra place to Africa, European nations were competing for only twelve places instead of thirteen. This made the European zone extremely competitive. Group 3 contained no less than four recent finalists in Spain, Denmark and the two Irelands. In the end it was the European champions Denmark who were the major casualties, a second-half goal by Spain in the last, crucial, match of the group knocking them out. The Spanish were accompanied to the finals by the Republic of Ireland, finalists for the second successive tournament.

Two other major footballing powers failed to qualify. England started as favourites to qualify along with Holland from group 2, but no-one had reckoned with Norway who started off with a 10-0 win over San Marino, the first time a European side had managed to score ten in a World Cup qualifier since 1969. With their confidence high, the Scandinavians followed up with victories over both Holland and England at home and ensured their qualification by drawing the away legs. This left a decider between the Dutch and English in Rotterdam to see who joined them. In a dramatic and controversial match, Holland won 2-0. England were out and, having feared the worst from the notorious English hooligans, the American organisers breathed another huge sigh of relief.

Just as dramatic was the exit of France from the tournament. Needing just one point from their last two games, the French looked to be coasting, especially as both games were at home against Israel and Bulgaria. In the first of those games the French were 2-1 up with only seven minutes to go but incredibly lost 3-2, Israel's first ever victory in a competitive match on European soil. Then against Bulgaria, the score stood at 1-1 in injury-time when Kostadinov broke away and scored a stunning goal to win the game and put the French out. It was small consolation that the group winners Sweden and Bulgaria finished third and fourth respectively in the final tournament.

Elsewhere the drama was harder to find. The Italians had a fright when they were held at home by Switzerland and then lost the return in Berne, but they muddled their way through, a late goal by Dino Baggio against Portugal ensuring that they qualified. The Swiss, one of the surprises of the qualifying tournament, secured their first appearance in the finals since 1966.

Group 4 in Europe was one of the closest with 3 points separating the top four sides. Belgium won their first six games, then faltered, but had done enough to see off the challenge of Czechoslovakia and Wales and qualify along with Romania. For Czechoslovakia it was the end of a World Cup story stretching back sixty years, two World Cup finals in 1934 and 1962 the highlights of a distinguished career in the tournament. The final game played by the team was a 0-0 draw in Belgium, before the Czechs and Slovaks went their separate ways.

Political changes in Eastern Europe seriously disrupted group five. The break-up of the old Soviet Union into independent countries, after the draw for the tournament had been made, caused a bitter dispute as to who should inherit the single place in the group. When it was decided that Russia should do so there was fury in the Ukraine, which had always been a huge source for players in the Soviet side. A compromise was reached whereby Ukrainians would be allowed to play for Russia in this tournament, but could represent Ukraine in future tournaments.

The situation was further complicated by the presence of Yugoslavia in the group. Sanctions against Belgrade meant that they were banned from international competition, with the result that there were only five teams in a weak group. It was only ever a two-horse race, and although Iceland put up a spirited performance, their best ever, they were no match for Greece and Russia. Greece made the finals for the first time in their history, but both qualifiers from group 5 failed to make it past the first round in America.

The Americans had six years to prepare for the finals and crucially no new stadia were needed. The Rose Bowl in Pasadena was chosen for the final, and with a capacity of over 90,000, it was the largest of the venues selected. The Pontiac Silverdome near Detroit was an interesting choice given that it provided the setting for the first World Cup match to be played indoors.

It was Soldier Field in Chicago, however, which hosted the opening ceremony. By American standards it was a rather subdued affair, as was the inaugural game between Germany and Bolivia, though it did show the first evidence of FIFA's strict instructions to referees to get tough on rule-breaking. The Bolivian Marco Etcheverry became the first of fifteen players to be sent off in the tournament. Much controversy would surround FIFA's efforts to clean up the game but they did lead to a reduction in bad tackles and, with the spectator in mind, time-wasting.

Jürgen Klinsmann scored the only goal of the game, and the Germans qualified for the second round with relative ease, though they were given a nasty shock by the South Koreans in their last game; 3-2 was the final score but it could have been worse for the Germans. The Koreans were undefeated until that point. They had staged a magnificent recovery against Spain in their opening game, scoring twice in the last ten minutes to force a 2-2 draw, but unfortunately could do no more than draw 0-0 against the hapless Bolivians. It was a key result. Spain beat Bolivia in their last game and finished in second place. Two points was not enough for Korea to qualify in third place.

There was no third qualifier either from group B, where Russia and Cameroon went home after the first round. In contrast to Italia '90, America was not a happy hunting ground for the Lions of Cameroon. Players were justifiably upset at unpaid bonuses and at one point before the tournament started FIFA were on the verge of awarding their place to another country after a dispute amongst officials following an election in the Cameroon Football Federation.

Russia too were racked by internal disputes which left them without such players as Shalimov, Kiriakov and Kanchelskis. If there was one consolation, it was in the 6-1 victory over Cameroon in their last game, and the setting of a new World Cup record. Oleg Salenko scored five goals, the first player ever to score more than four in a game in the finals. He also finished the tournament as joint top-scorer. Another record was set in the game when Roger Milla at 42 broke his own record as the oldest player to score in a final tournament.

The group winners were Brazil, ahead of Sweden. The Swedes had drawn their opening match with Cameroon, but victory over Russia meant that they had as good as qualified before they met Brazil in their final game. Brazil for their part were the pre-tournament favourites and they started their campaign with the belief that they really could win the cup for the first time since 1970. The problem lay in finding a balance between a style of play that was pleasing to watch and one which was capable of winning the tournament. As they cruised through the first round it looked as if they might have cracked the problem.

As for the host country, the USA, they finished third in one of the most exciting groups of the first round and along the way gave a massive boost to football in America by defeating one of the pre-tournament favourites to win the World Cup, Colombia. The South Americans turned out to be the biggest disappointment of the whole tournament as it all went disastrously wrong for them against Romania (1-3) and the USA (0-2). The latter result showed a sceptical American public that their side were no fools, but at the same time it dumped the Colombians out of the competition.

It also had far more serious consequences for one player in particular. Andres Escobar had scored an own goal in the first half to put the USA 1-0 ahead and after he returned home he was gunned down outside a restaurant in his home town of Medellin. His assassin is alleged to have shouted, "That's for the own goal." The murder cast a shadow over the tournament. Many of the Colombian team refused to fly back home and stayed on in America. They did win their final game, against Switzerland, but by then it was too late. The group was won by Romania, and with Georghe Hagi in inspirational form they were the major revelation of USA '94.

The other major talking point of the first round centred around Argentina and the possible return of Diego Maradona. He declared himself fit, and Argentine coach Alfio Basile was convinced enough to gamble on playing him. At first it seemed to have paid off; against Greece in their opening match, Argentina and Maradona were magnificent. He gave a display which ranked among his finest ever and capped it by scoring a delightful goal. Suddenly the Argentines looked potential champions. Boosted by the return from suspension of Claudio Caniggia and the emergence of Redondo as a world-class player, they beat Nigeria with another fine display. Then their world fell apart as Maradona failed a drugs test after the match.

As FIFA's medical expert put it, Maradona had used a 'cocktail' of ephedrine-based drugs in his campaign to get fit again. Maradona was withdrawn from the Argentine squad before he could be banned by FIFA, and although he admitted to using ephedrine-based drugs, he stated he did not realise they were a banned substance and claimed that he was a victim of a FIFA campaign to disgrace him. Certainly suspicion surrounded the fact that he should have been chosen randomly after the Nigerian game for the dope test, but whatever the circumstances, he had tested positive and had to go.

Having lit up the tournament in their first two games, Argentina now stumbled badly and were beaten 2-0 by Bulgaria. It was one of the most fascinating groups of the tournament. Having failed in sixteen attempts to win a game in the World Cup finals, the Bulgarians made it seventeen when they lost their opening game 3-0 to Nigeria, the newly-crowned African champions showing flair, skill and tactical awareness. The Bulgarians did bounce back in their next game, however, finally winning a match at the eighteenth attempt. Unsurprising perhaps that it should be against the hapless Greeks, the worst team in the tournament by some distance, but it was followed up by their second win on the trot against Argentina. With Nigeria also beating Greece, all three teams finished on six points, and by virtue of a stunning last-minute goal from Amokachi, Nigeria topped the group.

Ultimately it proved to be a misfortune for them because in the second round they faced Italy, who had scraped through group E in third place. The Italians had a torrid time in their first round matches. In one of the most eagerly anticipated games of the whole tournament they faced Ireland in the opening match of the group in New York, a centre of huge Irish and Italian immigration in the early years of the century. A 1-0 victory for Ireland sealed their reputation as great battlers, but for Italy it was a poor start that would colour the rest of their performances in the tournament.

The group was by far and away the worst of the first round. Goals were in short supply and if any team did emerge with credit it was Mexico, the eventual winners of the group. But it was a close-run thing. All four teams finished on four points and it was the defensive-minded Norwegians who failed to qualify for the next round. If there was some encouragement for Italy it was their brave performance against the Scandinavians. Down to ten men after their goalkeeper Pagliuca had been sent off, they managed to pull off a 1-0 win.

Group 6, seen as a straightforward affair for Holland and Belgium, did not prove to be so simple. Once again the Dutch preparations were hampered by the resurgence of that old chestnut, player power. Ruud Gullit stormed out of the training camp, refusing to travel to the States with the team, and with Marco Van Basten injured, Holland looked short of players capable of winning the World Cup. In their opening game, against Saudi Arabia, they were given a nasty shock before grabbing a late winner.

Belgium had just as much trouble overcoming supposedly weaker opposition in their first game against Morocco, but they managed to win 1-0 and repeated the scoreline in their next match against the Dutch. In the most sensational result of the group, however, the Belgians lost their final game to one of the most stunning goals the World Cup has ever seen, Saeed Owairan running three-quarters of the length of the pitch to score. Having already beaten the unlucky Moroccans, Saudi became the first Asian side since North Korea in 1966 to qualify from their group.

The last-minute goals in group D meant that the composition of the second round changed dramatically at the last moment. All four of the major nations, Argentina, Italy, Germany and Brazil would be kept apart until the semi-finals – if they qualified.

Germany and Belgium kicked off the second round at Soldier Field and set the tempo for much of the remaining knock-out games as three goals were scored in the first eleven minutes. Rudi Völler, recalled to the side after Stefan Effenberg had been sent home, made an immediate impact, opening the scoring after five minutes then setting up Klinsmann for Germany's second. By half-time the Germans were 3-1 up and cruising, but their poor second-half performances were a feature of the tournament and they were lucky to emerge victorious in this encounter. Albert pulled a last-minute goal back, but in a crucial incident earlier in the half, the Belgian striker Weber had been pulled down in the penalty area. The Swiss referee Röthlisberger did not award a penalty, a decision for which he was later sent home by FIFA.

Later in the day at RFK Stadium in Washington, Switzerland were victims of another controversial refereeing decision in their match against Spain. If a player is not interfering with play he should not be given off-side, the new FIFA directive said, as part of their attempts to give the benefit of doubt to the attackers. Hierro's opening goal for Spain saw the perfect interpretation of this. When he broke through, a team-mate was well off-side, but the goal stood. The match ended in a 3-0 victory for the Spaniards, but the scoreline did not do justice to the Swiss, who had surpassed all expectations.

Dallas was the venue the following day as Sweden took on Saudi Arabia. An early goal put the Swedes comfortably in command in the first half, and early in the second they increased their lead. The Saudis, however, slowly took control and by the end Sweden were on the rack. When Al Ghashiyan scored a superb individual goal four minutes from time, they looked certain to equalise, but in their efforts to score they conceded a third. Saudi had arrived in the States as complete unknowns, but they left with their reputation, and that of Asian football, considerably enhanced.

Later that afternoon, 90,000 fans in the Rose Bowl, Pasadena, were treated to the best match of the whole tournament, a thriller between Romania and Argentina. Once again the goals came early. A Dumitrescu free-kick opened the scoring for Romania, and although Batistuta scored from a penalty five minutes later, within two minutes the Romanians were back in front as Hagi set up Ilie Dumitrescu who finished exquisitely. Hagi scored the third himself with a magnificent shot but the excitement was not finished. With fifteen minutes to go Argentina, who had dominated the match and fallen to the counterattack, got the second goal their pressure deserved through Balbo, but despite coming close on several occasions, they could not level the scores and were out. Despite all of the trauma surrounding Maradona, they had won a host of admirers.

Independence Day saw the match that all America had been waiting for – the USA against Brazil – but first Ireland faced Holland in the heat of Orlando. The Dutch had won group F without ever having played well, but against the Irish they asserted their undoubted superiority, winning 2-0. It was the end of an Irish adventure that began to turn rather sour after their win against Italy. Defeat against Mexico, a tedious draw against Norway, and numerous problems with FIFA officials on the sidelines had taken the shine off their initial success. Against Holland they rarely threatened and the second goal was the result of a dreadful error by the usually excellent Packy Bonner in goal.

Stanford Stadium in San Francisco was the setting for the biggest game in the history of American soccer. For most of it the United States held the Brazilians at bay, and when just before half-time Leonardo was sent off for elbowing Ramos in the face, it seemed as though the impossible fairytale might just come true. With ten men, however, the Brazilians looked no less dangerous and fifteen minutes from time Bebeto scored the winner. That the Americans lost was no disgrace. They had averted the organisers' worst nightmare by qualifying from the first round, and the match against Brazil was watched by record television audiences.

The final day of the second round kicked off at Foxboro Stadium in Boston with a dramatic match as Nigeria came within a minute of eliminating Italy. A goal midway through the first half by Amunike put the Africans ahead and for the rest of the match, staunchly defending their goal, they kept the Italians at bay. Indeed, when Maldini pulled down Yekini with the Nigerian clean through, Italy were lucky not to be reduced to nine men, having already had Zola sent off moments before. But luck was certainly with the Italians in USA '94 and Roberto Baggio scored a last-gasp equaliser with a perfectly placed shot. Buoyed by this let-off, the Italians won the game with a penalty in extra-time.

There were criticisms of the standard of refereeing during the game, but they were nothing compared to those levelled against Al Sharif, the Syrian official in charge of the last game of the second round between Mexico and Bulgaria. By the end it had been turned into a farce. Stoichkov gave Bulgaria the lead with a brilliantly taken goal early on, but the Mexicans pulled level through a dubious penalty. The game was never bad-tempered and there were few serious fouls, but the referee was handing out so many cautions that inevitably in the second half two players were sent off for second offences. Not surprisingly the game petered out well before the end, and so for the first time in the tournament penalties were needed to decide a game. Penalty shoot-outs are not the Mexicans' strong point and yet again they failed to score more than one. Bulgaria qualified to meet Germany in the quarter-finals.

The schedule for the quarter-finals did not afford the Italians much rest. Their tie with Spain was the first played, and once again they got through a match they scarcely deserved to win thanks to Roberto Baggio. Throughout the tournament his overall contribution was negligible, yet his goals were magnificent, the angles so precise. Against the Spanish he scored another beauty with only two minutes remaining. Spain felt mightily aggrieved that they were not given a penalty just before the end when Tassotti viciously elbowed Luis Enrique in the face. The Spaniard had his nose broken and Tassotti later received an eight-match ban from FIFA, but Italy were in the semi-finals.

Brazil and Holland contested the second quarter-final at the Cotton Bowl in Dallas, and after a dreadful first 45 minutes, the game came alive. Having gone 2-0 ahead early in the second half, the Brazilians had their lead wiped out and might have crumbled, but they hit back through Branco's unstoppable free-kick from an outrageous distance. There had been a suspicion of off-side about Brazil's first two goals, but they survived their sternest test in the whole of the tournament to qualify for their first semi-final appearance since 1970.

The notable aspect of the quarter-final line-up was that seven of the eight teams were from Europe, and two of these were Eastern European nations. After so many World Cup embarrassments in the past, Bulgaria had now won three games on the trot but no-one gave them much chance against Germany. They responded by playing the game of their lives, as a brilliant Stoichkov free-kick and a superb Letchkov header sent the Germans home early. It was the first time they had lost at the quarter-final stage since 1962.

The last quarter-final was the second game to be decided on penalties, and it was the ebullient Romanians who lost out to Sweden in San Francisco. Before the game bets were being placed on an all-Eastern European final, but it was not to be. Raducioiu scored a last-gasp equaliser for Romania to send the game into extra-time and both sides scored again to make the final result 2-2. Ravelli in Sweden's goal was the hero in the shoot-out, saving from Belodedici.

It had been one of the most open tournaments in the history of the World Cup, but the semi-finals saw the end of the upsets. At Giants Stadium, Italy faced Bulgaria in what turned out to be an undistinguished match, apart, that is, from twenty minutes in the first half when the Italians ran their opponents ragged in an exhibition of football that was perhaps the best seen in the whole tournament. Roberto Baggio, inevitably, scored two superb goals in the space of five minutes to secure the win for Italy, but once Stoichkov scored from the penalty spot just before half time, the Italians went back into their defensive shell. They held on to reach the final for the fifth time in their history.

The second semi-final, a repeat of the 1958 final between Brazil and Sweden, was a disappointment. Exorbitant ticket prices meant that there were gaps in the Rose Bowl crowd and the match as a result seemed muted. The Brazilians again left it very late before scoring the only goal of the game, courtesy of Romario ten minutes from the end. The defensive Swedes looked intimidated by Brazil and gave up without much of a fight.

In the final Brazil could not manage to break down the Italian defence although Mazinho, Bebeto and Romario all came close. Baresi and Maldini both had fine games for Italy, but Baggio, suffering from a hamstring injury picked up in the semi-final, was never more than a passenger up front. His effort when clean through just before the end of extra-time was symptomatic of Italy's performance, as he shot weakly and hopelessly off target. In a tournament whose overall message was that positive football could win the day, it was ironic that the final should be goalless (the first ever) and have to be decided on penalties. It was Baggio, his touch deserting him after his goals had kept his side in the tournament, who missed the penalty which won the cup for Brazil.

It was a desperately unsatisfactory way in which to decide the world champions, but it did not detract from the overall impression the tournament had made. USA '94 will rank amongst the best ever staged, along with Mexico '70, Argentina '78 and Mexico '86. FIFA will be hoping that the standards set in the States will be built upon in France in 1998.

QUALIFYING TOURNAMENT

EUROPE

Group 1

	It	Sz	Pt	Sc	Ma	Es	Pl	W	D	L	F	A	Pts
ITALY	-	2-2	1-0	3-1	6-1	2-0	10	7	2	1	22	7	16
SWITZERLAND	1-0	-	1-1	3-1	3-0	4-0	10	6	3	1	23	6	15
PORTUGAL	1-3	1-0	-	5-0	4-0	3-0	10	6	2	2	18	5	14
SCOTLAND	0-0	1-1	0-0	-	3-0	3-1	10	4	3	3	14	13	11
MALTA	1-2	0-2	0-1	0-2	-	0-0	10	1	1	8	3	23	3
ESTONIA	0-3	0-6	0-2	0-3	0-1	-	10	0	1	9	1	27	1

Group 2

	No	Ho	En	Pd	Tu	SM	Pl	W	D	L	F	A	Pts
NORWAY	2-1	2-0	1-0	3-1	10-0		10	7	2	1	25	5	16
HOLLAND	0-0	-	2-0	2-2	3-1	6-0	10	6	3	1	29	9	15
ENGLAND	1-1	2-2	-	3-0	4-0	6-0	10	5	3	2	26	9	13
POLAND	0-3	1-3	1-1	-	1-0	1-0	10	3	2	5	10	15	8
TURKEY	2-1	1-3	0-2	2-1	-	4-1	10	3	1	6	11	19	7
SAN MARINO	0-2	0-7	1-7	0-3	0-0	-	10	0	1	9	2	46	1

Group 3

	Sp	Ri	Da	NI	Li	La	Al	Pl	W	D	L	F	A	Pts
SPAIN	-	0-0	1-0	3-1	5-0	5-0	3-0	12	8	3	1	27	4	19
REP. IRELAND	1-3	-	1-1	3-0	2-0	4-0	2-0	12	7	4	1	19	6	18
DENMARK	1-0	0-0	-	1-0	4-0	2-0	4-0	12	7	4	1	15	2	18
NTH. IRELAND	0-0	1-1	0-1	-	2-2	2-0	3-0	12	5	3	4	14	13	13
LITHUANIA	0-2	0-1	0-0	0-1	-	1-1	3-1	12	2	3	7	8	21	7
LATVIA	0-0	0-2	0-0	1-2	1-2	-	0-0	12	0	5	7	4	21	5
ALBANIA	1-5	1-2	0-1	1-2	1-0	1-1	-	12	1	2	9	6	26	4

Group 4

	Gr	Ru	Ic	Hu	Lu	Pl	W	D	L	F	A	Pts
GREECE	-	1-0	1-0	0-0	2-0	8	6	2	0	10	2	14
RUSSIA	1-1	-	1-0	3-0	2-0	8	5	2	1	15	4	12
ICELAND	0-1	1-1	-	2-0	1-0	8	3	2	3	7	6	8
HUNGARY	0-1	1-3	1-2	-	1-0	8	2	1	5	6	11	5
LUXEMBOURG	1-3	0-4	1-1	0-3	-	8	0	1	7	2	17	1

Group 5

	Ro	Be	Cz	Wa	Cy	Fl	Pl	W	D	L	F	A	Pts
ROMANIA	-	2-1	1-1	5-1	2-1	7-0	10	7	1	2	29	12	15
BELGIUM	1-0	-	0-0	2-0	1-0	3-0	10	7	1	2	16	5	15

							Pl	W	D	L	F	A	Pts
CZECHOSLOVAKIA	5-2	1-2	-	1-1	3-0	4-0	10	4	5	1	21	9	13
WALES	1-2	2-0	2-2	-	2-0	6-0	10	5	2	3	19	12	12
CYPRUS	1-4	0-3	1-1	0-1	-	3-1	10	2	1	7	8	18	5
FAEROE ISLANDS	0-4	0-3	0-3	0-3	0-2	-	10	0	0	10	1	38	0

Group 6

	Sd	Bu	Fr	Au	Fi	Is	Pl	W	D	L	F	A	Pts
SWEDEN	-	2-0	1-1	1-0	3-2	5-0	10	6	3	1	19	8	15
BULGARIA	1-1	-	2-0	4-1	2-0	2-2	10	6	2	2	19	10	14
FRANCE	2-1	1-2	-	2-0	2-1	2-3	10	6	1	3	17	10	13
AUSTRIA	1-1	3-1	0-1	-	3-0	5-2	10	3	2	5	15	16	8
FINLAND	0-1	0-3	0-2	3-1	-	0-0	10	2	1	7	9	18	5
ISRAEL	1-3	0-2	0-4	1-1	1-3	-	10	1	3	6	10	27	5

SOUTH AMERICA

Group A

	Co	Ar	Pa	Pe	Pl	W	D	L	F	A	Pts
COLOMBIA	-	2-1	0-0	4-0	6	4	2	0	13	2	10
ARGENTINA	0-5	-	0-0	2-1	6	3	1	2	7	9	7
PARAGUAY	1-1	1-3	-	2-1	6	1	4	1	6	7	6
PERU	0-1	0-1	2-2	-	6	0	1	5	4	12	1

Argentina qualified to face Australia in a play-off

Group B

	Br	Bo	Ur	Ec	Ve	Pl	W	D	L	F	A	Pts
BRAZIL	-	6-0	2-0	2-0	4-0	8	5	2	1	20	4	12
BOLIVIA	2-0	-	3-1	1-0	7-0	8	5	1	2	22	11	11
URUGUAY	1-1	2-1	-	0-0	4-0	8	4	2	2	10	7	10
ECUADOR	0-0	1-1	0-1	-	5-0	8	1	3	4	7	7	5
VENEZUELA	1-5	1-7	0-1	2-1	-	8	1	0	7	4	34	2

AFRICA

FIRST ROUND

Group A

	Al	Gh	Bu	Pl	W	D	L	F	A	Pts
ALGERIA	-	2-1	3-1	4	2	1	1	5	4	5
GHANA	2-0	-	1-0	4	2	0	2	4	3	4
BURUNDI	0-0	1-0	-	4	1	1	2	2	4	3

Group B

	Ca	Sw	Za	Pl	W	D	L	F	A	Pts
CAMEROON	-	5-0	0-0	4	2	2	0	7	1	6
SWAZILAND	0-0	-	1-0	3	1	1	1	1	5	3
ZAIRE	1-2	-	-	3	0	1	2	1	3	1

Group C

	Zi	Eg	An	To	Pl	W	D	L	F	A	Pts
ZIMBABWE	-	2-1	2-1	1-0	6	4	2	0	8	4	10
EGYPT	0-0	-	1-0	3-0	6	3	2	1	9	3	8
ANGOLA	1-1	0-0	-	-	5	1	2	2	3	4	4
TOGO	1-2	1-4	0-1	-	5	0	0	5	2	11	0

Group D

	Ni	SA	Co	Pl	W	D	L	F	A	Pts
NIGERIA	-	4-0	2-0	4	3	1	0	7	0	7
SOUTH AFRICA	0-0	-	1-0	4	2	1	1	2	4	5
CONGO	0-1	0-1	-	4	0	0	4	0	5	0

Group E

	CI	Ni	Bo	Pl	W	D	L	F	A	Pts
CÔTE D'IVOIRE	-	1-0	6-0	4	2	2	0	7	0	6
NIGER	0-0	-	2-1	4	2	1	1	3	2	5
BOTSWANA	0-0	0-1	-	4	0	1	3	1	9	1

Group F

	Mo	Tu	Et	Be	Pl	W	D	L	F	A	Pts
MOROCCO	-	0-0	5-0	5-0	6	4	2	0	13	1	10
TUNISIA	1-1	-	3-0	5-1	6	3	3	0	14	2	9
ETHIOPIA	0-1	0-0	-	3-1	6	1	1	4	3	11	3
BENIN	0-1	0-5	1-0	-	6	1	0	5	3	19	2

Group G

	Se	Ga	Mo	Pl	W	D	L	F	A	Pts
SENEGAL	-	1-0	6-1	4	3	0	1	10	4	6
GABON	3-2	-	3-1	4	2	1	1	7	5	5
MOZAMBIQUE	0-1	1-1	-	4	0	1	3	3	11	1

Group H

	Za	Ma	Na	Pl	W	D	L	F	A	Pts
ZAMBIA	-	3-1	4-0	4	3	0	1	11	3	6
MADAGASCAR	2-0	-	3-0	4	3	0	1	7	3	6
NAMIBIA	0-4	0-1	-	4	0	0	4	0	12	0

Group I

	Gu	Ke	Pl	W	D	L	F	A	Pts
GUINEA	-	4-0	2	1	0	1	4	2	2
KENYA	2-0	-	2	1	0	1	2	4	2

SECOND ROUND

Group 1

	Ni	CI	Al	Pl	W	D	L	F	A	Pts
NIGERIA	-	4-1	4-1	4	2	1	1	10	5	5
CÔTE D'IVOIRE	2-1	-	1-0	4	2	1	1	5	6	5
ALGERIA	1-1	1-1	-	4	0	2	2	3	7	2

Group 2

	Mo	Zm	Se	Pl	W	D	L	F	A	Pts
MOROCCO	-	1-0	1-0	4	3	0	1	6	3	6
ZAMBIA	2-1	-	4-0	4	2	1	1	6	2	5
SENEGAL	1-3	0-0	-	4	0	1	3	1	8	1

Group 3

	Cm	Zi	Gu	Pl	W	D	L	F	A	Pts
CAMEROON	-	3-1	3-1	4	3	0	1	7	3	6
ZIMBABWE	1-0	-	1-0	4	2	0	2	3	6	4
GUINEA	0-1	3-0	-	4	1	0	3	4	5	2

CENTRAL AND NORTH AMERICA

Pre-preliminary round

Dominican Republic .... 1-2 1-1 .... **Puerto Rico**
St Lucia .... 1-0 1-3 .... **St Vincent**

PRELIMINARY ROUND

Bermuda .... 1-0 1-2 .... Haiti
Jamaica .... 2-1 1-0 .... Puerto Rica
St Vincent .... W-O .... Cuba
Netherlands Antilles .... 1-1 0-3 .... **Antigua**
Guyana .... 1-2 1-1 .... **Surinam**
Barbados .... 1-2 0-3 .... **Trinidad**

FIRST ROUND

Antigua .... 0-3 1-2 .... **Bermuda**
Trinidad .... 1-2 1-1 .... **Jamaica**
Surinam .... 0-0 1-2 .... **St Vincent**
Guatemala .... 0-0 0-2 .... **Honduras**
Nicaragua .... 0-5 1-5 .... **El Salvador**
Panama .... 1-0 1-5 .... **Costa Rica**
Mexico .... Bye
Canada .... Bye

SECOND ROUND

Group A

	Me	Ho	CR	SV	Pl	W	D	L	F	A	Pts
MEXICO	-	2-0	4-0	11-0	6	4	1	1	22	3	9

					Pl	W	D	L	F	A	Pts
Honduras	1-1	-	2-1	4-0	6	4	1	1	14	6	9
Costa Rica	2-0	2-3	-	5-0	6	3	0	3	11	9	6
St Vincent	0-4	0-4	0-1	-	6	0	0	6	0	29	0

Group B

	ES	Ca	Ja	Be	Pl	W	D	L	F	A	Pts
El Salvador	-	1-1	2-1	4-1	6	4	1	1	12	6	9
Canada	2-3	-	1-0	4-2	6	2	3	1	9	7	7
Jamaica	0-2	1-1	-	3-2	6	1	2	3	6	9	4
Bermuda	1-0	0-0	1-1	-	6	1	2	3	7	12	4

THIRD ROUND

	Me	Ca	ES	Ho	Pl	W	D	L	F	A	Pts
MEXICO	-	4-0	3-1	3-0	6	5	0	1	17	5	10
Canada	1-2	-	2-0	3-1	6	3	1	2	10	10	7
El Salvador	2-1	1-2	-	2-1	6	2	0	4	6	11	4
Honduras	1-4	2-2	2-0	-	6	1	1	4	7	14	3

Canada qualified to meet the winners of Oceania, Australia, for the right to play-off against the runners-up of South America group A, Argentina, for a place in the finals

ASIA

FIRST ROUND

Group A Held in Amman, Jordan (lower left results) and Beijing, China (upper right results)

	Iq	Ch	Ye	Jo	Pa	Pl	W	D	L	F	A	Pts
Iraq	-	1-0	6-1	1-1	8-0	8	6	1	1	28	4	13
China	2-1	-	0-1	3-0	5-0	8	6	0	2	18	4	12
Yemen	0-3	0-1	-	1-1	5-1	8	3	2	3	12	13	8
Jordan	0-4	1-4	1-1	-	3-1	8	2	3	3	12	15	7
Pakistan	0-4	0-3	0-3	0-5	-	8	0	0	8	2	36	0

Group B Held in Tehran, Iran (upper right results) and Damascus, Syria (lower left results)

	Ir	Sy	Om	Ta	Pl	W	D	L	F	A	Pts
Iran	-	1-1	0-0	6-0	6	3	3	0	15	2	9
Syria	1-1	-	0-0	2-0	6	3	3	0	14	4	9
Oman	0-1	1-2	-	2-1	6	2	2	2	10	5	6
Taiwan	0-6	1-8	1-7	-	6	0	0	6	3	31	0

Group C Held in Doha, Qatar (upper right results) and Singapore (lower left results)

	NK	Qa	Si	In	Vi	Pl	W	D	L	F	A	Pts
North Korea	-	2-1	2-1	4-0	3-0	8	7	1	0	19	6	15
Qatar	2-2	-	4-1	3-1	4-0	8	5	1	2	22	8	11
Singapore	1-3	1-0	-	2-0	3-2	8	5	0	3	12	12	10
Indonesia	1-2	1-4	1-2	-	0-1	8	1	0	7	6	19	2
Vietnam	0-1	0-4	0-1	1-2	-	8	1	0	7	4	18	2

Group D Held in Beirut, Lebanon (lower left results) and Seoul, South Korea (upper right results)

	SK	Ba	Le	HK	In	Pl	W	D	L	F	A	Pts
South Korea	-	3-0	2-0	3-0	7-0	8	7	1	0	22	0	15
Bahrain	0-0	-	0-0	3-0	3-0	8	3	3	2	9	6	9
Lebanon	0-1	0-0	-	2-1	2-1	8	2	4	2	8	9	8
Hong Kong	0-3	2-1	2-2	-	1-3	8	2	1	5	8	18	5
India	0-3	1-2	2-2	1-2	-	8	1	1	6	8	22	3

Group E Held in Kuala Lumpur, Malaysia (lower left results) and Riyadh, Saudi Arabia (upper right results)

	SA	Ku	Ml	Mc	Pl	W	D	L	F	A	Pts
Saudi Arabia	-	2-0	3-0	8-0	6	4	2	0	20	1	10
Kuwait	0-0	-	2-0	8-0	6	2	3	1	21	4	7
Malaysia	1-1	1-1	-	5-0	6	2	2	2	16	7	6
Macao	0-6	1-10	0-9	-	6	0	0	6	1	46	0

Group F Held in Tokyo, Japan (upper right results) and Dubai, UAE (lower left results)

	Ja	AE	Th	Ba	SL	Pl	W	D	L	F	A	Pts
Japan	-	2-0	1-0	8-0	5-0	8	7	1	0	28	2	15
UAE	1-1	-	1-0	1-0	4-0	8	6	1	1	19	4	13
Thailand	0-1	1-2	-	4-1	1-0	8	4	0	4	13	7	8
Bangladesh	1-4	0-7	1-4	-	1-0	8	2	0	6	7	28	4
Sri Lanka	0-6	0-3	0-3	0-3	-	8	0	0	8	0	26	0

SECOND ROUND

Tournament held in Doha, Qatar

	SA	SK	Ja	Iq	Ir	NK	Pl	W	D	L	F	A	Pts
SAUDI ARABIA	-	1-1	0-0	1-1	4-3	2-1	5	2	3	0	8	6	7
SOUTH KOREA	-	-	0-1	2-2	3-0	3-0	5	2	2	1	9	4	6
Japan	-	-	-	2-2	1-2	3-0	5	2	2	1	7	4	6
Iraq	-	-	-	-	2-1	2-3	5	1	3	1	9	9	5
Iran	-	-	-	-	-	2-1	5	2	0	3	8	11	4
North Korea	-	-	-	-	-	-	5	1	0	4	5	12	2

OCEANIA

FIRST ROUND

Group 1

	Au	Ta	SI	Pl	W	D	L	F	A	Pts
Australia	-	2-0	6-1	4	4	0	0	13	2	8
Tahiti	0-3	-	4-2	4	1	1	2	5	8	3
Solomon Islands	1-2	1-1	-	4	0	1	3	5	13	1

Group 2

	NZ	Fi	Va	Pl	W	D	L	F	A	Pts
New Zealand	-	3-0	8-0	4	3	1	0	15	1	7
Fiji	0-0	-	3-0	4	2	1	1	6	3	5
Vanuatu	1-4	0-3	-	4	0	0	4	1	18	0

SECOND ROUND

New Zealand............................0-1 0-3 ....Australia

Australia qualified to meet the runners-up of CONCACAF, Canada, in a play-off to meet the runners-up of South America group A, Argentina, for a place in the finals

INTER REGIONAL PLAY-OFFS

Canada..................................2-1 1-2 1-4p ....Australia

Australia ....1-1 0-1 ....**ARGENTINA**

FINAL TOURNAMENT

HELD IN THE UNITED STATES, 17 JUNE - 17 JULY 1994

FIRST ROUND

Group A

Pontiac Silverdome, Detroit, 18-06-1994, 77,000

United States 1 (Wynalda 44)
Switzerland 1 (Bregy 39)

Pasadena Rose Bowl, Los Angeles, 18-06-1994, 91,000

Romania 3 (Raducioiu 16 89, Hagi 34)
Colombia 1 (Valencia 43)

Pontiac Silverdome, Detroit, 22-06-1994, 61,000

Switzerland 4 (Sutter.A 16, Chapuisat 52, Knup 65, Bregy 72)
Romania 1 (Hagi 35)

Pasadena Rose Bowl, Los Angeles, 22-06-1994, 93,000

United States 2 (Escobar OG 33, Stewart 51)
Colombia 1 (Valencia 89)

Pasadena Rose Bowl, Los Angeles, 26-06-1994, 93,000

Romania 1 (Petrescu 17)
United States 0

Stanford Stadium, San Francisco, 26-06-1994, 83,000
Colombia 2 (Gaviria 45, Lazano 90)
Switzerland 0

	Ro	Sz	US	Co	Pl	W	D	L	F	A	Pts
ROMANIA	-	1-4	1-0	3-1	3	2	0	1	5	5	6
SWITZERLAND	-	-	1-1	0-2	3	1	1	1	5	4	4
UNITED STATES	-	-	-	2-1	3	1	1	1	3	3	4
COLOMBIA	-	-	-	-	3	1	0	2	4	5	3

Group B

Pasadena Rose Bowl, Los Angeles, 19-06-1994, 83,000
Cameroon 2 (Embe 30, Oman-Biyik 47)
Sweden 2 (Ljung 9, Dahlin 74)

Stanford Stadium, San Francisco, 20-06-1994, 81,000
Brazil 2 (Romario 26, Rai 52p)
Russia 0

Stanford Stadium, San Francisco, 24-06-1994, 83,000
Brazil 3 (Romario 39, Marcio Santos 65, Bebeto 73)
Cameroon 0

Pontiac Silverdome, Detroit, 24-06-1994, 71,000
Sweden 3 (Brolin 39p, Dahlin 80 82)
Russia 1 (Salenko 4p)

Pontiac Siverdome, Detroit, 28-06-1994, 74,000
Russia 6 (Salenko 15 41 45p 72 75, Radchenko 82)
Cameroon 1 (Milla 47)

Stanford Stadium, San Francisco, 28-06-1994, 74,00
Brazil 1 (Romario 47)
Sweden 1 (Andersson.K 23)

	Br	Sd	Ru	Cm	Pl	W	D	L	F	A	Pts
BRAZIL	-	1-1	2-0	3-0	3	2	1	0	6	1	7
SWEDEN	-	-	3-1	2-2	3	1	2	0	6	4	5
RUSSIA	-	-	-	6-1	3	1	0	2	7	6	3
CAMEROON	-	-	-	-	3	0	1	2	3	11	1

Group C

Soldier Field, Chicago, 17-06-1994, 63,000
Germany 1 (Klinsmann 60)
Bolivia 0

Cotton Bowl, Dallas, 17-06-1994, 56,000
Spain 2 (Salinas 51, Goikoetxea, 56)
South Korea 2 (Myong-bo 84, Jung-won 90)

Soldier Field, Chicago, 21-06-1994, 63,000
Germany 1 (Klinsmann 47)
Spain 1 (Goikoetxea 14)

Foxboro Stadium, Boston, 23-06-1994, 53,000
South Korea 0
Bolivia 0

Soldier Field, Chicago, 27-06-1994, 63,000
Spain 3 (Guardiola 19p, Caminero 65 71)
Bolivia 1 (Sanchez 66)

Cotton Bowl, Dallas, 27-06-1994, 63,000
Germany 3 (Klinsmann 12 37, Riedle 20)
South Korea 2 (Sun-hong 52, Myong-bo 63)

	Ge	Sp	SK	Bo	Pl	W	D	L	F	A	Pts
GERMANY	-	1-1	3-2	1-0	3	2	1	0	5	3	7
SPAIN	-	-	2-2	3-1	3	1	2	0	6	4	5
SOUTH KOREA	-	-	-	0-0	3	0	2	1	4	5	2
BOLIVIA	-	-	-	-	3	0	1	2	1	4	1

Group D

Foxboro Stadium, Boston, 21-06-1994, 53,000
Argentina 4 (Batistuta 2 44 90p, Maradona 59)
Greece 0

Cotton Bowl, Dallas, 21-06-1994, 44,000
Nigeria 3 (Yekini 21, Amokachi 43, Amunike 54)
Bulgaria 0

Foxboro Stadium, Boston, 25-06-1994, 54,000
Argentina 2 (Caniggia 22 29)
Nigeria 1 (Siasia 8)

Soldier Field, Chicago, 26-06-1994, 63,000
Bulgaria 4 (Stoichkov 5p 56p, Lechkov 66, Boromirov 90)
Greece 0

Foxboro Stadium, Boston, 30-06-1994, 53,000
Nigeria 2 (George 45, Amokachi 90)
Greece 0

Cotton Bowl, Dallas, 30-06-1994, 63,000
Bulgaria 2 (Stoichkov 61, Sirakov 90)
Argentina 0

	Ng	Bu	Ar	Gr	Pl	W	D	L	F	A	Pts
NIGERIA	-	3-0	1-2	2-0	3	2	0	1	6	2	6
BULGARIA	-	-	2-0	4-0	3	2	0	1	6	3	6
ARGENTINA	-	-	-	4-0	3	2	0	1	6	3	6
GREECE	-	-	-	-	3	0	0	3	0	10	0

Group E

Giants Stadium, New York, 18-06-1994, 73,000
Rep. Ireland 1 (Houghton 11)
Italy 0

RFK Stadium, Washington, 19-06-1994, 52,000
Norway 1 (Rekdal 85)
Mexico 0

Giants Stadium, New York, 23-06-1994, 74,000
Italy 1 (Baggio.D 69)
Norway 0

Citrus Bowl, Orlando, 24-06-1994, 61,000
Mexico 2 (Garcia 42 66)
Rep. Ireland 1 (Aldridge 84)

RFK Stadium, Washington, 28-06-1990, 53,000
Italy 1 (Massaro 48)
Mexico 1 (Bernal 58)

Giants Stadium, New York, 28-06-1994, 76,000
Rep. Ireland 0
Norway 0

	Me	RI	It	No	Pl	W	D	L	F	A	Pts
MEXICO	-	2-1	1-1	0-1	3	1	1	1	3	3	4
REP. IRELAND	-	-	1-0	0-0	3	1	1	1	2	2	4
ITALY	-	-	-	1-0	3	1	1	1	2	2	4
NORWAY	-	-	-	-	3	1	1	1	1	1	4

Group F

Citrus Bowl, Orlando, 19-06-1994, 60,000
Belgium 1 (Degryse 11)
Morocco 0

RFK Stadium, Washington, 20-06-1994, 52,000
Holland 2 (Jonk 50, Taument 87)
Saudi Arabia 1 (Amin 19)

Giants Stadium, New York, 25-06-1994, 72,000
Saudi Arabia 2 (Al-Jaber 7p, Amin 45)
Morocco 1 (Chaouch 26)

Citrus Bowl, Orlando, 25-06-1994, 61,000
Belgium 1 (Albert 65)
Holland 0

Citrus Bowl, Orlando, 29-06-1994, 60,000
Holland 2 (Bergkamp 43, Roy 78)
Morocco 1 (Nader 47)

RFK Stadium, Washington, 29-06-1994, 52,000
Saudi Arabia 1 (Owairan 5)
Belgium 0

	Ho	SA	Be	Mo	Pl	W	D	L	F	A	Pts
HOLLAND	-	2-1	0-1	2-1	3	2	0	1	4	3	6
SAUDI ARABIA	-	-	1-0	2-1	3	2	0	1	4	3	6
BELGIUM	-	-	-	1-0	3	2	0	1	2	1	6
MOROCCO	-	-	-	-	3	0	0	3	2	5	0

SECOND ROUND

Stanford Stadium, San Francisco, 4-07-1994, 84,000
Brazil 1 (Bebeto 74)
United States 0

Citrus Bowl, Orlando, 4-07-1994, 61,000
Holland 2 (Bergkamp 11, Jonk 41)
Rep. Ireland 0

Pasadena Rose Bowl, Los Angeles, 3-07-1994, 90,000
Romania 3 (Dumitrescu 11 18, Hagi 58)
Argentina 2 (Batistuta 16p, Balbo 75)

Cotton Bowl, Dallas, 3-07-1994, 60,000
Sweden 3 (Dahlin 6, Andersson.K 51 88)
Saudi Arabia 1 (Al Ghashiyan 85)

Giants Stadium, New York, 5-07-1994, 71,000
Bulgaria 1 (Stoichkov 7)
Mexico 1 (Garcia Aspe 18p)
Bulgaria win 3-1 on pens

Soldier Field, Chicago, 2-07-1994, 60,000
Germany 3 (Völler 6 39, Klinsmann 11)
Belgium 2 (Grün 8, Albert 90)

RFK Stadium, Washington, 2-07-1994, 53,000
Spain 3 (Hierro 15, Luis Enrique 74, Beguiristain 87p)
Switzerland 0

Foxboro Stadium, Boston, 5-07-1994, 54,000
Italy 2 (Baggio.R 89 102p)
Nigeria 1 (Amunike 26)

QUARTER-FINALS

Cotton Bowl, Dallas, 9-07-1994, 63,000
Brazil 3 (Romario 52, Bebeto 62, Branco 81)
Holland 2 (Bergkamp 64, Winter 76)

Stanford Stadium, San Francisco, 10-07-1994, 81,000
Sweden 2 (Brolin 78, Andersson.K 114)
Romania 2 (Raducioiu 88 95)

Giants Stadium, New York, 10-07-1994, 72,000
Bulgaria 2 (Stoichkov 76, Letchkov 78)
Germany 1 (Matthäus 48p)

Foxboro Stadium, Boston, 9-07-1994, 61,000
Italy 2 (Baggio.D 26, Baggio.R 88)
Spain 1 (Caminero 59)

SEMI-FINALS

Pasadena Rose Bowl, Los Angeles, 13-07-1994, 88,000
Brazil 1 (Romario 80)
Sweden 0

Giants Stadium, New York, 13-07-1994,
Italy 2 (Baggio.R 21 26)
Bulgaria 1 (Stoichkov 44p)

3RD PLACE

Pasadena Rose Bowl, Los Angeles, 16-07-1994, 83,000
Sweden 4 (Brolin 8, Mild 30, Larsson.H 37, Andersson.K 39)
Bulgaria 0

FINAL

Pasadena Rose Bowl, Los Angeles, 17-07-1994, 94,000. Referee: Puhl, Hungary
BRAZIL 0
ITALY 0
Brazil won 3-2 on pens

Italy		**Brazil**	
Baresi	x	Marcio Santos	x
Albertini	1	Romario	1
Evani	1	Branco	1
Massaro	x	Dunga	1
Baggio.R	x		

Brazil - Taffarel - Jorginho (Cafu), Marcio Santos, Aldair, Branco - Mazinho, Mauro Silva, Dunga, Zinho (Viola) - Bebeto, Romario. Tr: Carlos Albert Parreira
Italy - Pagliuca - Mussi (Apolloni), Maldini, Baresi, Benarrivo - Donadoni, Albertini, Baggio.D (Evani), Berti - Baggio.R, Massaro. Tr: Sacchi

Top scorers: Oleg Salenko, Russia 6
Hristo Stoichkov, Bulgaria 6

THE FOOTBALL TOURNAMENT OF THE OLYMPIC GAMES

The football tournament of the Olympic Games has proved to be a major headache for the International Olympic Committee (IOC). There has been much argument about its status in the Games throughout the years because football is a sport dominated by professionalism while the tournament was, until recently, open only to amateur players.

There have been several distinct phases in its history: from 1896-1904 it was little more than a demonstration sport; from 1908-28 it could legitimately be regarded as the world championship; from 1952-76 it was the domain of the eastern European state amateurs; and post-1980 it was opened up to professional players who had not competed in World Cup games. The 1992 tournament in Barcelona heralded a further new phase. Olympic officials had wanted to turn it into a tournament open to everyone but, fearful that this would threaten the pre-eminence of the World Cup, FIFA insisted that it should become instead the official Under-23 world championship.

Year	Winner	Score	Runner-up
1896 *	Denmark	15-0	Izmir
1900 *	England	4-0	France
1904 *	Canada	7-0	United States
1906 *	Denmark	5-2	Izmir
1908	England	2-0	Denmark
1912	England	4-2	Denmark
1916	-		
1920	Belgium	2-0	Czechoslovakia
1924	Uruguay	3-0	Switzerland
1928	Uruguay	1-1 2-1	Argentina
1932	-		
1936	Italy	2-1	Austria
1940	-		
1944	-		
1948	Sweden	3-1	Yugoslavia
1952	Hungary	2-0	Yugoslavia
1956	Soviet Union	1-0	Yugoslavia
1960	Yugoslavia	3-1	Denmark
1964	Hungary	2-1	Czechoslovakia
1968	Hungary	4-1	Bulgaria
1972	Poland	2-1	Hungary
1976	East Germany	3-1	Poland
1980	Czechoslovakia	1-0	East Germany
1984	France	2-0	Brazil
1988	Soviet Union	2-1	Brazil
1992	Spain	3-2	Poland

* Unofficial tournaments

ORDER OF MERIT

	Country	G	S	B	Finals	S-Finals
1	Hungary	3	1	1	4	4
2	Soviet Union	2	-	3	2	4
3	England	2	-	-	2	2
4	Uruguay	2	-	-	2	2
5	Yugoslavia	1	3	1	4	6
6	Poland	1	2	-	3	3
7	East Germany	1	1	2	2	3
8	Czechoslovakia	1	1	-	3	3
9	Spain	1	1	-	1	1
10	Sweden	1	-	2	1	3
11	Italy	1	-	1	1	5
12	France	1	-	-	1	3
13	Belgium	1	-	-	1	1
14	Denmark	-	3	1	3	4
15	Brazil	-	2	-	2	3
16	Bulgaria	-	1	1	1	2
17	Argentina	-	1	-	1	1
	Austria	-	1	-	1	1
	Switzerland	-	1	-	1	1
20	Holland	-	-	3	-	4
21	West Germany	-	-	1	-	2
22	Ghana	-	-	1	-	1
	Japan	-	-	1	-	1
	Norway	-	-	1	-	1
25	Egypt	-	-	-	-	2
26	Australia	-	-	-	-	1
	Finland	-	-	-	-	1
	Great Britain	-	-	-	-	1
	India	-	-	-	-	1
	Mexico	-	-	-	-	1

From 1908-92, official tournaments only

I. OLYMPIAD, ATHENS 1896

6th - 15th April

Baron Pierre de Coubertin, the French educationalist, was the man mainly responsible for the revival of the Olympic Games. The first record of them being held was in 776 BC – although they certainly date from before then – and they continued through to AD 393 when they were abolished by the Christian Roman emperor Theodosius I, Greece having fallen under the influence of Rome. It is said he objected to the pagan rituals which accompanied the event. The Athens games of 1896 signalled a return after some 1503 years absence. De Coubertin believed strongly in the ideals of amateur sportsmanship and was of the opinion that the games would help promote peace among athletes and nations.

The first games of the modern era, the 294th in all on record, were staged at Athens in a new arena, the Panathenaic Stadium, built for the occasion and containing room for 80,000 people. As would be the case with future celebrations, the main heroes came from the athletics events held in the stadium. Sadly there was no such excitement surrounding the football competition. Quite where it was staged is unknown, as are the scores of all but one match – Denmark beating an Izmir select XI 15-0. The results involving the Athens select XI have been lost over the years. Denmark was credited with just one gold medal at the games and it was not for the football.

II. OLYMPIAD, PARIS 1900

20th May - 28th October

The 1900 Olympic Games in Paris were a disaster. Held on a haphazard basis from May until the end of October to coincide with the World Exhibition being held in the same city, they passed off almost unnoticed. Once again football was not considered as anything but a demonstration sport, despite the great progress being made in the game's organisation on the continent at the time. Three teams entered: a French XI, a Belgian XI and, representing Great Britain, Upton Park FC of London.

Upton Park were a moderately well-known side who had won the inaugural London Senior Cup in 1883 (and again the following year) and the Essex Senior Cup in 1895. With football in Great Britain still light years ahead of its rivals on the continent, they met the winners of a play-off in which the French beat Belgium 6-2 and duly became, somewhat dubiously, champions of the world. Olympic gold did not do much for the club, which folded not long afterwards.

Upton Park's victory was very much in keeping with the tempo of the rest of the Games. It is said that many competitors in Paris were unaware that they were actually taking part in the Olympics. "We have made a hash of it," were De Coubertin's words – and that was before the Games had even begun. Five months later no-one was disputing his verdict.

DEMONSTRATION GAME
23-09-1900, Velodrome Municipal de Vincennes, Paris, 1500. Referee: Wood, England
Club Français, Paris 7
Belgian Student XI 4

FINAL
20-09-1900, Velodrome Municipal de Vincennes, Paris, 500. Referee: Moignard, France
Upton Park FC, London 4 (Nicholas 2, Turner, Zealey)
Club Français, Paris 0
Great Britain - Jones - Grosling, Buckenham - Quash, Burridge, Chalk - Haslom, Zealley, Nicholas, Spackman, Turner
France - Huteau - Bach, Allemane - Gaillard, Bloch, Macaire - Fraysse, Garnier, Lambert, Grandjean, Canelle

III. OLYMPIAD, ST LOUIS 1904

1st July - 23rd November

Like the 1900 edition, the 1904 Olympic Games were also held in conjunction with a World Trade Fair - The Louisiana Purchase Exhibition - this time in St Louis in the United States, although they had initially been awarded to Chicago. And like the Paris Games, they were a disaster that nearly killed off the Olympic movement. St Louis was not a good choice; its remoteness from Europe meant only 13 nations bothered to enter, the number of athletes taking part fell from 1330 to 625, and of these 533 were Americans. Quite how seriously the whole event was taken was shown when it transpired that the winner of the marathon had taken a 10-mile lift in a car!

Competition was held over a period of five months with the football tournament taking place at the end, in November. There is some dispute as to whether it should be listed as an official or demonstration sport, but either way it consisted of just five matches involving three teams, all of them from North America. Played on a league basis, the tournament was won by Galt FC of Ontario representing Canada, ahead of Christian Brothers College, St Louis representing USA (I) and St Rose Kickers, St Louis representing USA (II). The next time the Olympics came to America in 1932, there would not even be a football tournament.

	Ca	UI	UII	Pl	W	D	L	F	A	Pts
Canada	-	7-0	4-0	2	2	0	0	11	0	4
USA (I)	-	-	2-0*	2	1	0	1	2	7	2
USA (II)	-	-	-	2	0	0	2	0	6	0

* After two 0-0 draws

Deciding game. 16-11-1904, St. Louis. Referee: McSweeney, USA
Galt FC, Canada 7 (Hall 3, Steep, McDonald 2, Taylor)
Christian Brothers, USA 0
Canada - Linton - Ducker, Gourlay - Lane, Johnston, Fraser - Taylor, Steep, Hall, McDonald, Twaits
USA - Menges - Brockmeyer, January.J - January.T, January.C, Ratican - Brittingham, Cudmore, Bartliff, Lawler, Lydon

17-11-1904, St. Louis. Referee: McSweeney, USA
Galt FC, Canada 4 (Taylor 2, Henderson, OG)
St. Rose, USA 0

20-11-1904, St. Louis
Christian Brothers, USA 0
St. Rose, USA 0

21-11-1904, St. Louis
Christian Brothers, USA 0
St. Rose, USA 0

23-11-1904, St. Louis
Christian Brothers, USA 2
St. Rose, USA 0

INTERIM GAMES, ATHENS 1906

22nd April - 2nd May

The intercalated Olympic Games of 1906 were a curious affair. The Greeks had hoped to hold their own games every four years to alternate with the main event, and 1906 was the first date this had been possible. But de Coubertin opposed the idea, it was dropped for future years, and none of the events are listed as official. At least after the disasters of 1900 and 1904 these Athens games of 1906 helped to revive the Olympic spirit.

The football tournament consisted of the same three teams as in 1896 plus a select XI from Salonica, only this time the team playing under the banner of Izmir was an international one, consisting mainly of French and Englishmen. Again the Danes won, beating both Izmir and Athens in the process. More is known about this Danish team; three of its members appeared two years later in the London Games.

	De	Sa	Iz	At	Pl	W	D	L	F	A	Pts
Denmark XI	-	-	5-1	9-0	2	2	0	0	14	1	4
Salonica XI	-	-	-	6-0	2	1	0	1	6	3	2
Izmir XI	-	3-0	-	-	2	1	0	1	4	5	2
Athens XI	-	-	-	-	2	0	0	2	0	15	0

Deciding game, 23-04-1906, Podilatodromio, Athens
Denmark 5
Izmir 1
Denmark - Andersen.V - Petersen.P, Buchwald - Ferslew, Rasmussen, Andersen.A - Nielsen.O, Petersen.C, Fredriksen, Lundgren, Rambusch
Izmir - Charnaud - Kuyumtzian, Girard.E - Girard.J, Joly, De La Fontaine - Whittal.D, Whittal. A, Whittal.G, Whittal.H, Whittal.E

23-04-1906, Podilatodromio, Athens
Salonika XI 6
Athens XI 0

24-04-1906, Podilatodromio, Athens
Denmark 9
Athens XI 0

24-04-1906, Podilatodromio, Athens
Izmir XI 3
Salonika XI 0

IV. OLYMPIAD, LONDON 1908

1st Football tournament, 19th - 24th October

The 1908 Games helped launch the Olympics as a major occasion, as big crowds turned up to the new White City stadium in London to watch the events. They also marked the birth of the official football tournament, helped no doubt by the fact that the Games took place in the home of football. Held after the track & field had finished, it was won by the England amateur team, representing the United Kingdom. Containing many of the country's best players, the side could lay claim to being the first world champions, even if the entry was restricted to just five countries.

Political troubles had led Hungary and Bohemia to withdraw, which left just two first round games. England's biggest rivals were Denmark, and it was they who stole the show. While England easily dispatched Sweden by eleven clear goals, the Danes beat a French "B" team 9-0 and were in exhilarating form against the French "A" team in the next round. Sophus Nielsen scored 10 goals as Denmark recorded the biggest ever win in international football to date, 17-1.

Their performance in the final against England, who had beaten Holland 4-0 in the other semi-final, was very creditable. The Danes were roundly praised as they lost only by two goals, and some reports described them as unfortunate to have lost at all. On half a dozen occasions in the second half, only good keeping by Bailey or wild Danish finishing kept England in the match.

The England captain, Vivian Woodward, scored the goal that clinched the game for his side. One of the most famous players of the day, he was England's leading goalscorer until he was overtaken in the 1950s by Lofthouse and Finney. If one includes the goals he scored in the amateur side, he can be regarded as the most prolific Englishman ever.

FIRST ROUND

White City, London, 20-11-1908, 2000

England	12 (Stapley 2, Woodward 2, Berry, Chapman, Purnell 4, Hawkes 2)
Sweden	1 (Bergström)

White City, London, 19-10-1908, 2000

Denmark	9 (Middleboe 2, Wolfhagen 4, Bohr.H 2, Nielsen.S)
France 'B'	0

Holland and France 'A' received byes into the semi-finals

SEMI-FINALS

White City, London, 22-10-1908, 6000

England	4 (Stapley 37 60 64 75)
Holland	0

White City, London, 22-10-1908, 1000

Denmark	17 (Nielsen.S 3 4 6 39 46 48 52 64 66 76, Lindgren 18 37, Middleboe.N 68, Wolfhagen 60 72 82 89)
France 'A'	1 (Sartorious 16)

3RD PLACE

White City, London, 23-10-1908, 1000

Holland	2 (Reeman 6, Snethlage 58)
Sweden	0

FINAL

White City, London, 24-10-1908, 8,000. Referee: Lewis, England

ENGLAND	2 (Chapman 20, Woodward 46)
DENMARK	0

England - Bailey - Corbett, Smith - Hunt, Chapman, Hawkes - Berry, Woodward, Stapley, Purnell, Hardman

Denmark - Drescher - Buchwald, Hansen - Bohr, Middleboe.N, Middleboe.O Nielsen-Norland, Lindgren, Nielsen, Wolffhagen, Rasmussen

V. OLYMPIAD, STOCKHOLM 1912

The 2nd Football tournament, 29th June - 4th July

The newly built Stockholms Stadion provided the centrepiece to the 1912 Games, including a football tournament played in sweltering heat, although some games were held at the Råsunda. The English amateur side, again captained by Woodward, retained their title, this time beating Denmark more comfortably in the final. The entry more than doubled to eleven as the tournament established itself as one of the main attractions of the Games. Finland, Italy, Austria, Germany, Hungary, Norway and Russia entered for the first time.

The 1912 tournament saw the start of a practice subsequently followed at most pre-Second World War games: having a consolation tournament for the teams beaten early on so that they did not have to travel home having played only one game. It was during this event that the German Gottfried Fuchs equalled Sophus Nielsen's feat of scoring 10 goals in a match as his side equalled the greatest margin of victory in an international. On the receiving end of the 16-0 thrashing were the Russians, who did not reappear until the 1952 Helsinki Games.

In the preliminary round of the tournament proper there were two surprises, the elimination of the hosts by Holland and of the Italians by Finland. Having lost to the Dutch in the previous Olympics Sweden had hoped that home advantage would tell this time, but Holland along with Denmark were the most developed of the European nations and were on their way to a second successive bronze medal. Finland's victory was all the more surprising because the game against Italy was only their third ever international match, the previous two having been lost heavily to Sweden. Austria, altogether more advanced than their German neighbours, won the third of the preliminary round fixtures, but in their first round tie they faced the Dutch for the first time ever in international football and lost 3-1.

Finland disposed of the very weak Russians in their first round tie, while England easily overcame Hungary 7-0, a score which the Danes repeated over Norway. The semi-finals therefore pitted the Finns against England and Denmark against the Dutch. There was little doubt as to what the result of the first tie would be, but the match between Denmark and Holland pitted the best two continental sides against each other. The Danes were the acknowledged masters of the continent, however, and it was they who prevailed on the day, Emil Jorgensen, Poul Nielsen and Anthon Olsen scoring the goals.

So once again the final was between England and Denmark. Anthon Olsen pitched in with two more goals but England, through Berry, Walden and Hoare, scored four. The result was not a foregone conclusion, as two years previously the Danes had become the first non-British side to beat an England international XI, beating the same amateur team that they were facing in the final, 2-1 in Copenhagen. Two years later they would win 3-0 in Copenhagen but here they lost to the English to take silver again. England were perhaps fortunate that Buchwald of Denmark had to leave the game injured, as they capitalised on the advantage to score two quick goals and eventually won 4-2.

Unlike the team of four years previously when all but three were full internationals, only Knight, Berry, Woodward and Walden played for the full England side during their careers, whilst Denmark included Chelsea's Nils Middleboe. Woodward and Berry became double Olympic gold medallists. Only eight other footballers can boast such a feat, Dezso Novák of Hungary and seven Uruguayans: Andres Mazzali, José Nasazzi, Pedro Arispe, José Andrade, Santos Urdinaran, Hector Scarone, Pedro Petrone and Pedro Cea.

The tournament was on occasion very rough, especially in the final of the consolation event between Austria and Hungary. In contrast, the England–Finland semi-final was notable for the pleasant atmosphere, which extended to an act of sportsmanship unlikely today. Awarded a penalty, England thought this "altogether too severe a punishment", and the ball was ostentatiously put over the bar!

PRELIMINARY ROUND

Traneberg-Sportplatz, Stockholm, 29-06-1912, 600

Finland 3 (Öhman 2, Soinio 40, Wiberg 105)
Italy 2 (Bontadini 10, Sardi 25)

Stockholms Stadion, Stockholm, 29-06-1912, 14,000

Holland 4 (Bouvy 28 52, Vos 43 91)
Sweden 3 (Svensson 3 80, Börjesson 62 pen)

Råsunda, Stockholm, 29-06-1912, 2000

Austria 5 (Studnicka 58, Neubauer 62, Merz 75 81, Cimera 89)
Germany 1 (Jäger 35)

FIRST ROUND

Råsunda, Stockholm, 30-06-1912, 8000

England 7 (Walden 21 23 49 53 55 85, Woodward 45)
Hungary 0

Traneberg-Sportplatz, Stockholm, 30-06-1912, 200

Finland 2 (Wiberg 30, Öhman 80)
Russia 1 (Butusov 72)

Råsunda, Stockholm, 30-06-1912, 7000

Holland 3 (Bouvy 8, Ten Cate 12, Vos 30)
Austria 1 (Müller 41)

Råsunda, Stockholm, 30-06-1912, 700

Denmark 7 (Olsen.A 4 70 88, Wolfhagen 25, Middleboe 37, Nielsen.S 60 85)
Norway 0

SEMI-FINALS

Stockholms Stadion, Stockholm, 2-07-1912, 4000

England 4 (Woodward, Walden[2], Sharpe.I)
Finland 0

Stockholms Stadion, Stockholm, 2-07-1912, 6000

Denmark 4 (Jorgensen 7, Olsen.A 14 87, Nielsen.P 37)
Holland 1 (OG 85)

3RD PLACE

Råsunda, Stockholm, 4-07-1912, 1000

Holland 9 (Van der Sluis 24 57, De Groot 28 86, Vos 29 43 46 74 78)
Finland 0

FINAL

Stockholms Stadion, Stockholm, 4-07-1912, 25,000. Referee: Groothoff, Holland

ENGLAND 4 (Walden 10, Hoare 22 41, Berry 43)
DENMARK 2 (Olsen 27 81)

England - Brebner - Burn, Knight - McWhirter, Littlewort, Dines - Berry, Woodward, Walden, Hoare, Sharpe

Denmark - Hansen.S - Middleboe.N, Hansen.H - Buchwald, Jorgensen, Berth Nielsen-Norland, Thufvason, Olsen, Nielsen, Wolffhagen

CONSOLATION TOURNAMENT

First Round

Hungary Bye

Råsunda, Stockholm, 1-07-1912, 2000

Germany 16(Fuchs 2 9 21 28 34 46 51 55 65 69, Förderer 6 27 53 66, Burger 30, Oberle 58)
Russia 0

Råsunda, Stockholm, 1-07-1912, 2500

Italy 1 (Sardi 15)
Sweden 0

Traneberg-Sportplatz, Stockholm,1-07-1912, 200

Austria 1 (Neubauer 2)
Norway 0

SEMI-FINALS

Råsunda, Stockholm, 3-07-1912, 2000

Hungary 3 (Schlosser 3 39 82)
Germany 1 (Förderer 56)

Djurgården Stadion, Stockholm, 3-07-1912, 3500

Austria 5 (Müller30, Grunwald 40 89, Hussak 49, Studnicka 65)
Italy 1 (Berardo 81)

FINAL

Råsunda, Stockholm, 5-07-1912, 5000

Hungary 3 (Schlosser 32, Pataki 60, Bodnár 76)
Austria 0

VI. OLYMPIAD, BERLIN 1916

Cancelled

VII. OLYMPIAD, ANTWERP 1920

3rd Football tournament, 28th August - 5th September

The ravages of the Great European War meant the cancellation of the 1916 Games due to be held in Berlin, but in keeping with the four-year cycle they resumed once again in Antwerp in 1920. None of the defeated combatants - Germany, the Austro-Hungarian bloc and Turkey - were invited and the war still cast a shadow over the event. It was a very low-budget affair, yet still the organisers went bankrupt. Neither were the Games particularly memorable, although there was great controversy in the football tournament.

The centre for the Games, the Olympisch Stadion in the Kiel district of Antwerp – now known as the Kielstadion – was home to Beerschot, then one of the top teams in the Belgian league. A new main stand was built for the Games, but compared to the stadia built for 1908 and 1912 it was small beer, holding only 27,000 spectators. For the first time some of the matches in the football tournament were farmed out to other cities, including one of the quarter-final ties.

Many nations were making their international debuts in the football tournament, among them Yugoslavia, Czechoslovakia, Spain, Egypt and Greece, while Luxembourg's game against Holland was only their fourth ever. There was controversy on a number of fronts, however. Great Britain were furious about the flagrant abuse of the amateur definition laid down for the tournament by FIFA and vowed never to take part in the tournament again. Indeed, by 1928 the differing definitions of the term amateur led to the four British Associations withdrawing from FIFA in protest.

Britain was not against professionalism, but insisted on clear-cut rules so that everyone knew where they stood. Central to the issue were "broken time" payments, that is to say payments made to compensate players for loss of income from their regular jobs whilst they were taking part in the tournament. FIFA insisted that players receiving such payments could be considered as amateur; more than forty years' experience of dealing with the problem at home convinced the British that this position was unworkable.

In the event Britain, again represented by the England amateur side, were knocked out by one of the few other genuine amateur teams present, Norway. Of the debutants only Czechoslovakia and Spain made it past the first round, the Czechs' 7-0 win over Yugoslavia signalling the start of an era which was to see great success at club level and an appearance in the final of the 1934 World Cup. Herbert "Murren" Karlsson was the hero of the round, scoring five of Sweden's nine goals in their thrashing of Greece.

A goal by Patricio, the first ever scored by Spain, put an end to the proud Olympic record of Denmark. Until the previous year they had been beaten on only two occasions by opposition other than the English amateurs in over 30 matches. Defeats away from home against Norway and Sweden in late 1919 and against Holland in Amsterdam four months before the Olympics were perhaps signs that their dominance was coming to an end, but they never expected to lose to the Spaniards. In the other first round ties a few eyebrows were raised at the difficulty Italy had in beating Egypt, but there were no such problems for Holland as they dispatched Luxembourg.

Another brace of goals from Karlsson could not rescue Sweden in the quarter-finals as they lost out by the odd goal in nine to the Dutch, who went on to meet Belgium in the semis. The host nation had received a bye in the first round and now dispatched Spain in the quarter-finals coutesy of a hat-trick from their star player Robert Coppée. Norway, who had provided the real surprise of the tournament with their first round victory over England, collapsed against Czechoslovakia, letting in four without reply, while France made it a second miserable tournament in a row for the Italians with their 3-1 victory. The result was something of a surprise given that the French had been beaten 9-4 earlier in the year in Milan.

In the semi-finals Belgium produced one of the best results in their history, beating Holland 3-0, their first victory over their neighbours for ten years, and the Czechs continued to make one of the most impressive international debuts ever witnessed. Drawing on the experience of players from the former republic of Bohemia and of great clubs like Sparta and Slavia Prague, they beat France 4-1 to make it 15 goals in three games with only one conceded. Antonin Janda-Ocko led the scoring with six goals, although it was a hat-trick by Oto Mazal-Skvajn which saw off the French.

The final was a truly bad-tempered affair that was never finished. Belgium won the match but it ended in uproar not long after the home side scored their second goal. The Czechs walked off the pitch complaining of biased refereeing by the English official. They were promptly banned by FIFA and a tournament for the silver and bronze medals was hastily arranged. Spain, having won the consolation tournament, beat Holland in a play-off to decide the medal placings, consigning the Dutch to their third consecutive bronze. Ideally the second and third place play-off should have involved Holland and France but most of the French players had gone home after their semi-final defeat. The Belgians' gold medal represents the only success by their national side in any tournament, and signalled a decline in the game in that country that was to last nearly 50 years.

FIRST ROUND

Belgium Bye

Stade Union St Gilloise, Brussels, 28-08-1920, 3000

Spain 1 (Patricio 54)
Denmark 0

Stade Union St Gilloise, Brussels, 28-08-1920, 3000

Holland 3 (Bulder 30, Groosjohan 47 85)
Luxembourg 0

Olympisch Stadion, Antwerp, 28-08-1920, 5000

Sweden 9 (Olsson 4 79, Karlsson 15 20 21 51 85, Wicksell 25, Dahl 31)
Greece 0

France Bye

Stade AA La Gantoise, Gent, 28-08-1920, 2000

Italy 2 (Baloncieri 25, Brezzi 57)
Egypt 1 (Zaki Osman 30)

Olympisch Stadion, Antwerp, 28-08-1920, 5000

Norway 3 (Gundersen 13 51, Wilhelms 63)
England 1 (Nicholas 25)

Stade de Antwerp FC, Antwerp, 28-08-1920, 600

Czechoslovakia 7 (Vanik 20 46 79p, Janda 34 50 75, Sedlacek 43)
Yugoslavia 0

QUARTER-FINALS

Olympisch Stadion, Antwerp, 29-08-1920, 18000

Belgium 3 (Coppée 11 52 55)
Spain 1 (Arrate 62p)

Stade de Antwerp FC, Antwerp, 29-08-1920, 5000

Holland 5 (Groosjaohan 10 57, Bulder 44 88p, De Natris 115)
Sweden 4 (Karlsson 16 32, Olsson 20, Dahl 72)

Olympisch Stadion, Antwerp, 29-08-1920, 10000

France 3 (Bard 10 54, Boyer 14)
Italy 1 (Brezzi 33p)

Stade Union St Gilloise, Brussels, 29-08-1920, 4000

Czechoslovakia 4 (Vanik 8, Janda 17 66 77)
Norway 0

SEMI-FINALS

Olympisch Stadion, Antwerp, 31-08-1920, 22000

Belgium 3 (Larnoe 46, Van Hege 55, Bragard 85)
Holland 0

Olympisch Stadion, Antwerp, 31-08-1920, 12000

Czechoslovakia 4 (Mazal 18 75 87, Steiner 70)
France 1 (Boyer 79)

FINAL

Olympisch (Kielstadion), Antwerp, 5-09-1920, 35,000. Referee: Lewis, England

BELGIUM 2 (Coppée 6, Larnoe 30)
CZECHOSLOVAKIA 0

Belgium - De Bie - Swartenbroeks, Verbeeck - Musch, Hense, Fierens - Van Hege, Larnoe, Bragard, Coppee, Bastin

Czechoslovakia - Klapka - Hojer, Steiner - Kolenaty, Kada, Seifert - Sedlacek, Janda, Vanik, Mazal, Placek

Match abandoned after 39 minutes

PLAY-OFF FOR SECOND AND THIRD PLACES

FIRST ROUND

Stade de Antwerp FC, Antwerp, 1-09-1920, 1500

Spain 2 (Belauste 51, Acedo 53)
Sweden 1 (Dahl 28)

Stade de Antwerp FC, Antwerp, 1-09-1920, 500

Italy 2 (Sardi 46, Badini II 96)
Norway 1 (Andersen.A 40)

SECOND ROUND

Olympisch Stadion, Antwerp, 2-09-1920, 10000

Spain 2 (Sesumanga 43 72)
Italy 0

2ND/3RD PLACE FINAL

Olympisch Stadion, Antwerp, 6-09-1920, 4000

Spain 3 (Sesumanga 7 35, Pichichi 72)
Holland 1 (Groosjohan 68)

One game was played in a consolation tournament, but because of events surrounding the final the tournament was discontinued

Olympisch Stadion, Antwerp, 30-08-1920, 500

Egypt 4 (Sayd Abaza 2, Hussein Hegazi, Hassan Aloba)
Yugoslavia 2 (Dubravcic, Ruzic)

VIII. OLYMPIAD, PARIS 1924

The 4th Football tournament, 25th May - 9th June

Paris was given a second chance to stage the Olympic Games and unsurprisingly expended much more effort on the occasion than Antwerp had done four years previously or indeed than they had done themselves 24 years previously. The stadium at Colombes, home of the famous Racing Club rugby side, was enlarged to hold all the major events including 10 of the football matches, but the French crowds were criticised for their partisan behaviour which went as far as booing during the national anthems.

Happily the football tournament will be remembered as one of the best ever, to rank alongside that of Amsterdam in 1928. The 1920s would chiefly be remembered for the dazzling skills of the South Americans, which many Europeans were seeing for the first time – remarkably, 1924 was the first time any South American team had played on European soil. Indeed the impression made by Uruguay in these Paris Games helped create the legend of skilful South American football that Brazil were to build on in later years. In a wonderful display that took the European sides by surprise, Uruguay won the tournament with ease, a feat they repeated four years later.

A definite aura surrounds the Uruguayan teams of 1924 and 1928, owing partly to the fact that most of the players went on to win the first World Cup in 1930. Their style was new to the Europeans. They played with a flair and a joy that had rarely been witnessed before and their sheer skill on the ball took the breath away. For such a small country Uruguay had an outstanding record in international football. In 1923 they were crowned South American champions for the fourth time in only eight tournaments, two ahead of both Argentina and Brazil. It was a title they were to retain on their return from Paris.

The entry for the tournament grew from 14 to 22, but due to the amateur divide Great Britain were not present and neither were Denmark, the two finalists from 1908 and 1912. The Football Association in London had asked FIFA in 1923 to accept its definition of the word amateur, but this was refused. In 1921 Belgium, the Olympic champions, had legitimised the payment of players for income lost due to football commitments. France, Italy, Norway and Switzerland soon followed suit, whilst still defining these players as amateur. FIFA had no clear definition and it was left to individual countries to decide on the issue.

This left the IOC with a tricky problem, but given that football was by far and away the biggest attraction, providing over one third of the total income, FIFA's wish to bow to the will of the majority and the IOC's wish to see football included in the Games were perhaps understandable. The football final alone in 1924 provided the Games with one-twelfth of the total income, money essential for their financial survival and well-being.

Because of the high number of entrants a preliminary round had to be played, pitting many of the weaker nations against stronger opponents. This was not the case, however, in the Italy–Spain encounter. Both were rightly counted among the pre-tournament favourites. Spain had won eight games in a row between September 1920 and January 1923 and drawn 0-0 draw in Milan in March 1924, but over the years the Italians were to prove a bogey team for them, beating them in this tournament and in the 1928 Olympics and the 1934 World Cup. Here the Spaniards lost 1-0, and to make matters worse, they won their next nine games after the Olympics before losing in May 1927 – to Italy! The Spanish record speaks for itself - 19 wins in their first 23 international matches.

Other preliminary round matches saw the Uruguayans thrash Yugoslavia 7-0, a repeat for the Yugoslavs of their defeat at the hands of Czechoslovakia four years earlier. Pedro Petrone scored the first two of his eight goals in the tournament for Uruguay. Both of the finalists from 1920 were beaten in the first round, Belgium rather heavily at the hands of Sweden, Czechoslovakia by Switzerland who went on to reach the final. Hungary, one of the major powers of the time, were on the end of the tournament's biggest upset losing 3-0 to Egypt.

The two American entrants met in the first round, Uruguay easily beating the USA. The Uruguayans had little trouble reaching the final, beating the hosts in the quarter-finals and in the semis consigning Holland to their fourth consecutive semi-final defeat. The Dutch could not make it four bronze medals out of four, however, as Sweden beat them in the play-off.

The final was a terribly one-sided affair. Although they had beaten three strong sides to reach the final, the Swiss were not a great force and there was nothing the star of their side, Max Abegglen, could do to stop the South American champions, who scored once in the first half through Petrone and twice in the second through Cea and Romano. Cea, Nasazzi, Andrade and Scarone were all members of the World Cup winning side six years later, and this victory signalled the beginning of Uruguay's 10-year reign as world champions.

PRELIMINARY ROUND

Colombes, Paris, 26-05-1924, 1,000

Uruguay 7 (Cea 2, Petrone 2, Vidal, Romano, Scarone.H)
Yugoslavia 0

Paris, 25-05-1924

United States 1 (Straden)
Estonia 0

Paris, 26-05-1924, 3,000

Hungary 5 (Hirzer 2, Opata 2, Eisenhoffer)
Poland 0

Colombes, Paris, 25-05-1924, 20,000

Italy 1 (OG)
Spain 0

Bergere, Paris, 25-05-1924, 5,000

Czechoslovakia 5 (Sedlacek 2, Stapl, Novak, Capek)
Turkey 2 (Bekir 2)

Paris, 25-05-1924

Switzerland 9 (Sturzenegger 4, Abegglen.M 3, Ramseyer, Dietrich)
Lithuania 0

FIRST ROUND

Paris, 29-05-1924

Uruguay 3 (Petrone 3)
United States 0

Saint-Ouen, Paris, 27-05-1924

France 7 (Crut 3, Nicolas 2, Boyer 2)
Latvia 0

Paris, 27-05-1924, 1,000

Holland 6 (Pijl 4, De Natris, Hurgronje)
Romania 0

Colombes, Paris, 28-05-1924, 1,000

Rep. Ireland 1 (Duncan)
Bulgaria 0

Colombes, Paris, 29-05-1924, 8,000

Sweden 8 (Kock 3, Rydell 3, Brommesson, Kaufeldt)
Belgium 1 (Larnoe)

Paris, 29-05-1924, 8,000

Egypt 3 (Ighen 2, Riad)
Hungary 0

Stade Pershing, Paris, 29-05-1924, 2,000

Italy 2 (Baloncieri, Della Valle)
Luxembourg 0

Bergere, Paris, 28-05-1924, 12,000

Switzerland 1 (Dietrich)
Czechoslovakia 1 (Stapl)

Bergere, Paris, 30-05-1924, 10,000

Switzerland 1 (Pache)
Czechoslovakia 0

QUARTER-FINALS

Colombes, Paris, 1-06-1924, 45,000

Uruguay 5 (Scarone.H 2, Petrone 2, Romano)
France 1 (Nicolas)

Paris, 2-06-1924, 2,000

Holland 2 (Formenoy 2)
Rep. Ireland 1 (Farrell)

Pershing, Paris, 1-06-1924, 6,000

Sweden 5 (Kaufeldt 2, Brommesson 2, Rydell)
Egypt 0

Bergere, Paris, 2-06-1924, 12,000

Switzerland 2 (Sturzenegger, Abegglen.M)
Italy 1 (Della Valle)

SEMI-FINALS

Colombes, 6-06-1924, 40,000

Uruguay 2 (Scarone.H, Cea)
Holland 1 (Pijl)

Colombes, Paris, 5-06-1924, 7,000

Switzerland 2 (Abegglen.M 2)
Sweden 1 (Kock)

3RD PLACE

Colombes, Paris, 8-06-1924, 9,000

Sweden 1 (Kaufeldt)
Holland 1 (Le Fevre)

Colombes, Paris, 9-06-1924, 40,000
Sweden 3 (Rydell 2, Lundquist)
Holland 1 (Formenoy)

FINAL
Colombes, Paris. 9-06-1924, 41,000. Referee: Slawick, France
URUGUAY 3 (Petrone 27, Cea 63, Romano 81)
SWITZERLAND 0
Uruguay - Mazzali - Nasazzi, Arispe - Andrade, Vidal, Ghierra - Urdinaran, Scarone.H, Petrone, Cea, Romano
Switzerland - Pulver - Reymond, Ramseyer - Oberhauser, Schmiedlin, Pollitz Ehrenbolger, Pache, Dietrich, Abegglen, Fassler

IX. OLYMPIAD, AMSTERDAM 1928

The 5th Football tournament, 27th May - 13th June
For the third consecutive occasion the Olympics were staged in north-west Europe, the honour this time going to Amsterdam. The major innovation of the Games was the Olympic flame which has since come to symbolise the whole movement.

Setting the football tournament on fire again were the Uruguayans. This time they were joined by their South American rivals Argentina, who if anything were the more impressive of the two en route to the final. The Argentines scored 23 goals in their first three matches, Tarasconi getting ten of them with four each in the first two matches. The United States were overwhelmed in the first round and Belgium dispatched easily in the quarter-finals before Argentina met the real surprise of the tournament, Egypt, who had defeated Turkey and Portugal to reach the semi-finals. The Africans could progress no further as Argentina scored six more goals without reply.

The other half of the draw was certainly the stronger. Germany were back for the first time in 16 years but they were undone by Uruguay in the quarter-finals. In the semi-finals, the Uruguayans met Italy, who had been responsible for the demise of France and Spain and were many people's favourites for the title. In a close game the South Americans recorded their eighth straight win in Olympic competition to set up a classic encounter with their neighbours Argentina in the final, the first part of a double bill that would be resumed two years later in the World Cup final.

For the only time in the history of the competition the Olympic final was not settled in the first game and required a replay. The 1-1 draw in Amsterdam's Olympic stadium was the 102nd time the two teams had met. In the 103rd meeting the Argentines fell to the guile of Figueroa and Hector Scarone, the former playing his only game of the tournament. Against anyone else, Argentina would probably have become champions, but Uruguay knew them well and exploited that knowledge to the fullest.

The 1928 final was the last hurrah for football in the Olympic Games. Professionalism was rapidly spreading and by the time football was next held in the Games, in the Berlin Olympics of 1936, most of the major nations taking part could not send their full-strength squads. Indeed such were the problems this issue was causing that the 1932 Games in Los Angeles did not have a football tournament, the only Olympics not to do so.

PRELIMINARY ROUND
Olympisch Stadion, Amsterdam, 27-05-1928
Portugal 4 (José Soares 2, Vitor Silva, Waldemar Mota)
Chile 2 (Carbonell, Subiabre)

FIRST ROUND
Olympisch Stadion, Amsterdam, 30-05-1928, 40,000
Uruguay 2 (Urdinaran, Scarone.H)
Holland 0

Olympisch Stadion, Amsterdam, 28-05-1928,
Germany 4 (Hornauer, Hofmann 3)
Switzerland 0

Olympisch Stadion, Amsterdam, 29-05-1928, 8,000
Italy 4 (Rossetti, Levratto, Banchero, Baloncieri)
France 3 (Brouzes 2, Dauphin)

Olympisch Stadion, Amsterdam, 30-05-1928, 4,000
Spain 7 (Yermo 3, Luis Regueiro 2, Marculeta, Mariscal)
Mexico 1 (Carreño)

Olympisch Stadion, Amsterdam, 28-05-1928
Egypt 7
Turkey 1 (Bekir)

Olympisch Stadion, Amsterdam, 29-05-1928, 15,000
Portugal 2 (Vitor Silva, Augusto Silva)
Yugoslavia 1 (Bonacic)

Olympisch Stadion, Amsterdam, 27-05-1928, 10,000
Belgium 5 (Braine.R 2, Versyp, Moeschal 2)
Luxembourg 3 (Schutz, Weisgerber, Theissen)

Olympisch Stadion, Amsterdam, 29-05-1928
Argentina 11 (Tarasconi 4, Cherro 3, Orsi 2, Ferreyra.M 2)
United States 2 (Findlay 2)

QUARTER-FINALS
Olympisch Stadion, Amsterdam, 3-06-1928
Uruguay 4 (Petrone 3, Castro)
Germany 1 (Hofmann)

Olympisch Stadion, Amsterdam, 1-06-1928
Italy 1 (Baloncieri)
Spain 1 (Zaldua)

Olympisch Stadion, Amsterdam, 4-06-1928
Italy 7 (Magnozzi, Schiavio, Baloncieri, Bernardini, Rivolta, Levratto 2)
Spain 1 (Yermo)

Olympisch Stadion, Amsterdam, 4-06-1928
Egypt 2 (Mokltar, Riad)
Portugal 1 (Vitor Silva)

Olympisch Stadion, Amsterdam, 2-06-1928, 25,000
Argentina 6 (Tarasconi 4, Monti, Ferreyra.M)
Belgium 3 (Braine.R, Van Halme, Moeschal)

SEMI-FINALS

Olympisch Stadion, Amsterdam, 7-06-1928

Uruguay	3 (Cea, Campolo, Scarone.H)
Italy	2 (Baloncieri, Levratto)

Olympisch Stadion, Amsterdam, 6-06-1928

Argentina	6 (Tarasconi 2, Ferreyra.M 2, Cherro, Carricaberry)
Egypt	0

3RD PLACE

Olympisch Stadion, Amsterdam, 10-06-1928

Italy	11 (Schiavio 3, Baloncieri 2, Banchero 3, Magnozzi 3)
Egypt	3 (Riad 2, Hassan)

FINAL

Olympisch Stadion, Amsterdam, 10-06-1928. Referee: Mutter, Holland

URUGUAY	1 (Ferreyra.M)
ARGENTINA	1 (Petrone)

Uruguay - Mazzali - Nasazzi, Arispe - Andrade, Fernandez, Gestido Urdinarrain, Castro.H, Petrone, Cea, Campolo

Argentina - Bossio - Bidoglio, Paternoster - Medici, Monti, Evaristo.J Carricaberry, Tarasconi, Ferreyra.M, Gainzarain, Orsi

Replay. Olympisch Stadion, Amsterdam, 13-06-1928. Referee: Mutter, Holland

URUGUAY	2 (Figueroa, Scarone.H)
ARGENTINA	1 (Monti)

Uruguay - Mazzali - Nasazzi, Arispe - Andrade, Piriz, Gestido - Arremond, Scarone.H, Borjas, Cea, Figueroa

Argentina - Bossio - Bidoglio, Paternoster - Medici, Monti, Evaristo.J Carricaberry, Tarasconi, Ferreyra.M, Perducca, Orsi

CONSOLATION TOURNAMENT

FIRST ROUND

Het Kassel, Rotterdam, 5-06-1928, 22,000

Holland	3 (Smeets, Tap, Ghering)
Belgium	1 (Braine.P)

Arnhem, 5-06-1928

Chile	3 (Subiabre 3)
Mexico	1 (Sota.E)

FINAL

De Kuip, Rotterdam, 8-06-1928, 18,000

Holland	2 (Smeets, Ghering)
Chile	2 (Bravo, Alfaro)

Holland won on lots

POST-1928 OLYMPIC GAMES

After 1928 the Olympic football tournament gradually became an outdated concept for the nations of South America and Western Europe, and although they continued to enter teams, they had had no realistic chance of success against the state-sponsored amateur sides of post-war eastern Europe. Scandinavia, for so long a bastion of the amateur game, emerged as the only threat to the sides of the Communist bloc, none more so than Sweden, victors in 1948.

The 1952 tournament, the last not to be preceded by a qualifying round, was won by Hungary, and the Olympic title stands as the only major honour won by the Magic Magyars in their heyday. The side was almost identical to that which appeared in the 1954 World Cup final, but on no occasion after 1952 could the winners claim to be the best team in the world as the Hungarians could.

Yugoslavia won at the fourth attempt in 1960 in a tournament whose stucture was rapidly changing. The qualifying tournament for 1956 had involved only 10 games; for 1960 it was divided along continental lines and consisted of almost 100. Both Africa and Asia were given two entries each and in many respects the Olympic football tournament has been just as important to these countries as the World Cup, given the small number of professional players there.

In 1964 their allocation for the final tournament was increased to three entries each, compared to the World Cup, where they were allotted just one. It is not surprising to find that the Olympic tournament often attracted more entrants and became a regular feature on the fixture list for both continents.

The 1960s and 1970s were dominated by Hungary, Poland, Czechoslovakia and East Germany, who entered sides identical to those fielded in normal internationals, but for the 1984 tournament FIFA changed the eligibility rules to allow the selection of anyone who had not played in a World Cup qualifier. This was a bizarre rule at best, in that it actually stopped many amateurs from taking part in what was supposed to be an amateur tournament.

It did break the eastern European stranglehold, as France won the gold medal in Los Angeles, but it threw the tournament into disrepute. Had it not been for the huge crowds which attended matches at each Games, football might well have been jettisoned long before. At Los Angeles and Seoul for example, more spectators turned up to see the football than any other event, including track & field, and the revenue was important for the success of the Games as a whole.

The IOC tried to persuade FIFA to accept an Olympic tournament open to the full national sides of every country, but FIFA were not keen to see the status of the World Cup undermined and instead decided on an under-23 tournament open to all players, regardless of their professional status or past World Cup appearances. This was implemented for Barcelona in 1992.

The solution smacks of compromise, but at least the playing field is now level for all nations, for the first time since the 1920s. There are many who feel that with a gap of four years, the World Cup is not representative of the shifts in power among the top football nations, and that a full-strength Olympic Games football tournament would be a good idea. Accommodating the extra qualifying fixtures, however, might prove to be an insurmountable problem.

X. OLYMPIAD, LOS ANGELES 1932

30th July - 14th August. No football tournament was held

XI. OLYMPIAD, BERLIN 1936

The 6th Football tournament, 3rd - 15th August

FIRST ROUND

Italy	1-0	United States
Japan	3-2	Sweden
Germany	9-0	Luxembourg
Norway	4-0	Turkey
Poland	3-0	Hungary
Great Britain	2-0	China
Peru	7-3	Finland
Austria	3-1	Egypt

QUARTER-FINALS

Italy	8-0	Japan
Norway	2-0	Germany
Poland	5-4	Great Britain
Austria	2-4 *	Peru

* Match abandoned. Peru failed to turn up for rearranged game

SEMI-FINALS

Italy	2-1	Norway
Austria	3-1	Poland

3RD PLACE

Norway	3-2	Poland

FINAL

Olympiastadion, Berlin, 15-08-1936, 90,000. Referee: Bauwens, Germany

ITALY 2 (Frossi 70 92)
AUSTRIA 1 (Kainberger.K 80)

Italy - Venturini - Foni, Rava - Baldo, Piccini, Locatelli - Frossi, Marchini, Bertoni, Biagi, Gabriotti

Austria - Kainberger.E - Kunz, Kargl - Krenn, Wahlmuller, Hofmeister Warginz, Laudon, Steinmetz, Kainberger.K, Fuchsberger

XII. OLYMPIAD, TOKYO/HELSINKI 1940

Cancelled

XIII. OLYMPIAD, LONDON 1944

Cancelled

XIV. OLYMPIAD, LONDON 1948

The 7th Football tournament, 31st July - 13th August

PRELIMINARY ROUND

Holland	3-1	Rep. Ireland
Luxembourg	6-0	Afghanistan

FIRST ROUND

Sweden	3-0	Austria
Korea	5-3	Mexico
Denmark	3-1	Egypt
Italy	9-0	United States
Great Britain	4-3	Holland
France	2-1	India
Turkey	4-0	China
Yugoslavia	6-1	Luxembourg

QUARTER-FINALS

Sweden	12-0	Korea
Denmark	5-3	Italy
Great Britain	1-0	France
Yugoslavia	3-1	Turkey

SEMI-FINALS

Sweden	4-2	Denmark
Yugoslavia	3-1	Great Britain

3RD PLACE

Denmark	5-3	Great Britain

FINAL

Wembley, London, 13-08-1948, 60,000. Refere: Ling, England

SWEDEN 3 (Gren 24 67 Nordahl.G 48)
YUGOSLAVIA 1 (Bobek)

Sweden - Lindberg - Nordahl.K, Nilsson.E - Rosengren, Nordahl.B, Andersson Rosén, Gren, Nordahl.G, Carlsson, Liedholm

Yugoslavia - Lovric - Brozovic, Stankovic - Cajkovski.Ze, Jovanovic Atanackovic, Cimermancic, Mitic, Bobek, Cajkovski.Zl, Vukas

XV. OLYMPIAD, HELSINKI 1952

The 8th Football tournament, 15th July - 2nd August

PRELIMINARY ROUND

Hungary	2-1	Romania
Italy	8-0	United States
Egypt	5-4	Chile
Brazil	5-1	Holland
Luxembourg	5-3	Great Britain
Denmark	2-1	Greece
Poland	2-1	France
Soviet Union	2-1	Bulgaria
Yugoslavia	10-1	India

FIRST ROUND

Hungary	3-0	Italy
Turkey	2-1	Dutch W.Indies
Sweden	4-1	Norway
Austria	4-3	Finland
West Germany	3-1	Egypt
Brazil	2-1	Luxembourg
Denmark	2-0	Poland
Yugoslavia	5-5 3-1	Soviet Union

QUARTER-FINALS

Hungary	7-1	Turkey
Sweden	3-1	Austria
West Germany	4-2	Brazil
Yugoslavia	5-3	Denmark

SEMI-FINALS

Hungary	6-0	Sweden
Yugoslavia	3-1	West Germany

3RD PLACE

Sweden	2-0	West Germany

FINAL

Olympiastadion, Helsinki, 2-08-1952, 60,000. Referee: Ellis, England

HUNGARY 2 (Puskás 25, Czibor 88)
YUGOSLAVIA 0

Hungary - Grosics - Buzánszky, Lantos - Bozsik, Lóránt, Zakariás - Hidegkuti, Kocsis, Palotás, Puskás, Czibor

Yugoslavia - Beara - Stankovic, Crnkovic - Cajkovski.Zl, Horvat, Boskov Ognjanov, Mitic, Vukas, Bobek, Zebec

XVI. OLYMPIAD, MELBOURNE 1956

The 9th Football tournament, 24th November - 8th December

PRELIMINARY ROUND

Soviet Union 2-1 West Germany
Great Britain 9-0 Thailand
Australia 2-0 Japan

FIRST ROUND

Soviet Union 0-0 4-0 Indonesia
Bulgaria 6-1 Great Britain
India 4-2 Australia
Yugoslavia 9-1 United States

SEMI-FINALS

Soviet Union 2-1 Bulgaria
Yugoslavia 4-1 India

3RD PLACE

Bulgaria 3-0 India

FINAL

Melbourne Cricket Ground, Melbourne, 8-12-1956, 120,000. Referee: Wright, Australia

SOVIET UNION 1 (Ilyin 48)
YUGOSLAVIA 0

Soviet Union - Yachin - Baschaschkin, Ogognikov - Kuznetsov, Netto, Maslenkin - Tatushin, Isaev, Simonian ,Salinikov, Ilyin

Yugoslavia - Radenkovic - Koscak, Radovic - Santek, Spajic, Krstic Sekularac, Antic, Papek, Veselinovic, Mujic

XVII. OLYMPIAD, ROME 1960

The 10th Football tournament, 26th August - 10th September

FIRST ROUND

Group 1

	Yu	Bu	Eg	Tu	Pl	W	D	L	F	A	Pts
YUGOSLAVIA	-	3-3	6-1	4-0	3	2	1	0	13	4	5
BULGARIA	-	-	2-0	3-0	3	2	1	0	8	3	5
EGYPT	-	-	-	3-3	3	0	1	2	4	11	1
TURKEY	-	-	-	-	3	0	1	2	3	10	1

Group 2

	It	Br	GB	Ta	Pl	W	D	L	F	A	Pts
ITALY	-	3-1	2-2	4-1	3	2	1	0	9	4	5
BRAZIL	-	-	4-3	5-0	3	2	0	1	10	6	4
GREAT BRITAIN	-	-	-	3-2	3	1	1	1	8	8	3
TAIWAN	-	-	-	-	3	0	0	3	3	12	0

Group 3

	De	Ar	Po	Tu	Pl	W	D	L	F	A	Pts
DENMARK	-	3-2	2-1	3-1	3	3	0	0	8	4	6
ARGENTINA	-	-	2-0	2-1	3	2	0	1	6	4	4
POLAND	-	-	-	6-1	3	1	0	2	7	5	2
TUNISIA	-	-	-	-	3	0	0	3	3	11	0

Group 4

	Hu	Fr	Pe	In	Pl	W	D	L	F	A	Pts
HUNGARY	-	7-0	6-2	2-1	3	3	0	0	15	3	6
FRANCE	-	-	2-1	1-1	3	1	1	1	3	9	3
PERU	-	-	-	3-1	3	1	0	2	6	9	2
INDIA	-	-	-	-	3	0	1	2	3	6	1

SEMI-FINALS

Yugoslavia 1-1 * Italy
Denmark 2-0 Hungary

* Yugoslavia won on lots

3RD PLACE

Hungary 2-1 Italy

FINAL

Flamino, Rome, 10-09-1960, 40,000. Referee: Lo Bello, Italy

YUGOSLAVIA 3 (Galic, Matus, Kostic)
DENMARK 1 (Nielsen.F)

Yugoslavia - Vidinic - Roganovic, Jusufi - Perusic, Durkovic, Zanetic Ankovic, Matus, Galic, Knez, Kostic

Denmark - Froem - Andersen, Jensen - Hansen, Nielsen.Hn, Nielsen.F - Pedersen, Troelsen, Nielsen.Hr, Enoksen, Sorensen

XVIII. OLYMPIAD, TOKYO 1964

The 11th Football tournament, 11th - 23rd October

FIRST ROUND

Group 1

	EG	Ro	Me	Ir	Pl	W	D	L	F	A	Pts
EAST GERMANY	-	1-1	2-0	4-0	3	2	1	0	7	1	5
ROMANIA	-	-	3-1	1-0	3	2	1	0	5	2	5
MEXICO	-	-	-	1-1	3	0	1	2	2	6	1
IRAN	-	-	-	-	3	0	1	2	1	6	1

Group 2

	Hu	Yu	Mo	Pl	W	D	L	F	A	Pts
HUNGARY	-	6-5	6-0	2	2	0	0	12	5	4
YUGOSLAVIA	-	-	3-1	2	1	0	1	8	7	2
MOROCCO	-	-	-	2	0	0	2	1	9	0

Group 3

	Cz	Eg	Br	SK	Pl	W	D	L	F	A	Pts
CZECHOSLOVAKIA	-	5-1	1-0	6-1	3	3	0	0	12	2	6
EGYPT	-	-	1-1	10-0	3	1	1	1	12	6	3
BRAZIL	-	-	-	4-0	3	1	1	1	5	2	3
SOUTH KOREA	-	-	-	-	3	0	0	3	1	20	0

Group 4

	Gh	Ja	Ar	Pl	W	D	L	F	A	Pts
GHANA	-	3-2	1-1	2	1	1	0	4	3	3
JAPAN	-	-	3-2	2	1	0	1	5	5	2
ARGENTINA	-	-	-	2	0	1	1	3	4	1

QUARTER-FINALS

Hungary 2-0 Romania
Egypt 5-1 Ghana
East Germany 1-0 Yugoslavia
Czechoslovakia 4-0 Japan

SEMI-FINALS

Hungary 6-0 Egypt
Czechoslovakia 2-1 East Germany

5TH - 8TH PLACE

Romania 4-2 Ghana
Yugoslavia 6-1 Japan
Romania 3-0 Yugoslavia

3RD PLACE

East Germany 3-1 Egypt

FINAL

National Stadium, Tokyo, 23-10-1964. Referee: Ashkenazi, Israel

HUNGARY 2 (OG 47, Bene 60)
CZECHOSLOVAKIA 1 (Brumovsky 80)

Hungary - Szentimihályi (Gelei) - Novák, Ihász, Szepesi (Palotai), Orban, Nogradi, Farkas, Csernai, Bene, Komora, Katona

Czechoslovakia - Schmucker - Urban, Picman, Vojta, Weiss, Geleta, Brumovsky, Mraz, Lichtnegl, Masny, Valosek

XIX. OLYMPIAD, MEXICO CITY 1968

The 12th Football tournament, 13th - 26th October

FIRST ROUND

Group 1

	Fr	Me	Co	Gu	Pl	W	D	L	F	A	Pts
France	-	4-1	1-2	3-1	3	2	0	1	8	4	4
Mexico	-	-	1-0	4-0	3	2	0	1	6	4	4
Colombia	-	-	-	2-3	3	1	0	2	4	5	2
Guinea	-	-	-	-	3	1	0	2	4	9	2

Group 2

	Sp	Ja	Br	Ni	Pl	W	D	L	F	A	Pts
Spain	-	0-0	1-0	3-0	3	2	1	0	4	0	5
Japan	-	-	1-1	3-1	3	1	2	0	4	2	4
Brazil	-	-	-	3-3	3	0	2	1	4	5	2
Nigeria	-	-	-	-	3	0	1	2	4	9	1

Group 3

	Hu	Is	Gh	ES	Pl	W	D	L	F	A	Pts
Hungary	-	2-0	2-2	4-0	3	2	1	0	8	2	5
Israel	-	-	5-3	3-1	3	2	0	1	8	6	4
Ghana	-	-	-	1-1	3	0	2	1	6	8	2
El Salvador	-	-	-	-	3	0	1	2	2	8	1

Group 4

	Bu	Gu	Cz	Th	Pl	W	D	L	F	A	Pts
Bulgaria	-	2-1	2-2	7-0	3	2	1	0	11	3	5
Guatemala	-	-	1-0	4-1	3	2	0	1	6	3	4
Czechoslovakia	-	-	-	8-0	3	1	1	1	10	3	3
Thailand	-	-	-	-	3	0	0	3	1	19	0

QUARTER-FINALS

Hungary .... 1-0 .... Guatemala
Japan .... 3-1 .... France
Mexico .... 2-0 .... Spain
Bulgaria .... 1-1 * .... Israel
* Won on the toss of a coin

SEMI-FINALS

Hungary .... 5-0 .... Japan
Bulgaria .... 3-2 .... Mexico

3RD PLACE

Japan .... 2-0 .... Mexico

FINAL

Azteca, Mexico City, 26-10-1968. Referee: De Leo, Mexico

HUNGARY 4 (Menczel 40 48, Dunai.A 41 61)
BULGARIA 1 (Dimitrov 20)

Hungary - Fater - Novák, Dunai.L, Páncsics, Menczel, Szücs, Fazekas, Dunai.A, Nagy, Noskó, Juhász

Bulgaria - Yordanov - Guerov, Christakiev, Gadarski, Ivkov, Georgiev, Dimitrov, Yantchovski (Christov.K), Jekov, Christov.A, Donev (Ivanov)

XX. OLYMPIAD, MUNICH 1972

The 13th Football Tournament, 28th August - 10th September

FIRST ROUND

Group 1

	WG	Mo	Ma	US	Pl	W	D	L	F	A	Pts
West Germany	-	3-0	3-0	7-0	3	3	0	0	13	0	6
Morocco	-	-	6-0	0-0	3	1	1	1	6	3	3
Malaysia	-	-	-	3-0	3	1	0	2	3	9	2
United States	-	-	-	-	3	0	1	2	0	10	0

Group 2

	SU	Me	Bu	Su	Pl	W	D	L	F	A	Pts
Soviet Union	-	4-1	1-0	2-1	3	3	0	0	7	2	6
Mexico	-	-	1-0	1-0	3	2	0	1	3	4	4
Burma	-	-	-	2-0	3	1	0	2	2	2	2
Sudan	-	-	-	-	3	0	0	3	1	5	0

Group 3

	Hu	De	Ir	Br	Pl	W	D	L	F	A	Pts
Hungary	-	2-0	5-0	2-2	3	2	1	0	9	2	5
Denmark	-	-	4-0	3-2	3	2	0	1	7	4	4
Iran	-	-	-	1-0	3	1	0	2	1	9	2
Brazil	-	-	-	-	3	0	1	2	4	6	1

Group 4

	Po	EG	Co	Gh	Pl	W	D	L	F	A	Pts
Poland	-	2-1	5-1	4-0	3	3	0	0	11	2	6
East Germany	-	-	6-1	4-0	3	2	0	1	11	3	4
Colombia	-	-	-	3-1	3	1	0	2	5	12	2
Ghana	-	-	-	-	3	0	0	3	1	11	0

SECOND ROUND

Group A

	Hu	EG	WG	Me	Pl	W	D	L	F	A	Pts
Hungary	-	2-0	4-1	2-0	3	3	0	0	8	1	6
East Germany	-	-	3-2	7-0	3	2	0	1	10	4	4
West Germany	-	-	-	1-1	3	0	1	2	4	8	1
Mexico	-	-	-	-	3	0	1	2	1	10	1

Group B

	Po	SU	De	Mo	Pl	W	D	L	F	A	Pts
Poland	-	2-1	1-1	5-0	3	2	1	0	8	2	5
Soviet Union	-	-	4-0	3-0	3	2	0	1	8	2	4
Denmark	-	-	-	3-1	3	1	1	1	4	6	3
Morocco	-	-	-	-	3	0	0	3	1	11	0

3RD PLACE

Soviet Union .... 2-2 .... East Germany
Bronze medal shared

FINAL

Olympiastadion, Munich, 10-09-1972, 50,000. Referee: Tsechenscher, West Germany

POLAND 2 (Deyna 47 68)
HUNGARY 1 (Varadi 42)

Poland - Kostka - Gut, Cmikiewski, Gorgon, Anczok, Szoltyski, Deyna (Szymczak) Kraska, Maszczyk, Lubanski, Gadocha

Hungary - Géczi - Vépi, Pancsics, Juhasz, Szücs, Kozma, Dunai.A (Tóth), Kü (Kocsis), Varadi, Dunai.E, Bálint

XXI OLYMPIAD, MONTREAL 1976

The 14th Football tournament, 18th - 31st July

FIRST ROUND

Group 1

	Br	EG	Sp	Pl	W	D	L	F	A	Pts
Brazil	-	0-0	2-1	2	1	1	0	2	1	3
East Germany	-	-	1-0	2	1	1	0	1	0	3
Spain	-	-	-	2	0	0	2	1	3	0

Group 2

	Fr	Is	Me	Gu	Pl	W	D	L	F	A	Pts
France	-	1-1	4-1	4-1	3	2	1	0	9	3	5
Israel	-	-	2-2	0-0	3	0	3	0	3	3	3
Mexico	-	-	-	1-1	3	0	2	1	4	7	2
Guatemala	-	-	-	-	3	0	2	1	2	5	2

Group 3

	Po	Ir	Cu	Pl	W	D	L	F	A	Pts
Poland	-	3-2	0-0	2	1	1	0	3	2	3
Iran	-	-	1-0	2	1	0	1	3	3	2
Cuba	-	-	-	2	0	1	1	0	1	1

Group 4

	SU	NK	Ca	Pl	W	D	L	F	A	Pts
Soviet Union	-	3-0	2-1	2	2	0	0	5	1	4
North Korea	-	-	3-1	2	1	0	1	3	4	2
Canada	-	-	-	2	0	0	2	2	5	0

QUARTER-FINALS

East Germany .... 4-0 .... France
Soviet Union .... 2-1 .... Iran
Brazil .... 4-1 .... Israel
Poland .... 5-0 .... North Korea

SEMI-FINALS

East Germany .... 2-1 .... Soviet Union
Poland .... 2-0 .... Brazil

3RD PLACE

Soviet Union .... 2-0 .... Brazil

FINAL

Olympic Stadium, Montreal, 31-07-1976, 71,000. Referee: Barreto, Uruguay

EAST GERMANY 3 (Schade 7, Hoffmann 14, Hafner 79)
POLAND 1 (Lato 59)

East Germany - Croy - Lauck, Weise, Dorner, Kurbjuweit - Schade, Riediger (Bransch), Hafner - Kische, Lowe (Grobner), Hoffmann
Poland - Tomaszewski (Mowlik) - Symanowski, Wieczorek, Zmuda, Wawrowski Maszczyk, Deyna, Kasperczak - Lato, Szarmach, Kmiecik

XXII. OLYMPIAD, MOSCOW 1980

The 15th Football tournament, 20th July - 2nd August

FIRST ROUND

Group 1

	SU	Cu	Ve	Zm	Pl	W	D	L	F	A	Pts
Soviet Union	-	8-0	4-0	3-1	3	3	0	0	15	1	6
Cuba	-	-	2-1	1-0	3	2	0	1	3	9	4
Venezuela	-	-	-	2-1	3	1	0	2	3	7	2
Zambia	-	-	-	-	3	0	0	3	2	6	0

Group 2

	Cz	Ku	Co	Ni	Pl	W	D	L	F	A	Pts
Czechoslovakia	-	0-0	3-0	1-1	3	1	2	0	4	1	4
Kuwait	-	-	1-1	3-1	3	1	2	0	4	2	4
Colombia	-	-	-	1-0	3	1	1	1	2	4	3
Nigeria	-	-	-	-	3	0	1	2	2	5	1

Group 3

	EG	Al	Sp	Sy	Pl	W	D	L	F	A	Pts
East Germany	-	1-0	1-1	5-0	3	2	1	0	7	1	5
Algeria	-	-	1-1	3-0	3	1	1	1	4	2	3
Spain	-	-	-	0-0	3	0	3	0	2	2	3
Syria	-	-	-	-	3	0	1	2	0	8	1

Group 4

	Yu	Iq	Fi	CR	Pl	W	D	L	F	A	Pts
Yugoslavia	-	1-1	2-0	3-2	3	2	1	0	6	3	5
Iraq	-	-	0-0	3-0	3	1	2	0	4	1	4
Finland	-	-	-	3-0	3	1	1	1	3	2	3
Costa Rica	-	-	-	-	3	0	0	3	2	9	0

QUARTER-FINALS

Czechoslovakia .... 3-0 .... Cuba
Yugoslavia .... 3-0 .... Algeria
Soviet Union .... 2-1 .... Kuwait
East Germany .... 4-0 .... Iraq

SEMI-FINALS

Czechoslovakia .... 2-0 .... Yugoslavia
East Germany .... 1-0 .... Soviet Union

3RD PLACE

Soviet Union .... 2-0 .... Yugoslavia

FINAL

Centralny Lenina, Moscow, 2-08-1980, 70,000. Referee: Azim Zade, Soviet Union

CZECHOSLOVAKIA 1 (Svoboda 77)
EAST GERMANY 0

Czechoslovakia - Seman - Mazura, Macela, Radimec, Rygel - Rott, Berger, Stambachr - Vízek (Svoboda), Licka, Pokluda (Nemec)
East Germany - Rudwaleit - Muller, Hause (Liebers), Trieloff, Ullrich Schnuphase, Terletzki, Steinbach - Baum, Netz, Kuhn

XXIII. OLYMPIAD, LOS ANGELES 1984

The 16th Football tournament, 29th July - 11th August

FIRST ROUND

Group 1

	Fr	Ch	No	Qa	Pl	W	D	L	F	A	Pts
France	-	1-1	2-1	2-2	3	1	2	0	5	4	4
Chile	-	-	0-0	1-0	3	1	2	0	2	1	4
Norway	-	-	-	2-0	3	1	1	1	3	2	3
Qatar	-	-	-	-	3	0	1	2	2	5	1

Group 2

	Yu	Ca	Cm	Iq	Pl	W	D	L	F	A	Pts
Yugoslavia	-	1-0	2-1	4-2	3	3	0	0	7	3	6
Canada	-	-	3-1	1-1	3	1	1	1	4	3	3
Cameroon	-	-	-	1-0	3	1	0	2	3	5	2
Iraq	-	-	-	-	3	0	1	2	3	6	1

Group 3

	Br	WG	Mo	SA	Pl	W	D	L	F	A	Pts
Brazil	-	1-0	2-0	3-1	3	3	0	0	6	1	6
West Germany	-	-	2-0	6-0	3	2	0	1	8	1	4
Morocco	-	-	-	1-0	3	1	0	2	1	4	2
Saudi Arabia	-	-	-	-	3	0	0	3	1	10	0

Group 4

	It	Eg	US	CR	Pl	W	D	L	F	A	Pts
Italy	-	1-0	1-0	0-1	3	2	0	1	2	1	4
Egypt	-	-	1-1	4-1	3	1	1	1	5	3	3
United States	-	-	-	3-0	3	1	1	1	4	2	3
Costa Rica	-	-	-	-	3	1	0	2	2	7	2

QUARTER-FINALS

France .... 2-0 .... Egypt
Yugoslavia .... 5-2 .... West Germany
Italy .... 1-0 .... Chile
Brazil .... 1-1 4-2p .... Canada

SEMI-FINALS

France .... 4-2 .... Yugoslavia
Brazil .... 2-1 .... Italy

3RD PLACE

Yugoslavia .... 2-1 .... Italy

FINAL

Rose Bowl, Pasadena, 11-08-1984, 101,000. Referee: Keizer, Holland

FRANCE 2 (Brisson 55, Xuereb 62)
BRAZIL 0

France - Rust - Ayache, Bibard, Jeannol, Zanon - Lemoult, Rohr, Lacombe.G Bijotat, Xuereb (Cubaynes), Brisson (Garande)
Brazil - Gilmar.R - Ronaldo, Pinga, Mauro Galvao, André Luís - Ademir, Dunga, Gilmar - Tonho (Mílton Cruz), Kita (Chicao), Silvinho

XXIV. OLYMPIAD, SEOUL 1988

The 17th Football tournament, 17th September - 1st October

FIRST ROUND

Group 1

	Sd	WG	Tu	Ch	Pl	W	D	L	F	A	Pts
Sweden	-	2-1	2-2	2-0	3	2	1	0	6	3	5
West Germany	-	-	4-1	3-0	3	2	0	1	8	3	4
Tunisia	-	-	-	0-0	3	0	2	1	3	6	2
China	-	-	-	-	3	0	1	2	0	5	1

Group 2

	Zm	It	Iq	Gu	Pl	W	D	L	F	A	Pts
Zambia	-	4-0	2-2	4-0	3	2	1	0	10	2	5
Italy	-	-	2-0	5-2	3	2	0	1	7	6	4
Iraq	-	-	-	3-0	3	1	1	1	5	4	3
Guatemala	-	-	-	-	3	0	0	3	2	12	0

Group 3

	SU	Ar	SK	US	Pl	W	D	L	F	A	Pts
Soviet Union	-	2-1	0-0	4-2	3	2	1	0	6	3	5
Argentina	-	-	2-1	1-1	3	1	1	1	4	4	3
South Korea	-	-	-	0-0	3	0	2	1	1	2	2
United States	-	-	-	-	3	0	2	1	3	5	2

Group 4

	Br	Au	Yu	Ni	Pl	W	D	L	F	A	Pts
Brazil	-	3-0	2-1	4-0	3	3	0	0	9	1	6
Australia	-	-	1-0	1-0	3	2	0	1	2	3	4
Yugoslavia	-	-	-	3-1	3	1	0	2	4	4	2
Nigeria	-	-	-	-	3	0	0	3	1	8	0

QUARTER-FINALS

Soviet Union .... 3-0 .... Australia
Italy .... 2-1 .... Sweden
West Germany .... 4-0 .... Zambia
Brazil .... 1-0 .... Argentina

SEMI-FINALS

Soviet Union .... 3-2 .... Italy
Brazil .... 1-1 3-2p .... West Germany

3RD PLACE

West Germany .... 3-0 .... Italy

FINAL

Olympic Stadium, Seoul, 1-10-1988, 73,000. Referee: Biguet, France

SOVIET UNION 2 (Dobrovolski 62, Savichev 104)
BRAZIL 1 (Romario 30)

Soviet Union - Kharin - Ketashvili, Yarovenko, Gorlukvich, Losev - Kuznetsov, Dobrovolski, Mikhailichenko, Tatarchuk - Liuti (Skliyarov), Narbekovas (Savichev)

Brazil - Taffarel - Luís Carlos, Aloísio, André Cruz, Jorginho - Andrade, Milton, Neto (Edmar) - Careca II, Bebeto (Joao Paulo), Romario

XXV. OLYMPIAD, BARCELONA 1992

The 18th Football Tournament

QUALIFYING TOURNAMENT

EUROPE

The European Under-21 Championship doubled as the qualifying tournament for the Olympic Games. Spain qualified as hosts, whilst England, Scotland, San Marino and Luxembourg were not eligible to qualify

FIRST ROUND

Group 1

	Cz	Fr	Sp	Al	Ic	Pl	W	D	L	F	A	Pts
Czechoslovakia	-	1-0	3-1	3-0	7-0	8	7	1	0	23	4	15
France	1-2	-	0-1	3-0	2-1	8	3	2	3	7	5	8
Spain	1-1	0-0	-	1-0	2-0	7	3	2	2	6	5	8
Albania	1-5	0-0	-	-	2-1	7	1	2	4	3	13	4
Iceland	0-1	0-1	1-0	0-0	-	8	1	1	6	3	15	3

Group 2

	Sc	Bu	Ro	Sz	Pl	W	D	L	F	A	Pts
Scotland	-	1-0	2-0	4-2	4	5	0	1	13	5	10
Bulgaria	2-0	-	0-1	1-0	4	4	0	2	6	2	8
Romania	1-3	0-1	-	1-3	4	2	0	4	5	9	4
Switzerland	0-3	0-2	0-2	-	4	1	0	5	5	13	2

Group 3

	It	No	SU	Hu	Pl	W	D	L	F	A	Pts
Italy	-	2-1	1-0	1-0	6	4	1	1	6	8	9
Norway	6-0	-	0-1	3-1	6	3	1	2	13	6	7
Soviet Union	1-1	2-2	-	2-0	6	2	3	1	6	4	7
Hungary	0-1	0-1	0-0	-	6	0	1	5	1	8	1

Group 4

Preliminary matches

Liechtenstein .... 0-6 0-10 .... **Austria**

	De	Yu	Au	SM	Pl	W	D	L	F	A	Pts
Denmark	-	3-0	1-1	7-0	6	4	2	0	21	4	10
Yugoslavia	2-6	-	1-0	5-0	6	4	0	2	11	10	8
Austria	1-1	1-2	-	3-0	6	2	2	2	8	5	6
San Marino	0-3	0-1	0-2	-	6	0	0	6	0	21	0

Group 5

	Ge	Be	Lu	Pl	W	D	L	F	A	Pts
Germany	-	3-1	3-0	4	4	0	0	12	1	8
Belgium	0-3	-	2-0	4	2	0	2	5	6	4
Luxembourg	0-3	0-2	-	4	0	0	4	0	10	0

Group 6

	Ho	Pt	Fi	Ma	Pl	W	D	L	F	A	Pts
Holland	-	1-1	1-0	7-1	6	4	2	0	20	4	10
Portugal	0-0	-	2-0	2-0	6	4	2	0	9	2	10
Finland	1-7	0-1	-	3-1	6	2	0	4	7	13	4
Malta	1-4	1-3	1-3	-	6	0	0	6	5	22	0

Group 7

	Pd	En	Tu	RI	Pl	W	D	L	F	A	Pts
Poland	-	2-1	2-0	2-0	4	6	0	0	10	2	12
England	0-1	-	2-0	3-0	4	3	1	2	11	5	7
Turkey	0-1	2-2	-	2-1	4	1	1	4	6	11	3
Rep. Ireland	1-2	0-3	3-2	-	4	1	0	5	5	14	2

Group 8

	Sd	Is	Gr	Cy	Pl	W	D	L	F	A	Pts
Sweden	-	2-1	5-0	6-0	6	4	2	0	17	3	10
Israel	0-0	-	2-1	4-0	6	3	2	1	11	6	8
Greece	1-3	2-2	-	2-0	6	1	1	4	6	13	3
Cyprus	1-1	1-2	1-0	-	6	1	1	4	3	15	3

QUARTER-FINALS

Czechoslovakia .... 1-2 0-2 .... **Italy**
Denmark .... 5-0 1-1 .... **Poland**
Germany .... 1-1 3-4 .... Scotland
Holland .... 2-1 0-1 .... **Sweden**

Italy, Denmark, Sweden and Poland qualify for the finals. Holland qualify for play-off with Oceania winners, Australia.

SOUTH AMERICA

Tournament in Paraguay

FIRST ROUND

Group 1

	Co	Pa	Br	Pe	Ve	Pl	W	D	L	F	A	Pts
Colombia	-	0-0	2-0	4-1	4-0	4	3	1	0	10	1	7
Paraguay		-	0-1	7-1	1-0	4	2	1	1	8	2	5
Brazil			-	2-1	1-1	4	2	1	1	4	4	5
Peru				-	3-0	4	1	0	3	6	13	2
Venezuela					-	4	0	1	3	1	9	1

Group 2

	Ec	Ur	Ar	Ch	Bo	Pl	W	D	L	F	A	Pts
Ecuador	-	2-0	0-1	5-1	4-1	4	3	0	1	11	3	6
Uruguay		-	2-1	1-0	4-0	4	3	0	1	7	3	6
Argentina			-	1-1	1-0	4	2	1	1	4	3	5
Chile				-	0-0*	4	0	2	2	2	7	2
Bolivia					-	4	0	1	3	1	9	1

* Match not played

FINAL ROUND

	Pa	Co	Ur	Ec	Pl	W	D	L	F	A	Pts
Paraguay	-	1-0	0-0	1-0	3	2	1	0	2	0	5
Colombia	-	-	3-0	1-1	3	1	1	1	4	2	3
Uruguay	-	-	-	1-0	3	1	1	1	1	3	3
Ecuador	-	-	-	-	3	0	1	2	1	3	1

AFRICA

PRELIMINARY ROUND

Mauritius	1-0 1-2	**Somalia**
Mozambique	0-0 1-0	Swaziland
Botswana	0-0 1-2	**Gabon**
Ethiopia	W-O	Libya
Senegal	W-O	Burkina Faso
Sierra Leone	W-O	Mali
Mauritania	W-O	Gambia
Togo	W-O	Congo

FIRST ROUND

Sudan	1-2 0-2	**Egypt**
Mozambique	0-1 1-3	**Uganda**
Tunisia	3-1 0-1	Senegal
Algeria	0-0 0-1	**Sierra Leone**
Morocco	6-0 0-0	Mauritania
Togo	W-O	Liberia
Mauritius	W-O	Zambia
Malawi	W-O	Ethiopia
Cameroon	W-O	Gabon
Ivory Coast	W-O	Angola
Ghana	W-O	Guinea
Zimbabwe	W-O	Zaire

SECOND ROUND

Egypt	3-1 0-0	Malawi
Uganda	1-2 0-2	**Cameroon**
Tunisia	3-1 2-5	**Zimbabwe**
Ghana	2-1 2-2	Sierra Leone
Mauritius	W-O	Côte d'Ivoire
Morocco	W-O	Togo

THIRD ROUND

Cameroon	0-0 2-0	Morocco
Ghana	6-0 4-1	Mauritius
Egypt	3-0 1-1	Zimbabwe

ASIA

FIRST ROUND

Group 1

	Qa	Ir	AE	Ye	Pa	Pl	W	D	L	F	A	Pts
Qatar	-	2-0	2-1	3-0	2-0	8	6	1	1	16	4	13
Iran	2-0	-	2-2	2-1	5-0	8	5	2	1	19	6	12
Arab Emirates	0-2	0-1	-	2-1	2-0	8	3	2	3	8	8	8
Yemen	1-1	1-1	0-0	-	1-0	8	2	3	3	7	9	7
Pakistan	0-4	0-6	0-1	0-2	-	8	0	0	8	0	23	0

Group 2

Tournament in Hyderabad, India

	Ku	Sy	Om	Le	In	Pl	W	D	L	F	A	Pts
Kuwait	-	1-1	1-0	2-1	2-1	4	3	1	0	6	3	7
Syria	-	-	0-0	1-0	1-0	4	2	2	0	3	1	6
Oman	-	-	-	1-0	1-0	4	2	1	1	2	1	5
Lebanon	-	-	-	-	3-1	4	1	0	3	4	5	2
India	-	-	-	-	-	4	0	0	4	2	7	0

Group 3

Tournament in Bahrain

	Ba	SA	Jo	SL	Pl	W	D	L	F	A	Pts
Bahrain	-	0-2	4-0	6-0	3	2	0	1	10	2	4
Saudi Arabia	-	-	1-2	5-1	3	2	0	1	8	3	4
Jordan	-	-	-	7-0	3	2	0	1	9	5	4
Sri Lanka	-	-	-	-	3	0	0	3	1	18	0

Group 4

Tournaments in Seoul, South Korea and Kuala Lumpur, Malaysia

	SK	Th	Ma	Ba	Ph	Pl	W	D	L	F	A	Pts
South Korea	-	2-1	0-0	6-0	10-0	8	7	1	0	30	1	15
Thailand	0-2	-	4-1	3-2	7-1	8	5	0	3	25	9	10
Malaysia	0-2	1-0	-	0-1	5-0	8	4	1	3	13	7	9
Bangladesh	0-1	0-4	0-1	-	8-0	8	3	0	5	14	15	6
Philippines	0-7	0-6	0-5	0-3	-	8	0	0	8	1	51	0

Group 5

Tournaments in Pyongyang, North Korea and Beijing, China

	Ch	NK	Si	Md	Ne	Pl	W	D	L	F	A	Pts
China	-	1-0	3-0	17-0	10-0	8	7	1	0	51	1	15
North Korea	1-1	-	2-0	4-0	5-0	8	6	1	1	27	3	13
Singapore	0-3	1-3	-	1-1	4-1	8	3	1	4	14	16	7
Maldives	0-12	0-7	2-4	-	1-0	8	1	1	6	5	47	3
Nepal	0-4	0-5	1-4	2-1	-	8	1	0	7	4	34	2

Group 6

	Ja	HK	Id	Ta	Pl	W	D	L	F	A	Pts
Japan	-	3-0	3-1	2-0	6	5	0	1	14	5	10
Hong Kong	3-1	-	1-1	1-1	6	2	3	1	6	6	7
Indonesia	1-2	0-0	-	2-1	6	1	2	3	6	10	4
Taiwan	0-3	0-1	3-1	-	6	1	1	4	5	10	3

FINAL ROUND

Tournament in Kuala Lumpur

	Qa	SK	Ku	Ch	Ja	Ba	Pl	W	D	L	F	A	Pts
Qatar	-	1-0	0-3	1-0	1-0	1-0	5	4	0	1	4	3	8
South Korea	-	-	1-1	3-1	1-0	1-0	5	3	1	1	6	3	7
Kuwait	-	-	-	0-1	1-1	3-0	5	2	2	1	8	3	6
China	-	-	-	-	2-1	3-0	5	3	0	2	7	5	6
Japan	-	-	-	-	-	6-1	5	1	1	3	8	6	3
Bahrain	-	-	-	-	-	-	5	0	0	5	1	14	0

OCEANIA

	Au	NZ	Fi	PN	Pl	W	D	L	F	A	Pts
Australia	-	2-0	7-0	4-0	6	6	0	0	23	1	12
New Zealand	1-2	-	4-0	4-2	6	3	1	2	12	7	7
Fiji	0-3	0-0	-	1-1	6	1	2	3	3	15	4
Papua New Guinea	0-5	1-3	0-2	-	6	0	1	5	4	19	1

Play-off

Australia	1-1 2-2	Holland

CENTRAL AND NORTH AMERICA

PRELIMINARY ROUND

Puerto Rico	0-3 0-2	**Jamaica**
Haiti	1-1 2-2	Cuba
Aruba	0-0 0-9	**St. Lucia**
Antigua	0-0 0-5	**Barbados**
Neth. Antilles	0-1 0-0	**Surinam**

FIRST ROUND

Barbados 0-0 1-2 **Surinam**
Trinidad 1-0 0-1 2-1 Jamaica
St. Lucia 1-1 1-2 **Haiti**
Guatemala 2-2 0-2 **Honduras**
Belize 0-2 0-3 **El Salvador**
Panama W-O Costa Rica
Mexico Bye
Canada Bye
United States Bye

SECOND ROUND

Group 1

	Ho	Me	Su	Pl	W	D	L	F	A	Pts
Honduras	-	1-1	2-0	4	3	1	0	6	1	7
Mexico	0-1	-	6-0	4	1	2	1	8	3	4
Surinam	0-2	1-1	-	4	0	1	3	1	11	1

Group 2

	Ca	ES	Tr	Pl	W	D	L	F	A	Pts
Canada	-	4-0	3-0	4	3	0	1	11	4	6
El Salvador	3-1	-	2-0*	4	2	0	2	5	7	4
Trinidad	1-3	2-0	-	4	1	0	3	3	8	2

* El Salvador awarded the game 2-0

Group 3

	US	Pa	Ha	Pl	W	D	L	F	A	Pts
United States	-	7-1	8-0	4	3	1	0	18	2	7
Panama	1-1	-	2-2	3	0	2	1	4	10	2
Haiti	0-2	-	-	3	0	1	2	2	12	1

THIRD ROUND

	US	Me	Ca	Ho	Pl	W	D	L	F	A	Pts
United States	-	3-0	3-1	4-3	6	5	0	1	17	10	10
Mexico	1-2	-	4-1	5-1	6	3	1	2	14	9	7
Canada	2-1	1-1	-	2-2	6	1	2	3	7	12	4
Honduras	3-4	1-3	1-0	-	6	1	1	4	11	18	3

FINAL TOURNAMENT, 24TH JULY - 8TH AUGUST 1992

FIRST ROUND

Group 1

	Pd	It	US	Ku	Pl	W	D	L	F	A	Pts
Poland	-	3-0	2-2	2-0	3	2	1	0	7	2	5
Italy	-	-	2-1	1-0	3	2	0	1	3	4	4
United States	-	-	-	3-1	3	1	1	1	6	5	3
Kuwait	-	-	-	-	3	0	0	3	1	6	0

Group 2

	Gh	Au	Me	De	Pl	W	D	L	F	A	Pts
Ghana	-	3-1	1-1	0-0	3	1	2	0	4	2	4
Australia	-	-	1-1	3-0	3	1	1	1	5	4	3
Mexico	-	-	-	1-1	3	0	3	0	3	3	3
Denmark	-	-	-	-	3	0	2	1	1	4	2

Group 3

	Sp	Qa	Eg	Co	Pl	W	D	L	F	A	Pts
Spain	-	2-0	2-0	4-0	3	3	0	0	8	0	6
Qatar	-	-	1-0	1-1	3	1	1	1	2	3	3
Egypt	-	-	-	4-3	3	1	0	2	4	6	2
Colombia	-	-	-	-	3	0	1	2	4	9	1

Group 4

	Sd	Pa	SK	Mo	Pl	W	D	L	F	A	Pts
Sweden	-	0-0	1-1	4-0	3	1	2	0	5	1	4
Paraguay	-	-	0-0	3-1	3	1	2	0	3	1	4
South Korea	-	-	-	1-1	3	0	3	0	2	2	3
Morocco	-	-	-	-	3	0	1	2	2	8	1

QUARTER-FINALS

Spain 1-0 Italy
Ghana 4-2 Paraguay
Australia 2-1 Sweden
Poland 2-0 Qatar

SEMI-FINALS

Spain 2-0 Ghana
Poland 6-1 Australia

3RD PLACE

Ghana 1-0 Australia

FINAL

Nou Camp, Barcelona, 8-08-1992, 95,000. Referee: Jose Torres, Colombia

SPAIN 3 (Abelardo 65, Quico 72 90)
POLAND 2 (Kowalczyk 44, Staniek 76)

Spain - Toni - Abelardo - Lopez, Solozabal - Ferrere, Guardiola, Berges, Lasa (Amavisca) - Luis Enrique, Alfonso, Quico

Poland - Klak - Jalocha (Swierczewski), Kozminski, Waldoch, Lapinski - Gesior, Brzeczek, Kobylanski, Staniek - Kowalczyk, Juskowiak

THE FIFA UNDER-17 WORLD CHAMPIONSHIP

Aside from the World Cup for men and women and the football tournament of the Olympic Games, FIFA organises the Under-17 World Championship and the World Youth Cup for Under-20s.

FIFA is very keen to promote football at the grass-roots level and although often criticised for bringing competitive football to players at too young an age, it feels that the two junior tournaments serve that ideal. Both are relatively new tournaments, and the under-17 championship has shown that levels of skill are relatively even around the world. Africa has won three of the five editions and Asia one.

It is after that age that the disparity begins to show and the fact that the under-20 Youth Cup has been won on each occasion by a European or South American country shows how the more stable club situation on those two continents helps the development of players, many of whom are already established in a first division team at that age.

A major problem with the under-17 event especially has been the question of over-age players, and despite the heavy punishments handed out by FIFA, most notably the suspension of Mexico from the senior World Cup in 1990, accusations still fly after each event.

1985	Nigeria	2-0	West Germany
1987	Soviet Union	1-1 4-2p	Nigeria
1989	Saudi Arabia	2-2 5-4p	Scotland
1991	Ghana	1-0	Spain
1993	Nigeria	2-1	Ghana

	Country	G	S	B	Finals	S-Finals
1	Nigeria	2	1	-	3	3

2	Ghana	1	1	-	2	2
3	Saudi Arabia	1	-	-	1	1
	Soviet Union	1	-	-	1	1
5	Scotland	-	1	-	1	1
	Spain	-	1	-	1	1
	West Germany	-	1	-	1	1
8	Argentina	-	-	1	-	1
	Brazil	-	-	1	-	1
	Chile	-	-	1	-	1
	Côte d'Ivoire	-	-	1	-	1
	Portugal	-	-	1	-	1
13	Bahrain	-	-	-	-	1
	Guinea	-	-	-	-	1
	Italy	-	-	-	-	1
	Poland	-	-	-	-	1
	Qatar	-	-	-	-	1

To the end of the 1993 tournament

I. EDITION, CHINA. 31ST JULY - 11TH AUGUST 1985

FIRST ROUND

Group 1

	Ch	Gu	US	Bo	Pl	W	D	L	F	A	Pts
CHINA	-	2-1	3-1	1-1	3	2	1	0	6	3	5
GUINEA	-	-	1-0	3-0	3	2	0	1	5	2	4
UNITED STATES	-	-	-	2-1	3	1	0	2	3	5	2
BOLIVIA	-	-	-	-	3	0	1	2	2	6	1

Group 2

	Au	WG	Ar	Co	Pl	W	D	L	F	A	Pts
AUSTRALIA	-	1-0	1-0	2-1	3	3	0	0	4	1	6
WEST GERMANY	-	-	1-1	4-1	3	1	1	1	5	3	3
ARGENTINA	-	-	-	4-2	3	1	1	1	5	4	3
CONGO	-	-	-	-	3	0	0	3	4	10	0

Group 3

	SA	Ni	It	CR	Pl	W	D	L	F	A	Pts
SAUDI ARABIA	-	0-0	3-1	4-1	3	2	1	0	7	2	5
NIGERIA	-	-	1-0	3-0	3	2	1	0	4	0	5
ITALY	-	-	-	2-0	3	1	0	2	3	4	2
COSTA RICA	-	-	-	-	3	0	0	3	1	9	0

Group 4

	Hu	Br	Me	Qa	Pl	W	D	L	F	A	Pts
HUNGARY	-	1-0	0-0	3-0	3	2	1	0	4	0	5
BRAZIL	-	-	2-0	2-1	3	2	0	1	4	2	4
MEXICO	-	-	-	3-1	3	1	1	1	3	3	3
QATAR	-	-	-	-	3	0	0	3	2	8	0

QUARTER-FINALS

Nigeria.......3-1.......Hungary
Guinea.......0-0 4-2p.......Australia
Brazil.......2-1.......Saudi Arabia
West Germany.......4-2.......China

SEMI-FINALS

Nigeria.......1-1 4-2p.......Guinea
West Germany.......4-3.......Brazil

3RD PLACE

Brazil.......4-1.......Guinea

FINAL

Workers' Stadium, Beijing, 11-08-1985, 80,000. Referee: Bambridge, Australia

NIGERIA 2 (Akpoborire 4, Adamu 79)
WEST GERMANY 0

Nigeria - Agbonsevbage - Duere, Ugbade, Atere, Numa - Aikhionbore, Babatunde, Adamu, Akpoborie (Nakade) - Igbinoba, Momoh

Top scorer - Marcel Witeczek, West Germany.......8
Player of the tournament - William César de Oliveira, Brazil

II. EDITION. CANADA. 12TH - 25TH JULY 1987

FIRST ROUND

Group 1

	It	Qa	Eg	Ca	Pl	W	D	L	F	A	Pts
ITALY	-	1-1	1-0	3-0	3	2	1	0	5	1	5
QATAR	-	-	1-0	2-1	3	2	1	0	4	2	5
EGYPT	-	-	-	3-0	3	1	0	2	3	2	2
CANADA	-	-	-	-	3	0	0	3	1	8	0

Group 2

	CI	SK	Ec	US	Pl	W	D	L	F	A	Pts
CÔTE D'IVOIRE	-	1-1	1-0	1-0	3	2	1	0	3	1	5
SOUTH KOREA	-	-	0-1	4-2	3	1	1	1	5	4	3
ECUADOR	-	-	-	0-1	3	1	0	2	1	2	2
UNITED STATES	-	-	-	-	3	1	0	2	3	5	2

Group 3

	Au	Fr	SA	Br	Pl	W	D	L	F	A	Pts
AUSTRALIA	-	1-4	1-0	1-0	3	2	0	1	3	4	4
FRANCE	-	-	0-2	0-0	3	1	1	1	4	3	3
SAUDI ARABIA	-	-	-	0-0	3	1	1	1	2	1	3
BRAZIL	-	-	-	-	3	0	2	1	0	1	2

Group 4

	SU	Ni	Me	Bo	Pl	W	D	L	F	A	Pts
SOVIET UNION	-	1-1	7-0	4-2	3	2	1	0	12	3	5
NIGERIA	-	-	0-1	3-2	3	1	1	1	4	4	3
MEXICO	-	-	-	2-2	3	1	1	1	3	9	3
BOLIVIA	-	-	-	-	3	0	1	2	6	9	1

QUARTER-FINALS

Soviet Union.......3-2.......France
Côte d'Ivoire.......3-0.......Qatar
Italy.......2-0.......South Korea
Nigeria.......1-0.......Australia

SEMI-FINALS

Soviet Union.......5-1.......Côte d'Ivoire
Nigeria.......1-0.......Italy

3RD PLACE

Côte d'Ivoire.......2-1.......Italy

FINAL

Varsity Stadium, Toronto, 25-07-1987, 15,000

SOVIET UNION 1 (Nikiforov)
NIGERIA 1 (Osundu)
Soviet Union won 3-1 on penalties

Soviet Union - Okrosidze - Asadov, Mokritskij, Bezenar, Moroz - Matveev, Vysokos (Kadyrov), Muscinka, Nikiforov - Kasymov, Arutjunjan (Rusin)

Nigeria - Isa - Oyekale, Abdulahi, Duere (Jibrin), Fetuga - Peter, Enegwea, Nwosu, Mohammed - Osundo, Emoedofu

Top scorer - Moussa Traoré, Côte d'Ivoire.......5
Player of the tournament - Philip Osondu, Nigeria

III EDITION. SCOTLAND. 10TH - 24TH JUNE 1989

FIRST ROUND

Group 1

	Ba	Sc	Gh	Cu	Pl	W	D	L	F	A	Pts
Bahrain	-	1-1	1-0	3-0	3	2	1	0	5	1	5
Scotland	-	-	0-0	3-0	3	1	2	0	4	1	4
Ghana	-	-	-	2-2	3	0	2	1	2	3	2
Cuba	-	-	-	-	3	0	1	2	2	8	1

Group 2

	EG	Br	US	Au	Pl	W	D	L	F	A	Pts
East Germany	-	1-2	5-2	1-0	3	2	0	1	7	4	4
Brazil	-	-	0-1	3-1	3	2	0	1	5	3	4
United States	-	-	-	2-2	3	1	1	1	5	7	3
Australia	-	-	-	-	3	0	1	2	3	6	1

Group 3

	Ni	Ar	Ch	Ca	Pl	W	D	L	F	A	Pts
Nigeria	-	0-0	3-0	4-0	3	2	1	0	7	0	5
Argentina	-	-	0-0	4-1	3	1	2	0	4	1	4
China	-	-	-	1-0	3	1	1	1	1	3	3
Canada	-	-	-	-	3	0	0	3	1	9	0

Group 4

	Po	SA	Gu	Co	Pl	W	D	L	F	A	Pts
Portugal	-	2-2	1-1	3-2	3	1	2	0	6	5	4
Saudi Arabia	-	-	2-2	1-0	3	1	2	0	5	4	4
Guinea	-	-	-	1-1	3	0	3	0	4	4	3
Colombia	-	-	-	-	3	0	1	2	3	5	1

QUARTER-FINALS

Saudi Arabia .... 0-0 2-0p .... Nigeria
Bahrain .... 0-0 4-1p .... Brazil
Portugal .... 2-1 .... Argentina
Scotland .... 1-0 .... East Germany

SEMI-FINALS

Saudi Arabia .... 1-0 .... Bahrain
Scotland .... 1-0 .... Portugal

3RD PLACE

Portugal .... 3-0 .... Bahrain

FINAL

Hampden Park, Glasgow, 24-06-1989, 51,000
SAUDI ARABIA 2 (Al-Reshoudi 49, Al-Terair 65)
SCOTLAND 2 (Downie 7, Dickov 25)
Saudi Arabia won 5-4 on penalties
Saudi - Al Deayea - Abdulshkor, Burshaid, Al Theneyan, Al Alivi - Al Hammali, Al Hamdi, Al Reshoudi, Al Terair - Al Roaihi (Al Mosa), Al Shamrani
Scotland - Will - Bain, McMillan, Marshall, Beattie - Downie (Murray), Lindsay, O'Neill, Bollan - McGoldrick (McLaren), Dickov

Top scorer - Fodé Camara, Guinea 3
Player of the tournament - James Will, Scotland

IV EDITION. ITALY. 15TH - 31ST AUGUST 1991

FIRST ROUND

Group 1

	US	Ar	It	Ch	Pl	W	D	L	F	A	Pts
United States	-	1-0	1-0	3-1	3	3	0	0	5	1	6
Argentina	-	-	0-0	2-1	3	1	1	1	2	2	3
Italy	-	-	-	2-2	3	0	2	1	2	3	2
China	-	-	-	-	3	0	1	2	4	7	1

Group 2

	Au	Qa	Co	Me	Pl	W	D	L	F	A	Pts
Australia	-	0-1	2-0	4-3	3	2	0	1	6	4	4
Qatar	-	-	0-0	0-1	3	1	1	1	1	1	3
Congo	-	-	-	2-1	3	1	1	1	2	3	3
Mexico	-	-	-	-	3	1	0	2	5	6	2

Group 3

	Br	Ge	Su	Em	Pl	W	D	L	F	A	Pts
Brazil	-	2-0	1-0	4-0	3	3	0	0	7	0	6
Germany	-	-	3-1	2-2	3	1	1	1	5	5	3
Sudan	-	-	-	4-1	3	1	0	2	5	5	2
Arab Emirates	-	-	-	-	3	0	1	2	3	10	1

Group 4

	Sp	Gh	Ur	Cu	Pl	W	D	L	F	A	Pts
Spain	-	1-1	1-0	7-2	3	2	1	0	9	3	5
Ghana	-	-	2-0	2-1	3	2	1	0	5	2	5
Uruguay	-	-	-	1-0	3	1	0	2	1	3	2
Cuba	-	-	-	-	3	0	0	3	3	10	0

QUARTER-FINALS

Ghana .... 2-1 .... Brazil
Qatar .... 1-1 5-4p .... United States
Argentina .... 2-1 .... Australia
Spain .... 3-1 .... Germany

SEMI-FINALS

Ghana .... 0-0 4-2p .... Qatar
Spain .... 1-0 .... Argentina

3RD PLACE

Argentina .... 1-1 4-1p .... Qatar

FINAL

Comunale, Florence, 31-08-1991, 5,000. Referee: Sundell, Sweden
GHANA 1 (Duah 77)
SPAIN 0
Ghana - Owu - Nimo, Barnes, Asare, Mbeah - Lamptey, Opoku, Gargo, Duah - Preko (Brown), Addo. Tr: Pfister
Spain - Javier - Chocarro, Castro, Exposito, Juan Carlos - Gerardo, Vaqueriza (Gerardo), Sandro (Velasco), Emilio - Murgi, Toni. Tr: Troyano

Top scorer - Adriano Silva, Brazil 4
Player of the tournament - Nii Lamptey, Ghana

V EDITION. JAPAN. 31ST AUGUST - 4TH SEPTEMBER 1993

FIRST ROUND

Group 1

	Gh	Ja	Me	It	Pl	W	D	L	F	A	Pts
Ghana	-	1-0	4-1	4-0	3	3	0	0	9	1	6
Japan	-	-	2-1	0-0	3	1	1	1	2	2	3
Mexico	-	-	-	2-1	3	1	0	2	4	7	2
Italy	-	-	-	-	3	0	1	2	1	6	1

Group 2

	Ni	Au	Ar	Ca	Pl	W	D	L	F	A	Pts
Nigeria	-	2-0	4-0	8-0	3	3	0	0	14	0	6
Australia	-	-	2-2	5-0	3	1	1	1	7	4	3
Argentina	-	-	-	5-0	3	1	1	1	7	6	3
Canada	-	-	-	-	3	0	0	3	0	18	0

Group 3

	Cz	US	Co	Qa	Pl	W	D	L	F	A	Pts
Czechoslovakia	-	2-2	3-1	2-0	3	2	1	0	7	3	5
United States	-	-	1-2	5-1	3	1	1	1	8	5	3
Colombia	-	-	-	0-2	3	1	0	2	3	6	2
Qatar	-	-	-	-	3	1	0	2	3	7	2

Group 4

	Pd	Cl	Tu	Cn	Pl	W	D	L	F	A	Pts
POLAND	-	3-3	3-1	2-0	3	2	1	0	8	4	5
CHILE	-	-	2-0	2-2	3	1	2	0	7	5	4
TUNISIA	-	-	-	1-0	3	1	0	2	2	5	2
CHINA	-	-	-	-	3	0	1	2	2	5	1

QUARTER-FINALS

Nigeria .... 2-1 .... Japan
Poland .... 3-0 .... United States
Chile .... 4-1 .... Czechoslovakia
Ghana .... 1-0 .... Australia

SEMI-FINALS

Nigeria .... 2-1 .... Poland
Ghana .... 3-0 .... Chile

3RD PLACE

Chile .... 1-1 4-2p .... Poland

FINAL

National Stadium, Tokyo, 4-09-1993. Referee: Castrilli, Argentina

NIGERIA 2 (Oruma 3, Anosike 74)
GHANA 1 (Fameye 83)

Nigeria - Okhenoboh - Oparaku, Babayaro, Okenedo, Anyanwu - Ojigwe, Oruma, Kanu, Odini (Ogbebor) - Choji (Okougha), Anosike. Tr: Ikhayere

Ghana - Jarra - Barnes, Kuffour, Opoku, Edusei - Antwi (Muftawu), Fameye, Addo, Duah - Dadzie, Armah (Sarpong). Tr: Paha

Top scorer - Wilson Oruma, Nigeria 6
Player of the tournament - Daniel Addo, Ghana

THE FIFA WORLD YOUTH CUP FOR UNDER 20S

1977	Soviet Union	2-2 9-8p	Mexico
1979	Argentina	3-1	Soviet Union
1981	West Germany	4-0	Qatar
1983	Brazil	1-0	Argentina
1985	Brazil	1-0	Spain
1987	Yugoslavia	1-1 5-4p	West Germany
1989	Portugal	2-0	Nigeria
1991	Portugal	0-0 4-2p	Brazil
1993	Brazil	2-1	Ghana
1995	Argentina	2-0	Brazil

	Country	G	S	B	Finals	S-Finals
1	Brazil	3	2	2	5	7
2	Argentina	2	1	-	3	3
3	Portugal	2	-	1	2	3
4	Soviet Union	1	1	1	2	4
	West Germany	1	1	-	2	2
6	Yugoslavia	1	-	-	1	1
7	Nigeria	-	1	1	1	2
8	Spain	-	1	-	1	2
9	Ghana	-	1	-	1	1
	Mexico	-	1	-	1	1
	Qatar	-	1	-	1	1
12	England	-	-	1	-	2
	Poland	-	-	1	-	2
	Uruguay	-	-	1	-	2
15	East Germany	-	-	1	-	1
	Rumania	-	-	1	-	1
17	Australia	-	-	-	-	2
18	Chile	-	-	-	-	1
	South Korea	-	-	-	-	1
	United States	-	-	-	-	1

To the end of the 1995 tournament

I EDITION. TUNISIA. 27TH JUNE - 10TH JULY 1977

FIRST ROUND

Group 1

	Me	Sp	Fr	Tu	Pl	W	D	L	F	A	Pts
MEXICO	-	1-1	1-1	6-0	3	1	2	0	8	2	4
SPAIN	-	-	2-1	0-1	3	1	1	1	3	3	3
FRANCE	-	-	-	1-0	3	1	1	1	3	3	3
TUNISIA	-	-	-	-	3	1	0	2	1	7	2

Group 2

	Ur	Ho	Hu	Mo	Pl	W	D	L	F	A	Pts
URUGUAY	-	1-0	2-1	3-0	3	3	0	0	6	1	6
HONDURAS	-	-	2-0	1-0	3	2	0	1	3	1	4
HUNGARY	-	-	-	2-0	3	1	0	2	3	4	2
MOROCCO	-	-	-	-	3	0	0	3	0	6	0

Group 3

	Br	Ir	It	Cl	Pl	W	D	L	F	A	Pts
BRAZIL	-	5-1	2-0	1-1	3	2	1	0	8	2	5
IRAN	-	-	0-0	3-0	3	1	1	1	4	5	3
ITALY	-	-	-	1-1	3	0	2	1	1	3	2
CÔTE D'IVOIRE	-	-	-	-	3	0	2	1	2	5	2

Group 4

	SU	Pa	Iq	Au	Pl	W	D	L	F	A	Pts
SOVIET UNION	-	2-1	3-1	0-0	3	2	1	0	5	2	5
PARAGUAY	-	-	4-0	1-0	3	2	0	1	6	2	4
IRAQ	-	-	-	5-1	3	1	0	2	6	8	2
AUSTRIA	-	-	-	-	3	0	1	2	1	6	1

SEMI-FINALS

Soviet Union .... 0-0 4-3p .... Uruguay
Mexico .... 1-1 5-3p .... Brazil

3RD PLACE

Brazil .... 4-0 .... Uruguay

FINAL

Tunis, 10-07-1977, 5,000. Referee: Vautrot, France

SOVIET UNION 2 (Bessonov 43 52)
MEXICO 2 (Garduno 50, Manzo 59)
Soviet Union won 9-8 on penalties

Soviet Union - Novikov (Sivukha) - Krajacko, Baltaca, Kaplun, Ilijn - Bal, Bessonov, Khidiatullin, Byckov - Bodrov, Sopko. Tr: Mosjagin

Mexico - Paredes - Mora, Rubio, Alvarez, López - Rergis, Cosio, Rodriguez, Manzo - Garduño, Placencia. Tr: Portugal

Top scorer - Guina, Brazil 4
Player of the tournament - Vladimir Bessonov, Soviet Union

II EDITION. JAPAN. 25TH AUGUST - 7TH SEPTEMBER 1979

FIRST ROUND

Group 1

	Sp	Al	Me	Ja	Pl	W	D	L	F	A	Pts
SPAIN	-	0-1	2-1	1-0	3	2	0	1	3	2	4
ALGERIA	-	-	1-1	0-0	3	1	2	0	2	1	4
MEXICO	-	-	-	1-1	3	0	2	1	3	4	2
JAPAN	-	-	-	-	3	0	2	1	1	2	2

Group 2

	Ar	Po	Yu	Id	Pl	W	D	L	F	A	Pts
ARGENTINA	-	4-1	1-0	5-0	3	3	0	0	10	1	6
POLAND	-	-	2-0	6-0	3	2	0	1	9	4	4
YUGOSLAVIA	-	-	-	5-0	3	1	0	2	5	3	2
INDONESIA	-	-	-	-	3	0	0	3	0	16	0

Group 3

	Pa	Po	SK	Ca	Pl	W	D	L	F	A	Pts
Paraguay	-	0-1	3-0	3-0	3	2	0	1	6	1	4
Portugal	-	-	0-0	1-3	3	1	1	1	2	3	3
South Korea	-	-	-	1-0	3	1	1	1	1	3	3
Canada	-	-	-	-	3	1	0	2	3	5	2

Group 4

	Ur	SU	Hu	Gu	Pl	W	D	L	F	A	Pts
Uruguay	-	1-0	2-0	5-0	3	3	0	0	8	0	6
Soviet Union	-	-	5-1	3-0	3	2	0	1	8	2	4
Hungary	-	-	-	2-0	3	1	0	2	3	7	2
Guinea	-	-	-	-	3	0	0	3	0	10	0

QUARTER-FINALS

Argentina 5-0 Algeria
Uruguay 1-0 Portugal
Poland 0-0 4-3p Spain
Soviet Union 2-2 6-5p Paraguay

SEMI-FINALS

Argentina 2-0 Uruguay
Soviet Union 1-0 Poland

3RD PLACE

Uruguay 1-1 5-3p Poland

FINAL

National Stadium, Tokyo, 7-09-1979, 52,000. Referee: Wright, Brazil

ARGENTINA 3 (Alves 68, Diaz 71, Maradona 76)
SOVIET UNION 1 (Ponomarev 52)

Argentina - Garcia - Carabelli, Simön, Rossi, Alves - Barbas, Rinaldi (Meza), Maradona, Escudero (Torres) - Diaz, Calderön. Tr: Menotti

Soviet Union - Chanov - Yanushevski (Olefirenko), Khachatrian, Ovchinnikov, Polukarov - Dumanski (Mikhalevski), Ponomarev, Radenko, Gurinovich - Taran, Stukashev

Top scorer - Ramon Diaz, Argentina 8
Player of the tournament - Diego Maradona, Argentina

III EDITION. AUSTRALIA. 3RD - 18TH OCTOBER 1981

FIRST ROUND

Group 1

	Ur	Qa	Po	US	Pl	W	D	L	F	A	Pts
Uruguay	-	1-0	1-0	3-0	3	3	0	0	5	0	6
Qatar	-	-	1-0	1-1	3	1	1	1	2	2	3
Poland	-	-	-	4-0	3	1	0	2	4	2	2
United States	-	-	-	-	3	0	1	2	1	8	1

Group 2

	Br	Ro	SK	It	Pl	W	D	L	F	A	Pts
Brazil	-	1-1	3-0	1-0	3	2	1	0	5	1	5
Romania	-	-	1-0	1-0	3	2	1	0	3	1	5
South Korea	-	-	-	4-1	3	1	0	2	4	5	2
Italy	-	-	-	-	3	0	0	3	1	6	0

Group 3

	WG	Eg	Me	Sp	Pl	W	D	L	F	A	Pts
West Germany	-	1-2	1-0	4-2	3	2	0	1	6	4	4
Egypt	-	-	3-3	2-2	3	1	2	0	7	6	4
Mexico	-	-	-	1-1	3	0	2	1	4	5	2
Spain	-	-	-	-	3	0	2	1	5	7	2

Group 4

	En	Au	Ar	Cm	Pl	W	D	L	F	A	Pts
England	-	1-1	1-1	2-0	3	1	2	0	4	2	4
Australia	-	-	2-1	3-3	3	1	2	0	6	5	4
Argentina	-	-	-	1-0	3	1	1	1	3	3	3
Cameroon	-	-	-	-	3	0	1	2	3	6	1

QUARTER-FINALS

West Germany 1-0 Australia
Romania 2-1 Uruguay
England 4-2 Egypt
Qatar 3-2 Brazil

SEMI-FINALS

West Germany 1-0 Romania
Qatar 2-1 England

3RD PLACE

Romania 1-0 England

FINAL

Sydney Cricket Ground, Sydney, 18-10-1981, 19,000. Referee: Coelho, Brazil

WEST GERMANY 4 (Loose 26 66, Wohlfarth 42, Anthes 86)
QATAR 0

West Germany - Vollborn - Winklhofer, Zorc, Schmidkunz, Trieb - Sievers (Brunner), Schön, Loose, Anthes - Wohlfarth, Brummer (Herbst). Tr: Weise

Qatar - Ahmed Younes - Alsowaidi Mohd Duham, Ahmed Adil, Almas, Afifa - Beleal, Salem, Alsada, Maayouf - Mohamadi (Alsowaidi Khamis Duham), Almuhannadi. Tr: Evaristo

Top scorers - Five players with four
Player of the tournament - Romulus Gabor, Romania

IV EDITION. MEXICO. 2ND - 19TH JUNE 1983

FIRST ROUND

Group 1

	Sc	SK	Au	Me	Pl	W	D	L	F	A	Pts
Scotland	-	2-0	1-2	1-0	3	2	0	1	4	2	4
South Korea	-	-	2-1	2-1	3	2	0	1	4	4	4
Australia	-	-	-	1-1	3	1	1	1	4	4	3
Mexico	-	-	-	-	3	0	1	2	2	4	1

Group 2

	Ur	Pd	US	CI	Pl	W	D	L	F	A	Pts
Uruguay	-	3-1	3-2	0-0	3	2	1	0	6	3	5
Poland	-	-	2-0	7-2	3	2	0	1	10	5	4
United States	-	-	-	1-0	3	1	0	2	3	5	2
Côte d'Ivoire	-	-	-	-	3	0	1	2	2	8	1

Group 3

	Ar	Cz	Ch	Au	Pl	W	D	L	F	A	Pts
Argentina	-	2-0	5-0	3-0	3	3	0	0	10	0	6
Czechoslovakia	-	-	3-2	4-0	3	2	0	1	7	4	4
China	-	-	-	3-0	3	1	0	2	5	8	2
Austria	-	-	-	-	3	0	0	3	0	10	0

Group 4

	Br	Ho	Ni	SU	Pl	W	D	L	F	A	Pts
Brazil	-	1-1	3-0	2-1	3	2	1	0	6	2	5
Holland	-	-	0-0	3-2	3	1	2	0	4	3	4
Nigeria	-	-	-	1-0	3	1	1	1	1	3	3
Soviet Union	-	-	-	-	3	0	0	3	3	6	0

QUARTER-FINALS

Brazil 4-1 Czechoslovakia
South Korea 2-1 Uruguay
Poland 1-0 Scotland
Argentina 2-1 Holland

SEMI-FINALS

Brazil 2-1 South Korea
Argentina 1-0 Poland

3RD PLACE

Poland .... 2-1 .... South Korea

FINAL

Azteca, Mexico City, 19-06-1983, 110,000. Referee: Biguet, France

BRAZIL 1 (Geovani 39)
ARGENTINA 0

Brazil - Hugo - Heitor, Boni, Guto, Jorginho - Dunga, Geovani, Gilmar (Demétrio), Mauricinho - Marinho (Bebeto), Paulinho. Tr: Jair Pereira

Argentina - Islas - Basualdo, Borelli, Theiler, Oliveira - Gaona (Graciani), Vanemerak, Zarate, Garcia - Gabrich, Dezotti. Tr: Pachame

Top scorer - Geovani, Brazil 6
Player of the tournament - Geovani, Brazil

V EDITION. SOVIET UNION. 24TH AUGUST - 7TH SEPTEMBER 1985

FIRST ROUND

Group 1

	Bu	Co	Hu	Tu	Pl	W	D	L	F	A	Pts
Bulgaria	-	1-1	1-1	2-0	3	1	2	0	4	2	4
Colombia*	-	-	2-2	2-1	3	1	2	0	5	4	4
Hungary	-	-	-	2-1	3	1	2	0	5	4	4
Tunisia	-	-	-	-	3	0	0	3	2	6	0

* Colombia qualified on lots

Group 2

	Br	Sp	SA	RI	Pl	W	D	L	F	A	Pts
Brazil	-	2-0	1-0	2-1	3	3	0	0	5	1	6
Spain	-	-	0-0	4-2	3	1	1	1	4	4	3
Saudi Arabia	-	-	-	1-0	3	1	1	1	1	1	3
Rep. Ireland	-	-	-	-	3	0	0	3	3	7	0

Group 3

	SU	Ni	Au	Ca	Pl	W	D	L	F	A	Pts
Soviet Union	-	2-1	0-0	5-0	3	2	1	0	7	1	5
Nigeria	-	-	3-2	2-0	3	2	0	1	6	4	4
Australia	-	-	-	0-0	3	0	2	1	2	3	2
Canada	-	-	-	-	3	0	1	2	0	7	1

Group 4

	Me	Ch	Pa	En	Pl	W	D	L	F	A	Pts
Mexico	-	3-1	2-0	1-0	3	3	0	0	6	1	6
China	-	-	2-1	2-0	3	2	0	1	5	4	4
Paraguay	-	-	-	2-2	3	0	1	2	3	6	1
England	-	-	-	-	3	0	1	2	2	5	1

QUARTER-FINALS

Brazil .... 6-0 .... Colombia
Nigeria .... 2-1 .... Mexico
Soviet Union .... 1-0 .... China
Spain .... 2-1 .... Bulgaria

SEMI-FINALS

Brazil .... 2-0 .... Nigeria
Spain .... 2-2 4-3p .... Soviet Union

3RD PLACE

Nigeria .... 0-0 3-1p .... Soviet Union

FINAL

Centralny Lenina, Moscow, 7-09-1985, 45,000. Referee: Syme, Scotland

BRAZIL 1 (Henrique 92)
SPAIN 0

Brazil - Taffarel - Luciano, Luis Carlos, Henrique, Dida - João Antonio, Tostin, Silas (Marcal) - Muller, Gérson, Balalo. Tr: Gilson Nunes

Spain - Unzue - Tirado - Lizarralde, Arozarena, Mendiondo - Marcelino (Nayin), Paz, Gay, Fernando - Losada, Goicoechea. Tr: Pereda

Top scorers - Six players with three
Player of the tournament - Paulo Silas Pereira, Beazil

VI EDITION. CHILE. 10TH - 25TH OCTOBER 1987

FIRST ROUND

Group 1

	Yu	Ch	Au	To	Pl	W	D	L	F	A	Pts
Yugoslavia	-	4-2	4-0	4-1	3	3	0	0	12	3	6
Chile	-	-	2-0	3-0	3	2	0	1	7	4	4
Australia	-	-	-	2-0	3	1	0	2	2	6	2
Togo	-	-	-	-	3	0	0	3	1	9	0

Group 2

	It	Br	Ca	Ni	Pl	W	D	L	F	A	Pts
Italy	-	1-0	2-2	2-0	3	2	1	0	5	2	5
Brazil	-	-	1-0	4-0	3	2	0	1	5	1	4
Canada	-	-	-	2-2	3	0	2	1	4	5	2
Nigeria	-	-	-	-	3	0	1	2	2	8	1

Group 3

	EG	Sc	Co	Ba	Pl	W	D	L	F	A	Pts
East Germany	-	1-2	3-1	2-0	3	2	0	1	6	3	4
Scotland	-	-	2-2	1-1	3	1	2	0	5	4	4
Colombia	-	-	-	1-0	3	1	1	1	4	5	3
Bahrain	-	-	-	-	3	0	1	2	1	4	1

Group 4

	WG	Bu	US	SA	Pl	W	D	L	F	A	Pts
West Germany	-	3-0	2-1	3-0	3	3	0	0	8	1	6
Bulgaria	-	-	1-0	2-0	3	2	0	1	3	3	4
United States	-	-	-	1-0	3	1	0	2	2	3	2
Saudi Arabia	-	-	-	-	3	0	0	3	0	6	0

QUARTER-FINALS

Yugoslavia .... 2-1 .... Brazil
East Germany .... 2-0 .... Bulgaria
Chile .... 1-0 .... Italy
West Germany .... 1-1 4-3p .... Scotland

SEMI-FINALS

Yugoslavia .... 2-1 .... East Germany
West Germany .... 4-0 .... Chile

3RD PLACE

East Germany .... 1-1 3-1p .... Chile

FINAL

Estadio Nacional, Santiago. 25-10-1987, 68,000. Referee: Loustau, Argentina

YUGOSLAVIA 1 (Boban 85)
WEST GERMANY 1 (Witeczek 87)
Yugoslavia won 5-4 on penalties

Yugoslavia - Lekovic - Brnovic, Jarni, Pavlicic, Jankovic - Mijucic, Boban, Pavlovic (Zirojevic) - Suker, Petric, Skoric. Tr: Jozic

West Germany - Brunn - Luginger - Metz, Strehmel - Spyrka, Schneider, Reinhardt, Möller, Dammeier (Heidenreich) - Eichenauer (Epp), Witeczek. Tr: Vogts

Top scorer - Marcel Witeczek, West Germany 7
Player of the tournament - Robert Prosinecki, Yugoslavia

VII EDITION. SAUDI ARABIA. 16TH FEBRUARY - 3RD MARCH 1989

FIRST ROUND

Group 1

	Po	Ni	Cz	SA	Pl	W	D	L	F	A	Pts
Portugal	-	1-0	1-0	0-3	3	2	0	1	2	3	4
Nigeria	-	-	1-1	2-1	3	1	1	1	3	3	3
Czechoslovakia	-	-	-	1-0	3	1	1	1	2	2	3
Saudi Arabia	-	-	-	-	3	1	0	2	4	3	2

Group 2

	SU	Co	Sy	CR	Pl	W	D	L	F	A	Pts
Soviet Union	-	3-1	3-1	1-0	3	3	0	0	7	2	6
Colombia	-	-	2-0	0-1	3	1	0	2	3	4	2
Syria	-	-	-	3-1	3	1	0	2	4	6	2
Costa Rica	-	-	-	-	3	1	0	2	2	4	2

Group 3

	Br	US	EG	Ml	Pl	W	D	L	F	A	Pts
Brazil	-	3-1	2-0	5-0	3	3	0	0	10	1	6
United States	-	-	2-0	1-1	3	1	1	1	4	4	3
East Germany	-	-	-	3-0	3	1	0	2	3	4	2
Mali	-	-	-	-	3	0	1	2	1	9	1

Group 4

	Iq	Ar	No	Sp	Pl	W	D	L	F	A	Pts
Iraq	-	1-0	1-0	2-0	3	3	0	0	4	0	6
Argentina	-	-	2-0	1-2	3	1	0	2	3	3	2
Norway	-	-	-	4-2	3	1	0	2	4	5	2
Spain	-	-	-	-	3	1	0	2	4	7	2

QUARTER-FINALS

Portugal 1-0 Colombia
Brazil 1-0 Argentina
United States 2-1 Iraq
Nigeria 4-4 5-3p Soviet Union

SEMI-FINALS

Portugal 1-0 Brazil
Nigeria 2-1 United States

3RD PLACE

Brazil 2-0 United States

FINAL

King Fahd Stadium, Riyadh, 3-03-1989, 65,000. Referee: Schmidhuber, West Germany

PORTUGAL 2 (Abel 44, Jorge Couto 76)
NIGERIA 0

Portugal - Bizarro - Abel, Valido, Paulo Madeira, Morgado - Filipe, Hélio, Tozé, Amaral (Paulo Alvez) - João Pinto (Folha), Jorge Couto. Tr: Queiros

Nigeria - Amadi (Ikeji) - Elijah, Onyemachara, Chinedu, Charity - Oladimeji, Adepoju, Ogaba, Nwosu - Balogun (Osundo), Ohenhen. Tr: Disu

Top scorer - Oleg Salenko, Soviet Union 5
Player of the tournament - Bismarck, Brazil

VIII EDITION. PORTUGAL. 14TH - 30TH JUNE 1991

FIRST ROUND

Group 1

	Pt	Ko	RI	Ar	Pl	W	D	L	F	A	Pts
Portugal	-	1-0	2-0	3-0	3	3	0	0	6	0	6
Korea	-	-	1-1	1-0	3	1	1	1	2	2	3
Rep. Ireland	-	-	-	2-2	3	0	2	1	3	5	2
Argentina	-	-	-	-	3	0	1	2	2	6	1

Group 2

	Br	Me	Sd	CI	Pl	W	D	L	F	A	Pts
Brazil	-	2-2	2-0	2-1	3	2	1	0	6	3	5
Mexico	-	-	3-0	1-1	3	1	2	0	6	3	4
Sweden	-	-	-	4-1	3	1	0	2	4	6	2
Côte d'Ivoire	-	-	-	-	3	0	1	2	3	7	1

Group 3

	Au	SU	Eg	Tr	Pl	W	D	L	F	A	Pts
Australia	-	1-0	1-0	2-0	3	3	0	0	4	0	6
Soviet Union	-	-	1-0	4-0	3	2	0	1	5	1	4
Egypt	-	-	-	6-0	3	1	0	2	6	2	2
Trinidad	-	-	-	-	3	0	0	3	0	12	0

Group 4

	Sp	Sy	En	Ur	Pl	W	D	L	F	A	Pts
Spain	-	0-0	1-0	6-0	3	2	1	0	7	0	5
Syria	-	-	3-3	1-0	3	1	2	0	4	3	4
England	-	-	-	0-0	3	0	2	1	3	4	2
Uruguay	-	-	-	-	3	0	1	2	0	7	1

QUARTER-FINALS

Portugal 2-1 Mexico
Australia 1-1 5-4p Syria
Soviet Union 3-1 Spain
Brazil 5-1 Korea

SEMI-FINALS

Portugal 1-0 Australia
Brazil 3-0 Soviet Union

3RD PLACE

Soviet Union 1-1 5-4p Australia

FINAL

Estádio da Luz, Lisbon, 30-06-1991, 120,000. Referee: Lamolina, Argentina

PORTUGAL 0
BRAZIL 0
Portugal won 4-2 on penalties

Portugal - Brassard - Nélson (Tulipa) (Capucho), Rui Bento, Jorge Costa, Paulo Torres - Peixe, Rui Costa, Gil, Figo - Toni, João Pinto. Tr: Queiros

Brazil - Roger - Zelao, Andrei, Castro, Roberto Carlos - Rodrigao, Marquinhos, Djair - Luis Fernando (Serginho), Paulo Nuñes (Ramon), Elber. Tr: Ernesto Paulo

Top scorer - Sergei Cherbakov, Soviet Union 5
Player of the tournament - Peixe, Portugal

IX EDITION. AUSTRALIA. 5TH - 20TH MARCH 1993

FIRST ROUND

Group 1

	Ru	Au	Ca	Co	Pl	W	D	L	F	A	Pts
Russia	-	1-3	2-0	3-1	3	2	0	1	6	4	4
Australia	-	-	0-2	2-1	3	2	0	1	5	4	4
Cameroon	-	-	-	2-3	3	1	0	2	4	5	2
Colombia	-	-	-	-	3	1	0	2	5	7	2

Group 2

	Ur	Gh	Ge	Pt	Pl	W	D	L	F	A	Pts
Uruguay	-	1-1	2-1	2-1	3	2	1	0	5	3	5
Ghana	-	-	2-2	2-0	3	1	2	0	5	3	4
Germany	-	-	-	1-0	3	1	1	1	4	4	3
Portugal	-	-	-	-	3	0	0	3	1	5	0

Group 3

	En	US	SK	Tu	Pl	W	D	L	F	A	Pts
England	-	1-0	1-1	1-0	3	2	1	0	3	1	5
United States	-	-	2-2	6-0	3	1	1	1	8	3	3
South Korea	-	-	-	1-1	3	0	3	0	4	4	3
Turkey	-	-	-	-	3	0	2	1	1	8	1

Group 4

	Br	Me	SA	No	Pl	W	D	L	F	A	Pts
Brazil	-	2-1	0-0	2-0	3	2	1	0	4	1	5
Mexico	-	-	2-1	3-0	3	2	0	1	6	3	4
Saudi Arabia	-	-	-	0-0	3	0	2	1	1	2	2
Norway	-	-	-	-	3	0	1	2	0	5	1

QUARTER-FINALS

Brazil 3-0 United States
Australia 2-1 Uruguay
England 0-0 4-3p Mexico
Ghana 3-0 Russia

SEMI-FINALS

Brazil 2-0 Australia
Ghana 2-1 England

3RD PLACE

England 2-1 Australia

FINAL

Sydney, 20-03-1993, 40,000. Referee: Cakar, Turkey

BRAZIL 2 (Yan 50, Gian 88)
GHANA 1 (Duah 15)

Brazil - Dida - Juarez, Bruno, Gelson, Hermes - Pereira (Caico), Marcelinho, Yan - Cate, Adriano (Argel), Gian. Tr: Leal

Ghana - Owu - Kuffour, Nimo, Banini, Asare - Addo, Gargo, Lamptey, Akonnor (Boateng) - Ahinful, Duah. Tr: Duodu

Top scorer - Henry Zambrano, Colombia 3
Player of the tournament - Adriano, Brazil

X EDITION. QATAR. 14TH - 28TH APRIL 1995

FIRST ROUND

Group 1

	Br	Ru	Sy	Qa	Pl	W	D	L	F	A	Pts
Brazil	-	0-0	6-0	2-0	3	2	1	0	8	0	7
Russia	-	-	2-0	1-1	3	1	2	0	3	1	5
Syria	-	-	-	1-0	3	1	0	2	1	8	3
Qatar	-	-	-	-	3	0	1	2	1	4	1

Group 2

	Sp	Ja	Ch	Bu	Pl	W	D	L	F	A	Pts
Spain	-	2-1	6-3	5-1	3	3	0	0	13	5	9
Japan	-	-	2-2	2-0	3	1	1	1	5	4	4
Chile	-	-	-	1-1	3	0	2	1	6	9	2
Burundi	-	-	-	-	3	0	1	2	2	8	1

Group 3

	Po	Ar	Ho	Hd	Pl	W	D	L	F	A	Pts
Portugal	-	1-0	3-0	3-2	3	3	0	0	7	2	9
Argentina	-	-	1-0	4-2	3	2	0	1	5	3	6
Holland	-	-	-	7-1*	3	1	0	2	7	5	3
Honduras	-	-	-	-	3	0	0	3	5	14	0

*Match abandoned

Group 4

	Cm	Au	CR	Ge	Pl	W	D	L	F	A	Pts
Cameroon	-	3-2	3-1	1-1	3	2	1	0	7	4	7
Australia	-	-	2-0	1-1	3	1	1	1	5	4	4
Costa Rica	-	-	-	2-1	3	1	0	2	3	6	3
Germany	-	-	-	-	3	0	2	1	3	4	2

QUARTER-FINALS

Argentina 2-0 Cameroon
Spain 4-1 Russia
Portugal 2-1 Australia
Brazil 2-1 Japan

SEMI-FINALS

Argentina 3-0 Spain
Brazil 1-0 Portugal

3RD PLACE

Portugal 3-2 Spain

FINAL

Khalifa International Stadium, Doha, 28-04-1995, 50,000. Referee: Gallagher, England

ARGENTINA 2 (Biagini 25, Guerrero 83)
BRAZIL 0

Argentina - Irigoytia (Pezutti) - Lombardi, Pena, Sorin, Dominguez - Juan, Larrosa, Ibagaza, Coyette - Chaparro (Arangio), Biagini (Guererro). Tr: Pekerman

Brazil - Fabio - Cesar, Dedimar, Fabiano, Leonardo - Zé Elias, Elder (Luizao), Glaucio Ciao - Reinaldo (Denilson), Murilo (Claudinho). Tr: Jairo Leal

Top scorer - Joseba, Spain 5
Player of the tournament - Ciao, Brazil

THE WORLD CUP FOR WOMEN

The Women's World Cup, although only introduced in 1991, looks set to tap into one of the biggest growth sports in the world. It is not impossible that eventually the tournament will become an equal partner to the men's event as has happened in tennis and athletics.

Certainly, with half the world's population to account for, FIFA is taking the challenge seriously. If they can change football from being a bastion of male culture to a sport both played and watched by women as equal partners to men, it will be a magnificent achievement. It should certainly be one of their top priorities for the 21st century and the World Cup is just the first step on what promises to be a fruitful road.

I. EDITION

QUALIFYING TOURNAMENT

EUROPE

The fourth European Championship was used as the qualifying tournament. West Germany, Norway, Denmark, Italy and Sweden qualified for the finals.

SOUTH AMERICA

	Br	Ch	Ve	Pl	W	D	L	F	A	Pts
Brazil	-	6-1	6-0	2	2	0	0	12	1	4
Chile	-	-	1-0	2	1	0	1	2	6	2
Venezuela	-	-	-	2	0	0	2	0	7	0

CENTRAL AND NORTH AMERICA

FIRST ROUND

Group A

	US	Tr	Me	Ma	Pl	W	D	L	F	A	Pts
United States	-	0-0	12-0	12-0	3	2	1	0	24	0	5
Trinidad	-	-	3-1	1-1	3	1	2	0	4	2	4
Mexico	-	-	-	8-1	3	1	0	2	9	16	2
Martinique	-	-	-	-	3	0	1	2	2	21	1

Group B

	Ca	Ha	CR	Ja	Pl	W	D	L	F	A	Pts
Canada	-	2-0	6-0	9-0	3	3	0	0	17	0	6
Haiti	-	-	4-0	1-0	3	2	0	1	5	2	4
Costa Rica	-	-	-	2-1	3	1	0	2	2	11	2
Jamaica	-	-	-	-	3	0	0	3	1	12	0

SEMI-FINALS

United States 10-0 Haiti
Canada 6-0 Trinidad

3RD PLACE

Trinidad 4-2 Haiti

FINAL

UNITED STATES 5-0 Canada

AFRICA

FIRST ROUND

Nigeria 5-1 2-1 Ghana
Guinea W-O Senegal
Zambia W-O Zimbabwe
Cameroon W-O Congo

SEMI-FINALS

Nigeria 3-0 4-0 Guinea
Cameroon W-O Zambia

FINAL

NIGERIA 2-0 4-0 Cameroon

ASIA

FIRST ROUND

Group A

	Ch	Ta	Th	SK	Pl	W	D	L	F	A	Pts
China	-	3-0	10-1	10-0	3	3	0	0	23	1	6
Taiwan	-	-	0-0	9-0	3	1	1	1	9	3	3
Thailand	-	-	-	3-0	3	1	1	1	4	10	3
South Korea	-	-	-	-	3	0	0	3	0	22	0

Group B

	Ja	NK	HK	Ma	Si	Pl	W	D	L	F	A	Pts
Japan	-	1-0	4-1	12-0	10-0	4	4	0	0	27	1	8
North Korea	-	-	5-0	12-0	8-0	4	3	0	1	25	1	6
Hong Kong	-	-	-	0-0	2-0	4	1	1	2	3	9	3
Malaysia	-	-	-	-	1-0	4	1	1	2	1	24	3
Singapore	-	-	-	-	-	4	0	0	4	0	21	0

SEMI-FINALS

China 1-0 North Korea
Japan 0-0 5-4p Taiwan

3RD PLACE

Taiwan 0-0 5-4p North Korea

FINAL

CHINA 5-0 Japan

China, Japan and Taiwan qualified for the finals

OCEANIA

	NZ	Au	PN	Pl	W	D	L	F	A	Pts
NEW ZEALAND	-	1-0	11-0	4	3	0	1	28	1	6
Australia	1-0	-	12-0	4	3	0	1	21	1	6
Papua New Guinea	0-16	0-8	-	4	0	0	4	0	47	0

FINAL TOURNAMENT
HELD IN CHINA, 16TH - 30TH NOVEMBER 1991

FIRST ROUND

Group 1 (Guangzhou/Foshan/Punya)

	Ch	No	De	NZ	Pl	W	D	L	F	A	Pts
China	-	4-0	2-2	4-1	3	2	1	0	10	3	5
Norway	-	-	2-1	4-0	3	2	0	1	6	5	4
Denmark	-	-	-	3-0	3	1	1	1	6	4	3
New Zealand	-	-	-	-	3	0	0	3	1	11	0

Group 2 (Foshan/Punya)

	US	Sd	Br	Ja	Pl	W	D	L	F	A	Pts
United States	-	3-2	5-0	3-0	3	3	0	0	11	2	6
Sweden	-	-	2-0	8-0	3	2	0	1	12	3	4
Brazil	-	-	-	1-0	3	1	0	2	1	7	2
Japan	-	-	-	-	3	0	0	3	0	12	0

Group 3 (Jiangmen/Zhongshan)

	Ge	It	Ta	Ng	Pl	W	D	L	F	A	Pts
Germany	-	2-0	3-0	4-0	3	3	0	0	9	0	6
Italy	-	-	5-0	1-0	3	2	0	1	6	2	4
Taiwan	-	-	-	2-0	3	1	0	2	2	8	2
Nigeria	-	-	-	-	3	0	0	3	0	7	0

QUARTER-FINALS

United States 7-0 Taiwan
Germany 2-1 Denmark
Sweden 1-0 China
Norway 3-2 Italy

SEMI-FINALS

United States 5-2 Germany
Norway 4-1 Sweden

3RD PLACE

Sweden 4-0 Germany

FINAL

Tianhe Stadium, Guangzhou, 30-11-1991, 65,000. Referee: Zhuk, Soviet Union

UNITED STATES 2 (Akers-Stahl 20 77)
NORWAY 1 (Medalen 28)

United States - Harvey, Heinrichs, Higgins, Werden, Hamilton, Hamm, AkersStahl, Foudy, Jennings, Lilly, Biefeld. Tr: Dorrance
Norway - Seth - Zaborowski, Espeseth, Nyborg, Carleen - Haugen, Støre, Riise, Medalen - Hegstad, Svensson

II. EDITION

QUALIFYING ROUND

EUROPE

The sixth European Championship was used as a qualifying round. Sweden, England, Germany, Denmark and Norway qualified

SOUTH AMERICA

	Br	Ar	Ch	Ec	Bo	Pl	W	D	L	F	A	Pts
Brazil	-	8-0	6-1	13-0	15-0	4	4	0	0	42	1	12
Argentina	-	-	1-0	5-1	12-0	4	3	0	1	18	9	9
Chile	-	-	-	2-2	11-0	4	1	1	2	14	9	4
Ecuador	-	-	-	-	6-1	4	1	1	2	9	21	4
Bolivia	-	-	-	-	-	4	0	0	4	1	44	0

CONCACAF

	US	Ca	Me	Tr	Ja	Pl	W	D	L	F	A	Pts
United States	-	6-0	9-0	11-1	10-0	4	4	0	0	36	1	12
Canada	-	-	6-0	5-0	7-0	4	3	0	1	18	6	9
Mexico	-	-	-	3-3	3-1	4	1	1	2	6	19	4
Trinidad	-	-	-	-	2-1	4	1	1	2	6	20	4
Jamaica	-	-	-	-	-	4	0	0	4	2	22	0

AFRICA

FIRST ROUND

South Africa 5-3 6-2 Zambia
Nigeria 9-0 2-0 Sierra Leone
Angola W-O Cameroon
Ghana W-O Guinea

SEMI-FINALS

South Africa ....3-1 3-3....................Angola
Ghana....................0-3 0-2 ....Nigeria

FINAL

Nigeria ....4-1 7-1 ....South Africa

ASIA

1994 Asian Games football tournament

	Ja	Ch	Ta	SK	Pl	W	D	A	F	A	Pts
Japan	-	1-1	3-0	5-0	3	2	1	0	9	1	7
China	-	-	5-0	2-0	3	2	1	0	8	1	7
Taiwan	-	-	-	2-0	3	1	0	2	2	8	3
South Korea	-	-	-	-	3	0	0	3	0	9	0

China ....2-0 ....Japan

OCEANIA

	Au	NZ	PN	Pl	W	D	L	F	A	Pts
Australia	-	1-0	4-0	4	3	0	1	13	2	6
New Zealand	2-1	-	6-0	4	3	0	1	10	2	6
Papua N. Guinea	0-7	0-2	-	4	0	0	4	0	19	0

FINAL TOURNAMENT, SWEDEN.
5TH - 19TH JUNE 1995

FIRST ROUND

Group 1 (Karlstad, Helsingborg, Västerås)

	Ge	Sw	Ja	Br	Pl	W	D	L	F	A	Pts
Germany	-	2-3	1-0	6-1	3	2	0	1	9	4	6
Sweden	-	-	2-0	0-1	3	2	0	1	5	5	6
Japan	-	-	-	2-1	3	1	0	2	2	4	3
Brazil	-	-	-	-	3	1	0	2	3	8	3

Group 2 (Karlstad, Helsingborg, Gävle)

	No	En	Ca	Ng	Pl	W	D	L	F	A	Pts
Norway	-	2-0	7-0	8-0	3	3	0	0	17	0	9
England	-	-	3-2	3-2	3	2	0	1	6	6	6
Canada	-	-	-	3-3	3	0	1	2	5	13	1
Nigeria	-	-	-	-	3	0	1	2	5	14	1

Group 3 (Gävle, Västerås, Helsingborg)

	US	Ch	De	Au	Pl	W	D	L	F	A	Pts
United States	-	3-3	2-0	4-1	3	2	1	0	9	4	7
China	-	-	3-1	4-2	3	2	1	0	10	6	7
Denmark	-	-	-	5-0	3	1	0	2	6	5	3
Australia	-	-	-	-	3	0	0	3	3	13	0

QUARTER-FINALS

Norway ....3-1 ....Denmark
United States....................4-0 ....Japan
China....................1-1 ?-?p....................Sweden
Germany ....3-0....................England

SEMI-FINALS

Norway....................1-0 ....United States
Germany....................?-?....................China

3RD PLACE

United States ....2-0 ....China

FINAL

Råsunda, Stockholm, 18-06-1995, 17,000. Referee: Sweden

NORWAY 2 (Riise 37, Pettersen 41)
GERMANY 0

Norway - Nordby - Svensson, Nymark Andersen.N, Espeseth, Myklebust, Riise, Haugen, Nymark Andersen.A, Pettersen, Aarønes, Medalen. Tr: Pellerud

Germany - Goller - Bernhard, Austermühl, Lohn, Mohr, Neid, Wiegmann, Voss, Pohlman (Wunderlich), Meinert (Smisek), Prinz (Brocker). Tr: Bisanz

INTERCONTINENTAL CHAMPIONSHIP

If the World Cups since 1982 have proved anything, it is that the national sides of Asia and Africa are no longer pushovers for the rest. Gone are the days of Yugoslavia putting nine goals past Zaire. In 1982 Algeria beat West Germany, the eventual finalists, 1986 saw Morocco win their group, the exploits of the Cameroon in 1990 are legendary, and in 1994 the Saudis gave Asian football a massive boost.

The introduction in 1992 of the Intercontinental Championship, the winners of the world's regional championships for national sides competing in a tournament for the King Fahd Cup, was therefore a logical step. The European champions were absent from the first tournament in 1992, and it was Argentina who won the inaugural title by beating the Asian champions – and hosts – Saudi Arabia in the final.

The tournament does, however, have two major weaknesses. The oil-rich state of Saudi Arabia puts up millions of dollars to stage the tournament, including lavish prize money for all the participants. In 1992 the Saudi team were Asian champions but by the time of the second edition in 1995 they had no claim to be there at all. The fact that they took part anyway somewhat devalued the event.

The second problem relates to the timing of the continental championships which qualify teams for the intercontinental event. South America, CONCACAF and Africa stage theirs every two years, Europe and Asia theirs every four. Thus the 1995 winners Denmark, for example, could have taken part in the first two editions on the strength of having won just one edition of the European Championship in 1992.

The event as a concept does look set to stay, though whether or not it remains in Saudi Arabia is less certain. The 1995 tournament was surprisingly poorly attended, with the magnificent King Fahd stadium in Riyadh never more than half full. Matters were not helped by a lacklustre performance from the Saudi side which otherwise had an excellent year. Their World Cup performances in the States had impressed, while four months later they won the Gulf Cup for the first time.

A full-strength Denmark side beat Argentina in the final, handing Daniel Passarella his first defeat as Argentine coach. Denmark had earlier looked to be on their way out of the tournament, trailing Mexico late in the game in the last match of group 1. A Rasmussen equaliser two minutes from time, however, meant that both finished with identical records. Technically, lots should have been drawn to decide who proceeded to the final, but seeing as both teams were on the pitch a penalty shoot-out was quickly arranged. Never strong at penalties, the Mexicans missed out, reviving memories of the 1986 and 1994 World Cups when spot-kicks had also been their downfall.

FIRST EDITION. 1992

SEMI-FINALS

King Fahd Stadium, Riyadh, 16-10-1992, 15,000

Argentina 4 (Batistuta 2 10, Altamirano 67, Acosta 81)
Côte d'Ivoire 0

King Fahd Stadium, Riyadh, 16-10-1992, 70,000

Saudi Arabia 3 (Al Bishi 48p, Al Thunyan 74, Al Muwallid 84)
United States 0

3RD PLACE

King Fahd Stadium, Riyadh, 19-10-1992, 9,000

United States 5 (Balboa 12, Jones 31, Wynalda 56, Murray 67 83)
Côte d'Ivoire 2 (Traoré.A 16, Sie 76)

FINAL

King Fahd Stadium, Riyadh, 20-10-1992, 70,000

Argentina 3 (Rodriguez 18, Caniggia 24, Simeone 64)
Saudi Arabia 1 (Owairan 65)

SECOND EDITION. 1995

FIRST ROUND

Group 1

King Fahd Stadium, Riyadh, 6-1-1995, 22,000

Mexico 2 (Luis Garcia 65 84)
Saudi Arabia 0

King Fahd Stadium, Riyadh, 8-1-1995, 5,000

Denmark 2 (Laudrup.B 43, Wieghorst 90)
Saudi Arabia 0

King Fahd Stadium, Riyadh, 10-1-1995, 35,000

Denmark 1 (Rasmussen 88)
Mexico 1 (Luis Garcia 70)
Denmark qualified for the final by winning 4-2 on pens

Group 2

King Fahd Stadium, Riyadh, 6-1-1995, 22,000

Nigeria 3 (Siasia 5, Adepoju 54, Amokachi 64)
Japan 0

King Fahd Stadium, Riyadh, 8-1-1995, 5,000

Argentina 5 (Rambert 31, Ortega 45, Batistuta 47 85p, Chamot 53)
Japan 1 (Miura 57)

King Fahd Stadium, Riyadh, 10-1-1995, 35,000

Argentina 0
Nigeria 0

3RD PLACE

King Fahd Stadium, Riyadh, 13-1-1995, 25,000

Mexico 1 (Ramirez 20)
Nigeria 1 (Amokachi 31)
Mexico won 5-4 on pens

FINAL

King Fahd Stadium, Riyadh, 13-1-1995, 25,000

Denmark 2 (Laudrup.M 8p, Rasmussen 74)
Argentina 0

WORLD CLUB CHAMPIONSHIP

The World Club Championship is actually nothing of the sort as it involves only the winners of the European Champion Clubs' Cup and the Copa Libertadores. None of the African, Asian or CONCACAF champion teams are involved. Until this happens the title will remain a misnomer, despite the fact that in the event of a tournament involving all of the continents, a European or South American winner would be the most likely outcome.

A letter from Henri Delaunay, the general secretary of UEFA, to CONMEBOL suggesting a meeting between the winners of both the European Cup and any South American tournament they might organise was the spur the needed to get the Copa Libertadores off the ground.

At first the idea of an annual challenge match seemed a good one, but after a promising start the event became embroiled in controversy, and has only settled down as a worthwhile event since the fixture was move to Tokyo in 1980. Until that point games had been played on a home and away basis and more often than not resembled a battleground.

The tournament has gone through three distinct phases coinciding with the three decades of its existence. Real Madrid were unfortunately coming to the end of their supremacy when the tournament started but they appeared in the first edition and in a pulsating match in Madrid thrashed Peñarol 5–1. The following year Peñarol recovered their self-respect with a 5–0 victory over Benfica in the Centenario and a 2–1 win in the play-off two days later. Santos were responsible for another five-goal extravaganza against Benfica the following year, but the honeymoon was nearly over.

The 1963 Milan–Santos series was marred by several incidents and it became increasingly common for the intense rivalries between the two continents to spill over into violence on the field. There was no better example than in the 1967 and 1968 series, which involved Argentine and British clubs, and in 1969 when Milan played Estudiantes.

Feelings were running high in Argentina over their quarter-final exit in the 1966 World Cup against England, and in the play-off between Racing Club and Celtic a fight on the pitch led to five players being sent off after Basile had spat at Lennox. Manchester United and Estudiantes played a bad-tempered series the following year after which Stanley Rous, the president of FIFA, was moved to write a letter of complaint to the management of Estudiantes.

The whole justification of the tournament came into question the following year as Estudiantes embarked on a hostile campaign against the players of Milan, the net result of which was that three of their players landed up in jail for their behaviour in the second leg. Estudiantes were simply not concerned with playing football and their attitude ultimately led to the European sides giving the tournament the cold shoulder.

Throughout the 1970s the World Club Championship turned into a non-event as one after another of the European Cup winners decided they could not be bothered to play in the matches. Ajax, Bayern Munich and Liverpool on two occasions each refused to take part whilst Nottingham Forest in 1979 made it seven editions that had not contained the top European side.

Had it not been for the intervention in 1980 of the Japanese, who offered to stage the event, with Toyota as the sponsor, the World Club Championship would have almost certainly been consigned to the scrapheap. Instead it has become a stable annual event that has been contested over a single leg in the National Stadium in Tokyo.

Some of the games have even been entertaining, a feature not really in evidence since the first three series. South America has a better overall record, despite a succession of European wins in the late 1980s, and the fact that it is not uncommon to see a South American playing for a European side but not the other way around.

The World Club Championship looks set to stay. FIFA, who at the moment are not involved with the event, may wish to see it expanded to include Africa, Asia and Central America, at which point they would give it offical sanction, but that does not seem to be on the cards just yet.

ORDER OF MERIT

	Team	Country	G	S
1	Milan	ITA	3	3
2	Peñarol	URU	3	2
3	Nacional Montevideo	URU	3	-
4	Independiente	ARG	2	4
5	Internazionale	ITA	2	-
	Santos	BRA	2	-
	São Paulo FC	BRA	2	-
8	Estudiantes LP	ARG	1	2
9	Real Madrid	ESP	1	1
	Juventus	ITA	1	1
	Olimpia	PAR	1	1
12	Ajax	HOL	1	-
	Atlético Madrid	ESP	1	-
	Bayern München	FRG	1	-
	Boca Juniors	ARG	1	-
	Crvena Zvezda Beograd	YUG	1	-
	Feyenoord	HOL	1	-
	Flamengo	BRA	1	-
	Grêmio	BRA	1	-
	FC Porto	POR	1	-
	Racing Club	ARG	1	-
	River Plate	ARG	1	-
	Velez Sarsfield	ARG	1	-
24	Benfica	POR	-	2
	Liverpool	ENG	-	2
26	Argentinos Juniors	ARG	-	1
	Aston Villa	ENG	-	1
	Barcelona	ESP	-	1
	Bor. Mönchengladbach	FRG	-	1
	Glasgow Celtic	SCO	-	1
	Colo Colo	CHI	-	1
	Cruzeiro	BRA	-	1
	Manchester United	ENG	-	1
	At. Nacional Medellin	COL	-	1
	Malmö FF	SWE	-	1
	Nottingham Forest	ENG	-	1
	Panathinaikos	GRE	-	1
	PSV Eindhoven	HO	-	1
	Steaua Bucuresti	RUM	-	1
	Hamburger SV	FRG	-	1

	Country	G	S
1	Argentina	7	7
2	Italy	6	4
3	Uruguay	6	2
4	Brazil	6	1
5	Spain	2	2
6	Holland	2	1
7	Portugal	1	2
	West Germany	1	2
9	Paraguay	1	1
10	Yugoslavia	1	-
11	England	-	5
12	Chile	-	1
	Colombia	-	1
	Greece	-	1
	Rumania	-	1
	Scotland	-	1
	Sweden	-	1

1	South America	20	13
2	Europe	13	20

1960

1st leg. Centenario, Montevideo, 3-07-1960, 75,000. Referee: Praddaude, Argentina

PEÑAROL 0
REAL MADRID 0

Peñarol - Maidana - Martinez, Aguerre, Pino - Salvador, Gonçccalves Cubilla, Linazza, Hohberg, Spencer, Borges

Real Madrid - Dominguez - Marquitos, Santamaria, Pachín - Vidal, Zarraga Canario, Del Sol, Di Stéfano, Puskás, Bueno

2nd leg. Bernabeu, Madrid, 4-09-1960, 125,000. Referee: Aston, England

REAL MADRID 5 (Puskás 3 9, Di Stéfano 4, Herrera 44, Gento 54)
PEÑAROL 1 (Borges 69)

Real Madrid - Dominguez - Marquitos, Santamaria, Pachín - Vidal, Zarraga Herrera, Del Sol, Di Stéfano, Puskás, Gento. Tr: Munoz

Peñarol - Maidana - Pino, Mayewski, Martinez - Aguerre, Salvador - Cubilla, Linazza, Hohberg, Spencer, Borges. Tr: Scarone

1961

1st leg. Estádio da Luz, Lisbon, 4-09-1961, 50,000. Referee: Ebert, Switzerland

BENFICA 1 (Coluña 60)
PEÑAROL 0

Benfica - Costa Pereira - Angelo, Saravia, Joao - Neto, Cruz - Augusto, Santana, Aguas, Coluña, Cavem

Peñarol - Maidana - Gonzales, Martinez, Aguerre, Cano - Gonçalvez, Ledesma Spencer, Cubilla, Cabrera, Sasia

2nd leg. Centenario, Montevideo, 17-09-1961, 56,000. Referee: Nalfoino, Argentina

PENAROL 5 (Sasia 10, Joya 18 28, Spencer 42 60)
BEÑFICA 0

Peñarol - Maidana - Gonzales, Martinez, Cano, Aguerre - Goncalvez, Ledesma Cubilla, Sasia, Spencer, Joya

Benfica - Costa Pereira - Angelo, Saraiva, João - Neto, Cruz - Augusto, Santana, Mendes, Coluña, Cavem

Play-off. Centenario, Montevideo, 19-09-1961, 62,000. Referee: Praddaude, Argentina

PEÑAROL 2 (Sasia 6 41)
BENFICA 1 (Eusébio 35)

Peñarol - Maidana - Gonzales, Martinez, Aguerre, Cano - Goncalvez, Cabrera Cubilla, Ledesma, Sasia, Spencer

Benfica - Costa Pereira - Angelo, Humberto, Cruz - Neto, Coluna - Augusto, Eusébio, Aguas, Cavem, Simões. Tr: Guttmann

1962

1st leg. Maracana, Rio de Janeiro, 19-09-1962, 90,000. Referee: Ramirez, Paraguay

SANTOS 3 (Pelé 31 86, Coutinho 64)
BENFICA 2 (Santana 58 87)

Santos - Gilmar - Lima, Mauro, Calvet, Dalmo - Zito, Mengalvio - Dorval, Coutinho, Pelé, Pepe

Benfica - Costa Pereira - Jacinto, Raul, Humberto, Cruz - Cavem, Coluña Augusto, Santana, Eusébio, Simões

2nd leg. Estádio da Luz, Lisbon, 11-10-1962, 75,000. Referee: Scwinte, France

BENFICA 2 (Eusébio 87, Santana 89)
SANTOS 5 (Pelé 17 28 64, Coutinho 49, Pepe 77)

Benfica - Costa Pereira - Jacinto, Raul, Humberto, Cruz - Cavem, Coluña Augusto, Santana, Eusébio, Simões. Tr: Reira

Santos - Gilmar - Olavo, Mauro, Calvet, Dalmo - Lima, Zito - Dorval, Coutinho, Pelé, Pepe. Tr: Lula

1963

1st leg. San Siro, Milan, 16-10-1963, 80,000. Referee: Haberfellner, Austria

MILAN 4 (Trapattoni 4, Amarildo 15 65, Mora 80)
SANTOS 2 (Pelé 59 87)

Milan - Ghezzi - David, Maldini, Trapattoni, Trebbi - Pelagalli, Lodetti, Rivera - Mora, Altafini, Amarildo

Santos - Gilmar - Lima, Haroldo, Calvet, Geraldino - Zito, Mengalvio Dorval, Coutinho, Pelé, Pepe

2nd leg. Maracana, Rio de Janeiro, 14-11-1963, 150,000. Referee: Brozzi, Argentina

SANTOS 4 (Pepe 50 67, Almir 60, Lima 63)
MILAN 2 (Altafini 12, Mora 17)

Santos - Gilmar - Ismael, Dalmo, Mauro, Haroldo - Lima, Mengalvio - Dorval, Coutinho, Pelé, Pepe

Milan - Ghezzi - David, Maldini, Trapattoni, Trebbi - Pelagalli, Lodetti, Rivera - Mora, Altafini, Amarildo

Play-off. Maracana, Rio de Janeiro, 16-11-1963, 121,000. Referee: Brozzi, Argentina

SANTOS 1 (Dalmo 26)
MILAN 0

Santos - Gilmar - Ismael, Dalmo, Mauro, Haroldo - Lima, Mengalvio - Dorval, Coutinho, Almir, Pepe. Tr: Lula

Milan - Balzarini (Barluzzi) - Pelagalli, Maldini, Trebbi, Benitez Lodetti, Trapattoni - Mora, Altafini, Amarildo, Fortunato. Tr: Carniglia

1964

1st leg. Cordero, Avellaneda, 9-09-1964, 70,000. Referee: Marques, Brazil

INDEPENDIENTE 1 (Rodriguez 60)
INTERNAZIONALE 0

Independiente - Santoro - Ferreiro, Guzman, Maldonado, Rolan - Acevedo, Mura - Bernao, Prospitti, Rodriguez, Savoy.

Internazionale - Sarti - Burgnich, Guarneri, Picchi, Facchetti - Tagnin, Suárez, Corso - Jair, Mazzola, Peiro

2nd leg. San Siro, Milan, 23-09-1964, 70,000. Referee: Gere, Hungary

INTERNAZIONALE 2 (Mazzola 8, Corso 39)
INDEPENDIENTE 0

Internazionale - Sarti - Burgnich, Guarneri, Picchi, Facchetti - Malatrasi, Suárez, Corso - Jair, Mazzola, Milani

Independiente - Santoro - Ferreiro, Paflik, Maldonado, Decaria - Acevedo, Prospitti, Suarez - Mura, Rodriguez, Savoy

Play-off. Bernabeu, Madrid, 26-09-1964, 45,000. Referee: De Mendibil, Spain

INTERNAZIONALE 1 (Corso 120)
INDEPENDIENTE 0

Internazionale - Sarti - Malatrasi, Guarneri, Picchi, Facchetti - Tagnin, Suárez, Corso - Domenghini, Peiro, Milani. Tr: Herrera

Independiente - Santoro - Guzman, Paflik, Decaria, Maldonado - Acevedo, Prospitti, Suarez - Bernao, Rodriguez, Savoy. Tr: Guidice

1965

1st leg. San Siro, Milan, 8-09-1965, 70,000. Referee: Kreitlein, West Germany

INTERNAZIONALE 3 (Peiro 3, Mazzola 23 61)
INDEPENDIENTE 0

Internazionale - Sarti - Burgnich, Guarneri, Picchi, Facchetti - Bedin, Suárez, Corso - Jair, Mazzola, Peiro

Independiente - Santoro - Pavoni, Guzman, Navarro, Ferreiro - Acevedo, De La Mata, Avalay - Bernao, Rodriguez, Savoy.

2nd leg. Cordero, Avellaneda, 15-09-1965, 70,000. Referee: Yamasaki, Peru

INDEPENDIENTE 0
INTERNAZIONALE 0

Independiente - Santoro - Navarro, Pavoni, Guzman, Ferreiro - Rolan, Mori Bernao, Mura, Avalay, Savoy. Tr: Guidice

Internazionale - Sarti, Burgnich, Guarneri, Picchi, Facchetti - Bedin, Suárez, Corso - Jair, Mazzola, Peiro. Tr: Herrera

1966

1st leg. Centenario, Montevideo, 12-10-1966, 70,000. Referee: Vicuña, Chile

PEÑAROL 2 (Spencer 39 82)
REAL MADRID 0

Peñarol - Mazurkiewicz - Forlan, Lezcano, Varela, Gonzales - Gonçalvez, Cortes, Rocha - Abbadie, Spencer, Joya

Real Madrid - Betancort - Pachín, De Felipe, Zoco, Sanchís - Ruiz, Pirri, Velasquez - Serena, Amancio, Bueno

2nd leg. Bernabeu, Madrid, 26-10-1966, 70,000. Referee: Lo Bello, Italy

REAL MADRID 0
PEÑAROL 2 (Rocha 28, Spencer 37)

Real Madrid - Betancort - Calpe, De Felipe, Zoco, Sanchís - Pirri, Grosso, Velasquez - Serena, Amancio, Gento. Tr: Munoz

Peñarol - Mazurkiewicz - Gonzales, Lezcano, Varela, Caetano - Rocha, Gonçalvez, Cortes - Abbadie, Spencer, Joya. Tr: Maspoli

1967

1st leg. Hampden Park, Glasgow, 18-10-1967, 103,000. Referee: Gardeazabal, Spain

CELTIC 1 (McNeill 67)
RACING CLUB 0

Celtic - Simpson - Craig, McNeill, Gemmell - Murdoch, Clark - Johnstone, Lennox, Wallace, Auld, Hughes

Racing Club - Cejas - Martin, Perfumo, Basile, Diaz - Rulli, Mori, Maschio Cardenas, Rodriguez, Raffo

2nd leg. Mozart y Cuyo, Avellaneda, 1-11-1967, 80,000. Referee: Esteban, Spain
RACING CLUB 2 (Raffo 32, Cardenas 48)
CELTIC 1 (Gemmell 20)
Racing Club - Cejas - Perfumo, Chabay, Basile, Martin - Rulli, Maschio Raffo, Cardoso, Cardenas, Rodriguez
Celtic - Fallon - Craig, Clark, McNeill, Gemmell - Murdoch, O'Neill Johnstone, Wallace, Chalmers, Lennox

Play-off. Centenario, Montevideo, 4-11-1967, 65,000. Referee: Osorio, Paraguay
RACING CLUB 1 (Cardenas 55)
CELTIC 0
Racing Club - Cejas - Perfumo, Chabay, Martin, Basile - Rulli, Maschio Raffo, Cardoso, Cardenas, Rodriguez. Tr. Pizzuti
Celtic - Fallon - Craig, Clark, McNeill, Gemmell - Murdoch, Auld Johnstone, Lennox, Wallace, Hughes. Tr: Stein

1968

1st leg. Bombonera, Buenos Aires, 25-09-1968, 65,000. Referee: Miranda, Paraguay
ESTUDIANTES LP 1 (Conigliaro 28)
MANCHESTER UNITED 0
Estudiantes - Poletti - Malbernat, Aguirre - Suarez, Medina, Pachamé - Madero, Ribaudo, Bilardo - Togneri, Conigliaro, Veron
Manchester United - Stepney - Dunne, Sadler, Foulkes, Burns - Stiles, Crerand, Charlton - Morgan, Law, Best.

2nd leg. Old Trafford, Manchester, 16-10-1968, 60,000. Referee: Machin, France
MANCHESTER UNITED 1 (Morgan 8)
ESTUDIANTES LP 1 (Veron 5)
Manchester United - Stepney - Dunne, Foulkes, Brennan, Sadler - Crerand, Charlton - Morgan, Kidd, Law (Sartori), Best. Tr: Busby
Estudiantes - Poletti - Malbernat, Aguirre - Suarez, Medina, Bilardo - Pachamé, Madero - Togneri, Ribaudo, Conigliaro, Veron (Echecopar). Tr: Zubeldia

1969

1st leg. San Siro, Milan, 8-10-1969, 80,000. Referee: Machin, France
MILAN 3 (Sormani 8 73, Combin 44)
ESTUDIANTES LP 0
Milan - Cudicini - Malatrasi, Anquilletti, Rosato, Schnellinger - Lodetti, Rivera, Fogli - Sormani, Combin (Rognoni), Prati
Estudiantes - Poletti - Suarez, Manera, Madero, Malbernat - Bilardo, Togneri, Echecopar (Ribaudo) - Flores, Conigliaro, Veron

2nd leg. Bombonera, Buenos Aires, 22-10-1969, 65,000. Referee: Massaro, Chile
ESTUDIANTES LP 2 (Conigliaro 43, Suarez 44)
MILAN 1 (Rivera 30)
Estudiantes - Poletti - Manera, Aguirre - Suarez, Madero, Malbernat - Bilardo (Echecopar), Romero, Togneri - Conigliaro, Taverna, Veron. Tr: Zubeldia
Milan - Cudicini - Malatrasi (Maldera), Anquilletti, Rosato, Schnellinger Foglio, Lodetti, Rivera - Sormani, Combin, Prati (Rognoni). Tr: Rocco

1970

1st leg. Bombonera, Buenos Aires, 26-08-1970, 65,000. Referee: Glöckner, East Germany
ESTUDIANTES LP 2 (Echecopar 6, Veron 10)
FEYENOORD 2 (Kindvall 21, Van Hanegem 65)
Estudiantes - Errea - Pagnanini, Spadaro, Togneri, Malbernat - Bilardo (Solari), Pachamé, Echecopar (Rudzki) - Conigliaro, Flores, Veron
Feyenoord - Treytel - Romeyn, Israel, Laseroms, Van Duivenbode - Hasil, Jansen, Van Henegem (Boskamp) - Wery, Kindvall, Moulijn

2nd leg. Feyenoord Stadion, Rotterdam, 9-09-1970, 70,000. Referee: Tejada, Peru
FEYENOORD 1 (Van Deale 65)
ESTUDIANTES LP 0
Feyenoord - Treytel - Romeyn, Israel, Laseroms, Van Duivenbode - Hasil (Boskamp), Van Henegem, Jansen - Wery, Kindvall, Moulijn (Van Deale). Tr: Happel
Estudiantes - Pezzano - Malbernat, Spadaro, Togneri, Medina (Pagnanini) Bilardo, Pachamé, Romero - Conigliaro (Rudzki), Flores, Veron. Tr: Zubeldia

1971

European champions Ajax withrew. Their place was taken by the European Cup Finalists, Panathinaikos.

1st leg. Athens, 15-12-1971, 60,000
PANATHINAIKOS 1 (Filakouris 48)
NACIONAL MONTEVIDEO 1 (Artime 50)

2nd leg. Centenario, Montevideo, 29-12-1971, 70,000
NACIONAL MONTEVIDEO 2 (Artime 34 75)
PANATHINAIKOS 1 (Filakouris 89)

1972

1st leg. Mozart y Cuyo, Avellaneda, 6-09-1972, 65,000. Referee: Bakhramov, Soviet Union
INDEPENDIENTE 1 (Sa 82)
AJAX 1 (Cruyff 6)
Independiente - Santoro - Commisso, Lopez, Sa, Pavoni - Pastoriza, Semenewicz, Raimondo (Bulla) - Balbuena, Maglioni, Mircoli
Ajax - Stuy - Suurbier, Hulshoff, Blankenburg, Krol - Haan, Neeskens, Muhren.G - Swart, Cruyff (Muhren.A), Keizer

2nd leg. Olympisch Stadion, Amsterdam, 28-09-1972, 65,000. Referee: Romey, Paraguay
AJAX 3 (Neeskens 12, Rep 16 78)
INDEPENDIENTE 0
Ajax - Stuy - Suurbier, Hulshoff, Blankenburg, Krol - Haan, Neeskens, Muhren.G - Swart (Rep), Cruyff, Keizer. Tr: Kovacs
Independiente - Santoro - Commisso, Sa, Lopez, Pavoni - Pastoriza, Garisto (Magan), Semenewicz - Balbuena, Maglioni, Mircoli (Bulla)

1973

European champions Ajax withdrew. Their place was taken by the European Cup Finalists, Juventus.

Stadio Olimpico, Rome, 28-11-1973, 35,000
INDEPENDIENTE 1 (Bochini 40)
JUVENTUS 0

1974

European champions Bayern München withdrew. Their place was taken by the European Cup Finalists, Atlético Madrid.

1st leg. Mozart y Cuyo, Buenos Aires, 12-03-1975, 60,000
INDEPENDIENTE 1 (Balbuena 33)
ATLÉTICO MADRID 0

2nd leg. Vicente Calderón, Madrid, 10-04-1975, 45,000
ATLÉTICO MADRID 2 (Irureta 21, Ayala 86)
INDEPENDIENTE 0

1975

Independiente and Bayern München decided not to play each other

1976

1st leg. Olympiastadion, Munich, 23-11-1976, 22,000. Referee: Pestarino, Argentina
BAYERN MÜNCHEN 2 (Müller 80, Kapellmann 83)
CRUZEIRO 0

Bayern München - Maier - Andersson, Beckenbauer, Schwarzenbeck, Horsmann Durnberger, Kapellmann - Torstensson, Hoeness, Müller, Rummenigge
Cruzeiro - Raul - Nelinho, Moraes, Osiris, Vanderlay - Zé Carlos, Piazza, Eduardo - Jairzinho, Palinha, Joãozinho

2nd leg. Mineirao, Belo Horizonte, 21-12-1976, 114,000. Referee: Partridge, England
CRUZEIRO 0
BAYERN MÜNCHEN 0
Cruzeiro - Raul - Moraes, Osiris, Piazza (Eduardo), Nelinho - Vanderlay, Dirceu (Forlan) Zé Carlos - Jairzinho, Palinha, Joãozinho
Bayern München - Maier - Andersson, Beckenbauer, Schwarzenbeck, Horsmann Weiss, Hoeness, Kapellmann - Torstensson, Müller, Rummenigge. Tr: Lattek

1977

European champions Liverpool withdrew. Their place was taken by the European Cup Finalists, Borussia Mönchengladbach.

1st leg. Bombonera, Buenos Aires, 22-03-1978, 50,000
BOCA JUNIORS 2 (Mastrangelo 16, Ribolzi 51)
MÖNCHENGLADBACH 2 (Hannes 24, Bonhof 29)

2nd leg. Wildpark Stadion, Karlsruhe, 26-07-1978, 21,000
MÖNCHENGLADBACH 0
BOCA JUNIORS 3 (Zanabria 2, Mastrangelo 33, Salinas 35)

1978

Boca Juniors and Liverpool decided not to play each other.

1979

European champions, Nottingham Forest, withdrew. Their place was taken by European Cup Finalists, Malmö

1st leg. Malmö Stadion, Malmö, 18-11-1979, 4,000
MALMÖ FF 0
OLIMPIA 1 (Isasi 41)

2nd leg. Manuel Ferreira, Asuncion, 3-03-1980, 35,000
OLIMPIA 2 (Solalinde 40, Michelagnoli 71)
MALMÖ FF 1 (Earlandsson 48)

1980

National Stadium, Tokyo, 11-02-1981, 62,000. Referee: Klein, Israel
NACIONAL MONTEVIDEO 1 (Victorino 10)
NOTTINGHAM FOREST 0
Nacional - Rodriguez - Moreira, Blanco, Enriquez, Gonzalez - Milar, Esparrago, Luzardo, Morales - Bica, Victorino. Tr: Mujica
Nottingham Forest - Shilton - Anderson, Lloyd, Burns, Gray.F - Ponte (Ward), O'Neill, Gray.S, Robertson - Francis, Wallace. Tr: Clough

1981

National Stadium, Tokyo, 13-12-1981, 62,000. Referee: Vasquez, Mexico
FLAMENGO 3 (Nunes 13 41, Adilio 34)
LIVERPOOL 0
Flamengo - Raul - Leandro, Junior, Mozer, Marinho - Adilio, Tita, Andrade Zico, Lico, Nunes. Tr: Paolo Cesar Carpegiani
Liverpool - Grobbelaar - Neal, Lawrenson, Hansen, Thompson - Kennedy.R, Lee, McDermott (Johnson), Souness - Dalglish, Johnston. Tr: Paisley

1982

National Stadium, Tokyo, 12-12-1982, 62,000. Referee: Calderon, Costa Rica
PEÑAROL 2 (Jair 27, Charrua 68)
ASTON VILLA 0
Peñarol - Fernandez - Diogo, Oliveira, Morales, Gutierrez - Saralegui, Bossio, Jair - Ramos (Charrua), Morena, Silva. Tr: Bagnulo
Aston Villa - Rimmer - Jones, Evans, McNaught, Williams - Bremner, Mortimer, Cowans - Shaw, Withe, Morley. Tr: Barton

1983

National Stadium, Tokyo, 11-12-1983, 62,000. Referee: Vautrot, France
GRÊMIO 2 (Renato 37, 93)
HAMBURGER SV 1 (Schröder 85)
Grêmio - Mazaropi - Paulo Roberto, Baidek, De Leon, Magalhaes - Sergio, Paulo Cesar (Caio), Osvaldo (Bonamigo), China - Renato, Tarciso. Tr: Valdir Espinosa
Hamburg - Stein - Wehmeyer, Jakobs, Hieronymus, Schröder - Hartwig, Groh, Rolff, Magath - Wuttke, Hansen. Tr: Happel

1984

National Stadium, Tokyo, 9-12-1984, 62,000. Referee: Romualdo, Brazil
INDEPENDIENTE 1 (Percudani 6)
LIVERPOOL 0
Independiente - Goyen - Villaverde (Monzon), Enrique, Clausen, Trossero Marangoni, Burruchaga, Giusti, Bochini - Percudani, Barberon. Tr: Pastoriza
Liverpool - Grobbelaar - Neal, Kennedy.A, Gillespie, Hansen - Nicol, Dalglish, Molby, Wark (Whelan) - Rush, Johnston. Tr: Fagan

1985

National Stadium, Tokyo, 8-12-1985, 62,000. Referee: Roth, West Germany
JUVENTUS 2 (Platini 63, Laudrup 82)
ARGENTINOS JUNIORS 2 (Ereros 55, Castro 75)
Juventus won 4-2 on penalties
Juventus - Tacconi - Favero, Brio, Scirea (Pioli), Cabrini - Bonini, Manfredonia, Platini - Mauro (Briaschi), Serena, Laudrup. Tr: Trapattoni
Argentinos Juniors - Vidallé - Villalba, Pavoni, Olguin, Domenech - Videla, Batista, Commisso (Corsi) - Castro, Borghi, Ereros (Lopez). Tr: Yudica

1986

National Stadium, Tokyo, 14-12-1986, 62,000. Referee: Martinez-Bazan, Uruguay
RIVER PLATE 1 (Alzamendi 28)
STEAUA BUCURESTI 0
River Plate - Pumpido - Gordillo, Gutierrez, Montenegro, Ruggeri - Alfaro (Sperandio), Alonso, Enrique - Gallego, Alzamendi, Funes. Tr: Vieira
Steaua Bucuresti - Stimgaciu - Iovan, Bumbescu, Belodedici, Barbulescu (Majaru) - Weisenbacher, Stoica, Balint, Balan - Lacatus, Piturca. Tr: Iordanescu

1987

National Stadium, Tokyo, 13-12-1987, 45,000. Referee: Wöhrer, Austria
FC PORTO 2 (Gomes 41, Madjer 108)
PEÑAROL 1 (Viera 80)
Porto - Mlynarczyk - João Pinto, Geraldao, Lima Periera, Inacio - Rui Barros (Quim), Magalhaes, André, Sousa - Gomes, Madjer. Tr: Ivic
Peñarol - Periera - Herrera (Goncalves), Rotti, Trasante, Dominguez Perdomo, Viera, Aguirre, Cabrera (Matosas) - Vidal, Da Silva. Tr: Tabarez

1988

National Stadium, Tokyo, 11-12-1988, 62,000. Referee: Palacios, Colombia
NACIONAL MONTEVIDEO 2 (Ostolaza 7 119)
PSV EINDHOVEN 2 (Romario 75, Koeman 109)
Nacional won 7-6 on penalties
Nacional - Seré - Gómez, De Leon, Revelez, Saldaña - Ostolaza, Vargas (Morán), Lemos, De Lima - Cardaccio (Carreño), Castro. Tr: Fleitas

PSV Eindhoven - Van Breukelen - Gerets, Koot, Koeman, Heintze (Valckx) - Lerby, Van Aerle, Vanenburg (Gillhaus) - Romario, Kieft, Ellerman. Tr: Hiddink

1989

National Staium, Tokyo, 17-12-1989, 62,000. Referee: Fredriksson, Sweden

MILAN 1 (Evani 118)

AT. NACIONAL MEDELLIN 0

Milan - Galli - Baresi, Tassotti, Maldini, Fuser (Evani) - Costacurta, Donadoni, Rijkaard, Ancelotti - Van Basten, Massaro (Simone). Tr: Sacchi

Nacional - Higuita - Escobar, Gómez, Herrera, Cassiani - Pérez, Arango (Restrepo), Alvárez, Arboleda (Uzurriaga) - Garcia, Tréllez. Tr: Maturana

1990

National Stadium, Tokyo, 9-12-1990, 60,000. Referee: Wright, Brazil

MILAN 3 (Rijkaard 43 65, Stroppa 62)

OLIMPIA 0

Milan - Pazzagli - Baresi, Tassotti, Costacurta, Maldini (Galli) - Carbone, Donadoni (Guerreiri), Rijkaard, Stroppa - Gullit, Van Basten. Tr: Sacchi

Olimpia - Almeida - Fernandez, Caceres, Guasch, Ramirez (Chamac) - Suarez, Hoyn (Cubilla), Balbuena, Monzon - Amarilla, Samaniego. Tr: Cubilla

1991

National Stadium, Tokyo, 8-12-1991, 60,000. Referee: Röthlisberger, Switzerland

CRVENA ZVEZDA 3 (Jugovic 19 58, Pancev 72)

COLO COLO 0

Crvena Zvezda - Milojevic - Radinovic, Vasilijevic, Belodedic, Najdoski Jugovic, Stosic, Ratkovic, Savicevic - Mikhailovic, Pancev. Tr: Popovic

Colo Colo - Moron - Garrido, Margas, Ramirez.M, Salvatierra (Dabrowski) Mendoza, Vilches, Barticciotto, Pizarro - Yanez, Martinez (Rubio). Tr: Jozic

1992

National Stadium, Tokyo, 13-12-1992, 60,000. Referee: Loustau, Argentina

SÃO PAULO FC 2 (Rai 26 79)

BARCELONA 1 (Stoichkov 13)

São Paulo - Zetti - Victor, Adilson, Ronaldo, Cafú - Pintado, Ronaldo Luiz, Rai, Toninho Cerezo (Dinho) - Palinha, Muller. Tr: Santana

Barcelona - Zubizarreta - Ferrer, Koeman.R, Witschge - Guardiola, Eusebio, Amor, Bakero (Goikoetxea), Beguiristain (Nadal) - Laudrup.M, Stoichkov. Tr: Cruyff

1993

National Stadium, Tokyo, 12-12-1993, 60,000. Referee: Quiniou, France

SÃO PAULO FC 3 (Palinha 20, Toninho Cerezo 59, Muller 86)

MILAN 2 (Massaro 48, Papin 82)

São Paulo - Zetti - Cafú, Valber, Ronaldo, Doriva - André, Dinho, Leonardo, Toninho Cerezo - Palinha (Juninho), Muller. Tr: Santana

Milan - Rossi - Panucci, Costacurta, Baresi, Maldini - Donadoni, Desailly, Albertini (Tassotti), Massaro - Raducioiu (Orlando), Papin. Tr: Capello

1994

National Stadium, Tokyo, 1-12-1994, 55,000. Referee: Torres, Colombia

VELEZ SARSFIELD 2 (Trotta 50p, Asad 57)

MILAN 0

Velez - Chilavert - Almandoz, Trotta, Sotomayor, Cardozo - Gomez, Basualdo, Bassedas, Pompei - Asad, Flores. Tr: Bianchi

Milan - Rossi - Tassotti, Costacurta, Baresi, Maldini - Donadoni, Albertini, Desailly, Boban - Savicevic (Simone), Massaro (Panucci). Tr: Capello

COPA INTER AMERICA

The Inter-American Cup is an occasional series played between the winners of the Copa Libertadores and the winners of the CONCACAF Cup. The winners of the former have always been more interested in the annual challenge against the European champions and the fixture against their CONCACAF counterparts has suffered as a result. However, the South American champions have on occasion been persuaded to play, mainly when the financial incentives have been good enough. Mexican sides have provided the toughest opposition.

1968

1st leg. Mexico City, 13-02-1969

Toluca 1 (Linares)

Estudiantes LP 2 (Conigliaro, Bilardo)

2nd leg. La Plata, 19-02-1969

Estudiantes LP 1 (Veron)

Toluca 2 (Linares, Albino)

Play-off. Montevideo, 21-02-1969

Estudiantes LP 3 (Conigliaro 2, Flores.E)

Toluca 0

1971

1st leg. Mexico City, 15-07-1972

Cruz Azul 1 (Pulido)

Nacional Montevideo 1 (Mamelli)

2nd leg. Montevideo, 7-11-1972

Nacional Montevideo 2 (Mamelli, Castro.B)

Cruz Azul 1 (Bustos)

1972

1st leg. San Pedro Sula, 17-06-1973

Olimpia 1 (Brand)

Independiente 2 (Semenewicz, Maglioni)

2nd leg. Tegucigalpa, 20-06-1972

Olimpia 0

Independiente 2 (Maglioni, Balbuena)

1974

1st leg. Guatemala City, 24-11-1974

Municipal 0

Independiente 1 (Bochini)

2nd leg. Guatemala City, 26-11-1974

Municipal 1 (Mitrovich)

Independiente 0

Independiente won 4-2 on penalties

1976

1st leg. Caracus, 26-08-1976

Independiente 2 (Bochini, Villaverde)

Atletico Español 2 (Ramirez, Borbolla)

2nd leg. Caracus, 29-08-1976

Independiente 0

Atletico Español 0

Independiente won 4-2 on penalties

1977

1st leg. Buenos Aires, 28-03-1978

Boca Juniors 3 (Salinas 2, Mastrangelo)

América 0

2nd leg. Mexico City, 17-04-1978

América	1	(Kiese)
Boca Juniors	0	

Play-off. Mexico City, 19-04-1978

América	2	(Acevedo, Reynoso)
Boca Juniors	1	(Pavon)

1979

1st leg. San Salvador, 18-02-1980

Deportivo FAS	3	(Casadei 2, Abraham)
Olimpia	3	(Solalinde, Yaluk, Isasi)

2nd leg. Asuncion, 17-03-1980

Olimpia	5	(Aquino, Michelagnoli 2, Ortiz 2)
Deportivo FAS	0	

1980

1st leg. Mexico City, 25-03-1981

UNAM	3	(Sanchez 2, Ferreti)
Nacional Montevideo	1	(Esparrago)

2nd leg. Montevideo, 8-04-1981

Nacional Montevideo	3	(Cabrera.J 2, Cabrera.W)
UNAM	1	(Vargas)

Play-off. Los Angeles, 15-05-1981

UNAM	2	(Ferretti, Vargas)
Nacional Montevideo	1	(Cabrera.J)

1985

Port of Spain, 11-12-1986, 30,000

Argentinos Juniors	1	(Valdez)
Defence Force	0	

1986

1st leg. San Jose, 21-07-1987, 16,000

LD Alajuelense	0	
River Plate	0	

2nd leg. Buenos Aries, 16-08-1987, 20,000

River Plate	3	(Villazan, Funes, Enrique)
LD Alajeulense	0	

1988

1st leg. Tegucigalpa, 5-03-1989, 30,000

Olimpia	1	(Rivera)
Nacional Montevideo	1	(Fonseca)

2nd leg. Montevideo, 30-03-1989, 30,000

Nacional Montevideo	4	(Fonseca, Ostolaza, Noe 2)
Olimpia	0	

1989

1st leg. Medellin, 25-07-1990, 26,000

At. Nacional Medellin	2	(Fajardo, Galeano)
UNAM	0	

2nd leg. Mexico City, 1-08-1990, 15,000

UNAM	1	(Negrete)
At. Nacional Medellin	4	(OG, Restrepo, Galeano, Arango)

1990

1st leg. Asuncion, 1-10-1991, 40,000

Olimpia	1	(Gonzalez)
América	1	(Edu)

2nd leg. Mexico City, 12-10-1991, 60,000

América	2	(Toninho 2)
Olimpia	1	(Gonzalez)

1991

1st leg. Cuauhtemoc, Puebla, 9-09-1992, 8,000

Puebla	1	(Silmar)
Colo Colo	4	(Barticciotto 3, Adomaitis)

2nd leg. Santiago, 22-09-1992, 55,000

Colo Colo	3	(Rubio, Mendoza, Adomaitis)
Puebla	1	(Rotllan)

1993

1st leg. San José, 15-09-1994, 7,000

Deportivo Saprissa	3	(Myers, Fonseca, Wanchoppe)
Universidad Catolica	1	(Vazquez.S)

2nd leg. Santiago, 1-10-1994

Universidad Catolica	5	(Romero, Acosta, Olmos, Ardiman, Barrera)
Deportivo Saprissa	1	(Wanchoppe)

ORDER OF MERIT

	Team	G	S
1	Independiente	3	-
2	Nacional Montevideo	2	1
3	América	2	-
4	Olimpia Asuncion	1	1
	UNAM	1	1
6	Argentinos Juniors	1	-
	Colo Colo	1	-
	Estudiantes LP	1	-
	At. Nacional Medellin	1	-
	River Plate	1	-
	Universidad Catolica	1	-
12	Olimpia Tegucigalpa	-	2
13	*Ten other finalists*	-	1

	G	S
South America	12	3
CONCACAF	3	12

To the end of the 1993 edition

AFRO-ASIAN CLUB CUP

Denied an intercontinental club championship by the Europeans and South Americans, the African (CAF) and Asian (AFC) federations decided to organise their own annual event between the winners of the African Champions Cup and the Asian Champion Teams Cup. Not surprisingly, the African clubs have had much the better of things.

1985	Daewoo Royals	KOR	2-0	FAR Rabat	MOR
1986	Zamalek	EGY	2-0	Furukawa	JAP
1987	Al Ahly	EGY	3-1 1-0	Yomiuri	JAP
1988	Entente Sétif	ALG	2-0 3-1	Al Saad	QAT
1991	Club Africain	TUN	2-1 2-2	Al Hilal	KSA
1992	WAC Casablanca	MOR	0-0 2-0	Pass	IRN
1993	Thai Farmers Bank	THA	1-2 1-0	Zamalek	EGY

AFRO-ASIAN CUP OF NATIONS

At the same time as the Afro-Asian Club Cup was introduced, a tournament for the champions of both continents was also launched. As the Asian Cup is played every four years compared to every two for the African Nations Cup, the competition has had obvious logistical difficulties. One answer has been for the Asian Games winner to stand in to keep up the two-year cycle, and this happened for the 1987 edition, won by South Korea. Since then the tournament has been played only once.

1985	Cameroon	4-1 1-2	Saudi Arabia
1987	South Korea	1-1 4-3p	Egypt
1991	Algeria	1-2 1-0	Iran
1993	Japan	1-0	Côte d'Ivoire

EUROPE

Europe is without question the centre of world football. The game has been played there in its modern form for longer than anywhere else, it boasts six times more registered clubs than both South America and Asia, its nearest rivals, and for many years players from all over the world have migrated to Europe to play their football.

From very austere beginnings in the north of England, competitive club football in Europe has grown into a huge business that occupies many television hours a week, and not just within Europe – one can travel to almost anywhere in the world and still find the odd snippet of Italian, English, German or Spanish league football on the local television stations.

The British, having founded the modern game in 1863, were instrumental in its spread across the continent. Many of the great English amateur teams of the late 19th century, such as the Middlesex Wanderers, undertook continental tours, whilst British residents were always willing to play a game wherever they lived. It is perhaps fortunate that Britain and France, who took to the game from a very early stage, were the major world powers at the time rather than America, for otherwise we might all now be playing American football and baseball instead.

FIFA, at the time of its foundation, was very much a European affair, and it was perhaps this heavy European bias that delayed the formation of UEFA until 1954, fifty years after FIFA's birth. Although many international matches both at club and national level were played before 1954, the real growth of competitive games took place after that date. Tournaments like the British and Scandinavian Championships had been organised by the relevant national associations, whilst special committees were set up to run tournaments like the Mitropa Cup and the International (later Dr Gerö) Cup.

The introduction of the European Champion Clubs Cup, known commonly as the European Cup, was the real turning point in the history of European football, followed in 1958 by the European Nations Cup, later known as the European Football Championship. For the first time a rigid structure for both club and international football was set in place. National teams embarked on two-year playing schedules, alternately for the World Cup and European Championship.

The European Cup, the Cup-Winners Cup and the Fairs/UEFA Cup have also added a much more competitive edge to club football in each country. The chance to play in one of the European competitions is every footballer's ambition, but it also means more revenue for the clubs involved. All these competitions have helped keep European football in the limelight. Players' reputations are gained or lost in them, whilst the European Cup final every May is the highlight of the season's calendar.
Europe has seen many boundary changes in the 20th century but none have had as much impact on football as those of the early 1990s. Many new countries have emerged, others have disappeared. Gone are Czechoslovakia, East Germany and the Soviet Union, who between them won two European Championships and four Olympic titles. Welcomed into the fold, nations as diverse as Slovakia, Moldova and Azerbaijan. Membership of UEFA, which had remained largely constant since the war, stood at 34 in 1989. That number has now risen to 49, the Soviet Union alone spawning 12 new nations.

These changes have visibly affected the structure of European football. The European Championship has been enlarged to cope with the growing numbers. For many years most qualifying groups contained just four teams. Now six is the norm, which means space has to be found in an ever busier calendar for an extra four games. A qualifying competition involving 48 countries to produce just seven qualifiers was not thought worthwhile, and instead of the usual eight finalists, Euro '96 in England will have 16.

Club football has also undergone structural changes, none more so than the European Cup. With 49 champion teams the tournament was likely to become unwieldy, so for the 1994-95 edition only the 24 top-ranked nations were allowed to enter their champions. The others were accommodated in an ever-increasing UEFA Cup.

Another impact from the changes has been on UEFA's role within FIFA. With their say at the FIFA Congress enhanced by having more votes, the Europeans have begun to flex their muscles again in the world game. Yet UEFA also faces difficult problems itself. With an expanding European Community likely to include all the major footballing powers by the end of the decade, the federation's restrictions on the movement of players across national boundaries will almost certainly be challenged.

There is no doubt, however, that Europe will continue to be the central attraction in the world game. Its clubs are richer and its leagues more diverse than anywhere else. New powers will emerge, like Croatia, with sides that can match the best. Others will take longer to make an impact, held back, like Bosnia and Armenia, by political instability and civil war. With a territory that stretches over 5000 kilometres from Iceland in the north-west to Azerbaijan in the south-east, UEFA's Europe is now a continent as diverse as Asia and Africa – but containing the likes of Germany, Italy, England and Spain, no less dominant for it.

THE EUROPEAN GOVERNING BODY

Union of European Football Associations
Chemin de Redoute 54
Case Postale 303
Ch-1260 Nyon
Switzerland
Tel: + 41 22 9944444
Fax: + 41 22 9944488/90

Year of formation: 1954
Registered Clubs: 243,733
Registered Players 18,244,000
Registered referees: 386,392

MEMBERS - 49
Albania – Armenia – Austria – Azerbaijan – Belarus – Belgium – Bulgaria – Croatia – Cyprus – Czech Republic – Denmark – England – Estonia – Faeroe Islands – Finland – France – Georgia – Germany – Greece – Hungary – Iceland – Northern Ireland – Republic of Ireland – Israel – Italy – Latvia – Liechtenstein – Lithuania – Luxembourg – FYR Macedonia – Malta – Moldova – Netherlands – Norway – Poland – Portugal – Romania – Russia – San Marino – Scotland – Slovakia – Slovenia – Spain – Sweden – Switzerland – Turkey – Ukraine – Wales – Yugoslavia

NON MEMBERS - 11
Åland – Alderney – Andorra – Bosnia – Gibraltar – Greenland – Guernsey – Isle of Man – Jersey – Monaco – Vatican

Presidents of UEFA

Ebbe Schwartz	Denmark	1954-62
Gustav Wiederkehr	Switzerland	1962-72
Artemio Franchi	Italy	1972-83
Jacques Georges	France	1983-90
Lennart Johannsson	Sweden	1990

EUROPEAN FOOTBALLER OF THE YEAR

From 'France Football'

1956

1	Stanley Matthews	Blackpool	ENG	47
2	Alfredo Di Stéfano	Real Madrid	ESP	44
3	Raymond Kopa	Stade de Reims	FRA	33
4	Ferenc Puskas	Honved	HUN	32
5	Lev Yashin	Dynamo Moskva	URS	19
6	Jozsef Bozsik	Honved	HUN	15
7	Ernst Ocwirk	Sampdoria	AUT	9
8	Sandor Kocsis	Honved	HUN	6
9	Ivan Kolev	CDNA Sofia	BUL	4
	Billy Wright	Wolverhampton Wanderers	ENG	4
	Thadée Cisowski	Racing Club Paris	FRA	4

1957

1	Alfredo Di Stéfano	Real Madrid	ESP	72
2	Billy Wright	Wolverhampton Wndrs	ENG	19
3	Raymond Kopa	Real Madrid	FRA	16
	Duncan Edwards	Manchester United	ENG	16
5	Lazslo Kubala	Barcelona	ESP	15
6	John Charles	Juventus	WAL	14
7	Edward Strelitsov	Torpedo Moskva	URS	12
8	Tommy Taylor	Manchester United	ENG	10
9	Jozsef Bozsik	Honved	HUN	9
	Igor Netto	Dynamo Moskva	URS	9

1958

1	Raymond Kopa	Real Madrid	FRA	71
2	Helmut Rahn	Rot-Weiss Essen	FRG	40
3	Just Fontaine	Stade de Reims	FRA	23
4	Kurt Hamrin	Fiorentina	SWE	15
	John Charles	Juventus	WAL	15
6	Billy Wright	Wolverhampton Wndrs	ENG	9
7	Johnny Haynes	Fulham	ENG	7
8	Harry Gregg	Manchester United	IRE	6
	Horst Szymaniak	Wuppertaler SV	FRG	6
	Nils Liedholm	Milan	SWE	6

1959

1	Alfredo Di Stéfano	Real Madrid	ESP	80
2	Raymond Kopa	Stade de Reims	FRA	42
3	John Charles	Juventus	WAL	24
4	Luis Suárez	Barcelona	ESP	22
5	Agne Simonsson	Örgryte IS Göteborg	SWE	20
6	Lajos Tichy	Honved	HUN	18
7	Ferenc Puskas	Real Madrid	HUN	16
8	Francisco Gento	Real Madrid	ESP	12
9	Helmut Rahn	1.FC Köln	FRG	11
10	Horst Szymaniak	Karlsruher SC	FRG	8

1960

1	Luis Suárez	Barcelona	ESP	54
2	Ferenc Puskas	Real Madrid	HUN	37
3	Uwe Seeler	Hamburger SV	FRG	33
4	Alfredo Di Stéfano	Real Madrid	ESP	32
5	Lev Yashin	Dynamo Moskva	URS	28
6	Raymond Kopa	Stade de Reims	FRA	14
7	John Charles	Juventus	WAL	11
	Bobby Charlton	Manchester United	ENG	11
9	Omar Sivori	Juventus	ITA	9
	Horst Szymaniak	Karlsruher SC	FRG	9

1961

1	Omar Sivori	Juventus	ITA	46
2	Luis Suarez	Internazionale	ESP	40
3	Johnny Haynes	Fulham	ENG	22
4	Lev Yashin	Dynamo Moskva	URS	21
5	Ferenc Puskas	Real Madrid	ESP	16
6	Alfredo di Stéfano	Real Madrid	ESP	13
	Uwe Seeler	Hamburger SV	FRG	13
8	John Charles	Juventus	WAL	10
9	Francisco Gento	Real Madrid	ESP	8
10	Seven Players on 5 votes			

1962

1	Josef Masopust	Dukla Praha	TCH	65
2	Eusébio	Benfica	POR	
3	Karl-Heinz Schnellinger	1.FC Köln	FRG	
4	Dragoslav Sekularac	Crvena Zvezda Beograd	YUG	
5	Joseph Jurion	RSC Anderlecht	BEL	
6	Gianni Rivera	Milan	ITA	
7	Jimmy Greaves	Tottenham Hotspur	ENG	
8	John Charles	Roma	WAL	
	Milan Galic	Partizan Beograd	YUG	
10	Janos Gorocs	Ujpesti Dózsa	HUN	

1963

1	Lev Yashin	Dynamo Moskva	URS	73
2	Gianni Rivera	Milan	ITA	56
3	Jimmy Greaves	Tottenham Hotspur	ENG	51
4	Denis Law	Manchester United	SCO	45
5	Eusébio	Benfica	POR	19
6	Karl-Heinz Schnellinger	Mantova	FRG	16
7	Uwe Seeler	Hamburger SV	FRG	9
8	Luis Suárez	Internazionale	ESP	5
	Giovanni Trapattoni	Milan	ITA	5
	Bobby Charlton	Manchester United	ENG	5

1964

1	Denis Law	Manchester United	SCO	61
2	Luis Suárez	Internazionale	ESP	43
3	Amancio	Real Madrid	ESP	38
4	Eusébio	Benfica	POR	31
5	Paul Van Himst	RSC Anderlecht	BEL	28
6	Jimmy Greaves	Tottenhan Hotspur	ENG	19
7	Mario Corso	Internazionale	ITA	17
8	Lev Yashin	Dynamo Moskva	URS	15
9	Gianni Rivera	Milan	ITA	14
10	Valerie Voronin	Torpedo Moskva	URS	13

1965

	Player	Club	Country
1	Eusébio	Benfica	POR
2	Giacinto Facchetti	Internazionale	ITA
3	Luis Suárez	Internazionale	ITA
4	Paul Van Himst	RSC Anderlecht	BEL
5	Bobby Charlton	Manchester United	ENG
6	Florian Albert	Ferencváros	HUN
7	Gianni Rivera	Milan	ITA
8	Georgi Asparuchov	Levski Sofia	BUL
	Sandro Mazzola	Internazionale	ITA
	Valery Voronin	Torpedo Moskva	URS

1966

	Player	Club	Country	Points
1	Bobby Charlton	Manchester United	ENG	81
2	Eusébio	Benfica	POR	80
3	Franz Beckenbauer	Bayern München	FRG	59
4	Bobby Moore	West Ham United	ENG	31
5	Florian Albert	Ferencváros	HUN	23
6	Ferenc Bene	Ujpesti Dózsa	HUN	8
7	Lev Yashin	Dynamo Moskva	URS	6
	Alan Ball	Everton	ENG	6
	János Farkas	Vasas Budapest	HUN	6
10	José Torres	Benfica	POR	5

1967

	Player	Club	Country	Points
1	Florian Albert	Ferencváros	HUN	68
2	Bobby Charlton	Manchester United	ENG	40
3	Jimmy Johnstone	Glasgow Celtic	SCO	39
4	Franz Beckenbauer	Bayern München	FRG	37
5	Eusébio	Benfica	POR	26
6	Tommy Gemmell	Glasgow Celtic	SCO	21
7	Gerd Müller	Bayern München	FRG	19
8	George Best	Manchester United	NIR	18
9	Igor Chislenko	Torpedo Moskva	URS	9
10	3 players on 8 points			

1968

	Player	Club	Country	Points
1	George Best	Manchester United	NIR	61
2	Bobby Charlton	Manchester United	ENG	53
3	Dragan Dzajic	Crvena Zvezda Beograd	YUG	46
4	Franz Beckenbauer	Bayern München	FRG	36
5	Giacinto Facchetti	Internazionale	ITA	30
6	Gigi Riva	Cagliari	ITA	22
7	Amancio	Real Madrid	ESP	21
8	Eusébio	Benfica	POR	15
9	Gianni Rivera	Milan	ITA	13
10	Jimmy Greaves	Tottenham Hotspur	ENG	8
	Pirri	Real Madrid	ESP	8

1969

	Player	Club	Country	Points
1	Gianni Rivera	Milan	ITA	83
2	Gigi Riva	Cagliari	ITA	79
3	Gerd Müller	Bayern München	FRG	38
4	Johan Cruyff	Ajax	HOL	30
	Ove Kindvall	Feyenoord	SWE	30
6	George Best	Manchester United	NIR	21
7	Franz Beckenbauer	Bayern München	FRG	18
8	Pierino Prati	Milan	ITA	17
9	Peter Jekov	CSKA Sofia	BUL	14
10	Jackie Charlton	Leeds United	ENG	10

1970

	Player	Club	Country	Points
1	Gerd Müller	Bayern München	FRG	77
2	Bobby Moore	West Ham United	ENG	69
3	Gigi Riva	Cagliari	ITA	65
4	Franz Beckenbauer	Bayern München	FRG	32
5	Wolfgang Overath	1.FC Köln	FRG	29
6	Dragan Dzajic	Crvena Zvezda Beograd	YUG	24
7	Johan Cruyff	Ajax	HOL	
8	Gordon Banks	Stoke City	ENG	8
	Sandro Mazzola	Internazionale	ITA	8
10	4 players on 7 points			

1971

	Player	Club	Country	Points
1	Johan Cruyff	Ajax	HOL	116
2	Sandro Mazzola	Internazionale	ITA	57
3	George Best	Manchester United	NIR	56
4	Gunter Netzer	Bor. Mönchengladbach	FRG	30
5	Franz Beckenbauer	Bayern München	FRG	27
6	Gerd Müller	Bayern München	FRG	18
	Josip Skoblar	Olympique Marseille	YUG	18
8	Martin Chivers	Tottenham Hotspur	ENG	13
9	Piet Keizer	Ajax	HOL	9
10	Ferenc Bene	Ujpesti Dózsa	HUN	7
	Bobby Moore	West Ham United	ENG	7

1972

	Player	Club	Country	Points
1	Franz Beckenbauer	Bayern München	FRG	81
2	Gerd Müller	Bayern München	FRG	79
	Gunter Netzer	Bor. Mönchengladbach	FRG	79
4	Johan Cruyff	Ajax	HOL	73
5	Piet Keizer	Ajax	HOL	13
6	Kazimierz Deyna	Legia Warszawa	POL	6
7	Gordon Banks	Stoke City	ENG	4
	Barry Hulshoff	Ajax	HOL	4
	Wlodzmierz Lubánski	Gornik Zabrze	POL	4
	Bobby Moore	West Ham United	ENG	4

1973

	Player	Club	Country	Points
1	Johan Cruyff	Barcelona	HOL	96
2	Dino Zoff	Juventus	ITA	47
3	Gerd Müller	Bayern München	FRG	44
4	Franz Beckenbauer	Bayern München	FRG	30
5	Billy Bremner	Leeds United	SCO	22
6	Kazimierz Deyna	Legia Warszawa	POL	16
7	Eusébio	Benfica	POR	14
8	Gianni Rivera	Milan	ITA	12
9	Ralf Edström	PSV Eindhoven	SWE	11
	Uli Hoeness	Bayern München	FRG	11

1974

	Player	Club	Country	Points
1	Johan Cruyff	Barcelona	HOL	116
2	Franz Beckenbauer	Bayern München	FRG	105
3	Kazimierz Deyna	Legia Warszawa	POL	35
4	Paul Breitner	Real Madrid	FRG	32
5	Johan Neeskens	Barcelona	HOL	21
6	Grzegorz Lato	Stal Mielec	POL	16
7	Gerd Müller	Bayern München	FRG	14
8	Robert Gadocha	Legia Warszawa	POL	11
9	Billy Bremner	Leeds United	SCO	9
10	Ralf Edström	PSV Eindhoven	SWE	4
	Jurgen Sparwasser	1.FC Magdeburg	GDR	4
	Berti Vogts	Bor. Mönchengladbach	FRG	4

1975

	Player	Club	Country	Points
1	Oleg Blokhin	Dynamo Kiev	URS	122
2	Franz Beckenbauer	Bayern München	FRG	42
3	Johan Cruyff	Barcelona	HOL	27
4	Berti Vogts	Bor. Mönchengladbach	FRG	25
5	Sepp Maier	Bayern München	FRG	20
6	Ruud Geels	Ajax	HOL	18
7	Jupp Heynckes	Bor. Mönchengladbach	FRG	17
8	Paul Breitner	Real Madrid	FRG	14
9	Colin Todd	Derby County	ENG	12
10	Dudu Georgescu	Dinamo Bucuresti	RUM	11

1976

	Player	Club	Country	Points
1	Franz Beckenbauer	Bayern München	FRG	91
2	Robby Rensenbrink	RSC Anderlecht	HOL	75
3	Ivo Viktor	Dukla Praha	TCH	52
4	Kevin Keegan	Liverpool	ENG	32
5	Michel Platini	AS Nancy	FRA	19
6	Anton Ondrus	Slovan Bratislava	TCH	16
7	Johan Cruyff	Barcelona	HOL	12

	Ivan Curkovic	AS Saint Étienne	YUG	12
9	Rainer Bonhof	Bor. Mönchengladbach	FRG	9
	Marian Masny	Slovan Bratislava	TCH	9
	Gerd Müller	Bayern München	FRG	9

1977

1	Allan Simonsen	Bor. Mönchengladbach	DEN	74
2	Kevin Keegan	Liverpool	ENG	71
3	Michel Platini	AS Nancy	FRA	70
4	Roberto Bettega	Juventus	ITA	39
5	Johan Cruyff	Barcelona	HOL	23
6	Klaus Fischer	Schalke 04	FRG	21
7	Tibor Nyilasi	Ferencváros	HUN	13
	Robby Rensenbrink	RSC Anderlecht	HOL	13
9	Dudu Georgescu	Dinamo Bucuresti	RUM	6
10	Steve Heighway	Liverpool	ENG	5
	Emlyn Hughes	Liverpool	ENG	5
	Berti Vogts	Bor. Mönchengladbach	FRG	5

1978

1	Kevin Keegan	Hamburger SV	ENG	87
2	Hans Krankl	SK Rapid Wien	AUT	81
3	Robby Rensenbrink	RSC Anderlecht	HOL	50
4	Roberto Bettega	Juventus	ITA	28
5	Paolo Rossi	Lanerossi-Vicenza	ITA	23
6	Ronnie Hellstrom	1.FC Kaiserslautern	SWE	20
	Ruud Krol	Ajax	HOL	20
8	Kenny Dalglish	Liverpool	SCO	10
	Allan Simonsen	Bor. Mönchengladbach	DEN	10
10	Peter Shilton	Nottingham Forest	ENG	9

1979

1	Kevin Keegan	Hamburger SV	ENG	118
2	Karl-Heinz Rummenigge	Bayern München	FRG	52
3	Ruud Krol	Ajax	HOL	41
4	Manni Kaltz	Hamburger SV	FRG	27
5	Michel Platini	AS Saint Étienne	FRA	23
6	Paolo Rossi	Perugia	ITA	16
7	Liam Brady	Arsenal	IRL	13
	Trevor Francis	Nottingham Forest	ENG	13
9	Zbigniew Boniek	Wisla Krakow	POL	9
	Zdenek Nehoda	Dukla Praha	TCH	9

1980

1	Karl-Heinz Rummenigge	Bayern München	FRG	122
2	Bernd Schuster	Barcelona	FRG	34
3	Michel Platini	AS Saint Étienne	FRA	33
4	Wilfred Van Moer	SK Beveren	BEL	27
5	Jan Ceulemans	Club Brugge	BEL	20
6	Horst Hrubesch	Hamburger SV	FRG	18
7	Herbert Prohaska	Internazionale	AUT	16
8	Hansi Müller	VfB Stuttgart	FRG	11
	Liam Brady	Juventus	IRL	11
10	Manni Kaltz	Hamburger SV	FRG	10

1981

1	Karl-Heinz Rummenigge	Bayern München	FRG	106
2	Paul Breitner	Bayern München	FRG	64
3	Bernd Schuster	Barcelona	FRG	39
4	Michel Platini	AS Saint Étienne	FRA	36
5	Oleg Blokhin	Dynamo Kiev	URS	14
6	Dino Zoff	Juventus	ITA	13
7	Ramas Shengelia	Dynamo Tbilisi	URS	10
8	Alexander Chivadze	Dynamo Tbilisi	URS	9
9	Liam Brady	Juventus	IRL	7
	John Wark	Ipswich Town	SCO	7

1982

1	Paolo Rossi	Juventus	ITA	115
2	Alain Giresse	Girondins Bordeaux	FRA	64
3	Zbigniew Boniek	Juventus	POL	53
4	Karl-Heinz Rummenigge	Bayern München	FRG	51
5	Bruno Conti	Roma	ITA	48
6	Rinat Dasayev	Spartak Moskva	URS	17
7	Pierre Littbarski	1.FC Köln	FRG	10
8	Dino Zoff	Juventus	ITA	9
9	Michel Platini	Juventus	FRA	5
10	Bernd Schuster	Barcelona	FRG	4

1983

1	Michel Platini	Juventus	FRA	110
2	Kenny Dalglish	Liverpool	SCO	26
3	Allan Simonsen	Vejle BK	DEN	25
4	Gordon Strachan	Aberdeen	SCO	24
5	Felix Magath	Hamburger SV	FRG	20
6	Rinat Dasayev	Spartak Moskva	URS	15
	Jean-Marie Pfaff	Bayern München	BEL	15
8	Jesper Olsen	Ajax	DEN	14
	Karl-Heinz Rummenigge	Bayern München	FRG	14
10	Bryan Robson	Manchester United	ENG	13

1984

1	Michel Platini	Juventus	FRA	128
2	Jean Tigana	Girondins Bordeaux	FRA	57
3	Preben Elkjaer-Larsen	Hellas Verona	DEN	48
4	Ian Rush	Liverpool	WAL	44
5	Chalana	Girondins Bordeaux	POR	18
6	Graeme Souness	Sampdoria	SCO	16
7	Harald Schumacher	1.FC Köln	FRG	12
8	Karl-Heinz Rummenigge	Internazionale	FRG	10
9	Alain Giresse	Girondins Bordeaux	FRA	9
10	Bryan Robson	Manchester United	ENG	7

1985

1	Michel Platini	Juventus	FRA	127
2	Preben Elkjaer-Larsen	Hellas Verona	DEN	71
3	Bernd Schuster	Barcelona	FRG	46
4	Michael Laudrup	Juventus	DEN	14
5	Karl-Heinz Rummenigge	Internazionale	FRG	13
6	Zbigniew Boniek	Roma	POL	12
7	Oleg Protasov	Dnepr Dnepropetrovsk	URS	10
8	Hans-Peter Briegel	Hellas Verona	FRG	9
9	Rinat Dasayev	Spartak Moskva	URS	8
	Bryan Robson	Manchester United	ENG	8

1986

1	Igor Belanov	Dynamo Kiev	URS	84
2	Gary Lineker	Barcelona	ENG	62
3	Emilio Butragueño	Real Madrid	ESP	59
4	Manuel Amoros	AS Monaco	FRA	22
	Preben Elkjaer-Larsen	Hellas Verona	DEN	22
6	Ian Rush	Liverpool	WAL	20
	Alexander Zavarov	Dynamo Kiev	URS	20
8	Marco Van Basten	Ajax	HOL	10
	Helmut Ducadam	Steaua Bucuresti	ROM	10
10	Alessandro Altobelli	Internazionale	ITA	9

1987

1	Ruud Gullit	Milan	HOL	106
2	Paolo Futre	Atlético Madrid	POR	91
3	Emilio Butragueño	Real Madrid	ESP	61
4	Gonzales Michel	Real Madrid	ESP	29
5	Gary Lineker	Barcelona	ENG	13
6	John Barnes	Liverpool	ENG	10
	Marco Van Basten	Milan	HOL	10
8	Gianluca Vialli	Sampdoria	ITA	9
9	Bryan Robson	Manchester United	ENG	7
10	Klaus Allofs	Olympique Marseille	FRG	6
	Glen Hysen	Fiorentina	SWE	6

1988

1	Marco Van Basten	Milan	HOL	129
2	Ruud Gullit	Milan	HOL	88
3	Frank Rijkaard	Milan	HOL	45

4	Alexei Mikhailichenko	Dynamo Kiev	URS	41
5	Ronald Koeman	PSV Eindhoven	HOL	39
6	Lothar Matthäus	Bayern München	FRG	10
7	Gianluca Vialli	Sampdoria	ITA	7
8	Franco Baresi	Milan	ITA	5
	Jurgen Klinsmann	VfB Stuttgart	FRG	5
	Alexander Zavarov	Juventus	URS	5

1989

1	Marco Van Basten	Milan	HOL	119
2	Franco Baresi	Milan	HOL	80
3	Frank Rijkaard	Milan	HOL	43
4	Lothar Matthäus	Internazionale	FRG	24
5	Peter Shilton	Derby County	ENG	22
6	Dragan Stojkovic	Crvena Zvezda Beograd	YUG	19
7	Ruud Gullit	Milan	HOL	16
8	Georghe Hagi	Steaua Bucuresti	ROM	11
	Jürgen Klinsmann	Internazionale	FRG	11
10	Michel Preud'homme	KV Mechelen	BEL	10
	Jean-Pierre Papin	Olympique Marseille	FRA	10

1990

1	Lothar Matthäus	Internazionale	FRG	137
2	Salvadore Schillaci	Juventus	ITA	84
3	Andreas Brehme	Internazionale	FRG	68
4	Paul Gascoigne	Tottenham Hotspur	ENG	43
5	Franco Baresi	Milan	ITA	37
6	Jurgen Klinsmann	Internazionale	FRG	12
	Enzo Scifo	AJ Auxerre	BEL	12
8	Roberto Baggio	Juventus	ITA	8
9	Frank Rijkaard	Milan	HOL	7
10	Guido Buchwald	VfB Stuttgart	FRG	6

1991

1	Jean-Pierre Papin	Olympique Marseille	FRA	141
2	Darko Pancev	Crvena Zvezda Beograd	YUG	42
	Dejan Savicevic	Crvena Zvezda Beograd	YUG	42
	Lothar Matthäus	Internazionale	FRG	42
5	Robert Prosinecki	Real Madrid	YUG	34
6	Gary Lineker	Tottenham Hotspur	ENG	33
7	Gianluca Vialli	Sampdoria	ITA	18
8	Miodrag Belodedic	Crvena Zvezda Beograd	YUG	15
9	Mark Hughes	Manchester United	WAL	12
10	Chris Waddle	Olympique Marseille	ENG	11

1992

1	Marco Van Basten	Milan	HOL	98
2	Hristo Stoichkov	Barcelona	BUL	80
3	Dennis Bergkamp	Ajax	HOL	53
4	Thomas Hässler	Roma	GER	42
5	Peter Schmeichel	Manchester United	DAN	41
6	Brian Laudrup	Fiorentina	DAN	32
7	Michael Laudrup	Barcelona	DAN	22
8	Ronald Koeman	Barcelona	HOL	14
9	Stéphane Chapuisat	Borussia Dortmund	SUI	10
10	Frank Rijkaard	Milan	HOL	8
	Enzo Scifo	Torino	BEL	8

1993

1	Roberto Baggio	Juventus	ITA	142
2	Dennis Bergkamp	Internazionale	HOL	83
3	Eric Cantona	Manchester United	FRA	34
4	Alen Boksic	Lazio	CRO	29
5	Michael Laudrup	Barcelona	DAN	27
6	Franco Baresi	Milan	ITA	24
7	Paolo Maldini	Milan	ITA	19
8	Emil Kostadinov	FC Porto	BUL	11
9	Stéphane Chapuisat	Borussia Dortmund	SUI	9
	Ryan Giggs	Manchester United	WAL	9

1994

1	Hristo Stoichkov	Barcelona	BUL	210
2	Roberto Baggio	Juventus	ITA	136
3	Paolo Maldini	Milan	ITA	109
4	Tomas Brolin	Parma	SWE	68
	Georghe Hagi	Barcelona	ROM	68
6	Jürgen Klinsmann	Tottenham	GER	43
7	Thomas Ravelli	IFK Göteborg	SWE	21
8	Jari Litmanen	Ajax	FIN	12
9	Marcel Desailly	Milan	FRA	8
	Dejan Savicevic	Milan	YUG	8

THE EUROPEAN FOOTBALL CHAMPIONSHIP

1960	Soviet Union	2-1	Yugoslavia
1964	Spain	2-1	Soviet Union
1968	Italy	1-1 2-0	Yugoslavia
1972	West Germany	3-0	Soviet Union
1976	Czechoslovakia	2-2 5-4p	West Germany
1980	West Germany	2-1	Belgium
1984	France	2-0	Spain
1988	Holland	2-0	Soviet Union
1992	Denmark	2-0	Germany

Europe was the last continent to organise a championship for its members, just pipped to the post by Africa and Asia but some way behind both South and Central America. This seems odd given the opportunities that were available before it finally got underway in 1958. Odder still was the fact that West Germany, Italy, Belgium, Holland, Switzerland, Sweden, Finland, Luxembourg and the four British nations did not enter the first edition. Scotland and West Germany did not enter the second edition either.

Originally called the European Nations Cup, the trophy was named after Henri Delaunay, the French football administrator and former General Secretary of UEFA, whose idea the competition was. From humble beginnings the championship has grown steadily and is now without question the number two event in football after the World Cup.

The first two editions were played entirely on a knockout basis. Since then qualifying groups have been added and the final tournament has grown from having an initial four teams, through eight (1980-92) to the present sixteen (from 1996). For many years it was actually harder to qualify for the finals of the European Championship than it was for the World Cup, and the likes of Italy and Spain have missed out on more than one occasion. The list of winners, too, reflects this diversity. Only the Germans have won it more than once.

The early dominant powers were the countries of the Eastern bloc. Three of the four semi-finalists in 1960 were from behind the Iron Curtain, and the biggest of them all, the Soviet Union, won, beating Yugoslavia 2-1 in the final. France hosted the final stages, but despite home advantage lost a thrilling semi-final 5-4 to Yugoslavia.

The Soviet Union again reached the final four years later but lost to Spain. In 1960 the Spanish had pulled out of their quarter-final tie with the Soviets, who were regarded as politically unsuitable by the right-wing Franco government. Thankfully there were no such problems the second time around as Spain had been chosen to host the final tournament. Home advantage was made to count with a 2-1 extra-time victory over Hungary in the semi-finals and there was a repeat scoreline in the final against the Soviets.

The 1968 tournament saw the introduction of eight qualifying groups. Scotland at last entered, as did West Germany. The biggest surprise was the elimination of Portugal by Bulgaria, but the Bulgarians then lost in the quarter-finals to Italy, who were awarded the hosting of the final tournament. Italy's semi-final victory over the Soviet Union was somewhat fortuitous in that after a 0-0 draw, they won on the toss of a coin. Meanwhile, the world champions England were losing to a late goal against Yugoslavia and had to be content with a third-place victory over the Soviets. A replay was needed in the final but the Italians eventually triumphed, leaving the poor Yugoslavs to collect yet another runners-up medal.

The 1972 tournament again saw the eastern Europeans put in a strong challenge, and again the Soviet Union made it to the final. This was West Germany's tournament, however. They were at their very best and reached the final by beating England in the quarter-finals and Belgium in the semis. The Belgians had been chosen to host the tournament after beating Italy, but they were no match for the Germans. Gerd Müller was in devastating form, and his goals sealed the title for his team.

Neither Italy nor England made it past the qualifying stage in 1976, but as the tournament progressed it all looked set for a repeat of the World Cup final of two years previously between West Germany and Holland. Czechoslovakia, England's conquerors in the qualifying round, put a spanner in the works by defeating the Dutch in the semi-finals with two very late goals in extra time. West Germany also needed two goals in the second period of extra time to beat the hosts Yugoslavia, who earlier in the match had looked as if they would run away with the game. In the final the Germans left it very late again to score their equalising goal but lost in the penalty shoot-out – the first ever in the European Championships – to the Czechs, who were crowned as Europe's unlikely champions. In five tournaments, five different nations had won Europe's top prize.

A new format was adopted for the 1980 championship. The hosts, Italy, were chosen at the outset, instead of after the quarter-final round as had been the practice, and were given a bye to the final tournament. The quarter-finals were done away with, the seven group winners now proceeding to a final tournament consisting of two groups of four, the winners of which would contest the final. The Soviet Union was the surprise absentee, and Yugoslavia did not make the trip either. Greece made their first ever appearance in the finals of a major tournament, and West Germany became the only nation to win the competition twice when they beat the surprise package, Belgium, 2-1 in the final. Hrubesch's winning goal came two minutes from time.

The group matches were marred by violence on the terraces involving the English supporters, and it was to the great relief of the authorities that England were knocked out in the first round. They also headed the list of big names failing to qualify for the 1984 tournament, for which France were chosen as hosts. New stadia were built and old ones refurbished in preparation, and in the end it proved worthwhile as the public were treated to the best ever championship. The French, in particular, were brilliant, and their victory partially compensated for their semi-final loss in the 1982 World Cup. Michel Platini was inspired and his nine goals in five matches were the crucial factor in the hosts' success. It was Platini who scored the opening goal in the final, which France won 2-0, and the winner against Portugal in the dramatic semi-final at Marseille, one of the great matches of all time. Denmark also shone, but failed in a penalty shoot-out against Spain in the other semi-final.

The Dutch made it seven different winners in eight tournaments with victory in West Germany in 1988. France were notable absentees, but England were back, as were the Italians, whilst the Republic of Ireland made a surprise first appearance and exceeded all expectations. Despite being among the favourites, England were a massive disappointment and it was the Dutch and the Soviet Union who qualified from group 2 to meet West Germany and Italy respectively in the semi-finals. Marco Van Basten, the star of the tournament, put the hosts out with two minutes remaining in the semi-final and was on target again in the final against the Soviets. Playing football reminiscent of their golden age in the 1970s, Holland thrilled the crowd in Munich with their display, and at last won an international honour.

Four years later, in perhaps the most extraordinary championships ever, Denmark, to the surprise of everyone, won the tournament in neighbouring Sweden, having failed initially to qualify for the finals - Yugoslavia were expelled and their place given to the Danes, who had finished second to them in their qualifying group. Italy and Spain were absent and it was not a good tournament for the established powers as both France and England bowed out in the first round, while the Germans might easily have joined them. Holland, after a fine first round, fell under the Danish spell and were knocked out in the semi-finals. No-one believed that the injury-hit Danes could repeat the feat against Germany in the final, but they did. In a splendid display of defence and counter-attack, they ran out 2-0 winners.

1960

1ST EDITION

PRELIMINARY ROUND

Rep. Ireland	2-0 0-4	**Czechoslovakia**

FIRST ROUND

France	7-1 1-1	Greece
Soviet Union	3-1 1-0	Hungary
Romania	3-0 0-2	Turkey
Norway	0-1 2-5	**Austria**
Yugoslavia	2-0 1-1	Bulgaria
East Germany	0-2 2-3	**Portugal**
Denmark	2-2 1-5	**Czechoslovakia**
Poland	2-4 0-3	**Spain**

QUARTER-FINALS

Spain refused to travel to the Soviet Union and so withdrew

1st leg. Stadionul 23 August, Bucharest, 22-05-1960, 100,000
Romania 0
Czechoslovakia 2 (Masopust 9, Bubník 45)

2nd leg. Tehelné PoleBratislava, 29-05-1960, 45,000
Czechoslovakia 3 (Buberník I 15, Bubník 18)
Romania 0

1st leg. Colombes, Paris, 13-12-1959, 43,000
France 5 (Fontaine 7 18 70, Vincent 38 82)
Austria 2 (Horak 40, Pichler 65)

2nd leg. Praterstadion, Vienna, 27-03-1960, 38,000
Austria 2 (Nemec 26, Probst 64)
France 4 (Marcel 46, Rahis 59, Heutte 77, Kopa 83)

1st leg. Estádio Nacional, Lisbon, 8-05-1960, 50,000
Portugal 2 (Santana 30, Matateu 70)
Yugoslavia 1 (Kostic 81)

2nd leg. JNA Stadion, Belgrade, 22-05-1960, 55,000
Yugoslavia 5 (Sekularac 8, Cebinac 45, Galic 79, Kostic 50 88)
Portugal 1 (Cavém 29)

SEMI-FINALS

Vélodrome, Marseille, 6-07-1960, 23,000
Soviet Union 3 (Ivanov.V 35 58, Ponedelnik 64)
Czechoslovakia 0

Parc des Princes, Paris, 6-07-1990, 26,000
Yugoslavia 5 (Galic 11, Zanetic 55, Knez 75, Jerkovic 77 78)
France 4 (Vincent 12, Heutte 43 62, Wisnieski 52)

3RD PLACE

Vélodrome, Marseille, 9-07-1960, 9,000
Czechoslovakia 2 (Bubernik 58, Pavlovic 88)
France 0

FINAL

Parc des Princes, Paris, 10-07-1960, 18,000. Referee: Ellis, England
SOVIET UNION 2 (Metreveli 49, Ponedelnik 113)
YUGOSLAVIA 1 (Galic 41)

Soviet Union - Yashin - Tchekeli, Maslenkin, Kroutikov - Voinov, Netto, Metreveli, Ivanov.V, Ponedelnik, Bubukin, Meshki. Tr: Katchalin

Yugoslavia - Vidinic - Durkovic, Miladinovic, Jusufi - Zanetic, Perusic Sekularac, Jerkovic, Galic, Matus, Kostic. Tr: Ciric

1964

2ND EDITION

FIRST ROUND

Spain	6-0 1-3	Romania
Poland	0-2 0-2	**Nth. Ireland**
Denmark	6-1 3-1	Malta
East Germany	2-1 1-1	Czechoslovakia
Hungary	3-1 1-1	Wales
Italy	6-0 1-0	Turkey
Holland	3-1 1-1	Switzerland
Norway	0-2 1-1	**Sweden**
Rep. Ireland	4-2 1-1	Iceland
Yugoslavia	3-2 1-0	Belgium
Bulgaria	3-1 1-3 1-0*	Portugal
England	1-1 2-5	**France**
Albania	W-O	Greece
Austria	Bye	
Luxembourg	Bye	
Soviet Union	Bye	

* Play-off in Rome

SECOND ROUND

Spain	1-1 1-0	Nth. Ireland
Denmark	4-0 0-1	Albania
Austria	0-0 2-3	**Rep. Ireland**
East Germany	1-2 3-3	**Hungary**
Soviet Union	2-0 1-1	Italy
Holland	1-1 1-2	**Luxembourg**
Yugoslavia	0-0 2-3	**Sweden**
Bulgaria	1-0 1-3	**France**

QUARTER-FINALS

1st leg. Sanchez Pizjuan, Seville, 11-03-1964, 27,000
Spain 5 (Ammancio 5 29, Fuste 12, Marcelino 33 89)
Rep. Ireland 1 (McEvoy 18)

2nd leg. Dalymount Park, Dublin, 8-04-1964, 38,000
Rep. Ireland 0
Spain 2 (Zaballa 25 88)

1st leg. Colombes, Paris, 25-04-1964, 35,000
France 1 (Cossou 73)
Hungary 3 (Albert 15, Tichy 16 70)

2nd leg. Népstadion, Budapest, 23-05-1964, 80,000
Hungary 2 (Sipos 24, Bene 55)
France 1 (Combin 2)

1st leg. Municipal, Luxembourg City, 4-12-1963, 6,000
Luxembourg 3 (Pilot 1, Klein 23 51)
Denmark 3 (Madsen 9 31 46)

2nd leg. Idrætsparken, Copenhagen, 10-12-1963, 39,000
Denmark 2 (Madsen 16 70)
Luxembourg 2 (Leonard 13, Schmidt 84)

Play-off. Amsterdam, 18-12-1963, 5,000
Denmark 1 (Madsen 41)
Luxembourg 0

1st leg. Råsunda, Stockholm, 13-05-1964, 37,000
Sweden 1 (Hamrin 88)
Soviet Union 1 Ivanov.V 62)

2nd leg. Leninstadion, Moscow, 27-05-1964, 103,000
Soviet Union 3 (Pondelnik 32 56, Voronin 83)
Sweden 1 (Hamrin 78)

SEMI-FINALS

Bernabeu, Madrid, 17-06-1964, 75,000
Spain 2 (Pereda 39, Amancio 115)
Hungary 1 (Bene 85)

Nou Camp, Barcelona, 17-06-1964, 50,000
Soviet Union 3 (Voronin 19, Ponedelnik 40, Ivanov.V 88)
Denmark 0

3RD PLACE

Nou Camp, Barcelona, 20-06-1964, 3,000
Hungary 3 (Bene 11, Novák 107 110)
Denmark 1 (Bertelsen 81)

FINAL

Bernabeu, Madrid, 21-06-1964, 105,000. Referee: Holland, England
SPAIN 2 (Pereda 6, Marcelino 83)
SOVIET UNION 1 (Khusainov 8)

Spain - Iríbar - Rivilla, Olivella, Calleja - Zoco, Fusté - Amancio, Pereda, Marcelino, Suárez, Lapetra. Tr: Villalonga

Soviet Union - Yashin - Chustikov, Shesterniev, Anitchkin, Mudrik - Voronin, Korniev - Chislenko, Ivanov.V, Ponedelnik, Khusainov. Tr: Beskov

1968
3RD EDITION

QUALIFYING TOURNAMENT

Group 1

	Sp	Cz	RI	Tu	Pl	W	D	L	F	A	Pts
SPAIN	-	2-1	2-0	2-0	6	3	1	2	6	2	8
CZECHOSLOVAKIA	1-0	-	1-2	3-0	6	3	1	2	8	4	7
REP. IRELAND	0-0	0-2	-	2-1	6	2	1	3	5	8	5
TURKEY	0-0	0-0	2-1	-	6	2	1	3	3	8	4

Group 2

	Bu	Pt	Sd	No	Pl	W	D	L	F	A	Pts
BULGARIA	-	1-0	3-0	4-2	6	4	2	0	10	2	10
PORTUGAL	0-0	-	1-2	2-1	6	2	2	2	6	6	6
SWEDEN	0-2	1-1	-	5-2	6	2	1	3	9	12	5
NORWAY	0-0	1-2	3-1	-	6	1	1	4	9	14	3

Group 3

	SU	Gr	Au	Fi	Pl	W	D	L	F	A	Pts
SOVIET UNION	-	4-0	4-3	2-0	6	5	0	1	16	6	10
GREECE	0-1	-	4-1	2-1	6	2	2	2	8	9	6
AUSTRIA	1-0	1-1	-	2-1	6	2	2	2	8	10	6
FINLAND	2-5	1-1	0-0	-	6	0	2	4	5	12	2

Group 4

	Yu	WG	Al	Pl	W	D	L	F	A	Pts
YUGOSLAVIA	-	1-0	4-0	4	3	0	1	8	3	6
WEST GERMANY	3-1	-	6-0	4	2	1	1	9	2	5
ALBANIA	0-2	0-0	-	4	0	1	3	0	12	1

Group 5

	Hu	EG	Ho	De	Pl	W	D	L	F	A	Pts
HUNGARY	-	3-1	2-1	6-0	6	4	1	1	15	5	9
EAST GERMANY	1-0	-	4-3	3-2	6	3	1	2	10	10	7
HOLLAND	2-2	1-0	-	2-0	6	2	1	3	11	11	5
DENMARK	0-2	1-1	3-2	-	6	1	1	4	6	16	3

Group 6

	It	Ro	Sz	Cy	Pl	W	D	L	F	A	Pts
ITALY	-	3-1	4-0	5-0	6	5	1	0	17	3	11
ROMANIA	0-1	-	4-2	7-0	6	3	0	3	18	14	6
SWITZERLAND	2-2	7-1	-	5-0	6	2	1	3	17	13	5
CYPRUS	0-2	1-5	2-1	-	6	1	0	5	3	25	2

Group 7

	Fr	Be	Pd	Lu	Pl	W	D	L	F	A	Pts
FRANCE	-	1-1	2-1	3-1	6	4	1	1	14	6	9
BELGIUM	2-1	-	2-4	3-0	6	3	1	2	14	9	7
POLAND	1-4	3-1	-	4-0	6	3	1	2	13	9	7
LUXEMBOURG	0-3	0-5	0-0	-	6	0	1	5	1	18	1

Group 8

	En	Sc	Wa	NI	Pl	W	D	L	F	A	Pts
ENGLAND	-	2-3	5-1	2-0	6	4	1	1	15	5	9
SCOTLAND	1-1	-	3-2	2-1	6	3	2	1	10	8	8
WALES	0-3	1-1	-	2-0	6	1	2	3	6	12	4
NTH. IRELAND	0-2	1-0	0-0	-	6	1	1	4	2	8	3

QUARTER-FINALS

1st leg. Vasilij Levski, Sofia, 6-04-1968, 68,000
Bulgaria 3 (Kotkov 11, Dermendjiev 66, Jekov 73)
Italy 2 (OG 60, Prati 83)

2nd leg. San Paolo, Naples, 20-04-1968, 90,000
Italy 2 (Prati 14, Domenghini 55)
Bulgaria 0

1st leg. Népstadion, Budapest, 4-05-1968, 80,000
Hungary 2 (Farkas 21, Göröcs 85)
Soviet Union 0

2nd leg. Leninstadion, Moscow, 11-05-1968, 103,000
Soviet Union 3 (OG 22, Khurtzilava 59, Byshovets 73)
Hungary 0

1st leg. Wembley, London, 3-04-1968, 100,000
England 1 (Charlton.R 84)
Spain 0

2nd leg. Bernabeu, Madrid, 8-05-1968, 120,000
Spain 1 (Amancio 47)
England 2 (Peters 54, Hunter 81)

1st leg. Vélodrome, Marseille, 6-04-1968, 45,000
France 1 (Di Nallo 78)
Yugoslavia 1 (Musemic 65)

2nd leg. Crvena Zvezda, Belgrade, 24-04-1968, 47,000
Yugoslavia 5 (Petkovic 2 32, Musemic 13 79, Dzajic 14)
France 1 (Di Nallo 33)

SEMI-FINALS

San Paolo, Naples, 5-06-1968, 75,000
Italy 0
Soviet Union 0
Italy won on the toss of a coin

Comunale, Florence, 5-06-1968, 21,000
Yugoslavia 1 (Dzajic 85)
England 0

3RD PLACE

Stadio Olimpico, Rome, 8-06-1968, 50,000
England 2 (Charlton.R 39, Hurst 63)
Soviet Union 0

FINAL

Stadio Olimpico, Rome, 8-06-1968, 85,000. Referee: Dienst, Switzerland

ITALY 1 (Domenghini 80)
YUGOSLAVIA 1 (Dzajic 39)

Italy - Zoff - Burgnich, Guarneri, Facchetti - Ferrini, Castano - Domenghini, Juliano, Anastasi, Lodetti, Prati

Yugoslavia - Pantelic - Fazlagic, Paunovic, Holcer, Damjanovic - Pavlovic, Trivic - Petkovic, Musemic, Acimovic, Dzajic

Replay. Stadio Olimpico, Rome, 10-06-1968, 50,000. Referee: De Mendibil, Spain

ITALY 2 (Riva 11, Anastasi 32)
YUGOSLAVIA 0

Italy - Zoff - Burgnich, Guarneri, Facchetti - Rosato, Salvadore - Domenghini, Mazzola, Anastasi, De Sisti, Riva. Tr: Valcareggi

Yugoslavia - Pantelic - Fazlagic, Paunovic, Holcer, Damjanovic - Pavlovic, Trivic - Acimovic, Musemic, Hosic, Dzajic. Tr: Mitic

1972

4TH EDITION

QUALIFYING TOURNAMENT

Group 1

	Ro	Cz	Wa	Fi	Pl	W	D	L	F	A	Pts
ROMANIA	-	2-1	2-0	3-0	6	4	1	1	11	2	9
CZECHOSLOVAKIA	1-0	-	1-0	1-1	6	4	1	1	11	4	9
WALES	0-0	1-3	-	3-0	6	2	1	3	5	6	5
FINLAND	0-4	0-4	0-1	-	6	0	1	5	1	16	1

Group 2

	Hu	Bu	Fr	No	Pl	W	D	L	F	A	Pts
HUNGARY	-	2-0	1-1	4-0	6	4	1	1	12	5	9
BULGARIA	3-0	-	2-1	1-1	6	3	1	2	11	7	7
FRANCE	0-2	2-1	-	3-1	6	3	1	2	10	8	7
NORWAY	1-3	1-4	1-3	-	6	0	1	5	5	18	1

Group 3

	En	Sz	Gr	Ma	Pl	W	D	L	F	A	Pts
ENGLAND	-	1-1	3-0	5-0	6	5	1	0	15	3	11
SWITZERLAND	2-3	-	1-0	5-0	6	4	1	1	12	5	9
GREECE	0-2	0-1	-	2-0	6	1	1	4	3	8	3
MALTA	0-1	1-2	1-1	-	6	0	1	5	2	16	1

Group 4

	SU	Sp	NI	Cy	Pl	W	D	L	F	A	Pts
SOVIET UNION	-	2-1	1-0	6-1	6	4	2	0	13	4	10
SPAIN	0-0	-	3-0	7-0	6	3	2	1	14	3	8
NTH. IRELAND	1-1	1-1	-	5-0	6	2	2	2	10	6	6
CYPRUS	1-3	0-2	0-3	-	6	0	0	6	2	26	0

Group 5

	Be	Pt	Sc	De	Pl	W	D	L	F	A	Pts
BELGIUM	-	3-0	3-0	2-0	6	4	1	1	11	3	9
PORTUGAL	1-1	-	2-0	5-0	6	3	1	2	10	6	7
SCOTLAND	1-0	2-1	-	1-0	6	3	0	3	4	7	6
DENMARK	1-2	0-1	1-0	-	6	1	0	5	2	11	2

Group 6

	It	Au	Sd	RI	Pl	W	D	L	F	A	Pts
ITALY	-	2-2	3-0	3-0	6	4	2	0	12	4	10
AUSTRIA	1-2	-	1-0	6-0	6	3	1	2	14	6	7
SWEDEN	0-0	1-0	-	1-0	6	2	2	2	3	5	6
REP. IRELAND	1-2	1-4	1-1	-	6	0	1	5	3	17	1

Group 7

	Yu	Ho	EG	Lu	Pl	W	D	L	F	A	Pts
YUGOSLAVIA	-	2-0	0-0	0-0	6	3	3	0	7	2	9
HOLLAND	1-1	-	3-2	6-0	6	3	1	2	18	6	7
EAST GERMANY	1-2	1-0	-	2-1	6	3	1	2	11	6	7
LUXEMBOURG	0-2	0-8	0-5	-	6	0	1	5	1	23	1

Group 8

	WG	Pd	Tu	Al	Pl	W	D	L	F	A	Pts
WEST GERMANY	-	0-0	1-1	2-0	6	4	2	0	10	2	10
POLAND	1-3	-	5-1	3-0	6	2	2	2	10	6	6
TURKEY	0-3	1-0	-	2-1	6	2	1	3	5	13	5
ALBANIA	0-1	1-1	3-0	-	6	1	1	4	5	9	3

QUARTER-FINALS

1st leg. Wembley, London, 29-04-1972, 100,000

England 1 (Lee.F 78)
West Germany 3 (Hoeness 27, Netzer 84, Müller.G 88)

2nd leg. Olympiastadion, Berlin, 13-05-1972, 76,000

West Germany 0
England 0

1st leg. San Siro, Milan, 29-04-1972, 65,000

Italy 0
Belgium 0

2nd leg. Parc Astrid, Brussels, 13-05-1972, 26,000

Belgium 2 (Van Moer 23, Van Himst 71)
Italy 1 (Riva 86)

1st leg. Népstadion, Budapest, 29-04-1972, 70,000

Hungary 1 (Branikovits 11)
Romania 1 (Satmareanu 56)

2nd leg. Stadionul 23 August, Bucharest, 14-05-1972, 75,000

Romania 2 (Dobrin 14, Neagu 81)
Hungary 2 (Szöke 5, Kocsis.L 36)

Play-off. Belgrade, 17-05-1972, 32,000

Hungary 2 (Kocsis.L 27, Szöke 89)
Romania 1 (Neagu 34)

1st leg. Crvena Zvezda, Belgrade, 30-04-1972, 70,000

Yugoslavia 0
Soviet Union 0

2nd leg. Leninstadion, Moscow, 13-05-1972, 103,000

Soviet Union 3 (Kolotov 53, Banishevski 74, Kozinkevich 90)
Yugoslavia 0

SEMI-FINALS

Bosuil, Antwerp, 14-06-1972, 60,000

West Germany 2 (Müller 24 72)
Belgium 1 (Polleunis 83)

Parc Astrid, Brussels, 14-06-1972, 3,000

Soviet Union 1 (Konkov 53)
Hungary 0

3RD PLACE

Sclessin, Liège, 17-06-1972, 10,000

Belgium 2 (Lambert 24, Van Himst 28)
Hungary 1 (Kü 53)

FINAL

Heysel, Brussels, 18-06-1972, 65,000. Referee: Marschall, Austria

WEST GERMANY 3 (Muller 27 58, Wimmer 52)
SOVIET UNION 0

West Germany - Maier - Höttges, Schwarzenbeck, Beckenbauer, Breitner - Wimmer, Hoeness, Netzer - Heynckes, Müller, Kremers. Tr: Schön

Soviet Union - Rudakov - Dzodzuashvili, Khurtsilava, Kaplichny, Istomin, Kolotov, Troshkin, Konkov (Dolmatov) - Baidachni, Banishevski (Kozinkievits), Onishenko. Tr: Ponomarev

1976

5TH EDITION

QUALIFYING TOURNAMENT

Group 1

	Cz	En	Po	Cy	Pl	W	D	L	F	A	Pts
CZECHOSLOVAKIA	-	2-1	5-0	4-0	6	4	1	1	15	5	9
England	3-0	-	0-0	5-0	6	3	2	1	11	3	8
Portugal	1-1	1-1	-	1-0	6	2	3	1	5	7	7
Cyprus	0-3	0-1	0-2	-	6	0	0	6	0	16	0

Group 2

	Wa	Hu	Au	Lu	Pl	W	D	L	F	A	Pts
WALES	-	2-0	1-0	5-0	6	5	0	1	14	4	10
Hungary	1-2	-	2-1	8-1	6	3	1	2	15	8	7
Austria	2-1	0-0	-	6-2	6	3	1	2	11	7	7
Luxembourg	1-3	2-4	1-2	-	6	0	0	6	7	28	0

Group 3

	Yu	NI	Sd	No	Pl	W	D	L	F	A	Pts
YUGOSLAVIA	-	1-0	3-0	3-1	6	5	0	1	12	4	10
Nth. Ireland	1-0	-	1-2	3-0	6	3	0	3	8	5	6
Sweden	1-2	0-2	-	3-1	6	3	0	3	8	9	6
Norway	1-3	2-1	0-2	-	6	1	0	5	5	15	2

Group 4

	Sp	Ro	Sc	De	Pl	W	D	L	F	A	Pts
SPAIN	-	1-1	1-1	2-0	6	3	3	0	10	6	9
Romania	2-2	-	1-1	6-1	6	1	5	0	11	6	7
Scotland	1-2	1-1	-	3-1	6	2	3	1	8	6	7
Denmark	1-2	0-0	0-1	-	6	0	1	5	3	14	1

Group 5

	Ho	Pl	It	Fi	Pl	W	D	L	F	A	Pts
HOLLAND	-	3-0	3-1	4-1	6	4	0	2	14	8	8
Poland	4-1	-	0-0	3-0	6	3	2	1	9	5	8
Italy	1-0	0-0	-	0-0	6	2	3	1	3	3	7
Finland	1-3	1-2	0-1	-	6	0	1	5	3	13	1

Group 6

	SU	RI	Tu	Sz	Pl	W	D	L	F	A	Pts
SOVIET UNION	-	2-1	3-0	4-1	6	4	0	2	10	6	8
Rep. Ireland	3-0	-	4-0	2-1	6	3	1	2	11	5	7
Turkey	1-0	1-1	-	2-1	6	2	2	2	5	10	6
Switzerland	0-1	1-0	1-1	-	6	1	1	4	5	10	3

Group 7

	Be	EG	Fr	Ic	Pl	W	D	L	F	A	Pts
BELGIUM	-	1-2	2-1	1-0	6	3	2	1	6	3	8
East Germany	0-0	-	2-1	1-1	6	2	3	1	8	7	7
France	0-0	2-2	-	3-0	6	1	3	2	7	6	5
Iceland	0-2	2-1	0-0	-	6	1	2	3	3	8	4

Group 8

	WG	Gr	Bu	Ma	Pl	W	D	L	F	A	Pts
WEST GERMANY	-	1-1	1-0	8-0	6	3	3	0	14	4	9
Greece	2-2	-	2-1	4-0	6	2	3	1	12	9	7
Bulgaria	1-1	3-3	-	5-0	6	2	2	2	12	7	6
Malta	0-1	2-0	0-2	-	6	1	0	5	2	20	2

QUARTER-FINALS

1st leg. Tehelné Pole, Bratislava, 24-04-1976, 50,000
Czechoslovakia 2 (Móder 34, Panenka 47)
Soviet Union 0

2nd leg. Respublikansky Stadion, Kiev, 22-05-1976, 100,000
Soviet Union 2 (Burjak 53, Blokhin 87)
Czechoslovakia 2 (Móder 45 82)

1st leg. Feyenoord Stadion, Rotterdam, 25-04-1976, 58,000
Holland 5 (Rijsbergen 17, Rensenbrink 28 58 85, Neeskens 80)
Belgium 0

2nd leg. Heysel, Brussels, 22-05-1976, 45,000
Belgium 1 (Van Gool 27)
Holland 2 (Rep 62, Cruyff 78)

1st leg. Stadion Dinamo, Zagreb, 25-04-1976, 50,000
Yugoslavia 2 (Vukotic 1, Popivoda 55)
Wales 0

2nd leg. Ninian Park, Cardiff, 22-05-1976, 50,000
Wales 1 (Evans 38)
Yugoslavia 1 (Katalinski 19)

1st leg. Vicente Calderón, Madrid, 24-04-1976, 63,000
Spain 1 (Santillana 22)
West Germany 1 (Beer 60)

2nd leg. Olympiastadion, Munich, 22-05-1976, 77,000
West Germany 2 (Hoeness 17, Toppmöller 43)
Spain 0

SEMI-FINALS

Stadion Dinamo, Zagreb, 16-06-1976, 40,000
Czechoslovakia 3 (Ondrus 20, Nehoda 115, Vesely.F 118)
Holland 1 (OG 75)

Crvena Zvezda, Belgrade, 17-06-1976, 75,000
West Germany 4 (Flohe 65, Müller.D 80 114 119)
Yugoslavia 2 (Popivoda 20, Dzajic 30)

3RD PLACE

Stadion Dinamo, Zagreb, 19-06-1976, 18,000
Holland 3 (Geels 27 107, Van de Kerkof.W 39)
Yugoslavia 2 (Katalinski 43, Dzajic 82)

FINAL

Crvena Zvezda, Belgrade, 20-06-1976, 45,000. Referee: Gonella, Italy
CZECHOSLOVAKIA 2 (Svehlík 8, Dobiás 25)
WEST GERMANY 2 (Müller.D 28, Hölzenbein 89)
Czechoslovakia won 5-3 on penalties

Czechoslovakia		**West Germany**	
Masny	1	Bonhof	1
Nehoda	1	Flohe	1
Ondrus	1	Bongartz	1
Jurkemik	1	Hoeness	x
Panenka	1		

Czechoslovakia - Viktor - Pivarník, Ondrus, Capkovic, Gögh - Dobiás (Vesely.F), Móder, Panenka - Masny, Svehlík (Jurkemik), Nehoda. Tr: Jezek

West Germany - Maier - Vogts, Schwarzenbeck, Beckenbauer, Dietz - Wimmer (Flohe), Beer (Bongartz), Bonhof - Hoeness, Müller.D, Hölzenbein. Tr: Schoen

6TH EDITION

QUALIFYING TOURNAMENT

Group 1

	En	NI	RI	Bu	De	Pl	W	D	L	F	A	Pts
ENGLAND	-	4-0	2-0	2-0	1-0	8	7	1	0	22	5	15
Nth. Ireland	1-5	-	1-0	2-0	2-1	8	4	1	3	8	14	9

						Pl	W	D	L	F	A	Pts
Rep. Ireland	1-1	0-0	-	3-0	2-0	8	2	3	3	9	8	7
Bulgaria	0-3	0-2	1-0	-	3-0	8	2	1	5	6	14	7
Denmark	3-4	4-0	3-3	2-2	-	8	1	2	5	3	17	4

Group 2

	Be	Au	Pt	Sc	No	Pl	W	D	L	F	A	Pts
BELGIUM	-	1-1	2-0	2-0	1-1	8	4	4	0	12	5	12
Austria	0-0	-	1-2	3-2	4-0	8	4	3	1	14	7	11
Portugal	1-1	1-2	-	1-0	3-1	8	4	1	3	10	11	9
Scotland	1-3	1-1	4-1	-	3-2	8	3	1	4	15	13	7
Norway	1-2	0-2	0-1	0-4	-	8	0	1	7	5	20	1

Group 3

	Sp	Yu	Ro	Cy	Pl	W	D	L	F	A	Pts
SPAIN	-	0-1	1-0	5-0	6	4	1	1	13	5	9
Yugoslavia	1-2	-	2-1	5-0	6	4	0	2	14	6	8
Romania	2-2	3-2	-	2-0	6	2	2	2	9	8	6
Cyprus	1-3	0-3	1-1	-	6	0	1	5	2	19	1

Group 4

	Ho	Pd	EG	Sz	Ic	Pl	W	D	L	F	A	Pts
HOLLAND	-	1-1	3-0	3-0	3-0	8	6	1	1	20	6	13
Poland	2-0	-	1-1	2-0	2-0	8	5	2	1	13	4	12
East Germany	2-3	2-1	-	5-2	3-1	8	5	1	2	18	11	11
Switzerland	1-3	0-2	0-2	-	2-0	8	2	0	6	7	18	4
Iceland	0-4	0-2	0-3	1-2	-	8	0	0	8	2	21	0

Group 5

	Cz	Fr	Sd	Lu	Pl	W	D	L	F	A	Pts
CZECHOSLOVAKIA	-	2-0	4-1	4-0	6	5	0	1	17	4	10
France	2-1	-	2-2	3-0	6	4	1	1	13	7	9
Sweden	1-3	1-3	-	3-0	6	1	2	3	9	13	4
Luxembourg	0-3	1-3	1-1	-	6	0	1	5	2	17	1

Group 6

	Gr	Hu	Fi	SU	Pl	W	D	L	F	A	Pts
GREECE	-	4-1	8-1	1-0	6	3	1	2	13	7	7
Hungary	0-0	-	3-1	2-0	6	2	2	2	9	9	6
Finland	3-0	2-1	-	1-1	6	2	2	2	10	15	6
Soviet Union	2-0	2-2	2-2	-	6	1	3	2	7	8	5

Group 7

	WG	Tu	Wa	Ma	Pl	W	D	L	F	A	Pts
WEST GERMANY	-	2-0	5-1	8-0	6	4	2	0	17	1	10
Turkey	0-0	-	1-0	2-1	6	3	1	2	5	5	7
Wales	0-2	1-0	-	7-0	6	3	0	3	11	8	6
Malta	0-0	1-2	0-2	-	6	0	1	5	2	21	1

ITALY qualified as hosts

FINAL TOURNAMENT
ITALY, 11 - 22 JUNE 1980

FIRST ROUND

Group 1

Stadio Olimpico, Rome, 11-06-1980, 15,000
West Germany 1 (Rummenigge 55)
Czechoslovakia 0

San Paolo, Naples, 11-06-1980, 10,000
Holland 1 (Kist 56p)
Greece 0

San Paolo, Naples, 14-06-1980, 50,000
West Germany 3 (Allofs 15 60 67)
Holland 2 (Rep 75p, Van de Kerkof.W 86)

Stadio Olimpico, Rome, 14-06-1980, 7,000
Czechoslovakia 3 (Panenka 5, Vízek 25, Nehoda 63)
Greece 1 (Anastopoulos 11)

Giuseppe Meazza, Milan, 17-06-1980, 11,000
Czechoslovakia 1 (Nehoda 13)
Holland 1 (Kist 58)

Comunale, Turin, 17-06-1980, 13,000
West Germany 0
Greece 0

	WG	Cz	Ho	Gr	Pl	W	D	L	F	A	Pts
West Germany	-	1-0	3-2	0-0	3	2	1	0	4	2	5
Czechoslovakia	-	-	1-1	3-1	3	1	1	1	4	3	3
Holland	-	-	-	1-0	3	1	1	1	4	4	3
Greece	-	-	-	-	3	0	1	2	1	4	1

Group 2

Comunale, Turin, 12-06-1980, 7,000
Belgium 1 (Ceulemans 38)
England 1 (Wilkins 32)

Giuseppe Meazza, Milan, 12-06-1980, 55,000
Italy 0
Spain 0

Giuseppe Meazza, Milan, 15-06-1980, 11,000
Belgium 2 (Gerets 17, Cools 64)
Spain 1 (Quini 35)

Comunale, Turin, 15-06-1980, 59,000
Italy 1 (Tardelli 79)
England 0

San Paolo, Naples, 18-06-1980, 14,000
England 2 (Brooking 18, Woodcock 62)
Spain 1 (Dani 48p)

Stadio Olimpico, Rome, 18-06-1980, 69,000
Italy 0
Belgium 0

	Be	It	En	Sp	Pl	W	D	L	F	A	Pts
Belgium	-	0-0	1-1	2-1	3	1	2	0	3	2	4
Italy	-	-	1-0	0-0	3	1	2	0	1	0	4
England	-	-	-	2-1	3	1	1	1	3	3	3
Spain	-	-	-	-	3	0	1	2	2	4	1

3RD PLACE

San Paolo, Naples, 21-06-1980, 25,000
Czechoslovakia 1 (Jurkemik 48)
Italy 1 (Graziani 74)
Czechoslovakia won 9-8 on penalties

FINAL

Stadio Olimpico, Rome, 22-06-1980, 48,000. Referee: Rainea, Romania
WEST GERMANY 2 (Hrubesch 10 88)
BELGIUM 1 (Vandereycken 72)

West Germany - Schumacher - Kaltz, Stielike, Förster.K.H, Dietz - Schuster, Briegel (Cullmann), Müller.H -Rummenigge, Hrubesch, Allofs. Tr: Derwall

Belgium - Pfaff - Gerets, Millecamps, Meeuws, Renquin - Cools, Vandereycken,Van Moer - Mommens, Vander Elst, Ceulemans. Tr: Thys

1984
7TH EDITION

QUALIFYING TOURNAMENT

Group 1

	Be	Sz	EG	Sc	Pl	W	D	L	F	A	Pts
BELGIUM	-	3-0	2-1	3-2	6	4	1	1	12	8	9

					Pl	W	D	L	F	A	Pts
SWITZERLAND	3-1	-	0-0	2-0	6	2	2	2	7	9	6
EAST GERMANY	1-2	3-0	-	2-1	6	2	1	3	7	7	5
SCOTLAND	1-1	2-2	2-0	-	6	1	2	3	8	10	4

Group 2

	Pt	SU	Pd	Fi	Pl	W	D	L	F	A	Pts
PORTUGAL	-	1-0	2-1	5-0	6	5	0	1	11	6	10
SOVIET UNION	5-0	-	2-0	2-0	6	4	1	1	11	2	9
POLAND	0-1	1-1	-	1-1	6	1	2	3	6	9	4
FINLAND	0-2	0-1	2-3	-	6	0	1	5	3	14	1

Group 3

	De	En	Gr	Hu	Lu	Pl	W	D	L	F	A	Pts
DENMARK	-	2-2	1-0	3-1	6-0	8	6	1	1	17	5	13
ENGLAND	0-1	-	0-0	2-0	9-0	8	5	2	1	23	3	12
GREECE	0-2	0-3	-	2-2	1-0	8	3	2	3	8	10	8
HUNGARY	1-0	0-3	2-3	-	6-2	8	3	1	4	18	17	7
LUXEMBOURG	1-2	0-4	0-2	2-6	-	8	0	0	8	5	36	0

Group 4

	Yu	Wa	Bu	No	Pl	W	D	L	F	A	Pts
YUGOSLAVIA	-	4-4	3-2	2-1	6	3	2	1	12	11	8
WALES	1-1	-	1-0	1-0	6	2	3	1	7	6	7
BULGARIA	0-1	1-0	-	2-2	6	2	1	3	7	8	5
NORWAY	3-1	0-0	1-2	-	6	1	2	3	7	8	4

Group 5

	Ro	Sd	Cz	It	Cy	Pl	W	D	L	F	A	Pts
ROMANIA	-	2-0	0-1	1-0	3-1	8	5	2	1	9	3	12
SWEDEN	0-1	-	1-0	2-0	5-0	8	5	1	2	14	5	11
CZECHOSLOVAKIA	1-1	2-2	-	2-0	6-0	8	3	4	1	15	7	10
ITALY	0-0	0-3	2-2	-	3-1	8	1	3	4	6	12	5
CYPRUS	0-1	0-1	1-1	1-1	-	8	0	2	6	4	21	2

Group 6

	WG	NI	Au	Tu	Al	Pl	W	D	L	F	A	Pts
WEST GERMANY	-	0-1	3-0	5-1	2-1	8	5	1	2	15	5	11
NTH. IRELAND	1-0	-	3-1	2-1	1-0	8	5	1	2	8	5	11
AUSTRIA	0-0	2-0	-	4-0	5-0	8	4	1	3	15	10	9
TURKEY	0-3	1-0	3-1	-	1-0	8	3	1	4	8	16	7
ALBANIA	1-2	0-0	1-2	1-1	-	8	0	2	6	4	14	2

Group 7

	Sp	Ho	RI	Ic	Ma	Pl	W	D	L	F	A	Pts
SPAIN	-	1-0	2-0	1-0	12-1	8	6	1	1	24	8	13
HOLLAND	2-1	-	2-1	3-0	5-0	8	6	1	1	22	6	13
REP. IRELAND	3-3	2-3	-	2-0	8-0	8	4	1	3	20	10	9
ICELAND	0-1	1-1	0-3	-	1-0	8	1	1	6	3	13	3
MALTA	2-3	0-6	0-1	2-1	-	8	1	0	7	5	37	2

FRANCE qualified as hosts

FINAL TOURNAMENT.
FRANCE. 12 - 27 JUNE 1984

FIRST ROUND

Group 1

Parc des Princes, Paris, 12-06-1984, 47,000
France 1 (Platini 77)
Denmark 0

Félix Bollaert, Lens, 12-06-1984, 45,000
Belgium 2 (Vandenbergh 27, Grun 44)
Yugoslavia 0

Beaujoire, Nantes, 16-06-1984, 51,000
France 5 (Platini 3 74 88, Giresse 32, Fernandez 43)
Belgium 0

Gerland, Lyon, 16-06-1984, 25,000
Denmark 5 (OG 7, Berggren 16, Arnesen 68, Elkjaer 81, Lauridsen 83)
Yugoslavia 0

Geoffroy Guichard, Saint Etienne, 19-06-1984, 50,000
France 3 (Platini 59 61 76)
Yugoslavia 2 (Sestic 31, Stojkovic 80)

Meinau, Strasbourg, 19-06-1984, 36,000
Denmark 3 (Arnesen 40, Brylle 60, Elkjaer 83)
Belgium 2 (Ceulemans 25, Vercauteren 38)

	Fr	De	Be	Yu	Pl	W	D	L	F	A	Pts
FRANCE	-	1-0	5-0	3-2	3	3	0	0	9	2	6
DENMARK	-	-	3-2	5-0	3	2	0	1	8	3	4
BELGIUM	-	-	-	2-0	3	1	0	2	4	8	2
YUGOSLAVIA	-	-	-	-	3	0	0	3	2	10	0

Group 2

Meinau, Strasbourg, 14-06-1984, 47,000
Portugal 0
West Germany 0

Geoffroy Guichard, Saint Etienne, 14-06-1984, 15,000
Spain 1 (Carrasco 20)
Romania 1 (Bölöni 34)

Félix Bollaert, Lens, 17-06-1984, 35,000
West Germany 2 (Völler 24 65)
Romania 1 (Coras 46)

Vélodrome, Marseille, 17-06-1984, 30,000
Portugal 1 (Sousa 51)
Spain 1 (Santillana 72)

Parc des Princes, Paris, 20-06-1984, 40,000
Spain 1 (Maceda 89)
West Germany 0

Beaujoire, Nantes, 20-06-1984, 20,000
Portugal 1 (Nene 80)
Romania 0

	Sp	Pt	WG	Ro	Pl	W	D	L	F	A	Pts
SPAIN	-	1-1	1-0	1-1	3	1	2	0	3	2	4
PORTUGAL	-	-	0-0	1-0	3	1	2	0	2	1	4
WEST GERMANY	-	-	-	2-1	3	1	1	1	2	2	3
ROMANIA	-	-	-	-	3	0	1	2	2	4	1

SEMI-FINALS

Vélodrome, Marseille, 23-06-1984, 55,000
France 3 (Domergue 24 114, Platini 119)
Portugal 2 (Jordao 73 97)

Gerland, Lyon, 24-06-1984, 48,000
Spain 1 (Maceda 66)
Denmark 1 (Lerby 6)
Spain won 5-4 on penalties

FINAL

Parc des Princes, Paris, 27-06-1984, 47,000. Referee: Christov, Czechoslovakia
FRANCE 2 (Platini 57, Bellone 90)
SPAIN 0

France - Bats - Battiston (Amoros), Le Roux, Bossis, Domergue - Giresse, Tigana, Fernandez, Platini - Lacombe (Genghini), Bellone. Tr: Hidalgo

Spain - Arconada - Urquiaga, Salva (Roberto), Gallego - Señor, Francisco, Víctor, Camacho, Julio Alberto (Sarabia) - Santillana, Carrasco. Tr: Muñoz

1988

8TH EDITION

QUALIFYING TOURNAMENT

Group 1

	Sp	Ro	Au	Al	Pl	W	D	L	F	A	Pts
SPAIN	-	1-0	2-0	5-0	6	5	0	1	14	6	10
Romania	3-1	-	4-0	5-1	6	4	1	1	13	3	9
Austria	2-3	0-0	-	3-0	6	2	1	3	6	9	5
Albania	1-2	0-1	0-1	-	6	0	0	6	2	17	0

Group 2

	It	Sd	Pt	Sz	Ma	Pl	W	D	L	F	A	Pts
ITALY	-	2-1	3-0	3-2	5-0	8	6	1	1	16	4	13
Sweden	1-0	-	0-1	2-0	1-0	8	4	2	2	12	5	10
Portugal	0-1	1-1	-	0-0	2-2	8	2	4	2	6	8	8
Switzerland	0-0	1-1	1-1	-	4-1	8	1	5	2	9	9	7
Malta	0-2	0-5	0-1	1-1	-	8	0	2	6	4	21	2

Group 3

	SU	EG	Fr	Ic	No	Pl	W	D	L	F	A	Pts
SOVIET UNION	-	2-0	1-1	2-0	4-0	8	5	3	0	14	3	13
East Germany	1-1	-	0-0	2-0	3-1	8	4	3	1	13	4	11
France	0-2	0-1	-	2-0	1-1	8	1	4	3	4	7	6
Iceland	1-1	0-6	0-0	-	2-1	8	2	2	4	4	14	6
Norway	0-1	0-0	2-0	0-1	-	8	1	2	5	5	12	4

Group 4

	En	Yu	NI	Tu	Pl	W	D	L	F	A	Pts
ENGLAND	-	2-0	3-0	8-0	6	5	1	0	19	1	11
Yugoslavia	1-4	-	3-0	4-0	6	4	0	2	13	9	8
Nth. Ireland	0-2	1-2	-	1-0	6	1	1	4	2	10	3
Turkey	0-0	2-3	0-0	-	6	0	2	4	2	16	2

Group 5

	Ho	Gr	Hu	Pd	Cy	Pl	W	D	L	F	A	Pts
HOLLAND	-	1-1	2-0	0-0	4-0*	8	6	2	0	15	1	14
Greece	0-3	-	2-1	1-0	3-1	8	4	1	3	12	13	9
Hungary	0-1	3-0	-	5-3	1-0	8	4	0	4	13	11	8
Poland	0-2	2-1	3-2	-	0-0	8	3	2	3	9	11	8
Cyprus	0-2	2-4	0-1	0-1	-	8	0	1	7	3	16	1

* Original 8-0 victory declared void

Group 6

	De	Cz	Wa	Fi	Pl	W	D	L	F	A	Pts
DENMARK	-	1-1	1-0	1-0	6	3	2	1	4	2	8
Czechoslovakia	0-0	-	2-0	3-0	6	2	3	1	7	5	7
Wales	1-0	1-1	-	4-0	6	2	2	2	7	5	6
Finland	0-1	3-0	1-1	-	6	1	1	4	4	10	3

Group 7

	RI	Bu	Be	Sc	Lu	Pl	W	D	L	F	A	Pts
REP. IRELAND	-	2-0	0-0	0-0	2-1	8	4	3	1	10	5	11
Bulgaria	2-1	-	2-0	0-1	3-0	8	4	2	2	12	6	10
Belgium	2-2	1-1	-	4-1	3-0	8	3	3	2	16	8	9
Scotland	0-1	0-0	2-0	-	3-0	8	3	3	2	7	5	9
Luxembourg	0-2	1-4	0-6	0-0	-	8	0	1	7	2	23	1

WEST GERMANY qualified as hosts

FINAL TOURNAMENT.

WEST GERMANY. 10 - 25 JUNE 1988

FIRST ROUND

Group 1

Rheinstadion, Düsseldorf, 10-06-1988, 68,000

West Germany 1 (Brehme 55)
Italy 1 (Mancini 51)

Niedersachsenstadion, Hanover, 11-06-1988, 60,000

Spain 3 (Michel 5, Butragueño 52, Gordillo 67)
Denmark 2 (Laudrup M. 25, Povlsen 85)

Parkstadion, Gelsenkirchen, 14-06-1988, 70,000

West Germany 2 (Klinsmann 9, Thon 85)
Denmark 0

Waldstadion, Frankfurt, 14-06-1988, 51,000

Italy 1 (Vialli 73)
Spain 0

Olympiastadion, Munich, 17-06-1988, 72,000

West Germany 2 (Völler 30 51)
Spain 0

Müngersdorfer, Cologne, 17-06-1988, 60,000

Italy 2 (Altobelli 65, De Agostini 87)
Denmark 0

	WG	It	Sp	De	Pl	W	D	L	F	A	Pts
West Germany	-	1-1	2-0	2-0	3	2	1	0	5	1	5
Italy	-	-	1-0	2-0	3	2	1	0	4	1	5
Spain	-	-	-	3-2	3	1	0	2	3	5	2
Denmark	-	-	-	-	3	0	0	3	2	7	0

Group 2

Neckarstadion, Stuttgart, 12-06-1988, 53,000

Rep. Ireland 1 (Houghton 5)
England 0

Müngersdorfer, Cologne, 12-06-1988, 60,000

Soviet Union 1 (Rats 53)
Holland 0

Rheinstadion, Düsseldorf, 15-06-1988, 65,000

Holland 3 (Van Basten 23 71 75)
England 1 (Robson 53)

Niedersachsenstadion, Hanover, 15-06-1988, 52,000

Soviet Union 1 (Protasov 74)
Rep. Ireland 1 (Whelan 38)

Waldstadion, Frankfurt, 18-06-1988, 53,000

Soviet Union 3 (Aleinikov 3, Mikhailichenko 28, Pasulko 72)
England 1 (Adams 16)

Parkstadion, Gelsenkirchen, 18-06-1988, 70,000

Holland 1 (Kieft 81)
Rep. Ireland 0

	SU	Ho	RI	En	Pl	W	D	L	F	A	Pts
Soviet Union	-	1-0	1-1	3-1	3	2	1	0	5	2	5
Holland	-	-	1-0	3-1	3	2	0	1	4	2	4
Rep. Ireland	-	-	-	1-0	3	1	1	1	2	2	3
England	-	-	-	-	3	0	0	3	2	7	0

SEMI-FINALS

Volksparkstadion, Hamburg, 21-06-1988, 60,000

Holland 2 (Koeman.R 73, Van Basten 88)
West Germany 1 (Matthäus 54)

Neckarstadion, Stuttgart, 22-06-1988, 70,000

Soviet Union 2 (Litovchenko 59, Protasov 62)
Italy 0

FINAL

Olympiastadion, Munich, 25-06-1988, 72,000. Referee: Vautrot, France

HOLLAND 2 (Gullit 32, Van Basten 53)
SOVIET UNION 0

Holland - Van Breukelen - Van Aerle, Rijkaard, Koeman.R, Van Tiggelen, Vanenburg, Wouters, Muhren, Koeman.E - Gullit, Van Basten. Tr: Michels
Soviet Union - Dassaev - Demianenko, Aleinikov, Khidiatulin, Rats Litovchenko, Zavarov, Mikhailichenko, Gotsmanov (Baltacha) - Protasov (Pasulko), Belanov. Tr: Lobonovsky

1992

9TH EDITION

QUALIFYING TOURNAMENT

Group 1

	Fr	Cz	Sp	Ic	Al	Pl	W	D	L	F	A	Pts
FRANCE	-	2-1	3-1	3-1	5-0	8	8	0	0	20	6	16
Czechoslovakia	1-2	-	3-2	1-0	2-1	8	5	0	3	12	9	10
Spain	1-2	2-1	-	2-1	9-0	7	3	0	4	17	12	6
Iceland	1-2	0-1	2-0	-	2-0	8	2	0	6	7	10	4
Albania	0-1	0-2	-	1-0	-	7	1	0	6	2	21	2

Group 2

	Sc	Sz	Ro	Bu	SM	Pl	W	D	L	F	A	Pts
SCOTLAND	-	2-1	2-1	1-1	4-0	8	4	3	1	14	7	11
Switzerland	2-2	-	0-0	2-0	7-0	8	4	2	2	19	7	10
Romania	1-0	1-0	-	0-3	6-0	8	4	2	2	13	7	10
Bulgaria	1-1	2-3	1-1	-	4-0	8	3	3	2	15	8	9
San Marino	0-2	0-4	1-3	0-3	-	8	0	0	8	1	33	0

Group 3

	SU	It	No	Hu	Cy	Pl	W	D	L	F	A	Pts
SOVIET UNION	-	0-0	2-0	2-2	4-0	8	5	3	0	13	2	13
Italy	0-0	-	1-1	3-1	2-0	8	3	4	1	12	5	10
Norway	0-1	2-1	-	0-0	3-0	8	3	3	2	9	5	9
Hungary	0-1	1-1	0-0	-	4-2	8	2	4	2	10	9	8
Cyprus	0-3	0-4	0-3	0-2	-	8	0	0	8	2	25	0

Group 4

	Yu	De	NI	Au	FI	Pl	W	D	L	F	A	Pts
YUGOSLAVIA	-	1-2	4-1	4-1	7-0	8	7	0	1	24	4	14
Denmark	0-2	-	2-1	2-1	4-1	8	6	1	1	18	7	13
Nth. Ireland	0-2	1-1	-	2-1	1-1	8	2	3	3	11	11	7
Austria	0-2	0-3	0-0	-	3-0	8	1	1	6	6	14	3
Faeroe Isl.	0-2	0-4	0-5	1-0	-	8	1	1	6	3	26	3

Group 5

	Ge	Wa	Be	Lu	Pl	W	D	L	F	A	Pts
GERMANY	-	4-1	1-0	4-0	6	5	0	1	13	4	10
Wales	1-0	-	3-1	1-0	6	4	1	1	8	6	9
Belgium	0-1	1-1	-	3-0	6	2	1	3	7	6	5
Luxembourg	2-3	0-1	0-2	-	6	0	0	6	2	14	0

Group 6

	Ho	Pt	Gr	Fi	Ma	Pl	W	D	L	F	A	Pts
HOLLAND	-	1-0	2-0	2-0	1-0	8	6	1	1	17	2	13
Portugal	1-0	-	1-0	1-0	5-0	8	5	1	2	11	4	11
Greece	0-2	3-2	-	2-0	4-0	8	3	2	3	11	9	8
Finland	1-1	0-0	1-1	-	2-0	8	1	4	3	5	8	6
Malta	0-8	0-1	1-1	1-1	-	8	0	2	6	2	23	2

Group 7

	En	RI	Pd	Tu	Pl	W	D	L	F	A	Pts
ENGLAND	-	1-1	2-0	1-0	6	3	3	0	7	3	9
Rep. Ireland	1-1	-	0-0	5-0	6	2	4	0	13	6	8
Poland	1-1	3-3	-	3-0	6	2	3	1	8	6	7
Turkey	0-1	1-3	0-1	-	6	0	0	6	1	14	0

SWEDEN qualified as hosts

FINAL TOURNAMENT.

SWEDEN. 10 - 26 JUNE 1992

FIRST ROUND

Group 1

Råsunda, Stockholm, 10-06-1992, 29,000
Sweden 1 (Eriksson 26)
France 1 (Papin 59)

Malmö Stadion, Malmö, 11-06-1992, 26,000
Denmark 0
England 0

Malmö Stadion, Malmö, 14-06-1992, 26,000
France 0
England 0

Råsunda, Stockholm, 14-06-1992, 29,000
Sweden 1 (Brolin 58)
Denmark 0

Råsunda, Stockholm, 17-06-1992, 30,000
Sweden 2 (Eriksson 51, Brolin 84)
England 1 (Platt 3)

Malmö Stadion, Malmö, 17-06-1992, 17,000
Denmark 2 (Larsen 7, Elstrup 78)
France 1 (Papin 59)

	Sd	De	Fr	En	Pl	W	D	L	F	A	Pts
Sweden	-	1-0	1-1	2-1	3	2	1	0	4	2	5
Denmark	-	-	2-1	0-0	3	1	1	1	2	2	3
France	-	-	-	0-0	3	0	2	1	2	3	2
England	-	-	-	-	3	0	2	1	1	2	2

Group 2

Nya Ullevi, Gothenburg, 12-06-1992, 35,000
Holland 1 (Bergkamp 77)
Scotland 0

Idraetspark, Norrköping, 12-06-1992, 17,000
Germany 1 (Hässler 90)
CIS 1 (Dobrovolski 63)

Idraetspark, Norrköping, 15-06-1992, 17,000
Germany 2 (Riedle 29, Effenberg 47)
Scotland 0

Nya Ullevi, Gothenburg, 15-06-1992, 34,000
Holland 0
CIS 0

Idraetspark, Norrköping, 18-06-1992, 14,000
Scotland 3 (OG 7, McClair 17, McAllister 83)
CIS 0

Nya Ullevi, Gothenburg, 18-06-1992, 37,000
Holland 3 (Rijkaard 3, Witschge 15, Bergkamp 73)
Germany 1 (Klinsmann 53)

	Ho	Ge	Sc	CI	Pl	W	D	L	F	A	Pts
Holland	-	3-1	1-0	0-0	3	2	1	0	4	1	5
Germany	-	-	2-0	1-1	3	1	1	1	4	4	3
Scotland	-	-	-	3-0	3	1	0	2	3	3	2
CIS	-	-	-	-	3	0	2	1	1	4	2

SEMI-FINALS

Råsunda, Stockholm, 21-06-1992, 28,000
Germany 3 (Hässler 11, Riedle 59 88)
Sweden 2 (Brolin 64, Andersson 89)

Nya Ullevi, Gothenburg, 22-06-1992
Denmark 2 (Larsen H. 5 32)
Holland 2 (Bergkamp 23, Rijkaard 85)
Denmark won 5-4 on penalties

FINAL
Nya Ullevi, Gothenburg, 26-06-1992, 37,000. Referee: Galler, Switzerland
DENMARK 2 (Jensen J. 18, Vilfort 78)
GERMANY 0
Denmark - Schmeichel - Sivebaek (Christiansen), Nielsen.K, Olsen.L, Piechnik, Christofte, Jensen.J, Vilfort, Larsen.H - Povlsen, Laudrup.B. Tr: Möller Nielsen
Germany - Illgner - Helmer, Reuter, Kohler, Buchwald - Brehme, Hässler, Sammer (Doll), Effenberg (Thom) - Riedle, Klinsmann. Tr: Vogts

	Country	G	S	B	Finals	S-Finals
1	Germany	2	2	1	4	5
2	Soviet Union	1	3	-	4	5
3	Spain	1	1	-	2	2
4	Holland	1	-	2	1	3
5	Czechoslovakia	1	-	2	1	2
6	Denmark	1	-	1	1	3
7	Italy	1	-	1	1	2
8	France	1	-	-	1	2
9	Yugoslavia	-	2	-	2	3
10	Belgium	-	1	1	1	2
	Hungary	-	-	1	-	2
12	England	-	-	1	-	1
	Portugal	-	-	1	-	1
	Sweden	-	-	1	-	

OTHER SENIOR TOURNAMENTS

THE DR. GERÖ / INTERNATIONAL CUP

The International Cup, as it was originally known, was the brainchild of Hugo Meisl, one of the dominant personalities of inter-war European football administration. The competition brought together four of the most powerful European nations of the time, Italy, Austria, Czechoslovakia and Hungary, as well as Switzerland and, in the final edition, Yugoslavia. It was ranked with the British International Championships as the most important of the regional competitions of the time, ahead of the Scandinavian, Balkan and Baltic Cups.

Usually played over two years, six editions of the tournament were started but only five finished, the 1936-37 series being cut short by the hostile political climate of the time and the annexation of Austria by Germany. It was played twice after the Second World War, both tournaments taking a marathon five years to complete, but when the European Championship was introduced in 1958 the organisers felt that much of the justification for the event was gone, and it was discontinued in 1960.

Honours were evenly spread over the years. Italy were the only side to win twice, a fair reflection of their inter-war strength, whilst the Austrian "Wunderteam" gained just recognition for their good football by winning the second series. Not surprisingly the great Hungarian team of the late 1940s and early 1950s won the first post-war edition (1948-53) and it was the other Eastern bloc country, Czechoslovakia, who won the last title. Only Switzerland did not manage to win at least one tournament, finishing last in each series.

1927-29 Italy
1931-32 Austria
1933-35 Italy
1936-37 -
1948-53 Hungary
1955-60 Czechoslovakia

1ST EDITION. 1927 - 1930

	It	Au	Cz	Hu	Sz	Pl	W	D	L	F	A	Pts
ITALY	-	0-1	4-2	4-3	3-2	8	5	1	2	21	15	11
Austria	3-0	-	0-1	5-1	2-0	8	5	0	3	17	10	10
Czechoslovakia	2-2	2-0	-	1-1	5-0	8	4	2	2	17	10	10
Hungary	0-5	5-3	2-0	-	3-1	8	4	1	3	20	23	9
Switzerland	2-3	1-3	1-4	4-5	-	8	0	0	8	11	28	0

Decisive match. Ulloi ut, Budapest, 11-05-1930, 40,000
Hungary 0
Italy 5 (Meazza 17, 65, 70, Magnozzi 72, Costantino 84)
Hungary - Aknai - Korányi, Fogl - Borsányi, Turay, Vig - Markos, Takács, Opata, Hirzer, Titkos
Italy - Combi - Monzeglio, Caligaris - Colombari, Ferraris, Pitto Costantino, Baloncieri, Meazza, Magnozzi, Orsi

Champions: **ITALY**

2ND EDITION. 1931 - 1932

	Au	It	Hu	Cz	Sz	Pl	W	D	L	F	A	Pts
AUSTRIA	-	2-1	0-0	2-1	3-1	8	4	3	1	19	9	11
Italy	2-1	-	3-2	2-2	3-0	8	3	3	2	14	11	9
Hungary	2-2	1-1	-	2-1	6-2	8	2	4	2	17	15	8
Czechoslovakia	1-1	2-1	3-3	-	7-3	8	2	3	3	18	19	7
Switzerland	1-8	1-1	3-1	5-1	-	8	2	1	5	16	30	5

Decisive game. Prater, Vienna, 20-03-1932, 63,000
Austria 2 (Sindelar 56, 58)
Italy 1 (Meazza 66)
Austria - Hiden - Schramseis, Blum - Mock, Hoffmann, Nausch - Zischek, Gschweidl, Sindelar, Müller, Vogel
Italy - Sclavi - Rosetta, Allemandi - Pitto, Ferraris, Bertolini - Costantino, Sansone, Meazza, Magnozzi, Orsi

Champions: **AUSTRIA**

3RD EDITION. 1933 - 1935

	It	Au	Hu	Cz	Sz	Pl	W	D	L	F	A	Pts
ITALY	-	2-4	2-2	2-0	5-2	8	5	1	2	18	10	11
Austria	0-2	-	4-4	2-2	3-0	8	3	3	2	17	15	9
Hungary	0-1	3-1	-	1-0	3-0	8	3	3	2	17	16	9
Czechoslovakia	2-1	0-0	2-2	-	3-1	8	2	4	2	11	11	8
Switzerland	0-3	2-3	6-2	2-2	-	8	1	1	6	13	24	3

Decisive game. Prater, Vienna, 24-03-1935, 60,000
Austria 0
Italy 2 (Piola 51, 81)
Austria - Platzer - Pavlicek, Sesta - Wagner, Smistik, Skoumal - Zischek, Gschweidl, Sindelar, Kaburek, Pesser
Italy - Ceresoli - Monzeglio, Mascheroni - Pitto, Faccio, Corsi - Guaita, Demaria, Piola, Ferrari Giovanni, Orsi

Champions: **ITALY**

4TH EDITION. 1936 - 1937. UNFINISHED

	Hu	It	Cz	Au	Sz	Pl	W	D	L	F	A	Pts
Hungary	-	-	8-3	5-3	2-0	7	5	0	2	24	15	10
Italy	2-0	-	-	-	4-2	4	3	1	0	9	4	7
Czechoslovakia	5-2	0-1	-	2-1	5-3	7	3	1	3	16	20	7
Austria	1-2	-	1-1	-	4-3	6	2	1	3	13	14	5
Switzerland	1-5	2-2	4-0	1-3	-	8	1	1	6	16	25	3

5TH EDITION. 1948 - 1953

	Hu	Cz	Au	It	Sz	Pl	W	D	L	F	A	Pt
HUNGARY	-	2-1	6-1	1-1	7-4	8	5	1	2	27	17	11
Czechoslovakia	5-2	-	3-1	2-0	5-0	8	4	1	3	18	12	9
Austria	3-2	3-1	-	1-0	3-3	8	3	1	4	15	19	9
Italy	0-3	3-0	3-1	-	2-0	8	3	2	2	10	9	8
Switzerland	2-4	1-1	1-2	1-1	-	8	1	3	4	12	25	3

Decisive match. Ulloi ut, Budapest, 23-05-1948, 37,000

Hungary 2 (Egresi, Deák)
Czechoslovakia 1 (Subert)

Hungary - Henni - Rudas, Nagy - Balogh, Kovács (Kéri), Nagymarosi - Egresi, Szusza, Deák, Puskás, Tóth

Czechoslovakia - Havlícek (Capek) - Senecky, Vedral - Pokorny, Marko, Karel, Kokstein, Rygr, Malatinsky, Subert, Klimek

Champions: **HUNGARY**

6TH EDITION. 1955 - 1960

	Cz	Hu	Au	Yu	It	Sz	Pl	W	D	L	F	A	Pts
Czechoslovakia	-	1-3	3-2	1-0	2-1	3-2	10	7	2	1	25	15	16
Hungary	2-4	-	6-1	2-2	2-0	8-0	10	6	3	1	34	16	15
Austria	2-2	2-2	-	2-1	3-2	4-0	10	4	3	3	21	21	11
Yugoslavia	1-2	1-3	1-1	-	6-1	0-0	10	3	3	4	21	13	9
Italy	1-1	1-1	2-1	0-4	-	3-0	10	2	3	5	12	21	7
Switzerland	1-6	4-5	2-3	1-5	1-1	-	10	0	2	8	11	38	2

Decisive match. Nep, Budapest, 20-05-1956, 90,000

Hungary 2 (Machos 32, Bozsik 65)
Czechoslovakia 4 (Feureisl 8, Moravcík 27 55 Pazdera 75)

Hungary - Gellér - Kárpáti, Kotász, Szojka - Teleki, Bozsik - Budai (Tichy), Kocsis, Machos, Hidegkuti, Fenyvesi

Czechoslovakia - Dolejsí - Hertl, Hledik, Novík - Pluskal, Masopust - Pazdera, Moravcík, Feureisl (Práda), Borovicka, Kraus

Champions: **CZECHOSLOVAKIA**

THE MITROPA CUP

The Mitropa Cup was the most glamorous competition in Europe in the inter-war years and was the forerunner of today's European club competitions. The idea to have clubs from different countries playing a knock-out cup had been touted for some years and Hugo Meisl, as well as launching the International Cup for national sides, introduced the Mitropa Cup the same year. The name Mitropa is a shortened form of Mittel Europa, meaning middle Europe, and entry was restricted to Italy, Austria, Hungary, Czechoslovakia, Switzerland, and occasionally Romania and Yugoslavia. Initially only the champion team of each country was allowed to enter, but this was increased to the top two and, at one point, the top four.

The Mitropa Cup was suspended after 1939 and did not get underway again properly until 1955, but with the arrival of the European Cup, it lost much of its significance. None of the best sides were ever entered and in 1980 entry was restricted to the second division champions of the participating countries.

At its height in the inter-war years, the Mitropa Cup drew large crowds and sealed the reputations of many teams. The possibility of taking part certainly helped spice up club football in the area. Large fees were paid for players in a bid to win the tournament, especially by the Italian clubs, who apart from Bologna were surprisingly unsuccessful. Instead it was the cities of Prague, Budapest and Vienna which stole the honours, winning all but two of the titles. Slavia and Sparta Prague won three titles between them, Ferencváros and Ujpesti Budapest won two apiece, whilst Vienna clubs won the other four titles.

1927	Sparta Praha	TCH	6-2 1-2	Rapid Wien	AUT
1928	Ferencváros	HUN	7-1 3-5	Rapid Wien	AUT
1929	Ujpesti Dózsa	HUN	5-1 2-2	Slavia Praha	TCH
1930	Rapid Wien	AUT	2-0 2-3	Sparta Praha	TCH
1931	First Vienna	AUT	3-2 2-1	Wien AC	AUT
1932	Bologna	ITA	Walk-over		
1933	FK Austria	AUT	1-2 3-1	Ambrosiana-Inter	ITA
1934	Bologna	ITA	2-3 5-1	Admira Wien	AUT
1935	Sparta Praha	TCH	1-2 3-0	Ferencváros	HUN
1936	FK Austria	AUT	0-0 1-0	Sparta Praha	TCH
1937	Ferencváros	HUN	4-2 5-4	Lazio	ITA
1938	Slavia Praha	TCH	2-2 2-0	Ferencváros	HUN
1939	Ujpesti Dózsa	HUN	4-1 2-2	Ferencváros	HUN

THE LATIN CUP

Contested by the champions of Spain, Italy, Portugal and France, the Latin Cup replaced the Mitropa Cup as the top club competition in the immediate post-war period, but it too suffered from the arrival of the new UEFA-sponsored tournaments and was discontinued in 1957. Played in a single city every year, the tournament was curious in that there was not a cup presentation at the end of each edition. Instead, points were awarded – four to the winners down to one for the fourth-placed team – and after fours years the cup itself was awarded to the country with the highest number of combined points.

1949	Barcelona	ESP	2-1	Sporting CP	POR
1950	Benfica	POR	3-3 2-1	Bordeaux	FRA
1951	Milan	ITA	5-0	OSC Lille	FRA
1952	Barcelona	ESP	1-0	OGC Nice	FRA
1953	Stade de Reims	FRA	3-0	Milan	ITA
1954	-				
1955	Real Madrid	ESP	2-0	Stade de Reims	FRA
1956	Milan	ITA	2-1	Athletic Bilbao	ESP
1957	Real Madrid	ESP	1-0	Benfica	POR

The standings at the end of the first edition (1949-52) were

1	Spain	12
2	France	10
3	Italy	9
	Portugal	9

The standings at the end of the second edition (1953-57) were:

1	Spain	12
2	Italy	11
3	France	9
4	Portugal	8

THE BRITISH INTERNATIONAL CHAMPIONSHIP

Until England and Scotland decided in 1984 that they could no longer justify playing this annual championship with Northern Ireland and Wales, on the grounds of an overcrowded fixture list and dwindling attendances at the matches, the home internationals, as they were called, were the longest running of all the world's competitions.

Started in 1884 as a natural progression from the annual friendly matches that had taken place between the four British nations, the championship was the major feature in their fixture list until after the Second World War. Organised either over the length of the season or over a week at the end of it, the highlight was the England–Scotland game, played alternately in Glasgow and London.

1884	Scotland
1885	Scotland
1886	England / Scotland
1887	Scotland
1888	England
1889	Scotland
1890	Scotland / England
1891	England
1892	England
1893	England
1894	Scotland
1895	England
1896	Scotland
1897	Scotland
1898	England
1899	England
1900	Scotland
1901	England
1902	Scotland
1903	England / Ireland / Scotland
1904	England
1905	England
1906	England / Scotland
1907	Wales
1908	Scotland / England
1909	England
1910	Scotland
1911	England
1912	England / Scotland
1913	England
1914	Ireland
1915-19	-
1920	Wales
1921	Scotland
1922	Scotland
1923	Scotland
1924	Wales
1925	Scotland
1926	Scotland
1927	Scotland / England
1928	Wales
1929	Scotland
1930	England
1931	Scotland / England
1932	England
1933	Wales
1934	Wales
1935	England / Scotland
1936	Scotland
1937	Wales
1938	England
1939	England / Scotland / Wales
1940-46	-
1947	England
1948	England
1949	Scotland
1950	England
1951	Scotland
1952	Wales / England
1953	England / Scotland
1954	England
1955	England
1956	England / Scotland / Wales / Nth. Ireland
1957	England
1958	England / Nth. Ireland
1959	Nth. Ireland / England
1960	England / Scotland / Wales
1961	England
1962	Scotland
1963	Scotland
1964	Scotland / England / Nth. Ireland
1965	England
1966	England
1967	Scotland
1968	England
1969	England
1970	England / Scotland / Wales
1971	England
1972	England / Scotland
1973	England
1974	England
1975	England
1976	Scotland
1977	Scotland
1978	England
1979	England
1980	Nth. Ireland
1981	-
1982	England
1983	England
1984	Nth. Ireland

England	54 wins
Scotland	40 wins
Wales	12 wins
Ireland/Nth. Ire	8 wins

On two occasions the championship was used as a qualifying group for the World Cup (and once for the European Championship) but other members of UEFA were unhappy that this guaranteed Britain a World Cup place. Their complaints rather backfired when the British nations were duly placed in four separate groups for the 1958 World Cup and all four qualified for the finals in Sweden that year!

England and Scotland dominated the home internationals and after 1984 carried on their annual fixture under the guise of the Rous Cup in which another country, usually from South America, was invited to make up a threesome. But after repeated incidents of hooliganism between the English and the Scots, even this tournament went by the board, and in 1990, for the first time ever in peacetime, the most famous "derby" match of them all was not played.

THE SCANDINAVIAN CHAMPIONSHIP

Scandinavia boasted the strongest of the remaining regional tournaments, but this too was dropped as an ever-increasing fixture list crowded it out. Played consecutively from 1924 until 1971, each series lasted four years. Every nation played each other once a year, and when all had played their opponents twice at home and twice away, the winner was the nation with most points. Denmark, Norway and Finland all won one edition but Sweden were easily the strongest of the four as their tally of seven titles suggests.

1924-28	Denmark
1929-32	Norway
1933-36	Sweden
1937-47	Sweden
1948-51	Sweden
1952-55	Sweden
1956-59	Sweden
1960-63	Finland
1964-67	Sweden
1968-71	Sweden

THE BALTIC CUP

The Baltic Championships may have remained a historical curiosity had it not been for the re-emergence of Latvia, Lithuania and Estonia as independent nations in 1991. Played over the course of a few days in a designated city, the cup was never particularly notable as the three nations were always among the weakest in Europe.

1928	Latvia
1929	Estonia
1930	Lithuania
1931	Estonia
1932	Latvia
1935	Lithuania
1936	Latvia
1937	Latvia
1938	Estonia
1940	Latvia
1991	Lithuania
1992	Lithuania
1993	Latvia
1994	Lithuania
1995	Latvia

THE BALKAN CUP

The Balkan Cup, played in the 1930s and briefly revived in the 1970s, was a major factor in the development of the game in south-eastern Europe. Though none of the entrants were especially strong during the 1930s,

Yugoslavia, Romania and Bulgaria have all enjoyed successful spells since 1945. The tournament remains notable for affording Albania her only international honour to date.

1929-31	Romania	1946	Albania
1932	Bulgaria	1947	Hungary
1933	Romania	1948	Unfinished
1934	Yugoslavia	1973-76	Bulgaria
1934-35	Bulgaria	1977-80	Romania
1936	Romania		

EUROPEAN YOUTH TOURNAMENTS

One of the biggest growth areas in European football over the last 20 years has been the in the number of age-limited tournaments organised. A junior championship was launched in 1948 and until the start of the under-23 tournament in 1972 this was the main age-restricted competition in Europe. With the introduction of two FIFA-controlled world championships, Europe has had to fit in with the qualifying cycle for these tournaments. In 1982 an under-16 tournament was introduced to tie in with the World Under-16 championships, whilst the Under-18 Championships, which had grown out of the European Junior championship, was used to qualify teams foir the World Youth Championship. The other age-restricted tournament, the Under-23 championship, became an under-21 event and since the Barcelona Games has been used as a qualifying round for the Olympics.

EUROPEAN UNDER-16 CHAMPIONSHIP

1982	Italy	1-0	West Germany
1984	West Germany	2-0	Soviet Union
1985	Soviet Union	4-0	Greece
1986	Spain	2-1	Italy
1987	Italy *	1-0	Soviet Union
1988	Spain	0-0 4-2p	Portugal
1989	Portugal	4-1	East Germany
1990	Czechoslovakia	3-2	Yugoslavia
1991	Spain	2-0	Germany
1992	Germany		
1993	Poland	1-0	Italy
1994	Turkey	1-0	Denmark
1995	Portugal	2-0	Spain

* Italy's title was later taken away for fielding over-age players

EUROPEAN JUNIOR CHAMPIONSHIP

1948	England	1954	Spain
1949	France	1955	No final
1950	Austria	1956	No final
1951	Yugoslavia	1957	Austria
1952	Spain	1958	Italy
1953	Hungary	1959	Bulgaria
1960	Hungary	1971	England
1961	Portugal	1972	England
1962	Romania	1973	England
1963	England	1974	Bulgaria
1964	England	1975	England
1965	East Germany	1976	Soviet Union
1966	Soviet Union & Italy	1977	Belgium
1967	Soviet Union	1978	Soviet Union
1968	Czechoslovakia	1979	Yugoslavia
1969	Bulgaria	1980	England
1970	East Germany		

EUROPEAN YOUTH CHAMPIONSHIP - U18

1981	West Germany	1-0	Poland
1982	Scotland	3-1	Czechoslovakia
1983	France	1-0	Czechoslovakia
1984	Hungary	0-0 3-2p	Soviet Union
1986	East Germany	3-1	Italy
1988	Soviet Union	3-1	Portugal
1990	Soviet Union	0-0 4-2p	Portugal
1992	Turkey	2-1	Portugal
1993	England	1-0	Turkey
1994	Portugal	1-1 4-1p	Germany

EUROPEAN UNDER - 23 CHAMPIONSHIP

1972	Czechoslovakia	2-2 3-1	Soviet Union
1974	Hungary	2-3 4-0	East Germany
1976	Soviet Union	1-1 2-1	Hungary

EUROPEAN UNDER - 21 CHAMPIONSHIP

1978	Yugoslavia	1-0 4-4	East Germany
1980	Soviet Union	0-0 1-0	East Germany
1982	England	3-1 2-3	West Germany
1984	England	1-0 2-0	Spain
1986	Spain	1-2 2-1 3-0p	Italy
1988	France	0-0 3-0	Greece
1990	Soviet Union	4-2 3-1	Yugoslavia
1992	Italy	2-0 0-1	Sweden
1994	Italy	1-0	Portugal

EUROPEAN CHAMPIONSHIP FOR WOMEN

The European Championship for women, after an uncertain start, is now a flourishing event, and for two of the last three editions has doubled up as a qualifying tournament for the women's World Cup. Along with North America, Europe is where women's football is at its strongest. The US model is based around the college system, but in Europe the links with the men's game are much stronger. With a strong international calendar established, the next step is for the clubs in each country to venture beyond their own borders.

In Italy internationals have been played regularly since 1968, the same year as a national league for women was introduced. Many of the clubs like Lazio, Milan, Juventus and Bologna, bear the same name as their male counterparts. England also has a league and a cup competition, but the real power lies in Scandinavia. Norway won the second World Cup in 1995 having been runners-up in 1991, and Sweden was a major player in the rebirth of the women's game in the 1970s. Germany is also a power to be reckoned with. A championship has been contested there since 1974 and despite not playing their first international until 1982 they have been European champions three times and were World Cup semi-finalists in 1991.

Year	Winner	Score	Runner-up
1984	Sweden	1-0 0-1 4-3p	England
1987	Norway	2-1	Sweden
1989	West Germany	4-1	Norway
1991	West Germany	3-1	Norway
1993	Norway	1-0	Italy
1995	Germany	3-2	Sweden

1st EDITION 1982-84

FIRST ROUND

Group 1

	Sd	No	Fi	IC	Pl	W	D	L	F	A	Pts
SWEDEN	-	2-0	5-0	5-0	6	6	0	0	26	1	12
Norway	1-2	-	3-0	2-2	6	3	1	2	10	6	7
Finland	0-6	0-3	-	3-0	6	2	0	4	5	17	4
Iceland	0-6	0-1	0-2	-	6	0	1	5	2	19	1

Group 2

	En	Sc	RI	NI	Pl	W	D	L	F	A	Pts
ENGLAND	-	2-0	6-0	7-1	6	6	0	0	24	1	12
Scotland	0-4	-	3-0	3-0	6	3	1	2	9	8	7
Rep. Ireland	0-1	1-1	-	3-2	6	2	1	3	6	14	5
Nth. Ireland	0-4	1-2	1-2	-	6	0	0	6	5	21	0

Group 3

	It	Fr	Sz	Pt	Pl	W	D	L	F	A	Pts
ITALY	-	3-0	2-0	3-0	6	5	0	1	12	1	10
France	1-0	-	1-1	2-0	6	2	3	1	4	4	7
Switzerland	0-2	0-0	-	2-0	6	1	3	2	4	6	5
Portugal	0-2	0-0	1-1	-	6	0	2	4	1	10	2

Group 4

	De	Ho	WG	Be	Pl	W	D	L	F	A	Pts
DENMARK	-	2-0	1-0	1-0	6	3	2	1	8	5	8
Holland	2-1	-	2-2	5-0	6	2	2	2	12	9	6
West Germany	1-1	1-1	-	1-1	6	0	5	1	6	7	5
Belgium	2-2	3-2	1-1	-	6	1	3	2	7	12	5

SEMI-FINALS

Sweden.......................3-2 2-1 ....Italy
England.......................2-1 1-0 ....Denmark

FINAL

1st leg. Gothenburg, 21-05-1984, 5,000

Sweden 1 (Sundhage)
England 0

2nd leg. Luton, 27-05-1984, 2,000

England 1 (Curl)
Sweden 0

Sweden won 4-3 on penalties

Sweden - Leidinge - Jansson, Börjesson, Burevik, Kaberg, Svenjeby, Andersson, Hansson, Johannsson, Ahman-Svensson, Videkull, Sundhage

2nd EDITION 1985-87

FIRST ROUND

Group 1

	No	De	WG	Fi	Pl	W	D	L	F	A	Pts
NORWAY	-	2-2	0-0	2-0	6	3	3	0	12	6	7
Denmark	2-5	-	3-0	1-1	6	2	2	2	10	10	6
West Germany	2-3	2-0	-	1-0	6	2	1	3	5	7	5
Finland	0-0	0-2	1-0	-	6	1	2	3	2	6	4

Group 2

	En	Sc	RI	NI	Pl	W	D	L	F	A	Pts
ENGLAND	-	4-0	4-0	-	4	4	0	0	17	1	8
Scotland	1-3	-	-	7-0	4	2	0	2	17	8	4
Rep. Ireland	0-6	-	-	1-0	4	2	0	2	2	10	4
Nth. Ireland	-	1-9	0-1	-	4	0	0	4	1	18	0

Group 3

	Sd	Ho	Be	Fr	Pl	W	D	L	F	A	Pts
SWEDEN	-	2-0	5-0	1-0	6	5	0	1	14	3	10
Holland	2-0	-	3-0	1-0	6	4	0	2	12	8	8
Belgium	1-2	3-1	-	3-1	6	2	0	4	8	15	4
France	0-4	3-5	3-1	-	6	1	0	5	7	15	2

Group 4

	It	Hu	Sp	Sz	Pl	W	D	L	F	A	Pts
ITALY	-	1-0	1-1	3-0	6	5	1	0	13	6	11
Hungary	2-3	-	1-0	1-1	6	3	1	2	8	7	7
Spain	2-3	1-2	-	0-2	6	1	1	4	7	9	3
Switzerland	1-2	1-2	0-3	-	6	1	1	4	5	11	3

FINAL TOURNAMENT

Held in Norway 11-14 June 1987

SEMI-FINALS

Norway.......................2-0 ....Italy
Sweden.......................2-2 3-2p ....England

3RD PLACE

Italy.......................2-1 ....England

FINAL

Oslo, 14-06-1987, 8,000

Norway 2 (Stendal 2)
Sweden 1 (Videkull)

Norway - Andreassen - Hoch-Nielsen, Straedet, Storhaug, Mortensen, Scheel, Støre, Haugen, Stendal, Nyborg, Nielsen (Bakken)

3rd EDITION 1987-89

FIRST ROUND

Group 1

	De	No	En	Fi	Pl	W	D	L	F	A	Pts
DENMARK	-	3-2	2-0	3-1	6	5	0	1	12	6	10
NORWAY	0-1	-	2-0	0-2	6	2	1	3	10	10	5
England	2-1	1-3	-	1-1	6	2	1	3	6	10	5
Finland	1-2	3-3	1-2	-	6	1	2	3	9	11	4

Group 2

	Ho	Sd	RI	Pl	W	D	L	F	A	Pts
HOLLAND	-	1-0	2-0	4	3	1	0	4	0	7
SWEDEN	0-0	-	4-0	4	1	2	1	5	2	4
Rep. Ireland	0-1	1-1	-	4	0	1	3	1	8	1

Scotland withdrew mid-tournament. All their results were nullified

Group 3

	WG	It	Hu	Sz	Pl	W	D	L	F	A	Pts
WEST GERMANY	-	3-0	4-0	0-0	6	4	2	0	18	0	10

					Pl	W	D	L	F	A	Pts
ITALY	0-0	-	5-1	5-0	6	3	2	1	16	4	8
HUNGARY	0-1	0-0	-	7-1	6	1	1	4	8	14	3
SWITZERLAND	0-10	0-6	3-0	-	6	1	1	4	4	28	3

Group 4

	Fr	Cz	Be	Sp	Bu	Pl	W	D	L	F	A	Pts
FRANCE	-	2-2	0-0	0-0	5-0	8	4	4	0	14	3	12
CZECHOSLOV.	0-0	-	0-0	1-0	3-0	8	4	4	0	10	3	12
BELGIUM	0-2	1-1	-	1-0	5-0	8	2	4	2	7	4	8
SPAIN	1-3	0-2	1-0	-	1-0	8	2	2	4	4	8	6
BULGARIA	0-2	0-1	0-0	1-1	-	8	0	2	6	1	18	2

QUARTER-FINALS

Czechoslovakia .... 1-1 0-2 .... **West Germany**
Italy .... 2-0 2-1 .... France
Denmark .... 1-5 1-1 .... **Sweden**
Norway .... 2-1 3-0 .... Holland

FINAL TOURNAMENT

Held in West Germany 28 June - 2 July

SEMI-FINALS

West Germany .... 1-1 4-3p .... Italy
Norway .... 2-1 .... Sweden

3RD PLACE

Sweden .... 2-1 .... Italy

FINAL

Osnabruck, 2-07-1989, 22,000
West Germany 4 (Lohn 2, Mohr, Fehrmann)
Norway 1 (Grude)
West Germany - Isbert - Kuhlmann - Nardenbach, Raith - Haberlass (Bindl), Fitschen (Fehrmann), Neid, Damm - Voss, Mohr, Lohn

4TH EDITION 1989-91

FIRST ROUND

Group 1

	Ho	RI	NI	Pl	W	D	L	F	A	Pts
HOLLAND	-	2-0	9-0	4	3	1	0	17	0	7
REP. IRELAND	0-0	-	4-0	4	2	1	1	6	3	5
NTH. IRELAND	0-6	1-2	-	4	0	0	4	1	21	0

Group 2

	Sd	Fr	Pd	Pl	W	D	L	F	A	Pts
SWEDEN	-	4-1	4-	4	4	0	0	12	2	8
FRANCE	0-2	-	2-0	4	2	0	2	6	7	4
POLAND	0-2	1-3	-	4	0	0	4	2	11	0

Group 3

	No	En	Fi	Be	Pl	W	D	L	F	A	Pts
NORWAY	-	2-0	4-0	4-0	6	5	1	0	12	0	11
ENGLAND	0-0	-	0-0	1-0	6	2	3	1	4	2	7
FINLAND	0-1	0-0	-	3-0	6	1	2	3	3	6	4
BELGIUM	0-1	0-3	1-0	-	6	1	0	5	1	12	2

Group 4

	WG	Hu	Cz	Bu	Pl	W	D	L	F	A	Pts
WEST GERMANY	-	0-0	5-0	4-0	6	5	1	0	18	1	11
HUNGARY	0-4	-	2-0	2-0	6	3	1	2	7	7	7
CZECHOSLOVAKIA	0-1	3-0	-	2-0	6	3	0	3	8	10	6
BULGARIA	1-4	0-3	2-3	-	6	0	0	6	3	18	0

Group 5

	De	It	Sz	Sp	Pl	W	D	L	F	A	Pts
DENMARK	-	1-0	4-0	5-0	6	5	1	0	18	2	11
ITALY	1-1	-	4-1	3-1	6	3	2	1	12	4	8
SWITZERLAND	0-4	0-4	-	2-1	6	1	1	4	3	17	3
SPAIN	1-3	0-0	0-0	-	6	0	2	4	3	13	2

QUARTER-FINALS

England .... 1-4 0-2 .... West Germany
Sweden .... 1-1 0-0 .... Italy
Denmark .... 0-0 1-0 .... Holland
Norway .... 2-1 2-0 .... Hungary

FINAL TOURNAMENT

Held in Denmark 10-14 July 1991

SEMI-FINALS

West Germany .... 3-0 .... Italy
Norway .... 0-0 8-7p .... Denmark

3RD PLACE

Denmark .... 2-1 .... Italy

FINAL

Aalborg, 14-07-1991, 3,000
West Germany 3 (Mohr 2, Neid)
Norway 1 (Hegstad)
West Germany - Isbert - Fitschen - Nardenbach, Kuhlmann - Unsleber (Gottschlich), Neid, Damm, Raith - Voss (Bornschein), Mohr, Wiegmann

5TH EDITION 1991-93

FIRST ROUND

Group 1

	No	Be	Sz	Pl	W	D	L	F	A	Pts
NORWAY	-	8-0	6-0	4	3	1	0	24	0	7
BELGIUM	0-0	-	0-0	4	1	2	1	1	8	4
SWITZERLAND	0-10	0-1	-	4	0	1	3	0	17	1

Group 2

	De	Fr	Fi	Pl	W	D	L	F	A	Pts
DENMARK	-	4-1	5-0	4	3	1	0	14	2	7
FRANCE	0-4	-	5-1	4	1	1	2	7	10	3
FINLAND	1-1	1-1	-	4	0	2	2	3	12	2

Group 3

	En	Ic	Sc	Pl	W	D	L	F	A	Pts
ENGLAND	-	4-0	1-0	4	4	0	0	9	1	8
ICELAND	1-2	-	2-1	4	1	1	2	3	7	3
SCOTLAND	0-2	0-0	-	4	0	1	3	1	5	1

Group 4

	Sd	Sp	RI	Pl	W	D	L	F	A	Pts
SWEDEN	-	1-1	10-0	4	3	1	0	16	1	7
SPAIN	0-4	-	0-1	4	1	1	2	2	6	3
REP. IRELAND	0-1	0-1	-	4	1	0	3	1	12	2

Group 5

	Ho	Ro	Gr	Pl	W	D	L	F	A	Pts
HOLLAND	-	1-1	2-0	4	2	2	0	6	1	6
ROMANIA	0-0	-	1-0	4	1	3	0	2	1	5
GREECE	0-3	0-0	-	4	0	1	3	0	6	1

Group 6

Germany .... 3-0 .... Yugoslavia

Group 7

	It	Cz	Pd	Pl	W	D	L	F	A	Pts
ITALY	-	2-2	3-1	4	3	1	0	12	4	7
CZECHOSLOVAKIA	0-3	-	3-0	4	2	1	1	7	6	5
POLAND	1-4	1-2	-	4	0	0	4	3	12	0

Group 8

	IS	Hu	Bu	Pl	W	D	L	F	A	Pts
COMMONWLTH IS	-	2-1	3-0	4	3	1	0	7	2	7

HUNGARY	0-0	-	3-0	4	2	1	1	5	2	5
BULGARIA	1-2	0-1	-	4	0	0	4	1	9	0

QUARTER-FINALS

Norway 3-0 3-0 Holland
Commonwealth IS 0-7 0-0 **Germany**
Sweden 1-2 1-1 **Denmark**
Italy 3-2 3-0 England

FINAL TOURNAMENT

Held in Italy, 29 June - 4 July 1993

SEMI-FINALS

Norway 1-0 Denmark
Italy 1-1 4-3p Germany

3RD PLACE

Denmark 3-1 Germany

FINAL

Cesena, 4-07-1993

Norway 1 (Hegstadt)
Italy 0

Norway - Beth - Nysveen, Nymark.N, Zaborowski, Espeseth - Riise, Støre, Carleen, Andersen.A - Aarønes (Hegstad), Medalen (Sandberg)

6TH EDITION 1993-95

FIRST ROUND

Group 1

	No	Fi	Hu	Cz	Pl	W	D	L	F	A	Pts
NORWAY	-	4-0	8-0	6-1	6	5	1	0	33	3	11
Finland	2-2	-	1-1	4-0	6	2	3	1	8	7	7
Hungary	0-4	0-1	-	4-4	6	0	3	3	5	18	3
Czech Republic	0-9	0-0	0-0	-	6	0	3	3	5	23	3

Group 2

	Ru	Ro	Uk	Po	Pl	W	D	L	F	A	Pts
RUSSIA	-	1-0	2-1	0-0	6	4	2	0	9	4	10
Romania	2-2	-	5-0	3-0	6	3	2	1	16	5	8
Ukraine	0-2	2-2	-	3-0	6	2	1	3	9	12	5
Poland	1-2	0-4	1-3	-	6	0	1	5	2	15	1

Group 3

	De	Bu	Li	Pl	W	D	L	F	A	Pts
Denmark	-	6-1	11-0	4	4	0	0	32	1	8
Bulgaria	0-4	-	1-1	4	1	1	2	3	11	3
Lithuania	0-11	0-1	-	4	0	1	3	1	24	1

Group 4

	Sw	Sl	La	Pl	W	D	L	F	A	Pts
Sweden	-	6-0	9-0	4	4	0	0	22	0	8
Slovakia	0-2	-	3-1	4	2	0	2	4	9	4
Latvia	0-5	0-1	-	4	0	0	4	1	18	0

Group 5

	Ge	Cr	Sw	Wa	Pl	W	D	L	F	A	Pts
GERMANY	-	8-0	11-0	12-0	6	6	0	0	55	0	12
Croatia	0-7	-	1-1	3-0	6	3	1	2	8	18	7
Switzerland	0-5	1-2	-	4-2	6	2	1	3	9	23	5
Wales	0-12	1-2	2-3	-	6	0	0	6	5	36	0

Group 6

	It	Fr	Po	Sc	Pl	W	D	L	F	A	Pts
ITALY	-	2-0	1-2	4-0	6	4	1	1	15	4	9
France	1-1	-	3-0	1-0	6	4	1	1	9	3	9
Portugal	1-3	0-1	-	8-2	6	3	0	3	13	11	6
Scotland	0-4	0-3	1-2	-	6	0	0	6	3	22	0

Group 7

	En	Sp	Be	Sl	Pl	W	D	L	F	A	Pts
ENGLAND	-	0-0	6-0	10-0	6	4	2	0	29	0	10
Spain	0-0	-	4-0	17-0	6	3	3	0	29	0	9
Belgium	0-3	0-0	-	7-0	6	2	1	3	15	13	5
Slovenia	0-10	0-8	0-8	-	6	0	0	6	0	60	0

Group 8

	Ic	Ho	Gr	Pl	W	D	L	F	A	Pts
ICELAND	-	2-1	3-0	4	4	0	0	12	2	8
Holland	0-1	-	2-0	4	2	0	2	7	3	4
Greece	1-6	0-4	-	4	0	0	4	1	15	0

QUARTER-FINALS

Russia 0-1 4-0 **Germany**
Iceland 1-2 1-2 **England**
Italy 1-3 2-4 **Norway**
Denmark 2-0 0-3 **Sweden**

SEMI-FINALS

England 1-4 1-2 **Germany**
Norway 4-3 1-4 **Sweden**

FINAL

Kaiserslautern, 26-03-1995, 8,000

Germany 3 (Meinert 32, Prinz 64, Wiegmann 83)
Sweden 2 (Andersson 6, Andelen-Andersson 88)

Germany - Goller - Bernhard, Austermühl, Pohlmann, Lohn, Meinert, Voss (Wunderlich), Wiegmann, Mohr, Neid, Brocker-Grigoli (Prinz)

HISTORY OF THE EUROPEAN CUPS

Europe has three major club competitions. The European Cup is the premier event and until 1994 it was open to all of the continent's champion clubs. Since then, however, only the top 24 UEFA-ranked countries' champions have been allowed to compete. The other two tournaments are the Cup Winners Cup, reserved for the winners of the knock-out competition in each country, and the UEFA Cup, which is for the best of the rest. The number of entries allocated to individual countries in this last competition is determined by a UEFA coefficient table and is based upon past results in all three tournaments. Since 1994 the UEFA Cup, always the largest of the three tournaments, has been even further expanded, taking the overflow of champion clubs from the European Cup.

The European Champion Clubs' Cup, or European Cup as it is more usually known, was the first of the three to get underway. In early 1955, Gabriel Hanot, then editor of L'Equipe, a French daily sports paper, invited representatives to a meeting in Paris to sound out the idea of creating a championship for the major clubs of Europe. Fifteen clubs responded to his invitation by attending the meeting and it was agreed to organise a tournament for the 1955-56 season.

FIFA were willing to support the idea and so UEFA gave the tournament its blessing, and has organised it ever since. The first tournament was curious in that only half of the clubs which took part were the champions of their respective countries. Not until the following season did UEFA manage to restrict it to the current practice of champions (and the previous season's winners) only. Fortunately for the long-term success of the competition, Real Madrid were maturing into one of the best sides club football had ever seen, and in a feat which is almost certain never to be repeated, they won five consecutive editions of the tournament and wrote themselves into football folklore. Ever since these triumphs, the competition has had a special aura about it.

This was not the case with the other two tournaments. At roughly the same time as the meeting arranged by Hanot, Ernst Thommen, a Swiss vice-president of UEFA, invited representatives to Basle with a view to organising a tournament for representative sides from cities in Europe that regularly organised trade fairs. This may have been a somewhat tenuous reason for a tournament, but it was agreed upon, and the International Industries Fairs Inter-Cities Cup was launched in the autumn of 1955.

Commonly known as the Fairs Cup, it drew entrants from ten cities that organised such events. The original idea was for each of these cities to field a representative side from all of the teams located in their city, but this idea did not hold out for very long. Barcelona, the winners of the first edition, fielded a team based purely on players from CF Barcelona, whilst Birmingham simply entered Birmingham City. Originally conceived as a two-year tournament, the first edition lasted for three years during which time only 23 games were played.

The Cup Winners Cup did not have a particularly auspicious start either. To begin with, not every country in Europe had a cup competition. Many did not see the need for one, and it was only in countries like Britain, where the cup goes back further than the league, that they enjoyed any real support. Nevertheless the organising committee of the Mitropa Cup launched the competition for the 1960-61 season, and Europe's trio of cups was on the road.

From the early 1960s to the 1990s the tournament structures remained fairly stable. With there being 32 active members of UEFA for most of that period, the format for the European Cup and Cup Winners Cup was a simple knock-out on a home and away basis, with the highest aggregate scorers going through to the next round. If the scores were level, the team which had scored more goals away from home qualified, and if that could not separate the sides, the winner was decided on penalty kicks. The away-goals system was first used in 1967, before which time an extra game was often played. Penalty kicks were introduced in 1971 to replace the very arbitrary toss of a coin.

The only fixtures not played on a home and away basis are the European Cup final and the Cup Winners Cup final, which are played in a neutral city. Until 1984 the venues were selected at the start of the season, but there was always the danger that the 'home' side would reach the final and on the 10 occasions this happened only once did the visitors win, when Liverpool beat Roma in 1984. Now the venues are decided later in the season to ensure that the ground will be neutral whoever reaches the final.

The UEFA Cup final, by contrast, is played over two legs. Over the years this tournament has been regarded by many as the hardest of the three to win. With twice the number of teams taking part, there is more quality opposition to overcome, and the field very often includes many of the season's eventual domestic champions. Less than half the winners of the European Cup have managed to retain their league title in the same season.

There have been three distinct phases in these European competitions. The first, lasting until the late 1960s, was the period of domination by clubs from southern Europe, notably, Spain, Italy and Portugal. Not until Glasgow Celtic triumphed in 1967 was the European Cup won by a non-Latin side, whilst southern teams were also dominant in the Fairs Cup. Other than Real Madrid, the most notable sides of this period were Barcelona, Valencia and Real Zaragoza from Spain, the two Milan clubs and Roma from Italy, and the two Lisbon clubs, Benfica and Sporting, from Portugal.

The European Cup produced some exciting encounters in these early years, none better than the 1960 final between Real Madrid and Eintracht Frankfurt. Scorer of a hat-trick that day was Alfredo Di Stéfano, and he was without question the leading personality in the tournament until he left Real in 1964. His 49 goals from 58 matches in the European Cup, the only one of the competitions in which he competed, is a record never likely to be equalled.

Eusébio took over Di Stéfano's mantle in the 1960s as his Benfica side reached five finals, winning two of them. In the 1962 clash between Benfica and Real, Eusébio's two goals were instrumental in helping overcome the Madrid giants in what was another scintillating game. Eusébio's all-time goals tally in the Europeean Cup, 47, is second only to Di Stéfano.

Italy was not to be left out and for three seasons running in the first half of the 1960s, the city of Milan ruled Europe. Clubs from northern Europe were beginning to mount a challenge, however. In 1963 Tottenham Hotspur won the Cup Winners Cup and West Ham United matched them two years later. Then Celtic's European Cup win against Internazionale in 1967 signalled a dramatic decline for the established powers as Britain, Holland and Germany began to flex their muscles.

This second phase saw two hat-tricks of European Cup wins, first by Ajax of Holland and then Bayern Munich of West Germany. These followed wins by Manchester United in 1968 and Feyenoord in 1970. The same was happening in the Cup Winners Cup and Fairs Cup. Milan won the Cup Winners Cup in 1968 and 1973, but they were the only Latin side to do so from 1965 until Barcelona won it for the first time in 1979.

The Fairs Cup was becoming very much an English affair by the late 1960s with six victories on the trot. It was in the late 1970s, however, that English clubs really came into their own, especially in the European Cup. Seven victories in eight years by three teams from England, most notably Liverpool, represents the best run of any country in the European Cup, but this period also heralded a decline in the number of goals scored, especially in the finals. The first five finals produced 26 goals; it took 19 finals after 1975 for the same number to be reached.

The year 1985 marked a turning point in European football. For many years the game had been plagued by hooliganism from the supporters. The 1975 European Cup final in Paris was marred by supporters of Leeds United tearing the stadium to pieces as their team lost to Bayern Munich, whilst the previous year supporters of Tottenham and Feyenoord had wrecked the UEFA Cup final. Whenever the English travelled abroad they seemed to leave a trail of destruction behind them.

The whole sordid problem came to a head at the 1985 European Cup final between Liverpool and Juventus when 39 supporters, mainly Italians, were crushed to death in the Heysel stadium in Brussels. The English clubs paid the price and were banned from all European competitions indefinitely.

Though free of English hooligans, the European competitions suffered without the English clubs who had done so well until 1985. Goals in the final of the European Cup threatened to dry up all together as three finals finished 0-0 and had to be settled by penalties. The hooligan problem did not go away either, as there seemed to be an active element in most countries determined to copy the English.

However, this third phase in European club football was also marked by the rise of the Latin countries again, especially Italy, whose clubs, free from a ban on importing players, bought up the best. Milan most notably have revived past glories with three European Cup wins including two crushing 4-0 victories, but Juventus, Internazionale, Napoli, Parma and Sampdoria have all won one or other of the competitions.

The 1990s have seen wholesale changes in European club football. In 1991 English clubs were readmitted, and although they have not managed to reach the heights of previous years, there have been wins in the Cup Winners Cup for Manchester United and Arsenal. The increasing number of countries affiliated to UEFA has proved something of a headache, with extensive pre-qualifying now necessary in the UEFA Cup and Cup Winners Cup.

There is also a clear desire on the part of the continent's biggest clubs to reap the maximum reward from European competition. For many years the idea of a European Super League had been mooted, thwarted only by the adverse effect it would have on the national leagues. However, in 1992 a Champions League of two divisions replaced the knock-out stages of the European Cup from the quarter-finals onwards, and in 1995 the League was expanded to four groups of four teams and switched to replace the first and second rounds, with the knock-out format returning for the quarter-finals. For UEFA and the lucky 16 clubs, it meant that lucrative television contracts could no longer be compromised by an inconvenient early exit.

THE EUROPEAN CHAMPION CLUBS' CUP

Year	Winner	Score	Runner-up
1956	Real Madrid	4-3	Stade de Reims
1957	Real Madrid	2-0	Fiorentina
1958	Real Madrid	3-2	Milan
1959	Real Madrid	2-0	Stade de Reims
1960	Real Madrid	7-3	Eintracht Frankfurt
1961	Benfica	3-2	Barcelona
1962	Benfica	5-3	Real Madrid
1963	Milan	2-1	Benfica
1964	Internazionale	3-1	Real Madrid
1965	Internazionale	1-0	Benfica
1966	Real Madrid	2-1	Partizan Beograd
1967	Glasgow Celtic	2-1	Internazionale
1968	Manchester United	4-1	Benfica
1969	Milan	4-1	Ajax
1970	Feyenoord	2-1	Glasgow Celtic
1971	Ajax	2-0	Panathinaikos
1972	Ajax	2-0	Internazionale
1973	Ajax	1-0	Juventus
1974	Bayern München	1-1 4-0	Atlético Madrid
1975	Bayern München	2-0	Leeds United
1976	Bayerm München	1-0	AS Saint-Étienne
1977	Liverpool	3-1	Borussia M'gladbach
1978	Liverpool	1-0	Club Brugge
1979	Nottingham Forest	1-0	Malmö FF
1980	Nottingham Forest	1-0	Hamburger SV
1981	Liverpool	1-0	Real Madrid
1982	Aston Villa	1-0	Bayern München
1983	Hamburger SV	1-0	Juventus
1984	Liverpool	1-1 4-2p	Roma
1985	Juventus	1-0	Liverpool
1986	Steaua Bucuresti	0-0 2-0p	Barcelona
1987	FC Porto	2-1	Bayern München
1988	PSV Eindhoven	0-0 6-5p	Benfica
1989	Milan	4-0	Steaua Bucuresti
1990	Milan	1-0	Benfica
1991	Crvena Zvezda	0-0 5-3p	Olymp. Marseille
1992	Barcelona	1-0	Sampdoria
1993	Olympique Marseille	1-0	Milan
1994	Milan	4-0	Barcelona
1995	Ajax	1-0	Milan

THE EUROPEAN CUP WINNERS CUP

Year	Winner	Score	Runner-up
1961	Fiorentina	2-0 2-1	Glasgow Rangers
1962	Atlético Madrid	1-1 3-0	Fiorentina
1963	Tottenham Hotspur	5-1	Atlético Madrid
1964	Sporting CP	3-3 1-0	MTK Budapest
1965	West Ham United	2-0	TSV 1860 München
1966	Borussia Dortmund	2-1	Liverpool
1967	Bayern München	1-0	Glasgow Rangers
1968	Milan	2-0	Hamburger SV
1969	Slovan Bratislava	3-2	Barcelona
1970	Manchester City	2-1	Gornik Zabrze

1971	Chelsea	1-1 2-1	Real Madrid
1972	Glasgow Rangers	3-2	Dynamo Moskva
1973	Milan	1-0	Leeds United
1974	1.FC Magbeburg	2-0	Milan
1975	Dynamo Kiev	3-0	Ferencváros
1976	RSC Anderlecht	4-2	West Ham United
1977	Hamburger SV	2-0	RSC Anderlecht
1978	RSC Anderlecht	4-0	FK Austria
1979	Barcelona	4-3	Fortuna Düsseldorf
1980	Valencia	0-0 5-4p	Arsenal
1981	Dynamo Tbilisi	2-1	Carl Zeiss Jena
1982	Barcelona	2-1	Standard CL
1983	Aberdeen	2-1	Real Madrid
1984	Juventus	2-1	FC Porto
1985	Everton	3-1	SK Rapid Wien
1986	Dynamo Kiev	3-0	Atlético Madrid
1987	Ajax	1-0	Lokomotive Leipzig
1988	KV Mechelen	1-0	Ajax
1989	Barcelona	2-0	Sampdoria
1990	Sampdoria	2-0	RSC Anderlecht
1991	Manchester United	2-1	Barcelona
1992	Werder Bremen	2-0	AS Monaco
1993	Parma	3-1	Royal Antwerp FC
1994	Arsenal	1-0	Parma
1995	Real Zaragoza	2-1	Arsenal

THE INTER-CITIES FAIRS CUP

1958	Barcelona	2-2 6-0	London Select XI
1960	Barcelona	0-0 4-1	Birmingham City
1961	Roma	2-2 2-0	Birmingham City
1962	Valencia	6-2 1-1	Barcelona
1963	Valencia	2-1 2-0	Dinamo Zagreb
1964	Real Zaragoza	2-1	Valencia
1965	Ferencváros	1-0	Juventus
1966	Barcelona	0-1 4-2	Real Zaragoza
1967	Dinamo Zagreb	2-0 0-0	Leeds United
1968	Leeds United	1-0 0-0	Ferencváros
1969	Newcastle United	3-0 3-2	Ujpesti Dózsa
1970	Arsenal	1-3 3-0	RSC Anderlecht
1971	Leeds United	2-2 1-1	Juventus

THE UEFA CUP

1972	Tottenham Hotspur	2-1 1-1	Wolverhampton W
1973	Liverpool	3-0 0-2	Borussia M'gladbach
1974	Feyenoord	2-2 2-0	Tottenham Hotspur
1975	B. Mönchengladbach	0-0 5-1	Twente Enschede
1976	Liverpool	3-2 1-1	Club Brugge
1977	Juventus	1-0 1-2	Athletic Bilbao
1978	PSV Eindhoven	0-0 3-0	SEC Bastia
1979	B. Mönchengladbach	1-1 1-0	Crvena Zvezda
1980	Eintracht Frankfurt	2-3 1-0	Borussia M'gladbach
1981	Ipswich Town	3-0 2-4	AZ 67 Alkmaar
1982	IFK Göteborg	1-0 3-0	Hamburger SV
1983	RSC Anderlecht	1-0 1-1	Benfica
1984	Tottenham Hotspur	1-1 1-1 4-3p	Anderlecht
1985	Real Madrid	3-0 0-1	Videoton SC
1986	Real Madrid	5-1 0-2	1.FC Köln
1987	IFK Göteborg	1-0 1-1	Dundee United
1988	Bayer Leverkusen	0-3 3-0 3-2p	Español
1989	Napoli	2-1 3-3	VfB Stuttgart
1990	Juventus	3-1 0-0	Fiorentina
1991	Internazionale	2-0 0-1	Roma
1992	Ajax	2-2 0-0	Torino
1993	Juventus	3-1 3-0	Borussia Dortmund
1994	Internazionale	1-0 1-0	Austria Salzburg
1995	Parma	1-0, 1-1	Juventus

1955–56

Bold type shows the winner of each tie. See Appendix at the back of the book for each club's country of origin.

EUROPEAN CUP

FIRST ROUND

Servette FC	0-2 0-5	**Real Madrid**
Sporting CP	3-3 2-5	**Partizan Beograd**
SK Rapid Wien	6-1 0-1	PSV Eindhoven
Milan	3-4 4-1	1.FC Saarbrücken
Rot-Weiss Essen	0-4 1-1	**Hibernian Ed'burgh**
Djurgårdens IF	0-0 4-1	Gwardia Warszawa
Vörös Lobogó	6-3 4-1	RSC Anderlecht
ÅGF Åarhus	0-2 2-2	**Stade de Reims**

QUARTER-FINALS

Real Madrid	4-0 0-3	Partizan Beograd
SK Rapid Wien	1-1 2-7	**Milan**
Hibernian Edinburgh	3-1 1-0	Djurgårdens IF
Stade de Reims	4-2 4-4	Vörös Lobogó

SEMI-FINALS

Real Madrid	4-2 1-2	Milan
Stade de Reims	2-0 1-0	Hibernian Edinburgh

FINAL

Parc des Princes, Paris, 13-06-1956, 38,000. Referee: Ellis, England

REAL MADRID 4 (Di Stéfano 14, Rial 30 79, Marquitos 67)

STADE DE REIMS 3 (Leblond 6, Templin 10, Hidalgo 62)

Real Madrid - Alonso - Atienza, Marquitos, Lesmes - Muñoz, Zarraga Joseito, Marchal, Di Stéfano, Rial, Gento. Tr: Villalonga

Stade de Reims - Jacquet - Zimny, Jonquet, Giraudo - Leblond, Siatka Hidalgo, Glovacki, Kopa, Bliard, Templin. Tr: Batteux

Top scorers: Glovacki, Stade de Reims 7
Milutinovic, Partizan Beograd 7

1956–57

EUROPEAN CUP

PRELIMINARY ROUND

ÅGF Åarhus	1-1 1-5	**OGC Nice**
FC Porto	1-2 2-3	**Athletic Bilbao**
RSC Anderlecht	0-2 0-10	**Manchester United**
Borussia Dortmund	4-3 1-2 7-0	AC Spora
Dinamo Bucuresti	3-1 1-2	Galatasaray
Slovan Bratislava	4-0 0-2	CWKS Warszawa
Real Madrid	Bye	
SK Rapid Wien	Bye	
Glasgow Rangers	Bye	
Honvéd	Bye	
Rapid JC Heerlen	Bye	
Crvena Zvezda Beograd	Bye	
CDNA Sofia	Bye	
Grasshopper-Club	Bye	
IFK Norrköping	Bye	
Fiorentina	Bye	

FIRST ROUND

Real Madrid	4-2 1-3 2-0	SK Rapid Wien
Glasgow Rangers	2-1 1-2 1-3	**OGC Nice**
Athletic Bilbao	3-2 3-3	Honvéd
Manchester United	3-2 0-0	Borussia Dortmund
Rapid JC Heerlen	3-4 0-2	**Crvena Zvezda Beograd**
CDNA Sofia	8-1 2-3	Dinamo Bucuresti

Slovan Bratislava	1-0 0-2	**Grasshopper-Club**
Fiorentina	1-1 1-0	IFK Norrköping

QUARTER-FINALS

Real Madrid	3-0 3-2	OGC Nice
Athletic Bilbao	5-3 0-3	**Manchester United**
Crvena Zvezda Beograd	3-1 1-2	CDNA Sofia
Fiorentina	3-1 2-2	Grasshopper-Club

SEMI-FINALS

Real Madrid	3-1 2-2	Manchester United
Crvena Zvezda Beograd	0-1 0-0	**Fiorentina**

FINAL

Bernabeu, Madrid, 30-05-1957, 124,000. Referee: Horn, Holland

REAL MADRID 2 (Di Stéfano 70, Gento 76)
FIORENTINA 0

Real Madrid - Alonso - Torres, Marquitos, Lesmes - Muñoz, Zarraga - Kopa, Mateos, Di Stéfano, Rial, Gento. Tr: Villalonga

Fiorentina - Sarti - Magnini, Orzan, Cervato - Scaramucci, Segato - Julinho, Gratton, Virgili, Montuori, Bizzarri. Tr: Bernardini

Top scorer: Violet, Manchester United 9

1957–58

EUROPEAN CUP

PRELIMINARY ROUND

Sevilla	3-1 0-0	Benfica
ÅGF Åarhus	0-0 3-0	Glenavon
CDNA Sofia	2-1 1-6	**Vasas Budapest**
Gwardia Warszawa	3-1 1-3 1-1	**Wismut K-M-S**
Shamrock Rovers	0-6 2-3	**Manchester United**
Stade Dudelange	0-5 1-9	**Crvena Zvezda Beograd**
Glasgow Rangers	3-1 1-2	AS Saint-Étienne
Milan	4-1 2-5 4-2	SK Rapid Wien
Real Madrid	Bye	
Royal Antwerp FC	Bye	
Ajax	Bye	
BSC Young Boys	Bye	
Dukla Praha	Bye	
IFK Norrköping	Bye	
Borussia Dortmund	Bye	
CCA Bucuresti	Bye	

FIRST ROUND

Royal Antwerp FC	1-2 0-6	**Real Madrid**
Sevilla	4-0 0-2	ÅGF Åarhus
Wismut Karl-Marx-Stadt	1-3 0-1	**Ajax**
BSC Young Boys	1-1 1-2	**Vasas Budapest**
Manchester United	3-0 0-1	Dukla Praha
IFK Norrköping	2-2 1-2	**Crvena Zvezda Beograd**
Borussia Dortmund	4-2 1-3 3-1	CCA Bucuresti
Glasgow Rangers	1-4 0-2	**Milan**

QUARTER-FINALS

Real Madrid	8-0 2-2	Sevilla
Ajax	2-2 0-4	**Vasas Budapest**
Manchester United	2-1 3-3	Crvena Zvezda Beograd
Borussia Dortmund	1-1 1-4	**Milan**

SEMI-FINALS

Real Madrid	4-0 0-2	Vasas Budapest
Manchester United	2-1 0-4	**Milan**

FINAL

Heysel, Brussels, 28-05-1958, 67,000. Referee: Alsteen, Belgium

REAL MADRID 3 (Di Stéfano 74, Rial 79, Gento 107)
MILAN 2 (Schiaffino 69, Grillo 78)

Real Madrid - Alonso - Atienza, Santamaria, Lesmes - Santisteban, Zarraga - Kopa, Joseito, Di Stéfano, Rial, Gento. Tr: Carniglia

Milan - Soldan - Fontana, Maldini, Beraldo - Bergamaschi, Radice - Danova, Liedholm, Schiaffino, Grillo, Cucchiaroni. Tr: Viani

Top scorer: Di Stefano, Real Madrid 10

FAIRS CUP (1955-58)

FIRST ROUND

Group A

	Ba	St	Pl	W	D	L	F	A	Pts
Barcelona	-	6-2	2	1	1	0	7	3	3
Staevnet Select XI	1-1	-	2	0	1	1	3	7	1
Vienna Select XI	Withdrew								

Group B

	BC	In	Za	Pl	W	D	L	F	A	Pts
Birmingham City	-	2-1	3-0	4	3	1	0	6	1	7
Internazionale	0-0	-	4-0	4	2	1	1	6	2	5
Zagreb Select XI	0-1	0-1	-	4	0	0	4	0	9	0

Group C

	LS	Le	Pl	W	D	L	F	A	Pts
Lausanne-Sports	-	7-3	2	1	0	1	10	9	2
Leipzig Select XI	6-3	-	2	1	0	1	9	10	2
Cologne Select XI	Withdrew								

Group D

	Lo	Fr	Ba	Pl	W	D	L	F	A	Pts
London Select XI	-	3-2	1-0	4	3	0	1	9	3	6
Frankfurt Select XI	1-0	-	5-1	4	2	0	2	10	10	4
Basle Select XI	0-5	6-2	-	4	1	0	3	7	13	2

SEMI-FINALS

Birmingham City	4-3 0-1 1-2	**Barcelona**
Lausanne-Sports	2-1 0-2	**London Select XI**

FINAL

1st leg. Stamford Bridge, London, 5-03-1958, 45,000. Referee: Dusch, West Germany

LONDON SELECT XI 2 (Greaves 5, Langley 83)
BARCELONA 2 (Tejada 4, Martinez 43)

London - Kelsey, Sillett, Langley, Blanchflower, Norman, Koot, Groves, Greaves, Smith, Haynes, Robb

Barcelona - Estrems, Olivella, Segarra, Gracia, Gensana, Ribelles, Basora, Evaristo, Martinez, Villaverde, Tejada

2nd leg. Nou Camp, Barcelona, 1-05-1958, 62,000. Referee: Dusch, West Germany

BARCELONA 6 (Suárez 2, Evaristo 2, Martinez, Verges)
LONDON SELECT XI 0

Barcelona - Ramallets - Olivella, Segarra, Verges, Brugue, Gensana, Tejada, Evaristo, Martinez, Suárez, Basora

London - Kelsey - Wright, Cantwell, Blanchflower, Brown, Bowen, Medwin, Groves, Smith, Bloomfield, Lewis

1958–59

EUROPEAN CUP

PRELIMINARY ROUND

Real Madrid	Bye	
Besiktas	W-O	Olympiakos
Juventus	3-1 0-7	**Wiener Sport-Club**
Dinamo Zagreb	2-2 1-2	**Dukla Praha**
KB København	3-0 2-5 1-3	**FC Schalke 04**
Wolverhampton Wan	Bye	
CDNA Sofia	Bye	

Atlético Madrid 8-0 5-1 Drumcondra
Wismut K-M-S 4-2 0-2 4-0 Petrolul Ploiesti
IFK Göteborg 2-1 0-1 5-1 Jeunesse Esch
Polonia Bytom 0-3 0-3 **MTK Budapest**
DOS Utrecht 3-4 1-2 **Sporting CP**
BSC Young Boys W-O Manchester United
Standard CL 5-1 1-2 Heart of Midlothian
HPS Helsinki Bye
Ards 1-4 2-6 **Stade de Reims**

FIRST ROUND

Real Madrid 2-0 1-1 Besiktas
Weiner Sport-Club 3-1 0-1 Dukla Praha
Wolverhampton Wanderers 2-2 1-2 **FC Schalke 04**
Atlético Madrid 2-1 0-1 3-1 CDNA Sofia
MTK Budapest 1-2 1-4 **BSC Young Boys**
Wismut Karl-Marx-Stadt 4-0 2-2 IFK Göteborg
Sporting CP 2-3 0-3 **Standard CL**
Stade de Reims 4-0 3-0 HPS Helsinki

QUARTER-FINALS

Wiener Sport-Club 0-0 1-7 **Real Madrid**
Atlético Madrid 3-0 1-1 FC Schalke 04
BSC Young Boys 2-2 0-0 2-1 Wismut Karl-Marx-Stadt
Standard CL 2-0 0-3 **Stade de Reims**

SEMI-FINALS

Real Madrid 2-1 0-1 2-1 Atlético Madrid
BSC Young Boys 1-0 0-3 **Stade de Reims**

FINAL

Neckarstadion, Stuttgart, 3-06-1959, 80,000. Referee: Dusch, West Germany

REAL MADRID 2 (Mateos 2, Di Stéfano 47)
STADE DE REIMS 0

Real Madrid - Dominguez - Marquitos, Santamaria, Zarraga - Santisteban, Ruiz - Kopa, Mateos, Di Stéfano, Rial, Gento. Tr: Carniglia

Stade de Reims - Colonna - Rodzik, Jonquet, Giraudo - Penverne, Leblond, Lamartine, Bliard, Fontaine, Piantoni, Vincent. Tr: Batteux

Top scorer: Fontaine, Stade de Reims 10

1959–60

EUROPEAN CUP

PRELIMINARY ROUND

Real Madrid Bye
Jeunesse Esch 5-0 1-2 LKS Lódz
Fenerbahçe 1-1 3-2 Csepel SC
OGC Nice 3-2 1-1 Shamrock Rovers
Vorwärts Berlin 2-1 0-2 **Wolverhampton Wan.**
Crvena Zvezda Beograd Bye
Olympiakos 2-2 1-3 **Milan**
CDNA Sofia 2-2 2-6 **Barcelona**
Glasgow Rangers 5-2 2-0 RSC Anderlecht
CH Bratislava 2-1 2-0 FC Porto
Linfield 2-1 1-6 **IFK Göteborg**
Sparta Rotterdam Bye
Wiener Sport-Club 0-0 2-1 Petrolul Ploiesti
B 1909 Odense Bye
BSC Young Boys Bye
Eintracht Frankfurt W-O KuPS Kuopio

FIRST ROUND

Real Madrid 7-0 5-2 Jeunesse Esch
Fenerbahçe 2-1 1-2 1-5 **OGC Nice**
Crvena Zvezda Beograd 1-1 0-3 **Wolverhampton W.**
Milan 0-2 1-5 **Barcelona**
Glasgow Rangers 4-3 1-1 CH Bratislava
Sparta Rotterdam 3-1 1-3 3-1 IFK Göteborg
B 1909 Odense 0-3 2-2 **Wiener Sport-Club**
BSC Young Boys 1-4 1-1 **Eintracht Frankfurt**

QUARTER-FINALS

OGC Nice 3-2 0-4 **Real Madrid**
Barcelona 4-0 5-2 Wolverhampton W.
Sparta Rotterdam 2-3 1-0 2-3 **Glasgow Rangers**
Eintracht Frankfurt 2-1 1-1 Wiener Sport-Club

SEMI-FINALS

Real Madrid 3-1 3-1 Barcelona
Eintracht Frankfurt 6-1 6-3 Glasgow Rangers

FINAL

Hampden Park, Glasgow, 18-05-1960, 135,000. Referee: Mowat, Scotland

REAL MADRID 7 (Di Stéfano 27 30 75, Puskas 45 56 60 71)
EINTRACHT FRANKFURT 3 (Kress 10, Stein 64 72)

Real Madrid - Dominguez - Marquitos, Santamaria, Pachin - Vidal, Zarraga, Canario, Del Sol, Di Stéfano, Puskas, Gento. Tr: Munoz

Eintracht - Loy - Lutz, Eigenbrodt, Höfer - Weilbacher, Stinka - Kress, Lindner, Stein, Pfaff, Meier. Tr: Oswald

Top scorer: Puskas, Real Madrid 12

FAIRS CUP (1958-1960)

FIRST ROUND

Basle Select XI 1-2 2-5 **Barcelona**
Internazionale 7-0 1-1 Olympique Lyon
Frem København 1-3 1-4 **Chelsea**
Belgrade Select XI 6-1 5-3 Lausanne-Sports
Union St Gilloise 6-1 0-1 Leipzig Select XI
Hannover 96 1-3 1-1 **Roma**
Zagreb Select XI 4-2 0-1 Ujpesti Dózsa
Cologne Select XI 2-2 0-2 **Birmingham City**

QUARTER-FINALS

Barcelona 4-0 4-2 Internazionale
Chelsea 1-0 1-4 **Belgrade Select XI**
Union St Gilloise 2-0 1-1 Roma
Birmingham City 1-0 3-3 Zagreb Select XI

SEMI-FINALS

Belgrade Select XI 1-1 1-3 **Barcelona**
Union St Gilloise 2-4 2-4 **Birmingham City**

FINAL

1st leg. St. Andrews, Birmingham, 29-03-1960, 40,000. Referee: Van Nuffel, Belgium

BIRMINGHAM CITY 0
BARCELONA 0

Birmingham City - Schofield - Farmer, Allen, Watts, Smith, Neal, Astall, Gordon, Weston, Orritt, Hooper

Barcelona - Ramallets - Olivella, Gracia, Segarra, Rodri, Gensana, Coll, Kocsis, Martinez, Ribelles, Villaverde

2nd leg. Nou Camp, Barcelona, 4-05-1960, 70,000. Referee: Van Nuffel, Belgium

BARCELONA 4 (Martinez 3, Czibor 6 48, Coll 78)
BIRMINGHAM CITY 1 (Hooper 82)

Barcelona - Ramallets - Olivella, Gracia, Verges, Rodri, Segarra, Coll, Ribelles, Martinez, Kubala, Czibor

Birmingham City - Schofield - Farmer, Allen, Watts, Smith, Neal, Astall, Gordon, Weston, Murphy, Hooper

1960–61

EUROPEAN CUP

FIRST ROUND

Heart of Midlothian .... 1-2 0-3 .... **Benfica**
Crvena Zvezda Beograd .... 1-2 0-3 .... **Ujpesti Dózsa**
Fredrikstad FK .... 4-3 0-0 .... Ajax
ÅGF Åarhus .... 3-0 0-1 .... Legia Warszawa
Juventus .... 2-0 1-4 .... **CDNA Sofia**
HIFK Helsinki .... 1-3 1-2 .... **IFK Malmö**
Wismut K-M-S .... W-O .... Glenavon
SK Rapid Wien .... 4-0 0-1 .... Besiktas
Hamburger SV .... Bye
Limerick FC .... 0-5 2-4 .... **BSC Young Boys**
Stade de Reims .... 6-1 5-0 .... Jeunesse Esch
Burnley .... Bye
CCA Bucuresti .... 0-3 .... **Spartak Králové**
Panathinaikos .... Bye
Real Madrid .... Bye
Barcelona .... 2-0 3-0 .... Lierse SK

SECOND ROUND

Benfica .... 6-2 1-2 .... Ujpesti Dózsa
ÅGF Åarhus .... 3-0 1-0 .... Fredrikstad FK
IFK Malmö .... 1-0 1-1 .... CDNA Sofia
SK Rapid Wien .... 3-1 0-2 1-0 .... Wismut Karl-Marx-Stadt
BSC Young Boys .... 0-5 3-3 .... **Hamburger SV**
Burnley .... 2-0 2-3 .... Stade de Reims
Spartak Králové .... 1-0 0-0 .... Panathinaikos
Real Madrid .... 2-2 1-2 .... **Barcelona**

QUARTER-FINALS

Benfica .... 3-1 4-1 .... ÅGF Åarhus
SK Rapid Wien .... 2-0 2-0 .... IFK Malmö
Burnley .... 3-1 1-4 .... **Hamburger SV**
Barcelona .... 4-0 1-1 .... Spartak Králové

SEMI-FINALS

Benfica .... 3-0 1-1 .... SK Rapid Wien
Barcelona .... 1-0 1-2 1-0 .... Hamburger

FINAL

Wankdorf, Berne, 31-05-1961, 27,000. Referee: Dienst, Switzerland

BENFICA 3 (Aguas 30, OG 32, Coluna 55)
BARCELONA 2 (Kocsis 20, Czibor 75)

Benfica - Costa Pereira - João, Germano, Angelo - Neto, Cruz - Augusto, Santana, Aguas, Coluna, Cavém. Tr: Guttmann
Barcelona - Ramallets - Foncho, Gensana, Gracia - Verges, Garay - Kubala, Kocsis, Evaristo, Suárez, Czibor. Tr: Orizaola

Top scorer: José Aguas, Benfica 10

FAIRS CUP

FIRST ROUND

Union St Gilloise .... 0-0 1-4 .... **Roma**
Olympique Lyon .... 1-3 2-1 .... **1.FC Köln**
Zagreb Select XI .... 1-1 3-4 .... **Barcelona**
Lausanne-Sports .... 0-2 .... **Hibernian Edinburgh**
Internazionale .... 8-2 6-1 .... Hannover 96
Leipzig Select XI .... 5-2 1-4 0-2 .... **Belgrade Select XI**
Frem København .... 8-1 3-3 .... Basle Select XI
Birmingham City .... 3-2 2-1 .... Ujpesti Dózsa

QUARTER-FINALS

1.FC Köln .... 0-2 2-0 1-4 .... **Roma**
Barcelona .... 4-4 2-3 .... **Hibernian Edinburgh**
Internazionale .... 5-0 0-1 .... Belgrade Select XI
Frem København .... 4-4 0-5 .... **Birmingham City**

SEMI-FINALS

Hibernian Edinburgh .... 2-2 3-3 0-6 .... **Roma**
Internazionale .... 1-2 1-2 .... **Birmingham City**

FINAL

1st leg. St. Andrews, Birmingham, 27-09-1961, 21,000. Referee: Davidson, Scotland

BIRMINGHAM CITY 2 (Hellawell 78, Orritt 85)
ROMA 2 (Manfredini 30 56)

Birmingham City - Schofield - Farmer, Sissons, Hennessey, Foster, Beard, Hellawell, Bloomfield, Harris, Orritt, Auld
Roma - Cudicini - Fontana, Corsini, Guiliano, Losi, Carpanesi, Orlando, Da Costa, Manfredini, Angelillo, Menichelli

2nd leg. Stadio Olimpico, Rome, 11-10-1961, 60,000. Referee: Schwinte, France

ROMA 2 (OG 56, Pestrin 90)
BIRMINGHAM CITY 0

Roma - Cudicini - Fontana, Corsini, Carpanesi, Losi, Pestrin, Orlando, Angelillo, Manfredini, Lojacono, Menichelli
Birmingham City - Schofield - Farmer, Sissons, Hennessey, Smith, Beard, Hellawell, Bloomfield, Harris, Singer, Orritt

CUP WINNERS CUP

PRELIMINARY ROUND

Vorwärts Berlin .... 2-1 0-2 .... **Red Star Brno**
Glasgow Rangers .... 4-2 1-2 .... Ferencváros

QUARTER-FINALS

FC Luzern .... 0-3 2-6 .... **Fiorentina**
Red Star Brno .... 0-0 0-2 .... **Dinamo Zagreb**
FK Austria .... 2-0 0-5 .... **Wolverhampton W.**
B. Mönchengladbach .... 0-3 0-8 .... **Glasgow Rangers**

SEMI-FINALS

Fiorentina .... 3-0 1-2 .... Dinamo Zagreb
Glasgow Rangers .... 2-0 1-1 .... Wolverhampton W.

FINAL

1st leg. Ibrox, Glasgow, 17-05-1961, 80,000. Referee: Steiner, Austria

GLASGOW RANGERS 0
FIORENTINA 2 (Milani 12 88)

Rangers - Ritchie - Shearer, Caldow, Davis - Paterson, Baxter - Wilson, McMillan, Scott, Brand, Hume
Fiorentina - Albertosi - Robotti, Castelletti, Gonfiantini - Orzan, Rimbaldo - Hamrin, Micheli, Da Costa, Milani, Petris

2nd leg. Comunale, Florence, 27-05-1961, 50,000. Referee: Hernadi, Hungary

FIORENTINA 2 (Milani 12, Hamrin 86)
GLASGOW RANGERS 1 (Scott 60)

Fiorentina - Albertosi - Robotti, Castelletti, Gonfiantini - Orzan, Rimbaldo - Hamrin, Micheli, Da Costa, Milani, Petris
Rangers - Ritchie - Shearer, Caldow, Davis - Paterson, Baxter - Scott, McMillan, Millar, Brand, Wilson

Top scorers: Hamrin, Fiorentina 5
Brand, Rangers 5

1961–62

EUROPEAN CUP

FIRST ROUND

Benfica .... Bye

CCA Bucuresti .... 0-0 0-2 .... **FK Austria**
Fenerbahçe .... Bye
1.FC Nürnberg .... 5-0 4-1 .... Drumcondra
Servette FC .... 5-0 2-1 .... Hibernians Paola
CDNA Sofia .... 4-4 1-2 .... **Dukla Praha**
IFK Göteborg .... 0-3 2-8 .... **Feyenoord**
Górnik Zabrze .... 4-2 1-8 .... **Tottenham Hotspur**
Standard CL .... 2-1 2-0 .... Fredrikstad FK
Haka Valkeakoski .... Bye
Vorwärts Berlin .... 3-0 .... Linfield
AS Monaco .... 2-3 2-3 .... **Glasgow Rangers**
Sporting CP .... 1-1 0-2 .... **Partizan Beograd**
Panathinaikos .... 1-1 1-2 .... **Juventus**
AC Spora .... 0-6 2-9 .... **B 1913 Odense**
Vasas Budapest .... 0-2 1-3 .... **Real Madrid**

SECOND ROUND

FK Austria .... 1-1 1-5 .... **Benfica**
Fenerbahçe .... 1-2 0-1 .... **1.FC Nürnberg**
Servette FC .... 4-3 0-2 .... **Dukla Praha**
Feyenoord .... 1-3 1-1 .... **Tottenham Hotspur**
Vorwärts Berlin .... 1-2 1-4 .... **Glasgow Rangers**
Standard CL .... 5-1 2-0 .... Haka Valkeakoski
Partizan Beograd .... 1-2 0-5 .... **Juventus**
B 1913 Odense .... 0-3 0-9 .... **Real Madrid**

QUARTER-FINALS

1.FC Nürnberg .... 3-1 0-6 .... **Benfica**
Dukla Praha .... 1-0 1-4 .... **Tottenham Hotspur**
Standard CL .... 4-1 0-2 .... Glasgow Rangers
Juventus .... 0-1 1-0 1-3 .... **Real Madrid**

SEMI-FINALS

Benfica .... 3-1 1-2 .... Tottenham Hotspur
Real Madrid .... 4-0 2-0 .... Standard CL

FINAL

Olympisch Stadion, Amsterdam, 2-05-1962, 65,000. Referee: Horn, Holland

BENFICA 5 (Aguas 25, Cavém 34, Coluña 51, Eusébio 65 68)
REAL MADRID 3 (Puskás 17 23 38)

Benfica - Costa Pereira - João, Germano, Angelo - Cavém, Cruz - Augusto, Eusébio, Aguas, Coluña, Simões. Tr: Guttmann

Real Madrid - Araquistain - Casado, Santamaria, Miera - Felo, Pachin, Tejada, Del Sol, Di Stéfano, Puskás, Gento. Tr: Muñoz

Top scorer: Di Stéfano, Real Madrid 7
Puskás, Real Madrid 7
Tejada, Real Madrid 7

FAIRS CUP

FIRST ROUND

Valencia .... 2-0 5-1 .... Nottingham Forest
Lausanne-Sports .... Bye
Union St Gilloise .... 1-3 0-2 .... **Heart of Midlothian**
1.FC Köln .... 4-2 0-2 3-5 .... **Internazionale**
Milan .... 0-0 0-2 .... **Novi Sad Select XI**
Iraklis Salonica .... Bye
Spartak Brno .... 2-2 1-4 .... **Leipzig Select XI**
RC Strasbourg .... 1-3 2-10 .... **MTK Budapest**
Basle Select XI .... 1-1 1-4 .... **Crvena Zvezda Beograd**
OS Belenenses .... 3-3 1-3 .... **Hibernian Edinburgh**
Hannover 96 .... 0-1 0-2 .... **RCD Español**
Birmingham City .... Bye
Olympique Lyon .... 4-2 2-5 .... **Sheffield Wednesday**
Roma .... Bye
Dinamo Zagreb .... 7-2 2-2 .... Staevnet Select XI
West Berlin XI .... 1-0 0-3 .... **Barcelona**

SECOND ROUND

Lausanne-Sports .... 3-4 .... **Valencia**
Heart of Midlothian .... 0-1 0-4 .... **Internazionale**
Iraklis Salonica .... 2-1 1-9 .... **Novi Sad Select XI**
MTK Budapest .... 3-0 0-3 2-0 .... Leipzig Select XI
Crvena Zvezda Beograd .... 4-0 1-0 .... Hibernian Edinburgh
RCD Español .... 5-2 0-1 .... Birmingham City
Sheffield Wednesday .... 4-0 0-1 .... Roma
Barcelona .... 5-1 2-2 .... Dinamo Zagreb

QUARTER-FINALS

Valencia .... 2-0 3-3 .... Internazionale
Novi Sad Select XI .... 1-4 1-2 .... **MTK Budapest**
RCD Español .... 2-1 0-5 .... **Crvena Zvezda Beograd**
Sheffield Wednesday .... 3-2 0-2 .... **Barcelona**

SEMI-FINALS

Valencia .... 3-0 7-3 .... MTK Budapest
Barcelona .... 2-0 4-1 .... Crvena Zvezda Beograd

FINAL

1st leg. Luis Casanova, Valencia, 8-09-1962, 65,000. Referee: Barberan, France

VALENCIA 6 (Yosu 14 42, Guillot 35 54 67, Nuñez 74)
BARCELONA 2 (Kocsis 4 20)

Valencia - Zamora - Piquer, Mestre, Sastre, Quinçoces, Chicão, Nuñez, Ribelles, Waldo, Guillot, Yosu

Barcelona - Pesudo - Benitez, Rodri, Olivella, Verges, Gracia, Cubilla, Kocsis, Re, Villaverde, Camps

2nd leg. Nou Camp, Barcelona, 12-09-1962, 60,000. Referee: Campanati, Italy

BARCELONA 1 (Kocsis 46)
VALENCIA 1 (Guillot 87)

Barcelona - Pesudo - Benitez, Garay, Fuste, Verges, Gracia, Cubilla, Kocsis, Goyvaerts, Villaverde, Camps

Valencia - Zamora - Piquer, Mestre, Sastre, Quinçoces, Chicão, Nuñez, Urtiaga, Waldo, Guillot, Yosu

CUP WINNERS CUP

PRELIMINARY ROUND

FC Sedan .... 2-3 1-4 .... **Atlético Madrid**
Glenavon .... 1-4 1-3 .... **Leicester City**
La Chaux-de-Fonds .... 6-2 0-5 .... **Leixoes SC**
Swansea Town .... 2-2 1-5 .... **Motor Jena**
Floriana .... 2-5 2-10 .... **Ujpesti Dózsa**
Dunfermline Athletic .... 4-1 4-0 .... St Patrick's Athletic
SK Rapid Wien .... 0-0 5-2 .... Spartak Varna
Fiorentina .... Bye
Werder Bremen .... Bye
ÅGF Aarhus .... Bye
Alliance Dudelange .... Bye
Progresul Oradea .... Bye
Ajax .... Bye
Vardar Skopje .... Bye
Olympiakos .... Bye
Dynamo Zilina .... Bye

FIRST ROUND

Leicester City .... 1-1 0-2 .... **Atlético Madrid**
Werder Bremen .... 2-0 3-2 .... ÅGF Aarhus
Leixoes SC .... 1-1 1-0 .... Progresul Oradea
Motor Jena .... 7-0 2-2 .... Alliance Dudelange
Ajax .... 2-1 1-3 .... **Ujpesti Dózsa**
Dunfermline Athletic .... 5-0 0-2 .... Vardar Skopje
Olympiakos .... 2-3 0-1 .... **Dynamo Zilina**
Fiorentina .... 3-1 6-2 .... SK Rapid Wien

QUARTER-FINALS

Werder Bremen .... 1-1 1-3 .... **Atlético Madrid**
Motor Jena .... 1-1 3-1 .... Leixoes SC

Ujpesti Dózsa..........4-3 1-0 ....Dunfermline Athletic
Dynamo Zilina..........3-2 0-2 ....**Fiorentina**

SEMI-FINALS
Motor Jena..........0-1 0-4 ....**Atlético Madrid**
Fiorentina..........2-0 1-0 ....Ujpesti Dózsa

FINAL
Hampden Park, Glasgow, 10-05-1962, 27,000. Referee: Wharton, Scotland
ATLÉTICO MADRID 1 (Peiro 11)
FIORENTINA 1 (Hamrin 27)
Atlético - Madinabeytia - Rivilla, Calleja, Ramirez - Griffa, Glaria Jones, Adelardo, Mendonça, Peiro, Collar
Fiorentina - Albertosi - Robotti, Castelletti, Malatrasi - Orzan, Marchesi

Replay. Neckarstadion, Stuttgart, 5-09-1962, 38,000. Referee: Tschenscher, West Germany
ATLÉTICO MADRID 3 (Jones 8, Mendonca 27, Peiro 59)
FIORENTINA 0
Atlético - Madinabeytia - Rivilla, Calleja, Ramirez - Griffa, Glaria Jones, Adelardo, Mendonça, Peiro, Collar
Fiorentina - Albertozi - Robotti, Castelletti, Malatrasi - Orzan, Marchesi, Hamrin, Ferretti, Milani, Dell-Angelo, Petris

Top scorer: Göröcs, Ujpesti Dózsa..........8

1962–63

EUROPEAN CUP

FIRST ROUND
Milan..........8-0 6-0 ....Union Luxembourg
Floriana..........1-4 0-10 ....**Ipswich Town**
Dinamo Bucuresti..........1-1 0-3 ....**Galatasaray**
Polonia Bytom..........2-1 4-1 ....Panathinaikos
CDNA Sofia..........2-1 4-1 ....Partizan Beograd
Real Madrid..........3-3 0-1 ....**RSC Anderlecht**
Shelbourne..........0-2 1-5..........**Sporting CP**
Dundee..........8-1 0-4..........1.FC Köln
Servette FC..........1-3 3-1 1-3 ....**Feyenoord**
Fredrikstad FK..........1-4 0-7 ....**Vasas Budapest**
FK Austria..........5-3 2-0 ....HIFK Helsinki
Stade de Reims..........Bye
Vorwärts Berlin..........0-3 0-1 ....**Dukla Praha**
Linfield..........1-2 0-0 ....**Esbjerg FB**
IFK Norrköping..........2-0 1-1 ....Partizani Tiranë
Benfica..........Bye

SECOND ROUND
Milan..........3-0 1-2 ....Ipswich Town
Galatasaray..........4-1 0-1 ....Polonia Bytom
CDNA Sofia..........2-2 0-2..........**RSC Anderlecht**
Sporting CP..........1-0 1-4..........**Dundee**
Feyenoord..........1-1 2-2 1-0 ....Vasas Budapest
FK Austria..........3-2 0-5..........**Stade de Reims**
Esbjerg FB..........0-0 0-5..........**Dukla Praha**
IFK Norrköping..........1-1 1-5 ....**Benfica**

QUARTER-FINALS
Galatasaray..........1-3 0-5 ....**Milan**
RSC Anderlecht..........1-4 1-2..........**Dundee**
Stade de Reims..........0-1 1-1 ....**Feyenoord**
Benfica..........2-1 0-0..........Dukla Praha

SEMI-FINALS
Milan..........5-1 0-1 ....Dundee
Feyenoord..........0-0 1-3 ....**Benfica**

FINAL
Wembley, London, 22-05-1963, 45,000. Referee: Holland, England
MILAN 2 (Altafini 58 70)
BENFICA 1 (Eusébio 19)
Milan - Ghezzi - David, Maldini, Trebbi - Benitez, Trapattoni - Pivatelli, Sani, Altafini, Rivera, Mora. Tr: Rocco
Benfica - Costa Pereira - Cavém, Cruz, Humberto, Raul - Coluna, Santana, Augusto, Torres, Eusébio, Simões. Tr: Riera

Top scorer: Altafini, Milan..........14

FAIRS CUP

FIRST ROUND
Valencia..........4-2 2-2 ....Glasgow Celtic
Everton..........1-0 0-2 ....**Dunfermline Athletic**
Utrecht Select XI..........3-2 2-1..........Tasmania Berlin
Hibernian Edinburgh..........4-0 3-2 ....Staevnet Select XI
SK Rapid Wien..........1-1 0-1 ..**Crvena Zvezda Beograd**
Barcelona..........1-1 1-1 3-2 ....OS Belenenses
Glentoran..........0-2 2-6..........**Real Zaragoza**
Altay Izmir..........2-3 1-10 ....**Roma**
Viktoria Köln..........4-3 1-4 ....**Ferencváros**
Sampdoria..........1-0 2-0 ....Aris Bonnevoie
Vojvodina Novi Sad..........1-0 0-2..........**Leipzig Select XI**
Petrolul Ploiesti..........4-2 0-1 ....Spartak Brno
Basle Select XI..........0-3 ....**Bayern München**
Drumcondra..........4-1 2-4..........Odense Select XI
Olympique Marseille..........1-0 2-4..........**Union St Gilloise**
FC Porto..........1-2 0-0 ....**Dinamo Zagreb**

SECOND ROUND
Valencia..........4-0 2-6 1-0..........Dunfermline Athletic
Utrecht Select XI..........0-1 1-2..........**Hibernian Edinburgh**
Crvena Zvezda Beograd 3-2 0-1 1-0 ....Barcelona
Roma..........4-2 2-1 ....Real Zaragoza
Sampdoria..........1-0 0-6 ....**Ferencváros**
Petrolul Ploiesti..........1-0 0-1 1-0..........Leipzig Select XI
Bayern München..........6-0 0-1 ....Drumcondra
Dinamo Zagreb..........2-1 0-1 3-2 ....Union St Gilloise

QUARTER-FINALS
Valencia..........5-0 1-2 ....Hibernian Edinburgh
Roma..........3-0 0-2..........Crvena Zvezda Beograd
Ferencváros..........2-0 0-1 ....Petrolul Ploiesti
Bayern München..........0-0 1-4 ....**Dinamo Zagreb**

SEMI-FINALS
Valencia..........3-0 0-1 ....Roma
Ferencváros..........0-1 1-2 ....**Dinamo Zagreb**

FINAL
1st leg. Dinamo Stadion, Zagreb, 12-06-1963, 40,000. Referee: Adami, Italy
DINAMO ZAGREB 1 (Zambata 13)
VALENCIA 2 (Waldo 64, Urtiaga 67)
Dinamo Zagreb - Skoric - Belin, Braun, Biscam, Markovic, Perusic, Kobesnac, Zambata, Knez, Matus, Lamza
Valencia - Zamora - Piquer, Chicao, Paquito, Quincoces, Sastre, Manio, Sanchez-Lage, Waldo, Ribelles, Urtiaga

2nd leg. Luis Casanova, Valencia, 26-06-1963, 55,000. Referee: Howley, England
VALENCIA 2 (Manio 68, Nunez 78)
DINAMO ZAGREB 0
Valencia - Zamora - Piquer, Chicao, Paquito, Quincoces, Sastre, Manio, Sanchez-Lage, Waldo, Ribelles, Nunez
Dinamo Zagreb - Skoric - Belin, Braun, Matus, Markovic, Perusic, Kobesnac, Lamza, Raus, Zambata, Knez

CUP WINNERS CUP

PRELIMINARY ROUND

Tottenham Hotspur ......Bye
Glasgow Rangers ......4-0 0-2 ......Sevilla
Lausanne-Sports ......3-0 2-4 ......Sparta Rotterdam
Slovan Bratislava ......Bye
Bangor City ......2-0 1-3 1-2 ......**Napoli**
Ujpesti Dózsa ......5-0 0-0 ......Zaglebie Sosnowiec
Portadown ......Bye
OFK Beograd ......2-0 3-3 ......Chemie Halle
1.FC Nürnberg ......Bye
AS Saint-Étienne ......1-1 3-0 ......Vitória FC Setúbal
SK Sturm Graz ......Bye
Alliance Dudelange ......1-1 1-8 ......**B 1909 Odense**
Steaua Bucuresti ......3-2 1-5 ......**Botev Plovdiv**
Shamrock Rovers ......Bye
Hibernians Paola ......W-O ......Olympiakos
Atlético Madrid ......Bye

FIRST ROUND

Tottenham Hotspur ......5-2 3-2 ......Glasgow Rangers
Lausanne-Sports ......1-1 0-1 ......**Slovan Bratislava**
Ujpesti Dózsa ......1-1 1-1 1-3 ......**Napoli**
OFK Beograd ......5-1 2-3 ......Portadown
AS Saint-Étienne ......0-0 0-3 ......**1.FC Nürnberg**
SK Sturm Graz ......1-1 3-5 ......**B 1909 Odense**
Shamrock Rovers ......0-4 0-1 ......**Botev Plovdiv**
Atlético Madrid ......4-0 1-0 ......Hibernians Paola

QUARTER-FINALS

Slovan Bratislava ......2-0 0-6 ......**Tottenham Hotspur**
OFK Beograd ......2-0 1-3 3-1 ......Napoli
B 1909 Odense ......0-1 0-6 ......**1.FC Nürnberg**
Botev Plovdiv ......1-1 0-4 ......**Atlético Madrid**

SEMI-FINALS

OFK Beograd ......1-2 1-3 ......**Tottenham Hotspur**
1.FC Nürnberg ......2-1 0-2 ......**Atlético Madrid**

FINAL

Feyenoord Stadion, Rotterdam, 15-05-1963, 49,000. Referee: Van Leuwen, Holland

TOTTENHAM HOTSPUR 5 (Greaves 16 80, White 35, Dyson 67 85)
ATLÉTICO MADRID 1 (Collar 47)

Tottenham - Brown - Baker, Norman, Henry - Blanchflower, Marchi - Jones, White, Smith, Greaves, Dyson
Atlético - Madinabeytia - Rivilla, Griffa, Rodriguez - Ramiro, Glaria Jones, Adelardo, Chuzo, Mendonca, Collar

Top scorer: Greaves, Tottenham Hotspur 7

1963–64

EUROPEAN CUP

FIRST ROUND

Everton ......0-0 0-1 ......**Internazionale**
AS Monaco ......7-2 1-1 ......AEK Athens
Haka Valkeakoski ......4-1 0-4 ......**Jeunesse Esch**
Partizan Beograd ......3-0 3-1 ......Anorthosis F'gusta
Górnik Zabrze ......1-0 0-1 2-1 ......FK Austria
Dukla Praha ......6-0 2-0 ......Valletta
Distillery ......3-3 0-5 ......**Benfica**
SOFK Lyn Oslo ......2-4 1-3 ......**Borussia Dortmund**
Dundalk ......0-3 2-1 ......**FC Zürich**
Galatasaray ......4-0 0-2 ......Ferencváros
Partizani Tiranë ......1-0 1-3 ......**Spartak Plovdiv**
Esbjerg FB ......3-4 1-7 ......**PSV Eindhoven**
Milan ......Bye
Standard CL ......1-0 0-2 ......**IFK Norrköping**
Dinamo Bucuresti ......2-0 1-0 ......Motor Jena
Glasgow Rangers ......0-1 0-6 ......**Real Madrid**

SECOND ROUND

Internazionale ......1-0 3-1 ......AS Monaco
Jeunesse Esch ......2-1 2-6 ......**Partizan Beograd**
Górnik Zabrze ......2-0 1-4 ......**Dukla Praha**
Benfica ......2-1 0-5 ......**Borussia Dortmund**
FC Zürich ......2-0 0-2 2-2 ......Galatasaray
Spartak Plovdiv ......0-1 0-0 ......**PSV Eindhoven**
IFK Norrköping ......1-1 2-5 ......**Milan**
Dinamo Bucuresti ......1-3 3-5 ......**Real Madrid**

QUARTER-FINALS

Partizan Beograd ......0-2 1-2 ......**Internazionale**
Dukla Praha ......0-4 3-1 ......**Borussia Dortmund**
PSV Eindhoven ......1-0 1-3 ......**FC Zürich**
Real Madrid ......4-1 0-2 ......Milan

SEMI-FINALS

Borussia Dortmund ......2-2 0-2 ......**Internazionale**
FC Zürich ......1-2 0-6 ......**Real Madrid**

FINAL

Prater, Vienna, 27-05-1964, 72,000. Referee: Stoll, Austria

INTERNAZIONALE 3 (Mazzola 43 76, Milani 61)
REAL MADRID 1 (Felo 70)

Internazionale - Sarti - Burgnich, Guarneri, Facchetti - Tagnin, Picchi Jair, Mazzola, Milani, Suarez, Corso. Tr: Herrera
Real Madrid - Vicente - Isidro, Santamaria, Pachin - Zoco, Muller - Amancio, Felo, Di Stéfano, Puskás, Gento. Tr: Munoz

Top scorers: Kovacevic, Partizan Beograd 7
Mazzola, Internazionale 7
Puskas, Real Madrid 7

FAIRS CUP

FIRST ROUND

Real Zaragoza ......6-1 3-0 ......Iraklis Salonica
Lausanne-Sports ......2-2 4-4 3-2 ......Heart of Midlothian
Atlético Madrid ......2-1 0-0 ......FC Porto
Juventus ......2-1 1-2 1-0 ......OFK Beograd
Spartak Brno ......5-0 2-1 ......Servette FC
Glentoran ......1-4 0-3 ......**Partick Thistle**
Staevnet Select X ......1-7 3-2 ......**Arsenal**
Aris Bonnevoie ......0-2 0-0 ......**RFC Liège**
1.FC Köln ......3-1 1-1 ......AA Gent
DOS Utrecht ......1-4 1-4 ......**Sheffield Wednesday**
Tresnjevka Zagreb ......0-2 1-2 ......**OS Belenenses**
Hertha BSC Berlin ......1-3 0-2 ......**Roma**
Ujpesti Dózsa ......3-2 0-0 ......SC Leipzig
Steagul Rosu Brasov ......1-3 1-2 ......**Lokomotiv Plovdiv**
SK Rapid Wien ......1-0 3-2 ......Racing Club Paris
Shamrock Rovers ......0-1 2-2 ......**Valencia**

SECOND ROUND

Lausanne-Sports ......1-2 0-3 ......**Real Zaragoza**
Juventus ......1-0 2-1 ......Atlético Madrid
Partick Thistle ......3-2 0-4 ......**Spartak Brno**
Arsenal ......1-1 1-3 ......**RFC Liège**
1.FC Köln ......3-2 2-1 ......Sheffield Wednesday
Roma ......2-1 1-0 ......OS Belenenses
Ujpesti Dózsa ......0-0 3-1 ......Lokomotiv Plovdiv
SK Rapid Wien ......0-0 2-3 ......**Valencia**

QUARTER-FINALS

Real Zaragoza 3-2 0-0 Juventus
RFC Liège 2-0 0-2 1-0 Spartak Brno
Roma 3-1 0-4 **1.FC Köln**
Valencia 5-2 1-3 Ujpesti Dózsa

SEMI-FINALS

RFC Liège 1-0 1-2 0-2 **Real Zaragoza**
Valencia 4-1 0-2 1.FC Köln

FINAL

Nou Camp, Barcelona, 25-06-1964, 50,000. Referee, De Campos, Portugal

REAL ZARAGOZA 2 (Villa 40, Marcelino 83)
VALENCIA 1 (Urtiaga 42)

Real Zaragoza - Yarza, Cortizo, Santamaria, Reija, Isasi, Pais, Canario, Duca, Marcelino, Villa, Lapetra

Valencia - Zamora, Arnal, Villegani, Paquito, Quincoces, Roberto, Suco, Guillot, Waldo, Urtiaga, Ficha

CUP WINNERS CUP

FIRST ROUND

Atalanta 2-0 1-3 1-3 **Sporting CP**
Apoel Nicosia 6-0 0-1 Gjøvik Lyn
Tottenham Hotspur Bye
Willem II Tilburg 1-1 1-6 **Manchester United**
Hamburger SV 4-0 3-2 Union Luxembourg
Shelbourne 0-2 1-3 **Barcelona**
Olympiakos 2-1 0-1 2-0 Zaglebie Sosnowiec
Olympique Lyon 3-1 3-1 B 1913 Odense
FC Basel 1-5 0-5 **Glasgow Celtic**
Linzer ASK 1-0 0-1 1-1 **Dinamo Zagreb**
HPS Helsinki 1-4 1-8 **Slovan Bratislava**
Sliema Wanderers 0-0 0-2 **Borough United**
Fenerbahçe 4-1 0-1 Petrolul Ploiesti
Linfield Bye
Motor Zwickau Bye
MTK Budapest 1-0 1-1 Slavia Sofia

SECOND ROUND

Sporting CP 16-1 2-0 Apoel Nicosia
Tottenham Hotspur 2-0 1-4 **Manchester United**
Barcelona 4-4 0-0 2-3 **Hamburger SV**
Olympique Lyon 4-1 1-2 Olympiakos
Glasgow Celtic 3-0 1-2 Dinamo Zagreb
Borough United 0-1 0-3 **Slovan Bratislava**
Fenerbahçe 4-1 0-2 Linfield
Motor Zwickau 1-0 0-2 **MTK Budapest**

QUARTER-FINALS

Manchester United 4-1 0-5 **Sporting CP**
Hamburger SV 1-1 0-2 **Olympique Lyon**
Glasgow Celtic 1-0 1-0 Slovan Bratislava
MTK Budapest 2-0 1-3 1-0 Fenerbahçe

SEMI-FINALS

Olympique Lyon 0-0 1-1 0-1 **Sporting CP**
Glasgow Celtic 3-0 0-4 **MTK Budapest**

FINAL

Heysel, Brussels, 13-05-1964, 3,000. Referee: Van Nuffel, Belgium

SPORTING CLUB 3 (Mascaranha 40, Figueiredo 45 80)
MTK BUDAPEST 3 (Sandor 19 75, Kuti 73)

Sporting - Carvalho - Gomez, Perdis, Battista, Carlos - Geo, Mendes Oswaldo, Mascaranha, Figueiredo, Morais

MTK Budapest - Kovalik - Keszei, Dansky, Jenei - Nagy, Kovacs - Sandor, Vasas, Kuti, Bodor, Halapi

Replay. Bosuil, Antwerp, 15-05-1964, 19,000. Referee: Versyp, Belgium

SPORTING CLUB 1 (Morais 19)
MTK BUDAPEST 0

Sporting - Carvalho - Gomez, Perdis, Battista, Carlos - Geo, Mendes Oswaldo, Mascaranha, Figueiredo, Morais

MTK Budapest - Kovalik - Keszei, Dansky, Jenei - Nagy, Kovacs - Sandor, Vasas, Kuti, Bodor, Halapi

Top scorer: Mascaranha, Sporting CP 9

1964–65

EUROPEAN CUP

FIRST ROUND

Internazionale Bye
Sliema Wanderers 0-2 0-5 **Dinamo Bucuresti**
Glasgow Rangers 3-1 2-4 3-1 Crvena Zvezda Beograd.
SK Rapid Wien 3-0 2-0 Shamrock Rovers
Glentoran 2-2 2-3 **Panathinaikos**
Partizani Tiranë 0-0 0-2 **1.FC Köln**
RSC Anderlecht 1-0 1-2 0-0 Bologna
KR Reykjavík 0-5 1-6 **Liverpool**
Chemie Leipzig 0-2 2-4 **Vasas ETO Györ**
Lokomotiv Sofia 8-3 0-2 Malmö FF
DWS Amsterdam 3-1 1-0 Fenerbahçe
Reipas Lahti 2-1 0-3 **SOFK Lyn Oslo**
B 1909 Odense 2-5 0-4 **Real Madrid**
Dukla Praha 4-1 0-3 0-0 Górnik Zabrze
AS Saint-Étienne 2-2 1-2 **La Chaux-de-Fonds**
Aris Bonnevoie 1-5 1-5 **Benfica**

SECOND ROUND

Internazionale 6-0 1-0 Dinamo Bucuresti
Glasgow Rangers 1-0 2-0 SK Rapid Wien
Panathinaikos 1-1 1-2 **1.FC Köln**
Liverpool 3-0 1-0 RSC Anderlecht
Vasas ETO Györ 5-3 3-4 Lokomotiv Sofia
DWS Amsterdam 5-0 3-1 SOFK Lyn Oslo
Real Madrid 4-0 2-2 Dukla Praha
La Chaux-de-Fonds 1-1 0-5 **Benfica**

QUARTER-FINALS

Internazionale 3-1 0-1 Glasgow Rangers
1.FC Köln 0-0 0-0 2-2 **Liverpool**
DWS Amsterdam 1-1 0-1 **Vasas ETO Györ**
Benfica 5-1 1-2 Real Madrid

SEMI-FINALS

Liverpool 3-1 0-3 **Internazionale**
Vasas ETO Györ 0-1 0-4 **Benfica**

FINAL

San Siro, Milan, 27-05-1965, 85,000. Referee: Dienst, Switzerland

INTERNAZIONALE 1 (Jair 42)
BENFICA 0

Internazionale - Sarti - Burgnich, Guarneri, Facchetti - Bedin, Picchi Jair, Mazzola, Peiro, Suarez, Corso. Tr: Herrera

Benfica - Costa Pereira - Cavem, Cruz, Germano, Raul - Neto, Coluna, Augusto, Eusebio, Torres, Simoes. Tr: Schwartz

Top scorer: Torres, Benfica 9

FAIRS CUP

FIRST ROUND

Ferencváros 2-0 0-1 Spartak Brno
Wiener Sport-Club 2-1 1-0 SC Leipzig

Aris Salonica 0-0 0-3 **Roma**
NK Zagreb 3-2 6-0 Grazer AK
Dunfermline Athletic 4-2 0-0 Örgryte IS
B 1913 Odense 1-3 0-1 **VfB Stuttgart**
Hertha BSC Berlin 2-1 0-2 **Royal Antwerp FC**
Athletic Bilbao 2-2 2-0 OFK Beograd
Vålerengens Oslo 2-5 2-4 **Everton**
Eint. Frankfurt 3-0 1-5 **Kilmarnock**
Manchester United 6-1 1-1 Djurgårdens IF
Borussia Dortmund 4-1 0-2 Girondins Bordeaux
Leixoes SC 1-1 0-3 **Glasgow Celtic**
Barcelona 0-1 2-0 Fiorentina
RC Strasbourg 2-0 0-1 Milan
FC Basel 2-0 0-1 AC Spora
Servette FC 2-2 1-6 **Atlético Madrid**
OS Belenenses 1-1 0-0 1-2 **Shelbourne**
Valencia 1-1 1-3 **RFC Liège**
KB København 3-4 1-2 **DOS Utrecht**
Vojvodina Novi Sad 1-1 1-1 0-2 **Lokomotiv Plovdiv**
Göztepe Izmir 0-1 1-2 **Petrolul Ploiesti**
Real Betis 1-1 0-2 **Stade Français**
Union St Gilloise 0-1 0-1 **Juventus**

SECOND ROUND
Ferencváros 2-1 0-1 2-0 Wiener Sport-Club
NK Zagreb 1-1 0-1 **Roma**
Dunfermline Athletic 1-0 0-0 VfB Stuttgart
Athletic Bilbao 2-0 1-0 Royal Antwerp FC
Kilmarnock 0-2 1-4 **Everton**
Borussia Dortmund 1-6 0-4 **Manchester United**
Barcelona 3-1 0-0 Glasgow Celtic
FC Basel 0-1 2-5 **RC Strasbourg**
Shelbourne 0-1 0-1 **Atlético Madrid**
DOS Utrecht 0-2 0-2 **RFC Liège**
Petrolul Ploiesti 1-0 0-2 **Lokomotiv Plovdiv**
Stade Français 0-0 0-1 **Juventus**

THIRD ROUND
Roma 1-2 0-1 **Ferencváros**
Athletic Bilbao 1-0 0-1 2-1 Dunfermline Athletic
RC Strasbourg 0-0 2-2 0-0 Barcelona
Manchester United 1-1 2-1 Everton
RFC Liège 1-0 0-2 **Atlético Madrid**
Juventus 1-1 1-1 2-1 Lokomotiv Plovdiv

QUARTER-FINALS
Ferencváros 1-0 1-2 3-0 Athletic Bilbao
RC Strasbourg 0-5 0-0 **Manchester United**
Atlético Madrid Bye
Juventus Bye

SEMI-FINALS
Manchester United 3-2 0-1 1-2 Ferencváros
Atlético Madrid 3-1 1-3 1-3 Juventus

FINAL
Comunale, Turin, 23-06-1965, 25,000. Referee: Dienst, Switzerland
FERENCVAROS 1 (Fenyvesi 74)
JUVENTUS 0
Ferencváros - Geczi, Novak, Horvath, Juhasz, Matrai, Orosz, Karaba, Varga, Albert, Rakosi, Fenyvesi
Juventus - Anzolin, Gori, Sarti, Bercellino, Castano, Leoncini, Stachini, Del Sol, Combin, Mazzia, Menichelli

CUP WINNERS CUP

FIRST ROUND
AA Gent 0-1 1-1 **West Ham United**
Sparta Praha 10-0 6-0 Anorthosis Famagusta
Slavia Sofia 1-1 2-0 Cork Celtic
Lausanne-Sports 2-0 0-1 Honvéd
Esbjerg FB 0-0 0-1 **Cardiff City**
Sporting CP Bye
Dundee Bye
Valletta 0-3 1-5 **Real Zaragoza**
Torino 3-1 2-2 Fortuna 54 Geleen
FK Skeid Oslo 1-0 0-2 **Haka Valkeakoski**
AEK Athens 2-0 0-3 **Dinamo Zagreb**
Steaua Bucuresti 3-0 2-0 Derry City
Admira Wien 1-3 0-1 **Legia Warszawa**
Aufbau Magdeburg 1-1 1-1 1-1 **Galatasaray**
FC Porto 3-0 1-0 Olympique Lyon
Union Luxembourg 0-4 0-6 **TSV München 1860**

SECOND ROUND
West Ham United 2-0 1-2 Sparta Praha
Slavia Sofia 1-0 1-2 2-3 **Lausanne-Sports**
Sporting CP 1-2 0-0 **Cardiff City**
Dundee 2-2 1-2 **Real Zaragoza**
Torino 5-0 1-0 Haka Valkeakoski
Steaua Bucuresti 1-3 0-2 **Dinamo Zagreb**
Legia Warszawa 2-1 0-1 1-0 Galatasaray
FC Porto 0-1 1-1 **TSV München 1860**

QUARTER-FINALS
Lausanne-Sports 1-2 3-4 **West Ham United**
Real Zaragoza 2-1 1-0 Cardiff City
Torino 1-1 2-1 Dinamo Zagreb
Legia Warszawa 0-4 0-0 **TSV München 1860**

SEMI-FINALS
West Ham United 2-1 1-1 Real Zaragoza
Torino 2-0 1-3 0-2 **TSV München 1860**

FINAL
Wembley, London, 19-05-1965, 100,000. Referee: Zsolt, Hungary
WEST HAM UNITED 2 (Sealey 70 72)
TSV MUNCHEN 1860 0
West Ham - Standen - Kirkup, Burkett, Moore - Peters, Brown - Sealey, Boyce, Hurst, Dear, Sissons
München 1860 - Radenkovic - Wagner, Kohlars, Reich - Bena, Luttrop - Heiss, Küppers, Brunnenmeier, Grosser, Rebele

Top scorers: Masek & Mraz, Sparta Praha 6

1965–66

EUROPEAN CUP

FIRST ROUND
Feyenoord 2-1 0-5 **Real Madrid**
17 Nëntori Tiranë 0-0 0-1 **Kilmarnock**
Fenerbahçe 0-0 1-5 **RSC Anderlecht**
SOFK Lyn Oslo 5-3 1-5 **Derry City**
Panathinaikos 4-1 0-1 Sliema Wanderers
IBK Keflavík 1-4 1-9 **Ferencváros**
Dinamo Bucuresti 4-0 3-2 B 1909 Odense
Internazionale Bye
HJK Helsinki 2-3 0-6 **Manchester United**
Drumcondra 1-0 0-3 **Vorwärts Berlin**
Stade Dudelange 0-8 0-10 **Benfica**
Djurgårdens IF 2-1 0-6 **Levski Sofia**
Lausanne-Sports 0-0 0-4 **Sparta Praha**
Linzer ASK 1-3 1-2 **Górnik Zabrze**
Apoel Nicosia 0-5 0-5 **Werder Bremen**
Partizan Beograd 2-0 2-2 FC Nantes

SECOND ROUND
Kilmarnock 2-2 1-5 **Real Madrid**
RSC Anderlecht 9-0 Derry City
Ferencváros 0-0 3-1 Panathinaikos

Dinamo Bucuresti 2-1 0-2 **Internazionale**
Vorwärts Berlin 0-2 1-3 **Manchester United**
Levski Sofia 2-2 2-3 **Benfica**
Sparta Praha 3-0 2-1 Górnik Zabrze
Partizan Beograd 3-0 0-1 Werder Bremen

QUARTER-FINALS

RSC Anderlecht 1-0 2-4 **Real Madrid**
Internazionale 4-0 1-1 Ferencváros
Manchester United 3-2 5-1 Benfica
Sparta Praha 4-1 0-5 **Partizan Beograd**

SEMI-FINALS

Real Madrid 1-0 1-1 Internazionale
Partizan Beograd 2-0 0-1 Manchester United

FINAL

Heysel, Brussels, 11-05-1966, 55,000. Referee: Kreitlein, West Germany

REAL MADRID 2 (Amancio 70, Serena 75)
PARTIZAN BEOGRAD 1 (Vasovic 55)

Real Madrid - Araquistain - Pachin, De Felipe, Zoco, Sanchis - Pirri, Velazquez - Serena, Amancio, Grosso, Gento. Tr: Munoz

Partizan - Soskic - Jusufi, Rasovic, Vasovic, Milhailovic - Kovacevic, Becejac - Bajic, Hasanagic, Galic, Pirmajer. Tr: Gegic

Top scorer: Eusébio, Benfica 8

FAIRS CUP

FIRST ROUND

DOS Utrecht 0-0 1-7 **Barcelona**
Royal Antwerp FC 1-0 3-3 Glentoran
Stade Français 0-0 0-1 **FC Porto**
Girondins Bordeaux 0-4 1-6 **Sporting CP**
RFC Liège 1-0 0-2 **NK Zagreb**
Malmö FF 0-3 0-4 **TSV München 1860**
AIK Stockholm 3-1 0-0 Daring CB
Milan 1-0 1-2 1-1 RC Strasbourg
Wiener Sport-Club 6-0 1-2 PAOK Salonica
Chelsea 4-1 0-0 Roma
Leeds United 2-1 0-0 Torino
Hibernian Edinburgh 2-0 0-2 0-3 **Valencia**
Union Luxembourg 0-4 0-13 **1.FC Köln**
1.FC Nürnberg 1-1 0-1 **Everton**
Crvena Zvezda Beograd 0-4 1-3 **Fiorentina**
Spartak Brno 2-0 0-1 Lokomotiv Plovdiv
Hannover 96 Bye
RCD Español Bye
Steagul Rosu Brasov Bye
Göztepe Izmir Bye
Servette FC Bye
GD Cuf Barreiro Bye
SC Leipzig Bye
FC Basel Bye
Aris Salonica Bye
Ujpesti Dózsa Bye
Dunfermline Athletic. Bye
KB København Bye
Heart of Midlothian Bye
Vålerengens Oslo Bye
Shamrock Rovers Bye
Real Zaragoza Bye

SECOND ROUND

Royal Antwerp FC 2-1 0-2 **Barcelona**
Hannover 96 5-0 1-2 FC Porto
NK Zagreb 2-2 0-1 **Steagul Rosu Brasov**
Sporting CP 2-1 3-4 1-2 **RCD Español**
Göztepe Izmir 2-1 1-9 **TSV München 1860**
AIK Stockholm 2-1 1-4 **Servette FC**
GD Cuf Barreiro 2-0 0-2 0-1 **Milan**
Wiener Sport-Club 1-0 0-2 **Chelsea**
SC Leipzig 1-2 0-0 **Leeds United**
FC Basel 1-3 1-5 **Valencia**
Aris Salonica 2-1 0-2 **1.FC Köln**
Ujpesti Dózsa 3-0 1-2 Everton
Dunfermline Athletic 5-0 4-2 KB København
Fiorentina 2-0 0-4 **Spartak Brno**
Heart of Midlothian 1-0 3-1 Vålerengens IF Oslo
Shamrock Rovers 1-1 1-2 **Real Zaragoza**

THIRD ROUND

Hannover 96 2-1 0-1 1-1 **Barcelona**
RCD Español 3-1 2-4 1-0 Steagul Rosu Brasov
Servette FC 1-1 1-4 **TSV München 1860**
Milan 2-1 1-2 1-1 **Chelsea**
Leeds United 1-1 1-0 Valencia
1.FC Köln 3-2 0-4 **Ujpesti Dózsa**
Dunfermline Athletic 2-0 0-0 Spartak Brno
Heart of Midlothian 3-3 2-2 0-1 **Real Zaragoza**

QUARTER-FINALS

Barcelona 1-0 1-0 RCD Español
TSV München 1860 2-2 0-1 **Chelsea**
Leeds United 4-1 1-1 Ujpesti Dózsa
Dunfermline Athletic 1-0 2-4 **Real Zaragoza**

SEMI-FINALS

Barcelona 2-0 0-2 5-0 Chelsea
Real Zaragoza 1-0 1-2 3-1 Leeds United

FINAL

1st leg. Nou Camp, Barcelona, 14-09-1966, 70,000. Referee: Zsolt, Hungary

BARCELONA 0
REAL ZARAGOZA 1 (Canario 30)

Barcelona - Sadurni - Benitez, Eladio, Montesinos, Gallego, Torres, Zaballa, Muller, Zaldua, Fuste, Vidal

Real Zaragoza - Yarza - Irusquieta, Reija, Pais, Santamaria, Violeta, Canario, Santos, Marcelino, Villa, Lapetra

2nd leg. La Romareda, Zaragoza, 21-09-1966, 35,000. Referee: LoBello, Italy

REAL ZARAGOZA 2 (Marcelino 24 87)
BARCELONA 4 (Pujol 3 86 120, Zaballa 89)

Real Zaragoza - Yarza - Irusquieta, Reija, Pais, Santamaria, Violeta, Canario, Santos, Marcelino, Villa, Lapetra

Barcelona - Sadurni - Foncho, Eladio, Montesinos, Gallego, Torres, Zaballa, Mas, Zaldua, Fuste, Pujol

CUP WINNERS CUP

FIRST ROUND

Floriana 1-5 0-8 **Borussia Dortmund**
Limerick FC 1-2 0-2 **CSKA-CZ Sofia**
Wiener Neustadt 0-1 0-2 **Stiinta Cluj**
Atlético Madrid 4-0 1-0 Dinamo Zagreb
FC Sion 5-1 1-2 Galatasaray
1.FC Magdeburg 1-0 2-0 AC Spora
Omonia Nicosia 0-1 1-1 **Olympiakos**
West Ham United Bye
Go Ahead Deventer 0-6 0-1 **Glasgow Celtic**
ÅGF Åarhus 2-1 2-1 Vitória FC Setúbal
KR Reykjavík 1-3 1-3 **Rosenborg BK**
Coleraine 1-6 0-4 **Dinamo Kiev**
Reipas Lahti 2-10 0-6 **Honvéd**
Dukla Praha 2-0 0-0 Stade Rennes

Cardiff City 1-2 0-1 **Standard CL**
Juventus 1-0 0-2 **Liverpool**

SECOND ROUND
Borussia Dortmund 3-0 2-4 CSKA-CZ Sofia
Stiinta Cluj 0-2 0-4 **Atlético Madrid**
1.FC Magdeburg 8-1 2-2 FC Sion
West Ham United 4-0 2-2 Olympiakos
ÅGF Århus 0-1 0-2 **Glasgow Celtic**
Rosenborg BK 1-4 0-2 **Dynamo Kiev**
Dukla Praha 2-3 2-1 **Honvéd**
Liverpool 3-1 2-1 Standard Liege

QUARTER-FINALS
Atlético Madrid 1-1 0-1 **Borussia Dortmund**
West Ham United 1-0 1-1 1.FC Magdeburg
Glasgow Celtic 3-0 1-1 Dynamo Kiev
Honvéd 0-0 0-2 **Liverpool**

SEMI-FINALS
West Ham United 1-2 1-3 **Borussia Dortmund**
Glasgow Celtic 1-0 0-2 **Liverpool**

FINAL
Hampden Park, Glasgow, 5-05-1966, 41,000. Referee: Schwinte, France
BORUSSIA DORTMUND 2 (Held 62, Libuda 109)
LIVERPOOL 1 (Hunt 68)
Borussia - Tilkowski - Cyliax, Paul, Redder - Kurrat, Assauer - Libuda, Schmidt, Held, Sturm, Emmerich
Liverpool - Lawrence - Lawler, Yeats, Byrne - Milne, Stevenson - Callaghan, Hunt, St John, Smith, Thompson

Top scorer: Emmerich, Borussia Dortmund 14

1966–67

EUROPEAN CUP

PRELIMINARY ROUND
Sliema Wanderers 1-2 0-4 **CSKA-CZ Sofia**
Waterford FC 1-6 0-6 **Vorwärts Berlin**

FIRST ROUND
Glasgow Celtic 2-0 3-0 FC Zürich
KR Reykjavík 2-3 2-5 **FC Nantes**
Malmö FF 0-2 1-3 **Atlético Madrid**
Admira Wien 0-1 0-0 **Vojvodina Novi Sad**
Liverpool 2-0 1-3 2-0 Petrolul Ploiesti
Ajax 2-0 2-1 Besiktas
Haka Valkeakoski 1-10 0-2 **RSC Anderlecht**
Esbjerg FB 0-2 0-4 **Dukla Praha**
Aris Bonnevoie 3-3 1-6 **Linfield**
Vålerengens Oslo W-O 17 Nëntori Tiranë
Górnik Zabrze 2-1 1-2 3-1 Vorwärts Berlin
CSKA-CZ Sofia 3-1 0-1 Olympiakos
Real Madrid Bye
TSV München 1860 8-0 2-1 Omonia Nicosia
Vasas Budapest 5-0 2-0 Sporting CP
Internazionale 1-0 0-0 Torpedo Moskva

SECOND ROUND
FC Nantes 1-3 1-3 **Glasgow Celtic**
Vojvodina Novi Sad 3-1 0-2 3-2 Atlético Madrid
Ajax 5-1 2-2 Liverpool
Dukla Praha 4-1 2-1 RSC Anderlecht
CSKA-CZ Sofia 4-0 0-3 Górnik Zabrze
Vålerengens IF Oslo 1-4 1-1 **Linfield**
TSV München 1860 1-0 1-3 **Real Madrid**
Internazionale 2-1 2-0 Vasas Budapest

QUARTER-FINALS
Vojvodina Novi Sad 1-0 0-2 **Glasgow Celtic**
Ajax 1-1 1-2 **Dukla Praha**
Linfield 2-2 0-1 **CSKA-CZ Sofia**
Internazionale 1-0 2-0 Real Madrid

SEMI-FINALS
Glasgow Celtic 3-1 0-0 Dukla Praha
Internazionale 1-1 1-1 1-0 CSKA-CZ Sofia

FINAL
Estádio Nacional, Lisbon, 25-05-1967, 54,000. Referee: Tschenscher, West Germany
GLASGOW CELTIC 2 (Gemmell 63, Chalmers 85)
INTERNAZIONALE 1 (Mazzola 8)
Celtic - Simpson, Craig, McNeill, Gemmell - Murdoch, Clark - Johnstone, Wallace, Chalmers, Auld, Lennox. Tr: Stein
Internazionale - Sarti - Burgnich, Guarneri, Facchetti - Bedin, Picchi Domenghini, Mazzola, Cappellini, Bicicli, Corso. Tr: Herrera

Top scorers: Piepenburg, Vorwärts Berlin 6
Van Himst, Anderlecht 6

FAIRS CUP

FIRST ROUND
Spartak Brno 2-0 0-2 **Dinamo Zagreb**
Frigg SK Oslo 1-3 1-3 **Dunfermline Athletic**
Dinamo Pitesti 2-0 2-2 Sevilla
Juventus 5-0 2-0 Aris Salonica
Wiener Sport-Club 1-2 1-3 **Napoli**
VfB Stuttgart 1-1 0-2 **Burnley**
Olimpia Ljubljana 3-3 0-3 **Ferencváros**
OGC Nice 2-2 1-2 **Örgryte IS**
Drumcondra 0-2 1-6 **Eintracht Frankfurt**
FC Porto 2-1 1-2 **Girondins Bordeaux**
Union Luxembourg 0-1 0-1 **Royal Antwerp FC**
Djurgårdens IF 1-3 1-2 **Lokomotive Leipzig**
Bologna 2-1 3-1 Göztepe Izmir
DOS Utrecht 2-1 2-2 FC Basel
Crvena Zvezda Beograd 5-0 0-2 Athletic Bilbao
1.FC Nürnberg 1-2 0-2 **Valencia**
Toulouse FC Bye
Dundee United Bye
Barcelona Bye
Vitória FC Setúbal Bye
B 1909 Odense Bye
Lausanne-Sports Bye
Hvidovre BK Bye
AA Gent Bye
Kilmarnock Bye
Spartak Plovdiv Bye
Benfica Bye
RFC Liège Bye
Sparta Praha Bye
West Bromwich Albion Bye
DWS Amsterdam Bye
Leeds United Bye

SECOND ROUND
Dunfermline Athletic 4-2 0-2 **Dinamo Zagreb**
Toulouse FC 3-0 1-5 **Dinamo Pitesti**
Barcelona 1-2 0-2 **Dundee United**
Juventus 3-1 2-0 Vitória FC Setúbal
Lausanne-Sports 1-3 0-5 **Burnley**
B 1909 Odense 1-4 1-2 **Napoli**
Örgryte IS 0-0 1-7 **Ferencváros**

Eintracht Frankfurt 5-1 2-2 Hvidovre BK
Royal Antwerp FC 0-1 2-7 **Kilmarnock**
AA Gent 1-0 0-0 Girondins Bordeaux
Spartak Plovdiv 1-1 0-3 **Benfica**
Lokomotive Leipzig 0-0 2-1 RFC Liège
Sparta Praha 2-2 1-2 **Bologna**
DOS Utrecht 1-1 2-5 **West Bromwich Albion**
Valencia 1-0 2-1 Crvena Zvezda Beograd
DWS Amsterdam 1-3 1-5 **Leeds United**

THIRD ROUND
Dinamo Pitesti 0-1 0-0 **Dinamo Zagreb**
Juventus 3-0 0-1 Dundee United
Burnley 3-0 0-0 Napoli
Eintracht Frankfurt 4-1 1-2 Ferencváros
Kilmarnock 1-0 2-1 AA Gent
Lokomotive Leipzig 3-1 1-2 Benfica
Bologna 3-0 3-1 West Bromwich Albion
Leeds United 1-1 2-0 Valencia

QUARTER-FINALS
Juventus 2-2 0-3 **Dinamo Zagreb**
Eintracht Frankfurt 1-1 2-1 Burnley
Lokomotive Leipzig 1-0 0-2 **Kilmarnock**
Bologna 1-0 0-1 **Leeds United**

SEMI-FINALS
Eintracht Frankfurt 3-0 0-4 **Dinamo Zagreb**
Leeds United 4-2 0-0 Kilmarnock

FINAL
1st leg. Dinamo Stadion, Zagreb, 30-08-1967, 40,000. Referee: Bueno Perales, Spain
DINAMO ZAGREB 2 (Cercek 39 59)
LEEDS UNITED 0
Dinamo Zagreb - Skoric - Gracanin, Brncic, Belin, Ramljak - Blaskovic, Cercek - Piric, Zambata, Gucmirtl, Rora
Leeds Utd - Sprake - Reaney, Cooper, Bremner, Charlton, Hunter, Bates, Lorimer, Belfitt, Gray, O'Grady

2nd leg. Elland Road, Leeds, 6-09-1967, 35,000. Referee: Lo Bello, Italy
LEEDS UNITED 0
DINAMO ZAGREB 0
Leeds Utd - Sprake - Bell, Cooper, Bremner, Charlton, Hunter, Reaney, Belfitt, Greenhoff, Giles, O'Grady
Dinamo Zagreb - Skoric - Gracanin, Brncic, Belin, Ramljak - Blaskovic, Cercek - Piric, Zambata, Gucmirtl, Rora

CUP WINNERS CUP

PRELIMINARY ROUND
Valur Reykjavík 1-1 1-8 **Standard CL**

FIRST ROUND
Tatran Presov 1-1 2-3 **Bayern München**
Shamrock Rovers 4-1 4-1 AC Spora
OFK Beograd 1-3 0-3 **Spartak Moskva**
SK Rapid Wien 4-0 5-3 Galatasaray
Fiorentina 1-0 2-4 **Vasas ETO Györ**
AEK Athens 0-1 2-3 **Sporting Braga**
Chemie Leipzig 3-0 2-2 Legia Warszawa
Standard CL 5-1 1-0 Apollon Limassol
Swansea Town 1-1 0-4 **Slavia Sofia**
RC Strasbourg 1-0 1-1 Steaua Bucuresti
Floriana 1-1 0-6 **Sparta Rotterdam**
Servette FC 1-1 2-1 AIFK Abo
FK Skeid Oslo 3-2 1-3 **Real Zaragoza**
ÅAB Ålborg 0-0 1-2 **Everton**
Borussia Dortmund Bye
Glentoran 1-1 0-4 **Glasgow Rangers**

SECOND ROUND
Shamrock Rovers 1-1 2-3 **Bayern München**
Spartak Moskva 1-1 0-1 **SK Rapid Wien**
Vasas ETO Györ 3-0 0-2 Sporting Braga
Chemie Leipzig 2-1 0-1 **Standard CL**
RC Strasbourg 1-0 0-2 **Slavia Sofia**
Servette FC 2-0 0-1 Sparta Rotterdam
Real Zaragoza 2-0 0-1 Everton
Glasgow Rangers 2-1 0-0 Borussia Dortmund

QUARTER-FINALS
SK Rapid Wien 1-0 0-2 **Bayern München**
Vasas ETO Györ 2-1 0-2 **Standard CL**
Servette FC 1-0 0-3 **Slavia Sofia**
Glasgow Rangers 2-0 0-2 Real Zaragoza

SEMI-FINALS
Bayern München 2-0 3-1 Standard CL
Slavia Sofia 0-1 0-1 **Glasgow Rangers**

FINAL
Nürnbergerstadion, Nuremberg, 31-05-1967, 69,000. Referee: Lo Bello, Italy
BAYERN MUNCHEN 1 (Roth 108)
GLASGOW RANGERS 0
Bayern München - Maier - Nowak, Kupferschmidt, Beckenbauer, Olk - Roth, Koulmann - Nafziger, Ohlhauser, Müller, Brenninger
Rangers - Martin - Johansen, Provan, McKinnon, Greig - Jardine, Smith.D , Henderson, Hynd, Smith.A, Johnston

Top scorer: Müller, Bayern München 9

1967–68

EUROPEAN CUP

FIRST ROUND
Manchester United 4-0 0-0 Hibernians Paola
Olympiakos Nicosia 2-2 1-3 **FK Sarajevo**
Górnik Zabrze 3-0 1-0 Djurgårdens IF
Glasgow Celtic 1-2 1-1 **Dynamo Kiev**
Ajax 1-1 1-2 **Real Madrid**
FC Basel 1-2 3-3 **Hvidovre BK**
FK Skeid Oslo 0-1 1-1 **Sparta Praha**
FC Karl-Marx-Stadt 1-3 1-2 **RSC Anderlecht**
Olympiakos 0-0 0-2 **Juventus**
Botev Plovdiv 2-0 0-3 **Rapid Bucuresti**
Eintracht Braunschweig W-O Dinamo Tiranë
Besiktas 0-1 0-3 **SK Rapid Wien**
Dundalk 0-1 1-8 **Vasas Budapest**
Valur Reykjavík 1-1 3-3 Jeunesse Esch
AS Saint-Étienne 2-0 3-0 KuPS Kuopio
Glentoran 1-1 0-0 **Benfica**

SECOND ROUND
FK Sarajevo 0-0 1-2 **Manchester United**
Dynamo Kiev 1-2 1-1 **Górnik Zabrze**
Sparta Praha 3-2 3-3 RSC Anderlecht
Hvidovre 2-2 1-4 **Real Madrid**
Juventus 1-0 0-0 Rapid Bucuresti
SK Rapid Wien 1-0 0-2 **Eintracht Braunschweig**
Vasas Budapest 6-0 5-1 Valur Reykjavík
Benfica 2-0 0-1 AS Saint-Étienne

QUARTER-FINALS

Manchester United 2-0 0-1 Górnik Zabrze
Real Madrid 3-0 1-2 Sparta Praha
Eint. Braunschweig 3-2 0-1 0-1 **Juventus**
Vasas Budapest 0-0 0-3 **Benfica**

SEMI-FINALS

Manchester United 1-0 3-3 Real Madrid
Benfica 2-0 1-0 Juventus

FINAL

Wembley, London, 29-05-1968, 100,000. Referee: Lo Bello, Italy

MANCHESTER UNITED 4 (Charlton 53 99, Best 93, Kidd 94)
BENFICA 1 (Graca 75)

Manchester Utd - Stepney - Brennan, Stiles, Foulkes, Dunne - Crerand, Charlton, Sadler - Best, Kidd, Aston. Tr: Busby

Benfica - Henrique - Adolfo, Humberto, Jacinto, Cruz - Graca, Coluna, Augusto - Eusébio, Torres, Simoes. Tr: Otto Gloria

Top scorer: Eusébio, Benfica 6

FAIRS CUP

FIRST ROUND

AC Spora 0-9 0-7 **Leeds United**
Partizan Beograd 5-1 1-1 Lokomotiv Plovdiv
Hibernian Edinburgh 3-0 1-3 FC Porto
Napoli 4-0 1-1 Hannover 96
OGC Nice 0-1 0-4 **Fiorentina**
Club Brugge 0-0 1-2 **Sporting CP**
1.FC Köln 2-0 2-2 Slavia Praha
Dynamo Dresden 1-1 1-2 **Glasgow Rangers**
FC Zürich 3-1 0-1 Barcelona
Eintracht Frankfurt 0-1 0-4 **Nottingham Forest**
PAOK Salonica 0-2 2-3 **RFC Liège**
DWS Amsterdam 2-1 0-3 **Dundee**
Bologna 2-0 0-0 SOFK Lyn Oslo
Dinamo Zagreb 5-0 0-2 Petrolul Ploiesti
Wiener Sport-Club 2-5 1-2 **Atlético Madrid**
Royal Antwerp FC 1-2 0-0 **Göztepe Izmir**
Lokomotive Leipzig 5-1 0-1 Linfield
Vojvodina Novi Sad 1-0 3-1 GD Cuf Barreiro
Frem København 0-1 2-3 **Athletic Bilbao**
St. Patrick's Athletic 1-3 3-6 **Girondins Bordeaux**
Malmö FF 0-2 1-2 **Liverpool**
Servette FC 2-2 0-4 **TSV München 1860**
DOS Utrecht 3-2 1-3 **Real Zaragoza**
FC Arges Pitesti 3-1 0-4 **Ferencváros**

SECOND ROUND

Partizan Beograd 1-2 1-1 **Leeds United**
Napoli 4-1 0-5 **Hibernian Edinburgh**
Fiorentina 1-1 1-2 **Sporting CP**
Glasgow Rangers 3-0 1-3 1.FC Köln
Nottingham Forest 2-1 0-1 **FC Zürich**
Dundee 3-1 4-1 RFC Liège
Bologna 0-0 2-1 Dinamo Zagreb
Vojvodina Novi Sad 0-0 2-0 Lokomotive Leipzig
Atlético Madrid 2-0 0-3 **Göztepe Izmir**
Girondins Bordeaux 1-3 0-1 **Athletic Bilbao**
Liverpool 8-0 1-2 TSV München 1860
Real Zaragoza 2-1 0-3 **Ferencváros**

THIRD ROUND

Leeds United 1-0 1-1 Hibernian Edinburgh
Glasgow Rangers Bye
FC Zürich 3-0 0-1 Sporting CP
Dundee Bye
Bologna Bye
Vojvodina Novi Sad 1-0 1-0 Göztepe Izmir
Athletic Bilbao Bye
Ferencváros 1-0 1-0 Liverpool

QUARTER-FINALS

Glasgow Rangers 0-0 0-2 **Leeds United**
Dundee 1-0 1-0 FC Zürich
Bologna 0-0 2-0 Vojvodina Novi Sad
Ferencváros 2-1 2-1 Athletic Bilbao

SEMI-FINALS

Dundee 1-1 0-1 **Leeds United**
Ferencváros 3-2 2-2 Bologna

FINAL

1st leg. Elland Road, Leeds, 7-08-1968, 25,000. Referee: Scheurer, Switzerland

LEEDS UNITED 1 (Jones 41)
FERENCVAROS 0

Leeds Utd - Sprake - Reaney, Cooper, Bremner, Charlton, Hunter, Lorimer, Madeley, Jones (Belfitt), Giles (Greenhoff), Gray

Ferencváros - Geczi - Novak, Pancsics, Havasi, Juhasz, Szucs, Szoke, Varga, Albert, Rakosi, Fenyvesi (Balint)

2nd leg. Népstadion, Budapest, 11-09-1968, 76,000. Referee: Schulemburg, West Germany

FERENCVAROS 0
LEEDS UNITED 0

Ferencváros - Geczi - Novak, Pancsics, Havasi, Juhasz, Szucs, Rakosi, Szoke (Karaba), Varga, Albert, Katona

Leeds Utd - Sprake - Reaney, Cooper, Bremner, Charlton, Hunter, O'Grady, Lorimer, Jones, Madeley, Hibbitt (Bates)

CUP WINNERS CUP

FIRST ROUND

Milan 5-1 1-1 Levski Sofia
Vasas ETO Györ 5-0 4-0 Apollon Nicosia
Aberdeen 10-0 4-1 KR Reykjavík
Altay Izmir 2-3 0-0 **Standard CL**
Valencia 4-0 4-2 Crusaders
FK Austria 0-2 1-2 **Steaua Bucuresti**
Fredrikstad FK 1-5 1-2 **Vitória FC Setúbal**
Bayern München 5-0 2-1 Panathinaikos
Shamrock Rovers 1-1 0-2 **Cardiff City**
Floriana 1-2 0-1 **NAC Breda**
Lausanne-Sports 3-2 0-2 **Spartak Trnava**
Torpedo Moskva 0-0 1-0 Sach'ring Zwickau
Aris Bonnevoie 0-3 1-2 **Olympique Lyon**
Hajduk Split 0-2 3-4 **Tottenham Hotspur**
HJK Helsinki 1-4 0-4 **Wisla Kraków**
Hamburger SV 5-3 2-0 Randers Freja

SECOND ROUND

Vasas ETO Györ 2-2 1-1 **Milan**
Standard CL 3-0 0-2 Aberdeen
Valencia 3-0 0-1 Steaua Bucuresti
Bayern München 6-2 1-1 Vitória FC Setúbal
NAC Breda 1-1 1-4 **Cardiff City**
Torpedo Moskva 3-0 3-1 Spartak Trnava
Olympique Lyon 1-0 3-4 Tottenham Hotspur
Wisla Kraków 0-1 0-4 **Hamburger SV**

QUARTER-FINALS

Standard CL 1-1 1-1 0-2 **Milan**
Valencia 1-1 0-1 **Bayern München**
Cardiff City 1-0 0-1 1-0 Torpedo Moskva
Hamburger SV 2-0 0-2 2-0 Olympique Lyon

SEMI-FINALS

Milan 2-0 0-0 Bayern München
Hamburger SV 1-1 3-2 Cardiff City

FINAL

Feyenoord Stadion, Rotterdam, 23-05-1968, 53,000. Referee: Ortiz de Mendebil, Spain

MILAN 2 (Hamrin 3 19)
HAMBURGER SV 0

Milan - Cudicini - Anquilletti, Schnellinger, Rosato, Scala - Trapattoni, Lodetti - Hamrin, Sormani, Rivera, Prati
Hamburg - Özcan - Sandmann, Schulz, Horst, Kurbjuhn - Dieckmann, Krämer, Dörfel.B, Seeler, Honig, Dorfel.G

Top scorer: Seeler, Hamburger SV 6

1968–69

EUROPEAN CUP

FIRST ROUND

Malmö FF 2-1 1-4 **Milan**
Crvena Zvezda Beograd W-O Carl Zeiss Jena
AS Saint-Étienne 2-0 0-4 **Glasgow Celtic**
RSC Anderlecht 3-0 2-2 Glentoran
Waterford FC 1-3 1-7 **Manchester United**
Rosenborg BK 1-3 3-3 **SK Rapid Wien**
Real Madrid 6-0 6-0 AEL Limassol
Steaua Bucuresti 3-1 0-4 **Spartak Trnava**
Floriana 1-1 0-2 **Reipas Lahti**
AEK Athens 3-0 2-3 Jeunesse Esch
FC Zürich 1-3 2-1 **Akademisk Kob'havn**
Valur Reykjavík 0-0 1-8 **Benfica**
Manchester City 0-0 1-2 **Fenerbahçe**
1.FC Nürnberg 1-1 0-4 **Ajax**
Levski Sofia Withdrew
Ferencváros Withdrew
Dynamo Kiev Withdrew
Ruch Chorzów Withdrew

SECOND ROUND

Milan Bye
Glasgow Celtic 5-1 1-1 Crvena Zvezda Beograd
SK Rapid Wien 1-0 1-2 Real Madrid
Manchester United 3-0 1-3 RSC Anderlecht
Reipas Lahti 1-9 1-7 **Spartak Trnava**
AEK Athens 0-0 2-0 Akademisk København
Benfica Bye
Ajax 2-0 2-0 Fenerbahçe

QUARTER-FINALS

Milan 0-0 1-0 Glasgow Celtic
Manchester United 3-0 0-0 SK Rapid Wien
Spartak Trnava 2-1 1-1 AEK Athens
Ajax 1-3 3-1 3-0 Benfica

SEMI-FINALS

Milan 2-0 0-1 Manchester United
Ajax 3-0 0-2 Spartak Trnava

FINAL

Bernabeu, Madrid, 28-05-1969, 31,000. Referee: Ortiz de Mendebil, Spain

MILAN 4 (Prati 7 40 75, Sormani 67)
AJAX 1 (Vasovic 60)

Milan - Cudicini - Malatrasi, Anquilletti, Schnellinger, Rosato, Trapattoni - Lodetti, Rivera - Hamrin, Sormani, Prati. Tr: Rocco
Ajax - Bals - Suurbier (Muller), Hulshoff, Vasovic, Van Duivenbode - Pronk, Groot (Nuninga) - Swart, Cruyff, Danielsson, Keizer. Tr: Michels

Top scorer: Law, Manchester United 9

FAIRS CUP

FIRST ROUND

Newcastle United 4-0 0-2 Feyenoord
Sporting CP 4-0 1-4 Valencia
Slavia Sofia 0-0 0-2 **Aberdeen**
Trakia Plovdiv 3-1 0-2 **Real Zaragoza**
Dinamo Zagreb 1-1 1-2 **Fiorentina**
Hansa Rostock 3-0 1-2 OGC Nice
Olympique Lyon 1-0 0-1 Académica Coimbra
Vitória FC Setúbal 3-0 3-1 Linfield
Athletic Bilbao 2-1 1-2 Liverpool
Daring CB 2-1 0-2 **Panathinaikos**
Lausanne-Sports 0-2 0-2 **Juventus**
Wacker Innsbruck 2-2 0-3 **Eintracht Frankfurt**
Beerschot VAV 1-1 1-2 **DWS Amsterdam**
Chelsea 5-0 4-3 Morton
DOS Utrecht 1-1 1-2 **Dundalk**
Glasgow Rangers 2-0 0-1 Vojvodina Novi Sad
Göztepe Izmir 2-0 0-2 Olympique Marseille
Leixoes SC 1-1 0-0 **FC Arges Pitesti**
Bologna 4-1 2-1 FC Basel
Rapid Bucuresti 3-1 1-6 **OFK Beograd**
Olimpia Ljubljana 0-3 1-2 **Hibernian Edinburgh**
Lokomotive Leipzig W-O KB København
Wiener Sport-Club 1-0 0-5 **Slavia Praha**
FC Metz 1-4 2-3 **Hamburger SV**
Standard CL 0-0 2-3 **Leeds United**
Napoli 3-1 0-1 Grasshopper-Club
FK Skeid Oslo 1-1 1-2 **AIK Stockholm**
Hannover 96 3-2 1-0 B 1909 Odense
Legia Warszawa 6-0 3-2 TSV München 1860
Atlético Madrid 2-1 0-1 **KSV Waregem**
Aris Salonica 1-0 6-0 Hibernians Paola
Ujpesti Dózsa W-O Union Luxembourg

SECOND ROUND

Sporting CP 1-1 0-1 **Newcastle United**
Aberdeen 2-1 0-3 **Real Zaragoza**
Hansa Rostock 3-2 1-2 **Fiorentina**
Vitória FC Setúbal 5-0 2-1 Olympique Lyon
Panathinaikos 0-0 0-1 **Athletic Bilbao**
Juventus 0-0 0-1 **Eintracht Frankfurt**
Chelsea 0-0 0-0 **DWS Amsterdam**
Glasgow Rangers 6-1 3-0 Dundalk
Göztepe Izmir 3-0 2-3 FC Arges Pitesti
OFK Beograd 1-0 1-1 Bologna
Hibernian Edinburgh 3-1 1-0 Lokomotive Leipzig
Hamburger SV 4-1 1-3 Slavia Praha
Leeds United 2-0 0-2 Napoli
AIK Stockholm 4-2 2-5 **Hannover 96**
KSV Waregem 1-0 0-2 **Legia Warszawa**
Aris Salonica 1-2 1-9 **Ujpesti Dózsa**

THIRD ROUND

Real Zaragoza 3-2 1-2 **Newcastle United**
Vitória FC Setúbal 3-0 1-2 Fiorentina
Eintracht Frankfurt 1-1 0-1 **Athletic Bilbao**
DWS Amsterdam 0-2 1-2 **Glasgow Rangers**
OFK Beograd 3-1 0-2 **Göztepe Izmir**
Hamburger SV 1-0 1-2 Hibernian Edinburgh
Leeds United 5-1 2-1 Hannover 96
Legia Warszawa 0-1 2-2 **Ujpesti Dózsa**

QUARTER-FINALS

Newcastle United 5-1 1-3 Vitória FC Setúbal
Glasgow Rangers 4-1 0-2 Athletic Bilbao
Göztepe Izmir W-O Hamburger SV
Leeds United 0-1 0-2 **Ujpesti Dózsa**

SEMI-FINALS

Glasgow Rangers 0-0 0-2 **Newcastle United**
Göztepe Izmir 1-4 0-4 **Ujpesti Dózsa**

FINAL

1st leg. St. James' Park, Newcastle, 29-05-1969, 60,000. Referee: Hannet, France

NEWCASTLE UNITED 3 (Moncur 63 72, Scott 83)
UJPESTI DOZSA 0

Newcastle - McFaul, Craig, Clark, Gibb, Burton, Moncur, Scott, Robson, Davies, Arentoft, Sinclair (Foggon)

Ujpesti Dózsa - Szentmihalyi, Kaposzta, Solymosi, Bankuti, Nosko, Dunai.E, Fazekas, Gorocs, Bene, Dunai.A, Zambo

2nd leg. Budapest, 11-06-69, 37,000. Referee: Heymann, Switzerland

UJPESTI DOZSA 2 (Bene 31, Gorocs 44)
NEWCASTLE UNITED 3 (Moncur 46, Arentoft 50, Foggon 74)

Ujpesti Dózsa - Szentmihalyi, Kaposzta, Solymosi, Bankuti, Nosko, Dunai.E, Fazekas, Gorocs, Bene, Dunai.A, Zambo

Newcastle - McFaul, Craig, Clark, Gibb, Burton, Moncur, Scott (Foggon), Arentoft, Robson, Davies, Sinclair

CUP WINNERS CUP

FIRST ROUND

Slovan Bratislava 3-0 0-2 FK Bor
Cardiff City 2-2 1-2 **FC Porto**
Partizani Tiranë 1-0 1-3 **Torino**
Club Brugge 3-1 0-2 **West Bromwich Albion**
Dinamo Bucuresti W-O Vasas ETO Györ
Olympiakos 2-0 2-0 Fram Reykjavík
Dunfermline Athletic 10-1 2-0 Apoel Nicosia
Girondins Bordeaux 2-1 0-3 **1.FC Köln**
Altay Izmir 3-1 1-4 **SOFK Lyn Oslo**
US Rumelange 2-1 0-1 **Sliema Wanderers**
Randers Freja 1-0 2-1 Shamrock Rovers
ADO Den Haag 4-1 2-1 Grazer AK
Crusaders 2-2 1-4 **IFK Norrköping**
FC Lugano 0-1 0-3 **Barcelona**
Spartak Sofia Withdrew
Union Berlin Withdrew
Górnik Zabrze Withdrew
Dynamo Moskva Withdrew

SECOND ROUND

FC Porto 1-0 0-4 **Slovan Bratislava**
Torino Bye
Dinamo Bucuresti 1-1 0-4 **West Bromwich Albion**
Dunfermline Athletic 4-0 0-3 Olympiakos
ADO Den Haag 0-1 0-3 **1.FC Köln**
Randers Freja 6-0 2-0 Sliema Wanderers
SOFK Lyn Oslo 2-0 2-3 IFK Norrköping
Barcelona Bye

QUARTER-FINALS

Torino 0-1 1-2 **Slovan Bratislava**
Dunfermline Athletic 0-0 1-0 West Bromwich Albion
1.FC Köln 2-1 3-0 Randers Freja
Barcelona 3-2 2-2 SOFK Lyn Oslo

SEMI-FINALS

Dunfermline Athletic 1-1 0-1 **Slovan Bratislava**
1.FC Köln 2-2 1-4 **Barcelona**

FINAL

St. Jakob, Basle, 21-05-1969, 19,000. Referee: Van Raveszn, Holland

SLOVAN BRATISLAVA 3 (Cvetler 2, Hrivnak 30, Jan Capkovic 42)
BARCELONA 2 (Zaldua 16, Rexach 52)

Slovan - Vencel - Filo, Horvath, Hrivnak - Zlocha, Hrdlicka, Josef Capkovic - Cvetler, Moder (Macar), Jokl, Jan Capkovic

Barcelona - Sadurni - Franch (Pereda), Eladio, Rife - Olivella, Zabalza, Pellicer - Castro (Mendoza), Zaldua, Fuste, Rexach

Top scorer: Rühl, 1.FC Köln 6

1969–70

EUROPEAN CUP

PRELIMINARY ROUND

TPS Turku 0-1 0-4 **KB København**

FIRST ROUND

Feyenoord 12-2 4-0 KR Reykjavík
Milan 5-0 3-0 Avenir Beggen
Crvena Zvezda Beograd 8-0 4-2 Linfield
Vorwärts Berlin 2-0 1-1 Panathinaikos
Galatasaray 2-0 3-2 Waterford FC
Hibernians Paola 2-2 0-4 **Spartak Trnava**
Bayern München 2-0 0-3 **AS Saint-Étienne**
UT Arad 1-2 0-8 **Legia Warszawa**
Leeds United 10-0 6-0 SOFK Lyn Oslo
CSKA Sofia 2-1 1-4 **Ferencváros**
Real Madrid 8-0 6-1 Olympiakos Nicosia
Standard CL 3-0 1-1 17 Nëntori Tiranë
Fiorentina 1-0 2-1 Östers IF Växjö
FK Austria 1-2 1-3 **Dynamo Kiev**
Benfica 2-0 3-2 KB København
FC Basel 0-0 0-2 **Glasgow Celtic**

SECOND ROUND

Milan 1-0 0-2 **Feyenoord**
Vorwärts Berlin 2-1 2-3 Crvena Zvezda Beograd
Galatasaray 1-0 0-1 Spartak Trnava
Legia Warszawa 2-1 1-0 AS Saint-Étienne
Leeds United 3-0 3-0 Ferencváros
Standard CL 1-0 3-2 Real Madrid
Dynamo Kiev 1-2 0-0 **Fiorentina**
Glasgow Celtic 3-0 0-3 Benfica

QUARTER-FINALS

Vorwärts Berlin 1-0 0-2 **Feyenoord**
Galatasaray 1-1 0-2 **Legia Warszawa**
Standard CL 0-1 0-1 **Leeds United**
Glasgow Celtic 3-0 0-1 Fiorentina

SEMI-FINALS

Legia Warszawa 0-0 0-2 **Feyenoord**
Leeds United 0-1 1-2 **Glasgow Celtic**

FINAL

San Siro, Milan, 6-05-1970, 53,000. Referee: Lo Bello, Italy

FEYENOORD 2 (Israel 31, Kindvall 117)
GLASGOW CELTIC 1 (Gemmell 29)

Feyenoord - Pieters Graafland - Romeijn (Haak), Laseroms, Israel, Van Duivenbode - Hasil, Jansen - Van Hanegem, Wery, Kindvall, Moulijn. Tr: Happel

Celtic - Williams - Hay, Brogan, McNeill, Gemmell - Murdoch, Auld (Connelly) - Johnstone, Lennox, Wallace, Hughes. Tr: Stein

Top scorer: Jones, Leeds United 8

FAIRS CUP

FIRST ROUND

Arsenal 3-0 0-1 Glentoran
Sporting CP 4-0 2-2 Linzer ASK
RSC Charleroi 2-1 3-1 NK Zagreb

FC Rouen 2-0 0-1 FC Twente Enschede
FC Zürich 3-2 1-3 **Kilmarnock**
Slavia Sofia 2-0 1-1 Valencia
TSV München 1860 2-2 1-2 **FK Skeid Oslo**
Dinamo Bacau 6-0 1-0 Floriana
Carl Zeiss Jena 1-0 0-0 Altay Izmir
Aris Salonica 1-1 0-3 **Cagliari**
Partizan Beograd 2-1 0-2 **Ujpesti Dózsa**
FC Metz 1-1 1-2 **Napoli**
VfB Stuttgart 3-0 1-1 Malmö FF
Sabadell 2-0 1-5 **Club Brugge**
Wiener Sport-Club 4-2 1-4 **Ruch Chorzów**
Hannover 96 2-1 0-3 **Ajax**
Internazionale 3-0 1-0 Sparta Praha
Hansa Rostock 3-0 0-2 Panionios
Lausanne-Sports 1-2 1-2 **Rába ETO Györ**
Barcelona 4-0 2-0 B 1909 Odense
Vitória FC Setúbal 3-1 4-1 Rapid Bucuresti
Liverpool 10-0 4-0 Dundalk
Juventus 3-1 2-1 Lokomotiv Plovdiv
Las Palmas 0-0 0-1 **Hertha BSC Berlin**
Dundee United 1-2 0-1 **Newcastle United**
Hvidovre BK 1-2 0-2 **FC Porto**
Vitória Guimaraes 1-0 1-1 Baník Ostrava
Rosenborg BK 1-0 0-2 **Southampton**
Dunfermline Athletic 4-0 0-2 Girondins Bordeaux
Gwardia Warszawa 1-0 1-1 Vojvodina Novi Sad
Jeunesse Esch 3-2 0-4 **Coleraine**
Valur Reykjavík 0-6 0-2 **RSC Anderlecht**

SECOND ROUND

Sporting CP 0-0 0-3 **Arsenal**
RSC Charleroi 3-1 0-2 **FC Rouen**
Kilmarnock 4-1 0-2 Slavia Sofia
FK Skeid Oslo 0-0 0-2 **Dinamo Bacau**
Carl Zeiss Jena 2-0 1-0 Cagliari
Club Brugge 5-2 0-3 **Ujpesti Dózsa**
VfB Stuttgart 0-0 0-1 **Napoli**
Ajax 7-0 2-1 Ruch Chorzów
Hansa Rostock 2-1 0-3 **Internazionale**
Rába ETO Györ 2-3 0-2 **Barcelona**
Vitória FC Setúbal 1-0 2-3 Liverpool
Hertha BSC Berlin 3-1 0-0 Juventus
FC Porto 0-0 0-1 **Newcastle United**
Vitória SC Guimaraes 3-3 1-5 **Southampton**
Dunfermline Athletic 2-1 1-0 Gwardia Warszawa
RSC Anderlecht 6-1 7-3 Coleraine

THIRD ROUND

FC Rouen 0-0 0-1 **Arsenal**
Kilmarnock 1-1 0-2 **Dinamo Bacau**
Carl Zeiss Jena 1-0 3-0 Ujpesti Dózsa
Napoli 1-0 0-4 **Ajax**
Barcelona 1-2 1-1 **Internazionale**
Vitória FC Setúbal 1-1 0-1 **Hertha BSC Berlin**
Newcastle United 0-0 1-1 Southampton
RSC Anderlecht 1-0 2-3 Dunfermline Athletic

QUARTER-FINALS

Dinamo Bacau 0-2 1-7 **Arsenal**
Carl Zeiss Jena 3-1 1-5 **Ajax**
Hertha BSC Berlin 1-0 0-2 **Internazionale**
RSC Anderlecht 2-0 1-3 Newcastle United

SEMI-FINALS

Arsenal 3-0 0-1 Ajax
RSC Anderlecht 0-1 2-0 Internazionale

FINAL

1st leg. Parc Astrid, Brussels, 22-04-1970, 37,000. Referee: Scheurer, Switzerland

RSC ANDERLECHT 3 (Devrindt 25, Mulder 30 74)
ARSENAL 1 (Kennedy 82)

Anderlecht - Trappeniers, Heylens, Velkeneers, Kialunda, Cornelis (Peeters), Nordahl, Desanghere, Puis, Devrindt, Van Himst, Mulder
Arsenal - Wilson, Storey, McNab, Kelly, McLintock, Simpson, Armstrong, Sammels, Radford, George (Kennedy), Graham

2nd leg. Highbury, London, 28-04-1970, 51,000. Referee: Kunze, East Germany

ARSENAL 3 (Kelly 25, Radford 75, Sammels 76)
RSC ANDERLECHT 0

Arsenal - Wilson, Storey, McNab, Kelly, McLintock, Simpson, Armstrong, Sammels, Radford, George, Graham
Anderlecht - Trappeniers, Heylens, Velkeneers, Kialunda, Martens, Nordahl, Desanghere, Puis, Devrindt, Mulder, Van Himst

CUP WINNERS CUP

PRELIMINARY ROUND

SK Rapid Wien 0-0 1-1 Torpedo Moskva

FIRST ROUND

Athletic Bilbao 3-3 0-3 **Manchester City**
Lierse SK 10-1 1-0 Apoel Nicosia
1.FC Magdeburg 1-0 1-1 MTK Budapest
Académica Coimbra 0-0 1-0 KuPS Kuopio
Dinamo Zagreb 3-0 0-0 Slovan Bratislava
Dukla Praha 1-0 0-2 **Olympique Marseille**
IFK Norrköping 5-1 0-1 Sliema Wanderers
Shamrock Rovers 2-1 0-3 **FC Schalke 04**
Ards 0-0 1-3 **Roma**
SK Rapid Wien 1-2 2-4 **PSV Eindhoven**
Mjøndalen IF 1-7 1-5 **Cardiff City**
Göztepe Izmir 3-0 3-2 Union Luxembourg
IBV Vestmannaeyjar 0-4 0-4 **Levski-Spartak**
Frem København 2-1 0-1 **FC St. Gallen**
Glasgow Rangers 2-0 0-0 Steaua Bucuresti
Olympiakos 2-2 0-5 **Górnik Zabrze**

SECOND ROUND

Lierse SK 0-3 0-5 **Manchester City**
1.FC Magdeburg 1-0 0-2 **Académica Coimbra**
Olympique Marseille 1-1 0-2 **Dinamo Zagreb**
IFK Norrköping 0-0 0-1 **FC Schalke 04**
Roma 1-0 0-1 PSV Eindhoven
Göztepe Izmir 3-0 0-1 Cardiff City
Levski-Spartak 4-0 0-0 FC St. Gallen
Górnik Zabrze 3-1 3-1 Glasgow Rangers

QUARTER-FINALS

Académica Coimbra 0-0 0-1 **Manchester City**
Dinamo Zagreb 1-3 0-1 **FC Schalke 04**
Roma 2-0 0-0 Göztepe Izmir
Levski-Spartak 3-2 1-2 **Górnik Zabrze**

SEMI-FINALS

FC Schalke 04 1-0 1-5 **Manchester City**
Roma 1-1 2-2 1-1 **Górnik Zabrze**

FINAL

Prater, Vienna, 29-04-1970, 8,000. Referee: Schiller, Austria

MANCHESTER CITY 2 (Young 11, Lee 43)
GORNIK ZABRZE 1 (Oslizlo 70)

Manchester City - Corrigan - Book, Booth, Heslop, Pardoe - Doyle (Bowyer), Towers, Oakes - Bell, Lee, Young
Górnik Zabrze - Kostka - Oslizlo, Florenski (Deja), Gorgon, Olek - Latocha, Szoltysik, Wilczek (Skowronek) - Szarynski, Banas, Lubanski

Top scorer: Lubanski, Górnik Zabrze 8

1970–71

EUROPEAN CUP

PRELIMINARY ROUND

Levski-Spartak	3-1 0-3	**FK Austria**

FIRST ROUND

17 Nëntori Tiranë	2-2 0-2	**Ajax**
Spartak Moskva	3-2 1-2	**FC Basel**
Glentoran	1-3 0-1	**Waterford FC**
Glasgow Celtic	9-0 5-0	KPV Kokkola
IFK Göteborg	0-4 1-2	**Legia Warszawa**
Rosenborg BK	0-2 0-5	**Standard CL**
Cagliari	3-0 0-1	AS Saint-Étienne
Atlético Madrid	2-0 2-1	FK Austria
Ujpesti Dózsa	2-0 0-4	**Crvena Zvezda Beograd**
Feyenoord	1-1 0-0	**UT Arad**
Sporting CP	5-0 4-0	Floriana
Fenerbahçe	0-4 0-1	**Carl Zeiss Jena**
Everton	6-2 3-0	IBK Keflavík
B. Mönchengladbach	6-0 10-0	EPA Larnaca
Slovan Bratislava	2-1 2-2	B 1903 København
Jeunesse Esch	1-2 0-5	**Panathinaikos**

SECOND ROUND

Ajax	3-0 2-1	FC Basel
Waterford FC	0-7 2-3	**Glasgow Celtic**
Standard CL	1-0 0-2	**Legia Warszawa**
Cagliari	2-1 0-3	**Atlético Madrid**
Crvena Zvezda Beograd	3-0 3-1	UT Arad
Carl Zeiss Jena	2-1 2-1	Sporting CP
Borussia Mönchengladbach	1-1 1-1 3-4p	**Everton**
Panathinaikos	3-0 1-2	Slovan Bratislava

QUARTER-FINALS

Ajax	3-0 0-1	Glasgow Celtic
Atlético Madrid	1-0 1-2	Legia Warszawa
Carl Zeiss Jena	3-2 0-4	**Crvena Zvezda Beograd**
Everton	1-1 0-0	**Panathinaikos**

SEMI-FINALS

Atlético Madrid	1-0 0-3	**Ajax**
Crvena Zvezda Beograd	4-1 0-3	**Panathinaikos**

FINAL

Wembley, London, 2-06-1971, 83,000. Referee: Taylor, England

AJAX 2 (Van Dijk 5, OG 87)
PANATHINAIKOS 0

Ajax - Stuy - Neeskens, Hulshoff, Vasovic, Suurbier - Rijnders (Blankenburg), Muhren.G - Swart (Haan), Cruyff, Van Dijk, Keizer. Tr: Michels

Panathinaikos - Oeconomopoulos - Tomaras, Kapsis, Sourpis, Vlahos - Kamaras, Elefterakis - Grammos, Antoniadis, Domazos, Filakouris. Tr: Puskas

Top scorer: Antoniadis, Panathinaikos 10

FAIRS CUP

FIRST ROUND

FK Sarpsborg	0-1 0-5	**Leeds United**
Partizan Beograd	0-0 0-6	**Dynamo Dresden**
Dundee United	3-2 0-0	Grasshopper-Club
Sparta Praha	2-0 1-1	Athletic Bilbao
Zeljeznicar Sarajevo	3-4 4-5	**RSC Anderlecht**
Akademisk København	7-0 3-2	Sliema Wanderers
Hajduk Split	3-0 0-1	Slavia Sofia
Lausanne-Sports	0-2 1-2	**Vitória FC Setúbal**
Bayern München	1-0 1-1	Glasgow Rangers
Trakia Plovdiv	1-4 0-2	**Coventry City**
Coleraine	1-1 3-2	Kilmarnock
Sparta Rotterdam	6-0 9-0	IA Akranes
Hibernian Edinburgh	6-0 3-2	Malmö FF
Vitória Guimaraes	3-0 1-3	AS Angouleme
Dinamo Bucuresti	5-0 0-1	PAOK Salonica
Liverpool	1-0 1-1	Ferencváros
1.FC Köln	5-1 0-1	RCP Sedan
Ruch Chorzów	1-1 0-2	**Fiorentina**
B 1901 Nykobing	2-4 1-4	**Hertha BSC Berlin**
Spartak Trnava	2-0 0-2 4-3p	Olympique Marseille
Wiener Sport-Club	0-2 0-3	**SK Beveren**
Cork Hibernians	0-3 1-3	**Valencia**
Ilves Tampere	4-2 0-3	**SK Sturm Graz**
Lazio	2-2 0-2	**Arsenal**
AEK Athens	0-1 0-3	**FC Twente Enschede**
Sevilla	1-0 1-3	**Eskisehirspor**
AA Gent	0-1 1-7	**Hamburger SV**
FC Barreirense	2-0 1-6	**Dinamo Zagreb**
Universitatea Craiova	2-1 0-3	**Pécsi Dózsa**
Internazionale	1-1 0-2	**Newcastle United**
GKS Katowice	0-1 2-3	**Barcelona**
Juventus	7-0 4-0	Union Luxembourg

SECOND ROUND

Leeds United	1-0 1-2	Dynamo Dresden
Sparta Praha	3-1 0-1	Dundee United
Akademisk København	1-3 0-4	**RSC Anderlecht**
Vitória FC Setúbal	2-0 1-2	Hajduk Split
Bayern München	6-1 1-2	Coventry City
Sparta Rotterdam	2-0 2-1	Coleraine
Hibernian Edinburgh	2-0 1-2	Vitória SC Guimaraes
Liverpool	3-0 1-1	Dinamo Bucuresti
Fiorentina	1-2 0-1	**1.FC Köln**
Hertha BSC Berlin	1-0 1-3	**Spartak Trnava**
Valencia	0-1 1-1	**SK Beveren**
SK Sturm Graz	1-0 0-2	**Arsenal**
Eskisehirspor	3-2 1-6	**FC Twente Enschede**
Dinamo Zagreb	4-0 0-1	Hamburger SV
Newcastle United	2-0 0-2 3-5p	**Pécsi Dózsa**
Barcelona	1-2 1-2	**Juventus**

THIRD ROUND

Leeds United	6-0 3-2	Sparta Praha
RSC Anderlecht	2-1 1-3	**Vitória FC Setúbal**
Bayern München	2-1 3-1	Sparta Rotterdam
Hibernian Edinburgh	0-1 0-2	**Liverpool**
Spartak Trnava	0-1 0-3	**1.FC Köln**
Arsenal	4-0 0-0	SK Beveren
Dinamo Zagreb	2-2 0-1	**FC Twente Enschede**
Pécsi Dózsa	0-1 0-2	**Juventus**

QUARTER-FINALS

Leeds United	2-1 1-1	Vitória FC Setúbal
Liverpool	3-0 1-1	Bayern München
Arsenal	2-1 0-1	**1.FC Köln**
Juventus	2-0 2-2	FC Twente Enschede

SEMI-FINALS

Liverpool	0-1 0-0	**Leeds United**
1.FC Köln	1-1 0-2	**Juventus**

FINAL

1st leg. Comunale, Turin, 28-05-1971, 65,000. Referee: Van Ravens, Holland

JUVENTUS 2 (Bettega 27, Capello 55)
LEEDS UNITED 2 (Madeley 48, Bates 77)

Juventus - Piloni, Spinosi, Salvadore, Marchetti, Furino, Morini, Haller, Capello, Causio, Anastasi (Novellini), Bettega

Leeds Utd - Sprake, Reaney, Cooper, Bremner, Charlton, Hunter, Lorimer, Clarke, Jones (Bates), Giles, Madeley

2nd leg. Elland Road, Leeds, 3-06-1971, 42,000. Referee: Glöckner, East Germany

LEEDS UNITED 1 (Clarke 12)
JUVENTUS 1 (Anastasi 20)

Leeds Utd - Sprake, Reaney, Cooper, Bremner, Charlton, Hunter, Lorimer, Clarke, Jones, Giles, Madeley (Bates)
Juventus - Tancredi, Spinosi, Salvadore, Marchetti, Furino, Morini, Haller, Capello, Causio, Anastasi, Bettega

Top scorer: Anastasi, Juventus 10

CUP WINNERS CUP

PRELIMINARY ROUND

Bohemians Dublin..........1-2 2-2..........**TJ Gottwaldov**
Åtvidabergs FF..........1-1 0-2..........**Partizani Tiranë**

FIRST ROUND

Aris Salonica..........1-1 1-5..........**Chelsea**
CSKA Sofia..........9-0 2-1..........Haka Valkeakoski
IBA Akureyri..........1-7 0-7..........**FC Zürich**
Kickers Offenbach..........2-1 0-2..........**Club Brugge**
ÅAB Ålborg..........0-1 1-8..........**Górnik Zabrze**
Göztepe Izmir..........5-0 0-1..........Union Luxembourg
Aberdeen..........3-1 1-3 4-5p..........**Honvéd**
Manchester City..........1-0 1-2..........Linfield
TJ Gottwaldov..........2-1 0-1..........**PSV Eindhoven**
Steaua Bucuresti..........1-0 3-3..........Karpati Lvov
Olimpia Ljubljana..........1-1 1-8..........**Benfica**
Vorwärts Berlin..........0-0 1-1..........Bologna
Cardiff City..........8-0 0-0..........Pezoporikos
IF Strømsgodset..........0-5 3-2..........**FC Nantes**
Wacker Innsbruck..........3-2 2-1..........Partizani Tiranë
Hibernians Paola..........0-0 0-5..........**Real Madrid**

SECOND ROUND

CSKA Sofia..........0-1 0-1..........**Chelsea**
Club Brugge..........2-0 2-3..........FC Zürich
Göztepe Izmir..........0-1 0-3..........**Górnik Zabrze**
Honvéd..........0-1 0-2..........**Manchester City**
PSV Eindhoven..........4-0 3-0..........Steaua Bucuresti
Benfica..........2-0 0-2 3-5p..........**Vorwärts Berlin**
Cardiff City..........5-1 2-1..........FC Nantes
Real Madrid..........0-1 2-0..........Wacker Innsbruck

QUARTER-FINALS

Club Brugge..........2-0 0-4..........**Chelsea**
Manchester City..........2-0 0-2 3-1..........Górnik Zabrze
PSV Eindhoven..........2-0 0-1..........Vorwärts Berlin
Cardiff City..........1-0 0-2..........**Real Madrid**

SEMI-FINALS

Chelsea..........1-0 1-0..........Manchester City
PSV Eindhoven..........0-0 1-2..........**Real Madrid**

FINAL

Karaiskaki, Piraeus, 19-05-1971, 42,000. Referee: Scheurer, Switzerland

CHELSEA 1 (Osgood 55)
REAL MADRID 1 (Zoco 30)

Chelsea - Bonetti - Boyle, Dempsey, Webb, Harris - Hollins (Mulligan), Hudson, Cooke - Weller, Osgood (Baldwin), Housemann
Real Madrid - Borja - Jose Luis, Benito, Zoco, Zunzunegui - Pirri, Grosso, Velazquez - Perez (Fleitas), Amancio, Gento (Grande)

Replay. Karaiskaki, Piraeus, 21-05-1971, 35,000. Referee: Bucheli, Switzerland

CHELSEA 2 (Dempsey 32, Osgood 38)
REAL MADRID 1 (Fleitas 74)

Chelsea - Bonetti - Boyle, Dempsey, Webb, Harris - Cooke, Hudson, Weller Baldwin, Osgood (Smethurst), Housemann
Real Madrid - Borja - Jose Luis, Benito, Zoco, Zunzunegui - Pirri, Grosso, Velazquez (Gento) - Fleitas, Amancio, Bueno (Grande)

Top scorer: Lubanski, Górnik Zabrze 8

1971–72

EUROPEAN CUP

PRELIMINARY ROUND

Valencia..........3-1 1-0..........Union Luxembourg

FIRST ROUND

Ajax..........2-0 0-0..........Dynamo Dresden
Olympique Marseille..........2-1 1-1..........Górnik Zabrze
Reipas Lahti..........1-1 0-8..........**Grasshopper-Club**
IF Strømsgodset..........1-3 0-4..........**Arsenal**
Feyenoord..........8-0 9-0..........Olympiakos Nicosia
Dinamo Bucuresti..........0-0 2-2..........Spartak Trnava
CSKA Sofia..........3-0 1-0..........Partizani Tiranë
Wacker Innsbruck..........0-4 1-3..........**Benfica**
B 1903 København..........2-1 0-3..........**Glasgow Celtic**
IA Akranes..........0-4 0-0..........**Sliema Wanderers**
Valencia..........0-0 1-1..........Hajduk Split
Ujpesti Dózsa..........4-0 0-1..........Malmö FF
Standard CL..........2-0 3-2..........Linfield
Galatasaray..........1-1 0-3..........**CSKA Moskva**
Cork Hibernians..........0-5 1-2..........**B. Mönchengladbach**
Internazionale..........4-1 2-3..........AEK Athens

SECOND ROUND

Olympique Marseille..........1-2 1-4..........**Ajax**
Grasshopper-Club..........0-2 0-3..........**Arsenal**
Dinamo Bucuresti..........0-3 0-2..........**Feyenoord**
Benfica..........2-1 0-0..........CSKA Sofia
Glasgow Celtic..........5-0 2-1..........Sliema Wanderers
Valencia..........0-1 1-2..........**Ujpesti Dózsa**
CSKA Moskva..........1-0 0-2..........**Standard CL**
Internazionale..........4-2 0-0..........Borussia Mönchengladbach

QUARTER-FINALS

Ajax..........2-1 1-0..........Arsenal
Feyenoord..........1-0 1-5..........**Benfica**
Ujpesti Dózsa..........1-2 1-1..........**Glasgow Celtic**
Internazionale..........1-0 1-2..........Standard CL

SEMI-FINALS

Ajax..........1-0 0-0..........Benfica
Internazionale..........0-0 0-0 5-4p..........Glasgow Celtic

FINAL

Feyenoord Stadion, Rotterdam, 31-05-1972, 61,000. Referee: Héliès, France

AJAX 2 (Cruyff 47 78)
INTERNAZIONALE 0

Ajax - Stuy - Suurbier, Blankenburg, Hulshoff, Krol - Neeskens, Haan, Muhren.G - Swart, Cruyff, Keizer. Tr: Kovacs
Internazionale - Bordon - Burgnich, Facchetti, Bellugi, Oriali - Giubertoni (Bertini), Bedin, Frustalupi - Jair (Pellizarro), Mazzola, Boninsegna. Tr: Invernizzi

Top scorers: Cruyff, Ajax 5
Macari, Celtic 5
Takac, Standard CL 5

UEFA CUP

IBK Keflavík..........1-6 0-9..........**Tottenham Hotspur**
FC Porto..........0-2 1-1..........**FC Nantes**

FC Lugano	1-3 0-0	**Legia Warszawa**
Napoli	1-0 0-2	**Rapid Bucuresti**
Vitória FC Setúbal	1-0 1-2	Nîmes Olympique
Spartak Moskva	2-0 1-2	VSS Kosice
Zaglebie Walbrzych	1-0 3-2	Union Teplice
UT Arad	4-1 1-3	Austria Salzburg
Lierse SK	0-2 4-0	Leeds United
Rosenborg BK	3-0 1-0	HIFK Helsinki
FC Basel	1-2 1-2	**Real Madrid**
Chemie Halle	0-0	**PSV Eindhoven**
Dundee	4-2 1-0	Akademisk København
AS Saint-Étienne	1-1 1-2	**1.FC Köln**
Hertha BSC Berlin	3-1 4-1	IF Elfsborg Borås
Milan	4-0 3-0	Digenis Morphou
Fenerbahçe	1-1 1-3	**Ferencváros**
Atlético Madrid	2-1 0-1	**Panionios**
Southampton	2-1 0-2	**Athletic Bilbao**
Glentoran	0-1 1-6	**Eintracht Braunschweig**
Hamburger SV	2-1 0-3	**St. Johnstone**
Vasas Budapest	1-0 1-1	Shelbourne
Bologna	1-1 2-0	RSC Anderlecht
Zeljeznicar Sarajevo	3-0 1-3	Club Brugge
Marsa	0-6 0-5	**Juventus**
Celta	0-2 0-1	**Aberdeen**
Dinamo Zagreb	6-1 2-1	Botev Vratza
SK Rapid Wien	W-O	Vllaznia Shkodër
Carl Zeiss Jena	3-0 1-3	Lokomotiv Plovdiv
OFK Beograd	4-1 2-2	Djurgårdens IF
FC Den Haag	5-0 1-1	Aris Bonnevoie
Wolverhampton W.	3-0 4-1	Académica Coimbra

SECOND ROUND

FC Nantes	0-0 0-1	**Tottenham Hotspur**
Rapid Bucuresti	4-0 0-2	Legia Warszawa
Spartak Moskva	0-0 0-4	**Vitória FC Setúbal**
Zaglebie Walbrzych	1-1 1-2	**UT Arad**
Rosenborg BK	4-1 0-3	**Lierse SK**
Real Madrid	3-1 0-2	**PSV Eindhoven**
1.FC Köln	2-1 2-4	**Dundee**
Milan	4-2 1-2	Hertha BSC Berlin
Ferencváros	6-0	Panionios
Eintracht Braunschweig	2-1 2-2	Athletic Bilbao
St. Johnstone	2-0 0-1	Vasas Budapest
Zeljeznicar Sarajevo	1-1 2-2	Bologna
Juventus	2-0 1-1	Aberdeen
Dinamo Zagreb	2-2 0-0	**SK Rapid Wien**
OFK Beograd	1-1 0-4	**Carl Zeiss Jena**
FC Den Haag	1-3 0-4	**Wolverhampton W.**

THIRD ROUND

Tottenham Hotspur	3-0 2-0	Rapid Bucuresti
UT Arad	3-0 0-1	Vitória FC Setúbal
PSV Eindhoven	1-0 0-4	**Lierse SK**
Milan	3-0 0-2	Dundee
Eintracht Braunschweig	1-1 2-5	**Ferencváros**
St. Johnstone	1-0 1-5	**Zeljeznicar Sarajevo**
SK Rapid Wien	0-1 1-4	**Juventus**
Carl Zeiss Jena	0-1 0-3	**Wolverhampton W.**

QUARTER-FINALS

UT Arad	0-2 1-1	**Tottenham Hotspur**
Milan	2-0 1-1	Lierse SK
Ferencváros	1-2 2-1 5-4p	Zeljeznicar Sarajevo
Juventus	1-1 1-2	**Wolverhampton W.**

SEMI-FINALS

Tottenham Hotspur	2-1 1-1	Milan
Ferencváros	2-2 1-2	**Wolverhampton W.**

FINAL

1st leg. Molineux, Wolverhampton, 3-05-1972, 38,000. Referee: Bakhramov, Soviet Union

WOLVERHAMPTON W. 1 (McCalliog 72)
TOTTENHAM HOTSPUR 2 (Chivers 57 87)
Wolves - Parkes, Shaw, Taylor, Hegan, Munro, McAlle, McCalliog, Hibbitt, Richards, Dougan, Wagstaffe
Tottenham - Jennings, Kinnear, Knowles, Mullery, England, Beal, Gilzean, Perryman, Chivers, Peters, Coates (Pratt)

2nd leg. White Hart Lane, London, 17-05-1972, 54,000. Referee: Van Ravens, Holland

TOTTENHAM HOTSPUR 1 (Mullery 30)
WOLVERHAMPTON W. 1 (Wagstaffe 41)
Tottenham - Jennings, Kinnear, Knowles, Mullery, England, Beal, Gilzean, Perryman, Chivers, Peters, Coates
Wolves - Parkes, Shaw, Taylor, Hegan, Munro, McAlle, McCalliog, Hibbitt (Bailey), Richards, Dougan (Curran), Wagstaffe

Top scorer: Bründl, Eintracht Braunschweig 10

CUP WINNERS CUP

PRELIMINARY ROUND

B 1909 Odense	4-2 0-2	**FK Austria**
Hibernians Paola	3-0 0-2	Fram Reykjavík

FIRST ROUND

Stade Rennes	1-1 0-1	**Glasgow Rangers**
Sporting CP	4-0 3-0	SOFK Lyn Oslo
Dinamo Tiranë	1-1 0-1	**FK Austria**
Limerick FC	0-1 0-4	**Torino**
Hibernians Paola	0-0 0-1	**Steaua Bucuresti**
Distillery	1-3 0-4	**Barcelona**
Servette FC	2-1 0-2	**Liverpool**
Skoda Plzen	0-1 1-6	**Bayern München**
Dynamo Berlin	1-1 1-1 5-4p	Cardiff City
Beerschot VAV	7-0 1-0	Anorthosis Famagusta
Jeunesse Hautcharage	0-8 0-13	**Chelsea**
Zaglebie Sosnowiec	3-4 1-1	**Åtvidabergs FF**
Komló Bányász	2-7 2-1	**Crvena Zvezda Beograd**
Levski-Spartak	1-1 0-2	**Sparta Rotterdam**
MP Mikkeli	0-0 0-4	**Eskisehirspor**
Olympiakos	0-2 2-1	**Dynamo Moskva**

SECOND ROUND

Glasgow Rangers	3-2 3-4	Sporting CL
Torino	1-0 0-0	FK Austria
Barcelona	0-1 1-2	**Steaua Bucuresti**
Liverpool	0-0 1-3	**Bayern München**
Beerschot VAV	1-3 1-3	**Dynamo Berlin**
Åtvidabergs FF	0-0 1-1	Chelsea
Sparta Rotterdam	1-1 1-2	**Crvena Zvezda Beograd**
Eskisehirspor	0-1 0-1	**Dynamo Moskva**

QUARTER-FINALS

Torino	1-1 0-1	**Glasgow Rangers**
Steaua Bucuresti	1-1 0-0	**Bayern München**
Åtvidabergs FF	0-2 2-2	**Dynamo Berlin**
Crvena Zvezda Beograd	1-2 1-1	**Dynamo Moskva**

SEMI-FINALS

Bayern München	1-1 0-2	**Glasgow Rangers**
Dynamo Berlin	1-1 1-1 1-4p	**Dynamo Moskva**

FINAL

Nou Camp, Barcelona, 24-05-1972, 24,000. Referee: Ortiz de Mendebil, Spain

GLASGOW RANGERS 3 (Stein 23, Johnston 40 49)
DYNAMO MOSKVA 2 (Estrekov 60, Makovikov 87)
Rangers - McCloy - Jardine, Johnstone, Smith, Mathieson - Greig, Conn, MacDonald - McLean, Stein, Johnston
Dynamo Moskva - Pilgui - Basalev, Dolmatov, Zikov, Dobonosov

(Gerschkovitch) - Zhukov, Yakubik (Estrekov), Sabo - Baidatchini, Makovikov, Evriuschkin

Top scorer: Osgood, Chelsea ... 8

EUROPEAN SUPERCUP 1972

1st leg. Ibrox, Glasgow, 16-01-1973. Referee: MacKenzie, Scotland

GLASGOW RANGERS 1 (MacDonald 39)
AJAX 3 (Rep 31, Cruyff 43, Haan 44)

2nd leg. Amsterdam, 24-01-1973. Referee: Weyland, West Germany

AJAX 3 (Haan 9, Muhren 39, Cruyff 78)
GLASGOW RANGERS 2 (MacDonald 7 26)

1972–73

EUROPEAN CUP

FIRST ROUND

Ajax	Bye	
CSKA Sofia	2-1 2-0	Panathinaikos
Waterford FC	2-1 0-2	**Omonia Nicosia**
Galatasaray	1-1 0-6	**Bayern München**
Wacker Innsbruck	0-1 0-2	**Dynamo Kiev**
Sliema Wanderers	0-5 0-5	**Górnik Zabrze**
Aris Bonnevoie	0-2 0-4	**FC Arges Pitesti**
Real Madrid	3-0 1-0	IBK Keflavík
Derby County	2-0 2-1	Zeljeznicar Sarajevo
Malmö FF	1-0 1-4	**Benfica**
RSC Anderlecht	4-2 3-0	Vejle BK
Spartak Trnava	Bye	
Ujpesti Dózsa	2-0 2-3	FC Basel
Glasgow Celtic	2-1 3-1	Rosenborg BK
1.FC Magdeburg	6-0 3-1	TPS Turku
Olympique Marseille	1-0 0-3	**Juventus**

SECOND ROUND

CSKA Sofia	1-3 0-3	**Ajax**
Omonia Nicosia	0-9 0-4	**Bayern München**
Dynamo Kiev	2-0 1-2	Górnik Zabrze
FC Arges Pitesti	2-1 1-3	**Real Madrid**
Derby County	3-0 0-0	Benfica
Spartak Trnava	1-0 1-0	RSC Anderlecht
Glasgow Celtic	2-1 0-3	**Ujpesti Dózsa**
Juventus	1-0 1-0	1.FC Magdeburg

QUARTER-FINALS

Ajax	4-0 1-2	Bayern München
Dynamo Kiev	0-0 0-3	**Real Madrid**
Spartak Trnava	1-0 0-2	**Derby County**
Juventus	0-0 2-2	Ujpesti Dózsa

SEMI-FINALS

Ajax	2-1 1-0	Real Madrid
Juventus	3-1 0-0	Derby County

FINAL

Crvena Zvezda, Belgrade, 30-05-1973, 89,000. Referee: Gugulovic, Yugoslavia

AJAX 1 (Rep 4)
JUVENTUS 0

Ajax - Stuy - Suurbier, Hulshoff, Blankenburg, Krol - Neeskens, Muhren.G, Haan - Rep, Cruyff, Keizer. Tr: Kovacs

Juventus - Zoff - Salvadore, Marchetti, Morini, Longobucco - Causio (Cuccureddu), Furino, Capello - Altafini, Anastasi, Bettega (Haller). Tr: Vycpalek

Top scorer: Müller, Bayern München ... 11

UEFA CUP

FIRST ROUND

Liverpool	2-0 0-0	Eint. Frankfurt
AEK Athens	3-1 1-1	Salgótarján BTC
Universitatea Cluj	4-1 1-5	**Levski-Spartak**
SC Angers	1-1 1-2	**Dynamo Berlin**
FC Porto	3-1 1-0	Barcelona
Åtvidabergs FF	3-5 2-1	**Club Brugge**
Ruch Chorzów	3-0 0-1	Fenerbahçe
Dynamo Dresden	2-0 2-2	VÖEST Linz
Vitória FC Setúbal	6-1 0-1	Zaglebie Sosnowiec
Eskisehirspor	1-2 0-3	**Fiorentina**
UT Arad	1-2 0-2	**IFK Norrköping**
Internazionale	6-1 1-0	Valletta
Crvena Zvezda Beograd	5-1 2-3	Lausanne-Sports
Manchester City	2-2 1-2	**Valencia**
Olympiakos	2-1 1-0	Cagliari
SOFK Lyn Oslo	3-6 0-6	**Tottenham Hotspur**
Dynamo Tbilisi	3-2 0-2	**FC Twente Enschede**
FC Sochaux	1-3 1-2	**Frem København**
Slovan Bratislava	6-0 2-1	Vojvodina Novi Sad
Torino	2-0 0-4	**Las Palmas**
Beroe Stara Zagora	7-0 3-1	FK Austria
Honvéd	1-0 3-0	Partick Thistle
Feyenoord	9-0 12-0	US Rumelange
Dukla Praha	2-2 1-3	**OFK Beograd**
Stoke City	3-1 0-4	**1.FC Kaiserslautern**
Racing White	0-1 0-2	**GD Cuf Barreiro**
Grasshopper-Club	2-1 2-1	Nîmes Olympique
EPA Larnaca	0-1 0-1	**Ararat Yerevan**
1.FC Köln	2-1 3-0	Bohemians Dublin
Viking Stavanger	1-0 0-0	IBV Vestmannaeyjar
Hvidovre BK	W-O	HIFK Helsinki
Aberdeen	2-3 3-6	**B. Mönchengladbach**

SECOND ROUND

Liverpool	3-0 3-1	AEK Athens
Dynamo Berlin	3-0 0-2	Levski-Spartak
FC Porto	3-0 2-3	Club Brugge
Ruch Chorzów	0-1 0-3	**Dynamo Dresden**
Vitória FC Setúbal	1-0 1-2	Fiorentina
Internazionale	2-2 2-0	IFK Norrköping
Crvena Zvezda Beograd	3-1 1-0	Valencia
Tottenham Hotspur	4-0 0-1	Olympiakos
Frem København	0-5 0-4	**FC Twente Enschede**
Las Palmas	2-2 1-0	Slovan Bratislava
Beroe Stara Zagora	3-0 0-1	Honvéd
Feyenoord	4-3 1-2	**OFK Beograd**
GD Cuf Barreiro	1-3 1-0	**1.FC Kaiserslautern**
Grasshopper-Club	1-3 2-4	**Ararat Yerevan**
Viking FK Stavanger	1-0 1-9	**1.FC Köln**
B. Mönchengladbach	3-0 3-1	Hvidovre BK

THIRD ROUND

Dynamo Berlin	0-0 1-3	**Liverpool**
FC Porto	1-2 0-1	**Dynamo Dresden**
Vitória FC Setúbal	2-0 0-1	Internazionale
Tottenham Hotspur	2-0 0-1	Crvena Zvezda Beograd
FC Twente Enschede	3-0 1-2	Las Palmas
OFK Beograd	0-0 3-1	Beroe Stara Zagora
Ararat Yerevan	2-0 0-2 4-5p	**1.FC Kaiserslautern**
1.FC Köln	0-0 0-5	**B. Mönchengladbach**

QUARTER-FINALS

Liverpool	2-0 1-0	Dynamo Dresden
Tottenham Hotspur	1-0 1-2	Vitória FC Setúbal
OFK Beograd	3-2 0-2	**FC Twente Enschede**
1.FC Kaiserslautern	1-2 1-7	**B. Mönchengladbach**

SEMI-FINALS

Liverpool .... 1-0 1-2 .... Tottenham Hotspur
B. Mönchengladbach .... 3-0 2-1 .... FC Twente Enschede

FINAL

1st leg. Anfield, Liverpool, 10-05-1973, 41,000. Referee: Linemayr, Austria
LIVERPOOL 3 (Keegan 21 32, Lloyd 61)
B. MÖNCHENGLADBACH 0
Liverpool - Clemence, Lawler, Lindsay, Smith, Lloyd, Hughes, Keegan, Cormack, Toshack, Heighway (Hall), Callaghan
Borussia - Kleff, Michallik, Netzer, Bonhof, Vogts, Wimmer, Danner, Kulik, Jensen, Rupp (Simonsen), Heynckes

2nd leg. Bökelbergstadion, Mönchengladbach, 23-05-1973, 35,000. Referee: Kazakov, Soviet Union
B. MÖNCHENGLADBACH 2 (Heynckes 29 40)
LIVERPOOL 0
Borussia - Kleff, Surau, Netzer, Bonhof, Vogts, Wimmer, Danner, Kulik, Jensen, Rupp, Heynckes
Liverpool - Clemence, Lawler, Lindsay, Smith, Lloyd, Hughes, Keegan, Cormack, Heighway (Boersma), Toshack, Callaghan

Top scorer: Jeuring, FC Twente 12

CUP WINNERS CUP

FIRST ROUND

Red Boys .... 1-4 0-3 .... **Milan**
Víkingur Reykjavík .... 0-2 0-9 .... **Legia Warszawa**
SEC Bastia .... 0-0 1-2 .... **Atlético Madrid**
Spartak Moskva .... 1-0 0-0 .... FC Den Haag
FC Schalke 04 .... 2-1 3-1 .... Slavia Sofia
Pezoporikos .... 1-2 1-4 .... **Cork Hibernians**
Floriana .... 1-0 0-6 .... **Ferencváros**
Standard CL .... 1-0 2-4 .... **Sparta Praha**
Hajduk Split .... 1-0 1-0 .... Fredrikstad FK
FC Zürich .... 1-1 1-2 .... **Wrexham**
Fremad Amager .... 1-1 0-0 .... **Besa Kavajë**
Sporting CP .... 2-1 1-6 .... **Hibernian Edinburgh**
Rapid Bucuresti .... 3-0 0-1 .... Landskrona BoIS
SK Rapid Wien .... 0-0 2-2 .... PAOK Salonica
Carl Zeiss Jena .... 6-1 2-3 .... MP Mikkeli
MKE Ankaragücü .... 1-1 0-1 .... **Leeds United**

SECOND ROUND

Legia Warszawa .... 1-1 1-2 .... **Milan**
Atlético Madrid .... 3-4 2-1 .... **Spartak Moskva**
Cork Hibernians .... 0-0 0-3 .... **FC Schalke 04**
Ferencváros .... 2-0 1-4 .... **Sparta Praha**
Wrexham .... 3-1 0-2 .... **Hajduk Split**
Hibernian Edinburgh .... 7-1 1-1 .... Besa Kavajë
SK Rapid Wien .... 1-1 1-3 .... **Rapid Bucuresti**
Carl Zeiss Jena .... 0-0 0-2 .... **Leeds United**

QUARTER-FINALS

Spartak Moskva .... 0-1 1-1 .... **Milan**
FC Schalke 04 .... 2-1 0-3 .... **Sparta Praha**
Hibernian Edinburgh .... 4-2 0-3 .... **Hajduk Split**
Leeds United .... 5-0 3-1 .... Rapid Bucuresti

SEMI-FINALS

Milan .... 1-0 1-0 .... Sparta Praha
Leeds United .... 1-0 0-0 .... Hajduk Split

FINAL

Salonica, 16-05-73, 45,000. Referee: Michas, Greece
MILAN 1 (Chiarugi 5)
LEEDS UNITED 0
Milan - Vecchi - Sabadini, Zignoli, Anquilletti, Turone - Rosato (Dolci), Rivera, Benetti - Sogliano, Bigon, Chiarugi
Leeds Utd - Harvey - Reaney, Cherry, Bates, Madeley - Hunter, Gray.E, Yorath (McQueen) - Lorimer, Jordan, Jones

Top scorer: Chiarugi, Milan 7

EUROPEAN SUPERCUP 1973

1st leg. San Siro, Milan, 9-01-1974. Referee: Scheurer, Switzerland
MILAN 1 (Chiarugi 77)
AJAX 0
2nd leg. Amsterdam, 16-01-1974. Referee: Glöckner, East Germany
AJAX 6 (Mulder 26, Keizer 35, Neeskens 71, Rep 81, Muhren 84, Haan 87)
MILAN 0

1973–74

EUROPEAN CUP

FIRST ROUND

Bayern München .... 3-1 1-3 4-3p .... Åtvidabergs FF
Dynamo Dresden .... 2-0 2-3 .... Juventus
Ajax .... Bye
CSKA Sofia .... 3-0 1-0 .... Wacker Innsbruck
Viking Stavanger .... 1-2 0-1 .... **Spartak Trnava**
Zarja Voroschilovgrad .... 2-0 1-0 .... Apoel Nicosia
Benfica .... 1-0 1-0 .... Olympiakos
Waterford FC .... 2-3 0-3 .... **Ujpesti Dózsa**
TPS Turku .... 1-6 0-3 .... **Glasgow Celtic**
Vejle BK .... 2-2 1-0 .... FC Nantes
Club Brugge .... 8-0 2-0 .... Floriana
Fram Reykjavík .... 0-5 2-6 .... **FC Basel**
Crvena Zvezda Beograd .... 2-1 1-0 .... Stal Mielec
Jeunesse Esch .... 1-1 0-2 .... **Liverpool**
Crusaders .... 0-1 0-11 .... **Dinamo Bucuresti**
Atlético Madrid .... 0-0 1-0 .... Galatasaray

SECOND ROUND

Bayern München .... 4-3 3-3 .... Dynamo Dresden
Ajax .... 1-0 0-2 .... **CSKA Sofia**
Spartak Trnava .... 0-0 1-0 .... Zaria Voroschilovgrad
Benfica .... 1-1 0-2 .... **Ujpesti Dózsa**
Glasgow Celtic .... 0-0 1-0 .... Vejle BK
Club Brugge .... 2-1 4-6 .... **FC Basel**
Crvena Zvezda Beograd .... 2-1 2-1 .... Liverpool
Dinamo Bucuresti .... 0-2 2-2 .... **Atlético Madrid**

QUARTER-FINALS

Bayern München .... 4-1 1-2 .... CSKA Sofia
Spartak Trnava .... 1-1 1-1 3-4p .... **Ujpesti Dózsa**
FC Basel .... 3-2 2-4 .... **Glasgow Celtic**
Crvena Zvezda Beograd .... 0-2 0-0 .... **Atlético Madrid**

SEMI-FINALS

Ujpesti Dózsa .... 1-1 0-3 .... **Bayern München**
Glasgow Celtic .... 0-0 0-2 .... **Atlético Madrid**

FINAL

Heysel, Brussels, 15-05-1974, 49,000. Referee: Loraux, Belgium
BAYERN MUNCHEN 1 (Schwarzenbeck 119)
ATLÉTICO MADRID 1 (Luis 114)
Bayern - Maier - Hansen, Breitner, Schwarzenbeck, Beckenbauer - Roth, Zobel, Hoeness - Torstensson (Durnberger), Müller, Kapellmann
Atlético - Reina - Melo, Capon, Adelardo, Heredia - Luis, Eusebio, Irureta, Ufarte (Becerra), Garate, Salcedo (Alberto)

Replay. Heysel, Brussels, 17-05-1974, 23,000. Referee: Delcourt, Belgium

BAYERN MUNICH 4 (Hoeness 28 83, Müller 58 71)
ATLÉTICO MADRID 0

Bayern - Maier - Hansen, Breitner, Schwarzenbeck, Beckenbauer - Roth, Zobel, Hoeness - Torstensson, Müller, Kapellmann. Tr: Lattek
Atlético - Reina - Melo, Capon, Adelardo (Benegas), Heredia - Luis, Eusebio, Alberto (Ufarte) - Garate, Salcedo, Becerra. Tr: Lorenzo

Top scorer: Müller, Bayern München 9

UEFA CUP

FIRST ROUND

Östers IF Växjö ....1-3 1-2.... **Feyenoord**
Ferencváros ....0-1 1-2.... **Gwardia Warszawa**
Fiorentina ....0-0 0-1.... **Universitatea Craiova**
Ards ....3-2 1-6.... **Standard CL**
Sliema Wanderers ....0-2 0-1.... **Lokomotiv Plovdiv**
VSS Kosice ....1-0 2-5.... **Honvéd**
Carl Zeiss Jena ....3-0 3-0.... MP Mikkeli
Ruch Chorzów ....4-1 4-5.... Wuppertaler SV
Vitória FC Setúbal ....2-0 2-0.... Beerschot VAV
RCD Español ....0-3 2-1.... **RWD Molenbeek**
Hibernian Edinburgh ....2-0 1-1.... IBK Keflavík
IF Strømsgodset ....1-1 1-6.... **Leeds United**
Fredrikstad FK ....0-1 0-4.... **Dynamo Kiev**
B 1903 København ....2-1 1-1.... AIK Stockholm
Tatran Presov ....4-2 1-1.... Velez Mostar
VfB Stuttgart ....9-0 4-0.... Olympiakos Nicosia
Torino ....1-2 1-2.... **Lokomotive Leipzig**
OS Belenenses ....0-2 1-2.... **Wolverhampton W.**
Fortuna Düsseldorf ....1-0 2-2.... Naestved IF
Admira-Wacker ....1-0 1-2.... Internazionale
Panahaiki Patras ....2-1 1-0.... Grazer AK
Dundee ....1-3 2-4.... **FC Twente Enschede**
Lazio ....3-0 1-3.... FC Sion
Ipswich Town ....1-0 0-0.... Real Madrid
Union Luxembourg ....0-5 1-7.... **Olympique Marseille**
Eskisehirspor ....0-0 0-2.... **1.FC Köln**
Fenerbahçe ....5-1 1-1.... FC Arges Pitesti
OGC Nice ....3-0 0-2.... Barcelona
Dynamo Tbilisi ....4-1 0-2.... Slavia Sofia
Panathinaikos ....1-2 1-0.... **OFK Beograd**
Aberdeen ....4-1 3-1.... Finn Harps
Grasshopper-Club ....1-5 1-4.... **Tottenham Hotspur**

SECOND ROUND

Feyenoord ....3-1 0-1.... Gwardia Warszawa
Standard CL ....2-0 1-1.... Universitatea Craiova
Lokomotiv Plovdiv ....3-4 2-3.... **Honvéd**
Ruch Chorzów ....3-0 0-1.... Carl Zeiss Jena
Vitória FC Setúbal ....1-0 1-2.... RWD Molenbeek
Leeds United ....0-0 0-0 5-4p.... Hibernian Edinburgh
Dynamo Kiev ....1-0 2-1.... B 1903 København
VfB Stuttgart ....3-1 5-3.... Tatran Presov
Lokomotive Leipzig ....3-0 1-4.. Wolverhampton Wanderers
Admira-Wacker ....2-1 0-3.... **Fortuna Düsseldorf**
Panahaiki Patras ....1-1 0-7.... **FC Twente Enschede**
Ipswich Town ....4-0 2-4.... Lazio
Olympique Marseille ....2-0 0-6.... **1.FC Köln**
OGC Nice ....4-0 0-2.... Fenerbahçe
Dynamo Tbilisi ....3-0 5-1.... OFK Beograd
Aberdeen ....1-1 1-4.... **Tottenham Hotspur**

THIRD ROUND

Standard CL ....3-1 0-2.... **Feyenoord**
Honvéd ....2-0 0-5.... **Ruch Chorzów**
Leeds United ....1-0 1-3.... **Vitória FC Setúbal**
Dynamo Kiev ....2-0 0-3.... **VfB Stuttgart**
Fortuna Düsseldorf ....2-1 0-3.... **Lokomotive Leipzig**
Ipswich Town ....1-0 2-1.... FC Twente Enschede
OGC Nice ....1-0 0-4.... **1.FC Köln**
Dynamo Tbilisi ....1-1 1-5.... **Tottenham Hotspur**

QUARTER-FINALS

Ruch Chorzów ....1-1 1-3.... **Feyenoord**
VfB Stuttgart ....1-0 2-2.... Vitória FC Setúbal
Ipswich Town ....1-0 0-1 3-4p.... **Lokomotive Leipzig**
1.FC Köln ....1-2 0-3.... **Tottenham Hotspur**

SEMI-FINALS

Feyenoord ....2-1 2-2.... VfB Stuttgart
Lokomotive Leipzig ....1-2 0-2.... **Tottenham Hotspur**

FINAL

1st leg. White Hart Lane, London, 21-05-1974, 46,000. Referee: Scheurer, Switzerland

TOTTENHAM HOTSPUR 2 (England 39, OG 64)
FEYENOORD 2 (Van Hanegem 43, De Jong 85)

Tottenham - Jennings - Evans, Naylor, Pratt, England - Beal, McGrath, Perryman, Peters - Chivers, Coates
Feyenoord - Treytel - Rijsbergen, Van Daele, Israel, Vos - De Jong, Jansen, Van Hanegem, Ressel - Schoenmaker, Kristensen

2nd leg. Feyenoord Stadion, Rotterdam, 29-05-1974, 59,000. Referee: Lo Bello, Italy

FEYENOORD 2 (Rijsbergen 43, Ressel 84)
TOTTENHAM HOTSPUR 0

Feyenoord - Treytel - Rijsbergen, Van Daele, Israel, Vos - Ramljak, Jansen, De Jong, Ressel - Schoenmaker, Kristensen (Boskamp) (Wery)
Tottenham - Jennings - Evans, Naylor, Pratt (Holder), England - Beal, McGrath, Perryman Peters - Chivers, Coates

Top scorer: Schoenmaker, Feyenoord 10

CUP WINNERS CUP

FIRST ROUND

NAC Breda ....0-0 0-2.... **1.FC Magdeburg**
Baník Ostrava ....1-0 2-1.... Cork Hibernians
Torpedo Moskva ....0-0 0-2.... **Athletic Bilbao**
Fola Esch ....0-7 1-4.... **Beroe Stara Zagora**
RSC Anderlecht ....3-2 0-1.... **FC Zürich**
Pezoporikos ....0-0 0-11.... **Malmö FF**
Vasas Budapest ....0-2 0-1.... **Sunderland**
Cardiff City ....0-0 1-2.... **Sporting CP**
IBV Vestmannaeyjar ....0-7 1-9.... **B. Mönchengladbach**
MKE Ankaragücü ....0-2 0-4.... **Glasgow Rangers**
Gzira United ....0-2 0-7.... **SK Brann Bergen**
Chimea Rimnicu ....2-2 0-2.... **Glentoran**
Legia Warszawa ....1-1 0-1.... **PAOK Salonica**
Reipas Lahti ....0-0 0-2.... **Olympique Lyon**
Randers Freja ....0-0 1-2.... **SK Rapid Wien**
Milan ....3-1 1-0.... Dinamo Zagreb

SECOND ROUND

Baník Ostrava ....2-0 0-3.... **1.FC Magdeburg**
Beroe Stara Zagora ....3-0 0-1.... Athletic Bilbao
FC Zürich ....0-0 1-1.... Malmö FF
Sunderland ....2-1 0-2.... **Sporting CP**
B. Mönchengladbach ....3-0 2-3.... Glasgow Rangers
SK Brann Bergen ....1-1 1-3.... **Glentoran**
Olympique Lyon ....3-3 0-4.... **PAOK Salonica**
Milan ....0-0 2-0.... SK Rapid Wien

QUARTER-FINALS

1.FC Magdeburg ....2-0 1-1.... Beroe Stara Zagora
Glentoran ....0-2 0-5.... **B. Mönchengladbach**
Sporting CP ....3-0 1-1.... FC Zürich
Milan ....3-0 2-2.... PAOK Salonica

SEMI-FINALS

Sporting CP 1-1 1-2 **1.FC Magdeburg**
Milan 2-0 0-1 Borussia Mönchengladbach

FINAL

Feyenoord Stadion, Rotterdam, 8-05-1974, 4,000. Referee: Van Gemert, Holland

1.FC MAGDEBURG 2 (OG 43, Seguin 74)
MILAN 0

Magdeburg - Schulze - Enge, Zapf, Tyll, Abraham - Seguin, Pommerenke, Gaube - Raugust, Sparwasser, Hoffman

Milan - Pizzaballa - Sabadini, Anquilletti, Lanzi, Schnellinger - Benetti, Maldera, Rivera - Tresoldi, Bigon, Bergamaschi (Turini)

Top scorer: Heynckes, Borussia Mönchengladbach 10

1974–75

EUROPEAN CUP

FIRST ROUND

Bayern München Bye
1.FC Magdeburg Bye
Cork Celtic W-O Omonia Nicosia
Viking Stavanger 0-2 0-4 **Ararat Yerevan**
Hvidovre BK 0-0 1-2 **Ruch Chorzów**
Jeunesse Esch 2-3 0-2 **Fenerbahçe**
Hajduk Split 7-1 2-0 IBK Keflavík
AS Saint-Étienne 2-0 1-1 Sporting CP
VÖEST Linz 0-0 0-5 **Barcelona**
Feyenoord 7-0 4-1 Coleraine
Valletta 1-0 1-4 **HJK Helsinki**
Universitatea Craiova 2-1 1-3 **Åtvidabergs FF**
Slovan Bratislava 4-2 1-3 **RSC Anderlecht**
Glasgow Celtic 1-1 0-2 **Olympiakos**
Levski-Spartak 0-3 1-4 **Ujpesti Dózsa**
Leeds United 4-1 1-2 FC Zürich

SECOND ROUND

Bayern München 3-2 2-1 1.FC Magdeburg
Cork Celtic 1-2 0-5 **Ararat Yerevan**
Ruch Chorzów 2-1 2-0 Fenerbahçe
Hajduk Split 4-1 1-5 **AS Saint-Étienne**
Feyenoord 0-0 0-3 **Barcelona**
HJK Helsinki 0-3 0-1 **Åtvidabergs FF**
RSC Anderlecht 5-1 0-3 Olympiakos
Ujpesti Dózsa 1-2 0-3 **Leeds United**

QUARTER-FINALS

Bayern München 2-0 0-1 Ararat Yerevan
Ruch Chorzów 3-2 0-2 **AS Saint-Étienne**
Barcelona 2-0 3-0 Åtvidabergs FF
Leeds United 3-0 1-0 RSC Anderlecht

SEMI-FINALS

AS Saint-Étienne 0-0 0-2 **Bayern München**
Leeds United 2-1 1-1 Barcelona

FINAL

Parc des Princes, Paris, 28-05-1975, 48,000. Referee: Kitabdjian, France

BAYERN MUNCHEN 2 (Roth 71, Muller 81)
LEEDS UNITED 0

Bayern - Maier - Beckenbauer, Schwarzenbeck, Dürnberger, Andersson (Weiss), Zobel, Roth, Kapellmann - Hoeness (Wunder), Müller, Torstensson. Tr: Cramer

Leeds Utd - Stewart - Reaney, Gray.F, Madeley, Hunter - Bremner, Giles, Yorath (Gray.E) - Lorimer, Clarke, Jordan. Tr: Armfield

Top scorer: Müller, Bayern München 6

UEFA CUP

FIRST ROUND

Wacker Innsbruck 2-1 0-3 **B. Mönchengladbach**
Olympique Lyon 7-0 4-1 Red Boys
Grasshopper-Club 2-0 1-2 Panathinaikos
Vitória FC Setúbal 1-1 0-4 **Real Zaragoza**
Napoli 2-0 1-1 Videoton SC
FC Porto 4-1 1-3 Wolverhampton W.
FC Nantes 2-2 1-0 Legia Warszawa
Real Sociedad 0-1 0-4 **Baník Ostrava**
FC Amsterdam 5-0 7-0 Hibernians Paola
Etar Veliko Tarnovo 0-0 0-3 **Internazionale**
Lokomotiv Plovdiv 3-1 1-3 4-5p **Rába ETO Györ**
Torino 1-1 1-3 **Fortuna Düsseldorf**
Górnik Zabrze 2-2 0-3 **Partizan Beograd**
Valur Reykjavík 0-0 1-2 **Portadown**
Boluspor 0-1 0-3 **Dinamo Bucuresti**
1.FC Köln 5-1 4-1 KPV Kokkola
Vorwärts Frankfurt 2-1 0-3 **Juventus**
Rosenborg BK 2-3 1-9 **Hibernian Edinburgh**
SK Sturm Graz 2-1 0-1 **Royal Antwerp FC**
Stoke City 1-1 0-0 **Ajax**
Randers Freja 1-1 0-0 **Dynamo Dresden**
Östers IF Växjö 3-2 1-2 **Dynamo Moskva**
Besiktas 2-0 0-3 **Steagul Rosu Brasov**
Hamburger SV 3-0 1-0 Bohemians Dublin
Spartak Moskva 3-1 0-2 **Velez Mostar**
SK Rapid Wien 3-1 0-1 Aris Salonica
KB København 3-2 0-4 **Atlético Madrid**
Derby County 4-1 2-1 Servette FC
Dukla Praha W-O Pezoporikos
Start Kristiansand 1-2 0-5 **Djurgårdens IF**
RWD Molenbeek 1-0 4-2 Dundee
Ipswich Town 2-2 1-1 **FC Twente Enschede**

SECOND ROUND

B. Mönchengladbach 1-0 5-2 Olympique Lyon
Grasshopper-Club 2-1 0-5 **Real Zaragoza**
Napoli 1-0 1-0 FC Porto
FC Nantes 1-0 0-2 **Baník Ostrava**
Internazionale 1-2 0-0 **FC Amsterdam**
Rába ETO Györ 2-0 0-3 **Fortuna Düsseldorf**
Partizan Beograd 5-0 1-1 Portadown
Dinamo Bucuresti 1-1 2-3 **1.FC Köln**
Hibernian Edinburgh 2-4 0-4 **Juventus**
Ajax 1-0 1-2 Royal Antwerp FC
Dynamo Dresden 1-0 0-1 4-3p Dynamo Moskva
Hamburger SV 8-0 2-1 Steagul Rosu Brasov
SK Rapid Wien 1-1 0-1 **Velez Mostar**
Derby County 2-2 2-2 7-6p Atlético Madrid
Djurgårdens IF 0-2 1-3 **Dukla Praha**
FC Twente Enschede 2-1 1-0 RWD Molenbeek

THIRD ROUND

B. Mönchengladbach 5-0 4-2 Real Zaragoza
Napoli 0-2 1-1 **Baník Ostrava**
FC Amsterdam 3-0 2-1 Fortuna Düsseldorf
Partizan Beograd 1-0 1-5 **1.FC Köln**
Juventus 1-0 1-2 Ajax
Hamburger SV 4-1 2-2 Dynamo Dresden
Derby County 3-1 1-4 **Velez Mostar**
Dukla Praha 3-1 0-5 **FC Twente Enschede**

QUARTER-FINALS

Baník Ostrava 0-1 1-3 **B. Mönchengladbach**
1.FC Köln 5-1 3-2 FC Amsterdam
Juventus 2-0 0-0 Hamburger SV
Velez Mostar 1-0 0-2 **FC Twente Enschede**

SEMI-FINALS

I.FC Köln 1-3 0-1 **B. Mönchengladbach**
FC Twente Enschede 3-1 1-0 Juventus

FINAL

1st leg. Rheinstadion, Dusseldorf, 7-05-1975, 42,000. Referee: Palotai, Hungary

B. MÖNCHENGLADBACH 0
FC TWENTE ENSCHEDE 0

Borussia - Kleff - Wittkamp, Stielike, Vogts, Surau - Bonhof, Wimmer, Danner (Del'Haye), Kulik (Schaffer) - Simonsen, Jensen
FC Twente - Gross - Drost, Van Ierssel, Overweg, Oranen - Thijssen, Pahlplatz, Van der Vall, Bos - Jeuring (Achterberg), Zuidema

2nd leg. Diekman, Enschede, 21-05-1975, 21,000. Referee: Schiller, Austria

FC TWENTE ENSCHEDE 1 (Drost 76)
B. MÖNCHENGLADBACH 5 (Simonsen 2 86, Heynckes 9 50 60)

FC Twente - Gross - Drost, Van Ierssel, Overweg, Oranen, Bos (Muhren), Thijssen, Pahlplatz (Achterberg), Van der Vall, Jeuring, Zuidema
Borussia - Kleff - Wittkamp, Vogts, Surau (Schaffer), Klinkhammer - Bonhof, Wimmer (Koppel), Danner - Simonsen, Jensen, Heynckes

Top scorer: Heynckes, Borussia Mönchengladbach 11

CUP WINNERS CUP

FIRST ROUND

Dynamo Kiev 1-0 1-0 CSKA Sofia
Eintracht Frankfurt 3-0 2-2 AS Monaco
Dundee United 3-0 0-2 Jiul Petrosani
Bursaspor 4-2 0-0 Finn Harps
Benfica 4-0 4-1 Vanlose BK
Slavia Praha 1-0 0-1 2-3p **Carl Zeiss Jena**
Gwardia Warszawa 2-1 1-2 5-3p Bologna
PSV Eindhoven 10-0 4-1 Ards
PAOK Salonica 1-0 0-2 **Crvena Zvezda Beograd**
Avenir Beggen W-O Union Paralimni
KSV Waregem 2-1 1-4 **FK Austria**
Fram Reykjavík 0-2 0-6 **Real Madrid**
Malmö FF 1-0 0-1 5-4p FC Sion
Sliema Wanderers 2-0 1-4 **Reipas Lahti**
Liverpool 11-0 1-0 IF Strømsgodset
Ferencváros 2-0 4-1 Cardiff City

SECOND ROUND

Eintracht Frankfurt 2-3 1-2 **Dynamo Kiev**
Dundee United 0-0 0-1 **Bursaspor**
Carl Zeiss Jena 1-1 0-0 **Benfica**
Gwardia Warszawa 1-5 0-3 **PSV Eindhoven**
Avenir Beggen 1-6 1-5 **Crvena Zvezda Beograd**
Real Madrid 3-0 2-2 FK Austria
Malmö FF 3-1 0-0 Reipas Lahti
Liverpool 1-1 0-0 **Ferencváros**

QUARTER-FINALS

Bursaspor 0-1 0-2 **Dynamo Kiev**
PSV Eindhoven 0-0 2-1 Benfica
Real Madrid 2-0 0-2 5-6p **Crvena Zvezda Beo.**
Malmö FF 1-3 1-1 **Ferencváros**

SEMI-FINALS

Dynamo Kiev 3-0 1-2 PSV Eindhoven
Ferencváros 2-1 2-2 Crvena Zvezda Beograd

FINAL

St. Jakobs, Basle, 14-05-1975, 10,000. Referee, Davidson, Scotland

DYNAMO KIEV 3 (Onischenko 18 39, Blokhin 67)
FERENCVAROS 0

Dynamo Kiev - Rudakov - Troshkin, Matvienko, Reshko, Fomenko - Muntian, Konkov, Burjak, Kolotov - Onischenko, Blokhin
Ferencváros - Geczi - Martos, Megyesi, Pataki, Rab - Nyilasi (Onhaus), Juhasz, Mucha - Szabo, Mate, Magyar

Top scorer: Onishenko, Dynamo Kiev 7

EUROPEAN SUPERCUP 1975

1st leg. Olympiastadion, Munich, 9-09-1975. Referee: Gonella, Italy

BAYERN MÜNCHEN 0
DYNAMO KIEV 1 (Blokhin 66)

2nd leg. Republican Stadium, Kiev, 6-10-1975. Referee: Babaçan, Turkey

DYNAMO KIEV 2 (Blokhin 40 53)
BAYERN MÜNCHEN 0

1975–76

EUROPEAN CUP

FIRST ROUND

Jeunesse Esch 0-5 1-3 **Bayern München**
Malmö FF 2-1 1-2 2-1p 1.FC Magdeburg
Ujpesti Dózsa 4-0 1-5 FC Zürich
Benfica 7-0 0-1 Fenerbahçe
B. Mönchengladbach 1-1 6-1 Wacker Innsbruck
CSKA Sofia 2-1 0-2 **Juventus**
Slovan Bratislava 1-0 0-3 **Derby County**
Real Madrid 4-1 0-1 Dinamo Bucuresti
Linfield 1-2 0-8 **PSV Eindhoven**
Ruch Chorzów 5-0 2-2 KuPS Kuopio
RWD Molenbeek 3-2 1-0 Viking Stavanger
Floriana 0-5 0-3 **Hajduk Split**
Olympiakos 2-2 0-1 **Dynamo Kiev**
Omonia Nicosia 2-1 0-4 **IA Akranes**
Glasgow Rangers 4-1 1-1 Bohemians Dublin
KB København 0-2 1-3 **AS Saint-Étienne**

SECOND ROUND

Malmö FF 1-0 0-2 **Bayern München**
Benfica 5-2 1-3 Ujpesti Dózsa
B. Mönchengladbach 2-0 2-2 Juventus
Derby County 4-1 1-5 **Real Madrid**
Ruch Chorzów 1-3 0-4 **PSV Eindhoven**
Hajduk Split 4-0 3-2 RWD Molenbeek
Dynamo Kiev 3-0 2-0 IA Akranes
AS Saint-Étienne 2-0 2-1 Glasgow Rangers

QUARTER-FINALS

Benfica 0-0 1-5 **Bayern München**
Borussia Mönchengladbach 2-2 1-1 **Real Madrid**
Hajduk Split 2-0 0-3 **PSV Eindhoven**
Dynamo Kiev 2-0 0-3 **AS Saint-Étienne**

SEMI-FINALS

Real Madrid 1-1 0-2 **Bayern München**
AS Saint-Étienne 1-0 0-0 PSV Eindhoven

FINAL

Hampden Park, Glasgow, 12-05-1976, 63,000. Referee: Palotai, Hungary

BAYERN MÜNCHEN 1 (Roth 57)
AS SAINT-ÉTIENNE 0

Bayern - Maier - Hansen, Schwarzenbeck, Beckenbauer, Horsmann

- Roth, Dürnberger, Kapellmann, Rummenigge - Müller, Hoeness. Tr: Cramer
St-Étienne - Curkovic - Repellini, Piazza, Lopez, Janvion - Bathenay, Santini, Larque - Revelli.P, Revelli.H, Sarramagna (Rocheteau). Tr: Herbin

Top scorers: Heynckes, Borussia Mönchengladbach 6
Santillana, Real Madrid 6

UEFA CUP

FIRST ROUND

Hibernian Edinburgh .... 1-0 1-3 .... **Liverpool**
Grasshopper-Club .... 3-3 1-1 .... **Real Sociedad**
Royal Antwerp FC .... 4-1 1-0 .... Aston Villa
GAIS Göteborg .... 2-1 2-4 .... **Slask Wroclaw**
Torpedo Moskva .... 4-1 1-1 .... Napoli
SK Rapid Wien .... 1-0 1-3 .... **Galatasaray**
Bohemians Praha .... 1-2 1-1 .... **Honvéd**
ASA Tîrgu Mures .... 2-2 1-4 .... **Dynamo Dresden**
Levski-Spartak .... 3-0 4-1 .... Eskisehirspor
MSV Duisburg .... 7-1 3-2 .... Union Paralimni
Hertha BSC Berlin .... 4-1 2-1 .... HJK Helsinki
Glentoran .... 1-6 0-8 .... **Ajax**
VÖEST Linz .... 2-0 0-4 .... **Vasas Budapest**
Sliema Wanderers .... 1-2 1-3 .... **Sporting CP**
Chernomorets Odessa .... 1-0 0-3 .... **Lazio**
PAOK Salonica .... 1-0 1-6 .... **Barcelona**
BSC Young Boys .... 0-0 2-4 .... **Hamburger SV**
Universitatea Craiova .... 1-3 1-1 .. **Crvena Zvezda Beograd**
IBK Keflavík .... 0-2 0-4 .... **Dundee United**
FC Porto .... 7-0 3-0 .... Avenir Beggen
TJ Internacional .... 5-0 3-2 .... Real Zaragoza
Vojvodina Novi Sad .... 0-0 1-3 .... **AEK Athens**
Carl Zeiss Jena .... 3-0 1-0 .... Olympique Marseille
Holbaek BK .... 0-1 1-2 .... **Stal Mielec**
Everton .... 0-0 0-1 .... **Milan**
Athlone Town .... 3-1 1-1 .... Vålerengens Oslo
1.FC Köln .... 2-0 3-2 .... B 1903 København
AIK Stockholm .... 1-1 0-1 .... **Spartak Moskva**
Roma .... 2-0 0-1 .... Dunav Ruse
Molde FK .... 1-0 0-6 .... **Östers IF Växjö**
Feyenoord .... 1-2 0-2 .... **Ipswich Town**
Olympique Lyon .... 4-3 0-3 .... **Club Brugge**

SECOND ROUND

Real Sociedad .... 1-3 0-6 .... **Liverpool**
Slask Wroclaw .... 1-1 2-1 .... Royal Antwerp FC
Galatasaray .... 2-4 0-3 .... **Torpedo Moskva**
Honvéd .... 2-2 0-1 .... **Dynamo Dresden**
MSV Duisburg .... 3-2 1-2 .... **Levski-Spartak**
Hertha BSC Berlin .... 1-0 1-4 .... **Ajax**
Vasas Budapest .... 3-1 1-2 .... Sporting CP
Lazio .... 0-4 .... **Barcelona**
Crvena Zvezda Beograd .... 1-1 0-4 .... **Hamburger SV**
Dundee United .... 1-2 1-1 .... **FC Porto**
TJ Internacional .... 2-0 1-3 .... AEK Athens
Carl Zeiss Jena .... 1-0 0-1 2-3p .... **Stal Mielec**
Athlone Town .... 0-0 0-3 .... **Milan**
Spartak Moskva .... 2-0 1-0 .... 1.FC Köln
Östers IF Växjö .... 1-0 0-2 .... **Roma**
Ipswich Town .... 3-0 0-4 .... **Club Brugge**

THIRD ROUND

Slask Wroclaw .... 1-2 0-3 .... **Liverpool**
Dynamo Dresden .... 3-0 1-3 .... Torpedo Moskva
Ajax .... 2-1 1-2 3-5p .... **Levski-Spartak**
Barcelona .... 3-1 1-0 .... Vasas Budapest
Hamburger SV .... 2-0 1-2 .... FC Porto
TJ Internacional .... 1-0 0-2 .... **Stal Mielec**
Milan .... 4-0 0-2 .... Spartak Moskva
Club Brugge .... 1-0 1-0 .... Roma

QUARTER-FINALS

Dynamo Dresden .... 0-0 1-2 .... **Liverpool**
Barcelona .... 4-0 4-5 .... Levski-Spartak
Hamburger SV .... 1-1 1-0 .... Stal Mielec
Club Brugge .... 2-0 1-2 .... Milan

SEMI-FINALS

Barcelona .... 0-1 1-1 .... **Liverpool**
Hamburger SV .... 1-1 0-1 .... **Club Brugge**

FINAL

1st leg. Anfield, Liverpool, 28-04-1976, 49,000. Referee: Biwersi, Austria
LIVERPOOL 3 (Kennedy 59, Case 61, Keegan 65)
CLUB BRUGGE 2 (Lambert 5, Cools 15)
Liverpool - Clemence - Smith, Neal, Thompson, Hughes - Keegan, Kennedy, Callaghan - Fairclough, Heighway, Toshack (Case)
Brugge - Jensen - Bastijns, Krieger, Leekens, Volders - Cools, Vandereycken, Decubber - Van Gool, Lambert, Lefevre

2nd leg. Olympiastadion, Bruges, 19-05-1976, 32,000. Referee: Glöckner, East Germany
CLUB BRUGGE 1 (Lambert 11)
LIVERPOOL 1 (Keegan 15)
Brugge - Jensen - Bastijns, Krieger, Leekens, Volders - Cools, Vandereycken, Decubber (Hinderyckx) - Van Gool, Lambert (Sanders), Lefevre
Liverpool - Clemence - Smith, Neal, Thompson, Hughes, Keegan, Kennedy, Callaghan - Case, Heighway, Toshack (Fairclough)

Top scorer: Geels, Ajax 11

CUP WINNERS CUP

FIRST ROUND

Rapid Bucuresti .... 1-0 0-2 .... **RSC Anderlecht**
Borac Banja Luka .... 9-0 5-1 .... US Rumelange
FK Skeid Oslo .... 1-4 0-4 .... **Stal Rzeszów**
Wrexham .... 2-1 1-1 .... Djurgårdens IF
Valur Reykjavík .... 0-2 0-7 .... **Glasgow Celtic**
Spartak Trnava .... 0-0 0-3 .... **Boavista FC**
Besiktas .... 0-3 0-3 .... **Fiorentina**
Panathinaikos .... 0-0 0-2 .... **Sachsenring Zwickau**
Eintracht Frankfurt .... 5-1 6-2 .... Coleraine
FC Basel .... 1-2 1-1 .... **Atlético Madrid**
Haladás VSE .... 7-0 1-1 .... Valletta
SK Sturm Graz .... 3-1 0-1 .... Slavia Sofia
Vejle BK .... 0-2 0-2 .... **FC Den Haag**
Home Farm .... 1-1 0-6 .... **RC Lens**
Ararat Yerevan .... 9-0 1-1 .... Anorthosis Famagusta
Reipas Lahti .... 2-2 0-3 .... **West Ham United**

SECOND ROUND

RSC Anderlecht .... 3-0 0-1 .... Borac Banja Luka
Wrexham .... 2-0 1-1 .... Stal Rzeszów
Boavista FC .... 0-0 1-3 .... **Glasgow Celtic**
Fiorentina .... 1-0 0-1 4-5p .... **Sachsenring Zwickau**
Atlético Madrid .... 1-2 0-1 .... **Eintracht Frankfurt**
SK Sturm Graz .... 2-0 1-1 .... Haladás VSE Sombathely
FC Den Haag .... 3-2 3-1 .... RC Lens
Ararat Yerevan .... 1-1 1-3 .... **West Ham United**

QUARTER-FINALS

RSC Anderlecht .... 1-0 1-1 .... Wrexham
Glasgow Celtic .... 1-1 0-1 .... **Sachsenring Zwickau**
SK Sturm Graz .... 0-2 0-1 .... **Eintracht Frankfurt**
FC Den Haag .... 4-2 1-3 .... **West Ham United**

SEMI-FINALS

Sachsenring Zwickau .... 0-3 0-2 .... **RSC Anderlecht**
Eintracht Frankfurt .... 2-1 1-3 .... **West Ham United**

FINAL

Heysel, Brussels, 5-05-1976, 58,000. Referee: Wurtz, France

RSC ANDERLECHT 4 (Rensenbrink 42 73, Vander Elst 48 87)
WEST HAM UNITED 2 (Holland 28, Robson 68)

Anderlecht - Ruiter - Lomme, Van Binst, Thissen, Broos - Dockx, Coeck (Vercauteren), Haan, Vander Elst - Ressel, Rensenbrink

West Ham - Day - Coleman, Lampard (Taylor.A), Taylor.T, McDowell - Bonds, Brooking, Paddon - Holland, Jennings, Robson

Top scorer: Rensenbrink, Anderlecht 8

EUROPEAN SUPERCUP 1976

1st leg. Olympiastadion, Munich, 17-08-1976. Referee: Burns, England

BAYERN MÜNCHEN 2 (Müller 58 88)
RSC ANDERLECHT 1 (Haan 16)

2nd leg. Parc Astrid, Brussels, 30-08-1976. Referee: Schiller, Austria

RSC ANDERLECHT 4 (Rensenbrink 20 82, Vander Elst 25, Haan 59)
BAYERN MÜNCHEN 1 (Müller 63)

1976–77

EUROPEAN CUP

FIRST ROUND

Liverpool .... 2-0 5-0 .... Crusaders
IA Akranes .... 1-3 2-3 .... **Trabzonspor**
Dundalk .... 1-1 0-6 .... **PSV Eindhoven**
CSKA Sofia .... 0-0 0-1 .... **AS Saint-Étienne**
Dynamo Dresden .... 2-0 0-0 .... Benfica
Ferencváros .... 5-1 6-2 .... Jeunesse Esch
Sliema Wanderers .... 2-1 0-1 .... **TPS Turku**
Glasgow Rangers .... 1-1 0-1 .... **FC Zürich**
Dynamo Kiev .... 3-0 2-0 .... Partizan Beograd
Omonia Nicosia .... 0-2 1-1 .... **PAOK Salonica**
Viking Stavanger .... 2-1 0-2 .... **Baník Ostrava**
Koge BK .... 0-5 1-2 .... **Bayern München**
Club Brugge .... 2-1 1-1 .... Steaua Bucuresti
Stal Mielec .... 1-2 0-1 .... **Real Madrid**
Torino .... 2-1 1-1 .... Malmö FF
FK Austria .... 1-0 0-3 .... **B. Mönchengladbach**

SECOND ROUND

Trabzonspor .... 1-0 0-3 .... **Liverpool**
AS Saint-Étienne .... 1-0 0-0 .... PSV Eindhoven
Ferencváros .... 1-0 0-4 .... **Dynamo Dresden**
FC Zürich .... 2-0 1-0 .... TPS Turku
Dynamo Kiev .... 4-0 2-0 .... PAOK Salonica
Baník Ostrava .... 2-1 0-5 .... **Bayern München**
Real Madrid .... 0-0 0-2 .... **Club Brugge**
Torino .... 1-2 0-0 .... **B. Mönchengladbach**

QUARTER-FINALS

AS Saint-Étienne .... 1-0 1-3 .... **Liverpool**
FC Zürich .... 2-1 2-3 .... Dynamo Dresden
Bayern München .... 1-0 0-2 .... **Dynamo Kiev**
B. Mönchengladbach .... 2-2 1-0 .... Club Brugge

SEMI-FINALS

FC Zürich .... 1-3 0-3 .... **Liverpool**
Dynamo Kiev .... 1-0 0-2 .... **B. Mönchengladbach**

FINAL

Stadio Olimpico, Rome, 25-05-1977, 52,000. Referee: Wurtz, France

LIVERPOOL 3 (McDermott 29, Smith 67, Neal 85)
B. MÖNCHENGLADBACH 1 (Simonsen 50)

Liverpool - Clemence - Neal, Jones, Smith, Hughes - Case, Kennedy, Callaghan, McDermott - Keegan, Heighway. Tr: Paisley

Borussia - Kneib - Vogts, Klinkhammer, Wittkamp, Schaffer - Wohlers (Hannes), Wimmer (Kulik), Stielike, Bonhof - Simonsen, Heynckes. Tr: Lattek

Top scorerS: Cucinotta, FC Zürich 5
Müller, Bayern München 5

UEFA CUP

FIRST ROUND

Manchester City .... 1-0 0-2 .... **Juventus**
Ajax .... 1-0 0-2 .... **Manchester United**
Internazionale .... 0-1 1-1 .... **Honvéd**
Shachter Donetsk .... 3-0 1-1 .... Dynamo Berlin
Fenerbahçe .... 2-1 0-4 .... **Videoton SC**
Wacker Innsbruck .... 2-1 5-0 .... Start Kristiansand
ASA Tîrgu Mures .... 0-1 0-3 .... **Dinamo Zagreb**
1.FC Magdeburg .... 3-0 1-3 .... Cesena
Queen's Park Rangers .... 4-0 7-0 .... SK Brann Bergen
Fram Reykjavík .... 0-3 0-5 .... **Slovan Bratislava**
Grasshopper-Club .... 7-0 2-0 .... Hibernians Paola
1.FC Köln .... 2-0 1-1 .... GKS Tychy
Lokomotiv Plovdiv .... 2-1 1-4 .. **Crvena Zvezda Beograd**
Austria Salzburg .... 5-0 0-2 .... Adanaspor
Derby County .... 12-0 4-1 .... Finn Harps
AEK Athens .... 2-0 1-2 .... Dynamo Moskva
Naestved IF .... 0-3 0-4 .... **RWD Molenbeek**
Glasgow Celtic .... 2-2 0-2 .... **Wisla Kraków**
Sportul Studentesc .... 3-0 1-2 .... Olympiakos
FC Porto .... 2-2 2-3 .... **FC Schalke 04**
RCD Español .... 3-1 1-2 .... OGC Nice
Eintracht Braunschweig .... 7-0 0-1 .... Holbaek BK
Union Paralimni .... 1-3 0-8 .... **1.FC Kaiserslautern**
Feyenoord .... 3-0 1-2 .... Djurgårdens IF
OS Belenenses .... 2-2 2-3 .... **Barcelona**
Red Boys .... 0-3 1-3 .... **KSC Lokeren**
Hibernian Edinburgh .... 1-0 0-0 .... FC Sochaux
KuPS Kuopio .... 3-2 0-2 .... **Östers IF Växjö**
Dinamo Bucuresti .... 0-0 1-2 .... **Milan**
Slavia Praha .... 2-0 0-3 .... **Akademic Sofia**
Glentoran .... 3-2 0-3 .... **FC Basel**
Ujpesti Dózsa .... 1-0 0-5 .... **Athletic Bilbao**

SECOND ROUND

Manchester United .... 1-0 0-3 .... **Juventus**
Shachter Donetsk .... 3-0 3-2 .... Honvéd
Wacker Innsbruck .... 1-1 0-1 .... **Videoton SC**
1.FC Magdeburg .... 2-0 2-2 .... Dinamo Zagreb
Slovan Bratislava .... 3-3 2-5 .... **Queen's Park Rangers**
1.FC Köln .... 2-0 3-2 .... Grasshopper-Club
Austria Salzburg .... 2-1 0-1 .. **Crvena Zvezda Beograd**
AEK Athens .... 2-0 3-2 .... Derby County
Wisla Kraków .... 1-1 1-1 4-5p .... **RWD Molenbeek**
Sportul Studentesc .... 0-1 0-4 .... **FC Schalke 04**
Eintracht Braunschweig .... 2-1 0-2 .... **RCD Español**
1.FC Kaiserslautern .... 2-2 0-5 .... **Feyenoord**
Barcelona .... 2-0 1-2 .... KSC Lokeren
Hibernian Edinburgh .... 2-0 1-4 .... **Östers IF Växjö**
Akademic Sofia .... 4-3 0-2 .... **Milan**
FC Basel .... 1-1 1-3 .... **Athletic Bilbao**

THIRD ROUND

Juventus .... 3-0 0-1 .... Shachter Donetsk
1.FC Magdeburg .... 5-0 0-1 .... Videoton SC
Queen's Park Rangers .... 3-0 1-4 .... 1.FC Köln
AEK Athens .... 2-0 1-3 .... Crvena Zvezda Beograd
RWD Molenbeek .... 1-0 1-1 .... FC Schalke 04
RCD Español .... 0-1 0-2 .... **Feyenoord**

Östers IF Växjö 0-3 1-5 **Barcelona**
Athletic Bilbao 4-1 1-3 Milan

QUARTER-FINALS
1.FC Magdeburg 1-3 0-1 Juventus
Queen's Park Rangers 3-0 0-3 6-7p AEK Athens
Feyenoord 0-0 1-2 RWD Molenbeek
Athletic Bilbao 2-1 2-2 Barcelona

SEMI-FINALS
Juventus 4-1 1-0 AEK Athens
RWD Molenbeek 1-1 0-0 **Athletic Bilbao**

FINAL
1st leg. Comunale, Turin, 4-05-1977, 75,000. Referee: Corver, Holland
JUVENTUS 1 (Tardelli 15)
ATHLETIC BILBAO 0
Juventus - Zoff - Cuccureddu, Gentile, Scirea, Morini - Tardelli, Furino, Benetti - Causio, Boninsegna (Gori), Bettega
Athletic Bilbao - Iribar - Quaderra, Escalza, Guoicoechea, Guisasola Villar, Irureta, Rojo.M, Churruca - Dani, Rojo.J

2nd leg. San Mamés, Bilbao, 18-05-1977, 43,000. Referee: Linemayr, Austria
ATHLETIC BILBAO 2 (Churruca 11, Carlos 78)
JUVENTUS 1 (Bettega 7)
Athletic Bilbao - Iribar - Lasa (Carlos), Guisasola, Alesanco, Escalza Villar, Churruca, Irureta - Amarrortu, Dani, Rojo.J
Juventus - Zoff - Cuccureddu, Morini, Scirea, Gentile - Causio, Tardelli, Furino, Benetti - Boninsegna (Spinosi), Bettega

Top scorer: Bowles, Queens Park Rangers 11

CUP WINNERS CUP

PRELIMINARY ROUND
Cardiff City 1-0 1-2 Servette FC

FIRST ROUND
Hamburger SV 3-0 1-1 IBK Keflavík
Lokomotive Leipzig 2-0 1-5 **Heart of Midlothian**
Cardiff City 1-0 0-3 **Dynamo Tbilisi**
MTK-VM Budapest 3-1 1-1 Sparta Praha
Levski-Spartak 12-2 7-1 Reipas Lahti
CSU Galati 2-3 0-2 **Boavista FC**
Lierse SK 1-0 0-3 **Hajduk Split**
SK Rapid Wien 1-2 1-1 **Atlético Madrid**
SOFK Bodø-Glimt 0-2 0-1 **Napoli**
Iraklis Salonica 0-0 0-2 **Apoel Nicosia**
Bohemians Dublin 2-1 1-0 Esbjerg FB
Floriana 1-4 0-2 **Slask Wroclaw**
Southampton 4-0 1-2 Olympique Marseille
Carrick Rangers 3-1 1-2 Aris Bonnevoie
AIK Stockholm 1-2 1-1 **Galatasaray**
RSC Anderlecht 2-1 3-2 Roda JC Kerkrade

SECOND ROUND
Hamburger SV 4-2 4-1 Heart of Midlothian
Dynamo Tbilisi 1-4 0-1 **MTK-VM Budapest**
Boavista FC 3-1 0-2 **Levski-Spartak**
Atlético Madrid 1-0 2-1 Hajduk Split
Apoel Nicosia 1-1 0-2 **Napoli**
Slask Wroclaw 3-0 1-0 Bohemians Dublin
Carrick Rangers 2-5 1-4 **Southampton**
RSC Anderlecht 5-1 5-1 Galatasaray

QUARTER-FINALS
MTK-VM Budapest 1-1 1-4 **Hamburger SV**
Levski-Spartak 2-1 0-2 **Atlético Madrid**
Slask Wroclaw 0-0 0-2 **Napoli**
RSC Anderlecht 2-0 1-2 Southampton

SEMI-FINALS
Atlético Madrid 3-1 0-3 **Hamburger SV**
Napoli 1-0 0-2 **RSC Anderlecht**

FINAL
Olympisch Stadion, Amsterdam, 11-05-1977, 66,000. Referee: Partridge, England
HAMBURGER SV 2 (Volkert 78, Magath 88)
RSC ANDERLECHT 0
Hamburg - Kargus - Kaltz, Ripp, Nogly, Hidien - Memering, Magath, Keller Steffenhagen, Reimann, Volkert
Anderlecht - Ruiter - Van Binst, Van Den Daele, Thissen, Broos - Dockx (Van Poucke), Coeck, Haan, Vander Elst - Ressel, Rensenbrink

Top scorer: Milanov, Levski-Spartak 13

EUROPEAN SUPERCUP 1977

1st leg. Volksparkstadion, Hamburg, 22-11-1977. Referee: Da Silva Garrido, Portugal
HAMBURGER SV 1 (Keller 29)
LIVERPOOL 1 (Fairclough 65)
2nd leg. Anfield, Liverpool, 6-12-1977. Referee: Eriksson, Sweden
LIVERPOOL 6 (Thompson 21, McDermott 40 56 57, Fairclough 84, Dalglish 88)
HAMBURGER SV 0

1977-78

EUROPEAN CUP

FIRST ROUND
Liverpool Bye
Dynamo Dresden 2-0 1-2 Halmstad BK
Trabzonspor 1-0 0-2 **B 1903 København**
Benfica 0-0 0-0 4-1p Torpedo Moskva
FC Basel 1-3 1-0 **Wacker Innsbruck**
Glasgow Celtic 5-0 6-1 Jeunesse Esch
Crvena Zvezda Beograd 3-0 3-0 Sligo Rovers
Vasas Budapest 0-3 1-1 **B. Mönchengladbach**
Omonia Nicosia 0-3 0-2 **Juventus**
Valur Reykjavík 1-0 0-2 **Glentoran**
Levski-Spartak 3-0 2-2 Slask Wroclaw
Lillestrøm SK 2-0 0-4 **Ajax**
Dinamo Bucuresti 2-1 0-2 **Atlético Madrid**
Dukla Praha 1-1 0-0 **FC Nantes**
Floriana 1-1 0-4 **Panathinaikos**
KuPS Kuopio 0-4 2-5 **Club Brugge**

SECOND ROUND
Liverpool 5-1 1-2 Dynamo Dresden
Benfica 1-0 1-0 B 1903 København
Glasgow Celtic 2-1 0-3 **Wacker Innsbruck**
Crvena Zvezda Beograd 0-3 1-5 **B.Mönchengladbach**
Glentoran 0-1 0-5 **Juventus**
Levski-Spartak 1-2 1-2 **Ajax**
FC Nantes 1-1 1-2 **Atlético Madrid**
Club Brugge 2-0 0-1 Panathinaikos

QUARTER-FINALS
Benfica 1-2 1-4 **Liverpool**
Wacker Innsbruck 3-1 0-2 **B.Mönchengladbach**
Ajax 1-1 1-1 0-3p **Juventus**
Club Brugge 2-0 2-3 Atlético Madrid

SEMI-FINALS
Borussia Mönchengladbach......2-1 0-3 ......**Liverpool**
Juventus ......1-0 0-2 ......**Club Brugge**

FINAL
Wembley, London, 10-05-1978, 92,000. Referee: Corver, Holland
LIVERPOOL 1 (Dalglish 64)
CLUB BRUGGE 0
Liverpool - Clemence - Neal, Thompson, Hansen, Hughes - McDermott, Kennedy, Souness - Case (Heighway), Fairclough, Dalglish. Tr: Paisley
Brugge - Jensen - Bastijns, Krieger, Leekens, Maes (Volders) - Cools, Decubber, Vandereycken, Ku (Sanders) - Simoen, Sorensen. Tr: Happel

Top scorer: Simonsen, Borussia Mönchengladbach 5

UEFA CUP

FIRST ROUND
Glenavon ......2-6 0-5 ......**PSV Eindhoven**
Manchester City......2-2 0-0 ......**Widzew Lódz**
Start Kristiansand......6-0 2-0 ......Fram Reykjavík
Dynamo Kiev ......1-1 0-0......**Eintracht Braunschweig**
Boavista FC......1-0 0-5 ......**Lazio**
RC Lens......4-1 0-2 ......Malmö FF
Fiorentina......0-0 1-2 ......**FC Schalke 04**
Odra Opole......1-2 1-1 ......**1.FC Magdeburg**
Aston Villa......4-0 2-0 ......Fenerbahçe
Górnik Zabrze ......5-3 0-0 ......Haka Valkeakoski
Linzer ASK......3-2 0-7 ......**Ujpesti Dózsa**
Servette FC......1-0 0-2 ......**Athletic Bilbao**
Landskrona BoIS......0-1 0-5 ......**Ipswich Town**
Las Palmas......5-0 3-4 ......Sloboda Tuzla
AZ 67 Alkmaar ......11-1 5-0 ......Red Boys
Barcelona ......5-1 3-1 ......Steaua Bucuresti
Frem København......0-2 1-6 ......**Grasshopper-Club**
SK Rapid Wien ......1-0 0-3 ......**TJ Internacional**
Dundee United ......1-0 0-3 ......**KB København**
Internazionale......0-1 0-0 ......**Dynamo Tbilisi**
Bayern München......8-0 4-0 ......Mjøndalen IF
Marek Stanke Dimitrov......3-0 0-2 ......Ferencváros
FC Zürich......1-0 1-1 ......CSKA Sofia
Eintracht Frankfurt......5-0 0-0 ......Sliema Wanderers
RWD Molenbeek......0-0 2-1 ......Aberdeen
Carl Zeiss Jena......5-1 1-4 ......Altay Izmir
Standard CL ......1-0 2-3 ......Slavia Praha
ASA Tîrgu Mures ......1-0 0-3 ......**AEK Athens**
Torino......3-0 1-1 ......Apoel Nicosia
Olympiakos......3-1 1-5 ......**Dinamo Zagreb**
Bohemians Dublin......0-0 0-4 ......**Newcastle United**
SEC Bastia......3-2 2-1 ......Sporting CP

SECOND ROUND
Widzew Lódz......3-5 0-1 ......**PSV Eindhoven**
Start Kristiansand......1-0 0-4......**Eintracht Braunschweig**
Lazio ......2-0 0-6 ......**RC Lens**
1.FC Magdeburg ......4-2 3-1 ......FC Schalke 04
Aston Villa......2-0 1-1 ......Górnik Zabrze
Ujpesti Dózsa......2-0 0-3 ......**Athletic Bilbao**
Ipswich Town ......1-0 3-3 ......Las Palmas
AZ 67 Alkmaar......1-1 1-1 4-5p ......**Barcelona**
TJ Internacional ......1-0 1-5 ......**Grasshopper-Club**
KB København ......1-4 1-2 ......**Dynamo Tbilisi**
Bayern München......3-0 0-2 ......Marek Stanke Dimitrov
FC Zürich......0-3 3-4 ......**Eintracht Frankfurt**
RWD Molenbeek......1-1 1-1 5-6p......**Carl Zeiss Jena**
AEK Athens......2-2 1-4 ......**Standard CL**
Torino......3-1 0-1 ......Dinamo Zagreb
SEC Bastia......2-1 3-1 ......Newcastle United

THIRD ROUND
PSV Eindhoven......2-0 2-1 ......Eintracht Braunschweig
1.FC Magdeburg ......4-0 0-2 ......RC Lens
Aston Villa......2-0 1-1 ......Athletic Bilbao
Ipswich Town ......3-0 0-3 1-3p ......**Barcelona**
Dynamo Tbilisi......1-0 0-4......**Grasshopper-Club**
Eintracht Frankfurt......4-0 2-1 ......Bayern München
Carl Zeiss Jena......2-0 2-1 ......Standard CL
SEC Bastia......2-1 3-2 ......Torino

QUARTER-FINALS
1.FC Magdeburg......1-0 2-4......**PSV Eindhoven**
Aston Villa ......2-2 1-2 ......**Barcelona**
Eintracht Frankfurt ......3-2 0-1 ......**Grasshopper-Club**
SEC Bastia......7-2 2-4 ......Carl Zeiss Jena

SEMI-FINALS
PSV Eindhoven......3-0 1-3 ......Barcelona
Grasshopper-Club......3-2 0-1 ......**SEC Bastia**

FINAL
1st leg. Furiani, Bastia, 26-04-1978, 15,000. Referee: Maksimovis, Yugoslavia
SEC BASTIA 0
PSV EINDHOVEN 0
Bastia - Hiard - Burkhard, Guesdon, Orlanducci, Cazes - Papi, Lacuesta (Felix), Larios - Rep, Krimau, Mariot
PSV Eindhoven - Van Beveren - Van Kraay, Krijgh, Stevens, Brandts, Poortvliet - Van der Kuijlen, Van de Kerkhof.W, Deijkers - Van de Kerkhof.R Lubse

2nd leg. Philips Stadion, Eindhoven, 9-05-1978, 27,000. Referee: Rainea, Romania
PSV EINDHOVEN 3 (Van der Kerkhof.W 24, Deijkers 67, Van der Kuijlen 69)
SEC BASTIA 0
PSV Eindhoven - Van Beveren - Krijgh, Stevens, Van Kraay (Deacy), Brandts, Van de Kerkhof.W, Poortvliet, Van der Kuijlen - Lubse, Deijkers, Van de Kerkhof.R
Bastia - Hiard (Weller) - Marchioni, Orlanducci, Guesdon, Cazes - Lacuesta, Larios, Papi - Rep, Krimau, Mariot (De Zerbi)

Top scorers: Deijkers, PSV Eindhoven 8
Ponte, Grasshopper-Club 8

CUP WINNERS CUP

PRELIMINARY ROUND
Glasgow Rangers ......1-0 2-2......BSC Young Boys

FIRST ROUND
Lokomotiv Sofia......1-6 0-2......**RSC Anderlecht**
Hamburger SV ......8-1 5-2 ......Reipas Lahti
AS Saint-Étienne......1-1 0-2 ......**Manchester United**
1.FC Köln......2-2 0-1 ......**FC Porto**
Progres Niedercorn ......0-1 0-9 ......**Vejle BK**
PAOK Salonica ......2-0 2-0 ......Zaglebie Sosnowiec
SK Brann Bergen ......1-0 4-0 ......IA Akranes
Glasgow Rangers......0-0 0-3......**FC Twente Enschede**
Valletta......0-2 0-5 ......**Dynamo Moskva**
Olympiakos Nicosia......1-6 0-2......**Universitatea Craiova**
Coleraine ......1-4 2-2 ......**Lokomotive Leipzig**
Real Betis ......2-0 1-2 ......Milan
Dundalk......1-0 0-4 ......**Hajduk Split**
Besiktas......2-0 0-5 ......**Diósgyöri VTK**
Lokomotiva Kosice......0-0 2-2 ......Östers IF Växjö
Cardiff City......0-0 0-1 ......**FK Austria**

SECOND ROUND
Hamburger SV ......1-2 1-1 ......**RSC Anderlecht**
FC Porto......4-0 2-5 ......Manchester United

Vejle BK 3-0 1-2 PAOK Salonica
FC Twente Enschede 2-0 2-1 SK Brann Bergen
Dynamo Moskva 2-0 0-2 3-0p Universitatea Craiova
Lokomotive Leipzig 1-1 1-2 **Real Betis**
Diósgyöri VTK 2-1 1-2 3-4p **Hajduk Split**
FK Austria 0-0 1-1 Lokomotiva Kosice

QUARTER-FINALS

FC Porto 1-0 0-3 **RSC Anderlecht**
Vejle BK 0-3 0-4 **FC Twente Enschede**
Real Betis 0-0 0-3 **Dynamo Moskva**
FK Austria 1-1 1-1 3-0p Hajduk Split

SEMI-FINALS

FC Twente Enschede 0-1 0-2 **RSC Anderlecht**
Dynamo Moskva 2-1 1-2 4-5p **FK Austria**

FINAL

Parc des Princes, Paris, 3-05-1978, 48,000. Referee: Alginder, West Germany

RSC ANDERLECHT 4 (Rensenbrink 13 41, Van Binst 45 80)
FK AUSTRIA 0

Anderlecht - De Bree - Van Binst, Thissen, Dusbaba, Broos - Vander Elst, Haan, Nielsen, Coeck, Vercauteren (Dockx) - Rensenbrink
FK Austria - Baumgartner - Sara.R, Sara.J, Obermayer, Baumeister - Prohaska, Daxbacher (Martinez), Gasselich, Morales (Drazen) - Pirkner, Parits

Top scorer: Gritter, FC Twente Enschede 7

EUROPEAN SUPERCUP 1978

1st leg. Parc Astrid, Brussels, 4-12-1978. Referee: Palotai, Hungary

RSC ANDERLECHT 3 (Vercauteren 17, Vander Elst 38, Rensenbrink 87)
LIVERPOOL 1 (Case 27)

2nd leg. Anfield, Liverpool, 19-12-1978. Referee: Rainea, Romania

LIVERPOOL 2 (Hughes 13, Fairclough 85)
RSC ANDERLECHT 1 (Vander Elst 71)

1978–79

EUROPEAN CUP

PRELIMINARY ROUND

AS Monaco 3-0 0-2 Steaua Bucharesti

FIRST ROUND

Nottingham Forest 2-0 0-0 Liverpool
AEK Athens 6-1 1-4 FC Porto
Real Madrid 5-0 7-0 Progres Niedercorn
Grasshopper-Club 8-0 5-3 Valletta
Juventus 1-0 0-2 **Glasgow Rangers**
Fenerbahçe 2-1 1-6 **PSV Eindhoven**
B 1909 Odense 2-2 1-2 **Lokomotiv Sofia**
1.FC Köln 4-1 1-1 IA Akranes
Vllaznia Shkodër 2-0 1-4 **FK Austria**
Linfield 0-0 0-1 **Lillestrøm SK**
Omonia Nicosia 2-1 0-1 **Bohemians Dublin**
Partizan Beograd 2-0 0-2 4-5p **Dynamo Dresden**
Club Brugge 2-1 1-3 **Wisla Kraków**
Zbrojovka Brno 2-2 2-0 Ujpesti Dózsa
Haka Valkeakoski 0-1 1-3 **Dynamo Kiev**
Malmö FF 0-0 1-0 AS Monaco

SECOND ROUND

AEK Athens 1-2 1-5 **Nottingham Forest**
Real Madrid 3-1 0-2 **Grasshopper-Club**
Glasgow Rangers 0-0 3-2 PSV Eindhoven
Lokomotiv Sofia 0-1 0-4 **1.FC Köln**
FK Austria 4-1 0-0 Lillestrøm SK
Bohemians Dublin 0-0 0-6 **Dynamo Dresden**
Zbrojovka Brno 2-2 1-1 **Wisla Kraków**
Dynamo Kiev 0-0 0-2 **Malmö FF**

QUARTER-FINALS

Nottingham Forest 4-1 1-1 Grasshopper-Club
1.FC Köln 1-0 1-1 Glasgow Rangers
FK Austria 3-1 0-1 Dynamo Dresden
Wisla Kraków 2-1 1-4 **Malmö FF**

SEMI-FINALS

Nottingham Forest 3-3 1-0 1.FC Köln
FK Austria 0-0 0-1 **Malmö FF**

FINAL

Olympiastadion, Munich, 30-05-1979, 57,000. Referee: Linemayr, Austria

NOTTINGHAM FOREST 1 (Francis 45)
MALMÖ FF 0

Nottm. Forest - Shilton - Anderson, Lloyd, Burns, Clark - Francis, McGovern, Bowyer, Robertson - Woodcock, Birtles. Tr. Clough
Malmö - Moller - Andersson.R, Jonsson, Andersson.M, Erlandsson - Tapper (Malmberg), Ljungberg, Prytz, Kinnvall - Hansson (Andersson.T), Cervin. Tr: Houghton

Top scorer: Sulser, Grasshopper-Club 11

UEFA CUP

FIRST ROUND

B. Mönchengladbach 5-1 2-1 SK Sturm Graz
FC Nantes 0-2 0-0 **Benfica**
IBV Vestmannaeyjar 0-0 1-1 Glentoran
Pezoporikos 2-2 1-5 **Slask Wroclaw**
Milan 1-0 0-1 8-7p Lokomotiva Kosice
Olympiakos 2-1 1-3 **Levski-Spartak**
Standard CL 1-0 0-0 Dundee United
FC Twente Enschede 1-1 2-3 **Manchester City**
Honvéd 6-0 2-2 Adanaspor
Politechnica Timisoara 2-0 1-2 MTK-VM Budapest
Jeunesse Esch 0-0 0-2 **Lausanne-Sports**
Athletic Bilbao 2-0 0-3 **Ajax**
IF Elfsborg Borås 2-0 1-4 **RC Strasbourg**
Sporting Braga 5-0 2-3 Hibernians Paola
Carl Zeiss Jena 1-0 2-2 Lierse SK
MSV Duisburg 5-0 5-2 Lech Poznan
Hertha BSC Berlin 0-0 2-1 Trakia Plovdiv
Dynamo Tbilisi 2-0 1-1 Napoli
KuPS Kuopio 2-1 4-4 B 1903 København
Start Kristiansand 0-0 0-1 **Esbjerg FB**
FC Basel 2-3 1-4 **VfB Stuttgart**
Torpedo Moskva 4-0 3-3 Molde FK
Finn Harps 0-5 0-5 **Everton**
Dukla Praha 1-0 1-1 Lanerossi-Vicenza
Galatasaray 1-3 1-3 **West Bromwich Albion**
Hibernian Edinburgh 3-2 0-0 IFK Norrköping
FC Arges Pitesti 3-0 2-1 Panathinaikos
CSKA Sofia 2-1 1-4 **Valencia**
Hajduk Split 2-0 1-2 SK Rapid Wien
Arsenal 3-0 4-1 Lokomotive Leipzig
Sporting Gijón 3-0 0-1 Torino
Dynamo Berlin 5-2 1-4 **Crvena Zvezda Beograd**

SECOND ROUND

Benfica 0-0 0-2 **B. Mönchengladbach**
IBV Vestmannaeyjar 0-2 1-2 **Slask Wroclaw**
Levski-Spartak 1-1 0-3 **Milan**

Manchester City 4-0 0-2 Standard CL
Honvéd 4-0 0-2 Politehnica Timisoara
Ajax 1-0 4-0 Lausanne-Sports
RC Strasbourg 2-0 0-1 Hibernian Edinburgh
Carl Zeiss Jena 0-0 0-3 **MSV Duisburg**
Hertha BSC Berlin 2-0 0-1 Dynamo Tbilisi
KuPS Kuopio 0-2 1-4 **Esbjerg FB**
Torpedo Moskva 2-1 0-2 **VfB Stuttgart**
Everton 2-1 0-1 **Dukla Praha**
Sporting Braga 0-2 0-1 **West Bromwich Albion**
FC Arges Pitesti 2-1 2-5 **Valencia**
Hajduk Split 2-1 0-1 **Arsenal**
Sporting Gijón 0-1 1-1 **Crvena Zvezda Beograd**

THIRD ROUND
B. Mönchengladbach 1-1 4-2 Slask Wroclaw
Milan 2-2 0-3 **Manchester City**
Honvéd 4-1 0-2 Ajax
RC Strasbourg 0-0 0-4 **MSV Duisburg**
Esbjerg FB 2-1 0-4 **Hertha BSC Berlin**
VfB Stuttgart 4-1 0-4 **Dukla Praha**
Valencia 1-1 0-2 **West Bromwich Albion**
Crvena Zvezda Beograd 1-0 1-1 Arsenal

QUARTER-FINALS
Manchester City 1-1 1-3 **B. Mönchengladbach**
Honvéd 2-3 2-1 **MSV Duisburg**
Hertha BSC Berlin 1-1 2-1 Dukla Praha
Crvena Zvezda Beograd 1-0 1-1 West Bromwich Albion

SEMI-FINALS
MSV Duisburg 2-2 1-4 **B. Mönchengladbach**
Crvena Zvezda Beograd 1-0 1-2 Hertha BSC Berlin

FINAL
1st leg. Crvena Zvezda, Belgrade, 9-05-1979, 87,000. Referee: Foote, England
CRVENA ZVEZDA BEOGRAD 1 (Sestic 21)
BOR. MÖNCHENGLADBACH 1 (OG 60)
Red Star - Stojanovic - Jovanovic, Miletovic, Jurisic, Jovin - Muslin (Krmpotic), Petrovic, Blagojevic, Milosavljevic (Milovanovic) - Savic, Sestic
Borussia - Kneib - Vogts, Hannes, Schaffer, Ringels - Schäfer, Kulik, Nielsen (Danner), Wohlers (Gores) - Simonsen, Lienen

2nd leg. Rheinstadion, Dusseldorf, 23-05-1979, 45,000. Referee: Michelotti, Italy
BOR. MÖNCHENGLADBACH 1 (Simonsen 15)
CRVENA ZVEZDA BEOGRAD 0
Borussia - Kneib - Vogts, Hannes, Schaffer, Ringels - Schafer, Kulik (Koppel), Gores, Wohlers - Simonsen, Lienen
Red Star - Stojanovic - Jovanovic, Miletovic, Jurisic, Jovin - Muslin Petrovic, Blagojevic, Milovanovic (Sestic) - Savic, Milossavlevic

Top scorer: Simonsen, Borussia Mönchengladbach 9

CUP WINNERS CUP

FIRST ROUND
Barcelona 3-0 1-1 Shachter Donetsk
RSC Anderlecht Bye
Zaglebie Sosnowiec 2-3 1-1 **Wacker Innsbruck**
AZ 67 Alkmaar 0-0 0-2 **Ipswich Town**
Floriana 1-3 0-5 **Internazionale**
SOFK Bodø-Glimt 4-1 0-1 Union Luxembourg
NK Rijeka 3-0 0-2 Wrexham
SK Beveren 3-0 3-0 Ballymena United
Sporting CP 0-1 0-1 **Baník Ostrava**
Apoel Nicosia 0-2 0-1 **Shamrock Rovers**
Ferencváros 2-0 2-2 Kalmar FF
Valur Reykjavík 1-1 0-4 **1.FC Magdeburg**
PAOK Salonica 2-0 0-4 **Servette FC**
Frem København 2-0 0-4 **AS Nancy-Lorraine**
Marek Stanke Dimitrov 3-2 0-3 **Aberdeen**
Universitatea Craiova 3-4 1-1 **Fortuna Düsseldorf**

SECOND ROUND
RSC Anderlecht 3-0 0-3 1-4p **Barcelona**
Ipswich Town 1-0 1-1 Wacker Innsbruck
Internazionale 5-0 2-1 SOFK Bodø-Glimt
NK Rijeka 0-0 0-2 **SK Beveren**
Baník Ostrava 3-0 3-1 Shamrock Rovers
1.FC Magdeburg 1-0 1-2 Ferencváros
Servette FC 2-1 2-2 AS Nancy-Lorraine
Fortuna Düsseldorf 3-0 0-2 Aberdeen

QUARTER-FINALS
Ipswich Town 2-1 0-1 **Barcelona**
Internazionale 0-0 0-1 **SK Beveren**
1.FC Magdeburg 2-1 2-4 **Baník Ostrava**
Fortuna Düsseldorf 0-0 1-1 Servette FC

SEMI-FINALS
Barcelona 1-0 1-0 SK Beveren
Fortuna Düsseldorf 3-1 1-2 Baník Ostrava

FINAL
St. Jakobs, Basle, 16-05-1979, 58,000. Referee: Palotai, Hungary
BARCELONA 4 (Sanchez 5, Asensi 34, Rexach 104, Krankl 111)
FORTUNA DUSSELDORF 3 (Allofs.K 8, Seel 41 114)
Barcelona - Artola - Zuviria, Migueli, Costas (Martinez), Albaladejo (De la Cruz) - Sanchez, Neeskens, Asensi - Rexach, Krankl, Carrasco
Fortuna - Daniel - Baltes, Zewe, Zimmermann (Lund), Brei (Weikl) - Kohnen, Schmitz, Bommer - Allofs.T, Allofs.K, Seel

Top scorer: Altobelli, Internazionale 7

EUROPEAN SUPERCUP 1979

1st leg. City Ground, Nottingham, 30-01-1980. Referee: Prokop, East Germany
NOTTINGHAM FOREST 1 (George 9)
BARCELONA 0
2nd leg. Nou Camp, Barcelona, 5-02-1980. Referee: Eschweiler, West Germany
BARCELONA 1 (Roberto 25)
NOTTINGHAM FOREST 1 (Burns 42)

1979–80

EUROPEAN CUP

PRELIMINARY ROUND
Dundalk 1-1 2-0 Linfield

FIRST ROUND
Nottingham Forest 2-0 1-1 Östers IF Växjö
FC Arges Pitesti 3-0 0-2 AEK Athens
Servette FC 3-1 1-1 SK Beveren
Dynamo Berlin 4-1 0-0 Ruch Chorzów
Start Kristiansand 1-2 0-4 **RC Strasbourg**
Ujpesti Dózsa 3-2 0-2 **Dukla Praha**
Red Boys 2-1 1-6 **Omonia Nicosia**
HJK Helsinki 1-8 1-8 **Ajax**
Levski-Spartak 0-1 0-2 **Real Madrid**
FC Porto 0-0 1-0 Milan
Dundalk 2-0 0-1 Hibernians Paola
Partizani Tiranë 1-0 1-4 **Glasgow Celtic**

Hajduk Split 1-0 1-0 Trabzonspor
Vejle BK 3-2 1-1 FK Austria
Liverpool 2-1 0-3 **Dynamo Tbilisi**
Valur Reykjavík 0-3 1-2 **Hamburger SV**

SECOND ROUND

Nottingham Forest 2-0 2-1 FC Arges Pitesti
Dynamo Berlin 2-1 2-2 Servette FC
Dukla Praha 1-0 0-2 **RC Strasbourg**
Ajax 10-0 0-4 Omonia Nicosia
FC Porto 2-1 0-1 **Real Madrid**
Glasgow Celtic 3-2 0-0 Dundalk
Vejle BK 0-3 2-1 **Hajduk Split**
Hamburger SV 3-1 3-2 Dynamo Tbilisi

QUARTER-FINALS

Nottingham Forest 0-1 3-1 Dynamo Berlin
RC Strasbourg 0-0 0-4 **Ajax**
Glasgow Celtic 2-0 0-3 **Real Madrid**
Hamburger SV 1-0 2-3 Hajduk Split

SEMI-FINALS

Nottingham Forest 2-0 0-1 Ajax
Real Madrid 2-0 1-5 **Hamburger SV**

FINAL

Bernabeu, Madrid, 28-05-1980, 50,000. Referee: Garrido, Portugal

NOTTINGHAM FOREST 1 (Robertson 21)
HAMBURGER SV 0

Nottm. Forest - Shilton - Anderson, Gray (Gunn), Lloyd, Burns - O'Neill, McGovern, Bowyer, Mills (O'Hare), Robertson - Birtles. Tr: Clough

Hamburg - Kargus - Kaltz, Nogly, Buljan, Jakobs - Hieronymus (Hrubesch), Magath, Memering - Keegan, Reimann, Milewski. Tr: Zebec

Top scorer: Lerby, Ajax 10

UEFA CUP

FIRST ROUND

Aberdeen 1-1 0-1 **Eintracht Frankfurt**
Dinamo Bucuresti 3-0 9-0 Alki Larnaca
KuPS Kuopio 1-2 0-2 **Malmö FF**
Feyenoord 1-0 1-0 Everton
Glenavon 0-1 0-1 **Standard CL**
Napoli 2-0 0-1 Olympiakos
Kalmar FF 2-1 0-1 **IBK Keflavík**
Zbrojovka Brno 6-0 1-1 Esbjerg FB
FC Zürich 1-3 1-5 **1.FC Kaiserslautern**
Sporting CP 2-0 0-0 Bohemians Dublin
Dundee United 0-0 1-1 RSC Anderlecht
SK Rapid Wien 0-1 2-3 **Diósgyöri VTK**
Galatasaray 0-0 1-3 **Crvena Zvezda Beograd**
Carl Zeiss Jena 2-0 2-1 West Bromwich Albion
ÅGF Åarhus 1-1 1-0 Stal Mielec
Bohemians Praha 0-2 2-2 **Bayern München**
VfB Stuttgart 1-0 1-2 Torino
Atlético Madrid 1-2 0-3 **Dynamo Dresden**
FK Skeid Oslo 1-3 0-7 **Ipswich Town**
Progres Niedercorn 0-2 0-4 **Grasshopper-Club**
Dynamo Kiev 2-1 1-1 CSKA Sofia
Orduspor 2-0 0-6 **Baník Ostrava**
Shachter Donetsk 2-1 0-2 **AS Monaco**
Lokomotiv Sofia 3-0 0-2 Ferencváros
Widzew Lódz 2-1 0-3 **AS Saint-Étienne**
Sporting Gijón 0-0 0-1 **PSV Eindhoven**
Perugia 1-0 0-0 Dinamo Zagreb
Aris Salonica 3-1 1-2 Benfica
Wiener Sport-Club 0-0 1-3 **Universitatea Craiova**
Valletta 0-4 0-3 **Leeds United**
Internazionale 3-0 0-2 Real Sociedad
B. Mönchengladbach 3-0 1-1 Viking Stavanger

SECOND ROUND

Dinamo Bucuresti 2-0 0-3 **Eintracht Frankfurt**
Feyenoord 4-0 1-1 Malmö FF
Standard CL 2-1 1-1 Napoli
Zbrojovka Brno 3-1 2-1 IBK Keflavík
Sporting CP 1-1 0-2 **1.FC Kaiserslautern**
Dundee United 0-1 1-3 **Diósgyöri VTK**
Crvena Zvezda Beograd 3-2 3-2 Carl Zeiss Jena
ÅGF Åarhus 1-2 1-3 **Bayern München**
Dynamo Dresden 1-1 0-0 **VfB Stuttgart**
Grasshopper-Club 0-0 1-1 Ipswich Town
Baník Ostrava 1-0 0-2 **Dynamo Kiev**
Lokomotiv Sofia 4-2 1-2 AS Monaco
PSV Eindhoven 2-0 0-6 **AS Saint-Étienne**
Aris Salonica 1-1 3-0 Perugia
Universitatea Craiova 2-0 2-0 Leeds United
B. Mönchengladbach 1-1 3-2 Internazionale

THIRD ROUND

Eintracht Frankfurt 4-1 0-1 Feyenoord
Standard CL 1-2 2-3 **Zbrojovka Brno**
Diósgyöri VTK 0-2 1-6 **1.FC Kaiserslautern**
Bayern München 2-0 2-3 Crvena Zvezda Beograd
Grasshopper-Club 0-2 0-3 **VfB Stuttgart**
Lokomotiv Sofia 1-0 1-2 Dynamo Kiev
AS Saint-Étienne 4-1 3-3 Aris Salonica
B. Mönchengladbach 2-0 0-1 Universitatea Craiova

QUARTER-FINALS

Eintracht Frankfurt 4-1 2-3 Zbrojovka Brno
1.FC Kaiserslautern 1-0 1-4 **Bayern München**
VfB Stuttgart 3-1 1-0 Lokomotiv Sofia
AS Saint-Étienne 1-4 0-2 **B.Mönchengladbach**

SEMI-FINALS

Bayern München 2-0 1-5 **Eintracht Frankfurt**
VfB Stuttgart 2-1 0-2 **B.Mönchengladbach**

FINAL

1st leg. Bökelberg, Mönchengladbach, 7-05-80, 25,000. Referee: Gurucheta, Spain

BOR. MÖNCHENGLADBACH 3 (Kulik 44 88, Matthaus 76)
EINTRACHT FRANKFURT 2 (Karger 37, Holzenbein 71)

Borussia - Kneib - Hannes, Schäfer, Schaffer, Ringels - Matthäus, Kulik, Nielsen (Thychosen) - Del'Haye (Bödeker), Nickel, Lienen

Eintracht - Pahl - Pezzey, Neuberger, Körbel, Ehrmanntraut - Lorant, Hölzenbein (Nachtweih), Borchers, Nickel - Tscha, Karger (Trapp)

2nd leg. Waldstadion, Frankfurt, 21-05-1980, 59,000. Referee: Ponnet, Belgium

EINTRACHT FRANKFURT 1 (Schaub 81)
BOR. MÖNCHENGLADBACH 0

Eintracht - Pahl - Pezzey, Neuberger, Körbel, Ehrmanntraut - Lorant, Hölzenbein, Börchers, Nickel - Tscha, Nachtweih (Schaub)

Borussia - Kneib - Bödecker, Hannes, Schäfer, Ringels - Matthäus (Thychosen), Fleer, Kulik, Nielsen (Del'Haye) - Nickel, Lienen

Top scorers: Hoeness, Bayern München 7
Nickel, Borussia Mönchengladbach 7

CUP WINNERS CUP

PRELIMINARY ROUND

B 1903 København 6-0 1-0 Apoel Nicosia
Glasgow Rangers 1-0 2-0 Lillestrøm SK

FIRST ROUND

B 1903 København	2-2 0-4	**Valencia**
Glasgow Rangers	2-1 0-0	Fortuna Düsseldorf
Reipas Lahti	0-1 0-1	**Aris Bonnevoie**
IA Akranes	0-1 0-5	**Barcelona**
Dynamo Moskva	W-O	Vllaznia Shkodër
Sliema Wanderers	2-1 0-8	**Boavista FC**
BSC Young Boys	2-2 0-6	**Steaua Bucuresti**
Cliftonville	0-1 0-7	**FC Nantes**
Juventus	2-0 1-2	Rába ETO Györ
Arka Gdynia	3-2 0-2	**Beroe Stara Zagora**
Wacker Innsbruck	1-2 0-1	**Lokomotiva Kosice**
Beerschot VAV	0-0 1-2	**NK Rijeka**
IFK Göteborg	1-0 1-1	Waterford FC
Panionios	4-0 1-3	FC Twente Enschede
Wrexham	3-2 2-5	**1.FC Magdeburg**
Arsenal	2-0 0-0	Fenerbahçe

SECOND ROUND

Valencia	1-1 3-1	Glasgow Rangers
Aris Bonnevoie	1-4 1-7	**Barcelona**
Dynamo Moskva	0-0 1-1	Boavista FC
FC Nantes	3-2 2-1	Steaua Bucuresti
Beroe Stara Zagora	1-0 0-3	**Juventus**
Lokomotiva Kosice	2-0 0-3	**NK Rijeka**
Panionios	1-0 0-2	**IFK Göteborg**
Arsenal	2-1 2-2	1.FC Magdeburg

QUARTER-FINALS

Barcelona	0-1 3-4	**Valencia**
Dynamo Moskva	0-2 3-2	**FC Nantes**
NK Rijeka	0-0 0-2	**Juventus**
Arsenal	5-1 0-0	IFK Göteborg

SEMI-FINALS

FC Nantes	2-1 0-4	**Valencia**
Arsenal	1-1 1-0	Juventus

FINAL

Heysel, Brussels, 15-05-1980, 36,000. Referee: Christov, Czechoslovakia

VALENCIA 0
ARSENAL 0
Valencia won 5-4 on penalties

Valencia		**Arsenal**	
Kempes	x	Brady	x
Solsona	1	Stapleton	1
Pablo	1	Sunderland	1
Castellanos	1	Talbot	1
Bonhof	1	Hollins	1
Arias	1	Rix	x

Valencia - Pereira - Carrette, Botubot, Arias, Tendillo - Solsona, Saura, Bonhof, Subirates (Castellanos), Kempes, Pablo

Arsenal - Jennings - Rice, Nelson, O'Leary, Young - Rix, Talbot, Price (Hollins), Brady - Sunderland, Stapleton

Top scorer: Kempes, Valencia 9

EUROPEAN SUPERCUP 1980

1st leg. City Ground, Nottingham, 25-11-1980. Referee: Ponnet, Belgium

NOTTINGHAM FOREST 2 (Bowyer 57 89)
VALENCIA 1 (Felman 47)

2nd leg. Luis Casanova, Valencia, 17-12-1980. Referee: Wöhrer, Austria

VALENCIA 1 (Morena 51)
NOTTINGHAM FOREST 0

1980–81

EUROPEAN CUP

PRELIMINARY ROUND

Honvéd	8-0 3-0	Valletta

FIRST ROUND

OPS Oulu	1-1 1-10	**Liverpool**
Aberdeen	1-0 0-0	FK Austria
Trabzonspor	2-1 0-3	**Szombierki Bytom**
CSKA Sofia	1-0 1-0	Nottingham Forest
IBV Vestmannaeyjar	1-1 0-1	**Baník Ostrava**
Dynamo Berlin	3-0 1-2	Apoel Nicosia
Dinamo Tiranë	0-2 0-1	**Ajax**
Olympiakos	2-4 0-3	**Bayern München**
Internazionale	2-0 1-1	Universitatea Craiova
Linfield	0-1 0-2	**FC Nantes**
Club Brugge	0-1 1-4	**FC Basel**
Viking Stavanger	2-3 1-4	**Crvena Zvezda Beograd**
Jeunesse Esch	0-5 0-4	**Spartak Moskva**
Halmstad BK	0-0 2-3	**Esbjerg FB**
Sporting CP	0-2 0-1	**Honvéd**
Limerick United	1-2 1-5	**Real Madrid**

SECOND ROUND

Aberdeen	0-1 0-4	**Liverpool**
CSKA Sofia	4-0 1-0	Szombierki Bytom
Baník Ostrava	0-0 1-1	Dynamo Berlin
Bayern München	5-1 1-2	Ajax
FC Nantes	1-2 1-1	**Internazionale**
FC Basel	1-0 0-2	**Crvena Zvezda Beograd**
Spartak Moskva	3-0 0-2	Esbjerg FB
Real Madrid	1-0 2-0	Honvéd

QUARTER-FINALS

Liverpool	5-1 1-0	CSKA Sofia
Bayern München	2-0 4-2	Baník Ostrava
Internazionale	1-1 1-0	Crvena Zvezda Beograd
Spartak Moskva	0-0 0-2	**Real Madrid**

SEMI-FINALS

Liverpool	0-0 1-1	Bayern München
Real Madrid	2-0 0-1	Internazionale

FINAL

Parc des Princes, Paris, 27-05-1981, 48,000. Referee: Palotai, Hungary

LIVERPOOL 1 (Kennedy.A 82)
REAL MADRID 0

Liverpool - Clemence - Neal, Thompson, Hansen, Kennedy.A - Lee, McDermott, Souness, Kennedy.R - Dalglish (Case), Johnson. Tr: Paisley

Real Madrid - Agustin - Cortes (Pineda), Navajas, Sabido - Del Bosque, Angel, Camacho, Stielike - Juanito, Santillana, Cunningham. Tr: Boskov

Top scorers: Rummenigge, Bayern München 6
McDermott, Liverpool 6
Souness, Liverpool 6

UEFA CUP

FIRST ROUND

Ipswich Town	5-1 1-3	Aris Salonica
Bohemians Praha	3-1 1-2	Sporting Gijón
Juventus	4-0 2-4	Panathinaikos
Manchester United	1-1 0-0	**Widzew Lódz**
Hamburger SV	4-2 3-3	FK Sarajevo

PSV Eindhoven 3-1 0-1 Wolverhampton W.
IF Elfsborg Borås 1-2 0-0 **St. Mirren**
KuPS Kuopio 0-7 0-7 **AS Saint-Étienne**
Standard CL 1-1 2-1 Steaua Bucuresti
1.FC Kaiserslautern 1-0 2-3 RSC Anderlecht
FC Twente Enschede 5-1 0-2 IFK Göteborg
Dynamo Dresden 1-0 1-0 Napredak Krusevac
VfB Stuttgart 6-0 4-1 Pezoporikos
Ballymena United 2-1 0-3 **Vorwärts Frankfurt**
Sliema Wanderers 0-2 0-1 **Barcelona**
IA Akranes 0-4 0-6 **1.FC Köln**
FC Sochaux 2-0 1-2 Servette FC
Vasas Budapest 0-2 1-0 **Boavista FC**
FC Arges Pitesti 0-0 0-2 **FC Utrecht**
Shachter Donetsk 1-0 0-3 **Eintracht Frankfurt**
RWD Molenbeek 1-2 2-2 **Torino**
1.FC Magdeburg 2-1 3-2 Moss FK
FC Porto 1-0 0-0 Dundalk
Grasshopper-Club 3-1 5-2 B 1903 København
KSC Lokeren 1-1 1-0 Dynamo Moskva
Slask Wroclaw 0-0 2-7 **Dundee United**
Zbrojovka Brno 3-1 2-0 VÖEST Linz
Ujpesti Dózsa 1-1 0-1 **Real Sociedad**
Linzer ASK 1-2 1-4 **Radnicki Nis**
Fenerbahçe 0-1 1-2 **Beroe Stara Zagora**
Dynamo Kiev 1-1 0-0 **Levski-Spartak**
AZ 67 Alkmaar 6-0 4-0 Red Boys

SECOND ROUND

Ipswich Town 3-0 0-2 Bohemians Praha
Widzew Lódz 3-1 1-3 4-1p Juventus
PSV Eindhoven 1-1 1-2 **Hamburger SV**
St. Mirren 0-0 0-2 **AS Saint-Étienne**
1.FC Kaiserslautern 1-2 1-2 **Standard CL**
FC Twente Enschede 1-1 0-0 **Dynamo Dresden**
VfB Stuttgart 5-1 2-1 Vorwärts Frankfurt
1.FC Köln 0-1 4-0 Barcelona
FC Sochaux 2-2 1-0 Boavista FC
FC Utrecht 2-1 1-3 **Eintracht Frankfurt**
Torino 3-1 0-1 1.FC Magdeburg
FC Porto 2-0 0-3 **Grasshopper-Club**
Dundee United 1-1 0-0 **KSC Lokeren**
Zbrojovka Brno 1-1 1-2 **Real Sociedad**
Beroe Stara Zagora 0-1 1-2 **Radnicki Nis**
Levski-Spartak 1-1 0-5 **AZ 67 Alkmaar**

THIRD ROUND

Ipswich Town 5-0 0-1 Widzew Lódz
Hamburger SV 0-5 0-1 **AS Saint-Étienne**
Standard CL 1-1 4-1 Dynamo Dresden
VfB Stuttgart 3-1 1-4 **1.FC Köln**
Eintracht Frankfurt 4-2 0-2 **FC Sochaux**
Grasshopper-Club 2-1 1-2 4-3p Torino
KSC Lokeren 1-0 2-2 Real Sociedad
Radnicki Nis 2-2 0-5 **AZ 67 Alkmaar**

QUARTER-FINALS

AS Saint-Étienne 1-4 1-3 **Ipswich Town**
Standard CL 0-0 2-3 **1.FC Köln**
Grasshopper-Club 0-0 1-2 **FC Sochaux**
AZ 67 Alkmaar 2-0 0-1 KSC Lokeren

SEMI-FINALS

Ipswich Town 1-0 1-0 1.FC Köln
FC Sochaux 1-1 2-3 **AZ 67 Alkmaar**

FINAL

1st leg. Portman Road, Ipswich, 6-05-1981, 27,000. Referee: Prokop, East Germany

IPSWICH TOWN 3 (Wark 28, Thijssen 46, Mariner 56)
AZ 67 ALKMAAR 0

Ipswich Town - Cooper - Mills, Osman, Butcher, McCall - Thijssen, Wark, Muhren - Mariner, Brazil, Gates

AZ 67 Alkmaar - Treytel - Van der Meer, Spelbos, Metgod, Hovenkamp - Peters, Jonker, Arntz, Nygaard (Welzl) - Kist, Tol

2nd leg. Olympisch Stadion, Amsterdam, 20-05-1981, 28,000. Referee: Eschweiler, West Germany

AZ 67 ALKMAAR 4 (Welzl 7, Metgod 25, Tol 40, Jonker 74)
IPSWICH TOWN 2 (Thijssen 4, Wark 32)

AZ 67 Alkmaar - Treytel - Reijnders, Spelbos, Metgod, Hovenkamp - Peters, Arntz, Jonker, Nygaard - Welzl (Van den Dungen), Tol (Kist)
Ipswich Town - Cooper - Mills, Osman, Butcher, McCall - Thijssen, Wark, Muhren - Mariner, Brazil, Gates

Top scorer: Wark, Ipswich Town 14

CUP WINNERS CUP

PRELIMINARY ROUND

Glasgow Celtic 6-0 1-2 Diósgyöri VTK
Altay Izmir 0-0 0-4 **Benfica**

FIRST ROUND

Kastoria 0-0 0-2 **Dynamo Tbilisi**
Hibernians Paola 1-0 0-4 **Waterford FC**
Glasgow Celtic 2-1 0-1 **Politechnica Timisoara**
Castilla 3-1 1-5 **West Ham United**
Slavia Sofia 3-1 0-1 Legia Warszawa
AC Spora 0-6 0-6 **Sparta Praha**
Hvidovre BK 1-0 2-0 Fram Reykjavík
Ilves Tampere 1-3 2-4 **Feyenoord**
Dinamo Zagreb 0-0 0-2 **Benfica**
Malmö FF 1-0 0-0 Partizani Tiranë
Omonia Nicosia 1-3 0-4 **Waterschei THOR**
Fortuna Düsseldorf 5-0 3-0 Austria Salzburg
Newport County 4-0 0-0 Crusaders
FC Sion 1-1 0-2 **SK Haugar**
Valencia 2-0 3-3 AS Monaco
Roma 3-0 0-4 **Carl Zeiss Jena**

SECOND ROUND

Waterford 0-1 0-4 **Dynamo Tbilisi**
West Ham United 4-0 0-1 Politehnica Timisoara
Sparta Praha 2-0 0-3 **Slavia Sofia**
Hvidovre BK 1-2 0-1 **Feyenoord**
Malmö FF 1-0 0-2 **Benfica**
Waterschei THOR 0-0 0-1 **Fortuna Düsseldorf**
SK Haugar 0-0 0-6 **Newport County**
Carl Zeiss Jena 3-1 0-1 Valencia

QUARTER-FINALS

West Ham United 1-4 1-0 **Dynamo Tbilisi**
Slavia Sofia 3-2 0-4 **Feyenoord**
Fortuna Düsseldorf 2-2 0-1 **Benfica**
Carl Zeiss Jena 2-2 1-0 Newport County

SEMI-FINALS

Dynamo Tbilisi 3-0 0-2 Feyenoord
Carl Zeiss Jena 2-0 0-1 Benfica

FINAL

Rheinstadion, Dusseldorf, 13-05-1981, 9,000. Referee: Lattanzi, Italy

DYNAMO TBILISI 2 (Gutsayev 67, Daraselia 86)
CARL ZEISS JENA 1 (Hoppe 63)

Dynamo Tbilisi - Gabelia - Kostava, Chivadze, Khisanishvili, Tavadze Svanadze (Kakilashvili), Sulakvelidze, Daraselia - Gutsayev, Kipiani, Shengelia
Carl Zeiss Jena - Grapenthin - Brauer, Kurbjuweit, Schnuphase, Schilling, Hoppe (Overmann), Krause, Lindemann - Bielau (Topfer), Raab, Vogel

Top scorer: Cross, West Ham United 6

1981–82

EUROPEAN CUP

PRELIMINARY ROUND

AS Saint-Étienne 1-1 0-2 **Dynamo Berlin**

FIRST ROUND

Aston Villa 5-0 2-0 Valur Reykjavík
Dynamo Berlin 2-0 1-3 FC Zürich
FK Austria 3-1 0-1 Partizani Tiranë
Dynamo Kiev 1-0 1-1 Trabzonspor
Hibernians Paola 1-2 1-8 **Crvena Zvezda Beograd**
Ferencváros 3-2 0-3 **Baník Ostrava**
Glasgow Celtic 1-0 0-2 **Juventus**
Widzew Lódz 1-4 1-2 **RSC Anderlecht**
CSKA Sofia 1-0 0-0 Real Sociedad
Progres Niedercorn 1-1 0-4 **Glentoran**
Start Kristiansand 1-3 0-1 **AZ 67 Alkmaar**
OPS Oulu 0-1 0-7 **Liverpool**
Universitatea Craiova 3-0 0-2 Olympiakos
KB København 1-1 2-2 Athlone Town
Benfica 3-0 1-0 Omonia Nicosia
Östers IF Växjö 0-1 0-5 **Bayern München**

SECOND ROUND

Dynamo Berlin 1-2 1-0 **Aston Villa**
FK Austria 0-1 1-1 **Dynamo Kiev**
Baník Ostrava 3-1 0-3 **Crvena Zvezda Beograd**
RSC Anderlecht 3-1 1-1 Juventus
CSKA Sofia 2-0 1-2 Glentoran
AZ 67 Alkmaar 2-2 2-3 **Liverpool**
KB København 1-0 1-4 **Universitatea Craiova**
Benfica 0-0 1-4 **Bayern München**

QUARTER-FINALS

Dynamo Kiev 0-0 0-2 **Aston Villa**
RSC Anderlecht 2-1 2-1 Crvena Zvezda Beograd
Liverpool 1-0 0-2 **CSKA Sofia**
Universitatea Craiova 0-2 1-1 **Bayern München**

SEMI-FINALS

Aston Villa 1-0 0-0 RSC Anderlecht
CSKA Sofia 4-3 0-4 **Bayern München**

FINAL

Feyenoord, Rotterdam, 26-05-1982, 46,000. Referee: Konrath, France

ASTON VILLA 1 (Withe 67)
BAYERN MÜNCHEN 0

Aston Villa - Rimmer (Spink) - Swain, Evans, McNaught, Williams - Bremner, Cowans, Mortimer - Shaw, Withe, Morley. Tr: Barton

Bayern - Müller - Dremmler, Weiner, Augenthaler, Horsmann - Mathy (Güttler), Breitner, Kraus (Niedermayer), Dürnberger - Rummenigge, Hoeness. Tr: Csernai

Top scorers: Hoeness, Bayern München 7
Geurts, Anderlrcht 7

UEFA CUP

FIRST ROUND

Haka Valkeakoski 2-3 0-4 **IFK Göteborg**
SK Sturm Graz 1-0 1-2 CSKA Moskva
Adanaspor 1-3 1-4 **Internazionale**
Dinamo Bucuresti 3-0 1-2 Levski-Spartak
Hajduk Split 3-1 2-2 VfB Stuttgart
SK Beveren 3-0 5-0 Linfield
Boavista FC 4-1 1-3 Atlético Madrid
Bohemians Praha 0-1 0-1 **Valencia**
Tatabánya Bányász 2-1 0-1 **Real Madrid**
Dinamo Tiranë 1-0 0-4 **Carl Zeiss Jena**
PSV Eindhoven 7-0 1-2 Naestved IF
SK Rapid Wien 2-2 2-0 Videoton SC
FC Nantes 1-1 2-4 **KSC Lokeren**
Aris Salonica 4-0 4-2 Sliema Wanderers
Spartak Moskva 3-1 3-1 Club Brugge
1.FC Kaiserslautern 1-0 2-1 Akademic Sofia
Napoli 2-2 0-0 **Radnicki Nis**
Grasshopper-Club 1-0 3-1 West Bromwich Albion
Zenit Leningrad 1-2 1-4 **Dynamo Dresden**
Feyenoord 2-0 1-1 Szombierki Bytom
Byrne IL Stavanger 0-2 2-1 **SV Winterslag**
Panathinaikos 0-2 0-1 **Arsenal**
1.FC Magdeburg 3-1 0-2 **B. Mönchengladbach**
AS Monaco 2-5 2-1 **Dundee United**
Neuchâtel Xamax 4-0 2-3 Sparta Praha
Malmö FF 2-0 3-1 Wisla Kraków
Limerick United 0-3 1-1 **Southampton**
Sporting CP 4-0 7-0 Red Boys
Ipswich Town 1-1 1-3 **Aberdeen**
Apoel Nicosia 1-1 0-4 **FC Arges Pitesti**
Víkingur Reykjavík 0-4 0-4 **Girondins Bordeaux**
Hamburger SV 0-1 6-3 FC Utrecht

SECOND ROUND

SK Sturm Graz 2-2 2-3 **IFK Göteborg**
Internazionale 1-1 2-3 **Dinamo Bucuresti**
SK Beveren 2-3 2-1 **Hajduk Split**
Valencia 2-0 0-1 Boavista FC
Real Madrid 3-2 0-0 Carl Zeiss Jena
SK Rapid Wien 1-0 1-2 PSV Eindhoven
Aris Salonica 1-1 0-4 **KSC Lokeren**
Spartak Moskva 2-1 0-4 **1.FC Kaiserslautern**
Grasshopper-Club 2-0 0-2 0-3p **Radnicki Nis**
Feyenoord 2-1 1-1 Dynamo Dresden
SV Winterslag 1-0 1-2 Arsenal
Borussia Mönchengladbach 2-0 0-5 **Dundee United**
Malmö FF 0-1 0-1 **Neuchâtel Xamax**
Southampton 2-4 0-0 **Sporting CP**
Aberdeen 3-0 2-2 FC Arges Pitesti
Girondins Bordeaux 2-1 0-2 **Hamburger SV**

THIRD ROUND

IFK Göteborg 3-1 1-0 Dinamo Bucuresti
Valencia 5-1 1-4 Hajduk Split
SK Rapid Wien 0-1 0-0 **Real Madrid**
KSC Lokeren 1-0 1-4 **1.FC Kaiserslautern**
Radnicki Nis 2-0 0-1 Feyenoord
SV Winterslag 0-0 0-5 **Dundee United**
Sporting CP 0-0 0-1 **Neuchâtel Xamax**
Aberdeen 3-2 1-3 **Hamburger SV**

QUARTER-FINALS

Valencia 2-2 0-2 **IFK Göteborg**
Real Madrid 3-1 0-5 **1.FC Kaiserslautern**
Dundee United 2-0 0-3 **Radnicki Nis**
Hamburger SV 3-2 0-0 Neuchâtel Xamax

SEMI-FINALS

1.FC Kaiserslautern 1-1 1-2 **IFK Göteborg**
Radnicki Nis 2-1 1-5 **Hamburger SV**

FINAL

1st leg. Nya Ullevi, Gothenburg, 5-05-1982, 42,000. Referee: Carpenter, Ireland

IFK GÖTEBORG 1 (Tord Holmgren 87)
HAMBURGER SV 0

IFK Göteborg - Wernersson - Svensson, Hysen, Karlsson.C, Fredriksson - Tord Holmgren, Karlsson.J, Stromberg - Corneliusson, Nilsson (Sandberg), Tommy Holmgren (Schiller)

Hamburg - Stein - Kaltz, Jakobs, Hieronymus, Groh - Hartwig, Wehmeyer, Magath - Von Heesen (Memering), Bastrup, Hrubesch

2nd leg. Volksparkstadion, Hamburg, 19-05-1982, 60,000. Referee: Courtney, England
HAMBURGER SV 0
IFK GÖTEBORG 3 (Corneliusson 26, Nilsson 61, Fredriksson 63)
Hamburg - Stein - Kaltz (Hidien), Hieronymus, Groh, Wehmeyer - Hartwig, Memering, Magath, Von Heesen - Hrubesch, Bastrup
IFK Göteborg - Wernersson - Svensson, Hysen (Schiller), Karlsson.C, Fredriksson - Tord Holmgren, Stromberg, Karlsson.J - Corneliusson (Sandberg), Nilsson, Tommy Holmgren

Top scorer: Nilsson, IFK Göteborg.....9

CUP WINNERS CUP

PRELIMINARY ROUND

Politechnica Timisoara.....2-0 0-5.....**Lokomotive Leipzig**

FIRST ROUND

Barcelona.....4-1 0-1.....Trakia Plovdiv
Dukla Praha.....3-0 1-2.....Glasgow Rangers
Jeunesse Esch.....1-1 1-6.....**Velez Mostar**
Swansea City.....0-1 1-2.....**Lokomotive Leipzig**
Eintracht Frankfurt.....2-0 0-2 5-4p.....PAOK Salonica
SKA Rostov-na-Donu.....3-0 2-0.....MKE Ankaragücü
Fram Reykjavík.....2-1 0-4.....**Dundalk**
Ajax.....1-3 0-3.....**Tottenham Hotspur**
Dynamo Tbilisi.....2-0 2-2.....Grazer AK
KTP Kotka.....0-0 0-5.....**SEC Bastia**
Lausanne-Sports.....2-1 2-3.....Kalmar FF
Vålerengens Oslo.....2-2 1-4.....**Legia Warszawa**
Vejle BK.....2-1 0-3.....**FC Porto**
Ballymena United.....0-2 0-4.....**Roma**
Union Paralimni.....1-0 0-8.....**Vasas Budapest**
Floriana.....1-3 0-9.....**Standard CL**

SECOND ROUND

Dukla Praha.....1-0 0-4.....**Barcelona**
Lokomotive Leipzig.....1-1 1-1 3-0p.....Velez Mostar
SKA Rostov-na-Donu.....1-0 0-2.....**Eintracht Frankfurt**
Dundalk.....1-1 0-1.....**Tottenham Hotspur**
SEC Bastia.....1-1 1-3.....**Dynamo Tbilisi**
Legia Warszawa.....2-1 1-1.....Lausanne-Sports
FC Porto.....2-0 0-0.....Roma
Vasas Budapest.....0-2 1-2.....**Standard CL**

QUARTER-FINALS

Lokomotive Leipzig.....0-3 2-1.....**Barcelona**
Tottenham Hotspur.....2-0 1-2.....Eintracht Frankfurt
Legia Warszawa.....0-1 0-1.....**Dynamo Tbilisi**
Standard CL.....2-0 2-2.....FC Porto

SEMI-FINALS

Tottenham Hotspur.....1-1 0-1.....**Barcelona**
Dynamo Tbilisi.....0-1 0-1.....**Standard CL**

FINAL

Nou Camp, Barcelona, 12-05-1982, 100,000. Referee: Eschweiler, West Germany
BARCELONA 2 (Simonsen 44, Quini 63)
STANDARD CL 1 (Vandermissen 7)
Barcelona - Urruti - Gerardo, Migueli, Alesanco, Manolo - Sanchez, Moratalla, Esteban - Simonsen, Quini, Carrasco
Standard - Preud'homme - Gerets, Poel, Meeuws, Plessers - Vandermissen, Daerden, Haan, Botteron - Tahamata, Wendt

Top scorers: Shengelia, Dynamo Tbilisi.....6
Voordeckers, Standard CL.....6

EUROPEAN SUPERCUP 1982

1st leg. Nou Camp, Barcelona, 19-01-1983. Referee: Galler, Switzerland
BARCELONA 1 (Marcos 52)
ASTON VILLA 0
2nd leg. Villa Park, Birmingham, 26-01-1983. Referee: Ponnet, Belgium
ASTON VILLA 3 (Shaw 80, Cowans 99, McNaught 104)
BARCELONA 0

1982–83

EUROPEAN CUP

PRELIMINARY ROUND

Dinamo Bucuresti.....3-1 1-2.....Vålerengens Oslo

FIRST ROUND

Dynamo Berlin.....1-1 0-2.....**Hamburger SV**
Olympiakos.....2-0 0-1.....Östers IF Växjö
17 Nëntori Tiranë.....1-0 1-2.....Linfield
Grasshopper-Club.....0-1 0-3.....**Dynamo Kiev**
Dinamo Zagreb.....1-0 0-3.....**Sporting CP**
AS Monaco.....0-0 0-2.....**CSKA Sofia**
Glasgow Celtic.....2-2 2-1.....Ajax
Víkingur Reykjavík.....0-1 2-3.....**Real Sociedad**
Hibernians Paola.....1-4 1-3.....**Widzew Lódz**
Avenir Beggen.....0-5 0-8.....**SK Rapid Wien**
Omonia Nicosia.....2-0 0-3.....**HJK Helsinki**
Dundalk.....1-4 0-1.....**Liverpool**
Aston Villa.....3-1 0-0.....Besiktas
Dinamo Bucuresti.....2-0 1-2.....Dukla Praha
Standard CL.....5-0 0-3.....Rába ETO Györ
Hvidovre BK.....1-4 3-3.....**Juventus**

SECOND ROUND

Hamburger SV.....1-0 4-0.....Olympiakos
Dynamo Kiev.....W-O.....17 Nëntori Tiranë
CSKA Sofia.....2-2 0-0.....**Sporting CP**
Real Sociedad.....2-0 1-2.....Glasgow Celtic
SK Rapid Wien.....2-1 3-5.....**Widzew Lódz**
HJK Helsinki.....1-0 0-5.....**Liverpool**
Dinamo Bucuresti.....0-2 2-4.....**Aston Villa**
Standard CL.....1-1 0-2.....**Juventus**

QUARTER-FINALS

Dynamo Kiev.....0-3 2-1.....**Hamburger SV**
Sporting CP.....1-0 0-2.....**Real Sociedad**
Widzew Lódz.....2-0 2-3.....Liverpool
Aston Villa.....1-2 1-3.....**Juventus**

SEMI-FINALS

Real Sociedad.....1-1 1-2.....**Hamburger SV**
Juventus.....2-0 2-2.....Widzew Lódz

FINAL

Olympiako Stadio, Athens, 25-05-1983, 75,000. Referee: Rainea, Romania
HAMBURGER SV 1 (Magath 7)
JUVENTUS 0
Hamburg - Stein - Kaltz, Hieronymous, Jakobs, Wehmeyer - Groh, Rolff, Magath, Milewski - Bastrup (Von Heesen), Hrubesch. Tr: Happel
Juventus - Zoff - Gentile, Brio, Scirea, Cabrini - Bonini, Tardelli, Bettega - Platini, Rossi (Marocchino), Boniek. Tr: Trapattoni

Top scorer: Rossi, Juventus.....6

UEFA CUP

FIRST ROUND

RSC Anderlecht 3-0 3-1 Koparit Kuopio
FC Utrecht 0-1 0-2 **FC Porto**
Grazer AK 1-1 0-3 **Corvinul Hunedoara**
Slavia Sofia 2-2 2-4 **FK Sarajevo**
Spartak Moskva 3-2 5-2 Arsenal
Haarlem 2-1 3-3 AA Gent
Glentoran 1-3 0-1 **Baník Ostrava**
Manchester United 0-0 1-2 **Valencia**
Dundee United 1-1 2-0 PSV Eindhoven
Viking Stavanger 1-0 2-3 Lokomotive Leipzig
Lyngby BK 1-2 2-2 **IK Brage Borlange**
Vorwärts Frankfurt 1-3 2-0 **Werder Bremen**
Progres Niedercorn 0-1 0-3 **Servette FC**
Slask Wroclaw 2-2 1-0 Dynamo Moskva
AS Saint-Étienne 4-1 0-0 Tatabánya Bányász
Bohemians Praha 5-0 2-1 Admira-Wacker
Universitatea Craiova 3-1 0-1 Fiorentina
Fram Reykjavík 0-3 0-4 **Shamrock Rovers**
Zurrieq 1-4 0-4 **Hajduk Split**
Carl Zeiss Jena 3-1 0-5 **Girondins Bordeaux**
Sevilla 3-1 3-0 Levski-Spartak
PAOK Salonica 1-0 1-2 FC Sochaux
Dynamo Tbilisi 2-1 0-1 **Napoli**
1.FC Kaiserslautern 3-0 3-0 Trabzonspor
Roma 3-0 1-3 Ipswich Town
Southampton 2-2 0-0 **IFK Norrköping**
Borussia Dortmund 0-0 0-2 **Glasgow Rangers**
AEK Athens 0-1 0-5 **1.FC Köln**
Pezoporikos 2-2 0-1 **FC Zürich**
Ferencváros 2-1 1-1 Athletic Bilbao
Stal Mielec 1-1 0-0 **KSC Lokeren**
Benfica 2-1 2-1 Real Betis

SECOND ROUND

RSC Anderlecht 4-0 2-3 FC Porto
Corvinul Hunedoara 4-4 0-4 **FK Sarajevo**
Spartak Moskva 2-0 3-1 Haarlem
Valencia 1-0 0-0 Baník Ostrava
Viking FK Stavanger 1-3 0-0 **Dundee United**
Werder Bremen 2-0 6-2 IK Brage Borlange
Slask Wroclaw 0-2 1-5 **Servette FC**
AS Saint-Étienne 0-0 0-4 **Bohemians Praha**
Shamrock Rovers 0-2 0-3 **Universitatea Craiova**
Hajduk Split 4-1 0-4 **Girondins Bordeaux**
PAOK Salonica 2-0 0-4 **Sevilla**
Napoli 1-2 0-2 **1.FC Kaiserslautern**
Roma 1-0 0-1 4-2p IFK Norrkoping
Glasgow Rangers 2-1 0-5 **1.FC Köln**
Ferencváros 1-1 0-1 **FC Zürich**
Benfica 2-0 2-1 KSC Lokeren

THIRD ROUND

RSC Anderlecht 6-1 0-1 FK Sarajevo
Spartak Moskva 0-0 0-2 **Valencia**
Dundee United 2-1 1-1 Werder Bremen
Servette FC 2-2 1-2 **Bohemians Praha**
Girondins Bordeaux 1-2 0-2 **Universitatea Craiova**
Sevilla 1-0 0-4 **1.FC Kaiserslautern**
1.FC Köln 1-0 0-2 **Roma**
FC Zürich 1-1 0-4 **Benfica**

QUARTER-FINALS

Valencia 1-2 1-3 **RSC Anderlecht**
Bohemians Praha 1-0 0-0 Dundee United
1.FC Kaiserslautern 3-2 0-1 **Universitatea Craiova**
Roma 1-2 1-1 **Benfica**

SEMI-FINALS

Bohemians Praha 0-1 1-3 **RSC Anderlecht**
Benfica 0-0 1-1 Universitatea Craiova

FINAL

1st leg. Heysel, Brussels, 4-05-1983, 55,000. Referee: Dotschev, Bulgaria

RSC ANDERLECHT 1 (Brylle 29)
BENFICA 0

Anderlecht - Munaron - Hofkens, Peruzovic, Olsen, De Groote - Frimann, Coeck, Vercauteren, Lozano - Vandenbergh (Czerniatynski), Brylle

Benfica - Bento - Pietra, Alvaro, Humberto Coelho, Jose Luis - Sheu (Bastos Lopes), Frederico, Carlos Manuel, Chalana (Nene) - Diamantino, Filipovic

2nd leg. Estádio da Luz, Lisbon, 18-05-1983, 80,000. Referee: Corver, Holland

BENFICA 1 (Sheu 36)
RSC ANDERLECHT 1 (Lozano 38)

Benfica - Bento - Pietra, Humberto Coelho, Bastos Lopes, Veloso (Alves), Carlos Manuel, Stromberg, Sheu (Filipovic), Chalana - Nene, Diamantino

Anderlecht - Munaron - Peruzovic, De Greef, Broos, Olsen, De Groot Frimann, Lozano, Coeck, Vercauteren - Vandenbergh (Brylle)

Top scorers: Vandenbergh, Anderlecht 7
Giresse, Bordeaux 7

CUP WINNERS CUP

PRELIMINARY ROUND

Aberdeen 7-0 4-1 FC Sion
Swansea City 3-0 0-1 Sporting Braga

FIRST ROUND

Aberdeen 1-0 0-0 Dinamo Tiranë
IBV Vestmannaeyjar 0-1 0-3 **Lech Poznan**
Coleraine 0-3 0-4 **Tottenham Hotspur**
Torpedo Moskva 1-1 0-0 **Bayern München**
Lokomotiv Sofia 1-0 1-5 **Paris Saint-Germain**
Swansea City 12-0 5-0 Sliema Wanderers
Dynamo Dresden 3-2 1-2 **B 93 København**
Waterschei THOR 7-1 1-0 Red Boys
FK Austria 2-0 1-2 Panathinaikos
Galatasaray 2-1 1-1 Kuusysi Lahti
Lillestrøm SK 0-4 0-3 **Crvena Zvezda Beograd**
Barcelona 8-0 1-1 Apollon Limassol
Internazionale 2-0 1-2 Slovan Bratislava
Limerick United 1-1 0-1 **AZ 67 Alkmaar**
IFK Göteborg 1-1 1-3 **Ujpesti Dózsa**
FC Baia Mare 0-0 2-5 **Real Madrid**

SECOND ROUND

Aberdeen 2-0 1-0 Lech Poznan
Tottenham Hotspur 1-1 1-4 **Bayern München**
Swansea City 0-1 0-2 **Paris Saint-Germain**
B 93 København 0-2 1-4 **Waterschei THOR**
Galatasaray 2-4 1-0 **FK Austria**
Crvena Zvezda Beograd 2-4 1-2 **Barcelona**
AZ 67 Alkmaar 1-0 0-2 **Internazionale**
Real Madrid 3-1 1-0 Ujpesti Dózsa

QUARTER-FINALS

Bayern München 0-0 2-3 **Aberdeen**
Paris Saint-Germain 2-0 0-3 **Waterschei THOR**
FK Austria 0-0 1-1 Barcelona
Internazionale 1-1 1-2 **Real Madrid**

SEMI-FINALS

Aberdeen 5-1 0-1 Waterschei THOR
FK Austria 2-2 1-3 **Real Madrid**

FINAL

Nya Ullevi, Gothenburg, 11-05-1983, 17,000. Referee: Menegali, Italy

ABERDEEN 2 (Black 4, Hewitt 112)
REAL MADRID 1 (Juanito 15)

Aberdeen - Leighton - Rougvie, McLeish, Miller, McMaster - Cooper, Strachan, Simpson - McGhee, Black (Hewitt), Weir

Real Madrid - Agustin - Juan Jose, Metgod, Bonet, Camacho (San Jose) Angel, Gallego, Stielike, Isidro (Salguero) - Juanito, Santillana

Top scorer: Santillana, Real Madrid 8

EUROPEAN SUPERCUP 1983

1st leg. Volksparkstadion, Hamburg, 22-11-1983. Referee: Christov, Czechoslovakia

HAMBURGER SV 0
ABERDEEN 0

2nd leg. Pittodrie, Aberdeen, 20-12-1983. Referee: Brunmeier, Austria

ABERDEEN 2 (Simpson 47, McGhee 65)
HAMBURGER SV 0

1983-84

EUROPEAN CUP

FIRST ROUND

OB Odense 0-1 0-5 **Liverpool**
Lech Poznan 2-0 0-4 **Athletic Bilbao**
Ajax 0-0 0-2 **Olympiakos**
Benfica 3-0 3-2 Linfield
Dynamo Minsk 1-0 2-2 Grasshopper-Club
Rába ETO Györ 2-1 2-0 Víkingur Reykjavík
Hamburger SV W-O Vllaznia Shkodër
Kuusysi Lahti 0-1 0-3 **Dinamo Bucuresti**
Hamrun Spartans 0-3 0-3 **Dundee United**
Athlone Town 2-3 2-8 **Standard CL**
Fenerbahçe 0-1 0-4 **Bohemians Praha**
SK Rapid Wien 3-0 1-3 FC Nantes
Dynamo Berlin 4-1 2-0 Jeunesse Esch
Partizan Beograd 5-1 0-0 Viking Stavanger
CSKA Sofia 3-0 1-4 Omonia Nicosia
Roma 3-0 1-2 IFK Göteborg

SECOND ROUND

Liverpool 0-0 1-0 Athletic Bilbao
Olympiakos 1-0 0-3 **Benfica**
Rába ETO Györ 3-6 1-3 **Dynamo Minsk**
Dinamo Bucuresti 3-0 2-3 Hamburger SV
Standard CL 0-0 0-4 **Dundee United**
Bohemians Praha 2-1 0-1 **SK Rapid Wien**
Dynamo Berlin 2-0 0-1 Partizan Beograd
CSKA Sofia 0-1 0-1 **Roma**

QUARTER-FINALS

Liverpool 1-0 4-1 Benfica
Dynamo Minsk 1-1 0-1 **Dinamo Bucuresti**
SK Rapid Wien 2-1 0-1 **Dundee United**
Roma 3-0 1-2 Dynamo Berlin

SEMI-FINALS

Liverpool 1-0 2-1 Dinamo Bucuresti
Dundee United 2-0 0-3 **Roma**

FINAL

Stadio Olimpico, Rome, 30-05-1984, 69,000. Referee: Fredriksson, Sweden

LIVERPOOL 1 (Neal 13)
ROMA 1 (Pruzzo 42)
Liverpool won 4-2 on penalties

Liverpool		**Roma**	
Nicol	x	Di Bartolomei	1
Neal	1	Conti	x
Souness	1	Righetti	1
Rush	1	Graziani	x
Kennedy.A	1		

Liverpool - Grobbelaar - Neal, Lawrenson, Hansen, Kennedy.A - Johnston (Nicol), Lee, Souness, Whelan - Dalglish (Robinson), Rush. Tr: Fagan

Roma - Tancredi - Nappi, Bonetti, Righetti, Nela - Di Bartolomei, Falcao, Cerezo (Strukelj) - Conti, Pruzzo (Chierico), Graziani. Tr: Liedholm

Top scorer: Sokol, Dynamo Minsk 6

UEFA CUP

FIRST ROUND

Drogheda United 0-6 0-8 **Tottenham Hotspur**
St. Mirren 0-1 0-2 **Feyenoord**
Lokomotiv Plovdiv 1-2 1-3 **PAOK Salonica**
Anorthosis Famagusta 0-1 0-10 **Bayern München**
Trabzonspor 1-0 0-2 **Internazionale**
Atlético Madrid 2-1 0-3 **FC Groningen**
Dynamo Kiev 0-0 0-1 **Stade Laval**
Aris Bonnevoie 0-5 0-10 **FK Austria**
Sparta Praha 3-2 1-1 Real Madrid
Widzew Lódz 0-0 2-2 IF Elfsborg Borås
VfB Stuttgart 1-1 0-1 **Levski-Spartak**
1.FC Kaiserslautern 3-1 0-3 **Watford**
Radnicki Nis 3-0 2-1 FC St. Gallen
Rabat Ajax 0-10 0-6 **TJ Internacional**
Larissa 2-0 0-3 **Honvéd**
Universitatea Craiova 1-0 0-1 1-3p **Hajduk Split**
Nottingham Forest 2-0 1-0 Vorwärts Frankfurt
PSV Eindhoven 4-2 2-0 Ferencváros
Sevilla 1-1 2-3 **Sporting CP**
Glasgow Celtic 1-0 4-1 ÅGF Århus
Girondins Bordeaux 2-3 0-4 **Lokomotive Leipzig**
Werder Bremen 1-1 2-1 Malmö FF
Hellas-Verona 1-0 3-2 Crvena Zvezda Beograd
Sportul Studentesc 1-2 0-0 **SK Sturm Graz**
Spartak Moskva 2-0 5-0 HJK Helsinki
Vitoria Guimaraes 1-0 0-5 **Aston Villa**
IBV Vestmannaeyjar 0-0 0-3 **Carl Zeiss Jena**
Sparta Rotterdam 4-0 1-1 Coleraine
AA Gent 1-1 1-2 **RC Lens**
FC Zürich 1-4 2-4 **Royal Antwerp FC**
Baník Ostrava 5-0 1-1 B 1903 København
Byrne IL Stavanger 0-3 1-1 **RSC Anderlecht**

SECOND ROUND

Tottenham Hotspur 4-2 2-0 Feyenoord
PAOK Salonica 0-0 0-0 8-9p **Bayern München**
FC Groningen 2-0 1-5 **Internazionale**
FK Austria 2-0 3-3 Stade Laval
Widzew Lódz 1-0 0-3 **Sparta Praha**
Watford 1-1 3-1 Levski-Spartak
Radnicki Nis 4-0 2-3 TJ Internacional
Honvéd 3-2 0-3 **Hajduk Split**
PSV Eindhoven 1-2 0-1 **Nottingham Forest**
Sporting CP 2-0 0-5 **Glasgow Celtic**
Lokomotive Leipzig 1-0 1-1 Werder Bremen

Hellas-Verona 2-2 0-0 **SK Sturm Graz**
Spartak Moskva 2-2 2-1 Aston Villa
Sparta Rotterdam 3-2 1-1 Carl Zeiss Jena
RC Lens 2-2 3-2 Royal Antwerp FC
RSC Anderlecht 2-0 2-2 Baník Ostrava

THIRD ROUND
Bayern München 1-0 0-2 **Tottenham Hotspur**
FK Austria 2-1 1-1 Internazionale
Watford 2-3 0-4 **Sparta Praha**
Radnicki Nis 0-2 0-2 **Hajduk Split**
Nottingham Forest 0-0 2-1 Glasgow Celtic
SK Sturm Graz 2-0 0-1 Lokomotive Leipzig
Sparta Rotterdam 1-1 0-2 **Spartak Moskva**
RC Lens 1-1 0-1 **RSC Anderlecht**

QUARTER-FINALS
Tottenham Hotspur 2-0 2-2 FK Austria
Sparta Praha 1-0 0-2 **Hajduk Split**
Nottingham Forest 1-0 1-1 SK Sturm Graz
RSC Anderlecht 4-2 0-1 Spartak Moskva

SEMI-FINALS
Hajduk Split 2-1 0-1 **Tottenham Hotspur**
Nottingham Forest 2-0 0-3 **RSC Anderlecht**

FINAL
1st leg. Parc Astrid, Brussels, 9-05-1984, 35,000. Referee: Galler, Switzerland
RSC ANDERLECHT 1 (Olsen 85)
TOTTENHAM HOTSPUR 1 (Miller 57)
Anderlecht - Munaron - Grun, De Greef, Olsen, De Groot - Hofkens, Vandereycken, Scifo, Brylle - Vandenbergh (Arnesen), Czerniatynski (Vercauteren)
Tottenham - Parks - Thomas, Roberts, Hughton, Perryman - Miller, Stevens (Mabbutt), Hazard, Galvin - Archibald, Falco

2nd leg. White Hart Lane, London, 23-05-1984, 46,000. Referee: Roth, West Germany
TOTTENHAM HOTSPUR 1 (Roberts 84)
RSC ANDERLECHT 1 (Czerniatynski 60)
Tottenham - Parks - Thomas, Hughton, Roberts, Miller (Ardiles) - Mabbutt (Dick), Hazard, Stevens, Galvin - Archibald, Falco
Anderlecht - Munaron - Hofkens, Grun, De Greef, Olsen, De Groot - Arnesen (Gudjohnsen), Vercauteren, Scifo - Czerniatynski (Brylle), Vandereycken
Tottenham won 4-3 on penalties

Tottenham		**Anderlecht**	
Roberts	1	Olsen	x
Falco	1	Grun	1
Stevens	1	Scifo	1
Archibald	1	Vercauteren	1
Thomas	x	Gudjohnsen	x

Top scorer: Nyilasi, FK Austria 9

CUP WINNERS CUP

PRELIMINARY ROUND
Swansea City 1-1 0-1 **1.FC Magdeburg**

FIRST ROUND
Juventus 7-0 3-2 Lechia Gdansk
Glentoran 1-2 1-2 **Paris Saint-Germain**
Hammarby IF 4-0 1-2 17 Nëntori Tiranë
Sligo Rovers 0-1 0-3 **Haka Valkeakoski**
1.FC Magdeburg 1-5 0-2 **Barcelona**
NEC Nijmegen 1-1 1-0 SK Brann Bergen
Mersin Idman Yurdu 0-0 0-1 **Spartak Varna**
Manchester United 1-1 2-2 Dukla Praha
IA Akranes 1-2 1-1 **Aberdeen**
Union Paralimni 2-4 1-3 **SK Beveren**
Wacker Innsbruck 1-0 1-7 **1.FC Köln**
AEK Athens 2-0 1-4 **Ujpesti Dózsa**
B 1901 Nykobing 1-5 2-4 **Shachter Donetsk**
Servette FC 4-0 5-1 Avenir Beggen
Valletta 0-8 0-10 **Glasgow Rangers**
Dinamo Zagreb 2-1 0-1 **FC Porto**

SECOND ROUND
Paris Saint-Germain 2-2 0-0 **Juventus**
Hammarby IF 1-1 1-2 **Haka Valkeakoski**
NEC Nijmegen 2-3 0-2 **Barcelona**
Spartak Varna 1-2 0-2 **Manchester United**
SK Beveren 0-0 1-4 **Aberdeen**
Ujpesti Dózsa 3-1 2-4 1.FC Köln
Shachter Donetsk 1-0 2-1 Servette FC
Glasgow Rangers 2-1 0-1 **FC Porto**

QUARTER-FINALS
Haka Valkeakoski 0-1 0-1 **Juventus**
Barcelona 2-0 0-3 **Manchester United**
Ujpesti Dózsa 2-0 0-3 **Aberdeen**
FC Porto 3-2 1-1 Shachter Donetsk

SEMI-FINALS
Manchester United 1-1 1-2 **Juventus**
FC Porto 1-0 1-0 Aberdeen

FINAL
St. Jakobs, Basle, 16-05-1984, 60,000. Referee: Prokop, East Germany
JUVENTUS 2 (Vignola 12, Boniek 41)
FC PORTO 1 (Sousa 29)
Juventus - Tacconi - Gentile, Brio, Scirea, Cabrini - Tardelli, Bonini, Vignola (Caricola), Platini - Rossi, Boniek
Porto - Ze Beto - Joao Pinto, Lima Pereira, Enrico, Eduardo Luis (Costa), Magalhaes (Walsh), Frasco, Pacheco, Sousa - Gomes, Vermelinho

Top scorer: McGhee, Aberdeen 5

EUROPEAN SUPERCUP 1984

Comunale, Turin, 16-01-1985. Referee: Pauly, West Germany
JUVENTUS 2 (Boniek 39 79)
LIVERPOOL 0

1984–85

EUROPEAN CUP

FIRST ROUND
Ilves Tampere 0-4 1-2 **Juventus**
Grasshopper-Club 3-1 1-2 Honvéd
Labinoti Elbasan 0-3 0-3 **Lyngby BK**
Vålerengens Oslo 3-3 0-2 **Sparta Praha**
Trabzonspor 1-0 0-3 **Dnepr Dnepropetrovsk**
Levski-Spartak 1-1 2-2 VfB Stuttgart
Dinamo Bucuresti 4-1 1-2 Omonia Nicosia
Girondins Bordeaux 3-2 0-0 Athletic Bilbao
Feyenoord 0-0 1-2 **Panathinaikos**
Linfield 0-0 1-1 Shamrock Rovers
IA Akranes 2-2 0-5 **SK Beveren**
Avenir Beggen 0-8 0-9 **IFK Göteborg**
FK Austria 4-0 4-0 Valletta
Aberdeen 2-1 1-2 4-5p **Dynamo Berlin**
Crvena Zvezda Beograd 3-2 0-2 **Benfica**
Lech Poznan 0-1 0-4 **Liverpool**

SECOND ROUND

Juventus	2-0 4-2	Grasshopper-Club
Sparta Praha	0-0 2-1	Lyngby BK
Levski-Sofia	3-1 0-2	**Dnepr Dnepropetrovsk**
Girondins Bordeaux	1-0 1-1	Dinamo Bucuresti
Panathinaikos	2-1 3-3	Linfield
IFK Göteborg	1-0 1-2	SK Beveren
Dynamo Berlin	3-3 1-2	**FK Austria**
Liverpool	3-1 0-1	Benfica

QUARTER-FINALS

Juventus	3-0 0-1	Sparta Praha
Girondins Bordeaux	1-1 1-1 5-3p	Dnepr Dnepropetrovsk
IFK Göteborg	0-1 2-2	**Panathinaikos**
FK Austria	1-1 1-4	**Liverpool**

SEMI-FINALS

Juventus	3-0 0-2	Girondins Bordeaux
Liverpool	4-0 1-0	Panathinaikos

FINAL

Heysel, Brussels, 29-05-1985, 58,000. Referee: Daina, Switzerland

JUVENTUS 1 (Platini 56)
LIVERPOOL 0

Juventus - Tacconi - Favero, Cabrini, Brio, Scirea - Bonini, Platini, Tardelli - Briaschi (Prandelli), Rossi (Vignola), Boniek. Tr: Trapattoni
Liverpool - Grobbelaar - Neal, Beglin, Lawrenson (Gillespie), Hansen Nicol, Dalglish, Whelan, Wark - Rush, Walsh (Johnston). Tr: Fagan

Top scorers: Platini, Juventus 7
Nilsson, IFK Göteborg 7

UEFA CUP

FIRST ROUND

Real Madrid	5-0 0-2	Wacker Innsbruck
Real Valladolid	1-0 1-4	**NK Rijeka**
Fenerbahçe	0-1 0-2	**Fiorentina**
RSC Anderlecht	1-0 1-2	**Werder Bremen**
Bohemians Praha	6-1 2-2	Apollon Limassol
Red Boys	0-0 0-14	**Ajax**
Nottingham Forest	0-0 0-1	**Club Brugge**
Sporting Braga	0-3 0-6	**Tottenham Hotspur**
1.FC Köln	2-1 1-0	Pogon Szczecin
Glentoran	1-1 0-2	**Standard CL**
Lokomotive Leipzig	7-0 0-3	Lillestrøm SK
OB Odense	1-5 1-2	**Spartak Moskva**
Southampton	0-0 0-2	**Hamburger SV**
AS Monaco	2-2 1-2	**CSKA Sofia**
Bohemians Dublin	3-2 0-2	**Glasgow Rangers**
Sportul Studentesc	1-0 0-2	**Internazionale**
Sliven	1-0 1-5	**Zeljeznicar Sarajevo**
FC Sion	1-0 3-2	Atlético Madrid
Olympiakos	1-0 2-2	Neuchâtel Xamax
Real Betis	1-0 0-1 3-5p	**Universitatea Craiova**
Widzew Lódz	2-0 0-1	ÅGF Århus
Dukla Banska Bystrica	2-3 1-4	**B. Mönchengladbach**
Sporting CP	2-0 2-2	AJ Auxerre
Dynamo Minsk	4-0 6-0	HJK Helsinki
Manchester United	3-0 2-2	Rába ETO Györ
Vorwärts Frankfurt	2-0 0-3	**PSV Eindhoven**
Östers IF Växjö	0-1 0-1	**Linzer ASK**
AIK Stockholm	1-0 0-3	**Dundee United**
Rabat Ajax	0-2 0-2	**Partizan Beograd**
KR Reykjavík	0-3 0-4	**Queens Park Rangers**
Paris Saint-Germain	4-0 2-2	Heart of Midlothian
Videoton SC	1-0 0-0	Dukla Praha

SECOND ROUND

NK Rijeka	3-1 0-3	**Real Madrid**
Fiorentina	1-1 2-6	**RSC Anderlecht**
Ajax	1-0 0-1 2-4p	**Bohemians Praha**
Club Brugge	2-1 0-3	**Tottenham Hotspur**
Standard CL	0-2 1-2	**1.FC Köln**
Lokomotive Leipzig	1-1 0-2	**Spartak Moskva**
Hamburger SV	4-0 2-1	CSKA Sofia
Internazionale	3-0 1-3	Glasgow Rangers
Zeljeznicar Sarajevo	2-1 1-1	FC Sion
Universitatea Craiova	1-0 1-0	Olympiakos
Borussia Mönchengladbach	3-2 0-1	**Widzew Lódz**
Sporting CP	2-0 0-2 3-5p	**Dynamo Minsk**
PSV Eindhoven	0-0 0-1	**Manchester United**
Linzer ASK	1-2 1-5	**Dundee United**
Queens Park Rangers	6-2 0-4	**Partizan Beograd**
Paris Saint-Germain	2-4 0-1	**Videoton SC**

THIRD ROUND

RSC Anderlecht	3-0 1-6	**Real Madrid**
Tottenham Hotspur	2-0 1-1	Bohemians Praha
Spartak Moskva	1-0 0-2	**1.FC Köln**
Hamburger SV	2-1 0-1	**Internazionale**
Universitatea Craiova	2-0 0-4	**Zeljeznicar Sarajevo**
Widzew Lódz	0-2 1-0	**Dynamo Minsk**
Manchester United	2-2 3-2	Dundee United
Videoton SC	5-0 0-2	Partizan Beograd

QUARTER-FINALS

Tottenham Hotspur	0-1 0-0	**Real Madrid**
Internazionale	1-0 3-1	1.FC Köln
Zeljeznicar Sarajevo	2-0 1-1	Dynamo Minsk
Manchester United	1-0 0-1 4-5p	**Videoton SC**

SEMI-FINALS

Internazionale	2-0 0-3	**Real Madrid**
Videoton SC	3-1 1-2	Zeljeznicar Sarajevo

FINAL

1st leg. Sóstói, Székesfehérvár, 8-05-1985, 30,000. Referee: Vautrot, France

VIDEOTON SC 0
REAL MADRID 3 (Michel 31, Santillana 77, Valdano 89)

Videoton - Disztl.P - Borsanyi, Disztl.L, Csuhay, Horvath - Palkovics, Vegh, Wittman, Vadasz - Novath (Gyenti), Burcsa
Real Madrid - Miguel Angel - Chendo, Sanchis, Stielike, Camacho - San Jose, Michel, Gallego - Butragueno (Juanito), Santillana (Salguero), Valdano

2nd leg. Bernabeu, Madrid, 22-05-1985, 90,000. Referee: Ponnet, Belgium

REAL MADRID 0
VIDEOTON SC 1 (Majer 86)

Real Madrid - Miguel Angel - Chendo, Sanchis, Stielike, Camacho - San Jose, Michel, Gallego - Butragueno, Santillana, Valdano (Juanito)
Videoton - Disztl.P - Csuhay, Disztl.L, Vegh, Horvath - Burcsa, Csongradi (Wittman), Vadasz - Szabo, Majer, Novath (Palkovics)

Top scorers: Bannister, Queen's Park Rangers 7
Bahtic, Zeljeznicar 7

CUP WINNERS CUP

FIRST ROUND

University College Dublin	0-0 0-1	**Everton**
TJ Internacional	2-1 0-0	Kuusysi Lahti
Wisla Kraków	4-2 3-1	IBV Vestmannaeyjar
B 1903 København	0-0 0-3	**Fortuna Sittard**
Roma	1-0 0-0	Steaua Bucuresti
Wrexham	1-0 3-4	FC Porto

Trakia Plovdiv 4-0 1-1 Union Luxembourg
Bayern München 4-1 2-1 Moss FK
Dynamo Moskva 1-0 5-2 Hajduk Split
Ballymena United 0-1 1-2 **Hamrun Spartans**
Apoel Nicosia 0-3 1-3 **Servette FC**
Siófoki Bányász 1-1 0-2 **Larissa**
Malmö FF 2-0 1-4 **Dynamo Dresden**
FC Metz 2-4 4-1 Barcelona
AA Gent 1-0 0-3 **Glasgow Celtic**
SK Rapid Wien 4-1 1-1 Besiktas

SECOND ROUND

TJ Internacional 0-1 0-3 **Everton**
Fortuna Sittard 2-0 1-2 Wisla Kraków
Roma 2-0 1-0 Wrexham
Bayern München 4-1 0-2 Trakia Plovdiv
Dynamo Moskva 5-0 1-0 Hamrun Spartans
Larissa 2-1 1-0 Servette FC
Dynamo Dresden 3-1 0-0 FC Metz
SK Rapid Wien 3-1 1-0 Glasgow Celtic

QUARTER-FINALS

Everton 3-0 2-0 Fortuna Sittard
Bayern München 2-0 2-1 Roma
Larissa 0-0 0-1 **Dynamo Moskva**
Dynamo Dresden 3-0 0-5 **SK Rapid Wien**

SEMI-FINALS

Bayern München 0-0 1-3 **Everton**
SK Rapid Wien 3-1 1-1 Dynamo Moskva

FINAL

Feyenoord Stadion, Rotterdam, 15-05-1985, 50,000. Referee: Casarin, Italy

EVERTON 3 (Gray 57, Steven 72, Sheedy 85)
SK RAPID WIEN 1 (Krankl 83)

Everton - Southall - Stevens, Van den Hauwe, Ratcliffe, Mountfield - Reid, Steven, Bracewell, Sheedy - Gray, Sharp

Rapid - Konsel - Lainer, Weber, Garger, Brauneder - Hrstic, Kranjcar, Kienast, Weinhofer (Panenka) - Pacult (Gross), Krankl

Top scorers: Gray, Everton 5
Panenka, Rapid Wein 5
Gazaev, Dynamo Moskva 5

1985–86

EUROPEAN CUP

FIRST ROUND

Vejle BK 1-1 1-4 **Steaua Bucuresti**
Honvéd 2-0 3-1 Shamrock Rovers
Zenit Leningrad 2-0 2-0 Vålerengens Oslo
Kuusysi Lahti 2-1 2-1 FK Sarajevo
Górnik Zabrze 1-2 1-4 **Bayern München**
Dynamo Berlin 0-2 1-2 **FK Austria**
Rabat Ajax 0-5 0-5 **Omonia Nicosia**
RSC Anderlecht Bye
IFK Göteborg 3-2 2-1 Trakia Plovdiv
Girondins Bordeaux 2-3 0-0 **Fenerbahçe**
Linfield 2-2 1-2 **Servette FC**
IA Akranes 1-3 1-4 **Aberdeen**
Jeunesse Esch 0-5 1-4 **Juventus**
Hellas-Verona 3-1 2-1 PAOK Salonica
FC Porto 2-0 0-0 Ajax
Sparta Praha 1-2 1-0 **Barcelona**

SECOND ROUND

Honvéd 1-0 1-4 **Steaua Bucuresti**
Zenit Leningrad 2-1 1-3 **Kuusysi Lahti**
Bayern München 4-2 3-3 FK Austria
RSC Anderlecht 1-0 3-1 Omonia Nicosia
IFK Göteborg 4-0 1-2 Fenerbahçe
Servette FC 0-0 0-1 **Aberdeen**
Hellas-Verona 0-0 0-2 **Juventus**
Barcelona 2-0 1-3 FC Porto

QUARTER-FINALS

Steaua Bucuresti 0-0 1-0 Kuusysi Lahti
Bayern München 2-1 0-2 **RSC Anderlecht**
Aberdeen 2-2 0-0 **IFK Göteborg**
Barcelona 1-0 1-1 Juventus

SEMI-FINALS

RSC Anderlecht 1-0 0-3 **Steaua Bucuresti**
IFK Göteborg 3-0 0-3 4-5p **Barcelona**

FINAL

Sánchez Pizjuán, Sevilla, 7-05-1986, 70,000. Referee: Vautrot, France

STEAUA BUCURESTI 0
BARCELONA 0
Steaua won 2-0 on penalties

Steaua		**Barcelona**	
Majaru	x	Alesanco	x
Bolöni	x	Pedraza	x
Lacatus	1	Alonso	x
Balint	1	Marcos	x

Steaua - Ducadam - Iovan, Belodedici, Bumbescu, Barbulescu - Balint, Balan (Iordanescu), Boloni, Majaru - Lacatus, Piturca (Radu). Tr: Jenei

Barcelona - Urruti - Gerardo, Migueli, Alesanco, Julio Alberto - Victor, Marcos, Schuster (Moratalla), Pedraza - Archibald (Pichi Alonso), Carrasco. Tr: Venables

Top scorer: Nilsson, IFK Göteborg 6

UEFA CUP

FIRST ROUND

AEK Athens 1-0 0-5 **Real Madrid**
Chernomorets Odessa 2-1 2-3 Werder Bremen
Sparta Rotterdam 2-0 0-2 4-3p Hamburger SV
B. Mönchengladbach 1-1 2-0 Lech Poznan
Bohemians Dublin 2-5 2-2 **Dundee United**
Dinamo Bucuresti 2-1 0-1 **Vardar Skopje**
Apoel Nicosia 2-2 2-4 **Lokomotiv Sofia**
Neuchâtel Xamax 3-0 4-4 Sportul Studentesc
Valur Reykjavík 2-1 0-3 **FC Nantes**
Portimonense SC 1-0 0-4 **Partizan Beograd**
Boavista FC 4-3 1-3 **Club Brugge**
Spartak Moskva 1-0 3-1 TPS Turku
Legia Warszawa 3-0 1-1 Viking Stavanger
Videoton SC 1-0 2-3 Malmö FF
Linzer ASK 2-0 1-0 Baník Ostrava
Internazionale 5-1 0-0 FC St. Gallen
KSV Waregem 5-2 1-0 ÅGF Åarhus
Glasgow Rangers 1-0 0-2 **Osasuna**
Coleraine 1-1 0-5 **Lokomotive Leipzig**
AJ Auxerre 3-1 0-3 **Milan**
Wismut Aue 1-3 1-2 **Dnepr Dnepropetrovsk**
Avenir Beggen 0-2 0-4 **PSV Eindhoven**
Torino 2-1 1-1 Panathinaikos
Hajduk Split 5-1 2-2 FC Metz
Sporting CP 3-1 1-2 Feyenoord
Dinamo Tiranë 1-0 0-0 Hamrun Spartans
RFC Liège 1-0 3-1 Wacker Innsbruck
Athletic Bilbao 4-1 1-0 Besiktas

Pirin Blagoevgrad 1-3 0-4 **Hammarby IF**
Slavia Praha 1-0 0-3 **St. Mirren**
Rába ETO Györ 3-1 1-4 **Bohemians Praha**
1.FC Köln 0-0 2-1 Sporting Gijón

SECOND ROUND

Real Madrid 2-1 0-0 Chernomorets Odessa
Sparta Rotterdam 1-1 1-5 **B. Mönchengladbach**
Dundee United 2-0 1-1 Vardar Skopje
Lokomotiv Sofia 1-1 0-0 **Neuchâtel Xamax**
Partizan Beograd 1-1 0-4 **FC Nantes**
Spartak Moskva 1-0 3-1 Club Brugge
Videoton 0-1 1-1 **Legia Warszawa**
Linzer ASK 1-0 0-4 **Internazionale**
KSV Waregem 2-0 1-2 Osasuna
Milan 2-0 1-3 Lokomotive Leipzig
PSV Eindhoven 2-2 0-1 **Dnepr Dnepropetrovsk**
Torino 1-1 1-3 **Hajduk Split**
Dinamo Tiranë 0-0 0-1 **Sporting CP**
RFC Liège 0-1 1-3 **Athletic Bilbao**
Hammarby IF 3-3 2-1 St. Mirren
1.FC Köln 4-0 4-2 Bohemians Praha

THIRD ROUND

Borussia Mönchengladbach 5-1 0-4 **Real Madrid**
Dundee United 2-1 1-3 **Neuchâtel Xamax**
Spartak Moskva 0-1 1-1 **FC Nantes**
Internazionale 0-0 1-0 Legia Warszawa
KSV Waregem 1-1 2-1 Milan
Dnepr Dnepropetrovsk 0-1 0-2 **Hajduk Split**
Athletic Bilbao 2-1 0-3 **Sporting CP**
Hammarby 2-1 1-3 **1.FC Köln**

QUARTER-FINALS

Real Madrid 3-0 0-2 Neuchâtel Xamax
Internazionale 3-0 3-3 FC Nantes
Hajduk Split 1-0 0-1 4-5p **KSV Waregem**
Sporting CP 1-1 0-2 **1.FC Köln**

SEMI-FINALS

Internazionale 3-1 1-5 **Real Madrid**
1.FC Köln 4-0 3-3 KSV Waregem

FINAL

1st leg. Bernabeu, Madrid, 30-04-1986, 85,000. Referee: Courtney, England

REAL MADRID 5 (Sanchez 38, Gordillo 42, Valdano 51 84, Santillana 89)
1.FC KÖLN 1 (Allofs 29)

Real Madrid - Agustin - Salguero, Solana, Camacho - Martin Vazquez (Santillana), Michel, Juanito, Gordillo - Butragueno, Sanchez, Valdano

Köln - Schumacher - Geils, Gielchen, Steiner, Prestin - Geilenkirchen, Hönerbach, Bein (Hassler), Janssen - Littbarski (Dickel), Allofs

2nd leg. Olympiastadion, Berlin, 6-05-1986, 15,000. Referee: Valentine, Scotland

1.FC KÖLN 2 (Bein 22, Geilenkirchen 72)
REAL MADRID 0

Köln - Schumacher - Prestin, Gielchen, Geils (Schmitz) - Geilenkirchen, Steiner, Bein, Hönerbach - Janssen (Pisanti), Littbarski, Allofs

Real Madrid - Agustin - Chendo, Maceda, Solana, Camacho - Michel, Gallego, Valdano, Gordillo - Butragueno (Juanito), Sanchez (Santillana)

Top scorer: Allofs, 1.FC Köln 9

CUP WINNERS CUP

FIRST ROUND

FC Utrecht 2-1 1-4 **Dynamo Kiev**
AS Monaco 2-0 0-3 **Universitatea Craiova**
Fram Reykjavík 3-1 0-1 Glentoran
SK Rapid Wien 5-0 1-1 Tatabánya Bányász
Benfica Bye
Larissa 1-1 0-1 **Sampdoria**
AIK Stockholm 8-0 5-0 Red Boys
AEL Limassol 2-2 0-4 **Dukla Praha**
Zurrieq 0-3 0-9 **Bayer Uerdingen**
Galatasaray 1-0 1-2 Widzew Lódz
HJK Helsinki 3-2 2-1 Flamurtari Vlorë
Cercle Brugge 3-2 1-2 **Dynamo Dresden**
Crvena Zvezda Beograd 2-0 2-2 FC Aarau
Lyngby BK 1-0 3-2 Galway United
Fredrikstad FK 1-1 0-0 **Bangor City**
Atlético Madrid 1-1 2-1 Glasgow Celtic

SECOND ROUND

Universitatea Craiova 2-2 0-3 **Dynamo Kiev**
SK Rapid Wien 3-0 1-2 Fram Reykjavík
Benfica 2-0 0-1 Sampdoria
Dukla Praha 1-0 2-2 AIK Stockholm
Bayer Uerdingen 2-0 1-1 Galatasaray
HJK Helsinki 1-0 2-7 **Dynamo Dresden**
Lyngby BK 2-2 1-3 **Crvena Zvezda Beograd**
Bangor City 0-2 0-1 **Atlético Madrid**

QUARTER-FINALS

SK Rapid Wien 1-4 1-5 **Dynamo Kiev**
Dukla Praha 1-0 1-2 Benfica
Dynamo Dresden 2-0 3-7 **Bayer Uerdingen**
Crvena Zvezda Beograd 0-2 1-1 **Atlético Madrid**

SEMI-FINALS

Dynamo Kiev 3-0 1-1 Dukla Praha
Atlético Madrid 1-0 3-2 Bayer Uerdingen

FINAL

Stade de Gerland, Lyon, 2-05-1986, 39,000. Referee: Wöhrer, Austria

DYNAMO KIEV 3 (Zavarov 5, Blokhin 85, Yevtushenko 88)
ATLÉTICO MADRID 0

Dynamo Kiev - Chanov - Baltacha (Bal), Bessanov, Kuznetsov, Demianenko, Rats, Yakovenko, Yaremchuk, Zavarov (Yevtushenko) - Belanov, Blokhin

Atlético - Fillol - Tomas, Arteche, Ruiz, Villaverde - Prieto, Ramos, Marina, Landaburu (Setien) - Cabrera, Da Silva

Top scorers: Yaremchuk, Dynamo Kiev 6
Funkel, Bayer Uerdingen 6

EUROPEAN SUPERCUP 1986

Stade Louis II, Monte Carlo, 24-02-1987. Referee: Agnolin, Italy

STEAUA BUCURESTI 1 (Hagi 44)
DYNAMO KIEV 0

1986–87

EUROPEAN CUP

FIRST ROUND

FC Porto 9-0 1-0 Rabat Ajax
Paris Saint-Germain 2-2 0-1 **TJ Vitkovice**
Örgryte IS 2-3 1-4 **Dynamo Berlin**
Brøndbyernes IF 4-1 2-2 Honvéd
Besiktas 2-0 1-0 Dinamo Tiranë
Apoel Nicosia 1-0 2-3 HJK Helsinki
Shamrock Rovers 0-1 0-2 **Glasgow Celtic**
Beroe Stara Zagora 1-1 0-2 **Dynamo Kiev**

BSC Young Boys 1-0 0-5 **Real Madrid**
Juventus 7-0 4-0 Valur Reykjavík
Rosenborg BK 1-0 1-1 Linfield
Crvena Zvezda Beograd 3-0 1-2 Panathinaikos
RSC Anderlecht 2-0 1-1 Górnik Zabrze
Steaua Bucuresti Bye
Avenir Beggen 0-3 0-3 **FK Austria**
PSV Eindhoven 0-2 0-0 **Bayern München**

SECOND ROUND
TJ Vitkovice 1-0 0-3 **FC Porto**
Brøndbyernes IF 2-1 1-1 Dynamo Berlin
Besiktas W-O Apoel Nicosia
Glasgow Celtic 1-1 1-3 **Dynamo Kiev**
Real Madrid 1-0 0-1 3-1p Juventus
Rosenborg BK 0-3 1-4 **Crvena Zvezda Beograd**
RSC Anderlecht 3-0 0-1 Steaua Bucuresti
Bayern München 2-0 1-1 FK Austria

QUARTER-FINALS
FC Porto 1-0 1-1 Brøndbyernes IF
Besiktas 0-5 0-2 **Dynamo Kiev**
Crvena Zvezda Beograd 4-2 0-2 **Real Madrid**
Bayern München 5-0 2-2 RSC Anderlecht

SEMI-FINALS
FC Porto 2-1 2-1 Dynamo Kiev
Bayern München 4-1 0-1 Real Madrid

FINAL
Prater, Vienna, 27-05-1987, 56,000. Referee: Ponnet, Belgium
FC PORTO 2 (Madjer 77, Juary 79)
BAYERN MÜNCHEN 1 (Kogl 24)
Porto - Mlynaraczyk - Joao Pinto, Eduardo Luis, Celso, Inacio (Frasco), Quim (Juary), Magalhaes, Madjer, Sousa, Andre - Futre. Tr: Jorge
Bayern - Pfaff - Winklhofer, Nachtweih, Eder, Pflügner - Flick (Lunde), Brehme, Matthäus, Rummenigge - Hoeness, Kögl. Tr: Lattek

Top scorer: Cvetkovic, Crvena Zvezda Beograd 7

UEFA CUP

FIRST ROUND
Sigma Olomouc 1-1 0-4 **IFK Göteborg**
Coleraine 1-1 0-1 **Stahl Brandenburg**
Sportul Studentesc 1-0 1-1 Omonia Nicosia
Jeunesse Esch 1-2 1-1 **AA Gent**
Heart of Midlothian 3-2 0-1 **Dukla Praha**
Kalmar FF 1-4 0-3 **Bayer Leverkusen**
Legia Warszawa 0-0 1-0 Dnepr Dnepropetrovsk
Internazionale 2-0 1-0 AEK Athens
FC Nantes 0-4 1-1 **Torino**
Dynamo Minsk 2-4 1-0 **Rába ETO Györ**
Athletic Bilbao 2-0 0-1 1.FC Magdeburg
SK Beveren 1-0 0-0 Vålerengens Oslo
Spartak Moskva 0-0 1-0 FC Luzern
Napoli 1-0 0-1 3-4p **Toulouse FC**
NK Rijeka 0-1 1-1 **Standard CL**
FC Tirol 3-0 0-2 Sredets Sofia
B. Mönchengladbach 1-0 3-1 Partizan Beograd
Pécsi MSC 1-0 0-2 **Feyenoord**
Fiorentina 1-0 0-1 1-3p **Boavista FC**
Glasgow Rangers 4-0 0-2 Ilves Tampere
FC Groningen 5-1 3-1 Galway United
Neuchâtel Xamax 2-0 3-1 Lyngby BK
Atlético Madrid 2-0 1-2 Werder Bremen
Sparta Praha 1-1 1-2 **Vitória Guimaraes**
Flamurtari Vlorë 1-1 0-0 Barcelona
IA Akranes 0-9 0-6 **Sporting CP**
Linzer ASK 1-1 0-1 **Widzew Lódz**
Bayer Uerdingen 3-0 4-0 Carl Zeiss Jena
OFI Crete 1-0 0-4 **Hajduk Split**
Hibernians Paola 0-2 0-8 **Trakia Plovdiv**
Universitatea Craiova 2-0 1-2 Galatasaray
RC Lens 1-0 0-2 **Dundee United**

SECOND ROUND
IFK Göteborg 2-0 1-1 Stahl Brandenburg
Sportul Studentesc 0-3 1-1 **AA Gent**
Dukla Praha 0-0 1-1 Bayer Leverkusen
Legia Warszawa 3-2 0-1 **Internazionale**
Torino 4-0 1-1 Rába ETO Györ
SK Beveren 3-1 1-2 Athletic Bilbao
Toulouse FC 3-1 1-5 **Spartak Moskva**
FC Tirol 2-1 2-3 Standard CL
B. Mönchengladbach 5-1 2-0 Feyenoord
Glasgow Rangers 2-1 1-0 Boavista FC
FC Groningen 0-0 1-1 Neuchâtel Xamax
Vitória SC Guimaraes 2-0 0-1 Atlético Madrid
Barcelona 1-0 1-2 Sporting CP
Widzew Lódz 0-0 0-2 **Bayer Uerdingen**
Hajduk Split 3-1 2-2 Trakia Plovdiv
Dundee United 3-0 0-1 Universitatea Craiova

THIRD ROUND
AA Gent 0-1 0-4 **IFK Göteborg**
Dukla Praha 0-1 0-0 **Internazionale**
Torino 2-1 1-0 SK Beveren
Spartak Moskva 1-0 0-2 **FC Tirol**
Glasgow Rangers 1-1 0-0 **B. Mönchengladbach**
FC Groningen 1-0 0-3 **Vitória SC Guimaraes**
Bayer Uerdingen 0-2 0-2 **Barcelona**
Dundee United 2-0 0-0 Hajduk Split

QUARTER-FINALS
IFK Göteborg 0-0 1-1 Internazionale
Torino 0-0 1-2 **FC Tirol**
B Mönchengladbach 3-0 2-2 Vitória SC Guimaraes
Dundee United 1-0 2-1 Barcelona

SEMI-FINALS
IFK Göteborg 4-1 1-0 FC Tirol
Dundee United 0-0 2-0 Borussia Mönchengladbach

FINAL
1st leg. Nya Ullevi, Gothenburg, 6-05-1987, 50,000. Referee: Kirschen, East Germany
IFK GÖTEBORG 1 (Pettersson 38)
DUNDEE UNITED 0
IFK Göteborg - Wernersson - Carlsson, Hysen, Larsson, Fredriksson, Johansson (Nilsson.R), Tord Holmgren (Zetterlund), Andersson, Tommy Holmgren - Pettersson, Nilsson.L
Dundee United - Thompson - Malpas, Narey, Hegarty (Clark), Holt - McInally, Kirkwood, Bowman, Bannon - Sturrock (Beaumont), Redford

2nd leg. Tannadice Park, Dundee, 20-05-1987, 21,000. Referee: Igna, Romania
DUNDEE UNITED 1 (Clark 60)
IFK GÖTEBORG 1 (Nilsson.L 22)
Dundee United - Thompson - Malpas, Clark, Narey, Holt (Hegarty) - McInally, Ferguson, Kirkwood, Sturrock, Redford (Bannon), Gallacher
IFK Göteborg - Wernersson - Carlsson, Hysen, Larsson, Fredriksson Nilsson.R (Johansson), Tord Holmgren, Andersson, Tommy Holmgren (Mordt) Pettersson, Nilsson.L

Top scorers: Rantanen, IFK Göteborg 5
Houtman, FC Groningen 5
Kieft, Torino 5
Cascavel, Vitória SC Guimaraes 5

CUP WINNERS CUP

FIRST ROUND

Bursaspor 0-2 0-5 **Ajax**
Olympiakos 3-0 3-0 Union Luxembourg
17 Nëntori Tiranë 1-0 2-1 Dinamo Bucuresti
Malmö FF 6-0 1-2 Apollon Limassol
B 1903 København 1-0 0-2 **Vitosha Sofia**
Vasas Budapest 2-2 2-3 **Velez Mostar**
Zurrieq 0-3 0-4 **Wrexham**
Roma 2-0 0-2 3-4p **Real Zaragoza**
Waterford United 1-2 0-4 **Girondins Bordeaux**
Benfica 2-0 2-1 Lillestrøm SK
Haka Valkeakoski 2-2 1-3 **Torpedo Moskva**
VfB Stuttgart 1-0 0-0 Spartak Trnava
Aberdeen 2-1 0-3 **FC Sion**
Fram Reykjavík 0-3 0-1 **GKS Katowice**
SK Rapid Wien 4-3 3-3 Club Brugge
Glentoran 1-1 0-2 **Lokomotive Leipzig**

SECOND ROUND

Ajax 4-0 1-1 Olympiakos
17 Nëntori Tiranë 0-3 0-0 **Malmö FF**
Vitosha Sofia 2-0 3-4 Velez Mostar
Real Zaragoza 0-0 2-2 Wrexham
Benfica 1-1 0-1 **Girondins Bordeaux**
Torpedo Moskva 2-0 5-3 VfB Stuttgart
GKS Katowice 2-2 0-3 **FC Sion**
SK Rapid Wien 1-1 1-2 **Lokomotive Leipzig**

QUARTER-FINALS

Malmö FF 1-0 1-3 **Ajax**
Real Zaragoza 2-0 2-0 Vitosha Sofia
Girondins Bordeaux 1-0 2-3 Torpedo Moskva
Lokomotive Leipzig 2-0 0-0 FC Sion

SEMI-FINALS

Real Zaragoza 2-3 0-3 **Ajax**
Girondins Bordeaux 0-1 1-0 5-6p **Lokomotive Leipzig**

FINAL

Olympiako Stadio, Athens, 13-05-1987, 35,000. Referee: Agnolin, Italy

AJAX 1 (Van Basten 21)
LOKOMOTIVE LEIPZIG 0

Ajax - Menzo - Silooy, Rijkaard, Verlaat, Boeve - Wouters, Winter, Muhren (Scholten) - Van't Schip, Van Basten, Witschge (Bergkamp)
Lokomotive - Muller - Kreer, Baum, Lindner, Zotzsche - Scholz, Liebers (Kuhn), Bredow, Marschal - Richter, Edmond (Leitzke)

Top scorer: Bosman, Ajax 8

EUROPEAN SUPERCUP 1987

1st leg. Amsterdam, 24-11-1987. Referee: Valentine, Scotland

AJAX 0
FC PORTO 1 (Rui Barros 5)

2nd leg. Das Antas, Oporto, 13-01-1988. Referee: Schmidhuber, West Germany

FC PORTO 1 (Sousa 70)
AJAX 0

1987–88

EUROPEAN CUP

FIRST ROUND

PSV Eindhoven 3-0 0-2 Galatasaray
SK Rapid Wien 6-0 1-0 Hamrun Spartans
Lillestrøm SK 1-1 4-2 Linfield
Girondins Bordeaux 2-0 2-0 Dynamo Berlin
Bayern München 4-0 1-0 CFKA Sredets Sofia
Neuchâtel Xamax 5-0 1-2 Kuusysi Lahti
FC Porto 3-0 3-0 Vardar Skopje
Real Madrid 2-0 1-1 Napoli
Steaua Bucuresti 4-0 0-2 MTK-VM Budapest
Shamrock Rovers 0-1 0-0 **Omonia Nicosia**
Olympiakos 1-1 1-2 **Górnik Zabrze**
Dynamo Kiev 1-0 0-2 **Glasgow Rangers**
Malmö FF 0-1 1-1 **RSC Anderlecht**
Fram Reykjavík 0-2 0-8 **Sparta Praha**
ÅGF Åarhus 4-1 0-1 Jeunesse Esch
Benfica 4-0 Partizani Tiranë

SECOND ROUND

SK Rapid Wien 1-2 0-2 **PSV Eindhoven**
Lillestrøm SK 0-0 0-1 **Girondins Bordeaux**
Neuchâtel Xamax 2-1 0-2 **Bayern München**
Real Madrid 2-1 2-1 FC Porto
Steaua Bucuresti 3-1 2-0 Omonia Nicosia
Glasgow Rangers 3-1 1-1 Górnik Zabrze
Sparta Praha 1-2 0-1 **RSC Anderlecht**
ÅGF Åarhus 0-0 0-1 **Benfica**

QUARTER-FINALS

Girondins Bordeaux 1-1 0-0 **PSV Eindhoven**
Bayern München 3-2 0-2 **Real Madrid**
Steaua Bucuresti 2-0 1-2 Glasgow Rangers
Benfica 2-0 0-1 RSC Anderlecht

SEMI-FINALS

Real Madrid 1-1 0-0 **PSV Eindhoven**
Steaua Bucuresti 0-0 0-2 **Benfica**

FINAL

Neckarstadion, Stuttgart, 25-05-1988, 55,000. Referee: Agnolin, Italy

PSV EINDHOVEN 0
BENFICA 0

PSV Eindhoven won 6-5 on penalties

PSV		**Benfica**	
Koeman	I	Elzo	I
Kieft	I	Dito	I
Nielsen	I	Hajiri	I
Vanenburg	I	Pacheco	I
Lerby	I	Mozer	I
Jansson	I	Veloso	x

PSV Eindhoven - Van Breukelen - Gerets, Van Aerle, Koeman, Nielsen, Heintze - Vanenburg, Linskens, Lerby - Kieft, Gillhaus (Janssen). Tr: Hiddink
Benfica - Silvino - Veloso, Dito, Mozer, Alvaro - Elzo, Sheu, Chiquinho, Pacheco - Rui Aguas (Vando), Magnusson (Hajiri). Tr: Toni

Top scorers: Rui Aguas, Benfica 4
Ferreri, Bordeaux 4
Madjer, FC Porto 4
McCoist, Rangers 4
Michel, Real Madrid 4
Hagi, Steaua Bucharesti 4

UEFA CUP

FIRST ROUND

FK Austria 0-0 1-5 **Bayer Leverkusen**
Toulouse FC 5-1 1-0 Panionios
Bohemians Dublin 0-0 0-1 **Aberdeen**
Feyenoord 5-0 5-2 AC Spora

Flamurtari Vlorë 2-0 1-2 Partizan Beograd
Wismut Aue 0-0 1-1 Valur Reykjavík
Grasshopper-Club 0-4 0-1 **Dynamo Moskva**
Barcelona 2-0 0-1 OS Belenenses
Pogon Szczecin 1-1 1-3 **Hellas-Verona**
Linzer ASK 0-0 0-2 **FC Utrecht**
Brøndbyernes IF 2-1 0-0 IFK Göteborg
Sportul Studentesc 1-0 2-1 GKS Katowice
Lokomotiv Sofia 3-1 0-3 **Dynamo Tbilisi**
EPA Larnaca 0-1 0-3 **Victoria Bucuresti**
Spartak Moskva 3-0 0-1 Dynamo Dresden
Mjøndalen IF 0-5 1-0 **Werder Bremen**
Zenit Leningrad 2-0 0-5 **Club Brugge**
Crvena Zvezda Beograd 3-0 2-2 Trakia Plovdiv
Velez Mostar 5-0 0-3 FC Sion
Glasgow Celtic 2-1 0-2 **Borussia Dortmund**
Honvéd 1-0 0-0 KSC Lokeren
Universitatea Craiova 3-2 1-2 **GD Chaves**
Valletta 0-4 0-3 **Juventus**
Panathinaikos 2-0 2-3 AJ Auxerre
TJ Vitkovice 1-1 2-0 AIK Stockholm
Coleraine 0-1 1-3 **Dundee United**
SK Beveren 2-0 0-1 Bohemians Praha
Tatabánya Bányász 1-1 0-1 **Vitória Guimaraes**
Besiktas 0-0 1-3 **Internazionale**
TPS Turku 0-1 2-0 Admira-Wacker
Sporting Gijón 1-0 0-3 **Milan**
B. Mönchengladbach 0-1 1-4 **RCD Español**

SECOND ROUND

Toulouse FC 1-1 0-1 **Bayer Leverkusen**
Aberdeen 2-1 0-1 **Feyenoord**
Wismut Aue 1-0 0-2 **Flamurtari Vlorë**
Barcelona 2-0 0-0 Dynamo Moskva
FC Utrecht 1-1 1-2 **Hellas-Verona**
Brøndbyernes IF 3-0 0-3 0-3p **Sportul Studentesc**
Victoria Bucuresti 1-2 0-0 **Dynamo Tbilisi**
Spartak Moskva 4-1 2-6 **Werder Bremen**
Crvena Zvezda Beograd 3-1 0-4 **Club Brugge**
Borussia Dortmund 2-0 1-2 Velez Mostar
GD Chaves 1-2 1-3 **Honvéd**
Panathinaikos 1-0 2-3 Juventus
Dundee United 1-2 1-1 **TJ Vitkovice**
Vitória SC Guimaraes 1-0 0-1 5-4p SK Beveren
Internazionale 0-1 2-0 TPS Turku
Milan 0-2 0-0 **RCD Español**

THIRD ROUND

Feyenoord 2-2 0-1 **Bayer Leverkusen**
Barcelona 4-1 0-1 Flamurtari Vlorë
Hellas-Verona 3-1 1-0 Sportul Studentesc
Werder Bremen 2-1 1-1 Dynamo Tbilisi
Borussia Dortmund 3-0 0-5 **Club Brugge**
Honvéd 5-2 1-5 **Panathinaikos**
Vitória SC Guimaraes 2-0 0-2 4-5p **TJ Vitkovice**
Internazionale 1-1 0-1 **RCD Español**

QUARTER-FINALS

Bayer Leverkusen 0-0 1-0 Barcelona
Hellas-Verona 0-1 1-1 **Werder Bremen**
Panathinaikos 2-2 0-1 **Club Brugge**
RCD Español 2-0 0-0 TJ Vitkovice

SEMI-FINALS

Bayer Leverkusen 1-0 0-0 Werder Bremen
Club Brugge 2-0 0-3 **RCD Español**

FINAL

1st leg. Sarriá, Barcelona, 4-05-1988, 42,000. Referee: Krchnak, Czechoslovakia

ESPANOL 3 (Losada 45 56, Soler 49)
BAYER LEVERKUSEN 0

Español - N'Kono - Job, Miguel Angel, Gallart - Soler, Orejuela (Golobart), Urquiaga, Inaki - Valverde, Pichi Alonso (Lauridsen), Losada

Bayer - Vollborn - Rolff, De Kayser, Reinhardt.A, Hinterberger - Cha-Bum-Kun (Götz), Tita, Buncol, Falkenmayer (Reinhardt.K) - Waas, Tauber

2nd leg. Ulrich Haberland Stadion, Leverkusen, 18-05-1988, 22,000. Referee: Keizer, Holland

BAYER LEVERKUSEN 3 (Tita 57, Gotz 63, Cha-Bum-Kun 81)
ESPANOL 0

Bayer won 3-2 on penalties

Español		**Bayer**	
Alonso	I	Falkenmayer	x
Job	I	Rolff	I
Urquiaga	x	Waas	I
Zuniga	x	Tauber	I
Losada	x		

Bayer - Vollborn - Rolff, Seckler, Reinhardt.A, Reinhardt.K - Schreier (Waas), Buncol, Falkenmayer - Cha-Bum-Kun, Götz, Tita (Tauber)

Español - N'Kono - Miguel Angel, Golobart (Zuniga), Urquiaga - Job, Orejuela (Zubillaga), Inaki, Soler - Pichi Alonso, Losada

Top scorers: Brylle, Club Brugge 6
Saravakos, Panathinaikos 6

CUP WINNERS CUP

PRELIMINARY ROUND

AEL Limassol 0-1 1-5 **Dunajska Streda**

FIRST ROUND

KV Mechelen 1-0 2-0 Dinamo Bucuresti
St. Mirren 1-0 0-0 Tromsø IL
Real Sociedad 0-0 2-0 Slask Wroclaw
Dynamo Minsk 2-0 2-1 Gençlerbirligi
Sporting CP 4-0 2-4 FC Tirol
IA Akranes 0-0 0-1 **Kalmar FF**
Vitosha Sofia 1-0 1-3 **OFI Crete**
Merthyr Tydfil 2-1 0-2 **Atalanta**
Lokomotive Leipzig 0-0 0-1 **Olympique Marseille**
ÅAB Ålborg 1-0 0-1 2-4p **Hajduk Split**
Vllaznia Shkodër 2-0 4-0 Sliema Wanderers
RoPS Rovaniemi 0-0 1-1 Glentoran
Dunajska Streda 2-1 1-3 **BSC Young Boys**
Ujpesti Dózsa 1-0 1-3 **FC Den Haag**
Avenir Beggen 0-5 0-3 **Hamburger SV**
Ajax 4-0 2-0 Dundalk

SECOND ROUND

KV Mechelen 0-0 2-0 St. Mirren
Real Sociedad 1-1 0-0 **Dynamo Minsk**
Kalmar FF 1-0 0-5 **Sporting CP**
OFI Crete 1-0 0-2 **Atalanta**
Olympique Marseille 4-0 0-2 Hajduk Split
Vllaznia Shkodër 0-1 0-1 **RoPS Rovaniemi**
FC Den Haag 2-1 0-1 **BSC Young Boys**
Hamburger SV 0-1 0-2 **Ajax**

QUARTER-FINALS

KV Mechelen 1-0 1-1 Dynamo Minsk
Atalanta 2-0 1-1 Sporting CP
RoPS Rovaniemi 0-1 0-3 **Olympique Marseille**
BSC Young Boys 0-1 0-1 **Ajax**

SEMI-FINALS

KV Mechelen 2-1 2-1 Atalanta
Olympique Marseille 0-3 2-1 **Ajax**

FINAL

Stade de la Meinau, Strasbourg, 11-05-1988, 40,000. Referee: Pauly, West Germany

KV MECHELEN 1 (Den Boer 53)
AJAX 0
Mechelen - Preud'Homme - Clijsters, Sanders, Rutjes, Deferm - Hofkens (Theunis), Emmers, Koeman, De Wilde (Demesmeker) - Den Boer, Ohana
Ajax - Menzo - Blind, Wouters, Larsson, Verlaat (Meijer) - Van't Schip (Bergkamp), Winter, Muhren, Scholten - Bosman, Witschge

Top scorer: Cascavel, Sporting CP 6

EUROPEAN SUPERCUP 1988

1st leg. Achter de Kazerne, Mechelen, 1-02-1989. Referee: Kirschen, East Germany
KV MECHELEN 3 (Bosman 16 50, OG 17)
PSV EINDHOVEN 0
2nd leg. Philips Stadion, Eindhoven, 8-02-1989. Referee: Fredriksson, Sweden
PSV EINDHOVEN 1 (Gilhaus 78)
KV MECHELEN 0

1988–89

EUROPEAN CUP

FIRST ROUND
Vitosha Sofia 0-2 2-5 **Milan**
Dundalk 0-5 0-3 **Crvena Zvezda Beograd**
Honvéd 1-0 0-4 **Glasgow Celtic**
Dynamo Berlin 3-0 0-5 **Werder Bremen**
PSV Eindhoven Bye
FC Porto 3-0 0-2 HJK Helsinki
Górnik Zabrze 3-0 4-1 Jeunesse Esch
Real Madrid 3-0 1-0 Moss FK
SK Rapid Wien 2-1 0-2 **Galatasaray**
Larissa 2-1 1-2 0-3p **Neuchâtel Xamax**
Club Brugge 1-0 1-2 Brøndbyernes IF
Valur Reykjavík 1-0 0-2 **AS Monaco**
Pezoporikos 1-2 1-5 **IFK Göteborg**
Hamrun Spartans 2-1 0-2 **17 Nëntori Tiranë**
Spartak Moskva 2-0 1-1 Glentoran
Sparta Praha 1-5 2-2 **Steaua Bucuresti**

SECOND ROUND
Milan 1-1 1-1 4-2p Crvena Zvezda Beograd
Glasgow Celtic 0-1 0-0 **Werder Bremen**
PSV Eindhoven 5-0 0-2 FC Porto
Górnik Zabrze 0-1 2-3 **Real Madrid**
Neuchâtel Xamax 3-0 0-5 **Galatasaray**
Club Brugge 1-0 1-6 **AS Monaco**
17 Nëntori Tiranë 0-3 0-1 **IFK Göteborg**
Steaua Bucuresti 3-0 2-1 Spartak Moskva

QUARTER-FINALS
Werder Bremen 0-0 0-1 **Milan**
PSV Eindhoven 1-1 1-2 **Real Madrid**
AS Monaco 0-1 1-1 **Galatasaray**
IFK Göteborg 1-0 1-5 **Steaua Bucuresti**

SEMI-FINALS
Real Madrid 1-1 0-5 **Milan**
Steaua Bucuresti 4-0 1-1 Galatasaray

FINAL
Nou Camp, Barcelona, 24-05-1989, 97,000. Referee: Tritscher, West Germany
MILAN 4 (Gullit 17 38, Van Basten 26 46)
STEAUA BUCURESTI 0
Milan - Galli.G - Tassotti, Costacurta (Galli.F), Baresi, Maldini - Colombo, Rijkaard, Ancelotti, Donadoni - Gullit (Virdis), Van Basten. Tr: Sacchi
Steaua - Lung - Iovan, Petrescu, Bumbescu, Ungureanu - Hagi, Stoica, Minea, Rotariu (Balaci) - Lacatus, Piturca. Tr: Iordanescu

Top scorer: Van Basten, Milan 10

UEFA CUP

FIRST ROUND
Napoli 1-0 1-1 PAOK Salonica
FC Aarau 0-3 0-4 **Lokomotive Leipzig**
IA Akranes 0-0 1-2 **Ujpesti Dózsa**
Dnepr Dnepropetrovsk 1-1 1-2 **Girondins Bordeaux**
Union Luxembourg 1-7 0-4 **RFC Liège**
SCP Montpellier 0-3 1-3 **Benfica**
AEK Athens 1-0 0-2 **Athletic Bilbao**
Otelul Galati 1-0 0-5 **Juventus**
St. Patrick's Athletic 0-2 0-2 **Heart of Midlothian**
First Vienna FC 1-0 1-2 Ikast BK
Velez Mostar 1-0 5-2 Apoel Nicosia
Bayer Leverkusen 0-1 0-1 **OS Belenenses**
Internazionale 2-1 2-1 Sporting Braga
Malmö FF 2-0 1-2 Torpedo Moskva
Östers IF Växjö 2-0 0-6 **Dunajska Streda**
Bayern München 3-1 7-3 Legia Warszawa
Aberdeen 0-0 0-2 **Dynamo Dresden**
Molde FK 0-0 1-5 **KSV Waregem**
Partizan Beograd 5-0 5-0 Slavia Sofia
Roma 1-2 3-1 1.FC Nürnberg
TPS Turku 0-0 1-1 Linfield
Zalgiris Vilnius 2-0 2-5 **FK Austria**
Trakia Plovdiv 1-2 0-0 **Dynamo Minsk**
Sliema Wanderers 0-2 1-6 **Victoria Bucuresti**
Real Sociedad 2-1 2-3 Dukla Praha
Sporting CP 4-2 2-1 Ajax
Glasgow Rangers 1-0 4-2 GKS Katowice
Royal Antwerp FC 2-4 1-2 **1.FC Köln**
FC Groningen 1-0 1-2 Atlético Madrid
Servette FC 1-0 0-0 SK Sturm Graz
Besiktas 1-0 0-2 **Dinamo Zagreb**
VfB Stuttgart 2-0 1-2 Tatabánya Bányász

SECOND ROUND
Lokomotive Leipzig 1-1 0-2 **Napoli**
Ujpesti Dózsa 0-1 0-1 **Girondins Bordeaux**
RFC Liège 2-1 1-1 Benfica
Juventus 5-1 2-3 Athletic Bilbao
Heart of Midlothian 0-0 1-0 First Vienna FC
Velez Mostar 0-0 0-0 4-3p OS Belenenses
Malmö FF 0-1 1-1 **Internazionale**
Bayern München 3-1 2-0 Dunajska Streda
Dynamo Dresden 4-1 1-2 KSV Waregem
Partizan Beograd 4-2 0-2 **Roma**
FK Austria 2-1 0-1 **TPS Turku**
Dynamo Minsk 2-1 0-1 **Victoria Bucuresti**
Sporting CP 1-2 0-0 **Real Sociedad**
1.FC Köln 2-0 1-1 Glasgow Rangers
FC Groningen 2-0 1-1 Servette FC
Dinamo Zagreb 1-3 1-1 **VfB Stuttgart**

THIRD ROUND
Girondins Bordeaux 0-1 0-0 **Napoli**
RFC Liège 0-1 0-1 **Juventus**
Heart of Midlothian 3-0 1-2 Velez Mostar
Bayern München 0-2 3-1 Internazionale
Dynamo Dresden 2-0 2-0 Roma
Victoria Bucuresti 1-0 2-3 TPS Turku
Real Sociedad 1-0 2-2 1.FC Köln
FC Groningen 1-3 0-2 **VfB Stuttgart**

QUARTER-FINALS

Juventus 2-0 0-3 **Napoli**
Heart of Midlothian 1-0 0-2 **Bayern München**
Victoria Bucuresti 1-1 0-4 **Dynamo Dresden**
VfB Stuttgart 1-0 0-1 4-2p Real Sociedad

SEMI-FINALS

Napoli 2-0 2-2 Bayern München
VfB Stuttgart 1-0 1-1 Dynamo Dresden

FINAL

1st leg. San Paolo, Naples, 3-05-1989, 83,000. Referee: Germanakos, Greece

NAPOLI 2 (Maradona 68, Careca 87)
VfB STUTTGART 1 (Gaudino 17)

Napoli - Giuliani - Renica, Ferrera, Francini, Corradini (Crippa) - Alemao, Fusi, De Napoli - Careca, Maradona, Carnevale

Stuttgart - Immel - Allgöwer, Schmaler.N, Hartmann, Buchwald - Schäfer, Katanec, Sigurvinnson, Schröder - Walter (Zietsch), Gaudino

2nd leg. Neckarstadion, Stuttgart, 17-05-1989, 67,000. Referee: Sanchez Arminio,Spain

VfB STUTTGART 3 (Klinsmann 27, OG 70, Schmaler.O 89)
NAPOLI 3 (Alemao 18, Ferrera 39, Careca 62)

Stuttgart - Immel - Allgöwer, Schmaler.N, Hartmann - Schäfer, Katanec, Sigurvinnson, Schröder - Walter (Schmaler.O), Klinsmann, Gaudino

Napoli - Giuliani - Renica, Ferrera, Francini, Corradini - Alemao (Carranante), Fusi, De Napoli - Careca (Bigliardi), Maradona, Carnevale

Top scorers: Careca, Napoli 6
Gutschow, Dynamo Dresden 6

CUP WINNERS CUP

PRELIMINARY ROUND

Békéscaba ESSC 3-0 1-2 Byrne IL Stavanger

FIRST ROUND

Fram Reykjavík 0-2 0-5 **Barcelona**
Flamurtari Vlorë 2-3 0-1 **Lech Poznan**
Derry City 0-0 0-4 **Cardiff City**
Glenavon 1-4 1-3 **ÅGF Åarhus**
Roda JC Kerkrade 2-0 0-1 Vitória Guimaraes
Borac Banja Luka 2-0 0-4 **Metalist Kharkov**
Omonia Nicosia 0-1 0-2 **Panathinaikos**
Internacional ZTS 2-3 0-5 **CFKA Sredets Sofia**
KV Mechelen 5-0 3-1 Avenir Beggen
FC Metz 1-3 0-2 **RSC Anderlecht**
Sakaryaspor 2-0 0-1 Békéscaba ESSC
Grasshopper-Club 0-0 0-1 **Eintracht Frankfurt**
Dinamo Bucuresti 3-0 3-0 Kuusysi Lahti
Floriana 0-0 0-1 **Dundee United**
Carl Zeiss Jena 5-0 0-1 Kremser SC
IFK Norrköping 2-1 0-2 **Sampdoria**

SECOND ROUND

Barcelona 1-1 1-1 5-4p Lech Poznan
Cardiff City 1-2 0-4 **ÅGF Åarhus**
Roda JC Kerkrade 1-0 0-0 Metalist Kharkov
CFKA Sredets Sofia 2-0 1-0 Panathinaikos
KV Mechelen 1-0 2-0 RSC Anderlecht
Eintracht Frankfurt 3-1 3-0 Sakaryaspor
Dundee United 0-1 1-1 **Dinamo Bucuresti**
Carl Zeiss Jena 1-1 1-3 **Sampdoria**

QUARTER-FINALS

ÅGF Åarhus 0-1 0-0 **Barcelona**
CFKA Sredets Sofia 2-1 1-2 4-3p Roda JC Kerkrade
Eintracht Frankfurt 0-0 0-1 **KV Mechelen**
Dinamo Bucuresti 1-1 0-0 **Sampdoria**

SEMI-FINALS

Barcelona 4-2 2-1 CFKA Sredets Sofia
KV Mechelen 2-1 0-3 **Sampdoria**

FINAL

Wankdorf, Berne, 10-05-1989, 45,000. Referee: Courtney, England

BARCELONA 2 (Salinas 4, Recarte 79)
SAMPDORIA 0

Barcelona - Zubizarreta - Aloisio, Alexanco, Urbano - Milla (Soler), Amor, Eusebio, Roberto - Lineker, Salinas, Beguiristain (Recarte)

Sampdoria - Pagliuca - Pellegrini.L (Bonomi), Mannini (Pellegrini.S), Lanna, Salsano - Pari, Victor, Cerezo, Dossena - Vialli, Mancini

Top scorer: Stoichkov, CFKA Sredets Sofia 7

EUROPEAN SUPERCUP 1989

1st leg. Nou Camp, Barcelona, 23-11-1989. Referee: Quiniou, France

BARCELONA 1 (Amor 67)
MILAN 1 (Van Basten 44)

2nd leg. Giuseppe Meazza, Milan, 7-12-1989. Referee: Kohl, Austria

MILAN 1 (Evani 55)
BARCELONA 0

1989–90

EUROPEAN CUP

FIRST ROUND

Milan 4-0 1-0 HJK Helsinki
AC Spora 0-3 0-6 **Real Madrid**
Malmö FF 1-0 1-1 Internazionale
Rosenborg BK 0-0 0-5 **KV Mechelen**
PSV Eindhoven 3-0 2-0 FC Luzern
Steaua Bucuresti 4-0 1-0 Fram Reykjavík
Sliema Wanderers 1-0 0-5 **17 Nëntori Tiranë**
Glasgow Rangers 1-3 0-0 **Bayern München**
Olympique Marseille 3-0 1-1 Brøndbyernes IF
Dynamo Dresden 1-0 3-5 **AEK Athens**
Sparta Praha 3-1 2-1 Fenerbahçe
Ruch Chórzow 1-1 1-5 **CSKA Sofia**
Linfield 1-2 0-1 **Dnepr Dnepropetrovsk**
FC Tirol 6-0 3-2 Omonia Nicosia
Honvéd 1-0 1-2 Vojvodina Novi Sad
Derry City 1-2 0-4 **Benfica**

SECOND ROUND

Milan 2-0 0-1 Real Madrid
Malmö FF 0-0 1-4 **KV Mechelen**
Steaua Bucuresti 1-0 1-5 **PSV Eindhoven**
Bayern München 3-1 3-0 17 Nëntori Tiranë
Olympique Marseille 2-0 1-1 AEK Athens
Sparta Praha 2-2 0-3 **CSKA Sofia**
Dnepr Dnepropetrovsk 2-0 2-2 FC Tirol
Honvéd 0-2 0-7 **Benfica**

QUARTER-FINALS

KV Mechelen 0-0 0-2 **Milan**
Bayern München 2-1 1-0 PSV Eindhoven
CSKA Sofia 0-1 1-3 **Olympique Marseille**
Benfica 1-0 3-0 Dnepr Dnepropetrovsk

SEMI-FINALS

Milan 1-0 1-2 Bayern München
Olympique Marseille 2-1 0-1 **Benfica**

FINAL

Prater, Vienna, 23-05-1990, 57,000. Referee: Kohl, Austria

MILAN 1 (Rijkaard 68)
BENFICA 0

Milan - Galli.G - Tassotti, Costacurta, Baresi, Maldini - Colombo (Galli.F), Rijkaard, Ancelotti (Massaro), Evani - Gullit, Van Basten. Tr: Sacchi

Benfica - Silvino - Jose Carlos, Aldair, Ricardo, Samuel - Vitor Paneira (Garcia), Valdo, Thern, Hernani - Magnusson, Pacheco (Brito). Tr: Eriksson

Top scorers: Papin, Olympique Marseille 6
Romario, PSV Eindhoven 6

UEFA CUP

PRELIMINARY ROUND

AJ Auxerre 0-1 3-1 Dinamo Zagreb

FIRST ROUND

Górnik Zabrze 0-1 2-4 **Juventus**
Kuusysi Lahti 0-0 2-3 **Paris Saint-Germain**
Iraklis Salonica 1-0 0-2 **FC Sion**
FC Karl-Marx-Stadt 1-0 2-2 Boavista FC
FC Porto 2-0 2-1 Flacara Moreni
Valencia 3-1 1-1 Victoria Bucuresti
Apollon Limassol 0-3 1-1 **Real Zaragoza**
Örgryte IS 1-2 1-5 **Hamburger SV**
Levski Sofia 0-0 3-4 **Royal Antwerp FC**
Glentoran 1-3 0-2 **Dundee United**
Zenit Leningrad 3-1 0-0 Naestved IF
VfB Stuttgart 2-0 1-2 Feyenoord
Galatasaray 1-1 0-2 **Crvena Zvezda Beograd**
Zalgiris Vilnius 2-0 0-1 IFK Göteborg
Atalanta 0-0 0-2 **Spartak Moskva**
1.FC Köln 4-1 1-0 Plastika Nitra
Lillestrøm SK 1-3 0-2 **Werder Bremen**
FK Austria 1-0 1-1 Ajax
FC Wettingen 3-0 2-0 Dundalk
Sporting CP 0-0 0-0 3-4p **Napoli**
Aberdeen 2-1 0-1 **SK Rapid Wien**
FC Twente Enschede 0-0 1-4 **Club Brugge**
Hibernian Edinburgh 1-0 3-0 Videoton SC
IA Akranes 0-2 1-4 **RFC Liège**
AJ Auxerre 5-0 3-0 Apolonia Fier
RoPS Rovaniemi 1-1 1-0 GKS Katowice
Valletta 1-4 0-3 **First Vienna FC**
Rad Beograd 2-1 0-2 **Olympiakos**
Dynamo Kiev 4-0 2-1 MTK-VM Budapest
Hansa Rostock 2-3 0-4 **Baník Ostrava**
FC Sochaux 7-0 5-0 Jeunesse Esch
Atlético Madrid 1-0 0-1 1-3p **Fiorentina**

SECOND ROUND

Paris Saint-Germain 0-1 1-2 **Juventus**
FC Sion 2-1 1-4 **FC Karl-Marx-Stadt**
FC Porto 3-1 2-3 Valencia
Real Zaragoza 1-0 0-2 **Hamburger SV**
Royal Antwerp FC 4-0 2-3 Dundee United
Zenit Leningrad 0-1 0-5 **VfB Stuttgart**
Crvena Zvezda Beograd 4-1 1-0 Zalgiris Vilnius
1.FC Köln 3-1 0-0 Spartak Moskva
Werder Bremen 5-0 0-2 FK Austria
FC Wettingen 0-0 1-2 **Napoli**
Club Brugge 1-2 3-4 **SK Rapid Wien**
Hibernian Edinburgh 0-0 0-1 **RFC Liège**
RoPS Rovaniemi 0-5 0-3 **AJ Auxerre**
First Vienna FC 2-2 1-1 **Olympiakos**
Dynamo Kiev 3-0 1-1 Baník Ostrava
Fiorentina 0-0 1-1 FC Sochaux

THIRD ROUND

Juventus 2-1 1-0 FC Karl-Marx-Stadt
Hamburger SV 1-0 1-2 FC Porto
Royal Antwerp FC 1-0 1-1 VfB Stuttgart
Crvena Zvezda Beograd 2-0 0-3 **1.FC Köln**
Napoli 2-3 1-5 **Werder Bremen**
SK Rapid Wien 1-0 1-3 **RFC Liège**
Olympiakos 1-1 0-0 **AJ Auxerre**
Fiorentina 1-0 0-0 Dynamo Kiev

QUARTER-FINALS

Hamburger SV 0-2 2-1 **Juventus**
1.FC Köln 2-0 0-0 Royal Antwerp FC
RFC Liège 1-4 2-0 **Werder Bremen**
Fiorentina 1-0 1-0 AJ Auxerre

SEMI-FINALS

Juventus 3-2 0-0 1.FC Köln
Werder Bremen 1-1 0-0 **Fiorentina**

FINAL

1st leg. Comunale, Turin, 2-05-1990, 45,000. Referee: Soriano Aladren, Spain

JUVENTUS 3 (Galia 3, Casiraghi 59, De Agostini 73)
FIORENTINA 1 (Buso 10)

Juventus - Tacconi - Napoli, De Agostini, Galia, Bruno (Alessio) - Bonetti, Aleinikov, Barros, Marocchi - Casiraghi, Schillaci

Fiorentina - Landucci - Dell'Oglio, Volpecina, Pin, Battistini - Dunga, Nappi, Kubik (Malusci), Baggio - Buso, Di Chiara

2nd leg. Stadio Partenio, Avellino, 16-05-1990, 32,000. Referee: Schmidhuber, West Germany

FIORENTINA 0
JUVENTUS 0

Fiorentina - Landucci - Dell'Oglio, Volpecina, Pin, Battistini - Dunga, Nappi (Zironelli), Kubik, Baggio - Buso, Di Chiara

Juventus - Tacconi - Napoli, De Agostini, Galia, Bruno - Alessio, Aleinikov, Barros (Avallone), Marocchi - Casiraghi (Rosa), Schillaci

Top scorers: Gotz, 1.FC Köln 6
Riedle, Werder Bremen 6

CUP WINNERS CUP

PRELIMINARY ROUND

Chernomorets Burgas 3-1 0-4 **Dinamo Tiranë**

FIRST ROUND

SK Brann Bergen 0-2 0-1 **Sampdoria**
Besiktas 0-1 1-2 **Borussia Dortmund**
Torpedo Moskva 5-0 1-0 Cork City
Slovan Bratislava 3-0 0-4 **Grasshopper-Club**
Real Valladolid 5-0 1-0 Hamrun Spartans
Union Luxembourg 0-0 0-5 **Djurgårdens IF**
Valur Reykjavík 1-2 1-2 **Dynamo Berlin**
OS Belenenses 1-1 0-3 **AS Monaco**
Dinamo Tiranë 1-0 0-2 **Dinamo Bucuresti**
Panathinaikos 3-2 3-3 Swansea City
FC Groningen 1-0 2-1 Ikast BK
Partizan Beograd 2-1 4-5 Glasgow Celtic
Admira-Wacker 3-0 0-1 AEL Limassol
Ferencváros 5-1 1-1 Haka Valkeakoski
Barcelona 1-1 1-0 Legia Warszawa
RSC Anderlecht 6-0 4-0 Ballymena United

SECOND ROUND

Borussia Dortmund 1-1 0-2 **Sampdoria**
Torpedo Moskva 1-1 0-3 **Grasshopper-Club**
Real Valladolid 2-0 2-2 Djurgårdens IF
AS Monaco 0-0 1-1 Dynamo Berlin
Panathinaikos 0-2 1-6 **Dinamo Bucuresti**
FC Groningen 4-3 1-3 **Partizan Beograd**
Admira-Wacker 1-0 1-0 Ferencváros
RSC Anderlecht 2-0 1-2 Barcelona

QUARTER-FINALS

Sampdoria 2-0 2-1 Grasshopper-Club
Real Valladolid 0-0 0-0 1-3p **AS Monaco**
Dinamo Bucuresti 2-1 2-0 Partizan Beograd
RSC Anderlecht 2-0 1-1 Admira-Wacker

SEMI-FINALS

AS Monaco 2-2 0-2 **Sampdoria**
RSC Anderlecht 1-0 1-0 Dinamo Bucuresti

FINAL

Nya Ullevi, Gothenburg, 9-05-1990, 20,000. Referee: Galler, Switzerland

SAMPDORIA 2 (Vialli 105 107)
RSC ANDERLECHT 0

Sampdoria - Pagliuca - Pellegrini.L, Mannini, Vierchwood, Carboni - Pari, Katanec (Salsano), Invernizzi (Lombardo), Dossena - Vialli, Mancini

Anderlecht - De Wilde - Grun, Marchoul, Keshi, Kooiman - Vervoort, Musonda, Gudjohnson, Jankovic (Oliveira) - Degryse (Nilis), Van der Linden

Top scorer: Vialli, Sampdoria 7

EUROPEAN SUPERCUP 1990

1st leg. Luigi Ferraris, Genoa, 10-10-1990

SAMPDORIA 1 (Mikhailichenko 31)
MILAN 1 (Evani 31)

2nd leg. Giuseppe Meazza, Milan, 29-11-1990

MILAN 2 (Gullit 45, Rijkaard 76)
SAMPDORIA 0

1990–91

EUROPEAN CUP

FIRST ROUND

Crvena Zvezda Beograd 1-1 4-1 Grasshopper-Club
Valletta 0-4 0-6 **Glasgow Rangers**
Malmö FF 3-2 2-2 Besiktas
Union Luxembourg 1-3 0-3 **Dynamo Dresden**
FC Porto 5-0 8-1 Portadown
Dinamo Bucuresti 4-0 1-1 St. Patrick's Athletic
KA Akureyri 1-0 0-3 **CSKA Sofia**
Apoel Nicosia 2-3 0-4 **Bayern München**
Sparta Praha 0-2 0-2 **Spartak Moskva**
Napoli 3-0 2-0 Ujpesti Dózsa
FC Tirol 5-0 2-1 Kuusysi Lahti
OB Odense 1-4 0-6 **Real Madrid**
Milan Bye
Lillestrøm SK 1-1 0-2 **Club Brugge**
Lech Poznan 3-0 2-1 Panathinaikos
Olympique Marseille 5-1 0-0 Dinamo Tiranë

SECOND ROUND

Crvena Zvezda Beograd 3-0 1-1 Glasgow Rangers
Dynamo Dresden 1-1 1-1 5-4p Malmö FF
Dinamo Bucuresti 0-0 0-4 **FC Porto**
Bayern München 4-0 3-0 CSKA Sofia
Napoli 0-0 0-0 3-5p **Spartak Moskva**
Real Madrid 9-1 2-2 FC Tirol
Milan 0-0 1-0 Club Brugge
Lech Poznan 3-2 1-6 **Olympique Marseille**

QUARTER-FINALS

Crvena Zvezda Beograd 3-0 2-1 Dynamo Dresden
Bayern München 1-1 2-0 FC Porto
Spartak Moskva 0-0 3-1 Real Madrid
Milan 1-1 0-1 **Olympique Marseille**

SEMI-FINALS

Bayern München 1-2 2-2 **Crvena Zvezda Beograd**
Spartak Moskva 1-3 1-2 **Olympique Marseille**

FINAL

San Nicola, Bari, 29-05-1991, 50,000. Referee: Lanese, Italy

CRVENA ZVEZDA BEOGRAD 0
OLYMPIQUE MARSEILLE 0

Red Star Belgrade won 5-3 on penalties

Red Star		**Marseille**	
Prosinecki	I	Amoros	x
Binic	I	Casoni	I
Belodedici	I	Papin	I
Mihajlovic	I	Mozer	I
Pancev	I		

Red Star - Stojanovic - Belodedici, Najdoski, Sabanadzovic, Jugovic, Marovic, Mihajlovic - Binic, Savicevic (Stosic), Prosinecki - Pancev. Tr: Petrovic

Marseille - Olmeta - Amoros, Boli, Mozer, Di Meco (Stojkovic) - Fournier (Vercruysse), Germain, Casoni, Pele - Papin, Waddle. Tr: Goethals

Top scorer: Papin, Olympique Marseille 6
Pacult, FC Tirol 6

UEFA CUP

FIRST ROUND

SK Rapid Wien 2-1 1-3 **Internazionale**
Aston Villa 3-1 2-1 Baník Ostrava
Lausanne-Sports 3-2 0-1 **Real Sociedad**
Hibernians Paola 0-3 0-2 **Partizan Beograd**
IFK Norrköping 0-0 1-3 **1.FC Köln**
Avenir Beggen 2-1 0-5 **Internacional ZTS**
Fenerbahçe 3-0 3-2 Vitória Guimaraes
Atalanta 0-0 1-1 Dinamo Zagreb
Zaglebie Lubin 0-1 0-1 **Bologna**
Dnepr Dnepropetrovsk 1-1 1-3 **Heart of Midlothian**
MTK-VM Budapest 1-1 1-2 **FC Luzern**
Vejle BK 0-1 0-3 **Admira-Wacker**
Derry City 0-1 0-0 **Vitesse Arnhem**
FH Hafnarfjördur 1-3 2-2 **Dundee United**
Politechnica Timisoara 2-0 0-1 Atlético Madrid
Sporting CP 1-0 2-2 KV Mechelen
Brøndbyernes IF 5-0 1-4 Eintracht Frankfurt
Royal Antwerp FC 0-0 1-3 **Ferencváros**
GKS Katowice 3-0 1-0 TPS Turku
Bayer Leverkusen 1-0 1-1 FC Twente Enschede
Roda JC Kerkrade 1-3 1-3 **AS Monaco**
Chernomorets Odessa 3-1 1-2 Rosenborg BK
Sevilla 0-0 0-0 4-3p PAOK Salonica
Torpedo Moskva 4-1 1-1 GAIS Göteborg
RSC Anderlecht 2-0 2-0 Petrolul Ploiesti
Slavia Sofia 2-1 2-4 **Omonia Nicosia**
Partizani Tiranë 0-1 0-1 **Universitatea Craiova**
Borussia Dortmund 2-0 2-0 Chemnitzer FC
Glenavon 0-0 0-2 **Girondins Bordeaux**
1.FC Magdeburg 0-0 1-0 RoPS Rovaniemi

Iraklis Salonica	0-0 0-2	**Valencia**
Roma	1-0 1-0	Benfica

SECOND ROUND

Aston Villa	2-0 0-3	**Internazionale**
Real Sociedad	1-0 0-1 4-5p	**Partizan Beograd**
1.FC Köln	0-1 2-0	Internacional ZTS
Fenerbahçe	0-1 1-4	**Atalanta**
Heart of Midlothian	3-1 0-3	**Bologna**
FC Luzern	0-1 1-1	**Admira-Wacker**
Vitesse Arnhem	1-0 4-0	Dundee United
Sporting CP	7-0 0-2	Politehnica Timisoara
Brøndbyernes IF	3-0 1-0	Ferencváros
GKS Katowice	1-2 0-4	**Bayer Leverkusen**
Chernomorets Odessa	0-0 0-1	**AS Monaco**
Torpedo Moskva	3-1 1-2	Sevilla
Omonia Nicosia	1-1 0-3	**RSC Anderlecht**
Universitatea Craiova	0-3 0-1	**Borussia Dortmund**
1.FC Magdeburg	0-1 0-1	**Girondins Bordeaux**
Valencia	1-1 1-2	**Roma**

THIRD ROUND

Internazionale	3-0 1-1	Partizan Beograd
1.FC Köln	1-1 0-1	**Atalanta**
Admira-Wacker	3-0 0-3 5-6p	**Bologna**
Vitesse Arnhem	0-2 1-2	**Sporting CP**
Brøndbyernes IF	3-0 0-0	Bayer Leverkusen
Torpedo Moskva	2-1 2-1	AS Monaco
RSC Anderlecht	1-0 1-2	Borussia Dortmund
Roma	5-0 2-0	Girondins Bordeaux

QUARTER-FINALS

Atalanta	0-0 0-2	**Internazionale**
Bologna	1-1 0-2	**Sporting CP**
Brøndbyernes IF	1-0 0-1 4-2p	Torpedo Moskva
Roma	3-0 3-2	RSC Anderlecht

SEMI-FINALS

Sporting CP	0-0 0-2	**Internazionale**
Brøndbyernes IF	0-0 1-2	**Roma**

FINAL

1st leg. Giuseppe Meazza, Milan, 8-05-1991, 75,000. Referee: Spirin, Soviet Union

INTERNAZIONALE 2 (Matthaus 55, Berti 67)
ROMA 0

Internazionale - Zenga - Bergomi, Brehme, Battistini, Ferri - Paganin (Baresi), Bianchi, Berti, Matthäus - Klinsmann, Serena (Pizzi)
Roma - Cervone - Tempestilli, Nela, Berthold, Aldair (Carboni) - Comi (Muzzi), Gerolin, Di Mauro, Giannini - Völler, Rizzitelli

2nd leg. Stadio Olimpico, Rome, 22-05-1991, 71,000. Referee: Quiniou, France

ROMA 1 (Rizzitelli 81)
INTERNAZIONALE 0

Roma - Cervone - Tempestilli (Salsano), Gerolin, Berthold, Aldair - Nela, Desideri (Muzzi), Di Mauro, Giannini - Völler, Rizzitelli
Internazionale - Zenga - Bergomi, Brehme, Battistini, Ferri - Paganin, Bianchi, Berti, Matthäus - Klinsmann, Pizzi (Mandorlini)

Top scorer: Völler, Roma 10

CUP WINNERS CUP

PRELIMINARY ROUND

Bray Wanderers	1-1 0-2	**Trabzonspor**

FIRST ROUND

Manchester United	2-0 1-0	Pécsi MSC
Wrexham	0-0 1-0	Lyngby BK
Glentoran	1-1 0-5	**Steaua Bucuresti**
SCP Montpellier	1-0 0-0	PSV Eindhoven
1.FC Kaiserslautern	1-0 0-2	**Sampdoria**
Olympiakos	3-1 2-0	Flamurtari Vlorë
NEA Salamis	0-2 0-3	**Aberdeen**
Legia Warszawa	3-0 3-0	Swift Hesperange
Sliven	0-2 1-6	**Juventus**
PSV Schwerin	0-2 0-0	**FK Austria**
Estrela da Amadora	1-1 1-1 4-3p	Neuchâtel Xamax
Viking Stavanger	0-2 0-3	**RFC Liège**
KuPS Kuopio	2-2 0-4	**Dynamo Kiev**
Sliema Wanderers	1-2 0-2	**Dukla Praha**
Fram Reykjavík	3-0 1-1	Djurgårdens IF
Trabzonspor	1-0 2-7	**Barcelona**

SECOND ROUND

Manchester United	3-0 2-0	Wrexham
SCP Montpellier	5-0 3-0	Steaua Bucuresti
Olympiakos	0-1 1-3	**Sampdoria**
Aberdeen	0-0 0-1	**Legia Warszawa**
FK Austria	0-4 0-4	**Juventus**
RFC Liège	2-0 0-1	Estrela da Amadora
Dynamo Kiev	1-0 2-2	Dukla Praha
Fram Reykjavík	1-2 0-3	**Barcelona**

QUARTER-FINALS

Manchester United	1-1 2-0	SCP Montpellier
Legia Warszawa	1-0 2-2	Sampdoria
RFC Liège	1-3 0-3	**Juventus**
Dynamo Kiev	2-3 1-1	**Barcelona**

SEMI-FINALS

Legia Warszawa	1-3 1-1	**Manchester United**
Barcelona	3-1 0-1	Juventus

FINAL

Feyenoord Stadion, Rotterdam, 15-05-1991, 42,000. Referee: Karlsson, Sweden

MANCHESTER UNITED 2 (Bruce 67, Hughes 74)
BARCELONA 1 (Koeman 79)

Manchester United - Sealey, Irwin, Bruce, Pallister, Blackmore - Phelan, Robson, Ince, Sharpe - Hughes, McClair
Barcelona - Busquets - Alexanco (Pinilla), Nando, Koeman.R, Ferrer Goikoetxea, Eusebio, Baquero, Beguiristain - Salinas, Laudrup.M

Top scorer: Baggio, Juventus 9

EUROPEAN SUPERCUP 1991

Old Trafford, Manchester, 19-11-1991. Referee: Vander Ende, Holland

MANCHESTER UNITED 1 (McClair 67)
CRVENA ZVEZDA BEOGRAD 0

1991–92

EUROPEAN CUP

FIRST ROUND

Barcelona	3-0 0-1	Hansa Rostock
1.FC Kaiserslautern	2-0 1-1	Etar Veliko Tirnovo
Union Luxembourg	0-5 0-5	**Olymp. Marseille**
Sparta Praha	1-0 1-2	Glasgow Rangers
Hamrun Spartans	0-6 0-4	**Benfica**
Arsenal	6-1 0-1	FK Austria
Brøndbyernes IF	3-0 1-2	Zaglebie Lubin
HJK Helsinki	0-1 0-3	**Dynamo Kiev**
Fram Reykjavík	2-2 0-0	**Panathinaikos**
IFK Göteborg	0-0 1-1	Flamurtari

Besiktas 1-1 1-2 **PSV Eindhoven**
RSC Anderlecht 1-1 3-0 Grasshopper-Club
Crvena Zvezda Beograd 4-0 4-0 Portadown
Universitatea Craiova 2-0 0-3 **Apollon Limassol**
Kispest-Honvéd 1-1 2-0 Dundalk
Sampdoria 5-0 2-1 Rosenborg BK

SECOND ROUND

Barcelona 2-0 1-3 1.FC Kaiserslautern
Olympique Marseille 3-2 1-2 **Sparta Praha**
Benfica 1-1 3-1 Arsenal
Dynamo Kiev 1-1 1-0 Brøndbyernes IL
Panathinaikos 2-0 2-2 IFK Göteborg
PSV Eindhoven 0-0 0-2 **RSC Anderlecht**
Crvena Zvezda Beograd 3-1 2-0 Apollon Limassol
Kispest-Honved 2-1 1-3 **Sampdoria**

QUARTER-FINAL GROUPS

GROUP 1

	Sa	CZ	An	Pa	Pl	W	D	L	F	A	Pts
Sampdoria	-	2-0	2-0	1-1	6	3	2	1	10	5	8
Crvena Zvezda Beograd	1-3	-	3-2	1-0	6	3	0	3	9	10	6
Anderlecht	3-2	3-2	-	0-0	6	2	2	2	8	9	6
Panathinaikos	0-0	0-2	0-0	-	6	0	4	2	1	4	4

GROUP 2

	Ba	SP	Be	DK	Pl	W	D	L	F	A	Pts
Barcelona	-	3-2	2-1	3-0	6	4	1	1	10	4	9
Sparta Praha	1-0	-	1-1	2-1	6	2	2	2	7	7	6
Benfica	0-0	1-1	-	5-0	6	1	3	2	8	5	5
Dynamo Kiev	0-2	1-0	1-0	-	6	2	0	4	3	12	4

FINAL

Wembley, London, 20-05-1992, 71,000. Referee: Schmidhuber, Germany

BARCELONA 1 (Koeman.R 112)
SAMPDORIA 0

Barcelona - Zubizarreta - Eusebio, Ferrer, Koeman, Muñoz, Juan Carlos, Baquero, Guardiola (Alexanco), Laudrup.M - Salinas (Goikoetxea), Stoichkov. Tr: Cruyff

Sampdoria - Pagliuca - Mannini, Lanna, Vierchowod, Katanec - Lombardo, Pari, Cerezo, Bonetti.I (Invernizzi) - Vialli (Buso), Mancini. Tr: Boskov

Top scorer: Papin, Olympique Marseille 7

UEFA CUP

FIRST ROUND

Ajax 3-0 0-1 Örebro SK
FC Groningen 0-1 0-1 **Rot-Weiss Erfurt**
VfB Stuttgart 4-1 2-2 Pecsi MSC
Slavia Sofia 1-0 0-4 **Osasuna**
Vaci Izzo MTE 1-0 1-4 **Dynamo Moskva**
SC Salgueiros 1-0 0-1 2-4p **AS Cannes**
Eintracht Frankfurt 6-1 5-0 AC Spora
AA Gent 0-1 1-0 4-1p Lausanne-Sports
Liverpool 6-1 0-1 Kuusysi Lahti
Ikast FS 0-1 1-5 **AJ Auxerre**
PAOK Salonica 1-1 1-0 KV Mechelen
FC Tirol 2-1 1-1 Tromsø IL
Anorthosis Famagusta 1-2 2-2 **Steaua Bucuresti**
Sporting Gijón 2-0 0-2 3-2p Partizan Beograd
Sporting CP 0-0 0-2 **Dinamo Bucuresti**
Real Oviedo 1-0 1-3 **Genoa 1893**
Slovan Bratislava 1-2 1-1 **Real Madrid**
SK Sturm Graz 0-1 1-3 **FC Utrecht**
Glasgow Celtic 2-0 1-1 Germinal Ekeren
Neuchâtel Xamax 2-0 0-0 Floriana
Hamburger SV 1-1 3-0 Górnik Zabrze
CSKA Sofia 0-0 1-1 Parma
Hallescher FC 2-1 0-3 **Torpedo Moskva**
Bangor 0-3 0-3 **Sigma Olomouc**
Aberdeen 0-1 0-2 **B 1903 København**
Cork City 1-1 0-2 **Bayern München**
Olympique Lyon 1-0 1-1 Östers IF Växjö
HASK Gradanski 2-3 1-1 **Trabzonspor**
Vllaznia Shkoder 0-1 0-2 **AEK Athens**
MP Mikkeli 0-2 1-3 **Spartak Moskva**
Boavista FC 2-1 0-0 Internazionale
KR Reykjavík 0-2 1-6 **Torino**

SECOND ROUND

Rot-Weiss Erfurt 1-2 0-3 **Ajax**
Osasuna 0-0 3-2 VfB Stuttgart
AS Cannes 0-1 1-1 **Dynamo Moskva**
AA Gent 0-0 1-0 Eintracht Frankfurt
AJ Auxerre 2-0 0-3 **Liverpool**
PAOK Salonica 0-2 0-2 **FC Tirol**
Sporting Gijón 2-2 0-1 **Steaua Bucuresti**
Genoa 1893 3-1 2-2 Dinamo Bucuresti
FC Utrecht 1-3 0-1 **Real Madrid**
Neuchâtel Xamax 5-1 0-1 Glasgow Celtic
Hamburger SV 2-0 4-1 CSKA Sofia
Sigma Olomouc 2-0 0-0 Torpedo Moskva
B 1903 København 6-2 0-1 Bayern München
Olympique Lyon 3-4 1-4 **Trabzonspor**
Spartak Moskva 0-0 1-2 **AEK Athens**
Torino 2-0 0-0 Boavista FC

THIRD ROUND

Osasuna 0-1 0-1 **Ajax**
AA Gent 2-0 0-0 Dynamo Moskva
FC Tirol 0-2 0-4 **Liverpool**
Steaua Bucuresti 0-1 0-1 **Genoa 1893**
Neuchâtel Xamax 1-0 0-4 **Real Madrid**
Hamburger SV 1-2 1-4 **Sigma Olomouc**
B 1903 København 1-0 0-0 Trabzonspor
AEK Athens 2-2 0-1 **Torino**

QUARTER-FINALS

AA Gent 0-0 0-3 **Ajax**
Genoa 1893 2-0 2-1 Liverpool
Sigma Olomouc 1-1 0-1 **Real Madrid**
B 1903 København 0-2 0-1 **Torino**

SEMI-FINALS

Genoa 1893 2-3 1-1 **Ajax**
Real Madrid 2-1 0-2 **Torino**

FINAL

1st leg. Delle Alpi, Turin, 29-04-1992, 65,000. Referee: Worral, England

TORINO 2 (Casagrande 65 82)
AJAX 2 (Jonk 17, Pettersson 73)

Torino - Marchegiani - Bruno, Annoni, Cravero (Bresciani), Mussi (Sordo) Benedetti, Scifo, Martin Vasquez, Venturin - Lentini, Casagrande

Ajax - Menzo - Silooy, Blind, Jonk, De Boer - Winter, Kreek, Bergkamp, Vant'Schip, Pettersson, Roy

2nd leg. Olympisch Stadion, Amsterdam, 13-05-1992, 42,000. Referee: Petrovic, Yugoslavia

AJAX 0
TORINO 0

Ajax - Menzo - Silooy, Blind, Jonk, De Boer - Winter, Kreek (Vink), Alflen, Van't Schip, Petersson, Roy (Van Loen)

Torino - Marchegiani - Mussi, Cravero (Sordo), Benedetti, Fusi, Policano, Martin Vasquez, Scifo (Bresciani), Venturin - Casagrande, Lentini

Top scorer: Saunders, Liverpool 9

CUP WINNERS CUP

PRELIMINARY ROUND

SV Stockerau 0-1 0-1 **Tottenham Hotspur**
Galway United 0-3 0-4 **OB Odense**

FIRST ROUND

FC Bacau 0-6 0-5 **Werder Bremen**
Levski Sofia 2-3 1-4 **Ferencváros**
OB Odense 0-2 1-2 **Baník Ostrava**
Stahl Eisenhüttenstadt 1-2 0-3 **Galatasaray**
Fyllingen IL 0-1 2-7 **Atlético Madrid**
Athinaikos 0-0 0-2 **Manchester United**
GKS Katowice 2-0 1-3 Motherwell
Omonia Nicosia 0-2 0-2 **Club Brugge**
Partizani Tiranë 0-0 0-1 **Feyenoord**
Valur Reykjavík 0-1 1-1 **FC Sion**
Valletta 0-3 0-1 **FC Porto**
Hajduk Split 1-0 0-2 **Tottenham Hotspur**
CSKA Moskva 1-2 1-0 **Roma**
Glenavon 3-2 0-1 **Ilves Tampere**
IFK Norrköping 4-0 2-1 Jeunesse Esch
Swansea City 1-2 0-8 **AS Monaco**

SECOND ROUND

Werder Bremen 3-2 1-0 Ferencváros
Galatasaray 0-1 2-1 Baník Ostrava
Atlético Madrid 3-0 1-1 Manchester United
GKS Katowice 0-1 0-3 **Club Brugge**
FC Sion 0-0 0-0 3-5p **Feyenoord**
Tottenham Hotspur 3-1 0-0 FC Porto
Ilves Tampere 1-1 2-5 **Roma**
IFK Norrköping 1-2 0-1 **AS Monaco**

QUARTER-FINALS

Werder Bremen 2-1 0-0 Galatasaray
Atlético Madrid 3-2 1-2 **Club Brugge**
Feyenoord 1-0 0-0 Tottenham Hotspur
Roma 0-0 0-1 **AS Monaco**

SEMI-FINALS

Club Brugge 1-0 0-2 **Werder Bremen**
AS Monaco 1-1 2-2 Feyenoord

FINAL

Estádio da Luz, Lisbon, 6-05-1992, 15,000. Referee: D'Elia, Italy

WERDER BREMEN 2 (Allofs 41, Rufer 54)
AS MONACO 0

Werder Bremen - Rollmann - Wolter (Schaaf), Borowka, Bratseth, Bode - Bockenfeld, Eilts, Votova, Neubarth - Rufer, Allofs

Monaco - Ettori - Valery (Djorkaeff), Petit, Mendy, Sonor - Dib, Gnako, Passi, Barros - Weah, Fofana (Clement)

Top scorer: Lipcsei, Ferencváros 6

EUROPEAN SUPERCUP 1992

1st leg. Weserstadion, Bremen, 10-02-1993, 40,000. Referee: Nielsen, Denmark

WERDER BREMEN 1 (Allofs.K 87)
BARCELONA 1 (Salinas 37)

2nd leg. Nou Camp, Barcelona, 10-03-1993, 60,000. Referee: Karlsson, Sweden

BARCELONA 2 (Stoichkov 32, Goikoetxea 48)
WERDER BREMEN 1 (Rufer 41)

1992–93

EUROPEAN CUP

PRELIMINARY ROUND

KI Klaksvik 1-2 0-3 **Skonto Riga**
Olimpija Ljubljana 3-0 2-0 Norma Tallinn
Shelbourne 0-0 1-2 **Tavria Simferopol**
Valletta 1-2 0-1 Maccabi Tel Aviv

FIRST ROUND

Glentoran 0-5 0-3 **Olympique Marseille**
Kuusysi Lahti 1-0 0-2 **Dinamo Bucuresti**
FK Austria 3-1 2-3 CSKA Sofia
Maccabi Tel Aviv 0-1 0-3 **Club Brugge**
Vikingur Reykjavík 0-1 0-4 ? **CSKA Moskva**
Barcelona 1-0 0-0 Viking Stavanger
VfB Stuttgart 3-0 1-4 1-2 * **Leeds United**
* Stuttgart fielded an ineligible player in the second game. A play-off in Barcelona was ordered
Glasgow Rangers 2-0 1-0 Lyngby BK
IFK Göteborg 2-0 1-2 Besiktas
Lech Poznan 2-0 0-0 Skonto Riga
AEK Athens 1-1 2-2 Apoel Nicosia
PSV Eindhoven 6-0 2-0 Zalgiris Vilnius
Union Luxembourg 1-4 0-5 **FC Porto**
FC Sion 4-1 3-1 Tavria Simferopol
Slovan Bratislava 4-1 0-0 Ferencváros
Milan 4-0 3-0 Olimpija Ljubljana

SECOND ROUND

Dinamo Bucuresti 0-0 0-2 **Olympique Marseille**
Club Brugge 2-0 1-3 FK Austria
CSKA Moskva 1-1 3-2 Barcelona
Glasgow Rangers 2-1 2-1 Leeds United
IFK Göteborg 1-0 3-0 Lech Poznan
AEK Athens 1-0 0-3 **PSV Eindhoven**
FC Sion 2-2 0-4 **FC Porto**
Slovan Bratislava 0-1 0-4 **Milan**

QUARTER-FINAL GROUPS

Group 1	OM	GR	CB	CM	Pl	W	D	L	F	A	Pts
Olympique Marseille	-	1-1	3-0	6-0	6	3	3	0	14	4	9
Glasgow Rangers	2-2	-	2-1	0-0	6	2	4	0	7	5	8
Club Brugge	0-1	1-1	-	1-0	6	2	1	3	5	8	5
CSKA Moskva	1-1	0-1	1-2	-	6	0	2	4	2	11	2

Group 2	Mi	IG	Po	PE	Pl	W	D	L	F	A	Pts
Milan	-	4-0	1-0	2-0	6	6	0	0	11	1	12
IFK Göteborg	0-1	-	1-0	3-0	6	3	0	3	7	8	6
FC Porto	0-1	2-0	-	2-2	6	2	1	3	5	5	5
PSV Eindhoven	1-2	1-3	0-1	-	6	0	1	5	4	13	1

FINAL

Olympiastadion, Munich, 26-05-1993, 72,000. Referee: Rothlisberger, Switzerland

OLYMPIQUE MARSEILLE 1 (Boli 43)
MILAN 0

Marseille - Barthez - Angloma (Durand), Boli, Desailly, Di Meco - Pelé, Sauzee, Deschamps, Eydelie - Boksic, Völler (Thomas). Tr: Goethals

Milan - Rossi - Tassotti, Costacurta, Baresi, Maldini - Donadoni (Papin), Rijkaard, Albertini, Lentini - Van Basten (Eranio), Massaro. Tr: Capello

Top Scorer: Romario, PSV Eindhoven 7

UEFA CUP

FIRST ROUND

Juventus 6-1 4-0 Anorthosis Famagusta
Electroputere Craiova 0-6 0-4 **Panathinaikos**
Fenerbahçe 3-1 2-2 Botev Plovdiv
Sigma Olomouc 1-0 2-1 Universitatea Craiova
Dynamo Moskva 5-1 0-2 Rosenborg BK Trondheim
IFK Norrköping 1-0 0-3 **Torino**
Vaci Izzo 1-0 1-1 FC Groningen
Benfica 3-0 5-0 Belvedur Isola
Politechnica Timisoara 1-1 0-4 **Real Madrid**
Manchester United 0-0 0-0 3-4p **Torpedo Moskva**
KV Mechelen 2-1 0-0 Örebro SK
Vitesse Arnhem 3-0 2-1 Derry City
Hibernian Edinburgh 2-2 1-1 **RSC Anderlecht**
Dynamo Kiev 1-0 2-3 SK Rapid Wien
Valencia 1-5 0-1 **Napoli**
Paris Saint-Germain 2-0 2-0 * PAOK Salonica
Lokomotiv Plovdiv 2-2 1-7 **AJ Auxerre**
FC København 5-0 5-1 MP Mikkeli
Slavia Praha 1-0 2-4 **Heart of Midlothian**
Standard CL 5-0 0-0 Portadown
Fram Reykjavík 0-3 0-4 **1.FC Kaiserslautern**
Sheffield Wednesday 8-1 2-1 Spora Luxembourg
Vitória Guimaraes 3-0 0-2 Real Sociedad
Austria Salzburg 0-3 1-3 **Ajax**
Wacker Innsbruck 1-4 0-1 **Roma**
Grasshopper-Club 1-2 3-1 Sporting CP
Widzew Lodz 2-2 0-9 **Eintracht Frankfurt**
GKS Katowice 0-0 1-2 **Galatasaray**
Caen 3-2 0-2 **Real Zaragoza**
Neuchâtel Xamax 2-2 1-4 **Frem København**
1.FC Köln 2-0 0-3 **Glasgow Celtic**
Floriana 0-1 2-7 **Borussia Dortmund**
* Second match abandoned after 46 minutes. Result stood

SECOND ROUND

Panathinaikos 0-1 0-0 **Juventus**
Fenerbahçe 1-0 1-7 **Sigma Olomouc**
Torino 1-2 0-0 **Dynamo Moskva**
Benfica 5-1 1-0 Vaci Izzo
Real Madrid 5-2 2-3 Torpedo Moskva
Vitesse Arnhem 1-0 1-0 KV Mechelen
RSC Anderlecht 4-2 3-0 Dynamo Kiev
Napoli 0-2 0-0 **Paris Saint-Germain**
AJ Auxerre 5-0 2-0 FC København
Heart of Midlothian 0-1 0-1 **Standard CL**
1.FC Kaiserslautern 3-1 2-2 Sheffield Wednesday
Vitória Guimaraes 0-3 1-2 **Ajax**
Roma 3-0 3-4 Grasshopper-Club
Eintracht Frankfurt 0-0 0-1 **Galatasaray**
Frem København 0-1 1-5 **Real Zaragoza**
Borussia Dortmund 1-0 2-1 Glasgow Celtic

THIRD ROUND

Sigma Olomouc 1-2 0-5 **Juventus**
Dynamo Moskva 2-2 0-2 **Benfica**
Vitesse Arnhem 0-1 0-1 **Real Madrid**
Paris Saint-Germain 0-0 1-1 RSC Anderlecht
Standard CL 2-2 1-2 **AJ Auxerre**
Ajax 2-0 1-0 1FC Kaiserslautern
Roma 3-1 2-3 Galatasaray
Borussia Dortmund 3-1 1-2 Real Zaragoza

QUARTER-FINALS

Benfica 2-1 0-3 **Juventus**
Real Madrid 3-1 1-4 **Paris Saint-Germain**
AJ Auxerre 4-2 0-1 Ajax
Roma 1-0 0-2 **Borussia Dortmund**

SEMI-FINALS

Juventus 2-1 1-0 Paris Saint-Germain
Borussia Dortmund 2-0 0-2 6-5p AJ Auxerre

FINAL

1st leg. Westfalenstadion, Dortmund, 5-05-1993, 37,000. Referee: Puhl, Hungary
BORUSSIA DORTMUND 1 (Rummenigge.M 2)
JUVENTUS 3 (Baggio.D 27, Baggio.R 31 74)
Dortmund - Klos - Grauer, Reuter, Schmidt, Lusch - Franck (Mil), Zorc (Karl), Rummenigge, Poschner - Reinhardt, Chapuisat
Juventus - Peruzzi - Julio Cesar, Carrera, Kohler, De Marchi - Conte, Baggio.D, Baggio.R (Di Canio), Marocchi - Vialli, Möller (Galia)

2nd leg. Delle Alpi, Turin, 19-05-1993, 60,000. Referee: Blankenstein, Holland
JUVENTUS 3 (Baggio.D 5 40, Möller 65)
BORUSSIA DORTMUND 0
Juventus - Peruzzi - Carrera, Torricelli (Di Canio), De Marchi, Kohler, - Julio Cesar, Möller, Baggio.D, Baggio.R - Vialli (Ravanelli), Marocchi
Dortmund - Klos - Reinhardt, Schmidt, Schulz, Zelic - Poschner, Reuter (Lusch), Karl, Mil - Rummenigge (Franck), Sippel

Top scorer: Baticle, Auxerre 8

CUP WINNERS CUP

PRELIMINARY ROUND

Avenir Beggen 1-0 1-1 B'36 Tórshavn
FC Vaduz 0-5 1-7 **Chernomorets Odessa**
Branik Maribor 4-0 1-2 Hamrun Spartans
IF Strømgodset 0-2 0-2 **Hapoel Petah Tikva**

FIRST ROUND

Parma 1-0 1-1 Ujpesti TE
Valur Reykjavík 0-0 0-3 **Boavista**
Werder Bremen 3-1 1-2 Hannover 96
Airdrieonians 0-1 1-2 **Sparta Praha**
Olympiakos 0-1 3-0 Chernomorets Odessa
Miedz Legnica 0-1 0-0 **AS Monaco**
Trabzonspor 2-0 2-2 TPS Turku
Branik Maribor 0-3 1-6 **Atlético Madrid**
Spartak Moskva 0-0 5-1 Avenir Beggen
Liverpool 6-1 2-1 Apollon Limassol
Levski Sofia 2-1 0-1 **FC Luzern**
Feyenoord 1-0 1-2 Hapoel Petah Tikva
Bohemians Dublin 0-0 0-4 **Steaua Bucuresti**
AIK Stockholm 3-3 1-1 **ÅGF Århus**
Cardiff City 1-1 0-2 **Admira-Wacker**
Glenavon 1-1 1-1 1-3p **Royal Antwerp FC**

SECOND ROUND

Parma 0-0 2-0 Boavista
Werder Bremen 2-3 0-1 **Sparta Praha**
AS Monaco 0-1 0-0 **Olympiakos**
Trabzonspor 0-2 0-0 **Atlético Madrid**
Spartak Moskva 4-2 2-0 Liverpool
FC Luzern 1-0 1-4 **Feyenoord**
ÅGF Århus 3-2 1-2 **Steaua Bucuresti**
Admira-Wacker 2-4 4-3 **Royal Antwerp FC**

QUARTER-FINALS

Sparta Praha 0-0 0-2 **Parma**
Olympiakos 1-1 1-3 **Atlético Madrid**
Feyenoord 0-1 1-3 **Spartak Moskava**
Royal Antwerp FC 0-0 1-1 Steaua Bucuresti

SEMI-FINALS

Atlético Madrid 1-2 1-0 **Parma**
Spartak Moskva 1-0 1-3 **Royal Antwerp FC**

FINAL

Wembley, London, 12-05-1993, 37,000. Referee: Assenmacher, Germany

PARMA 3 (Minotti 9, Melli 30, Cuoghi 83)
ROYAL ANTWERP FC 1 (Severeyns 11)

Parma - Ballotta - Benarrivo, Di Chiara, Minotti, Apolloni, Grun - Zoratto (Pin), Cuoghi, Osio (Pizzi) - Melli, Brolin. Tr: Scala

Antwerp - Stojanovic - Brockaert, Taeymans, Smidts, Van Rethy, Segers (Moukrim) - Kiekens, Jakovljevic (Veirdeghem), Lehnhoff - Severeyns, Czerniatynski. Tr: Meeuws

Top scorer: Czerniatynski, Royal Antwerp 7

EUROPEAN SUPERCUP 1993

1st leg. Ennio Tardini, Parma, 12-01-1994. Referee: Diaz Vega, Spain

PARMA 0
MILAN 1 (Papin 43)

2nd leg. Giuseppe Meazza, Milan, 2-02-1994. Referee: Röthlisberger, Switzerland

MILAN 0
PARMA 2 (Sensini 23, Crippa 95)

1993–94

EUROPEAN CUP

PRELIMINARY ROUND

B'68 Toftir	0-5 0-6	**Croatia Zagreb**
Cwmbran Town	3-2 1-2	**Cork City**
Ekranas Panavezys	0-1 0-1	**Floriana**
HJK Helsinki	1-1 1-0	Norma Tallinn
Omonia Nicosia	2-1 0-2	**FC Aarau**
Avenir Beggen	0-2 0-1	**Rosenborg BK Trond.**
Skonto Riga	0-1 1-0 11-10p	Olimpija Ljubljana
Dynamo Tbilisi`	2-1 1-1	**Linfield**
Zimbru Kishinov	1-1 0-2	**Beitar Jerusalem**
Partizani Tiranë	0-0 0-3	**IA Akranes**

FIRST ROUND

FC Aarau	0-1 0-0	**Milan**
Linfield	3-0 0-4	**FC København**
AIK Stockholm	1-0 0-2	**Sparta Praha**
HJK Helsinki	0-3 0-3	**RSC Anderlecht**
Glasgow Rangers	3-2 1-2	**Levski Sofia**
Werder Bremen	5-2 1-1	Dynamo Minsk
IA Akranes	1-0 0-3	**Feyenoord**
FC Porto	2-0 0-0	Floriana
AS Monaco	1-0 1-1	AEK Athens
Steaua Buçuresti	1-2 3-2	Croatia Zagreb
Honved	2-3 1-2	**Manchester United**
Galatasaray	2-1 1-0	Cork City
Skonto Riga	0-5 0-4	**Spartak Moskva**
Lech Poznan	3-0 4-2	Beitar Jerusalem
Rosenborg BK Trondheim	3-1 1-4	**FK Austria**
Dynamo Kiev	3-1 1-4	**Barcelona**

SECOND ROUND

FC København	0-6 0-1	**Milan**
Levski Sofia	2-2 0-1	**Werder Bremen**
Sparta Praha	0-1 2-4	**RSC Anderlecht**
FC Porto	1-0 0-0	Feyenoord
AS Monaco	4-1 0-1	Steaua Buçuresti
Manchester United	3-3 0-0	**Galatasaray**
Lech Poznan	1-5 1-2	**Spartak Moskva**
Barcelona	3-0 2-1	FK Austria

QUARTER-FINAL GROUPS

Group A

	Ba	Mo	SM	Ga	Pl	W	D	L	F	A	Pts
Barcelona	-	2-0	5-1	3-0	6	4	2	0	13	3	10
AS Monaco	0-1	-	4-1	3-0	6	3	1	2	9	4	7
Spartak Moskva	2-2	0-0	-	0-0	6	1	3	2	6	12	5
Galatasaray	0-0	0-2	1-2	-	6	0	2	4	1	10	2

Group B

	Mi	Po	WB	An	Pl	W	D	L	F	A	Pts
Milan	-	3-0	2-1	0-0	6	2	4	0	6	2	8
FC Porto	0-0	-	3-2	2-0	6	3	1	2	10	6	7
Werder Bremen	1-1	0-5	-	5-3	6	2	1	3	11	15	5
RSC Anderlecht	0-0	1-0	1-2	-	6	1	2	3	5	9	4

SEMI-FINALS

Milan	3-0	AS Monaco
Barcelona	3-0	FC Porto

FINAL

Olympic Stadium, Athens, 18-05-1994, 75,000. Referee: Don, England

MILAN 4 (Massaro 22 45, Savicevic 47, Desailly 58)
BARCELONA 0

Milan - Rossi - Tassotti, Galli, Maldini (Nava), Panucci - Albertini, Desailly, Donadoni, Boban - Savicevic, Massaro. Tr: Capello

Barcelona - Zubiarreta - Ferrer, Nadal, Koeman.R, Sergi (Enrique) - Amor, Bakero, Guardiola, Beguiristain (Eusebio) - Romario, Stoichkov. Tr: Cruyff

Top scorers: Koeman.R, Barcelona 8
Rufer, Werder Bremen 8

UEFA CUP

FIRST ROUND

Internazionale	3-1 2-0	Rapid Bucharest
VAC FC	2-0 0-4	**Apollon Limassol**
FC Twente Enschede	3-4 0-3	**FC Bayern München**
Norwich City	3-0 0-0	Vitesse Arnhem
Brøndbyernes IF	2-0 1-3	Dundee United
Kuusysi Lahti	4-0 2-1	KSV Waregem
Gloria Bistrita	0-0 0-2	**Maribor Branik**
Borussia Dortmund	0-0 1-0	Spartak Vladikavkaz
Juventus	3-0 1-0	Lokomotiv Moskva
Östers IF Växjö	1-3 1-4	**Kongsvinger IL**
Botev Plovdiv	2-3 1-5	**Olympiakos**
Tenerife	2-2 1-0	AJ Auxerre
IFK Norrköping	0-1 1-1	**KV Mechelen**
KR Reykjavík	1-2 0-0	**MTK Budapest**
Trabzonspor	3-1 3-1	Valletta
Dinamo Bucuresti	3-2 0-2	**Cagliari**
Karlsruher SC	2-1 0-0	PSV Eindhoven
FC Nantes	1-1 1-3	**Valencia**
Crusaders	0-0 0-4	**Servette FC**
Bohemians Dublin	0-1 0-5	**Girondins Bordeaux**
Slavia Praha	1-1 0-1	**OFI Crete**
Heart of Midlothian	2-1 0-3	**Atlético Madrid**
Lazio	2-0 2-0	Lokomotiv Plovdiv
Union Luxembourg	0-1 0-4	**Boavista**
Dynamo Moskva	0-6 2-1	**Eintracht Frankfurt**
Dnepr Dnepropetrovsk	1-0 3-2	Admira Wacker
Slovan Bratislava	0-0 1-2	**Aston Villa**
AAB Aalborg	1-0 0-5	**Deportivo La Coruña**
Kocaelispor	0-0 0-2	**Sporting CP**
BSC Young Boys	0-0 0-1	**Glasgow Celtic**
Royal Antwerp FC	2-0 2-2	Maritimo
Austria Salzburg	2-0 2-0	DAC Dunajska Streda

SECOND ROUND

Internazionale 1-0 3-3 Apollon Limassol
FC Bayern München 1-2 1-1 **Norwich City**
Kuusysi Lahti 1-4 1-3 **Brøndbyernes IF**
Maribor Branik 0-0 1-2 **Borussia Dortmund**
Kongsvinger IL 1-1 0-2 **Juventus**
Tenerife 2-1 3-4 Olympiakos
KV Mechelen 5-0 1-1 MTK Budapest
Trabzonspor 1-1 0-0 **Cagliari**
Valencia 3-1 0-7 **Karlsruher SC**
Girondins Bordeaux 2-1 1-0 Servette FC
Atlético Madrid 1-0 0-2 **OFI Crete**
Lazio 1-0 0-2 **Boavista**
Eintracht Frankfurt 2-0 0-1 Dnepr Dnepropetrovsk
Deportivo La Coruña 1-1 1-0 Aston Villa
Glasgow Celtic 1-0 0-2 **Sporting CP**
Austria Salzburg 1-0 1-0 Royal Antwerp FC

THIRD ROUND

Norwich City 0-1 0-1 **Internazionale**
Brøndbyernes IF 1-1 0-1 **Borussia Dortmund**
Juventus 3-0 1-2 Tenerife
KV Mechelen 1-3 0-2 **Cagliari**
Girondins Bordeaux 1-0 0-3 **Karlsruher SC**
OFI Crete 1-4 0-2 **Boavista**
Eintracht Frankfurt 1-0 1-0 Deportivo La Coruña
Sporting CP 2-0 0-3 **Austria Salzburg**

QUARTER-FINALS

Borussia Dortmund 1-3 2-1 **Internazionale**
Cagliari 1-0 2-1 Juventus
Boavista 1-1 0-1 **Karlsruher SC**
Austria Salzburg 1-0 0-1 5-4p Eintracht Frankfurt

SEMI-FINALS

Cagliari 3-2 0-3 **Internazionale**
Austria Salzburg 0-0 1-1 Karlsruher SV

FINAL

1st leg. Ernst Happel Stadion, Vienna, 26-04-1994, 47,000. Referee: Nielsen, Denmark

AUSTRIA SALZBURG 0
INTERNAZIONALE 1 (Berti 35)

Salzburg - Konrad - Lainer, Weber, Winklhofer (Steiner), Furstaller - Aigner, Amerhauser (Muzek), Artner, Marquinho - Pfeifenberger, Stadler

Inter - Zenga - Paganin.A, Orlando, Jonk, Bergomi - Battistini, Bianchi, Manicone, Berti - Bergkamp (Dell'Anno), Sosa (Ferri)

2nd leg. Giuseppe Meazza, Milan, 11-05-1994, 80,000. Referee: McCluskey, Scotland

INTERNAZIONALE 1 (Jonk 63)
AUSTRIA SALZBURG 0

Inter - Zenga - Paganin.A, Fontolan (Ferri), Jonk, Bergomi - Battistini, Orlando, Manicone, Berti - Bergkamp (Paganin.M), Sosa. Tr: Bagnoli

Salzburg - Konrad - Winklhofer (Amerhauser), Lainer, Weber, Furstaller - Aigner, Jurcevic, Artner (Steiner), Hutter - Marquinho, Feiesinger. Tr: Baric

Top scorers: Bergkamp, Internazionale 8
Schmitt, Karlsruher SC 8

CUP WINNERS CUP

PRELIMINARY ROUND

FC Balzers 3-1 0-0 Albpetrol Patosi
RAF Jelgava 0-1* **HB Tórshavn**
Stade Dudelange 0-1 1-6 **Maccabi Haifa**
FC Lugano 5-0 1-2 Neman Grodno
Valur Reykjavík 3-1 0-1 MyPa Anjalankoski
Sliema Wanderers 1-3 0-3 **Degerfors IF**
Bangor 1-1 1-2 **Apoel Nicosia**
Nikol Tallinn 0-4 1-4 **Lillestrøm SK**
1.FC Kosice 2-0 0-1 Zalgiris Vilnius
Karpaty Lvov 1-0 1-3 **Shelbourne**
Publikum Celje 0-1 0-0 **OB Odense**
*HB received a bye after RAF failed to appear for the second leg

FIRST ROUND

OB Odense 1-2 1-1 **Arsenal**
Standard CL 5-2 3-1 Cardiff City
Valur Reykjavík 0-3 0-4 **Aberdeen**
Lillestrøm SK 0-2 2-1 **Torino**
Real Madrid 3-0 3-1 FC Lugano
FC Innsbruck Tirol 3-0 2-1 Ferencváros
Universitatea Craiova 4-0 3-0 HB Tórshavn
Apoel Nicosia 0-1 0-2 **Paris Saint-Germain**
Benfica 1-0 1-1 GKS Katowice
CSKA Sofia 8-0 3-1 FC Balzers
Panathinaikos 3-0 2-1 Shelbourne
Bayer Leverkusen 2-0 3-0 FC Boby Brno
Hajduk Split 1-0 0-6 **Ajax**
1.FC Kosice 2-1 0-2 **Besiktas**
Torpedo Moskva 1-0 1-3 **Maccabi Haifa**
Degerfors IF 1-2 0-2 **Parma**

SECOND ROUND

Arsenal 3-0 7-0 Standard CL
Torino 3-2 2-1 Aberdeen
FC Innsbruck Tirol 1-1 0-3 **Real Madrid**
Paris Saint-Germain 4-0 2-0 Universitatea Craiova
Benfica 3-1 3-1 CSKA Sofia
Panathinaikos 1-4 2-1 **Bayer Leverkusen**
Ajax 2-1 4-0 Besiktas
Maccabi Haifa 0-1 1-0 1-3p **Parma**

QUARTER-FINALS

Torino 0-0 0-1 **Arsenal**
Real Madrid 0-1 1-1 **Paris Saint-Germain**
Benfica 1-1 4-4 Bayer Leverkusen
Ajax 0-0 0-2 **Parma**

SEMI-FINALS

Paris Saint-Germain 1-1 0-1 **Arsenal**
Benfica 2-1 0-1 **Parma**

FINAL

Parkstadion, Copenhagen, 4-05-1994, 33,000. Referee: Krondl, Czech Republic

ARSENAL 1 (Smith 19)
PARMA 0

Arsenal - Seaman - Dixon, Winterburn, Davis, Bould, Adams - Campbell, Morrow, Smith, Merson (McGoldrick), Selley. Tr: Graham

Parma - Bucci - Benarrivo, Di Chiara, Minotti, Apolloni - Sensini, Brolin, Pin (Melli), Crippa - Zola, Asprilla. Tr: Scala

Top scorers: Andenov, CSKA Sofia 5
Jess, Aberdeen 5
Kirsten, Bayer Leverkusen 5
Mizrahi, Maccabi Haifa 5

EUROPEAN SUPERCUP 1994

1st leg. Highbury, London, 1-02-1995, 38,000. Referee: Van der Ende, Holland

Arsenal 0
Milan 0

2nd leg. Giuseppe Meazza, Milan, 8-02-1995, 23,000. Referee: Krug, Germany

Milan 2 (Boban 41, Massaro 66)
Arsenal 0

1994–95

EUROPEAN CUP

FIRST ROUND

AEK Athens	2-0 1-0	Glasgow Rangers
Avenir Beggen	1-5 0-4	**Galatasaray**
Legia Warszawa	0-1 0-4	**Hajduk Split**
Maccabi Haifa	1-2 1-3	**Austria Salzburg**
Paris Saint-Germain	3-0 2-1	FC Vac
Silkeborg IF	0-0 1-3	Dynamo Kiev
Sparta Praha	1-0 0-2	**IFK Göteborg**
Steaua Buçuresti	4-1 1-1	Servette FC

Ajax, Anderlecht, Barcelona, FC Bayern München, Benfica, Manchester United, Milan, Spartak Moskva all received byes to the Champions League

CHAMPIONS LEAGUE

Group A

	Go	Ba	MU	Ga	Pl	W	D	L	F	A	Pts
IFK Göteborg	-	2-1	3-1	1-0	6	4	1	1	10	7	9
Barcelona	1-1	-	4-0	2-1	6	2	2	2	11	8	6
Manchester United	4-2	2-2	-	4-0	6	2	2	2	11	11	6
Galatasaray	0-1	2-1	0-0	-	6	1	1	4	3	9	3

Group B

	PS	BM	SM	DK	Pl	W	D	L	F	A	Pts
Paris Saint-Germain	-	2-0	4-1	1-0	6	6	0	0	12	3	12
Bayern München	0-1	-	2-2	1-0	6	2	2	2	8	7	6
Spartak Moskva	1-2	1-1	-	1-0	6	1	2	3	8	12	4
Dynamo Kiev	1-2	1-4	3-2	-	6	1	0	5	5	11	2

Group C

	Be	HS	SB	An	Pl	W	D	L	F	A	Pts
Benfica	-	2-1	2-1	3-1	6	3	3	0	9	5	9
Hajduk Split	0-0	-	1-4	2-1	6	2	2	2	5	7	6
Steaua Bucuresti	1-1	0-1	-	1-1	6	1	3	2	7	6	5
Anderlecht	1-1	0-0	0-0	-	6	0	4	2	4	7	4

Group D

	Aj	Mi	AS	AA	Pl	W	D	L	F	A	Pts
Ajax	-	2-0	1-1	2-0	6	4	2	0	9	2	10
Milan	0-2	-	3-0*	2-1	6	3	1	2	6	5	5
Austria Salzburg	0-0	0-1	-	0-0	6	1	3	2	4	6	5
AEK Athens	1-2	0-0	1-3	-	6	0	2	4	3	9	2

*Milan deducted two points

QUARTER-FINALS

Hajduk Split	0-0 0-3	**Ajax**
Bayern München	0-0 2-2	IFK Göteborg
Barcelona	1-1 1-2	**Paris Saint-Germain**
Milan	2-0 0-0	Benfica

SEMI-FINALS

Bayern München	0-0 2-5	**Ajax**
Paris Saint-Germain	0-1 0-2	**Milan**

FINAL

Ernst Happel Stadion, Vienna, 24-05-1995, 49,000. Referee: Craciunescu, Romania

AJAX 1 (Kluivert 85)
MILAN 0

Ajax - Van der Sar - Reiziger, Blind, De Boer.F - Seedorf (Kanu), Rijkaard, Litmanen (Kluivert), Davids - George, De Boer.R, Overmars. Tr: Van Gaal

Milan - Rossi - Panucci, Costacurta, Baresi, Maldini - Donadoni, Albertini, Desailly, Boban - Massaro (Eranio), Simone. Tr: Capello

Top Scorer - Weah, Paris Saint-Germain 7

UEFA CUP

PRELIMINARY ROUND

SK Slavia Praha	2-0 4-0	Cork City
ROMAR Mazeikiai	0-2 0-2	**AIK Stockholm**
Anorthosis Famagusta	2-0 2-1	FC Shumen
Bangor City	1-2 0-2	**IA Akranes**
FH Hafnarfjördur	1-0 1-3	**Linfield**
OB Odense	3-0 3-0	Flora Tallinn
Vardar Skopje	1-1 0-1	**Békéscsaba**
Teuta Durrës	1-4 2-4	**Apollon Limassol**
Inter Cardiff	0-2 0-6	**GKS Katowice**
Aris Salonica	3-1 2-1	Hapoel Beer-Sheva
Lillestrøm SK	4-1 0-2	Shakhtyor Donetsk
Kispest-Honved	4-1 1-0	Zimbru Chisinau
Motherwell	3-0 4-1	HB Tórshavn
FC København	0-1 4-0	FC Jazz Pori
Portadown	0-2 0-3	**Slovan Bratislava**
Dynamo Tbilisi	2-0 2-1	Universitatea Craiova
CS Grevenmacher	1-2 0-6	**Rosenborg BK Trond.**
GI Gotu	0-1 2-3	**Trelleborgs FF**
Dynamo Minsk	3-1 3-4	Hibernians
Olimpija Ljubljana	3-2 2-1	Levski Sofia
Valletta	2-6 1-1	**Rapid Bucuresti**
Inter Bratislava	0-3 1-0	**MyPa**
Skonto Riga	0-0 1-1	Aberdeen
Górnik Zabrze	6-0 1-0	Shamrock Rovers
Fenerbahçe	5-0 2-0	Turan Tauz
FC Aarau	1-0 1-0	Mura Murska Sobota
CSKA Sofia	3-0 0-0	Ararat Yerevan

FIRST ROUND

Vitesse Arnhem	1-0 0-2	**Parma**
AIK Stockholm	0-0 2-2	SK Slavia Praha
Royal Antwerp FC	0-5 2-5	**Newcastle United**
Anorthosis Famagusta	2-0 0-3	**Athletic Bilbao**
Real Madrid	1-0 1-2	Sporting CP
RFC Seraing	3-4 1-0	**Dynamo Moskva**
IA Akranes	0-4 1-4	**1.FC Kaiserslautern**
Linfield	1-1 0-5	**OB Odense**
Rotor Volgograd	3-2 0-3	**FC Nantes**
Tekstilschik Kamyshin	6-1 0-1	Békéscsaba
Olympiakos	1-2 0-3	**Olympique Marseille**
Apollon Limassol	1-3 3-2	**FC Sion**
GKS Katowice	1-0 0-1 4-3p	Aris Salonica
Girondins Bordeaux	3-1 2-0	Lillestrøm SK
FC Twente Enschede	1-4 3-1	**Kispest-Honved**
Bayer Leverkusen	5-4 0-0	PSV Eindhoven
Borussia Dortmund	1-0 2-0	Motherwell
Slovan Bratislava	1-0 1-1	FC København
Dynamo Tbilisi	1-0 1-5	**FC Tirol Innsbruck**
Rosenborg BK Trondheim	1-0 1-4	**Deportivo La Coruña**
Trabzonspor	2-1 3-3	Dinamo Bucuresti
Internazionale	1-0 0-1 3-4p	**Aston Villa**
Blackburn Rovers	0-1 2-2	**Trelleborgs FF**
Dynamo Minsk	0-0 1-4	**Lazio**
Olimpija Ljubljana	1-1 0-2	**Eintracht Frankfurt**
Rapid Bucuresti	2-0 1-2	RSC Charleroi
Boavista	2-1 1-1	MyPa
Napoli	2-0 1-0	Skonto Riga
Admira Wacker	5-2 1-1	Gornik Zabrze
AS Cannes	4-0 5-1	Fenerbahçe
FC Aarau	0-0 0-1	**CS Maritimo**
CSKA Sofia	3-2 1-5	**Juventus**

SECOND ROUND

AIK Stockholm	0-1 0-2	**Parma**
Newcastle United	3-2 0-1	**Athletic Bilbao**
Dynamo Moskva	2-2 0-4	**Real Madrid**
1.FC Kaiserslautern	1-1 0-0	**OB Odense**

FC Nantes 2-0 2-1 Tekstilschik Kamyshin
FC Sion 2-0 1-3 Olympique Marseille
GKS Katowice 1-0 1-1 Girondins Bordeaux
Kispest-Honved 0-2 0-5 **Bayer Leverkusen**
Slovan Bratislava 2-1 0-3 **Borussia Dortmund**
FC Tirol Innsbruck 2-0 0-4 **Deportivo La Coruña**
Trabzonspor 1-0 1-2 Aston Villa
Trelleborgs FF 0-0 0-1 **Lazio**
Rapid Bucuresti 2-1 0-5 **Eintracht Frankfurt**
Boavista 1-1 1-2 **Napoli**
Admira-Wacker 1-1 4-2 AS Cannes
Maritimo 0-1 1-2 **Juventus**

THIRD ROUND

Athletic Bilbao 1-0 2-4 **Parma**
OB Odense 2-3 2-0 Real Madrid
FC Nantes 4-0 2-2 FC Sion
GKS Katowice 1-4 0-4 **Bayer Leverkusen**
Deportivo La Coruña 1-0 1-3 **Borussia Dortmund**
Trabzonspor 1-2 1-2 **Lazio**
Entracht Frankfurt 1-0 1-0 Napoli
Admira-Wacker 1-3 1-2 **Juventus**

QUARTER-FINALS

Parma 1-0 0-0 OB Odense
Bayer Leverkusen 5-1 0-0 FC Nantes
Lazio 1-0 0-2 **Borussia Dortmund**
Eintracht Frankfurt 1-1 0-3 **Juventus**

SEMI-FINALS

Bayer Leverkusen 1-2 0-3 **Parma**
Juventus 2-2 2-1 Borussia Dortmund

FINAL

1st leg. Ennio Tardini, Parma, 3-05-1995, 22,000. Referee: Lopez Nieto, Spain

PARMA 1 (Baggio.D 5)
JUVENTUS 0

Parma - Bucci - Benarrivo (Mussi), Minotti, Apolloni, Fernando Couto, Di Chiara - Pin, Baggio.D, Sensini, Zola (Fiore), Asprilla

Juventus - Rampulla - Fusi (Del Piero), Tacchinardi, Carrera (Marocchi), Jarni - Paulo Sousa, Di Livio, Deschamps - Vialli, Baggio.R, Ravanelli

2nd leg. Giuseppe Meazza, Milan, 17-05-1995, 80,000. Referee: Van der Wijngaert, Belgium

JUVENTUS 1 (Vialli 33)
PARMA 1 (Baggio.D 54)

Juventus - Peruzzi - Ferrara, Porrini, Torricelli, Jarni - Paulo Sousa, Di Livio (Carrera), Marocchi (Del Piero), Baggio.R - Vialli, Ravanelli. Tr Lippi

Parma - Bucci - Benarrivo (Mussi), Susic, Minotti, Di Chiara (Castellini) - Couto, Fiore, Baggio.D, Crippa - Zola. Tr: Scala

Top scorer - Kirsten, Bayer Leverkusen

CUP WINNERS CUP

PRELIMINARY ROUND

Bangor 0-1 0-4 **Tatran Presov**
IBK Keflavik 1-2 1-4 **Maccabi Tel Aviv**
Barry Town 0-1 0-6 **Zalgiris Vilnius**
Floriana 2-2 0-1 **Sligo Rovers**
Pirin Blagoevgrad 3-0 1-0 FC Schaan
FC Norma Tallinn 1-4 0-10 **Maribor Branik**
Viktoria Zizkov 1-0 3-3 IFK Norrköping
FK Bodø-Glimt 6-0 0-0 Olimpija Riga
Ferencváros 6-1 6-1 F91 Dudelange
B 71 Sandur 0-5 0-2 **HJK Helsinki**
Fandok Bobruisk 4-1 0-3 **SK Tiranë**
Tiligul Tiraspol 0-1 1-3 **Omonia Nicosia**

FIRST ROUND

Gloria Bistrita 2-1 0-4 **Real Zaragoza**
Dundee United 3-2 1-3 **Tatran Presov**
Maccabi Tel Aviv 0-0 0-2 **Werder Bremen**
Zagiris Vilnius 1-1 1-2 **Feyenoord**
Sligo Rovers 1-2 1-3 **Club Brugge**
Pirin Blagoevgrad 0-2 1-6 **Panathinaikos**
Maribor Branik 1-1 0-3 **FK Austria**
Chelsea 4-2 0-0 Viktoria Zizkov
FK Bodø-Glimt 3-2 0-2 **Sampdoria**
Grasshopper-Club 3-0 0-1 Chernomorets Odessa
CSKA Moskva 2-1 1-2 6-7p Ferencváros
FC Porto 2-0 1-0 LKS Lodz
Croatia Zagreb 3-1 0-3 **AJ Auxerre**
Besiktas 2-0 1-1 HJK Helsinki
Brøndbyernes IF 3-0 1-0 SK Tiranë
Omonia Nicosia 1-3 0-3 **Arsenal**

SECOND ROUND

Tatran Presov 0-4 1-2 **Real Zaragoza**
Feyenoord 1-0 4-3 Werder Bremen
Club Brugge 1-0 0-0 Panathinaikos
Chelsea 0-0 1-1 FK Austria
Sampdoria 3-0 2-3 Grasshopper-Club
FC Porto 6-0 0-2 Ferencváros
Besiktas 2-2 0-2 **AJ Auxerre**
Brøndbyernes IF 1-2 2-2 **Arsenal**

QUARTER-FINALS

Feyenoord 1-0 0-2 **Real Zaragoza**
Club Brugge 1-0 0-2 **Chelsea**
Sampdoria 0-1 1-0 5-3p FC Porto
Arsenal 1-1 1-0 AJ Auxerre

SEMI-FINALS

Real Zaragoza 3-0 1-3 Chelsea
Arsenal 3-2 2-3 3-2p Sampdoria

FINAL

Parc des Princes, Paris, 10-05-1995, 42,000. Referee: Ceccarini, Italy

REAL ZARAGOZA 2 (Esnaider 68, Nayim 119)
ARSENAL 1 (Hartson 77)

Zaragoza - Cedrun - Belsue, Aguado, Caceres, Solana - Aragon, Nayim, Parseza, Poyet, Higuera (Garcia Sanjuan) (Geli) - Esnaider. Tr: Fernandez

Arsenal - Seaman - Dixon, Adams, Linighan, Winterburn (Morrow) - Schwarz, Keown (Hillier), Parlour, Merson - Wright, Hartson. Tr: Houston

Top scorer - Wright, Arsenal 9

COMBINED EUROPEAN CLUB RECORDS

	Team	Country	G	S	B
1	Real Madrid	ESP	8	5	8
2	Barcelona	ESP	7	6	4
3	Milan	ITA	7	4	2
4	Ajax	HOL	6	2	2
	Liverpool	ENG	6	2	2
6	Juventus	ITA	5	5	5
7	Bayern München	FRG/GER	4	2	9
8	Internazionale	ITA	4	2	6
9	RSC Anderlecht	BEL	3	4	2
10	Tottenham Hotspur	ENG	3	1	3
11	Valencia	ESP	3	1	-
12	Benfica	POR	2	6	3
13	Bor. Mönchengladbach	FRG/GER	2	3	3

14	Hamburger SV	FRG/GER	2	3	2
	Leeds United	ENG	2	3	2
16	Arsenal	ENG	2	2	-
17	Real Zaragoza	ESP	2	1	2
18	Parma	ITA	2	1	-
19	Manchester United	ENG	2	-	6
20	Feyenoord	HOL	2	-	3
	PSV Eindhoven	HOL	2	-	3
22	Dynamo Kiev	URS/UKR	2	-	2
23	Nottingham Forest	ENG	2	-	1
	IFK Göteborg	SWE	2	-	1
25	Atlético Madrid	ESP	1	3	5
26	Fiorentina	ITA	1	3	-
27	Ferencváros	HUN	1	2	2
	Glasgow Rangers	SCO	1	2	2
	Roma	ITA	1	2	2
30	Sampdoria	ITA	1	2	1
31	Glasgow Celtic	SCO	1	1	4
	Crvena Zvezda Beograd	YUG	1	1	4
33	Borussia Dortmund	FRG/GER	1	1	2
	Eintracht Frankfurt	FRG/GER	1	1	2
	Olympique Marseille	FRA	1	1	2
36	HASK Gradanski Zagreb	YUG/CRO	1	1	1
	Steaua Bucuresti	ROM	1	1	1
	West Ham United	ENG	1	1	1
	FC Porto	POR	1	1	1
40	Chelsea	ENG	1	-	2
	Sporting CP	POR	1	-	2
	Werder Bremen	FRG	1	-	2
43	Aberdeen	SCO	1	-	1
	Bayer Leverkusen	FRG/GER	1	-	1
	Dynamo Tbilisi	URS/GEO	1	-	1
	Manchester City	ENG	1	-	1
	KV Mechelen	BEL	1	-	1
	Napoli	ITA	1	-	1
49	Aston Villa	ENG	1	-	-
	Everton	ENG	1	-	-
	Ipswich Town	ENG	1	-	-
	1.FC Magdeburg	GDR/GER	1	-	-
	Newcastle United	ENG	1	-	-
	Slovan Bratislava	TCH/SLK	1	-	-
55	Club Brugge	BEL	-	2	2
56	Birmingham City	ENG	-	2	1
57	Stade de Reims	FRA	-	2	-
58	1.FC Köln	FRG/GER	-	1	7
59	Standard CL	BEL	-	1	2
	FK Austria	AUT	-	1	2
	FC Twente Enschede	HOL	-	1	2
	AS Monaco	FRA	-	1	2
	Dynamo Moskva	URS/RUS	-	1	2
	VfB Stuttgart	FRG/GER	-	1	2
	Ujpesti TE	HUN	-	1	2
66	Carl Zeiss Jena	GDR/GER	-	1	1
	Dundee United	SCO	-	1	1
	VfB Leipzig	GDR/GER	-	1	1
	MTK-VM Budapest	HUN	-	1	1
	Panathinaikos	GRE	-	1	1
	SK Rapid Wien	AUT	-	1	1
	AS Saint-Etienne	FRA	-	1	1
	Torino	ITA	-	1	1
	Wolverhampton W.	ENG	-	1	1
75	AZ Alkmaar	HOL	-	1	-
	Royal Antwerp FC	BEL	-	1	-
	Athletic Bilbao	ESP	-	1	-
	Austria Salzburg	AUT	-	1	-
	SEC Bastia	FRA	-	1	-
	RCD Español	ESP	-	1	-
	Fortuna Düsseldorf	FRG/GER	-	1	-
	Górnik Zabrze	POL	-	1	-
	Malmö FF	SWE	-	1	-
	TSV München 1860	FRG/GER	-	1	-
	Partizan Beograd	YUG	-	1	-
	Videoton SC	HUN	-	1	-
	London Select XI	ENG	-	1	-
88	CSKA Sofia	BUL	-	-	3
	Paris Saint-Germain	FRA	-	-	3
90	Girondins Bordeaux	FRA	-	-	2
	Dinamo Bucuresti	ROM	-	-	2
	Dukla Praha	TCH	-	-	2
	Dundee	SCO	-	-	2
	Legia Warszawa	POL	-	-	2
	Hajduk Split	YUG/CRO	-	-	2
	Hibernian Edinburgh	SCO	-	-	2
	Spartak Moskva	URS/RUS	-	-	2
	FC Zürich	SUI	-	-	2
99	AEK Athens	GRE	-	-	1
	Atalanta	ITA	-	-	1
	AJ Auxerre	FRA	-	-	1
	Baník Ostrava	TCH	-	-	1
	Bayer Uerdingen	FRG/GER	-	-	1
	Belgrade Select XI	YUG	-	-	1
	SK Beveren	BEL	-	-	1
	Bologna	ITA	-	-	1
	Brøndbyernes IF	DEN	-	-	1
	Cagliari	ITA	-	-	1
	Cardiff City	WAL	-	-	1
	Derby County	ENG	-	-	1
	MSV Duisburg	FRG/GER	-	-	1
	Bohemians Praha	TCH	-	-	1
	Dunfermline Athletic	SCO	-	-	1
	Berliner FC	GDR/GER	-	-	1
	1.FC Dynamo Dresden	GDR/GER	-	-	1
	Galatasaray	TUR	-	-	1
	Genoa 1893	ITA	-	-	1
	Göztepe Izmir	TUR	-	-	1
	Grasshopper-Club	SUI	-	-	1
	Hertha BSC Berlin	FRG/GER	-	-	1
	Karlsruher SC	FRG/GER	-	-	1
	1.FC Kaiserslautern	FRG/GER	-	-	1
	Kilmarnock	SCO	-	-	1
	Lausanne-Sports	SUI	-	-	1
	RFC Liège	BEL	-	-	1
	Olympique Lyon	FRA	-	-	1
	RWD Molenbeek	BEL	-	-	1
	FC Nantes	FRA	-	-	1
	1.FC Nürnberg	FRG	-	-	1
	OFK Beograd	YUG	-	-	1
	Radnicki Nis	YUG	-	-	1
	Real Sociedad	ESP	-	-	1
	FSV Zwickau	GDR/GER	-	-	1
	FC Schalke 04	FRG	-	-	1
	Slavia Sofia	BUL	-	-	1
	FC Sochaux	FRA	-	-	1
	Sparta Praha	TCH	-	-	1
	Spartak Trnava	TCH/SLK	-	-	1
	FC Tirol	AUT	-	-	1
	Union St. Gilloise	BEL	-	-	1
	Universitatea Craiova	ROM	-	-	1
	Vasas Budapest	HUN	-	-	1
	Rába ETO Györ	HUN	-	-	1
	KSV Waregem	BEL	-	-	1
	Racing Club Genk	BEL	-	-	1
	Widzew Lódz	POL	-	-	1
	BSC Young Boys Berne	SUI	-	-	1
	Zeljeznicar Sarajevo	YUG/BOS	-	-	1

To the end of the 1994-95 season

COMBINED EUROPEAN COUNTRY RECORDS

		G	S	B	Finals	S-Finals
1	England	24	13	21	37	58
2	Italy	22	20	22	42	62
3	Spain	21	18	20	39	58
4	Germany	12	14	37	26	63
5	Holland	10	4	10	14	24
6	Belgium	4	8	13	12	25
7	Portugal	4	7	6	11	17
8	Scotland	3	4	14	7	21
9	Soviet Union	3	1	6	4	10
10	Yugoslavia	2	3	11	5	16
11	Sweden	2	1	1	3	4
12	France	1	6	14	7	20
13	Hungary	1	5	7	6	13
14	East Germany	1	2	5	3	8
15	Romania	1	1	4	2	6
16	Czechoslovakia	1	-	6	1	7
17	Austria	-	3	4	3	7
18	Poland	-	1	3	1	4
19	Greece	-	1	2	1	3
20	Switzerland	-	-	5	-	5
21	Bulgaria	-	-	4	-	4
22	Turkey	-	-	2	-	2
23	Denmark	-	-	1	-	1
	Wales	-	-	1	-	1
	Russia			1		1

CLUB RECORDS IN THE EUROPEAN CUP

			G	S	B
1	Real Madrid	ESP	6	3	7
2	Milan	ITA	5	3	1
3	Ajax	HOL	4	1	1
	Liverpool	ENG	4	1	1
5	Bayern München	FRG/GER	3	2	4
6	Benfica	POR	2	5	1
7	Internazionale	ITA	2	2	2
8	Nottingham Forest	ENG	2	-	-
9	Barcelona	ESP	1	3	2
10	Juventus	ITA	1	2	2
11	Glasgow Celtic	SCO	1	1	2
12	Hamburger SV	FRG/GER	1	1	1
	Olympique Marseille	FRA	1	1	1
	Steaua Bucuresti	ROM	1	1	1
15	Manchester United	ENG	1	-	4
16	Crvena Zvezda Beograd	YUG	1	-	2
17	Feyenoord	HOL	1	-	1
	FC Porto	POR	1	-	1
	PSV Eindhoven	HOL	1	-	1
20	Aston Villa	ENG	1	-	-
21	Stade de Reims	FRA	-	2	-
22	Atlético Madrid	ESP	-	1	2
23	Bor. Mönchengladbach	FRG/GER	-	1	1
	Leeds United	ENG	-	1	1
	Panathinaikos	GRE	-	1	1
	AS Saint-Étienne	FRA	-	1	1
27	Eintracht Frankfurt	FRG/GER	-	1	-
	Club Brugge	BEL	-	1	-
	Fiorentina	ITA	-	1	-
	Malmö FF	SWE	-	1	-
	Partizan Beograd	YUG	-	1	-
	Roma	ITA	-	1	-
	Sampdoria	ITA	-	1	-
34	RSC Anderlecht	BEL	-	-	2
	CSKA Sofia	BUL	-	-	2
	Dynamo Kiev	URS/UKR	-	-	2
	FC Zürich	SUI	-	-	2
38	FK Austria	AUT	-	-	1
	Girondins Bordeaux	FRA	-	-	1
	Borussia Dortmund	FRG/GER	-	-	1
	1.FC Köln	FRG/GER	-	-	1
	Derby County	ENG	-	-	1
	Dinamo Bucuresti	ROM	-	-	1
	Dukla Praha	TCH	-	-	1
	Dundee	SCO	-	-	1
	Dundee United	SCO	-	-	1
	Galatasaray	TUR	-	-	1
	IFK Göteborg	SWE	-	-	1
	Hibernian Edinburgh	SCO	-	-	1
	Legia Warszawa	POL	-	-	1
	AS Monaco	FRA	-	-	1
	Paris Saint-Germain	FRA	-	-	1
	Glasgow Rangers	SCO	-	-	1
	SK Rapid Wien	AUT	-	-	1
	Real Sociedad	ESP	-	-	1
	Spartak Moskva	URS/RUS	-	-	1
	Spartak Trnava	TCH/SLK	-	-	1
	Standard CL	BEL	-	-	1
	Tottenham Hotspur	ENG	-	-	1
	Ujpesti TE	HUN	-	-	1
	Vasas Budapest	HUN	-	-	1
	Rába ETO Györ	HUN	-	-	1
	Widzew Lódz	POL	-	-	1
	BSC Young Boys Berne	SUI	-	-	1

COUNTRIES IN THE EUROPEAN CUP

		G	S	B	Finals	S-Finals
1	Italy	8	10	5	18	21
2	England	8	2	8	10	18
3	Spain	7	7	12	14	25
4	Holland	6	1	3	7	10
5	Germany	4	5	8	9	17
6	Portugal	3	5	2	8	10
7	France	1	4	5	5	9
8	Scotland	1	1	6	2	8
9	Romania	1	1	2	2	4
	Yugoslavia	1	1	2	2	4
11	Belgium	-	1	3	1	4
12	Greece	-	1	1	1	2
	Sweden	-	1	1	1	2
14	Hungary	-	-	3	-	3
	Soviet Union	-	-	3	-	3
	Switzerland	-	-	3	-	3
17	Austria	-	-	2	-	2
	Bulgaria	-	-	2	-	2
	Czechoslovakia	-	-	2	-	2
	Poland	-	-	2	-	2
21	Turkey	-	-	1	-	1

CLUB RECORDS IN THE EUROPEAN CUP WINNERS CUP

	Team	Country	G	S	B
1	Barcelona	ESP	3	2	-
2	RSC Anderlecht	BEL	2	2	-
3	Milan	ITA	2	1	-
4	Dynamo Kiev	URS/UKR	2	-	-
5	Atlético Madrid	ESP	1	2	2
6	Arsenal	ENG	1	2	-
	Glasgow Rangers	SCO	1	2	-
8	Sampdoria	ITA	1	1	1

	West Ham United	ENG	1	1	1
10	Ajax	HOL	1	1	-
	Fiorentina	ITA	1	1	-
	Hamburger SV	FRG/GER	1	1	-
	Parma	ITA	1	1	-
14	Bayern München	FRG/GER	1	-	3
15	Juventus	ITA	1	-	2
	Real Zaragoza	ESP	1	-	2
17	Aberdeen	SCO	1	-	1
	Chelsea	ENG	1	-	1
	Dynamo Tbilisi	URS/GEO	1	-	1
	Manchester City	ENG	1	-	1
	Manchester United	ENG	1	-	1
	KV Mechelen	BEL	1	-	1
	Sporting CP	POR	1	-	1
	Tottenham Hotspur	ENG/GER	1	-	1
25	Borussia Dortmund	FRG/GER	1	-	-
	Everton	ENG	1	-	-
	1.FC Magdeburg	GDR/GER	1	-	-
	Slovan Bratislava	TCH/SLK	1	-	-
	Valencia	ESP	1	-	-
	Werder Bremen	FRG/GER	1	-	-
31	Real Madrid	ESP	-	2	-
32	Dynamo Moskva	URS/RUS	-	1	2
33	FK Austria	AUT	-	1	1
	Carl Zeiss Jena	GDR/GER	-	1	1
	AS Monaco	FRA	-	1	1
	Standard CL	BEL	-	1	1
37	Ferencváros	HUN	-	1	-
	Fortuna Düsseldorf	FRG/GER	-	1	-
	Górnik Zabrze	POL	-	1	-
	Leeds United	ENG	-	1	-
	Liverpool	ENG	-	1	-
	VfB Leipzig	GDR/GER	-	1	-
	MTK-VM Budapest	HUN	-	1	-
	TSV München 1860	FRG/GER	-	1	-
	FC Porto	POR	-	1	-
	SK Rapid Wien	AUT	-	1	-
	Royal Antwerp FC	BEL	-	1	-
48	Benfica	POR	-	-	2
	Glasgow Celtic	SCO	-	-	2
	Feyenoord	HOL	-	-	2
	PSV Eindhoven	HOL	-	-	2
52	Atalanta	ITA	-	-	1
	Baník Ostrava	TCH	-	-	1
	Bayer Uerdingen	FRG/GER	-	-	1
	SK Beveren	BEL	-	-	1
	Girondins Bordeaux	FRA	-	-	1
	Bor. Mönchengladbach	FRG/GER	-	-	1
	Cardiff City	WAL	-	-	1
	Club Brugge	BEL	-	-	1
	CSKA Sofia	BUL	-	-	1
	1.FC Köln	FRG/GER	-	-	1
	Dukla Praha	TCH	-	-	1
	Dunfermline Athletic	SCO	-	-	1
	Berliner FC	GDR/GER	-	-	1
	Dinamo Bucuresti	ROM	-	-	1
	HASK Gradanski Zagreb	YUG/CRO	-	-	1
	Eintracht Frankfurt	FRG/GER	-	-	1
	Hajduk Split	YUG/CRO	-	-	1
	Legia Warszawa	POL	-	-	1
	Olympique Lyon	FRA	-	-	1
	Olympique Marseille	FRA	-	-	1
	FC Nantes	FRA	-	-	1
	Napoli	ITA	-	-	1
	1.FC Nürnberg	FRG/GER	-	-	1
	OFK Beograd	YUG	-	-	1
	Paris Saint-Germain	FRA	-	-	1
	Crvena Zvezda Beograd	YUG	-	-	1
	Roma	ITA	-	-	1
	FSV Zwickau	GDR/GER	-	-	1
	FC Schalke 04	FRG/GER	-	-	1
	Slavia Sofia	BUL	-	-	1
	Sparta Praha	TCH	-	-	1
	Spartak Moskva	RUS	-	-	1
	Torino	ITA	-	-	1
	FC Twente Enschede	HOL	-	-	1
	Ujpesti TE	HUN	-	-	1
	Racing Club Genk	BEL	-	-	1
	Wolverhampton Wand.	ENG	-	-	1

COUNTRIES IN THE EUROPEAN CUP WINNERS CUP

	Team	G	S	B	Finals	S-Finals
1	England	7	5	6	12	18
2	Spain	6	6	4	12	16
3	Italy	6	4	7	10	17
4	Germany	4	3	9	7	16
5	Belgium	3	4	5	7	12
6	Soviet Union	3	1	3	4	7
7	Scotland	2	2	4	4	8
8	East Germany	1	2	3	3	6
9	Holland	1	1	5	2	7
10	Portugal	1	1	3	2	5
11	Czechoslovakia	1	-	3	1	4
12	Austria	-	2	1	2	3
	Hungary	-	2	1	2	3
14	France	-	1	6	1	7
15	Poland	-	1	1	1	2
16	Yugoslavia	-	-	4	-	4
17	Bulgaria	-	-	2	-	2
18	Romania	-	-	1	-	1
	Wales	-	-	1	-	1
	Russia	-	-	1	-	1

CLUB RECORDS IN FAIRS CUP AND UEFA CUP

			G	S	B
1	Juventus	ITA	3	3	1
2	Barcelona	ESP	3	1	2
3	Bor. Mönchengladbach	FRG/GER	2	2	1
4	Leeds United	ENG	2	1	1
	Tottenham Hotspur	ENG	2	1	1
6	Valencia	ESP	2	1	-
7	Internazionale	ITA	2	-	4
8	Liverpool	ENG	2	-	1
	Real Madrid	ESP	2	-	1
10	IFK Göteborg	SWE	2	-	-
11	RSC Anderlecht	BEL	1	2	-
12	Ferencváros	HUN	1	1	2
13	Roma	ITA	1	1	1
14	HASK Gradanski Zagreb	YUG/CRO	1	1	-
	Real Zaragoza	ESP	1	1	-
16	Ajax	HOL	1	-	1
	Bayer Leverkusen	FRG/GER	1	-	1
	Eintracht Frankfurt	FRG/GER	1	-	1
19	Arsenal	ENG	1	-	-
	Feyenoord	HOL	1	-	-
	Ipswich Town	ENG	1	-	-
	Napoli	ITA	1	-	-
	Newcastle United	ENG	1	-	-
	Parma	ITA	1	-	-
	PSV Eindhoven	HOL	1	-	-
26	Birmingham City	ENG	-	2	1
27	1.FC Köln	FRG/GER	-	1	5
28	VfB Stuttgart	FRG/GER	-	1	2

29	Borussia Dortmund	FRG/GER	-	1	1
	Club Brugge	BEL	-	1	1
	Hamburger SV	FRG/GER	-	1	1
	Crvena Zvezda Beograd	YUG	-	1	1
	FC Twente Enschede	HOL	-	1	1
34	Austria Salzburg	AUT	-	1	-
	AZ Alkmaar	HOL	-	1	-
	Athletic Bilbao	ESP	-	1	-
	SEC Bastia	FRA	-	1	-
	Benfica	POR	-	1	-
	Dundee United	SCO	-	1	-
	RCD Español	ESP	-	1	-
	Fiorentina	ITA	-	1	-
	London Select XI	ENG	-	1	-
	Torino	ITA	-	1	-
	Ujpesti TE	HUN	-	1	-
	Videoton SC	HUN	-	1	-
	Wolverhampton Wand.	ENG	-	1	-
47	Bayern München	FRG/GER	-	-	2
	Werder Bremen	FRG/GER	-	-	2
49	AEK Athens	GRE	-	-	1
	AJ Auxerre	FRA	-	-	1
	Atlético Madrid	ESP	-	-	1
	Belgrade Select XI	YUG	-	-	1
	Bologna	ITA	-	-	1
	Brøndbyernes IF	DEN	-	-	1
	Cagliari	ITA	-	-	1
	Chelsea	ENG	-	-	1
	MSV Duisburg	FRG/GER	-	-	1
	Bohemians Praha	TCH	-	-	1
	Dundee	SCO	-	-	1
	1.FC Dynamo Dresden	GDR/GER	-	-	1
	Genoa 1893	ITA	-	-	1
	Grasshopper-Club	SUI	-	-	1
	Göztepe Izmir	TUR	-	-	1
	Hibernian Edinburgh	SCO	-	-	1
	Hajduk Split	YUG/CRO	-	-	1
	Hertha BSC Berlin	FRG/GER	-	-	1
	1.FC Kaiserslautern	FRG/GER	-	-	1
	Karlsruher SC	FRG/GER	-	-	1
	Kilmarnock	SCO	-	-	1
	RFC Liège	BEL	-	-	1
	Lausanne-Sports	SUI	-	-	1
	VfB Leipzig	GDR/GER	-	-	1
	Manchester United	ENG	-	-	1
	Milan	ITA	-	-	1
	MTK-VM Budapest	HUN	-	-	1
	RWD Molenbeek	BEL	-	-	1
	Nottingham Forest	ENG	-	-	1
	Paris Saint-Germain	FRA	-	-	1
	Radnicki Nis	YUG	-	-	1
	Glasgow Rangers	SCO	-	-	1
	FC Sochaux	FRA	-	-	1
	Sporting CP	POR	-	-	1
	FC Tirol	AUT	-	-	1
	Universitatea Craiova	ROM	-	-	1
	Union St. Gilloise	BEL	-	-	1
	KSV Waregem	BEL	-	-	1
	Zeljeznicar Sarajevo	YUG/BOS	-	-	1

COUNTRIES IN THE FAIRS CUP AND UEFA CUP

		G	S	B	Finals	S-Finals
1	England	9	6	7	15	22
2	Italy	8	6	10	14	24
3	Spain	8	5	4	13	17
4	Germany	4	6	20	10	30
5	Holland	3	2	2	5	7
6	Sweden	2	-	-	2	2
7	Belgium	1	3	5	4	9
8	Hungary	1	3	3	4	7
9	Yugoslavia	1	2	5	3	8
10	Scotland	-	1	4	1	5
11	France	-	1	3	1	4
12	Austria	-	1	1	1	2
	Portugal	-	1	1	1	2
14	East Germany	-	-	2	-	2
	Switzerland	-	-	2	-	2
	Czechoslovakia	-	-	1	-	1
	Denmark	-	-	1	-	1
	Greece	-	-	1	-	1
	Romania	-	-	1	-	1
	Turkey	-	-	1	-	1

To the end of the 1994-95 season

ALBANIA

In 1946 on their international debut, the Albanians won their only honour to date, the Balkan Cup, defeating both Romania and Bulgaria to lift the trophy on their own soil. Since then success has been muted to say the least, and despite impressive victories over Czechoslovakia in 1952 and Belgium in 1984, Albania have amassed one of the poorest records in international football.

This small Balkan country does hold one curious record in world football, however. A 1980s study on attendances found that, as a percentage of the population as a whole, more people went to football matches in Albania than anywhere else.

Like her Balkan neighbours, Albania was for centuries under Turkish rule, and at the beginning of the 20th century, although football was played by foreign residents in Tirana, the Turks did all they could to stop the locals playing. It was not until 1930 therefore, that an association was formed and a league competition introduced.

The stability was short-lived however; in 1939 Mussolini annexed Albania and all competition stopped. In the turbulent year of 1944, the country was taken over by the Communists under Enver Hoxha, and until the death of Stalin in 1953, Albania looked to be entering into the mainstream of European football. Hoxha fell out with the new Soviet leaders, however, and so Albania cut herself off from the Eastern bloc as well, and between 1954 and 1963 played only one international in Europe, against East Germany, preferring instead the company of the equally hard-line Communist Chinese. Many matches were played between the two countries, but as the Chinese were not members of FIFA, only one of these 'full' internationals is recognised as such.

In 1963, Albania unexpectedly entered the European Nations Cup but unfortunately for the organisers were drawn against Greece, historically their bitter rivals, who refused to play them. Albania were given a walkover to the next round where they met Denmark, losing 4-0 in Copenhagen before a consolation 1-0 triumph at home in the return. The following year a 2-0 defeat in Rotterdam marked their first World Cup experience. Although they were fairly regular competitors at international level for the rest of the decade and into the early 1970s, the Albanians then went back into their shell until the early 1980s, since when they have not missed a qualifying campaign for either World Cup or European Championship.

THE ORDER OF MERIT

		All			League			Cup		Europe		
	Team	G	S	B	G	S	B	G	S	G	S	B
1	Partizani Tiranë	28	26	4	15	18	4	13	8	-	-	-
2	Dinamo Tiranë	27	11	7	15	8	7	12	3	-	-	-
3	SK Tiranë	22	14	11	15	9	11	7	5	-	-	-
4	Vllaznia Shkodër	12	11	12	7	7	12	5	4	-	-	-
5	Flamurtari Vlorë	3	12	2	1	6	2	2	6	-	-	-
6	SK Elbasani	3	1	1	1	-	1	2	1	-	-	-
7	Teuta Durrës	2	6	4	1	3	4	1	3	-	-	-
8	Skënderbeu Korçë	1	6	2	1	3	2	-	3	-	-	-
9	Besa Kavajë	-	7	9	-	1	9	-	6	-	-	-
10	Albpetrol Patosi	-	1	-	-	-	-	-	1	-	-	-
	Luftëtari Gijrokas.	-	1	-	-	1	-	-	-	-	-	-
	Tomori Berat	-	1	-	-	-	-	-	1	-	-	-
	Traktori Lushnjë	-	1	-	-	-	-	-	1	-	-	-

The club sides in Albania have followed much the same pattern in terms of European participation. In 1988 Flamurtari enjoyed the best-ever run by an Albanian club in Europe when they reached the third round of the UEFA Cup, knocking out Partizan Belgrade and winning the home leg of their tie against Barcelona.

Domestically, since the fall of the communist government, clubs from Tirana have not been so dominant, but the loss of state patronage has meant that increasingly, clubs are following the age-old pattern of selling their best players abroad. The modern generation of exports includes Sulejman Demollari, Albania's most capped player, who started a very successful career with Dinamo Bucharest in Romania.

Population: 3,262,000
Area, sq km: 28,748
% in urban areas: 35.8%
Capital city: Tirana

Federata Shqiptarë e Futbollit
Rruga Dervish Hima #31
Tirana
Albania
Tel: + 355 42 27877
Fax: + 355 42 27877

Year of formation	1930
Affiliation to FIFA	1932
Affiliation to UEFA	1954
Registered clubs	52
Registered players	3700
Registered coaches	191
Registered referees	430
National stadium	Qemal Stafa, Tirana 20 000
National colours	Red shirts, Red shorts, Red socks
Reserve colours	White shirts, White shorts, White socks
Season	September - May

THE RECORD

WORLD CUP

1930-62	Did not enter
1966	QT 4th/4 in group 5
1970	Did not enter
1974	QT 4th/4 in group 4
1978	Did not enter
1982	QT 4th/5 in group 1
1986	QT 3rd/4 in group 1
1990	QT 4th/4 in group 2
1994	QT 7th/7 in group 3

EUROPEAN CHAMPIONSHIP

1960	Did not enter
1964	2nd round
1968	QT 3rd/3 in group 4
1972	QT 4th/4 in group 8
1976	Did not enter
1980	Did not enter
1984	QT 5th/5 in group 6
1988	QT 4th/4 in group 1
1992	QT 5th/5 in group 1
1996	QT group 7

BALKAN CUP

1946 Winners

EUROPEAN CLUB COMPETITIONS

European Cup
2nd round - 17 Nëntori 1983 1989 1990

Cup Winners Cup
2nd round - Partizani 1971, Besa Kavajë 1973, 17 Nëntori 1987, Vllaznia 1988

UEFA Cup
3rd round - Flamurtari 1988

CLUB DIRECTORY

TIRANE (Population - 238,000)

Klubi Sportiv Dinamo Tiranë (1950)
Dinamo 12,000 – Blue, white trim

Klubi Sportiv Partizani Tiranë (1946)
Qemal Stafa 20,000 – Red, white trim

Klubi Sportiv Tiranë (1920)
Qemal Stafa 20,000 – Blue & white stripes/White
Previous names - Agmi 1920-27, SK Tiranë 1927-39, Shprefeja 1939-45, 17 Nëntori 1945-50, Tiranë 1950-51, Puna Tiranë 1951-58, 17 Nëntori 1958-91

DURRES (Population - 82,000)

Klubi Sportiv Teuta Durrës (1925)
Teuta 10,000 – Blue, white trim
Previous names - Teuta 1925-45, Yllikuq 1945-49, Puna 1950-57, Lokomotiva 1957-91

ELBASAN (Population - 80,000)

Klubi Sportiv Elbasani (1923)
Elbasani 11,000 – Yellow/Blue
Previous names - Urani 1923-34, Bashkimi 1934-49, Puna 1950-56, Labinoti 1956-91

SHKODER (Population - 79,000)

Clubi Sportiv Vllaznia Shkodër (1919)
Vllaznia 16,000 – Blue & red stripes/Blue
Previous names - Bashkimi 1919-35, Vllaznia 1935-49, Puna 1950-57

VLORE (Population - 71,000)

Klubi Sportiv Flamurtari Vlorë (1923)
Flamurtari 15,000 – White, red trim
Previous names - Vlorë 1923-35, Ismail Qemali 1935-45, Flamurtari 1945-49, Puna 1950-57

KORCE (Population 57,000)

Klubi Sportiv Skendërbeu Korce (1926)
Skendërbeu – Red & white stripes/White
Previous names - Skendëderbeu 1923-46, Dinamo 1946-49, Puna 1950-57

KAVAJE

Klubi Sportiv Besa Kavajë (1925)
Besa 10,000 – Yellow & black stripes/Black
Previous names - Adriaticu 1930-35, Besa 1935-49, Puna 1950-57

FIER

Klubi Sportiv Apolonia Fier (1925)
Apolonia 10,000 – Green & white stripes/White
Previous names - Apolonia 1925-49, Puna 1950-57

LEZHE

Klubi Sportiv Besëlidhja Lezhë (1930)
Besëlidhja 5,000 – White with black sleeves/Red
Previous names - Bardhyli 1930-37, Lezhë 1937-50, Puna 1950-57

GJIROKASTER
Klubi Sportiv Shqiponia Gjirokastër (1929)
Subi Bakiri 8,000 – Blue & black stripes/Black
Previous names - Luftëtari 1929-45, Shqiponja 1945-48, Luftëtari 1948-51, Puna 1951-57, Luftëtari 1958-92

BERAT
Klubi Sportiv Tomori Berat (1923)
Tomori 13,000 – White
Previous names - Muzeka 1923-31, Tomori 1931-49, Puna 1949-57

LUSHNJE
Klubi Sportiv Lushnjë (1926)
Lushnje 8,000 – Green/White
Previous names - Traktori 1926-49, Puna 1950-57, Traktori 1957-91

PATOSI
Klubi Sportiv Albpetrol Patosi (1947)
Patosi 5,000 – White with blue sleeves/Blue
Previous name – Punëtori 1947-92
All clubs with the exception of Dinamo Tiranë and Partizani were known only by the name of their town from 1949-50

ALBANIAN LEAGUE CHAMPIONSHIP

1930d*	SK Tiranë 14 Skënderbeu Korçë 14 Bashkimi Shkodër 13
1931	SK Tiranë 1-1 3-1 Teuta Durrës
1932c	SK Tiranë 13 Bashkimi Shkodër 11 Teuta Durrës 11
1933	Skënderbeu Korçë 12 Bashkimi Shkodër 10 Teuta Durrës 8
1934e	SK Tiranë 19 Skënderbeu Korçë 18 Bashkimi Shkodër 16
1935	-
1936f	SK Tiranë 25 Vllaznia Shkodër 23 Besa Kavajë 13
1937h	SK Tiranë 35 Vllaznia Shkodër 29 Besa Kavajë 22
1938-44	-
1945	Vllaznia Shkodër 2-1 2-1 SK Tiranë
1946	Vllaznia Shkodë 3-0 2-0 Flamurtari Vlorë
1947g	Partizani Tiranë 29 Vllaznia Shkodër 28 Dinamo Korçë 24
1948	Partizani Tiranë 6-2 Flamurtari Vlorë
1949	Partizani Tiranë 30 Vllaznia Shkodër 26 Yllikuq Durrës 20
1950g1	Dinamo Tiranë 29 Partizani Tiranë 29 Vllaznia Shkodër 23
1951n	Dinamo Tiranë 50 Partizani Tiranë 48 Puna Tiranë 35
1952d	Dinamo Tiranë 16 Partizani Tiranë 15 Puna Shkodër 12
1953h	Dinamo Tiranë 30 Partizani Tiranë 29 Puna Tiranë 29
1954k	Partizani Tiranë 43 Dinamo Tiranë 36 Puna Tiranë 31
1955q	Dinamo Tiranë 55 Partizani Tiranë 55 Puna Tiranë 37
1956g	Dinamo Tiranë 29 Partizani Tiranë 23 Puna Tiranë 17
1957f	Partizan Tiranë 23 Dinamo Tiranë 23 Puna Korçë 17
1958	Partizani Tiranë 19 Besa Kavajë 18 17 Nëntori Tiranë 17
1959	Partizani Tiranë 23 17 Nëntori Tiranë 19 Dinamo Tiranë 14
1960h	Dinamo Tiranë 32 Partizani Tiranë 28 17 Nëntori Tiranë 20
1961	Partizani Tiranë 30 Dinamo Tiranë 30 1 7Nëntori Tiranë 23
1962	-
1963k	Partizani Tiranë 36 Dinamo Tiranë 32 Besa Kavajë 31
1964	Partizani Tiranë 37 Dinamo Tiranë 32 Besa Kavajë 29
1965	17 Nëntori Tiranë 31 Partizani Tiranë 30 Dinamo Tiranë 30
1966	17 Nëntori Tiranë 38 Partizani Tiranë 38 Dinamo Tiranë 29
1967	Dinamo Tiranë 38 17 Nëntori Tiranë 33 Besa Kavajë 26
1968n	17 Nëntori Tiranë 45 Partizani Tiranë 44 Dinamo Tiranë 38
1969	-
1970	17 Nëntori Tiranë 44 Partizani Tiranë 38 Vllaznia Shkodër 35
1971	Partizani Tiranë 40 Dinamo Tiranë 39 Vllaznia Shkodër 34
1972	Vllaznia Shkodër 40 17 Nëntori Tiranë 37 Dinamo Tiranë 36
1973	Dinamo Tiranë 41 Partizani Tiranë 34 Besa Kavajë 34
1974	Vllaznia Shkodër 37 Partizani Tiranë 36 Besa Kavajë 30
1975	Dinamo Tiranë 44 Vllaznia Shkodër 39 Partizani Tiranë 34
1976k	Dinamo Tiranë 28 17 Nëntori Tiranë 26 Vllaznia Shkodër 25
1977r1	Dinamo Tiranë 44 Skënderbeu Korçë 40 Vllaznia Shkodër 37
1978k	Vllaznia Shkodër 29 Luftëtari Gijrokaster 26 Partizani Tiranë 25
1979n	Partizani Tiranë 36 17 Nëntori Tiranë 35 Besa Kavajë 31
1980	Dinamo Tiranë 37 17 Nëntori Tiranë 32 Vllaznia Shkodër 31
1981	Partizani Tiranë 37 Dinamo Tiranë 36 17 Nëntori Tiranë 35
1982	17 Nëntori Tiranë 37 Flamurtari Vlorë 33 Dinamo Tiranë 32
1983	Vllaznia Shkodër 34 Partizani Tiranë 34 17 Nëntori Tiranë 32
1984	Labinoti Elbasan 37 17 Nëntori Tiranë 34 Partizani Tiranë 30
1985	17 Nëntori Tiranë 39 Dinamo Tiranë 33 Vllaznia Shkodër 29
1986	Dinamo Tiranë 38 Flamurtari Vlorë 38 17 Nëntori Tiranë 37
1987	Partizani Tiranë 36 Flamurtari Vlorë 33 Vllaznia Shkodër 32
1988u1	17 Nëntori Tiranë 48 Flamurtari Vlorë 41 Labinoti Elbasan 39
1989r1	17 Nëntori Tiranë 48 Partizani Tiranë 45 Dinamo Tiranë 42
1990s	Dinamo Tiranë 50 Partizani Tiranë 49 Flamurtari Vlorë 39
1991w	Flamurtari Vlorë 54 Partizani Tiranë 48 Vllaznia Shkodër 45
1992q	Vllaznia Shkodër 44 Partizani Tiranë 38 Teuta Durrës 33
1993	Partizani Tiranë 43 Teuta Durrës 38 Besa Kavajë 37
1994n	Teuta Durrës 37 SK Tiranë 33 Flamurtari Vlorë 30
1995q	SK Tiranë 44 Teuta Durrës 32 Partizan Tiranë 32

* Play-off

1930	SK Tiranë	0-0 2-0	Skënderbeu Korçe

ALBANIAN CUP FINALS

1948	Partizani Tiranë	5-2	17 Nëntori Tiranë
1949	Partizani Tiranë	1-0	17 Nëntori Tiranë
1950	Dinamo Tiranë	2-1	Partizani Tiranë
1951	Dinamo Tiranë	3-2	Partizani Tiranë
1952	Dinamo Tiranë	4-1	Puna Tiranë
1953	Dinamo Tiranë	2-0	Partizani Tiranë
1954	Dinamo Tiranë	2-1	Partizani Tiranë
1955-56	-		
1957	Partizani Tiranë	2-0	Lokomotiva Durrës
1958	Partizani Tiranë	4-0	Skënderbeu Korçë
1959	-		
1960	Dinamo Tiranë	1-0 1-0	Flamurtari Vlorë
1961	Partizani Tiranë	1-1 1-0	Besa Kavajë
1962	-		
1963	17 Nëntori Tiranë	1-0 2-3	Besa Kavajë
1964	Partizani Tiranë	3-0	Tomori Berat
1965	Vllaznia Shkodër	1-0	Skënderbeu Korçë
1966	Partizani Tiranë	2-1 4-3	Vllaznia Shkodër
1967	-		
1968	Partizani Tiranë	4-1	Vllaznia Shkodër

1969	-			
1970	Partizani Tiranë	4-0 0-1	Vllaznia Shkodër	
1971	Dinamo Tiranë	2-0	Besa Kavajë	
1972	Vllaznia Shkodër	2-0 0-2	Besa Kavajë	
1973	Partizani Tiranë	1-0	Dinamo Tiranë	
1974	Dinamo Tiranë	1-0	Partizani Tiranë	
1975	Labinoti Elbasan	1-0 1-0	Lokomotiva Durrës	
1976	17 Nëntori Tiranë	3-1 1-0	Skënderbeu Korçë	
1977	17 Nëntori Tiranë	2-1 1-2	Dinamo Tiranë	
1978	Dinamo Tiranë	0-0 1-0	Traktori Lushnjë	
1979	Vllaznia Shkodër	1-1 2-1	Dinamo Tiranë	
1980	Partizani Tiranë	1-1 1-0	Labinoti Elbasan	
1981	Vllaznia Shkodër	5-1 1-2	Besa Kavajë	
1982	Dinamo Tiranë	1-0 2-3	17 Nëntori Tiranë	
1983	17 Nëntori Tiranë	1-0	Flamurtari Vlorë	
1984	17 Nëntori Tiranë	2-1	Flamurtari Vlorë	
1985	Flamurtari Vlorë	2-1	Partizani Tiranë	
1986	17 Nëntori Tiranë	3-1	Vllaznia Shkodër	
1987	Vllaznia Shkodër	3-0 1-3	Flamurtari Vlorë	
1988	Flamurtari Vlorë	1-0	Partizani Tiranë	
1989	Dinamo Tiranë	0-0 3-1	Partizani Tiranë	
1990	Dinamo Tiranë	1-1 4-2p	Flamurtari Vlorë	
1991	Partizani Tiranë	1-1 4-3p	Flamurtari Vlorë	
1992	SK Elbasani	2-1	Besa Kavajë	
1993	Partizani Tiranë	1-0	Albpetrol Patosi	
1994	SK Tiranë	0-0 1-0	Teuta Durrës	
1995	Teuta Durrës	0-0 4-3p	SK Tiranë	

LEADING INTERNATIONAL GOALSCORERS

9	Sokol Kushta	(Flamurtari,Iraklis Salonica, Apollon Kalamarias)
6	Qamil Teliti	
6	Loro Borici	(Vllaznia,Partizani)
5	Llir Pernaska	(Dinamo Tiranë)
4	Mirashi	(Vllaznia)
4	Altin Rraklli	(Besa Kavajë,SC Freiburg)
3	Zihni Gjinali	(Dinamo Tiranë)
3	Bedri Omuri	(17 Nëntori)
3	Panajot Pano	(Partizani)
3	Muhedin Targaj	(Dinamo Tiranë)

LEADING INTERNATIONAL APPEARANCES

43	Sulejman Demollari	(Dinamo Tiranë, Dinamo Bucuresti)
35	Hysen Zmijani	(Vllaznia,GFC Ajaco)
28	Arben Minga	(17 Nëntori)
27	Mirel Josa	(17 Nëntori)
27	Sokol Kushta	(Flamurtari,Iraklis Salonica)
26	Artur Lekbello	(Aris Salonica)
24	Loro Borici	(Vllaznia,Partizani)
24	Panajot Pano	(Partizani)
23	Perlat Musta	(Partizani,Dinamo Bucuresti)

INTERNATIONAL MATCHES PLAYED BY ALBANIA

Date	Opponents	Result	Venue	Competition	Scorers
7-10-1946	Yugoslavia	L 2-3	Tirana	BC	Begeja, Teliti
9-10	Bulgaria	W 3-1	Tirana	BC	Borici 2, Mirashi
13-10	Romania	W 1-0	Tirana	BC	Teliti
25-05-1947	Romania	L 0-4	Tirana	BCE	
15-06	Bulgaria	L 0-2	Sofia	BCE	
20-08	Hungary	L 0-3	Budapest	BCE	
14-09	Yugoslavia	L 2-4	Tirana	BCE	Borici,Parapani
2-05-1948	Romania	W 1-0	Bucharest	BCE	Mirashi
23-05	Hungary	D 0-0	Tirana	BCE	
27-06	Yugoslavia	D 0-0	Belgrade	BCE	
23-10-1949	Romania	D 1-1	Bucharest	Fr	Teliti
6-11	Poland	L 1-2	Warsaw	Fr	Gjinali
17-11	Bulgaria	D 0-0	Sofia	Fr	
29-11	Romania	L 1-4	Tirana	Fr	Mirashi
1-05-1950	Poland	D 0-0	Tirana	Fr	
4-06	Bulgaria	W 2-1	Tirana	Fr	Borici, Bichaku
1-09	Czechoslovakia	L 0-3	Prague	Fr	
24-09	Hungary	L 0-12	Budapest	Fr	
8-10	Romania	L 0-6	Bucharest	Fr	
29-11-1952	Czechoslovakia	W 3-2	Tirana	Fr	Gjinali, Teliti,Jareci
9-12	Czechoslovakia	W 2-1	Tirana	Fr	Gjinali, Borici
29-11-1953	Poland	W 2-0	Tirana	Fr	Borici, Resmja
15-09-1957	China	L 2-3	Beijing	Fr	Ndini, Kraja
1-05-1958	East Germany	D 1-1	Tirana	Fr	Kraga
2-06-1963	Bulgaria	L 0-1	Tirana	OGq	
16-06	Bulgaria	L 0-1	Sofia	OGq	
29-06	Denmark	L 0-4	Copenhagen	ECr2	
30-10	Denmark	W 1-0	Tirana	ECr2	Pana
24-05-1964	Holland	L 0-2	Rotterdam	WCq	
11-10	Algeria	W 2-0	Tirana	Fr	Haxhui, OG
25-10	Holland	L 0-2	Tirana	WCq	
11-04-1965	Switzerland	L 0-2	Tirana	WCq	
2-05	Switzerland	L 0-1	Geneva	WCq	
7-05	Nth. Ireland	L 1-4	Belfast	WCq	Gashari

24-11	Nth. Ireland	D 1-1	Tirana	WCq	Haxhiu
8-04-1967	West Germany	L 0-6	Dortmund	ECq	
14-05	Yugoslavia	L 0-2	Tirana	ECq	
12-11	Yugoslavia	L 0-4	Belgrade	ECq	
17-12	West Germany	D 0-0	Tirana	ECq	
14-10-1970	Poland	L 0-3	Chorzow	ECq	
13-12	Turkey	L 1-2	Istanbul	ECq	Ziu
17-02-1971	West Germany	L 0-1	Tirana	ECq	
18-04	Romania	L 1-2	Bucharest	OGq	
12-05	Poland	D 1-1	Tirana	ECq	Zegha
26-05	Romania	L 1-2	Tirana	OGq	
12-06	West Germany	L 0-2	Karlsruhe	ECq	
14-11	Turkey	W 3-0	Tirana	ECq	Pernaska 2, Pano
21-06-1972	Finland	L 0-1	Helsinki	WCq	
29-10	Romania	L 0-2	Bucharest	WCq	
7-04-1973	East Germany	L 0-2	Magdeburg	WCq	
6-05	Romania	L 1-4	Tirana	WCq	Bizi
10-10	Finland	W 1-0	Tirana	WCq	Ragani
3-11	East Germany	L 1-4	Tirana	WCq	Ghika
8-11	China	D 1-1	Tirana	Fr	Pano
10-10-1976	Algeria	W 3-0	Tirana	Fr	Ballgina,Pernaska 2
3-09-1980	Finland	W 2-0	Tirana	WCq	Braho, Baci
19-10	Bulgaria	L 1-2	Sofia	WCq	Pernaska
15-11	Austria	L 0-5	Vienna	WCq	
6-12	Austria	L 0-1	Tirana	WCq	
1-04-1981	West Germany	L 0-2	Tirana	WCq	
2-09	Finland	L 1-2	Kotka	WCq	Targaj
14-10	Bulgaria	L 0-2	Tirana	WCq	
18-11	West Germany	L 0-8	Dortmund	WCq	
22-09-1982	Austria	L 0-5	Vienna	ECq	
27-10	Turkey	L 0-1	Izmir	ECq	
15-12	Nth. Ireland	D 0-0	Tirana	ECq	
30-03-1983	West Germany	L 1-2	Tirana	ECq	Targaj
27-04	Nth. Ireland	L 0-1	Belfast	ECq	
11-05	Turkey	D 1-1	Tirana	ECq	OG
8-06	Austria	L 1-2	Tirana	ECq	Targaj
20-11	West Germany	L 1-2	Saarbrucken	ECq	Tomori
17-10-1984	Belgium	L 1-3	Brussels	WCq	Omuri
31-10	Poland	D 2-2	Mielic	WCq	Minga, Kola
22-12	Belgium	W 2-0	Tirana	WCq	Josa, Minga
27-02-1985	Greece	L 0-2	Athens	WCq	
28-03	Turkey	D 0-0	Tirana	Fr	
30-05	Poland	L 0-1	Tirana	WCq	
30-10	Greece	D 1-1	Tirana	WCq	Omuri
15-10-1986	Austria	L 0-3	Graz	ECq	
3-12	Spain	L 1-2	Tirana	ECq	Minga
25-03-1987	Romania	L 1-5	Bucharest	ECq	Muca
29-04	Austria	L 0-1	Tirana	ECq	
28-10	Romania	L 0-1	Vlore	ECq	
18-11	Spain	L 0-5	Seville	ECq	
6-08-1988	Cuba	D 0-0	Beirat	Fr	
20-09	Romania	L 0-3	Constantza	Fr	
19-10	Poland	L 0-1	Chorzow	WCq	
5-11	Sweden	L 1-2	Tirana	WCq	Shehu
18-01-1989	Greece	D 1-1	Tirana	Fr	Minga
8-03	England	L 0-2	Tirana	WCq	
26-04	England	L 0-5	London	WCq	
8-10	Sweden	L 1-3	Stockholm	WCq	Kushta
15-11	Poland	L 1-2	Tirana	WCq	Kushta
30-05-1990	Iceland	L 0-2	Reykjavik	ECq	
5-09	Greece	L 0-1	Patras	Fr	
17-11	France	L 0-1	Tirana	ECq	
19-12	Spain	L 0-9	Seville	ECq	
30-03-1991	France	L 0-5	Paris	ECq	
1-05	Czechoslovakia	L 0-2	Tirana	ECq	
26-05	Iceland	W1-0	Tirana	ECq	Abazi
4-09	Greece	W2-0	Athens	Fr	Kushta 2
16-10	Czechoslovakia	L 1-2	Olomouc	ECq	Zmijani
29-01-1992	Greece	W 1-0	Tirana	Fr	Rraklli

Date	Opponent	Result	Venue	Comp	Scorers
22-04	Spain	L 0-3	Seville	WCq	
26-05	Rep. Ireland	L 0-2	Dublin	WCq	
3-06	Lithuania	W 1-0	Tirana	WCq	Abazi
9-09	Nth. Ireland	L 0-3	Belfast	WCq	
11-11	Latvia	D 1-1	Tirana	WCq	Kepa
17-02-1993	Nth. Ireland	L 1-2	Tirana	WCq	Rraklli
14-04	Lithuania	L 1-3	Vilnius	WCq	Demollari
15-05	Latvia	D 0-0	Riga	WCq	
26-05	Rep. Ireland	L 1-2	Tirana	WCq	Kushta
2-06	Denmark	L 0-4	Copenhagen	WCq	
8-09	Denmark	L 0-1	Tirana	WCq	
22-09	Spain	L 1-5	Tirana	WCq	Kushta
14-05-1994	Macedonia	L 1-5	Tetovo	Fr	Rraklli
7-09	Wales	L 0-2	Cardiff	ECq	
16-11	Germany	L 1-2	Tirana	ECq	Zmijani
14-12	Georgia	L 0-1	Tirana	ECq	
18-12	Germany	L 1-2	Kaiserslautern	ECq	Rraklli
29-03-1995	Moldova	W 3-0	Tirana	ECq	Kushta 2, Kacaj
26-04	Georgia	L 0-2	Tbilisi	ECq	
7-06	Moldova	W 3-2	Chisinau	ECq	Kushta, Bellai, Vata

ARMENIA

Armenia was not totally unknown in football circles before the break-up of the Soviet Union, thanks to the top club in the country, Ararat Yerevan. Boasting Soviet internationals like Oganesian, Andreasian and Bondarenko, Ararat won the 'double' in 1973 and reached the quarter-finals of the 1975 European Cup where they lost to the eventual winners, Bayern Munich.

European competition returned to Yerevan in 1994 after Ararat won the 1993 Armenian championship, although with entry to the European Cup now restricted, they qualified only for the expanded UEFA Cup. They fell at the first hurdle, losing 3-0 on aggregate to Bulgaria's CSKA Sofia.

The national team made their international debut in May 1994 against the United States in Fullerton, and in September that year played their first competitive international, a 2-0 defeat in Brussels against Belgium. That was in the qualifying tournament for the 1996 European Championships, in which they were grouped with Spain, Belgium, Denmark, Macedonia and Cyprus.

Sadly, Armenia is a nation at war with another of the ex-Soviet republics, Azerbaijan. The two countries have fought a bitter battle over Nagorno-Karabakh, an Armenian enclave in Azeri territory, and UEFA will hopefully ensure that their paths do not cross in European competitions in the near future.

Population: 3,288,000
Area, sq km: 29,800
Capital city: Yerevan

Football Federation of Armenia
9 Abovian Street
375001 Yerevan
Armenia
Tel: + 7 8852 527582
Fax: + 7 8852 523376

Year of formation	1992
Affiliation to FIFA	1992
Affiliation to UEFA	1992
Registered clubs	956
Registered players	12 055
Registered referees	45
National stadium	Razdan, Yerevan 50 000
National colours	Orange/Blue/Red

THE RECORD

WORLD CUP

1930-94 Did not enter

EUROPEAN CHAMPIONSHIP

1960-92 Did not enter
1996 QT group 2

EUROPEAN CLUB COMPETITIONS

European Cup
Quarter-finalists - Ararat Yerevan 1975

Cup Winners Cup
2nd round - Ararat Yerevan 1976

UEFA Cup
3rd round - Ararat Yerevan 1973

CLUB DIRECTORY

YEREVAN (Population - 1,315,000)

Ararat Yerevan (1937)
Razdan 50,000 – Red/Blue
Previous names - Dynamo 1937-54, Spartak 1954-62

Homenetmen Yerevan (AOSS)

Van Yerevan

Yerazank Yerevan

Nairit Yerevan

Kanaz Yerevan

GYUMRI (Population - 228,000)

Previously Leninakam
Shirak Gyumri.

ABOVYAN

Banants Abovyan
Kotiak Abovyan

ARMENIAN LEAGUE CHAMPIONSHIP

1992k	Homenetmen Yerevan 37 Shirak Gyumri 37 Banants Abovyan 36
1993p	Ararat Yerevan 51 Shirak Gyumr 49 Banants Abovyan 48
1994q	Shirak Gyumri 52 Homenetmen Yerevan 47 Ararat Yerevan 47

ARMENIAN CUP FINALS

1992	Banants Abovyan		
1993	Ararat Yerevan	3-1	Shirak Gyumri
1994	Ararat Yerevan	1-0	Shirak Gyumri
1995	Ararat Yerevan	4-2	Kotiak Abovyan

INTERNATIONAL MATCHES PLAYED BY ARMENIA

15-05-1994	USA	L 0-1	Fullerton	Fr
7-09	Belgium	L 0-2	Brussels	ECq
8-10	Cyprus	D 0-0	Yerevan	ECq
16-11	Cyprus	L 0-2	Limassol	ECq
26-04-1995	Spain	L 0-2	Yerevan	ECq
10-05	Macedonia	D 2-2	Yerevan	ECq
	Scorers: Grigorian, Shakhgeloyan			
7-06	Spain	L 0-1	Seville	ECq

AUSTRIA

September 12th, 1991 will go down as a landmark in Austrian football. Before a handful of spectators in Landskrona, Sweden, the national side lost 1-0 to a Faeroe Islands team playing its very first competitive international match. How the mighty have fallen! For Vienna, in the first half of the 20th century, was at the very hub of European football. Now it is little more than a sideshow.

The very first international match on mainland Europe took place on Viennese soil and until the 1960s Austria lived up to this proud tradition. Vienna was one of the three great cities of the Austro-Hungarian empire along with Budapest and Prague, and the legend of the 'Danubian school of football' was born even before the three cities became the capitals of their own separate countries after the First World War. Austrian teams became synonymous with skilful ball-players who combined clever short passing movements with innovative tactics. Austria was also innovative off the field. The great Hugo Meisl was one of the game's greatest administrators, and it was largely due to his efforts that football became so popular in central Europe.

The large British community in Vienna formed the basis from which football developed. Naturally, English teams were invited to play there and in 1900 Southampton visited and gave a display that greatly encouraged the development of the game, beating a Vienna selection 6-0. A cup had been introduced for teams from Vienna three years previously, and as the name of the first winners, Cricketers, suggests, British influence was strong. It was to Budapest, however, that Austrian teams turned for more regular opposition. Hungarian clubs were invited to take part in Der Challenge-Cup, and on 12 October 1902 the most significant event to that date on mainland Europe took place. Before 500 spectators and an English referee, Austria beat Hungary 5-0 in an international match that was to be the first of thousands on the continent.

The Hungary match became an annual event but opposition was also found in matches against Germany and Italy. In 1912 Austria entered the Stockholm Olympics and although Germany were well beaten in the first round, a strong Dutch side beat the Austrians 3-1 in the quarter-finals. In a consolation tournament organised for the teams that did not reach the semi-finals, Austria lost in the final to Hungary.

At the same time that international football was gaining a foothold, clubs were being created across the country but especially in Vienna. Along with the Cricketers, who are no longer in existence, 1894 also saw the founding of First Vienna who to this day retain the English spelling of their name. In 1898 Sportklub Rapid arrived on the scene as a workers' club, and they were joined in 1911 by their greatest rivals Amateure, who later became known as FK Austria. The governing body of Austrian football was formed in 1904 and joined FIFA in 1905, a year after FIFA's own formation. A league was set up in 1911, taking over from Der Challenge-Cup as the source of competition in Vienna. The league was contested entirely by teams from Vienna, and it was not until 1949 that clubs from other cities were invited to take part. The same was true of the Vienna Cup introduced in 1919.

The inter-war period was Austria's most successful era. Success in the Mitropa Cup and the International Cup helped seal her reputation. The Mitropa Cup especially caught the imagination of the public and huge crowds turned up to see the annual games. Rapid, FK Austria and First Vienna all won the tournament, whilst in the International Cup, the national team finished as runners-up in the first tournament and won the second. Victory in the 1930-32 edition saw the Austrians at their very best. Dubbed as the 'Wunderteam' the exploits of this side are never likely to be equalled by another Austrian side. After losing to Italy in early 1931. Austria enjoyed a spell lasting until June 1934 when they took on all-comers and generally beat them convincingly - 101 goals were scored in 30 games, and though Austria did not stay undefeated in this time, one of the two defeats suffered was at the hands of England, in London, a game in which the English were lucky not to lose their unbeaten home record 20 years before they finally did.

The names of the members of the 'Wunderteam' will echo down through the ages. The forward line was one of the most fearsome ever fielded, spearheaded by a man called der Papierne, 'the man of paper', due to his slight build. This was Matthias Sindelar who until the emergence of Hans Krankl in the 1970s was Austria's most celebrated player. He scored 27 goals for his country as did his forward partner Schall, who along with Gschweidl, Zischek, Vogel and later Binder and Bican were the terror of defences across the continent. Sadly however, aside from the International Cup victory, there was to be no lasting honour to mark the quality of this side. The 1934 World Cup was there for the taking and had it been played anywhere other than Italy, Austria might well have won it.

Instead, after having disposed of both France and Hungary, they met Italy in the semi-finals in Milan. Home advantage and a muddy pitch settled the match 1-0 in favour of the more robust Italians. Demoralised by the defeat, the Austrians also lost the third place play-off to Germany four days later.

Italy were again Austria's downfall two years later in the 1936 Olympic Games, this time in the final. Playing without all their well-known players, who by this time were all professionals and therefore ineligible, the Austrians were not expected to progress far, and the fact that they reached the final owed much to a man who had helped mould the Austrian game for over 20 years – Jimmy Hogan, an Englishman who felt more at home away from England, a country that never appreciated his talents, had coached in Austria on and off since 1912, and worked in Germany and Hungary. His work as coach of the team for the 1936 Olympics was his crowning glory and to this day the Olympic Final remains the only major final the Austrians have ever played in.

Hitler soon put paid to any aspirations the Austrians may have had of winning the 1938 World Cup. United into a greater Germany in March 1938, 'Austrian' football ceased to exist, and although three international matches were played by the Germans in Vienna, all three were during the war. Austrian club sides were not so easily submerged, however. Rapid won the German Cup in 1938 and were German champions in 1941, whilst First Vienna won the Cup in 1943.

Remarkably, when the Austrians next took the field for an international match, on 19 August 1945 in a match against Hungary, four of the side were survivors from the previous game in October 1937 against Czechoslovakia. Sindelar was not amongst them, however. Contrary to some reports which had him dying in a concentration camp for Jews during the war, Sindelar was not Jewish and had in fact committed suicide in 1939. At his funeral, 20,000 people turned out to pay their respects to possibly the greatest Austrian footballer ever.

In 1948 Austria entered the London Olympics but there was no repeat of their previous success as they lost 3-0 in the first round against Sweden, who went on to win the tournament. Like many European countries, Austria shunned the 1950 World Cup, but in the meantime, under Walter Nausch a new team was being moulded. The dynamos of the side were Ernst Ocwirk and Gerhard Hanappi and they inspired the Austrians to the semi-finals of the 1954 World Cup. Portugal were beaten 9-1 in the qualifiers and in the final tournament the goals carried on flowing. That so many goals were scored in the tournament was in no small part due to a remarkable game between Austria and their hosts. The final score of 7-5 in favour of the Austrians is the highest ever score in the World Cup finals and is unlikely to be beaten. Their 6-1 defeat at the hands of Germany in the semi-finals, however, surprised even the Germans. Once again the Austrians had fallen at a hurdle they were expected to conquer with ease. There was to be no third attempt at winning a World Cup semi-final. From 1954 onwards, the Austrians became increasing happy just to qualify for the finals.

THE ORDER OF MERIT

		All			League			Cup		Europe		
	Team	G	S	B	G	S	B	G	S	G	S	B
1	FK Austria Wien	47	29	18	22	17	16	25	11	-	1	2
2	SK Rapid Wien	43	30	19	29	18	18	14	11	-	1	1
3	Admira-Wacker	15	17	11	9	13	11	6	4	-	-	-
4	FC Tirol Innsbruck	14	10	6	7	5	5	7	5	-	-	1
5	First Vienna FC	9	12	10	6	7	10	3	5	-	-	-
6	Wiener Sport-Club	4	14	5	3	7	5	1	7	-	-	-
7	SV Austria Salzburg	2	7	-	2	3	-	-	3	-	1	-
8	Linzer ASK	2	4	4	1	1	4	1	3	-	-	-
9	Wiener AF	2	2	3	1	2	3	1	-	-	-	-
10	FC Linz	1	4	1	1	2	1	-	2	-	-	-
11	Floridsdorfer AC	1	3	1	1	3	1	-	-	-	-	-
12	Grazer AK	1	2	2	-	-	2	1	2	-	-	-
13	Hakoah Wien	1	1	-	1	1	-	-	-	-	-	-
14	Kremser SC	1	-	-	-	-	-	1	-	-	-	-
	SV Stockerau	1	-	-	-	-	-	1	-	-	-	-
16	SK Sturm Graz	-	4	3	-	2	3	-	2	-	-	-
17	BAC Wien	-	2	-	-	1	-	-	1	-	-	-
18	Rudolfshugel FC	-	1	2	-	1	2	-	-	-	-	-
19	DSV Leoban	-	1	-	-	-	-	-	1	-	-	-
	FC Wien	-	1	-	-	1	-	-	-	-	-	-
	Slovan Wien	-	1	-	-	-	-	-	1	-	-	-
	Wiener Neustadt	-	1	-	-	-	-	-	1	-	-	-
	Vorwärts Steyr	-	1	-	-	-	-	-	1	-	-	-
24	I.SC Simmering	-	-	1	-	-	1	-	-	-	-	-

Austria's triumphs until the early 1950s are best seen in the light of what was still very much an amateur game, but at which they were professionals. With a population of only seven million, the increasing commercialisation of the game was bound to leave them behind. A none too happy outing at the 1958 World Cup was followed by failure to qualify again until 1978, and seven attempts to qualify for the European Championship finals have all ended in disappointment. Club football has suffered too. As the league was extended to include provincial teams, many of the great club sides of the 1920s and 1930s either fell by the wayside or merged with others in an effort to stay solvent. Austrian clubs have also fared badly in the European club competitions, although FK Austria and Rapid have both reached the final of the Cup Winners Cup and the provincial side Casino Salzburg were runners-up in the UEFA Cup.

Austria does, however, continue to produce fine players, although they rarely stay in Austria for their club football. The late 1970s and early 1980s saw some success at international level. Hans Krankl along with Walter Schachner, Herbert Prohaska, Bruno Pezzey and Kurt Jara led the Austrians to two World Cup qualifications, in 1978 and 1982. In the 1978 finals, victories over Spain and Sweden ensured a place in the second round, where despite beating the reigning champions West Germany, they lost to both the Dutch and the Italians. The 1982 tournament will always be remembered for the great Gijón swindle in which the West Germans and Austrians contrived a result that saw both teams through at the expense of Algeria. Once in the second round the Austrians came up against France who ensured their elimination with a 1-0 victory in Madrid.

Failure to qualify for the 1986 Mexico World Cup due to the presence of their eternal rivals Hungary, was followed by qualification for Italy in 1990. Though much was expected of a forward line that included Polster, Rodax and Ogris, Austria could not proceed beyond the first round. If that was perhaps to be expected, what happened the following September in their European Championship match against the Faeroes was not. The defeat at the hands of the part-timers was deeply embarrassing and ensured that once again the European Championship would bring no joy to the Austrians.

To cap a sorry period for the national side, they were never in the running for a place in the 1994 World Cup finals either. For Austrian football there was consolation only in Casino Salzburg's dazzling run to the final of the 1994 UEFA Cup. They defeated Sporting Lisbon, Eintracht Frankfurt and Karlsruhe on the way, but failed to overcome Internazionale and so missed out on being the first Austrian club side to land a European title.

Population: 7,623,000
Area, sq km: 83,856
% in urban areas: 57.7%
Capital city: Vienna

Österreichischer Fußball-Bund
Ernst Happel Stadion, Sektor A/F
Meiereistrasse, Postfach 340
A-1020 Wien
Austria
Tel: + 43 1 727180
Fax: + 43 1 7281632

Year of formation	1904
Affiliation to FIFA	1905
Affiliation to UEFA	1954
Registered clubs	2081
Registered players	252 000
Professional players	380
Registered coaches	2814
Registered referees	2200
National stadium	Ernst Happel
Stadion, Vienna	62 000
National colours	White shirts, Black shorts, Black socks
Reserve colours	Red shirts,
White shorts,	Red socks
Season	July - June, with a mid season break December-February

THE RECORD

WORLD CUP

1930	Did not enter
1934	QT 2nd/3 in group 8 - Final Tournament/ Semi-finalists/4th Place
1938	Did not enter
1950	Did not enter
1954	QT 1st/2 in group 5 - Final Tournament/ Semi-finalists/3rd Place
1958	QT 1st/3 in group 5 - Final Tournament/1st round
1962	Did not enter
1966	QT 3rd/3 in group 6
1970	QT 3rd/4 in group 7
1974	QT 2nd/4 in group 1
1978	QT 1st/4 in group 3 - Final Tournament/2nd round
1982	QT 2nd/5 in group 1 - Final Tournament/2nd round
1986	QT 3rd/4 in group 5
1990	QT 2nd/5 in group 3 - Final Tournament/1st round
1994	QT 4th/6 in group 6

EUROPEAN CHAMPIONSHIP

1960	Quarter-finalists
1964	Did not enter
1968	QT 3rd/4 in group 3
1972	QT 2nd/4 in group 6
1976	QT 3rd/4 in group 2
1980	QT 2nd/5 in group 2
1984	QT 3rd/5 in group 6
1988	QT 3rd/4 in group 1
1992	QT 4th/5 in group 4
1996	QT group 6

DR. GERÖ CUP

1929	2nd
1932	Winners
1935	2nd
1953	3rd
1960	3rd

EUROPEAN CLUB COMPETITIONS

European Cup
Semi-finalists - SK Rapid Wien 1961, FK Austria 1979

Cup Winners Cup
Finalists - FK Austria 1978, SK Rapid Wien 1985

UEFA Cup
Finalists - SV Casino Salzburg 1994

Mitropa Cup
Winners - SK Rapid Wien 1930, First Vienna 1931, FK Austria 1933 1936
Finalists - SK Rapid Wien 1927 1928, Wiener AC 1931, Admira 1934

CLUB DIRECTORY

VIENNA (Population - 1,875,000)

FC Admira-Wacker (1971)
Südstadt 12,000 – Black/Black, white trimmings
Previous names - Admira Wien (1905) and Wacker Wien (1908) merged in 1971

FK Austria (1911)
Franz Horr 10,000 – Violet with white sleeves/White
Previous names - Amateure until 1926. Merged with Wiener Athletik Club (WAC) (1896) in 1969

First Vienna FC (1894)
Hohe Warte 10,000 – Yellow/Blue

SK Rapid Wien (1898)
Gerhard Hanappi 19,000 – Green & white stripes/White

Wiener Sport-Club (1893)
Sport-Club Platz 8,000 – Black & white stripes/Black, orange trimmings

Vienna clubs that are no longer in existence: Cricket FV 1894-1939, Hakoah 1901-39, Hertha 1904-40, Rudolfshügel 1902-35, Wien AF 1912-35, FC Wien 1918-56 (Previously known as Nicholson 1918-32)

LINZ (Population - 335,000)

Linzer ASK (Athletik-Sport-Klub) (1908)
Linzer 27,000 – White/Black

FC Linz (1949)
Linzer 27,000 – Blue/Blue, white trimmings
Previous names - VÖEST merged with SV Stickstoff (1929) in 1964, SK VÖEST Linz 1964-91, FC Stahl Linz 1991-93

GRAZ (Population - 325,000)

Grazer AK (1902)
Liebenau 9,000 – Red/Red

SK Sturm Graz (1909)
Sturm-Platz 11,000 – White/Black, black trimmings

SALZBURG (Population 220,000)

SV Austria Salzburg (1933)
Lehen 14,000 – White/White, violet trimmings
Previous names - Formed when Hertha and Rapid Salzburg merged in 1933

INNSBRUCK (Population - 185,000)

FC Tirol Innsbruck (1913)

Tivoli 17,000 – Green & red stripes/Green, white trimmings

Previous names - Wacker Innsbruck 1913-86, FC Tirol 1986-92, Wacker Innsbruck 1992-93

KLAGENFURT (Population - 115,000)

SK Austria Klagenfurt (1920)

Wörthersee 12,000 – Violet/White

ST. PÖLTEN (Population - 67,000)

VSE St. Pölten (1920)

Voith-Platz 11,000 – Red/Red, white trimmings

STEYR (Population - 65,000)

SK Vorwärts Steyr (1919)

Steyr 9,000 – Red/White, white trimmings

WIENER NEUSTADT (Population - 35,000)

SC Wiener Neustadt (1908)

Sportstadion – White/Blue

KREMS (Population 23,000)

Kremser SC (1919)

Kremser 15,000 – White with black sleeves & shoulders/White

MÖDLING (Population - 19,000)

VfB Mödling (1911)

Sportplatz Mödling 6,000 – White/White, red trimmings

STOCKERAU

SV Stockerau (1907)

Stadion Alte 7,000 – Red/Black

AUSTRIAN LEAGUE CHAMPIONSHIP

1912i	SK Rapid Wien 31 Wiener Sport-Club 30 Wiener AF 29
1913h	SK Rapid Wien 33 Wiener AF 26 Wiener Sport-Club 21
1914	Wiener AF 27 SK Rapid Wien 27 Wiener AC 23
1915ae	Wiener AC 16 Wiener AF 15 SK Rapid Wien 10
1916h	SK Rapid Wien 31 Floridsdorfer AC 29 Wiener AF 26
1917	SK Rapid Wien 29 Floridsdorfer AC 27 Rudolfshügel FC 27
1918	Floridsdorfer AC 24 SK Rapid Wien 24 Wiener AF 22
1919	SK Rapid Wien 31 Rudolfshügel FC 24 Wiener AC 23
1920k	SK Rapid Wien 33 Amateure 33 Wiener Sport-Club 30
1921l	SK Rapid Wien 40 Amateure 34 Rudolfshügel FC 26
1922	Wiener Sport-Club 34 Hakoah Wien 32 SK Rapid Wien 31
1923	SK Rapid Wien 36 Amateure 32 Admira Wien 27
1924k	Amateure 36 First Vienna FC 32 Wiener Sport-Club 30
1925i	Hakoah Wien 26 Amateure 24 First Vienna FC 23
1926l	Amateure 35 First Vienna FC 31 I.SC Simmering 29
1927	Admira Wien 36 BAC Wien 33 SK Rapid Wien 31
1928	Admira Wien 39 SK Rapid Wien 36 First Vienna FC 32
1929k	SK Rapid Wien 33 Admira Wien 30 Wiener AC 30
1930i	SK Rapid Wien 30 Admira Wien 29 First Vienna FC 28
1931h	First Vienna FC 29 Admira Wien 27 SK Rapid Wien 26
1932k	Admira Wien 33 First Vienna FC 31 SK Rapid Wien 31
1933	First Vienna FC 35 SK Rapid Wien 32 Admira Wien 25
1934	Admira Wien 33 SK Rapid Wien 31 FK Austria 27
1935	SK Rapid Wien 40 Admira Wien 34 First Vienna FC 27
1936	Admira Wien 37 First Vienna FC 32 SK Rapid Wien 26
1937	Admira Wien 35 FK Austria 35 First Vienna FC 30
1938h	SK Rapid Wien 30 Wiener Sport-Club 23 FK Austria 21
1939	Admira Wien 28 Wacker Wien 26 SK Rapid Wien 25
1940f	SK Rapid Wien 20 Wacker Wien 17 Wiener Sport-Club 16
1941h	SK Rapid Wien 28 Wacker Wien 24 First Vienna FC24
1942g	First Vienna FC 25 FC Wien 21 SK Rapid Wien 19
1943i	First Vienna FC 30 Wiener AC 27 Floridsdorfer AC 25
1944g	First Vienna FC 27 Floridsdorfer AC 22 Wiener AC 16
1945	-
1946k	SK Rapid Wien 35 FK Austria 34 Wacker Wien 31
1947i	Wacker Wien 30 SK Rapid Wien 28 First Vienna FC 27
1948h	SK Rapid Wien 28 Wacker Wien 27 FK Austria 22
1949	FK Austria 27 SK Rapid Wien 25 Admira Wien 24
1950l	FK Austria 38 SK Rapid Wien 36 Wacker Wien 33
1951	SK Rapid Wien 43 Wacker Wien 38 FK Austria 32
1952n	SK Rapid Wien 41 FK Austria 39 First Vienna FC 32
1953	FK Austria 45 Wacker Wien 44 SK Rapid Wien 39
1954	SK Rapid Wien 39 FK Austria 38 Wacker Wien 31
1955	First Vienna FC 39 Wiener Sport-Club 39 SK Rapid Wien 36
1956	SK Rapid Wien 43 Wacker Wien 41 First Vienna FC 40
1957	SK Rapid Wien 40 First Vienna FC 39 FK Austria 38
1958	Wiener Sport-Club 45 SK Rapid Wien 43 First Vienna FC 30
1959	Wiener Sport-Club 46 SK Rapid Wien 44 First Vienna FC 32
1960	SK Rapid Wien 42 Wiener Sport-Club 38 Wiener AC 38
1961	FK Austria 39 First Vienna FC 32 Wiener AC 32
1962	FK Austria 42 Linzer ASK 38 Admira Wien 36
1963	FK Austria 38 Admira Wien 34 Wiener Sport-Club 33
1964	SK Rapid Wien 43 FK Austria 37 Linzer ASK 33
1965	Linzer ASK 36 SK Rapid Wien 35 Admira Wien 35
1966	Admira Wien 43 SK Rapid Wien 40 FK Austria 35
1967	SK Rapid Wien 41 Wacker Innsbruck 41 FK Austria 35
1968	SK Rapid Wien 44 Wacker Innsbruck 37 FK Austria 35
1969p	FK Austria 46 Wiener Sport-Club 38 SK Rapid Wien 35
1970q	FK Austria 45 Wiener Sport-Club 38 SK Sturm Graz 36
1971	Wacker Innsbruck 44 SV Austria Salzburg 43 SK Rapid Wien 41
1972p	Wacker Innsbruck 39 FK Austria 38 SK VÖEST Linz 35
1973q	Wacker Innsbruck 43 SK Rapid Wien 40 Grazer AK 36
1974r	SK VÖEST Linz 47 Wacker Innsbruck 46 SK Rapid Wien 45
1975u2	Wacker Innsbruck 51 SK VÖEST Linz 42 SK Rapid Wien 41
1976	FK Austria 52 Wacker Innsbruck 45 SK Rapid Wien 40
1977	Wacker Innsbruck 53 SK Rapid Wien 47 FK Austria 45
1978	FK Austria 56 SK Rapid Wien 42 Wacker Innsbruck 39
1979	FK Austria 55 Wiener Sport-Club 41 SK Rapid Wien 39
1980	FK Austria 50 SK VÖEST Linz 43 Linzer ASK 43
1981	FK Austria 46 SK Sturm Graz 45 SK Rapid Wien 43
1982	SK Rapid Wien 47 FK Austria 44 Grazer AK 38
1983q	SK Rapid Wien 48 FK Austria 48 Wacker Innsbruck 38
1984	FK Austria 47 SK Rapid Wien 47 Linzer ASK 42
1985	FK Austria 54 SK Rapid Wien 45 Linzer ASK 38
1986u3	FK Austria 58 SK Rapid Wien 56 Wacker Innsbruck 39
1987	SK Rapid Wien 52 FK Austria 52 FC Tirol 45
1988	SK Rapid Wien 54 FK Austria 46 SK Sturm Graz 42
1989u4	FC Tirol 39 Admira-Wacker 33 FK Austria 39
1990	FC Tirol 38 FK Austria 31 Admira-Wacker 29
1991	FK Austria 36 FC Tirol 35 SK Sturm Graz 32
1992	FK Austria 33 SV Austria Salzburg 33 FC Tiro 33
1993	FK Austria 36 SV Austria Salzburg 36 Admira-Wacker 28
1994u2	SV Austria Salzburg 51 FK Austria 49 Admira-Wacker 44
1995	SV Austria Salzburg 47 SK Sturm Graz 47 SK Rapid Wien 46

DER CHALLENGE-CUP

1897	Cricketers	3-2	First Vienna FC
1898	First Vienna FC	2-1	Cricketers

1899	First Vienna FC	1-0	Cricketers
1900	First Vienna FC	2-0	Cricketers
1901	Wiener AC	Lge	
1902	Cricketers	2-1	Budapest TC
1903	Wiener AC	5-1	Ferencvaros
1904	Wiener AC	7-0	Cricketers
1905	Wiener Sport-Club	2-1	Budapest Magyar
1906-08	-		
1909	Ferencvaros Budapest		
1910	Budapest TC	2-1	Wiener SC
1911	Wiener Sport-Club		

AUSTRIAN CUP FINALS

1919	SK Rapid Wien	3-0	Wiener Sport-Club
1920	SK Rapid Wien	5-2	Amateure
1921	Amateure	2-1	Wiener Sport-Club
1922	Wiener AF	2-1	Amateure
1923	Wiener Sport-Club	3-1	Wacker Wien
1924	Amateure	8-6	Slovan Wien
1925	Amateure	3-1	First Vienna FC
1926	Amateure	4-3	First Vienna FC
1927	SK Rapid Wien	3-0	FK Austria
1928	Admira Wien	2-1	Wiener AC
1929	First Vienna FC	3-2	SK Rapid Wien
1930	First Vienna FC	1-0	FK Austria
1931	Wiener AC declared winners		
1932	Admira Wien	6-1	Wiener AC
1933	FK Austria	1-0	BAC Wien
1934	Admira Wien	8-0	SK Rapid Wien
1935	FK Austria	5-1	Wiener AC
1936	FK Austria	3-0	First Vienna FC
1937	First Vienna FC	2-0	Wiener Sport-Club
1938	Wiener AC	1-0	Wiener Sport-Club
1939-45	-		
1946	SK Rapid Wien	2-1	First Vienna FC
1947	Wacker Wien	4-3	FK Austria
1948	FK Austria	2-0	SK Sturm Graz
1949	FK Austria	5-2	Vorwärts Steyr
1950-58	-		
1959	Wiener AC	2-0	SK Rapid Wien
1960	FK Austria	4-2	SK Rapid Wien
1961	SK Rapid Wien	3-1	First Vienna FC
1962	FK Austria	4-1	Grazer AK
1963	FK Austria	1-0	Linzer ASK
1964	Admira Wien	1-0	FK Austria
1965	Linzer ASK	1-1 1-0	Wiener Neustadt
1966	Admira Wien	1-0	SK Rapid Wien
1967	FK Austria	1-0	Linzer ASK
1968	SK Rapid Wien	2-0	Grazer AK
1969	SK Rapid Wien	2-1	Wiener Sport-Club
1970	Wacker Innsbruck	1-0	Linzer ASK
1971	FK Austria	2-1	SK Rapid Wien
1972	SK Rapid Wien	1-2 3-1	Wiener Sport-Club
1973	Wacker Innsbruck	1-0 1-2	SK Rapid Wien
1974	FK Austria	2-1 1-1	SV AustriaSalzburg
1975	Wacker Innsbruck	3-0 0-2	SK Sturm Graz
1976	SK Rapid Wien	1-0 1-2	Wacker Innsbruck
1977	FK Austria	1-0 3-0	Wiener Sport-Club
1978	Wacker Innsbruck	1-1 2-1	SK VÖEST Linz
1979	Wacker Innsbruck	1-0 1-1	Admira-Wacker
1980	FK Austria	0-1 2-0	SV Austria Salzburg
1981	Grazer AK	0-1 2-0	SV Austria Salzburg
1982	FK Austria	1-0 3-1	Wacker Innsbruck
1983	SK Rapid Wien	3-0 5-0	Wacker Innsbruck
1984	SK Rapid Wien	1-3 2-0	FK Austria
1985	SK Rapid Wien	3-3 6-5p	FK Austria
1986	FK Austria	6-4	SK Rapid Wien
1987	SK Rapid Wien	2-0 2-2	FC Tirol
1988	Kremser SC	2-0 1-3	FC Tirol
1989	FC Tirol	0-2 6-2	Admira-Wacker
1990	FK Austria	3-1	SK Rapid Wien
1991	SV Stockerau	2-1	SK Rapid Wien
1992	FK Austria	1-0	Admira-Wacker
1993	Wacker Innsbruck	3-1	SK Rapid Wien
1994	FK Austria	4-0	FC Linz
1995	SK Rapid Wien	1-0	DSV Leoben

LEADING INTERNATIONAL GOALSCORERS

34 Hans Krankl	(Rapid,Barcelona)	1973-85
32 Toni Polster	(FKAustria,Sevilla,Logroñes, Vallecano,Köln)	1982-
28 Erich Hof	(Wiener Sport-Club)	1957-68
28 Johann Horvath	(Simmering,Rapid,Wacker, FC Wien)	1924-34
27 Matthias Sindelar	(FK Austria)	1926-37
27 Anton Schall	(Admira)	1927-34
24 Karl Zischek	(Wacker)	1931-45
23 Walter Schachner	(DSVAlpine,FK Austria, Cesena,Torino, Pisa,Avellino)	1976-88
22 Theodor Wagner	(Wacker)	1946-57
19 Karl Decker	(First Vienna)	1945-52

Karl Decker also scored 8 goals in 8 games for Germany in 1942

LEADING INTERNATIONAL APPEARANCES

93 Gerhard Hanappi	(Wacker,Rapid)	1948-62
86 Karl Koller	(First Vienna)	1952-65
84 Friedrich Koncilia #	(Wattens,Innsbruck, Anderlecht,FK Austria)	1970-85
84 Bruno Pezzey	(Innsbruck,Ein Frank., Werder Br.,Tirol)	1975-90
83 Herbert Prohaska	(FK Austria,Internazionale,Roma)	1974-89
69 Hans Krankl	(Rapid,Barcelona)	1973-85
69 Toni Polster	(FK Austria,Sevilla, Logroñes,Vallecano,Köln)	1982-
68 Heribert Weber	(Sturm Graz,Rapid,Salzburg)	1976-89
63 Walter Schachner	(DSV Alpine,FK Austria, Cesena,Torino,Pisa,Avellino)	1976-88
62 Ernst Ocwirk	(Floridsdorfer,FK Austria)	1945-62

NATIONAL TEAM COACHES

1945-48	Edi Bauer
1948	Committee
1948-54	Walter Nausch
1954-55	Hans Kaulich
1955	Josef Molzer
1955-56	Karl Geyer
1956-58	Josef Argauer & Josef Molzer
1958	Committee
1958-64	Karl Decker
1964	Josef Walter & Bela Guttman
1964-67	Edi Frühwirth
1967-68	Erwin Alge & Hans Pesser
1968-75	Leopold Stastny
1975	Branko Elsner
1976-78	Helmut Senekowitsch
1978-81	Karl Stotz
1982	Georg Schmidt & Felix Latzke
1982-84	Erich Hof
1985-87	Branko Elsner
1988-90	Josef Hickersberger
1990-91	Alfred Riedl
1991	Didi Constantini
1991-92	Ernst Happel
1993-	Herbert Prohaska

INTERNATIONAL MATCHES PLAYED BY AUSTRIA

Date	Opponents	Result	Venue	Competition	Scorers
12-10-1902	Hungary	W 5-0	Vienna	Fr	Studnicka 3, Huber, Taurer
10-06-1903	Hungary	L 2-3	Budapest	Fr	Studnicka, Pulchert
11-10	Hungary	W 4-2	Vienna	Fr	Studnicka 3, Huber
2-06-1904	Hungary	L 0-3	Budapest	Fr	
9-11	Hungary	W 5-4	Vienna	Fr	Stansfield 4, Bugno
9-04-1905	Hungary	D 0-0	Budapest	Fr	
4-11-1906	Hungary	L 1-3	Budapest	Fr	Hussack
5-05-1907	Hungary	W 3-1	Vienna	Fr	Schediwy, Dünnmann, Wolf
3-11	Hungary	L 1-4	Budapest	Fr	Dünnmann
3-05-1908	Hungary	W 4-0	Vienna	Fr	Hussack, Kubik, Kohn, Andres
6-06	England	L 1-6	Vienna	Fr	Schmieger
7-06	Germany	W 3-2	Vienna	Fr	Dlabac, Studnicka, Andres
8-06	England	L 1-11	Vienna	Fr	Hirschl
1-11	Hungary	L 3-5	Budapest	Fr	Fischera 2, Studnicka
2-05-1909	Hungary	L 3-4	Vienna	Fr	Neubauer.L 2, Schmieger
30-05	Hungary	D 1-1	Budapest	Fr	Schrenk
1-06	England	L 1-8	Vienna	Fr	Neubauer.L
9-11	Hungary	D 2-2	Budapest	Fr	Schmieger 2
1-05-1910	Hungary	W 2-1	Vienna	Fr	Hussack, Fischera
6-11	Hungary	L 0-3	Budapest	Fr	
7-05-1911	Hungary	W 3-1	Vienna	Fr	Merz 2, Hussack
9-10	Germany	W 2-1	Dresden	Fr	Schmieger, Neumann
5-11	Hungary	L 0-2	Budapest	Fr	
5-05-1912	Hungary	D 1-1	Vienna	Fr	Fischera
29-06	Germany	W 5-1	Stockholm	OGr1	Merz 2, Cimera, Studnicka, Neubauer.L
30-06	Holland	L 1-3	Stockholm	OGqf	Muller.A
1-07	Norway	W 1-0	Stockholm	OGct	OG
3-07	Italy	W 5-1	Stockholm	OGct	Grundwald 2, Müller.A, Hussak, Studnicka
5-07	Hungary	L 0-3	Stockholm	OGct	
3-11	Hungary	L 0-4	Budapest	Fr	
22-12	Italy	W 3-1	Genoa	Fr	Schmieger, Kuthan, Kohn
27-04-1913	Hungary	L 1-4	Vienna	Fr	Studnicka
15-06	Italy	W 2-0	Vienna	Fr	Brandstätter 2
26-10	Hungary	L 3-4	Budapest	Fr	Merz, Schwarz.J, Dittrich
11-01-1914	Italy	D 0-0	Milan	Fr	
3-05	Hungary	W 2-0	Vienna	Fr	Fischera 2
4-10	Hungary	D 2-2	Budapest	Fr	Studnicka, Swatosch.F
8-11	Hungary	L 1-2	Vienna	Fr	Kuthan
2-05-1915	Hungary	W 5-2	Budapest	Fr	Studnicka 2, Swatosch.F, Ehrlich, Hoel
30-05	Hungary	L 1-2	Vienna	Fr	
3-10	Hungary	W 4-2	Vienna	Fr	Bauer.E 2, Heinzl 2
7-11	Hungary	L 2-6	Budapest	Fr	Studnicka, Kuthan
7-05-1916	Hungary	W 3-1	Vienna	Fr	Bauer.E 2, Studnicka
4-06	Hungary	L 1-2	Budapest	Fr	Bauer.E
1-10	Hungary	W 3-2	Budapest	Fr	Bauer.E 2, Grundwald
5-11	Hungary	D 3-3	Vienna	Fr	Bauer.E, Kraus.J
6-05-1917	Hungary	D 1-1	Vienna	Fr	
3-06	Hungary	L 2-6	Budapest	Fr	Bauer.E, Heinzl
15-07	Hungary	L 1-4	Vienna	Fr	Prousek
7-10	Hungary	L 1-2	Budapest	Fr	Sedlacek.J
4-11	Hungary	L 1-2	Vienna	Fr	Wilda
23-12	Switzerland	W 1-0	Basle	Fr	Bauer.E
26-12	Switzerland	L 2-3	Zurich	Fr	Bauer.E, Neubauer
14-04-1918	Hungary	L 0-2	Budapest	Fr	
9-05	Switzerland	W 5-1	Vienna	Fr	Wilda 2, Heinlein, Kozeluh, OG
2-06	Hungary	L 0-2	Vienna	Fr	
6-10	Hungary	L 0-3	Vienna	Fr	
6-04-1919	Hungary	L 1-2	Budapest	Fr	Wondrak
5-10	Hungary	W 2-0	Vienna	Fr	Uridil, Bauer.E
9-11	Hungary	L 2-3	Budapest	Fr	Hansl, Treml
2-05-1920	Hungary	D 2-2	Vienna	Fr	Swatosch, Wieser
26-09	Germany	W 3-2	Vienna	Fr	Swatosch 3
7-11	Hungary	W 2-1	Budapest	Fr	Swatosch, Kuthan
25-03-1921	Sweden	D 2-2	Vienna	Fr	Kuthan 2
24-04	Hungary	W 4-1	Budapest	Fr	Kuthan 2, Wondrak, Neubauer.K
1-05	Switzerland	D 2-2	St Gallen	Fr	Kuthan, Neubauer.K

Date	Opponents	Result	Venue	Competition	Scorers
5-05	Germany	D 3-3	Dresden	Fr	Kuthan, Wondrak, Uridil
24-07	Sweden	W 3-1	Stockholm	Fr	Kuthan 2, Uridil
31-07	Finland	W 3-2	Helsinki	Fr	Uridil 2, Neumann
15-01-1922	Italy	D 3-3	Milan	Fr	Hansl 2, Köck
23-04	Germany	L 0-2	Vienna	Fr	
30-04	Hungary	D 1-1	Budapest	Fr	Jiszda
11-06	Switzerland	W 7-1	Vienna	Fr	Uridil 3, Kuthan 2, Fischera 2
24-09	Hungary	D 2-2	Vienna	Fr	Kuthan, Wessely
26-11	Hungary	W 2-1	Budapest	Fr	Swatosch, Kowanda
21-12	Switzerland	L 0-2	Geneva	Fr	
15-04-1923	Italy	D 0-0	Vienna	Fr	
6-05	Hungary	W 1-0	Vienna	Fr	Swatosch
10-06	Sweden	L 2-4	Gothenburg	Fr	Swatosch, Wieser
15-08	Finland	W 2-1	Vienna	Fr	Wieser 2
23-09	Hungary	L 0-2	Budapest	Fr	
13-01-1924	Germany	L 3-4	Nuremberg	Fr	Swatosch, Seidl, Jiszda
20-01	Italy	W 4-0	Genoa	Fr	Wieser 2, Swatosch, Jiszda
10-02	Yugoslavia	W 4-1	Zagreb	Fr	Wieser 3, Hofbauer
4-05	Hungary	D 2-2	Budapest	Fr	Wieser, Horvath
20-05	Romania	W 4-1	Vienna	Fr	Kanhäuser 3, Häusler
21-05	Bulgaria	W 6-0	Vienna	Fr	Horvath 3, Grünwald, Danis
22-06	Egypt	W 3-1	Vienna	Fr	Horvath, Höss, Wessely
14-09	Hungary	W 2-1	Vienna	Fr	Horvath, Wessely
9-11	Sweden	D 1-1	Vienna	Fr	Wessely
21-12	Spain	L 1-2	Barcelona	Fr	Horvath
22-03-1925	Switzerland	W 2-0	Vienna	Fr	Horvath, Gschweidl
19-04	France	W 4-0	Paris	Fr	Swatosch 2, Wieser, Cutti
5-05	Hungary	W 3-1	Vienna	Fr	Haftl, Häusler
24-05	Czechoslovakia	L 1-3	Prague	Fr	Swatosch
5-07	Sweden	W 4-2	Stockholm	Fr	Horvath 3, Swatosch
10-07	Finland	W 2-1	Helsinki	Fr	Wessely, Dumser
20-09	Hungary	D 1-1	Budapest	Fr	OG
27-09	Spain	L 0-1	Vienna	Fr	
8-11	Switzerland	L 0-2	Berne	Fr	
13-12	Belgium	W 4-3	Liege	Fr	Cutti 2, Wieser, Hierländer
14-03-1926	Czechoslovakia	W 2-0	Vienna	Fr	Cutti, Hierländer
2-05	Hungary	W 3-0	Budapest	Fr	Cutti, Hanel, Eckl
30-05	France	W 4-1	Vienna	Fr	Hanel, Wesely, Ivramitsch 2
19-09	Hungary	L 2-3	Vienna	Fr	Wessely, Höss
28-09	Czechoslovakia	W 2-1	Prague	Fr	Sindelar, Wortmann
10-10	Switzerland	W 7-1	Vienna	Fr	Horvath 3, Sindelar 2, Wessely, Klima
7-11	Sweden	W 3-1	Vienna	Fr	Horvath, Sindelar, Klima
11-03-1927	Czechoslovakia	L 1-2	Vienna	Fr	Blum
10-04	Hungary	W 6-0	Vienna	Fr	Jiszda 2, Horvath, Sindelar, Wessely, Rappan
22-05	Belgium	W 4-1	Vienna	Fr	Schall 2, Wessely, Jiszda
29-05	Switzerland	W 4-1	Zurich	Fr	Jiszda, Blum, Giebisch, OG
18-09	Czechoslovakia	L 0-2	Prague	DGC	
25-09	Hungary	L 3-5	Budapest	DGC	Wessely 2, Siegl
6-11	Italy	W 1-0	Bologna	DGC	Runge
8-01-1928	Belgium	W 2-1	Brussels	Fr	Wessely, Hierländer
1-04	Czechoslovakia	L 0-1	Vienna	DGC	
6-05	Hungary	D 5-5	Budapest	Fr	Weselik 3, Wessely, Kirbes
29-07	Sweden	W 3-2	Stockholm	Fr	Gschweidl, Seidl, Smistik
7-10	Hungary	W 5-1	Vienna	DGC	Siegl 2, Weselik, Wessely, Gschweidl
28-10	Switzerland	W 2-0	Vienna	DGC	Tandler 2
11-11	Italy	D 2-2	Rome	Fr	Runge, Tandler
17-03-1929	Czechoslovakia	D 3-3	Prague	Fr	Weselik 2, Siegl
7-04	Italy	W 3-0	Vienna	DGC	Horvath 2, Weselik
5-05	Hungary	D 2-2	Vienna	Fr	Weselik, Siegl
15-09	Czechoslovakia	W 2-1	Vienna	Fr	Weselik, Gschweidl
6-10	Hungary	L 1-2	Budapest	Fr	Klima
27-10	Switzerland	W 3-1	Berne	DGC	Horvath, Schall, Stoiber
23-03-1930	Czechoslovakia	D 2-2	Prague	Fr	Horvath 2
14-05	England	D 0-0	Vienna	Fr	
1-06	Hungary	L 1-2	Budapest	Fr	Adelbrecht
21-09	Hungary	L 2-3	Vienna	Fr	Weselik, Gschweidl
16-11	Sweden	W 4-1	Vienna	Fr	Weselik, Wessely, Gschweidl, Schall
22-02-1931	Italy	L 1-2	Milan	DGC	Horvath
12-04	Czechoslovakia	W 2-1	Vienna	DGC	Horvath, Nausch

Date	Opponents	Result	Venue	Competition	Scorers
3-05	Hungary	D 0-0	Vienna	DGC	
16-05	Scotland	W 5-0	Vienna	Fr	Zischek 2, Sindelar, Schall, Vogl.A
24-05	Germany	W 6-0	Berlin	Fr	Schall 3, Vogl.A, Gschweidl, Zischek
16-06	Switzerland	W 2-0	Vienna	Fr	Gschweidl, Schall
13-09	Germany	W 5-0	Vienna	Fr	Sindelar 3, Schall, Gschweidl
4-10	Hungary	D 2-2	Budapest	DGC	Zischek 2
29-11	Switzerland	W 8-1	Basle	DGC	Schall 3, Vogl.A 2, Sindelar, Gschweidl, Zischek
20-03-1932	Italy	W 2-1	Vienna	DGC	Sindelar 2
24-04	Hungary	W 8-2	Vienna	Fr	Schall 4, Sindelar 3, Gschweidl
22-05	Czechoslovakia	D 1-1	Prague	DGC	Sindelar
17-07	Sweden	W 4-3	Stockholm	Fr	Sindelar, Vogl.A, Waitz, Molzer
2-10	Hungary	W 3-2	Budapest	Fr	Schall, Müller.H, Braun
23-10	Switzerland	W 3-1	Vienna	DGC	Schall 2, Müller.H
7-12	England	L 3-4	London	Fr	Zischek 2, Sindelar
11-12	Belgium	W 6-1	Brussels	Fr	Schall 4, Weselik, Zischek
12-02-1933	France	W 4-0	Paris	Fr	Sindelar, Zischek, Weselik, Vogl.A
9-04	Czechoslovakia	L 1-2	Vienna	Fr	Smistik
30-04	Hungary	D 1-1	Budapest	Fr	Ostermann
11-06	Belgium	W 4-1	Vienna	Fr	Binder.F 2, Sindelar, Erdl
17-09	Czechoslovakia	D 3-3	Prague	Fr	Sindelar 2, Müller.H
1-10	Hungary	D 2-2	Vienna	Fr	Schall, Müller.H
29-11	Scotland	D 2-2	Glasgow	Fr	Schall, Zischek
10-12	Holland	W 1-0	Amsterdam	Fr	Bican
11-02-1934	Italy	W 4-2	Turin	DGC	Zischek 3, Binder.F
25-03	Switzerland	W 3-2	Geneva	DGC	Bican 2, Kaburek.M
15-04	Hungary	W 5-2	Vienna	Fr	Bican 2, Schall, Zischek, Viertl
25-04	Bulgaria	W 6-1	Vienna	WCq	Horvath 3, Sindelar, Zischek, Viertl
27-05	France	W 3-2	Turin	WCr1	Sindelar, Schall, Bican
31-05	Hungary	W 2-1	Bologna	WCr2	Horvath, Zischek
3-06	Italy	L 0-1	Milan	WCsf	
7-06	Germany	L 2-3	Naples	WC3p	Horvath, Sesta
23-09	Czechoslovakia	D 2-2	Vienna	DGC	Binder.F, Vogl.A
7-10	Hungary	L 1-3	Budapest	DGC	Zischek
11-11	Switzerland	W 3-0	Vienna	DGC	Zischek, Skoumal, Kaburek.M
24-03-1935	Italy	L 0-2	Vienna	DGC	
14-04	Czechoslovakia	D 0-0	Prague	DGC	
12-05	Hungary	L 3-6	Budapest	Fr	Zischek 2, Durspekt
12-05	Poland	W 5-2	Vienna	Fr	Stoiber 2, Vogel.L, Pesser, Hahnemann
6-10	Hungary	D 4-4	Vienna	DGC	Bican 3, Hofmann.L
6-10	Poland	L 0-1	Warsaw	Fr	
19-01-1936	Spain	W 5-4	Madrid	Fr	Hanreiter 2, Zischek, Bican, Binder.F
26-01	Portugal	W 3-2	Oporto	Fr	Bican. Binder.F, Zischek
22-03	Czechoslovakia	D 1-1	Vienna	DGC	Bican
5-04	Hungary	L 3-5	Vienna	Fr	Bican 2, Zischek
6-05	England	W 2-1	Vienna	Fr	Viertl, Geiter
17-05	Italy	D 2-2	Rome	Fr	Jerusalem, Viertl
6-08	Egypt*	W 3-1	Berlin	OGr1	
9-08	Peru*	L 2-4	Berlin	OGqf	Werginz, Steinmetz
11-08	Poland*	W 3-1	Berlin	OGsf	
15-08	Italy*	L 1-2	Berlin	OGf	Kainberger
27-09	Hungary	L3-5	Budapest	DGC	Sindelar 2, Binder.F
8-11	Switzerland	W3-1	Zurich	DGC	Binder.F, Hahnemann
24-01-1937	France	W2-1	Paris	Fr	Stroh.J, Binder.F
21-03	Italy	W2-0	Vienna	Fr	Stroh, Jerusalem. Abandoned 73 mins
9-05	Scotland	D1-1	Vienna	Fr	Jerusalem
23-05	Hungary	D2-2	Budapest	Fr	Pesser 2
19-09	Switzerland	W4-3	Vienna	DGC	Jerusalem 2, Sindelar, Geiter
5-10	Latvia	W2-1	Vienna	WCq	Jerusalem, Binder.F
10-10	Hungary	L1-2	Vienna	DGC	Stroh.J
24-10	Czechoslovakia	L1-2	Prague	DGC	Neumer
19-08-1945	Hungary	L0-2	Budapest	Fr	
20-08	Hungary	L2-5	Budapest	Fr	Kominek, Decker
6-12	France	W4-1	Vienna	Fr	Decker 3, Neumer
14-04-1946	Hungary	W3-2	Vienna	Fr	Decker 2, Melchior.E
5-05	France	L1-3	Paris	Fr	Hahnemann
6-10	Hungary	L0-2	Budapest	Fr	
27-10	Czechoslovakia	L3-4	Vienna	Fr	Binder.F 2, Kaspirek
10-11	Switzerland	L0-1	Berne	Fr	
1-12	Italy	L2-3	Milan	Fr	Epp, Stojaspal

Date	Opponents	Result	Venue	Competition	Scorers
4-05-1947	Hungary	L 2-5	Budapest	Fr	Epp 2
14-09	Hungary	W 4-3	Vienna	Fr	Binder.F 2, Körner.A, Hahnemann
5-10	Czechoslovakia	L 2-3	Prague	Fr	Binder.F, Stojaspal
9-11	Italy	W 5-1	Vienna	Fr	Brinek.T 2, Körner.A, Ocwirk, Stojaspal
18-04-1948	Switzerland	W 3-1	Vienna	Fr	Epp 2, Melchior.E
2-05	Hungary	W 3-2	Vienna	DGC	Körner.A, Wagner.T, Melchior.E
30-05	Turkey	W 1-0	Istanbul	Fr	Körner.A
11-07	Sweden	L 2-3	Stockholm	Fr	Habitzl 2
2-08	Sweden	L 0-3	London	OGr1	
3-10	Hungary	L 1-2	Budapest	Fr	Melchior.E
31-10	Czechoslovakia	L 1-3	Bratislava	DGC	Stroh.J
14-11	Sweden	W 2-1	Vienna	Fr	Habitzl, Wagner.T
20-03-1949	Turkey	W 1-0	Vienna	Fr	Decker
3-04	Switzerland	W 2-1	Lausanne	DGC	Habitzl 2
8-05	Hungary	L 1-6	Budapest	DGC	Melchior.E
22-05	Italy	L 1-3	Florence	DGC	Huber.A
25-09	Czechoslovakia	W 3-1	Vienna	DGC	Decker 2, Huber.A
16-10	Hungary	L 3-4	Vienna	Fr	Decker 2, Dienst
13-11	Yugoslavia	W 5-2	Belgrade	Fr	Decker 3, Huber.A 2
19-03-1950	Switzerland	D 3-3	Vienna	DGC	Decker, Körner.R, Huber.A
2-04	Italy	W 1-0	Vienna	DGC	Melchior.E
14-05	Hungary	W 5-3	Vienna	Fr	Decker 2, Melchior.E, Dienst, Aurenik
8-10	Yugoslavia	W 7-2	Vienna	Fr	Stojaspal 2, Melchior.E 2, Decker, Wagner.T, Aurednik
29-10	Hungary	L 3-4	Budapest	Fr	Wagner.T 2, Melchior.E
5-11	Denmark	W 5-1	Vienna	Fr	Wagner.T 3, Melchior.E, Aurednik
13-12	Scotland	W 1-0	Glasgow	Fr	Melchior.E
27-05-1951	Scotland	W 4-0	Vienna	Fr	Wagner.T 2, Hanappi 2
17-06	Denmark	D 3-3	Copenhagen	Fr	Melchior.E, Wagner.T, Riegler.J
23-09	West Germany	L 0-2	Vienna	Fr	
14-10	Belgium	W 8-1	Brussels	Fr	Huber.A 3, Stojaspal 2, Melchior.E 2, Hanappi
1-11	France	D 2-2	Paris	Fr	Körner.A, Stojaspal
28-11	England	D 2-2	London	Fr	Melchior.E, Stojaspal
23-03-1952	Belgium	W 2-0	Vienna	Fr	Stojaspal 2
7-05	Rep. Ireland	W 6-0	Vienna	Fr	Huber.A 3, Dienst 2, Haummer
25-05	England	L 2-3	Vienna	Fr	Huber.A, Dienst
22-06	Switzerland	D 1-1	Geneva	Fr	Decker
21-09	Yugoslavia	L 2-4	Belgrade	Fr	Körner.A, Cejka.F
19-10	France	L 1-2	Vienna	Fr	Walzhofer.O
23-11	Portugal	D 1-1	Oporto	Fr	Halla
22-03-1953	West Germany	D 0-0	Cologne	Fr	
25-03	Rep. Ireland	L 0-4	Dublin	Fr	
26-04	Hungary	D 1-1	Budapest	Fr	Hinesser
27-09	Portugal	W 9-1	Vienna	WCq	Probst.E 5, Dienst, Wagner.T, Ocwirk, Happel
11-10	Hungary	L 2-3	Vienna	Fr	Wagner.T, Happel
29-11	Portugal	D 0-0	Lisbon	WCq	
11-04-1954	Hungary	L 0-1	Vienna	Fr	
9-05	Wales	W 2-0	Vienna	Fr	Dienst, Halla
30-05	Norway	W 5-0	Vienna	Fr	Probst.E 2, Happel, Schleger
16-06	Scotland	W 1-0	Zurich	WCr1	Probst.E
19-06	Czechoslovakia	W 5-0	Zurich	WCr1	Probst.E 3, Stojaspal 2
26-06	Switzerland	W 7-5	Lausanne	WCqf	Wagner.T 3, Körner.A 2, Probst.E, Ocwirk
30-06	West Germany	L 1-6	Basle	WCsf	Stojaspal
3-07	Uruguay	W 3-1	Zurich	WC3p	Stojaspal, Ocwirk, OG
3-10	Yugoslavia	D 2-2	Vienna	Fr	Walzhofer.O, Haummer
31-10	Sweden	L 1-2	Stockholm	Fr	Wagner.T
14-11	Hungary	L 1-4	Budapest	Fr	Hanappi
27-03-1955	Czechoslovakia	L 2-3	Brno	DGC	Probst.E, Dienst
24-04	Hungary	D 2-2	Vienna	DGC	Probst.E 2
1-05	Switzerland	W 3-2	Berne	DGC	Probst.E, Brousek.R, Hofbauer.O
19-05	Scotland	L 1-4	Vienna	Fr	Ocwirk
16-10	Hungary	L 1-6	Budapest	DGC	Grohs
30-10	Yugoslavia	W 2-1	Vienna	DGC	Hanappi, Grohs
23-11	Wales	W 2-1	Wrexham	Fr	Hanappi, Wagner.T
25-03-1956	France	L 1-3	Paris	Fr	Hanappi
15-04	Brazil	L 2-3	Vienna	Fr	Sabetzer 2
2-05	Scotland	D 1-1	Glasgow	Fr	Wagner.T
17-06	Yugoslavia	D 1-1	Zagreb	DGC	Koller
30-09	Luxembourg	W 7-0	Vienna	WCq	Wagner.T 2, Hanappi 2, Haummer, Walzhofer.O, Kozlicek.E

Date	Opponents	Result	Venue	Competition	Scorers
14-10	Hungary	L 0-2	Vienna	Fr	
9-12	Italy	L 1-2	Genoa	DGC	Körner.A
24-02-1957	Malta	W 3-2	Gzira	Fr	OG, Wagner, Haummer
10-03	West Germany	L 2-3	Vienna	Fr	Wagner.T, Buzek
14-04	Switzerland	W 4-0	Vienna	DGC	Buzek 2, Haummer, Koller
5-05	Sweden	W 1-0	Vienna	Fr	Dienst
26-05	Holland	W 3-2	Vienna	WCq	Buzek, Koller, Stotz
15-09	Yugoslavia	D 3-3	Belgrade	Fr	Dienst 2, Happel
25-09	Holland	D 1-1	Amsterdam	WCq	Hanappi
29-09	Luxembourg	W 3-0	Luxembourg	WCq	Dienst, Kozlicek.E, Senekowitsch
13-10	Czechoslovakia	D 2-2	Vienna	DGC	Körner.A, Senekowitsch
23-03-1958	Italy	W 3-2	Vienna	DGC	Kozlicek.P, Körner.A, Buzek
14-05	Rep. Ireland	W 3-1	Vienna	Fr	Körner.A, Buzek, Hamerl
8-06	Brazil	L 0-3	Uddevalla	WCr1	
11-06	Soviet Union	L 0-2	Boras	WCr1	
15-06	England	D 2-2	Boras	WCr1	Körner.A, Koller
14-09	Yugoslavia	L 3-4	Vienna	Fr	Körner.A, Happel, Ninaus.H
5-10	France	L 1-2	Vienna	Fr	Hof.E
19-11	West Germany	D 2-2	Berlin	Fr	Knoll, Horak
20-05-1959	Norway	W 1-0	Oslo	ECr1	Hof.E
24-05	Belgium	W 2-0	Brussels	Fr	Skerlan, Huberts
14-06	Belgium	W 4-2	Vienna	Fr	Hof.E 2, Horak, Skerlan
23-09	Norway	W 5-2	Vienna	ECr1	Hof.E 2, Nemec 2, Skerlan
22-11	Spain	L 3-6	Valencia	Fr	Hof.E, Knoll, Senekowitsch
13-12	France	L 2-5	Paris	ECqf	Horak, Pichler.R
27-03-1960	France	L 2-4	Vienna	ECqf	Nemec, Probst.E
1-05	Czechoslovakia	L 0-4	Prague	Fr	
29-05	Scotland	W 4-1	Vienna	Fr	Hof.E 2, Hanappi 2
22-06	Norway	W 2-1	Oslo	Fr	Hof.E, Hamerl
4-09	Soviet Union	W 3-1	Vienna	Fr	Hof.E 2, Flögel
30-10	Spain	W 3-0	Vienna	Fr	Hof.E, Senekowitsch, Nemec
20-11	Hungary	L 0-2	Budapest	Fr	
10-12	Italy	W 2-1	Naples	Fr	Hof.E, Kaltenbrunner.E
27-05-1961	England	W 3-1	Vienna	Fr	Hof.E, Senekowitsch, Nemec
11-06	Hungary	W 2-1	Budapest	Fr	Nemec, Rafreider
10-09	Soviet Union	W 1-0	Moscow	Fr	Rafreider
8-10	Hungary	W 2-1	Vienna	Fr	Hof.E, Oslansky
19-11	Yugoslavia	L 1-2	Zagreb	Fr	Nemec
5-01-1962	Egypt	L 0-1	Cairo	Fr	
4-04	England	L 1-3	London	Fr	Buzek
8-04	Rep. Ireland	W 3-2	Dublin	Fr	Hof.E, Buzek, Hirnschrodt
6-05	Bulgaria	W 2-0	Vienna	Fr	Hof.E, OG
24-06	Hungary	L 1-2	Vienna	Fr	Nemec
16-09	Czechoslovakia	L 0-6	Vienna	Fr	
28-10	Hungary	L 0-2	Budapest	Fr	
11-11	Italy	L 1-2	Vienna	Fr	Nemec
25-11	Bulgaria	D 1-1	Sofia	Fr	Nemec
24-04-1963	Czechoslovakia	W 3-1	Vienna	Fr	Nemec 3
8-05	Scotland	L 1-4	Glasgow	Fr	Linhart
9-06	Italy	L 0-1	Vienna	Fr	
25-09	Rep. Ireland	D 0-0	Vienna	ECr1	
13-10	Rep. Ireland	L 2-3	Dublin	ECr1	Koleznik, Flogel
27-10	Hungary	L 1-2	Budapest	Fr	Viehböck
14-12	Italy	L 0-1	Turin	Fr	
12-04-1964	Holland	D 1-1	Amsterdam	Fr	Flögel
3-05	Hungary	W 1-0	Vienna	Fr	Nemec
14-05	Uruguay	L 0-2	Vienna	Fr	
27-09	Yugoslavia	W 3-2	Vienna	Fr	Nemec 2, Hasil
11-10	Soviet Union	W 1-0	Vienna	Fr	Glechner
24-03-1965	France	W 2-1	Paris	Fr	Koller, Seitl
25-04	East Germany	D 1-1	Vienna	WCq	Hof.E
16-05	Soviet Union	D 0-0	Moscow	Fr	
13-06	Hungary	L 0-1	Vienna	WCq	
5-09	Hungary	L 0-3	Budapest	WCq	
9-10	West Germany	L 1-4	Stuttgart	Fr	Buzek
20-10	England	W 3-2	London	Fr	Fritsch 2, Flögel
31-10	East Germany	L 0-1	Leipzig	WCq	
24-04-1966	Soviet Union	L 0-1	Vienna	Fr	
22-05	Rep. Ireland	W 1-0	Vienna	Fr	Seitl

Date	Opponents	Result	Venue	Competition	Scorers
18-06	Italy	L 0-1	Milan	Fr	
18-09	Holland	W 2-1	Vienna	Fr	Sara, Viehböck
2-10	Finland	D 0-0	Helsinki	ECq	
5-10	Sweden	L 1-4	Stockholm	Fr	
30-10	Hungary	L 1-3	Budapest	Fr	Flögel
27-05-1967	England	L 0-1	Vienna	Fr	Wolny
11-06	Soviet Union	L 3-4	Moscow	ECq	Hof.E, Wolny, Siber
6-09	Hungary	L 1-3	Vienna	Fr	Hof.E
24-09	Finland	W 2-1	Vienna	ECq	Flögel, Grausam
4-10	Greece	L 1-4	Athens	ECq	Grausam
15-10	Soviet Union	W 1-0	Vienna	ECq	Grausam
5-11	Greece	D 1-1	Vienna	ECq	Siber
1-05-1968	Romania	D 1-1	Linz	Fr	Siber
19-05	Cyprus	W 7-1	Vienna	WCq	Hof.E 5, Redl, Siber
16-06	Soviet Union	L 1-3	Leningrad	Fr	Hof.E
22-09	Switzerland	L 0-1	Berne	Fr	
13-10	West Germany	L 0-2	Vienna	WCq	
6-11	Scotland	L 1-2	Glasgow	WCq	Starek
10-11	Rep. Ireland	D 2-2	Dublin	Fr	Hof.E, Redl
19-04-1969	Cyprus	W 2-1	Nicosia	WCq	Kreuz, Redl
23-04	Israel	D 1-1	Tel Aviv	Fr	Kreuz
27-04	Malta	W 3-1	Gzira	Fr	Köglberger 2, Kreuz
10-05	West Germany	L 0-1	Nuremberg	WCq	
21-09	West Germany	D 1-1	Vienna	Fr	Pirkner
5-11	Scotland	W 2-0	Vienna	WCq	Redl 2
8-04-1970	Yugoslavia	D 1-1	Sarajevo	Fr	Redl
12-04	Czechoslovakia	L 1-3	Vienna	Fr	OG
29-04	Brazil	L 0-1	Rio de Janeiro	Fr	
10-09	Yugoslavia	L 0-1	Graz	Fr	
27-09	Hungary	D 1-1	Budapest	Fr	Redl
7-10	France	W 1-0	Vienna	Fr	Kreuz
31-10	Italy	L 1-2	Vienna	ECq	Parits
4-04-1971	Hungary	L 0-2	Vienna	Fr	
26-05	Sweden	L 0-1	Stockholm	ECq	
30-05	Rep. Ireland	W 4-1	Dublin	ECq	Kodat, Starek, Schmidradner, OG
11-07	Brazil	D 1-1	Sao Paulo	Fr	Jara
4-09	Sweden	W 1-0	Vienna	ECq	Stering
10-10	Rep. Ireland	W 6-0	Linz	ECq	Parits 3, Jara 2, Pirkner
20-11	Italy	D 2-2	Rome	ECq	Jara, Sara
8-04-1972	Czechoslovakia	L 0-2	Brno	Fr	
30-04	Malta	W 4-0	Vienna	WCq	Hickersberger 3, Hof.N
10-06	Sweden	W 2-0	Vienna	WCq	Parits, Pumm
3-09	Romania	D 1-1	Craiova	Fr	Hickersberger
15-10	Hungary	D 2-2	Vienna	WCq	Hasil, Jara
25-11	Malta	W 2-0	Gzira	WCq	Köglberger, OG
28-03-1973	Holland	W 1-0	Vienna	Fr	Köglberger
29-04	Hungary	D 2-2	Budapest	WCq	Starek, Jara
23-05	Sweden	L 2-3	Gothenburg	WCq	Jara, Starek
13-06	Brazil	D 1-1	Vienna	Fr	Kreuz
26-09	England	L 0-7	London	Fr	
10-10	West Germany	L 0-4	Hanover	Fr	
27-11	Sweden	L 1-2	Gelsenkirchen	WCq	Hattenberger
27-03-1974	Holland	D 1-1	Rotterdam	Fr	Krankl
1-05	Brazil	D 0-0	Sao Paulo	Fr	
8-06	Italy	D 0-0	Vienna	Fr	
4-09	Wales	W 2-1	Vienna	ECq	Kreuz, Krankl
28-09	Hungary	W 1-0	Vienna	Fr	Krankl
13-11	Turkey	W 1-0	Istanbul	Fr	Stering
1-02-1975	Tunisia	D 3-3	Tunis	Fr	Fendler II 2, Jara
16-03	Luxembourg	W 2-1	Luxembourg	ECq	Köglberger, Krankl
2-04	Hungary	D 0-0	Vienna	ECq	
7-06	Czechoslovakia	D 0-0	Vienna	Fr	
3-09	West Germany	L 0-2	Vienna	Fr	
24-09	Hungary	L 1-2	Budapest	ECq	Krankl
15-10	Luxembourg	W 6-2	Vienna	ECq	Welzl 2, Krankl 2, Jara, Prohaska
19-11	Wales	L 0-1	Wrexham	ECq	
28-04-1976	Sweden	W 1-0	Vienna	Fr	Pirkner
12-06	Hungary	L 0-2	Budapest	Fr	
23-06	Soviet Union	L 1-2	Vienna	Fr	Rinker

Date	Opponents	Result	Venue	Competition	Scorers
22-09	Switzerland	W 3-1	Linz	Fr	Krankl, Köglberger, Kreuz (p)
13-10	Hungary	L 2-4	Vienna	Fr	Krankl 2
10-11	Greece	W 3-0	Kavala	Fr	Hickersberger, Krankl, Pezzey
5-12	Malta	W 1-0	Gzira	WCq	Krankl
15-12	Israel	W 3-1	Tel Aviv	Fr	Prohaska, Schachner, Krankl
9-03-1977	Greece	W 2-0	Vienna	Fr	Sara, Schachner
17-04	Turkey	W 1-0	Vienna	WCq	Schachner
30-04	Malta	W 9-0	Salzburg	WCq	Krankl 6, Stering 2, Pirkner
1-06	Czechoslovakia	D 0-0	Ostrava	Fr	
24-08	Poland	W 2-1	Vienna	Fr	Stering, Krankl
24-09	East Germany	D 1-1	Vienna	WCq	Kreuz
12-10	East Germany	D 1-1	Leipzig	WCq	Hattenberger
30-10	Turkey	W 1-0	Izmir	WCq	Prohaska
15-02-1978	Greece	D 1-1	Athens	Fr	Krankl
22-03	Belgium	L 0-1	Charleroi	Fr	
4-04	Switzerland	W 1-0	Basle	Fr	Jara
20-05	Holland	L 0-1	Vienna	Fr	
3-06	Spain	W 2-1	Buenos Aires	WCr1	Schachner, Krankl
7-06	Sweden	W 1-0	Buenos Aires	WCr1	Krankl
11-06	Brazil	L 0-1	Mar del Plata	WCr1	
14-06	Holland	L 1-5	Cordoba	WCr2	Obermayer
18-06	Italy	L 0-1	Buenos Aires	WCr2	
21-06	West Germany	W 3-2	Cordoba	WCr2	OG, Krankl 2
30-08	Norway	W 2-0	Oslo	ECq	Pezzey, Krankl
20-09	Scotland	W 3-2	Vienna	ECq	Pezzey, Schachner, Kreuz
15-11	Portugal	L 1-2	Vienna	ECq	Schachner
30-01-1979	Israel	W 1-0	Tel Aviv	Fr	Oberacher
28-03	Belgium	D 1-1	Brussels	ECq	Krankl
2-05	Belgium	D 0-0	Vienna	ECq	
13-06	England	W 4-3	Vienna	Fr	Pezzey 2, Welzl 2
29-08	Norway	W 4-0	Vienna	ECq	Jara, Prohaska, Kreuz, Krankl
26-09	Hungary	W 3-1	Vienna	Fr	Prohaska 2, Steinkogler
17-10	Scotland	D 1-1	Glasgow	ECq	Krankl
21-11	Portugal	W 2-1	Lisbon	ECq	Welzl, Schachner
2-04-1980	West Germany	L 0-1	Munich	Fr	
21-05	Argentina	L 1-5	Vienna	Fr	Jara
4-06	Hungary	D 1-1	Budapest	Fr	Jara
24-09	Finland	W 2-0	Helsinki	WCq	Jara, Welzl
8-10	Hungary	W 3-1	Vienna	Fr	Welzl, Keglevits 2
15-11	Albania	W 5-0	Vienna	WCq	Pezzey, Schachner 2, Welzl, Krankl
6-12	Albania	W 1-0	Tirana	WCq	Welzl
4-02-1981	Israel	L 0-1	Tel Aviv	Fr	
29-04	West Germany	L 0-2	Hamburg	WCq	
28-05	Bulgaria	W 2-0	Vienna	WCq	Krankl, Jara
17-06	Finland	W 5-1	Linz	WCq	Prohaska 2, Krankl, Welzl, Jurtin
23-09	Spain	D 0-0	Vienna	Fr	
14-10	West Germany	L 1-3	Vienna	WCq	Schachner
11-11	Bulgaria	D 0-0	Sofia	WCq	
24-03-1982	Hungary	W 3-2	Budapest	Fr	Krankl, Schachner, Hattenberger
28-04	Czechoslovakia	W 2-1	Vienna	Fr	Schachner 2
19-05	Denmark	W 1-0	Vienna	Fr	Degeorgi
17-06	Chile	W 1-0	Oviedo	WCr1	Schachner
21-06	Algeria	W 2-0	Oviedo	WCr1	Schachner, Krankl
25-06	West Germany	L 0-1	Gijon	WCr1	
28-06	France	L 0-1	Madrid	WCr2	
1-07	Nth. Ireland	D 2-2	Madrid	WCr2	Pezzey, Hintermaier
22-09	Albania	W 5-0	Vienna	ECq	Hagmayr, Gasselich, Weber, Brauneder, OG
13-10	Nth. Ireland	W 2-0	Vienna	ECq	Schachner 2
17-11	Turkey	W 4-0	Vienna	ECq	Polster, Pezzey, Prohaska, Schachner
27-04-1983	West Germany	D 0-0	Vienna	ECq	
17-05	Soviet Union	D 2-2	Vienna	Fr	Gasselich, Pezzey
8-06	Albania	W 2-1	Tirana	ECq	Schachner 2
21-09	Nth. Ireland	L 1-3	Belfast	ECq	Gasselich
5-10	West Germany	L 0-3	Gelsenkirchen	ECq	
16-11	Turkey	L 1-3	Istanbul	ECq	Baumeister
28-03-1984	France	L 0-1	Bordeaux	Fr	
18-04	Greece	D 0-0	Vienna	Fr	
2-05	Cyprus	W 2-1	Nicosia	WCq	Gisinger, Prohaska
7-06	Liechtenstein	W 6-0	Vaduz	Fr	Polster, Messlender, Willfurth, Prohaska 2, Keglevits

Date	Opponents	Result	Venue	Competition	Scorers
12-09	Denmark	L 1-3	Copenhagen	Fr	Gisinger
26-09	Hungary	L 1-3	Budapest	WCq	Schachner
14-11	Holland	W 1-0	Vienna	WCq	Jara
27-03-1985	Soviet Union	L 0-2	Tbilisi	Fr	
17-04	Hungary	L 0-3	Vienna	WCq	
1-05	Holland	D 1-1	Rotterdam	WCq	Schachner
7-05	Cyprus	W 4-0	Graz	WCq	Hrstic, Polster, Schachner, Willfurth
16-10	Yugoslavia	L 0-3	Linz	Fr	
20-11	Spain	D 0-0	Zaragoza	Fr	
26-03-1986	Italy	L 1-2	Udine	Fr	Polster
14-05	Sweden	W 1-0	Salzburg	Fr	Kienast
27-08	Switzerland	D 1-1	Innsbruck	Fr	Polster
10-09	Romania	L 0-4	Bucharest	ECq	
15-10	Albania	W 3-0	Graz	ECq	Ogris.A, Polster, Linzmaier
29-10	West Germany	W 4-1	Vienna	Fr	Polster 2, Kienast 2
8-02-1987	Tunisia	W 3-1	Tunis	Fr	Polster 2, Ogris
25-03	Yugoslavia	L 0-4	Banja Luka	Fr	
1-04	Spain	L 2-3	Vienna	ECq	Linzmaier, Polster
29-04	Albania	W 1-0	Tirana	ECq	Polster
18-08	Switzerland	D 2-2	St. Gallen	Fr	Ogris.A, Zsak
14-10	Spain	L 0-2	Seville	ECq	
18-11	Romania	D 0-0	Vienna	ECq	
2-02-1988	Morocco	L 1-3	Toulouse	Fr	Ogris
5-02	Switzerland	L 1-2	Monaco	Fr	OG
6-04	Greece	D 2-2	Athens	Fr	Zsak, Willfurth
27-04	Denmark	W 1-0	Vienna	Fr	OG
17-05	Hungary	W 4-0	Budapest	Fr	Marko 3, Hasenhüttl
3-08	Brazil	L 0-2	Vienna	Fr	
31-08	Hungary	D 0-0	Linz	Fr	
20-09	Czechoslovakia	L 2-4	Prague	Fr	Pacult, Willfurth
19-10	Soviet Union	L 0-2	Kiev	WCq	
2-11	Turkey	W 3-2	Vienna	WCq	Polster, Herzog 2
25-03-1989	Italy	L 0-1	Vienna	Fr	
11-04	Czechoslovakia	L 1-2	Graz	Fr	Herzog
20-05	East Germany	D 1-1	Leipzig	WCq	Polster
31-05	Norway	L 1-4	Oslo	Fr	Ogris.A
14-06	Iceland	D 0-0	Reykjavik	WCq	
23-08	Iceland	W 2-1	Salzburg	WCq	Pfeifenberger, Zsak
6-09	Soviet Union	D 0-0	Vienna	WCq	
4-10	Malta	W 2-1	Ta'Quali	Fr	Glatzmayer, Rodax
25-10	Turkey	L 0-3	Istanbul	WCq	
15-11	East Germany	W 3-0	Vienna	WCq	Polster 3
28-02-1990	Egypt	D 0-0	Cairo	Fr	
28-03	Spain	W 3-2	Malaga	Fr	Polster, Rodax, Hörtnagl
11-04	Hungary	W 3-0	Salzburg	Fr	Ogris.A, Artner, Keglevits
3-05	Argentina	D 1-1	Vienna	Fr	Zsak
30-05	Holland	W 3-2	Vienna	Fr	Zsak, Pecl, Pfeffer
9-06	Italy	L 0-1	Rome	WCr1	
15-06	Czechoslovakia	L 0-1	Florence	WCr1	
19-06	USA	W 2-1	Florence	WCr1	Rodax, Ogris.A
21-08	Switzerland	L 1-3	Vienna	Fr	Ogris.A
12-09	Faeroe Islands	L 0-1	Landskrona	ECq	
31-10	Yugoslavia	L 1-4	Belgrade	ECq	Ogris.A
14-11	Nth. Ireland	D 0-0	Vienna	ECq	
17-04-1991	Norway	D 0-0	Vienna	Fr	
1-05	Sweden	L 0-6	Stockholm	Fr	
22-05	Faeroe Islands	W 3-0	Salzburg	ECq	Pfeifenberger, Streiter, Wetl
5-06	Denmark	L 1-2	Odense	ECq	Ogris.E
4-09	Portugal	D 1-1	Oporto	Fr	Kockler
9-10	Denmark	L 0-3	Vienna	ECq	
16-10	Nth. Ireland	L 1-2	Belfast	ECq	Lainer
13-11	Yugoslavia	L 0-2	Vienna	ECq	
25-03-1992	Hungary	L 1-2	Budapest	Fr	Polster
14-04	Lithuania	W 4-0	Vienna	Fr	Ogris.A, Prosenik, Polster, Hutti
29-04	Wales	D 1-1	Vienna	Fr	Baur
19-05	Poland	L 2-4	Salzburg	Fr	Hasenhutti, Waldhoer
27-05	Holland	L 2-3	Sittard	Fr	Polster, Schinkels
19-08	Czechoslovakia	D 2-2	Bratislava	Fr	Stöger, Pfeifenberger
2-09	Portugal	D 1-1	Linz	Fr	Polster

14-10	France	L 0-2	Paris	WCq	
28-10	Israel	W 5-2	Vienna	WCq	Herzog 2, Polster, Stöger, Ogris
18-11	Germany	D 0-0	Nuremberg	Fr	
10-03-1993	Greece	W 2-1	Vienna	Fr	Pfeifenberger, Baur
27-03	France	L 0-1	Vienna	WCq	
14-04	Bulgaria	W 3-1	Vienna	WCq	Pfeifenberger, Kühbauer, Polster
13-05	Finland	L 1-3	Turku	WCq	Zisser
19-05	Sweden	L 0-1	Stockholm	WCq	
25-08	Finland	W 3-0	Vienna	WCq	Kühbauer, Pfeifenberger, Herzog
13-10	Bulgaria	L 1-4	Sofia	WCq	Herzog
27-10	Israel	D 1-1	Tel Aviv	WCq	Reinmayr
10-11	Sweden	D 1-1	Vienna	WCq	Herzog
23-03-1994	Hungary	D 1-1	Linz	Fr	Pfeifenberger
20-04	Scotland	L 1-2	Vienna	Fr	Hütter
17-05	Poland	W 4-3	Katowice	Fr	Stöger 3, Hochmaier
2-06	Germany	L 1-5	Vienna	Fr	Polster
17-08	Russia	L 0-3	Klagenfurt	Fr	
7-09	Liechtenstein	W 4-0	Eschen	ECq	Polster 3, Aigner
12-10	Northern Ireland	L 1-2	Vienna	ECq	Polster
13-11	Portugal	L 0-1	Lisbon	ECq	
29-03-1995	Latvia	W 5-0	Salzburg	ECq	Herzog 2, Pfeifenberger, Polster 2
26-04	Liechtenstein	W 7-0	Salzburg	ECq	Kühbauer, Polster 2, Sabitzer, Purk, Hütter 2
11-06	Rep. Ireland	W 3-1	Dublin	ECq	Polster 2, Ogris

AZERBAIJAN

Nestling on the northern border of Iran and on the western shores of the Caspian Sea, Azerbaijan seems a little out of place in 'Europe'. Countries such as Syria and Iraq all lie to the west, closer to the European heartland. But as a former member of the Soviet Union, oil-rich Azerbaijan has fallen into UEFA's sphere of influence. This predominantly moslem country is potentially one of the wealthiest in Europe, though the war with Armenia over the disputed territory of Nagorno-Karabakh has left it in some turmoil.

Football has very little tradition in Azerbaijan. Neftchi Baku, from the capital, were occasional participants in the Soviet first division but rarely shone, and since the country was accepted into the European football fold, little has gone right.

A 5-0 defeat at the hands of Malta was an ominously poor start to their international career, and Baku was not able to stage any of the home matches in the qualifying round of the 1996 European Championships because of the war. Instead, Trabzon in Turkey was the venue for Azerbaijan's first 'home' international match, against Israel.

Population: 7,300,000
Area, sq km: 86,600
Capital city: Baku

The Association of Football Feder-ations of Azerbaijan
H. Hagiev Kuc 42
370009 Baku
Azerbaijan
Tel: +994 12940542
Fax: +994 12989393

Year of formation	1991
Affiliation to FIFA	1994
Affiliation to UEFA	1994
National stadium	Republican, Baku 35 000
National colours	White shirts, White shorts, White socks
Season	May - November

THE RECORD

WORLD CUP

1930-94 Did not enter

EUROPEAN CHAMPIONSHIP

1960-92 Did not enter
1996 QT group 1

EUROPEAN CLUB COMPETITIONS

European Cup
Have never qualified

Cup Winners Cup
Have never qualified

UEFA Cup
Preliminary round - Turan Tauz 1995

CLUB DIRECTORY

BAKU (Population - 2,020,000)

Neftchi Baku (1937)
Republican 35,000 – White/Maroon
Previous name - Neftjanik 1937-68

Azneftyag Baku

Azeri Baku

Inshaatchi Baku

GYANDZHA (Population - 278,000)

Kyapaz Gyandzha

SUMGAIT (Population - 231,000)

Khazar Sumgait

AGDAM

Karabakh Agdam

TAUZ

Turan Tauz

MINGECHAUR

Kyur Mingechaur

AZERBAIJAN LEAGUE CHAMPIONSHIP

1992u8	Neftchi Baku 62 Khazar Sumgait 57 Turan Tauz 56
1993u9	Karabakh Agdam 1-0 Khazar Sumgait
1994	Turan Tauz

AZERBAIJAN CUP FINALS

1992 Inshaatchi Baku 2-1 Kyur Mingechaur
1993 Karabakh Agdam 1-0 Khazar Sumgait

INTERNATIONAL MATCHES PLAYED BY AZERBAIJAN

Date	Opponents	Result	Venue	Competition	Scorers
19-04-1994	Malta	L 0-5	Ta'Qali	Fr	
1-09	Moldova	L 1-2	Chisinau	Fr	Alekperov
7-09	Romania	L 0-3	Bucharest	ECq	
12-10	Poland	L 0-1	Mielec	ECq	
16-11	Israel	L 0-2	Trabzon	ECq	
13-12	France	L 0-2	Trabzon	ECq	
29-03-1995	Slovakia	L 1-4	Kosice	ECq	Sulemanov
26-04	Romania	L 1-4	Trabzon	ECq	Sulemanov

BELARUS

Belarus, bordered by Russia, Poland, Ukraine and the Baltic States, is one of the few republics to have a club side who were champions of the old Soviet league; Dinamo Minsk won the title in 1982, the last team from outside Russia and the Ukraine to do so. Not surprisingly, they won the first three titles after independence and in 1994, as a mark of their superiority, their second team were runners-up! Indeed the only two games they lost in that championship were to the reserve side.

Neman Grodno have been the only team to break Dinamo's monopoly, winning the Cup in 1993, but they failed to negotiate the preliminary round of the Cup Winners Cup the following season, losing heavily to the Swiss club Lugano. Dinamo reached the quarter-finals of all three European competitions in 1980s, but more recently they too have struggled.

The best-known Belarussian, Sergei Aleinikov, who was capped 77 times by the Soviet Union and played for Juventus, has helped the national side adapt to their new role. So far they have not been disgraced – they even beat Holland in the 1996 European Championship qualifiers.

Population: 10,200,000
Area, sq km: 207,600
Capital city: Minsk

Football Federation of Belarus
8-2 Kyrov Street
220600 Minsk
Belarus
Tel: + 7 0172 272920
Fax: + 7 0172 272920

Year of formation	1992
Affiliation to FIFA	1992
Affiliation to UEFA	1993
Registered clubs	48
Registered players	4920
Registered referees	489
National stadium	Dynamo, Minsk 50 000
National colours	White/Red/Red
Season	July - June, with a mid season break November - March

THE RECORD

WORLD CUP
1930-94 Did not enter

EUROPEAN CHAMPIONSHIP
1960-92 Did not enter
1996 QT group 5

EUROPEAN CLUB COMPETITIONS

European Cup
Quarter-finalists - Dynamo Minsk 1984

Cup Winners Cup
Quarter-finalists - Dynamo Minsk 1988

UEFA Cup
Quarter-finalists - Dynamo Minsk 1985

CLUB DIRECTORY

MINSK (Population - 1,650,000)
Dynamo Minsk (1928)
Dynamo 50,000 – Violet with white sleeves/White
Previous names - Dynamo 1935-54, Spartak 1954-59, Belarus 1959-62
Reserve team - Dynamo '93 Minsk (Previously called Belarus Minsk)

Torpedo Minsk (1947)
Torpedo 5,000 – White/Black

GOMEL (Population - 500,000)
Gomselmash Gomel (1959)
Gomselmash 10,000 – White/Black

MOGILEV (Population - 356,000)
Dnepr Mogilev (1960)
Spartak 10,000 – White/Blue

Torpedo Mogilev (1974)
Torpedo 7,000

VITEBSK (Population - 350,000)
Kim Vitebsk (1960)
Dynamo 5,000 – Red/Black

Lokomotiv Vitebsk (1986)
Dynamo 5,000

GRODNO (Population - 270,000)
Neman Grodno (1964)
Krasroyeznamya 14,000

BREST (Population - 258,000)
Dynamo Brest (1960)
Dynamo 10,000 – White/Blue

BOBRUJSK (Population - 223,000)
Fandok Bobrujsk (1984)
Spartak 3,000 – Yellow/Black

Shinnik Bobrujsk (1958)
Spartak 3,000

RECHITSA
Vedrich Rechitsa (1952)
Rechitsadrev 5,000

BELARUS LEAGUE CHAMPIONSHIP

1992fg	Dynamo Minsk 25 Dnepr Mogilev 24 Dynamo Brest 20
1993r	Dynamo Minsk 57 Kim Vitebsk 47 Belarus Minsk 46
1994q	Dynamo Minsk 52 Dynamo '93 Minsk 43 Kim Vitebsk 43
1995	Dynamo Minsk 48 Dvina 46 Dynamo '93 Minsk 42

BELARUS CUP FINALS

1992	Dynamo Minsk	6-1	DneprMogilev
1993	Neman Grodno	2-1	Vedrich Rechitsa
1994	Dynamo Minsk	3-1	FandokBobrujsk
1995	Dynamo '93	1-1 7-6p	Torpedo Mogilev

INTERNATIONAL MATCHES PLAYED BY BELARUS

28-10-1992	Ukraine	D 1-1	Minsk	Fr	Gotsmanov
27-01-1993	Ecuador	D 1-1	Guayaquil	Fr	Gerasimets
30-01	Peru	D 1-1	Lima	Fr	Orlovsky
25-05-1994	Ukraine	L 1-3	Kiev	Fr	Belkevich
17-08	Poland	D 1-1	Radom	Fr	Vergeichik
7-09	Norway	L 0-1	Oslo	ECq	
12-10	Luxembourg	W 2-0	Minsk	ECq	Romanschenko, Gerasimets
16-11	Norway	L 0-4	Minsk	ECq	
29-03-1995	Czech Republic	L 2-4	Ostrava	ECq	Gerasimets, Gurinovich
26-04	Malta	D 1-1	Minsk	ECq	Taikov
7-06	Holland	W 1-0	Gerisamets	ECq	Gerasimets

BELGIUM

Belgians have been playing football for longer than most; but, hidebound by tradition, they were held back for years from modernising their domestic game. Since the restrictions were removed in the 1960s, the Belgians have proved to be one of the more enduring forces of both European and world football. They are a divided nation – the north is largely Flemish-speaking, the south dominated by the French-speaking Walloons – but this rivalry has helped bring more passion to the club scene.

Belgium was at the forefront of organised football on the continent. The Association was formed in 1895, and a league started the following year, thus making it, along with Sweden, the oldest league in Europe outside of Great Britain. Naturally the Belgians were prime movers in the formation of FIFA in 1904, and in the same year played their first international, making their debut against France who were also playing their first game. The following year, Belgium met Holland in Antwerp. Over the course of the first half of the century, the Belgium-France match became an annual event, whilst the Belgium-Holland game was usually played twice a year, one at home and one away.

A large number of clubs had been formed by the turn of the century, the oldest of them, Royal Antwerp, having been founded in 1880. RFC Liège won the inaugural championship, and although some of the famous clubs of this time no longer survive as separate entities, they survive as combinations that have since merged. Although teams were very active in the league, they remained true to the amateur spirit. The sport was seen very much as a pastime, and this meant that progress at both club and national level was slow.

In 1920, Belgium won their only ever major honour, beating Czechoslovakia in the final of the Olympic Games. At the time only the British Isles were professional, so with some justification the Belgians regarded themselves as world champions. The fact that the tournament was held in Belgium and occurred in the immediate aftermath of World War I does take some shine off the honour, and in subsequent years Belgium did not live up to the reputation gained by winning the tournament.

Results in the inter-war period were poor and saw defeats in the first round of every tournament entered, with the exception of the 1928 Olympic Games where they beat Luxembourg in the first round only to lose heavily to Argentina in the quarter-finals. The Belgian FA was heavily involved in promoting the idea of the World Cup, and so when it was launched they were one of the few European nations to make the trip to Uruguay. They were spectacularly unsuccessful once there, but one Belgian did make an impression. Jean Langenus became the first man to referee the World Cup Final, resplendent as he was in knickerbockers and cap.

Very few players of this period can be regarded as of the highest class. Two who were, however, were the Braine brothers, Raymond and Pierre. Raymond has often been regarded as one of the all-time greats of Belgian football, and in its amateur state, it could not keep him. He helped Beerschot to four titles in five years in the 1920s, playing alongside his brother, and after being refused a work permit to play in England he joined Sparta Prague in 1931 as a professional, winning many honours.

The post-war years saw no dramatic improvement. Anderlecht became the dominant club and by the 1960s were at the forefront of a movement to modernise the game, which they felt was decaying at the roots. The newly introduced European Cup was an important influence, never more so than in 1956 when Anderlecht suffered an embarrassing 10-0 defeat at the hands of Manchester United. Semi-professionalism was grudgingly introduced and foreigners known as 'Independents' were brought in to pep up a flagging club scene.

In 1970 Anderlecht reached the final of the Fairs Cup, the first international success of note for a Belgian team. They lost to Arsenal but their achievement marked the beginning of a new era in Belgian football. The introduction of full professionalism in 1972 gave the country the final impetus it needed to perform at the highest level as Anderlecht, Club Brugge and Standard Liège all found that they could compete with the best when on an equal footing. In 1976 Anderlecht won the Cup Winners Cup, the first honour for any Belgian side since 1920, and followed up with victory in the same competition two years later and the UEFA Cup in 1983. In 1978 Club Brugge lost in the European Cup final to Liverpool, the closest any Belgian side has come to winning Europe's premier trophy. Perhaps the most surprising success was that of Mechelen, a small town in the north. They emerged in the late 1980s to break the big three's traditional stranglehold on honours and in the process lift the European Cup Winners Cup and the Super Cup.

The Belgian league can now claim to be one of the best in Europe, though it still lacks the strength in depth of Italy, Germany, England and Spain. It has overcome serious problems, none greater than the bribes scandal of 1984 involving Standard. It was discovered that that two years previously they had bought the vital league game against Waterschei which they won to clinch the title, and top players such as Eric Gerets and Michel Preud'homme were implicated along with coach Raymond Goethals.

Historically the national side has followed a similar pattern to the clubs. Although famous names such as Jef Mermans, Pol Anoul, Rik Coppens, Jef Jurion and especially Paul Van Himst represented Belgium during the 1950s and 1960s, they achieved little. Indeed the 1970 World Cup was the first time since 1954 that they had qualified for the final tournament, and once there they again made little impression.

THE ORDER OF MERIT

		All			League			Cup		Europe		
	Team	G	S	B	G	S	B	G	S	G	S	B
1	RSC Anderlecht	35	21	7	24	15	5	8	2	3	4	2
2	Club Brugge KV	15	17	11	9	11	9	6	4	-	2	2
3	Standard Club Liège	13	16	17	8	9	15	5	6	-	1	2
4	Union Saint Gilloise	13	8	8	11	8	7	2	-	-	-	1
5	Beerschot VAV	9	8	5	7	7	5	2	1	-	-	-
6	Racing CB	7	5	3	6	5	3	1	-	-	-	-
7	Royal Antwerp FC	6	14	7	4	12	7	2	1	-	1	-
8	KV Mechelen	6	8	4	4	5	3	1	3	1	-	1
9	RC Liègeois	6	4	5	5	3	4	1	1	-	-	1
10	Daring CB	5	5	4	5	4	4	-	1	-	-	-
11	Cercle Brugge	5	2	6	3	-	6	2	2	-	-	-
12	Lierse SK	4	3	2	3	2	2	1	1	-	-	-
13	SK Beveren	4	2	1	2	-	-	2	2	-	-	1
14	AA Gent	2	1	5	-	1	5	2	-	-	-	-
15	Racing Club Genk	2	1	2	-	-	1	2	1	-	-	1
16	KSV Waregem	1	1	1	-	-	-	1	1	-	-	1
17	RWD Molenbeek	1	-	4	1	-	3	-	-	-	-	1
18	Racing Tournai	1	-	-	-	-	-	1	-	-	-	-
19	Berchem Sport	-	3	1	-	3	1	-	-	-	-	-
20	RSC Charelroi	-	3	-	-	1	-	-	2	-	-	-
21	Racing Mechelen	-	2	4	-	1	4	-	1	-	-	-
22	FC Germinal Ekeren	-	2	-	-	-	-	-	2	-	-	-
	KSC Lokeren	-	2	-	-	1	-	-	1	-	-	-
	St. Truidense VV	-	2	-	-	1	-	-	1	-	-	-
25	Leopold CB	-	1	3	-	1	3	-	-	-	-	-
26	Olympic Charleroi	-	1	1	-	1	1	-	-	-	-	-
	Racing White	-	1	1	-	-	1	-	1	-	-	-
28	FC Beringen	-	1	-	-	1	-	-	-	-	-	-
	FC Diest	-	1	-	-	-	-	-	1	-	-	-
	Racing Gent	-	1	-	-	-	-	-	1	-	-	-
	Tubantia Borgerhout	-	1	-	-	-	-	-	1	-	-	-
	SK Tongeren	-	1	-	-	-	-	-	1	-	-	-
	CS Verviers	-	1	-	-	-	-	-	1	-	-	-
34	Athletic Brussels	-	-	1	-	-	1	-	-	-	-	-
	SC Brussels	-	-	1	-	-	1	-	-	-	-	-
	RFC Seraing	-	-	1	-	-	1	-	-	-	-	-

Two years later, however, Van Himst captained the team to third place in the European Championships and that marked the start of a successful run in that tournament. Belgium came through the qualifying round on four successive occasions and reached the final itself in 1980, losing 2-1 to West Germany in Rome. In the World Cup, Holland put paid to their hopes of reaching the finals in 1974 and 1978, but since then the Belgians have qualified every time. The national team has had just two coaches since 1976, Guy Thys until 1991 and, since then, Paul Van Himst. Consistency of selection has been vindicated by results, and rarely has a team been so closely moulded as that of Thys.

The side's greatest achievement came in the 1986 World Cup where they were eventually beaten in the semi-finals by two brilliant Maradona goals. For the association, reward for 25 years of progress finally came in 1995 when they were jointly awarded, with Holland, the staging of the 2000 European Championships.

Population: 9,958,000
Area, sq km: 30,518
% in urban areas: 96.5%
Capital city: Brussels

Union Royale Belge des Sociétés de Football-Association
Avenue Houba de Strooper #145
B-1020 Brussels
Belgium
Tel: + 32 2 4771211
Fax: + 32 2 4782391

Year of formation	1895
Affiliation to FIFA	1904
Affiliation to UEFA	1954
Registered clubs	2095
Registered players	468 000
Professional players	1260
Registered coaches	2765
Registered referees	6902

National stadium	Stade du Heysel 35 000
National colours	Red with white trimmings/Red/Red
Reserve colours	White with red trimmings/White/White
Season	August - May

THE RECORD

WORLD CUP

1930	QT Automatic - Final Tournament/1st round
1934	QT 2nd/3 in group 11 - Final Tournament/1st round
1938	QT 2nd/3 in group 8 - Final Tournament/1st round
1950	Did not enter
1954	QT 1st/3 in group 2 - Final Tournament/1st round
1958	QT 2nd/3 in group 2
1962	QT 3rd/3 in group 1
1966	QT 2nd/3 in group 1
1970	QT 1st/4 in group 6 - Final Tournament/1st round
1974	QT 2nd/4 in group 3
1978	QT 2nd/4 in group 4
1982	QT 1st/5 in group 2 - Final Tournament/2nd round
1986	QT 2nd/4 in group 1 - Final Tournament/Semi-finalists/4th place
1990	QT 1st/5 in group 7 - Final Tournament/2nd round
1994	QT 2nd/6 in group 5 - Final Tournament/2nd round

EUROPEAN CHAMPIONSHIP

1960	Did not enter
1964	1st round
1968	QT 2nd/4 in group 7

1972	QT 1st/4 in group 5 - Final Tournament/Semi-finalists/3rd place
1976	QT 1st/4 in group 7 - Final Tournament/Quarter-finalists
1980	QT 1st/5 in group 2 - Final Tournament/Finalists
1984	QT 1st/4 in group 1 - Final tournament/1st round
1988	QT 3rd/5 in group 7
1992	QT 3rd/4 in group 5
1996	QT group 2

EUROPEAN CLUB COMPETITIONS

European Cup
Finalists - Club Brugge 1978

Cup Winners Cup
Winners - RSC Anderlecht 1976 1978 KV Mechelen 1988
Finalists - RSC Anderlecht 1977 1990 Standard CL 1982 Royal Antwerp FC 1993

UEFA Cup
Winners - RSC Anderlecht 1983
Finalists - RSC Anderlecht 1970 1984 Club Brugge 1976

CLUB DIRECTORY

BRUSSELS (Population - 2,385,000)

RSC Anderlecht (1908)
Stade Constant Vanden Stock "Parc Astrid" 29,000 – White/White, violet trimmings

RWD Molenbeek (1973)
Edmond Machtens 18,000 – White/Black, red trimmings
Previous names - Merger in 1973 of Racing White Brussels (1963) and Daring CB (1895). Racing White was the result of a merger in 1963 between Racing CB (1891) and White Star AC (1910)

Royale Union St. Gilloise (1897)
Joseph Marien 'La Butte' 30,000 – Blue/Yellow

ANTWERP (Population - 1,100,000)

Royal Antwerp FC (1880)
Bosuil 20,000 – Red/Red, white trimmings

Beerschot VAV (1899
Kiel 25,000 – Violet/White

FC Germinal Ekeren (1920)
Veltwijkpark 6,000 – Red/Yellow - Red and yellow trimmings

LIEGE (Population - 750,000)

Standard Club Liège (1898)
Sclessin 25,000 – Red/White, white trimmings

RC Liègeois (1892)
Rocourt 25,000 – Red & blue stripes/Blue
Previous names - FC Liègeois 1892-1989, RFC Liège 1989-93

CHARLEROI (Population - 480,000)

RSC Charleroi (1904)
Mambour 23,000 – Black & white stripes/Black

Olympic Charleroi (1912)
La Neuville – White/Black
Previous name - Olympic Montignies 1971-80

GENT (Population - 465,000)

AA Gent (1898)
Jules Ottenstadion 20,000 – White/Blue - Blue trimmings

HASSELT (Population - 290,000)

Racing Club Genk (1988)
Thyl Geyselinck 19,000 – Yellow/White, white trimmings
Previous names - Merger in 1988 of SV Winterslag (1923) and Waterschei THOR (1925)

BRUGES (Population - 223,000)

Club Brugge KV (1891)
Olympiastadion 27,000 – Blue & black stripes/Black

KSV Cercle Brugge (1899)
Olympiastadion 27,000 – White, black & green stripes/Black

KORTRIJK (Population - 202,000)

KV Kortrijk (1971)
Gulden Sporen 16,000 – White/Red
Previous names - Merger in 1971 of Kortrijk Sport (1901) and Stade Kortrijk

MECHELEN (Population - 121,000)

KV Mechelen (1904)
Achter de Kazerne 14,000 – Red & yellow stripes/Black, black trimmings

Racing Club Mechelen (1904)
Oscar Vankesbeeckstadium 12,000 – Green/White

SERAING (Population - 62,000)

RFC Seraing (1900)
Stade Communal 15,000 – Red and black hoops/Black

BEVEREN

KSK Beveren (1934)
Freethiel 15,000 – Yellow/Blue, blue trimmings
Previous names - Formed when Amical and Standard merged in 1934

LOKEREN (Population - 33,000)

KSC Lokeren (1970)
Daknam 18,000 – White/black
Previous names - Merger in 1970 of Racing and Standard Lokeren

SINT-TRUIDEN

St. Truidense VV (1924)
Staaien 15,000 – Yellow/Blue, blue trimmings

WAREGEM

KSV Waregem (1946)
Regenboogstadion 12,000 – Red/Red, white trimmings
Previous names - Merger in 1946 of Red Star and Sportif

LIER (Population - 31,000)

Lierse SK (1906)
Herman Vanderpoortenstadium 14,000 – Yellow with black sleeves/Yellow, black trimmings

BELGIAN LEAGUE CHAMPIONSHIP

1896e	FC Liègeois 20 Royal Antwerp FC 14 SC Brussels 13
1897d	Racing CB 16 FC Liègeois 12 Royal Antwerp FC 11
1898	FC Liègeois 14 Racing CB 10 Leopold CB 6
1899c	FC Liègeois 16 Racing CB 8 Leopold CB 7
1900d*	Racing CB 14 Royal Antwerp FC 14 Athletic Brussels 12
1901g	Racing CB 26 Beerschot 25 Leopold CB 23
1902b*	Racing CB 9 Leopold CB 9 Union St. Gilloise 4
1903	Racing CB 11 Union St. Gilloise 6 Beerschot 6
1904	Union St. Gilloise 12 Racing CB 6 Club Brugge 4
1905i	Union St. Gilloise 35 Racing CB 30 Club Brugge 28
1906h	Union St. Gilloise 33 Club Brugge 29 Racing CB 24
1907	Union St. Gilloise 34 Racing CB 25 Club Brugge 24
1908	Racing CB 35 Union St. Gilloise 30 Club Brugge 26
1909k	Union St. Gilloise 41 Daring CB 34 Club Brugge 33
1910*	Union St. Gilloise 38 Club Brugge 38 Cercle Brugge 36
1911	Cercle Brugge 35 Club Brugge 34 Daring CB 27
1912	Daring CB 38 Union St. Gilloise 36 Racing CB 29
1913*	Union St. Gilloise 38 Daring CB 38 Racing CB 31
1914	Daring CB 36 Union St. Gilloise 33 Cercle Brugge 30
1915-19	-
1920	Club Brugge 34 Union St. Gilloise 32 Daring CB 31
1921	Daring CB 36 Union St. Gilloise 31 Beerschot 27
1922n*	Beerschot 39 Union St. Gilloise 39 Royal Antwerp FC 37
1923	Union St. Gilloise 42 Beerschot 37 Cercle Brugge 37
1924	Beerschot 38 Union St. Gilloise 37 Cercle Brugge 33
1925	Beerschot 40 Royal Antwerp FC 34 Union St. Gilloise 32
1926	Beerschot 40 Standard CL 33 Daring CB 32
1927	Cercle Brugge 35 Beerschot 33 Standard CL 32

1928 Beerschot 48 Standard CL 37 Cercle Brugge 34
1929* Royal Antwerp FC 39 Beerschot 39 Racing Mechelen 31
1930 Cercle Brugge 37 Royal Antwerp FC 36 Racing Mechelen 31
1931 Royal Antwerp FC 37 KV Mechelen 34 Berchem Sport 33
1932 Lierse SK 37 Royal Antwerp FC 36 Union St. Gilloise 29
1933 Union St. Gilloise 43 Royal Antwerp FC 36 Cercle Brugge 33
1934 Union St. Gilloise 43 Daring CB 35 Standard CL 35
1935 Union St. Gilloise 45 Lierse SK 40 Daring CB 35
1936 Daring CB 37 Standard CL 34 Union St. Gilloise 32
1937 Daring CB 39 Beerschot 38 Union St. Gilloise 36
1938 Beerschot 41 Daring CB 36 Union St. Gilloise 31
1939 Beerschot 41 Lierse SK 34 Olympic Charleroi 33
1940-41 -
1942 Lierse SK 39 Beerschot 35 Royal Antwerp FC 33
1943q KV Mechelen 46 Beerschot 44 Lierse SK 39
1944 Royal Antwerp FC 49 RSC Anderlecht 42 Beerschot 37
1945 -
1946u KV Mechelen 55 Royal Antwerp FC 49 RSC Anderlecht 46
1947 RSC Anderlecht 50 Olympic Charleroi 48 KV Mechelen 45
1948q KV Mechelen 43 RSC Anderlecht 38 FC Liègeois 36
1949 RSC Anderlecht 41 Berchem Sport 38 Standard CL 38
1950 RSC Anderlecht 45 Berchem Sport 40 Racing Mechelen 38
1951 RSC Anderlecht 38 Berchem Sport 38 Racing Mechelen 36
1952 FC Liègeois 44 Racing Mechelen 40 Royal Antwerp FC 40
1953 FC Liègeois 42 RSC Anderlecht 41 Beerschot 36
1954 RSC Anderlecht 37 KV Mechelen 36 AA Gent 36
1955 RSC Anderlecht 41 AA Gent 38 Standard CL 37
1956 RSC Anderlecht 42 Royal Antwerp FC 39 Union St. Gilloise 37
1957 Royal Antwerp FC 46 RSC Anderlecht 40 AA Gent 39
1958 Standard CL 44 Royal Antwerp FC 44 AA Gent 41
1959 RSC Anderlecht 44 FC Liègeois 43 Standard CL 42
1960 Lierse SK 38 RSC Anderlecht 37 Waterschei THOR 35
1961 Standard CL 45 FC Liègeois 41 RSC Anderlecht 37
1962 RSC Anderlecht 49 Standard CL 40 Royal Antwerp FC 40
1963 Standard CL 44 Royal Antwerp FC 40 RSC Anderlecht 37
1964 RSC Anderlecht 45 FC Beringen 41 Standard CL 40
1965 RSC Anderlecht 51 Standard CL 39 Beerschot 35
1966 RSC Anderlecht 47 St. Truidense VV 40 Standard CL 40
1967 RSC Anderlecht 47 Club Brugge 45 FC Liègeois 39
1968 RSC Anderlecht 46 Club Brugge 45 Standard CL 40
1969 Standard CL 45 RSC Charleroi 40 Lierse SK 36
1970 Standard CL 49 Club Brugge 45 AA Gent 39
1971 Standard CL 47 Club Brugge 46 RSC Anderlecht 41
1972 RSC Anderlecht 45 Club Brugge 45 Standard CL 41
1973 Club Brugge 45 Standard CL 38 Racing White 37
1974 RSC Anderlecht 41 Royal Antwerp FC 39 RWD Molenbeek 39
1975v RWD Molenbeek 61 Royal Antwerp FC 52 RSC Anderlecht 52
1976u Club Brugge 52 RSC Anderlecht 48 RWD Molenbeek 47
1977t Club Brugge 52 RSC Anderlecht 48 Standard CL 45
1978 Club Brugge 51 RSC Anderlecht 50 Standard CL 49
1979 SK Beveren 49 RSC Anderlecht 45 Standard CL 44
1980 Club Brugge 53 Standard CL 49 RWD Molenbeek 48
1981 RSC Anderlecht 57 KSC Lokeren 46 Standard CL 42
1982 Standard CL 48 RSC Anderlecht 46 AA Gent 45
1983 Standard CL 50 RSC Anderlecht 49 Royal Antwerp FC 46
1984 SK Beveren 51 RSC Anderlecht 47 Club Brugge 44
1985 RSC Anderlecht 59 Club Brugge 48 FC Liègeois 46
1986* RSC Anderlecht 52 Club Brugge 52 Standard CL 42
1987 RSC Anderlecht 57 KV Mechelen 55 Club Brugge 45
1988 Club Brugge 51 KV Mechelen 49 Royal Antwerp FC 49
1989 KV Mechelen 57 RSC Anderlecht 53 FC Liègeois 46
1990 Club Brugge 57 RSC Anderlecht 53 KV Mechelen 50
1991 RSC Anderlecht 53 KV Mechelen 50 Club Brugge 47
1992 Club Brugge 53 RSC Anderlecht 49 Standard CL 46
1993 RSC Anderlecht 58 Standard CL 45 KV Mechelen 42
1994 RSC Anderlecht 55 Club Brugge 53 RFC Seraing 43
1995 RSC Anderlecht 52 Standard CL 51 Club Brugge 49

Championship play-offs

1900	Racing CB	1-0	Royal Antwerp FC
1902	Racing CB	4-3	Leopold CB
1910	Union St. Gilloise	2-0	Club Brugge
1913	Union St. Gilloise	2-0	Daring CB
1922	Beerschot	2-0	Union St. Gilloise
1929	Royal Antwerp FC	3-1	Beerschot
1986	RSC Anderlecht	1-1 2-2	Club Brugge

Anderlecht won on away goals

BELGIAN CUP FINALS

1912	Racing CB	1-0	Racing Gent
1913	Union St. Gilloise	3-2	Cercle Brugge
1914	Union St. Gilloise	4-1	Club Brugge
1915-26	-		
1927	Cercle Brugge	2-1	Tubantia Borgerhout
1928-53	-		
1954	Standard CL	3-1	Racing Mechelen
1955	Royal Antwerp FC	4-0	Waterschei THOR
1956	Racing Tournai	2-1	CS Verviers
1957-63	-		
1964	AA Gent	4-2	FC Diest
1965	RSC Anderlecht	3-2	Standard CL
1966	Standard CL	1-0	RSC Anderlecht
1967	Standard CL	3-1	KV Mechelen
1968	Club Brugge	1-1 4-4 4-2p	Beerschot
1969	Lierse SK	2-0	Racing White
1970	Club Brugge	6-1	Daring CB
1971	Beerschot	2-1	St. Truidense VV
1972	RSC Anderlecht	1-0	Standard CL
1973	RSC Anderlecht	2-1	Standard CL
1974	KSV Waregem	4-1	SK Tongeren
1975	RSC Anderlecht	1-0	Royal Antwerp FC
1976	RSC Anderlecht	4-0	Lierse SK
1977	Club Brugge	4-3	RSC Anderlecht
1978	SK Beveren	2-0	RSC Charleroi
1979	Beerschot	1-0	Club Brugge
1980	Waterschei THOR	2-1	SK Beveren
1981	Standard CL	4-0	KSC Lokeren
1982	Waterschei THOR	2-0	KSV Waregem
1983	SK Beveren	3-1	Club Brugge
1984	AA Gent	2-0	Standard CL
1985	Cercle Brugge	1-1 5-4p	SK Beveren
1986	Club Brugge	3-0	Cercle Brugge
1987	KV Mechelen	1-0	FC Liègeois
1988	RSC Anderlecht	2-0	Standard CL
1989	RSC Anderlecht	2-0	Standard CL
1990	RFC Liège	2-1	FC Germinal Ekeren
1991	Club Brugge	3-1	KV Mechelen
1992	Royal Antwerp FC	2-2 9-8p	KV Mechelen
1993	Standard CL	2-0	RSC Charleroi
1994	RSC Anderlecht	2-0	Club Brugge
1995	Club Brugge	3-1	FC Germinal Ekeren

LEADING INTERNATIONAL GOALSCORERS

30 Bernard Voorhoof	(Lierse)	1928-40
30 Paul Van Himst	(Anderlecht)	1960-74
27 Jef Mermans	(Anderlecht)	1945-56
26 Robert De Veen	(Club Brugge)	1906-13
26 Raymond Braine	(Beerschot,Sparta Praha)	1925-39
23 Jan Ceulemans	(Club Brugge)	1977-91
22 Marc Degryse	(Club Brugge,Anderlecht)	1984-
21 Rik Coppens	(Beerschot)	1949-59
20 Pol Anoul	(Liege)	1947-54
20 Erwin Vandenbergh	(Lierse,Anderlecht,Lille,Gent)	1979-91

LEADING INTERNATIONAL APPEARANCES

96 Jan Ceulemans	(Club Brugge)	1977-91
86 Eric Gerets	(Standard,Milan,Maastricht,PSV)	1975-91
82 Paul Van Himst	(Anderlecht)	1960-74
75 Georges Grün	(Anderlecht,Parma)	1984-
69 Enzo Scifo	(Anderlecht,Inter,Bordeaux, Auxerre,Torino/Monaco)	1984-
69 Franky Vander Elst	(Club Brugge)	1984-
68 Vic Mees	(Antwerp)	1949-60
67 Georges Heylens	(Anderlecht)	1961-73
64 Jef Jurion	(Anderlecht)	1955-67
64 Jean-Marie Pfaff	(Beveren,Bayern München)	1976-87

NATIONAL TEAM COACHES

1912-28	F.W. Maxwell
1928-30	Victor Loewenfeld
1930-34	Hector Goetinck
1935	Jules Turnauer
1935-40	Jack Butler
1944-46	François Demol
1947-53	Bill Gormlie
1953-54	David Livingstone
1955-57	André Vandeweyer
1957	Louis Nicolay
1957-58	Geza Toldi
1958-68	Constant Vanden Stock
1968-76	Raymond Goethals
1976-91	Guy Thys
1989-90	Walter Meeuws
1990-91	Guy Thys
1991-	Paul Van Himst

INTERNATIONAL MATCHES PLAYED BY BELGIUM

1-05-1904	France	D 3-3	Brussels	Fr	Destrebecq, Quéritet 2
30-04-1905	Holland	L 1-4	Antwerp	Fr	OG
7-05	France	W 7-0	Brussels	Fr	Van Hoorden 2,Destrebecq 3,Theunen 2
14-05	Holland	L 0-4	Rotterdam	Fr	
22-04-1906	France	W 5-0	Paris	Fr	Feye 2, Van Hoorden, Deveen 2
29-04	Holland	W 5-0	Antwerp	Fr	Vanden Eynde.G, Goetinck, De Veen 3
13-05	Holland	W 3-2	Rotterdam	Fr	Cambier 2, Destrebecq
14-04-1907	Holland	L 1-3	Antwerp	Fr	Feye
21-04	France	L 1-2	Brussels	Fr	OG
9-05	Holland	W 2-1	Haarlem	Fr	Feye, Goetinck
29-03-1908	Holland	L 1-4	Antwerp	Fr	Vertongen
12-04	France	W 2-1	Paris	Fr	De Veen 2
18-04	England Am	L 2-8	Brussels	Fr	De Veen 2
26-04	Holland	L 1-3	Rotterdam	Fr	Saeys
26-10	Sweden	W 2-1	Brussels	Fr	Kavorkian, Goossens
21-03-1909	Holland	L 1-4	Antwerp	Fr	Poelmans
17-04	England Am	L 2-11	London	Fr	De Veen 2
25-04	Holland	L 1-4	Rotterdam	Fr	Goossens
9-05	France	W 5-2	Brussels	Fr	De Veen 3, Van Hoorden, Theunen
13-03-1910	Holland	W 3-2	Antwerp	Fr	De Veen 2, Six
26-03	England Am	D 2-2	Brussels	Fr	Six, Paternoster
3-04	France	W 4-0	Paris	Fr	Six 2, Saeys, De Veen
10-04	Holland	L 0-7	Haarlem	Fr	
16-05	Germany	W 3-0	Duisburg	Fr	Saeys 2, Van Staceghem
4-03-1911	England Am	L 0-4	London	Fr	
19-03	Holland	L 1-5	Antwerp	Fr	Paternoster
2-04	Holland	L 1-3	Dordrecht	Fr	Six
23-04	Germany	W 2-1	Liege	Fr	Van Houtte, Saeys
30-04	France	W 7-1	Brussels	Fr	De Veen 5, Saeys, Bouttiau
28-01-1912	France	D 1-1	Paris	Fr	Hubin
20-02	Switzerland	W 9-2	Antwerp	Fr	Van Cant 2, Saeys 3, Six 2, De Veen 2
10-03	Holland	L 1-2	Antwerp	Fr	Nizot
8-04	England Am	L 1-2	Brussels	Fr	Nizot
28-04	Holland	L 3-4	Dordrecht	Fr	Musch, Nizot 2
9-11	England Am	L 0-4	Swindon	Fr	
16-02-1913	France	W 3-0	Brussels	Fr	Nizot 2, Bessens
9-03	Holland	D 3-3	Antwerp	Fr	De Veen 2, Nizot
20-04	Holland	W 4-2	Zwolle	Fr	Suetens, Musch 2, Nizot
1-05	Italy	L 0-1	Turin	Fr	
4-05	Switzerland	W 2-1	Basle	Fr	Saeys, Brébart
2-11	Switzerland	W 2-0	Verviers	Fr	Wertz, Nizot
23-11	Germany	W 6-2	Antwerp	Fr	Brébart 3, Van Cant 3
25-01-1914	France	L 3-4	Lille	Fr	Van Cant, Brébart, Thys
24-02	England Am	L 1-8	Brussels	Fr	Brébart
15-03	Holland	L 2-4	Antwerp	Fr	Brébart 2
26-04	Holland	L 2-4	Amsterdam	Fr	Van Cant, Nizot

Date	Opponent	Result	Venue	Comp	Scorers
9-03-1919	France	D 2-2	Brussels	Fr	Coppée, Hebdin
17-02-1920	England Am	W 3-1	Brussels	Fr	Coppée 2, Van Hege
28-03	France	L 1-2	Paris	Fr	Vlaminck
29-08	Spain	W 3-1	Antwerp	OGqf	Coppée 3
31-08	Holland	W 3-0	Antwerp	OGsf	Larnoe, Van Hege, Bragard
2-09	Czechoslovakia	W 2-0	Antwerp	OGf	Coppée, Larnoe
6-03-1921	France	W 3-1	Brussels	Fr	Bragard 2, Van Hege
5-05	Italy	L 2-3	Antwerp	Fr	Larnoe, Bragard
15-05	Holland	D 1-1	Antwerp	Fr	Bragard
21-05	England	L 0-2	Brussels	Fr	
9-10	Spain	L 0-2	Bilbao	Fr	
15-01-1922	France	L 1-2	Paris	Fr	Michel
26-03	Holland	W 4-0	Antwerp	Fr	Larnoe 2, Vandevelde, Coppée
15-04	Denmark	D 0-0	Liege	Fr	
7-05	Holland	W 2-1	Amsterdam	Fr	OG, Michel
21-05	Italy	L 2-4	Milan	Fr	Larnoe, Thys
4-02-1923	Spain	W 1-0	Antwerp	Fr	Coppée
25-02	France	W 4-1	Brussels	Fr	Gillis 2, Larnoe 2
19-03	England	L 1-6	London	Fr	Vlaminck
29-04	Holland	D 1-1	Amsterdam	Fr	Thys
5-05	England Am	W 3-0	Brussels	Fr	Larnoe, Thys, Gillis
1-11	England	D 2-2	Antwerp	Fr	Larnoe, Schelstraete
13-01-1924	France	L 0-2	Paris	Fr	
23-03	Holland	D 1-1	Amsterdam	Fr	Coppée
27-04	Holland	D 1-1	Antwerp	Fr	Thys
29-05	Sweden	L 1-8	Paris	OGr1	Larnoe
10-06	Sweden*	W 5-0	Brussels	Fr	Gillis, Despae 2, Henderieckx 2
5-10	Denmark	L 1-2	Copenhagen	Fr	Adams
11-11	France	W 3-0	Brussels	Fr	Braine.P, Dupac 2
8-12	England	L 0-4	West Bromwich	Fr	
15-03-1925	Holland	L 0-1	Antwerp	Fr	
3-05	Holland	L 0-5	Amsterdam	Fr	
21-05	Hungary	W 3-1	Budapest	Fr	Houet, Adams, Thys
24-05	Switzerland	D 0-0	Lausanne	Fr	
6-09	Holland*	D 1-1	Antwerp	Fr	Thys
13-12	Austria	L 3-4	Liege	Fr	Thys, Gillis, Braine.P
14-02-1926	Hungary	L 0-2	Brussels	Fr	
14-03	Holland	D 1-1	Antwerp	Fr	Adams
11-04	France	L 3-4	Paris	Fr	Vanderbouwhelde, Thys, Devos
2-05	Holland	W 5-1	Amsterdam	Fr	Braine.R 2, Diddens, Adams, Gillis
24-05	England	L 3-5	Antwerp	Fr	Thys, Braine.R 2
20-06	France	D 2-2	Brussels	Fr	Gillis, Adams
29-08	Holland*	W 5-1	Rotterdam	Fr	Frenay, Devos, Despae 3
2-01-1927	Czechoslovakia	L 2-3	Liege	Fr	Bierna, Gillis
13-03	Holland	W 2-0	Antwerp	Fr	Bierna, Adams
3-04	Sweden	W 2-1	Brussels	Fr	Braine.R, Adams
1-05	Holland	L 2-3	Amsterdam	Fr	Diddens, Braine.R
11-05	England	L 1-9	Brussels	Fr	Van Halme
22-05	Austria	L 1-4	Vienna	Fr	Braine.P
26-05	Czechoslovakia	L 0-4	Prague	Fr	
4-09	Sweden	L 0-7	Stockholm	Fr	
8-01-1928	Austria	L 1-2	Brussels	Fr	Ledent
12-02	Rep. Ireland	L 2-4	Liege	Fr	Braine.R, Ledent
11-03	Holland	D 1-1	Amsterdam	Fr	Braine.R
1-04	Holland	W 1-0	Antwerp	Fr	Moeschal
15-04	France	W 3-2	Paris	Fr	Devos, Braine.R 2
19-05	England	L 1-3	Antwerp	Fr	Moeschal
27-05	Luxembourg	W 5-3	Amsterdam	OGr1	Braine.R 2, Versyp, Moeschal 2
2-06	Argentina	L 3-6	Amsterdam	OGqf	Braine.R, Van Halme, Moeschal
5-06	Holland	L 1-3	Rotterdam	OGct	Braine.P
4-11	Holland	D 1-1	Amsterdam	Fr	Braine.R
20-04-1929	Rep. Ireland	L 0-4	Dublin	Fr	
5-05	Holland	W 3-1	Antwerp	Fr	Braine.R 2, Vandenbawhede
11-05	England	L 1-5	Brussels	Fr	Moeschal
26-05	France	W 4-1	Liege	Fr	Vandenbawhede, Braine.R, Bastin 2
8-12	Holland*	L 0-1	Amsterdam	Fr	
13-04-1930	France	W 6-1	Paris	Fr	Versyp 2, Adams, Vandenbawhede 3
4-05	Holland	D 2-2	Amsterdam	Fr	Bastin, Adams
11-05	Rep. Ireland	L 1-3	Brussels	Fr	Bastin
18-05	Holland	W 3-1	Antwerp	Fr	Voorhoof, Bastin, OG
25-05	France	L 1-2	Liege	Fr	Adams

8-06	Portugal	W 2-1	Antwerp	Fr	Vandenbawhede, Bastin
13-07	United States	L 0-3	Montevideo	WCr1	
20-07	Paraguay	L 0-1	Montevideo	WCr1	
14-09	Holland*	W 4-1	Brussels	Fr	Vanderbawhede 2, Voorhoof, Moeschal
21-09	Czechoslovakia	L 2-3	Antwerp	Fr	Versyp, Voorhoof
28-09	Sweden	D 2-2	Liege	Fr	Secrétin, Braine.P
7-12	France	D 2-2	Paris	Fr	Van Beeck, Voorhoof
29-03-1931	Holland	L 2-3	Amsterdam	Fr	Versyp, Voorhoof
3-05	Holland	W 4-2	Antwerp	Fr	Voorhoof 2, Vanden Eynde.S, Versyp
16-05	England	L 1-4	Brussels	Fr	Capelle
31-05	Portugal	L 2-3	Lisbon	Fr	Van Beeck, Hellemans
11-10	Poland	W 2-1	Brussels	Fr	Hellemans, Voorhoof
6-12	Switzerland	W 2-1	Brussels	Fr	Capelle 2
14-02-1932	Holland*	W 3-2	Amsterdam	Fr	Versijp 2, Capelle
20-03	Holland	L 1-4	Antwerp	Fr	Bastin
17-04	Holland	L 1-2	Amsterdam	Fr	Capelle
1-05	France	W 5-2	Brussels	Fr	Brichaut, Vanden Eynde.S 2, Capelle, Van Beeck
5-06	Denmark	W 4-3	Copenhagen	Fr	Capelle 3, Van Beeck
12-06	Sweden	L 1-3	Stockholm	Fr	Vanden Eynde.S
16-10	Holland*	L 2-3	Brussels	Fr	Claessens, Capelle
11-12	Austria	L 1-6	Brussels	Fr	Van Landegem
12-02-1933	Italy	L 2-3	Brussels	Fr	Voorhoof 2
12-03	Switzerland	D 3-3	Zurich	Fr	Desmedt, Voorhoof 2
26-03	France	L 0-3	Paris	Fr	
9-04	Holland	L 1-3	Antwerp	Fr	Saeys.A
7-05	Holland	W 2-1	Amsterdam	Fr	Desmedt, Voorhoof
4-06	Poland	W 1-0	Warsaw	Fr	Brichaut
11-06	Austria	L 1-4	Vienna	Fr	Voorhoof
22-10	Germany	L 1-8	Duisburg	Fr	Lamoot
26-11	Denmark	D 2-2	Brussels	Fr	Versyp, Vanden Eynde.S
21-01-1934	France	L 2-3	Brussels	Fr	Voorhoof, Van Den Eynde.F
25-02	Rep. Ireland	D 4-4	Dublin	WCq	Capelle, Vanden Eynde.S, Van Den Eynde.F 2
11-03	Holland	L 3-9	Amsterdam	Fr	Voorhoof, Brichaut, Versyp
29-04	Holland	L 2-4	Antwerp	WCq	Grimonprez, Voorhoof
27-05	Germany	L 2-5	Florence	WCr1	Voorhoof 2
31-03-1935	Holland	L 2-4	Amsterdam	Fr	Van Beeck, Voorhoof
14-04	France	D 1-1	Brussels	Fr	Van Beeck
28-04	Germany	L 1-6	Brussels	Fr	Isemborghs
12-05	Holland	L 0-2	Brussels	Fr	
30-05	Switzerland	D 2-2	Brussels	Fr	OG 2
17-11	Sweden	W 5-1	Brussels	Fr	Van Caelenberghe, Capelle 2, Isemborghs 2
16-02-1936	Poland	L 0-2	Brussels	Fr	
8-03	France	L 0-3	Paris	Fr	
29-03	Holland	L 0-8	Amsterdam	Fr	
3-05	Holland	D 1-1	Brussels	Fr	Braine.R
9-05	England	W 3-2	Brussels	Fr	Isemborghs 2, Fiévez
24-05	Switzerland	D 1-1	Basle	Fr	Capelle
21-02-1937	France	W 3-1	Brussels	Fr	Braine.R, Ceuleers, Vanden Eynde.S
4-04	Holland	W 2-1	Antwerp	Fr	Ceuleers, Fiévez
18-04	Switzerland	L 1-2	Brussels	Fr	Voorhoof
25-04	Germany	L 0-1	Hanover	Fr	
2-05	Holland	L 0-1	Rotterdam	Fr	
6-06	Yugoslavia	D 1-1	Belgrade	Fr	Capelle
10-06	Romania	L 1-2	Bucharest	Fr	Voorhoof
30-01-1938	France	L 3-5	Paris	Fr	Braine.R, Voorhoof, Vanden Eynde.S
27-02	Holland	L 2-7	Rotterdam	Fr	Braine.R, Voorhoof
13-03	Luxembourg	W 3-2	Luxembourg	WCq	Voorhoof 2, Braine.R
3-04	Holland	D 1-1	Antwerp	WCq	Isemborghs
8-05	Switzerland	W 3-0	Lausanne	Fr	Voorhoof 2, Capelle
15-05	Italy	L 1-6	Milan	Fr	Capelle
29-05	Yugoslavia	D 2-2	Brussels	Fr	Capelle, Vandenwouwer
5-06	France	L 1-3	Paris	WCr1	Isemborghs
29-01-1939	Germany	L 1-4	Brussels	Fr	Stijnen
19-03	Holland	W 5-4	Antwerp	Fr	Capelle 3, Fievez, Braine.R
23-04	Holland	L 2-3	Amsterdam	Fr	Braine.R, Buyle
14-05	Switzerland	L 1-2	Liege	Fr	Voorhoof
18-05	France	L 1-3	Brussels	Fr	Lamoot
27-05	Poland	D 3-3	Lodz	Fr	Fiévez, Braine.R, Isemborghs
10-12	Holland*	L 2-5	Rotterdam	Fr	Buyle, Voorhoof
17-03-1940	Holland	W 7-1	Antwerp	Fr	Nelis, Voorhoof, Van Craen 3, Vandenwouwer, OG
21-04	Holland	L 2-4	Amsterdam	Fr	Van Craen, Nelis

24-12-1944	France	L 1-3	Paris	Fr	De Wael
13-05-1945	Luxembourg	L 1-4	Luxembourg	Fr	Gillaux
15-12	France	W 2-1	Brussels	Fr	Sermon 2
19-01-1946	England *	L 0-2	London	VI	
23-01	Scotland *	D 2-2	Glasgow	VI	Lemberechts, Chaves
23-02	Luxembourg	W 7-0	Charleroi	Fr	De Cleyn 5, Coppens.H, Lemberechts
12-05	Holland	L 3-6	Amsterdam	Fr	De Cleyn 2, Coppens.H
30-05	Holland	D 2-2	Antwerp	Fr	Lemberechts, Van Vaerenbergh
7-04-1947	Holland	L 1-2	Amsterdam	Fr	Thirifays
4-05	Holland	L 1-2	Antwerp	Fr	Anoul
18-05	Scotland	W 2-1	Brussels	Fr	Anoul 2
1-06	France	L 2-4	Paris	Fr	De Cleyn, Coppens.H
21-09	England	L 2-5	Brussels	Fr	Mermans, De Cleyn
2-11	Switzerland	L 0-4	Geneva	Fr	
14-03-1948	Holland	D 1-1	Antwerp	Fr	Van Steenlant
18-04	Holland	D 2-2	Rotterdam	Fr	Mermans, Van Steenlant
28-04	Scotland	L 0-2	Glasgow	Fr	
6-06	France	W 4-2	Brussels	Fr	Chaves 2, Govard, Mermans
17-10	France	D 3-3	Paris	Fr	Mermans, Anoul, Chaves
21-11	Holland	D 1-1	Antwerp	Fr	Chaves
2-01-1949	Spain	D 1-1	Barcelona	Fr	Coppens.H
13-03	Holland	D 3-3	Amsterdam	Fr	Mermans 2, OG
24-04	Rep. Ireland	W 2-0	Dublin	Fr	Lemberechts, Mermans
22-05	Wales	W 3-1	Liege	Fr	Govard 2, De Hert
2-10	Switzerland	W 3-0	Brussels	Fr	Verbruggen 2, Mermans
6-11	Holland	W 1-0	Rotterdam	Fr	Govard
23-11	Wales	L 1-5	Cardiff	Fr	Coppens.R
5-03-1950	Italy	L 1-3	Bologna	Fr	Chaves
16-04	Holland	W 2-0	Antwerp	Fr	Mermans, De Hert
10-05	Rep. Ireland	W 5-1	Brussels	Fr	Mermans 3, De Hert, Chaves
18-05	England	L 1-4	Brussels	Fr	Mermans
4-06	France	W 4-1	Brussels	Fr	Mermans 3, Mordant
1-11	France	D 3-3	Paris	Fr	Lemberechts, Mermans 2
12-11	Holland	W 7-2	Antwerp	Fr	Lemberechts 3, Mermans 2, Anoul 2
15-04-1951	Holland	L 4-5	Amsterdam	Fr	Mermans, Chaves, Vaillant
20-05	Scotland	L 0-5	Brussels	Fr	
10-06	Spain	D 3-3	Brussels	Fr	Van Gestel 2, Van Steenlant
17-06	Portugal	D 1-1	Lisbon	Fr	Givard
14-10	Austria	L 1-8	Brussels	Fr	Lemberechts
25-11	Holland	W 7-6	Rotterdam	Fr	Anoul 3, Verbruggen, Moës 2, Van Steen
24-02-1952	Italy	W 2-0	Brussels	Fr	Moës 2
23-03	Austria	L 0-2	Vienna	Fr	
6-04	Holland	W 4-2	Antwerp	Fr	Anoul, Coppens.R 2, Lemberechts
22-05	France	L 1-2	Brussels	Fr	Mermans
19-10	Holland	W 2-1	Antwerp	Fr	Anoul, Mermans
26-11	England	L 0-5	London	Fr	
25-12	France	W 1-0	Paris	Fr	Straetmans
19-03-1953	Spain	L 1-3	Barcelona	Fr	Lemberechts
19-04	Holland	W 2-0	Amsterdam	Fr	Coppens.R, Janssens.T
14-05	Yugoslavia	L 1-3	Brussels	Fr	Anoul
25-05	Finland	W 4-2	Helsinki	WCq	Coppens.R 3, Anoul
28-05	Sweden	W 3-2	Stockholm	WCq	Anoul, Straetmans, Lemberechts
23-09	Finland	D 2-2	Brussels	WCq	Bollen.M 2
8-10	Sweden	W 2-0	Brussels	WCq	Coppens.R, Mees
25-10	Holland	L 0-1	Rotterdam	Fr	
22-11	Switzerland	D 2-2	Zurich	Fr	Vanden Bosch.H 2
14-03-1954	Portugal	D 0-0	Brussels	Fr	
4-04	Holland	W 4-0	Antwerp	Fr	Mermans, Coppens.R 2, OG
9-05	Yugoslavia	W 2-0	Zagreb	Fr	Coppens.R, Mermans
30-05	France	D 3-3	Brussels	Fr	Mermans, Anoul 2
17-06	England	D 4-4	Basle	WCr1	Anoul 2, Coppens.R, OG
20-06	Italy	L 1-4	Lugano	WCr1	Anoul
26-09	West Germany	W 2-0	Brussels	Fr	Coppens.R, Anoul
24-10	Holland	W 4-3	Antwerp	Fr	Lemberechts, Coppens.R 2, Houf
11-11	France	D 2-2	Paris	Fr	OG, Lemberechts
16-01-1955	Italy	L 0-1	Bari	Fr	
3-04	Holland	L 0-1	Amsterdam	Fr	
5-06	Czechoslovakia	L 1-3	Brussels	Fr	OG
25-09	Czechoslovakia	L 2-5	Prague	Fr	Coppens.R, Orlans
28-09	Romania	L 0-1	Bucharest	Fr	
16-10	Holland	D 2-2	Rotterdam	Fr	Jacquemijns 2

25-12	France	W 2-1	Brussels	Fr	Jadot, Vanden Bosch.H
11-03-1956	Switzerland	L 1-3	Brussels	Fr	Mermans
8-04	Holland	L 0-1	Antwerp	Fr	
3-06	Hungary	W 5-4	Brussels	Fr	Van Kerkhoven, Vandewaeyer.R, Orlans 2, Houf
14-10	Holland	L 2-3	Antwerp	Fr	Willems.M, Houf
11-11	France	L 3-6	Paris	WCq	Houf, Willems.M 2
23-12	West Germany	L 1-4	Cologne	Fr	Moyson
31-03-1957	Spain	L 0-5	Brussels	Fr	
28-04	Holland	D 1-1	Amsterdam	Fr	Vandenberg.P
26-05	Romania	W 1-0	Brussels	Fr	Vandenberg.P
5-06	Iceland	W 8-3	Brussels	WCq	Orlans 2, Piters, Vandenberg.P, Coppens.R 2, Mees 2
4-09	Iceland	W 5-2	Reykjavik	WCq	Van Herpe, Vandenberg.P 3, Willems.M
27-10	France	D 0-0	Brussels	WCq	
17-11	Holland	L 2-5	Rotterdam	Fr	Vandenberg.P, Houf
8-12	Turkey	D 1-1	Ankara	Fr	Jurion
2-03-1958	West Germany	L 0-2	Brussels	Fr	
13-04	Holland	L 2-7	Antwerp	Fr	Coppens.R 2
26-05	Switzerland	W 2-0	Zurich	Fr	Stockman, Paeschen
28-09	Holland	L 2-3	Antwerp	Fr	Hanon, Piters
26-10	Turkey	D 1-1	Brussels	Fr	Piters
23-11	Hungary	L 1-3	Budapest	Fr	Mallants
1-03-1959	France	D 2-2	Paris	Fr	Lippens, Piters
19-04	Holland	D 2-2	Amsterdam	Fr	Wegria, Goyvaerts
24-05	Austria	L 0-2	Brussels	Fr	
14-06	Austria	L 2-4	Vienna	Fr	Vanden Voer, Coppens.R
4-10	Holland	L 1-9	Rotterdam	Fr	Delire
28-02-1960	France	W 1-0	Brussels	Fr	Piters
27-03	Switzerland	W 3-1	Brussels	Fr	Dirickx, Jadot, Ritzen
13-04	Chile	D 1-1	Brussels	Fr	Vandenberg.P
24-04	Holland	W 2-1	Antwerp	Fr	Lippens, Piters
22-05	Bulgaria	L 1-4	Sofia	Fr	Piters
2-10	Holland	L 1-4	Antwerp	Fr	Wegria
19-10	Sweden	L 0-2	Stockholm	WCq	
30-10	Hungary	W 2-1	Brussels	Fr	Van Himst, Hanon
20-11	Switzerland	L 2-4	Brussels	WCq	Van Himst, Paeschen
8-03-1961	West Germany	L 0-1	Frankfurt	Fr	
15-03	France	D 1-1	Paris	Fr	Paeschen
22-03	Holland	L 2-6	Rotterdam	Fr	Paeschen, Van Himst
20-05	Switzerland	L 1-2	Lausanne	WCq	Claessen.R
4-10	Sweden	L 0-2	Brussels	WCq	
18-10	France	W 3-0	Brussels	Fr	Hanon, Vandenberg.P, Claessen.R
12-11	Holland	W 4-0	Amsterdam	Fr	Claessen.R 2, Vandenberg.P, Van Himst
24-12	Bulgaria	W 4-0	Brussels	Fr	Stockman, Jurion, Van Himst 2
1-04-1962	Holland	W 3-1	Antwerp	Fr	Jurion, Vandenberg.P 2
13-05	Italy	L 1-3	Brussels	Fr	Van Himst
17-05	Portugal	W 2-1	Lisbon	Fr	Stockman, Jurion
23-05	Poland	L 0-2	Warsaw	Fr	
14-10	Holland	W 2-0	Antwerp	Fr	Stockman, Van Himst
4-11	Yugoslavia	L 2-3	Belgrade	ECr1	Stockman, Jurion
2-12	Spain	D 1-1	Brussels	Fr	Jurion
3-03-1963	Holland	W 1-0	Rotterdam	Fr	Vandenberg.P
31-03	Yugoslavia	L 0-1	Brussels	ECr1	
24-04	Brazil	W 5-1	Brussels	Fr	Stockman 3, Van Himst, OG
20-10	Holland	D 1-1	Amsterdam	Fr	Vandenberg.P
1-12	Spain	W 2-1	Valencia	Fr	Vandenberg.P, Puis
25-12	France	W 2-1	Paris	Fr	Van Himst 2
22-03-1964	Holland	D	0-0	Antwerp	Fr
15-04	Switzerland	L	0-2	Geneva	Fr
3-05	Portugal	L 1-2	Brussels	Fr	Vandenberg.P
30-09	Holland	W 1-0	Antwerp	Fr	Jurion
21-10	England	D 2-2	London	Fr	Cornelis, Van Himst
2-12	France	W 3-0	Brussels	Fr	Van Himst, Vermeyen 2
24-03-1965	Rep. Ireland	W 2-0	Dublin	Fr	OG, Jurion
7-04	Poland	D 0-0	Brussels	Fr	
9-05	Israel	W 1-0	Brussels	WCq	Jurion
2-06	Brazil	L 0-5	Rio de Janeiro	Fr	
26-09	Bulgaria	L 0-3	Sofia	WCq	
27-10	Bulgaria	W 5-0	Brussels	WCq	Van Himst 2, Thio 2, Stockman
10-11	Israel	W 5-0	Tel Aviv	WCq	Van Himst 3, Thio, Puis
29-12	Bulgaria	L 1-2	Florence	WCq	OG
17-04-1966	Holland	L 1-3	Rotterdam	Fr	Spronck

20-04	France	W 3-0	Paris	Fr	Lambert, Stockman, Thio
22-05	Soviet Union	L 0-1	Brussels	Fr	
25-05	Rep. Ireland	L 2-3	Liege	Fr	Van Himst, Vanden Boer
22-10	Switzerland	W 1-0	Bruges	Fr	Claessen.R
11-11	France	W 2-1	Brussels	ECq	Van Himst 2
19-03-1967	Luxembourg	W 5-0	Luxembourg	ECq	Van Himst 2, Stockman 3
16-04	Holland	W 1-0	Antwerp	Fr	Puis
21-05	Poland	L 1-3	Chorzow	ECq	Puis
8-10	Poland	L 2-4	Brussels	ECq	Devrindt 2
28-10	France	D 1-1	Nantes	ECq	Claessen.R
22-11	Luxembourg	W 3-0	Bruges	ECq	Thio 2, Claessen.R
10-01-1968	Israel	W 2-0	Tel Aviv	Fr	Devrindt, Puis
6-03	West Germany	L 1-3	Brussels	Fr	Devrindt
7-04	Holland	W 2-1	Amsterdam	Fr	Polleunis 2
24-04	Soviet Union	L 0-1	Moscow	Fr	
19-06	Finland	W 2-1	Helsinki	WCq	Devrindt, Polleunis
9-10	Finland	W 6-1	Waregem	WCq	Polleunis 3, Puis 2, Semmeling
16-10	Yugoslavia	W 3-0	Brussels	WCq	Devrindt 2, Polleunis
11-12	Spain	D 1-1	Madrid	WCq	Devrindt
23-02-1969	Spain	W 2-1	Liege	WCq	Devrindt 2
16-04	Mexico	W 2-0	Brussels	Fr	Puis, Van Himst
19-10	Yugoslavia	L 0-4	Skopje	WCq	
5-11	Mexico	L 0-1	Mexico City	Fr	
25-02-1970	England	L 1-3	Brussels	Fr	Dockx
3-06	El Salvador	W 3-0	Mexico City	WCr1	Van Moer 2, Lambert
6-06	Soviet Union	L 1-4	Mexico City	WCr1	Lambert
11-06	Mexico	L 0-1	Mexico City	WCr1	
15-11	France	L 1-2	Brussels	Fr	Van Moer
25-11	Denmark	W 2-0	Bruges	ECq	Devrindt 2
3-02-1971	Scotland	W 3-0	Liege	ECq	Van Himst 2, OG
17-02	Portugal	W 3-0	Brussels	ECq	Lambert 2, Denul
20-05	Luxembourg	W 4-0	Luxembourg	Fr	Denul, Van Himst, Semmeling, Van Moer
26-05	Denmark	W 2-1	Copenhagen	ECq	Devrindt 2
7-11	Luxembourg	W 1-0	Verviers	Fr	Van Den Daele
10-11	Scotland	L 0-1	Aberdeen	ECq	
21-11	Portugal	D 1-1	Lisbon	ECq	Lambert
29-04-1972	Italy	D 0-0	Milan	ECqf	
13-05	Italy	W 2-1	Brussels	ECqf	Van Moer, Van Himst
18-05	Iceland	W 4-0	Liege	WCq	Van Himst, Polleunis 3
22-05	Iceland	W 4-0	Bruges	WCq	Janssens.F, Lambert 2, Dockx
14-06	West Germany	L 1-2	Antwerp	ECsf	Polleunis
17-06	Hungary	W 2-1	Liege	EC3p	Lambert, Van Himst
4-10	Norway	W 2-0	Oslo	WCq	Dolmans, Lambert,
19-11	Holland	D 0-0	Antwerp	WCq	
18-04-1973	East Germany	W 3-0	Antwerp	Fr	Lambert 2, Dockx
31-10	Norway	W 2-0	Brussels	WCq	Dolmans, Lambert
18-11	Holland	D 0-0	Amsterdam	WCq	
13-03-1974	East Germany	L 0-1	Berlin	Fr	
17-04	Poland	D 1-1	Liege	Fr	Van Moer
1-05	Switzerland	W 1-0	Geneva	Fr	Van Herp
1-06	Scotland	W 2-1	Bruges	Fr	Henrotay, Lambert
8-09	Iceland	W 2-0	Reykjavik	ECq	Van Moer, Teugels
12-10	France	W 2-1	Brussels	ECq	Martens, Vander Elst
7-12	East Germany	D 0-0	Leipzig	ECq	
30-04-1975	Holland	W 1-0	Antwerp	Fr	Lambert
6-09	Iceland	W 1-0	Liege	ECq	Lambert
27-09	East Germany	L 1-2	Brussels	ECq	Pius
15-11	France	D 0-0	Paris	ECq	
25-04-1976	Holland	L 0-5	Rotterdam	ECqf	
22-05	Holland	L 1-2	Brussels	ECqf	Van Gool
5-09	Iceland	W 1-0	Reykjavik	WCq	Vander Elst
10-11	Nth. Ireland	W 2-0	Liege	WCq	Van Gool, Lambert
26-01-1977	Italy	L 1-2	Rome	Fr	Piot
26-03	Holland	L 0-2	Antwerp	WCq	
3-09	Iceland	W 4-0	Brussels	WCq	Van Binst, Martens, Courant, Lambert
26-10	Holland	L 0-1	Amsterdam	WCq	
16-11	Nth. Ireland	L 0-3	Belfast	WCq	
21-12	Italy	L 0-1	Liege	Fr	
22-03-1978	Austria	W 1-0	Charleroi	Fr	Geurts
19-04	East Germany	D 0-0	Magdeburg	Fr	
20-09	Norway	D 1-1	Lokeren	ECq	Cools

11-10	Portugal	D 1-1	Lisbon	ECq	Vercauteren
15-11	Israel	L 0-1	Tel Aviv	Fr	
28-03-1979	Austria	D 1-1	Brussels	ECq	Vandereycken
2-05	Austria	D 0-0	Vienna	ECq	
12-09	Norway	W 2-1	Oslo	ECq	Janssens.J, Vander Elst
26-09	Holland	L 0-1	Rotterdam	Fr	
17-10	Portugal	W 2-0	Brussels	ECq	Van Moer, Vander Elst
21-11	Scotland	W 2-0	Brussels	ECq	Vander Elst, Voordeckers
19-12	Scotland	W 3-1	Glasgow	ECq	Vandenbergh.E, Vander Elst 2
27-02-1980	Luxembourg	W 5-0	Brussels	Fr	Vandenbergh.E 2, Vandereyken, Vander Elst 2
18-03	Uruguay	W 2-0	Brussels	Fr	Verheyen, Vander Elst
2-04	Poland	W 2-1	Brussels	Fr	Coeck, Vandenbergh.E
6-06	Romania	W 2-1	Brussels	Fr	Ceulemans, Vander Elst
12-06	England	D 1-1	Turin	ECr1	Ceulemans
15-06	Spain	W 2-1	Milan	ECr1	Gerets, Cools
18-06	Italy	D 0-0	Rome	ECr1	
22-06	West Germany	L 1-2	Rome	ECf	Vandereycken
15-10	Rep. Ireland	D 1-1	Dublin	WCq	Cluytens
19-11	Holland	W 1-0	Brussels	WCq	Vandenbergh.E
21-12	Cyprus	W 2-0	Nicosia	WCq	Vandenbergh.E, Ceulemans
18-02-1981	Cyprus	W 3-2	Brussels	WCq	Plessers, Vandenbergh.E, Ceulemans
25-03	Rep. Ireland	W 1-0	Brussels	WCq	Ceulemans
29-04	France	L 2-3	Paris	WCq	Vandenbergh.E, Ceulemans
9-09	France	W 2-0	Brussels	WCq	Czerniatynski, Vandenbergh.E
14-10	Holland	L 0-3	Rotterdam	WCq	
16-12	Spain	L 0-2	Valencia	Fr	
24-03-1982	Romania	W 4-1	Brussels	Fr	Verheyen 2, Czerniatynski 2
28-04	Bulgaria	W 2-1	Brussels	Fr	Vandenbergh.E, Van Moer
27-05	Denmark	L 0-1	Copenhagen	Fr	
13-06	Argentina	W 1-0	Barcelona	WCr1	Vandenbergh.E
19-06	El Salvador	W 1-0	Elche	WCr1	Coeck
22-06	Hungary	D 1-1	Elche	WCr1	Czerniatynski
28-06	Poland	L 0-3	Barcelona	WCr2	
1-07	Soviet Union	L 0-1	Barcelona	WCr2	
22-09	West Germany	D 0-0	Munich	Fr	
6-10	Switzerland	W 3-0	Brussels	ECq	Vercauteren, Coeck, Vandenbergh.E
15-12	Scotland	W 3-2	Brussels	ECq	Vandenbergh.E, Vander Elst 2
30-03-1983	East Germany	W 2-1	Leipzig	ECq	Vander Elst, Vandenbergh.E
27-04	East Germany	W 2-1	Brussels	ECq	Ceulemans, Coeck
31-05	France	D 1-1	Luxembourg	Fr	Voordeckers
21-09	Holland	D 1-1	Brussels	Fr	Voordeckers
12-10	Scotland	D 1-1	Glasgow	ECq	Vercauteren
9-11	Switzerland	L 1-3	Berne	ECq	Vandenbergh.E
29-02-1984	West Germany	L 0-1	Brussels	Fr	
17-04	Poland	W 1-0	Warsaw	Fr	Czerniatynski
6-06	Hungary	D 2-2	Brussels	Fr	Ceulemans 2
13-06	Yugoslavia	W 2-0	Lens	ECr1	Vandenbergh.E, Grün
16-06	France	L 0-5	Nantes	ECr1	
19-06	Denmark	L 2-3	Strasbourg	ECr1	Ceulemans, Vercauteren
5-09	Argentina	L 0-2	Brussels	Fr	
17-10	Albania	W 3-1	Brussels	WCq	Claesen.N, Scifo, Voordeckers
19-12	Greece	D 0-0	Athens	WCq	
22-12	Albania	L 0-2	Tirana	WCq	
27-03-1985	Greece	W 2-0	Brussels	WCq	Vercauteren, Scifo
1-05	Poland	W 2-0	Brussels	WCq	Vandenbergh.E, Vercauteren
11-09	Poland	D 0-0	Chorzow	WCq	
16-10	Holland	W 1-0	Brussels	WCq	Vercauteren
20-11	Holland	L 1-2	Rotterdam	WCq	Grün
19-02-1986	Spain	L 0-3	Elche	Fr	
23-04	Bulgaria	W 2-0	Brussels	Fr	De Smet, Vandenbergh.E
19-05	Yugoslavia	L 1-3	Brussels	Fr	Claesen.N
3-06	Mexico	L 1-2	Mexico City	WCr1	Vandenbergh.E
8-06	Iraq	W 2-1	Toluca	WCr1	Scifo, Claesen.N
11-06	Paraguay	D 2-2	Toluca	WCr1	Vercauteren, Veyt
15-06	Soviet Union	W 4-3	Leon	WCr2	Scifo, Ceulemans, Demol, Claesen.N
22-06	Spain	D 1-1	Puebla	WCqf	Ceulemans
25-06	Argentina	L 0-2	Mexico City	WCsf	
28-06	France	L 2-4	Puebla	WC3p	Ceulemans, Claesen.N
10-09	Rep. Ireland	D 2-2	Brussels	ECq	Claesen.N, Scifo
14-10	Luxembourg	W 6-0	Luxembourg	ECq	Gerets, Claesen.N 3, Vercauteren, Ceulemans
19-11	Bulgaria	D 1-1	Brussels	ECq	Janssen

Date	Opponent	Result	Venue	Comp	Scorers
4-02-1987	Portugal	L 0-1	Braga	Fr	
1-04	Scotland	W 4-1	Brussels	ECq	Claesen.N 3, Vercauteren
29-04	Rep. Ireland	D 0-0	Dublin	ECq	
9-09	Holland	D 0-0	Rotterdam	Fr	
23-09	Bulgaria	L 0-2	Sofia	ECq	
14-10	Scotland	L 0-2	Glasgow	ECq	
11-11	Luxembourg	W 3-0	Brussels	ECq	Ceulemans, Degryse, Creve
19-01-1988	Israel	W 3-2	Tel Aviv	Fr	Degryse, Van der Linden, Grün
26-03	Hungary	W 3-0	Brussels	Fr	Ceulemans, OG, Severeyns
4-06	Denmark	L 1-3	Odense	Fr	Ceulemans
12-10	Brazil	L 1-2	Antwerp	Fr	Clijsters
19-10	Switzerland	W 1-0	Brussels	WCq	Vervoort
16-11	Czechoslovakia	D 0-0	Bratislava	WCq	
15-02-1989	Portugal	D 1-1	Lisbon	WCq	Gerets
29-04	Czechoslovakia	W 2-1	Brussels	WCq	Degryse 2
27-05	Yugoslavia	W 1-0	Brussels	Fr	Van der Linden
1-06	Luxembourg	W 5-0	Lille	WCq	Van der Linden 4, Vervoort
8-06	Canada	W 2-0	Ottawa	Fr	Ceulemans, Degryse
24-08	Denmark	W 3-0	Bruges	Fr	Degryse, Ceulemans 2
6-09	Portugal	W 3-0	Brussels	WCq	Ceulemans, Van der Linden 2
11-10	Switzerland	D 2-2	Basle	WCq	Degryse, OG
25-10	Luxembourg	D 1-1	Brussels	WCq	Versavel
17-01-1990	Greece	L 0-2	Athens	Fr	
21-02	Sweden	D 0-0	Brussels	Fr	
26-05	Romania	D 2-2	Brussels	Fr	Scifo, Clijsters
2-06	Mexico	W 3-0	Brussels	Fr	Degryse 2, Versavel
6-06	Poland	D 1-1	Brussels	Fr	Emmers
12-06	South Korea	W 2-0	Verona	WCr1	Degryse, De Wolf
17-06	Uruguay	W 3-1	Verona	WCr1	Clijsters, Scifo, Ceulemans
21-06	Spain	L 1-2	Verona	WCr1	Vervoort
26-06	England	L 0-1	Bologna	WCr2	
12-09	East Germany	L 0-2	Brussels	Fr	
17-10	Wales	L 1-3	Cardiff	ECq	Versavel
13-02-1991	Italy	D 0-0	Terni	Fr	
27-02	Luxembourg	W 3-0	Brussels	ECq	Vandenbergh.E, Ceulemans, Scifo
27-03	Wales	D 1-1	Brussels	ECq	Degryse
1-05	Germany	L 0-1	Hanover	ECq	
11-09	Luxembourg	W 2-0	Luxembourg	ECq	Scifo, Degryse
9-10	Hungary	W 2-0	Szekesfehervar	Fr	Emmens, Scifo
20-11	Germany	L 0-1	Brussels	ECq	
26-02-1992	Tunisia	L 1-2	Tunis	Fr	Oliveira
25-03	France	D 3-3	Paris	Fr	Albert, Scifo, Wilmots
22-04	Cyprus	W 1-0	Brussels	WCq	Wilmots
3-06	Faeroe Islands	W 3-0	Toftir	WCq	Albert, Wilmots 2
2-09	Czechoslovakia	W 2-1	Prague	WCq	OG, Czerniatynski
14-10	Romania	W 1-0	Brussels	WCq	Smidts
18-11	Wales	W 2-0	Brussels	WCq	Staelens, Degryse
13-02-1993	Cyprus	W 3-0	Nicosia	WCq	Scifo 2, Albert
31-03	Wales	L 0-2	Cardif	WCq	
22-05	Faeroe Islands	W 3-0	Brussels	WCq	Wilmots 2, Scifo
6-10	Gabon	W 2-1	Brussels	Fr	Wilmots 2
13-10	Romania	L 1-2	Bucharest	WCq	Scifo
17-11	Czechoslovakia	D 0-0	Brussels	WCq	
16-02-1994	Malta	L 0-1	Ta'Qali	Fr	
4-06	Zambia	W 9-0	Brussels	Fr	Weber 5, Degryse 3, Nilis
8-06	Hungary	W 3-1	Brussels	Fr	Weber, Degryse, Nilis
19-06	Morocco	W 1-0	Orlando	WCr1	Degryse
25-06	Holland	W 1-0	Orlando	WCr1	Albert
29-06	Saudi Arabia	L 0-1	Washington	WCr1	
2-07	Germany	L 2-3	Chicago	WCr2	Grün, Albert
7-09	Armenia	W 2-0	Brussels	ECq	OG, Degryse
12-10	Denmark	L 1-3	Copenhagen	ECq	Degryse
16-11	Macedonia	D 1-1	Brussels	ECq	Verheyen
17-12	Spain	L 1-4	Brussels	ECq	Degryse
29-03-1995	Spain	D 1-1	Seville	ECq	Degryse
22-04	United States	W 1-0	Brussels	Fr	Schepens
26-04	Cyprus	W 2-0	Brussels	ECq	Karagiannis, Schepens
7-06	Macedonia	W 5-0	Skopje	ECq	Grün, Scifo 2, Schepens, Versavel

BOSNIA-HERCEGOVINA

Bosnia is not a member of UEFA, nor is there much football played there at present, but the war-ravaged country has a proud football tradition from its time as part of the Yugoslav state. The capital Sarajevo had championship-winning sides in all three decades before the 1990s, whilst both Velez Mostar and Bora Banja Luka are former winners of the Yugoslav Cup.

There are Bosnians playing in leagues around Europe, the likes of Faruk Hadzibegic and Mehmed Bazdanovic, both regulars in the old Yugoslav side. However, the only football to be played in Sarajevo since independence is the occasional match against the United Nations peacekeepers.

Population: 4,479,000
Area, sq km: 51,129
Capital city: Sarajevo

THE RECORD

WORLD CUP
1930-94 Did not enter

EUROPEAN CHAMPIONSHIP
1960-96 Did not enter

EUROPEAN CLUB COMPETITIONS

European Cup
2nd round - FK Sarajevo 1968

Cup Winners Cup
2nd round - Borac Banja Luka 1976 Velez Mostar 1982 1987

UEFA Cup
Semi-finalists - Zeljeznicar Sarajevo 1985

CLUB DIRECTORY

SARAJEVO (Population - 479,000)

FK Sarajevo (1946)
Kosevo 45,000 – Claret/Claret

FK Zeljeznicar Sarajevo (1921)
Grbavica 26,000 – Sky Blue/Sky blue

BANJA LUKA (Population - 193,000)

FK Borac Banja Luka (1926)
Gradski 18,000 – Red/Blue

ZENICA (Population - 144,000)

FK Celik Zenica (1945)
Bilino Polje 22,000 – Red/Black

TUZLA (Population - 129,000)

FK Sloboda Tuzla (1919)
Tusanj 11,000 – Red and black stripes/Black

MOSTAR (Population - 110,000)

FK Velez Mostar (1922)
Gradski 21,000 – Red/Red

BULGARIA

As was the case in most Eastern bloc countries, Bulgarian football benefited enormously from the communist takeover in 1944. Before then, the standard was very poor and the game not taken very seriously. There had been a league and a cup for clubs, and the national team took part regularly in the Balkan Cup, but it was not until after 1944 that the first grass pitch was laid.

In typical communist fashion, football was organised from top to bottom. New training techniques were introduced and players became 'professionals', if not in name then in outlook. Yet this approach was ultimately to lead to the stagnation of the game. 'The system' produced many fine footballers, and the Bulgars were almost impossible to beat in Sofia in the 1960s, but as the leading players cast their eyes to the fabulous sums being earned by their counterparts in the West, a decline set in that left the game once again among the weakest on the continent.

Popular legend has it that football first made an appearance in the country when a certain Georges de Regibus came to Bulgaria in 1894. He was a Swiss physical education teacher, and he used football as part of his warm-up routine at the boys' middle school in Varna. Indeed the Black Sea resort of Varna has always been regarded as the hotbed of Bulgarian football in these early years.

Political events in the Balkan region, however, held up the development of the game. After independence in 1908, Bulgaria became involved in the two Balkan Wars of 1912 and 1913. The area was referred to as the 'powder keg of Europe', so it was not surprising that sport did not have a very high priority. Indeed any sports club was officially frowned upon, so great credit must go to players like Stefan Naumov, a prominent figure in Sofia, for their perseverance. He organised the first inter-town match in 1912, a team from Plovdiv beating his Sofia side 4-0.

Sofia, due to its size and importance, began to take over from Varna as the leading force behind the game. In 1913, a group of the leading Sofia players, led by Dimiter Blagoyev and Boris Sharankov, formed Slavia, the oldest surviving club in the league, whilst in 1914 a group of teenage enthusiasts started Levski, a team that was destined to become one of the most successful and best supported clubs in the country. By the early 1920s, the political situation in the Balkans had stabilised, and the mounting popularity of the game meant that proper organisation was required. In 1923 the Bulgarian National Sports Federation was founded, of which the Football Federation formed a part, and the following year a successful application to FIFA was submitted.

By 1923 numerous clubs had sprung up around the country and disorganised regional leagues had already been formed. On 31 July 1921, ten clubs in Sofia created the Sofia sports league, whilst on the same day the Northern league was formed in Varna. After an abortive attempt at a national championship in 1924, a competition took place the following year involving the winners of the leagues from Sofia, Plovdiv, Varna, Burgas, Kyustendil and Vratsa. It was won by Vladislav Varna.

This formula continued until 1937 when for the first time

a single league of the top 10 clubs was introduced. This lasted only 3 seasons, however, before the war forced a return to the regional leagues. In 1944 football was suspended altogether when Russian troops marched into the country, but that period from 1925 to 1943 was an era of great equality in terms of honours won in the league. No fewer than nine teams won the title, though all bar one of them came from either Sofia or Varna. In 1938 a knock-out competition was introduced. Formulated along the lines of the English cup in that any team could compete, it has, unlike those of many other countries, always been a very popular tournament. Five editions of it were played before it was suspended in 1943 and all five were won by teams from Sofia.

Bulgaria's baptism in international football can only be described as disastrous. They lost their first match 6-0 away to a powerful Austrian team, proceeded to lose their next six, and failed to win until their 15th game some six years later. Most of their games before 1943 were played against their neighbours in the Balkans and when they did venture out they were usually given sound thrashings by Europe's strongest nations. Results like the 13-0 defeat by Spain meant that the team were unwilling to take on the more advanced nations any more than necessary. Instead, the Balkan Cup proved a popular arena for games as Bulgaria won the tournament twice before the war.

The lure of the World Cup proved too strong to resist even though the Bulgarians knew they were one of the weakest sides. An application was made to take part in the second tournament in 1934 and they were drawn in a qualifying group that included Austria and Hungary, both major powers in Europe. The gulf in class was illustrated as the Bulgarians crashed twice to the Hungarians and once to the Austrians. In the 1938 competition their opponents were Czechoslovakia, the runners-up in 1934. The first match in Sofia was probably Bulgaria's finest pre-war result. They held the Czechs to a 1-1 draw but alas to no avail as they were humbled 6-0 in the return in Prague five months later. The most famous player of this era was Luibomir Angelov. Although he scored 25 goals Bulgaria's overall pre-war record was very poor.

After falling into the hands of the Nazis early on in the war, Bulgaria was 'liberated' by the Soviets in 1944. The high priority given by the Communist government to sport slowly transformed the football scene as large funds were made available for facilities and coaching. The championship was resumed in 1945, but in 1948 the whole system was reorganised. A single first division of 10 teams was established, though this has crept up over the years to 16. This formed the apex of a league pyramid that included every team in the country right down to the junior teams.

The other significant influence of state socialism could be seen in the actual composition of the clubs themselves. After the war each club came under the control of one official body or another. Each city had their representative for the Army, the Police, the railway workers and other industries, but Sofia clubs have always remained dominant. Levski, for a long time the team of the Interior Ministry, struggled to maintain a challenge to CSKA, the Army team, who, as they formed the basis of the national team, were given every advantage. In their first 15 years CSKA won the title a staggering 12 times. Indeed they have only once ever finished outside the top five, a disastrous 11th in 1964.

The CSKA side of the 1950s is regarded as the best club side the country has ever produced. It included such great names as Ivan Kolev, widely acclaimed as the best Bulgarian player of his time, as well as Stefan Bojkov, Manol Manolov, Georgy Naidenov and Dimiter Milanov. By the early 1960s CSKA were forced to rebuild, however, and the league briefly became an open affair. In five consecutive seasons five different teams triumphed, whilst in the space of seven years five different teams won the cup. By the end of the decade, however, events were back to normal with CSKA and Levski-Spartak passing the title back and forth between them.

Two events have shaped Bulgarian league football since then. First, after violent incidents in the 1985 Cup final between CSKA and Levski, both clubs were officially disbanded. They did resurface under different names, Sredets and Vitosha respectively, but are now back with their original names and continue to dominate the league. Of more lasting significance was the decision to let players move abroad, which has considerably weakened the league. There has, however, been a positive knock-on effect for the national side.

Since 1945 Bulgaria have taken great strides in international football. For a 15-year spell in the 1960s and 1970s, they were one of the top dozen countries in Europe. After the war, the Bulgarians were limited at first to matches against other communist countries - not until a World Cup match in 1957 against Norway did they leave the seclusion of Eastern Europe.

The Bulgarian approach was to build physically strong teams that could conform to a set pattern of play. As a result Bulgaria have always been tricky opponents but were thought to lack the flair and flexibility that could have made them a very successful team. Before the 1994 World Cup in America, they held one of the competition's most unwanted records: in five appearances in the finals, they failed to win a game in 16 attempts.

During the 1950s, the national team was in essence the CSKA team with Ivan Kolev, and Stefan Bojkov the captain, at the helm. Their results varied. Failure to qualify for the 1954 and 1958 World Cups was countered by a bronze medal at the Melbourne Olympics in 1956, but it was not until the end of the decade that the first real signs came that all the effort being afforded to football was beginning to pay off.

THE ORDER OF MERIT

	Team	All G	All S	All B	League G	League S	League B	Cup G	Cup S	SAC G	SAC S	Europe G	Europe S	Europe B
1	CSKA Sofia	47	22	4	27	13	1	6	3	14	6	-	-	3
2	Levski Sofia	45	33	7	19	25	7	9	2	17	6	-	-	-
3	Slavia Sofia	12	11	12	6	9	11	-	-	6	2	-	-	1
4	Lokomotiv Sofia	8	10	6	4	7	6	1	-	3	3	-	-	-
5	Botev Plovdiv	5	11	10	3	2	10	-	4	2	5	-	-	-
6	Ch. More Varna	4	8	2	4	6	2	-	-	-	2	-	-	-
7	Spartak Plovdiv	2	4	-	1	1	-	-	-	1	3	-	-	-
8	Et. Veliko Tarnovo	2	-	1	1	-	1	-	-	1	-	-	-	-
9	AC 23 Sofia	2	-	-	1	-	-	1	-	-	-	-	-	-
10	Lokomotiv Plovdiv	1	5	2	-	1	2	-	-	1	4	-	-	-
11	Ber. Stara Zagora	1	4	1	1	-	1	-	-	-	4	-	-	-
12	Spartak Varna	1	4	1	1	2	1	-	1	-	1	-	-	-
13	SC Sofia	1	1	-	1	1	-	-	-	-	-	-	-	-
14	Mar. St. Dimitrov	1	-	1	-	-	1	-	-	1	-	-	-	-
	Shipka Sofia	1	-	1	-	-	1	1	-	-	-	-	-	-
	Sliven	1	-	1	-	-	1	1	-	-	-	-	-	-
17	Dunav Ruse	-	5	-	-	1	-	-	3	-	1	-	-	-
18	Pirin Blagoevgrad	-	3	1	-	-	1	-	2	-	1	-	-	-
19	Sportclub Plovdiv	-	2	-	-	-	-	-	2	-	-	-	-	-
20	Akademic Sofia	-	1	2	-	-	2	-	-	-	1	-	-	-
21	Spartak Pleven	-	1	1	-	-	1	-	-	-	1	-	-	-
22	Chern. Burgas	-	1	-	-	-	-	-	1	-	-	-	-	-
	Chern. Popovo	-	1	-	-	-	-	-	-	-	1	-	-	-
	Chirpan	-	1	-	-	-	-	-	-	-	1	-	-	-
	Dorostol	-	1	-	-	-	-	-	-	-	1	-	-	-
	Macedonia Skoplje	-	1	-	-	1	-	-	-	-	-	-	-	-
	Mar. Istok Radnevo	-	1	-	-	-	-	-	-	-	1	-	-	-
	Minyor Pernik	-	1	-	-	-	-	-	-	-	1	-	-	-
	Neftokhimik Burgas	-	1	-	-	-	-	-	-	-	1	-	-	-
30	Botev Vratsa	-	-	1	-	-	1	-	-	-	-	-	-	-

To the end of the 1994-1995 season

Bulgaria qualified for the World Cup finals for the first time when a 1-0 win over France in a play-off sent them to Chile in 1962. It was to be the first of four consecutive appearances in the finals, but each time was to prove a severe disappointment. Their poor showing in Chile was put down to inexperience of the big occasion, but matters did not improve four years later in the finals in England. Bad tactics and an injury to the inspirational Georgi Asparuhov, who had scored their only goal in Chile four years previously, sent the team home after three defeats.

The late 1960s probably saw the side at its peak. The prolific Hristo Bonev broke into the team in this period along with players such as Petar Jekov. The disappointment of an unfortunate defeat at the hands of Italy in the quarter-finals of the 1968 European Championships was assuaged by a silver medal at the Mexico Olympics later that summer, and qualification for their third successive World Cup finals in Mexico in 1970 was greeted with real optimism and hope. Indeed Bulgaria's performance this time was far more creditable and although they again failed to win a match and progress beyond the first round, their tally of 5 goals from 3 games was an improvement. If Asparuhov, again carrying an injury, had been fully fit, matters may have turned out differently, but at least Bulgaria had made their contribution to the general spirit in which this tournament was played.

In 1971, however, Asparuhov was killed in a car crash along with his international team-mate Nikola Kotkov. Although the team still managed to qualify for the next World Cup in West Germany thanks largely to the presence of Bonev, they left the finals this time without much credit, again failing to win a match.

The game in Bulgaria entered a long period of decline after 1974 and after a particularly poor qualifying campaign for the 1980 European Championships the entire governing body was sacked. Despite making it to the finals of the 1986 World Cup in Mexico, the Bulgarians again came away without a win, though bizarrely this did not prevent them from qualifying for the second round.

The fall of the Communist government may have left the league in Bulgaria weaker, but since the mass emigration of the top players in the 1990s the national team has been the main beneficiary. Players such as Hristo Stoichkov have found fame and fortune outside Bulgaria – a European Cup winner with Barcelona in 1992, he was voted European Footballer of the Year in 1994.

The Bulgarians qualified for USA '94 thanks to a goal by Emil Kostadinov in the last minute of their final qualifiying match against France, but after a 3-0 defeat in their opening game of the finals against Nigeria, it looked as if yet more disappointment was in store. Instead, victory over Greece in the next game finally broke their infamous sequence and superb displays followed as both Argentina and Germany were beaten on the way to the semi-final. There the Bulgarians finally bowed out to Italy, but they had finally laid their World Cup jinx to rest.

Population: 8,997,000
Area, sq km: 110,994
% in urban areas: 67.6%
Capital city: Sofia

Bulgarski Futbolen Soius
ul. Karnigradska 19
1000 Sofia
Bulgaria
Tel: + 359 2 877490
Fax: + 359 2 803237

Year of formation	1923
Affiliation to FIFA	1924
Affiliation to UEFA	1954
Registered clubs	23 000
Registered players	441 300
Professional players	600
Registered coaches	2390
Registered referees	1124
National stadium	Vasilij Levski 70 000
National colours	White with green and red trimmings/ Green/Red
Reserve colours	Red/White/White
Season	August - June, with a mid season break December - February

THE RECORD

WORLD CUP

1930	Did not enter
1934	QT 3rd/3 in group 8
1938	QT Failed to qualify
1950	Did not enter
1954	QT 3rd/3 in group 8
1958	QT 2nd/3 in group 3
1962	QT 1st/3 in group 2 - Final Tournament/1st round
1966	QT 1st/3 in group 1 - Final Tournament/1st round

1970	QT 1st/4 in group 8 - Final Tournament/1st round
1974	QT 1st/4 in group 6 - Final Tournament/1st round
1978	QT 2nd/4 in group 5
1982	QT 3rd/5 in group 1
1986	QT 2nd/5 in group 4 - Final Tournament/2nd round
1990	QT 4th/4 in group 1
1994	QT 2nd/6 in group 6 - Final Tournament/Semi-finalists/4th place

EUROPEAN CHAMPIONSHIP

1960	1st round
1964	2nd round
1968	QT 1st/4 in group 2 - Final Tournament/Quarter-finalists
1972	QT 2nd/4 in group 2
1976	QT 3rd/4 in group 8
1980	QT 4th/5 in group 1
1984	QT 3rd/4 in group 4
1988	QT 2nd/5 in group 7
1992	QT 4th/5 in group 2
1996	QT group 7

EUROPEAN CLUB COMPETITIONS

European Cup
Semi-finalists - CSKA Sofia 1967 1982

Cup Winners Cup
Semi-finalists - Slavia Sofia 1967 CSKA Sofia 1989

UEFA Cup
Quarter-finalists - Levski-Spartak 1976 Lokomotiv Sofia 1980

CLUB DIRECTORY

SOFIA (Population - 1,217,000)

CSKA Sofia (1948)
Norodna Armia 30,000 – Red/White, white trimmings
Previous names - Septemvri CDW 1948-49, Narodna Voiska 1949-50, CDNA 1950-64, CSKA-CZ 1964-69, CSKA 1969-85, Sredets 1985-87, CFKA Sredets 1987-1989. Septemvri CDW split away in 1957 but rejoined in 1969

FC Levski Sofia (1914)
Georgi Asparuhov 60,000 – Blue/Blue, white trimmings
Previous names - Levski 1914-49, Dinamo 1949-57, Levski 1957-69, Levski-Spartak 1969-85, Vitosha 1985-1989. Spartak Sofia with whom Levski merged in 1969 were called Iskra 1907-11, Rakovski 1911-13, FK 13 1913-45, Rakovski 1945-47, Spartak 1947-69

FC Lokomotiv Sofia (1929)
Lokomotiv 25,000 – Red & black stripes/Black
Previous names - JSK Sofia 1929-45, Lokomotiv 1945-49, Torpedo 1949-50. In 1969 Lokomotiv merged with Slavia to become Lokomotiv JSK, but the two clubs separated in 1971

FC Slavia Sofia (1913)
Slavia 32,000 – White/White, black trimmings
Previous names - Slavia 1913-49, Strojtel 1949-51, Udarnik 1951-57

Akademik Sofia (1947)
Akademik 15,000 – Blue/Blue

PLOVDIV (Population - 364,000)

FC Botev Plovdiv (1912)
Cristo Botev 40,000 – Yellow & black chequered/Black
Previous names - Botev 1912-44, Shipka 1944-47, Botev 1947-51, DNW 1951-55, SKNA 1955-56, 1956-67 Botev, Trakia 1967-1990. Botev merged with Spartak and Akademik in 1967, but Spartak broke away in 1982

FC Lokomotiv Plovdiv (1936)
Lokomotiv 25,000 – Black & white stripes/Black
Previous names - JSK, JSK Levski, Slavia and Torpedo

FC Spartak Plovdiv (1947)
Spartak 12,000 – Blue and white stripes/Blue
Previous names - Levski and Udarnik. Merged with Botev as Trakia from 1967-82

VARNA (Population - 306,000)

FC Cherno More Varna (1913)
Cherno More 12,000 – Green/Green - White trimmings
Previous names - Ticha (1913) and Vladislav (1921) merged in 1945 to become TV'45. Botev Varna 1948-50, VUS 1950-56, SKNA 1956-57

FC Spartak Varna (1914)
Spartak 12,000 – Blue/Blue
Previous names - Shipenski Sokol. Merged in 1969 with Lokomotiv to become JSK Spartak, but broke away in 1986

BURGAS (Population - 200,000)

FC Chernomorets Burgas (1916)
Chernomorets 24,000 – Blue/Blue - White trimmings
Previous names - Merger in 1969 of Lokomotiv and Botev

FC Neftochimik Burgas (1932)
Neftochimik 12,000 – Green/Green

RUSE (Population - 190,000)

FC Dunav Ruse (1919)
Gradski 25,000 – Blue/Blue
Previous names - Cava, Levski and Napradek

STARA ZAGORA (Population - 158,000)

FC Beroe Stara Zagora (1916)
Beroe 24,000 – White with thick green stripe/White, red trimmings
Previous names - Merger (1956) of Botev, DNA & Spartak. Lokomotiv joined 1958.

PLEVEN (Population - 136,000)

FC Spartak Pleven (1919)
Slavi Aleksejev 20,000 – Blue/White
Previous names - Skobelev, Pobeda, SP'39

SLIVEN (Population - 104,000)

FC Sliven (1914)
Hadji Dimitar 25,000 – Orange/Blue
Previous names - Sportist, DNA, SKNA

PERNIK (Population - 96,000)

FC Minyor Pernik (1919)
Minyor 20,000 – Yellow/Black
Previous names - Minyor 1952-62, Krakara 1962-70, Pernik 1970-73

VELIKO TARNOVO (Population - 70,000)

FC Etar Veliko Tarnovo (1924)
Ivailo 18,000 – Violet/Violet, white trimmings
Previous names - Trapezita, Udarnik, Cerweno Zname, Spartak and DNA

GORNA ORIAHOVISTA

FC Lokomotiv GO (1922)
Lokomotiv 10,000 – Black & white stripes/Black
Previous names - Levski, JSK, Nikolo Petrov, Torpedo

BLAGOEVGRAD (Population - 67,000)

FC Pirin Blagoevgrad (1934)
Cristo Botev 20,000 – Green/Green, white trimmings
Previous names - Botev, Macedonia, Torpedo, Strojtel

VRATSA (Population - 77,000)

Botev Vratsa (1921)
Cristo Botev 28,000 – Red/Black

SHUMEN

FC Shumen (1919)
Panaiot Volov 30,000 – Yellow/Blue, blue trimmings

BULGARIAN LEAGUE CHAMPIONSHIP

1925	Vladislav Varna	2-0	Levski Sofia
1926	Vladislav Varna	1-1	Slavia Sofia
1927	-		
1928	Slavia Sofia	4-0	Vladislav Varna
1929	Botev Plovdiv	1-0	Levski Sofia
1930	Slavia Sofia	4-1	Vladislav Varna
1931	AC 23 Sofia	3-0	Shipenski Sokol
1932	Shipenski Sokol	2-1	Slavia Sofia
1933	Levski Sofia	3-1	Shipenski Sokol
1934	Vladislav Varna	2-0	Slavia Sofia
1935	SC Sofia	4-0	Ticha Varna

1936	Slavia Sofia	2-0	Ticha Varna
1937	Levski Sofia	1-1 3-0	Levski Ruse

	Champions	Runners-up	3rd
1938h	Ticha Varna 25	Vladislav Varna 22	Shipka Sofia 22
1939	Slavia Sofia 23	Vladislav Varna 22	Ticha Varna 22
1940	JSK Sofia 23	Levski Sofia 22	Slavia Sofia 22

1941	Slavia Sofia	0-0 2-1	JSK Sofia
1942	Levski Sofia	2-0 1-0	Macedonia Skoplje
1943	Slavia Sofia	1-0 1-0	Levski Sofia
1944	-		
1945	Lokomotiv Sofia	3-1 1-1	SC Sofia
1946	Levski Sofia	1-0 1-0	Lokomotiv Sofia
1947	Levski Sofia	1-1 1-0	Lokomotiv Sofia
1948	Septemvri CDW	1-2 3-1	Levski Sofia

	Champions	Runners-up	3rd
1949h	Levski Sofia 33	Septemvri CDW 24	Lokomotiv Sofia 21
1950	Dinamo Sofia 29	Strojtel Sofia 27	Akademic Sofia 22
1951k	CDNA Sofia 37	Spartak Sofia 36	Dinamo Sofia 26
1952	CDNA Sofia 33	Spartak Sofia 26	Lokomotiv Sofia 25
1953p	Dinamo Sofia 43	CDNA Sofia 42	VUS Varna 31
1954n	CDNA Sofia 45	Udarnik Sofia 38	Lokomotiv Sofia 36
1955	CDNA Sofia 37	Udarnik Sofia 31	Spartak Varna 28
1956k	CDNA Sofia 31	Dinamo Sofia 26	SKNA Plovdiv 25
1957	CDNA Sofia 34	Lokomotiv Sofia 33	Levski Sofia 30
1958af	CDNA Sofia 18	Levski Sofia 14	Spartak Pleven 14
1959k	CDNA Sofia 32	Slavia Sofia 27	Levski Sofia 24
1960	CDNA Sofia 32	Levski Sofia 28	Lokomoti Sofia 23
1961n	CDNA Sofia 40	Levski Sofia 30	Botev Plovdiv 29
1962	CDNA Sofia 41	Spartak Plovdiv 35	Levski Sofia 30
1963q	Spartak Plovdiv 43	Botev Plovdiv 40	CDNA Sofia 37
1964	Lokomotiv Sofia 44	Levski Sofia 41	Slavia Sofia 35
1965	Levski Sofia 42	Lokomotiv Sofia 39	Slavia Sofia 35
1966	CSKA-CZ Sofia 42	Levski Sofia 41	Slavia Sofia 39
1967	Botev Plovdiv 38	Slavia Sofia 37	Levski Sofia 36
1968	Levski Sofia 45	CSKA-CZ Sofia 42	Lokomotiv Sofia 40
1969p	CSKA Sofia 47	Levski-Spartak 40	Lokomotiv Plovdiv 39
1970	Levski-Spartak 50	CSKA Sofia 44	Slavia Sofia 34
1971q	CSKA Sofia 48	Levski-Spartak 48	Botev Vratsa 38
1972t	CSKA Sofia 58	Levski-Spartak 50	Beroe Stara Zagora 42
1973	CSKA Sofia 51	Lokomotiv Plovdiv 43	Slavia Sofia 43
1974q	Levski-Spartak 47	CSKA Sofia 46	Lokomotiv Plovdiv 34
1975	CSKA Sofia 39	Levski-Spartak 38	Slavia Sofia 36
1976	CSKA Sofia 43	Levski-Spartak 41	Akademic Sofia 37
1977	Levski-Spartak 43	CSKA Sofia 39	Marek St. Dimitrov 38
1978	Lokomotiv Sofia 42	CSKA Sofia 41	Levski-Spartak 38
1979	Levski-Spartak 43	CSKA Sofia 40	Lokomotiv Sofia 37
1980	CSKA Sofia 46	Slavia Sofia 45	Levski-Spartak 37
1981	CSKA Sofia 40	Levski-Spartak 36	Trakia Plovdiv 35
1982	CSKA Sofia 47	Levski-Spartak 46	Slavia Sofia 35
1983	CSKA Sofia 45	Levski-Spartak 42	Trakia Plovdiv 36
1984	Levski-Spartak 47	CSKA Sofia 45	Sliven 31
1985	Trakia Plovdiv 33	Lokomotiv Sofia 33	Pirin Blagoevgrad 31
1986	Beroe Stara Zagora 43	Trakia Plovdiv 41	Slavia Sofia 36
1987	CFKA Sredets 47	Vitosha Sofia 44	Trakia Plovdiv 39
1988	Vitosha Sofia 48	CFKA Sredets 46	Trakia Plovdiv 39
1989	CFKA Sredets 48	Vitosha Sofia 39	Etar Veliko Tarnovo 34
1990	CSKA Sofia 47	Levski Sofia 36	Slavia Sofia 36
1991	Etar Veliko Tarnovo 44	CSKA Sofia 37	Slavia Sofia 37
1992	CSKA Sofia 47	Levski Sofia 45	Botev Plovdiv 37
1993	Levski Sofia 50	CSKA Sofia 42	Botev Plovdiv 38
1994p5	Levski Sofia 71	CSKA Sofia 54	Botev Plovdiv 50
1995q3	Levski Sofia 79	Lokomotiv Sofia 68	Botev Plovdiv 60

BULGARIAN CUP FINALS

1938	FK 13 Sofia	3-0	Levski Ruse
1939	Shipka Sofia	2-0	Levski Ruse
1940	FK 13 Sofia	2-0	Sportclub Plovdiv
1941	AC 23 Sofia	4-2	Napradek Ruse
1942	Levski Sofia	3-0	Sportclub Plovdiv

BULGARIAN CUP OF THE REPUBLIC

1981	CSKA Sofia (League format)		
1982	Levski-Spartak	4-0	CSKA Sofia
1983	CSKA Sofia	4-0	Spartak Varna
1984	Levski-Spartak	1-0	Trakia Plovdiv
1985	CSKA Sofia	2-1	Levski-Spartak (Void)
1986	Vitosha Sofia	2-1	CFKA Sredets
1987	CFKA Sredets	2-1	Vitosha Sofia
1988	CFKA Sredets	4-1	Vitosha Sofia
1989	CFKA Sredets	3-0	Chernomorets Burgas
1990	Sliven	2-0	CSKA Sofia
1991	Levski Sofia	2-1	Botev Plovdiv
1992	Levski Sofia	5-0	Pirin Blagoevgrad
1993	CSKA Sofia	1-0	Botev Plovdiv
1994	Levski Sofia	1-0	Pirin Blagoevgrad
1995q3	Lokomotiv Sofia	4-2	Botev Plovdiv

SOVIET ARMY CUP

1946	Levski Sofia	4-1	Chernomorets Popovo
1947	Levski Sofia	1-0	Botev Plovdiv
1948	Lokomotiv Sofia	1-0	Slavia Plovdiv
1949	Dinamo Sofia	1-1 2-2 2-1	Narodna Voiska
1950	Dinamo Sofia	1-1 1-1 1-0	Narodna Voiska
1951	CDNA Sofia	1-0	Academic Sofia
1952	Udarnik Sofia	3-1	Spartak Sofia
1953	Lokomotiv Sofia	2-1	Dinamo Sofia
1954	CDNA Sofia	2-1	Udarnik Sofia
1955	CDNA Sofia	5-2	Spartak Plovdiv
1956	Dinamo Sofia	5-2	Botev Plovdiv
1957	Levski Sofia	2-1	Spartak Pleven
1958	Spartak Plovdiv	1-0	Minyor Pernik
1959	Levski Sofia	1-0	Spartak Plovdiv
1960	Septemvri CDW Sofia	4-3	Lokomotiv Plovdiv
1961	CDNA Sofia	3-0	Spartak Varna
1962	Botev Plovdiv	3-0	Dunav Ruse
1963	Slavia Sofia	2-0	Botev Plovdiv
1964	Slavia Sofia	3-2	Botev Plovdiv
1965	CSKA-CZ Sofia	3-2	Levski Sofia
1966	Slavia Sofia	1-0	CSKA-CZ Sofia

1967	Levski Sofia	3-0	Spartak Sofia
1968	Spartak Sofia	3-2	Beroe Stara Zagora
1969	CSKA Sofia	2-1	Levski-Spartak
1970	Levski-Spartak	2-1	CSKA Sofia
1971	Levski-Spartak	3-0	Lokomotiv Plovdiv
1972	CSKA Sofia	3-0	Slavia Sofia
1973	CSKA Sofia	2-1	Beroe Stara Zagora
1974	CSKA Sofia	2-1	Levski-Spartak
1975	Slavia Sofia	3-2	Lokomotiv Sofia
1976	Levski-Spartak	4-3	CSKA Sofia
1977	Levski-Spartak	2-1	Lokomotiv Sofia
1978	Marek St. Dimitrov	1-0	CSKA Sofia
1979	Levski-Spartak	4-1	Beroe Stara Zagora
1980	Slavia Sofia	3-1	Beroe Stara Zagora
1981	Trakia Plovdiv	1-0	Pirin Blagoevgrad
1982	Lokomotiv Sofia	2-1	Lokomotiv Plovdiv
1983	Lokomotiv Plovdiv	3-1	Chirpan
1984	Levski-Spartak	4-0	Dorostol
1985	CSKA Sofia	4-0	Cherno More Varna
1986	CFKA Sredets	2-0	Lokomotiv Sofia
1987	Vitosha Sofia	3-2	Spartak Plovdiv
1988	Vitosha Sofia	2-0	Cherno More Varna
1989	CFKA Sredets	6-1	Maritsa Istok Radnevo
1990	CSKA Sofia	2-1	Botev Plovdiv
1991	Etar Veliko Tarnovo	2-1	Neftokhimik Burgas

BULGARIAN LEAGUE CUP

1995	Etar Veliko Tarnovo	3-0	Dunav Ruse

LEADING INTERNATIONAL GOALSCORERS

47	Hristo Bonev	(Lokomotiv Plovdiv)	1967-79
25	Lubomir Angelov	(Shipka Sofia,AC 23, Chavdar Sofia)	1931-40
25	Ivan Kolev	(CSKA)	1950-63
25	Petar Jekov	(Beroe,CSKA)	1963-72
24	Hristo Stoichkov	(CSKA,Barcelona)	1987-
23	Atanas Mihailov	(Lokomotiv Sofia)	1967-79
22	Nasko Sirakov	(Levski,Real Zaragoza, Español,Levski,Lens,Levski)	1983-
20	Dimitar Milanov	(CSKA)	
19	Georgi Asparouhkov	(Levski)	1962-70
19	Dinko Dermendjiev	(Botev Plovdiv)	1962-77

LEADING INTERNATIONAL APPEARANCES

96	Hristo Bonev	(Lokomotiv Plovdiv)	1967-79
90	Dimitar Penev	(CSKA)	1964-77
83	Borislav Mikhailov #	(Levski,Belenenses,Mulhouse)	1983-
80	Anyo Sadkov	(Lokomotiv Plovdiv, Belenenses)	1982-91
76	Georgi Dimitrov	(CSKA,St-Étienne)	1978-88
75	Ivan Kolev	(CSKA)	1950-63
73	Dobromir Jetchev	(Spartak,Levski-Spartak)	1961-74
70	Ivan Dimitrov	(Lokomotiv Sofia,Spartak, Akademik)	1957-70
68	Nasko Sirakov	(as above)	1983-

INTERNATIONAL MATCHES PLAYED BY BULGARIA

21-05-1924	Austria	L 0-6	Vienna	Fr	
28-05	Rep. Ireland	L 0-1	Paris	OGr1	
10-04-1925	Turkey	L 1-2	Istanbul	Fr	Mutafchiev
31-05	Romania	L 2-4	Sofia	Fr	Ivanov.A, Dimitriev
25-04-1926	Romania	L 1-6	Bucharest	Fr	Denev.K
30-05	Yugoslavia	L 1-3	Zagreb	Fr	Staikov
15-05-1927	Yugoslavia	L 0-2	Sofia	Fr	
17-07	Turkey	D 3-3	Sofia	Fr	Liutzkanov 2, Stoyanov
14-10	Turkey	L 1-3	Istanbul	Fr	Manolov.D
21-04-1929	Romania	L 0-3	Bucharest	Fr	
30-06	Greece	D 1-1	Sofia	Fr	Staikov
15-09	Romania	L 2-3	Sofia	Fr	Staikov 2,
13-04-1930	Yugoslavia	L 1-6	Belgrade	Fr	Staikov
15-06	Yugoslavia	D 2-2	Sofia	Fr	Staikov, Stoyanov
12-10	Romania	W 5-3	Sofia	BC	Staikov 2, Stoyanov, Peshev, Vasilev.V
16-11	Yugoslavia	L 0-3	Sofia	BC	
7-12	Greece	L 1-6	Athens	BC	Peshev
19-04-1931	Yugoslavia	L 0-1	Belgrade	BC	
10-05	Romania	L 2-5	Bucharest	BC	Lozanov, Panchev
27-09	Turkey	W 5-1	Sofia	Fr	Panchev 2, Lozanov, Peshev, Stoyanov
4-10	Yugoslavia	W 3-2	Sofia	Fr	Lozanov, Angelov, Panchev
25-10	Greece	W 2-1	Sofia	BC	Peshev, Angelov
27-03-1932	Greece	W 2-1	Athens	Fr	Panchev, Angelov
9-06	France	L 3-5	Sofia	Fr	Panchev 3
26-06	Romania	W 2-0	Belgrade	BC	Panchev, Peshev
30-06	Yugoslavia	W 3-2	Belgrade	BC	Angelov, Panchev, Lozanov
2-07	Greece	W 2-0	Belgrade	BC	Peshev, Angelov
5-11	Turkey	W 3-2	Istanbul	Fr	Staikov, Peshev, Angelov
21-05-1933	Spain	L 0-13	Madrid	Fr	
4-06	Romania	L 0-7	Bucharest	BC	
7-06	Yugoslavia	L 0-4	Bucharest	BC	
10-06	Greece	W 2-0	Bucharest	BC	Todorov 2
4-02-1934	Greece	L 0-1	Athens	Fr	
18-03	Yugoslavia	L 1-2	Sofia	Fr	Angelov
25-03	Hungary	L 1-4	Sofia	WCq	Baikushev

1-04	Yugoslavia	W 3-2	Belgrade	Fr	Baikushev 2, Angelov
25-04	Austria	L 1-6	Vienna	WCq	Lozanov
29-04	Hungary	L 1-4	Budapest	WCq	Todorov
25-12	Yugoslavia	L 3-4	Athens	BC	Peshev, Todorov, Panchev
30-12	Romania	L 2-3	Athens	BC	Angelov 2
1-01-1935	Greece	W 2-1	Athens	BC	Lozanov, Panchev
16-06	Greece	W 5-2	Sofia	BC	Angelov 2, Yordanov.V 2, Peshev
19-06	Romania	W 4-0	Sofia	BC	Lozanov, Yordanov.V, Peshev, OG
24-06	Yugoslavia	D 3-3	Sofia	BC	Angelov 3
20-10	Germany	L 2-4	Leipzig	Fr	Panchev, Stoichkov.K
21-05-1936	Greece	W 5-4	Bucharest	BC	Panchev 2, Rafailov, Angelov, Lozanov
24-05	Romania	L 1-4	Bucharest	BC	Angelov
11-07-1937	Yugoslavia	W 4-0	Sofia	Fr	Angelov 2, Yordanov.V, Rafailov
12-09	Poland	D 3-3	Sofia	Fr	Iliev.K, Angelov, Yordanov.V
7-11	Czechoslovakia	D 1-1	Sofia	WCq	Pachedjiev
24-03-1938	France	L 1-6	Paris	Fr	Lozanov
24-04	Czechoslovakia	L 0-6	Prague	WCq	
24-05-1939	Latvia	W 3-0	Sofia	Fr	Bobev, Angelov, Pachedjiev
22-10	Germany	L 1-3	Sofia	Fr	Yordanov.V
6-06-1940	Slovakia	L 1-4	Sofia	Fr	Stoyanov
20-10	Germany	L 3-7	Munich	Fr	Evtimov 2, Angelov
11-04-1942	Croatia	L 0-6	Zagreb	Fr	
19-07	Germany	L 0-3	Sofia	Fr	
6-06-1943	Hungary	L 2-4	Sofia	Fr	Milev, Spassov.V
8-10-1946	Romania	D 2-2	Tirana	BC	Milev, OG
9-10	Albania	L 1-3	Tirana	BC	Spassov.V
12-10	Yugoslavia	L 1-2	Tirana	BC	Laskov
15-06-1947	Albania	W 2-0	Sofia	BCE	Stankov.T 2
6-07	Romania	L 2-3	Sofia	BCE	Stankov.T, Yordanov.V
17-08	Hungary	L 0-9	Budapest	BCE	
12-10	Yugoslavia	L 1-2	Zagreb	BCE	Stankov.T
4-04-1948	Poland	D 1-1	Sofia	BCE	Stankov.T
20-06	Romania	L 2-3	Bucharest	BCE	Argirov, Tzetkov
4-07	Yugoslavia	L 1-3	Sofia	BCE	Argirov
29-08	Czechoslovakia	W 1-0	Sofia	BCE	Milev
7-11	Hungary	W 1-0	Sofia	BCE	Milanov.D
4-09-1949	Czechoslovakia	W 3-1	Prague	Fr	Laskov, Spassov.V, Milanov.D
2-10	Poland	L 2-3	Warsaw	Fr	Spassov.V, Bojkov
30-10	Hungary	L 0-5	Budapest	Fr	
17-11	Albania	D 0-0	Sofia	Fr	
4-06-1950	Albania	L 1-2	Tirana	Fr	Spassov.V
27-08	Czechoslovakia	L 1-2	Sofia	Fr	Trandafilov
30-10	Poland	L 0-1	Sofia	Fr	
12-11	Hungary	D 1-1	Sofia	Fr	Dimitrov.A
18-05-1952	Poland	W 1-0	Warsaw	Fr	Milanov.D
15-07	Soviet Union	L 1-2	Kotka	OGr1	Kolev.I
14-06-1953	East Germany	D 0-0	Dresden	Fr	
28-06	Romania	L 1-3	Bucharest	WCq	Tashkov
6-09	Czechoslovakia	L 1-2	Sofia	WCq	Bojkov
13-09	Poland	D 2-2	Sofia	Fr	Dimitrov.G 2
4-10	Hungary	D 1-1	Sofia	Fr	Kolev.I
11-10	Romania	L 1-2	Sofia	WCq	Kolev.I
8-11	Czechoslovakia	D 0-0	Bratislava	WCq	
8-08-1954	Poland	D 2-2	Warsaw	Fr	Kolev.I, Milanov.D
24-10	East Germany	W 3-1	Sofia	Fr	Kolev.I 2, Yanev
7-01-1955	Egypt	L 0-1	Cairo	Fr	
23-01	Lebanon	W 3-2	Beirut	Fr	Milanov.D 3
22-05	Egypt	W 2-1	Sofia	Fr	Milanov.D, Gugalov
26-06	Poland	D 1-1	Sofia	Fr	Bojkov
9-10	Romania	D 1-1	Bucharest	Fr	Panayotov
23-10	Great Britain	W 2-0	Sofia	OGq	Stefanov, Yanev
13-11	Czechoslovakia	W 3-0	Sofia	Fr	Kolev.I, Bojkov, Diev
20-11	East Germany	L 0-1	Berlin	Fr	
12-05-1956	Great Britain	D 3-3	London	OGq	Milanov.D, OG, Dimitrov.G
26-08	Poland	W 2-1	Wroclaw	Fr	Milanov.D, Kolev.I
10-09	Romania	W 2-0	Sofia	Fr	Milanov.D, Yanev
14-10	East Germany	W 3-1	Sofia	Fr	Kolev.I 2, Panayotov
30-11	Great Britain	W 6-1	Melbourne	OGr2	Milanov.D 3, Dimitrov.G, Kolev.I 2
5-12	Soviet Union	L 1-2	Melbourne	OGsf	Kolev.I
7-12	India	W 3-0	Melbourne	OG3p	Diev 2, Milanov.D
22-05-1957	Norway	W 2-1	Oslo	WCq	Dimitrov.G 2

26-05	Denmark	D 1-1	Copenhagen	Fr	Kovachev
23-06	Hungary	L 1-4	Budapest	WCq	Dimitrov.G
21-07	Soviet Union	L 0-4	Sofia	Fr	
15-09	Hungary	L 1-2	Sofia	WCq	Diev
29-09	Poland	D 1-1	Sofia	Fr	Milanov.D
3-11	Norway	W 7-0	Sofia	WCq	Iliev.C 3, Panayotov 2, Yanev, Debarski
25-12	France	D 2-2	Paris	Fr	Diev, Nestorov
14-05-1958	Brazil	L 0-4	Rio de Janeiro	Fr	
18-05	Brazil	L 1-3	Sao Paulo	Fr	Diev
5-10	East Germany	D 1-1	Berlin	Fr	Milanov.D
12-10	Czechoslovakia	W 1-0	Ostrava	Fr	Milanov.D
7-12	Turkey	D 0-0	Ankara	Fr	
21-12	West Germany	L 0-3	Augsburg	Fr	
13-05-1959	Holland	W 3-2	Sofia	Fr	Vasilev.A 2, Kolev.I
31-05	Yugoslavia	L 0-2	Belgrade	ECr1	
27-06	Soviet Union	D 1-1	Moscow	OGq	Milanov.D
13-09	Soviet Union	W 1-0	Sofia	OGq	Kolev.I
11-10	France	W 1-0	Sofia	Fr	Kolev.I
25-10	Yugoslavia	D 1-1	Sofia	ECr1	Diev
8-11	Romania	L 0-1	Bucharest	OGq	
6-12	Denmark	W 2-1	Sofia	Fr	Abadjiev, Dimitrov.I
3-04-1960	Holland	L 2-4	Amsterdam	Fr	Yakimov, Panayotov
1-05	Romania	W 2-1	Sofia	OGq	Yordanov.D, Kovachev
22-05	Belgium	W 4-1	Sofia	Fr	Kolev.I 2, Yordanov.D, Diev
26-06	Poland	L 0-4	Chorzow	Fr	
10-07	East Germany	W 2-0	Sofia	Fr	Iliev.C, Yakimov
26-08	Turkey *	W 3-0	Grossetto	OGr1	Diev 2 Iliev.C
29-08	Egypt	W 2-0	Aquila	OGr1	Yordanov.D, Diev
1-09	Yugoslavia	D 3-3	Rome	OGr1	Debarski 2, Rakarov
23-11	West Germany	W 2-1	Sofia	Fr	Kolev.I 2
27-11	Turkey	W 2-1	Sofia	Fr	Kolev.I, Iliev.C
11-12	France	L 0-3	Paris	WCq	
14-05-1961	Poland	D 1-1	Warsaw	Fr	Kolev.I
16-06	Finland	W 2-0	Helsinki	WCq	Iliev.C, Kolev.I
29-10	Finland	W 3-1	Sofia	WCq	Yakimov, Diev, Velichkov.P
12-11	France	W 1-0	Sofia	WCq	Iliev.C
16-12	France	W 1-0	Milan	WCq	Yakimov
24-12	Belgium	L 0-4	Brussels	Fr	
6-05-1962	Austria	L 0-2	Vienna	Fr	
30-05	Argentina	L 0-1	Rancagua	WCr1	
3-06	Hungary	L 1-6	Rancagua	WCr1	Asparuhov
7-06	England	D 0-0	Rancagua	WCr1	
30-09	Poland	W 2-1	Sofia	Fr	Diev, Apostolov
7-11	Portugal	W 3-1	Sofia	ECr1	Asparuhov 2, Diev
25-11	Austria	D 1-1	Sofia	Fr	Kolev.I
16-12	Portugal	L 1-3	Lisbon	ECr1	Iliev.C
6-01-1963	Algeria	L 1-2	Algiers	Fr	Asparuhov
23-01	Portugal	W 1-0	Rome	ECr1	Asparuhov
28-04	Czechoslovakia	W 1-0	Sofia	Fr	Yakimov
2-06	Albania	W 1-0	Tirana	OGq	
16-06	Albania	W 1-0	Sofia	OGq	
4-09	East Germany	D 1-1	Magdeburg	Fr	Dermendjiev
18-09	Sudan	D 1-1	Sofia	Fr	Kotkov
29-09	France	W 1-0	Sofia	ECr2	Diev
26-10	France	L 1-3	Paris	ECr2	Yakimov
18-03-1964	Yugoslavia	L 0-1	Sofia	OGq	
1-04	Yugoslavia	L 0-1	Nis	OGq	
3-04	Romania	L 1-2	Bucharest	OGq	
31-05	Romania	L 0-1	Sofia	OGq	
29-11	Soviet Union	D 0-0	Sofia	Fr	
20-12	Turkey	D 0-0	Istanbul	Fr	
24-02-1965	Greece	W 2-1	Athens	Fr	Apostolov, Debarski
9-05	Turkey	W 4-1	Sofia	Fr	Debarski 3, Penev.D
16-05	Poland	D 1-1	Krakow	Fr	Debarski
13-06	Israel	W 4-0	Sofia	WCq	Kotkov 2, Asparuhov, Kitov
4-09	East Germany	W 3-2	Varna	Fr	Kotkov 2, Diev
26-09	Belgium	W 3-0	Sofia	WCq	Kotkov 2, Asparuhov
27-10	Belgium	L 0-5	Brussels	WCq	
21-11	Israel	W 2-1	Tel Aviv	WCq	Kolev.I, Asparuhov
29-12	Belgium	W 2-1	Florence	WCq	Asparuhov 2
25-02-1966	Egypt	D 2-2	Cairo	Fr	Kostov, Jekov

1-06	Yugoslavia	W 2-0	Belgrade	Fr	Jekov 2
14-06	Italy	L 1-6	Bologna	Fr	Asparuhov
12-07	Brazil	L 0-2	Liverpool	WCr1	
16-07	Portugal	L 0-3	Manchester	WCr1	
20-07	Hungary	L 1-3	Manchester	WCr1	Asparuhov
6-11	Yugoslavia	W 6-1	Sofia	Fr	Jekov 2, Dimitrov.Y 2, Vasilev.A, Dermendjiev
13-11	Norway	W 4-2	Sofia	ECq	Tzanev 2, Jekov 2
22-03-1967	West Germany	L 0-1	Hanover	Fr	
11-06	Sweden	W 2-0	Stockholm	ECq	Jekov, Dermendjiev
29-06	Norway	D 0-0	Oslo	ECq	
8-10	Soviet Union	L 1-2	Sofia	Fr	Dermendjiev
12-11	Sweden	W 3-0	Sofia	ECq	Kotkov, Mitkov, Asparuhov
26-11	Portugal	W 1-0	Sofia	ECq	Dermendjiev
17-12	Portugal	D 0-0	Lisbon	ECq	
6-04-1968	Italy	W 3-2	Sofia	ECqf	Kotkov, Dermendjiev, Jekov
10-04	East Germany *	W 4-1	Stara Zagora	OGq	
20-04	Italy	L 0-2	Naples	ECqf	
24-04	East Germany *	L 2-3	Leipzig	OGq	
9-10	Turkey	W 2-0	Istanbul	Fr	Dermendjiev, Bonev
14-10	Thailand *	W 7-0	Leon	OGr1	Christov 2, Giuonine, Jekov, Zafirov, Donev, Ivkov
16-10	Czechoslovakia *	D 2-2	Guadalajara	OGr1	Gueroguiev, Jekov
18-10	Guatemala *	W 2-1	Leon	OGr1	Donev, Jekov
20-10	Israel *	D 1-1	Leon	OGqf	Christakiev. Won on lots
22-10	Mexico *	W 3-2	Guadalajara	OGsf	Jekov, Christov, Dimitrov
26-10	Hungary *	L 1-4	Mexico City	OGf	Dimitrov
27-10	Holland	W 2-0	Sofia	WCq	Bonev, Asparuhov
11-12	England	D 1-1	London	Fr	Asparuhov
23-04-1969	Luxembourg	W 2-1	Sofia	WCq	Asparuhov 2
24-05	Italy	D 0-0	Turin	Fr	
15-06	Poland	W 4-1	Sofia	WCq	Bonev, Dermendjiev, Penev.D, Asparuhov
24-09	West Germany	L 0-1	Sofia	Fr	
22-10	Holland	D 1-1	Rotterdam	WCq	Bonev
9-11	Poland	L 0-3	Warsaw	WCq	
7-12	Luxembourg	W 3-1	Luxembourg	WCq	Dermendjiev, Yakimov, Bonev
28-12	Morocco	L 0-3	Casablanca	Fr	
15-02-1970	Mexico	D 1-1	Mexico City	Fr	Marashliev
18-02	Mexico	L 0-2	Leon	Fr	
21-02	Peru	W 3-1	Lima	Fr	Nikodimov, Marashliev, Mihailov
24-02	Peru	L 3-5	Lima	Fr	Dermendjiev, Asparuhov, Marashliev
8-04	France	D 1-1	Rouen	Fr	Jekov
5-05	Soviet Union	D 3-3	Sofia	Fr	Jekov 2, Bonev
6-05	Soviet Union	D 0-0	Sofia	Fr	
2-06	Peru	L 2-3	Leon	WCr1	Dermendjiev, Bonev
7-06	West Germany	L 2-5	Leon	WCr1	Nikodimov, Kolev.T
11-06	Morocco	D 1-1	Leon	WCr1	Jechev
15-11	Norway	D 1-1	Sofia	ECq	Atanasov
7-04-1971	Greece	W 1-0	Athens	Fr	Vasilev.M
28-04	Soviet Union	D 1-1	Sofia	Fr	Mitkov
19-05	Hungary	W 3-0	Sofia	ECq	Kolev.B, Petkov, Velichkov.S
9-06	Norway	W 4-1	Oslo	ECq	Bonev 2, Jekov, Vasilev.M
25-09	Hungary	L 0-2	Budapest	ECq	
10-11	France	L 1-2	Nantes	ECq	Bonev
17-11	Greece	D 2-2	Sofia	Fr	Vasiliev.M, Kirilov
4-12	France	W 2-1	Sofia	ECq	Jekov, Mihailov
29-03-1972	Soviet Union	D 1-1	Sofia	Fr	Bonev
16-04	Poland	W 3-1	Stara Zagora	OGq	Bonev 2, Dermendjiev
7-05	Poland	L 0-3	Warsaw	OGq	
7-06	Soviet Union	L 0-1	Moscow	Fr	
21-06	Italy	D 1-1	Sofia	Fr	Bonev
18-10	Nth. Ireland	W 3-0	Sofia	WCq	Bonev 2, Kolev.B
19-11	Cyprus	W 4-0	Nicosia	WCq	Mihailov, Bonev, Denev.G 2.
28-01-1973	Cyprus	W 3-0	Nicosia	Fr	Denev.G 2, Mihailov
31-01	Greece	D 2-2	Athens	Fr	Petkov, Bonev
4-02	Indonesia	W 4-0	Djakarta	Fr	Mihailov 2, Dermendjiev 2
8-02	New Caledonia	W 5-3	Noumea	Fr	Vasilev.G, Yakimov, Dermendjiev, Mihailov 2
14-02	Australia	D 2-2	Sydney	Fr	Vasilev.G, Mihailov
16-02	Australia	W 3-1	Adelaide	Fr	Bogomilov, Pritargov, Mihailov
18-02	Australia	W 2-0	Melbourne	Fr	Pritargov, Dermendjiev
28-03	Soviet Union	W 1-0	Plovdiv	Fr	Dermendjiev
18-04	Turkey	L 2-5	Izmir	BC	Panov, Milanov.K
2-05	Portugal	W 2-1	Sofia	WCq	Denev.G, Bonev

12-05	West Germany	L 0-3	Hamburg	Fr	
19-08	Poland	L 0-2	Varna	Fr	
26-09	Nth. Ireland	D 0-0	Sheffield	WCq	
13-10	Portugal	D 2-2	Lisbon	WCq	Bonev 2
18-11	Cyprus	W 2-0	Sofia	WCq	Kolev.B, Denev.G
6-02-1974	Cyprus	W 4-1	Morphou	Fr	Kolev.B, Bonev 3
8-02	Kuwait	W 3-1	Kuwait City	Fr	Denev.G, Bonev, Petkov
10-02	Kuwait	W 2-1	Kuwait City	Fr	Bonev 2
31-03	Hungary	L 1-3	Zalaegerzeg	Fr	Bonev
13-04	Czechoslovakia	L 0-1	Plovdiv	Fr	
14-04	Brazil	L 0-1	Rio de Janeiro	Fr	
8-05	Turkey	W 5-1	Sofia	BC	Bonev, OG, Jechev, Panov, Grigorov
25-05	North Korea	W 6-1	Sofia	Fr	Bonev 3, Mihailov, Panov, Borisov
1-06	England	L 0-1	Sofia	Fr	
15-06	Sweden	D 0-0	Dusseldorf	WCr1	
19-06	Uruguay	D 1-1	Hanover	WCr1	Bonev
23-06	Holland	L 1-4	Dortmund	WCr1	OG
25-09	Romania	D 0-0	Sofia	Fr	
13-10	Greece	D 3-3	Sofia	ECq	Bonev, Denev.G 2.
10-11	Hungary	D 0-0	Varna	Fr	
18-12	Greece	L 1-2	Athens	ECq	Kolev.B
29-12	Italy	D 0-0	Genoa	Fr	
26-03-1975	East Germany	D 0-0	Berlin	Fr	
27-04	West Germany	D 1-1	Sofia	ECq	Kolev.B
11-06	Malta	W 5-0	Sofia	ECq	Dimitrov.B, Denev.G, Panov, Bonev, Milanov.K
19-11	West Germany	L 0-1	Stuttgart	ECq	
21-12	Malta	W 2-0	Gzira	ECq	Panov, Yordanov.J
25-01-1976	Japan	W 3-1	Tokyo	Fr	Bonev, Tzvetkov.C, Iliev.S
28-01	Japan	D 1-1	Osaka	Fr	Bonev
1-02	Japan	W 3-0	Tokyo	Fr	Simov, Djevizov, Hristov
24-03	Soviet Union	L 0-3	Sofia	Fr	
5-05	North Korea	W 3-0	Sofia	Fr	Bonev 2, Jeliazkov
12-05	Romania	W 1-0	Veliko Tarnovo	BC	Vasilev.T
17-08	Switzerland	D 2-2	Lucerne	Fr	Vasilev.T, Yordanov.J
22-09	Turkey	D 2-2	Sofia	Fr	Bonev, Jeliazkov
9-10	France	D 2-2	Sofia	WCq	Bonev, Panov
27-10	East Germany	L 0-4	Sliven	Fr	
28-11	Romania	L 2-3	Bucharest	BC	Jeliazkov, Garabski
11-01-1977	Algeria	D 1-1	Algiers	Fr	Dermendjiev
23-01	Brazil	L 0-1	Sao Paulo	Fr	
30-01	Cyprus	W 2-1	Nicosia	Fr	Panov, Milanov.K
16-02	Turkey	L 0-2	Istanbul	BC	
13-04	Denmark	W 3-1	Sofia	Fr	Tzvetkov.C, Jeliazkov, Borsov
1-06	Rep. Ireland	W 2-0	Sofia	WCq	Panov, Jeliazkov
21-09	Turkey	W 3-1	Sofia	BC	Jeliazkov, Alexandrov.A, Djevizov
12-10	Rep. Ireland	D 0-0	Dublin	WCq	
26-10	Greece	D 0-0	Sofia	Fr	
16-11	France	L 1-3	Paris	WCq	Tzvetkov.C
22-02-1978	Scotland	L 1-2	Glasgow	Fr	Mladenov
29-03	Argentina	L 1-3	Buenos Aires	Fr	Grantcharov
1-04	Peru	D 1-1	Lima	Fr	Manolov.K
5-04	Mexico	L 0-3	Mexico City	Fr	
23-04	Czechoslovakia	D 0-0	Brno	Fr	
26-04	Poland	L 0-1	Warsaw	Fr	
26-04	Iran	D 1-1	Tehran	Fr	Sokolov
3-05	Romania	L 0-2	Bucharest	BC	
31-05	Romania	D 1-1	Sofia	BC	Mladenov
4-08	Romania*	W 2-0	Varna	Fr	Markov.P, Ivanov.A
30-08	East Germany	D 2-2	Erfurt	Fr	Panov, Stankov.A
20-09	Italy	L 0-1	Turin	Fr	
11-10	Denmark	D 2-2	Copenhagen	ECq	Panov, Iliev.I
29-11	Nth. Ireland	L 0-2	Sofia	ECq	
16-01-1979	Cyprus	W 1-0	Larnaca	Fr	Gochev
7-02	Romania*	D 1-1	Starke Dimitrov	Fr	Vasilev
14-02	Romania*	W 2-1	Blagoevgrad	Fr	Mladenov, Kerimov
26-02	East Germany	W 1-0	Burgas	Fr	R.Gochev
28-03	Soviet Union	L 1-3	Simferopol	Fr	Panov
25-04	Argentina	L 1-2	Buenos Aires	Fr	Bonev
2-05	Nth. Ireland	L 0-2	Belfast	ECq	
19-05	Rep. Ireland	W 1-0	Sofia	ECq	Tzvetkov.C
6-06	England	L 0-3	Sofia	ECq	

Date	Opponent	Result	Venue	Comp	Scorers
17-10	Rep. Ireland	L 0-3	Dublin	ECq	
31-10	Denmark	W 3-0	Sofia	ECq	Jeliazkov, Tzvetkov.C 2.
22-11	England	L 0-2	London	ECq	
8-03-1980	Kuwait	D 1-1	Kuwait City	Fr	Jeliazkov
26-03	Soviet Union	L 1-3	Sofia	Fr	Tzvetkov.C
14-05	Greece	D 0-0	Athens	Fr	
22-05	Norway	L 0-1	Oslo	Fr	
4-06	Finland	W 2-0	Helsinki	WCq	Markov.P, Kostadinov.K
10-09	Romania	L 1-2	Varna	Fr	Slavkov
24-09	Sweden	L 2-3	Burgas	Fr	Tzvetkov.C, Markov.P
9-10	Argentina	L 0-2	Buenos Aires	Fr	
19-10	Albania	W 2-1	Sofia	WCq	Jeliazkov, Slavkov
3-12	West Germany	L 1-3	Sofia	WCq	Yonchev
20-01-1981	Mexico	D 1-1	Mexico City	Fr	Kostadinov.K
27-01	Ecuador	W 3-1	Quito	Fr	Slavkov, Tzvetkov.C, Kostadinov.K
1-02	Bolivia	W 3-1	La Paz	Fr	Slavkov, Tzvetkov.C, Kostadinov.K
11-02	Peru	W 2-1	Lima	Fr	Zehtinski, Tzvetkov.C
25-03	Yugoslavia	L 1-2	Subotica	Fr	Slavkov
15-04	Portugal	D 1-1	Oporto	Fr	Tzvetkov.C
29-04	Norway	W 1-0	Pleven	Fr	Tzvetkov.P
13-05	Finland	W 4-0	Sofia	WCq	Slavkov 2, Kostadinov.K, Tzvetkov.C
28-05	Austria	L 0-2	Vienna	WCq	
12-08	Sweden	L 0-1	Uddevalla	Fr	
9-09	Romania	W 2-1	Bucharest	Fr	Yonchev, Kostadinov.K
23-09	Italy	L 2-3	Bologna	Fr	Mladenov, Blonghev
14-10	Albania	W 2-0	Tirana	WCq	Slavkov 2
28-10	Brazil	L 0-3	Porto Alegre	Fr	
11-11	Austria	D 0-0	Sofia	WCq	
22-11	West Germany	L 0-4	Dusseldorf	WCq	
16-12	Portugal	W 5-2	Haskovo	Fr	Yonchev 2, Zdravkov 2, OG
14-04-1982	Romania	L 1-2	Ruse	Fr	Lovtschev
28-04	Belgium	L 1-2	Brussels	Fr	Mladenov
5-05	Argentina	L 1-2	Buenos Aires	Fr	Mladenov
15-05	France	D 0-0	Lyon	Fr	
7-09	Switzerland	L 2-3	St. Gallen	Fr	Yonchev, Zdravkov
22-09	East Germany	D 2-2	Burgas	Fr	Zdravkov 2
14-10	Malta	W 7-0	Sofia	Fr	Kerimov, Blonghev, Velichkov.B, Dimitrov.G, Slavkov 3
27-10	Norway	D 2-2	Sofia	ECq	Velichkov.B, Nikolov
17-11	Yugoslavia	L 0-1	Sofia	ECq	
22-12	Turkey	W 1-0	Istanbul	Fr	Gospodinov
26-12	Malta	D 0-0	Ta'Qali	Fr	
7-03-1983	Switzerland	D 1-1	Varna	Fr	Getov
23-03	Poland	L 1-3	Lodz	Fr	Naidenov
13-04	East Germany	L 0-3	Gera	Fr	
27-04	Wales	L 0-1	Wrexham	ECq	
4-05	Cuba	W 5-2	Sofia	Fr	Valtchev, Spassov.E, Gospodinov 2, Pashev
8-08	Algeria	W 3-2	Paris	Fr	Zdravkov. Sadkov 2
7-09	Norway	W 2-1	Oslo	ECq	Mladenov, Sirakov
26-10	Czechoslovakia	W 2-1	Prague	Fr	Mladenov, Iskrenov
16-11	Wales	W 1-0	Sofia	ECq	Gochev
21-12	Yugoslavia	L 2-3	Split	ECq	Iskrenov, Dimitrov.G
4-02-1984	Morocco	D 1-1	Casablanca	Fr	Mladenov
15-02	West Germany	L 2-3	Varna	Fr	Iskrenov 2
4-04	Kuwait	D 1-1	Kuwait City	Fr	Gospodinov
8-06	Denmark	D 1-1	Copenhagen	Fr	Zdravkov
6-09	Portugal	L 0-1	Lisbon	Fr	
29-09	Yugoslavia	D 0-0	Belgrade	WCq	
16-10	Turkey	D 0-0	Istanbul	Fr	
21-11	France	L 0-1	Paris	WCq	
5-12	Luxembourg	W 4-0	Sofia	WCq	Sirakov, Velichkov.B, Mladenov, Dimitrov.G
5-02-1985	Switzerland	W 1-0	Queretaro	Fr	Zdravkov
7-02	Poland	D 2-2	Queretaro	Fr	Dimitrov.G, Zdravkov
6-04	East Germany	W 1-0	Sofia	WCq	Mladenov
17-04	West Germany	L 1-4	Augsburg	Fr	Zdravkov
2-05	France	W 2-0	Sofia	WCq	Dimitrov.G, Sirakov
1-06	Yugoslavia	W 2-1	Sofia	WCq	Getov 2
27-08	Mexico	D 1-1	Los Angeles	Fr	Iskrenov
4-09	Holland	L 0-1	Heerenveen	Fr	
25-09	Luxembourg	W 3-1	Luxembourg	WCq	Dimitrov.G, OG 2
16-10	Greece	W 2-0	Salonica	Fr	Kolev.H, Sadkov
16-11	East Germany	L 1-2	Karl-Marx-Stadt	WCq	Gochev
18-12	Spain	L 0-2	Valencia	Fr	

9-02-1986	East Germany	L 1-2	Queretaro	Fr	Pashev
19-02	Morocco	D 0-0	Rabat	Fr	
9-04	Denmark	W 3-0	Sofia	Fr	Sirakov 2, Velichkov.B
23-04	Belgium	L 0-2	Brussels	Fr	
30-04	North Korea	W 3-0	Sofia	Fr	Dragolov, Markov.A 2
31-05	Italy	D 1-1	Mexico City	WCr1	Sirakov
6-06	South Korea	D 1-1	Mexico City	WCr1	Getov
10-06	Argentina	L 0-2	Mexico City	WCr1	
15-06	Mexico	L 0-2	Mexico City	WCr2	
10-09	Scotland	D 0-0	Glasgow	ECq	
7-10	East Germany	W 2-0	Sofia	Fr	Stoichkov.H 2
29-10	Tunisia	D 3-3	Tunis	Fr	Alexandrov.P, Sirakov, Markov.P
19-11	Belgium	D 1-1	Brussels	ECq	Tanev
29-01-1987	China	W 4-0	Sofia	Fr	Dragolov, Penev.L 2, Eranosyan
1-04	Rep.of Ireland	W 2-1	Sofia	ECq	Sadkov, Tanev
30-04	Luxembourg	W 4-1	Luxembourg	ECq	Sadkov, Sirakov, Tanev, Kolev.H
20-05	Luxembourg	W 3-0	Sofia	ECq	Sirakov, Yordanov.G, Kolev.H
23-09	Belgium	W 2-0	Sofia	ECq	Sirakov, Tanev
14-10	Rep.of Ireland	L 0-2	Dublin	ECq	
11-11	Scotland	L 0-1	Sofia	ECq	
21-01-1988	UAE	W 3-2	Dubai	Fr	Kirov, Alexandrov.P, Stoichkov.H
23-01	UAE	W 3-0	Dubai	Fr	Iliev.N, Kolev.H, Sadkov
25-01	UAE	W 3-1	Sharjah	Fr	Sadkov, Kolev.H, Alexandrov.P
29-01	Egypt	L 0-1	Cairo	Fr	
23-03	Czechoslovakia	W 2-0	Sofia	Fr	Sirakov, Penev.L
13-04	East Germany	D 1-1	Burgas	Fr	Ivanov.T
24-05	Holland	W 2-1	Rotterdam	Fr	Ivanov.T, Penev.L
4-08	Finland	D 1-1	Vaasa	Fr	Pashev
7-08	Iceland	W 3-2	Reykjavik	Fr	Yordanov.G, Penev.L, Alexandrov.P
9-08	Norway	D 1-1	Oslo	Fr	Stoichkov.H
24-08	Poland	L 2-3	Bialystok	Fr	Stoichkov.H, Penev.L
19-10	Romania	L 1-3	Sofia	WCq	Kolev.H
2-11	Denmark	D 1-1	Copenhagen	WCq	Sadkov
22-12	UAE	W 1-0	Sharjah	Fr	Kostadinov.E
21-02-1989	Soviet Union	L 1-2	Sofia	Fr	Kostadinov.E
22-03	West Germany	L 1-2	Sofia	Fr	Stoichkov.H
26-04	Denmark	L 0-2	Sofia	WCq	
10-05	Romania	L 0-1	Bucharest	WCq	
23-08	East Germany	D 1-1	Erfurt	Fr	Yordanov.G
20-09	Italy	L 0-4	Cesena	Fr	
11-10	Greece	W 4-0	Varna	WCq	Ivanov.Z, Barkov, Iskrenov, Stoichkov.H
15-11	Greece	L 0-1	Athens	WCq	
5-05-1990	Brazil	L 1-2	Campinas	Fr	Kostadinov.E
12-09	Switzerland	L 0-2	Geneva	ECq	
26-09	Sweden	L 0-2	Stockholm	Fr	
17-10	Romania	W 3-0	Bucharest	ECq	Sirakov, Todorov 2
14-11	Scotland	D 1-1	Sofia	ECq	Todorov
27-03-1991	Scotland	D 1-1	Glasgow	ECq	Kostadinov.E
9-04	Denmark	D 1-1	Odense	Fr	Alexandrov.P
1-05	Switzerland	L 2-3	Sofia	ECq	Kostadinov.E, Sirakov
22-05	San Marino	W 3-0	Serravalle	ECq	Ivanov.Z, Sirakov, Penev.L
28-05	Brazil	L 0-3	Uberlandia	Fr	
21-08	Turkey	D 0-0	Stara Zagora	Fr	
25-09	Italy	W 2-1	Sofia	Fr	Kostadinov.E, Stoichkov.H
16-10	San Marino	W 4-0	Sofia	ECq	Penev.L, Stoichkov.H, Yankov, Iliev.N
20-11	Romania	D 1-1	Sofia	ECq	Sirakov
28-04-1992	Switzerland	W 2-0	Berne	Fr	Sirakov, Kostadinov.E
14-05	Finland	W 3-0	Helsinki	WCq	Balakov, Kostadinov.E 2
19-08	Mexico	D 1-1	Sofia	Fr	Stoichkov.H
26-08	Turkey	L 2-3	Trabzon	Fr	Stoilov 2
9-09	France	W 2-0	Sofia	WCq	Stoichkov.H, Balakov
7-10	Sweden	L 0-2	Stockholm	WCq	
11-11	Portugal	L 1-2	Saint-Ouen	Fr	Balakov
2-12	Israel	W 2-0	Tel Aviv	Fr	Sirakov, Penev.L
10-01-1993	Tunisia	L 0-3	Beja	Fr	
18-02	UAE	L 0-1	Dubai	Fr	
20-02	UAE	W 3-1	Dubai	Fr	Sirakov, Vidolov, Borimirov
14-04	Austria	L 1-3	Vienna	WCq	Ivanov.T
28-04	Finland	W 2-0	Sofia	WCq	Stoichkov.H, Yankov
12-05	Israel	D 2-2	Sofia	WCq	Stoichkov.H, Sirakov
8-09	Sweden	D 1-1	Sofia	WCq	Stoichkov.H
13-10	Austria	W 4-1	Sofia	WCq	Penev.L 2, Stoichkov.H, Lechkov

17-11	France	W 2-1	Paris	WCq	Kostadinov.E 2
19-01-1994	Mexico	D 1-1	San Diego	Fr	Balakov
15-04	Oman	D 1-1	Mascat	Fr	Yankov
28-04	Kuwiat	D 2-1	Kuwait City	Fr	Yankov, OG
3-06	Ukraine	D 1-1	Sofia	Fr	Sirakov
22-06	Nigeria	L 0-3	Dallas	WCr1	
26-06	Greece	W 4-0	Chicago	WCr1	Stoichkov.H 2, Lechkov, Borimirov
30-06	Argentina	W 2-0	Dallas	WCr1	Stoichkov.H, Sirakov
5-07	Mexico	D 1-1	New York	WCr2	Stoichkov.H. Won 3-1pens
10-07	Germany	W 2-1	New York	WCqf	Stoichkov.H, Lechkov
13-07	Italy	L 1-2	New York	WCsf	Stoichkov.H
16-07	Sweden	L 0-4	Los Angeles	WC3p	
12-10	Georgia	W 2-0	Sofia	ECq	Kostadinov 2
16-11	Moldova	W 4-1	Sofia	ECq	Stoichkov 2, Balakov, Kostadinov
14-12	Wales	W 3-0	Cardiff	ECq	Ivanov, Kostadinov, Stoichkov
15-02-1995	Argentina	L 1-4	Mendoza	Fr	Sirakov
12-04	Maecedonia	D 0-0	Strumica	Fr	
29-03-	Wales	W 3-1	Sofia	ECq	Balakov, Penev.L 2
26-04	Moldova	W 3-0	Chisinau	ECq	Balakov, Stoichkov 2
7-06	Germany	W 3-2	Sofia	ECq	Stoichkov 2, Kostadinov

CROATIA

When Croatia took the field against Romania in December 1990, it was their first international for nearly 50 years. During the Second World War the country had existed as an independent state with the backing of the German government. For four years internationals were played, with mixed success, against the Axis powers and their occupied territories, notably Slovakia.

A league was also contested and Gradanski Zagreb, five times Yugoslav champions in the 1920s and 1930s, won three of the four titles. With the war over and Tito, himself a Croatian, leading the government in Belgrade, the country became part of Yugoslavia again.

More titles followed for Croatian clubs including Dinamo Zagreb, a club which had its origins in Gradanski. Until Red Star Belgrade won the European Cup in 1991, Dinamo were the only Yugoslav club to have won a European title. Finalists in the Fairs Cup in 1963, they eventually won the tournament in 1967. They were not, however, the most successful Croatian club in the Yugoslav league: that honour went to Hajduk Split, seven times champions after the war, nine times in all. Hajduk also won nine Yugoslav Cups, one more than Dinamo.

Many of the best players in the Yugoslav national team were Croats, so it was no surprise that independent Croatia should immediately be such a football power. The Yugoslav victory in the 1987 World Youth Cup owed much to the talents of Robert Jarni, Janko Jankovic, Zvonimir Boban, Davor Suker and Robert Prosinecki – all Croatians.

The country has managed to avoid the worst of the troubles that have beset the region since the break-up of Yugoslavia and in October 1992 Zagreb played host to Mexico in the first international to be played on Croatian soil since 1944. Club football has suffered from the exodus of top players such as Boban and Alen Boksic, a European Cup winner with Marseille in 1993 before joining Lazio, but Hajduk and Croatia Zagreb, the renamed Dinamo, continue to produce players of class.

Population: 4,683,000
Area, sq km: 56,538
Capital city: Zagreb

Croatian Football Federation
Illica 31
CRO-41000 Zagreb
Croatia
Tel: + 385 41 424647
Fax: + 385 41 424639

Year of formation	1912 & 1991
Affiliation to FIFA	1992
Affiliation to UEFA	1992
Registered clubs	1579
Registered players	78 000
Registered referees	7563
National Stadium	Maksimir, Zagreg 60 000
National colours	Red/White/Blue
Season	August - June, with a mid season break December - February

THE RECORD

WORLD CUP

1930-94 Did not enter

EUROPEAN CHAMPIONSHIP

1960-92 Did not enter
1996 QT group 4

EUROPEAN CLUB COMPETITIONS

European Cup
Quarter-finalists - Hajduk Split 1976 1980

Cup Winners Cup
Semi-finalists - Dinamo Zagreb 1961 Hajduk Split 1973

UEFA Cup
Winners - Dinamo Zagreb 1967
Finalists - Dinamo Zagreb 1963

CLUB DIRECTORY

ZAGREB (Population - 697,000)

Croatia Zagreb (1945)
Maksimir 60,000 – Blue/Blue, white trimmings
Previous name - Merger in 1945 of HASK Zagreb and Gradanski Zagreb (1911), NK Dinamo Zagreb 1945-91, HASK Gradanski Zagreb 1991-92

NK Zagreb (1945)
Kranjcevicevoj 17,000 – Blue/Blue, white trimmings
Previous name - Borac 1946-52

Tresnjevka Zagreb (1926)
Tresnjevka 10,000 – Green/Green

RIJEKA (Population - 199,000)

NK Rijeka (1946)
Kantrida 25,000 – White/White, light blue trimmings

SPLIT (Population - 191,000)
NK Hajduk Split (1911)
Poljud 50,000 – White/Blue, blue trimmings

OSIJEK (Population - 162,000)
NK Osijek (1967)
Gradski 35,000 – White/White, blue trim
Previous names - Merger in 1967 of Proleter (1945) and Slavija (1929)

ZAPRESIC
INKER Zapresic (1929)
Inker 12,000 – Yellow/Blue, blue trimmings

CROATIAN LEAGUE CHAMPIONS

1941	Gradanski Zagreb		
1942	Concordia Zagreb		
1943	Gradanski Zagreb		
1944	Gradanski Zagreb		
1945-91	-		
1992k	Hajduk Split 36	NK Zagreb 33	NK Osijek 27
1993q	Croatia Zagreb 49	Hajduk Split 42	NK Zagreb 40
1994t	Hajduk Split 50	NK Zagreb 49	Croatia Zagreb 48
1995q	Hajduk Split 65	Croatia Zagreb 64	NK Osijek 59

CROATIAN CUP FINALS

1992	INKER Zapresic	1-1 1-0	HASKGradanski Zagreb
1993	Hajduk Split	4-1 1-2	Croatia Zagreb
1994	Croatia Zagreb	0-1 2-0	NK Rijeka
1995	Hajduk Split	3-2 1-0	Croatia Zagreb

INTERNATIONAL MATCHES PLAYED BY CROATIA

2-05-1940	Hungary	L	0-1	Budapest	Fr	
8-12	Hungary	D	1-1	Zagreb	Fr	Wolfl
15-06-1941	Germany	L	1-5	Vienna	Fr	Wolfl
7-09	Slovakia	D	1-1	Bratislava	Fr	
28-09	Slovakia	W	5-2	Zagreb	Fr	
18-01-1942	Germany	L	0-2	Zagreb	Fr	
5-04	Italy	L	0-4	Genoa	Fr	
11-04	Bulgaria	W	6-0	Zagreb	Fr	
7-06	Slovakia	W	2-1	Bratislava	Fr	
14-06	Hungary	D	1-1	Budapest	Fr	Plese
6-09	Slovakia	W	6-1	Zagreb	Fr	
11-10	Romania	D	2-2	Bucharest	Fr	Zimmermancici, Wolfl
1-11	Germany	L	1-5	Stuttgart	Fr	Wolfl
10-04-1943	Slovakia	W	1-0	Zagreb	Fr	
7-06	Slovakia	W	3-1	Bratislava	Fr	
9-04-1944	Slovakia	W	7-3	Zagreb	Fr	
22-12-1990	Romania	W	2-0	Fiume	Fr	Kranjcar, Bogdan
19-06-1991	Slovenia	W	1-0	Murska Sobotz	Fr	Komljenovic
5-07-1992	Australia	L	0-1	Melbourne	Fr	
8-07	Australia	L	1-3	Adelaide	Fr	Weber
12-07	Australia	D	0-0	Sydney	Fr	
22-10	Mexico	W	3-0	Zagreb	Fr	Suker 2, Racunica
25-06-1993	Ukraine	W	3-1	Zagreb	Fr	Suker, Adzic, Bicanic
23-03-1994	Spain	W	2-0	Valencia	Fr	Prosinec
20-04	Slovakia	L	1-4	Bratislava	Fr	Popovic
18-05	Hungary	D	2-2	Györ	Fr	Mladenovic 2
4-06	Argentina	D	0-0	Zagreb	Fr	
17-08	Israel	W	4-0	Tel Aviv	Fr	Cvitanovic 2, Jurcevic, Mumlek
4-09	Estonia	W	2-0	Tallinn	ECq	Suker 2
9-10	Lithuania	W	2-0	Zagreb	ECq	Jerkan, Kozniku
16-11	Italy	W	2-1	Palermo	ECq	Suker 2
25-03-1995	Ukraine	W	4-0	Zagreb	ECq	Boban, Suker 2, Prosinecki
29-03	Lithuania	D	0-0	Vilnius	ECq	
26-04	Slovenia	W	2-0	Zagreb	ECq	Prosinecki, Suker
11-06	Ukraine	L	0-1	Kiev	ECq	

CYPRUS

Until the expansion of UEFA in the early 1990s, Cyprus struggled to win international matches and only very rarely succeeded. But no longer! Victory against the Faroe Islands in June 1992 was the first by the national side in a competitive international for almost 20 years, and within two years they had achieved further wins over Greece, Malta and new members Georgia and Estonia.

Furthermore, their clubs have started to put together some good results in European competitions. In 1993/94 Apollon defeated the Hungarian side Vac FC in the first round of the UEFA Cup, then held mighty Inter to a 3-3 draw after losing only 1-0 in Milan. The Italians went on to win the cup.

Cyprus effectively operates as two separate countries. In 1974 Turkish troops invaded and occupied the north of the island, and inevitably the division had an effect on football as Greek clubs which found themselves on

Turkish territory had to up and move south. Famagusta, now in the northern sector of the island, was home to two Greek clubs, Anorthosis and Nea Salamis. Both relocated to Larnaca.

The Greeks have always been the more football-oriented of the two communities, and as a British colony, football caught on easily amongst the locals. The Cyprus Football Association was formed in 1934, and a league as well as a cup competition was introduced the following year. In 1948 this association was affiliated to the FA in London and membership of FIFA was granted. An international was played against Israel the following year, but it was not until the 1962 World Cup qualifiers that another Cypriot team took the field.

THE ORDER OF MERIT

	Team	All G	All S	All B	League G	League S	League B	Cup G	Cup S	Europe G	Europe S	Europe B
1	Apoel Nicosia	29	23	11	15	16	11	14	7	-	-	-
2	Omonia Nicosia	28	11	4	18	7	4	10	4	-	-	-
3	AEL Limassol	12	4	4	6	1	4	6	3	-	-	-
4	Anorthosis of Fam.	10	11	4	6	7	4	4	4	-	-	-
5	EPA Larnaca	7	9	4	2	6	4	5	3	-	-	-
6	Apollon Limassol	6	8	2	2	3	2	4	5	-	-	-
7	Olympiakos Nicosia	4	6	2	3	3	2	1	3	-	-	-
8	Trust AC	4	3	-	1	2	-	3	1	-	-	-
9	Pezoporikos Larnac	3	15	14	2	8	14	1	7	-	-	-
10	Chetin Kaya	3	4	3	1	1	3	2	3	-	-	-
11	NEA Salamina	1	1	4	-	-	4	1	1	-	-	-
12	Union Paralimni	-	5	2	-	1	2	-	4	-	-	-
13	Alki Larnaca	-	5	1	-	-	1	-	5	-	-	-
14	Aris Limassol	-	1	1	-	-	1	-	1	-	-	-
15	Digenis Morphou	-	1	-	-	1	-	-	-	-	-	-

To the end of the 1994-1995 season

Since Cyprus became a member of UEFA in 1962, they have regularly entered teams in competitions at both national and club level, but until very recently success in the European club competitions was as spectacularly absent as it was for the national side. Apoel, traditionally the strongest team on the island, were once on the receiving end of a 16-1 thrashing by Sporting from Portugal and have also conceded double figures to Dunfermline and Lierse SK.

Only one predominantly Turkish club, Chetin Kaya, ever achieved any success in the league or cup. But the northern state is not recognised by anyone outside Ankara and although an effort was made to join world football, FIFA would have nothing to do with it. To all intents and purposes, football lies dormant north of the green line.

Thankfully, given the bitterness which exists, only once has a Cypriot club been drawn against a side from Turkey. In 1987, Apoel beat HJK Helsinki and were drawn against Besiktas in the second round – and so promptly withdrew.

Population: 568,000
Area, sq km: 5,896
% in urban areas: 63.6%
Capital city: Nicosia

Cyprus Football Association
Stasinos Str #1, Engomi 152
PO Box 5071
Nicosia
Cyprus
Tel: + 357 2 445341
Fax: + 357 2 472544

Year of formation	1934
Affiliation to FIFA	1948
Affiliation to UEFA	1954
Registered clubs	84
Registered players	19 000
Registered coaches	250
Registered referees	189
National stadium	Makarion Athletic Centre 20 000
National colours	Blue/White/Blue
Reserve colours	White/Blue/White
Season	September - May

THE RECORD

WORLD CUP

1930-58	Did not enter
1962	QT 1st round in group 7
1966	QT 3rd/3 in group 2
1970	QT 4th/4 in group 7
1974	QT 4th/4 in group 6
1978	QT 4th/4 in group 1
1982	QT 5th/5 in group 2
1986	QT 4th/4 in group 5
1990	QT 5th/5 in group 5
1994	QT 5th/6 in group 4

EUROPEAN CHAMPIONSHIP

1960	Did not enter
1964	Did not enter
1968	QT 4th/4 in group 6
1972	QT 4th/4 in group 4
1976	QT 4th/4 in group 1
1980	QT 4th/4 in group 3
1984	QT 5th/5 in group 5
1988	QT 5th/5 in group 5
1992	QT 5th/5 in group 3
1996	QT group 2

EUROPEAN CLUB COMPETITIONS

European Cup
2nd round - Omonia 1973 1980 1986 1988 Apollon 1992

Cup Winners Cup
2nd round - Apoel 1964 1977

UEFA Cup
2nd round - Omonia 1991, Apollon 1994

CLUB DIRECTORY

NICOSIA (Population - 185,000 plus 37,000 in the Turkish sector)

Omonia Nicosia (1948)
Makarion 20,000 – White/White, green trimmings

Apoel Nicosia (1926)
Makarion 20,000 – Yellow/Blue, blue trimmings

Olympiakos Nicosia (1931)
Pancypria 10,000 – Green/Black, black trimmings

LIMASSOL (Population - 120,000)

AEL Limassol (1930)
Tsirion 22,000 – Yellow/Yellow, blue trimmings

Apollon Limassol (1954)
Tsirion 22,000 – Blue/Blue & white

Aris Limassol (1930)
Tsirion 22,000 – Green/Green, white trimmings

APEP Pitsilias (1979)
Municipal Kyperounta 6,000 – Blue and black stripes/Blue, white trimmings

LARNACA (Population - 48,000)

Anorthosis of Famagusta (1911)
Antonis Papadopoulos 8,000 – Blue & white stripes/Blue

AEK FC Larnaca (1927)
Zenon 8,000 – Green/Green, white trimmings
Previous name - Pezoporikos Larnaca 1927-94

Alki Larnaca (1948)
Zenon 8,000 – Blue with red sleeves/Red

EPA Larnaca (1932)
Zenon 8,000 – Black with yellow chest/Yellow

NEA Salamina FC of Famagusta (1948)
Antonis Papadopoulos 8,000 – Red/White, white trimmings

Trust AC (1896-1944)
Old Gymnastica – Blue/White

PARALIMNI

Union of Paralimni (1936)
Paralimni 7,000 – Claret with blue sleeves/White

PAPHOS (Population - 13,000)

APOP Paphos (1953)
Paphiako 8,000 – White/White

Evagoras Paphos (1961)
Paphiako 8,000 – Sky Blue/White

Digenis Morphou moved to Limassol after the invasion of the north of the island. Anorthosis and NEA Salamina moved to Larnaca.

CYPRIOT LEAGUE CHAMPIONSHIP

1935 Trust AC 24 LTSK Nicosia 16 Apoel Nicosia 15
1936 Apoel Nicosia 24 Trust AC 20 LTSK Nicosia 19
1937 Apoel Nicosia 20 Trust AC 19 LTSK Nicosia 16
1938 AEL Limassol 13 Apoel Nicosia 10 Aris Limassol 9
1939 Apoel Nicosia 20 EPA Larnaca 18 AEL Limassol 12
1940 Apoel Nicosia 16 Pezoporikos Larnaca 14 EPA Larnaca 11
1941 AEL Limassol 12Apoel Nicosia 12 EPA Larnaca 4
1942-44 -
1945 Apoel Nicosia 17 EPA Larnaca 17 AEL Limassol 13
1946 EPA Larnaca 17 Apoel Nicosia 15 Pezoporikos Larnaca 9
1947 Apoel Nicosia 24 EPA Larnaca 18 Pezoporikos Larnaca 11
1948 Apoel Nicosia 15 AEL Limassol 11 Olympiakos Nicosia 8
1949 Apoel Nicosia 28 Anorthosis Famagusta 21 Pezoporikos Larnaca 19
1950 Anorthosis Famagusta 23 EPA Larnaca 22 Apoel Nicosia 17
1951 LTSK Nicosia 20 Apoel Nicosia 18 Anorthosis Famagusta 17
1952 Apoel Nicosia 22 EPA Larnaca 17 Chetin Kaya 17
1953 AEL Limassol 23 Pezoporikos Larnaca 21 Apoel Nicosia 17
1954 Pezoporikos Larnaca 26 Apoel Nicosia 22 Anorthosis Famagusta 18
1955 AEL Limassol 29 Pezoporikos Larnaca 24 Apoel Nicosia 23
1956 AEL Limassol 23 Apoel Nicosia 21 NEA Salamina Famagusta 19
1957 Anorthosis Famagusta 29 Pezoporikos Larnaca 21 Omonia Nicosia 21
1958 Anorthosis Famagusta 27 Pezoporikos Larnaca 21 EPA Larnaca 20
1959 -
1960 Anorthosis Famagusta 30 Omonia Nicosia 29 Apoel Nicosia 23
1961 Omonia Nicosia 44 Anorthosis Famagusta 35 Pezoporikos Larnaca 29
1962 Anorthosis Famagusta 35 Omonia Nicosia 31 Pezoporikos Larnaca 30
1963 Anorthosis Famagusta 37 Apoel Nicosia 32 Omonia Nicosia 27
1964 -
1965 Apoel Nicosia 54 Olympiakos Nicosia 47 AEL Limassol 47
1966 Omonia Nicosia 50 Olympiakos Nicosia 49 NEA Salamina Famagusta 48
1967 Olympiakos Nicosia 55 Apoel Nicosia 55 Anorthosis Famagusta 54
1968 AEL Limassol 58 Omonia Nicosia 54 Pezoporikos Larnaca 52
1969 Olympiakos Nicosia 55 Omonia Nicosia 52 Pezoporikos Larnaca 50
1970 EPA Larnaca 53 Pezoporikos Larnaca 53 Omonia Nicosia 53
1971 Olympiakos Nicosia 31 Digenis Morphou 27 Apoel Nicosia 26
1972 Omonia Nicosia 32 EPA Larnaca 30 Union Paralimni 25
1973 Apoel Nicosia 42 Olympiakos Nicosia 34 Pezoporikos Larnaca 31
1974 Omonia Nicosia 44 Pezoporikos Larnaca 42 AEL Limassol 33
1975 Omonia Nicosia 43 Union Paralimni 39 Olympiakos Nicosia 39
1976 Omonia Nicosia 50 Apoel Nicosia 42 Union Paralimni 42
1977 Omonia Nicosia 54 Apoel Nicosia 51 Pezoporikos Larnaca 40
1978 Omonia Nicosia 51 Apoel Nicosia 41 Pezoporikos Larnaca 37
1979 Omonia Nicosia 45 Apoel Nicosia 44 Alki Larnaca 33
1980 Apoel Nicosia 48 Omonia Nicosia 48 Pezoporikos Larnaca 33
1981 Omonia Nicosia 38 Apoel Nicosia 36 Pezoporikos Larnaca 34
1982 Omonia Nicosia 44 Pezoporikos Larnaca 34 Apoel Nicosia 34
1983 Omonia Nicosia 36 Anorthosis Famagusta 35 Apoel Nicosia 32
1984 Omonia Nicosia 42 Apollon Limassol 37 Pezoporikos Larnaca 34
1985 Omonia Nicosia 43 Apoel Nicosia 34 Anorthosis Famagusta 33
1986 Apoel Nicosia 47 Omonia Nicosia 40 Apollon Limassol 37
1987 Omonia Nicosia 52 Apoel Nicosia 47 EPA Larnaca 43
1988 Pezoporikos Larnaca 48 Apoel Nicosia 47 Omonia Nicosia 37
1989 Omonia Nicosia 43 Apollon Limasso 40 Apoel Nicosia 34
1990 Apoel Nicosia 41 Omonia Nicosia 35 Pezoporikos Larnaca 31
1991 Apollon Limassol 44 Anorthosis Famagusta 41 Apoel Nicosia 35
1992 Apoel Nicosia 60 Anorthosis Famagusta 58 Apollon Limassol 53
1993 Omonia Nicosia 59 Apollon Limassol 57 NEA Salamina Famagusta 48
1994 Apollon Limassol 63 Anorthosis Famagusta 61 Apoel Nicosia 56
1995 Omonia Nicosia 48 Anorthosis Famagusta 47 NEA Salamina Famagusta 41

CYPRIOT CUP FINALS

1935 Trust AC..........0-0 1-0..........Apoel Nicosia
1936 Trust AC..........4-1..........LTSK Nicosia
1937 Apoel Nicosia..........2-1..........Trust AC
1938 Trust AC..........1-0..........LTSK Nicosia
1939 AEL Limassol..........3-1..........Apoel Nicosia
1940 AEL Limassol..........3-1..........Pezoporikos Larnaca

Year	Winner	Score	Runner-up
1941	Apoel Nicosia	2-1	AEL Limassol
1942-44	-		
1945	EPA Larnaca	3-1	Apoel Nicosia
1946	EPA Larnaca	2-1	Apoel Nicosia
1947	Apoel Nicosia	4-1	Anorthosis Famagusta
1948	AEL Limassol	2-0	Apoel Nicosia
1949	Anorthosis Famagusta	3-0	Apoel Nicosia
1950	EPA Larnaca	2-0	Anorthosis Famagusta
1951	Apoel Nicosia	7-0	EPA Larnaca
1952	Chetin Kaya	4-1	Pezoporikos Larnaca
1953	EPA Larnaca	2-1	Chetin Kaya
1954	Chetin Kaya	2-1	Pezoporikos Larnaca
1955	EPA Larnaca	2-1	Pezoporikos Larnaca
1956-1961	-		
1962	Anorthosis Famagusta	5-2	Olympiakos Nicosia
1963	Apoel Nicosia	1-1 2-0	Anorthosis Famagusta
1964	-		
1965	Omonia Nicosia	5-1	Apollon Limassol
1966	Apollon Limassol	4-2	NEA Salamina Famagusta
1967	Apollon Limassol	1-0	Alki Larnaca
1968	Apoel Nicosia	2-1	EPA Larnaca
1969	Apoel Nicosia	1-0	Omonia Nicosia
1970	Pezoporikos Larnaca	2-1	Alki Larnaca
1971	Anorthosis Famagusta	1-1 1-0	Omonia Nicosia
1972	Omonia Nicosia	3-1	Pezoporikos Larnaca
1973	Apoel Nicosia	1-0	Pezoporikos Larnaca
1974	Omonia Nicosia	3-2	Union Paralimni
1975	Anorthosis Famagusta	3-2	Union Paralimni
1976	Apoel Nicosia	6-0	Alki Larnaca
1977	Olympiakos Nicosia	2-0	Alki Larnaca
1978	Apoel Nicosia	3-0	Olympiakos Nicosia
1979	Apoel Nicosia	1-0	AEL Limassol
1980	Omonia Nicosia	3-1	Alki Larnaca
1981	Omonia Nicosia	1-1 3-0	Union Paralimni
1982	Omonia Nicosia	2-2 4-1	Apollon Limassol
1983	Omonia Nicosia	2-1	Union Paralimni
1984	Apoel Nicosia	1-1 3-1	Pezoporikos Larnaca
1985	AEL Limassol	1-0	EPA Larnaca
1986	Apollon Limassol	2-0	Apoel Nicosia
1987	AEL Limassol	1-0	Apollon Limassol
1988	Omonia Nicosia	2-1	AEL Limassol
1989	AEL Limassol	3-2	Aris Limassol
1990	NEA Salamina Famagusta	3-2	Omonia Nicosia
1991	Omonia Nicosia	1-0	Olympiakos Nicosia
1992	Apollon Limassol	1-0	Omonia Nicosia
1993	Apoel Nicosia	4-1	Apollon Limassol
1994	Omonia Nicosia	1-0	Anorthosis Famagusta
1995	Apoel Nicosia	4-2	Apollon Limassol

LEADING INTERNATIONAL APPEARANCES

68 Yiannakis Yiangoudakis
55 Floros Nicolaou
48 Pambos Pittas
46 Nicos Pantziaras
40 George Savvides
37 Andreas Stylianou
35 Michael Stefanis
33 Kostas Miamiliotis
32 Andros Sotiriou
30 Klitos Erotocritou
30 Avram Socratous

LEADING INTERNATIONAL SCORERS

8 Phivos Vrahimis
8 Andros Sotiriou
6 Sotiris Kaifas
6 Pambos Pittas
5 Pambos Papadopoulos

INTERNATIONAL MATCHES PLAYED BY CYPRUS

Date	Opponent	Result	Venue	Comp	Scorers
30-07-1949	Israel	L 1-3	Tel Aviv	Fr	Yiasemis
13-11-1960	Israel	D 1-1	Nicosia	WCq	Yiasemis
27-11	Israel	L 1-6	Tel Aviv	WCq	Yiasemis
27-11-1963	Greece	W 3-1	Nicosia	Fr	Pakkos 2, Kristallis
20-03-1965	Lebanon	W 2-0	Nicosia	Fr	Pakkos, Kristallis
24-04	West Germany	L 0-5	Karlsruhe	WCq	
5-05	Sweden	L 0-3	Norrkoping	WCq	
7-11	Sweden	L 0-5	Famagusta	WCq	
14-11	West Germany	L 0-6	Nicosia	WCq	
3-12-1966	Romania	L 1-5	Nicosia	ECq	Pierides
22-03-1967	Italy	L 0-2	Nicosia	ECq	
23-04	Romania	L 0-7	Bucharest	ECq	
1-11	Italy	L 0-5	Cosenza	ECq	
8-11	Switzerland	L 0-5	Lugano	ECq	
17-02-1968	Switzerland	W 2-1	Nicosia	ECq	Asproy, Papadopoulos
19-05	Austria	L 1-7	Vienna	WCq	Kantzilieris
23-11	West Germany	L 0-1	Nicosia	WCq	
11-12	Scotland	L 0-5	Nicosia	WCq	
25-03-1969	Greece	L 0-1	Athens	Fr	
19-04	Austria	L 1-2	Nicosia	WCq	Efthymiadis
17-05	Scotland	L 0-8	Glasgow	WCq	
21-05	West Germany	L 0-12	Essen	WCq	
15-11-1970	Soviet Union	L 1-3	Nicosia	ECq	Charalambous
9-12	Greece	D 1-1	Athens	Fr	Pamboulis
3-02-1971	Nth. Ireland	L 0-3	Nicosia	ECq	
21-04	Nth. Ireland	L 0-5	Belfast	ECq	
9-05	Spain	L 0-2	Nicosia	ECq	

7-06	Soviet Union	L 1-6	Moscow	ECq	Stefanis
24-11	Spain	L 0-7	Granada	ECq	
29-03-1972	Portugal	L 0-4	Lisbon	WCq	
10-05	Portugal	L 0-1	Nicosia	WCq	
19-11	Bulgaria	L 0-4	Nicosia	WCq	
28-01-1973	Bulgaria	L 0-3	Nicosia	Fr	
14-02	Nth. Ireland	W 1-0	Nicosia	WCq	Antoniou
8-05	Nth. Ireland	L 0-3	London	WCq	
18-11	Bulgaria	L 0-2	Sofia	WCq	
6-02-1974	Bulgaria	L 1-4	Morphou	Fr	Haris
15-11	Greece	L 1-3	Athens	Fr	Papadopoulos
1-04-1975	Greece	L 1-2	Nicosia	Fr	Constantinou
16-04	England	L 0-5	London	ECq	
20-04	Czechoslovakia	L 0-4	Prague	ECq	
11-05	England	L 0-1	Limassol	ECq	
8-06	Portugal	L 0-2	Limassol	ECq	
23-11	Czechoslovakia	L 0-3	Limassol	ECq	
3-12	Portugal	L 0-1	Setubal	ECq	
23-05-1976	Denmark	L 1-5	Limassol	WCq	Stefanis
27-10	Denmark	L 0-5	Copenhagen	WCq	
31-10	Poland	L 0-5	Warsaw	WCq	
5-12	Portugal	L 1-2	Limassol	WCq	Stavros
30-01-1977	Bulgaria	L 1-2	Nicosia	Fr	Savva
15-05	Poland	L 1-3	Nicosia	WCq	Antoniou
16-11	Portugal	L 0-4	Lisbon	WCq	
11-01-1978	Greece	L 0-2	Limassol	Fr	
16-11	Saudi Arabia	D 2-2	Nicosia	Fr	Timotheoy, Economolis
13-12	Spain	L 0-5	Salamanca	ECq	
1-04-1979	Yugoslavia	L 0-3	Nicosia	ECq	
13-05	Romania	D 1-1	Limassol	ECq	Kaiafas
14-11	Yugoslavia	L 0-5	Novi Sad	ECq	
18-11	Romania	L 0-2	Bucharest	ECq	
9-12	Spain	L 1-3	Limassol	ECq	Vrahimis
16-01-1980	Greece	D 1-1	Nicosia	Fr	Kitzas
26-03	Rep. Ireland	L 2-3	Nicosia	WCq	Pantziaras, Kaiafas
11-10	France	L 0-7	Limassol	WCq	
19-11	Rep. Ireland	L 0-6	Dublin	WCq	
21-12	Belgium	L 0-2	Nicosia	WCq	
18-02-1981	Belgium	L 2-3	Brussels	WCq	Lysandrou, Firos
22-02	Holland	L 0-3	Groningen	WCq	
15-04	Greece	L 0-1	Nicosia	Fr	
29-04	Holland	L 0-1	Nicosia	WCq	
5-12	France	L 0-4	Paris	WCq	
14-04-1982	Syria	W 1-0	Damascus	Fr	Vrahimis
1-05	Romania	L 1-3	Hunedoara	ECq	Vrahimis
27-10	Greece	D 1-1	Nicosia	Fr	Yiangoudakis
13-11	Sweden	L 0-1	Nicosia	ECq	
22-12	Greece	L 0-1	Yanina	Fr	
12-02-1983	Italy	D 1-1	Limassol	ECq	Mavris
27-03	Czechoslovakia	D 1-1	Nicosia	ECq	Theofanus
16-04	Czechoslovakia	L 0-6	Prague	ECq	
15-05	Sweden	L 0-5	Malmo	ECq	
12-11	Romania	L 0-1	Limassol	ECq	
22-12	Italy	L 1-3	Perugia	ECq	Tsingis
11-04-1984	Greece	D 1-1	Athens	Fr	Theofanus
2-05	Austria	L 1-2	Nicosia	WCq	Christophorou
30-09	Greece	L 0-2	Limassol	Fr	
30-10	Canada	D 0-0	Nicosia	Fr	
17-11	Hungary	L 1-2	Limassol	WCq	Fotis
17-12	Luxembourg	W 1-0	Nicosia	Fr	Tsikos
23-12	Holland	L 0-1	Nicosia	WCq	
27-02-1985	Holland	L 1-7	Amsterdam	WCq	Marangos
3-04	Hungary	L 0-2	Budapest	WCq	
7-05	Austria	L 0-4	Graz	WCq	
19-02-1986	Greece	D 0-0	Athens	Fr	
3-12	Greece	L 2-4	Nicosia	ECq	Christofidis, Savvides
21-12	Holland	L 0-2	Nicosia	ECq	
14-01-1987	Greece	L 1-3	Athens	ECq	Savva
8-02	Hungary	L 0-1	Nicosia	ECq	
25-03	Jordan	L 1-2	Amman	Fr	Taziadoros
12-04	Poland	D 0-0	Gdansk	ECq	

28-10	Holland	L 0-8	Rotterdam	ECq	Declared Void
11-11	Poland	L 0-1	Limassol	ECq	
2-12	Hungary	L 0-1	Budapest	ECq	
9-12	Holland	L 0-4	Amsterdam	ECq	
12-10-1988	Malta	L 0-1	Limassol	Fr	
22-10	France	D 1-1	Nicosia	WCq	Pittas
2-11	Norway	L 0-3	Limassol	WCq	
23-11	Malta	D 1-1	Ta'Qali	Fr	Ioannou
11-12	Yugoslavia	L 0-4	Belgrade	WCq	
8-02-1989	Scotland	L 2-3	Limassol	WCq	Koliandris, Ioannou
26-04	Scotland	L 1-2	Glasgow	WCq	Nicolaou
21-05	Norway	L 1-3	Oslo	WCq	Koliandris
11-10	Malta	D 0-0	Nicosia	Fr	
28-10	Yugoslavia	L 1-2	Athens	WCq	Pittas
18-11	France	L 0-2	Toulouse	WCq	
31-10-1990	Hungary	L 2-4	Budapest	ECq	Xiourouppas, Tsolakis
14-11	Norway	L 0-3	Nicosia	ECq	
22-12	Italy	L 0-4	Limassol	ECq	
27-02-1991	Greece	D 1-1	Limassol	Fr	Nicolaou
3-04	Hungary	L 0-2	Limassol	ECq	
1-05	Norway	L 0-3	Oslo	ECq	
29-05	Soviet Union	L 0-4	Moscow	ECq	
16-10	Iceland	D 1-1	Larnaca	Fr	Pittas
13-11	Soviet Union	L 0-3	Larnaca	ECq	
21-12	Italy	L 0-3	Foggia	ECq	
3-03-1992	Israel	L 1-2	Tel Aviv	Fr	Pittas
25-03	Greece	L 1-3	Limassol	Fr	Elia
22-04	Belgium	L 0-1	Brussels	WCq	
17-06	Faeroe Islands	W 2-0	Toftir	WCq	Sotiriou, Papavassiliou
2-09	Greece	W 3-2	Salonica	Fr	Charalambous, Sotiriou, Andreou
7-10	Malta	W 3-0	Limassol	Fr	Hadjilucas, Costa, Ioannou.D
14-10	Wales	L 0-1	Limassol	WCq	
18-11	Slovenia	D 1-1	Larnaca	Fr	Savvides
29-11	Romania	L 1-4	Larnaca	WCq	Pittas
22-12	Georgia	W 1-0	Larnaca	Fr	Ioannou.D
1-02-1993	Poland	D 0-0	Nicosia	Fr	
13-02	Belgium	L 0-3	Nicosia	WCq	
24-03	Czechoslovakia	D 1-1	Limassol	WCq	Sotiriou
14-04	Romania	L 1-2	Bucharest	WCq	Sotiriou
25-04	Faeroe Islands	W 3-1	Limassol	WCq	Xiourouppas, Sotiriou, Ioannou.Y
6-10	Israel	D 2-2	Limassol	Fr	Pittas, Sotiriou
13-10	Wales	L 0-2	Cardiff	WCq	
27-10	Czechoslovakia	L 0-3	Kosice	WCq	
9-03-1994	Estonia	W 2-0	Paralimni	Fr	Agathocleous, Andreou
27-04	Slovenia	L 0-3	Maribor	Fr	
7-09	Spain	L 1-2	Limassol	ECq	Sotiriou
8-10	Armenia	D 0-0	Yerevan	ECq	
16-11	Armenia	W 2-0	Limassol	ECq	Sotiriou, Phasiouliotis
29-11	Israel	L 3-4	Jerusalem	Fr	OG, Gogic, Hadjilucas
17-12	Macedonia	L 0-3	Skopje	ECq	
25-01-1995	Greece	L 2-3	Larnaca	Fr	
8-02	Norway	L 0-2	Larnaca	Fr	
15-02	Estonia	W 3-1	Limassol	Fr	Gogic, Engomitis, Larkov
8-03	Sweden	D 3-3	Limassol	Fr	Agathocleous, Hadjilucas, Engomitis
29-03	Denmark	D 1-1	Limassol	ECq	Agathocleos
26-04	Belgium	L 0-2	Brussels	ECq	
7-06	Denmark	L 0-4	Copenhagen	ECq	

THE CZECH REPUBLIC

The Czech Republic is the heartland of the former state of Czechoslovakia and heads towards the next century with great hope. Its capital Prague has been at the centre of a great economic success story since the fall of Communism and the football federation will be hoping for a similar revival.

In 1993 came the introduction of a new Czech League and the first championship had familiar winners, Sparta Prague. However, it also saw the regeneration of a few names from the past. Slavia Prague, a club born in the days before Czechoslovakia even existed, have become a force again, whilst Viktoria Zizkov, champions in 1928, won the Czech Cup. At the same time the old Army team Dukla Prague, a club which had always received special patronage from the Communist rulers, went the other way. They were relegated in 1994 after winning just one game all season and losing in the Cup to a fifth division side.

The Czech league is not a new concept. Dating originally from 1896, it has been played in various forms over the years, depending on which territories came under the auspices of the governing body at the time. The Stredocesky League, a popular tournament in the early 1920s, was restricted to clubs around the former Bohemian capital Prague, whilst the Ceskomoravska League, played during the war, was open to all of Bohemia and Moravia, the regions which make up the present Czech Republic. It has not been unknown for the Stredocesky Cup to run alongside the Czech Cup, while after 1970 the Czechoslovakian Cup final took the form of a play-off between the winners of the Czech Cup and Slovak Cup.

Both Sparta and Slavia were formed in 1893 and they dominated football in Prague from the very start, Slavia winning three of the five Czech leagues played between 1896 and 1902. The Charity Cup in 1906 was the next major tournament to be launched and results confirmed the Sparta-Slavia axis as the dominant force in the capital, so that they were the only serious title contenders when the Czech League was launched in 1912 and the Stredocesky League in 1918. Both clubs also made their mark internationally, Slavia in particular scoring heavy wins in the early years of the century over First Vienna (11-0), Nuremburg (12-2), Bayern Munich (13-0) and Budapest Torna Club (12-0).

A Bohemian national side took to the field in 1903 against Hungary and over the next five years six further internationals were played, all against the same opponents apart from one game against England in 1908. Bohemia were due to enter the 1908 Olympics in London but withdrew at the last moment and played no more internationals until they entered the 1920 Games – as Czechoslovakia.

Czech sides were always the more dominant in the new Czechoslovakian league, the Slavia-Sparta hegemony continuing throughout the inter-war years. During the war Czech clubs again played in their own league but when forces were joined again afterwards, the decline of Slavia allowed Slovak clubs such as Slovan Bratislava and later Spartak Trnava to challenge Sparta.

The wheel has turned full circle and Czech football now looks set to be dominated by Sparta and Slavia again. It is hoped that the success of the country's economy will have a positive effect on the game and enable Sparta and Slavia to compete with the best in Europe.

Population: 10,298,000
Area, sq km: 78,864
% in urban areas: 75.7%
Capital city: Prague

Ceskoslovensky Fotbalovy Svaz
NA Porici #12
11530 Prague 1
Czechoslovakia
Tel: + 42 2 356913
Fax: + 42 2 352784

Year of formation	1901-22, 1990
Affiliation to FIFA	1906-22, 1994
Affiliation to UEFA	1993
Registered clubs	3562
Registered players	237 000
Registered referees	9500
National stadium	Strahov, Prague 19 000
National colours	Red/White/Blue
Reserve colours	White/White/White
Season	August - June, with a mid season break December - February

THE RECORD

WORLD CUP
1930-94 Entered as Czechoslovakia

EUROPEAN CHAMPIONSHIP
1960-92 Entered as Czechoslovakia
1996 QT group 5

EUROPEAN CLUB COMPETITIONS
European Cup
Semi-finalists - Dukla Praha 1967

European Cup Winners Cup
Semi-finalists - Sparta Praha 1973 Banik Ostrava 1979 Dukla Praha 1986

UEFA Cup
Semi-finalists - Bohemians Praha 1983

Mitropa Cup
Winners - Sparta 1927 1935 Slavia 1938
Finalists - Slavia 1929 Sparta 1930 1936

CLUB DIRECTORY

PRAGUE (Population - 1,325,000)
FC Bohemians Praha (1905)
Vrsovice 14,000 – White/Green, green trimmings
Previous names - AFK Vrsovice 1905-27, Bohemians 1927-39, AFK Bohemia 1939-49, Zeleznicari 1949-51, Spartak Stalingrad 1951-61, Bohemians CKD 1961-90

FK Dukla Praha (1948)
Juliska 28,000 – Yellow/Yellow, red trimmings
Previous names - ATK 1948-52, UDA 1952-56

SK Slavia Praha (1893)
Dr Vacka 16,000 – Red & white halves/White
Previous names - SK Slavia 1893-1949, Dynamo Slavia 1949-51, TJ Slavia 1951-90

AC Sparta Praha (1893)
Strahov 19,000 – Red/White, white trimmings
Previous names - AC Sparta 1893-1949, Sparta Bratrstvi 1949-51, Sparta Sokolovo 1951-53, Spartak Sokolovo 1953-64, TJ Sparta CKD 1964-90

FK Viktoria Zizkov (1903)
FK Viktoria 10,000 – Red & white stripes/White

OSTRAVA (Population - 760,000)
FC Baník Ostrava OKD (1922)
Bazaly 32,000 – Light blue/Blue
Previous names - Slezska 1922-48, Trojice 1948-50, OKD 1950-53, TJ Baník OKD 1953-90

FC Vitkovice (1922)
Vitkovice 23,000 – White/Blue, red & blue trimmings
Previous names - Zelezarni 1934-39 & 1945-52, Baník Vitkovice 1952-57, TJ Vitkovice 1957-92

BRNO (Population - 450,000)
FC Boby Brno (1913)
Za Luzankami 35,000 – Red with white sleeves/Red
Previous names - Zidenice 1913-49, Zbrojovka Zidenice 1949-52, MEZ Zidenice 1952-53, Red Star 1953-61, Spartak 1961-65, TJ Zbrojovka 1965-90, FC Zbrojovka 1990-92

PLZEN (Population - 210,000)
FC Viktoria Plzen (1911)
Struncovy Sady 35,000 – Red/Red, white trimmings
Previous names - Viktoria 1911-48, Skoda 1948-53, Spartak 1953-65, TJ Skoda 1965-92

OLOMOUC (Population - 126,000)
SK Sigma Olomouc MZ (1919)
Andruv 14,000 – Blue with white sleeves/Blue
Previous names - Sokol Moravska Zelezarny 1919-53, Banik 1953-56, Spartak 1956-61, Moravske Zelezarny 1961-66, TJ Sigma ZTS 1966-90

ZLIN (Population - 124,000)
FC Svit Zlin (1919)
Letna 12,000 – Yellow/Black, black trimmings
Previous names - FK Zlin 1919-24, Bata Zlin 1924-48, Botostroj Zlin 1948-49, Svit Gottwaldov 1949-53, Iskra Gottwaldov 1953-58, TJ Gottwaldov 1958-90

HRADEC KRALOVE (Population - 113,000)
SK Spartak Hradec Králové (1905)
Vsesportovni 25,000 – White with black sleeves/White
Previous names - SK 1905-48, Sokol Skoda 1948-53, RH Spartak ZVU 1953-90

PARDUBICE (Population - 95,000)
SK Pardubice (1925)
VCHZ – Blue/White
Previous name - Explosie 1925-49, VCHZ Pardubice 1949-90, Synthesia 1990-93

TEPLICE (Population - 94,000)
Sklo Union Teplice (1945)
Na Stinadlech – Yellow/Blue
Previous names - Technomat 1945-51, Vodotechna 1951-52, Ingstav 1952, Tatran 1952-60, Slovan 1960-66

CHEB
SKP Union Cheb (1950)
Lokomotiva 14,000 – Blue/Blue, white trimmings
Previous names - Sokolovo 1951-53, Red Star 1953-66, Dukla Hranicar 1966-71, Red Star Cheb (Rudá Hvezda) 1971-90

CZECH LEAGUE CHAMPIONS

Czech League (Mistrovstvi Cech)

1896	FC Kickers & DFC Praha
1897	Slavia Praha
1898	Slavia Praha
1899	Slavia Praha
1902	CAFC Vinohrady

Czech League (Mistrovstvi CSF)

1912	Sparta Praha 1-1 4-0	AFK Kolín	
1913	Slavia Praha 2-0	Moravska Slavia Brno	
1917	Sparta Praha	Slavia Praha	Viktoria Zizkov
1919	Sparta Praha 6	SK Kladno 3	Olympia Plzen 3
1922	Sparta Praha 7-0	SK Hradec Králové	

Stredocesky League (Mistrovstvi Stredoceske Zupy)

1918	Slavia Praha 16	Sparta Praha 15	AFK Vrsovice 9
1919	Sparta Praha 14	Slavia Praha 14	Union Zizkov 12
1920	Sparta Praha 22	AFK Vrsovice 15	Viktoria Zizkov 14
1921	Sparta Praha 22	Slavia Praha 16	Union Zizkov 16
1922	Sparta Praha 26	Slavia Praha 24	Cechie Karlín 16
1923	Sparta Praha 30	Slavia Praha 25	Cechie Karlín 19
1924	Slavia Praha 22	Viktoria Zizkov 21	CAFC Vinohrady 14

Ceskomoravska liga

1939i	Sparta Praha 32	Slavia Praha 31	SK Pardubice 28
1940k	Slavia Praha 36	Sparta Praha 35	SK Pardubice 23
1941	Slavia Praha 32	SK Plzen 26	SK Pardubice 24
1942	Slavia Praha 37	SK Prostejov 28	SK Plzen 24
1943	Slavia Praha 32	Sparta Praha 29	Bata Zlin 25
1944n	Sparta Praha 48	Slavia Praha 45	Bata Zlin 32

Ceskomoravska Liga

1994q	Sparta Praha 45	Slavia Praha 39	Banik Ostrava 36
1995q3	Sparta Praha 70	Slavia Praha 64	FC Boby Brno 54

CZECH CUP FINALS

Pohár Dobrocinnosti (Charity Cup)

Year	Winners	Score	Runners-up
1906	SK Smichov	?	Sparta Praha
1907	SK Smichov	3-1	Sparta Praha "B"
1908	Slavia Praha "B"	?	Sparta Praha
1909	Sparta Praha	3-1	SK Smichov
1910	Slavia Praha	5-2	SK Smichov
1911	Slavia Praha	4-1	AFK Kolín
1912	Slavia Praha	4-3	Viktoria Zizkov
1913	Viktoria Zizkov	2-0	Slavia Praha
1914	Viktoria Zizkov	1-0	Slavia Praha
1915	Sparta Praha	6-2	Sparta Kladno
1916	Viktoria Zizkov	3-0	Sparta Praha

Stredocesky Cup

1918	Sparta Praha	4-1	Slavia Praha
1919	Sparta Praha	2-0	Viktoria Zizkov
1920	Sparta Praha	5-1	Viktoria Zizkov
1921	Viktoria Zizkov	3-0	Sparta Praha
1922	Slavia Praha	3-2	Cechie Karlin
1923	Sparta Praha	3-1	Slavia Praha
1924	Sparta Praha	5-1	AFK Vrsovice
1925	Sparta Praha	7-0	CAFC Vinohrady
1926	Slavia Praha	10-0	CAFC Vinohrady
1927	Slavia Praha	1-0	Sparta Praha
1928	Slavia Praha	1-1 1-1 3-2	Sparta Praha
1929	Viktoria Zizkov	3-1	SK Liben
1930	Slavia Praha	4-2	SK Kladno
1931	Sparta Praha	3-1	Slavia Praha
1932	Slavia Praha	2-1	Sparta Praha
1933	Viktoria Zizkov	2-1	Sparta Praha
1934	Sparta Praha	6-0	SK Kladno
1935	Slavia Praha	4-1	Bohemians Praha
1936	Sparta Praha	1-1 1-0	Slavia Praha
1937-39	-		
1940	Viktoria Zizkov	5-3	Sparta Praha
1941	Slavia Praha	13-2	SS Plincner
1942	Bohemians Praha	8-6	Sparta Praha

Czech Cup

1940	ASO Olomouc	3-1 2-1	SK Prostejov
1941	Slavia Praha	2-3 6-3	Sparta Praha
1942	Slavia Praha	5-2 5-5	Bohemians Praha
1943	Sparta Praha	3-1 7-1	Viktoria Plzen
1944	Sparta Praha	4-2 4-3	Viktoria Plzen
1945	Slavia Praha	1-1 5-2	SK Rakovnik
1946	Sparta Praha	6-0 3-0	Slezka Ostrava
1947-69	-		
1970	TJ Gottwaldov	2-2 4-0	LIAZ Jablonec
1971	Skoda Plzen	1-1 3-3 5-5p	Sparta Praha "B"
1972	Sparta Praha	2-1 2-1	Dukla Praha
1973	Banik Ostrava	2-1 0-1 5-4p	Union Teplice
1974	Slavia Praha	1-1 3-1	Sparta Praha
1975	Sparta Praha	1-0 2-1	Banik Ostrava
1976	Sparta Praha	4-1 1-0	SONP Kladno
1977	Union Teplice	1-0 2-1	Sparta Praha
1978	Banik Ostrava	0-1 2-0	Mladá Boleslav
1979	Banik Ostrava	2-0 1-0	Skoda Plzen
1980	Sparta Praha	1-1 4-2	Bohemians Praha
1981	Dukla Praha	3-1 2-3	Bohemians Praha
1982	Bohemians Praha	4-0	Dukla Praha

Year	Winners	Score	Runners-up
1983	Bohemians Praha	2-1 1-1	Dukla Praha
1984	Sparta Praha	3-0 3-0	Dukla Praha
1985	Dukla Praha	3-1	Dynamo Ceske Bud.
1986	Sparta Praha	4-2	Dukla Praha
1987	Sparta Praha	1-1 4-3p	Slavia Praha
1988	Sparta Praha	3-0	TJ Vitkovice
1989	Sparta Praha	1-0	Slavia Praha
1990	Dukla Praha	5-3	Uherske Hradiste
1991	Banik Ostrava	4-2	Dynamo Ceske Budejovice
1992	Sparta Praha	2-1	Banik Ostrava
1993	Sparta Praha	2-0	FC Boby Brno
1994	Viktoria Zizkov	2-2 6-5p	Sparta Praha
1995	Spartak Hradec Králové	0-0 3-1p	Viktoria Zizkov

INTERNATIONAL MATCHES PLAYED BY BOHEMIA

Date	Opponent	Result	Venue	Comp	Scorers
5-04-1903	Hungary	L 1-2	Budapest	Fr	Resek
1-04-1906	Hungary	D 1-1	Budapest	Fr	Setela
7-10	Hungary	D 4-4	Prague	Fr	Horvath, Baumruk, Vanek, Kosek
7-04-1907	Hungary	L 2-5	Budapest	Fr	Pelikan, Milka
6-10	Hungary	W 5-3	Prague	Fr	Kosek 3, Belka 2
5-04-1908	Hungary	L 2-5	Budapest	Fr	Belka 2
13-06	England	L 0-4	Prague	Fr	

INTERNATIONAL MATCHES PLAYED BY THE CZECH REPUBLIC

Date	Opponent	Result	Venue	Comp	Scorers
23-02-1994	Turkey	W 4-1	Istanbul	Fr	Novotny, Látal, Siegl 2
20-04	Switzerland	L 0-3	Zurich	Fr	
25-05	Lithuania	W 5-3	Ostrava	Fr	Kuka 2, Frydek, Kubik, Postulka
5-06	Rep. Ireland	W 3-1	Dublin	Fr	Kuka 2, Suchoparek
17-08	France	D 2-2	Bordeaux	Fr	Skuhravy, Smejkal
6-09	Malta	W 6-1	Prague	ECq	Smejkal,Kubik, Siegl 3, Berger
12-10	Malta	D 0-0	Ta'Qali	ECq	
16-11	Holland	D 0-0	Rotterdam	ECq	
8-03-1995	Finland	W 4-1	Brno	Fr	Berger 2, Samec 2
29-03-	Belarus	W 4-2	Ostrava	ECq	Kadlec, Berger 2, Kuka
26-04	Holland	W 3-1	Prague	ECq	Skuhravy, Nemecek, Berger
8-05	Slovakia	D 1-1	Bratislava	Fr	Smejkal
7-06	Luxembourg	L 0-1	Luxembourg	ECq	

THE FORMER CZECHOSLOVAKIA

In November 1993 Czechoslovakia quietly slipped into footballing history, a 0-0 draw in a World Cup qualifier in Brussels proving the last act of a once great footballing nation. Henceforth the Czech Republic and Slovakia would both play as independent states again.

Czechoslovakia was itself born as an independent state in 1918 but it was not until 1925 that a national league was set up catering for all three republics of Bohemia, Moravia and Slovakia. The national team entered the Olympic Games in 1920 and reached the first of the four major finals they have appeared in, but they lost 2-0 to the hosts, Belgium, and were not even awarded the silver medal as they walked off the field after half an hour, complaining about the bias of the referee.

Throughout the 1920s and 1930s, Czechoslovakia produced some fabulous players and sides. Sparta Prague won the first Mitropa Cup in 1927, a feat they repeated in 1935, whilst their city rivals Slavia were victorious in 1938. Both clubs dominated the league at home, winning 13 of the 14 championships played before the war. Success in the Mitropa Cup meant that both Slavia and Sparta could bring famous players, the likes of the Belgian Raymond Braine, to Prague.

In the 1934 World Cup the national side contained players such as Antonin Puc, the all-time leading goalscorer for Czechoslovakia, Frantisek Planicka, regarded as the finest goalkeeper of the pre-war era, and Oldrich Nejedly, another prolific goalscorer. They played some of the best football of the tournament but lost 2-1 to Italy in the final in Rome. The 1938 World Cup was not such a success as they were eliminated by Brazil after the infamous Battle of Bordeaux in the quarter-finals, Planicka breaking an arm and Nejedly a leg.

After the Second World War and the Communist takeover all clubs were incorporated into various government bodies such as the army and police and the immediate effect was to break the Sparta-Slavia stranglehold. Dukla Prague, the team of the army, and sides from Bratislava and other provincial towns began to make their presence felt. Slavia went into a decline from which they have only just recovered. Clubs such as Slovan Bratislava, Banik Ostrava, and Spartak Trnava all had successful spells in the league and cup. Slovan won the Cup Winners Cup in 1969, but it was the only European title ever won by a Czechslovakian club.

THE ORDER OF MERIT

	Team	All G	All S	All B	League G	League S	League B	Cup G	Cup S	Europe G	Europe S	Europe B
1	Sparta Praha	27	21	8	19	16	7	8	5	-	-	1
2	Dukla Praha	19	9	5	11	7	3	8	2	-	-	2
3	Slovan Bratislava	14	16	3	8	10	3	5	6	1	-	-
4	Slavia Praha	9	11	7	9	9	7	-	2	-	-	-
5	Spartak Trnava	9	2	2	5	1	1	4	1	-	-	1
6	Baník Ostrava	6	7	2	3	6	1	3	1	-	-	1
7	Lokomotiva Kosice	2	1	2	-	-	2	2	1	-	-	-
8	TJ Internacional	1	6	5	1	3	5	-	3	-	-	-
9	1.FC Kosice	1	4	2	-	1	2	1	3	-	-	-
10	Bohemians Praha	1	2	12	1	1	11	-	1	-	-	1
11	Viktoria Zizkov	1	1	3	1	1	3	-	-	-	-	-
12	Zbrojovka Brno	1	1	1	1	1	1	-	-	-	-	-
	TJ Vítkovice	1	1	-	1	1	-	-	-	-	-	-
14	DAC Dunajská Streda	1	-	1	-	-	1	1	-	-	-	-
15	SK Zlin	1	-	-	-	-	-	1	-	-	-	-
	Spartak Hradec Králové	1	-	-	1	-	-	-	-	-	-	-
17	Tatran Presov	-	4	1	-	2	1	-	2	-	-	-
18	Jednota Trencin	-	2	1	-	1	1	-	1	-	-	-
19	Sklo Union Teplice	-	1	2	-	-	2	-	1	-	-	-
20	Skoda Plzen	-	1	1	-	-	1	-	1	-	-	-
	FC Nitra	-	1	1	-	1	1	-	-	-	-	-
22	Synthesia Pardubice	-	1	-	-	-	-	-	1	-	-	-
	SK Zilina	-	1	-	-	-	-	-	1	-	-	-
	Dukla Banská Bystrica	-	1	-	-	-	-	-	1	-	-	-
25	SONP Kladno	-	-	2	-	-	2	-	-	-	-	-
	SK Prostejov	-	-	2	-	-	2	-	-	-	-	-
	SK Zidenice	-	-	2	-	-	2	-	-	-	-	-
28	Sigma Olomouc	-	-	1	-	-	1	-	-	-	-	-

The final standings for Czechoslovakia 1925-1993

For a decade after the war it looked as if the national side had been permanently weakened. Poor performances in the 1954 and 1958 World Cups were followed, however, by an upturn in fortunes. Based now around the powerful Dukla team, Czechoslovakia finished third in the inaugural European Championship and followed this success by reaching the World Cup Final again in 1962. In that side was Josef Masopust, one of the most famous Czechoslovakian footballers of all time.

There were those who claimed that the post-war generation did not match up to their illustrious predecessors, and there was a grain of truth in this. Failure to qualify for the 1966 World Cup as well as defeat in the first round of the 1964 European Championship by East Germany lent credence to the idea that had it not been for Viliam Schroif, their goalkeeper who was in inspirational form up until the final in Chile, the team would not have got as far as they did.

The slide continued throughout the 1970s despite one heroic interlude. In the 1976 European Championship, England were beaten into second place in the qualifying group and the quarter-finals saw victory over the Soviet Union. Czechoslovakia were unfancied when they travelled to Yugoslavia for the final stages, but in the semi-finals they beat Holland 3-1 to qualify for their fourth major final. They now faced the world champions West Germany and the match was a classic, a 2-2 draw after extra-time. The championship was decided on penalty kicks and the Czechs prevailed, ultimately deserving of their title in what had proved to be an entertaining final tournament.

Once again the team's success owed much to outstanding goalkeeping and Ivo Viktor went on to win the European Footballer of the Year award, the only player from Czechoslovakia to do so. In defence Anton Ondrus was particularly strong whilst in midfield Antonin Panenka and Karol Dobias combined well. Zdenek Nehoda in attack was a prolific goalscorer, and finished his career only three short of Puc's record tally, at a time when goals were much harder to come by. Third place was achieved at the 1980 European Championships but although the team qualified for two more World Cups neither was a spectacular success.

The Velvet Revolution of 1989 which saw the Communists swept from power also signalled the end of Czechoslovakia as an entity. The Slovaks voted to become independent, and the 1992/93 domestic season was Czechoslovakia's last.

THE RECORD

Year of formation	1922-93
Affiliation to FIFA	1923-94
Affiliation to UEFA	1954-93

WORLD CUP

1930	Did not enter	
1934	QT 1st/2 in group 9	Final Tournament/Finalists
1938	QT 1st/2 in group 6	Final Tournament/Quarter-finalists
1950	Did not enter	
1954	QT 1st/3 in group 8	Final Tournament/1st round
1958	QT 1st/3 in group 4	Final Tournament/1st round
1962	QT 1st/3 in group 8	Final Tournament/Finalists
1966	QT 2nd/4 in group 4	
1970	QT 1st/4 in group 2	Final Tournament/1st round
1974	QT 2nd/3 in group 8	
1978	QT 2nd/3 in group 7	
1982	QT 2nd/5 in group 3	Final Tournament/1st round
1986	QT 4th/5 in group 2	
1990	QT 2nd/5 in group 7	Final Tournament/Quarter-finalists
1994	QT 3rd/6 in group 4	

EUROPEAN CHAMPIONSHIP

1960	Semi-finalists/3rd place	
1964	1st round	
1968	QT 2nd/4 in group 1	
1972	QT 2nd/4 in group 1	
1976	QT 1st/4 in group 1	Final Tournament/Winners
1980	QT 1st/4 in group 5	Final Tournament/3rd place
1984	QT 3rd/5 in group 5	
1988	QT 2nd/4 in group 6	
1992	QT 2nd/5 in group 1	

DR. GERÖ / INTERNATIONAL CUP

1929	3rd
1932	4th
1935	4th
1953	2nd
1960	Winners

EUROPEAN CLUB COMPETITIONS

European Cup
Semi-finalists - Dukla Praha 1967, Spartak Trnava 1969

European Cup Winners Cup
Winners - Slovan Bratislava 1969

UEFA Cup
Semi-finalists - Bohemians Praha 1983

Mitropa Cup
Winners - Sparta 1927 1935 Slavia 1938
Finalists - Slavia 1929 Sparta 1930 1936

CZECHOSLOVAKIAN LEAGUE CHAMPIONSHIP

1925ae	Slavia Praha 15 Sparta Praha 15 Viktoria Zizkov 11
1926k	Sparta Praha 39 Slavia Praha 38 Viktoria Zizkov 35
1927ad	Sparta Praha 13 Slavia Praha 11 AFK Vrsovice8
1928e	Viktoria Zizkov 18 Slavia Praha 16 Sparta Praha 14
1929	Slavia Praha 21 Viktoria Zizkov 18 Sparta Praha 13
1930f	Slavia Praha 28 Sparta Praha 18 Viktoria Zizkov 16
1931	Slavia Praha 24 Sparta Praha 21 Bohemians Praha 18
1932g	Sparta Praha 27 Slavia Praha 22 Bohemians Praha 18
1933h	Slavia Praha 26 Sparta Praha 24 Viktoria Plzen 22
1934	Slavia Praha 30 Sparta Praha 25 SK Kladno 21
1935k	Slavia Praha 36 Sparta Praha 35 SK Zidenice 26
1936n	Sparta Praha 41 Slavia Praha 41 SK Prostejov 36
1937k	Slavia Praha 38 Sparta Praha 31 SK Prostejov 29
1938	Sparta Praha 36 Slavia Praha 29 SK Zidenice 26
1939-45	-
1946	Sparta Praha 4-2 5-0 Slavia Praha
1947n	Slavia Praha 40 Sparta Praha 39 SK Kladno 32
1948i	Sparta Praha 27 Slavia Praha 27 SK Bratislava 24
1948*	Dynamo Slavia 18 Viktoria Plzen 18 Bratrstvi Sparta 17
1949n	NV Bratislava 41 Bratrstvi Sparta 37 Zeleznicari 33
1950	NV Bratislava 35 Bratrstvi Sparta 35 Zeleznicari 35
1951	NV Bratislava 33 Sparta Sokolovo 33 Dynamo Kosice 33
1952	Sparta Sokolovo 41 NV Bratislava 40 Ingstav Teplice 33
1953ag	UDA Praha 22 Sparta Sokolovo 19 CH Bratislava 18
1954k	Spartak Sokolovo 30 Baník Ostrava 28 CH Bratislava 27
1955	Slovan Bratislava 31 UDA Praha 29 Spartak Sokolovo 27
1956	Dukla Praha 32 Slovan Bratislava 27 Spartak Sokolovo 26
1957	-
1958s	Dukla Praha 40 Spartak Sokolovo 40 CH Bratislava 38
1959n	CH Bratislava 40 Dukla Praha 31 Dynamo Praha 31
1960	Spartak Hr. Králóve 34 Slovan Bratislava 32 Dukla Praha 32
1961	Dukla Praha 39 CH Bratislava 32 Slovan Bratislava 29
1962	Dukla Praha 35 Slovan Nitra 32 CH Bratislava 30
1963	Dukla Praha 35 Jednota Trencin 32 Baník Ostrava 31
1964	Dukla Praha 37 Slovan Bratislava 35 Tatran Presov 31
1965	Sparta Praha 42 Tatran Presov 33 VSS Kosice 30
1966	Dukla Praha 33 Sparta Praha 33 Slavia Praha 33
1967	Sparta Praha 39 Slovan Bratislava 35 Spartak Trnava 34
1968	Spartak Trnava 35 Slovan Bratislava 30 Jednota Trencin 30
1969	Spartak Trnava 39 Slovan Bratislava 34 Sparta Praha 29
1970q	Slovan Bratislava 43 Spartak Trnava 40 Sparta Praha 38
1971	Spartak Trnava 40 VSS Kosice 36 Union Teplice 35
1972	Spartak Trnava 44 Slovan Bratislava 42 Dukla Praha 35
1973	Spartak Trnava 39 Tatran Presov 38 VSS Kosice 35
1974	Slovan Bratislava 37 Dukla Praha 35 Slavia Praha 34
1975	Slovan Bratislava 39 TJ Internacional 37 Bohemians Praha 36
1976	Baník Ostrava 37 Slovan Bratislava 36 Slavia Praha 36
1977	Dukla Praha 42 TJ Internacional 38 Slavia Praha 36
1978	Zbrojovka Brno 43 Dukla Praha 41 Lokomotiva Kosice 39
1979	Dukla Praha 41 Baník Ostrava 41 Zbrojovka Brno 35
1980	Baník Ostrava 41 Zbrojovka Brno 36 Bohemians Praha 34
1981	Baník Ostrava 40 Dukla Praha 38 Bohemians Praha 36
1982	Dukla Praha 42 Baník Ostrava 38 Bohemians Praha 38
1983	Bohemians Praha 42 Baník Ostrava 40 Sparta Praha 36
1984	Sparta Praha 46 Dukla Praha 44 Bohemians Praha 40
1985	Sparta Praha 43 Bohemians Praha 43 Slavia Praha 39
1986	TJ Vítkovice 40 Sparta Praha 37 Dukla Praha 34
1987	Sparta Praha 42 TJ Vítkovice 37 Bohemians Praha 35
1988	Sparta Praha 49 Dukla Praha 39 Dunajská Streda 35
1989	Sparta Praha 45 Baník Ostrava 42 Plastika Nitra 34
1990	Sparta Praha 46 Baník Ostrava 41 Internacional ZTS 36
1991	Sparta Praha 39 Slovan Bratislava 38 Sigma Olomouc 37
1992	Slovan Bratislava 51 Sparta Praha 47 Slavia Praha 43
1993	Sparta Praha 48 Slavia Praha 43 Slovan Bratislava 42

* Unofficial tournament

CZECHOSLOVAKIAN CUP FINALS

1961	Dukla Praha	3-0	Dynamo Zilina
1962	Slovan Bratislava	1-1 4-1	Dukla Praha
1963	Slovan Bratislava	0-0 9-0	Dynamo Praha
1964	Sparta Sokolovo	4-1	VSS Kosice
1965	Dukla Praha	0-0 5-3p	Slovan Bratislava
1966	Dukla Praha	2-1 4-0	Tatran Presov
1967	Spartak Trnava	2-4 2-0 5-4p	Sparta Praha
1968	Slovan Bratislava	0-1 2-0	Dukla Praha
1969	Dukla Praha	1-1 1-0	VCHZ Pardubice
1970	TJ Gottwaldov	3-3 0-0 4-3p	Slovan Bratislava
1971	Spartak Trnava	2-1 5-1	Skoda Plzen
1972	Sparta Praha	0-1 4-3 4-2p	Slovan Bratislava
1973	Baník Ostrava	1-2 3-1	VSS Kosice
1974	Slovan Bratislava	0-1 1-0 4-3p	Slavia Praha
1975	Spartak Trnava	3-1 1-0	Sparta Praha
1976	Sparta Praha	3-2 1-0	Slovan Bratislava
1977	Lokomotiva Kosice	2-1	Union Teplice
1978	Baník Ostrava	1-0	Jednota Trencin
1979	Lokomotiva Kosice	2-1	Baník Ostrava
1980	Sparta Praha	2-0	ZTS Kosice
1981	Dukla Praha	4-1	Dukla Banská Bystrica
1982	Slovan Bratislava	0-0 4-2p	Bohemians Praha
1983	Dukla Praha	2-1	Slovan Bratislava
1984	Sparta Praha	4-2	TJ Internacional
1985	Dukla Praha	3-2	Lokomotiva Kosice
1986	Spartak Trnava	1-1 4-3p	Sparta Praha
1987	DAC Dunajská Streda	0-0 3-2p	Sparta Praha
1988	Sparta Praha	2-0	Internacional ZTS
1989	Sparta Praha	3-0	Slovan Bratislava
1990	Dukla Praha	1-1 5-4p	Internacional ZTS
1991	Baník Ostrava	6-1	Spartak Trnava
1992	Sparta Praha	2-1	Tatran Presov
1993	1.FC Kosice	5-1	Sparta Praha

Two unofficial tournaments were also held

1951	Kovosmalt Trnava	1-0	Armaturka Usti
1952	ATK Praha	4-3	Skoda Hradec Králové

LEADING INTERNATIONAL GOALSCORERS

34	Antonín Puc	(Slavia Praha)	1926-38
31	Zdenek Nehoda	(Dukla Praha, Amaliendorf)	1971-87
28	Oldrich Nejedly	(Sparta Praha)	1931-38
28	Josef Silny	(Slavia Praha, Sparta Praha)	1925-34
22	Adolf Scherer	(CH Bratislava, Slovnaft Bratislava)	1958-64
21	Frantisek Svoboda	(Slavia Praha)	1927-37

18 Marián Masny	(Slovan Bratislava)	1974-82
17 Ladislav Vízek	(Dukla Praha)	1977-86
17 Antonín Panenka	(Bohemians Praha,Rapid Wien)	1973-82
14 Tomás Skuhravy	(Cheb, Sparta,Genoa	1985-

LEADING INTERNATIONAL APPEARANCES

90 Zdenek Nehoda	(Dukla Praha, Amaliendorf)	1971-87
75 Ladislav Novák	(Dukla Praha)	1952-66
75 Marián Masny	(Slovan Bratislava)	1974-82
73 Frantisek Plánicka	(Slavia Praha)	1926-38
67 Karol Dobiás	(Spartak Trnava, Bohemians Praha)	1967-80
63 Josef Masopust	(Dukla Praha)	1954-66
63 Ivo Viktor	(Dukla Praha)	1966-77
62 Ján Popluhár	(Slovan Bratislava)	1958-67
59 Anton Ondrus	(Slovan Bratislava)	1974-87
59 Antonin Puc	(Slavia Praha)	1926-38

INTERNATIONAL MATCHES PLAYED BY CZECHOSLOVAKIA

28-08-1920	Yugoslavia	W 7-0	Antwerp	OGr1	Janda 3, Vaník 3, Sedlácek
29-08	Norway	W 4-0	Brussels	OGqf	Janda 3, Vaník
31-08	France	W 4-1	Antwerp	OGsf	Mazal 3, Steiner
2-09	Belgium	L 0-2	Antwerp	OGf	
28-10-1921	Yugoslavia	W 6-1	Prague	Fr	Vaník 4, Janda 2
13-11	Sweden	D 2-2	Prague	Fr	Janda 2
26-02-1922	Italy	D 1-1	Turin	Fr	Janda
11-06	Denmark	W 3-0	Copenhagen	Fr	Dvorácek 2, Pilat
28-06	Yugoslavia	L 3-4	Zagreb	Fr	Plodr, Vaník, Dvorácek
13-08	Sweden	W 2-0	Stockholm	Fr	Stapl, Dvorácek
6-05-1923	Denmark	W 2-0	Prague	Fr	Stapl, Císar
27-05	Italy	W 5-1	Prague	Fr	Sedlácek 3, Kozeluh.K, Dvorácek
1-07	Romania	W 6-0	Cluj	Fr	Stapl 2, Capek 2, Vlcek 2
28-10	Yugoslavia	D 4-4	Prague	Fr	Stapl 2, Capek 2
25-05-1924	Turkey	W 5-2	Paris	OGr1	Sedlácek 2, Stapl, Novák.J, Capek
28-05	Switzerland	D 1-1	Paris	OGr2	Stapl
30-05	Switzerland	L 0-1	Paris	OGr2	
31-08	Romania	W 4-1	Prague	Fr	Rysavy, Dvorácek, Zd'ársky.K, Kolenaty
28-09	Yugoslavia	W 2-0	Zagreb	Fr	Lastovicka, Jelínek
23-05-1925	Poland	W 2-1	Prague	Fr	Mraz, Polacek
24-05	Austria	W 3-1	Prague	Fr	Sedlácek, Capek, Severin
11-10	Hungary	W 2-0	Prague	Fr	Dvorácek, Perner
28-10	Yugoslavia	W 7-0	Prague	Fr	Dvorácek 3, Silny, Soltys, Wimmer, Steiner
17-01-1926	Italy	L 1-3	Turin	Fr	Kristál
14-03	Austria	L 0-2	Vienna	Fr	
6-06	Poland	W 2-1	Krakow	Fr	Polacek, Dolejsi
6-06	Hungary	L 1-2	Budapest	Fr	Silny
13-06	Sweden	D 2-2	Stockholm	Fr	Novák.O 2
28-06	Yugoslavia	W 6-2	Zagreb	Fr	Silny 4, Puc, Wimmer
3-07	Sweden	W 4-2	Prague	Fr	Jelínek, Meduna, Novák.O, Mares
28-09	Austria	L 1-2	Prague	Fr	Jelínek
28-10	Italy	W 3-1	Prague	Fr	Capek 2, Puc
2-01-1927	Belgium	W 3-2	Liege	Fr	Svoboda 2, Podrazil
20-02	Italy	D 2-2	Milan	Fr	Puc, Silny
11-03	Austria	W 2-1	Vienna	Fr	Puc, Maloun
24-04	Hungary	W 4-1	Prague	Fr	Puc, Silny, Svoboda, Steiner
26-05	Belgium	W 4-0	Prague	Fr	Puc 2, Silny, Fleischmann
30-07	Yugoslavia	D 1-1	Belgrade	Fr	Puc
18-09	Austria	W 2-0	Prague	DGC	Kratochvíl, Podrazil
9-10	Hungary	W 2-1	Budapest	Fr	Silny, Podrazil
23-10	Italy	D 2-2	Prague	DGC	Svoboda 2
28-10	Yugoslavia	W 5-3	Prague	Fr	Bejbl 2, Svoboda 2, Soltys
1-04-1928	Austria	W 1-0	Vienna	DGC	Silny
22-04	Hungary	L 0-2	Budapest	DGC	
13-05	France	W 2-0	Paris	Fr	Puc 2
23-09	Hungary	W 6-1	Prague	Fr	Bejbl 2, Kratochvíl, Puc, Podrazil, Káda
27-10	Poland	W 3-2	Prague	Fr	Puc 2, Bejbl
28-10	Yugoslavia	W 7-1	Prague	Fr	Puc 2, Silny 2, Bejbl 2, Soltys
3-03-1929	Italy	L 2-4	Bologna	DGC	Silny, Svoboda
17-03	Austria	D 3-3	Prague	Fr	Silny, Svoboda, Soltys
5-05	Switzerland	W 4-1	Lausanne	DGC	Silny 2, Puc, Podrazil
28-06	Yugoslavia	D 3-3	Zagreb	Fr	Silny, Madelon, Hojer.A
8-09	Hungary	D 1-1	Prague	DGC	Hojer.A
15-09	Austria	L 1-2	Vienna	Fr	Kratochvíl
6-10	Switzerland	W 5-0	Prague	DGC	Puc 2, Kratochvíl, Svoboda, Junek
28-10	Yugoslavia	W 4-3	Prague	Fr	Silny 2, Kloz, Thaut
1-01-1930	Spain	L 0-1	Barcelona	Fr	

12-01	Portugal	L 0-1	Lisbon	Fr	
23-03	Austria	D 2-2	Prague	Fr	Junek, Svoboda
1-05	Hungary	D 1-1	Prague	Fr	Hojer.A
11-05	France	W 3-2	Paris	Fr	Silny, Kostálek, Junek
14-06	Spain	W 2-0	Prague	Fr	Svoboda, Hojer.A
21-09	Belgium	W 3-2	Antwerp	Fr	Hejma, Soltys, Junek
26-10	Hungary	D 1-1	Budapest	Fr	Soltys
15-02-1931	France	W 2-1	Paris	Fr	Novák.A 2
22-03	Hungary	D 3-3	Prague	DGC	Svoboda 2, Junek
12-04	Austria	L 1-2	Vienna	DGC	Silny
13-06	Switzerland	W 7-3	Prague	DGC	Bejbl 3, Silny 2, Bradác.V 2
14-06	Poland	W 4-0	Warsaw	Fr	Pelcner 2, Bára, Nejedly
2-08	Yugoslavia	L 1-2	Belgrade	Fr	Puc
20-09	Hungary	L 0-3	Budapest	Fr	
15-11	Italy	D 2-2	Rome	DGC	Svoboda 2
20-03-1932	Hungary	L 1-3	Prague	Fr	Silny
17-04	Switzerland	L 1-5	Zurich	DGC	Bradác.V
22-05	Austria	D 1-1	Prague	DGC	Svoboda
29-05	Holland	W 2-1	Amsterdam	Fr	Silny, Nejedly
18-09	Hungary	L 1-2	Budapest	DGC	Puc
9-10	Yugoslavia	W 2-1	Prague	Fr	Puc, Nejedly
28-10	Italy	W 2-1	Prague	DGC	Nejedly, Bradác.V
19-03-1933	Hungary	L 0-2	Budapest	Fr	
9-04	Austria	W 2-1	Vienna	Fr	Puc 2
7-05	Italy	L 0-2	Florence	DGC	
10-06	France	W 4-0	Prague	Fr	Puc, Nejedly, Svoboda, Junek
6-08	Yugoslavia	L 1-2	Zagreb	Fr	Kocsis
17-09	Austria	D 3-3	Prague	Fr	Puc 2, Silny
15-10	Poland	W 2-1	Warsaw	WCq	Silny, Pelcner
25-03-1934	France	W 2-1	Paris	Fr	Sobotka, Svoboda
29-04	Hungary	D 2-2	Prague	DGC	Puc, Subotka
16-05	England	W 2-1	Prague	Fr	Puc, Nejedly
27-05	Romania	W 2-1	Trieste	WCr1	Puc, Nejedly
31-05	Switzerland	W 3-2	Turin	WCqf	Nejedly, Svoboda, Sobotka
3-06	Germany	W 3-1	Rome	WCsf	Nejedly 3
10-06	Italy	L 1-2	Rome	WCf	Puc
2-09	Yugoslavia	W 3-1	Prague	Fr	Nejedly, Sobotka, Junek
23-09	Austria	D 2-2	Vienna	DGC	Cech 2
14-10	Switzerland	D 2-2	Geneva	DGC	Nejedly 2
17-03-1935	Switzerland	W 3-1	Prague	DGC	Nejedly 2, Horák
14-04	Austria	D 0-0	Prague	DGC	
26-05	Germany	L 1-2	Dresden	Fr	Hruska
6-09	Yugoslavia	D 0-0	Belgrade	Fr	
22-09	Hungary	L 0-1	Budapest	DGC	
27-10	Italy	W 2-1	Prague	DGC	Horák 2
9-02-1936	France	W 3-0	Paris	Fr	Puc, Nejedly, Boucek
22-03	Austria	D 1-1	Vienna	DGC	Zajícek
26-04	Spain	W 1-0	Prague	Fr	Zajícek
27-09	Germany	L 1-2	Prague	Fr	Cech
18-10	Hungary	W 5-2	Prague	DGC	Kloz 4, Kopecky
13-12	Italy	L 0-2	Genoa	Fr	
21-02-1937	Switzerland	W 5-3	Prague	DGC	Kopecky 2, Puc, Svoboda, Horák
18-04	Romania	D 1-1	Bucharest	Fr	Nejedly
22-05	Scotland	L 1-3	Prague	Fr	Puc
23-05	Italy	L 0-1	Prague	DGC	
19-09	Hungary	L 3-8	Budapest	DGC	Nejedly, Rulc, Ríha
3-10	Yugoslavia	W 5-4	Prague	Fr	Nejedly, Rulc, Sobotka, Senecky, Ríha
13-10	Latvia	W 4-0	Prague	Fr	Sobotka 3, Senecky
24-10	Austria	W 2-1	Prague	DGC	Kloz, Ríha
7-11	Bulgaria	D 1-1	Sofia	WCq	Ríha
1-12	England	L 4-5	London	Fr	Nejedly 2, Puc, Zeman
8-12	Scotland	L 0-5	Glasgow	Fr	
3-04-1938	Switzerland	L 0-4	Basle	DGC	
24-04	Bulgaria	W 6-0	Prague	WCq	Simunek 3, Nejedly 2, Ludl
18-05	Rep. Ireland	D 2-2	Prague	Fr	Nejedly 2
5-06	Holland	W 3-0	Le Havre	WCr1	Nejedly, Zeman, Kostálek
12-06	Brazil	D 1-1	Bordeaux	WCqf	Nejedly
14-06	Brazil	L 1-2	Bordeaux	WCqf	Kopecky
7-08	Sweden	W 6-2	Stockholm	Fr	Bican 3, Senecky 2, Horák
28-08	Yugoslavia	W 3-1	Zagreb	Fr	Bican, Bradác.V, Seneky
4-12	Romania	W 6-2	Prague	Fr	Bican 4, Ludl, Kopecky

Date	Opponent	Result	Venue	Competition	Scorers
7-04-1946	France	L 0-3	Paris	Fr	
9-05	Yugoslavia	L 0-2	Prague	Fr	
14-09	Switzerland	W 3-2	Prague	Fr	Janík, Ríha, Klimek
29-09	Yugoslavia	L 2-4	Belgrade	Fr	Klimek, Plánicky
27-10	Austria	W 4-3	Vienna	Fr	Cejp 2, Zechar 2
11-05-1947	Yugoslavia	W 3-1	Prague	Fr	Bican 2, Cejp
20-06	Denmark	D 2-2	Copenhagen	Fr	Zachar 2
22-06	Holland	W 2-1	Amsterdam	Fr	Kubala 2
31-08	Poland	W 6-3	Prague	Fr	Kubala 2, Bican 2, Cejp, Ludl
21-09	Romania	W 6-2	Bucharest	Fr	Kubala 2, Cejp 2, Simansky 2
5-10	Austria	W 3-2	Prague	Fr	Ríha 2, Balázi
14-12	Italy	L 1-3	Bari	Fr	Ríha
18-04-1948	Poland	L 1-3	Warsaw	BCE	Kokstein
23-05	Hungary	L 1-2	Budapest	BCE/DGC	Subert
12-06	France	L 0-4	Prague	Fr	
4-07	Romania	L 1-2	Bucharest	BCE	Menclík
29-08	Bulgaria	L 0-1	Sofia	BCE	
10-10	Switzerland	D 1-1	Basle	DGC	Cejp
31-10	Austria	W 3-1	Bratislava	DGC	Hemele 2, Hlavácek
23-03-1949	Luxembourg	D 2-2	Bratislava	Fr	Hemele 2
10-04	Hungary	W 5-2	Prague	DGC	Hlavácek 2, Pazicky, Preis, Simansky
22-05	Romania	W 3-2	Prague	Fr	Pazicky, Preis, Simansky
4-09	Bulgaria	L 1-3	Prague	Fr	Marko
25-09	Austria	L 1-3	Vienna	DGC	Simansky
30-10	Poland	W 2-0	Vitkovice	Fr	Pazicky, Preis
13-11	France	L 0-1	Paris	Fr	
30-04-1950	Hungary	L 0-5	Budapest	Fr	
21-05	Romania	D 1-1	Bucharest	Fr	Zd'ársky.J
27-08	Bulgaria	W 2-1	Sofia	Fr	Hlavácek, Preis
1-09	Albania	W 3-0	Prague	Fr	Zd'ársky, Hlavácek, Cejp
22-10	Poland	W 4-1	Warsaw	Fr	Preis 3, Cejp
20-05-1951	Romania	D 2-2	Prague	Fr	Vlk, Cejp
14-10	Hungary	L 1-2	Vitkovice	Fr	Vejvoda
11-05-1952	Romania	L 1-3	Bucharest	Fr	Pluskal
14-09	Poland	D 2-2	Prague	Fr	Zd'ársky, Müller
19-10	Hungary	L 0-5	Budapest	Fr	
29-11	Albania	L 2-3	Tirana	Fr	Müller, Kvapil
9-12	Albania	L 1-2	Tirana	Fr	Dvorák
26-04-1953	Italy	W 2-0	Prague	DGC	Pazicky 2
10-05	Poland	D 1-1	Wroclaw	Fr	Simansky
14-06	Romania	W 2-0	Prague	WCq	Vlk, Pazicky
6-09	Bulgaria	W 2-1	Sofia	WCq	Vlk 2
20-09	Switzerland	W 5-0	Prague	DGC	Trnka 2, Kraus, Hertl, Pazicky
4-10	Hungary	L 1-5	Prague	Fr	Kacáni
25-10	Romania	W 1-0	Bucharest	WCq	Safránek
8-11	Bulgaria	D 0-0	Bratislava	WCq	
13-12	Italy	L 0-3	Genoa	DGC	
16-06-1954	Uruguay	L 0-2	Berne	WCr1	
19-06	Austria	L 0-5	Zurich	WCr1	
24-10	Hungary	L 1-4	Budapest	Fr	Pazdera
27-03-1955	Austria	W 3-2	Brno	DGC	Procházka, Crha, Pesek
5-06	Belgium	W 3-1	Brussels	Fr	Trnka, Crha, Kraus
25-09	Belgium	W 5-2	Prague	Fr	Práda 2, Pazdera, Crha, Simansky
2-10	Hungary	L 1-3	Prague	DGC	Práda
13-11	Bulgaria	L 0-3	Sofia	Fr	
21-04-1956	Brazil	D 0-0	Prague	Fr	
10-05	Switzerland	W 6-1	Geneva	DGC	Feureisl 4, Masopust, Borovicka
20-05	Hungary	W 4-2	Budapest	DGC	Moravcík 2, Feureisl, Pazdera
5-08	Brazil	W 1-0	Rio de Janeiro	Fr	Moravcík
8-08	Brazil	L 1-4	Sao Paulo	Fr	Moravcík
12-08	Uruguay	L 1-2	Montevideo	Fr	Masopust
19-08	Argentina	L 0-1	Buenos Aires	Fr	
26-08	Chile	L 0-3	Santiago	Fr	
30-09	Yugoslavia	W 2-1	Belgrade	DGC	Práda
25-11	Turkey	D 1-1	Prague	Fr	Feureisl
1-05-1957	Wales	L 0-1	Cardiff	WCq	
18-05	Yugoslavia	W 1-0	Bratislava	DGC	Borovicka
26-05	Wales	W 2-0	Prague	WCq	Kraus, OG
16-06	East Germany	W 3-1	Brno	WCq	Bubník, Molnár, Kraus
13-10	Austria	D 2-2	Vienna	DGC	Moravcík 2
27-10	East Germany	W 4-1	Leipzig	WCq	Kraus 2, Moravcík, Novák.L

13-12	Egypt	W 2-1	Cairo	Fr	Moravcík, Kacáni
2-04-1958	West Germany	W 3-2	Prague	Fr	Molnár
8-06	Nth. Ireland	L 0-1	Halmstad	WCr1	
11-06	West Germany	D 2-2	Helsingborg	WCr1	Zikán, Dvorák
15-06	Argentina	W 6-1	Helsingborg	WCr1	Zikán 2, Hovorka 2, Feureisl, Dvorák
17-06	Nth. Ireland	L 1-2	Malmo	WCr1	Zikán
30-08	Soviet Union	L 1-2	Prague	Fr	Masopust
20-09	Switzerland	W 2-1	Bratislava	DGC	Moravcík, Scherer
12-10	Bulgaria	L 0-1	Ostrava	Fr	
13-12	Italy	D 1-1	Genoa	DGC	Masopust
18-12	Turkey	L 0-1	Istanbul	Fr	
5-04-1959	Rep. Ireland	L 0-2	Dublin	ECpr	
10-05	Rep. Ireland	W 4-0	Bratislava	ECpr	Dolinsky, Pavlovic.L, Buberník, Stacho
6-09	Soviet Union	L 1-3	Moscow	Fr	Molnár
23-09	Denmark	D 2-2	Copenhagen	ECr1	Dolinsky, Kacáni
18-10	Denmark	W 5-1	Brno	ECr1	Buberník 2, Scherer 2, Dolinsky
1-11	Italy	W 2-1	Prague	DGC	Dolinsky, Scherer
1-05-1960	Austria	W 4-0	Prague	Fr	Dolinsky, Kvasnák, Moravcík, Masopust
22-05	Romania	W 2-0	Bucharest	ECqf	Masopust, Bubník
29-05	Romania	W 3-0	Bratislava	ECqf	Buberník 2, Bubník
6-07	Soviet Union	L 0-3	Marseille	ECsf	
9-07	France	W 2-0	Marseille	EC3p	Bubník, Pavlovic.L
30-10	Holland	W 4-0	Prague	Fr	Scherer 3, Kadraba
26-03-1961	Sweden	W 2-1	Prague	Fr	Adamec, Kadraba
29-04	Mexico	W 2-1	Ostrava	Fr	Scherer, Kadraba
14-05	Scotland	W 4-0	Bratislava	WCq	Pospíchal 2, Kadraba, Kvasnák
19-06	Argentina	D 3-3	Brno	Fr	Masek, Kadraba, Kvasnák
26-09	Scotland	L 2-3	Glasgow	WCq	Scherer, Kvasnák
8-10	Rep. Ireland	W 3-1	Dublin	WCq	Kvasnák 2, Scherer
29-10	Rep. Ireland	W 7-1	Prague	WCq	Scherer 2, Kvasnák 2, Masopust, Pospíchal, Jelínek (II)
29-11	Scotland	W 4-2	Brussels	WCq	Scherer, Pospíchal, Kvasnák, Hledík
7-04-1962	Sweden	L 1-3	Gothenburg	Fr	Pospíchal
22-04	Uruguay	W 3-1	Prague	Fr	Scherer, Kadraba, Jelínek (II)
31-05	Spain	W 1-0	Viña del Mar	WCr1	Stibrányi
2-06	Brazil	D 0-0	Viña del Mar	WCr1	
7-06	Mexico	L 1-3	Viña del Mar	WCr1	Masek
10-06	Hungary	W 1-0	Rancagua	WCqf	Scherer
13-06	Yugoslavia	W 3-1	Vina del Mar	WCsf	Scherer 2, Kadraba
17-06	Brazil	L 1-3	Santiago	WCf	Masopust
16-09	Austria	W 6-0	Vienna	Fr	Masopust 2, Kucera 2, Scherer, Kadraba
28-10	Poland	W 2-1	Bratislava	Fr	Scherer, Láfa
21-11	East Germany	L 1-2	Berlin	ECr1	Kucera
31-03-1963	East Germany	D 1-1	Prague	ECr1	Masek
24-04	Austria	L 1-3	Vienna	Fr	Masek
28-04	Bulgaria	L 0-1	Sofia	Fr	
29-05	England	L 2-4	Bratislava	Fr	Scherer, Kadraba
2-06	Hungary	D 2-2	Prague	Fr	Scherer, Kvasnák
3-11	Yugoslavia	L 0-2	Zagreb	Fr	
11-04-1964	Italy	D 0-0	Florence	Fr	
29-04	West Germany	W 4-3	Ludwigshafen	Fr	Mráz 2, Pospíchal, Scherer
17-05	Yugoslavia	L 2-3	Prague	Fr	Mráz, Masny
13-09	Poland	L 1-2	Warsaw	Fr	Masek
11-10	Hungary	D 2-2	Budapest	Fr	Pospíchal 2
25-04-1965	Portugal	L 0-1	Bratislava	WCq	
30-05	Romania	L 0-1	Bucharest	WCq	
19-09	Romania	W 3-1	Prague	WCq	Knebort, Jokl
9-10	Turkey	W 6-0	Istanbul	WCq	Knebort 2, Jokl 2, Kabát, Kvasnák
31-10	Portugal	D 0-0	Oporto	WCq	
21-11	Turkey	W 3-1	Brno	WCq	Mráz 2, Horváth
18-05-1966	Soviet Union	L 1-2	Prague	Fr	Adamec
12-06	Brazil	L 1-2	Rio de Janeiro	Fr	Masny
15-06	Brazil	D 2-2	Rio de Janeiro	Fr	Popluhár, Szikora
19-10	Yugoslavia	L 0-1	Belgrade	Fr	
2-11	England	D 0-0	London	Fr	
6-11	Holland	W 2-1	Amsterdam	Fr	Hrdlicka, Geleta
3-05-1967	Switzerland	W 2-1	Basle	Fr	Jokl, Geleta
21-05	Rep. Ireland	W 2-0	Dublin	ECq	Masny.V, Szikora
18-06	Turkey	W 3-0	Bratislava	ECq	Adamec 2, Jurkanin
1-10	Spain	W 1-0	Prague	ECq	Horváth
22-10	Spain	L 1-2	Madrid	ECq	Kuna
15-11	Turkey	D 0-0	Ankara	ECq	

22-11	Rep. Ireland	L 1-2	Prague	ECq	OG
27-04-1968	Yugoslavia	W 3-0	Bratislava	Fr	Adamec, Kuna, Jokl
23-06	Brazil	W 3-2	Bratislava	Fr	Adamec 3
25-09	Denmark	W 3-0	Copenhagen	WCq	Jokl, Kuna, Hagara
20-10	Denmark	W 1-0	Bratislava	WCq	Jokl
16-04-1969	Holland	L 0-2	Rotterdam	Fr	
4-05	Rep. Ireland	W 2-1	Dublin	WCq	Kabát, Adamec
25-05	Hungary	L 0-2	Budapest	WCq	
14-09	Hungary	D 3-3	Prague	WCq	Hagara, Kvasnák, Kuna
7-10	Rep. Ireland	W 3-0	Prague	WCq	Adamec 3
3-12	Hungary	W 4-1	Marseille	WCq	Kvasnák, Vesely.B, Adamec, Jokl
12-04-1970	Austria	W 3-1	Vienna	Fr	Adamec, Albrecht, Hrdlicka
9-05	Luxembourg	W 1-0	Luxembourg	Fr	Jurkanin
13-05	Norway	W 2-0	Oslo	Fr	Kuna, Horváth
3-06	Brazil	L 1-4	Guadalajara	WCr1	Petrás
6-06	Romania	L 1-2	Guadalajara	WCr1	Petrás
11-06	England	L 0-1	Guadalajara	WCr1	
5-09	France	L 0-3	Nice	Fr	
7-10	Finland	D 1-1	Prague	ECq	Albrecht
25-10	Poland	D 2-2	Prague	Fr	Stratil 2
21-04-1971	Wales	W 3-1	Swansea	ECq	Capkovic.J 2, Táborsky
16-05	Romania	W 1-0	Bratislava	ECq	Vesely.F
16-06	Finland	W 4-0	Helsinki	ECq	Karkó 2, Capkovic.J, Pollák
14-07	Brazil	L 0-1	Rio de Janeiro	Fr	
25-09	East Germany	D 1-1	Berlin	Fr	Kuna
27-10	Wales	W 1-0	Prague	ECq	Kuna
14-11	Romania	L 1-2	Bucharest	ECq	Capkovic.J
8-04-1972	Austria	W 2-0	Brno	Fr	Petrás, Térnenyi
26-04	Luxembourg	W 6-0	Plzen	Fr	Kuna 2, Capkovic.J 2, Jokl, Dobiás
14-05	Sweden	W 2-1	Gothenburg	Fr	Jokl 2
28-06	Brazil	D 0-0	Rio de Janeiro	Clr2	
2-07	Scotland	D 0-0	Porto Alegre	Clr2	
6-07	Yugoslavia	L 1-2	Sao Paulo	Clr2	Hrusecky
30-08	Holland	L 1-2	Prague	Fr	Hagara
15-10	Poland	L 0-3	Bydgoszcz	Fr	
1-11	East Germany	L 1-3	Bratislava	Fr	Pekárik
28-03-1973	West Germany	L 0-3	Dusseldorf	Fr	
2-05	Denmark	D 1-1	Copenhagen	WCq	Petrás
27-05	England	D 1-1	Prague	Fr	Novák.I
6-06	Denmark	W 6-0	Prague	WCq	Nehoda, Vesely.B 3, Bicovsky, Hagara
26-09	Scotland	L 1-2	Glasgow	WCq	Nehoda
17-10	Scotland	W 1-0	Bratislava	WCq	Nehoda
27-03-1974	East Germany	L 0-1	Dresden	Fr	
7-04	Brazil	L 0-1	Rio de Janeiro	Fr	
13-04	Bulgaria	W 1-0	Plovdiv	Fr	Dobiás
27-04	France	D 3-3	Prague	Fr	Pivarník, Bicovsky, Panenka
20-05	Soviet Union	W 1-0	Odessa	Fr	Nehoda
25-09	East Germany	W 3-1	Prague	Fr	Bicovsky 2, Ondrus
13-10	Sweden	W 4-0	Bratislava	Fr	Svehlík 2, Masny.M, Bicovsky
30-10	England	L 0-3	London	ECq	
13-11	Poland	D 2-2	Prague	Fr	Svehlík, Masny.M
8-12	Indonesia	D 1-1	Djakarta	Fr	Kroupa
20-12	Iran	W 1-0	Tehran	Fr	Ondrus
31-03-1975	Romania	D 1-1	Prague	Fr	Nehoda
20-04	Cyprus	W 4-0	Prague	ECq	Panenka 3, Masny.M
30-04	Portugal	W 5-0	Prague	ECq	Bicovsky 2, Nehoda 2, Petrás
7-06	Austria	D 0-0	Vienna	Fr	
24-09	Switzerland	D 1-1	Brno	Fr	Masny.M
15-10	Hungary	D 1-1	Bratislava	Fr	Nehoda
30-10	England	W 2-1	Bratislava	ECq	Nehoda, Gallis
12-11	Portugal	D 1-1	Oporto	ECq	Ondrus
19-11	East Germany	D 1-1	Brno	OGq	Bicovsky
23-11	Cyprus	W 3-0	Limassol	ECq	Nehoda, Bicovsky, Masny.M
10-03-1976	Soviet Union	D 2-2	Kosice	Fr	Ondrus, Nehoda
27-03	France	D 2-2	Paris	Fr	Ondrus, Dobiás
7-04	East Germany	D 0-0	Leipzig	OGq	
24-04	Soviet Union	W 2-0	Bratislava	ECqf	Móder, Panenka
22-05	Soviet Union	D 2-2	Kiev	ECqf	Móder 2
16-06	Holland	W 3-1	Zagreb	ECsf	Ondrus, Nehoda, Vesely.F
20-06	West Germany	D 2-2	Belgrade	ECf	Svehlík, Dobiás. Won 5-3 pens
22-09	Romania	D 1-1	Bucharest	Fr	Panenka

6-10	Romania	W 3-2	Prague	Fr	Panenka, Dobiás, Ondrus
13-10	Scotland	W 2-0	Prague	WCq	Panenka, Petrás
17-11	West Germany	L 0-2	Hanover	Fr	
23-03-1977	Greece	W 4-0	Prague	Fr	Panenka, Nehoda, Gögh, Masny.M
30-03	Wales	L 0-3	Wrexham	WCq	
20-04	Hungary	L 0-2	Budapest	Fr	
24-05	Switzerland	L 0-1	Basle	Fr	
1-06	Austria	D 0-0	Ostrava	Fr	
7-09	Turkey	W 1-0	Bratislava	Fr	Gajdusek
21-09	Scotland	L 1-3	Glasgow	WCq	Gajdusek
9-11	Hungary	D 1-1	Prague	Fr	Nehoda
16-11	Wales	W 1-0	Prague	WCq	Nehoda
22-03-1978	Greece	W 1-0	Salonika	Fr	Kroupa
15-04	Hungary	L 1-2	Budapest	Fr	Kroupa
23-04	Bulgaria	D 0-0	Brno	Fr	
17-05	Brazil	L 0-2	Rio de Janeiro	Fr	
21-05	Sweden	D 0-0	Stockholm	Fr	
6-09	East Germany	L 1-2	Leipzig	Fr	Ondrus
4-10	Sweden	W 3-1	Stockholm	ECq	Masny 2, Nehoda
11-10	West Germany	L 3-4	Prague	Fr	Stambachr 2, Masny
8-11	Italy	W 3-0	Bratislava	Fr	Jarusek, Panenka, Masny
29-11	England	L 0-1	London	Fr	
14-03-1979	Spain	W 1-0	Bratislava	Fr	Masny
4-04	France	W 2-0	Bratislava	ECq	Panenka, Stambachr
1-05	Luxembourg	W 3-0	Luxembourg	ECq	Masny, Gajdusek, Stambachr
5-05	Soviet Union	L 0-3	Moscow	Fr	
12-09	Hungary	L 1-2	Nyiregyhaza	Fr	Panenka
26-09	Rep. Ireland	W 4-1	Prague	Fr	Ondrus, Nehoda, Kroupa, Masny
10-10	Sweden	W 4-1	Prague	ECq	Nehoda, Kozák, Vízek 2
17-11	France	L 1-2	Paris	ECq	Kozák
24-11	Luxembourg	W 4-0	Prague	ECq	Panenka, Masny 2, Vízek
23-01-1980	Mexico	L 0-1	Leon	Fr	
27-01	Australia	W 4-0	Canberra	Fr	Jurkemik, Vízek, Nehoda, Kozák
3-02	Australia	W 5-0	Sydney	Fr	Masny 2, Gajdusek, Kroupa, Kozák
9-02	Australia	D 2-2	Melbourne	Fr	Dobiás, Nehoda
26-03	Switzerland	L 0-2	Basle	Fr	
16-04	Spain	D 2-2	Gijon	Fr	Nehoda 2
30-04	Hungary	W 1-0	Kosice	Fr	Nehoda
16-05	Romania	W 2-1	Brno	Fr	Vízek 2
11-06	West Germany	L 0-1	Rome	ECr1	
14-06	Greece	W 3-1	Rome	ECr1	Panenka, Vízek, Nehoda
17-06	Holland	D 1-1	Milan	ECr1	Nehoda
21-06	Italy	D 1-1	Naples	EC3p	Jurkemik. Won 9-8 pens
24-09	Poland	D 1-1	Chorzow	Fr	Nehoda
8-10	East Germany	L 0-1	Prague	Fr	
15-10	Argentina	L 0-1	Buenos Aires	Fr	
19-11	Wales	L 0-1	Cardiff	WCq	
3-12	Turkey	W 2-0	Prague	WCq	Nehoda 2
25-01-1981	Bolivia	L 1-2	La Paz	Fr	Janecka
30-01	Bolivia	W 5-2	Santa Cruz	Fr	Daneska, Nehoda 2, Kozák, Vízek
4-02	Peru	W 3-1	Lima	Fr	Vízek 2, Jakubec
24-03	Switzerland	L 0-1	Bratislava	Fr	
15-04	Turkey	W 3-0	Istanbul	WCq	Janecka, Kozák, Vízek
29-04	Rep. Ireland	L 1-3	Dublin	Fr	Masny
27-05	Iceland	W 6-1	Bratislava	WCq	Vízek, Panenka, Nehoda, Kozák 2, Janecka
9-09	Wales	W 2-0	Prague	WCq	OG, Licka
23-09	Iceland	D 1-1	Reykjavik	WCq	Kozák
28-10	Soviet Union	L 0-2	Tbilisi	WCq	
11-11	Argentina	D 1-1	Buenos Aires	Fr	Valek
29-11	Soviet Union	D 1-1	Bratislava	WCq	Vojacek
3-03-1982	Brazil	D 1-1	Sao Paulo	Fr	Janecka
9-03	Argentina	D 0-0	Mar del Plata	Fr	
24-03	Greece	W 2-1	Prague	Fr	Radimec, Jarolim
14-04	West Germany	L 1-2	Cologne	Fr	Bicovsky
28-04	Austria	L 1-2	Vienna	Fr	Jakkubec
17-06	Kuwait	D 1-1	Valladolid	WCr1	Panenka
20-06	England	L 0-2	Bilbao	WCr1	
24-06	France	D 1-1	Valladolid	WCr1	Panenka
6-10	Sweden	D 2-2	Bratislava	ECq	Janecka 2
27-10	Denmark	W 3-1	Copenhagen	Fr	Cermak, Fiala, Choupka
13-11	Italy	D 2-2	Milan	ECq	Sloup, Chaloupka

Date	Opponent	Result	Venue	Comp	Scorers
27-03-1983	Cyprus	D 1-1	Nicosia	ECq	Bicovsky
16-04	Cyprus	W 6-0	Prague	ECq	Danek 2, Vízek 2, Prokes, Jurkemik
15-05	Romania	W 1-0	Bucharest	ECq	Vízek
7-09	Switzerland	D 0-0	Neuchatel	Fr	
21-09	Sweden	L 0-1	Stockholm	ECq	
26-10	Bulgaria	L 1-2	Prague	Fr	Stambacher
16-11	Italy	W 2-0	Prague	ECq	Rada 2
30-11	Romania	D 1-1	Bratislava	ECq	Luhovy
28-03-1984	East Germany	L 1-2	Erfurt	Fr	Griga
7-04	Italy	D 1-1	Verona	Fr	Griga
16-05	Denmark	W 1-0	Prague	Fr	Knoflicek
5-09	Greece	W 1-0	Athens	Fr	Berger
14-10	Portugal	L 1-2	Oporto	WCq	Jarolim
31-10	Malta	W 4-0	Prague	WCq	Janecka 2, Jarolim, Berger
27-03-1985	Switzerland	L 0-2	Sion	Fr	
21-04	Malta	D 0-0	Ta'Qali	WCq	
30-04	West Germany	L 1-5	Prague	WCq	Griga
5-06	Sweden	L 0-2	Stocholm	WCq	
4-09	Poland	W 3-1	Brno	Fr	Berger, Kubik, OG
25-09	Portugal	W 1-0	Prague	WCq	Hruska
16-10	Sweden	W 2-1	Prague	WCq	Vízek 2
17-11	West Germany	D 2-2	Munich	WCq	Novák.J, Lauda
23-04-1986	East Germany	W 2-0	Nitra	Fr	Knoflicek, Luhovy
27-05	Rep. Ireland	L 0-1	Reykjavik	Fr	
29-05	Iceland	W 2-1	Reykjavik	Fr	Kula, Chovanec
3-08	Australia	D 1-1	Melbourne	Fr	Novák.J
6-08	Australia	W 1-0	Adelaide	Fr	Griga
10-08	Australia	W 3-0	Sydney	Fr	Kula, Kubik 2
10-09	Holland	W 1-0	Prague	Fr	Knoflicek
15-10	Finland	W 3-0	Brno	ECq	Janecka, Knoflicek, Kula
12-11	Denmark	D 0-0	Bratislava	ECq	
25-03-1987	Switzerland	W 2-1	Bellinzona	Fr	Kubik 2
29-04	Wales	D 1-1	Wrexham	ECq	Knoflicek
13-05	East Germany	L 0-2	Brandenburg	Fr	
3-06	Denmark	D 1-1	Copenhagen	ECq	Hasek
9-09	Finland	L 0-3	Helsinki	ECq	
27-10	Poland	W 3-1	Bratislava	Fr	Danek, Micinec, Bilek
11-11	Wales	W 2-0	Prague	ECq	Knoflicek, Bilek
12-01-1988	Finland	L 0-2	Las Palmas	Fr	
15-01	East Germany	W 1-0	Las Palmas	Fr	Hasek
24-02	Spain	W 2-1	Malaga	Fr	Knoflicek, Kubik
23-03	Bulgaria	L 0-2	Sofia	Fr	
27-04	Soviet Union	D 1-1	Trnava	Fr	Vlk
1-06	Denmark	W 1-0	Copenhagen	Fr	Kubik
24-08	France	D 1-1	Paris	Fr	Danek
20-09	Austria	W 4-2	Prague	Fr	Luhovy, Bilek, Danek 2
18-10	Luxembourg	W 2-0	Esch	WCq	Hasek, Chovanec
4-11	Norway	W 3-2	Bratislava	Fr	Griga, Weiss, Luhovy
16-11	Belgium	D 0-0	Bratislava	WCq	
11-04-1989	Austria	W 2-1	Graz	Fr	Griga 2
29-04	Belgium	L 1-2	Brussels	WCq	Luhovy
9-05	Luxembourg	W 4-0	Prague	WCq	Griga, Skuhravy 2, Bilek
7-06	Switzerland	W 1-0	Berne	WCq	Skuhravy
5-09	Romania	W 2-0	Nitra	Fr	Vlk, Bilek
6-10	Portugal	W 2-1	Prague	WCq	Bilek 2
25-10	Switzerland	W 3-0	Prague	WCq	Skuhravy, Bilek, Moravcik
15-11	Portugal	D 0-0	Lisbon	WCq	
21-02-1990	Spain	L 0-1	Alicante	Fr	
4-04	Egypt	L 0-1	Brno	Fr	
25-04	England	L 2-4	London	Fr	Skuhravy, Kubik
26-05	West Germany	L 0-1	Dusseldorf	Fr	
10-06	United States	W 5-1	Florence	WCr1	Skuhravy 2, Bilek, Hasek, Luhovy
15-06	Austria	W 1-0	Florence	WCr1	Bilek
19-06	Italy	L 0-2	Rome	WCr1	
23-06	Costa Rica	W 4-1	Bari	WCr2	Skuhravy 3, Kubik
1-07	West Germany	L 0-1	Milan	WCqf	
29-08	Finland	D 1-1	Kuusankoski	Fr	Kuka
26-09	Iceland	W 1-0	Kosice	ECq	Danek
13-10	France	L 1-2	Paris	ECq	Skuhravy
14-11	Spain	W 3-2	Prague	ECq	Danek 2, Moravcik
30-01-1991	Australia	W 1-0	Melbourne	Fr	Kristofik

6-02	Australia	W 2-0	Sydney	Fr	Kula, Grussmann
27-03	Poland	W 4-0	Olomouc	Fr	Kuka, Moravcik, Pecko, Danek
1-05	Albania	W 2-0	Tirana	ECq	Kubik, Kuka
5-06	Iceland	W 1-0	Reykjavik	ECq	Hasek
21-08	Switzerland	D 1-1	Prague	Fr	Luhovy
4-09	France	L 1-2	Bratislava	ECq	OG
25-09	Norway	W 3-2	Oslo	Fr	Nemecek, Moravcik, Kuka
16-10	Albania	W 2-1	Olomouc	ECq	Kula, Lancz
13-11	Spain	L 1-2	Seville	ECq	Nemecek
18-12	Brazil	L 1-2	Goiana	Fr	Skuhravy
4-01-1992	Egypt	L 0-2	Cairo	Fr	
25-03	England	D 2-2	Prague	Fr	Skuhravy, Nemecek
22-04	Germany	D 1-1	Prague	Fr	Bilek
27-05	Poland	L 0-1	Jastrzebie	Fr	
19-08	Austria	D 2-2	Bratislava	Fr	Chovanec, Moravcik
2-09	Belgium	L 1-2	Prague	WCq	Kadlec
23-09	Faeroe Islands	W 4-0	Kosice	WCq	Nemecek, Kuka 2, Dubovsky
14-11	Romania	D 1-1	Bucharest	WCq	Nemecek
24-03-1993	Cyprus	D 1-1	Limassol	WCq	Moravcik
28-04	Wales	D 1-1	Ostrava	WCq	Látal
2-06	Romania	W 5-2	Kosice	WCq	Vrabec, Látal, Dubovsky 3
16-06	Faeroe Islands	W 3-0	Tóftir	WCq	Hasek, Postulka 2
8-09	Wales	D 2-2	Cardiff	WCq	Kuka, Dubovsky
27-10	Cyprus	W 3-0	Kosice	WCq	Dubovsky, Hapal, Skuhravy
17-11	Belgium	D 0-0	Brussels	WCq	

DENMARK

The Danes were among the very first continental nations to take up football, and of these early proponents of the game they were certainly the best. Yet before long they were left behind, firmly ensconced in the amateur tradition. Fortunately, a collection of fine players all come to prominence in the late 1970s and early 1980s and their success at international level forced change at home. Club football was reorganised in an attempt to give the clubs the same opportunity for success, and the recent exploits of the likes of Brondby and Odense suggest it is paying off.

Scandinavia was a popular location for tours by British sides at the turn of the century. Staevnet, a combination of the four main Copenhagen sides, KB, B93, Akademisk and Frem, were specially formed to take on these tourists and the experience gained launched Denmark to the forefront of the European game. KB Copenhagen, formed in 1876, are even older than most English and Scottish clubs, but although there were numerous clubs by the turn of the century, a league did not come into operation until 1913.

The 1908 and 1912 Olympics were a particular triumph for the Danish national side. As a fortress of the amateur game, their players came from unlikely backgrounds. Harald Bohr, who played in all three games at the 1908 Games in London, became a mathematician of international renown, whilst his brother Niels, who made one appearance for the national side, later won the Nobel prize for physics! In 1908, coached by Charlie Williams, the Manchester City goalkeeper, the Danes beat France 17-1 and 9-0 to qualify for the final. In the first of those games, Sophus Nielsen scored 10 goals, a record for an international that stands to this day. Against England in the final at White City, Denmark played very well and the hosts struggled to win 2-0.

Four years later in the final in Stockholm, the same two teams faced each other again. In the semi-finals, the Danes had disposed of their biggest rivals, Holland, with an easy victory and in the final they had their fair share of the play, eventually losing 4-2. These early Danish teams included Nils Middleboe, who joined Chelsea in 1913 and became one of their most famous players.

As professionalism was adopted in parts of Europe in the 1920s, the focus of football shifted towards Central and Southern Europe and away from Scandinavia. The decline in Denmark's performances in the inter-war period was startling, as even Norway caught up and for a while overtook them in terms of success on the field. Of the Scandinavian countries only Finland remained weaker, and even victory against them was no longer assured.

With a number of talented individuals such as Karl and John Hansen and Karl Praest, the Danes staged a mini-revival after the war and achieved third place at the 1948 Olympics. However, all three players were subsequently signed by Juventus, and a rule which kept foreign-based professionals out of the Danish national side meant that no lasting progress was made. Twelve years later, after Denmark had finished runners-up in the Rome Olympics, the same happened again. Club football as a result was not exactly vibrant. Copenhagen's hegemony was broken in the 1950s as the provincial clubs began to win honours, but the game was seen as little more than a pastime and attendances were poor.

The 1970s saw the beginnings of change, and the national side gave the lead. One player in particular, Allan Simonsen, seemed to set an example for others to follow.

Playing for Borussia Mönchengladbach and Barcelona, his profile was higher than any Dane before him. There followed a flood of players leaving Denmark for the clubs of Western Europe. The likes of Michael Laudrup, Preben Elkjaer-Larsen, John Sivebaek, Jesper Olsen, Jan Molby and Soren Lerby all left home to play professional football abroad.

With the rule barring these players from representing Denmark thrown out in 1976, the effect on the national team was not long in coming. In the 1984 European Championships, England were knocked out in the qualifying round, beaten 1-0 at Wembley. This Danish victory was all the more remarkable in that it represented one of only three competitive defeats that England had ever suffered at home.

THE ORDER OF MERIT

		All			League			Cup		Europe		
	Team	G	S	B	G	S	B	G	S	G	S	B
1	KB København	16	19	8	15	15	8	1	4	-	-	-
2	ÅGF Åarhus	13	7	10	5	4	10	8	3	-	-	-
3	B 93 København	11	5	9	10	5	9	1	-	-	-	-
4	Vejle BK	11	3	2	5	2	2	6	1	-	-	-
5	Akademisk K'havn	9	13	9	9	11	9	-	2	-	-	-
6	B 1903 København	9	10	8	7	8	8	2	2	-	-	-
7	Frem København	8	15	9	6	12	9	2	3	-	-	-
8	Esbjerg FB	7	7	1	5	3	1	2	4	-	-	-
9	Brøndbyernes IF	7	4	3	5	3	2	2	1	-	-	1
10	OB Odense	6	4	3	3	3	3	3	1	-	-	-
11	Lyngby BK	5	5	3	2	3	3	3	2	-	-	-
12	B 1909 Odense	4	1	1	2	-	1	2	1	-	-	-
	Hvidovre BK	4	1	1	3	1	1	1	-	-	-	-
14	ÅAB Åalborg	3	4	2	1	-	2	2	4	-	-	-
15	Randers Freja	3	1	-	-	1	-	3	-	-	-	-
16	Koge BK	2	3	-	2	1	-	-	2	-	-	-
17	FC København	2	1	-	1	1	-	1	-	-	-	-
18	B 1913 Odense	1	2	1	-	2	1	1	-	-	-	-
19	Silkeborg IF	1	-	1	1	-	1	-	-	-	-	-
20	Vanlose BK	1	-	-	-	-	-	1	-	-	-	-
21	Fremad Amager	-	3	1	-	2	1	-	1	-	-	-
	Ikast BK	-	3	1	-	1	1	-	2	-	-	-
23	Naestved IF	-	3	4	-	2	4	-	1	-	-	-
24	Holbaek BK	-	3	-	-	1	-	-	2	-	-	-
25	B 1901 Nykobing	-	2	-	-	-	-	-	2	-	-	-
	Åalborg Chang	-	1	-	-	-	-	-	1	-	-	-
	Frem Sakskobing	-	1	-	-	-	-	-	1	-	-	-
	Odense KFUM	-	1	-	-	-	-	-	1	-	-	-
	Skovshoved IF	-	1	-	-	1	-	-	-	-	-	-
30	Horsens FS	-	-	1	-	-	1	-	-	-	-	-

To the end of the 1994-95 season

In the finals, the Danes won many admirers for their skilful and entertaining brand of football, as did their supporters who added much colour and humour to the event. Following a semi-final appearance in France where they lost on penalties to Spain, Denmark qualified for what remains their only World Cup finals appearance to date, the 1986 Mexico tournament. A stunning 6-1 victory over Uruguay in the first round saw the team being talked about as possible world champions. Once again, however, Spain put paid to their hopes as the Danes collapsed in the second round. With the original generation of players who had been part of this revolution now starting to retire, many thought that Denmark's heyday was over.

This has not happened, however, as talented players have continued to emerge. The national team reached the European Championship finals again in 1988, and although they failed to impress then, the best was yet to come. Beaten into second place by Yugoslavia in the qualifying round of the same competition four years later, the Danes found themselves drafted into the finals at the last minute when the Yugoslavs were expelled. There they progressed to the last four at the expense of England and France, defeated Holland on penalties to reach the final, and upset Germany 2-0 to become European champions.

It was an extraordinary achievement and a massive boost for the domestic game's professional Super League, introduced in 1991. Professionalism had been introduced in 1978 but never properly exploited until the new league's arrival. Results in European club competitions improved dramatically in the 1990s as Brondby reached the semi-finals of the UEFA Cup and such giants as Real Madrid and Bayern Munich fell victim to Danish clubs. Meanwhile the national team's success story continued when they won the 1995 Intercontinental Cup, beating Argentina in the final. The world is waiting to see just what the Danes are going to do next.

Population: 5,139,000
Area, sq km: 43,093
% in urban areas: 86.4%
Capital city: Copenhagen

Dansk Boldspil-Union
Ved Amagerbanen #15
DK-2300 Copenhagen S
Denmark
Tel: + 45 31 950511
Fax: + 45 31 950588

Year of formation	1889
Affiliation to FIFA	1904
Affiliation to UEFA	1954
Registered clubs	1555
Registered players	338 000
Professional players	350
Registered coaches	4800
Registered referees	7969
National stadium	Idrætsparken, Copenhagen 40 000
National colours	Red/White/Red
Reserve colours	White/White/Red
Season	1st phase (Grundspil) August - November 2nd phase (Slutspil) March - June

THE RECORD

WORLD CUP

1930-54	Did not enter
1958	QT 3rd/3 in group 1
1962	Did not enter
1966	QT 4th/4 in group 7
1970	QT 3rd/4 in group 2
1974	QT 3rd/3 in group 8
1978	QT 3rd/4 in group 1
1982	QT 3rd/5 in group 5
1986	QT 1st/5 in group 6 - Final Tournament/2nd round
1990	QT 2nd/4 in group 1
1994	QT 3rd/7 in group 3

EUROPEAN CHAMPIONSHIP

1960	1st round
1964	Semi-finalists/4th place
1968	QT 4th/4 in group 5
1972	QT 4th/4 in group 5
1976	QT 4th/4 in group 4
1980	QT 5th/5 in group 1

1984 QT 1st/5 in group 3 - Final Tournament/Semi-finalists
1988 QT 1st/4 in group 6 - Final Tournament/1st round
1992 QT 2nd/5 in group 4 - Final Tournament/Winners
1996 QT group 2

EUROPEAN CLUB COMPETITIONS

European Cup
Quarter-finalists - ÅGF Århus 1961

Cup Winners Cup
Quarter-finalists - Randers Freja 1969 Vejle BK 1978 ÅGF Århus 1989

UEFA Cup
Semi-finalists - Brøndbyernes IF 1991

CLUB DIRECTORY

COPENHAGEN (Population - 1,685,000)

Akademisk Boldklub København (1889)
Gladsaxe Idrætspark 10,000 – Green and white stripes/White

B 93 København (Boldklubben 93) (1893)
Osterbrö 7,000 – White/Blue

Brøndbyernes Idrætsförening (1964)
Brøndby Stadion 22,000 – Yellow with blue sleeves/Blue

FC København (1992)
Idrætsparken 40,000 – White/White
Previous name - Formed in 1992 from a merger of KB København (1876) and B 1903 København (1903)

Boldklubben Frem København (1886)
Valby Idrætspark 12,000 – Blue with two red hoops/White

BK Fremad Amager (1910)
Sundby Idrætspark 8,000 – Blue with white sleeves/White

Hvidovre Boldklub (1925)
Hvidovre Stadion 15,000 – Red/Blue

Lyngby Boldklub (1921)
Lyngby Stadion 15,000 – Blue/White, red trimmings

Vanlose Boldklub (1921)
Vanlose Idrætspark 8,000 – White/Black

ÅARHUS (Population - 258,000)

ÅGF Åarhus (Åarhus Gimnastic Förening) (1880)
Århus 20,000 – White/Blue, blue trimmings

ODENSE (Population - 178,000)

B 1909 Odense (Boldklubben 1909) (1909)
Odense Stadion 20,000 – Red/White, white trimmings

B 1913 Odense (Boldklubben 1913) (1913)
Campusvej – Blue/White

OB Odense (Odense Boldklub) (1887)
Odense Stadion 20,000 – Blue and white stripes/Blue

ÅALBORG (Population - 154,000)

ÅAB Åalborg (Åalborg Boldspilklub) (1885)
Åalborg Stadion 22,000 – Red and white stripes/White

ESBJERG (Population - 81,000)

Esbjerg Förenede Boldklub (1924)
Esbjerg Idrætsparken 20,000 – Blue and white stripes/Blue

RANDERS (Population - 61,000)

Randers Freja (1898)
Randers Stadion 20,000 – Blue and white stripes/Blue

VEJLE (Population - 50,000)

Vejle Boldklub (1891)
Vejle Stadion 18,000 – Red/White

NAESTVED (Population - 38,000)

Naestved Idræts Förening (1939)
Naestved Stadion 20,000 – Green/White

KOGE (Population - 35,000)

Koge Boldklub (1927)
Koge 14,000 – Black and white stripes/Black

SILKEBORG (Population - 33,000)

Silkeborg Idræts Förening (1917)
Silkeborg Stadion 12,000 – Red/White, white trimmings

HOLBAEK (Population - 21,000)

Holbaek BK (1931)
Holbaek Stadion 10,000 – Blue/White

NYKOBING FALSTER (Population - 18,000)

B 1901 Nykobing (1901)
Idrætspark 8,000 – Blue and white stripes/Blue

IKAST

Ikast Forenede Sportsklubber (1935)
Ikast Stadion 15,000 – Yellow/Blue, blue trimmings

DANISH LEAGUE CHAMPIONSHIP

1913d KB København 17 B 93 København 14 Frem København 10
1914 KB København 18 B 93 København 12 Frem København 12
1915 -
1916 B 93 København 15 KB København 15 Akademisk 15
1917 KB København 15 Akademisk 13 B 93 København 12
1918 KB København 17 Frem København 12 B 93 København 11
1919e Akademisk 22 B 93 København 18 KB København 17
1920 B 1903 København 17 KB København 16 Akademisk 16
1921c Akademisk 11 B 1903 København 11 B 93 København 10
1922 KB København 14 Frem København 8 B 1903 København 8
1923 Frem København 12 B 93 København 10 KB København 10
1924d B 1903 København 15 KB København 13 B 93 København 12
1925 KB København 18 Akademisk 12 B 93 København 10
1926 B 1903 København 15 B 93 København 13 Frem København 12
1927 B 93 København 18 B 1903 København 12 Akademisk 9
1928al B 93 København 6 Frem København 6 B 1903 København 6
1929 B 93 København 7 KB København 5 Akademisk 3
1930ae B 93 København 17 Frem København 15 B 1903 København 14
1931 Frem København 17 KB København 13 B 93 København 12
1932 KB København 18 Akademisk 15 B 93 København 12
1933 Frem København 16 B 1903 København 14 ÅGF Århus 12
1934 B 93 København 14 B 1903 København 14 Frem København 13
1935 B 93 København 13 Frem København 12 KB København 12
1936 Frem København 15 Akademisk 15 ÅAB Åalborg 10
1937h Akademisk 28 Frem København 26 B 93 København 25
1938 B 1903 København 27 Frem København 27 KB København 22
1939 B 93 København 31 KB København 24 Akademisk 20
1940 KB København 24 Fremad Amager 22 B 93 København20
1941 Frem København 4-2 Fremad Amager
1942 B 93 København.................3-2 ....Akademisk
1943 Akademisk...........................2-1 ....KB København
1944 Frem København ....4-2 ....Akademisk
1945 Akademisk.........................1-1 3-2 ....ÅAF Åarhus
1946h B 93 København 28 KB København 24 Akademisk 21
1947 Akademisk 28 KB København 26 Fremad Amager 22
1948 KB København 33 Frem København 29 Akademisk 26
1949 KB København 27 Akademisk 22 ÅGF Åarhus 19
1950 KB København 28 Akademisk 27 ÅGF Åarhus 26
1951 Akademisk 28 OB Odense 19 ÅGF Åarhus 18
1952 Akademisk 26 Koge BK 21 B 1909 Odense 20

1953 KB København 30 Skovshoved IF 23 OB Odense 21
1954 Koge BK 23 KB København 20 Akademisk 19
1955 ÅGF Åarhus 25 Akademisk 23 Frem København 21
1956 ÅGF Åarhus 26 Esbjerg FB 22 Akademisk 22
1957o ÅGF Åarhus 39 Akademisk 37 Frem København 32
1958k Vejle BK 30 Frem København 29 OB Odense 28
1959 B 1909 Odense 33 KB København 31 Vejle BK 29
1960 ÅGF Åarhus 32 KB København 29 Vejle BK 29
1961 Esbjerg FB 33 KB København 33 B 1913 Odense 28
1962 Esbjerg FB 37 B 1913 Odense 29 ÅGF Åarhus 27
1963 Esbjerg FB 33 B 1913 Odense 25 B 1903 København 25
1964 B 1909 Odense 31 ÅGF Åarhus 30 KB København 29
1965 Esbjerg FB 31 Vejle BK 30 B 1903 København 28
1966 Hvidovre BK 31 Frem København 27 KB København 25
1967 Akademisk 31 Frem København 29 Horsens FS 28
1968 KB København 29 Esbjerg FB 29 Frem København 29
1969 B 1903 København 34 KB København 30 ÅAB Åalborg 29
1970 B 1903 København 27 Akademisk 27 Hvidovre BK 26
1971 Vejle BK 29 Hvidovre BK 24 Frem København 24
1972 Vejle BK 33 B 1903 København 27 Naestved IF 26
1973 Hvidovre BK 27 Randers Freja 26 KB København 26
1974 KB København 33 Vejle BK 25 B 1903 København 24
1975q Koge BK 41 Holbaek BK 41 Naestved IF 38
1976 B 1903 København 40 Frem København 39 KB København 39
1977 OB Odense 47 B 1903 København 39 Esbjerg FB 34
1978 Vejle BK 44 Esbjerg FB 40 ÅGF Åarhus 39
1979 Esbjerg FB 46 KB København 40 B 1903 København 38
1980 KB København 40 Naestved IF 40 OB Odense 38
1981 Hvidovre BK 40 Lyngby BK 39 Naestved IF 38
1982 OB Odense 41 ÅGF Åarhus 40 B 1903 København 35
1983 Lyngby BK 40 OB Odense 38 ÅGF Åarhus 36
1984 Vejle BK 41 ÅGF Åarhus 40 Lyngby BK 38
1985 Brøndbyernes IF 43 Lyngby BK 37 ÅGF Åarhus 36
1986n ÅGF Åarhus 41 Brøndbyernes IF 37 Naestved IF 35
1987 Brøndbyernes IF 47 Ikast BK 38 ÅGF Åarhus 36
1988 Brøndbyernes IF 40 Naestved IF 35 Lyngby BK 35
1989 OB Odense 41 Brøndbyernes IF 38 Lyngby BK 38
1990 Brøndbyernes IF 42 B 1903 København 31 Ikast BK 30
1991h Brøndbyernes IF 26 Lyngby BK 24 ÅGF Åarhus 20
1992f4 Lyngby BK 32 B 1903 København 29 Frem København 26
1993 FC København 32 OB Odense 31 Brøndbyernes IF 30
1994 Silkeborg IF 31 FC København 29 Brøndbyernes IF 27
1995 ÅAB Åalborg 31 Brøndbyernes IF 29 Silkeborg IF 24

DANISH CUP FINALS

1955	ÅGF Åarhus	4-0	Aalborg Chang
1956	Frem København	1-0	Akademisk
1957	ÅGF Åarhus	2-0	Esbjerg FB
1958	Vejle BK	3-2	ÅGF Åarhus
1959	Vejle BK	1-1 2-0	ÅGF Åarhus
1960	ÅGF Åarhus	2-0	Frem Sakskobing
1961	ÅGF Åarhus	2-0	KB København
1962	B 1909 Odense	1-0	Esbjerg FB
1963	B 1913 Odense	2-1	Koge BK
1964	Esbjerg FB	2-1	Odense KFUM
1965	ÅGF Åarhus	1-0	KB København
1966	ÅAB Åalborg	3-1	KB København
1967	Randers Freja	1-0	ÅAB Åalborg
1968	Randers Freja	3-1	Vejle BK
1969	KB København	3-0	Frem København
1970	ÅAB Åalborg	2-1	Lyngby BK
1971	B 1909 Odense	1-0	Frem København
1972	Vejle BK	2-0	Fremad Amager
1973	Randers Freja	2-0	B 1901 Nykobing
1974	Vanlose BK	5-2	OB Odense
1975	Vejle BK	1-0	Holbaek BK
1976	Esbjerg FB	2-1	Holbaek BK
1977	Vejle BK	2-1	B 1909 Odense
1978	Frem København	1-1 1-1 6-5p	Esbjerg FB
1979	B 1903 København	1-0	Koge BK
1980	Hvidovre BK	5-3	Lyngby BK
1981	Vejle BK	2-1	Frem København
1982	B 93 København	3-3 1-0	B 1903 København
1983	OB Odense	3-0	B 1901 Nykobing
1984	Lyngby BK	2-1	KB København
1985	Lyngby BK	3-2	Esbjerg FB
1986	B 1903 København	2-1	Ikast BK
1987	ÅGF Åarhus	3-0	ÅAB Åalborg
1988	ÅGF Åarhus	2-1	Brøndbyernes IF
1989	Brøndbyernes IF	6-3	Ikast BK
1990	Lyngby BK	0-0 6-1	ÅGF Åarhus
1991	OB Odense	0-0 0-0 4-3p	ÅAB Åalborg
1992	ÅGF Åarhus	3-0	B 1903 København
1993	OB Odense	2-0	ÅAB Åalborg
1994	Brøndbyernes IF	0-0 3-1p	Naestved IF
1995	FC København	5-0	Akademisk

LEADING INTERNATIONAL GOALSCORERS

52	Poul Nielsen	(KB)
44	Pauli Jorgensen	(Frem)
43	Ole Madsen	(HIK)
38	Preben Elkjaer-Larssen	(1.FC Köln,Lokeren,Verona)
31	Michael Laudrup	(Brøndby,Lazio,Juventus,Barcelona)
29	Henning Enoksen	(Vejle,AGF)
22	Michael Rohde	(B93)
21	Allan Simonsen	(Vejle,Mönchengladbach,Barcelona)
21	Flemming Povlsen	(AGF,Castilla, 1.FC Köln,PSV,Borussia Dortmund)

LEADING INTERNATIONAL APPEARANCES

102	Morten Olsen	(B1901, Cercle Brugge, Molenbeek, Anderlecht, 1.FC Köln)
87	John Sivebaek	(Vejle,Manchester United, St-Étienne, Monaco)
83	Lars Olsen	(Køge BK,Brøndby, Trabzonspor,Seraing)
80	Michael Laudrup	(Brøndby,Lazio,Juventus,Barcelona)
78	Peter Schmeichel	(Brøndby,Manchester United)
75	Per Rontved	(Bronshoj,Werder Bremen, Randers Freja)
70	Kim Vilfort	(Frem,Lille,Brøndby)
69	Jens Jorn Bertelsen	(Esbjerg,Seraing,Rouen,Aarau)
69	Preben Elkjaer-Larsen	(1.FC Köln,Lokeren,Verona)
68	John Jensen	(Brøndby,HamburgerSV,Arsenal)
67	Soren Lerby	(Ajax,Bayern München,Monaco,PSV)

INTERNATIONAL MATCHES PLAYED BY DENMARK

19-10-1908	France	W 9-0	London	OGr1	Wolfhagen 4, Middelboe.N 2, Bohr.H 2, Nielsen.So
22-10	France	W 17-1	London	OGsf	Nielsen.So 10,Wolfhagen 4, Lindgreen 2 Middelboe
24-10	England Am	L 0-2	London	OGf	
5-05-1910	England Am	W 2-1	Copenhagen	Fr	Lindgreen, Wolfhagen

Date	Opponent	Result	Venue	Comp	Scorers
21-10-1911	England Am	L 0-3	London	Fr	
30-06-1912	Norway	W 7-0	Stockholm	OGqf	Olsen.An 3, Nielsen.So 2, Middelboe.N, Wolfhagen
2-07	Holland	W 4-1	Stockholm	OGsf	Olsen.An 2, Jorgensen.E, Nielsen.P
4-07	England Am	L 2-4	Stockholm	OGf	Olsen.An 2
6-10	Germany	W 3-1	Copenhagen	Fr	Middelboe.N 2, Olsen.Al
25-05-1913	Sweden	W 8-0	Copenhagen	Fr	Gyldenstein 3, Olsen.An 2, Wolfhagen, Nielsen.P, Middelboe.N
5-10	Sweden	W 10-0	Stockholm	Fr	Nielsen.P 6, Knudsen 2, Wolfhagen 2
26-10	Germany	W 4-1	Hamburg	Fr	Nielsen.P 4
17-05-1914	Holland	W 4-3	Copenhagen	Fr	Nielsen.P 3, Nielsen.So
5-06	England Am	W 3-0	Copenhagen	Fr	Knudsen, Nielsen.So, Nielsen.P
6-06-1915	Sweden	W 2-0	Copenhagen	Fr	Olsen.An, Nielsen.P
19-09	Norway	W 8-1	Copenhagen	Fr	Nielsen.P 3, Olsen.An 3, Rohde, Castella
31-10	Sweden	W 2-0	Stockholm	Fr	Nielsen.P, Rohde
4-06-1916	Sweden	W 2-0	Copenhagen	Fr	Nielsen.P 2
25-06	Norway	W 2-0	Oslo	Fr	Rohde 2
8-10	Sweden	L 0-4	Stockholm	Fr	
15-10	Norway	W 8-0	Copenhagen	Fr	Nielsen.P 4, Rohde 3, Olsen.An
3-06-1917	Sweden	D 1-1	Copenhagen	Fr	Nielsen.So
17-06	Norway	W 2-1	Oslo	Fr	Olsen.Al, Wolfhagen
7-10	Norway	W 12-0	Copenhagen	Fr	Nielsen.P 5, Klein 3, Rohde 2, Berth, Olsen.Al
14-10	Sweden	W 2-1	Stockholm	Fr	Olsen.Al, Grothan
2-06-1918	Sweden	W 3-0	Copenhagen	Fr	Hansen.C 2, OG
16-06	Norway	L 1-3	Oslo	Fr	Grothan
6-10	Norway	W 4-0	Copenhagen	Fr	Hansen.C, Blicher, Olsen.Al, Nielsen.P
20-10	Sweden	W 2-1	Gothenburg	Fr	Laursen, Aaby
5-06-1919	Sweden	W 3-0	Copenhagen	Fr	Nielsen.P 2, Thorsteinsson
12-06	Norway	W 5-1	Copenhagen	Fr	Nielsen.P 3, Rohde 2
21-09	Norway	L 2-3	Oslo	Fr	Nielsen.P 2
12-10	Sweden	L 0-3	Stockholm	Fr	
5-04-1920	Holland	L 0-2	Amsterdam	Fr	
13-06	Norway	D 1-1	Oslo	Fr	Andersen.B
28-08	Spain	L 0-1	Brussels	OGr1	
10-10	Sweden	W 2-0	Stockholm	Fr	Hansen.Ha, Rohde
12-06-1921	Holland	D 1-1	Copenhagen	Fr	Hansen.Ha
2-10	Norway	W 3-1	Copenhagen	Fr	Nielsen.P 3
9-10	Sweden	D 0-0	Stockholm	Fr	
15-04-1922	Belgium	D 0-0	Liege	Fr	
17-04	Holland	L 0-2	Amsterdam	Fr	
11-06	Czechoslovakia	L 0-3	Copenhagen	Fr	
10-09	Norway	D 3-3	Fredrikstad	Fr	Grothan, Nielsen.P 2
1-10	Sweden	L 1-2	Copenhagen	Fr	Nielsen.P
6-05-1923	Czechoslovakia	L 0-2	Prague	Fr	
17-06	Switzerland	W 3-2	Copenhagen	Fr	Olsen.Al, Blicher 2
30-09	Norway	W 2-1	Copenhagen	Fr	Blicher, Jorgensen.V
14-10	Sweden	W 3-1	Stockholm	Fr	Jorgensen.V, Nilsson.E, Wilhelmsen
21-04-1924	Switzerland	L 0-2	Basle	Fr	
15-06	Sweden	L 2-3	Copenhagen	Fr	Olsen.Al, Nilsson.E
14-09	Norway	W 3-1	Oslo	Fr	Olsen.Al, Nielsen.P 2
5-10	Belgium	W 2-1	Copenhagen	Fr	Nielsen.P 2
14-06-1925	Sweden	W 2-0	Stockholm	Fr	Larsen.E, Nielsen.P
21-06	Norway	W 5-1	Copenhagen	Fr	Nilsson.E 2, Nielsen.P, Rohde, Larsen.E
27-09	Finland	D 3-3	Aarhus	Fr	OG, Jorgensen.P 2
25-10	Holland	L 2-4	Amsterdam	Fr	Nilsson.E, Jorgensen.V
13-06-1926	Holland	W 4-1	Copenhagen	Fr	Blicher, Jorgensen.V 3
20-06	Finland	L 2-3	Helsinki	Fr	Petersen.S, Boge
19-09	Norway	D 2-2	Oslo	Fr	Rohde 2
3-10	Sweden	W 2-0	Copenhagen	Fr	Bendixen, Rohde
29-05-1927	Norway	W 1-0	Oslo	Fr	Uldaler
12-06	Holland	D 1-1	Copenhagen	Fr	Hansen.He
19-06	Sweden	D 0-0	Stockholm	Fr	
2-10	Germany	W 3-1	Copenhagen	Fr	Rohde 2, Hansen.He
30-10	Norway	W 3-1	Copenhagen	Fr	Jorgensen.P, Rohde, Hansen.He
22-04-1928	Holland	L 0-2	Amsterdam	Fr	
17-06	Norway	W 3-2	Oslo	Fr	Hansen.He, Rohde, Jorgensen.P
16-09	Germany	L 1-2	Nuremberg	Fr	Jorgensen
7-10	Sweden	W 3-1	Copenhagen	Fr	Rohde, Jorgensen.P, Nilsson.E
16-06-1929	Sweden	L 2-3	Gothenburg	Fr	Larsen.E, Uldaler
23-06	Norway	L 2-5	Copenhagen	Fr	Jorgensen.P, Christophersen
13-10	Finland	W 8-0	Copenhagen	Fr	Jorgensen.P 3, Hansen.He 2, Uldaler, Eriksen.S, Rohde
16-06-1930	Finland	W 6-1	Helsinki	Fr	Hansen.He, Uldaler 3, Eriksen.S, Jorgensen.P

22-06	Sweden	W 6-1	Copenhagen	Fr	Jorgensen.P 3, Eriksen.S, Kleven, Christophersen
7-09	Germany	W 6-3	Copenhagen	Fr	Kleven, Jorgensen.P 3, Nilsson.E, Christophersen
21-09	Norway	L 0-1	Oslo	Fr	
25-05-1931	Norway	W 3-1	Copenhagen	Fr	Jorgensen.P 2, Christophersen
14-06	Holland	L 0-2	Copenhagen	Fr	
28-06	Sweden	L 1-3	Stockholm	Fr	Jorgensen.P
27-09	Germany	L 2-4	Hanover	Fr	Nilsson.E, Jorgensen.P
11-10	Finland	L 2-3	Copenhagen	Fr	Uldaler, OG
5-06-1932	Belgium	L 3-4	Copenhagen	Fr	Hansen.He, Christophersen, Jorgensen.P
19-06	Sweden	W 3-1	Copenhagen	Fr	Hansen.He, Petersen.S, Jorgensen.P
30-08	Finland	L 2-4	Helsinki	Fr	Jorgensen.P 2
25-09	Norway	W 2-1	Oslo	Fr	Jorgensen.P, Hansen.He
9-10	Scotland	W 3-1	Copenhagen	Fr	Jorgensen.P, Christophersen, Taarup
11-06-1933	Norway	D 2-2	Copenhagen	Fr	Thielsen 2
18-06	Sweden	W 3-2	Stockholm	Fr	Jorgensen.P, Kleven 2
8-10	Finland	W 2-0	Copenhagen	Fr	Taarup, Uldaler
26-11	Belgium	D 2-2	Brussels	Fr	Uldaler 2
21-05-1934	Poland	W 4-2	Copenhagen	Fr	Uldaler 2, Jorgensen.P 2
17-06	Sweden	L 3-5	Copenhagen	Fr	Uldaler, Jorgensen.P 2
3-07	Finland	L 1-2	Helsinki	Fr	Lundsteen
23-09	Norway	L 1-3	Oslo	Fr	Lundsteen
7-10	Germany	L 2-5	Copenhagen	Fr	Lundsteen, Stoltz
16-06-1935	Sweden	L 1-3	Gothenburg	Fr	Jorgensen.P
23-06	Norway	W 1-0	Copenhagen	Fr	Stoltz
6-10	Finland	W 5-1	Copenhagen	Fr	Thielsen, Uldaler 2, Sorensen.K, Kleven
3-11	Holland	L 0-3	Amsterdam	Fr	
14-06-1936	Sweden	W 4-3	Copenhagen	Fr	Sobirk, OG, Jorgensen.P, Thielsen
30-06	Finland	W 4-1	Helsinki	Fr	Jorgensen.P 2, Kleven, Hansen.K
30-09	Norway	D 3-3	Oslo	Fr	Sobirk 2, Jorgensen.P
4-10	Poland	W 2-1	Copenhagen	Fr	Stoltz 2
16-05-1937	Germany	L 0-8	Breslau	Fr	
13-06	Norway	W 5-1	Copenhagen	Fr	Kleven, Sobirk 2, Hansen.K, Rasmussen.Pe
12-09	Poland	L 1-3	Warsaw	Fr	Iversen
3-10	Sweden	W 2-1	Stockholm	Fr	Sobirk, Andersen.Kn
17-10	Finland	W 2-1	Copenhagen	Fr	Andersen.Kn, Friedmann
21-06-1938	Sweden	L 0-1	Copenhagen	Fr	
31-08	Finland	L 1-2	Helsinki	Fr	Sorensen.A
18-09	Norway	D 1-1	Oslo	Fr	Hansen.K
23-10	Holland	D 2-2	Copenhagen	Fr	Uldaler, Christensen.R
15-06-1939	Finland	W 5-0	Copenhagen	Fr	Thielsen, Hansen.K 2, Sobirk 2
18-06	Norway	W 6-3	Copenhagen	Fr	Jorgensen.P 3, Thielsen, Sorensen.A, Christensen.W
25-06	Germany	L 0-2	Copenhagen	Fr	
17-09	Finland	W 8-1	Copenhagen	Fr	Theisen 3, Nielsen.A, Jorgensen.P, Albrechtsen, Sobirk, OG
1-10	Sweden	L 1-4	Stockholm	Fr	Jorgensen.P
22-10	Norway	W 4-1	Copenhagen	Fr	Jorgensen.P 2, Albrechtsen, Friedmann
6-10-1940	Sweden	D 1-1	Stockholm	Fr	Mathiessen
20-10	Sweden	D 3-3	Copenhagen	Fr	Hansen.K 3
17-11	Germany	L 0-1	Hamburg	Fr	
14-09-1941	Sweden	D 2-2	Stockholm	Fr	Ploger, Hansen.K
19-10	Sweden	W 2-1	Copenhagen	Fr	Ploger, Hansen.K
16-11	Germany	D 1-1	Dresden	Fr	Hansen.K
28-06-1942	Sweden	L 0-3	Copenhagen	Fr	
4-10	Sweden	L 1-2	Stockholm	Fr	Sorensen.A
20-06-1943	Sweden	W 3-2	Copenhagen	Fr	Christiansen.K 2, Ploger 2
24-06-1945	Sweden	L 1-2	Stockholm	Fr	Sobirk
1-07	Sweden	L 3-4	Copenhagen	Fr	Aage Hansen 2, Hansen.K
26-08	Norway	W 4-2	Copenhagen	Fr	Christiansen.K 2, Aage Hansen,Jensen.A
9-09	Norway	W 5-1	Oslo	Fr	Aage Hansen 2, Bronée, Jensen.V, Aage Praest
30-09	Sweden	L 1-4	Stockholm	Fr	Påhlsson
16-06-1946	Norway	L 1-2	Oslo	Fr	Sorensen.J
24-06	Sweden	W 3-1	Copenhagen	Fr	Ploger, Sorensen.J, Aage Praest
8-07	Norway	W 2-0	Copenhagen	Fr	Aage Praest, Sorensen.A
17-07	Iceland	W 3-0	Reykjavik	Fr	Aage Hansen, Christiansen.K, Sorensen.J
1-09	Finland	W 5-2	Helsinki	Fr	Sorensen.E 2, Jensen.I, Ploger, Aage Praest
6-10	Sweden	D 3-3	Gothenburg	Fr	Aage Praest, Sorensen.J, Aage Hansen
20-10	Norway	W 7-1	Copenhagen	Fr	Aage Hansen 4, Aage Praest 2, Sorensen.J
15-06-1947	Sweden	L 1-4	Copenhagen	Fr	Aage Hansen
20-06	Czechoslovakia	D 2-2	Copenhagen	Fr	Aage Praest, Aage Hansen
26-06	Sweden	L 1-6	Stockholm	Fr	Sorensen.J
21-09	Norway	W 5-3	Oslo	Fr	Aage Praest, Hansen.JW 2, OG

5-10	Finland	W 4-1	Aarhus	Fr	Aage Praest 2, Hansen.JW, Sorensen.J
12-06-1948	Norway	L 1-2	Copenhagen	Fr	Jensen.I
15-06	Finland	W 3-0	Helsinki	Fr	Hansen.Jo, Christiansen.K, Lyngsaa
26-06	Poland	W 8-0	Copenhagen	Fr	Aage Hansen 2, Aage Praest 3, Hansen.Jo 2, Ploger
31-07	Egypt	W 3-1	London	OGr1	Aage Hansen 2, Ploger
5-08	Italy *	W 5-3	London	OGqf	Hansen.Jo 4, Ploger
10-08	Sweden	L 2-4	London	OGsf	Seebach, Hansen.Jo
13-08	Great Britain	W 5-3	London	OG3p	Hansen.Jo 2, Aage Praest 2, Sorensen.J
26-09	England	D 0-0	Copenhagen	Fr	
10-10	Sweden	L 0-1	Stockholm	Fr	
12-06-1949	Holland	L 1-2	Copenhagen	Fr	Hansen.Sv
19-06	Poland	W 2-1	Warsaw	Fr	Rechendorff, Lundberg
7-08	Iceland	W 5-1	Aarhus	Fr	Hansen.Je 2, Lundberg, Frandsen, Rechendorff
11-09	Norway	W 2-0	Oslo	Fr	Rechendorff, Hansen.Je
11-09	Finland	L 0-2	Copenhagen	Fr	
23-10	Sweden	W 3-2	Copenhagen	Fr	Petersen.C, Hansen.JW, Hansen.Ed
11-12	Holland	W 1-0	Amsterdam	Fr	Lyngsaa
28-05-1950	Yugoslavia	L 1-5	Belgrade	Fr	Piilmark
22-06	Norway	W 4-0	Copenhagen	Fr	Petersen.P, Hansen.Ed, Hansen.Je, Jensen.A
25-06	Norway	L 1-4	Aarhus	Fr	Jensen.A
27-08	Finland	W 2-1	Helsinki	Fr	Petersen.P, Seebach
10-09	Yugoslavia	L 1-4	Copenhagen	Fr	Hansen.Ed
15-10	Sweden	L 0-4	Stockholm	Fr	
5-11	Austria	L 1-5	Vienna	Fr	Jensen.Er
12-05-1951	Scotland	L 1-3	Glasgow	Fr	Hansen.JW
17-06	Austria	D 3-3	Copenhagen	Fr	Jensen.A, Lundberg
16-09	Norway	L 0-2	Oslo	Fr	
30-09	Finland	W 1-0	Copenhagen	Fr	Staalgaard
21-10	Sweden	W 3-1	Copenhagen	Fr	Rasmussen.Po, Lundberg, Staalgaard
25-05-1952	Scotland	L 1-2	Copenhagen	Fr	Rasmussen.Po
11-06	Sweden	L 0-2	Oslo	Fr	
22-06	Sweden	L 3-4	Stockholm	Fr	Rasmussen.Po, Petersen.P, Seebach
15-07	Greece	W 2-1	Tammerfors	OGr1	Petersen.P, Seebach
21-07	Poland	W 2-0	Turku	OGr2	Seebach, Nielsen.Sv
25-07	Yugoslavia	L 3-5	Helsinki	OGqf	Lundberg, Seebach, Hansen.Je
21-09	Holland	W 3-2	Copenhagen	Fr	Nielsen.K, Petersen.P, Nielsen.Sv
5-10	Finland	L 1-2	Helsinki	Fr	Jensen.P
19-10	Norway	L 1-3	Copenhagen	Fr	Jensen.P
7-03-1953	Holland *	W 2-1	Rotterdam	Fr	Seebach 2
21-06	Sweden	L 1-3	Copenhagen	Fr	Seebach
27-06	Switzerland	W 4-1	Basle	Fr	Sorensen.KO, Jensen.A 2, Hansen.Je
9-08	Iceland	W 4-0	Copenhagen	Fr	Seebach 2, Nielsen.E, Hansen.Er
13-09	Norway	W 1-0	Oslo	Fr	Sorensen.B
4-10	Finland	W 6-1	Copenhagen	Fr	Hansen.Je 2, Petersen.P, Sorensen.KO, Nielsen.K 2
4-06-1954	Norway	L 1-2	Malmo	Fr	Kendzior
13-06	Finland	D 2-2	Helsinki	Fr	Kendzior 2
19-09	Switzerland	D 1-1	Copenhagen	Fr	Olesen
10-10	Sweden	L 2-5	Stockholm	Fr	Hansen.Je, Sorensen.B
31-10	Norway	L 0-1	Copenhagen	Fr	
13-03-1955	Holland	D 1-1	Amsterdam	Fr	Birkeland
15-05	Hungary	L 0-6	Copenhagen	Fr	
19-06	Finland	W 2-1	Copenhagen	Fr	Hansen.Je
3-07	Iceland	W 4-0	Reykjavik	Fr	Jensen.A, Hansen.Je, Pedersen.P 2
11-09	Norway	D 1-1	Oslo	Fr	Jacobsen
2-10	England	L 1-5	Copenhagen	Fr	Lundberg
16-10	Sweden	D 3-3	Copenhagen	Fr	Anderson.O 2, Lundberg
23-05-1956	Soviet Union	L 1-5	Moscow	Fr	Lundberg
24-06	Norway	L 2-3	Copenhagen	Fr	Lundberg, Pedersen.P
1-07	Soviet Union	L 2-5	Copenhagen	Fr	Andersen.O, Jensen.A
16-09	Finland	W 4-0	Helsinki	Fr	Andersen.O 2, Pedersen.P, Hansen.Jr
4-10	Rep. Ireland	L 1-2	Dublin	WCq	Jensen.A
21-10	Sweden	D 1-1	Stockholm	Fr	Hansen.Je
4-11	Holland	D 2-2	Copenhagen	Fr	Olesen, Lundberg
5-12	England	L 2-5	Wolverhampton	WCq	Nielsen.O 2
15-05-1957	England	L 1-4	Copenhagen	WCq	Jensen.J
26-05	Bulgaria	D 1-1	Copenhagen	Fr	Jensen.A
18-06	Finland	L 0-2	Helsinki	Fr	
19-06	Norway	W 2-0	Tammerfors	Fr	Jensen.Eg, Hansen.Jr
30-06	Sweden	L 1-2	Copenhagen	Fr	Hansen.Je
10-07	Iceland	W 6-2	Reykjavik	Fr	Jensen.Eg 3, Hansen.Je, Pedersen.P
22-09	Norway	D 2-2	Oslo	Fr	Pedersen.P, Kjaer

2-10	Rep. Ireland	L 0-2	Copenhagen	WCq	
13-10	Finland	W 3-0	Copenhagen	Fr	Hansen.Al, Nielsen.O, Machon
15-05-1958	Neth. Antilles	W 3-2	Aarhus	Fr	Pedersen.P, Enoksen 2
25-05	Poland	W 3-2	Copenhagen	Fr	Pedersen.P 2, Sorensen.Jo
29-06	Norway	L 1-2	Copenhagen	Fr	Pedersen.P
14-09	Finland	W 4-1	Helsinki	Fr	Pedersen.P, Machon, Danielsen 2
24-09	West Germany	D 1-1	Copenhagen	Fr	Enoksen
15-10	Holland	L 1-5	Rotterdam	Fr	Enoksen
26-10	Sweden	D 4-4	Stockholm	Fr	Madsen.O 3, Enoksen
21-06-1959	Sweden	L 0-6	Copenhagen	Fr	
26-06	Iceland	W 4-2	Reykjavik	OGq	Hansen.Je 2, Madsen.O 2
2-07	Norway	W 2-1	Copenhagen	OGq	Enoksen, Madsen.O
18-08	Iceland	D 1-1	Copenhagen	OGq	Enoksen
13-09	Norway	W 4-2	Oslo	OGq	Enoksen 2, Pedersen.P, Nielsen.H
23-09	Czechoslovakia	D 2-2	Copenhagen	ECr1	Pedersen.P, Hansen.B
4-10	Finland	W 4-0	Copenhagen	Fr	Nielsen.H 3, Kramer
18-10	Czechoslovakia	L 1-5	Brno	ECr1	Kramer
2-12	Greece	W 3-1	Athens	Fr	Enoksen 2, Pedersen.P
6-12	Bulgaria	L 1-2	Sofia	Fr	Enoksen
26-05-1960	Norway	W 3-0	Copenhagen	Fr	Pedersen.P, Nielsen.F 2
3-07	Greece	W 7-2	Copenhagen	Fr	Nielsen.H 3, Enoksen 3, Pedersen.P
27-07	Hungary	W 1-0	Copenhagen	Fr	Hansen.Jr
10-08	Finland	W 2-1	Copenhagen	Fr	Nielsen.H 2
26-08	Argentina *	W 3-2	Rome	OGr1	Nielsen.H 2, Sorensen.Jo
29-08	Poland	W 2-1	Livorno	OGr1	Nielsen.H, Pedersen.P
1-09	Tunisia	W 3-1	Aquilla	OGr1	Nielsen.H 2, Nielsen.F
6-09	Hungary	W 2-0	Rome	OGsf	Nielsen.H, Enoksen
10-09	Yugoslavia	L 1-3	Rome	OGf	Nielsen.F
23-10	Sweden	L 0-2	Gothenburg	Fr	
28-05-1961	East Germany	D 1-1	Copenhagen	Fr	Madsen.O
18-06	Sweden	L 1-2	Copenhagen	Fr	Madsen.O
17-09	Norway	W 4-0	Oslo	Fr	Danielsen 2, Madsen.O, Sorensen.O
20-09	West Germany	L 1-5	Dusseldorf	Fr	OG
15-10	Finland	W 9-1	Copenhagen	Fr	Sorensen.Jo 3, Danielsen 2, Madsen.O 2, Rasmussen.E 2
5-11	Poland	L 0-5	Chorzow	Fr	
23-05-1962	East Germany	L 1-4	Leipzig	Fr	Madsen.O
11-06	Norway	W 6-1	Copenhagen	Fr	Madsen.O 3, Enoksen, Bertelsen, Jorgensen.H
28-06	Malta	W 6-1	Copenhagen	ECr1	Madsen.O 3, Enoksen, Bertelsen, Clausen
11-09	Neth. Antilles	W 3-1	Odense	Fr	Enoksen 2, Madsen.O
16-09	Finland	W 6-1	Helsingfors	Fr	Enoksen 2, Madsen.O 2, Jorgensen.H, Clausen
26-09	Holland	W 4-1	Copenhagen	Fr	Enoksen 2, Madsen.O, Bertelsen
28-10	Sweden	L 2-4	Stockholm	Fr	Madsen.O, Bertelsen
8-12	Malta	W 3-1	Gzira	ECr1	Madsen.O, Bertelsen, Christiansen.C
12-12	Turkey	D 1-1	Istanbul	Fr	Madsen.O
19-05-1963	Hungary	L 0-6	Budapest	Fr	
3-06	Finland	D 1-1	Copenhagen	Fr	Enoksen
23-06	Romania	L 2-3	Copenhagen	OGq	Bruun, Enoksen
29-06	Albania	W 4-0	Copenhagen	ECr2	Petersen.J, Madsen.O, Clausen, Enoksen
15-09	Norway	W 4-0	Oslo	Fr	Thorst, Bertelsen 2, Enoksen
6-10	Sweden	D 2-2	Copenhagen	Fr	Madsen.O, Thorst
30-10	Albania	L 0-1	Tirana	ECr2	
3-11	Romania	W 3-2	Bucharest	OGq	Thorst 2, Bertelsen
28-11	Romania	L 1-2	Turin	OGq	Thorst
4-12	Luxembourg	D 3-3	Luxembourg	ECqf	Madsen.O 3
10-12	Luxembourg	D 2-2	Copenhagen	ECqf	Madsen.O 2
18-12	Luxembourg	W 1-0	Amsterdam	ECqf	Madsen.O
17-06-1964	Soviet Union	L 0-3	Barcelona	ECsf	
20-06	Hungary	L 1-3	Barcelona	EC3p	Bertelsen
28-06	Sweden	L 1-4	Malmo	Fr	Danielsen
6-09	Finland	L 1-2	Helsinki	Fr	Rasmussen.J
11-10	Norway	W 2-0	Copenhagen	Fr	Madsen.O 2
21-10	Wales	W 1-0	Copenhagen	WCq	Madsen.O
29-11	Greece	L 2-4	Athens	WCq	Madsen.O, Berg
1-12	Israel	W 1-0	Tel Aviv	Fr	Sondergaard
5-12	Italy	L 1-3	Bologna	Fr	Enoksen
9-06-1965	Finland	W 3-1	Copenhagen	Fr	Madsen.O 2, Sorensen.O
20-06	Sweden	W 2-1	Copenhagen	Fr	Madsen.O, Sorensen.O
27-06	Soviet Union	L 0-6	Moscow	WCq	
5-07	Iceland	W 3-1	Reykjavik	Fr	Madsen.O, Pedersen.K, Hansen.E
26-09	Norway	D 2-2	Oslo	Fr	Fritsen, Troelsen
17-10	Soviet Union	L 1-3	Copenhagen	WCq	Troelsen

Date	Opponent	Result	Venue	Comp	Scorers
27-10	Greece	D 1-1	Copenhagen	WCq	Fritsen
1-12	Wales	L 2-4	Wrexham	WCq	Poulsen, Fritsen
30-05-1966	Turkey	D 0-0	Copenhagen	Fr	
17-06	Argentina	L 0-2	Copenhagen	Fr	
21-06	Portugal	L 1-3	Esbjerg	Fr	Le Fevre
26-06	Norway	L 0-1	Copenhagen	Fr	
3-07	England	L 0-2	Copenhagen	Fr	
18-09	Finland	L 1-2	Helsinki	Fr	Jorgensen.J
21-09	Hungary	L 0-6	Budapest	ECq	
26-10	Israel	W 3-1	Copenhagen	Fr	Thorst, Moller, Hansen.J
6-11	Sweden	L 1-2	Stockholm	Fr	Wiberg
30-11	Holland	L 0-2	Rotterdam	ECq	
24-05-1967	Hungary	L 0-2	Copenhagen	ECq	
4-06	East Germany	D 1-1	Copenhagen	ECq	Bjerre
25-06	Sweden	D 1-1	Copenhagen	Fr	Bjerre
23-08	Iceland	W 14-2	Copenhagen	Fr	Bjerre 3, Laudrup.F 3, Le Fevre 3, Dyreborg 2, Olsen.JS 2, Sondergaard
24-09	Norway	W 5-0	Oslo	Fr	Dyreborg 5
4-10	Holland	W 3-2	Copenhagen	ECq	Bjerre 2, Sondergaard
11-10	East Germany	L 2-3	Leipzig	ECq	Sondergaard, Dyreborg
22-10	Finland	W 3-0	Copenhagen	Fr	Hansen.J, Bjerre, Laudrup.F
4-06-1968	Finland	W 3-1	Helsinki	Fr	Lund 2, Le Fevre
23-06	Norway	W 5-1	Copenhagen	Fr	Troelsen 3, Larsen.S 2
27-06	Sweden	L 1-2	Stockholm	Fr	OG
25-09	Czechoslovakia	L 0-3	Copenhagen	WCq	
16-10	Scotland	L 0-1	Copenhagen	Fr	
20-10	Czechoslovakia	L 0-1	Bratislava	WCq	
20-11	Luxembourg	W 5-1	Copenhagen	Fr	Wiberg 3, Jensen.B 2
4-12	Rep. Ireland	D 1-1	Dublin	WCq	Wiberg. Match abandoned
12-01-1969	Bermuda	W 5-1	Hamilton	Fr	Jensen.B 3, Sorensen.L, Holmstrom
15-01	Surinam	L 1-2	Paramaribo	Fr	Jensen.H
22-01	Mexico	L 0-3	Mexico City	Fr	
6-05	Mexico	W 3-1	Copenhagen	Fr	Madsen.O, Sorensen.L, Jensen.B
27-05	Rep. Ireland	W 2-0	Copenhagen	WCq	Sorensen.O 2
15-06	Hungary	W 3-2	Copenhagen	WCq	Sorensen.O, Le Fevre, Madsen.O
25-06	Sweden	L 0-1	Copenhagen	Fr	
1-07	Bermuda	W 6-0	Aalborg	Fr	Jensen.B 3, Sorensen.L, Sorensen.O, Michaelsen
10-09	Finland	W 5-2	Copenhagen	Fr	Jensen.B 3, Larsen.S 2
21-09	Norway	L 0-2	Oslo	Fr	
15-10	Rep. Ireland	D 1-1	Dublin	WCq	Jensen.B
22-10	Hungary	L 0-3	Budapest	WCq	
19-05-1970	Poland	L 0-2	Kopenhagen	Fr	
3-06	Finland	D 1-1	Helsinki	Fr	Pedersen.K
25-06	Sweden	D 1-1	Gothenburg	Fr	Pedersen.K
7-07	Iceland	D 0-0	Reykjavik	Fr	
2-09	Poland	L 0-5	Warsaw	Fr	
21-09	Norway	L 0-1	Copenhagen	Fr	
14-10	Portugal	L 0-1	Copenhagen	ECq	
11-11	Scotland	L 0-1	Glasgow	ECq	
25-11	Belgium	L 0-2	Bruges	ECq	
12-05-1971	Portugal	L 0-5	Oporto	ECq	
26-05	Belgium	L 1-2	Copenhagen	ECq	Bjerre
9-06	Scotland	W 1-0	Copenhagen	ECq	Laudrup.F
20-06	Sweden	L 1-3	Copenhagen	Fr	Bjerre
30-06	West Germany	L 1-3	Copenhagen	Fr	Bjerre
28-07	Japan	W 3-2	Copenhagen	Fr	Nygaard, Forsing, Schriver
8-09	Finland	D 0-0	Copenhagen	Fr	
26-09	Norway	W 4-1	Oslo	Fr	Schriver 2, Nyagaard, Rasmussen
7-06-1972	Finland	W 3-0	Copenhagen	Fr	Kristensen 2, Bjerre
29-06	Sweden	L 0-2	Malmo	Fr	
3-07	Iceland	W 5-2	Reykjavik	Fr	Simonsen.A 2, Bak, Hansen.H, Hansen.J
16-08	Mexico	W 3-0	Copenhagen	Fr	Nyagaard 3
4-10	Switzerland	D 1-1	Copenhagen	Fr	Hansen.H
18-10	Scotland	L 1-4	Copenhagen	WCq	Laudrup.F
15-11	Scotland	L 0-2	Glasgow	WCq	
26-04-1973	Sweden	L 1-2	Copenhagen	Fr	Dahl
2-05	Czechoslovakia	D 1-1	Copenhagen	WCq	Bjornmose
6-06	Czechoslovakia	L 0-6	Prague	WCq	
20-06	Norway	W 1-0	Copenhagen	Fr	Dahl
23-09	Norway	W 1-0	Trondheim	Fr	Hansen.H
13-10	Hungary	D 2-2	Copenhagen	Fr	Jensen.H, Stendahl
21-11	France	L 0-3	Paris	Fr	

Date	Opponent	Result	Venue	Comp	Scorers
6-03-1974	Togo	W 2-0	Lome	Fr	Pettersson 2
10-03	Benin	L 0-2	Cotonou	Fr	
3-06	Sweden	L 0-2	Copenhagen	Fr	
6-06	Finland	D 1-1	Oulu	Fr	Pettersson
3-09	Indonesia	W 9-0	Copenhagen	Fr	Holmstrom 3, Jensen.H 3, Nygaard, Simonsen, Sorensen.N
25-09	Spain	L 1-2	Copenhagen	ECq	Nygaard
9-10	Iceland	W 2-1	Aalborg	Fr	Lund, Le Fevre
13-10	Romania	D 0-0	Copenhagen	ECq	
10-05-1975	Romania	L 1-6	Bucharest	ECq	Dahl
25-06	Finland	W 2-0	Copenhagen	Fr	Bjornmose, OG
3-09	Scotland	L 0-1	Copenhagen	ECq	
25-09	Sweden	D 0-0	Malmo	Fr	
12-10	Spain	L 0-2	Barcelona	ECq	
29-10	Scotland	L 1-3	Glasgow	ECq	Bastrup
4-02-1976	Israel	W 1-0	Tel Aviv	Fr	Hansen.A
11-05	Sweden	W 2-1	Gothenburg	Fr	Bastrup, Bjerg
23-05	Cyprus	W 5-1	Limassol	WCq	Bastrup 2, Simonsen, Hansen.T, Rasmussen
24-06	Norway	D 0-0	Bergen	Fr	
25-08	Norway	W 3-0	Copenhagen	Fr	Rontved, Hansen.K, Hansen.H
1-09	France	D 1-1	Copenhagen	Fr	Rontved
22-09	Italy	L 0-1	Copenhagen	Fr	
27-10	Cyprus	W 5-0	Copenhagen	WCq	Jensen.H 2, Nielsen, Rontved, Kristensen
17-11	Portugal	L 0-1	Lisbon	WCq	
30-01-1977	Gambia	W 4-1	Banjul	Fr	Hansen.J, Sorensen.J, Hansen.A, Jorgensen
2-02	Senegal	W 3-2	Dakar	Fr	Christensen.S, Norregaard, Jorgensen
13-04	Bulgaria	L 1-3	Sofia	Fr	Sorensen
1-05	Poland	L 1-2	Copenhagen	WCq	Simonsen
1-06	Norway	W 2-0	Oslo	Fr	Lund, Sorensen
15-06	Sweden	W 2-1	Copenhagen	Fr	Simonsen
22-06	Finland	W 2-1	Helsinki	Fr	Elkjaer 2
21-09	Poland	L 1-4	Chorzow	WCq	Nygaard
5-10	Sweden	L 0-1	Malmo	Fr	
9-10	Portugal	L 2-4	Copenhagen	WCq	Rontved, Hansen.A
8-02-1978	Israel	L 0-2	Tel Aviv	Fr	
24-05	Rep. Ireland	D 3-3	Copenhagen	ECq	Jensen.H, Nielsen.B, Lerby
31-05	Norway	W 2-1	Oslo	Fr	Sorensen.J, Larsen
28-06	Iceland	D 0-0	Reykjavik	Fr	
16-08	Sweden	W 2-1	Copenhagen	Fr	Nielsen.B, Rontved
20-09	England	L 3-4	Copenhagen	ECq	Simonsen, Arnesen, Rontved
11-10	Bulgaria	D 2-2	Copenhagen	ECq	Nielsen.B, Lerby
25-10	Nth. Ireland	L 1-2	Belfast	ECq	Jensen.H
2-05-1979	Rep. Ireland	L 0-2	Dublin	ECq	
9-05	Sweden	D 2-2	Copenhagen	Fr	Nielsen.B, Lerby
6-06	Nth. Ireland	W 4-0	Copenhagen	ECq	Elkjaer 3, Simonsen
27-06	Soviet Union	L 1-2	Copenhagen	Fr	Andersson.T
29-08	Finland	D 0-0	Mikkeli	Fr	
12-09	England	L 0-1	London	ECq	
26-09	Finland	W 1-0	Copenhagen	Fr	Elkjaer
31-10	Bulgaria	L 0-3	Sofia	ECq	
14-11	Spain	W 3-1	Cadiz	Fr	Elkjaer 2, Bethelsen
7-05-1980	Sweden	W 1-0	Gothenburg	Fr	Steffensen
21-05	Spain	D 2-2	Copenhagen	Fr	Simonsen, Bastrup
4-06	Norway	W 3-1	Copenhagen	Fr	Nielsen.B, Arnesen, Elkjaer
12-07	Soviet Union	L 0-2	Moscow	Fr	
27-08	Switzerland	D 1-1	Lausanne	Fr	Bastrup
27-09	Yugoslavia	L 1-2	Ljubljana	WCq	Arnesen
15-10	Greece	L 0-1	Copenhagen	WCq	
1-11	Italy	L 0-2	Rome	WCq	
19-11	Luxembourg	W 4-0	Copenhagen	WCq	Arnesen 2, Elkjaer, Simonsen
15-04-1981	Romania	W 2-1	Copenhagen	Fr	Simonsen, Bastrup
1-05	Luxembourg	W 2-1	Luxembourg	WCq	Elkjaer, Arnesen
14-05	Sweden	W 2-1	Malmo	Fr	Bastrup, Elkjaer
3-06	Italy	W 3-1	Copenhagen	WCq	Rontved, Arnesen, Bastrup
12-08	Finland	W 2-1	Tammerfors	Fr	Madsen.Ol, Eigenbrod
26-08	Iceland	W 3-0	Copenhagen	Fr	Simonsen 2, Lundqvist
9-09	Yugoslavia	L 1-2	Copenhagen	WCq	Elkjaer
23-09	Norway	W 2-1	Copenhagen	Fr	Elkjaer, Arnesen
14-10	Greece	W 3-2	Salonika	WCq	Lerby, Arnesen, Elkjaer
5-05-1982	Sweden	D 1-1	Copenhagen	Fr	Arnesen
19-05	Austria	L 0-1	Vienna	Fr	
27-05	Belgium	W 1-0	Copenhagen	Fr	Larsen.E

15-06	Norway	L 1-2	Oslo	Fr	Laudrup.M
11-08	Finland	W 3-2	Copenhagen	Fr	Bastrup, Lerby, Busk
1-09	Romania	L 0-1	Bucharest	Fr	
22-09	England	D 2-2	Copenhagen	ECq	Hansen.A, Olsen.J
27-10	Czechoslovakia	L 1-3	Copenhagen	Fr	Laudrup.M
10-11	Luxembourg	W 2-1	Luxembourg	ECq	Lerby, Bergren
27-04-1983	Greece	W 1-0	Copenhagen	ECq	Busk
1-06	Hungary	W 3-1	Copenhagen	ECq	Elkjaer, Olsen.J, Simonsen
7-09	France	W 3-1	Copenhagen	Fr	Laudrup.M 2, Brylle
21-09	England	W 1-0	London	ECq	Simonsen
12-10	Luxembourg	W 6-0	Copenhagen	ECq	Laudrup.M 3, Elkjaer 2, Simonsen
26-10	Hungary	L 0-1	Budapest	ECq	
16-11	Greece	W 2-0	Athens	ECq	Elkjaer, Simonsen
14-03-1984	Holland	L 0-6	Amsterdam	Fr	
2-04	Spain	L 1-2	Valencia	Fr	Eriksen
16-05	Czechoslovakia	L 0-1	Prague	Fr	
6-06	Sweden	W 1-0	Gothenburg	Fr	Elkjaer
8-06	Bulgaria	D 1-1	Copenhagen	Fr	Laudrup.M
12-06	France	L 0-1	Paris	ECr1	
16-06	Yugoslavia	W 5-0	Lyon	ECr1	Arnesen 2, Berggreen, Elkjaer, Lauridsen
19-06	Belgium	W 3-2	Strasbourg	ECr1	Arnesen, Brylle, Elkjaer
24-06	Spain	D 1-1	Lyon	ECsf	Lerby. Lost 4-5 pens
12-09	Austria	W 3-1	Copenhagen	Fr	Laudrup.M, Christensen, Eigenbrod
26-09	Norway	W 1-0	Copenhagen	WCq	Elkjaer
17-10	Switzerland	L 0-1	Berne	WCq	
14-11	Rep. Ireland	W 3-0	Copenhagen	WCq	Elkjaer 2, Lerby
27-01-1985	Honduras	L 0-1	Tegucigalpa	Fr	
8-05	East Germany	W 4-1	Copenhagen	Fr	Laudrup.M 2, Lauridsen, Berggreen
5-06	Soviet Union	W 4-2	Copenhagen	WCq	Elkjaer 2, Laudrup.M 2
11-09	Sweden	L 0-3	Copenhagen	Fr	
25-09	Soviet Union	L 0-1	Moscow	WCq	
9-10	Switzerland	D 0-0	Copenhagen	WCq	
16-10	Norway	W 5-1	Oslo	WCq	Berggreen 2, Laudrup.M, Lerby, Elkjaer
13-11	Rep. Ireland	W 4-1	Dublin	WCq	Elkjaer 2, Laudrup, Sivabaek
26-03-1986	Nth. Ireland	D 1-1	Belfast	Fr	Christensen.F
9-04	Bulgaria	L 0-3	Sofia	Fr	
13-05	Norway	L 0-1	Oslo	Fr	
16-05	Poland	W 1-0	Copenhagen	Fr	Elkjaer
20-05	Paraguay	L 1-2	Bogota	Fr	Andersen
4-06	Scotland	W 1-0	Nezahualcoytl	WCr1	Elkjaer
8-06	Uruguay	W 6-1	Nezahualcoytl	WCr1	Elkjaer 3, Lerby, Laudrup.M, Olsen.J
13-06	West Germany	W 2-0	Queretaro	WCr1	Olsen.J, Eriksen
18-06	Spain	L 1-5	Queretaro	WCr2	Olsen.J
10-09	East Germany	W 1-0	Leipzig	Fr	Eriksen
24-09	West Germany	L 0-2	Copenhagen	Fr	
29-10	Finland	W 1-0	Copenhagen	ECq	Bertelsen
12-11	Czechoslovakia	D 0-0	Bratislava	ECq	
29-04-1987	Finland	W 1-0	Helsinki	ECq	Molby
3-06	Czechoslovakia	D 1-1	Copenhagen	ECq	Molby
26-08	Sweden	L 0-1	Stockholm	Fr	
9-09	Wales	L 0-1	Cardiff	ECq	
23-09	West Germany	L 0-1	Hamburg	Fr	
14-10	Wales	W 1-0	Copenhagen	ECq	Elkjaer
27-04-1988	Austria	L 0-1	Vienna	Fr	
10-05	Hungary	D 2-2	Budapest	Fr	Frimann, Eriksen
1-06	Czechoslovakia	L 0-1	Copenhagen	Fr	
4-06	Belgium	W 3-1	Odense	Fr	Eriksen 2, Olsen.M
11-06	Spain	L 2-3	Hanover	ECr1	Laudrup.M, Povlsen
14-06	West Germany	L 0-2	Gelsenkirchen	ECr1	
17-06	Italy	L 0-2	Cologne	ECr1	
31-08	Sweden	W 2-1	Stockholm	Fr	Elstrup 2
14-09	England	L 0-1	London	Fr	
28-09	Iceland	W 1-0	Copenhagen	Fr	Bartram
19-10	Greece	D 1-1	Athens	WCq	Povlsen
2-11	Bulgaria	D 1-1	Copenhagen	WCq	Elstrup
8-02-1989	Malta	W 2-0	Ta'Qali	Fr	Elstrup, Larsen.H
10-02	Finland	D 0-0	Ta'Qali	Fr	
12-02	Algeria	D 0-0	Ta'Qali	Fr	
22-02	Italy	L 0-1	Pisa	Fr	
12-04	Canada	W 2-0	Aalborg	Fr	Elstrup, Vilfort
26-04	Bulgaria	W 2-0	Sofia	WCq	Povlsen, Laudrup.B
17-05	Greece	W 7-1	Copenhagen	WCq	Laudrup.B, Bartram, Nielsen.K, Povlsen, Vilfort,

					Andersen.H, Laudrup.M
7-06	England	D 1-1	Copenhagen	Fr	Elstrup
14-06	Sweden	W 6-0	Copenhagen	Fr	Elstrup 2, Povlsen, Andersen.H, Bartram, Laudrup.M
18-06	Brazil	W 4-0	Copenhagen	Fr	Laudrup.M 2, Olsen.M, Olsen.L
24-08	Belgium	L 0-3	Bruges	Fr	
6-09	Holland	D 2-2	Amsterdam	Fr	Bartram, Heintze
11-10	Romania	W 3-0	Copenhagen	WCq	Nielsen.K, Laudrup.B, Povlsen
15-11	Romania	L 1-3	Bucharest	WCq	Povlsen
29-01-1990	Iraq	D 1-1	Baghdad	Fr	
1-02	Iraq	L 0-1	Baghdad	Fr	
5-02	UAE	D 1-1	Dubai	Fr	Larsen.J
9-02	UAE	W 5-0	Dubai	Fr	Jakobsen, Larsen.J, Svingaard, Risom, Hogh
12-02	Bahrain	W 2-1	Manama	Fr	Jakobsen 2
14-02	Egypt	D 0-0	Cairo	Fr	
11-04	Turkey	W 1-0	Copenhagen	Fr	Jakobsen
15-05	England	L 0-1	London	Fr	
30-05	West Germany	L 0-1	Gelsenkirchen	Fr	
6-06	Norway	W 2-1	Trondheim	Fr	Povlsen, Laudrup.M
5-09	Sweden	W 1-0	Vasteras	Fr	Christensen.B
11-09	Wales	W 1-0	Copenhagen	Fr	Laudrup.B
10-10	Faeroe Islands	W 4-1	Copenhagen	ECq	Laudrup.M 2, Elstrup, Povlsen
17-10	Nth. Ireland	D 1-1	Belfast	ECq	Bartram
14-11	Yugoslavia	L 0-2	Copenhagen	ECq	
9-04-1991	Bulgaria	D 1-1	Odense	Fr	Hoegh
1-05	Yugoslavia	W 2-1	Belgrade	ECq	Christensen.B 2
5-06	Austria	W 2-1	Odense	ECq	Christensen.B 2
12-06	Italy	L 0-2	Malmo	Fr	
15-06	Sweden	L 0-4	Norrkoping	Fr	
4-09	Iceland	D 0-0	Rejkjavik	Fr	
25-09	Faeroe Islands	W 4-0	Landskrona	ECq	Christofte, Christensen.B, Pingel, Vilfort
9-10	Austria	W 3-0	Vienna	ECq	OG, Povlsen, Christensen.B
13-11	Nth. Ireland	W 2-1	Odense	ECq	Povlsen 2
8-04-1992	Turkey	L 1-2	Ankara	Fr	Christensen.B
29-04	Norway	W 1-0	Aarhus	Fr	Elstrup
3-06	Commonw. IS	D 1-1	Copenhagen	Fr	Christensen.B
11-06	England	D 0-0	Malmo	ECr1	
14-06	Sweden	L 0-1	Stockholm	ECr1	
17-06	France	W 2-1	Malmo	ECr1	Larsen.L, Elstrup
22-06	Holland	D 2-2	Gothenburg	ECsf	Larsen.L 2. Won 5-4 pens
26-06	Germany	W 2-0	Gothenburg	ECf	Jensen.J, Vilfort
26-08	Latvia	D 0-0	Riga	WCq	
9-09	Germany	L 1-2	Copenhagen	Fr	Elstrup
23-09	Lithuania	D 0-0	Vilnius	WCq	
14-10	Rep. Ireland	D 0-0	Copenhagen	WCq	
18-11	Northern Ireland	W 1-0	Belfast	WCq	Larsen.H
30-01-1993	United States	D 2-2	Phoenix	Fr	Strudal, Kjeldbjerg
24-02	Argentina	D 1-1	Mar del Plata	AFT	OG. Lost 4-5 pens
31-03	Spain	W 1-0	Copenhagen	WCq	Povlsen
14-04	Latvia	W 2-0	Copenhagen	WCq	Vilfort, Strudal
28-04	Rep. Ireland	D 1-1	Dublin	WCq	Vilfort
2-06	Albania	W 4-0	Copenhagen	WCq	Jensen.J, Pingel 2, Møller
25-08	Lithuania	W 4-0	Copenhagen	WCq	Olsen.L, Pingel, Laudrup.B, Skarbalius
8-09	Albania	W 1-0	Tirana	WCq	Pingel
13-10	Northern Ireland	W 1-0	Copenhagen	WCq	Laudrup.B
17-11	Spain	L 0-1	Seville	WCq	
9-03-1994	England	L 0-1	London	Fr	
20-04	Hungary	W 3-1	Copenhagen	Fr	Laudrup.M 2, Povlsen
26-05	Sweden	W 1-0	Copenhagen	Fr	Laudrup.M
1-06	Norway	L 1-2	Oslo	Fr	Povlsen
17-08	Finland	W 2-1	Copenhagen	Fr	Laudrup.B, Wieghorst
7-09	Macedonia	D 1-1	Skopje	ECq	Povlsen
12-10	Belgium	W 3-1	Copenhagen	ECq	Vilfort, Jensen, Strudal
16-11	Spain	L 0-3	Seville	ECq	
8-01-1995	Saudi Arabia	W 2-0	Riyadh	ICr1	Laudrup.B, Wieghorst
10-01	Mexico	D 1-1	Riyadh	ICr1	Rasmussen. Won 4-2p
13-01	Argentina	W 2-0	Riyadh	ICf	Laudrup.M, Rasmussen
24-01	Canada	W 1-0	Toronto	Fr	Høyer-Nielsen
29-01	Portugal	L 0-1	Toronto	Fr	
29-03	Cyprus	D 1-1	Limassol	ECq	Schjønberg
26-04	Macedonia	W 1-0	Copenhagen	ECq	Nielsen.P
31-05	Finland	W 1-0	Helsinki	Fr	Beck
7-06	Cyprus	W 4-0	Copenhagen	ECq	Vilfort 2, Laudrup.B, Laudrup.M

ENGLAND

The playing fields of Eton and the other major Public Schools of 19th-century England should have a treasured place in the hearts of the world, for out of these exclusive establishments came the embryonic versions of all the major codes of modern-day football. For many centuries, in different parts of the world, a haphazard and often violent form of 'Foote-balle' had been practised by the population at large, but the Public Schools were the first to adopt binding rules and mark out a definitive area of play.

The rules varied from school to school but in 1848, pupils at Cambridge University, in an attempt to unify these different methods of play, drew up the 'Cambridge Rules'. Based primarily on the dribbling game, these laws formed the basis of those adopted in 1863 by the newly formed Football Association. The historic meeting on 26 October that year marks the birth of Association Football proper. The handling code went its separate way, giving rise to the birth of rugby, and although various regions like Sheffield did not immediately adopt the new rules, the new association gradually became the pre-eminent body in England. Four events of tremendous significance happened before the turn of the century. In 1871 the Football Association launched the Challenge Cup. In 1872 the first international match was played, between England and Scotland. In 1885 professionalism was legalised, whilst in 1888 league football was introduced.

The Football Association Challenge Cup, or FA Cup as it is more commonly known, is the oldest and still the most famous football tournament played in the world. The 'little tin idol', as the Cup itself was called, was instrumental in the development of the game. It brought into focus the issue of professionalism by pitting the 'old schoolboy' amateur sides of the South against the rapidly forming 'works' sides of the industrial North. Football, though initially a pastime of the privileged elite, was fast becoming a major recreation in the drab industrial cities. Factory workers enjoyed both playing and watching the game as a diversion from the harsh realities of 19th-century life. The increasingly widespread practice of finishing work at lunchtime on a Saturday left the afternoon free, and many workers used the time to watch football, a tradition that survives to this day in England. By 1880 rumours were rife that many of these Northern sides were paying members of their teams, and as they became more successful in the Cup, the issue of professionalism was brought to a head.

In 1883 Blackburn Olympic beat Old Etonians 2-1 in the final and never again would the amateur sides of the South triumph. In 1884 having just drawn with Preston North End in the fourth round of the Cup, Upton Park protested that Preston were employing professionals. Major Sudell, the architect of the great Preston side of the late 1880s, openly admitted that this was the case but maintained that it was common practice amongst all the Northern clubs. Preston were disqualified, but a year later, realising that fighting the tide was futile, the Football Association legalised professionalism.

Professionalism, once established, then had a big influence on the next major development in the game, the formation of the Football League in 1888. The regular payment of players necessitated playing regular fixtures. As the Cup did not afford this, William McGregor of the Aston Villa club proposed, in a letter to interested parties, the arranging of home and away fixtures each season as occurred in cricket. The idea was adopted at a meeting in the Anderton Hotel in Fleet Street on 22 March 1888. All of the 12 clubs involved in the new league were from the North or the Midlands, and not until the 1930s were any teams from the South to feature prominently in either the Cup or the League. Football had found its roots, and they lay mainly in the North.

On Saturday 30 November 1872 at the West of Scotland cricket ground in Glasgow, England met Scotland in the first ever international football match played in the world. It would be another 30 years before any non-British sides took up the idea. By then the annual fixture was equal in importance to any other sporting fixture in the calendar and served as an excellent model for these countries to follow. It also became a means whereby professionals could play alongside their amateur colleagues. After the events of 1885 this was crucial in uniting the game and keeping the Football Association as the ultimate governing body in English football. The first professional to play for England was the Blackburn Rovers half-back James Forrest, against Scotland in 1885, but despite the growing strength of the professional game, amateurs continued to represent England well into the next century.

In 1879 Wales were added to the fixture list as were Ireland in 1882. In 1884 these fixtures were formalised into the British International Championship, and until 1923 this was the basis of England's international programme. It was not until 1908, when the side made a tour of central Europe, that teams from outside Britain were first encountered, although representative English sides had toured Germany in 1896 and 1899, and France in the early years of the 20th century, whilst numerous English club sides had made trips to all four corners of the world in an effort to spread the game. The British Championship however, remained at the pinnacle of world football.

Many fine club sides emerged in these early years, the first being the Wanderers. They won the Cup five times in the first seven years. Their major rivals, the Old Etonians, won twice and were the losing side on four occasions. A leading figure of this time was the redoubtable Lord Kinnaird who appeared in nine of the first twelve finals for both the Wanderers and Old Etonians. His five winners' medals remains a record and he later went on to become president of the Football Association. Two teams emerged to take the limelight away from these Southern amateur sides. First Blackburn Rovers, who themselves won the Cup five times between 1884 and 1891. James Forrest appeared in all five of their triumphs, thus equalling the feat of both Wollaston of the Wanderers and Lord Kinnaird.

Along with Blackburn, Preston reinforced the supremacy of the North. Often labelled 'the Invincibles', Preston revolutionised the game in England. Using the 2-3-5 formation, they recognised the need for a more scientific approach to their play. The team became the most feared in the land and in 1889 they did the coveted League and Cup 'double' without losing a game. Their star player was undoubtedly John Goodall, the outstanding centre-forward of his generation. Soon, however, other teams from the North began to make their presence felt, notably Aston Villa, Sunderland and Newcastle United. Until 1921 only one team from the South managed to win a trophy: Tottenham Hotspur won the Cup in 1901 as a Southern League side.

Before the First World War, many great players helped spread the popularity of the game to the extent that by 1914 it had become the national sport. Crowds of over 100000 had watched the Cup Final, whilst even in the South the professional teams of the Southern League gained in popularity. Chief among these great players, curiously, was an amateur, GO Smith. He played for the last great amateur side, the Corinthians, and won 20 caps for England at a time when only three internationals were played every season. Steve Bloomer of Derby County, Billy Bassett of West Brom, Ernest Needham of Sheffield United and Vivian Woodward, an amateur with Tottenham, also stand out as the great pre-war players, the latter leading England to two Olympic gold medals in 1908 and 1912. Woodward was also the star of England's first official foreign tour in 1908 and again the next year. He scored 15 goals in the seven matches against Austria, Hungary and Bohemia.

Along with Scotland, there can be no doubt that England were a class above the rest of the football world during this period. Huge victories over Ireland (13-2 in 1899), Austria (11-1 in 1908), France (15-0, 12-0, 11-0 and 10-1 between 1906 and 1910) and Germany (9-0 in 1909) confirm this fact, to the extent that the last two victories were achieved by the England amateur side as opposed to the full team containing the professionals. The rivalry with Scotland, however, was a different matter, with the honours evenly shared. The Scots played an enormous part in the development of the game in England. Most notably they were responsible for the adoption of the passing game, which gradually took over from the dribbling game as the norm. This happened due to the large numbers of Scots who came to play their football south of the border. Successful teams such as Sunderland in the 1890s relied heavily on their contribution as did teams like Preston. Even William McGregor, the father of the Football League, originally hailed from north of the border.

When football resumed after the break caused by the war, it seemed as though things were back to normal. England and the rest of the Home Unions were, however, beginning on a course of gradual isolation. The world was taking up football with a passion, and becoming rather good at it. The Football Association had joined FIFA in 1905, but had always adopted a rather paternal attitude towards it. They withdrew in 1920 because they refused to fraternise with their wartime adversaries, and having rejoined in 1924 they withdrew again in 1928 over the definition of the word 'amateur' in relation to the Olympic Games. This action meant that England could not compete in any of the first three World Cups which were played during the inter-war period. Even if they had been members of FIFA it is doubtful that would have deigned to compete anyway. Judging by the interest shown in the English newspapers at the time of these tournaments, most Englishmen cannot have even been aware that they were being played.

The consequences of this self-imposed 'splendid isolation' did not immediately become apparent. England's first defeat against foreign opposition did not come until they were beaten by Spain in 1929 in Madrid. Defeats by France in 1930, Hungary and Czechoslovakia in 1934, Austria and Belgium in 1936, Switzerland in 1938 and Yugoslavia in 1939, all away from home, did little to dent England's self-belief, but the cracks were beginning to appear. Even the 4-3 victory over the Austrian 'Wunderteam' at Chelsea in 1932 only disguised the fact that the Austrians were the better team. Most Englishmen assume that they would have won the three World Cups of the 1930s, but even Vittorio Pozzo, the Italian manager and a great admirer of English football, stated that away from England, the English would have been lucky to have reached the quarter-finals of either the 1934 or 1938 tournaments.

The English League, however, continued to be strong between the wars. It produced two sides of outstanding quality, Huddersfield Town in the 1920s and Arsenal in the 1930s. Both won the League three years in succession, and both had a common guiding force, Herbert Chapman. He was a revolutionary figure, the first modern-day manager. He had an astute tactical brain with which he devised methods of play and then bought players who would fit into this system. Along with Charlie Buchan, his skilful centre-forward at Arsenal, he introduced the 'third-back game' following the change in the offside law in 1925. To counter the increased number of goals being scored as a result of this change, he pulled the centre-half back into the role of a stopper as well as introducing a deep-lying centre-forward, both of whose roles would be to initiate effective counter attacks. Arsenal played this system to great effect, the key player being Alex James. It often seemed that Arsenal were under pressure for most of a match but a key pass from James, deep in defence, regularly brought goals on the counter. Arsenal always had an excellent forward line with players like Ted Drake, Cliff Bastin and David Jack, along with Buchan, playing for them in the 1930s. Their five League Championships and two Cup wins are testament to the skills of Herbert Chapman, though he did not live to see all of his team's triumphs.

During the Second World War, the game went on. It was thought to be a good diversion during troubled times, though none of the international or domestic results are counted as official. The interest shown in the game directly after the war has never been surpassed. Huge crowds turned out every week, but what they were witnessing was a decline that had set in before the war, especially with regard to the national side. Again, however, results disguised the true state of the game. A 4-0 win over the World Cup holders Italy in Turin in 1948 was hailed as a world-beating performance, as was the 10-0 victory over Portugal in Lisbon the previous year.

The 1950 World Cup in Brazil did little to bring the team down to earth. Defeats by America and Spain were dismissed as flukes and it was not until one famous Wednesday afternoon in November 1953 that the English team realised that tactically they were stale, the state of coaching in the country was poor and that technically players from elsewhere were superior to them. The 6-3 victory by Hungary that day, the first by a foreign team on English soil, had far-reaching repercussions. Slowly the English began to learn from the experience, to adapt foreign methods and styles to the English game. This defeat and those that followed in the 1954, 1958, and 1962 World Cups paved the way for their triumph in the 1966 competition, by forcing the English team to find out where the faults lay and what their strengths were.

England was not devoid of talent in these post-war years. Stanley Matthews seemed to get better with age and there were players such as Tom Finney of Preston, Billy Wright of Wolves and Nat Lofthouse of Bolton who were all excellent players. Stan Cullis, the Wolves manager, built a successful team based more on hard work and rudimentary tactics than on skill, but one which dominated the league in the 1950s and achieved notable victories in friendly matches against Honved and Spartak Moscow. One team, however, paved the way for the English revival. Matt Busby, a former Scottish international, created the Manchester United legend. In his time at the club he moulded together four excellent sides, the greatest of which was possibly the 'Busby Babes' team. Spearheaded by Duncan Edwards, the boy genius, they seemed destined to become as fine a team as the famous Real Madrid who were dominating the European Cup in the latter half of the 1950s. Tragically, however, the team was wiped out by an air crash at Munich airport on their way back to England from a European Cup tie in February 1958. Duncan Edwards, Roger Byrne and Tommy Taylor, all established England internationals, perished in the disaster. One survivor who formed the link with the next great Manchester United team was Bobby Charlton. He also played a crucial role in England's re-emergence as a world power in the 1960s, playing alongside the likes of Jimmy Greaves, Gordon Banks, Bobby Moore and Martin Peters. Charlton and the rest of the England team, ably managed by the dour Alf Ramsey, won the World Cup at home in 1966.

England's victory formed the basis from which the game, especially at club level, developed. Manchester United's victory in the 1968 European Cup was not the first win by an English club in a European competition - Tottenham and West Ham had won the Cup Winners Cup in 1963 and 1965 respectively - but it fired a warning shot that the game in England was in a healthy state and that the World Cup victory was no fluke. For the next 17 years, clubs from England dominated the European scene. From 1977 until 1984 three different English teams won the European Cup in seven of the eight seasons. The UEFA Cup was won six years in succession, by five different clubs, between 1968 and 1974. The strength in depth of the Football League could not be matched by any other European nation. A very English style of game had emerged that was quick and penetrative and best epitomised by first Leeds United and then Liverpool. Between them they won nine European finals and appeared in 13.

This astounding success can partially be traced back to 1963, when the maximum wage limit imposed on English players was removed. It allowed the top clubs to sign and pay handsomely all the top players in the country. A league of superclubs began to emerge. Up until 1963 the championship and the Cup had been open affairs, and anybody had a chance to win. This allowed small clubs like Burnley to win the League as late as 1960. But by the late 1960s Liverpool, Everton, Manchester United, Arsenal, Leeds and Tottenham came to dominate the domestic scene. By the end of the 1980s Liverpool had become pre-eminent. A single statistic sums up their stunning success. Between 1973 and 1991 they finished outside of the top two in the league on only one occasion, a miserable fifth in 1980. During that time they won the championship an incredible 10 times.

Achievement at club level did not, however, translate itself into success at international level. Third place in the European Championship in 1968 and fourth place in the 1990 World Cup have been the only achievements of note since the World Cup victory in 1966. An unlucky defeat in the quarter-finals of the 1970 World Cup in Mexico, with what many rate as a better team than the 1966 side, proved to be the beginning of a traumatic time for the national side as England failed to qualify for both the 1974 and 1978 World Cup Finals. The irony of the situation was that England's side in the 1970s, though not world beaters, was never a bad one. Players such as Colin Bell, Tony Currie, Mike Channon and Kevin Keegan deserved to have their talents displayed on a World Cup stage.

By the 1980s the team had settled down and were unlucky not to progress further than they did in the 1982 World Cup, as was the case in 1986 when Maradona's 'Hand of God' sealed their fate in the quarter-finals. However, the events at the Heysel stadium in Brussels during the 1985 European Cup final between Liverpool and Juventus, where 39 Italians fans died as a result of hooliganism, left English clubs banned from European competition and isolated, and their consequent lack of European experience inevitably had its effect on the national side as the disastrous performance in the finals of the 1988 European

Championship showed. Indeed the game as a whole was seriously tarnished by a series of tragedies and continued hooliganism. In May 1985, 45 people lost their lives in a fire at Bradford City Football Club, whilst in April 1989 95 fans were crushed at Hillsborough in Sheffield at the FA Cup semi-final between Liverpool and Nottingham Forest.

Thankfully those grim events proved to be a watershed for the game in England. Hooliganism was gradually brought under control within stadiums with the help of security cameras and England has progressed from having some of the most rundown stadia in Europe to being able now to count its grounds among the best. With the award of the 1996 European Championships, the development of the stadia has been taken a stage further.

THE ORDER OF MERIT

		All			League			Cup		Europe			L Cup	
	Team	G	S	B	G	S	B	G	S	G	S	B	G	S
1	Liverpool	34	19	4	18	10	2	5	5	6	2	2	5	2
2	Manchester United	20	19	9	9	11	3	8	5	2	-	6	1	3
3	Arsenal	20	14	4	10	3	4	6	6	2	2	-	2	3
4	Aston Villa	19	14	2	7	10	2	7	2	1	-	-	4	2
5	Tottenham H.	15	7	12	2	4	9	8	1	3	1	3	2	1
6	Everton	15	16	7	9	7	7	5	7	1	-	-	-	2
7	Newcastle Utd	11	6	3	4	-	3	6	5	1	-	-	-	1
8	Wolv'hampton W	9	10	7	3	5	6	4	4	-	1	1	2	-
9	Manchester City	9	8	4	2	3	3	4	4	1	-	1	2	1
10	Nottingham Forest	9	5	5	1	2	4	2	1	2	-	1	4	2
11	Blackburn Rovers	9	3	3	3	1	3	6	2	-	-	-	-	-
12	Sunderland	8	8	8	6	5	8	2	2	-	-	-	-	1
13	Sheffield Wed.	8	5	7	4	1	7	3	3	-	-	-	1	1
14	Leeds United	7	11	3	3	5	1	1	3	2	3	2	1	-
15	West Bromwich	7	9	1	1	2	1	5	5	-	-	-	1	2
16	Sheffield United	5	4	-	1	2	-	4	2	-	-	-	-	-
17	The Wanderers	5	-	-	-	-	-	5	-	-	-	-	-	-
18	Preston North	4	11	2	2	6	2	2	5	-	-	-	-	-
19	Huddersfield T	4	7	3	3	3	3	1	4	-	-	-	-	-
20	West Ham Utd	4	4	2	-	-	1	3	1	1	1	1	-	2
21	Chelsea	4	4	5	1	-	3	1	3	1	-	2	1	1
22	Bolton Wan.	4	4	3	-	-	3	4	3	-	-	-	-	1
23	Derby County	3	6	5	2	3	4	1	3	-	-	1	-	-
24	Burnley	3	4	5	2	2	5	1	2	-	-	-	-	-
25	Ipswich Town	3	2	3	1	2	3	1	-	1	-	-	-	-
26	Portsmouth	3	2	1	2	-	1	1	2	-	-	-	-	-
27	Old Etonians	2	4	-	-	-	-	2	4	-	-	-	-	-
28	Norwich City	2	2	1	-	-	1	-	-	-	-	-	2	2
29	Bury	2	-	-	-	-	-	2	-	-	-	-	-	-
30	Leicester City	1	6	1	-	1	1	-	4	-	-	-	1	1
31	Birmingham City	1	4	1	-	-	-	-	2	-	2	1	1	-
32	Southampton	1	4	-	-	1	-	1	2	-	-	-	-	1
33	Blackpool	1	3	1	-	1	1	1	2	-	-	-	-	-
34	Oxford Univers	1	3	-	-	-	-	1	3	-	-	-	-	-
	Queens Park Rangers	1	3	-	-	1	-	-	1	-	-	-	1	1
	Royal Engineers	1	3	-	-	-	-	1	3	-	-	-	-	-
37	Cardiff	1	2	1	-	1	-	1	1	-	-	1	-	-
	Charlton Ath.	1	2	1	-	1	1	1	1	-	-	-	-	-
39	Luton Town	1	2	-	-	-	-	-	1	-	-	-	1	1
40	Notts County	1	1	2	-	-	2	1	1	-	-	-	-	-
41	Stoke City	1	1	-	-	-	-	-	-	-	-	-	1	1
	Clapham Rovers	1	1	-	-	-	-	1	1	-	-	-	-	-
	Barnsley	1	1	-	-	-	-	1	1	-	-	-	-	-
44	Swindon Town	1	-	-	-	-	-	-	-	-	-	-	1	-
	Old Carthusians	1	-	-	-	-	-	1	-	-	-	-	-	-
	Coventry City	1	-	-	-	-	-	1	-	-	-	-	-	-
	Oxford United	1	-	-	-	-	-	-	-	-	-	-	1	-
	Blackburn Olym.	1	-	-	-	-	-	1	-	-	-	-	-	-
	Bradford City	1	-	-	-	-	-	1	-	-	-	-	-	-
	Wimbledon	1	-	-	-	-	-	1	-	-	-	-	-	-
51	Watford	-	2	-	-	1	-	-	1	-	-	-	-	-
	Bristol City	-	2	-	-	1	-	-	1	-	-	-	-	-
	Oldham Ath.	-	2	-	-	1	-	-	-	-	-	-	-	1
	Queens Park	-	2	-	-	-	-	-	2	-	-	-	-	-
55	Crystal Palace	-	1	1	-	-	1	-	1	-	-	-	-	-
56	Fulham	-	1	-	-	-	-	-	1	-	-	-	-	-
	Brighton & Hove Albion	-	1	-	-	-	-	-	1	-	-	-	-	-
	London Select XI	-	1	-	-	-	-	-	-	-	1	-	-	-
	Rochdale	-	1	-	-	-	-	-	-	-	-	-	-	1
	Rotherham U	-	1	-	-	-	-	-	-	-	-	-	-	1
60	Middlesbrough	-	-	1	-	-	1	-	-	-	-	-	-	-

To the end of the 1994-1995 season

Likewise after six or seven years in the doldrums, English club football is flourishing again with large amounts of money from television, ever-increasing attendances and a fierce competitive spirit in the new Premier League, which has seen the re-emergence of teams such as Manchester United, Arsenal, Leeds United, Sheffield Wednesday, Aston Villa and especially Blackburn Rovers. Funded by steel baron Jack Walker and with a brand new multi-million pound stadium, Blackburn have set a new standard for top players' wages and others have had to follow. Success is also starting to return at European level with victories in the Cup Winners Cup by Manchester United and Arsenal.

Population: 47,254,000
Area, sq km: 130,439
% in urban areas: 91.5%
Capital city: London

The Football Association
16 Lancaster Gate
London, W2 3LW
England
Tel: + 44 171 2624542
Fax: + 44 171 4020486

Year of formation 1863

Affiliation to FIFA	1905-1920, 1924-28, 1946
Affiliation to UEFA	1954
Registered clubs	41 750
Registered players	3 258 000
Professional Players	5000
Registered coaches	41 600
Registered referees	31 500
National stadium	Empire Stadium, Wembley, London 80 000
National colours	White/Blue/White
Reserve colours	Red/White/Red
Season	August - May

THE RECORD

WORLD CUP

1930-38	Did not enter
1950	QT 1st/4 in group 1 - Final Tournament/1st round
1954	QT 1st/4 in group 3 - Final Tournament/Quarter-finalists
1958	QT 1st/3 in group 1 - Final Tournament/1st round
1962	QT 1st/3 in group 6 - Final Tournament/Quarter-finalists
1966	QT Automatic - Final Tournament/Winners

1970 QT Automatic - Final Tournament/Quarter-finalists
1974 QT 2nd/3 in group 5
1978 QT 2nd/4 in group 2
1982 QT 2nd/5 in group 4 - Final Tournament/2nd round
1986 QT 1st/5 in group 3 - Final Tournament/Quarter-finalists
1990 QT 2nd/4 in group 2 - Final Tournament/Semi-finalists/ 4th place
1994 QT 3rd/6 in group 2

EUROPEAN CHAMPIONSHIP

1960 Did not enter
1964 1st round
1968 QT 1st/4 in group 8 - Final Tournament/Semi-finalists/ 3rd place
1972 QT 1st/4 in group 3 - Final Tournament/Quarter-finalists
1976 QT 2nd/4 in group 1
1980 QT 1st/5 in group 1 - Final Tournament/1st round
1984 QT 2nd/5 in group 3
1988 QT 1st/4 in group 4 - Final Tournament/1st round
1992 QT 1st/4 in group 7 - Final Tournament/1st round
1996 QT Automatic

EUROPEAN CLUB COMPETITIONS

European Cup
Winners - Manchester United 1968, Liverpool 1977 1978 1981 1984, Nottingham Forest 1979 1980, Aston Villa 1982
Finalists - Leeds United 1975, Liverpool 1985

Cup Winners Cup
Winners - Tottenham Hotspur 1963, West Ham United 1965, Manchester City 1970, Chelsea 1971, Everton 1985, Manchester United 1991, Arsenal 1994
Finalists - Liverpool 1966, Leeds United 1973, West Ham United 1976, Arsenal 1980 1995

UEFA Cup
Winners - Leeds United 1968 1971, Newcastle United 1969, Arsenal 1970, Tottenham Hotspur 1972 1984, Liverpool 1973 1976, Ipswich Town 1981
Finalists - Birmingham City 1960 1961, Leeds United 1967, Wolverhampton Wanderers 1972, Tottenham Hotspur 1974

CLUB DIRECTORY

LONDON (Population - 11,100,000)

Arsenal (1886)
Highbury 38,000 – Red, white sleeves/ White
Previous names - Dial Square 1886, Royal Arsenal 1886-92, Woolwich Arsenal 1892-1913

Charlton Athletic (1905)
The Valley 14,000 – Red/White

Chelsea (1905)
Stamford Bridge 36,000 – Blue/Blue

Crystal Palace (1905)
Selhurst Park 17,000 – Red and blue stripes/Red

Millwall (1885)
The New Den 20,000 – Blue/White
Previous names - Millwall Rovers 1885, Millwall Athletic 1889

Queens Park Rangers (1885)
Loftus Road 19,000 – Blue & white hoops/White

Tottenham Hotspur (1882)
White Hart Lane 33,000 – White/Blue
Previous name - Hotspur FC 1882-85

Watford (1891)
Vicarage Road 16,000 – Yellow/Black

West Ham United (1895)
Upton Park 22,000 – Claret, blue sleeves/White
Previous name - Thames Ironworks 1895-1900

Wimbledon (1889)
Selhurst Park 17,000 – Blue/Blue, yellow trim
Previous name - Wimbledon Old Centrals 1889-1905

MANCHESTER (Population - 2,775,000)

Manchester City (1887)
Maine Road 21,000 – Sky blue/White
Previous name - Ardwick FC 1887-94

Manchester United (1878)
Old Trafford 43,000 – Red/White, black trim
Previous name - Newton Heath FC 1880-92

Oldham Athletic (1894)
Boundary Park 16,000 – Blue/Blue, red trim
Previous name - Pine Villa 1894

Bolton Wanderers (1874)
Burnden Park 20,000 – White/Blue
Previous name - Christ Church FC 1874-77

BIRMINGHAM (Population - 2,675,000)

Aston Villa (1874)
Villa Park 40,000 – Claret with thin blue stripes/White

Birmingham City (1875)
St Andrews 27,000 – Blue/White
Previous names - Small Heath Alliance 1875-88, Small Heath 1888-1905, Birmingham FC 1905-45

West Bromwich Albion (1879)
The Hawthorns 26,000 – Blue & white stripes/Blue

Wolverhampton Wanderers (1877)
Molineux 28,000 – Gold/Black

LEEDS (Population - 1,540,000)

Leeds United (1904)
Elland Road 43,000 – White with thin yelow,blue,yellow band on chest/White
Previous name - Leeds City 1904-19

LIVERPOOL (Population - 1,525,000)

Everton (1878)
Goodison Park 40,000 – Blue/White

Liverpool (1892)
Anfield 40,000 – Red/Red, white trim

NEWCASTLE UPON TYNE (Population - 1,300,000)

Newcastle United (1882)
St James' Park 32,000 – Black & white stripes/Black

SUNDERLAND

Sunderland (1879)
Roker Park 27,000 – Red and white stripes/Black

SHEFFIELD (Population - 710,000)

Sheffield United (1889)
Bramall Lane 23,000 – Red & white stripes/White

Sheffield Wednesday (1867)
Hillsborough 41,000 – Blue & white stripes/Blue

NOTTINGHAM (Population - 655,000)

Nottingham Forest (1865)
City Ground 28,000 – Red/White

Notts County (1862)
The oldest league club in the world
Meadow Lane 20,000 – Black & white stripes/Black, yellow trim

COVENTRY (Population - 645,000)

Coventry City (1883)
Highfield Road 22,000 – Sky blue/Sky blue

BRISTOL (Population - 630,000)

Bristol City (1894)
Ashton Gate 23,000 – Red/White - White trimmings

MIDDLESBROUGH (Population - 580,000)

Middlesbrough (1876)
Ayresome Park 26,000 – Red/White

LEICESTER (Population - 495,000)

Leicester City (1884)
Filbert Street 22,000 – Blue/Blue, white trim
Previous name - Leicester Fosse 1884-1919

PORTSMOUTH (Population - 485,000)

Portsmouth (1898)
Fratton Park 26,000 – Blue/White

STOKE-ON-TRENT (Population - 440,000)
Stoke City (1863)
Victoria Ground 25,000 – Red & white stripes/White

BRIGHTON (Population - 420,000)
Brighton and Hove Albion (1900)
Goldstone Ground 18,000 – Blue & white stripes/Blue

SOUTHAMPTON (Population - 415,000)
Southampton (1885)
The Dell 15,000 – Red & white stripes/Black
Previous name - Southampton St Mary's 1885-97

DERBY (Population - 275,000)
Derby County (1884)
Baseball Ground 19,000 – White, black sleeves/Black

NORWICH (Population - 230,000)
Norwich City (1905)
Carrow Road 21,000 – Yellow/Green

OXFORD (Population - 230,000)
Oxford United (1893)
Manor Ground 11,000 – Yellow, blue sleeves/Blue
Previous name - Headington United 1893-1960

BLACKBURN (Population - 221,000)
Blackburn Rovers (1875)
Ewood Park 30,000 – Blue & white halves/White

LUTON (Population - 220,000)
Luton Town (1885)
Kenilworth Road 11,000 – White/White, blue trim

BURNLEY (Population - 160,000)
Burnley (1882)
Turf Moor 22,000 – Claret with blue sleeves/White

IPSWICH (Population - 129,000)
Ipswich Town (1878)
Portman Road 22,000 – Blue, white sleeves/White

SWINDON (Population - 128,000)
Swindon Town (1881)
County Ground 16,000 – Red/White

CARLISLE (Population - 72,000)
Carlisle United (1904)
Brunton Park 13,000 – Blue/White

ENGLISH LEAGUE CHAMPIONSHIP

1889k Preston North End 40 Aston Villa 29 Wolverhampton Wanderers 28
1890 Preston North End 33 Everton 31 Blackburn Rovers 27
1891 Everton 29 Preston North End 27 Notts County 26
1892n Sunderland 42 Preston North End 37 Bolton Wanderers 36
1893q Sunderland 48 Preston North End 37 Everton 36
1894 Aston Villa 44 Sunderland 38 Derby County 36
1895 Sunderland 47 Everton 42 Aston Villa 39
1896 Aston Villa 45 Derby County 41 Everton 39
1897 Aston Villa 47 Sheffield United 36 Derby County 36
1898 Sheffield United 42 Sunderland 37 Wolverhampton Wanderers 35
1899t Aston Villa 45 Liverpool 43 Burnley 39
1900 Aston Villa 50 Sheffield United 48 Sunderland 41
1901 Liverpool 45 Sunderland 43 Notts County 40
1902 Sunderland 44 Everton 41 Newcastle United 37
1903 Sheffield Wednesday 42 Aston Villa 41 Sunderland 41
1904 Sheffield Wednesday 47 Manchester City 44 Everton 43
1905 Newcastle United 48 Everton 47 Manchester City 46
1906v Liverpool 51 Preston North End 47 Sheffield Wednesday 44
1907 Newcastle United 51 Bristol City 48 Everton 45
1908 Manchester United 52 Aston Villa 43 Manchester City 43
1909 Newcastle United 53 Everton 46 Sunderland 44
1910 Aston Villa 53 Liverpool 48 Blackburn Rovers 45
1911 Manchester United 52 Aston Villa 51 Sunderland 45
1912 Blackburn Rovers 49 Everton 46 Newcastle United 44
1913 Sunderland 54 Aston Villa 50 Sheffield Wednesday 49
1914 Blackburn Rovers 51 Aston Villa 44 Middlesbrough 43
1915 Everton 46 Oldham Athletic 45 Blackburn Rovers 43
1916-19 -
1920y West Bromwich Albion 60 Burnley 51 Chelsea 49
1921 Burnley 59 Manchester City 54 Bolton Wanderers 52
1922 Liverpool 57 Tottenham Hotspur 51 Burnley 49
1923 Liverpool 60 Sunderland 54 Huddersfield Town 53
1924 Huddersfield Town 57 Cardiff City 57 Sunderland 53
1925 Huddersfield Town 58 West Bromwich Albion 56 Bolton Wanderers 55
1926 Huddersfield Town 57 Arsenal 52 Sunderland 48
1927 Newcastle United 56 Huddersfield Town 51 Sunderland 49
1928 Everton 53 Huddersfield Town 51 Leicester City 48
1929 Sheffield Wednesday 52 Leicester City 51 Aston Villa 50
1930 Sheffield Wednesday 60 Derby County 50 Manchester City 47
1931 Arsenal 66 Aston Villa 59 Sheffield Wednesday 52
1932 Everton 56 Arsenal 54 Sheffield Wednesday 50
1933 Arsenal 58 Aston Villa 54 Sheffield Wednesday 51
1934 Arsenal 59 Huddersfield Town 56 Tottenham Hotspur 49
1935 Arsenal 58 Sunderland 54 Sheffield Wednesday 49
1936 Sunderland 56 Derby County 48 Huddersfield Town 48
1937 Manchester City 57 Charlton Athletic 54 Arsenal 52
1938 Arsenal 52 Wolverhampton Wanderers 51 Preston North End 49
1939 Everton 59 Wolverhampton Wanderers 55 Charlton Athletic 50
1940-46 -
1947 Liverpool 57 Manchester United 56 Wolverhampton Wanderers 56
1948 Arsenal 59 Manchester United 52 Burnley 52
1949 Portsmouth 58 Manchester United 53 Derby County 53
1950 Portsmouth 53 Wolverhampton Wanderers 53 Sunderland 52
1951 Tottenham Hotspur 60 Manchester United 56 Blackpool 50
1952 Manchester United 57 Tottenham Hotspur 53 Arsenal 53
1953 Arsenal 54 Preston North End 54 Wolverhampton Wanderers 51
1954 Wolverhampton Wanderers 57 West Bromwich Albion 53 Huddersfield Town 51
1955 Chelsea 52 Wolverhampton Wanderers 48 Portsmouth 48
1956 Manchester United 60 Blackpool 49 Wolverhampton Wanderers 49
1957 Manchester United 64 Tottenham Hotspur 56 Preston North End 56
1958 Wolverhampton Wanderers 64 Preston North End 59 Tottenham Hotspur 51
1959 Wolverhampton Wanderers 61 Manchester United 55 Arsenal 50
1960 Burnley 55 Wolverhampton Wanderers 54 Tottenham Hotspur 53
1961 Tottenham Hotspur 66 Sheffield Wednesday 58 Wolverhampton Wanderers 57
1962 Ipswich Town 56 Burnley 53 Tottenham Hotspur 52
1963 Everton 61 Tottenham Hotspur 55 Burnley 54
1964 Liverpool 57 Manchester United 53 Everton 52
1965 Manchester United 61 Leeds United 61 Chelsea 56
1966 Liverpool 61 Leeds United 55 Burnley 55
1967 Manchester United 60 Nottingham Forest 56 Tottenham Hotspur 56
1968 Manchester City 58 Manchester United 56 Liverpool 55
1969 Leeds United 67 Liverpool 61 Everton 57

1970 Everton 66 Leeds United 57 Chelsea 55
1971 Arsenal 65 Leeds United 64 Tottenham Hotspur 52
1972 Derby County 58 Leeds United 57 Liverpool 57
1973 Liverpool 60 Arsenal 57 Leeds United 53
1974 Leeds United 62 Liverpool 57 Derby County 48
1975 Derby County 53 Liverpool 51 Ipswich Town 51
1976 Liverpool 60 Queens Park Rangers 59 Manchester United 56
1977 Liverpool 57 Manchester City 56 Ipswich Town 52
1978 Nottingham Forest 64 Liverpool 57 Everton 55
1979 Liverpool 68 Nottingham Forest 60 West Bromwich Albion 59
1980 Liverpool 60 Manchester United 58 Ipswich Town 53
1981 Aston Villa 60 Ipswich Town 56 Arsenal 53
1982y1 Liverpool 87 Ipswich Town 83 Manchester United 78
1983 Liverpool 82 Watford 71 Manchester United 70
1984 Liverpool 80 Southampton 77 Nottingham Forest 74
1985 Everton 90 Liverpool 77 Tottenham Hotspur 77
1986 Liverpool 88 Everton 86 West Ham United 84
1987 Everton 86 Liverpool 77 Tottenham Hotspur 71
1988x1 Liverpool 90 Manchester United 81 Nottingham Forest 73
1989v1 Arsenal 76 Liverpool 76 Nottingham Forest 64
1990 Liverpool 79 Aston Villa 70 Tottenham Hotspur 63
1991 Arsenal 83 Liverpool 76 Crystal Palace 69
1992y1 Leeds United 82 Manchester United 78 Sheffield Wednesday 75
1993 Manchester United 84 Aston Villa 74 Norwich City 72
1994 Manchester United 92 Blackburn Rovers 84 Newcastle United 77
1995 Blackburn Rovers 89 Manchester United 88 Nottingham Forest 77

ENGLISH FA CUP FINALS

1872	Wanderers	1-0	Royal Engineers
1873	Wanderers	2-0	Oxford University
1874	Oxford University	2-0	Royal Engineers
1875	Royal Engineers	1-1 2-0	Old Etonians
1876	Wanderers	1-1 3-0	Old Etonians
1877	Wanderers	2-1	Oxford University
1878	Wanderers	3-1	Royal Engineers
1879	Old Etonians	1-0	Clapham Rovers
1880	Clapham Rovers	1-0	Oxford University
1881	Old Carthusians	3-0	Old Etonians
1882	Old Etonians	1-0	Blackburn Rovers
1883	Blackburn Olympic	2-1	Old Etonians
1884	Blackburn Rovers	2-1	Queen's Park Glasgow
1885	Blackburn Rovers	2-0	Queen's Park Glasgow
1886	Blackburn Rovers	0-0 2-0	West Bromwich Albion
1887	Aston Villa	2-0	West Bromwich Albion
1888	West Bromwich Albion	2-1	Preston North End
1889	Preston North End	3-0	Wolverhampton Wanderers
1890	Blackburn Rovers	6-1	Sheffield Wednesday
1891	Blackburn Rovers	3-1	Notts County
1892	West Bromwich Albion	3-0	Aston Villa
1893	Wolverhampton Wand	1-0	Everton
1894	Notts County	4-1	Bolton Wanderers
1895	Aston Villa	1-0	West Bromwich Albion
1896	Sheffield Wednesday	2-1	Wolverhampton Wanderers
1897	Aston Villa	3-2	Everton
1898	Nottingham Forest	3-1	Derby County
1899	Sheffield United	4-1	Derby County
1900	Bury	4-0	Southampton
1901	Tottenham Hotspur	2-2 3-1	Sheffield United
1902	Sheffield United	1-1 2-1	Southampton
1903	Bury	6-0	Derby County
1904	Manchester City	1-0	Bolton Wanderers
1905	Aston Villa	2-0	Newcastle United
1906	Everton	1-0	Newcastle United
1907	Sheffield Wednesday	2-1	Everton
1908	Wolverhampton Wand	3-1	Newcastle United
1909	Manchester United	1-0	Bristol City
1910	Newcastle United	1-1 2-0	Barnsley
1911	Bradford City	0-0 1-0	Newcastle United
1912	Barnsley	0-0 1-0	West Bromwich Albion
1913	Aston Villa	0-0 1-0	Sunderland
1914	Burnley	1-0	Liverpool
1915	Sheffield United	3-0	Chelsea
1916-19	-		
1920	Aston Villa	1-0	Huddersfield Town
1921	Tottenham Hotspur	1-0	Wolverhampton Wanderers
1922	Huddersfield Town	1-0	Preston North End
1923	Bolton Wanderers	2-0	West Ham United
1924	Newcastle United	2-0	Aston Villa
1925	Sheffield United	1-0	Cardiff City
1926	Bolton Wanderers	1-0	Manchester City
1927	Cardiff City	1-0	Arsenal
1928	Blackburn Rovers	3-1	Huddersfield Town
1929	Bolton Wanderers	2-0	Portsmouth
1930	Arsenal	2-0	Huddersfield Town
1931	West Bromwich Albion	2-1	Birmingham City
1932	Newcastle United	2-1	Arsenal
1933	Everton	3-0	Manchester City
1934	Manchester City	2-1	Portsmouth
1935	Sheffield Wednesday	4-2	West Bromwich Albion
1936	Arsenal	1-0	Sheffield United
1937	Sunderland	3-1	Preston North End
1938	Preston North End	1-0	Huddersfield Town
1939	Portsmouth	4-1	Wolverhampton Wanderers
1940-45	-		
1946	Derby County	4-1	Charlton Athletic
1947	Charlton Athletic	1-0	Burnley
1948	Manchester United	4-2	Blackpool
1949	Wolverhampton Wand.	3-1	Leicester City
1950	Arsenal	2-0	Liverpool
1951	Newcastle United	2-0	Blackpool
1952	Newcastle United	1-0	Arsenal
1953	Blackpool	4-3	Bolton Wanderers
1954	West Bromwich Albion	3-2	Preston North End
1955	Newcastle United	3-1	Manchester City
1956	Manchester City	3-1	Birmingham City
1957	Aston Villa	2-1	Manchester United
1958	Bolton Wanderers	2-0	Manchester United
1959	Nottingham Forest	2-1	Luton Town
1960	Wolverhampton Wand.	3-0	Blackburn Rovers
1961	Tottenham Hotspur	2-0	Leicester City
1962	Tottenham Hotspur	3-1	Burnley
1963	Manchester United	3-1	Leicester City
1964	West Ham United	3-2	Preston North End
1965	Liverpool	2-1	Leeds United
1966	Everton	3-2	Sheffield Wednesday
1967	Tottenham Hotspur	2-1	Chelsea
1968	West Bromwich Albion	1-0	Everton
1969	Manchester City	1-0	Leicester City
1970	Chelsea	2-2 2-1	Leeds United
1971	Arsenal	2-1	Liverpool
1972	Leeds United	1-0	Arsenal
1973	Sunderland	1-0	Leeds United
1974	Liverpool	3-0	Newcastle United

1975	West Ham United	2-0	Fulham
1976	Southampton	1-0	Manchester United
1977	Manchester United	2-1	Liverpool
1978	Ipswich Town	1-0	Arsenal
1979	Arsenal	3-2	Manchester United
1980	West Ham United	1-0	Arsenal
1981	Tottenham Hotspur	1-1 3-2	Manchester City
1982	Tottenhan Hotspur	1-1 1-0	Queens Park Rangers
1983	Manchester United	2-2 4-0	Brighton & Hove Albion
1984	Everton	2-0	Watford
1985	Manchester United	1-0	Everton
1986	Liverpool	3-1	Everton
1987	Coventry City	3-2	Tottenham Hotspur
1988	Wimbledon	1-0	Liverpool
1989	Liverpool	3-2	Everton
1990	Manchester United	3-3 1-0	Crystal Palace
1991	Tottenham Hotspur	2-1	Nottingham Forest
1992	Liverpool	2-0	Sunderland
1993	Arsenal	1-1 2-1	Sheffield Wednesday
1994	Manchester United	4-0	Chelsea
1995	Everton	1-0	Manchester United

ENGLISH LEAGUE CUP FINALS

1961	Aston Villa	0-2 3-0	Rotherham United
1962	Norwich City	3-0 1-0	Rochdale
1963	Birmingham City	3-1 0-0	Aston Villa
1964	Leicester City	1-1 3-2	Stoke City
1965	Chelsea	3-2 0-0	Leicester City
1966	West Bromwich Alb	1-2 4-1	West Ham United
1967	Queens Park Rangers	3-2	West Bromwich Albion
1968	Leeds United	1-0	Arsenal
1969	Swindon Town	3-1	Arsenal
1970	Manchester City	2-1	West Bromwich Albion
1971	Tottenham Hotspur	2-0	Aston Villa
1972	Stoke City	2-1	Chelsea
1973	Tottenham Hotspur	1-0	Norwich City
1974	Wolverhampton Wand	2-1	Manchester City
1975	Aston Villa	1-0	Norwich City
1976	Manchester City	2-1	Newcastle United
1977	Aston Villa	0-0 1-1 3-2	Everton
1978	Nottingahm Forest	0-0 1-0	Liverpool
1979	Nottingham Forest	3-2	Southampton
1980	Wolverhampton Wand	1-0	Nottingham Forest
1981	Liverpool	1-1 2-1	West Ham United
1982	Liverpool	3-1	Tottenham Hotspur
1983	Liverpool	2-1	Manchester United
1984	Liverpool	0-0 1-0	Everton
1985	Norwich City	1-0	Sunderland
1986	Oxford United	3-0	Queens Park Rangers
1987	Arsenal	2-1	Liverpool
1988	Luton Town	3-2	Arsenal
1989	Nottingham Forest	3-1	Luton Town
1990	Nottingham Forest	1-0	Oldham Athletic
1991	Sheffield Wednesday	1-0	Manchester United
1992	Manchester United	1-0	Nottingham Forest
1993	Arsenal	2-1	Sheffield Wednesday
1994	Aston Villa	3-1	Manchester United
1995	Liverpool	2-1	Bolton Wanderers

LEADING INTERNATIONAL GOALSCORERS

49	Bobby Charlton	(Manchester United)	1958-1970
48	Gary Lineker	(Leicester/Everton/Barcelona/ Tottenham)	1984-1992
44	Jimmy Greaves	(Chelsea/Tottenham)	1959-1967
30	Tom Finney	(Preston)	1946-1958
	Nat Lofthouse	(Bolton)	1950-1958
29	Vivian Woodward	(Tottenham/Chelsea)	1903-1911
28	Steve Bloomer	(Derby/Middlesbrough)	1895-1907
26	Bryan Robson	(West Brom/Manchester United)	1980-1991
26	David Platt	(Aston Villa/Bari/Juventus/ Sampdoria)	1989-
24	Geoff Hurst	(West Ham)	1966-1972
23	Stan Mortensen	(Blackpool)	1947-1953

LEADING INTERNATIONAL APPEARANCES

125	Peter Shilton	(Leicester/Stoke/Nottm Forest/Southampton/Derby)	1970-1990
108	Bobby Moore	(West Ham)	1962-1973
106	Bobby Charlton	(Manchester United)	1958-1970
105	Billy Wright	(Wolverhampton)	1946-1959
90	Bryan Robson	(West Brom/Manchester United)	1980-1991
86	Kenny Sansom	(Crystal Palace/Arsenal)	1979-1988
84	Ray Wilkins	(Chelsea/Manchester United/ Milan)	1976-1986
80	Gary Lineker	(Leicester/Everton/Barcelona/ Tottenham)	1984-1992
78	John Barnes	(Watford/Liverpool)	1983-
77	Terry Butcher	(Ipswich/Glasgow Rangers)	1980-1990
76	Tom Finney	(Preston)	1946-1958

NATIONAL TEAM COACHES

1946-1962	Walter Winterbottom
1962-1974	Sir Alf Ramsey
1974	Joe Mercer
1974-1977	Don Revie
1977-1982	Ron Greenwood
1982-1990	Bobby Robson
1990-1994	Graham Taylor
1994-	Terry Venables

INTERNATIONAL MATCHES PLAYED BY ENGLAND

5-03-1870	Scotland *	D 1-1	London	Fr	Baker
19-11	Scotland *	W 1-0	London	Fr	Walker
28-02-1871	Scotland *	D 1-1	London	Fr	Walker
18-11	Scotland *	W 2-1	London	Fr	Walker 2
24-02-1872	Scotland *	W 1-0	London	Fr	Clegg
30-11	Scotland	D 0-0	Glasgow	Fr	
8-03-1873	Scotland	W 4-2	London	Fr	Chenery, Bonsor, Kenyon-Slaney 2
7-03-1874	Scotland	L 1-2	Glasgow	Fr	Kingsford
6-03-1875	Scotland	D 2-2	London	Fr	Alcock, Wollaston

Date	Opponent	Result	Venue	Comp	Scorers
4-03-1876	Scotland	L 0-3	Glasgow	Fr	
3-03-1877	Scotland	L 1-3	London	Fr	Lyttleton
2-03-1878	Scotland	L 2-7	Glasgow	Fr	Cursham.A, Wylie
18-01-1879	Wales	W 2-1	London	Fr	Sorby, Whitfield
5-04	Scotland	W 5-4	London	Fr	Bailey, Goodyer, Mosforth, Bambridge.E 2
13-03-1880	Scotland	L 4-5	Glasgow	Fr	Sparks, Mosforth, Bambridge.E 2
15-03	Wales	W 3-2	Wrexham	Fr	Brindle, Sparks 2
26-02-1881	Wales	L 0-1	Blackburn	Fr	
12-03	Scotland	L 1-6	London	Fr	Bambridge.E
18-02-1882	Ireland	W 13-0	Belfast	Fr	Bambridge.E, Brown.A 4, Brown.J 2, Vaughton 5, Cursham.H
11-03	Scotland	L 1-5	Glasgow	Fr	Vaughton
13-03	Wales	L 3-5	Wrexham	Fr	Parry.E, Cursham.H, Mosforth
3-02-1883	Wales	W 5-0	London	Fr	Cursham.A, Mitchell 3, Bambridge.E
24-02	Ireland	W 7-0	Liverpool	Fr	Whateley 2, Pawson, Dunn 2, Cobbold 2
10-03	Scotland	L 2-3	Sheffield	Fr	Cobbold, Mitchell
23-02-1884	Ireland	W 8-1	Belfast	HC	Johnson.E 2, Bambridge.A, Bambridge.E 2, Cursham.H 3
15-03	Scotland	L 0-1	Glasgow	HC	
17-03	Wales	W 4-0	Wrexham	HC	Bailey, Gunn, Bromley-Davenport 2
28-02-1885	Ireland	W 4-0	Manchester	HC	Lofthouse.J, Spilsbury, Brown.J, Bambridge.E
14-03	Wales	D 1-1	Blackburn	HC	Mitchell
21-03	Scotland	D 1-1	London	HC	Bambridge.E
13-03-1886	Ireland	W 6-1	Belfast	HC	Spilsbury 4, Dewhurst, Lindley
27-03	Scotland	D 1-1	Glasgow	HC	Lindley
29-03	Wales	W 3-1	Wrexham	HC	Dewhurst, Bambridge.E, Lindley
5-02-1887	Ireland	W 7-0	Sheffield	HC	Cobbold 2, Lindley 3, Dewhurst 2
26-02	Wales	W 4-0	London	HC	Cobbold 2, Lindley 2
19-03	Scotland	L 2-3	Blackburn	HC	Dewhurst, Lindley
4-02-1888	Wales	W 5-1	Crewe	HC	Dewhurst 2, Woodhall, Goodall, Lindley
17-03	Scotland	W 5-0	Glasgow	HC	Lindley, Hodgetts, Dewhurst 2, Goodall
31-03	Ireland	W 5-1	Belfast	HC	Dewhurst, Allen.G 3, Lindley
23-02-1889	Wales	W 4-1	Stoke	HC	Bassett, Goodall, Southworth, Dewhurst
2-03	Ireland	W 6-1	Liverpool	HC	Weir, Yates 3, Lofthouse.J, Brodie
13-04	Scotland	L 2-3	London	HC	Bassett, Weir
15-03-1890	Wales	W 3-1	Wrexham	HC	Currey 2, Lindley
15-03	Ireland	W 9-1	Belfast	HC	Townley 2, Davenport 2, Geary 3, Lofthouse.J, Barton
5-04	Scotland	D 1-1	Glasgow	HC	Wood
7-03-1891	Wales	W 4-1	Sunderland	HC	Goodall, Southworth, Chadwick, Milward
7-03	Ireland	W 6-1	Wolverhampton	HC	Cotterill, Daft, Henfrey, Lindley 2, Bassett
6-04	Scotland	W 2-1	Blackburn	HC	Goodall, Chadwick
5-03-1892	Wales	W 2-0	Wrexham	HC	Henfrey, Sandilands
5-03	Ireland	W 2-0	Belfast	HC	Daft 2
2-04	Scotland	W 4-1	Glasgow	HC	Southworth, Goodall 2, Chadwick
25-02-1893	Ireland	W 6-1	Birmingham	HC	Sandilands, Gilliatt 3, Winckworth, Smith.G
13-03	Wales	W 6-0	Stoke	HC	Spiksley 2, Goodall, Bassett, Schofield, Reynolds
1-04	Scotland	W 5-2	London	HC	Spiksley 2, Gosling, Cotterill, Reynolds
3-03-1894	Ireland	D 2-2	Belfast	HC	Devey, Spiksley
12-03	Wales	W 5-1	Wrexham	HC	Veitch 3, Gosling, OG
7-04	Scotland	D 2-2	Glasgow	HC	Goodall, Reynolds
9-03-1895	Ireland	W 9-0	Derby	HC	Bloomer 2, Goodall 2, Bassett, Howell, Becton 2, OG
18-03	Wales	D 1-1	London	HC	Smith.G
6-04	Scotland	W 3-0	Liverpool	HC	Bloomer, Smith.G, OG
7-03-1896	Ireland	W 2-0	Belfast	HC	Bloomer, Smith.G
16-03	Wales	W 9-1	Cardiff	HC	Bloomer 5, Smith.G 2, Goodall, Bassett
4-04	Scotland	L 1-2	Glasgow	HC	Bassett
20-02-1897	Ireland	W 6-0	Nottingham	HC	Bloomer 2, Wheldon 3, Athersmith
29-03	Wales	W 4-0	Sheffield	HC	Bloomer, Needham, Milward 2
3-04	Scotland	L 1-2	London	HC	Bloomer
5-03-1898	Ireland	W 3-2	Belfast	HC	Morren, Athersmith, Smith.G
28-03	Wales	W 3-0	Wrexham	HC	Smith.G, Wheldon 2
2-04	Scotland	W 3-1	Glasgow	HC	Bloomer 2, Wheldon
18-02-1899	Ireland	W 13-2	Sunderland	HC	Forman.F (I), Bloomer 2, Athersmith, Settle 3, Smith.G 4, Forman.F (II) 2
20-03	Wales	W 4-0	Bristol	HC	Bloomer 2, Forman.F (II), Needham
8-04	Scotland	W 2-1	Birmingham	HC	Smith.G, Settle
17-03-1900	Ireland	W 2-0	Dublin	HC	Johnson.W, Sagar
26-03	Wales	D 1-1	Cardiff	HC	Wilson.G
7-04	Scotland	L 1-4	Glasgow	HC	Bloomer
9-03-1901	Ireland	W 3-0	Southampton	HC	Foster, Crawshaw
18-03	Wales	W 6-0	Newcastle	HC	Bloomer 4, Foster, Needham
30-03	Scotland	D 2-2	London	HC	Blackburn, Bloomer

Date	Opponent	Result	Venue	Comp	Scorers
21-09	Germany *	W 12-0	London	Fr	Foster 6, Smith.G 2, Farnfield 2, Ryder, Hales
3-03-1902	Wales	D 0-0	Wrexham	HC	
22-03	Ireland	W 1-0	Belfast	HC	Settle
5-04	Scotland *	D 1-1	Glasgow	HC	Settle
3-05	Scotland	D 2-2	Birmingham	HC	Wilkes, Settle
14-02-1903	Ireland	W 4-0	Wolverhampton	HC	Sharp, Davis.H, Woodward 2
2-03	Wales	W 2-1	Portsmouth	HC	Bache, Woodward
4-04	Scotland	L 1-2	Sheffield	HC	Woodward
29-02-1904	Wales	D 2-2	Wrexham	HC	Common, Bache
12-03	Ireland	W 3-1	Belfast	HC	Common, Bache, Davis.G
9-04	Scotland	W 1-0	Glasgow	HC	Bloomer
25-02-1905	Ireland	D 1-1	Middlesbrough	HC	Bloomer
27-03	Wales	W 3-1	Liverpool	HC	Woodward 2, Harris
1-04	Scotland	W 1-0	London	HC	Bache
17-02-1906	Ireland	W 5-0	Belfast	HC	Bond 2, Day, Harris, Brown.A
19-03	Wales	W 1-0	Cardiff	HC	Day
7-04	Scotland	L 1-2	Glasgow	HC	Shepherd
1-11	France *	W 15-0	Paris	Fr	Harris 7, Woodward 4, Day 2, Farnfield, Raine
16-02-1907	Ireland	W 1-0	Liverpool	HC	Hardman
18-03	Wales	D 1-1	London	HC	Stewart
1-04	Holland *	W 8-1	The Hague	Fr	Mansfield 2, Bell.A, Woodward, Foster, Hardman 2, Hawkes
6-04	Scotland	D 1-1	Newcastle	HC	Bloomer
21-12	Holland *	W 12-2	Darlington	Fr	Woodward 3, Stapley 5, Bell.A 3, Raine
15-02-1908	Ireland	W 3-1	Belfast	HC	Woodward, Hilsdon 2
16-03	Wales	W 7-1	Wrexham	HC	Wedlock, Windridge, Hilsdon 2, Woodward 3
23-03	France *	W 12-0	Ipswich	Fr	Jordan 6, Woodward 3, Hawkes, Berry, Raine
4-04	Scotland	D 1-1	Glasgow	HC	Windridge
18-04	Belgium *	W 8-2	Brussels	Fr	Purnell 2, Woodward 2, Stapley 3, OG
20-04	Germany *	W 5-1	Berlin	Fr	Woodward 2, Stapley 2, Purnell
6-06	Austria	W 6-1	Vienna	Fr	Hilsdon 2, Windridge 2, Bridgett, Woodward
8-06	Austria	W 11-1	Vienna	Fr	Woodward 4, Bridgett, Bradshaw 3, Warren, Rutherford, Windridge
10-06	Hungary	W 7-0	Budapest	Fr	Hilsdon 4, Windridge, Woodward, Rutherford
13-06	Bohemia	W 4-0	Prague	Fr	Hilsdon 2, Windridge, Rutherford
8-09	Sweden *	W 6-1	Gothenburg	Fr	Purnell, Berry 4, Louch
20-10	Sweden *	W 12-1	London	OGr1	Stapley 2, Woodward 2, Berry, Chapman, Purnell 4, Hawkes 2
22-10	Holland *	W 4-0	London	OGsf	Purnel, Stapley 3
24-10	Denmark *	W 2-0	London	OGf	Chapman, Woodward
13-02-1909	Ireland	W 4-0	Bradford	HC	Hilsdon 2, Woodward 2
16-03	Germany *	W 9-0	Oxford	Fr	Dunning 3, Hoare 2, Porter 3, Chapman
15-03	Wales	W 2-0	Nottingham	HC	Holley, Freeman
3-04	Scotland	W 2-0	London	HC	Wall 2
12-04	Holland *	W 4-0	Amsterdam	Fr	Dunning 2, Porter, Stapley
17-04	Belgium *	W 11-2	London	Fr	Chapman, Woodward 2, Raine, Stapley 3, Dunning 4
20-05	Switzerland *	W 9-0	Basle	Fr	Raine 2, Woodward 4, Stapley, Dunning 2
22-05	France *	W 11-0	Paris	Fr	Fayers 2, Raine 2, Stapley 2, Porter 3, Wright.E, OG
29-05	Hungary	W 4-2	Budapest	Fr	Woodward 2, Fleming, Bridgett
31-05	Hungary	W 8-2	Budapest	Fr	Woodward 4, Fleming 2, Holley 2
1-06	Austria	W 8-1	Vienna	Fr	Woodward 3, Warren, Halse 2, Holley 2
6-11	Sweden *	W 7-0	Hull	Fr	Owen 3, Stapley 3, Woodward
11-12	Holland *	W 9-1	London	Fr	Stapley 2, Woodward 5, Owen, Williams
12-02-1910	Ireland	D 1-1	Belfast	HC	Fleming
14-03	Wales	W 1-0	Cardiff	HC	Ducat
26-03	Belgium *	D 2-2	Brussels	Fr	Owen, Porter
2-04	Scotland	L 0-2	Glasgow	HC	
9-04	Switzerland *	W 6-1	London	Fr	Steer 2, Webb.G 2, Fayers, Corbett
16-04	France *	W 10-1	Brighton	Fr	Steer 4, Wilson 4, Berry, Chapman
5-05	Denmark *	L 1-2	Copenhagen	Fr	Steer
11-02-1911	Ireland	W 2-1	Derby	HC	Shepherd, Evans
4-03	Belgium *	W 4-0	London	Fr	OG, Webb.G 2, Woodward
13-03	Wales	W 3-0	London	HC	Woodward 2, Webb.G
23-03	France *	W 3-0	Paris	Fr	Hoare 2, Healey
1-04	Scotland	D 1-1	Liverpool	HC	Stewart
14-04	Germany *	D 2-2	Berlin	Fr	Webb.G, Wright.E
17-04	Holland *	W 1-0	Amsterdam	Fr	Webb.G
25-05	Switzerland *	W 4-1	Berne	Fr	Hoare, Sharp.G, Woodward, Healey
21-10	Denmark *	W 3-0	London	Fr	Webb.G, Hoare, ?
10-02-1912	Ireland	W 6-1	Dublin	HC	Fleming 3, Freeman, Holley, Simpson
11-03	Wales	W 2-0	Wrexham	HC	Holley, Freeman

16-03	Holland *	W 4-0	Hull	Fr	Woodward 2, Bailey, Wright.E
23-03	Scotland	D 1-1	Glasgow	HC	Holley
8-04	Belgium *	W 2-1	Brussels	Fr	Bailey 2
30-06	Hungary *	W 7-0	Stockholm	OGqf	Walden 5, Woodward 2
2-07	Finland *	W 4-0	Stockholm	OGsf	Woodward, Walden 2, Sharpe.I
4-07	Denmark *	W 4-2	Stockholm	OGf	Berry, Walden, Hoare 2
9-11	Belgium *	W 4-0	Swindon	Fr	Woodward 2, Wright.E, Healey
15-02-1913	Ireland	L 1-2	Belfast	HC	Buchan
27-02	France *	W 4-1	Paris	Fr	Berry, Hoare 2, Sanders
21-03	Germany *	W 3-0	Berlin	Fr	Woodward, Douglas 2
17-03	Wales	W 4-3	Bristol	HC	Flemming, McCall, Latheron, Hampton
24-03	Holland *	L 1-2	The Hague	Fr	Woodward
5-04	Scotland	W 1-0	London	HC	Hampton
15-11	Holland *	W 2-1	Hull	Fr	Knight, Woodward
14-02-1914	Ireland	L 0-3	Middlesbrough	HC	
24-02	Belgium *	W 8-1	Brussels	Fr	Sharp.G 2, Louch 3, Moore2, Woodward
16-03	Wales	W 2-0	Cardiff	HC	Smith.J (I), Wedlock
4-04	Scotland	L 1-3	Glasgow	HC	Fleming
5-06	Denmark *	L 0-3	Copenhagen	Fr	
10-06	Sweden *	W 5-1	Stockholm	Fr	Moore 2, Woodward, Sharpe.I, Prince
12-06	Sweden **	W 5-0	Stockholm	Fr	Prince 2, Woodward 2, Moore
25-10-1919	Ireland	D 1-1	Belfast	HC	Cock
17-02-1920	Belgium *	L 1-3	Brussels	Fr	Gardner
15-03	Wales	L 1-2	London	HC	Buchan
10-04	Scotland	W 5-4	Sheffield	HC	Kelly 2, Cock, Morris.F, Quantrill
28-08	Norway *	L 1-3	Antwerp	OGr1	Nicholas
23-10	Ireland	W 2-0	Sunderland	HC	Kelly, Walker
14-03-1921	Wales	D 0-0	Cardiff	HC	
9-04	Scotland	L 0-3	Glasgow	HC	
21-05	Belgium	W 2-0	Brussels	Fr	Buchan, Chambers
22-10	Ireland	D 1-1	Belfast	HC	Kirton
13-03-1922	Wales	W 1-0	Liverpool	HC	Kelly
8-04	Scotland	L 0-1	Birmingham	HC	
21-10	Ireland	W 2-0	West Bromwich	HC	Chambers 2
5-03-1923	Wales	D 2-2	Cardiff	HC	Chambers, Watson.V
19-03	Belgium	W 6-1	London	Fr	Hegan 2, Chambers, Mercer, Seed, Bullock
14-04	Scotland	D 2-2	Glasgow	HC	Kelly, Watson.V
5-05	Belgium *	L 0-3	Brussels	Fr	
10-05	France	W 4-1	Paris	Fr	Hegan 2, Buchan, Creek
21-05	Sweden	W 4-2	Stockholm	Fr	Walker 2, Moore.J, Thornewell
20-10	Ireland	L 1-2	Belfast	HC	Bradford.J
1-11	Belgium	D 2-2	Antwerp	Fr	Brown.W, Roberts.W
3-03-1924	Wales	L 1-2	Blackburn	HC	Roberts.W
12-04	Scotland	D 1-1	London	HC	Walker
17-05	France	W 3-1	Paris	Fr	Gibbins 2, Storer
22-10	Nth. Ireland	W 3-1	Liverpool	HC	Kelly, Bedford, Walker
8-12	Belgium	W 4-0	West Bromwich	Fr	Bradford.J 2, Walker 2
28-02-1925	Wales	W 2-1	Swansea	HC	Roberts.F 2
4-04	Scotland	L 0-2	Glasgow	HC	
21-05	France	W 3-2	Paris	Fr	Gibbins, Dorrell, OG
24-10	Nth. Ireland	D 0-0	Belfast	HC	
1-03-1926	Wales	L 1-3	London	HC	Walker
17-04	Scotland	L 0-1	Manchester	HC	
24-05	Belgium	W 5-3	Antwerp	HC	Osborne 3, Carter.J, Johnson.T
20-10	Nth. Ireland	D 3-3	Liverpool	HC	Brown.G, Spence, Bullock
12-02-1927	Wales	D 3-3	Wrexham	HC	Dean 2, Walker
2-04	Scotland	W 2-1	Glasgow	HC	Dean 2
11-05	Belgium	W 9-1	Brussels	Fr	Dean 3, Brown.G 2, Rigby 2, Page, Hulme
21-05	Luxembourg	W 5-2	Luxembourg	Fr	Dean 3, Kelly, Bishop
26-05	France	W 6-0	Paris	Fr	Dean 2, Brown.G 2, Rigby, OG
22-10	Nth. Ireland	L 0-2	Belfast	HC	
28-11	Wales	L 1-2	Burnley	HC	OG
31-03-1928	Scotland	L 1-5	London	HC	Kelly
17-05	France	W 5-1	Paris	Fr	Stephenson 2, Dean 2, Jack
19-05	Belgium	W 3-1	Antwerp	Fr	Dean 2, Matthews.V
22-10	Nth. Ireland	W 2-1	Liverpool	HC	Hulme, Dean
17-11	Wales	W 3-2	Swansea	HC	Hulme 2, Hine
13-04-1929	Scotland	L 0-1	Glasgow	HC	
9-05	France	W 4-1	Paris	Fr	Kail 2, Camsell 2
11-05	Belgium	W 5-1	Brussels	Fr	Camsell 4, Carter.J
15-05	Spain	L 3-4	Madrid	Fr	Carter.J 2, Bradford.J

Date	Opponent	Result	Venue	Type	Scorers
19-10	Nth. Ireland	W 3-0	Belfast	HC	Camsell 2, Hine
20-11	Wales	W 6-0	London	HC	Adcock, Camsell 3, Johnson.T 2,
5-04-1930	Scotland	W 5-2	London	HC	Jack, Watson.V 2, Rimmer 2
10-05	Germany	D 3-3	Berlin	Fr	Bradford.J 2, Jack
14-05	Austria	D 0-0	Vienna	Fr	
20-10	Nth. Ireland	W 5-1	Sheffield	HC	Burgess 2, Crooks, Hampson, Houghton
22-11	Wales	W 4-0	Wrexham	HC	Hodgson, Bradford.J, Hampson 2
28-03-1931	Scotland	L 0-2	Glasgow	HC	
14-05	France	L 2-5	Paris	Fr	Crooks, Waring
16-05	Belgium	W 4-1	Brussels	Fr	Burgess 2, Houghton, Roberts.H
17-10	Nth. Ireland	W 6-2	Belfast	HC	Waring 2, Smith.J (II), Hine,Houghton 2
18-11	Wales	W 3-1	Liverpool	HC	Smith.J (II), Crooks, Hine
9-12	Spain	W 7-1	London	Fr	Smith.J (II) 2, Johnson.T 2, Crooks 2, Dean
9-04-1932	Scotland	W 3-0	London	HC	Waring, Crooks, Barclay
17-10	Nth. Ireland	W 1-0	Blackpool	HC	Barclay
16-11	Wales	D 0-0	Wrexham	HC	
7-12	Austria	W 4-3	London	Fr	Hampson 2, Houghton, Crooks
1-04-1933	Scotland	L 1-2	Glasgow	HC	Hunt.G
13-05	Italy	D 1-1	Rome	Fr	Bastin
20-05	Switzerland	W 4-0	Berne	Fr	Bastin 2, Richardson 2
14-10	Nth. Ireland	W 3-0	Belfast	HC	Brook, Grosvenor, Bowers
15-11	Wales	L 1-2	Newcastle	HC	Brook
6-12	France	W 4-1	London	Fr	Camsell 2, Brook, Grosvenor
14-04-1934	Scotland	W 3-0	London	HC	Brook, Bastin, Bowers
10-05	Hungary	L 1-2	Budapest	Fr	Tilson
16-05	Czechoslovakia	L 1-2	Prague	Fr	Tilson
29-09	Wales	W 4-0	Cardiff	HC	Tilson 2, Brook, Matthews.S
14-11	Italy	W 3-2	London	Fr	Brook 2, Drake
6-02-1935	Nth. Ireland	W 2-1	Liverpool	HC	Bastin 2
6-04	Scotland	L 0-2	Glasgow	HC	
18-05	Holland	W 1-0	Amsterdam	Fr	Worrall
19-10	Nth. Ireland	W 3-1	Belfast	HC	Tilson 2, Brook
4-12	Germany	W 3-0	London	Fr	Camsell 2, Bastin
5-02-1936	Wales	L 1-2	Wolverhampton	HC	Bowden
4-04	Scotland	D 1-1	London	HC	Camsell
6-05	Austria	L 1-2	Vienna	Fr	Camsell
9-05	Belgium	L 2-3	Brussels	Fr	Camsell, Hobbis
17-10	Wales	L 1-2	Cardiff	HC	Bastin
18-11	Nth. Ireland	W 3-1	Stoke	HC	Carter.H, Bastin, Worrall
2-12	Hungary	W 6-2	London	Fr	Drake 3, Brook, Britton, Carter.H
17-04-1937	Scotland	L 1-3	Glasgow	HC	Steele
14-05	Norway	W 6-0	Oslo	Fr	Steele 2, Kirchen, Galley, Goulden, OG
17-05	Sweden	W 4-0	Stockholm	Fr	Steele 3, Johnson.J
20-05	Finland	W 8-0	Helsinki	Fr	Payne 2, Steele 2, Kirchen, Willingham, Johnson.J, Robinson
23-10	Nth. Ireland	W 5-1	Belfast	HC	Mills 3, Hall, Brook
17-11	Wales	W 2-1	Middlesbrough	HC	Matthews.S, Hall
1-12	Czechoslovakia	W 5-4	London	Fr	Crayston, Morton, Matthews.S 3
9-04-1938	Scotland	L 0-1	London	HC	
14-05	Germany	W 6-3	Berlin	Fr	Robinson 2, Bastin, Broome, Matthews.S, Goulden
21-05	Switzerland	L 1-2	Zurich	Fr	Bastin
26-05	France	W 4-2	Paris	Fr	Drake 2, Broome, Bastin
22-10	Wales	L 2-4	Cardiff	HC	Lawton, Matthews.S
9-11	Norway	W 4-0	Newcastle	Fr	Smith.J (III) 2, Dix, Lawton
16-11	Nth. Ireland	W 7-0	Manchester	HC	Hall 5, Lawton, Matthews.S
15-04-1939	Scotland	W 2-1	Glasgow	HC	Beasley, Lawton
13-05	Italy	D 2-2	Milan	Fr	Lawton, Hall
18-05	Yugoslavia	L 1-2	Belgrade	Fr	Broome
24-05	Romania	W 2-0	Bucharest	Fr	Goulden, Welsh
19-01-1946	Belgium *	W 2-0	London	VI	Brown.R, Pye
11-05	Switzerland *	W 4-1	London	VI	Carter.H 2, Brown.G, Lawton
19-05	France *	L 1-2	Paris	VI	
28-09	Nth. Ireland	W 7-2	Belfast	HC	Carter.H, Mannion 3, Finney, Lawton, Langton
30-09	Rep. Ireland	W 1-0	Dublin	Fr	Finney
13-11	Wales	W 3-0	Manchester	HC	Mannion 2, Lawton
27-11	Holland	W 8-2	Huddersfield	Fr	Lawton 4, Carter.H 2, Mannion, Finney
12-04-1947	Scotland	D 1-1	London	HC	Carter.H
3-05	France	W 3-0	London	Fr	Finney, Mannion, Carter.H
18-05	Switzerland	L 0-1	Zurich	Fr	
25-05	Portugal	W 10-0	Lisbon	Fr	Lawton 4, Mortensen 4, Finney, Matthews.S
21-09	Belgium	W 5-2	Brussels	Fr	Lawton 2, Mortensen, Finney 2

Date	Opponent	Result	Venue	Comp	Scorers
18-10	Wales	W 3-0	Cardiff	HC	Finney, Mortensen, Lawton
5-11	Nth. Ireland	D 2-2	Liverpool	HC	Mannion, Lawton
19-11	Sweden	W 4-2	London	Fr	Mortensen 3, Lawton
10-04-1948	Scotland	W 2-0	Glasgow	HC	Finney, Mortensen
16-05	Italy	W 4-0	Turin	Fr	Mortensen, Lawton, Finney 2
26-09	Denmark	D 0-0	Copenhagen	Fr	
9-10	Nth. Ireland	W 6-2	Belfast	HC	Matthews.S, Mortensen 3, Milburn, Pearson.S
10-11	Wales	W 1-0	Birmingham	HC	Finney
2-12	Switzerland	W 6-0	London	Fr	Haines 2, Hancocks 2, Rowley, Milburn
9-04-1949	Scotland	L 1-3	London	HC	Milburn
13-05	Sweden	L 1-3	Stockholm	Fr	Finney
18-05	Norway	W 4-1	Oslo	Fr	Mullen, Finney, OG, Morris.J
22-05	France	W 3-1	Paris	Fr	Morris.J 2, Wright
21-09	Rep. Ireland	L 0-2	Liverpool	Fr	
15-10	Wales	W 4-1	Cardiff	HC/WCq	Mortensen, Milburn 3
16-11	Nth. Ireland	W 9-2	Manchester	HC/WCq	Rowley 4, Froggatt.J, Pearson.S 2, Mortensen 2
30-11	Italy	W 2-0	London	Fr	Rowley, Wright
15-04-1950	Scotland	W 1-0	Glasgow	HC/WCq	Bentley
14-05	Portugal	W 5-3	Lisbon	Fr	Finney 4, Mortensen
18-05	Belgium	W 4-1	Brussels	Fr	Mullen, Mortensen, Mannion, Bentley
25-06	Chile	W 2-0	Rio de Janeiro	WCr1	Mortensen, Mannion
29-06	United States	L 0-1	Belo Horizonte	WCr1	
2-07	Spain	L 0-1	Rio de Janeiro	WCr1	
7-10	Nth. Ireland	W 4-1	Belfast	HC	Baily 2, Lee.J, Wright
15-11	Wales	W 4-2	Sunderland	HC	Baily 2, Mannion, Milburn
22-11	Yugoslavia	D 2-2	London	Fr	Lofthouse.N 2
14-04-1951	Scotland	L 2-3	London	HC	Hassall, Finney
9-05	Argentina	W 2-1	London	Fr	Mortensen, Milburn
19-05	Portugal	W 5-2	Liverpool	Fr	Nicholson, Milburn 2, Finney, Hassall
3-10	France	D 2-2	London	Fr	OG, Medley
20-10	Wales	D 1-1	Cardiff	HC	Baily
14-11	Nth. Ireland	W 2-0	Birmingham	HC	Lofthouse.N 2
28-11	Austria	D 2-2	London	Fr	Ramsey, Lofthouse.N
5-04-1952	Scotland	W 2-1	Glasgow	HC	Pearson.S 2
18-05	Italy	D 1-1	Florence	Fr	Broadis
25-05	Austria	W 3-2	Vienna	Fr	Lofthouse.N 2, Sewell
28-05	Switzerland	W 3-0	Zurich	Fr	Sewell, Lofthouse.N 2
4-10	Nth. Ireland	D 2-2	Belfast	HC	Lofthouse.N, Elliott
12-11	Wales	W 5-2	London	HC	Finney, Lofthouse.N 2, Froggatt.J, Bentley
26-11	Belgium	W 5-0	London	Fr	Elliott 2, Lofthouse.N 2, Froggatt.R
18-04-1953	Scotland	D 2-2	London	HC	Broadis 2
14-05	Argentina *	L 1-3	Buenos Aires	Fr	Taylor.T
17-05	Argentina	D 0-0	Buenos Aires	Fr	Abandoned after 21 minutes
24-05	Chile	W 2-1	Santiago	Fr	Taylor.T, Lofthouse.N
31-05	Uruguay	L 1-2	Montevideo	Fr	Taylor.T
8-06	United States	W 6-3	New York	Fr	Broadis, Finney 2, Lofthouse.N 2, Froggatt.R
10-10	Wales	W 4-1	Cardiff	HC/WCq	Wilshaw 2, Lofthouse.N 2
11-11	Nth. Ireland	W 3-1	Liverpool	HC/WCq	Hassall 2, Lofthouse.N
25-11	Hungary	L 3-6	London	Fr	Sewell, Mortensen, Ramsey
3-04-1954	Scotland	W 4-2	Glasgow	HC/WCq	Broadis, Nicholls, Allen.R, Mullen
16-05	Yugoslavia	L 0-1	Belgrade	Fr	
23-05	Hungary	L 1-7	Budapest	Fr	Broadis
20-06	Belgium	D 4-4	Basle	WCr1	Broadis 2, Lofthouse.N 2
26-06	Switzerland	W 2-0	Berne	WCr1	Wilshaw, Mullen
2-07	Uruguay	L 2-4	Basle	WCqf	Lofthouse.N, Finney
2-10	Nth. Ireland	W 2-0	Belfast	HC	Haynes, Revie
10-11	Wales	W 3-2	London	HC	Bentley 3
1-12	West Germany	W 3-1	London	Fr	Bentley, Allen.R, Shackleton
2-04-1955	Scotland	W 7-2	London	HC	Wilshaw 4, Lofthouse.N 2, Revie
15-05	France	L 0-1	Paris	Fr	
18-05	Spain	D 1-1	Madrid	Fr	Bentley
22-05	Portugal	L 1-3	Oporto	Fr	Bentley
2-10	Denmark	W 5-1	Copenhagen	Fr	Revie 2, Lofthouse.N 2, Bradford.G
22-10	Wales	L 1-2	Cardiff	HC	OG
2-11	Nth. Ireland	W 3-0	London	HC	Wilshaw 2, Finney
30-11	Spain	W 4-1	London	Fr	Atyeo, W.Perry 2, Finney
14-04-1956	Scotland	D 1-1	Glasgow	HC	Haynes
9-05	Brazil	W 4-2	London	Fr	Taylor.T 2, Grainger 2
16-05	Sweden	D 0-0	Stockholm	Fr	
20-05	Finland	W 5-1	Helsinki	Fr	Wilshaw, Haynes, Astall, Lofthouse.N 2
25-05	West Germany	W 3-1	Berlin	Fr	Edwards, Grainger, Haynes

6-10	Nth. Ireland	D 1-1	Belfast	HC	Matthews.S
14-11	Wales	W 3-1	London	HC	Haynes, Brooks, Finney
28-11	Yugoslavia	W 3-0	London	Fr	Brooks, Taylor.T 2
5-12	Denmark	W 5-2	Wolverhampton	WCq	Taylor.T 3, Edwards 2
6-04-1957	Scotland	W 2-1	London	HC	Kevan, Edwards
8-05	Rep. Ireland	W 5-1	London	WCq	Taylor.T 3, Atyeo 2
15-05	Denmark	W 4-1	Copenhagen	WCq	Haynes, Taylor.T 2, Atyeo
19-05	Rep. Ireland	D 1-1	Dublin	WCq	Atyeo
19-10	Wales	W 4-0	Cardiff	HC	OG, Haynes 2, Finney
6-11	Nth. Ireland	L 2-3	London	HC	A'Court, Edwards
27-11	France	W 4-0	London	Fr	Taylor.T 2, Robson.R
19-04-1958	Scotland	W 4-0	Glasgow	HC	Douglas, Kevan 2, Charlton.R
7-05	Portugal	W 2-1	London	Fr	Charlton.R 2
11-05	Yugoslavia	L 0-5	Belgrade	Fr	
18-05	Soviet Union	D 1-1	Moscow	Fr	Kevan
8-06	Soviet Union	D 2-2	Gothenburg	WCr1	Kevan, Finney
11-06	Brazil	D 0-0	Gothenburg	WCr1	
15-06	Austria	D 2-2	Boras	WCr1	Haynes, Kevan
17-06	Soviet Union	L 0-1	Gothenburg	WCr1	
4-10	Nth. Ireland	D 3-3	Belfast	HC	Charlton.R 2, Finney
22-10	Soviet Union	W 5-0	London	Fr	Haynes 3, Charlton.R, Lofthouse.N
26-11	Wales	D 2-2	Birmingham	HC	Broadbent 2
11-04-1959	Scotland	W 1-0	London	HC	Charlton.R
6-05	Italy	D 2-2	London	Fr	Charlton.R, Bradley
13-05	Brazil	L 0-2	Rio de Janeiro	Fr	
17-05	Peru	L 1-4	Lima	Fr	Greaves
24-05	Mexico	L 1-2	Mexico City	Fr	Kevan
28-05	United States	W 8-1	Los Angeles	Fr	Charlton.R 3, Flowers 2, Bradley, Kevan, Haynes
17-10	Wales	D 1-1	Cardiff	HC	Greaves
28-10	Sweden	L 2-3	London	Fr	Connelly, Charlton.R
18-11	Nth. Ireland	W 2-1	London	HC	Baker, Parry.R
9-04-1960	Scotland	D 1-1	Glasgow	HC	Charlton.R
11-05	Yugoslavia	D 3-3	London	Fr	Douglas, Greaves, Baker
15-05	Spain	L 0-3	Madrid	Fr	
22-05	Hungary	L 0-2	Budapest	Fr	
8-10	Nth. Ireland	W 5-2	Belfast	HC	Smith.R, Greaves 2, Charlton.R, Douglas
19-10	Luxembourg	W 9-0	Luxembourg	WCq	Greaves 3, Charlton.R 3, Smith.R 2, Haynes
26-10	Spain	W 4-2	London	Fr	Greaves, Douglas, Smith.R 2
23-11	Wales	W 5-1	London	HC	Greaves 2, Charlton.R, Smith.R, Haynes
15-04-1961	Scotland	W 9-3	London	HC	Robson.R, Greaves 3, Douglas, Smith.R 2, Haynes 2
10-05	Mexico	W 8-0	London	Fr	Hitchens, Charlton.R 3, Robson.R, Douglas 2, Flowers
21-05	Portugal	D 1-1	Lisbon	WCq	Flowers
24-05	Italy	W 3-2	Rome	Fr	Hitchens 2, Greaves
27-05	Austria	L 1-3	Vienna	Fr	Greaves
28-09	Luxembourg	W 4-1	London	WCq	Pointer, Viollet, Charlton.R 2
14-10	Wales	D 1-1	Cardiff	HC	Douglas
25-10	Portugal	W 2-0	London	WCq	Connelly, Pointer
22-11	Nth. Ireland	D 1-1	London	HC	Charlton.R
4-04-1962	Austria	W 3-1	London	Fr	Crawford, Flowers, Hunt.R
14-04	Scotland	L 0-2	Glasgow	HC	
9-05	Switzerland	W 3-1	London	Fr	Flowers, Hitchens, Connelly
20-05	Peru	W 4-0	Lima	Fr	Flowers, Greaves 3
31-05	Hungary	L 1-2	Rancagua	WCr1	Flowers
2-06	Argentina	W 3-1	Rancagua	WCr1	Flowers, Charlton.R, Greaves
7-06	Bulgaria	D 0-0	Rancagua	WCr1	
10-06	Brazil	L 1-3	Viña del Mar	WCqf	Hitchens
3-10	France	D 1-1	Sheffield	ECr1	Flowers
20-10	Nth. Ireland	W 3-1	Belfast	HC	Greaves, O'Grady 2
21-11	Wales	W 4-0	London	HC	Connelly, Peacock 2, Greaves
27-02-1963	France	L 2-5	Paris	ECr1	Smith.R, Tambling
6-04	Scotland	L 1-2	London	HC	Douglas
8-05	Brazil	D 1-1	London	Fr	Douglas
29-05	Czechoslovakia	W 4-2	Bratislava	Fr	Greaves 2, Smith.R, Charlton.R
2-06	East Germany	W 2-1	Leipzig	Fr	Hunt.R, Charlton.R
5-06	Switzerland	W 8-1	Basle	Fr	Charlton.R 3, Byrne 2, Douglas, Kay, Melia
12-10	Wales	W 4-0	Cardiff	HC	Smith.R 2, Greaves, Charlton.R
20-11	Nth. Ireland	W 8-3	London	HC	Greaves 4, Paine 3, Smith.R
11-04-1964	Scotland	L 0-1	Glasgow	HC	
6-05	Uruguay	W 2-1	London	Fr	Byrne 2
17-05	Portugal	W 4-3	Lisbon	Fr	Byrne 3, Charlton.R
24-05	Rep. Ireland	W 3-1	Dublin	Fr	Eastham, Byrne, Greaves

27-05	United States	W 10-0	New York	Fr	Hunt.R 4, Pickering 3, Paine 2, Charlton.R
30-05	Brazil	L 1-5	Rio de Janeiro	CN	Greaves
4-06	Portugal	D 1-1	Sao Paulo	CN	Hunt.R
6-06	Argentina	L 0-1	Rio de Janeiro	CN	
3-10	Nth. Ireland	W 4-3	Belfast	HC	Pickering, Greaves 3
21-10	Belgium	D 2-2	London	Fr	Pickering, Hinton
18-11	Wales	W 2-1	London	HC	Wignall 2
9-12	Holland	D 1-1	Amsterdam	Fr	Greaves
10-04-1965	Scotland	D 2-2	London	HC	Charlton.R, Greaves
5-05	Hungary	W 1-0	London	Fr	Greaves
9-05	Yugoslavia	D 1-1	Belgrade	Fr	Bridges
12-05	West Germany	W 1-0	Nuremberg	Fr	Paine
16-05	Sweden	W 2-1	Gothenburg	Fr	Ball, Connolly
2-10	Wales	D 0-0	Cardiff	HC	
20-10	Austria	L 2-3	London	Fr	Charlton.R, Connolly
10-11	Nth. Ireland	W 2-1	London	HC	Baker, Peacock
8-12	Spain	W 2-0	Madrid	Fr	Baker, Hunt.R
5-01-1966	Poland	D 1-1	Liverpool	Fr	Moore.R
23-02	West Germany	W 1-0	London	Fr	Stiles
2-04	Scotland	W 4-3	Glasgow	HC	Hurst, Hunt.R 2, Charlton.R
4-05	Yugoslavia	W 2-0	London	Fr	Greaves, Charlton.R
26-06	Finland	W 3-0	Helsinki	Fr	Peters, Hunt.R, Charlton.J
29-06	Norway	W 6-1	Oslo	Fr	Greaves 4, Connolly, Moore.R
3-07	Denmark	W 2-0	Copenhagen	Fr	Charlton.J, Eastham
5-07	Poland	W 1-0	Chorzow	Fr	Hunt.R
11-07	Uruguay	D 0-0	London	WCr1	
16-07	Mexico	W 2-0	London	WCr1	Charlton.R, Hunt.R
20-07	France	W 2-0	London	WCr1	Hunt.R 2
23-07	Argentina	W 1-0	London	WCqf	Hurst
26-07	Portugal	W 2-1	London	WCsf	Charlton.R 2
30-07	West Germany	W 4-2	London	WCf	Hurst 3, Peters
22-10	Nth. Ireland	W 2-0	Belfast	HC/ECq	Hunt.R, Peters
2-11	Czechoslovakia	D 0-0	London	Fr	
16-11	Wales	W 5-1	London	HC/ECq	Hurst 2, Charlton.R, Charlton.J, OG
15-04-1967	Scotland	L 2-3	London	HC/ECq	Charlton.J, Hurst
24-05	Spain	W 2-0	London	Fr	Greaves, Hunt.R
27-05	Austria	W 1-0	Vienna	Fr	Ball
21-10	Wales	W 3-0	Cardiff	HC/ECq	Peters, Charlton.R, Ball
22-11	Nth. Ireland	W 2-0	London	HC/ECq	Hurst, Charlton.R
6-12	Soviet Union	D 2-2	London	Fr	Ball, Peters
24-02-1968	Scotland	D 1-1	Glasgow	HC/ECq	Peters
3-04	Spain	W 1-0	London	ECqf	Charlton.R
8-05	Spain	W 2-1	Madrid	ECqf	Peters, Hunter
22-05	Sweden	W 3-1	London	Fr	Peters, Charlton.R, Hunt.R
1-06	West Germany	L 0-1	Hanover	Fr	
5-06	Yugoslavia	L 0-1	Florence	ECsf	
8-06	Soviet Union	W 2-0	Rome	EC3p	Charlton.R, Hurst
6-11	Romania	D 0-0	Bucharest	Fr	
11-12	Bulgaria	D 1-1	London	Fr	Hurst
15-01-1969	Romania	D 1-1	London	Fr	Charlton.J
12-03	France	W 5-0	London	Fr	Hurst 3, O'Grady, Lee.F
3-05	Nth. Ireland	W 3-1	Belfast	HC	Peters, Lee.F, Hurst
7-05	Wales	W 2-1	London	HC	Charlton.R, Lee.F
10-05	Scotland	W 4-1	London	HC	Peters 2, Hurst 2
1-06	Mexico	D 0-0	Mexico City	Fr	
8-06	Uruguay	W 2-1	Montevideo	Fr	Lee.F, Hurst
12-06	Brazil	L 1-2	Rio de Janeiro	Fr	Bell
5-11	Holland	W 1-0	Amsterdam	Fr	Bell
10-12	Portugal	W 1-0	London	Fr	Charlton.J
14-01-1970	Holland	D 0-0	London	Fr	
25-02	Belgium	W 3-1	Brussels	Fr	Ball, Hurst
18-04	Wales	D 1-1	Cardiff	HC	Lee.F
21-04	Nth. Ireland	W 3-1	London	HC	Peters, Hurst, Charlton.R
25-04	Scotland	D 0-0	Glasgow	HC	
20-05	Colombia	W 4-0	Bogota	Fr	Peters 2, Charlton.R, Ball
24-05	Ecuador	W 2-0	Quito	Fr	Lee.F, Kidd
2-06	Romania	W 1-0	Guadalajara	WCr1	Hurst
7-06	Brazil	L 0-1	Guadalajara	WCr1	
11-06	Czechoslovakia	W 1-0	Guadalajara	WCr1	Clarke
14-06	West Germany	L 2-3	Leon	WCqf	Mullery, Peters
25-11	East Germany	W 3-1	London	Fr	Lee.F, Peters, Clarke

Date	Opponent	Result	Venue	Comp	Scorers
3-02-1971	Malta	W 1-0	Gzira	ECq	Peters
21-04	Greece	W 3-0	London	ECq	Chivers, Hurst, Lee.F
12-05	Malta	W 5-0	London	ECq	Chivers 2, Lee.F, Clarke, Lawler
15-05	Nth. Ireland	W 1-0	Belfast	HC	Clarke
19-05	Wales	D 0-0	London	HC	
22-05	Scotland	W 3-1	London	HC	Peters, Chivers 2
13-10	Switzerland	W 3-2	Basle	ECq	Hurst, Chivers, OG
10-11	Switzerland	D 1-1	London	ECq	Summerbee
1-12	Greece	W 2-0	Athens	ECq	Hurst, Chivers
29-04-1972	West Germany	L 1-3	London	ECqf	Lee.F
13-05	West Germany	D 0-0	Berlin	ECqf	
20-05	Wales	W 3-0	Cardiff	HC	Hughes, Bell, Marsh
23-05	Nth. Ireland	L 0-1	London	HC	
27-05	Scotland	W 1-0	Glasgow	HC	Ball
11-10	Yugoslavia	D 1-1	London	Fr	Royle
15-11	Wales	W 1-0	Cardiff	WCq	Bell
24-01-1973	Wales	D 1-1	London	WCq	Hunter
14-02	Scotland	W 5-0	Glasgow	Fr	OG, Clarke 2, Channon, Chivers
12-05	Nth. Ireland	W 2-1	Liverpool	HC	Chivers 2
15-05	Wales	W 3-0	London	HC	Chivers, Channon, Peters
19-05	Scotland	W 1-0	London	HC	Peters
27-05	Czechoslovakia	D 1-1	Prague	Fr	Clarke
6-06	Poland	L 0-2	Chorzow	WCq	
10-06	Soviet Union	W 2-1	Moscow	Fr	OG, Chivers
14-06	Italy	L 0-2	Turin	Fr	
26-09	Austria	W 7-0	London	Fr	Channon 2, Clarke 2, Chivers, Currie, Bell
17-10	Poland	D 1-1	London	WCq	Clarke
14-11	Italy	L 0-1	London	Fr	
3-04-1974	Portugal	D 0-0	Lisbon	Fr	
11-05	Wales	W 2-0	Cardiff	HC	Bowles, Keegan
15-05	Nth. Ireland	W 1-0	London	HC	Weller
18-05	Scotland	L 0-2	Glasgow	HC	
22-05	Argentina	D 2-2	London	Fr	Channon, Worthington
29-05	East Germany	D 1-1	Leipzig	Fr	Channon
1-06	Bulgaria	W 1-0	Sofia	Fr	Worthington
5-06	Yugoslavia	D 2-2	Belgrade	Fr	Channon, Keegan
30-10	Czechoslovakia	W 3-0	London	ECq	Channon, Bell 2
20-11	Portugal	D 0-0	London	ECq	
12-03-1975	West Germany	W 2-0	London	Fr	Bell, Macdonald
16-04	Cyprus	W 5-0	London	ECq	Macdonald 5
11-05	Cyprus	W 1-0	Limassol	ECq	Keegan
17-05	Nth. Ireland	D 0-0	Belfast	HC	
21-05	Wales	D 2-2	London	HC	Johnson.D 2
24-05	Scotland	W 5-1	London	HC	Francis.G 2, Beattie, Bell, Johnson.D
3-09	Switzerland	W 2-1	Basle	Fr	Keegan, Channon
30-10	Czechoslovakia	L 1-2	Bratislava	ECq	Channon
19-11	Portugal	D 1-1	Lisbon	ECq	Channon
24-03-1976	Wales	W 2-1	Wrexham	Fr	Kennedy, Taylor.P
8-05	Wales	W 1-0	Cardiff	HC	Taylor.P
11-05	Nth. Ireland	W 4-0	London	HC	Francis.G, Channon 2, Pearson.J
15-05	Scotland	L 1-2	Glasgow	HC	Channon
23-05	Brazil	L 0-1	Los Angeles	Fr	
28-05	Italy	W 3-2	New York	Fr	Channon 2, Thompson
13-06	Finland	W 4-1	Helsinki	WCq	Keegan 2, Channon, Pearson.J
8-09	Rep. Ireland	D 1-1	London	Fr	Pearson.J
13-10	Finland	W 2-1	London	WCq	Tueart, Royle
17-11	Italy	L 0-2	Rome	WCq	
9-02-1977	Holland	L 0-2	London	Fr	
30-03	Luxembourg	W 5-0	London	WCq	Keegan, Francis.T, Kennedy,Channon 2
28-05	Nth. Ireland	W 2-1	Belfast	HC	Channon, Tueart
31-05	Wales	L 0-1	London	HC	
4-06	Scotland	L 1-2	London	HC	Channon
8-06	Brazil	D 0-0	Rio de Janeiro	Fr	
12-06	Argentina	D 1-1	Buenos Aires	Fr	Pearson.J
15-06	Uruguay	D 0-0	Montevideo	Fr	
7-09	Switzerland	D 0-0	London	Fr	
12-10	Luxembourg	W 2-0	Luxembourg	WCq	Kennedy, Mariner
16-11	Italy	W 2-0	London	WCq	Keegan, Brooking
22-02-1978	West Germany	L 1-2	Munich	Fr	Pearson.J
19-04	Brazil	D 1-1	London	Fr	Keegan
13-05	Wales	W 3-1	Cardiff	HC	Latchford, Currie, Barnes.P

Date	Opponent	Result	Venue	Comp	Scorers
16-05	Nth. Ireland	W 1-0	London	HC	Neal
20-05	Scotland	W 1-0	Glasgow	HC	Coppell
24-05	Hungary	W 4-1	London	Fr	Barnes.P, Neal, Francis.T, Currie
20-09	Denmark	W 4-3	Copenhagen	ECq	Keegan 2, Latchford, Neal
25-10	Rep. Ireland	D 1-1	Dublin	ECq	Latchford
29-11	Czechoslovakia	W 1-0	London	Fr	Coppell
7-02-1979	Nth. Ireland	W 4-0	London	ECq	Keegan, Latchford 2, Watson.D
19-05	Nth. Ireland	W 2-0	Belfast	HC	Watson.D, Coppell
23-05	Wales	D 0-0	London	HC	
26-05	Scotland	W 3-1	London	HC	Barnes.P, Coppell, Keegan,
6-06	Bulgaria	W 3-0	Sofia	ECq	Keegan, Watson.D, Barnes.P
10-06	Sweden	D 0-0	Stockholm	Fr	
13-06	Austria	L 3-4	Vienna	Fr	Keegan, Coppell, Wilkins
12-09	Denmark	W 1-0	London	ECq	Keegan
17-10	Nth. Ireland	W 5-1	Belfast	ECq	Francis.T 2, Woodcock 2, OG
22-11	Bulgaria	W 2-0	London	ECq	Watson.D, Hoddle
6-02-1980	Rep. Ireland	W 2-0	London	ECq	Keegan 2
26-03	Spain	W 2-0	Barcelona	Fr	Woodcock, Francis.T
13-05	Argentina	W 3-1	London	Fr	Johnson.D 2, Keegan
17-05	Wales	L 1-4	Wrexham	HC	Mariner
20-05	Nth. Ireland	D 1-1	London	HC	OG
24-05	Scotland	W 2-0	Glasgow	HC	Brooking, Coppell
31-05	Australia	W 2-1	Sydney	Fr	Hoddle, Mariner
12-06	Belgium	D 1-1	Turin	ECr1	Wilkins
15-06	Italy	L 0-1	Turin	ECr1	
18-06	Spain	W 2-1	Naples	ECr1	Brooking, Woodcock
10-09	Norway	W 4-0	London	WCq	McDermott 2, Woodcock, Mariner
15-10	Romania	L 1-2	Bucharest	WCq	Woodcock
19-11	Switzerland	W 2-1	London	WCq	OG, Mariner
25-03-1981	Spain	L 1-2	London	Fr	Hoddle
29-04	Romania	D 0-0	London	WCq	
12-05	Brazil	L 0-1	London	Fr	
20-05	Wales	D 0-0	London	HC	
23-05	Scotland	L 0-1	London	HC	
30-05	Switzerland	L 1-2	Basle	WCq	McDermott
6-06	Hungary	W 3-1	Budapest	WCq	Brooking 2, Keegan
9-09	Norway	L 1-2	Oslo	WCq	Robson.B
18-11	Hungary	W 1-0	London	WCq	Mariner
23-02-1982	Nth. Ireland	W 4-0	London	HC	Robson.B, Keegan, Wilkins, Hoddle
27-04	Wales	W 1-0	Cardiff	HC	Francis.T
25-05	Holland	W 2-0	London	Fr	Woodcock, Mariner
29-05	Scotland	W 1-0	Glasgow	HC	Mariner
2-06	Iceland	D 1-1	Reykjavik	Fr	Goddard
3-06	Finland	W 4-1	Helsinki	Fr	Mariner 2, Robson.B 2
16-06	France	W 3-1	Bilbao	WCr1	Robson.B 2, Mariner
20-06	Czechoslovakia	W 2-0	Bilbao	WCr1	Francis.T, Mariner
25-06	Kuwait	W 1-0	Bilbao	WCr1	Francis.T
29-06	West Germany	D 0-0	Madrid	WCr2	
5-07	Spain	D 0-0	Madrid	WCr2	
22-09	Denmark	D 2-2	Copenhagen	ECq	Francis.T 2
13-10	West Germany	L 1-2	London	Fr	Woodcock
17-11	Greece	W 3-0	Salonika	ECq	Woodcock 2, Lee.S
15-12	Luxembourg	W 9-0	London	ECq	OG, Coppell, Woodcock, Blissett 3, Chamberlain, Hoddle, Neal
23-02-1983	Wales	W 2-1	London	HC	Butcher, Neal
30-03	Greece	D 0-0	London	ECq	
27-04	Hungary	W 2-0	London	ECq	Francis.T, Withe
28-05	Nth. Ireland	D 0-0	Belfast	HC	
1-06	Scotland	W 2-0	London	HC	Robson.B, Cowans
12-06	Australia	D 0-0	Sydney	Fr	
15-06	Australia	W 1-0	Brisbane	Fr	Walsh
19-06	Australia	D 1-1	Melbourne	Fr	Francis.T
21-09	Denmark	L 0-1	London	ECq	
12-10	Hungary	W 3-0	Budapest	ECq	Hoddle, Lee.S, Mariner
16-11	Luxembourg	W 4-0	Luxembourg	ECq	Robson.B 2, Mariner, Butcher
29-02-1984	France	L 0-2	Paris	Fr	
4-04	Nth. Ireland	W 1-0	London	HC	Woodcock
2-05	Wales	L 0-1	Wrexham	HC	
26-05	Scotland	D 1-1	Glasgow	HC	Woodcock
2-06	Soviet Union	L 0-2	London	Fr	
10-06	Brazil	W 2-0	Rio de Janeiro	Fr	Barnes.J, Hateley

Date	Opponent	Result	Venue	Type	Scorers
13-06	Uruguay	L 0-2	Montevideo	Fr	
17-06	Chile	D 0-0	Santiago	Fr	
12-09	East Germany	W 1-0	London	Fr	Robson.B
17-10	Finland	W 5-0	London	WCq	Sansom, Robson.B, Hateley 2, Woodcock
14-11	Turkey	W 8-0	Istanbul	WCq	Anderson, Robson.B 3, Woodcock 2, Barnes.J 2
27-02-1985	Nth. Ireland	W 1-0	Belfast	WCq	Hateley
26-03	Rep. Ireland	W 2-1	London	Fr	Lineker, Steven
1-05	Romania	D 0-0	Bucharest	WCq	
22-05	Finland	D 1-1	Helsinki	WCq	Hateley
25-05	Scotland	L 0-1	Glasgow	Fr	
6-06	Italy	L 1-2	Mexico City	Fr	Hateley
9-06	Mexico	L 0-1	Mexico City	Fr	
12-06	West Germany	W 3-0	Mexico City	Fr	Robson.B, Dixon.K 2
16-06	United States	W 5-0	Los Angeles	Fr	Lineker 2, Dixon.K 2, Steven
11-09	Romania	D 1-1	London	WCq	Hoddle
16-10	Turkey	W 5-0	London	WCq	Waddle, Lineker 3, Robson.B
13-11	Nth. Ireland	D 0-0	London	WCq	
29-01-1986	Egypt	W 4-0	Cairo	Fr	Steven, OG, Wallace, Cowans
26-02	Israel	W 2-1	Tel Aviv	Fr	Robson.B 2
26-03	Soviet Union	W 1-0	Tbilisi	Fr	Waddle
23-04	Scotland	W 2-1	London	Fr	Butcher, Hoddle
17-05	Mexico	W 3-0	Los Angeles	Fr	Hateley 2, Beardsley
24-05	Canada	W 1-0	Burnaby	Fr	Hateley
3-06	Portugal	L 0-1	Monterrey	WCr1	
8-06	Morocco	D 0-0	Monterrey	WCr1	
11-06	Poland	W 3-0	Monterrey	WCr1	Lineker 3
18-06	Paraguay	W 3-0	Mexico City	WCr2	Lineker 2, Beardsley
22-06	Argentina	L 1-2	Mexico City	WCqf	Lineker
10-09	Sweden	L 0-1	Stockholm	Fr	
15-10	Nth. Ireland	W 3-0	London	ECq	Lineker 2, Waddle
12-11	Yugoslavia	W 2-0	London	ECq	Mabbutt, Anderson
18-02-1987	Spain	W 4-2	Madrid	Fr	Lineker 4
1-04	Nth. Ireland	W 2-0	Belfast	ECq	Robson.B, Waddle
29-04	Turkey	D 0-0	Izmir	ECq	
19-05	Brazil	D 1-1	London	Fr	Lineker
23-05	Scotland	D 0-0	Glasgow	Fr	
9-09	West Germany	L 1-3	Dusseldorf	Fr	Lineker
14-10	Turkey	W 8-0	London	ECq	Barnes.J 2, Lineker 3, Robson.B, Beardsley, Webb
11-11	Yugoslavia	W 4-1	Belgrade	ECq	Beardsley, Barnes.J, Robson.B, Adams
17-02-1988	Israel	D 0-0	Tel Aviv	Fr	
23-03	Holland	D 2-2	London	Fr	Lineker, Adams
27-04	Hungary	D 0-0	Budapest	Fr	
21-05	Scotland	W 1-0	London	Fr	Beardsley
24-05	Colombia	D 1-1	London	Fr	Lineker
28-05	Switzerland	W 1-0	Lausanne	Fr	Lineker
12-06	Rep. Ireland	L 0-1	Stuttgart	ECr1	
15-06	Holland	L 1-3	Dusseldorf	ECr1	Robson.B
18-06	Soviet Union	L 1-3	Frankfurt	ECr1	Adams
14-09	Denmark	W 1-0	London	Fr	Webb.N
19-10	Sweden	D 0-0	London	WCq	
16-11	Saudi Arabia	D 1-1	Riyadh	Fr	Adams
8-02-1989	Greece	W 2-1	Athens	Fr	Barnes.J, Robson.B
8-03	Albania	W 2-0	Tirana	WCq	Barnes.J, Robson.B
26-04	Albania	W 5-0	London	WCq	Lineker, Beardsley 2, Waddle, Gascoigne
23-05	Chile	D 0-0	London	Fr	
27-05	Scotland	W 2-0	Glasgow	Fr	Waddle, Bull
3-06	Poland	W 3-0	London	WCq	Lineker, Barnes.J, Webb.N
7-06	Denmark	D 1-1	Copenhagen	Fr	Lineker
6-09	Sweden	D 0-0	Stockholm	WCq	
11-10	Poland	D 0-0	Chorzow	WCq	
15-11	Italy	D 0-0	London	Fr	
13-12	Yugoslavia	W 2-1	London	Fr	Robson.B 2
28-03-1990	Brazil	W 1-0	London	Fr	Lineker
25-04	Czechoslovakia	W 4-2	London	Fr	Bull 2, Pearce, Gascoigne
15-05	Denmark	W 1-0	London	Fr	Lineker
22-05	Uruguay	L 1-2	London	Fr	Barnes.J
2-06	Tunisia	D 1-1	Tunis	Fr	Bull
11-06	Rep. Ireland	D 1-1	Cagliari	WCr1	Lineker
16-06	Holland	D 0-0	Cagliari	WCr1	
21-06	Egypt	W 1-0	Cagliari	WCr1	Wright.M
26-06	Belgium	W 1-0	Bologna	WCr2	Platt

1-07	Cameroon	W 3-2	Naples	WCqf	Lineker 2, Platt
4-07	West Germany	D 1-1	Milan	WCsf	Lineker. Lost 3-4 pens
7-07	Italy	L 1-2	Bari	WC3p	Platt
12-09	Hungary	W 1-0	London	Fr	Lineker
17-10	Poland	W 2-0	London	ECq	Lineker, Beardsley
14-11	Rep. Ireland	D 1-1	Dublin	ECq	Platt
6-02-1991	Cameroon	W 2-0	London	Fr	Lineker 2
27-03	Rep. Ireland	D 1-1	London	ECq	OG
1-05	Turkey	W 1-0	Izmir	ECq	Wise
21-05	Soviet Union	W 3-1	London	Fr	Smith.A, Platt 2
25-05	Argentina	D 2-2	London	Fr	Lineker, Platt
1-06	Australia	W 1-0	Sydney	Fr	OG
3-06	New Zealand	W 1-0	Auckland	Fr	Lineker
8-06	New Zealand	W 2-0	Wellington	Fr	Pearce, Hirst
12-06	Malaysia	W 4-2	Kuala Lumpur	Fr	Lineker 4
11-09	Germany	L 0-1	London	Fr	
16-10	Turkey	W 1-0	London	ECq	Smith.A
13-11	Poland	D 1-1	Poznan	ECq	Lineker
19-02-1992	France	W 2-0	London	Fr	Shearer, Lineker
25-03	Czechoslovakia	D 2-2	Prague	Fr	Merson, Keown
29-04	Commonw. IS	D 2-2	Moscow	Fr	Lineker, Steven
12-05	Hungary	W 1-0	Budapest	Fr	OG
17-05	Brazil	D 1-1	London	Fr	Platt
3-06	Finland	W 2-1	Helsinki	Fr	Platt 2
11-06	Denmark	D 0-0	Malmo	ECr1	
14-06	France	D 0-0	Malmo	ECr1	
17-06	Sweden	L 1-2	Stockholm	ECr1	Platt
9-09	Spain	L 0-1	Santander	Fr	
14-10	Norway	D 1-1	London	WCq	Platt
18-11	Turkey	W 4-0	London	WCq	Gascoigne 2, Shearer, Pearce
17-02-1993	San Marino	W 6-0	London	WCq	Platt 4, Palmer, Ferdinand
31-03	Turkey	W 2-0	Izmir	WCq	Platt, Gascoigne
28-04	Holland	D 2-2	London	WCq	Barnes, Platt
29-05	Poland	D 1-1	Chorzow	WCq	Wright.I
2-06	Norway	L 0-2	Oslo	WCq	
9-06	USA	L 0-2	Boston	Fr	
13-06	Brazil	D 1-1	Washington	Fr	Platt
19-06	Germany	L 1-2	Detroit	Fr	Platt
8-09	Poland	W 3-0	London	WCq	Ferdinand, Gascoigne, Pearce
13-10	Holland	L 0-2	Rotterdam	WCq	
17-11	San Marino	W 7-1	Bologna	WCq	Ince 2, Wright.I 4, Ferdinand
9-03-1994	Denmark	W 1-0	London	Fr	Platt
17-05	Greece	W 5-0	London	Fr	Anderton, Beardsley, Platt 2, Shearer
22-05	Norway	D 0-0	London	Fr	
7-09	USA	W 2-0	London	Fr	Shearer 2
12-10	Romania	D 1-1	London	Fr	Lee.R
16-11	Nigeria	W 1-0	London	Fr	Platt
15-02-1995	Rep. Ireland	L 0-1	Dublin	Fr	Match abandoned after 27 mins
29-03	Uruguay	D 0-0	London	Fr	
3-06	Japan	W 2-1	London	Fr	Anderton, Platt
8-06	Sweden	D 3-3	Leeds	Fr	Sheringham, Platt, Anderton
11-06	Brazil	L 1-3	London	Fr	Le Saux

ESTONIA

Estonia, along with their Baltic neighbours Lithuania and Latvia, enjoyed a brief period of independence in the inter-war years, and in that time they started a league and played international matches.

Shuffled backwards and forwards between Poland, Sweden, Germany, Denmark and Russia, the Estonian people, when finally given independence in 1918, celebrated by forming a national football association. A league was started and international fixtures arranged, although games were almost entirely confined to the Scandinavian area. There was, however, a brief visit to Paris for the 1924 Olympic Games, where they lost 1-0 to the United States in the first round.

Despite being the smallest of the three Baltic states, Estionia were the most prolific and successful. Friendly matches were played, with some success, against Finland, and with less success against Sweden, Poland, the Soviet Union, Norway, Turkey, the Republic of Ireland, Germany and Hungary. The mainstays of their fixture list, however, were their Baltic neighbours Lithuania and Latvia, both in friendly games and in the Baltic Cup, a competition Estonia won on three occasions in the 1930s.

Absorption into the Soviet Union in 1939 effectively killed football in the country, and the newly independent

Estonia emerged in the 1990s as the weakest of the Baltic states. A league of sorts carried on throughout the Soviet years, but the clubs bore little resemblance to those of the pre-war period. As none of the teams from Estonia made it to the higher echelons of the Soviet league system, the winners of the Estonian regional league were the de facto champions of Estonia. Sport Tallinn were the only Estonian entrants into the short-lived Baltic League in 1990 before the regional league took on the role of a national league in the wake of independence. Two of the most succesful teams of the Soviet era, Dünamo and Norma Tallinn, were prominent in the new league, the latter winning the first two recognised Estonian championships. They might have made it three in a row in 1994 but for a bizarre incident.

Three clubs entered the final week of the championship level on points, Norma, Tevalte and Flora Tallinn. The first two clubs are strongholds of the huge Russian community in Estonia, whilst Flora are the team of the Estonians. In a move seen by many as pure favouritism, the federation dissolved Tevalte for alleged match-fixing and corruption, a charge which was never proved. Both Norma and Flora won their last games and had to play-off for the title. Norma, in support of Tevalte, deliberately fielded their reserve team and lost 5-2 as a result. Tevalte, who earlier in the season had beaten Kalev Sillamae 24-0 in a league match, appealed to FIFA and were reinstated in the league for the 1995-96 season.

The episode did not bode well for the future of Estonian football. Many ethnic Russians who have lived in Estonia all their lives have been labelled as foreigners by the federation, and Flora players form the basis of the national side. Their first outing in the World Cup since 1938 was hardly impressive and the first three years of internationals since independence saw just two wins in 31 outings, the only victories coming against Lithuania and Liechtenstein.

Population: 1,571,000
Area, sq km: 45,100
Capital city: Tallinn

Eesti Jalgpalli Liit
Regati PST 1
Tallinn EE 0019
Tel: + 372 2 238253
Fax: +372 2 238387

Year of formation	1921-43 & 1989
Affiliation to FIFA	1923-43 & 1992
Affiliation to UEFA	1992
Registered clubs	40
Registered players	3000
Registered referees	75
National stadium	Kadriorg, Tallinn 6000
National colours	Blue/Black/White
Season	August - June, with a mid season break November - March

THE RECORD

WORLD CUP

1930	Did not enter
1934	QT 3rd/3 in group 5
1938	QT 3rd/4 in group 1
1950-90	Did not enter
1994	QT 6th/6 in group 1

EUROPEAN CHAMPIONSHIP

1960-92	Did not enter
1996	QT group 4

Baltic Cup
Winners 1929, 1931, 1938

EUROPEAN CLUB COMPETITIONS

European Cup
Preliminary round - Norma Tallinn 1993 1994
Cup Winners Cup
Preliminary round - Nikol Tallinn 1994, Norma Tallinn 1995
UEFA Cup
Preliminary round - Flora Tallinn 1995

CLUB DIRECTORY

TALLINN (Population - 478,000)

Dünamo Tallinn (1940)
Tuletbrje 1,000 – White/Blue

FC Flora Tallinn (1990)
Kadriorg 6,000 – Blue/White

FC Norma Tallinn (1959)
Norma 1,000 – Blue/Blue

FC Tevalte Tallinn (1993)
Kadriorg 6,000
Previous name - Vigri Tallinn 1980-93

FC VMK Nikol Tallinn (1951)
Kadriorg 6,000
Previous name - VMV Tallinn

TARTU (Population - 113,000)

Kalev Esdag Tartu (1910)
Tamme 3,000 – White/Black

Merkuur Tartu (1987)
Estre 1,000 – Red/Red

JOHVI

EP Johvi (1974)
(Eesti Polabkivi)
Kaevur 2,000 – Yellow/White

NARVA

Trans Narva (1979)
Kreenholm 2,000 – Yellow/Red

PARNU

Tervis Parnu (1992)
Kalev 2,000

ESTONIAN LEAGUE CHAMPIONS

1922an	LFLS Kaunas 26 LFLS Sanciai 18 Makabi Kaunas 14
1922	Sport Tallinn 4-2 Kalev Tallinn
1923	Kalev Tallinn 6-0 Tartu ASK
1924	Sport Tallinn 1-0 1-3 1-1 2-0 Kalev Tallinn
1925	Sport Tallinn 5-0 Kalev Tallinn
1926	Tallinn JK 4-1 Sport Tallinn
1927	Sport Tallinn 2-0 Tallinn JK
1928	Tallinn JK 4-1 Merkuur Tallinn
1929	Sport Tallinn 10 Tallinn JK 7 Kalev Tallinn 5
1930	Kalev Tallinn 5 Sport Tallinn 5 Tallinn JK 2
1931	Sport Tallinn 9 Kalev Tallinn 7 Tallinn JK 7
1932	Sport Tallinn 18 Puhkekodu Tallinn 13 Kalev Tallinn 11
1933	Sport Tallinn 16 Estonia Tallinn 15 Tallinn JK 14
1934	Estonia Tallinn 17 Sport Tallinn 15 Puhkekodu Tallinn 11
1935	Estonia Tallinn 13 Tallinn JK 8 Sport Tallinn 8
1936	Estonia Tallinn 23 Sport Tallinn 18 Puhkekodu Tallinn 17
1937	-
1938	Estonia Tallinn 22 Tallinn ESTA 19 Kalev Tallinn 18
1939	Estonia Tallinn 23 Tallinn JK 17 Sport Tallinn 15
1940	Olümpia Tartu 22 Estonia Tallinn 21 Tallinn ESTA 16

ESTONIAN REGIONAL LEAGUE CHAMPIONS

1942	PSR Tartu
1943	Estonia Tallinn

1944	-
1945	Dünamo Tallinn
1946	BL Tallinn
1947	Dünamo Tallinn
1948	BL Tallinn
1949	Dünamo Tallinn
1950	Dünamo Tallinn
1951	BL Tallinn
1952	BL Tallinn
1953	Dünamo Tallinn
1954	Dünamo Tallinn
1955	Kalev Tallinn
1956	BL Tallinn
1957	Ulemiste Kalev Tallinn
1958	Ulemiste Kalev Tallinn
1959	Ulemiste Kalev Tallinn
1960	BL Tallinn
1961	Kopli Kalev Tallinn
1962	Ulemiste Kalev Tallinn
1963	Tempo Tallinn
1964	Norma Tallinn
1965	BL Tallinn
1966	BL Tallinn
1967	Norma Tallinn
1968	BL Tallinn
1969	Dvigatel Tallinn
1970	Norma Tallinn
1971	Tempo Tallinn
1972	BL Tallinn
1973	Kreenholm Narva
1974	Baltika Narva
1975	Baltika Narva
1976	Dvigatel Tallinn
1977	Baltika Narva
1978	Dünamo Tallinn
1979	Norma Tallinn
1980	Dünamo Tallinn
1981	Dünamo Tallinn
1982	Tempo Tallinn
1983	Dünamo Tallinn
1984	Estonia Jöhvi
1985	KK Pärnu
1986	Zvezda Tallinn
1987	Tempo Tallinn
1988	Tempo Tallinn
1989	Norma Tallinn
1990	VMV Tallinn
1991	VMV Tallinn

ESTONIAN LEAGUE CHAMPIONS

1992	Norma Tallinn 12 EP Jöhvi 10 VMV Tallinn 8
1993	Norma Tallinn 42 Flora Tallinn 34 Nikol Tallinn 33
1994	Flora Tallinn 36 Norma Tallinn 36 Nikol Tallinn 33
1995	Flora Tallinn 41 FC Lantana 40 Trans Narva 26

Championship play-off
1994 Flora Tallinn 5-2 ..Norma Tallinn

ESTONIAN CUP WINNERS

1938	Sport Tallinn
1939	JK Tallinn
1940	JK Tallinn
1941	-
1942	Sport Tallinn
1943	PSR Tartu
1944-45	-
1946	Dünamo Tallinn
1947	Dünamo Tallinn
1948	VVS Tallinn
1949	Dünamo Tallinn
1950	BL Tallinn
1951	BL Tallinn
1952	BL Tallinn
1953	Dünamo Tallinn
1954	VVS Tallinn
1955	BL Tallinn
1956	BL Tallinn
1957	Spartak Viljandi
1958	Ulemiste Kalev Tallinn
1959	Ulemiste Kalev Tallinn
1960	BL Tallinn
1961	Ulemiste Kalev Tallinn
1962	Norma Tallinn
1963	Kreenholm Narva
1964	Ulemiste Kalev Tallinn
1965	Norma Tallinn
1966	Start Tallinn
1967	BL Tallinn
1968	BL Tallinn
1969	Dvigatel Tallinn
1970	Start Tallinn
1971	Norma Tallinn
1972	Kopli Dünamo Tallinn
1973	Norma Tallinn
1974	Norma Tallinn
1975	Baltika Narva
1976	SK Aseri
1977	Kalev Sillamäe
1978	Kalev Sillamäe
1979	Baltika Narva
1980	Dünamo Tallinn
1981	KK Pärnu
1982	KK Pärnu
1983	Dünamo Tallinn
1984	Tempo Tallinn
1985	Estonia Johvi
1986	Estonia Johvi
1987	Estonia Johvi
1988	KK Pärnu
1989	Norma Tallinn
1990	KK Pärnu
1991	VMV Tallinn

ESTONIAN CUP FINALS

1992 VMV Tallinn...0-0 4-3p..Keemik Kohtla
1993 Nikol Tallinn..0-0 4-2p...Norma Tallinn
1994 Norma Tallinn...4-1.........Trans Narva
1995 Flora Tallinn......2-0Lantana Morlekor

INTERNATIONAL MATCHES PLAYED BY ESTONIA

Date	Opponent	Result	Venue	Comp	Scorers
17-10-1920	Finland	L 0-6	Helsinki	Fr	
22-07-1921	Sweden	D 0-0	Tallinn	Fr	
28-08	Finland	L 0-3	Tallinn	Fr	
11-08-1922	Finland	L 2-10	Helsinki	Fr	Kuulman, Tell
24-09	Latvia	D 1-1	Riga	Fr	Üpraus
24-06-1923	Lithuania	W 5-0	Kaunas	Fr	Tell 3, Ellman, Paal
24-07	Latvia	D 1-1	Tallinn	Fr	Paal
18-09	Soviet Union	D 2-2	Tallinn	Fr	Kaljot 2
25-09	Poland	L 1-4	Tallinn	Fr	Joll
30-09	Finland	W 2-1	Tallinn	Fr	Tell, Joll
25-05-1924	United States	L 0-1	Paris	OGr1	
3-06	Rep. Ireland	L 1-3	Paris	Fr	Üpraus
19-06	Turkey	L 1-4	Tallinn	Fr	Üpraus
25-07	Sweden	L 2-5	Stockholm	Fr	Üpraus, Väli
24-08	Lithuania	L 1-2	Tallinn	Fr	Üpraus
14-09	Finland	L 0-4	Helsinki	Fr	
18-10	Latvia	L 0-2	Riga	Fr	
28-06-1925	Lithuania	W 1-0	Kaunas	Fr	Üpraus
5-07	Finland	W 2-0	Tallinn	Fr	Pihlak 2
26-08	Latvia	D 2-2	Tallinn	Fr	Pihlak 2
1-09	Poland	D 0-0	Tallinn	Fr	
13-06-1926	Lithuania	W 3-1	Tallinn	Fr	Ellman, Üpraus, Piklak
4-07	Poland	L 0-2	Warsaw	Fr	
23-07	Sweden	L 1-7	Tallinn	Fr	Räästas

5-09	Finland	D 1-1	Helsinki	Fr	Joll
19-09	Latvia	W 1-0	Riga	Fr	Ellman
16-06-1927	Latvia	W 4-1	Tallinn	Fr	Ellman, Pihlak 2, OG
1-07	Sweden	L 1-3	Norrkoping	Fr	Paal
10-08	Finland	W 2-1	Tallinn	Fr	Pihlak, Joll
13-08	Lithuania	W 5-0	Kaunas	Fr	Kipp, Kull 2, Ellman, Kaljot
25-09	Latvia	L 1-4	Riga	Fr	Pihlak
9-07-1928	Sweden	L 0-1	Tallinn	Fr	
26-07	Lithuania	W 6-0	Tallinn	BC	Pihlak 3, Räästas, Maurer 2
27-07	Latvia	L 0-1	Tallinn	BC	
12-08	Finland	D 2-2	Helsinki	Fr	Pihlak, Paal
23-09	Latvia	D 1-1	Riga	Fr	Pihlak
7-07-1929	Sweden	L 1-4	Landskrona	Fr	Idlane
25-07	Finland	D 1-1	Tallinn	Fr	Kull
15-08	Lithuania	W 5-2	Riga	BC	Einman 2, Pihlak, Ellman 2
16-08	Latvia	D 2-2	Riga	BC	Einman, Ellman
27-08	Finland	L 1-2	Helsinki	Fr	Pihlak
18-09	Latvia	W 4-1	Tallinn	Fr	Brenner, Ellman, Paal, Pihlak
27-06-1930	Latvia	D 1-1	Tallinn	Fr	Brenner
18-07	Sweden	L 1-5	Tallinn	Fr	Gerassimov
6-08	Finland	W 4-0	Tallinn	Fr	Karm 2, Brenner 2
15-08	Lithuania	L 1-2	Kaunas	BC	Karm
16-08	Latvia	L 2-3	Kaunas	BC	Einman, Karm
13-09	Lithuania	L 0-4	Klaipeda	Fr	
26-10	Poland	L 0-6	Warsaw	Fr	
28-05-1931	Latvia	W 1-0	Riga	Fr	Einman
9-06	Lithuania	W 4-1	Tallinn	Fr	Karm 3, Kass
17-06	Finland	L 1-3	Helsinki	Fr	Räästas
8-07	Sweden	L 1-3	Sandviken	Fr	Ellman
30-08	Lithuania	W 2-0	Tallinn	BC	Ellman, Kass
1-09	Latvia	W 3-1	Tallinn	BC	Ellman, Karm 2
27-09	Latvia	L 1-2	Riga	Fr	Kass
1-06-1932	Latvia	W 3-0	Tallinn	Fr	Laasner, Ellman, Kass
5-06	Norway	L 0-3	Oslo	Fr	
15-07	Sweden	L 1-3	Tallinn	Fr	Kass
6-08	Lithuania	L 0-1	Kaunas	Fr	
17-08	Finland	L 0-3	Tallinn	Fr	
29-08	Lithuania	L 1-2	Riga	BC	Mötlik
30-08	Latvia	L 0-1	Riga	BC	
28-05-1933	Latvia	L 0-2	Riga	Fr	
11-06	Sweden	L 2-6	Stockholm	WCq	Kass, Kuremaa
20-07	Lithuania	W 2-1	Tallinn	Fr	Idlane 2
9-08	Latvia	W 2-1	Tallinn	Fr	Ellman, Lassner
16-08	Finland	L 1-2	Helsinki	Fr	Ader
2-09	Lithuania	D 1-1	Kaunas	BC	Kuremaa
3-09	Latvia	L 0-1	Kaunas	BC	
5-09	Lithuania	W 5-0	Kaunas	Fr	Ellman 3, Siimenson, Kuremaa
29-06-1934	Lithuania	D 1-1	Kaunas	Fr	Parbo
8-08	Finland	D 1-1	Tallinn	Fr	Siimenson
10-08	Hungary	D 2-2	Tallinn	Fr	Kuremaa, Neeris
12-06-1935	Latvia	D 1-1	Riga	Fr	Siimenson
19-06	Lithuania	D 2-2	Tallinn	Fr	Kuremaa, Ellman
9-07	Sweden	L 1-2	Tallinn	Fr	Ellman
7-08	Finland	D 2-2	Helsinki	Fr	Uukkivi, Ellman
20-08	Lithuania	L 1-2	Tallinn	BC	Linberg
22-08	Latvia	D 1-1	Tallinn	BC	Ellman
15-09	Germany	L 0-5	Stettin	Fr	
18-09	Lithuania	D 2-2	Kaunas	Fr	Kuremaa 2
28-05-1936	Latvia	L 3-4	Tallinn	Fr	Linberg, Siimenson 2
30-06	Lithuania	L 0-2	Kaunas	Fr	
20-08	Finland	D 2-2	Tallinn	Fr	Uukkivi, Kuremaa
30-08	Lithuania	W 2-1	Riga	BC	Siimenson, Kuremaa
31-08	Latvia	L 1-2	Riga	BC	Kaljo
3-06-1937	Lithuania	W 2-1	Kaunas	Fr	Sillak, Uukkivi
20-06	Sweden	L 2-7	Stockholm	WCq	Siimenson, Uukkivi
14-07	Romania	W 2-1	Tallinn	Fr	Kaljo, Siimenson
19-08	Finland	W 1-0	Turku	WCq	Kuremaa
29-08	Germany	L 1-4	Konigsberg	WCq	Siimenson
4-09	Latvia	D 1-1	Kaunas	BC	Kuremaa
5-09	Lithuania	W 4-0	Kaunas	BC	Siimenson 2, Uukkivi, Sillandi
7-09	Latvia	L 0-2	Kaunas	BCpo	

19-09	Latvia	L 1-3	Riga	Fr	Kuremaa
31-05-1938	Norway	L 0-1	Oslo	Fr	
11-06	Lithuania	W 2-0	Kaunas	Fr	Kurmaa 2
22-06*	Hungary	L 2-3	Tallinn	Fr	Siimenson, Kuremaa
20-07	Latvia	L 0-2	Tallinn	Fr	
17-08	Finland	L 1-3	Tallinn	Fr	Siimenson
3-09	Lithuania	W 3-1	Tallinn	BC	Veidemann 2, Uukkivi
5-09	Latvia	D 1-1	Tallinn	BC	Kass
29-06-1939	Germany	L 0-2	Tallinn	Fr	
27-07	Latvia	D 3-3	Riga	Fr	Siimenson, Kuremaa, Veidemann
4-08	Finland	L 2-4	Helsinki	Fr	Uukkivi, Kass
27-08	Lithuania	L 0-1	Tallinn	Fr	
18-07-1940	Latvia	W 2-1	Tallinn	Fr	Kuremaa 2
11-08	Lithuania	L 0-2	Kaunas	Fr	
7-09	Lithuania	D 1-1	Riga	BC	
8-09	Latvia	D 2-2	Riga	BC	Uukkivi, Koslovski
3-08-1942	Latvia	L 0-4	Riga	Fr	
18-08	Latvia	L 1-6	Tallinn	Fr	Linberg
15-11-1991	Lithuania	L 1-4	Vilnius	BC	Kirs
16-11	Latvia	L 0-2	Vilnius	BC	
3-06-1992	Slovenia	D 1-1	Tallinn	Fr	Putsov
15-07	Latvia	L 1-2	Leipaja	BC	Olumets
16-07	Lithuania	D 1-1	Leipaja	BC	Olumets
16-08	Switzerland	L 0-6	Tallinn	WCq	
25-10	Malta	D 0-0	Ta'Qali	WCq	
20-02-1993	Finland	D 0-0	Vaanta	BC	
21-02	Latvia	L 0-2	Vaanta	BC	
7-04	Slovenia	L 0-2	Ljubljana	Fr	
14-04	Italy	L 0-2	Trieste	WCq	
12-05	Malta	L 0-1	Tallinn	WCq	
19-05	Scotland	L 0-3	Tallinn	WCq	
2-06	Scotland	L 1-3	Aberdeen	WCq	Bragin
2-07	Latvia	L 0-2	Parnu	BC	
4-07	Lithuania	W 2-1	Parnu	BC	Zamorski, Bragin
5-09	Portugal	L 0-2	Tallinn	WCq	
22-09	Italy	L 0-3	Tallinn	WCq	
26-10	Liechtenstein	W 2-0	Balzers	Fr	Bragin, Rajala
10-11	Portugal	L 0-3	Lisbon	WCq	
17-11	Switzerland	L 0-4	Zurich	WCq	
9-03-1994	Cyprus	L 0-2	Paralimni	Fr	
7-05	USA	L 0-4	Fullerton	Fr	
23-05	Wales	L 1-2	Tallinn	Fr	Reim
1-06	Macedonia	L 0-2	Skopje	Fr	
29-07	Lithuania	L 0-3	Vilnius	BC	
30-07	Latvia	L 0-2	Vilnius	BC	
16-08	Iceland	L 0-4	Akureyri	Fr	
4-09	Croatia	L 0-2	Tallinn	ECq	
8-10	Italy	L 0-2	Tallinn	ECq	
26-10	Finland	L 0-7	Tallinn	Fr	
6-11	Latvia	D 0-0	Ozolnieki	Fr	
13-11	Ukraine	L 0-3	Kiev	ECq	
4-01-1995	Vietnam	L 0-1	Ho Chi Minh	Fr	
6-02	Norway	L 0-7	Larnaca	Fr	
15-02	Cyprus	L 1-3	Limassol	Fr	Reim
25-03	Italy	L 1-4	Salerno	ECq	Reim
29-03	Slovenia	L 0-3	Maribor	ECq	
26-04	Ukraine	L 0-1	Tallinn	ECq	
19-05	Latvia	L 0-2	Riga	BC	
20-05	Lithuania	L 0-7	Riga	BC	
11-06	Slovenia	L 1-3	Tallinn	ECq	Reim

FAEROE ISLANDS

Geographically the Faeroe Islands could hardly be more remote from Europe, but they made quite an entrance in September 1990. Other 'minnows' such as Cyprus, Malta and Luxembourg had chalked up only a handful wins between them in years of international competition, yet the Faeroes, playing their first competitive game, won it. Austria were their victims, in the biggest shock the European Championships had ever seen, and they did not even enjoy home advantage, the game taking place in neutral Sweden.

The goalkeeper Knudsen, playing throughout the game in a bobble hat, became an instant hero, as did Nielsen, scorer of the winning goal. This result was followed up by an equally impressive draw away to Northern Ireland in Belfast, and the Faeroe Islanders finished the group with three completely unexpected points.

A league was started in the Faeroe Islands in 1942 and a cup competition has been played since 1967, but it was not until 1993 that any of the clubs took part in the European competitions. So far there has been no giant-killing to match that of the national team.

The Faeroes' first international match was actually played as long ago as 1930, with Iceland, the Shetland Islands, the Orkneys and Greenland having since contributed to one of the most bizarre fixture lists in world football, based on competitions such as the North Atlantic Cup and the Island Games.

A new pitch meeting UEFA standards has been laid in Tórshavn, and so the islanders can now look forward to some of the best players in the world visiting their shores.

Population: 46,986
Area, sq km: 1,339
% in urban areas: 30%
Capital city: Tórshavn

Fótbóltssambund Føroya
The Faroes' Football Association
Gundadalur
PO Box 1028
FR-110 Tórshavn
Faeroe Islands
Tel: + 298 16707
Fax: + 298 19079

Year of formation	1979
Affiliation to FIFA	1988
Affiliation to UEFA	1988
Registered clubs	172
Registered players	2900
Registered referees	61
National stadium	Gundadulur 8 000
National colours	White/Blue/White
Season	April - October

THE RECORD

WORLD CUP

1930-90	Did not enter
1994	QT 6th/6 in group 4

EUROPEAN CHAMPIONSHIP

1960-88	Did not enter
1992	QT 5th/5 in group 4
1996	QT group 8

EUROPEAN CLUB COMPETITIONS

European Cup
Preliminary round - KI Klaksvik 1993, B'68 Toftir 1994
Cup Winners Cup
First round - HB Tórshavn 1994
UEFA Cup
Preliminary round - HB Tóshavn 1995, GI Gotu 1995

CLUB DIRECTORY

TORSHAVN (Population - 14,000)

HB Tórshavn (1904)
(Havnar Boltfelag)
Gundadalur 8,000 – Black & red stripes/Black

B'36 Tórshavn (1936)
(Boltfelagid 36)
Gundadalur 8,000 – White/Black

EIDI

EB/Streymur (1993)
Streymes & Eidi both 1,000 – Red, brown sleeves/Red
Previous name - Merger in 1993 of Streymur Hvalvik and EB Eidi

FUGLAFJORDUR

IF Fuglafjordur (1946)
(Itrottarfelag Fuglafjordur)
Fuglafjordur 3,000 – White/Red

GOTU

GI Gotu (1926)
(Gotu Itrottarfelag)
Gotu 3,000 – Yellow/Blue

LEIRVIK

LIF Leirvik (1928)
(Leirvikar Itrottarfelag)
Leirvik 2,000 – Green/Green, black trim

KLAKSVIK

KI Klaksvik (1904)
(Klaksvikar Itrottarfelag)
Klaksvik 4,000 – Blue with white hoop/Blue

RUNAVIK

NSI Runavik (1957)
(Nes Soknar Itrottarfelag)
Runavik 2,000 – Yellow, red sleeves/Red

SANDUR

B'71 Sandur (1970)
Sandur 2,000 – Yellow/Blue

TOFTIR

B'68 Toftir (1962)
Svangaskard 6,000 – Red & black stripes/Black

TVOROYRI

TB Tvoroyri (1892)
(Tvoroyrar Boltfelag)
Sevmyra 4,000 – Black & white stripes/Black

VAGUR

VB Vagur (1905)
(Vags Boltfelag)
Vestri a Eidinum 3,000 – White with red V on chest/Blue

FAEROE ISLANDS LEAGUE CHAMPIONSHIP

1942	KI Klaksvik
1943	TB Tvoroyri
1944	-
1945	TB Tvoroyri
1946	B'36 Tórshavn
1947	SI Sorvag
1948	B'36 Tórshavn
1949	TB Tvoroyri
1950	B'36 Tórshavn
1951	TB Tvoroyri
1952	KI Klaksvik
1953	KI Klaksvik
1954	KI Klaksvik
1955	HB Tórshavn
1956	KI Klaksvik
1957	KI Klaksvik
1958	KI Klaksvik
1959	B'36 Tórshavn
1960	HB Tórshavn
1961	KI Klaksvik
1962	B'36 Tórshavn
1963	HB Tórshavn
1964	HB Tórshavn
1965	HB Tórshavn
1966	KI Klaksvik
1967	KI Klaksvik
1968	KI Klaksvik
1969	KI Klaksvik
1970	KI Klaksvik
1971	HB Tórshavn
1972	KI Klaksvik
1973	HB Tórshavn
1974	HB Tórshavn
1975	HB Tórshavn
1976	TB Tvoroyri
1977	TB Tvoroyri
1978	HB Tórshavn
1979	IF Fuglafjordur
1980	TB Tvoroyri
1981	HB Tórshavn
1982	HB Tórshavn
1983	GI Gotu
1984	B'68 Toftir
1985	B'68 Toftir
1986	GI Gotu
1987	GI Gotu
1988	HB Tórshavn
1989	B'71 Sandur
1990	HB Tórshavn
1991	KI Klaksvik
1992	B'68 Toftir
1993	GI Gotu
1994	GI Gotu

Number of League wins

KI Klaksvik	15
HB Tórshavn	14
TB Tvoroyri	7
B'36 Tórshavn	5
GI Gotu	5
B'68 Toftir	3
SI Sorvag	1
IF Fuglafjordur	1
B'71 Sandur	1

FAEROE ISLANDS CUP FINALS

1967	KI Klaksvik	6-2	B'36 Tórshavn
1968	HB Tórshavn	2-1	B'36 Tórshavn
1969-72	-		
1973	HB Tórshavn	2-1	KI Klaksvik
1974	VB Vagur	7-5	HB Tórshavn
1975	HB Tórshavn	7-2	IF Fuglafjordur
1976	HB Tórshavn	3-1	TB Tvoroyri
1977	TB Tvoroyri	4-3	VB Vagur
1978	TB Tvoroyri	5-2	HB Tórshavn
1979	TB Tvoroyri	5-0	KI Klaksvik
1980	TB Tvoroyri	2-1	NSI Runavik
1981	HB Tórshavn	5-2	TB Tvoroyri
1982	HB Tórshavn	2-1	IF Fuglafjordur
1983	GI Gotu	5-1	Royn Valba
1984	HB Tórshavn	2-0	GI Gotu
1985	GI Gotu	4-2	NSI Runavik
1986	NSI Runavik	3-1	LIF Lorvik
1987	HB Tórshavn	2-2 3-0	IF Fuglafjordur
1988	HB Tórshavn	1-0	NSI Runavik
1989	HB Tórshavn	1-1 2-0	B'71 Sandur
1990	KI Klaksvik	6-1	GI Gotu
1991	B'36 Tórshavn	1-0	HB Tórshavn
1992	HB Tórshavn	1-0	KI Klaksvik
1993	B'71 Sandur	2-0	HB Tórshavn
1994	KI Klaksvik	2-1	B'71 Sandur

Number of Cup wins

HB Tórshavn	11
TB Tvoroyri	4
KI Klaksvik	3
GI Gotu	2
NSI Runavik	1
VB Vagur	1
B'36 Tórshavn	1
B'71 Sandur	1

INTERNATIONAL MATCHES PLAYED BY THE FAEROE ISLANDS

Date	Opponents	Result	Venue	Compet	Scorers
1930-	Iceland	L 0-1	Tórshavn	Fr	
	Shetland Isl	L 1-5	Lerwick	Fr	
	Shetland Isl	D 1-1	Lerwick	Fr	
	Shetland Isl	L 0-3	Lerwick	Fr	
-1935	Shetland Isl	L 2-5	Lerwick	Fr	
29-07-1948	Shetland Isl	W 4-1	Tórshavn	Fr	Johansen.J 2, Mortensen.W, Hansen.A
9-07-1951	Shetland Isl	W 7-2	Lerwick	Fr	Lydersen 4, Johansen.J, Mortensen.M
7-04-1953	Shetland Isl	W 5-0	Tórshavn	Fr	Nolsoe.A 3, Lydersen, Johansen.J
9-07-1955	Shetland Isl	L 0-1	Lerwick	Fr	
21-07-1957	Shetland Isl	W 4-1	Tórshavn	Fr	Nolsoe.A 2, Eliasen 2
8-08-1959	Shetland Isl	W 4-1	Lerwick	Fr	Eliasen, Jensen.M, Nolsoe.P 2
20-08-1961	Shetland Isl	W 6-1	Tórshavn	Fr	Dam.E 5, Jacobsen.S
29-06-1963	Shetland Isl	W 3-2	Lerwick	Fr	Thomasen, Magnussen.T, Kallsberg
2-07-1967	Shetland Isl	W 1-0	Tórshavn	Fr	Baldvinsson
-06-1968	Orkney	L 0-2	Tórshavn	NAC	
14-07	Orkney	L 0-2	Tórshavn	Fr	
-06-1969	Shetland Isl	W 2-1	Tórshavn	NAC	
19-07	Shetland Isl	W 2-1	Tórshavn	Fr	Nolsoe.H 2
-06-1970	Shetland Isl	L 0-3	Lerwick	NAC	
-06	Orkney Isl	W 4-2	Kirkwall	NAC	
15-07	Shetland Isl	L 0-3	Lerwick	Fr	
20-06-1971	Orkney	D 1-1	Tórshavn	NAC	Mortensen.S
25-06-1972	Shetland Isl	W 6-2	Tórshavn	Fr	Nolsoe.H 2, Thomsen 2, Weyhe, Rasmussen.E
12-07	Iceland	L 0-3	Reykjavik	Fr	
8-06-1973	Iceland	L 0-4	Klaksvik	Fr	
13-06	Shetland Isl	L 1-5	Seafield	Fr	Augustinussen
18-06	Orkney Isl	L 1-2	Kirkwall	Fr	Petersen.D
3-07-1974	Iceland	L 2-3	Tórshavn	Fr	Jacobsen.S 2
23-06-1975	Iceland	L 0-6	Reykjavik	Fr	
16-06-1976	Iceland	L 1-6	Tórshavn	Fr	Eysturoy
10-07-1979	Orkney	W 4-3	Kirkwall	Fr	Nolsoe.H 3, Muller
30-06-1980	Iceland	L 1-2	Akureyri	Fr	Jacobsen.Su
2-07	Greenland	W 6-0	Akureyri	Fr	Nolsoe.A 3, Jacobsen.Su 2, Dalsgaro
2-07-1981	Shetland Isl	W 3-0	Tvaera	Fr	Bartalsstovu, Nolsoe.A, Jacobsen.Su
4-07	Shetland Isl	W 4-1	Fuglafjordor	Fr	Dalsgaro, Nielsen.K, Nolsoe.A, OG
5-07	Shetland Isl	D 2-2	Tórshavn	Fr	Nielsen.K, OG
1-08-1982	Iceland	L 1-4	Tórshavn	Fr	Nielsen.J
2-08	Iceland	L 0-4	Gotu	Fr	
29-06-1983	Greenland	D 0-0	Godthaab	Fr	
	Greenland	W 3-2	Godthaab	Fr	
8-08	Iceland	L 0-6	Njardvik	Fr	
1-08-1984	Iceland	D 0-0	Tórshavn	Fr	
5-08	Greenland	W 1-0	Klaksvik	Fr	Michelsen
7-08	Greenland	W 4-2	Tórshavn	Fr	Hansen.J, OG, Hojgaard, Bartalsstovu
11-06-1985	Shetland Isl	W 1-0	Lerwick	Fr	Thomsen
10-07	Iceland	L 0-9	Keflavik	Fr	

12-07	Iceland	L 0-1	Akranes	Fr	
24-08-1988	Iceland	L 0-1	Akranes	Fr	
14-04-1989	Canada	W 1-0	Tórshavn	Fr	Nielsen.T
16-04	Canada	L 0-1	Tórshavn	Fr	
6-07	Anglesey	W 6-0	Gotu	ISG	Magnussen.B 4, Jarnskor, Reynheim
7-07	Shetland Isl	W 4-0	Tórshavn	ISG	Morkore, Rasmussen.J, Magnussen.B, Nielsen.T
8-07	Greenland	W 3-0	Fuglefjord	ISG	Rasmussen.J 3
12-07	Aland Isl	W 7-1	Tórshavn	ISG	Magnussen.B 6, Danielson
12-06-1990	Shetland Isl	W 2-0	Lerwick	Fr	Nielsen.T, Dam.Ja
8-08	Iceland	L 2-3	Tórshavn	Fr	Morkore, Dam.Ja
12-09	Austria	W 1-0	Landskrona	ECq	Nielsen.T
10-10	Denmark	L 1-4	Copenhagen	ECq	Morkore
1-05-1991	Nth. Ireland	D 1-1	Belfast	ECq	Reynheim
16-05	Yugoslavia	L 0-7	Belgrade	ECq	
22-05	Austria	L 0-3	Salzburg	ECq	
24-06	Shetland Isl	W 3-0	Aland	ISG	Rasmussen.J, Jarnskor, Morkore
25-06	Greenland	W 3-2	Aland	ISG	Rasmussen.J 2, Jarnskor
26-06	Jersey	W 5-3	Aland	ISG	Reynheim, Thomassen.A, Rasmussen.J 2, Dam.Ja
29-06	Angelsey	W 2-0	Aland	ISG	Rasmussen.J, Davidsen.E
15-07	Turkey	D 1-1	Tórshavn	Fr	Jonsson
11-09	Nth. Ireland	L 0-5	Landskrona	ECq	
25-09	Denmark	L 0-4	Landskrona	ECq	
16-10	Yugoslavia	L 0-2	Landskrona	ECq	
6-05-1992	Romania	L 0-7	Bucharest	WCq	
13-05	Norway	L 0-2	Oslo	Fr	
3-06	Belgium	L 0-3	Toftir	WCq	
17-06	Cyprus	L 0-2	Toftir	WCq	
5-08	Israel	D 1-1	Toftir	Fr	Reynheim
9-09	Wales	L 0-6	Cardiff	WCq	
23-09	Czechoslovakia	L 0-4	Kosice	WCq	
25-04-1993	Cyprus	L 1-3	Limassol	WCq	Arge
22-05	Belgium	L 0-3	Brussels	WCq	
6-06	Wales	L 0-3	Toftir	WCq	
16-06	Czechoslovakia	L 0-3	Toftir	WCq	
11-08	Norway	L 0-7	Toftir	Fr	
8-09	Romania	L 0-4	Toftir	WCq	
7-09-1994	Greece	L 1-5	Toftir	ECq	Rasmussen.J
12-10	Scotland	L 1-5	Glasgow	ECq	Muller
16-11	Finland	L 0-5	Helsinki	ECq	
26-04-1995	Finland	L 0-4	Toftir	ECq	
6-05	Russia	L 0-3	Moscow	ECq	
25-05	San Marino	W 3-0	Toftir	ECq	Hansen.J, Rasmussen.J, Johnsson.J
7-06	Scotland	L 0-2	Toftir	ECq	

FINLAND

Football is not the national sport in Finland, and trails in popularity well behind the likes of skiing, ski-jumping, and ice hockey. Finnish athletes such as Lasse Viren, the world's best long-distance runner in the 1970s, have always received far more attention than footballers. Consequently, football is not up to much in the land of lakes, and does not look as though it ever will be.

The football association, formed in 1907, instigated a league in the following year, but this was based almost exclusively around Helsinki, the distances between towns being too great to allow the participation of provincial teams until later on.

In the international field Finland did not venture far either. Except for a tour to Austria, Hungary and Germany in 1923, the national side rarely left northern Europe and Scandinavia until after the Second World War. In 1912 Finland entered the Stockholm Olympic Games and reached the semi-finals, beating Italy and what was Tsarist Russia on the way. In the semis, however, they were drawn against England and lost, as they did in the bronze medal play-off match against Holland.

The achievements in Stockholm proved to be a false dawn and even high-scoring victories over the Baltic states could not disguise the weakness of the game. On five occasions since, the Finns have been on the receiving end of a double-figure defeat.

The Scandinavian Championship provided the Finns' staple diet of international games until well into the 1970s when World Cup and European Championship commitments forced its abandonment, and apart from the 1960-63 edition which they rather surprisingly won, Finland were accustomed to finishing last on most occasions. Playing football only in the summer months does not make playing fixtures against those countries who play on a winter timetable very easy, although tours abroad in the early months of the year are now common practice.

Finnish clubs have been involved in the European competitions from the earliest years and there have been some suprising successes, especially from the provincial clubs, who after the war began to make their presence felt both in the league and cup. In 1986, Kuusysi Lahti reached the quarter-finals of the European Cup with victories over Sarajevo and Zenit Leningrad and only lost to Steaua Bucharest, the eventual winners, by the odd goal.

THE ORDER OF MERIT

		All			League			Cup		Europe		
	Team	G	S	B	G	S	B	G	S	G	S	B
1	HJK Helsinki	23	12	10	18	9	10	5	3	-	-	-
2	Haka Valkeakoski	13	8	8	4	5	8	9	3	-	-	-
3	Reipas Lahti	10	10	3	3	6	3	7	4	-	-	-
4	HPS Helsinki	10	7	2	9	6	2	1	1	-	-	-
5	TPS Turku	10	14	5	8	12	5	2	2	-	-	-
6	HIFK Helsinki	7	8	4	7	7	4	-	1	-	-	-
7	KuPS Kuopio	7	8	1	5	8	1	2	-	-	-	-
8	Kuusysi Lahti	7	7	-	5	4	-	2	3	-	-	-
9	KTP Kotka	6	2	2	2	-	2	4	2	-	-	-
10	Åbo IFK	4	5	1	3	5	1	1	-	-	-	-
11	KIF Helsinki	4	2	3	4	1	3	-	1	-	-	-
12	Ilves Tampere	4	2	-	2	1	-	2	1	-	-	-
13	IFK Vaasa	3	2	2	3	2	2	-	-	-	-	-
14	VPS Vaasa	2	4	1	2	3	1	-	1	-	-	-
15	MP Mikkeli	2	3	-	-	3	-	2	-	-	-	-
16	OPS Oulu	2	-	-	2	-	-	-	-	-	-	-
17	KPV Kokkola	1	2	2	1	1	2	-	1	-	-	-
	RoPS Rovaniemi	1	2	2	-	-	2	1	2	-	-	-
19	MyPa Myllykoski	1	2	-	-	2	-	1	-	-	-	-
20	Sudet Kouvola	1	1	4	1	1	4	-	-	-	-	-
21	FC Jazz Pori	1	1	1	1	-	1	-	1	-	-	-
22	PP Voikka	1	1	-	-	-	-	1	1	-	-	-
	PUS Helsinki	1	1	-	1	1	-	-	-	-	-	-
	TPV Tampere	1	1	-	1	1	-	-	-	-	-	-
25	Helsinki Toverit	1	-	3	1	-	3	-	-	-	-	-
26	Pyrkiva Turku	1	-	1	1	-	1	-	-	-	-	-
27	Unitas Helsinki	1	-	-	1	-	-	-	-	-	-	-
	Drott	1	-	-	-	-	-	1	-	-	-	-
29	Koparit Kuopio	-	4	-	-	2	-	-	2	-	-	-
30	OTP Oulu	-	3	-	-	-	-	-	3	-	-	-
31	Assat Pori	-	2	-	-	1	-	-	1	-	-	-
	ViPS Viipuri	-	2	-	-	2	-	-	-	-	-	-
	SePS Seinajoken	-	2	-	-	-	-	-	2	-	-	-
34	Janteva Kotka	-	1	-	-	1	-	-	-	-	-	-
	Jaro Pietarsaari	-	1	-	-	-	-	-	1	-	-	-
	KePS Kemi	-	1	-	-	-	-	-	1	-	-	-
	LaPA Lappenranta	-	1	-	-	-	-	-	1	-	-	-
	IF Sport Vaasa	-	1	-	-	-	-	-	1	-	-	-
	Tapion Honka	-	1	-	-	-	-	-	1	-	-	-
	Turun Toverit	-	1	-	-	1	-	-	-	-	-	-
	TKT Tampere	-	1	-	-	-	-	-	1	-	-	-
42	TaPa Tampere	-	-	1	-	-	1	-	-	-	-	-
	TuPK Turku	-	-	1	-	-	1	-	-	-	-	-

To the end of the 1994 season plus 1995 Cup

More and more, however, the best Finnish players are moving abroad, following in the footsteps of Juhani Peltonen who spent a couple of seasons in the 1960s in Germany with Hamburg. Mika-Matti Paatelainen has spent many successful seasons in British club football whilst Ajax believe they have unearthed the best Finnish footballer of all time in Jari Litmanen.

The national side look increasingly capable of causing an upset or two, and in the 1980 European Championships were only one point off qualifying for the final tournament, finishing above the Soviet Union but behind Greece. Such exploits are what the Finns have come rely on for their entertainment, but they would still rather see their ice hockey heroes or their rally drivers in action than watch their local football side every week.

Population: 4,978,000
Area, sq km: 338,145
% in urban areas: 61.7%
Capital city: Helsinki

Suomen Palloliito Finlands Bollfoerbund
Kuparitie #1
PO Box 29
SF-00441 Helsinki
Finland
Tel: + 358 0 7010101
Fax: + 358 0 70101098

Year of formation	1907
Affiliation to FIFA	1908
Affiliation to UEFA	1954
Registered clubs	1092
Registered players	159 000
Registered coaches	4100
Registered referees	2400
National stadium	Olympiastadion 50 000
National colours	White/Blue/White
Reserve colours	Blue/White/Blue
Season	April - October

THE RECORD

WORLD CUP

1930	Did not enter
1934	Did not enter
1938	QT 4th/4 in group 1
1950	QT 3rd/3 in group 5
1954	QT 3rd/3 in group 2
1958	QT 3rd/3 in group 6
1962	QT 3rd/3 in group 2
1966	QT 4th/4 in group 8
1970	QT 4th/4 in group 6
1974	QT 3rd/4 in group 4
1978	QT 3rd/4 in group 2
1982	QT 5th/5 in group 1
1986	QT 4th/5 in group 3
1990	QT 3rd/4 in group 4
1994	QT 5th/6 in group 6

EUROPEAN CHAMPIONSHIP

1960	Did not enter
1964	Did not enter
1968	QT 4th/4 in group 3
1972	QT 4th/4 in group 1
1976	QT 4th/4 in group 5
1980	QT 3rd/4 in group 6
1984	QT 4th/4 in group 2
1988	QT 4th/4 in group 6
1992	QT 4th/5 in group 6
1996	QT group 8

EUROPEAN CLUB COMPETITIONS

European Cup
Quarter-finalists - Kuusysi Lahti 1986
Cup Winners Cup
Quarter-finalists - Haka Valkeakosken 1984 RoPS Rovaniemi 1988
UEFA Cup
3rd round - TPS Turku 1989

CLUB DIRECTORY

HELSINKI (Population - 990,000)

HIFK Helsinki (1897)
(Helsingen Idrotts Förening Kamraterna)
Helsingen Pallokenttä 7,000 – Red/White

HJK Helsinki (1907)
(Helsingin Jalkapallo Klubi)
Helsingen Pallokenttä 7,000 – Blue & white stripes/Blue

HPS Helsinki (1917)
(Helsingen Palloseura)
Helsingen Pallokenttä 7,000

FinnPa (1965)
(Finnairin Palloilijat)
Helsingen Pallokenttä 7,000 – White/White, red & blue trim

TAMPERE (Population - 241,000)
FC Ilves Tampere (1931)
Tammela 6,000 – Yellow/Yellow, black trim
Previous name - Ilves Kissat 1931-70

TPV Tampere (1930)
(Tampereen Pallo-Veikot)
Tammela 6,000 – Red/Red, white trim

TURKU (Population - 221,000)
TPS Turku (1922)
(Turun Palloseura)
Kupittaa 10,000 – Black & white stripes/White

Åbo IFK (1908)
(Åbo Idrotts Förening Kamraterna)
Kupittaa 10,000 – Yellow/Black

OULU (Population - 112,000)
FC Oulu (1992)
Raatti 10,000 – Yellow & red stripes/Black
Previous name - Merger in 1992 of OPS (1925) and OTP (1946)

LAHTI (Population - 109,000)
FC Kuusysi Lahti (1934)
Keskusurheilukenttä 15,000 – White/White, blue trim
Previous names - UP Lahti 1934-69, Lahti'69 1969-74

Reipas Lahti (1891)
Keskusurheilukenttä 15,000 – Orange and black stripes/Black

KUOPIO (Population -78,000)
KuPS Kuopio (1923)
(Kuopion Palloseura)
Väinölänniemi 12,000 – Yellow/Black

Koparit Kuopio (1931)
Väinölänniemi 12,000 – Green/White
Previous name - KPT 1931-82

PORI (Population - 77,000)
FC Jazz Pori (1934)
Porin 10,000 – Red/White
Previous name - PPT Pori 1934-1992

KOUVOLA (Population - 55,000)
Sudet Kouvola (1912)
Keskuskenttä – Red/White

VAASA (Population - 53,000)
Vassa IFK (1900)
(Idrotts Förening Kamraterna)
Vaskiluoto – Blue/White

KOTKA (Population - 60,000)
KTP Kotka (1927)
(Kotkan Työväen Palloillijat)
Ureheilukeskus 6,000 – Green & black stripes/White

MIKKELI (Population - 31,000)
MP Mikkeli (1929)
(Mikkelin Palloilijat)
Urheilupuisto 10,000 – Blue/White

KOKKOLA (Population - 34,000)
KPV Kokkola (1930)
(Kokkolan Palloveikot)
Keskuskenttä 6,000 – Green/Green, white trimmings

KEMI (Population - 26,000)
KePS Kemi (1932)
(Kemin Palloseura)
Sauvosaari 4,000 – Red/White

VALKEAKOSKI (Population - 22,000)
FC Haka (1932)
Tehtaan Kenttä 6,000 – White/Black

ROVANIEMI (Population - 31,000)
RoPS Rovaniemi (1950)
(Rovaniemen Palloseura)
Keskuskenttä 4,000 – White, blue trim

MYLLYKOSKI (Population -)
MyPa (1947)
(Myllykosken Pallo-47)
Saviniemi 8,000 – White, red & blue trim

FINNISH LEAGUE CHAMPIONSHIP

1908	Unitas Helsinki	4-1	PUS Helsinki
1909	PUS Helsinki	4-0	HIFK Helsinki
1910	Åbo IFK	4-2	ViPS Viipuri
1911	HJK Helsinki	7-1	Åbo IFK
1912	HJK Helsinki	7-1	HIFK Helsinki
1913	KIF Helsinki	5-3	Åbo IFK
1914	-		
1915	KIF Helsinki	1-0	Åbo IFK
1916	KIF Helsinki	3-2	Åbo IFK
1917	HJK Helsinki	4-2	Åbo IFK
1918	HJK Helsinki	3-0	ViPS Viipuri
1919	HJK Helsinki	1-0	Reipas Lahti
1920	Åbo IFK	2-1	HPS Helsinki
1921	HPS Helsinki	1-1 2-1	HJK Helsinki
1922	HPS Helsinki	4-2	Reipas Lahti
1923	HJK Helsinki	3-1	TPS Turku
1924	Åbo IFK	4-3	HPS Helsinki
1925	HJK Helsinki	3-2	TPS Turku
1926	HPS Helsinki	5-2	TPS Turku
1927	HPS Helsinki	6-0	Reipas Lahti
1928	TPS Turku	1-1 3-2	HIFK Helsinki
1929	HPS Helsinki	4-0	HIFK Helsinki

1930ad HIFK Helsinki 12 TPS Turku 12 HPS Helsinki 9
1931 HIFK Helsinki 14 HPS Helsinki 10 TPS Turku 8
1932f HPS Helsinki 20 VPS Vaasa 19 HIFK Helsinki 17
1933 HIFK Helsinki 27 HJK Helsinki 16 Sudet Kouvola 16
1934 HPS Helsinki 24 HIFK Helsinki 23 Helsinki Toverit 15
1935 HPS Helsinki 22 HIFK Helsinki 17 Helsinki Toverit 15
1936 HJK Helsinki 19 HPS Helsinki 17 HIFK Helsinki 16
1937 HIFK Helsinki 21 HJK Helsinki 20 Sudet Kouvola 16
1938 HJK Helsinki 20 TPS Turku 16 VPS Vaasa 16
1939 TPS Turku 20 HJK Helsinki 18 Helsinki Toverit 13
1940 Sudet Kouvola ....2-1 ....TPS Turku
1941 TPS Turku 21 VPS Vaasa 19 Sudet Kouvola 17
1942 Helsinki Toverit ....6-4 ....Sudet Kouvola
1943 -
1944ad IFK Vaasa 9 TPS Turku 9 Sudet Kouvola 9
1945 VPS Vaasa..........2-0..........HPS Helsinki
1946 IFK Vaasa ....5-2 0-1 5-1 ....TPV Tampere
1947ab HIFK Helsinki 4 Turun Toverit 4 KTP Kotka 2
1948ah VPS Vaasa 24 TPS Turku 24 HPS Helsinki 21
1949k TPS Turku 34 VPS Vaasa 33 KIF Helsinki 32
1950h Ilves Kissat 25 KuPS Kuopio 22 IFK Vaasa 20
1951 KTP Kotka 27 IFK Vaasa 26 TuPK Turku 23
1952 KTP Kotka 26 IFK Vaasa 22 Pyrkiva Turku 21
1953 IFK Vaasa 24 Janteva Kotka 24 KuPS Kuopio 21
1954 Pyrkiva Turku 26 KuPS Kuopio 22 HJK Helsinki 22
1955 KIF Helsinki 25 Haka Valkeakoski 23 IFK Vaasa 21
1956 KuPS Kuopio 27 HJK Helsinki 21 KIF Helsinki 20
1957 HPS Helsinki 26 Haka Valkeakoski 25 TPS Turku 21
1958 KuPS Kuopio 26 HPS Helsinki 26 HIFK Helsinki 21
1959 HIFK Helsinki 27 RU '38 Pori 25 Haka Valkeakoski 21
1960k Haka Valkeakoski 41 TPS Turku 28 KIF Helsinki 27
1961 HIFK Helsinki 31 KIF Helsinki 30 Haka Valkeakoski 29
1962 Haka Valkeakoski 32 Reipas Lahti 27 TaPA Tampere 26
1963 Reipas Lahti 32 Haka Valkeakoski 31 Åbo IFK 25
1964 HJK Helsinki 34 KuPS Kuopio 30 KTP Kotka 28
1965 Haka Valkeakoski 31 HJK Helsinki 29 Reipas Lahti 25
1966 KuPS Kuopio 29 HJK Helsinki 27 Haka Valkeakoski 24
1967 Reipas Lahti 32 KuPS Kuopio 30 TPS Turku 28
1968 TPS Turku 32 Reipas Lahti 30 HJK Helsinki 29
1969 KPV Kokkola 35 KuPS Kupio 32 HJK Helsinki 27

1970	Reipas Lahti 32 MP Mikkeli 29 HIFK Helsinki 28
1971n	TPS Turku 34 HIFK Helsinki 33 KPV Kokkola 33
1972k	TPS Turku 31 MP Mikkeli 30 Reipas Lahti 28
1973	HJK Helsinki 33 KPV Kokkola 31 Reipas Lahti 30
1974	KuPS Kuopio 33 Reipas Lahti 30 HJK Helsinki 28
1975	TPS Turku 32 KuPS Kupio 30 KPV Kokkola 27
1976	KuPS Kuopio 32 Haka Valkeakoski 30 HJK Helsinki 29
1977	Haka Valkeakoski 33 KuPS Kuopio 26 TPS Turku 25
1978	HJK Helsinki 33 KPT Kuopio 32 Haka Valkeakoski 31
1979p1	OPS Oulu 41 KuPS Kuopio 40 HJK Helsinki 35
1980p2	OPS Oulu 26 Haka Valkeakoski 25 HJK Helsinki 24
1981	HJK Helsinki 25 KPT Kuopio 23 Haka Valkeakoski 23
1982	Kuusysi Lahti 24 HJK Helsinki 22 Haka Valkeakoski 22
1983	Ilves Tampere 27 HJK Helsinki 25 Haka Valkeakoski 25
1984	Kuusysi Lahti ....4-0 4-4 ....TPS Turku
1985	HJK Helsinki ....4-1 0-1 ....Ilves Tampere
1986k	Kuusysi Lahti 32 TPS Turku 30 HJK Helsinki 30
1987	HJK Helsinki 33 Kuusysi Lahti 30 TPS Turku 28
1988o1	HJK Helsinki 43 Kuusysi Lahti 34 RoPS Rovaniemi 31
1989	Kuusysi Lahti 41 TPS Turku 39 RoPS Rovaniemi 34
1990	HJK Helsinki ....1-1 1-0........Kuusysi Lahti
1991s1	Kuusysi Lahti 59 MP Mikkeli 58 Haka Valkeakoski 54
1992	HJK Helsinki 66 Kuusysi Lahti 63 FC Jazz 63
1993p6	FC Jazz 58 MyPa 54 HJK Helsinki 49
1994n1	TPV Tampere 52 MyPa 50 HJK Helsinki 43

Play-offs

1944	IFK Vaasa	5-1	TPS Turku
1947	HIFK Helsinki	3-2	Turun Toverit
1953	IFK Vaasa	3-1	Janteva Kotka
1958	KuPS Kuopio	1-0	HPS Helsinki

FINNISH CUP FINALS

1955	Haka Valkeakoski	5-1	HPS Helsinki
1956	PP Voikka	2-1	TKT Tampere
1957	Drott	2-1	KPT Kuopio
1958	KTP Kotka	4-1	KIF Helsinki
1959	Haka Valkeakoski	2-1	HIFK Helsinki
1960	Haka Valkeakoski	3-1	RU '38 Pori
1961	KTP Kotka	5-2	PP Voikka
1962	HPS Helsinki	5-0	RoPS Rovaniemi
1963	Haka Valkeakoski	1-0	Reipas Lahti
1964	Reipas Lahti	1-0	LaPa Lappenranta
1965	Abo IFK	1-0	TPS Turku
1966	HJK Helsinki	6-1	KTP Kotka
1967	KTP Kotka	2-0	Reipas Lahti
1968	KuPS Kuopio	2-1	KTP Kotka
1969	Haka Valkeakoski	2-0	Tapion Honka
1970	MP Mikkeli	2-0	Reipas Lahti
1971	MP Mikkeli	4-1	IF Sport Vaasa
1972	Reipas Lahti	2-0	VPS Vaasa
1973	Reipas Lahti	1-0	SePS Seinajoki
1974	Reipas Lahti	1-0	OTP Oulu
1975	Reipas Lahti	6-2	HJK Helsinki
1976	Reipas Lahti	2-0	Ilves Tampere
1977	Haka Valkeakoski	3-1	SePS Seinajoki
1978	Reipas Lahti	1-1 3-1	KPT Kuopio
1979	Ilves Tampere	2-0	TPS Turku
1980	KTP Kotka	3-2	Haka Valkeakoski
1981	HJK Helsinki	4-0	Kuusysi Lahti
1982	Haka Valkeakoski	3-2	KPV Kokkola
1983	Kuusysi Lahti	2-0	Haka Valkeakoski
1984	HJK Helsinki	2-1	Kuusysi Lahti
1985	Haka Valkeakoski	1-0	Reipas Lahti
1986	RoPS Rovaniemi	2-0	KePS Kemi
1987	Kuusysi Lahti	5-4	OTP Oulu
1988	Haka Valkeakoski	1-0	OTP Oulu
1989	KuPS Kuopio	3-2	Haka Valkeakoski
1990	Ilves Tampere	2-1	HJK Helsinki
1991	TPS Turku	0-0 5-3p	Kuusysi Lahti
1992	MyPa	2-0	FF Jaro
1993	HJK Helsinki	2-0	RoPS Rovaniemi
1994	TPS Turku	2-1	HJK Helsinki
1995	HJK Helsinki	2-0	FC Jazz

LEADING INTERNATIONAL GOALSCORERS

19	Ari Hjelm	(Ilves,Stuttgart Kickers,Ilves, St Pauli)	1981-
17	Verner Eklöf	(HIFK,HJK)	1919-1927
16	Aulis Koponen	(HPS)	1924-1935
	Gunnar Aström	(HIFK)	1923-1937
13	Jorma Vaihela	(Turun Toverit,PoPa,RU-38 Pori)	1947-1954
	William Kanerva	(HJK,HPS)	1922-1938
13	Mixu Paatelainen	(PS-44,Haka,Dundee Utd, Aberdeen,Bolton Wanderers)	1983-
12	Kalevi Lehtovirta	(TuKv,TuPy,TuWe,Red Star,TPS, TuTo,TuPy)	1947-1959
12	Kai Pahlman	(HPS,HJK)	1954-1968

LEADING INTERNATIONAL APPEARANCES

91	Ari Hjelm	(Ilves,Stuttgart Kickers,Ilves, St. Pauli)	1981-
83	Erkka Petäjä	(TPS,Östers,Helsingborgs, Malmo,Yverdon)	1980-
76	Arto Tolsa	(KTP,Beerschot)	1962-1981
69	Esko Ranta	(Ilves,TPV,TaPa,Haka)	1972-1980
68	Juhani Peltonen	(Haka,Hamburger SV)	1954-1970
66	Hannu Turunen	(KTP,KuPS)	1978-1987
63	Miika Toivola	(PiTU,TPS,HJK)	1967-1980
61	Stig-Goran Myntti	(IFK Vaasa)	1945-1958
60	Olli Huttunen	(Haka)	1976-1992
58	Frans Karjagin	(HIFK)	1929-1942

INTERNATIONAL MATCHES PLAYED BY FINLAND

22-10-1911	Sweden	L 2-5	Helsinki	Fr	Lindback, Jerima
27-06-1912	Sweden	L 1-7	Stockholm	Fr	Wiberg
29-06	Italy	W 3-2	Stockholm	OGr1	Ohman.J, Soinio.E, Wiberg
30-06	Tsarist Russia	W 2-1	Stockholm	OGqf	Wiberg, Ohman.J
2-07	England *	L 0-4	Stockholm	OGsf	
4-07	Holland	L 0-9	Stockholm	OG3p	
24-05-1914	Sweden	L 3-4	Stockholm	Fr	Schybergsson 2, Johansson.K
29-05-1919	Sweden	L 0-1	Stockholm	Fr	
28-09	Sweden	D 3-3	Helsinki	Fr	Wickstrom 2, Thorn
30-05-1920	Sweden	L 0-4	Stockholm	Fr	
19-09	Sweden	W 1-0	Helsinki	Fr	Ohman.J

17-10	Estonia	W 6-0	Helsinki	Fr	Tanner 2, Eklof 2, Ohman.G, Osterholm
25-05-1921	Norway	L 2-3	Oslo	Fr	Eklof, Mantila
29-05	Sweden	W 3-0	Stockholm	Fr	Kelin, Ohman.G
31-07	Austria	L 2-3	Helsinki	Fr	Mantila, OG
28-08	Estonia	W 3-0	Tallinn	Fr	Grannas, Hirvonen, Eklof
18-09	Germany	D 3-3	Helsinki	Fr	Eklof, Thorn, Ohman.G
5-06-1922	Sweden	L 1-4	Helsinki	Fr	Kataiavoori
13-07	Hungary	L 1-5	Helsinki	Fr	Kelin
11-08	Estonia	W 10-2	Helsinki	Fr	Ohman.J 6, Mantila 2, Eklof 2
26-08	Norway	L 1-3	Helsinki	Fr	Eklof
17-06-1923	Norway	L 0-3	Oslo	Fr	
20-06	Sweden	L 4-5	Gavle	Fr	Linna 2, Kelin, Eklof
12-08	Germany	W 2-1	Dresden	Fr	Linna, OG
15-08	Austria	L 1-2	Vienna	Fr	Eklof
19-08	Hungary	L 1-3	Budapest	Fr	Linna
23-09	Poland	W 5-3	Helsinki	Fr	Eklof 2, Korma 2, Linna
30-09	Estonia	L 1-2	Tallinn	Fr	Österlund.T (I)
17-06-1924	Turkey	L 2-4	Helsinki	Fr	Kelin, Korma
28-07	Sweden	L 5-7	Helsinki	Fr	Korma 2, Eklof, Koponen, Karjagin.A
10-08	Poland	L 0-1	Warsaw	Fr	
14-08	Latvia	W 2-0	Riga	Fr	Korma, Koponen
23-08	Norway	W 2-0	Helsinki	Fr	Kanerva, Korma
14-09	Estonia	W 4-0	Helsinki	Fr	Koponen 2, Kanerva, Soinio
7-06-1925	Norway	L 0-1	Oslo	Fr	
9-06	Sweden	L 0-4	Gothenburg	Fr	
26-06	Germany	L 3-5	Helsinki	Fr	Koponen 2, Kelin
5-07	Estonia	L 0-2	Tallinn	Fr	
10-07	Austria	L 1-2	Helsinki	Fr	Eklof
9-08	Latvia	W 3-1	Helsinki	Fr	Korma 2, Eklof
30-08	Poland	D 2-2	Helsinki	Fr	Linna, Kulmala
27-09	Denmark	D 3-3	Aarhus	Fr	Eklof 2, Koponen
6-06-1926	Norway	L 2-5	Helsinki	Fr	Kanerva 2
20-06	Denmark	W 3-2	Helsinki	Fr	Lonnberg 2, Kelin
26-07	Sweden	L 2-3	Helsinki	Fr	Kanerva, Saario
8-08	Poland	L 1-7	Poznan	Fr	Laaksonen
12-08	Latvia	W 4-1	Riga	Fr	Koponen 2, Silve, Lonnberg
5-09	Estonia	D 1-1	Helsinki	Fr	Saario
12-06-1927	Sweden	L 2-6	Stockholm	Fr	Åström 2
15-06	Norway	L 1-3	Oslo	Fr	Åström
10-08	Estonia	L 1-2	Tallinn	Fr	Kulmala
11-09	Latvia	W 3-1	Helsinki	Fr	Korma, Koponen, OG
3-06-1928	Norway	L 0-6	Helsinki	Fr	
12-08	Estonia	D 2-2	Helsinki	Fr	Åström, Kanerva
19-08	Latvia	L 1-2	Riga	Fr	Lonnberg
2-09	Sweden	L 2-3	Helsinki	Fr	Kanerva, Malmgren
14-06-1929	Sweden	L 1-3	Stockholm	Fr	Koponen
18-06	Norway	L 0-4	Oslo	Fr	
25-07	Estonia	D 1-1	Tallinn	Fr	Koponen
27-08	Estonia	W 2-1	Helsinki	Fr	Koponen, Lonnberg
15-09	Latvia	W 3-1	Helsinki	Fr	Svanström, Närvänen, Suontausta
13-10	Denmark	L 0-8	Copenhagen	Fr	
20-10	Germany	L 0-4	Hamburg	Fr	
1-06-1930	Norway	L 2-6	Oslo	Fr	Åström, Saario
16-06	Denmark	L 1-6	Helsinki	Fr	Kanerva
4-08	Latvia	L 0-3	Riga	Fr	
6-08	Estonia	L 0-4	Tallinn	Fr	
28-09	Sweden	D 4-4	Helsinki	Fr	Lehtinen.L 3, Koponen
17-06-1931	Estonia	W 3-1	Helsinki	Fr	Åström 2, Strömsten
3-07	Sweden	L 2-8	Stockholm	Fr	Lintamo, Grönlund
19-08	Latvia	W 4-0	Helsinki	Fr	Grönlund 2, Malmgren, Åström
6-09	Norway	D 4-4	Helsinki	Fr	Åström 2, Kanerva, Salin
11-10	Denmark	W 3-2	Copenhagen	Fr	Strömsten 2, Åström
16-05-1932	Sweden	L 1-7	Stockholm	Fr	Kanerva
10-06	Sweden	L 1-3	Helsinki	Fr	Grönlund
17-06	Norway	L 1-2	Oslo	Fr	Grönlund
1-07	Germany	L 1-4	Helsinki	Fr	Åström
17-08	Estonia	W 3-0	Tallinn	Fr	Lintamo, Salin, OG
30-08	Denmark	W 4-2	Helsinki	Fr	Malmgren 2, Lintamo 2
14-07-1933	Sweden	L 0-2	Stockholm	Fr	
9-08	Lithuania	W 9-2	Helsinki	Fr	Ronkanen 2, Grönlund 2, Karjagin.L 2, Åström 2, Viinioksa

16-08	Estonia	W 2-1	Helsinki	Fr	Weckström, OG
3-09	Norway	L 1-5	Helsinki	Fr	Åström
8-10	Denmark	L 0-2	Copenhagen	Fr	
3-07-1934	Denmark	W 2-1	Helsinki	Fr	Salin, Taipale
8-08	Estonia	D 1-1	Tallinn	Fr	Taipale
14-08	Latvia	D 1-1	Riga	Fr	Kylmälä
16-08	Lithuania	L 0-1	Kaunas	Fr	
2-09	Norway	L 2-4	Oslo	Fr	Lonnberg 2
23-09	Sweden	W 5-4	Helsinki	Fr	Koponen 2, Lintamo 2, Åström
5-06-1935	Latvia	W 4-1	Helsinki	Fr	Weckström 2, Kanerva, Lintamo
12-06	Sweden	D 2-2	Stockholm	Fr	Weckström 2
7-08	Estonia	D 2-2	Helsinki	Fr	Larvo 2
18-08	Germany	L 0-6	Munich	Fr	
8-09	Norway	L 1-5	Helsinki	Fr	Larvo
6-10	Denmark	L 1-5	Copenhagen	Fr	Grönlund
30-06-1936	Denmark	L 1-4	Helsinki	Fr	Salin
6-08	Peru	L 3-7	Berlin	OGr1	Kanerva, Grönlund, Larvo
20-08	Estonia	D 2-2	Tallinn	Fr	Grönlund, Weckström
6-09	Norway	W 2-0	Oslo	Fr	Weckström, Lehtonen
27-09	Sweden	L 1-2	Helsinki	Fr	Kanerva
20-05-1937	England	L 0-8	Helsinki	Fr	
16-06	Sweden	L 0-4	Stockholm	WCq	
29-06	Germany	L 0-2	Helsinki	WCq	
19-08	Estonia	L 0-1	Turku	WCq	
5-09	Norway	L 0-2	Helsinki	Fr	
17-10	Denmark	L 1-2	Copenhagen	Fr	Mäkelä
15-06-1938	Sweden	L 0-2	Stockholm	Fr	
17-06	Norway	L 0-9	Oslo	Fr	
4-07	Sweden	L 2-4	Helsinki	Fr	Lintamo, Granström
17-08	Estonia	W 3-1	Tallinn	Fr	Weckström, Eronen, Lehtonen
31-08	Denmark	W 2-1	Helsinki	Fr	Lintamo, Lehtonen
18-09	Lithuania	W 3-1	Helsinki	Fr	Lehtonen 3
9-06-1939	Sweden	L 1-5	Stockholm	Fr	OG
15-06	Denmark	L 0-5	Copenhagen	Fr	
20-07	Italy	L 2-3	Helsinki	Fr	Lehtonen, Weckström
4-08	Estonia	W 4-2	Helsinki	Fr	Kylmälä 3, Eronen
3-09	Norway	L 1-2	Helsinki	Fr	Eronen
17-09	Denmark	L 1-8	Copenhagen	Fr	Granström
24-09	Latvia	L 0-3	Helsinki	Fr	
29-08-1940	Sweden	L 2-3	Helsinki	Fr	Weckström, Beijar
1-09	Germany	L 0-13	Leipzig	Fr	
22-09	Sweden	L 0-5	Stockholm	Fr	
5-10-1941	Germany	L 0-6	Helsinki	Fr	
15-09-1943	Hungary	L 0-3	Helsinki	Fr	
3-10	Sweden	D 1-1	Helsinki	Fr	Teräs
26-08-1945	Sweden	L 2-7	Gothenburg	Fr	Beijar 2
30-09	Sweden	L 1-6	Helsinki	Fr	Sotiola
28-06-1946	Norway	L 0-12	Bergen	Fr	
1-09	Denmark	L 2-5	Helsinki	Fr	Svahn, Beijar
15-09	Sweden	L 0-7	Helsinki	Fr	
26-06-1947	Norway	L 1-2	Helsinki	Fr	Hasso
24-08	Sweden	L 0-7	Boras	Fr	
7-09	Norway	D 3-3	Helsinki	Fr	Myntti 2, Reunanen
17-09	Poland	L 1-4	Helsinki	Fr	Forsman
5-10	Denmark	L 1-4	Aarhus	Fr	Stolpe
15-06-1948	Denmark	L 0-3	Helsinki	Fr	
2-07	Iceland	L 0-2	Reykjavik	Fr	
5-09	Norway	L 0-2	Oslo	Fr	
19-09	Sweden	D 2-2	Helsinki	Fr	Lehtovirta, Rytkönen
17-10	Poland	L 0-1	Warsaw	Fr	
16-06-1949	Holland	L 1-4	Helsinki	Fr	Reunanen
8-07	Norway	D 1-1	Helsinki	Fr	Vaihela
8-09	Rep. Ireland	L 0-3	Dublin	WCq	
11-09	Denmark	W 2-0	Copenhagen	Fr	Asikainen, Rytkönen
2-10	Sweden	L 1-8	Malmo	Fr	Vaihela
9-10	Rep. Ireland	D 1-1	Helsinki	WCq	Vaihela
11-06-1950	Holland	W 4-1	Helsinki	Fr	Myntti, Asikainen, Rytkönen, Vaihela
27-08	Denmark	L 1-2	Helsinki	Fr	Asikainen
7-09	Yugoslavia	W 3-2	Helsinki	Fr	Vaihela, Asikainen, Lehtovirta
10-09	Norway	L 1-4	Oslo	Fr	Lilja
24-09	Sweden	L 0-1	Helsinki	Fr	

16-08-1951	Norway	D 1-1	Helsinki	Fr	Vaihela
2-09	Sweden	L 2-3	Stockholm	Fr	Vaihela, Lehtovirta
30-09	Denmark	L 0-1	Copenhagen	Fr	
27-10	Holland	D 4-4	Rotterdam	Fr	Lehtovirta 2, Vaihela, Rytkonen
4-11	Luxembourg	L 0-3	Luxembourg	Fr	
18-11	Hungary	L 0-8	Budapest	Fr	
10-06-1952	Norway	W 2-1	Oslo	Fr	Rikberg 2
13-06	Sweden	W 3-1	Oslo	Fr	Rikberg 2, Vaihela
22-06	Hungary	L 1-6	Helsinki	Fr	Lehtovirta
4-08	China	W 4-0	Helsinki	Fr	Vaihela 2, Pelkonen, Stolpe
31-08	Norway	L 2-7	Oslo	Fr	Lehtovirta, Rikberg
21-09	Sweden	L 1-8	Helsinki	Fr	Pelkonen
5-10	Denmark	W 2-1	Helsinki	Fr	Rikberg, Rytkönen
25-05-1953	Belgium	L 2-4	Helsinki	WCq	Lehtovirta 2
5-08	Sweden	D 3-3	Helsinki	WCq	Lehtovirta, Lahtinen, Rikberg
16-08	Sweden	L 0-4	Stockholm	WCq	
30-08	Norway	L 1-4	Helsinki	Fr	Lahtinen
23-09	Belgium	D 2-2	Brussels	WCq	Lahtinen, Vaihela
4-10	Denmark	L 1-6	Copenhagen	Fr	OG
25-05-1954	Scotland	L 1-2	Helsinki	Fr	Lahtinen
4-06	Sweden	L 0-6	Gothenburg	Fr	
13-06	Denmark	D 2-2	Helsinki	Fr	Myntti, Hiltunen
15-08	Sweden	L 1-10	Helsinki	Fr	Lahtinen
29-08	Norway	L 1-3	Oslo	Fr	Hiltunen
19-05-1955	Hungary	L 1-9	Helsinki	Fr	Hiltunen
19-06	Denmark	L 1-2	Copenhagen	Fr	Lehmusvirta
14-08	Norway	L 1-3	Helsinki	Fr	Hiltunen
28-08	Sweden	L 0-3	Halsingborg	Fr	
11-09	Poland	L 1-3	Helsinki	Fr	Asikainen
20-05-1956	England	L 1-5	Helsinki	Fr	Forsgren
10-06	Sweden	L 1-3	Helsinki	Fr	Lahtinen
29-06	Iceland	W 2-1	Helsinki	Fr	Forsgren 2
26-08	Norway	D 1-1	Oslo	Fr	Forsgren
16-09	Denmark	L 0-4	Helsinki	Fr	
4-11	Poland	L 0-5	Krakow	Fr	
18-06-1957	Denmark	W 2-0	Helsinki	Fr	Pahlman, Vanhanen
19-06	Sweden	L 1-5	Helsinki	Fr	Myntti
5-07	Poland	L 1-3	Helsinki	WCq	Vanhanen
27-07	Soviet Union	L 1-2	Moscow	WCq	Lahtinen
15-08	Soviet Union	L 0-10	Helsinki	WCq	
1-09	Norway	L 0-4	Helsinki	Fr	
22-09	Sweden	L 1-5	Stockholm	Fr	Sundelin
13-10	Denmark	L 0-3	Copenhagen	Fr	
3-11	Poland	L 0-4	Warsaw	WCq	
15-06-1958	Norway	L 0-2	Oslo	Fr	
20-08	Sweden	L 1-7	Helsinki	Fr	Korpela
14-09	Denmark	L 1-4	Helsinki	Fr	Pahlman
28-06-1959	Norway	L 2-4	Helsinki	Fr	Kankkonen 2
2-08	Sweden	L 1-3	Malmo	Fr	Nevalainen
6-09	East Germany	W 3-2	Helsinki	Fr	Pahlman, Hiltunen, Rosqvist
4-10	Denmark	L 0-4	Copenhagen	Fr	
18-10	Poland	L 1-3	Helsinki	OGq	Kankkonen
8-11	Poland	L 2-6	Chorzow	OGq	Österlund.T (II), Peltonen
22-06-1960	Sweden	L 0-3	Helsinki	Fr	
10-08	Denmark	L 1-2	Copenhagen	Fr	OG
28-08	Norway	L 3-6	Oslo	Fr	Kankkonen 2, Pahlman
25-09	France	L 1-2	Helsinki	WCq	Pahlman
30-10	East Germany	L 1-5	Rostock	Fr	Rytkönen
16-06-1961	Bulgaria	L 0-2	Helsinki	WCq	
27-06	Norway	W 4-1	Helsinki	Fr	Pahlman, Holmqvist, Mäkelä, Nuovanen
9-08	Sweden	L 0-4	Norrkoping	Fr	
28-09	France	L 1-5	Paris	WCq	Pahlman
15-10	Denmark	L 1-9	Copenhagen	Fr	Österlund.T (II)
29-10	Bulgaria	L 1-3	Sofia	WCq	Pietiläinen
19-06-1962	Sweden	L 0-3	Helsinki	Fr	
26-08	Norway	L 1-2	Bergen	Fr	Mäkelä
16-09	Denmark	L 1-6	Helsinki	Fr	Virtanen
3-06-1963	Denmark	D 1-1	Copenhagen	Fr	Pahlman
27-06	Norway	W 2-0	Helsinki	Fr	Pahlman, Lyytikäinen
14-08	Sweden	D 0-0	Stockholm	Fr	
7-06-1964	West Germany	L 1-4	Helsinki	Fr	Peltonen

Date	Opponent	Result	Venue	Type	Scorers
2-08	Sweden	W 1-0	Helsinki	Fr	Järvi
20-08	Norway	L 0-2	Trondheim	Fr	
23-08	Iceland	W 2-0	Reykjavik	Fr	Järvi, Kestilä
6-09	Denmark	W 2-1	Helsinki	Fr	Järvi, Peltonen
21-10	Scotland	L 1-3	Glasgow	WCq	Peltonen
4-11	Italy	L 1-6	Genoa	WCq	Peltonen
27-05-1965	Scotland	L 1-2	Helsinki	WCq	Hyvärinen
9-06	Denmark	L 1-3	Copenhagen	Fr	Tolsa
23-06	Italy	L 0-2	Helsinki	WCq	
8-08	Norway	W 4-0	Helsinki	Fr	Pahlman, Mäkilä, Kumpulampi, Lindholm
22-08	Sweden	D 2-2	Lulea	Fr	Pahlman, Mäkilä
26-09	Poland	W 2-0	Helsinki	WCq	Peltonen, Nuoranen
24-10	Poland	L 0-7	Szczecin	WCq	
8-05-1966	Israel	L 0-3	Helsinki	Fr	
4-06	Sweden	W 1-0	Helsinki	Fr	Lindholm
26-06	England	L 0-3	Helsinki	Fr	
14-08	Norway	D 1-1	Stavanger	Fr	Lindholm
18-09	Denmark	W 2-1	Helsinki	Fr	Mäkipää, Laine
2-10	Austria	D 0-0	Helsinki	ECq	
16-10	Greece	L 1-2	Salonica	ECq	Mäkipää
10-05-1967	Greece	D 1-1	Helsinki	ECq	Peltonen
1-06	Norway	L 0-2	Helsinki	Fr	
10-08	Sweden	L 0-2	Stockholm	Fr	
30-08	Soviet Union	L 0-2	Moscow	ECq	
6-09	Soviet Union	L 2-5	Turku	ECq	Peltonen, Syriävaara
24-09	Austria	L 1-2	Vienna	ECq	Peltonen
22-10	Denmark	L 0-3	Copenhagen	Fr	
4-06-1968	Denmark	L 1-3	Helsinki	Fr	Tolsa
19-06	Belgium	L 1-2	Helsinki	WCq	Flink
18-08	Norway	L 1-4	Oslo	Fr	Tolsa
11-09	Sweden	L 0-3	Helsinki	Fr	
25-09	Yugoslavia	L 1-9	Belgrade	WCq	Tolsa
9-10	Belgium	L 1-6	Waregem	WCq	Lindholm
22-05-1969	Sweden	L 0-4	Vaxjo	Fr	
4-06	Yugoslavia	L 1-5	Helsinki	WCq	Tolsa
25-06	Spain	W 2-0	Helsinki	WCq	Lindholm, Tolsa
24-07	Iceland	W 3-1	Helsinki	Fr	Lindholm, Rissanen, OG
24-08	Norway	D 2-2	Helsinki	Fr	Lindholm, Tolsa
10-09	Denmark	L 2-5	Copenhagen	Fr	Lindholm, Tolsa
15-10	Spain	L 0-6	La Concepcion	WCq	
3-06-1970	Denmark	D 1-1	Helsinki	Fr	Tolsa
17-06	Norway	L 0-2	Bergen	Fr	
26-08	Sweden	L 1-2	Helsinki	Fr	Lindholm
7-10	Czechoslovakia	D 1-1	Prague	ECq	Paatelainen
11-10	Romania	L 0-3	Bucharest	ECq	
20-05-1971	Sweden	L 1-4	Boras	Fr	Paatelainen
26-05	Wales	L 0-1	Helsinki	ECq	
16-06	Czechoslovakia	L 0-4	Helsinki	ECq	
24-08	Norway	D 1-1	Helsinki	Fr	Suhonen
8-09	Denmark	D 0-0	Copenhagen	Fr	
22-09	Romania	L 0-4	Helsinki	ECq	
13-10	Wales	L 0-3	Swansea	ECq	
31-05-1972	Norway	D 0-0	Turku	Fr	
7-06	Denmark	L 0-3	Copenhagen	Fr	
21-06	Albania	W 1-0	Helsinki	WCq	Toivola
16-07	Soviet Union	D 1-1	Vaasa	Fr	Rissanen
20-09	Romania	D 1-1	Helsinki	WCq	Rissanen
7-10	East Germany	L 0-5	Dresden	WCq	
6-06-1973	East Germany	L 1-5	Tampere	WCq	Manninen
8-07	Sweden	D 1-1	Halmstad	Fr	Suomalainen
29-08	Sweden	L 1-2	Helsinki	Fr	Suhonen
10-10	Albania	L 0-1	Tirana	WCq	
14-10	Romania	L 0-9	Bucharest	WCq	
6-06-1974	Denmark	D 1-1	Oulu	Fr	Paatelainen
15-08	Norway	W 2-1	Oslo	Fr	Tiovola, Linholm
19-08	Iceland	D 2-2	Reykjavik	Fr	Paatelainen, Laine
1-09	Poland	L 1-2	Helsinki	ECq	Rahja
25-09	Holland	L 1-3	Helsinki	ECq	Rahja
9-10	Poland	L 0-3	Poznan	ECq	
5-06-1975	Italy	L 0-1	Helsinki	ECq	
25-05	Denmark	L 0-2	Copenhagen	Fr	

3-09	Holland	L 1-4	Nijmegen	ECq	Paatelainen
27-09	Italy	D 0-0	Rome	ECq	
19-05-1976	Switzerland	W 1-0	Kuopio	Fr	Jantunen
1-06	Sweden	L 0-2	Helsinki	Fr	
13-06	England	L 1-4	Helsinki	WCq	Paatelainen
14-07	Iceland	W 1-0	Helsinki	Fr	Heiskanen.H
11-08	Sweden	L 0-6	Malmo	Fr	
25-08	Turkey	W 2-1	Helsinki	Fr	Heiskanen.A, Paatelainen
8-09	Scotland	L 0-6	Glasgow	Fr	
22-09	Luxembourg	W 7-1	Helsinki	WCq	Rissanen 2, Heiskanen.E 2, Heiskanen.A, Heikkinen, Maekynen
13-10	England	L 1-2	London	WCq	Nieminen
6-04-1977	Turkey	W 2-1	Ankara	Fr	Paatelainen, Nieminen
26-05	Luxembourg	W 1-0	Luxembourg	WCq	Heiskanen.A
8-06	Italy	L 0-3	Helsinki	WCq	
22-06	Denmark	L 1-2	Helsinki	Fr	Nieminen
18-08	Norway	D 1-1	Oslo	Fr	Paatelainen
7-09	West Germany	L 0-1	Helsinki	Fr	
5-10	Switzerland	L 0-2	Zurich	Fr	
15-10	Italy	L 1-6	Turin	WCq	Haaskivi
5-04-1978	Soviet Union	L 2-10	Erevan	Fr	Heiskanen.A, Nieminen
3-05	Mexico	L 0-1	Helsinki	Fr	
24-05	Greece	W 3-0	Helsinki	ECq	Ismail 2, Nieminen
28-06	Sweden	L 1-2	Boras	Fr	Ismail
9-08	Norway	D 1-1	Helsinki	Fr	Ismail
30-08	Poland	L 0-1	Helsinki	Fr	
20-09	Hungary	W 2-1	Helsinki	ECq	Ismail, Pyykko
11-10	Greece	L 1-8	Athens	ECq	Heiskanen.A
5-02-1979	Iraq	L 0-1	Baghdad	Fr	
7-02	Iraq	L 0-2	Baghdad	Fr	
9-02	Bahrain	W 1-0	Manama	Fr	Backman
4-07	Soviet Union	D 1-1	Helsinki	ECq	Ismail
21-08	Norway	L 0-1	Kuopio	OGq	
29-08	Denmark	D 0-0	Mikkeli	Fr	
26-09	Denmark	L 0-1	Copenhagen	Fr	
17-10	Hungary	L 1-3	Debrecen	ECq	Toivola
26-10	Norway	D 1-1	Stavanger	OGq	Rautiainen
31-10	Soviet Union	D 2-2	Moscow	ECq	Hakala, Haaskivi
21-11	Mexico	D 1-1	Mexico City	Fr	Nieminen
26-11	Bermuda	W 2-0	Hamilton	Fr	Nieminen, Himanka
22-05-1980	Sweden	L 0-2	Helsinki	Fr	
4-06	Bulgaria	L 0-2	Helsinki	WCq	
25-06	Iceland	D 1-1	Reykjavik	Fr	Tissari
21-08	Norway	L 1-6	Oslo	Fr	Himanka
3-09	Albania	L 0-2	Tirana	WCq	
24-09	Austria	L 0-2	Helsinki	WCq	
30-11	Bolivia	L 0-3	La Paz	Fr	
4-12	Bolivia	D 2-2	Santa Cruz	Fr	Jaakonsaari, Valvee
8-12	Uruguay	L 0-6	Montevideo	Fr	
1-03-1981	Sweden	W 2-1	Lahti	Fr	
13-05	Bulgaria	L 0-4	Sofia	WCq	
24-05	West Germany	L 0-4	Lahti	WCq	
17-06	Austria	L 1-5	Linz	WCq	Valvee
2-07	Norway	W 3-1	Helsinki	Fr	Kousa, Rajaniemi, Turunen
29-07	Sweden	L 0-1	Halmstad	Fr	
12-08	Denmark	L 1-2	Tampere	Fr	Valvee
2-09	Albania	W 2-1	Kotka	WCq	Houtsonen, Kousa
23-09	West Germany	L 1-7	Bochum	WCq	Turunen
20-02-1982	Sweden	D 2-2	Lahti	Fr	Jaakonsaari 2
21-02	Sweden	W 2-1	Lahti	Fr	Jaakonsaari, Ikalainen
28-04	Norway	D 1-1	Stavanger	Fr	Nieminen
3-06	England	L 1-4	Helsinki	Fr	Haaskivi
11-07	Iceland	W 3-2	Helsinki	Fr	Ismail, Himanka, Kousa
11-08	Denmark	L 2-3	Copenhagen	Fr	Valvee, Turunen
8-09	Poland	L 2-3	Kuopio	ECq	Valvee, Kousa
22-09	Portugal	L 0-2	Helsinki	ECq	
13-10	Soviet Union	L 0-2	Moscow	ECq	
16-03-1983	East Germany	L 1-3	Magdeburg	Fr	Hjelm
17-04	Poland	D 1-1	Warsaw	ECq	OG
1-06	Soviet Union	L 0-1	Helsinki	ECq	
7-09	Sweden	L 0-3	Helsinki	Fr	

21-09	Portugal	L 0-5	Lisbon	ECq	
9-03-1984	Kuwait	L 0-1	Kuwait	Fr	
15-05	Soviet Union	L 1-3	Kouvola	Fr	Rantanen
27-05	Nth. Ireland	W 1-0	Pori	WCq	Valvee
16-08	Mexico	L 0-3	Helsinki	Fr	
12-09	Poland	L 0-2	Helsinki	Fr	
17-10	England	L 0-5	London	WCq	
31-10	Turkey	W 2-1	Antalya	WCq	Hjelm, Lipponen
14-11	Nth. Ireland	L 1-2	Belfast	WCq	Lipponen
20-11	Saudi Arabia	L 1-2	Jubayl	Fr	Hjelm
22-11	Qatar	D 2-2	Doha	Fr	Pekonen, Remes
24-11	Qatar	D 1-1	Doha	Fr	Hjelm
23-01-1985	Spain	L 1-3	Alicante	Fr	Lipponen
8-02	Chile	L 0-2	Viña del Mar	Fr	
14-02	Uruguay	L 1-2	Montevideo	Fr	Valvee
17-02	Ecuador	L 1-3	Ambato	Fr	Nieminen
26-02	Mexico	L 1-2	Acapulco	Fr	Pekonen
17-04	Poland	L 1-2	Opole	Fr	Ukkonen
22-05	England	D 1-1	Helsinki	WCq	Rantanen
6-06	Romania	D 1-1	Helsinki	WCq	Lipponen
28-08	Romania	L 0-2	Timisoara	WCq	
25-09	Turkey	W 1-0	Tampere	WCq	Rantenen
22-01-1986	Portugal	D 1-1	Leiria	Fr	Hjelm
22-02	Bahrain	D 0-0	Manama	Fr	
24-02	Bahrain	W 4-0	Manama	Fr	Valvee, Tornvall, Ikalainen, Rasimus
17-04	Brazil	L 0-3	Brasilia	Fr	
7-05	Soviet Union	D 0-0	Moscow	Fr	
6-08	Sweden	L 1-3	Helsinki	Fr	Lipponen
20-08	East Germany	W 1-0	Lahti	Fr	Hjelm
10-09	Wales	D 1-1	Helsinki	ECq	Hjelm
15-10	Czechoslovakia	L 0-3	Brno	ECq	
29-10	Denmark	L 0-1	Copenhagen	ECq	
18-03-1987	Poland	L 1-3	Rybnik	Fr	Ikalainen
1-04	Wales	L 0-4	Wrexham	ECq	
29-04	Denmark	L 0-1	Helsinki	ECq	
28-05	Brazil	L 2-3	Helsinki	Fr	Hjelm, Lius
9-09	Czechoslovakia	W 3-0	Helsinki	ECq	Hjelm, Lius, Tiainen
12-01-1988	Czechoslovakia	W 2-0	Las Palmas	Fr	Paatelainen.M, Alatensio
15-01	Sweden	L 0-1	Las Palmas	Fr	
7-02	Malta	L 0-2	Ta'Qali	Fr	
13-02	Tunisia	W 3-0	Ta'Qali	Fr	Lipponen 3
19-05	Colombia	L 1-3	Helsinki	Fr	Rantanen
4-08	Bulgaria	D 1-1	Vaasa	Fr	Myyry
17-08	Soviet Union	D 0-0	Turku	Fr	
31-08	West Germany	L 0-4	Helsinki	WCq	
19-10	Wales	D 2-2	Swansea	WCq	Ukkonen, Paatelainen.M
3-11	Kuwait	D 0-0	Kuwait City	Fr	
6-11	Kuwait	D 0-0	Kuwait City	Fr	
11-01-1989	Egypt	L 1-2	El Mehalla	Fr	Paatelainen.M
13-01	Egypt	L 1-2	Cairo	Fr	Tarkkio
8-02	Algeria	L 0-2	Ta'Qali	Fr	
10-02	Denmark	D 0-0	Ta'Qali	Fr	
12-02	Malta	D 0-0	Ta'Qali	Fr	
22-03	East Germany	D 1-1	Dresden	Fr	Lipponen
31-05	Holland	L 0-1	Helsinki	WCq	
23-08	Yugoslavia	D 2-2	Kuopio	Fr	Tarkkio, Ukkonen
6-09	Wales	W 1-0	Helsinki	WCq	Lipponen
4-10	West Germany	L 1-6	Dortmund	WCq	Lipponen
22-10	Trinidad	W 1-0	Port of Spain	Fr	Lius
25-10	Trinidad	L 0-2	Port of Spain	Fr	
15-11	Holland	L 0-3	Rotterdam	WCq	
12-02-1990	Arab Emirates	D 1-1	Dubai	Fr	Tiainen
15-02	Kuwait	W 1-0	Cairo	Fr	Aaltonen.M
1-03	USA	L 1-2	Tampa	Fr	Tarkkio
16-05	Rep. Ireland	D 1-1	Dublin	Fr	Tauriainen
27-05	Sweden	L 0-6	Stockholm	Fr	
29-08	Czechoslovakia	D 1-1	Kuusankoski	Fr	Jarvinen
12-09	Portugal	D 0-0	Helsinki	ECq	
11-11	Tunisia	W 2-1	Tunis	Fr	Paatelainen.M, Tegelberg
25-11	Malta	D 1-1	Ta'Qali	ECq	Holmgren
13-03-1991	Poland	D 1-1	Warsaw	Fr	Paatelainen.M
17-04	Holland	L 0-2	Rotterdam	ECq	

16-05	Malta	W 2-0	Helsinki	ECq	Jarvinen, Litmanen
5-06	Holland	D 1-1	Helsinki	ECq	Holmgren
11-09	Portugal	L 0-1	Oporto	ECq	
9-10	Greece	D 1-1	Helsinki	ECq	Ukkonen
30-10	Greece	L 0-2	Athens	ECq	
12-02-1992	Turkey	D 1-1	Adana	Fr	Karvinen
25-03	Scotland	D 1-1	Glasgow	Fr	Litmanen
15-04	Brazil	L 1-3	Cuiaba	Fr	Vanhala
14-05	Bulgaria	L 0-3	Helsinki	WCq	
3-06	England	L 1-2	Helsinki	Fr	Hjelm
26-08	Poland	D 0-0	Pietarsaari	Fr	
9-09	Sweden	L 0-1	Helsinki	WCq	
7-11	Tunisia	D 1-1	Tunis	Fr	Hjelm
14-11	France	L 1-2	Paris	WCq	Jarvinen
20-01-1993	India	D 0-0	Madras	Fr	
22-01	Cameroon	D 0-0	Madras	Fr	
26-01	India	W 2-0	Madras	Fr	Tauriainen, Rajamaki
28-01	Cameroon	L 0-2	Madras	Fr	
31-01	North Korea	L 2-3	Madras	Fr	Karvinen, Rajamaki
20-02	Estonia	D 0-0	Vantaa	BC	
21-02	Lithuania	W 3-0	Vantaa	BC	Gronholm, Ruhanen, Kinnunen
13-04	Poland	L 1-2	Radom	Fr	Heikkinen
28-04	Bulgaria	L 0-2	Sofia	WCq	
13-05	Austria	W 3-1	Turku	WCq	Paatelainen, Rajamaki, Hjelm
16-06	Israel	D 0-0	Lahti	WCq	
25-08	Austria	L 0-3	Vienna	WCq	
8-09	France	L 0-2	Tampere	WCq	
13-10	Sweden	L 2-3	Stockholm	WCq	Suominen, Litmanen
10-11	Israel	W 3-1	Tel Aviv	WCq	Hyrylainen, Paavola, Hjelm
25-01-1994	Qatar	L 0-1	Doha	Fr	
27-01	Qatar	D 0-0	Doha	Fr	
30-01	Oman	W 2-0	Muscat	Fr	Kanerva, Suominen
1-02	Oman	D 1-1	Muscat	Fr	Gronholm
23-02	Morocco	D 0-0	Casablanca	Fr	
27-05	Italy	L 0-2	Parma	Fr	
2-06	Spain	L 1-2	Tampere	Fr	Jarvinen
17-08	Denmark	L 1-2	Copenhagen	Fr	Suominen
7-09	Scotland	L 0-2	Helsinki	ECq	
12-10	Greece	0-4	Salonica	ECq	
26-10	Estonia	W 7-0	Tallinn	Fr	Eriksson, Ruhanen 2, Sumiala 2, Hjelm 2
16-11	Faeroe Islands	W 5-0	Helsinki	ECq	Sumiala, Litmanen 2, Paatelainen 2
30-11	Spain	L 0-2	Malaga	Fr	
14-12	San Marino	W 4-1	Helsinki	ECq	Paatelainen 4
8-03-1995	Czech Republic	L 1-4	Brno	ECq	Hjelm
29-03	San Marino	W 2-0	Serravalle	ECq	Litmanen, Sumiala
26-04	Faeroe Islands	W 4-0	Toftir	ECq	Hjelm, Paatelainen, Lindberg, Helin
31-05	Denmark	L 0-1	Helsinki	Fr	
11-06	Greece	W 2-1	Helsinki	ECq	Litmanen, Hjelm

FRANCE

France is a footballing enigma. Along with England, Italy, Germany, and Spain, Europe's other dominant countries, the French have the capability to become a world power, but so far they have not realised that potential. This has been particularly true at club level where low attendances and general apathy have left France trailing behind the likes of Sweden in the European club competitions.

The national side have had their moments, however. They finished in third place in the 1958 World Cup, and in the 1980s they produced one of the most exciting teams Europe has ever seen, peaking with a victory in the 1984 European Championship.

If the English were responsible for inventing modern football and bringing it to the world, we have the French to thank for organising it and creating both the World Cup and European Championship. It is somewhat surprising, therefore, that the prime movers behind the formation of both FIFA and UEFA should have produced nothing but chaos in the organisation of the game at home. No fewer than five different bodies vied for control of the game before the present federation was founded in 1918.

In France, rugby was by far the more popular game at the turn of the century and football clubs were often offshoots of rugby clubs. The oldest, Le Havre Athletic Club, was an example of this. It was founded in 1872, but it was not until 1892 that a football section was formed. Up until that point, only rugby was played. Racing Club de France were another such club. Formed in 1882, they remain the standard bearers of French rugby, but it was not until 1932 that they formed a professional football section, Racing Club de Paris, and became involved in the round-ball game. White Rovers, Gordon and Club Francais, the first clubs devoted entirely to football, were founded in 1892.

The north of France was a popular venue for tours by English teams before the turn of the century and it was here that the game was played most, but football (and rugby) soon spread throughout the country. Various leagues were formed by the different bodies who claimed responsibility for the game, but the first proper competition, the French Cup, was not launched until 1918 with the formation of the Federation Francaise de Football. Open to teams from the whole of France, the competition proved a huge success. Although attempts were made to form a national league in the late 1920s, it was not until the FFF sanctioned professionalism in 1932 that a proper league structure was set up.

France had more success in organising a national side in the early years. Many unofficial games had already taken place against sides from England, Belgium and Holland by the time of the first official match, against Belgium in Brussels in 1904. Four years later France entered the London Olympic Games only to be resoundingly thrashed 17-1 by Denmark. The turmoil in club football obviously did not help matters, but even after the war results did not improve. A new low was reached in 1927 when the national side lost 13-1 to Hungary in Budapest and all three pre-war World Cups brought disappointment for the French, not least in 1938 when they were chosen to host the event but made little impact.

The first signs of real progress in French football came after the war with the emergence of Stade de Reims, an outstanding team who boasted names like Albert Batteux, who in 1950 became their manager, Roger Marché, Robert Jonquet, Roger Piantoni, Jean Vincent, Raymond Kopa and Just Fontaine. Twice they lost to Real Madrid in the final of the European Cup, but these players also formed the basis for the national side that played so well to finish third in the 1958 World Cup.

However, this success was not built on and the game went into decline. France qualified for only one of the next four World Cups, and after reaching the semi-finals of the first European Championships in 1960 made little impression either in this tournament or the European club competitions. Saint-Étienne did their best to halt the decline, reaching the European Cup final in 1976, but not until the following decade was it really reversed.

Michel Platini had emerged in the late 1970s as the greatest player in French history and one of the best in the world. He soon left for the Italian league and an illustrious career with Juventus so the French championship did not see much of the benefit; but the national side did. At the 1978 World Cup, had they not been grouped with Argentina and Italy, who won the tournament and came fourth respectively, France would undoubtedly have progressed to the second phase. Four years later, the side was reaching maturity, with the midfield of Jean Tigana, Alain Giresse, Bernard Genghini and Platini being especially gifted. They should have beaten West Germany in the semi-final after leading 3-1 in extra-time, but in the penalty shoot-out that followed, poor Maxime Bossis fired his kick at Schumacher and France were out.

Two years later in the European Championships, justice was done as the national team won their first and only major honour. Admittedly they were playing at home, but the French at that time were without question the best side in Europe, and for Platini the tournament was a personal triumph that elevated his reputation to the level of players like Pele, Maradona, Beckenbauer and Cruyff. He scored nine goals in the five games that ultimately saw France beat Spain 2-0 in the final at Parc des Princes. In the same year he won the second of three European Footballer of the Year titles, the first of two World Footballer of the Year awards, and the Italian league and Cup Winners Cup with Juventus.

The 1986 World Cup in Mexico saw the French reach the semi-finals again, and once more they were undone by the Germans at the crucial stage, having already knocked out the holders Italy and many people's favourites Brazil. But failure to qualify for the 1988 European Championship finals and the 1990 World Cup seemed to signal another decline in French fortunes. The backbone of the 1980s team had gone and not been adequately replaced. For once, however, there was encouragement from the clubs both at home and in Europe.

THE ORDER OF MERIT

		All			League			Cup		Europe		
	Team	G	S	B	G	S	B	G	S	G	S	B
1	Olympique Mar.	19	13	5	8	6	3	10	6	1	1	-
2	AS Saint-Étienne	16	7	3	10	3	2	6	3	-	-	-
3	AS Monaco	10	8	8	5	4	6	5	3	-	1	2
4	FC Nantes	8	12	2	7	7	1	1	5	-	-	1
5	OSC Lille	8	10	1	3	6	1	5	4	-	-	-
6	Stade de Reims	8	6	4	6	3	4	2	1	-	2	-
7	Girondins Bord.	7	13	6	4	7	4	3	6	-	-	2
8	Racing Club Paris	6	4	5	1	2	5	5	2	-	-	-
9	OGC Nice	6	4	-	4	3	-	2	1	-	-	-
10	Paris Saint-Germain	6	3	6	2	2	3	4	1	-	-	3
11	Red Star Paris	5	1	-	-	-	-	5	1	-	-	-
12	FC Sète	4	4	1	2	-	1	2	4	-	-	-
13	FC Sochaux	3	6	5	2	3	4	1	3	-	-	1
14	Olympique Lyon	3	4	3	-	1	2	3	3	-	-	1
	Racing Club Strasb.	3	4	3	1	1	3	2	3	-	-	-
16	CO Roubaix-Tourc.	2	2	1	1	-	1	1	2	-	-	-
17	Stade Rennais	2	2	-	-	-	-	2	2	-	-	-
18	US Sedan-Torcy	2	1	2	-	-	2	2	1	-	-	-
19	FC Metz	2	1	1	-	-	1	2	1	-	-	-
20	CAS Generaux	2	-	-	-	-	-	2	-	-	-	-
21	SEC Bastia	1	2	1	-	-	1	1	1	-	1	-
22	AJ Auxerre	1	1	4	-	-	3	1	1	-	-	1
23	Le Havre AC	1	1	1	-	-	1	1	1	-	-	-
24	Montpellier HSC	1	1	1	-	-	1	1	1	-	-	-
	Toulouse FC	1	1	1	-	1	1	1	-	-	-	-
26	AS Cannes	1	1	-	-	1	-	1	-	-	-	-
	CA Paris	1	1	-	-	-	-	1	1	-	-	-
	SO Montpellier	1	1	-	-	-	-	1	1	-	-	-
29	Club Francais	1	-	-	-	-	-	1	-	-	-	-
	Nancy-Lorraine XI	1	-	-	-	-	-	1	-	-	-	-

	AS Nancy-Lorraine	1	-	-	-	-	-	1	-	-	-	-
	Olympique Pantin	1	-	-	-	-	-	1	-	-	-	-
33	Nîmes Olympique	-	6	1	-	4	1	-	2	-	-	-
34	Racing Club Lens	-	5	2	-	3	2	-	2	-	-	-
35	FC Nancy	-	2	-	-	-	-	-	2	-	-	-
	Olympique Paris	-	2	-	-	-	-	-	2	-	-	-
	US Valenciennes	-	1	2	-	-	2	-	1	-	-	-
38	SC Angers	-	1	1	-	-	1	-	1	-	-	-
39	US Charleville	-	1	-	-	-	-	-	1	-	-	-
	FC Lyon	-	1	-	-	-	-	-	1	-	-	-
	US Orléans	-	1	-	-	-	-	-	1	-	-	-
	US Quevilly	-	1	-	-	-	-	-	1	-	-	-
	Racing Club France	-	1	-	-	-	-	-	1	-	-	-
	Reims-Champagne XI	-	1	-	-	-	-	-	1	-	-	-
	FC Rouen	-	1	-	-	-	-	-	1	-	-	-
	FC Troyes-Aube	-	1	-	-	-	-	-	1	-	-	-
	AS Valentigney	-	1	-	-	-	-	-	1	-	-	-

To the end of the 1994-95 season

Transformed by the money and power of Bernard Tapie, Olympique Marseille won five consecutive league titles and, more important, became the first French side to win a European trophy. After losing on penalties to Red Star Belgrade in the 1991 European Cup final, they came back to win the tournament in 1993, upsetting the favourites Milan 1-0 in Munich. With Paris Saint-Germain finally giving Paris a club to be proud of, things had never been better in the league, while new players like Eric Cantona, Jean-Pierre Papin and Marcel Desailly were giving the national side renewed hope too. Under Platini, they qualified for the finals of the 1992 European Championships without dropping a point, the first team ever to do so. French football, it seemed, had arrived.

But things were about to go disastrously wrong. The national side's performances proved a false dawn and their failure in the finals in Sweden prompted Platini to resign. There was another setback in 1993/94 when France failed to qualify for the World Cup finals in America, while at the same time one of Europe's biggest bribery scandals was breaking over Marseille. It transpired that when OM played Valenciennes the week before the 1993 European Cup final, in a match which sealed another league championship for them, their opponents were paid to take things easy. Jacques Glassman blew the whistle on the whole 'affaire', as it became known, and his colleagues Jorge Burruchaga and Christophe Robert admitted to receiving money from Marseille's Jean-Jacques Eydelie. All received worldwide bans. Marseille were relegated, stripped of their 1993 title and forced to sell off their best players. Above all, they lost the patronage of Tapie, who was subsequently jailed. It was a sorry end to what had promised to be a proud era in French club football.

Population: 56,647,000
Area, sq km: 543,965
% in urban areas: 73.4%
Capital city: Paris

Fédération Française de Football
60 bis, Avenue d'léna
F-75783 Paris Cédex 16
France
Tel: + 33 1 44317300
Fax: + 33 1 47208296

Year of formation	1918
Affiliation to FIFA	1904
Affiliation to UEFA	1954
Registered clubs	21 186
Registered players	1 915 836
Professional Players	1400
Registered coaches	600
Registered referees	22 772
National stadium	Parc des Princes 49 000
National colours	Blue/White/Red
Reserve colours	White/Blue/Red
Season	August - June, with a mid season break December and January

THE RECORD

WORLD CUP

1930	QT Automatic Final Tournament/1st round
1934	QT 2nd/3 in group 12 - Final Tournament/1st round
1938	QT Automatic - Final Tournament/2nd round
1950	QT 2nd rd in group 3
1954	QT 1st/3 in group 4 - Final Tournament/1st round
1958	QT 1st/3 in group 2 - Final Tournament/Semi-finalists/3rd place
1962	QT 2nd/3 in group 2
1966	QT 1st/4 in group 3 - Final Tournament/1st round
1970	QT 2nd/3 in group 5
1974	QT 3rd/3 in group 9
1978	QT 1st/3 in group 5 - Final Tournament/1st round
1982	QT 2nd/5 in group 2 - Final Tournament/Semi-finalists/4th place
1986	QT 1st/5 in group 4 - Final Tournament/Semi-finalists/3rd place
1990	QT 3rd/5 in group 5
1994	QT 3rd/6 in group 6

EUROPEAN CHAMPIONSHIP

1960	Semi-finalists/4th place
1964	Quarter-finalists
1968	QT 1st/4 in group 7 - Final Tournament/Quarter-finalists
1972	QT 3rd/4 in group 2
1976	QT 3rd/4 in group 7
1980	QT 2nd/4 in group 5
1984	QT Automatic - Final Tournament/Winners
1988	QT 3rd/5 in group 3
1992	QT 1st/5 in group 1 - Final Tournament/1st round
1996	QT group 1

EUROPEAN CLUB COMPETITIONS

European Cup
Winners - Olympique Marseille 1993
Finalists - Stade de Reims 1956 1959 Saint-Étienne 1976 Olympique Marseille 1991

Cup Winners Cup
Finalists - AS Monaco 1992

UEFA Cup
Finalists - Bastia 1978

CLUB DIRECTORY

PARIS (Population - 9,775,000)

Paris Saint-Germain (1970)
Parc des Princes 48,000 – Red with blue stripes & sleeves/Blue
Previous name - Paris FC 1970-73

Racing Club de Paris
(1932-66 as the professional section of Racing Club de France)
Colombes 60,000 – Sky blue & white hoops/White
A separate club called Racing Club de Paris, also known as Matra Racing, was formed in 1982. It was reconstituted in 1991 as Racing 92

Red Star 93 (1897)
St Ouen 21,000 – Green/White
Previous names - Merged with Olympique de Paris to form Red Star Olympique 1926-46, Red Star Olympique Audonien 1946-48, Merged with Stade Français to form Stade Red Star 1948-50, Red Star Olympique Audonien 1950-67, Merged with FC Toulouse to form Red Star FC 1967-70

Stade Français (1883-1985)
Stade Mathieu – Blue/Red
Previous name - Stade Red Star 1948-50. Dissolved in 1985

Lyon (Population - 1,275,000)
Olympique Lyonnais (1950)
Stade de Gerland 45,000 – White, blue & red trim

MARSEILLE (Population - 1,225,000)
Olympique de Marseille (1898)
Stade Vélodrome 46,000 – White, light blue trim

LILLE (Population - 1,020,000)
Lille Olympique Sporting Club (1945)
Grimonprez-Jooris 24,000 – White, red trim
Previous names - Merger in 1945 of SC Fives (1908) and Olympique Lille (1910)

Club Olympique Roubaix-Tourcoing (1945)
Amade Prouvost – Red & black stripes/White
Previous name - Merger in 1945 of Racing, Excelsior and US Tourcoing

BORDEAUX (Population - 640,000)
Les Girondins de Bordeaux (1881)
Parc de Lescure 40,000 – White with a red V on chest/White

TOULOUSE (Population - 541,000)
Toulouse Football Club (1937)
Municipal 35,000 – White, violet trim
Previous name - Merged with Red Star as Red Star FC 1967-70

NANTES (Population - 464,000)
Football Club de Nantes (1943)
Stade de la Beaujoire 34,000 – Yellow & green stripes/Yellow

NICE (Population - 449,000)
Olympique Gymnaste Club de Nice (1904)
Municipal du Ray 12,000 – Red & blue stripes/Black

TOULON (Population - 410,000)
Sporting Club Toulon (1945)
Mayol 18,000 – Yellow/Blue

STRASBOURG (Population - 400,000)
Racing Club de Strasbourg (1906)
Stade de Meinau 45,000 – Blue/White

GRENOBLE (Population - 392,000)
Football Club Grenoble Dauphiné (1892)
Charles Berli – Red/Blue

ROUEN (Population - 379,000)
Football Club de Rouen (1923)
Robert Diochon – White/Red

VALENCIENNES (Population - 349,000)
Union Sportive Valenciennes-Anzin (1913)
Roland Nungesser 9,000 – Red/White

LENS (Population - 327,000)
Racing Club de Lens (1906)
Félix Bollaert 49,000 – Yellow/Red

SAINT-ÉTIENNE (Population - 317,000)
Association Sportive Saint-Étienne (1920)
Geoffroy Guichard 48,000 – Green/White

NANCY (Population 306,000)
Association Sportive Nancy-Lorraine (1935)
Marcel Picot 37,000 – White/White
Previous name - FC Nancy 1935-67

CANNES (Population - 295,000)
Association Sportive de Cannes (1902)
Pièrre de Coubertin 20,000 – Red, white trim

LE HAVRE (Population - 254,000)
Le Havre Athletic Club (1872)
Jules Deschaseaux 22,000 – Blue, light blue trim

RENNES (Population - 234,000)
Stade Rennais Football Club (1901)
Route de Lorient 21,000 – Red/White, black trim

MONTPELLIER (Population - 221,000)
Montpellier HSC (1974)
(Herault Sports-Club)
La Mosson 25,000 – Blue, white sleeves/Orange
Previous name - Sports Olympique Montpellier 1919-69. The club was dissolved in 1969, but was the forerunner of the present club

BREST (Population - 201,000)
Brest Amorique Football Club (1912)
Franci Le Blé – White/White
Previous name - Stade de Brest 1912-86

REIMS (Population - 199,000)
Stade de Reims (1931)
Auguste Delaune 18,000 – Red, white sleeves/White

ANGERS (Population - 195,000)
Sporting Club de l'Ouest Angers (1945)
Jean-Bouin 20,000 – White with a black V on chest/Black, red trim

ANGOULEME (Population - 103,000)
Angoulême Charente (1945)
Chazny – Blue/White

METZ (Population - 186,000)
Football Club Metz (1932)
Saint Symphorien 28,000 – Claret, white trim

CAEN (Population - 183,000)
Stade Malherbe de Caen (1913)
Michel d'Ornano 21,000 – Blue & red stripes/Blue

NIMES (Population - 132,000)
Nîmes Olympique (1901)
Stade des Costières 26,000 – Red/Red
Previous name - SC Nîmes 1901-37

MONTBELIARD (Population - 128,000)
Football Club Sochaux-Montbéliard (1928)
Auguste-Bonal 15,000 – Yellow/Blue

MONACO (Population - 87,000)
Association Sportive de Monaco (1924)
Louis II 18,000 – Red & white diagonal halves/Red

LAVAL (Population - 55,000)
Stade Lavallois (1902)
Francis Le Basser 18,000 – Tangerine/Black

BASTIA (Population - 50,000)
Sporting Club Bastia (1962)
Armand-Césari de Furiani 8,000 – Blue & white stripes/White

AUXERRE (Population - 40,000)
Association de la Jeunesse Auxerroise (1905)
Abbé-Deschamps 22,000 – White, blue trim

SETE (Population - 39,000)
Football Club de Sète (1914)
Georges Bayrou 11,000 – Green & white stripes/Black

SEDAN (Population - 23,000)
US Sedan-Torcy (1953)
Emile Albeau 15,000 – Green/Red

FRENCH LEAGUE CHAMPIONSHIP

1933	Olympique Lille 4-3 AS Cannes
1934n	FC Sete 34 SC Fives 33 Olympique Marseille 33
1935q	FC Sochaux 48 RC Strasbourg 47 Racing Club Paris 37
1936	Racing Club Paris 44 Olympique Lille 41 RC Strasbourg 39
1937	Olympique Marseille 38 FC Sochaux 38 Racing Club Paris 37
1938	FC Sochaux 44 Olympique Marseille 42 FC Sete 41
1939	FC Sète 42 Olympique Marseille 40 Racing Club Paris 38

1940-45	-
1946t	OSC Lille 45 AS Saint-Étienne 44 CO Roubaix 41
1947v	CO Roubaix 53 Stade de Reims 49 RC Strasbourg 49
1948t	Olympique Marseille 48 OSC Lille 47 Stade de Reims 46
1949	Stade de Reims 48 OSC Lille 47 Olympique Marseille 42
1950	Girondins Bordeaux 51 OSC Lille 45 Stade de Reims 44
1951	OGC Nice 41 OSC Lille 41 Le Havre AC 40
1952	OGC Nice 46 Girondins Bordeaux 45 OSC Lille 44
1953	Stade de Reims 48 FC Sochaux 44 Girondins Bordeaux 43
1954	OSC Lille 47 Stade de Reims 46 Girondins Bordeaux 46
1955	Stade de Reims 44 Toulouse FC 40 RC Lens 38
1956	OGC Nice 43 RC Lens 42 AS Monaco 41
1957	AS Saint-Étienne 49 RC Lens 45 Stade de Reims 43
1958	Stade de Reims 48 Nîmes Olympique 41 AS Monaco 41
1959v	OGC Nice 56 Nîmes Olympique 53 Racing Club Paris 49
1960	Stade de Reims 60 Nîmes Olympique 53 Racing Club Paris 49
1961	AS Monaco 57 Racing Club Paris 56 Stade de Reims 50
1962	Stade de Reims 48 Racing Club Paris 48 Nîmes Olympique 47
1963	AS Monaco 50 Stade de Reims 47 FC Sedan 46
1964t	AS Saint-Étienne 44 AS Monaco 41 RC Lens 40
1965	FC Nantes 43 Girondins Bordeaux 41 US Valenciennes 40
1966v	FC Nantes 60 Girondins Bordeaux 53 US Valenciennes 52
1967	AS Saint-Étienne 54 FC Nantes 50 SC Angers 44
1968	AS Saint-Étienne 57 OGC Nice 46 FC Sochaux 43
1969t	AS Saint-Étienne 53 Girondins Bordeaux 51 FC Metz 42
1970	AS Saint-Étienne 56 Olympique Marseille 45 RCP Sedan 42
1971v	Olympique Marseille 55 AS Saint-Étienne 51 FC Nantes 46
1972	Olympique Marseille 56 Nîmes Olympique 51 FC Sochaux 47
1973	FC Nantes 55 OGC Nice 50 Olympique Marseille 48
1974	AS Saint-Étienne 66 FC Nantes 58 Olympique Lyon 55
1975	AS Saint-Étienne 58 Olympique Marseille 49 Olympique Lyon 48
1976	AS Saint-Étienne 57 OGC Nice 54 FC Sochaux 52
1977	FC Nantes 58 RC Lens 49 SEC Bastia 47
1978	AS Monaco 53 FC Nantes 52 RC Strasbourg 50
1979	RC Strasbourg 56 FC Nantes 54 AS Saint-Étienne 54
1980	FC Nantes 57 FC Sochaux 54 AS Saint-Étienne 54
1981	AS Saint-Étienne 57 FC Nantes 55 Girondins Bordeaux 49
1982	AS Monaco 55 AS Saint-Étienne 54 FC Sochaux 49
1983	FC Nantes 58 Girondins Bordeaux 48 Paris Saint-Germain 47
1984	Girondins Bordeaux 54 AS Monaco 54 AJ Auxerre 49
1985	Girondins Bordeaux 59 FC Nantes 56 AS Monaco 48
1986	Paris Saint-Germain 56 FC Nantes 53 Girondins Bordeaux 49
1987	Girondins Bordeaux 53 Olympique Marseille 49 Toulouse FC 48
1988	AS Monaco 52 Girondins Bordeaux 46 SCP Montpellier 45
1989v1	Olympique Marseille 73 Paris Saint-Germain 70 AS Monaco 68
1990v	Olympique Marseille 53 Girondins Bordeaux 51 AS Monaco 46
1991	Olympique Marseille 55 AS Monaco 51 AJ Auxerre 48
1992	Olympique Marseille 58 AS Monaco 52 Paris Saint-Germain 47
1993	Olympique Marseille* 55 Paris Saint-Germain 51 AS Monaco 51
1994	Paris Saint-Germain 59 Olympique Marseille 51 AJ Auxerre 46
1995	FC Nantes 79 Olympique Lyon 69 Paris Saint-Germain 67

* Olympique Marseille stripped of title

FRENCH CUP FINALS

1918	Olympique de Pantin	3-0	FC Lyon
1919	CAS Generaux	3-2	Olympique Paris
1920	CA Paris	2-1	Le Havre AC
1921	Red Star Paris	2-1	Olympique Paris
1922	Red Star Paris	2-0	Stade Rennais
1923	Red Star Paris	4-2	FC Sète
1924	Olympique Marseille	3-2	FC Sète
1925	CAS Generaux	1-1 3-2	FC Rouen
1926	Olympique Marseille	4-1	AS Valentigney
1927	Olympique Marseille	3-0	US Quevilly
1928	Red Star Paris	3-1	CA Paris
1929	SO Montpellier	2-0	FC Sète
1930	FC Sete	3-1	Racing Club France
1931	Club Francais	3-0	SO Montpellier
1932	AS Cannes	1-0	Racing Club Roubaix
1933	Excelsior Roubaix	3-1	Racing Club Roubaix
1934	FC Sete	2-1	Olympique Marseille
1935	Olympique Marseille	3-0	Stade Rennais
1936	Racing Club Paris	1-0	US Charleville
1937	FC Sochaux	2-1	RC Strasbourg
1938	Olympique Marseille	2-1	FC Metz
1939	Racing Club Paris	3-1	Olympique Lille
1940	Racing Club Paris	2-1	Olympique Marseille
1941	Girondins Bordeaux	2-0	SC Fives
1942	Red Star Paris	2-0	FC Sète
1943	Olympique Marseille	2-2 4-0	Girondins Bordeaux
1944	Nancy-Lorraine XI	4-0	Reims-Champagne XI
1945	Racing Club Paris	3-0	OSC Lille
1946	OSC Lille	4-2	Red Star Paris
1947	OSC Lille	2-0	RC Strasbourg
1948	OSC Lille	3-2	RC Lens
1949	Racing Club Paris	5-2	OSC Lille
1950	Stade Rennais	2-0	Racing Club Paris
1951	RC Strasbourg	3-0	US Valenciennes
1952	OGC Nice	5-3	Girondins Bordeaux
1953	OSC Lille	2-1	FC Nancy
1954	OGC Nice	2-1	Olympique Marseille
1955	OSC Lille	5-2	Girondins Bordeaux
1956	FC Sedan	3-1	FC Troyes-Aube
1957	FC Toulouse	6-3	SC Angers
1958	Stade de Reims	3-1	Nîmes Olympique
1959	Le Havre AC	2-2 3-0	FC Sochaux
1960	AS Monaco	4-2	AS Saint-Étienne
1961	FC Sedan	3-1	Nîmes Olympique
1962	AS Saint-Étienne	1-0	FC Nancy
1963	AS Monaco	0-0 2-0	Olympique Lyon
1964	Olympique Lyon	2-0	Girondins Bordeaux
1965	Stade Rennais	2-2 3-1	FC Sedan
1966	RC Strasbourg	1-0	FC Nantes
1967	Olympique Lyon	3-1	FC Sochaux
1968	AS Saint-Étienne	2-1	Girondins Bordeaux
1969	Olympique Marseille	2-0	Girondins Bordeaux
1970	AS Saint-Étienne	5-0	FC Nantes
1971	Stade Rennais	1-0	Olympique Lyon
1972	Olympique Marseille	2-1	SEC Bastia
1973	Olympique Lyon	2-1	FC Nantes
1974	AS Saint-Étienne	2-1	AS Monaco
1975	AS Saint-Étienne	2-0	RC Lens
1976	Olympique Marseille	2-0	Olympique Lyon
1977	AS Saint-Étienne	2-1	Stade de Reims
1978	AS Nancy-Lorraine	1-0	OGC Nice
1979	FC Nantes	4-1	AJ Auxerre
1980	AS Monaco	3-1	US Orléans
1981	SEC Bastia	2-1	AS Saint-Étienne
1982	Paris Saint-Germain	2-2 6-5p	AS Saint-Étienne
1983	Paris Saint-Germain	3-2	FC Nantes
1984	FC Metz	2-0	AS Monaco
1985	AS Monaco	1-0	Paris Saint-Germain

1986	Girondins Bordeaux	2-1	Olympique Marseille
1987	Girondins Bordeaux	2-0	Olympique Marseille
1988	FC Metz	1-1 5-4p	FC Sochaux
1989	Olympique Marseille	4-3	AS Monaco
1990	SCP Montpellier	2-1	Racing Club Paris
1991	AS Monaco	1-0	Olympique Marseille
1992	-		
1993	Paris Saint-Germain	3-0	FC Nantes
1994	AJ Auxerre	3-0	Montpellier HSC
1995	Paris Saint-Germain	1-0	RC Strasbourg

LEADING INTERNATIONAL GOALSCORERS

41	Michel Platini	(Nancy,St-Étienne,Juventus)	1976-1987
30	Jean-Pierre Papin	(Valenciennes,Club Brugge, Marseille,Milan)	1986-
27	Just Fontaine	(Nice,Stade Rennais)	1956-1960
20	Jean Nicolas	(Rouen)	1933-1939
	Paul Nicolas	(Gallia,Red Star,Amiens)	1920-1931
	Jean Vincent	(Lille,Stade Rennais)	1954-1961
19	Eric Cantona	(Auxerre,Marseille,Leeds United, Manchester United)	1987-
	Jean Baratte	(Lille,Aix)	1944-1953
18	Roger Piantoni	(Nancy,Stade Rennais,Nice)	1952-1961
	Raymond Kopa	(Angers,Stade Rennais,Real Madrid)	1952-1962

LEADING INTERNATIONAL APPEARANCES

82	Manuel Amoros	(Monaco,Marseille)	1982-1992
76	Maxime Bossis	(Nantes,Racing Club Paris)	1976-1986
72	Michel Platini	(Nancy,St-Étienne,Juventus)	1976-1987
65	Marius Tresor	(Ajaccio,Marseille,Bordeaux)	1971-1983
63	Roger Marche	(Stade de Reims,Racing Club Paris)	1947-1959
60	Luis Fernandez	(Paris SG,Racing Club Paris, Cannes)	1982-1992
58	Robert Jonquet	(Stade de Reims,Strasbourg)	1948-1960
	Henri Michel	(Aix,Nantes)	1967-1980
56	Patrick Battiston	(Metz,St-Étienne,Bordeaux, Monaco)	1977-1989
54	Jean-Pierre Papin	(Valenciennes,Club Brugge, Marseille,Milan)	1986-

NATIONAL TEAM COACHES

1949-54	Pierre Pibarot
1955-62	Albert Batteux
1962-66	Henri Guérin
1966-67	José Arribas & Jean Snella
1967	Just Fontaine
1967-69	Louis Dugauguez
1969-73	Georges Boulogne
1973-75	Stefan Kovacs
1976-84	Michel Hidalgo
1985-88	Henri Michel
1988-92	Michel Platini
1992-93	Gérard Houllier
1993-	Aimé Jacquet

INTERNATIONAL MATCHES PLAYED BY FRANCE

1-05-1904	Belgium	D 3-3	Brussels	Fr	Mesnier, Royet, Cypres
12-02-1905	Switzerland	W 1-0	Paris	Fr	Cypres
7-05	Belgium	L 0-7	Brussels	Fr	
22-04-1906	Belgium	L 0-5	Paris	Fr	
1-11	England Am	L 0-15	Paris	Fr	
21-04-1907	Belgium	W 2-1	Brussels	Fr	Royet, Puget
8-03-1908	Switzerland	W 2-1	Geneva	Fr	Sartorius, Francois
23-03	England Am	L 0-12	London	Fr	
12-04	Belgium	L 1-2	Paris	Fr	Verlet
10-05	Holland	L 1-4	Rotterdam	Fr	Francois
19-10	Denmark	L 0-9	London	OGr1	
22-10	Denmark	L 1-17	London	OGsf	Sartorius
9-05-1909	Belgium	L 2-5	Brussels	Fr	Mouton, Rigal
22-05	England Am	L 0-11	Paris	Fr	
3-04-1910	Belgium	L 0-4	Paris	Fr	
16-04	England Am	L 1-10	Brighton	Fr	Mouton
15-05	Italy	L 2-6	Milan	Fr	Sellier, Ducret
1-01-1911	Hungary	L 0-3	Paris	Fr	
23-03	England Am	L 0-3	Paris	Fr	
9-04	Italy	D 2-2	Paris	Fr	Maes 2
23-04	Switzerland	L 2-5	Geneva	Fr	Triboulet, Maes
30-04	Belgium	L 1-7	Brussels	Fr	Maes
29-10	Luxembourg	W 4-1	Luxembourg	Fr	Mesnier 2, Viallemonteil, Gravier
28-01-1912	Belgium	D 1-1	Paris	Fr	Maes
18-02	Switzerland	W 4-1	Paris	Fr	Mesnier, Triboulet, Vialmonteil, Maes
17-03	Italy	W 4-3	Turin	Fr	Maes 3, Mesnier
12-01-1913	Italy	W 1-0	Paris	Fr	Maes
16-02	Belgium	L 0-3	Brussels	Fr	
27-02	England Am	L 1-4	Paris	Fr	Poulain
9-03	Switzerland	W 4-1	Geneva	Fr	Dubly 2, Montagne, Eloy
20-04	Luxembourg	W 8-0	Paris	Fr	Maes 5, Poulain 2, Romano
25-01-1914	Belgium	W 4-3	Lille	Fr	Hanot, Jourde 2, Dubly
8-02	Luxembourg	L 4-5	Luxembourg	Fr	Bard, Ducret, Geromini, Triboulet
8-03	Switzerland	D 2-2	Paris	Fr	Devic, Gastiger
29-03	Italy	L 0-2	Turin	Fr	

31-05	Hungary	L 1-5	Budapest	Fr	Brouzes
9-03-1919	Belgium	D 2-2	Brussels	Fr	Hanot 2
18-01-1920	Italy	L 4-9	Milan	Fr	Bard 2, Dubly, Nicolas.P
29-02	Switzerland	W 2-0	Geneva	Fr	Dewaquez, Nicolas.P
28-03	Belgium	W 2-1	Paris	Fr	Nicolas.P 2
29-08	Italy	W 3-1	Antwerp	OGqf	Bard 2, Boyer
31-08	Czechoslovakia	L 1-4	Antwerp	OGsf	Boyer
20-02-1921	Italy	L 1-2	Marseille	Fr	Devic
6-03	Belgium	L 1-3	Brussels	Fr	Dewaquez
13-11	Holland	L 0-5	Paris	Fr	
15-01-1922	Belgium	W 2-1	Paris	Fr	Darques, Dewaquez
30-04	Spain	L 0-4	Bordeaux	Fr	
28-01-1923	Spain	L 0-3	San Sebastian	Fr	
25-02	Belgium	L 1-4	Brussels	Fr	Isbecque
2-04	Holland	L 1-8	Amsterdam	Fr	Bard
22-04	Switzerland	D 2-2	Paris	Fr	Dubly, Nicolas.P
10-05	England	L 1-4	Paris	Fr	Dewaquez
28-10	Norway	L 0-2	Paris	Fr	
13-01-1924	Belgium	W 2-0	Paris	Fr	Gross, Renier
23-03	Switzerland	L 0-3	Geneva	Fr	
17-05	England	L 1-3	Paris	Fr	Dewaquez
27-05	Estonia	W 7-0	Paris	OGr1	Crut 3, Nicolas.P 2, Boyer 2
1-06	Uruguay	L 1-5	Paris	OGqf	Nicolas.P
4-06	Hungary	L 0-1	Le Havre	Fr	
11-11	Belgium	L 0-3	Brussels	Fr	
22-03-1925	Italy	L 0-7	Turin	Fr	
19-04	Austria	L 0-4	Paris	Fr	
21-05	England	L 2-3	Paris	Fr	Boyer, Dewaquez
11-04-1926	Belgium	W 4-3	Paris	Fr	Crut 2, Dewaquez, Leveugle
18-04	Portugal	W 4-2	Toulouse	Fr	Salvano, Brunel 2, Bonello
25-04	Switzerland	W 1-0	Paris	Fr	Nicolas.P
30-05	Austria	L 1-4	Vienna	Fr	Gallay
13-06	Yugoslavia	W 4-1	Paris	Fr	Gallay, Nicolas.P 3
20-06	Belgium	D 2-2	Brussels	Fr	Accard, Dewaquez
16-03-1927	Portugal	L 0-4	Lisbon	Fr	
24-04	Italy	D 3-3	Paris	Fr	Taisne 2, Sottiault
22-05	Spain	L 1-4	Paris	Fr	Boyer
26-05	England	L 0-6	Paris	Fr	
12-06	Hungary	L 1-13	Budapest	Fr	Dewaquez
11-03-1928	Switzerland	L 3-4	Lausanne	Fr	Lieb, Seyler, Nicolas.P
15-04	Belgium	L 2-3	Paris	Fr	Bardot
29-04	Portugal	D 1-1	Paris	Fr	Nicolas.P
13-05	Czechoslovakia	L 0-2	Paris	Fr	
17-05	England	L 1-5	Paris	Fr	Brouzes
29-05	Italy	L 3-4	Amsterdam	OGr1	Brouzes, Pavillard 2
24-02-1929	Hungary	W 3-0	Paris	Fr	Banide, Nicolas.P, Lieb
24-03	Portugal	W 2-0	Paris	Fr	Nicolas.P, Galey
14-04	Spain	L 1-8	Zaragoza	Fr	Veinante
9-05	England	L 1-4	Paris	Fr	Dewaquez
19-05	Yugoslavia	L 1-3	Paris	Fr	Cheuva
26-05	Belgium	L 1-4	Liege	Fr	Dewaquez
23-02-1930	Portugal	L 0-2	Oporto	Fr	
23-03	Switzerland	D 3-3	Paris	Fr	Cheuva, Anatol, Liberati
13-04	Belgium	L 1-6	Paris	Fr	Dubus
11-05	Czechoslovakia	L 2-3	Paris	Fr	Delfour, Korb
18-05	Scotland	L 0-2	Paris	Fr	
25-05	Belgium	W 2-1	Liege	Fr	Pinel 2
13-07	Mexico	W 4-1	Montevideo	WCr1	Langiller, Laurent.L, Maschinot 2
15-07	Argentina	L 0-1	Montevideo	WCr1	
19-07	Chile	L 0-1	Montevideo	WCr1	
7-12	Belgium	D 2-2	Paris	Fr	Pinel 2
25-01-1931	Italy	L 0-5	Bologna	Fr	
15-02	Czechoslovakia	L 1-2	Paris	Fr	Langiller
15-03	Germany	W 1-0	Paris	Fr	OG
14-05	England	W 5-2	Paris	Fr	Laurent.L, Mercier, Langiller, Delfour, Liberati
29-11	Holland	L 3-4	Paris	Fr	Veinante
20-03-1932	Switzerland	D 3-3	Berne	Fr	Liberati, Veinante, Bardot
10-04	Italy	L 1-2	Paris	Fr	Liberati
1-05	Belgium	L 2-5	Brussels	Fr	Pavillard, Cesember
8-05	Scotland	L 1-3	Paris	Fr	Langiller
5-06	Yugoslavia	L 1-2	Belgrade	Fr	Alcazar

Date	Opponent	Result	Venue	Comp	Scorers
9-06	Bulgaria	W 5-3	Sofia	Fr	Rodriguez, Cesember 4
12-06	Romania	L 3-6	Bucharest	Fr	Chardar, Rolhion
12-02-1933	Austria	L 0-4	Paris	Fr	
19-03	Germany	D 3-3	Berlin	Fr	Rio, Gerard 2
26-03	Belgium	W 3-0	Paris	Fr	Rio, Langiller, Nicolas.J
23-04	Spain	W 1-0	Paris	Fr	Nicolas.J
25-05	Wales	D 1-1	Paris	Fr	Nicolas.J
10-06	Czechoslovakia	L 0-4	Prague	Fr	
6-12	England	L 1-4	London	Fr	Veinante
21-01-1934	Belgium	W 3-2	Brussels	Fr	Nicolas.J 2, Veinante
11-03	Switzerland	L 0-1	Paris	Fr	
25-03	Czechoslovakia	L 1-2	Paris	Fr	Korb
15-04	Luxembourg	W 6-1	Luxembourg	WCq	Aston, Nicolas.J 4, Liberati
10-05	Holland	W 5-4	Amsterdam	Fr	Keller, Nicolas.J 3, Alcazar
27-05	Austria	L 2-3	Turin	WCr1	Nicolas.J, Verriest
16-12	Yugoslavia	W 3-2	Paris	Fr	Nicolas.J 2, Courtois
24-01-1935	Spain	L 0-2	Madrid	Fr	
17-02	Italy	L 1-2	Rome	Fr	Keller
17-03	Germany	L 1-3	Paris	Fr	Duhart
14-04	Belgium	D 1-1	Brussels	Fr	Courtois
19-05	Hungary	W 2-0	Paris	Fr	Courtois 2
27-10	Switzerland	L 1-2	Geneva	Fr	OG
10-11	Sweden	W 2-0	Paris	Fr	OG, Courtois
12-01-1936	Holland	L 1-6	Paris	Fr	Courtois
9-02	Czechoslovakia	L 0-3	Paris	Fr	
8-03	Belgium	W 3-0	Paris	Fr	Courtois 2, Rio
13-12	Yugoslavia	W 1-0	Paris	Fr	Keller
24-01-1937	Austria	L 1-2	Paris	Fr	Novicki
21-02	Belgium	L 1-3	Brussels	Fr	Rio
21-03	Germany	L 0-4	Stuttgart	Fr	
23-05	Rep. Ireland	L 0-2	Paris	Fr	
10-10	Switzerland	W 2-1	Paris	Fr	Veinante 2
31-10	Holland	W 3-2	Amsterdam	Fr	Nicolas.J, Langiller, Courtois
5-12	Italy	D 0-0	Paris	Fr	
30-01-1938	Belgium	W 5-3	Paris	Fr	Courtois, Veinante 2, Heisserer, Ignace
24-03	Bulgaria	W 6-1	Paris	Fr	Nicolas.J 2, Aston 2, Aznar, Veinante
26-05	England	L 2-4	Paris	Fr	Jordan, Nicolas.J
5-06	Belgium	W 3-1	Paris	WCr1	Veinante, Nicolas.J 2
12-06	Italy	L 1-3	Paris	WCqf	Heisserer
4-12	Italy	L 0-1	Naples	Fr	
22-01-1939	Poland	W 4-0	Paris	Fr	Veinante 2, Heisserer, Zatelli
16-03	Hungary	D 2-2	Paris	Fr	Ben Barek, Heisserer
18-05	Belgium	W 3-1	Brussels	Fr	Koranyi 2, Mathe
20-05	Wales	W 2-1	Paris	Fr	Bigot, Veinante
28-01-1940	Portugal	W 3-2	Paris	Fr	Koranyi 2, Hiltl
8-03-1942	Switzerland	L 0-2	Marseille	Fr	
15-03	Spain	L 0-4	Seville	Fr	
24-12-1944	Belgium	W 3-1	Paris	Fr	Simonyi, Arnaudeau, Aston
8-04-1945	Switzerland	L 0-1	Lausanne	Fr	
6-12	Austria	L 1-4	Vienna	Fr	Bongiorni
15-12	Belgium	L 1-2	Brussels	Fr	Aston
7-04-1946	Czechoslovakia	W 3-0	Paris	Fr	Ben Barek, Vaast, Heisserer
14-04	Portugal	L 1-2	Lisbon	Fr	Vaast
5-05	Austria	W 3-1	Paris	Fr	Vaast, Heisserer, Leduc
19-05	England	W 2-1	Paris	VI	Prouff, Vaast
23-03-1947	Portugal	W 1-0	Paris	Fr	Bihel
3-05	England	L 0-3	London	Fr	
26-05	Holland	W 4-0	Paris	Fr	Alpsteg, Baratte 2, Dard
1-06	Belgium	W 4-2	Paris	Fr	Vaast 2, Baratte, Dard
8-06	Switzerland	W 2-1	Lausanne	Fr	Alpsteg, Baratte
23-11	Portugal	W 4-2	Lisbon	Fr	Vaast 3, Ben Barek
4-04-1948	Italy	L 1-3	Paris	Fr	Baratte
23-05	Scotland	W 3-0	Paris	Fr	Bongiorne, Flamion, Baratte
6-06	Belgium	L 2-4	Brussels	Fr	Cuissard, Ben Barek
12-06	Czechoslovakia	W 4-0	Prague	Fr	Baillot, Baratte 2, Batteux
17-10	Belgium	D 3-3	Paris	Fr	Flamion 2, Baratte
23-04-1949	Holland	L 1-4	Rotterdam	Fr	Baratte
27-04	Scotland	L 0-2	Glasgow	Fr	
22-05	England	L 1-3	Paris	Fr	Moreel
4-06	Switzerland	W 4-2	Paris	Fr	Baillot, Grumellon, Baratte 2
19-06	Spain	L 1-5	Paris	Fr	Baratte

Date	Opponent	Result	Venue	Comp	Scorers
9-10	Yugoslavia	D 1-1	Belgrade	WCq	Baillot
30-10	Yugoslavia	D 1-1	Paris	WCq	Baillot
13-11	Czechoslovakia	W 1-0	Paris	Fr	Baratte
11-12	Yugoslavia	L 2-3	Forence	WCq	Walter, Luciano
27-05-1950	Scotland	L 0-1	Paris	Fr	
4-06	Belgium	L 1-4	Brussels	Fr	Kargu
1-11	Belgium	D 3-3	Paris	Fr	Doye, Baratte, Kargu
10-12	Holland	W 5-2	Paris	Fr	Flamion, Baratte 2, Doye
6-02-1951	Yugoslavia	W 2-1	Paris	Fr	Strappe, Flamion
12-05	Nth. Ireland	D 2-2	Belfast	Fr	Baratte, Bonifaci
16-05	Scotland	L 0-1	Glasgow	Fr	
3-06	Italy	L 1-4	Genoa	Fr	Grumellon
3-10	England	D 2-2	London	Fr	Doye, Alpsteg
14-10	Switzerland	W 2-1	Geneva	Fr	Doye, Grumellon
1-11	Austria	D 2-2	Paris	Fr	Grumellon 2
26-03-1952	Sweden	L 0-1	Paris	Fr	
20-04	Portugal	W 3-0	Paris	Fr	Alpsteg, Strappe 2
22-05	Belgium	W 2-1	Brussels	Fr	Doye, Deladeriere
5-10	West Germany	W 3-1	Paris	Fr	Ujlaki, Cisowski, Strappe
19-10	Austria	W 2-1	Vienna	Fr	Baratte, Penverne
11-11	Nth. Ireland	W 3-1	Paris	Fr	Ujlaki, Kopa
16-11	Rep. Ireland	D 1-1	Dublin	Fr	Piantoni
25-12	Belgium	L 0-1	Paris	Fr	
14-05-1953	Wales	W 6-1	Paris	Fr	Gardien 2, Kopa 2, Bonifaci, Ujlaki
11-06	Sweden	L 0-1	Stockholm	Fr	
20-09	Luxembourg	W 6-1	Luxembourg	WCq	Piantoni, Kopa, Cicci, Glovacki, Kargu, Flamion
4-10	Rep. Ireland	W 5-3	Dublin	WCq	Glovacki, Penverne, Ujlaki 2, Flamion
18-10	Yugoslavia	L 1-3	Zagreb	Fr	Marcel
11-11	Switzerland	L 2-4	Paris	Fr	Ujlaki 2
25-11	Rep. Ireland	W 1-0	Paris	WCq	Piantoni
17-12	Luxembourg	W 8-0	Paris	WCq	Desgranges 2, Vincent 2, Fontaine 3, Foix
11-04-1954	Italy	L 1-3	Paris	Fr	Piantoni
30-05	Belgium	D 3-3	Brussels	Fr	Vincent, OG, Kopa
16-06	Yugoslavia	L 0-1	Lausanne	WCr1	
19-06	Mexico	W 3-2	Geneva	WCr1	Vincent, OG, Kopa
16-10	West Germany	W 3-1	Hanover	Fr	Foix 2, Vincent
11-11	Belgium	D 2-2	Paris	Fr	Kopa 2
17-03-1955	Spain	W 2-1	Madrid	Fr	Kopa, Vincent
3-04	Sweden	W 2-0	Paris	Fr	Oliver, Glovacki
15-05	England	W 1-0	Paris	Fr	Kopa
9-10	Switzerland	W 2-1	Basle	Fr	Kopa, Piantoni
23-10	Soviet Union	D 2-2	Moscow	Fr	Kopa, Piantoni
11-11	Yugoslavia	D 1-1	Paris	Fr	Piantoni
25-12	Belgium	L 1-2	Brussels	Fr	Piantoni
15-02-1956	Italy	L 0-2	Bologna	Fr	
25-03	Austria	W 3-1	Paris	Fr	Leblond, Vincent, Piantoni
7-10	Hungary	L 1-2	Paris	Fr	Cisowski
21-10	Soviet Union	W 2-1	Paris	Fr	Tellechea, Vincent
11-11	Belgium	W 6-3	Paris	WCq	Cisowski 5, Vincent
24-03-1957	Portugal	W 1-0	Lisbon	Fr	Piantoni
2-06	Iceland	W 8-0	Nantes	WCq	Oliver 2, Vincent 2, Dereuddre, Piantoni 2, Brahimi
1-09	Iceland	W 5-1	Rejkjavik	WCq	Cisowski 2, Ujlaki 2, Wisnieski
6-10	Hungary	L 0-2	Budapest	Fr	
27-10	Belgium	D 0-0	Brussels	WCq	
27-11	England	L 0-4	London	Fr	
25-12	Bulgaria	D 2-2	Paris	Fr	Wisnieski, Douis
13-03-1958	Spain	D 2-2	Paris	Fr	Fontaine, Piantoni
16-04	Switzerland	D 0-0	Paris	Fr	
8-06	Paraguay	W 7-3	Norrkoping	WCr1	Fontaine 3, Piantoni, Wisnieski, Kopa, Vincent
11-06	Yugoslavia	L 2-3	Vasteras	WCr1	Fontaine 2,
15-06	Scotland	W 2-1	Orebro	WCr1	Kopa, Fontaine
19-06	Nth. Ireland	W 4-0	Norrkoping	WCqf	Wisnieski, Fontaine 2, Piantoni
24-06	Brazil	L 2-5	Stockholm	WCsf	Fontaine, Piantoni
28-06	West Germany	W 6-3	Gothenburg	WC3p	Fontaine 4, Kopa, Douis
1-10	Greece	W 7-1	Paris	ECr1	Kopa, Fontaine 2, Cisowski 2, Vincent2
5-10	Austria	W 2-1	Vienna	Fr	Deladeriere, Fontaine
26-10	West Germany	D 2-2	Paris	Fr	Deladeriere, Douis
9-11	Italy	D 2-2	Paris	Fr	Vincent, Fontaine
3-12	Greece	D 1-1	Athens	ECr1	Bruey
1-03-1959	Belgium	D 2-2	Paris	Fr	Vincent 2
11-10	Bulgaria	L 0-1	Sofia	Fr	

11-11	Portugal	W 5-3	Paris	Fr	Fontaine 3, Grillet, Muller
13-12	Austria	W 5-2	Paris	ECr2	Fontaine 3, Vincent 2
17-12	Spain	W 4-3	Paris	Fr	Muller, Fontaine, Vincent, Marche
28-02-1960	Belgium	L 0-1	Brussels	Fr	
16-03	Chile	W 6-0	Paris	Fr	Kaelbel, Vincent, Grillet, Fontaine 2, Muller
27-03	Austria	W 4-2	Vienna	ECr2	Marcel, Rahis, Heutte, Kopa
6-07	Yugoslavia	L 4-5	Paris	ECsf	Vincent, Heutte 2, Wisnieski
9-07	Czechoslovakia	L 0-2	Marseille	EC3p	
25-09	Finland	W 2-1	Helsinki	WCq	Wisnieski, Ujlaki
28-09	Poland	D 2-2	Warsaw	Fr	Guillas, Wisnieski
12-10	Switzerland	L 2-6	Basle	Fr	Goujon 2
30-10	Sweden	L 0-1	Stockholm	Fr	
11-12	Bulgaria	W 3-0	Paris	WCq	Wisnieski, Marcel, Cossou
15-03-1961	Belgium	D 1-1	Paris	Fr	Piantoni
2-04	Spain	L 0-2	Madrid	Fr	
28-09	Finland	W 5-1	Paris	WCq	Faivre 2, Wisnieski, Piantoni, Schultz
18-10	Belgium	L 0-3	Brussels	Fr	
12-11	Bulgaria	L 0-1	Sofia	WCq	
10-12	Spain	D 1-1	Paris	Fr	Heutte
16-12	Bulgaria	L 0-1	Milan	WCq	
11-04-1962	Poland	L 1-3	Paris	Fr	De Bourgoing
5-05	Italy	L 1-2	Florence	Fr	Piumi
20-10	England	D 1-1	Sheffield	ECr1	Goujon
24-10	West Germany	D 2-2	Stuttgart	Fr	Stako, Goujon
11-11	Hungary	L 2-3	Paris	Fr	Di Nallo
9-01-1963	Spain	D 0-0	Barcelona	Fr	
27-02	England	W 5-2	Paris	ECr1	Wisnieski 2, Douis, Cossou 2
17-04	Holland	L 0-1	Rotterdam	Fr	
28-04	Brazil	L 2-3	Paris	Fr	Wisnieski, Di Nallo
29-09	Bulgaria	L 0-1	Sofia	ECr2	
26-10	Bulgaria	W 3-1	Paris	ECr2	Goujon 2, Herbin
11-11	Switzerland	D 2-2	Paris	Fr	Buron, Lech
25-12	Belgium	L 1-2	Paris	Fr	Masnaghetti
25-04-1964	Hungary	L 1-3	Paris	ECqf	Cossou
23-05	Hungary	L 1-2	Budapest	ECqf	Combin
4-10	Luxembourg	W 2-0	Luxembourg	WCq	Guy, Artelesa
11-11	Norway	W 1-0	Paris	WCq	Rambert
2-12	Belgium	L 0-3	Brussels	Fr	
24-03-1965	Austria	L 1-2	Paris	Fr	Hausser
18-04	Yugoslavia	L 0-1	Belgrade	WCq	
3-06	Argentina	D 0-0	Paris	Fr	
15-09	Norway	W 1-0	Oslo	WCq	Combin
9-10	Yugoslavia	W 1-0	Paris	WCq	Gondet
6-11	Luxembourg	W 4-1	Marseille	WCq	Gondet 2, Combin 2
19-03-1966	Italy	D 0-0	Paris	Fr	
20-04	Belgium	L 0-3	Paris	Fr	
5-06	Soviet Union	D 3-3	Moscow	Fr	Blanchet, Gondet, Bonnel
13-07	Mexico	D 1-1	London	WCr1	Hausser
15-07	Uruguay	L 1-2	London	WCr1	De Bourgoing
20-07	England	L 0-2	London	WCr1	
28-09	Hungary	L 2-4	Budapest	Fr	Gondet, Revelli.H
22-10	Poland	W 2-1	Paris	ECq	Di Nallo, Lech
11-11	Belgium	L 1-2	Brussels	ECq	Lech
26-11	Luxembourg	W 3-0	Luxembourg	ECq	Herbet, Revelli.H, Lech
22-03-1967	Romania	L 1-2	Paris	Fr	Dogliani
3-06	Soviet Union	L 2-4	Paris	Fr	Gondet, Simon
17-09	Poland	W 4-1	Warsaw	ECq	Herbin, Di Nallo 2, Guy
27-09	West Germany	L 1-5	Berlin	Fr	Bosquier
28-10	Belgium	D 1-1	Nantes	ECq	Herbin
23-12	Luxembourg	W 3-1	Paris	ECq	Loubet 3
6-04-1968	Yugoslavia	D 1-1	Marseille	ECqf	Di Nallo
24-04	Yugoslavia	L 1-5	Belgrade	ECqf	Di Nallo
25-09	West Germany	D 1-1	Marseille	Fr	Bosquier
17-10	Spain	L 1-3	Lyon	Fr	Blanchet
6-11	Norway	L 0-1	Strasbourg	WCq	
12-03-1969	England	L 0-5	London	Fr	
10-09	Norway	W 3-1	Oslo	WCq	Revelli.H 3
15-10	Sweden	L 0-2	Stockholm	WCq	
1-11	Sweden	W 3-0	Paris	WCq	Bras 2, Djorkaeff
8-04-1970	Bulgaria	D 1-1	Rouen	Fr	Michel
28-04	Romania	W 2-0	Reims	Fr	Loubet, Djorkaeff

3-05	Switzerland	L 1-2	Basle	Fr	Revelli.H
5-09	Czechoslovakia	W 3-0	Nice	Fr	Gondet, Loubet, Bosquier
7-10	Austria	L 0-1	Vienna	Fr	
11-11	Norway	W 3-1	Lyon	ECq	Floch, Lech, Mezy
15-11	Belgium	W 2-1	Brussels	Fr	Molitor
8-01-1971	Argentina	W 4-3	Buenos Aires	Fr	Loubet, Djorkaeff, Lech, Revelli.H
13-01	Argentina	L 0-2	Mar del Plata	Fr	
17-03	Spain	D 2-2	Valencia	Fr	Revelli.H 2
24-04	Hungary	D 1-1	Budapest	ECq	Revelli.H
8-09	Norway	W 3-1	Oslo	ECq	Vergnes, Loubet, Blanchet
9-10	Hungary	L 0-2	Paris	ECq	
10-11	Bulgaria	W 2-1	Nantes	ECq	Lech, Loubet
4-12	Bulgaria	L 1-2	Sofia	ECq	Blanchet
8-04-1972	Romania	L 0-2	Bucharest	Fr	
18-06	Colombia	W 3-2	Salvador	Clr1	Loubet 2, Molitor
25-06	Argentina	D 0-0	Salvador	Clr1	
2-09	Greece	W 3-1	Athens	Fr	Michel Revelli.H, Larque
13-10	Soviet Union	W 1-0	Paris	WCq	Bereta
15-11	Rep. Ireland	L 1-2	Dublin	WCq	Larque
3-03-1973	Portugal	L 1-2	Paris	Fr	Molitor
19-05	Rep. Ireland	D 1-1	Paris	WCq	Chiesa
26-05	Soviet Union	L 0-2	Moscow	WCq	
8-09	Greece	W 3-1	Paris	Fr	Jouve, Berdoll, Chiesa
13-10	West Germany	L 1-2	Gelsenkirchen	Fr	Tresor
21-11	Denmark	W 3-0	Paris	Fr	Bereta, Revelli.P, Revelli.H
23-03-1974	Romania	W 1-0	Paris	Fr	Bereta
27-04	Czechoslovakia	D 3-3	Prague	Fr	Chiesa, Lacombe 2
18-05	Argentina	L 0-1	Paris	Fr	
7-09	Poland	W 2-0	Wroclaw	Fr	Coste, Jodar
12-10	Belgium	L 1-2	Brussels	ECq	Coste
16-11	East Germany	D 2-2	Paris	ECq	Guillou, Gallice
26-03-1975	Hungary	W 2-0	Paris	Fr	Michel, Parizon
26-04	Portugal	L 0-2	Paris	Fr	
25-05	Iceland	D 0-0	Reykjavik	ECq	
3-09	Iceland	W 3-0	Nantes	ECq	Guillou 2, Berdoll
12-10	East Germany	L 1-2	Leipzig	ECq	Bathenay
15-11	Belgium	D 0-0	Paris	ECq	
27-03-1976	Czechoslovakia	D 2-2	Paris	Fr	Soler, Platini
24-04	Poland	W 2-0	Lens	Fr	Pintenat, Revelli.P
22-05	Hungary	L 0-1	Budapest	Fr	
1-09	Denmark	D 1-1	Copenhagen	Fr	Platini
9-10	Bulgaria	D 2-2	Sofia	WCq	Platini, Lacombe
17-11	Rep. Ireland	W 2-0	Paris	WCq	Platini, Bathenay
23-02-1977	West Germany	W 1-0	Paris	Fr	Rouyer
30-03	Rep. Ireland	L 0-1	Dublin	WCq	
23-04	Switzerland	W 4-0	Geneva	Fr	Platini, Six, Rocheteau, Rouyer
26-06	Argentina	D 0-0	Buenos Aires	Fr	
30-06	Brazil	D 2-2	Rio de Janeiro	Fr	Six, Tresor
8-10	Soviet Union	D 0-0	Paris	Fr	
16-11	Bulgaria	W 3-1	Paris	WCq	Rocheteau, Platini, Dalger
8-02-1978	Italy	D 2-2	Naples	Fr	Bathenay, Platini
8-03	Portugal	W 2-0	Paris	Fr	Baronchelli, Berdoll
1-04	Brazil	W 1-0	Paris	Fr	Platini
11-05	Iran	W 2-1	Toulouse	Fr	Gemmrich, Six
19-05	Tunisia	W 2-0	Lille	Fr	Platini, Dalger
2-06	Italy	L 1-2	Mar del Plata	WCr1	Lacombe
6-06	Argentina	L 1-2	Buenos Aires	WCr1	Platini
10-06	Hungary	W 3-1	Mar del Plata	WCr1	Lopez, Berdoll, Rocheteau
1-09	Sweden	D 2-2	Paris	ECq	Berdoll, Six
7-10	Luxembourg	W 3-1	Luxembourg	ECq	Six, Tresor, Gemmrich
8-11	Spain	W 1-0	Paris	Fr	Specht
25-02-1979	Luxembourg	W 3-0	Paris	ECq	Petit, Emon, Larios
4-04	Czechoslovakia	L 0-2	Bratislava	ECq	
2-05	United States	W 6-0	New York	Fr	Lacombe 3, OG, Amisse, Six
5-09	Sweden	W 3-1	Stockholm	ECq	Lacombe, Platini, Battiston
10-10	United States	W 3-0	Paris	Fr	Platini, Wagner, Amisse
17-11	Czechoslovakia	W 2-1	Paris	ECq	Pecout, Rampillon
27-02-1980	Greece	W 5-1	Paris	Fr	Bathenay, Platini 2, Christophe, Stopyra
26-03	Holland	D 0-0	Paris	Fr	
23-05	Soviet Union	L 0-1	Moscow	Fr	
11-10	Cyprus	W 7-0	Limassol	WCq	Lacombe, Platini 2, Larios 2, Six, Zimako

28-10	Rep. Ireland	W 2-0	Paris	WCq	Platini, Zimako
19-11	West Germany	L 1-4	Hanover	Fr	Larios
18-02-1981	Spain	L 0-1	Madrid	Fr	
25-03	Holland	L 0-1	Rotterdam	WCq	
29-04	Belgium	W 3-2	Paris	WCq	Soler 2, Six
15-05	Brazil	L 1-3	Paris	Fr	Six
9-09	Belgium	L 0-2	Brussels	WCq	
14-10	Rep. Ireland	L 2-3	Dublin	WCq	Bellone, Platini
18-11	Holland	W 2-0	Paris	WCq	Platini, Six
5-12	Cyprus	W 4-0	Paris	WCq	Rocheteau, Lacombe 2, Genghini
23-02-1982	Italy	W 2-0	Paris	Fr	Platini, Bravo
24-03	Nth. Ireland	W 4-0	Paris	Fr	Zenier, Couriol, Larios, Genghini
28-04	Peru	L 0-1	Paris	Fr	
15-05	Bulgaria	D 0-0	Lyon	Fr	
2-06	Wales	L 0-1	Toulouse	Fr	
16-06	England	L 1-3	Bilbao	WCr1	Soler
21-06	Kuwait	W 4-1	Valladolid	WCr1	Genghini, Platini, Six, Bossis
24-06	Czechoslovakia	D 1-1	Valladolid	WCr1	Six
28-06	Austria	W 1-0	Madrid	WCr2	Genghini
4-07	Nth. Ireland	W 4-1	Madrid	WCr2	Giresse 2, Rocheteau 2
8-07	West Germany	D 3-3	Seville	WCsf	Platini, Tresor, Giresse. Lost 4-5 pens
10-07	Poland	L 2-3	Alicante	WC3p	Girard, Couriol
31-08	Poland	L 0-4	Paris	Fr	
6-10	Hungary	W 1-0	Paris	Fr	Roussey
10-11	Holland	W 2-1	Rotterdam	Fr	Battiston, Platini
16-02-1983	Portugal	W 3-0	Guimaraes	Fr	Stopyra 2, Ferreri
23-03	Soviet Union	D 1-1	Paris	Fr	Fernandez
23-04	Yugoslavia	W 4-0	Paris	Fr	Le Roux, Rocheteau 2, Toure
31-05	Belgium	D 1-1	Luxembourg	Fr	Six
7-09	Denmark	L 1-3	Copenhagen	Fr	Platini
5-10	Spain	D 1-1	Paris	Fr	Rocheteau
12-11	Yugoslavia	D 0-0	Zagreb	Fr	
29-02-1984	England	W 2-0	Paris	Fr	Platini 2
28-03	Austria	W 1-0	Bordeaux	Fr	Rocheteau
18-04	West Germany	W 1-0	Strasbourg	Fr	Genghini
1-06	Scotland	W 2-0	Marseille	Fr	Giresse, Lacombe
12-06	Denmark	W 1-0	Paris	ECr1	Platini
16-06	Belgium	W 5-0	Nantes	ECr1	Platini 3, Giresse, Fernandez
19-06	Yugoslavia	W 3-2	St-Etienne	ECr1	Platini 3
23-06	Portugal	W 3-2	Marseille	ECsf	Domergue 2, Platini
27-06	Spain	W 2-0	Paris	ECf	Platini, Bellone
13-10	Luxembourg	W 4-0	Luxembourg	WCq	Battiston, Platini, Stopyra 2
21-11	Bulgaria	W 1-0	Paris	WCq	Platini
8-12	East Germany	W 2-0	Paris	WCq	Stopyra, Anziani
3-04-1985	Yugoslavia	D 0-0	Sarajevo	WCq	
2-05	Bulgaria	L 0-2	Sofia	WCq	
21-08	Uruguay	W 2-0	Paris	AFT	Rocheteau, Toure
11-09	East Germany	L 0-2	Leipzig	WCq	
30-10	Luxembourg	W 6-0	Paris	WCq	Rocheteau 3, Toure, Giresse, Fernandez
16-11	Yugoslavia	W 2-0	Paris	WCq	Platini 2
26-02-1986	Nth. Ireland	D 0-0	Paris	Fr	
26-05	Argentina	W 2-0	Paris	Fr	Ferreri, Vercruysse
1-06	Canada	W 1-0	Leon	WCr1	Papin
5-06	Soviet Union	D 1-1	Leon	WCr1	Fernandez
9-06	Hungary	W 3-0	Leon	WCr1	Stopyra, Tigana, Rocheteau
17-06	Italy	W 2-0	Mexico City	WCr2	Platini, Stopyra
21-06	Brazil	D 1-1	Guadalajara	WCqf	Platini. Won 4-3 pens
25-06	West Germany	L 0-2	Guadalajara	WCsf	
28-06	Belgium	W 4-2	Puebla	WC3p	Ferreri, Papin, Genghini, Amoros
19-08	Switzerland	L 0-2	Lausanne	Fr	
10-09	Iceland	D 0-0	Reykjavik	ECq	
11-10	Soviet Union	L 0-2	Paris	ECq	
19-11	East Germany	D 0-0	Leipzig	ECq	
29-04-1987	Iceland	W 2-0	Paris	ECq	Micciche, Stopyra
16-06	Norway	L 0-2	Oslo	ECq	
12-08	West Germany	L 1-2	Berlin	Fr	Cantona
9-09	Soviet Union	D 1-1	Moscow	ECq	Toure
14-10	Norway	D 1-1	Paris	ECq	Fargeon
18-11	East Germany	L 0-1	Paris	ECq	
27-01-1988	Israel	D 1-1	Tel Aviv	Fr	Stopyra
2-02	Switzerland	W 2-1	Toulouse	Fr	Passi, Fargeon

5-02	Morocco	W 2-1	Monaco	Fr	OG, Stopyra
23-03	Spain	W 2-1	Bordeaux	Fr	Passi, Fernandez
27-04	Nth. Ireland	D 0-0	Belfast	Fr	
24-08	Czechoslovakia	D 1-1	Paris	Fr	Paille
28-09	Norway	W 1-0	Paris	WCq	Papin
22-10	Cyprus	D 1-1	Nicosia	WCq	Xuereb
19-11	Yugoslavia	L 2-3	Belgrade	WCq	Perez, Sauzee
7-02-1989	Rep. Ireland	D 0-0	Dublin	Fr	
8-03	Scotland	L 0-2	Glasgow	WCq	
29-04	Yugoslavia	D 0-0	Paris	WCq	
16-08	Sweden	W 4-2	Malmo	Fr	Cantona 2, Papin 2
5-09	Norway	D 1-1	Oslo	WCq	Papin
11-10	Scotland	W 3-0	Paris	WCq	Deschamps, Cantona, OG
18-11	Cyprus	W 2-0	Toulouse	WCq	Deschamps, Blanc
21-01-1990	Kuwait	W 1-0	Kuwait	Fr	Blanc
24-01	East Germany	W 3-0	Kuwait	Fr	Cantona 2, Deschamps
28-02	West Germany	W 2-1	Montpellier	Fr	Papin, Cantona
28-03	Hungary	W 3-1	Budapest	Fr	Cantona 2, Sauzee
15-08	Poland	D 0-0	Paris	Fr	
5-09	Iceland	W 2-1	Reykjavik	ECq	Papin, Cantona
13-10	Czechoslovakia	W 2-1	Paris	ECq	Papin 2
17-11	Albania	W 1-0	Tirana	ECq	Boli
20-02-1991	Spain	W 3-1	Paris	ECq	Sauzee, Papin, Blanc
30-03	Albania	W 5-0	Paris	ECq	Sauzee 2, Papin 2, OG
14-08	Poland	W 5-1	Poznan	Fr	Sauzee, Papin, Simba, Blanc, Perez
4-09	Czechoslovakia	W 2-1	Bratislava	ECq	Papin 2
12-10	Spain	W 2-1	Seville	ECq	Fernandez, Papin
20-11	Iceland	W 3-1	Paris	ECq	Simba, Cantona 2
19-02-1992	England	L 0-2	London	Fr	
25-03	Belgium	D 3-3	Paris	Fr	Papin 2, Vahirua
27-05	Switzerland	L 1-2	Lausanne	Fr	Divert
5-06	Holland	D 1-1	Lens	Fr	Papin
10-06	Sweden	D 1-1	Stockholm	ECr1	Papin
14-06	England	D 0-0	Malmo	ECr1	
17-06	Denmark	L 1-2	Malmo	ECr1	Papin
26-08	Brazil	L 0-2	Paris	Fr	
9-09	Bulgaria	L 0-2	Sofia	WCq	
14-10	Austria	W 2-0	Paris	WCq	Papin, Cantona
14-11	Finland	W 2-1	Paris	WCq	Papin, Cantona
17-02-1993	Israel	W 4-0	Tel Aviv	WCq	Cantona, Blanc 2, Roche
27-03	Austria	W 1-0	Vienna	WCq	Papin
28-04	Sweden	W 2-1	Paris	WCq	Cantona 2
28-07	Russia	W 3-1	Caen	Fr	Sauzee, OG, Papin
22-08	Sweden	D 1-1	Stockholm	WCq	Sauzee
8-09	Finland	W 2-0	Tampere	WCq	Blanc, Papin
13-10	Israel	L 2-3	Paris	WCq	Sauzee, Ginola
17-11	Bulgaria	L 1-2	Paris	WCq	Cantona
16-02-1994	Italy	W 1-0	Naples	Fr	Djorkaeff
22-03	Chile	W 3-1	Lyon	Fr	Papin, Djorkaeff, Martins
26-05	Australia	W 1-0	Kobe	Fr	Cantona
29-05	Japan	W 4-1	Tokyo	Fr	Djorkaeff, Papin,OG, Ginola
17-08	Czech Republic	D 2-2	Bordeaux	Fr	Zidane 2
7-09	Slovakia	D 0-0	Bratislava	ECq	
8-10	Romania	D 0-0	Saint-Etienne	ECq	
16-11	Poland	D 0-0	Zabrze	ECq	
14-12	Azerbaijan	W 2-0	Trabzon	ECq	Papin, Loko
18-01-1995	Holland	W 1-0	Utrecht	Fr	Loko
29-03	Israel	D 0-0	Tel Aviv	ECq	
26-04	Slovakia	W 4-0	Nantes	ECq	OG, Ginola, Blanc, Guérin

GEORGIA

The civil war in Georgia may have lost much of its ferocity since Abkhazia seceded from the new Republic, but the country's troubles are by no means over. Economic hardship and the threat that the civil war might erupt again at any time means that there has been little development since independence from the Soviet Union in 1991.

Georgia does, however, have a proud football tradition almost entirely as a result of the exploits of Dynamo Tbilisi. When they entered the European Cup as Georgia's representatives for the first time in 1994, it was Dynamo's eleventh European campaign. In 1981 they became the most easterly side to win a European club trophy when they beat Carl-Zeiss Jena in the final of the Cup Winners Cup. On the way they had beaten West Ham United and Feyenoord, while the previous season they had claimed their most famous ever scalp when they knocked out Liverpool in the first round of the European Cup.

Dynamo first won the Soviet championship in 1964, although they had been runners-up as early as 1939. Their second championship came in 1978 when they produced one of the all-time great Soviet club sides containing the likes of Alexander Chivadze, David Kipiani, Ramaz Shengalia and Tengiz Sulakvelidze, all Soviet internationals. Twice the Soviet Cup was won and Dynamo stood as the sixth most successful Soviet club of all time when the domestic competitions were finally wound up in 1993.

By then Dynamo were no longer involved. Georgia had been one of the leading forces behind the break-up of the Soviet Union and in 1990, a year before independence, formed its own league. Not surprisingly Dynamo, known for a time as Iberiya, won all of the first five championships played, but their return to Europe was marred by scandal. They were expelled from the European Cup after attempting to bribe the referee in their home tie against Linfield.

The national side made their bow, under the leadership of Chivadze, in 1994 at the Rothmans tournament in Malta. Results were mixed but a 5-0 drubbing of Wales in a European Championship qualifier in Tbilisi made the rest of Europe take note.

Population: 5,443,000
Area, sq km: 69,700
Capital city: Tbilisi

The Football Federation of Georgia
5 Shota Iamanidze Street
Tbilisi 380012
Georgia
Tel: + 7 8832 340744
Fax: + 431 16029695

Year of formation	1991
Affiliation to FIFA	1992
Affiliation to UEFA	1993
Registered clubs	12
Registered players	6372
Registered referees	736
National stadium	National, Tbilisi 75 000
National colours	White/Black/Grey

THE RECORD

WORLD CUP

1930-94 Did not enter

EUROPEAN CHAMPIONSHIP

1960-92 Did not enter
1996 QT group 7

EUROPEAN CLUB COMPETITIONS

European Cup
2nd round - Dynamo Tbilisi 1980
Cup Winners Cup
Winners - Dynamo Tbilisi 1981
UEFA Cup
3rd round - Dynamo Tbilisi 1974, 1978, 1988

CLUB DIRECTORY

TBILISI (Population - 1,460,000)

Dynamo Tbilisi (1925)
Dynamo 74,000 – White/Blue
Previous name - Dynamo 1925-1990, Iberiya 1990-93

Shevardeni-1906 Tbilisi

KUTAISI (Population - 235,000)

FC Torpedo Kutaisi
Previous name: Kutaisi FC 1990-92

RUSTAVI (Pop. - 159,000)

Metalurg Rustavi
Previous name: Gorda 1990-93

BATUMI (Pop. - 136,000)

Batumi FC

SUCHUMI (Pop. - 121,000)

Tskhumi Suchumi

GORI (Population - 62,000)

Dila Gori

POTI (Population - 54,000)

Kolkheti-1913 Poti

SAMTREDIA

Sonavardo Samtredia

LANCHKUTI

Guria Lanchkuti

GEORGIAN LEAGUE CHAMPIONSHIP

1990t2	Iberiya Tbilisi 78 Guriya Lanchkhuti 72 Gorda Rustavi 69
1991u10	Iberiya Tbilisi 47 Guriya Lanchkhuti 46 Kutaisi FC 35
1992v1	Iberiya Tbilisi 87 Tskhumi Suchumi 76 Gorda Rustavi 75
1993g3	Dynamo Tbilisi 40 Alazani Gurdzhaani 32 Margveti Zestafoni 32
1994h2	Dynamo Tbilisi 48 Kolkheti-1913 Poti 44 Torpedo Kutaisi 31

GEORGIAN CUP FINALS

1990	Guriya Lanchkhuti	1-0	Tskhumi Suchumi
1991	-		
1992	Iberiya Tbilisi	3-1	Tskhumi Suchumi
1993	Dynamo Tbilisi	4-2	Batumi FC
1994	Dynamo Tbilisi	1-0	Metalurg Rustavi

INTERNATIONAL MATCHES PLAYED BY GEORGIA

8-02-1994	Slovenia	L 0-1	Ta'Qali	Fr	
10-02	Malta	W 1-0	Ta'Qali	Fr	Ketsbaia
12-02	Tunisia	W 2-0	Ta'Qali	Fr	Kizilashvili, Kudinov
23-02	Israel	L 0-2	Tel Aviv	Fr	
11-06	Nigeria	L 1-5	Ibadan	Fr	Arveladze.R
26-06	Latvia	W 3-1	Riga	Fr	Janashia.D, Kacharava, Jamarauli
7-09	Moldova	L 0-1	Tbilisi	ECq	
12-10	Bulgaria	L 0-1	Sofia	ECq	
16-11	Wales	W 5-0	Tbilisi	ECq	Ketsbaia 2, Kinkladze, Goglichgani,Arveladze.S
14-12	Albania	W 1-0	Tirana	ECq	Arveladze.S
29-03-1995	Germany	L 0-2	Tbilisi	ECq	
2-04	Albania	W 2-0	Tbilisi	ECq	Arveladze.S, Ketsbaia
7-06	Wales	W 1-0	Cardiff	ECq	Kinkladze

GERMANY

It would be hard to find a more enduring force in world football than Germany. Only once, when they have entered, have the Germans failed to qualify for the finals of the World Cup or European Championship. That was in 1968 when they finished second in their group behind Yugoslavia. Indeed on only one other occasion have they failed to top their qualifying group – and they more than made up for that, in the 1990 World Cup, by winning the trophy in the end.

One of a select group of six countries that have won football's world championship, until 1994 the Germans had the best overall record with three wins and three runners-up spots. Such is the level of expectation that it was considered a national disaster when they were beaten by Bulgaria in the quarter-finals in America.

By the turn of the century football had been played in Germany for over 20 years and the majority of today's major clubs had been formed by then. In 1875 Oxford University made a tour of Germany, the first by a British side abroad, but football was sometimes given a hostile reception. As was common in East Germany in the second half of the 20th century, the emphasis was often on individual sports, especially in the gymnastic associations or '*Turner*' as they were known. The *Turner* were ultra-nationalistic bodies and in Bavaria they managed to get football banned until 1913, but this did not stop the growth of the game.

The first club devoted entirely to football was SC Germania Hamburg, formed in 1887. As in France, some clubs like TSV 1860 Munich were already in existence but did not start football sections until later. Hamburg, as the major port in the country, was the first centre of football, but the game soon spread to the other regions and Berlin especially became dominant. In 1896, in the first inter-city match, they beat Hamburg 13-0.

In 1898 regional leagues were set up in Southern Germany and Berlin, and to help create an organised structure the Deutscher Fussball-Bund was formed in 1900. Two years later it was decided to invite the winners of the regional leagues to take part in an end of season play-off to determine the national champions. This system remained in place until 1963, when rather belatedly the West Germans became the last European country to institute a single national league.

Prime movers behind the growth of football in Germany were Ferdinand Hueppe, the first president of the DFB, Konrad Koch, a teacher who drew up the first rules in German in 1876, and Walter Bensemann, another teacher who founded numerous clubs around the country including Kicker (later Eintracht) Frankfurt. He also founded Germany's major football newspaper *Kicker* in 1920.

It was Bensemann, too, who was behind the visit of the English amateur team to Germany in 1899 and the return visit in 1901, but it was not until 1908 that a proper national side was instituted and an official international played against Switzerland in Basle. The record leading up to the First World War was not very impressive with only six wins in 30 games. One game was remarkable, however: in the consolation tournament at the 1912 Stockholm Olympic Games, the Germans defeated Tsarist Russia 16-0 and Gottfried Fuchs scored 10 of the goals.

The inter-war period did not see an immediate rise in German fortunes and there was a surprising reluctance to join in with the main stream of European football, even allowing for Britain's opposition to Germany remaining a member of FIFA. It would have made sense for the Germans to have entered the International Cup or for the clubs to have joined in the Mitropa Cup. The two great club sides from this era, Schalke 04 and I.FC Nürnberg, would probably have been a match for the leading Austrian, Czech, Italian and Hungarian sides.

After Hitler came to power results for the national team began to improve dramatically, though it can be seen from the records that weaker teams were played to bolster the record. The 1934 World Cup was something of a triumph, with Germany winning a third place play-off against the 'Wunderteam' of the Austrians, but both the 1936 Olympic Games and the 1938 World Cup were a disaster as Germany were beaten by supposedly inferior opponents. In 1938 they failed to beat Switzerland despite having the pick of Austria's best players, who after the 'Anchluss' were now eligible to play for the fatherland.

The outbreak of war did not stop internationals being played. As the Germans conquered more and more of Europe, it was common for games to be played against both these countries and those that remained neutral. The aftermath of the war, however, brought about great change, not least in that there were now two Germanys. With Germany having been thrown out of FIFA in 1946, football all but ceased in the territory held by the Americans, British and French, which became known as West Germany, as it did in the Eastern sector held by the Soviet Union.

In 1948 the Deutscher Fussball-Verband der DDR (East Germany) was formed and a national championship was organised in the East. The East had never been very powerful in pre-war football and teams from that area had won only five championships, two of those in the war years. The pattern continued throughout the GDR's existence as a separate nation. Never did East Germany's footballers match the achievements of its athletes and swimmers, either at club or international level.

Their first international was played in 1952 against Poland and the 1958 World Cup was the first official competition entered by East Germany. Many countries were unhappy about the presence of the GDR in FIFA, however, and it was not until 1963 that a friendly game was played against a major Western power, with the visit of England to Leipzig.

During their 45-year history, the East Germans built up a phenomenal reputation in the sports field, but football never benefited from their emphasis on sporting achievement and in many ways suffered because of it. Not only were gifted athletes often syphoned off into other sports, but more important, the level of official interference in the clubs reached ludicrous proportions.

As in all Eastern bloc countries, football teams in the GDR were part of government institutions, and as none of them dated to pre-1945 there was very little identification with the supporters. Teams frequently changed their names and sometimes even moved towns. Dynamo Berlin in particular came to represent the worst side of East German football. As the team of the Stasi secret police, they were universally disliked but managed to 'win' 10 league championships in a row in the 1970s and 1980s. Derided as the 'offside champions' due to the number of opponents' goals that were mysteriously disallowed for that offence, even their players on occasions were known to be acutely embarrassed by events on the field.

The national side did see some success. They qualified for the 1974 World Cup finals in neighbouring West Germany, and as luck would have it, were drawn in the same group as their western counterparts. Jurgen Sparwasser's goal has gone down in history as the winner in the only game ever played between the two countries and East Germany won the group. In the second round, however, they were no match for the Dutch or the Brazilians who ended any hopes they may have had of reaching the final.

Two years later, in the Montreal Olympics, they won the gold medal, but by this time the Olympic football tournament had lost much of its credibility. A runners-up spot four years later did nothing to reverse the deteriorating image of East German football, and it was with little regret that with reunification in 1990 the East German association was disbanded, as was the national side and the league structure. The state that it was in was summed up by the award of just two places to East German clubs in the unified Bundesliga – and many felt that even that was too generous.

THE ORDER OF MERIT FOR EAST GERMANY

		All			League			Cup		Europe		
	Team	G	S	B	G	S	B	G	S	G	S	B
1	1.FC Dynamo Dresden	15	12	8	8	8	6	7	4	-	-	1
2	Berliner FC	13	10	4	10	4	3	3	6	-	-	1
3	1.FC Magdeburg	11	2	6	3	2	6	7	-	1	-	-
4	FC Victoria 91 Frankfurt	8	7	1	6	4	1	2	3	-	-	-
5	FC Carl Zeiss Jena	7	13	6	3	9	5	4	3	-	1	1
6	FSV Zwickau	5	1	4	2	-	3	3	1	-	-	1
7	VfB Leipzig	4	8	9	-	3	8	4	4	-	1	1
8	FC Wismut Aue	4	3	-	3	2	-	1	1	-	-	-
9	FC Sachsen Leipzig	4	2	4	2	1	4	2	1	-	-	-
10	Hallescher FC	4	1	1	2	1	1	2	-	-	-	-
11	FC Hansa Rostock	2	9	-	1	4	-	1	5	-	-	-
12	FC Rot-Weiss Erfurt	2	4	1	2	2	1	-	2	-	-	-
13	Chemnitzer FC	1	4	1	1	1	1	-	3	-	-	-
14	1.FC Union Berlin	1	1	-	-	-	-	1	1	-	-	-
15	SG Motor Dessau	1	-	1	-	-	1	1	-	-	-	-
16	EHW Thale	1	-	-	-	-	-	1	-	-	-	-
	FSV Lokomotive Dresden	1	-	-	-	-	-	1	-	-	-	-
18	BSG Aktivist Senftenberg	-	1	1	-	1	1	-	-	-	-	-
19	BSG Chemie Zeitz	-	1	-	-	-	-	-	1	-	-	-
	BSG Einheit Pankow	-	1	-	-	-	-	-	1	-	-	-
	Eisenhüttenstadt FC Stahl	-	1	-	-	-	-	-	1	-	-	-
	FSV Wismut Gera	-	1	-	-	-	-	-	1	-	-	-
	BSG Lokomotive Stendal	-	1	-	-	-	-	-	1	-	-	-
	SG Friederichstadt	-	1	-	-	1	-	-	-	-	-	-
	PSV Schwerin	-	1	-	-	-	-	-	1	-	-	-

To the end of the 1990-1991 season, the last in the history of East Germany

As East Germany excelled at the individual sports, what became known as West Germany excelled in team sports and in particular at football. They were readmitted to FIFA in 1950, and four years later were world champions. Relying on a few players from the pre-war era and managed by Sepp Herberger, West Germany entered the 1954 World Cup in Switzerland and pulled off one of the biggest shocks ever.

The Hungarian side of 1954 was the best the world had seen, and many would argue that it has not been bettered since, and yet the Germans managed to beat them in the World Cup final, inflicting on the Hungarians their only defeat in six years. Not only did they beat Hungary, they also disposed of the fancied Austrians and Yugoslavia. The hero of the team was Helmut Rahn, but their success was more down to teamwork and the presence of the Walter brothers, along with Morlock and the inspirational Turek in goal.

From 1954 the Germans did not look back. A comprehensive coaching network was set up throughout the country and the flow of excellent footballers has continued unabated. Semi-finalists in 1958 and quarter-finalists in the 1962 World Cup, they reached the final again in 1966, but this time lost controversially to the hosts, England, at Wembley. Along with Rahn, the most famous players of this era were Uwe Seeler, Hans Schäfer, Helmut Haller, Hans Tilkowski, and Karl-Heinz Schnellinger.

As their fortunes rose on the pitch, it became evident that the league structure of the German game was becoming out of date, and so in 1963 a new single national league was created along with a second division, instead of the regional leagues which were relegated to the status of third division. Just as importantly, full-time professionalism was introduced, remarkably for the first time in the history of German football. Until 1963, most players had played on a semi-professional basis.

This was the spur that the game needed and by the late 1960s one team in particular was showing the way forward. Bayern Munich won the Bundesliga in 1969 with a team of players that have since become household names. They have dominated club football since and formed the basis of the national side that was without question the dominant force in world football in the 1970s. In goal Sepp Maier has never been equalled, although the defence in front of him consisting of Schwarzenbeck, Beckenbauer and Breitner would have made any goalkeeper look good. Franz Beckenbauer, in particular, was regarded, along with Johan Cruyff, as the heir apparent to the title left vacant by Pele as the world's greatest player. His concept of an attacking sweeper or *libero* was a major tactical innovation.

It was not just in defence and midfield that Bayern and West Germany were blessed with gifted players. Along with Pele and Puskás, there has never been a more prolific goalscorer than Gerd Müller. His 68 goals in just 62 international matches was an extraordinary achievement that will take some beating. Also scoring goals for Bayern and Germany was Uli Hoeness. The other dominant club during the 1970s, Borussia Mönchengladbach, also contributed their share of players with the likes of Berti Vogts, Rainer Bonhof, Herbert Wimmer, Uli Stielike, Jupp Heynckes and Gunter Netzer.

In 1972 West Germany became European champions for the first time and only surrendered their title to Czechoslovakia four years later after a penalty shoot-out in the final. In between they had become world champions for a second time when they won the 1974 World Cup at home. Beckenbauer captained the side and by the time of his international retirement in 1977 he had become the first German to win 100 caps. *Der Kaiser*, as he was known, also led Bayern to three consecutive European Cup wins in the 1970s, a decade which brought two UEFA Cup wins for Borussia Mönchengladbach and a Cup Winners Cup title for Hamburg. The Germans, it seemed, could do no wrong.

They started the 1980s in style as well, with an all-German UEFA Cup final won by Eintracht Frankfurt and a second European Championship for the national team. But with the Bayern/Borussia axis broken, club success in Europe became harder to come by. Hamburg's win in the 1983 European Cup remains the last in that competition by a German side, and since then only Bayer Leverkusen and Werder Bremen have brought home a European title, the 1988 UEFA Cup and 1992 Cup Winners Cup respectively. For the first time, Germany's top players began to play their club football outside the Bundesliga, first in Spain and then in Italy's Serie A.

Despite reaching the World Cup final in 1982 and 1986, the national team was widely perceived as having lost much of its flair, and indeed on both occasions nobody was quite sure how they had managed to progress so far. The famous German 'tournament mentality' seemed to be their greatest weapon. Poor showings in both the 1984 and 1988 European Championships, the latter on home soil, brought more disappointment, but the 1990 World Cup in Italy was a different affair. Led by Lothar Matthäus, Germany's most capped player of all time, the team were breathtaking in the early rounds and although they rather lost their way in the latter stages, they were nonetheless worthy champions. Beckenbauer became the first man to win the World Cup both as a captain and as coach.

THE ORDER OF MERIT

		All			League			Cup		Europe		
	Team	G	S	B	G	S	B	G	S	G	S	B
1	FC Bayern München	25	7	12	13	4	3	8	1	4	2	
2	1.FC Nürnberg	12	5	1	9	3	-	3	2	-	-	1
3	Hamburger SV	11	16	2	6	9	-	3	4	2	3	2
4	Borussia Mönchengladbach	10	7	8	5	2	5	3	2	2	3	3
5	FC Schalke 04	9	11	1	7	5	-	2	6	-	-	1
6	1.FC Köln	7	15	9	3	8	2	4	6	-	1	7
7	Werder Bremen	7	7	4	3	5	2	3	2	1	-	2
8	Borussia Dortmund	7	6	4	4	4	2	2	1	1	1	2
9	VfB Stuttgart	6	5	5	4	3	3	2	1	-	1	2
10	Eintracht Frankfurt	6	3	7	1	1	5	4	1	1	1	2
11	1.FC Kaisersl'tern	4	8	3	3	4	2	1	4	-	-	1
12	VfB Leipzig	4	2	-	3	2	-	1	-	-	-	-
13	Dresdner SC	4	1	-	2	1	-	2	-	-	-	-
14	F. Düsseldorf	3	7	2	1	1	2	2	5	-	1	-
15	TSV München	3	3	-	1	2	-	2	-	-	1	-
16	Karlsruher SC	3	2	1	1	1	-	2	1	-	-	1
17	SpVgg Fürth	3	1	-	3	1	-	-	-	-	-	-
18	Hannover 96	3	-	-	2	-	-	1	-	-	-	-
19	Hertha BSC Berlin	2	7	4	2	5	3	-	2	-	-	1
20	Viktoria Berlin	2	2	-	2	2	-	-	-	-	-	-
21	Rot-Weiss Essen	2	1	-	1	-	-	1	1	-	-	-
22	Bayer Leverkusen	2	-	2	-	-	1	1	-	1	-	1
23	Rapid Wien (Austria)	2	-	-	1	-	-	1	-	-	-	-
24	Holstein Kiel	1	2	-	1	2	-	-	-	-	-	-
	Karlsruher FV	1	2	-	1	2	-	-	-	-	-	-
	Kickers Offenbach	1	2	-	-	2	-	1	-	-	-	-
27	First Vienna (Austria)	1	1	-	-	1	-	1	-	-	-	-
28	Bayer Uerdingen	1	-	2	-	-	1	1	-	-	-	1
29	Eintracht Braunschweig	1	-	1	1	-	1	-	-	-	-	-
	SC Freiburg	1	-	1	1	-	1	-	-	-	-	-
31	VfR Mannheim	1	-	-	1	-	-	-	-	-	-	-
	Schwarz-Weiss Essen	1	-	-	-	-	-	1	-	-	-	-
	Union 92 Berlin	1	-	-	1	-	-	-	-	-	-	-
34	MSV Duisburg	-	4	1	-	2	-	-	2	-	-	1
35	Alemania Aachen	-	3	-	-	1	-	-	2	-	-	-
36	VfL Bochum	-	2	-	-	-	-	-	2	-	-	-
	FSV Frankfurt	-	2	-	-	1	-	-	1	-	-	-
	1.FC Saarbrücken	-	2	-	-	2	-	-	-	-	-	-
	Stuttgarter Kickers	-	2	-	-	1	-	-	1	-	-	-
40	Fortuna Köln	-	1	-	-	-	-	-	1	-	-	-
	Borussia Neunkirchen	-	1	-	-	-	-	-	1	-	-	-
	Preussen Münster	-	1	-	-	1	-	-	-	-	-	-
	SV Waldhof Mann.	-	1	-	-	-	-	-	1	-	-	-
	Union Berlin	-	1	-	-	1	-	-	-	-	-	-
	BSC Berlin (Am)	-	1	-	-	-	-	-	1	-	-	-
	VfL Wolfsburg	-	1	-	-	-	-	-	1	-	-	-
	Vorwärts Berlin	-	1	-	-	1	-	-	-	-	-	-

Phorzheim	-	I	-	-	I	-	-	-	-	-	-
Admira Wien (Austria)	-	I	-	-	I	-	-	-	-	-	-
DFC Prague (Czechoslavakia)	-	I	-	-	I	-	-	-	-	-	-

To the end of the 1994-1995 season

The backbone of that side was the trio of Matthäus, Andreas Brehme and Jürgen Klinsmann, all of whom played in Milan for Inter. After the World Cup, German players were in even greater demand in Italy and one after another they left the Bundesliga. Not since the great Arminia Bielefeld bribery scandal of 1972 had the league been under such threat, but gradually the 'player drain' was reversed as money began to pour into the domestic game from television and sponsorship. The 1990 World Cup had revitalised the German public's interest in football and since then attendances have risen steadily to a point where they are now on average the highest in Europe, helped by the fact that the championship is more competitive now that Bayern's stranglehold has been broken. European trophies remain elusive, but Germany remains the perfect model of how to run football.

Population: 79,070,000
Area, sq km: 356,954
% in urban areas: 85.5%
Capital city: Berlin

Deutscher Fussball-Bund
Otto-Fleck-Schneise 6
Postfach 710265
D-6000 Frankfurt am Main
Germany
Tel: + 49 69 67880
Fax: + 49 69 6788266

Year of formation	1900 (1948 for the East German DFB)
Affiliation to FIFA	1904-1946, 1950 (1952-90 for the East German DFB)
Affiliation to UEFA	1954
Registered clubs	26 274
Registered players	373 700
Professional players	1100
Registered coaches	63,950
Registered referees	63 188
National stadium	Olympiastadion, Munich 64 000
National colours	White/Black/White
Reserve colours	Green/White/White
Season	August - May, with a mid season break December - February

THE RECORD FOR GERMANY AND WEST GERMANY

WORLD CUP

1930	Did not enter
1934	QT 1st/3 in group 12 - Final Tournament/Semi-finalists/ 3rd place
1938	QT 1st/4 in group 1 - Final Tournament/1st round
1950	Did not enter
1954	QT 1st/3 in group 1 - Final Tournament/Winners
1958	QT Automatic - Final Tournament/Semi-finalists/ 4th place
1962	QT 1st/3 in group 3 - Final Tournament/Quarter-finalists
1966	QT 1st/3 in group 2 - Final tournament/Finalists
1970	QT 1st/4 in group 7 - Final Tournament/Semi-finalists/ 3rd place
1974	QT Automatic - Final Tournament/Winners
1978	QT Automatic - Final Tournament/2nd round
1982	QT 1st/5 in group 1 - Final Tournament/Finalists
1986	QT 1st/5 in group 2 - Final Tournament/Finalists
1990	QT 2nd/4 in group 4 - Final Tournament/Winners
1994	QT Automatic - Final Tournament/Quarter-finalists

EUROPEAN CHAMPIONSHIP

1960	Did not enter
1964	Did not enter
1968	QT 2nd/3 in group 4
1972	QT 1st/4 in group 8 - Final Tournament/Winners
1976	QT 1st/4 in group 8 - Final Tournament/Finalists
1980	QT 1st/4 in group 7 - Final Tournament/Winners
1984	QT 1st/5 in group 6 - Final Tournament/1st round
1988	QT Automatic - Final Tournament/Semi-finalists
1992	QT 1st/4 in group 5 - Final Tournament/Finalists
1996	QT group 7

EUROPEAN CLUB COMPETITIONS

European Cup
Winners - Bayern Munich 1974 1975 1976 SV Hamburg 1983
Finalists - Eintracht Frankfurt 1960 Bor. Monchengladbach 1977 SV Hamburg 1980 Bayern Munich 1982 1987

Cup Winners Cup
Winners - Borussia Dortmund 1966 Bayern Munich 1967 SV Hamburg 1977 Werder Bremen 1992
Finalists - TSV Munich 1860 1965 SV Hamburg 1968 Fortuna Düsseldorf 1979

UEFA Cup
Winners - Bor. Monchengladbach 1975 1979 Eintracht Frankfurt 1980 Bayer Leverkusen 1988
Finalists - Bor. Monchengladbach 1973 1980 SV Hamburg 1982 1.FC Köln 1986 VfB Stuttgart 1989 Borussia Dortmund 1993

THE RECORD FOR EAST GERMANY

WORLD CUP

1950	Did not enter
1954	Did not enter
1958	QT 3rd/3 in group 4
1962	QT 3rd/3 in group 4
1966	QT 2nd/3 in group 6
1970	QT 2nd/3 in group 3
1974	QT 1st/4 in group 4 - Final Tournament/2nd round
1978	QT 2nd/4 in group 3
1982	QT 2nd/3 in group 7
1986	QT 3rd/5 in group 4
1990	QT 4th/5 in group 3

EUROPEAN CHAMPIONSHIP

1960	1st round
1964	2nd round
1968	QT 2nd/4 in group 5
1972	QT 3rd/3 in group 7
1976	QT 2nd/4 in group 7
1980	QT 3rd/5 in group 4
1984	QT 3rd/4 in group 1
1988	QT 2nd/5 in group 3

EUROPEAN CLUB COMPETITIONS

European Cup
Quarter-finalists - Wismut Karl-Marx-Stadt 1959 Vorwärts Berlin 1970 Carl Zeiss Jena 1971 Dynamo Dresden 1977 1979 Dynamo Berlin 1980 1984

Cup Winners Cup
Winners - 1.FC Magdeburg 1974
Finalists - Carl Zeiss Jena 1981 Lokomotive Leipzig 1987

UEFA Cup
Semi-finalists - Lokomotive Leipzig 1974 Dynamo Dresden 1989

CLUB DIRECTORY

BERLIN (Population - 5,061,000)

FC Berlin (1952)
Sportforum 15,000 – White, red trim
Previous name - BFC Dynamo Berlin 1952-90

Blau-Weiss 90 (1890)
Olympia-Stadion 76,000 – Blue/White
Previous name - Merger in 1925 of Union 92 and Vorwärts 90

Hertha BSC (1892)
(Berliner Sports Club)
Olympia-Stadion 76,000 – White/Blue

1.FC Union Berlin (1945)
Alte Försterei 25,000 – Red/White
Previous names - SG Union Oberschöneweide 1945-51, BSG Motor Oberschöneweide 1951-55, SC Motor Berlin 1955-57, TSC Oberschöneweide 195763, TSC Berlin 1963-66
Tennis Borussia Berlin (1902)
Mommsen-Stadion 16,000 – Violet/White

ESSEN (Population - 4,950,000)

VfL Bochum (1938)
(Verein für Leibesuebung)
Ruhrstadion 42,000 – Blue, red trim
Previous name - merger in 1938 of Bochum 08, TG Bochum and Germania

BV Borussia Dortmund (1909)
(Ballspiel Verein)
Westfalenstadion 42,000 – Yellow/Black

MSV Duisburg (1902)
(Meiderichher Sport Verein)
Wedaustadion 30,000 – Blue & white hoops/White

Rot-Weiss Essen (1907)
Georg Melches Stadion 36,000 – White/Red

FC Schalke 04 Gelsenkirchen (1904)
Parkstadion 70,000 – Blue/White

FC Bayer 05 Uerdingen (1905)
Grotenburg Kampfbahn 34,000 – Red with two blue stripes/Red

SG Wattenscheid 09 (1909)
Lohrheidestadion 19,000 – Black & red stripes/White

HAMBURG (Population - 2,225,000)

Hamburger SV (1887)
(Sport-Verein)
Volksparkstadion 61,000 – White/Red
Previous name - Merger in 1919 of Germania '87, Falke '87 and Hamburger SC '87

FC St Pauli (1910)
Wilhelm Koch Stadion 20,000 – White/White

MUNICH (Population - 1,955,000)

FC Bayern München (1900)
Olympiastadion 64,000 – Red, blue trim

TSV München 1860 (1899)
(Turn & Sport Verein)
Grünwalder Strasse 35,000 – Sky blue & white stripes/Blue

STUTTGART (Population 1,925,000)

VfB Stuttgart (1893)
(Verein für Ballspiele)
Gottlieb Daimler Stadion (Neckarstadion) 53,000 – White with a red band on chest/White
Previous names - Merger in 1912 of FV 93 and KC Cannstadt (1897)

Stuttgarter Kickers (1899)
Waldau Stadion 10,000 – Blue/Blue

FRANKFURT AM MAIN (Population - 1,885,000)

SG Eintracht Frankfurt (1899)
(Sport Gemeinde)
Waldstadion 61,000 – Red/Black, white trim
Previous names - Merger in 1911 of Kicker & Viktoria Frankfurt, Frankfurter FV 1911-18

OFC Kickers Offenbach (1901)
(Offenbacher Fussball Club)
Bieberer Berg 30,000 – Red/White

COLOGNE (Population - 1,760,000)

FC Bayer 04 Leverkusen (1904)
Ulrich Haberland Stadion 26,000 – Red, white trim

1.FC Köln (1948)
Müngersdorfer Stadion 60,000 – White, rd trim
Previous name - Merger in 1948 of Kölner BC (1901) and FC Sülz (1907)

MANNHEIM (Population - 1,400,000)

SV Waldhof Mannheim (1907)
Stadion am Alsenweg 30,000 – Blue & black stripes/Blue

DUSSELDORF (Population - 1,190,000)

Fortuna Düsseldorf (1895)
Rheinstadion 68,000 – White, red sleeves/Red

NUREMBERG (Population - 1,030,000)

1.FC Nürnberg (1900)
Frankenstadion 49,000 – Red & white stripes/Black

HANOVER (Population - 1,000,000)

SV Hannover '96 (1896)
Niedersachsenstadion 60,000 – Red/Black

BREMEN (Population - 800,000)

SV Werder Bremen (1899)
Weserstadion 40,000 – White/Green

LEIPZIG (Population - 700,000)

VfB Leipzig (1896)
Zentralstadion 39,000 – Blue/White
Previous names - VfB Leipzig 1894-1945 SG Probstheida 1945-48, BSG Erich Zeigner 1948, BSG Einheit Ost 1949-54, SC Rotation 1954-63, SC Leipzig 1963-66, 1.FC Lokomotive Leipzig 1966-91

FC Sachsen Leipzig (1945)
Alfred Kunze Sportpark 22,000 – White/Green
Previous names - SG Leipzig-Leutzsch 1945-48, ZSG Industrie 1948-50, BSG Chemie 1950-54, SC Lokomotive 1954-63, BSG Chemie Leipzig 1963-90

DRESDEN (Population - 670,000)

1.FC Dynamo Dresden (1953)
Rudolf Harbig Stadion 32,000 – Yellow/Black
Previous name - SG VP Dresden 1945-52, SG Dynamo Dresden 1953-90

FSV Lokomotive Dresden (1950)
Sportplatz Pieschener Allee 3,000 – White/Black
Previous names - SG Mickten 1950, BSG Sachsenverlag 1950, BSG Rotation Dresden 1951-54, SC Einheit Dresden 1954-65

BIELEFELD (Population - 515,000)

DSC Arminia (1905)
(Deutscher Sport Club)
Stadion der Alm 35,000 – Blue/White

KARLSRUHE (Population - 485,000)

Karlsruher SC (1894)
Wildparkstadion 42,000 – White/Blue
Previous name - Merger in 1952 of Mülburg and Phönix '94

HALLE (Population - 475,000)

Hallescher FC (1945)
Kurt Wabbel Stadion 23,000 – White/Red
Ptrevious names: SG Freiimfelde Halle 1945-49, ZSG Union Halle 1949-50, BSG Turbine Halle 1950-54, SC Chemie Halle-Leuna 1958-66, HFC Chemie 1966-91

CHEMNITZ (Population - 450,000)

Chemnitzer FC (1965)
Sportforum 24,000 – Sky blue/Sky Blue
Previous names - SG Chemnitz Nord until 1950, BSG Fewa 1950-51, BSG Chemie Chemnitz 1951-53, BSG Chemie Karl-Marx-Stadt 1953-56, SC Motor Karl-Marx-Stadt 1956-63, SC Karl-Marx-Stadt 1963-65, FC Karl-Marx-Stadt 1965-90

MÖNCHENGLADBACH (Population - 410,000)

VFL 1900 Borussia Mönchengladbach (1900)
Bökelberg 34,000 – White, green trim

MAGDEBURG (Population - 400,000)

1.FC Magdeburg (1965)
Ernst Grube Stadion 35,000 – White/White
Previous names - SG Einheit Sudenburg until 1951, BSG Krupp 1951, BSG Stahl 1951-52, BSG Motor Mitte 1952-57, SC Aufbau 1957-65

SAARBRUCKEN (Population - 385,000)
1.FC Saarbrücken (1903)
Ludwigsparkstadion 38,000 – Blue/White, black trim

BRUNSWICK (Population - 330,000)
Braunschweiger TSV Eintracht (1895)
Eintracht Stadion 32,000 – Yellow/Blue

DARMSTADT (Population - 305,000)
SV Darmstadt 98 (1898)
Böllenfalltor 30,000 – Blue/White

ROSTOCK (Population - 249,000)
FC Hansa Rostock (1965)
Ostseestadion 25,000 – White/White
Previous names - Rostock until 1949, Empor Lauter 1949-54, SC Empor 1954-65, FC Rostock 1965-66

ERFURT (Population - 217,000)
FC Rot-Weiss Erfurt (1946)
Steigerwaldstadion 28,000 – White/Red
Previous names - Erfurt West 1946-48, SG Fortuna Erfurt 1948-49, KWU Erfurt 1949-50, Turbine Erfurt 1950-54, SC Turbine 1954-65

ZWICKAU (Population - 165,000)
FSV Zwickau (1949)
Westsachsenstadion 35,000 – Red/White
Previous names - SG Planitz 1949, Horch Zwickau 1949-50, Motor Zwickau 1950-67, BSG Sachsenring Zwickau 1967-90

KAISERSLAUTERN (Population - 138,000)
1.FC Kaiserslautern (1900)
Fritz Walter Stadion 38,000 – Red, white & black trim

JENA (Population - 107,000)
FC Carl Zeiss Jena (1946)
Ernst Abbe Sportfeld 9,000 – Blue/White
Previous names - SG Ernst Abbe 1946-48, SG Stadion Jena 1948-49, BSG Carl Zeiss Jena 1949-51, BSG Mechanik Jena 1951, BSG Motor Jena 195154, SC Motor Jena 1954-66

BRANDENBURG (Population - 94,000)
BSV Stahl Brandenburg (1950)
Stadion am Quenz 15,000 – White/Blue

FRANKFURT AN DER ODER (Population - 86,000)
FC Victoria 91 (1951)
Freundschaft 16,000 – Yellow/White
Previous names - SV Vorwärts Leipzig 1951-53, ASK Vorwärts Berlin 1954-71, FC Vorwärts Frankfurt/Oder 1971-91

FREIBURG (Population - 51,000)
Sport-Club Freiburg (1904)
Dreisamstadion 15,000 – Red, white trim

HOMBURG (Population - 41,000)
FC 08 Homburg/Saar (1908)
Waldstadion 25,000 – Green/White

AUE
FC Erzgebirge Aue (1946)
Erzgebirgestadion 20,000 – Violet/White
Previous names - Pneumatik Aue 1946-49, Zentra Wismut Aue 1949-51, Wismut Aue 1951-54, SC Wismut Karl-Marx-Stadt 1954-63, BSG Wismut Aue 1963-90

THE GERMAN CHAMPIONSHIP

Year	Winner	Score	Runner-up
1903	VfB Leipzig	7-2	DFC Prague
1904	-		
1905	Union 92 Berlin	2-0	Karlsruher FV
1906	VfB Leipzig	2-1	Pforzheim
1907	SC Freiburg	3-1	Viktoria Berlin
1908	Viktoria Berlin	3-1	Stuttgarter Kickers
1909	Phönix Karlsruhe	4-2	Viktoria Berlin
1910	Karlsruher FV	1-0	Holstein Kiel
1911	Viktoria Berlin	3-1	VfB Leipzig
1912	Holstein Kiel	1-0	Karlsruher FV
1913	VfB Leipzig	3-1	MSV Duisburg
1914	SPVgg Fürth	3-2	VfB Leipzig
1915-19	-		
1920	1.FC Nürnberg	2-0	SPVgg Fürth
1921	1.FC Nürnberg	5-0	Vorwärts Berlin
1922	-		
1923	Hamburger SV	3-0	Union Berlin
1924	1.FC Nürnberg	3-0	Hamburger SV
1925	1.FC Nürnberg	1-0	FSV Frankfurt
1926	SPVgg Fürth	4-1	Hertha BSC Berlin
1927	1.FC Nürnberg	2-0	Hertha BSC Berlin
1928	Hamburger SV	5-2	Hertha BSC Berlin
1929	SPVgg Fürth	3-2	Hertha BSC Berlin
1930	Hertha BSC Berlin	5-4	Holstein Kiel
1931	Hertha BSC Berlin	3-2	TSV München 1860
1932	Bayern München	2-0	Eintracht Frankfurt
1933	Fortuna Düsseldorf	3-0	FC Schalke 04
1934	FC Schalke 04	2-1	1.FC Nürnberg
1935	FC Schalke 04	6-4	VfB Stuttgart
1936	1.FC Nürnberg	2-1	Fortuna Düsseldorf
1937	FC Schalke 04	2-0	1.FC Nürnberg
1938	Hannover 96	3-3 4-3	FC Schalke 04
1939	FC Schalke 04	9-0	Admira Wien
1940	FC Schalke 04	1-0	Dresdner SC
1941	Rapid Wien	4-3	FC Schalke 04
1942	FC Schalke 04	2-0	First Vienna FC
1943	Dresdner SC	3-0	1.FC Saarbrücken
1944	Dresdner SC	4-0	Hamburger SV

THE WEST GERMAN CHAMPIONSHIP

Year	Winner	Score	Runner-up
1945-47	-		
1948	1.FC Nürnberg	2-1	1.FC Kaiserslautern
1949	VfR Mannheim	3-2	Borussia Dortmund
1950	VfB Stuttgart	2-1	Kickers Offenbach
1951	1.FC Kaiserslautern	2-1	Preussen Münster
1952	VfB Stuttgart	3-2	1.FC Saarbrücken
1953	1.FC Kaiserslautern	4-1	VfB Stuttgart
1954	Hannover 96	5-1	1.FC Kaiserslautern
1955	Rot-Weiss Essen	4-3	1.FC Kaiserslautern
1956	Borussia Dortmund	4-2	Karlsruher SC
1957	Borussia Dortmund	4-1	Hamburger SV
1958	FC Schalke 04	3-0	Hamburger SV
1959	Eintracht Frankfurt	5-3	Kickers Offenbach
1960	Hamburger SV	3-2	1.FC Köln
1961	1.FC Nürnberg	3-0	Borussia Dortmund
1962	1.FC Köln	4-0	1.FC Nürnberg
1963	Borussia Dortmund	3-1	1.FC Köln

THE BUNDESLIGA

Year	Standings
1964q	1.FC Köln 45 MSV Duisburg 39 Eintracht Frankfurt 39
1965	Werder Bremen 41 1.FC Köln 38 Borussia Dortmund 36
1966t	TSV München 1860 50 Borussia Dortmund 47 Bayern München 47
1967	Eintracht Braunschweig 43 TSV München 1860 41 Borussia Dortmund 39
1968	1.FC Nürnberg 47 Werder Bremen 44 Borussia Mönchengladbach 42
1969	Bayern München 46 Alemania Aachen 38 Borussia Mönchengladbach 37
1970	Borussia Mönchengladbach 51 Bayern München 47 Hertha BSC Berlin 45
1971	Borussia Mönchengladbach 50 Bayern München 48 Hertha BSC Berlin 41
1972	Bayern München 55 FC Schalke 04 52 Borussia Mönchengladbach 43
1973	Bayern München 54 1.FC Köln 43 Fortuna Düsseldorf 42

1974 Bayern München 49 Borussia Mönchengladbach 48 Fortuna Düsseldorf 41

1975 Borussia Mönchengladbach 50 Hertha BSC Berlin 44 Eintracht Frankfurt 43

1976 Borussia. Mönchengladbach 45 Hamburger SV 41 Bayern München 40

1977 Borussia Mönchengladbach 44 FC Schalke 04 43 Eintracht Braunschweig 43

1978 1.FC Köln 48 Borussia Mönchengladbach 48 Hertha BSC Berlin 40

1979 Hamburger SV 49 VfB Stuttgart 48 1.FC Kaiserslautern 43

1980 Bayern München 50 Hamburger SV 48 VfB Stuttgart & 1.FC Kaiserslautern 41

1981 Bayern München 53 Hamburger SV 49 VfB Stuttgart 46

1982 Hamburger SV 48 1.FC Köln 45 Bayern München 43

1983 Hamburger SV 52 Werder Bremen 52 VfB Stuttgart 48

1984 VfB Stuttgart 48 Hamburger SV 48 Borussia Mönchengladbach 48

1985 Bayern München 50 Werder Bremen 46 1.FC Köln 40

1986 Bayern München 49 Werder Bremen 49 Bayer Uerdingen 45

1987 Bayern München 53 Hamburger SV 47 Borussia Mönchengladbach 43

1988 Werder Bremen 52 Bayern München 48 1.FC Köln 48

1989 Bayern München 50 1.FC Köln 45 Werder Bremen 44

1990 Bayern München 49 1.FC Köln 43 Eintracht Frankfurt 43

1991 1.FC Kaiserslautern 48 Bayern München 45 Werder Bremen 42

1992 VfB Stuttgart 52 Borussia Dortmund 52 Eintracht Frankfurt 50

1993 Werder Bremen 48 Bayern München 47 Eintracht Frankfurt 42

1994 Bayern München 44 1.FC Kaiserslautern 43 Bayer Leverkusen 39

1995 Borussia Dortmund 49 Werder Bremen 48 SC Freiburg 46

GERMAN CUP FINALS

1935	1.FC Nürnberg	2-0	FC Schalke 04
1936	VFB Leipzig	2-1	FC Schalke 04
1937	Schalke 04	2-1	Fortuna Düsseldorf
1938	Rapid Wien	3-1	FSV Frankfurt
1939	1.FC Nürnberg	2-0	SV Waldhof Mannheim
1940	Dresdner SC	2-1	1.FC Nürnberg
1941	Dresdner SC	2-1	FC Schalke 04
1942	TSV München 1860	2-0	FC Schalke 04
1943	First Vienna FC	3-2	Hamburger SV

WEST GERMAN CUP FINALS

1953	Rot-Weiss Essen	2-1	Alemania Aachen
1954	VfB Stuttgart	1-0	1.FC Köln
1955	Karlsruher SC	3-2	FC Schalke 04
1956	Karlsruher SC	3-1	Hamburger SV
1957	Bayern München	1-0	Fortuna Düsseldorf
1958	VfB Stuttgart	4-3	Fortuna Düsseldorf
1959	Schwarz-Weiss Essen	5-2	Borussia Neunkirchen
1960	B. Mönchengladbach	3-2	Karlsruher SC
1961	Werder Bremen	2-0	1.FC Kaiserslautern
1962	1.FC Nürnberg	2-1	Fortuna Düsseldorf
1963	Hamburger SV	3-0	Borussia Dortmund
1964	TSV München 1860	2-0	Eintracht Frankfurt
1965	Borussia Dortmund	2-0	Alemannia Aachen
1966	Bayern München	4-2	MSV Duisburg
1967	Bayern München	4-0	Hamburger SV
1968	1.FC Köln	4-1	VfL Bochum
1969	Bayern München	2-1	FC Schalke 04
1970	Kickers Offenbach	2-1	1.FC Köln
1971	Bayern München	2-1	1.FC Köln
1972	FC Schalke 04	5-0	1.FC Kaiserslautern
1973	B. Mönchengladbach	2-1	1.FC Köln
1974	Eintracht Frankfurt	3-1	Hamburger SV
1975	Eintracht Frankfurt	1-0	MSV Duisburg
1976	Hamburger SV	2-0	1.FC Kaiserslautern
1977	1.FC Köln	1-1 1-0	Hertha BSC Berlin
1978	1.FC Köln	2-0	Fortuna Düsseldorf
1979	Fortuna Düsseldorf	1-0	Hertha BSC Berlin
1980	Fortuna Düsseldorf	2-1	1.FC Köln
1981	Eintracht Frankfurt	3-1	1.FC Kaiserslautern
1982	Bayern München	4-2	1.FC Nürnberg
1983	1.FC Köln	1-0	Fortuna Köln
1984	Bayern München	1-1 7-6p	B. Mönchengladbach
1985	Bayer Uerdingen	2-1	Bayern München
1986	Bayern München	5-2	VfB Stuttgart
1987	Hamburger SV	3-1	Stuttgarter Kickers
1988	Eintracht Frankfurt	1-0	VfL Bochum
1989	Borussia Dortmund	4-1	Werder Bremen
1990	1.FC Kaiserslautern	3-2	Werder Bremen
1991	Werder Bremen	1-1 4-3p	1.FC Köln

GERMAN CUP FINALS

1992	Hannover 96	0-0 4-3p	B. Mönchengladbach
1993	Bayer Leverkusen	1-0	Hertha BSC Berlin (Am)
1994	Werder Bremen	3-1	Rot-Weiss Essen
1995	B. Mönchengladbach	3-0	VfL Wolfsburg

THE EAST GERMAN LEAGUE CHAMPIONSHIP

1948 SG Planitz 1-0 Freiimfelde Halle

1949 ZSG Halle 4-1 Fortuna Erfurt

1950n Horch Zwickau 41 SG Friederichstadt 39 Waggonbau Dessau 37

1951t Chemie Leipzig 50 Turbine Erfurt 50 Motor Zwickau 43

1952u Turbine Halle 53 Polizei Dresden 49 Chemie Leipzig 47

1953r Dynamo Dresden 38 Wismut Aue 38 Motor Zwickau 37

1954p Turbine Erfurt 39 Chemie Leipzig 35 Dynamo Dresden 34

1955n Turbine Erfurt 34 Wismut K-M-S 33 Rotor Leipzig 30

1956 Wismut K-M-S 38 Brieske-Senftenberg 36 SC Lokomotive Leipzig 34

1957 Wismut K-M-S 36 Vorwärts Berlin 33 Rotor Leipzig 32

1958 Vorwärts Berlin 38 Motor Jena 32 Brieske-Senftenberg 30

1959 Wismut K-M-S 39 Vorwärts Berlin 35 Dynamo Berlin 33

1960 Vorwärts Berlin 41 Dynamo Berlin 32 SC Lokomotive Leipzig 32

1961 -

1962w Vorwärts Berlin 50 Empor Rostock 47 Dynamo Berlin 45

1963n Motor Jena 39 Empor Rostock 33 Vorwärts Berlin 31

1964 Chemie Leipzig 35 Empor Rostock 33 SC Leipzig 32

1965 Vorwärts Berlin 37 Motor Jena 32 Chemie Leipzig 31

1966 Vorwärts Berlin 34 Motor Jena 32 Lokomotive Leipzig 28

1967 FC Karl-Marx-Stadt 37 Lokomotive Leipzig 30 Motor Zwickau 27

1968 Carl-Zeiss Jena 39 Hansa Rostock 34 1.FC Magdeburg 33

1969 Vorwärts Berlin 34 Carl-Zeiss Jena 32 1.FC Magdeburg 31

1970 Carl-Zeiss Jena 39 Vorwärts Berlin 32 Dynamo Dresden 31

1971 Dynamo Dresden 39 Carl-Zeiss Jena 33 Chemie Halle 30

1972 1.FC Magdeburg 38 Dynamo Berlin 35 Dynamo Dresden 33

1973 Dynamo Dresden 42 Carl-Zeiss Jena 39 I.FC Magdeburg 34
1974 I.FC Magdeburg 39 Carl-Zeiss Jena 36 Dynamo Dresden 35
1975 I.FC Magdeburg 41 Carl-Zeiss Jena 38 Dynamo Dresden 32
1976 Dynamo Dresden 43 Dynamo Berlin 37 I.FC Magdeburg 36
1977 Dynamo Dresden 38 I.FC Magdeburg 34 Carl-Zeiss Jena 33
1978 Dynamo Dresden 41 I.FC Magdeburg 38 Dynamo Berlin 35
1979 Dynamo Berlin 46 Dynamo Dresden 39 Carl-Zeiss Jena 34
1980 Dynamo Berlin 43 Dynamo Dresden 42 Carl-Zeiss Jena 32
1981 Dynamo Berlin 39 Carl-Zeiss Jena 36 I.FC Magdeburg 34
1982 Dynamo Berlin 41 Dynamo Dresden 34 Lokomotive Leipzig 33
1983 Dynamo Berlin 46 Vorwärts Frankfurt 34 Carl-Zeiss Jena 34
1984 Dynamo Berlin 39 Dynamo Dresden 37 Lokomotive Leipzig 37
1985 Dynamo Berlin 44 Dynamo Dresden 38 Lokomotive Leipzig 38
1986 Dynamo Berlin 34 Lokomotive Leipzig 32 Carl-Zeiss Jena 31
1987 Dynamo Berlin 42 Dynamo Dresden 36 Lokomotive Leipzig 34
1988 Dynamo Berlin 37 Lokomotive Leipzig 37 Dynamo Dresden 33
1989 Dynamo Dresden 40 Dynamo Berlin 32 FC Karl-Marx-Stadt 30
1990 Dynamo Dresden 36 Chemnitzer FC 36 I.FC Magdeburg 34
1991 Hansa Rostock 35 Dynamo Dresden 32 Rot-Weiss Erfurt 31

Play-offs

1951	Chemie Leipzig	2-0	Turbine Erfurt
1953	Dynamo Dresden	3-2	Wismut Aue

EAST GERMAN CUP FINALS

1949	Waggonbau Dessau	1-0	Gera Süd
1950	EHW Thale	4-0	KWU Erfurt
1951	-		
1952	VP Dresden	3-0	SC Einheit Pankow
1953	-		
1954	Vorwärts Berlin	2-1	Motor Zwickau
1955	Wismut K-M-S	3-2	Empor Rostock
1956	Chemie Halle	2-1	Vorwärts Berlin
1957	SC Lokomotive Leipzig	2-1	Empor Rostock
1958	Einheit Dresden	2-1	SC Lokomotive Leipzig
1959	Dynamo Berlin	0-0 3-2	Wismut K-M-S
1960	Motor Jena	3-2	Empor Rostock
1961	-		
1962	Chemie Halle	3-1	Dynamo Berlin
1963	Motor Zwickau	3-0	Chemie Zeitz
1964	Aufbau Magdeburg	3-2	SC Leipzig
1965	Aufbau Magdeburg	2-1	Motor Jena
1966	Chemie Leipzig	1-0	Lokomotive Stendal
1967	Motor Zwickau	3-0	Hansa Rostock
1968	I.FC Union Berlin	2-1	Carl-Zeiss Jena
1969	I.FC Magdeburg	4-0	FC Karl-Marx-Stadt
1970	Vorwärts Berlin	4-2	Lokomotive Leipzig
1971	Dynamo Dresden	2-1	Dynamo Berlin
1972	Carl-Zeiss Jena	2-1	Dynamo Dresden
1973	I.FC Magdeburg	3-2	Lokomotive Leipzig
1974	Carl-Zeiss Jena	3-1	Dynamo Dresden
1975	Sachsenring Zwickau	2-2 4-3p	Dynamo Dresden
1976	Lokomotive Leipzig	3-0	Vorwärts Frankfurt/Oder
1977	Dynamo Dresden	3-2	Lokomotive Leipzig
1978	I.FC Magdeburg	1-0	Dynamo Dresden
1979	I.FC Magdeburg	1-0	Dynamo Berlin
1980	Carl-Zeiss Jena	3-1	Rot-Weiss Erfurt
1981	Lokomotive Leipzig	4-1	Vorwärts Frankfurt/Oder
1982	Dynamo Dresden	1-1 5-4p	Dynamo Berlin
1983	I.FC Magdeburg	4-0	FC Karl-Marx-Stadt
1984	Dynamo Dresden	2-1	Dynamo Berlin
1985	Dynamo Dresden	3-2	Dynamo Berlin
1986	Lokomotive Leipzig	5-1	I.FC Union Berlin
1987	Lokomotive Leipzig	4-1	Hansa Rostock
1988	Dynamo Berlin	2-0	Carl-Zeiss Jena
1989	Dynamo Berlin	1-0	FC Karl-Marx-Stadt
1990	Dynamo Dresden	2-1	PSV Schwerin
1991	Hansa Rostock	1-0	Stahl Eisenhüttenstadt

INTERNATIONAL MATCHES PLAYED BY EAST GERMANY

21-09-1952	Poland	L 0-3	Warsaw	Fr	
26-10	Romania	L 1-3	Bucharest	Fr	Schnieke
14-06-1953	Bulgaria	D 0-0	Dresden	Fr	
8-05-1954	Romania	L 0-1	Berlin	Fr	
26-09	Poland	L 0-1	Rostock	Fr	
24-10	Bulgaria	L 1-3	Sofia	Fr	Meier
18-09-1955	Romania	W 3-2	Bucharest	Fr	Tröger 2, Wirth
20-11	Bulgaria	W 1-0	Berlin	Fr	Tröger
22-07-1956	Poland	W 2-0	Chorzow	Fr	Tröger, Assmy
20-09	Indonesia	W 3-1	Karl-Marx-Stadt	Fr	Tröger 2, Wirth
14-10	Bulgaria	L 1-3	Sofia	Fr	Wirth
10-03-1957	Luxembourg	W 3-0	Berlin	Fr	Tröger 2, Schröter
19-05	Wales	W 2-1	Leipzig	WCq	Wirth, Tröger
16-06	Czechoslovakia	L 1-3	Brno	WCq	Wirth
25-09	Wales	L 1-4	Cardiff	WCq	Kaiser
27-10	Czechoslovakia	L 1-4	Leipzig	WCq	Müller.H
1-05-1958	Albania	D 1-1	Tirana	Fr	Tröger
28-06	Poland	D 1-1	Rostock	Fr	Klingbiel
13-08	Norway	L 5-6	Oslo	Fr	Schröter, Wirth, Assmy

14-09	Romania	W 3-2	Leipzig	Fr	Schröter, Assmy, Wirth
5-10	Bulgaria	D 1-1	Berlin	Fr	Tröger
2-11	Norway	W 4-1	Leipzig	Fr	Müller.H 2, Assmy, Schröter
11-02-1959	Indonesia	D 2-2	Djakarta	Fr	Wirth, Ducke.R
1-05	Hungary	L 0-1	Dresden	Fr	
21-06	Portugal	L 0-2	Berlin	ECr1	
28-06	Portugal	L 2-3	Oporto	ECr1	Vogt, Kohle
6-09	Finland	L 2-3	Helsinki	Fr	Franz.R, Schröter
10-07-1960	Bulgaria	L 0-2	Sofia	Fr	
17-08	Soviet Union	L 0-1	Leipzig	Fr	
30-10	Finland	W 5-1	Rostock	Fr	Nöldner 2, Erler, Ducke.P, Heine
4-12	Tunisia	W 3-0	Tunis	Fr	Nöldner, Müller.H, Meyer
11-12	Morocco	W 3-2	Casablanca	Fr	Meyer, Ducke.P, Müller.H
16-04-1961	Hungary	L 0-2	Budapest	WCq	
14-05	Holland	D 1-1	Leipzig	WCq	Erler
28-05	Denmark	D 1-1	Copenhagen	Fr	Mühlbächer
21-06	Morocco	L 1-2	Erfurt	Fr	Nöldner
10-09	Hungary	L 2-3	Berlin	WCq	Erler, Ducke.P
22-10	Poland	L 1-3	Wroclaw	Fr	Erler
10-12	Morocco	L 0-2	Casablanca	Fr	
3-05-1962	Soviet Union	L 1-2	Moscow	Fr	Erler
16-05	Yugoslavia	L 1-3	Belgrade	Fr	Ducke.R
23-05	Denmark	W 4-1	Leipzig	Fr	Schröter 3, Ducke.R
16-09	Yugoslavia	D 2-2	Leipzig	Fr	Wirth, Schröter
14-10	Romania	W 3-2	Dresden	Fr	Wirth, Schröter, Nachtigall
21-11	Czechoslovakia	W 2-1	Berlin	ECr1	Erler, Liebrecht
9-12	Mali	W 2-1	Bamoko	Fr	Erler 2
16-12	Guinea	W 3-2	Conakry	Fr	Frenzel 2, Vogel
31-03-1963	Czechoslovakia	D 1-1	Prague	ECr1	Ducke.P
12-05	Romania	L 2-3	Bucharest	Fr	Ducke.P, Nöldner
2-06	England	L 1-2	Leipzig	Fr	Ducke.P
4-09	Bulgaria	D 1-1	Magdeburg	Fr	Nachtigall
19-10	Hungary	L 1-2	Berlin	ECr2	
3-11	Hungary	D 3-3	Budapest	ECr2	
17-12	Burma	W 5-1	Rangoon	Fr	Backhaus, Stöcker, Kleiminger, Körner, Frässdorf
12-01-1964	Ceylon	W 12-1	Colombo	Fr	Kleiminger 4, Stöcker 3, Barthels 2, Nöldner, Backhaus, Frässdorf
23-02	Ghana	L 0-3	Accra	Fr	
3-01-1965	Uruguay	W 2-0	Montevideo	Fr	Frenzel, Ducke.P
25-04	Austria	D 1-1	Vienna	WCq	Nöldner
23-05	Hungary	D 1-1	Leipzig	WCq	Vogel
4-09	Bulgaria	L 2-3	Varna	Fr	Vogel, Nöldner
9-10	Hungary	L 2-3	Budapest	WCq	Ducke.P 2
31-10	Austria	W 1-0	Leipzig	WCq	Nöldner
27-04-1966	Sweden	W 4-1	Leipzig	Fr	Nöldner 2, Ducke.R, Frenzel
2-07	Chile	W 5-2	Leipzig	Fr	Nöldner, Frenzel, Vogel, Frässdorf, Geisler
4-09	Egypt	W 6-0	Karl-Marx-Stadt	Fr	Erler 2, Pankau, Vogel, Irmscher, Engelhardt
11-09	Poland	W 2-0	Erfurt	Fr	Erler, Körner
21-09	Romania	W 2-0	Gera	Fr	Nöldner, Frenzel
23-10	Soviet Union	D 2-2	Moscow	Fr	Frässdorf, Nöldner
5-04-1967	Holland	W 4-3	Leipzig	ECq	Frenzel 3, Vogel
17-05	Sweden	W 1-0	Halsingborg	Fr	Nöldner
4-06	Denmark	D 1-1	Copenhagen	ECq	Löwe
13-09	Holland	L 0-1	Amsterdam	ECq	
27-09	Hungary	L 1-3	Budapest	ECq	Frenzel
11-10	Denmark	W 3-2	Leipzig	ECq	Pankau 2, Körner
29-10	Hungary	W 1-0	Leipzig	ECq	Frenzel
18-11	Romania	W 1-0	Berlin	OGq	Pankau
6-12	Romania	W 1-0	Bucharest	OGq	Irmscher
2-02-1968	Czechoslovakia*	D 2-2	Santiago	Fr	Irmscher, Kreische
20-10	Poland	D 1-1	Szczecin	Fr	Löwe
29-03-1969	Italy	D 2-2	Berlin	WCq	Vogel, Kreische
16-04	Wales	W 2-1	Dresden	WCq	Löwe, Rock
22-06	Chile	L 0-1	Magdeburg	Fr	
9-07	Egypt	W 7-0	Rostock	Fr	Frenzel 3, Sparwasser 2, Vogel, Löwe
25-07	Soviet Union	D 2-2	Leipzig	Fr	Löwe, Frenzel
22-10	Wales	W 3-1	Cardiff	WCq	Vogel, Löwe, Frenzel
22-11	Italy	L 0-3	Naples	WCq	
8-12	Iraq	D 1-1	Baghdad	Fr	Körner
19-12	Egypt	W 3-1	Cairo	Fr	Kreische 2, Sparwasser
16-05-1970	Poland	D 1-1	Krakow	Fr	Vogel

Date	Opponent	Result	Venue	Comp	Scorers
26-07	Iraq	W 5-0	Jena	Fr	Ducke.P 2, Kreische, Vogel, Weise
6-09	Poland	W 5-0	Rostock	Fr	Kreische 2, Stempel, Stein, Vogel
11-11	Holland	W 1-0	Dresden	ECq	Ducke.P
15-11	Luxembourg	W 5-0	Luxembourg	ECq	Kreische 4, Vogel
25-11	England	L 1-3	London	Fr	Vogel
2-02-1971	Chile	W 1-0	Santiago	Fr	Kreische
8-02	Uruguay	W 3-0	Montevideo	Fr	Stein 2, Richter
10-02	Uruguay	D 1-1	Montevideo	Fr	Frenzel
24-04	Luxembourg	W 2-1	Gera	ECq	Kreische, Frenzel
9-05	Yugoslavia	L 1-2	Leipzig	ECq	Löwe
16-08	Mexico	W 1-0	Guadalajara	Fr	Sparwasser
18-09	Mexico	D 1-1	Leipzig	Fr	Löwe
25-09	Czechoslovakia	D 1-1	Berlin	Fr	Streich
10-10	Holland	L 2-3	Rotterdam	ECq	Vogel 2
16-10	Yugoslavia	D 0-0	Belgrade	ECq	
27-05-1972	Uruguay	W 1-0	Leipzig	Fr	Irmscher
31-05	Uruguay	D 0-0	Rostock	Fr	
28-08	Ghana	W 4-0	Munich	OGr1	Kreische 2, Sparwasser, Streich
30-08	Colombia *	W 6-1	Passau	OGr1	
1-09	Poland	L 1-2	Nuremberg	OGr1	Streich
3-09	Hungary *	L 0-2	Passau	OGr2	
5-09	Mexico *	W 7-0	Ingolstadt	OGr2	
8-09	West Germany *	W 3-2	Munich	OGr2	
10-09	Soviet Union	D 2-2	Munich	OG3p	Kreische, Vogel
7-10	Finland	W 5-0	Dresden	WCq	Kreische, Sparwasser 2, Streich 2
1-11	Czechoslovakia	W 3-1	Bratislava	Fr	Kreische 2, Ducke.P
15-02-1973	Colombia	W 2-0	Bogota	Fr	Streich, Kurbjuweit
18-02	Ecuador	D 1-1	Quito	Fr	Kreische
7-04	Albania	W 2-0	Magdeburg	WCq	Streich, Sparwasser
18-04	Belgium	L 0-3	Antwerp	Fr	
16-05	Hungary	W 2-1	Karl-Marx-Stadt	Fr	Streich 2
27-05	Romania	L 0-1	Bucharest	WCq	
6-06	Finland	W 5-1	Tampere	WCq	Streich 2, Löwe, Ducke.P, Kreische
17-07	Iceland	W 2-1	Reykjavik	Fr	
19-07	Iceland	W 2-0	Reykjavik	Fr	
26-09	Romania	W 2-0	Leipzig	WCq	Bransch 2
17-10	Soviet Union	W 1-0	Leipzig	Fr	Streich
3-11	Albania	W 4-1	Tirana	WCq	Streich 2, Löwe, Sparwasser
21-11	Hungary	W 1-0	Budapest	Fr	Lauck
26-02-1974	Tunisia	W 4-0	Tunis	Fr	Lauck 2, Frenzel, Dörner
28-02	Algeria	W 3-1	Algiers	Fr	Streich, Matoul, Löwe
13-03	Belgium	W 1-0	Berlin	Fr	Streich
27-03	Czechoslovakia	W 1-0	Dresden	Fr	Streich
22-05	Norway	W 1-0	Rostock	Fr	Sparwasser
29-05	England	D 1-1	Leipzig	Fr	Streich
14-06	Australia	W 2-0	Hamburg	WCr1	OG, Streich
18-06	Chile	D 1-1	Berlin	WCr1	Hoffman
22-06	West Germany	W 1-0	Hamburg	WCr1	Sparwasser
26-06	Brazil	L 0-1	Hanover	WCr2	
30-06	Holland	L 0-2	Gelsenkirchen	WCr2	
3-07	Argentina	D 1-1	Gelsenkirchen	WCr2	Streich
4-09	Poland	W 3-1	Warsaw	Fr	Kurbjuweit, Vogel, Dörner
25-09	Czechoslovakia	L 1-3	Prague	Fr	Hoffman
9-10	Canada	W 2-0	Frankfurt	Fr	Hoffman, Dörner
12-10	Iceland	D 1-1	Magdeburg	ECq	Hoffman
30-10	Scotland	L 0-3	Glasgow	Fr	
16-11	France	D 2-2	Paris	ECq	Sparwasser, Kreische
7-12	Belgium	D 0-0	Leipzig	ECq	
26-03-1975	Bulgaria	D 0-0	Berlin	Fr	
28-05	Poland	L 1-2	Halle	Fr	Vogel
5-06	Iceland	L 1-2	Reykjavik	ECq	Pommerenke
29-07	Canada	W 3-0	Toronto	Fr	Vogel, OG, Bransch
31-07	Canada	W 7-1	Ottawa	Fr	Vogel 3, Streich 2, Riediger, Pommerenke
27-09	Belgium	W 2-1	Brussels	ECq	Ducke.P, Häfner
12-10	France	W 2-1	Leipzig	ECq	Streich, Vogel
19-11	Czechoslovakia	D 1-1	Brno	OGq	Weise
7-04-1976	Czechoslovakia	D 0-0	Leipzig	OGq	
21-04	Algeria	W 5-0	Cottbus	Fr	Kotte 2, Riediger, Heidler, Dörner
18-07	Brazil *	D 0-0	Toronto	OGr1	
22-07	Spain *	W 1-0	Montreal	OGr1	
25-07	France *	W 4-0	Ottawa	OGqf	

Date	Opponent	Result	Venue	Comp	Scorers
27-07	Soviet Union	W 2-1	Montreal	OGsf	Kurbjuweit, Dörner
31-07	Poland	W 3-1	Montreal	OGf	Häfner, Schade, Hoffmann
22-09	Hungary	D 1-1	Berlin	Fr	Riediger
27-10	Bulgaria	W 4-0	Sliven	Fr	Streich 2, Heidler, Schade
17-11	Turkey	D 1-1	Dresden	WCq	Kotte
2-04-1977	Malta	W 1-0	Gzira	WCq	Streich
27-04	Romania	D 1-1	Bucharest	Fr	Kurbjuweit
12-07	Argentina	L 0-2	Buenos Aires	Fr	
28-07	Soviet Union	W 2-1	Leipzig	Fr	Häfner, Sparwasser
17-08	Sweden	W 1-0	Stockholm	Fr	Dörner
7-09	Scotland	W 1-0	Berlin	Fr	Schade
24-09	Austria	D 1-1	Vienna	WCq	Hoffmann
12-10	Austria	D 1-1	Leipzig	WCq	Löwe
29-10	Malta	W 9-0	Babelsberg	WCq	Streich 3, Hoffmann 3, Weber, Schade, Sparwasser
16-11	Turkey	W 2-1	Izmir	WCq	Schade, Hoffmann
8-03-1978	Switzerland	W 3-1	Karl-Marx-Stadt	Fr	Riediger, Hoffmann 2
4-04	Sweden	L 0-1	Leipzig	Fr	
19-04	Belgium	D 0-0	Magdeburg	Fr	
30-08	Bulgaria	D 2-2	Erfurt	Fr	Eigendorf 2
6-09	Czechoslovakia	W 2-1	Leipzig	Fr	Pommerenke, Eigendorf
4-10	Iceland	W 3-1	Halle	ECq	Peter, Riediger, Hoffmann
15-11	Holland	L 0-3	Rotterdam	ECq	
9-02-1979	Iraq	D 1-1	Baghdad	Fr	Streich
12-02	Iraq	L 1-2	Baghdad	Fr	Kühn
26-02	Bulgaria	L 0-1	Burgas	Fr	
28-03	Hungary	L 0-3	Budapest	Fr	
18-04	Poland	W 2-1	Leipzig	ECq	Lindemann, Streich
5-05	Switzerland	W 2-0	St. Gallen	ECq	Lindemann, Streich
1-06	Romania	W 1-0	Berlin	Fr	Streich
5-09	Soviet Union	L 0-1	Moscow	Fr	
12-09	Iceland	W 3-0	Reykjavik	ECq	Weber 2, Streich
26-09	Poland	D 1-1	Chorzow	ECq	Häfner
13-10	Switzerland	W 5-2	Berlin	ECq	Hoffmann 3, Weber, Schnuphase
21-11	Holland	L 2-3	Leipzig	ECq	Schnuphase, Streich
13-02-1980	Spain	W 1-0	Malaga	Fr	Streich
2-04	Romania	D 2-2	Bucharest	Fr	Streich, Schmuck
16-04	Greece	W 2-0	Leipzig	Fr	Weber, Streich
7-05	Soviet Union	D 2-2	Rostock	Fr	Kühn, Terletzki
8-10	Czechoslovakia	W 1-0	Prague	Fr	Streich
15-10	Spain	D 0-0	Leipzig	Fr	
19-11	Hungary	W 2-0	Halle	Fr	Trocha, Streich
4-04-1981	Malta	W 2-1	Gzira	WCq	Schnuphase, Häfner
19-04	Italy	D 0-0	Udine	Fr	
2-05	Poland	L 0-1	Chorzow	WCq	
19-05	Cuba	W 5-0	Senftenberg	Fr	Heun 2, Schnuphase, Streich, OG
10-10	Poland	L 2-3	Leipzig	WCq	Schnuphase, Streich
11-11	Malta	W 5-1	Jena	WCq	Krause, Streich, Heun, Liebers, OG
26-02-1982	Brazil	L 1-3	Natal	Fr	Dörner
10-02	Greece	W 1-0	Athens	Fr	Liebers
2-03	Iraq	D 0-0	Baghdad	Fr	
14-04	Italy	W 1-0	Leipzig	Fr	Hause
5-05	Soviet Union	L 0-1	Moscow	Fr	
19-05	Sweden	D 2-2	Halmstad	Fr	Jarosin, Dörner
8-09	Iceland	W 1-0	Reykjavik	Fr	Streich
22-09	Bulgaria	D 2-2	Burgas	Fr	Dörner, Riediger
13-10	Scotland	L 0-2	Glasgow	ECq	
17-11	Romania	W 4-1	Karl-Marx-Stadt	Fr	Kühn 2, Schnuphase, Heun
10-02-1983	Tunisia	W 2-0	Tunis	Fr	Streich, Kühn
23-02	Greece	W 2-1	Dresden	Fr	Richter, Streich
16-03	Finland	W 3-1	Magdeburg	Fr	Streich, Richter 2
30-03	Belgium	L 1-2	Leipzig	ECq	Streich
13-04	Bulgaria	W 3-0	Gera	Fr	Steinbach, Streich, Busse
27-04	Belgium	L 1-2	Brussels	ECq	Streich
14-05	Switzerland	D 0-0	Geneva	ECq	
26-07	Soviet Union	L 1-3	Leipzig	Fr	Streich
24-08	Romania	L 0-1	Bucharest	Fr	
12-10	Switzerland	W 3-0	Berlin	ECq	Richter, Ernst, Streich
16-11	Scotland	W 2-1	Halle	ECq	Kreer, Streich
15-02-1984	Greece	W 3-1	Athens	Fr	Döschner, Raab, Gütschow
28-03	Czechoslovakia	W 2-1	Erfurt	Fr	Minge, Ernst
11-08	Mexico	D 1-1	Berlin	Fr	Backs

Date	Opponent	Result	Venue	Comp	Scorers
29-08	Romania	W 2-1	Dresden	Fr	Minge, Liebers
12-09	England	L 0-1	London	Fr	
12-09	Greece	W 1-0	Zwickau	Fr	Gütschow
10-10	Algeria	W 5-2	Aue	Fr	Ernst 2, Stahmann, Rohde, Streich
20-10	Yugoslavia	L 2-3	Leipzig	WCq	Glowatzky, Ernst
17-11	Luxembourg	W 5-0	Esch	WCq	Ernst 3, Minge 2
8-12	France	L 0-2	Paris	WCq	
29-01-1985	Uruguay	L 0-3	Montevideo	Fr	
6-02	Ecuador	W 3-2	Guayaquil	Fr	Ernst 2, Thom
13-03	Algeria	D 1-1	Batna	Fr	Schulz
6-04	Bulgaria	L 0-1	Sofia	WCq	
17-04	Norway	W 1-0	Frankfurt	Fr	Krause
8-05	Denmark	L 1-4	Copenhagen	Fr	Zötzsche
18-05	Luxembourg	W 3-1	Babelsberg	WCq	Minge 2, Ernst
14-08	Norway	W 1-0	Oslo	Fr	Kirsten
11-09	France	W 2-0	Leipzig	WCq	Ernst, Kreer
28-09	Yugoslavia	W 2-1	Belgrade	WCq	Thom 2
16-10	Scotland	D 0-0	Glasgow	Fr	
16-11	Bulgaria	W 2-1	Karl-Marx-Stadt	WCq	Zötzsche, Liebers
9-02-1986	Bulgaria	W 2-1	Queretaro	Fr	Liebers, Zötzsche
14-02	Mexico	W 2-1	San Jose	Fr	Zötzsche 2
19-02	Portugal	W 3-1	Braga	Fr	Thom, Kirsten, Ernst
12-03	Holland	L 0-1	Leipzig	Fr	
26-03	Greece	L 0-2	Athens	Fr	
8-04	Brazil	L 0-3	Goiana	Fr	
23-04	Czechoslovakia	L 0-2	Nitra	Fr	
20-08	Finland	L 0-1	Lahti	Fr	
10-09	Denmark	L 0-1	Leipzig	Fr	
24-09	Norway	D 0-0	Oslo	ECq	
7-10	Bulgaria	L 0-2	Sofia	Fr	
29-10	Iceland	W 2-0	Karl-Marx-Stadt	ECq	Thom, Kirsten
19-11	France	D 0-0	Leipzig	ECq	
25-03-1987	Turkey	L 1-3	Istanbul	Fr	Minge
29-04	Soviet Union	L 0-2	Kiev	ECq	
13-05	Czechoslovakia	W 2-0	Brandenburg	Fr	Raab, Ernst
3-06	Iceland	W 6-0	Reykjavik	ECq	Thom 3, Minge, Doll, Döschner
28-07	Hungary	D 0-0	Leipzig	Fr	
19-08	Poland	L 0-2	Lublin	Fr	
23-09	Tunisia	W 2-0	Gera	Fr	Doll, Kirsten
10-10	Soviet Union	D 1-1	Berlin	ECq	Kirsten
28-10	Norway	W 3-1	Magdeburg	ECq	Kirsten 2, Thom
18-11	France	W 1-0	Paris	ECq	Ernst
13-01-1988	Sweden	L 1-4	Las Palmas	Fr	Thom
15-01	Czechoslovakia	L 0-1	Las Palmas	Fr	
27-01	Spain	D 0-0	Valencia	Fr	
3-03	Morocco	L 1-2	Mohammedia	Fr	Ernst
30-03	Romania	D 3-3	Halle	Fr	Ernst, Zötzsche, Stahmann
13-04	Bulgaria	D 1-1	Burgas	Fr	Stübner
31-08	Greece	W 1-0	Berlin	Fr	Sammer
21-09	Poland	L 1-2	Cottbus	Fr	Ernst
19-10	Iceland	W 2-0	Berlin	WCq	Thom 2
30-11	Turkey	L 1-3	Istanbul	WCq	Thom
13-02-1989	Egypt	W 4-0	Cairo	Fr	Thom 2, Kirsten 2
8-03	Greece	L 2-3	Athens	Fr	Thom, Halata
22-03	Finland	D 1-1	Dresden	Fr	Trautmann
12-04	Turkey	L 0-2	Magdeburg	WCq	
26-04	Soviet Union	L 0-3	Kiev	WCq	
20-05	Austria	D 1-1	Leipzig	WCq	Kirsten
23-08	Bulgaria	D 1-1	Erfurt	Fr	Kirsten
6-09	Iceland	W 3-0	Reykjavik	WCq	Sammer, Ernst, Doll
8-10	Soviet Union	W 2-1	Karl-Marx-Stadt	WCq	Thom, Sammer
25-10	Malta	W 4-0	Ta'Qali	Fr	Doll 2, Steinmann 2
15-11	Austria	L 0-3	Vienna	WCq	
24-01-1990	France	L 0-3	Kuwait City	Fr	
26-01	Kuwait	W 2-1	Kuwait City	Fr	Wuckel 2
28-03	United States	W 3-2	Berlin	Fr	Kirsten 3
11-04	Egypt	W 2-0	Karl-Marx-Stadt	Fr	Peschke, Sammer
25-04	Scotland	W 1-0	Glasgow	Fr	Doll
13-05	Brazil	D 3-3	Rio de Janeiro	Fr	Doll, Ernst, Steinmann
28-07	United States	W 2-1	Milwaukee	Fr	Gerlach, Rische
12-09	Belgium	W 2-0	Brussels	Fr	Sammer 2

LEADING INTERNATIONAL APPEARANCES FOR EAST GERMANY

102	Joachim Streich	(Hansa Rostock,1.FC Magdeburg)	1969-1984
100	Hans-Jürgen Dörner	(Dynamo Dresden)	1969-1985
94	Jürgen Croy #	(Sachsenring Zwickau)	1967-1981
86	Konrad Weise	(Carl Zeiss Jena)	1970-1981
74	Eberhard Vogel	(Motor, SC & FC K-M-S, Carl Zeiss Jena)	1962-1976
72	Bernd Bransch	(HFC Chemie,Carl Zeiss Jena)	1967-1976
68	Peter Ducke	(Motor Jena & Carl Zeiss Jena)	1960-1975
66	Lothar Kurbjuweit	(Carl Zeiss Jena)	1970-1981
	Martin Hoffmann	(1.FC Magdeburg)	1973-1981
65	Ronald Kreer	(1.FC Lokomotive Leipzig)	1982-1989

LEADING INTERNATIONAL GOALSCORERS FOR EAST GERMANY

55	Joachim Streich	(Hansa Rostock,1.FC Magdeburg)	1969-1984
25	Hans-Jürgen Kreische	(Dynamo Dresden)	1968-1975
	Eberhard Vogel	(Motor, SC & FC K-M-S,Carl Zeiss Jena)	1962-1976
20	Rainer Ernst	(Dynamo Berlin)	1981-1990
19	Henning Frenzel	(SC Lok. Leipzig,SC & 1.FC Lok. Leip)	1961-1974
16	Andreas Thom	(Dynamo Berlin)	1984-1990
	Jürgen Nöldner	(Vorwärts Berlin)	1960-1969
	Martin Hoffmann	(1.FC Magdeburg)	1973-1981
15	Jürgen Sparwasser	(1.FC Magdeburg)	1969-1977
	Peter Ducke	(Motor Jena & Carl Zeiss Jena)	1960-1975

Andreas Thom (Bayer Leverkusen) has also scored 2 goals for Germany 1990-

LEADING INTERNATIONAL GOALSCORERS FOR GERMANY AND WEST GERMANY

68	Gerd Müller	(Bayern München)	1966-1974
47	Rudi Völler	(Werder Bremen,Roma, Marseille)	1982-
45	Karl-Heinz Rummenigge	(Bayern München, Internazionale)	1976-1986
43	Uwe Seeler	(Hamburger SV)	1954-1970
33	Fritz Walter	(1.FC Kaiserslautern)	1940-1958
32	Klaus Fischer	(Schalke 04,1.FC Köln)	1977-1982
31	Jürgen Klinsmann	(VfB Stuttgart,Internazionale, Monaco,Tottenham)	1987-
30	Ernst Lehner	(Schwaben Augsburg, Blau-Weiss Berlin)	1933-1942
27	Edmund Conen	(FV Saarbrücken,Stuttgarter Kickers)	1934-1942
24	Richard Hofmann	(Meerane 07,Dresdner SC)	1927-1933

LEADING INTERNATIONAL APPEARANCES FOR GERMANY AND WEST GERMANY

122	Lothar Matthäus	(Mönchengladbach, Bayern München, Internazionale)	1980-
103	Franz Beckenbauer	(Bayern München)	1965-1977
96	Berti Vogts	(Mönchengladbach)	1967-1978
95	Sepp Maier	(Bayern München)	1966-1979
	Karl-Heinz Rummenigge	(Bayern München, Internazionale)	1976-1986
90	Rudi Völler	(Werder Bremen,Roma, Marseille)	1982-
86	Andreas Brehme	(Kaiserslautern, Bayern München,Internazionale, Kaiserslautern)	1984-
81	Karl-Heinz Förster	(VfB Stuttgart)	1978-1986
	Wolfgang Overath	(1.FC Köln)	1963-1974
76	Guido Buchwald	(VfB Stuttgart)	1984-
	Harald Schumacher	(1.FC Köln)	1979-1986

NATIONAL TEAM COACHES

1926-36	Otto Nerz
1936-64	Josef Herberger
1964-78	Helmut Schoen
1978-84	Josef Derwall
1984-90	Franz Beckenbauer
1990-	Berti Vogts

INTERNATIONAL MATCHES PLAYED BY GERMANY

5-04-1908	Switzerland	L 3-5	Basle	Fr	Becker 2, Förderer
20-04	England *	L 1-5	Berlin	Fr	Förderer
7-06	Austria	L 2-3	Vienna	Fr	Jäger, Kipp
16-03-1909	England *	L 0-9	Oxford	Fr	
4-04	Hungary	D 3-3	Budapest	Fr	Worpitzky 2, Ugi
4-04	Switzerland	W 1-0	Karlsruhe	Fr	Kipp
3-04-1910	Switzerland	W 3-2	Basle	Fr	Kipp, Hiller
24-04	Holland	L 2-4	Arnhem	Fr	Kipp, Fick
16-05	Belgium	L 0-3	Duisburg	Fr	
16-10	Holland	L 1-2	Kleve	Fr	Queck
26-03-1911	Switzerland	W 6-2	Stuttgart	Fr	Förderer 2, Fuchs 2, Kipp, Breunig
14-04	England *	D 2-2	Berlin	Fr	Möller.E 2
23-04	Belgium	L 1-2	Liege	Fr	Förderer
18-06	Sweden	W 4-2	Stockholm	Fr	Dumke 3, Kipp
9-10	Austria	L 1-2	Dresden	Fr	Worpitzky
29-10	Sweden	L 1-3	Hamburg	Fr	Möller.E
17-12	Hungary	L 1-4	Munich	Fr	Worpitzky
24-03-1912	Holland	D 5-5	Zwolle	Fr	Hirsch 4, Fuchs
14-04	Hungary	D 4-4	Budapest	Fr	Worpitzky, Kipp, Möller.E, Jäger
5-05	Switzerland	W 2-1	St. Gallen	Fr	Kipp, Mechling
29-06	Austria	L 1-5	Stockholm	OGct	Jäger

1-07	Tzarist Russia	W 16-0	Stockholm	OGct	Fuchs 10, Förderer 4, Oberle, Burger
3-07	Hungary	L 1-3	Stockholm	OGct	Förderer
6-10	Denmark	L 1-3	Copenhagen	Fr	Jäger
17-11	Holland	L 2-3	Leipzig	Fr	Jäger 2
21-03-1913	England *	L 0-3	Berlin	Fr	
18-05	Switzerland	L 1-2	Freiburg	Fr	Kipp
26-10	Denmark	L 1-4	Hamburg	Fr	Jäger
23-11	Belgium	L 2-6	Antwerp	Fr	Fuchs
5-04	Holland	D 4-4	Amsterdam	Fr	Jäger, Wegele, Harder, Queck
27-06-1920	Switzerland	L 1-4	Zurich	Fr	Jäger
26-09	Austria	L 2-3	Vienna	Fr	Sutor, Seiderer
24-10	Hungary	W 1-0	Berlin	Fr	Jäger
5-05-1921	Austria	D 3-3	Dresden	Fr	Seiderer, Träg, Popp
5-06	Hungary	L 0-3	Budapest	Fr	
18-09	Finland	D 3-3	Helsinki	Fr	Herberger 2, Kalb
26-03-1922	Switzerland	D 2-2	Frankfurt	Fr	Seiderer, Franz
23-04	Austria	W 2-0	Vienna	Fr	Jäger, Weissenbacher
2-07	Hungary	D 0-0	Bochum	Fr	
1-01-1923	Italy	L 1-3	Milan	Fr	Seiderer
10-05	Holland	D 0-0	Hamburg	Fr	
3-06	Switzerland	W 2-1	Basle	Fr	Hartmann 2
28-06	Sweden	L 1-2	Stockholm	Fr	Seiderer
12-08	Finland	L 1-2	Dresden	Fr	Claus-Oehler
4-11	Norway	W 1-0	Hamburg	Fr	Harder
13-01-1924	Austria	W 4-3	Nuremberg	Fr	Franz 3, Auer
21-04	Holland	W 1-0	Amsterdam	Fr	Auer
15-06	Norway	W 2-0	Oslo	Fr	Sutor, Wieder
31-08	Sweden	L 1-4	Berlin	Fr	Harder
21-09	Hungary	L 1-4	Budapest	Fr	Harder
23-11	Italy	L 0-1	Duisburg	Fr	
14-12	Switzerland	D 1-1	Stuttgart	Fr	Harder
29-03-1925	Holland	L 1-2	Amsterdam	Fr	Voss
21-06	Sweden	L 0-1	Stockholm	Fr	
26-06	Finland	W 5-3	Helsinki	Fr	Paulsen 3, Ruch, Voss
25-10	Switzerland	W 4-0	Basle	Fr	Harder 3, Hochgesang
18-04-1926	Holland	W 4-2	Dusseldorf	Fr	Pöttinger 3, Harder
20-06	Sweden	D 3-3	Nuremberg	Fr	Harder 3
31-10	Holland	W 3-2	Amsterdam	Fr	Harder 2, Wieder
12-12	Switzerland	L 2-3	Munich	Fr	Hochgesang, K.Scherm
2-10-1927	Denmark	L 1-3	Copenhagen	Fr	Kiessling
23-10	Norway	W 6-2	Hamburg	Fr	Hochgesang 2, Pöttinger 2, Hofmann.L, Kalb
20-11	Holland	D 2-2	Cologne	Fr	Pöttinger 2
15-04-1928	Switzerland	W 3-2	Berne	Fr	Hofmann.R, Hornauer, Albrecht
28-05	Switzerland	W 4-0	Amsterdam	OGr1	Hofmann.R 3, Hornauer
3-06	Uruguay	L 1-4	Amsterdam	OGqf	Hofmann.R
16-09	Denmark	W 2-1	Nuremberg	Fr	Hofmann.L, Heidkamp
23-09	Norway	W 2-0	Oslo	Fr	Kuzorra, Schmitt.J
30-09	Sweden	L 0-2	Stockholm	Fr	
10-02-1929	Switzerland	W 7-1	Mannheim	Fr	Frank 4, Sobek 2, Pöttinger
28-04	Italy	W 2-1	Turin	Fr	Frank, Hornauer
1-06	Scotland	D 1-1	Berlin	Fr	Ruch
23-06	Sweden	W 3-0	Cologne	Fr	Hofmann.R 3
20-10	Finland	W 4-0	Hamburg	Fr	Sackenheim 2, Hofmann.R, Szepan
2-03-1930	Italy	L 0-2	Frankfurt	Fr	
4-05	Switzerland	W 5-0	Zurich	Fr	Kuzorra 3, Hofmann.R 2
10-05	England	D 3-3	Berlin	Fr	Hofmann.R 3
7-09	Denmark	L 3-6	Copenhagen	Fr	Hofmann.R, Kund, Hohmann
28-09	Hungary	W 5-3	Dresden	Fr	Hofmann.L 2, Hofmann.R, Ludwig, Lachner
2-11	Norway	D 1-1	Breslau	Fr	Hanke
15-03-1931	France	L 0-1	Paris	Fr	
26-04	Holland	D 1-1	Amsterdam	Fr	Schlösser
24-05	Austria	L 0-6	Berlin	Fr	
17-06	Sweden	D 0-0	Stockholm	Fr	
21-06	Norway	D 2-2	Oslo	Fr	Ludwig, Bergmaier
13-09	Austria	L 0-5	Vienna	Fr	
27-09	Denmark	W 4-2	Hanover	Fr	Hofmann.R 3, Kuzorra
6-03-1932	Switzerland	W 2-0	Leipzig	Fr	Hofmann.R 2
1-07	Finland	W 4-1	Helsinki	Fr	Hofmann.R 3, Rutz
25-09	Sweden	W 4-3	Nuremberg	Fr	Rohr 2, Kobierski, Krumm
30-10	Hungary	L 1-2	Budapest	Fr	Malik
4-12	Holland	L 0-2	Dusseldorf	Fr	

1-01-1933	Italy	L 1-3	Bologna	Fr	Rohr
19-03	France	D 3-3	Berlin	Fr	Rohr 2, Lachner
22-10	Belgium	W 8-1	Duisburg	Fr	Hohmann 3, Wigold 2, Kobierski, Rasselnberg, Albrecht
5-11	Norway	D 2-2	Magdeburg	Fr	Hohmann, Albrecht
19-11	Switzerland	W 2-0	Zurich	Fr	Hohmann, Lachner
3-12	Poland	W 1-0	Berlin	Fr	Rasselnberg
14-01-1934	Hungary	W 3-1	Frankfurt	Fr	Conen, Lachner, Stubb
11-03	Luxembourg	W 9-1	Luxembourg	WCq	Rasselnberg 4, Hohmann 3, Wigold, Albrecht
27-05	Belgium	W 5-2	Florence	WCr1	Conen 3, Kobierski, Siffling
31-05	Sweden	W 2-1	Milan	WCqf	Hohmann 2
3-06	Czechoslovakia	L 1-3	Rome	WCsf	Noack
7-06	Austria	W 3-2	Naples	WC3p	Lehner 2, E.Conen
9-09	Poland	W 5-2	Warsaw	Fr	Lehner 2, Hohmann, Siffling, Szepan
7-10	Denmark	W 5-2	Copenhagen	Fr	Fath 3, Hohmann, Rohwedder
27-01-1935	Switzerland	W 4-0	Stuttgart	Fr	Conen 3, Lehner
17-02	Holland	W 3-2	Amsterdam	Fr	Hohmann, Conen, Kobierski
17-03	France	W 3-1	Paris	Fr	Hohmann, Kobierski, Lehner
28-04	Belgium	W 6-1	Brussels	Fr	Lenz 2, Damminger 2, Fath 2
8-05	Rep. Ireland	W 3-1	Dortmund	Fr	Damminger 2, Lehner
12-05	Spain	L 1-2	Cologne	Fr	Conen
26-05	Czechoslovakia	W 2-1	Dresden	Fr	Lenz 2
27-06	Norway	D 1-1	Oslo	Fr	Lenz
30-06	Sweden	L 1-3	Stockholm	Fr	Rohwedder
18-08	Finland	W 6-0	Munich	Fr	Conen 3, Lehner 3
18-08	Luxembourg	W 1-0	Luxembourg	Fr	Günter
25-08	Romania	W 4-2	Erfurt	Fr	Lenz, Hohmann, Rasselnberg, Simetsreiter
15-09	Poland	W 1-0	Breslau	Fr	Conen
15-09	Estonia	W 5-0	Stettin	Fr	Simetsreiter 2, Rasselnberg, Damminger, Malecki
13-10	Latvia	W 3-0	Konigsberg	Fr	Langenbein, Lenz, Panse
20-10	Bulgaria	W 4-2	Leipzig	Fr	Simetsreiter 2, Lehner, Pörtgen
4-12	England	L 0-3	London	Fr	
23-02-1936	Spain	W 2-1	Barcelona	Fr	Fath 2
27-02	Portugal	W 3-1	Lisbon	Fr	Hohmann, Lehner, Kitzinger
15-03	Hungary	L 2-3	Budapest	Fr	Lenz, Urban
4-08	Luxembourg	W 9-0	Berlin	OGr1	Simetsreiter 3, Urban 3, Gauchel 2, Elbern
7-08	Norway	L 0-2	Berlin	OGqf	
13-09	Poland	D 1-1	Warsaw	Fr	Hohmann
27-09	Czechoslovakia	W 2-1	Prague	Fr	Elbern, Siffling
27-09	Luxembourg	W 7-2	Krefeld	Fr	Pörtgen 3, Kuzorra 2, Günter, Malecki
14-10	Scotland	L 0-2	Glasgow	Fr	
17-10	Rep. Ireland	L 2-5	Dublin	Fr	Kobierski, Szepan
15-11	Italy	D 2-2	Berlin	Fr	Siffling 2
31-01-1937	Holland	D 2-2	Dusseldorf	Fr	Lehner 2
21-03	France	W 4-0	Stuttgart	Fr	Urban 2, Lehner, Lenz
21-03	Luxembourg	W 3-2	Luxembourg	Fr	Striebinger 2, Pörtgen
25-04	Belgium	W 1-0	Hanover	Fr	Hohmann
2-05	Switzerland	W 1-0	Zurich	Fr	Kitzinger
16-05	Denmark	W 8-0	Breslau	Fr	Siffling 5, Urban, Szepan, Lehner
25-06	Latvia	W 3-1	Riga	Fr	Berndt 2, Hohmann
29-06	Finland	W 2-0	Helsinki	WCq	Lehner, Urban
29-08	Estonia	W 4-1	Konigsberg	WCq	Lehner 2, Gauchel 2
24-10	Norway	W 3-0	Berlin	Fr	Siffling 3
21-11	Sweden	W 5-0	Hamburg	WCq	Siffling 2, Schön 2, Szepan
6-02-1938	Switzerland	D 1-1	Cologne	Fr	Szepan
20-03	Hungary	D 1-1	Nuremberg	Fr	Siffling
20-03	Luxembourg	W 2-1	Wuppertal	Fr	Gauchel 2
24-04	Portugal	D 1-1	Frankfurt	Fr	Siffling
14-05	England	L 3-6	Berlin	Fr	Gellesch, Gauchel, Pesser
4-06	Switzerland	D 1-1	Paris	WCr1	Gauchel
9-06	Switzerland	L 2-4	Paris	WCr1	Hahnemann, OG
18-09	Poland	W 4-1	Chemnitz	Fr	Gauchel 3, Schön
25-09	Romania	W 4-1	Bucharest	Fr	Stroh, Schön, Pesser, OG
29-01-1939	Belgium	W 4-1	Brussels	Fr	Lehner, Hahnemann, Binder, Schön
26-02	Yugoslavia	W 3-2	Berlin	Fr	Janes, Urban, Biallas
26-03	Italy	L 2-3	Florence	Fr	Hahnemann, Janes
26-03	Luxembourg	L 1-2	Differdange	Fr	Hänel
23-05	Rep. Ireland	D 1-1	Bremen	Fr	Schön
22-06	Norway	W 4-0	Oslo	Fr	Schön 2, Urban, Janes
25-06	Denmark	W 2-0	Copenhagen	Fr	Conen, Gauchel
29-06	Estonia	W 2-0	Tallinn	Fr	Lehner, R.Schaletzki
27-08	Slovakia	L 0-2	Bratislava	Fr	

24-09	Hungary	L 1-5	Budapest	Fr	Lehner
15-10	Yugoslavia	W 5-1	Zagreb	Fr	Schön 3, Szepan 2
22-10	Bulgaria	W 2-1	Sofia	Fr	Conen, Urban
12-11	Bohemia	D 4-4	Breslau	Fr	Binder 3, Janes
26-11	Italy	W 5-2	Berlin	Fr	Binder 3, Lehner, Conen
3-12	Slovakia	W 3-1	Chemnitz	Fr	Schön, Lehner, Fiederer
7-04-1940	Hungary	D 2-2	Berlin	Fr	Binder, Gauchel
14-04	Yugoslavia	L 1-2	Vienna	Fr	Lehner
5-05	Italy	L 2-3	Milan	Fr	Binder 2
14-07	Romania	W 9-3	Frankfurt	Fr	Walter.F 3, Plener 2, Hahnemann 2, Fiederer 2
1-09	Finland	W 13-0	Leipzig	Fr	Hahnemann 6, Conen 4, Walter.F 2, Arlt
15-09	Slovakia	W 1-0	Bratislava	Fr	Durek
6-10	Hungary	D 2-2	Budapest	Fr	Hahnemann, Lehner
20-10	Bulgaria	W 7-3	Munich	Fr	Conen 4, Lehner, Kupfer, Gärtner
3-11	Yugoslavia	L 0-2	Zagreb	Fr	
17-11	Denmark	W 1-0	Hamburg	Fr	Schön
9-03-1941	Switzerland	W 4-2	Stuttgart	Fr	Schön 2, Walter.F, Kobierski
6-04	Hungary	W 7-0	Cologne	Fr	Schön 2, Hahnemann 2, Kobierski, Walter.F, Janes
20-04	Switzerland	L 1-2	Berne	Fr	Hahnemann
1-06	Romania	W 4-1	Bucharest	Fr	Willimowski 2, Walter.F, Kobierski
15-06	Croatia	W 5-1	Vienna	Fr	Walter.F 2, Lehner 2, Willinowski
5-10	Sweden	L 2-4	Stockholm	Fr	Walter.F, Lehner
5-10	Finland	W 6-0	Helsinki	Fr	Willimowski 3, Eppenhoff 3
16-11	Denmark	D 1-1	Dresden	Fr	Hahnemann
7-12	Slovakia	W 4-0	Breslau	Fr	Conen 2, Walter.F, Durek
18-01-1942	Croatia	W 2-0	Zagreb	Fr	Decker, OG
1-02	Switzerland	L 1-2	Vienna	Fr	Decker
12-04	Spain	D 1-1	Berlin	Fr	Decker
3-05	Hungary	W 5-3	Budapest	Fr	Walter.F 2, Dörfel.F, Janes, Sing
19-07	Bulgaria	W 3-0	Sofia	Fr	Decker 2, Arlt
16-08	Romania	W 7-0	Bytom	Fr	Walter.F 3, Willimowski, Klingler, Burdenski, Decker
20-09	Sweden	L 2-3	Berlin	Fr	Decker, Klingler
18-10	Switzerland	W 5-3	Berne	Fr	Willimowski 4, Walter.F
1-11	Croatia	W 5-1	Stuttgart	Fr	Willimowski 2, Walter.F, Klingler, Janes
22-11	Slovakia	W 5-2	Bratislava	Fr	Klingler 3, Decker, Adamkiewicz

INTERNATIONAL MATCHES PLAYED BY WEST GERMANY

22-11-1950	Switzerland	W 1-0	Stuttgart	Fr	Burdenski
15-04-1951	Switzerland	W 3-2	Zurich	Fr	Gerritzen, Walter.F, Walter.O
17-06	Turkey	L 1-2	Berlin	Fr	Haferkamp
23-09	Austria	W 2-0	Vienna	Fr	Haferkamp, Morlock
17-10	Rep. Ireland	L 2-3	Dublin	Fr	Morlock, Walter.F
21-11	Turkey	W 2-0	Istanbul	Fr	Morlock 2
23-12	Luxembourg	W 4-1	Essen	Fr	Rahn.H, Stollenwerk, Termath 2
20-04-1952	Luxembourg	W 3-0	Luxembourg	Fr	Klodt, Stollenwerk, Zeitler
4-05	Rep. Ireland	W 3-0	Cologne	Fr	Posipal, Walter.O, Termath
5-10	France	L 1-3	Paris	Fr	Walter.O
9-11	Switzerland	W 5-1	Augsburg	Fr	Morlock, Walter.O, Walter.F, Schäfer 2
21-12	Yugoslavia	W 3-2	Ludwigshafen	Fr	Rahn.H, Morlock, Walter.F
28-12	Spain	D 2-2	Madrid	Fr	Walter.O, Termath
22-03-1953	Austria	D 0-0	Cologne	Fr	
19-08	Norway	D 1-1	Oslo	WCq	Walter.F
11-10	Saar	W 3-0	Stuttgart	WCq	Morlock 2, Schade
22-11	Norway	W 5-1	Hamburg	WCq	Morlock 2, Rahn.H, Walter.O, Walter.F
28-03-1954	Saar	W 3-1	Saarbrucken	WCq	Morlock 2, Schäfer
25-04	Switzerland	W 5-3	Basle	Fr	Walter.F 2, Schäfer 2, Morlock
17-06	Turkey	W 4-1	Berne	WCr1	Klodt, Morlock, Walter.O, Schäfer
20-06	Hungary	L 3-8	Basle	WCr1	Rahn.H, Pfaff, Herrmann.R
23-06	Turkey	W 7-2	Zurich	WCr1	Morlock 3, Schäfer 2, Walter.O, Walter.F
27-06	Yugoslavia	W 2-0	Geneva	WCqf	Rahn.H, OG
30-06	Austria	W 6-1	Basle	WCsf	Walter.O 2, Walter.F 2, Morlock, Schäfer
4-07	Hungary	W 3-2	Berne	WCf	Rahn.H 2, Morlock
26-09	Belgium	L 0-2	Brussels	Fr	
16-10	France	L 1-3	Hanover	Fr	Stürmer
1-12	England	L 1-3	London	Fr	Beck
19-12	Portugal	W 3-0	Lisbon	Fr	Pfaff, Juskowiak, Erhardt
30-03-1955	Italy	L 1-2	Stuttgart	Fr	Juskowiak
28-05	Rep. Ireland	W 2-1	Hamburg	Fr	Mai, Waldner
21-08	Soviet Union	L 2-3	Moscow	Fr	Walter.F, Schäfer

25-09	Yugoslavia	L 1-3	Belgrade	Fr	Morlock
16-11	Norway	W 2-0	Karlsruhe	Fr	Walter.F, Röhrig
18-12	Italy	L 1-2	Rome	Fr	Röhrig
14-03-1956	Holland	L 1-2	Dusseldorf	Fr	OG
25-05	England	L 1-3	Berlin	Fr	Walter.F
13-06	Norway	W 3-1	Oslo	Fr	Bäumler, Biesinger, Schönhoft
30-06	Sweden	D 2-2	Stockholm	Fr	Schröder, Biesinger
15-09	Soviet Union	L 1-2	Hanover	Fr	Schröder
21-11	Switzerland	L 1-3	Frankfurt	Fr	Neuschäfer
25-11	Rep. Ireland	L 0-3	Dublin	Fr	
23-12	Belgium	W 4-1	Cologne	Fr	Kelbassa, Schröder, Vollmar, Wewers
10-03-1957	Austria	W 3-2	Vienna	Fr	Rahn.H 2, Kraus
3-04	Holland	W 2-1	Amsterdam	Fr	Schmidt, Siedl
22-05	Scotland	L 1-3	Stuttgart	Fr	Siedl
20-11	Sweden	W 1-0	Hamburg	Fr	Schmidt
22-12	Hungary	W 1-0	Hanover	Fr	Kelbassa
2-03-1958	Belgium	W 2-0	Brussels	Fr	Schmidt, Schäfer
19-03	Spain	W 2-0	Frankfurt	Fr	Klodt, Cieslarczyk
2-04	Czechoslovakia	L 2-3	Prague	Fr	Cieslarczyk, OG
8-06	Argentina	W 3-1	Malmo	WCr1	Rahn.H 2, Seeler
11-06	Czechoslovakia	D 2-2	Halsingborg	WCr1	Rahn.H, Schäfer
15-06	Nth. Ireland	D 2-2	Malmo	WCr1	Rahn.H, Seeler
19-06	Yugoslavia	W 1-0	Malmo	WCqf	Rahn.H
24-06	Sweden	L 1-3	Gothenburg	WCsf	Schäfer
28-06	France	L 3-6	Gothenburg	WC3p	Rahn.H, Schäfer, Cieslarczyk
24-09	Denmark	D 1-1	Copenhagen	Fr	Rahn.H
26-10	France	D 2-2	Paris	Fr	Rahn.H, Seeler
19-11	Austria	D 2-2	Berlin	Fr	Rahn.H 2
21-12	Bulgaria	W 3-0	Augsburg	Fr	Seeler 2, Waldner
28-12	Egypt	L 1-2	Cairo	Fr	Morlock
6-05-1959	Scotland	L 2-3	Glasgow	Fr	Seeler, Juskowiak
20-05	Poland	D 1-1	Hamburg	Fr	Stein
4-10	Switzerland	W 4-0	Berne	Fr	Rahn.H, Juskowiak, Brülls, Vollmar
21-10	Holland	W 7-0	Cologne	Fr	Seeler 3, Schmidt 2, Brülls, Siedl
8-11	Hungary	L 3-4	Budapest	Fr	Seeler 2, Brülls
20-12	Yugoslavia	D 1-1	Hanover	Fr	Schmidt
23-03-1960	Chile	W 2-1	Stuttgart	Fr	Haller, Seeler
27-04	Portugal	W 2-1	Ludwigshafen	Fr	Rahn.H, Seeler
11-05	Rep. Ireland	L 0-1	Dusseldorf	Fr	
3-08	Iceland	W 5-0	Reykjavik	Fr	Dörfel.G 2, Seeler, Marx, Reitgassl
26-10	Nth. Ireland	W 4-3	Belfast	WCq	Dörfel.G 2, Brülls, Seeler
20-11	Greece	W 3-0	Athens	WCq	Dörfel.G, Brülls, Haller
23-11	Bulgaria	L 1-2	Sofia	Fr	Vollmar
8-03-1961	Belgium	W 1-0	Frankfurt	Fr	Dörfel.G
26-03	Chile	L 1-3	Santiago	Fr	Herrmann.G
10-05	Nth. Ireland	W 2-1	Berlin	WCq	Brülls, Kress
20-09	Denmark	W 5-1	Dusseldorf	Fr	Seeler 3, Kress, Brülls
8-10	Poland	W 2-0	Warsaw	Fr	Brülls, Haller
22-10	Greece	W 2-1	Augsburg	WCq	Seeler 2
11-04-1962	Uruguay	W 3-0	Hamburg	Fr	Koslowski, Haller, Schäfer
31-05	Italy	D 0-0	Santiago	WCr1	
3-06	Switzerland	W 2-1	Santiago	WCr1	Seeler, Brülls
6-06	Chile	W 2-0	Santiago	WCr1	Seeler, Szymaniak
10-06	Yugoslavia	L 0-1	Santiago	WCqf	
30-09	Yugoslavia	W 3-2	Zagreb	Fr	Strehl
24-10	France	D 2-2	Stuttgart	Fr	Konietzka, Steinmann
23-12	Switzerland	W 5-1	Karlsruhe	Fr	Schütz 2, Küppers, Kraus, Werner
5-05-1963	Brazil	L 1-2	Hamburg	Fr	Werner
28-09	Turkey	W 3-0	Frankfurt	Fr	Seeler 3
3-11	Sweden	L 1-2	Stockholm	Fr	Dörfel.G
29-12	Morocco	W 4-1	Casablanca	Fr	Konietzka 2, Krämer, Schmidt
1-01-1964	Algeria	L 0-2	Algiers	Fr	
29-04	Czechoslovakia	L 3-4	Ludwigshafen	Fr	Seeler 2, Geiger
12-05	Scotland	D 2-2	Hanover	Fr	Seeler 2
7-06	Finland	W 4-1	Helsinki	Fr	Schmidt, Kraus, Geiger, Overath
4-11	Sweden	D 1-1	Berlin	WCq	Brunnenmeier
13-03-1965	Italy	D 1-1	Hamburg	Fr	Sieloff
24-04	Cyprus	W 5-0	Karlsruhe	WCq	Overath 2, Sieloff 2, Strehl
12-05	England	L 0-1	Nuremberg	Fr	
26-05	Switzerland	W 1-0	Basle	Fr	Rodekamp
6-06	Brazil	L 0-2	Rio de Janeiro	Fr	

26-09	Sweden	W 2-1	Stockholm	WCq	Seeler, Krämer
9-10	Austria	W 4-1	Stuttgart	Fr	Ulsass 3, Sieloff
14-11	Cyprus	W 6-0	Nicosia	WCq	Brunnenmeier 2, Szymaniak, Heiss, Krämer, OG
23-02-1966	England	L 0-1	London	Fr	
23-03	Holland	W 4-2	Rotterdam	Fr	Beckenbauer 2, Seeler, Emmerich
4-05	Rep. Ireland	W 4-0	Dublin	Fr	Overath 2, Beckenbauer, Haller
7-05	Nth. Ireland	W 2-0	Belfast	Fr	Seeler, Heiss
1-06	Romania	W 1-0	Ludwigshafen	Fr	Seeler
23-06	Yugoslavia	W 2-0	Hanover	Fr	Seeler, Overath
12-07	Switzerland	W 5-0	Sheffield	WCr1	Beckenbauer 2, Haller 2, Held
16-07	Argentina	D 0-0	Birmingham	WCr1	
20-07	Spain	W 2-1	Birmingham	WCr1	Seeler, Emmerich
23-07	Uruguay	W 4-0	Sheffield	WCqf	Haller 2, Seeler, Beckenbauer
25-07	Soviet Union	W 2-1	Liverpool	WCsf	Beckenbauer, Haller
30-07	England	L 2-4	London	WCf	Weber, Haller
12-10	Turkey	W 2-0	Ankara	Fr	Rupp, Küppers
19-11	Norway	W 3-0	Cologne	Fr	Ulsass 2, Seeler
22-02-1967	Morocco	W 5-1	Karlsruhe	Fr	Ulsass 2, Heynckes, Zaczyk, Löhr
22-03	Bulgaria	W 1-0	Hanover	Fr	Heynckes
8-04	Albania	W 6-0	Dortmund	ECq	Müller.G 4, Löhr 2
3-05	Yugoslavia	L 0-1	Belgrade	ECq	
27-09	France	W 5-1	Berlin	Fr	Siemensmeyer 2, Müller.G, Overath, Libuda
7-10	Yugoslavia	W 3-1	Hamburg	ECq	Seeler, Müller.G, Löhr
22-11	Romania	L 0-1	Bucharest	Fr	
17-12	Albania	D 0-0	Tirana	ECq	
6-03-1968	Belgium	W 3-1	Brussels	Fr	Volkert 2, Laumen
17-04	Switzerland	D 0-0	Basle	Fr	
8-05	Wales	D 1-1	Cardiff	Fr	Overath
1-06	England	W 1-0	Hanover	Fr	Beckenbauer
16-06	Brazil	W 2-1	Stuttgart	Fr	Dörfel.B, Held
25-09	France	D 1-1	Marseille	Fr	Overath
13-10	Austria	W 2-0	Vienna	WCq	Müller.G, OG
23-11	Cyprus	W 1-0	Nicosia	WCq	Müller.G
14-12	Brazil	D 2-2	Rio de Janeiro	Fr	Held, Gerwien
18-12	Chile	L 1-2	Santiago	Fr	Ulsass
22-12	Mexico	D 0-0	Mexico City	Fr	
26-03-1969	Wales	D 1-1	Frankfurt	Fr	Müller.G
16-04	Scotland	D 1-1	Glasgow	WCq	Müller.G
10-05	Austria	W 1-0	Nuremberg	WCq	Müller.G
21-05	Cyprus	W 12-0	Essen	WCq	Müller.G 4, Overath 3, Haller 2, Höttges, Lorenz, Held
21-09	Austria	D 1-1	Vienna	Fr	Müller.G
24-09	Bulgaria	W 1-0	Sofia	Fr	Dörfel.B
22-10	Scotland	W 3-2	Hamburg	WCq	Müller.G, Libuda, Fichtel
11-02-1970	Spain	L 0-2	Seville	Fr	
8-04	Romania	D 1-1	Stuttgart	Fr	Overath
9-05	Rep. Ireland	W 2-1	Berlin	Fr	Seeler, Löhr
13-05	Yugoslavia	W 1-0	Hanover	Fr	Seeler
3-06	Morocco	W 2-1	Leon	WCr1	Seeler, Müller.G
7-06	Bulgaria	W 5-2	Leon	WCr1	Müller.G 3, Seeler, Libuda
10-06	Peru	W 3-1	Leon	WCr1	Müller.G 3
14-06	England	W 3-2	Leon	WCqf	Müller.G, Seeler, Beckenbauer
17-06	Italy	L 3-4	Mexico City	WCsf	Müller.G 2, Schnellinger
20-06	Uruguay	W 1-0	Mexico City	WC3p	Overath
9-09	Hungary	W 3-1	Nuremberg	Fr	Müller.G 2, Sieloff
17-10	Turkey	D 1-1	Cologne	ECq	Müller.G
18-11	Yugoslavia	L 0-2	Zagreb	Fr	
22-11	Greece	W 3-1	Athens	Fr	Beckenbauer, Netzer, Grabowski
17-02-1971	Albania	W 1-0	Tirana	ECq	Müller.G
25-04	Turkey	W 3-0	Istanbul	ECq	Müller.G 2, Köppel
12-06	Albania	W 2-0	Karlsruhe	ECq	Netzer, Grabowski
22-06	Norway	W 7-1	Oslo	Fr	Müller.G 3, Netzer, Overath, Beckenbauer, Held
27-06	Sweden	L 0-1	Gothenburg	Fr	
30-06	Denmark	W 3-1	Copenhagen	Fr	Müller.G, Beckenbauer, Flohe
8-09	Mexico	W 5-0	Hanover	Fr	Müller.G 3, Netzer, Köppel
10-10	Poland	W 3-1	Warsaw	ECq	Müller.G 2, Grabowski
17-11	Poland	D 0-0	Hamburg	ECq	
29-03-1972	Hungary	W 2-0	Budapest	Fr	Hoeness.U, Breitner
29-04	England	W 3-1	London	ECqf	Müller.G, Hoeness.U, Netzer
13-05	England	D 0-0	Berlin	ECqf	
26-05	Soviet Union	W 4-1	Munich	Fr	Müller.G 4

14-06	Belgium	W 2-1	Antwerp	ECsf	Müller.G 2
18-06	Soviet Union	W 3-0	Brussels	ECf	Müller.G 2, Wimmer
15-11	Switzerland	W 5-1	Dusseldorf	Fr	Müller.G 4, Netzer
14-02-1973	Argentina	L 2-3	Munich	Fr	Heynckes, Cullmann
28-03	Czechoslovakia	W 3-0	Dusseldorf	Fr	Müller.G 2, Kremers
9-05	Yugoslavia	L 0-1	Munich	Fr	
12-05	Bulgaria	W 3-0	Hamburg	Fr	Cullmann, Beckenbauer, OG
16-06	Brazil	L 0-1	Berlin	Fr	
5-09	Soviet Union	W 1-0	Moscow	Fr	Müller.G
10-10	Austria	W 4-0	Hanover	Fr	Müller.G 2, Weber, Kremers
13-10	France	W 2-1	Gelsenkirchen	Fr	Müller.G 2
14-11	Scotland	D 1-1	Glasgow	Fr	Hoeness.U
24-11	Spain	W 2-1	Stuttgart	Fr	Heynckes 2
23-02-1974	Spain	L 0-1	Barcelona	Fr	
26-02	Italy	D 0-0	Rome	Fr	
27-03	Scotland	W 2-1	Frankfurt	Fr	Grabowski, Breitner
17-04	Hungary	W 5-0	Dortmund	Fr	Müller.G 2, Wimmer, Kremers, Hölzenbein
1-05	Sweden	W 2-0	Hamburg	Fr	Heynckes 2
14-06	Chile	W 1-0	Berlin	WCr1	Breitner
18-06	Australia	W 3-0	Hamburg	WCr1	Cullmann, Müller.G, Overath
22-06	East Germany	L 0-1	Hamburg	WCr1	
26-06	Yugoslavia	W 2-0	Dusseldorf	WCr2	Müller.G, Breitner
30-06	Sweden	W 4-2	Dusseldorf	WCr2	Bonhoff, Hoeness, Overath, Grabowski
3-07	Poland	W 1-0	Frankfurt	WCr2	Müller.G
7-07	Holland	W 2-1	Munich	WCf	Müller.G, Breitner
4-09	Switzerland	W 2-1	Basle	Fr	Cullmann, Geye
20-11	Greece	D 2-2	Athens	ECq	Cullmann, Wimmer
22-12	Malta	W 1-0	Gzira	ECq	Cullmann
12-03-1975	England	L 0-2	London	Fr	
27-04	Bulgaria	D 1-1	Sofia	ECq	Ritschel
17-05	Holland	D 1-1	Frankfurt	Fr	Wimmer
3-09	Austria	W 2-0	Vienna	Fr	Beer 2
11-10	Greece	D 1-1	Dusseldorf	ECq	Heynckes
19-11	Bulgaria	W 1-0	Stuttgart	ECq	Heynckes
20-12	Turkey	W 5-0	Istanbul	Fr	Heynckes 2, Worm 2, Beer
28-02-1976	Malta	W 8-0	Dortmund	ECq	Heynckes 2, Worm 2, Beer 2, Vogts, Hölzenbein
24-04	Spain	D 1-1	Madrid	ECqf	Beer
22-05	Spain	W 2-0	Munich	ECqf	Hoeness.U, Toppmöller
17-06	Yugoslavia	W 4-2	Belgrade	ECsf	Müller.D 3, Flohe
20-06	Czechoslovakia	D 2-2	Belgrade	ECf	Müller.D, Hölzenbein. L 3-5 on pens
6-10	Wales	W 2-0	Cardiff	Fr	Beckenbauer, Heynckes
17-11	Czechoslovakia	W 2-0	Hanover	Fr	Beer, Flohe
23-02-1977	France	L 0-1	Paris	Fr	
27-04	Nth. Ireland	W 5-0	Cologne	Fr	Fischer 2, Bonhof, Flohe, Müller.D
30-04	Yugoslavia	W 2-1	Belgrade	Fr	Müller.D, Bonhof
5-06	Argentina	W 3-1	Buenos Aires	Fr	Fischer 2, Hölzenbein
8-06	Uruguay	W 2-0	Montevideo	Fr	Müller.D, Flohe
12-06	Brazil	D 1-1	Rio de Janeiro	Fr	Fischer
14-06	Mexico	D 2-2	Mexico City	Fr	Fischer 2
7-09	Finland	W 1-0	Helsinki	Fr	Fischer
8-10	Italy	W 2-1	Berlin	Fr	Rummenigge, Kaltz
16-11	Switzerland	W 4-1	Stuttgart	Fr	Fischer 2, Flohe, OG
14-12	Wales	D 1-1	Dortmund	Fr	Fischer
22-02-1978	England	W 2-1	Munich	Fr	Bonhof, Worm
8-03	Soviet Union	W 1-0	Frankfurt	Fr	Rüssmann
5-04	Brazil	L 0-1	Hamburg	Fr	
19-04	Sweden	L 1-3	Stockholm	Fr	Bonhof
1-06	Poland	D 0-0	Buenos Aires	WCr1	
6-06	Mexico	W 6-0	Cordoba	WCr1	Rummenigge 2, Flohe 2, Müller.D, Müller.H
10-06	Tunisia	D 0-0	Cordoba	WCr1	
14-06	Italy	D 0-0	Buenos Aires	WCr2	
18-06	Holland	D 2-2	Cordoba	WCr2	Müller.D, Abramczik
21-06	Austria	L 2-3	Cordoba	WCr2	Hölzenbein, Rummenigge
11-10	Czechoslovakia	W 4-3	Prague	Fr	Bonhof 2, Müller.H, Abramczik
15-11	Hungary	D 0-0	Frankfurt	Fr	Abandoned after 60 mins
20-12	Holland	W 3-1	Dusseldorf	Fr	Bonhof, Fischer, Rummenigge
25-02-1979	Malta	D 0-0	Gzira	ECq	
1-04	Turkey	D 0-0	Izmir	ECq	
2-05	Wales	W 2-0	Wrexham	ECq	Fischer, Zimmermann
22-05	Rep. Ireland	W 3-1	Dublin	Fr	Rummenigge, Hoeness.D, Kelsch
26-05	Iceland	W 3-1	Reykjavik	Fr	Hoeness.D 2, Kelsch
12-09	Argentina	W 2-1	Berlin	Fr	Rummenigge, Allofs

17-10	Wales	W 5-1	Cologne	ECq	Fischer 2, Förster.K, Rummenigge, Kaltz
21-11	Soviet Union	W 3-1	Tbilisi	Fr	Rummenigge 2, Fischer
22-12	Turkey	W 2-0	Gelsenkirchen	ECq	Fischer, Zimmermann
27-02-1980	Malta	W 8-0	Bremen	ECq	Allofs 2, Fischer 2, Bonhof, Kelsch, Rummenigge, OG
2-04	Austria	W 1-0	Munich	Fr	Müller.H
13-05	Poland	W 3-1	Frankfurt	Fr	Allofs, Rummenigge, Schuster
11-06	Czechoslovakia	W 1-0	Rome	ECr1	Rummenigge
14-06	Holland	W 3-2	Naples	ECr1	Allofs 3
17-06	Greece	D 0-0	Turin	ECr1	
22-06	Belgium	W 2-1	Rome	ECf	Hrubesch 2
10-09	Switzerland	W 3-2	Basle	Fr	Müller.H 2, Magath
11-10	Holland	D 1-1	Eindhoven	Fr	Hrubesch
19-11	France	W 4-1	Hanover	Fr	Allofs, Hrubesch, Briegel, Kaltz
3-12	Bulgaria	W 3-1	Sofia	WCq	Kaltz 2, Rummenigge
1-01-1981	Argentina	L 1-2	Montevideo	ML	Hrubesch
7-01	Brazil	L 1-4	Montevideo	ML	Allofs
1-04	Albania	W 2-0	Tirana	WCq	Schuster 2
29-04	Austria	W 2-0	Hamburg	WCq	Fischer, OG
19-05	Brazil	L 1-2	Stuttgart	Fr	Fischer
24-05	Finland	W 4-0	Lahti	WCq	Fischer 2, Kaltz, Briegel
2-09	Poland	W 2-0	Chorzow	Fr	Fischer, Rummenigge
23-09	Finland	W 7-1	Bochum	WCq	Rummenigge 3, Breitner 2, Fischer, Dremmler
14-10	Austria	W 3-1	Vienna	WCq	Littbarski 2, Magath
18-11	Albania	W 8-0	Dortmund	WCq	Rummenigge 3, Fischer 2, Littbarski, Breitner, Kaltz
22-11	Bulgaria	W 4-0	Dusseldorf	WCq	Rummenigge 2, Fischer, Kaltz
17-02-1982	Portugal	W 3-1	Hanover	Fr	Fischer 2, OG
21-03	Brazil	L 0-1	Rio de Janeiro	Fr	
24-03	Argentina	D 1-1	Buenos Aires	Fr	Dremmler
14-04	Czechoslovakia	W 2-1	Cologne	Fr	Littbarski, Breitner
12-05	Norway	W 4-2	Oslo	Fr	Rummenigge 2, Littbarski 2
16-06	Algeria	L 1-2	Gijon	WCr1	Rummenigge
20-06	Chile	W 4-1	Gijon	WCr1	Rummenigge 3, Reinders
25-06	Austria	W 1-0	Gijon	WCr1	Hrubesch
29-06	England	D 0-0	Madrid	WCr2	
2-07	Spain	W 2-1	Madrid	WCr2	Fischer, Littbarski
8-07	France	D 3-3	Seville	WCsf	Fischer, Littbarski, Rummenigge.W5-4p
11-07	Italy	L 1-3	Madrid	WCf	Breitner
22-09	Belgium	D 0-0	Munich	Fr	
13-10	England	W 2-1	London	Fr	Rummenigge 2
17-11	Nth. Ireland	L 0-1	Belfast	ECq	
23-02-1983	Portugal	L 0-1	Lisbon	Fr	
30-03	Albania	W 2-1	Tirana	ECq	Rummenigge, Völler
23-04	Turkey	W 3-0	Izmir	ECq	Rummenigge 2, Dremmler
27-04	Austria	D 0-0	Vienna	ECq	
7-06	Yugoslavia	W 4-2	Luxembourg	Fr	Meier 2, Rummenigge, Schuster
7-09	Hungary	D 1-1	Budapest	Fr	Völler
5-10	Austria	W 3-0	Gelsenkirchen	ECq	Völler 2, Rummenigge
26-10	Turkey	W 5-1	Berlin	ECq	Völler 2, Rummenigge 2, Stielike
16-11	Nth. Ireland	L 0-1	Hamburg	ECq	
20-11	Albania	W 2-1	Saarbrucken	ECq	Rummenigge, Strack
15-02-1984	Bulgaria	W 3-2	Varna	Fr	Stielike 2, Völler
29-02	Belgium	W 1-0	Brussels	Fr	Völler
28-03	Soviet Union	W 2-1	Hanover	Fr	Völler, Brehme
18-04	France	L 0-1	Strasbourg	Fr	
22-05	Italy	W 1-0	Zurich	Fr	Briegel
14-06	Portugal	D 0-0	Strasbourg	ECr1	
17-06	Romania	W 2-1	Lens	ECr1	Völler 2
20-06	Spain	L 0-1	Paris	ECr1	
12-09	Argentina	L 1-3	Dusseldorf	Fr	Jakobs
17-10	Sweden	W 2-0	Cologne	WCq	Rummenigge, Rahn.U
16-12	Malta	W 3-2	Ta'Qali	WCq	Allofs 2, Förster.K
29-01-1985	Hungary	L 0-1	Hamburg	Fr	
24-02	Portugal	W 2-1	Lisbon	WCq	Littbarski, Völler
27-03	Malta	W 6-0	Saarbrucken	WCq	Rummenigge 2, Rahn.U 2, Littbarski, Magath
17-04	Bulgaria	W 4-1	Augsburg	Fr	Völler 2, Littbarski, Rahn.U
30-04	Czechoslovakia	W 5-1	Prague	WCq	Littbarski, Allofs, Matthäus, Herget, Berthold
12-06	England	L 0-3	Mexico City	Fr	
15-06	Mexico	L 0-2	Mexico City	Fr	
28-08	Soviet Union	L 0-1	Moscow	Fr	
25-09	Sweden	D 2-2	Stockholm	WCq	Völler, Herget
16-10	Portugal	L 0-1	Stuttgart	WCq	
17-11	Czechoslovakia	D 2-2	Munich	WCq	Rummenigge, Herget

5-02-1986	Italy	W 2-1	Avellino	Fr	Herget, Matthäus
12-03	Brazil	W 2-0	Frankfurt	Fr	Allofs, Briegel
9-04	Switzerland	W 1-0	Basle	Fr	Hoeness.D
11-05	Yugoslavia	D 1-1	Bochum	Fr	Völler
14-05	Holland	W 3-1	Dortmund	Fr	Völler 2, Herget
4-06	Uruguay	D 1-1	Queretaro	WCr1	Allofs
8-06	Scotland	W 2-1	Queretaro	WCr1	Völler, Allofs
13-06	Denmark	L 0-2	Queretaro	WCr1	
17-06	Morocco	W 1-0	Monterrey	WCr2	Matthäus
21-06	Mexico	D 0-0	Monterrey	WCqf	
25-06	France	W 2-0	Guadalajara	WCsf	Brehme, Völler
29-06	Argentina	L 2-3	Mexico City	WCf	Rummenigge, Völler
24-09	Denmark	W 2-0	Copenhagen	Fr	Allofs, Thon
15-10	Spain	D 2-2	Hanover	Fr	Rahn.U, Waas
29-10	Austria	L 1-4	Vienna	Fr	Völler
25-03-1987	Israel	W 2-0	Tel Aviv	Fr	Thon, Matthäus
18-04	Italy	D 0-0	Cologne	Fr	
12-08	France	W 2-1	Berlin	Fr	Völler 2
9-09	England	W 3-1	Dusseldorf	Fr	Littbarski 2, Wuttke
23-09	Denmark	W 1-0	Hamburg	Fr	Völler
13-10	Sweden	D 1-1	Gelsenkirchen	Fr	Littbarski
18-11	Hungary	D 0-0	Budapest	Fr	
12-12	Brazil	D 1-1	Brasilia	Fr	Reuter
16-12	Argentina	L 0-1	Buenos Aires	Fr	
31-03-1988	Sweden	D 1-1	Berlin	Fr	Allofs
2-04	Argentina	W 1-0	Berlin	Fr	Matthäus
27-04	Switzerland	W 1-0	Kaiserslautern	Fr	Klinsmann
4-06	Yugoslavia	D 1-1	Bremen	Fr	Matthäus
10-06	Italy	D 1-1	Dusseldorf	ECr1	Brehme
14-06	Denmark	W 2-0	Gelsenkirchen	ECr1	Thon, Klinsmann
17-06	Spain	W 2-0	Munich	ECr1	Völler 2
21-06	Holland	L 1-2	Hamburg	ECsf	Matthäus
31-08	Finland	W 4-0	Helsinki	WCq	Völler 2, Matthäus, Riedle
21-09	Soviet Union	W 1-0	Dusseldorf	Fr	OG
19-10	Holland	D 0-0	Munich	WCq	
22-03-1989	Bulgaria	W 2-1	Sofia	Fr	Völler, Littbarski
26-04	Holland	D 1-1	Rotterdam	WCq	Riedle
31-05	Wales	D 0-0	Cardiff	WCq	
6-09	Rep. Ireland	D 1-1	Dublin	Fr	Dorfner
4-10	Finland	W 6-1	Dortmund	WCq	Möller.A 2, Littbarski, Völler, Klinsmann, Matthäus
15-11	Wales	W 2-1	Cologne	WCq	Völler, Hassler
28-02-1990	France	L 1-2	Montpellier	Fr	Möller.A
25-04	Uruguay	D 3-3	Stuttgart	Fr	Matthäus, Völler, Klinsmann
26-05	Czechoslovakia	W 1-0	Dusseldorf	Fr	Bein
30-05	Denmark	W 1-0	Gelsenkirchen	Fr	Völler
10-06	Yugoslavia	W 4-1	Milan	WCr1	Matthäus 2, Klinsmann, Völler
15-06	UAE	W 5-1	Milan	WCr1	Völler 2, Klinsmann, Matthäus, Bein
19-06	Colombia	D 1-1	Milan	WCr1	Littbarski
24-06	Holland	W 2-1	Milan	WCr2	Klinsmann, Brehme
1-07	Czechoslovakia	W 1-0	Milan	WCqf	Matthäus
4-07	England	D 1-1	Turin	WCsf	Brehme. Won 4-3 on pens
8-07	Argentina	W 1-0	Rome	WCf	Brehme
29-08	Portugal	D 1-1	Lisbon	Fr	Matthäus
10-10	Sweden	W 3-1	Stockholm	Fr	Klinsmann, Völler, Brehme

INTERNATIONAL MATCHES PLAYED BY GERMANY

31-10-1990	Luxembourg	W 3-2	Luxembourg	ECq	Klinsmann, Bein, Völler
19-12	Switzerland	W 4-0	Stuttgart	Fr	Völler, Riedle, Thom, Matthäus
27-03-1991	Soviet Union	W 2-1	Frankfurt	Fr	Reuter, Matthäus
1-05	Belgium	W 1-0	Hanover	ECq	Matthäus
5-06	Wales	L 0-1	Cardiff	ECq	
11-09	England	W 1-0	London	Fr	Riedle
16-10	Wales	W 4-1	Nuremberg	ECq	Möller.A, Völler, Riedle, Doll
20-11	Belgium	W 1-0	Brussels	ECq	Völler
18-12	Luxembourg	W 4-0	Leverkusen	ECq	Matthäus, Buchwald, Riedle, Hässler
25-03-1992	Italy	L 0-1	Turin	Fr	
22-04	Czechoslovakia	D 1-1	Prague	Fr	Hässler
30-05	Turkey	W 1-0	Gelsenkirchen	Fr	Völler
2-06	Nth. Ireland	D 1-1	Bremen	Fr	Binz

12-06	Common. IS	D 1-1	Norrkoping	ECr1	Hässler
15-06	Scotland	W 2-0	Norrkoping	ECr1	Riedle, Effenberg
18-06	Holland	L 1-3	Gothenburg	ECr1	Klinsmann
21-06	Sweden	W 3-2	Stockholm	ECsf	Hässler, Riedle 2
26-06	Denmark	L 0-2	Gothenburg	ECf	
9-09	Denmark	W 2-1	Copenhagen	Fr	Riedle, Effenberg
14-10	Mexico	D 1-1	Dresden	Fr	Völler
18-11	Austria	D 0-0	Nuremberg	Fr	
16-12	Brazil	L 1-3	Porto Alegre	Fr	Sammer
20-12	Uruguay	W 4-1	Montevideo	Fr	Buchwald, Möller.A, Hässler, Klinsmann
24-03-1993	Scotland	W 1-0	Glasgow	Fr	Riedle
14-04	Ghana	W 6-1	Bochum	Fr	Kirsten, Effenberg 2, Klinsmann 2, Möller.A
10-06	Brazil	D 3-3	Washington	Fr	Klinsmann 2, Möller.A
13-06	USA	W 4-3	Chicago	Fr	Klinsmann, Riedle 3
19-06	England	W 2-1	Detroit	Fr	Effenberg, Klinsmann
22-09	Tunisia	D 1-1	Tunis	Fr	Möller.A
13-10	Uruguay	W 5-0	Karlsruhe	Fr	Buchwald, Möller.A 2, Riedle, Kirsten
17-11	Brazil	W 2-1	Cologne	Fr	Buchwald, Möller.A
15-12	Argentina	L 1-2	Miami	Fr	Möller.A
18-12	USA	W 3-0	San Francisco	Fr	Möller.A, Kuntz, Thom
22-12	Mexico	D 0-0	Mexico City	Fr	
23-03-1994	Italy	W 2-1	Stuttgart	Fr	Klinsmann 2
27-04	UAE	W 2-0	Abu Dhabi	Fr	Kirsten, Gaudino
29-05	Rep. Ireland	L 0-2	Hanover	Fr	
2-06	Austria	W 5-1	Vienna	Fr	Sammer, Möller.A 2, Klinsmann, Basler
8-06	Canada	W 2-0	Toronto	Fr	Sammer, Völler
17-06	Bolivia	W 1-0	Chicago	WCr1	Klinsmann
21-06	Spain	D 1-1	Chicago	WCr1	Klinsmann
27-06	South Korea	W 3-2	Dallas	WCr1	Klinsmann 2, Riedle
2-07	Belgium	W 3-2	Chicago	WCr2	Völler 2, Klinsmann
10-07	Bulgaria	L 1-2	New York	WCqf	Matthäus
7-09	Russia	W 1-0	Moscow	Fr	Kuntz
12-10	Hungary	D 0-0	Budapest	Fr	
16-11	Albania	W 2-1	Tirana	ECq	Klinsmann, Kirsten
14-12	Moldova	W 3-0	Chisinau	ECq	Kirsten, Klinsmann, Matthäus
18-12	Albania	W 2-1	Kaiserslautern	ECq	Matthäus, Klinsmann
22-02-1995	Spain	D 0-0	Jerez	Fr	
29-03	Georgia	W 2-0	Tbilisi	ECq	Klinsmann 2
26-04	Wales	D 1-1	Dusseldorf	ECq	Herrlich
7-06	Bulgaria	L 2-3	Sofia	ECq	Klinsmann, Strunz

GREECE

The history of Greek football is a curious affair. Greece is amongst the most passionate of footballing nations, yet success for the national team has been non-existent. The clubs spend large amounts of money on foreign players, yet have nothing to show for it. So far, qualification for the 1980 European Championship and 1994 World Cup finals are the only successes of note.

Civil war and political instability in the first half of the 20th century certainly did not help the situation and it was not until 1926 that the football association was formed. A league championship was started two years later, based on clubs from Athens and Salonica, but not until 1960 was there a single national league. Instead, play-offs between various league winners were organised to determine the national champions in what was surely one of Europe's most complicated league structures.

Steeped in the history of the Olympic Games, Greek clubs reflected this heritage, not only through names of clubs like Olympiakos but also in their adherence to the amateur ethic. Full-time professionalism was introduced as late as 1979. The giants of the club game, Panathinaikos and AEK from Athens, Olympiakos from Piraeus, and Aris and PAOK from Salonica are all now very much professional outfits, but they, like the game in Greece generally, have been seriously affected by hooliganism. Until this problem is alleviated, progress can only be limited.

Immediately after World War II, civil war broke out as the communists tried to seize power. The fighting lasted until their defeat in 1950, but it left Greece on a limb in south-eastern Europe. Surrounded by communist countries, as well as Turkey, their traditional foe, the Greeks looked to the near-east for international matches. The Mediterranean Games was a popular source of competition, but most of these matches did not count as full internationals. Greece have entered every World Cup since 1954 and every European Championship since its inception, but it was not until the 1970s that regular friendly matches were played against top sides.

Qualification for the 1980 European Championship finals seemed to herald the dawn of a new age and their performances in Italy won them many friends, but that success was not built upon. When at last the Greeks did qualify for the World Cup, after 12 fruitless attempts, it owed more to the expulsion of Yugoslavia from their group. Alketas Panagoulias, who coached the 1980 European Championship side, also led the 1994 team to the USA, but their time there was not a happy one as they lost all three games.

THE ORDER OF MERIT

	All			League			Cup		Europe		
Team	G	S	B	G	S	B	G	S	G	S	B
1 Olympiakos Piraeus	44	23	9	25	15	9	19	8	-	-	-
2 Panathinaikos Athens	32	21	12	17	14	11	15	6	-	-	-
3 AEK Athens	19	17	10	11	12	9	8	5	-	-	-
4 PAOK Salonica	4	16	7	2	4	7	2	12	-	-	-
5 Aris Salonica	4	7	8	3	3	8	1	4	-	-	-
6 Larissa	2	3	-	1	1	-	1	2	-	-	-
7 Iraklis Salonica	1	7	2	-	3	2	1	4	-	-	-
8 Panionios Athens	1	6	3	-	2	3	1	4	-	-	-
9 OFI Crete	1	2	1	-	1	1	1	1	-	-	-
10 Ethnikos Piraeus	1	2	-	-	2	-	1	-	-	-	-
11 Kastoria	1	-	-	-	-	-	1	-	-	-	-
12 Doxa Drama	-	3	-	-	-	-	-	3	-	-	-
13 Apollon Athens	-	2	5	-	2	5	-	-	-	-	-
14 Athinaikos Athens	-	1	-	-	-	-	-	1	-	-	-
Pierikos Katerini	-	1	-	-	-	-	-	1	-	-	-
16 Atromitos Athens	-	-	1	-	-	1	-	-	-	-	-

To the end of the 1994-1995 season

Since professionalism was introduced there has not been the expected upturn in club fortunes either. The only appearance by a Greek side in a European final was back in 1971 when Panathinaikos, coached by Ferenc Puskás, lost in the European Cup to Ajax. The Olympic Stadium in Athens plays host to European glory only as one of UEFA's favoured 'neutral' locations for finals.

Population: 10,038,000
Area, sq km: 131,957
% in urban areas: 57.7%
Capital city: Athens

Elliniki Podosfairiki Omnospondia
Singrou Avenue #137
Athens GR17121
Greece
Tel: + 30 1 9338850
Fax: + 30 1 9359666

Year of formation	1926
Affiliation to FIFA	1927
Affiliation to UEFA	1954
Registered clubs	4136
Registered players	402 500
Professional players	500
Registered coaches	3950
Registered referees	4100
National stadium	OAKA 'Spiros Louis' Athens 74 000
National colours	White/Blue/White
Reserve colours	Blue/White/Blue
Season	September - June

THE RECORD

WORLD CUP

1930	Did not enter
1934	QT 2nd/2 in group 7
1938	QT 2nd/3 in group 5
1950	Did not enter
1954	QT 2nd/3 in group 10
1958	QT 3rd/3 in group 7
1962	QT 3rd/3 in group 3
1966	QT 3rd/4 in group 7
1970	QT 2nd/4 in group 1
1974	QT 3rd/3 in group 7
1978	QT 3rd/3 in group 9
1982	QT 4th/5 in group 5
1986	QT 4th/4 in group 1
1990	QT 3rd/4 in group 1
1994	QT 1st/5 in group 5 - Final Tournament/1st round

EUROPEAN CHAMPIONSHIP

1960	1st round
1964	Did not enter
1968	QT 2nd/4 in group 3
1972	QT 3rd/4 in group 3
1976	QT 2nd/4 in group 8
1980	QT 1st/4 in group 6 - Final Tournament/1st round
1984	QT 3rd/5 in group 3
1988	QT 2nd/5 in group 5
1992	QT 3rd/5 in group 6
1996	QT group 8

EUROPEAN CLUB COMPETITIONS

European Cup
Finalists - Panathinaikos 1971

Cup Winners Cup
Quarter-finalists - PAOK Salonica 1974, Larissa 1985

UEFA Cup
Semi-finalists - AEK Athens 1977

CLUB DIRECTORY

ATHENS (Population - 3,027,000)

AEK Athens (1924)
Nea Filadelphia 33,000 – Yellow/Black

Apollon Athens (1891)
Gipedo Rizopoleos 17,000 – Blue & white stripes/Blue

Athinaikos (1917)
Virono 6,000 – Red, yellow trim

Atromitos Athens (1923)
Gipedo Peristeriou – Blue/White

Ethnikos Piraeus (1925)
Karaiskakis 38,000 – Blue/White

Olympiakos Piraeus (1925)
Karaiskakis 38,000 – Red & white stripes/White

Panathinaikos Athens (1908)
Apostolos Nikolaidis 26,000 – Green & white stripes/Green

Panionios Athens (1890)
Nea Smyrni 16,000 – Blue/Red

SALONICA (Population - 706,000)

Apollon Kalamarias (1926)
Kalamarias 11,000 – Red & black stripes/Black

Aris Salonica (1914)
Harilaou 27,000 – Yellow/Black

Iraklis Salonica (1908)
Kaftantzoglio 45,000 – White, blue trim

PAOK Salonica (1926)
Toumbas 41,000 – Black & white stripes/White

PATRAS (Population - 154,000)

Panahaiki Patras (1923)
Panahaiki 20,000 – Red & black stripes/Black

IRAKLION (Population - 110,000)

OFI Crete (1925)
OFI 12,000 – Black, white trim

VOLOS (Population - 107,000)

Olympiakos Volos (1934)
Volos 15,000 – Red & white stripes/White

LARISSA (Population - 102,000)

Larissa FC (1964)
Alkazar 18,000 – White, mauve trim

RHODES (Population - 40,000)

Diagoras Rhodes (1905)
Diagoras 20,000 – Claret/Blue

VEROIA (Population - 37,000)

Veroia (1958)
Verias 10,000 – Red/Red

DRAMA (Population - 36,000)

Doxa Drama (1918)
Dramas 10,000 – Black & white stripes/White

LIVADIA
Levadiakos (1926)
Livadias 7,000 – Green, blue trim

SERRES (Population - 46,000)
Panserraikos (1964)
Serron 12,000 – Red, white sleeves/Red

KASTORIA (Population - 53,000)
Kastoria (1962)
Kastoria 6,000 – Red & yellow stripes/Red

GREEK CHAMPIONSHIP PLAY-OFFS

1928	Aris Salonica 6 Ethnikos Piraeus 5 Atromitos Athens 1
1929	-
1930	Panathinaikos 7 Aris Salonica 3 Olympiakos 2
1931	Olympiakos 24 Panathinaikos 19 Aris Salonica 19
1932	Aris Salonica 22 Panathinaikos 18 Apollon Athens 16
1933	Olympiakos 8 Aris Salonica 2 AEK Athens 0
1934	Olympiakos 3-2 2-1 Iraklis Salonica
1935	-
1936	Olympiakos 37 Panathinaikos 33 Apollon Athens 31
1937	Olympiakos 12 PAOK Salonica 6 Panathinaikos 4
1938	Olympiakos 12 Apollon Athens 8 Aris Salonica 4
1939	AEK Athens 3-1 4-2 Iraklis Salonica
1940	AEK Athens 1-0 4-3 PAOK Salonica
1941-1945	-
1946	Aris Salonica 9 AEK Athens 8 Olympiakos 7
1947	Olympiakos 25 Iraklis Salonica 24 Panionios 23
1948	Olympiakos 11 Apollon Athens 8 PAOK Salonica 5
1949	Panathinaikos 9 Olympiakos 9 Aris Salonica 4
1950	-
1951	Olympiakos 11 Panionios 8 Iraklis Salonica 2
1952	-
1953	Panathinaikos 10 Olympiakos 9 Aris Salonica 5
1954	Olympiakos 28 Panathinaikos 25 AEK Athens 21
1955	Olympiakos 29 Panathinaikos 25 Apollon Athens 22
1956	Olympiakos 23 Ethnikos Piraeus 22 Panathinaikos 22
1957	Olympiakos 46 Panathinaikos 46 Apollon Athens 42
1958	Olympiakos 55 AEK Athens 53 Panathinaikos 53
1959	Olympiakos 48 AEK Athens 46 Panionios 37

GREEK NATIONAL LEAGUE

1960q1	Panathinaikos 79 AEK Athens 79 Olympiakos 70
1961	Panathinaikos 80 Olympiakos 73 Panionios 70
1962	Panathinaikos 81 Olympiakos 78 Apollon Athens 74
1963	AEK Athens 77 Panathinaikos 77 Olympiakos 75
1964	Panathinaikos 84 Olympiakos 77 AEK Athens 71
1965	Panathinaikos 79 AEK Athens 76 Olympiakos 71
1966	Olympiakos 80 Panathinaikos 79 AEK Athens 71
1967	Olympiakos 79 AEK Athens 76 Panathinaikos 71
1968t1	AEK Athens 84 Olympiakos 80 Panathinaikos 79
1969	Panathinaikos 90 Olympiakos 88 Aris Salonica 79
1970	Panathinaikos 93 AEK Athens 85 Olympiakos 84
1971	AEK Athens 88 Panionios 83 Panathinaikos 82
1972	Panathinaikos 88 Olympiakos 83 AEK Athens 82
1973	Olympiakos 94 PAOK Salonica 92 Panathinaikos 82
1974t	Olympiakos 59 Panathinaikos 56 Aris Salonica 48
1975	Olympiakos 57 AEK Athens 55 PAOK Salonica 46
1976q	PAOK Salonica 49 AEK Athens 44 Olympiakos 41
1977t	Panathinaikos 54 Olympiakos 54 PAOK Salonica 52
1978	AEK Athens 53 PAOK Salonica 46 Panathinaikos 45
1979	AEK Athens 56 Olympiakos 56 Aris Salonica 50
1980	Olympiakos 47 Aris Salonica 47 Panathinaikos 45
1981	Olympiakos 49 AEK Athens 44 Aris Salonica 43
1982	Olympiakos 50 Panathinaikos 50 PAOK Salonica 46
1983	Olympiakos 50 Larissa 45 AEK Athens 45
1984q	Panathinaikos 46 Olympiakos 43 Iraklis Salonica 42
1985	PAOK Salonica 46 Panathinaikos 43 AEK Athens 43
1986	Panathinaikos 43 OFI Crete 38 AEK Athens 36
1987	Olympiakos 49 Panathinaikos 39 OFI Crete 38
1988	Larissa 43 AEK Athens 40 PAOK Salonica 39
1989	AEK Athens 44 Olympiakos 41 Panathinaikos 37
1990t	Panathinaikos 53 AEK Athens 50 PAOK Salonica 46
1991	Panathinaikos 54 Olympiakos 46 AEK Athens 42
1992	AEK Athens 54 Olympiakos 51 Panathinaikos 48
1993t2	AEK Athens 78 Panathinaikos 77 Olympiakos 68
1994	AEK Athens 79 Panathinaikos 72 Olympiakos 68
1995	Panathinaikos 83 Olympiakos 67 PAOK Salonica 65

GREEK CUP FINALS

1932	AEK Athens	5-3	Aris Salonica
1933	Ethnikos Piraeus	2-2 2-1	Aris Salonica
1934-38	-		
1939	AEK Athens	2-1	PAOK Salonica
1940	Panathinaikos	3-1	Aris Salonica
1941-46	-		
1947	Olympiakos	5-0	Iraklis Salonica
1948	Panathinaikos	2-1	AEK Athens
1949	AEK Athens	0-0 2-1	Panathinaikos
1950	AEK Athens	4-0	Aris Salonica
1951	Olympiakos	4-0	PAOK Salonica
1952	Olympiakos	2-2 2-0	Panionios
1953	Olympiakos	3-2	AEK Athens
1954	Olympiakos	2-0	Doxa Drama
1955	Panathinaikos	2-0	PAOK Salonica
1956	AEK Athens	2-1	Olympiakos
1957	Olympiakos	2-0	Iraklis Salonica
1958	Olympiakos	5-1	Doxa Drama
1959	Olympiakos	2-1	Doxa Drama
1960	Olympiakos	1-1 3-0	Panathinaikos
1961	Olympiakos	3-0	Panionios
1962	-		
1963	Olympiakos	3-0	Pierikos Katerini
1964	-		
1965	Olympiakos	1-0	Panathinaikos
1966	AEK Athens	2-0	Olympiakos
1967	Panathinaikos	1-0	Panionios
1968	Olympiakos	1-0	Panathinaikos
1969	Panathinaikos *	1-1	Olympiakos
1970	Aris Salonica	1-0	PAOK Salonica
1971	Olympiakos	3-1	PAOK Salonica
1972	PAOK Salonica	2-1	Panathinaikos
1973	Olympiakos	1-0	PAOK Salonica
1974	PAOK Salonica	2-2 4-3p	Olympiakos
1975	Olympiakos	1-0	Panathinaikos
1976	Iraklis Salonica	4-4 6-5p	Olympiakos
1977	Panathinaikos	2-1	PAOK Salonica
1978	AEK Athens	2-0	PAOK Salonica
1979	Panionios	3-1	AEK Athens
1980	Kastoria	5-2	Iraklis Salonica
1981	Olympiakos	3-1	PAOK Salonica
1982	Panathinaikos	1-0	Larissa
1983	AEK Athens	2-0	PAOK Salonica
1984	Panathinaikos	2-0	Larissa
1985	Larissa	4-1	PAOK Salonica
1986	Panathinaikos	4-0	Olympiakos
1987	OFI Crete	1-1 3-1p	Iraklis Salonica
1988	Panathinaikos	2-2 4-3p	Olympiakos
1989	Panathinaikos	3-1	Panionios
1990	Olympiakos	4-2	OFI Crete
1991	Panathinaikos	3-0 2-1	Athinaikos
1992	Olympiakos	1-1 2-0	PAOK Salonica
1993	Panathinaikos	1-0	Olympiakos
1994	Panathinaikos	3-3 4-2p	AEK Athens
1995	Panathinaikos	1-0	AEK Athens

* won on toss of coin

LEADING INTERNATIONAL GOALSCORERS

29	Nikolaos Anastopoulos	(Panionios,Olympiakos, Avellino)	1977-1988
22	Dimitrios Saravakos	(Panionios,Panathinaikos)	1982-21
21	Dimitrios Papaioanou	(AEK)	1963-1978
14	Georgios Sideris	(Atromitos,Olympiakos)	1958-1969
14	Panayotis Tsaluhidis	(Veria,Olympiakos)	1987-
11	Thomas Mavros	(Panionios,AEK)	1972-1984
8	Anastasios Mitropoulos	(Ethnikos,Olympiakos,AEK)	1978-1994
	Nikos Mahlas	(OFI)	1993-
7	Georgios Dedes	(Panionios)	1966-1973
	Georgios Delikaris	(PAOK)	1971-1981
	Konstandinos Kuis	(Aris)	1979-1984
	Andreas Papaemanuil	(Panathinaikos)	1958-1965
	Stavros Sarafis	(PAOK)	1969-1977
	Konstandinos Humis	(Ethnikos)	1934-1936

LEADING INTERNATIONAL APPEARANCES

78	Dimitrios Saravakos	(Panionios,Panathinaikos)	1982-
76	Anastasios Mitropoulos	(Ethnikos,Olympiakos, AEK)	1978-1994
73	Nikolaos Anastopoulos	(Panionios,Olympiakos/ Avellino)	1977-1988
71	Stratos Apostolakis	(Olympiakos, Panathinaikos)	1986-
70	Stelios Manolas	(AEK)	1982-
	Panayotis Tsaluhidis	(Veria,Olympiakos)	1987-
65	Savas Kofidis	(Iraklis,Olympiakos,Aris)	1982-
	Dimitrios Papaioanou	(AEK)	1963-1978
58	Nikolaos Sarganis #	(Olympiakos,Panathinaikos Athinaikos)	1980-1991
52	Georgios Firos	(Aris)	1974-1982

INTERNATIONAL MATCHES PLAYED BY GREECE

28-08-1920	Sweden	L 0-9	Antwerp	OGr1	
30-06-1929	Bulgaria	D 1-1	Sofia	Fr	Andrianopoulos.V
26-01-1930	Yugoslavia	W 2-1	Athens	BC	Andrianopoulos.Y, Andrianopoulos.K
25-05	Rumania	L 1-8	Bucharest	BC	Andrianopoulos.V
7-12	Bulgaria	W 6-1	Athens	BC	Tsolinas 4, Mesaris 2
15-03-1931	Yugoslavia	L 1-4	Belgrade	BC	Miyakis
25-10	Bulgaria	L 1-2	Sofia	BC	Kitsos
29-11	Rumania	L 2-4	Athens	BC	Angelakis 2
27-03-1932	Bulgaria	L 1-2	Athens	Fr	Simeonidis
26-06	Yugoslavia	L 1-7	Belgrade	BC	Kitsos
28-06	Rumania	L 0-3	Belgrade	BC	
2-07	Bulgaria	L 0-2	Belgrade	BC	
3-06-1933	Yugoslavia	L 3-5	Bucharest	BC	Simeonidis, Ragos, Pierakos
6-06	Rumania	L 0-1	Bucharest	BC	
10-06	Bulgaria	L 0-2	Bucharest	BC	
4-02-1934	Bulgaria	W 1-0	Athens	Fr	Danelian
25-03	Italy	L 0-4	Milan	WCq	
23-12	Yugoslavia	W 2-1	Athens	BC	Vazos, Andrianopoulos.L
27-12	Rumania	D 2-2	Athens	BC	Andrianopoulos.L, Humis
1-01-1935	Bulgaria	L 1-2	Athens	BC	Vazos
16-06	Bulgaria	L 2-5	Sofia	BC	Humis 2
21-06	Yugoslavia	L 1-6	Sofia	BC	Baltasis
24-06	Rumania	D 2-2	Sofia	BC	Humis 2
17-05-1936	Rumania	L 2-5	Bucharest	BC	Vazos, Simeonidis
21-05	Bulgaria	L 4-5	Bucharest	BC	Miyakis, Humis, Vazos, Simeonidis
19-06	Egypt	L 1-3	Cairo	Fr	Humis
22-01-1938	Palestine	W 3-1	Tel Aviv	WCq	Vikelidis 2, Miyakis
20-02	Palestine	W 1-0	Athens	WCq	Vikelidis
25-03	Hungary	L 1-11	Budapest	WCq	Makris
23-04-1948	Turkey	L 1-3	Athens	Fr	Vikelidis
28-11	Turkey	L 1-2	Istanbul	Fr	Filaktos
15-05-1949	Turkey	L 1-2	Athens	MC	Xenos
18-05	Egypt	L 1-3	Athens	MC	Hatzistavridis
25-11	Syria	W 8-0	Athens	MC	Papandoniou 3, Vasiliadis 2, Maropoulos, Nembidis 2
17-02-1950	Egypt	L 0-2	Cairo	Fr	
14-10-1951	Syria	W 4-0	Alexandria	Fr	Lekatsas 3, Muratis
18-10	Egypt	W 2-0	Alexandria	Fr	Kotridis, Lekatsas
21-10	Egypt	L 0-3	Cairo	Fr	
25-11	Egypt	W 1-0	Athens	Fr	Darivas
15-07-1952	Denmark	L 1-2	Tammerfors	OGr1	Emanuilidis
9-05-1953	Yugoslavia	L 0-1	Belgrade	WCq	
1-11	Israel	W 1-0	Athens	WCq	Bembis
8-03-1954	Israel	W 2-0	Tel Aviv	WCq	Kokinakis, Kamaras
28-03	Yugoslavia	L 0-1	Athens	WCq	
7-11	Egypt	D 1-1	Athens	Fr	Kuirukidis
21-01-1955	Egypt	D 1-1	Cairo	Fr	Panakis
5-05-1957	Yugoslavia	D 0-0	Athens	WCq	
16-06	Rumania	L 1-2	Athens	WCq	Panakis

Date	Opponent	Result	Venue	Comp	Scorers
3-11	Romania	L 0-3	Bucharest	WCq	
10-11	Yugoslavia	L 1-4	Belgrade	WCq	Nestoridis
1-10-1958	France	L 1-7	Paris	ECr1	Ifandis
3-12	France	D 1-1	Athens	ECr1	Papaemanuil
15-11-1959	Yugoslavia	L 0-4	Belgrade	OGq	
2-12	Denmark	L 1-3	Athens	Fr	Serafidis
6-03-1960	Israel	L 1-2	Tel Aviv	OGq	Linoxilakis
3-04	Israel	W 2-1	Athens	OGq	Serafidis 2
24-04	Yugoslavia	L 0-5	Athens	OGq	
3-07	Denmark	L 2-7	Copenhagen	Fr	Lukanidis 2
20-11	West Germany	L 0-3	Athens	WCq	
3-05-1961	Nth. Ireland	W 2-1	Athens	WCq	Papaemanuil 2
17-10	Nth. Ireland	L 0-2	Belfast	WCq	
22-10	West Germany	L 1-2	Augsburg	WCq	Papaemanuil
18-10-1962	Ethiopia	W 3-2	Athens	Fr	Papaemanuil, Nestoridis, Deimezis
22-05-1963	Poland	L 0-4	Warsaw	Fr	
16-10	Poland	W 3-1	Athens	Fr	Lukanidis, Sideris, Petridis
27-11	Cyprus	L 1-3	Nicosia	Fr	Domazos
13-05-1964	Ethiopia	W 3-1	Athens	Fr	Papazoglou 2, Taktikos
29-11	Denmark	W 4-2	Athens	WCq	Sideris 2, Papaioanou 2
9-12	Wales	W 2-0	Athens	WCq	Papaioanou, Papaemanuil
24-02-1965	Bulgaria	L 1-2	Athens	Fr	Papaemanuil
17-03	Wales	L 1-4	Cardiff	WCq	Papaioanou
23-05	Soviet Union	L 1-3	Moscow	WCq	Papaioanou
3-10	Soviet Union	L 1-4	Athens	WCq	Papaioanou
27-10	Denmark	D 1-1	Copenhagen	WCq	Sideris
16-10-1966	Finland	W 2-1	Salonica	ECq	Alexiadis 2
15-02-1967	Libya	W 4-0	Athens	Fr	Sideris 2, Yutsos 2
8-03	Romania	L 1-2	Bucharest	Fr	Sideris
10-05	Finland	D 1-1	Helsinki	ECq	Haitas
16-07	Soviet Union	L 0-4	Tbilisi	ECq	
4-10	Austria	W 4-1	Athens	ECq	Sideris 3, Papaioanou
31-10	Soviet Union	L 0-1	Athens	ECq	
5-11	Austria	D 1-1	Vienna	ECq	Sideris
12-10-1968	Switzerland	L 0-1	Basle	WCq	
20-11	Egypt	W 4-1	Athens	Fr	Papaioanou, Aidiniou, Dedes 2
11-12	Portugal	W 4-2	Athens	WCq	Papaioanou, Dedes, OG, Sideris
12-03-1969	Israel	D 3-3	Tel Aviv	Fr	Yutsos 3
25-03	Cyprus	W 1-0	Athens	Fr	
16-04	Romania	D 2-2	Athens	WCq	Sideris, Dedes
4-05	Portugal	D 2-2	Oporto	WCq	Botinos, Eleftherakis
19-07	Australia	L 0-1	Sydney	Fr	
23-07	Australia	D 2-2	Brisbane	Fr	Dedes 2
26-07	Australia	W 2-0	Melbourne	Fr	Dedes, Papaioanou
15-10	Switzerland	W 4-1	Salonica	WCq	Kudas, Botinos 2, Sideris
16-11	Romania	D 1-1	Bucharest	WCq	Domazos
11-10-1970	Malta	D 1-1	Gzira	ECq	Kritikopoulos
28-10	Spain	L 1-2	Zaragoza	Fr	Papaioanou
19-11	Australia	L 1-3	Athens	Fr	Eleftherakis
22-11	West Germany	L 1-3	Athens	Fr	Yutsos
9-12	Cyprus	D 1-1	Athens	Fr	Papaioanou
16-12	Switzerland	L 0-1	Athens	ECq	
7-04-1971	Bulgaria	L 0-1	Athens	Fr	
21-04	England	L 0-3	London	ECq	
12-05	Switzerland	L 0-1	Berne	ECq	
18-06	Malta	W 2-0	Athens	ECq	Davurlis, Aidiniou
6-07	Mexico	D 1-1	Mexico City	Fr	Davurlis
30-09	Mexico	L 0-1	Salonica	Fr	
17-11	Bulgaria	D 2-2	Sofia	Fr	Andoniadis, Papaioanou
1-12	England	L 0-2	Athens	ECq	
16-02-1972	Holland	L 0-5	Athens	Fr	
4-03	Italy	W 2-1	Athens	Fr	Andoniadis, Pomonis
12-04	Spain	D 0-0	Salonica	Fr	
7-05	Ethiopia	W 1-0	Addis Ababa	Fr	Spiridon
2-09	France	L 1-3	Athens	Fr	Sarafis
19-11	Yugoslavia	L 0-1	Belgrade	WCq	
17-01-1973	Spain	L 2-3	Athens	WCq	Kudas, Domazos
31-01	Bulgaria	D 2-2	Athens	Fr	Sarafis, Eleftherakis
21-02	Spain	L 1-3	Malaga	WCq	Andoniadis
8-09	France	L 1-3	Paris	Fr	Aidiniou
19-12	Yugoslavia	L 2-4	Athens	WCq	Eleftherakis, OG

28-04-1974	Brazil	D 0-0	Rio de Janeiro	Fr	
15-05	Poland	L 0-2	Warsaw	Fr	
29-05	Romania	L 1-3	Bucharest	BC	Sarafis
13-10	Bulgaria	D 3-3	Sofia	ECq	Andoniadis, Papaioanou, Glezos
15-11	Cyprus	W 3-1	Athens	Fr	Papaioanou, Sarafis, Terzanidis
20-11	West Germany	D 2-2	Athens	ECq	Delikaris, Eleftherakis
18-12	Bulgaria	W 2-1	Athens	ECq	Sarafis, Andoniadis
23-02-1975	Malta	L 0-2	Gzira	ECq	
1-04	Cyprus	W 2-1	Nicosia	Fr	Kritikopoulos, Anastasiadis
4-06	Malta	W 4-0	Salonica	ECq	Mavros, Andoniadis, Iosifidis, Papaioanou
24-09	Romania	D 1-1	Salonica	BC	Sarafis
11-10	West Germany	D 1-1	Dusseldorf	ECq	Delikaris
30-12	Italy	L 2-3	Florence	Fr	Kritikopoulos, Sarafis
6-05-1976	Poland	W 1-0	Athens	Fr	Kudas
22-09	Israel	L 0-1	Patras	Fr	
9-10	Hungary	D 1-1	Athens	WCq	Papaioanou
10-11	Austria	L 0-3	Kavala	Fr	
26-01-1977	Israel	D 1-1	Tel Aviv	Fr	Galakos
9-03	Austria	L 0-2	Vienna	Fr	
23-03	Czechoslovakia	L 0-4	Prague	Fr	
24-04	Soviet Union	L 0-2	Moscow	WCq	
10-05	Soviet Union	W 1-0	Salonica	WCq	Papaioanou
28-05	Hungary	L 0-3	Budapest	WCq	
21-09	Romania	L 1-6	Bucharest	Fr	Karavitis
26-10	Bulgaria	D 0-0	Sofia	Fr	
16-11	Yugoslavia	D 0-0	Salonica	BC	
11-01-1978	Cyprus	W 2-0	Limassol	Fr	Delikaris, Livathinos
15-02	Austria	D 1-1	Athens	Fr	Galakos
22-03	Czechoslovakia	L 0-1	Salonica	Fr	
5-04	Poland	L 2-5	Poznan	Fr	Karavitis, Mavros
24-05	Finland	L 0-3	Helsinki	ECq	
11-06	Australia	W 2-1	Melbourne	Fr	Ifandidis 2
14-06	Australia	W 1-0	Adelaide	Fr	Ifandidis
17-06	Australia	D 1-1	Sydney	Fr	Karavitis
20-09	Soviet Union	L 0-2	Erevan	ECq	
11-10	Finland	W 8-1	Athens	ECq	Mavros 4, Delikaris 2, Nikoludis, Galakos
29-10	Hungary	W 4-1	Salonica	ECq	Galakos 2, Ardizoglou, Mavros
15-11	Yugoslavia	L 1-4	Skoplje	BC	Mavros
13-12	Romania	W 2-1	Athens	Fr	Kudas, Nikoludis
14-02-1979	Israel	L 1-4	Tel Aviv	Fr	Delikaris
21-03	Romania	L 0-3	Bucharest	Fr	
2-05	Hungary	D 0-0	Budapest	ECq	
12-09	Soviet Union	W 1-0	Athens	ECq	Nikoludis
16-01-1980	Cyprus	D 1-1	Nicosia	Fr	Anastopoulos
27-02	France	L 1-5	Paris	Fr	Mavros
1-04	Switzerland	L 0-2	Zurich	Fr	
16-04	East Germany	L 0-2	Leipzig	Fr	
14-05	Bulgaria	D 0-0	Athens	Fr	
11-06	Holland	L 0-1	Naples	ECr1	
14-06	Czechoslovakia	L 1-3	Rome	ECr1	Anastopoulos
17-06	West Germany	D 0-0	Turin	ECr1	
15-10	Denmark	W 1-0	Copenhagen	WCq	Kuis
11-11	Australia	D 3-3	Athens	Fr	Damanakis, Domazos, Delikaris
6-12	Italy	L 0-2	Athens	WCq	
28-01-1981	Luxembourg	W 2-0	Salonica	WCq	Kuis, Kostikos
11-03	Luxembourg	W 2-0	Luxembourg	WCq	Kuis, Mavros
15-04	Cyprus	W 1-0	Nicosia	Fr	Iosifidis
29-04	Yugoslavia	L 1-5	Split	WCq	Kostikos
23-09	Sweden	W 2-1	Salonica	Fr	Anastopoulos, Kuis
14-10	Denmark	L 2-3	Salonica	WCq	Anastopoulos, Kuis
14-11	Italy	D 1-1	Turin	WCq	Kuis
29-11	Yugoslavia	L 1-2	Athens	WCq	Mavros
20-01-1982	Portugal	L 1-2	Athens	Fr	Anastopoulos
10-02	East Germany	L 0-1	Athens	Fr	
10-03	Soviet Union	L 0-2	Athens	Fr	
24-03	Czechoslovakia	L 1-2	Prague	Fr	Kuis
14-04	Holland	L 0-1	Eindhoven	Fr	
9-10	Luxembourg	W 2-0	Luxembourg	ECq	Anastopoulos 2
27-10	Cyprus	D 1-1	Nicosia	Fr	Mavros
17-11	England	L 0-3	Salonica	ECq	
1-12	Switzerland	L 1-3	Athens	Fr	Anastopoulos

22-12	Cyprus	W 1-0	Yanina	Fr	Semertzidis
2-02-1983	Romania	L 1-3	Larissa	Fr	Kusulakis
23-02	East Germany	L 1-2	Dresden	Fr	Ardizoglou
30-03	England	D 0-0	London	ECq	
27-04	Denmark	L 0-1	Copenhagen	ECq	
15-05	Hungary	W 3-2	Budapest	ECq	Anastopoulos, Kostikos, Papaioanou.A
5-10	Italy	L 0-3	Bari	Fr	
16-11	Denmark	L 0-2	Athens	ECq	
3-12	Hungary	D 2-2	Salonica	ECq	Anastopoulos 2
14-12	Luxembourg	W 1-0	Athens	ECq	Saravakos
15-02-1984	East Germany	L 1-3	Athens	Fr	Anastopoulos
7-03	Romania	L 0-2	Craiova	Fr	
11-04	Cyprus	D 1-1	Athens	Fr	Anastopoulos
18-04	Austria	D 0-0	Vienna	Fr	
5-09	Czechoslovakia	L 0-1	Athens	Fr	
12-09	East Germany	L 0-1	Zwickau	Fr	
30-09	Cyprus	W 2-0	Limassol	Fr	Mitsimbonas, Anastopoulos
9-10	Israel	D 2-2	Athens	Fr	Semertzidis, Manolas
17-10	Poland	L 1-3	Zabrze	WCq	Mitropoulos
19-12	Belgium	D 0-0	Athens	WCq	
9-01-1985	Israel	W 2-0	Tel Aviv	Fr	Anastopoulos, Kofidis
27-02	Albania	W 2-0	Athens	WCq	Saravakos, Antoniou
13-03	Italy	D 0-0	Athens	Fr	
27-03	Belgium	L 0-2	Brussels	WCq	
19-05	Poland	L 1-4	Athens	WCq	Anastopoulos
16-10	Bulgaria	L 0-2	Salonica	Fr	
30-10	Albania	D 1-1	Tirana	WCq	Skartados
17-01-1986	Qatar	W 1-0	Doha	Fr	Saravakos
19-02	Cyprus	D 0-0	Athens	Fr	
26-03	East Germany	W 2-0	Athens	Fr	Anastopoulos, Saravakos
1-05	Sweden	D 0-0	Malmo	Fr	
24-09	Spain	L 1-3	Gijon	Fr	Skartados
8-10	Italy	L 0-2	Bologna	Fr	
15-10	Poland	L 1-2	Poznan	ECq	Anastopoulos
12-11	Hungary	W 2-1	Athens	ECq	Mitropoulos, Anastopoulos
3-12	Cyprus	W 4-2	Nicosia	ECq	Antoniou, Batsinilas, Anastopoulos, Papaioanou.A
7-01-1987	Portugal	D 1-1	Portalegre	Fr	Batsinilas
14-01	Cyprus	W 3-1	Athens	ECq	Anastopoulos 2, Bonovas
11-03	Romania	D 1-1	Athens	Fr	Saravakos
25-03	Holland	D 1-1	Rotterdam	ECq	Saravakos
29-04	Poland	W 1-0	Athens	ECq	Saravakos
23-09	Soviet Union	L 0-3	Moscow	Fr	
7-10	Romania	D 2-2	Bucharest	Fr	Anastopoulos, Xanthopoulos
14-10	Hungary	L 0-3	Budapest	ECq	
16-12	Holland	L 0-3	Rhodes	ECq	
17-02-1988	Nth. Ireland	W 3-2	Athens	Fr	Manolas 2, Mitropoulos
23-03	Soviet Union	L 0-4	Athens	Fr	
6-04	Austria	D 2-2	Athens	Fr	Saravakos, Skartados
19-05	Canada	W 1-0	Montreal	Fr	Tsiolis
21-05	Canada	W 3-0	Toronto	Fr	Anastopoulos 2, Mitropoulos
23-05	Chile	W 1-0	Toronto	Fr	Anastopoulos
28-05	Canada	D 0-0	Toronto	Fr	
31-08	East Germany	L 0-1	Berlin	Fr	
21-09	Turkey	L 1-3	Istanbul	Fr	Anastopoulos
19-10	Denmark	D 1-1	Athens	WCq	Mitropoulos
2-11	Romania	L 0-3	Bucharest	WCq	
15-11	Hungary	W 3-0	Athens	Fr	Tsaluhidis 2, Lagonidis
18-01-1989	Albania	D 1-1	Tirana	Fr	Tsiandakis
25-01	Portugal	L 1-2	Athens	Fr	Borbokis
8-02	England	L 1-2	Athens	Fr	Saravakos
22-02	Norway	W 4-2	Athens	Fr	Samaras, Vakalopoulos, Tsaluhidis, Saravkos
8-03	East Germany	W 3-2	Athens	Fr	Saravakos 2, OG
29-03	Turkey	L 0-1	Athens	Fr	
5-04	Yugoslavia	L 1-4	Athens	Fr	Mitropoulos
26-04	Romania	D 0-0	Athens	WCq	
17-05	Denmark	L 1-7	Copenhagen	WCq	Mavridis
23-08	Norway	D 0-0	Oslo	Fr	
5-09	Poland	L 0-3	Warsaw	Fr	
20-09	Yugoslavia	L 0-3	Novi Sad	Fr	
11-10	Bulgaria	L 0-4	Varna	WCq	
25-10	Hungary	D 1-1	Budapest	Fr	Borbokis
15-11	Bulgaria	W 1-0	Athens	WCq	Nioplias

17-01-1990	Belgium	W 2-0	Athens	Fr	Tsaluhidis, Apostolakis
28-03	Israel	W 2-1	Athens	Fr	Manolas 2
30-05	Italy	D 0-0	Perugia	Fr	
5-09	Albania	W 1-0	Patras	Fr	Dimitriadis
10-10	Egypt	W 6-1	Athens	Fr	Tsaluhidis, Saravakos 5
31-10	Malta	W 4-0	Athens	ECq	Tsiandakis, Karapialis, Saravakos, Borbokis
21-11	Holland	L 0-2	Rotterdam	ECq	
19-12	Poland	L 1-2	Volos	Fr	Tsaluhidis
23-01-1991	Portugal	W 3-2	Athens	ECq	Borbokis, Manolas, Tsaluhidis
27-02	Cyprus	D 1-1	Limassol	Fr	Saravakos
27-03	Morocco	D 0-0	Rabat	Fr	
17-04	Sweden	D 2-2	Athens	Fr	OG, Borbokis
4-09	Albania	L 0-2	Athens	Fr	
9-10	Finland	D 1-1	Helsinki	ECq	Tsaluhidis
30-10	Finland	W 2-0	Athens	ECq	Saravakos, Borbokis
21-11	Portugal	L 0-1	Lisbon	ECq	
4-12	Holland	L 0-2	Salonica	ECq	
22-12	Malta	D 1-1	Ta'Qali	ECq	Marinakis
29-01-1992	Albania	L 0-1	Tirana	Fr	
12-02	Romania	W 1-0	Athens	Fr	Tsaluhidis
25-03	Cyprus	W 3-1	Limassol	Fr	Tursunidis, Karapialis, Donis
13-05	Iceland	W 1-0	Athens	WCq	Sofianopoulos
2-09	Cyprus	L 2-3	Salonica	Fr	Tsaluhidis, Donis
7-10	Iceland	W 1-0	Reykjavik	WCq	Tsaluhidis
11-11	Hungary	D 0-0	Salonica	WCq	
17-02-1993	Luxembourg	W 2-0	Athens	WCq	Dimitriadis, Mitropoulos
10-03	Austria	L 1-2	Vienna	Fr	Mahlas
31-03	Hungary	W 1-0	Budapest	WCq	Apostolakis
23-05	Russia	D 1-1	Moscow	WCq	Mitropoulos
12-10	Luxembourg	W 3-1	Luxembourg	WCq	Mahlas, Apostolakis, Saravakos
17-11	Russia	W 1-0	Athens	WCq	Mahlas
23-03-1994	Poland	D 0-0	Salonica	Fr	
27-04	Saudi Arabia	W 5-1	Athens	Fr	Mahlas 2, Alexoudis, Kostis, Tountziaris
9-05	Cameroon	L 0-3	Athens	Fr	
13-05	Bolivia	D 0-0	Athens	Fr	
17-05	England	L 0-5	London	Fr	
28-05	USA	D 1-1	New Haven	Fr	Hantzidis
5-06	Colombia	L 0-2	New York	Fr	
21-06	Argentina	L 0-4	Boston	WCr1	
26-06	Bulgaria	L 0-4	Chicago	WCr1	
30-06	Nigeria	L 0-2	Boston	WCr1	
7-09	Faeroe Islands	W 5-1	Toftir	ECq	Saravakos, Tsaluhidis 2, Alexandris 2
12-10	Finland	W 4-0	Salonica	ECq	Markou, Batista, Mahlas 2
16-11	San Marino	W 2-0	Athens	ECq	Mahlas, Frantzeskos
18-12	Scotland	W 1-0	Athens	ECq	Apostolakis
25-01-1995	Cyprus	W 3-2	Larnaca	Fr	Georgiadis, Frantzeskos, Vrizas
8-02	Romania	W 1-0	Kalamata	Fr	Tsaluhidis
8-03	Switzerland	D 1-1	Athens	Fr	Vrizas
26-04	Russia	L 0-3	Salonica	ECq	
17-05	Lithuania	L 1-2	Vilnius	Fr	Tsartas
11-06	Finland	L 1-2	Helsinki	ECq	Nikolaidis

HOLLAND

At once the best, and at another time among the worst, the Dutch it seems are capable of anything. Along with Denmark they were the first European country to play the game with any degree of success and reached the semi-finals of four successive Olympic Games from 1908. As the amateur ideal started to fade in the 1920s, a long period of decline set in, reaching its nadir with the national side's elimination by Luxembourg in the 1964 European Nations Cup. It was reversed thanks only to the emergence of one of the finest generations of footballers the world has ever known.

Proximity to Great Britain ensured the early development of the game in Holland and by the turn of the century there were numerous clubs playing either football or rugby. In 1889 the football association was formed, making it, after Denmark, the second oldest on mainland Europe. Tours by English sides were common, and in 1898 a league championship was instituted, along with a cup competition the following year. Of the original clubs which made an impact only Sparta Rotterdam remain of any consequence. Ajax were not formed until 1900 and did not win their first championship until 1918, Feyenoord were formed in 1908 and became champions for the first time in 1924, whilst PSV Eindhoven were formed as late as 1913. They did not win the league until 1929.

If the club scene was somewhat confused, the national team were very quick to set their stall out, and until the early 1920s were one of the best sides in Europe. After playing their first match against Belgium in 1905, the Dutch entered the 1908 Olympic Games in London. Given a bye to the semi-finals, they lost against the hosts but won the third place play-off against Sweden. Four years later in Stockholm they again won the bronze medal, having lost to Denmark in the semi-finals. When the Olympics resumed after the First World War, Holland once again reached the last four, this time losing to Belgium. In Paris in 1924, for the fourth consecutive tournament, they lost in the semi-finals, 2-1 to Uruguay. When Amsterdam was chosen to host the 1928 tournament it looked as if the Dutch might at last reach the final. Unfortunately they drew Uruguay in the first round, lost 2-0, and their Olympic dream was over for good.

Apart from twice-yearly matches against Belgium, Holland's international programe was very limited until the 1960s. Defeats in the first round of both the 1934 and 1938 World Cups did little to encourage the game. After World War II, a dreadful sequence of results – just one win in over five years – helped to bring about the modernisation of the game. Fas Wilkes, perhaps the first great name in Dutch football, left to play for Valencia in Spain, and it was felt that if change was not instituted more would leave; so in 1957, along with the creation of a national league for the first time, professionalism was sanctioned.

The immediate effect was the rise of the big clubs, Feyenoord, Ajax and PSV, who have dominated Dutch football ever since. In an attempt to stay alive in the new professional league, there were a spate of mergers between clubs who could not face the challenge alone, but none have managed to rise to the levels of the big three. Who, after all, remembers HVV and HBS Den Haag, who between them won eleven championships in the early years? The new professional league eventually began to sow the seeds of success and in 1970 Feyenoord won the European Cup. The following year it was won by their great rivals Ajax, in the first of three consecutive wins. The Dutch had arrived. Feyenoord won the UEFA Cup in 1974 and PSV did the same in 1978.

Of the many talented footballers who appeared for Holland in the 1970s the most famous was Johan Cruyff, but he was not the only Dutch star at the time. At Ajax, Johan Neeskens, Ruud Krol, Arie Haan, Johnny Rep, Willem Suurbier, Barrie Hulshoff and Gerry Muhren all joined him in the national side at one time or another. Along with the Feyenoord pair of Van Hanegem and Jansen they formed the basis of the team which so nearly won the 1974 World Cup. Under manager Rinus Michels, a key figure in modern Dutch football, the team played 'Total football'. They were all comfortable on the ball, could play in most positions on the pitch, and were highly skilful individuals who moulded well into a team structure.

A consequence of their impressive display was the dispersal of the team around Europe. Cruyff had gone to Barcelona in the first million-dollar deal in 1973, and the rest of the team soon followed, tempted by large offers from Italian and Spanish clubs. Despite this, Holland very nearly won the following World Cup in Argentina, but once again lost to the hosts in the final. Had Cruyff made the trip they might well have won. If ever a team deserved to win a major title it was that Dutch side of the 1970s, but they could not even manage a win in the European Championship, finishing third in 1976 after losing to Czechoslovakia in the semi-finals.

THE ORDER OF MERIT

		All			League			Cup		Europe		
	Team	G	S	B	G	S	B	G	S	G	S	B
1	Ajax Amsterdam	43	23	11	25	16	9	12	5	6	2	2
2	Feyenoord Rotterdam	25	19	9	13	17	6	10	2	2	-	3
3	PSV Eindhoven	21	13	14	13	9	11	6	4	2	-	3
4	HVV Den Haag	9	3	-	8	-	-	1	3	-	-	-
5	Sparta Rotterdam	9	1	5	6	-	5	3	1	-	-	-
6	HBS Den Haag	5	5	-	3	-	-	2	5	-	-	-
7	Willem II Tilburg	5	-	5	3	-	5	2	-	-	-	-
8	Quick Den Haag	5	-	-	1	-	-	4	-	-	-	-
9	FC Den Haag	4	6	4	2	-	4	2	6	-	-	-
	Go Ahead Eagles Deventer	4	6	4	4	5	4	-	1	-	-	-
11	AZ Alkmaar	4	2	3	1	1	3	3	-	-	1	-
12	RCH Haarlem	4	-	-	2	-	-	2	-	-	-	-
13	Haarlem	3	3	1	1	-	1	2	3	-	-	-
14	RAP Amsterdam	3	1	-	2	-	-	1	1	-	-	-
15	HFC Haarlem	3	-	-	-	-	-	3	-	-	-	-
16	NAC Breda	2	7	2	1	4	2	1	3	-	-	-
17	FC Twente Enschede	2	5	12	1	2	10	1	2	-	1	2
18	VOC Rotterdam	2	3	-	-	1	-	2	2	-	-	-
19	FC Utrecht	2	2	2	1	1	2	1	1	-	-	-
20	Fortuna Sittard	2	2	1	-	1	1	2	1	-	-	-
21	Eindhoven VV	2	2	-	1	2	-	1	-	-	-	-
	DFC Dordrecht	2	2	-	-	-	-	2	2	-	-	-
23	Heracles Almelo	2	1	1	2	1	1	-	-	-	-	-
24	Wageningen	2	-	-	-	-	-	2	-	-	-	-
25	Roda JC Kerkrade	1	5	-	1	2	-	-	3	-	-	-
26	DWS Amsterdam	1	3	1	1	3	1	-	-	-	-	-
27	SC Telstar	1	2	1	-	1	1	1	1	-	-	-
28	FC Den Bosch	1	2	-	1	1	-	-	1	-	-	-
	Be Quick Groningen	1	2	-	1	2	-	-	-	-	-	-
	VUC Den Haag	1	2	-	-	1	-	1	1	-	-	-
31	Velocitas Breda	1	1	-	-	1	-	1	-	-	-	-
	Quick Nijmegan	1	1	-	-	1	-	1	-	-	-	-
33	LONGA Lichtenvoorde	1	-	1	-	-	1	1	-	-	-	-
	VVV Venlo	1	-	1	-	-	1	1	-	-	-	-
	Velocitas Groningen	1	-	1	-	-	1	1	-	-	-	-
36	De Volewijckers	1	-	-	1	-	-	-	-	-	-	-
	Limburg Brunssue	1	-	-	1	-	-	-	-	-	-	-
	SVV Schiedam	1	-	-	1	-	-	-	-	-	-	-
	Concordia	1	-	-	-	-	-	1	-	-	-	-
	CVV	1	-	-	-	-	-	1	-	-	-	-
	Roermund	1	-	-	-	-	-	1	-	-	-	-
	Schoten	1	-	-	-	-	-	1	-	-	-	-
	ZFC	1	-	-	-	-	-	1	-	-	-	-
44	Vitesse Arnhem	-	8	-	-	5	-	-	3	-	-	-
	Plus 31 teams with combined total	-	46	12	-	20	12	-	26	-	-	-

To the end of the 1994-95 season

It seemed as if the Dutch dream was coming to an end with the failure to qualify for the 1982 and 1986 World Cups, but further success was just around the corner. PSV won the European Cup in 1988, whilst Ajax won their first European trophy for 14 years, the Cup Winners Cup, in 1987. In 1992 they became only the second team, after Juventus, to have won all three European trophies with their victory in the UEFA Cup, and they won the European Cup for a fourth time in 1995 beating Milan 1-0 in the final.

Starring in that final for Ajax against his old club was Frank Rijkaard, who together with Ruud Gullit and Marco Van Basten had formed a powerful Dutch trio in the dominant Milan side of the late 1980s. Spearheading a new generation of players brought up on the success of the Cruyff era, they also led Holland to victory in the 1988 European Championships in Germany. Once again under Rinus Michels, the Dutch stuttered in the first round but beat the Germans in the semi-finals and then destroyed the Soviet Union in a scintillating final in Munich. After years of coming so close, they had at last won a major title.

After a disappointing 1990 World Cup in which they lost to their old bogey team West Germany in the second round, the Dutch came close to retaining their European crown in 1992. With Dennis Bergkamp added to the side they played some of the best football seen in the finals in Sweden but fell to the Danes in the semi-final after a penalty shoot-out. In the 1994 World Cup, having eliminated England in the qualifiers, they reached the quarter-finals but lost to Brazil, to complete a remarkable sequence: in every post-war tournament for which they have qualified, Holland have been knocked out by the eventual winners! Except in 1988, that is.

Population: 14,934,000
Area, sq km: 41,863
% in urban areas: 88.6%
Capital city: Amsterdam, The Hague

Koninklijke Nederlandsche Voetbalbond (KNVB)
Woudenbergseweg #56
Postbus 515
NL-3700 Am Zeist
Netherlands
Tel: + 31 34399211
Fax: + 31 34391397

Year of formation	1889
Affiliation to FIFA	1904
Affiliation to UEFA	1954
Registered clubs	5900
Registered players	973 000
Professional players	600
Registered coaches	4100
Registered referees	11 991
National stadium	Olympisch Stadion Amsterdam 59 000
National colours	Orange/White/ Orange
Reserve colours	White/White/White
Season	August - May

THE RECORD

WORLD CUP

1930	Did not enter
1934	QT 1st/3 in group 11 - Final Tournament/1st round
1938	QT 1st/3 in group 8 - Final Tournament/1st round
1950	Did not enter
1954	Did not enter
1958	QT 2nd/3 in group 5
1962	QT 2nd/3 in group 4
1966	QT 3rd/4 in group 5
1970	QT 3rd/4 in group 8
1974	QT 1st/4 in group 3 - Final Tournament/Finalists
1978	QT 1st/4 in group 4 - Final Tournament/Finalists
1982	QT 4th/5 in group 2
1986	QT 2nd/4 in group 5
1990	QT 1st/4 in group 4 - Final Tournament/2nd round
1994	QT 2nd/6 in group 2 - Final Tournament/Quarter-finals

EUROPEAN CHAMPIONSHIP

1960	Did not enter
1964	2nd round
1968	QT 3rd/4 in group 5
1972	QT 2nd/4 in group 7
1976	QT 1st/4 in group 5 - Final Tournament/Semi-finalists/ 3rd place
1980	QT 1st/5 in group 4 - Final Tournament/1st round
1984	QT 2nd/5 in group 7
1988	QT 1st/5 in group 5 - Final Tournament/Winners
1992	QT 1st/5 in group 6 - Final Tournament/Semi-finalists
1996	QT group 5

EUROPEAN CLUB COMPETITIONS

European Cup
Winners - Feyenoord 1970 Ajax 1971 1972 1973 1995 PSV Eindhoven 1988 1995
Finalists - Ajax 1969

Cup Winners Cup
Winners - Ajax 1987
Finalists - Ajax 1988

UEFA Cup
Winners - Feyenoord 1974 PSV Eindhoven 1978 Ajax 1992
Finalists - Twente Enschede 1975 AZ 67 Alkmaar 1981

CLUB DIRECTORY

AMSTERDAM (Population - 1,860,000)

Ajax (1900)
De Meer 19,000 – White, red stripe/White

FC Amsterdam (1972-1983)
Olympisch Stadion 59,000 – White/Red
Previous names - Merger in 1972 of Blauw Wit (1902), DWS (1907) and Volewijckers (1920). The club was dissolved in 1983 when all three teams split away to operate as amateurs

Haarlem (1889)
Haarlem Stadion 14,000 – Blue, red sleeves/Red

SC Telstar Ijmuiden (1962)
Schoonenberg – White/White
Previous names - Merger in 1962 of Stormvogels and VSV

ROTTERDAM (Population - 1,110,000)

Excelsior (1902)
Woudensteyn – Red/Black

Feyenoord (1908)
Feyenoord Stadion 63,000 – Red & white halves/Black
Previous names - Wilhelmina 1908-10, Hellesluis 1910-11, Celeritas 1911-12

Sparta Rotterdam (1888)
Spangen 14,000 – Red & white stripes/Black

THE HAGUE (Population - 770,000)

FC Den Haag (1971)
Zuiderparkstadion 9,000 – Yellow/Green
Previous names - Merger in 1971 of ADO Den Haag (1905) and Holland Sport (1954)

UTRECHT (Population - 511,000)

FC Utrecht (1970)
Nieuw Galgenwaard 14,000 – Red, white sash/White
Previous names - Merger in 1970 of DOS Utrecht (1902), Velox and Elinkwijk (1919)

EINDHOVEN (Population - 376,000)

PSV Eindhoven (1913)
(Philips Sport Vereniging)
Philips Stadion 27,000 – Red, thin white stripes/White

Eindhoven (1909)
Aalsterweg – Blue & white stripes/Black

ARNHEM (Population - 294,000)
Vitesse Arnhem (1892)
Monnikenhuize 12,000 – Yellow, thin black stripes/White

ENSCHEDE (Population - 288,000)
FC Twente Enschede (1965)
Het Diekman 18,000 – Red, white trim
Previous names - Merger in 1965 of SC Enschede (1910) and Enschede Boys Honours

HEERLEN (Population - 266,000)
Roda JC Kerkrade (1914)
Kaalheide 23,000 – Yellow/Black
Previous names - Merged with Rapid Heerlen (1954) in 1962

NIJMEGEN (Population - 238,000)
NEC Nijmegan (1900)
(Nijmegan Eendracht Combinatie)
De Goffert Stadion 29,000 – Red, green hoop/Black

TILBURG (Population - 223,000)
Willem II Tilburg (1896)
Willem II 13,000 – Red white & blue stripes/White
Previous name - Tilburgia 1896-1908

GRONINGEN (Population - 207,000)
FC Groningen (1921)
Oosterpark 18,000 – Green & white stripes/White
Previous name - GVAV 1921-71

DORDRECHT (Population - 200,000)
SVV Dordrecht '90 (1904)
Krommedijk 9,000 – White, green trim
Previous names - DFC until 1974, FC Dordrecht 1974-79, DS '79 1979-1990. Merged with Schiedamse Voetbal Vereniging (SVV) (1904) in 1990

HERTOGENBOSCH (Population - 189,000)
FC Den Bosch (1967)
De Vliert 23,000 – White/White
Previous name - BVV 1906-67

GELEEN (Population - 177,000)
Fortuna Sittard (1968)
De Baandert 14,000 – Yellow/Green
Previous names - Merger of Fortuna 54 Geleen and Sittardia (1950) in 1968 to form FSC, FSC 1968-79

MAASTRICHT (Population - 158,000)
MVV Maastricht (1902)
(Maastrichtse Voetbal Vereniging)
De Geusselt 10,000 – Red/White

BREDA (Population - 154,000)
NAC Breda (1912)
(Noad Advendo Combinatie)
NAC Stadion 12,000 – Yellow/Black

ALKMAAR (Population - 121,000)
AZ Alkmaar (1967)
(Alkmaar-Zaanstreek)
Alkmaarderhout 18,000 – Red/White
Previous name - Almaar 1954-67, AZ 67 Alkmaar 1967-86

ZWOLLE (Population - 88,000)
FC Zwolle (1910)
Gemeentelijk 14,000 – Green/White
Previous name - PEC Zwolle 1910-90

VENLO (Population - 87,000)
VVV Venlose (1903)
(Venlose Voetbal Vereniging)
De Koel 18,000 – Yellow, thin black stripes/Black

DEVENTER (Population 64,000)
Go Ahead Eagles (1902)
De Adelaarshorst 11,000 – Yellow & red stripes/Red, white trim
Previous name - Go Ahead Deventer 1902-71

HELMOND (Population - 63,000)
Helmond Sport (1967)
De Braak – Red/White
Previous name - Helmondia until 1967

VOLENDAM (Pop. – 24,000)
FC Volendam (1920)
Sportpark Volendam 12,000 – Orange, white trim

DUTCH LEAGUE CHAMPIONSHIP

1898aa RAP Amsterdam 4 Vitesse Arnhem 0
1899 RAP Amsterdam 4 PW Enschede 0
1900 HVV Den Haag 2 Victoria Wageningen 2
1901 HVV Den Haag 2 Victoria Wageningen 2
1902 HVV Den Haag 3 Victoria Wageningen 1
1903a HVV Den Haag 8 Vitesse Arnhem 2 Volharding 2
1904 HBS Den Haag 5 Velocitas Breda 4 PW Enschede 3
1905aa HVV Den Haag 4 PW Enschede 0
1906 HBS Den Haag 4 PW Enschede 0
1907 HVV Den Haag 4 PW Enschede 0
1908 Quick Den Haag 2 UD 2
1909 Sparta Rotterdam 4 Wilhelmina 0
1910 HVV Den Haag 4 Quick Nijmegen 0
1911 Sparta Rotterdam 4 GVC 0
1912 Sparta Rotterdam 4 GVC 0
1913 Sparta Rotterdam 4 Vitesse Arnhem 0
1914 HVV Den Haag 6 Vitesse Arnhem 6
1915 Sparta Rotterdam 2 Vitesse Arnhem 2
1916a Willem II Tilburg 5 Go Ahead Deventer 4 Sparta Rotterdam 3
1917b Go Ahead Deventer 11 UVV 7 Willem II Tilburg 5
1918c Ajax 13 Go Ahead Deventer 10 Willem II Tilburg 9
1919 Ajax 13 Go Ahead Deventer 9 AFC Amsterdam 9
1920b Be Quick Groningen 10 VOC Rotterdam 7 Go Ahead Deventer 5
1921 NAC Breda 8 Be Quick Groningen 7 Ajax 6
1922 Go Ahead Deventer 7 Blauw-Wit Amst'dam 7 NAC Breda 6
1923 RCH Haarlem 8 Be Quick Groningen 5 Go Ahead Deventer 5
1924c Feyenoord 13 Stormvogels Velsen 12 NAC Breda 7
1925 HBS Den Haag 15 NAC Breda 11 Sparta Rotterdam 9
1926 SC Enschede 14 MVV Maastricht 10 Feyenoord 8
1927 Heracles Almelo 14 NAC Breda 10 Ajax 8
1928 Feyenoord 12 Ajax 10 NOAD Tilburg 8
1929 PSV Eindhoven 12 Go Ahead Deventer 10 Feyenoord 8
1930 Go Ahead Deventer 10 Ajax 9 Velocitas Groningen 9
1931 Ajax 12 Feyenoord 8 PSV Eindhoven 8
1932 Ajax 13 Feyenoord 12 SC Enschede 9
1933 Go Ahead Deventer 11 Feyenoord 10 Stormvogels Velsen 8
1934 Ajax 10 KFC Alkmaar 10 Willem II Tilburg 10
1935 PSV Eindhoven 13 Go Ahead Deventer 12 Ajax 8
1936 Feyenoord 12 Ajax 10 SC Enschede 10
1937 Ajax 14 Feyenoord 10 PSV Eindhoven 6
1938 Feyenoord 14 Heracles Almelo 12 DWS Amsterdam 7
1939 Ajax 12 DWS Amsterdam 10 SC Nijmegen 8
1940 Feyenoord 11 Blauw-Wit Amsterdam 9 Heracles Almelo 9
1941 Heracles Almelo 13 PSV Eindhoven 9 ADO Den Haag 7
1942 ADO Den Haag 10 Eindhoven VV 9 AGOVV 8
1943 ADO Den Haag 11 Feyenoord 9 Willem II Tilburg 8
1944 De Volewijckers 12 VUC Den Haag 10 LONGA Lichtenvoorde 9
1945 -
1946d Haarlem 15 Ajax 14 SC Heerenveen 10
1947 Ajax 17 SC Heerenveen 14 SC Nijmegen 9
1948 BVV Hertogenbosch 14 SC Heerenveen 13 Go Ahead Deventer 12
1949 SVV Schiedam 15 BVV Hertogenbosch 13 AGOVV 11
1950 Limburg Brunssue 15 Blauw-Wit Amsterdam 14 Maurits 10
1951c PSV Eindhoven 13 DWS Amsterdam 10 Willem II Tilburg 9

1952b	Willem II Tilburg 12 Hermes Schiedam 7 Haarlem 4
1953	RCH Haarlem 7 Eindhoven 7 Sparta Rotterdam 6
1954	Eindhoven 8 DOS Utrecht 6 PSV Eindhoven 5
1955	Willem II Tilburg 8 NAC Breda 6 PSV Eindhoven 6
1956	Rapid JC Heerlen 8 NAC Breda 8 Elikwijk Utrecht 5

DUTCH EREDIVISIE

1957t	Ajax 49 Fortuna '54 Geleen 45 SC Enschede 41
1958	DOS Utrecht 47 SC Enschede 47 Ajax 42
1959	Sparta Rotterdam 51 Rapid JC Heerlen 48 Fortuna '54 Geleen 44
1960	Ajax 50 Feyenoord 50 PSV Eindhoven 45
1961	Feyenoord 53 Ajax 51 VVV Venlo 42
1962	Feyenoord 50 PSV Eindhoven 49 Blauw-Wit Amsterdam 41
1963q	PSV Eindhoven 42 Ajax 39 Sparta Rotterdam 39
1964	DWS Amsterdam 43 PSV Eindhoven 41 SC Enschede 39
1965	Feyenoord 45 DWS Amsterdam 40 ADO Den Haag 33
1966	Ajax 52 Feyenoord 45 ADO Den Haag 39
1967t	Ajax 56 Feyenoord 51 Sparta Rotterdam 48
1968	Ajax 58 Feyenoord 55 Go Ahead Deventer 42
1969	Feyenoord 57 Ajax 54 FC Twente Enschede 47
1970	Ajax 60 Feyenoord 55 PSV Eindhoven 46
1971	Feyenoord 57 Ajax 53 ADO Den Haag 50
1972	Ajax 63 Feyenoord 55 FC Twente Enschede 48
1973	Ajax 60 Feyenoord 58 FC Twente Enschede 50
1974	Feyenoord 56 FC Twente Enschede 54 Ajax 51
1975	PSV Eindhoven 55 Feyenoord 53 Ajax 49
1976	PSV Eindhoven 53 Feyenoord 52 Ajax 50
1977	Ajax 52 PSV Eindhoven 47 AZ 67 Alkmaar 46
1978	PSV Eindhoven 53 Ajax 49 AZ 67 Alkmaar 47
1979	Ajax 54 Feyenoord 51 PSV Eindhoven 49
1980	Ajax 50 AZ 67 Alkmaar 47 PSV Eindhoven 44
1981	AZ 67 Alkmaar 60 Ajax 48 FC Utrecht 45
1982	Ajax 56 PSV Eindhoven 51 AZ 67 Alkmaar 47
1983	Ajax 58 Feyenoord 54 PSV Eindhoven 51
1984	Feyenoord 57 PSV Eindhoven 52 Ajax 51
1985	Ajax 54 PSV Eindhoven 48 Feyenoord 48
1986	PSV Eindhoven 60 Ajax 52 Feyenoord 44
1987	PSV Eindhoven 59 Ajax 53 Feyenoord 42
1988	PSV Eindhoven 59 Ajax 50 FC Twente Enschede 41
1989	PSV Eindhoven 53 Ajax 50 FC Twente Enschede 40
1990	Ajax 49 PSV Eindhoven 48 FC Twente Enschede 42
1991	PSV Eindhoven 53 Ajax 53 FC Groningen 46
1992	PSV Eindhoven 58 Ajax 55 Feyenoord 49
1993	Feyenoord 53 PSV Eindhoven 51 Ajax 49
1994	Ajax 54 Feyenoord 51 PSV Eindhoven 44
1995	Ajax 61 Roda JC Kerkrade 54 PSV EIndhoven 47

Championship play-offs

1900	HVV Den Haag	1-0	Victoria Wageningen
1901	HVV Den Haag	2-1	Victoria Wageningen
1908	Quick Den Haag	4-1	UD
1922	Go Ahead Eagles	1-0	Blauw-Wit Amsterdam
1934	Ajax won a three way play-off		
1953	RCH Haarlem	2-1	Eindhoven VV
1956	Rapid JC Heerlen	3-0	NAC Breda
1958	DOS Utrecht	1-0	SC Enschede
1960	Ajax	5-1	Feyenoord

DUTCH CUP FINALS

1899	RAP Amsterdam	1-0	HVV Den Haag
1900	Velocitas Breda	3-1	Ajax
1901	HBS Den Haag	4-3	RAP Amsterdam
1902	Haarlem	2-1	HBS Den Haag
1903	HVV Den Haag	6-1	HBS Den Haag
1904	HFC Haarlem	3-1	HVV Den Haag
1905	VOC Rotterdam	3-0	HBS Den Haag
1906	Concordia	3-2	Volharding
1907	VOC Rotterdam	4-3	Voorwaarts
1908	HBS Den Haag	3-1	VOC Rotterdam
1909	Quick Den Haag	2-0	VOC Rotterdam
1910	Quick Den Haag	2-0	HVV Den Haag
1911	Quick Den Haag	1-0	Haarlem
1912	Haarlem	2-0	Vitesse Arnhem
1913	HFC Haarlem	4-1	DFC Dordrecht
1914	DFC Dordrecht	3-2	Haarlem
1915	HFC Haarlem	1-0	HBS Den Haag
1916	Quick Den Haag	2-1	HBS Den Haag
1917	Ajax	5-0	VSV Velsen
1918	RCH Haarlem	2-1	VVA
1919	-		
1920	CVV	2-1	VUC Den Haag
1921	Schoten	2-1	RFC
1922-24	-		
1925	ZFC	5-1	Xerxes
1926	LONGA Lichtenvoorde	5-2	De Spartan
1927	VUC Den Haag	3-1	Vitesse Arnhem
1928	RCH Haarlem	2-0	PEC Zwolle
1929	-		
1930	Feyenoord	1-0	Excelsior
1931	-		
1932	DFC Dordrecht	5-4	PSV Eindhoven
1933	-		
1934	Velocitas Groningen	3-2	Feyenoord
1935	Feyenoord	5-2	Helmondia
1936	Roermond	4-2	KFC Alkmaar
1937	Eindhoven	1-0	De Spartan
1938	VSV Velsen	4-1	AGOVV
1939	Wageningen	2-1	PSV Eindhoven
1940-42	-		
1943	Ajax	3-2	DFC Dordrecht
1944	Willem II Tilburg	9-2	Groene Ster
1945-47	-		
1948	Wageningen	0-0*	DWV
1949	Quick Nijmegen	1-1*	Helmondia
1950	PSV Eindhoven	4-3	Haarlem
1951-56	-		
1957	Fortuna '54 Geleen	4-2	Feyenoord
1958	Sparta Rotterdam	4-3	Volendam
1959	VVV Venlo	4-1	ADO Den Haag
1960	-		
1961	Ajax	3-0	NAC Breda
1962	Sparta Rotterdam	1-0	DHC
1963	Willem II Tilburg	3-0	ADO Den Haag
1964	Fortuna '54 Geleen	0-0*	ADO Den Haag
1965	Feyenoord	1-0	Go Ahead Deventer
1966	Sparta Rotterdam	1-0	ADO Den Haag
1967	Ajax	2-1	NAC Breda
1968	ADO Den Haag	2-1	Ajax
1969	Feyenoord	1-1 2-0	PSV Eindhoven
1970	Ajax	2-0	PSV Eindhoven
1971	Ajax	2-2 2-1	Sparta Rotterdam
1972	Ajax	3-2	FC Den Haag
1973	NAC Breda	2-0	NEC Nijmegen
1974	PSV Eindhoven	6-0	NAC Breda
1975	FC Den Haag	1-0	FC Twente Enschede
1976	PSV Eindhoven	1-0	Roda JC Kerkrade
1977	FC Twente Enschede	3-0	PEC Zwolle
1978	AZ 67 Alkmaar	1-0	Ajax
1979	Ajax	1-1 3-0	FC Twente Enschede
1980	Feyenoord	3-1	Ajax
1981	AZ 67 Alkmaar	3-1	Ajax

1982	AZ 67 Alkmaar	5-1 0-1	FC Utrecht
1983	Ajax	3-1 3-1	NEC Nijmegan
1984	Feyenoord	1-0	Fortuna Sittard
1985	FC Utrecht	1-0	Helmond Sport
1986	Ajax	3-0	RBC Roosendaal
1987	Ajax	4-2	FC Den Haag
1988	PSV Eindhoven	3-2	Roda JC Kerkrade
1989	PSV Eindhoven	4-1	FC Groningen
1990	PSV Eindhoven	1-0	Vitesse Arnhem
1991	Feyenoord	1-0	BVV Den Bosch
1992	Feyenoord	3-0	Roda JC Kerkrade
1993	Ajax	6-2	SC Heerenveen
1994	Feyenoord	2-1	NEC Nijmegan
1995	Feyenoord	2-1	FC Volendam

* Won on penalties

LEADING INTERNATIONAL SCORERS

35 Faas Wilkes	(Xerxes,Valencia,VVV, Fortuna '54)	1946-1961
33 Abe Lenstra	(Heerenveen,SC Enschede)	1940-1959
Johan Cruyff	(Ajax,Barcelona)	1966-1977
28 Bep Bakhuys	(ZAC,HBS Den Haag)	1928-1937
26 Kick Smit	(Haarlem)	1934-1946
24 Marco Van Basten	(Ajax,Milan)	1983-
23 Dennis Bergkamp	(Ajax,Internazionale)	1990-
19 Leen Vente	(Neptunus,Feyenoord)	1933-1940
17 Mannes Francken	(HFC Haarlem)	1906-1914
Tonny Van der Linden	(DOS Utrecht)	1957-1963
Wim Tap	(ADO Den Haag)	1925-1931
Johan Neeskens	(Ajax,Barcelona,NY Cosmos)	1970-1981

LEADING INTERNATIONAL APPEARANCES

83 Ruud Krol	(Ajax,Vancouver Whitecaps, Napoli)	1969-1983
77 Ronald Koeman	(FC Groningen,Ajax,PSV Eindhoven,Barcelona)	1983-
73 Frank Rijkaard	(Ajax,Sporting CL,Milan,Ajax)	1981-1994
72 Hans Van Breukelen #	(FC Utrecht,Nottm. Forest,PSV)	1980-1992
70 Jan Wouters	(FC Utrecht,Ajax)	1982-
65 Ruud Gullit	(Haarlem,Feyenoord, PSV Eindhoven,Milan,Sampdoria)	1981-
Wim Jansen	(Feyenoord)	1967-1980
64 Puck Van Heel	(Feyenoord)	1925-1938
63 Willy Van de Kerkhof	(PSV Eindhoven)	1974-1985
60 Wim Suurbier	(Ajax,Metz,Schalke 04)	1966-1978

NATIONAL TEAM COACHES

1908-12	Edgar Chadwick
1912-14	Edgar Chadwick, Fred Warburton, T. Bradchow & J. Hunter
1914-23	Fred Warburton
1924	W. Townley
1924-40	Bob Glendenning
1940-47	Karel Kaufman & Otto Bonsema
1947-48	Jesse Carver
1948-49	Tom Sneddon & Karel Kaufman
1949-54	Jaap van der Leck
1954-55	Friedrich Donenfeld
1955-56	Max Merkel
1957	George Hardwick
1957-64	Elek Schwartz
1964-65	Dennis Neville
1965-70	Georg Kessler
1970-74	Frantisek Fadrhonc & Rinus Michels
1974-76	George Knobel
1976-81	Jan Zwartkruis & Ernst Happel (1977-78)
1981-84	Kees Rijvers
1984-88	Rinus Michels & Leo Beenhakker (1985-86)
1988-90	Thijs Libregts
1990	Leo Beenhakker
1990-92	Rinus Michels
1992-94	Dick Advocaat
1995-	Guus Hiddink

INTERNATIONAL MATCHES PLAYED BY HOLLAND

30-04-1905	Belgium	W 4-1	Antwerp	Fr	De Neve 4
14-05	Belgium	W 4-0	Rotterdam	Fr	De Neve 2, Hesselink, Lutjens
29-04-1906	Belgium	L 0-5	Antwerp	Fr	
13-05	Belgium	L 2-3	Rotterdam	Fr	Vinne, Muller
1-04-1907	England Am	L 1-8	The Hague	Fr	Blume
14-04	Belgium	W 3-1	Antwerp	Fr	Van Gogh 2, Feith
9-05	Belgium	L 1-2	Haarlem	Fr	Feith
21-12	England	L 2-12	Darlington	Fr	Ruffelse 2
29-03-1908	Belgium	W 4-1	Antwerp	Fr	Thomée 2, Ruffelse, De Korver
26-04	Belgium	W 3-1	Rotterdam	Fr	Thomée 2, Snethlage,
10-05	France	W 4-1	Rotterdam	Fr	Snethlage 2, Thomée, Akkersdijk
22-10	England Am	L 0-4	London	OGsf	
23-10	Sweden	W 2-0	London	OG3p	Snethlage, Reeman
25-10	Sweden	W 5-3	The Hague	Fr	Snethlage 2, Welcker, Francken, Thomée
21-03-1909	Belgium	W 4-1	Antwerp	Fr	Snethlage, Welcker, Lutjens, Kessler.J
12-04	England Am	L 0-4	Amsterdam	Fr	
25-04	Belgium	W 4-1	Rotterdam	Fr	Snethlage 3, Lutjens
11-12	England Am	L 1-9	London	Fr	Kessler.H (I)
13-03-1910	Belgium	L 2-3	Antwerp	Fr	Lutjens, Kessler.J
10-04	Belgium	W 7-0	Haarlem	Fr	Francken 3, Thomée 2, Welcker 2
24-04	Germany	W 4-2	Arnhem	Fr	Thomée 2, Lutjens, OG
16-10	Germany	W 2-1	Kleve	Fr	Thomée, Van Berckel
19-03-1911	Belgium	W 5-1	Antwerp	Fr	Francken 3, Thomée, Welcker
2-04	Belgium	W 3-1	Dordrecht	Fr	Francken 2, Van Breda Kolff

17-04	England Am	L 0-1	Amsterdam	Fr	
10-03-1912	Belgium	W 2-1	Antwerp	Fr	Thomée 2
16-03	England Am	L 0-4	Hull	Fr	
24-03	Germany	D 5-5	Zwolle	Fr	Thomée 2, Francken 2, OG
28-04	Belgium	W 4-3	Dordrecht	Fr	Francken 3, Van Berckel
29-06	Sweden	W 4-3	Stockholm	OGr1	Vos 2, Bouvy 2
30-06	Austria	W 3-1	Stockholm	OGqf	Vos, Bouvy, Ten Cate
2-07	Denmark	L 1-4	Stockholm	OGsf	OG
4-07	Finland	W 9-0	Stockholm	OG3p	Vos 5, De Groot 2, Sluis 2
17-11	Germany	W 3-2	Leipzig	Fr	Francken 2, Haak
9-03-1913	Belgium	D 3-3	Antwerp	Fr	Francken, Haak, Bosschart
24-03	England Am	W 2-1	The Hague	Fr	De Groot 2
20-04	Belgium	L 2-4	Zwolle	Fr	De Groot, Bouvy
15-11	England Am	L 1-2	Hull	Fr	Boutmy
15-03-1914	Belgium	W 4-2	Antwerp	Fr	Kessler.J 2, Francken, Van Holthe
5-04	Germany	D 4-4	Amsterdam	Fr	Buitenweg 2, Vos, ?
26-04	Belgium	W 4-2	Amsterdam	Fr	Buitenweg 2, Vos, Kessler.J
17-05	Denmark	L 3-4	Copenhagen	Fr	Buitenweg 2, De Groot
9-06-1919	Sweden	W 3-1	Amsterdam	Fr	Kessler.J, Gupffert, Brokmann
24-08	Sweden	L 1-4	Stockholm	Fr	Buitenweg
31-08	Norway	D 1-1	Oslo	Fr	Buitenweg
5-04-1920	Denmark	W 2-0	Amsterdam	Fr	Kessler.H (II), De Natris
13-05	Italy	D 1-1	Genoa	Fr	Kessler.J
16-05	Switzerland	L 1-2	Basle	Fr	De Natris
28-08	Luxembourg	W 3-0	Brussels	OGr1	Groosjohan 2, Bulder
29-08	Sweden	W 5-4	Antwerp	OGqf	Groosjohan 2, Bulder 2, De Natris
31-08	Belgium	L 0-3	Antwerp	OGsf	
5-09	Spain	L 1-3	Antwerp	OG2p	Groosjohan
28-03-1921	Switzerland	W 2-0	Amsterdam	Fr	Kessler.J, Gupffert
8-05	Italy	D 2-2	Amsterdam	Fr	Kessler.J, Van Gendt
15-05	Belgium	D 1-1	Antwerp	Fr	Kessler.J
12-06	Denmark	D 1-1	Copenhagen	Fr	Van Gendt
13-11	France	W 5-0	Paris	Fr	Van Gendt 3, Rodermond 2
26-03-1922	Belgium	L 0-4	Antwerp	Fr	
17-04	Denmark	W 2-0	Amsterdam	Fr	Rodermond, Groen
7-05	Belgium	L 1-2	Amsterdam	Fr	Bulder
19-11	Switzerland	L 0-5	Berne	Fr	
2-04-1923	France	W 8-1	Amsterdam	Fr	Bulder 2, Addicks 2, Roetert 2, Van Linge 2
29-04	Belgium	D 1-1	Amsterdam	Fr	Heijnen
10-05	Germany	D 0-0	Hamburg	Fr	
25-11	Switzerland	W 4-1	Amsterdam	Fr	Verlegh 2, Sigmond, Krom
23-03-1924	Belgium	D 1-1	Amsterdam	Fr	Pijl
21-04	Germany	L 0-1	Amsterdam	Fr	
27-04	Belgium	D 1-1	Antwerp	Fr	Visser
27-05	Romania	W 6-0	Paris	OGr2	Pijl 4, De Natris, Hurgronje
2-06	Rep. Ireland	W 2-1	Paris	OGqf	Formenoy 2
6-06	Uruguay	L 1-2	Paris	OGsf	Pijl
8-06	Sweden	D 1-1	Paris	OG3p	Le Fèvre
9-06	Sweden	L 1-3	Paris	OG3p	Formenoy
2-11	South Africa	W 2-1	Amsterdam	Fr	De Natris, Volkers
15-03-1925	Belgium	W 1-0	Antwerp	Fr	Volkers
29-03	Germany	W 2-1	Amsterdam	Fr	Volkers, De Haas
19-04	Switzerland	L 1-4	Zurich	Fr	Buitenweg
3-05	Belgium	W 5-0	Amsterdam	Fr	Buitenweg 3, Van Slangenburgh 2
25-10	Denmark	W 4-2	Amsterdam	Fr	Van Slangenburgh 2, Buitenweg, Tap
14-03-1926	Belgium	D 1-1	Antwerp	Fr	Tap
28-03	Switzerland	W 5-0	Amsterdam	Fr	Ruisch 2, Pijl, Gielens, Van Linge
18-04	Germany	L 2-4	Dusseldorf	Fr	Tap, Küchlin
2-05	Belgium	L 1-5	Amsterdam	Fr	Tap
13-06	Denmark	L 1-4	Copenhagen	Fr	Buitenweg
31-10	Germany	L 2-3	Amsterdam	Fr	Tap 2
13-03-1927	Belgium	L 0-2	Antwerp	Fr	
1-05	Belgium	W 3-2	Amsterdam	Fr	Tap 2, Massy
12-06	Denmark	D 1-1	Copenhagen	Fr	Elfring
13-11	Sweden	W 1-0	Amsterdam	Fr	Ghering
20-11	Germany	D 2-2	Cologne	Fr	Smeets, Weber
11-03-1928	Belgium	D 1-1	Amsterdam	Fr	Tap
1-04	Belgium	L 0-1	Antwerp	Fr	
22-04	Denmark	W 2-0	Amsterdam	Fr	Elfring, Kools
6-05	Switzerland	L 1-2	Basle	Fr	Smeets
30-05	Uruguay	L 0-2	Amsterdam	OGr1	
5-06	Belgium	W 3-1	Rotterdam	OGct	Tap, Smeets, Ghering

Date	Opponent	Result	Venue	Comp	Scorers
8-06	Chile	D 2-2	Rotterdam	OGct	Smeets, Ghering. Won on lots
14-06	Egypt	L 1-2	Rotterdam	Fr	Grobbe
4-11	Belgium	D 1-1	Amsterdam	Fr	Van Kol
2-12	Italy	L 2-3	Milan	Fr	Tap 2
17-03-1929	Switzerland	W 3-2	Amsterdam	Fr	Van Kol, Bakhuys, OG
5-05	Belgium	L 1-3	Antwerp	Fr	Bakhuys
4-06	Scotland	L 0-2	Amsterdam	Fr	
9-06	Sweden	L 2-6	Stockholm	Fr	Smeets 2
12-06	Norway	D 4-4	Oslo	Fr	Kools 2, Tap, Landaal
3-11	Norway	L 1-4	Amsterdam	Fr	Broek
6-04-1930	Italy	D 1-1	Amsterdam	Fr	Broek
4-05	Belgium	D 2-2	Amsterdam	Fr	Tap, Van Kol
18-05	Belgium	L 1-3	Antwerp	Fr	Broek
8-06	Hungary	L 2-6	Budapest	Fr	Landaal, Heijden
2-11	Switzerland	L 3-6	Zurich	Fr	Van Nellen, Mulders, Lagendaal
29-03-1931	Belgium	W 3-2	Amsterdam	Fr	Lagendaal 2, Formenoy
26-04	Germany	D 1-1	Amsterdam	Fr	Tap
3-05	Belgium	L 2-4	Antwerp	Fr	Van Kol, Adam
14-06	Denmark	W 2-0	Copenhagen	Fr	Lagendaal 2
29-11	France	W 4-3	Paris	Fr	Lagendaal 3, Mol
20-03-1932	Belgium	W 4-1	Antwerp	Fr	Lagendaal 4
17-04	Belgium	W 2-1	Amsterdam	Fr	Adam 2
8-05	Rep. Ireland	L 0-2	Amsterdam	Fr	
29-05	Czechoslovakia	L 1-2	Amsterdam	Fr	Bonsema
4-12	Germany	W 2-0	Dusseldorf	Fr	Adam 2
22-01-1933	Switzerland	L 0-2	Amsterdam	Fr	
5-03	Hungary	L 1-2	Amsterdam	Fr	Broek
9-04	Belgium	W 3-1	Antwerp	Fr	Bonsema 2, Van Nellen
7-05	Belgium	L 1-2	Amsterdam	Fr	Adam
10-12	Austria	L 0-1	Amsterdam	Fr	
11-03	Belgium	W 9-3	Amsterdam	Fr	Vente 5, Smit 2, Bakhuys 2
8-04-1934	Rep. Ireland	W 5-2	Amsterdam	WCq	Smit 2, Bakhuys 2, Vente
29-04	Belgium	W 4-2	Antwerp	WCq	Bakhuys 2, Smit, Vente
10-05	France	L 4-5	Amsterdam	Fr	Bakhuys 2, Smit, Vente
27-05	Switzerland	L 2-3	Milan	WCr1	Smit, Vente
4-11	Switzerland	W 4-2	Berne	Fr	Bakhuys 2, Smit, Van Gelder
17-02-1935	Germany	L 2-3	Amsterdam	Fr	Smit, Bakhuys
31-03	Belgium	W 4-2	Amsterdam	Fr	Bakhuys 3, Lagendaal
12-05	Belgium	W 2-0	Brussels	Fr	Bakhuys, Smit
18-05	England	L 0-1	Amsterdam	Fr	
3-11	Denmark	W 3-0	Amsterdam	Fr	Bakhuys, Smit, Wels
8-12	Rep. Ireland	W 5-3	Dublin	Fr	Van Nellen 2, Bakhuys, Smit, Drok
12-01-1936	France	W 6-1	Paris	Fr	Bakhuys 3, Wels, Drok, Van Nellen
29-03	Belgium	W 8-0	Amsterdam	Fr	Bakhuys 3, Van Nellen 2, Smit, Wels,Drok
3-05	Belgium	D 1-1	Brussels	Fr	Bakhuys
1-11	Norway	D 3-3	Amsterdam	Fr	Bakhuys, Smit, De Bock
31-01-1937	Germany	D 2-2	Dusseldorf	Fr	Van Spaandonck 2
7-03	Switzerland	W 2-1	Amsterdam	Fr	Bakhuys, Vrauwdeunt
4-04	Belgium	L 1-2	Antwerp	Fr	Wels
2-05	Belgium	W 1-0	Rotterdam	Fr	Vente
31-10	France	L 2-3	Amsterdam	Fr	Smit 2
28-11	Luxembourg	W 4-0	Rotterdam	WCq	De Boer 3, Smit
27-02-1938	Belgium	W 7-2	Rotterdam	Fr	Smit 4, Vente, Wels, Van Spaandonck
3-04	Belgium	D 1-1	Antwerp	WCq	Van Spaandonck
21-05	Scotland	L 1-3	Amsterdam	Fr	Vente
5-06	Czechoslovakia	L 0-3	Le Havre	WCr1	
23-10	Denmark	D 2-2	Copenhagen	Fr	Van Leur, Veen
26-02-1939	Hungary	W 3-2	Rotterdam	Fr	Vente 2, De Harder
19-03	Belgium	L 4-5	Antwerp	Fr	Vente 2, Smit, Dräger
23-04	Belgium	W 3-2	Amsterdam	Fr	Vente 2, Dräger
7-05	Switzerland	L 1-2	Berne	Fr	Smit
17-03-1940	Belgium	L 1-7	Antwerp	Fr	Smit
31-03	Luxembourg	L 4-5	Rotterdam	Fr	Lenstra, Bergman, Drok, Paauwe
21-04	Belgium	W 4-2	Amsterdam	Fr	De Harder 2, Vente, Engel
10-03-1946	Luxembourg	W 6-2	Luxembourg	Fr	Wilkes 4, Rijvers, Bergman
12-05	Belgium	W 6-3	Amsterdam	Fr	Wilkes 3, Smit, Rijvers, Dräger
30-05	Belgium	D 2-2	Antwerp	Fr	Wilkes 2
27-11	England	L 2-8	Huddersfield	Fr	Smit, Bergman
7-04-1947	Belgium	W 2-1	Amsterdam	Fr	Bergman 2
4-05	Belgium	W 2-1	Antwerp	Fr	Dräger, Roozen
26-05	France	L 0-4	Paris	Fr	
22-06	Czechoslovakia	L 1-2	Amsterdam	Fr	

Date	Opponent	Result	Venue	Comp	Scorers
21-09	Switzerland	W 6-2	Amsterdam	Fr	Wilkes 2, Rijvers 2, Dräger, Lenstra
14-03-1948	Belgium	D 1-1	Antwerp	Fr	Lenstra
18-04	Belgium	D 2-2	Rotterdam	Fr	Lenstra, Engelsman
26-05	Norway	W 2-1	Oslo	Fr	Clavan, Tuyn
9-06	Sweden	W 1-0	Amsterdam	Fr	Wilkes
21-11	Belgium	D 1-1	Antwerp	Fr	Clavan
13-03-1949	Belgium	D 3-3	Amsterdam	Fr	Lenstra, Clavan, Brandes
23-04	France	W 4-1	Rotterdam	Fr	Timmermans 3, Wilkes
12-06	Denmark	W 2-1	Copenhagen	Fr	Wilkes, Lenstra
16-06	Finland	W 4-1	Helsinki	Fr	Van Roessel 2, Schaap, Van Schijndel
6-11	Belgium	L 0-1	Rotterdam	Fr	
11-12	Denmark	L 0-1	Amsterdam	Fr	
16-04-1950	Belgium	L 0-2	Antwerp	Fr	
8-06	Sweden	L 1-4	Stockholm	Fr	Clavan
11-06	Finland	L 1-4	Helsinki	Fr	Lenstra
15-10	Switzerland	L 5-7	Basle	Fr	Clavan, Rijvers, Van Melis, De Graaf, OG
12-11	Belgium	L 2-7	Antwerp	Fr	Van Melis, De Graaf
10-12	France	L 2-5	Paris	Fr	Van Melis, Tuyn
15-04-1951	Belgium	W 5-4	Amsterdam	Fr	Van Melis 3, Lenstra 2
6-06	Norway	L 2-3	Rotterdam	Fr	Van Melis, Lenstra
27-10	Finland	D 4-4	Rotterdam	Fr	Van Melis 3, Lenstra
25-11	Belgium	L 6-7	Rotterdam	Fr	Lenstra 3, Van Melis, Clavan, Bennaars
6-04-1952	Belgium	L 2-4	Antwerp	Fr	Van Melis, Clavan
14-05	Sweden	D 0-0	Amsterdam	Fr	
16-07	Brazil	L 1-5	Turku	OGr1	Van Roessel
21-09	Denmark	L 2-3	Copenhagen	Fr	Lenstra, Van Roessel
19-10	Belgium	L 1-2	Antwerp	Fr	Lenstra
7-03-1953	Denmark	L 1-2	Rotterdam	Fr	Lenstra
22-03	Switzerland	L 1-2	Amsterdam	Fr	Lenstra
19-04	Belgium	L 0-2	Amsterdam	Fr	
27-09	Norway	L 0-4	Oslo	Fr	
25-10	Belgium	W 1-0	Rotterdam	Fr	Van Beurden
4-04-1954	Belgium	L 0-4	Antwerp	Fr	
19-05	Sweden	L 1-6	Stockholm	Fr	Louer
30-05	Switzerland	L 1-3	Zurich	Fr	Dillen
24-10	Belgium	L 3-4	Antwerp	Fr	Dillen, De Bruyckere, Gijp
13-03-1955	Denmark	D 1-1	Amsterdam	Fr	Lenstra
3-04	Belgium	W 1-0	Amsterdam	Fr	Dillen
1-05	Rep. Ireland	L 0-1	Dublin	Fr	
19-05	Switzerland	W 4-1	Rotterdam	Fr	Wilkes 2, Timmermans, De Bruyckere
16-10	Belgium	D 2-2	Rotterdam	Fr	Appel 2
6-11	Norway	W 3-0	Amsterdam	Fr	Bosselaar 2, Appel
16-11	Saar	W 2-1	Saarbrucken	Fr	Brusselers, Hart
14-03-1956	West Germany	W 2-1	Dusseldorf	Fr	Lenstra 2
8-04	Belgium	W 1-0	Antwerp	Fr	Koopal
10-05	Rep. Ireland	L 1-4	Rotterdam	Fr	Appel
6-06	Saar	W 3-2	Amsterdam	Fr	Lenstra, Wilkes, Koopal
15-09	Switzerland	W 3-2	Lausanne	Fr	Lenstra, Bosselaar, Gijp
14-10	Belgium	W 3-2	Antwerp	Fr	Appel 2, Notermans
4-11	Denmark	D 2-2	Copenhagen	Fr	Appel 2
30-01-1957	Spain	L 1-5	Madrid	Fr	Bosselaar
20-03	Luxembourg	W 4-1	Rotterdam	WCq	Gijp 2, Dillen, Brusselers
3-04	West Germany	L 1-2	Amsterdam	Fr	Wilkes
28-04	Belgium	D 1-1	Amsterdam	Fr	Carlier
26-05	Austria	L 2-3	Vienna	WCq	Van Melis 2
11-09	Luxembourg	W 5-2	Rotterdam	WCq	Lenstra 2, Wilkes, Van Melis, Rijvers
25-09	Austria	D 1-1	Amsterdam	WCq	Lenstra
17-11	Belgium	W 5-2	Rotterdam	Fr	Wilkes 2, Kruiver, Carlier, Van Wissen
13-04-1958	Belgium	W 7-2	Antwerp	Fr	Wilkes 2, Lenstra 2, Moulijn, Van Wissen, Notermans
23-04	Curacao	W 8-1	Rotterdam	Fr	Wilkes 2, Lenstra 2, Van Wissen 2, Moulijn, Kuil
4-05	Turkey	L 1-2	Amsterdam	Fr	Wilkes
28-05	Norway	D 0-0	Oslo	Fr	
28-09	Belgium	W 3-2	Antwerp	Fr	Linden, Kruiver, Hart
15-10	Denmark	W 5-1	Rotterdam	Fr	Lenstra 2, Linden, Kruiver, Kuil
2-11	Switzerland	W 2-0	Rotterdam	Fr	Kruiver 2
19-04-1959	Belgium	D 2-2	Amsterdam	Fr	Lenstra, Linden
10-05	Turkey	D 0-0	Istanbul	Fr	
13-05	Bulgaria	L 2-3	Sofia	Fr	Canjels 2
27-05	Scotland	L 1-2	Amsterdam	Fr	Gijp
4-10	Belgium	W 9-1	Rotterdam	Fr	Wilkes 3, Kuil 3, Linden, Rijvers, Klaassens
21-10	West Germany	L 0-7	Cologne	Fr	
4-11	Norway	W 7-1	Rotterdam	Fr	Linden 3, Wilkes 2, Rijvers, Kuil

Date	Opponent	Result	Venue	Comp	Scorers
3-04-1960	Bulgaria	W 4-2	Amsterdam	Fr	Linden 3, Groot
24-04	Belgium	L 1-2	Antwerp	Fr	Rijvers
18-05	Switzerland	L 1-3	Zurich	Fr	Rijvers
26-06	Mexico	L 1-3	Mexico City	Fr	Gijp
29-06	Neth. Antilles	D 0-0	Willemstad	Fr	
3-07	Surinam	W 4-3	Paramaribo	Fr	Kruiver 3, Swart
2-10	Belgium	W 4-1	Antwerp	Fr	Groot 2, Kuil, OG
30-10	Czechoslovakia	L 0-4	Prague	Fr	
22-03-1961	Belgium	W 6-2	Rotterdam	Fr	Groot 2, Kruiver 2, Swart, Moulijn
19-04	Mexico	L 1-2	Amsterdam	Fr	Wilkes
30-04	Hungary	L 0-3	Rotterdam	WCq	
14-05	East Germany	D 1-1	Leipzig	WCq	Groot
22-10	Hungary	D 3-3	Budapest	WCq	Linden 2, Groot
12-11	Belgium	L 0-4	Amsterdam	Fr	
1-04-1962	Belgium	L 1-3	Antwerp	Fr	Linden
9-05	Nth. Ireland	W 4-0	Rotterdam	Fr	Linden 2, Swart, Kuil
16-05	Norway	L 1-2	Oslo	Fr	Linden
5-09	Neth. Antilles	W 8-0	Amsterdam	Fr	Groot 3, Prins 2, Swart 2, Keizer
26-09	Denmark	L 1-4	Copenhagen	Fr	Prins
14-10	Belgium	L 0-2	Antwerp	Fr	
11-11	Switzerland	W 3-1	Amsterdam	ECr1	Linden, Groot, Swart
3-03-1963	Belgium	L 0-1	Rotterdam	Fr	
31-03	Switzerland	D 1-1	Berne	ECr1	Kruiver
17-04	France	W 1-0	Rotterdam	Fr	Groot
2-05	Brazil	W 1-0	Amsterdam	Fr	Petersen
11-09	Luxembourg	D 1-1	Amsterdam	ECr2	Nuninga
20-10	Belgium	D 1-1	Amsterdam	Fr	Keizer
30-10	Luxembourg	L 1-2	Rotterdam	ECr2	Kruiver
22-03-1964	Belgium	D 0-0	Antwerp	Fr	
12-04	Austria	D 1-1	Amsterdam	Fr	Nuninga
29-04	Sweden	L 0-1	Rotterdam	Fr	
24-05	Albania	W 2-0	Rotterdam	WCq	Schrijvers, Muller
30-09	Belgium	L 0-1	Antwerp	Fr	
25-10	Albania	W 2-0	Tirana	WCq	Van Nee, Geurtsen
9-12	England	D 1-1	Amsterdam	Fr	Moulijn
26-01-1965	Israel	W 1-0	Tel Aviv	Fr	Fransen
17-03	Nth. Ireland	L 1-2	Belfast	WCq	Van Nee
7-04	Nth. Ireland	D 0-0	Rotterdam	WCq	
17-10	Switzerland	D 0-0	Amsterdam	WCq	
14-11	Switzerland	L 1-2	Berne	WCq	Laseroms
23-03-1966	West Germany	L 2-4	Rotterdam	Fr	Nuninga, Swart
17-04	Belgium	W 3-1	Rotterdam	Fr	Keizer, Muller, Kuijlen
11-05	Scotland	W 3-0	Glasgow	Fr	Kuijlen 2, Nuninga
7-09	Hungary	D 2-2	Rotterdam	ECq	Cruyff, Pijs
18-09	Austria	L 1-2	Vienna	Fr	OG
6-11	Czechoslovakia	L 1-2	Amsterdam	Fr	Swart
30-11	Denmark	W 2-0	Rotterdam	ECq	Swart, Kuijlen
5-04-1967	East Germany	L 3-4	Leipzig	ECq	Keizer 2, Mulder
16-04	Belgium	L 0-1	Antwerp	Fr	
10-05	Hungary	L 1-2	Budapest	ECq	Suurbier
13-09	East Germany	W 1-0	Amsterdam	ECq	Cruyff
4-10	Denmark	L 2-3	Copenhagen	ECq	Suurbier, Israël
1-11	Yugoslavia	L 1-2	Rotterdam	Fr	Swart
29-11	Soviet Union	W 3-1	Rotterdam	Fr	Wery 2, Romeijn
7-04-1968	Belgium	L 1-2	Amsterdam	Fr	Klijnjan
1-05	Poland	D 0-0	Warsaw	Fr	
30-05	Scotland	D 0-0	Amsterdam	Fr	
5-06	Romania	D 0-0	Bucharest	Fr	
4-09	Luxembourg	W 2-0	Rotterdam	WCq	Van Hanegem, Jansen
27-10	Bulgaria	L 0-2	Sofia	WCq	
26-03-1969	Luxembourg	W 4-0	Rotterdam	WCq	Pahlplatz 2, Cruyff, Van Dijk
16-04	Czechoslovakia	W 2-0	Rotterdam	Fr	Roggeveen 2
7-05	Poland	W 1-0	Rotterdam	WCq	Roggeveen
7-09	Poland	L 1-2	Chorzow	WCq	Wery
22-10	Bulgaria	D 1-1	Rotterdam	WCq	Veenstra
5-11	England	L 0-1	Amsterdam	Fr	
14-01-1970	England	D 0-0	London	Fr	
28-01	Israel	W 1-0	Tel Aviv	Fr	Brokamp
11-10	Yugoslavia	D 1-1	Rotterdam	ECq	Israël
11-11	East Germany	L 0-1	Dresden	ECq	
2-12	Romania	W 2-0	Amsterdam	Fr	Cruyff 2
24-02-1971	Luxembourg	W 6-0	Rotterdam	ECq	Cruyff 2, Keizer 2, Lippens, Suurbier

4-04	Yugoslavia	L 0-2	Split	ECq	
10-10	East Germany	W 3-2	Rotterdam	ECq	Keizer 2, Hulshoff
17-11	Luxembourg	W 8-0	Eindhoven	ECq	Cruyff 3, Keizer, Hoekema, Pahlplatz, Hulshoff, Israël
1-12	Scotland	W 2-1	Amsterdam	Fr	Cruyff, Hulshoff
16-02-1972	Greece	W 5-0	Athens	Fr	Cruyff 2, Hulshoff 2, Neeskens
3-05	Peru	W 3-0	Rotterdam	Fr	Van Hanegem, Klijnjan, Schneider
30-08	Czechoslovakia	W 2-1	Prague	Fr	Cruyff, Neeskens
1-11	Norway	W 9-0	Rotterdam	WCq	Neeskens 3, Cruyff 2, Brokamp 2, Keizer, De Jong
19-11	Belgium	D 0-0	Antwerp	WCq	
28-03-1973	Austria	L 0-1	Vienna	Fr	
2-05	Spain	W 3-2	Amsterdam	Fr	Cruyff, Rep, OG
22-08	Iceland	W 5-0	Amsterdam	WCq	Cruyff 2, Haan, Van Hanegem, Brokamp
29-08	Iceland	W 8-1	Deventer	WCq	Cruyff 2, Brokamp 2, Neeskens, Van Hanegem, Van de Kerkhof.R,Schneider
12-09	Norway	W 2-1	Oslo	WCq	Cruyff, Hulshoff
10-10	Poland	D 1-1	Rotterdam	Fr	De Jong
18-11	Belgium	D 0-0	Amsterdam	WCq	
27-03-1974	Austria	D 1-1	Rotterdam	Fr	Krol
26-05	Argentina	W 4-1	Amsterdam	Fr	Neeskens, Rensenbrink, Strik, Haan
5-06	Romania	D 0-0	Rotterdam	Fr	
15-06	Uruguay	W 2-0	Hanover	WCr1	Rep 2
19-06	Sweden	D 0-0	Dortmund	WCr1	
23-06	Bulgaria	W 4-1	Dortmund	WCr1	Neeskens 2, Rep, De Jong
26-06	Argentina	W 4-0	Gelsenkirchen	WCr2	Cruyff 2, Krol, Rep
30-06	East Germany	W 2-0	Gelsenkirchen	WCr2	Neeskens, Rensenbrink
3-07	Brazil	W 2-0	Dortmund	WCr2	Neeskens, Cruyff
7-07	West Germany	L 1-2	Munich	WCf	Neeskens
4-09	Sweden	W 5-1	Stockholm	Fr	Neeskens 3, Cruyff, Rensenbrink
25-09	Finland	W 3-1	Helsinki	ECq	Cruyff 2, Neeskens
9-10	Switzerland	W 1-0	Rotterdam	Fr	Geels
20-11	Italy	W 3-1	Rotterdam	ECq	Cruyff 2, Rensenbrink
30-04-1975	Belgium	L 0-1	Antwerp	Fr	
17-05	West Germany	D 1-1	Frankfurt	Fr	Van Hanegem
31-05	Yugoslavia	L 0-3	Belgrade	Fr	
3-09	Finland	W 4-1	Nijmegen	ECq	Van der Kuylen 3, Lubse
10-09	Poland	L 1-4	Chorzow	ECq	Van de Kerkhof.R
15-10	Poland	W 3-0	Amsterdam	ECq	Neeskens, Geels, Thijssen
22-11	Italy	L 0-1	Rome	ECq	
25-04-1976	Belgium	W 5-0	Rotterdam	ECqf	Rensenbrink 3, Rijsbergen, Neeskens
22-05	Belgium	W 2-1	Brussels	ECqf	Rep, Cruyff
16-06	Czechoslovakia	L 1-3	Zagreb	ECsf	OG
19-06	Yugoslavia	W 3-2	Zagreb	EC3p	Geels 2, Van de Kerkhof.W
8-09	Iceland	W 1-0	Reykjavik	WCq	Geels
13-10	Nth. Ireland	D 2-2	Rotterdam	WCq	Krol, Cruyff
9-02-1977	England	W 2-0	London	Fr	Peters 2
26-03	Belgium	W 2-0	Antwerp	WCq	Rep, Cruyff
31-08	Iceland	W 4-1	Nijmegen	WCq	Geels 2, Van Hanegem, Rep
5-10	Soviet Union	D 0-0	Rotterdam	Fr	
12-10	Nth. Ireland	W 1-0	Belfast	WCq	Van de Kerkhof.W
26-10	Belgium	W 1-0	Amsterdam	WCq	Van de Kerkhof.R
22-02-1978	Israel	W 2-1	Tel Aviv	Fr	Rensenbrink, La Ling
5-04	Tunisia	W 4-0	Tunis	Fr	Nanninga 2, Van Leeuwen, OG
20-05	Austria	W 1-0	Vienna	Fr	Haan
3-06	Iran	W 3-0	Mendoza	WCr1	Rensenbrink 3
7-06	Peru	D 0-0	Mendoza	WCr1	
11-06	Scotland	L 2-3	Mendoza	WCr1	Rensenbrink, Rep
14-06	Austria	W 5-1	Cordoba	WCr2	Rep 2, Brandts, Rensenbrink, Van de Kerkhof.W
18-06	West Germany	D 2-2	Cordoba	WCr2	Haan, Van de Kerkhof.R
21-06	Italy	W 2-1	Buenos Aires	WCr2	Brandts, Haan
25-06	Argentina	L 1-3	Buenos Aires	WCf	Nanninga
20-09	Iceland	W 3-0	Nijmegen	ECq	Krol, Brandts, Rensenbrink
11-10	Switzerland	W 3-1	Berne	ECq	Wildschut, Brandts, Geels
15-11	East Germany	W 3-0	Rotterdam	ECq	Geels 2, OG
20-12	West Germany	L 1-3	Dusseldorf	Fr	La Ling
24-02-1979	Italy	L 0-3	Milan	Fr	
28-03	Switzerland	W 3-0	Eindhoven	ECq	Kist, Metgod, Peters
2-05	Poland	L 0-2	Chorzow	ECq	
22-05	Argentina	D 0-0	Berne	Fr	
5-09	Iceland	W 4-0	Reykjavik	ECq	Nanninga 2, Metgod, Van de Kerkhof.W
26-09	Belgium	W 1-0	Rotterdam	Fr	Poortvliet
17-10	Poland	D 1-1	Amsterdam	ECq	Stevens
21-11	East Germany	W 3-2	Leipzig	ECq	Thijssen, Kist, Van de Kerkhof.R

Date	Opponent	Result	Venue	Comp	Scorers
23-01-1980	Spain	L 0-1	Vigo	Fr	
26-03	France	D 0-0	Paris	Fr	
11-06	Greece	W 1-0	Naples	ECr1	Kist
14-06	West Germany	L 2-3	Naples	ECr1	Rep, Van de Kerkhof.W
17-06	Czechoslovakia	D 1-1	Milan	ECr1	Kist
10-09	Rep. Ireland	L 1-2	Dublin	WCq	Tahamata
11-10	West Germany	D 1-1	Eindhoven	Fr	Brandts
19-11	Belgium	L 0-1	Brussels	WCq	
30-12	Uruguay	L 0-2	Montevideo	ML	
6-01-1981	Italy	D 1-1	Montevideo	ML	Peters
22-02	Cyprus	W 3-0	Groningen	WCq	Hovenkamp, Schapendonk, Nanninga
25-03	France	W 1-0	Rotterdam	WCq	Muhren
29-04	Cyprus	W 1-0	Nicosia	WCq	Van Kooten
1-09	Switzerland	L 1-2	Zurich	Fr	Metgod
9-09	Rep. Ireland	D 2-2	Rotterdam	WCq	Thijssen, Muhren
14-10	Belgium	W 3-0	Rotterdam	WCq	Metgod, Van Kooten, Geels
18-11	France	L 0-2	Paris	WCq	
23-03-1982	Scotland	L 1-2	Glasgow	Fr	Kieft
14-04	Greece	W 1-0	Eindhoven	Fr	Ophof
25-05	England	L 0-2	London	Fr	
1-09	Iceland	D 1-1	Reykjavik	ECq	Schoenaker
22-09	Rep. Ireland	W 2-1	Rotterdam	ECq	Schoenaker, Gullit
10-11	France	L 1-2	Rotterdam	Fr	Tahamata
19-12	Malta	W 6-0	Aachen	ECq	Van Kooten 2, Schoenaker 2, Ophof, Hovenkamp
16-02-1983	Spain	L 0-1	Seville	ECq	
27-04	Sweden	L 0-3	Utrecht	Fr	
7-09	Iceland	W 3-0	Groningen	ECq	Koeman.R, Gullit, Houtman
21-09	Belgium	D 1-1	Brussels	Fr	Van Basten
12-10	Rep. Ireland	W 3-2	Dublin	ECq	Gullit 2, Van Basten
16-11	Spain	W 2-1	Rotterdam	ECq	Houtman, Gullit
17-12	Malta	W 5-0	Rotterdam	ECq	Rijkaard 2, Vanenburg, Wijnstekers, Houtman
14-03-1984	Denmark	W 6-0	Amsterdam	Fr	Van der Gijp 2, Houtman 2, Kieft, Hoekstra
17-10	Hungary	L 1-2	Rotterdam	WCq	Kieft
14-11	Austria	L 0-1	Vienna	WCq	
23-12	Cyprus	W 1-0	Nicosia	WCq	Houtman
27-02-1985	Cyprus	W 7-1	Amsterdam	WCq	Kieft 2, Schoenaker 2, Koeman.E, Van Basten, OG
1-05	Austria	D 1-1	Rotterdam	WCq	Kieft
14-05	Hungary	W 1-0	Budapest	WCq	De Wit
4-09	Bulgaria	W 1-0	Heerenven	Fr	De Wit
16-10	Belgium	L 0-1	Brussels	WCq	
20-11	Belgium	W 2-1	Rotterdam	WCq	Houtman, De Wit
12-03-1986	East Germany	W 1-0	Leipzig	Fr	Van Basten
29-04	Scotland	D 0-0	Eindhoven	Fr	
14-05	West Germany	L 1-3	Dortmund	Fr	Van der Gijp
10-09	Czechoslovakia	L 0-1	Prague	Fr	
15-10	Hungary	W 1-0	Budapest	ECq	Van Basten
19-11	Poland	D 0-0	Amsterdam	ECq	
21-12	Cyprus	W 2-0	Nicosia	ECq	Gullit, Bosman
21-01-1987	Spain	D 1-1	Barcelona	Fr	Gullit
25-03	Greece	D 1-1	Rotterdam	ECq	Van Basten
29-04	Hungary	W 2-0	Rotterdam	ECq	Gullit, Muhren
9-09	Belgium	D 0-0	Rotterdam	Fr	
14-10	Poland	W 2-0	Zabrze	ECq	Gullit 2
28-10	Cyprus	W 8-0	Rotterdam	ECq	Bosman 5, Gullit, Spelbos, Van't Schip
	Match declared void				
9-12	Cyprus	W 4-0	Amsterdam	ECq	Bosman 3, Koeman.R
16-12	Greece	W 3-0	Rhodes	ECq	Gillhaus 2, Koeman.R
23-03-1988	England	D 2-2	London	Fr	Bosman, OG
24-05	Bulgaria	L 1-2	Rotterdam	Fr	Wouters
1-06	Romania	W 2-0	Amsterdam	Fr	Bosman, Kieft
12-06	Soviet Union	L 0-1	Cologne	ECr1	
15-06	England	W 3-1	Dusseldorf	ECr1	Van Basten 3
18-06	Rep. Ireland	W 1-0	Gelsenkirchen	ECr1	Kieft
21-06	West Germany	W 2-1	Hamburg	ECsf	Koeman.R, Van Basten
25-06	Soviet Union	W 2-0	Munich	ECf	Gullit, Van Basten
14-09	Wales	W 1-0	Amsterdam	WCq	Gullit
19-10	West Germany	D 0-0	Munich	WCq	
16-11	Italy	L 0-1	Rome	Fr	
4-01-1989	Israel	W 2-0	Tel Aviv	Fr	Wouters, Van Loen
22-03	Soviet Union	W 2-0	Eindhoven	Fr	Van Basten, Koeman.R
26-04	West Germany	D 1-1	Rotterdam	WCq	Van Basten
31-05	Finland	W 1-0	Helsinki	WCq	Kieft

6-09	Denmark	D 2-2	Amsterdam	Fr	Koeman.R, Wouters
11-10	Wales	W 2-1	Wrexham	WCq	Rutjers, Bosman
15-11	Finland	W 3-0	Rotterdam	WCq	Bosman, Koeman.E, Koeman.R
20-12	Brazil	L 0-1	Rotterdam	Fr	
21-02-1990	Italy	D 0-0	Rotterdam	Fr	
28-03	Soviet Union	L 1-2	Kiev	Fr	Koeman.R
30-05	Austria	L 2-3	Vienna	Fr	Koeman.R, Van Basten
3-06	Yugoslavia	W 2-0	Zagreb	Fr	Rijkaard, Van Basten
12-06	Egypt	D 1-1	Palermo	WCr1	Kieft
16-06	England	D 0-0	Cagliari	WCr1	
21-06	Rep. Ireland	D 1-1	Palermo	WCr1	Gullit
24-06	West Germany	L 1-2	Milan	WCr2	Koeman.R
26-09	Italy	L 0-1	Palermo	Fr	
17-10	Portugal	L 0-1	Oporto	ECq	
21-11	Greece	W 2-0	Rotterdam	ECq	Bergkamp, Van Basten
19-12	Malta	W 8-0	Ta'Qali	ECq	Van Basten 5, Winter, Bergkamp 2
13-03-1991	Malta	W 1-0	Rotterdam	ECq	Van Basten
17-04	Finland	W 2-0	Rotterdam	ECq	Van Basten, Gullit
5-06	Finland	D 1-1	Helsinki	ECq	De Boer
11-09	Poland	D 1-1	Eindhoven	Fr	Bergkamp
16-10	Portugal	W 1-0	Rotterdam	ECq	Witschge
4-12	Greece	W 2-0	Salonica	ECq	Bergkamp, Blind
12-02-1992	Portugal	L 0-2	Faro	Fr	
25-03	Yugoslavia	W 2-0	Amsterdam	Fr	Kieft, Wouters
27-05	Austria	W 3-2	Sittard	Fr	Rijkaard, Bergkamp, Gullit
30-05	Wales	W 4-0	Utrecht	Fr	Roy, Van Basten, Winter, Jonk
5-06	France	D 1-1	Lens	Fr	Roy
12-06	Scotland	W 1-0	Gothenburg	ECr1	Bergkamp
15-06	Common. IS	D 0-0	Gothenburg	ECr1	
18-06	Germany	W 3-1	Gothenburg	ECr1	Rijkaard, Witschge, Bergkamp
22-06	Denmark	D 2-2	Gothenburg	ECsf	Bergkamp, Rijkaard. Lost 4-5 pens
9-09	Italy	L 2-3	Eindhoven	Fr	Bergkamp 2
23-09	Norway	L 1-2	Oslo	WCq	Bergkamp
14-10	Poland	D 2-2	Rotterdam	WCq	Van Vossen 2
16-12	Turkey	W 3-1	Istanbul	WCq	Van Vossen 2, Gullit
24-02-1993	Turkey	W 3-1	Utrecht	WCq	Overmars, Witschge 2
24-03	San Marino	W 6-0	Utrecht	WCq	Van den Brom, OG, De Wolf 2, De Boer.R, Van Vossen
28-04	England	D 2-2	London	WCq	Bergkamp, Van Vossen
9-06	Norway	D 0-0	Rotterdam	WCq	
22-09	San Marino	W 7-0	Bologna	WCq	Bosman 3, Jonk 2, De Boer.R, Koeman.R
13-10	England	W 2-0	Rotterdam	WCq	Koeman.R, Bergkamp
17-11	Poland	W 3-1	Poznan	WCq	Bergkamp 2, De Boer.R
19-01-1994	Tunisia	D 2-2	Tunis	Fr	Rijkaard, Koeman.R
23-03	Scotland	W 1-0	Glasgow	Fr	Roy
20-04	Rep. Ireland	L 0-1	Tilburg	Fr	
27-05	Scotland	W 3-1	Utrecht	Fr	Roy, Van Vossen, OG
1-06	Hungary	W 7-1	Eindhoven	Fr	Bergkamp 2, Roy, Koeman.R, Taument, Rijkaard 2
12-06	Canada	W 3-0	Toronto	Fr	Bergkamp, Overmars, Rijkaard
21-06	Saudi Arabia	W 2-1	Washington	WCr1	Jonk, Taument
25-06	Belgium	L 0-1	Orlando	WCr1	
29-06	Morocco	W 2-1	Orlando	WCr1	Bergkamp, Roy
4-07	Rep. Ireland	W 2-0	Orlando	WCr2	Bergkamp, Jonk
9-07	Brazil	L 2-3	Dallas	WCqf	Bergkamp, Winter
7-09	Luxembourg	W 4-0	Luxembourg	ECq	Roy, De Boer.R 2, Jonk
12-10	Norway	D 1-1	Oslo	ECq	Roy
16-11	Czech Republic	D 0-0	Rotterdam	ECq	
14-12	Luxembourg	W 5-0	Rotterdam	ECq	Mulder, Roy, Jonk, De Boer.R, Seedorf
18-01-1995	France	L 0-1	Utrecht	Fr	
22-02	Portugal	L 0-1	Eindhoven	Fr	
29-03	Malta	W 4-0	Rotterdam	ECq	Seedorf, Bergkamp, Winter, Kluivert
26-04	Czech Republic	L 1-3	Prague	ECq	Jonk
7-06	Belarus	L 0-1	Minsk	ECq	

HUNGARY

Proud Hungary! Never has a country come so close to winning the World Cup and yet been so cruelly denied as the Hungarians were in 1954. Regarded as the best team the world had ever seen the 'Magic Magyars', as they were known, lost only one game in six years of international football, and that game was the World Cup final. That team will always be the one all Hungarian national sides are compared to, a burden that will not go away until a team of equal stature is built. Given the state that Hungarian football finds itself in now, that could be a long time in coming.

Hungarian football was very quick to develop, especially in Budapest which along with Vienna and Prague formed the first focus of organised football in central Europe. Among the first clubs formed were Ujpesti in 1885, MTK in 1888 and Ferencváros in 1899, all of whom remain in the forefront of Hungarian football today, but as was traditional in central Europe, football sections were often added on to already existing sports clubs; in Hungary, these tended to be Gymnastic clubs.

In 1901 the football association was formed and Southampton, the first English professional club to travel abroad, came to Hungary. Although they defeated Budapest selections 8-0 and 13-0, it was the spur the Hungarians needed to develop their game. A league was formed in the same year, whilst the following year a national selection travelled to Vienna to take part in the very first international match on the continent.

Although beaten 5-0 on that historic day, the Hungarians developed into a highly original and prolific side, noted for some remarkable individuals. The first of the great Hungarian players was Imre Schlosser. His 58 goals either side of and during the First World War made him the outstanding player of his time and the leading scorer on mainland Europe, a position he held for many years.

Hungarian football flourished in the inter-war period, especially after professionalism was introduced in 1926. Ferencváros, Ujpesti and Hungaria, who had changed their name from MTK in 1927, were among the most feared clubs on the continent. MTK won a staggering 10 consecutive championships in the years up until 1925, but it was in the Mitropa Cup in the 1930s that Ferencváros and Ujpesti, especially, made their mark, with two wins apiece.

With the demise of the national side that had contained Schlosser and the great Alfred Schaffer, who had moved to Germany where he became known as the 'Fussballkönig' - Football king - by his fans at I.FC Nürnberg, another fine team was not long in developing. France were beaten 13-1 in Budapest in 1927, and by the 1934 World Cup Hungary were regarded as being among the favourites. However, they came up against the Austrian 'Wunderteam' and lost to them in the quarter-finals.

In 1938 they reached the final. The stars of this side were Gyorgy Sarosi and Gyula Zsengeller. Sarosi in particular was an influential figure. He had scored in a victory over England in Budapest just prior to the 1934 World Cup and hit a remarkable seven goals against Czechoslovakia in 1937. Zsengeller had scored five as Hungary put eleven past Greece to qualify for the 1938 tournament, and he netted five times in the lead-up to the final against Italy. There, however, the Hungarians were never in the match and lost 4-2.

After that defeat, Hungary, who were much more gifted than the Italians, were accused of being too pretty and lacking the steel to win. It was a lesson learned, and after the war they produced yet another great side to uphold the tradition started by Schlosser and continued by Sarosi.

Despite interference by the communist authorities in the club structure, football flourished after the war. Indeed it was seen by them as a propaganda weapon and no club epitomised this more than Honved in the 1950s. They formed the basis of the national side that went for six years and 48 games with only one defeat, a truly remarkable record.

There was the reliable Grosics in goal, with Jeno Buzansky and Mihaly Lantos in defence; the midfield had Gyula Lorant at centre-half along with Jozsef Bozsik, the captain and record cap winner; whilst the forward line was truly fearsome. Zoltan Czibor and Jozsef Toth operated down the wings whilst Nandor Hidegkuti operated slightly behind Sandor Kocsis and Ferenc Puskás, probably the most deadly striking partnership football has ever seen. Between them they scored an extraordinary 158 goals for the national side, more than some countries have scored full stop! After winning the 1952 Olympic title in Helsinki, Hungary sealed their reputation with a 6-3 victory at Wembley, England's first defeat on home soil by a non-British side. A 7-1 victory in the return in Budapest the following year confirmed them as overwhelming favourites to win the World Cup.

In Switzerland, Hungary played brilliantly. They began with a 9-0 victory over South Korea and followed this up with an 8-3 thrashing of West Germany marred only by a crucial injury to Puskás. In the quarter-finals the notorious Battle of Berne encounter with Brazil left the side battered and bruised, but it did not affect their semi-final performance against the reigning champions Uruguay. In what commentators at the time described as the best match they had ever seen, the Hungarians ran out 4-2 winners in extra-time. It was the first time Uruguay had been beaten in a World Cup match. Koscis, who netted twice, had scored a record 11 goals on the way to the final.

There had never been greater favourites than Hungary as they went into the World Cup final, and when they found themselves 2-0 up against the West Germans early in the match, it seemed they could do no wrong. Questions had been asked as to whether it was wise to bring back a half-fit Puskás, but he seemed to answer them by scoring the first goal. West Germany, however, fought back against all expectations to level the match and then took the lead seven minutes from time. Puskás had what looked a perfectly good goal disallowed shortly after, but the Hungarians had somehow contrived to lose the game. In their six-year run they had played many better sides than the Germans and beaten them with consummate ease. To lose only one match in six years and for that match to be the World Cup Final was a cruel disappointment, and as it transpired, they would not get a second opportunity.

The Hungarian uprising and its subsequent crushing by the Soviet army split the side up. Puskás, Kocsis and Czibor all decided to make their fortunes in the West, Puskás with Real Madrid, the others with Barcelona. If one person had epitomised Hungary at this time it was Puskás, the 'Galloping Major' as he was known due to his rank in the army. He was without question the greatest Hungarian player of all time.

In spite of this loss of the heart of the team, the football infrastructure in the country was such that by the early 1960s another supremely gifted side had emerged. Talented players, it seemed, simply poured off the production line - chief among the new generation were Florian Albert and Ferenc Bene. Added to this was the reputation Hungary had built up as a nation of top coaches. Bela Guttmann, for example, was only a modestly known player, yet he coached the successful Benfica side of the early 1960s. Hungary were quarter-finalists at both the 1962 and 1966 World Cups, which did not do them justice on either occasion. The shadow of their predecessors always limited the recognition given to this side.

THE ORDER OF MERIT

		All			League			Cup		Europe		
	Team	G	S	B	G	S	B	G	S	G	S	B
1	Ferencváros	44	39	21	25	29	19	18	8	1	-	-
2	MTK-VM Budapest	28	21	14	19	18	13	9	2	-	-	-
3	Ujpesti TE	26	23	18	19	17	16	7	5	-	-	-
4	Kispest-Honvéd	17	20	5	13	12	5	4	8	-	-	-
5	Vasas Budapest	10	3	11	6	2	10	4	1	-	-	1
6	Rába ETO Györ	7	4	4	3	2	3	4	2	-	-	1
7	Csepel SC	4	-	2	4	-	2	-	-	-	-	-
8	Diósgyöri VTK	2	3	1	-	-	1	2	3	-	-	-
9	Budapest TC	2	2	3	2	1	3	-	1	-	-	-
10	Vac FC Samsung	1	5	-	1	2	-	-	3	-	-	-
11	Pécsi MSC	1	3	1	-	1	1	1	2	-	-	-
12	Nagyváradi AC	1	1	-	1	1	-	-	-	-	-	-
13	Békéscsaba ESC	1	-	1	-	-	1	1	-	-	-	-
14	Bocskai Debrecen	1	-	1	-	-	1	1	-	-	-	-
	Szolnoki MAV	1	-	1	-	-	1	1	-	-	-	-
16	Siófoki Bányász	1	-	-	-	-	-	1	-	-	-	-
	Soroksár Erzsebet	1	-	-	-	-	-	1	-	-	-	-
	111 Kerület TVE	1	-	-	-	-	-	1	-	-	-	-
19	Tatabánya Bányász	-	4	4	-	2	4	-	2	-	-	-
20	Magyar AC	-	4	1	-	2	1	-	2	-	-	-
	Salgótárjan BTC	-	4	1	-	-	1	-	4	-	-	-
22	Videoton-Waltham SC	-	3	2	-	1	2	-	1	-	1	-
23	VSC Budapest	-	2	-	-	1	-	-	1	-	-	-
	Haladás VSE	-	2	-	-	-	-	-	2	-	-	-
	Komló Bányász	-	2	-	-	-	-	-	2	-	-	-
26	Törekvés SE	-	1	3	-	1	3	-	-	-	-	-
27	Budapest AK	-	1	1	-	-	1	-	1	-	-	-
	Szeged SC	-	1	1	-	-	1	-	1	-	-	-
	Kolozsvári AC	-	1	1	-	-	1	-	1	-	-	-
30	Atilla Miskolc	-	1	-	-	-	-	-	1	-	-	-
	Budapest EAC	-	1	-	-	-	-	-	1	-	-	-
	Dorogi AC	-	1	-	-	-	-	-	1	-	-	-
	Magyar UE	-	1	-	-	1	-	-	-	-	-	-
34	Debreceni VSE	-	-	1	-	-	1	-	-	-	-	-
	Nemzeti SC	-	-	1	-	-	1	-	-	-	-	-
	33 FC	-	-	1	-	-	1	-	-	-	-	-

To the end of the 1994-1995 season

Club football had been dominated by Honved in the 1950s, but Ferencváros managed to regain some of their former glories with four titles and a UEFA Cup victory in the 1960s. The 1970s, however, belonged to Ujpesti, who won a remarkable 9 titles in 11 years. The national side did not fare so well and having failed to qualify for the 1970 World Cup they entered a period of decline from which they have yet to escape. Fourth place in the 1972 European Championships remains the last Hungarian performance of note as three successive World Cup appearances from 1978 to 1986 all resulted in first round elimination, although they did catch the eye in 1982 with a record 10-1 win over El Salvador.

Hungary still produces players of high quality, such as Tibor Nyilasi and Lajos Detari, but the game seems to have lost its way. Betting scandals, match fixing and general apathy have characterised recent years. Since the fall of the Communist government in the early 1990s, Hungary has increasingly looked to the West in an attenpt to drag itself out of the mire. Videoton, UEFA Cup finalists in 1985, have been taken over and renamed by Parmalat, the Italian food company while Honved also have new sponsors.

Hungarians will be hoping that if the clubs can make progress they will drag the national side along as well, for the nineties have seen some desperately poor results: two draws with Malta in the 1990 World Cup qualifiers being topped in 1994 by defeat home and away to Iceland and a 7-1 thrashing by Holland. Hungary have never gone more than two World Cups without qualifying - but failure to reach France in 1998 would break that record.

Population: 10,437,000
Area, sq km: 93,031
% in urban areas: 62.0%
Capital city: Budapest

Magyar Labdarugó Szövetség
Népstadion, Toronyépület
'Tower Bldg', Istvánm. ut 3-5
H-1146 Budapest
Hungary
Tel: + 36 1 2529296
Fax: + 36 1 2529986

Year of formation	1901
Affiliation to FIFA	1906
Affiliation to UEFA	1954

Registered clubs	2503
Registered players	144 000
Professional players	700
Registered referees	4670
National stadium	Népstadion Budapest 72 000
National colours	Red/White/Green
Reserve colours	White/White/White
Season	August - June, with a mid season break Dec – Feb

THE RECORD

WORLD CUP

1930	Did not enter
1934	QT 1st/3 in group 8 - Final Tournament/Quarter-finalists
1938	QT 1st/3 in group 5 - Final Tournament/Runners-up
1950	Did not enter
1954	QT Walk-over - Final Tournament/Runners-up
1958	QT 1st/3 in group 3 - Final Tournament/1st round
1962	QT 1st/3 in group 4 - Final Tournament/Quarter-finalists
1966	QT 1st/3 in group 6 - Final Tournament/Quarter-finalists
1970	QT 2nd/4 in group 2
1974	QT 3rd/4 in group 1

1978	QT 1st/3 in group 9 - Final Tournament/1st round
1982	QT 1st/5 in group 4 - Final Tournament/1st round
1986	QT 1st/4 in group 5 - Final Tournament/1st round
1990	QT 3rd/5 in group 6
1994	QT 4th/5 in group 5

EUROPEAN CHAMPIONSHIP

1960	1st round
1964	Semi-finalists/3rd place
1968	QT 1st/4 in group 5 - Final Tournament/Quarter-finalists
1972	QT 1st/4 in group 2 - Final Tournament/Semi-finalists/ 4th place
1976	QT 2nd/4 in group 2
1980	QT 2nd/4 in group 6
1984	QT 4th/5 in group 3
1988	QT 3rd/5 in group 5
1992	QT 4th/5 in group 3
1996	QT group 3

Dr. Gerö Cup

1929	4th
1932	3rd
1935	3rd
1953	Winners
1960	2nd

EUROPEAN CLUB COMPETITIONS

European Cup
Semi-finalists - Vasas Budapest 1958 Vasas ETO Györ 1965 Ujpest Dózsa 1974
Cup Winners Cup
Finalists - MTK Budapest 1964 Ferencváros 1975
UEFA Cup
Winners - Ferencváros 1965
Finalists - Ferencváros 1968 Ujpest Dózsa 1969 Videoton 1985
Mitropa Cup
Winners - Ferencváros 1928 1937 Ujpest Dózsa 1929 1939
Finalists - Ferencváros 1935 1938 1939

CLUB DIRECTORY

BUDAPEST (Population - 2,565,000)

Csepel SC (1912)
Béke téri 14,000 – Blue & cherry halves/Red

Ferencváros Torna Club (1899)
Üllöi út 18,000 – Green & white hoops/White
Previous names - Ferencváros TC 1899-1950, ÉDOSZ 1950-51, Kinizsi 1951-56

Kispest-Honvéd FC (1909)
József Bozsik Stadion 15,000 – Red & black stripes/White
Previous names - Kispest AC 1909-49, Honvéd SE 1949-91

MTK Budapest (1888)
(Magyar Testgyakorlók Köre)
Hungária úti 24,000 – Blue/Blue, white trim
Previous names - MTK 1888-1926, Hungária 1926-40, MTK 1940-50, Textilés 195051, Bástya 1951-53, Vörös Lobogó 1953-56, MTK 1956-75. Merged with VM Egyetértés in 1975 to become MTK-VM 1975-91

Újpesti Torna Egylet (1885)
Megyeri úti 32,000 – Violet/White
Previous names - Ujpest TE 1885-1949, Budapest Dózsa 1949-57, Ujpesti Dózsa SC 1957-90

Vasas SC (1911)
Fáy utcai 18,000 – Red & white chequered/Blue
Previous names - Vasas 1911-43, Kinizsi Vasas 1943-45

DEBRECEN (Population 219,000)

Debreceni VSC (1902)
(Vasutas Sport Club)
Nagyerdei 20,000 – Red & white chequered/Red
Previous names - Merger in 1979 of Debrecen VSE and Debrecen MTE

MISKOLC (Population - 207,000)

Diósgyöri VTK (1910)
(Vasgyárak Testgyakorlo Köre)
Vasgyári Sporttélep 30,000 – Red/Red
Previous name - Diósgyör 1910-38, DIMAVAG 1938-45

SZEGED (Population - 189,000)

Szeged SC (1899)
Felsötiszaparti 18,000 – Blue & black stripes/Blue
Previous names - Szak 1899-1926, Bástya Szeged 1926-31, Szeged FC 1931-40, Szeged AK 1940-49, Petöfi 1950-57, Szak 1957-77. In 1977 Szak merged with SZEOL (1921) under SZEOL. SZEOL Became Szeged in 1987

PECS (Population - 183,000)

Pécsi MSC (1973)
(Munkas Sport Club)
PMSC 16,000 – Red/Black, white trim
Previous names - Merger in 1973 of Pécsi Dózsa, Pécs Bányász, Ercbányász, Helypar and Pécs Epitök

GYÖR (Population - 131,000)

ETO FC Györ (1904)
(Egyetértés Torna Osztálya)
Rába ETO Stadion 22,000 – White, green trim
Previous names - ETO Györ 1904-46, Vasas ETO Györ 1946-68, Györi Rába ETO 1968-93

SZÉKESFEHÉRVAR (Population - 113,000)

Parmalat FC (1941)
Sóstói 23,000 – Red & blue stripes/Blue
Previous names - Vadásztölténygyár 1941-48, Dolgozók 1949-50, Vasas 1950-68, Videoton SC 1968-89, Videoton-Waltham Sport Club 1989-93

SZOMBATHELY (Population - 87,000)

Haladás VSE (1919)
(Vasutas Sport Egytemi)
Haladás 18,000 – White, green & black trim
Previous names - Haladás 1919-26, Szombathely MAV 1926-36, Haladás 1936-48, Szombathely VSE 1948-49, Lokomotiv 1949-54, Törekvés 1954-56

SZOLNOK (Population - 87,000)

Szolnoki MAV MTE (1910)
Tiszaligeti – Blue/White
Previous names - Szolnok MAV 1910-49 1956-79, Lokomotiv 1949-55, Törekvés 195556. Merged with Szolnok MTE in 1979

KAPOSVAR (Population - 76,000)

Kaposvári Rákóczi SC (1923)
Rákóczi 18,000 – Red/White
Previous names - Kinizsi Kaposvár 1951-56 & 1957-70

TATABANYA (Population - 76,000)

Tatabányai Bányász SC (1910)
Bányász Stadion 22,000 – White/White
Previous name - Tatabánya SC 1910-49

BÉKÉSCSABA (Population - 70,000)

Békéscsabai Elöre FC (1912)
Békéscsaba 18,000 – Violet & white chequered/Violet

VESZPRÉM (Population 66,000)

Veszprémi FC (1912)
Municipal 10,000 – White/White

ZALAEGERSZEG (Population - 63,000)

Zalaegerszegi Torna Egylet (1920)
Zalaegerszegi 20,000 – Sky blue/White

SALGOTARJAN (Population - 48,000)

Salgótárjan BTC (1920)
(Bányász Torna Club)
Malinovszkij – White/Black

VAC (Population - 36,000)

Vác FC Samsung (1889)
Városi 15,000 – Red/Blue, white trim
Previous name - Váci Izzö MTE 1951-91

SIOFOK

Siófoki Bányász SE (1921)
Siófok 12,000 – Red & black hoops/Black

KOMLO

Komló Bányász
Komló 10,000
(1922) – Blue/White

HUNGARIAN LEAGUE CHAMPIONSHIP

1901c	Budapest TC 16 Magyar UE 10 Ferencváros 7
1902	Budapest TC 15 Ferencváros 9 33 FC 9
1903f	Ferencváros 21 Budapest TC 19 MTK Budapest 18
1904g	MTK Budapest 25 Ferencváros 24 Budapest TC 22
1905	Ferencváros 26 Postás Budapest 26 MTK Budapest 23
1906	-
1907f	Ferencváros 24 Magyar AC 22 MTK Budapest 22
1908g	MTK Budapest 28 Ferencváros 25 Magyar AC 24
1909	Ferencváros 28 Magyar AC 22 Budapest TC 21
1910	Ferencváros 27 MTK Budapest 25 Nemzeti SC 18
1911h	Ferencváros 32 MTK Budapest 24 Törekvés SE 22
1912	Ferencváros 30 MTK Budapest 22 Budapest AK 20
1913	Ferencváros 33 MTK Budapest 26 Budapest TC 24
1914	MTK Budapest 33 Ferencváros 27 Törekvés SE 23
1915-16	-
1917k	MTK Budapest 42 Törekvés SE 34 Ujpesti TE 27
1918	MTK Budapest 43 Ferencváros 31 Törekvés SE 30
1919	MTK Budapest 39 Ferencváros 35 Ujpesti TE 30
1920p	MTK Budapest 53 Kispest AC 43 Ferencváros 40
1921l	MTK Budapest 44 Ujpesti TE 36 Ferencváros 30
1922k	MTK Budapest 37 Ferencváros 36 Ujpesti TE 32
1923	MTK Budapest 37 Ujpesti TE 34 Ferencváros 32
1924	MTK Budapest 40 Ferencváros 30 Ujpesti TE 28
1925	MTK Budapest 38 Ferencváros 30 Vasas Budapest 27
1926	Ferencváros 33 MTK Budapest 31 Vasas Budapest 29
1927h	Ferencváros 30 Ujpesti TE 23 Hungária 19
1928k	Ferencváros 39 Hungária 35 Ujpesti TE 34
1929	Hungária 37 Ferencváros 36 Ujpesti TE 30
1930	Ujpesti TE 38 Ferencváros 36 Hungária 27
1931	Ujpesti TE 35 Hungária 30 Ferencváros 29
1932	Ferencváros 44 Ujpesti TE 36 Hungária 35
1933	Ujpesti TE 37 Hungária 36 Ferencváros 35
1934	Ferencváros 39 Ujpesti TE 37 Bocskai Debrecen 27
1935	Ujpesti TE 35 Ferencváros 33 Hungária 29
1936n	Hungária 48 Ujpesti TE 43 Ferencváros 39
1937	Hungária 43 Ferencváros 42 Ujpesti TE 37
1938	Ferencváros 47 Ujpesti TE 44 Hungária 40
1939	Ujpesti TE 44 Ferencváros 43 Hungária 41
1940	Ferencváros 39 Hungária 39 Ujpesti TE 38
1941	Ferencváros 45 Ujpesti TE 34 Szeged AK 32
1942q	Csepel SC 48 Ujpesti TE 44 Szolnoki MAV 41
1943	Csepel SC 45 Nagyváradi AC 42 Ferencváros 36
1944	Nagyváradi AC 49 Ferencváros 36 Kolozsvári AC 36
1945	Ujpesti TE 37 Ferencváros 34 Csepel SC 32
1946h	Ujpesti TE 31 Vasas Budapest 24 Csepel SC 20
1947q	Ujpesti TE 47 Kispest AC 41 Vasas Budapest 39
1948r	Csepel SC 52 Vasas Budapest 51 Ferencváros 50
1949q	Ferencváros 53 MTK Budapest 42 Kispest AC 41
1950	Honvéd 50 EDOSZ 46 Textiles Budapest 44
1950ah	Honvéd 27 Textiles Budapest 24 Budapest Dózsa 21
1951n	Bástya Budapest 46 Honvéd 42 Budapest Dózsa 31
1952	Honvéd 47 Bástya Budapest 45 Budapest Dózsa 36
1953	Vörös Lobogó 46 Honvéd 43 Vasas Budapest 32
1954	Honvéd 40 Vörös Lobogó 35 Kinizsi 33
1955	Honvéd 45 Vörös Lobogó 41 Kinizsi 37
1956	-
1957af	Vasas Budapest 17 MTK Budapest 16 Ujpesti Dózsa 14
1958n	MTK Budapest 35 Honvéd 34 Ferencváros 33
1959	Csepel SC 34 MTK Budapest 34 Honvéd 33
1960	Ujpesti Dózsa 40 Ferencváros 35 Vasas Budapest 32
1961	Vasas Budapest 38 Ujpesti Dózsa 34 MTK Budapest 32
1962	Vasas Budapest 38 Ujpesti Dózsa 36 Ferencváros 33
1963	Ferencváros 37 MTK Budapest 31 Ujpesti Dózsa 30
1963ag	Györ Vasas ETO 17 Honvéd 17 Ferencváros 17
1964n	Ferencváros 41 Honvéd 38 Tatabánya Bányász 33
1965	Vasas Budapest 39 Ferencváros 36 Ujpesti Dózsa 33
1966	Vasas Budapest 43 Ferencváros 37 Tatabánya Bányász 32
1967q	Ferencváros 52 Ujpesti Dózsa 44 Györ Vasas ETO 39
1968	Ferencváros 49 Ujpesti Dózsa 48 Vasas Budapest 42
1969	Ujpesti Dózsa 48 Honvéd 44 Ferencváros 39
1970f2	Ujpesti Dózsa 23 Ferencváros 20 Honvéd 18
1971	Ujpesti Dózsa 51 Ferencváros 49 Vasas Budapest 47
1972q	Ujpesti Dózsa 46 Honvéd 39 Salgótarján BTC 39
1973	Ujpesti Dózsa 46 Ferencváros 41 Vasas Budapest 40
1974	Ujpesti Dózsa 42 Ferencváros 39 Rába ETO Györ 38
1975p	Ujpesti Dózsa 45 Honvéd 42 Ferencváros 33
1976q	Ferencváros 46 Videoton SC 44 Ujpesti Dózsa 42
1977t	Vasas Budapest 53 Ujpesti Dózsa 50 Ferencváros 47
1978	Ujpesti Dózsa 51 Honvéd 50 MTK-VM Budapest 47
1979	Ujpesti Dózsa 52 Ferencváros 47 Diósgyöri VTK 44
1980	Honvéd 48 Ujpesti Dózsa 45 Vasas Budapest 44
1981	Ferencváros 51 Tatabánya Bányász 48 Vasas Budapest 46
1982	Rába ETO Györ 49 Ferencváros 44 Tatabánya Bányász 43
1983q	Rába ETO Györ 44 Ferencváros 43 Honvéd 42
1984	Honvéd 45 Rába ETO Györ 37 Videoton SC 37
1985	Honvéd 46 Rába ETO Györ 36 Videoton SC 36
1986	Honvéd 45 Pécsi MSC 39 Rába ETO Györ 37
1987	MTK-VM Budapest 43 Ujpesti Dózsa 40 Tatabánya Bányász 35
1988	Honvéd 41 Tatábanya Bányász 37 Ujpesti Dózsa 37
1989q2	Honvéd 61 Ferencváros 59 MTK-VM Budapest 59
1990q3	Ujpesti Dózsa 58 MTK-VM Budapest 58 Ferencváros 48
1991q	Honvéd 45 Ferencváros 40 Pécsi MSC 37
1992	Ferencváros 46 Vac FC Samsung 45 Kispest-Honvéd 40
1993	Kispest-Honvéd 43 Vac FC Samsung 42 Ferencváros 41
1994	Vac FC Samsung 46 Kispest-Honvéd 43 Békéscsaba 41
1995	Ferencváros 59 Ujpesti TE 52 Debreceni VSC 49

* The 1970 championship was played in two groups. Ujpesti beat Ferencváros 3-2 and 1-1 in a play-off to take first place, whilst Honvéd beat MTK 3-1 and 3-1 to take third place

HUNGARIAN CUP FINALS

1910	MTK Budapest	1-1 3-1	Budapest TC
1911	MTK Budapest	1-0	Magyar AC
1912	MTK Budapest	W-O	Ferencváros
1913	Ferencváros	2-1	Budapest AK
1914	MTK Budapest	4-0	Magyar AC
1915-21	-		
1922	Ferencváros	2-2 1-0	Ujpesti TE
1923	MTK Budapest	4-1	Ujpesti TE
1924	-		
1925	MTK Budapest	4-0	Ujpesti TE
1926	Kispest AC	1-1 3-2	Budapest EAC
1927	Ferencváros	3-0	Ujpesti TE
1928	Ferencváros	5-1	Attila Miskolc
1929	-		
1930	Bocskai Debrecen	5-1	Bástya Szeged
1931	III Kerület TVE	4-1	Ferencváros
1932	Hungária	1-1 4-3	Ferencváros
1933	Ferencváros	11-1	Ujpesti TE
1934	Soroksár	2-2 1-1 2-0	BSZKRT
1935	Ferencváros	2-1	Hungária
1936-40	-		
1941	Szolnoki MAV	3-0	Salgótarján BTC
1942	Ferencváros	6-2	DIMAVAG
1943	Ferencváros	3-0	Salgótarján BTC
1944	Ferencváros	2-2 3-1	Kolozsvári AC
1945-51	-		
1952	Bástya Budapest	3-2	Dorogi AC
1953-54	-		
1955	Vasas Budapest	3-2	Honvéd
1956	Ferencváros	2-1	Salgótarján BTC
1957-63	-		
1964	Honvéd	1-0	Vasas ETO Györ
1965	Vasas ETO Györ	4-0	Diósgyöri VTK
1966	Vasas ETO Györ	1-1 3-2	Ferencváros

1967	Vasas ETO Györ	1-0	Salgótarján BTC
1968	MTK Budapest	2-1	Honvéd
1969	Ujpesti Dózsa	3-1	Honvéd
1970	Ujpesti Dózsa	3-2	Komló Bányász
1971	-		
1972	Ferencváros	2-1	Tatabánya Bányász
1973	Vasas Budapest	4-3	Honvéd
1974	Ferencváros	3-1	Komló Bányász
1975	Ujpesti Dózsa	3-2	Haladás VSE
1976	Ferencváros	1-0	MTK-VM Budapest
1977	Diósgyöri VTK	*	Ferencváros
1978	Ferencváros	4-2	Pécsi MSC
1979	Rába ETO Györ	1-0	Ferencváros
1980	Diósgyöri VTK	3-1	Vasas Budapest
1981	Vasas Budapest	1-0	Diósgyöri VTK
1982	Ujpesti Dózsa	2-0	Videoton SC
1983	Ujpesti Dózsa	3-2	Honvéd
1984	Siófoki Bányász	2-1	Rába ETO Györ
1985	Honvéd	5-0	Tatabánya Bányász
1986	Vasas Budapest	0-0 5-4p	Ferencváros
1987	Ujpesti Dózsa	3-2	Pécsi MSC
1988	Békéscsaba ESSC	3-2	Honvéd
1989	Honvéd	1-0	Ferencváros
1990	Pécsi MSC	2-0	Honvéd
1991	Ferencváros	1-0	Vaci Izzo MTE
1992	Ujpesti TE	1-0	Vac FC Samsung
1993	Ferencváros	1-1 1-1 5-3p	Haladas VSE
1994	Ferencváros	2-1 3-0	Kispest-Honved
1995	Ferencváros	4-3	Vac FC Samsung

* League format used for the final rounds of the 1977 competition

LEADING INTERNATIONAL GOALSCORERS

83	Ferenc Puskás	(Kispest,Honvéd)
75	Sándor Kocsis	(Ferencváros,Honvéd)
58	Imre Schlosser	(Ferencváros,MTK,Wiener AC)
49	Lajos Tichy	(Honvéd)
42	György Sárosi	(Ferencváros)
39	Nandor Hidegkuti	(HAC,MTK)
36	Ferenc Bene	(Ujpesti)
32	Gyula Zsengellér	(Ujpesti)
	Tibor Nyilasi	(Ferencváros,FK Austria)
31	Flórián Albert	(Ferencváros)

LEADING INTERNATIONAL APPEARANCES

100	József Bozsik	(Kispest,Honvéd)
92	László Fazekas	(Ujpesti,Royal Antwerp)
86	Gyula Grosics	(MATEOSZ,Honvéd,Tatabánya)
84	Ferenc Puskás	(Kispest,Honvéd)
82	Imre Garaba	(Honvéd,Stade Rennes,Charleroi SC)
80	Sándor Mátrai	(Ferencváros)
77	Ferenc Sipos	(MTK,Honvéd)
76	Máté Fenyvesi	(Ferencváros)
	Ferenc Bene	(Ujpesti)
	László Bálint	(Ferencváros,Club Brugge,Toulouse)

NATIONAL TEAM COACHES

1902-04	Ferenc Gillemot
1904-06	Ferenc Stobbe
1906	Alfréd Hajós
1907-08	Ferenc Stobbe
1908-11	Frigyes Minder
1911-14	Ede Herczog
1914-17	Frigyes Minder
1918-19	Akos Fehéry
1919	Frigyes Minder
1920	József Harsády
1920	Lajos Tibor
1921-24	Gyula Kiss
1924	Ödön Holits
1924-26	Lajos Máriássy
1926-28	Gyula Kiss
1928	Tivadar Kiss
1928-29	János Földessy
1930	Mihály Pataki
1930	Frigyes Minder
1930-32	Lajos Máriássy
1932-34	Ödön Nádas
1934-39	Károly Dietz
1939-41	Dénes Ginzery
1941-42	József Fábián
1942-43	Kálmán Vághy
1945-48	Tibor Gallowits
1949-56	Gusztáv Sebes
1956-57	Márton Bukovi
1957	Lajos Baróti, Károly Sós & Károly Lakat
1957-66	Lajos Baróti
1966-67	Rudolf Illovszky
1968-69	Károly Sós
1970-71	József Hoffer
1971-74	Rudolf Illovszky
1974	József Bozsik
1974-75	Ede Moór
1975	János Szöcs
1975-78	Lajos Baróti
1978-79	Ferenc Kovács
1979-80	Károly Lakat
1980-83	Kálmán Mészöly
1983-86	György Mezey
1986	Imre Komora
1986-87	József Verebes
1988	László Bálint
1988-89	Georgy Mezey
1989-90	Bertalan Bicskei
1990-91	Kalman Mészöly
1991	Robert Glazier
1991-93	Emerich Jenei
1993	Ferenc Puskas
1993-94	Joszef Verebes
1994-	Kalman Mészöly

INTERNATIONAL MATCHES PLAYED BY HUNGARY

12-10-1902	Austria	L 0-5	Vienna	Fr	
5-04-1903	Bohemia	W 2-1	Budapest	Fr	Borbás, Minder
10-06	Austria	W 3-2	Budapest	Fr	Pokorny 2, Buda
11-10	Austria	L 2-4	Vienna	Fr	Borbás 2
2-06-1904	Austria	W 3-0	Budapest	Fr	Pokorny, Koch, Borbás
9-10	Austria	L 4-5	Vienna	Fr	Pokorny 2, Borbás, Károly
9-04-1905	Austria	D 0-0	Budapest	Fr	
1-04-1906	Bohemia	D 1-1	Budapest	Fr	Borbás
7-10	Bohemia	D 4-4	Prague	Fr	Horváth 2, Károly, Molnár.I
4-11	Austria	W 3-1	Budapest	Fr	Molnár.I, Schlosser, Károly
7-04-1907	Bohemia	W 5-2	Budapest	Fr	Horváth 3, Borbás, Molnár.I

5-05	Austria	L 1-3	Vienna	Fr	Károly
6-10	Bohemia	L 3-5	Prague	Fr	Gorszky, Szednicsek, Weisz
3-11	Austria	W 4-1	Budapest	Fr	Borbás 2, Károly, OG
5-04-1908	Bohemia	W 5-2	Budapest	Fr	Károly 3, Schlosser 2
3-05	Austria	L 0-4	Vienna	Fr	
10-06	England	L 0-7	Budapest	Fr	
1-11	Austria	W 5-3	Budapest	Fr	Krempels, Koródy, Schlosser 2, OG
4-04-1909	Germany	D 3-3	Budapest	Fr	Borbás, Schlosser, Sebestyén
2-05	Austria	W 4-3	Vienna	Fr	Schlosser 3, Biró.G
29-05	England	L 2-4	Budapest	Fr	Késmárky, Grósz
30-05	Austria	D 1-1	Budapest	Fr	Borbás
31-05	England	L 2-8	Budapest	Fr	Schlosser, Mészáros
9-11	Austria	D 2-2	Budapest	Fr	Schlosser 2
1-05-1910	Austria	L 1-2	Vienna	Fr	Dobó
26-05	Italy	W 6-1	Budapest	Fr	Schlosser 2, Weisz, Károly, Dobó, Koródy
6-11	Austria	W 3-0	Budapest	Fr	Koródy 2, Bodnár
1-01-1911	France	W 3-0	Paris	Fr	Schlosser 3
6-01	Italy	W 1-0	Milan	Fr	Schlosser
8-01	Switzerland	L 0-2	Zurich	Fr	
7-05	Austria	L 1-3	Vienna	Fr	Bodnár
29-10	Switzerland	W 9-0	Budapest	Fr	Schlosser 6, Koródy, Biró.G, Bodnár
5-11	Austria	W 2-0	Budapest	Fr	Koródy, Bodnár
17-12	Germany	W 4-1	Munich	Fr	Schlosser 2, Sebestyén, Bodnár
14-04-1912	Germany	D 4-4	Budapest	Fr	Bodnár 3, Schlosser
5-05	Austria	D 1-1	Vienna	Fr	Bodnár
20-06	Sweden	D 2-2	Gothenburg	Fr	Bodnár, Pataki
23-06	Norway	W 6-0	Oslo	Fr	Bodnár 3, Schlosser 2, Tóth.I
30-06	England *	L 0-7	Stockholm	OGqf	
3-07	Germany	W 3-1	Stockholm	OGct	Schlosser 3
5-07	Austria	W 3-0	Stockholm	OGct	Schlosser, Pataki, Bodnár
12-07	Tsarist Russia	W 9-0	Moscow	Fr	Pataki 4, Kertész.V 3, Schlosser 2
14-07	Tsarist Russia	W 12-0	Moscow	Fr	Schlosser 5, Kertész.V 3, Pataki 2, Tóth.I, Bródy
3-11	Austria	W 4-0	Budapest	Fr	Schlosser 2, Bodnár, Pataki
27-04-1913	Austria	W 4-1	Vienna	Fr	Pataki 2, Tóth.I, Biró.G
18-05	Sweden	W 2-0	Budapest	Fr	Pataki, Schlosser
26-10	Austria	W 4-3	Budapest	Fr	Kertész.V 2, Hlavay, Pataki
3-05-1914	Austria	L 0-2	Vienna	Fr	
31-05	France	W 5-1	Budapest	Fr	Bodnár 3, Payer, Pataki
21-06	Sweden	D 1-1	Stockholm	Fr	Schlosser
4-10	Austria	D 2-2	Budapest	Fr	Pótz, Schlosser
8-11	Austria	W 2-1	Vienna	Fr	Konrád II, Bodnár
2-05-1915	Austria	L 2-5	Budapest	Fr	Patakai, OG
30-05	Austria	W 2-1	Vienna	Fr	Schlosser, Borbás
3-10	Austria	L 2-4	Vienna	Fr	Schlosser, Kertész II
7-11	Austria	W 6-2	Budapest	Fr	Schaffer 3, Tóth 2, Kertész
7-05-1916	Austria	L 1-3	Vienna	Fr	Kertész II
4-06	Austria	W 2-1	Budapest	Fr	Schaffer, Schlosser
1-10	Austria	L 2-3	Budapest	Fr	Tóth, Schaffer
5-11	Austria	D 3-3	Vienna	Fr	Schaffer, Konrád II, Schlosser
6-05-1917	Austria	D 1-1	Vienna	Fr	Schlosser
3-06	Austria	W 6-2	Budapest	Fr	Schaffer 2, Schlosser 2, Urik, Weisz
15-07	Austria	W 4-1	Vienna	Fr	Schaffer 3, Schlosser
7-10	Austria	W 2-1	Budapest	Fr	Schaffer, Taussig
4-11	Austria	W 2-1	Vienna	Fr	Schaffer 2
14-04-1918	Austria	W 2-0	Budapest	Fr	Schlosser, Schaffer
12-05	Switzerland	W 2-1	Budapest	Fr	Schaffer, Schlosser
2-06	Austria	W 2-0	Vienna	Fr	Schlosser, Schaffer
6-10	Austria	W 3-0	Vienna	Fr	Payer 2, Braun
6-04-1919	Austria	W 2-1	Budapest	Fr	Orth, Braun
5-10	Austria	L 0-2	Vienna	Fr	
9-11	Austria	W 3-2	Budapest	Fr	Pataki 2, Orth
2-05-1920	Austria	D 2-2	Vienna	Fr	Tóth.I, Pataki
24-10	Germany	L 0-1	Berlin	Fr	
7-11	Austria	L 1-2	Budapest	Fr	Braun
24-04-1921	Austria	L 1-4	Vienna	Fr	Orth
5-06	Germany	W 3-0	Budapest	Fr	Schlosser, Guttmann, Braun
6-11	Sweden	W 4-2	Budapest	Fr	Orth 3, Schlosser
18-12	Poland	W 1-0	Budapest	Fr	Szabó.J
30-04-1922	Austria	D 1-1	Budapest	Fr	Molnár.G
14-05	Poland	W 3-0	Krakow	Fr	Solti.M 2, OG
15-06	Switzerland	D 1-1	Budapest	Fr	Blum

2-07	Germany	D 0-0	Bochum	Fr	
9-07	Sweden	D 1-1	Stockholm	Fr	Hirzer
13-07	Finland	W 5-1	Helsinki	Fr	Schwarz 2, Pataki 2, Fogel
24-09	Austria	D 2-2	Vienna	Fr	Priboj 2
26-11	Austria	L 1-2	Budapest	Fr	Molnár.G
4-03-1923	Italy	D 0-0	Genoa	Fr	
11-03	Switzerland	W 6-1	Lausanne	Fr	Orth 2, Molnár.G 2, Hirzer 2
6-05	Austria	L 0-1	Vienna	Fr	
19-08	Finland	W 3-1	Budapest	Fr	Braun 2, Hirzer
23-09	Austria	W 2-0	Budapest	Fr	Molnár.G, Jeszmás
28-10	Sweden	W 2-1	Budapest	Fr	Eisenhoffer 2
6-04-1924	Italy	W 7-1	Budapest	Fr	Molnár.G 3, Braun 2, Eisenhoffer, Opata
4-05	Austria	D 2-2	Budapest	Fr	Eisenhoffer 2
18-05	Switzerland	L 2-4	Zurich	Fr	Braun, Opata
26-05	Poland	W 5-0	Paris	OGr1	Hirzer 2, Opata 2, Eisenhoffer
29-05	Egypt	L 0-3	Paris	OGr2	
4-06	France	W 1-0	Le Havre	Fr	Eisenhoffer
31-08	Poland	W 4-0	Budapest	Fr	Takács 2, Orth, OG
14-09	Austria	L 1-2	Vienna	Fr	Orth
21-09	Germany	W 4-1	Budapest	Fr	Takács 2, Szentmiklóssy, OG
18-01-1925	Italy	W 2-1	Milan	Fr	Spitz, Takács
25-03	Switzerland	W 5-0	Budapest	Fr	Molnár.G 2, Jeny 2, Takács
5-05	Austria	L 1-3	Vienna	Fr	Takács
21-05	Belgium	L 1-3	Budapest	Fr	Jeny
12-07	Sweden	L 2-6	Stockholm	Fr	Takács 2
19-07	Poland	W 2-0	Krakow	Fr	Winkler, Holzbauer
20-09	Austria	D 1-1	Budapest	Fr	Priboj
4-10	Spain	L 0-1	Budapest	Fr	
11-10	Czechoslovakia	L 0-2	Prague	Fr	
8-11	Italy	D 1-1	Budapest	Fr	Molnár.G
14-02-1926	Belgium	W 2-0	Brussels	Fr	Pipa, Rémay
2-05	Austria	L 0-3	Budapest	Fr	
6-06	Czechoslovakia	W 2-1	Budapest	Fr	Takács, Kohut
20-08	Poland	W 4-1	Budapest	Fr	Kautzky, Horváth, Fogel, Senkey
19-09	Austria	W 3-2	Vienna	Fr	Holzbauer, Jeszmás, Kohut
14-11	Sweden	W 3-1	Budapest	Fr	Braun, Opata, Kohut
19-12	Spain	L 2-4	Vigo	Fr	Opata, Braun
26-12	Portugal	D 3-3	Oporto	Fr	
10-04-1927	Austria	L 0-6	Vienna	Fr	
10-04	Yugoslavia	W 3-0	Budapest	Fr	Siklóssy, Orth, Szabó.P
24-04	Czechoslovakia	L 1-4	Prague	Fr	Mészáros
12-06	France	W 13-1	Budapest	Fr	Takács 6, Kohut 2, Orth 2, Skvarek 2, OG
25-09	Austria	W 5-3	Budapest	DGC	Takács, Kohut, Ströck, Holzbauer, Hirzer
9-10	Czechoslovakia	L 1-2	Budapest	Fr	
25-03-1928	Italy	L 3-4	Rome	DGC	Kohut, Hirzer, Takács
25-03	Yugoslavia	W 2-1	Budapest	Fr	Stofián 2
22-04	Czechoslovakia	W 2-0	Budapest	DGC	Hirzer, Kohut
6-05	Austria	D 5-5	Budapest	Fr	Kohut 3, Hirzer, Ströck
23-09	Czechoslovakia	L 1-6	Prague	Fr	
7-10	Austria	L 1-5	Vienna	DGC	Hirzer
1-11	Switzerland	W 3-1	Budapest	DGC	Turay, Hirzer, Stöck
24-02-1929	France	L 0-3	Paris	Fr	
14-04	Switzerland	W 5-4	Berne	DGC	Takács 2, Toldi, Hirzer, OG
5-05	Austria	D 2-2	Vienna	Fr	Takács 2
8-09	Czechoslovakia	D 1-1	Prague	DGC	Kalmár
6-10	Austria	W 2-1	Budapest	Fr	Takács, Avar
13-04-1930	Switzerland	D 2-2	Basle	Fr	Toldi 2
1-05	Czechoslovakia	D 1-1	Prague	Fr	Hirzer
11-05	Italy	L 0-5	Budapest	DGC	
1-06	Austria	W 2-1	Budapest	Fr	Kohut, Turay
8-06	Holland	W 6-2	Budapest	Fr	Avar 3, Turay 2, Toldi
21-09	Austria	W 3-2	Vienna	Fr	Turay 2, Titkos
28-09	Germany	L 3-5	Dresden	Fr	Takács 3
26-10	Czechoslovakia	D 1-1	Budapest	Fr	Titkos
22-03-1931	Czechoslovakia	D 3-3	Prague	DGC	Avar 3
12-04	Switzerland	W 6-2	Budapest	DGC	Avar 3, Szabó.P, Kalmár, Táncos
3-05	Austria	D 0-0	Vienna	DGC	
21-05	Yugoslavia	L 2-3	Belgrade	Fr	Avar 2
20-09	Czechoslovakia	W 3-0	Budapest	Fr	Turay, Avar, Kalmár
4-10	Austria	D 2-2	Budapest	DGC	Szabó.P, Spitz
8-11	Sweden	W 3-1	Budapest	Fr	Avar 2, Spitz

13-12	Italy	L 2-3	Turin	DGC	Avar 2
19-02-1932	Egypt	D 0-0	Cairo	Fr	
20-03	Czechoslovakia	W 3-1	Prague	Fr	Turay, Závodi, Toldi
24-04	Austria	L 2-8	Vienna	Fr	Cseh 2
8-05	Italy	D 1-1	Budapest	DGC	Toldi
19-06	Switzerland	L 1-3	Berne	DGC	OG
18-09	Czechoslovakia	W 2-1	Budapest	DGC	Titkos, Toldi
2-10	Austria	L 2-3	Budapest	Fr	Kalmár, Déri
30-10	Germany	W 2-1	Budapest	Fr	Déri, Turay
27-11	Italy	L 2-4	Milan	Fr	Bihámy, Markos
29-01-1933	Portugal	L 0-1	Lisbon	Fr	
5-03	Holland	W 2-1	Amsterdam	Fr	Bihámy, Teleki
19-03	Czechoslovakia	W 2-0	Budapest	Fr	Turay, Cseh
30-04	Austria	D 1-1	Budapest	Fr	Markos
2-07	Sweden	L 2-5	Stockholm	Fr	Toldi, Sárosi.G
17-09	Switzerland	W 3-0	Budapest	DGC	Avar 2, OG
1-10	Austria	D 2-2	Vienna	Fr	Avar, Polgár
22-10	Italy	L 0-1	Budapest	DGC	
14-01-1934	Germany	L 1-3	Frankfurt	Fr	Polgár
25-03	Bulgaria	W 4-1	Sofia	WCq	Sárosi.G, Toldi, Szabó.P, Markos
15-04	Austria	L 2-5	Vienna	Fr	Sárosi.G 2
29-04	Bulgaria	W 4-1	Budapest	WCq	Szabó.P 2, Solti.J 2
29-04	Czechoslovakia	D 2-2	Prague	DGC	Sárosi.G 2
10-05	England	W 2-1	Budapest	Fr	Sárosi.G, Avar
27-05	Egypt	W 4-2	Naples	WCr1	Toldi 2, Teleki, Vincze.J
31-05	Austria	L 1-2	Bologna	WCqf	Sárosi.G
7-10	Austria	W 3-1	Budapest	DGC	Sárosi.G 2, Toldi
9-12	Italy	L 2-4	Milan	Fr	Sárosi.G, Avar
15-12	Rep. Ireland	W 4-2	Dublin	Fr	Avar 2, Vincze.J, Markos
14-04-1935	Switzerland	L 2-6	Zurich	DGC	Cseh 2
12-05	Austria	W 6-3	Budapest	Fr	Sárosi.G 3, Titkos 2, Toldi
19-05	France	L 0-2	Paris	Fr	
22-09	Czechoslovakia	W 1-0	Budapest	DGC	Markos
6-10	Austria	D 4-4	Vienna	DGC	Vincze.J 2, Sárosi.G, Toldi
10-11	Switzerland	W 6-1	Budapest	Fr	Sárosi.G 2, Vincze.J 2, Toldi, Cseh
24-11	Italy	D 2-2	Milan	DGC	Sárosi.G 2
15-03-1936	Germany	W 3-2	Budapest	Fr	Titkos, Cseh, Sárosi.G
5-04	Austria	W 5-3	Vienna	Fr	Kállai 3, Cseh 2
3-05	Rep. Ireland	D 3-3	Budapest	Fr	Sárosi.G 2, Sas
31-05	Italy	L 1-2	Budapest	Fr	Turay
27-09	Austria	W 5-3	Budapest	DGC	Toldi 3, Cseh, Titkos
4-10	Romania	W 2-1	Bucharest	Fr	Lázár, Toldi
18-10	Czechoslovakia	L 2-5	Prague	DGC	Titkos, Toldi
2-12	England	L 2-6	London	Fr	Vincze.J, Cseh
6-12	Rep. Ireland	W 3-2	Dublin	Fr	Titkos, Cseh, Toldi
11-04-1937	Switzerland	W 5-1	Basle	DGC	Zsengellér 3, Sárosi.G, Dudás
25-04	Italy	L 0-2	Turin	DGC	
9-05	Yugoslavia	D 1-1	Budapest	Fr	Cseh
23-05	Austria	D 2-2	Budapest	Fr	Sas, Cseh
19-09	Czechoslovakia	W 8-3	Budapest	DGC	Sárosi.G 7, Zsengellér
10-10	Austria	W 2-1	Vienna	DGC	Sárosi.G, Cseh
14-11	Switzerland	W 2-0	Budapest	DGC	Sárosi.G, Toldi
9-01-1938	Portugal	L 0-4	Lisbon	Fr	
16-01	Luxembourg	W 6-0	Luxembourg	Fr	Szendrödi 3, Kállai, Zsengellér, Miklósi
20-03	Germany	D 1-1	Nuremberg	Fr	Toldi
25-03	Greece	W 11-1	Budapest	WCq	Zsengellér 5, Nemes 3, Titkos 2, Vincze.J
5-06	Dutch East Indies	W 6-0	Reims	WCr1	Sárosi.G 2, Zsengellér 2, Kohut, Toldi
12-06	Switzerland	W 2-0	Lille	WCqf	Sárosi.G, Zsengellér
16-06	Sweden	W 5-1	Paris	WCsf	Zsengellér 2, Titkos, Sárosi.G, OG
19-06	Italy	L 2-4	Paris	WCf	Titkos, Sárosi.G
7-12	Scotland	L 1-3	Glasgow	Fr	Sárosi.G
26-02-1939	Holland	L 2-3	Rotterdam	Fr	Zsengellér, Gyetvai
16-03	France	D 2-2	Paris	Fr	Kiszely 2
19-03	Rep. Ireland	D 2-2	Cork	Fr	Zsengellér, Kolláth
2-04	Switzerland	L 1-3	Zurich	Fr	Déri
18-05	Rep. Ireland	D 2-2	Budapest	Fr	Kolláth 2
8-06	Italy	L 1-3	Budapest	Fr	Kiszely
27-08	Poland	L 2-4	Warsaw	Fr	Zsengellér, Adám
24-09	Germany	W 5-1	Budapest	Fr	Zsengellér 3, Kincses, Dudás
22-10	Romania	D 1-1	Bucharest	Fr	Tóth.M
12-11	Yugoslavia	W 2-0	Belgrade	Fr	Sárosi.G, Tóth.M

31-03-1940	Switzerland	W 3-0	Budapest	Fr	Sárosi.G 2, Sütö
7-04	Germany	D 2-2	Berlin	Fr	Toldi, Sárosi.B
2-05	Croatia	W 1-0	Budapest	Fr	Dudás
19-05	Romania	W 2-0	Budapest	Fr	Sárosi.G, Gyetvai
29-09	Yugoslavia	D 0-0	Budapest	Fr	
6-10	Germany	D 2-2	Budapest	Fr	
1-12	Italy	D 1-1	Genoa	Fr	Bodola
8-12	Croatia	D 1-1	Zagreb	Fr	Sárvári
23-03-1941	Yugoslavia	D 1-1	Belgrade	Fr	Gyetvai
6-04	Germany	L 0-7	Cologne	Fr	
16-11	Switzerland	W 2-1	Zurich	Fr	Kovacs I, Olajkár II
3-05-1942	Germany	L 3-5	Budapest	Fr	Nagymarosi, Zsengellér, Tihanyi II
14-06	Croatia	D 1-1	Budapest	Fr	Szusza
1-11	Switzerland	W 3-0	Budapest	Fr	Bodola, Németh, Tóth.M
16-05-1943	Switzerland	W 3-1	Geneva	Fr	Bodola 2, Zsengellér
6-06	Bulgaria	W 4-2	Sofia	Fr	Zsengellér 4
12-09	Sweden	W 3-2	Stockholm	Fr	Zsengellér, Sárvári, OG
15-09	Finland	W 3-0	Helsinki	Fr	Tóth.M 2, Sárvári
7-11	Sweden	L 2-7	Budapest	Fr	Szusza 2
19-08-1945	Austria	W 2-0	Budapest	Fr	Rudas, Zsengellér
20-08	Austria	W 5-2	Budapest	Fr	Szusza 2, Puskás, Zsengellér, Vincze.G
30-09	Romania	W 7-2	Budapest	Fr	Hidgekuti 2, Puskás 2, Zsengellér, Rudas, Nyers
14-04-1946	Austria	L 2-3	Vienna	Fr	Nyers, Zsengellér
6-10	Austria	W 2-0	Budapest	Fr	Deák 2
30-10	Luxembourg	W 7-2	Esch	Fr	Deák 3, Puskás 3, Nagymarosi
4-05-1947	Austria	W 5-2	Budapest	Fr	Szusza 2, Puskás, Egresi, OG
11-05	Italy	L 2-3	Turin	Fr	Szusza, Puskás
29-06	Yugoslavia	W 3-2	Belgrade	BCE	Szilágy, Puskás, Mike
17-08	Bulgaria	W 9-0	Budapest	BCE	Deák 4, Hidegkuti 3, Zsolnai, Nagymarosi
20-08	Albania	W 3-0	Budapest	BCE	Zsolnai, Egresi, Deák
14-09	Austria	L 3-4	Vienna	Fr	Szusza 3
12-10	Romania	W 3-0	Bucharest	BCE	Puskás 2, Egresi
21-04-1948	Switzerland	W 7-4	Budapest	DGC	Puskás 2, Deák 2, Göcze, Egresi, Szusza
2-05	Austria	L 2-3	Vienna	DGC	Szusza, Deák
23-05	Czechoslovakia	W 2-1	Budapest	DGC/BCE	Egresi, Deák
23-05	Albania	D 0-0	Tirana	BCE	
6-06	Romania	W 9-0	Budapest	BCE	Egresi 3, Mészáros 2, Puskás 2, Kocsis 2
19-09	Poland	W 6-2	Warsaw	BCE	Hidegkuti 2, Bozsik, Szusza, Deák, Tóth.M
3-10	Austria	W 2-1	Budapest	Fr	Deák, Szusza
24-10	Romania	W 5-1	Bucharest	BCE	Puskás 3, Deák 2
7-11	Bulgaria	L 0-1	Sofia	BCE	
10-04-1949	Czechoslovakia	L 2-5	Prague	DGC	Puskás, Szusza
8-05	Austria	W 6-1	Budapest	DGC	Puskás 3, Deák 2, Kocsis
12-06	Italy	D 1-1	Budapest	DGC	Deák
19-06	Sweden	D 2-2	Stockholm	Fr	Budai, Kocsis
10-07	Poland	W 8-2	Debrecen	Fr	Deák 4, Puskás 2, Egresi, Keszthelyi
16-10	Austria	W 4-3	Vienna	Fr	Puskás 2, Deák 2
30-10	Bulgaria	W 5-0	Budapest	Fr	Puskás 2, Deák, Budai, Rudas
20-11	Sweden	W 5-0	Budapest	Fr	Kocsis 3, Puskás, Deák
30-04-1950	Czechoslovakia	W 5-0	Budapest	Fr	Puskás 2, Kocsis 2, Szilágyi
14-05	Austria	L 3-5	Vienna	Fr	Kocsis, Puskás, Szilágyi
4-06	Poland	W 5-2	Warsaw	Fr	Szilágyi 3, Puskás 2
24-09	Albania	W 12-0	Budapest	Fr	Puskás 4, Budai 4, Palotás 2, Kocsis 2
29-10	Austria	W 4-3	Budapest	Fr	Puskás 3, Szilágyi
12-11	Bulgaria	D 1-1	Sofia	Fr	Szilágyi
27-05-1951	Poland	W 6-0	Budapest	Fr	Kocsis 2, Puskás 2, Sándor, Czibor
14-10	Czechoslovakia	W 2-1	Vitkovice	Fr	Kocsis 2
18-11	Finland	W 8-0	Budapest	Fr	Hidegkuti 3, Kocsis 2, Puskás 2, Czibor
15-06-1952	Poland	W 5-1	Warsaw	Fr	Kocsis 2, Puskás 2, Hidegkuti
22-06	Finland	W 6-1	Helsinki	Fr	Kocsis 3, Puskás, Bozsik, Palotás
15-07	Romania	W 2-1	Turku	OGr1	Kocsis, Czibor
21-07	Italy *	W 3-0	Helsinki	OGr2	Palotás 2, Kocsis
24-07	Turkey *	W 7-1	Kotka	OGqf	Kocsis 2, Puskás 2, Palotás, Lantos, Bozsik
28-07	Sweden	W 6-0	Helsinki	OGsf	Kocsis 2, Puskás, Palotás, Hidegkuti, OG
2-08	Yugoslavia	W 2-0	Helsinki	OGf	Puskás, Czibor
20-09	Switzerland	W 4-2	Berne	DGC	Puskás 2, Kocsis, Hidegkuti
19-10	Czechoslovakia	W 5-0	Budapest	Fr	Kocsis 3, Egresi, Hidegkuti
26-04-1953	Austria	D 1-1	Budapest	Fr	Czibor
17-05	Italy	W 3-0	Rome	DGC	Puskás 2, Hidegkuti
5-07	Sweden	W 4-2	Stockholm	Fr	Puskás, Budai, Kocsis, Hidegkuti
4-10	Czechoslovakia	W 5-1	Prague	Fr	Csordás 2, Hidegkuti, Tóth.M (II), Puskás

4-10	Bulgaria	D 1-1	Sofia	Fr	Szilágy
11-10	Austria	W 3-2	Vienna	Fr	Hidegkuti 2, Csordás
15-11	Sweden	D 2-2	Budapest	Fr	Palotás, Czibor
25-11	England	W 6-3	London	Fr	Hidegkuti 3, Puskás 2, Bozsik
12-02-1954	Egypt	W 3-0	Cairo	Fr	Puskás 2, Hidegkuti
11-04	Austria	W 1-0	Vienna	Fr	OG
23-05	England	W 7-1	Budapest	Fr	Puskás 2, Kocsis 2, Lantos, Hidegkuti, Tóth.J
17-06	South Korea	W 9-0	Zurich	WCr1	Kocsis 3, Puskás 2, Palotás 2, Lantos, Czibor
20-06	West Germany	W 8-3	Basle	WCr1	Kocsis 4, Hidegkuti 2, Puskás, Tóth.J
27-06	Brazil	W 4-2	Berne	WCqf	Kocsis 2, Hidegkuti, Lantos
30-06	Uruguay	W 4-2	Lausanne	WCsf	Kocsis 2, Czibor, Hidegkuti
4-07	West Germany	L 2-3	Berne	WCf	Puskás, Czibor
19-09	Romania	W 5-1	Budapest	Fr	Kocsis 2, Hidegkuti 2, Budai
26-09	Soviet Union	D 1-1	Moscow	Fr	Kocsis
10-10	Switzerland	W 3-0	Budapest	Fr	Kocsis 2, Bozsik
24-10	Czechoslovakia	W 4-1	Budapest	Fr	Kocsis 3, Sándor
14-11	Austria	W 4-1	Budapest	Fr	Czibor, Palotás, Kocsis, Sándor
8-12	Scotland	W 4-2	Glasgow	Fr	Bozsik, Hidegkuti, Sándor, Kocsis
24-04-1955	Austria	D 2-2	Vienna	DGC	Fenyvesi, Hidegkuti
8-05	Norway	W 5-0	Oslo	Fr	Palotás 2, Kocsis, Puskás, Tichy
11-05	Sweden	W 7-3	Stockholm	Fr	Kocsis 3, Puskás 2, Szojka, Hidegkuti
15-05	Denmark	W 6-0	Copenhagen	Fr	Sándor 3, Kocsis 2, Palotás
19-05	Finland	W 9-1	Helsinki	Fr	Palotás 3, Csordás 2, Tichy 2, Puskás, Tóth.J
29-05	Scotland	W 3-1	Budapest	Fr	Hidegkuti, Kocsis, Fenyvesi
17-09	Switzerland	W 5-4	Lausanne	DGC	Machos 2, Puskás 2, Kocsis
25-09	Soviet Union	D 1-1	Budapest	Fr	Puskás
2-10	Czechoslovakia	W 3-1	Prague	DGC	Kocsis, Czibor, Tichy
16-10	Austria	W 6-1	Budapest	DGC	Czibor 2, Tichy, Kocsis, Tóth.J, Puskás
13-11	Sweden	W 4-2	Budapest	Fr	Czibor 2, Tichy, Puskás
27-11	Italy	W 2-0	Budapest	DGC	Puskás, Tóth.J
19-02-1956	Turkey	L 1-3	Istanbul	Fr	Puskás
29-04	Yugoslavia	D 2-2	Budapest	DGC	Fenyvesi, Bozsik
20-05	Czechoslovakia	L 2-4	Budapest	DGC	Machos, Bozsik
3-06	Belgium	L 4-5	Brussels	Fr	Kocsis 2, Puskás, Budai
9-06	Portugal	D 2-2	Lisbon	Fr	Kocsis 2
15-07	Poland	W 4-1	Budapest	Fr	Kocsis 2, Szusza, Machos
16-09	Yugoslavia	W 3-1	Belgrade	DGC	Czibor, Kocsis, Puskás
23-09	Soviet Union	W 1-0	Moscow	Fr	Czibor
7-10	France	W 2-1	Paris	Fr	Machos, Kocsis
14-10	Austria	W 2-0	Vienna	Fr	Puskás, Sándor
12-06-1957	Norway	L 1-2	Oslo	WCq	Tichy
16-06	Sweden	D 0-0	Stockholm	Fr	
23-06	Bulgaria	W 4-1	Budapest	WCq	Machos 3, Bozsik
15-09	Bulgaria	W 2-1	Sofia	WCq	Hidegkuti 2
22-09	Soviet Union	L 1-2	Budapest	Fr	Hidegkuti
6-10	France	W 2-0	Budapest	Fr	Aspirány 2
10-11	Norway	W 5-0	Budapest	WCq	Csordás 2, Sándor, Machos, OG
22-12	West Germany	L 0-1	Hanover	Fr	
20-04-1958	Yugoslavia	W 2-0	Budapest	Fr	Sándor, Vasas
7-05	Scotland	D 1-1	Glasgow	Fr	Fenyvesi
8-06	Wales	D 1-1	Sandviken	WCr1	Bozsik
12-06	Sweden	L 1-2	Stockholm	WCr1	Tichy
15-06	Mexico	W 4-0	Sandviken	WCr1	Tichy 2, Sándor, Bencsics
17-06	Wales	L 1-2	Stockholm	WCr1	Tichy
14-09	Poland	W 3-1	Chorzow	Fr	Csordás, Tichy, Budai
28-09	Soviet Union	L 1-3	Moscow	ECr1	Göröcs
5-10	Yugoslavia	D 4-4	Zagreb	Fr	Sándor 3, Tichy
26-10	Romania	W 2-1	Bucharest	Fr	Vasas, Tichy
23-11	Belgium	W 3-1	Budapest	Fr	Tichy 2, Göröcs
19-04-1959	Yugoslavia	W 4-0	Budapest	Fr	Tichy 2, Sándor, Pál
1-05	East Germany	W 1-0	Dresden	Fr	Göröcs
28-06	Sweden	W 3-2	Budapest	Fr	Göröcs 2, Sándor
27-09	Soviet Union	L 0-1	Budapest	ECr1	
11-10	Yugoslavia	W 4-2	Belgrade	Fr	Albert 3, Bundzsák
25-10	Switzerland	W 8-0	Budapest	DGC	Tichy 4, Göröcs, Sándor, Albert
8-11	West Germany	W 4-3	Budapest	Fr	Tichy 2, Albert, Sándor
29-11	Italy	D 1-1	Florence	DGC	Tichy
22-05-1960	England	W 2-0	Budapest	Fr	Albert 2
5-06	Scotland	D 3-3	Budapest	Fr	Sándor, Göröcs, Tichy
27-07	Denmark	L 0-1	Copenhagen	Fr	
9-10	Yugoslavia	D 1-1	Budapest	Fr	Göröcs

30-10	Belgium	L 1-2	Brussels	Fr	Tichy
13-11	Poland	W 4-1	Budapest	Fr	Monostori 2, Göröcs, Sándor
20-11	Austria	W 2-0	Budapest	Fr	Göröcs, Machos
17-02-1961	Egypt	W 2-0	Cairo	Fr	Albert 2
16-04	East Germany	W 2-0	Budapest	WCq	Albert, Göröcs
30-04	Holland	W 3-0	Rotterdam	WCq	Sándor, Fenyvesi, Tichy
7-05	Yugoslavia	W 4-2	Belgrade	Fr	Tichy 2, Albert, OG
28-05	Wales	W 3-2	Budapest	Fr	Tichy 2, Solymosi
11-06	Austria	L 1-2	Budapest	Fr	Göröcs
10-09	East Germany	W 3-2	Berlin	WCq	Solymosi, Sándor, Tichy
8-10	Austria	L 1-2	Vienna	Fr	Tichy
22-10	Holland	D 3-3	Budapest	WCq	Monostori, Göröcs, Tichy
9-12	Chile	L 1-5	Santiago	Fr	Tichy
13-12	Chile	D 0-0	Santiago	Fr	
23-12	Uruguay	D 1-1	Montevideo	Fr	Solymosi
18-04-1962	Uruguay	D 1-1	Budapest	Fr	Bozsik
29-04	Turkey	W 2-1	Budapest	Fr	Solymosi, Göröcs
31-05	England	W 2-1	Rancagua	WCr1	Tichy, Albert
3-06	Bulgaria	W 6-1	Rancagua	WCr1	Albert 3, Tichy 2, Solymosi
6-06	Argentina	D 0-0	Rancagua	WCr1	
10-06	Czechoslovakia	L 0-1	Rancagua	WCqf	
24-06	Austria	W 2-1	Vienna	Fr	Tichy 2
2-09	Poland	W 2-0	Poznan	Fr	Tichy, Göröcs
14-10	Yugoslavia	L 0-1	Budapest	Fr	
28-10	Austria	W 2-0	Budapest	Fr	Göröcs, Sándor
7-11	Wales	W 3-1	Budapest	ECr1	Albert, Tichy, Sándor
11-11	France	W 3-2	Paris	Fr	Tichy 2, Rákosi
20-03-1963	Wales	D 1-1	Cardiff	ECr1	Tichy
5-05	Sweden	L 1-2	Stockholm	Fr	Albert
19-05	Denmark	W 6-0	Budapest	Fr	Göröcs, Fenyvesi, Monostori, Albert, Rákosi, Solymosi
2-06	Czechoslovakia	D 2-2	Prague	Fr	Tichy, Machos
22-09	Soviet Union	D 1-1	Moscow	Fr	Machos
6-10	Yugoslavia	L 0-2	Belgrade	Fr	
19-10	East Germany	W 2-1	Berlin	ECr2	Bene, Rákosi
27-10	Austria	W 2-1	Budapest	Fr	Albert, Sándor
3-11	East Germany	D 3-3	Budapest	ECr2	Bene, Sándor, Solymosi
25-04-1964	France	W 3-1	Paris	ECqf	Tichy 2, Albert
3-05	Austria	L 0-1	Vienna	Fr	
23-05	France	W 2-1	Budapest	ECqf	Sipos, Bene
17-06	Spain	L 1-2	Madrid	ECsf	Bene
20-06	Denmark	W 3-1	Barcelona	EC3p	Novák 2, Bene
4-10	Switzerland	W 2-0	Berne	Fr	Albert 2
11-10	Czechoslovakia	D 2-2	Budapest	Fr	Albert 2
25-10	Yugoslavia	W 2-1	Budapest	Fr	Albert 2
5-05-1965	England	L 0-1	London	Fr	
23-05	East Germany	D 1-1	Leipzig	WCq	Bene
13-06	Austria	W 1-0	Vienna	WCq	Fenyvesi
27-06	Italy	W 2-1	Budapest	Fr	Albert, Bene
5-09	Austria	W 3-0	Budapest	WCq	Farkas, Fenyvesi, Mészöly
9-10	East Germany	W 3-2	Budapest	WCq	Rákosi, Novák, Farkas
3-05-1966	Poland	D 1-1	Chorzow	Fr	Bene
8-05	Yugoslavia	L 0-2	Zagreb	Fr	
5-06	Switzerland	W 3-1	Budapest	Fr	Bene 2, Farkas
13-07	Portugal	L 1-3	Manchester	WCr1	Bene
15-07	Brazil	W 3-1	Liverpool	WCr1	Bene, Farkas, Mészöly
20-07	Bulgaria	W 3-1	Manchester	WCr1	Meszoly, Bene, OG
23-07	Soviet Union	L 1-2	Sunderland	WCqf	Bene
7-09	Holland	D 2-2	Rotterdan	ECq	Molnár.D, Mészöly
21-09	Denmark	W 6-0	Budapest	ECq	Albert 2, Mészöly, Bene, Farkas, Varga.Z
28-09	France	W 4-2	Budapest	Fr	Farkas 4
30-10	Austria	W 3-1	Budapest	Fr	Farkas 3
23-04-1967	Yugoslavia	W 1-0	Budapest	Fr	Bene
10-05	Holland	W 2-1	Budapest	ECq	Mészöly, Farkas
24-05	Denmark	W 2-0	Copenhagen	ECq	Albert, Bene
6-09	Austria	W 3-1	Vienna	Fr	Bene, Farkas, Varga.Z
27-09	East Germany	W 3-1	Budapest	ECq	Farkas 3
29-10	East Germany	L 0-1	Leipzig	ECq	
4-05-1968	Soviet Union	W 2-0	Budapest	ECqf	Farkas, Göröcs
11-05	Soviet Union	L 0-3	Moscow	ECqf	
25-05-1969	Czechoslovakia	W 2-0	Budapest	WCq	Dunai, Albert
8-06	Rep. Ireland	W 2-1	Dublin	WCq	Dunai, Bene

15-06	Denmark	L 2-3	Copenhagen	WCq	Bene, Farkas
14-09	Czechoslovakia	D 3-3	Prague	WCq	Bene, Dunai, Fazekas
24-09	Sweden	L 0-2	Stockholm	Fr	
22-10	Denmark	W 3-0	Budapest	WCq	Bene 2, Szücs
5-11	Rep. Ireland	W 4-0	Budapest	WCq	Halmosi, Bene, Puskás.L, Kocsis.L
3-12	Czechoslovakia	L 1-4	Marseille	WCq	Kocsis.L
12-04-1970	Yugoslavia	D 2-2	Belgrade	Fr	Fazekas, Bene
2-05	Poland	W 2-0	Budapest	Fr	Fazekas, Karsai
16-05	Sweden	L 1-2	Budapest	Fr	Fazekas
9-09	West Germany	L 1-3	Nuremberg	Fr	Fazekas
27-09	Austria	D 1-1	Budapest	Fr	Vidáts
7-10	Norway	W 3-1	Oslo	ECq	Bene, Nagy.L, OG
15-11	Switzerland	W 1-0	Basle	Fr	Fazekas
4-04-1971	Austria	W 2-0	Vienna	Fr	Bene
24-04	France	D 1-1	Budapest	ECq	Kocsis.L
19-05	Bulgaria	L 0-3	Sofia	ECq	
21-07	Brazil	D 0-0	Rio de Janeiro	Fr	
1-09	Yugoslavia	W 2-1	Budapest	Fr	Szöke, OG
25-09	Bulgaria	W 2-0	Budapest	ECq	Juhász.P, Vidáts
9-10	France	W 2-0	Paris	ECq	Bene, Zámbó
27-10	Norway	W 4-0	Budapest	ECq	Bene 2, Dunai, Szücs
14-11	Malta	W 2-0	Gzira	WCq	Bene 2
12-01-1972	Spain	L 0-1	Madrid	Fr	
29-03	West Germany	L 0-2	Budapest	Fr	
29-04	Romania	D 1-1	Budapest	ECqf	Branikovits
6-05	Malta	W 3-0	Budapest	WCq	Kocsis.L, Bene, Juhász.I
14-05	Romania	D 2-2	Bucharest	ECqf	Szöke, Kocsis.L
17-05	Romania	W 2-1	Belgrade	ECqf	Kocsis.L, Szöke
25-05	Sweden	D 0-0	Stockholm	WCq	
14-06	Soviet Union	L 0-1	Brussels	ECsf	
17-06	Belgium	L 1-2	Liege	EC3p	Kü
15-10	Austria	D 2-2	Vienna	WCq	Dunai, Kocsis.L
29-04-1973	Austria	D 2-2	Budaest	WCq	Zámbó, Bálint
16-05	East Germany	L 1-2	Karl-Marx-Stadt	Fr	OG
13-06	Sweden	D 3-3	Budapest	WCq	Kozma, Vidáts, Zámbó
26-09	Yugoslavia	D 1-1	Belgrade	Fr	Bene
13-10	Denmark	D 2-2	Copenhagen	Fr	Fazekas 2
21-11	East Germany	L 0-1	Budapest	Fr	
31-03-1974	Bulgaria	W 3-1	Zalaegerszeg	Fr	Fazekas 2, Bene
17-04	West Germany	L 0-5	Dortmund	Fr	
29-05	Yugoslavia	W 3-0	Szekesfehervar	Fr	Máté 2, Fazekas
28-09	Austria	L 0-1	Vienna	Fr	
13-10	Luxembourg	W 4-2	Luxembourg	ECq	Nagy.L 2, Horváth, Bálint
30-10	Wales	L 0-2	Cardiff	ECq	
10-11	Bulgaria	D 0-0	Varna	Fr	
4-12	Switzerland	W 1-0	Szolnok	Fr	Fazekas
26-03-1975	France	L 0-2	Paris	Fr	
2-04	Austria	D 0-0	Vienna	ECq	
16-04	Wales	L 1-2	Budapest	ECq	Branikovits
10-08	Iran	W 2-1	Tehran	Fr	Váradi, Nagy.L
24-09	Austria	W 2-1	Budapest	ECq	Nyilasi, Pusztai
8-10	Poland	L 2-4	Lodz	Fr	Nagy.L, Pusztai
15-10	Czechoslovakia	D 1-1	Bratislava	Fr	Váradi
19-10	Luxembourg	W 8-1	Szombathely	ECq	Nyilasi 5, Pintér, Wollek, Váradi
27-03-1976	Argentina	W 2-0	Budapest	Fr	Nyilasi, Fazekas
17-04	Yugoslavia	D 0-0	Banja Luka	Fr	
30-04	Switzerland	W 1-0	Lausanne	Fr	Fazekas
22-05	France	W 1-0	Budapest	Fr	Fekete
26-05	Soviet Union	D 1-1	Budapest	Fr	Fekete
12-06	Austria	W 2-0	Budapest	Fr	Magyar, Váradi
8-09	Sweden	D 1-1	Stockholm	Fr	Ebedli
22-09	East Germany	D 1-1	Berlin	Fr	Fazekas
9-10	Greece	D 1-1	Athens	WCq	Kereki
13-10	Austria	W 4-2	Vienna	Fr	Nyilasi 2, Kereki 2
9-02-1977	Peru	L 2-3	Lima	Fr	Töröcsik, Kereki
22-02	Mexico	D 1-1	Mexico City	Fr	Töröcsik
27-02	Argentina	L 1-5	Buenos Aires	Fr	Zombori
15-03	Iran	W 2-0	Tehran	Fr	Fazekas, Nyilasi
27-03	Spain	D 1-1	Alicante	Fr	Pusztai
13-04	Poland	W 2-1	Budapest	Fr	Nyilasi 2
20-04	Czechoslovakia	W 2-0	Budapest	Fr	Váradi, Kovács.I

Date	Opponent	Result	Venue	Comp	Scorers
30-04	Soviet Union	W 2-1	Budapest	WCq	Nyilasi, Kereki
18-05	Soviet Union	L 0-2	Tbilisi	WCq	
28-05	Greece	W 3-0	Budapest	WCq	Pusztai, Nyilasi, Fazekas
5-10	Yugoslavia	W 4-3	Budapest	Fr	Töröcsik 2, Váradi, Kereki
12-10	Sweden	W 3-0	Budapest	Fr	Nyilasi, Váradi, Töröcsik
29-10	Bolivia	W 6-0	Budapest	WCq	Nyilasi, Töröcsik, Zombori, Váradi, Pintér, Nagy.L
9-11	Czechoslovakia	D 1-1	Prague	Fr	Halász
30-11	Bolivia	W 3-2	La Paz	WCq	Töröcsik, Halász, OG
15-04-1978	Czechoslovakia	W 2-1	Budapest	Fr	Nyilasi, OG
24-05	England	L 1-4	London	Fr	Nagy.L
2-06	Argentina	L 1-2	Buenos Aires	WCr1	Csapó
6-06	Italy	L 1-3	Mar del Plata	WCr1	Tóth.A
10-06	France	L 1-3	Mar del Plata	WCr1	Zombori
20-09	Finland	L 1-2	Helsinki	ECq	Tieber
11-10	Soviet Union	W 2-0	Budapest	ECq	Váradi, Szokolai
29-10	Greece	L 1-4	Salonica	ECq	Váradi
15-11	West Germany	D 0-0	Frankfurt	Fr	Abandoned after 60 mins
28-03-1979	East Germany	W 3-0	Budapest	Fr	Töröcsik, Tieber, Tatar
4-04	Poland	D 1-1	Chorzow	Fr	Tatár
2-05	Greece	D 0-0	Budapest	ECq	
19-05	Soviet Union	D 2-2	Tbilisi	ECq	Tatár, Pusztai
12-09	Czechoslovakia	W 2-1	Nyiregyhaza	Fr	Tatár, Kuti
26-09	Austria	L 1-3	Vienna	Fr	Fekete
17-10	Finland	W 3-1	Debrecen	ECq	Fekete 2, Tatár
26-10	United States	L 0-2	Budapest	Fr	
26-03-1980	Poland	W 2-1	Budapest	Fr	Fazekas, Töröcsik
30-04	Czechoslovakia	L 0-1	Kosice	Fr	
31-05	Scotland	W 3-1	Budapest	Fr	Töröcsik 2, Kereki
4-06	Austria	D 1-1	Budapest	Fr	Kiss.L
20-08	Sweden	W 2-0	Budapest	Fr	Burcsa, OG
27-08	Soviet Union	L 1-4	Budapest	Fr	Pásztor
24-09	Spain	D 2-2	Budapest	Fr	Kiss.L, Bodonyi
8-10	Austria	L 1-3	Vienna	Fr	Bodonyi
19-11	East Germany	L 0-2	Halle	Fr	
15-04-1981	Spain	W 3-0	Valencia	Fr	Kiss.L, Bodonyi, Nyilasi
28-04	Switzerland	D 2-2	Lucerne	WCq	Bálint, Müller
13-05	Romania	W 1-0	Budapest	WCq	Fazekas
20-05	Norway	W 2-1	Oslo	WCq	Kiss.L 2
6-06	England	L 1-3	Budapest	WCq	Garaba
23-09	Romania	D 0-0	Bucharest	WCq	
14-10	Switzerland	W 3-0	Budapest	WCq	Nyilasi 2, Fazekas
31-10	Norway	W 4-1	Budapest	WCq	Kiss.L 2, Bálint, Fazekas
18-11	England	L 0-1	London	WCq	
11-02-1982	New Zealand	W 2-1	Auckland	Fr	Izsó, Bodonyi
14-02	New Zealand	W 2-1	Christchurch	Fr	Pölöskei, Izsó
24-03	Austria	L 2-3	Budapest	Fr	Váradi, Nyilasi
18-04	Peru	L 1-2	Budapest	Fr	Szentes
15-06	El Salvador	W 10-1	Elche	WCr1	Kiss.L 3, Fazekas 2, Nyilasi 2, Tóth.J, Szentes, Pölöskei
18-06	Argentina	L 1-4	Alicante	WCr1	Pölöskei
22-06	Belgium	D 1-1	Elche	WCr1	Varga.J
22-09	Turkey	W 5-0	Gyor	Fr	Garaba, Burcsa, Budavári, Kiss.S, Póczik
6-10	France	L 0-1	Paris	Fr	
27-03-1983	Luxembourg	W 6-2	Luxembourg	ECq	Póczik 3, Nyilasi, Pölöskei, Hannich
13-04	Portugal	D 0-0	Coimbra	Fr	
17-04	Luxembourg	W 6-2	Budapest	ECq	Nyilasi 2, Hajszán, Kiss.L, Szentes, Burcsa
27-04	England	L 0-2	London	ECq	
15-05	Greece	L 2-3	Budapest	ECq	Nyilasi, Hajszán
1-06	Denmark	L 1-3	Copenhagen	ECq	Nyilasi
7-09	West Germany	D 1-1	Budapest	Fr	Nyilasi
12-10	England	L 0-3	Budapest	ECq	
26-10	Denmark	W 1-0	Budapest	ECq	Kiss.S
3-12	Greece	D 2-2	Salonica	ECq	Kardos.J, Töröcsik
18-01-1984	Spain	W 1-0	Cadiz	Fr	Garaba
31-03	Yugoslavia	L 1-2	Subotica	Fr	Gyimesi
4-04	Turkey	W 6-0	Istanbul	Fr	Mészáros 2, Esterházy 2, Kardos.J, Bodonyi
23-05	Norway	D 0-0	Szekesfehervar	Fr	
31-05	Spain	D 1-1	Budapest	Fr	Nagy.A
6-06	Belgium	D 2-2	Brussels	Fr	Hajszán, Nyilasi
22-08	Switzerland	W 3-0	Budapest	Fr	Esterházy 2, Bodonyi
25-08	Mexico	L 0-2	Budapest	Fr	

26-09	Austria	W 3-1	Budapest	WCq	Nagy.A, Esterházy, Kardos.J
17-10	Holland	W 2-1	Rotterdam	WCq	Détári, Esterházy
17-11	Cyprus	W 2-1	Limassol	WCq	Róth, Nyilasi
29-01-1985	West Germany	W 1-0	Hamburg	Fr	Péter
3-04	Cyprus	W 2-0	Budapest	WCq	Nyilasi, Szokolai
17-04	Austria	W 3-0	Vienna	WCq	Kiprich 2, Détári
14-05	Holland	L 0-1	Budapest	WCq	
16-10	Wales	W 3-0	Cardiff	Fr	Esterházy, Hajszan, Détári
8-12	South Korea	W 1-0	Irapuato	Fr	Kiprich
11-12	Algeria	W 3-1	Monterrey	Fr	Zoltan, Kovács.K, Détári
14-12	Mexico	L 0-2	Mexico City	Fr	
2-02-1986	Qatar	W 3-0	Doha	Fr	Hannich, Kiprich, Détári
16-03	Brazil	W 3-0	Budapest	Fr	Détári, Kovács.K, Esterházy
2-06	Soviet Union	L 0-6	Irapuato	WCr1	
6-06	Canada	W 2-0	Irapuato	WCr1	Esterházy, Détári
9-06	France	L 0-3	Leon	WCr1	
9-09	Norway	D 0-0	Oslo	Fr	
15-10	Holland	L 0-1	Budapest	ECq	
12-11	Greece	L 1-2	Athens	ECq	Boda
8-02-1987	Cyprus	W 1-0	Nicosia	ECq	Boda
29-04	Holland	L 0-2	Rotterdam	ECq	
17-05	Poland	W 5-3	Budapest	ECq	Détári 2, Vincze.I, Péter, Preszeller
28-07	East Germany	D 0-0	Leipzig	Fr	
9-09	Scotland	L 0-2	Glasgow	Fr	
23-09	Poland	L 2-3	Warsaw	ECq	Bognár, Mészáros
14-10	Greece	W 3-0	Budapest	ECq	Détári, Bognár, Mészáros
18-11	West Germany	D 0-0	Budapest	Fr	
2-12	Cyprus	W 1-0	Budapest	ECq	Kiprich
16-03-1988	Turkey	W 1-0	Budapest	Fr	Kiprich
26-03	Belgium	L 0-3	Brussels	Fr	
27-04	England	D 0-0	Budapest	Fr	
4-05	Iceland	W 3-0	Budapest	Fr	Vincze.I, Sallai, Kovács.K
10-05	Denmark	D 2-2	Budapest	Fr	Kiprich, Bognár
17-05	Austria	L 0-4	Budapest	Fr	
31-08	Austria	D 0-0	Linz	Fr	
21-09	Iceland	W 3-0	Reykjavik	Fr	Kiprich 2, Vincze.I
19-10	Nth. Ireland	W 1-0	Budapest	WCq	Vincze.I
15-11	Greece	L 0-3	Athens	Fr	
11-12	Malta	D 2-2	Ta'Qali	WCq	Vincze.I, Kiprich
8-03-1989	Rep. Ireland	D 0-0	Budapest	WCq	
4-04	Switzerland	W 3-0	Budapest	Fr	Détári, Kovács.E, Bognár
12-04	Malta	D 1-1	Budapest	WCq	Boda
26-04	Italy	L 0-4	Taranto	Fr	
4-06	Rep. Ireland	L 0-2	Dublin	WCq	
6-09	Nth. Ireland	W 2-1	Belfast	WCq	Kovács.K, Bognár
11-10	Spain	D 2-2	Budapest	WCq	Pinter 2
25-10	Greece	D 1-1	Budapest	Fr	Szekeres
15-11	Spain	L 0-4	Seville	WCq	
20-03-1990	United States	W 2-0	Budapest	Fr	Petres, Limperger
28-03	France	L 1-3	Budapest	Fr	Pinter
11-04	Austria	L 0-3	Salzburg	Fr	
28-05	Arab Emirates	W 3-0	Nimes	Fr	Kovács.K 3
2-06	Colombia	W 3-1	Budapest	Fr	Kovács.K 2, Bognár
5-09	Turkey	W 4-1	Budapest	Fr	Kovács.K, Kozma, Kiprich 2
12-09	England	L 0-1	London	Fr	
10-10	Norway	D 0-0	Bergen	ECq	
17-10	Italy	D 1-1	Budapest	ECq	Disztl
31-10	Cyprus	W 4-2	Budapest	ECq	Lorincz, OG, Kiprich 2
19-02-1991	Argentina	L 0-2	Rosario	Fr	
27-03	Spain	W 4-2	Santander	Fr	Kiprich 2, Lórincz 2
3-04	Cyprus	W 2-0	Limassol	ECq	Szalma, Kiprich
17-04	Soviet Union	L 0-1	Budapest	ECq	
1-05	Italy	L 1-3	Salerno	ECq	Bognár
11-09	Rep. Ireland	L 1-2	Gyor	Fr	Kovacs.K
25-09	Soviet Union	D 2-2	Moscow	ECq	Kiprich 2
9-10	Belgium	L 0-2	Szekesfehervar	Fr	
30-10	Norway	D 0-0	Szombathely	ECq	
5-12	Mexico	L 0-3	Leon	Fr	
8-12	El Salvador	D 1-1	San Salvador	Fr	Hamori
25-03-1992	Austria	W 2-1	Budapest	Fr	Kiprich, Kovacs.K
29-04	Ukraine	W 3-1	Uzgorod	Fr	Sallai, Kiprich 2

12-05	England	L 0-1	Budapest	Fr	
3-06	Iceland	L 1-2	Budapest	WCq	Kiprich
26-08	Ukraine	W 2-1	Nyiregyhaza	Fr	Kovacs.K, Nagy
9-09	Luxembourg	W 3-0	Luxembourg	WCq	Detari, Kovacs.K 2
23-09	Israel	D 0-0	Budapest	Fr	
11-10	Qatar	W 4-1	Doha	Fr	Kiprich 3, Kovacs.K
13-10	Qatar	D 1-1	Doha	Fr	Kovacs.K
11-11	Greece	D 0-0	Salonica	WCq	
7-03-1993	Japan	W 1-0	Fukuoka	Fr	Kiprich
10-03	USA	D 0-0	Nagoya	Fr	
31-03	Greece	L 0-1	Budapest	WCq	
15-04	Sweden	L 0-2	Budapest	Fr	
28-04	Russia	L 0-3	Moscow	WCq	
29-05	Rep. Ireland	W 4-2	Dublin	Fr	Hamar 2, Balog, Urban
16-06	Iceland	L 0-2	Reykjavik	WCq	
8-09	Russia	L 1-3	Budapest	WCq	OG
27-10	Luxembourg	W 1-0	Budapest	WCq	Detari
9-03-1994	Switzerland	L 1-2	Budapest	Fr	Eszenyi
23-03	Austria	D 1-1	Linz	Fr	Illes
6-04	Slovenia	L 0-1	Szombathely	Fr	
20-04	Denmark	L 1-3	Copenhagen	Fr	Vincze
4-05	Poland	L 2-3	Krakow	Fr	Vincze, Klausz
18-05	Croatia	D 2-2	Gyor	Fr	Kereszturi
1-06	Holland	L 1-7	Eindhoven	Fr	Illes
8-06	Belgium	L 1-3	Brussels	Fr	Jagodics
7-09	Turkey	D 2-2	Budapest	ECq	Kiprich, Halmai
12-10	Germany	D 0-0		Fr	
16-11	Sweden	L 0-2	Stockholm	ECq	
10-12	Mexico	L 1-5	Los Angeles	Fr	Klaus
29-03-1995	Switzerland	D 2-2	Budapest	ECq	Kiprich, Illés
26-04	Sweden	W 1-0	Budapest	ECq	Halmai
11-06	Iceland	L 1-2	Reykjavik	ECq	Vincze

ICELAND

A small population in a remote island closer to Greenland than mainland Europe, where football can only be played in the summer months because it is otherwise too cold or too dark, would seem to be a poor recipe for football success. For years this stereotype did hold true of Iceland, but recently the national team have emerged, if not as a footballing power, then as likely to cause more than the odd upset.

THE ORDER OF MERIT

		All			League			Cup		Europe		
	Team	G	S	B	G	S	B	G	S	G	S	B
1	KR Reykjavík	28	25	12	20	22	12	8	3	-	-	-
2	Valur Reykjavík	27	19	17	19	16	17	8	3	-	-	
3	Fram Reykjavík	25	23	15	18	17	15	7	6	-	-	-
4	IA Akranes	21	19	8	15	11	8	6	8	-	-	-
5	Víkingur Reykjavík	6	8	8	5	7	8	1	1	-	-	-
6	IBK Keflavík	5	7	7	4	2	7	1	5	-	-	-
7	IBV Vestmannaeyjar	4	6	6	1	3	6	3	3	-	-	-
8	KA Akureyri	1	1	-	1	-	-	-	1	-	-	-
9	IBA Akureyri	1	-	4	-	-	4	1	-	-	-	-
10	FH Hafnarfjördhur	-	5	-	-	3	-	-	2	-	-	-
11	UBK Kópavogur	-	1	1	-	-	1	-	1	-	-	-
12	Grindavík	-	1	-	-	-	-	-	1	-	-	-
	Vídir Gardur	-	1	-	-	-	-	-	1	-	-	-
13	Thór Akureyri	-	-	2	-	-	2	-	-	-	-	-

To the end of the 1994 season

Its league football, however, though predating the formation of the national side by some 34 years, has never been of a very high standard. Reykjavik, dominating the island as it does, provided all of the winners until IA Akranes broke the stranglehold in 1951, and since then teams from the smaller towns have fared quite reasonably. Football is a very popular game and crowds of over 2,000 are not uncommon for league games, though the average is nearer 500.

For international matches it is not uncommon to see the Laugardalsvöllur full to capacity, and in recent years they have been treated to some excellent games. The national side first made an appearance in a match against Denmark in 1946, but for the next quarter of a century matches were sporadic. The 1958 World Cup and 1964 European Championship were both entered, but it was not until the 1970s that Iceland regularly took part in these two competitions.

Results were not impressive at first, but as experience was gained they began to improve. East Germany, Wales, Northern Ireland, Norway, Austria, Turkey and most recently Spain and Hungary have all been beaten in Reykjavik. Some very good players have played for the national side, and most are eager to join clubs in the rest of Europe. Arnor Gudjohnsen appeared in the UEFA Cup final for Anderlecht in 1984 and Asgeir Sigurvinsson did so in 1990 for Stuttgart. He was joined there in 1989 by Eyjölfur Sverrisson, who was part of the team which won the 1992 Bundesliga. Others who have made it abroad include Iceland's most capped player, Atli Edvaldsson, who spent eight years in Germany.

Iceland have not come close to qualifying for a major tournament, but more and more they are affecting the outcome of the qualifying groups. Their progress serves as a model for countries such as Malta, Luxembourg and Cyprus as to how the future of their game could be.

Population: 256,000
Area, sq km: 103,000
% in urban areas: 90.5%
Capital city: Reykjavík

Knattspyrnusamband Island
PO Box 8511
IS-104 Reykjavík
Iceland
Tel: + 354 1 814444
Fax: + 354 1 689793

Year of formation	1947
Affiliation to FIFA	1929
Affiliation to UEFA	1954
Registered clubs	110
Registered players	20,400
Registered coaches	120
Registered referees	524
National stadium	Laugardalsvöllur, Reykjavik 14,000
National colours	Blue/White/Blue
Reserve colours	White/Blue/White
Season	April - October

THE RECORD

WORLD CUP

1930-54	Did not enter
1958	QT 3rd/3 in group 2
1962-70	Did not enter
1974	QT 4th/4 in group 3
1978	QT 4th/4 in group 4
1982	QT 4th/5 in group 3
1986	QT 4th/4 in group 7
1990	QT 5th/5 in group 3
1994	QT 3rd/5 in group 5

EUROPEAN CHAMPIONSHIP

1960	Did not enter
1964	1st round
1968	Did not enter
1972	Did not enter
1976	QT 4th/4 in group 7
1980	QT 5th/5 in group 4
1984	QT 4th/5 in group 7
1988	QT 4th/5 in group 3
1992	QT 4th/5 in group 1
1996	QT group 3

EUROPEAN CLUB COMPETITIONS

European Cup
2nd round - Valur 1968 IA Akranes 1976
Cup Winners Cup
2nd round - Fram 1986 1991
UEFA Cup
2nd round - IBV Vestmannaeyjar 1979 IBK Keflavik 1980

CLUB DIRECTORY

REYKJAVIK (Population - 137,000)

Knattspyrnufélagid Fram (1908)
Laugardalsvöllur 14,000 – Blue/White

Fylkir (1967)
Fylkisvöllur 1,000 – Orange/White
IR Reykjavík (1907)
(Idróttafélag Reykjavikur)
IR-völlur – White/Blue

KR Reykjavík (1899)
(Knattspyrnufélag Reykjavikur)
KR-völlur 2,000 – Black & white stripes/Black

Thróttur (1949)
Thróttur-völlur – Red and white stripes/White

Knattspyrnufélagid Valur (1911)
Hlidarendi 3,000 – Red/White

Knattspyrnufélagid Víkingur (1908)
Víkingsvöllur 2,000 – Red & black stripes/Black

KOPAVOGUR (Population - 15,000)

UBK Kópavogur (1950)
(Ungmennafélagid Breidablik Kópavogur)
Idróttsvöllur – Green/White

AKUREYRI (Population - 14,000)

KA Akureyri (1974)
(Knattspyrnufélag Akureyri)
Akureyrivöllur 4,000 – Yellow/Blue
Previous name - IBA Akureyri until 1974

Idrottafélagid Thór (1974)
Akureyrivöllur 4,000 – White/Red
Previous name - IBA Akureyri until 1974

HAFNARFJÖRDUR (Population - 14,000)

FH Hafnarfjördur (1929)
(Fimleikafélag Hafnarfjördur)
Kaplakriki 3,000 – White/Black, red & black trim
Previous name - IBH Hafnarfjördur until 1961

Hauker (1961)
Idróttsvöllur – Red/White
Previous name - IBH Hafnarfjördur until 1961

KEFLAVIK (Population - 13,000)

IBK Keflavík (1946)
(Idrótta Bandelag Keflavíkur)
Keflavíkurvöllur 5,000 – Blue/White

VESTMANNAEYJAR

IBV Vestmannaeyjar (1946)
(Idrótta Bandelag Vestmannaeyjar)
Hásteinvöllur 1,000 – White, black trim

AKRANES

IA Akranes (1946)
(Idróttabandalag Akranes)
Akranesvöllur 3,000 – Yellow/Black

OLAFSFJÖRDUR

Idróttafélagig Leiftur (1931)
Idróttsvöllur 1,000 – Yellow/Green

GARDUR

Knattspyrnufélagid Vidir (1936)
Gardurvöllur 1,000 – Blue/White

HUSAVIK

Idróttafélagid Völsungur (1927)
Idróttsvöllur 2,000 – Green & white halves/Green

GARDABÆR

Ungemennafélagid Stjarnan (1960)
Stjarnanvöllur 2,000 – Blue/White

ICELANDIC LEAGUE CHAMPIONSHIP

1912aj	KR Reykjavik 3 Fram Reykjavík 3 IBV Vestmannaeyjar 0
1913	Fram Reykjavík declared winners
1914	Fram Reykjavík declared winners
1915aj	Fram Reykjavík 4 KR Reykjavík 2 Valur Reykjavík 0
1916	Fram Reykjavík 3 KR Reykjavík 3 Valur Reykjavík 0
1917	Fram Reykjavík 4 KR Reykjavík 2 Valur Reykjavík 0
1918ab	Fram Reykjavík 6 Víkingur Reykjavík 4 Valur Reykjavík 2
1919	KR Reykjavík 5 Fram Reykjavík 4 Víkingur Reykjavík 3
1920aj	Víkingur Reykjavík 4 KR Reykjavík 2 Fram Reykjavík 0
1921	Fram Reykjavík 4 Víkingur Reykjavík 2 KR Reykjavík 0
1922	Fram Reykjavík 4 Víkingur Reykjavík 1 KR Reykjavík 1
1923ab	Fram Reykjavík 6 KR Reykjavík 4 Valur Reykjavík 1
1924	Víkingur Reykjavík 6 Fram Reykjavík 4 KR Reykjavík 1
1925	Fram Reykjavík 5 Víkingur Reykjavík 4 KR Reykjavík 3
1926al	KR Reykjavík 7 Fram Reykjavík 7 Víkingur Reykjavík 4
1927ab	KR Reykjavík 6 Valur Reykjavík 4 Víkingur Reykjavík 2
1928aj	KR Reykjavík 4 Valur Reykjavík 2 Fram Reykjavík 0
1929a3	KR Reykjavík 8 Valur Reykjavík 4 IBV Vestmannaeyjar 4
1930al	Valur Reykjavík 8 KR Reykjavík 6 IBV Vestmannaeyjar 4
1931ab	KR Reykjavík 6 Valur Reykjavík 4 Víkingur Reykjavík 2
1932al	KR Reykjavík 7 Valur Reykjavík 5 IBA Akureyri 4
1933ab	Valur Reykjavík 6 KR Reykjavík 4 Fram Reykjavík 2
1934al	KR Reykjavík 7 Valur Reykjavík 6 Fram Reykjavík 5
1935ab	Valur Reykjavík 5 KR Reykjavík 4 Fram Reykjavík 3
1936	Valur Reykjavík 5 KR Reykjavík 4 Fram Reykjavík 3
1937aj	Valur Reykjavík 4 KR Reykjavík 2 Fram Reykjavík 0
1938ab	Valur Reykjavík 5 Víkingur Reykjavík 3 Fram Reykjavík 2
1939	Fram Reykjavík 4 KR Reykjavík 3 Víkingur Reykjavík 3
1940	Valur Reykjavík 5 Víkingur Reykjavík 4 KR Reykjavík 2
1941al	KR Reykjavík 7 Valur Reykjavík 6 Víkingur Reykjavík 3
1942	Valur Reykjavík 6 Fram Reykjavík 6 KR Reykjavík 4
1943	Valur Reykjavík 8 KR Reykjavík 4 Fram Reykjavík 4
1944ab	Valur Reykjavík 5 KR Reykjavík 4 Víkingur Reykjavík 2
1945	Valur Reykjavík 6 KR Reykjavík 4 Fram Reykjavík 1
1946ac	Fram Reykjavík 9 KR Reykjavík 8 Valur Reykjavík 7

1947a1 Fram Reykjavík 7 Valur Reykjavík 6 KR Reykjavík 5
1948ab KR Reykjavík 5 Víkingur Reykjavík 4 Valur Reykjavík 2
1949a1 KR Reykjavík 5 Fram Reykjavík 5 Valur Reykjavík 4
1950 KR Reykjavík 6 Fram Reykjavík 5 IA Akranes 3
1951 IA Akranes 6 Valur Reykjavík 4 KR Reykjavík 4
1952 KR Reykjavík 7 IA Akranes 6 Fram Reykjavík 4
1953 IA Akranes * Valur Reykjavík
1954ac IA Akranes 9 KR Reykjavík 8 Fram Reykjavík 5
1955 KR Reykjavík 9 IA Akranes 8 Valur Reykjavík 6
1956 Valur Reykjavík 9 KR Reykjavík 8 IA Akranes 7
1957 IA Akranes 10 Fram Reykjavík 7 Valur Reykjavík 6
1958 IA Akranes 9 KR Reykjavík 8 Valur Reykjavík 6
1959d KR Reykjavík 20 IA Akranes 11 Valur Reykjavík 11
1960 IA Akranes 15 KR Reykjavík 13 Fram Reykjavík 11
1961 KR Reykjavík 17 IA Akranes 15 Valur Reykjavík 12
1962 Fram Reykjavík 13 Valur Reykjavík 13 IA Akranes 12
1963 KR Reykjavík 15 IA Akranes 13 Valur Reykjavík 10
1964 IBK Keflavík 15 IA Akranes 12 KR Reykjavík 10
1965 KR Reykjavík 13 IA Akranes 13 IBK Keflavík 11
1966 Valur Reykjavík 14 IBK Keflavík 14 IBA Akureyri 12
1967 Valur Reykjavík 14 Fram Reykjavík 14 IBA Akureyri 13
1968 KR Reykjavík 15 Fram Reykjavík 12 IBA Akureyri 10
1969e IBK Keflavík 15 IA Akranes 14 KR Reykjavík 12
1970f IA Akranes 20 Fram Reykjavík 16 IBK Keflavík 16
1971 IBK Keflavík 20 IBV Vestmannaeyjar 20 Fram Reykjavík 15
1972 Fram Reykjavík 22 IBV Vestmannaeyjar 18 IBK Keflavík 15
1973 IBK Keflavík 26 Valur Reykjavík 21 IBV Vestmannaeyjar 17
1974 IA Akranes 23 IBK Keflavík 19 Valur Reykjavík 14
1975 IA Akranes 19 Fram Reykjavík 17 Valur Reykjavík 16
1976g Valur Reykjavík 25 Fram Reykjavík 24 IA Akranes 21
1977h IA Akranes 28 Valur Reykjavík 27 IBV Vestmannaeyjar 21
1978 Valur Reykjavík 35 IA Akranes 28 IBK Keflavík 20
1979 IBV Vestmannaeyjar 24 IA Akranes 23 Valur Reykjavík 23
1980 Valur Reykjavík 28 Fram Reykjavík 25 Víkingur Reykjavík 20
1981 Víkingur Reykjavík 25 Fram Reykjavík 23 IA Akranes 22
1982 Víkingur Reykjavík 23 IBV Vestmannaeyjar 22 KR Reykjavík 21
1983 IA Akranes 24 KR Reykjavík 20 UBK Kópavogur 19
1984h2 IA Akranes 38 Valur Reykjavík 28 IBK Keflavík 27
1985 Valur Reykjavík 38 IA Akranes 36 Thór Akureyri 35
1986 Fram Reykjavík 38 Valur Reykjavík 38 IA Akranes 30
1987 Valur Reykjavík 37 Fram Reykjavík 32 IA Akranes 30
1988 Fram Reykjavík 49 Valur Reykjavík 41 IA Akranes 32
1989 KA Akureyri 34 FH Hafnarfjördhur 32 Fram Reykjavík 32
1990 Fram Reykjavík 38 KR Reykjavík 38 IBV Vestmannaeyjar 37
1991 Víkingur Reykjavík 37 Fram Reykjavík 37 KR Reykjavík 28
1992 IA Akranes 40 KR Reykjavík 37 Thór Akureyri 35
1993 IA Akranes 49 FH Hafnarfjördhur 40 IBK Keflavík 27
1994 IA Akranes 39 FH Hafnarfjördhur 33 IBK Keflavík 31

* Championship play-off matches

1912	KR	3-1	Fram
1916	Fram	3-1	KR
1926	KR	8-2	Fram
1942	Valur	0-0 1-0	Fram
1949	KR	2-1	Fram
1953	IA Akranes	3-2	Valur
1962	Fram	1-0	Valur
1965	KR	2-1	IA Akranes
1966	Valur	2-2 2-1	IB Keflavík
1967	Valur	2-0	Fram
1971	IB Keflavík	4-0	IB Vestmannaeyjar

ICELANDIC CUP FINALS

1960	KR Reykjavík	2-0	Fram Reykjavík
1961	KR Reykjavík	4-3	IA Akranes
1962	KR Reykjavík	3-0	Fram Reykjavík
1963	KR Reykjavík	4-1	IA Akranes
1964	KR Reykjavík	4-0	IA Akranes
1965	Valur Reykjavík	5-3	IA Akranes
1966	KR Reykjavík	1-0	Valur Reykjavík
1967	KR Reykjavík	3-0	Víkingur Reykjavík
1968	IBV Vestmannaeyjar	2-1	KR Reykjavík
1969	IBA Akureyri	1-1 3-2	IA Akranes
1970	Fram Reykjavík	2-1	IBV Vestmannaeyjar
1971	Víkingur Reykjavík	1-0	UBK Kópavogur
1972	IBV Vestmannaeyjar	2-0	FH Hafnarfjördhur
1973	Fram Reykjavík	2-1	IBK Keflavík
1974	Valur Reykjavík	4-1	IA Akranes
1975	IBK Keflavík	1-0	IA Akranes
1976	Valur Reykjavík	3-0	IA Akranes
1977	Valur Reykjavík	2-1	Fram Reykjavík
1978	IA Akranes	1-0	Valur Reykjavík
1979	Fram Reykjavík	1-0	Valur Reykjavík
1980	Fram Reykjavík	2-1	IBV Vestmannaeyjar
1981	IBV Vestmannaeyjar	3-2	Fram Reykjavík
1982	IA Akranes	2-1	IBK Keflavík
1983	IA Akranes	2-1	IBV Vestmannaeyjar
1984	IA Akranes	2-1	Fram Reykjavík
1985	Fram Reykjavík	3-1	IBK Keflavík
1986	IA Akranes	2-1	Fram Reykjavík
1987	Fram Reykjavík	5-0	Vídir Gardur
1988	Valur Reykjavík	1-0	IBK Keflavík
1989	Fram Reykjavík	3-1	KR Reykjavík
1990	Valur Reykjavík	1-1 0-0 5-4p	KR Reykjavík
1991	Valur Reykjavík	2-1	FH Hafnarfjördhur
1992	Valur Reykjavík	5-2	KA Akureyri
1993	IA Akranes	2-1	IBK Keflavík
1994	KR Reyjavik	2-0	Grindavik

LEADING INTERNATIONAL GOALSCORERS

17	Rikhardur Jónsson	(Fram,IA)	1947-1965
12	Arnór Gudjohnsen	(Lokeren,Anderlecht, Bordeaux,Hacken,Örebro)	1979-
11	Pétur Pétursson	(IA,Feyenoord,Anderlecht, Antwerp,Hercules,KR)	1978-1990
	Matthías Hallgrímsson	(IA,IS Halmia)	1968-1977
9	Thórdur Thórdarson	(IA)	1951-1958
	Teitur Thórdarson	(IA,Jönköping Södra,Östers, Lens,Yverdon-Sports)	1972-1985
8	Sigurdur Grétarsson	(UBK,Iraklis,Luzern, Grasshoppers)	1980-1992
	Gudmundur Steinsson	(Fram,Kickers Offenbach)	1980-1988
	Atli Edvaldsson	(Valur,B.Dortmund,F.Düssel-dorf,B.Uerdingen,KR)	1976-1991
	Marteinn Geirsson	(Fram,Union St. Gilloise)	1971-1982

LEADING INTERNATIONAL APPEARANCES

70	Atli Edvaldsson	(Valur,B.Dortmund,F.Düssel-dorf,B.Uerdingen,KR)	1976-1991
69	Saevar Jónsson	(Valur,C. Brugge,Brann,Valur	1980-92
67	Marteinn Geirsson	(Fram,Union St. Gilloise)	1971-1982
61	Gudni Bergsson	(Valur,Tottenham)	1984-
59	Arnór Gudjohnsen	(Lokeren,Anderlecht, Bordeaux,Hacken,Örebro)	1979-
58	Olafur Thórdarson	(IA,Brann,Lyn Oslo,IA)	1984-
50	Gunnar Gislason	(KA,KR,Moss,Häcken)	1982-1991
	Arni Sveinsson	(IA)	1975-1985
46	Ragnar Margeirsson	(IBK,Cercle Brugge,Waterschei, Fram,KR)	1981-1992
	Sigurdur Grétarsson	(UBK,Iraklis,Luzern, Grasshoppers)	1980-1992
	Rúnar Kristinsson	(KR)	1987-

INTERNATIONAL MATCHES PLAYED BY ICELAND

Date	Opponent	Result	Venue	Type	Scorers
17-07-1946	Denmark	L 0-3	Reykjavik	Fr	
24-07-1947	Norway	L 2-4	Reykjavik	Fr	Gudmundsson.A 2
2-07-1948	Finland	W 2-0	Reykjavik	Fr	Jónsson.R 2
7-08-1949	Denmark	L 1-5	Aarhus	Fr	Halldórsson
29-06-1951	Sweden	W 4-3	Reykjavik	Fr	Jónsson.R 4
26-07	Norway	L 1-3	Trondheim	Fr	Jónsson.R
9-08-1953	Denmark	L 0-4	Copenhagen	Fr	
13-08	Norway	L 1-3	Bergen	Fr	Gunnarsson.G
4-07-1954	Norway	W 1-0	Reykjavik	Fr	Thórdarson.Th
24-08	Sweden	L 2-3	Kalmar	Fr	Thórdarson.Th, Jónsson.R
3-07-1955	Denmark	L 0-4	Reykjavik	Fr	
25-08	USA	W 3-2	Reykjavik	Fr	Gudmannsson.G 2, Thórdarson.Th
29-06-1956	Finland	L 1-2	Helsinki	Fr	Jónsson.R
2-06-1957	France	L 0-8	Nantes	WCq	
5-06	Belgium	L 3-8	Brussels	WCq	Thórdarson.Th 2, Jónsson.R
8-07	Norway	L 0-3	Reykjavik	Fr	
10-07	Denmark	L 2-6	Reykjavik	Fr	Jónsson.R, Thórdarson.Th
1-09	France	L 1-5	Reykjavik	WCq	Jónsson.T
4-09	Belgium	L 2-5	Reykjavik	WCq	Jónsson.R, Thórdarson.Th
26-06-1959	Denmark	L 2-4	Reykjavik	OGq	Beck, Jónsson.S
7-07	Norway	W 1-0	Reykjavik	OGq	Jónsson.R
18-08	Denmark	D 1-1	Copenhagen	OGq	Teitsson
21-08	Norway	L 1-2	Oslo	OGq	Steinsen
9-06-1960	Norway	L 0-4	Oslo	Fr	
3-08	West Germany	L 0-5	Reykjavik	Fr	
9-07-1962	Norway	L 1-3	Reykjavik	Fr	Jónsson.R
12-08	Rep. Ireland	L 2-4	Dublin	ECr1	Jónsson.R 2
2-09	Rep. Ireland	D 1-1	Reykjavik	ECr1	Arnason
10-08-1964	Bermuda	W 4-3	Reykjavik	Fr	Beck 2, Schram 2
23-08	Finland	L 0-2	Reykjavik	Fr	
5-07-1965	Denmark	L 1-3	Reykjavik	Fr	Baldvinsson
23-08-1967	Denmark	L 2-14	Copenhagen	Fr	Gunnarsson.H, Numason
18-07-1968	Norway	L 0-4	Reykjavik	Fr	
23-06-1969	Bermuda	W 2-1	Reykjavik	Fr	Schram, Hallgrimsson
21-07	Norway	L 1-2	Trondheim	Fr	Schram
24-07	Finland	L 1-3	Helsinki	Fr	Schram
11-11	Bermuda	L 2-3	Hamilton	Fr	Hallgrimsson, Lárusson
7-07-1970	Denmark	D 0-0	Reykjavik	Fr	
20-07	Norway	W 2-0	Reykjavik	Fr	Gunnarsson.H 2
26-05-1971	Norway	L 1-3	Bergen	Fr	Gunnarsson.H
13-08	Japan	L 0-2	Reykjavik	Fr	
18-05-1972	Belgium	L 0-4	Liege	WCq	
22-05	Belgium	L 0-4	Bruges	WCq	
3-07	Denmark	L 2-5	Reykjavik	Fr	Pálsson.T, Hafsteinsson
12-07	Faeroe Islands	W 3-0	Reykjavik	Fr	Hafsteinsson, Pálsson.T, OG
3-08	Norway	L 1-4	Stavanger	WCq	Öskarsson
8-06-1973	Faeroe Islands	W 4-0	Klakksvik	Fr	Geirsson.M 2, Jóhannson.S, Hallgrimsson
11-07	Sweden	L 0-1	Uddevalla	Fr	
17-07	East Germany	L 1-2	Reykjavik	Fr	Juliusson
19-07	East Germany	L 0-2	Reykjavik	Fr	
2-08	Norway	L 0-4	Reykjavik	WCq	
22-08	Holland	L 0-5	Amsterdam	WCq	
29-08	Holland	L 1-8	Deventer	WCq	Geirsson.E
3-07-1974	Faeroe Islands	W 3-2	Torshavn	Fr	Björnsson.K, Eliásson, Hallgrimsson
19-08	Finland	D 2-2	Reykjavik	Fr	Geirsson.M, Thórdarson.Te
8-09	Belgium	L 0-2	Reykjavik	ECq	
9-10	Denmark	L 1-2	Aalborg	Fr	Hallgrimsson
12-10	East Germany	D 1-1	Magdeburg	ECq	Hallgrimsson
25-05-1975	France	D 0-0	Reykjavik	ECq	
5-06	East Germany	W 2-1	Reykjavik	ECq	Edvaldsson.J, Sigurvinsson.A
23-06	Faeroe Islands	W 6-0	Reykjavik	Fr	Thórdarson.Te 3, Hallgrimsson 2, Hilmarsson
7-07	Norway	D 1-1	Reykjavik	OGq	Sveinsson
17-07	Norway	L 2-3	Bergen	OGq	Thórdarson.Te, Edvaldsson.J
3-09	France	L 0-3	Nantes	ECq	
6-09	Belgium	L 0-1	Liege	ECq	
19-05-1976	Norway	W 1-0	Oslo	Fr	Sigurvinsson.A
16-06	Faeroe Islands	W 6-1	Torshavn	Fr	Thorbjörnsson 2, Hallgrimsson 2, Danivalsson, Thórdarson.Te

14-07	Finland	L 0-1	Helsinki	Fr	
21-08	Luxembourg	W 3-1	Reykjavik	Fr	Thorbjörnsson 2, Sveinsson
5-09	Belgium	L 0-1	Reykjavik	WCq	
8-09	Holland	L 0-1	Reykjavik	WCq	
11-06-1977	Nth. Ireland	W 1-0	Reykjavik	WCq	Albertsson
30-06	Norway	W 2-1	Reykjavik	Fr	Albertsson, Thórdarson.Te
20-07	Sweden	L 0-1	Reykjavik	Fr	
31-08	Holland	L 1-4	Nijmegen	WCq	Sigurvinsson
3-09	Belgium	L 0-4	Brussels	WCq	
21-09	Nth. Ireland	L 0-2	Belfast	WCq	
28-06-1978	Denmark	D 0-0	Reykjavik	Fr	
3-09	USA	D 0-0	Reykjavik	Fr	
6-09	Poland	L 0-2	Reykjavik	ECq	
20-09	Holland	L 0-3	Nijmegen	ECq	
4-10	East Germany	L 1-3	Halle	ECq	Pétursson.P
22-05-1979	Switzerland	L 0-2	Berne	ECq	
26-05	West Germany	L 1-3	Reykjavik	Fr	Edvaldsson.E
9-06	Switzerland	L 1-2	Reykjavik	ECq	Gudlaugsson
5-09	Holland	L 0-4	Reykjavik	ECq	
12-09	East Germany	L 0-3	Reykjavik	ECq	
10-10	Poland	L 0-2	Krakow	ECq	
2-06-1980	Wales	L 0-4	Reykjavik	WCq	
25-06	Finland	D 1-1	Reykjavik	Fr	Pétursson.P
30-06	Faeroe Islands	W 2-1	Akureyri	Fr	Geirsson.M, Thorleifsson
3-07	Greenland	W 4-1	Husavik	Fr	Geirsson.M, Ölafsson.P, Gudmundsson.L, Steinsson
14-07	Norway	L 1-3	Oslo	Fr	Thorleifsson
17-07	Sweden	D 1-1	Halmstad	Fr	Thorbjörnsson
3-09	Soviet Union	L 1-2	Reykjavik	WCq	Sveinsson
24-09	Turkey	W 3-1	Izmir	WCq	Gudlaugsson, Gudmundsson.A, Thórdarson.Te
15-10	Soviet Union	L 0-5	Moscow	WCq	
27-05-1981	Czechoslovakia	L 1-6	Bratislava	WCq	Bergs
22-08	Nigeria	W 3-0	Reykjavik	Fr	Sveinsson, Geirsson.M, Gudmundsson.L
26-08	Denmark	L 0-3	Copenhagen	Fr	
9-09	Turkey	W 2-0	Reykjavik	WCq	Gudmundsson.L, Edvaldsson.A
23-09	Czechoslovakia	D 1-1	Reykjavik	WCq	Ormslev
14-10	Wales	D 2-2	Swansea	WCq	Sigurvinsson.A 2
14-03-1982	Kuwait	D 0-0	Kuwait City	Fr	
2-06	England	D 1-1	Reykjavik	Fr	Gudjohnsen.A
5-06	Malta	L 1-2	Messina	ECq	Geirsson.M
11-07	Finland	L 2-3	Helsinki	Fr	Geirsson.M, Edvaldsson.A
1-08	Faeroe Islands	W 4-1	Torshavn	Fr	Grétarsson.S 2, Karlsson.H, Kristjánsson
2-08	Faeroe Islands	W 4-0	Gotu	Fr	Grétarsson.S 2, Kristjánsson
1-09	Holland	D 1-1	Reykjavik	ECq	Edvaldsson.A
8-09	East Germany	L 0-1	Reykjavik	Fr	
13-10	Rep. Ireland	L 0-2	Dublin	ECq	
27-10	Spain	L 0-1	Malaga	ECq	
29-05-1983	Spain	L 0-1	Reykjavik	ECq	
5-06	Malta	W 1-0	Reykjavik	ECq	Edvaldsson.A
8-08	Faeroe Islands	W 6-0	Njardvik	Fr	Magnusson 2, Gudmundsson.S 2, Gislason, Margeirsson
17-08	Sweden	L 0-4	Reykjavik	Fr	
7-09	Holland	L 0-3	Groningen	ECq	
21-09	Rep. Ireland	L 0-3	Reykjavik	ECq	
20-06-1984	Norway	L 0-1	Reykjavik	Fr	
1-08	Faeroe Islands	D 0-0	Torshavn	Fr	
3-08	Greenland	W 1-0	Fuglafirdi	Fr	Birgirsson
12-09	Wales	W 1-0	Reykjavik	WCq	Bergs
25-09	Saudi Arabia	W 2-1	Dhahran	Fr	Gislason, Steinsson
17-10	Scotland	L 0-3	Glasgow	WCq	
14-11	Wales	L 1-2	Cardiff	WCq	Pétursson.P
31-03-1985	Kuwait	D 1-1	Kuwait City	Fr	Steinsson
24-04	Luxembourg	D 0-0	Ettelbruck	Fr	
28-05	Scotland	L 0-1	Reykjavik	WCq	
12-06	Spain	L 1-2	Reykjavik	WCq	Thórdarson.Te
10-07	Faeroe Islands	W 9-0	Keflavik	Fr	Margeirsson 3, Steinsson 2, Gislason, Hákonarson, Thorbjörnsson, Jónsson.Sa
12-07	Faeroe Islands	W 1-0	Akranes	Fr	Pétursson.P
25-09	Spain	L 1-2	Seville	WCq	Thorbjörnsson
11-03-1986	Bahrian	L 1-2	Manama	Fr	Askelsson
15-03	Bahrain	W 2-0	Manama	Fr	Askelsson, Steinsson
19-03	Kuwait	L 0-1	Kuwait City	Fr	
25-05	Rep. Ireland	L 1-2	Reykjavik	Fr	Gudjohnsen.A

29-05	Czechoslovakia	L 1-2	Reykjavik	Fr	Steinsson
10-09	France	D 0-0	Reykjavik	ECq	
24-09	Soviet Union	D 1-1	Reykjavik	ECq	Gudjohnsen.A
29-10	East Germany	L 0-2	Karl-Marx-Stadt	ECq	
26-02-1987	Kuwait	D 1-1	Kuwait City	Fr	Askelsson
28-02	Kuwait	W 1-0	Kuwait City	Fr	Olafsson.L
29-04	France	L 0-2	Paris	ECq	
3-06	East Germany	L 0-6	Reykjavik	ECq	
9-09	Norway	W 2-1	Reykjavik	ECq	Pétursson.P, Ormslev
23-09	Norway	W 1-0	Oslo	ECq	Edvaldsson.A
28-10	Soviet Union	L 0-2	Simferopol	ECq	
4-05-1988	Hungary	L 0-3	Budapest	Fr	
7-08	Bulgaria	L 2-3	Reykjavik	Fr	Ormslev 2
24-08	Faeroe Islands	W 1-0	Akranes	Fr	Torfason
31-08	Soviet Union	D 1-1	Reykjavik	WCq	Grétarsson.S
21-09	Hungary	L 0-3	Reykjavik	Fr	
12-10	Turkey	D 1-1	Istanbul	WCq	Torfason
19-10	East Germany	L 0-2	Berlin	WCq	
31-05-1989	Soviet Union	D 1-1	Moscow	WCq	Askelsson
14-06	Austria	D 0-0	Reykjavik	WCq	
23-08	Austria	L 1-2	Salzburg	WCq	Margeirsson
6-09	East Germany	L 0-3	Reykjavik	WCq	
20-09	Turkey	W 2-1	Reykjavik	WCq	Pétursson.P 2
28-03-1990	Luxembourg	W 2-1	Esch	Fr	Pétursson.P, Thórdarson.O
3-04	Bermuda	W 4-0	Hamilton	Fr	Pétursson.P 2, Ormslev, Einarsson
8-04	USA	L 1-4	St. Louis	Fr	Pétursson.P
30-05	Albania	W 2-0	Reykjavik	ECq	Gudjohnsen.A, Edvaldsson.A
8-08	Faeroe Islands	W 3-2	Torshafn	Fr	Gregory 2, Gudjohnsen.A
5-09	France	L 1-2	Reykjavik	ECq	Edvaldsson.A
26-09	Czechoslovakia	L 0-1	Kosice	ECq	
10-10	Spain	L 1-2	Seville	ECq	Jónsson.Si
1-05-1991	Wales	L 0-1	Cardiff	Fr	
7-05	Malta	W 4-1	Ta'Qali	Fr	Kristinsson 2, Grétarsson.S, Marteinsson
26-05	Albania	L 0-1	Tirana	ECq	
5-06	Czechoslovakia	L 0-1	Reykjavik	ECq	
17-07	Turkey	W 5-1	Reykjavik	Fr	Grétarsson.S, Gudjohnsen.A 4
4-09	Denmark	D 0-0	Reykjavik	Fr	
25-09	Spain	W 2-0	Reykjavik	ECq	Örlygsson, Sverrisson
16-10	Cyprus	D 1-1	Larnaca	Fr	Örlygsson
20-11	France	L 1-3	Paris	ECq	Sverrisson
10-02-1992	Malta	L 0-1	Ta'Qali	Fr	
2-03	UAE	W 1-0	Dubai	Fr	Helgason
8-04	Israel	D 2-2	Tel Aviv	Fr	Grétarsson.S, Grétarsson.A
13-05	Greece	L 0-1	Athens	WCq	
3-06	Hungary	W 2-1	Budapest	WCq	Örlygsson, Magnusson
9-08	Israel	L 0-2	Reykjavik	Fr	
7-10	Greece	L 0-1	Reykjavik	WCq	
14-10	Russia	L 0-1	Moscow	WCq	
17-04-1993	USA	D 1-1	Costa Mesa	Fr	Stefánsson
20-05	Luxembourg	D 1-1	Luxembourg	WCq	Gudjohnsen.A
2-06	Russia	D 1-1	Reykjavik	WCq	Sverrisson
16-06	Hungary	W 2-0	Reykjavik	WCq	Sverrisson, Gudjohnsen.A
31-08	USA	L 0-1	Reykjavik	Fr	
8-09	Luxembourg	W 1-0	Reykjavik	WCq	Ingólfsson
17-10	Tunisia	L 1-2	Tunis	Fr	Birgisson
20-04-1994	Saudi Arabia	L 0-2	Toulon	Fr	
24-04	USA	W 2-1	Chula Vista	Fr	Sigurdsson, Gunnlaugsson.B
4-05	Brazil	L 0-3	Florianopolis	Fr	
19-05	Bolivia	W 1-0	Reykjavik	Fr	Örlygsson
16-08	Estonia	W 4-0	Akureyri	Fr	Örlysson 3, Gudjónsson
7-09	Sweden	L 0-1	Reykjavik	ECq	
12-10	Turkey	L 0-5	Istanbul	ECq	
29-10	Kuwait	W 1-0	Kuwait City	Fr	Ingólfsson
16-11	Switzerland	L 0-1	Lausanne	ECq	
22-04-95	Chile	D 1-1	Temuco	Fr	Gunnlaugsson
1-06	Sweden	D 1-1	Stockholm	ECq	Gunnlaugsson
11-06	Hungary	W 2-1	Reykjavik	ECq	Bergsson, Jónsson.Si

ISRAEL

Israel was for many years among the strongest of nations in Asia, but since the rise to prominence in the 1970s of the Arab states, the Israelis have led a strange and often lonely existence. Cast out from the Asian Confederation in 1976 'with regret' - but no doubt considerable relief - Israel has flitted from Europe to Oceania in search of a home, and is the only country to have played a World Cup qualifying match in every continent of the world.

Thankfully the Israelis seem to have a permanent home at last, with both the clubs and the national side accepted into European competitions on a permanent basis. Visits to Israel, often seen by touring sides as a chance to bask in some winter sunshine, will now take on a far more serious aspect.

How Israel will fare in this new competitive environment remains to be seen. Their years in the wilderness have not had a healthy effect on the development of the game, as the association has struggled to maintain a regular fixture list for the national side, whilst nothing was seen of the club sides after their brief flurry in the Asian Champion Teams' Cup in the late 1960s until Maccabi Tel Aviv entered the 1993 European Cup. And with only four million inhabitants, Israel is unlikely ever to become a major power.

Israel did not exist as a nation until 1948 when the United Nations founded the state in what was then Palestine, but football predates that. Growing Jewish immigration to Palestine from Europe had encouraged the growth of the game and in 1928 the Palestine Football Association was formed in Tel Aviv. The presence of British soldiers and officials also gave the game a boost and the winners of the first championship in 1932 were the British Police.

The National Cup competition preceded the championship by four years, during which time it was won by both Hapoel and Maccabi Tel Aviv, who have been a major force in the game since. Domestic football in Israel has been relatively unaffected by the constant state of hostilities with her neighbours, although the invasion by the Arabs in 1948 and the Suez crisis of 1956 did bring about a temporary halt to the game.

A Palestinian side, made up entirely of Jews, took part in the 1934 World Cup and were drawn against Egypt in the qualifiers. These two games, along with the unsuccessful attempt to qualify for the 1938 World Cup and a friendly against the Lebanon, were the only games that Palestine played and it was not until 1949 that the national side was revived, as Israel.

The Israelis always knew it would be difficult to find opponents among their neighbours, and in the first few years after 1948 matches were confined to World Cup qualifying games and the odd friendly. This World Cup experience did give Israel an advantage when they took part in the 1956 Asian Cup, but although they were regarded as favourites for the tournament, South Korea proved too clever for them and they had to be content with second place, a position they secured again four years later.

The 1958 World Cup saw the first hint of the disruption that Israel's position was to cause world football when each of their opponents withdrew from the Asia-Africa section. This left the Israelis as the winners without having played a match, but a new FIFA law that no side except the holders and hosts could qualify without playing a game forced a play-off against Wales. Both matches were lost 2-0. Had the original games taken place, Israel may well have qualified without the need to play Wales, who were thus the unwitting benificiaries of Middle East politics.

Further controversy surrounded Israel's involvement at the 1962 Asian Games. The Indonesian hosts, mindful of their large Moslem population, refused to invite an Israeli team for any of the sports, in a move that nearly broke the Asian Games movement apart. The decision of the Asian Confederation to award Israel the staging of the 1964 Asian Cup may have been foolhardy in such circumstances, but the Israelis made full use of home advantage to win their only honour to date, beating India, a weakened South Vietnamese team and their fierce rivals South Korea.

Although this was not Israel's last appearance - they came third in 1968 - the emergence of the Arab states as a footballing bloc suggested that the Israelis were to become a fading power in Asian football. From the mid-1960s, Israel began to rely on visits by touring European sides for their players to gain experience, although there was a final hurrah in Asian football when they finished second behind Iran at the 1974 Asian Games in Tehran. Even here, controversy abounded. In their semi-final group, both North Korea and Kuwait refused to take the field against Israel and as a result forfeited the points and their hopes of making it to the final.

The Asian Football Confederation clearly needed to sort out the situation and in 1976 Israel were thrown out. The AFC faced a dilema. Either they bowed to pressure from a vocal section of their members or they stood firm and put at risk the future development of the game in the continent, which Israel's presence was beginning to disrupt. They took the former course to howls of protest from the world football community who regarded the decision as a political act. But it is difficult to see how else the AFC could have acted, and in the long run their decision may actually benefit the Israelis. Asia is the weakest of all the continents and Israel's national side and clubs will face a much higher standard of opposition in Europe.

THE ORDER OF MERIT

		All			League			Cup		Asia		
	Team	G	S	B	G	S	B	G	S	G	S	B
1	Maccabi Tel Aviv	38	17	5	18	7	5	18	10	2	--	-
2	Hapoel Tel Aviv	21	14	5	12	6	5	8	7	1	1	-
3	Maccabi Haifa	9	8	4	5	2	4	4	6	-	-	-
4	Hapoel Petah Tikva	8	14	3	6	8	3	2	6	-	-	-
5	Beitar Jerusalem	7	7	2	2	6	2	5	1	-	-	-
6	Maccabi Netanya	6	4	4	5	2	4	1	2	-	-	-
7	Bnei Yehuda Tel Aviv	4	5	2	1	3	2	3	2	-	-	-
8	Hakoah Ramat Gan	4	2	1	2	-	1	2	2	-	-	-
9	Hapoel Kfar Sava	4	-	-	1	-	-	3	-	-	-	-

10 Hapoel Haifa	3	6	6	-	2	6	3	4	-	-	-
11 Maccabi Petah Tikva	2	3	-	-	2	-	2	1	-	-	-
12 Beitar Tel Aviv	2	2	1	-	-	1	2	2	-	-	-
13 Hapoel Beer Sheva	2	1	4	2	-	4	-	1	-	-	-
14 British Police	2	-	-	1	-	-	1	-	-	-	-
15 Hapoel Jerusalem	1	1	1	-	-	1	1	1	-	-	-
16 Hapoel Lod	1	-	-	-	-	-	1	-	-	-	-
Hapoel Ramat Gan	1	-	-	1	-	-	-	-	-	-	-
18 Shimshon Tel Aviv	-	6	2	-	2	2	-	4	-	-	-
19 Maccabi Jaffa	-	4	2	-	3	2	-	1	-	-	-
20 Maccabi Hashmonaeem	-	2	-	-	-	-	-	2	-	-	-
21 48th Regiment	-	1	-	-	-	-	-	1	-	-	-
Hapoel Darom Tel Aviv	-	1	-	-	-	-	-	1	-	-	-
Hapoel Rishon Lezion	-	1	-	-	-	-	-	1	-	-	-
Maccabi Ramat Amidar	-	1	-	-	-	-	-	1	-	-	-
25 Maccabi Tveria	-	-	1	-	-	1	-	-	-	-	-

To the end of the 1994-1995 season

Not until 1992, however, was Israel formally welcomed into Europe and for fifteen years the national side led a nomadic existence. In 1970 Israel had qualified for the World Cup finals in Mexico, confirming their status as one of the strongest nations in Asia. That side was probably the best Israel has ever produced and they came away from Mexico with two draws, losing only to Uruguay. Mordecai Spiegler scored their only goal and he remains Israel's top scorer and most capped player. That Israel have not qualified since is largely due to the fact that they were adopted as an associate member of Oceania, which was not afforded an automatic berth in the finals.

In the 1990 World Cup, for instance, they were forced to play off against Colombia after winning the Oceania section, and it was no surprise when the stronger South Americans won through. Israel's future prospects for qualification do not look much better in Europe, but with more regular competition the hope is that they can emulate a small country like Denmark and make their presence felt. In the 1994 World Cup they beat France 3-2 in Paris, for their first competititve win on European soil.

Population: 4,666,000
Area, sq km: 20,700
% in urban areas: 89%
Capital city: Jerusalem

Hitachdut Lekaduregel Beisrael
Israel Football Association
12 Carlibach Street
PO Box 20188
Tel Aviv 61201
Israel
Tel: + 972 3 5709059
Fax: + 972 3 5702044

Year of formation	1928
Affiliation to FIFA	1929
Affiliation to UEFA	1992
Registered clubs	283
Registered players	28 000
Registered referees	700
National stadium	Ramat Gan, Tel Aviv 55 000
National colours	White/Blue/White
Reserve colours	Blue/White/White
Season	September - June

THE RECORD

WORLD CUP

1930	Did not enter
1934	QT 2nd/2 in group 4
1938	QT 3rd/3 in group 5
1950	QT 3rd/3 in group 3
1954	QT 3rd/3 in group 10
1958	QT Lost play-off - Asia
1962	QT 2nd/4 in group 7 - Europe
1966	QT 3rd/3 in group 1 - Europe
1970	QT R1 1st/2, R2 1st/2 - Asia - Final tournament/1st round
1974	QT 2nd/7 in group B - Asia
1978	QT 2nd/3 in group 2 - Asia
1982	QT 5th/5 in group 6 - Europe
1986	QT R1 2nd/4 - Oceania
1990	QT R1 -, R2 1st/3, R3 2nd/2 - Oceania/CONMEBOL
1994	QT 6th/6 in group 6 - Europe

EUROPEAN CHAMPIONSHIP

1996	QT group 1

ASIAN CHAMPIONSHIP

1956	QT Walk-over in group 1 - Final tournament/2nd place
1960	QT 1st/4 in group 1 - Final tournament/2nd place
1964	QT Automatic - Final tournament/Winners
1968	QT Automatic - Final tournament/3rd place
1972-92	Did not enter

ASIAN GAMES

1951	Did not enter
1954	Did not enter
1958	Quarter-finalists
1962-70	Did not enter
1974	Finalists
1978-94	Did not enter

OLYMPIC GAMES

1908-52	Did not enter
1956	QT Failed to qualify
1960	QT 2nd/3 in group 4 - Europe
1964	QT 1st round - Asia
1968	QT 1st/2 in group 3 - Asia Final tournament/Quarter-finalists
1972	QT 2nd/6 in group 2 - Asia
1976	QT 1st/6 in group 3 - Asia Final tournament/Quarter-finalists
1980	QT 3rd/4 in group 3 - Europe
1984	QT 5th/6 in group 4 - Europe
1988	QT R1 -, R2 2nd/4 - Oceania
1992	QT 2nd/4 in group 8 - Europe

CLUB COMPETITIONS

Asian Champions Club Cup
Winners - Hapoel Tel Aviv 1967, Maccabi Tel-Aviv 1969 1971
Finalists - Hapoel Tel-Aviv 1970
European Cup
1st round - Maccabi Tel Aviv 1993, Beitar Jerusalem 1994, Maccabi Haifa 1995
European Cup Winners Cup
2nd round - Maccabi Haifa 1994
UEFA Cup
Preliminary round - Hapoel Beer-Sheva 1995

CLUB DIRECTORY

TEL AVIV (Pop. - 1,553,000)

Beitar Tel Aviv (1940)
Ramat-Gan 46,000 – Blue, white sleeves/Blue

Bney Yehuda Tel Aviv (1935)
Shchonat Htikva 8,000 – White, red trim

Hakoah Maccabi Ramat Gan

Hapoel Kfar-Saba (1928)
Kfar-Saba 7,000 – Green & white hoops/Green

Hapoel Petah Tikva (1930)
Hapoel Petah-Tikva 7,000 – Blue & black stripes/Black

Hapoel Tel Aviv (1927)
Bloomfield 20,000 – Red/White

Maccabi Tel Aviv (1906)
Ramat-Gan 46,000 – White, blue sleeves/Blue, orange trim

Maccabi Petah Tikva (1912)
Hapoel Petah-Tikva 7,000 – Green/White

Shimshon Tel Aviv (1951)

JERUSALEM (Population - 493,000)
Beitar Jerusalem (1939)
Teddi Malcha 13,000 – Yellow & black stripes/Black

Hapoel Jerusalem (1927)
White/Red

HAIFA (Population - 435,000)
Hapoel Haifa (1930)
Kiriat Eliezer 17,000 – Red, white sleeves/White

Maccabi Haifa (1919)
Kiriat Eliezer 17,000 – Green, white trim

NETANYA (Pop. - 117,000)
Maccabi Netanya (1942)
Maccabi Netanya 14,000 – Yellow/Black

BEER SHEVA (Pop. - 113,000)
Hapoel Beer Sheva (1949)
Municipal 17,000 – Red, white sleeves/Red

ISRAELI LEAGUE CHAMPIONSHIP

1932 British Police
1933 -
1934 Hapoel Tel Aviv
1935 Hapoel Tel Aviv
1936 Hapoel Tel Aviv
1937 Maccabi Tel Aviv
1938 Hapoel Tel Aviv
1939 Maccabi Tel Aviv
1940 Hapoel Tel Aviv
1941 Maccabi Tel Aviv
1942 -
1943 Hapoel Tel Aviv
1944-46 -
1947 Maccabi Tel Aviv
1948 -
1949 Maccabi Tel Aviv
1950 Maccabi Tel Aviv 43 Hapoel Tel Aviv 37 Hapoel Haifa 36
1951 -
1952 Maccabi Tel Aviv 38 Maccabi Petah Tikva 30 Hapoel Haifa 29
1953 -
1954 Maccabi Tel Aviv 38 Maccabi Petah Tikva 32 Hapoel Petah Tikva 27
1955 Hapoel Petah Tikva 40 Maccabi Tel Aviv 38 Hapoel Tel Aviv 33
1956 Maccabi Tel Aviv 32 Hapoel Petah Tikva 29 Hapoel Tel Aviv 29
1957 Hapoel Tel Aviv 28 Hapoel Petah Tikva 24 Maccabi Tel Aviv 23
1958 Maccabi Tel Aviv 35 Hapoel Petah Tikva 34 Maccabi Haifa 27
1959 Hapoel Petah Tikva 32 Hapoel Haifa 31 Maccabi Tel Aviv 30
1960 Hapoel Petah Tikva 31 Maccabi Tel Aviv 30 Hapoel Haifa 26
1961 Hapoel Petah Tikva 36 Hapoel Tel Aviv 30 Hapoel Haifa 29
1962 Hapoel Petah Tikva 28 Maccabi Jaffa 26 Hapoel Tveria 25
1963 Hapoel Petah Tikva 32 Hapoel Tel Aviv 27 Maccabi Jaffa 24
1964 Hapoel Ramat Gan 40 Maccabi Jaffa 39 Hapoel Petah Tikva 38
1965 Hakoah Ramat Gan 37 Hapoel Petah Tikva 37 Hapoel Tel Aviv 36
1966 Hapoel Tel Aviv 38 Maccabi Tel Aviv 34 Hapoel Petah Tikva 34
1967 Maccabi Tel Aviv
1968 Maccabi Tel Aviv 78 Hapoel Petah Tikva 75 Hapoel Haifa 70
1969 Hapoel Tel Aviv 44 Maccabi Tel Aviv 43 Maccabi Netanya 41
1970 Maccabi Tel Aviv 39 Hapoel Tel Aviv 39 Maccabi Haifa 33
1971 Maccabi Netanya 47 Shimshon Tel Aviv 36 Hapoel Tel Aviv 35
1972 Maccabi Tel Aviv 45 Beitar Jerusalem 41 Hakoah Ramat Gan 39
1973 Hakoah Ramat Gan 42 Hapoel Tel Aviv 37 Hapoel Jerusalem 36
1974 Maccabi Netanya 37 Maccabi Tel Aviv 35 Beitar Jerusalem 34
1975 Hapoel Beer Sheva 40 Hapoel Haifa 37 Maccabi Netanya 37
1976 Hapoel Beer Sheva 42 Beitar Jerusalem 40 Hapoel Haifa 38
1977 Maccabi Tel Aviv 42 Maccabi Jaffa 39 Beitar Jerusalem 33
1978 Maccabi Netanya 38 Beitar J'salem 33 Mac'bi Tel Aviv 32
1979 Maccabi Tel Aviv 44 Beitar Jerusalem 40 Maccabi Netanya 36
1980 Maccabi Netanya 46 Hapoel Tel Aviv 36 Shimshon Tel Aviv 32
1981 Hapoel Tel Aviv 38 Bnei Yehuda 35 Maccabi Jaffa 34
1982 Hapoel Kfar Sava 42 Maccabi Netanya 41 Bnei Yehuda 35
1983 Maccabi Netanya 61 Shimshon Tel Aviv 47 Hapoel Beer Sheva 46
1984 Maccabi Haifa 57 Beitar Jerusalem 56 Hapoel Tel Aviv 47
1985 Maccabi Haifa 65 Beitar Jerusalem 60 Shimshon Tel Aviv 49
1986 Hapoel Tel Aviv 59 Maccabi Haifa 57 Maccabi Tel Aviv 57
1987 Beitar Jerusalem 66 Bnei Yehuda 51 Maccabi Tel Aviv 47
1988 Hapoel Tel Aviv 66 Maccabi Netanya 60 Hapoel Beer Sheva 52
1989 Maccabi Haifa 57 Hapoel Petah Tikva 54 Maccabi Netanya 52
1990 Bnei Yehuda 62 Hapoel Petah Tikva 58 Maccabi Haifa 51
1991 Maccabi Haifa 71 Hapoel Petah Tikva 70 Beitar Tel Aviv 50
1992 Maccabi Tel Aviv 71 Bnei Yehuda 56 Maccabi Haifa 45
1993 Beitar Jerusalem 71 Maccabi Tel Aviv 62 Bnei Yehuda 56
1994 Maccabi Haifa 95 Maccabi Tel Aviv 88 Hapoel Beer Sheva 65
1995 Maccabi Tel Aviv 63 Maccabi Haifa 58 Hapoel Beer Sheva 47

ISRAELI CUP FINALS

1928 Hapoel Tel Aviv ....2-0................Maccabi Hashmonaeem
1929 Maccabi Tel Aviv..............4-0................Maccabi Hashmonaeem
1930 Maccabi Tel Aviv..............2-1................48th Regiment
1931 -
1932 British Police ....3-0................Hapoel Haifa
1933 Maccabi Tel Aviv..............1-0................Hapoel Tel Aviv
1934 Hapoel Tel Aviv ....3-2................Maccabi Tel Aviv
1935 Maccabi Petah Tikva........1-0................Hakoah Ramat Gan
1936 -
1937 Hapoel Tel Aviv ....3-0................Hapoel Darom Tel Aviv
1938 Hapoel Tel Aviv ....2-1................Maccabi Tel Aviv
1939 Hapoel Tel Aviv ....2-1................Maccabi Petah Tikva
1940 Beitar Tel Aviv..................3-1................Maccabi Tel Aviv
1941 Maccabi Tel Aviv..............2-1................Hapoel Tel Aviv
1942 Beitar Tel Aviv ....12-1..............Maccabi Haifa
1943-45 -
1946 Maccabi Tel Aviv..........3-0 3-1............Hapoel Rishon Lezion
1947 Maccabi Tel Aviv..............3-2................Beitar Tel Aviv
1948-51 -
1952 Maccabi Petah Tikva........1-0................Maccabi Tel Aviv
1953 -
1954 Maccabi Tel Aviv..............4-0................Maccabi Netanya
1955 Maccabi Tel Aviv..............3-1................Hapoel Petah Tikva
1956 -
1957 Hapoel Petah Tikva..........2-1................Maccabi Jaffa
1958 Maccabi Tel Aviv..............2-0................Hapoel Haifa
1959 Maccabi Tel Aviv..............4-3................Hapoel Petah Tikva
1960 Hapoel Tel Aviv ....2-1................Hapoel Petah Tikva
1961 -
1962 Maccabi Haifa ....0-0 5-2............Maccabi Tel Aviv

1963	Hapoel Haifa	1-0	Maccabi Haifa
1964	Maccabi Tel Aviv	1-1 1-1 2-1	Hapoel Haifa
1965	Maccabi Tel Aviv	2-1	Bnei Yehuda
1966	Hapoel Haifa	2-1	Shimshon Tel Aviv
1967	Maccabi Tel Aviv	2-1	Hapoel Tel Aviv
1968	Bnei Yehuda	1-0	Hapoel Petah Tikva
1969	Hakoah Ramat Gan	1-0	Shimshon Tel Aviv
1970	Maccabi Tel Aviv	2-1	Maccabi Netanya
1971	Hakoah Ramat Gan	2-1	Maccabi Haifa
1972	Hapoel Tel Aviv	1-0	Hapoel Jerusalem
1973	Hapoel Jerusalem	2-0	Hakoah Ramat Gan
1974	Hapoel Haifa	1-0	Hapoel Petah Tikva
1975	Hapoel Kfar Sava	3-1	Beitar Jerusalem
1976	Beitar Jeusalem	2-1	Maccabi Tel Aviv
1977	Maccabi Tel Aviv	1-0	Beitar Tel Aviv
1978	Maccabi Netanya	2-1	Bnei Yehuda
1979	Beitar Jerusalem	2-1	Maccabi Tel Aviv
1980	Hapoel Kfar Sava	4-1	Maccabi Ramat Amidar
1981	Bnei Yehuda	2-2 4-3p	Hapoel Tel Aviv
1982	Bnei Yehuda	1-0	Hapoel Tel Aviv
1983	Hapoel Tel Aviv	3-2	Maccabi Tel Aviv
1984	Hapoel Lod	0-0 3-2p	Hapoel Beer Sheva
1985	Beitar Jerusalem	1-0	Maccabi Haifa
1986	Beitar Jerusalem	2-1	Shimshon Tel Aviv
1987	Maccabi Tel Aviv	3-3 4-3p	Maccabi Haifa
1988	Maccabi Tel Aviv	2-1	Hapoel Tel Aviv
1989	Beitar Jerusalem	3-3 4-3p	Maccabi Haifa
1990	Hapoel Kfar Sava	1-0	Shimshon Tel Aviv
1991	Maccabi Haifa	3-1	Hapoel Petah Tikva
1992	Hapoel Petah Tikvah	3-1	Maccabi Tel Aviv
1993	Maccabi Haifa	1-0	Maccabi Tel Aviv
1994	Maccabi Tel Aviv	2-0	Hapoel Tel Aviv
1995	Maccabi Haifa	2-0	Hapoel Haifa

LEADING INTERNATIONAL GOALSCORERS

24	Mordechai Spiegler	(Mac Netanya)	1963-1977
22	Nahum Stelmach	(Hap Petah-Tikva)	1956-1968
	Yoshua Feygenbaum	(Hap T.A.)	1966-1977
17	Gideon Damti	(Shimshon T.A.)	1971-1981
16	Yeoshua Glazer	(Mac. T.A).	1949-1961
	Uri Malmilian	(Beitar Jerusalem)	1975-1988
15	Ronen Harazi	(Beitar Jerusalem)	1992-
13	Gyora Spiegel	(Mac T.A.)	1965-1980
	Eli Ohana	(Beitar Jerusalem)	1984-
11	Ronny Rosenthal	(Maccabi Haifa,Club Brugge, Standard Cl,Liverpool, Tottenham)	1983-

LEADING INTERNATIONAL APPEARANCES

79	Mordechai Spiegler	(Mac Netanya)	1963-1977
75	Itzak Shum	(Hap Kfar Sava)	1969-1981
68	Itzak Visoker #	(Hap. Petah Tikva,Mac Net'ya)	1963-1976
	Nir Klinger	(Mac T.A.)	1987-
67	Gideon Damti	(Shimshon T.A.)	1971-1981
63	Avi Cohen	(Mac T.A.,Liverpool)	1976-1992
61	Nahum Stelmach	(Mac T.A.)	1956-1968
	Uri Malmilian	(Beitar Jerusalem)	1975-1988
	Bonny Ginzburg	(Irony Ashdad)	1984-

INTERNATIONAL MATCHES PLAYED BY ISRAEL

16-03-1934	Egypt	L 1-7	Cairo	WCq	Neudelmann
6-04	Egypt	L 1-4	Tel Aviv	WCq	Suknik
22-01-1938	Greece	L 1-3	Tel Aviv	WCq	Neufeld
20-02	Greece	L 0-1	Athens	WCq	
27-04-1940	Lebanon	W 5-1	Tel Aviv	Fr	Meitner, Scheindrowitch, Maclis, Caspi 2
30-07-1949	Cyprus	W 3-1	Tel Aviv	Fr	Weinberger 2, Yalovski
21-08	Yugoslavia	L 0-6	Belgrade	WCq	
18-09	Yugoslavia	L 2-5	Tel Aviv	WCq	Glazer 2
28-10-1950	Turkey	W 5-1	Tel Aviv	Fr	Gambasch 2, Glazer 3
3-12	Turkey	L 2-3	Istanbul	Fr	Glazer 2
1-11-1953	Greece	L 0-1	Athens	WCq	
8-11	Yugoslavia	L 0-1	Skoplje	WCq	
8-03-1954	Greece	L 0-2	Tel Aviv	WCq	
21-03	Yugoslavia	L 0-1	Tel Aviv	WCq	
1-05	South Africa	L 1-2	Johannesburg	Fr	Glazer
11-07-1956	Soviet Union	L 0-5	Moscow	OGq	
31-07	Soviet Union	L 1-2	Tel Aviv	OGq	Stelmach
1-09	Hong Kong	W 3-2	Hong Kong	AC	Glazer 2, Stelmach
8-09	South Korea	L 1-2	Hong Kong	AC	Stelmach
12-09	South Vietnam	W 2-1	Hong Kong	AC	Stelmach 2
15-01-1958	Wales	L 0-2	Tel Aviv	WCq	
5-02	Wales	L 0-2	Cardiff	WCq	
26-05	Iran	W 4-0	Tokyo	AGr1	Glazer, Stelmach 2, Reznik
28-05	Singapore	W 2-1	Tokyo	AGr1	Nahari, Stelmach
30-05	Taiwan	L 0-2	Tokyo	AGqf	
21-06-1959	Poland	L 2-7	Wroclaw	Fr	Goldstein, Stelmach
21-10	Yugoslavia	D 2-2	Tel Aviv	OGq	Stelmach 2
29-11	Poland	D 1-1	Tel Aviv	Fr	Levy.R
5-12	Iran	L 0-3	Cochin	ACq	
8-12	India	W 3-1	Cochin	ACq	Levy.R 3
10-12	Pakistan	W 2-0	Cochin	ACq	Levy.R, Stelmach
12-12	Iran	D 1-1	Cochin	ACq	Mentchel
14-12	India	W 2-1	Cochin	ACq	Stelmach, Levy.R
17-12	Pakistan	D 2-2	Cochin	ACq	Mentchel, Ratzabi

Date	Opponent	Result	Venue	Comp	Scorers
6-03-1960	Greece	W 2-1	Tel Aviv	OGq	Mentchel, Glazer
3-04	Greece	L 1-2	Athens	OGq	Glazer
10-04	Yugoslavia	W 2-1	Belgrade	OGq	Levy.R 2
17-10	South Korea	L 0-3	Seoul	AC	
19-10	South Vietnam	W 5-1	Seoul	AC	Levy.R, Stelmach, Levy.S, Mentchel, Aaronskind
20-10	Taiwan	W 1-0	Seoul	AC	Levy.S
13-11	Cyprus	D 1-1	Nicosia	WCq	Kaufmann
27-11	Cyprus	W 6-1	Tel Aviv	WCq	Levy.S 3, Nahari, Stelmach 2
14-03-1961	Ethiopia	W 1-0	Tel Aviv	WCq	Glazer
19-03	Ethiopia	W 3-2	Tel Aviv	WCq	Glazer 2, Stelmach
15-10	Italy	L 2-4	Tel Aviv	WCq	Stelmach, Young
22-10	South Korea	D 1-1	Tel Aviv	Fr	Stelmach
4-11	Italy	L 0-6	Turin	WCq	
14-12	Yugoslavia	L 0-2	Tel Aviv	Fr	
16-05-1962	Turkey	L 0-1	Istanbul	Fr	
7-10	Ethiopia	W 3-0	Tel Aviv	Fr	Levkowitch, Mentchel, Stelmach
13-11	Sweden	L 0-4	Tel Aviv	Fr	
25-11	Turkey	L 0-2	Tel Aviv	Fr	
19-05-1963	Brazil	L 0-5	Tel Aviv	Fr	
28-12	South Vietnam	W 1-0	Saigon	OGq	Young
2-01-1964	Hong Kong	W 3-0	Hong Kong	Fr	Mahalal 2, Spiegler
17-03	South Vietnam	L 0-2	Tel Aviv	OGq	
26-05	Hong Kong	W 1-0	Tel Aviv	AC	Spiegler
29-05	India	W 2-0	Tel Aviv	AC	Spiegler, Aharoni
3-06	South Korea	W 2-1	Tel Aviv	AC	Leon, Tisch
28-10	Yugoslavia	W 2-0	Tel Aviv	Fr	Spiegler, Cohen.S
1-12	Denmark	L 0-1	Tel Aviv	Fr	
26-01-1965	Holland	L 0-1	Tel Aviv	Fr	
9-05	Belgium	L 0-1	Brussels	WCq	
13-06	Bulgaria	L 0-4	Sofia	WCq	
10-11	Belgium	L 0-5	Tel Aviv	WCq	
21-11	Bulgaria	L 1-2	Tel Aviv	WCq	Talbi
8-05-1966	Finland	W 3-0	Helsinki	Fr	Young, Stelmach 2
15-06	Uruguay	L 1-2	Tel Aviv	Fr	Spiegler
12-10	Yugoslavia	L 1-3	Tel Aviv	Fr	Spiegler
26-10	Denmark	L 1-3	Copenhagen	Fr	Assis
7-12	Romania	L 1-2	Tel Aviv	Fr	Borba
10-01-1968	Belgium	L 0-2	Tel Aviv	Fr	
14-02	Switzerland	W 2-1	Tel Aviv	Fr	Spiegler 2
19-02	Sweden	L 0-3	Tel Aviv	Fr	
17-03	Ceylon	W 7-0	Tel Aviv	OGq	Borba 2, Spiegler 3, OG, Spiegel
22-03	Ceylon	W 4-0	Tel Aviv	OGq	Spiegel, Talbi, Rosenthal, Borba
12-05	Hong Kong	W 6-1	Tehran	AC	Spiegler 2, Spiegel 2, Romano 2
14-05	Burma	L 0-1	Tehran	AC	
17-05	Taiwan	W 4-1	Tehran	AC	Romano 2, Rosenthal, Spiegel
19-05	Iran	L 1-2	Tehran	AC	Spiegel
10-09	Nth. Ireland	L 2-3	Tel Aviv	Fr	Spiegler, Talbi
13-10	Ghana	W 5-3	Leon	OGr1	Spiegel 2, Feygenbaum 3
15-10	El Salvador	W 3-1	Leon	OGr1	Talbi, Spiegler, Bar.S
17-10	Hungary	L 0-2	Guadalajara	OGr1	
20-10	Bulgaria	D 1-1	Leon	OGqf	Feygenbaum. Lost on toss of coin
19-02-1969	Sweden	L 2-3	Tel Aviv	Fr	Spiegel, Young
12-03	Greece	D 3-3	Tel Aviv	Fr	Young, Talbi, Feygenbaum
23-04	Austria	D 1-1	Tel Aviv	Fr	Feygenbaum
25-08	Sweden	L 1-3	Stockholm	Fr	Talbi
28-09	New Zealand	W 4-0	Tel Aviv	WCq	Spiegler, Spiegel, Feygenbaum 2
1-10	New Zealand	W 2-0	Tel Aviv	WCq	Spiegler, Spiegel
4-12	Australia	W 1-0	Tel Aviv	WCq	Spiegel
14-12	Australia	D 1-1	Sydney	WCq	Spiegler
28-01-1970	Holland	L 0-1	Tel Aviv	Fr	
22-03	Ethiopia	W 5-1	Addis Ababa	Fr	Feygenbaum 3, Spiegler 2
2-06	Uruguay	L 0-2	Puebla	WCr1	
7-06	Sweden	D 1-1	Toluca	WCr1	Spiegler
11-06	Italy	D 0-0	Toluca	WCr1	
10-11	Australia	L 0-1	Tel Aviv	Fr	
12-03-1971	Sweden	W 2-1	Tel Aviv	Fr	Feygenbaum, Spiegel
11-11	Australia	D 2-2	Brisbane	Fr	Borba, Spiegler
14-11	Australia	L 0-1	Sydney	Fr	
21-11	Australia	W 3-1	Melbourne	Fr	Rosen, Sharabani 2
16-02-1972	Norway	W 2-1	Tel Aviv	Fr	Bar Nur 2
22-03	Ceylon	W 3-0	Rangoon	OGq	Calderon, Bar Nur, Borba
28-03	India	W 1-0	Rangoon	OGq	Spiegler

30-03	Indonesia	W 1-0	Rangoon	OGq	Sarussi
1-04	Thailand	D 0-0	Rangoon	OGq	L 2-4 pens
20-02-1973	Argentina	D 1-1	Tel Aviv	Fr	Shum
16-05	Japan	W 2-1	Seoul	WCq	Onana 2
19-05	Malaysia	W 3-0	Seoul	WCq	Farkas, Shum, Onana
21-05	Thailand	W 6-0	Seoul	WCq	Borba, Spiegler, Shum, Rosen 2, Onana
23-05	South Korea	D 0-0	Seoul	WCq	
26-05	Japan	W 1-0	Seoul	WCq	Onana
28-05	South Korea	L 0-1	Seoul	WCq	
19-07	Uruguay	L 1-2	Tel Aviv	Fr	Damti
13-11	United States	W 3-1	Tel Aviv	Fr	Peretz, Rosen, Macmel
15-11	United States	W 2-0	Beersheba	Fr	Damti, Peretz
28-05-1974	Australia	W 2-1	Tel Aviv	Fr	Feygenbaum 2
3-09	Malaysia	W 8-3	Tehran	AGr1	Onana 2, Schwartz, Feygenbaum, Damti 3, Massuari
5-09	Philippines	W 6-0	Tehran	AGr1	Schweitzer 2, Damti, Shum, Onana, Feygenbaum
7-09	Japan	W 3-1	Tehran	AGr1	Feygenbaum 2, Damti
10-09	Burma	W 3-0	Tehran	AGr2	Feygenbaum, Schweitzer, Damti
12-09	North Korea	W 2-0		AGr2	North Korea refused to play. Israel awarded game 2-0
14-09	Kuwait	W 2-0		AGr2	Kuwait refused to play. Israel awarded game 2-0
16-09	Iran	L 0-1	Tehran	AGf	
4-12	Romania	L 0-1	Tel Aviv	Fr	
20-10-1975	Mexico	W 1-0	Tel Aviv	Fr	Schweitzer
4-02-1976	Denmark	L 0-1	Tel Aviv	Fr	
3-03	Nth. Ireland	D 1-1	Tel Aviv	Fr	Damti
31-03	Japan	W 3-0	Seoul	OGq	Damti, Peretz, Oz
4-04	South Korea	W 3-1	Seoul	OGq	Schweitzer, Damti 2
11-04	Japan	W 4-1	Tel Aviv	OGq	Schweitzer, Damti, Shum 2
28-04	South Korea	D 0-0	Tel Aviv	OGq	
19-07	Guatemala	D 0-0	Toronto	OGr1	
21-07	Mexico *	D 2-2	Montreal	OGr1	Oz, Shum
23-07	France *	D 1-1	Montreal	OGr1	Peretz
25-07	Brazil *	L 1-4	Toronto	OGqf	Peretz
22-09	Greece	W 1-0	Patras	Fr	Tabak
3-11	Australia	D 1-1	Tel Aviv	Fr	Damti
15-12	Austria	L 1-3	Tel Aviv	Fr	Peretz
26-01-1977	Greece	D 1-1	Tel Aviv	Fr	Schweitzer
12-02	Australia	D 1-1	Melbourne	Fr	Damti
16-02	Australia	D 1-1	Sydney	Fr	Schweitzer
27-02	South Korea	D 0-0	Tel Aviv	WCq	
6-03	Japan	W 2-0	Tel Aviv	WCq	Machness.O, Bar.H
10-03	Japan	W 2-0	Tel Aviv	WCq	Machness.O, Peretz
20-03	South Korea	L 1-3	Seoul	WCq	Malmilian
8-02-1978	Denmark	W 2-0	Tel Aviv	Fr	Cohen.Y, Machness.G
22-02	Holland	L 1-2	Tel Aviv	Fr	Peretz
15-11	Belgium	W 1-0	Tel Aviv	Fr	Peretz
19-12	Romania	D 1-1	Tel Aviv	Fr	Malmilian
30-01-1979	Austria	L 0-1	Tel Aviv	Fr	
14-02	Greece	W 4-1	Tel Aviv	Fr	Shum, Peretz 3
26-03-1980	Nth Ireland	D 0-0	Tel Aviv	WCq	
18-06	Sweden	D 1-1	Stockholm	WCq	Damti
12-11	Sweden	D 0-0	Tel Aviv	WCq	
2-12	Australia	L 0-1	Beersheba	Fr	
17-12	Portugal	L 0-3	Lisbon	WCq	
25-02-1981	Scotland	L 0-1	Tel Aviv	WCq	
8-04	Romania	W 2-1	Tel Aviv	Fr	Sinai, Mizrahi
28-04	Scotland	L 1-3	Glasgow	WCq	Sinai
28-10	Portugal	W 4-1	Tel Aviv	WCq	Tabak 3, Damti
18-11	Nth Ireland	L 0-1	Belfast	WCq	
26-09-1983	Uruguay	D 2-2	Tel Aviv	Fr	Armeli, Levy.S
8-11	Romania	D 1-1	Tel Aviv	Fr	Malmilian
4-04-1984	Rep. Ireland	W 3-0	Tel Aviv	Fr	Ohana, Armeli, Sinai
11-04	Romania	D 0-0	Oradea	Fr	
10-06	Wales	D 0-0	Tel Aviv	Fr	
6-09	Malta	W 2-1	Tel Aviv	Fr	Malmilian 2
9-10	Greece	D 2-2	Athens	Fr	Cohen.Av, Ohana
16-10	Nth. Ireland	L 0-3	Belfast	Fr	
21-11	Romania	D 1-1	Tel Aviv	Fr	Ohana
19-12	Luxembourg	W 2-0	Tel Aviv	Fr	Malmilian, Ohana
9-01-1985	Greece	L 0-2	Tel Aviv	Fr	
27-02	Rep. Ireland	D 0-0	Tel Aviv	Fr	
1-05	Sweden	D 1-1	Tel Aviv	Fr	Ohana

Date	Opponent	Result	Venue	Comp	Scorers
3-09	Taiwan	W 6-0	Tel Aviv	WCq	Turk 3, Armeli, Malmilian 2
8-09	Taiwan	W 5-0	Tel Aviv	WCq	Cohen.Av, Armeli, Ohana 3
8-10	Australia	L 1-2	Tel Aviv	WCq	Armeli
20-10	Australia	D 1-1	Melbourne	WCq	Malmilian
26-10	New Zealand	L 1-3	Auckland	WCq	Armeli
10-11	New Zealand	D 3-3	Tel Aviv	WCq	Cohen.N, Selekter, Armeli
28-01-1986	Scotland	L 0-1	Tel Aviv	Fr	
26-02	England	L 1-2	Tel Aviv	Fr	Ohana
4-05	Argentina	L 2-7	Tel Aviv	Fr	Sinai, Malmilian
8-10	Romania	L 2-4	Tel Aviv	Fr	Malmilian, Cohen.N
18-02-1987	Nth. Ireland	D 1-1	Tel Aviv	Fr	Marili
25-03	West Germany	L 0-2	Tel Aviv	Fr	
8-04	Romania	L 2-3	Brasov	Fr	Brailovsky, Tikva
19-05	Switzerland	L 0-1	Aarau	Fr	
1-06	Brazil	L 0-4	Tel Aviv	Fr	
10-11	Rep. Ireland	L 0-5	Dublin	Fr	
2-12	Malta	D 1-1	Tel Aviv	Fr	Ovadia
16-12	Switzerland	L 0-2	Tel Aviv	Fr	
19-01-1988	Belgium	L 2-3	Tel Aviv	Fr	Malmilian, Tikva
27-01	France	D 1-1	Tel Aviv	Fr	Cohen.Ab
3-02	Romania	L 0-2	Haifa	Fr	
10-02	Poland	L 1-3	Tel Aviv	Fr	Rosenthal.R
17-02	England	D 0-0	Tel Aviv	Fr	
7-03	Australia	L 0-2	Melbourne	OGq	
9-03	New Zealand	W 2-0	Adelaide	OGq	Cohen.E, Iwanir
13-03	Taiwan	W 5-1	Sydney	OGq	Brailovsky 2, Malmilian 2, Levin
20-03	Australia	D 0-0	Christchurch	OGq	
23-03	Taiwan	W 9-0	Wellington	OGq	Tikva 3, Levin 3, Rosenthal.R, Cohen.E, Malmilian
27-03	New Zealand	W 1-0	Auckland	OGq	Levin
18-10	Malta	W 2-0	Beersheba	Fr	Sinai, Dryks
23-11	Romania	L 0-3	Sibiu	Fr	
4-01-1989	Holland	L 0-2	Tel Aviv	Fr	
11-01	Malta	W 2-1	Ta'Qali	Fr	Menahem, Sinai
8-02	Wales	D 3-3	Tel Aviv	Fr	Klinger, Alon, Dryks
5-03	New Zealand	W 1-0	Tel Aviv	WCq	Rosenthal.R
19-03	Australia	D 1-1	Tel Aviv	WCq	Ohana
9-04	New Zealand	D 2-2	Auckland	WCq	Rosenthal.R, Klinger
16-04	Australia	D 1-1	Sydney	WCq	Ohana
15-10	Colombia	L 0-1	Barranquilla	WCq	
30-10	Colombia	D 0-0	Tel Aviv	WCq	
28-03-1990	Greece	L 1-2	Athens	Fr	Sinai
25-04	Romania	L 1-4	Haifa	Fr	Aharoni
16-05	Soviet Union	W 3-2	Tel Aviv	Fr	Malmilian, Levin, Banin
22-05	Argentina	L 1-2	Tel Aviv	Fr	Banin
9-10	Soviet Union	L 0-3	Moscow	Fr	
12-02-1992	Commonwealth of. IS	L 1-2	Tel Aviv	Fr	Dricks
3-03	Cyprus	W 2-1	Tel Aviv	Fr	Berkovitz, Cohen.A
8-04	Iceland	D 2-2	Tel Aviv	Fr	Zohar, Cohen.A
5-08	Faeroe Islands	D 1-1	Torshavn	Fr	Banin
9-08	Iceland	W 2-0	Iceland	Fr	Berkovitch, Tikva
9-09	Poland	D 1-1	Mielec	Fr	Rosenthal.R
23-09	Hungary	D 0-0	Budapest	Fr	
28-10	Austria	L 2-5	Vienna	WCq	Zohar 2
11-11	Sweden	L 1-3	Tel Aviv	WCq	Banin
2-12	Bulgaria	L 0-2	Tel Aviv	WCq	
3-02-1993	Poland	D 0-0	Haifa	Fr	
17-02	France	L 0-4	Tel Aviv	WCq	
25-03	Russia	D 2-2	Haifa	Fr	Mizrahi 2
27-04	Ukraine	D 1-1	Odessa	Fr	Harazi.R
12-05	Bulgaria	D 2-2	Sofia	WCq	Harazi.R, Rosenthal.R
2-06	Sweden	L 0-5	Stockholm	WCq	
16-06	Finland	D 0-0	Lahti	WCq	
22-09	Romania	L 0-1	Bucharest	Fr	
5-10	Cyprus	D 2-2	Limassol	Fr	Harazi.R 2
13-10	France	W 3-2	Paris	WCq	Harazi.R, Berkovitch, Atar
27-10	Austria	D 1-1	Tel Aviv	WCq	Rosenthal.R
10-11	Finland	L 1-3	Tel Aviv	WCq	Harazi.R
23-02-1994	Georgia	W 2-0	Ashdod	Fr	Ohana 2
15-03	Ukraine	W 1-0	Haifa	Fr	Banin
20-04	Lithuania	D 1-1	Vilnius	Fr	Harazi.R
31-05	Argentina	L 0-3	Tel Aviv	Fr	
17-08	Croatia	L 0-4	Tel Aviv	Fr	

4-09	Poland	W 2-1	Tel Aviv	ECq	Harazi.R 2
12-10	Slovakia	D 2-2	Tel Aviv	ECq	Harazi.R, Banin
16-11	Azerbaijan	W 2-0	Trabzon	ECq	Harazi.R, Rosenthal.R
29-11	Cyprus	W 4-3	Jerusalem	Fr	Hazan 2, Harazi.R, Rosenthal.R
14-12	Romania	D 1-1	Tel Aviv	ECq	Rosenthal.R
14-02-1995	Luxembourg	W 4-2	Ashdod	Fr	Harazi.R,Hazan, Turgeman, OG
29-03	France	D 0-0	Tel Aviv	ECq	
25-04	Poland	L 3-4	Zabrze	ECq	Rosenthal.R, Revivo, Zohar
17-05	Brazil	L 1-2	Tel Aviv	Fr	Brumer
7-06	Romania	L 1-2	Bucharest	ECq	Berkovitch

ITALY

The Italians will always be big news in football. Their league has more players of quality than any other, their fans are amongst the most passionate in the world, and they have won the World Cup three times. Yet they are not universally popular in the football world: South America in particular has had cause to rue the agents of the big Italian clubs as player after player has been lured away from Argentina, Brazil and Uruguay. Italian football was also held accountable for the demise of the game as an entertaining spectacle when, during the 1960s and 1970s, its *catenaccio*, or defensive football motivated by the fear of defeat, spread right across the globe.

Despite this, Italy can be the perfect setting for football and has contributed greatly to the development of the game. The first clubs were formed in the three main cultural and industrial centres in Northern Italy. Internazionale Torino, the forerunners of the present day Torino, were formed in 1890; Genoa were formed in 1893 as Genoa Cricket and Football Club; whilst in Milan, Milan Football and Cricket Club, later simply known as Milan, were formed in 1899. The English influence was obvious, and some clubs to this day still retain the title Football Club rather than the Italian Associazione Calcio.

To call Genoa the first league champions is perhaps stretching the point in that the first competition in 1898 consisted of only three games, and until 1910 the number of matches played in each championship remained limited. It was the common practice to play eliminating games by region, often between only two clubs, to qualify for a round robin play-off.

The year 1910 proved to be a watershed for the Italians. Not only did the football association try to set league football on a more firm footing, but a national side was fielded for the first time. Although an impressive debut saw a 6-0 win over France, results well into the 1920s were not outstanding. Italy's first official competition, the 1912 Olympic Games, ended with first round defeat at the hands of Finland.

The 1910 league championship saw a dramatic increase in the number of games played and for the first time a single league was used, but the following year it reverted to regional groupings. As more and more clubs were formed and wanted to join in, these regional leagues became ever more complicated, but not until 1930 was a single national league reintroduced. When it was, it proved to be exactly the boost the game needed to project itself to the Italian population, and neither has had cause to look back since.

These early years were often marked by disorganisation. Although an association had been formed in 1898, its authority was always being challenged, whilst rivalries between the different towns meant that at various times it had its headquarters in Turin, Milan, Turin again and Bologna, before finally settling in Rome in 1929. In 1921 matters seemed to have got out of hand as the championship consisted of 18 regional leagues of vastly different strengths. The big clubs felt at the mercy of their smaller counterparts and in 1922 set up a rival organisation, but that only lasted a year.

The 1930s were exciting times for Italian football. Under the guidance of Vittorio Pozzo the national team reached dizzy heights of success that they have been hard pressed to match since. They won the 1934 World Cup, then won the gold medal at the 1936 Olympics before setting the seal on a remarkable decade with victory in the 1938 World Cup. Only seven games were lost throughout the whole of the 1930s.

The game was still deemed amateur, though for the most part it was nothing of the sort. Huge incentives were given to players, especially at club level where the Mitropa Cup was proving to be a rewarding challenge both on the field and financially. Clubs like Juventus, in a bid to give themselves an advantage in the championship, started to import players from abroad in a tradition that persists to this day. Luisito Monti and Raimundo Orsi were perhaps the most famous. Both were Argentinian, Monti having played in the 1930 World Cup final. That he subsequently played for Italy in the 1934 final gives a small indication why among some nations there was no little resentment of the Italians!

The greatest star of the period was Giuseppe Meazza, one of only two players - the other being Ferrari - who played in both World Cup winning teams. Meazza played for Internazionale, who along with Bologna and Juventus dominated league football at this time. Bologna, however, were the only ones who could turn this domination into success in the Mitropa Cup, winning it in 1932 and 1934. The first victory was achieved by a walk-over after a riot in the other semi-final between Juventus and Slavia Prague led to both teams being disqualified. In the 1934 final however, after losing 3-2 in the first leg to Admira Wien, Bologna pulled off a 5-1 victory, inspired by another of Italy's great players, Angelo Schiavio.

The immediate post-war football story is dominated by the Superga aircrash in 1949. Torino were, at the time, probably the best team Italy had seen and almost without exception formed the national side. On a return trip from Lisbon, however, the aircraft carrying the team crashed into the Superga hill in the suburbs of Turin, killing everyone on board. Among those killed were 10 Italian internationals, the most famous of whom was Valentin Mazzola, father of Sandro Mazzola who would achieve such fame in the 1960s.

Neither the national side nor Torino recovered quickly from the tragedy, and throughout the 1950s Italy faltered. Poor performances in the 1950 and 1954 World Cups were followed by failure to qualify for the 1958 tournament in Sweden, in what was seen as a national disaster. Although they qualified for both the 1962 and 1966 World Cups, on both occasions the performances were once again extremely disappointing. The defeat by North Korea in 1966 was especially humiliating.

Many blamed the number of *stranieri*, or foreigners, that were playing in the league. Throughout the 1950s, Swedes, Danes, Argentinians, Uruguayans, Brazilians, Englishmen and more were tempted into the Italian game by the vast salaries on offer. Milan had forced their way back to the top of the league after years in the wilderness, largely on the back of the Gre-No-Li trio of Swedes, Gren, Nordahl and Liedholm, whilst Juventus sealed their reputation as the biggest club in the country with players such as John Charles of Wales and the Danish pair Hansen and Praest.

In 1964 it was decided to ban the import of any more foreigners in order to allow Italian players to develop. For so long in the shadow of their foreign counterparts, they were no less skilful but they simply did not get the attention they deserved. The effect of the ban was twofold. Over the period of more than 20 years that the ban was in place, a new generation of Italian stars came to the fore, which ultimately led to the World Cup win in 1982.

On the domestic scene, however, a little of the gloss was taken off the large clubs who, with their foreigners, had looked as if they would dominate European football for good. Milan had won the European Cup in 1963, and were emulated by their local rivals Internazionale the following two years. Inter, in particular, relied heavily on the likes of the Brazilian Jair and Suarez of Spain. For Italian clubs, denied access to players like this, the 1970s proved to be a relatively barren time in European competitions.

Tactics did not help the cause either. Because of the money at stake in the Italian league, and the prestige that went with winning the title, ever more pressure was put on coaches. Catenaccio became the accepted style of play, reinforcing the image of the Italian game as sterile and moribund.

This description applied less to the national side. In the 1970 World Cup, the Italians proved that given the motivation they were as good if not better than most teams. After scoring just one goal in the three group matches, they turned on the style in the quarter and semi-finals, scoring eight goals against the hosts and West Germany. To lose in the final to Brazil was no disgrace. The same thing happened when they finally won the World Cup again in 1982. After three tedious perfomances in the opening group matches, they played four brilliant games and in the end were deserving winners.

The 1990 World Cup, which they hosted, saw the reverse happen. Starting off the tournament as if their very lives depended on winning, they were superb up until the semi-final against Argentina. Clearly the far superior side in that game, they took an early lead but then seemed to want to protect their advantage rather than reinforce their superiority. That age-old cautiousness finally undid them when it mattered most, and they had only themselves to blame as Argentina equalised and then won the penalty shoot-out.

THE ORDER OF MERIT

		All			League			Cup		Europe		
	Team	G	S	B	G	S	B	G	S	G	S	B
1	Juventus	37	23	16	23	16	11	9	2	5	5	5
2	Milan	25	21	15	14	12	13	4	5	7	4	2
3	Internazionale	20	16	17	13	11	11	3	3	4	2	6
4	Torino	13	17	7	8	9	6	5	7	-	1	1
5	Roma	10	10	7	2	5	5	7	3	1	2	2
6	Genoa 1893	10	5	2	9	4	1	1	1	-	-	1
7	Bologna	9	4	4	7	4	3	2	-	-	-	1
8	Fiorentina	7	10	4	2	5	4	4	2	1	3	-
9	Pro Vercelli	7	1	-	7	1	-	-	-	-	-	-
10	Napoli	6	7	7	2	4	6	3	3	1	-	1
11	Sampdoria	6	5	4	1	1	3	4	2	1	2	1
12	Parma	3	2	2	-	-	2	1	1	2	1	-
13	Lazio	2	6	2	1	5	2	1	1	-	-	-
14	Hellas-Verona	1	3	-	1	-	-	-	3	-	-	-
15	Venezia	1	2	1	-	1	1	1	1	-	-	-
16	Atalanta	1	1	1	-	-	-	1	1	-	-	1
	Cagliari	1	1	1	1	1	-	-	-	-	-	1
18	Casale	1	-	-	1	-	-	-	-	-	-	-
	Novese	1	-	-	1	-	-	-	-	-	-	-
	Vado	1	-	-	-	-	-	1	-	-	-	-
21	US Milanese	-	2	1	-	2	1	-	-	-	-	-
22	Alba	-	2	-	-	2	-	-	-	-	-	-
	Livorno	-	2	-	-	2	-	-	-	-	-	-
	Palermo	-	2	-	-	-	-	-	2	-	-	-
	Udinese	-	2	-	-	1	-	-	1	-	-	-
	Lanerossi Vicenza	-	2	-	-	2	-	-	-	-	-	-
27	Alessandria	-	1	1	-	-	1	-	1	-	-	-
	Padova	-	1	1	-	-	1	-	1	-	-	-
29	Ancona	-	1	-	-	-	-	-	1	-	-	-
	Catanzaro	-	1	-	-	-	-	-	1	-	-	-
	Fortitudo	-	1	-	-	1	-	-	-	-	-	-
	Novara	-	1	-	-	-	-	-	1	-	-	-
	Perugia	-	1	-	-	1	-	-	-	-	-	-
	Pisa	-	1	-	-	1	-	-	-	-	-	-
	Savoia	-	1	-	-	1	-	-	-	-	-	-
	SPAL Ferrara	-	1	-	-	-	-	-	1	-	-	-
37	Modena	-	-	1	-	-	1	-	-	-	-	-

To the end of the 1994-1995 season

With the relaxation of the ban on foreigners, the 1980s saw a tremendous boom in club football as Italian teams once again sought the cream of the world's footballers. Michel Platini was signed by Juventus and led them to many honours both at home and in Europe in the first half of the decade, while perhaps most significantly Diego Maradona was lured by Napoli from Barcelona. The Italians could now claim justifiably that theirs was the strongest league in the world, for without question they had most of the world's top players there. In the 1960s, they had failed to engage Pele, but with Maradona they now had the best player in the world.

As the number of foreigners allowed grew from one per team to the present three, a tradition started with the Gre-No-Li trio was continued as Milan went Dutch with Gullit, Rijkaard and Van Basten, and Internazionale went German with Klinsmann, Brehme and Matthäus. The influence of the *stranieri* - and perhaps the ban on English clubs - saw the Italians at their most prolific in Europe. Milan won the European Cup three times, whilst Napoli, Juventus, Internazionale, Parma and Sampdoria were all winners of one of the other two competitions.

Whether another decline in the national side has set in due to the emergence of the *stranieri* is open to debate, but failure to qualify for the 1992 European Championships was not an encouraging sign for the Italians. With freedom of movement for labour in the European Community, in no country will the battle between club and country be more pronounced in the future. Perhaps Italian players ought to buck the trend and move abroad themselves to countries like Spain, Germany or England, in order to increase their profile!

Population: 57,512,000
Area, sq km: 301,277
% in urban areas: 65.0%
Capital city: Rome

Federazione Italiana Giuoco Calcio
Via Gregorio Allegri #14
CP 2450
I-00198 Rome
Italy
Tel: + 39 6 8491111
Fax: + 39 6 84912239

Year of formation	1898
Affiliation to FIFA	1905
Affiliation to UEFA	1954
Registered clubs	19 966
Registered players	1 143 000
Professional players	3200
Registered coaches	33 057
Registered referees	28 455
National stadium	Stadio Olimpico, Rome 80 000
National colours	Blue/White/Blue
Reserve colours	White/Blue/Blue
Season	September - June

THE RECORD

WORLD CUP

1930	Did not enter
1934	QT 1st/2 in group 7 Final Tournament/Winners
1938	QT Automatic Final Tournament/Winners
1950	QT Automatic Final Tournament/1st round
1954	QT 1st/2 in group 9 Final Tournament/1st round
1958	QT 2nd/3 in group 8
1962	QT 1st/4 in group 7 Final Tournament/1st round
1966	QT 1st/4 in group 8 Final Tournament/1st round
1970	QT 1st/3 in group 3 Final Tournament/Finalists
1974	QT 1st/4 in group 2 Final Tournament/1st round
1978	QT 1st/4 in group 2 Final Tournament/2nd round/ 4th place
1982	QT 2nd/5 in group 4 Final Tournament/Winners
1986	QT Automatic Final Tournament/2nd round
1990	QT Automatic Final Tournament/Semi-finalists/ 3rd place
1994	QT 1st/6 in group 1 Final Tournament/Finalists

EUROPEAN CHAMPIONSHIP

1960	Did not enter
1964	2nd round
1968	QT 1st/4 in group 6 Final Tournament/Winners
1972	QT 1st/4 in group 6 Final Tournament/Quarter-finalists
1976	QT 3rd/4 in group 5
1980	QT Automatic Final Tournament/4th place
1984	QT 4th/5 in group 5
1988	QT 1st/5 in group 2 Final Tournament/Semi-finalists
1992	QT 2nd/5 in group 3
1996	QT group 4

Dr. Gerö Cup

1929	Winners
1932	2nd
1935	Winners
1953	4th
1960	5th

EUROPEAN CLUB COMPETITIONS

European Cup
Winners - Milan 1963 1969 1989 1990 1994 Internazionale 1964 1965, Juventus 1985
Finalists - Fiorentina 1957 Milan 1958 1993 1995 Internazionale 1967 1972 Juventus 1973 1983 Roma 1984 Sampdoria 1992

Cup Winners Cup
Winners - Fiorentina 1961 Milan 1968 1973 Juventus 1984 Sampdoria 1990 Parma 1993
Finalists - Fiorentina 1962 Milan 1974 Sampdoria 1989 Parma 1994

UEFA Cup
Winners - Roma 1961 Juventus 1977 1990 1993 Napoli 1989 Internazionale 1991 1994 Parma 1995
Finalists - Juventus 1965 1971 1995 Fiorentina 1990 Roma 1991 Torino 1992

Mitropa Cup
Winners - Bologna 1932 1934
Finalists - Ambrosiana-Inter 1933 Lazio 1937

CLUB DIRECTORY

ROME (Population - 3,175,000)

Lazio SS (1900)
Olimpico 82,000 – Sky blue/White
Previous name - SP Lazio 1900-25

Roma AS (1927)
Olimpico 82,000 – Red, yellow trim
Previous names - Merger in 1927 of Fortitudo, Pro Roma, Roman and Alba

MILAN (Population - 3,750,000)

Internazionale Milano FC (1908)
Giuseppe Meazza 76,000 – Black & blue stripes/Black
Previous name - Ambrosiana-Inter 1929-46

Milan AC (1899)
Giuseppe Meazza 76,000 – Red & black stripes/White
Previous name - Milan Cricket and Football Club 1899-1905, Milan Football Club 1905-38

NAPLES (Population - 2,875,000)

Napoli SSC (1926)
San Paolo 85,000 – Sky blue/White
Previous names - Merger in 1926 of Internaples and Naples

TURIN (Population - 1,550,000)

Juventus FC (1897)
Delle Alpi 71,000 – Black & white stripes/White
Previous name - SC Juventus 1897-99

Torino Calcio (1906)
Delle Alpi 71,000 – Grenadine/White
Previous names - Merger in 1906 of FC Torinense and dissatified members of Juventus. FC Torinense had merged with Internazionale Torino in 1900. FC Torino 1906-36

GENOA (Population - 805,000)
Genoa 1893 (1893)
Luigi Ferraris 41,000 – Red & blue halves/Blue
Previous names - Genoa Football and Cricket Club 1893-99, Genoa FC 1899-1929, Genova 1893 1929-45

Sampdoria UC (1946)
Luigi Ferraris 41,000 – Blue with hoops of white, red, black & white/White
Previous names - Merger in 1946 of Andrea Doria and Sampierdarenese

PALERMO (Population - 723,000)
Palermo US (1898)
Della Favorita 40,000 – Pink/Black
Previous names - US Palermo 1892-42, Palermo-Juve 1942-45, SSC Palermo 1945-87

FLORENCE (Population - 640,000)
Fiorentina AS (1926)
Artemio Franchi 47,000 – Violet, white trim
Previous manes: Merger in 1926 of Polisportiva and CS Firenze

CATANIA (Population - 550,000)
Catania Calcio (1946)
Cibali 12,000 – Red & blue stripes/Blue
Previous names - Merger in 1946 of Virtus and US Catanese (1908)

BOLOGNA (Population - 525,000)
Bologna FC (1909)
Renato Dall'Aria 40,000 – Red & blue stripes/White

BARI (Population - 475,000)
Bari AS (1928)
San Nicola 58,000 – White, red trim
Previous names - Merger in 1928 of FC Bari and US Ideale as US Bari. US Bari 1928-45

VENICE (Population - 420,000)
Venezia Calcio (1907)
Penzo 16,000 – Green, black & orange stripes/Black
Previous names - Venezia Mestre 1980-89

BERGAMO (Population - 345,000)
Atalanta Bergamasca Calcio (1907)
Comunale 33,000 – Black & blue stripes/Black

CAGLIARI (Population - 305,000)
Cagliari Calcio (1920)
Sant'Elia 41,000 – Red & blue halves/Blue
Previous names - Cagliari FC 1920-24, CS Cagliari 1924-34

PADUA (Population - 270,000)
Padova Calcio (1910)
Silvio Appiani 22,000 – White, red trim

MESSINA (Population - 268,000)
Messina AC Riunite (1945)
Giovanni Celeste 15,000 – Red/Black, yellow trim

VERONA (Population - 259,000)
Hellas-Verona (1903)
Bentegodi 50,000 – Blue, yellow trim
Previous names - Hellas 1903-19, Hellas-Verona 1919-28, AC Verona 1928-69

SALERNO (Population - 250,000)
Salernitana Sport (1919)
Stadio Vestuti 12,000 – Grenadine/Grenadine
Previous name - US Salernitana 1919-79

TARANTO (Population - 244,000)
Taranto FC (1926)
Erasmo Jacovone 29,000 – Red & blue stripes/Blue

TRIESTE (Population - 239,000)
Triestina USC (1918)
Nereo Rocco 40,000 – Red/White

BRESCIA (Population - 199,000)
Brescia Calcio (1911)
Mario Rigamonti 25,000 – Blue/White

MODENA (Population - 176,000)
Modena FC (1912)
Alberto Braglia 20,000 – Yellow/Blue
Previous name - Zenit Modena 1957-59

PARMA (Population - 175,000)
Parma AC (1968)
Ennio Tardini 20,000 – White, yellow & blue trim

LIVORNO (Population - 174,000)
Pro Livorno Calcio (1915)
Armando Picchi 20,000 – Cherry/White
Previous name - US Livorno 1915-88

COMO (Population - 165,000)
Como Calcio (1907)
Giuseppe Sinigaglia 23,000 – Blue/White
Previous names - FC Como 1907-25, AC Comense 1925-37

FOGGIA (Population - 155,000)
Foggia Calcio (1920)
Pino Zaccheria 25,000 – Red & black stripes/Black
Previous names - SC Foggia 1920-24, US Foggia 1924-85

PERUGIA (Population - 146,000)
Perugia AC (1905)
Renato Curi 40,000 – Red/White
Previous name - SS Perugia 1913-19

FERRARA (Population - 143,000)
Societa Polisportiva Ars et Labor (SPAL) (1907)
Paolo Mezzza 21,000 – Blue & white stripes/White

PESCARA (Population - 131,000)
Pescara Calcio (1936)
Adriatico 26,000 – White/Blue

UDINE (Population - 126,000)
Udinese Calcio (1896)
Friuli 42,000 – Black & white stripes/White

TERNI (Population - 111,000)
Ternana Polisportiva Calcio (1929)
Libero Liberati 38,000 – Red/Green

VICENZA (Population - 110,000)
Lanerossi-Vicenza SS (1902)
Romeo Menti 28,000 – Red & white stripes/White
Previous name - AC Vicenzia 1902-53

PISA (Population - 104,000)
Pisa Sporting Club (1909)
Arena Garibaldi 30,000 – Blue & black stripes/Black
Previous name - AC Pisa 1931-43

CATANZARO (Population - 102,000)
Catanzaro US (1929)
Nicola Ceravolo 30,000 – Red & yellow stripes/White

NOVARA (Population - 102,000)
Novara Calcio (1908)
Comunale 14,000 – Blue/Blue
Previous names - Novara FC 1908-34. Merged with US Novarese as Novara Calcio in 1934

LEECE (Population - 100,000)
Leece US (1908)
Via del Mare 55,000 – Red & yellow stripes/Red

ALESSANDRIA (Population - 96,000)
Alessandria USC (1920)
Moccagatta 12,000 – Grey/Black
Previous names - Merger in 1920 of US Alessandria and Alessandria FC

CESENA (Population - 90,000)
Cesena AC (1940)
Dino Manuzzi 27,000 – White/Black

PISTOIA (Population - 90,000)
Nuova Pistoiese (1921)
Comunale – Orange/Orange
Previous name - US Pistoiese 1921-88

LUCCA (Population - 88,000)
Lucchese-Libertas AS (1905)
Porta Elisa 9,000 – Red & black stripes/Black

VARESE (Population - 88,000)
Varese FC (1910)
Franco Ossola 23,000 – White/Red
Previous names - AS Varesina 1924-26, Varese Sportiva 1926-46

BUSTO ARSIZIO (Population 78,000)
Pro Patria et Libertate (1919)
Carlo Speroni 20,000 – Blue & white hoops/White

CREMONA (Population - 76,000)
Cremonese US (1903)
Giovanni Zini 14,000 – Grey & red stripes/Red
Previous name - AC Cremona 1903-13

AVELLINO (Population - 56,000)
Avellino US (1912)
Partenio 33,000 – Green/White

MANTOVA (Population - 56,000)
Mantova Nuova AC (1911)
Danilo Martelli 25,000 – Red/White

ASCOLI (Population – 53,000)
Ascoli Calcio 1898 (1898)
Cino e Lillo Del Duca 34,000 – Black & white stripes/White
Previous names - SS Vigor 1898-05, CS Vigor 1905-11, SS Ascoli 1911-55

VERCELLI (Population - 51,000)
Pro Vercelli USC (1892)
Leonida Robbiano 12,000 – White/White

LECCO (Population - 48,000)
Lecco Calcio (1910)
Rigamonti Ceppi 9,000 – White/White

LEGNANO (Population 48,000)
Legnano AC (1913)
Giovanni Mari 7,000 – Lilac/Lilac

EMPOLI (Population - 43,000)
Empoli FC (1921)
Carlo Castellani 19,000 – Blue/White

CASALE (Population – 41,000)
Casale AS (1909)
Natale Palli 8,000 – Black/Black

ITALIAN LEAGUE CHAMPIONSHIP

Year	Champions		Runners up
1898	Genoa	2-1	Internazionale
			Torino
1899	Genoa	2-0	Internazionale
			Torino
1900	Genoa	1-0	FC Torinese
1901	Milan	1-0	Genoa
1902	Genoa	2-0	Milan
1903	Genoa	3-0	Juventus
1904	Genoa	1-0	Juventus
1905	Juventus	*	Genoa
1906	Milan	*	Juventus
1907	Milan	*	Torino
1908	Pro Vercelli	*	US Milanese
1909	Pro Vercelli	2-0 1-1	US Milanese
1910	Internazionale	*	Pro Vercelli
1911	Pro Vercelli	3-0 2-1	Vicenza
1912	Pro Vercelli	6-0 7-0	Venezia
1913	Pro Vercelli	6-0	Lazio
1914	Casale	7-1 2-0	Lazio
1915	Genoa declared winners		
1916-19	-		
1920	Internazionale	3-2	Livorno
1921	Pro Vercelli	2-1	Pisa
1922	Novese	0-0 0-0 2-1	Sampierdarenese
1922	Pro Vercelli	3-0 5-2	Fortitudo
1923	Genoa	4-1 2-0	Lazio
1924	Genoa	3-1 1-1	Savoia
1925	Bologna	4-0 2-0	Alba
1926	Juventus	7-1 5-0	Alba
1927	Torino	*	Bologna
1928	Torino	*	Genoa
1929	Bologna	3-1 0-1 1-0	Torino

* Play-off league positions and points

1905	Juventus 6 Genoa 5 US Milanese 1
1906	Milan 5 Juventus 5 Genoa 2
1907	Milan 6 Torino 5 Andrea Doria 1
1908	Pro Vercelli 6 US Milanese 5 Andrea Doria 1
1910	Internazionale 25 Pro Vercelli 25 Juventus 20
	Internazionale won the play-off with Pro Vercelli 10-3
1927	Torino 14 Bologna 12 Juventus 11
1928	Torino 19 Genoa 17 Juventus/Alessandria 16

SERIE A

1930t	Ambrosiana-Inter 50 Genova 48 Juventus 45
1931	Juventus 55 Roma 51 Bologna 48
1932	Juventus 54 Bologna 50 Roma 40
1933	Juventus 54 Ambrosiana-Inter 46 Bologna 42
1934	Juventus 53 Ambrosiana-Inter 49 Napoli 46
1935q	Juventus 44 Ambrosiana-Inter 42 Fiorentina 39
1936	Bologna 40 Roma 39 Torino 38
1937	Bologna 42 Lazio 39 Torino 38
1938	Ambrosiana-Inter 41 Juventus 39 Milan 38
1939	Bologna 42 Torino 38 Ambrosiana-Inter 37
1940	Ambrosiana-Inter 44 Bologna 41 Juventus 36
1941	Bologna 39 Ambrosiana-Inter 35 Milan 34
1942	Roma 42 Torino 39 Venezia 38
1943	Torino 44 Livorno 43 Juventus 37
1944-45	-
1946f	Torino 22 Juventus 21 Milan 16
1947v	Torino 63 Juventus 53 Modena 51
1948x	Torino 65 Milan 49 Juventus 49
1949v	Torino 60 Internazionale 55 Milan 50
1950	Juventus 62 Milan 57 Internazionale 49
1951	Milan 60 Internazionale 59 Juventus 54
1952	Juventus 60 Milan 53 Internazionale 49
1953t	Internazionale 47 Juventus 45 Milan 43
1954	Internazionale 51 Juventus 50 Milan 44
1955	Milan 48 Udinese 44 Roma 41
1956	Fiorentina 53 Milan 41 Internazionale 39
1957	Milan 48 Fiorentina 42 Lazio 41
1958	Juventus 51 Fiorentina 43 Padova 42
1959	Milan 52 Fiorentina 49 Internazionale 46
1960	Juventus 55 Fiorentina 47 Milan 44
1961	Juventus 49 Milan 45 Internazionale 44
1962	Milan 53 Internazionale 48 Fiorentina 46
1963	Internazionale 49 Juventus 45 Milan 43
1964	Bologna 54 Internazionale 54 Milan 51
1965	Internazionale 54 Milan 51 Torino 44
1966	Internazionale 50 Bologna 46 Napoli 45
1967	Juventus 49 Internazionale 48 Bologna 45
1968q	Milan 46 Napoli 37 Juventus 36
1969	Fiorentina 45 Cagliari 41 Milan 41
1970	Cagliari 45 Internazionale 41 Juventus 38
1971	Internazionale 46 Milan 42 Napoli 39
1972	Juventus 43 Milan 42 Torino 42
1973	Juventus 45 Milan 44 Lazio 43
1974	Lazio 43 Juventus 41 Napoli 36
1975	Juventus 43 Napoli 41 Roma 39
1976	Torino 45 Juventus 43 Milan 38
1977	Juventus 51 Torino 50 Fiorentina 35
1978	Juventus 44 Lanerossi Vicenza 39 Torino 39
1979	Milan 44 Perugia 41 Juventus 37
1980	Internazionale 41 Juventus 38 Milan 36
1981	Juventus 44 Roma 42 Napoli 38
1982	Juventus 46 Fiorentina 45 Roma 38
1983	Roma 43 Juventus 39 Internazionale 38
1984	Juventus 43 Roma 41 Fiorentina 36
1985	Hellas-Verona 43 Torino 39 Internazionale 38
1986	Juventus 45 Roma 41 Napoli 39

1987 Napoli 42 Juventus 39 Internazionale 38
1988 Milan 45 Napoli 42 Roma 38
1989t Internazionale 58 Napoli 47 Milan 46
1990 Napoli 51 Milan 49 Internazionale 44
1991 Sampdoria 51 Milan 46 Internazionale 46
1992 Milan 56 Juventus 48 Torino 43
1993 Milan 50 Internazionale 46 Parma 41
1994 Milan 50 Juventus 47 Sampdoria 44
1995t2 Juventus 73 Lazio 63 Parma 63

Championship play-off
1964 Bologna..............................2-0................Internazionale

ITALIAN CUP FINALS

1922 Vado ....1-0................Udinese
1923-35 -
1936 Torino ....5-1 ....Alessandria
1937 Genoa ....1-0................Roma
1938 Juventus..........................3-1 2-1 ....Torino
1939 Ambrosiana-Inter ....2-1 ....Novara
1940 Fiorentina ....1-0................Genova
1941 Venezia ....3-3 1-0............Roma
1942 Juventus..........................1-1 4-1 ....Milan
1943 Torino ....4-0................Venezia
1944-57 -
1958 Lazio ....1-0................Fiorentina
1959 Juventus ....4-1 ....Internazionale
1960 Juventus ....3-2................Fiorentina
1961 Fiorentina ....2-0................Lazio
1962 Napoli ....2-1 ....SPAL Ferrara
1963 Atalanta ....3-1 ....Torino
1964 Roma ....0-0 1-0............Torino
1965 Juventus ....1-0................Internazionale
1966 Fiorentina ....2-1 ....Catanzaro
1967 Milan ....1-0................Padova
1968 Torino.................................. *
1969 Roma .... *
1970 Bologna .... *
1971 Torino............................0-0 5-3p ....Milan
1972 Milan ....2-0................Napoli
1973 Milan ....1-1 5-2p ....Juventus
1974 Bologna ....0-0 5-4p ....Palermo
1975 Fiorentina ....3-2................Milan
1976 Napoli ....4-0................Hellas-Verona
1977 Milan ....2-0................Internazionale
1978 Internazionale....................2-1 ....Napoli
1979 Juventus ....2-1 ....Palermo
1980 Roma ....0-0 3-2p ....Torino
1981 Roma ....1-1 1-1 5-3p.........Torino
1982 Internazionale................1-0 1-1 ....Torino
1983 Juventus..........................0-2 3-0 ....Hellas-Verona
1984 Roma ....1-1 1-0............Hellas-Verona
1985 Sampdoria ....1-0 2-1 ....Milan
1986 Roma ....1-2 2-0............Sampdoria
1987 Napoli..............................3-0 1-0............Atalanta
1988 Sampdoria ....2-0 1-2 ....Torino
1989 Sampdoria ....0-1 4-0............Napoli
1990 Juventus..........................0-0 1-0............Milan
1991 Roma ....3-1 1-1 ....Sampdoria
1992 Parma ....0-1 2-0............Juventus
1993 Torino..............................3-0 2-5 ....Roma
1994 Sampdoria ....0-0 6-1 ....Ancona
1995 Juventus..........................1-0 2-0 ....Parma

* Played on a league basis

LEADING INTERNATIONAL GOALSCORERS

35	Luigi Riva	(Cagliari)	1965-1974
33	Giuseppe Meazza	(Internazionale)	1930-1939
30	Silvio Piola	(Lazio,Juventus,Novara)	1935-1952
25	Adolfo Baloncieri	(Alessandria,Torino)	1920-1930
	Alessandro Altobelli	(Internazionale)	1980-1988
24	Roberto Baggio	(Fiorentina,Juventus)	1988-
23	Francesco Graziani	(Torino,Fiorentina)	1975-1983
22	Alessandro Mazzola	(Internazionale)	1963-1974
20	Paolo Rossi	(Vicenza,Perugia,Juventus, Milan)	1977-1986
19	Roberto Bettega	(Juventus)	1975-1983

LEADING INTERNATIONAL APPEARANCES

112	Dino Zoff #	(Napoli,Juventus)	1968-1983
94	Giacinto Facchetti	(Internazionale)	1963-1977
81	Marco Tardelli	(Juventus)	1976-1985
81	Franco Baresi	(Milan)	1982-1994
78	Gaetano Scirea	(Juventus)	1975-1986
77	Giuseppe Bergomi	(Internazionale)	1982-1991
73	Giancarlo Antognoni	(Fiorentina)	1974-1983
	Antonio Cabrini	(Juventus)	1978-1987
71	Claudio Gentile	(Juventus)	1975-1984
70	Alessandro Mazzola	(Internazionale)	1963-1974

NATIONAL TEAM COACHES

1910-12	Committee
1912	Vittorio Pozzo
1912-24	Committee
1924	Vittorio Pozzo
1924-25	Committee
1925-28	Augusto Rangone
1928-29	Carlo Carcano
1929-48	Vittorio Pozzo
1949-50	Novo, Bardelli, Copernico & Biancone
1951	Beretta, Busini & Combi
1952-53	Beretta & G. Meazza
1953-54	Czeizler, Schiavio & Piola
1954-56	Marmo, Pasquale, Tentorio, Schiavio & Foni
1957-58	Foni, Pasquale, Schiavio, Tentorio, Marmo, Biancone
1958-59	Ferrari, Mocchetti & Biancone
1960	Giuseppe Viani
1960-61	Giovanni Ferrari
1962	Giovanni Ferrari & P. Mazza
1962-66	Edmondo Fabbri
1966-67	Helenio Herrera & Ferruccio Valcareggi
1967-74	Ferruccio Valcareggi
1974-75	Fulvio Bernardini
1975-77	Fulvio Bernardini & Enzo Bearzot
1977-86	Enzo Bearzot
1986-91	Azeglio Vicini
1991-	Arrigo Sacchi

INTERNATIONAL MATCHES PLAYED BY ITALY

Date	Opponents	Result	Venue	Compet	Scorers
15-05-1910	France	W 6-2	Milan	Fr	Lana 3, Fossati, Rizzi, Debernardi
26-05	Hungary	L 1-6	Budapest	Fr	Rizzi

6-01-1911	Hungary	L 0-1	Milan	Fr	
9-04	France	D 2-2	Paris	Fr	Rampini, Boiocchi
7-05	Switzerland	D 2-2	Milan	Fr	Carrer, Boiocchi
21-05	Switzerland	L 0-3	Chaux-de-Fonds	Fr	
17-03-1912	France	L 3-4	Turin	Fr	Rampini 2, Cevenini.A
29-06	Finland	L 2-3	Stockholm	OGr1	Bontadini, Sardi
1-07	Sweden	W 1-0	Stockholm	OGct	Bontadini
3-07	Austria	L 1-5	Stockholm	OGct	Berardo
22-12	Austria	L 1-3	Genoa	Fr	Sardi
12-01-1913	France	L 0-1	Paris	Fr	
1-05	Belgium	W 1-0	Turin	Fr	Ara
15-06	Austria	L 0-2	Vienna	Fr	
11-01-1914	Austria	D 0-0	Milan	Fr	
29-03	France	W 2-0	Turin	Fr	Berardo, Cevenini.A
5-04	Switzerland	D 1-1	Genoa	Fr	Mattea
17-05	Switzerland	W 1-0	Berne	Fr	Barbesino
31-01-1915	Switzerland	W 3-1	Turin	Fr	Cevenini.A 2, Cevenini.L
18-01-1920	France	W 9-4	Milan	Fr	Cevenini.L 2, Aebi 3, Brezzi 3, Carcano
28-03	Switzerland	L 0-3	Berne	Fr	
13-05	Holland	D 1-1	Genoa	Fr	Sardi
28-08	Egypt	W 2-1	Ghent	OGr1	Baloncieri, Brezzi
29-08	France	L 1-3	Antwerp	OGqf	Brezzi
31-08	Norway	W 2-1	Antwerp	OGct	Sardi, Badini
2-09	Spain	L 0-2	Antwerp	OGct	
20-02-1921	France	W 2-1	Marseille	Fr	Cevenini.L, Santamaria
6-03	Switzerland	W 2-1	Milan	Fr	Migliavacca, Cevenini.L
5-05	Belgium	W 3-2	Antwerp	Fr	Migliavacca, Forlivesi, Ferraris.P (I)
8-05	Holland	D 2-2	Amsterdam	Fr	Forlivesi, Cevenini.L
6-11	Switzerland	D 1-1	Geneva	Fr	Moscardini
15-01-1922	Austria	D 3-3	Milan	Fr	Moscardini 2, Santamaria
26-02	Czechoslovakia	D 1-1	Turin	Fr	Baloncieri
21-05	Belgium	W 4-2	Milan	Fr	Baloncieri 2, Moscardini, Burlando
3-12	Switzerland	D 2-2	Bologna	Fr	Cevenini.L 2
1-01-1923	Germany	W 3-1	Milan	Fr	Cevenini.L, Santamaria, Migliavacca
4-03	Hungary	D 0-0	Genoa	Fr	
15-04	Austria	D 0-0	Vienna	Fr	
27-05	Czechoslovakia	L 1-5	Prague	Fr	Moscardini
20-01-1924	Austria	L 0-4	Genoa	Fr	
9-03	Spain	D 0-0	Milan	Fr	
6-04	Hungary	L 1-7	Budapest	Fr	Cevenini.L
25-05	Spain	W 1-0	Paris	OGr1	OG
29-05	Luxembourg	W 2-0	Paris	OGr2	Baloncieri, Della Valle
2-06	Switzerland	L 1-2	Paris	OGqf	Della Valle
16-11	Sweden	D 2-2	Milan	Fr	Magnozzi 2
23-11	Germany	W 1-0	Duisburg	Fr	Janni
18-01-1925	Hungary	L 1-2	Milan	Fr	Conti.L
22-03	France	W 7-0	Turin	Fr	Conti.L, Baloncieri 2, Levratto 2, Moscardini 2
14-06	Spain	L 0-1	Valencia	Fr	
18-06	Portugal	L 0-1	Lisbon	Fr	
4-11	Yugoslavia	W 2-1	Padua	Fr	Schiavio 2
8-11	Hungary	D 1-1	Budapest	Fr	Della Valle
17-01-1926	Czechoslovakia	W 3-1	Turin	Fr	Della Valle, Conti.L, Magnozzi
21-03	Rep. Ireland	W 3-0	Turin	Fr	Baloncieri, Magnozzi, Bernardini
18-04	Switzerland	D 1-1	Zurich	Fr	Magnozzi
9-05	Switzerland	W 3-2	Milan	Fr	Della Valle 2, Schiavio
18-07	Sweden	L 3-5	Stockholm	Fr	Levratto 2, Cevenini.L
28-10	Czechoslovakia	L 1-3	Prague	Fr	Levratto
30-01-1927	Switzerland	W 5-1	Geneva	Fr	Baloncieri 3, Libonatti, Rossetti
20-02	Czechoslovakia	D 2-2	Milan	Fr	Libonatti, Baloncieri
17-04	Portugal	W 3-1	Turin	Fr	Levratto 2, Baloncieri
24-04	France	D 3-3	Paris	Fr	Libonatti 2, Conti.L
29-05	Spain	W 2-0	Bologna	Fr	Baloncieri, OG
23-10	Czechoslovakia	D 2-2	Prague	DGC	Libonatti 2
6-11	Austria	L 0-1	Bologna	DGC	
1-01-1928	Switzerland	W 3-2	Genoa	DGC	Libonatti 2, Magnozzi
25-03	Hungary	W 4-3	Rome	DGC	Conti.L 2, Rossetti, Libonatti
15-04	Portugal	L 1-4	Oporto	Fr	Libonatti
22-04	Spain	D 1-1	Gijon	Fr	Libonatti
29-05	France	W 4-3	Amsterdam	OGr1	Rossetti, Levratto, Banchero, Baloncieri
1-06	Spain	D 1-1	Amsterdam	OGqf	Baloncieri
4-06	Spain	W 7-1	Amsterdam	OGqf	Magnozzi, Schiavio, Baloncieri, Bernardini, Rivolta, Levratto 2

7-06	Uruguay	L 2-3	Amsterdam	OGsf	Baloncieri, Levratto
10-06	Egypt	W 11-3	Amsterdam	OG3p	Schiavio 3, Baloncieri 2, Banchero 3, Magnozzi 3
14-10	Switzerland	W 3-2	Zurich	DGC	Rossetti 2, Baloncieri
11-11	Austria	D 2-2	Rome	Fr	Conti.L 2
2-12	Holland	W 3-2	Milan	Fr	Libonatti 2, Baloncieri
3-03-1929	Czechoslovakia	W 4-2	Bologna	DGC	Rossetti 3, Libonatti
7-04	Austria	L 0-3	Vienna	DGC	
28-04	Germany	L 1-2	Turin	Fr	Rossetti
1-12	Portugal	W 6-1	Milan	Fr	Mihalic 2, Orsi 2, Baloncieri, Sallustro
9-02-1930	Switzerland	W 4-2	Rome	Fr	Magnozzi, Orsi, Meazza 2
2-03	Germany	W 2-0	Frankfurt	Fr	Baloncieri, Meazza
6-04	Holland	D 1-1	Amsterdam	Fr	Baloncieri
11-05	Hungary	W 5-0	Budapest	DGC	Meazza 3, Magnozzi, Costantino
22-06	Spain	L 2-3	Bologna	Fr	Costantino 2
25-01-1931	France	W 5-0	Bologna	Fr	Meazza 3, Cesarini, Cattaneo
22-02	Austria	W 2-1	Milan	DGC	Meazza, Orsi
29-03	Switzerland	D 1-1	Berne	DGC	Cesarini
12-04	Portugal	W 2-0	Oporto	Fr	Orsi, Ferrari
19-04	Spain	D 0-0	Bilbao	Fr	
20-05	Scotland	W 3-0	Rome	Fr	Costantino, Meazza, Orsi
15-11	Czechoslovakia	D 2-2	Rome	DGC	Pitto, Bernardini
13-12	Hungary	W 3-2	Turin	DGC	Libonatti, Orsi, Cesarini
14-02-1932	Switzerland	W 3-0	Naples	DGC	Fedullo 3
20-03	Austria	L 1-2	Vienna	DGC	Meazza
10-04	France	W 2-1	Paris	Fr	Magnozzi, Costantino
8-05	Hungary	D 1-1	Budapest	DGC	Costantino
28-10	Czechoslovakia	L 1-2	Prague	DGC	Ferrari
27-11	Hungary	W 4-2	Milan	Fr	Orsi 2, Meazza, Ferrari
1-01-1933	Germany	W 3-1	Bologna	Fr	Meazza, Costantino, Schiavio
12-02	Belgium	W 3-2	Brussels	Fr	Meazza 2, Costantini
2-04	Switzerland	W 3-0	Geneva	DGC	Schiavio 2, Meazza
7-05	Czechoslovakia	W 2-0	Florence	DGC	Ferrari, Schiavio
13-05	England	D 1-1	Rome	Fr	Ferrari
22-10	Hungary	W 1-0	Budapest	DGC	Borel
3-12	Switzerland	W 5-2	Florence	DGC	Ferrari, Pizziolo, Orsi, Meazza, Monti
11-02-1934	Austria	L 2-4	Turin	DGC	Guaita 2
25-03	Greece	W 4-0	Milan	WCq	Guarisi, Meazza 2, Ferrari
27-05	USA	W 7-1	Rome	WCr1	Schiavio 3, Orsi 2, Ferrari, Meazza
31-05	Spain	D 1-1	Florence	WCqf	Ferrari
1-06	Spain	W 1-0	Florence	WCqf	Meazza
3-06	Austria	W 1-0	Milan	WCsf	Guaita
10-06	Czechoslovakia	W 2-1	Rome	WCf	Orsi, Schiavio
14-11	England	L 2-3	London	Fr	Meazza 2
9-12	Hungary	W 4-2	Milan	Fr	Guaita 2, Ferrari, Meazza
17-02-1935	France	W 2-1	Rome	Fr	Meazza 2
24-03	Austria	W 2-0	Vienna	DGC	Piola
27-10	Czechoslovakia	L 1-2	Prague	DGC	Pitto
24-11	Hungary	D 2-2	Milan	DGC	Colaussi, Ferrari
5-04-1936	Switzerland	W 2-1	Zurich	Fr	Demaria, Colaussi
17-05	Austria	D 2-2	Rome	Fr	Demaria, Pasinati
31-05	Hungary	W 2-1	Budapest	Fr	Pasinati, Meazza
3-08	United States	W 1-0	Berlin	OGr1	Frossi
7-08	Japan	W 8-0	Berlin	OGqf	Frossi 3, Biagi 4, Cappelli
10-08	Norway	W 2-1	Berlin	OGsf	Negro, Frossi
15-08	Austria *	W 2-1	Berlin	OGf	Frossi 2
25-10	Switzerland	W 4-2	Milan	DGC	Meazza, Piola 2, Pasinati
15-11	Germany	D 2-2	Berlin	Fr	Colaussi, Ferrari
13-12	Czechoslovakia	W 2-0	Genoa	Fr	Pasinati, Ferrari
25-04-1937	Hungary	W 2-0	Turin	DGC	Colaussi, Frossi
23-05	Czechoslovakia	W 1-0	Prague	DGC	Piola
27-05	Norway	W 3-1	Oslo	Fr	Meazza, Piola 2
31-10	Switzerland	D 2-2	Geneva	DGC	Piola 2
5-12	France	D 0-0	Paris	Fr	
15-05-1938	Belgium	W 6-1	Milan	Fr	Meazza, Andreolo, Pasinati, Piola 3
22-05	Yugoslavia	W 4-0	Genoa	Fr	Colaussi, Piola, Meazza, Ferrari
5-06	Norway	W 2-1	Marseille	WCr1	Ferraris.P (II), Piola
12-06	France	W 3-1	Paris	WCqf	Colaussi, Piola 2
16-06	Brazil	W 2-1	Marseille	WCsf	Colaussi, Meazza
19-06	Hungary	W 4-2	Paris	WCf	Colaussi 2, Piola 2
20-11	Switzerland	W 2-0	Bologna	Fr	Colaussi, OG
4-12	France	W 1-0	Naples	Fr	Biavati

26-03-1939	Germany	W 3-2	Florence	Fr	Piola 2, Biavati
13-05	England	D 2-2	Milan	Fr	Biavati, Piola
4-06	Yugoslavia	W 2-1	Belgrade	Fr	Piola, Colaussi
8-06	Hungary	W 3-1	Budapest	Fr	Piola, Colaussi 2
11-06	Romania	W 1-0	Bucharest	Fr	Colaussi
20-07	Finland	W 3-2	Helsinki	Fr	Piola 3
12-11	Switzerland	L 1-3	Zurich	Fr	Puricelli
26-11	Germany	L 2-5	Berlin	Fr	Neri, Demaria
3-03-1940	Switzerland	D 1-1	Turin	Fr	Corbelli
14-04	Romania	W 2-1	Rome	Fr	Biavati, Piola
5-05	Germany	W 3-2	Milan	Fr	Colaussi, Bertoni.I, Biavati
1-12	Hungary	D 1-1	Genoa	Fr	Trevisan
5-04-1942	Croatia	W 4-0	Genoa	Fr	Gabetto, Ferraris.P (II), Biavati, OG
19-04	Spain	W 4-0	Milan	Fr	Mazzola.V, Ferraris.P (II), Piola, Loik
11-11-1945	Switzerland	D 4-4	Zurich	Fr	Piola, Loik, Biavati 2
1-12-1946	Austria	W 3-2	Milan	Fr	Castigliano, Mazzola.V, Piola
27-04-1947	Switzerland	W 5-2	Florence	Fr	Mazzola.V, Loik, Menti 3
11-05	Hungary	W 3-2	Turin	Fr	Gabetto 2, Loik
9-11	Austria	L 1-5	Vienna	Fr	Carapellese
14-12	Czechoslovakia	W 3-1	Bari	Fr	Menti, Gabetto, Carapellese
4-04-1948	France	W 3-1	Paris	Fr	Carapellese 2, Gabetto
16-05	England	L 0-4	Turin	Fr	
27-02-1949	Portugal	W 4-1	Genoa	Fr	Menti, Carapellese, Mazzola.V, Maroso
27-03	Spain	W 3-1	Madrid	Fr	Lorenzi, Carapellese, Amadei
22-05	Austria	W 3-1	Florence	DGC	Cappello, Amadei, Boniperti
12-06	Hungary	D 1-1	Budapest	DGC	Carapellese
30-11	England	L 0-2	London	Fr	
5-03-1950	Belgium	W 3-1	Bologna	Fr	Muccinelli 2, Amadei
2-04	Austria	L 0-1	Vienna	DGC	
25-06	Sweden	L 2-3	Sao Paulo	WCr1	Carapellese, Muccinelli
2-07	Paraguay	W 2-0	Sao Paulo	WCr1	Carapellese, Pandolfini
8-04-1951	Portugal	W 4-1	Lisbon	Fr	Pandolfini, Burini, Amadei, Cappello
6-05	Yugoslavia	D 0-0	Milan	Fr	
3-06	France	W 4-1	Genoa	Fr	Lorenzi 2, Amadei, Cappello
11-11	Sweden	D 1-1	Florence	Fr	Amadei
25-11	Switzerland	D 1-1	Lugano	DGC	Boniperti
24-02-1952	Belgium	L 0-2	Brussels	Fr	
18-05	England	D 1-1	Florence	Fr	Amadei
26-10	Sweden	D 1-1	Stockholm	Fr	Vivolo
28-12	Switzerland	W 2-0	Palermo	DGC	Pandolfini, Frignani
26-04-1953	Czechoslovakia	L 0-2	Prague	DGC	
17-05	Hungary	L 0-3	Rome	DGC	
13-11	Egypt	W 2-1	Cairo	WCq	Frignani, Muccinelli
13-12	Czechoslovakia	W 3-0	Genoa	DGC	Cervato, Ricagni, Pandolfini
24-01-1954	Egypt	W 5-1	Milan	WCq	Pandolfini, Frignani, Boniperti 2, Ricagni
11-04	France	W 3-1	Paris	Fr	Pandolfini, Galli 2
17-06	Switzerland	L 1-2	Lausanne	WCr1	Boniperti
20-06	Belgium	W 4-1	Lugano	WCr1	Pandolfini, Galli, Frignani, Lorenzi
23-06	Switzerland	L 1-4	Basle	WCr1	Nesti
5-12	Argentina	W 2-0	Rome	Fr	Frignani, Galli
16-01-1955	Belgium	W 1-0	Bari	Fr	Boniperti
30-03	West Germany	W 2-1	Stuttgart	Fr	Frignani, Pivatelli
29-05	Yugoslavia	L 0-4	Turin	DGC	
27-11	Hungary	L 0-2	Budapest	DGC	
18-12	West Germany	W 2-1	Rome	Fr	OG, Boniperti
15-02-1956	France	W 2-0	Bologna	Fr	Carapellese, Gratton
25-04	Brazil	W 3-0	Milan	Fr	Virgili 2, OG
24-06	Argentina	L 0-1	Buenos Aires	Fr	
1-07	Brazil	L 0-2	Rio de Janeiro	Fr	
11-11	Switzerland	D 1-1	Berne	DGC	Firmani
9-12	Austria	W 2-1	Genoa	DGC	Longoni 2
25-04-1957	Nth. Ireland	W 1-0	Rome	WCq	Cervato
12-05	Yugoslavia	L 1-6	Zagreb	DGC	Cervato
26-05	Portugal	L 0-3	Lisbon	WCq	
4-12	Nth. Ireland	D 2-2	Belfast	Fr	Ghiggia, Montuori
22-12	Portugal	W 3-0	Milan	WCq	Gratton 2, Pivatelli
15-01-1958	Nth. Ireland	L 1-2	Belfast	WCq	Da Costa
23-03	Austria	L 2-3	Vienna	DGC	Petris, Firmani
9-11	France	D 2-2	Paris	Fr	Nicole 2
13-12	Czechoslovakia	D 1-1	Genoa	DGC	Galli
28-02-1959	Spain	D 1-1	Rome	Fr	Lojacono

Date	Opponent	Result	Venue	Type	Scorers
6-05	England	D 2-2	London	Fr	Brighenti, Mariani
1-11	Czechoslovakia	L 1-2	Prague	DGC	Lojacono
29-11	Hungary	D 1-1	Florence	DGC	Cervato
6-01-1960	Switzerland	W 3-0	Naples	DGC	OG, Stacchini, Montuori
13-03	Spain	L 1-3	Barcelona	Fr	Lojacono
10-12	Austria	L 1-2	Naples	Fr	Boniperti
25-04-1961	Nth. Ireland	W 3-2	Bologna	Fr	Stacchini 2, Sivori
24-05	England	L 2-3	Rome	Fr	Sivori, Brighenti
15-06	Argentina	W 4-1	Florence	Fr	Lojacono, Sivori 2, Mora
15-10	Israel	W 4-2	Tel Aviv	WCq	Lojacono, Altafini, Corso 2
4-11	Israel	W 6-0	Turin	WCq	Sivori 4, Corso, Angelillo
5-05-1962	France	W 2-1	Florence	Fr	Altafini 2
13-05	Belgium	W 3-1	Brussels	Fr	Menichelli, Altafini 2
31-05	West Germany	D 0-0	Santiago	WCr1	
2-06	Chile	L 0-2	Santiago	WCr1	
7-06	Switzerland	W 3-0	Santiago	WCr1	Mora, Bulgarelli 2
11-11	Austria	W 2-1	Vienna	Fr	Pascutti 2
2-12	Turkey	W 6-0	Bologna	ECr1	Rivera 2, Orlando 4
27-03-1963	Turkey	W 1-0	Istanbul	ECr1	Sormani
12-05	Brazil	W 3-0	Milan	Fr	Sormani, Mazzola.A, Bulgarelli
9-06	Austria	W 1-0	Vienna	Fr	Trapattoni
13-10	Soviet Union	L 0-2	Moscow	ECr2	
10-11	Soviet Union	D 1-1	Rome	ECr2	Rivera
14-12	Austria	W 1-0	Turin	Fr	Rivera
11-04-1964	Czechoslovakia	D 0-0	Florence	Fr	
10-05	Switzerland	W 3-1	Lausanne	Fr	Mazzola.A, Corso, Rivera
4-11	Finland	W 6-1	Genoa	WCq	Facchetti, OG, Rivera, Bulgarelli, Mazzola.A 2
5-12	Denmark	W 3-1	Bologna	Fr	Pascutti 2, Bulgarelli
13-03-1965	West Germany	D 1-1	Hamburg	Fr	Mazzola.A
18-04	Poland	D 0-0	Warsaw	WCq	
1-05	Wales	W 4-1	Florence	Fr	Lodetti 2, Barison, Nocera
16-06	Sweden	D 2-2	Malmo	Fr	Pascutti, Mazzola.A
23-06	Finland	W 2-0	Helsinki	WCq	Mazzola.A 2
27-06	Hungary	L 1-2	Budapest	Fr	Mazzola.A
1-11	Poland	W 6-1	Rome	WCq	Mazzola.A, Barison 3, Rivera, Mora
9-11	Scotland	L 0-1	Glasgow	WCq	
7-12	Scotland	W 3-0	Naples	WCq	Pascutti, Facchetti, Mora
19-03-1966	France	D 0-0	Paris	Fr	
14-06	Bulgaria	W 6-1	Bologna	Fr	Mazzola.A, Perani, Rizzo 2, Barison, Meroni
18-06	Austria	W 1-0	Milan	Fr	Burgnich
22-06	Argentina	W 3-0	Turin	Fr	Pascutti 2, Meroni
29-06	Mexico	W 5-0	Florence	Fr	Bulgarelli 2, Rivera 2, Mazzola.A
13-07	Chile	W 2-0	Sunderland	WCr1	Mazzola.A, Barison
16-07	Soviet Union	L 0-1	Sunderland	WCr1	
19-07	North Korea	L 0-1	Middlesbrough	WCr1	
1-11	Soviet Union	W 1-0	Milan	Fr	Guarneri
26-11	Romania	W 3-1	Naples	ECq	Mazzola.A 2, Depaoli
22-03-1967	Cyprus	W 2-0	Nicosia	ECq	Domenghini, Facchetti
27-03	Portugal	D 1-1	Rome	Fr	Cappellini
25-06	Romania	W 1-0	Bucharest	ECq	Bertini
1-11	Cyprus	W 5-0	Cosenza	ECq	Mazzola.A 2, Riva 3
18-11	Switzerland	D 2-2	Berne	ECq	Riva 2
23-12	Switzerland	W 4-0	Cagliari	ECq	Mazzola.A, Riva, Domenghini
6-04-1968	Bulgaria	L 2-3	Sofia	ECqf	OG, Prati
20-04	Bulgaria	W 2-0	Naples	ECqf	Prati, Domenghini
5-06	Soviet Union	D 0-0	Naples	ECsf	
8-06	Yugoslavia	D 1-1	Rome	ECf	Domenghini
10-06	Yugoslavia	W 2-0	Rome	ECf	Riva, Anastasi
23-10	Wales	W 1-0	Cardiff	WCq	Riva
1-01-1969	Mexico	W 3-2	Mexico City	Fr	Riva 2, Anastasi
5-01	Mexico	D 1-1	Mexico City	Fr	Bertini
29-03	East Germany	D 2-2	Berlin	WCq	Riva
24-05	Bulgaria	D 0-0	Turin	Fr	
4-11	Wales	W 4-1	Rome	WCq	Riva 3, Mazzola.A
22-11	East Germany	W 3-0	Naples	WCq	Mazzola.A, Domenghini, Riva
21-02-1970	Spain	D 2-2	Madrid	Fr	Anastasi, Riva
10-05	Portugal	W 2-1	Lisbon	Fr	Riva 2
3-06	Sweden	W 1-0	Toluca	WCr1	Domenghini
6-06	Uruguay	D 0-0	Puebla	WCr1	
11-06	Israel	D 0-0	Toluca	WCr1	
14-06	Mexico	W 4-1	Toluca	WCqf	OG, Riva 2, Rivera

Date	Opponent	Result	Venue	Competition	Scorers
17-06	West Germany	W 4-3	Mexico City	WCsf	Boninsegna, Burgnich, Riva, Rivera
21-06	Brazil	L 1-4	Mexico City	WCf	Boninsegna
17-10	Switzerland	D 1-1	Berne	Fr	Mazzola.A
31-10	Austria	W 2-1	Vienna	ECq	De Sisti, Mazzola.A
8-12	Rep. Ireland	W 3-0	Florence	ECq	De Sisti, Boninsegna, Prati
20-02-1971	Spain	L 1-2	Cagliari	Fr	De Sisti
10-05	Rep. Ireland	W 2-1	Dublin	ECq	Boninsegna, Prati
9-06	Sweden	D 0-0	Stockholm	ECq	
25-09	Mexico	W 2-0	Genoa	Fr	Boninsegna 2
9-10	Sweden	W 3-0	Milan	ECq	Riva 2, Boninsegna
20-11	Austria	D 2-2	Rome	ECq	Prati, De Sisti
4-03-1972	Greece	L 1-2	Athens	Fr	Boninsegna
29-04	Belgium	D 0-0	Milan	ECqf	
13-05	Belgium	L 1-2	Brussels	ECqf	Riva
17-06	Romania	D 3-3	Bucharest	Fr	Prati 2, Causio
21-06	Bulgaria	D 1-1	Sofia	Fr	Chinaglia
20-09	Yugoslavia	W 3-1	Turin	Fr	Riva, Chinaglia, Anastasi
7-10	Luxembourg	W 4-0	Luxembourg	WCq	Chinaglia, Riva 2, Capello
21-10	Switzerland	D 0-0	Berne	WCq	
13-01-1973	Turkey	D 0-0	Naples	WCq	
25-02	Turkey	W 1-0	Istanbul	WCq	Anastasi
31-03	Luxembourg	W 5-0	Genoa	WCq	Riva 4, Rivera
9-06	Brazil	W 2-0	Rome	Fr	Riva, Capello
14-06	England	W 2-0	Turin	Fr	Anastasi, Capello
29-09	Sweden	W 2-0	Milan	Fr	Anastasi, Riva
20-10	Switzerland	W 2-0	Rome	WCq	Rivera, Riva
14-11	England	W 1-0	London	Fr	Cappelo
26-02-1974	West Germany	D 0-0	Rome	Fr	
8-06	Austria	D 0-0	Vienna	Fr	
15-06	Haiti	W 3-1	Munich	WCr1	Rivera, OG, Anastasi
19-06	Argentina	D 1-1	Stuttgart	WCr1	OG
23-06	Poland	L 1-2	Stuttgart	WCr1	Capello
28-09	Yugoslavia	L 0-1	Zagreb	Fr	
20-11	Holland	L 1-3	Rotterdam	ECq	Boninsegna
29-12	Bulgaria	D 0-0	Genoa	Fr	
19-04-1975	Poland	D 0-0	Rome	ECq	
5-06	Finland	W 1-0	Helsinki	ECq	Chinaglia
8-06	Soviet Union	L 0-1	Moscow	Fr	
27-09	Finland	D 0-0	Rome	ECq	
26-10	Poland	D 0-0	Warsaw	ECq	
22-11	Holland	W 1-0	Rome	ECq	Capello
30-12	Greece	W 3-2	Florence	Fr	Pulici 2, Savoldi
7-04-1976	Portugal	W 3-1	Turin	Fr	Antognoni, Graziani, Pulici
28-05	England	L 2-3	New York	Fr	Graziani 2
31-05	Brazil	L 1-4	New Haven	Fr	Capello
5-06	Romania	W 4-2	Milan	Fr	Graziani, Antognoni, Bettega 2
22-09	Denmark	W 1-0	Copenhagen	Fr	Pulici
25-09	Yugoslavia	W 3-0	Rome	Fr	Bettega 2, Graziani
16-10	Luxembourg	W 4-1	Luxembourg	WCq	Graziani, Bettega 2, Antognoni
17-11	England	W 2-0	Rome	WCq	Antognoni, Bettega
22-12	Portugal	L 1-2	Lisbon	Fr	Bettega
26-01-1977	Belgium	W 2-1	Rome	Fr	Graziani, OG
8-06	Finland	W 3-0	Helsinki	WCq	Gentile, Bettega, Benetti
8-10	West Germany	L 1-2	Berlin	Fr	Antognoni
15-10	Finland	W 6-1	Turin	WCq	Bettega 4, Graziani, Zaccarelli
16-11	England	L 0-2	London	WCq	
3-12	Luxembourg	W 3-0	Rome	WCq	Bettega, Graziani, Causio
21-12	Belgium	W 1-0	Liege	Fr	Antognoni
25-01-1978	Spain	L 1-2	Madrid	Fr	Tardelli
8-02	France	D 2-2	Naples	Fr	Graziani 2
18-05	Yugoslavia	D 0-0	Rome	Fr	
2-06	France	W 2-1	Mar del Plata	WCr1	Rossi, Zaccarelli
6-06	Hungary	W 3-1	Mar del Plata	WCr1	Rossi, Bettega, Benetti
10-06	Argentina	W 1-0	Buenos Aires	WCr1	Bettega
14-06	West Germany	D 0-0	Buenos Aires	WCr2	
18-06	Austria	W 1-0	Buenos Aires	WCr2	Rossi
21-06	Holland	L 1-2	Buenos Aires	WCr2	OG
24-06	Brazil	L 1-2	Buenos Aires	WC3p	Causio
20-09	Bulgaria	W 1-0	Turin	Fr	Cabrini
23-09	Turkey	W 1-0	Florence	Fr	Graziani
8-11	Czechoslovakia	L 0-3	Bratislava	Fr	

21-12	Spain	W 1-0	Rome	Fr	Rossi
24-02-1979	Holland	W 3-0	Milan	Fr	Bettega, Rossi, Tardelli
26-05	Argentina	D 2-2	Rome	Fr	Causio, Rossi
13-06	Yugoslavia	L 1-4	Zagreb	Fr	Rossi
26-09	Sweden	W 1-0	Florence	Fr	Oriali
17-11	Switzerland	W 2-0	Udinese	Fr	Graziani, Tardelli
16-02-1980	Romania	W 2-1	Naples	Fr	Collovati, Causio
15-03	Uruguay	W 1-0	Milan	Fr	Graziani
19-04	Poland	D 2-2	Turin	Fr	Causio, Scirea
12-06	Spain	D 0-0	Milan	ECr1	
15-06	England	W 1-0	Turin	ECr1	Tardelli
18-06	Belgium	D 0-0	Rome	ECr1	
21-06	Czechoslovakia	D 1-1	Naples	EC3p	Graziani. Lost 8-9 pens
24-09	Portugal	W 3-1	Genoa	Fr	Altobelli 2, Graziani
11-10	Luxembourg	W 2-0	Luxembourg	WCq	Collovati, Bettega
1-11	Denmark	W 2-0	Rome	WCq	Graziani 2
15-11	Yugoslavia	W 2-0	Turin	WCq	Cabrini, Conti.B
6-12	Greece	W 2-0	Athens	WCq	Antognoni, Scirea
3-01-1981	Uruguay	L 0-2	Montevideo	ML	
6-01	Holland	D 1-1	Montevideo	ML	Ancelotti
19-04	East Germany	D 0-0	Udine	Fr	
3-06	Denmark	L 1-3	Copenhagen	WCq	Graziani
23-09	Bulgaria	W 3-2	Bologna	Fr	Graziani 2, Dossena
17-10	Yugoslavia	D 1-1	Belgrade	WCq	Bettega
14-11	Greece	D 1-1	Turin	WCq	Conti.B
5-12	Luxembourg	W 1-0	Naples	WCq	Collovati
23-02-1982	France	L 0-2	Paris	Fr	
14-04	East Germany	L 0-1	Leipzig	Fr	
28-05	Switzerland	D 1-1	Geneva	Fr	Cabrini
14-06	Poland	D 0-0	Vigo	WCr1	
18-06	Peru	D 1-1	Vigo	WCr1	Conti.B
23-06	Cameroon	D 1-1	Vigo	WCr1	Graziani
29-06	Argentina	W 2-1	Barcelona	WCr2	Tardelli, Cabrini
5-07	Brazil	W 3-2	Barcelona	WCr2	Rossi 3
8-07	Poland	W 2-0	Barcelona	WCsf	Rossi 2
11-07	West Germany	W 3-1	Madrid	WCf	Rossi, Tardelli, Altobelli
27-10	Switzerland	L 0-1	Rome	Fr	
13-11	Czechoslovakia	D 2-2	Milan	ECq	Altobelli, OG
4-12	Romania	D 0-0	Florence	ECq	
12-02-1983	Cyprus	D 1-1	Limassol	ECq	OG
16-04	Romania	L 0-1	Bucharest	ECq	
29-05	Sweden	L 0-2	Gothenburg	ECq	
5-10	Greece	W 3-0	Bari	Fr	Giordano, Cabrini, Rossi
15-10	Sweden	L 0-3	Naples	ECq	
16-11	Czechoslovakia	L 0-2	Prague	ECq	
22-12	Cyprus	W 3-1	Perugia	ECq	Altobelli, Cabrini, Rossi
4-02-1984	Mexico	W 5-0	Rome	Fr	Bagni, Rossi 3, Conti.B
3-03	Turkey	W 2-1	Istanbul	Fr	Altobelli, Cabrini
7-04	Czechoslovakia	D 1-1	Verona	Fr	Bagni
22-05	West Germany	L 0-1	Zurich	Fr	
26-05	Canada	W 2-0	Toronto	Fr	Altobelli, Battistini
30-05	USA	D 0-0	New York	Fr	
26-09	Sweden	W 1-0	Milan	Fr	Cabrini
3-11	Switzerland	D 1-1	Lausanne	Fr	Cabrini
8-12	Poland	W 2-0	Pescara	Fr	Altobelli, Di Gennaro
5-02-1985	Rep. Ireland	W 2-1	Dublin	Fr	Rossi, Altobelli
13-03	Greece	D 0-0	Athens	Fr	
3-04	Portugal	W 2-0	Ascoli	Fr	Conti.B, Rossi
2-06	Mexico	D 1-1	Mexico City	Fr	Di Gennaro
6-06	England	W 2-1	Mexico City	Fr	Bagni, Altobelli
25-09	Norway	L 1-2	Lecce	Fr	Altobelli
16-11	Poland	L 0-1	Chorzow	Fr	
5-02-1986	West Germany	L 1-2	Avellino	Fr	Serena
26-03	Austria	W 2-1	Udine	Fr	Altobelli, Di Gennaro
11-05	China	W 2-0	Naples	Fr	Di Gennaro, Altobelli
31-05	Bulgaria	D 1-1	Mexico City	WCr1	Altobelli
5-06	Argentina	D 1-1	Puebla	WCr1	Altobelli
10-06	South Korea	W 3-2	Puebla	WCr1	Altobelli 2, OG
17-06	France	L 0-2	Mexico City	WCr2	
8-10	Greece	W 2-0	Bologna	Fr	Bergomi 2
15-11	Switzerland	W 3-2	Milan	ECq	Donadoni, Altobelli 2
6-12	Malta	W 2-0	Ta'Qali	ECq	Ferri, Altobelli

24-01-1987	Malta	W 5-0	Bergamo	ECq	Bagni, Bergomi, Altobelli 2, Vialli
14-02	Portugal	W 1-0	Lisbon	ECq	Altobelli
18-04	West Germany	D 0-0	Cologne	Fr	
28-05	Norway	D 0-0	Oslo	Fr	
3-06	Sweden	L 0-1	Stockholm	ECq	
10-06	Argentina	W 3-1	Zurich	Fr	De Napoli, OG, Vialli
23-09	Yugoslavia	W 1-0	Pisa	Fr	Altobelli
17-10	Switzerland	D 0-0	Berne	ECq	
14-11	Sweden	W 2-1	Naples	ECq	Vialli 2
5-12	Portugal	W 3-0	Milan	ECq	Vialli, Giannini, De Agostini
20-02-1988	Soviet Union	W 4-1	Bari	Fr	Baresi, Vialli 2, Bergomi
31-03	Yugoslavia	D 1-1	Split	Fr	Vialli
27-04	Luxembourg	W 3-0	Luxembourg	Fr	Ferri, Bergomi, L.De Agostini
4-06	Wales	L 0-1	Brescia	Fr	
10-06	West Germany	D 1-1	Dusseldorf	ECr1	Mancini
14-06	Spain	W 1-0	Frankfurt	ECr1	Vialli
17-06	Denmark	W 2-0	Cologne	ECr1	Altobelli, De Agostini
22-06	Soviet Union	L 0-2	Stuttgart	ECsf	
19-10	Norway	W 2-1	Pescara	Fr	Giannini, Ferri
16-11	Holland	W 1-0	Rome	Fr	Vialli
22-12	Scotland	W 2-0	Perugia	Fr	Giannini, Berti
22-02-1989	Denmark	W 1-0	Pisa	Fr	Bergomi
25-03	Austria	W 1-0	Vienna	Fr	Berti
29-03	Romania	L 0-1	Sibiu	Fr	
22-04	Uruguay	D 1-1	Verona	Fr	Baggio.R
26-04	Hungary	W 4-0	Taranto	Fr	Vialli, Ferri, Berti, Carnevale
20-09	Bulgaria	W 4-0	Cesena	Fr	Baggio.R 2, Carnevale, OG
14-10	Brazil	L 0-1	Bologna	Fr	
11-11	Algeria	W 1-0	Vicenza	Fr	Serena
15-11	England	D 0-0	London	Fr	
21-12	Argentina	D 0-0	Cagliari	Fr	
21-02-1990	Holland	D 0-0	Rotterdam	Fr	
31-03	Switzerland	W 1-0	Basle	Fr	De Agostini
30-05	Greece	D 0-0	Perugia	Fr	
9-06	Austria	W 1-0	Rome	WCr1	Schillaci
14-06	USA	W 1-0	Rome	WCr1	Giannini
19-06	Czechoslovakia	W 2-0	Rome	WCr1	Schillaci, Baggio.R
25-06	Uruguay	W 2-0	Rome	WCr2	Schillaci, Serena
30-06	Rep. Ireland	W 1-0	Rome	WCqf	Schillaci
3-07	Argentina	D 1-1	Naples	WCsf	Schillaci. Lost 3-4 pens
7-07	England	W 2-1	Bari	WC3p	Baggio.R, Schillaci
26-09	Holland	W 1-0	Palermo	Fr	Baggio.R
17-10	Hungary	D 1-1	Budapest	ECq	Baggio.R
3-11	Soviet Union	D 0-0	Rome	ECq	
22-12	Cyprus	W 4-0	Limassol	ECq	Vierchowod, Serena 2, Lombardo
13-02-1991	Belgium	D 0-0	Terni	Fr	
1-05	Hungary	W 3-1	Salerno	ECq	Donadoni 2, Vialli
5-06	Norway	L 1-2	Oslo	ECq	Schillaci
12-06	Denmark	W 2-0	Malmo	Fr	Rizzitelli, Vialli
16-06	Soviet Union	D 1-1	Stockholm	Fr	Giannini
25-09	Bulgaria	L 1-2	Sofia	Fr	Giannini
12-10	Soviet Union	D 0-0	Moscow	ECq	
13-11	Norway	D 1-1	Genoa	ECq	Rizzitelli
21-12	Cyprus	W 2-0	Foggia	ECq	Vialli, Baggio.R
19-02-1992	San Marino	W 4-0	Cesena	Fr	Baggio.R 2, Donadoni, Casiraghi
25-03	Germany	W 1-0	Turin	Fr	Baggio.R
31-05	Portugal	D 0-0	New Haven	Fr	
4-06	Rep. Ireland	W 2-0	Boston	Fr	Signori, Costacurta
6-06	United States	D 1-1	Chicago	Fr	Baggio.R
9-09	Holland	W 3-2	Eindhoven	Fr	Eranio, Baggio.R, Vialli
14-10	Switzerland	D 2-2	Cagliari	WCq	Baggio.R, Eranio
18-11	Scotland	D 0-0	Glasgow	WCq	
16-12	Malta	W 2-1	Ta'Qali	WCq	Vialli, Signori
20-01-1993	Mexico	W 2-0	Florence	Fr	Baggio.R, Maldini
24-02	Portugal	W 3-1	Oporto	WCq	Baggio.R, Casiraghi, Baggio.D
24-03	Malta	W 6-1	Palermo	WCq	Baggio.D, Signori, Vierchowod, Mancini 2, Maldini
14-04	Estonia	W 2-0	Trieste	WCq	Baggio.R, Signori
1-05	Switzerland	L 0-1	Berne	WCq	
22-09	Estonia	W 3-0	Tallinn	WCq	Baggio.R 2, Mancini
13-10	Scotland	W 3-1	Rome	WCq	Donadoni, Casiraghi, Eranio
17-11	Portugal	W 1-0	Milan	WCq	Baggio.D
6-02-1994	France	L 0-1	Naples	Fr	

23-03	Germany	L 1-2	Stuttgart	Fr	Baggio.D
27-05	Finland	W 2-0	Parma	Fr	Signori, Casiraghi
3-06	Switzerland	W 1-0	Rome	Fr	Signori
11-06	Costa Rica	W 1-0	New Haven	Fr	Signori
18-06	Rep. Ireland	L 0-1	New York	WCr1	
23-06	Norway	W 1-0	New York	WCr1	Baggio.D
28-06	Mexico	D 1-1	Washington	WCr1	Massaro
5-07	Nigeria	W 2-1	Boston	WCr2	Baggio.R 2
9-07	Spain	W 2-1	Boston	WCqf	Baggio.D, Baggio.R
13-07	Bulgaria	W 2-1	New York	WCsf	Baggio.R 2
17-07	Brazil	D 0-0	Los Angeles	WCf	Lost 2-3 pens
7-09	Slovenia	D 1-1	Maribor	ECq	Costacurta
8-10	Estonia	W 2-0	Tallinn	ECq	Panucci, Casiraghi
16-11	Croatia	L 1-2	Palermo	ECq	Baggio.D
21-12	Turkey	W 3-1	Pescara	Fr	Crippa, Lombardo, Apolloni
25-03-1995	Estonia	W 4-1	Salerno	ECq	Zola 2, Albertini, Ravanelli
29-03	Ukraine	W 2-0	Kiev	ECq	Zola
26-04	Lithuania	W 1-0	Vilnius	ECq	Zola
19-06	Switzerland	W 1-0	Lausanne	Fr	Casiraghi
21-06	Germany	L 0-2	Zurich	Fr	

LATVIA

Of the three Baltic countries who enjoyed a brief period of independence during the inter-war years, Latvia were the most successful. Winners of the Baltic Cup on five occasions, they even managed to beat Sweden in one match, although the Swedes were represented by a very inexperienced side on that occasion. As if to prove the point, Sweden won the next encounter 12-0!

Independent once again since 1991, Latvia do not look to be in a very strong position. Only Daugava Riga, formed in 1948 after Latvia's absorption into the Soviet Union, ever appeared in the Soviet first division. In 1949 they finished second from bottom and were not seen again in the top flight. Little remains of the inter-war set-up and much has changed since Soviet times. Skonto Riga have emerged as the top team of the post-independence era, winning the first four championships. In the 1995 UEFA Cup they even managed to knock out Aberdeen, former winners of the Cup Winners Cup.

In 1993 Latvia won the Baltic Cup and the previous year they entered the World Cup for the first time in 54 years, finishing one off the bottom of their qualifying group. But with a growing interest in the game and a population of over three million, they may never qualify for a major tournament, but there is no reason why they should not enter into the mainstream of European football.

Population: 2,673,000
Area, sq km: 64,500
Capital city: Riga

Latvijas Futbola Federacija
Augsiela 1
Riga, LV-1009
Latvia
Tel: + 371 2 292988
Fax: + 371 8828331

Year of formation:	1921
Affiliation to FIFA	1923-43 & 1991
Affiliation to UEFA	1992
Registered clubs	50
Registered players	12 000
Registered referees	155
National stadium	Daugavas, Riga 15 000
National colours	Claret with blue sleeves/Blue/White
Season	April - October

THE RECORD

WORLD CUP

1930	Did not enter
1934	Did not enter
1938	QT 2nd/3 in group 7
1950-90	Did not enter
1994	QT 6th/7 in group 3

EUROPEAN CHAMPIONSHIP

1960-92	Did not enter
1996	QT group 4

Baltic Cup
Winners 1928, 1932, 1936, 1937, 1940, 1993 1995

EUROPEAN CLUB COMPETITIONS

European Cup
1st round - Skonto Riga 1993 1994
Cup Winners Cup
Preliminary round - RAF Jelgava 1994, Olimpija Riga 1995
UEFA Cup
First round - Skonto Riga 1995

CLUB DIRECTORY

RIGA (Population - 900,000)

FC Dag Riga
Stadium - Yurnieks 2,000
Merger in 1993 of VEF and Zenta

Olimpija Riga
Stadium - Vagonbuvetays 1,000

Pardaugava Riga
Stadium - Energoautomatikas 1,000

Skonto Riga
Stadium - Daugava 15,000
Reserve team: Interskonto

Vidus Riga
Stadium - Lu 6,000

DAUGAVPILS (Population - 128,000)

Auseklis Daugavpils
Stadium - Tseltnieks 3,000

FC Khimikis Daugavpils
Stadium - Tseltnieks 3,000
Previous name - FC Baltnet Daugavpils

LIEPAJA (Population - 114,000)

FC Liepaja
Stadium - Daugava 8,000
Previous name - Olimpija Liepaja until 1994

JELGAVA (Population - 72,000)

RAF Jelgava
Stadium - Daugava 3,000

Inter-war clubs included RFK Riga (Rigas Futbola Klubs) and SKA Riga (Armijas Sporta Klubs Riga)

LEAGUE CHAMPIONS OF LATVIA

1922 Kaiserwood Riga 18 JSK Riga 15 LJS Riga 10
1923 Kaiserwood Riga 4-0 LNJS Liepaja
1924 RFK Riga 5-1 Cesu Viesiga Biedriba
1925 RFK Riga 4-3 Olimpija Liepaja
1926 RFK Riga 8 Olimpija Liepaja 6 SKA Daugavpils 4
1927 Olimpija Liepaja 10 RFK Riga 6 LSB Riga 5
1928 Olimpija Liepaja 13 RFK Riga 9 LSB Riga 7
1929 Olimpija Liepaja 14 RFK Riga 12 Amatieris Riga 8
1930 RFK Riga 19 Olimpija Liepaja 17 RV Riga 14
1931 RFK Riga 21 Olimpija Liepaja 20 RV Riga 15
1932 SKA Riga 20 RV Riga 20 RFK Riga 19
1933 Olimpija Liepaja 22 RFK Riga 20 SKA Riga 17
1934 RFK Riga 24 RV Riga 18 SKA Riga 17
1935 RFK Riga 24 Olimpija Liepaja 18 US Riga 16
1936 Olimpija Liepaja 26 SKA Riga 23 RFK Riga 19
1937 -
1938 Olimpija Liepaja 21 RFK Riga 18 SKA Riga 13
1939 Olimpija Liepaja 23 SKA Riga 21 RFK Riga 21
1940 RFK Riga 23 Olimpija Liepaja 21 SKA Riga 16

Play-off
1932 SKA Riga............................3-1 ....RV Riga

REGIONAL LEAGUE CHAMPIONS OF LATVIA

1942 SKA Riga
1943 SKA Riga
1944 SKA Riga
1945 Dinamo Riga
1946 Daugava Liepaja
1947 Daugava Liepaja
1948 Komanda Zhmyleva
1949 Sarkanajs Metalurgs Liepaja
1950 ODO Riga
1951 Sarkanajs Metalurgs Liepaja
1952 ODO Riga
1953 Sarkanajs Metalurgs Liepaja
1954 Sarkanajs Metalurgs Liepaja
1955 Trudovye Reservy Riga
1956 Sarkanajs Metalurgs Liepaja
1957 Sarkanajs Metalurgs Liepaja
1958 Sarkanajs Metalurgs Liepaja
1959 REZ Riga
1960 SKA Riga
1961 SKA Riga
1962 SKA Riga
1963 SKA Riga
1964 SKA Riga
1965 SKA Riga
1966 Energija Riga
1967 Energija Riga
1968 Start Brotseny
1969 Venta Ventspils
1970 VEF Riga
1971 VEF Riga
1972 Jurnieks Riga
1973 VEF Riga
1974 VEF Riga
1975 VEF Riga
1976 Energija Riga
1977 Energija Riga
1978 Khimik Daugavpils
1979 Elektron Riga
1980 Khimik Daugavpils
1981 Elektron Riga
1982 Elektron Riga
1983 VEF Riga
1984 Torpedo Riga
1985 Alfa Riga
1986 Torpedo Riga
1987 Torpedo Riga
1988 RAF Jelgava
1989 RAF Jelgava
1990 Gauja Valmiera

LEAGUE CHAMPIONS OF LATVIA

1991h Skonto Riga 32 Pardaugava Riga 26 Olimpija Leipaja 25
1992k Skonto Riga 38 RAF Jelgava 38 VEF Riga 33
1993h Skonto Riga 34 Olimpija Riga 26 RAF Jelgava 26
1994k Skonto Riga 42 RAF Jelgava 33 FC Dag Riga 29

Play-off
1992 Skonto Riga.........................3-1 ....RAF Jelgava

LATVIAN REGIONAL CUP WINNERS

1945 Daugava Liepaja
1946 Daugava Liepaja
1947 Daugava Liepaja
1948 Sarkanajs Metalurgs Liepaja
1949 Sarkanajs Metalurgs Liepaja
1950 ODO Riga
1951 ODO Riga
1952 ODO Riga
1953 Sarkanajs Metalurgs Liepaja
1954 Sarkanajs Metalurgs Liepaja
1955 Sarkanajs Metalurgs Liepaja
1956 VEF Riga
1957 Dinamo Riga
1958 REZ Riga
1959 SKA Riga
1960 SKA Riga
1961 Start Brotseny
1962 Selmash Liepaja
1963 Selmash Liepaja
1964 Vulkan Kuldiga
1965 Baltija Liepaja
1966 SKA Riga
1967 Venta Ventspils
1968 Start Brotseny
1969 Elektron Riga
1970 Jurnieks Riga
1971 VEF Riga
1972 Jurnieks Riga
1973 Pilot Riga
1974 Elektron Riga
1975 Lijelupe Jurmala
1976 Khimik Daugavpils
1977 Elektron Riga
1978 Elektron Riga
1979 Khimik Daugavpils
1980 Elektron Riga
1981 Elektron Riga
1982 Energija Riga
1983 Elektron Riga
1984 Celtnieks Riga
1985 Celtnieks Riga
1986 Celtnieks Riga
1987 VEF Riga
1988 RAF Jelgava
1989 Torpedo Riga
1990 Daugava Riga

LATVIAN CUP FINALS

1991	Celtnieks Daugavpils	0-0 3-1p	Skonto Riga
1992	Skonto Riga	1-0	Kompar/Daugava Riga
1993	RAF Jelgava	1-0	Pardaugava Riga
1994	Olimpija Riga	2-0	FC Dag Riga
1995	Skonto Riga	3-0	FC Dag Riga

LEADING INTERNATIONAL GOALSCORERS

24	Eriks Pétersons	(RFK Riga)	1929-1940
14	Alberts Seibelis	(RFK Riga,RV Riga, Vilhelms Kuze Riga)	1925-1939
13	Aleksandrs Vanags	(ASK Riga)	1937-1942
	Ilja Vestermans	(Hakoah Riga)	1935-1938
10	Arnolds Taurins	(RFK Riga)	1925-1935
9	Voldemárs Plade	(Kaiserwood Riga,RFK Riga, RV Riga)	1923-1929
8	Fricis Kaneps	(RFK Riga)	1937-1940
	Arkadijs Pavlovs	(RFK Riga)	1924-1933
7	Vaclavs Bordusko	(RV Riga,ASK Riga)	1934-1939
	Jánis Rozitis	(RFK Riga,VEF Riga)	1934-1939

LEADING INTERNATIONAL APPEARANCES

64	Eriks Pétersons	(RFK Riga)	1929-1940
58	Jánis Lidmanis	(RFK Riga)	1931-1940
54	Alberts Seibelis	(RFK Riga,RV Riga, Vilhelms Kuze Riga)	1925-1939
41	Péteris Lauks	(Amatieris Riga, RFK Riga)	1927-1940
	Voldemárs Bérzins	(RFK Riga)	1927-1936
39	Arnolds Taurins	(RFK Riga)	1925-1935
37	Voldemárs Grávelis	(RFK Riga)	1925-1932
	Arkadijs Pavlovs	(RFK Riga)	1924-1933
36	Rúdolfs Slavisens	(RFK Riga)	1932-1938
35	Arvids Jurgens	(RFK Riga, RV Riga, ASK Riga)	1924-1935

INTERNATIONAL MATCHES PLAYED BY LATVIA

24-09-1922	Estonia	D 1-1	Riga	Fr	
24-07-1923	Estonia	D 1-1	Tallinn	Fr	Bárda.A
27-05-1924	France	L 0-7	Paris	OGr1	
22-06	Turkey	L 1-3	Riga	Fr	Bárda.A
6-08	Lithuania	W 4-2	Kaunas	Fr	Stanciks, Bárda.A, Abrams, Plade
13-08	Finland	L 0-2	Riga	Fr	
18-10	Estonia	W 2-0	Riga	Fr	Abrams, Bárda.E
9-08-1925	Finland	L 1-3	Helsinki	Fr	Taurins
26-08	Estonia	D 2-2	Tallinn	Fr	Taurins 2
20-09	Lithuania	D 2-2	Riga	Fr	Bárda.E 2
20-07-1926	Sweden	W 4-1	Riga	Fr	Strazdins, Seibelis, Taurins, Pavlovs
12-08	Finland	L 1-4	Riga	Fr	Strazdins
21-08	Lithuania	W 3-2	Kaunas	Fr	Pavlovs 2, Stanciks
19-09	Estonia	L 0-1	Riga	Fr	
29-05-1927	Sweden	L 0-12	Stockholm	Fr	
16-06	Estonia	L 1-4	Tallinn	Fr	Urbans
27-07	Lithuania	W 6-3	Riga	Fr	Plade 2, Zins 3, Bradins
11-09	Finland	L 1-3	Helsinki	Fr	Seibelis
25-09	Estonia	W 4-1	Riga	Fr	Zins, Urbans, Plade 2
6-07-1928	Sweden	L 0-4	Riga	Fr	
25-07	Lithuania	W 3-0	Tallinn	BC	Pavlovs, Vaters 2
27-07	Estonia	W 1-0	Tallinn	BC	Taurins
19-08	Finland	W 2-1	Riga	Fr	Pavlovs 2
1-09	Lithuanaia	D 1-1	Kaunas	Fr	Urbans
23-09	Estonia	D 1-1	Riga	Fr	Plade
28-07-1929	Sweden	L 0-10	Malmö	Fr	
14-08	Lithuania	W 3-1	Riga	BC	Plade 3
16-08	Estonia	D 2-2	Riga	BC	Priede, Pavlovs
15-09	Finland	L 1-3	Helsinki	Fr	Pétersons
18-09	Estonia	L 1-4	Tallinn	Fr	Seibelis
27-06-1930	Estonia	D 1-1	Tallinn	Fr	Jénihs
22-07	Sweden	L 0-5	Riga	Fr	
4-08	Finland	W 3-0	Riga	Fr	Pétersons, Pavlovs, Dambrevics
16-08	Estonia	W 3-2	Kaunas	BC	Pétersons, Zins, Dambrevics
17-08	Lithuania	D 3-3	Kaunas	BC	Pétersons 3
26-10	Poland	L 0-6	Warsaw	Fr	
28-05-1931	Estonia	L 0-1	Riga	Fr	
30-06	Lithuania	W 5-2	Riga	Fr	Pétersons 4, Verners
26-07	Sweden	L 0-6	Vasteras	Fr	
5-08	Poland	L 0-5	Riga	Fr	
19-08	Finland	L 0-4	Helsinki	Fr	
31-08	Lithuania	W 1-0	Tallinn	BC	Pétersons
1-09	Estonia	L 1-3	Tallinn	BC	Skincs
27-09	Estonia	W 2-1	Riga	Fr	Skincs, Stauvers
1-06-1932	Estonia	L 0-3	Tallinn	Fr	
29-06	Lithuania	W 3-2	Kaunas	Fr	Seibelis, Jénihs 2

13-07	Sweden	D 0-0	Riga	Fr	
24-07	Lithuania	W 2-1	Liepaja	Fr	Pétersons, Taurins
28-08	Lithuania	W 4-1	Riga	BC	Pétersons, Seibelis, Jénihs, Taurins
30-08	Estonia	W 1-0	Riga	BC	Seibelis
2-10	Poland	L 1-2	Warsaw	Fr	Taurins
28-05-1933	Estonia	W 2-0	Riga	Fr	Taurins, Pétersons
12-06	Lithuania	W 6-2	Riga	Fr	Pétersons 3, Bréde, Seibelis, Taurins
4-07	Sweden	D 1-1	Riga	Fr	Pétersons
9-08	Estonia	L 1-2	Tallinn	Fr	Seibelis
3-09	Estonia	W 1-0	Kaunas	BC	Seibelis
4-09	Lithuania	D 2-2	Kaunas	BC	Pétersons 2
10-06-1934	Lithuania	L 0-2	Kaunas	Fr	
14-08	Finland	D 1-1	Riga	Fr	Priede
9-09	Lithuania	L 1-3	Riga	Fr	Bordusko
23-09	Sweden	L 1-3	Stockholm	Fr	Jénihs
14-10	Poland	L 2-6	Riga	Fr	Priede, Jénihs
30-05-1935	Lithuania	W 6-1	Riga	Fr	Raisters, Vitols 3, Vestermans 2
5-06	Finland	L 1-4	Helsinki	Fr	Vestermans
12-06	Estonia	D 1-1	Riga	Fr	Rozitis
5-07	Sweden	L 0-3	Riga	Fr	
21-08	Lithuania	D 2-2	Tallinn	BC	Vestermans 2
22-08	Estonia	D 1-1	Tallinn	BC	Pétersons
8-09	Lithuania	D 2-2	Kaunas	Fr	Lidmanis, Pétersons
15-09	Poland	D 3-3	Lodz	Fr	Skincs, Pétersons, Verners
13-10	Germany	L 0-3	Konigsberg	Fr	
28-05-1936	Estonia	W 4-3	Tallinn	Fr	Bordusko, Verners 2, Rozitis
14-06	Lithuania	W 5-1	Kaunas	Fr	Verners, Seibelis 2, Raisters, Pakalns
29-08	Lithuania	W 2-1	Riga	BC	Vestermans, Seibelis
31-08	Estonia	W 2-1	Riga	BC	Seibelis, Lidmanis
6-09	Poland	D 3-3	Riga	Fr	Pétersons, Rozitis
25-06-1937	Germany	L 1-3	Riga	Fr	Raisters
13-07	Romania	D 0-0	Riga	Fr	
29-07	Lithuania	W 4-2	Riga	WCq	Kaneps 3, Vestermans
3-09	Lithuania	W 5-1	Kaunas	WCq/BC	Kaneps 2, Bordusko 2, Vestermans
4-09	Estonia	D 1-1	Kaunas	BC	Vestermans
7-09	Estonia	W 2-0	Kaunas	BCpo	Rozitis, Vestermans
19-09	Estonia	W 3-1	Riga	Fr	Rozitis, Kaneps, Bordusko
5-10	Austria	L 1-2	Vienna	WCq	Vestermans
10-10	Poland	L 1-2	Katowice	Fr	Rozitis
13-10	Czechoslovakia	L 0-7	Prague	Fr	
17-05-1938	Lithuania	W 2-0	Riga	Fr	Vanags 2
10-06	Sweden	D 3-3	Stockholm	Fr	Krupss, Raisters, Bordusko
20-07	Estonia	W 2-0	Tallinn	Fr	Raisters, Vanags
4-09	Lithuania	D 1-1	Tallinn	BC	Krupss
5-09	Estonia	D 1-1	Tallinn	BC	Raisters
25-09	Poland	W 2-1	Riga	Fr	Vanags, Seibelis
18-05-1939	Romania	L 0-4	Bucharest	Fr	
24-05	Bulgaria	L 0-3	Sofia	Fr	
27-07	Estonia	D 3-3	Riga	Fr	Freimanis 2, Vanags
24-09	Finland	W 3-0	Helsinki	Fr	Vanags 2, Kaneps
18-07-1940	Estonia	L 1-2	Tallinn	Fr	Kaneps
6-09	Lithuania	W 1-0	Riga	BC	Lidmanis
8-09	Estonia	D 2-2	Riga	BC	Vanags 2
13-10	Lithuania	L 3-4	Kaunas	Fr	Freimanis, Aspens, Levitanus
3-08-1942	Estonia	W 4-0	Riga	Fr	Peicha, Jegers 2, Freimanis
18-08	Estonia	W 8-1	Tallinn	Fr	Freimanis 2, Peicha 2, Vanags 2, Jegers, Fischers
16-11-1991	Estonia	W 2-0	Vilnius	BC	Sprogis, Troitskis
17-11	Lithuania	D 1-1	Vilnius	BC	Teplovs
8-04-1992	Romania	L 0-2	Bucharest	Fr	
26-05	Malta	L 0-1	Ta'Qali	Fr	
15-07	Estonia	W 2-1	Leipaja	BC	Shitiks, Linards
17-07	Lithuania	L 2-3	Leipaja	BC	Teplovs, Popkovs
12-08	Lithuania	L 1-2	Riga	WCq	Linards
26-08	Denmark	D 0-0	Riga	WCq	
9-09	Rep. Ireland	L 0-4	Dublin	WCq	
23-09	Spain	D 0-0	Riga	WCq	
28-10	Lithuania	D 1-1	Vilnius	WCq	Linards
11-11	Albania	D 1-1	Tirana	WCq	Alexeyenko
18-11	Poland	L 0-1	Ilawa	Fr	
16-12	Spain	L 0-5	Seville	WCq	
14-04-1993	Denmark	L 0-2	Copenhagen	WCq	
15-05	Albania	D 0-0	Riga	WCq	
2-06	Northern Ireland	L 1-2	Riga	WCq	Linards
9-06	Rep. Ireland	L 0-2	Riga	WCq	
2-07	Estonia	W 2-0	Parnu	BC	Astafyev, Sharando

3-07	Lithuania	D 0-0	Parnu	BC	
8-09	Northern Ireland	L 0-2	Belfast	WCq	
3-06-1994	Malta	W 2-0	Riga	Fr	Droupass, Astafyev
26-06	Georgia	L 1-3	Riga	Fr	Astafyev
30-07	Estonia	W 2-0	Vilnius	BC	Astafyev, Boulders
31-07	Lithuania	L 0-1	Vilnius	BC	
7-09	Rep. Ireland	L 0-3	Riga	ECq	
9-10	Portugal	L 1-3	Riga	ECq	Milevsky
6-11	Estonia	D 0-0	Ozolniecki	Fr	
15-11	Liechtenstein	W 1-0	Vaduz	ECq	Babichev
8-03-1995	Hungary	L 1-3	Budapest	Fr	Zemlinsky
29-03	Austria	L 0-5	Salzburg	ECq	
26-04	Northern Ireland	L 0-1	Riga	ECq	
19-05	Estonia	W 2-0	Riga	BC	Zeiberlins, Ivanovs
21-05	Lithuania	W 2-0	Riga	BC	Zemlinsky, Astafyev
3-06	Portugal	L 2-3	Oporto	ECq	Babichev, Rimkus
7-06	Northern Ireland	W 2-1	Belfast	ECq	Zeiberlins, Astafyev

LIECHTENSTEIN

That this tiny principality, squeezed in between Austria and Switzerland, should have a national team at all is quite remarkable. The population is just 27,000, and its citizens are more usually concerned with banking and finance than playing football.

The country's football association dates back to 1933 and in 1974 they joined both FIFA and UEFA, but before 1994 few matches were played. In 1981 a trip was made to Korea and the results in the President's Cup were very impressive, especially the victory over Indonesia. The best result to date, however, is the 2-0 victory over China (population over 100 million!) in 1982.

There is no league in Liechtenstein and the seven LFV member teams compete in the lower divisons of Swiss football. There is, however, an annual Cup competition and the winners have entered the Cup Winners Cup since the 1993 edition. The national team also entered the European mainstream in 1994 when they played their first match in the European Championship, losing 4-1 to Northern Ireland in Belfast. It has to be expected, though, that if they continue to enter the major tournaments they will be on the receiving end of some big scores.

Population: 27,000
Area, sq km: 160
Capital city: Vaduz

Liechtensteiner Fussball-Verband
Postfach 165
FL-9490 Vaduz
Liechtenstein
Tel: + 41 75 2332428
Fax: + 41 75 2332430

Year of formation	1933
Affiliation to FIFA	1974
Affiliation to UEFA	1974
Registered clubs	7
Registered players	1290
Registered coaches	36
Registered referees	29
National colours	Blue/Red/Blue
Reserve colours	Yellow/Red/Yellow
Season	Teams compete in the Swiss league

THE RECORD

WORLD CUP
1930-94 Did not enter

EUROPEAN CHAMPIONSHIP
1960-92 Did not enter
1996 QT group 6

EUROPEAN CLUB COMPETITIONS
European Cup
Ineligible to compete

Cup Winners Cup
1st round - FC Balzers 1994

UEFA Cup
Ineligible to compete

LIECHTENSTEIN CUP WINNERS

1946	FC Triesen
1947	FC Triesen
1948	FC Triesen
1949	FC Vaduz
1950	FC Triesen
1951	FC Triesen
1952	FC Vaduz
1953	FC Vaduz
1954	FC Vaduz
1955	FC Schaan
1956	FC Vaduz
1957	FC Vaduz
1958	FC Vaduz
1959	FC Vaduz
1960	FC Vaduz
1961	FC Vaduz
1962	FC Vaduz
1963	FC Schaan
1964	FC Balzers
1965	FC Triesen
1966	FC Vaduz
1967	FC Vaduz
1968	FC Vaduz
1969	FC Vaduz
1970	FC Vaduz
1971	FC Vaduz
1972	FC Triesen
1973	FC Balzers
1974	FC Vaduz
1975	FC Triesen
1976	USV Eschen/Mauren
1977	USV Eschen/Mauren
1978	USV Eschen/Mauren
1979	FC Balzers
1980	FC Vaduz
1981	FC Balzers
1982	FC Balzers
1983	FC Balzers
1984	FC Balzers
1985	FC Vaduz
1986	FC Vaduz
1987	USV Eschen/Mauren
1988	FC Vaduz
1989	FC Balzers
1990	FC Vaduz
1991	FC Balzers
1992	FC Vaduz
1993	FC Balzers
1994	FC Schaan
1995	FC Vaduz

Number of cup wins to 1995

1	FC Vaduz	25
2	FC Balzers	10
3	FC Triesen	8
4	USV Eschen/Mauren	4
5	FC Schaan	3

INTERNATIONAL MATCHES PLAYED BY LIECHTENSTEIN

14-06-1981	Malta	D 1-1	Seoul	PC	
16-06	Thailand	L 0-2	Seoul	PC	
22-06	Indonesia	W 3-2	Seoul	PC	
6-10	Malaysia	W 1-0	Balzers	Fr	
6-06-1982	China	W 2-0	Vaduz	Fr	Moser 2
6-06-1984	Austria	L 0-6	Vaduz	Fr	
30-05-1990	United States	L 1-4	Eschen	Fr	Marxer
12-03-1991	Switzerland	L 0-6	Balzers	Fr	
26-10-1993	Estonia	L 0-2	Balzers	Fr	
20-04-1994	Northern Ireland	L 1-4	Belfast	ECq	Hasler
27-05	Switzerland	L 0-2	Basle	Fr	
7-09	Austria	L 0-4	Eschen	ECq	
12-10	Rep. Ireland	L 0-4	Dublin	ECq	
15-11	Latvia	L 0-1	Vaduz	ECq	
18-12	Portugal	L 0-8	Lisbon	ECq	
26-04-1995	Austria	L 0-7	Salzburg	ECq	
3-06	Rep. Ireland	D 0-0	Eschen	ECq	

LITHUANIA

Although the largest of the three Baltic republics, Lithuania was the weakest of the trio in the period of independence between the wars. Since the break-up of the Soviet Union, however, it has emerged as the strongest. Ethnically the most homogenous of the three states, the Lithuanians broke away from the Soviet league in 1990 and along with clubs from Estonia and Latvia formed the Baltic league. The Lithuanians even played an international against fellow secessionists Georgia in Tbilisi that year, drawing 2-2.

The Baltic league was won by Zalgiris Vilnius, and without question they are the top club in the region. In 1987 they finished third in the Soviet league, and they twice appeared in the UEFA Cup under the Soviet banner, the only Baltic club ever to do so. The Baltic league, however, lasted only one season and in 1991 Lithuania started its own championship, 52 years after the last one had finished. In a shortened season, Zalgiris won the title two points ahead of Banga Kaunas.

Vilnius and Kaunas are the two largest cities in Lithuania, but since independence they have had their predominance challenged by teams from the smaller cities. In the inter-war period, however, as the then capital, Kaunas dominated the championship (Vilnius at that time was in Poland), and for many years the football association was located in Kaunas. Only since the Soviet occupation in the war has Vilnius come on to the scene.

The Lithuanians entered both the inter-war World Cups held in Europe, but it was not until the 1994 tournament that they could enter again. In the qualifiers for USA '94 they finished above Latvia and Albania. They also won three of the first four editions of the revived Baltic Cup, reinforcing their position as the top nation in the Baltics.

For Zalgiris though, the task of remaining the top team in Lithuania looks more difficult. Increasingly, entrepreneurs are getting involved with clubs, none more so than the 1994 champions ROMAR Mazeikiai. In two years they have gone from being unknowns to champions as a result of a rich sponsor. There is still some way to go, however, before the clubs can begin to make headway in Europe. Ekranas Panevezys, champions in 1993, gave Malta a very rare night of celebration when they lost to Floriana in the first round of the European Cup the following season.

Population: 3,682,000
Area, sq km: 65,200
Capital city: Vilnius

Lithuanian Football Union
6 Zemaites Street
232675 Vilnius
Tel: + 370 2 353654
Fax: + 370 2 353651

Year of formation	1922
Affiliation to FIFA	1923-43 & 1992
Affiliation to UEFA	1992
Registered clubs	171
Registered players	9800
Registered referees	72

National stadium	Central stadium, Vilnius 15 000
National colours	Yellow/Green/Yellow
Season	August - May, with a mid season break from November - March

THE RECORD

WORLD CUP

1930	Did not enter
1934	QT 3nd/3 in group 5
1938	QT 3rd/3 in group 7
1950-90	Did not enter
1994	QT 5th/7 in group 3

EUROPEAN CHAMPIONSHIP

1960-92	Did not enter
1996	QT group 4

Baltic Cup
Winners 1930, 1935, 1991, 1992, 1994

EUROPEAN CLUB COMPETITIONS

European Cup
1st round - Zalgiris Vilnius 1993
Cup Winners Cup
1st round - Zalgiris Vilnius 1995
UEFA Cup
2nd round - Zalgiris Vilnius 1990

CLUB DIRECTORY

VILNIUS (Population - 582,000)
Zalgiris Vilnius (1947)
Zalgiris 15,000 – Green/White
Previous name - Dinamo 1947-48, Spartak 1948-62

Panerys Vilnius
Panerys 5,000

KAUNAS (Population - 423,000)
FBK Kaunas
Darius ir Girenas 12,000
Previous name - Banga Kaunas

Inkaras Kaunas
Inkaras 2,000

KLAIPEDA (Population 204,000)
Aras Klaipeda
Zalgiris 10,000

Sirijus Klaipeda
Zalgiris 10,000

SIAULIAI (Population - 145,000)
Siauliai-Sakalas
Siauliai 2,000

PANEVEZYS (Population - 126,000)
Ekranas Panevezys
Ekranas 5,000 – Red, white trim

MAZEIKIAI
FC ROMAR Mazeikiai (1947)
Mazeikiai 8,000 – Red/Red
Previous names - Atmosfera, Jovaras, FK Mazeikiai. Present name from 1993

Pre-war clubs
Lietuvos Fizinio Lavinimosi Sajunga Kaunas - LFLS
Sanciu sauliu Klubas Kovas, Kaunas - Kovas Kaunas
Klaipedos Sporto Sajunga - KSS Klaipeda
Maisto Sporto Klubas Kaunas - MSK Kaunas
Lietuvos Gimnastikos ir Sporto Federacija, Kaunas - LGSF Kaunas

LEAGUE CHAMPIONS OF LITHUANIA

1922an	LFLS Kaunas 26 LFLS Sanciai 18 Makabi Kaunas 14
1923ao	LFLS Kaunas 7 KSK Kaunas 5 Kovas Kaunas 4
1924	Kovas Kaunas 2-1 Sportverein Klaipeda
1925	Kovas Kaunas 2-0 LFLS Siauliai
1926	Kovas Kaunas 3-2 KSS Klaipeda
1927	LFLS Kaunas 3-1 Sportverein Pagegiai
1928	KSS Klaipeda 3-1 LFLS Kaunas
1929	KSS Klaipeda 4-2 LFLS Kaunas
1930	KSS Klaipeda 1-1 3-1 LFLS Kaunas
1931b1	KSS Klaipeda 10 Kovas Kaunas 8 Freya Klaipeda 7
1932ad	LFLS Kaunas 12 KSS Klaipeda 12 LGSF Kaunas 8
1933e	Kovas Kaunas 19 LFLS Kaunas 18 LGSF Kaunas 12
1934ap	MSK Kaunas 14 LFLS Kaunas 14 LGSF Kaunas 14
1935	Kovas Kaunas 3-2 KSS Klaipeda
1936ad	Kovas Kaunas 14 LFLS Kaunas 10 LGSF Kaunas 8
1937g	KSS Klaipeda 28 Kovas Kaunas 21 LFLS Kaunas 21
1938h	KSS Klaipeda 26 LGSF Kaunas 26 Svyturys Klaipeda 24
1939al	LGSF Kaunas 17 Kovas Kaunas 16 KSS Klaipeda 16
1939ad	LGSF Kaunas 12 Tauras Kaunas 9 LFLS Kaunas 8

Play-offs

1932	LFLS Kaunas 6-1 KSS Klaipeda
1934	MSK Kaunas 2-2 5-1 LFLS Kaunas
1938	KSS Klaipeda 3-1 LGSF Klaipeda

REGIONAL LEAGUE CHAMPIONS OF LITHUANIA

1942	LFLS Kaunas
1943	Tauras Kaunas
1944	-
1945	Spartaks Kaunas
1946	Dinamo Kaunas
1947	Lokomotiv Kaunas
1948	Elnias Siauliai
1949	Elnias Siauliai
1950	Inkaras Kaunas
1951	Inkaras Kaunas
1952	Saliutas Vilnius
1953	Elnias Siauliai
1954	Inkaras Kaunas
1955	Lima Kaunas
1956	Linu audiniai Plunge
1957	Elnias Siauliai
1958	Elnias Siauliai
1959	Raud Zhvaigzhde Vilnius
1960	Elnias Siauliai
1961	Elnias Siauliai
1962	Atletas Kaunas
1963	Statyba Panevzys
1964	Inkaras Kaunas
1965	Inkaras Kaunas
1966	Nevezis Kedainiai
1967	Saliutas Vilnius
1968	Statyba Panevzys
1969	Statybininkas Siauliai
1970	Atletas Kaunas
1971	Pazanga Vilnius
1972	Nevezis Kedainiai
1973	Nevezis Kedainiai
1974	Tauras Siauliai
1975	Dainava Alytus
1976	Atmosfera Mazeikiai
1977	Statybininkas Siauliai
1978	Granitas Klaipeda
1979	Atmosfera Mazeikiai
1980	Granitas Klaipeda
1981	Granitas Klaipeda
1982	Pazanga Vilnius
1983	Pazanga Vilnius
1984	Granitas Klaipeda
1985	Ekranas Panevzys
1986	Banga Kaunas
1987	Tauras Taurage
1988	SRT Vilnius
1989	Banga Kaunas
1990	Sirijus Klaipeda

LEAGUE CHAMPIONS OF LITHUANIA

1991	Zalgiris Vilnius 3-1 Lietuvos Vilnius
1992m1	Zalgiris Vilnius 39 Panerys Vilnius 38 Sirijus Klaipeda 33
1993o2	Ekranas Panevezys 46 Zalgiris Vilnius 43 Panerys Vilnius 36
1994k	ROMAR Mazeikiai 38 Zalgiris Vilnius 37 Ekranas Panevezys 31
1995	Inkaras Kaunas 36 Zalgiris Vilnius 36 ROMAR Mazeikiai 34 Play-off: Inkaras Kaunas 2-0 Zalgiris Vilnius

LITHUANIAN REGIONAL CUP WINNERS

1947	Lokomotiv Kaunas
1948	Inkaras Kaunas

1949	Inkaras Kaunas
1950	Elnias Siauliai
1951	Inkaras Kaunas
1952	Karininky Vilnius
1953	Lima Kaunas
1954	Inkaras Kaunas
1955	Politechnikos Kaunas
1956	Raudonasis Spalis Kaunas
1957	Elnias Siauliai
1958	Spartak Vilnius
1959	Elnias Siauliai
1960	Komanda Panemunes
1961	Cementininkas Akmenes
1962	Lima Kaunas
1963	Saliutas Vilnius
1964	Minija Kretingos
1965	Inkaras Kaunas
1966	Zalgiris Vilnius
1967	Nevezis Kedainiai
1968	Nevezis Kedainiai
1969	Inkaras Kaunas
1970	Nevezis Kedainiai
1971	Pazanga Vilnius
1972	Nevezis Kedainiai
1973	Nevezis Kedainiai
1974	Statybininkas Siauliai
1975	Vienybe Ukmerges
1976	Kelininkas Kaunas
1977	Granitas Klaipeda
1978	Kelininkas Kaunas
1979	Kelininkas Kaunas
1980	Kelininkas Kaunas
1981	Granitas Klaipeda
1982	Pazanga Vilnius
1983	Granitas Klaipeda
1984	SRT Vilnius
1985	Ekranas Panevzys
1986	Granitas Klaipeda
1987	SRT Vilnius
1988	Sirijus Klaipeda

LITHUANIAN CUP FINALS

1992	Lietuvos Vilnius	1-0	Zalgiris Vilnius
1993	Zalgiris Vilnius	1-0	Sirijus Klaipeda
1994	Zalgiris Vilnius	4-2	Ekranas Panevezys
1995	Inkaras Kaunas	2-1	Zalgiris Vilnius

LEADING INTERNATIONAL GOALSCORERS

13	Antanas Lingis	(LFLS,KSK,MSK)	1928-1938
8	Jaroslavas Citavicius	(Kovas)	1926-1933
6	Stepas Chmelevskis	(SP.Klaipeda,KSS Klaipeda)	1929-1932
	Zigmas Sabaliauskas	(Kovas)	1933-1940
5	Juozas Gudelis	(Kovas)	1935-1939
	Valdemaras Jaskevicius	(LGSF)	1934-1940

LEADING INTERNATIONAL APPEARANCES

41	Romualdas Marcinkus	(LFLS,Kovas)	1927-1938
34	Antanas Lingis	(LFLS,KSK,MSK)	1928-1938
29	Romualdas Zebrauskas	(Kovas)	1926-1936
28	Fridrichas Tepferis	(LGSF,KSK,MSK,LFLS)	1931-1936
26	Andrius Tereskinas	(Zalgiris)	1991-

INTERNATIONAL MATCHES PLAYED BY LITHUANIA

24-06-1923	Estonia	L 0-5	Kaunas	Fr	
25-05-1924	Switzerland	L 0-9	Paris	OGr1	
1-06	Egypt	L 0-10	Paris	Fr	
16-08	Latvia	L 2-4	Kaunas	Fr	Nopensas 2
24-08	Estonia	W 2-1	Tallinn	Fr	Krygas, Seidleris
28-06-1925	Estonia	L 0-1	Kaunas	Fr	
20-09	Latvia	D 2-2	Riga	Fr	Sabaliauskas.S, Zukauskas.L
13-06-1926	Estonia	L 1-3	Tallinn	Fr	Sabaliauskas.S
21-08	Latvia	L 2-3	Kaunas	Fr	Sabaliauskas.S, Zebrauskas
27-07-1927	Latvia	L 3-6	Riga	Fr	Marcinkus, Blatas, Trumpjonas
13-08	Estonia	L 0-5	Kaunas	Fr	
25-07-1928	Latvia	L 0-3	Tallinn	BC	
26-07	Estonia	L 0-6	Tallinn	BC	
1-09	Latvia	D 1-1	Kaunas	Fr	Skema
14-08-1929	Latvia	L 1-3	Riga	BC	Chmelevskis
15-08	Estonia	L 2-5	Riga	BC	Chmelevskis, Rutkauskas
15-08-1930	Estonia	W 2-1	Kaunas	BC	Citavicius, Lingis
17-08	Latvia	D 3-3	Kaunas	BC	Citavicius, Lingis Chmelevskis
13-09	Estonia	W 4-0	Klaipeda	Fr	Chmelevskis 2, Zekas, Lingis
9-06-1931	Estonia	L 1-4	Tallinn	Fr	Chmelevskis
30-06	Latvia	L 2-5	Riga	Fr	Citavicius, Dirgela
26-08	Romania	L 2-4	Kaunas	Fr	Raclauskas, Trumpjonas
30-08	Estonia	L 0-2	Tallinn	BC	
31-08	Latvia	L 0-1	Tallinn	BC	
27-06-1932	Latvia	L 2-3	Kaunas	Fr	Lingis, Citavicius
24-07	Latvia	L 1-2	Liepaja	Fr	Lingis
16-08	Estonia	W 1-0	Kaunas	Fr	Citavicius
28-08	Latvia	L 1-4	Riga	BC	Citavicius
29-08	Estonia	W 2-1	Riga	BC	Cizauskas, Lingis
11-09	Latvia	W 1-0	Kaunas	Fr	Lingis
25-09	Sweden	L 1-8	Stockholm	Fr	Efisovas
12-06-1933	Latvia	L 2-6	Riga	Fr	Sabaliauskas.Z, Dirgela
29-06	Sweden	L 0-2	Kaunas	Fr	
20-07	Estonia	L 1-2	Tallinn	Fr	Citavicius

9-08	Finland	L 2-9	Helsinki	Fr	Sabaliauskas.Z 2
2-09	Estonia	D 1-1	Kaunas	BC	Citavicius
4-09	Latvia	D 2-2	Kaunas	BC	Sabaliauskas.Z, Lingis
5-09	Estonia	L 0-5	Kaunas	Fr	
10-06-1934	Latvia	W 2-0	Kaunas	Fr	Baliulevicius 2
29-06	Estonia	D 1-1	Kaunas	Fr	Sabaliauskas.Z
16-08	Finland	W 1-0	Kaunas	Fr	Kersnauskas
9-09	Latvia	W 3-1	Riga	Fr	Bubnovas 2, Klimas
30-05-1935	Latvia	L 1-6	Riga	Fr	Buzinskas
19-06	Estonia	D 2-2	Tallinn	Fr	Kersnauskas, Buzinskas
20-08	Estonia	W 2-1	Tallinn	BC	Jaskevicius, Lingis
21-08	Latvia	D 2-2	Tallinn	BC	Lingis, Gudelis
8-09	Latvia	D 2-2	Kaunas	Fr	Lingis, Marcinkus
18-09	Estonia	D 2-2	Kaunas	Fr	Lingis, Kersnauskas
14-06-1936	Latvia	L 1-5	Kaunas	Fr	Kersnauskas
30-06	Estonia	W 2-0	Kaunas	Fr	Gudelis, Sabaliauskas.Z
29-08	Latvia	L 1-2	Riga	BC	Jaskevicius
30-08	Estonia	L 1-2	Riga	BC	Gudelis
3-06-1937	Estonia	L 1-2	Kaunas	Fr	Gudelis
9-07	Romania	L 0-2	Kaunas	Fr	
29-07	Latvia	L 2-4	Riga	WCq	Gudelis, Paulionis
3-09	Latvia	L 1-5	Kaunas	WCq/BC	Paulionis
5-09	Estonia	L 0-4	Kaunas	BC	
17-05-1938	Latvia	L 0-2	Riga	Fr	
11-06	Estonia	L 0-2	Kaunas	Fr	
3-09	Estonia	L 1-3	Tallinn	BC	Surkus
4-09	Latvia	D 1-1	Tallinn	BC	Jaskevicius
18-09	Finland	L 1-3	Helsinki	Fr	Jastevicius
11-06-1939	Sweden	L 0-7	Karlstad	Fr	
27-08	Estonia	W 1-0	Tallinn	Fr	Adomavicius
11-08-1940	Estonia	W 2-0	Kaunas	Fr	Skeivys, Adomavicius
6-09	Latvia	L 0-1	Riga	BC	
7-09	Estonia	D 1-1	Riga	BC	Geleziunas
13-10	Latvia	W 4-3	Kaunas	Fr	Saunoris 2, Jaskevicius, Adomavicius
15-11-1991	Estonia	W 4-1	Vilnius	BC	Vitkovskis, Ramelis, Urbonas, Magdishauskas
17-11	Latvia	D 1-1	Vilnius	BC	Skarbalius
25-03-1992	Poland	L 0-2	Katowice	Fr	
14-04	Austria	L 0-4	Vienna	Fr	
28-04	Nth. Ireland	D 2-2	Belfast	WCq	Narbekovas, Fridrikas
3-06	Albania	L 0-1	Tirana	WCq	
16-07	Estonia	D 1-1	Leipaja	BC	Apanovics
17-07	Latvia	W 3-2	Leipaja	BC	
12-08	Latvia	W 2-1	Riga	WCq	Poderis, Tereskinas
12-09	Georgia	W 1-0	Kaunas	Fr	Mika
23-09	Denmark	D 0-0	Vilnius	WCq	
14-10	Slovakia	L 0-1	Vilnius	Fr	
28-10	Latvia	D 1-1	Vilnius	WCq	Fridrikas
24-02-1993	Spain	L 0-5	Seville	WCq	
30-03	Slovakia	D 2-2	Dunajska Streda	Fr	Zdancius 2
31-03	Poland	D 1-1	Brzeszcze	Fr	Poderis
14-04	Albania	W 3-1	Vilnius	WCq	Baltusnikas, Sukristovas, Baranauskas
18-05	Ukraine	L 1-2	Vilnius	Fr	Zdancius
25-05	Northern Ireland	L 0-1	Vilnius	WCq	
2-06	Spain	L 0-2	Vilnius	WCq	
16-06	Rep. Ireland	L 0-1	Vilnius	WCq	
3-07	Latvia	D 0-0	Pärnu	BC	
4-07	Estonia	L 1-2	Pärnu	BC	Olsanskis
25-08	Denmark	L 0-4	Copenhagen	WCq	
8-09	Rep. Ireland	L 0-2	Dublin	WCq	
20-04-1994	Israel	D 1-1	Vilnius	Fr	Baltusnikas
25-05	Czech Republic	L 3-5	Ostrava	Fr	Narbekovas, Zalys, Stumbrys
29-07	Estonia	W 3-0	Vilnius	BC	Ivanauskas 2, Mikalajunas
31-07	Latvia	W 1-0	Vilnius	BC	Tereskinas
17-08	Sweden	L 2-4	Orebro	Fr	Vainekis, Skarbalius
7-09	Ukraine	W 2-0	Kiev	ECq	Ivanauskas, Skarbalius
9-10	Croatia	L 0-2	Zagreb	ECq	
16-11	Slovenia	W 2-1	Maribor	ECq	Sukristovas, Zuta
15-03-1995	Poland	L 1-4	Ostrowiec Swiet.	Fr	Pocius
29-03	Croatia	D 0-0	Vilnius	ECq	
26-04	Italy	L 0-1	Vilnius	ECq	
17-05	Greece	W 2-1	Vilnius	Fr	Maciulevicius, Preiksaitis
20-05	Estonia	W 7-0	Riga	BC	Skarbalius, Baltunikas, Preiksaitis, Upstas, Zuta, Zvingilas, Poderis
21-05	Latvia	L 0-2	Riga	BC	
7-06	Slovenia	W 2-1	Vilnius	ECq	Stonkas, Suika

LUXEMBOURG

Ten out of ten for effort, but Luxembourg fail to score at all for achievement. They have entered every World Cup bar the first and have without fail finished last in their qualifying group. Added to this is the fact that after two victories were gained against Thailand and South Korea in the 1980 Marah Halim Cup, Luxembourg set off on a stunning run of 78 games with only five draws to break the losing sequence, which at one point amounted to 32 straight losses.

THE ORDER OF MERIT

		All			League			Cup		Europe		
	Team	G	S	B	G	S	B	G	S	G	S	B
1	Jeunesse Esch/ Alzette	31	20	11	22	11	11	9	9	-	-	-
2	AC Spora Luxembourg	23	21	15	14	13	15	9	8	-	-	-
3	Red Boys Differdange	21	19	14	6	10	14	15	9	-	-	-
4	Union Luxembourg	20	19	11	11	10	11	9	9	-	-	-
5	Stade Dudeldange	14	13	6	10	6	6	4	7	-	-	-
6	Avenir Beggen	12	8	2	6	5	2	6	3	-	-	-
7	Fola Esch/Alzette	8	8	4	5	7	4	3	1	-	-	-
8	Progres Niedercorn	7	8	8	3	5	8	4	3	-	-	-
9	Aris Bonnevoie	4	6	2	3	1	2	1	5	-	-	-
10	US Rumelange	2	5	1	-	3	1	2	2	-	-	-
11	The National Schifflange	2	3	-	1	2	-	1	1	-	-	-
12	Alliance Dudelange	2	2	-	-	1	-	2	1	-	-	-
13	CS Grevenmacher	1	6	1	-	2	1	1	4	-	-	-
14	US Dudelange	1	5	3	-	4	3	1	1	-	-	-
15	Jeun Hautcharage	1	-	-	-	-	-	1	-	-	-	-
	Swift Hesperange	1	-	-	-	-	-	1	-	-	-	-
	SC Tetange	1	-	-	-	-	-	1	-	-	-	-
18	F'91 Dudelange	-	2	-	-	-	-	-	2	-	-	-
19	AS Differdange	-	1	-	-	-	-	-	1	-	-	-
	SC Differdange	-	1	-	-	1	-	-	-	-	-	-
	Olympique Eischen	-	1	-	-	-	-	-	1	-	-	-
	CS Petange	-	1	-	-	-	-	-	1	-	-	-
	Racing Rodange	-	1	-	-	-	-	-	1	-	-	-
	Red Star Merl	-	1	-	-	-	-	-	1	-	-	-

To the end of the 1994-1995 season

Leaving aside the Marah Halim Cup, which was of a dubious 'A' grade status anyway, the winless run included a further 22 matches and seven years. The night of 25 February 1994, however, was an historic one for Luxembourg as the national side left the field of the Ta'Qali stadium in Malta having beaten their hosts 1-0 in a European Championship qualifier. The barren run had come to an end exactly 21 years, 3 months and 21 days after they had last defeated European opposition, and 22 years, 4 months and 3 days after their last win in a competitive match. The scale of the triumph can be gauged by the fact that it was only their second ever victory in the European Championships, with a similar number of wins having been recorded in the World Cup. To cap that, four months later they beat the Czech Republic at home. It never rains but it pours!

The Federation Luxembourgeoise de Football was formed in 1908 and became a member of FIFA two years later, when a league was also started. Luxembourg is a small country, traditionally involved in both finance and heavy industry, and it was as a form of leisure for the latter's workers that football gained a hold. Nowadays the structure remains amateur, but a few players do manage to make a name for themselves abroad as professionals, usually in France or Belgium.

The three dominant towns in the league are Luxembourg itself, Differdange and Esch. The latter has produced the best known club in the country, Jeunesse Esch, and they remain the only club to have reached the second round of the European Cup, where in 1964 they managed to beat Partizan Belgrade 2-1 at home, although they lost the tie 4-7 on aggregate. Heavy defeats are the norm for most clubs in Europe.

The first international match was played in 1911 against France, and Luxembourg have been very active in international games since. Most of the games, however, have been played against amateur or 'B' selections, and therefore do not show up on their record. This was especially true in the years up until the 1960s, during which time regular matches were contested with both Holland and Belgium in particular, but also against selections from other European countries.

Just occasionally, before 1995, Luxembourg did taste success. France and Belgium were beaten in full internationals, but the most impressive victories came against Portugal in 1961 in the World Cup, and Holland in the 1964 European Championship, when a 2-2 draw in Amsterdam and a 2-1 win in Rotterdam saw Luxembourg qualify for the quarter-finals and a tie against Denmark. The Danes eventually won in a play-off in Amsterdam after a 3-3 and 2-2 draw.

The expansion of UEFA has given football in Luxembourg new hope. Traditionally the bottom seed in their qualifying group and therefore kept apart from sides of equal stature, Luxembourg should now find themselves grouped with opponents they have a chance of beating.

Population: 379,000
Area, sq km: 2,586
% in urban areas: 77.6%
Capital city: Luxembourg

Federation Luxembourgeoise de Football
50 Rue de Strasbourg
L-2560 Luxembourg
Tel: + 352 488665
Fax: + 352 400201

Year of formation	1908
Affiliation to FIFA	1910
Affiliation to UEFA	1954
Registered clubs	123
Registered players	23 700
Registered referees	247
National stadium	Stade Municipal 10 000
National colours	Red/White/Blue
Reserve colours	Blue/White/Blue
Season	August - May

THE RECORD

WORLD CUP

1930	Did not enter
1934	QT 3rd/3 in group 12
1938	QT 3rd/3 in group 8
1950	QT 2nd/2 in group 4
1954	QT 3rd/3 in group 4
1958	QT 3rd/3 in group 5

1962 QT 3rd/3 in group 6
1966 QT 4th/4 in group 3
1970 QT 4th/4 in group 8
1974 QT 4th/4 in group 2
1978 QT 4th/4 in group 2
1982 QT 5th/5 in group 5
1986 QT 5th/5 in group 4
1990 QT 5th/5 in group 7
1994 QT 5th/5 in group 5

EUROPEAN CHAMPIONSHIP

1960 Did not enter
1964 Quarter-finalists
1968 QT 4th/4 in group 7
1972 QT 4th/4 in group 7
1976 QT 4th/4 in group 2
1980 QT 4th/4 in group 5
1984 QT 5th/5 in group 3
1988 QT 5th/5 in group 7
1992 QT 4th/4 in group 5
1996 QT group 5

EUROPEAN CLUB COMPETITIONS

European Cup
2nd round - Jeunesse Esch 1964
Cup Winners Cup
2nd round - Alliance Dudelange 1962 Aris Bonnevoie 1980
UEFA Cup
Never past the first round

CLUB DIRECTORY

LUXEMBOURG CITY (Population - 133,000)

FC Aris Bonnevoie (1922)
Camille Polfer 3,000 – White/Black

FC Avenir Beggen (1915)
Beggen 5,000 – Yellow/Black

AC Spora Luxembourg (1923)
Municipal 9,000 – Yellow, blue trim
Previous names - Merger of Sporting Club (1908) and Racing Club (1907) in 1923

FC Union Sportive Luxembourg (1908)
Achille Hammerel 6,000 – White/Blue
Previous name - US Hollerich 1908-20

ESCH-SUR-ALZETTE (Population - 83,000)

CS FOLA Esch (1906)
(Football and Lawn Tennis Club)
Émile Mayrisch 10,000 – Red & white stripes/Red

AS La Jeunesse d'Esch (1907)
De La Frontière 7,000 – Black & white stripes/White

DIFFERDANGE (Population - 16,000)

AS Differdange (1921)
Henri Jungers – White/White

FA Red Boys Differdange (1907)
Thillenberg 6,000 – Red, black & white trim

DUDELANGE (Population - 14,000)

F'91 Dudelange (1991)
Jos Nosbaum 4,000 – Yellow, black trim
Previous names - Merger in 1991 of Alliance (1916), US Dudelange (1912) & Stade Dudelange (1913)

PÉTANGE (Population - 11,000)

CS Pétange (1909)
Antoine Nangeroni 3,000 – Blue & white stripes/White

FC Progrés Niedercorn (1919)
Jos Haupert 3,000 – Yellow/Blue

RUMELANGE

Union Sportive Rumelange (1908)
Municipal 3,000 – Blue/White

GREVENMACHER

CS Grevenmacher (1909)
Op Flohr 3,000 – Blue, white trim

HESPERANGE

FC Swift Hesperange (1916)
Holleschbierg 2,000 – Red, white trim

WILTZ

FC Wiltz 71 (1971)
Get'zt 3,000 – Red & white diagonal halves/Red

TETANGE

SC Tétange (1914)
Gommerwiese – Green/White

SCHIFFLANGE

The National Schifflange (1912)
National – Yellow/Black

HAUTCHARAGE

Jeunesse Hautcharage (1919)
Umbechel – White/Black

LUXEMBOURG LEAGUE CHAMPIONSHIP

1910 Racing Club 3-2 US Hollerich
1911b Sporting Club 9 SC Differdange 9 US Hollerich 6
1912 US Hollerich 8 Sporting Club 8 Racing Club 7
1913 -
1914d US Hollerich 16 Sporting Club 15 Racing Club 10
1915 US Hollerich 8-1 Jeunesse Esch
1916 US Hollerich 16 Sporting Club 12 Fola Esch 11
1917 US Hollerich 20 Fola Esch 12 Racing Club 8
1918 Fola Esch 16 US Hollerich 13 Sporting Club 10
1919 Sporting Club 16 Fola Esch 13 Jeunesse Esch 12
1920 Fola Esch 17 Stade Dudelange 13 Sporting Club 10
1921f Jeunesse Esch 20 Fola Esch 19 Union Luxembourg 18
1922 Fola Esch 22 Union Luxembourg 20 Jeunesse Esch 16
1923 Red Boys 23 Stade Dudelange 22 Fola Esch 16
1924 Fola Esch 23 AC Spora 20 Red Boys 18
1925 AC Spora 21 Stade Dudelange 20 Jeunesse Esch 18
1926 Red Boys 22 AC Spora 21 Fola Esch 18
1927 Union Luxembourg 21 Red Boys 18 AC Spora 17
1928 AC Spora 24 Stade Dudelange 16 Red Boys 15
1929 AC Spora 19 Fola Esch 18 Red Boys 17
1930 Fola Esch 20 AC Spora 19 Red Boys 17
1931 Red Boys 25 AC Spora 20 Progres Niedercorn 14
1932 Red Boys 21 Progres Niedercorn 21 AC Spora 14
1933 Red Boys 27 AC Spora 16 Progres Niedercorn 15
1934 AC Spora 23 Red Boys 18 US Dudelange 14
1935 AC Spora 20 Red Boys 17 Jeunesse Esch 14
1936h AC Spora 28 Jeunesse Esch 26 Red Boys 22
1937 Jeunesse Esch 26 Progres Niedercorn 26 US Dudelange 26
1938 AC Spora 26 Jeunesse Esch 24 Stade Dudelange 22
1939 Stade Dudelange 31 US Dudelange 28 AC Spora 23
1940 Stade Dudelange 31 US Dudelange 24 Progres Niedercorn 22
1941-44 -
1945 Stade Dudelange 6-0 AC Spora
1946h Stade Dudelange 32 US Dudelange 24 Progres Niedercorn 21
1947k Stade Dudelange 40 US Dudelange 28 Fola Esch 25
1948 Stade Dudelange 38 Union Luxembourg 27 Red Boys 27
1949 AC Spora 38 Fola Esch 34 Stade Dudelange 29
1950 Stade Dudelange 35 National Schifflange 34 AC Spora 25
1951 Jeunesse Esch 32 National Schifflange 30 Red Boys 26
1952h National Schifflange 24 AC Spora 23 Stade Dudelange 21
1953k Progres Niedercorn 32 Jeunesse Esch 31 Stade Dudelange 27
1954 Jeunesse Esch 33 Fola Esch 28 Progres Niedercorn 24
1955 Stade Dudelange 34 Fola Esch 25 Union Luxembourg 24
1956 AC Spora 33 Stade Dudelange 32 Progres Niedercorn 30
1957 Stade Dudelange 37 Jeunesse Esch 31 Red Boys 27
1958 Jeunesse Esch 35 Red Boys 30 Stade Dudelange 28
1959 Jeunesse Esch 32 AC Spora 26 Red Boys 26
1960 Jeunesse Esch 34 Stade Dudelange 28 CS Grevenmacher 26
1961 AC Spora 33 Jeunesse Esch 33 Union Luxembourg 30
1962 Union Luxembourg 39 Alliance Dudelange 32 AC Spora 24
1963 Jeunesse Esch 35 Union Luxembourg 29 Red Boys 28
1964 Aris Bonnevoie 33 Union Luxembourg 31 Stade Dudelange 30

1965 Stade Dudelange 32 Union Luxembourg 31 Jeunesse Esch 28
1966 Aris Bonnevoie 35 Union Luxembourg 28 US Dudelange 28
1967 Jeunesse Esch 36 AC Spora 30 Union Luxembourg 27
1968 Jeunesse Esch 35 US Rumelange 31 Union Luxembourg 28
1969 Avenir Beggen 34 Jeunesse Esch 34 Aris Bonnevoie 30
1970 Jeunesse Esch 36 US Rumelange 31 AC Spora 30
1971 Union Luxembourg 37 Aris Bonnevoie 29 Jeunesse Esch 29
1972 Aris Bonnevoie 31 US Rumelange 30 Red Boys 26
1973 Jeunesse Esch 38 Union Luxembourg 30 Red Boys 27
1974 Jeunesse Esch 38 Red Boys 32 AC Spora 30
1975 Jeunesse Esch 33 Avenir Beggen 31 Union Luxembourg 27
1976 Jeunesse Esch 34 Red Boys 30 US Rumelange 25
1977 Jeunesse Esch 34 Progres Niedercorn 32 Red Boys 27
1978 Progres Niedercorn 32 Jeunesse Esch 26 Red Boys 25
1979 Red Boys 34 Progres Niedercorn 34 Union Luxembourg 25
1980 Jeunesse Esch 33 Red Boys 32 Progres Niedercorn 30
1981 Progres Niedercorn 35 Red Boys 34 Jeunesse Esch 31
1982 Avenir Beggen 36 Progres Niedercorn 32 Jeunesse Esch 29
1983 Jeunesse Esch 34 Avenir Beggen 29 Aris Bonnevoie 28
1984 Avenir Beggen 33 Red Boys 32 Progres Niedercorn 27
1985 Jeunesse Esch 37 Red Boys 32 Avenir Beggen 28
1986 Avenir Beggen 33 Jeunesse Esch 32 AC Spora 31
1987 Jeunesse Esch 38 Avenir Beggen 35 AC Spora 30
1988p3 Jeunesse Esch 25 Avenir Beggen 23 Union Luxembourg 20.5
1989p4 AC Spora 29 Jeunesse Esch 25.5 Union Luxembourg 24
1990 Union Luxembourg 29.5 Avenir Beggen 27.5 Jeunesse Esch 26.5
1991 Union Luxembourg 28 Jeunesse Esch 25 AC Spora 22.5
1992 Union Luxembourg 26 Avenir Beggen 26 Jeunesse Esch 23
1993 Avenir Beggen 28.5 Union Luxembourg 27.5 Jeunesse Esch 23
1994 Avenir Beggen 28.5 CS Grevenmacher 24 Union Luxembourg 23
1995k Jeunesse Esch 35 CS Grevenmacher 35 Avenir Beggen 30

Play-off results

1911 Sporting Club 3-0 SC Differdange
1932 Red Boys 4-1 Progres Niedercorn
1937 Jeunesse Esch won a three way play-off
1961 AC Spora 1-0 Jeunesse Esch

LUXEMBOURG CUP FINALS

1922 Racing Club 2-0 Jeunesse Esch
1923 Fola Esch 3-0 Union Luxembourg
1924 Fola Esch 2-0 Red Boys
1925 Red Boys 1-1 3-0 AC Spora
1926 Red Boys 5-2 Union Luxembourg
1927 Red Boys 3-2 Jeunesse Esch
1928 AC Spora 2-2 3-3 5-2 Stade Dudelange
1929 Red Boys 5-3 AC Spora
1930 Red Boys 2-1 AC Spora
1931 Red Boys 5-3 AC Spora
1932 AC Spora 2-1 Red Boys
1933 Progres Niedercorn 4-1 Union Luxembourg
1934 Red Boys 5-2 AC Spora
1935 Jeunesse Esch 4-2 Red Boys
1936 Red Boys 2-0 Stade Dudelange
1937 Jeunesse Esch 3-0 Union Luxembourg
1938 Stade Dudelange 1-0 National Schifflange
1939 US Dudelange 2-1 Stade Dudelange
1940 AC Spora 6-2 Stade Dudelange
1941-44 -
1945 Progres Niedercorn 2-0 AC Spora
1946 Jeunesse Esch 3-1 Progres Niedercorn
1947 Union Luxembourg 2-1 Stade Dudelange
1948 Stade Dudelange 1-0 Red Boys
1949 Stade Dudelange 1-0 Racing Rodange
1950 AC Spora 5-1 Red Boys
1951 SC Tetange 1-1 2-0 CS Grevenmacher
1952 Red Boys 1-0 Red Star Merl
1953 Red Boys 2-1 CS Grevenmacher
1954 Jeunesse Esch 5-0 CS Grevenmacher
1955 Fola Esch 1-1 4-1 Red Boys
1956 Stade Dudelange 3-1 Progres Niedercorn
1957 AC Spora 2-1 Stade Dudelange
1958 Red Boys 3-1 US Dudelange
1959 Union Luxembourg 3-1 CS Grevenmacher
1960 National Schifflange 3-0 Stade Dudelange
1961 Alliance Dudelange 3-2 Union Luxembourg
1962 Alliance Dudelange 1-0 Union Luxembourg
1963 Union Luxembourg 2-1 AC Spora
1964 Union Luxembourg 1-0 Aris Bonnevoie
1965 AC Spora 1-0 Jeunesse Esch
1966 AC Spora 2-0 Jeunesse Esch
1967 Aris Bonnevoie 1-0 Union Luxembourg
1968 US Rumelange 0-0 1-0 Aris Bonnevoie
1969 Union Luxembourg 5-2 Alliance Dudelange
1970 Union Luxembourg 1-0 Red Boys
1971 Jeunesse Hautcharage 4-1 Jeunesse Esch
1972 Red Boys 4-3 Aris Bonnevoie
1973 Jeunesse Esch 3-2 Fola Esch
1974 Jeunesse Esch 4-1 Avenir Beggen
1975 US Rumelange 2-0 Jeunesse Esch
1976 Jeunesse Esch 2-1 Aris Bonnevoie
1977 Progres Niedercorn 4-4 3-1 Red Boys
1978 Progres Niedercorn 2-1 Union Luxembourg
1979 Red Boys 4-1 Aris Bonnevoie
1980 AC Spora 3-2 Progres Niedercorn
1981 Jeunesse Esch 5-0 Olympique Eischen
1982 Red Boys 2-1 US Rumelange
1983 Avenir Beggen 4-2 Union Luxembourg
1984 Avenir Beggen 4-1 US Rumelange
1985 Red Boys 1-0 Jeunesse Esch
1986 Union Luxembourg 4-1 Red Boys
1987 Avenir Beggen 6-0 AC Spora
1988 Jeunesse Esch 1-0 Avenir Beggen
1989 Union Luxembourg 2-0 Avenir Beggen
1990 Swift Hesperange 3-3 7-1 AS Differdange
1991 Union Luxembourg 3-0 Jeunesse Esch
1992 Avenir Beggen 1-0 CS Petange
1993 Avenir Beggen 5-2 F'91 Dudelange
1994 Avenir Beggen 3-1 F'91 Dudelange
1995 CS Grevenmacher 1-1 3-2 Jeunesse Esch

LEADING INTERNATIONAL GOALSCORERS

16 Léon Mart (Fola Esch)
15 Gustave Kemp (Differdange)
14 Camille Libar (Stade Dudelange)
13 Nicolas Kettel (Stade Dudelange,Diekirch)
12 François Muller (Merl/Grevenmacher)
11 Léon Letsch (Spora,Roubaix-Tourcoing)
9 Nico Braun (Union,Schalke,Metz,Charleroi SC)
Gilbert Dussier (Red Boys,Jeunesse,Völklingen,Lille)
Jules Gales (Spora)
Robert Theissen (Spora)
Roby Langers (Union.Mönchengladbach,Marseille,Metz, Quimper,Guingamp,Orleans,Nice, Cannes, Yverdon,Carouge)

LEADING INTERNATIONAL APPEARANCES

77 François Konter (Rodange,Anderlecht,AA Gent)
75 Carlo Weis (Spora,Metz,Winterslag,Reims, Thionville,Avenir)

67 Ernest Brenner (Stade Dudelange)
64 Marcel Bossi (Niedercorn,Jeunesse Esch)
63 Gilbert Dresch (Avenir Beggen)
58 Jean-Paul Girres (Union,Avenir Beggen,Hesperange)
58 Roby Langers (see goalscorers table)
57 Ferdinand Brosius (Spora)
56 Nicolas Kettel (Stade Dudelange,Diekirch)
54 Hubert Meunier (Niedercorn,Jeunesse Esch,Avenir Beggen)

All totals include 'B' internationals

INTERNATIONAL MATCHES PLAYED BY LUXEMBOURG

29-10-1911	France	L 1-4	Luxembourg	Fr	Elter
20-04-1913	France	L 0-8	Paris	Fr	
8-02-1914	France	W 5-4	Luxembourg	Fr	Massard 4, Bernard
28-08-1920	Holland	L 0-3	Brussels	OGr1	
29-05-1924	Italy	L 0-2	Paris	OGr2	
21-05-1927	England	L 2-5	Esch	Fr	Hubert, Lefevre
27-05-1928	Belgium	L 3-5	Amsterdam	OGr1	Schutz, Weisgerber, Theissen
28-06	Egypt	D 1-1	Esch	Fr	Theissen
11-03-1934	Germany	L 1-9	Luxembourg	WCq	Mengel
15-04	France	L 1-6	Luxembourg	WCq	Speicher
18-08-1935	Germany	L 0-1	Luxembourg	Fr	
9-05-1936	Rep. Ireland	L 1-5	Luxembourg	Fr	Mart
4-08	Germany	L 0-9	Berlin	OGr1	
27-09	Germany	L 2-7	Krefeld	Fr	Kemp 2
21-03-1937	Germany	L 2-3	Luxembourg	Fr	Kemp, Stamet
28-11	Holland	L 0-4	Rotterdam	WCq	
16-01-1938	Hungary	L 0-6	Luxembourg	Fr	
13-03	Belgium	L 2-3	Luxembourg	WCq	Libar, Kemp
20-03	Germany	L 1-2	Wuppertal	Fr	Libar
26-03-1939	Germany	W 2-1	Differdange	Fr	Mart 2
31-03-1940	Holland	W 5-4	Rotterdam	Fr	Kemp 2, Libar, Feller.P, Everard
13-05-1945	Belgium	W 4-1	Luxembourg	Fr	Mart 2, Libar, Kemp
23-02-1946	Belgium	L 0-7	Charleroi	Fr	
10-03	Holland	L 2-6	Luxembourg	Fr	Lahure, Feller.P
28-07	Norway	W 3-2	Luxembourg	Fr	Schumacher 2, Pauly
30-10	Hungary	L 2-7	Esch	Fr	
24-05-1947	Scotland	L 0-6	Luxembourg	Fr	
26-07-1948	Afghanistan	W 6-0	London	OGr1	Konter 2, Kremer 2, Wagner, Feller.V
31-07	Yugoslavia	L 1-6	London	OGr2	Schammel
23-03-1949	Czechoslovakia	D 2-2	Bratislava	Fr	Letsch, Paulus
26-06	Switzerland	L 2-5	Zurich	WCq	Wagner, Reuter
18-09	Switzerland	L 2-3	Luxembourg	WCq	Muller, Kremer
15-08-1950	Norway	D 2-2	Bergen	Fr	Letsch, Muller
4-11-1951	Finland	W 3-0	Luxembourg	Fr	Muller, Nurenberg.V, OG
23-12	West Germany	L 1-4	Essen	Fr	Muller
20-04-1952	West Germany	L 0-3	Luxembourg	Fr	
20-09-1953	France	L 1-6	Luxembourg	WCq	Kohn
28-10	Rep. Ireland	L 0-4	Dublin	WCq	
17-12	France	L 0-8	Paris	WCq	
7-03-1954	Rep. Ireland	L 0-1	Luxembourg	WCq	
30-09-1956	Austria	L 0-7	Vienna	WCq	
20-03-1957	Holland	L 1-4	Rotterdam	WCq	Halsdorf
11-09	Holland	L 2-5	Rotterdam	WCq	Fiedler, Letsch
29-09	Austria	L 0-3	Luxembourg	WCq	
17-06-1959	Norway	L 0-1	Oslo	Fr	
19-10-1960	England	L 0-9	Luxembourg	WCq	
19-03-1961	Portugal	L 0-6	Lisbon	WCq	
28-09	England	L 1-4	London	WCq	Dimmer
8-10	Portugal	W 4-2	Luxembourg	WCq	Schmit 3, Hoffmann
11-04-1962	Soviet Union	L 1-3	Luxembourg	Fr	Schmit
11-09-1963	Holland	D 1-1	Amsterdam	ECr2	May
30-10	Holland	W 2-1	Rotterdam	ECr2	Dimmer 2
4-12	Denmark	D 3-3	Luxembourg	ECqf	Pilot, Klein.H 2
10-12	Denmark	D 2-2	Copenhagen	ECqf	Leonard, Schmit
18-12	Denmark	L 0-1	Amsterdam	ECqf	
20-09-1964	Yugoslavia	L 1-3	Belgrade	WCq	Schmit
4-10	France	L 0-2	Luxembourg	WCq	
8-11	Norway	L 0-2	Luxembourg	WCq	
27-05-1965	Norway	L 2-4	Trondheim	WCq	Brenner, Dublin
19-09	Yugoslavia	L 2-5	Luxembourg	WCq	Pilot 2
6-11	France	L 1-4	Marseille	WCq	Pilot
2-10-1966	Poland	L 0-4	Szezecin	ECq	

26-11	France	L 0-3	Luxembourg	ECq	
19-03-1967	Belgium	L 0-5	Luxembourg	ECq	
16-04	Poland	D 0-0	Luxembourg	ECq	
22-11	Belgium	L 0-3	Bruges	ECq	
23-12	France	L 1-3	Paris	ECq	Klein.J
4-09-1968	Holland	L 0-2	Rotterdam	WCq	
20-11	Denmark	L 1-5	Copenhagen	Fr	Klein.J
26-03-1969	Holland	L 0-4	Rotterdam	WCq	
10-04	Mexico	W 2-1	Luxembourg	Fr	Leonard, Philipp
20-04	Poland	L 1-8	Krakow	WCq	Leonard
23-04	Bulgaria	L 1-2	Sofia	WCq	Leonard
12-10	Poland	L 1-5	Luxembourg	WCq	
7-12	Bulgaria	L 1-3	Luxembourg	WCq	Philipp
4-01-1970	Malta	D 1-1	Gzira	Fr	Hoffmann.N
9-05	Czechoslovakia	L 0-1	Luxembourg	Fr	
14-10	Yugoslavia	L 0-2	Luxembourg	ECq	
15-11	East Germany	L 0-5	Luxembourg	ECq	
24-02-1971	Holland	L 0-6	Rotterdam	ECq	
24-04	East Germany	L 1-2	Gera	ECq	Dussier
20-05	Belgium	L 0-4	Luxembourg	Fr	
27-10	Yugoslavia	D 0-0	Titograd	ECq	
7-11	Belgium	L 0-1	Verviers	Fr	
17-11	Holland	L 0-8	Eindhoven	ECq	
26-04-1972	Czechoslovakia	L 0-6	Pilsen	Fr	
7-10	Italy	L 0-4	Luxembourg	WCq	
22-10	Turkey	W 2-0	Esch	WCq	Dussier, Braun
10-12	Turkey	L 0-3	Istanbul	WCq	
31-03-1973	Italy	L 0-5	Genoa	WCq	
8-04	Switzerland	L 0-1	Luxembourg	WCq	
26-09	Switzerland	L 0-1	Lucerne	WCq	
7-10	Canada	L 0-2	Luxembourg	Fr	
4-11	Norway	W 2-1	Luxembourg	Fr	Monacelli, Langers
13-10-1974	Hungary	L 2-4	Luxembourg	ECq	Dussier 2
20-11	Wales	L 0-5	Swansea	ECq	
16-03-1975	Austria	L 1-2	Luxembourg	ECq	Braun
1-05	Wales	L 1-3	Luxembourg	ECq	Philipp
15-10	Austria	L 2-6	Vienna	ECq	Braun, Philipp
19-10	Hungary	L 1-8	Szombathely	ECq	Dussier
21-08-1976	Iceland	L 1-3	Reykjavik	Fr	Braun
22-09	Finland	L 1-7	Helsinki	WCq	Zender.G
16-10	Italy	L 1-4	Luxembourg	WCq	Braun
30-03-1977	England	L 0-5	London	WCq	
26-05	Finland	L 0-1	Luxembourg	WCq	
12-10	England	L 0-2	Luxembourg	WCq	
3-12	Italy	L 0-3	Rome	WCq	
22-03-1978	Poland	L 1-3	Luxembourg	Fr	Reiter
7-10	France	L 1-3	Luxembourg	ECq	Michaux
25-02-1979	France	L 0-3	Paris	ECq	
1-05	Czechoslovakia	L 0-3	Luxembourg	ECq	
7-06	Sweden	L 0-3	Malmo	ECq	
23-10	Sweden	D 1-1	Esch	ECq	Braun
24-11	Czechoslovakia	L 0-4	Prague	ECq	
27-02-1980	Belgium	L 0-5	Brussels	Fr	
26-03	Uruguay	L 0-1	Esch	Fr	
1-05	Thailand	W 1-0	Medan	Fr	Clemens
9-05	South Korea	W 3-2	Medan	Fr	Di Domenico, Reiter 2
11-05	Japan	L 0-1	Medan	Fr	
13-05	Burma	L 0-2	Medan	Fr	
14-05	South Korea	L 0-3	Medan	Fr	
10-09	Yugoslavia	L 0-5	Luxembourg	WCq	
4-10	USA	L 0-2	Dudelange	Fr	
11-10	Italy	L 0-2	Luxembourg	WCq	
19-11	Denmark	L 0-4	Copenhagen	WCq	
28-01-1981	Greece	L 0-2	Salonica	WCq	
11-03	Greece	L 0-2	Luxembourg	WCq	
1-05	Denmark	L 1-2	Luxembourg	WCq	Nurenberg.A
14-10	Spain	L 0-3	Valencia	Fr	
21-11	Yugoslavia	L 0-5	Novi Sad	WCq	
5-12	Italy	L 0-1	Naples	WCq	
9-10-1982	Greece	L 0-2	Luxembourg	ECq	
10-11	Denmark	L 1-2	Luxembourg	ECq	Di Domenico

15-12	England	L 0-9	London	ECq	
27-03-1983	Hungary	L 2-6	Luxembourg	ECq	Reiter, Schreiner
17-04	Hungary	L 2-6	Budapest	ECq	Reiter, Malget
12-10	Denmark	L 0-6	Copenhagen	ECq	
16-11	England	L 0-4	Luxembourg	ECq	
14-12	Greece	L 0-1	Athens	ECq	
29-02-1984	Spain	L 0-1	Luxembourg	Fr	
11-03	Turkey	L 1-3	Esch	Fr	Dresch
1-05	Norway	L 0-2	Ettelbruck	Fr	
9-06	Portugal	L 1-2	Luxembourg	Fr	Wagner
13-10	France	L 0-4	Luxembourg	WCq	
17-11	East Germany	L 0-5	Esch	WCq	
5-12	Bulgaria	L 0-4	Sofia	WCq	
17-12	Cyprus	L 0-1	Nicosia	Fr	
19-12	Israel	L 0-2	Tel Aviv	Fr	
22-12	Turkey	L 0-1	Istanbul	Fr	
27-03-1985	Yugoslavia	L 0-1	Zenica	WCq	
24-04	Iceland	D 0-0	Ettelbruck	Fr	
1-05	Yugoslavia	L 0-1	Luxembourg	WCq	
18-05	East Germany	L 1-3	Babelsberg	WCq	Langers.R
25-09	Bulgaria	L 1-3	Luxembourg	WCq	Langers.R
30-10	France	L 0-6	Paris	WCq	
5-02-1986	Portugal	L 0-2	Portimao	Fr	
14-10	Belgium	L 0-6	Luxembourg	ECq	
12-11	Scotland	L 0-3	Glasgow	ECq	
30-04-1987	Bulgaria	L 1-4	Luxembourg	ECq	Langers.R
20-05	Bulgaria	L 0-3	Sofia	ECq	
28-05	Rep. Ireland	L 0-2	Luxembourg	ECq	
9-09	Rep. Ireland	L 1-2	Dublin	ECq	Krings
23-09	Spain	L 0-2	Castellon	Fr	
11-11	Belgium	L 0-3	Brussels	ECq	
2-12	Scotland	D 0-0	Esch	ECq	
27-04-1988	Italy	L 0-3	Luxembourg	Fr	
21-09	Switzerland	L 1-4	Luxembourg	WCq	Langers.R
18-10	Czechoslovakia	L 0-2	Esch	WCq	
16-11	Portugal	L 0-1	Oporto	WCq	
9-05-1989	Czechoslovakia	L 0-4	Prague	WCq	
1-06	Belgium	L 0-5	Lille	WCq	
11-10	Portugal	L 0-3	Saarbrucken	WCq	
25-10	Belgium	D 1-1	Brussels	WCq	Hellers
15-11	Switzerland	L 1-2	St. Gallen	WCq	Malget
28-03-1990	Iceland	L 1-2	Esch	Fr	Malget
31-10	Germany	L 2-3	Luxembourg	ECq	Girres, Langers.R
14-11	Wales	L 0-1	Luxembourg	ECq	
27-02-1991	Belgium	L 0-3	Brussels	ECq	
11-09	Belgium	L 0-2	Luxembourg	ECq	
12-10	Portugal	D 1-1	Luxembourg	Fr	Weis
13-11	Wales	L 0-1	Cardiff	ECq	
18-12	Germany	L 0-4	Leverkusen	ECq	
25-03-1992	Turkey	L 2-3	Luxembourg	Fr	Girres, Wolf
9-09	Hungary	L 0-3	Luxembourg	WCq	
28-10	Russia	L 0-2	Moscow	WCq	
17-02-1993	Greece	L 0-2	Athens	WCq	
14-04	Russia	L 0-4	Luxembourg	WCq	
20-05	Iceland	D 1-1	Luxembourg	WCq	OG
8-09	Iceland	L 0-1	Reykjavik	WCq	
12-10	Greece	L 1-3	Luxembourg	WCq	Fanelli
27-10	Hungary	L 0-1	Budapest	WCq	
23-03-1994	Morocco	L 1-2	Luxembourg	Fr	Wolf
7-09	Holland	L 0-4	Luxembourg	ECq	
12-10	Belarus	L 0-2	Minsk	ECq	
14-12	Holland	L 0-5	Rotterdam	ECq	
14-02-1995	Israel	L 2-4	Ashdod	ECq	Langers 2
22-02	Malta	W 1-0	Ta'Qali	ECq	Langers
29-03	Norway	L 0-2	Luxembourg	ECq	
26-04	Norway	L 0-5	Oslo	ECq	
7-06	Czech Republic	W 1-0	Luxembourg	ECq	Hellers

MACEDONIA

Macedonia was the 49th of the current 49 members to be admitted to UEFA, only just meeting the deadline for entry into the 1996 European Championships. Technically known as the Former Yugoslav Republic of Macedonia - after complaints from the Greeks who wanted it to be known as the Republic of Skopje so as not to conflict with their own territory of the same name - Macedonia has emerged relatively unscathed from the troubles affecting Yugoslavia.

Vardar Skopje, Yugoslav Cup winners in 1961, are the biggest team in Macedonia and they won the first two championships after independence. In 1987 they thought they had won the Yugoslav league title, but when a court order overruled a 6-point penalty which had been imposed on 12 clubs at the start of the season, Partizan became champions. It was hard on Vardar, but they did enter the European Cup the following season.

Star of that side was Macedonia's most famous player, Darko Pancev, who subsequently played for Red Star, winning the European Cup in 1991. Runner-up to Jean-Pierre Papin in the European Footballer of the Year poll that year, Pancev moved on to join Internazionale in Italy and captained Macedonia in their first competitive international, a 1-1 draw with Denmark in a European Championship qualifier in 1994. Indeed the Macedonians, seeded in the fourth tier of six for Euro '96, were only three minutes away from beating the holders, despite having a player (Pancev!) sent off.

Population: 2,111,000
Area, sq km: 25,713
Capital city: Skopje

Football Union of Macedonia
8-ma Udarna brigada 31-a
9100 Skopje
Macedonia
Tel: + 91 236943
Fax: + 91 235448

Year of formation	1992
Affiliation to FIFA	1994
Affiliation to UEFA	1994
National stadium	Gradski, Skopje 25 000
National colours	Red/Red/Red

THE RECORD

WORLD CUP
1930-94 Did not enter

EUROPEAN CHAMPIONSHIP
1960-92 Did not enter
1996 QT ???/6 in group 2

EUROPEAN CLUB COMPETITIONS
European Cup
First round - Vardar Skopje 1988
Cup Winners Cup
First round - Vardar Skopje 1962
UEFA Cup
Second round - Vardar Skopje 1986

CLUB DIRECTORY

SKOPJE (Population - 547,000)
FK Vardar Skoplje (1947)
Gradski 25,000 – Red & black stripes/Black
Previous names - Gradjanski 1922-39, Pobeda 1939-47

Balkan Stokokomerc Skopje

Sloga Jugomagnat Skopje

FCU-55 Skopje

BITOLA (Population - 143,000)
Pelister Bitola (1945)
Gradski 15,000 – Green & white stripes/Green

PRILEP (Population - 99,000)
Pobeda Vitaminka Prilep

KRATOVO (Population - 99,000)
Sileks Kratovo

TETOVO
Ljuboten Tetovo

TITOVO VELES
Borec Titovo Veles

STRUMICA
Belasica Strumica

MACEDONIAN LEAGUE CHAMPIONSHIP

1993t	Vardar Skopje 61 Sileks Kratovo 40 Balkan Stokokomerc 40
1994q	Vardar Skopje 51 Sileks Kratovo 44 Balkan Stokokomerc 37
1995q3	Vardar Skopje 76 Sileks Kratovo 60 Sloga Jugomagnat 58

MACEDONIAN CUP FINALS

1993	Vardar Skopje	1-0	Pelister Bitola
1994	Sileks Kratovo	1-1 3-0p	Pelister Bitola
1995	Vardar Skopje	2-1	Sileks Kratovo

INTERNATIONAL MATCHES PLAYED BY MACEDONIA

13-10-1993	Slovenia	W 4-1	Kranj	Fr	Boskovski, Pancev, Janevski, Kanatlarovski
23-03-1994	Slovenia	W 2-0	Skopje	Fr	Serafimovski, Boskovski
14-05	Albania	W 5-1	Tetovo	Fr	Nedzmeden, Micevski.V 2, Boskovski, Stojkovski.M
1-06	Estonia	W 2-0	Skopje	Fr	Boskovski, Kanatlarovski
31-08	Turkey	L 2-0	Skopje	Fr	
7-09	Denmark	D 1-1	Skopje	ECq	Stojkovski.M
12-10	Spain	L 0-2	Skopje	ECq	
16-11	Belgium	D 1-1	Brussels	ECq	Boskovski
17-12	Cyprus	W 3-0	Skopje	ECq	Djurovski.B 3
12-04-1995	Bulgaria	D 0-0	Strumica	Fr	
26-04	Denmark	L 0-1	Copenhagen	ECq	
10-05	Armenia	D 2-2	Yerevan	ECq	Hristo,Markovski
7-06	Belgium	L 0-5	Skopje	ECq	

MALTA

With a population of only 300,000 Malta will never be able to call upon a large pool of players, but it is disappointing that they have not done better. Almost all of their victories have come from games against African or Asian opposition, and of the middle-ranking European powers only Greece and Belgium have been defeated.

The Malta Football Association was formed as far back as 1900, and as a British colony, was affiliated to the Football Association in London. The obvious British influence led to the formation of a league in 1910, with a cup competition introduced in 1935. In 1959, with the permission of the FA in London, Malta decided the time was right to start playing international football and they were granted membership of FIFA. They entered the African section of the 1960 Olympic Games qualifiers but the venture did not turn out successfully; although they held both Morocco and Tunisia to draws at home, they lost to both away.

It was not until the 1970s that Malta began regularly entering the World Cup and European Championship, but Maltese clubs have been steadfast competitors in the three European club competitions since the early 1960s. As would be expected, results have not been good despite the professional status of many of the players, with double-figure aggregate defeats not uncommon.

The club scene has traditionally been dominated by Floriana and Sliema Wanderers, although Valletta FC, Hamrun Spartans and Hibernians Paola make up the traditional big five. Since the inauguration of the Ta'Qali national stadium in 1980, all of the games in the premier league take place there, so technically there are no home games. There is little justification in having any more stadia given that the island is only 316 square kilometres big and that full to capacity, Ta'Qali will hold one tenth of the island's population.

THE ORDER OF MERIT

		All			League			Cup		Europe		
	Team	G	S	B	G	S	B	G	S	G	S	B
1	Floriana	43	22	11	25	11	11	18	11	-	-	-
2	Sliema Wanderers	39	41	17	22	26	17	17	15	-	-	-
3	Valletta	21	23	18	14	13	18	7	10	-	-	-
4	Hamrun Spartans	13	12	13	7	10	13	6	2	-	-	-
5	Hibernians	13	18	7	8	9	7	5	9	-	-	-
6	Rabat Ajax	3	2	1	2	1	1	1	1	-	-	-
7	St. Georges	1	6	5	1	4	5	-	2	-	-	-
8	Zurrieq	1	2	2	-	-	2	1	2	-	-	-
9	Melita St. Julians	1	2	1	-	1	1	1	1	-	-	-
10	Gzira United	1	-	1	-	-	1	1	-	-	-	-
11	KOMR Militia	1	-	-	1	-	-	-	-	-	-	-
12	Birkirkara Luxol	-	3	-	-	1	-	-	2	-	-	-
13	Marsa	-	2	-	-	2	-	-	-	-	-	-
14	Hamrun Liberty	-	1	-	-	-	-	-	1	-	-	-
	Hamrun United	-	1	-	-	1	-	-	-	-	-	-
	Sengla Athletic	-	1	-	-	-	-	-	1	-	-	-
	Vittoriosa Rovers	-	1	-	-	1	-	-	-	-	-	-
18	ASC Militia	-	-	1	-	-	1	-	-	-	-	-
	Civil Police	-	-	1	-	-	1	-	-	-	-	-
	St. Joseph's	-	-	1	-	-	1	-	-	-	-	-

To the end of the 1994-95 season

If there has been little to cheer about at club level, the record of the Maltese national eleven brings little relief either. Bottom of every qualifying group they have ever taken part in, they have occasionally achieved an honourable draw against the likes of Czechoslovakia and Portugal. Until 1980 the Maltese had the 'advantage' of what was considered to be the worst pitch in Europe at the old Empire stadium in Gzira, but that has gone with the completion of the Ta'Qali. With the expansion of UEFA, however, Malta beat Estonia in Tallinn in the 1994 World Cup qualifiers, their first win in a competitive international in over 10 years and within a year they had also beaten Belgium 1-0 at home and seen off Azerbaijan 5-0, their biggest ever win in an international. They also have a player of genuine class in Carmen Busuttil, Malta's all-time top scorer with 20 goals, who has spent many seasons with Genk in Belgium.

Population: 353,000
Area, sq km: 316
% in urban areas: 85.3%
Capital city: Valletta

Malta Football Association
280 St. Paul Street
Valletta
Malta
Tel: + 356 222697
Fax: + 356 245136

Year of formation	1900
Affiliation to FIFA	1959
Affiliation to UEFA	1960
Registered clubs	272
Registered players	7,100
Professional players	370
Registered coaches	71
Registered referees	75
National stadium	Ta'Qali Stadium 18,000

National colours	Red/White/Red
Reserve colours	White/White/Red
Season	September - May

THE RECORD

WORLD CUP

1930-70	Did not enter
1974	QT 4th/4 in group 1
1978	QT 4th/4 in group 3
1982	QT 3rd/3 in group 7
1986	QT 5th/5 in group 2
1990	QT 5th/5 in group 6
1994	QT 5th/6 in group 1

EUROPEAN CHAMPIONSHIP

1960	Did not enter
1964	1st round
1968	Did not enter
1972	QT 4th/4 in group 3
1976	QT 4th/4 in group 8
1980	QT 4th/4 in group 7
1984	QT 5th/5 in group 7
1988	QT 5th/5 in group 2
1992	QT 5th/5 in group 6
1996	QT group 5

EUROPEAN CLUB COMPETITIONS

European Cup
2nd round - Sliema Wanderers 1972

Cup Winners Cup
2nd round - Hibernians 1963 1972 Sliema Wanderers 1969 Hamrun Spartans 1985

UEFA Cup
Never past the first round

CLUB DIRECTORY

VALLETTA (Population - 9,000)

Valletta FC (1904)
Ta'Qali 18,000 – White/White
Previous names - Valletta United 1904-32, Valletta City 1932-39

BIRKIRKARA (Population - 20,000)
Birkirkara Luxol (1934)
Ta'Qali 18,000 – Red, yellow trim
Previous names - Merger in 1994 of Birkirkara FC and Luxol St Andrews

HAMRUM (Population - 13,000)
Hamrun Spartans FC (1907)
Ta'Qali 18,000 – Red & black stripes/Red

SLIEMA (Population - 13,000)
Sliema Wanderers FC (1909)
Ta'Qali 18,000 – Blue/Black

FLORIANA
Floriana FC (1900)
Ta'Qali 18,000 – Green & white stripes/Green

PAOLA (Population - 12,000)
Hibernians FC (1931)
Ta'Qali 18,000 – White/Black

RABAT
Rabat Ajax FC (1930)
Ta'Qali 18,000 – Black & white stripes/White
Previous name - Rabat FC 1929-1981

ZURRIEQ
Zurrieq FC (1949)
Ta'Qali 18,000 – Red/White

COSPICUA
St Georges FC (1899)
Ta'Qali 18,000 – Sky blue/White
Previous names - Merged in 1930 with Old St. Georges

MSIDA
St Joseph's FC (1911)
Ta'Qali 18,000 – Red/White
Previous name - Merged with Msida Rovers in 1924 as St. Joseph's

ST JULIANS
Melita St Julians FC (1906)
Ta'Qali 18,000 – Red/White
Previous name - BEL St. Julian's

MARSA
Marsa Football Club (1910)
Ta'Qali 18,000 – Blue & red stripes/Blue
Previous name - Marsa United 1910-31

GZIRA
Gzira United Football Club (1950)
Ta'Qali 18,000 – Brown/White

MALTESE LEAGUE CHAMPIONSHIP

1910al	Floriana 8 Sliema Wanderers 5 St. Joseph's 4
1911	-
1912	Floriana 8 Hamrun Spartans 4 St. George's 3
1913bl	Floriana 12 Hamrun Spartans 10 Sliema Wanderers 8
1914	Hamrun Spartans 10 St. George's 10 Valletta United 8
1915ac	Valletta United 9 Hamrun Spartans 7 Sliema Wanderers 6
1916	-
1917	St. George's 8 Sliema Wanderers 8 Hamrun Spartans 7
1918ad	Hamrun Spartans 12 St. George's 12 Sliema Wanderers 11
1919al	KOMR Militia 8 Hamrun United 6 ASC Militia 2
1920ac	Sliema Wanderers 9 Hamrun Spartans 7 Valletta United 6
1921cl	Floriana 16 Marsa United 13 Hamrun Spartans 13
1922bl	Floriana 10 Sliema Wanderers 9 Civil Police 8
1923ac	Sliema Wanderers 10 Floriana 8 Sliema Rangers 4
1924al	Sliema Wanderers 8 Vittoriosa Rovers 4 Valletta United 4
1925ad	Floriana 13 Sliema Wanderers 11 Valletta United 8
1926bl	Sliema Wanderers 12 Floriana 9 Valletta United 6
1927ab	Floriana 5 Sliema Wanderers 3 St. George's 2
1928bl	Floriana 10 Valletta United 9 St. George's 6
1929a	Floriana 7 Sliema Wanderers 4 Valletta United 1
1930al	Sliema Wanderers 7 Old St. George's 7 Valletta United 3
1931b	Floriana 12 Sliema Wanderers 6 Valletta United 4
1932ab	Valletta United 5 Sliema Wanderers 4 Sliema Rangers 2
1933	Sliema Wanderers 5 Hibernians 5 Sliema Rangers 2
1934a4	Sliema Wanderers 5 Hibernians 3
1935bl	Floriana 11 Sliema Wanderers 10 Hibernians 9
1936a	Sliema Wanderers 6 Floriana 5 Hibernians 1
1937b	Floriana 8 Hibernians 6 Sliema Wanderers 5
1938	Sliema Wanderers 10 Floriana 8 Valletta 3
1939	Sliema Wanderers 11 Melita St. Julians 5 St. George's 4
1940d	Sliema Wanderers 16 St. George's 16 Melita St. Julians 10
1941-44	-
1945ab	Valletta 4 Sliema Wanderers 3 Floriana 3
1946e	Valletta 19 Sliema Wanderers 17 Floriana 16
1947f	Hamrun Spartans 21 Valletta 20 Floriana 17
1948	Valletta 23 Hamrun Spartans 21 Sliema Wanderers 19
1949	Sliema Wanderers 22 Hamrun Spartans 20 Valletta 19
1950	Floriana 23 Hamrun Spartans 22 Sliema Wanderers 19
1951	Floriana 23 Hibernians 20 Valletta 18
1952	Floriana 24 Hamrun Spartans 20 Sliema Wanderers 19
1953	Floriana 21 Birkirkara United 20 Valletta 19
1954	Sliema Wanderers 20 Floriana 19 Hamrun Spartans 16
1955	Floriana 26 Sliema Wanderers 21 Hamrun Spartans 18
1956	Sliema Wanderers 24 Floriana 19 Hamrun Spartans 14
1957	Sliema Wanderers 26 Valletta 20 Floriana 19
1958	Floriana 24 Sliema Wanderers 21 Hamrun Spartans 19
1959	Valletta 23 Sliema Wanderers 18 Hamrun Spartans 15
1960	Valletta 24 Hibernians 20 Floriana 16
1961	Hibernians 25 Valletta 22 Sliema Wanderers 20
1962	Floriana 28 Valletta 24 Sliema Wanderers 17
1963	Valletta 23 Hibernians 21 Sliema Wanderers 21
1964	Sliema Wanderers 26 Valletta 22 Hibernians 17
1965e	Sliema Wanderers 20 Valletta 18 Hibernians 16
1966d	Sliema Wanderers 17 Floriana 11 Hibernians 10
1967	Hibernians 17 Sliema Wanderers 16 Floriana 10
1968f	Floriana 25 Sliema Wanderers 20 Hibernians 18
1969	Hibernians 21 Valletta 18 Floriana 18
1970	Floriana 22 Sliema Wanderers 19 Valletta 17
1971	Sliema Wanderers 20 Marsa 20 Gzira United 17
1972h	Sliema Wanderers 26 Floriana 26 Valletta 24
1973	Floriana 26 Sliema Wanderers 25 Hamrun Spartans 25
1974	Valletta 28 Hibernians 24 Sliema Wanderers 21
1975	Floriana 31 Sliema Wanderers 24 St. George's 23
1976	Sliema Wanderers 26 Floriana 25 Hibernians 20
1977	Floriana 33 Sliema Wanderers 27 Valletta 25
1978	Valletta 28 Hibernians 26 Sliema Wanderers 24
1979b2	Hibernians 11 Valletta 6 Sliema Wanderers 4
1980h	Valletta 31 Sliema Wanderers 28 Floriana 28
1981f	Hibernians 26 Sliema Wanderers 23 Floriana 15
1982	Hibernians 26 Sliema Wanderers 18 Floriana 16
1983	Hamrun Spartans 24 Valletta 16 Rabat Ajax 16
1984ak	Valletta 11 Rabat Ajax 10 Hamrun Spartans 9
1985al	Rabat Ajax 17 Hamrun Spartans 16 Sliema Wanderers 15
1986f	Rabat Ajax 23 Hibernians 18 Hamrun Spartans 17
1987	Hamrun Spartans 25 Valletta 16 Zurrieq 16
1988	Hamrun Spartans 22 Sliema Wanderers 19 Zurrieq 18
1989g	Sliema Wanderers 26 Valletta 23 Hamrun Spartans 20
1990	Valletta 28 Sliema Wanderers 24 Hamrun Spartans 23
1991	Hamrun Spartans 24 Valletta 19 Floriana 18
1992h	Valletta 33 Floriana 24 Hamrun Spartans 23
1993	Floriana 29 Hamrun Spartans 24 Valletta 24
1994	Hibernians 31 Floriana 28 Valletta 27
1995h2	Hibernians 43 Sliema Wanderers 39 Valletta 37

MALTESE CUP FINALS

1935	Sliema Wanderers	4-0	Floriana
1936	Sliema Wanderers	2-1	Floriana
1937	Sliema Wanderers	2-1	St. George's
1938	Floriana	2-1	Sliema Wanderers
1939	Melita St. Julians	4-0	Sliema Wanderers
1940	Sliema Wanderers	3-2	Melita St. Julians
1941-44	-		
1945	Floriana	2-1	Sliema Wanderers
1946	Sliema Wanderers	2-1	Hamrun Liberty

1947	Floriana	3-0	Valletta
1948	Sliema Wanderers	2-2 1-0	Hibernians
1949	Floriana	5-1	Sliema Wanderers
1950	Floriana	3-1	St. George's
1951	Sliema Wanderers	5-0	Hibernians
1952	Sliema Wanderers	3-3 1-1 1-0	Hibernians
1953	Floriana	1-0	Sliema Wanderers
1954	Floriana	5-1	Rabat FC
1955	Floriana	1-0	Sliema Wanderers
1956	Sliema Wanderers	1-0	Floriana
1957	Floriana	2-0	Valletta
1958	Floriana	2-0	Sliema Wanderers
1959	Sliema Wanderers	1-1 1-0	Valletta
1960	Valletta	3-0	Floriana
1961	Floriana	2-0	Hibernians
1962	Hibernians	1-0	Valletta
1963	Sliema Wanderers	2-0	Hibernians
1964	Valletta	1-0	Sliema Wanderers
1965	Sliema Wanderers	4-2	Floriana
1966	Floriana	2-1	Hibernians
1967	Floriana	1-0	Hibernians
1968	Sliema Wanderers	3-2	Hibernians
1969	Sliema Wanderers	3-1	Hamrun Spartans
1970	Hibernians	1-1 2-1	Valletta
1971	Hibernians	1-1 2-0	Sliema Wanderers
1972	Floriana	3-1	Sliema Wanderers
1973	Gzira United	0-0 0-0 2-0	Birkirkara United
1974	Sliema Wanderers	1-0	Floriana
1975	Valletta	1-0	Hibernians
1976	Floriana	2-0	Valletta
1977	Valletta	1-0	Floriana
1978	Valletta	3-2	Floriana
1979	Sliema Wanderers	2-1	Floriana
1980	Hibernians	2-1	Sliema Wanderers
1981	Floriana	2-1	Senglea Athletic
1982	Hibernians	2-0	Sliema Wanderers
1983	Hamrun Spartans	2-0	Valletta
1984	Hamrun Spartans	0-0 1-0	Zurrieq
1985	Zurrieq	0-0 2-1	Valletta
1986	Rabat Ajax	2-0	Zurrieq
1987	Hamrun Spartans	2-1	Sliema Wanderers
1988	Hamrun Spartans	4-2	Floriana
1989	Hamrun Spartans	1-0	Floriana
1990	Sliema Wanderers	1-0	Birkirkara United
1991	Valletta	2-1	Sliema Wanderers
1992	Hamrun Spartans	3-3 2-1p	Valletta
1993	Floriana	5-0	Sliema Wanderers
1994	Floriana	2-1	Valletta
1995	Valletta	1-0	Hamrun Spartans

LEADING INTERNATIONAL GOALSCORERS

20	Carmel Busuttil	(Rabat Ajax,Verbania,RC Genk)	1982-
6	Raymond Xuereb	(Floriana,Hamrun Spartans)	1971-85
5	Hubert Suda	(Sliema Wanderers)	1988-

LEADING INTERNATIONAL APPEARANCES

72	Carmel Busuttil	(Rabat,Verbania,RC Genk)	1982-
70	John Buttigieg	(Sliema Wanderers,Brentford)	1984-
69	Michael Degeorgio	(Hamrun Spartans)	1981-93
65	Raymond Vella	(Marsa,Hamrun Spartans, St. Andrews)	1984-94
62	Charles Scerri	(Rabat Ajax, Hibernians)	1986-
62	Martin Gregory	(Sliema Wanderers)	1985-

INTERNATIONAL MATCHES PLAYED BY MALTA

8-03-1959	Tunisia	D 0-0	Tunis	Fr	
8-12-1960	Tunisia	W 1-0	Gzira	Fr	Borg
5-11-1961	Norway	D 1-1	Gzira	Fr	Demanuele.P
28-06-1962	Denmark	L 1-6	Copenhagen	ECr1	Theobald
3-07	Norway	L 0-5	Trondheim	Fr	
8-12	Denmark	L 1-3	Gzira	ECr1	Urpani
20-09-1963	Egypt	L 0-6	Caserta	MG	
23-09	Lebanon	L 0-2	Salerno	MG	
13-02-1966	Libya	W 1-0	Gzira	Fr	Aquilina.E
27-03	Libya	W 1-0	Tripoli	Fr	Cocks
27-04-1969	Austria	L 1-3	Gzira	Fr	Cini
4-01-1970	Luxembourg	D 1-1	Gzira	Fr	Cini
11-10	Greece	D 1-1	Gzira	ECq	Vassallo
20-12	Switzerland	L 1-2	Gzira	ECq	Theobald
3-02-1971	England	L 0-1	Gzira	ECq	
21-04	Switzerland	L 0-5	Lucerne	ECq	
12-05	England	L 0-5	London	ECq	
18-06	Greece	L 0-2	Athens	ECq	
14-11	Hungary	L 0-2	Gzira	WCq	
8-12	Algeria	D 1-1	Gzira	Fr	Vassallo
15-03-1972	Algeria	L 0-1	Algiers	Fr	
30-04	Austria	L 0-4	Vienna	WCq	
6-05	Hungary	L 0-3	Budapest	WCq	
15-10	Sweden	L 0-7	Gothenburg	WCq	
25-11	Austria	L 0-2	Gzira	WCq	
28-09-1973	Canada	W 2-0	Gzira	Fr	Xuereb.R, Arpa
11-11	Sweden	L 1-2	Gzira	WCq	Camilleri
24-08-1974	Libya	L 0-1	Gzira	Fr	
4-09	Libya	D 0-0	Tripoli	Fr	
22-12	West Germany	L 0-1	Gzira	ECq	
23-02-1975	Greece	W 2-0	Gzira	ECq	Aquilina.R, Magro
4-06	Greece	L 0-4	Salonica	ECq	

11-06	Bulgaria	L 0-5	Sofia	ECq	
21-12	Bulgaria	L 0-2	Gzira	ECq	
28-02-1976	West Germany	L 0-8	Dortmund	ECq	
10-03	Libya	D 2-2	Gzira	Fr	Losco 2
31-10	Turkey	L 0-4	Istanbul	WCq	
24-11	Tunisia	D 1-1	Gzira	Fr	Magro
5-12	Austria	L 0-1	Gzira	WCq	
5-03-1977	Tunisia	W 1-0	Tunis	Fr	Xuereb.R
2-04	East Germany	L 0-1	Gzira	WCq	
30-04	Austria	L 0-9	Salzburg	WCq	
6-09	Tunisia	L 1-2	Tunis	Fr	Xuereb.G
29-10	East Germany	L 0-9	Babelsberg	WCq	
27-11	Turkey	L 0-3	Gzira	WCq	
14-05-1978	Libya	L 0-1	Tripoli	Fr	
25-10	Wales	L 0-7	Wrexham	ECq	
25-02-1979	West Germany	D 0-0	Gzira	ECq	
18-03	Turkey	L 1-2	Izmir	ECq	Spiteri-Gonzi
2-06	Wales	L 0-2	Gzira	ECq	
28-08	Tunisia	L 0-4	Tunis	Fr	
28-10	Turkey	L 1-2	Gzira	ECq	Farrugia.Em
27-02-1980	West Germany	L 0-8	Bremen	ECq	
7-12	Poland	L 0-2	Gzira	WCq	Abandoned after 82 mins
4-04-1981	East Germany	L 1-2	Gzira	WCq	Fabri
14-06	Liechtenstein	D 1-1	Seoul	PC	
23-06	Indonesia	W 1-0	Seoul	PC	
27-06	Thailand	W 2-0	Seoul	PC	
24-10	Tunisia	W 1-0	Tunis	Fr	Tortell
11-11	East Germany	L 1-5	Jena	WCq	Spiteri-Gonzi
15-11	Poland	L 0-6	Wroclaw	WCq	
5-06-1982	Iceland	W 2-1	Messina	ECq	Spiteri-Gonzi, Fabri
14-10	Bulgaria	L 0-7	Sofia	Fr	
19-12	Holland	L 0-6	Aachen	ECq	
1-02-1983	Tunisia	L 1-2	Marsa	Fr	Fabri
30-03	Rep. Ireland	L 0-1	Ta'Qali	ECq	
15-05	Spain	L 2-3	Ta'Qali	ECq	Busuttil 2
5-06	Iceland	L 0-1	Reykjavik	ECq	
9-10	Libya	L 0-4	Tripoli	Fr	
16-11	Rep. Ireland	L 0-8	Dublin	ECq	
17-12	Holland	L 0-5	Rotterdam	ECq	
21-12	Spain	L 1-12	Seville	ECq	Demanuele.S
23-05-1984	Sweden	L 0-4	Norrkoping	WCq	
6-09	Israel	L 1-2	Tel Aviv	Fr	Muscat
31-10	Czechoslovakia	L 0-4	Prague	WCq	
16-12	West Germany	L 2-3	Ta'Qali	WCq	Busuttil, Xuereb.R
10-02-1985	Portugal	L 1-3	Ta'Qali	WCq	Farrugia.N
27-03	West Germany	L 0-6	Saarbrucken	WCq	
3-04	Jordan	W 3-1	Ta'Qali	Fr	Xuereb.R 3
21-04	Czechoslovakia	D 0-0	Ta'Qali	WCq	
12-10	Portugal	L 2-3	Lisbon	WCq	Degiorgio, OG
17-11	Sweden	L 1-2	Ta'Qali	WCq	Farrugia.N
16-11-1986	Sweden	L 0-5	Ta'Qali	ECq	
6-12	Italy	L 0-2	Ta'Qali	ECq	
24-01-1987	Italy	L 0-5	Bergamo	ECq	
29-03	Portugal	D 2-2	Funchal	ECq	Mizzi, Busuttil
15-04	Switzerland	L 1-4	Neuchatel	ECq	Busuttil
24-05	Sweden	L 0-1	Gothenburg	ECq	
15-11	Switzerland	D 1-1	Ta'Qali	ECq	Busuttil
2-12	Israel	D 1-1	Tel Aviv	Fr	Mizzi
20-12	Portugal	L 0-1	Ta'Qali	ECq	
7-02-1988	Finland	W 2-0	Ta'Qali	Fr	Busuttil 2
10-02	Tunisia	W 2-1	Ta'Qali	Fr	Vella.R, Busuttil
22-03	Scotland	D 1-1	Ta'Qali	Fr	Busuttil
21-05	Nth. Ireland	L 0-3	Belfast	WCq	
1-06	Wales	L 2-3	Ta'Qali	Fr	Busuttil 2
12-10	Cyprus	W 1-0	Limassol	Fr	Busuttil
18-10	Israel	L 0-2	Beersheba	Fr	
23-11	Cyprus	D 1-1	Ta'Qali	Fr	Carabott
11-12	Hungary	D 2-2	Ta'Qali	WCq	Busuttil 2
11-01-1989	Israel	L 1-2	Ta'Qali	Fr	Carabott
22-01	Spain	L 0-2	Ta'Qali	WCq	
8-02	Denmark	L 0-2	Ta'Qali	Fr	
10-02	Algeria	L 0-1	Ta'Qali	Fr	

12-02	Finland	D 0-0	Ta'Qali	Fr	
23-03	Spain	L 0-4	Seville	WCq	
12-04	Hungary	D 1-1	Budapest	WCq	Busuttil
26-04	Nth. Ireland	L 0-2	Ta'Qali	WCq	
28-05	Rep. Ireland	L 0-2	Dublin	WCq	
4-10	Austria	L 1-2	Ta'Qali	Fr	Zarb
11-10	Cyprus	D 0-0	Nicosia	Fr	
25-10	East Germany	L 0-4	Ta'Qali	Fr	
15-11	Rep. Ireland	L 0-2	Ta'Qali	WCq	
7-02-1990	Norway	D 1-1	Ta'Qali	Fr	Scerri
10-02	South Korea	L 1-2	Ta'Qali	Fr	Laferla
5-05	United States	L 0-1	Piscataway	Fr	
28-05	Scotland	L 1-2	Ta'Qali	Fr	Degiorgio
2-06	Rep. Ireland	L 0-3	Ta'Qali	Fr	
31-10	Greece	L 0-4	Athens	ECq	
25-11	Finland	D 1-1	Ta'Qali	ECq	Suda
19-12	Holland	L 0-8	Ta'Qali	ECq	
9-02-1991	Portugal	L 0-1	Ta'Qali	ECq	
20-02	Portugal	L 0-5	Oporto	ECq	
13-03	Holland	L 0-1	Rotterdam	ECq	
7-05	Iceland	L 1-4	Ta'Qali	Fr	Suda
16-05	Finland	L 0-2	Helsinki	ECq	
7-06	Indonesia	W 3-0	Seoul	PC	Degiorgio, Scerri, Suda
9-06	Egypt	L 2-5	Seoul	PC	Brincat, Suda
11-06	South Korea	D 1-1	Seoul	PC	Suda
27-11	Libya	W 2-0	Psyala	Fr	Brincat, Sultana
22-12	Greece	D 1-1	Ta'Qali	Fr	Sultana
10-02-1992	Iceland	W 1-0	Ta'Qali	Fr	Zerafa
26-05	Latvia	W 1-0	Ta'Qali	Fr	Saliba
7-10	Cyprus	L 0-3	Limassol	Fr	
25-10	Estonia	D 0-0	Ta'Qali	WCq	
18-11	Switzerland	L 0-3	Berne	WCq	
19-12	Italy	L 1-2	Ta'Qali	WCq	Gregory
24-01-1993	Portugal	L 0-1	Ta'Qali	WCq	
17-02	Scotland	L 0-3	Glasgow	WCq	
24-03	Italy	L 1-6	Palermo	WCq	Busuttil
17-04	Switzerland	L 0-2	Ta'Qali	WCq	
12-05	Estonia	W 1-0	Tallinn	WCq	Laferla
19-06	Portugal	L 0-4	Oporto	WCq	
5-11	Egypt	L 0-3	Tunis	Fr	
7-11	Gabon	W 2-1	Tunis	Fr	Brincat, Busuttil
17-11	Scotland	L 0-2	Ta'Qali	WCq	
8-02-1994	Tunisia	D 1-1	Ta'Qali	Fr	Vella.S
10-02	Georgia	L 0-1	Ta'Qali	Fr	
12-02	Slovenia	L 0-1	Ta'Qali	Fr	
16-02	Belgium	W 1-0	Ta'Qali	Fr	Busuttil
30-03	Slovakia	L 1-2	Ta'Qali	Fr	Laferla
19-04	Azerbaijan	W 5-0	Ta'Qali	Fr	Saliba, Laferla, Busuttil, Camilleri.J, Scerri
2-06	Latvia	L 0-2	Riga	Fr	
16-08	Slovakia	D 1-1	Bratislava	Fr	Laferla
6-09	Czech Republic	L 1-6	Prague	ECq	Laferla
12-10	Czech Republic	D 0-0	Ta'Qali	ECq	
14-12	Norway	L 0-1	Ta'Qali	ECq	
22-02-1995	Luxembourg	L 0-1	Ta'Qali	ECq	
29-03	Holland	L 0-4	Rotterdam	ECq	
26-04	Belarus	D 1-1	Minsk	ECq	Carabott
7-06	Norway	L 0-2	Oslo	ECq	

MOLDOVA

For years Moldova was a figment of the novelist's imagination, a fairytale land of princes and vampires. But in 1994 under its Romanian name, Moldova was an independent European country playing its first game in the 1996 European Championship. Furthermore, after two games they led their group ahead of Germany and Bulgaria!

For centuries under Polish, Turkish, Russian and finally Romanian rule, Moldova achieved independence from the Soviet Union in 1991. Nesting between the Ukraine and Romania, the country is made up largely of Romanian speakers. Fighting has occurred however in the Trans Donestr region of the country where the majority want independence from Moldova and this has meant a difficult baptism for the new state.

Zimbru, from the capital Chisinau, are the biggest club in the country and have won the first three championships since independence, successfully staged despite the problems in the country. Their great rivals Tigilul Tiraspol have been runners-up on all three occasions but won two of the first three cup competitions played.

Population: 4,338,000
Area, sq km: 33,700
Capital city: Chisinau

Federatia Moldoveneasca de Fotbal
Bd Stefan cel Mare 73
277001 Chisinau
Moldova
Tel: + 3732 224498
Fax: + 3732 222244

Year of formation	1990
Affiliation to FIFA	1994
Affiliation to UEFA	1994
Registered clubs	45
Registered players	33 600
Registered referees	180
National stadium	Republican, Chisinau 22 000
National colours	Blue/Red/Yellow

THE RECORD

WORLD CUP
1930-94 Did not enter

EUROPEAN CHAMPIONSHIP
1960-92 Did not enter
1996 QT group 7

EUROPEAN CLUB COMPETITIONS
European Cup
Preliminary round - Zimbru Chisinau 1994
Cup Winners Cup
Preliminary round - Tiligul Tiraspol 1995
UEFA Cup
Preliminary round - Zimbru Chisinau 1995

CLUB DIRECTORY

CHISINAU (Population - 665,000)
Zimbru Chisinau (1947)
Republican 22,000 – Yellow/Yellow
Previous names - Dinamo, Burevestnik, Moldova, Avintul and Nistru. Present name from 1991

Torentul Chisinau

FC Agro Chisinau

Sportul Chisinau

TIRASPOL (Population - 182,000)
Tiligul Tiraspol
Colours - Red/Red

COMRAT
Bugeac Comrat

CALARASI
Codru Calarasi

BOROSENI
Moldova Boroseni

OTACI
Nistru Otaci

MOLDOVAN LEAGUE CHAMPIONSHIP

1992	Zimbru Chisinau 35	Tiligul Tiraspol 35	Bugeac Comrat 33
1993q	Zimbru Chisinau 50	Tiligul Tiraspol 47	Moldova Boroseni 41
1994	Zimbru Chisinau 52	Tiligul Tiraspol 49	Codru Calarasi 40
1995n1	Zimbru Chisinau 67	Tiligul Tiraspol 66	Olimpia Balti 57

MOLDOVAN CUP FINALS

1992	Bugeac Comrat	5-0	Tiligul Tiraspol
1993	Tiligul Tiraspol	1-0	Dinamo Christina
1994	Tiligul Tiraspol	1-0	Nistru Otaci
1995	Tiligul Tiraspol	1-0	Zimbru Chisinau

INTERNATIONAL MATCHES PLAYED BY MOLDOVA

16-04-1994	USA	D 1-1	Jacksonville	Fr	Kosse
20-04	USA	L 0-3	Davidson	Fr	
1-09	Azerbaijan	W 2-1	Chisinau	Fr	Kleshchenko 2
7-09	Georgia	W 1-0	Tbilisi	ECq	Oprea
12-10	Wales	W 3-2	Chisinau	ECq	Belous,Secu,Pogorelov
16-11	Bulgaria	L 1-4	Sofia	ECq	Clescenko
14-12	Germany	L 0-3	Chisinau	ECq	
29-03-1995	Albania	L 0-3	Tirana	ECq	
26-04	Bulgaria	L 0-3	Chisinau	ECq	
7-06	Albania	L 2-3	Chisinau	ECq	Curtianu,Clescenko

NORTHERN IRELAND

The fourth oldest football association in the world; a permanent seat on the International Board, the world's rule-making body; the third oldest league in the world and a history of international matches that stretches back 110 years. This is the heritage of football in Northern Ireland but one which is increasingly under threat. How long will a Northern Ireland team last before it is either swallowed up into a British XI or a United Ireland XI?

The Irish Football Association, not to be confused with the Football Association of Ireland which rules the game in the Republic, until 1923 controlled football throughout the island of Ireland. Until that time, however, the game was a predominantly Northern sport. The association was based in Belfast, and on only six occasions in 40 years did the Irish team play a match in Dublin. Shelbourne and Bohemians of Dublin had the odd cup success, but the real football base was in the North.

The civil war in the early 1920s and the partition of the country led to bitter disputes between the association in the North and its new rival in the South. There were major defections to the Southern body, even from those clubs located in the six provinces which constituted Northern Ireland. A meeting of the four British associations in 1923 decided to recognise the Dublin association, but ordered that clubs located within the six provinces should rejoin the association in Belfast. With the Irish Free State in the South embarking on international matches and running its own league and cup, Irish football was split into two camps, although it was not until 1948 that the North abstained from selecting players for the national side who were from the South.

Along with Wales, Ireland has had to compete fiercely with rugby for the affections of the public. The first foot ball playing club was Ulster FC, a rugby club who formed a football section after an exhibition match between two Scottish clubs, Queen's Park and Caledonian, in 1878 in Belfast. Soon football clubs began to spring up in and around Belfast. The first of these devoted entirely to football, Cliftonville FC, was formed in 1879 by JM McAlery, who was instrumental in the formation of the Irish Football Association in the following year.

Club football in Ireland has never been particularly strong and has always suffered from the loss of its best players to either England or Scotland, but in these early years most of the players appearing for Irish clubs were Scottish. That not many Irish people were playing football can be seen from their early results in international matches. A match against England was organised for 1882 in Belfast and the 13-0 defeat remains their record loss. Heavy defeats were the order of the day until the turn of the century, and although the Irish fairly soon reached the standard of the Welsh, who had had a four year headstart in international matches, it was not until 1903 that Scotland were beaten for the first time, whilst a further ten years were needed to inflict a defeat on England.

For 68 years the Home International Championship for provided Ireland and subsequently Northern Ireland with their only international opposition. Not until 1951 when France visited Belfast did they play a non-British side. During these years, the Home International Championship was won just twice. In 1914 Ireland won it outright, whilst in 1903 it was shared with both England and Scotland.

After 1951, the increase in competitive matches revitalised the Irish and until the competition's demise in 1984, Northern Ireland either won or shared the title on six occasions. Most importantly, in 1958, victories over Italy and Portugal saw them qualify for the World Cup Finals in Sweden. With perhaps the best international team the country has ever had, the Irish reached the quarter-finals, further than either England or Scotland. Danny Blanchflower, the man who led Tottenham to the English League and Cup double three years later, was the linchpin of the side which also contained Billy Bingham, who later achieved great feats as manager of the side, Jimmy McIlroy, Jackie Blanchflower, Danny's brother, a very young Derek Dougan and Peter McParland whose goals in Sweden contributed so greatly to the fine results achieved there.

Of the World Cup team only Peacock did not play his club football in England, and he was a regular for Glasgow Celtic. This highlights the weakness of the league in Northern Ireland. Another weakness that in many ways is even more damaging is the sectarian nature of football in the country. The most successful club, Linfield, are associated with the Protestant community, and in a country where religious violence has been an everyday occurrence, this leads football down a very dangerous path. Before the Second World War, the main challenge to the supremacy of Linfield came from Belfast Celtic, which as the name suggests was a Catholic-based club, modelled on their mentors from Glasgow.

The matches between Linfield and Celtic became the scene of increasing violence between the two sets of supporters and after a particularly nasty incident in 1948, Celtic withdrew from the league and stopped playing soon after, although they still technically exist as a club. They are not the only victims of the Troubles. Derry City withdrew from the league in 1972, and now play in the Republic of Ireland's league. In recent years Cliftonville have become the focus for Catholic support, but trouble has also occurred in games between Linfield and another staunchly Protestant club Glentoran. Glentoran supporters have even been known to wear the green and white of Celtic to goad their opponents.

THE ORDER OF MERIT

		All			League			Europe		
	Team	G	S	B	G	S	B	G	S	B
1	Linfield	77	35	13	42	16	13	-	-	-
2	Glentoran	34	37	20	19	20	20	-	-	-
3	Belfast Celtic	22	8	8	14	4	8	-	-	-
4	Distillery	18	15	8	6	8	8	-	-	-
5	Cliftonville	10	13	4	2	5	4	-	-	-
6	Glenavon	7	17	5	3	9	5	-	-	-
7	Ballymena United	6	10	5	-	2	5	-	-	-
8	Coleraine	5	11	8	1	7	8	-	-	-
9	Ards	5	3	8	1	1	8	-	-	-
10	Crusaders	5	2	2	3	1	2		-	-
11	Derry City	4	10	3	1	7	3	-	-	-
12	Portadown	3	11	4	2	7	4	-	-	-
13	Shelbourne Dublin	3	4	1	-	1	1	-	-	-
14	Queen's Island	3	3	-	1	3	-	-	-	-
15	Bohemians Dublin	1	5	-	-	-	-	-	-	-
16	Bangor	1	3	2	-	1	2	-	-	-
17	Ulster FC	1	3	-	-	1	-	-	-	-
18	Carrick Rangers	1	2	-	-	-	-	-	-	-
	Willowfield	1	1	-	-	-	-	-	-	-
20	Dundela	1	-	-	-	-	-	-	-	-
	Moyola Park	1	-	-	-	-	-	-	-	-
	Gordon Highlanders	1	-	-	-	-	-	-	-	-
23	Larne	-	4	1	-	-	1	-	-	-
24	Limavady	-	2	-	-	-	-	-	-	-
25	The Black Watch	-	1	-	-	-	-	-	-	-
	Derry Celtic	-	1	-	-	-	-	-	-	-
	Freebooters	-	1	-	-	-	-	-	-	-
	St. Columbs Hall Celtic	-	1	-	-	-	-	-	-	-
	Sherwood Forest.	-	1	-	-	-	-	-	-	-
	Wellington Park	-	1	-	-	-	-	-	-	-
	YMCA Belfast	-	1	-	-	-	-	-	-	-
32	Lancashire Fusiliers	-	-	1	-	-	1	-	-	-
	Newry Town	-	-	1	-	-	1	-	-	-

To the end of the 1994-95 season

Amidst all this, the Irish Football Association has striven to remain neutral in the conflict, and it is perhaps fortunate for them that the best players do play abroad, thus avoiding disputes with clubs alleging biased selection policy for the national side. One player who would have been picked no matter where he played was George Best, the most talented Irishman ever to have played football. Indeed he would have walked into the national side of any country in the world. It is unfortunate for him that at his peak he was denied a world stage to display his talents, for the Northern Irish team of the late 1960s was perhaps at its lowest ebb.

The 1980s saw a dramatic rise in their fortunes, but by then it was too late for Best. Outright champions in the Home International Championship for only the second time in 1980, Northern Ireland qualified for the 1982 World Cup thanks largely to the increase in the number of places given to Europe after the expansion of the final tournament. Once there, however, they impressed everyone with their spirit which saw them finish top of their first round group after beating the hosts, Spain, 1-0 in Valencia. Unfortunately they were drawn in the same group as France in the second round and lost 4-1 against them in the decisive match.

They qualified again for the 1986 World Cup in Mexico, and although drawn again with Spain they could not repeat the victory of four years previously, whilst a defeat by Brazil saw to it that they did not qualify for the second round. Since 1986 the Northern Irish team has been in decline. In 1984 they had won the last Home International Championship, but deprived of the income from the folding of the championship, times are hard, and matches now consist mainly of European Championship and World Cup qualifiers.

Financial pressure, and the rise of football in the Republic of Ireland, has led to calls for the unification of Irish football. There is a united team in rugby union so why not for football? Such a move would seem to make sense, but whether football in this troubled island could rise above the fighting and sectarian hatreds like rugby is open to question.

Population: 1,567,000
Area, sq km: 14,120
% in urban areas: 91.5%
Capital city: Belfast

Irish Football Association
20 Winsor Avenue
Belfast BT9 6EG
Northern Ireland
Tel: + 44 232 669458
Fax: + 44 232 667620

Year of formation	1880
Affiliation to FIFA	1911-1920, 1924-1928, 1946
Affiliation to UEFA	1954
Registered clubs	1000
Registered players	20 000
Professional players	230
Registered coaches	90
Registered referees	400
National stadium	Windsor Park 28 000
National colours	Green/White/Green
Reserve colours	White/Green/Green
Season	September - May

THE RECORD

WORLD CUP

1930-38	Did not enter
1950	QT 4th/4 in group 1
1954	QT 3rd/4 in group 2
1958	QT 1st/3 in group 8 - Final Tournament/Quarter-finalists
1962	QT 2nd/3 in group 3
1966	QT 2nd/4 in group 5
1970	QT 2nd/3 in group 4
1974	QT 3rd/4 in group 6
1978	QT 3rd/4 in group 4
1982	QT 2nd/5 in group 6 - Final Tournament/2nd round
1986	QT 2nd/5 in group 3 - Final Tournament/1st round
1990	QT 4th/5 in group 6
1994	QT 4th/7 in group 3

EUROPEAN CHAMPIONSHIP

1960	Did not enter
1964	2nd round
1968	QT 4th/4 in group 8
1972	QT 3rd/4 in group 4
1976	QT 2nd/4 in group 3
1980	QT 2nd/5 in group 1
1984	QT 2nd/5 in group 6
1988	QT 3rd/4 in group 4
1992	QT 3rd/5 in group 4
1996	QT group 6

EUROPEAN CLUB COMPETITIONS

European Cup
Quarter-finals - Linfield 1967
Cup Winners Cup
Quarter-finals - Glentoran 1974
UEFA Cup
2nd round - Coleraine 1970 1971 Portadown 1975

CLUB DIRECTORY

BELFAST (Population - 303,000)

Belfast Celtic (1891)
Celtic Park – Green/White
Stopped playing in 1949

Crusaders FC (1909)
Seaview 9,000 – Red & black stripes/Black

Distillery FC (1880)
New Grosvenor 14,000 – White, blue trim

Glentoran FC (1882)
The Oval 30,000 – Green, red sleeves/Black

Linfield FC (1886)
Windsor Park 28,000 – Blue/White

LONDONDERRY (Population - 97,000)

Derry City FC (1928)
Brandywell Park 11,000 – Red & white stripes/Black
Previous name - Derry Celtic 1892-1915
Derry City now play in the Republic of Ireland League

NEWTOWNABBEY (Population - 72,000)

Cliftonville FC (1879)
Solitude 17,000 – Red/White

BANGOR (Population - 70,000)

Bangor FC (1918)
Clandeboye Park 5,000 – White/Blue, yellow & blue trim

BALLYMENA (Population - 28,000)

Ballymena United (1928)
The Showgrounds 8,000 – Blue, white trim
Previous name - Ballymena FC 1928-34

CARRICKFERGUS (Population - 17,000)

Carrick Rangers FC (1939)
Taylor's Avenue 5,000 – Red/Black

COLERAINE (Population - 14,000)

Coleraine FC (1927)
The Showgrounds 8,000 – Blue & white stripes/Blue

LARNE (Population - 18,000)

Larne FC (1889)
Inver Park 12,000 – Red/White

LURGAN (Population - 63,000)

Glenavon FC (1889)
Mourneview Park 15,000 – Blue/White

NEWRY (Population - 11,000)

Newry Town FC (1923)
The Showgrounds 15,000 – Blue & white stripes/White

NEWTOWNARDS (Population - 15,000)

Ards FC (1902)
Castlereagh Park 10,000 – Red & blue stripes/Blue

PORTADOWN

Portadown FC (1924)
Shamrock Park 15,000 – Red, white trim

OMAGH (Population - 14,000)

Omagh Town FC (1964)
St. Julian's Road 8,000 – White/Black

UNITED IRELAND LEAGUE CHAMPIONSHIP

1891f Linfield 25 Distillery 21 Glentoran 19
1892g Linfield 30 Ulster 24 Lancashire Fusiliers 23
1893d Linfield 18 Cliftonville 15 Distillery 11
1894 Glentoran 16 Linfield 14 Cliftonville 10
1895b Linfield 10 Distillery 7 Glentoran 4
1896 Distillery 8 Cliftonville 8 Linfield 5
1897d Glentoran 17 Cliftonville 11 Linfield 11
1898 Linfield 17 Cliftonville 13 Glentoran 13
1899 Distillery 15 Linfield 15 Cliftonville 12
1900c Celtic 11 Linfield 10 Cliftonville 9
1901d Distillery 16 Glentoran 15 Celtic 10
1902f Linfield 24 Glentoran 21 Distillery 19
1903 Distillery 20 Linfield 19 Glentoran 17
1904 Linfield 26 Distillery 20 Glentoran 20
1905 Glentoran 21 Celtic 21 Linfield 16
1906 Cliftonville 19 Linfield 17 Distillery 19
1907 Linfield 23 Shelbourne 19 Distillery 16
1908 Linfield 22 Cliftonville 17 Glentoran 17
1909 Linfield 21 Glentoran 19 Shelbourne 15
1910 Cliftonville 20 Celtic 18 Linfield 15
1911 Linfield 22 Glentoran 22 Celtic 15
1912 Glentoran 24 Distillery 21 Celtic 20
1913h Glentoran 26 Distillery 24 Linfield 23
1914f Linfield 24 Glentoran 19 Celtic 17
1915 Celtic 23 Glentoran 21 Linfield 17
1916-19 -
1920 Celtic 23 Distillery 20 Glentoran 19

NORTHERN IRISH LEAGUE CHAMPIONSHIP

1921c Glentoran 14 Glenavon 12 Linfield 9
1922d Linfield 17 Glentoran 13 Distillery 11
1923 Linfield 16 Queen's Island 12 Glentoran 11
1924h Queen's Island 26 Distillery 20 Glenavon 20
1925k Glentoran 37 Queen's Island 32 Celtic 27
1926 Celtic 33 Glentoran 30 Larne 27
1927 Celtic 37 Queen's Island 30 Distillery 29
1928n Celtic 45 Linfield 41 Newry Town 33
1929 Celtic 48 Linfield 39 Glentoran 33
1930 Linfield 42 Glentoran 36 Coleraine 32
1931 Glentoran 47 Linfield 38 Celtic 36
1932 Linfield 42 Derry City 38 Celtic 32
1933 Celtic 41 Distillery 39 Linfield 38
1934 Linfield 46 Celtic 37 Glentoran 35
1935 Linfield 46 Derry City 40 Celtic 37
1936 Celtic 43 Derry City 41 Linfield 38
1937 Celtic 44 Derry City 43 Linfield 42
1938 Celtic 41 Derry City 41 Portadown 37
1939 Celtic 40 Ballymena United 35 Derry City 33
1940 Celtic 45 Portadown 41 Glentoran 39
1941-47 -
1948k Celtic 39 Linfield 35 Ballymena United 27
1949 Linfield 36 Celtic 31 Glentoran 29
1950 Linfield 38 Glentoran 38 Distillery 29
1951 Glentoran 38 Linfield 34 Glenavon 31
1952 Glenavon 37 Glentoran 27 Coleraine 27
1953 Glentoran 33 Linfield 31 Ballymena United 29
1954 Linfield 36 Glentoran 35 Glenavon 28
1955 Linfield 36 Glenavon 36 Ards 24
1956 Linfield 40 Glenavon 29 Bangor City 27
1957 Glenavon 35 Linfield 34 Ards 30
1958 Ards 36 Glenavon 34 Ballymena United 28
1959 Linfield 34 Glenavon 31 Glentoran 27
1960 Glenavon 35 Glentoran 32 Distillery 29
1961 Linfield 32 Portadown 32 Ards 31
1962 Linfield 31 Portadown 31 Ballymena United 29
1963 Distillery 31 Linfield 29 Portadown 28
1964 Glentoran 33 Coleraine 32 Derry City 29
1965 Derry City 35 Coleraine 30 Crusaders 27
1966 Linfield 34 Derry City 32 Glentoran 32
1967 Glentoran 34 Linfield 33 Derry City 27
1968 Glentoran 37 Linfield 36 Coleraine 35
1969 Linfield 35 Derry City 32 Glentoran 30
1970 Glentoran 34 Coleraine 28 Ards 27
1971 Linfield 38 Glentoran 35 Distillery 30
1972 Glentoran 33 Portadown 30 Ards 29
1973 Crusaders 32 Ards 31 Portadown 29
1974 Coleraine 35 Portadown 30 Crusaders 30
1975 Linfield 37 Coleraine 32 Glentoran 31
1976 Crusaders 36 Glentoran 32 Coleraine 31
1977 Glentoran 36 Glenavon 31 Linfield 28
1978 Linfield 40 Glentoran 34 Glenavon 28
1979 Linfield 34 Glenavon 28 Ards 27
1980 Linfield 39 Ballymena United 30 Glentoran 27
1981 Glentoran 37 Linfield 35 Ballymena United 28
1982 Linfield 37 Glentoran 33 Coleraine 31
1983 Linfield 35 Glentoran 30 Coleraine 28
1984n Linfield 45 Glentoran 42 Cliftonville 31
1985 Linfield 39 Coleraine 36 Glentoran 34
1986 Linfield 43 Coleraine 35 Ards 31
1987n1 Linfield 57 Coleraine 53 Ards 48
1988 Glentoran 62 Linfield 60 Coleraine 52
1989 Linfield 65 Glentoran 55 Coleraine 50
1990 Portadown 55 Glenavon 54 Glentoran 44
1991q3 Portadown 71 Bangor City 61 Glentoran 60
1992 Glentoran 77 Portadown 65 Linfield 60
1993 Linfield 66 Crusaders 66 Bangor 64
1994 Linfield 70 Portadown 68 Glenavon 68
1995 Crusaders 67 Glenavon 60 Portadown 50

Championship play-offs

1889 Distillery .... 2-1 .... Linfield
1905 Glentoran .... bt .... Celtic
1911 Linfield .... bt .... Glentoran
1938 Celtic .... bt .... Derry City
1950 Linfield .... 2-0 .... Glentoran
1955 Linfield .... 3-0 .... Glenavon
1961 Linfield .... 3-2 .... Portadown
1962 Linfield .... 3-1 .... Portadown

UNITED IRELAND CUP FINALS

1881 Moyola Park .... 1-0 .... Cliftonville
1882 Queen's Island .... 2-1 .... Cliftonville
1883 Cliftonville .... 5-0 .... Ulster
1884 Distillery .... 5-0 .... Wellington Park
1885 Distillery .... 2-0 .... Limavady
1886 Distillery .... 1-0 .... Limavady
1887 Ulster .... 3-0 .... Cliftonville
1888 Cliftonville .... 2-1 .... Distillery
1889 Distillery .... 5-4 .... YMCA
1890 Gordon Highlanders .... 3-1 .... Cliftonville
1891 Linfield .... 4-2 .... Ulster
1892 Linfield .... 7-0 .... The Black Watch
1893 Linfield .... 5-1 .... Cliftonville
1894 Distillery .... 3-2 .... Linfield
1895 Linfield .... 10-1 .... Bohemians
1896 Distillery .... 3-1 .... Glentoran
1897 Cliftonville .... 3-1 .... Sherwood Foresters
1898 Linfield .... 2-0 .... St. Columbs Hall Celtic
1899 Linfield .... 2-1 .... Glentoran
1900 Cliftonville .... 2-1 .... Bohemians
1901 Cliftonville .... 1-0 .... Freebooters

Year	Winner	Score	Runner-up
1902	Linfield	5-1	Distillery
1903	Distillery	3-1	Bohemians
1904	Linfield	5-1	Derry Celtic
1905	Distillery	3-0	Shelbourne
1906	Shelbourne	2-0	Celtic
1907	Cliftonville	1-0	Shelbourne
1908	Bohemians	3-1	Shelbourne
1909	Cliftonville	2-1	Bohemians
1910	Distillery	1-0	Cliftonville
1911	Shelbourne	2-1	Bohemians
1912	Linfield	W-O	
1913	Linfield	2-0	Glentoran
1914	Glentoran	3-1	Linfield
1915	Linfield	1-0	Celtic
1916	Linfield	1-0	Glentoran
1917	Glentoran	2-0	Celtic
1918	Celtic	2-0	Linfield
1919	Linfield	2-1	Glentoran
1920	Shelbourne	W-O	
1921	Glentoran	2-0	Glenavon

NORTHERN IRISH CUP FINALS

Year	Winner	Score	Runner-up
1922	Linfield	2-0	Glenavon
1923	Linfield	2-0	Glentoran
1924	Queen's Island	1-0	Willowfield
1925	Distillery	2-1	Glentoran
1926	Celtic	3-2	Linfield
1927	Ards	3-2	Cliftonville
1928	Willowfield	1-0	Larne
1929	Ballymena United	2-1	Celtic
1930	Linfield	4-3	Ballymena United
1931	Linfield	3-0	Ballymena United
1932	Glentoran	2-1	Linfield
1933	Glentoran	3-1	Distillery
1934	Linfield	5-0	Cliftonville
1935	Glentoran	1-0	Larne
1936	Linfield	2-1	Derry City
1937	Celtic	3-0	Linfield
1938	Celtic	2-0	Bangor City
1939	Linfield	2-0	Ballymena United
1940	Ballymena United	2-0	Glenavon
1941	Celtic	1-0	Linfield
1942	Linfield	3-1	Glentoran
1943	Celtic	1-0	Glentoran
1944	Celtic	3-1	Linfield
1945	Linfield	4-2	Glentoran
1946	Linfield	3-0	Distillery
1947	Celtic	1-0	Glentoran
1948	Linfield	3-0	Coleraine
1949	Derry City	3-1	Glentoran
1950	Linfield	2-1	Distillery
1951	Glentoran	3-1	Ballymena United
1952	Ards	1-0	Glentoran
1953	Linfield	5-0	Coleraine
1954	Derry City	2-2 0-0 1-0	Glentoran
1955	Dundela	3-0	Glenavon
1956	Distillery	2-2 0-0 1-0	Glentoran
1957	Glenavon	2-0	Derry City
1958	Ballymena United	2-0	Linfield
1959	Glenavon	1-1 2-0	Ballymena United
1960	Linfield	5-1	Ards
1961	Glenavon	5-1	Linfield
1962	Linfield	4-0	Portadown
1963	Linfield	2-1	Distillery
1964	Derry City	2-0	Glentoran
1965	Coleraine	2-1	Glenavon
1966	Glentoran	2-0	Linfield
1967	Crusaders	3-1	Glentoran
1968	Crusaders	2-0	Linfield
1969	Ards	0-0 4-2	Distillery
1970	Linfield	2-1	Ballymena United
1971	Distillery	3-0	Derry City
1972	Coleraine	2-1	Portadown
1973	Glentoran	3-2	Linfield
1974	Ards	2-1	Ballymena United
1975	Coleraine	1-1 0-0 1-0	Linfield
1976	Carrick Rangers	2-1	Linfield
1977	Coleraine	4-1	Linfield
1978	Linfield	3-1	Ballymena United
1979	Cliftonville	3-2	Portadown
1980	Linfield	2-0	Crusaders
1981	Ballymena United	1-0	Glenavon
1982	Linfield	2-1	Coleraine
1983	Glentoran	1-1 2-1	Linfield
1984	Ballymena United	4-1	Carrick Rangers
1985	Glentoran	1-1 1-0	Linfield
1986	Glentoran	2-1	Coleraine
1987	Glentoran	1-0	Larne
1988	Glentoran	1-0	Glenavon
1989	Ballymena United	1-0	Larne
1990	Glentoran	3-0	Portadown
1991	Portadown	2-1	Glenavon
1992	Glenavon	2-1	Linfield
1993	Bangor	1-0	Ards
1994	Linfield	2-0	Bangor
1995	Linfield	3-1	Carrick Rangers

LEADING INTERNATIONAL GOALSCORERS

Goals	Player	Clubs	Years
13	Colin Clarke	(Bournemouth,Southampton, Portsmouth)	1986-
12	Gerry Armstrong	(Tottenham,Watford, Mallorca,West Brom,Chester-field)	1977-1986
	Joe Bambrick	(Linfield,Chelsea)	1929-1938
	Billy Gillespie	(Sheffield United)	1913-1931
11	Jimmy Quinn	(Blackburn,Swindon, West Ham,Leicester,Bradford, Bournemouth,Reading)	1984-
10	Billy Bingham	(Sunderland,Luton,Everton, Port Vale)	1951-1964
	Johnny Crossan	(Sparta Rotterdam,Sunderland, Man City,Middlesbrough)	1960-1968
	Jimmy McIlroy	(Burnley,Stoke)	1952-1966
	Peter McParland	(Aston Villa,Wolverhampton)	1954-1962
9	George Best	(Manchester United,Fulham)	1964-1978
	Martin O'Neill	(Distillery,Nottm Forest,Norwich, Man City,Notts Cty)	1972-1985
	Olphie Stanfield	(Distillery)	1887-1897
	Norman Whiteside	(Manchester United)	1982-1988

LEADING INTERNATIONAL APPEARANCES

Caps	Player	Clubs	Years
119	Pat Jennings	(Watford,Tottenham,Arsenal)	1964-1986
91	Mal Donaghy	(Luton Town,Manchester United, Chelsea)	1980-
88	Sammy McIlroy	(Man.United,Stoke,Man.City, Örgryte)	1972-1987
73	Jimmy Nichol	(Man.United,Toronto,Sunderland, Rangers,West Brom)	1976-1986
67	David McCreery	(Man.United,QPR,Tulsa, Newcastle,Hearts)	1976-1990
64	Martin O'Neill	(Distillery,Nottm Forest, Norwich,Man City, Notts Cty)	1972-1985
63	Gerry Armstrong	(Tottenham,Watford,Mallorca, West Brom,Chesterfield)	1977-1986
59	Terry Neill	(Arsenal,Hull City)	1961-1973
56	Billy Bingham	(Sunderland,Luton,Everton, Port Vale)	1951-1964
	Danny Blanchflower	(Barnsley,Aston Villa,Tottenham)	1950-1963
56	Nigel Worthington	(Sheffield Wednesday)	1984-

INTERNATIONAL MATCHES PLAYED BY THE UNITED IRISH TEAM

Date	Opponent	Result	Venue	Comp	Scorers
18-02-1882	England	L 0-13	Belfast	Fr	
25-02	Wales	L 1-7	Wrexham	Fr	Johnston.S
24-02-1883	England	L 0-7	Liverpool	Fr	
17-03	Wales	D 1-1	Belfast	Fr	Morrow
26-01-1884	Scotland	L 0-5	Belfast	HC	
9-02	Wales	L 0-6	Wrexham	HC	
23-02	England	L 1-8	Belfast	HC	McWha
28-02-1885	England	L 0-4	Manchester	HC	
14-03	Scotland	L 2-8	Glasgow	HC	Gibb.J 2
11-04	Wales	L 2-8	Belfast	HC	Molyneux, Dill
27-02-1886	Wales	L 0-5	Wrexham	HC	
13-03	England	L 1-6	Belfast	HC	Williams
20-03	Scotland	L 2-7	Belfast	HC	Condy, Johnston.S
5-02-1887	England	L 0-7	Sheffield	HC	
19-02	Scotland	L 1-4	Glasgow	HC	Browne
12-03	Wales	W 4-1	Belfast	HC	Stanfield, Browne, Peden, Sherrard
3-03-1888	Wales	L 0-11	Wrexham	HC	
24-03	Scotland	L 2-10	Belfast	HC	Lemon, Dalton
31-03	England	L 1-5	Belfast	HC	Crone
2-03-1889	England	L 1-6	Liverpool	HC	Wilton
9-03	Scotland	L 0-7	Glasgow	HC	
27-04	Wales	L 1-3	Belfast	HC	Lemon
8-02-1890	Wales	L 2-5	Shrewsbury	HC	Dalton 2
15-03	England	L 1-9	Belfast	HC	Reynolds
29-03	Scotland	L 1-4	Belfast	HC	Peden
7-02-1891	Wales	W 7-2	Belfast	HC	Dalton 3, Stanfield 2, Gaffikin 2
7-03	England	L 1-6	Wolverhampton	HC	Whiteside.T
28-03	Scotland	L 1-2	Glasgow	HC	Stanfield
27-02-1892	Wales	D 1-1	Bangor	HC	Stanfield
5-03	England	L 0-2	Belfast	HC	
19-03	Scotland	L 2-3	Belfast	HC	Williamson, Gaffikin
25-02-1893	England	L 1-6	Birmingham	HC	Gaffikin
25-03	Scotland	L 1-6	Glasgow	HC	Gaffikin
5-04	Wales	W 4-3	Belfast	HC	Peden 3, Wilton
24-02-1894	Wales	L 1-4	Swansea	HC	Stanfield
3-03	England	D 2-2	Belfast	HC	Stanfield, Gibson
31-03	Scotland	L 1-2	Belfast	HC	Stanfield
9-03-1895	England	L 0-9	Derby	HC	
16-03	Wales	D 2-2	Belfast	HC	Gawkrodger, Sherrard
30-03	Scotland	L 1-3	Glasgow	HC	Sherrard
29-02-1896	Wales	L 1-6	Wrexham	HC	Turner
7-03	England	L 0-2	Belfast	HC	
28-03	Scotland	D 3-3	Belfast	HC	Barron 2, Milne
20-02-1897	England	L 0-6	Nottingham	HC	
6-03	Wales	W 4-3	Belfast	HC	Barron, Stanfield, Pyper.J (1), Peden
27-03	Scotland	L 1-5	Glasgow	HC	Pyper.J (11)
19-02-1898	Wales	W 1-0	Llandudno	HC	Peden
5-03	England	L 2-3	Belfast	HC	Pyper.J (11), Mercer
26-03	Scotland	L 0-3	Belfast	HC	
18-02-1899	England	L 2-13	Sunderland	HC	McAllen, Campbell.J
4-03	Wales	W 1-0	Belfast	HC	Meldon
25-03	Scotland	L 1-9	Glasgow	HC	Goodall
24-02-1900	Wales	L 0-2	Llandudno	HC	
3-03	Scotland	L 0-3	Belfast	HC	
17-03	England	L 0-2	Dublin	HC	
23-02-1901	Scotland	L 0-11	Glasgow	HC	
9-03	England	L 0-3	Southampton	HC	
23-03	Wales	L 0-1	Belfast	HC	
22-02-1902	Wales	W 3-0	Cardiff	HC	Gara 3
1-03	Scotland	L 1-3	Belfast	HC	Milne
22-03	England	L 0-1	Belfast	HC	
14-02-1903	England	L 0-4	Wolverhampton	HC	
21-03	Scotland	W 2-0	Glasgow	HC	Connor, Kirwan
28-03	Wales	W 2-0	Belfast	HC	Goodall, Sheridan
12-03-1904	England	L 1-3	Belfast	HC	Kirwan
21-03	Wales	W 1-0	Bangor	HC	McCracken
26-03	Scotland	D 1-1	Dublin	HC	Sheridan
25-02-1905	England	D 1-1	Middlesbrough	HC	OG

18-03	Scotland	L 0-4	Glasgow	HC	
8-04	Wales	D 2-2	Belfast	HC	Murphy, O'Hagan
17-02-1906	England	L 0-5	Belfast	HC	
17-03	Scotland	L 0-1	Dublin	HC	
2-04	Wales	D 4-4	Wrexham	HC	Maxwell 2, Sloan 2
16-02-1907	England	L 0-1	Liverpool	HC	
23-02	Wales	L 2-3	Belfast	HC	O'Hagan, Sloan
16-03	Scotland	L 0-3	Glasgow	HC	
15-02-1908	England	L 1-3	Belfast	HC	Hannon
14-03	Scotland	L 0-5	Dublin	HC	
11-04	Wales	W 1-0	Aberdare	HC	Sloan
13-02-1909	England	L 0-4	Bradford	HC	
15-03	Scotland	L 0-5	Glasgow	HC	
20-03	Wales	L 2-3	Belfast	HC	Lacey, Hunter.A (I)
12-02-1910	England	D 1-1	Belfast	HC	Thompson
19-03	Scotland	W 1-0	Belfast	HC	Thompson
11-04	Wales	L 1-4	Wrexham	HC	Darling
28-01-1911	Wales	L 1-2	Belfast	HC	Halligan
11-02	England	L 1-2	Derby	HC	McAuley
18-03	Scotland	L 0-2	Glasgow	HC	
10-02-1912	England	L 1-6	Dublin	HC	Hamill
16-03	Scotland	L 1-4	Belfast	HC	McKnight
13-04	Wales	W 3-2	Cardiff	HC	McCandless 2, Brennan.B
18-01-1913	Wales	L 0-1	Belfast	HC	
15-02	England	W 2-1	Belfast	HC	Gillespie 2
15-03	Scotland	L 1-2	Dublin	HC	McKnight
19-01-1914	Wales	W 2-1	Wrexham	HC	Young, Gillespie
14-02	England	W 3-0	Middlesbrough	HC	Lacey 2, Gillespie
14-03	Scotland	D 1-1	Belfast	HC	Young
25-10-1919	England	D 1-1	Belfast	HC	Ferris.J
14-02-1920	Wales	D 2-2	Belfast	HC	McCandless, Emerson
13-03	Scotland	L 0-3	Glasgow	HC	
23-10	England	L 0-2	Sunderland	HC	
26-02-1921	Scotland	L 0-2	Belfast	HC	
9-04	Wales	L 1-2	Swansea	HC	Chambers
22-10	England	D 1-1	Belfast	HC	Gillespie
4-03-1922	Scotland	L 1-2	Glasgow	HC	Gillespie
1-04	Wales	D 1-1	Belfast	HC	Gillespie
21-10	England	L 0-2	West Bromwich	HC	
3-03-1923	Scotland	L 0-1	Belfast	HC	
14-04	Wales	W 3-0	Wrexham	HC	Irvine.R 2, Gillespie

INTERNATIONAL MATCHES PLAYED BY NORTHERN IRELAND

20-10-1923	England	W 2-1	Belfast	HC	Gillespie, Croft
1-03-1924	Scotland	L 0-2	Glasgow	HC	
15-03	Wales	L 0-1	Belfast	HC	
22-10	England	L 1-3	Liverpool	HC	Gillespie
28-02-1925	Scotland	L 0-3	Belfast	HC	
18-04	Wales	D 0-0	Wrexham	HC	
24-10	England	D 0-0	Belfast	HC	
13-02-1926	Wales	W 3-0	Belfast	HC	Gillespie, Curran 2
27-02	Scotland	L 0-4	Glasgow	HC	
20-10	England	D 3-3	Liverpool	HC	Gillespie, Davey, Irvine.R
26-02-1927	Scotland	L 0-2	Belfast	HC	
9-04	Wales	D 2-2	Cardiff	HC	Johnston.H 2
22-10	England	W 2-0	Belfast	HC	OG, Mahood
4-02-1928	Wales	L 1-2	Belfast	HC	Chambers
25-02	Scotland	W 1-0	Glasgow	HC	Chambers
22-10	England	L 1-2	Liverpool	HC	Bambrick
2-02-1929	Wales	D 2-2	Wrexham	HC	Mahood, McCluggage
23-02	Scotland	L 3-7	Belfast	HC	Bambrick 2, Rowley
19-10	England	L 0-3	Belfast	HC	
1-02-1930	Wales	W 7-0	Belfast	HC	Bambrick 6, McCluggage
22-02	Scotland	L 1-3	Glasgow	HC	McCaw
20-10	England	L 1-5	Sheffield	HC	Dunne
21-02-1931	Scotland	D 0-0	Belfast	HC	
22-04	Wales	L 2-3	Wrexham	HC	Dunne, Rowley
19-09	Scotland	L 1-3	Glasgow	HC	Dunne
17-10	England	L 2-6	Belfast	HC	Dunne, Kelly

5-12	Wales	W 4-0	Belfast	HC	Kelly 2, Millar, Bambrick
17-09-1932	Scotland	L 0-4	Belfast	HC	
17-10	England	L 0-1	Blackpool	HC	
7-12	Wales	L 1-4	Wrexham	HC	English
16-09-1933	Scotland	W 2-1	Glasgow	HC	Martin 2
14-10	England	L 0-3	Belfast	HC	
4-11	Wales	D 1-1	Belfast	HC	Jones.S
20-10-1934	Scotland	W 2-1	Belfast	HC	Martin, Coulter
6-02-1935	England	L 1-2	Liverpool	HC	Stevenson
27-03	Wales	L 1-3	Wrexham	HC	Bambrick
19-10	England	L 1-3	Belfast	HC	Brown
13-11	Scotland	L 1-2	Edinburgh	HC	Kelly
11-03-1936	Wales	W 3-2	Belfast	HC	Gibb.T, Stevenson, Kernaghan
31-10	Scotland	L 1-3	Belfast	HC	Kernaghan
18-11	England	L 1-3	Stoke	HC	Davis
17-03-1937	Wales	L 1-4	Wrexham	HC	Stevenson
23-10	England	L 1-5	Belfast	HC	Stevenson
10-11	Scotland	D 1-1	Aberdeen	HC	Doherty.P
16-03-1938	Wales	W 1-0	Belfast	HC	Bambrick
8-10	Scotland	L 0-2	Belfast	HC	
16-11	England	L 0-7	Manchester	HC	
15-03-1939	Wales	L 1-3	Wrexham	HC	Milligan
28-09-1946	England	L 2-7	Belfast	HC	Lockhart 2
27-11	Scotland	D 0-0	Glasgow	HC	
16-04-1947	Wales	W 2-1	Belfast	HC	Stevenson, Doherty.P
4-10	Scotland	W 2-0	Belfast	HC	Smyth 2
5-11	England	D 2-2	Liverpool	HC	Doherty.P, Walsh
10-03-1948	Wales	L 0-2	Wrexham	HC	
9-10	England	L 2-6	Belfast	HC	Walsh 2
17-11	Scotland	L 2-3	Glasgow	HC	Walsh 2
9-03-1949	Wales	L 0-2	Belfast	HC	
1-10	Scotland	L 2-8	Belfast	HC/WCq	Smyth 2
16-11	England	L 2-9	Manchester	HC/WCq	Smyth, Brennan.R
8-03-1950	Wales	D 0-0	Wrexham	HC/WCq	
7-10	England	L 1-4	Belfast	HC	McMorran
1-11	Scotland	L 1-6	Glasgow	HC	McGarry
7-03-1951	Wales	L 1-2	Belfast	HC	Simpson
12-05	France	D 2-2	Belfast	Fr	Ferris.R, Simpson
6-10	Scotland	L 0-3	Belfast	HC	
14-11	England	L 0-2	Birmingham	HC	
19-03-1952	Wales	L 0-3	Swansea	HC	
4-10	England	D 2-2	Belfast	HC	Tully 2
5-11	Scotland	D 1-1	Glasgow	HC	D'Arcy
11-11	France	L 1-3	Paris	Fr	Tully
15-04-1953	Wales	L 2-3	Belfast	HC	McMorran 2
3-10	Scotland	L 1-3	Belfast	HC/WCq	Lockhart
11-11	England	L 1-3	Liverpool	HC/WCq	McMorran
31-03-1954	Wales	W 2-1	Wrexham	HC/WCq	McParland 2
2-10	England	L 0-2	Belfast	HC	
3-11	Scotland	D 2-2	Glasgow	HC	Bingham, McAdams
20-04-1955	Wales	L 2-3	Belfast	HC	Crossan.E, Walker
8-10	Scotland	W 2-1	Belfast	HC	Blanchflower.J, Bingham
2-11	England	L 0-3	London	HC	
11-04-1956	Wales	D 1-1	Cardiff	HC	Jones.J
6-10	England	D 1-1	Belfast	HC	McIlroy.J
7-11	Scotland	L 0-1	Glasgow	HC	
16-01-1957	Portugal	D 1-1	Lisbon	WCq	Bingham
10-04	Wales	D 0-0	Belfast	HC	
25-04	Italy	L 0-1	Rome	WCq	
1-05	Portugal	W 3-0	Belfast	WCq	Simpson, McIlroy.J, Casey
5-10	Scotland	D 1-1	Belfast	HC	Bingham
6-11	England	W 3-2	London	HC	McIlroy.J, McCrory, Simpson
4-12	Italy	D 2-2	Belfast	Fr	Cush 2
15-01-1958	Italy	W 2-1	Belfast	WCq	McIlroy.J, Cush
16-04	Wales	D 1-1	Cardiff	HC	Simpson
8-06	Czechoslovakia	W 1-0	Halmstad	WCr1	Cush
11-06	Argentina	L 1-3	Halmstad	WCr1	McParland
15-06	West Germany	D 2-2	Malmo	WCr1	McParland 2
17-06	Czechoslovakia	W 2-1	Malmo	WCr1	McParland 2
19-06	France	L 0-4	Norrkoping	WCqf	
4-10	England	D 3-3	Belfast	HC	Cush, Peacock, Casey

15-10	Spain	L 2-6	Madrid	Fr	Bingham, McIlroy.J
5-11	Scotland	D 2-2	Glasgow	HC	OG, McIlroy.J
22-04-1959	Wales	W 4-1	Belfast	HC	McParland 2, Peacock, McIlroy.J
3-10	Scotland	L 0-4	Belfast	HC	
18-11	England	L 1-2	London	HC	Bingham
6-04-1960	Wales	L 2-3	Wrexham	HC	Bingham, Blanchflower.D
8-10	England	L 2-5	Belfast	HC	McAdams 2
26-10	West Germany	L 3-4	Belfast	WCq	McAdams 3
9-11	Scotland	L 2-5	Glasgow	HC	Blanchflower.D, McParland
12-04-1961	Wales	L 1-5	Belfast	HC	Dougan
25-04	Italy	L 2-3	Bologna	Fr	Dougan, McAdams
3-05	Greece	L 1-2	Athens	WCq	McIlroy.J
10-05	West Germany	L 1-2	Berlin	WCq	McIlroy.J
7-10	Scotland	L 1-6	Belfast	HC	McLaughlin
17-10	Greece	W 2-0	Belfast	WCq	McLaughlin 2
22-11	England	D 1-1	London	HC	McIlroy.J
11-04-1962	Wales	L 0-4	Cardiff	HC	
9-05	Holland	L 0-4	Rotterdam	Fr	
10-10	Poland	W 2-0	Chorzow	ECr1	Dougan, Humphries
20-10	England	L 1-3	Belfast	HC	Barr
7-11	Scotland	L 1-5	Glasgow	HC	Bingham
28-11	Poland	W 2-0	Belfast	ECr1	Crossan.J, Bingham
3-04-1963	Wales	L 1-4	Belfast	HC	Harvey
30-05	Spain	D 1-1	Bilbao	ECr2	Irvine.W
12-10	Scotland	W 2-1	Belfast	HC	Bingham, Wilson.S
30-10	Spain	L 0-1	Belfast	ECr2	
20-11	England	L 3-8	London	HC	Crossan.J, Wilson.S 2
15-04-1964	Wales	W 3-2	Swansea	HC	McLaughlin, Wilson.S, Harvey
29-04	Uruguay	W 3-0	Belfast	Fr	Crossan.J 2, Wilson.S
3-10	England	L 3-4	Belfast	HC	Wilson.S, McLaughlin 2
14-10	Switzerland	W 1-0	Belfast	WCq	Crossan.J
14-11	Switzerland	L 1-2	Lausanne	WCq	Best
25-11	Scotland	L 2-3	Glasgow	HC	Best, Irvine.W
17-03-1965	Holland	W 2-1	Belfast	WCq	Crossan.J, Neill
31-03	Wales	L 0-5	Belfast	HC	
7-04	Holland	D 0-0	Rotterdam	WCq	
7-05	Albania	W 4-1	Belfast	WCq	Crossan.J, Best
2-10	Scotland	W 3-2	Belfast	HC	Dougan, Crossan.J, Irvine.W
10-11	England	L 1-2	London	HC	Irvine.W
24-11	Albania	D 1-1	Tirana	WCq	Irvine.W
30-03-1966	Wales	W 4-1	Cardiff	HC	Irvine.W, Wilson.S, Welsh, Harvey
7-05	West Germany	L 0-2	Belfast	Fr	
22-06	Mexico	W 4-1	Belfast	Fr	Johnston.W, Elder, Nicholson, Ferguson
22-10	England	L 0-2	Belfast	HC/ECq	
16-11	Scotland	L 1-2	Glasgow	HC/ECq	Nicholson
12-04-1967	Wales	D 0-0	Belfast	HC/ECq	
21-10	Scotland	W 1-0	Belfast	HC/ECq	Clements
22-11	England	L 0-2	London	HC/ECq	
28-02-1968	Wales	L 0-2	Wrexham	HC/ECq	
10-09	Israel	W 3-2	Tel Aviv	Fr	Irvine.W 2, Dougan
23-10	Turkey	W 4-1	Belfast	WCq	Best, McMordie, Dougan, Campbell.W
11-12	Turkey	W 3-0	Istanbul	WCq	Harkin 2, Nicholson
3-05-1969	England	L 1-3	Belfast	HC	McMordie
6-05	Scotland	D 1-1	Glasgow	HC	McMordie
10-05	Wales	D 0-0	Belfast	HC	
10-09	Soviet Union	D 0-0	Belfast	WCq	
22-10	Soviet Union	L 0-2	Moscow	WCq	
18-04-1970	Scotland	L 0-1	Belfast	HC	
21-04	England	L 1-3	London	HC	Best
25-04	Wales	L 0-1	Swansea	HC	
11-11	Spain	L 0-3	Seville	ECq	
3-02-1971	Cyprus	W 3-0	Nicosia	ECq	Nicholson, Dougan, Best
21-04	Cyprus	W 5-0	Belfast	ECq	Dougan, Best 3, Nicholson
15-05	England	L 0-1	Belfast	HC	
18-05	Scotland	W 1-0	Glasgow	HC	OG
22-05	Wales	W 1-0	Belfast	HC	Hamilton.B
22-09	Soviet Union	L 0-1	Moscow	ECq	
13-10	Soviet Union	D 1-1	Belfast	ECq	Nicholson
16-02-1972	Spain	D 1-1	Hull	ECq	Morgan
20-05	Scotland	L 0-2	Glasgow	HC	
23-05	England	W 1-0	London	HC	Neill

Date	Opponent	Result	Venue	Comp	Scorers
27-05	Wales	D 0-0	Wrexham	HC	
18-10	Bulgaria	L 0-3	Sofia	WCq	
14-02-1973	Cyprus	L 0-1	Nicosia	WCq	
28-03	Portugal	D 1-1	Coventry	WCq	O'Neill.M (I)
8-05	Cyprus	W 3-0	London	WCq	Morgan, Anderson 2
12-05	England	L 1-2	Liverpool	HC	Clements
16-05	Scotland	W 2-1	Glasgow	HC	O'Neill.M (I), Anderson
19-05	Wales	W 1-0	Liverpool	HC	Hamilton.B
26-09	Bulgaria	D 0-0	Sheffield	WCq	
14-11	Portugal	D 1-1	Lisbon	WCq	O'Kane
11-05-1974	Scotland	W 1-0	Glasgow	HC	Cassidy
15-05	England	L 0-1	London	HC	
18-05	Wales	L 0-1	Wrexham	HC	
4-09	Norway	L 1-2	Oslo	ECq	Finney
30-10	Sweden	W 2-0	Stockholm	ECq	O'Neill.M (I), Nicholl.C
16-03-1975	Yugoslavia	W 1-0	Belfast	ECq	Hamilton.B
17-05	England	D 0-0	Belfast	HC	
20-05	Scotland	L 0-3	Glasgow	HC	
23-05	Wales	W 1-0	Belfast	HC	Finney
3-09	Sweden	L 1-2	Belfast	ECq	Hunter.A (II)
29-10	Norway	W 3-0	Belfast	ECq	Morgan, McIlroy.S, Hamilton.B
19-11	Yugoslavia	L 0-1	Belgrade	ECq	
3-03-1976	Israel	D 1-1	Tel Aviv	Fr	OG
8-05	Scotland	L 0-3	Glasgow	HC	
11-05	England	L 0-4	London	HC	
14-05	Wales	L 0-1	Swansea	HC	
13-10	Holland	D 2-2	Rotterdam	WCq	McGrath, Spence
10-11	Belgium	L 0-2	Liege	WCq	
27-04-1977	West Germany	L 0-5	Cologne	Fr	
28-05	England	L 1-2	Belfast	HC	McGrath
1-06	Scotland	L 0-3	Glasgow	HC	
3-06	Wales	D 1-1	Belfast	HC	Nelson
11-06	Iceland	L 0-1	Reykjavik	WCq	
21-09	Iceland	W 2-0	Belfast	WCq	McGrath, McIlroy.S
12-10	Holland	L 0-1	Belfast	WCq	
16-11	Belgium	W 3-0	Belfast	WCq	Armstrong 2, McGrath
13-05-1978	Scotland	D 1-1	Glasgow	HC	O'Neill.M (I)
16-05	England	L 0-1	London	HC	
19-05	Wales	L 0-1	Wrexham	HC	
20-09	Rep. Ireland	D 0-0	Dublin	ECq	
25-10	Denmark	W 2-1	Belfast	ECq	Spence, Anderson
29-11	Bulgaria	W 2-0	Sofia	ECq	Armstrong, Nicholl.J
7-02-1979	England	L 0-4	London	ECq	
2-05	Bulgaria	W 2-0	Belfast	ECq	Nicholl.C, Armstrong
19-05	England	L 0-2	Belfast	HC	
22-05	Scotland	L 0-1	Glasgow	HC	
26-05	Wales	D 1-1	Belfast	HC	Spence
6-06	Denmark	L 0-4	Copenhagen	ECq	
17-10	England	L 1-5	Belfast	ECq	Moreland
21-11	Rep. Ireland	W 1-0	Belfast	ECq	Armstrong
26-03-1980	Israel	D 0-0	Tel Aviv	WCq	
16-05	Scotland	W 1-0	Belfast	HC	Hamilton.W
20-05	England	D 1-1	London	HC	Cochrane
23-05	Wales	W 1-0	Cardiff	HC	Brotherston
11-06	Australia	W 2-1	Sydney	Fr	Nicholl.C, O'Neill.M (I)
15-06	Australia	D 1-1	Melbourne	Fr	O'Neill.M (I)
18-06	Australia	W 2-1	Adelaide	Fr	Brotherston, McCurdy
15-10	Sweden	W 3-0	Belfast	WCq	Brotherston, McIlroy.S, Nicholl.J
19-11	Portugal	L 0-1	Lisbon	WCq	
25-03-1981	Scotland	D 1-1	Glasgow	WCq	Hamilton.W
29-04	Portugal	W 1-0	Belfast	WCq	Armstrong
19-05	Scotland	L 0-2	Glasgow	HC	
3-06	Sweden	L 0-1	Stockholm	WCq	
14-10	Scotland	D 0-0	Belfast	WCq	
18-11	Israel	W 1-0	Belfast	WCq	Armstrong
23-02-1982	England	L 0-4	London	HC	
24-03	France	L 0-4	Paris	Fr	
28-04	Scotland	D 1-1	Belfast	HC	McIlroy.S
27-05	Wales	L 0-3	Wrexham	HC	
17-06	Yugoslavia	D 0-0	Zaragoza	WCr1	
21-06	Honduras	D 1-1	Zaragoza	WCr1	Armstrong
25-06	Spain	W 1-0	Valencia	WCr1	Armstrong

Date	Opponent	Result	Venue	Comp	Scorers
1-07	Austria	D 2-2	Madrid	WCr2	Hamilton.W 2
4-07	France	L 1-4	Madrid	WCr2	Armstrong
13-10	Austria	L 0-2	Vienna	ECq	
17-11	West Germany	W 1-0	Belfast	ECq	Stewart
15-12	Albania	D 0-0	Tirana	ECq	
30-03-1983	Turkey	W 2-1	Belfast	ECq	O'Neill.M (I), McClelland
27-04	Albania	W 1-0	Belfast	ECq	Stewart
24-05	Scotland	D 0-0	Glasgow	HC	
28-05	England	D 0-0	Belfast	HC	
31-05	Wales	L 0-1	Belfast	HC	
21-09	Austria	W 3-1	Belfast	ECq	Hamilton.W, Whiteside.N, O'Neill.M (I)
12-10	Turkey	L 0-1	Ankara	ECq	
16-11	West Germany	W 1-0	Hamburg	ECq	Whiteside.N
13-12	Scotland	W 2-0	Glasgow	HC	Whiteside.N, McIlroy.S
4-04-1984	England	L 0-1	London	HC	
22-05	Wales	D 1-1	Swansea	HC	Armstrong
27-05	Finland	L 0-1	Pori	WCq	
12-09	Romania	W 3-2	Belfast	WCq	Whiteside.N, O'Neill.M (I), OG
16-10	Israel	W 3-0	Belfast	Fr	Whiteside.N, Doherty.L, Quinn
14-11	Finland	W 2-1	Belfast	WCq	O'Neill.J, Armstrong
27-02-1985	England	L 0-1	Belfast	WCq	
27-03	Spain	D 0-0	Palma	Fr	
1-05	Turkey	W 2-0	Belfast	WCq	Whiteside.N 2
11-09	Turkey	D 0-0	Izmir	WCq	
16-10	Romania	W 1-0	Bucharest	WCq	Quinn
13-11	England	D 0-0	London	WCq	
26-02-1986	France	D 0-0	Paris	Fr	
26-03	Denmark	D 1-1	Belfast	Fr	McDonald
23-04	Morocco	W 2-1	Belfast	Fr	Clarke, Quinn
3-06	Algeria	D 1-1	Guadalajara	WCr1	Whiteside.N
7-06	Spain	L 1-2	Guadalajara	WCr1	Clarke
12-06	Brazil	L 0-3	Guadalajara	WCr1	
15-10	England	L 0-3	London	ECq	
12-11	Turkey	D 0-0	Izmir	ECq	
18-02-1987	Israel	D 1-1	Tel Aviv	Fr	Penney
1-04	England	L 0-2	Belfast	ECq	
29-04	Yugoslavia	L 1-2	Belfast	ECq	Clarke
14-10	Yugoslavia	L 0-3	Sarajevo	ECq	
11-11	Turkey	W 1-0	Belfast	ECq	Quinn
17-02-1988	Greece	L 2-3	Athens	Fr	Clarke 2
23-03	Poland	D 1-1	Belfast	Fr	Wilson.D
27-04	France	D 0-0	Belfast	Fr	
21-05	Malta	W 3-0	Belfast	WCq	Clarke, Penney, Quinn
14-09	Rep. Ireland	D 0-0	Belfast	WCq	
19-10	Hungary	L 0-1	Budapest	WCq	
21-12	Spain	L 0-4	Seville	WCq	
8-02-1989	Spain	L 0-2	Belfast	WCq	
26-04	Malta	W 2-0	Ta'Qali	WCq	Clarke, O'Neill.M (II)
26-05	Chile	L 0-1	Belfast	Fr	
6-09	Hungary	L 1-2	Belfast	WCq	Whiteside.N
11-10	Rep. Ireland	L 0-3	Dublin	WCq	
27-03-1990	Norway	L 2-3	Belfast	Fr	Quinn, Wilson.K
18-05	Uruguay	W 1-0	Belfast	Fr	Wilson.K
12-09	Yugoslavia	L 0-2	Belfast	ECq	
17-10	Denmark	D 1-1	Belfast	ECq	Clarke
14-11	Austria	D 0-0	Vienna	ECq	
6-02-1991	Poland	W 3-1	Belfast	Fr	Taggart 2, Magilton
27-03	Yugoslavia	L 1-4	Belgrade	ECq	Hill
1-05	Faeroe Islands	D 1-1	Belfast	ECq	Clarke
11-09	Faeroe Islands	W 5-0	Landskrona	ECq	Wilson.K, Clarke 3, McDonald
16-10	Austria	W 2-1	Belfast	ECq	Dowie, Black
13-11	Denmark	L 1-2	Odense	ECq	Taggart
19-02-1992	Scotland	L 0-1	Glasgow	Fr	
28-04	Lithuania	D 2-2	Belfast	WCq	Wilson.K, Taggart
2-06	Germany	D 1-1	Bremen	Fr	Hughes
9-09	Albania	W 3-0	Belfast	WCq	Clarke, Wilson.K, Magilton
14-10	Spain	D 0-0	Belfast	WCq	
18-11	Denmark	L 0-1	Belfast	WCq	
17-02-1993	Albania	W 2-1	Tirana	WCq	Magilton, McDonald
31-03	Rep. Ireland	L 0-3	Dublin	WCq	
28-04	Spain	L 1-3	Seville	WCq	Wilson.K
25-05	Lithuania	W 1-0	Vilnius	WCq	Dowie

2-06	Latvia	W 2-1	Riga	WCq	Magilton, Taggart
8-09	Latvia	W 2-0	Belfast	WCq	Quinn, Gray
13-10	Denmark	L 0-1	Copenhagen	WCq	
17-11	Rep. Ireland	D 1-1	Belfast	WCq	Quinn
20-03-1994	Romania	W 2-0	Belfast	Fr	Morrow, Gray
20-04	Liechtenstein	W 4-1	Belfast	ECq	Quinn 2, Lomas, Dowie
4-06	Colombia	L 0-2	Boston	Fr	
12-06	Mexico	L 0-3	Miami	Fr	
7-09	Portugal	L 1-2	Belfast	ECq	Quinn
12-10	Austria	W 2-1	Vienna	ECq	Gillespie, Gray
16-11	Rep. Ireland	L 0-4	Belfast	ECq	
29-03-1995	Rep. Ireland	D 1-1	Dublin	ECq	Dowie
26-04	Latvia	W 1-0	Riga	ECq	Dowie
22-05	Canada	L 0-2	Edmonton	Fr	
25-05	Chile	L 1-2	Edmonton	Fr	Dowie
7-06	Latvia	L 1-2	Belfast	ECq	Dowie

NORWAY

Norway have always been one of Europe's perennial underdogs. For years they lived in the shadow of Sweden and Denmark, both a rich source of players for the professional teams of Western Europe. Norwegians by contrast very rarely ventured abroad - until recently, that is. Now, with the exposure of their exiles to top quality league football, the Norwegians have become a force at international level. They ended Italy's hopes of qualifying for the 1992 European Championship finals with victory in Oslo, and in 1994 topped their World Cup qualifying group ahead of Holland and England to reach the finals for the first time since 1938.

Norway is a large elongated country in which mountains make communications difficult. It is therefore surprising to see how well distributed football is when it might have been expected to have developed only in and around the capital. Oslo, Bergen, Trondheim and Stavanger of the major towns all have successful clubs whilst even smaller and more remote towns have played a part in the development of the game.

The Norges Fotballforbund initiated a cup competition in 1902, the year in which it was founded, and for the next 34 years this remained the sole source of competition. Norway's oldest club, Odds BK of Skein, founded in 1894, were the dominant force in the early years of the competition and set the trend for the success of non-Oslo clubs.

The national team first took to the field in 1908. An 11-3 defeat at the hands of Sweden was not the best of starts and it was not until ten years later that Norway won their first game. Throughout the years, matches against their Scandinavian neighbours, especially in the Scandinavian Championship, have provided the bulk of the international programme. The 1930s saw the Norwegians at their height as they won the 1929-32 edition.

The 1936 Olympic Games represents Norway's greatest achievement. Against all the odds they reached the semi-finals and only lost to the Italian 'professionals' in extra-time. On the way they caused one of the biggest upsets ever in football by beating the hosts, Germany. Given the backdrop to the game the victory is remarkable. With the Germans roared on by a fanatical crowd which included Hitler, Norway, according to the script, should have crumbled. Instead they played the game of their lives to win 2-0. In a scene reminiscent of the snub to Jesse Owens in the same Games, Hitler stormed out of the stadium in a rage. A 3-2 victory over Poland in the third place play-off gave Norway the bronze medal. Qualification for the 1938 World Cup saw them have the misfortune to draw Italy in the first round. They lost in extra-time by the same score as they had done two years previously in Berlin.

THE ORDER OF MERIT

	Team	G	S	B	G	S	B	G	S	G	S	B
1	Fredrikstad FK	19	15	1	9	8	1	10	7	-	-	-
2	Rosenborg BK Trondheim	17	9	1	10	5	1	7	4	-	-	-
3	Viking FK Stavanger	12	6	4	8	2	4	4	4	-	-	-
4	Odd SK Skien	11	9	-	-	2	-	11	7	-	-	-
5	SOFK Lyn Oslo	10	9	2	2	4	2	8	5	-	-	-
6	Lillestrøm SK	9	13	3	5	6	3	4	7	-	-	-
7	FK Skeid Oslo	9	8	1	1	5	1	8	3	-	-	-
8	SK Brann Bergen	7	8	1	2	2	1	5	6	-	-	-
9	FK Sarpsborg	6	6	2	-	-	2	6	6	-	-	-
10	Vålerengens IF Oslo	5	3	2	4	1	2	1	2	-	-	-
11	IF Stromsgodset	5	1	2	1	-	2	4	1	-	-	-
12	Ørn FK Horten	4	4	-	-	-	-	4	4	-	-	-
13	Mjöndalen IF	3	7	-	-	2	-	3	5	-	-	-
14	Frigg SK Oslo	3	3	-	-	-	-	3	3	-	-	-
15	Larvik Turn IF	3	1	-	3	-	-	-	1	-	-	-
16	FK Bodø-Glimt	2	3	-	-	2	-	2	1	-	-	-
17	FK Moss	2	2	-	1	1	-	1	1	-	-	-
18	Mercantile	2	1	-	-	-	-	2	1	-	-	-
19	IK Start Kristiansand	2	-	8	2	-	8	-	-	-	-	-
20	Molde FK	1	4	3	-	2	3	1	2	-	-	-
21	Bryne IL Stavanger	1	2	-	-	2	-	1	-	-	-	-
	Kvik Halden	1	2	-	-	-	-	1	2	-	-	-
23	Tromsø IL	1	1	1	-	1	1	1	-	-	-	-
24	Fram Larvik	1	1	-	1	-	-	-	1	-	-	-
	Gjøvik Lyn	1	1	-	-	-	-	1	1	-	-	-
	Grane Nordstrand	1	1	-	-	-	-	1	1	-	-	-
	Sparta Sarpsborg	1	1	-	-	1	-	1	-	-	-	-
28	Freidig SK Trondheim	1	-	-	1	-	-	-	-	-	-	-
29	Kongsvinger IL	-	2	2	-	2	2	-	-	-	-	-
30	SK Haugar	-	2	-	-	-	-	-	2	-	-	-

	Sandefjord BK	-	2	-	-	-	-	-	2	-	-	-
	IF Uradd	-	2	-	-	-	-	-	2	-	-	-
	SK Vard Haugesund	-	2	-	-	-	-	-	2	-	-	-
34	Akademisk SK Oslo	-	1	-	-	-	-	-	1	-	-	-
	Asker	-	1	-	-	-	-	-	1	-	-	-
	Drafn SK Drammen	-	1	-	-	-	-	-	1	-	-	-
	Drammens BK	-	1	-	-	-	-	-	1	-	-	-
	IF Eik Tönsberg	-	1	-	-	1	-	-	-	-	-	-
	Fyllingen Bergen	-	1	-	-	-	-	-	1	-	-	-
	Sogndal IL	-	1	-	-	-	-	-	1	-	-	-
	Solberg	-	1	-	-	-	-	-	1	-	-	-
	Steinkjer IFK	-	1	-	-	1	-	-	-	-	-	-
43	Hamarkameratene	-	-	1	-	-	1	-	-	-	-	-

To the end of the 1994 season

Olympic year, 1936, had seen the introduction of a national league for the clubs, although the winner was decided in a series of knock-out games until 1961, at which point a single league was introduced. Not many Norwegians made their name abroad at this time and this was one of the strengths of the league. Thorbjorn Svenssen, for example, was in the 1950s one of the most famous names in Europe, representing his country on 104 occasions, yet he played all his football for Sandefjord BK. Likewise, Jurgen Juve, the most prolific scorer for the national team with 30 goals, played only for SOFK Lyn Oslo.

Only since the early 1980s have the best Norwegian players moved abroad. It started as a trickle but has become a flood. The most famous export has been their national captain Rune Bratseth. Playing for Werder Bremen in Germany, he helped them to two Bundesliga titles, two German Cups and a Cup Winners Cup triumph. Following the lead given by Norway's most capped goalkeeper Erik Thorstvedt, who joined Tottenham in 1988, England has become the most popular destination. Of the 17 foreign-based players used by the national side in 1994, 12 were based with English clubs. After the victories over Holland and England much was expected of the team in America, but over-cautious tactics were their undoing and despite beating Mexico, they were eliminated on goal difference in the first round.

The league in Norway is still amateur and their clubs have struggled in European competitions, only very occasionally making it past the first round. The most successful team of recent years has been Rosenborg of Trondheim, one of the most northerly clubs in the world. The actual holder of that distinction, however, is Tromso - where for two months in the summer you can play a game at two o'clock in the morning without needing to turn the floodlights on!

Population: 4,246,000
Area, sq km: 323,878
% in urban areas: 72.8%
Capital city: Oslo

Norges Fotballforbund
Ullevål Stadion
Postboks 3823
Ullevål Hageby
N-0805 Oslo 8
Norway
Tel: + 47 22 951000
Fax: + 47 22 951010

Year of formation	1902
Affiliation to FIFA	1908
Affiliation to UEFA	1954
Registered clubs	1857
Registered players	573 500
Registered coaches	9222
Registered referees	3866
National stadium	Ullevål Stadion 23,000
National colours	Red with white sleeves/White/Blue
Reserve colours	Blue/White/Blue
Season	May - October

THE RECORD

WORLD CUP

1930	Did not enter
1934	Did not enter
1938	QT 1st/2 in group 2 - Final Tournament/1st round
1950	Did not enter
1954	QT 3rd/3 in group 1
1958	QT 3rd/3 in group 3
1962	QT 3rd/3 in group 5
1966	QT 2nd/4 in group 3
1970	QT 3rd/3 in group 5
1974	QT 3rd/4 in group 3
1978	QT 2nd/3 in group 6
1982	QT 5th/5 in group 4
1986	QT 5th/5 in group 6
1990	QT 4th/5 in group 5
1994	QT 1st/6 in group 2 - Final tournament/1st round

EUROPEAN CHAMPIONSHIP

1960	1st round
1964	1st round
1968	QT 4th/4 in group 2
1972	QT 4th/4 in group 2
1976	QT 4th/4 in group 3
1980	QT 5th/5 in group 2
1984	QT 4th/4 in group 4
1988	QT 5th/5 in group 3
1992	QT 3rd/5 in group 3
1996	QT group 5

EUROPEAN CLUB COMPETITIONS

European Cup
2nd round - Fredrikstad 1961 Lyn Oslo 1965 Vålerengens 1967 Lillestrøm 1979 Rosenborg 1987
Cup Winners Cup
Quarter-finals - Lyn Oslo 1969
UEFA Cup
2nd round - Vålerengens 1966 Skeid Oslo 1970 Rosenborg 1972 Viking Stavanger 1973 1983 Start Kristiansand 1978, Kongsvinger IL 1994

CLUB DIRECTORY

OSLO (Population - 720,000)

Frigg SK Oslo (1904)
(Sport Klubben)
Voldsløkka 4,000 – Blue/White

SOFK Lyn Oslo (1896)
(Ski og Fotball Klubb)
Ullevål 26,000 – Red, broad white stripe/Blue

FK Skeid Oslo (1915)
(Fotball Klubben)
Ullevål 26,000 – Red/Black

Vålerengens IF Oslo (1913)
(Idrettsførening)
Ullevål 26,000 – Blue/White, red trim

BERGEN (Population - 239,000)

SK Brann Bergen (1908)
Brann 25,000 – Red, white sleeves/White

Fyllingen IL (1946)
(Idrettslag)
Varden Kunstgressbane 8,000 – Yellow/Blue

TRONDHEIM (Population - 134,000)

Rosenborg BK Trondheim (1917)
(Ball Klubb)
Lerkendal 28,000 – White/Black

STAVANGER (Population - 132,000)

Bryne IL Stavanger (1926)
Bryne 12,000 – Red with white sleeves/White

Viking FK Stavanger (1899)
Stavanger 18,000 – Blue/White

SKIEN (Population - 77,000)
Odd SK Skien (1894)
Falkum – White/Black

DRAMMEN (Population - 73,000)
Strømgodset IF (1907)
Marienlyst 15,000 – Blue/White

KRISTIANSAND (Population - 62,000)
IK Start Kristiansand (1905)
(Idretts Klubben)
Kristiansand 15,000 – Yellow/Black

FREDRIKSTAD (Population 52,000)
Fredrikstad FK (1903)
Fredrikstad 16,000 – White/Red

TROMSO (Population - 47,000)
Tromsø IL (1920)
Alfheim 10,000 – Red & white stripes/White

LILLESTROM
Lillestrøm SK (1917)
Åråsen 12,000 – Yellow/Black

MOSS (Population - 24,000)
Moss FK (1906)
Melløs 12,000 – Yellow/Black

KONGSVINGER
Kongsvinger IL (1892)
Gjemselund 7,000 – Red/White

MJONDALEN
Mjøndalen IF (1910)
Nedre Eiker 15,000 – Brown/White

MOLDE (Population - 21,000)
Molde FK (1911)
Molde 14,000 – Blue/White

SARPSBORG
FK Sarpsborg (1903)
Sarpsborg 20,000 – Blue/White

BODO (Population - 35,000)
SOFK Bodø-Glimt (1916)
Aspmyra 10,000 – Yellow/Black

HORTEN
Ørn FK (1904)
Lystlunden – Brown/White

GJOVIK
Gjøvik Lyn (1902)
Gjövik – Red/White

LARVIK
Larvik Turn IF (1906)
Luisenlund – White/Blue

HAUGESUND (Population - 27,000)
SK Haugar (1947)
Haugersund 15,000 – Blue/White

NORWEGIAN LEAGUE CHAMPIONSHIP

1938 Fredrikstad FK ....0-0 4-0 ....SOFK Lyn Oslo
1939 Fredrikstad FK ....2-1 ....FK Skeid Oslo
1940-47 -
1948 Freidig SK.........................2-1 ....Sparta Sarpsborg
1949 Fredrikstad FK ....3-1 3-0 ....Vålerengens IF Oslo
1950 Fram Larvik....................1-1 1-0 ....Fredrikstad FK
1951 Fredrikstad FK ....4-2 3-1 ....Odd SK Skien
1952 Fredrikstad FK ....3-1 ....SK Brann Bergen
1953 Larvik Turn IF...................3-2 ....FK Skeid Oslo
1954 Fredrikstad FK ....2-1 ....FK Skeid Oslo
1955 Larvik Turn IF...................4-2 ....Fredrikstad FK
1956 Larvik Turn IF...................3-2 ....Fredrikstad FK
1957 Fredrikstad FK ....6-1 ....Odd SK Skien
1958 Viking FK Stavanger ....2-0 ....FK Skeid Oslo
1959 Lillestrøm SK..................2-2 4-1 ....Fredrikstad FK
1960 Fredrikstad FK ....6-2 ....Lillestrøm SK
1961 Fredrikstad FK ....2-0 ....IF Eik

1962q SK Brann Bergen 46 Steinkjer IFK 41 Fredrikstad FK 41
1963h SK Brann Bergen 24 SOFK Lyn Oslo 23 FK Skeid Oslo 20
1964 SOFK Lyn Oslo 26 Fredrikstad FK 24 FK Sarpsborg 23
1965 Vålerengens IF Oslo 27 SOFK Lyn Oslo 26 FK Sarpsborg 23
1966 FK Skeid Oslo 25 Fredrikstad FK 24 SOFK Lyn Oslo 21
1967 Rosenborg BK 25 FK Skeid Oslo 22 SOFK Lyn Oslo 21
1968 SOFK Lyn Oslo 28 Rosenborg BK 24 Viking FK Stavanger 21
1969 Rosenborg BK 27 Fredrikstad FK 22 IF Stromgodset 22
1970 IF Stromgodset 25 Rosenborg BK 24 Hamarkameratene 23
1971 Rosenborg BK 24 SOFK Lyn Oslo 23 Viking FK Stavanger 22
1972k Viking FK Stavanger 34 Fredrikstad FK 34 IF Stromgodset 27
1973 Viking FK Stavanger 32 Rosenborg BK 27 Start Kristiansand 26
1974 Viking FK Stavanger 31 Molde FK 30 Vålerengens IF Oslo 28
1975 Viking FK Stavanger 30 SK Brann Bergen 27 Start Kristiansand 27
1976 Lillestrøm SK 31 Mjondalen IF 30 SK Brann Bergen 28
1977 Lillestrøm SK 36 SOFK Bodø-Glimt 28 Molde FK 27
1978 Start Kristiansand 33 Lillestrøm SK 31 Viking FK Stavanger 31
1979 Viking FK Stavanger 32 Moss FK 30 Start Kristiansand 27
1980 Start Kristiansand 29 Bryne IL 29 Lillestrøm SK 27
1981 Vålerengens IF Oslo 29 Viking FK Stavanger 28 Rosenborg BK 26
1982 Viking FK Stavanger 29 Bryne IL 26 Lillestrøm SK 25
1983 Vålerengens IF Oslo 31 Lillestrøm SK 28 Start Kristiansand 27
1984 Vålerengens IF Oslo 32 Viking FK Stavanger 25 Start Kristiansand 25
1985 Rosenberg BK 33 Lillestrøm SK 32 Vålerengens IF Oslo 24
1986 Lillestrøm SK 33 Mjondalen IF 27 Kongsvinger IL 27
1987k2 Moss FK 44 Molde FK 41 Kongsvinger IL 39
1988k3 Rosenborg BK 47 Lillestrøm SK 40 Molde FK 39
1989 Lillestrøm SK 52 Rosenborg BK 44 Tromsø IL 37
1990 Rosenborg BK 44 Tromsø IL 42 Molde FK 40
1991 Viking FK Stavanger 41 Rosenborg BK 36 Start Kristiansand 34
1992 Rosenborg BK 46 Kongsvinger IL 40 Start Kristiansand 39
1993 Rosenborg BK 47 FK Bodø/Glimt 45 Lillestrøm SK 42
1994 Rosenborg BK 49 Lillestrøm SK 41 Viking FK Stavanger 39

NORWEGIAN CUP FINALS

1902 Grane Nordstrand..........2-0 ....Odd SK Skien
1903 Odd SK Skien....................1-0 ....Grand Nordstrand
1904 Odd SK Skien....................4-0 ....IF Uradd
1905 Odd SK Skien....................2-1 ....Akademisk FK Oslo
1906 Odd SK Skien....................1-0 ....FK Sarpsborg
1907 Mercantile ....3-0 ....FK Sarpsborg
1908 SOFK Lyn Oslo ....3-2 ....Odd SK Skien
1909 SOFK Lyn Oslo ....4-3 ....Odd SK Skien
1910 SOFK Lyn Oslo ....4-2 ....Odd SK Skien
1911 SOFK Lyn Oslo ....5-2 ....IF Uradd
1912 Mercantile ....6-0 ....Fram Larvik
1913 Odd SK Skien....................2-1 ....Mercantile
1914 Frigg SK Oslo ....4-2 ....Gjøvik Lyn
1915 Odd SK Skien....................2-1 ....Kvik Halden
1916 Frigg SK Oslo ....2-0 ....Ørn FK Horten
1917 FK Sarpsborg.....................4-1 ....SK Brann Bergen
1918 Kvik Halden ....4-0 ....SK Brann Bergen
1919 Odd SK Skien....................1-0 ....Frigg SK Oslo
1920 Örn FK Horten ....1-0 ....Frigg SK Oslo
1921 Frigg SK Oslo ....2-0 ....Odd SK Skien
1922 Odd SK Skien....................5-1 ....Kvik Halden
1923 SK Brann Bergen ....2-1 ....SOFK Lyn Oslo
1924 Odd SK Skien....................3-0 ....Mjøndalen IF
1925 SK Brann Bergen ....3-0 ....FK Sarpsborg

1926	Odd SK Skien	3-0	Örn FK Horten
1927	Örn FK Horten	4-0	Drafn SK
1928	Örn FK Horten	2-1	SOFK Lyn Oslo
1929	FK Sarpsborg	2-1	Orn FK Horten
1930	Örn FK Horten	4-2	Drammens BK
1931	Odd SK Skien	3-1	Mjøndalen IF
1932	Fredrikstad FK	6-1	Örn FK Horten
1933	Mjøndalen IF	3-1	Viking FK Stavanger
1934	Mjøndalen IF	2-1	FK Sarpsborg
1935	Fredrikstad FK	4-0	FK Sarpsborg
1936	Fredrikstad FK	2-0	Mjøndalen IF
1937	Mjøndalen IF	4-2	Odd SK Skien
1938	Fredrikstad FK	3-2	Mjøndalen IF
1939	FK Sarpsborg	2-1	FK Skeid Oslo
1940	Fredrikstad FK	3-0	FK Skeid Oslo
1941-44	-		
1945	SOFK Lyn Oslo	1-1 1-1 4-0	Fredrikstad FK
1946	SOFK Lyn Oslo	3-2	Fredrikstad FK
1947	FK Skeid Oslo	2-0	Viking FK Stavanger
1948	FK Sarpsborg	1-0	Fredrikstad SK
1949	FK Sarpsborg	3-1	FK Skeid Oslo
1950	Fredrikstad FK	3-0	SK Brann Bergen
1951	FK Sarpsborg	3-2	Asker
1952	Sparta Sarpsborg	3-2	Solberg
1953	Viking FK Stavanger	2-1	Lillestrøm SK
1954	FK Skeid Oslo	3-0	Fredrikstad FK
1955	FK Skeid Oslo	5-0	Lillestrøm SK
1956	FK Skeid Oslo	2-1	Larvik Turn IF
1957	Fredrikstad FK	4-0	Sandefjord BK
1958	FK Skeid Oslo	1-0	Lillestrøm SK
1959	Viking FK Stavanger	2-1	Sandefjord BK
1960	Rosenborg BK	3-3 3-2	Odd SK Skien
1961	Fredrikstad FK	7-0	SK Haugar
1962	Gjøvik Lyn	2-0	SK Vard Haugesund
1963	FK Skeid Oslo	2-1	Fredrikstad FK
1964	Rosenborg BK	2-1	FK Sarpsborg
1965	FK Skeid Oslo	2-2 1-1 2-1	Frigg SK Oslo
1966	Fredrikstad FK	3-2	SOFK Lyn Oslo
1967	SOFK Lyn Oslo	4-1	Rosenberg BK
1968	SOFK Lyn Oslo	3-0	Mjøndalen IF
1969	IF Stromsgodset	2-2 5-3	Fredrikstad FK
1970	IF Stromsgodset	4-2	SOFK Lyn Oslo
1971	Rosenborg BK	4-1	Fredrikstad FK
1972	SK Brann Bergen	1-0	Rosenborg BK
1973	IF Stromsgodset	1-0	Rosenborg BK
1974	FK Skeid Oslo	3-1	Viking FK Stavanger
1975	SOFK Bodø-Glimt	2-0	SK Vard Haugesund
1976	SK Brann Bergen	2-1	Sogndal IL
1977	Lillestrøm SK	1-0	SOFK Bodø-Glimt
1978	Lillestrøm SK	2-1	SK Brann Bergen
1979	Viking FK Stavanger	2-1	SK Haugar
1980	Vålerengens IF Oslo	4-1	Lillestrøm SK
1981	Lillestrøm SK	3-1	Moss FK
1982	SK Brann Bergen	3-2	Molde FK
1983	Moss FK	2-0	Vålerengens IF Oslo
1984	Fredrikstad FK	3-3 3-2	Viking FK Stavanger
1985	Lillestrøm SK	4-1	Vålerengens IF Oslo
1986	Tromsø IL	4-1	Lillestrøm SK
1987	Bryne IL Stavanger	1-0	SK Brann Bergen
1988	Rosenberg BK	2-2 2-0	SK Brann Bergen
1989	Viking FK Stavanger	2-2 2-1	Molde FK
1990	Rosenborg BK	5-1	Fyllingen
1991	IF Stromsgodset	3-2	Rosenborg BK
1992	Rosenborg BK	3-2	Lillestrøm SK
1993	FK Bodø/Glimt	2-0	IF Stromsgodset
1994	Molde FK	3-2	SOFK Lyn Oslo

LEADING INTERNATIONAL GOALSCORERS

33	Jørgen Juve	(SOFK Lyn)	1928-1937
26	Einar Gundersen	(Tonsberg Turn,Odd BK)	1917-1928
25	Harald Hennum	(Frigg FK,Skeid)	1949-1960
22	Gunnar Thoresen	(Larvik Turn IF)	1946-1958
20	Jan Åge Fjørtoft	(Hamarkameratene, Lillestrøm,Rapid Wein, Swindon)	1986-
19	Odd Iversen	(Rosenborg BK,RC Mechelen, Vålerengens)	1967-1979
	Olav Nilsen	(Viking)	1962-1971
18	Odd Wang Sørensen	(Sparta Sarpsborg)	1947-1955
17	Arne Brustad	(SOFK Lyn)	1921-1933
	Reidar Kvammen	(Viking FK)	1933-1949
15	Gøran Sørloth	(Rosenborg,Mönchengladbach, Rosenborg,Bursaspor)	1985-

LEADING INTERNATIONAL APPEARANCES

104	Thorbjørn Svenssen	(Sandefjord BK)	1947-1962
92	Erik Thorstvedt	(Viking FK,Bor. Mönchenglad, IFK Gøteborg,Tottenham)	1982-
77	Svein Grondalen	(Raufoss IL,Rosenborg BK, Moss FK)	1973-1984
66	Terje Kojedal	(Hamarkameratene,Mulhouse, Valenciennes)	1981-1989
64	Gunnar Thoresen	(Larvik Turn IF)	1946-1958
62	Olav Nilsen	(Viking FK)	1962-1971
61	Roar Johansen	(Fredrikstad FK)	1958-1967
60	Rune Bratseth	(Rosenborg BK,Werder Bremen)	1986-1994
60	Jan Åge Fjørtoft	(Hamarkamertatene,Lillestrøm, Rapid Wien,Swindon)	1986-
58	Harry Boye Karlsen	(Orn FK,SOFK Lyn,Larvik Turn IF)	1946-1956

INTERNATIONAL MATCHES PLAYED BY NORWAY

12-07-1908	Sweden	L 3-11	Gothenburg	Fr	Enderud, Bøhn 2
11-09-1910	Sweden	L 0-4	Oslo	Fr	
17-09-1911	Sweden	L 1-4	Stockholm	Fr	Nysted
16-06-1912	Sweden	L 1-2	Oslo	Fr	Maartmann.R
23-06	Hungary	L 0-6	Oslo	Fr	
30-06	Denmark	L 0-7	Stockholm	OGqf	
1-07	Austria	L 0-1	Stockholm	OGct	
3-11	Sweden	L 2-4	Gothenburg	Fr	Ditlev-Simonsen.H 2
8-06-1913	Sweden	L 0-9	Stockholm	Fr	
14-09	Tsarist Russia	D 1-1	Moscow	Fr	Lauritzen
26-10	Sweden	D 1-1	Oslo	Fr	Skou
28-06-1914	Sweden	L 0-1	Oslo	Fr	

Date	Opponent	Result	Venue	Type	Scorers
12-07	Tsarist Russia	D 1-1	Oslo	Fr	Maartmann.R
25-10	Sweden	L 0-7	Stockholm	Fr	
27-06-1915	Sweden	D 1-1	Oslo	Fr	Engebretsen
19-09	Denmark	L 1-8	Copenhagen	Fr	Ditlev-Simonsen.H
24-10	Sweden	L 2-5	Stockholm	Fr	Ditlev-Simonsen.H, Wold
25-06-1916	Denmark	L 0-2	Oslo	Fr	
2-07	Sweden	L 0-6	Stockholm	Fr	
3-09	USA	D 1-1	Oslo	Fr	Engebretsen
1-10	Sweden	D 0-0	Oslo	Fr	
15-10	Denmark	L 0-8	Copenhagen	Fr	
17-06-1917	Denmark	L 1-2	Oslo	Fr	Helgesen
19-08	Sweden	D 3-3	Halsingborg	Fr	Gundersen.E 2, Aas
16-09	Sweden	L 0-2	Oslo	Fr	
7-10	Denmark	L 0-12	Copenhagen	Fr	
26-05-1918	Sweden	L 0-2	Stockholm	Fr	
16-06	Denmark	W 3-1	Oslo	Fr	Helgesen, Helsing, Gundersen.E
15-09	Sweden	W 2-1	Oslo	Fr	Gundersen.E 2
6-10	Denmark	L 0-4	Copenhagen	Fr	
12-06-1919	Denmark	L 1-5	Copenhagen	Fr	Helgesen
29-06	Sweden	W 4-3	Oslo	Fr	Engebretsen 2, Wold, Gundersen.E
31-08	Holland	D 1-1	Oslo	Fr	Engebretsen
14-09	Sweden	W 5-1	Gothenburg	Fr	Engebretsen 3, Wold, Gundersen.E
21-09	Denmark	W 3-2	Oslo	Fr	Gundersen.E 2, Helgesen
13-06-1920	Denmark	D 1-1	Oslo	Fr	Gundersen.E
27-06	Sweden	L 0-3	Oslo	Fr	
28-08	England *	W 3-1	Antwerp	OGr1	Gundersen.E 2, Wilhelms
29-08	Czechoslovakia	L 0-4	Brussels	OGqf	
31-08	Italy	L 1-2	Antwerp	OGct	Andersen.A
26-09	Sweden	D 0-0	Stockholm	Fr	
25-05-1921	Finland	W 3-2	Oslo	Fr	Paulsen.M, Berstad 2
19-06	Sweden	W 3-1	Oslo	Fr	Gundersen.E, Resberg, Strøm
18-09	Sweden	W 3-0	Stockholm	Fr	Gundersen.E, Wilhelms, Holm
2-10	Denmark	L 1-3	Copenhagen	Fr	Helgesen
23-08-1922	Sweden	D 0-0	Stockholm	Fr	
26-08	Finland	W 3-1	Helsinki	Fr	Gundersen.E, Strøm, Nielsen.W
10-09	Denmark	D 3-3	Fredrikstad	Fr	Gundersen.E, Aas, Wilhelms
24-09	Sweden	L 0-5	Oslo	Fr	
17-06-1923	Finland	W 3-0	Oslo	Fr	Strøm 2, Johnsen
21-06	Switzerland	D 2-2	Oslo	Fr	Berstad, Johnsen
16-09	Sweden	L 2-3	Oslo	Fr	Wilhelms, Ulrichsen
30-09	Denmark	L 1-2	Copenhagen	Fr	Johnsen
28-10	France	W 2-0	Paris	Fr	Berstad, Wilhelms
4-11	Germany	L 0-1	Hamburg	Fr	
15-06-1924	Germany	L 0-2	Oslo	Fr	
23-08	Finland	L 0-2	Helsinki	Fr	
14-09	Denmark	L 1-3	Oslo	Fr	Berstad
21-09	Sweden	L 1-6	Stockholm	Fr	Berstad
7-06-1925	Finland	W 1-0	Oslo	Fr	Olsen.A
21-06	Denmark	L 1-5	Copenhagen	Fr	Lunde
23-08	Sweden	L 3-7	Oslo	Fr	Berstad 2, Lunde
6-06-1926	Finland	W 5-2	Helsinki	Fr	Gundersen.E 3, Andersen.A, Jacobsen.E
9-06	Sweden	L 2-3	Stockholm	Fr	Andersen.A, Gundersen.E
19-09	Denmark	D 2-2	Oslo	Fr	Gundersen.E, Berstad
7-10	Poland	L 3-4	Fredrikstad	Fr	Andersen.A, Steen 2
29-05-1927	Denmark	L 0-1	Oslo	Fr	
15-06	Finland	W 3-1	Oslo	Fr	Møller, Strøm, Berstad
26-06	Sweden	L 3-5	Oslo	Fr	Berstad 2, Gundersen.E
23-10	Germany	L 2-6	Hamburg	Fr	Dahl, Gundersen.E
30-10	Denmark	L 1-3	Copenhagen	Fr	Gundersen.E
3-06-1928	Finland	W 6-0	Helsinki	Fr	Gundersen.E 2, Andersen.E (I) 2, Andersen.S, Helgesen
7-06	Sweden	L 1-6	Stockholm	Fr	Helgesen
17-06	Denmark	L 2-3	Oslo	Fr	Berstad, Andersen.S
23-09	Germany	L 0-2	Oslo	Fr	
28-05-1929	Scotland	L 3-7	Oslo	Fr	Kongsvik 2, Berg-Johannesen
12-06	Holland	D 4-4	Oslo	Fr	Juve 3, Andersen.E (I)
18-06	Finland	W 4-0	Oslo	Fr	Juve 2, Berg-Johannesen, Andersen.E (II)
23-06	Denmark	W 5-2	Copenhagen	Fr	Juve 2, Berg-Johannesen, Andersen.E (II)
29-09	Sweden	W 2-1	Oslo	Fr	Juve, Gundersen.O
3-11	Holland	W 4-1	Amsterdam	Fr	Juve 2, Berg-Johannesen 2
1-06-1930	Finland	W 6-2	Oslo	Fr	Juve 3, Pettersen.M 2, Pettersen.H
19-06	Switzerland	W 3-0	Oslo	Fr	Juve 2, Krupp

Date	Opponent	Result	Venue	Comp	Scorers
6-07	Sweden	L 3-6	Stockholm	Fr	Juve 3
21-09	Denmark	W 1-0	Oslo	Fr	Kongsvik
2-11	Germany	D 1-1	Breslau	Fr	Nielsen.A
25-05-1931	Denmark	L 1-3	Copenhagen	Fr	Juve
21-06	Germany	D 2-2	Oslo	Fr	Moe 2
6-09	Finland	D 4-4	Helsinki	Fr	Børresen.A, Børresen.L, Pettersen.M, Johannesen.F
27-09	Sweden	W 2-1	Oslo	Fr	Juve, Andersen.E (I)
5-06-1932	Estonia	W 3-0	Oslo	Fr	Juve 2, Pedersen
17-06	Finland	W 2-1	Oslo	Fr	Johannesen.F 2
1-07	Sweden	W 4-1	Gothenburg	Fr	Juve 2, Moe 2
25-09	Denmark	L 1-2	Oslo	Fr	Juve
11-06-1933	Denmark	D 2-2	Copenhagen	Fr	Pedersen 2
3-09	Finland	W 5-1	Helsinki	Fr	Juve 3, Hansen.F, OG
24-09	Sweden	L 0-1	Oslo	Fr	
5-11	Germany	D 2-2	Magdeburg	Fr	Juve, Kvammen.A
1-07-1934	Sweden	D 3-3	Stockholm	Fr	Pettersen.M, Pedersen.B Svendsen
2-09	Finland	W 4-2	Oslo	Fr	Kvammen, Hansen.S, Berglie 2
23-09	Denmark	W 3-1	Oslo	Fr	Hansen.S 2, Berglie
23-06-1935	Denmark	L 0-1	Copenhagen	Fr	
27-06	Germany	D 1-1	Oslo	Fr	Hoel
8-09	Finland	W 5-1	Helsinki	Fr	Hoel 3, Jamissen, Kvammen
22-09	Sweden	L 0-2	Oslo	Fr	
3-11	Switzerland	L 0-2	Zurich	Fr	
18-06-1936	Switzerland	L 1-2	Oslo	Fr	Hansen.S
5-07	Sweden	L 0-2	Gothenburg	Fr	
26-07	Sweden	W 4-3	Stockholm	Fr	Kvammen 3, Isaksen
3-08	Turkey	W 4-0	Berlin	OGr1	Martinsen 2, Kvammen, Brustad
7-08	Germany	W 2-0	Berlin	OGqf	Isaksen 2
10-08	Italy	L 1-2	Berlin	OGsf	Brustad
13-08	Poland	W 3-2	Berlin	OG3p	Brustad 3
6-09	Finland	L 0-2	Oslo	Fr	
30-09	Denmark	D 3-3	Oslo	Fr	Frantzen 2, Brustad
1-11	Holland	D 3-3	Amsterdam	Fr	Martinsen, Brustad 2
14-05-1937	England	L 0-6	Oslo	Fr	
27-05	Italy	L 1-3	Oslo	Fr	Danielsen
13-06	Denmark	L 1-5	Copenhagen	Fr	Martinsen
5-09	Finland	W 2-0	Helsinki	Fr	Martinsen 2
19-09	Sweden	W 3-2	Oslo	Fr	Kvammen, Brustad, Isaksen
10-10	Rep. Ireland	W 3-2	Oslo	WCq	Kvammen 2, Martinsen
24-10	Germany	L 0-3	Berlin	Fr	
7-11	Rep. Ireland	D 3-3	Dublin	WCq	Kvammen 2, Martinsen
31-05-1938	Estonia	W 1-0	Oslo	Fr	Brustad
5-06	Italy	L 1-2	Marseilles	WCr1	Brustad
17-06	Finland	W 9-0	Oslo	Fr	Brustad 4, Kvammen 2, Arnesen, Isaksen, Andersen.T
4-09	Sweden	W 2-1	Oslo	Fr	Arnesen, Brynildsen
18-09	Denmark	D 1-1	Oslo	Fr	Arnesen
2-10	Sweden	W 3-2	Stockholm	Fr	Brustad, Brynildsen, Nordahl
23-10	Poland	D 2-2	Warsaw	Fr	Martinsen, Nordahl
9-11	England	L 0-4	Newcastle	Fr	
3-06-1939	Sweden	L 2-3	Stockholm	Fr	Frantzen 2
14-06	Sweden	W 1-0	Copenhagen	Fr	Martinsen
18-06	Denmark	L 3-6	Copenhagen	Fr	Brustad, Kvammen, Frantzen
22-06	Germany	L 0-4	Oslo	Fr	
3-09	Finland	W 2-1	Helsinki	Fr	Andersen.T 2
17-09	Sweden	L 2-3	Oslo	Fr	Navestad, Yven
22-10	Denmark	L 1-4	Copenhagen	Fr	Brynildsen
26-08-1945	Denmark	L 2-4	Copenhagen	Fr	Spydevold, Moe.K
9-09	Denmark	L 1-5	Oslo	Fr	Brynildsen
21-10	Sweden	L 0-10	Stockholm	Fr	
16-06-1946	Denmark	W 2-1	Oslo	Fr	Nordahl, Osnes
28-06	Finland	W 12-0	Bergen	Fr	Thoresen 3, Sätrange 3, Kvammen 2, Osnes 2, Nordahl 2
8-07	Denmark	L 0-2	Copenhagen	Fr	
28-07	Luxembourg	L 2-3	Luxembourg	Fr	Dahlen.K, Johannessen
15-09	Sweden	L 0-3	Oslo	Fr	
20-10	Denmark	L 1-7	Copenhagen	Fr	Brynildsen
11-06-1947	Poland	W 3-1	Oslo	Fr	Brynildsen 2, Arnesen
26-06	Finland	W 2-1	Helsinki	Fr	Karlsen, Johannessen
28-06	Sweden	L 1-5	Helsinki	Fr	Brynildsen
24-07	Iceland	W 4-2	Reykjavik	Fr	Thoresen 2, Brynildsen, Sätrang
7-09	Finland	D 3-3	Helsinki	Fr	Brynildsen, Sørensen, Dahlen.G

Date	Opponent	Result	Venue	Comp	Scorers
21-09	Denmark	L 3-5	Oslo	Fr	Osnes 2, Thoresen
5-10	Sweden	L 1-4	Stockholm	Fr	Kvammen
26-05-1948	Holland	L 1-2	Oslo	Fr	Sørensen
12-06	Denmark	W 2-1	Copenhagen	Fr	Sørdahl
6-08	United States	W 11-0	Oslo	Fr	Sørensen 5, Thoresen 3, Sørdahl 2, Dahlen.G
5-09	Finland	W 2-0	Oslo	Fr	Sørensen 2
19-09	Sweden	L 3-5	Oslo	Fr	Thoresen, Sørdahl, Dahlen.G
24-12	Egypt	D 1-1	Cairo	Fr	Sørensen
18-05-1949	England	L 1-4	Oslo	Fr	Andresen
19-06	Yugoslavia	L 1-3	Oslo	Fr	Bredesen
8-07	Finland	D 1-1	Helsinki	Fr	Sørensen
11-09	Denmark	L 0-2	Oslo	Fr	
2-10	Sweden	D 3-3	Stockholm	Fr	Bredesen 2, Hennum
22-06-1950	Denmark	L 0-4	Copenhagen	Fr	
15-08	Luxembourg	D 2-2	Bergen	Fr	Thoresen, Andersen.H
10-09	Finland	W 4-1	Oslo	Fr	Andresen 2, Bredesen, Thoresen
24-09	Sweden	L 1-3	Oslo	Fr	Karlsen
5-11	Yugoslavia	L 0-4	Belgrade	Fr	
26-11	Rep. Ireland	D 2-2	Dublin	Fr	Bredesen, Andresen
30-05-1951	Rep. Ireland	L 2-3	Oslo	Fr	Hvidsten, Sørensen
6-06	Holland	W 3-2	Rotterdam	Fr	Johannessen 2, Sørensen
26-07	Iceland	W 3-1	Trondheim	Fr	Hennum, Hvidsten, OG
16-08	Finland	D 1-1	Helsinki	Fr	Bredesen
23-08	Yugoslavia	L 2-4	Oslo	Fr	Dybwad 2
16-09	Denmark	W 2-0	Oslo	Fr	Thoresen, OG
30-09	Sweden	W 4-3	Gothenburg	Fr	Karlsen 2, Bredesen, Dahlen.G
10-06-1952	Finland	L 1-2	Oslo	Fr	Johannessen
25-06	Yugoslavia	L 1-4	Zagreb	Fr	Sørensen
21-07	Sweden	L 1-4	Tammerfors	OGr1	Sørensen
31-08	Finland	W 7-2	Oslo	Fr	Kristiansen 3, Sørensen 2, Thoresen 2
5-10	Sweden	L 1-2	Oslo	Fr	Johannessen
19-10	Denmark	W 3-1	Copenhagen	Fr	Nordahl, Sørensen, Jevne
24-06-1953	Saar	L 2-3	Oslo	WCq	Thoresen, Dahlen.K
13-08	Iceland	W 3-1	Bergen	Fr	Dybwad, Kristiansen, Thoresen
19-08	West Germany	D 1-1	Oslo	WCq	Hennum
30-08	Finland	W 4-1	Helsinki	Fr	Thoresen 2, Hennum, Hansen.PA
13-09	Denmark	L 0-1	Oslo	Fr	
27-09	Holland	W 4-0	Oslo	Fr	Thoresen 2, Dybwad, Nordahl
18-10	Sweden	D 0-0	Stockholm	Fr	
8-11	Saar	D 0-0	Saarbrucken	WCq	
22-11	West Germany	L 1-5	Hamburg	WCq	Nordahl
5-05-1954	Scotland	L 0-1	Glasgow	Fr	
19-05	Scotland	D 1-1	Oslo	Fr	Kure
30-05	Austria	L 0-5	Vienna	Fr	
4-06	Denmark	W 2-1	Malmo	Fr	Kure, Ljostveit
7-06	Sweden	L 0-3	Stockholm	Fr	
4-07	Iceland	L 0-1	Reykjavik	Fr	
29-08	Finland	W 3-1	Oslo	Fr	Hennum, Dybwad, Johannessen
19-09	Sweden	D 1-1	Oslo	Fr	Sundby
31-10	Denmark	W 1-0	Copenhagen	Fr	Hennum
8-11	Rep. Ireland	L 1-2	Dublin	Fr	Olsen.W
8-05-1955	Hungary	L 0-5	Oslo	Fr	
25-05	Rep. Ireland	L 1-3	Oslo	Fr	Kotte
12-06	Romania	L 0-1	Oslo	Fr	
14-08	Finland	W 3-1	Helsinki	Fr	Hennum 2, Kure
11-09	Denmark	D 1-1	Oslo	Fr	OG
25-09	Sweden	D 1-1	Stockholm	Fr	OG
6-11	Holland	L 0-3	Amsterdam	Fr	
16-11	West Germany	L 0-2	Karlsruhe	Fr	
30-05-1956	Poland	D 0-0	Oslo	Fr	
13-06	West Germany	L 1-3	Oslo	Fr	Dybwad
24-06	Denmark	W 3-2	Copenhagen	Fr	Sandengen 2, Dybwad
26-06	Romania	L 0-2	Bucharest	Fr	
26-08	Finland	D 1-1	Oslo	Fr	Hølvik
16-09	Sweden	W 3-1	Oslo	Fr	Gundersen.F 2, Kure
28-10	Poland	L 3-5	Warsaw	Fr	Dybwad 2, Kure
22-05-1957	Bulgaria	L 1-2	Oslo	WCq	Hennum
12-06	Hungary	W 2-1	Oslo	WCq	Hennum, Kristiansen
18-06	Sweden	D 0-0	Turku	Fr	
19-06	Denmark	L 0-2	Tammerfors	Fr	
8-07	Iceland	W 3-0	Reykjavik	Fr	Dybwad, Kristiansen, Legernes

1-09	Finland	W 4-0	Helsinki	Fr	Kristiansen 2, Hennum, Kristoffersen
22-09	Denmark	D 2-2	Oslo	Fr	Kristoffersen
13-10	Sweden	L 2-5	Stockholm	Fr	Hennum, Thoresen
3-11	Bulgaria	L 0-7	Sofia	WCq	
10-11	Hungary	L 0-5	Budapest	WCq	
28-05-1958	Holland	D 0-0	Oslo	Fr	
15-06	Finland	W 2-0	Oslo	Fr	Hennum, Pedersen.A
29-06	Denmark	W 2-1	Copenhagen	Fr	Borgen, Pedersen.A
13-08	East Germany	W 6-5	Oslo	Fr	Hennum 4, Pedersen.A 2
14-09	Sweden	L 0-2	Oslo	Fr	
2-11	East Germany	L 1-4	Leipzig	Fr	Hennum
20-05-1959	Austria	L 0-1	Oslo	ECr1	
17-06	Luxembourg	W 1-0	Oslo	Fr	Hennum
28-06	Finland	W 4-2	Helsinki	Fr	Hennum 2, Borgen, Larsen.R (I)
2-07	Denmark	L 1-2	Copenhagen	OGq	Pedersen.RB
7-07	Iceland	L 0-1	Reykjavik	OGq	
21-08	Iceland	W 2-1	Oslo	OGq	Kristiansen, Backe
13-09	Denmark	L 2-4	Oslo	OGq	Sørensen.A, Kristiansen
23-09	Austria	L 2-5	Vienna	ECr1	Ødegarrd 2
18-10	Sweden	L 2-6	Gothenburg	Fr	Backe, Hennum
4-11	Holland	L 1-7	Rotterdam	Fr	Kristoffersen
26-05-1960	Denmark	L 0-3	Copenhagen	Fr	
9-06	Iceland	W 4-0	Oslo	Fr	Larsen.R (II), Backe, Dybwad, Borgen
22-06	Austria	L 1-2	Oslo	Fr	Backe
28-08	Finland	W 6-3	Oslo	Fr	Berg.A 2, Pedersen.RB 2, Hennum, Jensen
18-09	Sweden	W 3-1	Oslo	Fr	Borgen, Pedersen.RB, Hennum
6-11	Rep. Ireland	L 1-3	Dublin	Fr	Hennum
16-05-1961	Mexico	D 1-1	Bergen	Fr	Backe
1-06	Turkey	L 0-1	Oslo	WCq	
27-06	Finland	L 1-4	Helsinki	Fr	Pedersen.RB
1-07	Soviet Union	L 2-5	Moscow	WCq	Borgen, Hansen.E
23-08	Soviet Union	L 0-3	Oslo	WCq	
17-09	Denmark	L 0-4	Oslo	Fr	
22-10	Sweden	L 0-2	Gothenburg	Fr	
29-10	Turkey	L 1-2	Istanbul	WCq	Jensen
5-11	Malta	D 1-1	Gzira	Fr	Kotte
16-05-1962	Holland	W 2-1	Oslo	Fr	Borgen, Jensen
11-06	Denmark	L 1-6	Copenhagen	Fr	Andersen.T
21-06	Sweden	L 0-2	Oslo	ECr1	
3-07	Malta	W 5-0	Trondheim	Fr	Nilsen 3, Pedersen.A, Krogh
9-07	Iceland	W 3-1	Reykjavik	Fr	Nilsen 2, Pedersen.A
26-08	Finland	W 2-1	Bergen	Fr	Nilsen, Larsen.R (II)
16-09	Sweden	W 2-1	Oslo	Fr	Jensen, Johansen.E
4-11	Sweden	D 1-1	Malmo	ECr1	Krogh
15-05-1963	Poland	L 2-5	Oslo	Fr	Krogh, Pedersen.A
4-06	Scotland	W 4-3	Bergen	Fr	Krogh, Nilsen, Pedersen.A, Johansen.E
27-06	Finland	L 0-2	Helsinki	Fr	
14-08	Sweden	D 0-0	Gothenburg	Fr	
4-09	Poland	L 0-9	Szezecin	Fr	
15-09	Denmark	L 0-4	Oslo	Fr	
3-11	Switzerland	W 2-0	Zurich	Fr	Jensen, Johansen.E
7-11	Scotland	L 1-6	Glasgow	Fr	Kristoffersen
13-05-1964	Rep. Ireland	L 1-4	Oslo	Fr	Eriksen
1-07	Switzerland	W 3-2	Bergen	Fr	Larsen.EB, Nilsen, Johansen.E
20-08	Finland	W 2-0	Trondheim	Fr	Seeman, Berg.H
20-09	Sweden	D 1-1	Oslo	Fr	Seeman
11-10	Denmark	L 0-2	Copenhagen	Fr	
8-11	Luxembourg	W 2-0	Luxembourg	WCq	Berg.H, Johansen.E
11-11	France	L 0-1	Paris	WCq	
19-05-1965	Thailand	W 7-0	Bergen	Fr	Berg.H 3, Nilsen, Johansen.E, Pedersen.A, Kaspersen
27-05	Luxembourg	W 4-2	Trondheim	WCq	Pedersen.A, Johansen.E, Sjødberg, Kristoffersen
16-06	Yugoslavia	W 3-0	Oslo	WCq	Seeman, Nilsen, Berg.H
8-08	Finland	L 0-4	Helsinki	Fr	
15-09	France	L 0-1	Oslo	WCq	
26-09	Denmark	D 2-2	Oslo	Fr	Johansen.E, Stavrum
31-10	Sweden	D 0-0	Stockholm	Fr	
7-11	Yugoslavia	D 1-1	Belgrade	WCq	Stavrum
12-06-1966	Portugal	L 0-4	Lisbon	Fr	
26-06	Denmark	W 1-0	Copenhagen	Fr	Johansen.E
29-06	England	L 1-6	Oslo	Fr	Sunde
14-08	Finland	D 1-1	Stavanger	Fr	Pedersen.A

18-09	Sweden	L 2-4	Oslo	Fr	Berg.H, Hasund
13-11	Bulgaria	L 2-4	Sofia	ECq	Hasund 2
19-11	West Germany	L 0-3	Cologne	Fr	
1-06-1967	Finland	W 2-0	Helsinki	Fr	Nilsen 2
8-06	Portugal	L 1-2	Oslo	ECq	Iversen
29-06	Bulgaria	D 0-0	Oslo	ECq	
3-09	Sweden	W 3-1	Oslo	ECq	Berg.H, Sunde, Birkeland
24-09	Denmark	L 0-5	Oslo	Fr	
5-11	Sweden	L 2-5	Stockholm	ECq	Iversen, Nilsen
12-11	Portugal	L 1-2	Oporto	ECq	Nilsen
9-06-1968	Poland	L 1-6	Oslo	Fr	Sunde
23-06	Denmark	L 1-5	Copenhagen	Fr	Presberg
18-07	Iceland	W 4-0	Reykjavik	Fr	Berg.H 2, Olsen.OD, Nilsen
18-08	Finland	W 4-1	Oslo	Fr	Iversen 2, Berg.H, Olsen.OD
15-09	Sweden	D 1-1	Oslo	Fr	Olsen.OD
9-10	Sweden	L 0-5	Stockholm	WCq	
6-11	France	W 1-0	Strasbourg	WCq	Iversen
8-05-1969	Mexico	L 0-2	Oslo	Fr	
1-06	Sweden	L 2-4	Gothenburg	Fr	Iversen, Berg.H
19-06	Sweden	L 2-5	Oslo	WCq	Olsen.OD 2
3-07	Bermuda	W 3-0	Stavanger	Fr	Iversen 2, Olsen.OD
21-07	Iceland	W 2-1	Trondheim	Fr	Iversen, Nilsen
24-08	Finland	D 2-2	Helsinki	Fr	Iversen 2
27-08	Poland	L 1-6	Lodz	Fr	Iversen
10-09	France	L 1-3	Oslo	WCq	Olsen.OD
21-09	Denmark	W 2-0	Oslo	Fr	Olsen.OD, Säthrang
11-11	Mexico	L 0-4	Mexico City	Fr	
16-11	Guatemala	W 3-1	Guatemala City	Fr	Hestad 2, Spydevold
13-05-1970	Czechoslovakia	L 0-2	Oslo	Fr	
17-06	Finland	W 2-0	Bergen	Fr	Paulsen, Seemann
20-07	Iceland	L 0-2	Reykjavik	Fr	
13-09	Sweden	L 2-4	Oslo	Fr	Nilsen, Fuglset.T
21-09	Denmark	W 1-0	Copenhagen	Fr	Iversen
7-10	Hungary	L 1-3	Oslo	ECq	Iversen
11-11	France	L 1-3	Lyon	ECq	Nilsen
15-11	Bulgaria	D 1-1	Sofia	ECq	Fuglset.T
26-05-1971	Iceland	W 3-1	Bergen	Fr	Fuglset.J 2, Espeseth
9-06	Bulgaria	L 1-4	Oslo	ECq	Iversen
22-06	West Germany	L 1-7	Oslo	Fr	Iversen
8-08	Sweden	L 0-3	Malmo	Fr	
24-08	Finland	D 1-1	Helsinki	Fr	Fuglset.J
8-09	France	L 1-3	Oslo	ECq	Olsen.OD
26-09	Denmark	L 1-4	Oslo	Fr	Fuglset.J
27-10	Hungary	L 0-4	Budapest	ECq	
23-02-1972	Israel	L 1-2	Tel Aviv	Fr	Johansen.TE
31-05	Finland	D 0-0	Turku	Fr	
14-06	Uruguay	L 0-1	Oslo	Fr	
3-08	Iceland	W 4-1	Stavanger	WCq	Fuglset.J, Lund, Hestad, Johansen.TE
17-09	Sweden	L 1-3	Oslo	Fr	Fuglset.J
4-10	Belgium	L 0-2	Oslo	WCq	
1-11	Holland	L 0-9	Rotterdam	WCq	
6-06-1973	Rep. Ireland	D 1-1	Oslo	Fr	Paulsen
20-06	Denmark	L 0-1	Copenhagen	Fr	
25-07	North Korea	W 3-0	Bergen	Fr	Vold, Kvia, Johansen.TE
2-08	Iceland	W 4-0	Reykjavik	WCq	Sunde, Lund, Pettersen, Johannessen
12-09	Holland	L 1-2	Oslo	WCq	Hestad
23-09	Denmark	L 0-1	Trondheim	Fr	
31-10	Belgium	L 0-2	Brussels	WCq	
4-11	Luxembourg	L 1-2	Luxembourg	Fr	Sunde
22-05-1974	East Germany	L 0-1	Rostock	Fr	
6-06	Scotland	L 1-2	Oslo	Fr	Lund
8-08	Sweden	L 1-2	Gothenburg	Fr	Hestad
15-08	Finland	L 1-2	Oslo	Fr	Johansen.TE
4-09	Nth. Ireland	W 2-1	Oslo	ECq	Lund 2
30-10	Yugoslavia	L 1-3	Belgrade	ECq	Lund
9-06-1975	Yugoslavia	L 1-3	Oslo	ECq	Thunberg
30-06	Sweden	L 1-3	Stockholm	ECq	Olsen.EJ
7-07	Iceland	D 1-1	Reykjavik	OGq	Høyland
17-07	Iceland	W 3-2	Bergen	OGq	Slinning, Høyland, Skuseth
13-08	Sweden	L 0-2	Oslo	ECq	
29-10	Nth. Ireland	L 0-3	Belfast	ECq	

Date	Opponent	Result	Venue	Comp	Scorers
24-03-1976	Rep. Ireland	L 0-3	Dublin	Fr	
19-05	Iceland	L 0-1	Oslo	Fr	
16-06	Sweden	L 0-2	Stockholm	WCq	
24-06	Denmark	D 0-0	Bergen	Fr	
25-08	Denmark	L 0-3	Copenhagen	Fr	
8-09	Switzerland	W 1-0	Oslo	WCq	Lund
22-09	Sweden	W 3-2	Oslo	Fr	Thunberg 2, Jacobsen.P
26-05-1977	Sweden	L 0-1	Gothenburg	Fr	
1-06	Denmark	L 0-2	Oslo	Fr	
30-06	Iceland	L 1-2	Reykjavik	Fr	Iversen
18-08	Finland	D 1-1	Oslo	Fr	Iversen
7-09	Sweden	W 2-1	Oslo	WCq	Ottensen, Iversen
30-10	Switzerland	L 0-1	Berne	WCq	
29-03-1978	Spain	L 0-3	Gijon	Fr	
21-05	Rep. Ireland	D 0-0	Oslo	Fr	
31-05	Denmark	L 1-2	Oslo	Fr	Thoresen
9-08	Finland	D 1-1	Helsinki	Fr	Johansen.TE
30-08	Austria	L 0-2	Oslo	ECq	
20-09	Belgium	D 1-1	Lokeren	ECq	Larsen-Økland
25-10	Scotland	L 2-3	Glasgow	ECq	Aas, Larsen-Økland
9-05-1979	Portugal	L 0-1	Oslo	ECq	
7-06	Scotland	L 0-4	Oslo	ECq	
28-06	Sweden	L 0-2	Gothenburg	Fr	
15-08	Sweden	W 2-0	Oslo	Fr	Mathiesen, Larsen-Økland
21-08	Finland	W 1-0	Kuopio	OGq	Davidsen
29-08	Austria	L 0-4	Vienna	ECq	
12-09	Belgium	L 1-2	Oslo	ECq	Jacobsen.P
26-10	Finland	D 1-1	Stavanger	OGq	Rein
1-11	Portugal	L 1-3	Lisbon	ECq	Hammer
22-05-1980	Bulgaria	W 1-0	Oslo	Fr	Jacobsen.P
4-06	Denmark	L 1-3	Copenhagen	Fr	Kollshaugen
14-07	Iceland	W 3-1	Oslo	Fr	Kollshaugen, Jacobsen.P, Erlandsen
21-08	Finland	W 6-1	Oslo	Fr	Jacobsen.P 4, Dokken, Aas
10-09	England	L 0-4	London	WCq	
24-09	Rumania	D 1-1	Oslo	WCq	Hareide
29-10	Switzerland	W 2-1	Berne	WCq	Hareide, Mathiesen
28-02-1981	Sweden	L 2-4	Lahti	Fr	Hareide, Davidsen
29-04	Bulgaria	L 0-1	Pleven	Fr	
20-05	Hungary	L 1-2	Oslo	WCq	Thoresen
3-06	Rumania	L 0-1	Bucharest	WCq	
17-06	Switzerland	D 1-1	Oslo	WCq	Davidsen
2-07	Finland	L 1-3	Helsinki	Fr	Davidsen
12-08	Nigeria	D 2-2	Oslo	Fr	Jacobsen.P, Lund
9-09	England	W 2-1	Oslo	WCq	Albertsen, Thoresen
23-09	Denmark	L 1-2	Copenhagen	Fr	Kojedal
31-10	Hungary	L 1-4	Budapest	WCq	Lund
28-04-1982	Finland	D 1-1	Stavanger	Fr	Thoresen
12-05	West Germany	L 2-4	Oslo	Fr	LarsenØkland, Albertsen
15-06	Denmark	W 2-1	Oslo	Fr	Hareide, Hansen.V
11-08	Sweden	W 1-0	Olso	Fr	Lund
22-09	Wales	L 0-1	Swansea	ECq	
13-10	Yugoslavia	W 3-1	Oslo	ECq	Lund, Larsen-Økland, Hareide
27-10	Bulgaria	D 2-2	Sofia	ECq	Larsen-Økland, Thoresen
13-11	Kuwait	L 0-1	Kuwait City	Fr	
10-08-1983	Rumania	D 0-0	Oslo	Fr	
7-09	Bulgaria	L 1-2	Oslo	ECq	Hareide
21-09	Wales	D 0-0	Oslo	ECq	
12-10	Yugoslavia	L 1-2	Belgrade	ECq	Thoresen
1-05-1984	Luxembourg	W 2-0	Ettelbruck	Fr	Thoresen, Dokken
23-05	Hungary	D 0-0	Szekesfehervar	Fr	
6-06	Wales	W 1-0	Trondheim	Fr	Larsen-Økland
20-06	Iceland	W 1-0	Reykjavik	Fr	Johansen.E
29-08	Poland	D 1-1	Drammen	Fr	Davidsen
12-09	Switzerland	L 0-1	Oslo	WCq	
26-09	Denmark	L 0-1	Copenhagen	WCq	
10-10	Soviet Union	D 1-1	Oslo	WCq	Thoresen
17-10	Rep. Ireland	W 1-0	Oslo	WCq	Jacobsen.P
18-12	Egypt	W 1-0	Cairo	Fr	Davidsen
21-12	Egypt	W 1-0	Ismailia	Fr	Seland
26-02-1985	Wales	D 1-1	Wrexham	Fr	Ahlsen
17-04	East Germany	L 0-1	Frankfurt	Fr	
1-05	Rep. Ireland	D 0-0	Dublin	WCq	

22-05	Sweden	L 0-1	Gothenburg	Fr	
5-06	Wales	W 4-2	Bergen	Fr	Sollied, Larsen-Økland, Jacobsen.P, OG
14-08	East Germany	L 0-1	Oslo	Fr	
10-09	Egypt	W 3-0	Oslo	Fr	Andersen.J, Soler, Jacobsen.P
25-09	Italy	W 2-1	Leece	Fr	Larsen-Økland, Davidsen
16-10	Denmark	L 1-5	Oslo	WCq	Sundby
30-10	Soviet Union	L 0-1	Moscow	WCq	
13-11	Switzerland	D 1-1	Lucerne	WCq	Sundby
26-02-1986	Grenada	W 2-1	St George's	Fr	Sundby, Skogheim
30-04	Argentina	W 1-0	Oslo	Fr	Osvold
13-05	Denmark	W 1-0	Oslo	Fr	Thoresen
4-06	Romania	L 1-3	Bucharest	Fr	Sundby
20-08	Romania	D 2-2	Oslo	Fr	Larsen-Økland 2
9-09	Hungary	D 0-0	Oslo	Fr	
24-09	East Germany	D 0-0	Oslo	ECq	
29-10	Soviet Union	L 0-4	Simferopol	ECq	
24-03-1987	Poland	L 1-4	Wroclaw	Fr	Sundby
28-05	Italy	D 0-0	Oslo	Fr	
3-06	Soviet Union	L 0-1	Oslo	ECq	
16-06	France	W 2-0	Oslo	ECq	Mordt, Andersen.J
12-08	Sweden	D 0-0	Oslo	Fr	
9-09	Iceland	L 1-2	Reykjavik	ECq	Andersen.J
23-09	Iceland	L 0-1	Oslo	ECq	
14-10	France	D 1-1	Paris	ECq	Sundby
28-10	East Germany	L 1-3	Magdeburg	ECq	Fjerestad
1-06-1988	Rep. Ireland	D 0-0	Oslo	Fr	
28-07	Brazil	D 1-1	Oslo	Fr	Fjørtoft
9-08	Bulgaria	D 1-1	Oslo	Fr	Sørloth
14-09	Scotland	L 1-2	Oslo	WCq	Fjørtoft
28-09	France	L 0-1	Paris	WCq	
19-10	Italy	L 1-2	Pescara	Fr	Brandhaug
2-11	Cyprus	W 3-0	Limassol	WCq	Sørloth 2, Osvold
4-11	Czechoslovakia	L 2-3	Bratislava	Fr	Sørloth, Adgestein
22-02-1989	Greece	L 2-4	Athens	Fr	Bratseth, Sørloth
2-05	Poland	L 0-3	Oslo	Fr	
21-05	Cyprus	W 3-1	Oslo	WCq	Osvold, Sørloth, Bratseth
31-05	Austria	W 4-1	Oslo	Fr	Halle, Fjørtoft, Løken, Kojedal
14-06	Yugoslavia	L 1-2	Oslo	WCq	Fjørtoft
23-08	Greece	D 0-0	Oslo	Fr	
5-09	France	D 1-1	Oslo	WCq	Bratseth
11-10	Yugoslavia	L 0-1	Sarajevo	WCq	
25-10	Kuwait	D 2-2	Kuwait City	Fr	Sørloth, Fjørtoft
15-11	Scotland	D 1-1	Glasgow	WCq	Johnsen.E
5-02-1990	South Korea	W 3-2	Ta'Qali	Fr	Berg.Ø, Skammelsrud, Tangen
7-02	Malta	D 1-1	Ta'Qali	Fr	Fjørtoft
27-03	Nth. Ireland	W 3-2	Belfast	Fr	Skammelsrud, Andersen.J, Johnsen.E
6-06	Denmark	L 1-2	Trondheim	Fr	Andersen.J
22-08	Sweden	L 1-2	Stavanger	Fr	Ahlsen
12-09	Soviet Union	L 0-2	Moscow	ECq	
10-10	Hungary	D 0-0	Bergen	ECq	
31-10	Cameroon	W 6-1	Oslo	Fr	Bratseth, Bohinen, Dahlum, Fjørtoft 2, Sørloth
7-11	Tunisia	W 3-1	Bizerte	Fr	Dahlum 2, Ingebrigtsen
14-11	Cyprus	W 3-0	Nicosia	ECq	Sørloth, Bohinen, Brandhaug
17-04-1991	Austria	D 0-0	Vienna	Fr	
1-05	Cyprus	W 3-0	Oslo	ECq	Lydersen, Dahlum, Sørloth
22-05	Rumania	W 1-0	Oslo	Fr	Fjørtoft
5-06	Italy	W 2-1	Oslo	ECq	Dahlum, Bohinen
8-08	Sweden	L 1-2	Oslo	Fr	Leonhardsen
28-08	Soviet Union	L 0-1	Oslo	ECq	
25-09	Czechoslovakia	L 2-3	Oslo	Fr	Jakobsen, Fjørtoft
30-10	Hungary	D 0-0	Szombathely	ECq	
13-11	Italy	D 1-1	Genoa	ECq	Jakobsen
7-01-1992	Egypt	D 0-0	Cairo	Fr	
4-02	Bermuda	W 3-1	Hamilton	Fr	Leonhardsen 3
29-04	Denmark	L 0-1	Aarhus	Fr	
13-05	Faeroe Islands	W 2-0	Oslo	Fr	Sørloth, Bohinen
3-06	Scotland	D 0-0	Oslo	Fr	
26-08	Sweden	D 2-2	Oslo	Fr	Leonhardsen, Nilsen
9-09	San Marino	W 10-0	Oslo	WCq	Rekdal 2, Halle 3, Sørloth 2, Nilsen 2, Mykland
23-09	Holland	W 2-1	Oslo	WCq	Rekdal, Sørloth
7-10	San Marino	W 2-0	Serravalle	WCq	Jakobsen, Flo

14-10	England	D 1-1	London	WCq	Rekdal
2-12	China	L 1-2	Guangzhou	Fr	Flo
10-02-1993	Portugal	D 1-1	Faro	Fr	Sørloth
30-03	Qatar	W 6-1	Doha	Fr	Leonhardsen, Flo, Fjørtoft 3, Jakobsen
28-04	Turkey	W 3-1	Oslo	WCq	Rekdal, Fjørtoft, Jakobsen
2-06	England	W 2-0	Oslo	WCq	Leonhardsen, Bohinen
9-06	Holland	D 0-0	Rotterdam	WCq	
11-08	Faeroe Islands	W 7-0	Toftir	Fr	Bohinen, Leonhardsen, Mjelde 2, Østenstad 2, Pedersen.J
8-09	USA	W 1-0	Oslo	Fr	Bjørnebye
22-09	Poland	W 1-0	Oslo	WCq	Flo
13-10	Poland	W 3-0	Poznan	WCq	Flo, Fjørtoft, Johnsen.R
10-11	Turkey	L 1-2	Istanbul	WCq	Bohinen
15-01-1994	USA	L 1-2	Tempe	Fr	Strandli
19-01	Costa Rica	D 0-0	San Diego	Fr	
9-03	Wales	W 3-1	Cardiff	Fr	Flo, Mykland, Jakobsen
20-04	Portugal	D 0-0	Oslo	Fr	
22-05	England	D 0-0	London	Fr	
1-06	Denmark	W 2-1	Oslo	Fr	Jakobsen, Berg.H
5-06	Sweden	L 0-2	Stockholm	Fr	
19-06	Mexico	W 1-0	Washington	WCr1	Rekdal
23-06	Italy	L 0-1	New York	WCr1	
28-06	Rep. Ireland	D 0-0	New York	WCr1	
7-09	Belarus	W 1-0	Oslo	ECq	Frigård
12-10	Holland	D 1-1	Oslo	ECq	Rekdal
16-11	Belarus	W 4-0	Minsk	ECq	Berg, Leonhardsen, Bohinen, Rekdal
14-12	Malta	W 1-0	Ta'Qali	ECq	Fjørtoft
6-02-1995	Estonia	W 7-0	Larnaca	Fr	Jakobsen 2, Bohinen 2, Brattbakk 2, Halle
8-02	Cyprus	W 2-0	Larnaca	Fr	Leonhardsen, Flo
29-03	Luxembourg	W 2-0	Luxembourg	ECq	Leonhardsen, Aase
26-04	Luxembourg	W 5-0	Oslo	ECq	Jakobsen, Fjørtoft, Brattbakk, Berg, Rekdal
25-05	Ghana	W 3-2	Oslo	Fr	Rekdal, Fjørtoft 2
7-06	Malta	W 2-0	Oslo	ECq	Fjørtoft, Flo

POLAND

Poland is a country whose boundaries have chopped and changed more than any other European country in recent history. In the 17th century Poland was roughly three times the size it is today and stretched south to include even Kiev, whilst in the 19th century it had shrunk to include only the area around Warsaw, Krakow and Lublin. In the period from 1874 to 1918, when football first started on the continent, it did not even exist at all.

Poland was part of both the German and Russian Empires at this time, and it was the German areas that took most to football at the turn of the century. Königsberg (now Kalliningrad in the Soviet Union), Danzig (now Gdansk), Stettin (now Szczecin) and Breslau (now Wroclaw) were all centres of German football prior to 1945. Warsaw, Lodz, Lwow and Lublin, as part of Russia until 1918, formed the basis of the Polish state that was created in 1921, along with Krakow from Germany.

The Polish Football Federation was formed in 1919 and admitted to FIFA four years later. In 1921 a championship was started, and as if to prove the transient nature of politics at the time, one of the early dominant clubs, Pogon Lwow, would today find itself in the Ukraine. A number of clubs from around this time still exist: Wisla Krakow and LKS Lodz, formed in 1906 and 1908 respectively, remain two of the oldest clubs still playing football at the highest level in Poland, and along with Legia Warsaw, formed in 1916, and Ruch Chorzow, in 1920, they dominated football until the Second World War.

In December 1921 a national side took to the field for the first time in a match against Hungary, and although the record up to 1939 was not outstanding, the Poles managed to hold their own against most sides. The finest player of this generation was Ernst Wilimowski of Ruch Chorzow and he will always be remembered for what turned out to be a personal duel with the Brazilian Leonidas in the 1938 World Cup match in Strasbourg. Both scored four goals, but sadly for Wilimowski and his team-mates, Poland lost 6-5. Two years previously they had reached the semi-finals of the Berlin Olympics only to lose to Austria. In the event, their disappointment was not eased with a bronze medal as they also lost the third place play-off to Norway.

The war and its aftermath brought wholesale changes not only to the boundaries of Poland once again, setting them as they remain to this day, but also to the set-up of club football. In true communist fashion, football was organised from head to toe. The control of clubs passed to various government bodies, whilst at the same time new clubs were created. One of these, Górnik Zabrze, dominated the league from the late 1950s to early 1970s. In 1963 a young Wlodzimierz Lubanski made his debut for Górnik, joining Ernest Pol, who until Lubanski took over his mantle was Poland's most prolific marksman. Lubanski was the spark that ignited Polish football which in the post-war period had progressed steadily but not spectacularly.

By the end of the 1960s Poland had embarked on an era of success that lasted the best part of 15 years and included Olympic gold and silver medals as well as third place in the 1974 World Cup and a semi-final appearance in 1982.

Central to the side that won the 1972 Olympic Games was Lubanski, but alongside him were Kazimierz Deyna and Robert Gadocha, both prolific goalscorers. Unfortunately for Poland, Lubanski was injured and did not play in the 1974 World Cup but Deyna and Gadocha were joined by Grzegorz Lato and Andrzej Szarmach, two more players who seemed to be able to score with ease. Not only was the attack formidable, the defence was also particularly strong, dominated as it was by the giant Jan Tomaszewski in goal along with Wladislav Zmuda and Jerzy Gorgon in front of him. Lato especially emerged as a star after the World Cup where his seven goals were instrumental in taking Poland to third place.

THE ORDER OF MERIT

		All			League			Cup		Europe		
	Team	G	S	B	G	S	B	G	S	G	S	B
1	Górnik Zabrze	20	11	7	14	4	7	6	6	-	1	-
2	Legia Warszawa	17	11	10	6	6	8	11	5	-	-	2
3	Ruch Chorzów	15	9	6	13	5	6	2	4	-	-	-
4	Wisla Kraków	8	12	8	6	8	8	2	4	-	-	-
5	Lech Poznan	8	1	3	5	-	3	3	1	-	-	-
6	Cracovia	5	2	-	5	2	-	-	-	-	-	-
7	Zaglebie Sosnowiec	4	5	2	-	4	2	4	1	-	-	-
8	Pogon Lwow	4	3	-	4	3	-	-	-	-	-	-
9	GKS Katowice	3	8	3	-	4	3	3	4	-	-	-
10	Widzew Lódz	3	6	4	2	6	3	1	-	-	-	1
11	Slask Wroclaw	3	2	1	1	2	1	2	-	-	-	-
12	Polonia Bytom	2	7	2	2	4	2	-	3	-	-	-
13	Warta Poznan	2	5	6	2	5	6	-	-	-	-	-
14	Stal Mielec	2	2	3	2	1	3	-	1	-	-	-
15	LKS Lódz	2	2	2	1	1	2	1	1	-	-	-
16	Polonia Warszawa	2	2	-	1	2	-	1	-	-	-	-
17	Gwardia Warszawa	1	2	2	-	1	2	1	1	-	-	-
18	Lechia Gdansk	1	1	1	-	-	1	1	1	-	-	-
	Szombierki Bytom	1	1	1	1	1	1	-	-	-	-	-
20	Garbarnia Kraków	1	1	-	1	1	-	-	-	-	-	-
	Zaglebie Lubin	1	1	-	1	1	-	-	-	-	-	-
22	Arka Gdynia	1	-	-	-	-	-	1	-	-	-	-
	Miedz Legnica	1	-	-	-	-	-	1	-	-	-	-
	Stal Rzeszów	1	-	-	-	-	-	1	-	-	-	-
25	Pogon Szczecin	-	3	1	-	1	1	-	2	-	-	-
26	Piast Gliwice	-	2	-	-	-	-	-	2	-	-	-
27	AKS Chorzów	-	1	2	-	1	2	-	-	-	-	-
28	Czarni Zagan	-	1	-	-	-	-	-	1	-	-	-
	Górnik Radlin	-	1	-	-	1	-	-	-	-	-	-
	Jagiellonia Bialystok	-	1	-	-	-	-	-	1	-	-	-
	I.FC Katowice	-	1	-	-	1	-	-	-	-	-	-
	Rakow Czestochowa	-	1	-	-	-	-	-	1	-	-	-
	ROW II Rybnik	-	1	-	-	-	-	-	1	-	-	-
	Sparta Lwow	-	1	-	-	-	-	-	1	-	-	-
	GKS Tychy	-	1	-	-	1	-	-	-	-	-	-
	Wawel Kraków	-	1	-	-	1	-	-	-	-	-	-
37	Odra Opole	-	-	1	-	-	1	-	-	-	-	-
	Zaglebie Walbrzych	-	-	1	-	-	1	-	-	-	-	-

Remarkably the team kept together for most of the 1970s. Lubanski finally bowed out after the 1978 World Cup, but by this time Zbigniew Boniek, perhaps Poland's best known player, had made his debut, and the side that entered the World Cup in Argentina was perhaps the strongest ever to represent Poland. However, although they reached the second round, they were disappointing against both Brazil and Argentina. The 1982 World Cup side fared better, reaching the semi-finals before losing to Italy, but the achievement to a large extent papered over the cracks that were appearing in Polish football.

Many of the well-known players were given permission to move abroad, Boniek to Juventus, Zmuda to Verona, Lato to Lokeren and Szarmach to Auxerre for example, and this exodus left the domestic game in a poor state. Since the fall of the communist government, matters have, if anything, become worse. For clubs left to fight for their existence in the commercial world, the sole source of money seems to be the sale of players to clubs in the West, and this in turn lessens interest. On only three occasions in 1994 and 1995 was there a crowd of 20,000 in the league. The majority of games attracted less than 5,000. With so many players gaining experience abroad, the national side may well regain some of their former stature in time, but they have not qualified for a major tournament since 1986.

Given the size of the country, there is no reason why clubs such as Górnik Zabrze and Legia Warsaw should not be up there with the best on the continent. The main problem is that the regions of heavy industry and mining were always the heartland of soccer in Poland, and it is these very areas that have borne the brunt of the post-communism modernisation process. The Katowice conurbation containing Chorzow, Bytom and Zabrze, along with Lodz, Krakow, Poznan and Wroclaw, once burgeoning cities, are now wracked by unemployment. There is simply no money to be spent on what at the moment is a poor standard of football.

Matters have not been helped by scandals on the field, none more so than the match-fixing affair of 1993 which saw Legia Warsaw stripped of their title. Both Legia and LKS Lodz went into the last day of the season level on points with Legia having a goal difference advantage of three. LKS duly won their last game 7-1 at home to Olimpia Poznan and surprise, surprise, Legia won 6-0 away to Wisla Krakow. Smelling a rat, the Polish FA deducted 2 points from all four teams leaving Lech Poznan as champions.

Population: 38,064,000
Area, sq km: 312,683
% in urban areas: 61.2%
Capital city: Warsaw

Polski Zwiazek Pilki Noznej
Al. Ujazdowskie #22
00-478 Warsaw
Poland

Tel: + 48 2 6289344
Fax: + 48 2 6219175

Year of formation	1919
Affiliation to FIFA	1923
Affiliation to UEFA	1954
Registered clubs	5880
Registered players	269 000
Registered coaches	3918
Professional players	320
Registered referees	7215
National stadium	Stadion Slaski, Chorzów, 70 000
National colours	White/Red/White
Reserve colours	Red/White/Red
Season	August - June, with a mid season break December - Feb

THE RECORD

WORLD CUP

1930 Did not enter
1934 QT 2nd/2 in group 9
1938 QT 1st/2 in group 2 - Final Tournament/1st round
1950 Did not enter
1954 Did not enter
1958 QT 2nd/3 in group 6
1962 QT 1st rd in group 10
1966 QT 3rd/4 in group 8
1970 QT 2nd/4 in group 8
1974 QT 1st/3 in group 5 - Final Tournament/2nd round/ 3rd place
1978 QT 1st/4 in group 1 - Final Tournament/2nd round
1982 QT 1st/3 in group 7 - Final Tournament/Semi-finalists/ 3rd place
1986 QT 1st/4 in group 1 - Final Tournament/2nd round
1990 QT 3rd/4 in group 2
1994 QT 4th/6 in group 2

EUROPEAN CHAMPIONSHIP

1960 1st round
1964 1st round
1968 QT 3rd/4 in group 7
1972 QT 2nd/4 in group 8
1976 QT 2nd/4 in group 5
1980 QT 2nd/5 in group 4
1984 QT 3rd/4 in group 2
1988 QT 4th/5 in group 5
1992 QT 3rd/4 in group 7
1996 QT group 1

EUROPEAN CLUB COMPETITIONS

European Cup
Semi-finalists - Legia Warszawa 1970 Widzew Lódz 1983
Cup Winners Cup
Finalists - Górnik Zabrze 1970
UEFA Cup
Quarter-finalists - Ruch Chorzów 1974 Stal Mielec 1976

CLUB DIRECTORY

WARSAW (Population - 2,323,000)

Legia Warszawa (1916)
Wojska Polskiego 21,000 – Red, white trim
Previous names - WKS 1016-20, Legia 1920-50, CWKS 1950-57

Gwardia Warszawa (1948)
Gwardia 12,000 – Blue/White

Polonia Warszawa (1946)
Polonia 15,000 – Red/Black, red & white trim
Previous name - Kolejarz 1948-56

KATOWICE (Population - 2,778,000)

AKS Chorzów (1910)
(Amatorski Klub Sportowy)
1 Maja – Green/White
Previous name - Budowlani 1948-55

GKS Katowice (1964)
(Górniczy Klub Sportowy)
GKS 11,000 – Yellow/Black

Górnik Zabrze (1948)
Górnik 23,000 – Red, white trim

Polonia Bytom (1920)
Koniewa – Blue/Red
Previous name - Ogniwo 1948-55

Ruch Chorzów (1920)
Ruch 40,000 – Blue, white trim
Previous name - Unia 1950-55

Szombierki Bytom (1919)
Frycza Modrzewskiego – Green & black stripes/Black
Previous names - Górnik Bytom 1948-56

GKS Tichy (1971)
Tichy 18,000 – Green & black stripes/Red

LODZ (Population - 1,061,000)

LKS Lódz (1908)
(Lodzkie Klub Sportowy)
LKS 35,000 – Red, white trim
Previous names - Wlokniarz 1948-54

Widzew Lódz (1910)
Widzew 22,000 – White, red trim

GDANSK (Population - 909,000)

Lechia Gdansk (1945)
Lechia 18,000 – White/Green
Previous names - Budowlany 1949-56

Arka Gdynia (1929)
Gdynia 16,000 – Yellow/Blue

KRAKOW (Population - 828,000)

KS Cracovia (1906)
Cracovia 12,000 – Red & white stripes/White
Previous names - Ogniwo 1949-54, Sparta 1954-55

Garbarnia Kraków (1921)
Parkowa – Claret/White
Previous names - Zwiazkowiec 1949-50, Wlokniarz 1950-55

Hutnik Kraków (1950)
Hutnik 14,000 – Blue/White

Wisla Kraków (1906)
Wisla 18,000 – Red, blue sash/White
Previous names - Gwardia 1949-55

POZNAN (Population - 672,000)

Lech Poznan (1922)
Lech 23,000 – Blue, white trim
Previous names - Kolejarz 1947-56

GKS Olimpia Poznan (1945)
Olimpia 22,000 – Blue, white trim

KS Warta Poznan (1912)
Warta 50,000 – Green/Green
Previous names - Zwiazkowiec 1949-55

WROCLAW (Population - 640,000)

Slask Wroclaw (1947)
Slask 14,000 – Green/White
Previous names - Ogniwo 1948-56

SZCZECIN (Population - 449,000)

Pogon Szczecin (1948)
Pogon 17,000 – Red, white trim

LUBLIN (Population - 389,000)

Motor Lublin (1950)
Motor 20,000 – Yellow/Blue

BYDGOSZCZ (Population - 372,000)

Zawisza Bydgoszcz (1946)
Zawisza 43,000 – Blue/Black, black & white trim
Previous names - OWKS 1948-56

BIALYSTOK (Population - 259,000)

Jagiellonia Bialystok (1927)
Jagiellonia 5,000 – Yellow/Orange

SOSNOWIEC (Population - 258,000)

Zaglebie Sosnowiec (1906)
Ludowy 34,000 – Red/Green
Previous names - Milowice 1906-08, Union 1908-1918, Sosnowiec 1918-21, Victoria 1921-31, Unia 1931-39, RKU 1939-48, Stal 1948-63

WALBRZYCH (Population - 207,000)

Górnik Walbrzych (1946)
Górnik 30,000 – Blue/White

Zaglebie Walbrzych (1946)
Walbrzych 25,000 – Green/Black

RZESZOW (Population - 147,000)

Stal Rzeszów (1944)
White/Blue

OPOLE (Population - 128,000)

Odra Opole (1945)
Opole 20,000 – Blue/Red

LEGNICA (Population - 100,000)

Miedz Legnica (1971)
Ulica Orla Bialengo 8,000 – White/Red

LUBIN (Population - 77,000)

Zaglebie Lubin (1946)
Zaglebie 34,000 – Red & white stripes/Red

MIELEC (Population - 56,000)

Stal Mielec (1939)
Stal 30,000 – Blue, white trim

POLISH LEAGUE CHAMPIONSHIP

1921c Cracovia 15 Polonia Warszawa 10 Warta Poznan 8
1922 Pogon Lwow 4-3 1-1 Warta Poznan
1923 Pogon Lwow 3-0 1-2 2-1 Wisla Kraków
1924 -
1925a Pogon Lwow 7 Warta Poznan 3 Wisla Kraków 2
1926 Pogon Lwow 6 Polonia Warszawa 3 Warta Poznan 3
1927n Wisla Kraków 40 1.FC Katowice 36 Warta Poznan 32
1928p Wisla Kraków 42 Warta Poznan 40 Legia Warszawa 36
1929l Warta Poznan 33 Garbarnia Kraków 32 Wisla Kraków 30
1930k Cracovia 33 Wisla Kraków 32 Legia Warszawa 30
1931 Garbarnia Krakow 30 Wisla Kraków 29 Legia Warszawa 29
1932 Cracovia 29 Pogon Lwow 28 Warta Poznan 27
1933d Ruch Chorzów 14 Pogon Lwow 13 Wisla Kraków 13
1934k Ruch Chorzów 36 Cracovia 29 Wisla Kraków 28
1935i Ruch Chorzów 26 Pogon Lwow 25 Warta Poznan 24
1936h Ruch Chorzów 24 Wisla Kraków 22 Warta Poznan 21
1937 Cracovia 26 AKS Chorzów 24 Ruch Chorzów 23
1938 Ruch Chorzów 27 Warta Poznan 21 Wisla Kraków 20
1939-45 -
1946b Polonia Warszawa 9 Warta Poznan 6 AKS Chorzów 5
1947 Warta Poznan 8 Wisla Kraków 4 AKS Chorzów 0
1948n Cracovia 38 Wisla Kraków 38 Ruch Chorzów 30
1949k Gwardia Kraków 30 Ogniwo Kraków 29 Kolejarz Poznan 27
1950 Gwardia Kraków 33 Unia Chorzów 32 Kolejarz Poznan 26
1951 Gwardia Kraków 32 Górnik Radlin 29 CWKS Warszawa 27
1952 Unia Chorzów 7-0 0-0 Ogniwo Bytom
1953k Unia Chorzów 38 Wawel Kraków 28 Gwardia Kraków 27
1954i Ogniwo Bytom 24 Wlokniarz Lódz 24 Unia Chorzów 24
1955k CWKS Warszawa 28 Stal Sosnowiec 27 Unia Chorzów 25
1956 CWKS Warszawa 34 Unia Chorzów 29 Budowlani Gdansk 27
1957 Górnik Zabrze 33 Gwardia Warszawa 32 LKS Lódz 29
1958 LKS Lódz 32 Polonia Bytom 31 Górnik Zabrze 27
1959 Górnik Zabrze 36 Polonia Bytom 30 Gwardia Warszawa 25
1960 Ruch Chorzów 30 Legia Warszawa 29 Górnik Zabrze 28
1961n Górnik Zabrze 43 Polonia Bytom 35 Legia Warszawa 32
1962 Polonia Bytom 4-1 1-2 Górnik Zabrze
1963n Górnik Zabrze 42 Ruch Chorzów 37 Stal Sosnowiec 36
1964 Górnik Zabrze 40 Zaglebie Sosnowiec 31 Odra Opole 31
1965 Górnik Zabrze 37 Szombierki Bytom 32 Zaglebie Sosnowiec 31
1966 Górnik Zabrze 42 Wisla Kraków 32 Polonia Bytom 31
1967 Górnik Zabrze 37 Zaglebie Sosnowiec 34 Ruch Chorzów 30
1968 Ruch Chorzów 38 Legia Warszawa 35 Górnik Zabrze 33
1969 Legia Warszawa 39 Górnik Zabrze 37 Polonia Bytom 28
1970 Legia Warszawa 40 Ruch Chorzów 35 Górnik Zabrze 35
1971 Górnik Zabrze 39 Legia Warszawa 34 Zaglebie Walbrzych 27
1972 Górnik Zabrze 37 Zaglebie Sosnowiec 33 Legia Warszawa 32
1973 Stal Mielec 36 Ruch Chorzów 33 Gwardia Warszawa 30
1974q Ruch Chorzów 41 Górnik Zabrze 38 Stal Mielec 37
1975 Ruch Chorzów 44 Stal Mielec 38 Slask Wroclaw 36
1976 Stal Mielec 38 GKS Tychy 38 Wisla Kraków 37
1977 Slask Wroclaw 41 Widzew Lódz 38 Górnik Zabrze 37
1978 Wisla Kraków 39 Slask Wroclaw 38 Lech Poznan 37
1979 Ruch Chorzów 39 Widzew Lódz 39 Stal Mielec 36
1980 Szombierki Bytom 39 Widzew Lódz 36 Legia Warszawa 36
1981 Widzew Lódz 39 Wisla Kraków 37 Szombierki Bytom 36
1982 Widzew Lódz 39 Slask Wroclaw 39 Stal Mielec 35
1983 Lech Poznan 39 Widzew Lódz 38 Ruch Chorzów 35
1984 Lech Poznan 42 Widzew Lódz 42 Pogon Szczecin 38
1985 Górnik Zabrze 42 Legia Warszawa 41 Widzew Lódz 38
1986 Górnik Zabrze 46 Legia Warszawa 42 Widzew Lódz 41
1987q5 Górnik Zabrze 49 Pogon Szczecin 44 GKS Katowice 43
1988 Górnik Zabrze 51 GKS Katowice 40 Legia Warszawa 39
1989 Ruch Chorzów 52 GKS Katowice 47 Górnik Zabrze 45
1990 Lech Poznan 42 Zaglebie Lubin 40 GKS Katowice 40
1991q Zaglebie Lubin 44 Górnik Zabrze 40 Wisla Kraków 40
1992t Lech Poznan 49 GKS Katowice 44 Widzew Lódz 43
1993 Lech Poznan * 47 Legia Warszawa 47 LKS Lódz 47
1994 Legia Warszawa 48 GKS Katowice 48 Górnik Zabrze 46
1995 Legia Warszawa 51 Widzew Lódz 45 GKS Katowice 42

* Lech Poznan declared champions after match fixing by Legia and LKS, both of whom were deducted two points

Play-offs
1948 Cracovia ....3-1 ....Wisla Krakow

POLISH CUP FINALS

1926 Wisla Kraków ....2-1 ....Sparta Lvov
1927-50 -
1951 Unia Chorzów ....2-0 ....Gwardia Kraków
1952 Kolejarz Warszawa ....1-0 ....CWKS Warszawa
1953 -
1954 Gwardia Warszawa ......0-0 3-1 ....Gwardia Kraków
1955 CWKS Warszawa ....5-0 ....Budowlani Gdansk
1956 CWKS Warszawa ....3-0 ....Górnik Zabrze
1957 LKS Lódz ....2-1 ....Górnik Zabrze
1958-61 -
1962 Zaglebie Sosnowiec ....2-1 ....Górnik Zabrze
1963 Zaglebie Sosnowiec ....2-0 ....Ruch Chorzów
1964 Legia Warszawa ....2-1 ....Polonia Bytom
1965 Górnik Zabrze ....4-0 ....Czarni Zagan
1966 Legia Warszawa ....2-1 ....Górnik Zabrze
1967 Wisla Kraków ....2-0 ....Rakow Czestochowa
1968 Górnik Zabrze ....3-0 ....Ruch Chorzów
1969 Górnik Zabrze ....2-0 ....Legia Warszawa
1970 Górnik Zabrze ....3-1 ....Ruch Chorzów
1971 Górnik Zabrze ....3-1 ....Zaglebie Sosnowiec
1972 Górnik Zabrze ....5-2 ....Legia Warszawa
1973 Legia Warszawa ....0-0 4-2p ....Polonia Bytom
1974 Ruch Chorzów ....2-0 ....Gwardia Warszawa
1975 Stal Rzeszów ....0-0 3-2p ....ROW II Rybnik
1976 Slask Wroclaw ....2-0 ....Stal Mielec
1977 Zaglebie Sosnowiec ....1-0 ....Polonia Bytom
1978 Zaglebie Sosnowiec ....2-0 ....Piast Gliwice
1979 Arka Gdynia ....2-1 ....Wisla Kraków
1980 Legia Warszawa ....5-0 ....Lech Poznan
1981 Legia Warszawa ....1-0 ....Pogon Szczecin
1982 Lech Poznan ....1-0 ....Pogon Szczecin
1983 Lechia Gdansk ....2-1 ....Piast Gliwice
1984 Lech Poznan ....3-0 ....Wisla Kraków
1985 Widzew Lódz ....0-0 3-1p ....GKS Katowice
1986 GKS Katowice ....4-1 ....Górnik Zabrze
1987 Slask Wroclaw ....0-0 4-3p ....GKS Katowice
1988 Lech Poznan ....1-1 3-2p ....Legia Warszawa
1989 Legia Warszawa ....5-2 ....Jagiellonia Bialystok
1990 Legia Warszawa ....2-0 ....GKS Katowice
1991 GKS Katowice ....1-0 ....Legia Warszawa
1992 Miedz Legnica ....1-1 4-3p ....Gornik Zabrze
1993 GKS Katowice ....1-1 5-4p ....Ruch Chorzów
1994 Legia Warszawa ....2-0 ....LKS Lódz
1995 Legia Warszawa ....2-0 ....GKS Katowice

LEADING INTERNATIONAL APPEARANCES

104 Grzegorz Lato (Stal Mielec, Lokeren, Atalanta)
102 Kazimierz Deyna (Legia Warszawa)

92	Wladyslaw Zmuda	(Gwardia,Slask,Widzew, Verona,Cosmos)
87	Antoni Szymanowski	(Wisla Krakow,Gwardia Warszawa)
80	Wlodzimierz Lubanski	(Gornik Zabrze,Lokeren)
	Zbigniew Boniek	(Widzew Lodz,Juventus,Roma)
66	Roman Kosecki	(Legia,Galatarasaray,Osasuna, Atletico Madrid)
65	Robert Gadocha	(Legia Warszawa,Nantes)
	Jan Tomaszewski	(Legia,LKS Lodz,Beerschot, Hercules)
63	Henryk Kasperczak	(Stal Mielec)
62	Dariusz Dziekanowski	(Gwardia,Widzew,Legia,Celtic)

LEADING INTERNATIONAL GOALSCORERS

50	Wlodzimierz Lubanski	(Gornik Zabrze,Lokeren)
45	Grzegorz Lato	(Stal Mielec,Lokeren,Atalanta)
	Kazimierz Deyna	(Legia Warszawa)
40	Ernest Pol	(Legia Warzawa,Gornik Zabrze)
33	Andrzej Szarmach	(Gornik Zabrze,Stal Mielec,Auxerre)
27	Gerard Cieslik	(Ruch Chorzow)
24	Zbigniew Boniek	(Widzew Lodz,Juventus,Roma)
21	Ernest Wilimowski	(Ruch Chorzow)
20	Robert Gadocha	(Legia Warszawa,Nantes)
19	Dariusz Dziekanowski	(Gwardia,Widzew,Legia,Celtic)
	Roman Kosecki	(see appearances list)

Ernst Willimowski also scored 13 goals in 8 games for Germany between 1939 and 1942

INTERNATIONAL MATCHES PLAYED BY POLAND

18-12-1921	Hungary	L 0-1	Budapest	Fr	
14-05-1922	Hungary	L 0-3	Krakow	Fr	
28-05	Sweden	W 2-1	Stockholm	Fr	Klotz, Garbien
3-09	Romania	D 1-1	Czernowitz	Fr	Dluzniak
1-10	Yugoslavia	W 3-1	Zagreb	Fr	Kaluza 2, Garbien
3-06-1923	Yugoslavia	L 1-2	Krakow	Fr	Kaluza
2-09	Romania	D 1-1	Lwow	Fr	Kuchar.W
23-09	Finland	L 3-5	Helsinki	Fr	Stalinski 2, Miller.J
25-09	Estonia	W 4-1	Tallinn	Fr	Kowalski.W 2, Stalinski, Batsch
1-11	Sweden	D 2-2	Krakow	Fr	Stalinski 2
18-05-1924	Sweden	L 1-5	Stockholm	Fr	Batsch
26-05	Hungary	L 0-5	Paris	OGr1	
10-06	United States	L 2-3	Warsaw	Fr	Czulak, Chruscinski
29-06	Turkey	W 2-0	Lodz	Fr	Balcer, Reyman (I)
10-08	Finland	W 1-0	Warsaw	Fr	Reyman (I)
31-08	Hungary	L 0-4	Budapest	Fr	
23-05-1925	Czechoslovakia	L 1-2	Prague	Fr	Batsch
19-07	Hungary	L 0-2	Krakow	Fr	
30-08	Finland	D 2-2	Helsinki	Fr	Stalinski, Kaluza
2-09	Estonia	D 0-0	Tallinn	Fr	
2-10	Turkey	W 2-1	Istanbul	Fr	Adamek, Sperling
1-11	Sweden	L 2-6	Krakow	Fr	Kuchar.W, Sperling
6-06-1926	Czechoslovakia	L 1-2	Krakow	Fr	Kuchar.W
4-07	Estonia	W 2-0	Warsaw	Fr	Tupalski, Sobota
8-08	Finland	W 7-1	Poznan	Fr	Batsch 4, Stalinski 3
20-08	Hungary	L 1-4	Budapest	Fr	Stalinski
12-09	Turkey	W 6-1	Lwow	Fr	Steuermann 3, Batsch 2, Balcer
3-10	Sweden	L 1-3	Stockholm	Fr	Adamek
7-10	Norway	W 4-3	Fredrikstad	Fr	Kaluza 2, Balcer 2
19-06-1927	Romania	D 3-3	Bucharest	Fr	Kaluza, Wojcik, Pazurek.K
10-06-1928	United States	D 3-3	Warsaw	Fr	Kuchar.W 2, Steuermann
1-07	Sweden	W 2-1	Katowice	Fr	Kuchar.W, Stalinski
27-10	Czechoslovakia	L 2-3	Prague	Fr	Reyman (I) 2
28-09-1930	Sweden	W 3-0	Stockholm	Fr	Ciszewski 2, Smoczek
26-10	Latvia	W 6-0	Warsaw	Fr	Nawrot 4, Malik, Balcer
14-06-1931	Czechoslovakia	L 0-4	Warsaw	Fr	
5-08	Latvia	W 5-0	Riga	Fr	Kossok.K 2, Kisielinski 2, Reyman (I)
23-08	Romania	L 2-3	Warsaw	Fr	Wypijewski, Nawrot
11-10	Belgium	L 1-2	Brussels	Fr	Wypijewski
25-10	Yugoslavia	W 6-3	Poznan	Fr	Balcer 3, Kniola 2, Martyna
29-05-1932	Yugoslavia	W 3-0	Zagreb	Fr	Nawrot 2, Ciszewski
10-07	Sweden	W 2-0	Warsaw	Fr	Nawrot, Bator
2-10	Romania	W 5-0	Bucharest	Fr	Nawrot 3, Urban, Matyas.M
2-10	Latvia	W 2-1	Warsaw	Fr	Kossok.K, Radojewski
4-06-1933	Belgium	L 0-1	Warsaw	Fr	
10-09	Yugoslavia	W 4-3	Warsaw	Fr	Nawrot 2, Majowski, Król
15-10	Czechoslovakia	L 1-2	Warsaw	WCq	Martyna
3-12	Germany	L 0-1	Berlin	Fr	
21-05-1934	Denmark	L 2-4	Copenhagen	Fr	Nawrot 2
23-05	Sweden	L 2-4	Stockholm	Fr	Nawrot, Wilimowski

Date	Opponent	Result	Venue	Comp	Scorers
26-08	Yugoslavia	L 1-4	Belgrade	Fr	Wilimowski
9-09	Germany	L 2-5	Warsaw	Fr	Wilimowski, Pazurek
14-10	Romania	D 3-3	Lwow	Fr	Martyna 2, Urban
14-10	Latvia	W 6-2	Riga	Fr	Wodarz, Lysakowski, Peterek, Pazurek
12-05-1935	Austria	L 2-5	Vienna	Fr	Matyas.M 2
18-08	Yugoslavia	L 2-3	Katowice	Fr	Matyas.M, Peterek
15-09	Germany	L 0-1	Breslau	Fr	
15-09	Latvia	D 3-3	Lodz	Fr	Malczyk.S, Smoczek, ?
6-10	Austria	W 1-0	Warsaw	Fr	Matyas.M
3-11	Romania	L 1-4	Bucharest	Fr	Pazurek
16-02-1936	Belgium	W 2-0	Brussels	Fr	Piec.T, God
5-08	Hungary *	W 3-0	Berlin	OGr1	God 2, Wodarz
8-08	Great Britain*	W 5-4	Berlin	OGqf	Wodarz 3, God, Piec.T
11-08	Austria *	L 1-3	Berlin	OGsf	God
13-08	Norway	L 2-3	Berlin	OG3p	Wodarz, Peterek
6-09	Yugoslavia	L 3-9	Belgrade	Fr	Peterek 2, Wodarz
6-09	Latvia	D 3-3	Riga	Fr	Matyas.M, Wostal, Schwarz
13-09	Germany	D 1-1	Warsaw	Fr	Wodarz
4-10	Denmark	L 1-2	Copenhagen	Fr	God
23-06-1937	Sweden	W 3-1	Warsaw	Fr	Wilimowski, Wodarz, Piontek
4-07	Romania	L 2-4	Lodz	Fr	Piontek, Matyas.M
12-09	Denmark	W 3-1	Warsaw	Fr	Wilimowski, Król, Piec.T
12-09	Bulgaria	D 3-3	Sofia	Fr	Korbas 3
10-10	Yugoslavia	W 4-0	Warsaw	WCq	Piontek 2, Wilimowski, Wostal
10-10	Latvia	W 2-1	Katowice	Fr	Piec.T, Pytel
13-03-1938	Switzerland	D 3-3	Zurich	Fr	Wilimowski, Piontek, Wostal
3-04	Yugoslavia	L 0-1	Belgrade	WCq	
22-05	Rep. Ireland	W 6-0	Warsaw	Fr	Piontek 2, Wodarz 2, Wilimowski, Wasiewicz
5-06	Brazil	L 5-6	Strasbourg	WCr1	Wilimowski 4, Scherfke
18-09	Germany	L 1-4	Chemnitz	Fr	Peterek
25-09	Yugoslavia	D 4-4	Warsaw	Fr	Wilimowski 2, Piontek, Korbas
25-09	Latvia	L 1-2	Riga	Fr	Habowski
23-10	Norway	D 2-2	Warsaw	Fr	Wilimowski, Piec.T
13-11	Rep. Ireland	L 2-3	Dublin	Fr	Wilimowski, Piontek
22-01-1939	France	L 0-4	Paris	Fr	
27-05	Belgium	D 3-3	Lodz	Fr	Wilimowski 2, Wostal
4-06	Switzerland	D 1-1	Warsaw	Fr	Piontek
27-08	Hungary	W 4-2	Warsaw	Fr	Wilimowski 3, Piontek
11-06-1947	Norway	L 1-3	Oslo	Fr	Jablonski
19-07	Romania	L 1-2	Warsaw	Fr	Cieslik
31-08	Czechoslovakia	L 3-6	Prague	Fr	Cieslik 2, Hogendorf
14-09	Sweden	L 4-5	Stockholm	Fr	Gracz 2, Cieslik, Hogendorf
17-09	Finland	W 4-1	Helsinki	Fr	Cieslik 2, Spodzieja 2
19-10	Yugoslavia	L 1-7	Belgrade	Fr	Cieslik
26-10	Romania	D 0-0	Bucharest	Fr	
4-04-1948	Bulgaria	D 1-1	Sofia	BCE	Parpan.T
18-04	Czechoslovakia	W 3-1	Warsaw	BCE	Cieslik, Gracz, Spodzieja
26-06	Denmark	L 0-8	Copenhagen	Fr	
25-08	Yugoslavia	L 0-1	Warsaw	BCE	
19-09	Hungary	L 2-6	Warsaw	BCE	Cieslik, Kohut.J
10-10	Romania	D 0-0	Chorzow	BCE	
17-10	Finland	W 1-0	Warsaw	Fr	Cieslik
8-05-1949	Romania	L 1-2	Bucharest	Fr	Mamon
19-06	Denmark	L 1-2	Warsaw	Fr	Kokot.A
10-07	Hungary	L 2-8	Debrecen	Fr	Mamon, Spodzieja
2-10	Bulgaria	W 3-2	Warsaw	Fr	Cieslik 2, Alszer
30-10	Czechoslovakia	L 0-2	Vitkovice	Fr	
6-11	Albania	W 2-1	Warsaw	Fr	Cieslik, Kohut.J
1-05-1950	Albania	D 0-0	Tirana	Fr	
14-05	Romania	D 3-3	Wroclaw	Fr	Cieslik 3
4-06	Hungary	L 2-5	Warsaw	Fr	Cieslik, Mordarski
22-10	Czechoslovakia	L 1-4	Warsaw	Fr	Gracz
30-10	Bulgaria	W 1-0	Sofia	Fr	Cieslik
27-05-1951	Hungary	L 0-6	Budapest	Fr	
18-05-1952	Bulgaria	L 0-1	Warsaw	Fr	
25-05	Romania	L 0-1	Bucharest	Fr	
15-06	Hungary	L 1-5	Warsaw	Fr	Alszer
21-07	Denmark	L 0-2	Turku	OGr2	
14-09	Czechoslovakia	D 2-2	Prague	Fr	Mordarski, Wisniewski
21-09	East Germany	W 3-0	Warsaw	Fr	Aniola.T 2, Trampisz
10-05-1953	Czechoslovakia	D 1-1	Wroclaw	Fr	Kohut.J

Date	Opponent	Result	Venue	Comp	Scorers
13-09	Bulgaria	D 2-2	Sofia	Fr	Sobek, Wisniewski
29-11	Albania	L 0-2	Tirana	Fr	
8-08-1954	Bulgaria	D 2-2	Warsaw	Fr	Trampisz 2
26-09	East Germany	W 1-0	Rostock	Fr	Cieslik
29-05-1955	Romania	D 2-2	Bucharest	Fr	Cieslik, Hachorek
26-06	Bulgaria	D 1-1	Sofia	Fr	Brychczy
11-09	Finland	W 3-1	Helsinki	Fr	Cieslik 2, Kempny
30-05-1956	Norway	D 0-0	Oslo	Fr	
15-07	Hungary	L 1-4	Budapest	Fr	Kempny
22-07	East Germany	L 0-2	Chorzow	Fr	
26-08	Bulgaria	L 1-2	Wroclaw	Fr	Pol.E
28-10	Norway	W 5-3	Warsaw	Fr	Pol.E 4, Kempny
4-11	Finland	W 5-0	Krakow	Fr	Kempny 2, Brychczy, Kowal, Baszkiewicz
16-11	Turkey	D 1-1	Istanbul	Fr	Pol.E
19-05-1957	Turkey	L 0-1	Warsaw	Fr	
23-06	Soviet Union	L 0-3	Moscow	WCq	
5-07	Finland	W 3-1	Helsinki	WCq	Jankowski 3
29-09	Bulgaria	D 1-1	Sofia	Fr	Brychczy
20-10	Soviet Union	W 2-1	Chorzow	WCq	Cieslik 2
3-11	Finland	W 4-0	Warsaw	WCq	Brychczy 2, Jankowski, Gawlik
24-11	Soviet Union	L 0-2	Leipzig	WCq	
11-05-1958	Rep. Ireland	D 2-2	Chorzow	Fr	Cieslik, Zientara
25-05	Denmark	L 2-3	Copenhagen	Fr	Cieslik, Lentner
1-06	Scotland	L 1-2	Warsaw	Fr	Cieslik
28-06	East Germany	D 1-1	Rostock	Fr	Kempny
14-09	Hungary	L 1-3	Chorzow	Fr	OG
5-10	Rep. Ireland	D 2-2	Dublin	Fr	Pol.E 2
20-05-1959	West Germany	D 1-1	Hamburg	Fr	Baszkiewicz
21-06	Israel	W 7-2	Wroclaw	Fr	Liberda 2, Hachorek 2, Szarzynski 2, Baszkiewicz
28-06	Spain	L 2-4	Chorzow	ECr1	Pol.E, Brychczy
30-08	Romania	L 2-3	Warsaw	Fr	Pol.E 2
14-10	Spain	L 0-3	Madrid	ECr1	
18-10	Finland	W 3-1	Helsinki	OGq	Pol.E, Hachorek, Gawronski
8-11	Finland	W 6-2	Chorzow	OGq	Pol.E 3, Hachorek, Sykta, Szarzynski
29-11	Israel	D 1-1	Tel Aviv	Fr	Pol.E
4-05-1960	Scotland	W 3-2	Glasgow	Fr	Pol.E, Brychczy, Baszkiewicz
19-05	Soviet Union	L 1-7	Moscow	Fr	Pol.E
26-06	Bulgaria	W 4-0	Chorzow	Fr	Hachorek 2, Lentner, Zientara
26-08	Tunisia	W 6-1	Rome	OGr1	Pol.E 5, Hachorek
29-08	Denmark	L 1-2	Livorno	OGr1	Gadecki
1-09	Argentina *	L 0-2	Naples	OGr1	
28-09	France	D 2-2	Warsaw	Fr	Faber, Norkowski.M
13-11	Hungary	L 1-4	Budapest	Fr	Pol.E
21-05-1961	Soviet Union	W 1-0	Warsaw	Fr	Pol.E
4-06	Yugoslavia	L 1-2	Belgrade	WCq	Brychczy
25-06	Yugoslavia	D 1-1	Chorzow	WCq	Schmidt.J
8-10	West Germany	L 0-2	Warsaw	Fr	
22-10	East Germany	W 3-1	Wroclaw	Fr	Pol.E 2, Lentner
5-11	Denmark	W 5-0	Chorzow	Fr	Pol.E 3, Gajda 2
11-04-1962	France	W 3-1	Paris	Fr	Pol.E, Lentner, Brychczy
15-04	Morocco	W 3-1	Casablanca	Fr	Brychczy, Jarek, Wilczek
23-05	Belgium	W 2-0	Warsaw	Fr	Brychczy, Lentner
2-09	Hungary	L 0-2	Poznan	Fr	
30-09	Bulgaria	L 1-2	Sofia	Fr	Faber
10-10	Nth. Ireland	L 0-2	Chorzow	ECr1	
11-10	Morocco	D 1-1	Warsaw	Fr	Wilczek
28-10	Czechoslovakia	L 1-2	Bratislava	Fr	Lentner
28-11	Nth. Ireland	L 0-2	Belfast	ECr1	
15-05-1963	Norway	W 5-2	Oslo	Fr	Faber 2, Brychczy 2, Galeczka
22-05	Greece	W 4-0	Warsaw	Fr	Brychczy 2, Galeczka 2
2-06	Romania	D 1-1	Chorzow	Fr	Faber
4-09	Norway	W 9-0	Szczecin	Fr	Faber 2, Bazan 2, Szoltysik 2, Blaut.B, Lubanski, Galeczka
22-09	Turkey	D 0-0	Poznan	Fr	
16-10	Greece	L 1-3	Athens	Fr	Musialek
10-05-1964	Rep. Ireland	W 3-1	Krakow	Fr	Faber, Szoltysik, Wilim (I)
13-09	Czechoslovakia	W 2-1	Warsaw	Fr	Pol.E 2
27-09	Turkey	W 3-2	Istanbul	Fr	Pol.E, Lubanski, Banas
7-10	Sweden	D 3-3	Stockholm	Fr	Liberda 2, Pol.E
25-10	Rep. Ireland	L 2-3	Dublin	Fr	Pol.E, Lubanski
7-04-1965	Belgium	D 0-0	Brussels	Fr	

18-04	Italy	D 0-0	Warsaw	WCq	
16-05	Bulgaria	D 1-1	Krakow	Fr	Pol.E
23-05	Scotland	D 1-1	Chorzow	WCq	Lentner
26-09	Finland	L 0-2	Helsinki	WCq	
13-10	Scotland	W 2-1	Glasgow	WCq	Pol.E, Sadek
24-10	Finland	W 7-0	Szczecin	WCq	Lubanski 4, Sadek 2, Pol.E
1-11	Italy	L 1-6	Rome	WCq	Lubanski
5-01-1966	England	D 1-1	Liverpool	Fr	Sadek
3-05	Hungary	D 1-1	Chorzow	Fr	Lubanski
18-05	Sweden	D 1-1	Wroclaw	Fr	Oslizlo
5-06	Brazil	L 1-4	Belo Horizonte	Fr	Liberda
8-06	Brazil	L 1-2	Rio de Janeiro	Fr	Liberda
11-06	Argentina	D 1-1	Buenos Aires	Fr	Liberda
5-07	England	L 0-1	Chorzow	Fr	
11-09	East Germany	L 0-2	Erfurt	Fr	
2-10	Luxembourg	W 4-0	Szczecin	ECq	Sadek, Liberda, Jarosik, Grzegorczyk
22-10	France	L 1-2	Paris	ECq	Grzegorczyk
17-11	Romania	L 3-4	Ploiesti	Fr	Galeczka, Jarosik, Strzalkowski
16-04-1967	Luxembourg	D 0-0	Luxembourg	ECq	
21-05	Belgium	W 3-1	Chorzow	ECq	Lubanski 2, Szoltysik
20-07	Soviet Union	L 0-1	Warsaw	OGq	
4-08	Soviet Union	L 1-2	Moscow	OGq	Lubanski
17-09	France	L 1-4	Warsaw	ECq	Brychczy
8-10	Belgium	W 4-2	Brussels	ECq	Zmijewski 3, Brychczy
29-10	Romania	D 0-0	Krakow	Fr	
24-04-1968	Turkey	W 8-0	Chorzow	Fr	Faber 3, Lubanski 3, Bula, Zmijewski
1-05	Holland	D 0-0	Warsaw	Fr	
15-05	Rep. Ireland	D 2-2	Dublin	Fr	Lubanski, Jarosik
9-06	Norway	W 6-1	Oslo	Fr	Jarosik 3, Zmijewski 2, Lubanski
20-06	Brazil	L 3-6	Warsaw	Fr	Sadek, Zmijewski, Blaut.B
20-10	East Germany	D 1-1	Szczecin	Fr	Gadocha
30-10	Rep. Ireland	W 1-0	Chorzow	Fr	Lubanski
20-04-1969	Luxembourg	W 8-1	Krakow	WCq	Lubanski 5, Deyna 2, Wilim
30-04	Turkey	W 3-1	Ankara	Fr	Wilim 2, Lubanski
7-05	Holland	L 0-1	Rotterdam	WCq	
15-06	Bulgaria	L 1-4	Sofia	WCq	Deyna
27-08	Norway	W 6-1	Lodz	Fr	Lubanski 2, Marx 2, Deyna, Brychczy
7-09	Holland	W 2-1	Chorzow	WCq	Lubanski, Jarosik
12-10	Luxembourg	W 5-1	Luxembourg	WCq	Deyna 2, Lubanski, Jarosik, Bula
9-11	Bulgaria	W 3-0	Warsaw	WCq	Jarosik 2, Deyna
2-05-1970	Hungary	L 0-2	Budapest	Fr	
6-05	Rep. Ireland	W 2-1	Poznan	Fr	Kozerski, Szoltysik
16-05	East Germany	D 1-1	Krakow	Fr	Deyna
19-05	Denmark	W 2-0	Copenhagen	Fr	Jarosik, Banas
22-07	Iraq	W 2-0	Szczecin	Fr	Banas, Szoltysik
2-09	Denmark	W 5-0	Warsaw	Fr	Marx 3, Lubanski, Deyna
6-09	East Germany	L 0-5	Rostock	Fr	
23-09	Rep. Ireland	W 2-0	Dublin	Fr	Szoltysik, Stachurski
14-10	Albania	W 3-0	Chorzow	ECq	Lubanski, Gadocha, Szoltysik
25-10	Czechoslovakia	D 2-2	Prague	Fr	Blaut.B, Kozerski
5-05-1971	Switzerland	W 4-2	Lausanne	Fr	Lubanski, Deyna, Szoltysik, Banas
12-05	Albania	D 1-1	Tirana	ECq	Banas
22-09	Turkey	W 5-1	Krakow	ECq	Lubanski 3, Gadocha, Bula
10-10	West Germany	L 1-3	Warsaw	ECq	Gadocha
17-11	West Germany	D 0-0	Hamburg	ECq	
5-12	Turkey	L 0-1	Izmir	ECq	
16-04-1972	Bulgaria	L 1-3	Stara Zagora	OGq	Lubanski
7-05	Bulgaria	W 3-0	Warsaw	OGq	Banas 2, Marx
10-05	Switzerland	D 0-0	Poznan	Fr	
28-08	Colombia *	W 5-1	Ingolstadt	OGr1	Gadocha 3, Deyna 2
30-08	Ghana	W 4-0	Regensburg	OGr1	Gadocha 2, Lubanski, Deyna
1-09	East Germany	W 2-1	Nuremberg	OGr1	Gorgon 2
3-09	Denmark	D 1-1	Regensburg	OGr2	Deyna
5-09	Soviet Union	W 2-1	Augsburg	OGr2	Deyna, Szoltysik
8-09	Morocco	W 5-0	Nuremberg	OGr2	Deyna 2, Kmiecik, Lubanski, Gadocha
10-09	Hungary *	W 2-1	Munich	OGf	Deyna 2
15-10	Czechoslovakia	W 3-0	Bydgoszcz	Fr	Deyna 2, Gadocha
20-03-1973	United States	W 4-0	Lodz	Fr	Lubanski 3, Kasperczak
28-03	Wales	L 0-2	Cardiff	WCq	
13-05	Yugoslavia	D 2-2	Warsaw	Fr	Lubanski, Masztaler
16-05	Rep. Ireland	W 2-0	Wroclaw	Fr	Lubanski 2

6-06	England	W 2-0	Chorzow	WCq	Lubanski, Banas
1-08	Canada	W 3-1	Toronto	Fr	Gadocha 2, Gorgon
3-08	United States	W 1-0	Chicago	Fr	Kasperczak
5-08	Mexico	W 1-0	Los Angeles	Fr	Gorgon
8-08	Mexico	W 2-1	Monterrey	Fr	Gadocha, Gorgon
10-08	United States	W 4-0	San Francisco	Fr	Kmiecik 2, Kasztelan, Szarmach
12-08	United States	L 0-1	New Britain	Fr	
19-08	Bulgaria	W 2-0	Varna	Fr	Lato 2
26-09	Wales	W 3-0	Chorzow	WCq	Lato, Gadocha, Domarski
10-10	Holland	D 1-1	Rotterdam	Fr	Deyna
17-10	England	D 1-1	London	WCq	Domarski
21-10	Rep. Ireland	L 0-1	Dublin	Fr	
17-04-1974	Belgium	D 1-1	Liege	Fr	Deyna
15-05	Greece	W 2-0	Warsaw	Fr	Lato, Jakobczak
15-06	Argentina	W 3-2	Stuttgart	WCr1	Lato 2, Szarmach
19-06	Haiti	W 7-0	Munich	WCr1	Szarmach 3, Lato 2, Deyna, Gorgon
23-06	Italy	W 2-1	Stuttgart	WCr1	Deyna, Szarmach
26-06	Sweden	W 1-0	Stuttgart	WCr2	Lato
30-06	Yugoslavia	W 2-1	Frankfurt	WCr2	Lato, Deyna
3-07	West Germany	L 0-1	Frankfurt	WCr2	
6-07	Brazil	W 1-0	Munich	WC3p	Lato
1-09	Finland	W 2-1	Helsinki	ECq	Lato, Szarmach
4-09	East Germany	L 1-3	Warsaw	Fr	Lato
7-09	France	L 0-2	Wroclaw	Fr	
9-10	Finland	W 3-0	Poznan	ECq	Lato, Gadocha, Kasperczak
31-10	Canada	W 2-0	Warsaw	Fr	Kasalik, Jakobczak
13-11	Czechoslovakia	D 2-2	Prague	Fr	Szarmach, Gadocha
26-03-1975	United States	W 7-0	Poznan	Fr	Deyna 3, Lato 2, Szarmach 2
19-04	Italy	D 0-0	Rome	ECq	
28-05	East Germany	W 2-1	Halle	Fr	Lato, Marx
24-06	United States	W 4-0	Seattle	Fr	Lato, Szarmach, Bula, Wyrobek
6-07	Canada	W 8-1	Montreal	Fr	Lato 3, Deyna 2, Szarmach, Marx, Bula
9-07	Canada	W 4-1	Toronto	Fr	Szarmach 2, Deyna, Kwiatkowski
10-09	Holland	W 4-1	Chorzow	ECq	Szarmach 2, Gadocha, Lato
8-10	Hungary	W 4-2	Lodz	Fr	Marx 2, Kmiecik, Kasperczak
15-10	Holland	L 0-3	Amsterdam	ECq	
26-10	Italy	D 0-0	Warsaw	ECq	
24-03-1976	Argentina	L 1-2	Chorzow	Fr	Kmiecik
24-04	France	L 0-2	Lens	Fr	
6-05	Greece	L 0-1	Athens	Fr	
11-05	Switzerland	L 1-2	Basle	Fr	Boniek
26-05	Rep. Ireland	L 0-2	Poznan	Fr	
18-07	Cuba	D 0-0	Montreal	OGr1	
22-07	Iran	W 3-2	Montreal	OGr1	Szarmach 2, Deyna
25-07	North Korea	W 5-0	Montreal	OGqf	Szarmach 2, Lato 2, Szymanowski
27-07	Brazil *	W 2-0	Toronto	OGsf	Szarmach 2
30-07	East Germany	L 1-3	Montreal	OGf	Lato
16-10	Portugal	W 2-0	Oporto	WCq	Lato 2
31-10	Cyprus	W 5-0	Warsaw	WCq	Deyna 2, Boniek, Szarmach, Terlecki
13-04-1977	Hungary	L 1-2	Budapest	Fr	Nawalka
24-04	Rep. Ireland	D 0-0	Dublin	Fr	
1-05	Denmark	W 2-1	Copenhagen	WCq	Lubanski 2
15-05	Cyprus	W 3-1	Limassol	WCq	Lato, Terlecki, Mazur
29-05	Argentina	L 1-3	Buenos Aires	Fr	Lato
10-06	Peru	W 3-1	Lima	Fr	Szarmach, Deyna, Kasperczak
12-06	Bolivia	W 2-1	La Paz	Fr	Lato, Kapka
19-06	Brazil	L 1-3	Sao Paulo	Fr	Boniek
24-08	Austria	L 1-2	Vienna	Fr	Kmiecik
7-09	Soviet Union	L 1-4	Volgograd	Fr	Lato
21-09	Denmark	W 4-1	Chorzow	WCq	Lato, Deyna, Szarmach, Masztaler
29-10	Portugal	D 1-1	Chorzow	WCq	Deyna
12-11	Sweden	W 2-1	Wroclaw	Fr	Deyna, Kusto
22-03-1978	Luxembourg	W 3-1	Luxembourg	Fr	Szarmach 2, Lubanski
5-04	Greece	W 5-2	Poznan	Fr	Deyna 2, Lato, Boniek, Zmuda
12-04	Rep. Ireland	W 3-0	Lodz	Fr	Deyna, Boniek, Mazur
26-04	Bulgaria	W 1-0	Warsaw	Fr	Lato
1-06	West Germany	D 0-0	Buenos Aires	WCr1	
6-06	Tunisia	W 1-0	Rosario	WCr1	Lato
10-06	Mexico	W 3-1	Rosario	WCr1	Boniek 2, Deyna
14-06	Argentina	L 0-2	Rosario	WCr2	
18-06	Peru	W 1-0	Mendoza	WCr2	Szarmach

21-06	Brazil	L 1-3	Mendoza	WCr2	Lato
30-08	Finland	W 1-0	Helsinki	Fr	Majewski.S
6-09	Iceland	W 2-0	Reykjavik	ECq	Lato, Kusto
11-10	Romania	L 0-1	Bucharest	Fr	
15-11	Switzerland	W 2-0	Wroclaw	ECq	Boniek, Ogaza
18-02-1979	Tunisia	W 2-0	Tunis	Fr	Ogaza 2
21-03	Algeria	W 1-0	Algiers	Fr	Lato
4-04	Hungary	D 1-1	Chorzow	Fr	Lato
18-04	East Germany	L 1-2	Leipzig	ECq	Boniek
2-05	Holland	W 2-0	Chorzow	ECq	Boniek, Mazur
19-08	Libya	W 5-0	Slupsk	Fr	Kmiecik, Terlecki, Faber, Janas, Wieczorek
29-08	Romania	W 3-0	Warsaw	Fr	Lato, Boniek, Terlecki
12-09	Switzerland	W 2-0	Lausanne	ECq	Terlecki 2
26-09	East Germany	D 1-1	Chorzow	ECq	Wieczorek
10-10	Iceland	W 2-0	Krakow	ECq	Ogaza 2
17-10	Holland	D 1-1	Amsterdam	ECq	Rudy
27-02-1980	Iraq	D 1-1	Baghdad	Fr	Palasz
26-03	Hungary	L 1-2	Budapest	Fr	Lato
2-04	Belgium	L 1-2	Brussels	Fr	Lato
19-04	Italy	D 2-2	Turin	Fr	Szarmach, Sybis
26-04	Yugoslavia	L 1-2	Borovo	Fr	Sybis
13-05	West Germany	L 1-3	Frankfurt	Fr	Boniek
28-05	Scotland	W 1-0	Poznan	Fr	Boniek
22-06	Iraq	W 3-0	Warsaw	Fr	Lato, Kmiecik, Iwan
29-06	Brazil	D 1-1	Sao Paulo	Fr	Lato
2-07	Bolivia	W 1-0	Santa Cruz	Fr	Iwan
9-07	Colombia	W 4-1	Bogota	Fr	Iwan 3, Terlecki
24-09	Czechoslovakia	D 1-1	Chorzow	Fr	Lubanski
12-10	Argentina	L 1-2	Buenos Aires	Fr	Ciolek
12-11	Spain	W 2-1	Barcelona	Fr	Iwan 2
19-11	Algeria	W 5-1	Krakow	Fr	Iwan 2, Ciolek, Kupcewicz, Dziuba
7-12	Malta	W 2-0	Gzira	WCq	Smolarek, Lipka
25-03-1981	Romania	L 0-2	Bucharest	Fr	
2-05	East Germany	W 1-0	Chorzow	WCq	Buncol
24-05	Rep. Ireland	W 3-0	Bydgoszcz	Fr	Iwan, Ogaza, OG
2-09	West Germany	L 0-2	Chorzow	Fr	
23-09	Portugal	L 0-2	Lisbon	Fr	
10-10	East Germany	W 3-2	Leipzig	WCq	Szarmach 2, Smolarek
28-10	Argentina	W 2-1	Buenos Aires	Fr	Boniek, Buncol
15-11	Malta	W 6-0	Wroclaw	WCq	Smolarek 2, Boniek, Buncol, Majewski.S, Dziekanowski
18-11	Spain	L 2-3	Lodz	Fr	Boniek, Palasz
14-06-1982	Italy	D 0-0	Vigo	WCr1	
19-06	Cameroon	D 0-0	La Coruna	WCr1	
22-06	Peru	W 5-1	La Coruna	WCr1	Lato, Boniek, Buncol, Smolarek, Ciolek
28-06	Belgium	W 3-0	Barcelona	WCr2	Boniek 3
4-07	Soviet Union	D 0-0	Barcelona	WCr2	
8-07	Italy	L 0-2	Barcelona	WCsf	
10-07	France	W 3-2	Alicante	WC3p	Szarmach, Kupcewicz, Majewski.S
31-08	France	W 4-0	Paris	Fr	Kupcewicz 2, Buncol, Locha
8-09	Finland	W 3-2	Kuopio	ECq	Smolarek, Dziekanowski, Kupcewicz
10-10	Portugal	L 1-2	Lisbon	ECq	Król
23-03-1983	Bulgaria	W 3-1	Lodz	Fr	Majewski, Dziekanowski, Okonski
17-04	Finland	D 1-1	Warsaw	ECq	Smolarek
22-05	Soviet Union	D 1-1	Chorzow	ECq	Boniek
7-09	Romania	D 2-2	Krakow	Fr	Ciolek, Iwan
9-10	Soviet Union	L 0-2	Moscow	ECq	
28-10	Portugal	L 0-1	Wroclaw	ECq	
11-01-1984	India	W 2-1	Calcutta	Fr	Dziekanowski, Pawlak
15-01	China	W 1-0	Calcutta	Fr	Adamiec
17-01	Argentina	D 1-1	Calcutta	Fr	Buncol
27-01	China	W 1-0	Calcutta	Fr	Wójcicki
27-03	Switzerland	D 1-1	Zurich	Fr	Boniek
17-04	Belgium	L 0-1	Warsaw	Fr	
23-05	Rep. Ireland	D 0-0	Dublin	Fr	
29-08	Norway	D 1-1	Drammen	Fr	Tarasiewicz
12-09	Finland	W 2-0	Helsinki	Fr	Dziekanowski, Palasz
26-09	Turkey	W 2-0	Slupsk	Fr	Dziekanowski 2
17-10	Greece	W 3-1	Zabrze	WCq	Dziekanowski 2, Smolarek
31-10	Albania	D 2-2	Mielec	WCq	Palasz, Smolarek
8-12	Italy	L 0-2	Pescara	Fr	

Date	Opponent	Result	Venue	Comp	Scorers
5-02-1985	Mexico	L 0-5	Queretaro	Fr	
7-02	Bulgaria	D 2-2	Queretaro	Fr	Dziekanowski, Prusik
10-02	Colombia	W 2-1	Bogota	Fr	Palasz 2
14-02	Colombia	L 0-1	Cali	Fr	
27-03	Romania	D 0-0	Sibiu	Fr	
17-04	Finland	W 2-1	Opole	Fr	Palasz, Zmuda
1-05	Belgium	L 0-2	Brussels	WCq	
19-05	Greece	W 4-1	Athens	WCq	Boniek, Smolarek, Dziekanowski, Ostrowski
30-05	Albania	W 1-0	Tirana	WCq	Boniek
21-08	Sweden	L 0-1	Malmo	Fr	
4-09	Czechoslovakia	L 1-3	Brno	Fr	Prusik
11-09	Belgium	D 0-0	Chorzow	WCq	
16-11	Italy	W 1-0	Chorzow	Fr	Dziekanowski
8-12	Tunisia	L 0-1	Tunis	Fr	
11-12	Turkey	D 1-1	Adana	Fr	Furtok
16-02-1986	Uruguay	D 2-2	Montevideo	Fr	Baran.K 2
26-03	Spain	L 0-3	Cadiz	Fr	
16-05	Denmark	L 0-1	Copenhagen	Fr	
2-06	Morocco	D 0-0	Monterrey	WCr1	
7-06	Portugal	W 1-0	Monterrey	WCr1	Smolarek
11-06	England	L 0-3	Monterrey	WCr1	
16-06	Brazil	L 0-4	Guadalajara	WCr2	
7-10	North Korea	D 2-2	Bydgoszcz	Fr	Karas, Tarasiewicz
15-10	Greece	W 2-1	Poznan	ECq	Dziekanowski 2
12-11	Rep. Ireland	W 1-0	Warsaw	Fr	Koniarek
19-11	Holland	D 0-0	Amsterdam	ECq	
18-03-1987	Finland	W 3-1	Rybnik	Fr	Lesniak, Furtok, Urban
24-03	Norway	W 4-1	Wroclaw	Fr	Furtok, Urban, Prusik, Król
12-04	Cyprus	D 0-0	Gdansk	ECq	
29-04	Greece	L 0-1	Athens	ECq	
17-05	Hungary	L 3-5	Budapest	ECq	Smolarek, Wójcicki, Marciniak
19-08	East Germany	W 2-0	Lublin	Fr	Prusik, Król
2-09	Romania	W 3-1	Bydgoszcz	Fr	Lesniak 2, Rudy.A
23-09	Hungary	W 3-2	Warsaw	ECq	Lesniak, Dziekanowski, Tarasiewicz
14-10	Holland	L 0-2	Zabrze	ECq	
27-10	Czechoslovakia	L 1-3	Bratislava	Fr	Tarasiewicz
11-11	Cyprus	W 1-0	Limassol	ECq	Lesniak
6-02-1988	Romania	D 2-2	Haifa	Fr	Cisek 2
10-02	Israel	W 3-1	Tel Aviv	Fr	Prusik, Kosecki, Kubicki
23-03	Nth. Ireland	D 1-1	Belfast	Fr	Dziekanowski
22-05	Rep. Ireland	L 1-3	Dublin	Fr	Warzycha.R
1-06	Soviet Union	L 1-2	Moscow	Fr	Dziekanowski
13-07	United States	W 2-0	New Britain	Fr	Kosecki 2
15-07	Canada	W 2-1	Toronto	Fr	Rudy.A, Tarasiewicz
24-08	Bulgaria	W 3-2	Bialystok	Fr	Furtok, Rudy.A, OG
21-09	East Germany	W 2-1	Cottbus	Fr	Furtok 2
19-10	Albania	W 1-0	Chorzow	WCq	Warzycha.K
8-02-1989	Costa Rica	W 2-4	San Jose	Fr	Warzycha.K 2, Kosecki, Urban
12-02	Guatemala	W 1-0	Guatemala City	Fr	Warzycha.K
14-02	Mexico	L 1-3	Puebla	Fr	Kosecki
12-04	Romania	W 2-1	Warsaw	Fr	Urban, Tarasiewicz
2-05	Norway	W 3-0	Oslo	Fr	Furtok 2, Wdowczyk
3-06	England	L 0-3	London	WCq	
7-07	Sweden	L 1-2	Stockholm	WCq	Tarasiewicz
23-08	Soviet Union	D 1-1	Lublin	Fr	Wdowczyk
5-09	Greece	W 3-0	Warsaw	Fr	Warzycha.R, Dziekanowski, Ziober
20-09	Spain	L 0-1	La Coruña	Fr	
11-10	England	D 0-0	Chorzow	WCq	
25-10	Sweden	L 0-2	Chorzow	WCq	
15-11	Albania	W 2-1	Tirana	WCq	Tarasiewicz, Ziober
2-02-1990	Iran	W 2-0	Tehran	Fr	Ziober 2
4-02	Iran	W 1-0	Tehran	Fr	Szewczyk
11-02	Kuwait	D 1-1	Cairo	Fr	Kosecki
28-03	Yugoslavia	D 0-0	Lodz	Fr	
4-05	Colombia	L 1-2	Chicago	Fr	Kosecki
6-05	Costa Rica	W 2-0	Chicago	Fr	Pisz, Nowak
10-05	United States	L 1-3	Hershey	Fr	Ziober
19-05	Scotland	D 1-1	Glasgow	Fr	OG
21-05	Arab Emirates	W 4-0	Marseille	Fr	Dziekanowski, Kosecki, Warzycha.R 2
6-06	Belgium	D 1-1	Brussels	Fr	Ziober
15-08	France	D 0-0	Paris	Fr	

26-09	Romania	L 1-2	Bucharest	Fr	Warzycha.R
10-10	United States	L 2-3	Warsaw	Fr	Kosecki, Ziober
17-10	England	L 0-2	London	ECq	
14-11	Turkey	W 1-0	Istanbul	ECq	Dziekanowski
19-12	Greece	W 2-1	Volos	Fr	Soczynski, Kosecki
6-02-1991	Nth. Ireland	L 1-3	Belfast	Fr	Warzycha.R
13-03	Finland	D 1-1	Warsaw	Fr	Lesiak
27-03	Czechoslovakia	L 0-4	Olomouc	Fr	
17-04	Turkey	W 3-0	Warsaw	ECq	Tarasiewicz, Urban, Kosecki
1-05	Rep. Ireland	D 0-0	Dublin	ECq	
29-05	Wales	D 0-0	Radom	Fr	
14-08	France	L 1-5	Poznan	Fr	Ziober
21-08	Sweden	W 2-0	Gdynia	Fr	Kowalczyk, Trzeciak
11-09	Holland	D 1-1	Eindhoven	Fr	Ziober
16-10	Rep. Ireland	D 3-3	Poznan	ECq	Czachowski, Furtok, Urban
13-11	England	D 1-1	Poznan	ECq	Szewczyk
25-03-1992	Lithuania	W 2-0	Katowice	Fr	Kraus, Lesiak
7-05	Sweden	L 0-5	Stockholm	Fr	
19-05	Austria	W 4-2	Salzburg	Fr	Kosecki 2, Warzycha.K, Kowalczyk
27-05	Czechoslovakia	W 1-0	Jastrzebie	Fr	Warzycha.K
26-08	Finaland	D 0-0	Pietarsaari	Fr	
9-09	Israel	D 1-1	Mielec	Fr	Szewczyk
23-09	Turkey	W 1-0	Poznan	WCq	Waldoch
14-10	Holland	D 2-2	Rotterdam	WCq	Kozminski, Kowalczyk
18-11	Latvia	W 1-0	Ilawa	Fr	Mielcarski
26-11	Argentina	L 0-2	Buenos Aires	Fr	
29-11	Uruguay	W 1-0	Montevideo	Fr	Gesior
1-02-1993	Cyprus	D 0-0	Nicosia	Fr	
3-02	Israel	D 0-0	Haifa	Fr	
17-03	Brazil	D 2-2	Ribeiro Preto	Fr	Brzeczek, Warzycha.R
13-04	Finland	W 2-0	Radom	Fr	Lesniak 2
28-04	San Marino	W 1-0	Lodz	WCq	Furtok
19-05	San Marino	W 3-0	Serravalle	WCq	Lesniak 2, Warzycha.K
29-05	England	D 1-1	Chorzow	WCq	Adamczuk
8-09	England	L 0-3	London	WCq	
22-09	Norway	L 0-1	Oslo	WCq	
27-10	Turkey	L 1-2	Istanbul	WCq	Kowalczyk
17-11	Holland	L 1-3	Poznan	WCq	Lesniak
9-02-1994	Spain	D 1-1	Tenerife	Fr	Kosecki
23-03	Greece	D 0-0	Salonica	Fr	
13-04	Saudi Arabia	W 1-0	Cannes	Fr	Wieszczycki
4-05	Hungary	W 3-2	Krakow	Fr	OG, Baluszynski, Fedoruk
17-05	Austria	L 3-4	Katowice	Fr	Juskowiak, Brzeczek, Moskal
17-08	Belarus	D 1-1	Radom	Fr	Bak
4-09	Israel	L 1-2	Tel Aviv	ECq	Kosecki
12-10	Azerbaijan	W 1-0	Mielec	ECq	Juskowiak
16-11	France	D 0-0	Zabrze	ECq	
7-12	Saudi Arabia	W 2-0	Riyadh	Fr	Dembinski, Lapinski
10-12	Saudi Arabia	W 2-1	Riyadh	Fr	Baluszynski, Rzasa
15-03-1995	Lithuania	W 4-1	Osrtowiec Swiet.	Fr	Czereszewski, Waldoch, Wieszczycki, Jaskulski
29-03	Romania	L 1-2	Bucharest	ECq	Juskowiak
25-04	Israel	W 4-3	Zabrze	ECq	Nowak, Juskowiak, Kowalczyk, Kosecki
7-06	Slovakia	W 5-0	Zabrze	ECq	Juskowiak 2, Swierczewski, Kosecki, Nowak
26-06	Brazil	L 1-2	Recife	Fr	Juskowiak

PORTUGAL

Portugal's football fame rests on three laurels: the continued excellence of Benfica, Sporting and FC Porto, the 1966 World Cup, and Eusébio. The Portuguese were without doubt one of the great nations of the 1960s. Benfica appeared in five European Cup finals, winning two of them, whilst the national side, based as it was on these Benfica players, enjoyed its most successful era. The Portuguese will always produce players of talent - they have won the World Youth Cup twice - but for the senior team, a record of just three appearances in the finals of a major tournament is a woeful statistic.

The Federaçao Portuguesa de Futebol was formed in 1914, but it was not until eight years later that it organised a competition for the numerous clubs that had been formed. Until this time, clubs had taken part in local competitions, with the major centres in Lisbon and Oporto. Indeed the Portuguese Federation was formed as a result of the merger of the two associations from these cities.

Most of the clubs still prominent today were formed around the turn of the century. Benfica were founded in 1904 whilst their great rivals Sporting and FC Porto appeared two years later. FC Porto were the winners of the first cup competition in 1922, and since then Portuguese football has been dominated by these three teams in a way that is unique in European football. The league championship, introduced in 1935, has only ever been won by four teams. Apart from the big three, Belenenses in 1948 are the only other team to have won the major prize.

THE ORDER OF MERIT

		All			League			Cup		Europe		
	Team	G	S	B	G	S	B	G	S	G	S	B
1	Benfica	57	34	12	30	20	9	25	8	2	6	3
2	Sporting Clube Portugal	33	28	21	16	14	19	16	14	1	-	2
3	FC Porto	27	34	10	14	21	9	12	12	1	1	1
4	OS Belenenses	7	10	14	1	3	14	6	7	-	-	-
5	Boavista FC	4	2	2	-	1	2	4	1	-	-	-
6	Vitória FC Setúbal	2	8	3	-	1	3	2	7	-	-	-
7	Académica Coimbra	1	5	-	-	1	-	1	4	-	-	-
8	Atlético Clube Portugal	1	3	2	-	-	2	1	3	-	-	-
9	Sporting Clube Braga	1	2	-	-	-	-	1	2	-	-	-
10	CS Marítimo	1	1	-	-	-	-	1	1	-	-	-
	SC Olhanense	1	1	-	-	-	-	1	1	-	-	-
12	Estrela da Amadora	1	-	-	-	-	-	1	-	-	-	-
	Leixoes SC	1	-	-	-	-	-	1	-	-	-	-
14	Vitória SC Guimaraes	-	4	2	-	-	2	-	4	-	-	-
15	FC Barreirense	-	2	-	-	-	-	-	2	-	-	-
16	SC Beira Mar	-	1	-	-	-	-	-	1	-	-	-
	GD Estoril Praia	-	1	-	-	-	-	-	1	-	-	-
	SC Farense	-	1	-	-	-	-	-	1	-	-	-
	FC Rio Ave	-	1	-	-	-	-	-	1	-	-	-
	Sporting Clube Covilha	-	1	-	-	-	-	-	1	-	-	-
	SC Uniao Torriense	-	1	-	-	-	-	-	1	-	-	-
	GD Quimgal	-	-	1	-	-	1	-	-	-	-	-

To the end of the 1994-95 season

The national team did not have an auspicious start. In December 1921, a friendly match was organised against neighbours Spain. It was not a success and throughout the next three decades matches were fairly infrequent, with Spain providing the only regular opposition. This reluctance to get a national team together more often still persists today. In 1988 only two games were played whilst 1990 saw only four, far too few to achieve anything at the highest level.

Club football has traditionally been the strength of the Potuguese game. By the mid 1930s Benfica, Sporting and Porto had wrested control of the Cup from other pretenders, and they dominated the new league from the outset. With big memberships, all three clubs built large stadia which in turn attracted bigger crowds and so the cycle continued. For many years Benfica's Stadium of Light in Lisbon was the biggest club ground in Europe. Clubs like Belenenses, Boavista and teams from provincial towns such as Setubal and Guimaraes were simply unable to compete. It is a remarkable statistic that only 10 sides have ever managed to finish in the top three in Portugal, and five of those have done so on two occasions or fewer.

The early 1960s saw Portugal finally make an impact on the European game. In 1961 Benfica won the European Cup, beating Barcelona in the final. The following year they won it again, this time beating Real Madrid in a thriller in Amsterdam. A third final the year after that ended in defeat at the hands of Milan at Wembley, whilst the losses in the 1965 and 1968 finals had more to do with the fact that both games were effectively played away rather than on neutral territory. In 1965 they lost to a sterile Internazionale by the only goal in the San Siro, whilst in 1968, Wembley was the scene of another defeat for them, this time at the hands of Manchester United.

The basis of the Benfica side was also the core of the national side in the 1960s, and the central figure was Eusébio, who along with Mario Coluña was Mozambiquan by birth. Both were spotted young, brought over to Portugal, and qualified to play for the mother country. The use of players from their colonies gave Portuguese sides an aura of mystique, as European crowds in the 1960s were still unused to black footballers. Jose Aguas was another African-born player, from Angola, and he scored two goals, one in each of the finals, that helped Benfica in their European Cup triumphs. The other great players for both Benfica and Portugal in the 1960s included Costa Pereira in goal and Germano, who is often rated as the best centre-half of his generation, with Cavem and Jose Augusto on either wing keeping Eusébio, Coluña and Torres well supplied in the centre. Eusébio, however, was the undoubted star.

Qualification for the 1966 World Cup reversed a trend that had seen six previous unsuccessful attempts to qualify, but once there the Portuguese played some of the best football of that or any other tournament, beating Hungary, Bulgaria and Brazil with great style in the first round. The quarter-finals saw them pitted against the North Koreans. Three goals down after half an hour, Portugal looked in serious danger, but one of the most inspired individual performances ever witnessed in the World Cup saw Eusébio score four goals as his side came back to win 5-3. It is often said that it is worse to lose a semi-final than a final, and for Eusébio, the defeat by England at Wembley provoked the most publicised tears until Paul Gascoigne was moved to the same 24 years later. Despite his nine goals, Eusébio was denied the opportunity to appear in the World Cup final, a stage he richly deserved.

The Portuguese have struggled to live up to the great reputation of this side and the 1970s saw a decline both of the national team and the club sides. Not until 1983, when Benfica lost to Anderlecht in the UEFA Cup, did a Portuguese side appear in another European club final. It sparked a mini-revival as the following year FC Porto reached the Cup Winners Cup final and the national team were unlucky to lose a thrilling semi-final to France in the European Championships. Qualification for only their second World Cup in 1986 followed, but although the trip to Mexico proved to be a disaster, FC Porto then became the third club from Portugal to win a European honour when they won the 1987 European Cup, beating Bayern Munich in the final.

Portuguese football has the makings of being among the best in Europe. Two more European Cup final appearances by Benfica in 1988 and 1990 are testament to the strength of the top Portuguese clubs, and victories in the 1989 and 1991 World Youth Cups show that quality players are still being produced in Portugal. The challenge is to blend the native Portuguese players with the numerous foreign stars playing their league football in Portugal, as well as achieving the right balance between club and country. Until the national team is more consistent and given a proper programme which will allow it to fulfil its capabilities, Portugal will remain a curiosity on the European scene.

Population: 10,388,000
Area, sq km: 92,389
% in urban areas: 29.6%
Capital city: Lisbon

Federaçao Portuguesa de Futebol
Praça de Alegría #25
Apartado 21.100
P-1128 Lisbon Codex
Portugal
Tel: + 351 1 3428207
Fax: + 351 1 3467231

Year of formation	1914
Affiliation to FIFA	1926
Affiliation to UEFA	1954
Registered clubs	1420
Registered players	81 200
Professional players	1650
Registered coaches	571
Registered referees	208
National stadium	Estádio Nacional 60 000
National colours	Red/Green/Red
Reserve colours	White/Red/White
Season	August - June

THE RECORD

WORLD CUP

1930	Did not enter
1934	QT 2nd/2 in group 6
1938	QT 2nd/2 in group 4
1950	QT 2nd/2 in group 6
1954	QT 2nd/2 in group 5
1958	QT 3rd/3 in group 8
1962	QT 2nd/3 in group 6
1966	QT 1st/4 in group 4 - Final Tournament/Semi-finalists/ 3rd place
1970	QT 4th/4 in group 1
1974	QT 2nd/4 in group 6
1978	QT 2nd/4 in group 1
1982	QT 4th/5 in group 6
1986	QT 2nd/5 in group 2 - Final Tournament/1st round
1990	QT 3rd/5 in group 7
1994	QT 3rd/6 in group 1

EUROPEAN CHAMPIONSHIP

1960	Quarter-finalists
1964	1st round
1968	QT 2nd/4 in group 2
1972	QT 2nd/4 in group 5
1976	QT 3rd/4 in group 1
1980	QT 3rd/5 in group 2
1984	QT 1st/4 in group 2 - Final Tournament/Semi-finalists
1988	QT 3rd/5 in group 2
1992	QT 2nd/5 in group 6
1996	QT group 6

EUROPEAN CLUB COMPETITIONS

European Cup
Winners - Benfica 1961 1962 FC Porto 1987
Finalists - Benfica 1963 1965 1968 1988 1990

Cup Winners Cup
Winners - Sporting CP 1964
Finalists - FC Porto 1984

UEFA Cup
Finalists - Benfica 1983

CLUB DIRECTORY

LISBON (Population - 2,250,000)

Atlético Clube Portugal (1942)
Tapadinha – Yellow & blue stripes/Blue
Previous names - Formed when Carcavelinhos and Uniao merged in 1942

FC Barreirense (1911)
(Futebol Clube)
Manuel de Melo – Red & white chequered/White

CF "OS Belenenses" (1919)
(Clube de Futebol)
Estádio do Restelo 42,000 – Blue/White

Sport Lisboa e Benfica (1904)
Estádio da Luz 120,000 – Red/White

CF Estrela da Amadora (1932)
José Gomes 25,000 – Red, green & thin white stripes/White

Grupo Desportivo Quimigal (1937)
Alfiedo da Silva – Green/White
Previous names - Unidos FC 1937-44, GD Cuf Barreiro 1944-78

Sporting Clube de Portugal (1906)
José Alvalade 70,000 – Green & white hoops/Black

OPORTO (Population - 1,225,000)

Boavista FC (1903)
Estádio do Bessa 26,000 – Black & white checks/Black

FC do Porto (1906)
Estádio das Antas 76,000 – Blue & white stripes/Blue

Sport Commércio e Salgueiros (1911)
Campo Vidal Pinheiro 20,000 – Red, white trim

Leixoes Sport Club (1907)
Estádio do Mar 20,000 – Red & white stripes/White

FUNCHAL, Madeira (Population - 273,000)

Clube Sport Marítimo (1910)
Estádio dos Barreiros 16,000 – Red & green stripes/White

Clube Desportivo Nacional (1910)
Estádio dos Barreiros 16,000 – Black & white stripes/Black

CF Uniao (1913)
Estádio dos Barreiros 16,000 – Yellow & blue stripes/Blue

SETUBAL (Population - 77,000)

Vitória FC Setúbal (1910)
Estádio do Bonfim 30,000 – Green & white stripes/White

COIMBRA (Population - 74,000)

Associacao Académica de Coimbra (1876)
Municipal 35,000 – Black/Black

BRAGA (Population - 63,000)

Sporting Club de Braga (1921)
Primeiro de Maio 40,000 – Red, white sleeves/White

FC de Famalicao (1931)
22 de Julho 25,000 – White/Blue

GUIMARAES (Population - 22,000)

Vitória SC Guimarães (1922)
Vitória Sport Clube 33,000 – White, black trim

OLHAO (Population - 19,000)

SC Olhanense (1912)
(Sporting Clube)
Padinho – Red & black stripes/White

CHAVES (Population - 12,000)

Grupo de Desportivo de Chaves (1949)
Municipal 25,000 – Red & blue stripes/Blue

PORTIMAO (Population - 19,000)

Portimonense SC (1914)
Estádio do Portimonense 17,000 – Black & white stripes/Black

PORTUGUESE LEAGUE CHAMPIONSHIP

1935f	FC Porto 22 Sporting CP 20 Benfica 19
1936	Benfica 21 FC Porto 20 Sporting CP 18
1937	Benfica 24 OS Belenenses 23 Sporting CP 20
1938	Benfica 23 FC Porto 23 Sporting CP 22
1939	FC Porto 23 Sporting CP 22 Benfica 21
1940h	FC Porto 34 Sporting CP 32 OS Belenenses 25
1941f	Sporting CP 23 FC Porto 20 OS Belenenses 19
1942k	Benfica 38 Sporting CP 34 OS Belenenses 30
1943h	Benfica 30 Sporting CP 29 OS Belenenses 28
1944	Sporting CP 31 Benfica 26 Atletico CP 24
1945	Benfica 30 Sporting CP 27 OS Belenenses 27
1946k	OS Belenenses 38 Benfica 37 Sporting CP 32
1947n	Sporting CP 47 Benfica 41 FC Porto 33
1948	Sporting CP 41 Benfica 41 OS Belenenses 37
1949	Sporting CP 42 Benfica 37 OS Belenenses 35
1950	Benfica 45 Sporting CP 39 Atletico CP 30
1951	Sporting CP 45 FC Porto 34 Benfica 30
1952	Sporting CP 41 Benfica 40 FC Porto 36
1953	Sporting CP 43 Benfica 39 OS Belenenses 36
1954	Sporting CP 43 FC Porto 36 Benfica 32
1955	Benfica 39 OS Belenenses 39 Sporting CP 37
1956	FC Porto 43 Benfica 43 OS Belenenses 37
1957	Benfica 41 FC Porto 40 OS Belenenses 33
1958	Sporting CP 43 FC Porto 43 Benfica 36
1959	FC Porto 41 Benfica 41 OS Belenenses 38
1960	Benfica 45 Sporting CP 43 OS Belenenses 36
1961	Benfica 46 Sporting CP 42 FC Porto 33
1962	Sporting CP 43 FC Porto 41 Benfica 36
1963	Benfica 48 FC Porto 42 Sporting CP 38
1964	Benfica 46 FC Porto 40 Sporting CP 34
1965	Benfica 43 FC Porto 37 CUF Barreiro 34
1966	Sporting CP 42 Benfica 41 FC Porto 34
1967	Benfica 43 Académica Coimbra 40 FC Porto 39
1968	Benfica 41 Sporting CP 37 FC Porto 36
1969	Benfica 39 FC Porto 37 Vitória Guimaraes 36
1970	Sporting CP 46 Benfica 38 Vitória Setúbal 36
1971	Benfica 41 Sporting CP 38 FC Porto 37
1972q	Benfica 55 Vitória Setúbal 45 Sporting CP 43
1973	Benfica 58 OS Belenenses 40 Vitória Setúbal 38
1974	Sporting CP 49 Benfica 47 Vitória Setúbal 45
1975	Benfica 49 FC Porto 44 Sporting CP 43
1976	Benfica 50 Boavista FC 48 OS Belenenses 40
1977	Benfica 51 Sporting CP 42 FC Porto 41
1978	FC Porto 51 Benfica 51 Sporting CP 42
1979	FC Porto 50 Benfica 49 Sporting CP 42
1980	Sporting CP 52 FC Porto 50 Benfica 45
1981	Benfica 50 FC Porto 48 Sporting CP 37
1982	Sporting CP 46 Benfica 44 FC Porto 43
1983	Benfica 51 FC Porto 47 Sporting CP 42
1984	Benfica 52 FC Porto 49 Sporting CP 42
1985	FC Porto 55 Sporting CP 47 Benfica 43
1986	FC Porto 49 Benfica 47 Sporting CP 46
1987	Benfica 49 FC Porto 46 Vitória Guimaraes 41
1988v	FC Porto 66 Benfica 51 OS Belenenses 48
1989	Benfica 63 FC Porto 56 Boavista FC 49
1990t	FC Porto 59 Benfica 55 Sporting CP 46
1991v	Benfica 69 FC Porto 67 Sporting CP 56
1992t	FC Porto 56 Benfica 46 Boavista 44
1993	FC Porto 54 Benfica 52 Sporting CP 45
1994	Benfica 54 FC Porto 52 Sporting CP 51
1993	FC Porto 62 Sporting CP 53 Benfica 49

PORTUGUESE CUP FINALS

1922	FC Porto	3-1	Sporting CP
1923	Sporting CP	3-0	Académica Coimbra
1924	SC Olhanense	4-2	FC Porto
1925	FC Porto	2-1	Sporting CP
1926	CS Marítimo	2-0	OS Belenenses
1927	OS Belenenses	3-0	Vitória Setúbal
1928	Carcavelinhos	3-1	Sporting CP
1929	OS Belenenses	2-1	Uniao Lisbon
1930	Benfica	3-1	FC Barreirense
1931	Benfica	3-0	FC Porto
1932	FC Porto	2-0	OS Belenenses
1933	OS Belenenses	3-1	Sporting CP
1934	Sporting CP	4-3	FC Barreirense
1935	Benfica	2-1	Sporting CP
1936	Sporting CP	3-1	OS Belenenses
1937	FC Porto	3-2	Sporting CP
1938	Sporting CP	3-1	Benfica
1939	Académica Coimbra	4-3	Benfica
1940	Benfica	3-1	OS Belenenses
1941	Sporting CP	4-1	OS Belenenses
1942	OS Belenenses	2-0	Vitória Guimaraes
1943	Benfica	5-1	Vitória Setúbal
1944	Benfica	8-0	GD Estoril Praia
1945	Sporting CP	1-0	SC Olhanense
1946	Sporting CP	4-2	Atletico CP
1947	-		
1948	Sporting CP	3-1	OS Belenenses
1949	Benfica	2-1	Atletico CP
1950	-		
1951	Benfica	5-1	Académica Coimbra
1952	Benfica	5-4	Sporting CP
1953	Benfica	5-0	FC Porto
1954	Sporting CP	3-2	Vitória Setúbal
1955	Benfica	2-1	Sporting CP
1956	FC Porto	3-0	SC Uniao Torriense
1957	Benfica	3-1	Sporting Covilha
1958	FC Porto	1-0	Benfica
1959	Benfica	1-0	FC Porto
1960	OS Belenenses	2-1	Sporting CP
1961	Leixoes SC	2-0	FC Porto
1962	Benfica	3-0	Vitória Setúbal
1963	Sporting CP	4-0	Vitória Guimaraes
1964	Benfica	6-2	FC Porto
1965	Vitória Setúbal	3-1	Benfica
1966	Sporting Braga	1-0	Vitória Setúbal
1967	Vitória Setúbal	3-2	Académica Coimbra
1968	FC Porto	2-1	Vitória Setúbal
1969	Benfica	2-1	Académica Coimbra
1970	Benfica	3-1	Sporting CP
1971	Sporting CP	4-1	Benfica
1972	Benfica	3-2	Sporting CP
1973	Sporting CP	3-2	Vitória Setúbal
1974	Sporting CP	2-1	Benfica
1975	Boavista FC	2-1	Benfica
1976	Boavista FC	2-1	Vitória Guimaraes
1977	FC Porto	2-1	Sporting Braga
1978	Sporting CP	1-1 2-1	FC Porto
1979	Boavista FC	1-1 1-0	Sporting CP
1980	Benfica	1-0	FC Porto
1981	Benfica	3-1	FC Porto
1982	Sporting CP	4-0	Sporting Braga
1983	Benfica	1-0	FC Porto
1984	FC Porto	4-1	FC Rio Ave
1985	Benfica	3-1	FC Porto
1986	Benfica	2-0	OS Belenenses
1987	Benfica	2-1	Sporting CP
1988	FC Porto	1-0	Vitória Guimaraes
1989	OS Belenenses	2-1	Benfica
1990	Estrela da Amadora	2-0	SC Farense
1991	FC Porto	3-1	SC Beira Mar
1992	Boavista FC	2-1	FC Porto
1993	Benfica	5-2	Boavista FC
1994	FC Porto	0-0 2-1	Sporting CP
1995	Sporting CP	2-0	Maritimo

LEADING INTERNATIONAL GOALSCORERS

41	Eusébio Ferreira	(Benfica)	1961-1973
22	Tamanini Nené	(Benfica)	1971-1984
15	Fernando Peyroteo	(Sporting CP)	1938-1949
	Rui Jordao	(Benfica,Sporting CP)	1972-1989
14	José Torres	(Benfica,Vitória Setúbal)	1963-1973
13	Lucas da Fonseca 'Matateu'	(Belenenses)	1952-1960
	Fernando Gomes	(FC Porto)	1975-1987
11	José Aguas	(Benfica)	1952-1962
10	Rui Aguas	(Portimonense,Benfica)	1985-

LEADING INTERNATIONAL APPEARANCES

69	Joao Pinto I	(FC Porto)	1983-
66	Tamanini Nené	(Benfica)	1971-1984
64	Eusébio Ferreira	(Benfica)	1961-1973
	Humberto Coelho	(Benfica,Paris St.Germain)	1968-1983
63	Manuel Bento #	(Benfica)	1976-1986
57	Mário Coluna	(Benfica)	1955-1968
48	Fernando Gomes	(FC Porto)	1975-1987
46	Antonio Simoes	(Benfica)	1962-1973
45	José Augusto P. Almeida	(Barreirense,Benfica)	1958-1968
43	Rui Jordao	(Benfica,Sporting CP)	1972-1989

INTERNATIONAL MATCHES PLAYED BY PORTUGAL

18-12-1921	Spain	L 1-3	Madrid	Fr	Alberto Augusto
17-12-1922	Spain	L 1-2	Lisbon	Fr	Jaime Gonçalves
16-12-1923	Spain	L 0-3	Seville	Fr	
15-05-1925	Spain	L 0-2	Lisbon	Fr	
18-06	Italy	W 1-0	Lisbon	Fr	Joao Maia
18-04-1926	France	L 2-4	Toulouse	Fr	Augusto Silva, Joao Santos
26-12	Hungary	D 3-3	Oporto	Fr	Joao Santos, José Martins, Tiago
16-03-1927	France	W 4-0	Lisbon	Fr	José Martins 2, José Soares 2
17-04	Italy	L 1-3	Turin	Fr	Cambalacho
29-05	Spain	L 0-2	Madrid	Fr	
8-01-1928	Spain	D 2-2	Lisbon	Fr	Jose Martins, Joao Santos
1-04	Argentina	D 0-0	Lisbon	Fr	
15-04	Italy	W 4-1	Oporto	Fr	Waldemar Mota 3, Vitor Silva
29-04	France	D 1-1	Paris	Fr	Armando Martins
27-05	Chile	W 4-2	Amsterdam	OGr1	José Soares 2, Vitor Silva, Waldemar Mota
29-05	Yugoslavia	W 2-1	Amsterdam	OGr2	Vitor Silva, Augusto Silva
4-06	Egypt	L 1-2	Amsterdam	OGqf	Vitor Silva
17-03-1929	Spain	L 0-5	Seville	Fr	
24-03	France	L 0-2	Paris	Fr	
1-12	Italy	L 1-6	Milan	Fr	Vitor Silva
12-01-1930	Czechoslovakia	W 1-0	Lisbon	Fr	José Soares
23-02	France	W 2-0	Oporto	Fr	José Soares 2
8-06	Belgium	L 1-2	Antwerp	Fr	Armando Martins
30-11	Spain	L 0-1	Oporto	Fr	
12-04-1931	Italy	L 0-2	Oporto	Fr	
31-05	Belgium	W 3-2	Lisbon	Fr	Armando Martins, Vitor Silva, Artur Sousa
3-05-1932	Yugoslavia	W 3-2	Lisbon	Fr	Artur Sousa, Alfredo Valadas, Soeiro Vasques
29-01-1933	Hungary	W 1-0	Lisbon	Fr	Artur Sousa
2-04	Spain	L 0-3	Vigo	Fr	
11-03-1934	Spain	L 0-9	Madrid	WCq	
18-03	Spain	L 1-2	Lisbon	WCq	Vitor Silva
5-05-1935	Spain	D 3-3	Lisbon	Fr	Artur Sousa 2, Soeiro Vasques
26-01-1936	Austria	L 2-3	Oporto	Fr	Ferreira Silva, Soeiro Vasques
27-02	Germany	L 1-3	Lisbon	Fr	Vitor Silva
9-01-1938	Hungary	W 4-0	Lisbon	Fr	Joao Cruz, Espirito Santo, Artur Sousa
24-04	Germany	D 1-1	Frankfurt	Fr	Artur Sousa
1-05	Switzerland	L 1-2	Milan	WCq	Peyroteo
6-11	Switzerland	L 0-1	Lausanne	Fr	
12-02-1939	Switzerland	L 2-4	Lisbon	Fr	Joao Cruz, Soeiro Vasques
28-01-1940	France	L 2-3	Paris	Fr	Peyroteo 2
12-01-1941	Spain	D 2-2	Lisbon	Fr	Peyroteo 2
16-03	Spain	L 1-5	Bilbao	Fr	Artur Sousa
1-01-1942	Switzerland	W 3-0	Lisbon	Fr	Alberto Gomes, Mourao
11-03-1945	Spain	D 2-2	Lisbon	Fr	Peyroteo 2
6-05	Spain	L 2-4	La Coruña	Fr	Peyroteo 2
21-05	Switzerland	L 0-1	Basle	Fr	
14-04-1946	France	W 2-1	Lisbon	Fr	Araujo, Peyroteo
16-06	Rep. Ireland	W 3-1	Lisbon	Fr	Rogério, Peyroteo 2
5-01-1947	Switzerland	D 2-2	Lisbon	Fr	Rogério, Moreira
26-01	Spain	W 4-1	Lisbon	Fr	Travassos 2, Araujo 2
23-03	France	L 0-1	Paris	Fr	
4-05	Rep. Ireland	W 2-0	Dublin	Fr	Jesus Correia, Araujo

Date	Opponent	Result	Venue	Comp	Scorers
25-05	England	L 0-10	Lisbon	Fr	
23-11	France	L 2-4	Lisbon	Fr	Peyroteo, Araujo
21-03-1948	Spain	L 0-2	Madrid	Fr	
23-05	Rep. Ireland	W 2-0	Lisbon	Fr	Peyroteo, Albano
27-02-1949	Italy	L 1-4	Genoa	Fr	Miguel Lourenço
20-03	Spain	D 1-1	Lisbon	Fr	Peyroteo
15-05	Wales	W 3-2	Lisbon	Fr	Demétrico, José Mota, M.Vasques
22-05	Rep. Ireland	L 0-1	Dublin	Fr	
2-04-1950	Spain	L 1-5	Madrid	WCq	Cabrita
9-04	Spain	D 2-2	Lisbon	WCq	Travassos, Jesus Correia
14-05	England	L 3-5	Lisbon	Fr	Ben-David 2, M.Vasques
21-05	Scotland	D 2-2	Lisbon	Fr	Travassos, Albano
8-04-1951	Italy	L 1-4	Lisbon	Fr	Jesus Correia
12-05	Wales	L 1-2	Cardiff	Fr	Ben-David
19-05	England	L 2-5	Liverpool	Fr	Demétrico, Albano
17-06	Belgium	D 1-1	Lisbon	Fr	Ben-David
20-04-1952	France	L 0-3	Paris	Fr	
23-11	Austria	D 1-1	Oporto	Fr	Travassos
14-12	Argentina	L 1-3	Lisbon	Fr	M.Vasques
27-09-1953	Austria	L 1-9	Vienna	WCq	José Aguas
22-11	South Africa	W 3-1	Lisbon	Fr	Hernâni, José Aguas, Matateu
29-11	Austria	D 0-0	Lisbon	WCq	
14-03-1954	Belgium	D 0-0	Brussels	Fr	
28-11	Argentina	L 1-3	Lisbon	Fr	Travassos
19-12	West Germany	L 0-3	Lisbon	Fr	
4-05-1955	Scotland	L 0-3	Glasgow	Fr	
22-05	England	W 3-1	Oporto	Fr	José Aguas 2, Matateu
20-11	Sweden	L 2-6	Lisbon	Fr	José Aguas 2
18-12	Turkey	L 1-3	Istanbul	Fr	Hernâni
23-12	Egypt	W 4-0	Cairo	Fr	José Aguas 2, Matateu 2
25-03-1956	Turkey	W 3-1	Lisbon	Fr	M.Vasques, Matateu, OG
8-04	Brazil	L 0-1	Lisbon	Fr	
3-06	Spain	W 3-1	Lisbon	Fr	Palmeiro 3
9-06	Hungary	D 2-2	Lisbon	Fr	José Aguas, M.Vasques
16-01-1957	Nth. Ireland	D 1-1	Lisbon	WCq	M.Vasques
24-03	France	L 0-1	Lisbon	Fr	
1-05	Nth. Ireland	L 0-3	Belfast	WCq	
26-05	Italy	W 3-0	Lisbon	WCq	M.Vasques, Teixeira, Matateu
11-06	Brazil	L 1-2	Rio de Janeiro	Fr	Matateu
16-06	Brazil	L 0-3	Sao Paulo	Fr	
22-12	Italy	L 0-3	Milan	WCq	
13-04-1958	Spain	L 0-1	Madrid	Fr	
7-05	England	L 1-2	London	Fr	Carlos Duarte
16-05-1959	Switzerland	L 3-4	Geneva	Fr	Hernâni, Cavém, Matateu
21-05	Sweden	L 0-2	Gothenburg	Fr	
3-06	Scotland	W 1-0	Lisbon	Fr	Matateu
21-06	East Germany	W 2-0	Berlin	ECr1	Matateu, Mário Coluna
28-06	East Germany	W 3-2	Oporto	ECr1	Cavém, Mário Coluna 2
11-11	France	L 3-5	Paris	Fr	Matateu 2, Cavém
27-04-1960	West Germany	L 1-2	Ludwigshaven	Fr	Cavém
8-05	Yugoslavia	W 2-1	Lisbon	ECqf	Santana, Matateu
22-05	Yugoslavia	L 1-5	Belgrade	ECqf	Cavém
19-03-1961	Luxembourg	W 6-0	Lisbon	WCq	José Aguas, Yauca 3, Mário Coluna, OG
21-05	England	D 1-1	Lisbon	WCq	José Aguas
4-06	Argentina	L 0-2	Lisbon	Fr	
8-10	Luxembourg	L 2-4	Luxembourg	WCq	Eusébio, Tauca
25-10	England	L 0-2	London	WCq	
6-05-1962	Brazil	L 1-2	Sao Paulo	Fr	Mário Coluna
9-05	Brazil	L 0-1	Rio de Janeiro	Fr	
17-05	Belgium	L 1-2	Lisbon	Fr	Eusébio
7-11	Bulgaria	L 1-3	Sofia	ECr1	Eusébio
16-12	Bulgaria	W 3-1	Lisbon	ECr1	Hernâni 2, Mário Coluna
23-01-1963	Bulgaria	L 0-1	Rome	ECr1	
21-04	Brazil	W 1-0	Lisbon	Fr	José Augusto
29-04-1964	Switzerland	W 3-2	Zurich	Fr	Torres, Simoes, José Augusto
3-05	Belgium	W 2-1	Brussels	Fr	Eusébio, José Augusto
17-05	England	L 3-4	Lisbon	Fr	Torres 2, Eusébio
31-05	Argentina	L 0-2	Rio de Janeiro	CN	
4-06	England	D 1-1	Sao Paulo	CN	Peres
7-06	Brazil	L 1-4	Rio de Janeiro	CN	Mário Coluna
15-11	Spain	W 2-1	Oporto	Fr	Eusebio 2

24-01-1965	Turkey	W 5-1	Lisbon	WCq	Mário Coluna, Eusébio 3, Jaime Graça
19-04	Turkey	W 1-0	Ankara	WCq	Eusébio
25-04	Czechoslovakia	W 1-0	Bratislava	WCq	Eusébio
13-06	Romania	W 2-1	Lisbon	WCq	Eusébio 2
24-06	Brazil	D 0-0	Oporto	Fr	
31-10	Czechoslovakia	D 0-0	Oporto	WCq	
21-11	Romania	L 0-2	Bucharest	WCq	
12-06-1966	Norway	W 4-0	Lisbon	Fr	Eusébio 2, José Augusto 2
18-06	Scotland	W 1-0	Glasgow	Fr	Torres
21-06	Denmark	W 3-1	Esbjerg	Fr	Eusébio, Torres 2
26-06	Uruguay	W 3-0	Lisbon	Fr	Torres 3
3-07	Romania	W 1-0	Oporto	Fr	Torres
13-07	Hungary	W 3-1	Manchester	WCr1	José Augusto 2, Torres
16-07	Bulgaria	W 3-0	Manchester	WCr1	Eusébio, Torres, OG
19-07	Brazil	W 3-1	Liverpool	WCr1	Simoes, Eusébio 2
23-07	North Korea	W 5-3	Liverpool	WCqf	Eusébio 4, José Augusto
26-07	England	L 1-2	London	WCsf	Eusébio
28-07	Soviet Union	W 2-1	London	WC3p	Eusébio, Torres
13-11	Sweden	L 1-2	Lisbon	ECq	Jaime Graça
27-03-1967	Italy	D 1-1	Rome	Fr	Eusébio
1-06	Sweden	D 1-1	Stockholm	ECq	Custódio Pinto
8-06	Norway	W 2-1	Oslo	ECq	Eusébio 2
12-11	Norway	W 2-1	Oporto	ECq	Torres, Jaime Graça
26-11	Bulgaria	L 0-1	Sofia	ECq	
17-12	Bulgaria	D 0-0	Lisbon	ECq	
30-06-1968	Brazil	L 0-2	Lourenco Marques	Fr	
27-10	Romania	W 3-0	Lisbon	WCq	Jacinto 2, Joao
11-12	Greece	L 2-4	Athens	WCq	José Augusto, Eusébio
6-04-1969	Mexico	D 0-0	Lisbon	Fr	
16-04	Switzerland	L 0-2	Lisbon	WCq	
4-05	Greece	D 2-2	Oporto	WCq	Eusébio, Peres
12-10	Romania	L 0-1	Bucharest	WCq	
2-11	Switzerland	D 1-1	Berne	WCq	Eusébio
10-12	England	L 0-1	London	Fr	
10-05-1970	Italy	L 1-2	Lisbon	Fr	Humberto Coelho
14-10	Denmark	W 1-0	Copenhagen	ECq	Joao
17-02-1971	Belgium	L 0-3	Brussels	ECq	
21-04	Scotland	W 2-0	Lisbon	ECq	Eusébio, OG
12-05	Denmark	W 5-0	Oporto	ECq	Rui Rodrigues, Eusébio, Batista 2, OG
13-10	Scotland	L 1-2	Glasgow	ECq	Rui Rodrigues
21-11	Belgium	D 1-1	Lisbon	ECq	Peres
29-03-1972	Cyprus	W 4-0	Lisbon	WCq	Humberto Coelho, Nené, Jorge, Jordao
10-05	Cyprus	W 1-0	Nicosia	WCq	Chico Faria
11-06	Ecuador	W 3-0	Natal	Clr1	Eusébio, Dinis, Nené
14-06	Iran	W 3-0	Recife	Clr1	Eusébio, Dinis, Toni
18-06	Chile	W 4-1	Recife	Clr1	Humberto Coelho, Dinis 2, Eusébio
25-06	Rep. Ireland	W 2-1	Recife	Clr1	Peres, Nené
29-06	Argentina	W 3-1	Rio de Janeiro	Clr2	Adolfo, Eusébio, Dinis
2-07	Uruguay	D 1-1	Sao Paulo	Clr2	Peres
6-07	Soviet Union	W 1-0	Belo Horizonte	Clr2	Jordao
9-07	Brazil	L 0-1	Rio de Janeiro	Clf	
3-03-1973	France	W 2-1	Paris	Fr	Eusebio 2
28-03	Nth. Ireland	D 1-1	Coventry	WCq	Eusebio
2-05	Bulgaria	L 1-2	Sofia	WCq	Nené
13-10	Bulgaria	D 2-2	Lisbon	WCq	Simoes, Quaresma
14-11	Nth. Ireland	D 1-1	Lisbon	WCq	Jordao
3-04-1974	England	D 0-0	Lisbon	Fr	
13-11	Switzerland	L 0-3	Berne	Fr	
20-11	England	D 0-0	London	ECq	
26-04-1975	France	W 2-0	Paris	Fr	Nené, Marinho
30-04	Czechoslovakia	L 0-5	Prague	ECq	
13-05	Scotland	L 0-1	Glasgow	Fr	
8-06	Cyprus	W 2-0	Limassol	ECq	Nené, Moinhos
12-11	Czechoslovakia	D 1-1	Oporto	ECq	Nené
19-11	England	D 1-1	Lisbon	ECq	Rui Rodrigues
3-12	Cyprus	W 1-0	Setubal	ECq	Alves
7-04-1976	Italy	L 1-3	Turin	Fr	Fraguito
16-10	Poland	L 0-2	Oporto	WCq	
17-11	Denmark	W 1-0	Lisbon	WCq	Manuel Fernandes
5-12	Cyprus	W 2-1	Limassol	WCq	Chalana, Nené
22-12	Italy	W 2-1	Lisbon	Fr	Nené 2

30-03-1977	Switzerland	W 1-0	Funchal	Fr	Alves
9-10	Denmark	W 4-2	Copenhagen	WCq	Jordao, Nené, Manuel Fernandes, Octavio
29-10	Poland	D 1-1	Chorzow	WCq	Manuel Fernandes
16-11	Cyprus	W 4-0	Lisbon	WCq	Seninho, Chalana, Vital, Manuel Fernandes
8-03-1978	France	L 0-2	Paris	Fr	
20-09	United States	W 1-0	Setubal	Fr	Costa
11-10	Belgium	D 1-1	Lisbon	ECq	Fernando Gomes
15-11	Austria	W 2-1	Vienna	ECq	Nené, Alberto
29-11	Scotland	W 1-0	Lisbon	ECq	Alberto
9-05-1979	Norway	W 1-0	Oslo	ECq	Alves
26-09	Spain	D 1-1	Vigo	Fr	Nené
17-10	Belgium	L 0-2	Brussels	ECq	
1-11	Norway	W 3-1	Lisbon	ECq	Artur, Nené 2
21-11	Austria	L 1-2	Lisbon	ECq	Reinaldo
26-03-1980	Scotland	L 1-4	Glasgow	ECq	Fernando Gomes
24-09	Italy	L 1-3	Genoa	Fr	Jordao
7-10	United States	D 1-1	Lisbon	Fr	Carlos Manuel
15-10	Scotland	D 0-0	Glasgow	WCq	
19-11	Nth. Ireland	W 1-0	Lisbon	WCq	Jordao
17-12	Israel	W 3-0	Lisbon	WCq	Humberto Coelho 2, Jordao
15-04-1981	Bulgaria	D 1-1	Oporto	Fr	Oliveira
29-04	Nth. Ireland	L 0-1	Belfast	WCq	
20-06	Spain	W 2-0	Oporto	Fr	Nené, Nogueira
24-06	Sweden	L 0-3	Stockholm	WCq	
23-09	Poland	W 2-0	Lisbon	Fr	Nené, Sheu
14-10	Sweden	L 1-2	Lisbon	WCq	Pietra
28-10	Israel	L 1-4	Tel Aviv	WCq	Jordao
18-11	Scotland	W 2-1	Lisbon	WCq	Manuel Fernandes, Oliveira
16-12	Bulgaria	L 2-5	Haskovo	Fr	Oliveira 2
20-01-1982	Greece	W 2-1	Athens	Fr	Oliveira 2
17-02	West Germany	L 1-3	Hanover	Fr	De Matos
24-03	Switzerland	L 1-2	Lugano	Fr	Nené
5-05	Brazil	L 1-3	Sao Luiz	Fr	Nené
22-09	Finland	W 2-0	Helsinki	ECq	Nené, Oliveira
10-10	Poland	W 2-1	Lisbon	ECq	Nené, Fernando Gomes
16-02-1983	France	L 0-3	Guimaraes	Fr	
23-02	West Germany	W 1-0	Lisbon	Fr	Dito
13-04	Hungary	D 0-0	Coimbra	Fr	
27-04	Soviet Union	L 0-5	Moscow	ECq	
8-06	Brazil	L 0-4	Coimbra	Fr	
21-09	Finland	W 5-0	Lisbon	ECq	Jordao, Carlos Manuel, Luis, Oliveira, OG
28-10	Poland	W 1-0	Wroclaw	ECq	Carlos Manuel
13-11	Soviet Union	W 1-0	Lisbon	ECq	Jordao
2-06-1984	Yugoslavia	L 2-3	Lisbon	Fr	Jordao 2
9-06	Luxembourg	W 2-1	Luxembourg	Fr	Eurico, Diamantino
14-06	West Germany	D 0-0	Strasbourg	ECr1	
17-06	Spain	D 1-1	Marseille	ECr1	Sousa
20-06	Romania	W 1-0	Nantes	ECr1	Nené
23-06	France	L 2-3	Marseille	ECsf	Jordao 2
6-09	Bulgaria	W 1-0	Lisbon	Fr	Fernando Gomes
12-09	Sweden	W 1-0	Stockholm	WCq	Fernando Gomes
14-10	Czechoslovakia	W 2-1	Oporto	WCq	Diamantino, Carlos Manuel
14-11	Sweden	L 1-3	Lisbon	WCq	Jordao
30-01-1985	Romania	L 2-3	Lisbon	Fr	Futre, Carlos Manuel
10-02	Malta	W 3-1	Ta'Qali	WCq	Fernando Gomes 2, Carlos Manuel
24-02	West Germany	L 1-2	Lisbon	WCq	Diamantino
3-04	Italy	L 0-2	Ascoli	Fr	
25-09	Czechoslovakia	L 0-1	Pague	WCq	
12-10	Malta	W 3-2	Lisbon	WCq	Fernando Gomes 2, Rafael
16-10	West Germany	W 1-0	Stuttgart	WCq	Carlos Manuel
22-01-1986	Finland	D 1-1	Leiria	Fr	Diamantino
5-02	Luxembourg	W 2-0	Portimao	Fr	Frederico, Fernando Gomes
19-02	East Germany	L 1-3	Braga	Fr	Fernando Gomes
3-06	England	W 1-0	Monterrey	WCr1	Carlos Manuel
7-06	Poland	L 0-1	Monterrey	WCr1	
11-06	Morocco	L 1-3	Guadalajara	WCr1	Diamantino
12-10	Sweden	D 1-1	Lisbon	ECq	Jorge Coelho
29-10	Switzerland	D 1-1	Berne	ECq	Manuel Fernandes
7-01-1987	Greece	D 1-1	Portalegre	Fr	Jorge Coelho
4-02	Belgium	W 1-0	Braga	Fr	Frasco
14-02	Italy	L 0-1	Lisbon	ECq	

29-03	Malta	D 2-2	Funchal	ECq	Placido 2
23-09	Sweden	W 1-0	Stockholm	ECq	Fernando Gomes
11-11	Switzerland	D 0-0	Oporto	ECq	
5-12	Italy	L 0-3	Milan	ECq	
20-12	Malta	W 1-0	Ta'Qali	ECq	Frederico
12-10-1988	Sweden	D 0-0	Gothenburg	Fr	
16-11	Luxembourg	W 1-0	Oporto	WCq	Fernando Gomes
25-01-1989	Greece	W 2-1	Athens	Fr	Nunes, Paneira
15-02	Belgium	D 1-1	Lisbon	WCq	Paneira
29-03	Angola	W 6-0	Lisbon	Fr	Frederico 2, Domingos Oliveira, Andre, Nunes, Semedo
26-04	Switzerland	W 3-1	Lisbon	WCq	Joao Pinto, Frederico, Paneira
8-06	Brazil	L 0-4	Rio de Janeiro	Fr	
31-08	Romania	D 0-0	Setubal	Fr	
6-09	Belgium	L 0-3	Brussels	WCq	
20-09	Switzerland	W 2-1	Neuchatel	WCq	Futre, Rui Aguas
6-10	Czechoslovakia	L 1-2	Prague	WCq	Rui Aguas
11-10	Luxembourg	W 3-0	Saarbrucken	WCq	Rui Aguas 2, Rui Barros
15-11	Czechoslovakia	D 0-0	Lisbon	WCq	
29-08-1990	West Germany	D 1-1	Lisbon	Fr	Rui Aguas
12-09	Finland	D 0-0	Helsinki	ECq	
17-10	Holland	W 1-0	Oporto	ECq	Rui Aguas
19-12	United States	W 1-0	Oporto	Fr	Domingos
16-01-1991	Spain	D 1-1	Castellon	Fr	Oceano
23-01	Greece	L 2-3	Athens	ECq	Rui Aguas, Futre
9-02	Malta	W 1-0	Ta'Qali	ECq	Futre
20-02	Malta	W 5-0	Oporto	ECq	Rui Aguas, Leal, Paneira, OG, Cadete
4-09	Austria	D 1-1	Oporto	Fr	Rui Barros
11-09	Finland	W 1-0	Oporto	ECq	Cesar Brito
12-10	Luxembourg	D 1-1	Luxembourg	Fr	Nogueira
16-10	Holland	L 0-1	Rotterdam	ECq	
21-11	Greece	W 1-0	Lisbon	ECq	Joao Pinto II
15-01-1992	Spain	D 0-0	Torres Novas	Fr	
12-02	Holland	W 2-0	Faro	Fr	Oceano, Cesar Brito
31-05	Italy	D 0-0	New Haven	Fr	
3-06	USA	L 0-1	Chicago	Fr	
7-06	Rep. Ireland	L 0-2	Boston	Fr	
2-09	Austria	D 1-1	Linz	Fr	Hélder
14-10	Scotland	D 0-0	Glasgow	WCq	
11-11	Bulgaria	W 2-1	Saint-Ouen	Fr	Figo, Oceano
24-01-1993	Malta	W 1-0	Ta'Qali	WCq	Rui Aguas
10-02	Norway	D 1-1	Faro	Fr	Oceano
24-02	Italy	L 1-3	Oporto	WCq	Fernando Couto
31-03	Switzerland	D 1-1	Berne	WCq	Semedo
28-04	Scotland	W 5-0	Lisbon	WCq	Rui Barros 2, Cadete 2, Futre
19-06	Malta	W 4-0	Oporto	WCq	Nogueira, Rui Costa, João Pinto II, Cadete
5-09	Estonia	W 2-0	Tallinn	WCq	Rui Costa, Folha
13-10	Switzerland	W 1-0	Oporto	WCq	João Pinto II
10-11	Estonia	W 3-0	Lisbon	WCq	Futre, Oceano, Rui Aguas
17-11	Italy	L 0-1	Milan	WCq	
20-01-1994	Spain	D 2-2	Vigo	Fr	OG, Oceano
20-04	Norway	D 0-0	Oslo	Fr	
7-09	Nth. Ireland	W 2-1	Belfast	ECq	Rui Costa, Domingos Oliveira
9-10	Latvia	W 3-1	Riga	ECq	João Pinto 11 2, Figo
13-11	Austria	W 1-0	Lisbon	ECq	Figo
18-12	Liechtenstein	W 8-0	Lisbon	ECq	D. Oliveira 2,Oceano,João Pinto 11, F. Couto,P. Alves 2
26-01-1995	Canada	D 1-1	Toronto	Fr	Folha
29-01	Denmark	W 1-0	Toronto	Fr	Paulo Alves
22-02	Holland	W 1-0	Eindhoven	Fr	Pedro Barbosa
26-04	Rep. Ireland	L 0-1	Dublin	ECq	
3-06	Latvia	W 3-2	Oporto	ECq	Figo, Secretario, Domingos Oliveira

REPUBLIC OF IRELAND

For many years the Republic of Ireland's footballers struggled along, not only in the shadow of their neighbours in the North but also as poor cousins of rugby union and the indigenous sports of the island such as Gaelic football and hurling. But ever since Jackie Charlton, a World Cup winner with the English in 1966, took over as manager of the national side in 1986, football in the South has risen to a prominence that it did not previously enjoy.

Football had never been traditionally strong in the South. The Irish Football Association was located in Belfast and from the area that now constitutes the Republic, only

Shelbourne, Bohemians of Dublin and Shamrock Rovers regularly took part in either the league or the cup before partition in 1921.

A championship and a cup were initiated the following year but the league has been characterised by the departure of all its best players to either England or Scotland, and has therefore not had the chance to develop. Financial crises and the closure and reformation of clubs have for a long time been the order of the day. Cork, the second largest city in the country, has been represented by five different clubs called by 14 different names, in so far as it is possible to connect all the different teams.

THE ORDER OF MERIT

		All			League			Cup		Europe		
	Team	G	S	B	G	S	B	G	S	G	S	B
1	Shamrock Rovers	39	19	11	15	12	11	24	7	-	-	-
2	Dundalk	17	15	6	9	10	6	8	5	-	-	-
3	Shelbourne	15	21	9	8	9	9	7	12	-	-	-
4	Bohemians Dublin	13	20	11	7	10	11	6	10	-	-	-
5	Cork Athletic	13	9	2	7	2	2	6	7	-	-	-
6	Home Farm Drum.	11	9	4	5	5	4	6	4	-	-	-
7	Waterford United	8	10	8	6	4	8	2	6	-	-	-
8	St. Patrick's Athletic	6	6	1	4	2	1	2	4	-	-	-
9	Sligo Rovers	4	7	4	2	2	4	2	5	-	-	-
10	Limerick City	4	5	3	2	2	3	2	3	-	-	-
11	St. James' Gate	4	3	-	2	1	-	2	2	-	-	-
12	Derry City	3	4	1	1	2	1	2	2	-	-	-
13	Cork Hibernians	3	3	3	1	1	3	2	2	-	-	-
14	Athlone Town	3	1	3	2	1	3	1	-	-	-	-
15	Cork Celtic	1	7	2	1	4	2	-	3	-	-	-
16	Cork City	1	4	1	1	2	1	-	2	-	-	-
17	Finn Harps	1	3	1	-	3	1	1	-	-	-	-
18	Dolphin	1	3	-	1	1	-	-	2	-	-	-
19	Galway United	1	2	1	-	1	1	1	1	-	-	-
20	Alton United	1	-	-	-	-	-	1	-	-	-	-
	Bray Wanderers	1	-	-	-	-	-	1	-	-	-	-
	Transport	1	-	-	-	-	-	1	-	-	-	-
	University College Dublin	1	-	-	-	-	-	1	-	-	-	-
24	Drogheda United	-	3	3	-	1	3	-	2	-	-	-
25	Brideville	-	2	-	-	-	-	-	2	-	-	-
26	St. Francis	-	1	-	-	-	-	-	1	-	-	-
27	Jacobs	-	-	1	-	-	1	-	-	-	-	-

To the end of the 1994-95 season. The totals for Shelbourne and Bohemians include honours won in the All Ireland League pre-1922.

With a great many professionals playing in England and Scotland, the Republic were always 'on the verge' of becoming a good side. Their first match was in the 1924 Olympic Games in Paris and saw a 1-0 victory over Bulgaria. Holland, however, won the quarter-final tie, and although Ireland have entered the World Cup on every occasion since 1934, international fixtures were the exception rather than the rule until after the Second World War.

At times the results of these international matches were encouraging. West Germany, for example, were defeated twice in the late 1950s and early 1960s. West Ham and Manchester United's Noel Cantwell, who played at this time, emerged as perhaps the first major star from the Republic, but was followed soon by Johnny Giles, the linchpin of the very successful Leeds United side of the 1960s and early 1970s.

The depth of the squad was never quite sufficient, however, to qualify for the final tournament of either the World Cup or European Championship. Despite the presence of Liam Brady and Frank Stapleton, this trend continued right through to the late 1980s when, in a bold move, the Football Association of Ireland appointed Charlton as manager. Designing a set of tactics based very much on the more robust side of the English game, which all the players were used to, Charlton gave the team a belief in itself. They qualified for the 1988 European Championship finals in West Germany and their performance there set the scene for furure years. The Irish supporters brought a refreshing dose of good humour to the tournament, whilst the team, despite the absence of Brady, came close to making the semi-finals after beating England in their opening game.

Two years later the Irish qualified for the World Cup finals for the first time and reached the last eight before losing to Italy in Rome. A curious fact about their performance was that they got so far by scoring only two goals and indeed without actually winning a match! With limited resources, Ireland relied to a large degree on their fighting spirit in adversity and this was certainly evident in Italy. They were criticised in some quarters for their policy of poaching English and Scottish players with tenuous Irish links, but there could be no doubt that the policy had paid off.

Despite not qualifying for the 1992 European Championships, Ireland proved that their success was well founded by making it to USA '94 where they did win a game - sensationally, in their opening game against the eventual finalists Italy. But in the heat of Orlando the team struggled for the rest of the tournament. They qualified for the second round but lost emphatically to Holland. The national team has been a remarkable success: the challenge now facing the FAI is how to develop club football in Ireland.

Population: 3,509,000
Area, sq km: 70,285
% in urban areas: 57.0%
Capital city: Dublin

The Football Association of Ireland
Cumann Peile Na H-Eirean
80 Merrion Square
South Dublin 2
Republic of Ireland

Tel: + 353 1 6766864
Fax: + 353 1 6610931

Year of formation	1921
Affiliation to FIFA	1923
Affiliation to UEFA	1954
Registered clubs	3290
Registered players	157 000
Professional players	388
Registered coaches	20
Registered referees	1332
National stadium	Dalymount Park 22 000
Other major stadia	Landsdowne Road (Irish Rugby Football Union) 49 000
National colours	Green/White/Green
Reserve colours	White/Green/White
Season	August - April

THE RECORD

WORLD CUP

1930 Did not enter
1934 QT 3rd/3 in group 11
1938 QT 2nd/2 in group 2
1950 QT 2nd/3 in group 5
1954 QT 2nd/3 in group 4
1958 QT 2nd/3 in group 1
1962 QT 3rd/3 in group 8
1966 QT 2nd/2 in group 9
1970 QT 4th/4 in group 2
1974 QT 2nd/3 in group 9
1978 QT 3rd/3 in group 5
1982 QT 3rd/5 in group 2
1986 QT 4th/5 in group 6
1990 QT 2nd/5 in group 6 - Final Tournament/Quarter-finalists
1994 QT 2nd/7 in group 3 - Final Tournament/2nd round

EUROPEAN CHAMPIONSHIP

1960 Preliminary round
1964 Quarter-finalists
1968 QT 4th/4 in group 1
1972 QT 4th/4 in group 6
1976 QT 2nd/4 in group 6
1980 QT 3rd/5 in group 1
1984 QT 3rd/5 in group 7
1988 QT 1st/5 in group 7 - Final Tournament/1st round
1992 QT 2nd/4 in group 7
1996 QT group 6

EUROPEAN CLUB COMPETITIONS

European Cup
2nd round - Waterford 1971 Cork Celtic 1975 Bohemians 1979 Dundalk 1980

Cup Winners Cup
2nd round - Shamrock Rovers 1963 1967 1979 Cork Hibernians 1973 Bohemians 1977 Waterford 1981 Dundalk 1982

UEFA Cup
2nd round - Drumcondra 1963 Shelbourne 1965 Shamrock Rovers 1966 1983 Athlone Town 1976

CLUB DIRECTORY

DUBLIN (Population - 1,140,000)

Bohemians FC (1890)
Dalymount Park 25,000 – Red & black stripes/Black

Home Farm FC (1928)
Tolka Park 9,000 – Blue & white hoops/White
Previous name - Home Farm and Drumcondra merged in 1972 as Home Farm

St. James' Gate FC (1913)
Iveagh Grounds – Black & white hoops/White

St. Patrick's Athletic FC (1929)
Harold's Cross 10,000 – Red/White

Shamrock Rovers FC (1899)
Royal Dublin Society Showgrounds 22,000 – Green & white hoops/Green

Shelbourne FC (1895)
Tolka Park 9,000 – Red/White
Previous name - Reds United 1934-36

University College Dublin FC (1895)
Belfield 10,000 – Sky blue/White

CORK (Population - 173,000)

Cork City FC (1984)
Bishopstown 12,000 – White, red & green stripes/Green

There have been five other clubs from Cork all of which no longer exist. They were:
1: **Cork Athletic** folded in 1957. They were previously known as Fordsons 1912-30, Cork FC 1930-38, Cork City 1938-40, Cork United 1940-48, Cork Athletic 1948-57
2: **Cork Celtic** folded in 1979. They were previously known as Evergreen United from 1935-59, Cork Celtic 1959-79
3: **Cork United** folded in 1982. They were previously known as Albert Rovers 1946-77, Cork Alberts 1977-79, Cork United 1979-82
4: **Cork Bohemians** 1920-34
5: **Cork Hibernians** folded in 1976. They were previously known as AOH. (Ancient Order of the Hibernians)

LIMERICK (Population - 76,000)

Limerick FC (1983)
Rathbane 10,000 – Blue/White
Previous names - Limerick FC 1937-79, Limerick United 1979-83, Limerick City 1983-92

GALWAY (Population - 47,000)

Galway United FC (1976)
Terryland Park 5,000 – Maroon/White
Previous name - Galway Rovers 1976-81

WATERFORD (Population - 41,000)

Waterford United FC (1921)
Kilcohan Park 12,000 – Blue/Blue
Previous name - Waterford FC 1921-82

ATHLONE (Population - 9,000)

Athlone Town FC (1887)
St. Mels Park 6,000 – Blue & black stripes/Black

BALLYBOFEY

Finn Harps FC (1954)
Finn Park 10,000 – White/Blue

BRAY (Population - 22,000)

Bray Wanderers FC (1942)
Carlisle Grounds 10,000 – Green & white stripes/Green

DROGHEDA (Population - 23,000)

Drogheda United FC (1919)
United Park 10,000 – Blue/White, claret trim
Previous name - Drogheda FC 1919-75

DUNDALK (Population - 26,000)

Dundalk FC (1919)
Oriel Park 20,000 – White/Black

SLIGO (Population - 56,000)

Sligo Rovers FC (1908)
The Showgrounds 10,000 – Red & white stripes/White

REPUBLIC OF IRELAND LEAGUE CHAMPIONSHIP

1922f St. James' Gate 23 Bohemians 21 Shelbourne 18
1923k Shamrock Rovers 39 Shelbourne 34 Bohemians 32
1924h Bohemians 32 Shelbourne 28 Jacobs 24
1925 Shamrock Rovers 31 Bohemians 28 Shelbourne 27
1926 Shelbourne 31 Shamrock Rovers 29 Fordsons 27
1927 Shamrock Rovers 32 Shelbourne 29 Bohemians 25
1928 Bohemians 31 Shelbourne 28 Shamrock Rovers 25
1929 Shelbourne 33 Bohemians 32 Shamrock Rovers 24
1930 Bohemians 30 Shelbourne 29 Shamrock Rovers 26
1931k Shelbourne 31 Dundalk 28 Bohemians 27
1932 Shamrock Rovers 32 Cork FC 29 Waterford 28
1933h Dundalk 29 Shamrock Rovers 24 Shelbourne 23
1934 Bohemians 27 Cork FC 26 Shamrock Rovers 22
1935 Dolphin 28 St. James' Gate 27 Sligo Rovers 20
1936k Bohemians 36 Dolphin 33 Cork FC 31
1937 Sligo Rovers 34 Dundalk 24 Waterford 24
1938 Shamrock Rovers 32 Waterford 31 Dundalk 30
1939 Shamrock Rovers 36 Sligo Rovers 27 Dundalk 27
1940 St. James' Gate 36 Shamrock Rovers 30 Sligo Rovers 28
1941i Cork United 30 Waterford 30 Bohemians 23
1942h Cork United 30 Shamrock Rovers 28 Shelbourne 21
1943 Cork United 27 Dundalk 26 Drumcondra 23
1944f Shelbourne 21 Limerick United 20 Shamrock Rovers 15
1945 Cork United 22 Limerick United 17 Shamrock Rovers 17
1946 Cork United 21 Drumcondra 19 Waterford 16
1947 Shelbourne 19 Drumcondra 18 Shamrock Rovers 17
1948 Drumcondra 18 Dundalk 17 Shelbourne 17
1949h Drumcondra 29 Shelbourne 23 Dundalk 23
1950 Cork Athletic 25 Drumcondra 24 Shelbourne 21
1951 Cork Athletic 26 Sligo Rovers 25 Drumcondra 23

1952k	St. Patrick's Ath 34 Shelbourne 31 Shamrock Rovers 29
1953	Shelbourne 30 Drumcondra 29 Shamrock Rovers 27
1954	Shamrock Rovers 30 Evergreen United 28 Drumcondra 27
1955	St. Patrick's Ath 36 Waterford 33 Shamrock Rovers 28
1956	St. Patrick's Ath 34 Shamrock Rovers 31 Waterford 30
1957	Shamrock Rovers 36 Drumcondra 31 Sligo Rovers 29
1958	Drumcondra 33 Shamrock Rovers 31 Evergreen United 29
1959	Shamrock Rovers 34 Evergreen United 29 Waterford 29
1960	Limerick FC 30 Cork Celtic 28 Shelbourne 28
1961	Drumcondra 33 St. Patrick's Ath 32 Waterford 29
1962	Shelbourne 35 Cork Celtic 35 Shamrock Rovers 31
1963h	Dundalk 24 Waterford 23 Drumcondra 23
1964k	Shamrock Rovers 35 Dundalk 30 Limerick United 30
1965	Drumcondra 32 Shamrock Rovers 31 Bohemians 27
1966	Waterford 36 Shamrock Rovers 34 Bohemians 27
1967	Dundalk 34 Bohemians 27 Sligo Rovers 27
1968	Waterford 34 Dundalk 30 Cork Celtic 30
1969	Waterford 36 Shamrock Rovers 33 Cork Hibernians 30
1970n	Waterford 38 Shamrock Rovers 36 Cork Hibernians 35
1971	Cork Hibernians 35 Shamrock Rovers 35 Waterford 34
1972	Waterford 44 Cork Hibernians 40 Bohemians 37
1973	Waterford 42 Finn Harps 41 Bohemians 37
1974	Cork Celtic 42 Bohemians 38 Cork Hibernians 38
1975	Bohemians 42 Athlone Town 33 Finn Harps 30
1976	Dundalk 40 Finn Harps 36 Waterford 34
1977	Sligo Rovers 39 Bohemians 38 Drogheda United 35
1978q	Bohemians 44 Finn Harps 42 Drogheda United 40
1979	Dundalk 45 Bohemians 43 Drogheda United 42
1980	Limerick United 47 Dundalk 46 Athlone Town 39
1981	Athlone Town 51 Dundalk 45 Limerick United 41
1982q6	Dundalk 80 Shamrock Rovers 76 Bohemians 72
1983n1	Athlone Town 65 Drogheda United 49 Dundalk 48
1984n	Shamrock Rovers 42 Bohemians 36 Athlone Town 34
1985q	Shamrock Rovers 49 Bohemians 43 Athlone Town 40
1986k	Shamrock Rovers 33 Galway United 31 Dundalk 30
1987	Shamrock Rovers 39 Dundalk 30 Bohemians 29
1988s	Dundalk 46 St. Patrick's Ath 45 Bohemians 45
1989	Derry City 53 Dundalk 51 Limerick City 45
1990	St. Patrick's Ath 52 Derry City 49 Dundalk 42
1991	Dundalk 52 Cork City 50 St. Patrick's Ath 44
1992	Shelbourne 49 Derry City 44 Cork City 43
1993r1	Cork City 40 Bohemians 40 Shelbourne 40
1994r3	Shamrock Rovers 66 Cork City 59 Galway United 50
1995	Dundalk 51 Shelbourne 49 Derry City 46

Championship play-off

1962	Shelbourne	1-0	Cork Celtic
1993	Cork City won a 3 way play-off		

REPUBLIC OF IRELAND CUP FINALS

1922	St. James's Gate	1-1 1-0	Shamrock Rovers
1923	Alton United	1-0	Shelbourne
1924	Athlone Town	1-0	Fordsons
1925	Shamrock Rovers	2-1	Shelbourne
1926	Fordsons	3-2	Shamrock Rovers
1927	Drumcondra	1-1 1-0	Brideville
1928	Bohemians	2-1	Drumcondra
1929	Shamrock Rovers	0-0 3-0	Bohemians
1930	Shamrock Rovers	1-0	Brideville
1931	Shamrock Rovers	1-1 1-0	Dundalk
1932	Shamrock Rovers	1-0	Dolphin
1933	Shamrock Rovers	3-3 3-0	Dolphin
1934	Cork FC	2-1	St. James's Gate
1935	Bohemians	4-3	Dundalk
1936	Shamrock Rovers	2-1	Cork FC
1937	Waterford	2-1	St. James's Gate
1938	St. James's Gate	2-1	Dundalk
1939	Shelbourne	1-1 1-0	Sligo Rovers
1940	Shamrock Rovers	3-0	Sligo Rovers
1941	Cork United	2-2 3-1	Waterford
1942	Dundalk	3-1	Cork United
1943	Drumcondra	2-1	Cork United
1944	Shamrock Rovers	3-2	Shelbourne
1945	Shamrock Rovers	1-0	Bohemians
1946	Drumcondra	2-1	Shamrock Rovers
1947	Cork United	2-2 2-0	Bohemians
1948	Shamrock Rovers	2-1	Drumcondra
1949	Dundalk	3-0	Shelbourne
1950	Transport	2-2 2-2 3-1	Cork Athletic
1951	Cork Athletic	1-1 1-0	Shelbourne
1952	Dundalk	1-1 3-0	Cork Athletic
1953	Cork Athletic	2-2 2-1	Evergreen United
1954	Drumcondra	1-0	St. Patrick's Athletic
1955	Shamrock Rovers	1-0	Drumcondra
1956	Shamrock Rovers	3-2	Cork Athletic
1957	Drumcondra	2-0	Shamrock Rovers
1958	Dundalk	1-0	Shamrock Rovers
1959	St. Patrick's Athletic	2-2 2-1	Waterford
1960	Shelbourne	2-0	Cork Hibernians
1961	St. Patrick's Athletic	2-1	Drumcondra
1962	Shamrock Rovers	4-1	Shelbourne
1963	Shelbourne	2-0	Cork Hibernians
1964	Shamrock Rovers	1-1 2-1	Cork Celtic
1965	Shamrock Rovers	1-1 1-0	Limerick
1966	Shamrock Rovers	2-0	Limerick
1967	Shamrock Rovers	3-2	St. Patrick's Athletic
1968	Shamrock Rovers	3-0	Waterford
1969	Shamrock Rovers	1-1 4-1	Cork Celtic
1970	Bohemians	0-0 0-0 2-1	Sligo Rovers
1971	Limerick FC	0-0 3-0	Drogheda United
1972	Cork Hibernians	3-0	Waterford
1973	Cork Hibernians	0-0 1-0	Shelbourne
1974	Finn Harps	3-1	St. Patrick's Athletic
1975	Home Farm	1-0	Shelbourne
1976	Bohemians	1-0	Drogheda United
1977	Dundalk	2-0	Limerick
1978	Shamrock Rovers	1-0	Sligo Rovers
1979	Dundalk	2-0	Waterford
1980	Waterford	1-0	St. Patrick's Athletic
1981	Dundalk	2-0	Sligo Rovers
1982	Limerick United	1-0	Bohemians
1983	Sligo Rovers	2-1	Bohemians
1984	University College	0-0 2-1	Shamrock Rovers
1985	Shamrock Rovers	1-0	Galway United
1986	Shamrock Rovers	2-0	Waterford
1987	Shamrock Rovers	3-0	Dundalk
1988	Dundalk	1-0	Derry City
1989	Derry City	0-0 1-0	Cork City
1990	Bray Wanderers	3-0	St. Francis
1991	Galway United	1-0	Shamrock Rovers
1992	Bohemians	1-0	Cork City
1993	Shelbourne	1-0	Dundalk
1994	Sligo Rovers	1-0	Derry City
1995	Derry City	2-1	Shelbourne

LEADING INTERNATIONAL GOALSCORERS

20	Frank Stapleton	(Arsenal,Man United,Ajax, Derby,Le Havre,Blackburn)	1977-1990
19	Don Givens	(Man United,Luton,QPR, Birmingham City,Xamax FC)	1969-1982
14	John Aldridge	(Oxford,Liverpool, Real Sociedad,Tranmere)	1986-
	Noel Cantwell	(West Ham,Man United)	1954-1967
13	Jimmy Dunne	(Sheff United,Arsenal, South-ampton, Shamrock Rovers)	1930-39
	Gerry Daly	(Man United,Derby,Coventry, B'ham City,Shrewsbury)	1973-1987

12 Tony Cascarino	(Gillingham,Millwall, Aston Villa,Celtic,Chelsea)	1986-
10 Niall Quinn	(Arsenal,Manchester City)	1986-
9 Kevin Sheedy	(Everton,Newcastle)	1984-
Liam Brady	(Arsenal,Juventus,Sampdoria, Inter,Ascoli,West Ham)	1975-1990
68 David O'Leary	(Arsenal)	1977-1993
64 Ray Houghton	(Oxford,Liverpool,Aston Villa)	1986-
John Aldridge	(Oxford,Liverpool, Real Sociedad,Tranmere)	1986-
59 Johnny Giles	(Man United,Leeds, West Bromwich,Shamrock Rovers)	1960-1979
59 Steve Staunton	(Liverpool,Aston Villa)	1988-

LEADING INTERNATIONAL APPEARANCES

78 Pat Bonner #	(Celtic)	1981-1994
76 Paul McGrath	(Man United,Aston Villa)	1985-
72 Liam Brady	(Arsenal,Juventus,Sampdoria, Inter,Ascoli,West Ham)	1975-1990
71 Kevin Moran	(Man United,Sporting Gijon, Blackburn)	1980-1994
Frank Stapleton	(Arsenal,Man United,Ajax, Derby,Le Havre,Blackburn)	1977-1990

NATIONAL TEAM COACHES

1969-71	Mick Meagan
1971-73	Liam Tuohy
1973	Sean Thomas
1973-80	Johnny Giles
1980	Alan Kelly
1980-85	Eoin Hand
1986-	Jack Charlton

INTERNATIONAL MATCHES PLAYED BY THE REPUBLIC OF IRELAND

Date	Opponent	Result	Venue	Comp	Scorers
28-05-1924	Bulgaria *	W 1-0	Paris	OGr1	Duncan
2-06	Holland *	L 1-2	Paris	OGqf	
3-06	Estonia *	W 3-1	Paris	Fr	Duncan, Muldoon
16-06-1925	United States *	W 3-1	Dublin	Fr	Brooks 3
21-03-1926	Italy	L 0-3	Turin	Fr	
12-02-1928	Belgium	W 4-2	Liege	Fr	White 2, Lacey, Sullivan
20-04-1929	Belgium	W 4-0	Dublin	Fr	Flood 3, Byrne
11-05-1930	Belgium	W 3-1	Brussels	Fr	Dunne 2, Flood
26-04-1931	Spain	D 1-1	Barcelona	Fr	Moore
13-12	Spain	L 0-5	Dublin	Fr	
8-05-1932	Holland	W 2-0	Amsterdam	Fr	O'Reilly, Moore
25-02-1934	Belgium	D 4-4	Dublin	WCq	Moore 4
8-04	Holland	L 2-5	Amsterdam	WCq	Moore, Squires
15-12	Hungary	L 2-4	Dublin	Fr	Donnelly, Bermingham
5-05-1935	Switzerland	L 0-1	Basle	Fr	
8-05	Germany	L 1-3	Dortmund	Fr	Dunne
8-12	Holland	L 3-5	Dublin	Fr	Ellis, Horlacher 2
17-03-1936	Switzerland	W 1-0	Dublin	Fr	Dunne
3-05	Hungary	D 3-3	Budapest	Fr	Dunne 2, Madden
9-05	Luxembourg	W 5-1	Luxembourg	Fr	Dunne 3, Donnelly, O'Reilly
17-10	Germany	W 5-2	Dublin	Fr	Davis 2, Donnelly 2, Geoghegan
6-12	Hungary	L 2-3	Dublin	Fr	Fallon, Davis
17-05-1937	Switzerland	W 1-0	Berne	Fr	Dunne
23-05	France	W 2-0	Paris	Fr	Jordan, Brown
10-10	Norway	L 2-3	Oslo	WCq	Geoghegan, Dunne
7-11	Norway	D 3-3	Dublin	WCq	Dunne, O'Flanagan, Duggan
18-05-1938	Czechoslovakia	D 2-2	Prague	Fr	Davis, Dunne
22-05	Poland	L 0-6	Warsaw	Fr	
18-09	Switzerland	W 4-0	Dublin	Fr	Bradshaw 2, Dunne, Donnelly
13-11	Poland	W 3-2	Dublin	Fr	Fallon, Carey, Dunne
19-03-1939	Hungary	D 2-2	Cork	Fr	Bradshaw, Carey
18-05	Hungary	D 2-2	Budapest	Fr	O'Flanagan 2
23-05	Germany	D 1-1	Bremen	Fr	Bradshaw
16-06-1946	Portugal	L 1-3	Lisbon	Fr	O'Reilly
23-06	Spain	W 1-0	Madrid	Fr	Sloan
30-09	England	L 0-1	Dublin	Fr	
2-03-1947	Spain	W 3-2	Dublin	Fr	Walshe 2, Coad
4-05	Portugal	L 0-2	Dublin	Fr	
23-05-1948	Portugal	L 0-2	Lisbon	Fr	
30-05	Spain	L 1-2	Barcelona	Fr	Walshe
5-12	Switzerland	L 0-1	Dublin	Fr	
24-04-1949	Belgium	L 0-2	Dublin	Fr	
22-05	Portugal	W 1-0	Dublin	Fr	Coad
2-06	Sweden	L 1-3	Stockholm	WCq	Walshe
12-06	Spain	L 1-4	Dublin	Fr	Martin.C
8-09	Finland	W 3-0	Dublin	WCq	Martin.C 2, Gavin
21-09	England	W 2-0	Liverpool	Fr	Martin,C Farrell
9-10	Finland	D 1-1	Helsinki	WCq	Farrell

13-11	Sweden	L 1-3	Dublin	WCq	Martin.C
10-05-1950	Belgium	L 1-5	Brussels	Fr	Duffy
26-11	Norway	D 2-2	Dublin	Fr	Carey, Walshe
13-05-1951	Argentina	L 0-1	Dublin	Fr	
30-05	Norway	W 3-2	Oslo	Fr	Ringstead, Farrell, Coad
17-10	West Germany	W 3-2	Dublin	Fr	OG, Fitzsimons, Glynn
4-05-1952	West Germany	L 0-3	Cologne	Fr	
7-05	Austria	L 0-6	Vienna	Fr	
1-06	Spain	L 0-6	Madrid	Fr	
16-11	France	D 1-1	Dublin	Fr	Fallon
25-03-1953	Austria	W 4-0	Dublin	Fr	Ringstead 2, Eglinton, O'Farrell
4-10	France	L 3-5	Dublin	WCq	Ryan, Walsh, O'Farrell
28-10	Luxembourg	W 4-0	Dublin	WCq	Fitzsimons 2, Ryan, Eglinton
25-11	France	L 0-1	Paris	WCq	
7-03-1954	Luxembourg	W 1-0	Luxembourg	WCq	Cummins
8-11	Norway	W 2-1	Dublin	Fr	Martin.C, Ryan
1-05-1955	Holland	W 1-0	Dublin	Fr	Fitzgerald
25-05	Norway	W 3-1	Oslo	Fr	Cummins 2, Ringstead
28-05	West Germany	L 1-2	Hamburg	Fr	Fallon
19-09	Yugoslavia	L 1-4	Dublin	Fr	Fitzsimons
27-11	Spain	D 2-2	Dublin	Fr	Fitzsimons, Ringstead
10-05-1956	Holland	W 4-1	Rotterdam	Fr	Fitzsimons 2, Haverty, Ringstead
3-10	Denmark	W 2-1	Dublin	WCq	Curtis, Gavin
25-11	West Germany	W 3-0	Dublin	Fr	Cantwell, McCann, Haverty
8-05-1957	England	L 1-5	London	WCq	Curtis
19-05	England	D 1-1	Dublin	WCq	Ringstead
2-10	Denmark	W 2-0	Copenhagen	WCq	Fitzsimons, Cummins
11-05-1958	Poland	D 2-2	Chorzow	Fr	Curtis, Cummins
14-05	Austria	L 1-3	Vienna	Fr	Curtis
5-10	Poland	D 2-2	Dublin	Fr	Cantwell 2
5-04-1959	Czechoslovakia	W 2-0	Dublin	ECpr	Tuohy, Cantwell
10-05	Czechoslovakia	L 0-4	Bratislava	ECpr	
1-11	Sweden	W 3-2	Dublin	Fr	Giles, Curtis 2
30-03-1960	Chile	W 2-0	Dublin	Fr	Cantwell, Curtis
11-05	West Germany	W 1-0	Dusseldorf	Fr	Fagan
18-05	Sweden	L 1-4	Malmo	Fr	Fagan
28-09	Wales	L 2-3	Dublin	Fr	Fagan
6-11	Norway	W 3-1	Dublin	Fr	Fitzgerald 2, Fagan
3-05-1961	Scotland	L 1-4	Glasgow	WCq	Haverty
7-05	Scotland	L 0-3	Dublin	WCq	
8-10	Czechoslovakia	L 1-3	Dublin	WCq	Giles
29-10	Czechoslovakia	L 1-7	Prague	WCq	Fogarty
8-04-1962	Austria	L 2-3	Dublin	Fr	Cantwell, Tuohy
12-08	Iceland	W 4-2	Dublin	ECr1	Cantwell, Tuohy, Fogarty
2-09	Iceland	D 1-1	Reykjavik	ECr1	Tuohy
9-06-1963	Scotland	W 1-0	Dublin	Fr	Cantwell
25-09	Austria	D 0-0	Vienna	ECr2	
13-10	Austria	W 3-2	Dublin	ECr2	Cantwell 2, OG
11-03-1964	Spain	L 1-5	Seville	ECqf	McEvoy
8-04	Spain	L 0-2	Dublin	ECqf	
10-05	Poland	L 1-3	Krakow	Fr	Ambrose
13-05	Norway	W 4-1	Oslo	Fr	Hurley, McEvoy, Giles
24-05	England	L 1-3	Dublin	Fr	Strahan
25-10	Poland	W 3-2	Dublin	Fr	McEvoy 2, Mooney
24-03-1965	Belgium	L 0-2	Dublin	Fr	
5-05	Spain	W 1-0	Dublin	WCq	OG
27-10	Spain	L 1-4	Seville	WCq	McEvoy
10-11	Spain	L 0-1	Paris	WCq	
4-05-1966	West Germany	L 0-4	Dublin	Fr	
22-05	Austria	L 0-1	Vienna	Fr	
25-05	Belgium	W 3-2	Liege	Fr	Cantwell 2, Fullam
23-10	Spain	D 0-0	Dublin	ECq	
16-11	Turkey	W 2-1	Dublin	ECq	O'Neill, McEvoy
7-12	Spain	L 0-2	Valencia	ECq	
22-02-1967	Turkey	L 1-2	Ankara	ECq	Cantwell
21-05	Czechoslovakia	L 0-2	Dublin	ECq	
22-11	Czechoslovakia	W 2-1	Prague	ECq	Treacy, O'Connor
15-05-1968	Poland	D 2-2	Dublin	Fr	
30-10	Poland	L 0-1	Chorzow	Fr	
10-11	Austria	D 2-2	Dublin	Fr	Rogers, Hale
4-12	Denmark	D 1-1	Dublin	WCq	Abandoned 51 mins

Date	Opponent	Result	Venue	Comp	Scorers
4-05-1969	Czechoslovakia	L 1-2	Dublin	WCq	Rogers
27-05	Denmark	L 0-2	Copenhagen	WCq	
8-06	Hungary	L 1-2	Dublin	WCq	Givens
21-09	Scotland	D 1-1	Dublin	Fr	Givens
7-10	Czechoslovakia	L 0-3	Prague	WCq	
15-10	Denmark	D 1-1	Dublin	WCq	Givens
5-11	Hungary	L 0-4	Budapest	WCq	
6-05-1970	Poland	L 1-2	Poznan	Fr	Givens
9-05	West Germany	L 1-2	Berlin	Fr	Mulligan
23-09	Poland	L 0-2	Dublin	Fr	
14-10	Sweden	D 1-1	Dublin	ECq	Carroll
28-10	Sweden	L 0-1	Stockholm	ECq	
8-12	Italy	L 0-3	Florence	ECq	
10-05-1971	Italy	L 1-2	Dublin	ECq	Conway
30-05	Austria	L 1-4	Dublin	ECq	Rogers
10-10	Austria	L 0-6	Linz	ECq	
11-06-1972	Iran	W 2-1	Recife	Clr1	Leech, Givens
18-06	Ecuador	W 3-2	Natal	Clr1	Rogers, Martin.M O'Connor
21-06	Chile	L 1-2	Recife	Clr1	Rogers
25-06	Portugal	L 1-2	Recife	Clr1	Leech
18-10	Soviet Union	L 1-2	Dublin	WCq	Conroy
15-11	France	W 2-1	Dublin	WCq	Conroy, Treacy
13-05-1973	Soviet Union	L 0-1	Moscow	WCq	
16-05	Poland	L 0-2	Wroclaw	Fr	
19-05	France	D 1-1	Paris	WCq	Martin.M
6-06	Norway	D 1-1	Oslo	Fr	Dennehy
21-10	Poland	W 1-0	Dublin	Fr	Dennehy
5-05-1974	Brazil	L 1-2	Rio de Janerio	Fr	Mancini
8-05	Uruguay	L 0-2	Montevideo	Fr	
12-05	Chile	W 2-1	Santiago	Fr	Hand, Conway
30-10	Soviet Union	W 3-0	Dublin	ECq	Givens 3
20-11	Turkey	D 1-1	Izmir	ECq	Givens
10-05-1975	Switzerland	W 2-1	Dublin	ECq	Martin.M, Treacy
18-05	Soviet Union	L 1-2	Kiev	ECq	Hand
21-05	Switzerland	L 0-1	Berne	ECq	
29-10	Turkey	W 4-0	Dublin	ECq	Givens 4
24-03-1976	Norway	W 3-0	Dublin	Fr	Brady, Holmes, Walsh
26-05	Poland	W 2-0	Poznan	Fr	Givens 2
8-09	England	D 1-1	London	Fr	Daly
13-10	Turkey	D 3-3	Ankara	Fr	Stapleton, Daly, Waters
17-11	France	L 0-2	Paris	WCq	
9-02-1977	Spain	L 0-1	Dublin	Fr	
30-03	France	W 1-0	Dublin	WCq	Brady
24-04	Poland	D 0-0	Dublin	Fr	
1-06	Bulgaria	L 0-2	Sofia	WCq	
12-10	Bulgaria	D 0-0	Dublin	WCq	
5-04-1978	Turkey	W 4-2	Dublin	Fr	Giles, McGee, Treacy 2
12-04	Poland	L 0-3	Lodz	Fr	
21-05	Norway	D 0-0	Oslo	Fr	
24-05	Denmark	D 3-3	Copenhagen	ECq	Stapleton, Grealish, Daly
20-09	Nth. Ireland	D 0-0	Dublin	ECq	
25-10	England	D 1-1	Dublin	ECq	Daly
2-05-1979	Denmark	W 2-0	Dublin	ECq	Daly, Givens
19-05	Bulgaria	L 0-1	Sofia	ECq	
22-05	West Germany	L 1-3	Dublin	Fr	Ryan
29-05	Argentina *	D 0-0	Dublin	Fr	
11-09	Wales	L 1-2	Swansea	Fr	OG
26-09	Czechoslovakia	L 1-4	Prague	Fr	McGee
17-10	Bulgaria	W 3-0	Dublin	ECq	Martin.M, Grealish, Stapleton
29-10	United States	W 3-2	Dublin	Fr	Grealish, Givens, Anderson
21-11	Nth. Ireland	L 0-1	Belfast	ECq	
6-02-1980	England	L 0-2	London	ECq	
26-03	Cyprus	W 3-2	Nicosia	WCq	Lawrenson, McGee 2
30-04	Switzerland	W 2-0	Dublin	Fr	Givens, Daly
16-05	Argentina	L 0-1	Dublin	Fr	
10-09	Holland	W 2-1	Dublin	WCq	Daly, Lawrenson
15-10	Belgium	D 1-1	Dublin	WCq	Grealish
28-10	France	L 0-2	Paris	WCq	
19-11	Cyprus	W 6-0	Dublin	WCq	Daly 2, Grealish, Robinson, Stapleton, Hughton
24-02-1981	Wales	L 1-3	Dublin	Fr	Grealish
25-03	Belgium	L 0-1	Brussels	WCq	

29-04	Czechoslovakia	W 3-1	Dublin	Fr	Moran 2, Stapleton
24-05	Poland	L 0-3	Bydgoszcz	Fr	
9-09	Holland	D 2-2	Rotterdam	WCq	Robinson, Stapleton
14-10	France	W 3-2	Dublin	WCq	OG, Stapleton, Robinson
28-04-1982	Algeria	L 0-2	Algiers	Fr	
22-05	Chile	L 0-1	Santiago	Fr	
27-05	Brazil	L 0-7	Uberlandia	Fr	
30-05	Trinidad	L 1-2	Port of Spain	Fr	Brady
22-09	Holland	L 1-2	Rotterdam	ECq	Daly
13-10	Iceland	W 2-0	Dublin	ECq	Stapleton, Grealish
17-11	Spain	D 3-3	Dublin	ECq	Grimes, Stapleton 2
30-03-1983	Malta	W 1-0	Ta'Qali	ECq	Stapleton
27-04	Spain	L 0-2	Zaragoza	ECq	
21-09	Iceland	W 3-0	Reykjavik	ECq	Waddock, Robinson, Walsh
12-10	Holland	L 2-3	Dublin	ECq	Waddock, Brady
16-11	Malta	W 8-0	Dublin	ECq	Lawrenson 2, Brady 2, Stapleton, O'Callaghan, Sheedy, Daly
4-04-1984	Israel	L 0-3	Tel Aviv	Fr	
23-05	Poland	D 0-0	Dublin	Fr	
3-06	China	W 1-0	Sapporo	Fr	O'Keefe
8-08	Mexico	D 0-0	Dublin	Fr	
12-09	Soviet Union	W 1-0	Dublin	WCq	Walsh
17-10	Norway	L 0-1	Oslo	WCq	
14-11	Denmark	L 0-3	Copenhagen	WCq	
5-02-1985	Italy	L 1-2	Dublin	Fr	Waddock
27-02	Israel	D 0-0	Tel Aviv	Fr	
26-03	England	L 1-2	London	Fr	Brady
1-05	Norway	D 0-0	Dublin	WCq	
26-05	Spain	D 0-0	Cork	Fr	
2-06	Switzerland	W 3-0	Dublin	WCq	Stapleton, Grealish, Sheedy
11-09	Switzerland	D 0-0	Berne	WCq	
16-10	Soviet Union	L 0-2	Moscow	WCq	
13-11	Denmark	L 1-4	Dublin	WCq	Stapleton
26-03-1986	Wales	L 0-1	Dublin	Fr	
23-04	Uruguay	D 1-1	Dublin	Fr	Daly
27-04	Iraq	L 0-1	Baghdad	Fr	
25-05	Iceland	W 2-1	Reykjavik	Fr	Daly, McGrath
27-05	Czechoslovakia	W 1-0	Reykjavik	Fr	Stapleton
10-09	Belgium	D 2-2	Brussels	ECq	Stapleton, Brady
15-10	Scotland	D 0-0	Dublin	ECq	
12-11	Poland	L 0-1	Warsaw	Fr	
18-02-1987	Scotland	W 1-0	Glasgow	ECq	Lawrenson
1-04	Bulgaria	L 1-2	Sofia	ECq	Stapleton
29-04	Belgium	D 0-0	Dublin	ECq	
23-05	Brazil	W 1-0	Dublin	Fr	Brady
28-05	Luxembourg	W 2-0	Luxembourg	ECq	Galvin, Whelan
9-09	Luxembourg	W 2-1	Dublin	ECq	Stapleton, McGrath
14-10	Bulgaria	W 2-0	Dublin	ECq	McGrath, Moran
10-11	Israel	W 5-0	Dublin	Fr	Byrne, Kelly.D 3, Quinn
23-03-1988	Romania	W 2-0	Dublin	Fr	Moran, Kelly.D
27-04	Yugoslavia	W 2-0	Dublin	Fr	McCarthy, Moran
22-05	Poland	W 3-1	Dublin	Fr	Sheedy, Cascarino, Sheridan
1-06	Norway	D 0-0	Oslo	Fr	
12-06	England	W 1-0	Stuttgart	ECr1	Houghton
15-06	Soviet Union	D 1-1	Hanover	ECr1	Whelan
18-06	Holland	L 0-1	Gelsenkirchen	ECr1	
14-09	Nth. Ireland	D 0-0	Belfast	WCq	
19-10	Tunisia	W 4-0	Dublin	Fr	Cascarino 2, Aldridge, Sheedy
16-11	Spain	L 0-2	Seville	WCq	
7-02-1989	France	D 0-0	Dublin	Fr	
8-03	Hungary	D 0-0	Budapest	WCq	
26-04	Spain	W 1-0	Dublin	WCq	OG
28-05	Malta	W 2-0	Dublin	WCq	Houghton, Moran
4-06	Hungary	W 2-0	Dublin	WCq	McGrath, Cascarino
6-09	West Germany	D 1-1	Dublin	Fr	Stapleton
11-10	Nth. Ireland	W 3-0	Dublin	WCq	Whelan, Cascarino, Houghton
15-11	Malta	W 2-0	Ta'Qali	WCq	Aldridge 2
28-03-1990	Wales	W 1-0	Dublin	Fr	Slaven
25-04	Soviet Union	W 1-0	Dublin	Fr	Staunton
16-05	Finland	D 1-1	Dublin	Fr	Sheedy
27-05	Turkey	D 0-0	Izmir	Fr	

2-06	Malta	W 3-0	Ta'Qali	Fr	Quinn, Townsend, Stapleton
11-06	England	D 1-1	Cagliari	WCr1	Sheedy
17-06	Egypt	D 0-0	Palermo	WCr1	
21-06	Holland	D 1-1	Palermo	WCr1	Quinn
25-06	Romania	D 0-0	Genoa	WCr2	Won 5-4 pens
30-06	Italy	L 0-1	Rome	WCqf	
12-09	Morocco	W 1-0	Dublin	Fr	Kelly.D
17-10	Turkey	W 5-0	Dublin	ECq	Aldridge 3, O'Leary, Quinn
14-11	England	D 1-1	Dublin	ECq	Cascarino
6-02-1991	Wales	W 3-0	Wrexham	Fr	Quinn 2, Byrne
27-03	England	D 1-1	London	ECq	Quinn
1-05	Poland	D 0-0	Dublin	ECq	
22-05	Chile	D 1-1	Dublin	Fr	Kelly.D
1-06	USA	D 1-1	Boston	Fr	Cascarino
11-09	Hungary	W 2-1	Gyor	Fr	Kelly.D, Aldridge
16-10	Poland	D 3-3	Poznan	ECq	McGrath, Townsend, Cascarino
13-11	Turkey	W 3-1	Istanbul	ECq	Byrne 2, Cascarino
19-02-1992	Wales	L 0-1	Dublin	Fr	
25-03	Switzerland	W 2-1	Dublin	Fr	Coyne, Aldridge
29-04	USA	W 4-1	Dublin	Fr	Townsend, Irwin, Quinn, Cascarino
26-05	Albania	W 2-0	Dublin	WCq	Aldridge, McGrath
30-05	USA	L 1-3	Washington	Fr	McCarthy
4-06	Italy	L 0-2	Boston	Fr	
7-06	Portugal	W 2-0	Boston	Fr	Staunton, Coyne
9-09	Latvia	W 4-0	Dublin	WCq	Sheedy, Aldridge 3
14-10	Denmark	D 0-0	Copenhagen	WCq	
18-11	Spain	D 0-0	Seville	WCq	
17-02-1993	Wales	W 2-1	Dublin	Fr	Sheedy, Coyne
31-03	Nth. Ireland	W 3-0	Dublin	WCq	Townsend, Quinn, Staunton
28-04	Denmark	D 1-1	Dublin	WCq	Quinn
26-05	Albania	W 2-1	Tirana	WCq	Staunton, Cascarino
9-06	Latvia	W 2-0	Riga	WCq	Aldridge, McGrath
16-06	Lithuania	W 1-0	Vilnius	WCq	Staunton
8-09	Lithuania	W 2-0	Dublin	WCq	Aldridge, Kernaghan
13-10	Spain	L 1-3	Dublin	WCq	Sheridan
17-11	Nth. Ireland	D 1-1	Belfast	WCq	McLoughlin
23-03-1994	Russia	D 0-0	Dublin	Fr	
20-04	Holland	W 1-0	Tilburg	Fr	Coyne
24-05	Bolivia	W 1-0	Dublin	Fr	Sheridan
29-05	Germany	W 2-0	Hanover	Fr	Cascarino, Kelly.G
5-06	Czech Republic	L 1-3	Dublin	Fr	Townsend
18-06	Italy	W 1-0	New York	WCr1	Houghton
24-06	Mexico	L 1-2	Orlando	WCr1	
28-06	Norway	D 0-0	New York	WCr1	
4-07	Holland	L 0-2	Orlando	WCr2	
7-09	Latvia	W 3-0	Riga	ECq	Aldridge 2, Sheridan
12-10	Liechtenstein	W 4-0	Dublin	ECq	Coyne 2, Quinn 2
16-11	Nth. Ireland	W 4-0	Belfast	ECq	Aldridge, Keane, Sheridan, Townsend
15-02-1995	England	W 1-0	Dublin	Fr	Kelly.D
29-03	Nth. Ireland	D 1-1	Dublin	ECq	Quinn
26-04	Portugal	W 1-0	Dublin	ECq	OG
3-06	Liechtenstein	D 0-0	Eschen	ECq	
11-06	Austria	L 1-3	Dublin	ECq	Houghton

ROMANIA

Romania took to football before most of her Balkan neighbours. The Federatia Romana de Fotbal was formed in 1908, a full 15 years before neighbours Bulgaria sought to do the same. The initial impulse to organise football came from the growing number of teams that were playing the game at that time, not only in Bucharest but in the rich oil fields of Ploiesti. Here a growing number of industries, such as textiles, had sprung up and many of them were run by English companies.

At first the indigenous population were hesitant about taking up the game, but in Prince Carol, the heir to the Romanian throne, they had a perfect role model, and it was at his instigation that the football federation was formed. In 1910, Prince Carol formed the larger Federation of Romanian Sports Societies, which the football body immediately joined. So keen was the prince on sport, and football in particular, that he became the first General Secretary of the Federation.

A championship was started in 1910, and the first champions, Olimpia Bucharest, contained several Britons in their side, but the First World War nearly killed the game. As the popularity of the game declined, so did the popularity of Carol, who was by now King, and in 1925 he abdicated. The ethnically Hungarian Transylvania, in the north-west of the country, was left as the main area where football was still played. Timisoara in particular was a stronghold and remained so throughout the inter-war period.

In June 1922 a match was played against Yugoslavia in a game that represented Romania's first ever and Yugoslavia's first on home soil. The Yugoslavs provided regular opposition in the inter-war years, and in the 1930s the Balkan Cup gave a competitive edge to the games. Bulgaria and Greece also took part in these tournaments, and of the four nations, Romania was the most successful with three titles.

King Carol was back in business in 1930, and he insisted Romania take part in the first World Cup in Uruguay. He selected a squad of players and then persuaded their employers to allow them leave to travel to South America. As one of only four European teams to make the journey, they were given a splendid welcome by the hosts although the hospitality did not extend to the pitch. Having beaten Peru, Romania lost 4-0 to Uruguay in the crucial match of the group and so failed to qualify for the semi-finals.

Romania entered all of the first three World Cups, but luckily did not have to travel so far for the 1934 and 1938 tournaments because they did not reach the second round in either. The eventual finalists Czechoslovakia ended their hopes in 1934, but it was a much more unlikely source, Cuba, who knocked the Romanians out in 1938, even if they did need a replay. Two players stand out from this time, the captain Emeric Vogel and the prolific scorer Iuliu Bodola, who to this day remains the top scorer for the national side.

The communists took control of the government in 1944, and as was standard practice they reorganised the game from top to bottom. Of all the Eastern Bloc countries, however, Romania was the last to benefit from the new system. In fact, the extraordinary thing was that when its allies were at their strongest, Romania was at its weakest, and whilst football has fallen into disrepair in the late 1980s in Poland, Hungary, Bulgaria and Czechoslovakia, Romania has embarked on its most successful era ever.

Two clubs have dominated Romanian football in the post-war period, Dinamo Bucharest, the team of the despised Securitate police, and Steaua Bucharest, the team of the army. At no time was this dominance more marked than in the 1988 season, when out of 34 games, both won 30 and the only separating factor was that Steaua had beaten Dinamo at home and drawn away.

Steaua, known as CCA Bucharest in the 1950s, won their first championship in 1951, Dinamo in 1955. Since then, apart from the occasional success of provincial teams like Petrolul Ploiesti, UT Arad, Arges Pitesti and Universitatea Craiova, the championship has remained a stronghold for these Bucharest teams.

Until the 1980s Romanian football was generally unremarkable. A few good players such as Florea Dumitrache, who scored two goals in the 1970 World Cup Finals, did emerge but not in any great numbers. Qualification for the 1970 World Cup, their first post-war, was followed by their reaching the quarter-finals of the 1972 European Championships before losing to Hungary after a play-off, but the upswing in fortunes was only temporary. Despite the presence of Dudu Georgescu and Anghel Iordanescu, two of the great names in Romanian football, it was not until 1984 that the Romanians qualified for a major tournament again.

THE ORDER OF MERIT

		All			League			Cup		Europe		
	Team	G	S	B	G	S	B	G	S	G	S	B
1	Steaua Bucuresti	36	17	7	17	9	6	18	7	1	1	1
2	Dinamo Bucuresti	22	27	8	15	17	6	7	10	-	-	2
3	Rapid Bucuresti	10	15	3	1	11	3	9	4	-	-	-
4	Universitatea Craiova	10	8	8	4	5	7	6	3	-	-	1
5	UT Arad	8	3	1	6	1	1	2	2	-	-	-
6	Venus Bucuresti	8	1	1	8	-	1	-	1	-	-	-
7	Petrolul Ploiesti	6	4	2	4	3	2	2	1	-	-	-
	Ripensia Timisoara	6	4	2	4	2	2	2	2	-	-	-
9	Chinezul Timisoara	6	1	-	6	-	-	-	1	-	-	-
10	Politehnica Timisoara	2	4	5	-	-	5	2	4	-	-	-
11	FC Arges Pitesti	2	3	3	2	2	3	-	1	-	-	-
12	FC Bihor Oradea	2	3	1	1	2	1	1	1	-	-	-
13	CSM Resita	2	1	-	1	1	-	1	-	-	-	-
14	Colentina Bucuresti	2	-	-	2	-	-	-	-	-	-	-
	Olimpia Bucuresti	2	-	-	2	-	-	-	-	-	-	-
	Prahova Ploiesti	2	-	-	2	-	-	-	-	-	-	-
17	Universitatea Cluj	1	4	1	-	1	1	1	3	-	-	-
18	Jiul Petroseni	1	3	1	-	2	1	1	1	-	-	-
19	Progresul Bucuresti	1	1	2	-	-	2	1	1	-	-	-
20	Coltea Brasov	1	1	-	1	1	-	-	-	-	-	-
21	Chimea Vîlcea	1	-	-	-	-	-	1	-	-	-	-
	Ariesul Turda	1	-	-	-	-	-	1	-	-	-	-
	Gloria Bistrita	1	-	-	-	-	-	1	-	-	-	-
	Romano-American Bucuresti	1	-	-	1	-	-	-	-	-	-	-
	Tirnu Severin	1	-	-	-	-	-	1	-	-	-	-
26	Sportul Studentesc	-	4	3	-	1	3	-	3	-	-	-
27	Victoria Cluj	-	3	-	-	3	-	-	-	-	-	-
28	CFR Timisoara	-	2	1	-	1	1	-	1	-	-	-
29	FC Maramures Baia Mare	-	2	-	-	-	-	-	2	-	-	-
30	AMEFA Arad	-	1	1	-	1	1	-	-	-	-	-
	Steagul Rosu Brasov	-	1	1	-	1	1	-	-	-	-	-
	ASA Tîrgu Mures	-	1	1	-	1	1	-	-	-	-	-

To the end of the 1994-95 season

The early 1980s saw the government of Nicolae Ceausescu become even more murderous than before and the two implements of his power, the army and the police, both used their football clubs to enhance their reputations even further. If Steaua and Dinamo had been powerful before, they were now transformed into sides that were almost unbeatable. This helped the national side, and led by Ladislau Bölöni, Romania's most capped player, they pulled themselves out of the doldrums. Though the 1984 European Championship in France was not a success, it proved to be the launching pad for Romania's emergence as a first-class football nation.

The late 1980s were an extraordinary time for Steaua in particular. Not only did they remain unbeaten for three consecutive seasons but in 1986 they became the only team from behind the Iron Curtain to win Europe's top prize, the European Cup, beating Barcelona 2-0 on penalties in the final. Three years later they were back again, but were on the end of a sound thrashing by Milan.

Not only were Steaua rampant at this time, the national side enjoyed a renaissance which included qualification for the World Cup in 1990. Steaua players were well represented in the side as it was common practice for all the best players to be recruited into either the Dinamo or Steaua camps.

The best known Romanian player of the 1980s has been Georghe Hagi, but he has been well supported by players such as Silviu Lung in goal, Mircea Rednic, Michael Klein, Dorin Mateut, Gheorghe Popescu, Rodion Camataru and Marius Lacatus, all of whom have been in demand in the West since the downfall of Ceausescu. Generally acknowledged to be one of the better sides in the World Cup in Italy, they were unlucky to lose on penalties in the second round to the Republic of Ireland.

Better was to come in the 1994 World Cup. With a side built around Hagi, Romania almost made it to the semi-finals. In a scintillating display in their first match they beat one of the pre-tournament favourites, Colombia, in style, whilst in the second round, in what was by far the best match of the tournament, they beat Argentina 3-2 with Ilie Dumitrescu outstanding. Despite losing to Sweden on penalties in the quarter-finals, they returned home to a huge reception.

Population: 23,265,000
Area, sq km: 237,500
% in urban areas: 51.3%
Capital city: Bucharest

Federatia Romana de Fotbal
Vasile Conta #16
Bucharest 70130
Romania

Year of formation	1908
Affiliation to FIFA	1930
Affiliation to UEFA	1954
Registered clubs	4900
Registered players	207 500
Professional players	650
Registered coaches	10 346
Registered referees	5597
National stadium	Stadionul 23 August, Bucharest, 65 000
National colours	Yellow/Blue/Red
Reserve colours	Blue/Yellow/Red
Season	August - June with a mid season break in January and February

THE RECORD

WORLD CUP

1930	QT Automatic - Final Tournament/1st round
1934	QT 2nd/3 in group 10 - Final Tournament/1st round
1938	QT Walk-over - Final Tournament/1st round
1950	Did not enter
1954	QT 2nd/3 in group 8
1958	QT 2nd/3 in group 7
1962	Did not enter
1966	QT 3rd/4 in group 4
1970	QT 1st/4 in group 1 - Final Tournament/1st round
1974	QT 2nd/4 in group 4
1978	QT 2nd/3 in group 8
1982	QT 3rd/5 in group 4
1986	QT 3rd/5 in group 3
1990	QT 1st/4 in group 1 - Final Tournament/2nd round
1994	QT 1st/6 in group 4 - Final Tournament/Quarter-finalists

EUROPEAN CHAMPIONSHIP

1960	Quarter-finalists
1964	1st round
1968	QT 2nd/4 in group 6
1972	QT 1st/4 in group 1 - Final Tournament/Quarter-finalists
1976	QT 2nd/4 in group 4
1980	QT 3rd/4 in group 3
1984	QT 1st/5 in group 5 - Final Tournament/1st round
1988	QT 2nd/4 in group 1
1992	QT 3rd/5 in group 2
1996	QT group 1

EUROPEAN CLUB COMPETITIONS

European Cup
Winners - Steaua Bucharest 1986
Finalists - Steaua Bucharest 1989
Cup Winners Cup
Semi-finalists - Dinamo Bucharest 1990
UEFA Cup
Semi-finalists - Universitatea Craiova 1983
Mitropa Cup
Quarter-finalists - Ripensia Timisoara 1938, Rapid Bucharest 1938

CLUB DIRECTORY

BUCHAREST (Population - 2,250,000)

Dinamo Bucuresti (1948)
Dinamo 18,000 – Red/Red
Previous names - Merger of Unirea and Tricolor in 1926 to form Unirea Tricolor, who merged with Ciocanul in 1948 to form Dinamo

Progresul Bucuresti (1934)
National 70,000 – White, blue trim
Previous names - Lafayette until 1948, Grafica 1948-50, Spartac 1950-54

Rapid Bucuresti (1923)
Rapid 15,000 – White, maroon chest band/White
Previous names - Casa Ferovarilul Rapid 1923-36 & 1946-50, Rapid 1936-46, Locomotiva 1950-58

Sportul Studentesc Bucuresti (1916)
Sportul Studentesc 15,000 – White/Black
Previous names - Universitar 1916-19, Sportul Studentesc 1919-44, Sparta 1944-48, Central Universitar 1948-54, Stiinta 1954-67, Politehnica 1967-69

Steaua Bucuresti (1947)
Steaua 30,000 – Blue/Red
Previous names - Armata 1947-48, CSCA 1948-50, CCA 1950-62

Clubs from Bucharest no longer in existence: Venus Bucuresti (1915-49) - Olimpia Bucuresti - Colentina Bucuresti - Victoria Bucuresti (1971-90)

BRASOV (Population - 351,000)

FC Brasov (1937)
Tineretului 15,000 – Yellow & black stripes/Black
Previous names - AS UAB Brasov 1937-50, Steagul Rosu 1950-79

CONSTANTA (Population - 327,000)

FC Farul Constanta (1949)
Farul 20,000 – Blue & white stripes/White
Previous names - Locomotiva 1950-57, Farul 1957-72, FC Constanta 1972-90

TIMISOARA (Population - 325,000)

Poletehnica Timisoara (1921)
1 mai 40,000 – Violet & white stripes/White
Previous names - UCAS 1921-30, CSU 1930-50, Stiinta 1950-66
Clubs from Timisoara that are no longer in existence:
1: CAMT Timisoara 1913-48. Known as Chinezul 1913-29, RGMT 1929-33, Chinezul 1933-39, CAMT 1939-48
2: Ripensia 1928-48

IASI (Population - 313,000)
Politehnica Iasi (1958)
23 August – Blue/White
Previous names - CSMS Iasi 1958-67

CLUJ-NAPOCA (Population - 310,000)
Universitatea Cluj-Napoca (1919)
Municipal 30,000 – White/White
Previous names - CSR 1919-23, Universitatea 1923-48, CSU 1948-49, Stiinta 1949-66

Victoria Cluj 1920-47 were known as Romania Cluj from 1920-36

PLOIESTI (Population - 300,000)
Petrolul Ploiesti (1924)
Petrolul 16,000 – Yellow/Yelow
Previous names - Juventus Bucuresti 1924-44, Distributia Bucuresti 1944-48, Petrolul Bucuresti 1948-49, Partizanul Bucuresti 1949-50, Flacara Bucuresti 1950-52, Flacara Ploiesti 1952-57, Energia Ploiesti 1957

Prahova Ploiesti (1909)
Municipal – Red/White
Previous names - United Ploiesti 1909-14, Prahova 1914-47, Concordia 1947-50, Partizanul 1950-56, Metalul 1956-58

GALATI (Population - 295,000)
Otelul Galati (1964)
Otelul 15,000 – Red & blue stripes/Red
Previous name - Metalosport Galati until 1982

CRAIOVA (Population - 281,000)
Universitatea Craiova (1948)
Central 35,000 – White, blue stripes/White
Previous name - Stiinta 1950-66

Electroputere Craiova (1949)
Valea Rosie 10,000 – White, red trim

BRAILA (Population - 235,000)
FCM Progresul Braila (1960)
Municipal 8,000 – White/Blue

ORADEA (Population - 213,000)
FC Bihor Oradea (1972)
Bihor 20,000 – Blue & red stripes/Blue
Previous names - Nagyvarad 1911-20 1940-44, CAO 1920-40, Libertatea 1944-48, ICO 1948-51, Progresul 1951-57, CSO 1957-61, Crisana 1961-72

ARAD (Population - 187,000)
UTA Arad (1943)
UTA 15,000 – Red/Red
Previous name - IT Arad 1943-50, Flamura Rosie 1950-58

BACAU (Population - 179,000)
FC Selena Bacau (1950)
Municipal 34,000 – White/Red
Previous names - Dinamo Bacau 1950-70, SC Bacau 1970-90, FC Bacau 1990-92

SIBIU (Population - 177,000)
FC Inter Sibiu (1982)
Municipal 15,000 – Red & blue stripes/White

TIRGU MURES (Population - 158,000)
ASA Tîrgu Mures (1962)
Municipal 12,000 – Blue/Red

PITESTI (Population - 157,000)
FC Arges Pitesti (1953)
Trivale 18,000 – Violet/White
Previous name - Dinamo Pitesti 1953-67

BAIA MARE (Population - 139,000)
FC Maramures Baia Mare (1962)
Dealul Florilor 20,000 – Yellow/Blue
Previous names - FC Baia Mare 1962-85

RESITA (Population - 105,000)
CSM Resita (1922)
Valea Domanului – Red/Black
Previous names - UDR 1922-45, Otelul 1945-48, Metalochimic 1948-50, Metalul 1950-58

RIMNICU VILCEA (Population - 96,000)
Chîmea Rimnicu Vîlcea (1924)
1 Mai 13,000 – White/Blue
Previous names - Vilceana 1924-44, CSM 1944-55, Flamura Rosie 1955-57, Unirea 1957-58 1962-66, Saniterul 1958-59, Chîmea 1959-62, Oltul 1966-67

HUNEDOARA (Population - 88,000)
Corvinul Hunedoara (1921)
Corvinul 15,000 – Blue, white sleeves/Blue
Previous names - Corvinul 1921-46 1957-63, UF 1946-48, IMS 1948-52, Metalul 1952-57 1964-70, Siderurgistul 1963-64

PETROSANI (Population - 74,000)
Jiul Petrosani (1919)
Jiul 25,000 – Black & white stripes/Black
Previous names - Minerilor 1919-24, UCAS 1924-30, Merger with CS Lupeni in 1930 to form Jiul 1930-50, Partizanul 1950, Flacara 1950-53, Minerul 1953-58

BISTRITA (Population - 57,000)
Gloria Bistrita (1926)
Municipal 12,000 – Blue, white trim

ROMANIAN LEAGUE CHAMPIONSHIP

1910	Olimpia Bucuresti
1911	Olimpia Bucuresti
1912	United Ploiesti
1913	Colentina Bucuresti
1914	Colentina Bucuresti
1915	Romano-Americana
1916	Prahova Ploiesti
1917-19	-
1920	Venus Bucuresti
1921	Venus Bucuresti

1922	Chinezul Timisoara	5-1	Victoria Cluj
1923	Chinezul Timisoara	3-0	Victoria Cluj
1924	Chinezul Timisoara	4-1	CAO Oradea
1925	Chinezul Timisoara	5-1	UCAS Petrosani
1926	Chinezul Timisoara	3-0	Juventus Bucuresti
1927	Chinezul Timisoara	2-2 4-3	Coltea Brasov
1928	Coltea Brasov	3-2	Jiul Lupeni
1929	Venus Bucuresti	3-2	Romania Cluj
1930	Juventus Bucuresti	3-0	Gloria CFR Arad
1931	UDR Resita	2-0	SG Sibiu
1932	Venus Bucuresti	3-0	UDR Resita
1933	Ripensia Timisoara	5-3 0-0	Universitatea Cluj
1934	Venus Bucuresti	3-2 5-3	Ripensia Timisoara

1935	Ripensia Timisoara 32 CAO Oradea 29 Venus Bucuresti 29
1936	Ripensia Timisoara 30 AMEFA Arad 28 Juventus Bucuresti 24
1937	Venus Bucuresti 32 Rapid Bucuresti 30 Ripensia Timisoara 27
1938	Ripensia Timisoara 2-0 2-0 Rapid Bucuresti
1939	Venus Bucuresti 35 Ripensia Timisoara 26 AMEFA Arad 25
1940	Venus Bucuresti 31 Rapid Bucuresti 29 Sportul Studentesc 27
1941	Unirea Tricolor 38 Rapid Bucuresti 35 Ripensia Timisoara 32
1942-46	-
1947	IT Arad 44 Carmen Bucuresti 33 CFR Timisoara 33
1948	IT Arad 50 CFR Timisoara 45 CFR Bucuresti 42
1949	ICO Oradea 37 CFR Bucuresti 32 Jiul Petrosani 30
1950	Flamura Rosie 28 Lokomotiva Buchuresti 28 Stiinta Timisoara 25
1951	CCA Bucuresti 32 Dinamo Bucuresti 32 Progresul Oradea 26
1952	CCA Bucuresti 36 Dinamo Bucuresti 34 Cimpulung 25
1953	CCA Bucuresti 28 Dinamo Bucuresti 25 Flamura Rosie 24
1954	Flamura Rosie 35 CCA Bucuresti 34 Dinamo Bucuresti 33
1955	Dinamo Bucuresti 37 Flacara Ploiesti 34 Progresul Bucuresti 33
1956	CCA Bucuresti 33 Dinamo Bucuresti 29 Stiinta Timisoara 29

1957 -
1958 Petrolul Ploiesti 27 CCA Bucuresti 27 Stiinta Timisoara 27
1959 Petrolul Ploiesti 31 Dinamo Bucuresti 30 CCA Bucuresti 29
1960 CCA Bucuresti 34 Steagul Rosu Brasov 27 Petrolul Ploiesti 24
1961 CCA Bucuresti 37 Dinamo Bucuresti 32 Rapid Bucuresti 30
1962 Dinamo Bucuresti 36 Petrolul Ploiesti 33 Progresul Bucuresti 31
1963 Dinamo Bucuresti 37 Steaua Bucuresti 34 Stiinta Timisoara 29
1964 Dinamo Bucuresti 40 Rapid Bucuresti 33 Steaua Bucuresti 31
1965 Dinamo Bucuresti 38 Rapid Bucuresti 37 Steaua Bucuresti 31
1966 Petrolul Ploiesti 38 Rapid Bucuresti 32 Dinamo Bucuresti 28
1967 Rapid Bucuresti 34 Dinamo Bucuresti 32 Universitatea Craiova 30
1968 Steaua Bucuresti 35 FC Arges Pitesti 33 Dinamo Bucuresti 31
1969 UT Arad 38 Dinamo Bucuresti 35 Rapid Bucuresti 34
1970 UT Arad 39 Rapid Bucuresti 37 Steaua Bucuresti 34
1971 Dinamo Bucuresti 36 Rapid Bucuresti 35 Steaua Bucuresti 33
1972 FC Arges Pitesti 41 UT Arad 37 Universitatea Cluj 37
1973 Dinamo Bucuresti 39 Universitatea Craiova 39 FC Arges Pitesti 35
1974 Universitatea Craiova 45 Dinamo Bucuresti 44 Steagul Rosu Brasov 39
1975 Dinamo Bucuresti 43 ASA Tîrgu Mures 40 Universitatea Craiova 39
1976 Steaua Bucuresti 51 Dinamo Bucuresti 44 ASA Tîrgu Mures 38
1977 Dinamo Bucuresti 49 Steaua Bucuresti 45 Universitatea Craiova 41
1978 Steaua Bucuresti 41 FC Arges Pitesti 41 Politehnica Timisoara 38
1979 FC Arges Pitesti 45 Dinamo Bucuresti 41 Steaua Bucuresti 40
1980 Universitatea Craiova 44 Steaua Bucuresti 44 FC Arges Pitesti 39
1981 Universitatea Craiova 46 Dinamo Bucuresti 43 FC Arges Pitesti 42
1982 Dinamo Bucuresti 47 Universitatea Craiova 45 Corvinul Hunedoara 39
1983 Dinamo Bucuresti 49 Universitatea Craiova 46 Sportul Studentesc 44
1984 Dinamo Bucuresti 49 Steaua Bucuresti 47 Universitatea Craiova 43
1985 Steaua Bucuresti 54 Dinamo Bucuresti 52 Sportul Studentesc 48
1986 Steaua Bucuresti 57 Sportul Studentesc 48 Universitatea Craiova 46
1987 Steaua Bucuresti 59 Dinamo Bucuresti 44 Victoria Bucuresti 38
1988 Steaua Bucuresti 64 Dinamo Bucuresti 63 Victoria Bucuresti 40
1989 Steaua Bucuresti 65 Dinamo Bucuresti 62 Victoria Bucuresti 45
1990 Dinamo Bucuresti 57 Steaua Bucuresti 56 Universitatea Craiova 44
1991 Universitatea Craiova 50 Steaua Bucuresti 50 Dinamo Bucuresti 43
1992 Dinamo Bucuresti 55 Steaua Bucuresti 48 Electroputere Craiova 39
1993 Steaua Bucuresti 48 Dinamo Bucuresti 47 Universitatea Craiova 37
1994 Steaua Bucuresti 53 Universitatea Craiova 40 Dinamo Bucuresti 39
1995 Steaua Bucuresti 77 Universitatea Craiova 68 Dinamo Bucuresti 65

ROMANIAN CUP FINALS

1934 Ripensia Timisoara ....5-0 ....Universitatea Cluj
1935 CFR Bucuresti..................6-5 ....Ripensia Timisoara
1936 Ripensia Timisoara ....5-1 ....Unirea Tricolor
1937 Rapid Bucuresti................5-1 ....Ripensia Timisoara
1938 Rapid Bucuresti................3-2 ....CAMT Timisoara
1939 Rapid Bucuresti................2-0 ....Sportul Studentesc
1940 Rapid Bucuresti......2-2 4-4 2-2 2-1 ......Venus Bucuresti
1941 Rapid Bucuresti................4-3 ....Unirea Tricolor
1942 Rapid Bucuresti................7-1 ....Universitatea Cluj
1943 Tirnu Severin....................4-0 ....Sportul Studentesc
1944-47 -
1948 IT Arad ....3-2 ....CFR Timisoara
1949 CSCA Bucuresti ....2-1 ....CSU Cluj
1950 CCA Bucuresti ....3-1 ....Flamura Rosie
1951 CCA Bucuresti ....3-1 ....Flacara Medias
1952 CCA Bucuresti ....2-0 ....Flacara Ploiesti
1953 Flamura Rosie ....1-0 ....CCA Bucuresti
1954 Metalul Resita....................2-0 ....Dinamo Bucuresti
1955 CCA Bucuresti ....6-3 ....Progresul Oradea
1956 Progresul Oradea..............2-0 ....Metalul Turzii
1957 -
1958 Stiinta Timisoara..............1-0 ....Progresul Bucuresti
1959 Dinamo Bucuresti ....4-0 ....Minerul Baia Mare
1960 Ariesul Turda....................2-0 ....Dinamo Bucuresti
1961 Progresul Bucuresti..........2-1 ....Rapid Bucuresti
1962 Steaua Bucuresti..............5-1 ....Rapid Bucuresti
1963 Petrolul Ploiesti................6-1 ....Siderurgistul Galati
1964 Dinamo Bucuresti ....5-3 ....Steaua Bucuresti
1965 Stiinta Cluj ....2-1 ....Dinamo Pitesti
1966 Steaua Bucuresti..............4-0 ....UT Arad
1967 Steaua Bucuresti..............6-0 ....Foresta Falticeni
1968 Dinamo Bucuresti ....3-1 ....Rapid Bucuresti
1969 Steaua Bucuresti..............2-1 ....Dinamo Bucuresti
1970 Steaua Bucuresti..............2-1 ....Dinamo Bucuresti
1971 Steaua Bucuresti..............3-2 ....Dinamo Bucuresti
1972 Rapid Bucuresti................2-0 ....Jiul Petrosani
1973 Chimia Vîlcea................1-1 3-0 ....Constructorul Galatizi
1974 Jiul Petrosani....................4-2 ....Politehnica Timisoara
1975 Rapid Bucuresti................2-1 ....Universitatea Craiova
1976 Steaua Bucuresti..............1-0 ....CSU Galati
1977 Universitatea Craiova......2-1 ....Steaua Bucuresti
1978 Universitatea Craiova......3-1 ....Olimpia Satu Mare
1979 Steaua Bucuresti..............3-0 ....Sportul Studentesc
1980 Politehnica Timisoara......2-1 ....Steaua Bucuresti
1981 Universitatea Craiova......6-0 ....Politehnica Timisoara
1982 Dinamo Bucuresti ....3-2 ....FC Baia Mare
1983 Universitatea Craiova......2-1 ....Politehnica Timisoara
1984 Dinamo Bucuresti ....2-1 ....Steaua Bucuresti
1985 Steaua Bucuresti..............2-1 ....Universitatea Craiova
1986 Dinamo Bucuresti ....1-0 ....Steaua Bucuresti
1987 Steaua Bucuresti..............1-0 ....Dinamo Bucuresti
1988 Steaua Bucuresti..............2-1 ....Dinamo Bucuresti
1989 Steaua Bucuresti..............1-0 ....Dinamo Bucuresti
1990 Dinamo Bucuresti ....6-4 ....Steaua Bucuresti
1991 Universitatea Craiova......2-1 ....FC Bacau
1992 Steaua Bucuresti..........1-1 4-3p ....Politehnica Timisoara

1993	Universitatea Craiova	2-0	Dacia Unirea Braila	
1994	Gloria Bistrita	1-0	Universitatea Craiova	
1995	Petrolul Ploesti	1-1 6-4p	Rapid Bucuresti	

LEADING INTERNATIONAL GOALSCORERS

30 Iuliu Bodola	(CA Oradea, Venus)	1931-1939
26 Anghel Iordanescu	(Steaua)	1971-1981
25 Georghe Hagi	(Sportul Studentesc, Steaua, Real Madrid, Brescia)	1983-
25 Ladislau Bölöni	(Tîrgu Mures, Steaua, Racing Jette)	1975-1988
22 Rodion Camataru	(Univ. Craiova, Dinamo, Charleroi)	1978-1990
21 Dudu Georgescu	(Dinamo, SC Bacau)	1974-1984
20 Stefan Dobai	(Banatul Timisoara, Ripensia Timisoara)	1930-1939
Florin Raducioiu	(Dinamo, Bari, Verona, Brescia, Milan)	1990-
19 Ilie Dumitrescu	(Steaua)	1989-
15 Florea Dumitrache	(Dinamo)	1968-1974

LEADING INTERNATIONAL APPEARANCES

108 Ladislau Bölöni	(Tîrgu Mures, Steaua, Racing Jette)	1975-1988
91 Georghe Hagi	(Sportul Studentesc, Steaua, Real Madrid, Brescia)	1983-
90 Michael Klein	(Corvinul, Dinamo, Bayer Uerdingen)	1981-1991
83 Mircea Rednic	(Corvinul, Dinamo, Bursaspor)	1981-1991
77 Silvio Lung #	(Univ. Craiova, Steaua, Logrones, Elect. Craiova)	1979-1993
75 Cornel Dinu	(Dinamo)	1968-1981
Rodion Camataru	(Univ. Craiova, Dinamo, Charleroi)	1978-1990
70 Mircea Lucescu	(Stiinta, Polit. Bucuresti, Dinamo, Corvinul)	1966-1979
69 Ilie Balaci	(Univ. Craiova, FC Olt, Dinamo)	1974-1986
69 Marius Lacatus	(Steaua, Fiorentina, Real Oviedo)	1984-
66 Costica Stefanescu	(Univ. Craiova)	1977-1985

INTERNATIONAL MATCHES PLAYED BY ROMANIA

8-06-1922	Yugoslavia	W 2-1	Belgrade	Fr	Ronay, Guga
3-09	Poland	D 1-1	Czernowitz	Fr	Kozzovits
10-06-1923	Yugoslavia	L 1-2	Bucharest	Fr	Ronay
1-07	Czechoslovakia	L 0-6	Cluj	Fr	
2-09	Poland	D 1-1	Lwow	Fr	Guga
26-10	Turkey	D 2-2	Istanbul	Fr	Gansl 2
20-05-1924	Austria	L 1-4	Vienna	Fr	Ströck
27-05	Holland	L 0-6	Paris	OGr1	
31-05	Czechoslovakia	L 1-4	Prague	Fr	Semler
1-05-1925	Turkey	L 1-2	Bucharest	Fr	Brauchler
31-08	Bulgaria	W 4-2	Sofia	Fr	Wetzer 2, Semler 2
25-04-1926	Bulgaria	W 6-1	Bucharest	Fr	Guga, Gugelbauer 2, Csomag, Ströck, Auer I
7-05	Turkey	W 3-1	Istanbul	Fr	Semler 2, Matek
3-10	Yugoslavia	W 3-2	Zagreb	Fr	Semler, Kilianowici, Guga
10-05-1927	Yugoslavia	L 0-3	Bucharest	Fr	
19-06	Poland	D 3-3	Bucharest	Fr	Auer II 2, Tänzer
15-04-1928	Turkey	W 4-2	Arad	Fr	Wetzer, OG, Sepi, Csomag
6-05	Yugoslavia	L 1-3	Belgrade	Fr	Possak
21-04-1929	Bulgaria	W 3-0	Bucharest	Fr	Ciolac 3
10-05	Yugoslavia	L 2-3	Bucharest	Fr	Subasanu, Boross
15-09	Bulgaria	W 3-2	Sofia	Fr	Sepi, Kovacs.N, Desu
6-10	Yugoslavia	W 2-1	Bucharest	BC	Sepi, Ciolac
4-05-1930	Yugoslavia	L 1-2	Belgrade	Fr	Desu
25-05	Greece	W 8-1	Bucharest	BC	Wetzer 5, Vogl, Raffinski, Dobay
14-07	Peru	W 3-1	Montevideo	WCr1	Desu, Stanciu, Kovacs.N
20-07	Uruguay	L 0-4	Montevideo	WCr1	
12-10	Bulgaria	L 3-5	Sofia	BC	Wetzer 2, OG
10-05-1931	Bulgaria	W 5-2	Bucharest	BC	Sepi, Bodola 2, Stanciu 2
28-06	Yugoslavia	W 4-2	Zagreb	BC	Glanzman, Kovacs.N, Bodola 2
23-08	Poland	W 3-2	Warsaw	Fr	Sepi 2, Kocsis
26-08	Lithuania	W 4-2	Kaunas	Fr	Bodola 3, Sepi
29-11	Greece	W 4-2	Athens	BC	Bodola 3, Sepi
12-06-1932	France	W 6-3	Bucharest	Fr	Bodola 2, Wetzer 2, Schwartz 2
26-06	Bulgaria	L 0-2	Belgrade	BC	
28-06	Greece	W 3-0	Belgrade	BC	Ciolac, Schwartz, Bodola
3-07	Yugoslavia	L 1-3	Belgrade	BC	Kovacs.N
2-10	Poland	L 0-5	Bucharest	Fr	
4-06-1933	Bulgaria	W 7-0	Bucharest	BC	Vîlcov 2, Dobay 2, Ciolac 3
6-06	Greece	W 1-0	Bucharest	BC	Dobay
11-06	Yugoslavia	W 5-0	Bucharest	BC	Bindea, Ciolac, Bodola 2, Dobay
29-10	Switzerland	D 2-2	Berne	WCq	Sepi, Dobay
29-04-1934	Yugoslavia	W 2-1	Bucharest	WCq	Schwartz, Dobay

27-05	Czechoslovakia	L 1-2	Trieste	WCr1	Dobay
14-10	Poland	D 3-3	Lwow	Fr	Dobay 2, Ciolac
24-12	Greece	D 2-2	Athens	BC	Dobay, Ciolac
30-12	Bulgaria	W 3-2	Athens	BC	Bodola 2, Ciolac
1-01-1935	Yugoslavia	L 0-4	Athens	BC	
17-06	Yugoslavia	L 0-2	Sofia	BC	
19-06	Bulgaria	L 0-4	Sofia	BC	
24-06	Greece	D 2-2	Sofia	BC	Bodola, Gruim
25-08	Germany	L 2-4	Erfurt	Fr	Vîlcov 2
1-09	Sweden	L 1-7	Stockholm	Fr	Georgescu.G
3-11	Poland	W 4-1	Bucharest	Fr	Schileru, Bindea 2, Sepi
10-05-1936	Yugoslavia	W 3-2	Bucharest	BC	Bodola 3
17-05	Greece	W 5-2	Bucharest	BC	Bodola 2, Schwartz 2, Dobay
24-05	Bulgaria	W 4-1	Bucharest	BC	Schwartz 2, Ciolac, Dobay
4-10	Hungary	L 1-2	Bucharest	Fr	Bindea
18-04-1937	Czechoslovakia	D 1-1	Bucharest	Fr	Bodola
10-06	Belgium	W 2-1	Bucharest	Fr	Baratky 2
27-06	Sweden	D 2-2	Bucharest	Fr	Baratky 2
4-07	Poland	W 4-2	Lodz	Fr	Dobay, Baratky 2, Bodola
9-07	Lithuania	W 2-0	Kaunas	Fr	Bogdan, Bodola
13-07	Latvia	D 0-0	Riga	Fr	
15-07	Estonia	L 1-2	Tallinn	Fr	Bodola
6-09	Yugoslavia	L 1-2	Belgrade	Fr	Baratky
8-05-1938	Yugoslavia	L 0-1	Bucharest	Fr	
5-06	Cuba	D 3-3	Toulouse	WCr1	Bindea, Baratky, Dobay
9-06	Cuba	L 1-2	Toulouse	WCr1	Dobay
6-09	Yugoslavia	D 1-1	Belgrade	Fr	Bindea
25-09	Germany	L 1-4	Bucharest	Fr	Orza
4-12	Czechoslovakia	L 2-6	Prague	Fr	Baratky, Bodola
7-05-1939	Yugoslavia	W 1-0	Bucharest	Fr	Dobay
18-05	Latvia	W 4-0	Bucharest	Fr	Bodola 2, Dobay, OG
24-05	England	L 0-2	Bucharest	Fr	
11-06	Italy	L 0-1	Bucharest	Fr	
22-10	Hungary	D 1-1	Bucharest	Fr	Spielmann
31-03-1940	Yugoslavia	D 3-3	Bucharest	Fr	Bindea 2, Baratky
14-04	Italy	L 1-2	Rome	Fr	Baratky
19-05	Hungary	L 0-2	Budapest	Fr	
14-07	Germany	L 3-9	Frankfurt	Fr	Baratky 2, Ploesteanu
22-09	Yugoslavia	W 2-1	Belgrade	Fr	Popescu, Bogdan
1-06-1941	Germany	L 1-4	Bucharest	Fr	Niculescu
12-10	Slovakia	W 3-2	Bucharest	Fr	Humis, Bindea 2
16-08-1942	Germany	L 0-7	Bytom	Fr	
23-08	Slovakia	L 0-1	Bratislava	Fr	
11-10	Croatia	D 2-2	Bucharest	Fr	Florian, Bogdan
13-06-1943	Slovakia	D 2-2	Bucharest	Fr	Marian, Kovacs.I
30-09-1945	Hungary	L 2-7	Budapest	Fr	Pecsovsky, Fabian
8-10-1946	Bulgaria	D 2-2	Tirana	BC	Reuter, Toth
11-10	Yugoslavia	W 2-1	Tirana	BC	Reuter, Fabian
13-10	Albania	L 0-1	Tirana	BC	
25-05-1947	Albania	W 4-0	Tirana	BCE	Farkas 3, Kovacs.I
22-06	Yugoslavia	L 1-3	Bucharest	BCE	Farkas
6-07	Bulgaria	W 3-2	Sofia	BCE	Bacut, Pecsovsky
20-07	Poland	W 2-1	Warsaw	Fr	Spielmann 2
21-09	Czechoslovakia	L 2-6	Bucharest	Fr	Spielmann, Dumitrescu
12-10	Hungary	L 0-3	Bucharest	BCE	
26-10	Poland	D 0-0	Bucharest	Fr	
2-05-1948	Albania	L 0-1	Bucharest	BCE	
6-06	Hungary	L 0-9	Budapest	BCE	
20-06	Bulgaria	W 3-2	Bucharest	BCE	Farkas 2, Dumitrescu
4-07	Czechoslovakia	W 2-1	Bucharest	BCE	Iordache, Bartha
10-10	Poland	D 0-0	Chorzow	BCE	
24-10	Hungary	L 1-5	Bucharest	BCE	Pecsovsky
8-05-1949	Poland	W 2-1	Bucharest	Fr	Pecsovsky 2
22-05	Czechoslovakia	L 2-3	Prague	Fr	Vaczi, Lungu
23-10	Albania	D 1-1	Bucharest	Fr	Pecsovsky
29-11	Albania	W 4-1	Tirana	Fr	Lungu 2, Vaczi, Filote
14-05-1950	Poland	D 3-3	Wroclaw	Fr	Mircea, Vaczi, Bodo
21-05	Czechoslovakia	D 1-1	Bucharest	Fr	Bodo
8-10	Albania	W 6-0	Bucharest	Fr	Pecsovsky 2, Radulescu 2, Mercea, Suru
20-05-1951	Czechoslovakia	D 2-2	Prague	Fr	Vaczi 2
11-05-1952	Czechoslovakia	W 3-1	Bucharest	Fr	Paraschiva, Serfözö, Ozon
25-05	Poland	W 1-0	Bucharest	Fr	Paraschiva

15-07	Hungary	L 1-2	Turku	OGpr	Suru
26-10	East Germany	W 3-1	Bucharest	Fr	Vaczi 3
14-06-1953	Czechoslovakia	L 0-2	Prague	WCq	
28-06	Bulgaria	W 3-1	Bucharest	WCq	Pecsovsky 2, Ene
11-10	Bulgaria	W 2-1	Sofia	WCq	Serfözö, Calinoiu
25-10	Czechoslovakia	L 0-1	Bucharest	WCq	
8-05-1954	East Germany	W 1-0	Berlin	Fr	Ozon
19-09	Hungary	L 1-5	Budapest	Fr	Ozon
29-05-1955	Poland	D 2-2	Bucharest	Fr	Ozon, Georgescu.N
12-06	Norway	W 1-0	Oslo	Fr	Ozon
15-06	Sweden	L 1-4	Gothenburg	Fr	Georgescu.N
18-09	East Germany	L 2-3	Bucharest	Fr	Georgescu.N
28-09	Belgium	W 1-0	Bucharest	Fr	Georgescu.N
9-10	Bulgaria	D 1-1	Bucharest	Fr	Georgescu.N
22-04-1956	Yugoslavia	W 1-0	Belgrade	Fr	Cacoveanu
17-06	Sweden	L 0-2	Bucharest	Fr	
26-06	Norway	W 2-0	Bucharest	Fr	Zaharia, David
10-09	Bulgaria	L 0-2	Sofia	Fr	
26-05-1957	Belgium	L 0-1	Brussels	Fr	
1-06	Soviet Union	D 1-1	Moscow	Fr	Ene
16-06	Greece	W 2-1	Athens	WCq	Ene, Ozon
29-09	Yugoslavia	D 1-1	Bucharest	WCq	Ene
3-11	Greece	W 3-0	Bucharest	WCq	Pecsovsky, Tataru I, Cacoveanu
17-11	Yugoslavia	L 0-2	Belgrade	WCq	
14-09-1958	East Germany	L 2-3	Leipzig	Fr	Constantin, Ene
26-10	Hungary	L 1-2	Bucharest	Fr	Dinulescu
2-11	Turkey	W 3-0	Bucharest	ECr1	Oaida, Constantin, Dinulescu
26-04-1959	Turkey	L 0-2	Istanbul	ECr1	
19-07	Soviet Union	L 0-2	Moscow	OGq	
2-08	Soviet Union	D 0-0	Bucharest	OGq	
30-08	Poland	W 3-2	Warsaw	Fr	Dridea 3
8-11	Bulgaria	W 1-0	Bucharest	OGq	Constantin
1-05-1960	Bulgaria	L 1-2	Sofia	OGq	Tataru I
22-05	Czechoslovakia	L 0-2	Bucharest	ECr1	
29-05	Czechoslovakia	L 0-3	Prague	ECr1	
14-05-1961	Turkey	W 1-0	Ankara	Fr	Dridea
8-10	Turkey	W 4-0	Bucharest	Fr	Seredai 2, Constantin 2
30-09-1962	Morocco	W 4-0	Bucharest	Fr	Voinea, Ozon, Seredai
14-10	East Germany	L 2-3	Dresden	Fr	Emil 2
1-11	Spain	L 0-6	Madrid	ECr1	
25-11	Spain	W 3-1	Bucharest	ECr1	Tataru I, Manolache, Constantin
23-12	Morocco	L 1-3	Casablanca	Fr	Constantin
12-05-1963	East Germany	W 3-2	Bucharest	Fr	Pavlovici, Haidu, Pîrcalab
2-06	Poland	D 1-1	Chorzow	Fr	Haidu
23-06	Denmark	W 3-2	Copenhagen	OGq	Constantin, Manolache 2
9-10	Turkey	D 0-0	Ankara	Fr	
27-10	Yugoslavia	W 2-1	Bucharest	Fr	Tircovnicu, Haidu
3-11	Denmark	L 2-3	Bucharest	OGq	Emil 2
28-11	Denmark	W 2-1	Turin	OGq	Creiniceanu, Sasu
3-05-1964	Bulgaria	W 2-1	Bucharest	OGq	Constantin 2
31-05	Bulgaria	W 1-0	Sofia	OGq	Kozska
17-06	Yugoslavia	W 2-1	Belgrade	Fr	Georgescu.N, Ionescu.I
11-10	Mexico *	W 3-1	Omiya	OGr1	Creiniceanu, Pircalab, Ionescu.I
13-10	East Germany *	D 1-1	Omiya	OGr1	Pavlovici
15-10	Iran	W 1-0	Omiya	OGr1	Pavlovici
18-10	Hungary *	L 0-2	Yokohama	OGqf	
20-10	Ghana	W 4-2	Osaka	OG5p	Pavlovici 3, Creiniceanu
22-10	Yugoslavia	W 3-0	Osaka	OG5p	Pavlovici, Pircalab, Constantin
2-05-1965	Turkey	W 3-0	Bucharest	WCq	Georgescu.N, Mateianu, Creiniceanu
30-05	Czechoslovakia	W 1-0	Bucharest	WCq	Mateianu
13-06	Portugal	L 1-2	Lisbon	WCq	Avram
19-09	Czechoslovakia	L 1-3	Prague	WCq	Coe
23-10	Turkey	L 1-2	Ankara	WCq	Georgescu.N
21-11	Portugal	W 2-0	Bucharest	WCq	Pîrcalab, Badea
1-06-1966	West Germany	L 0-1	Ludwigshafen	Fr	
19-06	Uruguay	W 1-0	Bucharest	Fr	Iancu
3-07	Portugal	L 0-1	Oporto	Fr	
21-09	East Germany	L 0-2	Gera	Fr	
2-11	Switzerland	W 4-2	Bucharest	ECq	Fratila 3, Dridea
17-11	Poland	W 4-3	Ploiesti	Fr	OG, Gergely, Fratila, Coe
26-11	Italy	L 1-3	Naples	ECq	Dobrin
3-12	Cyprus	W 5-1	Nicosia	ECq	Dridea 2, Lucescu, Fratila 2

7-12	Israel	W 2-1	Tel Aviv	Fr	Badea, Pîrcalab
4-01-1967	Uruguay	D 1-1	Montevideo	Fr	OG
8-03	Greece	W 2-1	Athens	Fr	Ionescu.I
22-03	France	W 2-1	Paris	Fr	Fratila, Dridea
23-04	Cyprus	W 7-0	Bucharest	ECq	Lucescu, Martinovici, Dumitriu 3, Ionescu.I 2
24-05	Switzerland	L 1-7	Zurich	ECq	Dobrin
25-06	Italy	L 0-1	Bucharest	ECq	
29-10	Poland	D 0-0	Krakow	Fr	
18-11	East Germany	L 0-1	Berlin	OGq	
22-11	West Germany	W 1-0	Bucharest	Fr	Gergely
6-12	East Germany	L 0-1	Bucharest	OGq	
24-12	Zaire	D 1-1	Kinshasa	Fr	Sasu
1-05-1968	Austria	D 1-1	Linz	Fr	Kallo
5-06	Holland	D 0-0	Bucharest	Fr	
27-10	Portugal	L 0-3	Lisbon	WCq	
6-11	England	D 0-0	Bucharest	Fr	
23-11	Switzerland	W 2-0	Bucharest	WCq	Dumitrache, Domide
15-01-1969	England	D 1-1	London	Fr	Dumitrache
16-04	Greece	D 2-2	Athens	WCq	Dumitrache 2
14-05	Switzerland	W 1-0	Lausanne	WCq	OG
3-09	Yugoslavia	D 1-1	Belgrade	Fr	Dembrowski
12-10	Portugal	W 1-0	Bucharest	WCq	Dobrin
16-11	Greece	D 1-1	Bucharest	WCq	Dembrowski
9-02-1970	Peru	L 0-2	Lima	Fr	
8-04	West Germany	D 1-1	Stuttgart	Fr	Neagu
28-04	France	L 0-2	Reims	Fr	
6-05	Yugoslavia	D 0-0	Bucharest	Fr	
2-06	England	L 0-1	Guadalajara	WCr1	
6-06	Czechoslovakia	W 2-1	Guadalajara	WCr1	Neagu, Dumitrache
10-06	Brazil	L 2-3	Guadalajara	WCr1	Dumitrache, Dembrowski
11-10	Finland	W 3-0	Bucharest	ECq	Dumitrache, Nunweiller
11-11	Wales	D 0-0	Cardiff	ECq	
2-12	Holland	L 0-2	Amsterdam	Fr	
18-04-1971	Albania	W 2-1	Bucharest	OGq	Iordanescu, Salceanu
21-04	Yugoslavia	W 1-0	Novi Sad	Fr	Dembrowski
16-05	Czechoslovakia	L 0-1	Bratislava	ECq	
26-05	Albania	W 2-1	Tirana	OGq	Tataru II 2
22-09	Finland	W 4-0	Helsinki	ECq	Iordanescu, Lupescu I, Dembrowski, Lucescu
10-10	Denmark	L 1-2	Copenhagen	OGq	Dembrowski
14-11	Czechoslovakia	W 2-1	Bucharest	ECq	Dembrowski, Dobrin
24-11	Wales	W 2-0	Bucharest	ECq	Lupescu I, Lucescu
31-01-1972	Morocco	W 4-2	Casablanca	Fr	Kun, Radu, Brosowski, Domide
8-04	France	W 2-0	Bucharest	Fr	Iordanescu, Dinu
23-04	Peru	D 2-2	Bucharest	Fr	Tataru II, Marcu
29-04	Hungary	D 1-1	Budapest	ECqf	Satmareanu
14-05	Hungary	D 2-2	Bucharest	ECqf	Dobrin, Neagu
17-05	Hungary	L 1-2	Belgrade	ECqf	Neagu
21-05	Denmark	L 2-3	Bucharest	OGq	Gyorfi, Dumitru
17-06	Italy	D 3-3	Bucharest	Fr	Dobrin, Hainal, OG
3-09	Austria	D 1-1	Craiova	Fr	Dembrowski
20-09	Finland	D 1-1	Helsinki	WCq	Nunweiller
29-10	Albania	W 2-0	Bucharest	WCq	Dobrin, Dembrowski
18-04-1973	Soviet Union	L 0-2	Kiev	Fr	
6-05	Albania	W 4-1	Tirana	WCq	Dumitru, Troi, Dumitrache, Taralunga
27-05	East Germany	W 1-0	Bucharest	WCq	Dumitrache
26-09	East Germany	L 0-2	Leipzig	WCq	
14-10	Finland	W 9-0	Bucharest	WCq	Marcu 2, Mircea 2, Dumitrache 2, Dumitru, Pantea, Georgescu.D
23-03-1974	France	L 0-1	Paris	Fr	
17-04	Brazil	L 0-2	Sao Paulo	Fr	
22-04	Argentina	L 1-2	Buenos Aires	Fr	Kun
29-05	Greece	W 3-1	Bucharest	BC	Iordanescu 2, Lucescu
5-06	Holland	D 0-0	Rotterdam	Fr	
28-07	Japan	W 4-1	Constanza	Fr	Dumitrache 2, Dumitru, Hainal
25-09	Bulgaria	D 0-0	Sofia	Fr	
13-10	Denmark	D 0-0	Copenhagen	ECq	
4-12	Israel	W 1-0	Tel Aviv	Fr	Samas
19-03-1975	Turkey	D 1-1	Istanbul	Fr	Lucescu
31-03	Czechoslovakia	D 1-1	Prague	Fr	Kun
17-04	Spain	D 1-1	Madrid	ECq	Crisan
10-05	Denmark	W 6-1	Bucharest	ECq	Georgescu.D 2, Crisan 2, Lucescu, Dinu
1-06	Scotland	D 1-1	Bucharest	ECq	Georgescu.D

24-09	Greece	D 1-1	Salonica	BC	Dimitru
12-10	Turkey	D 2-2	Bucharest	Fr	Iordanescu, Dinu
16-11	Spain	D 2-2	Bucharest	ECq	Georgescu.D, Iordanescu
29-11	Soviet Union	D 2-2	Bucharest	Fr	Troi, Hainal
17-12	Scotland	D 1-1	Glasgow	ECq	Crisan
12-05-1976	Bulgaria	L 0-1	Veliko Tarnovo	BC	
5-06	Italy	L 2-4	Milan	Fr	Lucescu, Georgescu.D
2-07	Iran	D 2-2	Tehran	Fr	Bölöni, Sandu
22-09	Czechoslovakia	D 1-1	Bucharest	Fr	Georgescu.D
6-10	Czechoslovakia	L 2-3	Prague	Fr	Balaci, Georgescu.D
28-11	Bulgaria	W 3-2	Bucharest	BC	Troi 2, Multescu
23-03-1977	Turkey	W 4-0	Bucharest	BC	Georgescu.D, Dumitru, Vigu, Iordanescu
16-04	Spain	W 1-0	Bucharest	WCq	OG
27-04	East Germany	D 1-1	Bucharest	Fr	Dumitru
8-05	Yugoslavia	W 2-0	Zagreb	WCq	Georgescu.D, Iordanescu
5-08	Iran	D 0-0	Tehran	Fr	
21-09	Greece	W 6-1	Bucharest	Fr	Dumitru 3, Bölöni 2, Georgescu.D
26-10	Spain	L 0-2	Madrid	WCq	
13-11	Yugoslavia	L 4-6	Bucharest	WCq	Vigu, Iordanescu, Bölöni, Georgescu.D
22-03-1978	Turkey	D 1-1	Istanbul	BC	Georgescu.D
5-04	Argentina	L 0-2	Buenos Aires	Fr	
3-05	Bulgaria	W 2-0	Bucharest	BC	Iordanescu, Balaci
14-05	Soviet Union	L 0-1	Bucharest	Fr	
31-05	Bulgaria	D 1-1	Sofia	BC	Iordanescu
11-10	Poland	W 1-0	Bucharest	Fr	Iordanescu
25-10	Yugoslavia	W 3-2	Bucharest	ECq	Sames 2, Iordanescu
15-11	Spain	L 0-1	Valencia	ECq	
13-12	Greece	L 1-2	Athens	Fr	Romila
19-12	Israel	D 1-1	Tel Aviv	Fr	Stan
21-03-1979	Greece	W 3-0	Bucharest	Fr	Dimitru, Balaci, Georgescu.D
4-04	Spain	D 2-2	Craiova	ECq	Georgescu.D 2
13-05	Cyprus	D 1-1	Limassol	ECq	Augustin
1-06	East Germany	L 0-1	Berlin	Fr	
29-08	Poland	L 0-3	Warsaw	Fr	
14-10	Soviet Union	L 1-3	Moscow	Fr	Nicolae
31-10	Yugoslavia	L 1-2	Kosovo	ECq	Raducanu
18-11	Cyprus	W 2-0	Bucharest	ECq	Raducanu, Multescu
16-02-1980	Italy	L 1-2	Naples	Fr	Bölöni
30-03	Yugoslavia	L 0-2	Belgrade	BC	
2-04	East Germany	D 2-2	Bucharest	Fr	Sandu, OG
16-05	Czechoslovakia	L 1-2	Brno	Fr	Ionescu
6-06	Belgium	L 1-2	Brussels	Fr	Camataru
27-08	Yugoslavia	W 4-1	Bucharest	BC	Iordanescu 3, Camataru
10-09	Bulgaria	W 2-1	Varna	Fr	Beldeanu, Iordanescu
24-09	Norway	D 1-1	Oslo	WCq	Iordanescu
15-10	England	W 2-1	Bucharest	WCq	Raducanu, Iordanescu
25-03-1981	Poland	W 2-0	Bucharest	Fr	Camataru, Iordanescu
8-04	Israel	L 1-2	Tel Aviv	Fr	Sandu
15-04	Denmark	L 1-2	Copenhagen	Fr	Camataru
29-04	England	D 0-0	London	WCq	
13-05	Hungary	L 0-1	Budapest	WCq	
3-06	Norway	W 1-0	Bucharest	WCq	Ticleanu
9-09	Bulgaria	L 1-2	Bucharest	Fr	Balaci
23-09	Hungary	D 0-0	Bucharest	WCq	
10-10	Switzerland	L 1-2	Bucharest	WCq	Balaci
11-11	Switzerland	D 0-0	Berne	WCq	
24-03-1982	Belgium	L 1-4	Brussels	Fr	Ticleanu
14-04	Bulgaria	W 2-1	Ruse	Fr	Camataru, Bölöni
1-05	Cyprus	W 3-1	Hunedoara	ECq	Vaetus, Camataru, Bölöni
12-05	Argentina	L 0-1	Rosario	Fr	
17-05	Peru	L 0-2	Lima	Fr	
19-05	Chile	W 3-2	Santiago	Fr	Klein 2, Augustin
14-07	Japan	W 4-0	Suceava	Fr	Klein, Turcu, Bölöni, Georgescu.D
18-07	Japan	W 3-1	Bucharest	Fr	Georgescu.D 2, Bölöni
1-09	Denmark	W 1-0	Bucharest	Fr	Balaci
8-09	Sweden	W 2-0	Bucharest	ECq	Andone, Klein
17-11	East Germany	L 1-4	Karl-Marx-Stadt	Fr	Bölöni
4-12	Italy	D 0-0	Florence	ECq	
29-01-1983	Turkey	D 1-1	Istanbul	Fr	Gabor
2-02	Greece	W 3-1	Larissa	Fr	Camataru 2, Bölöni
9-03	Turkey	W 3-1	Tirgu Mures	Fr	Balaci 2, Bölöni
30-03	Yugoslavia	L 0-2	Timisoara	Fr	

Date	Opponent	Result	Venue	Comp	Scorers
16-04	Italy	W 1-0	Bucharest	ECq	Bölöni
15-05	Czechoslovakia	L 0-1	Bucharest	ECq	
1-06	Yugoslavia	L 0-1	Sarajevo	Fr	
9-06	Sweden	W 1-0	Stockholm	ECq	Camataru
10-08	Norway	D 0-0	Oslo	Fr	
24-08	East Germany	W 1-0	Bucharest	Fr	Negrila
7-09	Poland	D 2-2	Krakow	Fr	Movila, Irimescu
12-10	Wales	L 0-5	Wrexham	Fr	
8-11	Israel	D 1-1	Tel Aviv	Fr	Coras
12-11	Cyprus	W 1-0	Limassol	ECq	Bölöni
30-11	Czechoslovakia	D 1-1	Bratislava	ECq	Geolgau
22-01-1984	Ecuador	W 3-1	Guayaquil	Fr	Bölöni, Iorgulescu, Camataru
7-02	Algeria	D 1-1	Algiers	Fr	OG
7-03	Greece	W 2-0	Craiova	Fr	Coras, Mateus
11-04	Israel	D 0-0	Oradea	Fr	
14-06	Spain	D 1-1	Saint Etienne	ECr1	Bölöni
17-06	West Germany	L 1-2	Lens	ECr1	Coras
20-06	Portugal	L 0-1	Nantes	ECr1	
29-07	China	W 4-2	Iasi	Fr	Rednic, Camataru, Orac, Balint
1-08	China	W 1-0	Buzau	Fr	Balint
29-08	East Germany	L 1-2	Dresden	Fr	Irimescu
12-09	Nth. Ireland	L 2-3	Belfast	WCq	Hagi, Geolgau
21-11	Israel	D 1-1	Tel Aviv	Fr	Lacatus
30-01-1985	Portugal	W 3-2	Lisbon	Fr	Lacatus 2, Hagi
27-03	Poland	D 0-0	Sibiu	Fr	
3-04	Turkey	W 3-0	Craiova	WCq	Camataru 2, Hagi
1-05	England	D 0-0	Bucharest	WCq	
6-06	Finland	D 1-1	Helsinki	WCq	Hagi
7-08	Soviet Union	L 0-2	Moscow	Fr	
28-08	Finland	W 2-0	Timisoara	WCq	Hagi, Mateut
11-09	England	D 1-1	London	WCq	Camataru
16-10	Nth. Ireland	L 0-1	Bucharest	WCq	
13-11	Turkey	W 3-1	Izmir	WCq	Iorgulescu, Coras, Iovan
28-02-1986	Egypt	D 2-2	Alexandria	Fr	Coras, Iorgulescu
2-03	Egypt	W 1-0	Alexandria	Fr	Gabor
14-03	Iraq	D 1-1	Baghdad	Fr	Augustin
17-03	Iraq	D 0-0	Baghdad	Fr	
26-03	Scotland	L 0-3	Glasgow	Fr	
23-04	Soviet Union	W 2-1	Timisoara	Fr	Hagi, Camataru
4-06	Norway	W 3-1	Bucharest	Fr	Piturca 2, Mateut
20-08	Norway	D 2-2	Oslo	Fr	Hagi, OG
10-09	Austria	W 4-0	Bucharest	ECq	Iovan 2, Lacatus, Hagi
8-10	Israel	W 4-2	Tel Aviv	Fr	Piturca 2, Bölöni, Camaratu
12-11	Spain	L 0-1	Seville	ECq	
4-03-1987	Turkey	W 3-1	Ankara	Fr	Belodedici, Bölöni, OG
11-03	Greece	D 1-1	Athens	Fr	Hagi
25-03	Albania	W 5-1	Bucharest	ECq	Piturca, Bölöni, Hagi, Belodedici, Bumbescu
8-04	Israel	W 3-2	Brasov	Fr	Cimpeanu, Belodedici, Kramer
29-04	Spain	W 3-1	Bucharest	ECq	Piturca, Mateut, Ungureanu
2-09	Poland	L 1-3	Bydgoszcz	Fr	Bölöni
7-10	Greece	D 2-2	Bucharest	Fr	Tîrlea, Bölöni
28-10	Albania	W 1-0	Vlore	ECq	Klein
18-11	Austria	D 0-0	Vienna	ECq	
3-02-1988	Israel	W 2-0	Haifa	Fr	Bölöni, Ciuca
6-02	Poland	D 2-2	Haifa	Fr	Coras, Sabau
23-03	Rep. Ireland	L 0-2	Dublin	Fr	
30-03	East Germany	D 3-3	Halle	Fr	Andone, Geolgau, Bölöni
1-06	Holland	L 0-2	Amsterdam	Fr	
20-09	Albania	W 3-0	Constanta	Fr	Belodedici, Hagi, Camataru
19-10	Bulgaria	W 3-1	Sofia	WCq	Mateut, Camataru 2
2-11	Greece	W 3-0	Bucharest	WCq	Mateut, Hagi, Sabau
23-11	Israel	W 3-0	Sibiu	Fr	Mateut 2, Camataru
29-03-1989	Italy	W 1-0	Sibiu	Fr	Sabau
12-04	Poland	L 1-2	Warsaw	Fr	Sabau
26-04	Greece	D 0-0	Athens	WCq	
10-05	Bulgaria	W 1-0	Bucharest	WCq	Popescu
31-08	Portugal	D 0-0	Setubal	Fr	
5-09	Czechoslovakia	L 0-2	Nitra	Fr	
11-10	Denmark	L 0-3	Copenhagen	WCq	
15-11	Denmark	W 3-1	Bucharest	WCq	Balint 2, Sabau
4-02-1990	Algeria	D 0-0	Algiers	Fr	
28-03	Egypt	W 3-1	Cairo	Fr	Timofte I 2, Balint

3-04	Switzerland	L 1-2	Lucerne	Fr	Hagi
25-04	Israel	W 4-1	Haifa	Fr	Hagi, Sabau, Balint, OG
21-05	Egypt	W 1-0	Bucharest	Fr	Camataru
26-05	Belgium	D 2-2	Brussels	Fr	Rednic, Lacatus
9-06	Soviet Union	W 2-0	Bari	WCr1	Lacatus 2
14-06	Cameroon	L 1-2	Bari	WCr1	Balint
18-06	Argentina	D 1-1	Naples	WCr1	Balint
25-06	Rep. Ireland	D 0-0	Genoa	WCr2	Lost 4-5 pens
29-08	Soviet Union	W 2-1	Moscow	Fr	Lacatus, Lupescu
12-09	Scotland	L 1-2	Glasgow	ECq	Camaturu
26-09	Poland	W 2-1	Bucharest	Fr	Lazar, Rotariu
17-10	Bulgaria	L 0-3	Bucharest	ECq	
5-12	San Marino	W 6-0	Bucharest	ECq	Sabau, Mateut, Raducioiu, Lupescu, Badea, Petrescu
27-03-1991	San Marino	W 3-1	Serravalle	ECq	Hagi, Raducioiu, Timofte
3-04	Switzerland	D 0-0	Neuchatel	ECq	
17-04	Spain	W 2-0	Caceres	Fr	Timofte II, Balint
22-05	Norway	L 0-1	Oslo	Fr	
28-08	USA	L 0-2	Brasov	Fr	
16-10	Scotland	W 1-0	Bucharest	ECq	Hagi
13-11	Switzerland	W 1-0	Bucharest	ECq	Mateut
20-11	Bulgaria	D 1-1	Sofia	ECq	Popescu
25-12	Egypt	L 0-3	Cairo	Fr	
28-12	Egypt	D 1-1	Port Said	Fr	Munteanu
12-02-1992	Greece	L 0-1	Athens	Fr	
8-04	Latvia	W 2-0	Bucharest	Fr	Badea, Petrescu
6-05	Faeroe Islands	W 7-0	Bucharest	WCq	Balint 3, Hagi, Lacatus, Lupescu, Pana
20-05	Wales	W 5-1	Bucharest	WCq	Hagi 2, Lupescu 2, Balint
26-08	Mexico	W 2-0	Bucharest	Fr	Varga, Dumitrescu
14-10	Belgium	L 0-1	Brussels	WCq	
14-11	Czechoslovakia	D 1-1	Bucharest	WCq	Dumitrescu
29-11	Cyprus	W 4-1	Larnaca	WCq	Popescu, Raducioiu, Hagi, Hanganu
31-01-1993	Ecuador	L 0-3	Guayaquil	Fr	
3-02	Peru	W 2-0	Lima	Fr	Hanganu, Dumitrescu
6-02	USA	D 1-1	Santa Barbara	Fr	Dumitrescu
10-02	Mexico	L 0-2	Monterrey	Fr	
14-04	Cyprus	W 2-1	Bucharest	WCq	Dumitrescu 2
2-06	Czechoslovakia	L 2-5	Kosice	WCq	Raducioiu 2
8-09	Faeroe Islands	W 4-0	Toftir	WCq	Raducioiu 4
22-09	Israel	W 1-0	Bucharest	Fr	Panduru
13-10	Belgium	W 2-1	Bucharest	WCq	Raducioiu, Dumitrescu
17-11	Wales	W 2-1	Cardiff	WCq	Hagi, Raducioiu
10-02-1994	Hong Kong	D 1-1	Hong Kong	Fr	Dumitrescu
13-02	USA	W 2-1	Hong Kong	Fr	Dumitrescu 2
16-02	South Korea	W 2-1	Chong Won	Fr	Dumitrescu 2
23-03	Nth. Ireland	L 0-2	Belfast	Fr	
20-04	Bolivia	W 3-0	Bucharest	Fr	Dumitrescu 2, Niculescu
25-05	Nigeria	W 2-0	Bucharest	Fr	Dumitrescu, Petrescu
1-06	Slovenia	D 0-0	Bucharest	Fr	
12-06	Sweden	D 1-1	Mission Viejo	Fr	Hagi
18-06	Colombia	W 3-1	Los Angeles	WCr1	Raducioiu 2, Hagi
22-06	Switzerland	L 1-4	Detroit	WCr1	Hagi
26-06	USA	W 1-0	Los Angeles	WCr1	Petrescu
3-07	Argentina	W 3-2	Los Angeles	WCr2	Dumitrescu 2, Hagi
10-07	Sweden	D 2-2	San Francisco	WCqf	Raducioiu 2. Lost 4-5 pens
7-09	Azerbaijan	W 3-0	Bucharest	ECq	Belodedici, Petrescu, Raducioiu
8-10	France	D 0-0	St. Etienne	ECq	
12-10	England	D 1-1	London	Fr	Dumitrescu
12-11	Slovakia	W 3-2	Bucharest	ECq	Popescu, Hagi, Prodan
14-12	Israel	D 1-1	Tel Aviv	ECq	Lacatus
21-12	Argentina	L 0-1	Buenos Aires	Fr	
8-02-1995	Greece	L 0-1	Kalamata	Fr	
15-02	Turkey	D 1-1	Izmir	Fr	Sabau
29-03	Poland	W 2-1	Bucharest	ECq	Raducioiu, OG
26-04	Azerbaijan	W 4-1	Trabzon	ECq	Raducioiu 3, Dumitrescu
7-06	Israel	W 2-1	Bucharest	ECq	Lacatus, Munteanu

RUSSIA

The Soviet Union may have passed into history, broken up into 15 independent states, but the largest of those, Russia, is still the biggest country in the world and has a population of nearly 150 million to draw on in its attempt to build on the strong Soviet football tradition. Other than the Baltic states, Russia was the only ex-Soviet country already to have played international football under its own banner. Eight games were played before 1917 and all were lost, two of them rather heavily. A 16-0 defeat at the 1912 Olympics by Germany was followed two weeks later by a 12-0 thrashing at the hands of Hungary. Thankfully for Russia their second venture into international football has not been quite so traumatic on the field, although off it they have again grabbed the headlines.

Although vast tracts of Russia lie in Asia, almost all of the football activity has been centred in the European area, and it was here that the game first took root. The first known side was formed by the English managers of the Morozov cotton mills in Orekhovo, Harry and Clement Charnock. Clad in the colours of Blackburn Rovers, the Charnocks' favoured team, Morozov were the leading light of football in the Moscow area, and when football was reorganised in 1923 on Soviet lines they became Dynamo Moscow, the team of the Electrical Trades Union.

By the early years of the 20th century, leagues had sprung up in many of the major cities of the Russian Empire, most notably in St Petersburg, which was then the capital. In 1897 the Amateur Sports Club of St Petersburg formed a football team which led to the creation of the league in that city. It was not until 1912 that the All Russian Football Union was created and a short-lived championship for representative sides introduced. Though widely played, football was largely a pastime of the privileged classes, and as a result there was not much strength in depth nor an eagerness to develop the game, as was shown in the ill-fated trip to the Stockholm Olympics. Indeed, football remained low key until after 1945, held back by political considerations, the vast size of the country and the harsh weather conditions throughout much of the year.

Following the dissolution of the Soviet Union, 1992 saw the first Russian championship and in August that year the national side played their first game. Immediately there was controversy as the Russians were given the World Cup berth allocated to the Soviet Union, to howls of protest from the Ukraine which had always provided its fair share of players for the Soviet national team. Further controversy dogged that World Cup campaign as a players' revolt led to most of them refusing to go to USA '94. Tactical differences with coach Pavel Sadyrin were cited as the reason, but it owed more to their wanting the return of Anatoly Byshovets, who as coach had taken the players' side in a dispute with the federation over payments. Not surprisingly, without their best players Russia were eliminated in the first round in America, but striker Oleg Salenko did set a record by scoring five goals in the 6-1 win over Cameroon, the most ever in a single match at the World Cup finals.

As for the health of the domestic game, much will depend on how the Russian economy fares. Crowds have dwindled as the stars have gone abroad, and the top clubs will face a tough task shaking off Russia's record of never having won a European club title (Ukraine's Dynamo Kiev and Georgia's Dynamo Tbilisi were the only such Soviet successes) However, there were signs of promise when in 1993 CSKA Moscow knocked holders Barcelona out of the European Cup and Spartak reached the semi-finals of the Cup Winners Cup. Indeed, Spartak have emerged as the strongest club in the new league, winning the first three championships and each time qualifying for the European Champions League.

Population: 147,400,000
Area, sq km: 17,075,400
Capital city: Moscow

The Russian Football Federation
Luzhnetskaja Naberzhnaja #8
119871GSP-3 Moscow
Russia
Tel: + 7 095 2010834
Fax: + 7 095 2011303

Year of formation	1912
Affiliation to FIFA	1946
Affiliation to UEFA	1954
Registered clubs	43 700
Registered players	2 174 000
Registered referees	102 600
National stadium	Luzhniki, Moscow 96 000
National colours	White/Blue/White
Season	March - November

THE RECORD

WORLD CUP

1930-90	Did not enter
1994	QT 2nd/5 in group 5 - Final Tournament/1st round

EUROPEAN CHAMPIONSHIP

1960-92	Did not enter
1996	QT group 8

EUROPEAN CLUB COMPETITIONS

European Cup
Semi-finalists - Spartak Moscow 1991
Cup Winners Cup
Finalists - Dynamo Moscow 1972
UEFA Cup
Quarter-finalists - Spartak Moscow 1984
Torpedo Moscow 1991

CLUB DIRECTORY

MOSCOW (Population - 13,100,000)

Asmaral Moskva (1990)
Krasnaya Presnya 5,000

CSKA Moskva (1923)
(Centralnyi Sportivny Klub Armii)
Dynamo 51,000 – Red & white hoops/Red
Previous names - Olls 1923, OPPV 1923-28, CDKA 1928-50, CDSA 1950-58, CSK-MO 1958-59

Dynamo Moskva (1923)
Dynamo 51,000 – White/Blue

Lokomotiv Moskva (1923)
Lokomotiv 30,000 – Red/White
Previous name - Kor 1923-36

Spartak Moskva (1922)
Luzhniki 96,000 – Red/Red
Previous name - Moskovski Klub Sporta 1922-35

Torpedo Moskva (1924)
Torpedo 21,000 – White/Black
Previous name - Proletarskkaja Kuznica 1924-36

ST PETERSBURG (Population - 5,825,000)

Zenit St Petersburg (1931)
Kirova 75,000 – Violet/White
Previous names - Stalin Leningrad 1931-40, Zenit Leningrad 1940-91

Smena-Saturn St Petersburg

NIZHNI NOVGOROD (Population - 2,025,000)

Volga Nizhni Novgorod (1963)

Volga – White/White
Previous names - Merger in 1963 of Torpedo and Rakieta Sormovo, Volga Gorky 1963-91

Lokomotiv Nizhni Novgorod (1987)
Lokomotiv 13,000

YEKATERINBURG (Population - 1,620,000)
Uralmash Yekaterinburg (1928)
Central 25,000 – Red/White
Previous names - ODO 1950-60, Uralmash Sverdlovsk 1960-91

NOVOSIBIRSK (Population - 1,600,000)
Tchkalovets Novosibirsk

SAMARA (Population - 1,505,000)
Kriliya Sovjetov Samara (1942)
Metallurg 37,000 – Blue/White
Previous name - Kriliya Sovjetov Kuybyshev 1943-91

VOLGOGRAD (Population - 1,360,000)
Rotor Volgograd (1929)
Central 40,000 – Blue/Blue
Previous names - Traktor Stalingrad 1933-48, Torpedo Stalingrad 1948-57, Stal Stalingrad 1957-61, Stal Volgograd 1961-71

CHEYLABINSK (Population - 1,325,000)
Zenit Cheylabinsk

OMSK (Population - 1,175,000)
Irtysh Omsk

ROSTOV-NA-DONU (Population - 1,165,000)
SKA Rostov-Na-Donu (1938)
Central 35,000 – Red/Green
Previous name - SKVO 1938-60

Rostselmash Rostov-Na-Donu (1930)
Rostselmash 17,000Colours -

SARATOV (Population - 1,155,000)
Sokol Saratov

KAZAN (Population - 1,140,000
Rubin Kazan

UFA (Population - 1,100,000)
Gastello Ufa

PERM (Population - 1,091,000)
Zvezda Perm

KRASNOYARSK (Population - 912,000)
Metallurg Krasnoyarsk

VORONEZH (Population - 887,000)
Fakel Voronezh

YAROSLAVL (Population - 633,000)
Shinnik Yaroslavl (1957)

KRASNODAR (Population - 620,000)
Kuban Krasnodar (1954)

TYUMEN (Population - 477,000)
Dinamo-Gazovik Tyumen

STAVROPOL (Population - 318,000)
Dynamo Stavropol

VLADIKAVKAZ (Population - 300,000)
Spartak Vladikavkaz (1921)
Spartak 38,000 – Red/White
Previous name - Spartak Ordzhonikidze 1961-91

ORECHOVO-ZUJEVO (Population - 205,000)
FK Orechovo Orechovo-Zujevo

NAKHODKA (Population - 165,000)
Okean Nakhodka (1966)

KAMYSHIN (Population - 122,000)
Tekstilschik Kamyshin (1958)
Tekstilschik 7,000

RUSSIAN LEAGUE CHAMPIONS

1992f3 Spartak Moskva 24 Spartak Vladikavkaz 17 Dynamo Moskva 16
1993t Spartak Moskva 53 Rotor Volgograd 42 Dynamo Moskva 42
1994q Spartak Moskva 50 Dynamo Moskva 39 Lokomotiv Moskva 36

RUSSIAN CUP FINALS

1993	Torpedo Moskva	1-1 5-3p	CSKA Moskva
1994	Spartak Moskva	2-2 4-2p	CSKA Moskva
1995	Dynamo Moskva	0-0 7-6p	Rotor Volgograd

LEADING INTERNATIONAL GOALSCORERS

7	Dmitri Radchenko	(Spartak Moskva,Racing Santander)	1992-
6	Oleg Salenko	(Logrones)	1993-
5	Sergei Kiriakov	(Karlsruhe)	1992-
4	Aleksandr Borodyuk	(Schalke 04,Freiburg)	1992-

LEADING INTERNATIONAL APPEARANCES

27	Victor Onopko	(Spartak Moskva)	1992-
22	Dmitri Radchenko	(Spartak Moskva,Racing Santander)	1992-
20	Valeri Karpin	(Spartak Moskva)	1992-
17	Stanislav Cherchesov	(Spartak Moskva, Dynamo Dresden)	1992-
	Dmitri Khlestov	(Spartak Moskva)	1992-
16	Vasili Kulkov	(Benfica)	1992-
15	Sergei Gorlukovich	(Bayer Uerdingen)	1993-

NATIONAL TEAM COACHES

1992-94 Pavel Sadyrin
1994- Oleg Romantsev

INTERNATIONAL MATCHES PLAYED BY RUSSIA

30-06-1912	Finland	L 1-2	Stockholm	OGqf	Butusov
1-07	Germany	L 0-16	Stockholm	OGct	
12-07	Hungary	L 0-9	Moscow	Fr	
14-07	Hungary	L 0-12	Moscow	Fr	
4-05-1913	Sweden	L 1-4	Moscow	Fr	Zhitarev
14-09	Norway	D 1-1	Moscow	Fr	Sisoyev
5-07-1914	Sweden	D 2-2	Stockholm	Fr	Zhitarev 2
12-07	Norway	D 1-1	Oslo	Fr	Krotov

16-11-1924	Turkey	W 3-0	Moscow	Fr	Butusov 2, Spakovski
15-05-1925	Turkey	W 2-1	Ankara	Fr	Selin, Butusov
17-08-1992	Mexico	W 2-0	Moscow	Fr	Karpin, Popov
14-10	Iceland	W 1-0	Moscow	WCq	Yuran
28-10	Luxembourg	W 2-0	Moscow	WCq	Yuran, Radchenko
13-02-1993	USA	W 1-0	Orlando	Fr	Sergeyev
18-02	El Salvador	W 2-1	Los Angeles	Fr	Onopko, Tedeyev
21-02	USA	D 0-0	San Jose	Fr	
25-03	Israel	D 2-2	Haifa	Fr	Popov 2
14-04	Luxembourg	W 4-0	Luxembourg	WCq	Kiriakov 2, Shalimov, Kulkov
28-04	Hungary	W 3-0	Moscow	WCq	Kanchelskis, Kolyvanov, Yuran
23-05	Greece	D 1-1	Moscow	WCq	Dobrovolsky
2-06	Iceland	D 1-1	Reykjavik	WCq	Kiriakov
28-07	France	L 1-3	Caen	Fr	OG
8-09	Hungary	W 3-1	Budapest	WCq	Pyatnitski, Kiriakov, Borodyuk
6-10	Saudi Arabia	L 2-4	Riyadh	Fr	Mostovoi 2
17-11	Greece	L 0-1	Athens	WCq	
29-01-1994	USA	D 1-1	Seattle	Fr	Radchenko
2-02	Mexico	W 4-1	Oakland	Fr	Borodyuk 3, Radchenko
23-03	Rep. Ireland	D 0-0	Dublin	Fr	
20-04	Turkey	W 1-0	Bursa	Fr	Radchenko
29-05	Slovakia	W 2-1	Moscow	Fr	Pyatnitski, Tsymbalar
20-06	Brazil	L 0-2	San Francisco	WCr1	
24-06	Sweden	L 1-3	Detroit	WCr1	Salenko
28-06	Cameroon	W 6-1	San Francisco	WCr1	Salenko 5, Radchenko
17-08	Austria	W 3-0	Klagenfurt	Fr	Beschastnykh, Nikiforov, Simutenkov
7-09	Germany	L 0-1	Moscow	Fr	
12-10	San Marino	W 4-0	Moscow	ECq	Karpin, Kolyvanov, Nikiforov, Radchenko
16-11	Scotland	D 1-1	Glasgow	ECq	Radchenko
8-03-1995	Slovakia	L 1-2	Bratislava	Fr	Karpin
29-03	Scotland	D 0-0	Moscow	ECq	
26-04	Greece	W 3-0	Salonica	ECq	Nikiforov, OG, Beschastnykh
6-05	Faeroe Islands	W 3-0	Moscow	ECq	Kechinov, Mukhamadiev, Pisarev
31-05	Yugoslavia	W 2-1	Belgrade	Fr	Karpin, Beschastnykh
7-06	San Marino	W 7-0	Serravalle	ECq	Dobrovolski, OG, Kiriakov, Shalimov, Beschastnykh, Kolyvanov, Chernyshov

SAN MARINO

San Marino is the smallest independent country in Europe. With a population of just 22,000 it is located entirely within northern Italy 50 miles to the east of Florence. It was to the general surprise therefore that San Marino sought and gained membership of both FIFA and UEFA in 1988 and entered the 1992 European Championship.

The experience was not an especially happy one but there were no rugby scores, and the qualifying campaign for the 1994 World Cup not only brought their first point, from a 0-0 draw with Turkey, but also a place in the record books, Davide Gualtieri's goal after nine seconds against England being the fastest ever in the World Cup.

A league has been in operation in San Marino since 1986, the same year a cup competition was launched. Made up of ten clubs, the league is played over 18 games after which the top four, plus the second division champions, play-off for the title. In 1994 the second division side almost won it, La Fiorita losing in the final to Tre Fiori. San Marino have never entered a team in the European club cups, the only member of UEFA not to have done so.

Something historians will be looking out for is how long it will take San Marino to gain their first international win, and whether they will match Luxembourg's record of games without a win in the process.

Population: 22,000
Area, sq km: 61
Capital city: San Marino

Federazione Sammarinese Giuoco Calcio
Via Ca dei Lunghi #18
CailungoMarzo #11
47031 San Marino
Tel: + 39 549 990515
Fax: + 39 549 992348

Year of formation	1931
Affiliation to FIFA	1988
Affiliation to UEFA	1988

Registered clubs	17
Registered players	1026
Registered referees	26
National stadium	Serravalle 7000
National colours	Sky Blue/Sky Blue/Sky Blue
Season	October - May with a break in January

THE RECORD

WORLD CUP

1930-90	Did not enter
1994	QT 6th/6 in group 6

EUROPEAN CHAMPIONSHIP

1960-88	Did not enter
1992	QT 5th/5 in group 2
1996	QT group 8

EUROPEAN CLUB COMPETITIONS

Have never entered

LEAGUE CHAMPIONSHIP OF SAN MARINO

1986	Faetano 26 San Giovanni 25 La Fiorita 24			
1987	La Fiorita	2-1	Faetano	
1988	Tre Fiori	3-3 6-5p	Virtus	
1989	Domagnano	2-1	La Fiorita	
1990	La Fiorita	1-0	Cosmos	
1991	Faetano	1-0	Tre Fiori	
1992	Montevito	4-2	Libertas	
1993	Tre Fiori	2-0	Domagnano	
1994	Tre Fiori	2-0	La Fiorita	
1995	Tre Fiori	1-0	La Fiorita	

SAN MARINO CUP FINALS

1986	La Fiorita	6-1	Tre Fiori
1987	Libertas	0-0 5-3p	Tre Penne
1988	Domagnano	2-1	La Fiorita
1989	Libertas	2-0	La Fiorita
1990	Domagnano	2-0	Juvenes
1991	Libertas	2-0	Faetano
1992	Domagnano	1-1 5-3p	Tre Fiori
1993	Faetano	1-0	Libertas
1994	Faetano	3-1	Folgore
1995	Cosmos	0-0 3-1p	Faetano

INTERNATIONAL MATCHES PLAYED BY SAN MARINO

14-11-1990	Switzerland	L 0-4	Serravalle	ECq	
5-12	Romania	L 0-6	Bucharest	ECq	
27-03-1991	Romania	L 1-3	Serravalle	ECq	Pasolini
1-05	Scotland	L 0-2	Serravalle	ECq	
22-05	Bulgaria	L 0-3	Serravalle	ECq	
5-06	Switzerland	L 0-7	St. Gallen	ECq	
16-10	Bulgaria	L 0-4	Sofia	ECq	
13-11	Scotland	L 0-4	Glasgow	ECq	
19-02-1992	Italy	L 0-4	Cesena	Fr	
9-09	Norway	L 0-10	Oslo	WCq	
7-10	Norway	L 0-2	Saerravalle	WCq	
28-10	Turkey	L 1-4	Ankara	WCq	Bacciocchi
17-02-1993	England	L 0-6	London	WCq	
10-03	Turkey	D 0-0	Serravalle	WCq	
24-03	Holland	L 0-6	Utrecht	WCq	
28-04	Poland	L 0-1	Lodz	WCq	
19-05	Poland	L 0-3	Serravalle	WCq	
22-09	Holland	L 0-7	Bologna	WCq	
17-11	England	L 1-7	Bologna	WCq	Gualtieri
12-10-1994	Russia	L 0-4	Moscow	ECq	
16-11	Greece	L 0-2	Athens	ECq	
14-12	Finland	L 1-4	Helsinki	ECq	Della Valle
29-03-1995	Finland	L 0-2	Serravalle	ECq	
26-04	Scotland	L 0-2	Serravalle	ECq	
25-05	Faeroe Islands	L 0-3	Toftir	ECq	
7-06	Russia	L 0-7	Serravalle	ECq	

SCOTLAND

Scotland may not have invented football, but the country contributed hugely in the development, spread and rise in popularity of the game. More often than not it was Scottish immigrant workers who showed the locals how the game was played as it spread abroad, whilst in Britain, both Irish and English teams regularly featured large numbers of Scots before the turn of the century.

England in particular has continued in this vein as Scottish players continue to go south to further their careers. From great early teams like Preston North End and Sunderland to modern-day Liverpool, Scots have made their mark not only as players but also as managers. Much of the current reputation of both Manchester United and Liverpool is due to two Scots, Matt Busby and Bill Shankly, and it is a tradition carried on today by the likes of Alex Ferguson at United.

To look at Scottish football only in terms of its contribution in other countries, however, would be to miss out on a proud history within its own borders. Queen's Park Football Club, formed in 1867 by members of a Glasgow YMCA, was the first Scottish club to be formed. Named after the park in which the members used to play, they were the standard bearers of football in Scotland before the turn of the century. Devoutly amateur, even to this day, their home, Hampden Park, remains the spiritual home of Scottish football.

A great many of the present-day clubs were formed in the 1870s, and in 1873 it was felt necessary to form a Scottish Football Association to regulate the game north of the border. Although part of the United Kingdom, Scotland did not come under the control of the Football Association in London, and in respect of its contribution to the world game it has remained a separate entity to this date, still keeping its permanent seat on the world's rule-making body, the International Board.

Glasgow was chosen as the location for the association in preference to the capital Edinburgh, where the Scottish Rugby Union was founded in the same year. Over the years Glasgow has come to be regarded as the football capital of Scotland. Edinburgh, on the other hand, with Murrayfield as the second 'National Stadium' and home to the Scottish rugby team, has never been regarded as a football city, despite the presence of Hibernian and Heart of Midlothian, the city's two football teams.

A year after its formation, the Scottish FA launched a cup competition based on the English model. Naturally, Queen's Park were the first winners, and in the great amateur era before professionalism was adopted in 1893, they won the competition on ten occasions. Their victory in the 1893 tournament was a watershed in the development of the game. In the year that professionalism was introduced, it was the last honour they won. Their opponents that day, Celtic, though defeated, had the last laugh. They represented the new face of Scottish football, and along with their fierce rivals Rangers, soon started on a course of total domination of the domestic game.

This two-club domination stands no comparison elsewhere in world football, with the exception of the Montevideo giants, Peñarol and Nacional. The similarities with Uruguay do not end there either. Both countries have remarkably small populations in relation to their impact on the game. Though Scotland have never been crowned world champions like their South American counterparts, they were for 30 or so years the top national side in the world. Not until the turn of the century did England begin to match them.

The England-Scotland rivalry on the international field dates back to 30 November 1872, when the first ever international match took place. England, represented by players from teams like the 1st Surrey Rifles, Oxford University, Wanderers and Sheffield Wednesday, faced a team of Scots who - surprise, surprise - all came from the Queen's Park club. The 0-0 scoreline seems somewhat surprising in that of the 22 players on the the pitch, 14 were forwards! The England-Scotland game remained an annual encounter and, apart from the war years, took place every year until 1990. Wales were added to the fixture list in 1876, and with the inclusion in 1884 of Ireland, the Home International Championship was launched. Scotland's total of 41 victories in this tournament, although 13 less than England's, ranks as a considerable achievement.

The matches against England provided the first tactical breakthrough in the game, and it was a Scottish innovation. In the very early years, football consisted of a player receiving the ball and dribbling with it until he lost it or scored. In the 1870s, the Scottish national side introduced the concept of passing, and the results in the international matches of this time show that they were the masters of this new style. The Scots were also at the forefront of the next great tactical leap in the 1880s, with the introduction of the 2-3-5 formation.

While the British Isles was the focus of world football Scotland played an important part in the development of the game, but by the end of the First World War they were becoming increasingly isolated. Scottish club sides had been amongst the first British sides to make tours abroad, especially to Scandinavia, but it was not until a tour in 1929 to Scandinavia and Germany that Scotland played an international match against anyone other than a British side.

It soon became apparent that valuable ground had been lost when in 1931, in the space of four days, they were beaten 5-0 by Austria and 3-0 by Italy. Three years previously a false light had been cast on the Scottish game when a team called the 'Wembley Wizards' thrashed England 5-1 on their own territory. That Wembley team was a good one, but it highlighted a major problem that the Scots have had to deal with down the years: the loss of their best players to English clubs.

In that side were three of the greatest names of Scottish football: Hughie Gallacher, Alex James and Alec Jackson. Gallacher played for Newcastle, James for Preston and later notably for Arsenal, whilst Jackson plied his trade with Huddersfield. Between them they could only muster 45 caps. James in particular suffered through refusals to release him for internationals as well as the inbred reluctance of the Scottish FA to select 'Anglo-Scots'. His eight caps belie his reputation as one of the most influential figures in football at that time. The other of the giants of the Scottish game at the time, Alan 'the Wee Blue Devil' Morton, by contrast stayed in Scotland and won 31 caps.

Faced with an exodus on such a large scale, it is surprising that league football managed to survive in Scotland. That it did was largely the result of a continual flow of talented players and two clubs, Celtic and Rangers. In religion, Scotland is a divided country with very active Protestant and Catholic traditions. Founded in 1888 to help finance soup kitchens for the poor of the city, Celtic are the standard bearers of the largely Irish-descended Catholic community, and the Irish tricolour is still flown at the ground today.

Rangers on the other hand have been fierce proponents of the Protestant community since they were founded in 1873. It took over 100 years for them to sign a recognised Catholic. When Mo Johnston joined Rangers in 1989 it was breaking new ground in that not only was he a Catholic, he had also played for Celtic in the past. The rivalry is strong, its intensity matched perhaps only elsewhere in the world by the Real Madrid-Barcelona encounters in Spain, and it has kept Scottish football on its feet, where in different circumstances it might have withered away.

Rangers and Celtic have completely dominated the league and cup. Between them they have won the title in 81 of 99 league seasons, and they have faced each other in the Cup final on 13 occasions. This hegemony has at various times been tested, most notably in recent years with the rise to prominence of Aberdeen and Dundee United and the continuing presence of Hearts and Hibs from Edinburgh, but it will never be broken as long as the set-up in Scottish football remains as it is at present.

THE ORDER OF MERIT

		All			League			Cup		Europe			LgeC	
	Team	G	S	B	G	S	B	G	S	G	S	B	G	S
1	Glasgow Rangers	91	47	18	45	23	16	26	16	1	2	2	19	6
2	Glasgow Celtic	75	51	21	35	22	17	30	16	1	1	4	9	12
3	Aberdeen	16	26	7	4	13	6	7	7	1	-	1	4	6
4	Heart of Midlothian	13	19	11	4	13	11	5	5	-	-	-	4	1
5	Queen's Park	10	2	-	-	-	-	10	2	-	-	-	-	-
6	Hibernian	8	19	13	4	6	11	2	8	-	-	2	2	5
7	Dundee	5	9	3	1	4	1	1	3	-	-	2	3	2
8	Motherwell	4	10	6	1	5	6	2	4	-	-	-	1	1
9	East Fife	4	2	2	-	-	2	1	2	-	-	-	3	-
10	Kilmarnock	3	12	4	1	4	3	2	5	-	-	1	-	3
11	Dundee United	4	9	7	1	-	6	1	6	-	1	1	2	2
12	Third Lanark	3	5	2	1	-	2	2	4	-	-	-	-	1
13	Dumbarton	3	5	-	2	-	-	1	5	-	-	-	-	-
14	St. Mirren	3	4	2	-	-	2	3	3	-	-	-	-	1
15	Vale of Levan	3	4	-	-	-	-	3	4	-	-	-	-	-
16	Clyde	3	3	3	-	-	3	3	3	-	-	-	-	-
17	Partick Thistle	2	4	3	-	-	3	1	1	-	-	-	1	3
18	Falkirk	2	3	1	-	2	1	2	-	-	-	-	-	1
19	Dunfermline Athletic	2	3	3	-	-	2	2	1	-	-	1	-	2
20	Renton	2	3	-	-	-	-	2	3	-	-	-	-	-
21	Airdrieonians	1	7	1	-	4	1	1	3	-	-	-	-	-
22	Morton	1	3	2	-	1	2	1	1	-	-	-	-	1
23	Raith Rovers	1	2	1	-	-	1	-	1	-	-	-	1	1
24	St. Bernard's	1	-	1	-	-	1	1	-	-	-	-	-	-
25	St. Johnstone	-	1	1	-	-	1	-	-	-	-	-	-	1
26	Hamilton Academicals	-	2	-	-	-	-	-	2	-	-	-	-	-
27	Albion Rovers	-	1	-	-	-	-	-	1	-	-	-	-	-
	Cambuslang	-	1	-	-	-	-	-	1	-	-	-	-	-
	Clydesdale	-	1	-	-	-	-	-	1	-	-	-	-	-
	Thornley Bank	-	1	-	-	-	-	-	1	-	-	-	-	-

To the end of the 1994-1995 season

The post-war years were troubled ones for the national side. Despite qualifying for the 1950 World Cup, a competition which up until that point they had refused to enter, in a fit of pique the Scots withdrew, feeling that as they had finished only second in their group a place was not merited. Such arrogance did not deter them from travelling to Switzerland four years later, as they again finished second behind England in the Home International tournament which was used as a qualifying group.

The Scots must have wished they had stayed away again after a 7-0 humiliation by Uruguay ensured an early exit from the tournament. Since then, the national side has been no more than a medium power in European football. Five times in a row from 1974 they reached the World Cup finals, but never managed to progress beyond the first round. Qualification for the 1992 European Championships marked the first such success in seven outings, but qualifying for the final tournaments of the World Cup and European Championship would seem to be the limit of what the Scots can achieve. To actually win either of them is probably beyond their reach.

The same could be said of Scotland's club football. The late 1960s saw it at its strongest. In 1967, Celtic became the first British side to win the European Cup and were losing finalists three years later, whilst in 1972, Rangers won the Cup Winners Cup. In a country where all of the stars seemed to play abroad, Jimmy Johnstone, a crucial figure in the success at Celtic at the time, bucked the trend and stayed at home. He was part of a side which won a staggering nine consecutive championships, only one short of the world record. The players of true international class who left, however, still outnumbered those who stayed and included such famous names as Denis Law at Manchester United, Ian St John and Kenny Dalglish at Liverpool, Billy Bremner at Leeds . . . the list goes on.

Scottish clubs inevitably suffered and although Aberdeen won the Cup Winners Cup in 1983 and Dundee United reached the final of the UEFA Cup in 1987, Scottish influence in European competitions has waned. In the late 1980s, Rangers, having set themselves up with one of the most modern stadiums in Europe, not only started to reverse the southward flow of players by buying English internationals, but also recruited from the continent in a bid to revitalise their European ambitions. In the long run the policy may work, but success has not been forthcoming as yet. At home they are unchallenged, and since the late 1980s have won seven consecutive championships.

There is potential in Scottish football. An unusually high percentage of the population either follows or takes part in the game, and this is a key factor in helping to overcome the disadvantage of a relatively small population; whether the lead given by Rangers in facing the future will bring any more success is open to debate.

Population: 5,094,000
Area, sq km: 78,783
% in urban areas: 91.5%
Capital city: Edinburgh

The Scottish Football Association
6 Park Gardens
Glasgow, G3 7YF
Scotland
Tel: + 44 141 3326372
Fax: + 44 141 3327559

Year of formation	1873
Affiliation to FIFA	1910-1920, 1924-1928, 1946
Affiliation to UEFA	1954
Registered clubs	6148
Registered players	140 300
Professional Players	3200
Registered coaches	260
Registered referees	2200
National stadium	Hampden Park, Glasgow 38 000

National colours	Blue/White/Red
Reserve colours	White/Blue/Red
Season	August - May

THE RECORD

WORLD CUP

1930-38	Did not enter
1950	QT 2nd/4 in group 1 - Withdrew

1954 QT 2nd/4 in group 3 - Final Tournament/1st round
1958 QT 1st/3 in group 9 - Final Tournament/1st round
1962 QT 2nd/3 in group 8
1966 QT 2nd/4 in group 8
1970 QT 2nd/4 in group 7
1974 QT 1st/3 in group 8 - Final Tournament/1st round
1978 QT 1st/3 in group 7 - Final Tournament/1st round
1982 QT 1st/5 in group 6 - Final Tournament/1st round
1986 QT 2nd/4 in group 7 - Final Tournament/1st round
1990 QT 2nd/5 in group 5 - Final Tournament/1st round
1994 QT 4th/6 in group 1

EUROPEAN CHAMPIONSHIP

1960 Did not enter
1964 Did not enter
1968 QT 2nd/4 in group 8
1972 QT 3rd/4 in group 5
1976 QT 3rd/4 in group 4
1980 QT 4th/5 in group 2
1984 QT 4th/4 in group 1
1988 QT 4th/5 in group 7
1992 QT 1st/5 in group 2 - Final Tournament/Ist round
1996 QT group 8

EUROPEAN CLUB COMPETITIONS

European Cup
Winners - Glasgow Celtic 1967
Finalists - Glasgow Celtic 1970
Cup Winners Cup
Winners - Glasgow Rangers 1972, Aberdeen 1983
Finalists - Glasgow Rangers 1961 1967
UEFA Cup
Finalists - Dundee United 1987

CLUB DIRECTORY

EDINBURGH (Population - 630,000)

Heart of Midlothian FC (1874)
Tynecastle Park 25,000 – Maroon/White

Hibernian FC (1875)
Easter Road 22,000 – Green, white sleeves/White

GLASGOW (Population - 1,800,000)

The Celtic FC (1888)
Celtic Park 'Parkhead' 53,000 – Green & white hoops/White

Clyde FC (1878)
Firhill Park 20,000 – White/Black

Clydebank FC (1965)
Kilbowie Park 9,000 – White, red diagonal stripe/White

Hamilton Academical FC (1875)
Douglas Park 14,000 – Red & white hoops/White

Motherwell FC (1886)
Fir Park 18,000 – Yellow, claret hoop/Claret

Partick Thistle FC (1876)
Firhill Park 20,000 – Yellow & red stripes, black sleeves/Black

Queen's Park FC (1867)
Hampden Park 74,000 – Black & white hoops/White

Rangers FC (1873)
Ibrox 44,000 – Blue/White

St. Mirren FC (1877)
Love Street 21,000 – Black & white stripes/White

ABERDEEN (Population - 186,000)

Aberdeen FC (1903)
Pittodrie 21,000 – Red, white trim

DUNDEE (Population - 172,000)

Dundee FC (1893)
Dens Park 22,000 – Blue, with white-blue-red hoop/White

Dundee United FC (1909)
Tannadice Park 22,000 – Tangerine/Black
Previous name - Dundee Hibernians 1909-23

FALKIRK (Population - 148,000)

East Stirlingshire FC (1881)
Firs Park 6,000 – White, black chest band/Black

Falkirk FC (1876)
Brockville Park 18,000 – Blue/White, red trim

KIRKCALDY (Population - 148,000)

Raith Rovers FC (1883)
Stark's Park 9,000 – Blue/White

DUNFERMLINE (Population - 125,000)

Dunfermline Athletic FC (1885)
East End Park 19,000 – Black & white stripes/Black

GREENOCK (Population - 101,000)

Greenock Morton FC (1874)
Cappielow Park 16,000 – Blue & white hoops/White

AYR (Population - 100,000)

Ayr United FC (1910)
Somerset Park 18,000 – White, black chest band/Black

KILMARNOCK (Population - 84,000)

Kilmarnock FC (1869)
Rugby Park 17,000 – White/Blue

STIRLING (Population - 61,000)

Stirling Albion FC (1945)
Annfield Park 4,000 – Red, white sleeves/White

COATBRIDGE (Population - 50,000)

Albion Rovers FC (1882)
Clifton Hall 1,000 – Yellow/Red

PERTH (Population - 41,000)

St. Johnstone FC (1884)
McDiarmid Park 10,000 – Blue/White

AIRDRIE

Airdrieonians FC (1878)
Broomfield Park 11,000 – White/White

DUMBARTON (Population - 23,000)

Dumbarton FC (1872)
Boghead Park 10,000 – Gold, white chest band/Black

METHIL FIFE

East Fife FC (1903)
Bayview Park 14,000 – Black & gold stripes/Black

SCOTTISH LEAGUE CHAMPIONSHIP

1891h* Dumbarton 29 Rangers 29 Celtic 21
1892k Dumbarton 37 Celtic 35 Heart of Midlothian 34
1893h Celtic 29 Rangers 28 St. Mirren 20
1894 Celtic 29 Heart of Midlothian 26 St. Bernard's 23
1895 Heart of Midlothian 31 Celtic 26 Rangers 22
1896 Celtic 30 Rangers 26 Hibernian 24
1897 Heart of Midlothian 28 Hibernian 26 Rangers 25
1898 Celtic 33 Rangers 29 Hibernian 22
1899 Rangers 36 Heart of Midlothian 26 Celtic 24
1900 Rangers 32 Celtic 25 Hibernian 24
1901i Rangers 35 Celtic 29 Hibernian 25
1902h Rangers 28 Celtic 26 Heart of Midlothian 22
1903k Hibernian 37 Dundee 31 Rangers 29
1904n Third Lanark 43 Heart of Midlothian 39 Celtic 38
1905 Celtic 41 Rangers 41 Third Lanark 35
1906q Celtic 49 Heart of Midlothian 43 Airdrieonians 38
1907t Celtic 55 Dundee 48 Rangers 45
1908 Celtic 55 Falkirk 51 Rangers 50
1909 Celtic 51 Dundee 50 Clyde 48
1910 Celtic 54 Falkirk 52 Rangers 46
1911 Rangers 52 Aberdeen 48 Falkirk 44

1912 Rangers 51 Celtic 45 Clyde 42
1913 Rangers 53 Celtic 49 Heart of Midlothian 41
1914v Celtic 65 Rangers 59 Heart of Midlothian 54
1915 Celtic 65 Heart of Midlothian 61 Rangers 50
1916 Celtic 67 Rangers 56 Morton 51
1917 Celtic 64 Morton 54 Rangers 53
1918t Rangers 56 Celtic 55 Kilmarnock 43
1919 Celtic 58 Rangers 57 Morton 47
1920y Rangers 71 Celtic 68 Motherwell 57
1921 Rangers 76 Celtic 66 Heart of Midlothian 50
1922 Celtic 67 Rangers 66 Raith Rovers 51
1923v Rangers 55 Airdrieonians 50 Celtic 46
1924 Rangers 59 Airdrieonians 50 Celtic 46
1925 Rangers 60 Airdrieonians 57 Hibernian 52
1926 Celtic 58 Airdrieonians 50 Heart of Midlothian 50
1927 Rangers 56 Motherwell 51 Celtic 49
1928 Rangers 60 Celtic 55 Motherwell 55
1929 Rangers 67 Celtic 51 Motherwell 50
1930 Rangers 60 Motherwell 55 Aberdeen 53
1931 Rangers 60 Celtic 58 Motherwell 56
1932 Motherwell 66 Rangers 61 Celtic 48
1933 Rangers 62 Motherwell 59 Heart of Midlothian 50
1934 Rangers 66 Motherwell 62 Celtic 47
1935 Rangers 55 Celtic 52 Heart of Midlothian 50
1936 Celtic 66 Rangers 61 Aberdeen 61
1937 Rangers 61 Aberdeen 54 Celtic 52
1938 Celtic 61 Heart of Midlothian 58 Rangers 49
1939 Rangers 59 Celtic 48 Aberdeen 46
1940-46 -
1947q Rangers 46 Hibernian 44 Aberdeen 39
1948 Hibernian 48 Rangers 46 Partick Thistle 36
1949 Rangers 46 Dundee 45 Hibernian 39
1950 Rangers 50 Hibernian 49 Heart of Midlothian 43
1951 Hibernian 48 Rangers 38 Dundee 38
1952 Hibernian 45 Rangers 41 East Fife 37
1953 Rangers 43 Hibernian 43 East Fife 39
1954 Celtic 43 Heart of Midlothian 38 Partick Thistle 35
1955 Aberdeen 49 Celtic 46 Rangers 41
1956t Rangers 52 Aberdeen 46 Heart of Midlothian 45
1957 Rangers 55 Heart of Midlothian 53 Kilmarnock 42
1958 Heart of Midlothian 62 Rangers 49 Celtic 46
1959 Rangers 50 Heart of Midlothian 48 Motherwell 44
1960 Heart of Midlothian 54 Kilmarnock 50 Rangers 42
1961 Rangers 51 Kilmarnock 50 Third Lanark 42
1962 Dundee 54 Rangers 51 Celtic 46
1963 Rangers 57 Kilmarnock 48 Partick Thistle 46
1964 Rangers 55 Kilmarnock 49 Celtic 47
1965 Kilmarnock 50 Heart of Midlothian 50 Dunfermline 49
1966 Celtic 57 Rangers 55 Kilmarnock 45
1967 Celtic 58 Rangers 55 Clyde 46
1968 Celtic 63 Rangers 61 Hibernian 45
1969 Celtic 54 Rangers 49 Dunfermline 45
1970 Celtic 57 Rangers 45 Hibernian 44
1971 Celtic 56 Aberdeen 54 St. Johnstone 44
1972 Celtic 60 Aberdeen 50 Rangers 44
1973 Celtic 57 Rangers 56 Hibernian 45
1974 Celtic 53 Hibernian 49 Rangers 48
1975 Rangers 56 Hibernian 49 Celtic 45
1976u2 Rangers 54 Celtic 48 Hibernian 43
1977 Celtic 55 Rangers 46 Aberdeen 43
1978 Rangers 55 Aberdeen 53 Dundee United 40
1979 Celtic 48 Rangers 45 Dundee United 44
1980 Aberdeen 48 Celtic 47 St. Mirren 42
1981 Celtic 56 Aberdeen 49 Rangers 44
1982 Celtic 55 Aberdeen 53 Rangers 43
1983 Dundee United 56 Celtic 55 Aberdeen 55
1984 Aberdeen 57 Celtic 50 Dundee United 47
1985 Aberdeen 59 Celtic 52 Dundee United 47
1986 Celtic 50 Heart of Midlothian 50 Dundee United 47
1987z Rangers 69 Celtic 63 Dundee United 60
1988 Celtic 72 Heart of Midlothian 62 Rangers 60
1989u2 Rangers 56 Aberdeen 50 Celtic 46
1990 Rangers 51 Aberdeen 44 Heart of Midlothian 44
1991 Rangers 55 Aberdeen 53 Celtic 41
1992z Rangers 72 Heart of Midlothian 63 Celtic 62
1993 Rangers 73 Aberdeen 64 Celtic 60
1994 Rangers 58 Aberdeen 55 Motherwell 54
1995u11 Rangers 69 Motherwell 54 Hibernian 53
*championship shared

SCOTTISH CUP FINALS

Year	Winner	Score	Runner-up
1874	Queen's Park	2-0	Clydesdale
1875	Queen's Park	3-0	Renton
1876	Queen's Park	1-1 2-0	Third Lanark
1877	Vale of Levan	0-0 1-1 3-2	Rangers
1878	Vale of Levan	1-0	Third Lanark
1879	Vale of Levan	1-1 W-O	Rangers
1880	Queen's Park	3-0	Thornley Bank
1881	Queen's Park	3-1	Dumbarton
1882	Queen's Park	2-2 4-1	Dumbarton
1883	Dumbarton	2-2 2-1	Vale of Levan
1884	Queen's Park	W-O	Vale of Levan
1885	Renton	0-0 3-1	Vale of Levan
1886	Queen's Park	3-1	Renton
1887	Hibernian	2-1	Dumbarton
1888	Renton	6-1	Cambuslang
1889	Third Lanark	2-1	Celtic
1890	Queen's Park	1-1 2-1	Vale of Levan
1891	Heart of Midlothian	1-0	Dumbarton
1892	Celtic	5-1	Queen's Park
1893	Queen's Park	2-1	Celtic
1894	Rangers	3-1	Celtic
1895	St. Bernard's	2-1	Renton
1896	Heart of Midlothian	3-1	Hibernian
1897	Rangers	5-1	Dumbarton
1898	Rangers	2-0	Kilmarnock
1899	Celtic	2-0	Rangers
1900	Celtic	4-3	Queen's Park
1901	Heart of Midlothian	4-3	Celtic
1902	Hibernian	1-0	Celtic
1903	Rangers	1-1 0-0 2-0	Heart of Midlothian
1904	Celtic	3-2	Rangers
1905	Third Lanark	0-0 3-1	Rangers
1906	Heart of Midlothian	1-0	Third Lanark
1907	Celtic	3-0	Heart of Midlothian
1908	Celtic	5-1	St. Mirren
1909	Cup witheld. Celtic	2-2 1-1	Rangers
1910	Dundee	2-2 0-0 2-1	Clyde
1911	Celtic	0-0 2-0	Hamilton Academicals
1912	Celtic	2-0	Clyde
1913	Falkirk	2-0	Raith Rovers
1914	Celtic	0-0 4-1	Hibernian
1915-19	-		
1920	Kilmarnock	3-2	Albion Rovers
1921	Partick Thistle	1-0	Rangers
1922	Morton	1-0	Rangers
1923	Celtic	1-0	Hibernian
1924	Airdrieonians	2-0	Hibernian
1925	Celtic	2-1	Dundee
1926	St. Mirren	2-0	Celtic
1927	Celtic	3-1	East Fife
1928	Rangers	4-0	Celtic
1929	Kilmarnock	2-0	Rangers
1930	Rangers	0-0 2-1	Partick Thistle
1931	Celtic	2-2 4-2	Motherwell
1932	Rangers	1-1 3-0	Kilmarnock
1933	Celtic	1-0	Motherwell
1934	Rangers	5-0	St. Mirren
1935	Rangers	2-1	Hamilton Academicals

1936	Rangers	1-0	Third Lanark
1937	Celtic	2-1	Aberdeen
1938	East Fife	1-1 4-2	Kilmarnock
1939	Clyde	4-0	Motherwell
1940-46	-		
1947	Aberdeen	2-1	Hibernian
1948	Rangers	1-1 1-0	Morton
1949	Rangers	4-1	Clyde
1950	Rangers	3-0	East Fife
1951	Celtic	1-0	Motherwell
1952	Motherwell	4-0	Dundee
1953	Rangers	1-1 1-0	Aberdeen
1954	Celtic	2-1	Aberdeen
1955	Clyde	1-1 1-0	Celtic
1956	Heart of Midlothian	3-1	Celtic
1957	Falkirk	1-1 2-1	Kilmarnock
1958	Clyde	1-0	Hibernian
1959	St. Mirren	3-1	Aberdeen
1960	Rangers	2-0	Kilmarnock
1961	Dunfermline Athletic	0-0 2-0	Celtic
1962	Rangers	2-0	St. Mirren
1963	Rangers	1-1 3-0	Celtic
1964	Rangers	3-1	Dundee
1965	Celtic	3-2	Dunfermline Athletic
1966	Rangers	0-0 1-0	Celtic
1967	Celtic	2-0	Aberdeen
1968	Dunfermline Athletic	3-1	Heart of Midlothian
1969	Celtic	4-0	Rangers
1970	Aberdeen	3-1	Celtic
1971	Celtic	1-1 2-1	Rangers
1972	Celtic	6-1	Hibernian
1973	Rangers	3-2	Celtic
1974	Celtic	3-0	Dundee United
1975	Celtic	3-1	Airdrieonians
1976	Rangers	3-1	Heart of Midlothian
1977	Celtic	1-0	Rangers
1978	Rangers	2-1	Aberdeen
1979	Rangers	0-0 0-0 3-2	Hibernian
1980	Celtic	1-0	Rangers
1981	Rangers	0-0 4-1	Dundee United
1982	Aberdeen	4-1	Rangers
1983	Aberdeen	1-0	Rangers
1984	Aberdeen	2-1	Celtic
1985	Celtic	2-1	Dundee United
1986	Aberdeen	3-0	Heart of Midlothian
1987	St. Mirren	1-0	Dundee United
1988	Celtic	2-1	Dundee United
1989	Celtic	1-0	Rangers
1990	Aberdeen	0-0 9-8p	Celtic
1991	Motherwell	4-3	Dundee United
1992	Rangers	2-1	Airdrieonians
1993	Rangers	2-1	Aberdeen
1994	Dundee United	1-0	Rangers
1995	Celtic	1-0	Airdrieonians

SCOTTISH LEAGUE CUP FINALS

1947	Rangers	4-0	Aberdeen
1948	East Fife	0-0 4-1	Falkirk
1949	Rangers	2-0	Raith Rovers
1950	East Fife	3-0	Dunfermline Athletic
1951	Motherwell	3-0	Hibernian
1952	Dundee	3-2	Rangers
1953	Dundee	2-0	Kilmarnock
1954	East Fife	3-2	Partick Thistle
1955	Heart of Midlothian	4-2	Motherwell
1956	Aberdeen	2-1	St. Mirren
1957	Celtic	0-0 3-0	Partick Thistle
1958	Celtic	7-1	Rangers
1959	Heart of Midlothian	5-1	Partick Thistle
1960	Heart of Midlothian	2-1	Third Lanark
1961	Rangers	2-0	Kilmarnock
1962	Rangers	1-1 3-1	Heart of Midlothian
1963	Heart of Midlothian	1-0	Kilmarnock
1964	Rangers	5-0	Morton
1965	Rangers	2-1	Celtic
1966	Celtic	2-1	Rangers
1967	Celtic	1-0	Rangers
1968	Celtic	5-3	Dundee
1969	Celtic	6-2	Hibernian
1970	Celtic	1-0	St. Johnstone
1971	Rangers	1-0	Celtic
1972	Partick Thistle	4-1	Celtic
1973	Hibernian	2-1	Celtic
1974	Dundee	1-0	Celtic
1975	Celtic	6-3	Hibernian
1976	Rangers	1-0	Celtic
1977	Aberdeen	2-1	Celtic
1978	Rangers	2-1	Celtic
1979	Rangers	2-1	Aberdeen
1980	Dundee United	0-0 3-0	Aberdeen
1981	Dundee United	3-0	Dundee
1982	Rangers	2-1	Dundee United
1983	Celtic	2-1	Rangers
1984	Rangers	3-2	Celtic
1985	Rangers	1-0	Dundee United
1986	Aberdeen	3-0	Hibernian
1987	Rangers	2-1	Celtic
1988	Rangers	3-3 5-3p	Aberdeen
1989	Rangers	3-2	Aberdeen
1990	Aberdeen	2-1	Rangers
1991	Rangers	2-1	Celtic
1992	Hibernian	2-0	Dunfermline
1993	Rangers	2-1	Aberdeen
1994	Rangers	2-1	Hibernian
1995	Raith Rovers	2-2 6-5p	Celtic

LEADING INTERNATIONAL GOALSCORERS

30	Kenny Dalglish	(Celtic,Liverpool)	1972-1987
	Dennis Law	(Huddersfield,Man City, Torino,Man Utd)	1959-1974
23	Hughie Gallacher	(Airdrie,Newcastle,Chelsea, Derby)	1924-1935
22	Lawrie Reilly	(Hibernian)	1949-1957
15	Ally McCoist	(Rangers)	1986-
14	Robert Hamilton	(Rangers,Dundee)	1899-1911
	Maurice Johnston	(Watford,Celtic,Nantes, Rangers)	1984-1992
13	Bob McColl	(Queen's Park,Newcastle)	1896-1908
	Andrew Wilson	(Dunfermline,Middlesbrough)	1920-1922

LEADING INTERNATIONAL APPEARANCES

102	Kenny Dalglish	(Celtic,Liverpool)	1972-1987
77	Alex McLeish	(Aberdeen)	1980-1993
72	Paul McStay	(Celtic)	1984-
67	Jim Leighton	(Aberdeen,Manchester United, Hibernian)	1983-
65	Willie Miller	(Aberdeen)	1975-1990
62	Danny McGrain	(Celtic)	1973-1982
61	Richard Gough	(Dundee United,Tottenham, Rangers)	1983-

NATIONAL TEAM COACHES

1954-	Andy Beattie	1960-65	Ian McColl	1967-71	Bobby Brown	1978-85	Jock Stein
1958	Matt Busby	1965	Jock Stein	1971-72	Tommy Docherty	1985-86	Alex Ferguson
1958	Dawson Walker	1966	John Prentice	1973-77	Willie Ormond	1986-93	Andy Roxburgh
1959-60	Andy Beattie	1966-67	Malcolm MacDonald	1977-78	Ally McLeod	1993-	Craig Brown

INTERNATIONAL MATCHES PLAYED BY SCOTLAND

19-11-1870	England *	L 0-1	London	Fr	
28-02-1871	England *	D 1-1	London	Fr	
18-11	England *	L 1-2	London	Fr	
24-02	England *	L 0-1	London	Fr	
30-11-1872	England	D 0-0	Glasgow	Fr	
8-03-1873	England	L 2-4	London	Fr	Renny-Tailyour, Gibb
7-03-1874	England	W 2-1	Glasgow	Fr	McKinnon.A, Anderson.F
6-03-1875	England	D 2-2	London	Fr	McNeil, Andrews
4-03-1876	England	W 3-0	Glasgow	Fr	McKinnon.W, McNeil, Highet
25-03	Wales	W 4-0	Glasgow	Fr	Ferguson, Lang, McKinnon.W, McNeil
3-03-1877	England	W 3-1	London	Fr	Ferguson 2, Richmond
5-03	Wales	W 2-0	Wrexham	Fr	Campbell.C, OG
2-03-1878	England	W 7-2	Glasgow	Fr	McDougall 3, McGregor, McNeil 2, McKinnon.W
23-03	Wales	W 9-0	Glasgow	Fr	Campbell.P, Weir.J 2, Ferguson 3, Baird.J, Watson, Anon
5-04-1879	England	L 4-5	London	Fr	McKinnon.W 2, McDougall, Smith.J (I)
7-04	Wales	W 3-0	Wrexham	Fr	Campbell.P, Smith.J (I) 2
13-03-1880	England	W 5-4	Glasgow	Fr	Ker 3, Baird.J, Kay
27-03	Wales	W 5-1	Glasgow	Fr	Davidson.D, Beveridge, Lindsay, McAdam, Campbell.J (I)
12-03-1881	England	W 6-1	London	Fr	Smith.J (I) 3, Ker 2, McGuire
14-03	Wales	W 5-1	Wrexham	Fr	Smith.J (I) 2, Ker 2, Lindsay
11-03-1882	England	W 5-1	Glasgow	Fr	Harrower, Ker 2, Kay, McPherson.R
25-03	Wales	W 5-0	Glasgow	Fr	Kay, Ker, Fraser 2, McAulay
10-03-1883	England	W 3-2	Sheffield	Fr	Smith.J (I) 2, Fraser
12-03	Wales	W 3-0	Wrexham	Fr	Smith.J (I), Fraser, Anderson.W
26-01-1884	Ireland	W 5-0	Belfast	HC	Goudie, Harrower 2, Gossland 2
15-03	England	W 1-0	Glasgow	HC	Smith.J (I)
29-03	Wales	W 4-1	Glasgow	HC	Kay 2, Lindsay, Shaw
14-03-1885	Ireland	W 8-2	Glasgow	HC	Higgins.A (I) 4, Kelso, Barbour, McPherson.J (I), Calderwood
21-03	England	D 1-1	London	HC	Lindsay
23-03	Wales	W 8-1	Wrexham	HC	Anderson.W 3, Lindsay 2, Allan.D 2, Calderwood
20-03-1886	Ireland	W 7-2	Belfast	HC	Heggie 5, Dunbar, Gourlay
27-03	England	D 1-1	Glasgow	HC	Somerville
10-04	Wales	W 4-1	Glasgow	HC	Harrower 2, Allan.D 2
19-02-1887	Ireland	W 4-1	Glasgow	HC	Watt.W, Jenkinson, Johnstone.W, Lowe.J (I)
19-03	England	W 3-2	Blackburn	HC	McCall, Allan.J 2
21-03	Wales	W 2-0	Wrexham	HC	Robertson.W, Marshall.J
10-03-1888	Wales	W 5-1	Edinburgh	HC	Paul.W 2, McPherson.J (II) 2, Groves
17-03	England	L 0-5	Glasgow	HC	
24-03	Ireland	W 10-2	Belfast	HC	Dewar.G, Dickson, Aitken, McCallum, Brackenridge, OG, Anon 4
9-03-1889	Ireland	W 7-0	Glasgow	HC	Watt.F, McInnes 2, Black.D, Groves 3
13-04	England	W 3-2	London	HC	McLaren.J, Oswald, Munro.N
15-04	Wales	D 0-0	Wrexham	HC	
22-03-1890	Wales	W 5-0	Glasgow	HC	Paul.W 4, Wilson.H
29-03	Ireland	W 4-1	Belfast	HC	Wylie, Rankin.G 2, McPherson.J (II)
5-04	England	D 1-1	Glasgow	HC	McPherson.J (II)
21-03-1891	Wales	W 4-3	Wrexham	HC	Logan, Buchanan.R, Boyd.R 2
28-03	Ireland	W 2-1	Glasgow	HC	Waddell.T, Lowe.J (II)
6-04	England	L 1-2	Blackburn	HC	Watt.F
19-03-1892	Ireland	W 3-2	Belfast	HC	Keillor, Lambie, Ellis
26-03	Wales	W 6-1	Edinburgh	HC	Thomson.W, Hamilton.J 2, McPherson.J (II), Baird.D 2
2-04	England	L 1-4	Glasgow	HC	Bell
18-03-1893	Wales	W 8-0	Wrexham	HC	Madden 4, Barker 3, Lambie
25-03	Ireland	W 6-1	Glasgow	HC	Sellar 2, Kelly, McMahon, Hamilton.J, OG
1-04	England	L 2-5	London	HC	Sellar 2
24-03-1894	Wales	W 5-2	Kilmarnock	HC	Berry, Barker, Chambers, Alexander, Johnstone.J (I)
31-03	Ireland	W 2-1	Belfast	HC	Taylor, OG
7-04	England	D 2-2	Glasgow	HC	Lambie, McMahon
23-03-1895	Wales	D 2-2	Wrexham	HC	Madden, Divers

30-03	Ireland	W 3-1	Glasgow	HC	Lambie, Walker.J 2
6-04	England	L 0-3	Liverpool	HC	
21-03-1896	Wales	W 4-0	Dundee	HC	Neil 2, Keillor 2
28-03	Ireland	D 3-3	Belfast	HC	McColl 2, Drummond
4-04	England	W 2-1	Glasgow	HC	Lambie, Bell
20-03-1897	Wales	D 2-2	Wrexham	HC	Ritchie, OG
27-03	Ireland	W 5-1	Glasgow	HC	McPherson.J (II) 2, Gibson.N, McColl, King.A
3-04	England	W 2-1	London	HC	Hyslop, Millar
19-03-1898	Wales	W 5-2	Motherwell	HC	Gillespie 3, McKie 2
26-03	Ireland	W 3-0	Belfast	HC	Robertson.T, McColl, Stewart.W
2-04	England	L 1-3	Glasgow	HC	Millar
18-03-1899	Wales	W 6-0	Wrexham	HC	Campbell.J (II) 2, McColl 3, Marshall.H
25-03	Ireland	W 9-1	Glasgow	HC	McColl 3, Hamilton.R 2, Campbell.J (II) 2, Bell, Christie
8-04	England	L 1-2	Birmingham	HC	Hamilton.R
3-02-1900	Wales	W 5-2	Aberdeen	HC	Bell, Wilson.D (I) 2, Hamilton.R, Smith.A
3-03	Ireland	W 3-0	Belfast	HC	Campbell.J (III) 2, Smith.A
7-04	England	W 4-1	Glasgow	HC	McColl 3, Bell
23-02-1901	Ireland	W 11-0	Glasgow	HC	Campbell.J (III) 2, McMahon 4, Hamilton.R 4, Russell
2-03	Wales	D 1-1	Wrexham	HC	Robertson.J (I)
30-03	England	D 2-2	London	HC	Campbell.J (III), Hamilton.R
1-03-1902	Ireland	W 5-1	Belfast	HC	Hamilton.R 3, Buick, Walker.R
15-03	Wales	W 5-1	Greenock	HC	Smith.A 3, Buick, Drummond
5-04	England *	D 1-1	Glasgow	HC	Brown.A
3-05	England	D 2-2	Birmingham	HC	Templeton, Orr.R
9-03-1903	Wales	W 1-0	Cardiff	HC	Speedie
21-03	Ireland	L 0-2	Glasgow	HC	
4-04	England	W 2-1	Sheffield	HC	Speedie, Walker.R
12-03-1904	Wales	D 1-1	Dundee	HC	Walker.R
26-03	Ireland	D 1-1	Dublin	HC	Hamilton.R
9-04	England	L 0-1	Glasgow	HC	
6-03-1905	Wales	L 1-3	Wrexham	HC	Robertson.J (I)
18-03	Ireland	W 4-0	Glasgow	HC	Thomson.C 2, Walker.R, Quinn.J
1-04	England	L 0-1	London	HC	
3-03-1906	Wales	L 0-2	Edinburgh	HC	
17-03	Ireland	W 1-0	Dublin	HC	Fitchie
7-04	England	W 2-1	Glasgow	HC	Howie.J 2
4-03-1907	Wales	L 0-1	Wrexham	HC	
16-03	Ireland	W 3-0	Glasgow	HC	O'Rourke, Walker.R, Thomson.C
6-04	England	D 1-1	Newcastle	HC	OG
7-03-1908	Wales	W 2-1	Dundee	HC	Bennett, Lennie
14-03	Ireland	W 5-0	Dublin	HC	Quinn.J 4, Galt
4-04	England	D 1-1	Glasgow	HC	Wilson.A (I)
1-03-1909	Wales	L 2-3	Wrexham	HC	Walker.R, Paul.H
15-03	Ireland	W 5-0	Glasgow	HC	McMenemy 2, McFarlane, Thomson.A, Paul.H
3-04	England	L 0-2	London	HC	
5-03-1910	Wales	W 1-0	Kilmarnock	HC	Devine
19-03	Ireland	L 0-1	Belfast	HC	
2-04	England	W 2-0	Glasgow	HC	McMenemy, Quinn.J
6-03-1911	Wales	D 2-2	Cardiff	HC	Hamilton.R 2
18-03	Ireland	W 2-0	Glasgow	HC	Reid, McMenemy
1-04	England	D 1-1	Liverpool	HC	Higgins.A (II)
2-03-1912	Wales	W 1-0	Edinburgh	HC	Quinn.J
16-03	Ireland	W 4-1	Belfast	HC	Aitkenhead 2, Reid, Walker.R
23-03	England	D 1-1	Glasgow	HC	Wilson.A (I)
3-03-1913	Wales	D 0-0	Wrexham	HC	
15-03	Ireland	W 2-1	Dublin	HC	Reid, Bennett
5-04	England	L 0-1	London	HC	
28-02-1914	Wales	D 0-0	Glasgow	HC	
14-03	Ireland	D 1-1	Belfast	HC	Donnachie
4-04	England	W 3-1	Glasgow	HC	Thomson.C, McMenemy, Reid
26-02-1920	Wales	D 1-1	Cardiff	HC	Cairns
13-03	Ireland	W 3-0	Glasgow	HC	Wilson.A (II), Morton, Cunningham
10-04	England	L 4-5	Sheffield	HC	Miller.T 2, Wilson.A (II), Donaldson
12-02-1921	Wales	W 2-1	Aberdeeen	HC	Wilson.A (II) 2
26-02	Ireland	W 2-0	Belfast	HC	Wilson.A (II), Cassidy
9-04	England	W 3-0	Glasgow	HC	Wilson.A (II), Morton, Cunningham
4-02-1922	Wales	L 1-2	Wrexham	HC	Archibald.A
4-03	Ireland	W 2-1	Glasgow	HC	Wilson.A (II) 2
8-04	England	W 1-0	Birmingham	HC	Wilson.A (II)
3-03-1923	Ireland	W 1-0	Belfast	HC	Wilson.A (II)
17-03	Wales	W 2-0	Glasgow	HC	Wilson.A (II) 2

14-04	England	D 2-2	Glasgow	HC	Cunningham, Wilson.A (II)
16-02-1924	Wales	L 0-2	Cardiff	HC	
1-03	Nth. Ireland	W 2-0	Glasgow	HC	Cunningham, Morris.D
12-04	England	D 1-1	London	HC	OG
14-02-1925	Wales	W 3-1	Edinburgh	HC	Meiklejohn, Gallacher.H 2
28-02	Nth. Ireland	W 3-0	Belfast	HC	Meiklejohn, Gallacher.H, Dunn
4-04	England	W 2-0	Glasgow	HC	Gallacher.H 2
31-10	Wales	W 3-0	Cardiff	HC	Duncan.J, McLean.A, Clunas
27-02-1926	Nth. Ireland	W 4-0	Glasgow	HC	Gallacher.H 3, Cunningham
17-04	England	W 1-0	Manchester	HC	Jackson.A
30-10	Wales	W 3-0	Glasgow	HC	Gallacher.H, Jackson.A 2
26-02-1927	Nth. Ireland	W 2-0	Belfast	HC	Morton 2
2-04	England	L 1-2	Glasgow	HC	Morton
29-10	Wales	D 2-2	Wrexham	HC	Gallacher.H, Hutton
25-02-1928	Nth. Ireland	L 0-1	Glasgow	HC	
31-03	England	W 5-1	London	HC	Jackson.A 3, James, Gibson.J
27-10	Wales	W 4-2	Glasgow	HC	Gallacher.H 3, Dunn
23-02-1929	Nth. Ireland	W 7-3	Belfast	HC	Gallacher.H 4, Jackson.A, James
13-04	England	W 1-0	Glasgow	HC	Cheyne
28-05	Norway	W 7-3	Oslo	Fr	Cheyne 3, Nisbet 2, Craig, Rankin
1-06	Germany	D 1-1	Berlin	Fr	Imrie
4-06	Holland	W 2-0	Amsterdam	Fr	Fleming.J, Rankin.R
26-10	Wales	W 4-2	Cardiff	HC	Gallacher.H 2, James, Gibson.J
22-02-1930	Nth. Ireland	W 3-1	Glasgow	HC	Gallacher.H 2, Stevenson
5-04	England	L 2-5	London	HC	Fleming.J 2
18-05	France	W 2-0	Paris	Fr	Gallacher.H 2
25-10	Wales	D 1-1	Glasgow	HC	Battles
21-02-1931	Nth. Ireland	D 0-0	Belfast	HC	
28-03	England	W 2-0	Glasgow	HC	Stevenson, McGrory
16-05	Austria	L 0-5	Vienna	Fr	
20-05	Italy	L 0-3	Rome	Fr	
24-05	Switzerland	W 3-2	Geneva	Fr	Easson, Boyd.W, Love
19-09	Nth. Ireland	W 3-1	Glasgow	HC	Stevenson, McGrory, McPhail.R
31-10	Wales	W 3-2	Wrexham	HC	Stevenson, Thomson.R, McGrory
9-04-1932	England	L 0-3	London	HC	
8-05	France	W 3-1	Paris	Fr	Dewar.N 3
17-09	Nth. Ireland	W 4-0	Belfast	HC	McPhail.R 2, King.J, McGrory
26-10	Wales	L 2-5	Edinburgh	HC	Dewar.N, Duncan.D (I)
1-04-1933	England	W 2-1	Glasgow	HC	McGrory 2
16-09	Nth. Ireland	L 1-2	Glasgow	HC	McPhail.R
4-10	Wales	L 2-3	Cardiff	HC	Duncan.D (I), McFadyen
29-11	Austria	D 2-2	Glasgow	Fr	Meiklejohn, McFadyen
14-04-1934	England	L 0-3	London	HC	
20-10	Nth. Ireland	L 1-2	Belfast	HC	Gallacher.P
21-11	Wales	W 3-2	Aberdeen	HC	Duncan.D (I), Napier 2
6-04-1935	England	W 2-0	Glasgow	HC	Duncan.D (I) 2
5-10	Wales	D 1-1	Cardiff	HC	Duncan.D (I)
13-11	Nth. Ireland	W 2-1	Edinburgh	HC	Walker.T, Duncan.D (I)
4-04-1936	England	D 1-1	London	HC	Walker.T
14-10	Germany	W 2-0	Glasgow	Fr	Delaney 2
31-10	Nth. Ireland	W 3-1	Belfast	HC	Napier, Munro.A, McCulloch
2-12	Wales	L 1-2	Dundee	HC	Walker.T
17-04-1937	England	W 3-1	Glasgow	HC	O'Donnell, McPhail.R 2
9-05	Austria	D 1-1	Vienna	Fr	O'Donnell
22-05	Czechoslovakia	W 3-1	Prague	Fr	Simpson, McPhail.R, Gillick
30-10	Wales	L 1-2	Cardiff	HC	Massie
10-11	Nth. Ireland	D 1-1	Aberdeen	HC	Smith.J (II)
8-12	Czechoslovakia	W 5-0	Glasgow	Fr	McCulloch 2, Black.A, Buchanan.P, Kinnear
9-04-1938	England	W 1-0	London	HC	Walker.T
21-05	Holland	W 3-1	Amsterdam	Fr	Black.A, Murphy, Walker.T
8-10	Nth. Ireland	W 2-0	Belfast	HC	Delaney, Walker.T
9-11	Wales	W 3-2	Edinburgh	HC	Walker.T 2, Gillick
7-12	Hungary	W 3-1	Glasgow	Fr	Black.A, Walker.T, Gillick
15-04-1939	England	L 1-2	Glasgow	HC	Dougall
23-01-1946	Belgium *	D 2-2	Glasgow	VI	Delaney 2
15-05	Switzerland *	W 3-1	Glasgow	VI	Liddell 2, Delaney
19-10	Wales	L 1-3	Wrexham	HC	Waddell.W
27-11	Nth. Ireland	D 0-0	Glasgow	HC	
12-04-1947	England	D 1-1	London	HC	McLaren.A
18-05	Belgium	L 1-2	Brussels	Fr	Steel
24-05	Luxembourg	W 6-0	Luxembourg	Fr	McLaren.A 2, Steel 2, Flavell 2

4-10	Nth. Ireland	L 0-2	Belfast	HC	
12-11	Wales	L 1-2	Glasgow	HC	McLaren.A
10-04-1948	England	L 0-2	Glasgow	HC	
28-04	Belgium	W 2-0	Glasgow	Fr	Combe, Duncan.D (II)
17-05	Switzerland	L 1-2	Berne	Fr	Johnston.L
23-05	France	L 0-3	Paris	Fr	
23-10	Wales	W 3-1	Cardiff	HC	Howie.H, Waddell.W 2
17-11	Nth. Ireland	W 3-2	Glasgow	HC	Houliston 2, Mason
9-04-1949	England	W 3-1	London	HC	Mason, Steel, Reilly
27-04	France	W 2-0	Glasgow	Fr	Steel 2
1-10	Nth. Ireland	W 8-2	Belfast	HC/WCq	Morris.H 3, Waddell.W 2, Steel, Reilly, Mason
9-11	Wales	W 2-0	Glasgow	HC/WCq	McPhail.J, Linwood
15-04-1950	England	L 0-1	Glasgow	HC/WCq	
26-04	Switzerland	W 3-1	Glasgow	Fr	Bauld, Campbell.R, Brown
21-05	Portugal	D 2-2	Lisbon	Fr	Brown, W.Bauld
27-05	France	W 1-0	Paris	Fr	Brown
21-10	Wales	W 3-1	Cardiff	HC	Reilly 2, Liddell
1-11	Nth. Ireland	W 6-1	Glasgow	HC	McPhail.J 2, Steel 4
13-12	Austria	L 0-1	Glasgow	Fr	
14-04-1951	England	W 3-2	London	HC	Johnstone.R, Reilly, Liddell
12-05	Denmark	W 3-1	Glasgow	Fr	Steel, Reilly, Mitchell
16-05	France	W 1-0	Glasgow	Fr	Reilly
20-05	Belgium	W 5-0	Brussels	Fr	Hamilton.G 3, Mason, Waddell.W
27-05	Austria	L 0-4	Vienna	Fr	
6-10	Nth. Ireland	W 3-0	Belfast	HC	Johnstone.R 2, Orr.T
14-11	Wales	L 0-1	Glasgow	HC	
5-04-1952	England	L 1-2	Glasgow	HC	Reilly
30-04	USA	W 6-0	Glasgow	Fr	Reilly 3, McMillan 2, OG
25-05	Denmark	W 2-1	Copenhagen	Fr	Thornton, Reilly
30-05	Sweden	L 1-3	Stockholm	Fr	Liddell
18-10	Wales	W 2-1	Cardiff	HC	Brown, Liddell
5-11	Nth. Ireland	D 1-1	Glasgow	HC	Reilly
18-04-1953	England	D 2-2	London	HC	Reilly 2
6-05	Sweden	L 1-2	Glasgow	Fr	Johnstone.R
3-10	Nth. Ireland	W 3-1	Belfast	HC/WCq	Fleming.C 2, Henderson.J
4-11	Wales	D 3-3	Glasgow	HC/WCq	Brown, Johnstone.R, Reilly
3-04-1954	England	L 2-4	Glasgow	HC/WCq	Brown, OG
5-05	Norway	W 1-0	Glasgow	Fr	Hamilton.G
19-05	Norway	D 1-1	Oslo	Fr	MacKenzie
25-05	Finland	W 2-1	Helsinki	Fr	Ormond, Johnstone.R
16-06	Austria	L 0-1	Zurich	WCr1	
19-06	Uruguay	L 0-7	Basle	WCr1	
16-10	Wales	W 1-0	Cardiff	HC	Buckley
3-11	Nth. Ireland	D 2-2	Glasgow	HC	Davidson.J, Johnstone.R
8-12	Hungary	L 2-4	Glasgow	Fr	Ring, Johnstone.R
2-04-1955	England	L 2-7	London	HC	Reilly, Docherty
4-05	Portugal	W 3-0	Glasgow	Fr	Reilly, Gemmell.T (I), Liddell
15-05	Yugoslavia	D 2-2	Belgrade	Fr	Reilly, Smith.G
19-05	Austria	W 4-1	Vienna	Fr	Robertson.A, Smith.G, Liddell, Reilly
29-05	Hungary	L 1-3	Budapest	Fr	Smith.G
8-10	Nth. Ireland	L 1-2	Belfast	HC	Reilly
9-11	Wales	W 2-0	Glasgow	HC	Johnstone.R
14-04-1956	England	D 1-1	Glasgow	HC	Leggat
2-05	Austria	D 1-1	Glasgow	Fr	Conn
20-10	Wales	D 2-2	Cardiff	HC	Fernie, Reilly
7-11	Nth. Ireland	W 1-0	Glasgow	HC	Scott
21-11	Yugoslavia	W 2-0	Glasgow	Fr	Mudie, Baird.S
6-04-1957	England	L 1-2	London	HC	Ring
8-05	Spain	W 4-2	Glasgow	WCq	Mudie 3, Hewie
19-05	Switzerland	W 2-1	Basle	WCq	Mudie, Collins.R
22-05	West Germany	W 3-1	Stuttgart	Fr	Collins.R 2, Mudie
26-05	Spain	L 1-4	Madrid	WCq	Smith.G
5-10	Nth. Ireland	D 1-1	Belfast	HC	Leggat
6-11	Switzerland	W 3-2	Glasgow	WCq	Robertson.A, Mudie, Scott
13-11	Wales	D 1-1	Glasgow	HC	Collins.R
19-04-1958	England	L 0-4	Glasgow	HC	
7-05	Hungary	D 1-1	Glasgow	Fr	Mudie
1-06	Poland	W 2-1	Warsaw	Fr	Collins.R 2
8-06	Yugoslavia	D 1-1	Vasteras	WCr1	Murray
11-06	Paraguay	L 2-3	Norrkoping	WCr1	Mudie, Collins.R
15-06	France	L 1-2	Orebro	WCr1	Baird.S

18-10	Wales	W 3-0	Cardiff	HC	Leggat, Law, Collins.R
5-11	Nth. Ireland	D 2-2	Glasgow	HC	Herd, Collins.R
11-04-1959	England	L 0-1	London	HC	
6-05	West Germany	W 3-2	Glasgow	Fr	White, Weir.A, Leggat
27-05	Holland	W 2-1	Amsterdam	Fr	Collins.R, Leggat
3-06	Portugal	L 0-1	Lisbon	Fr	
3-10	Nth. Ireland	W 4-0	Belfast	HC	Leggat, Hewie, White, Mulhall
14-11	Wales	D 1-1	Glasgow	HC	Leggat
9-04-1960	England	D 1-1	Glasgow	HC	Leggat
4-05	Poland	L 2-3	Glasgow	Fr	Law, St John
29-05	Austria	L 1-4	Vienna	Fr	Mackay.D
5-06	Hungary	D 3-3	Budapest	Fr	Hunter, Herd, Young
8-06	Turkey	L 2-4	Ankara	Fr	Caldow, Young
22-10	Wales	L 0-2	Cardiff	HC	
9-11	Nth. Ireland	W 5-2	Glasgow	HC	Law, Caldow, Young, Brand 2
15-04-1961	England	L 3-9	London	HC	Mackay.D, Wilson.D (II), Quinn.P
3-05	Rep. Ireland	W 4-1	Glasgow	WCq	Brand 2, Herd 2
7-05	Rep. Ireland	W 3-0	Dublin	WCq	Young 2, Brand
14-05	Czechoslovakia	L 0-4	Bratislava	WCq	
26-09	Czechoslovakia	W 3-2	Glasgow	WCq	St John, Law 2
7-10	Nth. Ireland	W 6-1	Belfast	HC	Wilson.D (II), Scott 3, Brand 2
8-11	Wales	W 2-0	Glasgow	HC	St John 2
29-11	Czechoslovakia	L 2-4	Brussels	WCq	St John 2
14-04-1962	England	W 2-0	Glasgow	HC	Wilson.D (II), Caldow
2-05	Uruguay	L 2-3	Glasgow	Fr	Baxter, Brand
20-10	Wales	W 3-2	Cardiff	HC	Caldow, Law, Henderson.W
7-11	Nth. Ireland	W 5-1	Glasgow	HC	Law 4, Henderson.W
6-04-1963	England	W 2-1	London	HC	Baxter 2
8-05	Austria	W 4-1	Glasgow	Fr	Wilson.D (II) 2, Law 2, abandoned after 79 mins
4-06	Norway	L 3-4	Bergen	Fr	Law 3
9-06	Rep. Ireland	L 0-1	Dublin	Fr	
13-06	Spain	W 6-2	Madrid	Fr	St John, Wilson.D (II), Law, Henderson.W, Gibson.D, McLintock
12-10	Nth. Ireland	L 1-2	Belfast	HC	St John
7-11	Norway	W 6-1	Glasgow	Fr	Law 4, Mackay.D 2
20-11	Wales	W 2-1	Glasgow	HC	White, Law
11-04-1964	England	W 1-0	Glasgow	HC	Gilzean
12-05	West Germany	D 2-2	Hanover	Fr	Gilzean 2
3-10	Wales	L 2-3	Cardiff	HC	Chalmers, Gibson.D
21-10	Finland	W 3-1	Glasgow	WCq	Law, Chalmers, Gibson.D
25-11	Nth. Ireland	W 3-2	Glasgow	HC	Wilson.D (II) 2, Gilzean
10-04-1965	England	D 2-2	London	HC	Law, St John
8-05	Spain	D 0-0	Glasgow	Fr	
23-05	Poland	D 1-1	Chorzow	WCq	Law
27-05	Finland	W 2-1	Helsinki	WCq	Wilson.D (II), Greig
2-10	Nth. Ireland	L 2-3	Belfast	HC	Gilzean 2
13-10	Poland	L 1-2	Glasgow	WCq	McNeill
9-11	Italy	W 1-0	Glasgow	WCq	Greig
24-11	Wales	W 4-1	Glasgow	HC	Murdoch 2, Henderson.W, Greig
7-12	Italy	L 0-3	Naples	WCq	
2-04-1966	England	L 3-4	Glasgow	HC	Law, Johnstone.J (II) 2
11-05	Holland	L 0-3	Glasgow	Fr	
18-06	Portugal	L 0-1	Glasgow	Fr	
25-06	Brazil	D 1-1	Glasgow	Fr	Chalmers
22-10	Wales	D 1-1	Cardiff	HC/ECq	Law
16-11	Nth. Ireland	W 2-1	Glasgow	HC/ECq	Murdoch, Lennox
15-04-1967	England	W 3-2	London	HC/ECq	Law, Lennox, McCalliog
10-05	Soviet Union	L 0-2	Glasgow	Fr	
21-10	Nth. Ireland	L 0-1	Belfast	HC/ECq	
22-11	Wales	W 3-2	Glasgow	HC/ECq	Gilzean 2, McKinnon.R
24-02-1968	England	D 1-1	Glasgow	HC/ECq	Hughes
30-05	Holland	D 0-0	Amsterdam	Fr	
16-10	Denmark	W 1-0	Copenhagen	Fr	Lennox
6-11	Austria	W 2-1	Glasgow	WCq	Law, Bremner
11-12	Cyprus	W 5-0	Nicosia	WCq	Gilzean 2, Stein 2, Murdoch
16-04-1969	West Germany	D 1-1	Glasgow	WCq	Murdoch
3-05	Wales	W 5-3	Wrexham	HC	McNeill, Stein, Gilzean, Bremner, McLean.T
6-05	Nth. Ireland	D 1-1	Glasgow	HC	Stein
10-05	England	L 1-4	London	HC	Stein
17-05	Cyprus	W 8-0	Glasgow	WCq	Gray.E, McNeill, Stein 4, Henderson.W, Gemmell.T (II)

21-09	Rep. Ireland	D 1-1	Dublin	Fr	Stein
22-10	West Germany	L 2-3	Hamburg	WCq	Johnstone.J (II), Gilzean
5-11	Austria	L 0-2	Vienna	WCq	
18-04-1970	Nth. Ireland	W 1-0	Belfast	HC	O'Hare
22-04	Wales	D 0-0	Glasgow	HC	
25-04	England	D 0-0	Glasgow	HC	
11-11	Denmark	W 1-0	Glasgow	ECq	O'Hare
3-02-1971	Belgium	L 0-3	Liege	ECq	
21-04	Portugal	L 0-2	Lisbon	ECq	
15-05	Wales	D 0-0	Cardiff	HC	
18-05	Nth. Ireland	L 0-1	Glasgow	HC	
22-05	England	L 1-3	London	HC	Curran
9-06	Denmark	L 0-1	Copenhagen	ECq	
14-06	Soviet Union	L 0-1	Moscow	Fr	
13-10	Portugal	W 2-1	Glasgow	ECq	O'Hare, Gemmill
10-11	Belgium	W 1-0	Aberdeen	ECq	O'Hare
1-12	Holland	L 1-2	Amsterdam	Fr	Graham.G
26-04-1972	Peru	W 2-0	Glasgow	Fr	O'Hare, Law
20-05	Nth. Ireland	W 2-0	Glasgow	HC	Law, Lorimer
24-05	Wales	W 1-0	Glasgow	HC	Lorimer
27-05	England	L 0-1	Glasgow	HC	
29-06	Yugoslavia	D 2-2	Belo Horizonte	Clr2	Macari 2
2-07	Czechoslovakia	D 0-0	Porto Alegre	Clr2	
5-07	Brazil	L 0-1	Rio de Janeiro	Clr2	
18-10	Denmark	W 4-1	Copenhagen	WCq	Macari, Bone, Harper, Morgan
15-11	Denmark	W 2-0	Glasgow	WCq	Dalglish, Lorimer
14-02-1973	England	L 0-5	Glasgow	Fr	
12-05	Wales	W 2-0	Wrexham	HC	Graham.G 2
16-05	Nth. Ireland	L 1-2	Glasgow	HC	Dalglish
19-05	England	L 0-1	London	HC	
22-06	Switzerland	L 0-1	Berne	Fr	
30-06	Brazil	L 0-1	Glasgow	Fr	
26-09	Czechoslovakia	W 2-1	Glasgow	WCq	Holton, Jordan
17-10	Czechoslovakia	L 0-1	Bratislava	WCq	
14-11	West Germany	D 1-1	Glasgow	Fr	Holton
27-03-1974	West Germany	L 1-2	Frankfurt	Fr	Dalglish
11-05	Nth. Ireland	L 0-1	Glasgow	HC	
14-05	Wales	W 2-0	Glasgow	HC	Dalglish, Jardine
18-05	England	W 2-0	Glasgow	HC	Jordan, OG
1-06	Belgium	L 1-2	Bruges	Fr	Johnstone.J (II)
6-06	Norway	W 2-1	Oslo	Fr	Jordan, Dalglish
14-06	Zaire	W 2-0	Dortmund	WCr1	Lorimer, Jordan
18-06	Brazil	D 0-0	Frankfurt	WCr1	
22-06	Yugoslavia	D 1-1	Frankfurt	WCr1	Jordan
30-10	East Germany	W 3-0	Glasgow	Fr	Hutchison, Burns, Dalglish
20-11	Spain	L 1-2	Glasgow	ECq	Bremner
5-02-1975	Spain	D 1-1	Valencia	ECq	Jordan
16-04	Sweden	D 1-1	Gothenburg	Fr	Macdougall
13-05	Portugal	W 1-0	Glasgow	Fr	OG
17-05	Wales	D 2-2	Cardiff	HC	Jackson.C, Rioch
20-05	Nth. Ireland	W 3-0	Glasgow	HC	Macdougall, Dalglish, Parlane
24-05	England	L 1-5	London	HC	Rioch
1-06	Romania	D 1-1	Bucharest	ECq	McQueen
3-09	Denmark	W 1-0	Copenhagen	ECq	Harper
29-10	Denmark	W 3-1	Glasgow	ECq	Dalglish, Rioch, Macdougall
17-12	Romania	D 1-1	Glasgow	ECq	Rioch
7-04-1976	Switzerland	W 1-0	Glasgow	Fr	Pettigrew
6-05	Wales	W 3-1	Glasgow	HC	Pettigrew, Rioch, Gray.E
8-05	Nth. Ireland	W 3-0	Glasgow	HC	Gemmill, Masson, Dalglish
15-05	England	W 2-1	Glasgow	HC	Masson, Dalglish
8-09	Finland	W 6-0	Glasgow	Fr	Rioch, Masson, Dalglish, Gray.A 2, Gray.E
13-10	Czechoslovakia	L 0-2	Prague	WCq	
17-11	Wales	W 1-0	Glasgow	WCq	OG
27-04-1977	Sweden	W 3-1	Glasgow	Fr	Hartford, Dalglish, Craig
28-05	Wales	D 0-0	Wrexham	HC	
1-06	Nth. Ireland	W 3-0	Glasgow	HC	Dalglish 2, McQueen
4-06	England	W 2-1	London	HC	McQueen, Dalglish
15-06	Chile	W 4-2	Santiago	Fr	Dalglish, Macari 2, Hartford
18-06	Argentina	D 1-1	Buenos Aires	Fr	Masson
23-06	Brazil	L 0-2	Rio de Janeiro	Fr	
7-09	East Germany	L 0-1	Berlin	Fr	
21-09	Czechoslovakia	W 3-1	Glasgow	WCq	Jordan, Hartford, Dalglish

12-10	Wales	W 2-0	Liverpool	WCq	Masson, Dalglish
22-02-1978	Bulgaria	W 2-1	Glasgow	Fr	Gemmill, Wallace
13-05	Nth. Ireland	D 1-1	Glasgow	HC	Johnstone.D
17-05	Wales	D 1-1	Glasgow	HC	Johnstone.D
20-05	England	L 0-1	Glasgow	HC	
3-06	Peru	L 1-3	Cordoba	WCr1	Jordan
7-06	Iran	D 1-1	Cordoba	WCr1	OG
11-06	Holland	W 3-2	Mendoza	WCr1	Dalglish, Gemmill 2
20-09	Austria	L 2-3	Vienna	ECq	McQueen, Gray.A
25-10	Norway	W 3-2	Glasgow	ECq	Dalglish 2, Gemmill
29-11	Portugal	L 0-1	Lisbon	ECq	
19-05-1979	Wales	L 0-3	Cardiff	HC	
22-05	Nth. Ireland	W 1-0	Glasgow	HC	Graham.A
26-05	England	L 1-3	London	HC	Wark
2-06	Argentina	L 1-3	Glasgow	Fr	Graham
7-06	Norway	W 4-0	Oslo	ECq	Jordan, Dalglish, Robertson.J (II), McQueen
12-09	Peru	D 1-1	Glasgow	Fr	OG
17-10	Austria	D 1-1	Glasgow	ECq	Gemmill
21-11	Belgium	L 0-2	Brussels	ECq	
19-12	Belgium	L 1-3	Glasgow	ECq	Robertson.J (II)
26-03-1980	Portugal	W 4-1	Glasgow	ECq	Dalglish, Gray.A, Archibald.S, Gemmill
16-05	Nth. Ireland	L 0-1	Belfast	HC	
21-05	Wales	W 1-0	Glasgow	HC	Miller.W
24-05	England	L 0-2	Glasgow	HC	
28-05	Poland	L 0-1	Poznan	Fr	
31-05	Hungary	L 1-3	Budapest	Fr	Archibald.S
10-09	Sweden	W 1-0	Stockholm	WCq	Strachan
15-10	Portugal	D 0-0	Glasgow	WCq	
25-02-1981	Israel	W 1-0	Tel Aviv	WCq	Dalglish
25-03	Nth. Ireland	D 1-1	Glasgow	WCq	Wark
28-04	Israel	W 3-1	Glasgow	WCq	Robertson.J (II) 2, Provan
16-05	Wales	L 0-2	Swansea	HC	
19-05	Nth. Ireland	W 2-0	Glasgow	HC	Stewart.R, Archibald.S
23-05	England	W 1-0	London	HC	Robertson.J (II) (p)
9-09	Sweden	W 2-0	Glasgow	WCq	Jordan, Robertson.J (II)
14-10	Nth. Ireland	D 0-0	Belfast	WCq	
18-11	Portugal	L 1-2	Lisbon	WCq	Sturrock
24-02-1982	Spain	L 0-3	Valencia	Fr	
23-03	Holland	W 2-1	Glasgow	Fr	Gray.F, Dalglish
28-04	Nth. Ireland	D 1-1	Belfast	HC	Wark
24-05	Wales	W 1-0	Glasgow	HC	Hartford
29-05	England	L 0-1	Glasgow	HC	
15-06	New Zealand	W 5-2	Malaga	WCr1	Dalglish, Wark 2, Robertson.J (II), Archibald.S
18-06	Brazil	L 1-4	Seville	WCr1	Narey
22-06	Soviet Union	D 2-2	Malaga	WCr1	Jordan, Souness
13-10	East Germany	W 2-0	Glasgow	ECq	Wark, Sturrock
17-11	Switzerland	L 0-2	Berne	ECq	
15-12	Belgium	L 2-3	Brussels	ECq	Dalglish 2
30-03-1983	Switzerland	D 2-2	Glasgow	ECq	Wark, Nicholas
24-05	Nth. Ireland	D 0-0	Glasgow	HC	
28-05	Wales	W 2-0	Cardiff	HC	Gray.A, Brazil
1-06	England	L 0-2	London	HC	
12-06	Canada	W 2-0	Vancouver	Fr	Strachan, McGhee
16-06	Canada	W 3-0	Edmonton	Fr	Nicholas, Gough, Souness
20-06	Canada	W 2-0	Toronto	Fr	Gray.A 2
21-09	Uruguay	W 2-0	Glasgow	Fr	Robertson.J (II), Dodds
12-10	Belgium	D 1-1	Glasgow	ECq	Nicholas
16-11	East Germany	L 1-2	Halle	ECq	Bannon
13-12	Nth. Ireland	L 0-2	Belfast	HC	
28-02-1984	Wales	W 2-1	Glasgow	HC	Cooper, Johnston.M
26-05	England	D 1-1	Glasgow	HC	McGhee
1-06	France	L 0-2	Marseille	Fr	
12-09	Yugoslavia	W 6-1	Glasgow	Fr	Souness, Dalglish, Sturrock, Johnston.M, Cooper, Nicholas
17-10	Iceland	W 3-0	Glasgow	WCq	Nicholas, McStay 2
14-11	Spain	W 3-1	Glasgow	WCq	Dalglish, Johnston.M 2
27-02-1985	Spain	L 0-1	Seville	WCq	
27-03	Wales	L 0-1	Glasgow	WCq	
25-05	England	W 1-0	Glasgow	Fr	Gough
28-05	Iceland	W 1-0	Reykjavik	WCq	Bett
10-09	Wales	D 1-1	Cardiff	WCq	Cooper
16-10	East Germany	D 0-0	Glasgow	Fr	

20-11	Australia	W 2-0	Glasgow	WCq	McAvennie, Cooper
4-12	Australia	D 0-0	Melbourne	WCq	
28-01-1986	Israel	W 1-0	Tel Aviv	Fr	McStay
26-03	Romania	W 3-0	Glasgow	Fr	Gough, Strachan, Aitken
23-04	England	L 1-2	London	Fr	Souness
29-04	Holland	D 0-0	Eindhoven	Fr	
4-06	Denmark	L 0-1	Nezahualcoyotl	WCr1	
8-06	West Germany	L 1-2	Queretaro	WCr1	Strachan
13-06	Uruguay	D 0-0	Nezahualcoyotl	WCr1	
10-09	Bulgaria	D 0-0	Glasgow	ECq	
15-10	Rep. Ireland	D 0-0	Dublin	ECq	
12-11	Luxembourg	W 3-0	Glasgow	ECq	Cooper 2, Johnston.M
18-02-1987	Rep. Ireland	L 0-1	Glasgow	ECq	
1-04	Belgium	L 1-4	Brussels	ECq	McStay
23-05	England	D 0-0	Glasgow	Fr	
26-05	Brazil	L 0-2	Glasgow	Fr	
9-09	Hungary	W 2-0	Glasgow	Fr	McCoist 2
14-10	Belgium	W 2-0	Glasgow	ECq	McStay, McCoist
11-11	Bulgaria	W 1-0	Sofia	ECq	Mackay.G
2-12	Luxembourg	D 0-0	Esch	ECq	
17-02-1988	Saudi Arabia	D 2-2	Riyadh	Fr	Johnston.M, Collins.J
22-03	Malta	D 1-1	Ta'Qali	Fr	Sharp
27-04	Spain	D 0-0	Madrid	Fr	
17-05	Colombia	D 0-0	Glasgow	Fr	
21-05	England	L 0-1	London	Fr	
14-09	Norway	W 2-1	Oslo	WCq	McStay, Johnston.M
19-10	Yugoslavia	D 1-1	Glasgow	WCq	Johnston.M
22-12	Italy	L 0-2	Perugia	Fr	
8-02-1989	Cyprus	W 3-2	Limassol	WCq	Johnston.M, Gough 2
8-03	France	W 2-0	Glasgow	WCq	Johnston.M 2
26-04	Cyprus	W 2-1	Glasgow	WCq	Johnston.M, McCoist
27-05	England	L 0-2	Glasgow	Fr	
30-05	Chile	W 2-0	Glasgow	Fr	McInally, McLeod
6-09	Yugoslavia	L 1-3	Zagreb	WCq	Durie
11-10	France	L 0-3	Paris	WCq	
15-11	Norway	D 1-1	Glasgow	WCq	McCoist
28-03-1990	Argentina	W 1-0	Glasgow	Fr	McKimmie
25-04	East Germany	L 0-1	Glasgow	Fr	
16-05	Egypt	L 1-3	Aberdeen	Fr	McCoist
19-05	Poland	D 1-1	Glasgow	Fr	Johnston.M
28-05	Malta	W 2-1	Ta'Qali	Fr	McInally 2
11-06	Costa Rica	L 0-1	Genoa	WCr1	
16-06	Sweden	W 2-1	Genoa	WCr1	McCall, Johnston.M
20-06	Brazil	L 0-1	Turin	WCr1	
12-09	Romania	W 2-1	Glasgow	ECq	Robertson, McCoist
17-10	Switzerland	W 2-1	Glasgow	ECq	Robertson, McAllister
14-11	Bulgaria	D 1-1	Sofia	ECq	McCoist
6-02-1991	Soviet Union	L 0-1	Glasgow	Fr	
27-03	Bulgaria	D 1-1	Glasgow	ECq	Collins
1-05	San Marino	W 2-0	Serravalle	ECq	Strachan, Durie
11-09	Switzerland	D 2-2	Berne	ECq	Durie, McCoist
16-10	Romania	L 0-1	Bucharest	ECq	
13-11	San Marino	W 4-0	Glasgow	ECq	McStay, Gough, Durie, McCoist
19-02-1992	Nth. Ireland	W 1-0	Glasgow	Fr	McCoist
25-03	Finland	D 1-1	Glasgow	Fr	McStay
17-05	USA	W 1-0	Denver	Fr	Nevin
20-05	Canada	W 3-1	Toronto	Fr	McAllister, McCoist, Malpas
3-06	Norway	D 0-0	Olso	Fr	
12-06	Holland	L 0-1	Gothenburg	ECr1	
15-06	Germany	L 0-2	Norrkoping	ECr1	
18-06	CIS	W 3-0	Norrkoping	ECr1	OG, McClair, McAllister
9-09	Switzerland	L 1-3	Berne	WCq	McCoist
14-10	Portugal	D 0-0	Glasgow	WCq	
18-11	Italy	D 0-0	Glasgow	WCq	
17-02-1993	Malta	W 3-0	Glasgow	WCq	McCoist 2, Nevin
24-03	Germany	L 0-1	Glasgow	Fr	
28-04	Portugal	L 0-5	Lisbon	WCq	
19-05	Estonia	W 3-0	Tallinn	WCq	Gallacher, Collins, Booth
2-06	Estonia	W 3-1	Aberdeen	WCq	McClair, Nevin 2
8-09	Switzerland	D 1-1	Aberdeen	WCq	Collins
13-10	Italy	L 1-3	Rome	WCq	Gallacher
17-11	Malta	W 2-0	Ta'Qali	WCq	McKinlay, Hendry

23-03-1994	Holland	L 0-1	Glasgow	Fr	
20-04	Austria	W 2-1	Vienna	Fr	McGinlay, McKinlay
27-05	Holland	L 1-3	Utrecht	Fr	Shearer
7-09	Finland	W 2-0	Helsinki	ECq	Shearer, Collins
12-10	Faeroe Islands	W 5-1	Glasgow	ECq	McGinley, Booth, Collins 2, McKinley
16-11	Russia	D 1-1	Glasgow	ECq	Booth
18-12	Greece	L 0-1	Athens	ECq	
29-03-1995	Russia	D 0-0	Moscow	ECq	
26-04	San Marino	W 2-0	Serravalle	ECq	Collins, Calderwood
21-05	Japan	D 0-0	Hiroshima	KC	
24-05	Ecuador	W 2-1	Tokyo	KC	Robertson.D, Crawford
7-06	Faeroe Islands	W 2-0	Toftir	ECq	McKinlay, McGinlay

SLOVAKIA

It was pressure from Slovakia that led to the split with the Czech Republic at the beginning of 1993, but the Slovaks were not able to start their own championship until later in the year and did not play their first international until 1994. The Slovaks have always had a very proud sense of national identity, and it meant a great deal to the people to see a Slovak XI take the field for an international in Bratislava over 50 years after the city had last witnessed such an event. Of the two new countries, Slovakia is much the weaker economically but has a football tradition that is in many ways the equal of the Czech Republic.

Football took longer to catch on in Bratislava than in Prague, however, and it was not until the post-1945 period that any serious challenge was made in the Czechoslovakian league. A brief period of independence during the Second World War had seen Slovan Bratislava - then called SK Bratislava - emerge as the strongest team in the republic. From 1949 to 1951, back in Czechoslovakia, they won a hat-trick of titles, the first time the championship had gone outside Czech territory. They were champions eight times in all before 1993, but were not the only team from Slovakia to win the league. Their crosstown neighbours Inter won one title, while most remarkably Spartak, from the small town of Trnava, were victorious on five occasions.

Slovan were also the only Czechoslovakian side to win a European club title when they won the Cup Winners Cup in 1969. Having beaten Porto and Torino on the way to the final, they defeated Barcelona 3-2 in Basle to lift the trophy. The Slovak presence in the national side was also very influential. Of the 13 who played against West Germany in the 1976 European Championship final, nine were from Slovak clubs.

Not surprisingly, Slovan won the first championship after 1993, but the season was characterised by poor crowds; it is hard to see Slovak clubs making an impression in Europe in the immediate future.

Population: 5,268,000
Area, sq km: 49,036
Capital city: Bratislava

Slovensky Futbalovy Zvaz
Junacka 6
832 80 Bratislava
Slovakia
Tel: + 42 7 2790151
Fax: + 42 7 2790554

Year of formation	1990
Affiliation to FIFA	1993
Affiliation to UEFA	1993
Registered clubs	2410
Registered players	141 000
Registered referees	2700
National Stadium	Tehelné pole, Bratislava 33 000
National colours	Blue/Blue/Blue
Season	August - June, with a mid season break December - February

THE RECORD

WORLD CUP

1930-90 Entered as Czechoslovakia

EUROPEAN CHAMPIONSHIP

1960-92 Entered as Czechoslovakia
1996 QT group 1

EUROPEAN CLUB COMPETITIONS

European Cup
Semi-finalists - Spartak Trnava 1969
Cup Winners Cup
Winners - Slovan Bratislava 1969
UEFA Cup
Third round - TJ Internacional 1976

CLUB DIRECTORY

BRATISLAVA (Population - 435,000)

ASK Inter Slovnaft Bratislava (1942)
Pasienky 17,000 – Yellow/Black
Previous names - CH Bratislava 1942-62, Slovnaft 1962-65, TJ Internacionál 1965-86. Merged in 1986 with ZTS Petrzalka (1892) to become Internacionál ZTS. Adopted present name in 1990

SK Slovan Bratislava (1919)
Tehelné Pole 33,000 – Blue/White
Previous names - ICSSK 1919-40, SK 1940-49, NV 1949-52, TJ Slovan CHZJD 1952-90

KOSICE (Population - 232,000)

FK Lokomotiva Kosice (1946)
Jeho Cermell 28,000 – Blue & white stripes/White
Previous names - Zeleznicari 1946-48, Sparta 1948-49, Dynamo 1949-52. Merged with VSZ in 1963, but remained Lokomotiva

1.FC Kosice (1952)
Vsesportovy areál 30,000 – Orange/Blue
Previously names: Spartak Kosice 1952-56, Jednota Kosice 1956-62, VSS Kosice 1962-77, ZTS Kosice 1977-90, Jednota VSS Kosice 1990-92

ZILINA (Population - 96,000)

SK Zilina (1908)
Pod Dubnom 15,000 – Yellow/Green
Previous names - ZTK 1908-19, SK 1919-48, Slovena 1948-53, ISKRA 1953-56, Dynamo 1956-63, Jednota 1963-67, TJ ZVL Zilina 1967-90

NITRA (Population - 89,000)

FC Nitra (1911)
Nitra 13,000 – White, sky blue trim
Pevious names: NTVE 1911-19, NSE 1919-23, AC 1923-48, Sokol 1948-53, Slavoj 1953-56, Slovan 1956-66, AC 1966-76, TJ Plastika 1976-90

PRESOV (Population - 87,000)
FC Tatran Presov (1931)
Tatran 14,000 – Green/White
Previous names - Slavia 1931-45, PTS 1945-47, Sparta 1947-50, Dukla 1950-53, TJ Tatran 1953-89

BANSKA BYSTRICA (Population - 85,000)
FK Dukla Banská Bystrica (1965)
SNP Stiavnicky 11,000 – Red, two white hoops/Red

TRNAVA (Population - 72,000)
FC Spartak Trnava (1925)
Spartak 20,000 – Red & black stripes/Black
Previous names - Rapid 1925-39, TSS Trnava 1939-48, Kovosmalt 1948-53

DUNAJSKA STREDA
DAC Dunajská Streda (1905)
DAC 12,000 – Yellow/Blue

SLOVAK LEAGUE CHAMPIONSHIP

1939cl	AC Bystrica 15 SK Bratislava 15 SK Zilina 12
1940k	SK Bratislava 37 AC Bystrica 33 SK Zilina 28
1941	SK Bratislava 32 Vrutky 31 AC Bystrica 26
1942	SK Bratislava 31 Vrutky 29 SK Zilina 24
1943	OAP Bratislava 37 SK Bratislava 30 AC Bystrica 26
1944	SK Bratislava 38 OAP Bratislava 31 TSS Trnava 25
1945-93	-
1994r4	Slovan Bratislava 50 Inter Bratislava 40 DAC Dunajská Streda 36
1995r5	Slovan Bratislava 72 FC Kosice 52 Inter Bratislava 50

SLOVAK CUP WINNERS

1970	Slovan Bratislava	2-2 1-0	Dukla Banska Bystrica
1971	Spartak Trnava	2-0 0-1	Slovan Bratislava
1972	Slovan Bratislava	1-2 4-1	Spartak Trnava
1973	VSS Kosice	3-0 3-3	Tatran Presov
1974	Slovan Bratislava	0-0 2-2 6-5p	Spartak Trnava
1975	Spartak Trnava	2-0 1-2	AC Nitra
1976	Slovan Bratislava	1-0 2-1	TJ Internacional
1977	Lokomotiva Kosice	0-2 4-0	ZVL Zilina
1978	Jednota Trencin	1-0 3-1	Slovan Bratislava
1979	Lokomotiva Kosice	2-2 3-0	TJ Internacional
1980	ZTS Kosice	2-4 5-0	ZVL Zilina
1981	Dukla Banska Bystrica	1-1 1-0	ZTS Kosice
1982	Slovan Bratislava	0-0 3-1	ZTS Petrzalka
1983	Slovan Bratislava	0-0 1-1	TJ Plastica Nitra
1984	TJ Internacional	1-1 2-0	Dukla Banska Byst.
1985	Lokomotiva Kosice	1-1 1-0	Tatran Presov
1986	Spartak Trnava	1-0	ZVL Zilina
1987	DAC Dunajská Streda	0-0 6-5p	TJ Plastica Nitra
1988	Internacional ZTS	1-0	Spartak Trnava
1989	Slovan Bratislava	2-1	Povazska Bystrica
1990	Internacional ZTS	6-0	ZVL Zilina
1991	Spartak Trnava	1-0	FC Nitra
1992	Tatran Presov	2-0	Lokomotiva Kosice
1993	1.FC Kosice	0-0 5-4p	DAC Dunajská Streda
1994	Slovan Bratislava	2-1	Tatran Presov
1995	Inter Bratislava	1-1 3-1p	DAC Dunajská Str.

INTERNATIONAL MATCHES PLAYED BY SLOVAKIA

27-08-1939	Germany	W 2-0	Bratislava	Fr	Arpas, Luknar
3-12	Germany	L 1-3	Chemnitz	Fr	Luknar
6-06-1940	Bulgaria	W 4-1	Sofia	Fr	Bolcek, Foldes, Luknar, Vysocky
15-09	Germany	L 0-1	Bratislava	Fr	
7-09-1941	Croatia	D 1-1	Bratislava	Fr	Vysocky
28-09	Croatia	L 2-5	Zagreb	Fr	Besina, Bolcek
14-10	Romania	L 2-3	Bucharest	Fr	Kuchar, Bolcek
7-12	Germany	L 0-4	Breslau	Fr	
7-06-1942	Croatia	L 1-2	Bratislava	Fr	Fabian
23-08	Romania	W 1-0	Bratislava	Fr	Bolcek
6-09	Croatia	L 1-6	Zagreb	Fr	Podhradsky
22-11	Germany	L 2-5	Bratislava	Fr	Luknar, Biro
10-04-1943	Croatia	L 0-1	Zagreb	Fr	
7-06	Croatia	L 1-3	Bratislava	Fr	Danko
13-06	Romania	D 2-2	Bucharest	Fr	Balazi, Bolcek
9-04	Croatia	L 3-7	Zagreb	Fr	Arpas 3
16-11-1993	Slovenia	W 2-0	Prievidza	Fr	Faktor, Luhovy
2-02-1994	Arab Emirates	W 1-0	Dubai	Fr	Weiss
4-02	Egypt	L 0-1	Dubai	Fr	
6-02	Morocco	L 1-2	Dubai	Fr	Faktor
30-03	Malta	W 2-1	Ta'Qali	Fr	Timko, Hyravy
20-04	Croatia	W 4-1	Bratislava	Fr	Dubovsky 2, Kinder, Moravcik
29-05	Russia	L 1-2	Moscow	Fr	Tittel
16-08	Malta	D 1-1	Bratislava	Fr	Hipp
7-09	France	D 0-0	Bratislava	ECq	
12-10	Israel	D 2-2	Tel Aviv	ECq	Rusnák, Moravcik
12-11	Romania	L 2-3	Bucharest	ECq	Dubovsky, Chvila
22-02-1995	Brazil	L 0-5	Fortaleza	Fr	
8-03	Russia	W 2-1	Bratislava	Fr	Dubovsky 2
29-03	Azerbaijan	W 4-1	Kosice	ECq	Tittel, Timko 2, Dubovsky
26-04	France	L 0-4	Nantes	ECq	
8-05	Czech Republic	D 1-1	Bratislava	Fr	Timko
7-06	Poland	L 0-5	Zabrze	ECq	
22-06	Argentina	L 0-6	Mendoza	Fr	
25-06	Peru	L 0-1	Lima	Fr	

SLOVENIA

In football terms, Slovenia was the weakest of all the republics that made up Yugoslavia. Only Olimpija from the capital Ljubljana ever appeared in the Yugoslav first division, and their only moment of note came when they held Red Star to a draw in the 1970 Cup final before losing in the replay.

Over the years two Slovenians of international class have emerged. Branko Oblak won 46 caps for Yugoslavia between 1970 and 1977, while Srecko Katanec appeared 31 times between 1983 and 1990. He also won an Italian championship medal in 1991 with Sampdoria.

In truth, however, football is not a major passion in Slovenia, especially in Ljubljana where ice hockey dominates. Since independence, Maribor Bronik have threatened Olimpija's pre-eminence and it was in Maribor that the Slovenians made their competitive debut in international football against Italy. They were very unlucky not to beat the World Cup finalists that day, which saw Katanec make his farewell appearance.

Population: 1,948,000
Area, sq km: 20,251
Capital city: Ljubljana

Nagometna Zveza Slovenije
Tabor 14, PP47
61004 Ljubljana
Slovenia
Tel: + 38 61 311888
Fax: + 38 61 302337

Year of formation	1920
Affiliation to FIFA	1992
Affiliation to UEFA	1993
Registered clubs	337
Registered players	15 000
Registered referees	645
National Stadium	Bezigrad, Ljubljana 22 000
National colours	Green/Blue
Season	August - June, with a mid season break December - February

THE RECORD

WORLD CUP

1930-94 Did not enter

EUROPEAN CHAMPIONSHIP

1960-92 Did not enter
1996 QT group 4

EUROPEAN CLUB COMPETITIONS

European Cup
1st round - Olimpia Ljubljana 1993
Cup Winners Cup
1st round - Olimpia Ljubljana 1971, Maribor Branik 1993 1995
UEFA Cup
2nd round - Maribor Branik 1994

CLUB DIRECTORY

LJUBLJANA (Population - 316,000)

NK Zeleznicar Am Cosmos Ljubljana (1910)
ZSD Ljubljana 10,000 – Blue, white trim

NK Olimpija Ljubljana (1911)
Bezigrad 18,000 – Green, white trim
Previous names - Merger in 1962 of Enotnost and Odred

NK Svoboda Ljubljana (1947)
Svoboda 3,000 – Red/White

MARIBOR (Population - 187,000)

Maribor Branik (1958)
Ljudski Vrt 15,000 – Violet, yellow trim

NOVA GORICA (Population - 42,000)

NK HIT Gorica (1947)
Nova Gorica 5,000 – Orange/Orange

KOPER (Population - 41,000)

NK Koper (1950)
Bonifica 10,000 – Blue, yellow trim

VELENJE (Population - 38,000)

Rudar Velenje (1948)
Ob Jezeru 7,000 – Green & black stripes/Green

ISOLA

NK Isola (1946)
Isola 6,000 – Light blue/Blue
Previous name - Belvedur Isola until 1994

MURSKA SOBOTA

Mura Murska Sobota (1946)
Fazanerija 5,000 – Black, white sleeves/Black

ROGASKA SLATINA

Steklar Rogaska Slatina
Comunale 3,000 – White/White

AJDOVSCINA

Primorje Ajdovscina (1924)
Primorje 5,000 – Red/Black

CELJE

Publicum Celje (1946)
Skalna Klet 5,000 – White, light blue sleeves/White, yellow trim

SLOVENIAN LEAGUE CHAMPIONSHIP

1992	Olimpija Ljubljana 66 Maribor Branik 59 Belvedur Isola 56
1993	Olimpija Ljubljana 52 Maribor Branik 48 Mura Murska Sobota 46
1994	Olimpija Ljubljana 51 Mura Murska Sobota 45 Maribor Branik 42
1995	Olimpia Ljubljana 44 Maribor Branik 42 HIT Gorica 41

SLOVENIAN CUP FINALS

1992	Branik Maribor	0-0 4-3p	Olimpija Ljubljana
1993	Olimpija Ljubljana	2-1	Publikum Celje
1994	Maribor Branik	0-1 3-1	Mura Murska Sobota
1995	Mura Murska Sobota	1-1 1-0	Publikum Celje

INTERNATIONAL MATCHES PLAYED BY SLOVENIA

19-06-1991	Croatia	L 0-1	Murska Sobota	Fr	
3-06-1992	Estonia	D 1-1	Tallinn	Fr	Benedejcic
18-11	Cyprus	D 1-1	Larnaca	Fr	Milosevic
7-04-1993	Estonia	W 2-0	Ljubljana	Fr	Zulic, Udovic
13-10	Macedonia	L 1-4	Kranj	Fr	Pate
16-11	Slovakia	L 0-2	Prievidza	Fr	

8-02-1994	Georgia	W 1-0	Ta'Qali	Fr	Gliha
10-02	Tunisia	D 2-2	Ta'Qali	Fr	Jermanis, Binkovski
12-02	Malta	W 1-0	Ta'Qali	Fr	Gliha
22-03	Macedonia	L 0-2	Skopje	Fr	
6-04	Hungary	W 1-0	Szombathely	Fr	Katanec
27-04	Cyprus	W 3-0	Maribor	Fr	Pate 2, Udovic
1-06	Romania	D 0-0	Bucharest	Fr	
7-09	Italy	D 1-1	Maribor	ECq	Udovic
12-10	Ukraine	D 0-0	Kiev	ECq	
16-11	Lithuania	L 1-2	Maribor	ECq	Zahovic
29-03-1995	Estonia	W 3-0	Maribor	ECq	Zahovic, Gliha, Kokol
26-04	Croatia	L 0-2	Zagreb	ECq	
7-06	Lithuania	L 1-2	Vilnius	ECq	Gliha
11-06	Estonia	W 3-1	Tallinn	ECq	Novak, Zahovic

THE FORMER SOVIET UNION

In 1992, the national team of the already defunct Soviet Union, playing under the banner of the Commonwealth of Independent States (CIS), was consigned to history. If not always remembered with affection, the teams from the Soviet era will always command respect.

After the Russian revolution in 1917, which gave birth to the Soviet Union, football came under the control of the state's Committee of Physical Culture and Sport. It meant, as the name suggests, that the game was thoroughly organised along lines that suited the new political masters. Sports clubs were founded for the workers of various organisations and within them a whole host of sports were catered for. The idea was that sport would help in the cultural emancipation of the population, a fundamental tenet of communism. Interestingly, in light of later events, the original idea was not to build athletes capable of taking on the world; that came later, in the 1950s. Football and other sports were used as a mechanism to build the character of individuals and train them in the benefits of working in a group, which was considered vital for the development of the country. In the meantime, the Soviet Union became an international recluse.

The main clubs in Moscow, which after the revolution had become the capital, were the Dynamo club, the Spartak club for the producers' cooperative (formed in 1922), the Torpedo club for workers in the automobile industry (1924), the Lokomotive club for the railway workers (1923) and the army club, known eventually as CSKA, formed in 1923. The same type of organisation was repeated over the whole country. The development of these clubs was important, because although the idea of general sports clubs was not new, having long traditions in the German gymnastic clubs, the Soviet Union was the first country to actively promote them, and the system within which they functioned served as a role model for numerous countries around the world.

Competition did creep into this highly structured system in the 1930s and in 1936 a national football league was formed. Right from the start, the clubs from Moscow dominated the competition, and it was not until Dynamo Kiev's win in 1961 that a club from outside the capital won the championship. Soviet sides did play in friendly matches whenever the occasion merited, but despite the increase in international competition in the rest of Europe, the Soviet Union remained aloof.

Quite how far they had developed became apparent when Dynamo Moscow toured Sweden and Great Britain in 1945 in a gesture of friendship and to celebrate the victory over fascism. IFK Norrköping were beaten 5-0, the matches against Chelsea and Glasgow Rangers ended in draws, Cardiff City were beaten 10-1, whilst in the final match, Arsenal were beaten 4-3 on a foggy day at Highbury. Dynamo were shown to be a methodical team and highly trained, if lacking in flair, and as the Soviet Union began to open up to the West, this type of approach was to become a familar sight. A team travelled to Finland for the 1952 Olympic Games, but after beating Bulgaria in the first round and drawing 5-5 with Yugoslavia in a remarkable game in Tampere, they lost the replay and disappeared from sight for a further two years.

Only in 1955 did the Soviet Federation start to organise a proper international fixture list. A tour was made of India and in August that year, in an historic match, West Germany, the world champions, travelled to Moscow and were beaten 3-2 in the Soviets' first meeting with a major Western power. The following year they won the gold medal in the Melbourne Olympic Games, but due to a very poor field, the title did not carry a great deal of weight. Hopes were high for the 1958 World Cup, the first time they had entered the world's premier tournament. With a good if unspectacular side, they dumped England out of the competition before losing to the hosts Sweden in the quarter-finals.

The most notable names in the side at the time were the captain Igor Netto, Valentin Ivanov, Nikita Simonyan and the brilliant Lev Yashin in goal. This was the basis of the side that won the first European Championship two years later, along with the talented Slava Metreveli and Viktor Ponedelnik. Having beaten Yugoslavia in the final of the 1956 Olympic Games, they consigned the poor Yugoslavs to yet another runners-up spot, this time by a score of 2-1 in Paris. This victory was to be the only major title ever won by the Soviet Union in its entire history.

With a remarkably stable side, which was perhaps to be expected from a country that took its sport so seriously, the Soviet Union did consistently well in the 1960s without ever shining, and it was this lack of extra sparkle that perhaps cost them the chance of more titles. They lost in the final of the 1964 European Championship to Spain, and again to West Germany in 1972, whilst reaching the semi-finals in between in 1968. Had the coin landed on the other side after the semi-final draw with Italy that year, they would have appeared in a remarkable four consecutive finals. Finishing as quarter-finalists in the 1962 World Cup and semi-finalists in England four years later further reinforced the belief that the Soviets just did not have what it took to win a tournament, and it should not be forgotten that none of the major powers took part in the first European Championship which they won.

THE ORDER OF MERIT

		All			League			Cup		Europe		
	Team	G	S	B	G	S	B	G	S	G	S	B
1	Dynamo Kiev	24	13	5	13	11	3	9	2	2	-	2
2	Spartak Moskva	22	17	10	12	12	9	10	5	-	-	1
3	Dynamo Moskva	17	17	7	11	11	5	6	5	-	1	2
4	CSKA Moskva	12	7	6	7	4	6	5	3	-	-	-
5	Torpedo Moskva	9	12	6	3	3	6	6	9	-	-	-
6	Dynamo Tbilisi	5	11	14	2	5	13	2	6	1	-	1
7	Shachter Donetsk	4	6	2	-	2	2	4	4	-	-	-
8	Ararat Yerevan	3	4	-	1	2	-	2	2	-	-	-
9	Dnepr Dnepropetrovsk	3	2	2	2	2	2	1	-	-	-	-
10	Zenit Leningrad	2	3	1	1	-	1	1	3	-	-	-
11	Lokomotiv Moskva	2	2	-	-	1	-	2	1	-	-	-
12	SKA Rostov-na-Donu	1	3	-	-	1	-	1	2	-	-	-
13	Zarja Lugansk	1	2	-	1	-	-	-	2	-	-	-
14	Dynamo Minsk	1	1	3	1	-	3	-	1	-	-	-
15	Metalist Kharkov	1	1	-	-	-	-	1	1	-	-	-
16	SKA Karpati Lvov	1	-	-	-	-	-	1	-	-	-	-
17	Kriliya Kuybyshev	-	2	-	-	-	-	-	2	-	-	-
18	Komanda Kalilin	-	1	-	-	-	-	-	1	-	-	-
	Pachtakor Tashkent	-	1	-	-	-	-	-	1	-	-	-
	ZT Orechovo-Zujevo	-	1	-	-	-	-	-	1	-	-	-
21	Chernomorets Odessa	-	-	1	-	-	1	-	-	-	-	-
	Metallurg Moskva	-	-	1	-	-	1	-	-	-	-	-
	Neftchi Baku	-	-	1	-	-	1	-	-	-	-	-
	Zalgiris Vilnius	-	-	1	-	-	1	-	-	-	-	-

Final standings for the Soviet Union

At club level, the 1960s saw the rise of teams from outside Moscow, especially from the Ukraine which was establishing itself as a major football base. Leading the challenge were Dynamo Kiev and also very successful were the top side from Georgia, Dynamo Tbilisi. They share with Kiev the honour of being the only Soviet sides to win a European club competition. Dynamo Moscow lost in the 1972 Cup Winners Cup final to Glasgow Rangers, but Kiev went one better in 1975 when they beat the Hungarians Ferencváros 3-0 in Basle. Dynamo Tbilisi won the same tournament six years later before a poor crowd in Dusseldorf against Carl Zeiss Jena. Five years after that, and once again in the Cup Winners Cup, Kiev won with an impressive 3-0 victory over Atlético Madrid in Lyon.

The European Cup and UEFA Cup were different stories altogether and the record in both dismal. Three semi-final appearances in the European Cup is a record similar to a country like Switzerland, whilst in the UEFA Cup, the furthest a Soviet side reached is the quarter-finals, and then only on three occasions. Why they performed so poorly, despite the capacity to generate huge crowds, is a mystery that can not be explained away with the same reasons as for the failure of the national side.

The 1970s was a curious time for Soviet football, failing to qualify as they did for both the 1974 and 1978 World Cups. In 1974 they refused to play Chile in the Estadio Nacional in Santiago which had been used as a prison after the coup there in 1973, and were forced to withdraw, whilst in 1978 they finished second in their group behind Hungary. But in 1972 the first real star of Soviet football, Oleg Blokhin, made his debut for the national side, and despite missing out in 1974 and 1978, he was able to display his talents on the world stage in 1982 in Spain and again four years later in Mexico. He will go down in history as the most capped player in the history of the Soviet side as well as their top scorer. Voted European Footballer of the Year in 1975, along with Lev Yashin he is probably the finest footballer his country has ever produced.

In the 1988 European Championships, the Soviets once again reached the final and once again found themselves playing a minor role next to the real stars of the show. In 1964 it was the Spain of Suárez, Amancio and Zoco. In 1972 it was the Germans of Beckenbauer, Netzer and Müller, whilst in 1988 it was as sidekicks to Gullit, Van Basten and Rijkaard of Holland. Never again as the Soviet Union, however, will they have the chance to prove that they can be the main event.

THE RECORD

WORLD CUP

1930-54	Did not enter
1958	QT 1st/3 in group 6 - Final Tournament/Quarter-finalists
1962	QT 1st/3 in group 5 - Final Tournament/Quarter-finalists
1966	QT 1st/4 in group 7 - Final Tournament/Semi-finalists/ 4th place
1970	QT 1st/3 in group 4 - Final Tournament/Quarter-finalists
1974	QT 1st/3 in group 9 (Withdrew)
1978	QT 2nd/3 in group 9
1982	QT 1st/5 in group 3 - Final Tournament/2nd round
1986	QT 2nd/5 in group 6 - Final Tournament/2nd round
1990	QT 1st/5 in group 3 - Final Tournament/1st round

EUROPEAN CHAMPIONSHIP

1960	Winners
1964	Finalists
1968	QT 1st/4 in group 3 - Final Tournament/Semi-finalists/ 4th place
1972	QT 1st/4 in group 4 - Final Tournament/Finalists
1976	QT 1st/4 in group 6 - Final Tournament/Quarter-finalists
1980	QT 4th/4 in group 6
1984	QT 2nd/4 in group 2
1988	QT 1st/5 in group 3 - Final Tournament/Finalists
1992	QT 1st/5 in group 3 - Final Tournament/1st round

EUROPEAN CLUB COMPETITIONS

European Cup

Semi-finalists - Dynamo Kiev 1977 1987 Spartak Moscow 1991

Cup Winners Cup

Winners - Dynamo Kiev 1975, 1986 Dynamo Tbilisi 1981

Finalists - Dynamo Moscow 1972

UEFA Cup

Quarter-finalists - Spartak Moscow 1984 Dynamo Minsk 1985 Torpedo Moscow 1991

SOVIET LEAGUE CHAMPIONSHIP

1936b3	Dynamo Moskva 18 Dynamo Kiev 14 Spartak Moskva 13
1936am	Spartak Moskva 17 Dynamo Moskva 16 Dynamo Tbilisi 16
1937g2	Dynamo Moskva 38 Spartak Moskva 37 Dynamo Kiev 36
1938m	Spartak Moskva 39 CDKA Moskva 37 Metallurg Moskva 37
1939n	Spartak Moskva 37 Dynamo Tbilisi 33 CDKA Moskva 32
1940l	Dynamo Moskva 36 Dynamo Tbilisi 34 Spartak Moskva 31
1941-44	-
1945k	Dynamo Moskva 40 CDKA Moskva 39 Torpedo Moskva 27
1946	CDKA Moskva 37 Dynamo Moskva 33 Dynamo Tbilisi 33
1947l	CDKA Moskva 40 Dynamo Moskva 40 Dynamo Tbilisi 33
1948n	CDKA Moskva 41 Dynamo Moskva 40 Spartak Moskva 37
1949t	Dynamo Moskva 57 CDKA Moskva 51 Spartak Moskva 49
1950u	CDKA Moskva 53 Dynamo Moskva 50 Dynamo Tbilisi 47
1951p	CDSA Moskva 43 Dynamo Tbilisi 36 Shachter Stalino 34
1952ag	Spartak Moskva 20 Dynamo Kiev 17 Dynamo Moskva 17
1953i	Spartak Moskva 29 Dynamo Tbilisi 27 Torpedo Moskva 25
1954l	Dynamo Moskva 35 Spartak Moskva 32 Spartak Minsk 31
1955k	Dynamo Moskva 34 Spartak Moskva 33 CDSA Moskva 31
1956	Spartak Moskva 34 Dynamo Moskva 28 CDSA Moskva 25
1957	Dynamo Moskva 36 Torpedo Moskva 28 Spartak Moskva 28
1958	Spartak Moskva 32 Dynamo Moskva 31 CSK Moskva 27
1959	Dynamo Moskva 31 Lokomotiv Moskva 29 Dynamo Tbilisi 27
1960d	Torpedo Moskva 14 Dynamo Kiev 11 Dynamo Moskva 11
1961q4	Dynamo Kiev 45 Torpedo Moskva 41 Spartak Moskva 40
1962k	Spartak Moskva 32 Dynamo Moskva 29 Dynamo Tbilisi 28
1963v	Dynamo Moskva 55 Spartak Moskva 52 Dynamo Minsk 48
1964r	Dynamo Tbilisi 46 Torpedo Moskva 46 CSKA Moskva 43
1965	Torpedo Moskva 51 Dynamo Kiev 50 CSKA Moskva 38
1966u	Dynamo Kiev 56 SKA Rostov-na-Donu 47 Neftchi Baku 45
1967	Dynamo Kiev 54 Dynamo Moskva 48 Dynamo Tbilisi 45
1968v	Dynamo Kiev 57 Spartak Moskva 52 Torpedo Moskva 50
1969n	Spartak Moskva 43 Dynamo Kiev 39 Dynamo Tbilisi 35
1970r	CSKA Moskva 45 Dynamo Moskva 45 Spartak Moskva 38
1971q	Dynamo Kiev 44 Ararat Yerevan 37 Dynamo Tbilisi 36
1972	Zarja Vorosch'grad 40 Dynamo Kiev 35 Dynamo Tbilisi 35
1973	Ararat Yerevan 39 Dynamo Kiev 36 Dynamo Moskva 33
1974	Dynamo Kiev 40 Spartak Moskva 39 Chernomorets Odessa 35
1975	Dynamo Kiev 43 Shachter Donetsk 38 Dynamo Moskva 38
1976ah	Dynamo Moskva 22 Ararat Yerevan 19 Dynamo Tbilisi 18
1976	Torpedo Moskva 20 Dynamo Kiev 18 Dynamo Tbilisi 17
1977q	Dynamo Kiev 43 Dynamo Tbilisi 39 Torpedo Moskva 37
1978	Dynamo Tbilisi 42 Dynamo Kiev 38 Shachter Donetsk 37
1979t	Spartak Moskva 50 Shachter Donetsk 48 Dynamo Kiev 47
1980	Dynamo Kiev 51 Spartak Moskva 45 Zenit Leningrad 42
1981	Dynamo Kiev 53 Spartak Moskva 46 Dynamo Tbilisi 42
1982	Dynamo Minsk 47 Dynamo Kiev 46 Spartak Moskva 41
1983	Dnepr Dnepropetrovsk 49 Spartak Moskva 45 Dynamo Minsk 43
1984	Zenit Leningrad 47 Spartak Moskva 45 Dnepr Dnepropetrovsk 42
1985	Dynamo Kiev 48 Spartak Moskva 46 Dnepr Dnepropetrovsk 42
1986q	Dynamo Kiev 39 Dynamo Moskva 38 Spartak Moskva 37
1987	Spartak Moskva 42 Dnepr Dnepropetrovsk 39 Zalgiris Vilnius 36
1988	Dnepr Dnepropetrovsk 46 Dynamo Kiev 43 Torpedo Moskva 42
1989	Spartak Moskva 44 Dnepr Dnepropetrovsk 42 Dynamo Kiev 38
1990l	Dynamo Kiev 34 CSKA Moskva 31 Dynamo Moskva 31
1991q	CSKA Moskva 43 Spartak Moskva 41 Torpedo Moskva 36

SOVIET CUP FINALS

1936	Lokomotiv Moskva	2-0	Dynamo Tbilisi
1937	Dynamo Moskva	5-2	Dynamo Tbilisi
1938	Spartak Moskva	3-2	Elektrik Leningrad
1939	Spartak Moskva	3-1	Stalinets Leningrad
1940-43	-		
1944	Zenit Leningrad	2-1	CDKA Moskva
1945	CDKA Moskva	2-1	Dynamo Moskva
1946	Spartak Moskva	3-2	Dynamo Tbilisi
1947	Spartak Moskva	2-0	Torpedo Moskva
1948	CDKA Moskva	3-0	Spartak Moskva
1949	Torpedo Moskva	2-1	Dynamo Moskva
1950	Spartak Moskva	3-0	Dynamo Moskva
1951	CDSA Moskva	2-1	Komanda Kalinin
1952	Torpedo Moskva	1-0	Spartak Moskva
1953	Dynamo Moskva	1-0	Kriliya Kuybyshev
1954	Dynamo Kiev	2-1	Spartak Yerevan
1955	CDSA Moskva	2-1	Dynamo Moskva
1956	-		
1957	Lokomotiv Moskva	1-0	Spartak Moskva
1958	Spartak Moskva	1-0	Torpedo Moskva
1959	-		
1960	Torpedo Moskva	4-3	Dynamo Tbilisi
1961	Shachter Donetsk	3-1	Torpedo Moskva
1962	Shachter Donetsk	2-0	ZT Orechovo-Zujevo
1963	Spartak Moskva	2-1	Shachter Donetsk
1964	Dynamo Kiev	1-0	Kriliya Kuybyshev
1965	Spartak Moskva	0-0 2-1	Dynamo Minsk
1966	Dynamo Kiev	2-0	Torpedo Moskva
1967	Dynamo Moskva	3-0	CSKA Moskva
1968	Torpedo Moskva	1-0	Pakhtakor Tashkent
1969	SKA Karpati Lvov	2-1	SKA Rostov-na-Donu
1970	Dynamo Moskva	2-1	Dynamo Tbilisi
1971	Spartak Moskva	2-1	SKA Rostov-na-Donu
1972	Torpedo Moskva	0-0 1-1 4-1p	Spartak Moskva
1973	Ararat Yerevan	2-1	Dynamo Kiev
1974	Dynamo Kiev	3-0	Zarja Voroshilovgrad
1975	Ararat Yerevan	2-1	Zarja Voroshilovgrad
1976	Dynamo Tbilisi	3-0	Ararat Yerevan
1977	Dynamo Moskva	1-0	Torpedo Moskva
1978	Dynamo Kiev	2-1	Shachter Donetsk
1979	Dynamo Tbilisi	0-0 5-4p	Dynamo Moskva
1980	Shachter Donetsk	2-1	Dynamo Tbilisi
1981	SKA Rostov-na-Donu	1-0	Spartak Moskva
1982	Dynamo Kiev	1-0	Torpedo Moskva
1983	Shachter Donetsk	1-0	Metalist Kharkov
1984	Dynamo Moskva	2-0	Zenit Leningrad
1985	Dynamo Kiev	2-1	Shachter Donetsk
1986	Torpedo Moskva	1-0	Shachter Donetsk
1987	Dynamo Kiev	3-3 4-3p	Dynamo Minsk
1988	Metalist Kharkov	2-0	Torpedo Moskva
1989	Dnepr Dnepropetrovsk	1-0	Torpedo Moskva
1990	Dynamo Kiev	6-1	Lokomotiv Moskva
1991	CSKA Moskva	3-2	Torpedo Moskva
1992	Spartak Moskva	2-0	CSKA Moskva

LEADING INTERNATIONAL GOALSCORERS

39	Oleg Blokhin	(Dynamo Kiev)	1972-1988
29	Oleg Protasov	(Dnepr,Dinamo Kiev, Olympiakos)	1984-1992
26	Valentin Ivanov	(Torpedo Moskva)	1955-1965
24	Eduard Strelitsov	(Torpedo Moskva)	1955-1967
22	Viktor Kolotov	(Rubin Kazan,Dynamo Kiev)	1970-1978
20	Viktor Ponedelnik	(SKA Rostov-Na-Donu, Spartak Moskva)	1960-1966
19	Anatoly Banishevski	(Neftchi Baku)	1965-1972
	Igor Chislenko	(Dynamo Moskva)	1961-1968
15	Anatoly Byshovets	(Dynamo Kiev)	1966-1972
	Anatoly Ilyin	(Spartak Moskva)	1952-1959

LEADING INTERNATIONAL APPEARANCES

109	Oleg Blokhin	(Dynamo Kiev)	1972-1988
94	Rinat Dasayev	(Spartak Moskva/Sevilla)	1979-1990
89	Albert Shesternev	(CSKA Moskva)	1961-1971
82	Vladimir Bessonov	(Dynamo Kiev)	1977-1990
80	Anatoly Demyanenko	(Dynamo Kiev)	1981-1990
77	Sergei Aleinikov	(Dynamo Minsk,Juventus, Lecce)	1984-1992
75	Lev Yashin	(Dynamo Moskva)	1954-1967
68	Oleg Protasov	(Dnepr,Dinamo Kiev, Olympiakos)	1984-1992
67	Murtaz Khurtsilava	(Dynamo Tbilisi)	1965-1973
65	Valery Voronin	(Torpedo Moskva)	1960-1968

Complete record 1952-1992

NATIONAL TEAM COACHES

B.Arkadev	1952
B.Sokolov	1954
Gavril Katchalin	1955-58
G.Glazkov	1959
Mikhail Yakushin	1959
Gavril Katchalin	1960-62
Konstantin Beskov & N.Simonyan	1963-64
N.Morozov	1964-66
Mikhail Yakushin	1967-68
Gavril Katchalin	1969-70
Valentin Nikolaev	1970-71
N.Gylyaev	1972
G.Zonin	1972
E.Goryanski	1973
Konstantin Beskov	1974
Valery Lobanovski	1975-76
Valentin Nikolaev	1976
Nikita Simonyan	1976-79
O.Basilevich	1979
Konstantin Beskov	1979-82
Valery Lobanovski	1982-83
Eduard Malofeev	1984-86
Valery Lobanovski	1986-90
Anatoly Byshovets	1990-92

INTERNATIONAL MATCHES PLAYED BY THE SOVIET UNION

15-07-1952	Bulgaria	W 2-1	Kotka	OGr1	Bobrov, Trofimov
20-07	Yugoslavia	D 5-5	Tampere	OGr2	Bobrov 3, Trofimov, Petrov
22-07	Yugoslavia	L 1-3	Tampere	OGr2	Bobrov
8-09-1954	Sweden	W 7-0	Moscow	Fr	Simonyan 2, Ilyin, OG, Gogoberidze, Salinikov 2
26-09	Hungary	D 1-1	Moscow	Fr	Salinikov
6-02-1955	India	W 4-0	Dehli	Fr	Kuznetsov.U 3, Voinov
27-02	India	W 3-0	Bombay	Fr	Simonyan 2, Tatushin
2-03	India	W 3-0	Calcutta	Fr	Tatushin 2, Voinov
26-06	Sweden	W 6-0	Stockholm	Fr	Strelitsov 3, Tatushin, Salinikov, Ivanov.V
21-08	West Germany	W 3-2	Moscow	Fr	Parshin, Maslenkin, Ilyin
16-09	India	W 11-1	Moscow	Fr	Shabrov 2, Strelitsov 3, Salinikov 3, Kuznetsov.U 2, Netto
25-09	Hungary	D 1-1	Budapest	Fr	Kuznetsov.U
23-10	France	D 2-2	Moscow	Fr	Strelitsov, Simonyan
23-05-1956	Denmark	W 5-1	Moscow	Fr	Ivanov.V, Salinikov 2, Strelitsov, Ilyin
1-07	Denmark	W 5-2	Copenhagen	Fr	Ilyin 3, Isaev, Tatushin
11-07	Israel	W 5-0	Moscow	OGq	Tatushin, Ivanov.V 2, Simonyan 2
31-07	Israel	W 2-1	Tel Aviv	OGq	Ilyin, Tatushin
15-09	West Germany	W 2-1	Hanover	Fr	Strelitsov, Ivanov.V
23-09	Hungary	L 0-1	Moscow	Fr	
21-10	France	L 1-2	Paris	Fr	Isaev
29-11	Indonesia	D 0-0	Melbourne	OGqf	
1-12	Indonesia	W 4-0	Melbourne	OGqf	Salinikov 2, Ivanov.V, Netto
5-12	Bulgaria	W 2-1	Melbourne	OGsf	Strelitsov, Tatushin
8-12	Yugoslavia	W 1-0	Melbourne	OGf	Ilyin
1-06-1957	Romania	D 1-1	Moscow	Fr	Strelitsov
23-06	Poland	W 3-0	Moscow	WCq	Tatushin, Simonyan, Ilyin
21-07	Bulgaria	W 4-0	Sofia	Fr	Strelitsov 2, Ilyin, Isaev
27-07	Finland	W 2-1	Moscow	WCq	Voinov, Netto
15-08	Finland	W 10-0	Helsinki	WCq	Netto, Simonyan 3, Isaev 2, Strelitsov 2, Ilyin 2
22-09	Hungary	W 2-1	Budapest	Fr	Tatushin, Strelitsov
20-10	Poland	L 1-2	Chorzow	WCq	Ivanov.V
24-11	Poland	W 2-0	Leipzig	WCq	Strelitsov, Fedosov
18-05-1958	England	D 1-1	Moscow	Fr	Ivanov.V
8-06	England	D 2-2	Gothenburg	WCr1	Simonyan, Ivanov.A
11-06	Austria	W 2-0	Boras	WCr1	Ilyin, Ivanov.V
15-06	Brazil	L 0-2	Gothenburg	WCr1	
17-06	England	W 1-0	Gothenburg	WCr1	Ilyin
19-06	Sweden	L 0-2	Stockholm	WCqf	
30-08	Czechoslovakia	W 2-1	Prague	Fr	Voroshilov, Voinov

28-09	Hungary	W 3-1	Moscow	ECr1	Ilyin, Metreveli, Ivanov.V
22-10	England	L 0-5	London	Fr	
27-06-1959	Bulgaria	D 1-1	Moscow	OGq	Korolenkov
19-07	Romania	W 2-0	Moscow	OGq	Yurin, Metreveli
2-08	Romania	D 0-0	Bucharest	OGq	
6-09	Czechoslovakia	W 3-1	Moscow	Fr	Bubukin, Meshi, Ivanov.V
13-09	Bulgaria	L 0-1	Sofia	OGq	
27-09	Hungary	W 1-0	Budapest	ECr1	Voinov
3-10	China	W 1-0	Peking	Fr	Ilyin
19-05-1960	Poland	W 7-1	Moscow	Fr	Ivanov 2, Bubukin, Ponedelnik 3, Metreveli
	Spain		Walk-over	ECqf	Spain withdrew
6-07	Czechoslovakia	W 3-0	Marseille	ECsf	Ivanov.V 2, Ponedelnik
10-07	Yugoslavia	W 2-1	Paris	ECf	Metreveli, Ponedelnik
17-08	East Germany	W 1-0	Leipzig	Fr	Ponedelnik
4-09	Austria	L 1-3	Vienna	Fr	Ponedelnik
21-05-1961	Poland	L 0-1	Warsaw	Fr	
18-06	Turkey	W 1-0	Moscow	WCq	Voronin
24-06	Argentina	D 0-0	Moscow	Fr	
1-07	Norway	W 5-2	Moscow	WCq	Metreveli, Ponedelnik, Bubukin 2, Meshi
23-08	Norway	W 3-0	Oslo	WCq	Ponedelnik, Meshi, Metreveli
10-09	Austria	L 0-1	Moscow	Fr	
12-11	Turkey	W 2-1	Istanbul	WCq	Gusarov, Mamikin
18-11	Argentina	W 2-1	Buenos Aires	Fr	Ponedelnik 2
22-11	Chile	W 1-0	Santiago	Fr	Mamikin
29-11	Uruguay	W 2-1	Montevideo	Fr	Gusarov, Ponedelnik
11-04-1962	Luxembourg	W 3-1	Luxembourg	Fr	Mamikin 2, Gusarov
18-04	Sweden	W 2-0	Stockholm	Fr	Ponedelnik, Mamikin
27-04	Uruguay	W 5-0	Moscow	Fr	Mamikin 3, Chislenko, Ivanov.V
3-05	East Germany	W 2-1	Moscow	Fr	Ponedelnik, Chislenko
31-05	Yugoslavia	W 2-0	Arica	WCr1	Ivanov.V, Ponedelnik
3-06	Colombia	D 4-4	Arica	WCr1	Ivanov.V 2, Chislenko, Ponedelnik
6-06	Uruguay	W 2-1	Arica	WCr1	Mamikin, Ivanov.V
10-06	Chile	L 1-2	Arica	WCqf	Chislenko
22-05-1963	Sweden	L 0-1	Moscow	Fr	
22-09	Hungary	D 1-1	Moscow	Fr	Ivanov.V
13-10	Italy	W 2-0	Moscow	ECr2	Ponedelnik, Chislenko
10-11	Italy	D 1-1	Rome	ECr2	Gusarov
1-12	Morocco	D 1-1	Casablanca	Fr	OG
13-05-1964	Sweden	D 1-1	Stockholm	ECqf	Ivanov.V
20-05	Uruguay	W 1-0	Moscow	Fr	Mudrik
27-05	Sweden	W 3-1	Moscow	ECqf	Pondelnik 2, Voronin
17-06	Denmark	W 3-0	Barcelona	ECsf	Voronin, Pondelnik, Ivanov.V
21-06	Spain	L 1-2	Madrid	ECf	Khusainov
11-10	Austria	L 0-1	Vienna	Fr	
4-11	Algeria	D 2-2	Algiers	Fr	Mateev, Khusainov
22-11	Yugoslavia	D 1-1	Belgrade	Fr	Serebrjanikov
29-11	Bulgaria	D 0-0	Sofia	Fr	
16-05-1965	Austria	D 0-0	Moscow	Fr	
23-05	Greece	W 3-1	Moscow	WCq	Kazakov, Ivanov.V 2
30-05	Wales	W 2-1	Moscow	WCq	Ivanov.V, OG
27-06	Denmark	W 6-0	Moscow	WCq	Khusainov, Metreveli, Voronin, Barkaj 2, Meshi
4-07	Brazil	L 0-3	Moscow	Fr	
4-09	Yugoslavia	D 0-0	Moscow	Fr	
3-10	Greece	W 4-1	Athens	WCq	Metreveli, Banishevski 3
17-10	Denmark	W 3-1	Copenhagen	WCq	Metreveli, Malofiev, Sabo
27-10	Wales	L 1-2	Cardiff	WCq	Banishevski
21-11	Brazil	D 2-2	Rio de Janeiro	Fr	Banishevski, Metreveli
1-12	Argentina	D 1-1	Buenos Aires	Fr	Banishevski
4-12	Uruguay	W 3-1	Montevideo	Fr	Khusainov, Banishevski, Osynin
23-02-1966	Chile	W 2-0	Santiago	Fr	Sabo 2
20-04	Switzerland	D 2-2	Basle	Fr	Chislenko, Ponedelnik
24-04	Austria	W 1-0	Vienna	Fr	Voronin
18-05	Czechoslovakia	W 2-1	Prague	Fr	Banishevski 2
22-05	Belgium	W 1-0	Brussels	Fr	Serebrjanikov
5-06	France	D 3-3	Moscow	Fr	Metreveli, Banishevski, Chislenko
12-07	North Korea	W 3-0	Middlesbrough	WCr1	Malofiev 2, Banishevski
16-07	Italy	W 1-0	Sunderland	WCr1	Chislenko
20-07	Chile	W 2-1	Sunderland	WCr1	Porkujan 2
23-07	Hungary	W 2-1	Sunderland	WCqf	Chislenko, Porkujan
25-07	West Germany	L 1-2	Liverpool	WCsf	Porkujan
28-07	Portugal	L 1-2	London	WC3p	Metreveli

18-09	Yugoslavia	W 2-1	Belgrade	Fr	Krasnitski, Mateev
16-10	Turkey	L 0-2	Moscow	Fr	
23-10	East Germany	D 2-2	Moscow	Fr	Strelitsov, Chislenko
1-11	Italy	L 0-1	Milan	Fr	
10-05-1967	Scotland	W 2-0	Glasgow	Fr	OG, Medvidi
28-05	Mexico	W 2-0	Leningrad	Fr	Chislenko, Byshovets
3-06	France	W 4-2	Paris	Fr	Chislenko 2, Byshovets, Strelitsov
11-06	Austria	W 4-3	Moscow	ECq	Malofiev, Byshovets, Chislenko, Strelitsov
16-07	Greece	W 4-0	Tbilisi	ECq	Banishevski 2, Sabo, Chislenko
20-07	Poland	W 1-0	Warsaw	OGq	Chislenko
4-08	Poland	W 2-1	Moscow	OGq	Chislenko, Banishevski
30-08	Finland	W 2-0	Moscow	ECq	Khurtzilava, Chislenko
6-09	Finland	W 5-2	Turku	ECq	Sabo 2, Maslov, Banishevski, Malofiev
1-10	Switzerland	D 2-2	Moscow	Fr	Khurtzilava, OG
8-10	Bulgaria	W 2-1	Sofia	Fr	Strelitsov, Banishevski
15-10	Austria	L 0-1	Vienna	ECq	
31-10	Greece	W 1-0	Athens	ECq	Malofiev
29-11	Holland	L 1-3	Rotterdam	Fr	Maslov
6-12	England	D 2-2	London	Fr	Chislenko 2
17-12	Chile	W 4-1	Santiago	Fr	OG, Strelitsov 3
3-03-1968	Mexico	D 0-0	Mexico City	Fr	
7-03	Mexico	D 1-1	Leon	Fr	Byshovets
10-03	Mexico	D 0-0	Mexico City	Fr	
24-04	Belgium	W 1-0	Moscow	Fr	Sabo
4-05	Hungary	L 0-2	Budapest	ECqf	
11-05	Hungary	W 3-0	Moscow	ECqf	OG, Khurtzilava, Byshovets
5-06	Italy	D 0-0	Naples	ECsf	Italy won on toss of coin
8-06	England	L 0-2	Rome	EC3p	
16-06	Austria	W 3-1	Leningrad	Fr	Vyun, Gershkovich, Asatiani
1-08	Sweden	D 2-2	Gothenburg	Fr	Gershkovich, Khurtzilava
20-02-1969	Colombia	W 3-1	Bogota	Fr	Gershkovich, Kmelnitski 2
25-07	East Germany	D 2-2	Leipzig	Fr	Puzach, Kmelnitski
6-08	Sweden	L 0-1	Moscow	Fr	
10-09	Nth. Ireland	D 0-0	Belfast	WCq	
24-09	Yugoslavia	W 3-1	Belgrade	Fr	Asatiani, Nodija, Byshovets
15-10	Turkey	W 3-0	Kiev	WCq	Muntjan 2, Nodija
22-10	Nth. Ireland	W 2-0	Moscow	WCq	Nodija, Byshovets
16-11	Turkey	W 3-1	Istanbul	WCq	Asianti 2, Kmelnitski
14-02-1970	Peru	D 0-0	Lima	Fr	
20-02	Peru	W 2-0	Lima	Fr	Byshovets 2
22-02	El Salvador	W 2-0	San Salvador	Fr	Puzach, Serebrjanikov
26-02	Mexico	D 0-0	Mexico City	Fr	
5-05	Bulgaria	D 3-3	Sofia	Fr	Evrushihin, Byshovets, Nodija
6-05	Bulgaria	D 0-0	Sofia	Fr	
31-05	Mexico	D 0-0	Mexico City	WCr1	
6-06	Belgium	W 4-1	Mexico City	WCr1	Byshovets 2, Asatiani, Kmelnitski
10-06	El Salvador	W 2-0	Mexico City	WCr1	Byshovets 2
14-06	Uruguay	L 0-1	Mexico City	WCqf	
28-10	Yugoslavia	W 4-0	Moscow	Fr	Shevchenko, Fedotov, Kolotov, Nodija
15-11	Cyprus	W 3-1	Nicosia	ECq	Kolotov, Evrushihin, Shevchenko
17-02-1971	Mexico	D 0-0	Guadalajara	Fr	
19-02	Mexico	D 0-0	Mexico City	Fr	
28-02	El Salvador	W 1-0	San Salvador	Fr	OG
28-04	Bulgaria	D 1-1	Sofia	Fr	Shevchenko
30-05	Spain	W 2-1	Moscow	ECq	Kolotov, Shevchenko
7-06	Cyprus	W 6-1	Moscow	ECq	Fedotov 2, Evrushihin 2, Kolotov, Banishevski
14-06	Scotland	W1-0	Moscow	Fr	Evrushihin
18-09	India	W 5-0	Moscow	Fr	Kolotov 3, Kmelnitski 2
22-09	Nth. Ireland	W 1-0	Moscow	ECq	Muntjan
13-10	Nth. Ireland	D 1-1	Belfast	ECq	Byshovets
27-10	Spain	D 0-0	Seville	ECq	
29-03-1972	Bulgaria	D 1-1	Sofia	Fr	Kolotov
19-04	Peru	W 2-0	Kiev	Fr	Banishevski, Konkov
30-04	Yugoslavia	D 0-0	Belgrade	ECqf	
13-05	Yugoslavia	W 3-0	Moscow	ECqf	Kolotov, Banishevski, Kozinkevich
26-05	West Germany	L 1-4	Munich	Fr	Kolotov
7-06	Bulgaria	W 1-0	Moscow	Fr	Muntjan
14-06	Hungary	W 1-0	Brussels	ECsf	Konkov
18-06	West Germany	L 0-3	Brussels	ECf	
29-06	Uruguay	W 1-0	Sao Paulo	Clr2	Onishenko
2-07	Argentina	L0-1	Belo Horizonte	Clr2	

Date	Opponent	Result	Venue	Comp	Scorers
6-07	Portugal	L 0-1	Belo Horizonte	Clr2	
16-07	Finland	D 1-1	Vaasa	Fr	Blokhin
6-08	Sweden	D 4-4	Stockholm	Fr	Yeliseev, Andreasjan, Semenov, Blokhin
28-08	Burma	W 1-0	Regensburg	OGr1	Kolotov
30-08	Sudan	W 2-1	Munich	OGr1	Evrushihin, Zanazanyan
1-09	Mexico *	W 4-1	Regensburg	OGr1	Blokhin 3, Semenov
3-09	Morocco	W 3-0	Munich	OGr2	Semenov, Kolotov, Yeliseev
5-09	Poland	L 1-2	Augsburg	OGr2	Blokhin
8-09	Denmark *	W 4-0	Augsburg	OGr2	Kolotov, Semenov, Blokhin, Sabo
10-09	East Germany	D 2-2	Munich	OG3p	Blokhin, Khurtsilava
13-10	France	L 0-1	Paris	WCq	
18-10	Rep. Ireland	W 2-1	Dublin	WCq	Fedotov, Kolotov
28-03-1973	Bulgaria	L 0-1	Plovdiv	Fr	
18-04	Romania	W 2-0	Kiev	Fr	Onishenko, Muntjan
13-05	Rep. Ireland	W 1-0	Moscow	WCq	Onishenko
26-05	France	W 2-0	Moscow	WCq	Blokhin, Onishenko
10-06	England	L 1-2	Moscow	Fr	Muntjan
21-06	Brazil	L 0-1	Moscow	Fr	
5-08	Sweden	D 0-0	Moscow	Fr	
5-09	West Germany	L 0-1	Moscow	Fr	
26-09	Chile	D 0-0	Moscow	WCq	
17-10	East Germany	L 0-1	Leipzig	Fr	
21-11	Chile	L 0-2	Santiago	WCq	Soviet Union withdrew. Chile awarded game
17-04-1974	Yugoslavia	W 1-0	Zenica	Fr	Kipiani
20-05	Czechoslovakia	L 0-1	Odessa	Fr	
30-10	Rep. Ireland	L 0-3	Dublin	ECq	
2-04-1975	Turkey	W 3-0	Kiev	ECq	Kolotov 2, Blokhin
18-05	Rep. Ireland	W 2-1	Kiev	ECq	Blokhin, Kolotov
8-06	Italy	W 1-0	Moscow	Fr	Konkov
12-10	Switzerland	W 1-0	Zurich	ECq	Muntjan
12-11	Switzerland	W 4-1	Kiev	ECq	Konkov, Onishenko 2, Veremejev
23-11	Turkey	L 0-1	Izmir	ECq	
29-11	Romania	D 2-2	Bucharest	Fr	Kolotov, Konkov
10-03-1976	Czechoslovakia	D 2-2	Kosice	Fr	Blokhin, Troshkin
20-03	Argentina	L 0-1	Kiev	Fr	
24-03	Bulgaria	W 3-0	Sofia	Fr	Onischenko, Minaev, Blokhin
24-04	Czechoslovakia	L 0-2	Bratislava	ECqf	
22-05	Czechoslovakia	D 2-2	Kiev	ECqf	Burjak, Blokhin
26-05	Hungary	D 1-1	Budapest	Fr	Nazarenko
23-06	Austria	W 2-1	Vienna	Fr	Minaev 2
19-07	Canada	W 2-1	Montreal	OGr1	Onishenko 2
23-07	North Korea	W 3-0	Ottawa	OGr1	Kolotov, Veremejev, Blokhin
25-07	Iran	W 2-1	Sherbrooke	OGqf	Minaev, Zvagintzev
27-07	East Germany	L 1-2	Montreal	OGsf	Kolotov
29-07	Brazil *	W 2-0	Montreal	OG3p	Onishenko, Nazarenko
28-11	Argentina	D 0-0	Buenos Aires	Fr	
1-12	Brazil	L 0-2	Rio de Janeiro	Fr	
10-12	Indonesia	D 0-0	Djakarta	Fr	
20-03-1977	Tunisia	W 3-0	Tunis	Fr	Maksimenkov, Lobchev, Onishenko
23-03	Yugoslavia	W 4-2	Belgrade	Fr	Blokhin 2, Kipiani, Burjak
24-04	Greece	W 2-0	Moscow	WCq	Konkov, Kipiani
30-04	Hungary	L 1-2	Budapest	WCq	Kipiani
10-05	Greece	L 0-1	Salonica	WCq	
18-05	Hungary	W 2-0	Tbilisi	WCq	Burjak, OG
28-07	East Germany	L 1-2	Leipzig	Fr	Bubnov
7-09	Poland	W 4-1	Volgograd	Fr	Burjak, Blokhin 2, Chesnokov
5-10	Holland	D 0-0	Rotterdam	Fr	
8-10	France	D 0-0	Paris	Fr	
26-02-1978	Morocco	W 3-2	Marrakech	Fr	Blokhin, Konkov, Chesnokov
8-03	West Germany	L 0-1	Frankfurt	Fr	
5-04	Finland	W 10-2	Yerevan	Fr	Konkov, Kipiani, Chesnokov,Blokhin 3, Kolotov 2, Burjak, Petrakov
14-05	Romania	W 1-0	Bucharest	Fr	Blokhin
6-09	Iran	W 1-0	Tehran	Fr	Khidyatulin
20-09	Greece	W 2-0	Yerevan	ECq	Chesnokov, Bessonov
5-10	Turkey	W 2-0	Ankara	Fr	Gutsaev, Blokhin
11-10	Hungary	L 0-2	Budapest	ECq	
19-11	Japan	W 4-1	Tokyo	Fr	Daraselia, Gazzaev 2, Gavrilov
23-11	Japan	W 4-1	Tokyo	Fr	Kipiani 2, Khidyatulin, Kostava
26-11	Japan	W 3-0	Osaka	Fr	Gazzaev, Gavrilov, Bessonov
28-03-1979	Bulgaria	W 3-1	Simferopol	Fr	Blokhin, Shengelia, Gavrilov

19-04	Sweden	W 2-0	Tbilisi	Fr	Shengelia, Khidyatulin
5-05	Czechoslovakia	W 3-0	Moscow	Fr	Koridze, Shengelia, Khidyatulin
19-05	Hungary	D 2-2	Tbilisi	ECq	Chesnokov, Shengelia
27-06	Denmark	W 2-1	Copenhagen	Fr	Daraselia, OG
4-07	Finland	D 1-1	Helsinki	ECq	Kapsalis
5-09	East Germany	W 1-0	Moscow	Fr	Gavrilov
12-09	Greece	L 0-1	Athens	ECq	
14-10	Romania	W 3-1	Moscow	Fr	Khidyatulin, Burjak, Yurchishin
31-10	Finland	D 2-2	Moscow	ECq	Andreev, Gavrilov
21-11	West Germany	L 1-3	Tbilisi	Fr	Makhovikov
26-03-1980	Bulgaria	W 3-1	Sofia	Fr	Cherenkov, Chelebadze 2
29-04	Sweden	W 5-1	Malmo	Fr	Andreev 2, Gavrilov, Chelebadze, Fedorenko
7-05	East Germany	D 2-2	Rostock	Fr	Gassaev, Burjak
23-05	France	W 1-0	Moscow	Fr	Cherenkov
15-06	Brazil	W 2-1	Rio de Janeiro	Fr	Cherenkov, Andreev
12-07	Denmark	W 2-0	Moscow	Fr	Cherenkov, Gassaev
27-08	Hungary	W 4-1	Budapest	Fr	Blokhin, Sulakvelidze, Burjak, Rodionov
3-09	Iceland	W 2-1	Reykjavik	WCq	Gavrilov, Andreev
15-10	Iceland	W 5-0	Moscow	WCq	Andreev 2, Oganesian 2, Bessanov
4-12	Argentina	D 1-1	Mar del Plata	Fr	Oganesian
30-05-1981	Wales	D 0-0	Wrexham	WCq	
23-09	Turkey	W 4-0	Moscow	WCq	Chivadze, Demyanenko, Blokhin, Shengelia
7-10	Turkey	W 3-0	Izmir	WCq	Shengelia, Blokhin 2
28-10	Czechoslovakia	W 2-0	Tbilisi	WCq	Shengelia 2
18-11	Wales	W 3-0	Tbilisi	WCq	Daraselia, Blokhin, Gavrilov
29-11	Czechoslovakia	D 1-1	Bratislava	WCq	Blokhin
10-03-1982	Greece	W 2-0	Athens	Fr	Cherenkov, Burjak
14-04	Argentina	D 1-1	Buenos Aires	Fr	Oganesian
5-05	East Germany	W 1-0	Moscow	Fr	Shengelia
3-06	Sweden	D 1-1	Stockholm	Fr	Blokhin
14-06	Brazil	L 1-2	Seville	WCr1	Bal
19-06	New Zealand	W 3-1	Malaga	WCr1	Gavrilov, Blokhin, Baltacha
22-06	Scotland	D 2-2	Malaga	WCr1	Chivadze, Shengelia
1-07	Belgium	W 1-0	Barcelona	WCr2	Oganesian
4-07	Poland	D 0-0	Barcelona	WCr2	
13-10	Finland	W 2-0	Moscow	ECq	Baltacha, Andreev
23-03-1983	France	D 1-1	Paris	Fr	Cherenkov
13-04	Switzerland	W 1-0	Lausanne	Fr	Blokhin
27-04	Portugal	W 5-0	Moscow	ECq	Cherenkov 2, Rodionov, Demyanenko, Larionov
17-05	Austria	D 2-2	Vienna	Fr	Rodionov, Blokhin
22-05	Poland	D 1-1	Chorzow	ECq	OG
1-06	Finland	W 1-0	Helsinki	ECq	Blokhin
26-07	East Germany	W 3-1	Leipzig	Fr	Blokhin, Oganesian, Yevtushenko
9-10	Poland	W 2-0	Moscow	ECq	Demyanenko, Blokhin
13-11	Portugal	L 0-1	Lisbon	ECq	
28-03-1984	West Germany	L 1-2	Hanover	Fr	Litovchenko
15-05	Finland	W 3-1	Kuovola	Fr	Rodionov, Chivadze, Protasov
2-06	England	W 2-0	London	Fr	Gotsmanov, Protasov
19-08	Mexico	W 3-0	Leningrad	Fr	Rodionov 2, Blokhin
12-09	Rep. Ireland	L 0-1	Dublin	WCq	
10-10	Norway	D 1-1	Oslo	WCq	Litovchenko
21-01-1985	China	W 3-2	Cochin	Fr	Stukasov, Litovchenko
25-01	Yugoslavia	L 1-2	Cochin	Fr	Larionov
28-01	Iran	W 2-0	Cochin	Fr	Sigmantovich, Protasov
2-02	Morocco	W 1-0	Cochin	Fr	Dmitriev
4-02	Yugoslavia	W 2-1	Cochin	Fr	Aleinikov, Kondratiev
27-03	Austria	W 2-0	Tbilisi	Fr	Demyanenko, Protasov
17-04	Switzerland	D 2-2	Berne	WCq	Gavrilov, Demyanenko
2-05	Switzerland	W 4-0	Moscow	WCq	Protasov 2, Kondratiev 2
5-06	Denmark	L 2-4	Copenhagen	WCq	Protasov, Gotsmanov
7-08	Romania	W 2-0	Moscow	Fr	Protasov, Cherenkov
28-08	West Germany	W 1-0	Moscow	Fr	Sigmantovic
25-09	Denmark	W 1-0	Moscow	WCq	Protasov
16-10	Rep. Ireland	W 2-0	Moscow	WCq	Cherenkov, Protasov
30-10	Norway	W 1-0	Moscow	WCq	Kondratiev
22-01-1986	Spain	L 0-2	Las Palmas	Fr	
19-02	Mexico	L 0-1	Mexico City	Fr	
26-03	England	L 0-1	Tbilisi	Fr	
23-04	Romania	L 1-2	Timisoara	Fr	Rodionov
7-05	Finland	D 0-0	Moscow	Fr	
2-06	Hungary	W 6-0	Irapuato	WCr1	Yakovenko, Aleinikov, Belanov, Yaremchuk, OG, Rodionov

Date	Opponent	Result	Venue	Comp	Scorers
5-06	France	D 1-1	Leon	WCr1	Rats
9-06	Canada	W 2-0	Irapuato	WCr1	Blokhin, Zavarov
15-06	Belgium	L 3-4	Leon	WCr2	Belanov 3
20-08	Sweden	D 0-0	Gothenburg	Fr	
24-09	Iceland	D 1-1	Reykjavik	ECq	Sulakvelidze
11-10	France	W 2-0	Paris	ECq	Belanov, Rats
29-10	Norway	W 4-0	Simferopol	ECq	Litovchenko, Belanov, Blokhin, Khidyatulin
18-02-1987	Wales	D 0-0	Swansea	Fr	
18-04	Sweden	L 1-3	Tbilisi	Fr	OG
29-04	East Germany	W 2-0	Kiev	ECq	Zavarov, Belanov
3-06	Norway	W 1-0	Oslo	ECq	Zavarov
29-08	Yugoslavia	W 1-0	Belgrade	Fr	Dobrovolski
9-09	France	D 1-1	Moscow	ECq	Mikhailichenko
23-09	Greece	W 3-0	Moscow	Fr	Dobrovolski, Protasov, Yaremchuk
10-10	East Germany	D 1-1	Berlin	ECq	Aleinikov
28-10	Iceland	W 2-0	Simferopol	ECq	Belanov, Protasov
20-02-1988	Italy	L 1-4	Bari	Fr	Litovchenko
23-03	Greece	W 4-0	Athens	Fr	Protasov 3, Litovchenko
31-03	Argentina	W 4-2	Berlin	Fr	Zavarov, Litovchenko, Protasov 2
2-04	Sweden	L 0-2	Berlin	Fr	
27-04	Czechoslovakia	D 1-1	Trnava	Fr	Protasov
1-06	Poland	W 2-1	Moscow	Fr	Litovchenko, Protasov
12-06	Holland	W 1-0	Cologne	ECr1	Rats
15-06	Rep. Ireland	D 1-1	Hanover	ECr1	Protasov
18-06	England	W 3-1	Frankfurt	ECr1	Aleinikov, Mikhailichenko, Pasulko
22-06	Italy	W 2-0	Stuttgart	ECsf	Litovschenko, Protasov
25-06	Holland	L 0-2	Munich	ECf	
17-08	Finland	D 0-0	Turku	Fr	
31-08	Iceland	D 1-1	Reykjavik	WCq	Litovschenko
21-09	West Germany	L 0-1	Dusseldorf	Fr	
19-10	Austria	W 2-0	Kiev	WCq	Mikhailichenko, Zavarov
21-11	Syria	W 2-0	Damascus	Fr	Demyanenko, Gorlukovitch
23-11	Kuwait	W 1-0	Kuwait City	Fr	Mikhailichenko
27-11	Kuwait	W 2-0	Kuwait City	Fr	Protasov, Aleinikov
21-02-1989	Bulgaria	W 2-1	Sofia	Fr	Borodyuk, Rats
22-03	Holland	L 0-2	Eindhoven	Fr	
26-04	East Germany	W 3-0	Kiev	WCq	Dobrovolski, Litovchenko, Protasov
10-05	Turkey	W 1-0	Istanbul	WCq	Mikhailichenko
31-05	Iceland	D 1-1	Moscow	WCq	Dobrovolski
23-08	Poland	D 1-1	Lublin	Fr	Kiryakov
6-09	Austria	D 0-0	Vienna	WCq	
8-10	East Germany	L 1-2	Karl-Marx-Stadt	WCq	Litovchenko
15-11	Turkey	W 2-0	Simferopol	WCq	Protasov 2
22-02-1990	Costa Rica	W 2-1	Los Angeles	Fr	Litovchenko, Cherenkov
24-02	USA	W 3-1	Palo Alto	Fr	Bessonov, Cherenkov, Protasov
28-03	Holland	W 2-1	Kiev	Fr	Protasov, Lyuty
25-04	Rep. Ireland	L 0-1	Dublin	Fr	
16-05	Israel	L 2-3	Tel Aviv	Fr	Litovchenko, Mikhailichenko
9-06	Romania	L 0-2	Bari	WCr1	
13-06	Argentina	L 0-2	Naples	WCr1	
18-06	Cameroon	W 4-0	Bari	WCr1	Protasov, Zygmantovich, Zavarov, Dobrovolski
29-08	Romania	L 1-2	Moscow	Fr	Mikhailichenko
12-09	Norway	W 2-0	Moscow	ECq	Kanchelskis, Kuznetsov.O
9-10	Israel	W 3-0	Moscow	Fr	Yuran 2, Litovchenko
3-11	Italy	D 0-0	Rome	ECq	
21-11	United States	D 0-0	Port of Spain	Fr	
24-11	Trinidad	W 2-0	Port of Spain	Fr	Shalimov, Tsveyba
30-11	Guatemala	W 3-0	Guatemala City	Fr	Mostovoy, Dobrovolski, Kolyvanov
6-02-1991	Scotland	W 1-0	Glasgow	Fr	Kuznetsov.D
27-03	Germany	L 1-2	Frankfurt	Fr	Dobrovolski
17-04	Hungary	W 1-0	Budapest	ECq	Mikhailichenko
21-05	England	L 1-3	London	Fr	Tatarchuk
23-05	Argentina	D 1-1	Manchester	Fr	Kolyvanov
29-05	Cyprus	W 4-0	Moscow	ECq	Mostovoy, Mikhailichenko, Korneev, Aleinikov
13-06	Sweden	W 3-2	Gothenburg	Fr	Yuran, Kuznetsov.D, Korneev
16-06	Italy	D 1-1	Stockholm	Fr	Korneev
28-08	Norway	W 1-0	Oslo	ECq	Mostovoy
25-09	Hungary	D 2-2	Moscow	ECq	Shalimov, Kanchelskis
12-10	Italy	D 0-0	Moscow	ECq	
13-11	Cyprus	W 3-0	Larnaca	ECq	Protasov, Yuran, Mikhailichenko

INTERNATIONAL MATCHES OF THE COMMONWEALTH OF INDEPENDENT STATES

Date	Opponent	Result	Venue	Type	Scorers
25-01-1992	United States	W 1-0	Miami	Fr	Tsveyba
29-01	El Salvador	W 3-0	San Salvador	Fr	Chernishev 2, Khlestov
2-02	USA	L 1-2	Michigan	Fr	Sergeyev
12-02	Israel	W 2-1	Tel Aviv	Fr	Piatnitski, Kiriakov
19-02	Spain	D 1-1	Valencia	Fr	Kiriakov
8-03	Mexico	L 0-4	Mexico City	Fr	
11-03	Mexico	D 1-1	Tampico	Fr	Smirnov
29-04	England	D 2-2	Moscow	Fr	Chadadze, Kiriakov
3-06	Denmark	D 1-1	Copenhagen	Fr	Kolivanov
12-06	Germany	D 1-1	Norrkoping	ECr1	Dobrovolski
15-06	Holland	D 0-0	Gothenburg	ECr1	
18-06	Scotland	L 0-3	Norrkoping	ECr1	

SPAIN

Spain are one of the giants of world football. Their league is one of the top half dozen in the world, and although they have never won the World Cup, the national team play to a consistently high standard which has seen them crowned European champions. The real strength, however, lies with the club sides, especially Real Madrid and Barcelona who have few rivals in the top echelons of European football. In the all-time rankings for European club competitions they stand first and second respectively with eight and seven titles won, and in the Estadio Bernabeu in Madrid and Camp Nou in Barcelona they have two of the biggest and best club stadia in the world.

Football first made an appearance in Spain in the Basque region in the north of the country in the 1890s. British mining engineers were responsible according to some sources, British sailors according to others, but the game soon spread through the country, especially to the cities of Madrid, Barcelona and Valencia. The first club formed was the Athletic Club de Bilbao in 1898 and to this day they retain the English spelling in their name. Later in the same year Real Madrid were formed by students in the capital, though the club was not formalised until four years later and did not attain the Royal (Real) prefix until 1920 when it was granted by King Alfonso XIII.

By 1910 most of the major present-day clubs had been formed, spurred on by the presence of a cup competition that was introduced in 1902. Until the formation of a league in 1929, the Cup was the only national competition in the country and the winners were regarded as the champions of Spain. Bilbao featured strongly in the intial competitions. A combined Athletic Bilbao and Bilbao FC team called Vizcaya won the initial tournament, whilst Athletic won the next two and lost in the final of the following two. The city soon saw its dominance challenged when first Real Madrid then Barcelona had dominant spells before the First World War - and they have not relinquished this pre-eminence since. Athletic Bilbao, Atlético Madrid, Valencia and to a lesser extent Sevilla have all challenged at one time or another, but the Real-Barcelona fixture remains the biggest of them all, compounded by the intense regional rivalry between Catalonia, in which Barcelona is located, and the capital city.

In 1913, nine years after Spain joined FIFA, the Real Federacion Española de Fútbol was formed, unifying all the regional organisations, but not until 1920 did it field a representative side. The programme of international matches remained light until well into the second half of the century even though the first signs were encouraging. Up until the outbreak of civil war in 1936, Spain's record was very good, and it included victories over some of Europe's stronger nations, most notably the 4-3 win in Madrid in 1929 over England. The Spaniards thus became the first nation outside of the British Isles to beat the English in a full international game. Star of that side was Ricardo Zamora, their goalkeeper, but Zamora could do nothing to help beat Spain's bogey team, Italy. In the 1924 and 1928 Olympics and in the 1934 World Cup, Spain's hopes were dashed each time by the Italians.

The combination of the Civil War and then the Second World War effectively stopped international football for close on ten years, although club football carried on with an interruption only in the years when the fighting in the Civil War was at its worst. It was in the early years of the 1940s that the league competition grew in stature. Introduced in 1929 along with professionalism, it grew from 10 clubs in its first few years to 16 by 1951. Political undertones helped reinforce the stature of the game. During the civil war, Catalonia, and Barcelona in particular, had been the main area of resistance to Franco's Fascist forces. Defeated, the Catalan people were banned from organising political meetings and the only place they could meet for such discussions was at football matches. The same was true for the Basques and other regions of Spain. The 1940s therefore were boom years for football.

The 1950s saw even more rapid growth as these rivalries intensified. Foreigners were brought in to help build winning teams, most notably Alfredo Di Stéfano at Real Madrid and later the great Hungarian trio of Kubala, Kocsis and Czibor at Barcelona, and a trend was started that holds true to this day. Over the years many great players have been tempted into Spanish football by the high wages and the level of competition on offer.

Naturally there was concern about the effect on local players and after the initial influx a ban was imposed that lasted from 1963 to 1973, although many players in the league at this time were from South America and were considered, like Di Stéfano, as naturalised Spaniards.

Once the gates were opened again in 1973 the big names of world football reappeared in Spain, amongst them Cruyff and Neeskens at Barcelona, Breitner and Netzer at Real, and Rep and Keita, the first winner of the African Footballer of the Year award, at Valencia. Only Athletic Bilbao and Real Sociedad, with their Basque-only rule, did not have any foreigners on their books. Since then players like Kempes, Maradona, Lineker, Schuster and Hugo Sanchez have all made their mark in the Spanish league.

The fifties belonged to one team in particular, Real Madrid. They wrote themselves into football folklore by winning the first five European Cups. But it was not just the fact that they won five in a row, a feat unlikely ever to be equalled; it was style in which they did it. Central to the side was Di Stéfano, a player many rate as the best of all time. He appeared in all five triumphs along with Francisco Gento and Jose Maria Zarraga. Gento was also in the side when Real won the Cup again in 1966, as well as appearing in two more, losing, finals.

Real's crowning glory came in in the 1960 final against Eintracht Frankfurt. By then the Hungarian Ferenc Puskás had joined them and he scored four goals that day, while Di Stéfano hit a hat-trick as Real thrashed Eintracht 7-3. Real were not the only Spanish winners in Europe in the 1960s. Barcelona won the initial Fairs Cup in 1960 and again in 1966. In between there were wins in the same competition for Valencia and Zaragoza, while Atletico Madrid won the Cup Winners Cup in 1962. To cap it all, the national side won the 1964 European Nations Cup. Chosen to host the final tournament after reaching the last four, they defeated a good Hungarian side 2-1 in the semi-final then and saw off the defending champions, the Soviet Union, by the same score in the final, inspired by the brilliant Luis Suarez.

From the mid-fifties until the late sixties it seemed the Spanish could do no wrong, but there then followed a strange slump in fortunes in the 1970s. If there had been a weakness in Spanish football, it was with the national team; the 1964 side apart, they achieved little. A major problem was that with such strong regional identities existing in Spain, the national side was poorly supported; a Catalan or a Basque considers himself just that, not 'Spanish'. Barcelona has only ever staged 15 internationals, just five of them at Camp Nou, and there have been none at all in the Catalan capital since 1987. As a centre of Basque nationalism, Bilbao has fared even worse, with only six internationals in all, none since 1967.

During the 1950s the Spanish had given little priority to the national side, a fact borne out by their elimination from both the 1954 and 1958 World Cup qualifiers at the hands of Turkey and Scotland respectively. Taken more seriously in the 1960s, the team qualified for both Chile and England but did not get past the first round in either. The ban on foreigners, designed to improve Spain's chances, seemed eventually to have the reverse effect. Failure to qualify for either the 1970 or 1974 World Cups was compounded by poor results at club level in the European competitions. Real's 1966 European Cup triumph was the last title won by a Spanish team until Barcelona won the Cup Winners Cup in 1979. The Spanish football association was persuaded to lift the ban in 1973 and although there was no tangible benefit at first, Spain have since clawed their way back up the international ladder.

THE ORDER OF MERIT

		All			League			Cup		Europe		
1	Real Madrid	51	36	14	26	14	6	17	17	8	5	8
2	Barcelona	43	32	14	14	18	10	22	8	7	6	4
3	Athletic Bilbao	31	18	10	8	6	10	23	11	-	1	-
4	Atlético Madrid	17	17	17	8	8	12	8	6	1	3	5
5	Valencia	12	15	5	4	5	5	5	9	3	1	-
6	Real Zaragoza	6	6	6	-	1	4	4	4	2	1	2
7	Sevilla	4	6	2	1	4	2	3	2	-	-	-
	Real Sociedad	4	6	2	2	2	1	2	4	-	-	1
9	Real Union Irún	3	1	-	-	-	-	3	1	-	-	-
10	RCD Español	2	6	4	-	-	4	2	5	-	1	-
11	Real Betis Balompié	2	1	2	1	-	2	1	1	-	-	-
12	Deportivo La Coruña	1	3	1	-	3	1	1	-	-	-	-
	Arenas Guecho Bilbao	1	3	1	-	-	1	1	3	-	-	-
14	Vizcaya Bilbao	1	1	-	-	-	-	1	1	-	-	-
15	Racing Irún	1	-	-	-	-	-	1	-	-	-	-
16	Real Sporting Gijón	-	3	1	-	1	1	-	2	-	-	-
17	Las Palmas	-	2	1	-	1	1	-	1	-	-	-
18	Celta Vigo	-	2	-	-	-	-	-	2	-	-	-
	Español Madrid	-	2	-	-	-	-	-	2	-	-	-
	Real Valladolid	-	2	-	-	-	-	-	2	-	-	-
21	Racing Santander	-	1	1	-	1	1	-	-	-	-	-

To the end of the 1994-95 season

Real Madrid, Barcelona and Valencia all had their share of success in the 1980s but most disappointing for the Spaniards was their dreadful failure in the World Cup of 1982, when as hosts they were amongst the favourites. Seldom has a host nation fared so badly, and in five games they recorded only one victory. Two years later, with much the same side, they reached the final of the European Championships where they lost 2-0 to France in Paris. Spain have qualified for every World Cup since 1978 and have only missed out on two Euro finals, but they rarely progress beyond the last eight.

The club scene in Spain, however, is back to its best. Between 1961 and 1980, as Real Madrid won 14 championships and Barcelona just one, lack of competition was driving the standard of the league down. Since 1980, however, wins for Real Sociedad, Athletic Bilbao and Barcelona have all helped revive the championship. The four consecutive victories by Barcelona in the 1990s, under the leadership of Johan Cruyff, were especially welcome to the success-starved Catalans. Even better, they also managed to at last come out of the shadow of Real by winning the European Cup in 1992, the first win by a Spanish team for 26 years. Crowds are at their highest for some time and Spanish clubs provided most of the stars of the 1994 World Cup. The hope is that one day it will be native Spanish players returning home as world champions.

Population: 39,618,000
Area, sq km: 504,750
% in urban areas: 75.8%
Capital city: Madrid

Real Federación Española de Fútbol
Calle Alberto Bosch #13
Apartado Postal 347
E-28014 Madrid
Spain
Tel: + 34 1 4201362
Fax: + 34 1 4202094

Year of formation	1913
Affiliation to FIFA	1904
Affiliation to UEFA	1954
Registered clubs	12 421
Registered players	470 500
Professional players	2300
Registered coaches	4600
Registered referees	7822
National Stadium	None
National colours	Red/Blue/Black
Reserve colours	Blue/Blue/Black
Season	September - June

THE RECORD

WORLD CUP

1930	Did not enter
1934	QT 1st/2 in group 6 - Final Tournament/Quarter-finalists
1938	Did not enter
1950	QT 1st/2 in group 6 - Final Tournament/2nd round/ 4th place
1954	QT 2nd/2 in group 6
1958	QT 2nd/3 in group 9
1962	QT 1st/5 in group 9 - Final Tournament/1st round
1966	QT 1st/2 in group 9 - Final Tournament/1st round
1970	QT 3rd/4 in group 6
1974	QT 2nd/3 in group 7
1978	QT 1st/3 in group 8 - Final Tournament/1st round
1982	QT Automatic - Final Tournament/2nd round
1986	QT 1st/4 in group 7 - Final Tournament/Quarter-finalists
1990	QT 1st/5 in group 6 - Final Tournament/2nd round
1994	QT 1st/7 in group 3 - Final Tournament/Quarter-finalists

EUROPEAN CHAMPIONSHIP

1960	Quarter-finalists
1964	Winners
1968	QT 1st/4 in group 1 - Final Tournament/Quarter-finalists
1972	QT 2nd/4 in group 4
1976	QT 1st/4 in group 4 - Final Tournament/Quarter-finalists
1980	QT 1st/4 in group 3 - Final Tournament/1st round
1984	QT 1st/5 in group 7 - Final Tournament/Finalists
1988	QT 1st/4 in group 1 - Final Tournament/1st round
1992	QT 3rd/5 in group 1
1996	QT group 2

EUROPEAN CLUB COMPETITIONS

European Cup
Winners - Real Madrid 1956 1957 1958 1959 1960 1966 Barcelona 1992
Finalists - Barcelona 1961 1986 1994 Real Madrid 1962 1964 1981 Atlético Madrid 1974

Cup Winners Cup
Winners - Atlético Madrid 1962 Barcelona 1979 1982 1989 Valencia 1980 Real Zaragoza 1995
Finalists - Atlético Madrid 1963 1986 Barcelona 1969 1991 Real Madrid 1971 1983

UEFA Cup
Winners - Barcelona 1958 1960 1966 Valencia 1962 1963 Real Zaragoza 1964 Real Madrid 1985 1986
Finalists - Barcelona 1962 Valencia 1964 Real Zaragoza 1966 Athletic Bilbao 1977 Español 1988

CLUB DIRECTORY

MADRID (Population - 4,650,000)

Club Atlético de Madrid (1903)
Vicente Calderón 62,000 – Red & white stripes/Blue
Previous name - Atlético Aviación 1939-46
Reserve team: Atlético Madridleño Club de Fútbol (1963)

Real Madrid CF (1902)
(Club de Fútbol)
Santiago Bernabeu 90,000 – White, violet trim
Reserve team: Castilla Club de Fútbol (1942)

AD Rayo Vallecano (1940)
(Agrupacion Deportiva)
Nuevo Estadio de Vallecas 19,000 – White, red sash/White

BARCELONA (Pop. - 4,040,000)

FC Barcelona (1899)
(Fútbol Club)
Camp Nou 115,000 – Red & blue stripes/Blue
Reserve teams: Barcelona Atletic (1970) & Barcelona Amateur (1967)

RCD Español (1900)
(Real Club Deportivo)
Sarriá 41,000 – Blue & white stripes/Blue

Centre D'Esports Sabadell FC (1903)
Nova Creu Alta 20,000 – Blue & white quarters/Blue

VALENCIA (Pop. - 1,270,000)

Levante UD (1909)
(Unión Deportiva)
Levante 29,000 – Red & blue stripes/Blue

Valencia CF (1910)
Luis Casanova 49,000 – White/White

BILBAO (Pop. - 985,000)

Athletic Club de Bilbao (1898)
San Mamés 46,000 – Red & white stripes/Black
Reserve team: Bilbao Athletic Club (1918)

Arenas Guecho (1909)
Gobele – Red & black stripes/Black

SEVILLE (Pop. - 945,000)

Real Betis Balompié (1907)
Benito Villamarín 47,000 – Green & white stripes/White
Reserve team: Betis Deportivo Balompié (1968)

Sevilla FC (1905)
Sánchez Pizjuán 70,000 – White, red trim
Reserve team: Sevilla Atletico Club (1958)

ZARAGOZA (Pop. - 575,000)

Real Zaragoza CD (1932)
La Romareda 43,000 – White/Blue
Reserve team: Club Deportivo Aragón (1966)

MALAGA (Pop. - 566,000)

CD Málaga (1933)
La Rosaleda 42,000 – Sky blue & white stripes/Sky blue
Previous names - Merger in 1933 of Málaga & Malagueño

LAS PALMAS (Pop. - 358,000)

UD Las Palmas (1949)
Insular 20,000 – Yellow/Blue

VALLADOLID (Pop. - 329,000)

Real Valladolid Deportivo (1928)
Nuevo José Zorrilla 37,000 – Violet & white stripes/White

MURCIA (Pop. - 305,000)

Real Murcia CF (1924)
La Condomina 24,000 – Red/White

CORDOBA (Pop. - 298,000)

Córdoba CF (1951)
El Arcángel 18,000 – Green & white stripes/White

PALMA (Pop. - 306,000)
RCD Mallorca (1916)
Luis Sitjar 31,000 – Red/Black

ALICANTE (Pop. - 258,000)
Hércules CF (1922)
José Rico Pérez 40,000 – Blue & white stripes/Black

VIGO (Pop. - 262,000)
Real Club Celta de Vigo (1923)
Balaídos 33,000 – Sky blue/White

GRANADA (Pop. - 256,000)
Granada CF (1932)
Los Cármenes 25,000 – Red & white stripes/Blue

GIJON (Pop. - 255,000)
Real Sporting de Gijón (1905)
El Molinón 38,000 – Red & white stripes/Blue

LA CORUÑA (Pop. - 242,000)
Real Club Deportivo de La Coruña (1904)
Riazor 28,000 – Blue & white stripes/Blue

CADIZ (Pop. - 240,000)
Cádiz CF (1910)
Ramón de Carranza 22,000 – Yellow/Blue

SANTA CRUZ DE TENERIFE (Pop. - 211,000)
CD Tenerife (1922)
Heliodoro Rodríguez 24,000 – White/Blue

SANTANDER (Pop. - 163,000)
Real Racing Club Santander (1913)
El Sardinero 25,000 – White/Black, green trim

OVIEDO (Pop. - 186,000)
Real Oviedo CF (1926)
Carlos Tartiere 22,000 – Blue/White
Reserve team: Real Oviedo Aficionados (1941)

PAMPLONA (Pop. - 178,000)
Club Atlético Osasuna (1920)
El Sadar 25,000 – Red/Blue
Reserve team: Osasuna Promesas (1962)

ELCHE (Pop. - 177,000)
Elche CF (1923)
Manuel Martínez Valero 38,000 – White, green chest band/White

SAN SEBASTIAN (Pop. - 176,000)
Real Sociedad de Fútbol (1909)
Anoeta 30,000 – Blue & white stripes/White
Previous name - Ciclista de San Sebastián, Donostia 1931-40

LEON (Pop. - 159,000)
Cultural y Deportiva Leonesa (1928)
Antonio Amilibia 10,000 – White/White

BURGOS (Pop. - 158,000)
Real Burgos CF (1983)
El Plantío 20,000 – Red, maroon stripe on left side/White
Previous name - Burgos Club de Fútbol 1922-83

SALAMANCA (Pop. - 155,000)
UD Salamanca (1923)
El Helmántico 25,000 – White/Black

ALMERIA (Pop. - 154,000)
Club Polideportivo Almeirá (1982)
Antonio Franco Navarro – Red & white stripes/Blue

HUELVA (Pop. - 135,000)
Real Club Recreativo de Huelva (1880)
Colombino 13,000 – Blue & white stripes/White

ALBACETE (Pop. - 125,000)
Albacete Balompié (1939)
Carlos Belmonte 19,000 – White, red trim

LOGRONO (Pop. - 116,000)
CD Logroñes (1940)
Las Gaunas 16,000 – Red & white stripes/Black

LERIDA (Pop. - 108,000)
Unió Esportiva Lleida (1939)
Camp d'Esports 12,000 – Blue/White

TARRAGONA (Pop. - 107,000)
Gimnasia de Tarragona (1886)
Nou Estadi 15,000 – Red/White

JAEN (Pop. - 103,000)
Real Jaén CF (1922)
La Victoria 10,000 – White/White

ALCOY (Pop. - 66,000)
CD Alcoyano (1927)
El Collao 7,000 – Blue & white stripes/Blue

IRUN (Pop. - 54,000)
Real Union Irún (1915)
Gal – White/Black

CASTELLON (Pop. - 129,000)
CD Castellón (1931)
Castalia 14,000 – Black & white stripes/White

SANTIAGO DE COMPOSTELA (Pop. - 91,000)
Sociedad Deportiva Compostela (1962)
San Lazaro 12,000 – Blue & white halves/White

PONTEVEDRA (Pop. - 70,000)
Pontevedra CF (1941)
Municipal Pasarón – Claret/Blue

SPANISH PRIMERA DIVISIÓN

1929h	Barcelona 25 Real Madrid 23 Athletic Bilbao 20
1930	Athletic Bilbao 30 Barcelona 23 Arenas Guecho Bilbao20
1931	Athletic Bilbao 22 Racing Santander 22 Real Sociedad 22
1932	Real Madrid 28 Athletic Bilbao 25 Barcelona 24
1933	Real Madrid 28 Athletic Bilbao 26 RCD Español 22
1934	Athletic Bilbao 24 Real Madrid 22 Racing Santander 19
1935k	Real Betis 34 Real Madrid 33 Oviedo 26
1936	Athletic Bilbao 31 Real Madrid 29 Oviedo 28
1937-39	-
1940	Atlético Aviación 29 Sevilla 28 Athletic Bilbao 26
1941	Atlético Aviación 33 Athletic Bilbao 31 Valencia 27
1942n	Valencia 40 Real Madrid 33 Atlético Aviación 33
1943	Athletic Bilbao 36 Sevilla 33 Barcelona 32
1944	Valencia 40 Atlético Aviación 34 Sevilla 32
1945	Barcelona 39 Real Madrid 38 Atlético Aviación 31
1946	Sevilla 36 Barcelona 35 Athletic Bilbao 33
1947	Valencia 34 Athletic Bilbao 34 Atlético Madrid 32
1948	Barcelona 37 Valencia 34 Atlético Madrid 33
1949	Barcelona 37 Valencia 35 Real Madrid 34
1950	Atlético Madrid 33 Deportivo La Coruña 32 Valencia 31
1951q	Atlético Madrid 40 Sevilla 38 Valencia 37
1952	Barcelona 43 Athletic Bilbao 40 Real Madrid 38
1953	Barcelona 42 Valencia 40 Real Madrid 39
1954	Real Madrid 40 Barcelona 36 Valencia 34
1955	Real Madrid 46 Barcelona 41 Athletic Bilbao 39
1956	Athletic Bilbao 48 Barcelona 47 Real Madrid 38
1957	Real Madrid 44 Sevilla 39 Barcelona 39
1958	Real Madrid 45 Atlético Madrid 42 Barcelona 38
1959	Barcelona 51 Real Madrid 47 Athletic Bilbao 36
1960	Barcelona 46 Real Madrid 46 Athletic Bilbao 39
1961	Real Madrid 52 Atlético Madrid 40 Real Zaragoza 33
1962	Real Madrid 43 Barcelona 40 Atlético Madrid 36
1963	Real Madrid 49 Atlético Madrid 37 Oviedo 33
1964	Real Madrid 46 Barcelona 42 Real Betis 37
1965	Real Madrid 47 Atlético Madrid 43 Real Zaragoza 40
1966	Atlético Madrid 44 Real Madrid 43 Barcelona 38
1967	Real Madrid 47 Barcelona 42 RCD Español 37
1968	Real Madrid 42 Barcelona 39 Las Palmas 38
1969	Real Madrid 47 Las Palmas 38 Barcelona 36
1970	Atlético Madrid 42 Athletic Bilbao 41 Sevilla 35
1971	Valencia 43 Barcelona 43 Atlético Madrid 42

1972t Real Madrid 47 Valencia 45 Barcelona 43
1973 Atlético Madrid 48 Barcelona 46 RCD Español 45
1974 Barcelona 50 Atlético Madrid 42 Real Zaragoza 40
1975 Real Madrid 50 Real Zaragoza 38 Barcelona 37
1976 Real Madrid 48 Barcelona 43 Atlético Madrid 42
1977 Atlético Madrid 46 Barcelona 45 Athletic Bilbao 38
1978 Real Madrid 47 Barcelona 41 Athletic Bilbao 40
1979 Real Madrid 47 Sporting Gijón 43 Atlético Madrid 41
1980 Real Madrid 53 Real Sociedad 52 Sporting Gijón 39
1981 Real Sociedad 45 Real Madrid 45 Atlético Madrid 42
1982 Real Sociedad 47 Barcelona 45 Real Madrid 44
1983 Athletic Bilbao 50 Real Madrid 49 Atlético Madrid 46
1984 Athletic Bilbao 49 Real Madrid 49 Barcelona 48
1985 Barcelona 53 Atlético Madrid 43 Athletic Bilbao 41
1986 Real Madrid 56 Barcelona 45 Athletic Bilbao 43
1987zl Real Madrid 66 Barcelona 63 RCD Español 51
1988v Real Madrid 62 Real Sociedad 51 Atlético Madrid 48
1989 Real Madrid 62 Barcelona 57 Valencia 49
1990 Real Madrid 62 Valencia 53 Barcelona 51
1991 Barcelona 57 Atlético Madrid 47 Real Madrid 46
1992 Barcelona 55 Real Madrid 54 Atlético Madrid 53
1993 Barcelona 58 Real Madrid 57 Deportivo La Coruña 54
1994 Barcelona 56 Deportivo La Coruña 56 Real Zaragoza 46
1995 Real Madrid 55 Deportivo La Coruña 51 Real Betis 46

SPANISH CUP FINALS

1902 Vizcaya Bilbao....................2-1 ....Barcelona
1903 Athletic Bilbao ....3-2................Real Madrid
1904 Athletic Bilbao................W-O
1905 Real Madrid ....1-0................Athletic Bilbao
1906 Real Madrid ....4-1 ....Athletic Bilbao
1907 Real Madrid ....1-0................Vizcaya Bilbao
1908 Real Madrid ....2-1 ....Vigo Sporting
1909 Ciclista San Sebastian......3-1 ....Español Madrid
1910 Athletic Bilbao ....1-0................Basconia
1910 Barcelona..........................3-2................Español Madrid
1911 Athletic Bilbao ....3-1 ....RCD Español
1912 Barcelona..........................2-0................Gimnástica Madrid
1913 Barcelona...................2-2 0-0 2-1..........Real Sociedad
1913 Racing Irún....................2-2 1-0 ....Athletic Bilbao
1914 Athletic Bilbao ....2-1 ....Espana Barcelona
1915 Athletic Bilbao ....5-0................RCD Español
1916 Athletic Bilbao ....4-0................Real Madrid
1917 Real Madrid...................0-0 2-1 ....Arenas Guecho Bilbao
1918 Real Union Irún ....2-0................Real Madrid
1919 Arenas Guecho Bilbao....5-2................Barcelona
1920 Barcelona..........................2-0................Athletic Bilbao
1921 Athletic Bilbao ....4-1 ....Atlético Madrid
1922 Barcelona..........................5-1 ....Real Union Irún
1923 Athletic Bilbao ....1-0................Europa Barcelona
1924 Real Union Irún ....1-0................Real Madrid
1925 Barcelona..........................2-0................Arenas Guecho Bilbao
1926 Barcelona..........................3-2................Atlético Madrid
1927 Real Union Irún ....1-0................Arenas Guecho Bilbao
1928 Barcelona...................1-1 1-1 3-1..........Real Sociedad
1929 RCD Español.....................2-1 ....Real Madrid
1930 Athletic Bilbao ....3-2................Real Madrid
1931 Athletic Bilbao ....3-1 ....Real Betis
1932 Athletic Bilbao ....1-0................Barcelona
1933 Athletic Bilbao ....2-1 ....Real Madrid
1934 Real Madrid ....2-1 ....Valencia
1935 Sevilla ....3-0................Sabadell
1936 Real Madrid ....2-1 ....Barcelona
1937-38 -
1939 Sevilla ....6-2................Racing Ferrol
1940 RCD Español.....................3-2................Real Madrid
1941 Valencia.............................3-1 ....RCD Español
1942 Barcelona..........................4-3................Athletic Bilbao
1943 Athletic Bilbao ....1-0................Real Madrid
1944 Athletic Bilbao ....2-0................Valencia
1945 Athletic Bilbao ....3-2................Valencia
1946 Real Madrid ....3-1 ....Valencia
1947 Real Madrid ....2-0................RCD Español
1948 Sevilla ....4-1 ....Celta Vigo
1949 Valencia.............................1-0................Athletic Bilbao
1950 Athletic Bilbao ....4-1 ....Real Valladolid
1951 Barcelona..........................3-0................Real Sociedad
1952 Barcelona..........................4-2................Valencia
1953 Barcelona..........................2-1 ....Athletic Bilbao
1954 Valencia.............................3-0................Barcelona
1955 Athletic Bilbao ....1-0................Sevilla
1956 Athletic Bilbao ....2-1 ....Atlético Madrid
1957 Barcelona..........................1-0................RCD Español
1958 Athletic Bilbao ....2-0................Real Madrid
1959 Barcelona..........................4-1 ....Granada
1960 Atlético Madrid ....3-1 ....Real Madrid
1961 Atlético Madrid ....3-2................Real Madrid
1962 Real Madrid ....2-1 ....Sevilla
1963 Barcelona..........................3-1 ....Real Zaragoza
1964 Real Zaragoza ....2-1 ....Atlético Madrid
1965 Atlético Madrid ....1-0................Real Zaragoza
1966 Real Zaragoza ....2-0................Athletic Bilbao
1967 Valencia.............................2-1 ....Athletic Bilbao
1968 Barcelona..........................1-0................Real Madrid
1969 Athletic Bilbao ....1-0................Elche
1970 Real Madrid ....3-1 ....Valencia
1971 Barcelona..........................4-3................Valencia
1972 Atlético Madrid ....2-1 ....Valencia
1973 Athletic Bilbao ....2-0................Castellón
1974 Real Madrid ....4-0................Barcelona
1975 Real Madrid.................0-0 4-3p ....Atlético Madrid
1976 Atlético Madrid ....1-0................Real Zaragoza
1977 Real Betis ....2-2 11-9p...........Athletic Bilbao
1978 Barcelona..........................3-1 ....Las Palmas
1979 Valencia.............................2-0................Real Madrid
1980 Real Madrid ....6-1 ....Castilla
1981 Barcelona..........................3-1 ....Sporting Gijón
1982 Real Madrid ....2-1 ....Sporting Gijón
1983 Barcelona..........................2-1 ....Real Madrid
1984 Athletic Bilbao ....1-0................Barcelona
1985 Atlético Madrid ....2-1 ....Athletic Bilbao
1986 Real Zaragoza ....1-0................Barcelona
1987 Real Sociedad..............2-2 4-3p ....Atlético Madrid
1988 Barcelona..........................1-0................Real Sociedad
1989 Real Madrid ....1-0................Real Valladolid
1990 Barcelona..........................2-0................Real Madrid
1991 Atlético Madrid ....1-0................RCD Mallorca
1992 Atlético Madrid ....2-0................Real Madrid
1993 Real Madrid ....2-0................Real Zaragoza
1994 Real Zaragoza.............0-0 5-4p ....Celta Vigo
1995 Deportivo La Coruña .....2-1 ....Valencia

LEADING INTERNATIONAL GOALSCORERS

26	Emilio Butragueño	(Real Madrid)	1984-1992
23	Alfredo Di Stefáno	(Real Madrid)	1957-1961
21	Miguel Gonzalez 'Míchel'	(Real Madrid)	1985-1993
21	Julio Salinas	(Atlético Madrid, Barcelona,La Coruña)	1986-
20	Telmo Zarraonandia 'Zarra'	(Athletic Bilbao)	1945-1951
17	Isidro Lángara	(Oviedo)	1932-1936
16	Luis Regueirdo	(Real Union Irún, Real Madrid)	1927-1936
16	Jose Martinez 'Pirri'	(Real Madrid)	1966-1978
15	Carlos Alonso 'Santillana'	(Real Madrid)	1975-1985
14	Luis Súarez	(Barcelona,Internazionale, Sampdoria)	1957-1972

Di Stéfano also scored 3 goals in 8 appearances for Argentina

LEADING INTERNATIONAL APPEARANCES

101 Andoni Zubizarreta #	(Athletic Bilbao, Barcelona,Valencia)	1983-
81 Jose Antonio Camacho	(Real Madrid)	1975-1988
75 Rafael Gordillo	(Real Betis,Real Madrid)	1978-1988
69 Emilio Butragueño	(Real Madrid)	1984-1992
68 Luis Arconada #	(Real Sociedad)	1977-1985
66 Miguel Gonzalez 'Míchel'	(Real Madrid)	1985-1993
60 Víctor Munoz	(Real Zaragoza, Barcelona)	1981-1988
56 Carlos Alonso 'Santillana'	(Real Madrid)	1975-1985
54 Julio Salinas	(Atlético Madrid, Barcelona,La Coruña)	1986-
49 Jose Angel Iríbar #	(Athletic Bilbao)	1964-1976
48 Manuel Sanchís (II)	(Real Madrid)	1986-1992
46 Ricardo Zamora	(Barcelona, Español, Real Madrid)	1920-36

INTERNATIONAL MATCHES PLAYED BY SPAIN

28-08-1920	Denmark	W 1-0	Brussels	OGr1	Patricio
29-08	Belgium	L 1-3	Antwerp	OGqf	Arrate
1-09	Sweden	W 2-1	Antwerp	OGct	Belauste, Acedo
2-09	Italy	W 2-0	Antwerp	OGct	Sesúmaga 2
5-09	Holland	W 3-1	Antwerp	OG2p	Sesúmaga 2, Pichichi
9-10-1921	Belgium	W 2-0	Bilbao	Fr	Alcántara 2
18-12	Portugal	W 3-1	Madrid	Fr	Alcántara 2, Meana
30-04-1922	France	W 4-0	Bordeaux	Fr	Travieso 2, Alcántara 2
17-12	Portugal	W 2-1	Lisbon	Fr	Pieira, Monjardín
28-01-1923	France	W 3-0	San Sebastian	Fr	Monjardín 2, Zabala
4-02	Belgium	L 0-1	Antwerp	Fr	
16-12	Portugal	W 3-0	Seville	Fr	Zabala 3
9-03-1924	Italy	D 0-0	Milan	Fr	
25-05	Italy	L 0-1	Paris	OGr1	
21-12	Austria	W 2-1	Barcelona	Fr	Juantegui, Samieiter
15-05-1925	Portugal	W 2-0	Lisbon	Fr	Carmelo, Piera
1-06	Switzerland	W 3-0	Berne	Fr	Errazquin 3
14-06	Italy	W 1-0	Valencia	Fr	Errazquin
27-09	Austria	W 1-0	Vienna	Fr	Cubells
4-10	Hungary	W 1-0	Budapest	Fr	Carmelo
19-12-1926	Hungary	W 4-2	Vigo	Fr	Errazquin 2, Carmelo, Goiburu
17-04-1927	Switzerland	W 1-0	Santander	Fr	Oscar
22-05	France	W 4-1	Paris	Fr	Zaldúa 2, Yermo, Olaso
29-05	Italy	L 0-2	Bologna	Fr	
29-05	Portugal	W 2-0	Madrid	Fr	Moraleda, Oscar
8-01-1928	Portugal	D 2-2	Lisbon	Fr	Zaldúa, Goiburu
22-04	Italy	D 1-1	Gijon	Fr	Quesada
30-05	Mexico	W 7-1	Amsterdam	OGr1	Yermo 3, Regueiro 2, Marculeta, Mariscal
1-06	Italy	D 1-1	Amsterdam	OGqf	Zaldua
4-06	Italy	L 1-7	Amsterdam	OGqf	Yermo
17-03-1929	Portugal	W 5-0	Seville	Fr	Rubio 3, Padrón 2
14-04	France	W 8-1	Zaragoza	Fr	Rubio 4, Bienzobas 2, Goiburu 2
15-05	England	W 4-3	Madrid	Fr	Rubio 2, Lazcano, Goiburu
1-01-1930	Czechoslovakia	W 1-0	Barcelona	Fr	Sastre
14-06	Czechoslovakia	L 0-2	Prague	Fr	
22-06	Italy	W 3-2	Bologna	Fr	Luis Regueiro 2, Ventolra
30-11	Portugal	W 1-0	Oporto	Fr	Peña
19-04-1931	Italy	D 0-0	Bilbao	Fr	
26-04	Rep. Ireland	D 1-1	Barcelona	Fr	Arocha
9-12	England	L 1-7	London	Fr	Gorostiza
13-12	Rep. Ireland	W 5-0	Dublin	Fr	Luis Regueiro 2, Arocha, Samitier, Vantolrá
24-04-1932	Yugoslavia	W 2-1	Oviedo	Fr	Lángara, Luis Regueiro
2-04-1933	Portugal	W 3-0	Vigo	Fr	Elícegui 2, Larrinaga
23-04	France	L 0-1	Paris	Fr	
30-04	Yugoslavia	D 1-1	Belgrade	Fr	Goiburu
21-05	Bulgaria	W 13-0	Madrid	Fr	Chacho 6, Elícegui 3, Luis Regueiro 2, Bosch, OG
11-03-1934	Portugal	W 9-0	Madrid	WCq	Lángara 5, Luis Regueiro 2, Vantolrá, Chacho
18-03	Portugal	W 2-1	Lisbon	WCq	Lángara 2
27-05	Brazil	W 3-1	Genoa	WCr1	Lángara 2, Iraragorri
31-05	Italy	D 1-1	Florence	WCqf	Luis Regueiro
1-06	Italy	L 0-1	Florence	WCqf	
24-01-1935	France	W 2-0	Madrid	Fr	Luis Regueiro, Hilario
5-05	Portugal	D 3-3	Lisbon	Fr	Lángara 2, Gorostiza
12-05	Germany	W 2-1	Cologne	Fr	Lángara 2
19-01-1936	Austria	L 4-5	Madrid	Fr	Lángara 2, Luis Regueiro 2
23-02	Germany	L 1-2	Barcelona	Fr	Luis Regueiro
26-04	Czechoslovakia	L 0-1	Prague	Fr	

3-05	Switzerland	W 2-0	Berne	Fr	Lángara, Lecue
12-01-1941	Portugal	D 2-2	Lisbon	Fr	Campanal, Escolá
16-03	Portugal	W 5-1	Bilbao	Fr	Epi 2, Herrerita, Campanal, Campos
28-12	Switzerland	W 3-2	Valencia	Fr	Mundo 2, Campos
15-03-1942	France	W 4-0	Seville	Fr	Campos 2, Mundo, Epi
12-04	Germany	D 1-1	Berlin	Fr	Campos
19-04	Italy	L 0-4	Milan	Fr	
11-03-1945	Portugal	D 2-2	Lisbon	Fr	César, Epi
6-05	Portugal	W 4-2	La Coruña	Fr	Zarra 2, Herrerita, César
23-06-1946	Rep. Ireland	L 0-1	Madrid	Fr	
26-01-1947	Portugal	L 1-4	Lisbon	Fr	Iriondo
2-03	Rep. Ireland	L 2-3	Dublin	Fr	Zarra 2
21-03-1948	Portugal	W 2-0	Madrid	Fr	César, Gaínza
30-05	Rep. Ireland	W 2-1	Barcelona	Fr	Igoa 2
20-06	Switzerland	D 3-3	Zurich	Fr	Igoa 2, Pahíño
2-01-1949	Belgium	D 1-1	Barcelona	Fr	Silva
20-03	Portugal	D 1-1	Lisbon	Fr	Zarra
27-03	Italy	L 1-3	Madrid	Fr	Gaínza
12-06	Rep. Ireland	W 4-1	Dublin	Fr	Zarra 2, Basora, Igoa
19-06	France	W 5-1	Paris	Fr	Basora 3, Gaínza 2
2-04-1950	Portugal	W 5-1	Madrid	WCq	Zarra 2, Basora, Molowny, Panizo
9-04	Portugal	D 2-2	Lisbon	WCq	Zarra, Gaínza
25-06	USA	W 3-1	Curitiba	WCr1	Igoa, Basora, Zarra
29-06	Chile	W 2-0	Rio de Janeiro	WCr1	Basora, Zarra
2-07	England	W 1-0	Rio de Janeiro	WCr1	Zarra
9-07	Uruguay	D 2-2	Sao Paulo	WCr2	Basora 2
13-07	Brazil	L 1-6	Rio de Janeiro	WCr2	Igoa
16-07	Sweden	L 1-3	Sao Paulo	WCr2	Zarra
18-02-1951	Switzerland	W 6-3	Madrid	Fr	Zarra 4, Gaínza, César
10-06	Belgium	D 3-3	Brussels	Fr	Zarra 2, Gonzalvo (III)
17-06	Sweden	D 0-0	Stockholm	Fr	
1-06-1952	Rep. Ireland	W 6-0	Madrid	Fr	Basora 2, Coque, César, Panizo, Gaínza
8-06	Turkey	D 0-0	Istanbul	Fr	
7-12	Argentina	L 0-1	Madrid	Fr	
28-12	West Germany	D 2-2	Madrid	Fr	Gaínza, César
19-03-1953	Belgium	W 3-1	Barcelona	Fr	Marcet 2, Venancio
5-07	Argentina	L 0-1	Buenos Aires	Fr	
12-07	Chile	W 2-1	Santiago	Fr	Venancio, Kubala
8-11	Sweden	D 2-2	Bilbao	Fr	Venancio, Molowny
6-01-1954	Turkey	W 4-1	Madrid	WCq	Venancio, Gaínza, Miguel, Rafael Alsúa
14-03	Turkey	L 0-1	Istanbul	WCq	
17-03	Turkey	D 2-2	Rome	WCq	Arteche, Escudero
17-03-1955	France	L 1-2	Madrid	Fr	Gaínza
18-05	England	D 1-1	Madrid	Fr	Rial
19-06	Switzerland	W 3-0	Geneva	Fr	Collar, Arieta, Maguregui
27-11	Rep. Ireland	D 2-2	Dublin	Fr	Pahíño 2
30-11	England	L 1-4	London	Fr	Arieta
3-06-1956	Portugal	L 1-3	Lisbon	Fr	Peiró
30-01-1957	Holland	W 5-1	Madrid	Fr	Di Stéfano 3, Kubala, Garay
10-03	Switzerland	D 2-2	Madrid	WCq	Suárez, Miguel
31-03	Belgium	W 5-0	Brussels	Fr	Di Stéfano 2, Suárez, Mateos
8-05	Scotland	L 2-4	Glasgow	WCq	Kubala, Suárez
26-05	Scotland	W 4-1	Madrid	WCq	Basora 2, Mateos, Kubala
6-11	Turkey	W 3-0	Madrid	Fr	Kubala 3
24-11	Switzerland	W 4-1	Lausanne	WCq	Di Stéfano 2, Kubala 2
13-03-1958	France	D 2-2	Paris	Fr	Kubala, Suárez
19-03	West Germany	L 0-2	Frankfurt	Fr	
13-04	Portugal	W 1-0	Madrid	Fr	Di Stéfano
15-10	Nth. Ireland	W 6-2	Madrid	Fr	Tejada 4, Kubala, Suárez
28-02-1959	Italy	D 1-1	Rome	Fr	Di Stéfano
28-06	Poland	W 4-2	Chorzow	ECr1	Di Stéfano 2, Suárez 2
14-10	Poland	W 3-0	Madrid	ECr1	Di Stéfano, Gensana, Gento
22-11	Austria	W 6-3	Valencia	Fr	Di Stéfano 2, Suárez 2, Martínez, Mateos
17-12	France	L 3-4	Paris	Fr	Suárez, Martínez, Vergés
13-03-1960	Italy	W 3-1	Barcelona	Fr	Vergés, Di Stéfano, Martínez
15-05	England	W 3-0	Madrid	Fr	Martínez 2, Peiró
	Soviet Union	Walk-over		ECqf	Spain withdrew. Tie awarded to Soviet Union
10-07	Peru	W 3-1	Lima	Fr	Suárez 2, Di Stéfano
14-07	Chile	W 4-0	Santiago	Fr	Di Stéfano 2, Martínez, Collar
17-07	Chile	W 4-1	Santiago	Fr	Di Stéfano 2, Pereda Peiró
24-07	Argentina	L 0-2	Buenos Aires	Fr	

26-10	England	L 2-4	London	Fr	Del Sol, Suárez
30-10	Austria	L 0-3	Vienna	Fr	
2-04-1961	France	W 2-0	Madrid	Fr	Gensana, Gento
19-04	Wales	W 2-1	Cardiff	WCq	Foncho, Di Stéfano
18-05	Wales	D 1-1	Madrid	WCq	Peiró
11-06	Argentina	W 2-0	Seville	Fr	Del Sol, Di Stéfano
12-11	Morocco	W 1-0	Casablanca	WCq	Del Sol
23-11	Morocco	W 3-2	Madrid	WCq	Marcelino, Di Stéfano, Collar
10-12	France	D 1-1	Paris	Fr	Félix Ruiz
31-05-1962	Czechoslovakia	L 0-1	Viña del Mar	WCr1	
3-06	Mexico	W 1-0	Viña del Mar	WCr1	Peiró
6-06	Brazil	L 1-2	Viña del Mar	WCr1	Adelardo
1-11	Romania	W 6-0	Madrid	ECr1	Guillot 3, Veloso, Collar, OG
25-11	Romania	L 1-3	Bucharest	ECr1	Veloso
2-12	Belgium	D 1-1	Brussels	Fr	Guillot
9-01-1963	France	D 0-0	Barcelona	Fr	
30-05	Nth. Ireland	D 1-1	Bilbao	ECr2	Amancio
13-06	Scotland	L 2-6	Madrid	Fr	Adelardo, Veloso
30-10	Nth. Ireland	W 1-0	Belfast	ECr2	Gento
1-12	Belgium	L 1-2	Valencia	Fr	Zoco
11-03-1964	Rep. Ireland	W 5-1	Seville	ECqf	Amancio 2, Fusté, Marcelino 2
8-04	Rep. Ireland	W 2-0	Dublin	ECqf	Zaballa 2
17-06	Hungary	W 2-1	Madrid	ECsf	Pereda, Amancio
21-06	Soviet Union	W 2-1	Madrid	ECf	Pereda, Marcelino
15-11	Portugal	L 1-2	Oporto	Fr	Fusté
5-05-1965	Rep. Ireland	L 0-1	Dublin	WCq	
8-05	Scotland	D 0-0	Glasgow	Fr	
27-10	Rep. Ireland	W 4-1	Seville	WCq	Pereda 3, Lapetra
10-11	Rep. Ireland	W 1-0	Paris	WCq	Ufarte
8-12	England	L 0-2	Madrid	Fr	
23-06-1966	Uruguay	D 1-1	La Coruña	Fr	Gento
13-07	Argentina	L 1-2	Birmingham	WCr1	Pirri
15-07	Switzerland	W 2-1	Sheffield	WCr1	Sanchís, Amancio
20-07	West Germany	L 1-2	Birmingham	WCr1	Fusté
23-10	Rep. Ireland	D 0-0	Dublin	ECq	
7-12	Rep. Ireland	W 2-0	Valencia	ECq	José María, Pirri
1-02-1967	Turkey	D 0-0	Istanbul	ECq	
24-05	England	L 0-2	London	Fr	
31-05	Turkey	W 2-0	Bilbao	ECq	Grosso, Gento
1-10	Czechoslovakia	L 0-1	Prague	ECq	
22-10	Czechoslovakia	W 2-1	Madrid	ECq	Pirri, Garáte
28-02-1968	Sweden	W 3-1	Seville	Fr	Amancio 2, Rifé
3-04	England	L 0-1	London	ECqf	
2-05	Sweden	D 1-1	Malmo	Fr	Castellano
8-05	England	L 1-2	Madrid	ECqf	Amancio
17-10	France	W 3-1	Lyon	Fr	Pirri, Ufarte, Luis
27-10	Yugoslavia	D 0-0	Belgrade	WCq	
11-12	Belgium	D 1-1	Madrid	WCq	Gárate
23-02-1969	Belgium	L 1-2	Liege	WCq	Asensi
26-03	Switzerland	W 1-0	Valencia	Fr	Bustillo
23-04	Mexico	D 0-0	Seville	Fr	
30-04	Yugoslavia	W 2-1	Barcelona	WCq	Bustillo, Amancio
25-06	Finland	L 0-2	Helsinki	WCq	
15-10	Finland	W 6-0	La Concepcion	WCq	Gárate 2, Pirri, Velázquez, Amancio, Quino
11-02-1970	West Germany	W 2-0	Seville	Fr	Arieta 2
21-02	Italy	D 2-2	Madrid	Fr	Arieta 2
22-04	Switzerland	W 1-0	Lausanne	Fr	Rojo
28-10	Greece	W 2-1	Zaragoza	Fr	Luis, Quini
11-11	Nth. Ireland	W 3-0	Seville	ECq	Rexach, Pirri, Luis
20-02-1971	Italy	W 2-1	Cagliari	Fr	Pirri, Uriarte
17-03	France	D 2-2	Valencia	Fr	Pirri 2
9-05	Cyprus	W 2-0	Nicosia	ECq	Pirri, Violeta
30-05	Soviet Union	L 1-2	Moscow	ECq	Rexach
27-10	Soviet Union	D 0-0	Seville	ECq	
24-11	Cyprus	W 7-0	Granada	ECq	Pirri 2, Quini 2, Aguilar, Lora, Rojo
12-01-1972	Hungary	W 1-0	Madrid	Fr	Arieta
16-02	Nth. Ireland	D 1-1	Hull	ECq	Rojo
12-04	Greece	D 0-0	Salonica	Fr	
23-05	Uruguay	W 2-0	Madrid	Fr	Valdez, Gárate
11-10	Argentina	W 1-0	Madrid	Fr	Asensi
19-10	Yugoslavia	D 2-2	Las Palmas	WCq	Amancio, Asensi

Date	Opponent	Result	Venue	Comp	Scorers
17-01-1973	Greece	W 3-2	Athens	WCq	Valdez 2, Claramunt
21-02	Greece	W 3-1	Malaga	WCq	Claramunt, Sol, Roberto Martínez
2-05	Holland	L 2-3	Amsterdam	Fr	Valdez 2
17-10	Turkey	D 0-0	Istanbul	Fr	
21-10	Yugoslavia	D 0-0	Zagreb	WCq	
24-11	West Germany	L 1-2	Stuttgart	Fr	Claramunt
13-02-1974	Yugoslavia	L 0-1	Frankfurt	WCq	
23-02	West Germany	W 1-0	Barcelona	Fr	Asensi
25-09	Denmark	W 2-1	Copenhagen	ECq	Claramunt, Roberto Martínez
12-10	Argentina	D 1-1	Buenos Aires	Fr	Pirri
20-11	Scotland	W 2-1	Glasgow	ECq	Quini 2
5-02-1975	Scotland	D 1-1	Valencia	ECq	Megido
17-04	Romania	D 1-1	Madrid	ECq	Velázquez
12-10	Denmark	W 2-0	Barcelona	ECq	Pirri, Capón
16-11	Romania	D 2-2	Bucharest	ECq	Villar, Santillana
24-04-1976	West Germany	D 1-1	Madrid	ECqf	Santillana
22-05	West Germany	L 0-2	Munich	ECqf	
10-10	Yugoslavia	W 1-0	Seville	WCq	Pirri
9-02-1977	Rep. Ireland	W 1-0	Dublin	Fr	Satrústegui
27-03	Hungary	D 1-1	Alicante	Fr	Juanito
16-04	Romania	L 0-1	Bucharest	WCq	
21-09	Switzerland	W 2-1	Berne	Fr	Rubén Cano, López Ufarte
26-10	Romania	W 2-0	Madrid	WCq	Leal, Rubén Cano
30-11	Yugoslavia	W 1-0	Belgrade	WCq	Rubén Cano
25-01-1978	Italy	W 2-1	Madrid	Fr	Pirri, Dani
29-03	Norway	W 3-0	Gijon	Fr	Quini, Villar, Dani
26-04	Mexico	W 2-0	Granada	Fr	Quini, Dani
24-05	Uruguay	D 0-0	Montevideo	Fr	
3-06	Austria	L 1-2	Buenos Aires	WCr1	Dani
7-06	Brazil	D 0-0	Mar del Plata	WCr1	
11-06	Sweden	W 1-0	Buenos Aires	WCr1	Asensi
4-10	Yugoslavia	W 2-1	Zagreb	ECq	Juanito, Santillana
8-11	France	L 0-1	Paris	Fr	
15-11	Romania	W 1-0	Valencia	ECq	Asensi
13-12	Cyprus	W 5-0	Salamanca	ECq	Santillana 2, Asensi, Rubén Cano, Del Bosque
21-12	Italy	L 0-1	Rome	Fr	
14-03-1979	Czechoslovakia	L 0-1	Bratislava	Fr	
4-04	Romania	D 2-2	Craiova	ECq	Dani 2
26-09	Portugal	D 1-1	Vigo	Fr	Dani
10-10	Yugoslavia	L 0-1	Valencia	ECq	
14-11	Denmark	L 1-3	Cadiz	Fr	Mesa
9-12	Cyprus	W 3-1	Limassol	ECq	Villar, Santillana, Saura
23-01-1980	Holland	W 1-0	Vigo	Fr	Dani
13-02	East Germany	L 0-1	Malaga	Fr	
26-03	England	L 0-2	Barcelona	Fr	
16-04	Czechoslovakia	D 2-2	Gijon	Fr	Migueli, Quini
21-05	Denmark	D 2-2	Copenhagen	Fr	Saura, Alexanco
12-06	Italy	D 0-0	Milan	ECr1	
15-06	Belgium	L 1-2	Milan	ECr1	Quini
18-06	England	L 1-2	Naples	ECr1	Dani
24-09	Hungary	D 2-2	Budapest	Fr	Juanito, Satrústegui
15-10	East Germany	D 0-0	Leipzig	Fr	
12-11	Poland	L 1-2	Barcelona	Fr	Dani
18-02-1981	France	W 1-0	Madrid	Fr	Juanito
25-03	England	W 2-1	London	Fr	Satrústegui, Zamora
15-04	Hungary	L 0-3	Valencia	Fr	
20-06	Portugal	L 0-2	Oporto	Fr	
24-06	Mexico	W 3-1	Mexico City	Fr	Juanito 2, Zamora
28-06	Venezuela	W 2-0	Caracus	Fr	Juanito, Satrústegui
2-07	Colombia	D 1-1	Bogota	Fr	Alexanco
5-07	Chile	D 1-1	Santiago	Fr	Satrústegui
8-07	Brazil	L 0-1	Bahia	Fr	
23-09	Austria	D 0-0	Vienna	Fr	
14-10	Luxembourg	W 3-0	Valencia	Fr	López Ufarte 2, Saura
18-11	Poland	W 3-2	Lodz	Fr	López Ufarte, Alexanco, Alonso
16-12	Belgium	W 2-0	Valencia	Fr	Satrústegui 2
24-02-1982	Scotland	W 3-0	Valencia	Fr	Víctor, Quini, Gallego
24-03	Wales	D 1-1	Valencia	Fr	Satrústegui
28-04	Switzerland	W 2-0	Valencia	Fr	Tendillo, Alexanco
16-06	Honduras	D 1-1	Valencia	WCr1	López Ufarte
20-06	Yugoslavia	W 2-1	Valencia	WCr1	Juanito, Saura
25-06	Nth. Ireland	L 0-1	Valencia	WCr1	

2-07	West Germany	L 1-2	Madrid	WCr2	Zamora
5-07	England	D 0-0	Madrid	WCr2	
27-10	Iceland	W 1-0	Malaga	ECq	Pedraza
17-11	Rep. Ireland	D 3-3	Dublin	ECq	Maceda, Víctor, OG
16-02-1983	Holland	W 1-0	Seville	ECq	Señor
27-04	Rep. Ireland	W 2-0	Zaragoza	ECq	Santillana, Rincón
15-05	Malta	W 3-2	Ta'Qali	ECq	Señor, Carrasco, Gordillo
29-05	Iceland	W 1-0	Reykjavik	ECq	Maceda
5-10	France	D 1-1	Paris	Fr	Señor
16-11	Holland	L 1-2	Rotterdam	ECq	Santillana
21-12	Malta	W 12-1	Sevilla	ECq	Santillana 4, Rincón 4, Maceda 2, Sarabia, Señor
18-01-1984	Hungary	L 0-1	Cadiz	Fr	
29-02	Luxembourg	W 1-0	Luxembourg	Fr	Maceda
2-04	Denmark	W 2-1	Valencia	Fr	Santillana, Señor
26-05	Switzerland	W 4-0	Geneva	Fr	Santillana 2, OG, Gallego
31-05	Hungary	D 1-1	Budapest	Fr	Rincón
7-06	Yugoslavia	L 0-1	La Linea	Fr	
14-06	Romania	D 1-1	Saint Etienne	ECr1	Carrasco
17-06	Portugal	D 1-1	Marseille	ECr1	Sousa
20-06	West Germany	W 1-0	Paris	ECr1	Maceda
24-06	Denmark	D 1-1	Lyon	ECsf	Maceda
27-06	France	L 0-2	Paris	ECf	
17-10	Wales	W 3-0	Seville	WCq	Rincón, Carrasco, Butragueño
14-11	Scotland	L 1-3	Glasgow	WCq	Goicoechea
23-01-1985	Finland	W 3-1	Alicante	Fr	Rincón, Butragueño 2
27-02	Scotland	W 1-0	Seville	WCq	Clos
27-03	Nth. Ireland	D 0-0	Palma	Fr	
30-04	Wales	L 0-3	Wrexham	WCq	
26-05	Rep. Ireland	D 0-0	Cork	Fr	
12-06	Iceland	W 2-1	Reykjavik	WCq	Sarabia, Marcos
25-09	Iceland	W 2-1	Seville	WCq	Rincón, Gordillo
20-11	Austria	D 0-0	Zaragoza	Fr	
18-12	Bulgaria	W 2-0	Valencia	Fr	Michel, Calderé
22-01-1986	Soviet Union	W 2-0	Las Palmas	Fr	Salinas, Eloy
19-02	Belgium	W 3-0	Elche	Fr	Butragueño, Salinas, Macedo
26-03	Poland	W 3-0	Cadiz	Fr	Butragueño, Calderé, Salinas
1-06	Brazil	L 0-1	Guadalajara	WCr1	
7-06	Nth. Ireland	W 2-0	Guadalajara	WCr1	Butragueño, Salinas
12-06	Algeria	W 3-0	Monterrey	WCr1	Calderé 2, Eloy
18-06	Denmark	W 5-1	Queretaro	WCr2	Butragueño 4, Goicoechea
22-06	Belgium	D 1-1	Puebla	WCqf	Señor
24-09	Greece	W 3-1	Gijon	Fr	Salinas, Víctor, Francisco
15-10	West Germany	D 2-2	Hanover	Fr	Butragueño, Goicoechea
12-11	Romania	W 1-0	Seville	ECq	Michel
3-12	Albania	W 2-1	Tirana	ECq	Arteche, Joaquín
21-01-1987	Holland	D 1-1	Barcelona	Fr	Calderé
18-02	England	L 2-4	Madrid	Fr	Butragueño, Ramón
1-04	Austria	W 3-2	Vienna	ECq	Eloy 2, Carrasco
29-04	Romania	L 1-3	Bucharest	ECq	Calderé
23-09	Luxembourg	W 2-0	Castellon	Fr	Carrasco, Butragueño
14-10	Austria	W 2-0	Seville	ECq	Michel, Sanchís
18-11	Albania	W 5-0	Seville	ECq	Baquero 3, Michel, Llorente
27-01-1988	East Germany	D 0-0	Valencia	Fr	
24-02	Czechoslovakia	L 1-2	Malaga	Fr	Salinas
23-03	France	L 1-2	Bordeaux	Fr	Calderé
27-04	Scotland	D 0-0	Madrid	Fr	
1-06	Sweden	L 1-3	Salamanca	Fr	Butragueño
5-06	Switzerland	D 1-1	Basle	Fr	Andrinúa
11-06	Denmark	W 3-2	Hanover	ECr1	Michel, Butragueño, Gordillo
14-06	Italy	L 0-1	Frankfurt	ECr1	
17-06	West Germany	L 0-2	Munich	ECr1	
14-09	Yugoslavia	L 1-2	Oviedo	Fr	Michel
12-10	Argentina	D 1-1	Seville	Fr	Butragueño
16-11	Rep. Ireland	W 2-0	Seville	WCq	Manolo, Butragueño
21-12	Nth. Ireland	W 4-0	Seville	WCq	OG, Butragueño, Michel, Roberto
22-01-1989	Malta	W 2-0	Ta'Qali	WCq	Michel, Beguiristain
8-02	Nth. Ireland	W 2-0	Belfast	WCq	Andrinúa, Manolo
23-03	Malta	W 4-0	Seville	WCq	Michel 2, Manolo
26-04	Rep. Ireland	L 0-1	Dublin	WCq	
20-09	Poland	W 1-0	La Coruña	Fr	Michel
11-10	Hungary	D 2-2	Budapest	WCq	Salinas, Michel
15-11	Hungary	W 4-0	Seville	WCq	Manolo, Butragueño, Juanito, Gomez

13-12	Switzerland	W 2-1	Tenerife	Fr	Michel, Minambres
21-02-1990	Czechoslovakia	W 1-0	Alicante	Fr	Manolo
28-03	Austria	L 2-3	Malaga	Fr	Manolo, Butragueño
26-05	Yugoslavia	W 1-0	Ljubljana	Fr	Butrageuño
13-06	Uruguay	D 0-0	Udine	WCr1	
17-06	South Korea	W 3-1	Udine	WCr1	Michel 3
21-06	Belgium	W 2-1	Verona	WCr1	Michel, Gorriz
26-06	Yugoslavia	L 1-2	Verona	WCr2	Salinas
12-09	Brazil	W 3-0	Gijon	Fr	Carlos, Fernando, Michel
10-10	Iceland	W 2-1	Seville	ECq	Butragueño, Carlos
14-11	Czechoslovakia	L 2-3	Prague	ECq	Roberto, Carlos
19-12	Albania	W 9-0	Seville	ECq	Amor, Carlos 2, Butragueño 4, Hierro, Baquero
16-01-1991	Portugal	D 1-1	Castellon	Fr	Moya
20-02	France	L 1-3	Paris	ECq	Baquero
27-03	Hungary	L 2-4	Santander	Fr	Manolo, Carlos
17-04	Romania	L 0-2	Caceres	Fr	
1-09	Uruguay	W 2-1	Oviedo	Fr	Martin Vazquez, Manolo
25-09	Iceland	L 0-2	Reykjavik	ECq	
12-10	France	L 1-2	Seville	ECq	Abelardo
13-11	Czechoslovakia	W 2-1	Seville	ECq	Abelardo, Michel
15-01-1992	Portugal	D 0-0	Torres Novas	Fr	
19-02	CIS	D 1-1	Valencia	Fr	Hierro
11-03	USA	W 2-0	Valladolid	Fr	Beguiristain, Hierro
22-04	Albania	W 3-0	Seville	WCq	Michel 2, Hierro
9-09	England	W 1-0	Santander	Fr	Fonseca
23-09	Latvia	D 0-0	Riga	WCq	
14-10	Northern Ireland	D 0-0	Belfast	WCq	
18-11	Rep. Ireland	D 0-0	Seville	WCq	
16-12	Latvia	W 5-0	Seville	WCq	Bakero, Guardiola, Alfonso, Beguiristáin 2
27-01-1993	Mexico	D 1-1	Las Palmas	Fr	Toni
24-02	Lithuania	W 5-0	Seville	WCq	Cristóbal, Bakero, Beguiristáin, Christiansen, Aldana
31-03	Denmark	L 0-1	Copenhagen	WCq	
28-04	Northern Ireland	W 3-1	Seville	WCq	Salinas 2, Hierro
2-06	Lithuania	W 2-0	Vilnius	WCq	Guerrero 2
8-09	Chile	W 2-0	Alicante	Fr	Guerrero 2
22-09	Albania	W 5-1	Tirana	WCq	Salinas 3, Toni, Caminero
13-10	Rep. Ireland	W 3-1	Dublin	WCq	Caminero, Salinas 2
17-11	Denmark	W 1-0	Seville	WCq	Hierro
20-01-1994	Portugal	D 2-2	Vigo	Fr	Salinas, Juanele
9-02	Poland	D 1-1	Tenerife	Fr	Sergei
23-03	Croatia	L 0-2	Valencia	Fr	
2-06	Finland	W 2-1	Tampere	Fr	Felipe, Salinas
10-06	Canada	W 2-0	Montreal	Fr	Salinas, Juanele
17-06	South Korea	D 2-2	Dallas	WCr1	Salinas, Goikoetxea
21-06	Germany	D 1-1	Chicago	WCr1	Goikoetxea
27-06	Bolivia	W 3-1	Chicago	WCr1	Guardiola, Caminero 2
2-07	Switzerland	W 3-0	Washington	WCr2	Hierro, Luis Enrique, Beguiristáin
9-07	Italy	L 1-2	Boston	WCqf	Caminero
7-09	Cyprus	W 2-1	Limassol	ECq	Higuera 2
12-10	Macedonia	W 2-0	Skopje	ECq	Salinas 2
16-11	Denmark	W 3-0	Seville	ECq	Nadal, Donato, Luis Enrique
30-11	Finland	W 2-0	Malaga	Fr	Nadal, Goikoetxea
17-12	Belgium	W 4-1	Brussels	ECq	Hierro, Donato, Salinas, Luis Enrique
18-01-1995	Uruguay	D 2-2	La Coruña	Fr	Pizzi, Donato
22-02	Germany	D 0-0	Jerez	Fr	
29-03	Belgium	D 1-1	Seville	ECq	Guerrero
26-04	Armenia	W 2-0	Yerevan	ECq	Amavisca, Goikoetxea
7-06	Armenia	W 1-0	Seville	ECq	Hierro

SWEDEN

Though second best to Denmark in the early years of the century, by the 1920s Sweden had taken over the role of the leading Scandinavian football nation, a role they have been hard pressed to hold onto since the rebirth of the Danes in the 1980s. If Sweden does still hold an edge it is in a stronger club scene, which has seen IFK Göteborg crowned as UEFA Cup winners on two occasions, the only Scandinavian club to achieve such a feat.

Gothenburg was the early centre of Swedish football and it remains the city that is most passionate about the game; not surprisingly it is also the most successful. The oldest club in existence today, Örgryte IS, was formed there in 1887, as was the game's first governing body, the Swedish Sports and Athletic Association in 1895. They organised a championship open only to Gothenburg clubs and in 1896 Örgryte became the first champions. In 1900 the tournament was opened up to clubs from Stockholm, in 1902 an unofficial national body based in Stockholm was formed and in 1904, a few months after Sweden joined FIFA as one of the founding members, the current Swedish football association was formed. They took over the running of the championship which continued as a knock-out competition until 1925 when a national league was instituted. These early years of competition were dominated by clubs from Gothenburg and Stockholm, especially Örgryte, IFK, GAIS, AIK and Djurgårdens. Although IFK Eskilstuna became the first provincial club to win the championship in 1921, it was not until the thirties and forties that other provincial teams such Helsingborg IF, IFK Norrköping and Malmö FF made their presence felt.

Sweden's national side first took the field in July 1908 and recorded the most impressive international debut to date, beating Norway 11-3 in Gothenburg. Until 1920, however, results were mixed. A heavy defeat against the English amateurs at the 1908 Olympic Games was followed by another first round exit in the 1912 tournament. Despite hosting the games the Swedes lost 4-3 to Holland and it was left to Denmark to fly the flag for Scandinavia. In the Antwerp games of 1920, the Dutch were responsible for Sweden's demise once again, this time in the quarter-finals. One thing the Swedes did not find difficult, however, was scoring goals. In the two games they played in the competition proper they scored 13! Seven were scored by Herbert Karlsson, who along with Karl Gustafsson was one of the early stars of the Swedish game.

Sweden has consistently produced good players, and few have been better than Sven Rydell, the Örgryte inside forward whose 49 goals in 43 games between 1923 and 1932 remains a Swedish record. Along with players like Harry and Albin Dahl, Knut Kroon, Per Kaufeldt and Sigfrid Lindberg in goal, the Swedes built a strong reputation for themselves in the 1920s and early 1930s. In 1924 they laid the Dutch ghost to rest, beating them 3-1 to clinch a deserved bronze medal at the Paris Olympics, but it was not until the 1934 World Cup that another major competition was entered.

At this time the Scandinavian Championship was the major feature of the fixture list, though curiously the 1924-29 tournament was won by Denmark and the 1929-32 edition by Norway. Not until the third edition (1933-36) did Sweden prove triumphant, when the national side was arguably inferior to the team of the 1920s and early 1930s. Sven Jonasson, Tore Keller and Eric Persson led the Swedes to fourth place in the 1938 World Cup, but this was achieved with a bye in the first round and a relatively easy quarter-final tie against Cuba.

The late 1940s saw Sweden at perhaps their best ever, boasting one of the most famous forward lines ever in football. Gunnar Gren, Gunnar Nordahl and Nils Liedholm formed the famous Gre-No-Li trio that was instrumental in winning the Swedes the gold medal at the 1948 Olympic Games in London. So impressed were the scouts of AC Milan that all three were signed up in 1949, and all three made a huge impact on the Italian game, between them scoring 329 goals for Milan alone over subsequent years.

Suddenly Swedish players were fashionable and over the years the exodus to the major European leagues has continued unabated. Of the side that won the Olympic title in such style, only two remained in Sweden for the 1950 World Cup qualifiers, but with Karl Palmer and Nacka Skoglund drafted into the side, even without the exiles - who were ineligible to play for their country due to the strict amateur rules of the Swedish association - they qualified and eventually finished third in the final tournament. On the way they defeated the defending champions Italy 3-2 in Sao Paulo, which was good news for the players, eight of whom were signed up by Italian teams!

The supply of class players continued, among them Kurt Hamrin, who also made his name in Italy, and so it was with some relief that the football association overturned its rule forbidding the use of foreign-based players in time for the 1958 World Cup, which Sweden had the honour of staging. A home side without all of these stars would have been unimaginable, and certainly Sweden would not have reached the final as they did without them. Apart from Agne Simonsson and Gren, who had returned from Italy, the other forwards, Liedholm, Hamrin and Skogland, were all still based there.

A common factor running through the triumphant sides of 1948, 1950 and 1958 was George Raynor, their English manager, but even he could do nothing to overcome their opponents in the final. Having surpassed themselves by beating the strong Soviets and West Germans in the quarter- and semi-finals, the Swedes now found themselves facing Brazil and were simply no match for the talented South Americans, succumbing 5-2 despite taking a third-minute lead. The defeat still meant, however, that the Swedes remain as one of only ten countries to have appeared in a World Cup Final, an honour in itself. Raynor remained as manager until Switzerland qualified for Chile at the Swedes' expense after a play-off between the two countries in Berlin, and the rest of the 1960s proved to be a big disappointment. Both the national and club sides did not find the new competitions that were springing up easy going.

The 1970s were far more successful, with qualification for three World Cups. In 1974 a side including Ralf Edström and Ove Kindvall, both of whom were based in Holland, Ronnie Hellström in goal and Bjorn Nordqvist in defence, reached the second round of the World Cup in West Germany, but they were outclassed by the Germans and the Poles and finished third in the group. Though they qualified for Argentina in 1978 and Italy in 1990, the Swedes lacked consistency. The 1992 European Championship finals saw them appear for the first time in seven attempts only because as hosts they were given a free passage. One of the few pillars of stability was

THE ORDER OF MERIT

	Team	All G	All S	All B	League G	League S	League B	Cup G	Cup S	Europe G	Europe S	Europe B
1	Malmö FF	28	16	4	14	13	4	14	2	-	1	-
2	IFK Göteborg	21	8	12	15	7	11	4	1	2	-	1
3	IFK Norrköping	18	14	4	12	10	4	6	4	-	-	-
4	Örgryte IS Göteborg	14	5	4	14	5	4	-	-	-	-	-
5	AIK Stockholm	13	15	7	9	10	7	4	5	-	-	-
6	Djurgårdens IF Stockholm	9	13	7	8	10	7	1	3	-	-	-
7	GAIS Göteborg	7	5	3	6	4	3	1	1	-	-	-
8	Helsingborg IF	6	8	7	5	6	7	1	2	-	-	-
9	Östers IF Växjö	5	7	4	4	3	4	1	4	-	-	-
10	IF Elfsborg Borås	4	7	3	4	5	3	-	2	-	-	-
11	Åtvidabergs FF	4	5	-	2	2	-	2	3	-	-	-
12	Halmstad BK	3	1	-	2	1	-	1	-	-	-	-
13	Kalmar FF	2	1	1	-	-	1	2	1	-	-	-
14	IK Sleipner Norrköping	1	4	1	1	3	1	-	1	-	-	-
	Landskrona BoIS	1	4	1	-	-	1	1	4	-	-	-
16	Degerfors IF	1	2	2	-	2	2	1	-	-	-	-
17	IFK Eskilstuna	1	1	-	1	1	-	-	-	-	-	-
	Råå IF Helsingborg	1	1	-	-	1	-	1	-	-	-	-
19	Brynäs IF Gävle	1	-	-	1	-	-	-	-	-	-	-
	Fassbergs IF	1	-	-	1	-	-	-	-	-	-	-
	Göteborg IF	1	-	-	1	-	-	-	-	-	-	-
22	Hammarby IF Stockholm	-	4	-	-	2	-	-	2	-	-	-
23	IFK Uppsala	-	3	-	-	3	-	-	-	-	-	-
24	Göteborg FF	-	2	-	-	2	-	-	-	-	-	-
	Örgryte II	-	2	-	-	2	-	-	-	-	-	-
26	Örebro SK	-	2	1	-	1	1	-	1	-	-	-
27	Sandvikens IF	-	1	1	-	-	1	-	1	-	-	-
28	IK Brage	-	1	-	-	-	-	-	1	-	-	-
	Derby BK Linköping	-	1	-	-	1	-	-	-	-	-	-
	IV Göteborg	-	1	-	-	1	-	-	-	-	-	-
	Häcken BK Göteborg	-	1	-	-	-	-	-	1	-	-	-
	Jonköpings AIF	-	1	-	-	1	-	-	-	-	-	-
	Jonköping Södra	-	1	-	-	1	-	-	-	-	-	-
	BK Kenty Linköping	-	1	-	-	-	-	-	1	-	-	-
	IFK Malmö	-	1	-	-	1	-	-	-	-	-	-
	Sirius Uppsala	-	1	-	-	1	-	-	-	-	-	-
	IFK Stockholm	-	1	-	-	1	-	-	-	-	-	-

To the end of 1994 season for the Championship, 1995 for the Cup

Nordqvist, who between 1963 and 1978 made 115 appearances for his country. In 1978 he overtook the world record held by Bobby Moore, a position he held until he in turn was overtaken by, among others, Pat Jennings, Peter Shilton and Heinz Hermann.

At club level, Malmö FF somewhat surprisingly reached the final of the 1979 European Cup but lost to Nottingham Forest. Swedish clubs have never adopted full-time professionalism and virtually all the top names appear abroad, with Britain, Portugal, Holland, Belgium, Germany and Italy being the favoured destinations. IFK Göteborg did manage to go one better than Malmö by winning the UEFA Cup in 1982 and 1987 and lost to Barcelona in the semi-finals of the 1986 European Cup only after penalties, and all as a part-time side!

Sweden continues to produce quality players, but until full-time professionalism is introduced in the league, following the example of Denmark, clubs will not be able to hang on to the players they have nurtured. It is to the national team that the Swedish public looks for their greatest thrills, and this was never better illustrated than at the 1994 World Cup. Having reached the semi-finals of the European Championships two years earlier on home soil, the Swedes matched that in America in admirable fashion. With a forward line including Tomas Brolin, Martin Dahlin and Kennet Andersson, they were the top scorers in the tournament with 15 goals, and in goalkeeper Thomas Ravelli, their record cap-winner, they had one of the characters of the tournament. Having taken third place, the team returned home to a heroes' welcome.

Population: 8,529,000
Area, sq km: 449,964
% in urban areas: 83.4%
Capital city: Stockholm

Svenska Fotbollfoerbundet
Box 1216
S-17123 Solna
Sweden
Tel: + 46 8 7350900
Fax: + 46 8 275147

Year of formation	1904
Affiliation to FIFA	1904
Affiliation to UEFA	1954
Registered clubs	3242
Registered players	188 100
Registered referees	11 600
National stadium	Råsunda Stadion 33 000
National colours	Yellow/Blue/Yellow
Reserve colours	Blue/Blue/Blue
Season	April - October

THE RECORD

WORLD CUP

1930	Did not enter
1934	QT 1st/3 in group 5 - Final Tournament/Quarter-finalists
1938	QT 2nd/4 in group 1 - Final Tournament/Semi-finalists/ 4th place
1950	QT 1st/3 in group 5 - Final Tournament/2nd round/ 3rd place
1954	QT 2nd/3 in group 2
1958	QT Automatic - Final Tournament/Finalists
1962	QT 2nd/3 in group 1
1966	QT 2nd/3 in group 2
1970	QT 1st/3 in group 5 - Final Tournament/1st round
1974	QT 1st/4 in group 1 - Final Tournament/2nd round
1978	QT 1st/3 in group 6 - Final Tournament/1st round
1982	QT 3rd/5 in group 6
1986	QT 3rd/5 in group 2
1990	QT 1st/4 in group 2 - Final Tournament/1st round
1994	QT 1st/6 in group 6 - Final Tournament/Semi-finalists/ 3rd place

EUROPEAN CHAMPIONSHIP

1960	Did not enter
1964	Quarter-finalists
1968	QT 3rd/4 in group 2
1972	QT 3rd/4 in group 6
1976	QT 3rd/4 in group 3
1980	QT 3rd/4 in group 5
1984	QT 2nd/5 in group 5
1988	QT 2nd/5 in group 2
1992	QT Automatic - Final Tournament/Semi-finalists
1996	QT group 3

EUROPEAN CLUB COMPETITIONS

European Cup
Finalists - Malmö FF 1979
Cup Winners Cup
Quarter-finalists - Atvidabergs FF 1972 Malmö FF 1975 1987 IFK Göteborg 1980
UEFA Cup
Winners - IFK Göteborg 1982 1987

CLUB DIRECTORY

STOCKHOLM (Population - 1,449,000)

AIK Stockholm (1891)
(Allmänna Idrottsklubben)
Råsunda 30,000 – Black/White

Djurgårdens IF (1891)
(Idrottsförening)
Stockholms Stadion 22,000 – Light & dark blue stripes/Blue

Hammarby IF (1897)
Söderstadion 10,000 – White/Green

GOTHENBURG (Pop. - 710,000)

GAIS Göteborg (1894)
(Göteborgs Atlet & Idrottssälskap)
Nya Ullevi 52,000 – Green & black stripes/White

Häcken BK (1940)
(Bollklubben)
Rambergsvallen – Yellow/Black

IFK Göteborg (1904)
(Idrottsföreningen Kamraterna)
Nya Ullevi 52,000 – Blue & white stripes/Blue

Örgryte Idrottssälskap (1887)
Nya Ullevi 52,000 – Red/Blue

MALMÖ (Pop. - 445,000)

Malmö FF (1910)
(Fotboll Förening)
Malmö 26,000 – Sky blue/White

IFK Malmö (1899)
Malmö 26,000 – Yellow/White

ÖREBRO (Pop. - 119,000)

Örebro Sportklubb (1908)
Eyravallen 13,000 – White/Black

NORRKÖPING (Pop. - 119,000)

IFK Norrköping (1897)
Idrottspark 15,000 – White/Blue, black trim

HELSINGBORG (Pop. - 106,000)

Helsingborg IF (1907)
Olympia 16,000 – Red/Blue, black trim

Råå IF (1921)
Gamla Heden – Blue/White

BORÅS (Pop. - 100,000)

IF Elfsborg (1904)
Ryavallen 18,000 – Yellow/Black

ESKILSTUNA (Pop. - 88,000)

IFK Eskilstuna (1897)
Tunavallen – Blue/White

GÄVLE (Pop. - 87,000)

Brynäs IF (1912)
Geflering – Black/Black

HALMSTAD (Pop. - 77,000)

Halmstads BK (1914)
(Bollklubb)
Örjans Vall 20,000 – Blue/White

VÄXJÖ (Pop. - 67,000)

Östers IF (1930)
Vårendsvallen 15,000 – White/Blue, red trim

LULEA (Pop. - 66,000)

Lulea FF/IFK (1895)
Skogsvallen – Blue/White

ÅTVIDABERG

Åtvidabergs FF (1907)
Kopparvallen 11,000 – Blue/White

BORLANGE (Pop. - 46,000)

IK Brage (1925)
Domnarvsvallen 14,000 – Green/White

DEGERFORS

Degerfors IF (1907)
Stora Valla 15,000 – Red/White

KALMAR (Pop. - 53,000)

Kalmar FF (1910)
Fredriksskans 15,000 – Red/Red

SANDVIKEN (Pop. - 41,000)

Sandvikens IF (1918)
Jernvallen 21,000 – Red, white sleeves/White

LANDSKRONA (Pop. - 35,000)

Landskrona BoIS (1915)
(Boll & Idrottssällskap)
Idrottsparken 10,000 – Black & white stripes/Black

TRELLEBORG (Pop. - 34,000)

Trelleborgs FF (1926)
Idrottsplats 10,000 – Blue/White

SWEDISH LEAGUE CHAMPIONSHIP

Year	Winner	Score	Runner-up
1896	Örgryte IS	3-0	IV Göteborg
1897	Örgryte IS	1-0	Örgryte II
1898	Örgryte IS	3-0	AIK Stockholm
1899	Örgryte IS	4-0	Göteborg FF
1900	AIK Stockholm	1-0	Örgryte IS
1901	AIK Stockholm	W-O	Örgryte II
1902	Örgryte IS	9-0	Jonköpings AIF
1903	Göteborg IF	5-2	Göteborg FF
1904	Örgryte IS	2-1	Djurgårdens IF
1905	Örgryte IS	2-1	IFK Stockholm
1906	Örgryte IS	4-3	Djurgårdens IF
1907	Örgryte IS	4-1	IFK Uppsala
1908	IFK Göteborg	4-3	IFK Uppsala
1909	Örgryte IS	8-2	Djurgårdens IF
1910	IFK Göteborg	3-0	Djurgårdens IF
1911	AIK Stockholm	3-2	IFK Uppsala
1912	Djurgårdens IF	3-1	Örgryte IS
1913	Örgryte IS	3-2	Djurgårdens IF
1914	AIK Stockholm	7-2	Helsingborg IF
1915	Djurgårdens IF	4-1	Örgryte IS
1916	AIK Stockholm	3-1	Djurgårdens IF
1917	Djurgårdens IF	3-1	AIK Stockholm
1918	IFK Göteborg	5-0	Helsingborg IF
1919	GAIS Göteborg	4-1	Djurgårdens IF
1920	Djurgårdens IF	1-0	IK Sleipner
1921	IFK Eskilstuna	2-1	IK Sleipner
1922	GAIS Göteborg	3-1	Hammarby IF
1923	AIK Stockholm	5-1	IFK Eskilstuna
1924	Fassbergs IF	5-0	Sirius Uppsala
1925	Brynäs IF Gävle	4-2	Derby BK Linköping

1925k GAIS Göteborg 38 IFK Göteborg 36 Örgryte IS 35
1926 Örgryte IS 35 GAIS Göteborg 34 IFK Göteborg 33
1927 GAIS Göteborg 36 IFK Göteborg 33 Helsingborg IF 32
1928 Örgryte IS 33 Helsingborg IF 33 GAIS Göteborg 28
1929 Helsingborg IF 35 Örgryte IS 33 IFK Göteborg 32
1930 Helsingborg IF 31 IFK Göteborg 30 IK Sleipner 29
1931 GAIS Göteborg 36 AIK Stockholm 30 IFK Göteborg 30
1932 AIK Stockholm 33 Örgryte IS 31 GAIS Göteborg 30
1933 Helsingborg IF 35 GAIS Göteborg 34 IFK Göteborg 25
1934i Helsingborg IF 27 GAIS Göteborg 26 IFK Göteborg 25
1935k IFK Göteborg 33 AIK Stockholm 28 IF Elfsborg 28
1936 IF Elfsborg 34 AIK Stockholm 30 Sandvikens IF 27
1937 AIK Stockholm 36 IK Sleipner 27 Örgryte IS 25
1938 IK Sleipner 30 Helsingborg IF 26 Landskrona BoIS 26
1939 IF Elfsborg 34 AIK Stockholm 25 Malmö FF 25
1940 IF Elfsborg 32 IFK Göteborg 32 Helsingborg IF 27
1941 Helsingborg IF 31 Degerfors IF 29 AIK Stockholm 26
1942 IFK Göteborg 31 GAIS Göteborg 27 IFK Norrköping 26
1943 IFK Norrköping 31 IF Elfsborg 30 Helsingborg IF 30
1944 Malmö FF 37 IF Elfsborg 32 AIK Stockholm 32
1945 IFK Norrköping 37 IF Elfsborg 32 Malmö FF 28
1946 IFK Norrköping 35 Malmö FF 30 IFK Göteborg 30
1947 IFK Norrköping 36 AIK Stockholm 30 Malmö FF 28
1948 IFK Norrköping 33 Malmö FF 29 AIK Stockholm 27
1949 Malmö FF 29 Helsingborg IF 29 GAIS Göteborg 27
1950 Malmö FF 42 Jonköping Södra 27 Helsingborg IF 26

1951 Malmö FF 37 Råå IF Helsingborg 28 Degerfors IF 27
1952 IFK Norrköping 35 Malmö FF 32 Helsingborg IF 26
1953 Malmö FF 31 IFK Norrköping 27 Djurgårdens IF 26
1954 GAIS Göteborg 27 Helsingborg IF 26 Degerfors IF 25
1955 Djurgårdens IF 33 Halmstad BK 29 AIK Stockholm 28
1956 IFK Norrköping 35 Malmö FF 32 Djurgårdens IF 27
1957 IFK Norrköping 35 Malmö FF 28 Helsingborg IF 27
1958s IFK Göteborg 47 IFK Norrköping 47 Djurgårdens IF 42
1959k Djurgårdens IF 32 IFK Norrköping 31 IFK Göteborg 31
1960 IFK Norrköping 38 IFK Malmö 31 Örgryte IS 24
1961 IF Elfsborg 31 IFK Norrköping 26 IFK Göteborg 26
1962 IFK Norrköping 32 Djurgårdens IF 30 IFK Göteborg 24
1963 IFK Norrköping 31 Degerfors IF 29 AIK Stockholm 28
1964 Djurgårdens IF 31 Malmö FF 31 Örgryte IS 31
1965 Malmö FF 34 IF Elfsborg 32 AIK Stockholm 30
1966 Djurgårdens IF 33 IFK Norrköping 29 IF Elfsborg 29
1967 Malmö FF 33 Djurgårdens IF 28 Helsingborg IF 26
1968 Östers IF Växjö 27 Malmö FF 27 IFK Norrköping 27
1969 IFK Göteborg 31 Malmö FF 28 Djurgårdens IF 27
1970 Malmö FF 29 Åtvidabergs FF 28 Djurgårdens IF 24
1971 Malmö FF 30 Åtvidabergs FF 28 IFK Norrköping 26
1972 Åtvidabergs FF 33 AIK Stockholm 32 Östers IF Växjö 26
1973n Åtvidabergs FF 37 Östers IF Växjö 31 Djurgårdens IF 31
1974 Malmö FF 43 AIK Stockholm 34 Östers IF Växjö 33
1975 Malmö FF 42 Östers IF Växjö 37 Djurgårdens IF 34
1976 Halmstad BK 38 Malmö FF 35 Östers IF Växjö 32
1977 Malmö FF 38 IF Elfsborg 31 Kalmar FF 31
1978 Östers IF Växjö 38 Malmö FF 32 IFK Göteborg 31
1979 Halmstad BK 36 IFK Göteborg 35 IF Elfsborg 33
1980 Östers IF Växjö 37 Malmö FF 35 IFK Göteborg 34
1981 Östers IF Växjö 40 IFK Göteborg 36 IFK Norrköping 32
1982 IFK Göteborg..........1-2 3-1..........Hammarby IF
1983 IFK Göteborg..........1-1 3-0..........Östers IF Växjö
1984 IFK Göteborg..........5-1 2-0..........IFK Norrköping
1985 Örgryte IS..........4-2 2-3..........IFK Göteborg
1986 Malmö FF..........5-2 0-1..........AIK Stockholm
1987 IFK Göteborg..........1-0 1-2..........Malmö FF
1988 Malmö FF..........0-0 7-3..........Djurgårdens IF
1989 IFK Norrköping0-2 1-0 0-0 4-3p..........Malmö FF
1990 IFK Göteborg..........3-0 0-0..........IFK Norrköping

1991p4 IFK Göteborg 36 IFK Norrköping 31 Örebro SK 28
1992 AIK Stockholm 34 IFK Norrköping 32 Östers IF Växjö 30
1993n1 IFK Göteborg 59 IFK Norrköping 54 AIK Stockholm 46
1994 IFK Göteborg 54 Örebro SK 52 Malmö FF 49

SWEDISH CUP FINALS

1941 Helsingborg IF..........3-1..........IK Sleipner
1942 GAIS Göteborg..........2-1..........IF Elfsborg
1943 IFK Norrköping..........0-0 5-2..........AIK Stockholm
1944 Malmö FF..........4-3..........IFK Norrköping
1945 IFK Norrköping..........4-1..........Malmö FF
1946 Malmö FF..........3-0..........Åtvidabergs FF
1947 Malmö FF..........3-2..........AIK Stockholm
1948 Råå IF Helsingborg..........6-0..........BK Kenty Linköping
1949 AIK Stockholm..........1-0..........Landskrona BoIS
1950 AIK Stockholm..........3-2..........Helsingborg IF
1951 Malmö FF..........2-1..........Djurgårdens IF
1952 -
1953 Malmö FF..........3-2..........IFK Norrköping
1954-66 -
1967 Malmö FF..........2-0..........IFK Norrköping
1968 -
1969 IFK Norrköping..........1-0..........AIK Stockholm
1970 Åtvidabergs FF..........2-0..........Sandvikens IF
1971 Åtvidabergs FF..........3-2..........Malmö FF
1972 Landskrona BoIS..........0-0 3-2..........IFK Norrköping
1973 Malmö FF..........7-0..........Åtvidabergs FF
1974 Malmö FF..........2-0..........Östers IF Växjö
1975 Malmö FF..........1-0..........Djurgårdens IF
1976 AIK Stockholm..........1-1 3-0..........Landskrona BoIS
1977 Östers IF Växjö..........1-0..........Hammarby IF
1978 Malmö FF..........2-0..........Kalmar FF
1979 IFK Göteborg..........6-1..........Åtvidabergs FF
1980 Malmö FF..........3-3 4-3p..........IK Brage
1981 Kalmar FF..........4-0..........IF Elfsborg
1982 IFK Göteborg..........3-2..........Östers IF Växjö
1983 IFK Göteborg..........1-0..........Hammarby IF
1984 Malmö FF..........1-0..........Landskrona BoIS
1985 AIK Stockholm..........1-1 3-2p..........Östers IF Växjö
1986 Malmö FF..........2-1..........IFK Göteborg
1987 Kalmar FF..........2-0..........GAIS Göteborg
1988 IFK Norrköping..........3-1..........Örebro SK
1989 Malmö FF..........3-0..........Djurgårdens IF
1990 Djurgårdens IF..........2-0..........Häcken BK
..........Göteborg
1991 IFK Norrköping..........4-1..........Östers IF Växjö
1992 IFK Göteborg..........3-2..........AIK Stockholm
1993 Degerfors IF..........3-0..........Landskrona BoIS
1994 IFK Norrköping..........4-3..........Helsingborg IF
1995 Halmstads BK..........3-1..........AIK Stockholm

LEADING INTERNATIONAL GOALSCORERS

49	Sven Rydell	(Örgryte IS,Redberglids IK)
43	Gunnar Nordahl	(Degerfors IF,IFK Norrköping)
32	Gunnar Gren	(Garda BK,IFK Göteborg,Örgryte IS)
27	Agne Simonsson	(Örgryte IS,Real Madrid,Real Sociedad)
25	Tomas Brolin	(IFK Norrköping,Parma)
23	Per Kaufeldt	(AIK Stockholm
22	Karl Gustafsson	(IFK Köping,Köpings IF,Djurgårdens IF)
22	Martin Dahlin	(Malmö FF,Bor. Mönchengladbach)
	Kennet Andersson	(IFK Göteborg,Mechelen,Lille,Caen)
21	Albin Dahl	(Landskrona BoIS,Helsingborgs IF)
20	Nils-Ake Sandell	(Malmö FF,Lunds BK)
	Erik Persson	(AIK Stockholm)
	Sven Johansson	(IF Elfsborg)

LEADING INTERNATIONAL APPEARANCES

127	Thomas Ravelli	(Östers IF,IFK Göteborg)	1981-
115	Björn Nordqvist	(IFK Norrköping,PSV, IFK Göteborg)	1963-1978
94	Orvar Bergmark	(Örebro SK,AIK Stockholm, Roma)	1951-196
77	Ronnie Hellström	(Hammarby IF,Kaiserslautern)	1966-1980
75	Roland Nilsson	(IFK Göteborg,Sheffield Wednesday,Helsingborgs)	1986-
73	Karl Svensson	(Helsingborgs IF)	1949-1958
70	Bo Larsson	(Malmö FF,VfB Stuttgart)	1964-1978
69	Ingemar Erlandsson	(Malmö FF)	
68	Glenn Hysén	(IFK Göteborg,PSV,Fiorentina, Liverpool)	1980-1991

INTERNATIONAL MATCHES PLAYED BY SWEDEN

12-07-1908 Norway..........W 11-3..........Gothenburg..........Fr..........Gustafsson 2, Börjesson.E 4, Bergström.E 4, Lindman
8-09 England Am..........L 1-6..........Gothenburg..........Fr..........Bergström.E

Date	Opponent	Result	Venue	Competition	Scorers
20-10	England Am	L 1-12	London	OGr1	Bergström.G
23-10	Holland	L 0-2	London	OG3p	
25-10	Holland	L 3-5	The Hague	Fr	Gustafsson 2, Ohlson
26-10	Belgium	L 1-2	Brussels	Fr	Gustafsson
6-11-1909	England Am	L 0-7	Hull	Fr	
11-09-1910	Norway	W 4-0	Oslo	Fr	Myhrberg 2, Gustafsson 2
18-06-1911	Germany	L 2-4	Stockholm	Fr	Gustafsson 2
17-09	Norway	W 4-1	Stockholm	Fr	Ekroth 2, Börjesson.E, Dahlström
22-10	Finland	W 5-2	Helsinki	Fr	Eriksson, Persson.K, Brolin 2, Andersson.R
29-10	Germany	W 3-1	Hamburg	Fr	Börjesson.E 2, Olsson.J
16-06-1912	Norway	W 2-1	Oslo	Fr	Ekroth 2
20-06	Hungary	D 2-2	Gothenburg	Fr	Bergström.E, Swenson
27-06	Finland	W 7-1	Stockholm	Fr	Lorichs 3, Dahlström 2, Persson.K 2
29-06	Holland	L 3-4	Stockholm	OGr1	Swenson 2, Börjesson.E
1-07	Italy	L 0-1	Stockholm	OGct	
3-11	Norway	W 4-2	Gothenburg	Fr	Frykman, Swenson 2, Ekroth
4-05-1913	Russia	W 4-1	Moscow	Fr	Howander 2, Gustafsson, Swenson
18-05	Hungary	L 0-2	Budapest	Fr	
25-05	Denmark	L 0-8	Copenhagen	Fr	
8-06	Norway	W 9-0	Stockholm	Fr	Swenson 2, Bergström.R, Gustafsson 5, Ekroth
5-10	Denmark	L 0-10	Stockholm	Fr	
26-10	Norway	D 1-1	Oslo	Fr	Ohlsson.C
24-05-1914	Finland	W 4-3	Stockholm	Fr	Bergström.R, Swenson 2, Gunnarsson
10-06	England Am	L 1-5	Stockholm	Fr	Börjesson.E
21-06	Hungary	D 1-1	Stockholm	Fr	Börjesson.E
28-06	Norway	W 1-0	Oslo	Fr	Hjelm
5-07	Russia	D 2-2	Stockholm	Fr	Wicksell, Swenson
25-10	Norway	W 7-0	Stockholm	Fr	Ekroth 3, Söderberg 3, Johansson.G
6-06-1915	Denmark	L 0-2	Copenhagen	Fr	
27-06	Norway	D 1-1	Oslo	Fr	Gunnarsson
24-10	Norway	W 5-2	Stockholm	Fr	Swenson 3, Gunnarsson 2
31-10	Denmark	L 0-2	Stockholm	Fr	
4-06-1916	Denmark	L 0-2	Copenhagen	Fr	
2-07	Norway	W 6-0	Stockholm	Fr	Karlstrand, Gustafsson 3, Wicksell, Swenson,
20-08	United States	L 2-3	Stockholm	Fr	Törnqvist 2
1-10	Norway	D 0-0	Oslo	Fr	
8-10	Denmark	W 4-0	Stockholm	Fr	Karlstrand, Gustafsson, Swenson, Bergström.R
3-06-1917	Denmark	D 1-1	Copenhagen	Fr	Börjesson.E
19-08	Norway	D 3-3	Helsingborg	Fr	Ström 2, Malm
16-09	Norway	W 2-0	Oslo	Fr	Ekroth, Gustafsson
14-10	Denmark	L 1-2	Stockholm	Fr	Gustafsson
26-05-1918	Norway	W 2-0	Stockholm	Fr	Gustafsson, Sterne
2-06	Denmark	L 0-3	Copenhagen	Fr	
15-09	Norway	L 1-2	Oslo	Fr	Börjesson.E
20-10	Denmark	L 1-2	Gothenburg	Fr	Hjelm
29-05-1919	Finland	W 1-0	Stockholm	Fr	Svedberg
5-06	Denmark	L 0-3	Copenhagen	Fr	
9-06	Holland	L 1-3	Amsterdam	Fr	Karlsson.H
29-06	Norway	L 3-4	Oslo	Fr	Karlsson.H, OG, Bergström.R
24-08	Holland	W 4-1	Stockholm	Fr	Karlsson.H 3, Svedberg
14-09	Norway	L 1-5	Gothenburg	Fr	Svedberg
28-09	Finland	D 3-3	Helsinki	Fr	Kock 2, Arontzon
12-10	Denmark	W 3-0	Stockholm	Fr	Karlsson.H 3
30-05-1920	Finland	W 4-0	Stockholm	Fr	Dahl.A 2, Krantz 2
6-06	Switzerland	L 0-1	Stockholm	Fr	
27-06	Norway	W 3-0	Oslo	Fr	Karlsson.H, Bergström.R, Andersson.S
28-08	Greece	W 9-0	Antwerp	OGr1	Olsson.A 2, Karlsson.H 5, Wicksell, Dahl.A
29-08	Holland	L 4-5	Antwerp	OGqf	Karlsson.H 2, Olsson.A, Dahl.A
1-09	Spain	L 1-2	Antwerp	OGct	Dahl.A
19-09	Finland	L 0-1	Helsinki	Fr	
26-09	Norway	D 0-0	Stockholm	Fr	
10-10	Denmark	L 0-2	Stockholm	Fr	
25-03-1921	Austria	D 2-2	Vienna	Fr	Horndahl, Andersson.E
29-05	Finland	L 0-3	Stockholm	Fr	
19-06	Norway	L 1-3	Oslo	Fr	Kock
22-07	Estonia	D 0-0	Tallinn	Fr	
24-07	Austria	L 1-3	Stockholm	Fr	Dahl.A
18-09	Norway	L 0-3	Stockholm	Fr	
9-10	Denmark	D 0-0	Stockholm	Fr	
6-11	Hungary	L 2-4	Budapest	Fr	Karlsson.H 2
13-11	Czechoslovakia	D 2-2	Prague	Fr	Karlsson.H, Edlund

Date	Opponent	Result	Venue	Comp	Scorers
28-05-1922	Poland	L 1-2	Stockholm	Fr	Svedberg
5-06	Finland	W 4-1	Helsinki	Fr	Edlund 2, Kaufeldt 2
9-07	Hungary	D 1-1	Stockholm	Fr	Börjesson.E
13-08	Czechoslovakia	L 0-2	Stockholm	Fr	
23-08	Norway	D 0-0	Stockholm	Fr	
24-09	Norway	W 5-0	Oslo	Fr	Malm 2, Dahl.A 3
1-10	Denmark	W 2-1	Copenhagen	Fr	Dahl.H, Dahl.A
21-05-1923	England	L 2-4	Stockholm	Fr	Dahl.H 2
10-06	Austria	W 4-2	Gothenburg	Fr	Dahl.H, Olsson.G, Dahl.A 2
20-06	Finland	W 5-4	Gavle	Fr	Rydell, Paulsson 3, Carlsson.B
28-06	Germany	W 2-1	Stockholm	Fr	Dahl.H, Dahl.A
16-09	Norway	W 3-2	Oslo	Fr	Kaufeldy, Kock, Rydell
14-10	Denmark	L 1-3	Stockholm	Fr	Sundberg
28-10	Hungary	L 1-2	Budapest	Fr	Detter
1-11	Poland	D 2-2	Krakow	Fr	Dahl.H, Helgesson
18-05-1924	Poland	W 5-1	Stockholm	Fr	Rydell 3, Olsson.G, Svensson.T
29-05	Belgium	W 8-1	Paris	OGr2	Kock 3, Rydell 3, Brommesson, Kaufeldt
1-06	Egypt	W 5-0	Paris	OGqf	Kaufeldt 2, Brommesson 2, Rydell
5-06	Switzerland	L 1-2	Paris	OGsf	Kock
8-06	Holland	D 1-1	Paris	OG3p	Kaufeldt
9-06	Holland	W 3-1	Paris	OG3p	Rydell 2, Lundquist
15-06	Denmark	W 3-2	Copenhagen	Fr	Kaufeldt, Rydell 2
29-06	Egypt	W 5-0	Stockholm	Fr	Keller, Rydell 4
25-07	Estonia	W 5-2	Stockholm	Fr	Haglund, Keller, Kaufeldt 2, Kock
28-07	Finland	W 7-5	Helsinki	Fr	Haglund 2, Kock 3, Karlsson.B 2
31-08	Germany	W 4-1	Berlin	Fr	Wenzel, Malm, Rydberg, Carlsson.B
21-09	Norway	W 6-1	Stockholm	Fr	Keller, Kaufeldt 2, Rydell 3
9-11	Austria	D 1-1	Vienna	Fr	Paulsson
16-11	Italy	D 2-2	Milan	Fr	Kaufeldt, Malm
9-06-1925	Finland	W 4-0	Gothenburg	Fr	Johansson.F 4
14-06	Denmark	L 0-2	Stockholm	Fr	
21-06	Germany	W 1-0	Stockholm	Fr	Johansson.F
5-07	Austria	L 2-4	Stockholm	Fr	Rydell, Keller
12-07	Hungary	W 6-2	Stockholm	Fr	Johansson.F 3, Rydell 2, Kaufeldt
23-08	Norway	W 7-3	Oslo	Fr	Rydell 4, Kaufeldt 2, Haglund
1-11	Poland	W 6-2	Krakow	Fr	Dahl.A 2, Johansson.F 3, Rydberg
9-06-1926	Norway	W 3-2	Stockholm	Fr	Kaukeldt, Rydell 2
13-06	Czechoslovakia	D 2-2	Stockholm	Fr	Kaufeldt, Holmberg
20-06	Germany	D 3-3	Nuremberg	Fr	Hallbäck 2, Olsson.G
3-07	Czechoslovakia	L 2-4	Prague	Fr	Johansson.F, Holmberg
18-07	Italy	W 5-3	Stockholm	Fr	Rydberg, Holmberg, Kroon, Johansson.F 2
20-07	Latvia	L 1-4	Riga	Fr	Hedström
23-07	Estonia	W 7-1	Tallinn	Fr	Kling 3, Hedström 2, Lööf 2
26-07	Finland	W 3-2	Helsinki	Fr	Hedström 2, Sundberg
3-10	Denmark	L 0-2	Copenhagen	Fr	
3-10	Poland	W 3-1	Stockholm	Fr	Rydberg 2, Keller
7-11	Austria	L 1-3	Vienna	Fr	Rydberg
14-11	Hungary	L 1-3	Budapest	Fr	Svensson.T
3-04-1927	Belgium	L 1-2	Brussels	Fr	Rydell
29-05	Latvia	W 12-0	Stockholm	Fr	Hallbäck 6, Rydell 3, Johansson.T, Kaufeldt, Andersson.K
12-06	Finland	W 6-2	Stockholm	Fr	Hallbäck 2, Kaufeldt, Johansson.B 2, Dahl.H
19-06	Denmark	D 0-0	Stockholm	Fr	
26-06	Norway	W 5-3	Oslo	Fr	Rydell 3, Olsson.A 2
1-07	Estonia	W 3-1	Norrkoping	Fr	Keller 3
4-09	Belgium	W 7-0	Stockholm	Fr	Kroon 2, Kaufeldt 2, Brommesson, Persson.J, Holmberg
6-11	Switzerland	D 2-2	Zurich	Fr	Rydell, Kroon
13-11	Holland	L 0-1	Amsterdam	Fr	
7-06-1928	Norway	W 6-1	Stockholm	Fr	Keller 2, Lundahl 2, Kroon 2
1-07	Poland	L 1-2	Katowice	Fr	Persson.E
6-07	Latvia	W 4-0	Riga	Fr	Lööf 3, Pettersson
9-07	Estonia	W 1-0	Tallinn	Fr	Pettersson
29-07	Austria	L 2-3	Stockholm	Fr	Lundahl 2
2-09	Finland	W 3-2	Helsinki	Fr	Andersson.H 2, Bergström.E
30-09	Germany	W 2-0	Stockholm	Fr	Lundahl, Olsson.G
7-10	Denmark	L 1-3	Copenhagen	Fr	Rydell
9-06-1929	Holland	W 6-2	Stockholm	Fr	Dahl.A, Rydell 3, OG, Nilsson.J
14-06	Finland	W 3-1	Stockholm	Fr	Lundahl 2, Holmberg
16-06	Denmark	W 3-2	Gothenburg	Fr	Nilsson.J, Kaufeldt, Kroon
23-06	Germany	L 0-3	Cologne	Fr	
7-07	Estonia	W 4-1	Landskrona	Fr	Lundahl 2, Kroon, Dahl.H
28-07	Latvia	W 10-0	Malmo	Fr	Dahl.A, Rydell, Kroon 2, Andersson.R 3, Helgesson, Nilsson.J

Date	Opponent	Result	Venue	Comp	Scorers
29-09	Norway	L 1-2	Oslo	Fr	Kroon
15-06-1930	Switzerland	W 1-0	Stockholm	Fr	Kroon
22-06	Denmark	L 1-6	Copenhagen	Fr	Nilsson.J
6-07	Norway	W 6-3	Stockholm	Fr	Lundahl 3, Kroon 2, Dahl.A
18-07	Estonia	W 5-1	Tallinn	Fr	Sundberg 3, Thörn, Johansson.K
22-07	Latvia	W 5-0	Riga	Fr	Nilsson.A 2, Johansson.K, Lööf, Dunker
28-09	Belgium	D 2-2	Liege	Fr	Dahl.A 2
28-09	Finland	D 4-4	Helsinki	Fr	Karlsson.B 3, Andersson.A
28-09	Poland	L 0-3	Stockholm	Fr	
16-11	Austria	L 1-4	Vienna	Fr	Engdahl
17-06-1931	Germany	D 0-0	Stockholm	Fr	
28-06	Denmark	W 3-1	Stockholm	Fr	Gardtman, Rydell 2
3-07	Finland	W 8-2	Stockholm	Fr	Gardtman, Zetterberg 4, Hansson.E 3
8-07	Estonia	W 3-1	Sandviken	Fr	Jacobsson.R, Zetterberg 2
26-07	Latvia	W 6-0	Vasteras	Fr	Sundberg 3, Roos 2, Rydell
27-09	Norway	L 1-2	Oslo	Fr	Hansson.E
8-11	Hungary	L 1-3	Budapest	Fr	Rydell
16-05-1932	Finland	W 7-1	Stockholm	Fr	Rydell 3, OG, Persson.E, Nilsson.J, Holmberg
10-06	Finland	W 3-1	Helsinki	Fr	Nilsson.J, Holmberg, Gardtman
12-06	Belgium	W 3-1	Stockholm	Fr	Sundberg 2, Hansson.E
19-06	Denmark	L 1-3	Copenhagen	Fr	Kroon
1-07	Norway	L 1-4	Gothenburg	Fr	Holmberg
10-07	Poland	L 0-2	Warsaw	Fr	
13-07	Latvia	D 0-0	Riga	Fr	
15-07	Estonia	W 3-1	Tallinn	Fr	Johansson.T 2, Dunker
17-07	Austria	L 3-4	Stockholm	Fr	Nilsson.J (II) 2, Svensson.G
25-09	Germany	L 3-4	Nuremberg	Fr	Lundahl, Kempe, Persson.E
25-09	Lithuania	W 8-1	Stockholm	Fr	Gustavsson 2, Johansson.H 2, Nilsson.J (II) 4
6-11	Switzerland	L 1-2	Basle	Fr	Olsson.G
11-06-1933	Estonia	W 6-2	Stockholm	WCq	Kroon, Bunke.L, Ericsson 2, Bunke.T, Andersson.S
18-06	Denmark	L 2-3	Stockholm	Fr	Ericsson 2
29-06	Lithuania	W 2-0	Kaunas	WCq	Hansson.K 2
2-07	Hungary	W 5-2	Stockholm	Fr	Persson.E, Karlsson.H, Bunke.L 2, Nilsson.J
4-07	Latvia	D 1-1	Riga	Fr	Hansson.K
14-07	Finland	W 2-0	Stockholm	Fr	Kroon, Bunke.L
24-09	Norway	W 1-0	Oslo	Fr	Dunker
23-05-1934	Poland	W 4-2	Stockholm	Fr	Jonasson.S, Keller 3
27-05	Argentina	W 3-2	Bologna	WCr1	Jonasson.S 2, Kroon
31-05	Germany	L 1-2	Milan	WCqf	Dunker
17-06	Denmark	W 5-3	Copenhagen	Fr	Ericsson 4, Persson.E
1-07	Norway	D 3-3	Stockholm	Fr	Karlsson.E, Andersson.S, Ericsson
23-09	Finland	L 4-5	Helsinki	Fr	Persson.E 3, Keller
23-09	Latvia	W 3-1	Stockholm	Fr	Andersson.S, Carlsson.R, Gustavsson
12-06-1935	Finland	D 2-2	Stockholm	Fr	Persson.E, Nyberg
16-06	Denmark	W 3-1	Gothenburg	Fr	Grahn, Jonasson.S, Hallman
30-06	Germany	W 3-1	Stockholm	Fr	Hallman 2, Jonasson.S
5-07	Latvia	W 3-0	Riga	Fr	Carlsson.R, Jonasson.S, Samuelsson
9-07	Estonia	W 2-1	Tallinn	Fr	Samuelsson 2
1-09	Romania	W 7-1	Stockholm	Fr	Bergsten, Keller, Nilsson.A 3, Jonasson.S, Persson.E
22-09	Norway	W 2-0	Oslo	Fr	Nilsson.A, Grahn
10-11	France	L 0-2	Paris	Fr	
17-11	Belgium	L 1-5	Brussels	Fr	Nilsson.A
14-06-1936	Denmark	L 3-4	Copenhagen	Fr	OG Jonasson.S, Josefsson
21-06	Switzerland	W 5-2	Stockholm	Fr	Hallman 2, Jonasson.S 3
5-07	Norway	W 2-0	Gothenburg	Fr	Jonasson.S 2
26-07	Norway	L 3-4	Stockholm	Fr	Persson.E 2, Jonasson.S
4-08	Japan	L 2-3	Berlin	OGr1	Persson.E 2
27-09	Finland	W 2-1	Helsinki	Fr	Jonasson.S, Ericsson
17-05-1937	England	L 0-4	Stockholm	Fr	
16-06	Finland	W 4-0	Stockholm	WCq	Bunke.L 2, Persson.E, Svanström
20-06	Estonia	W 7-2	Stockholm	WCq	Josefsson 2, Bunke.L, Jonasson.S, Wetterström 3
23-06	Poland	L 1-3	Warsaw	Fr	Wetterström
27-06	Romania	D 2-2	Bucharest	Fr	Jonasson.S 2
19-09	Norway	L 2-3	Oslo	Fr	Bunke.L, Johansson.G
3-10	Denmark	L 1-2	Stockholm	Fr	Persson.E
21-11	Germany	L 0-5	Hamburg	WCq	
10-06-1938	Latvia	D 3-3	Stockholm	Fr	Hansson.K 2, Bergström.G
12-06	Cuba	W 8-0	Antibes	WCqf	Wetterstrom 3, Andersson 3, Keller, Nyberg
15-06	Finland	W 2-0	Stockholm	Fr	Bergström.G, Lagercrantz
16-06	Hungary	L 1-5	Paris	WCsf	Nyberg
19-06	Brazil	L 2-4	Bordeaux	WC3p	Jonasson.S, Nyberg

Date	Opponent	Result	Venue	Comp	Scorers
21-06	Denmark	W 1-0	Copenhagen	Fr	Nyberg
4-07	Finland	W 4-2	Helsinki	Fr	Lagercrantz 2, Nyberg, Bergström.G
7-08	Czechoslovakia	L 2-6	Stockholm	Fr	Nyberg, Bergström.G
4-09	Norway	L 1-2	Oslo	Fr	Hansson.K
2-10	Norway	L 2-3	Stockholm	Fr	Nyberg, Persson.E
3-06-1939	Norway	W 3-2	Stockholm	Fr	Martinsson, Andersson.A, Persson.E
9-06	Finland	W 5-1	Stockholm	Fr	Andersson.A, Persson.E 3, Grahn
11-06	Lithuania	W 7-0	Karlstad	Fr	Larsson.R, Hjelm 2, Nyström, Lundin, Karlsson.W
14-06	Norway	L 0-1	Copenhagen	Fr	
17-09	Norway	W 3-2	Oslo	Fr	Nyström 2, Lennartsson
1-10	Denmark	W 4-1	Stockholm	Fr	Lennartsson, Johansson.K, Nyström, Dahl.G
29-08-1940	Finland	W 3-2	Helsinki	Fr	Johansson.K 3
22-09	Finland	W 5-0	Stockholm	Fr	Persson.E, Johansson.K 3, Gren
6-10	Denmark	D 1-1	Stockholm	Fr	Emanuelsson
20-10	Denmark	D 3-3	Copenhagen	Fr	Jonasson.S, Holmqvist.E 2
14-09-1941	Denmark	D 2-2	Stockholm	Fr	Carlsson.H, Jacobsson.S
5-10	Germany	W 4-2	Stockholm	Fr	Carlsson.H 3, Mårtensson
19-10	Denmark	L 1-2	Copenhagen	Fr	Holmqvist.E
28-06-1942	Denmark	W 3-0	Copenhagen	Fr	OG, Nordahl, Carlsson.H
20-09	Germany	W 3-2	Berlin	Fr	Nyberg, Carlsson.H, Mårtensson
4-10	Denmark	W 2-1	Stockholm	Fr	Gren, Nordahl.G
15-11	Switzerland	L 1-3	Zurich	Fr	Leander
14-06-1943	Switzerland	W 1-0	Stockholm	Fr	Sandberg
20-06	Denmark	L 2-3	Copenhagen	Fr	Gren, Nordahl.G
12-09	Hungary	L 2-3	Stockholm	Fr	Nordahl.G 2
3-10	Finland	D 1-1	Helsinki	Fr	Johansson.K
7-11	Hungary	W 7-2	Budapest	Fr	Carlsson.H, Nyberg 2, Nilsson.S 2, Nordahl.G 2
24-06-1945	Denmark	W 2-1	Stockholm	Fr	Nordahl.G, Holmqvist
1-07	Denmark	W 4-3	Copenhagen	Fr	Åhlund 2, Nordahl.G, Gren
26-08	Finland	W 7-2	Gothenburg	Fr	Nyberg 2, Gren 3, Carlsson.H, Grahn
30-09	Denmark	W 4-1	Stockholm	Fr	Nordahl.G, Carlsson.H, OG, Nilsson.S
30-09	Finland	W 6-1	Helsinki	Fr	Tapper 5, Holmqvist.E
21-10	Norway	W 10-0	Stockholm	Fr	Persson.V, Nordahl.G 4, Carlsson.H 2, Nyberg 2, Gren
25-11	Switzerland	L 0-3	Geneva	Fr	
24-06-1946	Denmark	L 1-3	Copenhagen	Fr	Gren
7-07	Switzerland	W 7-2	Stockholm	Fr	Gren 4, Nyström, Nordahl.G, OG
15-09	Finland	W 7-0	Helsinki	Fr	Nilsson.G 3, Jönsson.E 2, Karlsson.B, Rosén
15-09	Norway	W 3-0	Oslo	Fr	Nyberg, Gren, Karlsson.E
6-10	Denmark	D 3-3	Gothenburg	Fr	Gren, Nordahl.K, Nordahl.G
15-06-1947	Denmark	W 4-1	Copenhagen	Fr	Nordahl.G 2, Liedholm, Lindskog
26-06	Denmark	W 6-1	Stockholm	Fr	Leander 2, Andersson.S, Nordahl.G, Nyström, Mårtenson
28-06	Norway	W 5-1	Helsinki	Fr	Nordahl.G 4, Persson.S
24-08	Finland	W 7-0	Boras	Fr	Liedholm 2, Nordahl.G 3, Gren, OG
14-09	Poland	W 5-4	Stockholm	Fr	Nordahl.G 2, Nyström, Tapper, Liedholm
5-10	Norway	W 4-1	Stockholm	Fr	Liedholm, Nordahl.G 2, Gren
19-11	England	L 2-4	London	Fr	Nordahl.G. Gren
9-06-1948	Holland	L 0-1	Amsterdam	Fr	
11-07	Austria	W 3-2	Stockholm	Fr	Liedholm, Gren 2
2-08	Austria	W 3-0	London	OGr1	Nordahl.G 2, Rosén
5-08	Korea	W 12-0	London	OGqf	Liedholm 2, Nordahl.G 4, Gren, Carlsson.H 3, Rosén 2
10-08	Denmark	W 4-2	London	OGsf	Carlsson.H 2, Rosén 2
13-08	Yugoslavia	W 3-1	London	OGf	Gren 2, Nordahl.G
19-09	Norway	W 5-3	Oslo	Fr	Nordahl.G 5
19-09	Finland	D 2-2	Helsinki	Fr	Tapper, Mårtensson
10-10	Denmark	W 1-0	Stockholm	Fr	Liedholm
14-11	Austria	L 1-2	Vienna	Fr	Gren
13-05-1949	England	W 3-1	Stockholm	Fr	Carlsson.H, Jeppson, Johnsson.E
2-06	Rep. Ireland	W 3-1	Stockholm	WCq	Andersson, Jeppson, Liedholm
19-06	Hungary	D 2-2	Stockholm	Fr	Jeppson, Gren
2-10	Finland	W 8-1	Malmo	Fr	Jönsson.E 3, Rydell.I 3, Palmér, Jakobsson
2-10	Norway	D 3-3	Stockholm	Fr	Lindskog, Jeppson, Simonsson.C
23-10	Denmark	L 2-3	Copenhagen	Fr	Jeppson, Mellberg
13-11	Rep. Ireland	W 3-1	Dublin	WCq	Palmér 3
20-11	Hungary	L 0-5	Budapest	Fr	
8-06-1950	Holland	W 4-1	Stockholm	Fr	Jeppson 2, Palmér, Nilsson.S
25-06	Italy	W 3-2	Sao Paulo	WCr1	Jeppson 2, Andersson.S
29-06	Paraguay	D 2-2	Curitiba	WCr1	Sundkvist, Palmér
9-07	Brazil	L 1-7	Rio de Janeiro	WCr2	Andersson.S
13-07	Uruguay	L 2-3	Sao Paulo	WCr2	Palmér, Sundkvist

Date	Opponent	Result	Venue	Comp	Scorers
16-07	Spain	W 3-1	Sao Paulo	WCr2	Sundkvist, Mellberg, Palmér
3-09	Yugoslavia	L 1-2	Stockholm	Fr	Lindskog
24-09	Finland	W 1-0	Helsinki	Fr	Rosén
24-09	Norway	W 3-1	Oslo	Fr	Jönsson.E 2, Palmér
15-10	Denmark	W 4-0	Stockholm	Fr	Granqvist, Jönsson.E, Bengtsson, OG
12-11	Switzerland	L 2-4	Geneva	Fr	Palmér, Leander
10-06-1951	Turkey	W 3-1	Stockholm	Fr	Sandin 2, Lundkvist
17-06	Spain	D 0-0	Stockholm	Fr	
29-06	Iceland	L 3-4	Reykjavik	Fr	Larsson.P, Jönsson.A 2
2-09	Yugoslavia	L 1-2	Belgrade	Fr	Rydell.I
2-09	Finland	W 3-2	Stockholm	Fr	Lundkvist 2, Eriksson.J
30-09	Norway	L 3-4	Gothenburg	Fr	Rydell.I 2, Lindh
21-10	Denmark	L 1-3	Copenhagen	Fr	Jönsson.E
11-11	Italy	D 1-1	Florence	Fr	Löfgren
14-11	Turkey	L 0-1	Istanbul	Fr	
26-03-1952	France	W 1-0	Paris	Fr	Westerberg
14-05	Holland	D 0-0	Amsterdam	Fr	
30-05	Scotland	W 3-1	Stockholm	Fr	Sandberg, Löfgren, Bengtsson
11-06	Denmark	W 2-0	Oslo	Fr	Löfgren, Brodd
13-06	Finland	L 1-3	Oslo	Fr	Lindh
22-06	Denmark	W 4-3	Stockholm	Fr	Bengtsson, Brodd, Sandberg, Sandell
21-07	Norway	W 4-1	Tammerfors	OGr1	Brodd 2, Rydell.I, Bengtsson
23-07	Austria *	W 3-1	Helsinki	OGqf	Sandberg, Brodd, Rydell
28-07	Hungary	L 0-6	Helsinki	OGsf	
1-08	West Germany *	W 2-0	Helsinki	OG3p	Rydell.I, Löfgren
21-09	Finland	W 8-1	Helsinki	Fr	Råberg 3, Persson.H 3, Sandin, Sandberg
5-10	Norway	W 2-1	Oslo	Fr	Jakobsson.K, Persson.H
26-10	Italy	D 1-1	Stockholm	Fr	Persson.H
6-05-1953	Scotland	W 2-1	Glasgow	Fr	Löfgren, Eriksson.L
28-05	Belgium	L 2-3	Stockholm	WCq	Bengtsson, Selmosson
11-06	France	W 1-0	Stockholm	Fr	Sandell
21-06	Denmark	W 3-1	Copenhagen	Fr	Thillberg 2, Eriksson.L
5-07	Hungary	L 2-4	Stockholm	Fr	Sandberg, Sandell
5-08	Finland	D 3-3	Helsinki	WCq	Sandell 2, Persson.H
16-08	Finland	W 4-0	Stockholm	WCq	Sandberg, Sandell 2, Sandin
8-10	Belgium	L 0-2	Brussels	WCq	
18-10	Norway	D 0-0	Stockholm	Fr	
8-11	Spain	D 2-2	Bilbao	Fr	Eriksson.J, Jacobsson.F
15-11	Hungary	D 2-2	Budapest	Fr	Källgren, Hamrin
19-05-1954	Holland	W 6-1	Stockholm	Fr	Thillberg 2, Sandell 2, Svensson.S 2
4-06	Finland	W 6-0	Gothenburg	Fr	Sandell, Svensson.S 2, Liander, Hamrin, Jakobsson.K
7-06	Norway	W 3-0	Stockholm	Fr	Svensson.S, Jakobsson.K, Sandell
15-08	Finland	W 10-1	Helsinki	Fr	Hamrin 3, Eklund 3, Thillberg 2, Eriksson.J
24-08	Iceland	W 3-2	Kalmar	Fr	Eriksson.J 2, Sandberg
8-09	Soviet Union	L 0-7	Moscow	Fr	
19-09	Norway	D 1-1	Oslo	Fr	Eriksson.J
10-10	Denmark	W 5-2	Stockholm	Fr	Eriksson.J, Sandell 3, OG
31-10	Austria	W 2-1	Stockholm	Fr	Sandell, Eriksson.J
3-04-1955	France	L 0-2	Paris	Fr	
11-05	Hungary	L 3-7	Stockholm	Fr	Löfgren, Svensson.S, Isgren
15-06	Romania	W 4-1	Gothenburg	Fr	Bengtsson, Hamrin 2, Svensson.S
26-06	Soviet Union	L 0-6	Stockholm	Fr	
28-08	Finland	W 3-0	Helsingborg	Fr	Sandell 2, Lindskog
25-09	Norway	D 1-1	Stockholm	Fr	Nilsson.B
16-10	Denmark	D 3-3	Copenhagen	Fr	Nilsson.B, Sandell, Hamrin
13-11	Hungary	L 2-4	Budapest	Fr	Svensson.S, Löfgren
20-11	Portugal	W 6-2	Lisbon	Fr	Hamrin, Nilsson.B, Löfgren 2, Jonsson.T, Sandell
16-05-1956	England	D 0-0	Stockholm	Fr	
10-06	Finland	W 3-1	Helsinki	Fr	Ekström, Löfgren, Sandell
17-06	Romania	W 2-0	Bucharest	Fr	Thillberg, Johansson.A
30-06	West Germany	D 2-2	Stockholm	Fr	Sandberg, Bengtsson
16-09	Norway	L 1-3	Oslo	Fr	Sandberg
21-10	Denmark	D 1-1	Stockholm	Fr	Löfgren
5-05-1957	Austria	L 0-1	Vienna	Fr	
16-06	Hungary	D 0-0	Stockholm	Fr	
18-06	Norway	D 0-0	Turku	Fr	
19-06	Finland	W 5-1	Helsinki	Fr	Källgren 3, Sandberg, Löfgren
30-06	Denmark	W 2-1	Copenhagen	Fr	Källgren 2
22-09	Finland	W 5-1	Helsinki	Fr	OG 2, Källgren, Jonsson.T, Gren
13-10	Norway	W 5-2	Stockholm	Fr	Simonsson.A 2, Sandberg, Ekström, Gren
20-11	West Germany	L 0-1	Hamburg	Fr	

Date	Opponent	Result	Venue	Comp	Scorers
7-05-1958	Switzerland	W 3-2	Helsingborg	Fr	Löfgren, Simonsson.A 2
8-06	Mexico	W 3-0	Stockholm	WCr1	Simonsson.A 2, Liedholm
12-06	Hungary	W 2-1	Stockholm	WCr1	Hamrin 2
15-06	Wales	D 0-0	Stockholm	WCr1	
19-06	Soviet Union	W 2-0	Stockholm	WCqf	Hamrin, Simonsson.A
24-06	West Germany	W 3-1	Gothenburg	WCsf	Skoglund, Gren, Hamrin
29-06	Brazil	L 2-5	Stockholm	WCf	Liedholm, Simonsson.A
20-08	Finland	W 7-1	Helsinki	Fr	Jonsson.T 3, Börjesson.R 2, Källgren, Simonsson.A
14-09	Norway	W 2-0	Oslo	Fr	Börjesson.R, Simonsson.A
26-10	Denmark	D 4-4	Stockholm	Fr	Berndtsson.B, Börjesson.R, Gren 2
21-05-1959	Portugal	W 2-0	Gothenburg	Fr	Simonsson.A, Ohlsson.O
21-06	Denmark	W 6-0	Copenhagen	Fr	Bild 2, Simonsson.A, Berndtsson.B 2, Backman
28-06	Hungary	L 2-3	Budapest	Fr	Jonsson.T, Backman
2-08	Finland	W 3-1	Malmo	Fr	Bild, Börjesson.R, Simonsson.A
18-10	Norway	W 6-2	Gothenburg	Fr	Simonsson.A 2, Berndtsson.B, Börjesson.R 2, Thillberg
28-10	England	W 3-2	London	Fr	Simonsson.A 2, Salomonsson
1-11	Rep. Ireland	L 2-3	Dublin	Fr	Börjesson.R, Berndtsson.B
18-05-1960	Rep. Ireland	W 4-1	Malmo	Fr	OG 2, Simonsson.A, Börjesson.R
22-06	Finland	W 3-0	Helsinki	Fr	Börjesson.R 2, Simonsson.A
18-09	Norway	L 1-3	Oslo	Fr	Börjesson.R
19-10	Belgium	W 2-0	Stockholm	WCq	Börjesson.R, Brodd
23-10	Denmark	W 2-0	Gothenburg	Fr	Börjesson.R, Bild
30-10	France	W 1-0	Stockholm	Fr	Jonsson.T
26-03-1961	Czechoslovakia	L 1-2	Prague	Fr	Jonsson.T
28-05	Switzerland	W 4-0	Stockholm	WCq	Jonsson.T, Börjesson.R 2, Simonsson.A
18-06	Denmark	W 2-1	Copenhagen	Fr	Börjesson.R 2
9-08	Finland	W 4-0	Norrkoping	Fr	Svahn 2, Bild, Backman
4-10	Belgium	W 2-0	Brussels	WCq	Brodd 2
22-10	Norway	W 2-0	Gothenburg	Fr	Råberg, Wendt
29-10	Switzerland	L 2-3	Berne	WCq	Simonsson.A, Brodd
12-11	Switzerland	L 1-2	Berlin	WCq	Brodd
7-04-1962	Czechoslovakia	W 3-1	Gothenburg	Fr	Öberg 2, Bild
18-04	Soviet Union	L 0-2	Stockholm	Fr	
19-06	Finland	W 3-0	Helsinki	Fr	Grahn.O, Brodd, Ohlsson.O
21-06	Norway	W 2-0	Oslo	ECr1	Martinsson 2
16-09	Norway	L 1-2	Oslo	Fr	Skiöld
28-10	Denmark	W 4-2	Stockholm	Fr	Ohlsson.O 2, Martinsson, Eriksson.L
4-11	Norway	D 1-1	Malmo	ECr1	Eriksson.L
13-11	Israel	W 4-0	Tel Aviv	Fr	Ohlsson.O, Skiöld 3
16-11	Thailand	W 2-1	Bangkok	Fr	Ohlsson.O, Nilsson.B
5-05-1963	Hungary	W 2-1	Stockholm	Fr	Mild, Brodd
22-05	Soviet Union	W 1-0	Moscow	Fr	Martinsson
19-06	Yugoslavia	D 0-0	Belgrade	ECr2	
14-08	Norway	D 0-0	Gothenburg	Fr	
14-08	Finland	D 0-0	Stockholm	Fr	
18-09	Yugoslavia	W 3-2	Malmo	ECr2	Persson.O 2, Bild
6-10	Denmark	D 2-2	Copenhagen	Fr	Bild, Öberg
3-11	West Germany	W 2-1	Stockholm	Fr	Simonsson.A, Bild
29-04-1964	Holland	W 1-0	Rotterdam	Fr	Simonsson.A
13-05	Soviet Union	D 1-1	Stockholm	ECqf	Hamrin
27-05	Soviet Union	L 1-3	Moscow	ECqf	Hamrin
28-06	Denmark	W 4-1	Malmo	Fr	Öberg, Bild, Martinsson, Magnusson.R
2-08	Finland	L 0-1	Helsinki	Fr	
20-09	Norway	D 1-1	Oslo	Fr	Larsson.B
7-10	Poland	D 3-3	Stockholm	Fr	Öberg, Magnusson.R, Larsson.B
4-11	West Germany	D 1-1	Berlin	WCq	Hamrin
5-05-1965	Cyprus	W 3-0	Norrkoping	WCq	Simonsson.A 2, Jonsson.T
16-05	England	L 1-2	Gothenburg	Fr	Eriksson.L
16-06	Italy	D 2-2	Malmo	Fr	Larsson.B, Persson.O
20-06	Denmark	L 1-2	Copenhagen	Fr	Persson.O
30-06	Brazil	L 1-2	Stockholm	Fr	Bild
22-08	Finland	D 2-2	Lulea	Fr	Bild, Simonsson.A
26-09	West Germany	L 1-2	Stockholm	WCq	Jonsson.T
31-10	Norway	D 0-0	Stockholm	Fr	
7-11	Cyprus	W 5-0	Famagusta	WCq	Granström 2, Kinvdall, Larsson.B 2
27-04-1966	East Germany	L 1-4	Leipzig	Fr	Kindvall
18-05	Poland	D 1-1	Wroclaw	Fr	Larsson.B
4-06	Finland	L 0-1	Helsinki	Fr	
27-06	Yugoslavia	D 1-1	Malmo	Fr	Nildén
30-06	Brazil	L 2-3	Gothenburg	Fr	Kindvall 2
18-09	Norway	W 4-2	Oslo	Fr	Karlsson.J, Turesson 3

5-10	Austria	W 4-1	Stockholm	Fr	Lundblad, Kindvall, Turesson 2
6-11	Denmark	W 2-1	Stockholm	Fr	Simonsson.A, Danielsson
13-11	Portugal	W 2-1	Lisbon	ECq	Danielsson 2
17-05-1967	East Germany	L 0-1	Helsingborg	Fr	
1-06	Portugal	D 1-1	Stockholm	ECq	Svensson.I
11-06	Bulgaria	L 0-2	Stockholm	ECq	
25-06	Denmark	D 1-1	Copenhagen	Fr	Selander
10-08	Finland	W 2-0	Stockholm	Fr	Eriksson.L, Danielsson
3-09	Norway	L 1-3	Oslo	ECq	Nordahl.T
5-11	Norway	W 5-2	Stockholm	ECq	Turesson 2, Danielsson, Eriksson.L 2
12-11	Bulgaria	L 0-3	Sofia	ECq	
19-02-1968	Israel	W 3-0	Tel Aviv	Fr	Ejderstedt 3
28-02	Spain	L 1-3	Seville	Fr	Ejderstedt
2-05	Spain	D 1-1	Malmo	Fr	Nordahl.T
22-05	England	L 1-3	London	Fr	Andersson.R
27-06	Denmark	W 2-1	Stockholm	Fr	Lindman, Nordahl.T
1-08	Soviet Union	D 2-2	Gothenburg	Fr	Eriksson.L, Grahn.O
11-09	Finland	W 3-0	Helsinki	Fr	Eriksson.L, Andersson.R, Selander
15-09	Norway	D 1-1	Oslo	Fr	Eriksson.L
9-10	Norway	W 5-0	Stockholm	WCq	Kindvall 3, Larsson.B 2
19-02-1969	Israel	W 3-2	Tel Aviv	Fr	Ejderstedt, Selander, Andersson.R
26-02	Yugoslavia	L 1-2	Split	Fr	Magnusson.R
1-05	Mexico	W 1-0	Malmo	Fr	Kindvall
22-05	Finland	W 4-0	Vaxjo	Fr	Johansson.H 2, Svensson.T, OG
1-06	Norway	W 4-2	Gothenburg	Fr	Pålsson, Ejderstadt 2, Andersson.R
19-06	Norway	W 5-2	Oslo	WCq	Persson.O, Eriksson.L, Kindvall, Grahn.O, Grip
25-06	Denmark	W 1-0	Copenhagen	Fr	Eklund
6-08	Soviet Union	W 1-0	Moscow	Fr	Eklund
25-08	Israel	W 3-1	Stockholm	Fr	Danielsson 2, Eriksson.L
24-09	Hungary	W 2-0	Stockholm	Fr	Nicklasson, Grahn.O
15-10	France	W 2-0	Stockholm	WCq	Kindvall 2
1-11	France	L 0-3	Paris	WCq	
22-02-1970	Mexico	D 0-0	Mexico City	Fr	
1-03	Mexico	W 1-0	Puebla	Fr	Eriksson.L
16-05	Hungary	W 2-1	Budapest	Fr	Persson.O, Ejderstedt
3-06	Italy	L 0-1	Toluca	WCr1	
7-06	Israel	D 1-1	Toluca	WCr1	Turesson
10-06	Uruguay	W 1-0	Puebla	WCr1	Grahn.O
25-06	Denmark	D 1-1	Gothenburg	Fr	Pålsson
26-08	Finland	W 2-1	Helsinki	Fr	Almqvist, Brzokoupil
13-09	Norway	W 4-2	Oslo	Fr	Danielsson, Brzokoupil, Svensson.T
14-10	Rep. Ireland	D 1-1	Dublin	ECq	Brzokoupil
28-10	Rep. Ireland	W 1-0	Stockholm	ECq	Turesson
12-03-1971	Israel	L 1-2	Tel Aviv	Fr	Eklund
20-05	Finland	W 4-1	Boras	Fr	Larsson.B, Svensson.T, Persson.O, Pålsson
26-05	Austria	W 1-0	Stockholm	ECq	Olsson.J
9-06	Italy	D 0-0	Stockholm	ECq	
20-06	Denmark	W 3-1	Copenhagen	Fr	Grahn.O 2, Eklund
27-06	West Germany	W 1-0	Gothenburg	Fr	Kindvall
8-08	Norway	W 3-0	Malmo	Fr	Sandberg, Pålsson, Larsson.B
4-09	Austria	L 0-1	Vienna	ECq	
9-10	Italy	L 0-3	Milan	ECq	
26-04-1972	Switzerland	D 1-1	Geneva	Fr	Hult
14-05	Czechoslovakia	L 1-2	Gothenburg	Fr	Hult
25-05	Hungary	D 0-0	Stockholm	WCq	
10-06	Austria	L 0-2	Vienna	WCq	
29-06	Denmark	W 2-0	Malmo	Fr	Larsson.B, Sandberg
6-08	Soviet Union	D 4-4	Stockholm	Fr	Edström 3, Pålsson
17-09	Norway	W 3-1	Oslo	Fr	Edström 2, Larsson.B
15-10	Malta	W 7-0	Gothenburg	WCq	Edström 3, Larsson.B 2, Sandberg, Szepanski
26-04-1973	Denmark	W 2-1	Copenhagen	Fr	Sandberg, Kindvall
23-05	Austria	W 3-2	Gothenburg	WCq	Sandberg 2, Grahn.O
13-06	Hungary	D 3-3	Budapest	WCq	Kindvall, Sandberg, Edström
25-06	Brazil	W 1-0	Stockholm	Fr	Sandberg
8-07	Finland	D 1-1	Halmstad	Fr	Leback
11-07	Iceland	W 1-0	Uddevalla	Fr	Tapper
5-08	Soviet Union	D 0-0	Moscow	Fr	
29-08	Finland	W 2-1	Helsinki	Fr	Torstensson, Svensson.H
29-09	Italy	L 0-2	Milan	Fr	
11-11	Malta	W 2-1	Gzira	WCq	Kindvall, Larsson.B
27-11	Austria	W 2-1	Gelsenkirchen	WCq	Sandberg, Larsson.B
1-05-1974	West Germany	L 0-2	Hamburg	Fr	

3-06	Denmark	W 2-0	Copenhagen	Fr	Sandberg, Torstensson
9-06	Switzerland	D 0-0	Malmo	Fr	
15-06	Bulgaria	D 0-0	Dusseldorf	WCr1	
19-06	Holland	D 0-0	Dortmund	WCr1	
23-06	Uruguay	W 3-0	Dusseldorf	WCr1	Edström 2, Sandberg
26-06	Poland	L 0-1	Stuttgart	WCr2	
30-06	West Germany	L 2-4	Dusseldorf	WCr2	Edström, Sandberg
3-07	Yugoslavia	W 2-1	Dusseldorf	WCr2	Edström, Torstensson
8-08	Norway	W 2-1	Gothenburg	Fr	Fredriksson, Tapper
4-09	Holland	L 1-5	Stockholm	Fr	Larsson.B
13-10	Czechoslovakia	L 0-4	Bratislava	Fr	
30-10	Nth. Ireland	L 0-2	Stockholm	ECq	
16-04-1975	Scotland	D 1-1	Gothenburg	Fr	Sjöberg
19-05	Algeria	W 4-0	Halmstad	Fr	Edström, Sandberg, Grahn.O, Sjöberg
4-06	Yugoslavia	L 1-2	Stockholm	ECq	Edström
30-06	Norway	W 3-1	Stockholm	ECq	Nordahl.T 2, Grahn.O
13-08	Norway	W 2-0	Oslo	ECq	Sandberg, Sjöberg
3-09	Nth. Ireland	W 2-1	Belfast	ECq	Sjöberg, Torstensson
25-09	Denmark	D 0-0	Malmo	Fr	
15-10	Yugoslavia	L 0-3	Zagreb	ECq	
28-02-1976	Tunisia	D 1-1	Tunis	Fr	Fredriksson
2-03	Algeria	W 2-0	Algiers	Fr	Fredriksson, Tapper
28-04	Austria	L 0-1	Vienna	Fr	
11-05	Denmark	L 1-2	Gothenburg	Fr	Sandberg
1-06	Finland	W 2-0	Helsinki	Fr	Torstensson, Linderoth
16-06	Norway	W 2-0	Stockholm	WCq	Andersson.B, Sjöberg
11-08	Finland	W 6-0	Malmo	Fr	Sjöberg 2, Ljungberg, Werner, Nilsson.T, Börjesson.B
8-09	Hungary	D 1-1	Stockholm	Fr	Torstensson
22-09	Norway	L 2-3	Oslo	Fr	Torstensson, Sjöberg
9-10	Switzerland	W 2-1	Basle	WCq	Börjesson.B, Sjöberg
27-04-1977	Scotland	L 1-3	Glasgow	Fr	Wendt
26-05	Norway	W 1-0	Gothenburg	Fr	Linderoth
8-06	Switzerland	W 2-1	Stockholm	WCq	Sjöberg, Börjesson.B
15-06	Denmark	L 1-2	Copenhagen	Fr	Nordin
20-07	Iceland	W 1-0	Reykjavik	Fr	Johansson.S
17-08	East Germany	L 0-1	Stockholm	Fr	
7-09	Norway	L 1-2	Oslo	WCq	Sjöberg
5-10	Denmark	W 1-0	Malmo	Fr	Larsson.L
12-10	Hungary	L 0-3	Budapest	Fr	
12-11	Poland	L 1-2	Wroclaw	Fr	Åslund
4-04-1978	East Germany	W 1-0	Leipzig	Fr	Åslund
19-04	West Germany	W 3-1	Stockholm	Fr	OG, Larsson.L 2
21-05	Czechoslovakia	D 0-0	Stockholm	Fr	
3-06	Brazil	D 1-1	Mar del Plata	WCr1	Sjöberg
7-06	Austria	L 0-1	Buenos Aires	WCr1	
11-06	Spain	L 0-1	Buenos Aires	WCr1	
28-06	Finland	W 2-1	Boras	Fr	Nilsson.T, Andersson.M
16-08	Denmark	L 1-2	Copenhagen	Fr	Berggren
1-09	France	D 2-2	Paris	ECq	Nordgren, Grönhagen
4-10	Czechoslovakia	L 1-3	Stockholm	ECq	Borg
19-04-1979	Soviet Union	L 0-2	Tbilisi	Fr	
9-05	Denmark	D 2-2	Copenhagen	Fr	Erlandsson, Ohlsson.B
7-06	Luxembourg	W 3-0	Malmo	ECq	Grönhagen, Cervin, Borg
10-06	England	D 0-0	Stockholm	Fr	
28-06	Norway	W 2-0	Gothenburg	Fr	Borg, Nordin
15-08	Norway	L 0-2	Oslo	Fr	
5-09	France	L 1-3	Stockholm	ECq	Backe
26-09	Italy	L 0-1	Florence	Fr	
10-10	Czechoslovakia	L 1-4	Prague	ECq	Svensson.J
23-10	Luxembourg	D 1-1	Esch	ECq	Grönhagen
14-11	Malaysia	W 3-1	Kuala Lumpur	Fr	Nilsson.P, Grönhagen, Andersson.M
17-11	Singapore	W 5-0	Singapore	Fr	Nilsson.T 3, Svensson.J 2
29-04-1980	Soviet Union	L 1-5	Malmo	Fr	Nordgren
7-05	Denmark	L 0-1	Gothenburg	Fr	
22-05	Finland	W 2-0	Helsinki	Fr	Nordgren, Sjöberg
18-06	Israel	D 1-1	Stockholm	WCq	Ramberg
17-07	Iceland	D 1-1	Halmstad	Fr	Backe
20-08	Hungary	L 0-2	Budapest	Fr	
10-09	Scotland	L 0-1	Stockholm	WCq	
24-09	Bulgaria	W 3-2	Burgas	Fr	Ramberg, Ohlsson.B, Holmgren
15-10	Nth. Ireland	L 0-3	Belfast	WCq	
12-11	Israel	D 0-0	Tel Aviv	WCq	

28-02-1981	Norway	W 4-2	Lahti	Fr	Nilsson.Tb, Rönnberg, Larsson.L, Nilsson.T
1-03	Finland	L 1-2	Lahti	Fr	Nilsson.Tb
14-05	Denmark	L 1-2	Malmo	Fr	Börjesson.B
3-06	Nth. Ireland	W 1-0	Stockholm	WCq	Borg
24-06	Portugal	W 3-0	Stockholm	WCq	Börjesson.B, Hysén, Svensson.J
29-07	Finland	W 1-0	Halmstad	Fr	Björklund
12-08	Bulgaria	W 1-0	Uddevalla	Fr	Sjöberg
9-09	Scotland	L 0-2	Glasgow	WCq	
23-09	Greece	L 1-2	Salonica	Fr	Larsson.T
14-10	Portugal	W 2-1	Lisbon	WCq	Larsson.T, Persson.T
28-10	Saudi Arabia	W 2-1	Riyadh	Fr	Larsson.T 2
20-02-1982	Finland	D 2-2	Lahti	Fr	Ahlström 2
21-02	Finland	L 1-2	Lahti	Fr	Dahlkvist
5-05	Denmark	D 1-1	Copenhagen	Fr	Larsson.T
19-05	East Germany	D 2-2	Halmstad	Fr	Persson.T, Larsson.T
3-06	Soviet Union	D 1-1	Stockholm	Fr	Nilsson.B
11-08	Norway	L 0-1	Oslo	Fr	
8-09	Romania	L 0-2	Bucharest	ECq	
6-10	Czechoslovakia	D 2-2	Bratislava	ECq	Jingblad, Eriksson.U
13-11	Cyprus	W 1-0	Nicosia	ECq	Corneliusson
27-04-1983	Holland	W 3-0	Utrecht	Fr	Corneliusson 2, Prytz
15-05	Cyprus	W 5-0	Malmo	ECq	Prytz 2, Corneliusson, Hysén, Ravelli
29-05	Italy	W 2-0	Gothenburg	ECq	Sandberg, Strömberg
9-06	Romania	L 0-1	Stockholm	ECq	
22-06	Brazil	D 3-3	Gothenburg	Fr	Corneliusson 2, Hysén
17-08	Iceland	W 4-0	Reykjavik	Fr	Jingblad, Ramberg, Hysén, Fredriksson.S
7-09	Finland	W 3-0	Helsinki	Fr	Eriksson.U 2, Sunesson
21-09	Czechoslovakia	W 1-0	Stockholm	ECq	Corneliusson
15-10	Italy	W 3-0	Naples	ECq	Strömberg 2, Sunesson
16-11	Trinidad	W 5-0	Port of Spain	Fr	Dahlqvist, Jingblad 3, Sunesson
19-11	Barbados	W 4-0	Bridgetown	Fr	Dahlqvist, Jingblad 3
22-11	Mexico	L 0-2	Morelia	Fr	
2-05-1984	Switzerland	D 0-0	Berne	Fr	
23-05	Malta	W 4-0	Norrkoping	WCq	Sunesson 2, Corneliusson, Erlandsson
6-06	Denmark	L 0-1	Gothenburg	Fr	
22-08	Mexico	D 1-1	Malmo	Fr	Prytz
12-09	Portugal	L 0-1	Stockholm	WCq	
26-09	Italy	L 0-1	Milan	Fr	
17-10	West Germany	L 0-2	Cologne	WCq	
14-11	Portugal	W 3-1	Lisbon	WCq	Prytz 2, Nilsson.Tb
1-05-1985	Israel	D 1-1	Tel Aviv	Fr	Prytz
22-05	Norway	W 1-0	Gothenburg	Fr	Prytz
5-06	Czechoslovakia	W 2-0	Stockholm	WCq	Prytz, Larsson.L
21-08	Poland	W 1-0	Malmo	Fr	Ravelli
11-09	Denmark	W 3-0	Copenhagen	Fr	Prytz, Corneliusson, Magnusson.M
25-09	West Germany	D 2-2	Stockholm	WCq	Corneliusson, Magnusson.M
16-10	Czechoslovakia	L 1-2	Prague	WCq	Corneliusson
17-11	Malta	W 2-1	Ta'Qali	WCq	Prytz, Strömberg
1-05-1986	Greece	D 0-0	Malmo	Fr	
14-05	Austria	L 0-1	Salzburg	Fr	
6-08	Finland	W 3-1	Helsinki	Fr	Prytz 2, Ekström
20-08	Soviet Union	D 0-0	Gothenburg	Fr	
10-09	England	W 1-0	Stockholm	Fr	Ekström
24-09	Switzerland	W 2-0	Stockholm	ECq	Ekström 2
12-10	Portugal	D 1-1	Lisbon	ECq	Strömberg
16-11	Malta	W 5-0	Ta'Qali	ECq	Ekström 2, Magnusson.M, Hysén, Fredriksson.S
18-04-1987	Soviet Union	W 3-1	Tbilisi	Fr	Limpár, Magnusson.M 2
24-05	Malta	W 1-0	Gothenburg	ECq	Ekström
3-06	Italy	W 1-0	Stockholm	ECq	Larsson.P
17-06	Switzerland	D 1-1	Lausanne	ECq	Ekström
12-08	Norway	D 0-0	Oslo	Fr	
26-08	Denmark	W 1-0	Stockholm	Fr	Magnusson.M
23-09	Portugal	L 0-1	Stockholm	ECq	
13-10	West Germany	D 1-1	Gelsenkirchen	Fr	Hysén
14-11	Italy	L 1-2	Naples	ECq	Larsson.P
13-01-1988	East Germany	W 4-1	Las Palmas	Fr	Thern 2, Truedsson, Rehn
15-01	Finland	W 1-0	Las Palmas	Fr	Thern
31-03	West Germany	D 1-1	Berlin	Fr	Truedsson. Won 4-2 on pens
2-04	Soviet Union	W 2-0	Berlin	Fr	Eskilsson, Holmqvist.H
27-04	Wales	W 4-1	Stockholm	Fr	Holmqvist.H 2, Strömberg, Eskilsson
1-06	Spain	W 3-1	Salamanca	Fr	Nilsson.J, Magnusson.M, Hysén
31-07	Brazil	D 1-1	Stockholm	Fr	Hellstrom

Date	Opponent	Result	Venue	Comp	Scorers
31-08	Denmark	L 1-2	Stockholm	Fr	Pettersson
12-10	Portugal	D 0-0	Gothenburg	Fr	
19-10	England	D 0-0	London	WCq	
5-11	Albania	W 2-1	Tirana	WCq	Holmqvist, Ekstrom
26-04-1989	Wales	W 2-0	Wrexham	Fr	Schiller, OG
7-05	Poland	W 2-1	Stockholm	WCq	Ljung, Larsson.N
31-05	Algeria	W 2-0	Orebro	Fr	Ingesson 2
14-06	Denmark	L 0-6	Copenhagen	Fr	
16-06	Brazil	W 2-1	Copenhagen	Fr	Ljung, Rehn
16-08	France	L 2-4	Malmo	Fr	Thern, Lindqvist
6-09	England	D 0-0	Stockholm	WCq	
8-10	Albania	W 3-1	Stockholm	WCq	Ingesson, Magnusson.M, Engkvist
25-10	Poland	W 2-0	Chorzow	WCq	Larsson.P, Ekström
14-02-1990	Arab Emirates	L 1-2	Dubai	Fr	Schwarz
17-02	Arab Emirates	W 2-0	Dubai	Fr	Rehn, Ingesson
21-02	Belgium	D 0-0	Brussels	Fr	
11-04	Algeria	D 1-1	Algiers	Fr	Schwarz
25-04	Wales	W 4-2	Stockholm	Fr	Brolin 2, Ingesson 2
27-05	Finland	W 6-0	Stockholm	Fr	Brolin 2, Magnusson.M, Limpár, Larsson.P, Thern
10-06	Brazil	L 1-2	Turin	WCr1	Brolin
16-06	Scotland	L 1-2	Genoa	WCr1	Strömberg
20-06	Costa Rica	L 1-2	Genoa	WCr1	Ekström
22-08	Norway	W 2-1	Stavanger	Fr	Engqvist, Fjellstrom
5-09	Denmark	L 0-1	Vasteras	Fr	
26-09	Bulgaria	W 2-0	Stockholm	Fr	Corneliusson, Andersson.K
10-10	West Germany	L 1-3	Stockholm	Fr	Rehn
17-04-1991	Greece	D 2-2	Athens	Fr	Erlingburg, Mild
1-05	Austria	W 6-0	Stockholm	Fr	Andersson.K 3, Rehn, Dahlin 2
5-06	Colombia	D 2-2	Stockholm	Fr	Brolin, Andersson.K
13-06	Soviet Union	L 2-3	Gothenburg	Fr	Brolin 2
15-06	Denmark	W 4-0	Norrkoping	Fr	Dahlin 2, Andersson.K, Brolin
8-08	Norway	W 2-1	Oslo	Fr	Nilsson.R, Limpár
21-08	Poland	L 0-2	Gdynia	Fr	
4-09	Yugoslavia	W 4-3	Stockholm	Fr	Dahlin 2, Limpar, Thern
9-10	Switzerland	L 1-3	Lucerne	Fr	Eriksson.J
25-01-1992	Australia	D 0-0	Sydney	Fr	
29-01	Australia	L 0-1	Adelaide	Fr	
2-02	Australia	L 0-1	Melbourne	Fr	
22-04	Tunisia	W 1-0	Tunis	Fr	Andersson.K
7-05	Poland	W 5-0	Stockholm	Fr	Andersson.K 2, Ingesson, Dahlin, Pettersson
27-05	Hungary	W 2-1	Stockholm	Fr	Schwarz 2
10-06	France	D 1-1	Stockholm	ECr1	Eriksson.J
14-06	Denmark	W 1-0	Stockholm	ECr1	Brolin
17-06	England	W 2-1	Stockholm	ECr1	Eriksson.J, Brolin
21-06	Germany	L 2-3	Stockholm	ECsf	Brolin, Andersson.K
26-08	Norway	D 2-2	Oslo	Fr	Dahlin, Pettersson
9-09	Finland	W 1-0	Helsinki	WCq	Ingesson
7-10	Bilgaria	W 2-0	Stockholm	WCq	Dahlin, Pettersson
11-11	Israel	W 3-1	Tel Aviv	WCq	Limpar, Dahlin, Ingesson
15-04-1993	Hungary	W 2-0	Budapest	Fr	Ekström, Rehn
28-04	France	L 1-2	Paris	WCq	Dahlin
19-05	Austria	W 1-0	Stockholm	WCq	Eriksson.J
2-06	Israel	W 5-0	Stockholm	WCq	Brolin 3, Zetterberg, Landberg
11-08	Switzerland	L 1-2	Boras	Fr	Dahlin
22-08	France	D 1-1	Stockholm	WCq	Dahlin
8-09	Bulgaria	D 1-1	Sofia	WCq	Dahlin
13-10	Finland	W 3-2	Stockholm	WCq	Dahlin 2, Larsson.H
10-11	Austria	D 1-1	Vienna	WCq	Mild
18-04-1994	Colombia	D 0-0	Fort Lauderdale	Fr	
20-02	Sweden	W 3-1	Miami	Fr	Larsson.H, Andersson.K, Lilienberg
25-02	Mexico	L 1-2	Fresno	Fr	Mild
20-04	Wales	W 2-0	Wrexham	Fr	Larsson.H, Brolin
5-05	Nigeria	W 3-1	Stockholm	Fr	Schwarz, Larsson.H, Ingesson
26-05	Denmark	L 0-1	Copenhagen	Fr	
5-06	Norway	W 2-0	Stockholm	Fr	Brolin 2
12-06	Romania	D 1-1	Mission Viejo	Fr	Ingesson
19-06	Cameroon	D 2-2	Los Angeles	WCr1	Ljung, Dahlin
24-06	Russia	W 3-1	Detroit	WCr1	Brolin, Dahlin 2
28-06	Brazil	D 1-1	Detroit	WCr1	Andersson.K
3-07	Saudi Arabia	W 3-1	Dallas	WCr2	Dahlin, Andersson.K 2
10-07	Romania	D 2-2	San Francisco	WCqf	Brolin, Andersson.K. Won 5-4pens
13-07	Brazil	L 0-1	Los Angeles	WCsf	

16-07	Bulgaria	W 4-0	Los Angeles	WC3p	Brolin, Mild, Larsson.H, Andersson.K
17-08	Lithuania	W 4-2	Orebro	Fr	Brolin 2, Andersson.P, Larsson.H
7-09	Iceland	W 1-0	Reykjavik	ECq	Ingesson
12-10	Switzerland	L 2-4	Berne	ECq	Andersson.K, Dahlin
16-11	Hungary	W 2-0	Stockholm	ECq	Brolin, Dahlin
8-03-1995	Cyprus	D 3-3	Limassol	Fr	Ekström, Andersson.K, Alexandersson
29-03	Turkey	L 1-2	Istanbul	ECq	Andersson.K
26-04	Hungary	L 0-1	Budapest	ECq	
1-06	Iceland	D 1-1	Stockholm	ECq	Brolin
4-06	Brazil	L 0-1	Birmingham	Fr	
8-06	England	D 3-3	Leeds	Fr	Mild 2, Andersson.K
10-06	Japan	D 2-2	Nottingham	Fr	Andersson.K 2

SWITZERLAND

Though never actually a force to be reckoned with, the Swiss were useful competitors in the first half of the century, but as a small and on the whole affluent society, they struggled to keep pace with the larger and more successful European nations since. Only with the emergence of a talented generation of players in the 1990s has Swiss football been able to regain some of its lost pride.

The Swiss Football Association, formed in 1895, was one of the first on mainland Europe and over the years the Swiss have proved themselves adept in the organisational field. Noted for its neutrality and situated in central Europe, Switzerland, one of the founding members of FIFA, became one of the centres for world football when it was decided to locate the FIFA organisation in Zürich. Fifty years later in 1954, the founders of UEFA decided that Switzerland should also be home to their body and so located themselves in Berne.

Football is recorded as having been played in Switzerland as early as 1869 by English students at La Châtelaine College in Geneva, and in 1879 St Gallen, the oldest surviving club, was formed. As the names of some of the clubs like Grasshoppers and Young Boys suggest, the British influence was strong. Three years after the formation of the association a championship was instituted, and by this time the majority of the clubs still active today had been formed. The first competition was won by Grasshoppers after a play-off between the winners of the three regional leagues. This was the system used until the introduction of a single national league in 1934. Grasshoppers, Servette and Young Boys, representing Zürich, Geneva and Berne respectively, were amongst the most successful teams in the early years and remain so. There is, however, a strong rivalry between the cities, and in recent years FC Zurich, FC Basel and regional clubs like Neuchâtel Xamax have all experienced periods of success at the expense of the established clubs.

In 1905 a national side was fielded for the first time with a match against France in Paris. Defeat that day was to become a familar experience, though notable victories were occasionally scored on home territory. Even the emergence of the amazing Abegglen footballing family could not alter the overall poor record of the national side. Max and André Abegglen fetaured in the side for nearly two decades and between them they scored over 60 goals for their country. Although the overall results remained poor, the Swiss continually made their mark upon the major tournaments in the 1920s and 1930s. Max Abegglen inspired them to a silver medal in the 1924 Olympic Games in Paris, where they succumbed to the dazzling Uruguayans in the final. They also reached the quarter-finals of both the 1934 and 1938 World Cups. Their 4-2 victory over Germany in the first round in 1938, in which André, the younger Abegglen brother by seven years, scored twice, was particularly impressive.

The Swiss finished last in every Dr Gerö Cup that was played, in perhaps a truer indication of the level of the game, and were often on the end of some heavy defeats. Aside from the victory over Germany in the World Cup, their finest moment pre-war was the 3-2 victory over England a month before the German game. Responsible for the national side at the time was one of the key figures in Swiss football history, Karl Rappan. The inventor of the 'Swiss Bolt' system, Rappan instigated a major tactical innovation which saw the initial use of a free man in defence, along the lines of a sweeper. Under him the Swiss experienced an immediate rise in their fortunes after the war, and as their manager on and off until he retired in 1968, he was responsible for Switzerland's continued presence as a international force.

Helped by players like Hügi, Ballaman, Fatton and Bickel, Switzerland took part in four of the first five World Cups after the war. As hosts in 1954 they reached the quarter-finals before losing to Austria in one of the most bizarre games ever staged in the tournament. Three-nil up after 23 minutes, they eventually lost 7-5 with all of the goals being scored within an hour. The 1950, 1962 and 1966 tournaments all saw elimination in the first round, but not much more was expected of the team and in light of later achievements, reaching the final tournament was success in itself.

From 1966 to 1994, though always difficult opponents, the national side failed to reach the finals of either the World Cup or European Championships. The 1992 European Championship saw them come close to breaking the sequence, finishing a point behind Scotland after losing their final match against Romania in Bucharest, and two years later they made it to the World Cup in America. Under English coach Roy Hodgson they served notice of their intentions by beating Italy in the qualifiers, and in the finals they sensationally thrashed the impressive Romanians, 4-1. The German-based quartet of Stéphane Chapuisat, Ciriaco Sforza, Adrian Knup and Alain Sutter provided the backbone of the side as they went through to the second round only to come unstuck against Spain, losing 3-0.

THE ORDER OF MERIT

	Team	All			League			Cup		Europe		
		G	S	B	G	S	B	G	S	G	S	B
1	Grasshopper-Club Zürich	41	27	11	23	17	10	18	10	-	-	1
2	Servette FC Geneve	22	26	11	16	15	11	6	11	-	-	-
3	BSC Young Boys Bern	17	17	9	11	12	8	6	5	-	-	1
4	Lausanne-Sports	14	13	7	7	7	6	7	6	-	-	1
5	FC Zürich	14	9	8	9	8	6	5	1	-	-	2
6	FC Basel	13	9	3	8	3	3	5	6	-	-	-
7	FC La Chaux-de-Fonds	9	4	7	3	3	7	6	1	-	-	-
8	FC Sion	8	1	5	1	1	5	7	-	-	-	-
9	FC Lugano	6	8	9	3	4	9	3	4	-	-	-
10	FC Aarau	4	3	3	3	1	3	1	2	-	-	-
11	Neuchâtel Xamax FC	3	6	7	3	2	7	-	4	-	-	-
12	FC Winterthur	3	4	1	3	2	1	-	2	-	-	-
13	FC Luzern	3	1	1	1	1	1	2	-	-	-	-
14	FC St. Gallen	2	2	2	1	-	2	1	2	-	-	-
15	FC Grenchen	1	7	1	-	4	1	1	3	-	-	-
16	Young Fellows Zurich	1	4	2	-	3	2	1	1	-	-	-
17	FC Bern	1	4	1	1	3	1	-	1	-	-	-
18	FC Biel	1	3	2	1	2	2	-	1	-	-	-
19	Urania Geneva Sport	1	2	1	-	1	1	1	1	-	-	-
20	AC Bellinzona	1	2	-	1	-	-	-	2	-	-	-
21	Etoile La Chaux de-Fonds	1	1	-	1	1	-	-	-	-	-	-
22	Anglo-American FC Zurich	1	-	-	1	-	-	-	-	-	-	-
	SC Brühl St. Gallen	1	-	-	1	-	-	-	-	-	-	-
24	Nordstern Basel	-	5	-	-	3	-	-	2	-	-	-
25	BSC Old Boys Basel	-	3	1	-	3	1	-	-	-	-	-
26	FC Schaffhausen	-	2	-	-	-	-	-	2	-	-	-
27	FC Chiasso	-	1	2	-	1	2	-	-	-	-	-
28	Chatelaine	-	1	-	-	1	-	-	-	-	-	-
	FC Fribourg	-	1	-	-	-	-	-	1	-	-	-
	FC Locarno	-	1	-	-	-	-	-	1	-	-	-
	FC Thun	-	1	-	-	-	-	-	1	-	-	-
32	Blue Stars Zürich	-	-	1	-	-	1	-	-	-	-	-
	FC Etoile Carouge	-	-	1	-	-	1	-	-	-	-	-
	Villa Longchamp	-	-	1	-	-	1	-	-	-	-	-

To the end of the 1994-95 season

Swiss club football, however, still has a much lower profile. For an important international match it is not unusual to see the Wankdorf stadium full to capacity, but the league does not have the glamour of those in neighbouring countries, though it does boast professionalism. The European club tournaments have not been particularly happy hunting grounds; FC Zürich have reached the semi-final of the European Cup twice, but on neither occasion were they serious contenders to win the tournament.

Population: 6,756,000
Area, sq km: 41,293
% in urban areas: 60.2%
Capital city: Berne

Schweizerischer Fussballverband
Laubeggstrasse #70
Postfach 24
CH-3000 Berne 32
Switzerland
Tel: + 41 31 9508111
Fax: + 41 31 9508181

Year of formation	1895
Affiliation to FIFA	1904
Affiliation to UEFA	1954
Registered clubs	473
Registered players	182 000
Professional Players	150
Registered coaches	7036
Registered referees	4500
National stadium	Wankdorf, Berne 28 000
National colours	Red/White/Red
Reserve colours	White/White/Red
Season	August - June

THE RECORD

WORLD CUP

1930	Did not enter
1934	QT 1st/3 in group 10 - Final Tournament/Quarter-finalists
1938	QT 1st/2 in group 4 - Final Tournament/Quarter-finalists
1950	QT 1st/2 in group 4 - Final Tournament/1st round
1954	QT Automatic - Final Tournament/Quarter-finalists
1958	QT 3rd/3 in group 9
1962	QT 1st/3 in group 1 - Final Tournament/1st round
1966	QT 1st/4 in group 5 - Final Tournament/1st round
1970	QT 3rd/4 in group 1
1974	QT 3rd/4 in group 2
1978	QT 3rd/3 in group 6
1982	QT 4th/5 in group 4
1986	QT 3rd/5 in group 6
1990	QT 4th/5 in group 7
1994	QT 2nd/6 in group 1 - Final Tournament/2nd round

EUROPEAN CHAMPIONSHIP

1960	Did not enter
1964	1st round
1968	QT 3rd/4 in group 6
1972	QT 2nd/4 in group 3
1976	QT 4th/4 in group 6
1980	QT 4th/5 in group 4
1984	QT 2nd/4 in group 1
1988	QT 4th/5 in group 2
1992	QT 2nd/5 in group 2
1996	QT group 3

Dr. Gerö Cup

1929	5th
1932	5th
1935	5th
1953	5th
1960	6th

EUROPEAN CLUB COMPETITIONS

European Cup
Semi-finalists - BSC Young Boys 1959 FC Zürich 1964 1977

Cup Winners Cup
Quarter-finalists - Lausanne-Sports 1965 Servette FC 1967 1979 FC Zürich 1974 FC Sion 1987 BSC Young Boys 1988 Grasshopper-Club 1990

UEFA Cup
Semi-finalists - Lausanne-Sports 1958 Grasshopper-Club 1978

Mitropa Cup
Quarter-finalists - Grasshopper-Club 1937

CLUB DIRECTORY

BERNE (Population - 298,000)
BSC Young Boys (1898)
(Berner Sportclub)
Wankdorf 28,000 – Yellow, black trim

ZURICH (Pop. - 860,000)
Grasshopper-Club Zürich (1886)
Hardturm 30,000 – Blue & white halves/White

Fussball-Club Zürich (1896)
Letzigrund 27,000 – White, blue trim

BASLE (Pop. - 575,000)
Fussball-Club Basel (1893)
St. Jakob 40,000 – Red/Blue, white trim

BSC Old Boys (1894)
(Basel Sportclub)
Schützenmatte 12,000 – Yellow/Black

GENEVA (Pop. - 460,000)
Servette Football Club Genève (1890)
Charmilles 30,000 – Grenadine, white trim

Urania Genève Sport (1896)
Frontenex 4,000 – Violet/White

LAUSANNE (Pop. - 259,000)
Lausanne-Sports (1896)
Olympique 26,000 – Blue, white trim
Previous name - Merger in 1920 of Montriond '96 and Hygrénique

LUCERNE (Pop. - 159,000)
Fussball-Club Luzern (1901)
Allmend 24,000 – Blue/White

ST. GALLEN (Pop. - 125,000)
St. Gallen Fussball-Club (1879)
Espenmoos 14,000 – Green, white trim

WINTERTHUR (Pop. - 107,000)
Fussball-Club Winterthur (1896)
Schützenwiese 15,000 – White/White

LUGANO (Pop. - 94,000)
Football-Club Lugano (1908)
Comunale Cornaredo 26,000 – Black, white chest 'V'/White

BIEL (Pop. - 81,000)
Fussball-Club Biel (1896)
Gorzellen – Blue/Yellow

THUN (Pop. - 77,000)
Fussball-Club Thun (1898)
Lachen – Red/White

NEUCHATEL (Pop. - 65,000)
Neuchâtel Xamax Football Club (1970)
Maladière 20,000 – Red & black stripes/Black
Previous names - Merger in 1970 of Cantonal and FC Neuchâtel

AARAU (Pop. - 57,000)
Fussball-Club Aarau (1902)
Brügglifeld 14,000 – White/Black

SCHAFFHAUSEN (Pop. - 53,000)
Fussball-Club Schaffhausen (1896)
Breite 7,000 – Yellow/Black

LOCARNO (Pop. - 42,000)
Football-Club Locarno (1906)
Del Lido 11,000 – White/Blue

LA CHAUX-DE-FONDS (Pop. - 35,000)
Football-Club La Chaux-de-Fonds (1894)
Charrière 14,000 – Yellow/Blue

SION (Pop. - 23,000)
Football-Club Sion (1909)
Tourbillon 19,000 – White, red trim

BELLINZONA (Pop. - 16,000)
Associazione Calcio Bellinzona (1904)
Comunale 20,000 – Red/Blue

WETTINGEN
Fussball-Club Wettingen (1931)
Altenburg 9,000 – White, blue trim

SWISS LEAGUE CHAMPIONSHIP

Regional League Play-offs

1898aj Grasshopper-Club 4 Chatelaine 0 Villa Longchamp 0

1899	Anglo-American	7-0	Old Boys Basel
1900	Grasshopper-Club	2-0	FC Bern
1901	Grasshopper-Club	2-0	FC Bern

1902aj FC Zürich 4 BSC Young Boys 1 FC Bern 1
1903 BSC Young Boys 4 FC Zürich 0 FC Neuchâtel 0
1904 FC St. Gallen 3 Old Boys Basel 1 Servette FC 1
1905 Grasshopper-Club 4 La Chaux-de-Fonds 1 BSC Young Boys 1
1906 FC Winterthur 4 Servette FC 2 BSC Young Boys 0
1907 Servette FC 4 Young Fellows Zürich 2 FC Basel 0
1908 FC Winterthur 4-1 BSC Young Boys
1909 BSC Young Boys 1-0 FC Winterthur
1910aj BSC Young Boys 4 Servette FC 2 FC Aarau 0
1911 BSC Young Boys 4 FC Zürich 2 Servette FC 0
1912 FC Aarau 4 Et. Chaux-de-Fonds 2 Servette FC 0
1913 Montriond Lausanne 4 Old Boys Basel 2 FC Aarau 0
1914 FC Aarau 3 BSC Young Boys 2 Cantonal Neuchâtel 1
1915 Brühl St. Gallen 3-0 Servette FC
1916aj Cantonal Neuchâtel 4 FC Winterthur 1 Old Boys Basel 1
1917 FC Winterthur 4 La Chaux-de-Fonds 1 BSC Young Boys 1
1918 Servette FC 4 BSC Young Boys 2 FC St. Gallen 0
1919 Et. Chaux-de-Fonds 4 Servette FC 1 FC Winterthur 1
1920 BSC Young Boys 3 Servette FC 2 Grasshopper-Club 1
1921 Grasshopper-Club 4 BSC Young Boys 2 Servette FC 0
1922 Servette FC 4 FC Luzern 2 Blue Stars Zürich 0
1923 FC Bern 3 Young Fellows Zürich 2 Servette FC 1
1924 FC Zürich 4 Nordstern Basel 2 Servette FC 0
1925 Servette FC 3 FC Bern 2 Young Fellows Zürich 1
1926 Servette FC 3 Grasshopper-Club 3 BSC Young Boys 0
1927 Grasshopper-Club 4 Nordstern Basel 2 FC Biel 0
1928 Grasshopper-Club 4 Nordstern Basel 2 FC Etoile Carouge 0
1929 BSC Young Boys 3 Grasshopper-Club 2 Urania Genève 1
1930ac Servette FC 8 Grasshopper-Club 5 FC Biel 5
1931 Grasshopper-Club 7 Urania Genève 6 La Chaux-de-Fonds 4
1932ab Lausanne-Sports 4 FC Zürich 4 Grasshopper-Club 3
1933 Servette FC 5 Grasshopper-Club 5 BSC Young Boys 2

National league

1934q Servette FC 49 Grasshopper-Club 46 FC Lugano 38
1935n Lausanne-Sports 41 Servette FC 40 FC Lugano 35
1936 Lausanne-Sports 41 Young Fellows Zürich 38 Grasshopper-Club 36
1937l Grasshopper-Club 36 BSC Young Boys 29 Young Fellows Zürich 28
1938k FC Lugano 30 Grasshopper-Club 29 BSC Young Boys 28
1939 Grasshopper-Club 31 FC Grenchen 27 FC Lugano 27
1940 Servette FC 41 FC Grenchen 28 Grasshopper-Club 26
1941 FC Lugano 37 BSC Young Boys 35 Servette FC 33
1942n Grasshopper-Club 36 FC Grenchen 36 Servette FC 35
1943 Grasshopper-Club 44 FC Lugano 35 Lausanne-Sports 34
1944 Lausanne-Sports 38 Servette FC 32 FC Lugano 30
1945 Grasshopper-Club 41 FC Lugano 34 BSC Young Boys 34
1946 Servette FC 36 FC Lugano 35 Lausanne-Sports 30
1947 FC Biel 36 Lausanne-Sports 35 FC Lugano 31
1948 AC Bellinzona 38 FC Biel 37 Lausanne-Sports 34
1949 FC Lugano 40 FC Basel 33 La Chaux-de-Fonds 29
1950 Servette FC 35 FC Basel 33 Lausanne-Sports 32
1951 Lausanne-Sports 34 FC Chiasso 31 La Chaux-de-Fonds 30
1952 Grasshopper-Club 38 FC Zürich 37 FC Chiasso 35
1953 FC Basel 42 BSC Young Boys 38 Grasshopper-Club 32
1954 La Chaux-de-Fonds 42 Grasshopper-Club 41 Lausanne-Sports 36
1955 La Chaux-de-Fonds 42 Lausanne-Sports 38 Grasshopper-Club 33
1956 Grasshopper-Club 42 La Chaux-de-Fonds 34 BSC Young Boys 32
1957 BSC Young Boys 45 Grasshopper-Club 41 La Chaux-de-Fonds 38

1958 BSC Young Boys 43 Grasshopper-Club 35 FC Chiasso 35
1959 BSC Young Boys 38 FC Grenchen 32 FC Zürich 30
1960 BSC Young Boys 42 FC Biel 36 La Chaux-de-Fonds 32
1961 Servette FC 46 BSC Young Boys 36 FC Zürich 35
1962 Servette FC 40 Lausanne-Sports 35 La Chaux-de-Fonds 34
1963 FC Zürich 44 Lausanne-Sports 40 La Chaux-de-Fonds 32
1964 La Chaux-de-Fonds 39 FC Zürich 38 FC Grenchen 38
1965 Lausanne-Sports 36 BSC Young Boys 32 Servette FC 31
1966 FC Zürich 42 Servette FC 35 Lausanne-Sports 32
1967 FC Basel 40 FC Zürich 39 FC Lugano 39
1968 FC Zürich 38 Grasshopper-Club 38 FC Lugano 38
1969 FC Basel 36 Lausanne-Sports 35 FC Zürich 30
1970 FC Basel 37 Lausanne-Sports 36 FC Zürich 34
1971 Grasshopper-Club 42 FC Basel 42 FC Lugano 31
1972 FC Basel 43 FC Zürich 39 Grasshopper-Club 38
1973 FC Basel 39 Grasshopper-Club 35 FC Sion 33
1974 FC Zürich 45 Grasshopper-Club 33 Servette FC 32
1975 FC Zürich 39 BSC Young Boys 33 Grasshopper-Club 33
1976 FC Zürich 44 Servette FC 39 FC Basel 34
1977r2 FC Basel 29 Servette FC 29 FC Zürich 27
1978 Grasshopper-Club 29 Servette FC 28 FC Basel 27
1979 Servette FC 35 FC Zürich 29 Grasshopper-Club 23
1980u5 FC Basel 33 Grasshopper-Club 31 Servette FC 31
1981n FC Zürich 40 Grasshopper-Club 34 Neuchâtel Xamax 34
1982q Grasshopper-Club 49 Servette FC 46 FC Zürich 46
1983 Grasshopper-Club 49 Servette FC 48 FC St. Gallen 40
1984 Grasshopper-Club 44 Servette FC 44 FC Sion 43
1985 Servette FC 46 FC Aarau 42 Neuchâtel Xamax 39
1986 BSC Young Boys 44 Neuchâtel Xamax 42 FC Luzern 41
1987 Neuchâtel Xamax 48 Grasshopper-Club 43 FC Sion 42
1988u4 Neuchâtel Xamax 32 Servette FC 30 FC Aarau 30
1989 FC Luzern 33 Grasshopper-Club 30 FC Sion 29
1990 Grasshopper-Club 31 Lausanne-Sports 31 Neuchâtel Xamax 30
1991 Grasshopper-Club 33 FC Sion 29 Neuchâtel Xamax 29
1992 FC Sion 33 Neuchâtel Xamax 31 Grasshopper-Club 30
1993 FC Aarau 34 BSC Young Boys 28 FC Lugano 27
1994 Servette FC 34 Grasshopper-Club 33 FC Sion 31
1995 Grasshopper-Club 37 FC Lugano 30 Neuchâtel Xam. 28

Championship Play-offs

1926	Servette FC	3-2	Grasshopper-Club
1932	Lausanne-Sports	5-2	FC Zürich
1933	Servette FC	3-2	Grasshopper-Club
1942*	Grasshopper-Club	0-0 1-1	FC Grenchen
1968	FC Zürich	2-0	Grasshopper-Club
1971	Grasshopper-Club	4-3	FC Basel
1977	FC Basel	2-1	Servette FC
1984	Grasshopper-Club	1-0	Servette FC

* Grasshoppers won on away goals

SWISS CUP FINALS

1926	Grasshopper-Club	2-1	FC Bern
1927	Grasshopper-Club	3-1	Young Fellows Zürich
1928	Servette FC	5-1	Grasshopper-Club
1929	Urania Genève	1-0	BSC Young Boys
1930	BSC Young Boys	1-0	FC Aarau
1931	FC Lugano	2-1	Grasshopper-Club
1932	Grasshopper-Club	5-1	Urania Genève
1933	FC Basel	4-3	Grasshopper-Club
1934	Grasshopper-Club	2-0	Servette FC
1935	Lausanne-Sports	10-0	Nordstern Basel
1936	Young Fellows Zürich	2-0	Servette FC
1937	Grasshopper-Club	10-0	Lausanne-Sports
1938	Grasshopper-Club	2-2 5-1	Servette FC
1939	Lausanne-Sports	2-0	Nordstern Basel
1940	Grasshopper-Club	3-0	FC Grenchen
1941	Grasshopper-Club	1-1 2-0	Servette FC
1942	Grasshopper-Club	0-0 2-1	FC Basel
1943	Grasshopper-Club	2-1	FC Lugano
1944	Lausanne-Sports	3-0	FC Basel
1945	BSC Young Boys	2-0	FC St. Gallen
1946	Grasshopper-Club	3-0	Lausanne-Sports
1947	FC Basel	3-0	Lausanne-Sports
1948	La Chaux-de-Fonds	2-2 2-2 4-0	FC Grenchen
1949	Servette FC	3-0	Grasshopper-Club
1950	Lausanne-Sports	1-1 4-0	Cantonal Neuchâtel
1951	La Chaux-de-Fonds	3-2	FC Locarno
1952	Grasshopper-Club	2-0	FC Lugano
1953	BSC Young Boys	1-1 3-1	Grasshopper-Club
1954	La Chaux-de-Fonds	2-0	FC Fribourg
1955	La Chaux-de-Fonds	3-1	FC Thun
1956	Grasshopper-Club	1-0	BSC Young Boys
1957	La Chaux-de-Fonds	3-1	Lausanne-Sports
1958	BSC Young Boys	1-1 4-1	Grasshopper-Club
1959	FC Grenchen	1-0	Servette FC
1960	FC Luzern	1-0	FC Grenchen
1961	La Chaux-de-Fonds	1-0	FC Biel
1962	Lausanne-Sports	4-0	AC Bellinzona
1963	FC Basel	2-0	Grasshopper-Club
1964	Lausanne-Sports	2-0	La Chaux-de-Fonds
1965	FC Sion	2-1	Servette FC
1966	FC Zürich	2-0	Servette FC
1967	FC Basel *	2-1	Lausanne-Sports
1968	FC Lugano	2-1	FC Winterthur
1969	FC St. Gallen	2-0	AC Bellinzona
1970	FC Zürich	4-1	FC Basel
1971	Servette FC	2-0	FC Lugano
1972	FC Zürich	1-0	FC Basel
1973	FC Zürich	2-0	FC Basel
1974	FC Sion	3-2	Neuchâtel Xamax
1975	FC Basel	2-1	FC Winterthur
1976	FC Zürich	1-0	Servette FC
1977	BSC Young Boys	1-0	FC St. Gallen
1978	Servette FC	2-2 1-0	Grasshopper-Club
1979	Servette FC	1-1 3-2	BSC Young Boys
1980	FC Sion	2-1	BSC Young Boys
1981	Lausanne-Sports	4-3	FC Zürich
1982	FC Sion	1-0	FC Basel
1983	Grasshopper-Club	2-2 3-0	Servette FC
1984	Servette FC	1-0	Lausanne-Sports
1985	FC Aarau	1-0	Neuchâtel Xamax
1986	FC Sion	3-1	Servette FC
1987	BSC Young Boys	4-2	Servette FC
1988	Grasshopper-Club	2-0	FC Schaffhausen
1989	Grasshopper-Club	2-1	FC Aarau
1990	Grasshopper-Club	2-1	Neuchâtel Xamax
1991	FC Sion	3-2	BSC Young Boys
1992	FC Luzern	3-1	FC Lugano
1993	FC Lugano	4-1	Grasshopper-Club
1994	Grasshopper-Club	4-0	FC Schaffhausen
1995	FC Sion	4-2	Grasshopper-Club

* FC Basel were later awarded the match 3-0

LEADING INTERNATIONAL GOALSCORERS

32	Max Abegglen	(Lausanne-Sports, Grasshoppers)	1922-1937
30	André Abegglen	(Etoile Carouge,Cantonal, Grasshoppers,Sochaux, Servette,Chaux-de-Fonds)	1927-1943
29	Jacques Fatton	(Servette,Olympique Lyonnais)	1946-1955
23	Josef Hügi	(FC Basel)	1951-1961
	Adrian Knup	(FC Luzern,VfB Stuttgart)	1989-
22	Charles Antenen	(Chaux-de-Fonds, Lausanne-Sports)	1948-1962

21 Lauro Amadò	(FC Lugano,Grasshoppers)	1935-1948
18 Georges Brégy	(FC Sion,BSC Young Boys)	1984-
18 Robert Ballaman	(FC Biel,Grasshoppers)	1948-1941
16 Kubilay Türkyilmaz	(Bellinzona,Servette,Bologna, Galatasaray)	1988-
15 Fritz Künzli	(FC Zürich,Lausanne-Sports)	1965-1977
15 Alfred Bickel	(Grasshoppers)	1936-1954
65 René Botteron	(FC Zürich,1.FC Köln, Standard CL,Basel)	1974-1986
64 Erich Burgener#	(Lausanne-Sports,Servette)	1973-1986
63 Jakob Kuhn	(FC Zürich)	1962-1976

LEADING INTERNATIONAL APPEARANCES

117 Heinz Hermann	(Grasshopers,Xamax,Servette)	1978-1991
107 Alain Geiger	(FC Sion,Servette,Xamax, St-Étienne,FC Sion)	1980-
80 Severino Minelli	(Servette,Grasshoppers)	1930-1943
77 André Egli	(Grasshoppers,B.Dortmund, Xamax)	1979-
71 Alfred Bickel	(Grasshoppers)	1936-1954
68 Max Abegglen	(Lausanne-Sports, Grasshoppers)	1922-1937
68 Roger Wehrli	(Grasshoppers,FC Luzern)	1978-1989

NATIONAL TEAM COACHES

Francois Degerine	1905-09
Committee	1910-24
Teddy Duckworth	1924
Committee	1924-33
Henry Müller	1933-37
Karl Rappan	1937-38
Henry Müller	1938-42
Karl Rappan	1942-49
Committee	1950-53
Karl Rappan	1953-54
Hans Rüegsegger	1954
Committee	1954-56
Jacques Spagnoli	1956-58
Willibald Hahn	1958-59
Committee	1960
Karl Rappan	1960-63
Georges Soboyka	1964
Alfredo Foni	1964-67
Erwin Ballabio	1967-69
René Hüssy	1970
Louis Maurer	1970-72
Bruno Michaud	1972-73
René Hüssy	1973-76
Miroslav Blazevic	1976
Roger Vonlanthen	1977-79
Leon Walker	1979-80
Paul Wolfisberg	1981-85
Daniel Jeandupeux	1986-89
Ulli Stielike	1989-91
Roy Hodgson	1991-

INTERNATIONAL MATCHES PLAYED BY SWITZERLAND

12-02-1905	France	L 0-1	Paris	Fr	
8-03-1908	France	L 1-2	Geneva	Fr	Frenken
5-04	Germany	W 5-3	Basle	Fr	Pfeiffer 2, Kämpfer 2, Hug
4-04-1909	Germany	L 0-1	Karlsruhe	Fr	
20-05	England Am	L 0-9	Basle	Fr	
3-04-1910	Germany	L 2-3	Basle	Fr	Müller.H, Renand
9-04	England Am	L 1-6	London	Fr	Sydler.H
8-01-1911	Hungary	W 2-0	Zurich	Fr	Wyss.P, Collet
26-03	Germany	L 2-6	Stuttgart	Fr	Weiss, Collet
23-04	France	W 5-2	Geneva	Fr	Rubli 2, Wyss.P 2, Sydler III
7-05	Italy	D 2-2	Milan	Fr	Hassler, Sydler III
21-05	Italy	W 3-0	Chaux de Fonds	Fr	Wyss.P, Sydler.H, Sydler III
25-05	England Am	L 1-4	Berne	Fr	Wyss.P
29-10	Hungary	L 0-9	Budapest	Fr	
18-02-1912	France	L 1-4	Paris	Fr	Wyss.P
20-02	Belgium	L 2-9	Antwerp	Fr	Weiss, Wyss.P
5-05	Germany	L 1-2	St. Gallen	Fr	Weiss
9-03-1913	France	L 1-4	Geneva	Fr	Rubli
4-05	Belgium	L 1-2	Basle	Fr	Wydler
18-05	Germany	W 2-1	Freiburg	Fr	Märki, Collet
2-11	Belgium	L 0-2	Verviers	Fr	
8-03-1914	France	D 2-2	Paris	Fr	Schreyer, Albicker
5-04	Italy	D 1-1	Genoa	Fr	Wyss.P
17-05	Italy	L 0-1	Berne	Fr	
31-01-1915	Italy	L 1-3	Turin	Fr	Wyss.P
23-12-1917	Austria	L 0-1	Basle	Fr	
26-12	Austria	W 3-2	Zurich	Fr	Haas 2, Huber
9-05-1918	Austria	L 1-5	Vienna	Fr	Keller
12-05	Hungary	L 1-2	Budapest	Fr	Keller
29-02-1920	France	L 0-2	Geneva	Fr	
28-03	Italy	W 3-0	Berne	Fr	Merkt 2, Kramer.G
16-05	Holland	W 2-1	Basle	Fr	Friedrich, Merkt
6-06	Sweden	W 1-0	Stockholm	Fr	Martenet
27-06	Germany	W 4-1	Zurich	Fr	Meyer 2, Merkt, Afflerbach
6-03-1921	Italy	L 1-2	Milan	Fr	Fontana
28-03	Holland	L 0-2	Amsterdam	Fr	
1-05	Austria	D 2-2	St. Gallen	Fr	Brand, Friedrich
6-11	Italy	D 1-1	Geneva	Fr	Pache
26-03-1922	Germany	D 2-2	Frankfurt	Fr	Sturzenegger, Merkt
11-06	Austria	L 1-7	Vienna	Fr	Leiber
15-06	Hungary	D 1-1	Budapest	Fr	Merkt
19-11	Holland	W 5-0	Berne	Fr	Abegglen.M 3, Pache, Leiber
3-12	Italy	D 2-2	Bologna	Fr	Pache, Ramseyer

21-12	Austria	W 2-0	Geneva	Fr	Leiber, Pache
11-03-1923	Hungary	L 1-6	Lausanne	Fr	Abegglen.M
22-04	France	D 2-2	Paris	Fr	Afflerbach 2
3-06	Germany	L 1-2	Basle	Fr	Pache
17-06	Denmark	L 2-3	Copenhagen	Fr	Pache, Abegglen.M
21-06	Norway	D 2-2	Oslo	Fr	Afflerbach, Charpillod
25-11	Holland	L 1-4	Amsterdam	Fr	De Lavallaz
23-03-1924	France	W 3-0	Geneva	Fr	Kramer.E, Pache, Dietrich
21-04	Denmark	W 2-0	Basle	Fr	Abegglen.M, Dietrich
18-05	Hungary	W 4-2	Zurich	Fr	Abegglen.M, Dietrich, Sturzenegger 2
25-05	Lithuania	W 9-0	Paris	OGpr	Sturzenegger 4, Abegglen.M 3, Ramseyer, Dietrich
28-05	Czechoslovakia	D 1-1	Paris	OGr1	Dietrich
30-05	Czechoslovakia	W 1-0	Paris	OGr1	Pache
2-06	Italy	W 2-1	Paris	OGqf	Sturzenegger, Abegglen.M
5-06	Sweden	W 2-1	Paris	OGsf	Abegglen.M 2
9-06	Uruguay	L 0-3	Paris	OGf	
14-12	Germany	D 1-1	Stuttgart	Fr	Dietrich
22-03-1925	Austria	L 0-2	Vienna	Fr	
25-03	Hungary	L 0-5	Budapest	Fr	
19-04	Holland	W 4-1	Zurich	Fr	Hürzeler 2, Sturzenegger, Abegglen.J
24-05	Belgium	D 0-0	Lausanne	Fr	
1-06	Spain	L 0-3	Berne	Fr	
25-10	Germany	L 0-4	Basle	Fr	
8-11	Austria	W 2-0	Berne	Fr	Abegglen.M, Passello
28-03-1926	Holland	L 0-5	Amsterdam	Fr	
18-04	Italy	D 1-1	Zurich	Fr	Ehrenbolger
25-04	France	L 0-1	Paris	Fr	
9-05	Italy	L 2-3	Milan	Fr	Sturzenegger, Brand
10-10	Austria	L 1-7	Vienna	Fr	Poretti.A
12-12	Germany	W 3-2	Munich	Fr	Brand, Weiler.M, Fink
30-01-1927	Italy	L 1-5	Geneva	Fr	Weiler.W
17-04	Spain	L 0-1	Santander	Fr	
29-05	Austria	L 1-4	Zurich	Fr	Jäggi.W
6-11	Sweden	D 2-2	Zurich	Fr	Ramseyer, Abegglen.M
1-01-1928	Italy	L 2-3	Genoa	DGC	Abegglen.M 2
11-03	France	W 4-3	Lausanne	Fr	Jäggi.W 3, Romberg
15-04	Germany	L 2-3	Berne	Fr	Jäggi.W 2
6-05	Holland	W 2-1	Basle	Fr	Tschirren, Abegglen.M
28-05	Germany	L 0-4	Amsterdam	OGr1	
14-10	Italy	L 2-3	Zurich	DGC	Abegglen.M, Grimm
28-10	Austria	L 0-2	Vienna	DGC	
1-11	Hungary	L 1-3	Budapest	DGC	Weiler.W
10-02-1929	Germany	L 1-7	Mannheim	Fr	Abegglen.M
17-03	Holland	L 2-3	Amsterdam	Fr	Abegglen.A, Grimm
14-04	Hungary	L 4-5	Berne	DGC	Abegglen.A 2, Abegglen.A, Weiler.M
5-05	Czechoslovakia	L 1-4	Lausanne	DGC	Abegglen.M
6-10	Czechoslovakia	L 0-5	Prague	DGC	
27-10	Austria	L 1-3	Berne	DGC	Passello
9-02-1930	Italy	L 2-4	Rome	Fr	Poretti.A 2
23-03	France	D 3-3	Paris	Fr	Lehmann 2, Romberg
13-04	Hungary	D 2-2	Basle	Fr	Baumeister, Ramseyer
4-05	Germany	L 0-5	Zurich	Fr	
15-06	Sweden	L 0-1	Stockholm	Fr	
19-06	Norway	L 0-3	Oslo	Fr	
2-11	Holland	W 6-3	Zurich	Fr	Abegglen.A 3, Jäggi.W, Poretti.A, Grassi
29-03-1931	Italy	D 1-1	Berne	DGC	Abegglen.A
12-04	Hungary	L 2-6	Budapest	DGC	Abegglen.A 2
24-05	Scotland	L 2-3	Geneva	Fr	Büche, Faugel
13-06	Czechoslovakia	L 3-7	Prague	DGC	Fasson, Büche, Springer
16-06	Austria	L 0-2	Vienna	Fr	
29-11	Austria	L 1-8	Basle	DGC	Abegglen.A
6-12	Belgium	L 1-2	Brussels	Fr	Ehrismann
14-02-1932	Italy	L 0-3	Naples	DGC	
6-03	Germany	L 0-2	Leipzig	Fr	
20-03	France	D 3-3	Berne	Fr	Abegglen.M, Abegglen.A 2
17-04	Czechoslovakia	W 5-1	Zurich	DGC	Abegglen.A 2, Abegglen.M 2, Billeter
19-06	Hungary	W 3-1	Berne	DGC	Von Känel, Passello, Abegglen.A
23-10	Austria	L 1-3	Vienna	DGC	Abegglen.A
6-11	Sweden	W 2-1	Basle	Fr	Abegglen.M 2
22-01-1933	Holland	W 2-0	Amsterdam	Fr	Jäggi.W, Von Känel
12-03	Belgium	D 3-3	Zurich	Fr	Abegglen.A 2, Abegglen.M

2-04	Italy	L 0-3	Geneva	DGC	
7-05	Yugoslavia	W 4-1	Zurich	Fr	Abegglen.M 2, Von Känel, Jaeck
20-05	England	L 0-4	Berne	Fr	
17-09	Hungary	L 0-3	Budapest	DGC	
24-09	Yugoslavia	D 2-2	Belgrade	WCq	Jäggi.W, Frigerio
29-10	Romania	D 2-2	Berne	WCq	Hufschmid, Hochstrasser
19-11	Germany	L 0-2	Zurich	Fr	
3-12	Italy	L 2-5	Florence	DGC	Kielholz, Bossi
11-03-1934	France	W 1-0	Paris	Fr	Kielholz
25-03	Austria	L 2-3	Geneva	DGC	Bossi, Kielholz
27-05	Holland	W 3-2	Milan	WCr1	Kielholz 2, Abegglen.A
31-05	Czechoslovakia	L 2-3	Turin	WCqf	Jäggi.W, Kielholz
14-10	Czechoslovakia	D 2-2	Geneva	DGC	Kielholz 2
4-11	Holland	L 2-4	Berne	Fr	Spagnoli, Jäggi.W
11-11	Austria	L 0-3	Vienna	DGC	
27-01-1935	Germany	L 0-4	Stuttgart	Fr	
17-03	Czechoslovakia	L 1-3	Prague	DGC	Bösch
14-04	Hungary	W 6-2	Zurich	DGC	Kielholz 3, Abegglen.A 2, Jaeck
5-05	Rep. Ireland	W 1-0	Basle	Fr	Weiler.W
30-05	Belgium	D 2-2	Brussels	Fr	Kielholz, OG
27-10	France	W 2-1	Geneva	Fr	Abegglen.A, Jäggi.W
3-11	Norway	W 2-0	Zurich	Fr	Stelzer, Jäggi.W
10-11	Hungary	L 1-6	Budapest	Fr	Abegglen.A
17-03-1936	Rep. Ireland	L 0-1	Dublin	Fr	
5-04	Italy	L 1-2	Zurich	Fr	Weiler.W
3-05	Spain	L 0-2	Berne	Fr	
24-05	Belgium	D 1-1	Basle	Fr	Ciseri
18-06	Norway	W 2-1	Oslo	Fr	Abegglen.M 2
21-06	Sweden	L 2-5	Stockholm	Fr	Aebi, Bickel
25-10	Italy	L 2-4	Milan	DGC	Bickel, Diebold
8-11	Austria	L 1-3	Zurich	DGC	OG
21-02-1937	Czechoslovakia	L 3-5	Prague	DGC	Bickel 2, Wagner
7-03	Holland	L 1-2	Amsterdam	Fr	Abegglen.M
11-04	Hungary	L 1-5	Basle	DGC	Aeby.G
18-04	Belgium	W 2-1	Brussels	Fr	Abegglen.M, Bickel
2-05	Germany	L 0-1	Zurich	Fr	
17-05	Rep. Ireland	L 0-1	Berne	Fr	
19-09	Austria	L 3-4	Vienna	DGC	Walaschek, Aebi, Aeby.G
10-10	France	L 1-2	Paris	Fr	Rupf
31-10	Italy	D 2-2	Geneva	DGC	Walaschek, Wagner
14-11	Hungary	L 0-2	Budapest	DGC	
6-02-1938	Germany	D 1-1	Cologne	Fr	Aeby.G
13-03	Poland	D 3-3	Zurich	Fr	Amadò 2, Abegglen.A
3-04	Czechoslovakia	W 4-0	Basle	DGC	Monnard, Grassi, Aeby.G, Amadò
1-05	Portugal	W 2-1	Milan	WCq	Aeby.G, Amadò
8-05	Belgium	L 0-3	Lausanne	Fr	
21-05	England	W 2-1	Zurich	Fr	Abey.G, Abegglen.A
4-06	Germany	D 1-1	Paris	WCr1	Abegglen.A
9-06	Germany	W 4-2	Paris	WCr1	Abegglen.A 2, Walaschek, Bickel
12-06	Hungary	L 0-2	Lille	WCqf	
18-09	Rep. Ireland	L 0-4	Dublin	Fr	
6-11	Portugal	W 1-0	Lausanne	Fr	Aebi.P
20-11	Italy	L 0-2	Bologna	Fr	
12-02-1939	Portugal	W 4-2	Lisbon	Fr	Aeby.G 2, Bickel, Sydler.C
2-04	Hungary	W 3-1	Zurich	Fr	Aeby.G, Aebi, Walaschek
7-05	Holland	W 2-1	Berne	Fr	Amadò 2
14-05	Belgium	W 2-1	Liege	Fr	Abegglen.A, Amadò
4-06	Poland	D 1-1	Warsaw	Fr	Amadò
12-11	Italy	W 3-1	Zurich	Fr	Monnard, Aeby.G
3-03-1940	Italy	D 1-1	Turin	Fr	Bickel
31-03	Hungary	L 0-3	Budapest	Fr	
9-03-1941	Germany	L 2-4	Stuttgart	Fr	Monnard, OG
20-04	Germany	W 2-1	Berne	Fr	Monnard, Amadò
16-11	Hungary	L 1-2	Zurich	Fr	Monnard
28-12	Spain	L 2-3	Valencia	Fr	Kappenburger, Aeby.R
1-01-1942	Portugal	L 0-3	Lisbon	Fr	
1-02	Germany	W 2-1	Vienna	Fr	Kappenburger 2
8-03	France	W 2-0	Marseille	Fr	Amadò, Kappenburger
18-10	Germany	L 3-5	Berne	Fr	Bickel, Amadò, Kappenburger
1-11	Hungary	L 0-3	Budapest	Fr	
15-11	Sweden	W 3-1	Zurich	Fr	Friedländer, Amadò, Bickel

Date	Opponent	Result	Venue	Comp	Scorers
16-05-1943	Hungary	L 1-3	Geneva	Fr	Monnard
14-06	Sweden	L 0-1	Stockholm	Fr	
8-04-1945	France	W 1-0	Lausanne	Fr	Friedländer
21-05	Portugal	W 1-0	Basle	Fr	Friedländer
11-11	Italy	D 4-4	Zurich	Fr	Amadò 3, Aeby.G
25-11	Sweden	W 3-0	Geneva	Fr	Amadò 2, Friedländer
11-05-1946	England *	L 1-4	London	VI	Friedländer
25-05	Scotland*	L 1-3	Glasgow	VI	Aeby.G
7-07	Sweden	L 2-7	Stockholm	Fr	Lanz, Courtat
14-09	Czechoslovakia	L 2-3	Prague	Fr	Amadò 2
10-11	Austria	W 1-0	Berne	Fr	Pasteur
5-01-1947	Portugal	D 2-2	Lisbon	Fr	Fatton 2
27-04	Italy	L 2-5	Florence	Fr	Fatton, Bocquet
18-05	England	W 1-0	Zurich	Fr	Fatton
8-06	France	L 1-2	Lausanne	Fr	Fatton
21-09	Holland	L 2-6	Amsterdam	Fr	Maillard, Amadó
2-11	Belgium	W 4-0	Geneva	Fr	Tamini, Fatton, Lusenti, Maillard
18-04-1948	Austria	L 1-3	Vienna	Fr	Fatton
21-04	Hungary	L 4-7	Budapest	DGC	Lusenti, Amadò, Maillard, Tamini
17-05	Scotland	W 2-1	Berne	Fr	Maillard, Fatton
20-06	Spain	D 3-3	Zurich	Fr	OG, Friedländer, Antenen
10-10	Czechoslovakia	D 1-1	Basle	DGC	Friedländer
2-12	England	L 0-6	London	Fr	
5-12	Rep. Ireland	W 1-0	Dublin	Fr	Bickel
3-04-1949	Austria	L 1-2	Lausanne	DGC	Bickel
26-05	Wales	W 4-0	Berne	Fr	Fatton 2, Ballaman 2, Pasteur
4-06	France	L 2-4	Paris	Fr	Fatton 2
26-06	Luxembourg	W 5-2	Zurich	WCq	Fatton 2, Maillard, Ballaman, Antenen
18-09	Luxembourg	W 3-2	Luxembourg	WCq	Maillard, Oberer, Fatton
2-10	Belgium	L 0-3	Brussels	Fr	
19-03-1950	Austria	D 3-3	Vienna	DGC	Fatton, Tamini, Oberer
26-04	Scotland	L 1-3	Glasgow	Fr	Antenen
11-06	Yugoslavia	L 0-4	Berne	Fr	
25-06	Yugoslavia	L 0-3	Belo Horizonte	WCr1	
28-06	Brazil	D 2-2	Sao Paulo	WCr1	Fatton 2
2-07	Mexico	W 2-1	Porto Alegre	WCr1	Bader, Antenen
15-10	Holland	W 7-5	Basle	Fr	Fatton 3, Friedländer 2, Antenen 2
12-11	Sweden	W 4-2	Geneva	Fr	Fatton 2, Friedländer, Antenen
22-11	West Germany	L 0-1	Stuttgart	Fr	
18-02-1951	Spain	L 3-6	Madrid	Fr	Bickel 2, OG
15-04	West Germany	L 2-3	Zurich	Fr	Bocquet, Fatton
16-05	Wales	L 2-3	Wrexham	Fr	Ballaman, Antenen
24-06	Yugoslavia	L 3-7	Belgrade	Fr	Ballaman 2, Bickel
14-10	France	L 1-2	Geneva	Fr	Ballaman
25-11	Italy	D 1-1	Lugano	DGC	Riva
28-05-1952	England	L 0-3	Zurich	Fr	
1-06	Turkey	W 5-1	Ankara	Fr	Riva 2, Hügi.J 2, Pasteur
22-06	Austria	D 1-1	Geneva	Fr	Riva
20-09	Hungary	L 2-4	Berne	DGC	Hügi.J, Fatton
9-11	West Germany	L 1-5	Augsburg	Fr	Friedländer
28-12	Italy	L 0-2	Palermo	DGC	
22-03-1953	Holland	W 2-1	Amsterdam	Fr	Mauron, Hügi.J
25-05	Turkey	L 1-2	Berne	Fr	Meier
27-06	Denmark	L 1-4	Basle	Fr	Hügi.J
20-09	Czechoslovakia	L 0-5	Prague	DGC	
11-11	France	W 4-2	Paris	Fr	Antenen 3, Fatton
22-11	Belgium	D 2-2	Zurich	Fr	Fatton, Antenen
25-04-1954	West Germany	L 3-5	Basle	Fr	Fatton, Ballaman, Kernan
23-05	Uruguay	D 3-3	Lausanne	Fr	Casali, Ballaman, Antenen
30-05	Holland	W 3-1	Zurich	Fr	Vonlanthen 3
17-06	Italy	W 2-1	Lausanne	WCr1	Hügi.J, Ballaman
20-06	England	L 0-2	Berne	WCr1	
23-06	Italy	W 4-1	Basle	WCr1	Hügi.J 2, Ballaman, Fatton
26-06	Austria	L 5-7	Lausanne	WCqf	Hügi.J 3, Ballaman 2
19-09	Denmark	D 1-1	Copenhagen	Fr	Antenen
10-10	Hungary	L 0-3	Budapest	Fr	
1-05-1955	Austria	L 2-3	Berne	DGC	Hügi.J, Vonlanthen
19-05	Holland	L 1-4	Rotterdam	Fr	Hügi.J
19-06	Spain	L 0-3	Geneva	Fr	
26-06	Yugoslavia	D 0-0	Belgrade	DGC	
17-09	Hungary	L 4-5	Lausanne	DGC	Vonlanthen 2, Antenen 2

9-10	France	L 1-2	Basle	Fr	Mauron
11-03-1956	Belgium	W 3-1	Brussels	Fr	Pastega, Ballaman, Meier
11-04	Brazil	D 1-1	Zurich	Fr	OG
1-05	Saar	D 1-1	Saarbrucken	Fr	Riva
10-05	Czechoslovakia	L 1-6	Geneva	DGC	Ballaman
15-09	Holland	L 2-3	Lausanne	Fr	Antenen, Riva
11-11	Italy	D 1-1	Berne	DGC	Ballaman
21-11	West Germany	W 3-1	Frankfurt	Fr	Riva, Hügi.J, Ballaman
10-03-1957	Spain	D 2-2	Madrid	WCq	Hügi.J 2
14-04	Austria	L 0-4	Vienna	DGC	
19-05	Scotland	L 1-2	Basle	WCq	Vonlanthen
6-11	Scotland	L 2-3	Glasgow	WCq	Riva, Vonlanden
24-11	Spain	L 1-4	Lausanne	WCq	Ballaman
16-04-1958	France	D 0-0	Paris	Fr	
7-05	Sweden	L 2-3	Helsingborg	Fr	Allemann 2
26-05	Belgium	L 0-2	Zurich	Fr	
20-09	Czechoslovakia	L 1-2	Bratislava	DGC	Meier
2-11	Holland	L 0-2	Rotterdam	Fr	
26-04-1959	Yugoslavia	L 1-5	Basle	DGC	Rey
16-05	Portugal	W 4-3	Geneva	Fr	Burger 2, Hamel, Frey
4-10	West Germany	L 0-4	Berne	Fr	
25-10	Hungary	L 0-8	Budapest	DGC	
6-01-1960	Italy	L 0-3	Naples	DGC	
27-03	Belgium	L 1-3	Brussels	Fr	Allemann
6-04	Chile	W 4-2	Basle	Fr	OG, Hügi.J, Allemann, Vonlanthen
18-05	Holland	W 3-1	Zurich	Fr	Allemann 2, Hügi.J
12-10	France	W 6-2	Basle	Fr	Hügi.J 5, Weber.H
20-11	Belgium	W 4-2	Brussels	WCq	Antenen 3, Schneiter
20-05-1961	Belgium	W 2-1	Lausanne	WCq	Ballaman, OG
28-05	Sweden	L 0-4	Stockholm	WCq	
29-10	Sweden	W 3-2	Berne	WCq	Antenen, Wüthrich, Eschmann
12-11	Sweden	W 2-1	Berlin	WCq	Schneiter, Antenen
9-05-1962	England	L 1-3	London	Fr	Allemann
30-05	Chile	L 1-3	Santiago	WCr1	Wüthrich
3-06	West Germany	L 1-2	Santiago	WCr1	Schneiter
7-06	Italy	L 0-3	Santiago	WCr1	
11-11	Holland	L 1-3	Amsterdam	ECr1	Hertig
23-12	West Germany	L 1-5	Karlsruhe	Fr	Brodmann
13-01-1963	Morocco	L 0-1	Casablanca	Fr	
31-03	Holland	D 1-1	Berne	ECr1	Allemann
5-06	England	L 1-8	Basle	Fr	Bertschi
3-11	Norway	L 0-2	Zurich	Fr	
11-11	France	D 2-2	Paris	Fr	OG, Bosson
15-04-1964	Belgium	W 2-0	Geneva	Fr	Schindelholz, Bertschi
29-04	Portugal	L 2-3	Zurich	Fr	OG, Eschmann
10-05	Italy	L 1-3	Lausanne	Fr	Eschmann
1-07	Norway	L 2-3	Bergen	Fr	Grünig 2
4-10	Hungary	L 0-2	Berne	Fr	
14-10	Nth. Ireland	L 0-1	Belfast	WCq	
14-11	Nth. Ireland	W 2-1	Lausanne	WCq	Quentin, Kuhn
11-04-1965	Albania	W 2-0	Tirana	WCq	Quentin, Kuhn
2-05	Albania	W 1-0	Geneva	WCq	Kuhn
26-05	West Germany	L 0-1	Basle	Fr	
17-10	Holland	D 0-0	Amsterdam	WCq	
14-11	Holland	W 2-1	Berne	WCq	Allemann, Hosp
20-04-1966	Soviet Union	D 2-2	Basle	Fr	Hosp, Grobéty
5-06	Hungary	L 1-3	Budapest	Fr	Kuhn
19-06	Mexico	D 1-1	Lausanne	Fr	Odermatt
12-07	West Germany	L 0-5	Sheffield	WCr1	
15-07	Spain	L 1-2	Sheffield	WCr1	Quentin
19-07	Argentina	L 0-2	Sheffield	WCr1	
22-10	Belgium	L 0-1	Bruges	Fr	
2-11	Romania	L 2-4	Bucharest	ECq	Künzli, Odermatt
5-01-1967	Mexico	L 0-3	Mexico City	Fr	
3-05	Czechoslovakia	L 1-2	Basle	Fr	Odermatt
24-05	Romania	W 7-1	Zurich	ECq	Künzli 2, Blättler 2, Quentin, Odermatt, OG
1-10	Soviet Union	D 2-2	Moscow	Fr	Blättler, Perroud
8-11	Cyprus	W 5-0	Lugano	ECq	Blättler 2, Künzli, Dürr, Odermatt
18-11	Italy	D 2-2	Berne	ECq	Quentin, Künzli
23-12	Italy	L 0-4	Cagliari	ECq	
14-02-1968	Israel	L 1-2	Tel Aviv	Fr	Künzli, OG

17-02	Cyprus	L 1-2	Nicosia	ECq	OG
17-04	West Germany	D 0-0	Basle	Fr	
22-09	Austria	W 1-0	Berne	Fr	Quentin
12-10	Greece	W 1-0	Basle	WCq	Quentin
23-11	Romania	L 0-2	Bucharest	WCq	
26-03-1969	Spain	L 0-1	Valencia	Fr	
16-04	Portugal	W 2-0	Lisbon	WCq	Vuilleumier 2
14-05	Romania	L 0-1	Lausanne	WCq	
24-09	Turkey	L 0-3	Istanbul	Fr	
15-10	Greece	L 1-4	Salonica	WCq	Künzli
2-11	Portugal	D 1-1	Berne	WCq	Künzli
22-04-1970	Spain	L 0-1	Lausanne	Fr	
3-05	France	W 2-1	Basle	Fr	Blättler 2
17-10	Italy	D 1-1	Berne	Fr	Blättler
15-11	Hungary	L 0-1	Basle	Fr	
16-12	Greece	W 1-0	Athens	ECq	Müller.K
20-12	Malta	W 2-1	Gzira	ECq	Quentin, Künzli
21-04-1971	Malta	W 5-0	Lucerne	ECq	Blättler, Künzli, Quentin, Citherlet, Müller.K
5-05	Poland	L 2-4	Lausanne	Fr	Künzli, Kuhn
12-05	Greece	W 1-0	Berne	ECq	Odermatt
26-09	Turkey	W 4-0	Zurich	Fr	Boffi, Odermatt, Balmer, Blättler
13-10	England	L 2-3	Basle	ECq	Jeandupeux, Künzli
10-11	England	D 1-1	London	ECq	Odermatt
26-04-1972	Sweden	D 1-1	Geneva	Fr	Blättler
10-05	Poland	D 0-0	Poznan	Fr	
4-10	Denmark	D 1-1	Copenhagen	Fr	Balmer
21-10	Italy	D 0-0	Berne	WCq	
15-11	West Germany	L 1-5	Dusseldorf	Fr	Künzli
8-04-1973	Luxembourg	W 1-0	Luxembourg	WCq	Odermatt
9-05	Turkey	D 0-0	Basle	WCq	
22-06	Scotland	W 1-0	Berne	Fr	Mundschin
26-09	Luxembourg	W 1-0	Lucerne	WCq	Blättler
20-10	Italy	L 0-2	Rome	WCq	
18-11	Turkey	L 0-2	Izmir	WCq	
1-05-1974	Belgium	L 0-1	Geneva	Fr	
9-06	Sweden	D 0-0	Malmo	Fr	
4-09	West Germany	L 1-2	Basle	Fr	Müller.K
9-10	Holland	L 0-1	Rotterdam	Fr	
13-11	Portugal	W 3-0	Berne	Fr	Jeandupeux, Pfister, Schild
1-12	Turkey	L 1-2	Izmir	ECq	Schild
4-12	Hungary	L 0-1	Szolnok	Fr	
30-04-1975	Turkey	D 1-1	Zurich	ECq	OG
10-05	Rep. Ireland	L 1-2	Dublin	ECq	Müller.K
21-05	Rep. Ireland	W 1-0	Berne	ECq	Elsener
3-09	England	L 1-2	Basle	Fr	Müller.K
24-09	Czechoslovakia	D 1-1	Brno	Fr	Risi
12-10	Soviet Union	L 0-1	Zurich	ECq	
12-11	Soviet Union	L 1-4	Kiev	ECq	Risi
7-04-1976	Scotland	L 0-1	Glasgow	Fr	
30-04	Hungary	L 0-1	Lausanne	Fr	
11-05	Poland	W 2-1	Basle	Fr	Bizzini, Barberis
19-05	Finland	L 0-1	Kuopio	Fr	
17-08	Bulgaria	D 2-2	Lucerne	Fr	Müller.K, Künzli
8-09	Norway	L 0-1	Oslo	WCq	
22-09	Austria	L 1-3	Linz	Fr	Trinchero
9-10	Sweden	L 1-2	Basle	WCq	Trinchero
30-03-1977	Portugal	L 0-1	Funchal	Fr	
23-04	France	L 0-4	Geneva	Fr	
24-05	Czechoslovakia	W 1-0	Basle	Fr	Müller.K
8-06	Sweden	L 1-2	Stockholm	WCq	Risi
7-09	England	D 0-0	London	Fr	
21-09	Spain	L 1-2	Berne	Fr	Elsener
5-10	Finland	W 2-0	Zurich	Fr	Elsener, Küttel
30-10	Norway	W 1-0	Berne	WCq	Sulser
16-11	West Germany	L 1-4	Stuttgart	Fr	Meyer
8-03-1978	East Germany	L 1-3	Karl-Marx-Stadt	Fr	Sulser
4-04	Austria	L 0-1	Basle	Fr	
6-09	United States	W 2-0	Lucerne	Fr	Elsener, Schnyder
11-10	Holland	L 1-3	Berne	ECq	Tanner
15-11	Poland	L 0-2	Wroclaw	ECq	
28-03-1979	Holland	L 0-3	Eindhoven	ECq	

5-05	East Germany	L 0-2	St. Gallen	ECq	
22-05	Iceland	W 2-0	Berne	ECq	Zappa, Hermann.Hr
9-06	Iceland	W 2-1	Reykjavik	ECq	Hermann.H, Ponte
12-09	Poland	L 0-2	Lausanne	ECq	
13-10	East Germany	L 2-5	Berlin	ECq	Barberis, Pfister
17-11	Italy	L 0-2	Udine	Fr	
26-03-1980	Czechoslovakia	W 2-0	Basle	Fr	Sulser, Barberis
1-04	Greece	W 2-0	Zurich	Fr	Schnyder 2
30-04	Rep. Ireland	L 0-2	Dublin	Fr	
27-08	Denmark	D 1-1	Lausanne	Fr	Pfister
10-09	West Germany	L 2-3	Basle	Fr	Pfister, Botteron
29-10	Norway	L 1-2	Berne	WCq	Barberis
19-11	England	L 1-2	London	WCq	Pfister
16-12	Argentina	L 0-5	Cordoba	Fr	
18-12	Uruguay	L 0-4	Montevideo	Fr	
21-12	Brazil	L 0-2	Cuiaba	Fr	
24-03-1981	Czechoslovakia	W 1-0	Bratislava	Fr	Botteron
28-04	Hungary	D 2-2	Lucerne	WCq	Sulser 2
30-05	England	W 2-1	Basle	WCq	Scheiwilder, Sulser
17-06	Norway	D 1-1	Oslo	WCq	Barberis
1-09	Holland	W 2-1	Zurich	Fr	Favre, Elia
10-10	Romania	W 2-1	Bucharest	WCq	Zappa, Lüthi
14-10	Hungary	L 0-3	Budapest	WCq	
11-11	Romania	D 0-0	Berne	WCq	
24-03-1982	Portugal	W 2-1	Lugano	Fr	Zappa, Egli
28-04	Spain	L 0-2	Valencia	Fr	
19-05	Brazil	D 1-1	Recife	Fr	Sulser
28-05	Italy	D 1-1	Geneva	Fr	Barberis
7-09	Bulgaria	W 3-2	St. Gallen	Fr	Sulser, Elsener, OG
6-10	Belgium	L 0-3	Brussels	ECq	
27-10	Italy	W 1-0	Rome	Fr	Elsener
17-11	Scotland	W 2-0	Berne	ECq	Sulser, Egli
1-12	Greece	W 3-1	Athens	Fr	Sulser 2, Egli
7-03-1983	Bulgaria	D 1-1	Varna	Fr	Ponte
30-03	Scotland	D 2-2	Glasgow	ECq	Egli, Hermann.H
13-04	Soviet Union	L 0-1	Lausanne	Fr	
14-05	East Germany	D 0-0	Berne	ECq	
17-06	Brazil	L 1-2	Basle	Fr	Koller
7-09	Czechoslovakia	D 0-0	Neuchatel	Fr	
12-10	East Germany	L 0-3	Berlin	ECq	
26-10	Yugoslavia	W 2-0	Basle	Fr	Sutter.B, Brigger
9-11	Belgium	W 3-1	Berne	ECq	Schällibaum, Brigger, Geiger
30-11	Algeria	W 2-1	Algiers	Fr	Jaccard, Hermann.H
2-12	Ivory Coast	L 0-1	Abidjan	Fr	
4-12	Zimbabwe	L 2-3	Harare	Fr	In-Albon, Lüdi
6-12	Kenya	D 0-0	Mombasa	Fr	
27-03-1984	Poland	D 1-1	Zurich	Fr	Hermann.H
2-05	Sweden	D 0-0	Berne	Fr	
26-05	Spain	L 0-4	Geneva	Fr	
22-08	Hungary	L 0-3	Budapest	Fr	
1-09	Argentina	L 0-2	Berne	Fr	
12-09	Norway	W 1-0	Oslo	WCq	Egli
17-10	Denmark	W 1-0	Berne	WCq	Barberis
3-11	Italy	D 1-1	Lausanne	Fr	Bregy
1-02-1985	Colombia	D 2-2	Bogota	Fr	Hermann.H, Schällibaum
5-02	Bulgaria	L 0-1	Queretaro	Fr	
6-02	Mexico	W 2-1	Queretaro	Fr	Geiger, Bregy
8-02	United States	D 1-1	Tampa	Fr	Hermann.H
27-03	Czechoslovakia	W 2-0	Sion	Fr	Sulser 2
17-04	Soviet Union	D 2-2	Berne	WCq	Bregy, Egli
2-05	Soviet Union	L 0-4	Moscow	WCq	
2-06	Rep. Ireland	L 0-3	Dublin	WCq	
28-08	Turkey	D 0-0	St. Gallen	Fr	
11-09	Rep. Ireland	D 0-0	Berne	WCq	
9-10	Denmark	D 0-0	Copenhagen	WCq	
13-11	Norway	D 1-1	Lucerne	WCq	Matthey
12-03-1986	Turkey	L 0-1	Adana	Fr	
9-04	West Germany	L 0-1	Basle	Fr	
6-05	Algeria	W 2-0	Geneva	Fr	Hermann.H 2
19-08	France	W 2-0	Lausanne	Fr	Hermann.H, Sutter.B
27-08	Austria	D 1-1	Innsbruck	Fr	Bickel
24-09	Sweden	L 0-2	Stockholm	ECq	

29-10	Portugal	D 1-1	Berne	ECq	Bregy
15-11	Italy	L 2-3	Milan	ECq	Brigger, Webber
25-03-1987	Czechoslovakia	L 1-2	Bellinzona	Fr	Hermann.H
15-04	Malta	W 4-1	Neuchatel	ECq	Egli, Bregy 3
19-05	Israel	W 1-0	Aarau	Fr	Bonvin
17-06	Sweden	D 1-1	Lausanne	ECq	Halter
18-08	Austria	D 2-2	St. Gallen	Fr	Bonvin, Sutter.B
17-10	Italy	D 0-0	Berne	ECq	
11-11	Portugal	D 0-0	Oporto	ECq	
15-11	Malta	D 1-1	Ta'Qali	ECq	Zwicker
16-12	Israel	W 2-0	Tel Aviv	Fr	Sutter.B, Bonvin
2-02-1988	France	L 1-2	Toulouse	Fr	Sutter.B
5-02	Austria	W 2-1	Monaco	Fr	Koller, Sutter.B
27-04	West Germany	L 0-1	Kaiserslautern	Fr	
28-05	England	L 0-1	Lausanne	Fr	
5-06	Spain	D 1-1	Basle	Fr	Sutter.B
24-08	Yugoslavia	L 0-2	Lucerne	Fr	
21-09	Luxembourg	W 4-1	Luxembourg	WCq	Sutter.A, Türkyilmaz 2, Sutter.B
19-10	Belgium	L 0-1	Brussels	WCq	
14-12	Egypt	W 3-1	Cairo	Fr	Zuffi 2, Hermann.H
4-04-1989	Hungary	L 0-3	Budapest	Fr	
26-04	Portugal	L 1-3	Lisbon	WCq	Zuffi
7-06	Czechoslovakia	L 0-1	Berne	WCq	
21-06	Brazil	W 1-0	Basle	Fr	Türkyilmaz
20-09	Portugal	L 1-2	Neuchatel	WCq	Türkyilmaz
11-10	Belgium	D 2-2	Basle	WCq	Knup, Türkyilmaz
25-10	Czechoslovakia	L 0-3	Prague	WCq	
15-11	Luxembourg	W 2-1	St. Gallen	WCq	Bonvin, Türkyilmaz
13-12	Spain	L 1-2	Tenerife	Fr	Knup
31-03-1990	Italy	L 0-1	Basle	Fr	
3-04	Romania	W 2-1	Lucerne	Fr	Hermann.H, Chassot
8-05	Argentina	D 1-1	Berne	Fr	Türkyilmaz
2-06	United States	W 2-1	St. Gallen	Fr	Schepull, Knup
21-08	Austria	W 3-1	Vienna	Fr	Türkyilmaz 2, Knup
12-09	Bulgaria	W 2-0	Geneva	ECq	Hottiger, Bickel.T
17-10	Scotland	L 1-2	Glasgow	ECq	Knup
14-11	San Marino	W 4-0	Serravalle	ECq	Sutter.A, Chapuisat, Knup, Chassot
19-12	Germany	L 0-4	Stuttgart	Fr	
2-02-1991	United States	W 1-0	Miami	Fr	Knup
3-02	Colombia	W 3-2	Miami	Fr	Koller, Sutter.B 2
12-03	Liechtenstein	W 6-0	Balzers	Fr	Hermann.H, Knup 3, Türkyilmaz, Aeby
3-04	Romania	D 0-0	Neuchatel	ECq	
1-05	Bulgaria	W 3-2	Sofia	ECq	Knup 2, Türkyilmaz
5-06	San Marino	W 7-0	St. Gallen	ECq	Knup 2, Hottiger, Sutter.B, Hermann.H, Ohrel, Türkyilmaz
21-08	Czechoslovakia	D 1-1	Prague	Fr	Türkyilmaz
11-09	Scotland	D 2-2	Berne	ECq	Chapuisat, Hermann.H
9-10	Sweden	W 3-1	Lucerne	Fr	Chapuisat, Herr, Türkyilmaz
13-11	Romania	L 0-1	Bucharest	ECq	
29-01-1992	UAE	W 2-0	Dubai	Fr	Sutter.B, Bonvin
25-03	Rep. Ireland	L 1-2	Dublin	Fr	OG
28-04	Bulgaria	L 0-2	Berne	Fr	
27-05	France	W 2-1	Lausanne	Fr	Bonvin 2
16-08	Estonia	W 6-0	Tallinn	WCq	Chapuisat 2, Bregy, Knup 2, Sforza
9-09	Scotland	W 3-1	Berne	WCq	Knup 2, Bregy
14-10	Italy	D 2-2	Cagliari	WCq	Ohrel, Chapuisat
18-11	Malta	W 3-0	Berne	WCq	Bickel.T, Sforza, Chapuisat
23-01-1993	Japan	D 1-1	Hong Kong	Fr	Sutter.B
26-01	Hong Kong	W 3-2	Hong Kong	Fr	Bonvin, Sforza, Bregy
17-03	Tunisia	W 1-0	Tunis	Fr	Knup
31-03	Portugal	D 1-1	Berne	WCq	Chapuisat
17-04	Malta	W 2-0	Ta'Qali	WCq	Ohrel, Türkyilmaz
1-05	Italy	W 1-0	Berne	WCq	Hottiger
11-08	Sweden	W 2-1	Boras	Fr	Knup, Herr
8-09	Scotland	D 1-1	Aberdeen	WCq	Bregy
13-10	Portugal	L 0-1	Oporto	WCq	
17-11	Estonia	W 4-0	Zurich	WCq	Knup, Bregy, Ohrel, Chapuisat
21-01-1994	USA	D 1-1	Fullerton	Fr	Fournier
26-01	Mexico	W 5-1	Oakland	Fr	Subiat 2, Bonvin, Grassi 2
9-03	Hungary	W 2-1	Budapest	Fr	Sforza, Subiat
20-04	Czech Republic	W 3-0	Zurich	Fr	Chapuisat 2, Bregy
27-05	Liechtenstein	W 2-0	Basle	Fr	Herr, Hottiger

3-06	Italy	L 0-1	Rome	Fr	
11-06	Bolivia	D 0-0	Montreal	Fr	
18-06	USA	D 1-1	Detroit	WCr1	Bregy
22-06	Romania	W 4-1	Detroit	WCr1	Sutter.A, Chapuisat, Knup, Bregy
26-06	Colombia	L 0-2	San Francisco	WCr1	
2-07	Spain	L 0-3	Washington	WCr2	
6-09	Arab Emirates	W 1-0	Sion	Fr	Sutter.A
12-10	Sweden	W 4-2	Berne	ECq	Ohrel, Sforza, Türkyilmaz, OG
16-11	Iceland	W 1-0	Lausanne	ECq	Bickel.T
14-12	Turkey	W 2-1	Istanbul	ECq	Koller, Bickel.T
8-03-1995	Greece	D 1-1	Athens	Fr	Fernandez
29-03	Hungary	D 2-2	Budapest	ECq	Subiat 2
26-04	Turkey	L 1-2	Berne	ECq	Hottiger
19-06	Italy	L 0-1	Lausanne	Fr	
23-06	Germany	L 1-2	Berne	Fr	Knup

TURKEY

Turkiye, as they would prefer to be known, are Europe's major under-achievers; there is a football revolution just waiting to happen. The interest is there, and there is an enormous amount of talent to be unearthed. With a population of over 55 million Turkey should be at the forefront of the European game. (The vast majority of Turkey is in fact in Asia, but with Istanbul, the major footballing city, located partly in Europe, the Turks have always looked to European countries for competition.) Due to a poor record in the past, however, they are usually listed as lower seeds and therefore drawn against the top sides in both the World Cup and European Championship. Qualification for either of these events will always be difficult until the duck is eventually broken.

Football first came to Turkey along with the British and a game is recorded in 1895 between English and Greek residents in Izmir. At this time, however, the foundations of the Ottoman Empire were crumbling and in an attempt to reverse the decline, the authorities were quick to stamp out any movement they perceived as a threat and football was regarded as just that. In one bizarre incident, a group of players were arrested after soldiers discovered shirts which were described as uniforms, a ball which they assumed was a cannon ball and a set of the rules in English which they took to be subversive literature!

In 1905 eight boys of the Galatasaray High School formed a team and they, along with Fenerbahçe, formed in 1907, and the oldest club of them all, Besiktas, formed in 1903, remain the top clubs of today. Until 1908 and the Young Turk Revolution, all clubs in Turkey operated in near secrecy. Seen as less of a threat by the new régime, the game enjoyed a brief period of growth. A league of sorts had been started in 1905 in Istanbul, but the Balkan Wars, the First World War, Civil War and then war with Greece put paid to any real efforts to promote the game until a republic with the present boundaries was declared in 1923.

As some semblance of peace was restored to the country, the Turkish Football Federation was formed later that year. Proper regional championships were started the following year with a view to staging a tournament to find the national champions at the end of the season, but the latter was only ever a regular occurrence in the late 1930s and early 1940s and the winners of the Istanbul league were regarded as the top club until the formation of the professional national league in 1959.

In 1923 the Turks took on Romania in Istanbul in their first international match, but it was not until the 1960s that any great prominence was given to the national side. One player perhaps more than any other was responsible for the increased awareness of the game: Lefter Kücükandonyadis, from the Greek quarter of Istanbul, was Turkey's first player of genuine international class, and from his first appearance in 1948 he helped change the fortunes of the game in his country.

Turkey had entered the 1924, 1928 and 1936 Olympic Games but were knocked out in the first round of each. During these years there had been a few wins against their Balkan neighbours, but the overall record was poor. It reached the stage that between 1932 and 1948 only three games were played. In 1948 fortunes changed as the Federation once more fielded a side. The quarter-finals of the 1948 Olympic Games in London were reached and the following year the Turks qualified for the World Cup finals in Brazil. In the light of subsequent failures to qualify, their withdrawal before the tournament got underway, due to the high expenses anticipated and the time needed to make the trip to Brazil, seems ridiculous, but four years later they were present in Switzerland for the 1954 tournament.

The situation was helped by the introduction of professionalism in 1951, and in June of that year they pulled off the first of a remarkable series of victories for which they became famous down the years when they beat West Germany 2-1 in Berlin. Admittedly the German game had not fully recovered from the war, but in qualifying for the 1954 World Cup they defeated Spain in Istanbul and drew 2-2 with them in a play-off in Rome, where they won the ensuing lots. They had beaten Switzerland in Berne in 1953 but on their return for the World Cup the following year, despite scoring seven against the South Koreans, they could not beat the Germans for a second time and bowed out of their sole World Cup Finals appearance after a play-off.

More good results were to follow, however. Portugal were beaten at home in 1955, whilst most impressive of all, and inspired by Lefter who scored two goals, the Turks ended Hungary's two-year unbeaten run with a 3-2 victory in Istanbul in 1956. Both Poland and Holland were defeated away from home before the end of the decade, and although not members of UEFA until 1962, Turkey were invited to take part in the initial European Championship and were unlucky to lose out to Romania in the first round on goal average. Alongside Lefter in what still stand out as the best teams Turkey has fielded were players such as Metin Otkay and Burhan Sargin who between them scored 47 goals for the national side. Since the mid-1960s, however, instead of building on these foundations the national team has declined. Heavy defeats at home in recent years by both Hungary and England have not helped matters.

THE ORDER OF MERIT

		All			League			Cup		Europe		
	Team	G	S	B	G	S	B	G	S	G	S	B
1	Galatasaray Istanbul	20	11	14	10	7	13	10	4	-	-	1
2	Fenerbahçe Istanbul	16	15	4	12	12	4	4	3	-	-	-
3	Besiktas Istanbul	13	14	3	9	10	3	4	4	-	-	-
4	Trabzonspor	11	8	4	6	4	4	5	4	-	-	-
5	Altay Izmir	2	5	2	-	-	2	2	5	-	-	-
6	MKE Ankaragücü	2	3	-	-	-	-	2	3	-	-	-
7	Göztepe Izmir	2	1	2	-	-	1	2	1	-	-	1
8	Eskisehirspor	1	5	2	-	3	2	1	2	-	-	-
9	Bursaspor	1	3	-	-	-	-	1	3	-	-	-
10	Gençlerbirligi Ankara	1	-	1	-	-	1	1	-	-	-	-
11	Sakaryaspor Adapazari	1	-	-	-	-	-	1	-	-	-	-
12	Samsunspor	-	1	2	-	-	2	-	1	-	-	-
13	Boluspor	-	1	1	-	-	1	-	1	-	-	-
14	Adana Demirspor	-	1	-	-	-	-	-	1	-	-	-
	Adanaspor	-	1	-	-	1	-	-	-	-	-	-
	Mersin Idman Yurdu	-	1	-	-	-	-	-	1	-	-	-
17	Kocaelispor	-	-	1	-	-	1	-	-	-	-	-
	Malatyaspor	-	-	1	-	-	1	-	-	-	-	-
	Zonguldakspor	-	-	1	-	-	1	-	-	-	-	-

To the end of the 1994-1995 season.
Not including winners pre-1959

With declining international fortunes, attention has focused on the very competitive national league. Although professionalism was legalised in 1951, it was not until eight years later that the regional leagues were replaced by a single national league. Galatasaray, Besiktas and Fenerbahçe have continued to be the leading clubs, but a unified structure has allowed provincial clubs as well as those from Izmir and Ankara to rise from obscurity. Trabzonspor, from the small town of Trabzon, have fared particularly well and along with the big three from Istanbul are part of an elite group which have managed to win the national league.

The 1960s saw the formation of many clubs in the smaller cities of Turkey, and as they gain more experience, they will undoubtedly challenge for honours as Trabzonspor have done. In the meantime, Turkey's main challenge for European club honours seems set to come from Istanbul. In 1989 Galatasaray reached the semi-finals of the European Cup, the best performance to date from a Turkish club. The question is how long will it be before one of them goes one further and reaches the final?

Population: 56,941,000
Area, sq km: 779,452
% in urban areas: 45.9%
Capital city: Ankara

Türkiye Futbol Federasyönu
Konur Sokak #10
Kizilay-Ankara
Turkey
Tel: + 90 4 4259182
Fax: + 90 4 4171090

Year of formation	1923
Affiliation to FIFA	1923
Affiliation to UEFA	1962
Registered clubs	4602
Registered players	237 500
Professional players	300
Registered coaches	5107
Registered referees	3394
National stadium	Inönü Stadi, Ankara 30 000
National colours	White with a red band on chest/White/Red
Reserve colours	Red with a white band on chest/White/Red
Season	August - May

THE RECORD

WORLD CUP

1930-38	Did not enter
1950	QT 1st/2 in group 2 - Withdrew
1954	QT 1st/2 in group 6 - Final Tournament/1st round
1958	Did not enter
1962	QT 2nd/3 in group 5
1966	QT 4th/4 in group 4
1970	QT 3rd/3 in group 4
1974	QT 2nd/4 in group 2
1978	QT 3rd/4 in group 3
1982	QT 5th/5 in group 3
1986	QT 5th/5 in group 3
1990	QT 3rd/5 in group 3
1994	QT 5th/6 in group 2

EUROPEAN CHAMPIONSHIP

1960	1st round
1964	1st round
1968	QT 3rd/4 in group 1
1972	QT 3rd/4 in group 8
1976	QT 3rd/4 in group 6
1980	QT 2nd/4 in group 7
1984	QT 4th/5 in group 6
1988	QT 4th/4 in group 4
1992	QT 4th/4 in group 7
1996	QT group 3

EUROPEAN CLUB COMPETITIONS

European Cup
Semi-finalists - Galatasaray 1989

Cup Winners Cup
Quarter-finalists - Fenerbahce 1964 Göztepe Izmir 1970 Bursaspor 1975

UEFA Cup
Semi-finalists - Göztepe Izmir 1969

CLUB DIRECTORY

ANKARA (Population - 2,400,000)

MKE Ankaragücü Kulübü (1910)
19 Mayis 24,000 – Yellow & blue stripes/White

Genclerbirligi Spor Kulübü (1923)
19 Mayis 24,000 – Red & black stripes/Black

ISTANBUL (Pop. - 5,750,000)

Besiktas Jimnastik Kulübü (1903)
Inönü 38,000 – White, black trim

Fenerbahçe Spor Kulübü (1907)
Fenerbahçe 30,000 – Blue & yellow stripes/Yellow

Galatasaray Spor Kulübü (1905)
Ali Sami Yen 34,000 – Red & yellow halves/Red

Sariyer Genclik Kulübü (1940)
Yusuf Ziya Önis 8,000 – Blue, white trim

IZMIR (Pop. - 1,550,000)
Altay Spor Kulübü (1914)
Alsancak 17,000 – White, black trim

Göztepe Spor Kulübü (1925)
Alsancak 17,000 – Yellow & black stripes/Black

Karsiyaka Spor Kulübü (1912)
Alsancak 17,000 – Red & green halves/Red

ADANA (Pop. - 931,000)
Adana Demirspor Kulübü (1940)
5 Ocak 21,000 – Dark blue & light blue quarters/White

Adanaspor Kulübü (1954)
5 Ocak 21,000 – Orange/White

BURSA (Pop. - 838,000)
Bursaspor Kulübü (1963)
Atatürk 22,000 – Green & white stripes/White

GAZIANTEP (Pop. - 478,000)
Gaziantepspor Kulübü (1965)
Kamil Ocak 20,000 – Red & black stripes/White

KONYA (Pop. - 439,000)
Konyaspor Kulübü (1981)
Atatürk 35,000 – Green/Green

KAYSERI (Pop. - 373,000)
Kayserispor Kulübü (1966)
Atatürk 15,000 – Red & yellow stripes/White

ESKISEHIR (Pop. - 366,000)
Eskisehirspor Kulübü (1965)
Atatürk 16,000 – Red/Black

ICEL (Pop. - 314,000)
Mersin Idmanyurdu (1925)
Tefvik Siri Gur – Red & blue stripes/White

DIYARBAKIR (Pop. - 305,000)
Diyarbakirspor Kulübü (1968)
Atatürk – Red & green stripes/White

MALATYA (Pop. - 243,000)
Malatyaspor Kulübü (1966)
Inönü 18,000 – Red/Red

SAMSUM (Pop. - 240,000)
Samsumspor Kulübü (1965)
19 Mayis 20,000 – Red, white trim

IZMIT (Pop. - 233,000)
Kocaelispor Kulübü (1966)
Ismetpasa 20,000 – Green, white trim

ZONGULDAK (Pop. - 210,000)
Zonguldakspor Kulübü (1966)
Sehir 15,000 – Red & blue stripes/Red

DENIZLI (Pop. - 169,000)
Denizlispor Kulübü (1966)
Sehir 15,000 – Green & black stripes/Black

ADAPAZARI (Pop. - 152,000)
Sakaryaspor Kulübü (1965)
Atatürk 15,000 – White/White

TRABZON (Pop. - 142,000)
Trabzonspor Kulübü PK (1967)
Avni Aker 27,000 – Light blue, maroon trim

ORDU (Pop. - 80,000)
Orduspor Kulübü (1967)
Ordu 20,000 – Purple/White

BOLU (Pop. - 50,000)
Boluspor Kulübü (1965)
Sehir 12,000 – Red & white hoops/White

REGIONAL LEAGUE PLAY-OFFS

1937	Fenerbahçe 36 Galatasaray 34 Besiktas 30
1938	Günes Istanbul 33 Besiktas 29 Galatasaray 26
1939	Galatasaray 35 Ankara Demirspor 35 MKE Ankaragücü 33
1940	Fenerbahçe 38 Galatasaray 34 Muhafiz Gücü Ankara 28
1941	Besiktas 50 Galatasaray 46 Fenerbahçe 46
1942	-
1943	Fenerbahçe 38 Galatasaray 38 Besiktas 32
1944	Besiktas 39 Fenerbahçe 36 Gözteppe Izmir 28
1945	Fenerbahçe 37 Besiktas 34 Galatasaray 32
1946	Fenerbahçe 28 Besiktas 26 Izmir Karagücü 18
1947	Besiktas 37 Fenerbahçe 35 Galatasaray 31
1948-49	-
1950	Fenerbahçe 35 Galatasaray 35 Besiktas 34

ISTANBUL LEAGUE CHAMPIONS

1924	Besiktas
1925	Galatasaray
1926	Galatasaray
1927	Galatasaray
1928	-
1929	Galatasaray
1930	Fenerbahçe
1931	Galatasaray
1932	Istanbulspor
1933	Fenerbahçe
1934	Besiktas
1935	Fenerbahçe
1936	Fenerbahçe
1937	Fenerbahçe
1938	Günes
1939	Besiktas
1940	Besiktas
1941	Besiktas
1942	Besiktas
1943	Besiktas
1944	Fenerbahçe
1945	Besiktas
1946	Besiktas
1947	Fenerbahçe
1948	Fenerbahçe
1949	Galatasaray
1950	Besiktas
1951	Besiktas
1952	Besiktas
1953	Fenerbahçe
1954	Besiktas
1955	Galatasaray
1956	Galatasaray
1957	Galatasaray
1958	Galatasaray

TURKISH NATIONAL LEAGUE

1959	Fenerbahçe * Galatasaray
1960v	Besiktas 65 Fenerbahçe 60 Galatasaray 58
1961	Fenerbahçe 61 Galatasaray 60 Besiktas 55
1962	Galatasaray 57 Fenerbahçe 53 Besiktas 48
1963k	Galatasaray 35 Besiktas 34 Fenerbahçe 28
1964t	Fenerbahçe 53 Besiktas 52 Galatasaray 42
1965q	Fenerbahçe 47 Besiktas 41 Galatasaray 39
1966	Besiktas 48 Galatasaray 42 Gençlerbirligi 38
1967r	Besiktas 45 Fenerbahçe 43 Galatasaray 41
1968	Fenerbahçe 49 Besiktas 42 Galatasaray 36
1969q	Galatasaray 46 Eskisehirspor 43 Besiktas 38
1970	Fenerbahçe 44 Eskisehirspor 37 Altay Izmir 36
1971	Galatasaray 42 Fenerbahçe 41 Göztepe Izmir 37
1972	Galatasaray 42 Eskisehirspor 39 Fenerbahçe 39
1973	Galatasaray 47 Fenerbahçe 42 Eskisehirspor 36
1974	Fenerbahçe 43 Besiktas 40 Boluspor 39
1975	Fenerbahçe 43 Galatasaray 38 Eskisehirspor 35
1976	Trabzonspor 43 Fenerbahçe 40 Galatasaray 37
1977	Trabzonspor 43 Fenerbahçe 39 Altay Izmir 35
1978	Fenerbahçe 42 Trabzonspor 41 Galatasaray 38
1979	Trabzonspor 42 Galatasaray 41 Fenerbahçe 38
1980	Trabzonspor 39 Fenerbahçe 35 Zonguldakspor 33
1981	Trabzonspor 39 Adanaspor 34 Galatasaray 34
1982r	Besiktas 44 Trabzonspor 43 Fenerbahçe 41
1983t	Fenerbahçe 49 Trabzonspor 47 Galatasaray 44
1984	Trabzonspor 50 Fenerbahçe 45 Galatasaray 44
1985	Fenerbahçe 50 Besiktas 50 Trabzonspor 42
1986u	Besiktas 56 Galatasaray 56 Samsunspor 48
1987	Galatasaray 54 Besiktas 53 Samsunspor 49
1988v1	Galatasaray 90 Besiktas 78 Malatyaspor 62
1989u6	Fenerbahçe 90 Besiktas 80 Galatasaray 66
1990t2	Besiktas 75 Fenerbahçe 70 Trabzonspor 68
1991q3	Besiktas 69 Galatasaray 64 Trabzonspor 51
1992	Besiktas 76 Fenerbahçe 71 Galatasaray 60
1993	Galatasaray 68 Besiktas 64 Kocaelispor 62
1994	Galatasaray 70 Fenerbahçe 69 Trabzonspor 59
1995	Besiktas 79 Trabzonspor 76 Galatasaray 69

* Fenerbahçe won a play-off against Galatasaray

TURKISH CUP FINALS

1963	Galatasaray	2-1 2-1	Fenerbahçe
1964	Galatasaray	0-0 *	Altay Izmir
1965	Galatasaray	0-0 1-0	Fenerbahçe
1966	Galatasaray	1-0	Besiktas
1967	Altay Izmir	2-2	Göztepe Izmir
1968	Fenerbahçe	2-0 0-1	Altay Izmir
1969	Göztepe Izmir	1-0 1-1	Galatasaray
1970	Göztepe Izmir	1-2 3-1	Eskisehirspor
1971	Eskisehirspor	0-1 2-0	Bursaspor
1972	MKE Ankaragücü	0-0 3-0	Altay Izmir
1973	Galatasaray	3-1 1-1	MKE Ankaragücü
1974	Fenerbahçe	0-1 3-0	Bursaspor
1975	Besiktas	0-1 2-0	Trabzonspor
1976	Galatasaray	0-1 1-0 5-4p	Trabzonspor
1977	Trabzonspor	1-0 0-0	Besiktas
1978	Trabzonspor	3-0 0-0	Adana Demirspor
1979	Fenerbahçe	1-2 2-0	Altay Izmir
1980	Altay Izmir	1-0 1-1	Galatasaray
1981	MKE Ankaragücü	2-1 0-0	Boluspor
1982	Galatasaray	3-0 1-2	MKE Ankaragücü
1983	Fenerbahçe	2-0 2-1	Mersin Idman Yurdu
1984	Trabzonspor	2-0	Besiktas
1985	Galatasaray	0-0 2-1	Trabzonspor
1986	Bursaspor	2-0	Altay Izmir
1987	Gençlerbirligi	5-0 1-2	Eskisehirspor
1988	Sakaryaspor	1-1 2-0	Samsunspor
1989	Besiktas	1-0 2-1	Fenerbahçe
1990	Besiktas	2-0	Trabzonspor
1991	Galatasaray	3-1	MKE Ankaragücü
1992	Trabzonspor	0-3 5-1	Bursaspor
1993	Galatasaray	1-0 2-2	Besiktas
1994	Besiktas	0-0 3-2	Galatasaray
1995	Trabzonspor	3-2 1-0	Galatasaray

* Galatasaray awarded the game

LEADING INTERNATIONAL GOALSCORERS

21	Lefter Kücülandonyadis	(Fenerbahçe)
19	Cemil Turan	(Istanbulspor,Fenerbahçe)
19	Metin Oktay	(Galatasaray)
15	Zeki-Riza Sporel	(Fenerbahçe)
10	Tanju Colak	(Samsunspor,Galatasaray, Fenerbahçe)
10	Hakan Sükür	(Bursaspor, Galatasaray)
7	Feyyaz Uçar	(Besiktas)
7	Burhan Sargin	(Fenerbahçe)
7	Sedat Özden	(Bursaspor)
7	Hami Mandirali	(Trabzonspor)

LEADING INTERNATIONAL APPEARANCES

51	Fatih Terim	(Galatasaray)
47	Turgay Seren	(Galatasaray)
46	Lefter Kücülandonyadis	(Fenerbahçe)
46	Oguz Cetin	(Fenerbahçe)
44	Cemil Turan	(Istanbulspor,Fenerbahçe)
40	Gökhan Keskin	(Besiktas)
39	Seref Has	(Fenerbahçe)
39	Recep Cetin	(Besiktas)

INTERNATIONAL MATCHES PLAYED BY TURKEY

26-10-1923	Romania	D 2-2	Istanbul	Fr	Zeki Riza 2
25-05-1924	Czechoslovakia	L 2-5	Paris	OGr1	Bekir 2
17-06	Finland	W 4-2	Helsinki	Fr	Zeki Riza 4
19-06	Estonia	W 4-1	Tallinn	Fr	Sabih, Bedri, Zeki Riza 2
22-06	Latvia	W 3-1	Riga	Fr	Zeki Riza 3
29-06	Poland	L 0-2	Lodz	Fr	
16-11	Soviet Union	L 0-3	Moscow	Fr	
10-04-1925	Bulgaria	W 2-1	Istanbul	Fr	Mehmet.L, Sabih
1-05	Romania	W 2-1	Bucharest	Fr	Zeki Riza, Mehmet.L
15-05	Soviet Union	L 1-2	Ankara	Fr	Sabih
2-10	Poland	L 1-2	Istanbul	Fr	Zeki Riza
7-05-1926	Romania	L 1-3	Istanbul	Fr	Muslih
2-10	Poland	L 1-6	Lwow	Fr	Alaaddin
17-07-1927	Bulgaria	D 3-3	Sofia	Fr	Latif 2, Kemal Faruki
14-10	Bulgaria	W 3-1	Istanbul	Fr	Zeki Riza 2, Nihat
8-04-1928	Yugoslavia	L 1-2	Zagreb	Fr	Latif
15-04	Romania	L 2-4	Arad	Fr	Kemal Faruki, Burhan
28-05	Egypt	L 1-7	Amsterdam	OGr1	Bekir
27-09-1931	Bulgaria	L 1-5	Sofia	BC	Hakki
2-10	Yugoslavia	W 2-0	Sofia	BC	Rebii, Fikret.B
5-11-1932	Bulgaria	L 2-3	Istanbul	Fr	Esref, Salahaddin
12-07-1936	Yugoslavia	D 3-3	Istanbul	Fr	Seref, Niyazi, Fikret.B
3-08	Norway	L 0-4	Berlin	OGr1	
1-08-1937	Yugoslavia	L 1-3	Belgrade	Fr	Rasih
23-04-1948	Greece	W 3-1	Athens	Fr	Fikret.K, Lefter, Sükrü
30-05	Austria	L 0-1	Istanbul	Fr	
2-08	China	W 4-0	London	OGr1	Gündüz 2, Huseyin, Lefter
5-08	Yugoslavia	L 1-3	London	OGqf	Sükrü
28-11	Greece	W 2-1	Istanbul	Fr	Reha 2
20-03-1949	Austria	L 0-1	Vienna	Fr	
13-05	Egypt	W 3-2	Athens	Fr	Bülent.E, Sükrü 2
15-05	Greece	W 2-1	Athens	Fr	Gündüz, Bülent.E

20-11	Syria	W 7-0	Ankara	WCq	Fahreddin 3, Bülent.U, Lefter, Erol, Gündüz
28-05-1950	Iran	W 6-1	Istanbul	Fr	Reha 3, Halit, Lefter 2
28-10	Israel	L 1-5	Tel Aviv	Fr	Reha
3-12	Israel	W 3-2	Istanbul	Fr	Halit, Isfendiyar, Lefter
10-06-1951	Sweden	L 1-3	Stockholm	Fr	Lefter
17-06	West Germany	W 2-1	Berlin	Fr	Recep, Muzaffer
14-11	Sweden	W 1-0	Istanbul	Fr	Muhtar
21-11	West Germany	L 0-2	Istanbul	Fr	
1-06-1952	Switzerland	L 1-5	Ankara	Fr	Garbis.B
8-06	Spain	D 0-0	Istanbul	Fr	
25-05-1953	Switzerland	W 2-1	Berne	Fr	Garbis.B 2
5-06	Yugoslavia	D 2-2	Istanbul	Fr	Burhan, Fikret.K
6-01-1954	Spain	L 1-4	Madrid	WCq	Recep
14-03	Spain	W 1-0	Istanbul	WCq	Burhan
17-03	Spain	D 2-2	Rome	WCq	Burhan, Suat
17-06	West Germany	L 1-4	Berne	WCr1	Suat
20-06	South Korea	W 7-0	Geneva	WCr1	Suat 2, Lefter, Burhan 3, Erol
23-06	West Germany	L 2-7	Zurich	WCr1	Mustafa, Lefter
17-10	Yugoslavia	L 1-5	Sarajevo	Fr	Burhan
18-12-1955	Portugal	W 3-1	Istanbul	Fr	Lefter, Metin, Nazmi
19-02-1956	Hungary	W 3-1	Istanbul	Fr	Lefter 2, Metin.O
25-03	Portugal	L 1-3	Lisbon	Fr	Isfendiyar
1-05	Brazil	L 0-1	Istanbul	Fr	
16-11	Poland	D 1-1	Istanbul	Fr	Metin.O
25-11	Czechoslovakia	D 1-1	Prague	Fr	Ergun
5-04-1957	Egypt	W 4-0	Cairo	Fr	Lefter 3, Hilmi
19-05	Poland	W 1-0	Warsaw	Fr	Ali.B
6-11	Spain	L 0-3	Madrid	Fr	
8-12	Belgium	D 1-1	Ankara	Fr	Can
4-05-1958	Holland	W 2-1	Amsterdam	Fr	Metin.O 2
26-10	Belgium	D 1-1	Brussels	Fr	Metin.O
2-11	Romania	L 0-3	Bucharest	ECr1	
7-12	Bulgaria	D 0-0	Ankara	Fr	
18-12	Czechoslovakia	W 1-0	Istanbul	Fr	Seref
26-04-1959	Romania	W 2-0	Istanbul	ECr1	Lefter 2
10-05	Holland	D 0-0	Istanbul	Fr	
8-06-1960	Scotland	W 4-2	Ankara	Fr	Metin.O, Lefter 2, Senol
27-11	Bulgaria	L 1-2	Sofia	Fr	Metin.O
14-05-1961	Romania	L 0-1	Ankara	Fr	
1-06	Norway	W 1-0	Oslo	WCq	Metin.O
18-06	Soviet Union	L 0-1	Moscow	WCq	
8-10	Romania	L 0-4	Bucharest	Fr	
18-10	South Korea	W 1-0	Ankara	Fr	Tarik
29-10	Norway	W 2-1	Istanbul	WCq	Aydin, Metin.O
12-11	Soviet Union	L 1-2	Istanbul	WCq	Metin.O
29-04-1962	Hungary	L 1-2	Budapest	Fr	Talat
16-05	Israel	W 1-0	Istanbul	Fr	Lefter
10-10	Ethiopia	W 3-0	Ankara	Fr	Metin.O 3
25-11	Israel	W 2-0	Tel Aviv	Fr	Senol 2
2-12	Italy	L 0-6	Bologna	ECr1	
12-12	Denmark	D 1-1	Istanbul	Fr	Birol
16-12	Ethiopia	D 0-0	Addis Ababa	Fr	
27-03-1963	Italy	L 0-1	Istanbul	ECr1	
22-09	Poland	D 0-0	Poznan	Fr	
28-09	West Germany	L 0-3	Frankfurt	Fr	
9-10	Romania	D 0-0	Ankara	Fr	
27-09-1964	Poland	L 2-3	Istanbul	Fr	Aydin, Metin.O
1-11	Tunisia	W 4-1	Ankara	Fr	Aydin, Metin.O 2, Can
20-12	Bulgaria	D 0-0	Istanbul	Fr	
24-01-1965	Portugal	L 1-5	Lisbon	WCq	Fevzi
19-04	Portugal	L 0-1	Ankara	WCq	
2-05	Romania	L 0-3	Bucharest	WCq	
9-05	Bulgaria	L 1-4	Sofia	Fr	Metin.O
21-07	Pakistan	W 3-1	Tehran	Fr	Ogün 2, Gürsel
25-07	Iran	D 0-0	Tehran	Fr	
9-10	Czechoslovakia	L 0-6	Istanbul	WCq	
23-10	Romania	W 2-1	Ankara	WCq	Fevzi, Nedim
21-11	Czechoslovakia	L 1-3	Brno	WCq	Ayhan
16-03-1966	Iran	D 0-0	Tehran	Fr	
30-05	Denmark	D 0-0	Copenhagen	Fr	
12-10	West Germany	L 0-2	Ankara	Fr	
16-10	Soviet Union	W 2-0	Moscow	Fr	Fevzi, Ayhan

16-11	Rep. Ireland	L 1-2	Dublin	ECq	Ogün
22-01-1967	Tunisia	D 0-0	Tunis	Fr	
1-02	Spain	D 0-0	Istanbul	ECq	
22-02	Rep. Ireland	W 2-1	Ankara	ECq	Ayhan, Ogün
31-05	Spain	L 0-2	Bilbao	ECq	
18-06	Czechoslovakia	L 0-3	Bratislava	ECq	
15-11	Czechoslovakia	D 0-0	Ankara	ECq	
26-11	Iran	W 1-0	Dacca	Fr	Nevzat
28-11	Pakistan	W 7-4	Dacca	Fr	Fevzi 2, Ergün 2, Ogün, Ayhan, Sanli
13-03-1968	Tunisia	D 0-0	Izmir	Fr	
24-04	Poland	L 0-8	Chorzow	Fr	
9-10	Bulgaria	L 0-2	Istanbul	Fr	
23-10	Nth. Ireland	L 1-4	Belfast	WCq	Ogün
11-12	Nth. Ireland	L 0-3	Istanbul	WCq	
17-01-1969	Saudi Arabia	W 2-1	Riyadh	Fr	Faruk, Mesut
30-04	Poland	L 1-3	Ankara	Fr	Ergün
14-09	Pakistan	W 4-2	Ankara	Fr	Fevzi, Can 2, Sanli
17-09	Iran	W 4-0	Ankara	Fr	Ender 2, Can, Metin
24-09	Switzerland	W 3-0	Istanbul	Fr	Metin, Nihat, Can
15-10	Soviet Union	L 0-3	Kiev	WCq	
16-11	Soviet Union	L 1-3	Istanbul	WCq	Ender
17-10-1970	West Germany	D 1-1	Cologne	ECq	Kamuran
13-12	Albania	W 2-1	Istanbul	ECq	Metin, Kemil
25-04-1971	West Germany	L 0-3	Istanbul	ECq	
22-09	Poland	L 1-5	Krakow	ECq	Nihat
26-09	Switzerland	L 0-4	Zurich	Fr	
14-11	Albania	L 0-3	Tirana	ECq	
5-12	Poland	W 1-0	Izmir	ECq	Cemil
4-10-1972	Algeria	L 0-1	Algiers	Fr	
22-10	Luxembourg	L 0-2	Esch	WCq	
10-12	Luxembourg	W 3-0	Istanbul	WCq	Osman 2, Köksal
13-01-1973	Italy	D 0-0	Naples	WCq	
14-02	Algeria	W 4-0	Izmir	Fr	Mehmet.B, Cemil, Ziya, Osman
25-02	Italy	L 0-1	Istanbul	WCq	
18-04	Bulgaria	W 5-2	Izmir	BC	Mehmet.B, Cemil 3, Metin
9-05	Switzerland	D 0-0	Basle	WCq	
17-10	Spain	D 0-0	Istanbul	Fr	
18-11	Switzerland	W 2-0	Izmir	WCq	Mehmet.F, Metin
18-01-1974	Pakistan	D 2-2	Karachi	Fr	Melih 2
20-01	Iran	W 1-0	Karachi	Fr	Sinan
8-05	Bulgaria	L 1-5	Sofia	BC	Cemil
13-11	Austria	L 0-1	Istanbul	Fr	
20-11	Rep. Ireland	D 1-1	Izmir	ECq	OG
1-12	Switzerland	W 2-1	Izmir	ECq	Izmail, Mehmet.B
19-03-1975	Romania	D 1-1	Istanbul	Fr	Cemil
2-04	Soviet Union	L 0-3	Kiev	ECq	
30-04	Switzerland	D 1-1	Zurich	ECq	Alpaslan
12-10	Romania	D 2-2	Bucharest	Fr	Cemil, Gökmen
29-10	Rep. Ireland	L 0-4	Dublin	ECq	
23-11	Soviet Union	W 1-0	Izmir	ECq	OG
20-12	West Germany	L 0-5	Istanbul	Fr	
8-02-1976	Iraq	D 0-0	Baghdad	Fr	
25-08	Finland	L 1-2	Helsinki	Fr	Resit
22-09	Bulgaria	D 2-2	Sofia	Fr	OG, Ali Kemal
13-10	Rep. Ireland	D 3-3	Ankara	Fr	Cemil 2, Isa
31-10	Malta	W 4-0	Istanbul	WCq	Mehmet.K, Cemil 3
17-11	East Germany	D 1-1	Dresden	WCq	Cemil
16-02-1977	Bulgaria	W 2-0	Istanbul	BC	Ali Kemal, Cemil
23-03	Romania	L 0-4	Bucharest	BC	
6-04	Finland	L 1-2	Ankara	Fr	Mustafa.B
17-04	Austria	L 0-1	Vienna	WCq	
7-09	Czechoslovakia	L 0-1	Bratislava	Fr	
21-09	Bulgaria	L 1-3	Sofia	BC	Sedat
30-10	Austria	L 0-1	Izmir	WCq	
16-11	East Germany	L 1-2	Izmir	WCq	Volkan
27-11	Malta	W 3-0	Gzira	WCq	Sedat 2, Cemil
22-03-1978	Romania	D 1-1	Istanbul	BC	Sedat
5-04	Rep. Ireland	L 2-4	Dublin	Fr	Cemil, Onder
23-09	Italy	L 0-1	Florence	Fr	
5-10	Soviet Union	L 0-2	Ankara	Fr	
29-11	Wales	L 0-1	Wrexham	ECq	
28-02-1979	Algeria	L 0-1	Bursa	Fr	

Date	Opponent	Result	Venue	Comp	Scorers
18-03	Malta	W 2-1	Izmir	ECq	Fatih, Sedat
1-04	West Germany	D 0-0	Izmir	ECq	
28-10	Malta	W 2-1	Gzira	ECq	Sedat, Mustafa.B
21-11	Wales	W 1-0	Izmir	ECq	Onal
22-12	West Germany	L 0-2	Gelsenkirchen	ECq	
24-09-1980	Iceland	L 1-3	Izmir	WCq	Fatih
1-10	Libya	L 1-2	Izmir	Fr	Muhararrem
3-10	Saudi Arabia	W 3-0	Izmir	Fr	Tuncay, OG, Ibrahim
5-10	Malaysia	W 3-0	Izmir	Fr	Metin.B 2, Tuncay
15-10	Wales	L 0-4	Cardiff	WCq	
3-12	Czechoslovakia	L 0-2	Prague	WCq	
25-03-1981	Wales	L 0-1	Ankara	WCq	
15-04	Czechoslovakia	L 0-3	Istanbul	WCq	
9-09	Iceland	L 0-2	Reykjavik	WCq	
23-09	Soviet Union	L 0-4	Moscow	WCq	
7-10	Soviet Union	L 0-3	Izmir	WCq	
22-09-1982	Hungary	L 0-5	Gyor	Fr	
27-10	Albania	W 1-0	Izmir	ECq	Arif
17-11	Austria	L 0-4	Vienna	ECq	
29-01-1983	Romania	D 1-1	Istanbul	Fr	Selcuk
9-03	Romania	L 1-3	Tirgu Mures	Fr	Rasit
30-03	Nth. Ireland	L 1-2	Belfast	ECq	Hasan
23-04	West Germany	L 0-3	Izmir	ECq	
11-05	Albania	D 1-1	Tirana	ECq	Metin.T
12-10	Nth. Ireland	W 1-0	Ankara	ECq	Selcuk
26-10	West Germany	L 1-5	Berlin	ECq	Hasan
16-11	Austria	W 3-1	Istanbul	ECq	Tufekci, Selcuk 2
20-01-1984	Egypt	L 0-1	Cairo	Fr	
22-01	Egypt	W 1-0	Port Said	Fr	Chinal
3-03	Italy	L 1-2	Istanbul	Fr	Tufekci
11-03	Luxembourg	W 3-1	Esch	Fr	Sedat, Tufekci 2
4-04	Hungary	L 0-6	Istanbul	Fr	
26-09	Poland	L 0-2	Slupsk	Fr	
16-10	Bulgaria	D 0-0	Istanbul	Fr	
31-10	Finland	L 1-2	Antalya	WCq	Tufekci
14-11	England	L 0-8	Istanbul	WCq	
22-12	Luxembourg	W 1-0	Istanbul	Fr	Kayhan
28-03-1985	Albania	D 0-0	Tirana	Fr	
3-04	Romania	L 0-3	Craiova	WCq	
1-05	Nth. Ireland	L 0-2	Belfast	WCq	
28-08	Switzerland	D 0-0	St. Gallen	Fr	
11-09	Nth. Ireland	D 0-0	Izmir	WCq	
25-09	Finland	L 0-1	Tampere	WCq	
16-10	England	L 0-5	London	WCq	
13-11	Romania	L 1-3	Izmir	WCq	Metin.T
11-12	Poland	D 1-1	Adana	Fr	Tanju
12-03-1986	Switzerland	W 1-0	Adana	Fr	Yusef
29-10	Yugoslavia	L 0-4	Split	ECq	
12-11	Nth. Ireland	D 0-0	Izmir	ECq	
4-03-1987	Romania	L 1-3	Ankara	Fr	Tanju
25-03	East Germany	W 3-1	Istanbul	Fr	Keser, Kayhan, Tanju
29-04	England	D 0-0	Izmir	ECq	
14-10	England	L 0-8	London	ECq	
11-11	Nth. Ireland	L 0-1	Belfast	ECq	
16-12	Yugoslavia	L 2-3	Izmir	ECq	Yusef, Feyyaz
16-03-1988	Hungary	L 0-1	Budapest	Fr	
21-09	Greece	W 3-1	Istanbul	Fr	Tanju, Oguz, Ridvan
12-10	Iceland	D 1-1	Istanbul	WCq	Tanju
2-11	Austria	L 2-3	Vienna	WCq	Feyyaz, Tanju
30-12	East Germany	W 3-1	Istanbul	WCq	Tanju 2, Oguz
29-03-1989	Greece	W 1-0	Athens	Fr	Ridvan
12-04	East Germany	W 2-0	Magdeburg	WCq	Tanju, Ridvan
10-05	Soviet Union	L 0-1	Istanbul	WCq	
20-09	Iceland	L 1-2	Reykjavik	WCq	Feyyaz
25-10	Austria	W 3-0	Istanbul	WCq	Ridvan 2, Feyyaz
15-11	Soviet Union	L 0-2	Simferopol	WCq	
11-04-1990	Denmark	L 0-1	Copenhagen	Fr	
27-05	Rep. Ireland	D 0-0	Izmir	Fr	
5-09	Hungary	L 1-4	Budapest	Fr	Tanju
17-10	Rep. Ireland	L 0-5	Dublin	ECq	
14-11	Poland	L 0-1	Istanbul	ECq	
27-02-1991	Yugoslavia	D 1-1	Izmir	Fr	Ugur

27-03	Tunisia	D 0-0	Tunis	Fr	
17-04	Poland	L 0-3	Warsaw	ECq	
1-05	England	L 0-1	Izmir	ECq	
15-07	Faeroe Islands	D 1-1	Torshavn	Fr	Hami
17-07	Iceland	L 1-5	Reykjavik	Fr	Unal
21-08	Bulgaria	D 0-0	Stara Zagora	Fr	
4-09	USA	D 1-1	Istanbul	Fr	Erdal
16-10	England	L 0-1	London	ECq	
13-11	Rep. Ireland	L 1-3	Istanbul	ECq	Riza
12-02-1992	Finland	D 1-1	Adana	Fr	Orhan
25-03	Luxembourg	W 3-2	Luxembourg	Fr	Unal, Hami 2
8-04	Denmark	W 2-1	Ankara	Fr	Hami, Hakan
30-05	Germany	L 0-1	Gelsenkirchen	Fr	
26-08	Bulgaria	W 3-2	Trabzon	Fr	Hami, Hakan 2
23-09	Poland	L 0-1	Poznan	WCq	
28-10	San Marino	W 4-1	Ankara	WCq	Hakan 2, Orhan, Hami
18-11	England	L 0-4	London	WCq	
16-12	Holland	L 1-3	Istanbul	WCq	Feyyaz
24-02-1993	Holland	L 1-3	Utrecht	WCq	Feyyaz
10-03	San Marino	D 0-0	Serravalle	WCq	
31-03	England	L 0-2	Izmir	WCq	
28-04	Norway	L 1-3	Oslo	WCq	Feyyaz
27-10	Poland	W 2-1	Istanbul	WCq	Hakan, Bülent.U
10-11	Norway	W 2-1	Istanbul	WCq	Ertugrul 2
23-02-1994	Czech Republic	L 1-4	Istanbul	Fr	Ertugrul
20-04	Russia	L 0-1	Bursa	Fr	
31-08	Macedonia	W 2-0	Skopje	Fr	OG, Arif
7-09	Hungary	D 2-2	Budapest	ECq	Hakan, Bülent.K
12-10	Iceland	W 5-0	Istanbul	ECq	Saffet 2, Hakan 2, Sergen
14-12	Switzerland	L 1-2	Istanbul	ECq	Recep
21-12	Italy	L 1-3	Pescara	Fr	Tolunay
15-02-1995	Romania	D 1-1	Izmir	Fr	Saffet
8-03	Israel	W 2-1	Istanbul	Fr	Aykut, Suat
29-03	Sweden	W 2-1	Istanbul	ECq	Emre, Sergen
26-04	Switzerland	W 2-1	Berne	ECq	Hakan, Ogün.T
4-06	Canada	W 3-1	Toronto	Fr	Alpay, Ogün.T, Ertugrul
7-06	Canada	W 3-0	Montreal	Fr	Sergen, Ogün.T, Hami

UKRAINE

Of all the former Soviet republics that now have their independence, it was always expected that Ukraine, along with Russia, would be the strongest. Dynamo Kiev were the most successful team in Soviet history with 13 league titles and 9 cup wins, and they were not the only Ukrainian team winning honours. Others included Shachter Donetsk, Dnepr Dnepropetrovsk, Zarja Lugansk, Karpati Lvov and Metalist Kharkov.

Of the 30 leading Soviet cap-winners, thirteen played their football in the Ukraine, and in Oleg Blokhin not only did the Ukraine have the Soviet Union's most capped player and record goalscorer, but also one of only two Soviet players ever to win the European Footballer of the Year award. The other, Igor Belanov, was himself a Ukrainian.

The Ukraine has had a history of changing borders and was not recognised as an independent country under that name before the 19th century. Its capital, Kiev, has always been an important city but has found itself part of Poland, the Soviet Union, and even, at one point, Lithuania. Ukraine became independent in 1991 and is one of the largest countries in Europe, with a population of 51 million. Hopes were high that it could make a big impact on European football, but progress has been disappointing.

Matters did not get off to a happy start when Russia inherited the Soviet Union's place in the 1994 World Cup qualifying round, the Ukrainians arguing that their status at least merited the chance to play-off for the World Cup berth. To compound their disappointment, many of the top Ukrainian stars who were allowed to play for Russia in the qualifiers as a special concession, elected to carry on playing for them afterwards. Ukraine therefore kicked off their 1996 European Championship campaign without the likes of Kanchelskis, Yuran, Onopko and Salenko, and in their first game lost embarrassingly at home to Lithuania.

Domestically, 1992 saw the first Ukrainian league and cup played, and although Dynamo Kiev won neither, they have retained their status as the country's top club. But crowds are poor, and with heavy industry in the big cities, for so long the lifeblood of football clubs, being eroded, the Ukraine faces a difficult task living up to its glorious past on the football field, when Dynamo Kiev were one of the most feared teams in Europe. Since their debut in Europe under the Ukrainian banner, the clubs' performances have been disappointing. Dynamo did beat Barcelona 3-1 at home in the 1994 European Cup, but they lost the return 4-1, while other clubs have suffered embarrassing defeats in the early rounds against opposition from the likes of Norway and Ireland.

Population: 51,707,000
Area, sq km: 603,78,200
Capital city: Kiev

Football Federation of the Ukraine
42 Kuybysheva Street
252023 Kiev 23
Tel: + 7 0442201344
Fax: + 7 0442201294

Year of formation	1991
Affiliation to FIFA	1992
Affiliation to UEFA	1993
Registered clubs	30 460
Registered players	759 500
Registered referees	14 000
National stadium	Central Republican 100 000
National colours	Yellow/Blue/Yellow
Season	August - June, with a mid season break December - February

THE RECORD

WORLD CUP
1930-94 Did not enter

EUROPEAN CHAMPIONSHIP
1960-92 Did not enter
1996 QT group 4

EUROPEAN CLUB COMPETITIONS
European Cup
Semi-finalists - Dynamo Kiev 1977 1987
Cup Winners Cup
Winners - Dynamo Kiev 1975 1986
UEFA Cup
3rd round - Dynamo Kiev 1974 1980 Shachter Donetsk 1977 Dnepr Dneprpropetrovsk 1986

CLUB DIRECTORY

KIEV (Pop. - 2,900,000)
Dynamo Kiev (1927)
Central Republican 100,000 – White, blue trim

DONETSK (Pop. - 2,200,000)
Shachter Donetsk (1936)
Lokomotiv 40,000 – Orange & black stripes/Black
Previous names - Stachanovec Stalino 1935-47, Shachter Stalino 1947-61

KHARKOV (Pop. - 1,940,000)
Metalist Kharkov (1944)
Metalist 37,000 – White, blue shoulders & sleeves/Blue
Previous names - Lokomotiv 1944-56, Avangard 1956-66

DNEPROPETROVSK (Pop. - 1,600,000)
Dnepr Dnepropetrovsk (1936)
Meteor 30,000 – Red, white trim

ODESSA (Pop. - 1,185,000)
Chernomorets Odessa (1958)
Central 43,000 – White, blue trim

ZAPOROZHE (Pop. - 884,000)
Metallurg Zaporozhe (1949)
Metallurg 23,000 – Red & white stripes/White

Torpedo Zaporozhe (1982)
ZAZ 12,000 – Blue/White, yellow trim

LVOV (Pop. - 790,000)
SKA Karpati Lvov (1963)
Druzjba 50,000 – Green & white stripes/White

KRIVOY ROG (Pop. - 713,000)
Krivbass Krivoy Rog (1959)
Metallurg 40,000 – Red & white stripes/Red

NIKOLAYEV (Pop. - 503,000)
Evis Nikolayev (1936)
Evis 25,000 – White/Blue, red trim

LUGANSK (Pop. - 497,000)
Zarja Lugansk (1923)
Avangard 40,000 – Red, white trim
Previous name - Jerjinec 1938-64, Zarja Voroschilovgrad 1964-90

VINNITSA (Pop. - 374,000)
Niva Vinnitsa (1958)
Centrum 25,000 – Green/White

SIMFEROPOL (Pop. - 344,000)
Tavria Simferopol (1958)
Lokomotiv 23,000 – Red, yellow trim

CHERNOVTSY (Pop. - 257,000)
Bukovina Chernovtsy (1949)
Bukovina 16,000 – Green/Red, yellow trim

KREMENCHUG (Pop. - 236,000)
Kremen Kremenchug (1959)
Dnepr 11,000 – Blue & white stripes/Blue

IVANO-FRANKOVSK (Pop. - 214,000)
Prikarpatye Ivano-Frankovsk (1947)
Rukh 15,000 – Red/Black, white trim

TERNOPOL (Pop. - 205,000)
Niva Ternopol (1959)
Central 17,000 – Red & white stripes/Black

LUTSK (Pop. - 161,000)
Volyn Lutsk (1960)
Avangard 15,000 – White/Green

CHEPETOVKA
Temp Chepetovka (1990)
Temp 10,000 – Red, white trim

UKRAINIAN LEAGUE CHAMPIONSHIP

1992	Tavria Simferopol .... 1-0 .... Dynamo Kiev
1993q	Dynamo Kiev 44 Dnepr Dnepropetrovsk 44 Chernomorets Odessa 38
1994t	Dynamo Kiev 56 Shachter Donetsk 49 Chernomorets Odessa 48
1995t2	Dynamo Kiev 83 Chernomorets Odessa 73 Dnepr 65

UKRAINIAN CUP FINALS

1992	Chernomorets Odessa	1-0	Metalist Kharkov
1993	Dynamo Kiev	2-1	Karpaty Lvov
1994	Chernomorets Odessa	0-0 5-4p	Tavria Simferopol
1995	Shachter Donetsk	1-1 8-7p	Dnepr Dnepropetrovsk

INTERNATIONAL MATCHES PLAYED BY UKRAINE

29-04-1992	Hungary	L 1-3	Uzhgorod	Fr	Getsko
27-06	USA	D 0-0	Piscataway	Fr	
26-08	Hungary	L 1-2	Nyiregyhaza	Fr	Gudymenko
28-10	Belarus	D 1-1	Minsk	Fr	Maksimov
27-04-1993	Israel	D 1-1	Odessa	Fr	Konovalov
18-05	Lithuania	W 2-1	Vilnius	Fr	Leonenko, Mikhaylenko
26-06	Croatia	L 1-3	Zagreb	Fr	Gusin
16-10	USA	W 2-1	High Point	Fr	Leonenko 2
20-10	Mexico	L 1-2	San Diego	Fr	OG

23-10	USA	W 1-0	Bethlehem	Fr	Popov
15-03-1994	Israel	L 0-1	Haifa	Fr	
25-05	Belarus	W 3-1	Kiev	Fr	Leonenko, Bezhenar, Mikhaylenko
3-06	Bulgaria	D 1-1	Sofia	Fr	Sak
7-09	Lithuania	L 0-2	Kiev	ECq	
12-10	Slovenia	D 0-0	Kiev	ECq	
13-11	Estonia	W 3-0	Kiev	ECq	Konalov, OG, Guseynov
25-03-1995	Croatia	L 0-4	Zagreb	ECq	
29-03	Italy	L 0-2	Tallinn	ECq	
26-04	Estonia	W 1-0	Tallinn	ECq	Guseynov
11-06	Croatia	W 1-0	Kiev	ECq	Kalitvintsev

WALES

Unlike England, Scotland and Northern Ireland, the other trio in the United Kingdom quartet, in Wales football is not the national sport. The national stadium is Cardiff Arms Park, the home of the Welsh Rugby Football Union, and until recent times at least, the oval ball has far outstripped the round one in popularity. Since the 1980s, as rugby has declined, football has made progress, albeit without managing to shake off Wales' image as 'the nearly men'. So often they have had qualification for the World Cup or European Championship finals within their grasp, but with the exception of the 1958 World Cup it has always slipped away.

North Wales has always been regarded as being more devoted to football than the south, the heartland of rugby, and it was there that Welsh football started. A club called Druids, the first club in the country and based in Ruabon near Wrexham, were formed at some point before 1875, when the oldest club still in existence, Wrexham AFC, were formed. The following year, also in Wrexham, the Football Association of Wales was instituted, three months after a match between a Scottish and Welsh team had taken place in Glasgow. Wrexham was naturally the venue for the return game the following year, and although games against both Ireland and England followed, it was not until 1894 that Wales played in the south, when they met Ireland in Swansea; and it was a further two years before Cardiff was considered.

Northern domination in these early years was complete. The Welsh Cup was introduced in 1878 and until 1912 the north produced all of the winners. The major clubs of the time, Druids, Wrexham, Bangor City, Oswestry and Chirk, however, all had to face up to the challenge that was rising in the south, especially from Cardiff City, Swansea Town, as they were then known, and Newport County. As the majority of the population lived in South Wales, this was an inevitable trend.

The Cup has always been the premier event in Welsh football as there has never been a proper league in force. In the 1920s Wrexham, Cardiff, Swansea and Newport all joined the English league, and with the exception of Newport who folded in the 1980s, they remain there today. A Welsh national league was started in 1993, with the winners qualifying for Europe, but none of the three professional clubs joined and indeed neither did most of the English-based semi-professional teams like Merthyr Tydfil. All of them preferred to take their chances of qualifying for Europe via the Welsh Cup.

It was actually in the English version, the FA Cup, that Cardiff enjoyed their most famous triumph, in 1927 when they defeated Arsenal 1-0 at Wembley. But apart from Cardiff in the 1920s, Welsh clubs have had a relatively low profile in the English league, generally languishing in its lower echelons. But it would seem that they prefer to stay in England, in the hope of emulating the rise of Swansea in the 1980s. Under the coaching of John Toshack they rose from the Fourth Division to the First in quick succession, but when he left for Spain they slid all the way back down again, where they have remained ever since.

Despite this low profile, Wales has produced some world class players. The first of these was the great Manchester City and Manchester United winger Billy Meredith, who played for Wales when he was 46 in 1920, some 25 years after he made his debut. This remains a world record to this day. Unfortunately for him, Wales' fixture list was composed entirely of Home International Championship games in these years. Not until the 1933 match with France in Paris did Wales play a foreign opponent. Had they done so when Meredith was playing he could have doubled his 48 caps, but this was still a remarkable figure for the time.

Success in these championships for both Meredith and Wales was not easy to come by, but they won their first title in 1907 and followed this up with victory in 1920, a fitting tribute to the retiring Meredith. The 1920 victory was the first of six during the 1920s and '30s, five of them outright. Although England won on seven occasions over the same period, only three of them were outright victories, a testament to the fact that the inter-war period was perhaps the most successful in the history of the game in Wales.

The national side left the borders of the British Isles for only the second time in 1939 for another match in Paris, but after the war a more concerted effort was made to take on opponents from abroad. After failing to qualify for the 1950 and 1954 World Cups, the qualifiers for which doubled up as matches in the Home International Championship, Wales somewhat fortuitously qualified for the tournament in Sweden in 1958 by beating Israel in a play-off. Czechoslovakia had come first in Wales' group, but when Israel were ordered to play-off for a place after all of their opponents had withdrawn, Wales were the lucky winners of the lottery.

Once in Sweden they progressed further than either Scotland or England, coming second in their group behind the hosts. In the quarter-finals the Welsh were rather unlucky to face Brazil. They gave the South Americans their hardest match in the competition, with Kelsey particularly brilliant in goal. The others stars of that that side were Ivor Allchurch, Trevor Ford and the great John Charles who found so much fame with Juventus in Italy.

THE ORDER OF MERIT

	Team	Total			League			Cup		Europe		
		G	S	B	G	S	B	G	S	G	S	B
1	Wrexham	23	22	-	-	-	-	23	22	-	-	-
2	Cardiff City	22	10	1	-	-	-	22	10	-	-	1
3	Swansea City	10	8	-	-	-	-	10	8	-	-	-
4	Druids	8	5	-	-	-	-	8	5	-	-	-
5	Shrewsbury Town	6	3	-	-	-	-	6	3	-	-	-
6	Bangor City	5	6	-	2	-	-	3	6	-	-	-
7	Chirk	5	1	-	-	-	-	5	1	-	-	-
8	Chester City	3	10	-	-	-	-	3	10	-	-	-
9	Merthyr Tydfil	3	3	-	-	-	-	3	3	-	-	-
10	Oswestry	3	1	-	-	-	-	3	1	-	-	-
11	Wellington Town	3	-	-	-	-	-	3	-	-	-	-
12	Rhyl	2	4	-	-	-	-	2	4	-	-	-
13	Newtown	2	3	-	-	-	-	2	3	-	-	-
14	Barry Town	2	-	-	-	-	-	2	-	-	-	-
	Crewe Alexandra	2	-	-	-	-	-	2	-	-	-	-
16	Hereford United	1	3	-	-	-	-	1	3	-	-	-
17	Connah's Quay	1	2	-	-	-	-	1	2	-	-	-
	Newport County	1	2	-	-	-	-	1	2	-	-	-
19	Flint	1	1	-	-	-	-	1	1	-	-	-
	Lovell's Athletic	1	1	-	-	-	-	1	1	-	-	-
	Tranmere Rovers	1	1	-	-	-	-	1	1	-	-	-
22	Cwmbran Town	1	-	1	1	-	1	-	-	-	-	-
	Aberystwyth Town	1	-	1	-	-	1	1	-	-	-	-
24	Borough United	1	-	-	-	-	-	1	-	-	-	-
	Bristol City	1	-	-	-	-	-	1	-	-	-	-
	Ebbw Vale	1	-	-	-	-	-	1	-	-	-	-
	South Liverpool	1	-	-	-	-	-	1	-	-	-	-
28	Aberdare	-	3	-	-	-	-	-	3	-	-	-
	Pontypridd	-	3	-	-	-	-	-	3	-	-	-
30	Inter Cardiff	-	2	-	-	2	-	-	-	-	-	-
31	Kidderminster Harriers	-	2	-	-	-	-	-	2	-	-	-
	Northwich Victoria	-	2	-	-	-	-	-	2	-	-	-
	Westminster Rovers	-	2	-	-	-	-	-	2	-	-	-
	Whitchurch	-	2	-	-	-	-	-	2	-	-	-
35	Ton Pentre	-	1	1	-	-	1	-	1	-	-	-
36	Aberaman	-	1	-	-	-	-	-	1	-	-	-
	Afan Lido	-	1	-	-	1	-	-	-	-	-	-
	Davenham	-	1	-	-	-	-	-	1	-	-	-
	Hednesford Town	-	1	-	-	-	-	-	1	-	-	-
	Llanelly	-	1	-	-	-	-	-	1	-	-	-
	Newtown White Stars	-	1	-	-	-	-	-	1	-	-	-
	Ruthin	-	1	-	-	-	-	-	1	-	-	-
	Stourbridge	-	1	-	-	-	-	-	1	-	-	-

To the end of the 1994-1995 season

The national side has been the main focus of attention in Welsh football, but since the 1958 World Cup the team have steadily built up their 'nearly men' reputation. In the 1976 European Championships they won their qualifying group but fell in the quarter-finals to Yugoslavia and thus missed out on the final tournament. They had reason reason to curse the Yugoslavs again in 1984 when they came within a minute of qualifying for the finals in France but were cruelly denied. In the World Cup it has been much the same story, especially since 1978 when Scotland qualified at Wales' expense thanks to a dubious penalty decision. In 1982 the Welsh lost out on goal difference to Czechoslovakia, and in 1986 they were again denied at the death by a Scottish penalty. In 1994 they missed out on the finals in America by a whisker, missing a vital penalty against Romania in a match they needed to win but eventually lost 2-1. These failures have meant that a fine generation of footballers has missed out on playing on the world's greatest stage. John Toshack, Ian Rush, Mark Hughes and Neville Southall would all have graced such a stage, and the Welsh are now hoping that Ryan Giggs, who turned down England to represent Wales, will not be similarly denied.

Population: 2,857,000
Area, sq km: 20,768
% in urban areas: 91.5%
Capital city: Cardiff

The Football Association of Wales
Plymouth Chambers
3 Westgate Street
Cardiff CF1 1DD
Tel: + 44 222 372325
Fax: + 44 222 343961

Year of formation	1876
Affiliation to FIFA	1910-1920, 1924-28, 1946
Affiliation to UEFA	1954
Registered clubs	2400
Registered players	53,140
Professional players	140
Registered referees	901
National stadium	Cardiff Arms Park (Welsh Rugby Football Union) 58,000

National colours	Red/Red/Red
Reserve colours	Yellow/Yellow/Yellow
Season	August - May

THE RECORD

WORLD CUP

1930-38	Did not enter
1950	QT 3rd/4 in group 1
1954	QT 4th/4 in group 3
1958	QT 2nd/3 in group 4 - Final Tournament/Quarter-finalists
1962	QT Rnd 1 in group 9
1966	QT 2nd/4 in group 7
1970	QT 3rd/3 in group 3
1974	QT 3rd/3 in group 5
1978	QT 3rd/3 in group 7
1982	QT 3rd/5 in group 3
1986	QT 3rd/4 in group 7
1990	QT 4th/4 in group 4
1994	QT 4th/6 in group 4

EUROPEAN CHAMPIONSHIP

1960	Did not enter
1964	1st round
1968	QT 3rd/4 in group 8
1972	QT 3rd/4 in group 1
1976	QT 1st/4 in group 2 - Final Tournament/Quarter-finalists
1980	QT 3rd/4 in group 7
1984	QT 2nd/4 in group 4
1988	QT 3rd/4 in group 6
1992	QT 2nd/4 in group 5
1996	QT group 7

EUROPEAN CLUB COMPETITIONS

European Cup
Preliminary round - Cwmbran Town 1994

Cup Winners Cup
Semi-finalists - Cardiff City 1968

UEFA Cup
Preliminary round - Bangor City 1995, Inter Cardiff 1995

CLUB DIRECTORY

CARDIFF (Population - 625,000)
Cardiff City FC (1899)
Ninian Park 42,000 – Blue/White

SWANSEA (Pop. - 275,000)
Swansea City FC (1900)
Vetch Field 26,000 – White, black trim
Previous name - Swansea Town 1900-70

WREXHAM (Pop. - 39,000)
Wrexham Association FC (1875)
Racecourse Ground 28,000 – Red/White

MERTHYR TYDFIL (Pop. - 38,000)
Merthyr Tydfil FC (1908)
Penydarren Park 10,000 – White/Black

BANGOR (Pop. - 12,000)
Bangor City FC (1875)
Farrar Road 10,000 – Blue, red & white trim

ABERYSTWYTH
Aberystwyth Town FC (1884)
Park Avenue 3,000 – Green & black stripes/Black

PORT TALBOT
Afan Lido FC (1967)
Afan Lido 2,000 – Red/White

PENYLAN
Cwmbran Town AFC (1955)
Cwmbran 13,000 – White/Red, blue trim

EBBW VALE
Ebbw Vale AFC (1906)
Eugene Cross Park 18,000 – Gold/Black

FFLINT
Fflint Town United (1880)
Ca'er Castell 9,000 – Black & white stripes/Black

BRIDGEND
Inter Cardiff FC (1990)
Penydarren Park 8,000 – White/Black

LLANELLI
Llanelli AFC (1896)
Stebonheath Park 3,000 – Red, white trim

NEWTOWN
Newtown AFC (1875)
Latham Park 5,000 – Red/White

RHYL
Rhyl FC (1883)
Belle Vue 6,000 – White, thin blue stripes/White

BARRY
Barry Town FC (1912)
Jenner Park 8,000 – Yellow/Yellow

WELSH LEAGUE CHAMPIONSHIP

1993vl Cwmbran Town 87 Inter Cardiff 83 Aberystwyth Town 78
1994 Bangor City 83 Inter Cardiff 81 Ton Pentre 71
1995 Bangor City 82 Afan Lido 76 Cwmbran Town 66

WELSH CUP FINALS

Year	Winner	Score	Runner-up
1878	Wrexham	1-0	Druids
1879	Newtown	1-0	Wrexham
1880	Druids	2-1	Ruthin
1881	Druids	2-0	Newtown White Stars
1882	Druids	2-1	Northwich Victoria
1883	Wrexham	1-0	Druids
1884	Oswestry	3-2	Druids
1885	Druids	2-0	Oswestry
1886	Druids	5-2	Newtown
1887	Chirk	4-2	Davenham
1888	Chirk	5-0	Newtown
1889	Bangor City	2-1	Northwich Victoria
1890	Chirk	1-0	Wrexham
1891	Shrewsbury Town	5-2	Wrexham
1892	Chirk	2-1	Westminster Rovers
1893	Wrexham	2-1	Chirk
1894	Chirk	2-0	Westminster Rovers
1895	Newtown	3-2	Wrexham
1896	Bangor City	3-1	Wrexham
1897	Wrexham	2-0	Newtown
1898	Druids	1-1 2-1	Wrexham
1899	Druids	2-2 1-0	Wrexham
1900	Aberystwyth Town	3-0	Druids
1901	Oswestry	1-0	Druids
1902	Wellington	1-0	Wrexham
1903	Wrexham	8-0	Aberaman
1904	Druids	3-2	Aberdare
1905	Wrexham	3-0	Aberdare
1906	Wellington	3-2	Whitchurch
1907	Oswestry	2-0	Whitchurch
1908	Chester	3-1	Connah's Quay
1909	Wrexham	1-0	Chester
1910	Wrexham	2-1	Chester
1911	Wrexham	6-1	Connah's Quay
1912	Cardiff City	0-0 3-0	Pontypridd
1913	Swansea Town	0-0 1-0	Pontypridd
1914	Wrexham	0-0 3-0	Llanelly
1915	Wrexham	1-1 1-0	Swansea Town
1916-19	-		
1920	Cardiff City	2-1	Wrexham
1921	Wrexham	1-1 3-1	Pontypridd
1922	Cardiff City	2-0	Ton Pentre
1923	Cardiff City	3-2	Aberdare
1924	Wrexham	2-2 1-0	Merthyr Tydfil
1925	Wrexham	3-1	Flint
1926	Ebbw Vale	3-2	Swansea Town
1927	Cardiff City	2-0	Rhyl
1928	Cardiff City	2-0	Bangor City
1929	Connah's Quay	3-0	Cardiff City
1930	Cardiff City	0-0 4-2	Rhyl
1931	Wrexham	7-0	Shrewsbury Town
1932	Swansea Town	1-1 2-0	Wrexham
1933	Chester	2-0	Wrexham
1934	Bristol City	1-1 3-0	Tranmere Rovers
1935	Tranmere Rovers	1-0	Chester
1936	Crewe Alexandra	2-0	Chester
1937	Crewe Alexandra	1-1 3-1	Rhyl
1938	Shrewsbury Town	2-1	Swansea Town
1939	South Liverpool	2-1	Cardiff City
1940	Wellington Town	4-0	Swansea Town
1941-46	-		
1947	Chester	0-0 5-1	Merthyr Tydfil
1948	Lovell's Athletic	3-0	Shrewsbury Town
1949	Merthyr Tydfil	2-0	Swansea Town
1950	Swansea Town	4-1	Wrexham
1951	Merthyr Tydfil	1-1 3-2	Cardiff City
1952	Rhyl	4-3	Merthyr Tydfil
1953	Rhyl	2-1	Chester
1954	Flint	2-0	Chester
1955	Barry Town	1-1 4-3	Chester
1956	Cardiff City	3-2	Swansea Town
1957	Wrexham	2-1	Swansea Town
1958	Wrexham	1-1 2-0	Chester
1959	Cardiff City	2-0	Lovell's Athletic
1960	Wrexham	1-1 1-0	Cardiff City
1961	Swansea Town	3-1	Bangor City
1962	Bangor City	0-3 2-0 3-1	Wrexham
1963	Borough United	2-1 0-0	Newport County
1964	Cardiff City	0-2 3-1 2-0	Bangor City

1965	Cardiff City	5-1 0-1 3-0	Wrexham
1966	Swansea Town	3-0 0-1 2-1	Chester
1967	Cardiff City	2-2 2-1	Wrexham
1968	Cardiff City	2-0 4-1	Hereford United
1969	Cardiff City	3-1 2-0	Swansea Town
1970	Cardiff City	1-0 4-0	Chester
1971	Cardiff City	1-0 3-1	Wrexham
1972	Wrexham	2-1 1-1	Cardiff City
1973	Cardiff City	0-1 5-0	Bangor City
1974	Cardiff City	1-0 1-0	Stourbridge
1975	Wrexham	2-1 3-1	Cardiff City
1976	Cardiff City	3-3 3-2	Hereford United
1977	Shrewsbury Town	1-2 3-0	Cardiff City
1978	Wrexham	0-0 3-1	Bangor City
1979	Shrewsbury Town	1-1 1-0	Wrexham
1980	Newport County	2-1 3-0	Shrewsbury Town
1981	Swansea City	1-0 1-1	Hereford United
1982	Swansea City	0-0 2-1	Cardiff City
1983	Swansea City	2-0 2-1	Wrexham
1984	Shrewsbury Town	2-1 0-0	Wrexham
1985	Shrewsbury Town	3-1 2-0	Bangor City
1986	Wrexham	1-1 2-1	Kidderminster Harriers
1987	Merthyr Tydfil	2-2 1-0	Newport County
1988	Cardiff City	2-0	Wrexham
1989	Swansea City	5-0	Kidderminster Harriers
1990	Hereford United	2-1	Wrexham
1991	Swansea City	2-0	Wrexham
1992	Cardiff City	1-0	Hednesford Town
1993	Cardiff City	5-0	Rhyl
1994	Barry Town	2-1	Cardiff City
1995	Wrexham	2-1	Cardiff City

LEADING INTERNATIONAL GOALSCORERS

28 Ian Rush	(Liverpool,Juventus,Liverpool)	1980-
23 Ivor Allchurch	(Swansea,Newcastle,Cardiff)	1951-1966
23 Trevor Ford	(Swansea,Aston Villa,Sunderland, Cardiff)	1947-1957
16 Dean Saunders	(Brighton,Oxford,Derby, Liverpool,Aston Villa)	1986-
15 John Charles	(Leeds,Juventus,Cardiff)	1950-1965
15 Cliff Jones	(Swansea,Tottenham,Fulham)	1954-1969
13 John Toshack	(Cardiff,Liverpool,Swansea)	1969-1980
12 Mark Hughes	(Manchester United,Barcelona)	1984-
12 Dai Astley	(Charlton,Aston Villa,Derby, Blackpool)	1931-1939
11 William Lewis	(Bangor,Crewe,Chester, Manchester City)	1885-1898
11 Billy Meredith	(Manchester City,Manchester United)	1895-1920

LEADING INTERNATIONAL APPEARANCES

81 Neville Southall	(Everton)	1982-
73 Peter Nicholas	(C. Palace,Arsenal,Luton, Aberdeen, Chelsea,Watford)	1979-1992
72 Joey Jones	(Liverpool,Wrexham,Chelsea, Huddersfield)	1976-1986
71 Ian Rush	(Liverpool,Juventus,Liverpool)	1980-
68 Ivor Allchurch	(Swansea,Newcastle,Cardiff)	1951-1966
66 Brian Flynn	(Burnley,Leeds)	1975-1984
59 Cliff Jones	(Swansea,Tottenham,Fulham)	1954-1969
59 Terry Yorath	(Leeds,Coventry,Tottenham, Vancouver)	1970-1981
59 Kevin Ratcliffe	(Everton)	1981-
59 David Phillips	(Plymouth,Man City,Coventry, Norwich, Nott'm Forest)	1984-
58 Leighton Phillips	(Cardiff,A.Villa,Swansea, Charlton)	1971-82
57 Mark Hughes	(Manchester United,Barcelona)	1984-
54 Leighton James	(Burnley,Derby,QPR,Swansea, Sunderland)	1972-83

INTERNATIONAL MATCHES PLAYED BY WALES

25-03-1876	Scotland	L 0-4	Glasgow	Fr	
5-03-1877	Scotland	L 0-2	Wrexham	Fr	
23-03-1878	Scotland	L 0-9	Glasgow	Fr	
18-01-1879	England	L 1-2	London	Fr	Davies.W (I)
7-04	Scotland	L 0-3	Wrexham	Fr	
15-03-1880	England	L 2-3	Wrexham	Fr	Roberts.J (I), Roberts.W (I)
27-03	Scotland	L 1-5	Glasgow	Fr	Roberts.W (I)
26-02-1881	England	W 1-0	Blackburn	Fr	Vaughan
14-03	Scotland	L 1-5	Wrexham	Fr	Cross
25-02-1882	Ireland	W 7-1	Wrexham	Fr	Price.J 4, Morgan, Owen.W (I) 2
13-03	England	W 5-3	Wrexham	Fr	Owen.W (I) 2, Morgan, Vaughan, OG
25-03	Scotland	L 0-5	Glasgow	Fr	
3-02-1883	England	L 0-5	London	Fr	
12-03	Scotland	L 0-3	Wrexham	Fr	
17-03	Ireland	D 1-1	Belfast	Fr	Roberts.W (II)
9-02-1884	Ireland	W 6-0	Wrexham	HC	Owen.W (I) 2, Shaw 2, Jones.R, Eyton-Jones
17-03	England	L 0-4	Wrexham	HC	
29-03	Scotland	L 1-4	Glasgow	HC	Roberts.R
14-03-1885	England	D 1-1	Blackburn	HC	Wilding
23-03	Scotland	L 1-8	Wrexham	HC	Jones.R
11-04	Ireland	W 8-2	Belfast	HC	Owen.W (II), Burke, Sisson 3, Roach 2, Jones.H
27-02-1886	Ireland	W 5-0	Wrexham	HC	Roberts.W (III), Wilding, Hersee, Sisson, Bryan
29-03	England	L 1-3	Wrexham	HC	Lewis.W (I)
10-04	Scotland	L 1-4	Glasgow	HC	OG
26-02-1887	England	L 0-4	London	HC	
12-03	Ireland	L 1-4	Belfast	HC	Sabine
21-03	Scotland	L 0-2	Wrexham	HC	

Date	Opponent	Result	Venue	Comp	Scorers
4-02-1888	England	L 1-5	Crewe	HC	Doughty.J
3-03	Ireland	W 11-0	Wrexham	HC	Doughty.J 4, Doughty.R 2, Wilding 2, Howell 2, Pryce-Jones
10-03	Scotland	L 1-5	Edinburgh	HC	Doughty.J
23-02-1889	England	L 1-4	Stoke	HC	Owen.W (II)
15-04	Scotland	D 0-0	Wrexham	HC	
27-04	Ireland	W 3-1	Belfast	HC	Jarrett 3
8-02-1890	Ireland	W 5-2	Shrewsbury	HC	Lewis.W 2 (I), Pryce-Jones 2, Owen.W (II)
15-03	England	L 1-3	Wrexham	HC	Lewis.W (I)
22-03	Scotland	D 0-0	Glasgow	HC	
7-02-1891	Ireland	L 2-7	Belfast	HC	Lewis.W (I) 2
7-03	England	L 1-4	Sunderland	HC	Howell
21-03	Scotland	L 3-4	Wrexham	HC	Bowdler 2, Owen.W (II)
27-02-1892	Ireland	D 1-1	Bangor	HC	Lewis.B
5-03	England	L 0-2	Wrexham	HC	
26-03	Scotland	L 1-6	Edinburgh	HC	Lewis.B
13-03-1893	England	L 0-6	Stoke	HC	
18-03	Scotland	L 0-8	Wrexham	HC	
5-04	Ireland	L 3-4	Belfast	HC	Owen.G 2, OG
24-02-1894	Ireland	W 4-1	Swansea	HC	Lewis.W (I) 2, James.E 2
12-03	England	L 1-5	Wrexham	HC	Bowdler
24-03	Scotland	L 2-5	Kilmarnock	HC	Morris.H 2
16-03-1895	Ireland	D 2-2	Belfast	HC	Trainer
18-03	England	D 1-1	London	HC	Lewis.W (I)
23-03	Scotland	D 2-2	Wrexham	HC	Lewis.W (I), Chapman
29-02-1896	Ireland	W 6-1	Wrexham	HC	Lewis.W (I) 2, Meredith 2, Pugh, Morris.A
16-03	England	L 1-9	Cardiff	HC	Chapman
21-03	Scotland	L 0-4	Dundee	HC	
6-03-1897	Ireland	L 3-4	Belfast	HC	Meredith 2, Jenkyns
20-03	Scotland	D 2-2	Wrexham	HC	Pugh, Morgan-Owen.M
29-03	England	L 0-4	Sheffield	HC	
19-02-1898	Ireland	L 0-1	Llandudno	HC	
19-03	Scotland	L 2-5	Motherwell	HC	Thomas.T, Morgan-Owen.M
28-03	England	L 0-3	Wrexham	HC	
4-03-1899	Ireland	L 0-1	Belfast	HC	
18-03	Scotland	L 0-6	Wrexham	HC	
20-03	England	L 0-4	Bristol	HC	
3-02-1900	Scotland	L 2-5	Aberdeen	HC	Butler, Parry
24-02	Ireland	W 2-0	Llandudno	HC	Parry, Meredith
26-03	England	D 1-1	Cardiff	HC	Meredith
2-03-1901	Scotland	D 1-1	Wrexham	HC	Parry
18-03	England	L 0-6	Newcastle	HC	
23-03	Ireland	W 1-0	Belfast	HC	Jones.J (I)
22-02-1902	Ireland	L 0-3	Cardiff	HC	
3-03	England	D 0-0	Wrexham	HC	
15-03	Scotland	L 1-5	Greenock	HC	Meredith
2-03-1903	England	L 1-2	Portsmouth	HC	Watkins
9-03	Scotland	L 0-1	Cardiff	HC	
28-03	Ireland	L 0-2	Belfast	HC	
29-02-1904	England	D 2-2	Wrexham	HC	Watkins, Davies.L (I)
12-03	Scotland	D 1-1	Dundee	HC	Atherton
21-03	Ireland	L 0-1	Bangor	HC	
6-03-1905	Scotland	W 3-1	Wrexham	HC	Morris.A, Meredith, Watkins
27-03	England	L 1-3	Liverpool	HC	Morris.A
8-04	Ireland	D 2-2	Belfast	HC	Watkins, Atherton
3-03-1906	Scotland	W 2-0	Edinburgh	HC	Jones.W, Jones.J (II)
19-03	England	L 0-1	Cardiff	HC	
2-04	Ireland	D 4-4	Wrexham	HC	Green 3, Morgan-Owen.H
23-02-1907	Ireland	W 3-2	Belfast	HC	Morris.R, Meredith, Jones.W
4-03	Scotland	W 1-0	Wrexham	HC	Morris.A
18-03	England	D 1-1	London	HC	Jones.W
7-03-1908	Scotland	L 1-2	Dundee	HC	Jones.W
16-03	England	L 1-7	Wrexham	HC	Davies.W (II)
11-04	Ireland	L 0-1	Aberdare	HC	
1-03-1909	Scotland	W 3-2	Wrexham	HC	Davies.W (II) 2, Jones.W
15-03	England	L 0-2	Nottingham	HC	
20-03	Ireland	W 3-2	Belfast	HC	Jones.W, Wynn, Meredith
5-03-1910	Scotland	L 0-1	Kilmarnock	HC	
14-03	England	L 0-1	Cardiff	HC	
11-04	Ireland	W 4-1	Wrexham	HC	Evans.R 2, Morris.A 2
28-01-1911	Ireland	W 2-1	Belfast	HC	Davies.W (II), Morris.A

6-03	Scotland	D 2-2	Cardiff	HC	Morris.A 2
13-03	England	L 0-3	London	HC	
2-03-1912	Scotland	L 0-1	Edinburgh	HC	
11-03	England	L 0-2	Wrexham	HC	
13-04	Ireland	L 2-3	Cardiff	HC	Davies.W (II), Davies.D
18-01-1913	Ireland	W 1-0	Belfast	HC	Roberts.J (II)
3-03	Scotland	D 0-0	Wrexham	HC	
17-03	England	L 3-4	Bristol	HC	Davies.W (III), Meredith, Peake
19-01-1914	Ireland	L 1-2	Wrexham	HC	Jones.E
28-02	Scotland	D 0-0	Glasgow	HC	
16-03	England	L 0-2	Cardiff	HC	
14-02-1920	Ireland	D 2-2	Belfast	HC	Davies.S 2
26-02	Scotland	D 1-1	Cardiff	HC	Evans.J
15-03	England	W 2-1	London	HC	Davies.S, Richards
12-02-1921	Scotland	L 1-2	Aberdeen	HC	Collier
14-03	England	D 0-0	Cardiff	HC	
9-04	Ireland	W 2-1	Swansea	HC	Hole, Davies.S
4-02-1922	Scotland	W 2-1	Wrexham	HC	Davies.S, Davies.L (II)
13-03	England	L 0-1	Liverpool	HC	
1-04	Ireland	D 1-1	Belfast	HC	Davies.L (II)
5-03-1923	England	D 2-2	Cardiff	HC	Keenor, Jones.I
17-03	Scotland	L 0-2	Glasgow	HC	
14-04	Ireland	L 0-3	Wrexham	HC	
16-02-1924	Scotland	W 2-0	Cardiff	HC	Davies.W (IV), Davies.L (II)
3-03	England	W 2-1	Blackburn	HC	Davies.W (IV), Vizard
15-03	Nth. Ireland	W 1-0	Belfast	HC	Russell
14-02-1925	Scotland	L 1-3	Edinburgh	HC	Williams.W
28-02	England	L 1-2	Swansea	HC	OG
18-04	Nth. Ireland	D 0-0	Wrexham	HC	
31-10	Scotland	L 0-3	Cardiff	HC	
13-02-1926	Nth. Ireland	L 0-3	Belfast	HC	
1-03	England	W 3-1	London	HC	Fowler 2, Davies.W (IV)
30-10	Scotland	L 0-3	Glasgow	HC	
12-02-1927	England	D 3-3	Wrexham	HC	Davies.L (II) 2, Lewis.W (II)
9-04	Nth. Ireland	D 2-2	Cardiff	HC	Williams.R 2
29-10	Scotland	D 2-2	Wrexham	HC	Curtis.E, OG
28-11	England	W 2-1	Burnley	HC	Lewis.W (II), OG
4-02-1928	Nth. Ireland	W 2-1	Belfast	HC	Davies.W (IV), Lewis.W (II)
27-10	Scotland	L 2-4	Glasgow	HC	Davies.W (IV) 2
17-11	England	L 2-3	Swansea	HC	Fowler, Keenor
2-02-1929	Nth. Ireland	D 2-2	Wrexham	HC	Mays, Warren
26-10	Scotland	L 2-4	Cardiff	HC	O'Callaghan, Davies.L (II)
20-11	England	L 0-6	London	HC	
1-02-1930	Nth. Ireland	L 0-7	Belfast	HC	
25-10	Scotland	D 1-1	Glasgow	HC	Bamford
22-11	England	L 0-4	Wrexham	HC	
22-04-1931	Nth. Ireland	W 3-2	Wrexham	HC	Phillips.C, Griffiths.T, Warren
31-10	Scotland	L 2-3	Wrexham	HC	Curtis.E 2
18-11	England	L 1-3	Liverpool	HC	Robbins
5-12	Nth. Ireland	L 0-4	Belfast	HC	
26-10-1932	Scotland	W 5-2	Edinburgh	HC	O'Callaghan 2, Griffiths.T, Astley, OG
16-11	England	D 0-0	Wrexham	HC	
7-12	Nth. Ireland	W 4-1	Wrexham	HC	Astley 2, Robbins 2
25-05-1933	France	D 1-1	Paris	Fr	Griffiths.T
4-10	Scotland	W 3-2	Cardiff	HC	Evans.W, Robbins, Astley
4-11	Nth. Ireland	D 1-1	Belfast	HC	Glover
15-11	England	W 2-1	Newcastle	HC	Mills, Astley
29-09-1934	England	L 0-4	Cardiff	HC	
21-11	Scotland	L 2-3	Aberdeen	HC	Phillips.C, Astley
27-03-1935	Nth. Ireland	W 3-1	Wrexham	HC	Jones.C (I), Phillips.C, Hopkins
5-10	Scotland	D 1-1	Cardiff	HC	Phillips.C
5-02-1936	England	W 2-1	Wolverhampton	HC	Astley, Jones.B (I)
11-03	Nth. Ireland	L 2-3	Belfast	HC	Astley, Phillips.C
17-10	England	W 2-1	Cardiff	HC	Morris.S, Glover
2-12	Scotland	W 2-1	Dundee	HC	Glover 2
17-03-1937	Nth. Ireland	W 4-1	Wrexham	HC	Glover 2, Jones.B (I), Warren
30-10	Scotland	W 2-1	Cardiff	HC	Jones.B (I), Morris.S
17-11	England	L 1-2	Middlesbrough	HC	Perry
16-03-1938	Nth. Ireland	L 0-1	Belfast	HC	
22-10	England	W 4-2	Cardiff	HC	Astley 2, Hopkins, Jones.B (I)
9-11	Scotland	L 2-3	Edinburgh	HC	Astley, Jones.L

Date	Opponent	Result	Venue	Comp	Scorers
15-03-1939	Nth. Ireland	W 3-1	Wrexham	HC	Cumner, Glover, Boulter
20-05	France	L 1-2	Paris	Fr	Astley
19-10-1946	Scotland	W 3-1	Wrexham	HC	Jones.B (I), Ford, OG
13-11	England	L 0-3	Manchester	HC	
16-04-1947	Nth. Ireland	L 1-2	Belfast	HC	Ford
18-10	England	L 0-3	Cardiff	HC	
12-11	Scotland	W 2-1	Glasgow	HC	Lowrie, Ford
10-03-1948	Nth. Ireland	W 2-0	Wrexham	HC	Lowrie, Edwards.G
23-10	Scotland	L 1-3	Cardiff	HC	Jones.B (I)
10-11	England	L 0-1	Birmingham	HC	
9-03-1949	Nth. Ireland	W 2-0	Belfast	HC	Edwards.G, Ford
15-05	Portugal	L 2-3	Lisbon	Fr	Ford 2
22-05	Belgium	L 1-3	Liege	Fr	Ford
26-05	Switzerland	L 0-4	Berne	Fr	
15-10	England	L 1-4	Cardiff	HC/WCq	Griffiths.M
9-11	Scotland	L 0-2	Glasgow	HC/WCq	
23-11	Belgium	W 5-1	Cardiff	Fr	Clarke, Paul, Ford 3
8-03-1950	Nth. Ireland	D 0-0	Wrexham	HC/WCq	
21-10	Scotland	L 1-3	Cardiff	HC	Powell.A
15-11	England	L 2-4	Sunderland	HC	Ford 2
7-03-1951	Nth. Ireland	W 2-1	Belfast	HC	Clarke 2
12-05	Portugal	W 2-1	Cardiff	Fr	Griffiths.M, Ford
16-05	Switzerland	W 3-2	Wrexham	Fr	Ford 2, Burgess
20-10	England	D 1-1	Cardiff	HC	Foulkes
14-11	Scotland	W 1-0	Glasgow	HC	Allchurch
19-03-1952	Nth. Ireland	W 3-0	Swansea	HC	Barnes, Allchurch, Clarke
18-10	Scotland	L 1-2	Cardiff	HC	Ford
12-11	England	L 2-5	London	HC	Ford 2
15-04-1953	Nth. Ireland	W 3-2	Belfast	HC	Charles.J 2, Ford
14-05	France	L 1-6	Paris	Fr	Allchurch
21-05	Yugoslavia	L 2-5	Belgrade	Fr	Ford 2
10-10	England	L 1-4	Cardiff	HC/WCq	Allchurch
4-11	Scotland	D 3-3	Glasgow	HC/WCq	Charles.J 2, Allchurch
31-03-1954	Nth. Ireland	L 1-2	Wrexham	HC/WCq	Charles.J
9-05	Austria	L 0-2	Vienna	Fr	
22-09	Yugoslavia	L 1-3	Cardiff	Fr	Allchurch
16-10	Scotland	L 0-1	Cardiff	HC	
10-11	England	L 2-3	London	HC	Charles.J 2
20-04-1955	Nth. Ireland	W 3-2	Belfast	HC	Charles.J 3
22-10	England	W 2-1	Cardiff	HC	Tapscott, Jones.C (II)
9-11	Scotland	L 0-2	Glasgow	HC	
23-11	Austria	L 1-2	Wrexham	Fr	Tapscott
11-04-1956	Nth. Ireland	D 1-1	Cardiff	HC	Clarke
20-10	Scotland	D 2-2	Cardiff	HC	Ford, Medwin
14-11	England	L 1-3	London	HC	Charles.J
10-04-1957	Nth. Ireland	D 0-0	Belfast	HC	
1-05	Czechoslovakia	W 1-0	Cardiff	WCq	Vernon
19-05	East Germany	L 1-2	Leipzig	WCq	Charles.M
26-05	Czechoslovakia	L 0-2	Prague	WCq	
25-09	East Germany	W 4-1	Cardiff	WCq	Palmer 3, Jones.C (II)
19-10	England	L 0-4	Cardiff	HC	
13-11	Scotland	D 1-1	Glasgow	HC	Medwin
15-01-1958	Israel	W 2-0	Tel Aviv	WCq	Allchurch, Bowen
5-02	Israel	W 2-0	Cardiff	WCq	Allchurch, Jones.C (II)
16-04	Nth. Ireland	D 1-1	Cardiff	HC	Hewitt
8-06	Hungary	D 1-1	Sandviken	WCr1	Charles.J
11-06	Mexico	D 1-1	Stockholm	WCr1	Allchurch
15-06	Sweden	D 0-0	Stockholm	WCr1	
17-06	Hungary	W 2-1	Stockholm	WCr1	Allchurch, Medwin
19-06	Brazil	L 0-1	Gothenburg	WCqf	
18-10	Scotland	L 0-3	Cardiff	HC	
26-11	England	D 2-2	Birmingham	HC	Tapscott, Allchurch
22-04-1959	Nth. Ireland	L 1-4	Belfast	HC	Tapscott
17-10	England	D 1-1	Cardiff	HC	Moore
4-11	Scotland	D 1-1	Glasgow	HC	Charles.J
6-04-1960	Nth. Ireland	W 3-2	Wrexham	HC	Medwin 2, Woosnam
28-09	Rep. Ireland	W 3-2	Dublin	Fr	Jones.C (II) 2, Woosnam
22-10	Scotland	W 2-0	Cardiff	HC	Vernon, Jones.C (II)
23-11	England	L 1-5	London	HC	Leek
12-04-1961	Nth. Ireland	W 5-1	Belfast	HC	Charles.M, Jones.C (II) 2, Allchurch, Leek
19-04	Spain	L 1-2	Cardiff	WCq	Woosnam

18-05	Spain	D 1-1	Madrid	WCq	Allchurch
28-05	Hungary	L 2-3	Budapest	Fr	Allchurch, Jones.C (II)
14-10	England	D 1-1	Cardiff	HC	Williams.G
8-11	Scotland	L 0-2	Glasgow	HC	
11-04-1962	Nth. Ireland	W 4-0	Cardiff	HC	Charles.M 4
12-05	Brazil	L 1-3	Rio de Janeiro	Fr	Allchurch
16-05	Brazil	L 1-3	Sao Paulo	Fr	Leek
22-05	Mexico	L 1-2	Mexico City	Fr	Charles.J
20-10	Scotland	L 2-3	Cardiff	HC	Allchurch, Charles.J
7-11	Hungary	L 1-3	Budapest	ECr1	Medwin
21-11	England	L 0-4	London	HC	
20-03-1963	Hungary	D 1-1	Cardiff	ECr1	Jones.C (II)
3-04	Nth. Ireland	W 4-1	Belfast	HC	Woosnam, Jones.C (II) 3
12-10	England	L 0-4	Cardiff	HC	
20-11	Scotland	L 1-2	Glasgow	HC	Jones.B (II)
15-04-1964	Nth. Ireland	L 2-3	Swansea	HC	Godfrey, Davies.R (I)
3-10	Scotland	W 3-2	Cardiff	HC	Davies.R (II), Leek 2
21-10	Denmark	L 0-1	Copenhagen	WCq	
18-11	England	L 1-2	London	HC	Jones.C (II)
9-12	Greece	L 0-2	Athens	WCq	
17-03-1965	Greece	W 4-1	Cardiff	WCq	Allchurch 2, England, Vernon
31-03	Nth. Ireland	W 5-0	Belfast	HC	Vernon 2, Jones.C (II), Williams.G, Allchurch
1-05	Italy	L 1-4	Florence	Fr	Godfrey
30-05	Soviet Union	L 1-2	Moscow	WCq	Davies.R (II)
2-10	England	D 0-0	Cardiff	HC	
27-10	Soviet Union	W 2-1	Cardiff	WCq	Vernon, Allchurch
24-11	Scotland	L 1-4	Glasgow	HC	Allchurch
1-12	Denmark	W 4-2	Wrexham	WCq	Vernon 2, Davies.R (II), Rees
30-03-1966	Nth. Ireland	L 1-4	Cardiff	HC	Davies.R (II)
14-05	Brazil	L 1-3	Rio de Janeiro	Fr	Davies.R (I)
18-05	Brazil	L 0-1	Belo Horizonte	Fr	
22-05	Chile	L 0-2	Santiago	Fr	
22-10	Scotland	D 1-1	Cardiff	HC/ECq	Davies.R (I)
16-11	England	L 1-5	London	HC/ECq	Davies.R (II)
12-04-1967	Nth. Ireland	D 0-0	Belfast	HC/ECq	
21-10	England	L 0-3	Cardiff	HC/ECq	
22-11	Scotland	L 2-3	Glasgow	HC/ECq	Davies.R (I), Durban
28-02-1968	Nth. Ireland	W 2-0	Wrexham	HC/ECq	Rees, Davies.R (II)
8-05	West Germany	D 1-1	Cardiff	Fr	Davies.R (II)
23-10	Italy	L 0-1	Cardiff	WCq	
26-03-1969	West Germany	D 1-1	Frankfurt	Fr	Jones.B (II)
16-04	East Germany	L 1-2	Dresden	WCq	Toshack
3-05	Scotland	L 3-5	Wrexham	HC	Davies.R (I) 2, Toshack
7-05	England	L 1-2	London	HC	Davies.R (I)
10-05	Nth. Ireland	D 0-0	Belfast	HC	
22-10	East Germany	L 1-3	Cardiff	WCq	Powell.D
4-11	Italy	L 1-4	Rome	WCq	England
18-04-1970	England	D 1-1	Cardiff	HC	Krzywicki
22-04	Scotland	D 0-0	Glasgow	HC	
25-04	Nth. Ireland	W 1-0	Swansea	HC	Rees
11-11	Romania	D 0-0	Cardiff	ECq	
21-04-1971	Czechoslovakia	L 1-3	Swansea	ECq	Davies.R (I)
15-05	Scotland	D 0-0	Cardiff	HC	
19-05	England	D 0-0	London	HC	
22-05	Nth. Ireland	L 0-1	Belfast	HC	
26-05	Finland	W 1-0	Helsinki	ECq	Toshack
13-10	Finland	W 3-0	Swansea	ECq	Durban, Toshack, Reece
27-10	Czechoslovakia	L 0-1	Prague	ECq	
24-11	Romania	L 0-2	Bucharest	ECq	
20-05-1972	England	L 0-3	Cardiff	HC	
24-05	Scotland	L 0-1	Glasgow	HC	
27-05	Nth. Ireland	D 0-0	Wrexham	HC	
15-11	England	L 0-1	Cardiff	WCq	
24-01-1973	England	D 1-1	London	WCq	Toshack
28-03	Poland	W 2-0	Cardiff	WCq	James.L, Hockey
12-05	Scotland	L 0-2	Wrexham	HC	
15-05	England	L 0-3	London	HC	
19-05	Nth. Ireland	L 0-1	Liverpool	HC	
26-09	Poland	L 0-3	Chorzow	WCq	
11-05-1974	England	L 0-2	Cardiff	HC	
14-05	Scotland	L 0-2	Glasgow	HC	

18-05	Nth. Ireland	W 1-0	Wrexham	HC	Smallman
4-09	Austria	L 1-2	Vienna	ECq	Griffiths.A
30-10	Hungary	W 2-0	Cardiff	ECq	Griffiths.A, Toshack
20-11	Luxembourg	W 5-0	Swansea	ECq	Toshack, England, Roberts.P, Griffiths.A, Yorath
16-04-1975	Hungary	W 2-1	Budapest	ECq	Toshack, Mahoney
1-05	Luxembourg	W 3-1	Luxembourg	ECq	Reece, James.L 2
17-05	Scotland	D 2-2	Cardiff	HC	Toshack, Flynn
21-05	England	D 2-2	London	HC	Toshack, Griffiths.A
23-05	Nth. Ireland	L 0-1	Belfast	HC	
19-11	Austria	W 1-0	Wrexham	ECq	Griffiths.A
24-03-1976	England	L 1-2	Wrexham	Fr	Curtis.A
24-04	Yugoslavia	L 0-2	Zagreb	ECqf	
6-05	Scotland	L 1-3	Glasgow	HC	Griffiths.A
8-05	England	L 0-1	Cardiff	HC	
14-05	Nth. Ireland	W 1-0	Swansea	HC	James.L
22-05	Yugoslavia	D 1-1	Cardiff	ECqf	Evans.I
6-10	West Germany	L 0-2	Cardiff	Fr	
17-11	Scotland	L 0-1	Glasgow	WCq	
30-03-1977	Czechoslovakia	W 3-0	Wrexham	WCq	James.L 2, Deacy
28-05	Scotland	D 0-0	Wrexham	HC	
31-05	England	W 1-0	London	HC	James.L
3-06	Nth. Ireland	D 1-1	Belfast	HC	Deacy
6-09	Kuwait	D 0-0	Wrexham	Fr	
20-09	Kuwait	D 0-0	Kuwait City	Fr	
12-10	Scotland	L 0-2	Liverpool	WCq	
16-11	Czechoslovakia	L 0-1	Prague	WCq	
14-12	West Germany	D 1-1	Dortmund	Fr	Jones.D
18-04-1978	Iran	W 1-0	Tehran	Fr	Dwyer
13-05	England	L 1-3	Cardiff	HC	Dwyer
17-05	Scotland	D 1-1	Glasgow	HC	OG
19-05	Nth. Ireland	W 1-0	Wrexham	HC	Deacy
25-10	Malta	W 7-0	Wrexham	ECq	Edwards.R 4, O'Sullivan, Thomas.M, Flynn
29-11	Turkey	W 1-0	Wrexham	ECq	Deacy
2-05-1979	West Germany	L 0-2	Wrexham	ECq	
19-05	Scotland	W 3-0	Cardiff	HC	Toshack 3
23-05	England	D 0-0	London	HC	
26-05	Nth. Ireland	D 1-1	Belfast	HC	James.R
2-06	Malta	W 2-0	Gzira	ECq	Nicholas, Flynn
11-09	Rep. Ireland	W 2-1	Swansea	Fr	Walsh, Curtis.A
17-10	West Germany	L 1-5	Cologne	ECq	Curtis.A
21-11	Turkey	L 0-1	Izmir	ECq	
17-05-1980	England	W 4-1	Wrexham	HC	Thomas.M, Walsh, James.R, OG
21-05	Scotland	L 0-1	Glasgow	HC	
23-05	Nth. Ireland	L 0-1	Cardiff	HC	
2-06	Iceland	W 4-0	Reykjavik	WCq	Walsh 2, Giles, Flynn
15-10	Turkey	W 4-0	Cardiff	WCq	Flynn, James.L 2, Walsh
19-11	Czechoslovakia	W 1-0	Cardiff	WCq	Giles
24-02-1981	Rep. Ireland	W 3-1	Dublin	Fr	Price.P, Boyle, Yorath
25-03	Turkey	W 1-0	Ankara	WCq	Harris
16-05	Scotland	W 2-0	Swansea	HC	Walsh 2
20-05	England	D 0-0	London	HC	
30-05	Soviet Union	D 0-0	Wrexham	WCq	
9-09	Czechoslovakia	L 0-2	Prague	WCq	
14-10	Iceland	D 2-2	Swansea	WCq	James.R, Curtis.A
18-11	Soviet Union	L 0-3	Tbilisi	WCq	
24-03-1982	Spain	D 1-1	Valencia	Fr	James.R
27-04	England	L 0-1	Cardiff	HC	
24-05	Scotland	L 0-1	Glasgow	HC	
27-05	Nth. Ireland	W 3-0	Wrexham	HC	Curtis.A, Rush, Nicholas
2-06	France	W 1-0	Toulouse	Fr	Rush
22-09	Norway	W 1-0	Swansea	ECq	Rush
15-12	Yugoslavia	D 4-4	Titograd	ECq	Flynn, Rush, Jones.J (III), James.R
23-02-1983	England	L 1-2	London	HC	Rush
27-04	Bulgaria	W 1-0	Wrexham	ECq	Charles.J (II)
28-05	Scotland	L 0-2	Cardiff	HC	
31-05	Nth. Ireland	W 1-0	Belfast	HC	Davies.G
12-06	Brazil	D 1-1	Cardiff	Fr	Flynn
21-09	Norway	D 0-0	Oslo	ECq	
12-10	Romania	W 5-0	Wrexham	Fr	Rush 2, Thomas.M, James.R, Curtis.A
16-11	Bulgaria	L 0-1	Sofia	ECq	
14-12	Yugoslavia	D 1-1	Cardiff	ECq	James.R

28-02-1984	Scotland	L 1-2	Glasgow	HC	James.R
2-05	England	W 1-0	Wrexham	HC	Hughes
22-05	Nth. Ireland	D 1-1	Swansea	HC	Hughes
6-06	Norway	L 0-1	Trondheim	Fr	
10-06	Israel	D 0-0	Tel Aviv	Fr	
12-09	Iceland	L 0-1	Reykjavik	WCq	
17-10	Spain	L 0-3	Seville	WCq	
14-11	Iceland	W 2-1	Cardiff	WCq	Thomas.M, Hughes
26-02-1985	Norway	D 1-1	Wrexham	Fr	Rush
27-03	Scotland	W 1-0	Glasgow	WCq	Rush
30-04	Spain	W 3-0	Wrexham	WCq	Rush 2, Hughes
5-06	Norway	L 2-4	Bergen	Fr	Hughes, Lovell
10-09	Scotland	D 1-1	Cardiff	WCq	Hughes
16-10	Hungary	L 0-3	Cardiff	Fr	
25-02-1986	Saudi Arabia	W 2-1	Dhahran	Fr	Slatter, Davies.G
26-03	Rep. Ireland	W 1-0	Dublin	Fr	Rush
21-04	Uruguay	D 0-0	Wrexham	Fr	
10-05	Canada	L 0-2	Toronto	Fr	
19-05	Canada	W 3-0	Vancouver	Fr	Saunders 2, Allen
10-09	Finland	D 1-1	Helsinki	ECq	Slatter
18-02-1987	Soviet Union	D 0-0	Swansea	Fr	
1-04	Finland	W 4-0	Wrexham	ECq	Rush, Hodges, Phillips.D, Jones.A
29-04	Czechoslovakia	D 1-1	Wrexham	ECq	Rush
9-09	Denmark	W 1-0	Cardiff	ECq	Hughes
14-10	Denmark	L 0-1	Copenhagen	ECq	
11-11	Czechoslovakia	L 0-2	Prague	ECq	
23-03-1988	Yugoslavia	L 1-2	Swansea	Fr	Saunders
27-04	Sweden	L 1-4	Stockholm	Fr	Hodges
1-06	Malta	W 3-2	Ta'Qali	Fr	Rush, Hughes, Horne
4-06	Italy	W 1-0	Brescia	Fr	Rush
14-09	Holland	L 0-1	Amsterdam	WCq	
19-10	Finland	D 2-2	Swansea	WCq	Saunders, OG
8-02-1989	Israel	D 3-3	Tel-Aviv	Fr	Allen, Horne, OG
26-04	Sweden	L 0-2	Wrexham	Fr	
31-05	West Germany	D 0-0	Cardiff	WCq	
6-09	Finland	L 0-1	Helsinki	WCq	
11-10	Holland	L 1-2	Wrexham	WCq	Bowen
15-11	West Germany	L 1-2	Cologne	WCq	Allen
28-03-1990	Rep. Ireland	L 0-1	Dublin	Fr	
25-04	Sweden	L 2-4	Stockholm	Fr	Saunders 2
19-05	Costa Rica	W 1-0	Cardiff	Fr	Saunders
11-09	Denmark	L 0-1	Copenhagen	Fr	
17-10	Belgium	W 3-1	Cardiff	ECq	Rush, Saunders, Hughes
14-11	Luxembourg	W 1-0	Luxembourg	ECq	Rush
6-02-1991	Rep. Ireland	L 0-3	Wrexham	Fr	
27-03	Belgium	D 1-1	Brussels	ECq	Saunders
1-05	Iceland	W 1-0	Cardiff	Fr	Bodin
29-05	Poland	D 0-0	Radom	Fr	
5-06	Germany	W 1-0	Cardiff	ECq	Rush
11-09	Brazil	W 1-0	Cardiff	Fr	Saunders
16-10	Germany	L 1-4	Nuremberg	ECq	Bodin
13-11	Luxembourg	W 1-0	Cardiff	ECq	Bodin
19-02-1992	Rep. Ireland	W 1-0	Dublin	Fr	Pembridge
29-04	Austria	D 1-1	Vienna	Fr	Coleman
20-05	Romania	L 1-5	Bucharest	WCq	Rush
30-05	Holland	L 0-4	Utrecht	Fr	
3-06	Argentina	L 0-1	Gifu	KC	
7-06	Japan	W 1-0	Matsuyama	KC	Bowen
9-09	Faeroe Islands	W 6-0	Cardiff	WCq	Rush 3, Saunders, Bowen, Blackmore
14-10	Cyprus	W 1-0	Limassol	WCq	Hughes
18-11	Belgium	L 0-2	Brussels	WCq	
17-02-1993	Rep. Ireland	L 1-2	Dublin	Fr	Hughes
31-03	Belgium	W 2-0	Cardiff	WCq	Giggs, Rush
28-04	Czechoslovakia	D 1-1	Ostrava	WCq	Hughes
6-06	Faeroe Islands	W 3-0	Toftir	WCq	Saunders, Young, Rush
8-09	Czechoslovakia	D 2-2	Cardiff	WCq	Giggs, Rush
13-10	Cyprus	W 2-0	Cardiff	WCq	Saunders, Rush
17-11	Romania	L 1-2	Cardiff	WCq	Saunders
9-03-1994	Norway	L 1-3	Cardiff	Fr	Coleman
20-04	Sweden	L 0-2	Wrexham	Fr	
23-05	Estonia	W 2-1	Tallinn	Fr	Rush, Phillips.D

7-09	Albania	W 2-0	Cardiff	ECq	Coleman, Giggs
12-10	Moldova	L 2-3	Chisinau	ECq	
16-11	Georgia	L 0-5	Tbilisi	ECq	
14-12	Bulgaria	L 0-3	Cardiff	ECq	
29-03-1995	Bulgaria	L 1-3	Sofia	ECq	Saunders
26-04	Germany	D 1-1	Dusseldorf	ECq	Saunders
7-06	Georgia	L 0-1	Cardiff	ECq	

YUGOSLAVIA

Of the four Eastern bloc countries that have broken up since the fall of communism, Yugoslavia is the only name that survives to fight another day on the football field. But it is a much diminished state after its violent disintegration. Having once encompassed Slovenia, Croatia, Macedonia, Bosnia-Hercegovina, Montenegro, Vojvodina, Kosovo and Serbia, it now consists of only the last four. One of the first indications that such a collapse might happen came in the league games between Red Star Belgrade and Dinamo Zagreb in the years leading up to the civil war. These matches were constantly marred by fierce fighting between supporters of the Serbian Red Star and Croatian Dinamo, as the old nationalist tensions surfaced.

It proved to be the end of the road for a country loved the world over for its football. In the 1960s, the phrase 'often the bridesmaid but never the bride' summed up Yugoslavia's habit of finishing as runners-up rather than winners, but over the years they have dazzled the world with some beautiful football played by some of the world's most skilful players. Out of the bitterness of the civil war, football has returned, and in Croatia it is flourishing, but it is unlikely now that the national team of Yugoslavia will ever win that elusive title. Thrown out of the 1992 European Championships after qualifying, Yugoslavia were banned from international football until the end of 1994, and when they do make a return to competition one can only hope that they will not be drawn in the same group as any of their former territories.

As in all of the Balkan nations, the development of the game was held up by the turbulent nature of the region at the beginning of the century. Yugoslavia did not exist as a state until after the First World War and it is to this prewar situation that the country has returned. Split, the Adriatic seaport in Croatia, saw the first club when Hajduk Split were formed in 1911, named after local fighters who had resisted the Ottoman Empire in the previous century. It was eleven years before they could take part in a proper league. An association for the newly-formed state was founded in 1919 and a national league started four years later. The standard of the game was not particularly high and many of the clubs that took part in the new competition no longer exist.

In 1920 the Yugoslavs took on another newly-formed country, Czechoslovakia, in the Antwerp Olympic Games, but the difference in experience told as they lost 7-0. A 4-2 defeat at the hands of Egypt in the consolation tournament did little to raise spirits and it was not until the late 1920s that the team began to perform better. In the 1924 Olympic Games, Uruguay inflicted another 7-0 defeat on them, whilst in 1928 an inexperienced Portugal side made sure that it was three first round exits in a row in the the world's premier football tournament of the time. The 1930 World Cup saw the first signs of development. As one of only four European countries to make the trip to Uruguay, Yugoslavia did commendably well to reach the semi-finals, but although the victory over Brazil looks good on paper, the Brazilians were not performing well at the time and were certainly not of the same calibre as the sides after the war. That Yugoslavia's success in Montevideo was a flash in the pan was proved by their failure to qualify for both the 1934 and 1938 tournaments, after defeats by Romania and Poland respectively.

In the early 1930s, the Balkan Cup provided much of the international interest and Yugoslavia's record was generally good, coming second in the first three editions and winning the fourth in 1934. It was not until after the Second World War that the Yugoslavs really began to make progress and move ahead of their Balkan neighbours. The war had once again caused a rift in the country as a German-backed government was installed in Croatia. A Croatian team was even able to travel widely during the war years and play international matches against Germany and her allies.

As a communist state, Yugoslavia, reunited again, could have been expected to go the same way as all the other Eastern bloc countries, but like their president, Tito, in his politics, Yugoslav football followed a peculiarly independent line. In fact they could perhaps have done with some of the teamwork so renowned of the communist countries, for despite producing players with outstanding skill, the main criticism levelled was one of inconsistency, and it was this that led to so many runner-up positions.

After the war, club football was completely reorganised along the lines of that in the Soviet Union. In 1945 Gradanski Zagreb, the first ever champions, and their rivals HASK formed the basis of the Dinamo club that was to become a dominant power, whilst in Belgrade, BSK, champions on five occasions in the 1930s and along with Hajduk the oldest club in the country, were reorganised as OFK. A new army team called Partizan were formed in 1945 whilst perhaps the most famous team of them all, Crvena Zvezda or Red Star, were formed as the University club in the same year. These five clubs have dominated the league, and the new cup competition introduced in 1947, ever since.

The standard was quick to improve, though it was mainly for the achievements of the national side that the Yugoslavs became famous. As an 'amateur' country they entered the 1948 Olympic Games with their full international side, and by finishing as runners-up started a remarkable sequence. In four consecutive Olympic tournaments, the Yugoslav team appeared in the final. Hungary beat them 2-0 in Helsinki in the 1952 final, the Soviet Union won 1-0 in 1956 in Melbourne before at last, in the 1960 Rome Olympics, the gold medal was won. Their opponents that day were poor Denmark, who in turn collected their third silver medal after having lost in the 1908 and 1912 finals. That win was the only title at senior level to be won by the national side, but unfortunately it carries little weight due to the lack of any Western-based professionals in the tournament. Two months previously in a similarly depleted first European Championship, Yugoslavia attained their customary second place after losing 2-1 in the final to the Soviet Union in Paris, having beaten both Portugal and France along the way.

THE ORDER OF MERIT

		All			League			Cup		Europe		
	Team	G	S	B	G	S	B	G	S	G	S	B
1	**Crvena Zvedza Beograd**	35	20	11	20	10	7	14	9	1	1	4
2	**Partizan Beograd**	20	17	8	13	11	8	7	5	-	1	-
3	Hajduk Split	18	15	12	9	10	10	9	5	-	-	2
4	Dinamo Zagreb	13	21	7	4	12	6	8	8	1	1	1
5	**OFK Beograd**	9	6	5	5	6	4	4	-	-	-	1
6	Gradanski Zagreb	5	2	3	5	2	3	-	-	-	-	-
7	Velez Mostar	2	5	4	-	3	4	2	2	-	-	-
8	**Vojvodina Novi Sad**	2	4	5	2	3	5	-	1	-	-	-
9	FK Sarajevo	2	4	-	2	2	-	-	2	-	-	-
10	**Jugoslavia Beo.**	2	3	3	2	3	3	-	-	-	-	-
11	Concordia Zagreb	2	1	-	2	1	-	-	-	-	-	-
12	NK Rijeka	2	1	-	-	-	-	2	1	-	-	-
13	Zeljeznicar Sarajevo	1	2	3	1	1	2	-	1	-	-	1
14	Borac Banja Luka	1	1	-	-	-	-	1	1	-	-	-
15	HASK Zagreb	1	-	1	1	-	1	-	-	-	-	-
16	Vardar Skopje	1	-	-	-	-	-	1	-	-	-	-
17	**Buducnost Pod.**	-	2	-	-	-	-	-	2	-	-	-
	Nasa Krila Zem.	-	2	-	-	-	-	-	2	-	-	-
	Spartak Subotica	-	2	-	-	-	-	-	2	-	-	-
20	**Radnicki Beograd**	-	1	2	-	-	2	-	1	-	-	-
21	Slavia Sarajevo	-	1	1	-	1	1	-	-	-	-	-
	Sloboda Tuzla	-	1	1	-	-	1	-	1	-	-	-
23	**FK Bor**	-	1	-	-	-	-	-	1	-	-	-
	Obilic Beograd	-	1	-	-	-	-	-	1	-	-	-
	Olimpija Ljubljana	-	1	-	-	-	-	-	1	-	-	-
	SASK Sarajevo	-	1	-	-	1	-	-	-	-	-	-
	Trepca Mitrovica	-	1	-	-	-	-	-	1	-	-	-
	Varteks Varazdin	-	1	-	-	-	-	-	1	-	-	-
29	**Radnicki Nis**	-	-	3	-	-	2	-	-	-	-	1
30	Lokomotiva Zagreb	-	-	1	-	-	1	-	-	-	-	-
	Belgrade Sel. XI	-	-	1	-	-	-	-	-	-	-	1

To the end of the 1994-95 season.

Clubs in bold remain under the banner of Yugoslavia.

In the World Cup the habit was to reach the quarter-finals before bowing out to West Germany. This happened in both 1954 and 1958, but when they were paired with the Germans in the quarter-finals for the third successive tournament, in 1962 in Chile, it was third time lucky and they won 1-0. Czechoslovakia were generally considered the weaker of the two teams in the semi-finals, but once again a lack of consistency let Yugoslavia down as they lost 3-1 in Viña del Mar and had to settle for fourth place after losing the third place play-off to the hosts.

Many fine players represented Yugoslavia in these post-war years. Stejpan Bobek was instrumental in helping the team reach the first two Olympic finals, and the 38 goals he scored between 1946 and 1956 remains a record. Branco Zebec, a team-mate of Bobek for most of those years, was another great player and after he retired in 1961, his 65 caps remained a record for over 10 years until broken by Dragan Dzajic. The two most important goalscorers who took over the role vacated by Bobek were Milan Galic and Bora Kostic, the former falling just one short of his predecessor's goal tally. Both were key elements in both the Olympic triumph of 1960 and the second place in the European Championship of that year. The outstanding player of the time though was Dragoslav Sekularac, and it was he who inspired his team to fourth place in the World Cup in Chile.

The mid-1960s were not a very happy time for the national side and they did not make the journey to England for the 1966 World Cup. Two years later, though, they defeated the world champions England in the semi-finals of the European Championship to reach yet another final. Surprise, surprise, it ended in defeat, though it took the hosts Italy two games to seal the victory. The star of this side was Dzajic, the most capped Yugoslav of all time, but despite his presence in the side until the late 1970s Yugoslavia's form continued to baffle.

In 1970, for the second consecutive World Cup, the team failed to qualify. When they did in 1974, they were very disappointing despite reaching the second round and beating Zaire 9-0. The European Championships has always been a different story. They have never finished lower than second in their qualifying group and in 1976 had a glorious opportunity to win the tournament when it was staged in Yugoslavia. Home advantage could not be made to count and they lost to the powerful West Germany in the semi-final.

It is sad that just as the country was mounting a serious challenge for honours once again, it should have fallen apart to wreck these hopes. The 1991 win by Red Star in the European Cup, though not Yugoslavia's first in a European competition, was the first in the premier event. Despite a dreadful final, they had played some scintillating football to get that far and once again Yugoslav footballers have become the fashion. For years they had been in high demand with clubs in the West, but the federation was always able to control the exodus, in most cases not allowing them to leave until they were past their prime. The team which won the 1987 World Youth Championship contained some of the most talented players in Yugoslavia's history and it was on these that the upsurge in fortunes in the late eighties and early nineties was based. Most of them, however, were Croatians and they jumped ship at the first available opportunity. Under different circumstances, it could have been Yugoslavia rather than Denmark who emerged as European champions in 1992.

In 1992 the recognition of both Slovenia and Croatia as separate states saw both organising their first championship, with Macedonia following suit the year after. The withdrawal of the Croatian clubs effectively ended the Yugoslav championship in any recognisable form, and with the withdrawal of the Bosnian teams it has become very much a Serbian affair. The final ignominy for Yugoslav football came with the forced withdrawal of the national side from the 1992 European Championship finals. It marked a sad end to a proud footballing history at a time when Yugoslav football was perhaps at its strongest.

Population: 10,337,000
Area, sq km: 102,173
% in urban areas: 46.5%
Capital city: Belgrade

Fudbalski Savez Jugoslavije
PO Box 263
Terazije #35
11000 Belgrade
Yugoslavia
Tel: + 38 11 333447
Fax: + 38 11 333433

Year of formation	1919
Affiliation to FIFA	1919
Affiliation to UEFA	1954
Registered clubs	2699
Registered players	117 800
Registered referees	6665
National Stadium	No national stadium
National colours	Blue/White/Red
Reserve colours	White/White/White
Season	August - May

THE RECORD

WORLD CUP

1930	QT Automatic - Final Tournament/Semi-finalists
1934	QT 3rd/3 in group 10
1938	QT 2nd/2 in group 2
1950	QT 1st/3 in group 3 - Final Tournament/1st round
1954	QT 1st/3 in group 10 - Final Tournament/Quarter-finalists
1958	QT 1st/3 in group 7 - Final Tournament/Quarter-finalists
1962	QT 1st/4 in group 10 - Final Tournament/Semi-finalists/ 4th place
1966	QT 3rd/4 in group 3
1970	QT 2nd/4 in group 6
1974	QT 1st/3 in group 7 - Final Tournament/2nd round
1978	QT 3rd/3 in group 8
1982	QT 1st/5 in group 5 - Final Tournament/1st round
1986	QT 4th/5 in group 4
1990	QT 1st/5 in group 5 - Final Tournament/Quarter-finalists
1994	Did not compete

EUROPEAN CHAMPIONSHIP

1960	Finalists
1964	2nd round
1968	QT 1st/3 in group 4 - Final Tournament/Finalists
1972	QT 1st/4 in group 7 - Final Tournament/Quarter-finalists
1976	QT 1st/4 in group 3 - Final Tournament/Semi-finalists/ 4th place
1980	QT 2nd/4 in group 3
1984	QT 1st/4 in group 4 - Final Tournament/1st round
1988	QT 2nd/4 in group 4
1992	QT 1st/5 in group 4
1996	Did not compete

Dr Gero Cup

1929-53	Did not enter
1960	4th

EUROPEAN CLUB COMPETITIONS

European Cup
Winners - Crvena Zvezda Beograd 1991
Finalists - Partizan Beograd 1966
Cup Winners Cup
Semi-finalists - Dinamo Zagreb 1961 OFK Beograd 1963 Hajduk Split 1973 Crvena Zvezda Beograd 1975
UEFA Cup
Winners - Dinamo Zagreb 1967
Finalists - Dinamo Zagreb 1963 Crvena Zvezda Beograd 1979
Mitropa Cup
Semi-finalists - SK Beograd 1939

CLUB DIRECTORY

BELGRADE (Pop. - 1,400,000)
OFK Beograd (1911)
Omladinski 25,000 – White, blue trim
Previous names - BSK 1911-40 & 1950-57, Metalac 1940-50

FK Crvena Zvezda (Red Star) Beograd (1945)
Crvena Zvezda 97,000 – Red & white stripes/Red

FK Partizan Beograd (1945)
JNA 50,000 – Black & white stripes/White

FK Rad Beograd (1958)
Rad 13,000 – White/Red

NOVI SAD (Pop. - 266,000)
FK Vojvodina Novi Sad (1914)
Gradski 22,000 – Red & white halves/White
Previous name - Sloga 1945-51

PRISTINA (Pop. - 244,000)
FK Pristina (1922)
Gradski 30,000 – Blue/White

NIS (Pop. - 240,000)
FK Radnicki Nis (1923)
Cair 20,000 – Blue, white sleeves/Blue

SUBOTICA (Pop. - 153,000)
FK Spartak Subotica (1945)
Gradski 28,000 – Blue/Blue

PODGORICA (Pop. - 145,000)
FK Budocnost Podgorica (1925)
Pod Goricom 15,000 – Blue & white stripes/Blue
Previous name - FK Budocnost Titograd 1946-92

ZRENJANIN (Pop. - 140,000)
FK Proleter Zrenjanin (1947)
Karadordevom 33,000 – Red, white trim

BOR (Pop. - 56,000)
FK Bor (1934)
Borovo 15,000 – Blue/Blue

KRUSEVAK
Napredak Krusevak (1926)
Mladost 25,000 – Red/White

YUGOSLAV LEAGUE CHAMPIONSHIP

1923	Gradanski Zagreb 1-1 4-2 SASK Sarajevo
1924	Jugoslavia Beograd 2-1 Hajduk Split
1925	Jugoslavia Beograd 3-2 Gradanski Beograd
1926	Gradanski Zagreb 2-1 Jugoslavia Beograd
1927ac	Hajduk Split 8 BSK Beograd 6 HASK Zagreb 5
1928	Gradanski Zagreb 9 Hajduk Split 6 BSK Beograd 6
1929c	Hajduk Split 12 BSK Beograd 10 Jugoslavia Beograd 8
1930d	Concordia Zagreb 15 Jugoslavia Beograd 13 Hajduk Split 13
1931	BSK Beograd 20 Concordia Zagreb 11 Gradanski Zagreb 10
1932	Concordia Zagreb 2-1 2-1 Hajduk Split
1933i	BSK Beograd 31 Hajduk Split 28 Jugoslavia Beograd 23

1934	-
1935h	BSK Beograd 24 Jugoslavia Beograd 22 Gradanski Zagreb 22
1936	BSK Beograd 1-0 1-1 Slavia Sarajevo
1937h	Gradanski Zagreb 28 Hajduk Split 21 BSK Beograd 21
1938	HASK Zagreb 26 BSK Beograd 26 Gradanski Zagreb 25
1939k	BSK Beograd 37 Gradanski Zagreb 32 Jugoslavia Beograd 28
1940d	Gradanski Zagreb 16 BSK Beograd 15 Slavia Sarajevo 14
1941-46	-
1947n	Partizan Beograd 47 Dinamo Zagreb 42 Crvena Zvezda 39
1948h	Dinamo Zagreb 29 Hajduk Split 24 Partizan Beograd 24
1949	Partizan Beograd 29 Crvena Zvezda 26 Hajduk Split 25
1950	Hajduk Split 28 Crvena Zvezda 26 Partizan Beograd 26
1951k	Crvena Zvezda 35 Dinamo Zagreb 35 Hajduk Split 32
1952b	Hajduk Split 9 Crvena Zvezda 8 Lokomotiva Zagreb 4
1953k	Crvena Zvezda 31 Hajduk Split 29 Partizan Beograd 25
1954n	Dinamo Zagreb 42 Partizan Beograd 41 Crvena Zvezda 38
1955	Hajduk Split 38 BSK Beograd 36 Dinamo Zagreb 34
1956	Crvena Zvezda 40 Partizan Beograd 35 Radnicki Beograd 31
1957	Crvena Zvezda 39 Vojvodina Novi Sad 35 Hajduk Split 30
1958	Dinamo Zagreb 37 Partizan Beograd 33 Radnicki Beograd 28
1959k	Crvena Zvezda 31 Partizan Beograd 31 Vojvodina Novi Sad 30
1960	Crvena Zvezda 33 Dinamo Zagreb 32 Partizan Beograd 27
1961	Partizan Beograd 32 Crvena Zvezda 31 Hajduk Split 30
1962	Partizan Beograd 31 Vojvodina Novi Sad 26 Dinamo Zagreb 25
1963n	Partizan Beograd 40 Dinamo Zagreb 35 Zeljeznicar Sarajevo 29
1964	Crvena Zvezda 36 OFK Beograd 33 Dinamo Zagreb 33
1965p	Partizan Beograd 43 FK Sarajevo 35 Crvena Zvezda 35
1966q	Vojvodina Novi Sad 43 Dinamo Zagreb 35 Velez Mostar 35
1967	FK Sarajevo 42 Dinamo Zagreb 40 Partizan Beograd 38
1968	Crvena Zvezda 43 Partizan Beograd 38 Dinamo Zagreb 35
1969t	Crvena Zvezda 48 Dinamo Zagreb 45 Partizan Beograd 40
1970	Crvena Zvezda 46 Partizan Beograd 44 Velez Mostar 43
1971	Hajduk Split 49 Zeljeznicar Sarajevo 45 Dinamo Zagreb 43
1972	Zeljeznicar Sarajevo 51 Crvena Zvezda 49 OFK Beograd 45
1973	Crvena Zvezda 52 Velez Mostar 46 OFK Beograd 45
1974	Hajduk Split 45 Velez Mostar 45 Crvena Zvezda 43
1975	Hajduk Split 48 Vojvodina Novi Sad 45 Crvena Zvezda 40
1976	Partizan Beograd 50 Hajduk Split 49 Dinamo Zagreb 44
1977	Crvena Zvezda 50 Dinamo Zagreb 41 Sloboda Tuzla 39
1978	Partizan Beograd 54 Crvena Zvezda 49 Hajduk Split 39
1979	Hajduk Split 50 Dinamo Zagreb 50 Crvena Zvezda 41
1980	Crvena Zvezda 48 FK Sarajevo 41 Radnicki Nis 39
1981	Crvena Zvezda 44 Hajduk Split 42 Radnicki Nis 41
1982	Dinamo Zagreb 49 Crvena Zvezda 44 Hajduk Split 44
1983	Partizan Beograd 45 Dinamo Zagreb 43 Hajduk Split 43
1984	Crvena Zvezda 44 Partizan Beograd 42 Zeljeznicar Sarajevo 42
1985	FK Sarajevo 48 Hajduk Split 44 Partizan Beograd 39
1986	Partizan Beograd 47 Crvena Zvezda 47 Velez Mostar 39
1987	Partizan Beograd 43 Velez Mostar 42 Crvena Zvezda 41
1988	Crvena Zvezda 45 Partizan Beograd 44 Velez Mostar 42
1989t3	Vojvodina Novi Sad 41 Crvena Zvezda 38 Hajduk Split 36
1990	Crvena Zvezda 51 Dinamo Zagreb 42 Hajduk Split 38
1991u7	Crvena Zvezda 54 Dinamo Zagreb 46 Partizan Beograd 41
1992s2	Crvena Zvezda 50 Partizan Beograd 46 Vojvodina Novi Sad 42
1993	Partizan Beograd 65 Crvena Zvezda 51 Vojvodina Novi Sad 46
1994u12	Partizan Beograd 42 Crvena Zvezda 37 Vojvodina Novi Sad 31
1995	Crvena Zvezda 42 Partizan Beograd 38 Vojvodina Novi Sad 37

YUGOSLAV CUP FINALS

1947	Partizan Beograd	2-0	Nasa Krila Zemun
1948	Crvena Zvezda	3-0	Partizan Beograd
1949	Crvena Zvezda	3-2	Nasa Krila Zemun
1950	Crvena Zvezda	1-1 3-0	Dinamo Zagreb
1951	Dinamo Zagreb	2-0 2-0	Vojvodina Novi Sad
1952	Partizan Beograd	6-0	Crvena Zvezda
1953	BSK Beograd	2-0	Hajduk Split
1954	Partizan Beograd	4-1	Crvena Zvezda
1955	BSK Beograd	2-0	Hajduk Split
1956	-		
1957	Partizan Beograd	5-3	Radnicki Belgrade
1958	Crvena Zvezda	4-0	Velez Mostar
1959	Crvena Zvezda	3-1	Partizan Belgrade
1960	Dinamo Zagreb	3-2	Partizan Beograd
1961	Vardar Skopje	2-1	Varteks Varazdin
1962	OFK Beograd	4-1	Spartak Subotica
1963	Dinamo Zagreb	4-1	Hajduk Split
1964	Crvena Zvezda	3-0	Dinamo Zagreb
1965	Dinamo Zagreb	2-1	Buducnost Titograd
1966	OFK Beograd	6-2	Dinamo Zagreb
1967	Hajduk Split	2-1	FK Sarajevo
1968	Crvena Zvezda	7-0	FK Bor
1969	Dinamo Zagreb	3-3 3-0	Hajduk Split
1970	Crvena Zvezda	2-2 1-0	Olimpija Ljubljana
1971	Crvena Zvezda	2-0 4-0	Sloboda Tuzla
1972	Hajduk Split	2-1	Dinamo Zagreb
1973	Dinamo Zagreb	2-1	Crvena Zvezda
1974	Hajduk Split	1-1 2-1	Crvena Zvezda
1975	Hajduk Split	1-0	Borac Banja Luka
1976	Hajduk Split	1-0	Dinamo Zagreb
1977	Hajduk Split	2-0	Buducnost Titograd
1978	NK Rijeka	1-0	Trepca Mitrovica
1979	NK Rijeka	0-0 2-1	Partizan Beograd
1980	Dinamo Zagreb	1-1 1-0	Crvena Zvezda
1981	Velez Mostar	3-2	Zeljeznicar Sarajevo
1982	Crvena Zvezda	2-2 4-2	Dinamo Zagreb
1983	Dinamo Zagreb	3-2	FK Sarajevo
1984	Hajduk Split	0-0 2-1	Crvena Zvezda
1985	Crvena Zvezda	1-1 2-1	Dinamo Zagreb
1986	Velez Mostar	3-1	Dinamo Zagreb
1987	Hajduk Split	1-1 9-8p	NK Rijeka
1988	Borac Banja Luka	1-0	Crvena Zvezda
1989	Partizan Beograd	6-1	Velez Mostar
1990	Crvena Zvezda	1-0	Hajduk Split
1991	Hajduk Split	1-0	Crvena Zvezda
1992	Partizan Beograd	1-0 2-2	Crvena Zvezda
1993	Crvena Zvezda	0-1 1-0 5-4p	Partizan Beograd
1994	Partizan Beograd	3-2 6-1	Spartak Subotica
1995	Crvena Zvezda	4-0 0-0	Obilic Beograd

LEADING INTERNATIONAL GOALSCORERS

38	Stjepan Bobek	(Partizan)	1946-1956
37	Milan Galic	(Partizan)	1959-1965
36	Blagoje Marjanovic	(BSK Beograd)	1926-1938
32	Rajko Mitic	(Crvena Zvezda)	1946-1957
29	Dusan Bajevic	(Velez Mostar)	1970-1977
28	Todor Veselinovic	(Vojvodina)	1953-1961
26	Bora Kostic	(Crvena Zvezda)	1956-1963
24	Zlatko Vujovic	(Hajduk Split,Bordeaux, Cannes,Paris SG)	1979-1990
23	Dragan Dzajic	(Crvena Zvezda,SEC Bastia)	1964-1979
22	Bernard Vukas	(Hajduk Split)	1948-1957

LEADING INTERNATIONAL APPEARANCES

85 Dragan Dzajic	(Crvena Zvezda,SEC Bastia)	1964-1979
70 Zlatko Vujovic	(Hajduk Split,Bordeaux, Cannes,Paris SG)	1979-1990
65 Branko Zebec	(Borac Zagreb,Partizan, Crvena Zvezda)	1951-1961
63 Stjepan Bobek	(Partizan)	1946-1956
61 Faruk Hadzibegic	(FK Sarajevo,Real Betis, Sochaux)	1982-1992
61 Branko Stankovic	(Crvena Zvezda)	1946-1956
60 Ivan Horvat	(Dinamo Zagreb)	1946-1956
59 Bernard Vukas	(Hajduk Split)	1948-1957
59 Rajko Mitic	(Crvena Zvezda)	1946-1957
59 Vladimir Beara #	(Hajduk Split,Crvena Zvezda)	1950-1959

INTERNATIONAL MATCHES PLAYED BY YUGOSLAVIA

28-08-1920	Czechoslovakia	L 0-7	Antwerp	OGr1	
2-09	Egypt	L 2-4	Antwerp	OGct	Dubravcic, Ruzic
28-10-1921	Czechoslovakia	L 1-6	Prague	Fr	Zinaja
8-06-1922	Romania	L 1-2	Belgrade	Fr	Sifer
28-06	Czechoslovakia	W 4-3	Zagreb	Fr	Saraz-Abraham 2, Zinaja 2
1-10	Poland	L 1-3	Zagreb	Fr	Vinek
3-06-1923	Poland	W 2-1	Krakow	Fr	Perska, Zinaja
10-06	Romania	W 2-1	Bucharest	Fr	Vinek 2
28-10	Czechoslovakia	D 4-4	Prague	Fr	Jovanovic 2, Petkovic, Babic
10-02-1924	Austria	L 1-4	Zagreb	Fr	Jovanovic
26-05	Uruguay	L 0-7	Paris	OGr1	
28-09	Czechoslovakia	L 0-2	Zagreb	Fr	
28-10-1925	Czechoslovakia	L 0-7	Prague	Fr	
4-11	Italy	L 1-2	Padua	Fr	Bencic
30-05-1926	Bulgaria	W 3-1	Zagreb	Fr	Cindric 3
13-06	France	L 1-4	Paris	Fr	Bonacic.M
28-06	Czechoslovakia	L 2-6	Zagreb	Fr	Giler, Petkovic
3-10	Romania	L 2-3	Zagreb	Fr	Percl 2
10-04-1927	Hungary	L 0-3	Budapest	Fr	
10-05	Romania	W 3-0	Bucharest	Fr	Luburic, Bonacic.A, Giler
15-05	Bulgaria	W 2-0	Sofia	Fr	Marjanovic 2
31-07	Czechoslovakia	D 1-1	Belgrade	Fr	Perska
28-10	Czechoslovakia	L 3-5	Prague	Fr	Bencic, Bonacic.M, Jovanovic
25-03-1928	Hungary	L 1-2	Budapest	Fr	
8-04	Turkey	W 2-1	Zagreb	Fr	Babic, Giler
6-05	Romania	W 3-1	Belgrade	Fr	Sotirovic 2, Marjanovic
29-05	Portugal	L 1-2	Amsterdam	OGr1	Bonacic.M
28-10	Czechoslovakia	L 1-7	Prague	Fr	Beleslin
10-05-1929	Romania	W 3-2	Bucharest	Fr	Pavelic, Hitrec, Lemesic
19-05	France	W 3-1	Paris	Fr	Hitrec, Marjanovic, Lajnert
28-06	Czechoslovakia	D 3-3	Zagreb	Fr	Marjanovic 2, Hitrec
6-10	Romania	L 1-2	Bucharest	BC	Marjanovic
28-10	Czechoslovakia	L 3-4	Prague	Fr	Hitrec 2, Lajnert
26-01-1930	Greece	L 1-2	Athens	BC	Vujadinovic
13-04	Bulgaria	W 6-1	Belgrade	Fr	Vujadinovic 2, Marjanovic 2, Tirnanic, Hrnjicek
4-05	Romania	W 2-1	Belgrade	Fr	Premeri, Bonacic.A
15-06	Bulgaria	D 2-2	Sofia	Fr	Tirnanic, Najdanovic
14-07	Brazil	W 2-1	Montevideo	WCr1	Tirnanic, Bek
17-07	Bolivia	W 4-0	Montevideo	WCr1	Bek 2, Marjanovic, Vujadinovic
27-07	Uruguay	L 1-6	Montevideo	WCsf	Vujadinovic
3-08	Argentina	L 1-3	Buenos Aires	Fr	Marjanovic
10-08	Brazil	L 1-4	Rio de Janeiro	Fr	
16-11	Bulgaria	W 3-0	Sofia	BC	Lemesic, Marjanovic, Praunsberger
15-03-1931	Greece	W 4-1	Belgrade	BC	Tomasevic 3, Hitrec
19-04	Bulgaria	W 1-0	Belgrade	BC	Marjanovic
21-05	Hungary	W 3-2	Belgrade	Fr	Marjanovic, Hitrec, Lemesic
28-06	Romania	L 2-4	Zagreb	BC	Zecevic, Marjanovic
2-08	Czechoslovakia	W 2-1	Belgrade	Fr	Zivkovic, Marjanovic
2-10	Turkey	L 0-2	Sofia	Fr	
4-10	Bulgaria	L 2-3	Sofia	Fr	Tirnanic, Marjanovic
25-10	Poland	L 3-6	Poznan	Fr	Bek 2, Hitrec
24-04-1932	Spain	L 1-2	Oviedo	Fr	Vujadinovic
3-05	Portugal	L 2-3	Lisbon	Fr	Vujadinovic 2
29-05	Poland	L 0-3	Zagreb	Fr	
5-06	France	W 2-1	Belgrade	Fr	Glisovic 2
26-06	Greece	W 7-1	Belgrade	BC	Zivkovic 2, Zecevic 2, Tirnanic, Vujadinovic, Glisovic
30-06	Bulgaria	L 2-3	Belgrade	BC	Zivkovic 2
3-07	Romania	W 3-1	Belgrade	BC	Zecevic, Zivkovic, Vujadinovic

9-10	Czechoslovakia	L 1-2	Prague	Fr	Zivkovic
30-04-1933	Spain	D 1-1	Belgrade	Fr	Marjanovic
7-05	Switzerland	L 1-4	Zurich	Fr	Hitric
3-06	Greece	W 5-3	Bucharest	BC	Kodrnja 3, Zivkovic 2
7-06	Bulgaria	W 4-0	Bucharest	BC	Kokotovic 3, Zivkovic
11-06	Romania	L 0-5	Bucharest	BC	
6-08	Czechoslovakia	W 2-1	Zagreb	Fr	Kragic, Kodrnja
10-09	Poland	L 3-4	Warsaw	Fr	Vujadinovic 2, Tirnanic
24-09	Switzerland	D 2-2	Belgrade	WCq	Marjanovic, Kragic
18-03-1934	Bulgaria	W 2-1	Sofia	Fr	Marjanovic 2
1-04	Bulgaria	L 2-3	Belgrade	Fr	Kragic, Zivkovic
29-04	Romania	L 1-2	Bucharest	WCq	Kragic
3-06	Brazil	W 8-4	Belgrade	Fr	Marjanovic 3, Glisovic 2, Stevovic, Tirnanic, Petrak
26-08	Poland	W 4-1	Belgrade	Fr	Sekulic 3, Marjanovic
2-09	Czechoslovakia	L 1-3	Prague	Fr	Sekulic
16-12	France	L 2-3	Paris	Fr	Marjanovic, Vujadinovic
23-12	Greece	L 1-2	Athens	BC	Sekulic
25-12	Bulgaria	W 4-3	Athens	BC	Tirnanic 2, Sekulic, Tomasevic
1-01-1935	Romania	W 4-0	Athens	BC	Tomasevic 2, Tiranic, Marjanovic
17-06	Romania	W 2-0	Sofia	BC	Marjanovic, Sekulic
21-06	Greece	W 6-1	Sofia	BC	Zivkovic 2, Glisovic 2, Marjanovic, Vujadinovic
24-06	Bulgaria	D 3-3	Sofia	BC	Vujadinovic 2, Marjanovic
18-08	Poland	W 3-2	Katowice	Fr	Zivkovic 2, Sekulic
6-09	Czechoslovakia	D 0-0	Belgrade	Fr	
10-05-1936	Romania	L 2-3	Bucharest	Fr	Vujadinovic, Tomasevic
12-07	Turkey	D 3-3	Istanbul	Fr	Marjanovic, Tirnanic, Tomasevic
6-09	Poland	W 9-3	Belgrade	Fr	Marjanovic 4, Bozovic 2, Perlic 2, Tirnanic
13-12	France	L 0-1	Paris	Fr	
9-05-1937	Hungary	D 1-1	Budapest	Fr	Lesnik
6-06	Belgium	D 1-1	Belgrade	Fr	Lesnik
11-07	Bulgaria	L 0-4	Sofia	Fr	
1-08	Turkey	W 3-1	Belgrade	Fr	Plese, Bozovic, Lesnik
6-09	Romania	W 2-1	Belgrade	Fr	Vujadinovic, Lesnik
3-10	Czechoslovakia	L 4-5	Prague	Fr	Plese 2, Valjarevic, OG
10-10	Poland	L 0-4	Warsaw	WCq	
3-04-1938	Poland	W 1-0	Belgrade	WCq	Marjanovic
8-05	Romania	W 1-0	Bucharest	Fr	Matosic
22-05	Italy	L 0-4	Genoa	Fr	
29-05	Belgium	D 2-2	Brussels	Fr	Petrovic, Matosic
28-08	Czechoslovakia	L 1-3	Zagreb	Fr	Sipos
6-09	Romania	D 1-1	Belgrade	Fr	Petrovic
25-09	Poland	D 4-4	Warsaw	Fr	Velfl 2, Velker, Kokotovic
26-02-1939	Germany	L 2-3	Berlin	Fr	Petrovic, Klodt
7-05	Romania	L 0-1	Bucharest	Fr	
18-05	England	W 2-1	Belgrade	Fr	Glisovic, Perlic
4-06	Italy	L 1-2	Belgrade	Fr	Petrovic
15-10	Germany	L 1-5	Zagreb	Fr	Antolkovic
12-11	Hungary	L 0-2	Belgrade	Fr	
31-03-1940	Romania	D 3-3	Bucharest	Fr	Valjarevic 2, Bozovic
14-04	Germany	W 2-1	Vienna	Fr	Glisovic, Velfl
22-09	Romania	L 1-2	Belgrade	Fr	Petrovic
29-09	Hungary	D 0-0	Budapest	Fr	
3-11	Germany	W 2-0	Zagreb	Fr	Bozovic, Cimerancic
23-03-1941	Hungary	D 1-1	Belgrade	Fr	Valjarevik
9-05-1946	Czechoslovakia	W 2-0	Prague	Fr	Tomasevic, Mitic
29-09	Czechoslovakia	W 4-2	Belgrade	Fr	Matosic 2, Mitic, Bobek
7-10	Albania	W 3-2	Tirana	BC	Matosic, Bobek, Cajkovski
11-10	Romania	L 1-2	Tirana	BC	Simonovski
13-10	Bulgaria	W 2-1	Tirana	BC	Sandic 2
11-05-1947	Czechoslovakia	L 1-3	Prague	Fr	Bobek
22-06	Romania	W 3-1	Bucharest	BCE	Bobek 2, Jezerkic
29-06	Hungary	L 2-3	Belgrade	BCE	Cimermancic, Mihajlovic
14-09	Albania	W 4-2	Tirana	BCE	Bobek, Mitic, Krnic, Cimermancic
12-10	Bulgaria	W 2-1	Zagreb	BCE	Mihajlovic 2
19-10	Poland	W 7-1	Belgrade	Fr	Jezerkic 4, Bobek 2, Mitic
27-06-1948	Albania	D 0-0	Belgrade	BCE	
4-07	Bulgaria	W 3-1	Sofia	BCE	Velfl, Mitic, Cajkovski
31-07	Luxembourg	W 6-1	London	OGr1	Cajkovski 2, Stankovic, Mihajlovic, Mitic, Bobek
5-08	Turkey	W 3-1	London	OGqf	Cajkovski, Bobek, Velfl
11-08	Great Britain*	W 3-1	London	OGsf	Mitic, Bobek, Velfl
13-08	Sweden	L 1-3	London	OGf	Bobek

25-08	Poland	W 1-0	Warsaw	BCE	Mitic
19-06-1949	Norway	W 3-1	Oslo	Fr	Mitic, Bobek, Cajkovski
21-08	Israel	W 6-0	Belgrade	WCq	Pajevic 3, Sencar, Cajkovski, Bobek
18-09	Israel	W 5-2	Tel Aviv	WCq	Valok 2, Bobek, Cajkovski, Cajkovski
9-10	France	D 1-1	Belgrade	WCq	Cajkovski
30-10	France	D 1-1	Paris	WCq	Bobek
13-11	Austria	L 2-5	Belgrade	Fr	Cajkovski, Bobek
11-12	France	W 3-2	Florence	WCq	Mihajlovic 2, Cajkovski
28-05-1950	Denmark	W 5-1	Belgrade	Fr	Mitic 3, Vukas, Hocevar
11-06	Switzerland	W 4-0	Berne	Fr	Cajkovski, Tomasevic, Bobek, Atanackovic
25-06	Switzerland	W 3-0	Belo Horizonte	WCr1	Mitic, Tomasevic, Ognjanov
29-06	Mexico	W 4-1	Porto Alegre	WCr1	Cajkovski 2, Bobek, Tomasevic
1-07	Brazil	L 0-2	Rio de Janeiro	WCr1	
3-09	Sweden	W 2-1	Stockholm	Fr	Valok, Herceg
7-09	Finland	L 2-3	Helsinki	Fr	Bobek, Vukas
10-09	Denmark	W 4-1	Copenhagen	Fr	Zivanovic, Bobek, Mitic, Herceg
8-10	Austria	L 2-7	Vienna	Fr	Mitic, Zivanovic
5-11	Norway	W 4-0	Belgrade	Fr	Ognjanov 2, Mitic, Rupnik
22-11	England	D 2-2	London	Fr	Zivanovic, OG
6-02-1951	France	L 1-2	Paris	Fr	Tomasevic
6-05	Italy	D 0-0	Milan	Fr	
24-06	Switzerland	W 7-3	Belgrade	Fr	Bobek 2, Mitic 2, Zebec 2, Rajkov
23-08	Norway	W 4-2	Oslo	Fr	Bobek 2, Vukas, Zebec
2-09	Sweden	W 2-1	Belgrade	Fr	Bobek, Ognjanov
25-06-1952	Norway	W 4-1	Zagreb	Fr	Vukas 2, Mitic, Zebec
15-07	India	W 10-1	Helsinki	OGr1	Zebec 4, Mitic 3, Vukas 2, Ognjanov
20-07	Soviet Union	D 5-5	Tampere	OGr2	Zebec 2, Ognjanov, Mitic, Bobek
22-07	Soviet Union	W 3-1	Tampere	OGr2	Mitic, Bobek, Cajkovski
25-07	Denmark	W 5-3	Helsinki	OGqf	Cajkovski, Bobek, Zebec, Ognjanovic, Vukas
29-07	West Germany*	W 3-1	Helsiki	OGsf	Mitic 2, Cajkovski
2-08	Hungary	L 0-2	Helsinki	OGf	
21-09	Austria	W 4-2	Belgrade	Fr	Bobek 3, Vukas
2-11	Egypt	W 5-0	Belgrade	Fr	Jocic 2, Rajkov, Cocic, Vukas
21-12	West Germany	L 2-3	Ludwigshafen	Fr	Cajkovski, Bobek
16-01-1953	Egypt	W 3-1	Cairo	Fr	Vukas 2, Mitic
9-05	Greece	W 1-0	Belgrade	WCq	Matosic
14-05	Belgium	W 3-1	Brussels	Fr	Vukas 2, Rajkov
21-05	Wales	W 5-2	Belgrade	Fr	Mitic 3, Vukas, Rajkov
5-06	Turkey	D 2-2	Istanbul	Fr	Rajkov, Mitic
18-10	France	W 3-1	Zagreb	Fr	Veselinovic, Rajkov, Dvornic
8-11	Israel	W 1-0	Skoplje	WCq	Milutinovic
21-03-1954	Israel	W 1-0	Tel Aviv	WCq	Zebec
28-03	Greece	W 1-0	Athens	WCq	Veselinovic
9-05	Belgium	L 0-2	Zagreb	Fr	
16-05	England	W 1-0	Belgrade	Fr	Mitic
16-06	France	W 1-0	Lausanne	WCr1	Milutinovic
19-06	Brazil	D 1-1	Lausanne	WCr1	Zebec
27-06	West Germany	L 0-2	Geneva	WCqf	
22-09	Wales	W 3-1	Cardiff	Fr	Veselinovic 3
26-09	Saar	W 5-1	Saarbrucken	Fr	Vukas 3, Bobek, Veselinovic
3-10	Austria	D 2-2	Vienna	Fr	Stankovic, Bobek
17-10	Turkey	W 5-1	Sarajevo	Fr	Bobek 3, Pasic, Markovic
15-05-1955	Scotland	D 2-2	Belgrade	Fr	Veselinovic, Vukas
29-05	Italy	W 4-0	Turin	DGC	Veselinovic, Zebec, Vukas, OG
26-06	Switzerland	D 0-0	Belgrade	DGC	
25-09	West Germany	W 3-1	Belgrade	Fr	Milutinovic, Rajkov, Veselinovic
19-10	Rep. Ireland	W 4-1	Dublin	Fr	Milutinovic 3, Veselinovic
30-10	Austria	L 1-2	Vienna	DGC	Milutinovic
11-11	France	D 1-1	Paris	Fr	Veselinovic
22-04-1956	Romania	L 0-1	Belgrade	Fr	
29-04	Hungary	D 2-2	Budapest	DGC	Vukas, Veselinovic
17-06	Austria	D 1-1	Zagreb	DGC	Rajkov
9-09	Indonesia	W 4-2	Belgrade	Fr	Milutinovic 3, Kostic
16-09	Hungary	L 1-3	Belgrade	DGC	Petakovic
30-09	Czechoslovakia	L 1-2	Belgrade	DGC	Stankovic
21-11	Scotland	L 0-2	Glasgow	Fr	
28-11	England	L 0-3	London	Fr	
28-11	United States	W 9-1	Melbourne	OGqf	Mujic 3, Veselinovic 3, Antic 2, Papec
4-12	India	W 4-1	Melbourne	OGsf	Papec 2, Veselinovic, OG
8-12	Soviet Union	L 0-1	Melbourne	OGf	
23-12	Indonesia	W 5-1	Djarkarta	Fr	Veselinovic 2, Liposinovic, Papec, Radovic

5-05-1957	Greece	D 0-0	Athens	WCq	
12-05	Italy	W 6-1	Zagreb	DGC	Milutinovic 2, Zebec, Liposinovic, Rajkov, Vukas
18-05	Czechoslovakia	L 0-1	Bratislava	DGC	
15-09	Austria	D 3-3	Belgrade	Fr	Rajkov, Milutinovic, OG
29-09	Romania	D 1-1	Bucharest	WCq	Mujic
10-11	Greece	W 4-1	Belgrade	WCq	Mujic 2, Petakovic, Krstic
17-11	Romania	W 2-0	Belgrade	WCq	Milutinovic 2
20-04-1958	Hungary	L 0-2	Budapest	Fr	
11-05	England	W 5-0	Belgrade	Fr	Petakovic 3, Milutinovic, Veselinovic
8-06	Scotland	D 1-1	Vasteras	WCr1	Petakovic
11-06	France	W 3-2	Vasteras	WCr1	Veselinovic 2, Petakovic
15-06	Paraguay	D 3-3	Eskilstuna	WCr1	Ognjanovic, Veselinovic, Rajkov
19-06	West Germany	L 0-1	Malmo	WCqf	
14-09	Austria	W 4-3	Vienna	Fr	Veselinovic 3, Mujic
5-10	Hungary	D 4-4	Zagreb	Fr	Zebec 2, Petakovic, Veselinovic
19-04-1959	Hungary	L 0-4	Budapest	Fr	
26-04	Switzerland	W 5-1	Basle	DGC	Sekularac 2, Veselinovic 2, Liposinovic
31-05	Bulgaria	W 2-0	Belgrade	ECr1	Galic, Tasic
11-10	Hungary	L 2-4	Belgrade	Fr	Mujic, Kostic
21-10	Israel	D 2-2	Tel Aviv	OGq	Kostic 2
25-10	Bulgaria	D 1-1	Sofia	ECr1	Mujic
15-11	Greece	W 4-0	Belgrade	OGq	Mujic 2, Mihajlovic, Kostic
20-12	West Germany	D 1-1	Hanover	Fr	Mujic
1-01-1960	Morocco	W 5-0	Casablanca	Fr	Kostic 2, Mihajlovic, Maravic, Ankovic
3-01	Tunisia	W 5-1	Tunis	Fr	Kostic, Knez, Maravic, Mihajlovic, Cebinac
8-01	Egypt	W 1-0	Cairo	Fr	Mihajlovic
10-04	Israel	L 1-2	Belgrade	OGq	Mujic
24-04	Greece	W 5-0	Athens	OGq	Kostic, Zanetic, Takac, Galic, Knez
8-05	Portugal	L 1-2	Lisbon	ECqf	Kostic
11-05	England	D 3-3	London	Fr	Galic 2, Kostic
22-05	Portugal	W 5-1	Belgrade	ECqf	Kostic 2, Sekularac, Cebinac, Galic
6-07	France	W 5-4	Paris	ECsf	Jerkovic 2, Galic, Zanetic, Knez
10-07	Soviet Union	L 1-2	Paris	ECf	Galic
6-08	Tunisia	W 7-0	Belgrade	Fr	Knez 3, Kostic 2, Galic, Maravic
26-08	Egypt	W 6-1	Pescara	OGr1	Kostic 4, Galic, Knez
29-08	Turkey *	W 4-0	Florence	OGr1	Kostic 2, Galic, Knez
1-09	Bulgaria	D 3-3	Rome	OGr1	Galic 3
5-09	Italy *	D 1-1	Naples	OGsf	Galic
10-09	Denmark	W 3-1	Rome	OGf	Galic, Matus, Kostic
9-10	Hungary	D 1-1	Budapest	Fr	Kostic
7-05-1961	Hungary	L 2-4	Belgrade	Fr	Kostic, Matus
4-06	Poland	W 2-1	Belgrade	WCq	Kaloperovic, Kostic
18-06	Morocco	W 3-2	Belgrade	Fr	Mujic 2, Matus
25-06	Poland	D 1-1	Chorzow	WCq	Galic
8-10	South Korea	W 5-1	Belgrade	WCq	Sekularac 2, Cebinac, Radakovic, Galic
19-11	Austria	W 2-1	Zagreb	Fr	Jerkovic 2
26-11	South Korea	W 3-1	Seoul	WCq	Galic 2, Jerkovic
29-11	Japan	W 1-0	Tokyo	Fr	Cebinac
2-12	Hong Kong	W 2-1	Hong Kong	Fr	Mujic, Bego
7-12	Indonesia	W 5-1	Djakarta	Fr	Radakovic, Galic, Sekularac, Mujic, Bego
14-12	Israel	W 2-0	Tel Aviv	Fr	Galic 2
16-05-1962	East Germany	W 3-1	Belgrade	Fr	Galic 2, Skoblar
31-05	Soviet Union	L 0-2	Arica	WCr1	
2-06	Uruguay	W 3-1	Arica	WCr1	Skoblar, Galic, Jerkovic
7-06	Colombia	W 5-0	Arica	WCr1	Galic 2, Jerkovic 2, Melic
10-06	West Germany	W 1-0	Santiago	WCqf	Radakovic
13-06	Czechoslovakia	L 1-3	Viña del Mar	WCsf	Jerkovic
16-06	Chile	L 0-1	Santiago	WC3p	
16-09	East Germany	D 2-2	Leipzig	Fr	Zambata, Jerkovic
19-09	Ethiopia	W 5-2	Belgrade	Fr	Matus 2, Zambata 2, Lukaric
30-09	West Germany	L 2-3	Zagreb	Fr	Galic 2
14-10	Hungary	W 1-0	Budapest	Fr	Galic
4-11	Belgium	W 3-2	Belgrade	ECr1	Skoblar 2, Vasovic
31-03-1963	Belgium	W 1-0	Brussels	ECr1	Galic
19-06	Sweden	D 0-0	Belgrade	ECr2	
18-09	Sweden	L 2-3	Malmo	ECr2	Galic, Zambata
6-10	Hungary	W 2-0	Belgrade	Fr	Skoblar, Samardzic
27-10	Romania	L 1-2	Bucharest	Fr	Smailovic
3-11	Czechoslovakia	W 2-0	Zagreb	Fr	Zambata, Skoblar
17-05-1964	Czechoslovakia	W 3-2	Prague	Fr	Skoblar, Samardzic, Zambata
17-06	Romania	L 1-2	Belgrade	Fr	Takac

20-09	Luxembourg	W 3-1	Belgrade	WCq	Kovacevic, Jerkovic, Galic
27-09	Austria	L 2-3	Vienna	Fr	Melic, Skoblar
13-10	Morocco	W 3-1	Tokyo	OGr1	Belin 2, Samardzic
15-10	Hungary *	L 5-6	Tokyo	OGr1	Belin 2, Osim 2, Zambata
18-10	East Germany *	L 0-1	Tokyo	OGqf	
20-10	Japan	W 6-1	Osaka	OG5p	Zambata 4, Osim 2
22-10	Romania	L 0-3	Osaka	OG5p	
25-10	Hungary	L 1-2	Budapest	Fr	Skoblar
28-10	Israel	L 0-2	Tel Aviv	Fr	
22-11	Soviet Union	D 1-1	Belgrade	Fr	Zambata
18-04-1965	France	W 1-0	Belgrade	WCq	Galic
9-05	England	D 1-1	Belgrade	Fr	Kovacevic
16-06	Norway	L 0-3	Oslo	WCq	
4-09	Soviet Union	D 0-0	Moscow	Fr	
19-09	Luxembourg	W 5-2	Luxembourg	WCq	Galic 2, Dzajic 2, Musovic
9-10	France	L 0-1	Paris	WCq	
7-11	Norway	D 1-1	Belgrade	WCq	Vasovic
4-05-1966	England	L 0-2	London	Fr	
8-05	Hungary	W 2-0	Zagreb	Fr	Gugleta, Skoblar
1-06	Bulgaria	L 0-2	Belgrade	Fr	
23-06	West Germany	L 0-2	Hanover	Fr	
27-06	Sweden	D 1-1	Malmo	Fr	Santrac
18-09	Soviet Union	L 1-2	Belgrade	Fr	Musovic
12-10	Israel	W 3-1	Tel Aviv	Fr	Bukal 2, Zambata
19-10	Czechoslovakia	W 1-0	Belgrade	Fr	Dzajic
6-11	Bulgaria	L 1-6	Sofia	Fr	Gugleta
23-04-1967	Hungary	L 0-1	Budapest	Fr	
3-05	West Germany	W 1-0	Belgrade	ECq	Skoblar
14-05	Albania	W 2-0	Tirana	ECq	Zambata 2
7-10	West Germany	L 1-3	Hamburg	ECq	Zambata
1-11	Holland	W 2-1	Rotterdam	Fr	Belin, Osim
12-11	Albania	W 4-0	Belgrade	ECq	Osim 2, Lazarevic, Spreco
6-04-1968	France	D 1-1	Marseille	ECqf	Musemic
24-04	France	W 5-1	Belgrade	ECqf	Petkovic 2, Musemic 2, Dzajic
27-04	Czechoslovakia	L 0-3	Bratislava	Fr	
5-06	England	W 1-0	Florence	ECsf	Dzajic
8-06	Italy	D 1-1	Rome	ECf	Dzajic
10-06	Italy	L 0-2	Rome	ECf	
25-06	Brazil	L 0-2	Belgrade	Fr	
25-09	Finland	W 9-1	Belgrade	WCq	Zambata 3, Musemic 3, Dzajic 2, Osim
16-10	Belgium	L 0-3	Brussels	WCq	
27-10	Spain	D 0-0	Belgrade	WCq	
17-12	Brazil	D 3-3	Rio de Janeiro	Fr	Spasovski, Dzajic, Bukal
19-12	Brazil	L 2-3	Belo Horizonte	Fr	Musemic, Bjekovic
22-12	Argentina	D 1-1	Mar del Plata	Fr	Musemic
26-02-1969	Sweden	W 2-1	Split	Fr	Bjekovic, Musemic
30-04	Spain	L 1-2	Barcelona	WCq	Pavlovic
4-06	Finland	W 5-1	Helsinki	WCq	Bukal 2, Dzajic, Spreco, Piric
3-09	Romania	D 1-1	Belgrade	Fr	Mujkic
24-09	Soviet Union	L 1-3	Belgrade	Fr	Dzajic
19-10	Belgium	W 4-0	Skoplje	WCq	Spasovski 2, Belin, Dzajic
8-04-1970	Austria	D 1-1	Sarajevo	Fr	Bajevic
12-04	Hungary	D 2-2	Belgrade	Fr	Gracanin, OG
6-05	Romania	D 0-0	Bucharest	Fr	
13-05	West Germany	L 0-1	Hanover	Fr	
10-09	Austria	W 1-0	Graz	Fr	Bajevic
11-10	Holland	D 1-1	Rotterdam	ECq	Dzajic
14-10	Luxembourg	W 2-0	Luxembourg	ECq	Bukal 2
28-10	Soviet Union	L 0-4	Moscow	Fr	
18-11	West Germany	W 2-0	Zagreb	Fr	Bukal, Dzajic
4-04-1971	Holland	W 2-0	Split	ECq	Jerkovic, Dzajic
21-04	Romania	L 0-1	Novi Sad	Fr	
9-05	East Germany	W 2-1	Leipzig	ECq	Filipovic, Dzajic
18-07	Brazil	D 2-2	Rio de Janeiro	Fr	Dzajic, Jerkovic
1-09	Hungary	L 1-2	Budapest	Fr	Oblak
22-09	Mexico	W 4-0	Sarajevo	Fr	Bukal 2, Acimovic, Oblak
16-10	East Germany	D 0-0	Belgrade	ECq	
27-10	Luxembourg	D 0-0	Titograd	ECq	
30-04-1972	Soviet Union	D 0-0	Belgrade	ECqf	
13-05	Soviet Union	L 0-3	Moscow	ECqf	
14-06	Venezuela	W 10-0	Curitiba	Clr1	Bajevic 5, Popivoda, Dzajic, Acimovic,Stepanovic, Katalinski

Date	Opponent	Result	Venue	Comp	Scorers
18-06	Bolivia	D 1-1	Campo Grande	Clr1	Katalinski
22-06	Paraguay	W 2-1	Manaus	Clr1	Bajevic 2
25-06	Peru	W 2-1	Manaus	Clr1	Bajevic 2
29-06	Scotland	D 2-2	Belo Horizonte	Clr2	Bajevic, Jerkovic
2-07	Brazil	L 0-3	Sao Paulo	Clr2	
6-07	Czechoslovakia	W 2-1	Sao Paulo	Clr2	Bajevic, Dzajic
9-07	Argentina	W 4-2	Rio de Janeiro	Cl3p	Bajevic 2, Katalinski, Dzajic
20-09	Italy	L 1-3	Turin	Fr	Vukotic
11-10	England	D 1-1	London	Fr	Vladic
19-10	Spain	D 2-2	Las Palmas	WCq	Bajevic 2
19-11	Greece	W 1-0	Belgrade	WCq	Acimovic
4-02-1973	Tunisia	W 5-0	Tunis	Fr	Bajevic 2, Petkovic 2, Vladic
9-05	West Germany	W 1-0	Munich	Fr	Bajevic
13-05	Poland	D 2-2	Warsaw	Fr	Pavlovic, Bjekovic
26-09	Hungary	D 1-1	Belgrade	Fr	Bjekovic
21-10	Spain	D 0-0	Zagreb	WCq	
19-12	Greece	W 4-2	Athens	WCq	Karasi 2, Bajevic, Surjak
13-02-1974	Spain	W 1-0	Frankfurt	WCq	Katalinski
17-04	Soviet Union	L 0-1	Zenicar	Fr	
29-05	Hungary	L 0-3	Szekesfehervar	Fr	
5-06	England	D 2-2	Belgrade	Fr	Petkovic, Oblak
13-06	Brazil	D 0-0	Frankfurt	WCr1	
18-06	Zaire	W 9-0	Gelsenkirchen	WCr1	Bajevic 3, Dzajic, Surjak, Katalinski, Bogicevic, Oblak, Petkovic
22-06	Scotland	D 1-1	Frankfurt	WCr1	Karasi
26-06	West Germany	L 0-2	Dusseldorf	WCr2	
30-06	Poland	L 1-2	Frankfurt	WCr2	Karasi
3-07	Sweden	L 1-2	Dusseldorf	WCr2	Surjak
28-09	Italy	W 1-0	Zagreb	Fr	Surjak
30-10	Norway	W 3-1	Belgrade	ECq	Katalinski 2, Vukotic
16-03-1975	Nth. Ireland	L 0-1	Belfast	ECq	
31-05	Holland	W 3-0	Belgrade	Fr	Savic, Popivoda, Ivezic
4-06	Sweden	W 2-1	Stockholm	ECq	Katalinski, Ivezic
9-06	Norway	W 3-1	Oslo	ECq	Buljan, Bogicevic, Surjak
15-10	Sweden	W 3-0	Zagreb	ECq	Oblak, Vladic, Vabec
19-11	Nth. Ireland	W 1-0	Belgrade	ECq	Oblak
18-02-1976	Tunisia	L 1-2	Tunis	Fr	Surjak
24-02	Algeria	W 2-1	Algiers	Fr	Vukotic, Sljivo
17-04	Hungary	D 0-0	Banja Luka	Fr	
24-04	Wales	W 2-0	Zagreb	ECqf	Vukotic, Popivoda
22-05	Wales	D 1-1	Cardiff	ECqf	Katalinski
17-06	West Germany	L 2-4	Belgrade	ECsf	Popivoda, Dzajic
19-06	Holland	L 2-3	Zagreb	EC3p	Katalinski, Dzajic
25-09	Italy	L 0-3	Rome	Fr	
10-10	Spain	L 0-1	Seville	WCq	
30-01-1977	Colombia	W 1-0	Bogota	Fr	Bajevic
1-02	Mexico	L 1-5	Leon	Fr	Bajevic
8-02	Mexico	W 1-0	Monterrey	Fr	Bajevic
23-03	Soviet Union	L 2-4	Belgrade	Fr	Bajevic, Jerkovic
30-04	West Germany	L 1-2	Belgrade	Fr	Bajevic
8-05	Romania	L 0-2	Zagreb	WCq	
26-06	Brazil	D 0-0	Belo Horizonte	Fr	
3-07	Argentina	L 0-1	Buenos Aires	Fr	
5-10	Hungary	L 3-4	Budapest	Fr	Susic 2, Nikolic
13-11	Romania	W 6-4	Bucharest	WCq	Susic 3, Muzinic, Trifunovic, Filipovic
16-11	Greece	D 0-0	Salonica	BC	
30-11	Spain	L 0-1	Belgrade	WCq	
5-04-1978	Iran	D 0-0	Tehran	Fr	
18-05	Italy	D 0-0	Rome	Fr	
4-10	Spain	L 1-2	Zagreb	ECq	Halilhodzic
25-10	Romania	L 2-3	Bucharest	ECq	Petrovic, Desnica
15-11	Greece	W 4-1	Skoplje	BC	Halilhodzic 3, Savic
1-04-1979	Cyprus	W 3-0	Nicosia	ECq	Vujovic.Z 2, Surjak
13-06	Italy	W 4-1	Zagreb	Fr	Susic 3, Zajec
16-09	Argentina	W 4-2	Belgrade	Fr	Susic 3, Sliskovic
10-10	Spain	W 1-0	Valencia	ECq	Surjak
31-10	Romania	W 2-1	Titova Mitrovica	ECq	Vujovic.Z, Sliskovic
14-11	Cyprus	W 5-0	Novi Sad	ECq	Kranjcar 2, Vujovic.Z, Petrovic, Savic
22-03-1980	Uruguay	W 2-1	Sarajevo	Fr	Klincarski, Vujovic.Z
30-03	Romania	W 2-0	Belgrade	BC	Krsticevic, Susic
26-04	Poland	W 2-1	Borovo	Fr	Mirocevic 2

27-08	Romania	L 1-4	Bucharest	BC	Susic
10-09	Luxembourg	W 5-0	Luxembourg	WCq	Vujovic.Z 2, Susic, Petrovic, Buljan
27-09	Denmark	W 2-1	Ljubjana	WCq	Vujovic.Zo, Pantelic
15-11	Italy	L 0-2	Turin	WCq	
25-03-1981	Bulgaria	W 2-1	Subotica	Fr	Halilhodzic, Sliskovic
29-04	Greece	W 5-1	Split	WCq	Vujovic.Z 2, Sljivo, Halilhodzic, Pantelic
9-09	Denmark	W 2-1	Copenhagen	WCq	Vujovic.Z, Petrovic
17-10	Italy	D 1-1	Belgrade	WCq	Vujovic.Z
21-11	Luxembourg	W 5-0	Novi Sad	WCq	Halilhodzic 2, Surjak, Pasic, Vujovic.Z
29-11	Greece	W 2-1	Athens	WCq	Surjak, Jerkovic
17-06-1982	Nth. Ireland	D 0-0	Zaragoza	WCr1	
20-06	Spain	L 1-2	Valencia	WCr1	Gudelj
24-06	Honduras	W 1-0	Zaragoza	WCr1	Petrovic
13-10	Norway	L 1-3	Oslo	ECq	Savic
17-11	Bulgaria	W 1-0	Sofia	ECq	Stojkovic.N,
15-12	Wales	D 4-4	Titograd	ECq	Cvetkovic, Zivkovic, Kranjcar, Jesic
30-03-1983	Romania	W 2-0	Timisoara	Fr	Dzeko, Trifunovic
23-04	France	L 0-4	Paris	Fr	
1-06	Romania	W 1-0	Sarajevo	Fr	OG
7-06	West Germany	L 2-4	Luxembourg	Fr	Jesic, Miljanovic
12-10	Norway	W 2-1	Belgrade	ECq	Vujovic.Z, Susic
26-10	Switzerland	L 0-2	Basle	Fr	
12-11	France	D 0-0	Zagreb	Fr	
14-12	Wales	D 1-1	Cardiff	ECq	Bazdarevic
21-12	Bulgaria	W 3-2	Split	ECq	Susic 2, Radanovic
31-03-1984	Hungary	W 2-1	Subotica	Fr	Durovski, Radanovic
2-06	Portugal	W 3-2	Lisbon	Fr	Susic, Halilovic, Stojkovic.D
7-06	Spain	W 1-0	La Linea	Fr	Susic
13-06	Belgium	L 0-2	Lens	ECr1	
16-06	Denmark	L 0-5	Lyon	ECr1	
19-06	France	L 2-3	St. Etienne	ECr1	Sestic, Stojkovic.D
12-09	Scotland	L 1-6	Glasgow	Fr	Vokri
29-09	Bulgaria	D 0-0	Belgrade	WCq	
20-10	East Germany	W 3-2	Leipzig	WCq	Bazdarevic, Vokri, Sestic
20-01-1985	Iran	W 3-1	Cochin	Fr	Baljic 2, Mlinaric
25-01	Soviet Union	W 2-1	Cochin	Fr	Hadzibegic, Vujovic.Z
29-01	China	D 1-1	Cochin	Fr	Zivkovic
1-02	South Korea	W 3-1	Cochin	Fr	Vokri, Gudelj, Vujovic.Zo
4-02	Soviet Union	L 1-2	Cochin	Fr	Hadzibegic
27-03	Luxembourg	W 1-0	Zenica	WCq	Gudelj
3-04	France	D 0-0	Sarajevo	WCq	
1-05	Luxembourg	W 1-0	Luxembourg	WCq	Vokri
1-06	Bulgaria	L 1-2	Sofia	WCq	Durovski
28-09	East Germany	L 1-2	Belgrade	WCq	Skoro
16-10	Austria	W 3-0	Linz	Fr	Vujovic.Z 2, Mrkela
16-11	France	L 0-2	Paris	WCq	
30-04-1986	Brazil	L 2-4	Recife	Fr	Gracan, Jankovic
11-05	West Germany	D 1-1	Bochum	Fr	Skoro
19-05	Belgium	W 3-1	Brussels	Fr	Skoro, Gracan, Vujovic.Z
29-10	Turkey	W 4-0	Split	ECq	Vujovic.Z 3, Savicevic
12-11	England	L 0-2	London	ECq	
25-03-1987	Austria	W 4-0	Banja Luka	Fr	Pancev 2, Stojkovic.D, Tuce
29-04	Nth. Ireland	W 2-1	Belfast	ECq	Stojkovic.D, Vujovic.Z
29-08	Soviet Union	L 0-1	Belgrade	Fr	
23-09	Italy	L 0-1	Pisa	Fr	
14-10	Nth. Ireland	W 3-0	Sarajevo	ECq	Vokri 2, Hadzibegic
11-11	England	L 1-4	Belgrade	ECq	Katanec
16-12	Turkey	W 3-2	Izmir	ECq	Radanovic, Katanec, Hadzibegic
23-03-1988	Wales	W 2-1	Swansea	Fr	Stojkovic.D, Jakovljevic
31-03	Italy	D 1-1	Split	Fr	Jakovljevic
27-04	Rep. Ireland	L 0-2	Dublin	Fr	
4-06	West Germany	D 1-1	Bremen	Fr	Baljic
24-08	Switzerland	W 2-0	Lucerne	Fr	Mihajlovic, Djukic
14-09	Spain	W 2-1	Oviedo	Fr	Bazdarevic, Cvetkovic
19-10	Scotland	D 1-1	Glasgow	WCq	Katanec
19-11	France	W 3-2	Belgrade	WCq	Spasic, Susic, Stojkovic.D
11-12	Cyprus	W 4-0	Belgrade	WCq	Savicevic 3, Hadzibegic
5-04-1989	Greece	W 4-1	Athens	Fr	Vujovic.Z 2, Tuce, Jakovljevic
29-04	France	D 0-0	Paris	WCq	
27-05	Belgium	L 0-1	Brussels	Fr	
14-06	Norway	W 2-1	Oslo	WCq	Stojkovic.D, Vujovic.Z

23-08	Finland	D 2-2	Kuopio	Fr	Pancev, Savicevic
6-09	Scotland	W 3-1	Zagreb	WCq	Katanec, OG 2
20-09	Greece	W 3-0	Novi Sad	Fr	Brnovic, Prosinecki, Pancev
11-10	Norway	W 1-0	Sarajevo	WCq	Hadzibegic
28-10	Cyprus	W 2-1	Athens	WCq	Stanojkovic, Pancev
14-11	Brazil	D 0-0	Joao Pessoa	Fr	
13-12	England	L 1-2	London	Fr	Skoro
28-03-1990	Poland	D 0-0	Lodz	Fr	
26-05	Spain	L 0-1	Ljubljana	Fr	
3-06	Holland	L 0-2	Zagreb	Fr	
10-06	West Germany	L 1-4	Milan	WCr1	Jozic
14-06	Colombia	W 1-0	Bologna	WCr1	Jozic
19-06	UAE	W 4-1	Bologna	WCr1	Susic, Pancev 2, Prosinecki
26-06	Spain	W 2-1	Verona	WCr2	Stojkovic 2
30-06	Argentina	D 0-0	Florence	WCqf	Lost 2-3 pens
12-09	Nth. Ireland	W 2-0	Belfast	ECq	Pancev, Prosinecki
31-10	Austria	W 4-1	Belgrade	ECq	Pancev 3, Katanec
14-11	Denmark	W 2-0	Copenhagen	ECq	Bazdarevic, Jarni
27-02-1991	Turkey	D 1-1	Izmir	Fr	Savicevic
27-03	Nth. Ireland	W 4-1	Belgrade	ECq	Binic, Pancev 3
1-05	Denmark	L 1-2	Belgrade	ECq	Pancev
16-05	Faeroe Islands	W 7-0	Belgrade	ECq	Najdoski, Prosinecki, Pancev 2, Vulic, Boban, Suker
4-09	Sweden	L 3-4	Stockholm	Fr	Savicevic 2, OG
16-10	Faeroe Islands	W 2-0	Landskrona	ECq	Jugovic, Savicevic
30-10	Brazil	L 1-3	Varginha	Fr	Lukic
13-11	Austria	W 2-0	Vienna	ECq	Lukic, Savicevic
25-03-1992	Holland	L 0-2	Amsterdam	Fr	
23-12-1994	Brazil	L 0-2	Porto Alegre	Fr	
27-12	Argentina	L 0-1	Buenos Aires	Fr	
4-02-1995	South Korea	W 1-0	Hong Kong	Fr	Kovacevic
31-03	Uruguay	W 1-0	Hong Kong	Fr	Milosevic
31-05	Russia	L 1-2	Belgrade	Fr	Petkovic

SOUTH AMERICA

Known for many years in football as the 'new world', South America is now very much part of the establishment of world football. CONMEBOL is the oldest continental confederation, having been in existence almost 40 years longer than UEFA, and of its ten members, three have been crowned world champions.

Through the organisation of the South American Championships, CONMEBOL has played a crucial role in the development of the game on the continent. Aside from the big three of Argentina, Brazil and Uruguay, until the last twenty years or so, almost all of the competitive matches played by the other seven countries were in CONMEBOL-sponsored tournaments. At club level, it organises both the Copa Libertadores as well as the recently introduced Super Copa and CONMEBOL Cup.

The Copa Libertadores is reserved for the champions and runners-up in each of the ten leagues and has been played since 1960. The Super Copa, introduced in 1988, is for all of the previous winners of the Copa Libertadores, whilst the CONMEBOL Cup, first played for in 1992, is, like the UEFA Cup and CAF Cup, for the best of the rest. In this tournament countries are ranked according to their past record and size. As a result Brazil has four places, Argentina three, Uruguay two, each of the others just one. The other major tournament is the Recopa, played between the winners of the Copa Libertadores and the Super Copa. Any excuse for a game!

South America covers a very large area, of which Brazil and Argentina occupy a sizeable proportion. Due to trading and cultural links with the east coast of America and Europe, the countries on the Atlantic coastline have been more prosperous than their neighbours who border on the Pacific, and this has helped make football in Brazil, Uruguay and Argentina more successful than in Chile, Peru, Paraguay, Bolivia or Ecuador.

In the other two members of CONMEBOL, Colombia and Venezuela, local factors have helped retard the growth of the game. In Venezuela, football is far less popular than a host of imported American sports such as baseball, whilst Colombia, who are prone to flout the regulations of FIFA, have often found themselves ostracised from the world game. The presence of the drug cartels has not helped the situation there either. Though situated in South America, Guyana and Surinam are members of CONCACAF, whilst French Guiana is affiliated to the French Football Federation.

Nine World Cup victories are testament to the strength of the national sides in South America, but club football seems to be in a permanent state of crisis. The deteriorating economic state of the continent has meant a constant flow of players to Europe, as clubs try to balance their books and players look for a secure living. Until the clubs are in a position to keep their players, perhaps even compete with the Europeans in the transfer market, the situation is unlikely to improve.

The basis is there, however. The biggest clubs can draw on large support, and the idea of a super league for the top twenty or so clubs is rapidly gaining momentum. Should that happen, who knows, we may indeed witness European players moving to South America to play their football for a change.

THE GOVERNING BODY

Confederación Sudamericana de Fútbol
Ed. Banco do Brasil - Piso 4
Nuestra Señora de la Asunción
540 Asunción
Paraguay
Tel: + 595 21 94628
Fax: + 595 21 92967

Year of formation - 1916

Members - 10
Argentina – Bolivia – Brazil – Chile – Colombia – Ecuador – Paraguay – Peru – Uruguay – Venezuela

Presidents of CONMEBOL

Héctor Rivadavia Gómez (Honorary Director)	Uruguay	1916-20
León Payrou (Hon. Director)	Uruguay	1920-21
Alfredo V.Viera (Hon. Director)	Uruguay	1921-36
Luis O.Salessi	Argentina	1936-39
Luis A.Valenzuela	Chile	1939-55
Carlos Dittborn Pinto	Chile	1955-57
José Ramos de Freitas	Brazil	1957-59
Fermin Sorhueta	Uruguay	1959-61
Raul H.Colombo	Argentina	1961-66
Teófilo Salinas Fuller	Peru	1966-86
Nicolás Leoz	Paraguay	1986-

SOUTH AMERICAN FOOTBALLER OF THE YEAR

From 'El Mundo' Caracas

1971

1	Tostão	Cruzeiro	BRA
2	Omar Pastoriza	Independiente	ARG
3	Luis Artime	Nacional Montevideo	ARG
4	Teófilo Cubillas	Alianza	PER
5	Gerson	São Paulo FC	BRA
6	Pelé	Santos	BRA
7	Ladislao Mazurkiewicz	Atlético Mineiro	URU
8	Jairzinho	Botafogo	BRA
9	Roberto Rivelino	Corinthians	BRA
10	Hector Chumpitaz	Universitario	PAR

1972

1	Teófilo Cubillas	Alianza	PER
2	Pelé	Santos	BRA
3	Jairzinho	Botafogo	BRA
4	Tostão	Vasco da Gama	BRA
5	Ademir da Guia	Palmeiras	BRA
	Julio Montero Castillo	Peñarol	URU
7	Norberto Alonso	River Plate	ARG
	Elias Figueroa	Internacional	CHI
9	Rodolfo Fischer	Botafogo	ARG
10	Carlos Reinoso	América Mexico City	CHI

1973

1	Pelé	Santos	BRA
2	Miguel Brindisi	Huracán	ARG
3	Roberto Rivelino	Corinthians	BRA
4	Fernando Morena	Peñarol	URU
5	Carlos Caszely	Colo Colo	CHI
6	Elias Figueroa	Internacional	CHI
7	Jairzinho	Botafogo	BRA
	Hugo Sotil	Barcelona (Spain)	PER
	Ruben Ayala	Atlético Madrid	ARG
10	Alberto Quintano	Cruz Azul	CHI
	Saturnino Arrua	Real Zaragoza	PAR

1974

1	Elias Figueroa	Internacional	CHI
2	Francisco Marinho	Botafogo	BRA
3	Carlos Babington	Wattenschied	ARG
4	Luis Pereira	Palmeiras	BRA
5	Pelé		BRA
6	Fernando Morena	Peñarol	URU
	Ricardo Bochini	Independiente	ARG
8	Rene Houseman	Huracán	ARG
9	Carlos Caszely	Levante	CHI
10	Roberto Rivelino	Fluminense	BRA

1975

1	Elias Figueroa	Internacional	CHI
2	Norberto Alonso	River Plate	ARG
3	Fernando Morena	Peñarol	URU
4	Nelinho	Cruzeiro	BRA
5	Luis Pereira	Atlético Madrid	BRA
6	Hugo Sotil	Barcelona (Spain)	ARG
7	Horacio Scotta	San Lorenzo	ARG
8	Teófilo Cubillas	FC Porto	PER
	Ricardo Bochini	Independiente	ARG
10	Leivinha	Atlético Madrid	BRA

1976

1	Elias Figueroa	Palestino	CHI
2	Zico	Flamengo	BRA
3	Rivelino	Fluminense	BRA
4	Hugo Gatti	Boca Juniors	ARG
5	Luis Pereira	Atlético Madrid	BRA
6	Fernando Morena	Peñarol	URU
7	Daniel Passarella	River Plate	ARG
	Paulo Cesar	Fluminense	BRA
	Norberto Alonso	River Plate	ARG
10	Leivinha	Atlético Madrid	BRA

1977

1	Zico	Flamengo	BRA
2	Roberto Rivelino	Fluminense	BRA
3	Elias Figueroa	Palestino	CHI
4	Pelé	New York Cosmos	BRA
5	Ubaldo Fillol	River Plate	ARG
6	Ricardo Bochini	Independiente	ARG
7	Teófilo Cubillas	Alianza	PER
8	Hugo Gatti	Boca Juniors	ARG
9	Daniel Bertoni	Independiente	ARG
10	Rene Houseman	Huracán	ARG

1978

1	Mario Kempes	Valencia	ARG
2	Ublado Fillol	River Plate	ARG
3	Dirceu Guimaraes	América Mexico City	BRA
4	Daniel Passarella	River Plate	ARG
5	Teofilo Cubillas	Alianza	PER
6	Elias Figueroa	Palestino	CHI
7	Ricardo Bochini	Independiente	ARG
8	César Cueto	Alianza	PER
9	Rivelino	Fluminense	BRA
10	Osvaldo Ardiles	Tottenham Hotspur	ARG

1979

1	Diego Maradona	Argentinos Juniors	ARG
2	Julio Romero	Sportivo Luqueño	PAR
3	Roberto Falcão	Internacional	BRA
4	Ubaldo Fillol	River Plate	ARG
5	Zico	Flamengo	BRA
6	Fernando Morena	Rayo Vallecano	URU
7	Carlos Caszely	Colo Colo	CHI
8	Daniel Passarella	River Plate	ARG
9	Mario Kempes	Valencia	ARG
10	Ramon Diaz	River Plate	ARG

1980

1	Diego Maradona	Argentinos Juniors	ARG
2	Zico	Flamengo	BRA
3	Waldemar Victorino	Nacional Montevideo	URU
4	Ubaldo Fillol	River Plate	ARG
5	Ruben Paz	Peñarol	URU
6	Daniel Passarella	River Plate	ARG
7	Toninho Cerezo	Atlético Mineiro	BRA
8	Sócrates	Corinthians	BRA
9	Rodolfo Rodrigues	Nacional Montevideo	URU
10	Julio Romero	New York Cosmos	PAR

1981

1	Zico	Flamengo	BRA
2	Diego Maradona	Boca Juniors	ARG
3	Junior	Flamengo	BRA
4	Julio Uribe	Sporting Cristal	PER
5	Patricio Yañez	San Luis Quillota	CHI
6	Daniel Passarella	River Plate	ARG
7	Roberto Falcão	Roma	BRA
8	Sócrates	Corinthians	BRA
9	Elias Figueroa	Fort Lauderdale Strikers	CHI
10	Ruben Paz	Peñarol	URU

1982

1	Zico	Flamengo	BRA
2	Roberto Falcão	Roma	BRA
3	Diego Maradona	Barcelona (Spain)	ARG
4	Fernando Morena	Peñarol	URU
5	Junior	Flamengo	BRA
6	Sócrates	Corinthians	BRA
7	Daniel Passarella	Fiorentina	ARG
8	Hugo Sanchez	Atlético Madrid	MEX
9	Julio Cesar Arzu	Racing Santander	HON
	Alberto Tarantini	River Plate	ARG
	Julio Uribe	Cagliari	PER

1983

1	Sócrates	Corinthians	BRA
2	Ubaldo Fillol	Argentinos Juniors	ARG
3	Eder	Atlético Mineiro	BRA
4	Fernando Morena	Peñarol	URU
5	Victor Diogo	Peñarol	URU

6	Ricardo Gareca	Boca Juniors	ARG
7	Rodolfo Rodriguez	Santos	URU
8	Ramon Aguilera	Nacional Montevideo	URU
9	Junior	Flamengo	BRA
10	Ruben Paz	Peñarol	URU
	Jorge Aravena	Universidad Catolica	CHI

1984

1	Enzo Francescoli	River Plate	URU
2	Ubaldo Fillol	Flamengo	ARG
3	Ricardo Bochini	Independiente	ARG
4	Rodolfo Rodriguez	Santos	URU
5	Ricardo Gareca	Boca Juniors	ARG
	Hugo De Leon	Grêmio	URU
7	Jorge Burruchaga	Independiente	ARG
8	Alberto Marcico	Ferrocarril Oeste	ARG
9	Victor Diogo	Palmeiras	URU
10	Fernando Morena	Peñarol	URU
	Eder	Atlético Mineiro	BRA

1985

1	Julio Romero	Fluminense	PAR
2	Enzo Francescoli	River Plate	URU
3	Claudio Borghi	Argentinos Juniors	ARG
4	Roberto Cabañas	América Cali	PAR
5	Walter Casagrande	Corinthians	BRA
6	Roberto Fernandez	América Cali	PAR
	Zico	Flamengo	BRA
8	Daniel Batista	Argentinos Juniors	ARG
	Renato Gaucho	Grêmio	BRA
	Rodolfo Rodriguez	Santos	URU

1986

1	Diego Maradona	Napoli	ARG
2	Careca	São Paulo FC	BRA
3	Hugo Sanchez	Real Madrid	MEX
4	Jorge Burruchaga	FC Nantes	ARG
5	Julio Romero	Fluminense	PAR
6	Jorge Valdano	Real Madrid	ARG
7	Enzo Francescoli	Racing Club Paris	URU
8	Josimar	Botafogo	BRA
9	Oscar Ruggeri	River Plate	ARG
10	Manuel Negrete	Sporting CL	MEX
	Antonio Alzamendi	River Plate	ARG

1987

1	Carlos Valderrama	Deportivo Cali	COL
2	Roberto Cabañas	América Cali	PAR
3	Antonio Alzamendi	River Plate	URU
4	Diego Aguirre	Peñarol	URU
5	Roberto Rojas	Colo Colo	CHI
6	Claudio Marangoni	Independiente	ARG
7	Jose Perdomo	Peñarol	URU
8	Juan Carlos Letelier	Cobreloa	CHI
9	Bernardo Redin	Deportivo Cali	COL
	Rodolfo Rodriguez	Santos	URU

1988

1	Ruben Paz	Racing Club	URU
2	Hugo De León	Nacional Montevideo	URU
3	Geovani Silva	Vasco da Gama	BRA
	Claudio Taffarel	Internacional	BRA
5	Nestor Fabbri	Racing Club	ARG
6	Bernardo Redin	Deportivo Cali	COL
7	Daniel Batista	River Plate	ARG
8	Julio Uribe	Sporting Cristal	PER
9	Polilla	River Plate	BRA
10	Paulo Evair	Guarani Campinas	BRA
	Yubert Lemos	Nacional Montevideo	URU

1989

1	Diego Maradona	Napoli	ARG
2	Ruben Sosa	Lazio	URU
3	Bebeto	Vasco da Gama	BRA
4	Romario	PSV Eindhoven	BRA
5	Careca	Napoli	BRA
6	Rene Higuita	At. Nacional Medellin	COL
7	Daniel Batista	River Plate	ARG
8	Alemão	Napoli	BRA
	Dunga	Fiorentina	BRA
10	Bernardo Redin	Deportivo Cali	COL

1990

1	Diego Maradona	Napoli	ARG
2	Claudio Caniggia	Atalanta	ARG
3	Rene Higuita	At. Nacional Medellin	COL
4	Careca	Napoli	BRA
5	Alemão	Napoli	BRA
	Sergio Goycochea	Racing Club	ARG
7	Hugo Sanchez	Real Madrid	MEX
8	Luis Conejo	Albacete	CRC
9	Carlos Valderrama	Montpellier	COL
10	Ruben Sosa	Lazio	URU
	Diego Latorre	Boca Juniors	ARG

1991

1	Gabriel Batistuta	Fiorentina	ARG
2	Claudio Caniggia	Atalanta	ARG
3	Ivan Zamorano	Sevilla	CHI
4	Ricardo Rocha	Real Madrid	BRA
5	Oscar Ruggeri	Velez Sarsfield	ARG
6	Leonardo Rodriguez	SC Toulon	ARG
7	Diego Latorre	Boca Juniors	ARG
8	Carlos Valderrama	Real Valladolid	COL
9	Daniel Fonseca	Cagliari	URU
	Diego Simeone	Pisa	ARG
	Mario Tilio	Cruzeiro	BRA

1992

1	Diego Maradona	Sevilla	ARG
2	Bebeto	Deportivo La Coruña	BRA
3	Rai	São Paulo FC	BRA
4	Gabriel Batistuta	Fiorentina	ARG
5	Claudio Caniggia	Roma	ARG
6	Daniel Fonseca	Napoli	URU
7	Romario	PSV Eindhoven	BRA
8	Roberto Cabañas	Boca Juniors	PAR
9	Ivan Zamorano	Real Madrid	CHI
10	Muller	São Paulo FC	BRA

SOUTH AMERICAN FOOTBALLER OF THE YEAR

From 'El Pais' Montevideo

1986

1	Antonio Alzamendi	URU
2	Careca	BRA
3	Romero	PAR

1987

1	Carlos Valderrama		COL

1988

1	Ruben Paz	Racing Club	URU
2	Hugo de Leon	Nacional Montevideo	URU
3	J. Pintos Saldanha	Nacional Montevideo	URU

1989

1	Bebeto	Vasco da Gama	BRA
2	Mazinho	Vasco da Gama	BRA
3	Rene Higuita	Atlético Nacional	COL

1990

1	Raul Vicente Amarilla	Olimpia	PAR
2	Ruben Da Silva	River Plate	URU
3	Rene Higuita	Atlético Nacional	COL
	Leonel Alvarez	Atlético Nacional	COL

1991

1	Oscar Ruggeri	Velez Sarsfield	ARG
2	Ramon Diaz	River Plate	ARG
3	Patricio Toledo	Universidad Catolica	CHI

1992

1	Rai	São Paulo FC	BRA
2	Sergio Goycochea	Olimpia	ARG
3	Fernando Gamboa	Newell's Old Boys	ARG
	Alberto Acosta	San Lorenzo	ARG

1993

1	Carlos Valderrama	Junior Barranquilla	COL
2	Marco Etcheverry	Colo Colo	BOL
3	Cafu	São Paulo FC	BRA
	Freddy Rincon	América Cali	COL

1994

1	Cafu	São Paulo FC	BRA
2	José Luis Chilavert	Velez Sarsfield	PAR
3	Gustavo Lopez	Independiente	ARG

THE SOUTH AMERICAN CHAMPIONSHIP

The South American Championship is now the longest running tournament in world football, and has been since the demise of the British International Championship in 1984. Played by the national teams of the ten members of CONMEBOL, the Copa America, as it has been known since the 1975 edition, predates its European counterpart by nearly fifty years, and played a crucial part in facilitating the spread of football in South America.

Between 1910 and 1959 it was played on average once every two years, but with the ever increasing fixture list, as well as the constant flow of players to Europe, it became more difficult to organise on such a regular basis. Between 1959 and 1987 it was held just five times, and there was a period of eight years in the late 1960s and early 1970s when it was not played at all. Since 1987, however, it has reverted back to the two-year formula.

Given that South America is dominated by Argentina, Brazil and Uruguay, one would expect the honours to have been evenly divided between these 'Big Three.' This has not been the case, however. Since 1922, Brazil have won the tournament on only two occasions, in 1959 and 1989. As there have been 30 tournaments played in this time, it can be seen just how poor their record is. Instead, Argentina and Uruguay have dominated the competition, between them winning 28 of the 37 editions played.

The first South American Championship took place in 1910. Though not an official competition, taking place as it did six years before the founding of CONMEBOL, it was acclaimed as such by the newspapers of the time. With Montevideo just over the River Plate from Buenos Aires, matches between Argentina and Uruguay in the Lipton and Newton Cups had been a regular feature for over five years. As transport was rapidly improving, both countries looked further afield for opposition. The opening of the Trans-Andine Railway between Argentina and Chile encouraged the Argentines to organise a tournament involving themselves, Uruguay, Brazil and Chile. Brazil withdrew, but at the end of May 1910 the tournament got underway, Uruguay defeating Chile, who had no experience of international football at all, 3-0 on the grounds of the Gimnasia club at Palermo in Buenos Aires. To Peñarol's Jose Piendibene, the star of Uruguayan football at that time, fell the honour of scoring the first goal in the championship's history.

A week later Argentina defeated the Chileans with even greater ease, setting up what over the years was to become the familar sight of Uruguay playing Argentina on the final day to decide the championship. Nearly 40,000 spectators turned up to see the game, such was the interest, and the occasion showed that some things never change in football. Excited fans burned down one of the stands at Gimnasia's ground and there were reports of shootings. The match was abandoned before it had even started, postponed until the following day and relocated to Racing Club's ground. There a much smaller crowd of 8,000, strictly controlled by the police, saw Argentina crowned as the first unofficial champions of South America. Leading 2-0 at half-time, they completely dominated the game and won 4-1.

The second tournament is also listed as an unofficial event, even though during it CONMEBOL was founded. Played in 1916 to celebrate Argentina's centenary as an independent nation, it saw Uruguay gain revenge for the defeat of six years previously. In the entire history of the championship there have only ever been six proper final ties, in 1975, 1979, 1983, 1987, 1993 and 1995. All the other tournaments were on a league basis. However, it was a practice of the organisers to try an predict which game would be the decider and leave that fixture until last! This became more complicated as more countries entered the tournament, and over the years the 'deciding game' has often occurred early on in the tournament.

Uruguay were the early force in the championship, winning six of the first 11 series, and they have carried on winning with surprising regularity ever since. Argentina, however, really came into their own from the mid 1920s until the end of the 1950s, winning 11 of 18. Brazil's record is lamentable. They have never won the championship outside their own country and have only won four overall. There is a small element of truth in the theory that they do not take the championship as seriously as the other countries, in that they have only staged the tournament on four occasions while there have been eight in Argentina, six in Uruguay, six in Chile and five in Peru. Their lack of success is better explained, though, by the fact that the majority of the championships were played before the 1960s, when the Brazilians were not as strong as either Argentina or Uruguay. Conversely, it was Brazil's misfortune that when they were at their best, from the mid 1950s, there were not that many championships played!

The 1960s saw a decline in the championship as the Copa Libertadores became an ever more popular tournament, and this, combined with an increased desire of the Big Three to play more lucrative friendlies in Europe, nearly killed off the competition for good. Bolivia were chosen to host the 1963 tournament and remarkably won it; but the Argentine and Brazilian selections, while by no means weak sides, were not full strength teams.

An eight-year gap after the 1967 edition, the longest in the championship's history, was followed by the introduction of a new format for 1975. Three qualifying groups were played, and for the first time the championship was not held in a single country. Instead, a home and away system was used to find the three qualifiers for the semi-finals, who were joined there by the previous year's winners. Peru and Paraguay seemed to adapt well to this new system as they carried off the title in 1975 and 1979 respectively. For both, it was only their second ever series win.

The 1975 edition was the first to attract the full complement of ten CONMEBOL members, a difficult number to work with, hence the bye to the semi-finals for the holders. In 1987 the same format was kept but the tournament was held in a single country, Argentina; it was not a satisfactory arrangement and in 1989 two groups of five were used, the top two in each group qualifying for a final round played on a league basis. This tournament provided Brazil with their first win in forty years, whilst in 1991, Argentina won for the first time in 32 years.

The 1993 tournament, held in Ecuador, was notable for the fact that both Mexico and the United States were invited to take part. The format was changed again so that there were three groups of four from which eight proceeded to the knock-out stage. The Mexicans made it all the way to the final, only to lose against Argentina. For the 1995 edition, CONMEBOL even tried to persuade first Spain and then Italy to take part! Thankfully, they declined, thus maintaining the regional integrity of the tournament.

THE ORDER OF MERIT

	Country	G	S	B
1	Argentina	15	10	4
2	Uruguay	14	6	6
3	Brazil	4	11	7
4	Paraguay	2	5	8
5	Peru	2	-	4
6	Bolivia	1	-	-
7	Chile	-	4	6
8	Colombia	-	1	3
9	Mexico	-	1	1

To the end of the 1995 championship

THE WINNERS

1910	Argentina
1916	Uruguay
1917	Uruguay
1919	Brazil
1920	Uruguay
1921	Argentina
1922	Brazil
1923	Uruguay
1924	Uruguay
1925	Argentina
1926	Uruguay
1927	Argentina
1929	Argentina
1935	Uruguay
1937	Argentina
1939	Peru
1941	Argentina
1942	Uruguay
1945	Argentina
1946	Argentina
1947	Argentina
1949	Brazil
1953	Paraguay
1955	Argentina
1956	Uruguay
1957	Argentina
1959	Argentina
1959	Uruguay
1963	Bolivia
1967	Uruguay
1975	Peru
1979	Paraguay
1983	Uruguay
1987	Uruguay
1989	Brazil
1991	Argentina
1993	Argentina
1995	Uruguay

ALL-TIME TOP SCORERS

17	Norberto Mendez	Argentina
17	Zizinho	Brazil
15	Teodoro Fernandez	Peru
15	Severino Varela	Uruguay
13	Ademir de Menezes	Brazil
13	Gabriel Batistuta	Argentina
13	Jair R. Pinto	Brazil
13	Jose Moreno	Argentina
13	Hector Scarone	Uruguay
12	Roberto Porta	Uruguay
12	Angel Romano	Uruguay
10	Javier Ambrois	Uruguay
10	Hector Castro	Uruguay
10	Oscar Gomez-Sanchez	Peru
10	Enrique Hormazabal	Chile
10	Angel Labruna	Argentina
10	Herminio Masantonio	Ar gentina
10	Pedro Petrone	Uruguay
10	Arnoldo Iguaran	Colombia

1910

1ST EDITION

Buenos Aires 29 May - 12 June. Unofficial tournament

Gimnasia Club, Buenos Aires, 29-05-1910, 5,000

Uruguay 3 (Piendibene, Brachi, Buck)
Chile 0

Gimnasia Club, Buenos Aires, 5-06-1910

Argentina 5 (Brown.E 2, Susan 2, Brown ER)
Chile 1 (Campbell)

Racing Club, Buenos Aires, 12-06-1910, 8,000

Argentina 4 (Vialle, Hayes, Hutton, Susan)
Uruguay 1 (Piendibene)

Argentina - Wilson - Brown.J, Brown.G - Brown.E, Ginocchio, Jacobs - Vialle, Hutton, Hayes, Susan, Gonzales

Uruguay - Saporiti - Bertone, Benincasa - Suazu, Apostegui, Pena - Brachi, Raymonda, Piendibene, Dacal, Buck

	Ar	Ur	Ch	Pl	W	D	L	F	A	Pts
ARGENTINA	-	4-1	5-1	2	2	0	0	9	2	4
URUGUAY	-	-	3-0	2	1	0	1	4	4	2
CHILE	-	-	-	2	0	0	2	1	8	0

Top scorer Susan, Argentina 3

1916

2ND EDITION

Buenos Aires 2 - 17 July. Unofficial tournament

Gimnasia y Esgrima, Buenos Aires, 2-07-1916, 30,000
Uruguay 2 (Piendibene 2, Gradín 2)
Chile 0

Gimnasia y Esgrima, Buenos Aires, 6-07-1916, 15,000
Argentina 6 (Ohaco 2, Brown.J 2, Marcovecchio 2)
Chile 1 (Báez)

Gimnasia y Esgrima, Buenos Aires, 8-07-1916, 15,000
Chile 1 (Salazar)
Brazil 1 (Demóstenes)

Gimnasia y Esgrima, Buenos Aires, 10-07-1916, 20,000
Argentina 1 (Laguna)
Brazil 1 (Aléncar)

Gimnasia y Esgrima, Buenos Aires, 12-07-1916, 20,000
Uruguay 2 (Gradín, Tognola)
Brazil 1 (Friedenreich)

Racing Club, Buenos Aires, 17-07-1916, 30,000. Referee: Fanta, Chile
Argentina 0
Uruguay 0
Argentina - Isola - Diaz, Reyes.A - Martínez, Olazar, Badaracco - Heissinger, Ohaco, Hayes.H, Reyes.E, Perinetti
Uruguay - Saporiti - Benincasa, Foglino - Zibechi, Delgado, Varela - Somma, Tognola Piendibene, Gradín, Marán

	Ur	Ar	Br	Ch	Pl	W	D	L	F	A	Pts
URUGUAY	-	0-0	2-1	4-0	3	2	1	0	6	1	5
ARGENTINA	-	-	1-1	6-1	3	1	2	0	7	2	4
BRAZIL	-	-	-	1-1	3	0	2	1	3	4	2
CHILE	-	-	-	-	3	0	1	2	2	11	1

Top scorer Isabelino Gradín, Uruguay 3

3RD EDITION

Montevideo 30 September - 14 October

Parque Central, Montevideo, 30-09-1917, 22,000
Uruguay 4 (Romano 2, Scarone.C 2)
Chile 0

Parque Central, Montevideo, 3-10-1917, 20,000
Argentina 4 (Ohaco 2, Calomino, Martinez)
Brazil 2 (Neco, Lagreca)

Parque Central, Montevideo, 6-10-1917, 12,000
Argentina 1 (OG)
Chile 0

Parque Central, Montevideo, 7-10-1917, 21,000
Uruguay 4 (Romano 2, Scarone.C, Scarone.H)
Brazil 0

Parque Central, Montevideo, 12-10-1917, 10,000
Brazil 5 (Haroldo 2, Amilcar, Caetano, Neco)
Chile 0

Parque Central, Montevideo, 14-10-1917, 40,000. Referee: Livingstone, Chile
Uruguay 1 (Scarone.H)
Argentina 0
Uruguay - Saporiti - Varela.M, Foglino - Pacheco, Rodriguez.G, Vanzzino - Perez.J, Scarone.H, Romano, Scarone.C, Somma
Argentina - Isola - Ferro, Reyes.A - Mattozzi, Olazar, Martinez - Calomino, Ohaco, Martin, Hayes.E, Perinetti

	Ur	Ar	Br	Ch	0Pl	W	D	L	F	A	Pts
URUGUAY	-	1-0	4-0	4-0	3	3	0	0	9	0	6
ARGENTINA	-	-	4-2	1-0	3	2	0	1	5	3	4
BRAZIL	-	-	-	5-0	3	1	0	2	7	8	2
CHILE	-	-	-	-	3	0	0	3	0	10	0

Top scorer Angel Romano, Uruguay 4

4TH EDITION

Rio de Janeiro 11 - 29 May

Alvaro Chaves, Rio de Janeiro, 11-05-1919, 25,000
Brazil 6 (Friedenreich 3, Neco 2, Haroldo)
Chile 0

Alvaro Chaves, Rio de Janeiro, 13-05-1919, 25,000
Uruguay 3 (Gradín, Scarone.C, Scarone.H)
Argentina 2 (Izaguirre, Calomino)

Alvaro Chaves, Rio de Janeiro, 17-05-1919, 7,000
Uruguay 2 (Perez.J, Scarone.C)
Chile 0

Alvaro Chaves, Rio de Janeiro, 18-05-1919, 28,000
Brazil 3 (Amilcar, Millon, Heitor Domingues)
Argentina 1 (Izaguirre)

Alvaro Chaves, Rio de Janeiro, 22-05-1919, 5,000
Argentina 4 (Clarke 3, Izaguirre)
Chile 1 (France)

Alvaro Chaves, Rio de Janeiro, 26-05-1919, 25,000
Uruguay 2 (Gradín, Scarone.C)
Brazil 2 (Neco 2)

Play-off. Alvaro Chaves, Rio de Janeiro, 29-05-1919, 28,000. Referee: Barbera, Argentina
Brazil 1 (Friedenreich)
Uruguay 0
Brazil - Marcos - Pindaro, Bianco - Sergio, Amilcar, Fortes - Millon, Neco, Friedenreich, Heitor Dominguez, Arnaldo
Uruguay - Saporiti - Varela.M, Foglino - Naguil, Zibechi, Vanzzino - Pérez.J, Scarone.H, Romano, Gradin, Marín

	Br	Ur	Ar	Ch	Pl	W	D	L	F	A	Pts
BRAZIL	-	2-2	3-1	6-0	3	2	1	0	11	3	5
URUGUAY	-	-	3-2	2-0	3	2	1	0	7	4	5
ARGENTINA	-	-	-	4-1	3	1	0	2	7	7	2
CHILE	-	-	-	-	3	0	0	3	1	12	0

Top scorers Neco, Brazil 4
Artur Friedenreich, Brazil 4

1920

5TH EDITION

Viña del Mar. 11 - 26 September

Sporting Club, Viña del Mar, 11-09-1920, 15,000
Brazil 1 (Alvariza)
Chile 0

Sporting Club, Viña del Mar, 12-09-1920, 20,000. Referee: Fanta, Chile
Uruguay 1 (Piendibene)
Argentina 1 (Etcheverria)
Uruguay - Legnazzi - Urdinarán, Foglino - Ruotta, Zibechi, Ravera - Somma, Pérez.J, Piendibene, Romano, Campolo
Argentina - Tesorieri - Cortella, Bearzotti - Frumento, Dellavalle, Uslenghi - Calomino, Libonatti, Badalini, Etcheverria, Miguel

Sporting Club, Viña del Mar, 17-09-1920, 16,000
Argentina 1 (Dellavalle)
Chile 1 (Dominguez)

Sporting Club, Viña del Mar, 18-09-1920, 16,000
Uruguay 6 (Romano 2, Pérez.J 2, Urdinarán, Campolo)
Brazil 0

Sporting Club, Viña del Mar, 25-09-1920, 12,000
Argentina 2 (Etchverria, Libonatti)
Brazil 0

Sporting Club, Viña del Mar, 26-09-1920, 16,000
Uruguay 2 (Perez.J, Romano)
Chile 1 (Bolados)

	Ur	Ar	Br	Ch	Pl	W	D	L	F	A	Pts
URUGUAY	-	1-1	6-0	2-1	3	2	1	0	9	2	5
ARGENTINA	-	-	2-0	1-1	3	1	2	0	4	2	4
BRAZIL	-	-	-	1-0	3	1	0	2	1	8	2
CHILE	-	-	-	-	3	0	1	2	2	4	1

Top scorers José Perez Uruguay 4
Angel Romano, Uruguay 4

6TH EDITION

Buenos Aires 2 - 30 October

Sportivo Barracas, Buenos Aires, 2-10-1921, 20,000
Argentina 1 (Libonatti)
Brazil 0

Sportivo Barracas, Buenos Aires, 9-10-1921, 18,000
Paraguay 2 (Rivas.G, López.E)
Uruguay 1 (Piendibene)

Sportivo Barracas, Buenos Aires, 12-10-1921, 25,000
Brazil 3 (Machado 2, Candiota)
Paraguay 0

Sportivo Barracas, Buenos Aires, 16-10-1921, 25,000
Argentina 3 (Libonatti, Etcheverria, Saruppo)
Paraguay 0

Sportivo Barracas, Buenos Aires, 23-10-1921, 18,000
Uruguay 2 (Romano 2)
Brazil 1 (Zezé I)

Sportivo Barracas, Buenos Aires, 30-10-1921, 30,000. Referee: Santos, Brazil
Argentina 1 (Libonatti)
Uruguay 0
Argentina - Tesorieri - Celli, Bearzotti - López.A, Dellavalle, Solari - Calomino, Libonatti,, Saruppo, Etcheverria, González.V
Uruguay - Beloutas - Benincasa, Foglino - Molinari, Zibechi, Broncini - Somma, Romano, Pendibene, Casanello, Campolo

	Ar	Br	Ur	Pa	Pl	W	D	L	F	A	Pts
ARGENTINA	-	1-0	1-0	3-0	3	3	0	0	5	0	6
BRAZIL	-	-	1-2	3-0	3	1	0	2	4	3	2
URUGUAY	-	-	-	1-2	3	1	0	2	3	4	2
PARAGUAY	-	-	-	-	3	1	0	2	2	7	2

Top scorer Julio Libonatti, Argentina 3

1922

7TH EDITION

Rio de Janeiro 17 September - 22 October

Alvaro Chaves, Rio de Janeiro, 17-09-1922, 30,000
Brazil 1 (Tatú)
Chile 1 (Bravo)

Alvaro Chaves, Rio de Janeiro, 23-09-1922, 6,000
Uruguay 2 (Heguy, Urdinarán)
Chile 0

Alvaro Chaves, Rio de Janeiro, 24-09-1922, 25,000
Brazil 1 (Amilcar)
Paraguay 1 (Rivas.G)

Alvaro Chaves, Rio de Janeiro, 28-09-1922, 6,000
Argentina 4 (Francia 2, Chiessa, Gaslini)
Chile 0

Alvaro Chaves, Rio de Janeiro, 1-10-1922, 30,000
Brazil 0
Uruguay 0

Alvaro Chaves, Rio de Janeiro, 5-10-1922, 1,000
Paraguay 3 (Ramirez.C, López.I, Fretes)
Chile 0

Alvaro Chaves, Rio de Janeiro, 8-10-1922, 7,000
Uruguay 1 (Buffoni)
Argentina 0

Alvaro Chaves, Rio de Janeiro, 12-10-1922, 3,000
Paraguay 1 (Elizeche)
Uruguay 0

Alvaro Chaves, Rio de Janeiro, 15-10-1922, 25,000
Brazil 2 (Amilcar, Neco)
Argentina 0

Alvaro Chaves, Rio de Janeiro, 18-10-1922, 8,000
Argentina 2 (Francia 2)
Paraguay 0

Play-off. Alvaro Chaves, Rio de Janeiro, 22-10-1922, 20,000. Referee: Guevara, Chile
Brazil 3 (Formiga 2, Neco)
Paraguay 1 (Rivas.G)
Brazil - Kuntz - Palamone, Barto - Lais, Amilcar, Fortes - Formiga, Neco, Heitor Domingues, Tatú, Rodriguez
Paraguay - Denis - Mena, Porta - Miranda, Fleitas Solich, Benitez.I - Capdevilla, Schaerer, Lopez.I, Rivas.G, Fretes

	Br	Pa	Ur	Ar	Ch	Pl	W	D	L	F	A	Pts
BRAZIL	-	1-1	0-0	2-0	1-1	4	1	3	0	4	2	5
PARAGUAY	-	-	1-0	0-2	3-0	4	2	1	1	5	3	5
URUGUAY	-	-	-	1-0	2-0	4	2	1	1	3	1	5
ARGENTINA	-	-	-	-	4-0	4	2	0	2	6	3	4
CHILE	-	-	-	-	-	4	0	1	3	1	10	1

Uruguay withdrew after the last match in protest over decisions in her match with Paraguay. This left a play-off between Brazil and Paraguay to decide the title.

Top scorer Juan Francia, Argentina 4

1923

8TH EDITION

Montevideo 29 October - 2 December

Parque Central, Montevideo, 29-10-1923, 20,000
Argentina 4 (Aguirre 3, Seruppo)
Paraguay 3 (Rivas.G, Zelada, Fretes)

Parque Central, Montevideo, 4-11-1923, 20,000
Uruguay 2 (Scarone.H, Petrone)
Paraguay 0

Parque Central, Montevideo, 11-11-1923, 15,000
Paraguay 1 (López.I)
Brazil 0

Parque Central, Montevideo, 18-11-1923, 15,000
Argentina 2 (Onzari, Saruppo)
Brazil 1 (Nilo)

Parque Central, Montevideo, 25-11-1923, 20,000
Uruguay 2 (Petrone, Cea)
Brazil 1 (Nilo)

Parque Central, Montevideo, 2-12-1923, 22,000. Referee: Campos, Brazil
Uruguay 2 (Petrone, Somma)
Argentina 0
Uruguay - Casella - Nasazzi, Uriarte - Andrade, Vidal, Ghierra - Pérez.L, Petrone, Scarone.H, Cea, Somma
Argentina - Tesorieri - Bidoglio, Iribarren - Médici, Vaccaro, Solari - Loizo, Miguel, Saruppo, Aguirre, Onzari

	Ur	Ar	Pa	Br	Pl	W	D	L	F	A	Pts
URUGUAY	-	2-0	2-0	2-1	3	3	0	0	6	1	6
ARGENTINA	-	-	4-3	2-1	3	2	0	1	6	6	4
PARAGUAY	-	-	-	1-0	3	1	0	2	4	6	2
BRAZIL	-	-	-	-	3	0	0	3	2	5	0

Top scorers Valdino Aguirre, Argentina 3
Pedro Petrone, Uruguay 3

1924

9TH EDITION

Montevideo 12 October - 2 November

Parque Central, Montevideo. 12-10-1924, 8,000
Paraguay 0
Argentina 0

Parque Central, Montevideo. 19-10-1924, 15,000
Uruguay 5 (Petrone 3, Zingone, Romano)
Chile 0

Parque Central, Montevideo. 25-10-1924, 4,000
Argentina 2 (Loyarte, Sosa.G)
Chile 0

Parque Central, Montevideo. 26-10-1924, 14,000
Uruguay 3 (Petrone, Romano, Cea)
Paraguay 1 (Sosa.U)

Parque Central, Montevideo. 1-11-1924, 1,000
Paraguay 3 (López.I 2, Rivas.G)
Chile 1 (Arellano)

Parque Central, Montevideo. 2-11-1924, 20,000. Referee: Fanta, Chile
Uruguay 0
Argentina 0
Uruguay - Mazzali - Nasazzi, Arispe - Alzugaray, Zibechi, Ghierra - Urdinarán, Barlocco, Petrone, Cea, Romano
Argentina - Tesorieri - Cochrane, Bearzotti - Médici, Bidoglio, Solari - Tarasconi, Loyarte, Sosa.G, Seoane, Onzari

	Ur	Ar	Pa	Ch	Pl	W	D	L	F	A	Pts
URUGUAY	-	0-0	3-1	5-0	3	2	1	0	8	1	5
ARGENTINA	-	-	0-0	2-0	3	1	2	0	2	0	4
PARAGUAY	-	-	-	3-1	3	1	1	1	4	4	3
CHILE	-	-	-	-	3	0	0	3	1	10	0

Top scorer Pedro Petrone, Uruguay 4

1925

10TH EDITION

Buenos Aires 29 November - 25 December

Sportivo Barracas, Buenos Aires, 29-11-1925, 12,000
Argentina 2 (Seoane, Sánchez.M)
Paraguay 0

La Bombonera, Buenos Aires, 6-12-1925, 18,000
Brazil 5 (Lagarto 2, Friedenreich, Moderato, Nilo)
Paraguay 2 (Rivas.G, Fretes)

Sportivo Barracas, Buenos Aires, 13-12-1925, 25,000
Argentina 4 (Seoane 3, Garasino)
Brazil 1 (Nilo)

La Bombonera, Buenos Aires, 17-12-1925, 14,000
Brazil 3 (Lagarto 2, Nilo)
Paraguay 1 (Fretes)

Sportivo Barracas, Buenos Aires, 20-12-1925, 25,000
Argentina 3 (Tarasconi, Seoane, Irurierta)
Paraguay 1 (Fleitas Solich)

La Bombonera, Buenos Aires, 25-12-1925, 18,000. Referee: Vallarino, Uruguay
Argentina 2 (Cerrutti, Seoane)
Brazil 2 (Friedenreich, Nilo)
Argentina - Tesorieri - Muttis, Bidoglio - Fortunato, Vaccaro, Médici - Tarascone, Cerrutti, Seoane, De Los Santos, Bianchi
Brazil - Tuffy - Penaforte, Helcio - Nascimeinto, Rueda, Pamplona - Filó, Lagarto, Friedenreich, Nilo, Moderato

	Ar	Br	Pa	Pl	W	D	L	F	A	Pts
ARGENTINA	-	4-1	2-0	4	3	1	0	11	4	7
BRAZIL	2-2	-	5-2	4	2	1	1	11	9	5
PARAGUAY	1-3	1-3	-	4	0	0	4	4	13	0

Top scorer Manuel Seoane, Argentina....................6

1926

11TH EDITION

Santiago 12 October - 3 November

Sport de Nuñoa, Santiago, 12-10-1926, 12,000

Chile 7 (Arellano 4, Subiabre, Ramirez.M, Moreno)
Bolivia 1 (Aguilar)

Sport de Nuñoa, Santiago, 16-10-1926, 8,000

Argentina 5 (Cherro 2, Sosa.G, Delgado, Miguel)
Bolivia 0

Sport de Nuñoa, Santiago, 17-10-1926, 13,000

Uruguay 3 (Borjas, Castro.H, Scarone.H)
Chile 1 (Subiabre)

Sport de Nuñoa, Santiago, 20-10-1926, 3,000

Argentina 8 (Sosa.G 4, Delgado 2, Cherro, Miguel)
Paraguay 0

Sport de Nuñoa, Santiago, 23-10-1926, 2,000

Paraguay 6 (Ramirez.J 3, Ramirez.C 2, López.I)
Bolivia 1 (Soto)

Sport de Nuñoa, Santiago, 24-10-1926, 15,000. Referee: Barba, Paraguay

Uruguay 2 (Castro.H, Borjas)
Argentina 0

Uruguay - Batignani - Nasazzi, Recoba - Andrade, Fernández.L, Vanzzino - Urdinarán, Scarone.H, Borjas, Castro.H, Saldombide
Argentina - Diaz - Bidoglio, Cochrane - Medici, Vaccaro, Monti - Tarasconi, Cherro, Sosa.G, Miguel, Delgado

Sport de Nuñoa, Santiago, 28-10-1926, 8,000

Uruguay 6 (Scarone.H 5, Romano)
Bolivia 0

Sport de Nuñoa, Santiago, 31-10-1926, 8,000

Chile 1 (Saavedra)
Argentina 1 (Tarasconi)

Sport de Nuñoa, Santiago, 1-11-1926, 12,000

Uruguay 6 (Castro.H 4, Saldombide 2)
Paraguay 1 (Fretes)

Sport de Nuñoa, Santiago, 3-11-1926, 6,000

Chile 5 (Subiabre 3, Ramirez.M 2)
Paraguay 1 (Vargas)

	Ur	Ar	Ch	Pa	Bo	Pl	W	D	L	F	A	Pts
URUGUAY	-	2-0	3-1	6-1	6-0	4	4	0	0	17	2	8
ARGENTINA	-	-	1-1	8-0	5-0	4	2	1	1	14	3	5
CHILE	-	-	-	5-1	7-1	4	2	1	1	14	6	5
PARAGUAY	-	-	-	-	6-1	4	1	0	3	8	20	2
BOLIVIA	-	-	-	-	-	4	0	0	4	2	24	0

Top scorers Hector Scarone, Uruguay 6
Hector Castro, Uruguay 6
Guillermo Subiabre, Chile 6

12TH EDITION

Lima 30 October - 27 November

Estadio Nacional, Lima, 30-10-1927, 15,000

Argentina 7 (Carricaberry, Seoane 2, Ferreyra.M, Luna 2, Recanattini)
Bolivia 1 (Algorta)

Estadio Nacional, Lima, 1-11-1927, 22,000

Uruguay 4 (Sacco, Castro.H, OG)
Peru 0

Estadio Nacional, Lima, 6-11-1927, 6,000

Uruguay 9 (Petrone 3, Figueroa 3, Arremón, Castro.H, Scarone.H)
Bolivia 0

Estadio Nacional, Lima, 13-11-1927, 15,000

Peru 3 (Montellanos, Neyra, Sarmiento)
Bolivia 2 (Bustamante 2)

Estadio Nacional, Lima, 20-11-1927, 26,000. Referee: Theurner, England

Argentina 3 (Recanattini, Luna, Carricaberry)
Uruguay 2 (Scarone.H 2)

Argentina - Diaz - Recanattini, Bidoglio - Evaristo.J, Zumelzú, Monti - Carricaberry, Maglio, Ferreira, Seoane, Luna
Uruguay - Capuccini - Canavessi, Tejera - Andrade, Fernández.L, Vanzzino - Arremón, Scarone.H, Petrone, Castro.H, Figueroa

Estadio Nacional, Lima, 27-11-1927, 15,000

Argentina 5 (Maglio, Seoane, Ferreira, Orsi, Carricaberry)
Peru 1 (Villaneuva)

	Ar	Ur	Pe	Bo	Pl	W	D	L	F	A	Pts
ARGENTINA	-	3-2	5-1	7-1	3	3	0	0	15	4	6
URUGUAY	-	-	4-0	9-0	3	2	0	1	15	3	4
PERU	-	-	-	3-2	3	1	0	2	4	11	2
BOLIVIA	-	-	-	-	3	0	0	3	3	19	0

Top scorers Alfredo Carricaberry, Argentina 3
Segundo Luna, Argentina 3
Pedro Petrone, Uruguay 3
Roberto Figueroa, Uruguay 3
Hector Scarone, Uruguay 3
Manuel Seoane, Argentina 3

1929

13TH EDITION

Buenos Aires 1 - 17 November

River Plate, Buenos Aires, 1-11-1929, 40,000

Paraguay 3 (González.A 2, Sosa.L)
Uruguay 0

San Lorenzo, Buenos Aires, 3-11-1929, 20,000

Argentina 3 (Zumelzú 2, Peucelle)
Peru 0

San Lorenzo, Buenos Aires, 10-11-1929, 20,000. Referee: Bonelli, Peru

Argentina 4 (Ferreira 2, Evaristo, Cherro)
Paraguay 1 (Dominguez)

Argentina - Bossio - Tarrio, Paternóster - Evaristo.J, Zumelzú, Chivirini - Peucelle, Rivarola, Ferreira, Cherro, Evaristo.M
Paraguay - Brunetti - Olmedo, Flores - Viccini, Diaz, Etcheverry - Nessi, Dominguez, González.A, Caceres, Sosa.U

River Plate, Buenos Aires, 11-11-1929, 22,000

Uruguay 4 (Fernández.L 3, Andrade.J)
Peru 1 (Bulnes)

Cordero, Buenos Aires, 16-11-1929, 8,000

Paraguay 5 (González.A 3, Nessi, Dominguez)
Peru 0

San Lorenzo, Buenos Aires, 17-11-1929, 60,000
Argentina 2 (Ferreira, Evaristo.M)
Uruguay 0

	Ar	Pa	Ur	Pe	Pl	W	D	L	F	A	Pts
ARGENTINA	-	4-1	2-0	3-0	3	3	0	0	9	1	6
PARAGUAY	-	-	3-0	5-0	3	2	0	1	9	4	4
URUGUAY	-	-	-	4-1	3	1	0	2	4	6	2
PERU	-	-	-	-	3	0	0	3	1	12	0

Top scorer Aurelio González, Paraguay 5

1935

14TH EDITION

Lima 6 - 27 January. Unofficial tournament

Estadio Nacional, Lima, 6-01-1935, 25,000
Argentina 4 (Lauri, Garcia.D, Arrieta, Masantonio)
Chile 1 (Carmona)

Estadio Nacional, Lima, 13-01-1935, 28,000
Uruguay 1 (Castro.H)
Peru 0

Estadio Nacional, Lima, 18-01-1935, 13,000
Uruguay 2 (Ciocca 2)
Chile 1 (Giúdici)

Estadio Nacional, Lima, 20-01-1935, 28,000
Argentina 4 (Masantonio 3, Garcia.D)
Peru 1 (Fernández.T)

Estadio Nacional, Lima, 26-01-1935, 12,000
Peru 1 (Montellanos)
Chile 0

Estadio Nacional, Lima, 27-01-1935, 25,000. Referee: Reginatto, Chile
Uruguay 3 (Castro.H, Taboada, Ciocca)
Argentina 0
Uruguay - Ballesteros - Nasazzi, Muñiz - Zunino (Denis), Fernandez.L, Pérez.M - Taboada, Ciocca, Castro.H, Fernandez.E, Castro.B
Argentina - Bello (Gualco) - Wilson, Scarcella - De Jonge, Minella, Demare - Lauri, Sastre, Masantonio, Garcia.D (Zito), Arrieta

	Ur	Ar	Pe	Ch	Pl	W	D	L	F	A	Pts
URUGUAY	-	3-0	1-0	2-1	3	3	0	0	6	1	6
ARGENTINA	-	-	4-1	4-1	3	2	0	1	8	5	4
PERU	-	-	-	1-0	3	1	0	2	2	5	2
CHILE	-	-	-	-	3	0	0	3	2	7	0

Top scorer Hermino Masantonio, Argentina 4

1937

15TH EDITION

Buenos Aires 27 December 1936 - 1 February 1937

San Lorenzo, Buenos Aires, 27-12-1936, 20,000
Brazil 3 (Alfonsinho, Roberto, Niginho)
Peru 2 (Fernández.T, Villaneuva)

San Lorenzo, Buenos Aires, 30-12-1936, 35,000
Argentina 2 (Varallo 2)
Chile 1 (Toro)

San Lorenzo, Buenos Aires, 2-01-1937, 25,000
Paraguay 4 (González.A 2, Erico, Ortega.A)
Uruguay 2 (Varela.S 2)

La Bombonera, Buenos Aires, 3-01-1937, 20,000
Brazil 6 (Luiz M.Oliveira 2, Patesko 2, Carvalho Leite, Roberto)
Chile 4 (Toro, Avendaño 2, Riveros)

San Lorenzo, Buenos Aires, 6-01-1937, 20,000
Uruguay 4 (Varela.S 2, Piriz, Camaiti)
Peru 2 (Fernandez.T, Magallanes)

La Bombonera, Buenos Aires, 9-01-1937, 25,000
Argentina 6 (Zozaya 3, Scopelli 2, Garcia.E)
Paraguay 1 (Gonzalez.A)

San Lorenzo, Buenos Aires, 10-01-1937, 18,000
Chile 3 (Toro 2, Arancibia)
Uruguay 0

San Lorenzo, Buenos Aires, 13-01-1937, 20,000
Brazil 5 (Luiz M.Oliveira 2, Patesko 2, Carvalho Leite)
Paraguay 0

San Lorenzo, Buenos Aires, 16-01-1937, 40,000
Argentina 1 (Zozaya)
Peru 0

San Lorenzo, Buenos Aires, 17-01-1937, 12,000
Paraguay 3 (Amarilla, Nuñez, Flor)
Chile 2 (Toro 2)

San Lorenzo, Buenos Aires, 19-01-1937, 35,000
Brazil 3 (Bahia, Niginho, Carvalho Leite)
Uruguay 2 (Villadoniga, Piriz)

San Lorenzo, Buenos Aires, 21-01-1937, 8,000
Peru 2 (Alcade.J 2)
Chile 2 (Torres, Arancibia)

San Lorenzo, Buenos Aires, 23-01-1937, 70,000
Uruguay 3 (Villadóniga, Piriz, Varela.S)
Argentina 2 (Varallo, Zozaya)

San Lorenzo, Buenos Aires, 24-01-1937, 8,000
Peru 1 (Lavalle)
Paraguay 0

Monumental, Buenos Aires, 30-01-1937, 80,000
Argentina 1 (Garcia.E)
Brazil 0

Play-off. San Lorenzo, Buenos Aires, 1-02-1937, 80,000. Referee: Macias, Argentina
Argentina 2 (De la Mata 2)
Brazil 0
Argentina - Bello - Tarrio, Fazio - Sastre, Lazzatti, Martinez - Guaita, Varallo (De La Mata), Zozaya (Ferreira), Cherro (Peucelle), Garcia.E
Brazil - Jurandir - Carnera, Jaú - Britto, Brandao, Afonsinho - Roberto I (Carreiro), Luiz M.Oliveira (Bahia), Cardeal (Carvalho Leite), Tim, Patesko

	Ar	Br	Ur	Pa	Ch	Pe	Pl	W	D	L	F	A	Pts
ARGENTINA	-	1-0	2-3	6-1	2-1	1-0	5	4	0	1	12	5	8
BRAZIL	-	-	3-2	5-0	6-4	3-2	5	4	0	1	17	9	8
URUGUAY	-	-	-	2-4	0-3	4-2	5	2	0	3	11	14	4
PARAGUAY	-	-	-	-	3-2	0-1	5	2	0	3	8	16	4
CHILE	-	-	-	-	-	2-2	5	1	1	3	12	13	3
PERU	-	-	-	-	-	-	5	1	1	3	7	10	3

Top scorer Raul Toro, Chile 7

1939

16TH EDITION

Lima. 15 January - 12 February

Estadio Nacional, Lima, 15-01-1939, 10,000
Paraguay 5 (Godoy 2, Barrios 2, Aquino)
Chile 1 (Sorrel)

Estadio Nacional, Lima, 15-01-1939, 10,000
Peru 5 (Fernández.T 3, Alcalde.J 2)
Ecuador 2 (Herrera, Suarez)

Estadio Nacional, Lima, 22-01-1939, 6,000
Uruguay 6 (Varela.S 3, Lago 2, Porta)
Ecuador 0

Estadio Nacional, Lima, 22-01-1939, 6,000
Peru 3 (Fernández.T 2, Alcalde.J)
Chile 1 (Dominguez)

Estadio Nacional, Lima, 29-01-1939, 15,000
Uruguay 3 (Varela.S, Camaiti, Chirimini)
Chile 2 (Muñoz, Luco)

Estadio Nacional, Lima, 29-01-1939, 15,000
Peru 3 (Fernández.T 2, Alcalde.J)
Paraguay 0

Estadio Nacional, Lima, 5-02-1939, 10,000
Chile 4 (Avendaño 2, Toro, Sorrel
Ecudor 1 (Arenas)

Estadio Nacional, Lima, 5-02-1939, 10,000
Uruguay 3 (Lago, Varela.S, Porta)
Paraguay 1 (Barrios)

Estadio Nacional, Lima, 12-02-1939, 15,000
Paraguay 3 (Mingo, Bareiro, Godoy)
Ecuador 1 (Herrera)

Estadio Nacional, Lima, 12-02-1939, 15,000. Referee: Vargas, Chile
Peru 2 (Alcalde.J 7, Bielich 35)
Uruguay 1 (Porta 44)
Peru - Honores - Chapell, Fernandez.A - Tovar, Pasache, Castillo - Alcade.T, Fernandez.T, Alcade.J, Bielich (Ibanez) (Quispe), Paredes
Uruguay - Granero - Sanguinetti (Zaccour), Mascheroni - Zunino, Galvalisi, Viana - Porta, Ciocca (Camaiti), Lago, Varela.S (Chirimini), Rodriguez

	Pe	Ur	Pa	Ch	Ec	Pl	W	D	L	F	A	Pts
PERU	-	2-1	3-0	3-1	5-2	4	4	0	0	13	4	8
URUGUAY	-	-	3-1	3-2	6-0	4	3	0	1	13	5	6
PARAGUAY	-	-	-	5-1	3-1	4	2	0	2	9	8	4
CHILE	-	-	-	-	4-1	4	1	0	3	8	12	2
ECUADOR	-	-	-	-	-	4	0	0	4	4	18	0

Top scorer Teodoro Fernández, Peru 7

1941

17TH EDITION

Santiago 2 February - 4 March. Unofficial tournament

Estadio Nacional, Santiago, 2-02-1941, 40,000
Chile 5 (Sorrel 2, Toro, Contreras.A, Arancibia)
Ecuador 0

Estadio Nacional, Santiago, 9-02-1941, 70,000
Uruguay 6 (Rivero 3, Porta, Gambetta, OG)
Ecuador 0

Estadio Nacional, Santiago, 9-02-1941, 70,000
Chile 1 (Pérez.R)
Peru 0

Estadio Nacional, Santiago, 12-02-1941, 45,000
Argentina 2 (Moreno.J 2)
Peru 1 (Socarraz)

Estadio Nacional, Santiago, 16-02-1941, 70,000
Argentina 6 (Marvezzi 5, Minella)
Ecuador 1 (Freire)

Estadio Nacional, Santiago, 16-02-1941, 70,000
Uruguay 2 (Cruche, Chirimini)
Chile 0

Estadio Nacional, Santiago, 23-02-1941, 48,000
Peru 4 (Fernández.T 3, Vallejos)
Ecuador 0

Estadio Nacional, Santiago, 23-02-1941, 48,000. Referee: Vargas, Chile
Argentina 1 (Sastre 54)
Uruguay 0
Argentina - Estrada - Salomón (Coletta), Alberti - Sbarra, Minella (Videla), Colombo Pedernera, Moreno.J, Marvezzi, Sastre, Garcia.E
Uruguay - Paz - Romero, Cadilla - Martinez, Varela.O (González.S), Gambetta - Medina (Chirimini), Porta, Rivero, Riephoff, Magliano

Estadio Nacional, Santiago, 26-02-1941, 20,000
Uruguay 2 (Riephoff, Varela.O)
Peru 0

Estadio Nacional, Santiago, 4-03-1941, 70,000
Argentina 1 (Garcia.E)
Chile 0

	Ar	Ur	Ch	Pe	Ec	Pl	W	D	L	F	A	Pts
ARGENTINA	-	1-0	1-0	2-1	6-1	4	4	0	0	10	2	8
URUGUAY	-	-	2-0	2-0	6-0	4	3	0	1	10	1	6
CHILE	-	-	-	1-0	5-0	4	2	0	2	6	3	4
PERU	-	-	-	-	4-0	4	1	0	3	5	5	2
ECUADOR	-	-	-	-	-	4	0	0	4	1	21	0

Top scorer Marvezzi, Argentina 5

1942

18TH EDITION

Montevideo 10 January - 7 February

Estadio Centenario, Montevideo, 10-01-1942, 40,000
Uruguay 6 (Castro.L 2, Varela.O, Ciocca, Zapirain, Porta)
Chile 1 (Contreras)

Estadio Centenario, Montevideo, 11-01-1942, 20,000
Argentina 4 (Masantonio 2, Sandoval, Perucca)
Paraguay 3 (Aveiro 2, Sánchez.V)

Estadio Centenario, Montevideo, 14-01-1942, 10,000
Brazil 6 (Pirilo 3, Patesko 2, Claudio C.Pinto)
Chile 1 (Dominguez)

Estadio Centenario, Montevideo, 17-01-1942, 30,000
Argentina 2 (Garcia.E, Masantonio)
Brazil 1 (Servílio I)

Estadio Centenario, Montevideo, 18-01-1942, 45,000
Uruguay 7 (Varela.S 3, Porta 2, Zapirain, Gambetta)
Ecuador 0

Estadio Centenario, Montevideo, 18-01-1942, 45,000
Paraguay 1 (Barrios)
Peru 1 (Magallanes)

Estadio Centenario, Montevideo, 21-01-1942, 10,000
Brazil 2 (Amorim 2)
Peru 1 (Fernández.L)

Estadio Centenario, Montevideo, 22-01-1942, 25,000
Paraguay 2 (Barrios, Franco)
Chile 0

Estadio Centenario, Montevideo, 22-01-1942, 25,000
Argentina 12 (Moreno.J 5, Masantonio 4, Garcia.E, Pedernera, Perucca)
Ecuador 0

Estadio Centenario, Montevideo, 24-01-1942, 55,000
Uruguay 1 (Varela.S)
Brazil 0

Estadio Centenario, Montevideo, 25-01-1942, 12,000
Paraguay 3 (Franco, Mingo, Ibarrola)
Ecuador 1 (Herrera)

Estadio Centenario, Montevideo, 25-01-1942, 12,000
Argentina 3 (Moreno.J 2, Heredia)
Peru 1 (Fernández.T)

Estadio Centenario, Montevideo, 28-01-1942, 40,000
Peru 2 (Quiñones, Morales)
Ecuador 1 (Jiminez)

Estadio Centenario, Montevideo, 28-01-1942, 40,000
Uruguay 3 (Varela.S, Porta, Ciocca)
Paraguay 1 (Barrios)

Estadio Centenario, Montevideo, 31-01-1942, 15,000
Argentina 0
Chile 0
Chile walked off the field after 43 minutes. Argentina were awarded the points

Estadio Centenario, Montevideo, 31-01-1942, 40,000
Brazil 5 (Pirilo 3, Tim, Zizinho)
Ecuador 1 (Alvarez)

Estadio Centenario, Montevideo, 1-02-1942, 40,000
Uruguay 3 (Chirimini, Castro.L, Porta)
Peru 0

Estadio Centenario, Montevideo, 5-02-1942, 15,000
Chile 2 (Dominguez, Casanoya)
Ecuador 1 (Alcibar)

Estadio Centenario, Montevideo, 5-02-1942, 15,000
Brazil 1 (Zizinho)
Paraguay 1 (Franco)

Estadio Centenario, Montevideo, 7-02-1942, 70,000
Peru 0
Chile 0

Estadio Centenario, Montevideo, 7-02-1942, 70,000. Referee: Rojas, Paraguay
Uruguay 1 (Zapirain)
Argentina 0

Uruguay - Paz - Ramero, Muñiz - Rodriguez, Varela.O, Gambetta - Castro, Varela.S (Chirimini) (Faltando), Ciocca, Porta, Zapirain
Argentina - Gualco - Salomón, Valussi (Montañez) - Esperón, Perucca, Ramos - Heredia (Pedernera), Sandoval, Masantonio, Moreno, Garcia (Ferreyra)

	Ur	Ar	Br	Pa	Pe	Ch	Ec	Pl	W	D	L	F	A	Pts
URUGUAY	-	1-0	1-0	3-1	3-0	6-1	7-0	6	6	0	0	21	2	12
ARGENTINA	-	-	2-1	4-3	3-1	0-0	12-0	6	5	0	1	21	6	10
BRAZIL	-	-	-	1-1	2-1	6-1	5-1	6	3	1	2	15	7	7
PARAGUAY	-	-	-	-	1-1	2-0	3-1	6	2	2	2	11	10	6
PERU	-	-	-	-	-	0-0	2-1	6	1	2	3	5	10	4
CHILE	-	-	-	-	-	-	2-1	6	1	1	4	4	15	3
ECUADOR	-	-	-	-	-	-	-	6	0	0	6	4	31	0

Top scorers José Moreno, Argentina 5
Herminio Masantonio, Argentina 5

1945

19TH EDITION

Santiago. 14 January - 28 February. Unofficial tournament

Estadio Nacional, Santiago, 14-01-1945, 65,000
Chile 6 (Alcántara 2, Hormazábal, Vera, Clavero 2)
Ecuador 3 (Raymondi 2, Mendoza)

Estadio Nacional, Santiago, 18-01-1945, 35,000
Argentina 4 (Pontoni, Martino, Loustau, De La Mata)
Bolivia 0

Estadio Nacional, Santiago, 21-01-1945, 60,000
Brazil 3 (Jorginho, Heleno de Freitas, Jaime)
Colombia 0

Estadio Nacional, Santiago, 24-01-1945, 70,000
Uruguay 5 (Garcia.A 3, Porta, Varela.O)
Ecuador 1 (Aguayo)

Estadio Nacional, Santiago, 24-01-1945, 70,000
Chile 5 (Clavero 3, Alcántara, Medina)
Bolivia 0

Estadio Nacional, Santiago, 28-01-1945, 28,000
Brazil 2 (Ademir de Menezes, Tesourinha)
Bolivia 0

Estadio Nacional, Santiago, 28-01-1945, 28,000
Uruguay 7 (Garcia.A 2, Garcia.J 2, Ortiz, Porta, Riephoff)
Colombia 0

Estadio Nacional, Santiago, 31-01-1945, 60,000
Argentina 4 (Pontoni, De La Mata, Martino, Pellegrina)
Ecuador 2 (Aguayo, Acevedo)

Estadio Nacional, Santiago, 31-01-1945, 60,000
Chile 2 (Medina, Piñero)
Colombia 0

Estadio Nacional, Santiago, 7-02-1945, 60,000
Argentina 9 (Pontoni 2, Méndez 2, Martino, Boyé, Ferraro 2, Loustau)
Colombia 1 (Mendoza)

Estadio Nacional, Santiago, 7-02-1945, 60,000
Brazil 3 (Heleno de Freitas 2, Rui)
Uruguay 0

Estadio Nacional, Santiago, 11-02-1945, 70,000
Bolivia 0
Ecuador 0

Estadio Nacional, Santiago, 11-02-1945, 70,000
Chile 1 (Medina)
Argentina 1 (Méndez)

Estadio Nacional, Santiago, 15-02-1945, 65,000
Uruguay 2 (Falero, Porta)
Bolivia 0

Estadio Nacional, Santiago, 15-02-1945, 65,000. Referee: Valentini, Uruguay
Argentina 3 (Méndez 3)
Brazil 1 (Ademir Menezes)

Argentina - Ricardo - Salomón, De Zorzi (Palma) - Sosa, Perucca, Colombo - Muñoz, Méndez (De la Mata), Pontoni, Martino (Farro), Loustau

Brazil - Oberdan - Domingos da Guia, Begliomini (Newton) - Biguá, Ruy, Jaime (Alfredo) Tesourinha, Zizinho, Heleno de Freitas (Servilio), Jair R.Pinto, Ademir Menezes

Estadio Nacional, Santiago, 18-02-1945, 65,000
Colombia 3 (Berdugo, Rubio, Gamez)
Ecuador 1 (Aguayo)

Estadio Nacional, Santiago, 18-02-1945, 65,000
Chile 1 (Medina)
Uruguay 0

Estadio Nacional, Santiago, 21-02-1945, 22,000
Bolivia 3 (Orozco, Romero, Fernández.R)
Colombia 3 (Rubio, Berdugo, Gamez)

Estadio Nacional, Santiago, 21-02-1945, 22,000
Brazil 9 (Ademir Menezes 3, Heleno de Freitas 2, Jair R.Pinto 2, Zizinho 2)
Ecuador 2 (Aguayo, Albornoz)

Estadio Nacional, Santiago, 25-02-1945, 45,000
Argentina 1 (Martino)
Uruguay 0

Estadio Nacional, Santiago, 28-02-1945, 80,000
Brazil 1 (Heleno de Freitas)
Chile 0

	Ar	Br	Ch	Ur	Co	Bo	Ec	Pl	W	D	L	F	A	Pts
ARGENTINA	-	3-1	1-1	1-0	9-1	4-0	4-2	6	5	1	0	22	5	11
BRAZIL	-	-	1-0	3-0	3-0	2-0	9-2	6	5	0	1	19	5	10
CHILE	-	-	-	1-0	2-0	5-0	6-3	6	4	1	1	15	5	9
URUGUAY	-	-	-	-	7-0	2-0	5-1	6	3	0	3	14	6	6
COLOMBIA	-	-	-	-	-	3-3	3-1	6	1	1	4	7	25	3
BOLIVIA	-	-	-	-	-	-	0-0	6	0	2	4	3	16	2
ECUADOR	-	-	-	-	-	-	-	6	0	1	5	9	27	1

Top scorers Norberto Méndez, Argentina 6
Helenio de Fretes, Brazil 6

1946

20TH EDITION

Buenos Aires. 12 January - 10 February. Unofficial tournament

Monumental, Buenos Aires, 12 01-1946, 70,000
Argentina 2 (De la Mata, Martino)
Paraguay 0

San Lorenzo, Buenos Aires, 16-01-1946, 70,000
Brazil 3 (Heleno de Freitas 2, Zizinho)
Bolivia 0

San Lorenzo, Buenos Aires, 16-01-1946, 70,000
Uruguay 1 (Medina)
Chile 0

San Lorenzo, Buenos Aires, 19-01-1946, 65,000
Chile 2 (Araya, Cremaschi)
Paraguay 1 (Rolón)

San Lorenzo, Buenos Aires, 19-01-1946, 65,000
Argentina 7 (Méndez 2, Labruna 2, Salvini 2, Loustau)
Bolivia 1 (Peredo)

San Lorenzo, Buenos Aires, 23-01-1946, 40,000
Brazil 4 (Jair R.Pinto 2, Heleno de Freitas, Chico)
Uruguay 3 (Medina 2, Vázquez)

Monumental, Buenos Aires, 26-01-1946, 80,000
Paraguay 4 (Villalba 2, Genes, Benitez Cáceres)
Bolivia 2 (OG, Ortega)

Monumental, Buenos Aires, 26-01-1946, 80,000
Argentina 3 (Labruna 2, Pedernera)
Chile 1 (Medina)

Cordero, Buenos Aires, 29-01-1946, 30,000
Uruguay 5 (Medina 4, Garcia.J)
Bolivia 0

Cordero, Buenos Aires, 29-01-1946, 30,000
Brazil 1 (Norival)
Paraguay 1 (Villalba)

San Lorenzo, Buenos Aires, 2-02-1946, 80,000
Argentina 3 (Pedernera, Labruna, Méndez)
Uruguay 1 (Riephoff)

San Lorenzo, Buenos Aires, 3-02-1946, 22,000
Brazil 5 (Zizinho 4, Chico)
Chile 1 (Salfate)

San Lorenzo, Buenos Aires, 8-02-1946, 18,000
Chile 4 (Araya 2, Cremaschi 2)
Bolivia 1 (OG)

San Lorenzo, Buenos Aires, 8-02-1946, 18,000
Paraguay 2 (Villalba, Rodriguez.A)
Uruguay 1 (OG)

Monumental, Buenos Aires, 10-02-1946, 80,000. Referee: Valentini, Uruguay
Argentina 2 (Méndez 2)
Brazil 0

Argentina - Vacca - Salomón (Marante), Sobrero - Fonda, Strembell (Ongaro), Pescia De la Mata, Méndez, Pedernera, Labruna, Loustau

Brazil - Luiz Borracha - Domingos da Guia, Norival - Zezé Procopio, Danilo Alvim, Jaime (Ruy) - Tesourinha (Eduardo Lima), Zizinho (Ademir Menezes), Heleno de Freitas, Jair R.Pinto, Chico

	Ar	Br	Pa	Ur	Ch	Bo	Pl	W	D	L	F	A	Pts
ARGENTINA	-	2-0	2-0	3-1	3-1	7-1	5	5	0	0	17	3	10
BRAZIL	-	-	1-1	4-3	5-1	3-0	5	3	1	1	13	7	7
PARAGUAY	-	-	-	2-1	1-2	4-2	5	2	1	2	8	8	5
URUGUAY	-	-	-	-	1-0	5-0	5	2	0	3	11	9	4
CHILE	-	-	-	-	-	4-1	5	2	0	3	8	11	4
BOLIVIA	-	-	-	-	-	-	5	0	0	5	4	23	0

Top scorer Medina, Uruguay 7

21ST EDITION

Guayaquil 30 November - 30 December

Capwell, Guayaquil, 30-11-1947, 30,000
Ecuador 2 (Jiménez.J 2)
Bolivia 2 (Gutiérrez 2)

Capwell, Guayaquil, 2-12-1947, 20,000
Uruguay 2 (Falero, Britos)
Colombia 0

Capwell, Guayaquil, 2-12-1947, 20,000. Referee: Rivas, Chile
Argentina 6 (Pontoni 3, Moreno.J, Loustau, Méndez)
Paraguay 0
Argentina - Cozzi - Marante (Colman), Sobrero - Yácono, Prucca, Pescia - Boyé, Méndez, Pontoni, Moreno, Loustau
Paraguay - Garcia.S - Hugo, Caciano - Céspedes, Gavilán, Ocampos - Cantero, Fernández.P, López Fretes (Rivas), Marin, Genés, Villalba

Capwell, Guayaquil, 4-12-1947, 30,000
Argentina 7 (Méndez 2, Boyé 2, Pontoni, Di Stéfano, Loustau)
Bolivia 0

Capwell, Guayaquil, 4-12-1947, 30,000
Ecuador 0
Colombia 0

Capwell, Guayaquil, 6-12-1947, 20,000
Peru 2 (Castillo, Mosquera)
Paraguay 2 (Villalba, Marin)

Capwell, Guayaquil, 6-12-1947, 20,000
Uruguay 6 (Sarro 2, Falero, Magliano, Gambetta, Puente)
Chile 0

Capwell, Guayaquil, 9-12-1947, 15,000
Chile 2 (Varela.C, Saéz)
Peru 1 (López.V)

Capwell, Guayaquil, 9-12-1947, 15,000
Uruguay 3 (Falero 2, Magliano)
Bolivia 0

Capwell, Guayaquil, 11-12-1947, 11,000
Chile 3 (López.P 2, Peñaloza)
Ecuador 0

Capwell, Guayaquil, 11-12-1947, 11,000
Argentina 3 (Moreno.J, Di Stéfano, Boyé)
Peru 2 (Gómez Sánchez, López.V)

Capwell, Guayaquil, 13-12-1947, 18,000
Colombia 0
Bolivia 0

Capwell, Guayaquil, 13-12-1947, 18,000
Paraguay 4 (Genés 2, Marin, Villalba)
Uruguay 2 (Magliano, Britos)

Capwell, Guayaquil, 16-12-1947, 30,000
Uruguay 6 (Falero 2, Sarro 2, Magliano, Puente)
Ecuador 1 (Garnica)

Capwell, Guayaquil, 16-12-1947, 30,000
Argentina 1 (Di Stéfano)
Chile 1 (Riera)

Capwell, Guayaquil, 18-12-1947, 12,000
Paraguay 3 (Marin, Avalos, Genés)
Bolivia 1 (Tapia)

Capwell, Guayaquil, 18-12-1947, 12,000
Argentina 6 (Di Stéfano 3, Fernandez.M, Boyé, Loustau)
Colombia 0

Capwell, Guayaquil, 20-12-1947, 20,000
Ecuador 0
Peru 0

Capwell, Guayaquil, 20-12-1947, 20,000
Paraguay 2 (Villalba 2)
Colombia 0

Capwell, Guayaquil, 23-12-1947, 5,000
Peru 5 (Mosquera 2, Valdivieso, López.V, Guzmán)
Colombia 1 (Arango)

Capwell, Guayaquil, 23-12-1947, 5,000
Paraguay 1 (Villalba)
Chile 0

Capwell, Guayaquil, 25-12-1947, 25,000
Argentina 2 (Moreno.J, Méndez)
Ecuador 0

Capwell, Guayaquil, 26-12-1947, 6,000
Uruguay 1 (Falero)
Peru 0

Capwell, Guayaquil, 27-12-1947, 5,000
Peru 2 (Gómez Sánchez, Valdivieso)
Bolivia 0

Capwell, Guayaquil, 28-12-1947, 25,000
Argentina 3 (Méndez 2, Loustau)
Uruguay 1 (Britos)

Capwell, Guayaquil, 29-12-1947, 5,000
Paraguay 4 (Marin 3, Genés)
Ecuador 0

Capwell, Guayaquil, 29-12-1947, 5,000
Chile 4 (Sáez, Prieto, Infante, Riera)
Colombia 1 (Rubio)

Capwell, Guayaquil, 31-12-1947, 5,000
Chile 4 (OG, López.P, Sáez, Riera)
Bolivia 3 (Tapia 2, Orgaz)

	Ar	Pa	Ur	Ch	Pe	Ec	Bo	Co	Pl	W	D	L	F	A	Pts
ARGENTINA	-	6-0	3-1	1-1	3-2	2-0	7-0	6-0	7	6	1	0	28	4	13
PARAGUAY	-	-	4-2	1-0	2-2	4-0	3-1	2-0	7	5	1	1	16	11	11
URUGUAY	-	-	-	6-0	1-0	6-1	3-0	2-0	7	5	0	2	21	8	10
CHILE	-	-	-	-	2-1	3-0	4-3	4-1	7	4	1	2	14	13	9
PERU	-	-	-	-	-	0-0	2-0	5-1	7	2	2	3	12	9	6
ECUADOR	-	-	-	-	-	-	2-2	0-0	7	0	3	4	3	17	3
BOLIVIA	-	-	-	-	-	-	-	0-0	7	0	2	5	6	21	2
COLOMBIA	-	-	-	-	-	-	-	-	7	0	2	5	2	19	2

Top scorer Nicolas Falero, Uruguay..........7

1949

22ND EDITION

Brazil 3 April - 8 May

Sao Januario, Rio de Janeiro, 3-04-1949, 70,000
Brazil 9 (Jair R.Pinto 2, Simao 2, Tesourinha 2, Ademir Menezes, Otávio, Zizinho)
Ecuador 1 (Chuchuca)

Pacaembu, São Paulo, 6-04-1949, 60,000
Bolivia 3 (Mena, Algañaraz, Godoy.B)
Chile 2 (Salamanca, Riera)

Pacaembu, São Paulo, 6-04-1949, 60,000
Paraguay 3 (López Fretes 2, Benitez.D)
Colombia 0

Sao Januario, Rio de Janeiro, 10-04-1949, 15,000
Peru 4 (Drago, Salinas, Pedraza 2)
Colombia 0

Sao Januario, Rio de Janeiro, 10-04-1949, 15,000
Paraguay 1 (Barrios.R)
Ecuador 0

Pacaembu, São Paulo, 10-04-1949, 40,000
Brazil 10 (Nininho 3, Claudio C.Pinho 2, Zizinho 2, Simao 2, Jair R.Pinto)
Bolivia 1 (Ugarte)

Pacaembu, São Paulo, 13-04-1949, 35,000
Brazil 2 (Claudio C.Pinho, Zizinho)
Chile 1 (López.P)

Sao Januario, Rio de Janeiro, 13-04-1949, 30,000
Uruguay 3 (Castro.R 2, Moreno)
Ecuador 2 (Arteaga, Vargas)

Sao Januario, Rio de Janeiro, 13-04-1949, 30,000
Paraguay 3 (Barrios.R, Arce, López Fretes)
Peru 1 (Drago)

Pacaembu, São Paulo, 17-04-1949, 45,000
Brazil 5 (Ademir Menezes 2, Orlando, Tesourinha, Canhotinho)
Colombia 0

Sao Januario, Rio de Janeiro, 17-04-1949, 8,000
Chile 1 (Rojas.C)
Ecuador 0

Sao Januario, Rio de Janeiro, 17-04-1949, 8,000
Bolivia 3 (Ugarte, Algañaraz, Gutierrez.B)
Uruguay 2 (Moll, Suarez)

Sao Januario, Rio de Janeiro, 20-04-1949, 7,000
Peru 4 (Drago 2, Gómez Sánchez, Castillo)
Ecuador 0

Sao Januario, Rio de Janeiro, 20-04-1949, 7,000
Chile 1 (López.P)
Colombia 1 (Pérez.A)

Pacaembu, São Paulo, 20-04-1949, 20,000
Uruguay 2 (Garcia.J 2)
Paraguay 1 (Vazquez)

Pacaembu, São Paulo, 24-04-1949, 14,000
Bolivia 2 (Algañaraz, Mena)
Ecuador 0

Pacaembu, São Paulo, 24-04-1949, 45,000
Colombia 2 (Gastelbondo, Pérez.A)
Uruguay 2 (Martinez.M, Ayala)

Sao Januario, Rio de Janeiro, 24-04-1949, 45,000
Brazil 7 (Jair R.Pinto 2, Simao, OG, Augusto, Orlando, Ademir Menezes)
Peru 1 (Salinas)

Vila Belmiro, Santos, 27-04-1949, 12,000
Peru 3 (Salinas 2, Lavalle)
Bolivia 0

Pacaembu, São Paulo, 27-04-1949, 1,000
Paraguay 4 (Arce 3, Benitez.D)
Chile 2 (Cremaschi, Ramos)

Sao Januario, Rio de Janeiro, 30-04-1949, 45,000
Paraguay 7 (Benitez.D 4, Arce 2, Avalos)
Bolivia 0

Sao Januario, Rio de Janeiro, 30-04-1949, 45,000
Brazil 5 (Jair R.Pinto 2, Danilo Alvim, Tesourinha, Zizinho)
Uruguay 1 (Castro.R)

Pacaembu, São Paulo, 30-04-1949, 1,000
Peru 3 (Castillo 2, Mosquera)
Chile 0

Sao Januario, Rio de Janeiro, 3-05-1949, 3,000
Ecuador 3 (Cantos, Vargas, Maldonado)
Colombia 2 (Garcia.R, Berdugo)

Caio Martins, Rio de Janeiro, 4-05-1949, 30,000
Peru 4 (Gómez Sánchez 2, Mosquera, Castillo)
Uruguay 3 (Moll, Castro.R, Ayala)

Caio Martins, Rio de Janeiro, 6-05-1949, 12,000
Bolivia 4 (Godoy 3, Rojas.N)
Colombia 0

America, Belo Horizonte, 8-05-1949, 5,000
Chile 3 (Infante 2, Cremaschi)
Uruguay 1 (Ayala)

Sao Januario, Rio de Janeiro, 8-05-1949, 50,000
Paraguay 2 (Avalos, Benitez.D)
Brazil 1 (Tesourinha)

Play-off. Sao Januario, Rio de Janeiro, 11-05-1949, 55,000. Referee: Berrick, England
Brazil 7 (Ademir Menezes 3, Tesourinha 2, Jair R.Pinto 2)
Paraguay 0

Brazil - Barbosa - Augusto, Mauro R.Oliveira - Ely, Danilo Alvim, Noronha - Tesourinha, Zizinho, Ademir Menezes, Jair R.Pinto, Simao

Paraguay - Garcia.S - González, Céspedes - Gavilán, Nardelli, Cantero - Fernández (Barrios), López Fretes (Romero), Arce, Benitez.D, Vázquez

	Br	Pa	Pe	Bo	Ch	Ur	Ec	Co	Pl	W	D	L	F	A	Pts
BRAZIL	-	1-2	7-1	10-1	2-1	5-1	9-1	5-0	7	6	0	1	39	7	12
PARAGUAY	-	-	3-1	7-0	4-2	1-2	1-0	3-0	7	6	0	1	21	6	12
PERU	-	-	-	3-0	3-0	4-3	4-0	4-0	7	5	0	2	20	13	10
BOLIVIA	-	-	-	-	3-2	3-2	2-0	4-0	7	4	0	3	13	24	8
CHILE	-	-	-	-	-	3-1	1-0	1-1	7	2	1	4	10	14	5
URUGUAY	-	-	-	-	-	-	3-2	2-2	7	2	1	4	14	20	5
ECUADOR	-	-	-	-	-	-	-	3-2	7	1	0	6	6	22	2
COLOMBIA	-	-	-	-	-	-	-	-	7	0	2	5	5	22	2

Top scorer Jair R.Pinto, Brazil 9

1953

23RD EDITION

Lima 22 February - 2 April

Estadio Nacional, Lima, 22-02-1953, 50,000
Bolivia 1 (OG)
Peru 0

Estadio Nacional, Lima, 25-02-1953, 45,000
Paraguay 3 (Fernández.R 2, Berni)
Chile 0

Estadio Nacional, Lima, 25-02-1953, 45,000
Uruguay 2 (Puente, Romero.C)
Bolivia 0

Estadio Nacional, Lima, 28-02-1953, 50,000
Peru 1 (Villamares)
Ecuador 0

Estadio Nacional, Lima, 1-03-1953, 45,000
Brazil 8 (Julinho 4, Pinga 2, Rodrigues 2)
Bolivia 1 (Ugarte)

Estadio Nacional, Lima, 1-03-1953, 45,000
Chile 3 (Molina 3)
Uruguay 2 (Morel, Balseiro)

Estadio Nacional, Lima, 4-03-1953, 45,000
Paraguay 0
Ecuador 0

Estadio Nacional, Lima, 4-03-1953, 45,000
Chile 0
Peru 0

Estadio Nacional, Lima, 8-03-1953, 45,000
Bolivia 1 (Alcón)
Ecuador 1 (Guzmán.E)

Estadio Nacional, Lima, 8-03-1953, 45,000
Peru 2 (Gómez Sánchez, Terry)
Paraguay 2 (Fernández.R, Berni)

Estadio Nacional, Lima, 12-03-1953, 35,000
Paraguay 2 (López.A, Berni)
Uruguay 2 (Balseiro 2)

Estadio Nacional, Lima, 12-03-1953, 35,000
Brazil 2 (Ademir Menezes, Claudio C.Pinho)
Ecuador 0

Estadio Nacional, Lima, 15-03-1953, 45,000
Brazil 1 (Ipojucan)
Uruguay 0

Estadio Nacional, Lima, 16-03-1953, 15,000
Paraguay 2 (Romero.J, Berni)
Bolivia 1 (Ugarte)

Estadio Nacional, Lima, 19-03-1953, 55,000
Chile 3 (Molina 2, Cremaschi)
Ecuador 0

Estadio Nacional, Lima, 19-03-1953, 55,000
Peru 1 (Navarrete)
Brazil 0

Estadio Nacional, Lima, 23-03-1953, 35,000
Brazil 3 (Baltazar, Julinho, Zizinho)
Chile 2 (Molina 2)

Estadio Nacional, Lima, 23-03-1953, 35,000
Uruguay 6 (Méndez, Peláez, Morel, Romero.C, Puente, Balseiro)
Ecuador 0

Estadio Nacional, Lima, 27-03-1953, 35,000
Paraguay 2 (López.A, León)
Brazil 1 (Nilton Santos)

Estadio Nacional, Lima, 28-03-1953, 45,000
Chile 2 (Meléndez, Diaz.G)
Bolivia 2 (Alcón, Santos)

Estadio Nacional, Lima, 28-03-1953, 45,000
Uruguay 3 (Peláez 2, Romero.C)
Peru 0

Play-off. Estadio Nacional, Lima, 1-04-1953, 35,000. Referee: Dean, England
Paraguay 3 (López.A, Gavilán, Fernández.R)
Brazil 2 (Baltazar 2)

Paraguay - Riquelme - Herrera, Olmedo, Gavilán, Leguizamón - Hermosilla, Berni - López.A (Parodi), Fernández.R, Romero (Lacasia), Gómez (González)

Brazil - Castilho - Djalma Santos, Haroldo II, Nilton Santos (Alfredo II) - Bauer, Brandaozinho, Didi - Julinho, Baltazar, Pinga (Ipojucan), Claudio C.Pinho

	Pa	Br	Ur	Ch	Pe	Bo	Ec	Pl	W	D	L	F	A	Pts
PARAGUAY	-	2-1	2-2	3-0	2-2*	2-1	0-0	6	3	3	0	11	6	8
BRAZIL	-	-	1-0	3-2	0-1	8-1	2-0	6	4	0	2	15	6	8
URUGUAY	-	-	-	2-3	3-0	2-0	6-0	6	3	1	2	15	6	7
CHILE	-	-	-	-	0-0	2-2*	3-0	6	2	2	2	10	10	7
PERU	-	-	-	-	-	0-1	1-0	6	2	2	2	4	6	7
BOLIVIA	-	-	-	-	-	-	1-1	6	1	1	4	6	15	3
ECUADOR	-	-	-	-	-	-	-	6	0	2	4	1	13	2

* 1. Chile awarded both points in 2-2 draw with Bolivia
* 2. Peru awarded both points in 2-2 draw with Paraguay

Top scorer Francisco Molina, Chile 7

24TH EDITION

Santiago 27 February - 30 March

Estadio Nacional, Santiago, 27-02-1955, 40,000
Chile 7 (Hormazábal 3, Diaz.G 2, Robledo.J, Meléndez)
Ecuador 1 (Villacreces)

Estadio Nacional, Santiago, 2-03-1955, 35,000
Argentina 5 (Michelli 4, Borello)
Paraguay 3 (Rolón, Villalba), Parodi)

Estadio Nacional, Santiago, 6-03-1955, 50,000
Chile 5 (Robledo.J 2, Hormazábal, Muñoz, Ramirez)
Peru 4 (Castillo, Barbadillo, Heredia, Gomez Sanchez)

Estadio Nacional, Santiago, 9-03-1955, 48,000
Uruguay 3 (Borges, Miguez, Abbadie)
Paraguay 1 (Rolón)

Estadio Nacional, Santiago, 9-03-1955, 48,000
Argentina 4 (Bonelli, Grillo, Michelli, Borello)
Ecuador 0

Estadio Nacional, Santiago, 13-03-1955, 50,000
Chile 2 (Muñoz, Hormazábal)
Uruguay 2 (Galván 2)

Estadio Nacional, Santiago, 13-03-1955, 50,000
Peru 4 (Gómez Sánchez 2, OG 2)
Ecuador 2 (Matute 2)

Estadio Nacional, Santiago, 16-03-1955, 35,000
Paraguay 2 (Rolón 2)
Ecuador 0

Estadio Nacional, Santiago, 16-03-1955, 35,000
Argentina 2 (Grillo, Cecconato)
Peru 2 (Gómez Sánchez 2)

Estadio Nacional, Santiago, 20-03-1955, 55,000
Chile 5 (Melendez 2, Muñoz 2, Hormazábal)
Paraguay 0

Estadio Nacional, Santiago, 23-03-1955, 25,000
Paraguay 1 (Rolón)
Peru 1 (Terry)

Estadio Nacional, Santiago, 23-03-1955, 25,000
Uruguay 5 (Abbadie 2, Galván, Miguez, Pérez)
Ecuador 1 (Matute)

Estadio Nacional, Santiago, 27-03-1955, 45,000
Argentina 6 (Labruna 3, Michelli 2, Borello)
Uruguay 1 (Miguez)

Estadio Nacional, Santiago, 30-03-1955, 65,000
Peru 2 (Castillo, Gómez Sánchez)
Uruguay 1 (Morel)

Estadio Nacional, Santiago, 30-03-1955, 65,000. Referee: Rodriguez, Uruguay
Argentina 1 (Michelli)
Chile 0
Argentina - Mussimessi - Dellacha, Balay, Vairo - Lombardo, Gutiérrez - Michelli (Vernazza), Cecconato, Borello, Labruna, Cucchiaroni
Chile - Escuti - Almeyda, Cortes, Carrasco - Alvarez, Robledo.E - Hormazábal, Melendez (Espinoza), Robledo.J, Muñoz (Diaz.G), Ramirez

	Ar	Ch	Pe	Ur	Pa	Ec	Pl	W	D	L	F	A	Pts
ARGENTINA	-	1-0	2-2	6-1	5-3	4-0	5	4	1	0	18	6	9
CHILE	-	-	5-4	2-2	5-0	7-1	5	3	1	1	19	8	7
PERU	-	-	-	2-1	1-1	4-2	5	2	2	1	13	11	6
URUGUAY	-	-	-	-	3-1	5-1	5	2	1	2	12	12	5
PARAGUAY	-	-	-	-	-	2-0	5	1	1	3	7	14	3
ECUADOR	-	-	-	-	-	-	5	0	0	5	4	22	0

Top scorer Rodolfo Micheli, Argentina 8

25TH EDITION

Montevideo 24 January - 15 February Unofficial tournament

Estadio Centenario, Montevideo, 21-01-1956, 55,000
Uruguay 4 (Escalada 2, Miguez, Roque)
Paraguay 2 (Gómez.A 2)

Estadio Centenario, Montevideo, 22-01-1956, 16,000
Argentina 2 (Sivori, Vairo)
Peru 1 (Drago)

Estadio Centenario, Montevideo, 24-01-1956, 18,000
Chile 4 (Hormazábal 2, Meléndez.R, Sánchez.L)
Brazil 1 (Maurinho)

Estadio Centenario, Montevideo, 28-01-1956, 70,000
Uruguay 2 (Escalada, Miguez.O)
Peru 0

Estadio Centenario, Montevideo, 29-01-1956, 45,000
Brazil 0
Paraguay 0

Estadio Centenario, Montevideo, 29-01-1956, 45,000
Argentina 2 (Labruna 2)
Chile 0

Estadio Centenario, Montevideo, 1-02-1956, 20,000
Brazil 2 (Alvaro, Zezinho)
Peru 1 (Drago)

Estadio Centenario, Montevideo, 1-02-1956, 20,000
Argentina 1 (Cecconato)
Paraguay 0

Estadio Centenario, Montevideo, 5-02-1956, 25,000
Paraguay 1 (Rolón)
Peru 1 (Andrade)

Estadio Centenario, Montevideo, 5-02-1956, 25,000
Brazil 1 (Luizinho)
Argentina 0

Estadio Centenario, Montevideo, 6-02-1956, 30,000
Uruguay 2 (Miguez.O, Borges)
Chile 1 (Ramirez.J)

Estadio Centenario, Montevideo, 9-02-1956, 5,000
Chile 4 (Hormazábal, Muñoz, Fernández.J, Sánchez.L)
Peru 3 (Castillo, Mosquera, Gómez Sánchez)

Estadio Centenario, Montevideo, 10-02-1956, 80,000
Uruguay 0
Brazil 0

Estadio Centenario, Montevideo, 12-02-1956, 4,000
Chile 2 (Hormazábal, Ramirez.J)
Paraguay 0

Estadio Centenario, Montevideo, 15-02-1956, 80,000. Referee: Nicola, Paraguay
Uruguay 1 (Ambrois)
Argentina 0
Uruguay - Maceiras - Martinez, Carranza, Brazionis - Rodriguez Andrade, Miramontes Borges (Pirez), Ambrois, Miguez.O, Escalada (Auscarriaga), Roque
Argentina - Mussimessi - Dellacha, Mouriño, Vairo - Lombardo, Gutiérrez - Pentrelli, Sivori, Grillo, Labruna, Zárate

	Ur	Ch	Ar	Br	Pa	Pe	Pl	W	D	L	F	A	Pts
URUGUAY	-	2-1	1-0	0-0	4-2	2-0	5	4	1	0	9	3	9
CHILE	-	-	0-2	4-1	2-0	4-3	5	3	0	2	11	8	6
ARGENTINA	-	-	-	0-1	1-0	2-1	5	3	0	2	5	3	6
BRAZIL	-	-	-	-	0-0	2-1	5	2	2	1	4	5	6
PARAGUAY	-	-	-	-	-	1-1	5	0	2	3	3	8	2
PERU	-	-	-	-	-	-	5	0	1	4	6	11	1

Top scorer Enrique Hormazabal, Chile 4

1957

26TH EDITION

Lima 7 March - 6 April

Estadio Nacional, Lima, 7-03-1957, 50,000
Uruguay 5 (Ambrois 4, Sasia)
Ecuador 2 (Cantos, Larraz)

Estadio Nacional, Lima, 10-03-1957, 55,000
Peru 2 (Terry 2)
Ecuador 1 (Cantos)

Estadio Nacional, Lima, 13-03-1957, 42,000
Argentina 8 (Maschio 4, Angelillo 2, Cruz, Corbatta)
Colombia 2 (Gamboa, Valencia)

Estadio Nacional, Lima, 13-03-1957, 42,000
Brazil 4 (Didi 3, Pepe)
Chile 2 (Ramirez.J, Fernández.J)

Estadio Nacional, Lima, 16-03-1957, 60,000
Peru 1 (Mosquera)
Chile 0

Estadio Nacional, Lima, 17-03-1957, 50,000
Colombia 1 (Arango)
Uruguay 0

Estadio Nacional, Lima, 17-03-1957, 50,000
Argentina 3 (Angelillo 2, Sivori)
Ecuador 0

Estadio Nacional, Lima, 20-03-1957, 40,000
Argentina 4 (Maschio 2, Angelillo, Sanfilippo)
Uruguay 0

Estadio Nacional, Lima, 21-03-1957, 45,000
Brazil 7 (Evaristo 2, Joel 2, Indio, Pepe, Zizinho)
Ecuador 1 (Larraz)

Estadio Nacional, Lima, 21-03-1957, 45,000
Chile 3 (Verdejo 2, Espinoza.S)
Colombia 2 (Arango, Carrillo)

Estadio Nacional, Lima, 23-03-1957, 55,000
Uruguay 5 (Ambrois 4, Carranza)
Peru 3 (Terry, Seminario, Mosquera)

Estadio Nacional, Lima, 24-03-1957, 45,000
Chile 2 (Ramirez.J 2)
Ecuador 2 (Larraz, Cantos)

Estadio Nacional, Lima, 24-03-1957, 45,000
Brazil 9 (Evaristo 5, Didi 2, Zizinho, Pepe)
Colombia 0

Estadio Nacional, Lima, 27-03-1957, 55,000
Peru 4 (Rivera 2, Terry, Bassa)
Colombia 1 (Arango)

Estadio Nacional, Lima, 28-03-1957, 50,000
Argentina 6 (Angelillo 2, Maschio 2, Sivori, Corbatta)
Chile 2 (Fernández.J 2)

Estadio Nacional, Lima, 28-03-1957, 50,000
Uruguay 3 (Campero 2, Ambrois)
Brazil 2 (Evaristo, Didi)

Estadio Nacional, Lima, 31-03-1957, 55,000
Brazil 1 (Didi)
Peru 0

Estadio Nacional, Lima, 1-04-1957, 40,000
Colombia 4 (Gamboa 2, Alvarez, Gutiérrez.J)
Ecuador 1 (Larraz)

Estadio Nacional, Lima, 1-04-1957, 40,000
Uruguay 2 (Campero, Roque)
Chile 0

Estadio Nacional, Lima, 3-04-1957, 55,000. Referee: Turner, England
Argentina 3 (Angelillo, Maschio, Cruz)
Brazil 0
Argentina - Dóminguez - Dellacha, Vairo, Giménez - Rossi.N, Schandlein - Corbatta, Maschio, Angelillo, Sivori, Cruz
Brazil - Gilmar (Castilho) - Djalma Santos, Edson, Olavo, Zózimo - Roberto Belangero, Didi - Joel, Evaristo (Indio), Zizinho (Dino Sani), Pepe

Estadio Nacional, Lima, 3-04-1957, 55,000
Peru 2 (Mosquera, Terry)
Argentina 1 (Sivori)

	Ar	Br	Ur	Pe	Co	Ch	Ec	Pl	W	D	L	F	A	Pts
ARGENTINA	-	3-0	4-0	1-2	8-2	6-2	3-0	6	5	0	1	25	6	10
BRAZIL	-	-	2-3	1-0	9-0	4-2	7-1	6	4	0	2	23	9	8
URUGUAY	-	-	-	5-3	0-1	2-0	5-2	6	4	0	2	15	12	8
PERU	-	-	-	-	4-1	1-0	2-1	6	4	0	2	12	9	8
COLOMBIA	-	-	-	-	-	2-3	4-1	6	2	0	4	10	25	4
CHILE	-	-	-	-	-	-	2-2	6	1	1	4	9	17	3
ECUADOR	-	-	-	-	-	-	-	6	0	1	5	7	23	1

Top scorers Humberto Maschio, Argentina 9
Javier Ambrois, Uruguay 9

1959

27TH EDITION

Buenos Aires 7 March - 4 April

Monumental, Buenos Aires. 7-03-1959, 70,000
Argentina 6 (Manfredini 2, Pizzutti 2, Callá, Belén)
Chile 1 (Alvarez.L)

Monumental, Buenos Aires. 8-03-1959, 35,000
Uruguay 7 (Borges, Sasia 2, Escalada, Guaglianone, Douksas, Pérez.D)
Bolivia 0

Monumental, Buenos Aires. 10-03-1959, 45,000
Brazil 2 (Didi, Pelé)
Peru 2 (Seminario 2)

Monumental, Buenos Aires. 11-03-1959, 45,000
Paraguay 2 (Aveiro 2)
Chile 1 (Sánchez.L)

Monumental, Buenos Aires. 11-03-1959, 45,000
Argentina 2 (Corbatta, Callá)
Bolivia 0

Monumental, Buenos Aires. 14-03-1959, 40,000
Peru 5 (Loayza 3, Joya, Gómez Sánchez)
Uruguay 3 (Demarco, Sasia, Douksas)

Monumental, Buenos Aires. 15-03-1959, 40,000
Paraguay 5 (Cayetano Ré 3, Sanabria.I, Aveiro)
Bolivia 0

Monumental, Buenos Aires. 15-03-1959, 40,000
Brazil 3 (Pelé 2, Didi)
Chile 0

Monumental, Buenos Aires. 18-03-1959, 70,000
Uruguay 3 (Demarco, Douksas, Sasia)
Paraguay 1 (Aveiro)

Monumental, Buenos Aires. 18-03-1959, 70,000
Argentina 3 (Corbatta, Sosa.R, OG)
Peru 1 (Loayza)

Monumental, Buenos Aires. 21-03-1959, 50,000
Brazil 4 (Paulo Valentim 2, Pelé, Didi)
Bolivia 2 (Garcia.A, Alcón)

Monumental, Buenos Aires. 21-03-1959, 50,000
Chile 1 (Moreno)
Peru 1 (Loayza)

Monumental, Buenos Aires. 22-03-1959, 50,000
Argentina 3 (Corbatta, Sosa.R, Cap)
Paraguay 1 (Sanabria.C)

Monumental, Buenos Aires. 26-03-1959, 70,000
Chile 5 (Soto.J 2, Soto.M 2, Sánchez.L)
Bolivia 1 (Alcócer 2)

Monumental, Buenos Aires. 26-03-1959, 70,000
Brazil 3 (Paulo Valentim 3)
Uruguay 1 (Escalada)

Monumental, Buenos Aires. 29-03-1959, 40,000
Peru 0
Bolivia 0

Monumental, Buenos Aires. 29-03-1959, 40,000
Brazil 4 (Pelé 3, Chinezinho)
Paraguay 1 (Parodi)

Monumental, Buenos Aires. 30-03-1959, 80,000
Argentina 4 (Belén 2, Sosa.R 2)
Uruguay 1 (Demarco)

Monumental, Buenos Aires. 2-03-1959, 5,000
Paraguay 2 (Aveiro 2)
Peru 1 (Gómez Sánchez)

Monumental, Buenos Aires. 2-03-1959, 5,000
Chile 1 (Moreno)
Uruguay 0

Monumental, Buenos Aires. 4-04-1959, 100,000. Referee: Robles, Chile
Argentina 1 (Pizzuti)
Brazil 1 (Pelé)
Argentina - Negri - Lombardo (Simeone), Griffa (Cardozo), Murúa - Mouriño, Cap Nardiello, Pizzuti, Sosa, Calá (Rodriguez.J), Belén
Brazil - Gilmar - Djalma Santos, Bellini, Orlando Pecanha, Coronel - Dino Sani, Didi Garrincha, Paulo Valentim (Almir Albuquerque), Pelé, Chinezinho

	Ar	Br	Pa	Pe	Ch	Ur	Bo	Pl	W	D	L	F	A	Pts
ARGENTINA	-	1-1	3-1	3-1	6-1	4-1	2-0	6	5	1	0	19	5	11
BRAZIL	-	-	4-1	2-2	3-0	3-1	4-2	6	4	2	0	17	7	10
PARAGUAY	-	-	-	2-1	2-1	1-3	5-0	6	3	0	3	12	12	6
PERU	-	-	-	-	1-1	5-3	0-0	6	1	3	2	10	11	5
CHILE	-	-	-	-	-	1-0	5-2	6	2	1	3	9	14	5
URUGUAY	-	-	-	-	-	-	7-0	6	2	0	4	15	14	4
BOLIVIA	-	-	-	-	-	-	-	6	0	1	5	4	23	1

Top scorer Pelé, Brazil 8

1959

28TH EDITION

Guayaquil 5 - 25 December. Unofficial tournament

Estadio Modelo, Guayaquil, 5-12-1959, 35,000
Brazil 3 (Paulo.PE 2, Zé de Mello)
Paraguay 2 (Parodi, Benitez.G)

Estadio Modelo, Guayaquil, 6-12-1959, 55,000
Uruguay 4 (Silveira, Escalada, Bergara, Pérez.D)
Ecuador 0

Estadio Modelo, Guayaquil, 9-12-1959, 55,000
Argentina 4 (Sanfilippo 3, Sosa.R)
Paraguay 2 (Lezcano.J, Cabral)

Estadio Modelo, Guayaquil, 12-12-1959, 55,000
Uruguay 3 (Escalada, Bergara, Sasia)
Brazil 0

Estadio Modelo, Guayaquil, 12-12-1959, 55,000
Ecuador 1 (Raffo)
Argentina 1 (Sosa.R)

Estadio Modelo, Guayaquil, 16-12-1959, 50,000. Referee: Sobrinho, Brazil
Uruguay 5 (Silveira 2, Bergara, Sasia, Douksas)
Argentina 0
Uruguay - Sosa - Méndez, González, Troche - Mesias, Silveira - Pérez.D, Bergara, Sasia, Douksas, Escalada
Argentina - Negri - Arredondo, Guidi, Grigoul - Murua, Bettinotti (Rattin) - Boggio, Pizzuti, Sosa (Ruiz), Sanfilippo (Rodriguez.J), Belén

Estadio Modelo, Guayaquil, 19-12-1959, 55,000
Brazil 3 (Geraldo, Paulo.PE, Zé de Mello)
Ecuador 1 (Raffo)

Estadio Modelo, Guayaquil, 22-12-1959, 45,000
Argentina 4 (Sanfilippo 3, Garcia.O)
Brazil 1 (Geraldo)

Estadio Modelo, Guayaquil, 22-12-1959, 45,000
Uruguay 1 (Sasia)
Paraguay 1 (Parodi)

Estadio Modelo, Guayaquil, 25-12-1959, 50,000
Ecuador 3 (Spencer, Balseca, Cañarte)
Paraguay 1 (OG)

	Ur	Ar	Br	Ec	Pa	Pl	W	D	L	F	A	Pts
URUGUAY	-	5-0	3-0	4-0	1-1	4	3	1	0	13	1	7
ARGENTINA	-	-	4-1	1-1	4-2	4	2	1	1	9	9	5
BRAZIL	-	-	-	3-1	3-2	4	2	0	2	7	10	4
ECUADOR	-	-	-	-	3-1	4	1	0	3	5	9	2
PARAGUAY	-	-	-	-	-	4	0	1	3	6	11	1

Top scorer José Sanfilippo, Argentina 6

1963

29TH EDITION

Bolivia. 10 - 31 March

Hernán Siles, La Paz, 10-03-1963, 15,000
Bolivia 4 (Lopez.R, Castillo, Camacho, Alcócer)
Ecuador 4 (Raymondi 2, Raffo, Bolaños)

Félix Capriles, Cochabamba, 10-03-1963, 18,000
Argentina 4 (Zárate 2, Rodriguez.M, Fernández.J)
Colombia 2 (Campillo, Aceros)

Félix Capriles, Cochabamba, 10-03-1963, 18,000
Brazil 1 (Flavio)
Peru 0

Félix Capriles, Cochabamba, 13-03-1963, 10,000
Peru 2 (Tenemás, Gallardo)
Argentina 1 (Zárate)

Hernán Siles, La Paz, 14-03-1963, 15,000
Paraguay 3 (Zarate.E 2, Quiñones)
Ecuador 1 (Raffo)

Hernán Siles, La Paz, 14-03-1963, 15,000
Brazil 5 (Flavio 2, Marco Antônio, Oswaldo, Fernando)
Colombia 1 (Gamboa)

Félix Capriles, Cochabamba, 17-03-1963, 18,000
Bolivia 2 (Alcócer, Castillo)
Colombia 1 (Botero)

Hernán Siles, La Paz, 17-03-1963, 8,000
Peru 2 (León, Mosquera)
Ecuador 1 (Raffo)

Hernán Siles, La Paz, 17-03-1963, 8,000
Paraguay 2 (Navarte, Ayala)
Brazil 0

Félix Capriles, Cochabamba, 20-03-1963, 10,000
Paraguay 3 (Cabrera.C 2, Valdez)
Colombia 2 (Campilo, Gamboa)

Félix Capriles, Cochabamba, 20-03-1963, 10,000
Argentina 4 (Savoy 3, Rodriguez.M)
Ecuador 2 (Pineda, Palacios)

Hernán Siles, La Paz, 21-03-1963, 20,000
Bolivia 3 (Camacho, Alcócer, Garcia.A)
Peru 2 (Gallardo, León)

Hernán Siles, La Paz, 24-03-1963, 10,000
Peru 1 (Gallardo)
Colombia 1 (González.F)

Hernán Siles, La Paz, 24-03-1963, 10,000
Argentina 3 (Rodriguez.M, Savoy, Juárez)
Brazil 0

Félix Capriles, Cochabamba, 24-03-1963, 18,000
Bolivia 2 (Castillo, Garcia.A)
Paraguay 0
Bolivia - López.A - Ramirez.M, Zabalaga, Cainzo - Camacho, Herbas - Garcia.A, Aramayo (Blacutt), Alcócer, Ugarte (López.R), Castillo
Paraguay - González.V - Insfran.A, Calonga (Cabrera), Bobadilla (Barbarolli) - Amarilla, Osorio, - Martinez, Lezcano, Zárate (Valdéz), Insfrán.E, Arambulo

Félix Capriles, Cochabamba, 27-03-1963, 20,000
Brazil 2 (Oswaldo 2)
Ecuador 2 (Gando, Raffo)

Félix Capriles, Cochabamba, 27-03-1963, 20,000
Paraguay 4 (Martinez.D 2, Cabrera.C, Zárate.E)
Peru 1 (Gallardo)

Hernán Siles, La Paz, 28-03-1963, 20,000
Bolivia 3 (Castillo, Blacutt, Camacho)
Argentina 2 (Rodriguez.M 2)

Hernán Siles, La Paz, 31-03-1963, 15,000
Ecuador 4 (Raffo 2, Raymondi, Bolaños)
Colombia 3 (Aceros, Bolero, González.F)

Hernán Siles, La Paz, 31-03-1963, 15,000
Argentina 1 (Lallana)
Paraguay 1 (Cabrera.C)

Félix Capriles, Cochabamba, 31-03-1963, 25,000
Bolivia 5 (Ugarte 2, Camacho, Garcia.A, Alcócer)
Brazil 4 (Flavio 2, Almir, Marco Antônio)

	Bo	Pa	Ar	Br	Pe	Ec	Co	Pl	W	D	L	F	A	Pts
BOLIVIA	-	2-0	3-2	5-4	3-2	4-4	2-1	6	5	1	0	19	13	11
PARAGUAY	-	-	1-1	2-0	4-1	3-1	3-2	6	4	1	1	13	7	9
ARGENTINA	-	-	-	3-0	1-2	4-2	4-2	6	3	1	2	15	10	7
BRAZIL	-	-	-	-	1-0	2-2	5-1	6	2	1	3	12	13	5
PERU	-	-	-	-	-	2-1	1-1	6	2	1	3	8	11	5
ECUADOR	-	-	-	-	-	-	4-3	6	1	2	3	14	18	4
COLOMBIA	-	-	-	-	-	-	-	6	0	1	5	10	19	1

Top scorer Carlos Raffo, Ecuador 6

1967

30TH EDITION

Montevideo 17 January - 2 February

Estadio Centenario, Montevideo, 17-01-1967, 15,000
Uruguay 4 (Rocha, Castillo, OG, Oyarbide)
Bolivia 0

Estadio Centenario, Montevideo, 18-01-1967, 15,000
Chile 2 (Marcos 2)
Venezuela 0

Estadio Centenario, Montevideo, 18-01-1967, 15,000
Argentina 4 (Mas, Artime, Bernao, Albrecht)
Paraguay 1 (Mora)

Estadio Centenario, Montevideo, 21-01-1967, 9,000
Uruguay 4 (Urruzmendi 2, Oyarbide, OG)
Venezuela 0

Estadio Centenario, Montevideo, 22-01-1967, 6,000
Argentina 1 (Bernao)
Bolivia 0

Estadio Centenario, Montevideo, 22-01-1967, 6,000
Chile 4 (Gallardo 2, Araya 2)
Paraguay 2 (Riveiro, Apocada)

Estadio Centenario, Montevideo, 25-01-1967, 5,000
Paraguay 1 (Del Puerto)
Bolivia 0

Estadio Centenario, Montevideo, 25-01-1967, 5,000
Argentina 5 (Artime 3, Carone, Marzolini)
Venezuela 1 (Santana)

Estadio Centenario, Montevideo, 26-01-1967, 30,000
Uruguay 2 (Rocha, Oyarbide)
Chile 2 (Gallardo, Marcos)

Estadio Centenario, Montevideo, 28-01-1967, 14,000
Venezuela 3 (Scovino, Santana, González.P)
Bolivia 0

Estadio Centenario, Montevideo, 28-01-1967, 14,000
Argentina 2 (Sarnari, Artime)
Chile 0

Estadio Centenario, Montevideo, 29-01-1967, 17,000
Uruguay 2 (Pérez.D, Urruzmendi)
Paraguay 0

Estadio Centenario, Montevideo, 1-02-1967, 1,000
Bolivia 0
Chile 0

Estadio Centenario, Montevideo, 1-02-1967, 1,000
Paraguay 5 (Rojas.J 2, Garay, Mora 2)
Venezuela 3 (Mendoza, Santana, Scovino)

Estadio Centenario, Montevideo, 2-02-1967, 70,000. Referee: Gasc, Chile
Uruguay 1 (Rocha)
Argentina 0
Uruguay - Mazurkiewicz - Baeza, Paz.J, Varela.L - Cincunegui

(Forlan), Mujica - Pérez.D, Rocha, Oyarbide (Viera), Salvá (Techera), Urruzmendi

Argentina - Roma - Calics, Rattin, Marzolini - Acevedo, Albrecht - Bernao (Raffo), González.A, Artime, Sarnari (Rojas.A), Mas (Carone)

	Ur	Ar	Ch	Pa	Ve	Bo	Pl	W	D	L	F	A	Pts
URUGUAY	-	1-0	2-2	2-0	4-0	4-0	5	4	1	0	13	2	9
ARGENTINA	-	-	2-0	4-1	5-1	1-0	5	4	0	1	12	3	8
CHILE	-	-	-	4-2	2-0	0-0	5	2	2	1	8	6	6
PARAGUAY	-	-	-	-	5-3	1-0	5	2	0	3	9	13	4
VENEZUELA	-	-	-	-	-	3-0	5	1	0	4	7	16	2
BOLIVIA	-	-	-	-	-	-	5	0	1	4	0	9	1

Top scorer Luis Artime, Argentina........5

1975

31ST EDITION

July - October

FIRST ROUND

Group 1

Olimpico, Caracas, 31-07-1975, 30,000

Venezuela 0
Brazil 4 (Palinha 2, Romeu, Danival)

Olimpico, Caracas, 3-08-1975, 30,000

Venezuela 1 (Iriarte)
Argentina 5 (Luque 3, Kempes, Ardiles)

Minerao, Belo Horizonte, 6-08-1975, 80,000

Brazil 2 (Nelinho 2)
Argentina 1 (Asad)

Rosario Central, Rosario, 10-08-1975, 50,000

Argentina 11 (Killer 3, Kempes 2, Zanabria 2, Gallego, Ardiles, Bóveda, Luque)
Venezuela 0

Minerao, Belo Horizonte, 13-08-1975, 32,000

Brazil 6 (Batata 2, Nelinho, Danival, Campos, Palinha)
Venezuela 0

Rosario Central, Rosario, 16-08-1975, 50,000

Argentina 0
Brazil 1 (Danival)

	Br	Ar	Ve	Pl	W	D	L	F	A	Pts
BRAZIL	-	2-1	6-0	4	4	0	0	13	1	8
ARGENTINA	0-1	-	11-0	4	2	0	2	17	4	4
VENEZUELA	0-4	1-5	-	4	0	0	4	1	26	0

Group 2

Estadio Nacional, Santiago, 17-07-1975, 50,000

Chile 1 (Crisosto)
Peru 1 (Rojas.P)

Jesus Bermudez, Oruro, 20-07-1975, 18,000

Bolivia 2 (Mezza.O 2)
Chile 1 (Gamboa)

Jesus Bermudez, Oruro, 27-07-1975, 18,000

Bolivia 0
Peru 1 (Ramirez.O)

Estadio Nacional, Lima, 7-08-1975, 40,000

Peru 3 (Ramirez.O, Cueto, Oblitas)
Bolivia 1 (Mezza.O)

Estadio Nacional, Santiago, 13-08-1975, 15,000

Chile 4 (Araneda 2, Ahumada, Gamboa)
Bolivia 0

Villaneuva, Lima, 20-08-1975, 40,000

Peru 3 (Rojas.P, Oblitas, Cubillas)
Chile 1 (Reinoso)

	Pe	Ch	Bo	Pl	W	D	L	F	A	Pts
PERU	-	3-1	3-1	4	3	1	0	8	3	7
CHILE	1-1	-	4-0	4	1	1	2	7	6	3
BOLIVIA	0-1	2-1	-	4	1	0	3	3	9	2

Group 3

El Campin, Bogota, 20-07-1975, 60,000

Colombia 1 (Diaz.E)
Paraguay 0

Estadio Modelo, Guayaquil, 24-07-1975, 50,000

Ecuador 2 (Carrera, Lasso)
Paraguay 2 (Kiese.H 2)

Atahualpa, Quito, 27-07-1975, 45,000

Ecuador 1 (Carrera)
Colombia 3 (Ortiz, Retat, Castro.P)

Defensores del Chaco, Asuncion, 30-07-1975, 50,000

Paraguay 0
Colombia 1 (Diaz.E)
Abandoned after 45 minutes

El Campin, Bogota, 7-08-1975, 50,000

Colombia 2 (Diaz.E, Calero)
Ecuador 0

Defensores del Chaco, Asuncion, 10-08-1975

Paraguay 3 (Rolón 2, Baez)
Ecuador 1 (Castañeda)

	Co	Pa	Ec	Pl	W	D	L	F	A	Pts
COLOMBIA	-	1-0	2-0	4	4	0	0	7	1	8
PARAGUAY	0-1	-	3-1	4	1	1	2	5	5	3
ECUADOR	1-3	2-2	-	4	0	1	3	4	10	1

SEMI-FINALS

1st leg. El Campin, Bogota, 21-09-1975, 55,000

Colombia 3 (Angulo, Ortiz, Diaz.E)
Uruguay 0

1st leg. Minerao, Belo Horizonte, 30-09-1975

Brazil 1 (Batata)
Peru 3 (Cubillas 2, Casaretto)

2nd leg. Estadio Centenario, Montevideo, 1-10-1975, 70,000

Uruguay 1 (Morena)
Colombia 0
Colombia qualified on goal difference

2nd leg. Villaneuva, Lima, 4-10-1975, 55,000

Peru 0
Brazil 2 (Ze Carlos, Campos)
Peru qualified on lots

FINAL

1st leg. El Campin, Bogota, 16-10-1975, 50,000

COLOMBIA 1 (Castro.P)
PERU 0

Colombia - Zape - Segovia, Zárate (González), Escobar, Bolaños - Calero, Retat, Umaña Rendón (Diaz.E), Londero, Castro.P

Peru - Sartor - Soria, Meléndez, Chumpitaz, Diaz.T - Quesada, Ojeda, Rojas (Ruiz) Barbadillo, Ramirez.O (Casaretto), Oblitas

2nd leg. Estadio Nacional, Lima, 22-10-1975, 50,000
PERU 2 (Oblitas, Ramirez.O)
COLOMBIA 0
Peru - Sartor - Soria, Meléndez, Chumpitaz, Diaz - Quesada, Ojeda, Rojas.P - Barbadillo (Ruiz), Ramirez.O, Oblitas
Colombia - Zape - Segovia, Zárate, Escobar, Bolaños - Calero, Retat, Umaña - Arboleda (Diaz), Londero, Castro.P (Angulo)

Play-off. Olimpico, Caracas, 28-10-1975, 30,000. Referee: Barreto, Uruguay
PERU 1 (Sotil)
COLOMBIA 0
Peru - Sartor - Soria, Meléndez, Chumpitaz, Diaz - Cubillas, Ojeda, Quesada - Rojas.P (Ramirez) Sotil, Oblitas
Colombia - Zape - Segovia, Zárate, Escobar, Bolaños - Ortiz, Calero, Umaña (Retat) Arboleda, Diaz (Castro.P), Campaz

Top scorers Ernesto Diaz, Colombia....4
Leopold Luque, Argentina....4

Final positions:
1 PERU
2 Colombia
3 Brazil
4 Uruguay
5 Argentina
6 Chile
7 Paraguay
8 Bolivia
9 Ecuador
10 Venezuela

1979

32ND EDITION

July - October

FIRST ROUND

Group 1

Pueblo Neuvo, San Cristobal, 1-08-1979, 40,000
Venezuela 0
Colombia 0

Pueblo Nuevo, San Cristobal, 8-08-1979, 14,000
Venezuela 1 (Carbajal)
Chile 1 (Peredo)

El Campin, Bogota, 15-08-1979, 45,000
Colombia 1 (Diaz.E)
Chile 0

El Campin, Bogota, 22-08-1979, 40,000
Colombia 4 (Iguarán, Valverde, Chaparro, Morón)
Venezuela 0

Estadio Nacional, Santiago, 29-08-1979, 70,000
Chile 7 (Peredo 2, Rivas 2, Veliz, Soto.M, Yañez.P)
Venezuela 0

Estadio Nacional, Santiago, 5-09-1979, 85,000
Chile 2 (Caszely, Peredo)
Colombia 0

	Ch	Co	Ve	Pl	W	D	L	F	A	Pts
CHILE	-	2-0	7-0	4	2	1	1	10	2	5
COLOMBIA	1-0	-	4-0	4	2	1	1	5	2	5
VENEZUELA	1-1	0-0	-	4	0	2	2	1	12	-2

Group 2

Hernán Siles, La Paz, 18-07-1979, 40,000
Bolivia 2 (Reynaldo 2)
Argentina 1 (López.C)

Hernán Siles, La Paz, 26-07-1979, 40,000
Bolivia 2 (Aragonés 2)
Brazil 1 (Roberto Dinamite)

Maracana, Rio de Janeiro, 2-08-1979, 130,000
Brazil 2 (Zico, Tita)
Argentina 1 (Coscia)

Jose Amalfitani, Buenos Aires, 8-08-1979, 30,000
Argentina 3 (Passarella, Gáspari, Maradona)
Bolivia 0

Morumbi, São Paulo, 16-08-1979, 50,000
Brazil 2 (Tita, Zico)
Bolivia 0

Monumental, Buenos Aires, 23-08-1979, 68,000
Argentina 2 (Passarella, Diaz.R)
Brazil 2 (Sócrates 2)

	Br	Bo	Ar	Pl	W	D	L	F	A	Pts
BRAZIL	-	2-0	2-1	4	2	1	1	7	5	5
BOLIVIA	2-1	-	2-1	4	2	0	2	4	7	4
ARGENTINA	2-2	3-0	-	4	1	1	2	7	6	3

Group 3

Atahualpa, Quito, 29-08-1979, 45,000
Ecuador 1 (Torres Garcés)
Paraguay 2 (Talavera, Solalinde)

Atahualpa, Quito, 5-09-1979, 30,000
Ecuador 2 (Tenorio, Alarcón)
Uruguay 1 (Victorino)

Defensores del Chaco, Asuncion, 13-09-1979, 25,000
Paraguay 2 (Morel.E, Osorio.J)
Ecuador 0

Centenario, Montevideo, 16-09-1979, 25,000
Uruguay 2 (Bica, Victorino)
Ecuador 1 (Klinger)

Defensores del Chaco, Asuncion, 20-09-1979, 25,000
Paraguay 0
Uruguay 0

Centenario, Montevideo, 26-09-1979, 18,000
Uruguay 2 (Milar, Paz.R)
Paraguay 2 (Morel.E 2)

	Pa	Ur	Ec	Pl	W	D	L	F	A	Pts
PARAGUAY	-	0-0	2-0	4	2	2	0	6	3	6
URUGUAY	2-2	-	2-1	4	1	2	1	5	5	4
ECUADOR	1-2	2-1	-	4	1	0	3	4	7	2

SEMI-FINALS

1st.leg. Estadio Nacional, Lima, 17-10-1979, 50,000
Peru 1 (Mosquera)
Chile 2 (Caszely 2)

2nd leg. Estadio Nacional, Santiago, 24-10-1979, 75,000
Chile 0
Peru 0

1st leg. Defensores del Chaco, Asuncion, 24-10-1979
Paraguay 2 (Morel.E, Talavera)
Brazil 1 (Palinha)

2nd leg. Maracana, Rio de Janeiro, 31-10-1979, 80,000
Brazil 2 (Falcao, Sócrates)
Paraguay 2 (Morel.M, Romero.C)

FINAL

1st leg. Defensores del Chaco, Asuncion, 28-11-1979. Referee: Da Rosa, Uruguay
PARAGUAY 3 (Romero.C 2, Morel.M)
CHILE 0
Paraguay - Fernández.R - Espinola, Sosa.F, Paredes (Cibils), Torales - Torres (Florentin), Kiese.C, Romero - Isasi, Morel.M, Morel.E
Chile - Osbén - Galindo, Quintano, Valenzuela, Escobar.E - Rivas, Soto, Bonvallet (Estay) - Caszely, Fabbiani, Rojas.M

2nd leg. Estadio Nacional, Santiago, 5-12-1979, 55,000. Referee: Barreto, Uruguay
CHILE 1 (Rivas)
PARAGUAY 0
Chile - Osbén - Galindo, Valenzuela, Figueroa, Escobar.E - Rivas, Bonvallet, Rojas.M (Neira) - Caszely, Fabbiani (Estay), Véliz
Paraguay - Fernández.R - Solalinde, Sosa.F, Paredes, Torales - Kiese (Florentin), Talavera, Romero.C - Isasi, Morel.M, Morel.E

Play-off. Jose Amalfitani, Buenos Aires, 11-12-1979, 6,000. Referee: Cesar Coelho, Brazil
PARAGUAY 0
CHILE 0
Paraguay - Fernández.R - Espinola, Paredes, Sosa.F, Torales - Florentin, Kiese, Romero.C Perez (Cibils), Morel.M, Aquino (Torres)
Chile - Osbén - Galindo, Valenzuela, Figueroa, Escobar.E - Rojas.M, Dubó (Estay), Rivas Caszely, Fabbiani (Yañez), Véliz
Paraguay won on goal difference

Top scorers Jorge Peredo, Chile 4
Eugenio Morel, Paraguay 4

Final positions:
1 PARAGUAY
2 Chile
3 Brazil
4 Peru
5 Colombia
6 Uruguay
7 Bolivia
8 Argentina
9 Ecuador
10 Venezuela

1983

33RD EDITION

August - November

FIRST ROUND

Group 1
Atahualpa, Quito, 10-08-1983, 50,000
Ecuador 2 (Vázquez, Vega)
Argentina 2 (Burruchaga 2)

Atahualpa, Quito, 17-08-1983, 50,000
Ecuador 0
Brazil 1 (Roberto Dinamite)

Monumental, Buenos Aires, 24-08-1983, 56,000
Argentina 1 (Gareca)
Brazil 0

Serra Dourada, Gôiania, 1-09-1983, 35,000
Brazil 5 (Roberto Dinamite 2, Renato Gaucho, Éder, Tita)
Ecuador 0

Monumental, Buenos Aires, 7-09-1983, 20,000
Argentina 2 (Ramos, Burruchaga)
Ecuador 2 (Quiñones, Maldonado)

Maracana, Rio de Janeiro, 14-09-1983, 75,000
Brazil 0
Argentina 0

	Br	Ar	Ec	Pl	W	D	L	F	A	Pts
BRAZIL	-	0-0	5-0	4	2	1	1	6	1	5
ARGENTINA	1-0	-	2-2	4	1	3	0	5	4	5
ECUADOR	0-1	2-2	-	4	0	2	2	4	10	2

Group 2
Hernán Siles, La Paz, 14-08-1983, 40,000
Bolivia 0
Colombia 1 (Valderrama.D)

Estadio Nacional, Lima, 17-08-1983, 30,000
Peru 1 (Navarro)
Colombia 0

Hernán Siles, La Paz, 21-08-1983, 45,000
Bolivia 1 (Romero.E)
Peru 1 (Navarro)

El Campin, Bogota, 28-08-1983, 50,000
Colombia 2 (Prince, Fiorillo)
Peru 2 (Malásquez 2)

El Campin, Bogota, 31-08-1983, 45,000
Colombia 2 (Valderrama.D, Molina)
Bolivia 2 (Melgar, Rojas.S)

Estadio Nacional, Lima, 4-09-1983, 50,000
Peru 2 (Leguia, Caballero)
Bolivia 1 (Panaguia)

	Pe	Co	Bo	Pl	W	D	L	F	A	Pts
PERU	-	1-0	2-1	4	2	2	0	6	4	6
COLOMBIA	2-2	-	2-2	4	1	2	1	5	5	4
BOLIVIA	1-1	0-1	-	4	0	2	2	4	6	2

Group 3
Centenario, Montevideo, 1-09-1983, 30,000
Uruguay 2 (Acevedo, Moreno.F)
Chile 1 (Orellana)

Centenario, Montevideo, 4-09-1983, 60,000
Uruguay 3 (Cabrera, Morena.F, Luzardo)
Venezuela 0

Estadio Nacional, Santiago, 8-09-1983, 20,000
Chile 5 (Aravena 2, Arriza, Dubó, Espinoza)
Venezuela 0

Estadio Nacional, Santiago, 11-09-1983, 55,000
Chile 2 (Dubó, Letelier)
Uruguay 0

Olimpico, Caracus, 18-09-1983, 3,000
Venezuela 1 (Febles)
Uruguay 2 (Santelli, Aguilera)

Brigido Iriarte, Caracus, 21-09-1983, 3,000
Venezuela 0
Chile 0

	Ur	Ch	Ve	Pl	W	D	L	F	A	Pts
URUGUAY	-	2-1	3-0	4	3	0	1	7	4	6
CHILE	2-0	-	5-0	4	2	1	1	8	2	5
VENEZUELA	1-2	0-0	-	4	0	1	3	1	10	1

SEMI-FINALS

1st leg. Estadio Nacional, Lima, 13-10-1983, 28,000

Peru 0
Uruguay 1 (Aguilera)

1st leg. Defensores del Chaco, Asuncion, 13-10-1983, 55,000

Paraguay 1 (Morel.M)
Brazil 1 (Eder)

2nd leg. Centenario, Montevideo, 20-10-1983, 58,000

Uruguay 1 (Cabrera)
Peru 1 (Malásquez)

2nd leg. Parque de Sabia, Uberlandia, 20-10-1983, 75,000

Brazil 0
Paraguay 0
Brazil win on away goals

FINAL

1st leg. Centenario, Montevideo, 27-10-1983, 65,000. Referee: Ortiz, Paraguay

URUGUAY 2 (Francescoli 42, Diogo 80)
BRAZIL 0

Uruguay - Rodriguez.R - Diogo, Gutiérrez.N, Acevedo, Agresta - González.W, Barrios, Cabrera - Aguilera (Bossio), Francescoli, Acosta (Ramos)

Brazil - Leao - Leandro, Márcio, Mozer, Junior - Jorginho, China (Tita), Renato Frederico - Renato Gaúcho, Roberto Dinamite, Éder

2nd leg. Fonte Nova, Salvador, 4-11-1983, 95,000. Referee: Perez, Peru

BRAZIL 1 (Jorginho 23)
URUGUAY 1 (Aguilera 75)

Brazil - Leao - Paulo Roberto, Márcio, Mozer, Junior - Jorginho, China, Sócrates - Tita (Renato Gaúcho), Roberto Dinamite (Careca), Éder

Uruguay - Rodriguez.R - Diogo, Gutiérrez.N, Acevedo, González.W - Barrios, Agresta, Cabrera - Aguilera (Bossio), Francescoli, Acosta (Ramos)

Top scorers Jorge Burruchaga, Argentina 3
Roberto Dinamite, Brazil 3
Carlos Aguilera, Uruguay 3
Eduardo Malasquez, Peru 3

Final positions:

1 URUGUAY
2 Brazil
3 Paraguay
4 Peru
5 Chile
6 Argentina
7 Colombia
8 Bolivia
9 Ecuador
10 Venezuela

1987

34TH EDITION

Argentina 27 June - 12 July

FIRST ROUND

Group 1

Monumental, Buenos Aires, 27-06-1987, 40,000

Argentina 1 (Maradona)
Peru 1 (Reyna)

Monumental, Buenos Aires, 2-07-1987, 30,000

Argentina 3 (Caniggia, Maradona 2)
Ecuador 0

Monumental, Buenos Aires, 4-07-1987, 10,000

Peru 1 (La Rosa)
Ecuador 1 (Cuvi)

	Ar	Pe	Ec	Pl	W	D	L	F	A	Pts
ARGENTINA	-	1-1	3-0	2	1	1	0	4	1	3
PERU	-	-	1-1	2	0	2	0	2	2	2
ECUADOR	-	-	-	2	0	1	1	1	4	1

Group 2

Estadio Cordoba, Cordoba, 28-06-1987, 8,000

Brazil 5 (Edú Marangón, OG, Careca, Nelsinho, Romario)
Venezuela 0

Estadio Cordoba, Cordoba, 30-06-1987, 5,000

Chile 3 (Letelier, Contreras, Salgado)
Venezuela 1 (Acosta)

Estadio Cordoba, Cordoba, 3-07-1989, 15,000

Chile 4 (Basay 2, Letelier 2)
Brazil 0

	Ch	Br	Ve	Pl	W	D	L	F	A	Pts
CHILE	-	4-0	3-1	2	2	0	0	7	1	4
BRAZIL	-	-	5-0	2	1	0	1	5	4	2
VENEZUELA	-	-	-	2	0	0	2	1	8	0

Group 3

Rosario Central, Rosario, 28-06-1987, 5,000

Paraguay 0
Bolivia 0

Rosario Central, Rosario, 1-07-1987, 5,000

Colombia 2 (Valderrama.C, Iguarán)
Bolivia 0

Rosario Central, Rosario, 5-07-1987, 10,000

Colombia 3 (Iguarán 3)
Paraguay 0

	Co	Bo	Pa	Pl	W	D	L	F	A	Pts
COLOMBIA	-	2-0	3-0	2	2	0	0	5	0	4
BOLIVIA	-	-	0-0	2	0	1	1	0	2	1
PARAGUAY	-	-	-	2	0	1	1	0	3	1

SEMI-FINALS

Estadio Cordoba, Cordoba, 8-07-1987, 10,000

Chile 2 (Astengo, Vera)
Colombia 1 (Redin)

Monumental, Buenos Aires, 9-07-1987, 65,000

Uruguay 1 (Alzamendi)
Argentina 0

3RD PLACE

Monumental, Buenos Aires, 11-07-1987, 15,000

Colombia 2 (Gómez.G, Galeano)
Argentina 1 (Canigga)

FINAL

Monumental, Buenos Aires, 12-07-1987, 35,000. Referee: Do Arppi, Brazil

URUGUAY 1 (Bengoechea.P 56)
CHILE 0

Uruguay - Pereira - Dominguez, Gutiérrez.N, Trasante, Saldaña - Matosas, Perdomo, Bengoechea.P - Alzamendi (Peña), Francescoli, Sosa.R

Chile - Rojas.R - Reyes, Gomez.E, Astengo, Hormazábal - Mardonez, Contreras, Puebla (Torro) (Rubio) - Letelier, Basay

Top scorer Arnaldo Iguarán, Colombia..4

Final Positions:

1	URUGUAY
2	Chile
3	Colombia
4	Argentina
5	Brazil
6	Peru
7	Bolivia
8	Ecuador
9	Paraguay
10	Venezuela

1989

35TH EDITION

Brazil 1 - 16 July

FIRST ROUND

Group 1

Fonte Nova, Salvador, 1-07-1989, 5,000
Paraguay 5 (Cañete 2, Neffa, Mendoza, OG)
Peru 2 (Hirano, Reinoso)

Fonte Nova, Salvador, 1-07-1989, 18,000
Brazil 3 (Bebeto, Geovani, Baltazar)
Venezuela 1 (Maldonado)

Fonte Nova, Salvador, 3-07-1989, 4,000
Colombia 4 (Higuita, Iguarán 2, De Avila)
Venezuela 2 (Maldonado 2)

Fonte Nova, Salvador, 3-07-1989, 8,000
Brazil 0
Peru 0

Fonte Nova, Salvador, 5-07-1989, 1,000
Peru 1 (Navarro)
Venezuela 1 (Maldonado)

Fonte Nova, Salvador, 5-07-1989, 1,000
Paraguay 1 (Mendoza)
Colombia 0

Fonte Nova, Salvador, 7-07-1989, 3,000
Paraguay 3 (Neffa, Ferreira 2)
Venezuela 0

Fonte Nova, Salvador, 7-07-1989, 9,000
Brazil 0
Colombia 0

Arruda, Recife, 9-07-1989, 60,000
Colombia 1 (Iguarán)
Peru 1 (Hirano)

Arruda, Recife, 9-07-1989, 76,000
Brazil 2 (Bebeto 2)
Paraguay 0

	Pa	Br	Co	Pe	Ve	Pl	W	D	L	F	A	Pts
PARAGUAY	-	0-2	1-0	5-2	3-0	4	3	0	1	9	4	6
BRAZIL	-	-	0-0	0-0	3-1	4	2	2	0	5	1	6
COLOMBIA	-	-	-	1-1	4-2	4	1	2	1	5	4	4
PERU	-	-	-	-	1-1	4	0	3	1	4	7	3
VENEZUELA	-	-	-	-	-	4	0	1	3	4	11	1

Group 2

Serra Dourada, Gôiania, 2-07-1989, 19,000
Ecuador 1 (Benitez)
Uruguay 0

Serra Dourada, Gôiania, 2-07-1989, 40,000
Argentina 1 (Caniggia)
Chile 0

Serra Dourada, Gôiania, 4-07-1989, 8,000
Uruguay 3 (Ostolaza 2, Sosa.R)
Bolivia 0

Serra Dourada, Gôiania, 4-07-1989, 12,000
Argentina 0
Ecuador 0

Serra Dourada, Gôiania, 6-07-1989, 3,000
Ecuador 0
Bolivia 0

Serra Dourada, Gôiania, 6-07-1989, 3,000
Uruguay 3 (Sosa.R, Alzamendi, Francescoli)
Chile 0

Serra Dourada, Gôiania, 8-07-1989, 3,000
Chile 5 (Olmis, Ramirez.J, Astengo, Pizarro, Reyes)
Bolivia 0

Serra Dourada, Gôiania, 8-07-1989, 18,000
Argentina 1 (Caniggia)
Uruguay 0

Serra Dourada, Gôiania, 10-07-1989, 2,000
Chile 2 (Olmis, Letelier)
Ecuador 1 (Aviles)

Serra Dourada, Gôiania, 10-07-1989, 5,000
Argentina 0
Bolivia 0

	Ar	Ur	Ch	Ec	Bo	Pl	W	D	L	F	A	Pts
ARGENTINA	-	1-0	1-0	0-0	0-0	4	2	2	0	2	0	6
URUGUAY	-	-	3-0	0-1	3-0	4	2	0	2	6	2	4
CHILE	-	-	-	2-1	5-0	4	2	0	2	7	5	4
ECUADOR	-	-	-	-	0-0	4	1	2	2	2	2	4
BOLIVIA	-	-	-	-	-	4	0	2	2	0	8	2

FINAL GROUP

Maracana, Rio de Janeiro, 12-07-1989, 60,000
Uruguay 3 (Francescoli, Alzamendi, Paz)
Paraguay 0

Maracana, Rio de Janeiro, 12-07-1989, 110,000
Brazil 2 (Bebeto, Romario)
Argentina 0

Maracana, Rio de Janeiro, 14-07-1989, 45,000
Uruguay 2 (Sosa.R 2)
Argentina 0

Maracana, Rio de Janeiro, 14-07-1989, 64,000
Brazil 3 (Bebeto 2, Romario)
Paraguay 0

Maracana, Rio de Janeiro, 16-07-1989, 90,000
Argentina 0
Paraguay 0

Maracana, Rio de Janeiro. 16-07-1989, 170,000. Referee: Silva, Chile

Brazil	1	(Romario 49)
Uruguay	0	

Brazil - Taffarel - Mazinho, Aldair, Mauro Galvao, Ricardo - Silas (Alemão), Dunga, Branco - Valdo (Josimar), Bebeto, Romario
Uruguay - Zeoli - Herrera, De León, Gutiérrez.N, Dominguez - Ostolaza (Correa), Perdomo, Francescoli - Paz.R (Da Silva), Alzamendi, Sosa.R

	Br	Ur	Ar	Pa	Pl	W	D	L	F	A	Pts
BRAZIL	-	1-0	2-0	3-0	3	3	0	0	6	0	6
Uruguay	-	-	2-0	3-0	3	2	0	1	5	1	4
Argentina	-	-	-	0-0	3	0	1	2	0	4	1
Paraguay	-	-	-	-	3	0	1	2	0	6	1

Top scorer Bebeto, Brazil 6

Final Positions

1	BRAZIL
2	Uruguay
3	Argentina
4	Paraguay
5	Chile
6	Colombia
7	Ecuador
8	Peru
9	Bolivia
10	Venezuela

1991

36TH EDITION

Chile 6 - 21 July

FIRST ROUND

Group 1

Estadio Nacional, Santiago, 6-07-1991, 50,000

Chile	2	(Vilches, Zamorano)
Venezuela	0	

Estadio Nacional, Santiago, 6-07-1991, 50,000

Paraguay	1	(Monzon)
Peru	0	

Collado, Concepcion, 8-07-1991, 21,000

Chile	4	(Rubio, Contreras, Zamorano 2)
Peru	2	(Maestri, Del Solar)

Estadio Nacional, Santiago, 8-07-1991, 2,000

Argentina	3	(Batistuta 2, Caniggia)
Venezuela	0	

Estadio Nacional, Santiago, 10-07-1991, 70,000

Paraguay	5	(Neffa, Guirland, Monzon 2, Sanabria)
Venezuela	0	

Estadio Nacional, Santiago, 10-07-1991, 70,000

Argentina	1	(Batistuta)
Chile	0	

Estadio Nacional, Santiago, 12-07-1991, 4,000

Peru	5	(La Rosa 2, OG, Del Solar, Hirano)
Venezuela	1	(OG)

Collado, Concepcion, 12-07-1991, 4,000

Argentina	4	(Batistuta, Simeone, Astrada, Caniggia)
Paraguay	1	(Cardozo)

Estadio Nacional, Santiago, 14-07-1991, 80,000

Argentina	3	(Latorre, Craviotto, Garcia)
Peru	2	(Yanez, Hirano)

Estadio Nacional, Santiago, 14-07-1991, 80,000

Chile	4	(Rubio, Zamorano, Estay, Vera)
Paraguay	0	

	Ar	Ch	Pa	Pe	Ve	Pl	W	D	L	F	A	Pts
ARGENTINA	-	1-0	4-1	3-2	3-0	4	4	0	0	11	3	8
CHILE	-	-	4-0	4-2	2-0	4	3	0	1	10	3	6
Paraguay	-	-	-	1-0	5-0	4	2	0	2	7	8	4
Peru	-	-	-	-	5-1	4	1	0	3	9	9	2
Venezuela	-	-	-	-	-	4	0	0	4	1	15	0

Group 2

Playa Ancha, Valparaiso, 7-07-1991, 15,000

Colombia	1	(De Avila)
Ecuador	0	

Playa Ancha, Valparaiso, 7-07-1991, 15,000

Bolivia	1	(Suarez.J)
Uruguay	1	(Castro)

Sausalito, Viña del Mar, 9-07-1991, 17,000

Uruguay	1	(Mendez.P)
Ecuador	1	(Aguinaga)

Sausalito, Viña del Mar, 9-07-1991, 17,000

Brazil	2	(Neto, Branco)
Bolivia	1	(Sanchez.E)

Sausalito, Viña del Mar, 11-07-1991, 15,000

Colombia	0	
Bolivia	0	

Sausalito, Viña del Mar, 11-07-1991, 15,000

Brazil	1	(Joao Paulo)
Uruguay	1	(Mendez.P)

Sausalito, Viña del Mar, 13-07-1991, 15,000

Ecuador	4	(Aguinaga, Aviles 2, Ramirez)
Bolivia	0	

Sausalito, Viña del Mar, 13-07-1991, 15,000

Colombia	2	(De Avila, Iguarán)
Brazil	0	

Sausalito, Viña del Mar, 15-07-1991, 30,000

Uruguay	1	(Mendez.P)
Colombia	0	

Sausalito, Viña del Mar, 15-07-1991, 30,000

Brazil	3	(Mazinho II, Santos, Henrique)
Ecuador	1	(Muñoz)

	Co	Br	Ur	Ec	Bo	Pl	W	D	L	F	A	Pts
COLOMBIA	-	2-0	0-1	1-0	0-0	4	2	1	1	3	1	5
BRAZIL	-	-	1-1	3-1	2-1	4	2	1	1	6	5	5
Uruguay	-	-	-	1-1	1-1	4	1	3	0	4	3	5
Ecuador	-	-	-	-	4-0	4	1	1	2	6	5	3
Bolivia	-	-	-	-	-	4	0	2	2	2	7	2

FINAL ROUND

Estadio Nacional, Santiago, 17-07-1991, 50,000. Referee: Maciel, Paraguay

Argentina	3	(Franco 1 39, Batistuta 46)
Brazil	2	(Branco 4, Joao Paulo 52)

Argentina - Goycochea - Basualdo, Ruggeri, Vazquez, Enrique - Astrada, Simeone, Franco, Rodriguez.L (Giunta) - Batistuta, Caniggia
Brazil - Taffarel - Mazinho I, Santos, Rocha, Branco - Henrique, Mauro Silva, Silvio Cesar (Renato), Neto - Marcio, Joao Paulo (Careca)

Estadio Nacional, Santiago, 17-07-1991, 50,000
Chile 1 (Zamorano)
Colombia 1 (Iguarán)

Estadio Nacional, Santiago, 19-07-1991, 65,000
Chile 0
Argentina 0

Estadio Nacional, Santiago, 19-07-1991, 65,000
Brazil 2 (Renato, Branco)
Colombia 0

Estadio Nacional, Santiago, 21-07-1991, 50,000
Brazil 2 (Mazinho II, Henrique)
Chile 0

Estadio Nacional, Santiago, 21-07-1991, 50,000
Argentina 2 (Simeone, Batistuta)
Colombia 1 (De Avila)

	Ar	Br	Ch	Co	Pl	W	D	L	F	A	Pts
ARGENTINA	-	3-2	0-0	2-1	3	2	1	0	5	3	5
BRAZIL	-	-	2-0	2-0	3	2	0	1	6	3	4
CHILE	-	-	-	1-1	3	0	2	1	1	3	2
COLOMBIA	-	-	-	-	3	0	1	2	2	5	1

Top scorer Batistuta, Argentina..........6

Final positions
1 ARGENTINA
2 Brazil
3 Chile
4 Colombia
5 Uruguay
6 Paraguay
7 Ecuador
8 Peru
9 Bolivia
10 Venezuela

1993

37TH EDITION

Ecuador 15 June - 4 July

FIRST ROUND

Group A

Atahualpa, Quito, 15-06-1993, 45,000
Ecuador 6 (Muñoz 21, Noriega 33, Fernandez 58 81, Hurtado.E 65, Aguinaga 84)
Venezuela 1 (Dolgetta 80)

Bellavista, Ambato, 16-06-1993, 22,000
Uruguay 1 (Ostolaza 51)
United States 0

Atahualpa, Quito, 19-06-1993, 45,000
Ecuador 2 (Aviles 9, Hurtado.E 37)
United States 0

Bellavista, Ambato, 19-06-1993, 15,000
Uruguay 2 (Saralegui 23, Kanapakis 80)
Venezuela 2 (Dolgetta 10, Rivas 73)

Atahualpa, Quito, 22-06-1993, 45,000
Venuzuela 3 (Dolgetta 66 78, Echenausi 89)
United States 3 (Henderson 21, Lalas 37, Kinnear 52)

Atahualpa, Quito, 22-06-1993, 45,000
Ecuador 2 (Aviles 28, Aguinaga 88)
Uruguay 1 (Kanapkis 65)

	Ec	Ur	Ve	US	Pl	W	D	L	F	A	Pts
ECUADOR	-	2-1	6-1	2-0	3	3	0	0	10	2	6
URUGUAY	-	-	2-2	1-0	3	1	1	1	4	4	3
VENEZUELA	-	-	-	3-3	3	0	2	1	6	11	2
UNITED STATES	-	-	-	-	3	0	1	2	3	6	1

Group B

Alejandro Serrano, Cuenca, 18-06-1993, 25,000
Paraguay 1 (Cabanas 7)
Chile 0

Alejandro Serrano, Cuenca, 18-06-1993, 25,000
Brazil 0
Peru 0

Alejandro Serrano, Cuenca, 21-06-1993, 15,000
Paraguay 1 (Monzon 38)
Peru 1 (Del Solar 77)

Alejandro Serrano, Cuenca, 21-06-1993, 23,000
Chile 3 (Sierra 16, Zambrano 52 59)
Brazil 2 (Muller 36, Palinha 55)

Alejandro Serrano, Cuenca, 24-06-1993, 25,000
Peru 1 (Del Solar 15)
Chile 0

Alejandro Serrano, Cuenca, 24-06-1993, 25,000
Brazil 3 (Palinha 15 71, Edmundo 61)
Paraguay 0

	Pe	Br	Pa	Ch	Pl	W	D	L	F	A	Pts
PERU	-	0-0	1-1	1-0	3	1	2	0	2	1	4
BRAZIL	-	-	3-0	2-3	3	1	1	1	5	3	3
PARAGUAY	-	-	-	1-0	3	1	1	1	2	4	3
CHILE	-	-	-	-	3	1	0	2	3	4	2

9 de Mayo, Machala, 16-06-1993, 20,000
Colombia 2 (Valencia 35, Aristizabal 89)
Mexico 1 (Alves 58)

Monumental, Guayaquil, 17-06-1993, 15,000
Argentina 1 (Batistuta 54)
Bolivia 0

9 de Mayo, Machala, 20-06-1993, 12,000
Bolivia 1 (Etcheverry 15)
Colombia 1 (Maturana 19)

Monumental, Guayaquil, 20-06-1993, 22,000
Argentina 1 (Ruggeri 28)
Mexico 1 (Patino 14)

Reales Tamarindos, Portoviejo, 23-06-1993, 25,000
Bolivia 0
Mexico 0

Monumental, Guayaquil, 23-06-1993, 65,000
Argentina 1 (Simeone 2)
Colombia 1 (Rincon 5)

	Co	Ar	Me	Bo	Pl	W	D	L	F	A	Pts
COLOMBIA	-	1-1	2-1	1-1	3	1	2	0	4	3	4
ARGENTINA	-	-	1-1	1-0	3	1	2	0	3	2	4
MEXICO	-	-	-	0-0	3	0	2	1	2	3	2
BOLIVIA	-	-	-	-	3	0	2	1	1	2	2

QUARTER-FINALS

Monumental, Guayaquil, 27-06-1993, 25,000
Argentina 1 (Rodriguez 69)
Brazil 1 (Muller 37)
Argentina won 6-5 on pens

Monumental, Guayaquil, 26-06-1993, 15,000
Colombia 1 (Perea 88)
Uruguay 1 (Saralegui 68)
Colombia won 5-3 on pens

Atahualpa, Quito, 26-06-1993, 45,000
Ecuador 3 (Hurtado.E 34, OG 44, Aviles 82)
Paraguay 0

Atahualpa, Quito, 27-06-1993, 15,000
Mexico 4 (Garcia Aspe 22 45, Alves 43, Patino 50)
Peru 2 (Del Solar 65, Barco 83)

SEMI-FINALS

Monumental, Guayaquil, 1-07-1993, 15,000
Argentina 0
Colombia 0
Argentina won 6-5 on pens

Atahualpa, Quito, 30-06-1993, 45,000
Mexico 2 (Sanchez.H 24, Ramirez.R 55)
Ecuador 0

3RD PLACE

Reales Tamarindos, Portoviejo, 3-07-1993, 20,000
Colombia 1 (Valencia 84)
Ecuador 0

FINAL

Monumental, Guayaquil, 4-07-1993, 40,000, Referee: Marcio Rezende, Brazil
Argentina 2 (Batistuta 65 85)
Mexico 1 (Galindo 76)

Argentina - Goycochea - Basualdo, Borelli, Ruggeri (Caceres) - Altamirano, Zapata, Redondo, Gorosito (Rodriguez.L) - Simeone, Acosta, Batistuta. Tr: Basile

Mexico - Campos - Gutierrez (Flores), Suarez, Ramirez.J, Ramirez.F - Patino (Garcia.L), Ambriz, Galindo, Garcia Aspe - Sanchez.H, Alves. Tr: Baron

Top scorer Dolgetta, Venezuela 4

1995

38TH EDITION

Uruguay 5 - 23 July

FIRST ROUND

Group A

Centenario, Montevideo, 5-07-1995, 32,000
Uruguay 4 (Fonseca 14, Otero 25, Francescoli 74p, Poyet 83)
Venezuela 1 (Dolgetta 53)

Municipal, Maldonado, 7-07-1995, 5,000
Paraguay 2 (Cardozo 62, Samaniego 74)
Mexico 1 (Garcia.L 44)

Centenario, Montevideo, 9-07-1995, 45,000
Uruguay 1 (Francescoli 14)
Paraguay 0

Municipal, Maldonado, 9-07-1995, 700
Mexico 3 (Garcia.L 41p 58p, Espinoza 77)
Venezuela 1 (Campos OG 61)

Municipal, Maldonado, 12-07-1995, 500
Paraguay 3 (Cardozo 35, Villamayor 63, Gamarra 82)
Venezuela 2 (Miranda 13, Dolguetta 68)

Centenario, Montevideo, 13-07-1995, 15,000
Uruguay 1 (Saralegui 79)
Mexico 1 (Garcia.L 67)

	Ur	Pa	Me	Ve	Pl	W	D	L	F	A	Pts
URUGUAY	-	1-0	1-1	4-1	3	2	1	0	6	2	7
PARAGUAY	-	-	2-1	3-2	3	2	0	1	5	4	6
MEXICO	-	-	-	3-1	3	1	1	1	5	4	4
VENEZUELA	-	-	-	-	3	0	0	3	4	10	0

Group B

Atilio Paiva Olivera, Rivera, 7-07-1995, 9,000
Colombia 1 (Asprilla 67)
Peru 1 (Palacios 79)

Atilio Paiva Olivera, Rivera, 7-07-1995, 9,000
Brazil 1 (Ronaldao 74)
Ecuador 0

Atilio Paiva Olivera, Rivera, 10-07-1995, 8,000
Colombia 1 (Rincon 45)
Ecuador 0

Atilio Paiva Olivera, Rivera, 10-07-1995, 10,000
Brazil 2 (Zinho 77p, Edmundo 82)
Peru 0

Atilio Paiva Olivera, Rivera, 13-07-1995, 15,000
Ecuador 2 (Diaz.E 62, Mora.J 77)
Peru 1 (Tenorio 84)

Atilio Paiva Olivera, Rivera, 13-07-1995, 24,000
Brazil 3 (Leonardo 31, Tulio 76, Juninho 83)
Colombia 0

	Br	Co	Ec	Pe	Pl	W	D	L	F	A	Pts
BRAZIL	-	3-0	1-0	2-0	3	3	0	0	6	0	9
COLOMBIA	-	-	1-0	1-1	3	1	1	1	2	4	4
ECUADOR	-	-	-	2-1	3	1	0	2	2	3	3
PERU	-	-	-	-	3	0	1	2	2	5	1

Group C

Artigas, Paysandu, 8-07-1995, 18,000
United States 2 (Wynalda 14 20)
Chile 1 (Rozental 63)

Artigas, Paysandu, 8-07-1995, 15,000
Argentina 2 (Batistuta 69, Balbo 82)
Bolivia 1 (Angola 79)

Artigas, Paysandu, 11-07-1995, 8,000
Bolivia 1 (Etcheverry 23)
United States 0

Artigas, Paysandu, 11-07-1995, 15,000
Argentina 4 (Batistuta 2 52, Simeone 6, Balbo 54)
Chile 0

Artigas, Paysandu, 14-07-1995
Bolivia 2 (Mercado 78, Ramos.M 87)
Chile 2 (Basay.I 55 61)

Artigas, Paysandu, 14-07-1995, 15,000
United States 3 (Klopas 21, Lalas 31, Wynalda 58)
Argentina 0

	US	Ar	Bo	Ch	Pl	W	D	L	F	A	Pts
UNITED STATES	-	3-0	0-1	2-1	3	2	0	1	5	2	6
ARGENTINA	-	-	2-1	4-0	3	2	0	1	6	4	6
BOLIVIA	-	-	-	2-2	3	1	1	1	4	4	4
CHILE	-	-	-	-	3	0	1	2	3	8	1

QUARTER-FINALS

Centenario, Montevideo, 16-07-1995, 25,000
Colombia 1 (Rincon 53)
Paraguay 1 (Villamayor 27)
Colombia won 5-4 on pens

Centenario, Montevideo, 16-07-1995, 40,000
Uruguay 2 (Otero 2, Fonseca 30)
Bolivia 1 (Sanchez.O 70)

Paysandu, 17-07-1995, 7,000
United States 0
Mexico 0
United States won 4-1 on pens

Atilio Paiva Olivera, Rivera, 17-07-1995, 20,000
Brazil 2 (Edmundo 9, Tulio 81)
Argentina 2 (Balbo 2, Batistuta 30)
Brazil won 4-2 on pens

SEMI-FINALS

Centenario, Montevideo, 19-07-1995
Uruguay 2 (Adinolfi 51, Otero 70
Colombia 0

Municipal, Maldonado, 20-07-1995, 10,000
Brazil 1 (Aldair 13)
United States 0

3RD PLACE

Municipal, Maldonado, 22-07-1995, 1,000
Colombia 4 (Quinonez 31, Valderrama 38, Asprilla 50, Rincon 76
United States 1 (Moore 53p)

FINAL

Centenario, Montevideo, 23-07-1995, 60,000. Referee: Brizio, Mexico
Uruguay 1 (Bengoechea.P 50)
Brazil 1 (Tulio 30)
Uruguay won 5-3 on pens

Uruguay - Alvez - Mendez, Herrera, Moas, Silva (Adinolfi) - Gutierrez.A, Dorta (Bengoechea.P), Poyet, Francescoli - Fonseca, (Martinez.S), Otero. Tr: Nuñez

Brazil - Taffarel - Jorginho (Beto), André Cruz, Aldair, Roberto Carlos - Cesar Sampaio, Zinho, Dunga, Juninho - Tulio, Edmundo. Tr: Zagalo

Top scorers Gabriel Batistuta, Argentina 4
Luis Garcia, Mexico 4

THE PAN-AMERICAN CHAMPIONSHIPS

The Confederación Panamericana de Football was formed in 1946 in Barranquilla, Colombia, in an attempt to unite all of the countries of the Americas. The motivation was more from the states of Central and North America in a bid to be associated with the more famous countries in South America. The body did not serve a particularly useful function aside from organising three championships before disappearing in the 1960s. The three tournaments do, however, represent the only continent-wide championships for the Americas, given that the football tournament of the Pan American Games is only open to amateurs, in a continent where professionalism is widespread.

1952

1st Panamerican Championship. Santiago 16 March - 20 April

	Br	Ch	Ur	Pe	Me	Pa	Pl	W	D	L	F	A	Pts
BRAZIL	-	3-0	4-2	0-0	2-0	5-0	5	4	1	0	14	2	9
CHILE	-	-	2-0	3-2	4-0	6-1	5	4	0	1	15	6	8
URUGUAY	-	-	-	5-2	3-1	6-1	5	3	0	2	16	10	6
PERU	-	-	-	-	3-0	7-1	5	2	1	2	14	9	5
MEXICO	-	-	-	-	-	4-2	5	1	0	4	5	14	2
PANAMA	-	-	-	-	-	-	5	0	0	5	5	28	0

1956

2nd Panamerican Championship. Mexico City 26 Feb - 18 March

	Br	Ar	CR	Pe	Me	Ch	Pl	W	D	L	F	A	Pts
BRAZIL	-	2-2	7-1	1-0	2-1	2-1	5	4	1	0	14	5	9
ARGENTINA	-	-	4-3	0-0	0-0	3-0	5	2	3	0	9	5	7
COSTA RICA	-	-	-	4-2	1-1	2-1	5	2	1	2	11	15	5
PERU	-	-	-	-	2-0	2-2	5	1	2	2	6	7	4
MEXICO	-	-	-	-	-	2-1	5	1	2	2	4	6	4
CHILE	-	-	-	-	-	-	5	0	1	4	5	11	1

1960

3rd Panamerican Championship. San Jose 7 - 20 March

	Ar	Br	Me	CR	Pl	W	D	L	F	A	Pts
ARGENTINA	-	2-1	3-2	2-0	6	4	1	1	9	4	9
BRAZIL	1-0	-	2-1	4-0	6	3	1	2	10	8	7
MEXICO	0-2	2-2	-	3-0	6	1	2	3	9	10	4
COSTA RICA	0-0	3-0	1-1	-	6	1	2	3	4	10	4

THE ATLANTIC CUP

The Atlantic Cup is an occasional series played between those countries which border the Atlantic Ocean. Of all the minor tournaments played in South America, this was the most important because it involved all the Big Three, Brazil, Argentina and Uruguay. Though not strictly an Atlantic nation, Paraguay were invited to take part in the second and third editions due to their proximity to the other three nations.

1956

1st Atlantic Cup 24 June - 8 July

	Br	Ar	Ur	Pl	W	D	L	F	A	Pts
BRAZIL	-	0-0	2-0	2	1	1	0	2	0	3
ARGENTINA	-	-	2-1	2	1	1	0	2	1	3
URUGUAY	-	-	-	2	0	0	2	1	4	0

1960

The 2nd Atlantic Cup. 3 - 17 August

	Br	Ar	Ur	Pa	Pl	W	D	L	F	A	Pts
BRAZIL	-	5-1	0-1	2-1	3	2	0	1	7	3	4
ARGENTINA	-	-	4-0	1-0	3	2	0	1	6	5	4
URUGUAY	-	-	-	2-1	3	2	0	1	3	5	4
PARAGUAY	-	-	-	-	3	0	0	3	2	5	0

1976

The 3rd Atlantic Cup. 25 February - 9 June

	Br	Ar	Pa	Ur	Pl	W	D	L	F	A	Pts
BRAZIL	-	2-0	3-1	2-1	6	5	1	0	12	5	11
ARGENTINA	1-2	-	2-2	4-1	6	3	1	2	13	9	7
PARAGUAY	1-1	2-3	-	1-0	6	1	3	2	9	11	5
URUGUAY	1-2	0-3	2-2	-	6	0	1	5	5	14	1

THE LIPTON AND NEWTON CUPS

Donated by the English tea baron, Sir Thomas Lipton, the Lipton Cup was the first regular tournament outside of the British Isles, and was contested between the national sides of Argentina and Uruguay. From 1905 until 1927 it was held on a regular basis, but since 1937 it has been played for on only eight occasions, as the fixture list of both countries has grown.

The Newton Cup, named after Richard Newton, a famous English settler in the mid-1800s, was introduced a year after the Lipton Cup. It too was contested by the national sides of Argentina and Uruguay, and like the Lipton Cup it was a regular event until the late 1920s. Since 1937 it has been played for on eight occasions.

Five other trophies have been contested between Argentina and Uruguay. From 1908 until 1923, both the Argentine and Uruguayan Ministries of Education presented a trophy; in 1913, in honour of Argentine president Roque Saenz Peña, a one-off tournament was played for a trophy bearing his name; and on four occasions in the 1930s and 1940s, the two sides met in matches played for the Copa Dr Hector Gomez and the Copa Juan Mignaburu.

Lipton Cup winners

1905	Shared
1906	Argentina
1907	Argentina
1908	Shared
1909	Argentina
1910	Uruguay
1911	Uruguay
1912	Uruguay
1913	Argentina
1915	Argentina
1916	Argentina
1917	Argentina
1918	Shared
1919	Uruguay
1922	Uruguay
1923	Shared
1927	Uruguay
1928	Shared
1929	Shared
1937	Argentina
1942	Shared
1945	Shared
1957	Shared
1962	Argentina
1968	Uruguay
1971	Shared
1973	Shared

Newton Cup winners

1906	Argentina
1907	Argentina
1908	Argentina
1909	Shared
1911	Argentina
1912	Shared
1913	Uruguay
1915	Uruguay
1916	Argentina
1917	Uruguay
1918	Argentina
1919	Uruguay
1920	Uruguay
1922	Shared
1924	Uruguay
1924	Argentina
1927	Argentina
1928	Argentina
1929	Uruguay
1930	Shared
1937	Argentina
1942	Argentina
1945	Argentina
1957	Shared
1968	Argentina
1971	Argentina
1973	Shared
1975	Argentina

THE ROCA CUP

Introduced in 1914, the Roca Cup is contested by the national sides of Brazil and Argentina. The last occasion it was played for, however, was in 1971. It is named after the Argentine general, Julio Roca.

1914	Brazil
1922	Brazil
1923	Argentina
1939	Argentina
1940	Argentina
1945	Brazil
1957	Brazil
1960	Brazil
1963	Brazil
1971	Shared

THE RIO BRANCO CUP

The Rio Branco Cup is contested by the national sides of Uruguay and Brazil. The first of the eight editions was in 1931, the last in 1967. It is named after the main border town between the two countries.

1931	Brazil
1932	Brazil
1940	Uruguay
1946	Uruguay
1947	Brazil
1948	Uruguay
1950	Brazil
1967	Shared

SOUTH AMERICAN YOUTH CUP

Since the introduction of the World Youth Cup in 1977, the South American Youth Cup for Under 20s has been used as a qualifying group for the world event. The first edition, however, was played in its own right as early as 1954.

1954	Uruguay
1958	Uruguay
1964	Uruguay
1967	Argentina
1971	Paraguay
1974	Brazil
1975	Uruguay
1977	Uruguay
1979	Uruguay
1981	Uruguay
1983	Brazil
1985	Brazil
1987	Colombia
1988	Brazil
1991	Brazil
1992	Brazil
1995	Brazil

SOUTH AMERICAN U-17 CHAMPIONSHIP

With the introduction of the World Cup for Under-17s in 1985, a tournament for that age group in South America was instituted, to qualify teams for the world event.

1985	Argentina
1986	Bolivia
1988	Brazil
1991	Brazil
1993	Colombia

OTHER SOUTH AMERICAN TOURNAMENTS

Of all the other irregular tournaments between South American countries, the most notable involve Chile and Paraguay. Chile have played in the Carlos Dittborn Cup against Argentina, the Bernardo O'Higgins Cup against Brazil, and the Juan Pinto Durán Cup against Uruguay. Paraguay have also played in the Rosa Chevallier Boutell Cup against Argentina, the Oswaldo Cruz Cup against Brazil, and the Artigas Cup against Uruguay. Other tournaments include the Pacific Cup between Chile and Peru and the Roque Gomez Peña Cup between Peru and Argentina. The least known perhaps is the Paz del Chaco Cup between Bolivia and Paraguay, played to celebrate the resolution of a border dispute between the two countries.

THE FOOTBALL TOURNAMENT OF THE PAN-AMERICAN GAMES

Open to all the countries of North, South and Central America, this tournament is for amateurs only and is only part of a much bigger tournament involving all sports. Despite them only sending amateur selections, it has still been dominated by countries from the south.

1937	Argentina
1951	Argentina
1955	Argentina
1959	Argentina
1963	Brazil
1967	Mexico
1971	Argentina
1975	Mexico
1979	Brazil
1983	Uruguay
1987	Brazil
1991	United States
1995	Argentina

SOUTH AMERICAN CLUB COMPETITIONS

The Copa Libertadores de América is the premier South American club event. Prior to its inception in 1960, there had been no continent-wide tournament organised by CONMEBOL. A still-born Campeonato Sudamericano de Campeones, organised by Colo Colo in Chile in 1948 and won by Vasco da Gama, attracted the champion teams from all but Colombia, Venezuela and Paraguay, but it was a financial disaster and was not repeated the following year. The success of the European Cup persuaded CONMEBOL to give the idea another try, and at a meeting in Brazil in 1958 the idea was approved in principle. That same year Henri Delaunay, the general secretary of UEFA, proposed an annual meeting between the winners of the European Cup and the winners of a South American tournament. The prospect of a World Club Championship was very appealing to the top clubs, and it was this more than anything else that got the idea off the ground.

The first series was organised in 1960, with seven of the continent's champions taking part. Missing were those of Ecuador, Peru and Venezuela. For the second tournament the following year, all bar the Venezuelans entered, but despite a weak club scene there, by 1964 they found the lure of the competition too hard to resist and entered for the first time.

The Copa Libertadores has had a rich and varied history and has not been without its moments of high drama. It has always been dominated by clubs from around the River Plate, and as in the South American Championship, Brazil's record is not very impressive. Argentina's is far and away the best, with twice as many wins as its nearest rival Uruguay, and in Independiente the Argentines have a team which has won it seven times, the same number as Brazil overall. There have been winners from six of the 10 South American confederations, and only Peru, Ecuador, Bolivia and Venezuela have yet to win, though the first two have been represented in the final on one occasion each.

The first two tournaments were played on a knock-out basis with home and away legs in each tie, including the final. Although the format of the earlier rounds has varied over the years, the final itself has always been played over two legs and is decided on a points basis, with goal difference only counting if the play-off has not produced a winner. Penalties have recently been introduced instead of the play-off.

The first two series were fairly low-key and both won by Peñarol. In 1960 the Uruguayan champions beat Olimpia of Paraguay in the final, the decisive goal coming from Alberto Spencer, their Ecuadoran forward. He remains the all-time top scorer in the Copa Libertadores with 54 goals, 50 for Peñarol and four for Barcelona of Guayaquil. In 1961 Peñarol beat Palmeiras of Brazil, and again Spencer scored the decisive goal. The following year they appeared in their third consecutive final, but this time faced Pelé and his Santos team. They lost, and it was

Santos who really gave the competition the boost it needed. Playing some of the best football the Copa Libertadores has ever seen, they retained their title the following year.

Santos' matches with Benfica and Milan in the World Club Championship also stirred up interest in the Copa Libertadores, and in 1966 it was decided to increase the eligibility to the champions and runners-up of each of the 10 nations. The knock-out system had been replaced in 1962 by three first round groups from which the top side in each qualified for the semi-finals; they were joined there by the previous year's winners. The increase in entrants in 1966 meant a huge number of games in the first round and Brazil withdrew their clubs in protest until 1968 and again from 1969 to 1970. Only when the first round was reorganised into five groups of four did they enter again.

After Santos relinquished their hold, the dominant force were the clubs from Argentina, most notably Independiente and Estudiantes. The latter, from the town of La Plata just south of Buenos Aires, became especially notorious for their rough tactics and gamesmanship. Winners for three successive years, based on one championship victory in 1967, their coach Osvaldo Zubeldia raised his team from an ordinary one to a winning combination by using tactics which found them no favour either among their South American or European opponents. Defensively almost impenetrable, Estudiantes used to goad the opposition into being sent off by a whole host of dirty tricks, and it worked. Unfortunately for the Copa Libertadores, after the positive image put across by Santos, Estudiantes undid most of the good work, especially with their displays in the World Club Championship.

Though never quite in the same league, Independiente did not do much to improve the image of the tournament with their four straight wins in the first half of the 1970s. Once again teamwork proved to be the key rather than the outstanding brilliance of a few players. Independiente, not as successful as either River Plate or Boca Juniors at home, remain the most successful club in the history of the tournament with seven wins. Boca Juniors eventually won in 1977 and again in 1978, but the second of those victories heralded a general decline in Argentina's dominance. Between Boca's final defeat by Santos in 1963 and their final defeat against Olimpia in 1979, an Argentine club appeared in all 17 finals played, winning 12 of them.

In 1979 Olimpia from Paraguay became the first club from one of the so-called smaller nations to win the title, and they repeated their success in 1990. The tournament became more even in its distribution, and in 1989, 1990 and 1991 the finals were notable for the absence of teams from Argentina, Brazil and Uruguay, the longest period in which none of their clubs made a final appearance.

In 1988 the structure of the tournament was changed yet again. The first round formula of five groups of four was kept, but instead of only one club qualifying to make up two semi-final groups of three with the previous years winners, as had been the format since 1971, the top two now went forward and the semi-final group system was replaced by a knock-out competition. The following year, the quite ridiculous system of *three* teams from the first round groups qualifying was introduced, to make the numbers up to a workable 16 teams for the knock-out stage. It means that sixty games are played to eliminate just five teams!

The last few years have seen a proliferation of club tournaments in South America. In 1988 the South American Super Copa was introduced. Played between former winners of the Copa Libertadores it was initially dismissed as just another excuse for a game, but it has the advantage that only the continent's top sides are included. Though it falls short of being a South American super league, the desperate financial position of many of the top sides may well see the Super Copa take over as the number one tournament on the continent, and it may yet progress from a knock-out tournament to one based on a league format.

Though the top sides from Argentina and Uruguay are well represented in the Super Copa, Brazilian teams are not. Of the big Rio de Janeiro clubs only Flamengo have won the Copa Libertadores, whilst from the São Paulo league only São Paulo FC and Santos are eligible to take part. The only other Brazilian clubs to have won the Copa Libertadores are Grêmio from Pôrto Alegre and Cruzeiro from Belo Horizonte.

With the Super Copa has come the Recopa, a play-off between the winners of the Copa Libertadores and the Super Copa. In 1993, as São Paulo FC had won both, the winners of South America's third competition, the CONMEBOL Cup, were invited to take part! The CONMEBOL Cup could be the most interesting development in South American club football since 1960, even though the first few editions were plagued by indifference. It is heavily weighted in favour of the 'Big Three', thus giving some of the larger clubs on the continent an outlet largely denied them at present.

A major problem for the Copa Libertadores over the years has been the movement of the top South American players to Europe. The tournament has undoubtedly lost some of the glamour of the early years, when the likes of Pelé were a regular feature. The irony of Argentinos Juniors' win in 1985 was that it was achieved with the money obtained from the sale of Diego Maradona, who in all his time at the club never appeared in the competition with them.

Another growing problem has been the ever-expanding fixture lists of clubs taking part. During the 1994 CONMEBOL Cup, São Paulo FC ended up playing two games on one day, one in the cup and one in the league. It was a season in which they were runners up in the Copa Libertadores, made it to the semi-finals of the Super Copa, and then won the CONMEBOL Cup!

The early 1990s has seen the rise to prominence again of Brazil and Argentina. São Paulo FC won two Copa Libertadores in a row and capped these performances by going on to win the World Club Championship twice as well, whilst in 1994 Velez Sarsfield became the first side from Argentina to win the Copa Libertadores since River Plate in 1986.

COPA LIBERTADORES

1960	Peñarol	1-0 1-1	Olimpia
1961	Peñarol	1-0 1-1	Palmeiras
1962	Santos	2-1 2-3 3-0	Peñarol
1963	Santos	3-2 2-1	Boca Juniors
1964	Independiente	0-0 1-0	Nacional Montevideo
1965	Independiente	1-0 1-3 4-1	Peñarol
1966	Peñarol	2-0 2-3 4-2	River Plate
1967	Racing Club	0-0 0-0 2-1	Nacional Montevideo
1968	Estudiantes LP	2-1 1-3 2-0	Palmeiras
1969	Estudiantes LP	1-0 2-0	Nacional Montevideo
1970	Estudiantes LP	1-0 0-0	Peñarol
1971	Nacional Montevideo	0-1 1-0 2-0	Estudiantes LP
1972	Independiente	0-0 2-1	Universitario
1973	Independiente	1-1 0-0 2-1	Colo Colo
1974	Independiente	1-2 2-0 1-0	São Paulo FC
1975	Independiente	0-1 3-1 2-0	Union Española
1976	Cruzeiro	4-1 1-2 3-2	River Plate
1977	Boca Juniors	1-0 0-1 0-0 5-4p	Cruzeiro
1978	Boca Juniors	0-0 4-0	Deportivo Cali
1979	Olimpia	2-0 0-0	Boca Juniors
1980	Nacional Montevideo	0-0 1-0	Internacional PA
1981	Flamengo	2-1 0-1 2-0	Cobreloa
1982	Peñarol	0-0 1-0	Cobreloa
1983	Grêmio	1-1 2-1	Peñarol
1984	Independiente	1-0 0-0	Grêmio
1985	Argentinos Juniors	1-0 0-1 1-1 5-4p	America Cali
1986	River Plate	2-1 1-0	America Cali
1987	Peñarol	0-2 2-1 1-0	America Cali
1988	Nacional Montevideo	0-1 3-0	Newell's Old Boys
1989	Nacional Medellín	0-2 2-0 5-4p	Olimpia
1990	Olimpia	2-0 1-1	Barcelona
1991	Colo Colo	0-0 3-0	Olimpia
1992	São Paulo FC	1-0 0-1 3-2p	Newell's Old Boys
1993	São Paulo FC	5-1 0-2	Universidad Catolica
1994	Velez Sarsfield	1-0 0-1 5-3p	São Paulo FC

SUPERCOPA

1988	Racing Club	2-1 1-1	Cruzeiro
1989	Boca Juniors	0-0 0-0 5-3p	Independiente
1990	Olimpia	3-0 3-3	Nacional Montevideo
1991	Cruzeiro	0-2 3-0	River Plate
1992	Cruzeiro	4-0 0-1	Racing Club
1993	São Paulo FC	2-2 2-2 5-3p	Flamengo
1994	Independiente	1-1 1-0	Boca Juniors

THE CONMEBOL CUP

1992	Atlético Mineiro	2-0 0-1	Olimpia
1993	Botafogo	1-1 2-2 3-1p	Peñarol
1994	São Paulo FC	6-1 0-3	Peñarol

THE RECOPA

1988	Nacional Montevideo	1-0 0-0	Racing Club
1989	Boca Juniors	1-0	Nacional Medellín
1990	Olimpia	*	
1991	Colo Colo	0-0 5-4p	Cruzeiro
1992	São Paulo FC	0-0 0-0 4-2p	Cruzeiro
1993	São Paulo FC	3-1	Botafogo
1994	Independiente	1-0	Velez Sarsfield

* Olimpia won both the Copa Libertadores and Super Cup and so were awarded the Recopa

1960

FIRST ROUND

Peñarol 7-1 1-1 Jorge Wilsterman
San Lorenzo 3-0 2-3 EC Bahia
Millonarios 1-0 6-0 Universidad de Chile
Olimpia Bye

SEMI-FINALS

Peñarol 0-0 1-1 2-1 San Lorenzo
Olimpia 5-1 0-0 Millonarios

FINAL

1st leg. Centenario, Montevideo, 12-06-1960. Referee: Robles, Chile

PEÑAROL 1 (Spencer 79)
OLIMPIA 0

Peñarol - Maidana - Martinez.W (Majewski), Pino - Salvador, Goncalvez, Aguerre - Cubilla, Linazza, Spencer, Crescio, Borges
Olimpia - Arias - Rojas.S, Lezcano.V - Rojas.A, Lezcano.C, Osorio - Rodriguez.V, Recalde, Roldan, Cabral, Melgarejo

2nd leg. Sajonia, Asuncion, 19-06-1960, 35,000. Referee: Praddaude, Argentina

OLIMPIA 1 (Recalde 28)
PEÑAROL 1 (Cubilla 83)

Olimpia - Arias - Arevalo, Peralta - Echague, Lezcano.C, Rojas.S - Rodriguez.V, Recalde, Roldan, Cabral, Malgarejo
Peñarol - Maidana - Martinez, Salvador - Pino, Goncalvez, Aguerre - Cubilla, Linazza, Spencer (Hoberg), Grieco, Borges. Tr: Scarone.R

Top scorer: Alberto Spencer, Peñarol 7

1961

FIRST ROUND

Independiente Santa Fé 2-2 3-0 Barcelona

QUARTER-FINALS

Peñarol 5-0 0-2 Universitario
Olimpia 5-2 1-2 Colo Colo
Independiente Santa Fé * 1-0 2-3 Jorge Wilsterman
Palmeiras 2-0 1-0 Independiente
* Santa Fé won on away goals

SEMI-FINALS

Peñarol 3-1 2-1 Olimpia
Palmeiras 4-1 2-2 Independiente Santa Fé

FINAL

1st leg. Centenario, Montevideo, 9-06-1961, 50,000. Referee: Praddaude, Argentina

PEÑAROL 1 (Spencer 89)
PALMEIRAS 0

Peñarol - Maidana - Martinez.W, Cano - Gonzalez.E, Matosas, Aguerre - Cubilla, Ledesma, Spencer, Sasia, Joya
Palmeiras - Waldir - Djalma Santos, Waldemar - Aldemar, Geraldo da Silva, Zequinha - Nilton Santos (Julinho), Humberto, Silva, Chinesinho, Romeiro

2nd leg. Pacaembú, São Paulo, 11-06-1961, 40,000. Referee: Praddaude, Argentina

PALMEIRAS 1 (Nardo 77)
PEÑAROL 1 (Sasia 2)

Palmeiras - Waldir - Djalma Santos, Waldemar - Geraldo da Silva, Zequinha, Aldemar - Julinho, Romeiro (Nardo), Geraldo Scotta, Chinesinho, Gildo. Tr: Zeze Moreira

Peñarol - Maidana - Martinez.W, Cano - Gonzalez.E, Matosas, Aguerre - Cubilla, Ledesma, Sasia, Spencer, Joya. Tr: Scarone.R

Top scorer Alberto Perazzo, Independiente Santa Fé 5

1962

FIRST ROUND

Group 1

	Sa	CP	Mu	Pl	W	D	L	F	A	Pts
Santos	-	9-1	4-3	4	3	1	0	20	6	7
Cerro Porteño	1-1	-	3-2	4	2	1	1	7	13	5
Deport. Municipal	1-6	1-2	-	4	0	0	4	7	15	0

Group 2

	Na	RC	SC	Pl	W	D	L	F	A	Pts
Nacional Montevideo	-	3-2	2-1	4	3	1	0	8	5	7
Racing Club	2-2	-	2-1	4	1	1	2	7	8	3
Sporting Cristal	0-1	2-1	-	4	1	0	3	4	6	2

Group 3

	UC	Em	Mi	Pl	W	D	L	F	A	Pts
Universidad Catolica	-	3-0	4-1	4	2	1	1	10	9	5
Emelec	7-2	-	4-2	4	2	0	2	12	10	4
Millonarios	1-1	3-1	-	4	1	1	2	7	10	3

SEMI-FINALS

Universidad Catolica ....1-1 0-1 ....**Santos**
Peñarol * ....3-1 1-2 1-1 ....Nacional Montevideo
* Peñarol qualified on goal difference

FINAL

1st leg. Centenario, Montevideo, 28-07-1962, 50,000. Referee: Robles, Chile

PEÑAROL 1 (Spencer 18)
SANTOS 2 (Coutinho 29 70)

Peñarol - Maidana - Lezcano, Cano - Gonzalez.E, Matosas, Caetano - Carranza (Moacir), Rocha, Sasia, Spencer, Joya

Santos - Gilmar - Lima, Mauro - Dalmao, Zito, Calvet - Dorval, Mengalvio, Pagao, Coutinho, Pepe (Osvaldo)

2nd leg. Villa Belmiro, Santos, 2-08-1962, 30,000. Referee: Robles, Chile

SANTOS 2 (Dorval 27, Mengalvio 50)
PEÑAROL 3 (Spencer 73, Sasia 18 48)

Santos - Gilmar - Lima, Mauro - Dalmao, Zito, Calvet - Dorval, Mengalvio, Pagao, Coutinho, Pepe

Peñarol - Maidana - Lezcano, Cano - Gonzalez.E, Matosas, Caetano - Carranza (Goncalvez), Rocha, Sasia, Spencer, Joya

Play-off. Monumental, Buenos Aires, 30-08-1962, 36,000. Referee: Horn, Holland

SANTOS 3 (OG 11, Pelé 48 89)
PEÑAROL 0

Santos - Gilmar - Lima, Mauro - Dalmo, Zito, Calvet - Dorval, Mengalvio, Coutinho, Pelé, Pepe

Peñarol - Maidana - Lezcano, Cano - Gonzalez.E, Goncalvez, Caetano - Rocha, Matosas, Spencer, Sasia, Joya

Top scorer Claudio Coutinho, Santos 6

1963

FIRST ROUND

Group 1

	Bo	Al	Mi	Pl	W	D	L	F	A	Pts
Botafogo	-	2-1	*	4	4	0	0	5	1	8
Alianza	0-1	-	0-0	4	1	1	2	2	3	3
Millonarios	0-2	0-1	-	4	0	1	3	0	3	1

* Game awarded to Botafogo 2-0

Group 2

	Pe	Ev	Pl	W	D	L	F	A	Pts
Peñarol	-	9-1	2	2	0	0	14	1	4
Everest	0-5	-	2	0	0	2	1	14	0

Group 3

	BJ	Ol	UC	Pl	W	D	L	F	A	Pts
Boca Juniors	-	5-3	1-0	4	3	0	1	9	6	6
Olimpia	1-0	-	2-1	4	2	0	2	7	10	4
Universidad de Chile	2-3	4-1	-	4	1	0	3	7	7	2

SEMI-FINALS

Santos ....1-1 4-0 ....Botafogo
Peñarol ....1-2 0-1 ....**Boca Juniors**

FINAL

1st leg. Maracanã, Rio de Janeiro, 3-09-1963, 55,000. Referee: Bois, France

SANTOS 3 (Coutinho 2 21, Lima 28)
BOCA JUNIORS 2 (Sanfilippo 43 89)

Santos - Gilmar - Mauro, Geraldino - Dalmao, Zito, Calvet - Dorval, Lima, Coutinho, Pelé, Pepe

Boca Juniors - Errea - Magdalena, Marzolini (Orlando) - Simeone, Rattin, Silveyra - Grillo, Rojas, Menendez, Sanfilippo, Gonzalez.A

2nd leg. La Bombonera, Buenos Aires, 11-09-1963, 50,000. Referee: Bois, France

BOCA JUNIORS 1 (Sanfilippo 46)
SANTOS 2 (Coutinho 50, Pelé 82)

Boca Juniors - Errea - Magdalena, Orlando - Simeone, Rattin, Silveyra - Grillo, Rojas, Menendez, Sanfilippo, Gonzalez.A. Tr: Pedernera

Santos - Gilmar - Mauro, Geraldino - Dalmao, Zito, Calvet - Dorval, Lima, Coutinho, Pelé, Pepe

Top scorer José Sanfilippo, Boca Juniors 7

1964

PRELIMINARY ROUND

Deportivo Italia ....0-0 2-1 ....EC Bahia

FIRST ROUND

Group 1

	Na	CP	Au	Pl	W	D	L	F	A	Pts
Nacional Montevideo	-	2-0	2-0	4	3	1	0	9	2	7
Cerro Porteñ	2-2	-	7-0	4	1	2	1	11	6	4
Aurora	0-3	2-2	-	4	0	1	3	2	14	1

Group 2

	In	Mi	Al	Pl	W	D	L	F	A	Pts
Independiente	-	5-1	4-0	4	3	1	0	11	3	7
Millonarios	*	-	3-2	4	2	0	2	6	8	4
Alianza	2-2	1-2	-	4	0	1	3	5	11	1

* Game awarded to Independiente

Group 3

	CC	Ba	DI	Pl	W	D	L	F	A	Pts
Colo Colo	-	3-2	4-0	4	3	0	1	9	7	6
Barcelona	4-0	-	1-0	4	2	0	2	7	6	4
Deportivo Italia	1-2	3-0	-	4	1	0	3	4	7	2

SEMI-FINALS

Santos ....2-3 1-2 ....**Independiente**
Nacional Montevideo ....4-2 4-2 ....Colo Colo

FINAL

1st leg. Centenario, Montevideo, 6-08-1964. Referee: Horn, Holland

NACIONAL MONTEVIDEO 0
INDEPENDIENTE 0

Nacional - Sosa - Baeza, Alvarez.Em - Ramos, Alvarez.El, Méndez - Pérez, Douksas, Jaburu, Arias (Bergara), Urruzmendi
Independiente - Santoro - Zerrillo, Rolan - Ferreiro, Acevedo, Maldonado - Bernao, Mura, Suarez, Rodriguez.M, Savoy

2nd leg. Cordero, Avellaneda, 12-08-1964. Referee: Larrosa, Paraguay

INDEPENDIENTE 1 (Rodriguez.M 35)
NACIONAL MONTEVIDEO 0

Independiente - Santoro - Guzman, Rolan - Ferreiro, Acevedo, Maldonado - Bernao, Prospitti, Suarez, Rodriguez.M, Savoy. Tr: Giudice
Nacional - Sosa - Baeza, Alvarez.Em - Ramos, Alvarez.El, Méndez - Oyarbide, Douksas, Jaburu, Pérez, Urruzmendi

Top scorers Celino Mora, Cerro Porteño 6
Mario Rodriguez, Independiente 6

1965

FIRST ROUND

Group 1

	BJ	TS	DQ	Pl	W	D	L	F	A	Pts
Boca Juniors	-	2-0	4-0	4	4	0	0	11	3	8
The Strongest	2-3	-	2-2	4	1	1	2	5	7	3
Deportivo Quito	1-2	0-1	-	4	0	1	2	3	9	1

Group 2

	Sa	UC	Un	Pl	W	D	L	F	A	Pts
Santos	-	1-0	2-1	4	4	0	0	10	3	8
Universidad de Chile	1-5	-	5-2	4	1	0	3	6	9	2
Universitario	1-2	1-0	-	4	1	0	3	5	9	2

Group 3

	Pe	Gu	Ga	Pl	W	D	L	F	A	Pts
Peñarol	-	2-0	2-0	4	3	0	1	5	2	6
Guarani Asuncion	2-1	-	2-0	4	3	0	1	6	4	6
Deportivo Galicia	0-0*	1-2	-	4	0	0	4	1	6	0

* Peñarol awarded both points after Deportivo fielded ineligible player

SEMI-FINALS

Independiente *................2-0 0-1 0-0....................Boca Juniors
Santos....................5-4 2-3 1-2 ....**Peñarol**
* Independiente qualified on goal difference

FINAL

1st leg. Cordero, Avellaneda, 9-04-1965. Referee: Yamasaki, Peru

INDEPENDIENTE 1 (Bernao 83)
PEÑAROL 0

Independiente - Santoro - Navarro, Decaria - Ferreiro, Acevedo, Guzman - Bernao, Mura, Suarez (De la Mata), Avallay, Savoy
Peñarol - Mazurkiewicz - Pérez, Varela - Forlan, Goncalvez, Caetano - Ledesma, Rocha, Silva, Sasia, Joya

2nd leg. Centenario, Montevideo, 12-04-1965. Referee: Yamasaki, Peru

PEÑAROL 3 (Goncalvez 14, Reznik 43, Rocha 46)
INDEPENDIENTE 1 (De la Mata 88)

Peñarol - Mazurkiewicz - Pérez, Varela - Forlan (Reznik), Goncalvez, Caetano - Ledesma, Rocha, Sasia, Silva, Joya
Independiente - Santoro - Navarro, Paflik - Ferreiro, Acevedo, Guzman - Bernao, Mura, Suarez, Avallay (De la Mata), Savoy

Play-off. Estadio Nacional, Santiago, 15-04-1965. Referee: Yamasaki, Peru

INDEPENDIENTE 4 (Acevedo 10, Bernao 27, Avallay 33, Mura 82)
PEÑAROL 1 (Joya 44)

Independiente - Santoro - Navarro, Decaria - Ferreiro, Acevedo, Guzman - Bernao, Mura, De la Mata (Mori), Avallay, Savoy. Tr: Giudice
Peñarol - Mazurkiewicz - Pérez, Varela - Forlan, Goncalvez, Caetano - Ledesma, Rocha, Reznik (Sasia), Silva, Joya

Top scorer Pelé, Santos 7

1966

FIRST ROUND

Group 1

	RP	BJ	DI	Un	Al	La	Pl	W	D	L	F	A	Pts
River Plate	-	2-1	2-1	5-0	3-2	3-0	10	8	1	1	23	8	17
Boca Juniors	2-0	-	5-2	2-0	1-0	2-1	10	7	0	3	19	9	14
Deportivo Italia	0-3	1-2	-	2-2	3-1	1-1	10	4	2	4	15	18	10
Universitario	1-1	2-1	1-2	-	2-0	1-0	10	3	4	3	10	14	10
Alianza	0-2	1-0	1-2	1-1	-	3-0	10	2	1	7	10	16	5
Deportivo Lara	1-2	0-3	0-1	0-0	2-1	-	10	1	2	7	5	17	4

Group 2

	UC	Gu	Ol	UC	Pl	W	D	L	F	A	Pts
Universidad Catolica	-	2-0	4-0	2-2	6	2	3	1	9	4	7
Guarani Asuncion	2-1	-	2-0	1-1	6	2	2	2	8	9	6
Olimpia	0-0	3-3	-	2-0	6	2	2	2	7	10	6
Universidad de Chile	0-0	2-0	1-2	-	6	1	3	2	6	7	5

Play-off
Guarani.................... 2-1 ....Olimpia

Group 3

	Pe	Na	Mu	JW	Em	NO	Pl	W	D	L	F	A	Pts
Peñarol	-	0-4	2-1	2-0	4-1	2-0	10	8	0	2	20	10	16
Nacional Montevideo	0-3	-	4-1	3-0	2-0	3-1	10	7	1	2	22	10	15
Deport. Municipal	1-3	3-2	-	1-1	4-1	5-1	10	4	2	4	22	20	10
Jorge Wilsterman	1-0	0-0	1-1	-	2-1	4-1	10	3	3	4	12	15	9
Emelec	1-2	0-1	2-1	3-1	-	2-1	10	4	0	6	16	18	8
Nueve de Octubre	1-2	2-3	3-4	3-2	0-5	-	10	1	0	9	13	32	2

SEMI-FINALS

Group 1

	RP	In	BJ	Gu	Pl	W	D	L	F	A	Pts
River Plate	-	4-2	2-2	3-1	6	3	2	1	13	8	8
Independiente	1-1	-	2-0	2-1	6	3	2	1	9	6	8
Boca Juniors	1-0	0-0	-	1-1	6	2	3	1	7	6	7
Guarani Asuncion	1-3	0-2	1-3	-	6	0	1	5	5	14	1

Play-off
River Plate ....2-1 ....Independiente

Group 2

	Pe	UC	Na	Pl	W	D	L	F	A	Pts
Peñarol	-	2-0	3-0	4	3	0	1	6	1	6
Universidad Catolica	1-0	-	1-0	4	2	0	2	4	5	4
Nacional Montevideo	0-1	3-2	-	4	1	0	3	3	7	2

FINAL

1st leg. Centenario, Montevideo, 12-05-1966, 49,000. Referee: Goicoechea, Argentina

PEÑAROL 2 (Abbadie 75, Joya 85)
RIVER PLATE 0

Peñarol - Mazurkiewicz - Lezcano, Diaz - Forlan, Goncalvez, Caetan - Abbadie, Rocha, Silva, Cortes, Joya
River Plate - Carrizo - Guzman, Vieitez - Sainz, Matosas, Bayo - Cubilla, Loayza (Onega.E), Onega.D, Sarnari, Solari

2nd leg. Monumental, Buenos Aires, 18-05-1966, 60,000. Referee: Codesal, Uruguay

RIVER PLATE 3 (Onega.D 38, Sarnari 52, Onega.E 73)
PEÑAROL 2 (Rocha 32, Spencer 50)
River Plate - Carrizo - Guzman, Vieitez - Sainz, Sarnari, Matosas - Cubilla, Solari, Onega.D (Lallana), Onega.E, Mas
Peñarol - Mazurkiewicz - Lezcano, Diaz - Forlan, Goncalvez, Caetano - Abbadie, Rocha, Spencer, Cortez, Joya

Play-off. Estadio Nacional, Santiago, 20-05-1966, 39,000. Referee: Vicuña, Chile
PEÑAROL 4 (Spencer 57 101, Abbadie 72, Rocha 109)
RIVER PLATE 2 (Onega.D 37, Solari 42)
Peñarol - Mazurkiewicz - Lezcano, Diaz (Gonzalez) - Forlan, Goncalvez, Caetano - Abbadie, Cortes, Spencer, Rocha, Joya
River Plate - Carrizo - Grispo, Vieytez - Sainz (Solari), Matosas, Sarnari - Cubilla, Onega.E, Lallana, Onega.D, Mas. Tr: Cesarini

Top scorer: Daniel Onega, River Plate 17

1967

FIRST ROUND

Group 1

	Cr	Un	SB	Ga	DI	Pl	W	D	L	F	A	Pts
Cruzeiro	-	4-1	3-1	3-1	3-0	8	7	1	0	22	6	15
Universitario	2-2	-	1-0	2-0	3-0	8	5	1	2	11	8	11
Sport Boys	1-2	0-1	-	2-0	5-2	8	2	1	5	10	11	5
Deportivo Galicia	0-1	2-0	2-1	-	0-0	8	2	1	5	5	10	5
Deportivo Italia	0-4	0-1	0-0	1-0	-	8	1	2	5	3	16	4

Group 2

	RC	RP	Me	Bo	SF	TO	Pl	W	D	L	F	A	Pts
Racing Club	-	2-0	5-2	6-0	4-1	6-0	10	8	1	1	29	7	17
River Plate	0-0	-	6-2	2-0	4-0	4-0	10	6	3	1	29	9	15
Independ. Medellín	0-2	0-1	-	2-2	4-0	3-0	10	4	1	5	17	19	9
Bolivar	0-2	3-3	0-2	-	2-2	1-0	10	2	4	4	12	22	8
Indep. Santa Fé	1-2	2-2	2-0	1-2	-	2-0	10	2	2	6	13	26	6
31 de Octubre	3-0	0-7	1-2	2-2	6-2	-	10	2	1	7	12	29	5

Group 3

	Na	CC	UC	Gu	Ba	Em	CP	Pl	W	D	L	F	A	Pts
Nacional Montevideo	-	5-2	3-0	3-1	2-0	4-1	4-1	12	9	1	2	34	12	19
Colo Colo	3-2	-	4-2	1-0	3-2	3-2	5-1	12	7	1	4	30	28	15
Universidad Catolica	0-0	5-2	-	1-1	2-1	5-2	3-1	12	5	3	4	22	18	13
Guarani Asuncion	0-1	4-2	1-1	-	4-1	3-0	1-2	12	4	2	6	18	15	10
Barcelona	2-1	1-1	0-2	2-1	-	2-1	1-2	12	4	1	7	14	23	9
Emelec	0-3	4-3	2-1	0-2	3-0	-	2-1	12	4	1	7	18	28	9
Cerro Porteño	2-6	0-1	1-0	1-0	1-2	1-1	-	12	4	1	7	14	26	9

SEMI-FINALS

Group 1

	RC	Un	RP	CC	Pl	W	D	L	F	A	Pts
Racing Club	-	1-2	3-1	2-0	6	4	1	1	11	5	9
Universitario	1-2	-	2-2	3-0	6	4	1	1	10	5	9
River Plate	0-0	0-1	-	1-1	6	0	3	3	4	8	3
Colo Colo	1-3	0-1	1-0	-	6	1	1	4	3	10	3

Play-off
Racing Club ....2-1 ....Universitario

Group 2

	Na	Cr	Pe	Pl	W	D	L	F	A	Pts
Nacional Montevideo	-	2-0	1-0	4	2	1	1	6	4	5
Cruzeiro	2-1	-	1-0	4	2	0	2	5	6	4
Peñarol	2-2	3-2	-	4	1	1	2	5	6	3

FINAL

1st leg. Mozart y Cuyo, Avellaneda, 15-08-1967, 54,000. Referee: Orozco, Peru
RACING CLUB 0
NACIONAL MONTEVIDEO 0
Racing - Cejas - Perfumo, Diaz - Martin, Mori, Basile - Martinoli, Rulli, Raffo, Rodriguez, Maschio
Nacional - Dominguez - Manicera, Alvarez.Em - Ubinas, Montero Castillo, Mujica - Esparrago, Viera, Celio, Sosa, Urruzmendi

2nd leg. Centenario, Montevideo, 25-08-1967, 62,000. Referee: Orozco, Peru
NACIONAL MONTEVIDEO 0
RACING CLUB 0
Nacional - Dominguez - Manicera, Alvarez.Em - Ubinas, Montero Castillo, Mujica - Esparrago, Viera, Celio, Sosa, Urruzmendi
Racing - Cejas - Perfumo, Diaz - Martin, Mori, Basile - Cardozo, Rulli, Cardenas, Raffo, Maschio

Play-off. Estadio Nacional, Santiago, 29-08-1967, 25,000. Referee: Orozco, Peru
RACING CLUB 2 (Cardozo 14, Raffo 43)
NACIONAL MONTEVIDEO 1 (Esparrago 79)
Racing - Cejas - Perfumo, Diaz - Martin, Mori, Basile - Cardozo (Parenti), Rulli, Cardenas, Raffo, Maschio. Tr: Pizzutti
Nacional - Dominguez - Manicera, Alvarez.Em - Ubinas, Montero Castillo, Mujica - Urruzmendi, Viera, Celio, Esparrago, Morales (Oyarbide)

Top scorer: Norberto Raffo, Racing Club 14

1968

FIRST ROUND

Group 1

	Es	In	DC	Mi	Pl	W	D	L	F	A	Pts
Estudiantes LP	-	2-0	3-0	0-0	6	5	1	0	12	3	11
Independiente	2-4	-	1-1	3-1	6	2	1	3	8	10	5
Deportivo Cali	1-2	1-0	-	1-0	6	2	1	3	6	10	5
Millonarios	0-1	1-2	4-2	-	6	1	1	4	6	9	3

Play-off for second place
Independiente ....3-2 ....Deportivo Cali

Group 2

	Un	SC	JW	AR	Pl	W	D	L	F	A	Pts
Universitario	-	1-1	5-1	6-0	6	3	3	0	17	4	9
Sporting Cristal	2-2	-	2-0	1-1	6	3	3	0	11	5	9
Jorge Wilsterman	0-0	0-1	-	3-0	5	1	1	3	4	8	3
Always Ready	0-3	1-4	-	-	5	0	1	4	2	17	1

Group 3

	UC	Em	Na	UC	Pl	W	D	L	F	A	Pts
Universidad Catolica	-	1-1	2-0	2-1	6	4	1	1	11	7	9
Emelec	1-2	-	0-0	2-1	6	2	3	1	5	4	7
Nacional Quito	2-1	0-1	-	3-1	6	2	1	3	5	6	5
Universidad de Chile	2-3	0-0	1-0	-	6	1	1	4	6	10	3

Group 4

	Pe	Gu	Na	Li	Pl	W	D	L	F	A	Pts
Peñarol	-	2-0	1-0	4-0	6	3	2	1	8	2	8
Guarani Asuncion	1-1	-	2-1	1-1	6	2	3	1	8	7	7
Nacional Montevideo	0-0	2-2	-	4-0	6	2	2	2	9	5	6
Libertad	1-0	0-2	0-2	-	6	1	1	4	2	13	3

Group 5

	Pa	PC	Ga	NR	Pl	W	D	L	F	A	Pts
Palmeiras	-	3-0	2-0	0-0	6	5	1	0	12	3	11
Portugues Caracas	1-2	-	1-0	1-1	6	2	1	3	5	11	5
Deportivo Galicia	1-2	2-0	-	2-1	6	2	0	4	5	7	4
Nautico Recife	1-3	3-2*	1-0	-	6	1	2	3	7	8	4

* Points awarded to Portugues. Nautico fielded ineligible players.

QUARTER-FINALS

Group 1

	Es	In	Un	Pl	W	D	L	F	A	Pts
Estudiantes LP	-	1-0	1-0	4	3	0	1	4	2	6
Independiente	1-2	-	3-0	4	2	0	2	7	3	4
Universitario	1-0	0-3	-	4	1	0	3	1	7	2

Group 2

	Pe	SC	Em	PC	Pl	W	D	L	F	A	Pts
Peñarol	-	1-1	2-0	4-0	6	4	2	0	11	1	11
Sporting Cristal	0-0	-	0-1	2-0	6	2	3	1	6	3	7
Emelec	0-1	0-2	-	2-0	6	1	1	4	3	7	4
Portugues Caracas	0-3	1-1	2-0	-	6	1	1	4	3	12	3

Group 3

	Pa	Gu	UC	Pl	W	D	L	F	A	Pts
Palmeiras	-	2-1	4-1	4	3	0	1	7	4	6
Guarani Asuncion	2-0	-	2-1	4	2	0	2	7	7	4
Universidad Catolica	0-1	4-2	-	4	1	0	3	6	9	2

SEMI-FINALS

Estudiantes LP *..........3-0 0-2 1-1 ....Racing Club
Palmeiras..........1-0 2-1 ....Peñarol
* Estudiantes qualified on goal difference

FINAL

1st leg. Estadio La Plata, La Plata, 2-05-1968. Referee: Marino, Uruguay

ESTUDIANTES LP 2 (Veron 83, Flores 87)
PALMEIRAS 1 (Servilio)

Estudiantes - Poletti - Fucceneco, Spadaro - Madero, Malbernat, Pachamé - Bilardo, Flores, Ribaudo (Lavezzi), Conigliaro, Veron

Palmeiras - Waldir - Geraldo da Silva, Baldochi - Osmar, Gilberto, Ademir da Guia - Dudu, Singue, Tupazinho, Servilio, Rinaldo

2nd leg. Pacaembú, São Paulo, 7-05-1968. Referee: Massaro, Chile

PALMEIRAS 3 (Tupazinho 10 68, Reinaldo 54)
ESTUDIANTES LP 1 (Veron 72)

Palmeiras - Waldir - Escalera, Baldochi - Osmar, Ferrari, Ademir da Guia - Dudu, Servilio (China), Tupazinho, Rinaldo, Singue

Estudiantes - Poletti - Spadaro, Madero - Fucceneco, Pachamé, Malbernat - Bilardo, Ribaudo, Flores (Togneri), Conigliaro, Veron

Play-off. Centenario, Montevideo, 16-05-1968. Referee: Orozio, Peru

ESTUDIANTES LP 2 (Ribaudo 13, Veron 82)
PALMEIRAS 0

Estudiantes - Poletti - Aguirre Suarez, Madero - Malbernat, Pachamé, Medina - Bilardo, Flores, Ribaudo, Conigliaro, Veron. Tr: Zubeldia

Palmeiras - Waldir - Escalera, Baldochi - Osmar, Ademir da Guia, Ferrari - Singue, Dudu, Tupazinho, Servilio (China), Rinaldo

Top scorer: Tupazinho, Palmeiras 11

1969

FIRST ROUND

Group 1

	DC	DI	UM	Ca	Pl	W	D	L	F	A	Pts
Deportivo Cali	-	3-0	3-1	2-0	6	3	2	1	12	6	8
Deportivo Italia	2-1	-	2-0	2-0	6	3	1	2	7	8	7
Union Magdalena	2-2	3-0	-	1-0	6	2	1	3	7	8	5
Canarias	1-1	1-1	1-0	-	6	1	2	3	3	7	4

Group 2

	Wa	SC	UC	JA	Pl	W	D	L	F	A	Pts
Wanderers	-	2-0	3-1	4-1	6	3	0	3	13	10	6
Sporting Cristal	2-1	-	2-0	2-2	6	2	2	2	11	11	6
Universidad Catolica	3-2	3-2	-	4-2	6	3	0	3	12	13	6
Juan Aurich	3-1	3-3	2-1	-	6	2	0	2	13	15	6

Group 2 play-off

	UC	Wa	SC	JA	Pl	W	D	L	F	A	Pts
Universidad Catolica	-	-	-	4-1	2	2	0	0	6	2	4
Wanderers	-	-	1-1	-	2	1	1	0	2	1	3
Sporting Cristal	1-2	-	-	-	2	0	1	1	2	3	1
Juan Aurich	-	0-1	-	-	2	0	0	2	1	5	0

Group 3

	CP	Ol	Bo	Li	Pl	W	D	L	F	A	Pts
Cerro Porteño	-	4-1	1-1	6-0	6	4	1	1	15	5	9
Olimpia	1-2	-	4-0	3-0	6	3	1	2	12	7	7
Bolivar	2-1	1-1	-	1-0	6	2	3	1	6	8	7
Litoral	0-1	0-2	1-1	-	6	0	1	5	1	14	1

Play-off
Olimpia..........2-1 ....Bolivar

Group 4

	Pe	Na	DQ	Ba	Pl	W	D	L	F	A	Pts
Peñarol	-	1-1	5-2	5-2	6	3	3	0	16	8	9
Nacional Montevideo	2-2	-	4-0	2-0	6	2	4	0	10	4	8
Deportivo Quito	1-1	0-0	-	1-0	6	1	3	2	4	10	5
Barcelona	0-2	1-1	0-0	-	6	0	2	4	3	11	2

QUARTER-FINALS

Group 1

	UC	CP	DI	Pl	W	D	L	F	A	Pts
Universidad Catolica	-	0-0	4-0	4	2	1	1	7	3	5
Cerro Porteño	0-1	-	1-0	4	1	2	1	1	1	4
Deportivo Italia	3-2	0-0	-	4	1	1	2	3	7	3

Group 2

	Na	DC	Wa	Pl	W	D	L	F	A	Pts
Nacional Montevideo	-	2-0	2-0	4	3	1	0	10	2	7
Deportivo Cali	1-5	-	5-1	4	1	1	2	9	11	3
Wanderers	1-1	3-3	-	4	0	2	2	5	11	2

Group 3

	Pe	Ol	Pl	W	D	L	F	A	Pts
Peñarol	-	1-1	2	1	1	0	2	1	3
Olimpia	0-1	-	2	0	1	1	1	2	1

SEMI-FINALS

Estudiantes LP..........3-1 3-1 ....Universidad Catolica
Nacional Montevideo *...2-0 0-1 0-0 ....Peñarol
* Nacional qualified on goal difference

FINAL

1st leg. Centenario, Montevideo, 15-05-1969, 50,000. Referee: Massaro, Chile

NACIONAL MONTEVIDEO 0
ESTUDIANTES LP 1 (Flores 66)

Nacional - Manga - Ancheta, Alvarez.Em - Ubinas, Montero Castillo, Mujica - Prieto, Maneiro (Esparrago), Cubilla, Celio, Morales (Taveira)

Estudiantes - Poletti - Togneri, Aguirre Suarez - Madero, Malbernat, Bilardo - Pachamé, Flores, Rudzki (Ribaudo), Conigliaro, Veron

2nd leg. Estadio La Plata, La Plata, 22-05-1969, 30,000. Referee: Delgado, Colombia

ESTUDIANTES LP 2 (Flores 22, Conigliaro 37)
NACIONAL MONTEVIDEO 0

Estudiantes - Poletti - Togneri, Aguirre Suarez - Madero, Malbernat, Bilardo - Pachamé, Flores, Rudzki, Conigliaro, Veron. Tr: Zubeldia

Nacional - Manga - Ubinas, Ancheta - Alvarez.Em, Mujica, Montero Castillo - Prieto, Esparrago, Cubilla, Garcia (Silveyra), Morales

Top scorers Alberto Ferrero, Wanderers Santiago 9

1970

FIRST ROUND

Group 1

	BJ	RP	Bo	Un	Pl	W	D	L	F	A	Pts
Boca Juniors	-	2-1	2-0	4-0	6	5	1	0	14	4	11
River Plate	1-3	-	1-0	9-0	6	3	1	2	15	6	7
Bolivar	2-3	1-1	-	2-0	6	1	2	3	7	9	4
Universitario	0-0	0-2	2-2	-	6	0	2	4	2	19	2

Group 2

	Na	Pe	Va	Ga	Pl	W	D	L	F	A	Pts
Nacional Montevideo	-	1-1	1-0	2-0	6	4	2	0	13	3	10
Peñarol	0-0	-	11-2	4-1	6	3	3	0	17	4	9
Valencia	2-5	0-0	-	3-1	6	2	1	3	9	18	5
Deportivo Galicia	0-4	0-1	0-2	-	6	0	0	6	2	16	0

Group 3

	Un	LQ	DA	AQ	Pl	W	D	L	F	A	Pts
Universitario	-	2-0	2-1	3-0	6	4	1	1	11	4	9
LDU Quito	2-0	-	1-2	4-1	6	3	1	2	10	6	7
Defensor Arica	1-1	0-0	-	0-1	6	1	3	2	5	6	5
America Quito	0-3	1-3	1-1	-	6	1	1	4	4	14	3

Group 4

	GU	UC	OI	DC	AC	Ra	Pl	W	D	L	F	A	Pts
Guarani Asuncion	-	1-0	1-0	1-1	4-1	2-0	10	5	5	0	12	4	15
Universidad de Chile	0-0	-	2-1	3-1	2-1	2-1	10	5	3	2	19	11	13
Olimpia	0-0	1-1	-	5-1	1-0	5-1	10	4	4	2	19	11	12
Deportivo Cali	0-0	2-0	0-1	-	4-2	3-2	10	5	2	3	18	16	12
America Cali	2-2	2-2	1-1	2-4	-	1-0	10	1	3	6	12	22	5
Rangers	0-1	1-7	4-4	0-2	2-0	-	10	1	1	8	11	27	3

QUARTER-FINALS

Group 1

	RP	BJ	Un	Pl	W	D	L	F	A	Pts
River Plate	-	1-1	5-3	4	3	1	0	9	5	7
Boca Juniors	0-1	-	1-0	4	2	1	1	5	3	5
Universitario	1-2	1-3	-	4	0	0	4	5	11	0

Group 2

	Pe	Gu	LQ	Pl	W	D	L	F	A	Pts
Peñarol	-	1-0	2-1	4	3	0	1	6	4	6
Guarani Asuncion	2-0	-	1-1	4	1	1	2	3	3	3
LDU Quito	1-3	1-0	-	4	1	1	2	4	6	3

Group 3

	UC	Na	Pl	W	D	L	F	A	Pts
Universidad de Chile	-	3-0	2	1	0	1	3	2	2
Nacional Montevideo	2-0	-	2	1	0	1	2	3	2

Play-off
Universidad de Chile ....2-1 ....Nacional Montevideo

SEMI-FINALS

Estudiantes LP......................3-1 1-0 ....River Plate
Peñarol *..............................2-0 0-1 2-2...........Universidad de Chile
* Peñarol qualified on goal difference

FINAL

1st leg. Estadio La Plata, La Plata, 21-05-1970, 36,000. Referee: Robles, Chile
ESTUDIANTES LP 1 (Togneri 87)
PEÑAROL 0
Estudiantes - Errea - Pagnanini, Spadaro, Togneri, Pachamé - Solari, Bilardo, Echecopar - Conigliaro, Flores (Rudzki), Veron
Peñarol - Pintos - Soria (Gonzalez), Figueroa - Peralta, Martinez, Goncalvez - Viera, Lamas (Caceres), Acuña, Onega.E, Lamberck

2nd leg. Centenario, Montevideo, 27-05-1970, 50,000. Referee: Larrosa, Paraguay
PEÑAROL 0
ESTUDIANTES LP 0
Peñarol - Pintos - Soria (Speranza), Figueroa - Peralta, Martinez, Viera - Goncalvez, Lamas, Onega.E, Lamberck, Acuña. Tr: Brandao
Estudiantes - Errea - Pagnanini, Spadaro - Togneri, Medina, Bilardo - Pachamé, Solari, Conigliaro (Aguilar), Echecopar (Rudzki), Veron. Tr: Zubeldia

Top scorer Francisco Bertocchi, LDU Quito 9

1971

FIRST ROUND

Group 1

	Un	RC	BJ	SC	Pl	W	D	L	F	A	Pts
Universitario	-	3-2	0-0	0-0	6	3	3	0	8	4	9
Rosario Central	2-2	-	*	4-0	6	3	1	2	11	8	7
Boca Juniors	*	2-1	-	2-2	6	1	2	3	4	5	4
Sporting Cristal	0-3	1-2	2-0	-	6	1	2	3	5	11	4

* Boca Juniors withdrew. Their opponents were awarded the points

Group 2

	Na	Pe	CP	St	Pl	W	D	L	F	A	Pts
Nacional Montevideo	-	2-1	3-0	5-0	6	5	1	0	14	2	11
Peñarol	0-2	-	1-0	9-0	6	3	1	2	14	6	7
Chaco Petrolero	0-1	1-1	-	3-1	6	1	1	4	5	9	3
The Strongest	1-1	1-2	2-1	-	6	1	1	4	5	21	3

Group 3

	Pa	Fl	DI	Ga	Pl	W	D	L	F	A	Pts
Palmeiras	-	3-1	1-0	3-0	6	5	0	1	13	5	10
Fluminense	2-0	-	6-0	3-1	6	4	0	2	16	6	8
Deportivo Italia	0-3	1-0	-	6-5	6	2	1	3	7	15	5
Deportivo Galicia	2-3	1-4	0-0	-	6	0	1	5	9	19	1

Group 4

	UE	CC	CP	Gu	Pl	W	D	L	F	A	Pts
Union Española	-	2-1	0-0	2-1	6	2	3	1	7	6	7
Colo Colo	1-1	-	1-0	3-2	6	2	2	2	6	7	6
Cerro Porteño	2-1	0-0	-	1-1	6	1	4	1	5	5	6
Guarani Asuncion	1-1	2-0	2-2	-	6	1	3	2	9	9	5

Group 5

	Ba	Em	DC	AJ	Pl	W	D	L	F	A	Pts
Barcelona	-	1-1	1-0	3-1	6	3	1	2	8	6	7
Emelec	1-0	-	3-1	1-1	6	2	3	1	6	4	7
Deportivo Cali	3-1	1-0	-	2-0	6	3	0	3	8	7	6
Atletico Junior	0-2	0-0	2-1	-	6	1	2	3	4	9	4

Play-off
Barcelona...3-0 ....Emelec

SEMI-FINALS

Group 1

	Na	Pa	Un	Pl	W	D	L	F	A	Pts
Nacional Montevideo	-	3-1	3-0	4	3	1	0	9	1	7
Palmeiras	0-3	-	3-0	4	2	0	2	6	7	4
Universitario	0-0	1-2	-	4	0	1	3	1	8	1

Group 2

	Es	Ba	UE	Pl	W	D	L	F	A	Pts
Estudiantes LP	-	0-1	2-1	4	3	0	1	4	2	6
Barcelona	0-1	-	1-0	4	2	0	2	3	4	4
Union Española	0-1	3-1	-	4	1	0	3	4	5	2

FINAL

1st leg. Estadio La Plata, La Plata, 26-05-1971, 32,000. Tr: Canessa, Chile

ESTUDIANTES LP 1 (Romeo 60)
NACIONAL MONTEVIDEO 0
Estudiantes - Leone - Aguirre Suarez, Togneri - Malbernat, Pachamé, Medina - Romeo, Echecopar, Rudzki (Bedogni), Verde, Veron
Nacional - Manga - Blanco, Ancheta - Masnik, Mujica, Montero Castillo - Esparrago (Mameli), Maneiro, Prieto (Bareno), Artime, Morales

2nd leg. Centenario, Montevideo, 2-06-1971, 62,000. Tr: Favilli Neto, Brazil
NACIONAL MONTEVIDEO 1 (Masnik 28)
ESTUDIANTES LP 0
Nacional - Manga - Ubinas, Anchetta - Masnik, Blanco, Montero Castillo - Esparrago, Maneiro, Cubilla (Prieto), Artime, Morales
Estudiantes - Leone - Malbernat, Aguirre Suarez - Togneri, Medina, Pachamé - Echecopar, Romeo, Verde, Rudzki (Bedogni), Veron

Play-off. Estadio Nacional, Lima, 9-06-1971, 42,000. Tr: Hormazabal, Chile
NACIONAL MONTEVIDEO 2 (OG 22, Artime 65)
ESTUDIANTES LP 0
Nacional - Manga - Ubinas, Anchetta - Masnik, Blanco, Montero Castillo - Esparrago, Maneiro (Mujica), Cubilla, Artime, Morales (Mameli). Tr: Echamendi
Estudiantes - Pezzano - Malbernat, Aguirre Suarez - Togneri, Medina, Pachamé - Romeo, Echecopar, Rudzki, Verde, Veron (Bedogni)

Top scorers Luis Artime, Nacional Montevideo 10
Raul Castronovo, Peñarol 10

1972

FIRST ROUND

Group 1

	In	RC	SF	NM	Pl	W	D	L	F	A	Pts
Independiente	-	2-0	4-2	2-0	6	4	2	0	13	5	10
Rosario Central	2-2	-	2-0	1-0	6	3	2	1	8	4	8
Indep. Santa Fé	0-2	0-0	-	1-1	6	1	2	3	4	9	4
At. Nacional Medellín	1-1	0-3	0-1	-	6	0	2	4	2	9	2

Group 2

	Ba	AQ	OP	Pe	Pl	W	D	L	F	A	Pts
Barcelona	-	3-1	1-1	3-0	6	3	3	0	9	3	9
America Quito	0-0	-	3-0	1-0	6	3	1	2	9	8	7
Oriente Petrolero	0-0	4-2	-	5-0	6	2	2	2	10	7	6
Chaco Petrolero	1-2	1-2	1-0	-	6	1	0	5	2	12	2

Group 3

	SP	OI	CP	AM	Pl	W	D	L	F	A	Pts
São Paulo FC	-	3-1	4-0	0-0	6	3	2	1	12	6	8
Olimpia	0-1	-	1-1	2-2*	6	1	3	2	7	8	6
Cerro Porteño	3-2	1-3	-	1-0	6	2	2	2	7	11	6
Atletico Mineiro	2-2	0-0	1-1	-	6	0	5	1	5	6	4

* Match abandoned. Olimpia awarded the points

Group 4

	Un	UC	Al	US	Pl	W	D	L	F	A	Pts
Universitario	-	2-1	2-1	3-1	6	3	2	1	9	6	8
Universidad de Chile	1-0	-	2-3	2-1	6	3	0	3	12	12	6
Alianza	2-2	3-4	-	1-0	6	2	2	2	10	10	6
Union San Felipe	0-0	3-2	0-0	-	6	1	2	3	5	8	4

Group 5

	Pe	DI	Va	Pl	W	D	L	F	A	Pts
Peñarol	-	1-0	2-1	4	4	0	0	12	3	8
Deportivo Italia	1-5	-	2-0	4	1	1	2	4	7	3
Valencia	1-4	1-1	-	4	1	0	3	3	9	1

SEMI-FINALS

Group 1

	Un	Na	Pe	Pl	W	D	L	F	A	Pts
Universitario	-	3-0	2-3	4	1	2	1	9	7	4
Nacional Montevideo	3-3	-	1-1	4	1	2	1	7	7	4
Peñarol	1-1	0-3	-	4	1	2	1	5	7	4

Group 2

	In	SP	Ba	Pl	W	D	L	F	A	Pts
Independiente	-	2-0	1-0*	4	2	1	1	4	2	5
São Paulo FC	1-0	-	1-1	4	1	2	1	2	3	4
Barcelona	1-1	0-0	-	4	0	3	1	2	3	3

* Match abandoned. Result stood

FINAL

1st leg. Estadio Nacional, Lima, 17-05-72, 45,000. Referee: Marques, Brazil
UNIVERSITARIO 0
INDEPENDIENTE 0
Universitario - Ballesteros - Soria, Cuellar - Chumpitaz, Luna, Techera - Carbonell, Castañeda, Ramirez, Rojas, Bailette
Independiente - Santoro - Comisso, Sa - Garisto, Pavoni, Pastoriza - Raimondo, Semenewicz, Balbuena, Mircoli, Saggioratto

2nd leg. Cordero, Avellaneda, 24-05-72, 65,000. Referee: Favilli Neto, Brazil
INDEPENDIENTE 2 (Maglioni 6 61)
UNIVERSITARIO 1 (Rojas 79)
Independiente - Santoro - Comisso, Sa - Garisto, Pavoni, Pastoriza - Raymundo, Semenewicz, Balbuena, Maglioni, Saggioratto. Tr: Dellacha
Universitario - Ballesteros - Soria, Cuellar - Chumpitaz, Luna, Techera (Alva) - Cruzado, Castaneda, Munante, Rojas, Ramirez

Top scorers Toninho, São Paulo FC 6
Teófilo Cubillas, Alianza 6

1973

FIRST ROUND

Group 1

	SL	JW	RP	OP	Pl	W	D	L	F	A	Pts
San Lorenzo	-	3-0	1-0	2-0	6	5	0	1	15	1	10
Jorge Wilsterman	1-0	-	1-0	1-0	6	3	1	2	6	8	7
River Plate	0-4	2-2	-	7-1	6	2	1	3	12	10	5
Oriente Petrolero	0-4	3-1	1-3	-	6	1	0	5	5	19	2

Group 2

	Bo	Pa	Na	Pe	Pl	W	D	L	F	A	Pts
Botafogo	-	2-0	3-2	4-1	6	4	1	1	15	9	9
Palmeiras	3-2	-	1-1	2-0	6	4	1	1	10	6	9
Nacional Montevideo	1-2	1-2	-	2-0	6	1	2	3	8	9	4
Peñarol	2-2	0-2	1-1	-	6	0	2	4	4	13	2

Play-off
Botafogo .... 2-1 .... SE Palmeiras

Group 3

	CC	Em	NQ	UE	Pl	W	D	L	F	A	Pts
Colo Colo	-	5-1	5-1	5-0	6	3	2	1	16	4	8
Emelec	1-0	-	2-0	1-0	6	3	1	2	6	7	7
Nacional Quito	1-1	1-0	-	1-0	6	2	1	3	5	10	5
Union Española	0-0	1-1	2-1	-	6	1	2	3	3	9	4

Group 4

	Mi	DC	Pl	W	D	L	F	A	Pts
Millonarios	-	6-2	2	1	1	0	6	2	3
Deportivo Cali	0-0	-	2	0	1	1	2	6	1

The Venezuelan entrants withdrew

Group 5

	CP	Ol	SC	Un	Pl	W	D	L	F	A	Pts
Cerro Porteño	-	4-2	5-0	1-0	6	4	1	1	14	5	9
Olimpia	2-1	-	1-0	1-0	6	3	0	3	7	8	6
Sporting Cristal	1-1	1-0	-	1-0	6	2	2	2	5	9	6
Universitario	0-2	2-1	2-2	-	6	1	1	4	4	8	3

SEMI-FINALS

Group 1

	In	SL	Mi	Pl	W	D	L	F	A	Pts
Independiente	-	1-0	2-0	4	2	1	1	5	3	5
San Lorenzo	2-2	-	2-0	4	1	2	1	4	3	4
Millonarios	1-0	0-0	-	4	1	1	2	1	4	3

Group 2

	CC	CP	Bo	Pl	W	D	L	F	A	Pts
Colo Colo	-	4-0	3-3	4	2	1	1	10	9	5
Cerro Porteño	5-1	-	3-2	4	2	0	2	8	9	4
Botafogo	1-2	2-0	-	4	1	1	2	8	8	3

FINAL

1st leg. Cordero, Avellaneda, 22-05-1973, 65,000. Referee: Lorenzo, Uruguay

INDEPENDIENTE 1 (Mendoza 75)
COLO COLO 1 (OG 71)

Independiente - Santoro - Comisso, Sa - Lopez, Pavoni, Semenewicz - Raymundo, Martinez, Balbuena (Bertoni), Giachello (Maglioni), Mendoza

Colo Colo - Neff - Galindo, Herrera - Gonzales, Silva, Paez - Valdés, Osorio (Caszely), Messen, Ahumada, Véliz

2nd leg. Estadio Nacional, Santiago, 29-05-1973, 77,000. Referee: Arpi Filho, Brazil

COLO COLO 0
INDEPENDIENTE 0

Colo Colo - Neff - Galindo, Herrera - Gonzales, Silva, Paez - Valdés, Osorio, Caszely, Messen, Véliz

Independiente - Santoro - Comisso, Sa - Lopez, Pavoni, Semenewicz - Raymundo, Martinez, Balbuena (Bertoni), Giachello (Maglioni), Mendoza

Play-off. Centenario, Montevideo, 6-06-1973, 45,000. Referee: Romei, Paraguay

INDEPENDIENTE 2 (Mendoza 25, Giachello 107)
COLO COLO 1 (Caszely 39)

Independiente - Santoro - Comisso, Sa - Lopez, Pavoni, Semenewicz - Raymundo, Galvan, Bertoni, Maglioni (Bochini), Mendoza (Giachello). Tr: Maschio

Colo Colo - Neff - Galindo, Herrera - Gonzales, Silva (Castañeda), Valdés - Paez, Messen, Caszely, Ahumada, Véliz (Lara)

Top scorer Carlos Caszely, Colo Colo 9

1974

FIRST ROUND

Group 1

	Hu	RC	UE	CC	Pl	W	D	L	F	A	Pts
Huracan	-	1-0	3-1	2-1	6	5	0	1	13	4	10
Rosario Central	1-0	-	4-0	2-0	6	5	0	1	11	2	10
Union Española	1-5	0-1	-	2-1	6	2	0	4	6	14	4
Colo Colo	0-2	1-3	0-2	-	6	0	0	6	3	13	0

Play-off
Huracan..4-0 ....Rosario Central

Group 2

	SP	Pa	JW	Mu	Pl	W	D	L	F	A	Pts
São Paulo FC	-	2-0	5-0	1-1	6	4	2	0	14	5	10
Palmeiras	1-2	-	2-0	3-0	6	3	0	3	7	5	6
Jorge Wilsterman	0-1	1-0	-	1-0	5	2	0	3	2	8	4
Deport. Municipal	3-3	0-1	-	-	5	0	2	3	4	9	2

Group 3

	Mi	NM	Po	Va	Pl	W	D	L	F	A	Pts
Millonarios	-	3-0	2-1	2-1	6	4	1	1	10	6	9
At. Nacional Medellín	1-2	-	3-0	2-1	6	3	1	2	8	7	7
Portuguesa	2-0	0-0	-	0-0	6	2	2	2	4	5	6
Valencia	1-1	1-2	0-1	-	6	0	2	4	4	8	2

Group 4

	DL	NQ	UC	SC	Pl	W	D	L	F	A	Pts
Defensor Lima	-	2-1	1-0	2-0	6	4	1	1	7	2	9
Nacional Quito	0-0	-	2-0	3-0	6	3	2	1	9	3	8
Universidad Catolica	1-0	0-0	-	0-0	6	1	2	3	2	5	4
Sporting Cristal	0-2	1-3	2-1	-	6	1	1	4	3	11	3

Group 5

	Pe	CP	Ol	Na	Pl	W	D	L	F	A	Pts
Peñarol	-	1-0	0-0	1-0	6	3	2	1	5	3	8
Cerro Porteño	1-1	-	1-0	2-1	6	2	3	1	7	6	7
Olimpia	0-2	1-1	-	2-0	6	1	3	2	4	5	5
Nacional Montevideo	2-0	2-2	1-1	-	6	1	2	3	6	8	4

SEMI-FINALS

Group 1

	In	Pe	Hu	Pl	W	D	L	F	A	Pts
Independiente	-	3-2	3-0	4	2	2	0	8	4	6
Peñarol	1-1	-	1-1	4	1	2	1	7	5	4
Huracan	1-1	0-3	-	4	0	2	2	2	8	2

Group 2

	SP	Mi	DL	Pl	W	D	L	F	A	Pts
São Paulo FC	-	4-0	4-0	4	3	1	0	9	0	7
Millonarios	0-0	-	1-0	4	2	1	1	5	5	5
Defensor Lima	0-1	1-4	-	4	0	0	4	1	10	0

FINAL

1st Leg. Morumbí, São Paulo, 12-10-1974, 51,000. Referee: Perex, Peru

SÃO PAULO FC 2 (Rocha 48, Mirandinha 50)
INDEPENDIENTE 1 (Saggioratto 28)

São Paulo - Valdir Perez - Nelson, Paranhos - Arlindo, Gilberto, Ademir da Guia - Zé Carlos (Mauro), Rocha, Terto, Mirandinha, Piau

Independiente - Gay - Comisso, Sa - Lopez, Pavoni, Galvan - Raimondo, Saggioratto, Balbuena, Bochini, Bertoni

2nd leg. Cordero, Avellaneda , 16-10-1974, 48,000. Referee: Barreto, Uruguay

INDEPENDIENTE 2 (Bochini 34, Balbuena 48)
SÃO PAULO FC 0

Independiente - Gay - Comisso, Sa - Lopez, Pavoni, Galvan - Raimondo, Saggioratto, Balbuena, Bochini, Bertoni (Semenewicz)

São Paulo - Valdir Perez - Nelson, Paranhos - Arlindo, Gilberto, Chicao - Zé Carlos, Rocha (Mauro), Terto, Mirandinha, Piau

Play-off. Estadio Nacional, Santiago, 19-10-1974, 27,000. Referee: Orozco, Peru

INDEPENDIENTE 1 (Pavoni 37)
SÃO PAULO FC 0

Independiente - Gay - Comisso, Sa - Lopez, Pavoni, Galvan - Raimondo, Semenewicz, Balbuena (Carrica), Bochini, Bertoni (Giribert). Tr: Ferreiro

São Paulo - Valdir Perez - Forlan, Paranhos - Arlindo, Gilberto (Nelson), Chicao - Zé Carlos (Silva), Rocha, Mauro, Mirandinha, Piau

Top scorers Terto, São Paulo FC 7
Pedro Rocha, São Paulo FC 7
Fernando Morena, Peñarol 7

1975

FIRST ROUND

Group 1

	RC	Ne	Ol	CP	Pl	W	D	L	F	A	Pts
Rosario Central	-	1-1	1-1	2-1	6	2	4	0	8	5	8
Newell's Old Boys	1-1	-	3-2	1-0	6	3	2	1	9	8	8
Olimpia	0-0	2-0	-	2-1	6	2	3	1	7	5	7
Cerro Porteño	1-3	2-3	0-0	-	6	0	1	5	5	11	1

Play-off

Rosario Central.............................1-0.......................Newell's Old Boys

Group 2

	UE	Hu	St	JW	Pl	W	D	L	F	A	Pts
Union Española	-	7-2	4-0	4-1	6	3	3	0	17	5	9
Huachipato	0-0	-	4-2	4-0	6	2	2	2	10	10	6
The Strongest	1-1	1-0	-	3-1	6	2	2	2	8	11	6
Jorge Wilsterman	1-1	0-0	1-1	-	6	0	3	3	4	13	3

Group 3

	Cr	DC	NM	VG	Pl	W	D	L	F	A	Pts
Cruzeiro	-	2-1	2-3	3-2	6	3	1	2	10	9	7
Deportivo Cali	1-0	-	0-0	2-1	6	2	2	2	5	5	6
At. Nacional Medellín	1-2	2-1	-	1-1	6	2	2	2	7	8	6
Vasco da Gama	1-1	0-0	2-0	-	6	1	3	2	7	7	5

Group 4

	LQ	Po	Ga	NQ	Pl	W	D	L	F	A	Pts
LDU Quito	-	1-1	4-2	3-1	6	3	3	0	11	6	9
Portuguesa	1-1	-	1-1	1-0	6	1	4	1	5	8	6
Deportivo Galicia	0-1	0-0	-	4-0	6	1	3	2	7	6	5
Nacional Quito	1-1	5-1	0-0	-	6	1	2	3	7	10	4

Group 5

	Un	Pe	Wa	UH	Pl	W	D	L	F	A	Pts
Universitario	-	3-2	3-1	1-1	6	4	2	0	12	6	10
Peñarol	0-1	-	1-0	5-2	6	4	0	2	13	7	8
Wanderers	0-2	1-2	-	4-0	6	1	1	4	8	10	3
Union Huaral	2-2	0-3	2-2	-	6	0	3	3	7	17	3

SEMI-FINALS

Group 1

	In	RC	Cr	Pl	W	D	L	F	A	Pts
Independiente	-	2-0	3-0	4	2	0	2	5	4	4
Rosario Central	2-0	-	3-1	4	2	0	2	5	5	4
Cruzeiro	2-0	2-0	-	4	2	0	2	5	6	4

Group 2

	UE	Un	LQ	Pl	W	D	L	F	A	Pts
Union Española	-	2-1	2-0	4	2	1	1	7	6	5
Universitario	1-1	-	2-1	4	1	2	1	4	4	4
LDU Quito	4-2	0-0	-	4	1	1	2	5	6	3

FINAL

1st leg. Estadio Nacional, Santiago, 18-06-1975, 43,000. Referee: Bazan, Uruguay

UNION ESPAÑOLA 1 (Ahumada 87)
INDEPENDIENTE 0

Union Española - Vallejos - Machuca, Soto - Arias, Palacios, Las Heras - Hinostroza, Trujillo, Spedaletti, Ahumada, Hoffman (Miranda)

Independiente - Pérez - Comisso, Sa - Semenewicz, Pavoni, Galvan - Bochini, Rojas, Balbuena, Ruiz Moreno, Bertoni (Giribert)

2nd leg. Cordero, Avellaneda , 25-06-1975, 52,000. Referee, Barreto, Uruguay

INDEPENDIENTE 3 (Rojas 1, Pavoni 58, Bertoni 83)
UNION ESPAÑOLA 1 (Las Heras 56)

Independiente - Pérez - Comisso, Sa - Semenewicz, Pavoni, Galvan - Bochini, Balbuena, Ruiz Moreno, Rojas, Bertoni

Union Española - Vallejos - Machuca, Berly - Soto, Arias, Palacios - Las Heras (Maldonado), Hinostroza, Spedaletti, Ahumada, Veliz (Trujillo)

Play-off. Defensores del Chaco, Asuncion, 29-06-1975, 45,000. Referee: Perez, Peru

INDEPENDIENTE 2 (Ruiz Moreno 29, Bertoni 65)
UNION ESPAÑOLA 0

Independiente - Pérez - Comisso, Sa - Lopez, Pavoni, Semenewicz - Galvan, Bochini, Balbuena, Ruiz Moreno, Bertoni (Saggioratto). Tr: Dellacha

Union Española - Vallejos - Machuca, Maldonado - Gaete, Arias, Palacios - Hinostroza (Las Heras), Veliz, Spedaletti, Trujillo, Ahumada. Tr: Santibañez

Top scorers Fernando Morena, Peñarol 8
Oswaldo Ramirez, Universitario 8

1976

FIRST ROUND

Group 1

	RP	Es	Po	DG	Pl	W	D	L	F	A	Pts
River Plate	-	1-0	2-1	4-1	6	5	0	1	10	3	10
Estudiantes LP	1-0	-	3-0	4-0	6	4	1	1	11	3	9
Portuguesa	0-2	2-2	-	3-1	6	2	1	3	8	11	5
Deportivo Galicia	0-1	0-1	1-2	-	6	0	0	6	3	15	0

Group 2

	LQ	DC	Bo	Gu	Pl	W	D	L	F	A	Pts
LDU Quito	-	1-1	2-1	4-0	6	3	2	1	10	5	8
Deportivo Cuenca	0-0	-	3-1	1-0	6	3	2	1	9	6	8
Bolivar	3-2	4-2	-	7-1	6	3	0	3	16	11	6
Guabirà	0-1	0-2	1-0	-	6	1	0	5	2	15	2

Play-off

LDU Quito.......................................2-1.........................Deportivo Cuenca

Group 3

	Cr	IP	Ol	SL	Pl	W	D	L	F	A	Pts
Cruzeiro	-	5-4	4-1	4-1	6	5	1	0	20	9	11
Internacional PA	0-2	-	1-0	3-0	6	3	1	2	10	8	7
Olimpia	2-2	1-1	-	2-3	6	1	2	3	7	11	4
Sportivo Luqueño	1-3	0-1	0-1	-	6	1	0	5	5	14	2

Group 4

	Al	Mi	AU	SF	Pl	W	D	L	F	A	Pts
Alianza	-	2-1	0-0	3-0	6	3	2	1	8	4	8
Millonarios	1-0	-	4-0	0-1	6	2	2	2	8	5	6
Alfonso Ugarte	0-0	1-1	-	2-1	6	1	4	1	5	8	6
Indep. Santa Fé	2-3	1-1	2-2	-	6	1	2	3	7	11	4

Group 5

	Pe	UE	Pa	Na	Pl	W	D	L	F	A	Pts
Peñarol	-	2-0	2-1	1-1	6	3	2	1	7	4	8
Union Española	0-0	-	1-0	2-0	6	3	2	1	5	3	8
Palestino	1-0	0-1	-	2-1	6	2	1	3	5	6	5
Nacional Montevideo	1-2	1-1	1-1	-	6	0	3	3	5	9	3

SEMI-FINALS

Group 1

	Cr	LQ	Al	Pl	W	D	L	F	A	Pts
Cruzeiro	-	4-1	7-1	4	4	0	0	18	3	8
LDU Quito	1-3	-	2-1	4	1	0	3	4	10	2
Alianza	0-4	2-0	-	4	1	0	3	4	13	2

Group 2

	RP	In	Pe	Pl	W	D	L	F	A	Pts
River Plate	-	0-0	3-0	4	2	1	1	4	1	5
Independiente	0-1	-	1-0	4	2	1	1	2	1	5
Peñarol	1-0	0-1	-	4	1	0	3	1	5	2

Play-off
River Plate .... 1-0 .... Independiente

FINAL

1st leg. Mineirao, Belo Horizonte, 21-07-76, 58,000. Referee: Llobregat, Venezuela

CRUZEIRO 4 (Nelinho 22, Palinha 29 40, Waldo 80)
RIVER PLATE 1 (Mas 63)

Cruzeiro - Raul - Nelinho, Morais - Menezes, Vanderlay, Wilson Piazza (Waldo) - Zé Carlos, Eduardo (Ronaldo), Palinha, Jairzinho, Joãzinho
River Plate - Fillol (Landaburu) - Comelles, Perfumo - Lonardi, Lopez.H, Merlo - Lopez.J, Gonzalez, Sabella, Luque, Mas

2nd leg. Monumental, Buenos Aires, 28-07-76, 45,000. Referee: Bazan, Uruguay

RIVER PLATE 2 (Lopez.J 10, Gonzalez 76)
CRUZEIRO 1 (Palinha 48)

River Plate - Landaburu - Comelles, Perfumo - Pasarella, Lopez.H (Artico), Lopez.J - Merlo, Alonso, Gonzalez, Luque, Mas (Sabella)
Cruzeiro - Raul - Nelinho, Morais - Menezes, Vanderlay, Zé Carlos - Wilson Piazza, Jairzinho, Eduardo (Ronaldo), Palinha, Joãzinho

Play-off. Estadio Nacional, Santiago, 30-07-76, 35,000. Referee: Martinez, Chile

CRUZEIRO 3 (Nelinho 24, Ronaldo 55, Joãzinho 88)
RIVER PLATE 2 (Mas 59, Urquiza 64)

Cruzeiro - Raul - Nelinho, Morais - Menezes, Vanderlay, Eduardo - Wilson Piazza (Osiris), Zé Carlos, Ronaldo, Palinha, Joãzinho. Tr: Moreyra
River Plate - Landaburu - Comelles, Lonardi - Artico, Urquiza, Sabella - Merlo, Alonso, Gonzalez, Luque, Mas (Crespo)

Top scorer: Palinha, Cruzeiro 13

1977

FIRST ROUND

Group 1

	BJ	RP	De	Pe	Pl	W	D	L	F	A	Pts
Boca Juniors	-	1-0	2-0	1-0	6	4	2	0	5	0	10
River Plate	0-0	-	1-1	2-1	6	1	4	1	5	5	6
Defensor	0-0	0-0	-	2-4	6	1	3	2	5	7	5
Peñarol	0-1	2-2	0-2	-	6	1	1	4	7	10	3

Group 2

	DC	Bo	OP	NM	Pl	W	D	L	F	A	Pts
Deportivo Cali	-	3-0	3-0	3-1	6	4	0	2	12	5	8
Bolivar	3-0	-	1-0	3-0	6	3	1	2	7	4	7
Oriente Petrolero	1-0	0-0	-	4-0	6	2	1	3	6	7	5
At. Nacional Medellín	0-3	1-0	3-1	-	6	2	0	4	5	14	4

Group 3

	IP	NQ	Co	DC	Pl	W	D	L	F	A	Pts
Internacional PA	-	2-0	1-0	3-1	6	4	1	1	9	4	9
Nacional Quito	2-0	-	2-1	0-0	6	3	1	2	6	6	7
Corinthians	1-1	3-0	-	4-0	6	2	1	3	10	6	5
Deportivo Cuenca	0-2	0-2	2-1	-	6	1	1	4	3	12	3

Group 4

	Li	UC	Ev	Ol	Pl	W	D	L	F	A	Pts
Libertad	-	3-0	2-1	2-2	6	3	2	1	10	5	8
Universidad de Chile	1-0	-	1-0	1-0	6	3	0	3	3	6	6
Everton	1-3	2-0	-	1-0	6	2	1	3	7	8	5
Olimpia	0-0	1-0	2-2	-	6	1	3	2	5	6	5

Group 5

	Po	UH	EM	SB	Pl	W	D	L	F	A	Pts
Portuguesa	-	2-0	3-0	0-0	6	4	2	0	10	2	10
Union Huaral	1-1	-	2-1	1-0	6	2	2	2	4	5	6
Estudiantes Merida	0-2	1-0	-	1-0	6	3	0	3	6	8	6
Sport Boys	1-2	0-0	1-3	-	6	0	2	4	2	7	2

SEMI-FINALS

Group 1

	BJ	DC	Li	Pl	W	D	L	F	A	Pts
Boca Juniors	-	1-1	1-0	4	2	2	0	4	2	6
Deportivo Cali	1-1	-	0-0	4	0	3	1	3	4	3
Libertad	0-1	2-1	-	4	1	1	2	2	3	3

Group 2

	Cr	IP	Po	Pl	W	D	L	F	A	Pts
Cruzeiro	-	0-0	2-1	4	3	1	0	7	1	7
Internacional PA	0-1	-	2-1	4	1	1	2	2	5	3
Portuguesa	0-4	3-0	-	4	1	0	3	5	8	2

FINAL

1st leg. La Bombonera, Buenos Aires, 6-09-77, 50,000. Referee: Cerullo, Uruguay

BOCA JUNIORS 1 (Veglio 3)
CRUZEIRO 0

Boca Juniors - Gatti - Pernia, Sa (Tesare) - Mouzo, Tarantini, Veglio - Suné, Zanabria, Mastrangelo, Pavon (Bernabitti), Felman
Cruzeiro - Raul - Nelinho, Morais - Menezes, Vanderlay, Zé Carlos - Eduardo, Eli Carlos, Méndez, Neca, Jaozinho

2nd leg. Mineirao, Belo Horizonte, 11-09-77, 55,000. Referee: Orozco, Peru

CRUZEIRO 1 (Nelinho 76)
BOCA JUNIORS 0

Cruzeiro - Raul - Nelinho, Morais - Menezes, Vanderlay, Zé Carlos - Eduardo, Eli Carlos (Livio), Méndez, Neca, Jaozinho
Boca Juniors - Gatti - Pernia, Tesare - Mouzo, Tarantini, Ribolzi - Suné, Veglio (Pavon), Zanabria, Mastrangelo, Felman (Ortiz)

Play-off. Centenario, Montevideo, 14-09-77, 45,000. Referee: Llobregat, Venezuela

BOCA JUNIORS 0
CRUZEIRO 0
Boca Juniors won 5-4 on penalties

Boca Juniors - Gatti - Pernia, Tesare - Mouzo, Tarantini, Benitez (Ribolzi) (Pavon) - Suné, Zanabria, Mastrangelo, Veglio, Felman. Tr: Lorenzo
Cruzeiro - Raul - Nelinho (Mariano), Morais - Menzezs, Vanderlay, Eduardo - Eli Carlos (Livio), Zé Carlos, Méndez, Neca, Jaozinho

Top scorer Nestor Scotta, Deportivo Cali 5

1978

FIRST ROUND

Group 1

	RP	In	LQ	NQ	Pl	W	D	L	F	A	Pts
River Plate	-	0-0	4-0	2-0	6	2	4	0	7	1	8
Independiente	0-0	-	2-0	2-0	6	3	2	1	6	2	8
LDU Quito	0-0	1-0	-	3-2	6	2	1	3	4	10	5
Nacional Quito	1-1	1-2	2-0	-	6	1	1	4	6	10	3

Play-off
River Plate .... 4-1 .... Independiente

Group 2

	Al	SC	St	OP	Pl	W	D	L	F	A	Pts
Alianza	-	4-1	2-0	5-1	6	5	1	0	19	5	11
Sporting Cristal	2-2	-	3-0	1-0	6	3	1	2	9	9	7
The Strongest	1-2	3-1	-	2-0	6	2	0	4	6	12	4
Oriente Petrolero	0-4	0-1	4-0	-	6	1	0	5	5	13	2

Group 3

	AM	UE	SP	Pa	Pl	W	D	L	F	A	Pts
Atletico Mineiro	-	5-1	2-1	2-0	6	4	2	0	16	8	10
Union Española	1-1	-	1-1	0-0	6	1	4	1	7	10	6
São Paulo FC	1-1	1-1	-	1-2	6	1	3	2	6	7	5
Palestino	4-5	2-3	0-1	-	6	1	1	4	8	12	3

Group 4

	DC	Pe	AJ	Da	Pl	W	D	L	F	A	Pts
Deportivo Cali	-	1-0	0-0	2-0	6	3	2	1	5	3	8
Peñarol	0-2	-	1-0	4-2	6	3	0	3	7	7	6
Atletico Junior	0-0	1-0	-	0-0	6	1	4	1	1	1	6
Danubio	3-0	1-2	0-0	-	6	1	2	3	6	8	4

Group 5

	CP	Po	EM	Li	Pl	W	D	L	F	A	Pts
Cerro Porteño	-	1-0	3-2	1-0	6	3	3	0	7	4	9
Portuguesa	1-1	-	1-2	2-1	6	2	2	2	5	5	6
Estudiantes Merida	1-1	0-0	-	1-1	6	1	3	2	7	8	5
Libertad	0-0	0-1	2-1	-	6	1	2	3	4	6	4

SEMI-FINALS

Group 1

	BJ	RP	AM	Pl	W	D	L	F	A	Pts
Boca Juniors	-	0-0	3-1	4	3	1	0	7	2	7
River Plate	0-2	-	1-0	4	1	1	2	1	3	3
Atletico Mineiro	1-2	1-0	-	4	1	0	3	3	6	2

Group 2

	DC	CP	Al	Pl	W	D	L	F	A	Pts
Deportivo Cali	-	1-1	3-2	4	3	1	0	12	4	7
Cerro Porteño	0-4	-	3-1	4	1	1	2	4	9	3
Alianza	1-4	3-0	-	4	1	0	3	7	10	2

FINAL

1st leg. Pascual Guerrero, Cali, 23-11-78. Referee: Ortiz, Paraguay

DEPORTIVO CALI 0
BOCA JUNIORS 0

Deportivo Cali - Zape - Ospina, Caicedo, Escobar, Castro (Correa) - Otero (Jaramillo), Landucci, Valverde - Torres, Scotta, Benitez

Boca Juniors - Rodriguez - Pernia, Sa, Mouzo, Bordon - Benitez, Suné, Zanabria Mastrangelo, Salinas, Perotti

2nd leg. La Bombonera, Buenos Aires, 28-11-78. Referee: Nuñez, Peru

BOCA JUNIORS 4 (Perotti 15 85, Mastrangelo 60, Salinas 71)
DEPORTIVO CALI 0

Boca Juniors - Gatti - Pernia, Sa, Mouzo, Bordon - Benitez (Veglio), Suné, Zanabria Mastrangelo, Salinas, Perotti

Deportivo Cali - Zape - Ospina (Castro), Caicedo, Escobar, Correa - Otero (Umana), Landucci, Valverde - Torres, Scotta, Benitez

Top scorers Guillermo La Rosa, Alianza 8
Nestor Scotta, Deportivo Cali 8

1979

FIRST ROUND

Group 1

	In	DC	Mi	Qu	Pl	W	D	L	F	A	Pts
Independiente	-	1-0	4-1	2-0	6	4	1	1	12	6	9
Deportivo Cali	1-0	-	2-0	3-2	6	3	1	2	8	7	7
Millonarios	3-3	1-1	-	1-0	6	2	2	2	8	11	6
Quilmes	1-2	3-1	1-2	-	6	1	0	5	7	11	2

Group 2

	Ol	Bo	SA	JW	Pl	W	D	L	F	A	Pts
Olimpia	-	3-0	1-0	4-2	6	5	0	1	12	4	10
Bolivar	2-1	-	4-1	4-0	6	4	1	1	18	7	9
Sol de America	0-1	2-2	-	2-1	6	2	1	3	8	11	5
Jorge Wilsterman	0-2	0-6	2-3	-	6	0	0	6	5	21	0

Group 3

	Gu	Un	Pa	Al	Pl	W	D	L	F	A	Pts
Guarani Campinas	-	6-1	1-0	2-1	6	5	0	1	16	6	10
Universitario	3-0	-	2-5	1-0	6	4	0	2	15	15	8
Palmeiras	1-4	1-2	-	4-0	6	3	0	3	15	11	6
Alianza	0-3	3-6	2-4	-	6	0	0	6	6	20	0

Group 4

	Pa	OH	Po	Ga	Pl	W	D	L	F	A	Pts
Palestino	-	1-0	6-0	5-0	6	4	2	0	16	2	10
O'Higgins	1-1	-	1-1	6-0	6	2	3	1	10	4	7
Portuguesa	0-2	1-1	-	1-1	6	0	4	2	4	12	4
Deportivo Galicia	1-1	0-1	1-1	-	6	0	3	3	3	15	3

Group 5

	Pe	Na	NQ	TU	Pl	W	D	L	F	A	Pts
Peñarol	-	1-1	2-1	4-0	6	4	2	0	10	2	10
Nacional Montevideo	0-0	-	3-0	2-0	6	2	3	1	7	3	7
Nacional Quito	0-2	1-0	-	2-1	6	2	1	3	6	10	5
Tecnico Universitari	0-1	1-1	2-2	-	6	0	2	4	4	12	2

SEMI-FINALS

Group 1

	Ol	Gu	Pa	Pl	W	D	L	F	A	Pts
Olimpia	-	2-1	3-0	4	3	1	0	8	2	7
Guarani Campinas	1-1	-	2-2	4	0	3	1	4	5	3
Palestino	0-2	0-0	-	4	0	2	2	2	7	2

Group 2

	BJ	In	Pe	Pl	W	D	L	F	A	Pts
Boca Juniors	-	2-0	1-0	4	2	1	1	3	1	5
Independiente	1-0	-	1-0	4	2	1	1	2	2	5
Peñarol	0-0	0-0	-	4	0	2	2	0	2	2

Play-off

Boca Juniors .... 1-0 .... Independiente

FINAL

1st leg. Defensores del Chaco, Asuncion, 22-07-1979, 45,000. Referee: Castro, Chile

OLIMPIA 2 (Aquino 3, Piazza 27)
BOCA JUNIORS 0

Olimpia - Almeida - Solalinde, Paredes, Giménez, Piazza - Torres, Kiese, Talavera - Isasi, Villalba, Aquino

Boca Juniors - Gatti - Pernia, Capurro, Sa, Bordon - Benitez (Palacios), Suné, Salinas Mastrangelo, Salguero, Rocha

2nd leg. La Bombonera, Buenos Aires, 27-07-1979, 50,000. Referee: Gardelino, Uruguay

BOCA JUNIORS 0
OLIMPIA 0

Boca Juniors - Gatti - Pernia, Sa, Capurro, Bordon - Benitez, Suné, Zanabria (Salguero) Mastrangelo, Salinas, Rocha (Palacios). Tr: Lorenzo

Olimpia - Almeida - Solalinde, Paredes, Giménez, Piazza - Torres (Guasch), Kiese, Talavera Isasi, Villalba, Aquino (Delgado). Tr: Cubilla

Top scorers Miltão, Guarani 6
Juan José Oré, Universitario 6

1980

FIRST ROUND

Group 1

	VS	RP	SC	AC	Pl	W	D	L	F	A	Pts
Velez Sarsfield	-	0-0	2-0	5-2	6	4	2	0	10	2	10
River Plate	0-0	-	3-2	3-0	6	4	2	0	10	3	10
Sporting Cristal	0-1	1-2	-	0-0	6	1	1	4	5	8	3
Atletico Chalaco	0-2	0-2	0-2	-	6	0	1	5	2	14	1

Play-off

Velez Sarsfield .... 1-1 .... River Plate

Velez Sarsfield qualify on goal difference

Group 2

	Na	St	De	OP	Pl	W	D	L	F	A	Pts
Nacional Montevideo	-	2-0	1-0	5-0	6	5	0	1	14	4	10
The Strongest	3-0	-	2-0	3-2	6	3	1	2	9	6	7
Defensor	0-3	1-1	-	1-1	6	1	2	3	3	8	4
Oriente Petrolero	1-3	1-0	0-1	-	6	1	1	4	5	13	3

Group 3

	IP	VG	Ga	Ta	Pl	W	D	L	F	A	Pts
Internacional PA	-	2-1	2-0	4-0	6	4	1	1	10	3	9
Vasco da Gama	0-0	-	4-0	1-0	6	3	2	1	7	2	8
Deportivo Galicia	2-1	0-0	-	1-0	6	3	1	2	4	7	7
Deportivo Tachira	0-1	0-1	0-1	-	6	0	0	6	0	9	0

Group 4

	AC	UC	SF	Em	Pl	W	D	L	F	A	Pts
America Cali	-	1-0	1-0	4-1	6	4	1	1	11	7	9
Universidad Catolica	4-2	-	1-0	5-0	6	3	0	3	10	5	6
Indep. Santa Fé	1-1	1-0	-	1-2	6	2	1	3	5	5	5
Emelec	1-2	1-0	0-2	-	6	2	0	4	5	14	4

Group 5

	OH	CP	CC	SA	Pl	W	D	L	F	A	Pts
O'Higgins	-	0-0	1-3	2-0	6	2	2	2	8	6	6
Cerro Porteño	1-0	-	5-3	0-0	6	2	2	2	8	7	6
Colo Colo	1-1	2-1	-	1-1	6	2	2	2	11	11	6
Sol de America	1-4	2-1	2-1	-	6	2	2	2	6	9	6

SEMI-FINALS

Group 1

	Na	Ol	OH	Pl	W	D	L	F	A	Pts
Nacional Montevideo	-	1-1	2-0	4	3	1	0	5	1	7
Olimpia	0-1	-	2-0	4	2	1	1	4	2	5
O'Higgins	0-1	0-1	-	4	0	0	4	0	6	0

Group 2

	IP	AC	VS	Pl	W	D	L	F	A	Pts
Internacional PA	-	0-0	3-1	4	2	2	0	4	1	6
America Cali	0-0	-	0-0	4	0	4	0	0	0	4
Velez Sarsfield	0-1	0-0	-	4	0	2	2	1	4	2

FINAL

1st leg. Beira-Rio, Porto Alegre, 30-07-80, 80,000. Referee: Romero, Argentina

INTERNACIONAL PORTO ALEGRE 0
NACIONAL MONTEVIDEO 0

Internacional - Gasperim - Toninho, Mauro Pastor, Mauro Galvao, Andrés - Tonho, Falcao, Batista, Jair - Chico Espina (Aldison), Mario Sergio

Nacional - Rodriguez - Moreira, De Leon, Blanco, Gonzalez - Luzardo, Esparrago, De la Pena - Bica, Victorino, Pérez

2nd leg. Centenario, Montevideo, 6-08-80, 75,000. Referee: Perez, Peru

NACIONAL MONTEVIDEO 1 (Victorino 35)
INTERNACIONAL PORTO ALEGRE 0

Nacional - Rodriguez - Moreira, Blanco, De Leon, Gonzalez - Esparrago, De la Pena, Luzardo - Bica, Victorino, Morales

Internacional - Gasperim - Toninho, Mauro Pastor, Mauro Galvao, Mineiro Jair (Bereta), Batista, Falcao, Chico Espina - Aldison, Mario Sergio

Top scorer Waldemar Victorino, Nacional Montevideo.............6

1981

FIRST ROUND

Group 1

	DC	RP	RC	AJ	Pl	W	D	L	F	A	Pts
Deportivo Cali	-	2-1	1-0	4-1	6	4	0	2	10	6	8
River Plate	1-2	-	3-2	3-0	6	3	1	2	9	6	7
Rosario Central	2-1	0-1	-	5-0	6	3	0	3	11	7	6
Atletico Junior	1-0	0-0	1-2	-	6	1	1	4	3	14	5

Group 2

	Co	SC	UC	AT	Pl	W	D	L	F	A	Pts
Cobreloa	-	6-1	1-0	6-1	6	3	3	0	14	3	9
Sporting Cristal	0-0	-	3-2	2-1	6	3	2	1	9	10	8
Universidad de Chile	0-0	1-1	-	3-0	6	2	2	2	8	6	6
Atletico Torino	1-1	0-2	1-2	-	6	0	1	5	4	16	1

Group 3

	Fl	AM	CP	Ol	Pl	W	D	L	F	A	Pts
Flamengo	-	2-2	5-2	1-1	6	2	4	0	14	9	8
Atletico Mineiro	2-2	-	1-0	1-0	6	2	4	0	8	6	8
Cerro Porteño	2-4	2-2	-	0-0	6	1	2	3	9	12	4
Olimpia	0-0	0-0	0-3	-	6	0	4	2	1	5	4

Play-off
Flamengo * ....0-0............................Atletico Mineiro
* Abandoned after 35 mins. Game awarded to Flamengo

Group 4

	JW	St	Ba	TU	Pl	W	D	L	F	A	Pts
Jorge Wilsterman	-	3-2	1-0	3-1	6	4	0	2	9	9	8
The Strongest	2-0	-	1-0	4-2	6	4	0	2	13	9	8
Barcelona	3-0	2-1	-	2-1	6	3	0	3	8	8	6
Tecnico Universitario	1-2	2-3	4-1	-	6	1	0	5	11	15	2

Play-off
Jorge Wilsterman............................4-1 ....The Strongest

Group 5

	Pe	BV	EM	Po	Pl	W	D	L	F	A	Pts
Peñarol	-	3-1	4-2	3-0	6	5	1	0	13	3	11
Bella Vista	0-0	-	3-1	4-0	6	4	1	1	16	5	9
Estudiantes Merida	0-2	1-4	-	1-1	6	0	2	4	5	14	2
Portuguesa	0-1	0-4	0-0	-	6	0	2	4	1	13	2

SEMI-FINALS

Group 1

	Co	Na	Pe	Pl	W	D	L	F	A	Pts
Cobreloa	-	2-2	4-2	4	3	1	0	9	5	7
Nacional Montevideo	1-2	-	1-1	4	0	3	1	5	6	3
Peñarol	0-1	1-1	-	4	0	2	2	4	7	2

Group 2

	Fl	DC	JW	Pl	W	D	L	F	A	Pts
Flamengo	-	3-0	4-1	4	4	0	0	10	2	8
Deportivo Cali	0-1	-	1-0	4	1	1	2	2	5	3
Jorge Wilsterman	1-2	1-1	-	4	0	1	3	3	8	1

FINAL

1st leg. Maracaná, Rio de Janeiro, 13-11-1981, 114,000. Referee: Esposito, Argentina

FLAMENGO 2 (Zico 12 30)
COBRELOA 1 (Merello 65)

Flamengo - Raul - Leandro, Figueiredo, Mozer, Junior - Andrade, Adilio, Zico Lico (Varoninho), Nunes, Tita

Cobreloa - Wirth - Tabilo, Rojas, Soto, Escobar - Alarcón, Jiménez, Merello Muñoz (Gómez), Siviero, Puebla

2nd leg. Estadio Nacional, Santiago, 20-11-1981, 61,000. Referee: Barreto, Uruguay

COBRELOA 1 (Merello 79)
FLAMENGO 0

Cobreloa - Wirth - Tabilo, Jiménez, Soto, Escobar - Merello, Alarcón, Gómez.R Puebla, Siviero, Olivera
Flamengo - Raul - Leandro, Figueiredo, Mozer, Junior - Adilio, Andrade, Zico, Lico, Nunes, Tita

Play-off. Centenario, Montevideo, 23-11-1981 35,000. Referee: Cerullo, Uruguay

FLAMENGO 2 (Zico 18 79)
COBRELOA 0

Flamengo - Raul - Leandro, Marinho, Mozer, Junior - Andrade, Adilio, Zico, Tita, Nunes (Anselmo), Lico
Cobreloa - Wirth - Tabilo, Páez (Munoz), Soto, Escobar - Merello, Jiménez, Alarcón - Puebla, Siviero, Olivera

Top scorer Zico, Flamengo 11

1982

FIRST ROUND

Group 1

	RP	St	BJ	JW	Pl	W	D	L	F	A	Pts
River Plate	-	4-1	1-0	3-0	6	4	1	1	9	2	11
The Strongest	1-0*	-	1-0	1-1	6	3	1	2	6	7	5
Boca Juniors	0-0	1-0	-	2-2	6	1	2	3	3	5	4
Jorge Wilsterman	0-1	1-2	1-0	-	6	1	2	3	5	9	4

* Points awarded to River Plate

Group 2

	Pe	SP	Gr	De	Pl	W	D	L	F	A	Pts
Peñarol	-	1-0	1-0	0-0	6	4	1	1	7	3	9
São Paulo FC	0-1	-	2-2	2-1	6	2	2	2	7	6	6
Gremio	3-1	0-0	-	-	5	1	3	1	5	4	5
Defensor	0-3	1-3	0-0	-	5	0	2	3	2	8	2

Group 3

	To	NM	EM	Ta	Pl	W	D	L	F	A	Pts
Deportes Tolima	-	0-0	1-0	2-2	6	3	3	0	9	3	9
At. Nacional Medellín	0-3	-	2-0	1-0	6	3	2	1	6	4	8
Estudiantes Merida	1-1	1-3	-	1-0	6	1	2	3	3	7	4
Deportivo Tachira	0-2	0-0	0-0	-	6	0	3	3	2	6	3

Group 4

	Co	CC	LQ	Ba	Pl	W	D	L	F	A	Pts
Cobreloa	-	2-0	3-1	3-0	6	3	3	0	9	2	9
Colo Colo	0-0	-	1-0	2-0	6	3	2	1	8	5	8
LDU Quito	0-0	2-2	-	4-2	6	1	2	3	8	12	4
Barcelona	1-1	1-3	4-1	-	6	1	1	4	8	14	3

Group 5

	Ol	Me	SA	DM	Pl	W	D	L	F	A	Pts
Olimpia	-	4-0	1-1	1-0	6	4	2	0	12	3	10
Mariano Melgar	0-3	-	3-2	2-1	6	4	0	2	9	10	8
Sol de America	1-1	0-2	-	2-1	6	2	2	2	9	8	6
Deportivo Municipal	1-2	0-2	0-3	-	6	0	0	6	3	12	0

SEMI-FINALS

Group 1

	Pe	Fl	RP	Pl	W	D	L	F	A	Pts
Peñarol	-	1-0	2-1	4	4	0	0	8	3	8
Flamengo	0-1	-	4-2	4	2	0	2	7	4	4
River Plate	2-4	0-3	-	4	0	0	4	5	13	0

Group 2

	Co	Ol	To	Pl	W	D	L	F	A	Pts
Cobreloa	-	1-0	3-0	4	2	1	1	5	2	5
Olimpia	1-1	-	2-0	4	1	2	1	4	3	4
Deportes Tolima	1-0	1-1	-	4	1	1	2	2	6	3

FINAL

1st leg. Centenario, Montevideo, 26-11-82, 70,000

PEÑAROL 0
COBRELOA 0

Peñarol - Fernández - Diogo, Olivera, Gutiérrez, Morales - Saralegui, Bossio, Jair - Walkir Silva (Rodriguez), Morena, Ramos
Cobreloa - Wirth - Tabilo, Gómez.E, Soto, Escobar - Alarcón, Merello (Puebla), Gómez.R - Siviero, Letelier, Olivera (Rubio)

2nd leg. Estadio Nacional, Santiago, 30-11-82, 70,000

COBRELOA 0
PEÑAROL 1 (Morena 89)

Cobreloa - Wirth - Tabilo (Martinez), Soto, Gómez.E, Escobar - Alarcón, Merello, Gómez.R - Rubio, Siviero, Olivera (Letelier)
Peñarol - Fernández - Diogo, Gutiérrez, Olivera, Morales - Bossio, Saralegui, Jair - Vargas, Morena, Ramos (Rodriguez)

Top scorer Fernando Morena, Peñarol 7

1983

FIRST ROUND

Group 1

	Es	Co	CC	FO	Pl	W	D	L	F	A	Pts
Estudiantes LP	-	2-0	4-1	0-0	6	3	1	2	8	6	7
Cobreloa	3-0	-	2-0	2-1	6	3	0	3	8	6	6
Colo Colo	1-0	2-1	-	1-0	6	3	0	3	5	8	6
Ferrocarril Oeste	1-2	1-0	1-0	-	6	2	1	3	4	5	5

Group 2

	Gr	Fl	Bo	Bl	Pl	W	D	L	F	A	Pts
Gremio	-	1-1	3-1	2-0	6	5	1	0	13	4	11
Flamengo	1-3	-	5-2	7-1	6	2	2	2	15	10	6
Bolivar	1-2	3-1	-	6-0	6	2	0	4	13	14	4
Blooming	0-2	0-0	3-0	-	6	1	1	4	4	17	3

Group 3

	AC	To	Un	Al	Pl	W	D	L	F	A	Pts
America Cali	-	1-1	2-0	2-0	6	4	2	0	10	3	10
Deportes Tolima	0-2	-	1-1	0-0	6	1	4	1	5	6	6
Universitario	1-1	2-2	-	0-0	6	0	4	2	5	8	4
Alianza	1-2	0-1	2-1	-	6	1	2	3	3	6	4

Group 4

	SC	NQ	Ba	Ta	Pl	W	D	L	F	A	Pts
At. San Cristobal	-	1-0	2-0	2-0	6	3	2	1	8	4	8
Nacional Quito	1-0	-	3-1	3-0	6	3	1	2	7	4	7
Barcelona	3-3	2-0	-	-	5	1	2	2	7	9	4
Deportivo Tachira	0-0	0-0	1-1	-	5	0	3	2	1	6	3

Group 5

	Na	Wa	NA	Ol	Pl	W	D	L	F	A	Pts
Nacional Montevideo	-	1-1	4-2	3-0	6	4	1	1	12	4	9
Wanderers	1-0	-	3-1	0-0	6	3	3	0	9	5	9
Nacional Asuncion	0-3	1-1	-	2-1	6	1	2	3	6	12	4
Olimpia	0-1	2-3	0-0	-	6	0	2	4	3	9	2

Play-off
Nacional Montevideo........2-0 ....Wanderers

SEMI-FINALS

Group 1

	Pe	Na	SC	Pl	W	D	L	F	A	Pts
Peñarol	-	2-0	1-0	4	3	1	0	5	1	7
Nacional Montevideo	1-2	-	5-1	4	2	0	2	8	6	4
Atletico San Cristobal	0-0	1-2	-	4	0	1	3	2	8	1

Group 2

	Gr	Es	AC	Pl	W	D	L	F	A	Pts
Gremio	-	2-1	2-1	4	2	1	1	7	6	5
Estudiantes LP	3-3	-	2-0	4	1	2	1	6	5	4
America Cali	1-0	0-0	-	4	1	1	2	2	4	3

FINAL

1st leg. Centenario, Montevideo, 22-07-83, 65,000. Referee: Nitti, Argentina

PEÑAROL 1 (Morena 35)
GREMIO 1 (Tita 12)

Peñarol - Fernández - Montelongo, Olivera, Gutiérrez, Diogo - Salazar, Bossio, Saralegui - Walkir Silva (Villareal), Morena, Ramos
Gremio - Mazaropi - Paulo Roberto, Baidek, De León, Casemiro - China, Osvaldo, Tita - Renato, Caio (César), Tarciso

2nd leg. Olimpico, Porto Alegre, 28-07-83, 75,000. Referee: Perez, Peru
GREMIO 2 (Caio 9, Cesar 87)
PEÑAROL 1 (Morena 70)
Grêmio - Mazaropi - Paulo Roberto, Baidek, De León, Casemiro - Osvaldo, China, Tita - Renato, Caio (César), Tarciso
Peñarol - Fernández - Montelongo, Olivera, Gutiérrez, Diogo - Saralegui, Bossio, Salazar - Walkir Silva (Peirano), Morena, Ramos

Top scorer Arsenio Luzardo, Nacional Montevideo 8

1984

FIRST ROUND

Group 1

	In	Ol	SL	Es	Pl	W	D	L	F	A	Pts
Independiente	-	3-2	2-0	4-1	6	4	1	1	11	5	9
Olimpia	1-0	-	0-0	2-1	6	4	1	1	8	5	9
Sportivo Luqueño	0-1	1-2	-	0-0	6	0	3	3	2	6	3
Estudiantes LP	1-1	0-1	1-1	-	6	0	3	3	4	9	3

Group 2

	UC	Bl	Bo	OH	Pl	W	D	L	F	A	Pts
Universidad Catolica	-	0-0	3-1	2-0	6	4	1	1	11	5	9
Blooming	1-2	-	2-1	3-0	6	3	2	1	10	6	8
Bolivar	3-2	0-0	-	5-1	6	2	2	2	10	8	6
O'Higgins	0-2	3-4	0-0	-	6	0	1	5	4	16	1

Group 3

	Fl	AC	AJ	Sa	Pl	W	D	L	F	A	Pts
Flamengo	-	4-2	3-1	4-1	6	5	1	0	19	6	11
America Cali	1-1	-	2-0	1-0	6	3	1	2	8	9	7
Atletico Junior	1-2	4-1	-	0-3	6	2	0	4	9	12	4
Santos	0-5	0-1	1-3	-	6	1	0	5	5	14	2

Group 4

	Na	NQ	Da	NO	Pl	W	D	L	F	A	Pts
Nacional Montevideo	-	1-1	1-0	6-0	6	4	1	1	13	5	9
Nacional Quito	3-1	-	3-0	3-1	6	3	2	1	12	6	8
Danubio	0-1	1-0	-	5-1	6	2	1	3	8	8	5
Nueve de Octubre	1-3	2-2	2-2	-	6	0	2	4	7	21	2

Group 5

	UM	SC	Po	Me	Pl	W	D	L	F	A	Pts
ULA Merida	-	0-1	2-0	1-0	6	4	0	2	6	4	8
Sporting Cristal	2-0	-	2-1	3-2	6	4	0	2	8	6	8
Portuguesa	1-2	1-0	-	4-0	6	3	0	3	9	7	6
Mariano Melgar	0-1	2-0	1-2	-	6	1	0	5	5	11	2

Play-off
ULA Merida ....2-1 ....Sporting Cristal

SEMI-FINALS

Group 1

	In	Na	UC	Pl	W	D	L	F	A	Pts
Independiente	-	1-0	2-1	4	2	2	0	4	2	6
Nacional Montevideo	1-1	-	2-0	3	1	1	1	3	2	3
Universidad Catolica	0-0	-	-	3	0	1	2	1	4	1

Group 2

	Gr	Fl	UM	Pl	W	D	L	F	A	Pts
Grêmio	-	5-1	6-1	4	3	0	1	14	5	6
Flamengo	3-1	-	2-1	4	3	0	1	9	7	6
ULA Merida	0-2	0-3	-	4	0	0	4	2	13	0

Play-off
Grêmio...0-0 ....Flamengo
Grêmio qualified due to a better goal difference

FINAL

1st leg. Olimpico, Porto Alegre, 24-07-84, 55,000
GREMIO 0
INDEPENDIENTE 1 (Burruchaga 24)
Grêmio - Joao Marcos - Casemiro, Baidek, De León, Paulo César - China, Luis Carlos, Osvaldo - Renato, Guilherme (Gilson), Tarciso
Independiente - Goyén - Clausen, Villaverde, Trossero, Enrique - Giusti, Marangoni, Bochini, Burruchaga - Bufarini, Barberón (Reinoso)

2nd leg. Cordero, Avellaneda, 27-07-84, 75,000
INDEPENDIENTE 0
GREMIO 0
Independiente - Goyén - Clausen, Villaverde, Trossero, Enrique - Giusti, Marangoni, Bochini (Zimmermann) - Bufarini, Burruchaga, Barberón
Grêmio - Joao Marcos - Casemiro, Baidek, De León, Paulo César - China, Luis Carlos, Osvaldo - Renato, Guilherme, Tarciso

Top scorer Tita, Flamengo 8

1985

FIRST ROUND

Group 1

	AJ	FO	Fl	VG	Pl	W	D	L	F	A	Pts
Argentinos Juniors	-	0-1	1-0	2-2	6	4	1	1	9	5	9
Ferrocarril Oeste	1-3	-	1-0	2-0	6	4	1	1	7	3	9
Fluminense	0-1	0-0	-	0-0	6	0	3	3	3	6	3
Vasco da Gama	1-2	0-2	3-3	-	6	0	3	3	6	11	3

Play-off
Argentinos Juniors...........................3-1 ....Ferrocarril Oeste

Group 2

	Bl	OP	Ta	DI	Pl	W	D	L	F	A	Pts
Blooming	-	1-1	6-3	8-0	6	5	1	0	20	4	11
Oriente Petrolero	0-1	-	3-2	3-1	6	3	2	1	11	6	8
Deportivo Tachira	0-1	1-1	-	0-0	6	1	2	3	9	12	4
Deportivo Italia	0-3	0-3	1-3	-	6	0	1	5	2	20	1

Group 3

	Pe	CC	Ma	BV	Pl	W	D	L	F	A	Pts
Peñarol	-	3-1	1-0	1-0	6	5	1	0	10	3	11
Colo Colo	1-2	-	2-0	2-0	6	3	0	3	10	8	6
Magallanes	1-1	1-3	-	2-1	6	2	1	3	5	8	5
Bella Vista	0-2	2-1	0-1	-	6	1	0	5	3	9	2

Group 4

	AC	CP	Mi	Gu	Pl	W	D	L	F	A	Pts
America Cali	-	2-0	0-0	2-1	6	2	4	0	5	2	8
Cerro Porteño	0-0	-	0-0	3-1	6	2	3	1	5	3	7
Millonarios	0-0	0-2	-	5-1	6	1	3	2	5	5	5
Guarani Asuncion	1-1	0-0	2-0	-	6	1	2	3	6	11	4

Group 5

	NQ	NO	Un	SB	Pl	W	D	L	F	A	Pts
Nacional Quito	-	3-1	4-1	2-0	5	5	0	0	12	3	10
Nueve de Octubre	0-1	-	1-0	4-0	4	2	0	2	6	4	4
Universitario	-	-	-	4-0	4	2	0	2	7	5	4
Sport Boys	1-2	-	0-2	-	5	0	0	5	1	14	0

SEMI-FINALS

Group 1

	AJ	In	Bl	Pl	W	D	L	F	A	Pts
Argentinos Juniors	-	2-2	1-0	4	2	2	0	6	4	6
Independiente	1-2	-	2-0	4	1	2	1	6	5	4
Blooming	1-1	1-1	-	4	0	2	2	2	5	2

Group 2

	AC	NQ	Pe	Pl	W	D	L	F	A	Pts
America Cali	-	5-0	4-0	4	2	1	1	10	3	5
Nacional Quito	2-0	-	2-0	4	2	0	2	4	7	4
Peñarol	1-1	2-0	-	4	1	1	2	3	7	3

FINAL

1st leg. Monumental, Buenos Aires, 17-10-85, 50,000. Referee: Escobar, Paraguay

ARGENTINOS JUNIORS 1 (Comisso 40)
AMERICA CALI 0

Argentinos - Vidallé - Villalba, Pavoni, Olguin, Domenech - Comisso, Batista, Corsi, Castro - Borghi, Ereros (Pellegrini)
America - Falcioni - Porras (Chaparro), Soto, Viafara, Valencia - Gonzáles Aquino, Cabañas, Penagos (Escobar) - De Avila, Ortiz, Gareca

2nd leg. Pascual Guerrero, Cali, 22-10-85, 50,000. Referee: Felix, Brazil

AMERICA CALI 1 (Ortiz 3)
ARGENTINOS JUNIORS 0

America - Falcioni - Valencia, Soto, Viafara, Chaparro - Sarmiento, Gonzáles Aquino, Cabanas - Ortiz (De Avila), Gareca, Bataglia (Herrera)
Argentinos - Vidallé - Villalba, Pavoni, Olguin, Domenech - Videla, Batista, Comisso - Castro (Lopez.J) - Borghi, Ereros (Valdez)

Play-off. Defensores del Chaco, Asuncion, 24-10-85, 35,000. Referee: Silva,Chile

ARGENTINOS JUNIORS 1 (Comisso 37)
AMERICA CALI 1 (Gareca 42)
Argentinos Juniors won 5-4 on penalties

Argentinos - Vidallé - Villalba (Mayor), Pellegrini (Lemme), Pavoni, Domenech Olguin, Batista, Corsi, Comisso - Borghi, Videla
America - Falcioni - Valencia, Soto, Viafara, Chaparro - Sarmiento, Gonzáles Aquino, Cabañas - Ortiz (De Avila), Gareca, Bataglia (Herrera)

Top scorer Juan Carlos Sánchez, Blooming 11

1986

FIRST ROUND

Group 1

	RP	Wa	BJ	Pe	Pl	W	D	L	F	A	Pts
River Plate	-	4-2	1-0	3-1	6	5	1	0	13	4	11
Wanderers	0-2	-	2-0	1-0	6	3	0	3	10	10	6
Boca Juniors	1-1	3-2	-	1-1	6	2	2	2	7	8	6
Peñarol	0-2	1-3	1-2	-	6	0	1	5	4	12	1

Group 2

	AC	DC	Co	UC	Pl	W	D	L	F	A	Pts
America Cali	-	0-0	0-0	2-1	6	3	3	0	8	4	9
Deportivo Cali	0-1	-	1-1	3-1	6	2	3	1	8	5	7
Cobresal	2-2	1-1	-	1-1	6	1	5	0	6	5	7
Universidad Catolica	1-3	1-3	0-1	-	6	0	1	5	5	13	1

Group 3

	Bo	JW	Un	UC	Pl	W	D	L	F	A	Pts
Bolivar	-	2-0	4-0	2-1	6	4	1	1	12	7	9
Jorge Wilsterman	1-2	-	4-0	2-0	6	3	0	3	11	8	6
Universitario	3-0	1-2	-	2-0	6	3	0	3	9	11	6
Universidad Cajamarca	2-2	3-2	1-3	-	6	1	1	4	7	13	3

Group 4

	Ba	DQ	Co	Ba	Pl	W	D	L	F	A	Pts
Barcelona	-	3-3	1-1	1-0	6	2	4	0	7	5	8
Deportivo Quito	0-0	-	2-1	3-1	6	2	3	1	12	11	7
Coritiba	0-0	3-1	-	-	5	1	3	1	6	5	5
Bangu	1-2	3-3	1-1	-	5	0	2	3	6	10	2

Group 5

	Ol	NA	Pl	W	D	L	F	A	Pts
Olimpia	-	3-1	2	2	0	0	5	2	4
Nacional Asuncion	1-2	-	2	0	0	2	2	5	0

The Venezuelan entrants withdrew

SEMI-FINALS

Group 1

	RP	AJ	Ba	Pl	W	D	L	F	A	Pts
River Plate	-	0-2	4-1	4	2	1	1	7	3	5
Argentinos Juniors	0-0	-	1-0	4	2	1	1	3	1	5
Barcelona	0-3	1-0	-	4	1	0	3	2	8	2

Play-off
River Plate ....0-0..........Argentinos Juniors
River Plate won due to a better goal difference

Group 2

	AC	Ol	Bo	Pl	W	D	L	F	A	Pts
America Cali	-	1-0	2-1	4	2	1	1	4	4	5
Olimpia	1-1	-	3-1	4	1	2	1	5	4	4
Bolivar	2-0	1-1	-	4	1	1	2	5	6	3

FINAL

1st leg. Pascual Guerrero, Cali, 22-10-1986, 55,000. Referee: Cardellino, Urug

AMERICA CALI 1 (Cabanas 47)
RIVER PLATE 2 (Funes 22, Alonso 25)

America - Falcioni - Valencia, Espinoza, Esterilla, Porras - Gonzáles Aquino, Ischia (De Avila), Cabañas - Ortiz (Escobar), Gareca, Bataglia
River Plate - Pumpido - Gordillo, Gutiérrez, Ruggeri, Montenegro - Enrique, Gallego, Alonso (Sperandio) - Alfaro (Troglio), Alzamendi, Funes

2nd leg. Monumental, Buenos Aires, 29-10-1986, 85,000. Referee: Wright, Brazil

RIVER PLATE 1 (Funes 70)
AMERICA CALI 0

River Plate - Pumpido - Gordillo, Gutiérrez, Ruggeri, Montenegro - Enrique, Gallego, Alonso - Alfaro (Gomez), Alzamendi (Sperandio), Funes. Tr: Viera
America - Falcioni - Valencia (De Avila), Espinoza, Luna, Porras - Gonzáles Aquino (Escobar), Ischia, Cabañas - Ortiz, Gareca, Bataglia

Top scorer Juan Carlos Lima, Deportivo Quito 9

1987

FIRST ROUND

Group 1

	In	RC	Ta	EM	Pl	W	D	L	F	A	Pts
Independiente	-	3-1	5-0	2-0	6	4	1	1	13	4	9
Rosario Central	0-0	-	3-2	5-2	6	3	2	1	12	7	8
Deportivo Tachira	3-2	0-0	-	3-2	6	3	1	2	11	12	7
Estudiantes Merida	0-1	0-3	0-3	-	6	0	0	6	4	17	0

Group 2

	AC	DC	St	OP	Pl	W	D	L	F	A	Pts
America Cali	-	1-0	6-0	3-1	6	3	2	1	13	5	8
Deportivo Cali	2-1	-	4-0	5-1	6	4	0	2	13	5	8
The Strongest	1-1	2-1	-	3-2	6	2	1	3	7	16	5
Oriente Petrolero	1-1	0-1	2-1	-	6	1	1	4	7	14	3

Play-off
America Cali ....0-0 4-2p ....Deportivo Cali

Group 3

	Co	CC	Gu	SP	Pl	W	D	L	F	A	Pts
Cobreloa	-	1-0	3-1	3-1	6	3	2	1	8	4	8
Colo Colo	0-0	-	2-0	2-2	6	2	3	1	6	4	7
Guarani Campinas	0-0	0-0	-	3-1	6	1	3	2	6	8	5
São Paulo FC	2-1	1-2	2-2	-	6	1	2	3	9	13	4

Group 4

	Ba	Ol	NQ	SA	Pl	W	D	L	F	A	Pts
Barcelona	-	3-2	2-1	1-0	6	4	0	2	8	7	8
Olimpia	1-0	-	2-0	2-1	6	3	1	2	9	10	7

					Pl	W	D	L	F	A	Pts
Nacional Quito	2-0	4-0	-	4-1	6	3	0	3	12	7	6
Sol de America	1-2	2-2	2-1	-	6	1	1	4	7	12	3

Group 5

	Pe	Pr	Al	SA	Pl	W	D	L	F	A	Pts
Peñarol	-	3-2	2-0	2-0	6	4	2	0	10	4	10
Progreso	1-1	-	0-0	3-0	6	1	3	2	7	7	5
Alianza	0-1	0-0	-	0-0	6	1	3	2	2	4	5
Colégio San Augustin	1-1	3-1	1-2	-	6	1	2	3	5	9	4

SEMI-FINALS

Group 1

	Pe	RP	In	Pl	W	D	L	F	A	Pts
Peñarol	-	0-0	3-0	4	2	1	1	7	3	5
River Plate	1-0	-	0-0	4	1	2	1	2	2	4
Independiente	2-4	2-1	-	4	1	1	2	4	8	3

Group 2

	AC	Co	Ba	Pl	W	D	L	F	A	Pts
America Cali	-	1-1	4-0	4	2	2	0	9	3	6
Cobreloa	2-2	-	3-0	4	2	2	0	8	3	6
Barcelona	0-2	0-2	-	4	0	0	4	0	11	0

FINAL

1st leg. Pascual Guerrero, Cali, 21-10-87, 45,000. Referee: Writh, Brazil

AMERICA CALI 2 (Bataglia, Cabañas)
PEÑAROL 0

America - Falcioni - Valencia, Espinosa, Aponte, Porras - Luna, Santin, Herrera (Escobar) - Cabañas, Gareca (Maturana), Bataglia
Peñarol - Preyra - Herrera, Trasante, Rotti, Dominguez - Perdomo, Matosas (Da Silva), Viera, Vidal (Villar) - Aguirre, Cabrera

2nd leg. Centenario, Montevideo, 28-10-87, 70,000. Referee: Calabria, Argentina

PEÑAROL 2 (Aguirre 58, Villar 86)
AMERICA CALI 1 (Cabañas 19)

Peñarol - Preyra - Rotti (Goncalvez), Trasante, Herrera, Perdomo - Dominguez, Vidal, Da Silva - Aguirre, Viera, Cabrera (Villar)
America - Falcioni - Aponte, Espinosa, Valencia, Luna - Porras, Bataglia, Santin - Gareca, Cabañas, Ortiz (Herrera)

Play-off. Estadio Nacional, Santiago, 31-10-87, 30,000. Referee: Silva, Chile

PEÑAROL 1 (Aguirre 119)
AMERICA CALI 0

Peñarol - Pereyra - Rotti, Trasante, Herrera, Dominguez - Da Silva, Perdomo (Goncalves), Viera, Vidal (Villar) - Aguirre, Cabrera
America - Falcioni - Valencia, Espinoza, Aponte, Ampudia - Luna, Santin, Cabañas - Ortiz, Gareca (Esterilla), Bataglia

Top scorer Ricardo Gareca, América Cali 7

1988

COPA LIBERTADORES

FIRST ROUND

Group 1

	UC	CC	Ma	Ta	Pl	W	D	L	F	A	Pts
Universidad Catolica	-	1-0	2-1	3-1	6	4	2	0	9	4	10
Colo Colo	2-2	-	1-0	2-0	6	4	1	1	7	3	9
Maritimo	0-0	0-1	-	1-1	6	0	3	3	2	5	3
Deportivo Tachira	0-1	0-1	0-0	-	6	0	2	4	2	8	2

Group 2

	Ne	SL	Ba	Fi	Pl	W	D	L	F	A	Pts
Newell's Old Boys	-	0-0	3-0	1-0	6	2	4	0	5	1	8
San Lorenzo	0-0	-	2-1	2-0	6	3	2	1	6	4	8
Barcelona	0-0	2-0	-	4-2	6	3	1	2	9	8	7
Filanbanco	1-1	1-2	1-2	-	6	0	1	5	5	12	1

Play-off to determine second round placement
Newell's Old Boys .... 1-0 .... San Lorenzo

Group 3

	AC	Na	Mi	Wa	Pl	W	D	L	F	A	Pts
America Cali	-	0-0	2-1	1-0	6	4	1	1	8	6	9
Nacional Montevideo	2-0	-	4-1	1-0	6	3	2	1	8	7	8
Millonarios	2-3	6-1	-	3-0	6	2	0	4	14	12	4
Wanderers	1-2	0-0	2-1	-	6	1	1	4	3	8	3

Group 4

	OP	Bo	CP	Ol	Pl	W	D	L	F	A	Pts
Oriente Petrolero	-	2-1	2-2	1-0	6	3	1	2	8	8	7
Bolivar	3-1	-	2-0	2-0	6	3	0	3	12	10	6
Cerro Porteño	1-0	3-2	-	0-0	6	2	2	2	6	7	6
Olimpia	1-2	4-2	1-0	-	6	2	1	3	6	7	5

Group 5

	Gu	Un	SR	Al	Pl	W	D	L	F	A	Pts
Guarani Campinas	-	1-1	4-1	1-0	6	3	2	1	9	5	8
Universitario	1-1	-	1-0	2-0	6	2	4	0	5	2	8
Sport Recife	0-1	0-0	-	5-0	6	2	1	3	7	6	5
Alianza	2-1	0-0	0-1	-	6	1	1	4	2	10	3

SECOND ROUND

Universidad Catolica .... 1-1 0-0 .... **Nacional Montevideo** *
America Cali .... 1-0 2-2 .... Universitario
Oriente Petrolero .... 2-1 0-0 .... Colo Colo
San Lorenzo .... 1-1 1-0 .... Guarani Campinas
Bolivar .... 1-0 0-1 2-3p .... **Newell's Old Boys**
Peñarol .... Bye

* Nacional qualified on away goals

QUARTER-FINALS

Newell's Old Boys .... 1-1 1-2 .... **Nacional Montevideo**
San Lorenzo .... 1-0 0-0 .... Peñarol
America Cali .... 2-0 1-1 .... Oriente Petrolero

SEMI-FINALS

Nacional Montevideo .... 1-0 1-1 .... America Cali
Newell's Old Boys .... 1-0 2-1 .... San Lorenzo

FINAL

1st leg. Cordoviola, Rosario, 19-10-88, 45,000. Referee: Silva, Chile

NEWELL'S OLD BOYS 1 (Gabrich 60)
NACIONAL MONTEVIDEO 0

Newell's - Scoponi - Llop, Theiler, Pautasso, Sensini - Martino (Fullana), Franco, Alfaro, Rossi - Batistuta, Almiron (Gabrich)
Nacional - Seré - Pintos Saldanha, Revelez, De León, Soca - Lemos, Ostolaza, Cardaccio, Castro - Vargas (Carreño), De Lima

2nd leg. Centenario, Montevideo, 26-10-88, 75,000. Referee: Coelho, Brazil

NACIONAL MONTEVIDEO 3 (Vargas 10, Ostolaza 30, De Leon 81)
NEWELL'S OLD BOYS 0

Nacional - Seré - Pintos Saldanha, Revelez, De León, Soca - Lemos, Ostolaza, Cardaccio, Castro (Moran) - Vargas (Carreño), De Lima. Tr: Fleitas
Newell's - Scoponi - Llop (Ramos), Theiler, Pautasso, Sensini - Martino, Alfaro (Almiron), Franco, Rossi - Batistuta, Gabrich. Tr: Yudica

Top scorer Arnoldo Iguaran, Millonarios 5

SUPER COPA

FIRST ROUND

Racing Club .... 2-0 0-0 .... Santos

Boca Juniors 1-0 0-2 **Grêmio**
Olimpia 2-0 0-4 **River Plate**
Nacional Montevideo Bye
Estudiantes LP 1-0 0-3 **Flamengo**
Peñaro 1-0 0-2 **Argentinos Juniors**
Independiente 1-2 0-1 **Cruzeiro**

QUARTER-FINALS

Racing Club Bye
Grêmio 1-0 1-3 **River Plate**
Nacional Montevideo 3-0 2-0 Flamengo
Cruzeiro 1-0 1-0 Argentinos Juniors

SEMI-FINALS

Racing Club 2-1 1-1 River Plate
Nacional Montevideo 3-2 0-1 **Cruzeiro** *
* Cruzeiro qualified on away goals

FINAL

1st leg. Mozart y Cuyo, Buenos Aires, 13-06-1988, 50,000
RACING CLUB 2 (Fernandez 44, Colombatti 89)
CRUZEIRO 1 (Robson 36)
Racing - Fillol - Vázquez, Fabbri, Acuña (Perez), Costas - Ludueña, Olarán, Fernandez - Colombatti, Paz, Catálan (Bello)
Cruzeiro - Wellington - Ronaldo, Heraldo, Heriberto, Gilmar - Ademir, Vladimir, Anderson (Denilson) - Eder, Careca II, Robson

2nd leg. Mineirao, Belo Horizonte, 18-06-1988
CRUZEIRO 1 (Robson 82)
RACING CLUB 1 (Catalan 44)
Cruzeiro - Wellington - Balu, Heraldo, Gilmar, Ademir - Eder, Vladimir, Anderson - Heriberto (Ramondal), Robson, Careca
Racing - Fillol - Vázquez, Fabbri, Acuña, Costas - Ludueña, Olarán, Fernandez Colombatti, Paz (Perez), Catálan (Bello). Tr: Basile

Top scorers Antonio Alzamendi, River Plate 4
Sergio Oliveira, Nacional Montivideo 4

RECOPA

1st leg, Centenario, Montevideo, 31-01-1989
Nacional Montevideo 1 (Fonseca)
Racing Club 0
2nd leg, Mozart y Cuyo, Buenos Aires, 6-02-1989
Racing Club 0
Nacional Montevideo 0

1989

COPA LIBERTADORES

FIRST ROUND

Group 1

	Co	SA	Ol	CC	Pl	W	D	L	F	A	Pts
Cobreloa	-	1-0	2-0	2-0	6	3	2	1	7	4	8
Sol de America	0-0	-	5-4	1-0	6	2	2	2	7	8	6
Olimpia	2-0	0-0	-	2-0	6	2	1	3	8	9	5
Colo Colo	2-2	3-1	2-0	-	6	2	1	3	7	8	5

Group 2

	Ba	Ta	IP	Ma	Pl	W	D	L	F	A	Pts
EC Bahia	-	4-1	1-0	3-2	6	4	2	0	11	5	10
Deportivo Tachira	1-1	-	1-0	2-0	6	3	1	2	7	8	7
Internacional PA	1-2	3-1	-	3-0	6	2	1	3	8	6	5
Maritimo	0-0	0-1	1-1	-	6	0	2	4	3	10	2

Group 3

	Mi	NM	DQ	Em	Pl	W	D	L	F	A	Pts
Millonarios	-	1-1	3-1	4-1	6	4	2	0	12	3	10
At. Nacional Medellín	0-2	-	2-1	3-1	6	2	3	1	8	7	7
Deportivo Quito	0-0	1-1	-	1-0	6	1	2	3	4	7	4
Emelec	0-2	1-1	1-0	-	6	1	1	4	4	11	3

Group 4

	BJ	RC	Un	SC	Pl	W	D	L	F	A	Pts
Boca Juniors	-	3-2	2-0	4-3	6	3	1	2	9	7	7
Racing Club	0-0	-	2-0	2-0	6	3	1	2	9	6	7
Universitario	1-0	2-1	-	4-0	6	3	0	3	7	6	6
Sporting Cristal	1-0	1-2	1-0	-	6	2	0	4	6	12	4

Play-off for second round placement
Boca Juniors 3-1 Racing Club

Group 5

	Pe	Da	Bo	St	Pl	W	D	L	F	A	Pts
Peñarol	-	2-0	5-0	1-1	6	3	1	2	11	9	7
Danubio	4-1	-	1-0	1-0	6	3	0	3	7	7	6
Bolivar	3-0	3-1	-	0-0	6	2	2	2	6	7	6
The Strongest	1-2	1-0	0-0	-	6	1	3	2	3	4	5

SECOND ROUND

At. Nacional Medellín 2-0 1-2 Racing Club
Bolivar 1-0 2-3 3-4p **Millonarios**
Deportivo Quito 0-0 0-1 **Cobreloa**
Nacional Montevideo 1-3 0-0 **Danubio**
Internacional PA 6-2 2-1 Peñarol
Universitario 1-1 1-2 **EC Bahia**
Sol de America 3-0 0-3 3-2p Deportivo Tachira
Olimpia 2-0 3-5 7-6p Boca Juniors

QUARTER-FINALS

At. Nacional Medellín 1-0 1-1 Millonarios
Cobreloa 0-2 1-2 **Danubio**
Internacional PA 1-0 0-0 EC Bahia
Olimpia 2-0 4-4 Sol de America

SEMI-FINALS

Danubio 0-0 0-6 **At. Nacional Medellín**
Olimpia 0-1 3-2 5-3p Internacional Porto Alegre

FINAL

1st leg. Defensores del Chaco, Asuncion, 24-05-89, 50,000. Referee: Wright, Brazil
OLIMPIA 2 (Bobadilla 36, Sanabria 60)
AT. NACIONAL MEDELLIN 0
Olimpia - Almeida - Miño, Benitez, Chamas, Krausemann - Sanabria (Balbuena), Guasch, Neffa, Bobadilla - Amarilla, Mendoza (Gonzalez)
Nacional - Higuita - Gómez, Perea, Escobar, Villa (Carmona) - Pérez, Alvárez, Fajardo, Garcia - Arango (Arboleda), Usurriaga

2nd leg. El Campin, Bogotá, 31-05-89, 50,000. Referee: Loustau, Argentina
AT. NACIONAL MEDELLIN 2 (OG 46, Usurriaga 64)
OLIMPIA 0
Nacional won 5-4 on penalties
Nacional - Higuita - Carmona, Perea, Escobar, Gómez - Alvárez, Garcia, Fajardo (Arboleda) - Arango (Pérez), Usurriaga, Trellez. Tr: Maturana
Olimpia - Almeida - Miño, Benitez, Chamas, Krausemann - Sanabria, Guasch, Bobadilla (Balbuena), Neffa - Amarilla, Mendoza. Tr: Cubilla

Top scorers Raul Amarilla, Olimpia 10
Carlos Aguilera, Peñarol 10

SUPER COPA

FIRST ROUND

Boca Juniors Bye
Racing Club Bye
Estudiantes LP 3-0 0-2 Peñarol

River Plate 2-1 1-2 1-4p **Grêmio**
Flamengo 0-1 1-2 **Argentinos Juniors**
Olimpia 2-0 0-3 **Cruzeiro**
Nacional Montevideo 2-1 0-2 **At. Nacional Medellín**
Santos 1-2 0-2 **Independiente**

QUARTER-FINALS

Boca Juniors 0-0 2-1 Racing Club
Grêmio 0-1 3-0 Estudiantes LP
Cruzeiro 1-1 0-2 **Argentinos Juniors**
At. Nacional Medellín 2-2 0-2 **Independiente**

SEMI-FINALS

Grêmio 0-0 0-2 **Boca Juniors**
Argentinos Juniors 0-1 1-2 **Independiente**

FINAL

1st leg. La Bombonera, Buenos Aires, 23-11-1989, 23,000
BOCA JUNIORS 0
INDEPENDIENTE 0
Boca Juniors - Navarro - Montoya, Simon, Cuciuffo, Stafuza - Giunta, Marchesini, Latorre - Marangoni, Graciani, Perazzo (Berti)
Independiente - Pereira - Morales, Delgado (Lozano), Bianco, Monzon - Ludueña, Altamirano, Moreno - Giusti, Insúa, Reggiardo (Ubaldi)

2nd leg. Cordero, Buenos Aires, 29-11-1989, 60,000
INDEPENDIENTE 0
BOCA JUNIORS 0
Independiente - Pereira - Morales, Delgado, Bianco, Monzon - Ludueña, Altamirano, Moreno (Artime) - Giusti, Insúa, Reggiardo (Bochini). Tr: Jorge Solari
Boca Juniors - Navarro - Montoya, Simon, Cuciuffo, Stafuza - Giunta, Marchesini, Perazzo (Berti) - Marangoni, Latorre, Graciani. Tr: Carlos Aimar
Boca Juniors won 5-3 on penalties

Top scorers Airez, Argentinos Juniors 3
Rubén Insúa, Independiente 3
John Trellez, At. Nacional 3

RECOPA

Orange Bowl, Miami, 17-03-1990, 9,000
Boca Juniors 1 (Latorre)
At. Nacional Medellin 0

1990

COPA LIBERTADORES

FIRST ROUND

Group 1

	Em	St	Ba	OP	Pl	W	D	L	F	A	Pts
Emelec	-	1-0	3-1	2-2	6	2	2	2	9	8	6
The Strongest	4-3	-	2-1	2-0	6	3	0	3	8	7	6
Barcelona	0-0	1-0	-	2-1	6	2	2	2	6	7	6
Oriente Petrolero	1-0	1-0	1-1	-	6	2	2	2	6	7	6

Play-off
Barcelona 3-1 2-3 Oriente Petrolero

Group 2

	In	RP	Pl	W	D	L	F	A	Pts
Independiente	-	1-0	2	1	1	0	1	0	3
River Plate	0-0	-	2	0	1	1	0	1	1

The Colombian representatives withdrew

Group 3

	CC	UC	UH	SC	Pl	W	D	L	F	A	Pts
Colo Colo	-	0-0	3-1	2-0	6	3	2	1	9	5	8
Universidad Catolica	2-1	-	2-2	2-0	6	2	3	1	6	4	7
Union Huaral	1-1	1-0	-	0-3	6	1	3	2	5	9	5
Sporting Cristal	1-2	0-0	0-0	-	6	1	2	3	4	6	4

Group 4

	Pr	De	Pe	MG	Pl	W	D	L	F	A	Pts
Progreso	-	1-1	2-0	1-1	6	2	3	1	7	4	7
Defensor	0-0	-	1-0	3-1	6	2	3	1	5	3	7
Pepeganga	1-0	1-0	-	2-1	6	3	0	3	4	5	6
Mineros Guyana	1-3	0-0	1-0	-	6	1	2	3	5	9	4

Play-off to determine second round placement
Progreso 4-0 Defensor

Group 5

	Ol	CP	VG	Gr	Pl	W	D	L	F	A	Pts
Olimpia	-	2-1	2-1	1-0	6	3	1	2	9	8	7
Cerro Porteño	3-2	-	1-1	3-1	6	2	2	2	8	8	6
Vasco da Gama	1-0	2-0	-	0-0	6	2	2	2	5	5	6
Grêmio	2-2	0-0	2-0	-	6	1	3	2	5	6	5

SECOND ROUND

Olimpia Bye
Universidad Catolica 3-1 1-1 The Strongest
Vasco da Gama 0-0 3-3 5-4p Colo Colo
Cerro Porteño 0-0 0-1 **At. Nacional Medellín**
Defensor 1-2 1-2 **River Plate**
Pepeganga 0-6 0-3 **Independiente**
Union Huaral 1-0 0-2 **Emelec**
Barcelona 2-0 2-2 Progreso

QUARTER-FINALS

Olimpia 2-0 4-4 Universidad Catolica
Vasco da Gama 0-0 0-1 **At. Nacional Medellín**
River Plate 2-0 1-1 Independiente
Emelec 0-0 0-1 **Barcelona**

SEMI-FINALS

At. Nacional Medellín 1-2 3-2 1-2p **Olimpia**
River Plate 1-0 0-1 3-4p **Barcelona**

FINAL

1st leg. Defensores del Chaco, Asuncion, 3-10-90, 35,000. Referee: Cardellino, Uruguay
OLIMPIA 2 (Amarilla 47, Samaniego 65)
BARCELONA 0
Olimpia - Almeida - Ramirez.J, Fernandez, Ramirez.M, Suarez - Guasch, Balbuena (Cubilla), Monzon, Gonzalez - Samaniego, Amarilla
Barcelona - Morales - Izquierdo, Martinez, Nacias, Bravo.F - Saralegui, Muñoz (Maldonado), Proano (Bravo.D), Trobbiani - Jimenez, Acosta

2nd leg. Modelo, Guayaquil, 10-10-90, 55,000. Referee: Montalban, Peru
BARCELONA 1 (Trobbiani 61)
OLIMPIA 1 (Amarilla 80)
Barcelona - Morales - Izquierdo, Bravo.F, Macias, Guzman (Proano) - Saralegui, Bravo.D, Trobbiani, Muñoz - Uquillas, Acosta. Tr: Brindisi
Olimpia - Almeida - Ramirez.J, Ramirez.M, Suarez, Fernandez (Gonzalez) - Guasch, Balbuena, Jara, Monzon - Amarilla (Sanabria), Samaniego. Tr: Cubilla

Top scorer Adriano Samaniego, Olimpia 7

SUPER COPA

FIRST ROUND

River Plate 3-0 0-3 3-4p **Olimpia**
Cruzeiro 1-0 0-1 2-4p **Racing Club**

Boca Juniors ... Bye
Peñarol ... 0-0 2-2 4-2p ... Santos
Grêmio ... 1-0 0-2 ... **Estudiantes LP**
Argentinos Juniors ... 3-1 1-3 4-3p ... Flamengo
Independiente ... 1-1 1-2 ... **Nacional Montevideo**

QUARTER-FINALS

Olimpia ... 1-1 3-0 ... Racing Club
Peñarol ... 0-1 2-0 ... Boca Juniors
Estudiantes LP ... Bye
Argentinos Juniors ... 2-1 1-3 ... **Nacional Montevideo**

SEMI-FINALS

Peñarol ... 2-1 0-6 ... **Olimpia**
Estudiantes LP ... 0-0 0-0 3-5p ... **Nacional Montevideo**

FINAL

1st leg. Montevideo, 5-01-1991, 45,000. Referee: Wright, Brazil

NACIONAL MONTEVIDEO 0
OLIMPIA 3 (Gonzalez 55, Amarilla 81, Samaniego 87)

Nacional - Seré - Gomez.T, Gomez.M, Revelez, Soca - Moran, Cardaccio, Lemos Valdez.D, Cabrera (Baez), Vargas (Ramos)
Olimpia - Almeida - Caceres, Ramirez, Fernandez, Suarez - Balbuena, Guasch, Monzon - Gonzalez, Amarilla, Samaniego

2nd leg. Asuncion, 11-01-1991, 40,000. Referee: Loustau, Argentina

OLIMPIA 3 (Samaniego 27, Amarilla 50, Monzon 69)
NACIONAL MONTEVIDEO 3 (Cardaccio 5, Moran 31, Wilson Nunez 34)

Olimpia - Almeida - Caceres, Ramirez, Fernandez, Suarez - Balbuena, Guasch, Monzon - Gonzalez (Villalba), Amarilla, Samaniego. Tr: Cubilla
Nacional - Seré - Maristal, Sarabia, Revelez, Mozo - Pena, Cardaccio, Moran Miranda (Cabrera), Wilson Nunez, Garcia (Ramos). Tr: Carlos Blanco

Top scorer Raul Amarilla, Olimpia ... 7

RECOPA

Olimpia were declared automatic winners after winning both the Libertadores and Super Cups

1991

COPA LIBERTADORES

FIRST ROUND

Group 1

	Bo	BJ	OP	RP	Pl	W	D	L	F	A	Pts
Bolivar	-	2-0	2-0	4-1	6	3	1	2	9	5	7
Boca Juniors	0-0	-	0-0	4-3	6	2	2	2	6	6	6
Oriente Petrolero	2-1	1-0	-	1-1	6	2	3	1	5	7	6
River Plate	2-0	0-2	3-1	-	6	2	1	3	10	12	5

Group 2

	CC	LQ	DC	Ba	Pl	W	D	L	F	A	Pts
Colo Colo	-	3-0	2-0	3-1	6	3	3	0	10	3	9
LDU Quito	0-0	-	4-0	0-0	6	2	2	2	5	6	6
Deportivo Concepcion	0-0	3-0	-	1-0	6	2	2	2	6	8	6
Barcelona	2-2	0-1	2-2	-	6	0	3	3	5	9	3

Group 3

	Fl	Co	Na	BV	Pl	W	D	L	F	A	Pts
Flamengo	-	2-0	4-0	1-1	6	3	3	0	11	4	9
Corinthians	1-1	-	0-0	4-1	6	1	4	1	7	6	6
Nacional Montevideo	0-1	1-1	-	3-0	6	2	2	2	7	6	6
Bella Vista	2-2	1-1	0-3	-	6	0	3	3	5	14	3

Group 4

	CP	AC	Un	SB	Pl	W	D	L	F	A	Pts
Cerro Porteño	-	1-1	0-0	3-0	6	2	4	0	9	4	8
Atletico Colegiales	1-1	-	2-0	4-1	6	2	4	0	10	5	8
Universitario	1-1	0-0	-	1-3	6	1	3	2	4	6	5
Sport Boys	1-3	2-2	0-2	-	6	1	1	4	7	15	3

Play-off to determine second round placement
Cerro Porteño ... 1-0 ... Atletico Colegiales

Group 5

	AC	NM	Ta	Ma	Pl	W	D	L	F	A	Pts
America Cali	-	1-0	3-2	2-0	6	5	1	0	10	3	11
At. Nacional Medellín	0-2	-	0-0	2-2	6	2	2	2	7	7	6
Deportivo Tachira	1-1	1-2	-	2-1	6	1	3	2	6	7	5
Maritimo	0-1	1-3	0-0	-	6	0	2	4	4	10	2

SECOND ROUND

Universitario ... 0-0 1-2 ... **Colo Colo**
Nacional Montevideo ... 4-1 1-1 ... Bolivar
Deportivo Tachira ... 2-3 0-5 ... **Flamengo**
Boca Juniors ... 3-1 1-1 ... Corinthians
LDU Quito ... 2-2 0-2 ... **At. Nacional Medellin**
Deportivo Concepcion ... 0-3 3-3 ... **America Cali**
Oriente Petrolero ... 1-1 0-2 ... **Cerro Porteño**
Atletico Colegiales ... 1-1 1-3 ... **Olimpia**

QUARTER-FINALS

Colo Colo ... 4-0 0-2 ... Nacional Montevideo
Flamengo ... 2-1 0-3 ... **Boca Juniors**
America Cali ... 0-0 0-2 ... **At. Nacional Medellin**
Cerro Porteño ... 1-0 0-3 ... **Olimpia**

SEMI-FINALS

Boca Juniors ... 1-0 1-3 ... **Colo Colo**
At. Nacional Medellin ... 0-0 0-1 ... **Olimpia**

FINAL

1st leg. Defensores del Chaco, Asuncion, 29-05-1991, 48,000. Referee: Filippi, Uruguay

OLIMPIA 0
COLO COLO 0

Olimpia - Battaglia - Caceres, Fernandez, Castro, Suarez - Balbuena, Guasch, Monzon, Guirland (Cubilla) - Samaniego, Gonzalez (Villalba)
Colo Colo - Moron - Garrido, Margas, Ramirez, Vilchez - Mendoza, Espinoza, Pizarro, Peralta - Barticciotto, Martinez

2nd leg. Estadio Nacional, Santiago, 5-06-1991, 64,000. Referee: Wright, Brazil

COLO COLO 3 (Perez 13 18, Herrera 85)
OLIMPIA 0

Colo Colo - Moron - Garrido, Ramirez, Margas, Vilchez - Peralta, Espinoza, Pizarro, Mendoza (Herrera) - Perez, Barticciotto. Tr: Jozic
Olimpia - Battaglia - Ramirez, Castro, Fernandez, Suarez - Jara (Guirland), Balbuena (Cubilla), Guasch, Monzon - Torres, Gonzalez. Tr: Cubilla

Top scorer Renato Gaucho, Flamengo ... 8

SUPER COPA

FIRST ROUND

Cruzeiro ... 0-0 0-0 5-4p ... Colo Colo
Boca Juniors ... 1-1 0-2 ... **Nacional Montevideo**

Argentinos Juniors ... 1-2 0-0 ... **Santos**
Peñarol ... 3-2 0-0 ... Racing Club
Flamengo ... 1-1 2-0 ... Estudiantes LP
River Plate ... 2-2 1-1 5-4p ... Grêmio

QUARTER-FINALS

Cruzeiro ... 4-0 0-3 ... Nacional Montevideo
Independiente ... 1-1 0-2 ... **Olimpia**
Peñarol ... 3-2 0-0 ... Santos
River Plate ... 1-0 1-2 4-3p ... Flamengo

SEMI-FINALS

Cruzeiro ... 1-1 0-0 5-3p ... Olimpia
River Plate ... 2-0 3-1 ... Peñarol

FINAL

1st leg. Monumental, Buenos Aires, 13-11-1991, 60,000. Referee: Orellana Ecuador

RIVER PLATE 2 (Rivarola 30, Higuain 90)
CRUZEIRO 0

River Plate - Comizzo - Gordillo, Higuain, Rivarola, Enrique - Diaz.H, Astrada (Zapata), Borrelli, Medina Bello - Diaz.R, Silvani
Cruzeiro - Paulo Cesar - Zelao, Vanderci, Adilson, Donato - Andrade, Ademir, Boiadeiro, Luis Fernando - Tilico (Paulinho), Charles (Macale)

2nd leg. Mineirao, Belo Horizonte, 20-11-1991, 80,000. Referee: Silva, Chile

CRUZEIRO 3 (Ademir 34, Tilico 52, Marquinhos 76)
RIVER PLATE 0

Cruzeiro - Paulo Cesar - Donato, Paulao, Adilson, Celio Gaucho - Ademir, Boiadeiro, Luis Fernando (Macale), Tilico - Charles, Marquinhos. Tr: Enio Andrade
River Plate - Comizzo - Gordillo, Higuain, Rivarola, Enrique - Diaz.H (Berti), Astrada, Borrelli, Zapata (Toresani) - Medina Bello, Diaz.R. Tr: Passarella

Top scorers Juan José Borrelli, River Plate ... 3
Charles, Cruzeiro ... 3
Renato Gaucho, Flamengo ... 3
Sergio Martinez, Peñarol ... 3

RECOPA

Kobe, Japan, 19-04-1992

Colo Colo 0
Cruzeiro 0
Colo Colo won 5-4 on penalties

1992

COPA LIBERTADORES

FIRST ROUND

Group 1

	NO	UC	SL	CC	Co	Pl	W	D	L	F	A	Pts
Newell's Old Boys	-	0-0	0-6	3-1	3-0	8	4	3	1	11	10	11
Universidad Catolica	1-1	-	4-0	0-0	5-1	8	2	5	1	15	8	9
San Lorenzo	0-1	2-2	-	1-0	3-0	8	4	1	3	13	8	9
Colo Colo	1-1	1-1	1-0	-	1-0	8	2	4	2	6	7	8
Coquimbo	1-2	3-2	0-1	1-1	-	8	1	1	6	6	18	3

Group 2

	Cr	SP	Bo	SJ	Pl	W	D	L	F	A	Pts
Criciuma	-	3-0	2-1	5-0	6	4	1	1	13	7	9
São Paulo FC	4-0	-	2-0	1-1	6	3	2	1	11	5	8
Bolivar	1-1	1-1	-	2-1	6	2	2	2	9	9	6
San Jose	1-2	0-3	2-4	-	6	0	1	5	5	17	1

Group 3

	Ba	Va	Ma	UM	Pl	W	D	L	F	A	Pts
Barcelona	-	0-0	3-1	5-1	6	4	2	0	11	3	10
Valdez	0-1	-	2-1	1-1	6	2	2	2	5	4	6
Maritimo	1-1	1-0	-	1-2	6	1	2	3	5	8	4
ULA Merida	0-1	0-2	0-0	-	6	1	2	3	4	10	4

Group 4

	NM	AC	SC	SB	Pl	W	D	L	F	A	Pts
Nacional Medellin	-	3-0	1-0	2-2	6	4	1	1	15	4	9
America Cali	2-0	-	1-0	2-0	6	4	0	2	8	7	8
Sporting Cristal	0-3	3-1	-	2-0	6	2	1	3	6	7	5
Sport Boys	0-6	1-2	1-1	-	6	0	2	4	4	15	2

Group 5

	CP	Na	De	SA	Pl	W	D	L	F	A	Pts
Cerro Porteño	-	1-1	1-1	2-0	6	3	3	0	9	4	9
Nacional Montevideo	0-0	-	1-0	2-2	6	2	3	1	9	7	6
Defensor	2-3	3-2	-	1-2	6	1	2	3	7	9	5
Sol de America	0-2	1-3	0-0	-	6	1	2	3	5	10	4

SECOND ROUND

Nacional Montevideo ... 0-2 0-2 ... **São Paulo FC**
Sporting Cristal ... 1-2 2-3 ... **Criciuma**
Bolivar ... 2-0 0-3 ... **Cerro Porteño**
Colo-Colo ... 1-0 0-2 ... **Barcelona**
Universidad Catolica ... 0-0 0-1 ... **America Cali**
Maritimo ... 0-0 0-3 ... **At. Nacional Medellin**
San Lorenzo ... 2-0 0-2 6-5p ... Valdez
Defensor ... 1-1 0-1 ... **Newell's Old Boys**

QUARTER-FINALS

São Paulo FC ... 1-0 1-1 ... Criciuma
Barcelona ... 1-1 1-1 4-3p ... Cerro Porteño
At. Nacional Medellin ... 0-1 2-4 ... **America Cali**
Newell's Old Boys ... 4-0 1-1 ... San Lorenzo

SEMI-FINALS

São Paulo FC ... 3-0 0-2 ... Barcelona
Newell's Old Boys ... 1-1 1-1 11-10p ... America Cali

FINAL

1st leg. Cordoviola, Rosario, 10-06-1992, 45,000. Referee: Silva, Chile

NEWELL'S OLD BOYS 1 (Berizzo 38)
SÃO PAULO FC 0

Newell's - Scoponi - Raggio, Gamboa, Pochettino, Saldanha - Berti, Berizzo, Martino (Garfagnoli) - Zamora, Lunari, Mendoza (Domizzi)
São Paulo - Zetti - Cafu, Antonio Carlos, Ronaldo, Ivan - Adilson, Pintado, Rai - Muller, Palinha (Macedo), Elivelton

2nd leg. Morumbi, São Paulo, 17-06-1992, 105,000. Referee: Cadena, Colombia

SÃO PAULO FC 1 (Rai 65)
NEWELL'S OLD BOYS 0

São Paulo - Zetti - Cafu, Antonio Carlos, Ronaldo, Ivan - Adilson, Pintado, Rai - Palinha, Muller (Macedo), Elivelton. Tr: Santana
Newell's - Scoponi - Saldana, Gamboa, Pochettino, Berizzo - Llop, Berti, Martino (Domizzi), Lunari - Zamora, Mendoza. Tr: Bielsa
São Paulo won 3-2 on penalties

Top scorer: Palinha, São Paulo FC ... 7

SUPER COPA

FIRST ROUND

At. Nacional Medellin ... 1-1 0-8 ... **Cruzeiro**
Argentinos Juniors ... 1-2 0-3 ... **River Plate**
Santos ... 1-1 1-4 ... **São Paulo FC**

Colo Colo ... 1-0 0-1 2-3p ... **Olimpia**
Grêmio ... 1-1 0-1 ... **Flamengo**
Boca Juniors ... 2-1 0-1 3-4p ... **Estudiantes LP**
Peñarol ... 2-2 0-1 ... **Nacional Montevideo**
Racing Club ... 2-1 0-0 ... Independiente

QUARTER-FINALS

Cruzeiro ... 2-0 0-2 5-4p ... River Plate
São Paulo ... 1-2 0-1 ... **Olimpia**
Flamengo ... 1-0 1-1 ... Estudiantes LP
Racing Club ... W-O ... Nacional Montevideo

SEMI-FINALS

Olimpia ... 0-1 2-2 ... **Cruzeiro**
Flamengo ... 3-3 0-1 ... **Racing Club**

FINAL

1st leg. Mineirao, Belo Horizonte, 18-11-1992, 77,000. Referee: Torres, Colombia

CRUZEIRO 4 (Roberto Gaucho 31 57, Luis Fernando 69, Boiadeiro 84)
RACING CLUB 0

Cruzeiro - Paulo Cesar - Paulo Roberto, Celio Lucio, Luizinho, Nonato - Douglas, Luis Fernando, Boiadeiro - Renato Gaucho, Betinho, Roberto Gaucho
Racing - Roa - Reinoso, Borelli, Zaccanti, Distefano - Matosas (Torres.F), Costas, Guendulain, Paz.R - Garcia, Graciani (Vallejos)

2nd leg. Buenos Aires, 25-11-1992. Referee: Escobar

RACING CLUB 1 (Garcia 85p)
CRUZEIRO 0

Racing - Roa - Reinoso, Vallejos (Torres.F), Distefano, Costas - Matosas (Cabrol), Paz.R Guendulain - Torres.C, Garcia, Graciani. Tr: Grondona
Cruzeiro - Paulo Cesar - Paulo Roberto, Celio Lucio, Luizinho, Nonato - Douglas, Luis Fernando, Boiadeiro - Renato Gaucho, Betinho, Roberto Gaucho (Arle).Tr: Jair Pereira

Top scorer Renato Gaucho, Cruzeiro ... 7

COPA CONMEBOL

FIRST ROUND

Fluminense ... 2-1 1-5 ... **Atletico Mineiro**
Atletico Junior ... 6-0 1-0 ... Maritimo
Bragantino ... 2-2 1-1 6-7p ... **Grêmio**
Nacional Quito ... 3-1 3-1 ... Universitario
O'Higgins ... 0-0 0-2 ... **Gimnasia y Esgrima**
Peñarol ... 0-0 1-1 7-6p ... Danubio
Velez Sarsfield ... 0-0 0-2 ... **Deportivo Español**
Oriente Petrolero ... 0-4 0-1 ... **Olimpia**

QUARTER-FINALS

Atletico Mineiro ... 2-2 3-0 ... Atletico Junior
Grêmio ... 1-0 1-4 ... **Nacional Quito**
Peñarol ... 0-0 1-3 ... **Gimnasia y Esgrima**
Olimpia ... 0-0 0-0 4-3p ... Deportivo Español

SEMI-FINALS

Nacional Quito ... 1-0 0-2 ... **Atletico Mineiro**
Olimpia ... 0-0 0-0 3-0p ... Gimnasia y Esgrima

FINAL

1st Leg. Mineirao, Belo Horizonte, 16-09-1992, 60,000. Referee: Silva, Chile

ATLÉTICO MINEIRO 2 (Negrini 30 58)
OLIMPIA 0

Atlético - Joao Leite (Humberto) - Alfinete, Luiz Eduardo, Ryuler, Paulo Roberto - Eder Lopes, Moacir, Negrini - Sergio Araujo, Ailton, Claudinho
Olimpia - Goycochea - Caceres, Ramirez, Nuñez, Suarez - Jara, Sanabria.V, Campos, Gonzalez (Meza) - Amarilla (Samaniego), Sanabria.M

2nd Leg. Asuncion, 23-09-1992, 35,000. Referee: Filippi, Uruguay

OLIMPIA 1 (Caballero 90)
ATLÉTICO MINEIRO 0

Olimpia - Goycochea - Caceres (Meza), Ramirez, Nuñez, Suarez - Jara, Sanabria.V, Campos (Caballero) - Gonzalez, Samaniego, Sanabria.M, Tr: Roberto Profumo
Atlético - Joao Leite - Alfinete, Luiz Eduardo, Ryuler, Paulo Roberto - Eder Lopes, Moacir, Negrini (Andre) - Sergio Araujo, Ailton (Toninho), Claudinho. Tr: Procopio Cardoso

Top scorer Ailton, Atlético Mineiro ... 6

RECOPA

1st leg. Saõ Paulo, 26-09-1993

Saõ Paulo 0
Cruzeiro 0

2nd leg. Belo Horizonte, 29-09-1993

Cruzeiro 0
Saõ Paulo 0
Saõ Paulo won 4-2 on penalties

1993

COPA LIBERTADORES

FIRST ROUND

Group 1

	Un	SC	Mi	Ca	Pl	W	D	L	F	A	Pts
Universitario	-	2-2	2-0	4-1	6	3	3	0	14	7	9
Sporting Cristal	1-3	-	6-2	0-1	6	3	1	2	13	9	7
Minerven	2-2	0-1	-	1-0	6	1	2	3	6	12	4
Caracas FC	1-1	1-3	1-1	-	6	1	2	3	5	10	4

Play-off
Minerven ... 1-0 ... Caracas FC

Group 2

	UC	Bo	Co	SJ	Pl	W	D	L	F	A	Pts
Universidad Catolica	-	3-0	1-1	4-1	6	3	2	1	15	8	8
Bolivar	3-1	-	3-0	3-1	6	3	1	2	10	7	7
Cobreloa	1-1	1-1	-	2-1	6	2	3	1	8	9	7
San Jose	2-5	1-0	2-3	-	6	1	0	5	8	17	2

Group 3

	NM	NQ	Ba	BV	Pl	W	D	L	F	A	Pts
Nacional Montevideo	-	5-1	3-0	2-2	6	3	2	1	12	6	8
Nacional Quito	2-0	-	1-0	5-0	6	3	0	3	9	11	6
Barcelona	1-1	4-0	-	2-0	6	2	1	3	8	7	5
Bella Vista	0-1	2-0	2-1	-	6	2	1	3	6	11	5

Group 4

	Fl	AC	NM	In	Pl	W	D	L	F	A	Pts
Flamengo	-	1-3	3-1	3-1	6	3	1	2	9	7	7
America Cali	2-1	-	0-3	4-2	6	3	1	2	12	11	7
Nacional Medellin	0-1	3-2	-	0-0	6	3	1	2	8	6	7
Internacional	0-0	1-1	0-1	-	6	0	3	3	4	9	3

Play-off for second round placement
America Cali ... 4-2 ... At. Nacional Medellin

Group 5

	CP	NO	OI	RP	Pl	W	D	L	F	A	Pts
Cerro Porteño	-	0-0	0-0	2-1	6	2	3	1	5	4	7

Newell's Old Boys	1-2 - 1-1 0-0	6	1	4	1	4	4	6
Olimpia	1-0 1-1 - 1-1	6	1	4	1	4	4	6
River Plate	1-1 0-1 1-0 -	6	1	3	2	4	5	5

SECOND ROUND

Newell's Old Boys ....2-0 0-4..........**São Paulo FC**
Flamengo ....8-2 1-0 ....Minerven
Nacional Montevideo..........1-2 0-3 ....**Olimpia**
Cerro Porteño ....1-1 2-0 ....Cobreloa
America Cali ....2-1 1-1..........Bolivar
National Quito..........3-0 0-4..........**Sporting Cristal**
Universitario..........2-1 0-3 ....**Barcelona**
Universidad Catolica..........2-0 1-2..........At. Nacional Medellin

QUARTER-FINALS

Flamengo..........1-1 0-2..........**São Paulo FC**
Cerro Porteño ....1-1 0-0 4-2p ....Olimpia
America Cali ....2-2 3-2 ....Sporting Cristal
Universidad Catolica..........3-1 1-0..........Barcelona

SEMI-FINALS

São Paulo FC..........1-0 0-0 ....Cerro Porteño
Universidad Catolica..........1-0 2-2 ....America Cali

FINAL

1st leg. Morumbi São Paulo, 19-05-1993, 85,000. Referee: Torres, Colombia

SÃO PAULO FC 5 (OG 31, Vitor 41, Gilmar 55, Rai 61, Muller 65)
UNIVERSIDAD CATOLICA 1 (Almada 85p)

São Paulo - Zetti - Vitor (Caté), Valber, Gilmar, Ronaldo Luiz (André) - Pintado, Dinho, Cafu - Palinha, Rai, Muller

Universidad - Wirth - Romero, Vazquez, Lopez (Barrera), Contreras - Parraguez, Lepe, Lunari, Tupper - Almada, Perez (Reynoso)

2nd leg. Estadio Nacional, Santiago, 26-05-1993, 40,000. Referee: Escobar, Paraguay

UNIVERSIDAD CATOLICA 2 (Lunari 9, Almada 15p)
SÃO PAULO FC 0

Universidad - Wirth - Romero, Vazquez, Contreras (Cardozo) - Tupper (Reynoso), Parraguez, Lepe, Perez - Barrera, Lunari, Almada. Tr: Prieto

São Paulo - Zetti - Vitor (Cerezo), Valber, Gilmar, Marcos Adriano - Pintado, Dinho, Cafu - Palinha, Rai, Muller. Tr: Santana

Top scorer Juan Carlos Almada, Universidad Catolica 9

SUPER COPA

FIRST ROUND

São Paulo FC..........2-0 1-1 ....Independiente
Peñarol..........1-0 0-2..........**Grêmio**
Cruzeiro..........6-1 3-3 ....Colo Colo
Nacional Montevideo ....1-1 3-1 ....Racing Club
Santos ....0-0 0-1 ....**At. Nacional Medellin**
Estudiantes LP..........2-0 3-1 ....Boca Juniors
River Plate..........2-1 2-1 ....Argentinos Juniors
Olimpia ....1-0 1-3 ....**Flamengo**

QUARTER-FINALS

São Paulo FC..........2-2 1-0..........Grêmio
Cruzeiro ....1-2 3-2 2-4p ....**Nacional Montevideo**
At. Nacional Medellin..........1-0 1-0..........Estudiantes LP
River Plate..........2-1 0-1 5-6p ....**Flamengo**

SEMI-FINALS

São Paulo FC..........1-0 1-2 5-4p ....At. Nacional Medellin
Flamengo ....2-1 3-0 ....Nacional Montevideo

FINAL

1st leg. Maracana, Rio de Janeiro, 17-11-1993, 50,000. Referee: Rezende, Brazil

FLAMENGO 2 (Marquinhos 35 47)
SÃO PAULO FC 2 (Leonardo 16, Juninho 87)

Flamengo - Gilmar - Charles, Junior Baiano, Rogerio, Marcos Adriano - Fabinho, Marquinhos, Nelio, Marcelinho - Renato Gaucho (Pia), Casagrande (Gelson)

Saõ Paulo - Zetti - Cafu, Valber, Ronaldo, Andre - Doriva, Dinho, Cerezo (Valdeir), Leonardo - Muller, Palhinha (Juninho)

2nd leg. Morumbi, São Paulo, 24-11-1993, 70,000. Referee: Marsiglia, Brazil

SÃO PAULO FC 2 (Leonardo 61, Juninho 80)
FLAMENGO 2 Renato Gaucho 9, Marquinhos 62

São Paulo - Zetti - Cafu, Valber, Ronaldo, Andre - Doriva, Dinho, Cerezo (Juninho), Leonardo - Muller, Palhinha (Gilherme). Tr. Santana

Flamengo - Gilmar - Charles, Gelson, Rogerio, Marcos Adriano - Fabinho, Marquinhos, Nelio, Marcelinho - Renato Gaucho (Eder Lopes), Casagrande (Magno). Tr: Junior

São Paulo won 5-3 on pens

Top scorer Ronaldo, Cruzeiro..........8

COPA CONMEBOL

FIRST ROUND

Botafogo..........3-1 3-2 ....Bragantino
Deportivo Tachira..........0-1 0-1 ....**Caracas FC**
Emelec ....1-0 2-3 3-4p ....**Deportivo Sipesa**
Atlético Mineiro..........2-0 0-2 4-2p ....Fluminense
Danubio..........0-0 0-2..........**San Lorenzo**
Sportivo Luqueño ....1-1 2-1..........Deportivo Español
Vasco da Gama..........2-0 2-4 2-4p..........**Colo Colo**
Peñarol ....1-0 1-1 ....Huracan

QUARTER-FINALS

Caracas FC..........0-1 0-3 ....**Botafogo**
Deportivo Sipesa..........1-1 0-1 ....**Atlético Mineiro**
Sportivo Luqueño ....3-0 1-4 2-4p ....**San Lorenzo**
Peñarol..........2-0 0-2 4-2p..........Colo Colo

SEMI-FINALS

Atlético Mineiro ....3-1 0-3 ....**Botafogo**
San Lorenzo..........0-1 2-1 2-4p ....**Peñarol**

FINAL

1st leg. Centenario, Montevideo, 22-09-1993, 18,000. Referee: Escobar, Paraguay

PEÑAROL 1 (Otero 37)
BOTAFOGO 1 (Perivaldo 4)

Peñarol - Rabajda - Tais, Gutierrez, De Los Santos, Da Silva - Reherman, Perdomo (Consani), Baltierra, Bengoechea (Ferreyra) - Otero, Rodriguez

Botafogo - William - Eliomar, André, Rogerio, Clei - China, Fabiano, Perivaldo - Alessio (Marcos Paulo), Sinval, Eliel

2nd leg. Maracana, Rio de Janeiro, 29-09-1993, 65,000. Referee: Lamolina, Argentina

BOTAFOGO 2 (Eliel 50, Sinval 70)
PEÑAROL 2 (Bengoechea 33, Otero 89)

Botafogo - William - Clei (Eliomar), André, Claudio, Perivaldo, - Nelson, Suelio, Eliel - Marcelo, Sinval, Alessio (Marcos Paulo). Tr. Carlos Alberto Torres

Peñarol - Rabajda - Tais, Gutierrez, De Los Santos, Da Silva - Dorta, Perdomo (Ferreyra), Baltierra, Bengoechea (Reherman) - Otero, Rodriguez. Tr. Perez

Botafogo won 3-1 on penalties

Top scorer Sinval, Botafogo 8

RECOPA

Kobe, 3-04-1994

São Paulo FC 3 (Leonardo 12, Guilherme 73, Euller 87)
Botafogo 1 (Cavalo 68)

1994

COPA LIBERTADORES

FIRST ROUND

Group 1

	IM	OI	AJ	CP	Pl	W	D	L	F	A	Pts
Independiente Medellin	-	0-0	0-1	3-0	6	3	2	1	6	1	8
Olimpia	0-2	-	1-0	1-0	6	3	2	1	5	3	8
Atlético Junior	0-1	0-0	-	3-2	6	2	1	3	4	5	5
Cerro Porteño	0-0	1-3	1-0	-	6	1	1	4	4	10	3

Group 2

	VS	Cr	Pa	BJ	Pl	W	D	L	F	A	Pts
Velez Sarsfield	-	2-0	1-0	1-1	6	3	2	1	8	7	8
Cruzeiro	1-1	-	2-1	2-1	6	3	1	2	7	8	7
Palmeiras	4-1	2-0	-	6-1	6	3	0	3	14	7	6
Boca Juniors	1-2	1-2	2-1	-	6	1	1	4	7	14	3

Group 3

	Em	Un	Ba	Al	Pl	W	D	L	F	A	Pts
Emelec	-	2-0	0-1	3-0	6	3	1	2	9	5	7
Universitario	2-1	-	0-0	0-1	6	2	2	2	4	5	6
Barcelona	0-1	0-0	-	3-0	6	2	2	2	5	3	6
Alianza	2-2	1-2	2-1	-	6	2	1	3	6	11	5

Group 4

	CC	UE	De	Na	Pl	W	D	L	F	A	Pts
Colo Colo	-	3-1	2-0	4-2	6	4	1	1	11	6	9
Union Española	1-2	-	1-0	1-0	6	3	1	2	6	6	7
Defensor	0-0	1-1	-	1-0	6	1	3	2	3	5	5
Nacional Montevideo	2-0	0-1	1-1	-	6	1	1	4	5	8	3

Group 5

	Bo	TS	Mi	Ma	Pl	W	D	L	F	A	Pts
Bolivar	-	0-0	4-0	2-1	6	3	3	0	9	9	9
The Strongest	0-0	-	7-1	5-0	6	2	3	1	13	7	7
Minerven	1-1	5-0	-	2-1	6	2	1	3	10	17	5
Maritimo	0-2	1-1	4-1	-	6	1	1	4	7	13	3

SECOND ROUND

Defensor .... 1-1 0-0 3-4p .... **Velez Sarsfield**
Minerven .... 2-0 1-3 4-0p .... Emelec
Universitario .... 2-1 0-2 .... **Independiente Medellin**
Atlético Junior .... 1-1 2-2 4-3p .... Colo Colo
Barcelona .... 0-1 1-2 .... **Olimpia**
Bolivar .... 2-1 4-0 .... The Strongest
Union Española .... 1-0 0-0 .... Cruzeiro
Palmeiras .... 0-0 1-2 .... **São Paulo FC**

QUARTER-FINALS

Minerven .... 0-0 2-0 .... **Velez Sarsfield**
Independiente Medellin .... 0-2 0-0 .... **Atlético Junior**
Olimpia .... 1-0 2-0 .... Bolivar
Union Española .... 1-1 3-4 .... **São Paulo FC**

SEMI-FINALS

Atlético Junior .... 2-1 1-2 4-5p .... **Velez Sarsfield**
São Paulo FC .... 2-1 0-1 4-3p .... Olimpia

FINAL

1st leg. Jose Amalfitani, Buenos Aires, 24-08-1994, 50,000. Referee: Torres, Colombia

VELEZ SARSFIELD 1 (Asad 35)
SÃO PAULO FC 0

Velez - Chilavert - Zandona, Trotta, Sotomayor, Cardozo - Basualdo, Gomez, Bassedas, Pompei - Asad (Husain), Flores (Fernandez)

São Paulo - Zetti - Vitor, Junior Baiano, Valber, Gilmar, André - Axel, Cafú, Palinha (Juninho) - Muller, Euller

2nd leg. Morumbi, São Paulo, 31-08-1994, 92,000. Referee: Filippi, Uruguay

SÃO PAULO FC 1 (Muller 32p)
VELEZ SARSFIELD 0

São Paulo - Zetti - Vitor, Junior Baiano, Gilmar, André - Valber, Axel, Cafú, Palinha (Juninho) - Euller, Muller. Tr: Santana

Velez - Chilavert - Almandoz, Trotta, Pellegrino, Cardozo - Zandona, Gomez, Basualdo, Bassedas, (Pompei) - Asad, Flores (Husain). Tr: Bianchi

Velez won 5-3 on pens

Top scorer Stalin Rivas, Minerven 7

SUPER COPA

FIRST ROUND

Santos .... 1-0 0-4 .... **Independiente**
Grêmio .... 1-1 2-1 .... Racing Club
Flamengo .... 0-0 0-2 .... **Estudiantes LP**
Olimpia .... 2-0 0-4 .... **Cruzeiro**
At. Nacional Medellin .... 0-2 1-1 .... **São Paulo FC**
Colo Colo .... 4-1 1-1 .... Argentinos Juniors
River Plate .... 2-2 1-0 .... Nacional Montevideo
Peñarol .... 1-0 1-4 .... **Boca Juniors**

QUARTER-FINALS

Grêmio .... 1-1 0-2 .... **Independiente**
Estudiantes LP .... 1-0 0-3 .... **Cruzeiro**
Colo Colo .... 2-1 1-4 .... **São Paulo FC**
River Plate .... 0-0 1-1 4-5p .... **Boca Juniors**

SEMI-FINALS

Cruzeiro .... 1-0 .... **Independiente**
Boca Juniors .... 2-0 .... São Paulo FC

FINAL

1st leg. Bombonera, Buenos Aires, 2-11-1994, 50,000. Referee: Ruscio, Argentina

BOCA JUNIORS 1 (Martinez 25)
INDEPENDIENTE 1 (Rambert 72)

Boca - Navarro Montoya - Vivas, Gamboa, Fabbri, MacAllister - Acuna, Mancuso, Marcico, Da Silva (Trellez) - Martinez (Carrizo), Carranza

Independiente - Islas - Craviotto, Arzeno, Serrizuela, Rios - Perez.H, Cagna, Garnero, Lopez.G (Gareca) - Usuriaga (Parodi), Rambert

2nd leg. Cordero, Buenos Aires, 9-11-1994, 60,000. Referee: Lamolina, Argentina

INDEPENDIENTE 1 (Rambert 55)
BOCA JUNIORS 0

Independiente - Islas - Craviotto (Gordillo), Arzeno, Serrizuela, Rios - Perez.H, Cagna, Garnero, Lopez.G - Usuriaga (Cascini), Rambert. Tr: Brindisi

Boca - Navarro Montoya - Vivas, Gamboa, Fabbri, MacAllister - Acuna, Carrizo (Pico), Marcico, Carranza (Trellez) - Da Silva, Martinez. Tr: Menotti

Top scorer Sebastian Rambert, Independiente 5

COPA CONMEBOL

FIRST ROUND

Grêmio 0-0 0-5 5-6p **São Paulo FC**
Sporting Cristal 2-1 1-0 Nacional Quito
Minerven 1-1 0-0 5-4p Botafogo
Corinthians 3-2 3-2 Vitória
Universidad de Chile 4-1 5-0 Oriente Petrolero
Lanus 1-1 2-2 2-4p **San Lorenzo**
Huracan 1-4 2-1 **Cerro Cora**
Peñarol 2-0 0-1 Danubio

QUARTER-FINALS

São Paulo FC 3-1 0-0 Sporting Cristal
Minerven 2-5 0-6 **Corinthians**
San Lorenzo 1-0 1-3 **Universidad de Chile**
Cerro Cora 3-1 1-6 **Peñarol**

SEMI-FINALS

Corinthians 3-4 3-2 4-5p **São Paulo FC**
Peñarol 2-0 1-1 Universidad de Chile

FINAL

1st leg. Morumbi, São Paulo, 14-12-1994, 30,000. Referee: Guerrero, Chile

SÃO PAULO FC 6 (Caio 35 80, Caté 58 83 89, Toninho 70)
PEÑAROL 1 (Aguilera 4)

São Paulo - Rogerio - Pavao, Nelson, Bordon, Ronaldo Luiz - Mona, Pereira, Caté, Denilson - Caio, Toninho

Peñarol - Ferro - Tais, Gutierrez, Aguirregaray, Lima - Dorta, Baltierra, De Los Santos, Bengoechea - Dario Silva, Aguilera

2nd leg. Centenario, Montevideo, 21-12-1994, 10,000. Referee: Castrilli, Argentina

PEÑAROL 3 (Rodriguez 57 73, Dario Silva 72)
SÃO PAULO FC 0

Peñarol - Ferro - Tais, De Los Santos, Aguirregaray, Romero - Pacheco, Dorta, Bengoechea (Martinez) Rodriguez - Dario Silva, Otero (Aguilera). Tr: Perez

São Paulo - Rogerio - Vitor, Nelson, Bordon, Correia - Ronaldo Luiz, Marcelo Moreira, Emerson - Caio, Girondo (Rodriguez), Denilson (Machado). Tr: Ramatho

Top scorers Martin Rodriguez, Peñarol 5
Juninho, São Paulo FC 5

RECOPA

National Stadium, Tokyo, 9-04-1995, 25,000

INDEPENDIENTE 1 (Serrizuela 69)
VELEZ SARSFIELD 0

COPA LIBERTADORES MEDALS TABLE

	Team	Country	G	S	B
1	Independiente	ARG	7	-	5
2	Peñarol	URU	5	4	10
3	Nacional Montevideo	URU	3	3	6
4	Estudiantes La Plata	ARG	3	1	1
5	Olimpia	PAR	2	3	5
6	Boca Juniors	ARG	2	2	3
7	São Paulo FC	BRA	2	2	1
8	Santos FC	BRA	2	-	2
9	River Plate	ARG	1	2	6
10	Colo Colo	CHI	1	1	2
11	Cruzeiro	BRA	1	1	2
12	Grêmio	BRA	1	1	-
13	Flamengo	BRA	1	-	2
	At. Nacional Medellín	COL	1	-	2
15	Racing Club Avellaneda	ARG	1	-	1
	Argentinos Juniors	ARG	1	-	1
	Vélez Sarsfield	ARG	1	-	1
18	America Cali	COL	-	3	5
19	Cobreloa	CHI	-	2	1
	SE Palmeiras	BRA	-	2	1
21	Newell's Old Boys	ARG	-	2	-
22	Barcelona	ECU	-	1	5
23	Universidad Catolica	CHI	-	1	4
24	Universitario	PER	-	1	3
25	SC Internacional Porto Alegre	BRA	-	1	2
	Deportivo Cali	COL	-	1	2
27	Union Española	CHI	-	1	1
28	Cerro Porteño	PAR	-	-	3
	San Lorenzo de Almagro	ARG	-	-	3
	Millonarios	COL	-	-	3
31	Botafogo	BRA	-	-	2
	Alianza	PER	-	-	2
	LDU Quito	ECU	-	-	2
34	Atlético Junior Barranquilla	COL	-	-	1
	Atlético Mineiro	BRA	-	-	1
	Blooming	BOL	-	-	1
	Bolivar	BOL	-	-	1
	Danubio	URU	-	-	1
	Defensor Lima	PER	-	-	1
	Guarani Asuncion	PAR	-	-	1
	Guarani Campinas	BRA	-	-	1
	Huracán	ARG	-	-	1
	Jorge Wilsterman	BOL	-	-	1
	Libertad	PAR	-	-	1
	Nacional Quito	ECU	-	-	1
	O'Higgins	CHI	-	-	1
	Palestino	CHI	-	-	1
	Portuguesa	VEN	-	-	1
	Rosario Central	ARG	-	-	1
	Atlético San Cristobal	VEN	-	-	1
	Independiente Santa Fé	COL	-	-	1
	Deportes Tolima	COL	-	-	1
	ULA Merida	VEN	-	-	1
	Universidad de Chile	CHI	-	-	1

COPA LIBERTADORES BY COUNTRY

	Country	G	S	B	Finals	S-Finals
1	Argentina	16	7	23	23	46
2	Uruguay	8	7	17	15	32
3	Brazil	7	7	14	14	28
4	Paraguay	2	3	10	5	15
5	Chile	1	5	11	6	17
6	Colombia	1	4	15	5	20
7	Ecuador	-	1	8	1	9
8	Peru	-	1	6	1	7
9	Bolivia	-	-	3	-	3
	Venezuela	-	-	3	-	3

To the end of the 1994 competition

SUPERCOPA MEDALS TABLE

	Team	Country	G	S	B
1	Cruzeiro	BRA	2	1	1
2	Boca Juniors	ARG	1	1	-
	Independiente	ARG	1	1	-
	Racing Club	ARG	1	1	-
5	Olimpia	PAR	1	-	2
6	São Paulo FC	BRA	1	-	1
7	Nacional Montevideo	URU	-	1	2

	Team	Country	G	S	B
8	Flamengo	BRA	-	1	1
	River Plate	ARG	-	1	1
10	Peñarol	URU	-	-	2
11	Argentinos Juniors	ARG	-	-	1
	Estudiantes LP	ARG	-	-	1
	Grêmio	BRA	-	-	1
	At. Nacional Medellin	COL	-	-	1

SUPERCOPA BY COUNTRY

	Country	G	S	B	Finals	S-Finals
1	Argentina	3	4	3	7	10
2	Brazil	3	2	4	5	9
3	Paraguay	1	-	2	1	3
4	Uruguay	-	1	4	1	5
5	Colombia	-	-	1	-	1

CONMEBOL CUP MEDALS TABLE

	Team	Country	G	S	B
1	Atlético Mineiro	BRA	1	-	1
2	Botafogo	BRA	1	-	-
	São Paulo FC	BRA	1	-	-
4	Peñarol	URU	-	2	-
5	Olimpia	PAR	-	1	-
	Corinthians	BRA	-	-	1
5	Gimnasia y Esgrima	ARG	-	-	1
	Nacional Quito	ECU	-	-	1
	San Lorenzo	ARG	-	-	1
	Universidad de Chile	CHI	-	-	1

CONMEBOL CUP BY COUNTRY

	Country	G	S	B	Finals	S-Finals
1	Brazil	3	-	2	3	5
2	Uruguay	-	2	-	2	3
3	Paraguay	-	1	-	1	1
4	Argentina	-	-	2	-	2
5	Chile	-	-	1	-	1
	Ecuador	-	-	1	-	1

To the end of the 1994 tournaments

ARGENTINA

Only the British have been playing the game longer, and few have ever played it better, than the Argentines. A championship was played there in 1891, a full five years before the first in mainland Europe, whilst their record of two World Cup victories is bettered only by Brazil, Germany and Italy. Had the Italians not continually swiped their best players - to play not only for their clubs but also for the national side until the rules were changed to forbid it - this figure would almost certainly be higher. After their initial entry in 1930 it was not until 1958 that Argentina made a serious bid to take part in the World Cup, and that collapsed around them as one of the best sides they had managed to put together was broken up by the unscrupulous Italian agents.

Argentina has produced more players of natural talent than almost any other country, as well as two of the greatest players ever in Alfredo di Stéfano and Diego Maradona. Both symbolise the excitement and the trauma Argentine football followers have had to endure. Di Stéfano left during the players' strike of 1948, never returned and ended up playing for Spain. Maradona left Argentina at the age of 21 having played four seasons with Argentinos Juniors and one with Boca, but that was all the Argentine public saw of him until he returned, past his prime, under the cloud of a drugs scandal. Both on their day were supreme footballers. Di Stéfano guided Real Madrid to countless honours in the 1950s, whilst Maradona not only guided Argentina to a World Cup victory in 1986 but also single-handedly transformed Napoli into one of the strongest teams in Europe.

The tragedy for Argentina is that these two were not the only ones to leave, and as a result the league, which by rights should be among the very best, often resembles the leftovers that the European clubs have rejected. Unfortunately, persistent economic pressures help reinforce this trend as players seek the higher wages on offer to them in Europe.

Football was brought to Argentina by the British, with whom the Argentines had very close links, and in May 1865 a team called Buenos Aires Football Club was founded. For many years the game was played exclusively by British residents in the capital, but by the end of the century it had been taken up by the locals. In 1887 Quilmes FC was formed by British railway workers, and they, along with Gimansia y Esgrima, formed five months previously in La Plata, 30 miles to the south of Buenos Aires, remain the two oldest clubs in the country. Not until after the turn of the century, however, did Gimnasia form a football section, a policy that had led disgruntled members to form Estudiantes de La Plata in 1905.

Many of the names of the clubs reflect the British involvement in the game. In 1889 Rosario Central were formed, whilst their great rivals from the same city are called Newell's Old Boys. In 1901 came the formation of River Plate, in 1903 Racing Club, in 1905 Boca Juniors and Independiente, and in 1908 Huracán; all had their origins in one or other of the migrant communities for which Argentina was famous. Boca Juniors, though founded by an Irishman, had their roots in the Italian community, Racing were named after the Paris-based club of the same name and wore the same light blue colours, whilst River Plate were formed by Englishmen. Of the current 'big five', only Independiente were formed by Argentines, all of whom worked for a store called City of London. The store already had a side but the Argentines wanted to play for a separate team, hence the name.

In 1891 Alexander Hutton, the director of the English High School, formed the Argentine Association Football League, and two years later this league was reformed as the Argentine Football Association. The winners of the first league in 1891, St Andrews, have since faded into the mists of time, as have Lomas Athletic and Alumni, the major powers until after the turn of the century. Alumni, made up of old boys from the English High School, were instrumental in popularising the game, but by the time of Racing's first championship in 1913, only a few British players remained and most teams were comprised of Argentinians. The Argentine championship was not a truly national competition. Only clubs from Buenos Aires, La Plata, Rosario and Santa Fe were ever invited to take part. The rest of the country had to make do with their own leagues, the first of which, the Liga Santiaguena de Futbol, was formed in 1906. Buenos Aires is, however, a large city, made up of 22 municipalities within which there are 50 *barrios*, or neighbourhoods. The identification of teams with either a municipality or *barrio* has ensured the survival of so many clubs in such a concentrated area, and the development of fierce rivalry between teams.

Not only was there a vibrant domestic scene in Argentine football, but along with Uruguay, Argentina were also at the forefront of the international game in South America. In 1901 a representative side took on a Uruguayan XI and a long rivalry was started that has seen more games than any other 'derby' encounter throughout the world. The match on 16 May was the first international played anywhere outside Great Britain. In 1905 these games were given a competitive edge when a cup was donated by Sir Thomas Lipton, the English tea baron. In these early years of international competition, the two countries played each other many times every year, and there is still confusion about which games should count as official internationals. Often two different 'national' teams took to the field on the same day. In 1910, Argentina organised a tournament between themselves, Uruguay and Chile, and although not strictly a South American Championship it was regarded as such at the time. Not until six years later, in celebration of Argentina's centenary, did the first recognised championship take place, and there began another rivalry with the Uruguayans to add to that of the Lipton and Newton Cups. Brazil very rarely threatened the Argentine-Uruguayan hegemony, except when the tournament was played on their home territory.

The game remained an amateur sport until the adoption of professionalism in 1931, but the years leading up to this event were often fraught with trouble as various different governing bodies were set up at the merest hint of an argument. In this pre-professional era, the most successful clubs were Racing Club and Huracán, the former a bastion of the amateur ideals. Neither adapted well to the new situation after 1931, and this was a factor that helped forge the success of both River Plate and Boca Juniors, the two most famous Argentine clubs. After 1931 the new professional league was the lifeblood of Argentine football until the 1960s when the Copa Libertadores caught the imagination. During this period the programme of the international side was very light, especially during the 1930s and 1950s when hardly any matches were played at all, further increasing the importance of the league.

The Boca Juniors side of the early 1930s and the River Plate side of the 1940s are counted among the greatest teams ever to have played in Argentina. Boca's side contained players such as Juan Evaristo, Cherro, Francisco Varallo, and the Brazilian Domingos da Guia, but perhaps the River Plate side was even better. At one time or another during their great decade, famous players like Bernabe Ferreyra, Carlos Peucelle, Angel Labruna, Jose Moreno and Adolfo Pedernera made River Plate the most famous club on the South American continent. The forward line containing Muñoz, Moreno, Pedernera and Loustau was referred to as *la máquina* - the machine - whilst the forward line of the 1947 championship winning side consisting of Reyes, Moreno, Di Stéfano, Labruna and Loustau was regarded as one of the best ever.

Up until the late 1950s Argentina remained an isolationist within the world game. Uruguay, Brazil and Paraguay were their only regular opponents outside the South American Championship which, along with Uruguay, they dominated from the start. Had they entered more than just the 1928 Olympic Games and the 1930 World Cup, Argentina might well have been world champions many years before they finally were in 1978. The national side's first excursion to Europe was for the 1928 Amsterdam Olympic Games. Domingo Tarasconi was in tremendous form and scored an amazing 12 goals in three games leading up to the final. It was Argentina's misfortune to meet Uruguay there, two sides who knew each other inside out. Tarasconi could not reproduce his form in the final and the Argentines lost after a replay. Two years later, Uruguay completed a double over them by winning the first World Cup final. This time Stabile was scoring the goals for Argentina, but despite taking a 2-1 half-time lead in Montevideo they succumbed to three second-half goals and went home runners-up yet again. A team did travel to the 1934 World Cup in Italy, but for fear of losing more players like Monti and Orsi to the Italian game, a third-rate side was sent that did not survive the first round. Not until the late 1950s did the national side resurface with any great enthusiasm.

The 1957 South American Championship saw the birth of a very good side containing another of Argentina's famous forward lines. Corbatta, Maschio, Angelillo, Sivori and Cruz caused a sensation in Lima, so much so that as soon as the tournament finished, Bologna signed Maschio, Juventus signed Sivori and Internazionale signed Angelillo. All three never played for Argentina again, appearing instead briefly for Italy. With a severely depleted side, the Argentines made the journey to Sweden for the 1958 World Cup and were promptly eliminated in the first round. Argentine football has now come to terms with the constant flow of players moving abroad and has used the extra experience gained by these players to its advantage. The rule introduced by FIFA forbidding the practice of playing for more than one country was crucial in this respect.

Argentina is lucky, though, in that there seems to be a

huge reservoir of very talented players in the country, and often the national side has not needed to rely on the foreign-based players. This was especially true in 1978 when at last Argentina won the World Cup. Of the winning side, only Mario Kempes played his football abroad. Argentina had been awarded the tournament after many failed attempts, but the deteriorating political situation nearly saw them lose it to the Low Countries. In the event, the 1978 tournament was notable for the superb atmosphere in which it was played, especially when Argentina took to the field and the stadium disappeared under a sea of sky blue and white tickertape. After winning their first two games, Argentina then lost to Italy which meant they had to overcome Brazil in their second round group. They made it through to the final only in somewhat controversial fashion.

When Brazil's victory over Poland left the Argentines needing to beat Peru 4-0, they scored six. The Brazilians cried foul, but this was an Argentine side desperate to please the home crowd and wipe out all the disappointments of the past. The front line of Kempes and Luque was in sparkling form, as were Ardiles and Bertoni in midfield. In defence they could rely on the towering presence of captain Daniel Passarella, later to become the national team coach. It was Passarella who lifted the trophy after the 3-1 victory against Holland in the final, but it was the performance of Kempes, who scored two excellent goals, which made it possible. There was much sympathy for Holland, losers in two consecutive finals, but Argentina were worthy winners, and it was just reward for all the fine footballers that they had produced in the past who had never had the opportunity to shine on the world stage.

Since 1978, along with Germany, Argentina have been the most potent force in international football. They have reached three of the last five World Cup finals, and in 1986 won the title for the second time. Central to the side was Diego Maradona, who along with Di Stéfano, Pelé and Cruyff ranks among the very best footballers the world has ever produced. Many rate him as the best ever. Home advantage may have been crucial to their victory in 1978, but in 1986, in what was a very open field, the Argentines were superb. Of the seven games played they won six, only the Italians holding them to a draw, and along the way they beat Uruguay, England, Belgium and West Germany. The final in the Azteca against the Germans was a classic encounter in which the winning goal from Jorge Burruchaga came just minutes from the end.

The side that won in Mexico contained some excellent players like Burruchaga, Valdano, Ruggeri and Pumpido, but Maradona was the undoubted star and it was to him that they looked for inspiration in their time of need. His second goal against England in the quarter-final is one of the best ever witnessed in the World Cup, though his first, the notorious 'Hand of God', will be remembered for different reasons. With Maradona Argentina appeared unstoppable, and although West Germany caused them a few heart-stopping moments towards the end of the final, it was no surprise that they finally won.

Four years later saw a repeat of 1986 when the Germans again faced Maradona and his Argentine side in the final, though this time Argentina lost in what is generally regarded as the worst final in the history of the tournament. Despite their reaching the final, Italia '90 was not a happy experience for Argentina. Their tactics were roundly condemned and they used penalty-kicks to excellent effect to reach a final that their form did not merit. They were up against the odds, however. Pumpido was carried off in the second game of the tournament with a broken leg, whilst Maradona was at half-speed due to injury.

Club football has remained remarkably buoyant despite the exodus of players, and in the Copa Libertadores Argentine clubs have a record second to none. Although they were slow to take to the competition, between 1964 and 1978 only three clubs from elsewhere could prise the trophy from Argentine hands. Two clubs have been especially pre-eminent, and surprisingly they were not Boca and River Plate but Independiente and Estudiantes de La Plata, neither of whom were particularly strong in the league at the time of their successes.

Unfortunately, Estudiantes were responsible for showing the world the dark side of Argentine football epitomised by their poor sportsmanship in the 1966 World Cup. It got to the stage where police were arresting players after the match for poor behaviour during it, notably after the World Club Championship match between Estudiantes and Milan in 1969 when three players from Estudiantes were imprisoned. Independiente won the Copa Libertadores four times in a row in the 1970s with a side including Ricardo Bochini, Daniel Bertoni and Ruben Galvan, the last two going on to star in Argentina's 1978 World Cup victory, and they remain the top club in the history of the competition with their record seven wins.

There was a major reorganisation of the league in 1967. Up until then the championship, though including all the major clubs, was not open to every team. It was renamed the Metropolitan League and a national championship, open to all of the clubs around the country, was started to run alongside it. Since the start of the 1970s, the stranglehold of the big Buenos Aires clubs has gradually been broken down as the two Rosario clubs and some of the less well-known clubs from the capital have begun to make their presence felt. Further reorganisation in 1985 saw, for the first time, a single national first division, as the national championship in its previous form was scrapped. There now exists a second division beneath which there are 32 regional leagues and three further leagues for clubs from Buenos Aires.

The Argentine league is unique in world football in that each year it produces two champions. For the 1992 season the league was broken up into two halves, the Apertura and the Clausura. Initially there was a play-off between the two winners, but after one season this was stopped. It is an experiment that has had mixed results; certainly crowd interest is sustained, but there is the feeling that no sooner has one season started than it finishes, demeaning the success of the sides who win it.

Argentina will always be at the centre of world football. In 1994 Velez Sarsfield, a relatively unsuccessful side in the Argentine league, beat AC Milan to become world club champions, but there was controversy for the national side at the World Cup finals in the USA. Having suffered four dreadful years in which he had flitted from club to club and served a fifteen-month ban for cocaine abuse, Maradona returned to the international stage looking like a new man. In their opening game against Greece, he and Argentina looked in stunning form and seemed to be on course for a third World Cup. Then, however, Maradona failed a drugs test and was banned once more. It was a sad end to an outstanding career.

Perhaps Argentina do not need him. In 1991 they were crowned South American champions for the first time since the 1950s, they retained the title in 1993 and were quarter-finalists in 1995. There is a still a constant flow of talented players emerging, such as Gabriel Batistuta who has equalled, and looks set to beat, Maradona's record of goals for the national team.

THE ORDER OF MERIT

		Total			League			Nat Champ			Sth Am		
	Team	G	S	B	G	S	B	G	S	B	G	S	B
1	River Plate	26	29	17	22	19	10	3	7	-	1	3	7
2	Boca Juniors	25	17	16	19	14	13	3	-	-	3	3	3
3	Independiente	23	15	14	12	13	9	3	1	-	8	1	5
4	Racing Club Avellaneda	17	7	10	15	6	8	-	-	1	2	1	1
5	San Lorenzo de Almagro	11	12	18	9	11	11	2	1	3	-	-	4
6	Alumni	9	2	-	9	2	-	-	-	-	-	-	-
7	Estudiantes La Plata	7	7	9	3	4	7	1	2	-	3	1	2
8	Huracán	5	5	8	5	5	7	-	-	-	-	-	1
9	Lomas Athletic	5	2	3	5	2	3	-	-	-	-	-	-
10	Newell's Old Boys	4	4	2	4	2	2	-	-	-	-	2	-
11	Rosario Central	4	3	2	1	1	1	3	2	-	-	-	1
12	Velez Sarsfield	3	7	7	1	6	4	1	1	2	1	-	1
13	Belgrano Athletic	3	3	3	3	3	3	-	-	-	-	-	-
14	Argentinos Juniors	3	2	3	1	2	1	1	-	-	1	-	2
15	Ferro Carril Oeste	2	3	1	-	2	1	2	1	-	-	-	-
16	AC Porteño	2	2	-	2	2	-	-	-	-	-	-	-
17	Quilmes	2	1	3	2	-	3	-	1	-	-	-	-
18	Estudiantil Porteño	2	-	-	2	-	-	-	-	-	-	-	-
19	Gimnasia y Esgrima LP	1	2	2	1	2	1	-	-	-	-	-	1
20	Chacarita Juniors	1	-	1	1	-	1	-	-	-	-	-	-
	Lomas Academic	1	-	1	1	-	1	-	-	-	-	-	-
	Sportivo Barracas	1	-	1	1	-	1	-	-	-	-	-	-
	Sportivo Dock Sud	1	-	1	1	-	1	-	-	-	-	-	-
24	English High School	1	-	-	1	-	-	-	-	-	-	-	-
	St. Andrew's	1	-	-	1	-	-	-	-	-	-	-	-

To the end of the 1995 season

Population: 31,963,000
Area, sq km: 2,780,092
% in urban areas: 85%
Capital city: Buenos Aires

Asociación del Fútbol Argentino
Viamonte #1366-76
1053 Buenos Aires
Argentina
Tel: + 54 1 404276
Fax: + 54 1 9533469

Year of formation	1893
Affiliation to FIFA	1912
Affiliation to CSF	1916
Registered clubs	3035
Registered players	386200
Professional players	3320
Registered coaches	5125
Registered referees	360
National stadium	Antonio Liberti 'Monumental' de Nunez 76 000
National colours	Light blue and white Stripes/Black/White
Reserve colours	Blue/Black/White
Season	August - December for Apertura February - May for Clausura

THE RECORD

WORLD CUP

1930	QT Automatic - Final Tournament/Runners-up
1934	QT W-O in group 3 - Final Tournament/1st round
1938-54	Did not enter
1958	QT 1st/3 in group 2 - Final Tournament/1st round
1962	QT 1st/2 in group 1 - Final Tournament/1st round
1966	QT 1st/3 in group 3 - Final Tournament/Quarter-finalists
1970	QT 3rd/3 in group 1
1974	QT 1st/3 in group 2 - Final Tournament/2nd round
1978	QT Automatic Final Tournament/Winners
1982	QT Automatic Final Tournament/2nd round
1986	QT 1st/4 in group 1 - Final Tournament/Winners
1990	QT Automatic Final Tournament/Finalists
1994	QT 2nd/4 in group 1 - Final Tournament/2nd round

SOUTH AMERICAN CHAMPIONSHIP

1910	1/3 - Winners
1916	2/4
1917	2/4
1919	3/4
1920	2/4
1921	1/4 - Winners
1922	4/5
1923	2/4
1924	2/4
1925	1/3 - Winners
1926	2/5
1927	1/4 - Winners
1929	1/4 - Winners
1935	2/4
1937	1/6 - Winners
1939	-
1941	1/5 - Winners
1942	2/7
1945	1/7 - Winners
1946	1/6 - Winners
1947	1/8 - Winners
1949	-
1953	-
1955	1/6 - Winners
1956	3/6
1957	1/7 - Winners
1959	1/7 - Winners
1959	2/5
1963	3/7
1967	2/6
1975	5/10 - 1st round
1979	8/10 - 1st round
1983	6/10 - 1st round
1987	4/10 - Semi-finalists
1989	3/10 - 2nd round
1991	1/10 - Winners
1993	1/12 - Winners
1995	5/12 - Quarter-finalists

SOUTH AMERICAN CLUB TOURNAMENTS

Copa Libertadores

Winners - Independiente 1964, 1965, 1972, 1973, 1974, 1975, 1984 Racing Club 1967, Estudiantes LP 1968, 1969, 1970, Boca Juniors 1977, 1978, Argentinos Juniors 1985, River Plate 1986, Velez Sarsfield 1994

Finalists - Boca Juniors 1963 1979, River Plate 1966 1976, Estudiantes LP 1971, Newell's Old Boys 1988 1992

Super Copa

Winners - Racing Club 1988, Boca Juniors 1989, Independiente 1994

Finalists - River Plate 1991, Racing Club 1992, Boca Juniors 1994

CONMEBOL Cup

Semi-finalists - Gimnasia y Esgrima 1992

CLUB DIRECTORY

BUENOS AIRES (Population - 10,750,000)

Club Almirante Brown (1922)
Estadio San Petesburgo 17,000 – Yellow & black stripes/Black

Asociacion Atlética Argentinos Juniors (1904)
Estadio Martin de Gainza 24,000 – Red, white trim

Club Deportivo Armenio (1962)
Estadio Vicente Lopez 15,000 – Green/Black

Club Atlético Atlanta (1904)
Estadio Humboldt 35,000 – Blue & yellow stripes/Blue

Club Atlético Banfield (1896)
Pena y Arenales 18,000 – Green & white stripes/green

Club Atlético Boca Juniors (1905)
La Bombonera 58,000 – Blue, yellow hoop/Blue

Club Atlético Chacarita Juniors (1906)
Estadio San Lartin 25,000 – Red, black & thin white stripes/Black

Club Deportivo Espanol (1956)
Estadio Espana 18,000 – Red/Blue, white trim

Club Ferrocarril Oeste (1904)
Estadio Martin de Gainza 24,000 – Green/White

Club Atlético Huracán (1908)
Estadio Tomas Aldolfo Duco 48,000 – White, red trim

Club Atlético Independiente (1905)
Cordero 68,000 – Red/Blue, white trim

Club Deportivo Italiano (1955)
Estadio Humbolt 35,000 – Blue, white trim

Club Atlético Lanús (1916)
Estadio General Arias 15,000 – Maroon/Maroon

Club Atlético Platense (1905)
Estadio Vicente Lopez 15,000 – White, black hoop/White

Quilmes Atlético Club (1887)
Estadio Sarmiento 20,000 – White/Blue

Racing Club (1903)
Mozart y Cuyo 70,000 – Sky blue & white stripes/Black

Club Atlético River Plate (1901)
Estadio Antonio Liberti 'Monumental' de Nunez 76,000 – White, red sash/Black

Club Atlético San Lorenzo de Almagro (1908)
Estadio San Lorenzo – Red & blue stripes/Blue

Club Atlético Temperley (1912)
Estadio Temperley 15,000 – Sky blue/Sky blue

Club Atlético Tigre (1902)
Estadio Victoria 25,000 – Red/Blue

Club Atlético Velez Sarsfield (1910)
Estadio José Amalfitani 49,000 – White, blue 'V'/Blue

CORDOBA (Pop. - 1,070,000)

Club Atlético Belgrano (1925)
Estadio Belgrano 20,000 – Sky Blue/White

Instituto Atlético Central (1918)
Estadio Instituto 21,000 – Red & white stripes/Black

Club Atlético Racing (1924)
Barrio Italia 20,000 – Sky blue & white stripes/Black

Club Atlético Talleres (1913)
Chateau Carreras 46,000 – Blue & white stripes/Blue

ROSARIO (Pop. - 1,045,000)

Club Atlético Newell's Old Boys (1903)
Parque Independencia 31,000 – Red & black halves/Black

Club Atlético Rosario Central (1889)
Estadio Cordoviola 41,000 – Blue & yellow stripes/Blue

MENDOZA (Pop. - 650,000)

Club Deportivo Maipu (1927)
Estadio San Martin 'Malvinas Argentinas' 50,000 – Red, white sash/Black

LA PLATA (Pop. - 560,000)

Club Estudiantes La Plata (1905)
Del Bosque 25,000 – Red & white stripes/Black

Gimnasia y Esgrima La Plata (1887)
Del Bosque 25,000 – White, blue hoop/Blue

SAN MIGUEL DE TUCUMAN (Pop. - 525,000)

Atlético Tucumán (1902)
La Ciudadela 20,000 – Sky blue & white stripes/Blue

San Martin Tucumán (1909)
La Ciudadela 20,000 – Red & white stripes/White

SANTA FE (Pop. - 292,000)

Club Atlético Colon Santa Fe (1905)
Estadio Centenario de los Elefantes 35,000 – Red & black halves/Black

Club Atlético Union Santa Fe (1907)
Lopez y Planes 22,000 – Red & white stripes/Black

SALTA (Pop. - 260,000)

Club Gimnasia y Tiro (1902)
Estadio Salta – Sky blue & white stripes/White

CORRIENTES (Pop. - 179,000)

Club Deportivo Mandiyu (1952)
Estadio Corrientes 15,000 – White, green trim

ARGENTINE AMATEUR LEAGUE CHAMPIONSHIP

1891	Saint Andrew's 13 Old Caledonians 13 Rosario Railway 7
1892	-
1893	Lomas Athletic 15 Flores AC 10 Quilmes Rowers 10
1894	Lomas Athletic 18 Rosario AC 14 Flores AC 12
1895	Lomas Athletic 12 Flores AC 8 Quilmes Rowers 4
1896	Lomas Academy 12 Flores AC 10 Lomas Athletic 9
1897	Lomas Athletic 20 Lanús AC 20 Belgrano 'A' 19
1898	Lomas Athletic 20 Lobos AC 20 Belgrano Athletic 17
1899	Belgrano Athletic 11 Lobos AC 9 Lomas Athletic 3
1900	English High School 11 Lomas Athletic 5 Belgrano Athletic 4
1901	Alumni 12 Belgrano Athletic 6 Quilmes 4
1902	Alumni 15 Barracas AC 10 Quilmes 7
1903	Alumni 18 Belgrano Atlhetic 15 Barracas AC 11
1904	Belgrano Athletic 19 Alumni 13 Lomas Athletic 11
1905	Alumni 21 Belgrano Athletic 18 Estudiantes Buenos Aires 17
1906	Alumni 4-0 Lomas Athletic
1907	Alumni 37 Estudiantes Buenos Aires 31 San Isidro 25
1908	Belgrano Athletic 31 Alumni 27 Argentino Quilmes 25
1909	Alumni 32 River Plate 24 Quilmes 20
1910	Alumni 25 CA Porteño 21 Belgrano Athletic 19 Estudiantes Buenos Aires 19

1911 Alumni 23 CA Porteño 23 San Isidro 18
1912 Quilmes 15 San Isidro 11 Racing Club 10
1912 CA Porteño 20 Independiente 20 Estudiantes LP 19
1913 Racing Club 2-0 San Isidro
1913 Estudiantes LP 31 Gimnasia y Esgrima BA 26 Argentino Quilmes 27
1914 Racing Club 23 Estudiantes Buenos Aires 21 Banfield 15 Boca Juniors 15
1914 CA Porteño 24 Estudiantes LP 21 Independiente 19
1915 Racing Club 46 San Isidro 46 River Plate 38
1916 Racing Club 34 Platense 30 River Plate 29
1917 Racing Club 35 River Plate 30 Huracán 28 Boca Juniors 28
1918 Racing Club 36 River Plate 35 Boca Juniors 24 San Isidro 24
1919 Boca Juniors 14 Estudiantes LP 7 Huracán 4
1919 Racing Club 26 Velez Sarsfield 18 Atlanta 16
1920 Boca Juniors 43 Banfield 31 Huracán 31
1920 River Plate 56 Racing Club 54 San Lorenzo 46
1921 Huracán 31 Del Plata 29 Boca Juniors 25
1921 Racing Club 66 River Plate 54 Independiente 53
1922 Huracán 28 Sportivo Palermo 25 Boca Juniors 22
1922 Independiente 65 River Plate 61 San Lorenzo 60
1923 Boca Juniors 51 Huracán 51 Sportivo Barracas 38
1923 San Lorenzo 35 Independiente 32 River Plate 31
1924 Boca Juniors 37 Temperley 32 Old Boys 29 Sportivo Dock Sud 29
1924 San Lorenzo 39 Gimnasia LP 37 Independiente 36 Platense 36
1925 Huracán 38 Nueva Chicago 38 El Porvenir 32
1925 Racing Club 39 San Lorenzo 36 Sportivo Almagro 32 Platense 32
1926 Boca Juniors 32 Argentinos Juniors 28 Huracán 24
1926 Independiente 46 San Lorenzo 45 Platense 37
1927 San Lorenzo 57 Boca Juniors 56 Lanús 50
1928 Huracán 58 Boca Juniors 57 Estudiantes LP 53
1929 Gimnasia LP 2-1 Boca Juniors
1930 Boca Juniors 61 Estudiantes LP 56 River Plate 52
1931 Estudiantil Porteño 26 Almagro 26 Sportivo Buenos Aires 22
1932 Sportivo Barracas 47 Colegiales 42 Barracas Central 42
1933 Sportivo Dock Sud 29 Nueva Chicago 28 Banfield 27
1934 Estudiantil Porteño 36 Banfield 33 Defensores Belgrano 32

ARGENTINE PROFESSIONAL LEAGUE CHAMPIONSHIP

1931 Boca Juniors 50 San Lorenzo 45 Estudiantes LP 44
1932 River Plate 50 Independiente 50 Racing Club 49
1933 San Lorenzo 50 Boca Juniors 49 Racing Club 47
1934 Boca Juniors 55 Independiente 54 San Lorenzo 51
1935 Boca Juniors 58 Independiente 55 San Lorenzo 49
1936 River Plate 4-2 San Lorenzo
1937 River Plate 58 Independiente 52 Boca Juniors 45
1938 Independiente 53 River Plate 51 San Lorenzo 43
1939 Independiente 56 River Plate 50 Huracán 50
1940 Boca Juniors 55 Independiente 47 Huracán 42
1941 River Plate 44 San Lorenzo 40 Newell's Old Boys 38
1942 River Plate 46 San Lorenzo 40 Huracán 37
1943 Boca Juniors 45 River Plate 44 San Lorenzo 35
1944 Boca Juniors 46 River Plate 44 Estudiantes LP 39
1945 River Plate 46 Boca Juniors 42 Independiente 41
1946 San Lorenzo 46 Boca Juniors 42 River Plate 41
1947 River Plate 48 Boca Juniors 42 Independiente 41
1948 Independiente 41 River Plate 37 Estudiantes LP 36
1949 Racing Club 49 River Plate 43 Platense 43
1950 Racing Club 47 Boca Juniors 39 Independiente 39
1951 Racing Club 44 Banfield 44 River Plate 43
1952 River Plate 40 Racing Club 39 Independiente 35
1953 River Plate 43 Velez Sarsfield 39 Racing Club 39
1954 Boca Juniors 45 Independiente 41 River Plate 38
1955 River Plate 45 Racing Club 38 Boca Juniors 37
1956 River Plate 43 Lanús 41 Boca Juniors 40
1957 River Plate 46 San Lorenzo 38 Racing Club 36
1958 Racing Club 41 Boca Juniors 38 San Lorenzo 38
1959 San Lorenzo 45 Racing Club 38 Independiente 33
1960 Independiente 41 River Plate 39 Argentinos Juniors 39
1961 Racing Club 47 San Lorenzo 41 River Plate 38
1962 Boca Juniors 43 River Plate 41 Gimnasia LP 38
1963 Independiente 37 River Plate 35 Racing Club 30
1964 Boca Juniors 44 Independiente 38 River Plate 37
1965 Boca Juniors 50 River Plate 49 Velez Sarsfield 40
1966 Racing Club 61 River Plate 56 Boca Juniors 48
1967 Estudiantes LP 3-0 Racing Club
1968 San Lorenzo 2-1 Estudiantes LP
1969 Chacarita Juniors 4-1 River Plate
1970 Independiente 27 River Plate 27 San lorenzo 25
1971 Independiente 50 Velez Sarsfield 49 Chacarita Juniors 46
1972 San Lorenzo 49 Racing Club 43 Huracán 40
1973 Huracán 46 Boca Juniors 42 San Lorenzo 40
1974 Newell's Old Boys 5 Rosario Central 3 Boca Juniors 2
1975 River Plate 55 Huracán 51 Boca Juniors 50
1976 Boca Juniors 19 Huracán 16 Estudiantes LP 14
1977 River Plate 63 Independiente 61 Velez Sarsfield 56
1978 Quilmes 54 Boca Juniors 53 Union Santa Fe 52
1979 River Plate 2-0 5-1 Velez Sarsfield
1980 River Plate 51 Argentinos Juniors 42 Talleres Cordoba 41
1981 Boca Juniors 50 Ferrocarril Oeste 49 Newell's Old Boys 39
1982 Estudiantes LP 54 Independiente 52 Boca Juniors 48
1983 Independiente 48 San Lorenzo 47 Ferrocarril Oeste 46
1984 Argentinos Juniors 51 Ferrocarril Oeste 50 Estudiantes LP 48
1985 -
1986 River Plate 56 Newell's Old Boys 46 Deportivo Español 46
1987 Rosario Central 49 Newell's Old Boys 48 Independiente 47
1988 Newell's Old Boys 55 San Lorenzo 49 Racing Club 48
1989 Independiente 84 Boca Juniors 76 Deportivo Español 68
1990 River Plate 53 Independiente 46 Boca Juniors 43
1991 Newell's Old Boys 28 River Plate 26 Velez Sarsfield 24
1991 Boca Juniors 32 San Lorenzo 27 Deportivo Mandiyu 23
1992 River Plate 31 Boca Juniors 24 San Lorenzo 22
1992 Newell's Old Boys 29 Velez Sarsfield 27 Deportivo Español 27
1993 Boca Juniors 27 River Plate 25 San Lorenzo 23
1993 Velez Sarsfield 27 Independiente 24 River Plate 22
1994 River Plate 24 Velez Sarsfield 23 Racing Club 23
1994 Independiente 26 Huracán 25 Rosario Central 23
1995 River Plate 31 San Lorenzo 26 Velez Sarsfield 24
1995 San Lorenzo 30 Gimnasia LP 29 Velez Sarsfield 28

Play-offs

1891	Saint Andrew's	3-1	Old Caledonians
1897	Lomas Athletic	1-1 0-0 1-0	Lanús AC
1898	Lomas Athletic	2-1	Lobos AC
1911	Alumni	2-1	Estudiantil Porteño
1912	Estudiantil Porteño	1-1 *	Independiente
1915	Racing Club	1-0	San Isidro
1923	Boca Juniors	3-0 0-2 0-0 2-0	Huracán
1925	Huracán	1-1 **	Nueva Chicago
1931	Estudiantil Porteño	3-1	Almagro
1932	River Plate	3-0	Independiente
1951	Racing Club	0-0 1-0	Banfield
1991	Newell's Old Boys	1-0 0-1 3-1p	Boca Juniors

* Awarded to Porteño after match suspended in the 87th minute
** Huracán declared winners after the match was suspended

ARGENTINE NATIONAL CHAMPIONSHIP

1967 Independiente 26 Estudiantes LP 24 Velez Sarsfield 20
1968 Velez Sarsfield 22 River Plate 22 Racing Club 22

1969 Boca Juniors 29 River Plate 27 San Lorenzo 27
1970 Boca Juniors 2-1 Rosario Central
1971 Rosario Central 2-1 San Lorenzo
1972 San Lorenzo 1-0 River Plate
1973 Rosario Central 5 River Plate 3 Atlanta/San Lorenzo 2
1974 San Lorenzo 11 Rosario Central 10 Velez Sarsfield 8
1975 River Plate 12 Estudiantes LP 11 San Lorenzo 9
1976 Boca Juniors 1-0 River Plate
1977 Independiente 1-1 2-2 Talleres Cordoba
1978 Independiente 0-0 2-0 River Plate
1979 River Plate 1-1 0-0 Union Santa Fe
1980 Rosario Central 5-1 0-2 Racing Cordoba
1981 River Plate 1-0 1-0 Ferrocarril Oeste
1982 Ferrocarril Oeste 0-0 2-0 Quilmes
1983 Estudiantes LP 2-0 1-2 Independiente
1984 Ferrocarril Oeste 3-0 1-0 River Plate
1985 Argentinos Juniors 1-1(4-3p) 2-1 Velez Sarsfield

LEADING INTERNATIONAL GOALSCORERS

33 Gabriel Batistuta (Newell's, River Plate, Boca, Fiorentina)
Diego Maradona (Argentinos Juniors, Boca Juniors, Barcelona, Napoli, Sevilla, Newell's, Boca Juniors)
24 Luis Artime (Atlanta, River Plate, Independiente)
23 Daniel Passarella (River Plate, Fiorentina)
22 Leopoldo Luque (River Plate)
20 José Sanfilippo (San Lorenzo)
19 Mario Kempes (Rosario Central, Valencia, River Plate)
Rinaldo Martino (San Lorenzo, Juventus, Boca Juniors)
René Pontoni (San Lorenzo)
17 Herminio Masantonio (Huracan)
José Manuel Moreno (River Plate, España)

LEADING INTERNATIONAL APPEARANCES

98 Oscar Ruggeri (Boca, River, Logrones, Real Madrid, Velez, Ancona, América, SanLorenzo)
90 Diego Maradona (Argentinos Juniors, Boca Juniors, Barcelona, Napoli, Sevilla, Newell's, Boca)
71 Amerigo Gallego (Newell's Old Boys)
69 Daniel Passarella (River Plate, Fiorentina)
60 Alberto Tarantini (Boca Juniors, Birmingham City, River Plate)
58 Jorgé Olguin
56 Ubaldo Fillol (Quilmes, River Plate)

INTERNATIONAL MATCHES PLAYED BY ARGENTINA

16-05-1901	Uruguay	W 3-2	Montevideo	Fr	
20-07-1902	Uruguay	W 6-0	Montevideo	Fr	Dickinson, Brown.J, Morgan, Anderson, OG 2
13-09-1903	Uruguay	L 2-3	Buenos Aires	Fr	Brown.J 2
15-08-1905	Uruguay	D 0-0	Buenos Aires	LC	
9-07-1906	South Africa	L 0-1	Buenos Aires	Fr	
15-08	Uruguay	W 2-0	Montevideo	LC	Brown.A, González.T
21-10	Uruguay	W 2-1	Buenos Aires	NC	Watson-Hutton, Brown.E
15-08-1907	Uruguay	W 2-1	Buenos Aires	LC	Brown.E, Jacobs
6-10	Uruguay	W 2-1	Montevideo	NC	Malbrán 2
15-08-1908	Uruguay	D 2-2	Montevideo	LC	Brown.EA, Susán
13-09	Uruguay	W 2-1	Buenos Aires	NC	Brown.E, Watson-Hutton
4-10	Uruguay	L 0-1	Buenos Aires	MEA	
15-08-1909	Uruguay	W 2-1	Buenos Aires	LC	Watson-Hutton, Brown.E
19-09	Uruguay	D 2-2	Montevideo	NC	Viale, OG
10-10	Uruguay	W 3-1	Buenos Aires	MEA	Brown.J, Brown.A 2
27-05-1910	Chile	W 3-1	Buenos Aires	Fr	Viale, Susán, Hayes.H
5-06	Chile	W 5-1	Buenos Aires	SC	Viale, Hayes.H 2, Weiss, Susán
12-06	Uruguay	W 4-1	Buenos Aires	SC	Viale, Hayes.H, Watson-Hutton, Susán
15-08	Uruguay	L 1-3	Montevideo	LC	Hayes.H
11-09	Chile	W 3-0	Viña del Mar	Fr	Gonzalez.M, Lawrie, Fernandez.E
13-11	Uruguay	D 1-1	Buenos Aires	MEA	Gonzalez.M
27-11	Uruguay	L 2-6	Buenos Aires	MEA	Gonzalez.M, Viale
30-04-1911	Uruguay *	W 2-1	Montevideo	Fr	Fernandez.E, Lennie
15-08	Uruguay	L 0-2	Buenos Aires	LC	
17-09	Uruguay	W 3-2	Montevideo	NC	Brown.A, Brown.E 2
8-10	Uruguay	D 1-1	Montevideo	MEU	Watson-Hutton
22-10	Uruguay	W 2-0	Buenos Aires	MEA	Piaggio 2
29-10	Uruguay	L 0-3	Montevideo	MEU	
25-02-1912	Uruguay *	W 2-0	Buenos Aires	Fr	Ohaco, Hayes.H
15-08	Uruguay	L 0-2	Montevideo	LC	
25-08	Uruguay	L 0-3	Montevideo	MEU	
22-09	Uruguay	L 0-1	Buenos Aires	MEA	
6-10	Uruguay	D 3-3	Buenos Aires	NC	Viale 2, Watson-Hutton
1-12	Uruguay	W 3-1	Montevideo	MC	Gonzalez.M, Marcovecchio, Viale
27-04-1913	Uruguay *	D 0-0	Buenos Aires	Fr	
15-06	Uruguay	D 1-1	Buenos Aires	SPC	Gonzalez.M
9-07	Uruguay	W 2-1	Buenos Aires	SPC	Gonzalez.M 2
13-07	Uruguay *	L 4-5	Montevideo	Fr	
15-08	Uruguay	W 4-0	Buenos Aires	LC	Susán 4
31-08	Uruguay	W 2-0	Buenos Aires	MEA	Polimeni, Hayes.H
21-09	Chile	W 2-0	Viña del Mar	Fr	

Date	Opponent	Result	Venue	Comp	Scorers
28-09	Uruguay *	W 4-0	Buenos Aires	Fr	
5-10	Uruguay	L 0-1	Montevideo	MEU	
26-10	Uruguay	L 0-1	Montevideo	NC	
30-08-1914	Uruguay	L 2-3	Montevideo	MEU	Calomino, Dannaher
13-09	Uruguay	W 2-1	Buenos Aires	MEA	Gallardo, Lazcano
20-09	Brazil	W 3-0	Buenos Aires	Fr	Izaguirre 2, Molfino
27-09	Brazil	L 0-1	Buenos Aires	RC	
18-07-1915	Uruguay	W 3-2	Montevideo	MEU	Marcovecchio 2, Hayes.H
15-08	Uruguay	W 2-1	Buenos Aires	LC	Marcovecchio, Hayes.H
12-09	Uruguay	L 0-2	Montevideo	NC	
6-07-1916	Chile	W 6-1	Buenos Aires	SC	Ohaco 2, Brown.J (II) 2, Marcovecchio 2
10-07	Brazil	D 1-1	Buenos Aires	SC	Laguna
12-07	Chile	W 1-0	Buenos Aires	Fr	Marcovecchio
17-07	Uruguay	D 0-0	Buenos Aires	SC	
15-08	Uruguay	W 2-1	Montevideo	LC	Hayes.E, Laiolo
15-08	Uruguay	W 3-1	Buenos Aires	NC	Ohaco 2, Hiller
1-10	Uruguay	W 1-0	Montevideo	MEU	Badalini
1-10	Uruguay	W 7-2	Buenos Aires	MEA	Simmons, Hiller 3, Cabano, Hayes.E 2
29-10	Uruguay	L 1-3	Montevideo	Fr	Guidi
18-07-1917	Uruguay	W 2-0	Montevideo	MEU	Marcovecchio 2
15-08	Uruguay	W 1-0	Buenos Aires	LC	Calomino
2-09	Uruguay	L 0-1	Montevideo	NC	
3-10	Brazil	W 4-2	Montevideo	SC	Calomino, Ohaco 2, Blanco.A
6-10	Chile	W 1-0	Montevideo	SC	OG
14-10	Uruguay	L 0-1	Montevideo	SC	
21-10	Chile	D 1-1	Buenos Aires	Fr	Matozzi
18-07-1918	Uruguay	D 1-1	Montevideo	MEU	Laiolo
28-07	Uruguay	L 1-3	Montevideo	MEU	Garcia.E
15-08	Uruguay	D 0-0	Buenos Aires	MEA	
25-08	Uruguay	W 2-1	Buenos Aires	MEA	Martin 2
20-09	Uruguay	D 1-1	Montevideo	LC	Calandra
29-09	Uruguay	W 2-0	Buenos Aires	NC	Vivaldo, Blanco.A
11-05-1919	Paraguay	W 5-1	Asuncion	Fr	Laguna 2, Ochandio 2, Polimeni
13-05	Uruguay	L 2-3	Rio de Janeiro	SC	Izaguirre, Calomino
15-05	Paraguay	W 3-0	Asuncion	Fr	Lazcano, Adet, Ochandio
18-05	Brazil	L 1-3	Rio de Janeiro	SC	Izaguirre
21-05	Paraguay	W 2-1	Asuncion	Fr	Adet, Ochandio
22-05	Chile	W 4-1	Rio de Janeiro	SC	Clarke 3, Izaguirre
24-05	Paraguay	W 2-1	Asuncion	Fr	Ochandio, Bianatti
1-06	Brazil	D 3-3	Rio de Janeiro	Fr	Clarke, Mattozzi, Laiolo
18-07	Uruguay	L 1-4	Montevideo	MEU	Hayes.H
24-08	Uruguay	L 1-2	Montevideo	NC	Olazar
7-09	Uruguay	L 1-2	Buenos Aires	LC	Badalini
19-10	Uruguay	W 6-1	Buenos Aires	MEA	Libonatti 3, Celli, Vivaldo, Chavín
7-12	Uruguay	L 2-4	Montevideo	Fr	Libonatti, Badalini
18-07-1920	Uruguay	L 0-2	Montevideo	MEU	
25-07	Uruguay	L 1-3	Buenos Aires	NC	Clarke
8-08	Uruguay	W 1-0	Buenos Aires	MEA	Calomino
12-09	Uruguay	D 1-1	Viña del Mar	SC	Etcheverria
17-09	Chile	D 1-1	Viña del Mar	SC	Dellavella
25-09	Brazil	W 2-0	Viña del Mar	SC	Etcheverria, Libonatti
12-10	Brazil	W 3-1	Buenos Aires	Fr	
7-04-1921	Paraguay *	L 1-3	Asuncion	Fr	Corbella
14-04	Paraguay *	D 2-2	Asuncion	Fr	Clarke, Calomino
25-09	Chile	W 4-1	Viña del Mar	Fr	Seoane 3, Caldas
2-10	Chile	D 1-1	Santiago	Fr	
2-10	Brazil	W 1-0	Buenos Aires	SC	Libonatti
16-10	Paraguay	W 3-0	Buenos Aires	SC	Libonatti, Saruppo, Etcheverria
30-10	Uruguay	W 1-0	Buenos Aires	SC	Libonatti
22-01-1922	Uruguay *	L 1-3	Buenos Aires	Fr	
22-07	Uruguay	D 2-2	Montevideo	Fr	
27-08	Uruguay *	D 3-3	Buenos Aires	Fr	
28-09	Chile	W 4-0	Rio de Janeiro	SC	Francia 2, Chiessa, Gaslini
8-10	Uruguay	L 0-1	Rio de Janeiro	SC	
15-10	Brazil	L 0-2	Rio de Janeiro	SC	
18-10	Paraguay	W 2-0	Rio de Janeiro	SC	Francia 2
22-10	Brazil	L 1-2	Sao Paulo	RC	Francia
22-10	Uruguay *	W 3-2	Buenos Aires	Fr	
22-10	Chile	W 1-0	Buenos Aires	Fr	
11-11	Uruguay *	W 4-0	La Plata	Fr	
12-11	Uruguay	L 0-1	Montevideo	LC	

10-12	Uruguay	L 0-1	Montevideo	MEU	
17-12	Uruguay	D 2-2	Buenos Aires	NC	Badalini 2
20-05-1923	Paraguay	L 0-2	Buenos Aires	RCB	
25-05	Paraguay	W 1-0	Buenos Aires	RCB	Izaguirre
25-05	Uruguay *	L 0-2	Montevideo	Fr	
24-06	Uruguay	D 0-0	Buenos Aires	LC	
15-07	Uruguay	D 2-2	Buenos Aires	MEA	
22-07	Uruguay	D 2-2	Montevideo	MEU	Tarascone, Irurieta
25-08	Uruguay *	D 1-1	Montevideo	Fr	Seoane
30-09	Uruguay	W 2-0	Montevideo	MEU	Saruppo, López.A
29-10	Paraguay	W 4-3	Montevideo	SC	Saruppo, Aguirre 3
18-11	Brazil	W 2-1	Montevideo	SC	Onzari, Saruppo
2-12	Uruguay	L 0-2	Montevideo	SC	
2-12	Brazil	L 0-2	Buenos Aires	RC	
3-12	Chile	W 6-0	Buenos Aires	Fr	
8-12	Uruguay	L 2-3	Buenos Aires	Fr	Anunziata, Acosta.L
9-12	Brazil	W 2-0	Buenos Aires	RC	Onzari, OG
15-05-1924	Paraguay	W 3-1	Asuncion	RCB	Onzari, Tarasconi, Seoane
18-05	Paraguay	L 1-2	Asuncion	RCB	Tarasconi
25-05	Uruguay	W 4-0	Buenos Aires	NC	Goicoechea 3, Aguirre
25-05	Uruguay	L 0-2	Montevideo	LC	
10-08	Uruguay	D 0-0	Buenos Aires	Fr	
31-08	Uruguay	W 3-2	Montevideo	MEU	Lacarelli 2, Monti.L
21-09	Uruguay	D 1-1	Montevideo	Fr	Tarascone
2-10	Uruguay	W 2-1	Buenos Aires	Fr	Onzari, Tarascone
12-10	Paraguay	D 0-0	Montevideo	SC	
25-10	Chile	W 2-0	Montevideo	SC	Loyarte, Sosa
2-11	Uruguay	D 0-0	Montevideo	SC	
16-11	Uruguay	L 0-1	Montevideo	Fr	
5-01-1925	Uruguay	W 1-0	Montevideo	Fr	
9-07	Paraguay	D 1-1	Buenos Aires	RCB	Evaristo.J
12-07	Paraguay	D 1-1	Buenos Aires	RCB	Gaslini
29-11	Paraguay	W 2-0	Buenos Aires	SC	Seoane, Sanchez
13-12	Brazil	W 4-1	Buenos Aires	SC	Seoane 3, Garasino
20-12	Paraguay	W 3-1	Buenos Aires	SC	Tarasconi, Seoane, Irurieta
25-12	Brazil	D 2-2	Buenos Aires	SC	Cerroti, Seoane
29-05-1926	Paraguay	W 2-1	Asuncion	RCB	Cherro, Stagnaro
3-06	Paraguay	W 2-1	Asuncion	RCB	Cesarini, Villagra
16-10	Bolivia	W 5-0	Santiago	SC	Cherro 2, Sosa, Delgado, Miguel
20-10	Paraguay	W 8-0	Santiago	SC	Sosa 4, Delgado 2, Cherro, Miguel
24-10	Uruguay	L 0-2	Santiago	SC	
31-10	Chile	D 1-1	Santiago	SC	Tarasconi
14-07-1927	Uruguay	W 1-0	Montevideo	NC	Carricaberry
30-08	Uruguay	L 0-1	Buenos Aires	LC	
30-10	Bolivia	W 7-1	Lima	SC	Luna 2, Carricaberry, Recanattini, Ferreyra.M, Seoane 2
20-11	Uruguay	W 3-2	Lima	SC	Recanattini, Luna, Carricaberry
27-11	Peru	W 5-1	Lima	SC	Ferreira, Maglio, Orsi, Carricaberry, Seoane
1-04-1928	Portugal	D 0-0	Lisbon	Fr	
29-05	United States	W 11-2	Amsterdam	OGr1	Tarasconi 4, Cherro 3, Orsi 2, Ferreyra.M 2
2-06	Belgium	W 6-3	Amsterdam	OGqf	Tarasconi 4, Monti.L, Ferreyra.M
6-06	Egypt	W 6-0	Amsterdam	OGsf	Tarasconi 2, Ferreyra.M 2, Cherro, Carricaberry
10-06	Uruguay	D 1-1	Amsterdam	OGf	Ferreyra.M
13-06	Uruguay	L 1-2	Amsterdam	OGf	Monti.L
30-08	Uruguay	W 1-0	Buenos Aires	NC	Seoane
21-09	Uruguay	D 2-2	Montevideo	LC	Alonso, Masrassi
16-06-1929	Uruguay	W 2-0	Buenos Aires	Fr	Peucelle, Scopelli
16-06	Uruguay	D 1-1	Montevideo	Fr	Maglio
20-09	Uruguay	L 1-2	Montevideo	NC	Maglio
28-09	Uruguay	D 0-0	Buenos Aires	LC	
3-11	Peru	W 3-0	Buenos Aires	SC	Zumelzu 2, Peucelle
10-11	Paraguay	W 4-1	Buenos Aires	SC	Ferreira 2, Evaristo.M, Cherro
17-11	Uruguay	W 2-0	Buenos Aires	SC	Ferreira, Evaristo.M
25-05-1930	Uruguay	D 1-1	Buenos Aires	NC	Varallo
15-07	France	W 1-0	Montevideo	WCr1	Monti.L
19-07	Mexico	W 6-3	Montevideo	WCr1	Stabile 3, Varallo 2, Zumelzu
22-07	Chile	W 3-1	Montevideo	WCr1	Stabile 2, Evaristo.M
26-07	United States	W 6-1	Montevideo	WCsf	Monti, Scopelli, Stabile 2, Peucelle 2
30-07	Uruguay	L 2-4	Montevideo	WCf	Peucelle, Stabile
3-08	Yugoslavia	W 3-1	Buenos Aires	Fr	Sponda 2, Trulillo
19-04-1931	Paraguay	W 1-0	Asuncion	Fr	Peucelle
25-04	Paraguay	D 1-1	Asuncion	Fr	

4-07	Paraguay	D 1-1	Buenos Aires	RCB	Monti.L
9-07	Paraguay	W 3-1	Buenos Aires	RCB	Castro 2, Spadaro
15-05-1932	Uruguay	W 2-0	Buenos Aires	Fr	Martinez.H, Cherro
18-05	Uruguay	L 0-1	Montevideo	Fr	
21-01-1933	Uruguay	L 1-2	Montevideo	Fr	Guaita
5-02	Uruguay	W 4-1	Buenos Aires	Fr	Cherro 4
14-12	Uruguay	W 1-0	Montevideo	Fr	Varallo
27-05-1934	Sweden	L 2-3	Bologna	WCr1	Belis, Galateo
18-07	Uruguay	D 2-2	Montevideo	Fr	Gonzales.T, Caceres
15-08	Uruguay	W 1-0	Buenos Aires	Fr	Peucelle
6-01-1935	Chile	W 4-1	Lima	SC	Lauri, Garcia.D, Arrieta, Masantonio
20-01	Peru	W 4-1	Lima	SC	Masantonio 3, Garcia.D
20-01	Uruguay *	D 2-2	Buenos Aires	Fr	Valentini, Pérez.J
27-01	Uruguay	L 0-3	Lima	SC	
18-07	Uruguay	D 1-1	Montevideo	HGC	Peucelle
15-08	Uruguay	W 3-0	Buenos Aires	JMC	Zozaya 2, Garcia.D
9-08-1936	Uruguay	W 1-0	Buenos Aires	JMC	Zozaya
20-09	Uruguay	L 1-2	Montevideo	HGC	Garcia.D
30-12	Chile	W 2-1	Buenos Aires	SC	Varallo.F 2
9-01-1937	Paraguay	W 6-1	Buenos Aires	SC	Zozaya 3, Scopelli, 2, Garcia.E
16-01	Peru	W 1-0	Buenos Aires	SC	Zozaya
23-01	Uruguay	L 2-3	Buenos Aires	SC	Varallo.F, Zozaya
30-01	Brazil	W 1-0	Buenos Aires	SC	Garcia.E
1-02	Brazil	W 2-0	Buenos Aires	SC	De La Matta 2
10-10	Uruguay	W 3-0	Montevideo	NC	Marvezzi, Fidel, Moreno
11-11	Uruguay	W 5-1	Buenos Aires	LC	Masantonio 3, Fidel, Garcia.E
18-06-1938	Uruguay	W 1-0	Buenos Aires	JMC	Moreno
12-10	Uruguay	W 3-2	Montevideo	HGC	Garcia.E, Cosso, Cavadini
15-01-1939	Brazil	W 5-1	Rio de Janeiro	RC	Masantonio 2, Moreno 2, Garcia.E
22-01	Brazil	L 2-3	Rio de Janeiro	RC	Rodolfi, Garcia.E
14-08	Paraguay	W 1-0	Asuncion	RCB	Fabrini
16-08	Paraguay	D 2-2	Asuncion	RCB	Sarlanga, Arrieta.L
18-02-1940	Brazil	D 2-2	Sao Paulo	RC	Cassán, Baldonedo
18-02	Paraguay	W 3-1	Buenos Aires	RCB	Ballesteros, Pedernera, Leguizamón
25-02	Paraguay	W 4-0	Buenos Aires	RCB	Laferrara 2, Masantonio 2
25-02	Brazil	W 3-0	Sao Paulo	RC	Baldonedo, Fidel, Sastre
2-03	Chile *	W 4-1	Buenos Aires	Fr	Laferrara 3, Maril
5-03	Brazil	W 6-1	Buenos Aires	RC	Peucelle 3, Masantonio 2, Baldonedo
9-03	Chile *	W 3-2	Buenos Aires	Fr	Arrieta.L 3
10-03	Brazil	L 2-3	Buenos Aires	RC	Baldonedo 2
17-03	Brazil	W 5-1	Buenos Aires	RC	Baldonedo 2, Masantonio, Peucelle, Cassán
18-07	Uruguay	L 0-3	Montevideo	HGC	
15-08	Uruguay	W 5-0	Buenos Aires	JMC	Sarlanga, Esperón, Moreno, Marvezzi 2
5-01-1941	Chile *	W 2-1	Santiago	Fr	Sastre, Arregui
9-01	Chile *	W 5-2	Santiago	Fr	Sastre 2, Arrieta.L 2, Arregui
19-01	Peru	D 1-1	Lima	RGP	Moreno
26-01	Peru	D 1-1	Lima	RGP	Belén
29-01	Peru	W 3-0	Lima	RGP	Moreno, Sastre, Marvezzi
12-02	Peru	W 2-1	Santiago	SC	Moreno 2
16-02	Ecuador	W 6-1	Santiago	SC	Marvezzi 5, Minella
23-02	Uruguay	W 1-0	Santiago	SC	Sastre
4-03	Chile	W 1-0	Santiago	SC	Garcia.E
11-01-1942	Paraguay	W 4-3	Montevideo	SC	Masantonio 2, Sandoval, Perucca
17-01	Brazil	W 2-1	Montevideo	SC	Garcia.E, Masantonio
22-01	Ecuador	W 12-0	Montevideo	SC	Moreno 5, Masantonio 4, Garcia.E, Pedernera, Perucca
25-01	Peru	W 3-1	Montevideo	SC	Moreno 2, Heredia
31-01	Chile	D 0-0	Montevideo	SC	Abandoned 43 mins
7-02	Uruguay	L 0-1	Montevideo	SC	
25-05	Uruguay	W 4-1	Buenos Aires	NC	Alberti, Pontoni 2, Martino
25-08	Uruguay	D 1-1	Montevideo	LC	Muñoz
6-01-1943	Uruguay *	W 1-0	Buenos Aires	Fr	Martino
9-01	Uruguay *	L 2-6	Montevideo	Fr	Alberti, Orleáns
28-03	Uruguay	D 3-3	Buenos Aires	JMC	Pontoni 2, Martino
4-04	Uruguay	W 1-0	Montevideo	HGC	Canteli
10-07	Paraguay	W 5-2	Asuncion	RCB	Sarlanga 2, Pellegrina, Martino, De La Mata
11-07	Paraguay	L 1-2	Asuncion	RCB	Sarlanga
5-01-1944	Uruguay *	W 3-1	Montevideo	Fr	Sued 2, Strembel
8-01	Uruguay *	D 3-3	Buenos Aires	Fr	Pontoni, De la Mata, Martino
29-01	Uruguay *	L 1-2	Montevideo	Fr	Labruna
29-01	Uruguay *	W 6-2	Buenos Aires	Fr	Pontoni 3, Martino, Salvini, Loustau
6-01-1945	Paraguay	W 5-2	Buenos Aires	RCB	Muñoz, Pontoni 2, Loustau, Martino

Date	Opponent	Result	Venue	Comp	Scorers
9-01	Paraguay	W 5-3	Buenos Aires	RCB	Pontoni 4, Martino
18-01	Bolivia	W 4-0	Santiago	SC	Pontoni, Martino, Loustau, De La Mata
31-01	Ecuador	W 4-2	Santiago	SC	Pontoni, De La Mata, Martino,Pellegrina
7-02	Colombia	W 9-1	Santiago	SC	Pontoni 2, Mendez.N 2, Martino, Boyé, Ferraro 2, Loustau
11-02	Chile	D 1-1	Santiago	SC	Mendez.N
15-02	Brazil	W 3-1	Santiago	SC	Mendez.N 3
25-02	Uruguay	W 1-0	Santiago	SC	Martino
7-07	Paraguay	L 1-5	Asuncion	RCB	Pontoni
9-07	Paraguay	W 3-1	Asuncion	RCB	Martino 2, Sued
18-07	Uruguay	D 2-2	Montevideo	LC	Martino, OG
15-08	Uruguay	W 6-2	Buenos Aires	NC	Loustau, Ferraro, Mendez.N, Martino 2, Pedernera
16-12	Brazil	W 4-3	Sao Paulo	RC	Pedernera, Boyé, Sued, Labruna
20-12	Brazil	L 2-6	Rio de Janeiro	RC	Pedernera, Martino
23-12	Brazil	L 1-3	Rio de Janeiro	RC	Martino
29-12	Uruguay *	D 1-1	Montevideo	Fr	Martino
12-01-1946	Paraguay	W 2-0	Buenos Aires	SC	De La Mata, Martino
19-01	Bolivia	W 7-1	Buenos Aires	SC	Mendez.N 2, Labruna 2, Salvini 2, Loustau
26-01	Chile	W 3-1	Buenos Aires	SC	Labruna 2, Pedernera
2-02	Uruguay	W 3-1	Buenos Aires	SC	Pedernera, Labruna, Mendez.N
10-02	Brazil	W 2-0	Buenos Aires	SC	Mendez.N 2
2-03-1947	Uruguay *	W 2-1	Buenos Aires	Fr	Pontoni, Caserio
9-03	Uruguay *	D 4-4	Montevideo	Fr	Mendez.N, Aguirre, Boyé, Ferraro
2-12	Paraguay	W 6-0	Guayaquil	SC	Pontoni 3, Moreno, Loustau, Mendez.N
4-12	Bolivia	W 7-0	Guayaquil	SC	Mendez.N 2, Boyé 2, Pontoni, Di Stéfano, Loustau
11-12	Peru	W 3-2	Guayaquil	SC	Moreno, Di Stéfano, Boyé
16-12	Chile	D 1-1	Guayaquil	SC	Di Stéfano
18-12	Colombia	W 6-0	Guayaquil	SC	Di Stéfano 3, Fernandez.M, Boyé, Loustau
25-12	Ecuador	W 2-0	Guayaquil	SC	Moreno, Mendez.N
28-12	Uruguay	W 3-1	Guayaquil	SC	Mendez.N 2, Loustau
18-05-1948	Uruguay *	W 1-0	Montevideo	Fr	Boyé
25-05	Uruguay *	L 0-2	Buenos Aires	Fr	
25-03-1950	Paraguay	D 2-2	Buenos Aires	RCB	Bravo, Vernazza
29-03	Paraguay	W 4-0	Buenos Aires	RCB	Labruna 2, Uñate 2
9-05-1951	England	L 1-2	London	Fr	Boyé
13-05	Rep. Ireland	W 1-0	Dublin	Fr	Labruna
7-12-1952	Spain	W 1-0	Madrid	Fr	Infante
14-12	Portugal	W 3-1	Lisbon	Fr	Loustau, Labruna 2
14-05-1953	England *	W 3-1	Buenos Aires	Fr	Grillo 2, Michelli
17-05	England	D 0-0	Buenos Aires	Fr	Abandoned after 23 mins.
5-07	Spain	W 1-0	Buenos Aires	Fr	Grillo
28-11-1954	Portugal	W 3-1	Lisbon	Fr	Michelli, Grillo, Cruz
5-12	Italy	L 0-2	Rome	Fr	
2-03-1955	Paraguay	W 5-3	Santiago	SC	Michelli 4, Borello
9-03	Ecuador	W 4-0	Santiago	SC	Bonelli, Grillo, Michelli, Borelo
16-03	Peru	D 2-2	Santiago	SC	Grillo, Cecconato
27-03	Uruguay	W 6-1	Santiago	SC	Labruna 3, Michelli 2, Borello
30-03	Chile	W 1-0	Santiago	SC	Michelli
22-01-1956	Peru	W 2-1	Montevideo	SC	Sivori, Vairo.J
29-01	Chile	W 2-0	Montevideo	SC	Labruna 2
1-02	Paraguay	W 1-0	Montevideo	SC	Cecconato
5-02	Brazil	L 0-1	Montevideo	SC	
15-02	Uruguay	L 0-1	Montevideo	SC	
28-02	Peru	D 0-0	Mexico City	PAC	
6-03	Costa Rica	W 4-3	Mexico City	PAC	Sivori 3, Maschio
11-03	Chile	W 3-0	Mexico City	PAC	Maschio 2, Sivori
13-03	Mexico	D 0-0	Mexico City	PAC	
18-03	Brazil	D 2-2	Mexico City	PAC	Yudica, Sivori
24-06	Italy	W 1-0	Buenos Aires	Fr	Conde
1-07	Uruguay	W 2-1	Montevideo	CA	Grillo 2
8-07	Brazil	D 0-0	Buenos Aires	CA	
15-08	Paraguay	W 1-0	Asuncion	RCB	Conde
19-08	Czechoslovakia	W 1-0	Buenos Aires	Fr	Angelillo
10-10	Uruguay	W 2-1	Paysandu	Fr	Garabal 2
14-11	Uruguay	D 2-2	Buenos Aires	Fr	Corbatta, Angelillo
13-03-1957	Colombia	W 8-2	Lima	SC	Maschio 4, Angelillo 2, Cruz.O, Corbatta
17-03	Ecuador	W 3-0	Lima	SC	Angelillo 2, Sivori
20-03	Uruguay	W 4-0	Lima	SC	Maschio 2, Angelillo, Sanfilippo
28-03	Chile	W 6-2	Lima	SC	Angelillo 2, Maschio 2, Sivori, Corbatta
3-04	Brazil	W 3-0	Lima	SC	Angelillo, Maschio, Cruz.O
6-04	Peru	L 1-2	Lima	SC	Sivori

9-04	Peru	W 4-1	Lima	Fr	Angelillo, Juárez, Castro, Cruz.O
23-05	Uruguay	D 0-0	Montevideo	NC	
5-06	Uruguay	D 1-1	Buenos Aires	LC	Angelillo
7-07	Brazil	W 2-1	Rio de Janeiro	RC	Labruna, Juárez
10-07	Brazil	L 0-2	Sao Paulo	RC	
6-10	Bolivia	L 0-2	La Paz	WCq	
13-10	Chile	W 2-0	Santiago	WCq	Conde, Menendez
20-10	Chile	W 4-0	Buenos Aires	WCq	Corbatta, Prado, Menendez, Zarate
27-10	Bolivia	W 4-0	Buenos Aires	WCq	Corbatta 2, Prado, Menendez
6-04-1958	Uruguay	L 0-1	Montevideo	Fr	
20-04	Paraguay	L 0-1	Asuncion	Fr	
28-04	Paraguay	W 2-0	Buenos Aires	Fr	Prado, Corbatta
30-04	Uruguay	W 2-0	Buenos Aires	Fr	Prado, Infante
8-06	West Germany	L 1-3	Malmo	WCr1	Corbatta
11-06	Nth. Ireland	W 3-1	Halmstad	WCr1	Corbatta, Menendez, Avio
15-06	Czechoslovakia	L 1-6	Halsingborg	WCr1	Corbatta
7-03-1959	Chile	W 6-1	Buenos Aires	SC	Manfredini 2, Pizzutti 2, Callá, Belén
11-03	Bolivia	W 2-0	Buenos Aires	SC	Corbatta, Callá
18-03	Peru	W 3-1	Buenos Aires	SC	Corbatta, Sosa.R, OG
22-03	Paraguay	W 3-1	Buenos Aires	SC	Corbatta, Sosa.R, Cap
30-03	Uruguay	W 4-1	Buenos Aires	SC	Belén 2, Sosa.R 2
4-04	Brazil	D 1-1	Buenos Aires	SC	Pizzutti
18-11	Chile	L 2-4	Santiago	Fr	Ruiz, Sanfilippo
9-12	Paraguay	W 4-2	Guayaquil	SC	Sanfilippo 3, Sosa.R
12-12	Ecuador	D 1-1	Guayaquil	SC	Sosa.R
16-12	Uruguay	L 0-5	Guayaquil	SC	
22-12	Brazil	W 4-1	Guayaquil	SC	Sanfilippo 3, Garcia.O
8-03-1960	Costa Rica	D 0-0	San Jose	PAC	
10-03	Mexico	W 3-2	San Jose	PAC	Belén 2, Nardiello
13-03	Brazil	W 2-1	San Jose	PAC	Belén, Nardiello
15-03	Costa Rica	W 2-0	San Jose	PAC	Onega, D'Ascenso
17-03	Mexico	W 2-0	San Jose	PAC	Jimenez, Nardiello
20-03	Brazil	L 0-1	San Jose	PAC	
26-05	Brazil	W 4-2	Buenos Aires	RC	Nardiello 2, D'Ascenso, Belén
29-05	Brazil	L 1-4	Buenos Aires	RC	Sosa.R
9-07	Paraguay	W 1-0	Buenos Aires	CA	Sosa.R
12-07	Brazil	L 1-5	Rio de Janeiro	CA	Sosa.R
24-07	Spain	W 2-0	Buenos Aires	Fr	Sanfilippo 2
17-08	Uruguay	W 4-0	Buenos Aires	CA	Sanfilippo 3, Jiménez.W
4-12	Ecuador	W 6-3	Guayaquil	WCq	Corbatta 2, Pando, Sosa.R, Ramaciotti, Sanfilippo
17-12	Ecuador	W 5-0	Buenos Aires	WCq	Sanfilippo, Corbatta 2, Sosa.R, Pando
17-05-1961	Paraguay	D 0-0	Asuncion	Fr	
4-06	Portugal	W 2-0	Lisbon	Fr	Pando, Sanfilippo
11-06	Spain	L 0-2	Seville	Fr	
15-06	Italy	L 1-4	Florence	Fr	Sacchi
19-06	Czechoslovakia	D 3-3	Brno	Fr	Sanfilippo 2, Artime
24-06	Soviet Union	D 0-0	Moscow	Fr	
12-10	Paraguay	W 5-1	Buenos Aires	Fr	Corbatta 2, Artime, Pagani, Sanfilippo
18-11	Soviet Union	L 1-2	Buenos Aires	Fr	Belén
13-03-1962	Uruguay	D 1-1	Montevideo	Fr	Belén
28-03	Mexico	W 1-0	Buenos Aires	Fr	OG
30-05	Bulgaria	W 1-0	Rancagua	WCr1	Facundo
2-06	England	L 1-3	Rancagua	WCr1	Sanfilippo
6-06	Hungary	D 0-0	Rancagua	WCr1	
15-08	Uruguay	W 3-1	Buenos Aires	LC	Pagani, Willington, Gonzalez.A
7-11	Chile	D 1-1	Santiago	CDC	Artime
21-11	Chile	W 1-0	Buenos Aires	CDC	Artime
10-03-1963	Colombia	W 4-2	Cochabamba	SC	Zárate 2, Rodriguez.M, Fernández.J
13-03	Peru	L 1-2	Cochabamba	SC	Zárate
20-03	Ecuador	W 4-2	Cochabamba	SC	Savoy 3, Rodriguez.M
24-03	Brazil	W 3-0	La Paz	SC	Rodriguez.M, Savoy, Juarez
28-03	Bolivia	L 2-3	La Paz	SC	Rodriguez.M 2
31-03	Paraguay	D 1-1	La Paz	SC	Lallana
13-04	Brazil	W 3-2	Sao Paulo	RC	Lallana 2, Juarez
16-04	Brazil	L 2-5	Rio de Janeiro	RC	Fernández.E, Rodriguez.M
15-10	Paraguay	W 4-0	Asuncion	RCB	Artime 2, Savoy, Onega.E
29-10	Paraguay	L 2-3	Buenos Aires	RCB	Menotti, Artime
31-05-1964	Portugal	W 2-0	Rio de Janeiro	CN	Rojas.A, Rendo
3-06	Brazil	W 3-0	Sao Paulo	CN	Onega.E, Telch 2
6-06	England	W 1-0	Rio de Janeiro	CN	Rojas.A
24-09	Chile	W 5-0	Buenos Aires	CDC	Artime 2, Onega.E, Rendo, Bielli

14-10	Chile	D 1-1	Santiago	CDC	Rattin
25-11	Paraguay	L 0-3	Asuncion	RCB	
8-12	Paraguay	W 8-1	Buenos Aires	RCB	Artime 4, Onega.E 2, Prospitti 2
3-06-1965	France	D 0-0	Paris	Fr	
9-06	Brazil	D 0-0	Rio de Janeiro	Fr	
14-07	Chile	W 1-0	Buenos Aires	CDC	Rojas.A
21-07	Chile	D 1-1	Santiago	CDC	Más
1-08	Paraguay	W 3-0	Buenos Aires	WCq	OG, Onega.E, Artime
8-08	Paraguay	D 0-0	Asuncion	WCq	
17-08	Bolivia	W 4-1	Buenos Aires	WCq	Bernao 2, Onega.E 2
29-08	Bolivia	W 2-1	La Paz	WCq	Artime 2
1-12	Soviet Union	D 1-1	Buenos Aires	Fr	Onega.E
11-06-1966	Poland	D 1-1	Buenos Aires	Fr	Más
17-06	Denmark *	W 2-0	Copenhagen	Fr	Solari, Onega.E
22-06	Italy	L 0-3	Turin	Fr	
13-07	Spain	W 2-1	Birmingham	WCr1	Artime 2
16-07	West Germany	D 0-0	Birmingham	WCr1	
19-07	Switzerland	W 2-0	Sheffield	WCr1	Artime, Onega.E
23-07	England	L 0-1	London	WCqf	
18-01-1967	Paraguay	W 4-1	Montevideo	SC	Más, Artime, Bernao, Albrecht
22-01	Bolivia	W 1-0	Montevideo	SC	Bernao
25-01	Venezuela	W 5-1	Montevideo	SC	Artime 3, Carone, Marzolini
28-01	Chile	W 2-0	Montevideo	SC	Sarnari, Artime
2-02	Uruguay	L 0-1	Montevideo	SC	
15-08	Chile	L 0-1	Santiago	Fr	
22-08	Mexico	L 1-2	Mexico City	Fr	Gennoni
13-10	Paraguay	D 1-1	Asuncion	Fr	Fischer
8-11	Chile	L 1-3	Santiago	Fr	Carone
15-05-1968	Paraguay	L 0-2	Asuncion	Fr	
5-06	Uruguay	W 2-0	Buenos Aires	NC	Avallay, Fischer
20-06	Uruguay	L 1-2	Montevideo	LC	OG
7-08	Brazil	L 1-4	Rio de Janeiro	Fr	Basile
11-08	Brazil	L 2-3	Belo Horizonte	Fr	Rendo, Silva
18-08	Colombia	W 1-0	Cali	Fr	Savoy
29-08	Peru	D 2-2	Lima	Fr	Yazalde, Savoy
1-09	Peru	D 1-1	Lima	Fr	Veglio
27-11	Chile	W 4-0	Rosario	CDC	Veglio, Fischer 2, Minitti
4-12	Chile	L 1-2	Santiago	CDC	Rendo
22-12	Yugoslavia	D 1-1	Mar del Plata	Fr	Olmedo
19-03-1969	Paraguay	D 1-1	Rosario	Fr	Cocco
9-04	Paraguay	D 0-0	Asuncion	Fr	
28-05	Chile	D 1-1	Santiago	Fr	OG
11-06	Chile	W 2-1	La Plata	Fr	Fischer, Brindisi
27-07	Bolivia	L 1-3	La Paz	WCq	Tarabini
3-08	Peru	L 0-1	Lima	WCq	
24-08	Bolivia	W 1-0	Buenos Aires	WCq	Albrecht
31-08	Peru	D 2-2	Buenos Aires	WCq	Albrecht, Rendo
4-03-1970	Brazil	W 2-0	Porto Alegre	Fr	Mas, Conigliaro
8-03	Brazil	L 1-2	Rio de Janeiro	Fr	Brindisi
8-04	Uruguay	W 2-1	Buenos Aires	Fr	Conigliaro, Mas
15-04	Uruguay	L 1-2	Montevideo	Fr	Giribet
22-10	Paraguay	D 1-1	Asuncion	Fr	Brindisi
8-01-1971	France	L 3-4	Buenos Aires	Fr	Brindisi, Nicolau, Laraaigneé
13-01	France	W 2-0	Mar del Plata	Fr	Laraigneé, Madurga
4-07	Paraguay	D 1-1	Asuncion	RCB	Marcos
9-07	Paraguay	W 1-0	Rosario	RCB	Laraigneé
14-07	Uruguay	W 1-0	Buenos Aires	NC	Madurga
18-07	Uruguay	D 1-1	Montevideo	LC	Bianchi
21-07	Chile	D 2-2	Santiago	CDC	Bianchi 2
28-07	Brazil	D 1-1	Buenos Aires	RC	Madurga
31-07	Brazil	D 2-2	Buenos Aires	RC	Fischer 2
4-08	Chile	W 1-0	Buenos Aires	CDC	Fischer
25-05-1972	Paraguay	D 0-0	Salta	Fr	
31-05	Chile	W 4-3	Santiago	CDC	Mas 2, Raimondo, Mastrángelo
22-06	Colombia	W 4-1	Salvador	Clr1	Bianchi 3, Vargas
25-06	France	D 0-0	Salvador	Clr1	
29-06	Portugal	L 1-3	Rio de Janeiro	Clr2	Brindisi
2-07	Soviet Union	W 1-0	Belo Horizonte	Clr2	Pastoriza
6-07	Uruguay	W 1-0	Porto Alegre	Clr2	Más
9-07	Yugoslavia	L 2-4	Rio de Janeiro	Cl3p	Brindisi 2
25-09	Chile	W 2-0	Buenos Aires	CDC	Brindisi, Ayala

11-10	Spain	L 0-1	Madrid	Fr	
25-10	Peru	W 2-0	Lima	RCC	Ayala 2
6-02-1973	Mexico	L 0-2	Mexico City	Fr	
14-02	West Germany	W 3-2	Munich	Fr	Ghiso, Alonso, Brindisi
20-02	Israel	D 1-1	Tel Aviv	Fr	Heredia
17-05	Uruguay	D 1-1	Buenos Aires	LC	Brindisi
23-05	Uruguay	D 1-1	Montevideo	NC	Babington
13-07	Chile	W 5-4	Buenos Aires	CDC	Guerini, Ayala 2, Brindisi 2
18-07	Chile	L 1-3	Santiago	CDC	Brindisi
27-07	Peru	W 3-1	Buenos Aires	RCC	Guerini 2, Brindisi
9-09	Bolivia	W 4-0	Buenos Aires	WCq	Brindisi 2, Ayala 2
16-09	Paraguay	D 1-1	Asuncion	WCq	Ayala
23-09	Bolivia	W 1-0	La Paz	WCq	Fornari
7-10	Paraguay	W 3-1	Buenos Aires	WCq	Ayala 2, Guerini
22-04-1974	Rumania	W 2-1	Buenos Aires	Fr	Houseman, Kempes
18-05	France	W 1-0	Paris	Fr	Kempes
22-05	England	D 2-2	London	Fr	Kempes 2
26-05	Holland	L 1-4	Amsterdam	Fr	Wolff
15-06	Poland	L 2-3	Stuttgart	WCr1	Heredia, Babington
19-06	Italy	D 1-1	Stuttgart	WCr1	Houseman
23-06	Haiti	W 4-1	Munich	WCr1	Yazalde 2, Houseman, Ayala
26-06	Holland	L 0-4	Gelsenkirchen	WCr2	
30-06	Brazil	L 1-2	Hanover	WCr2	Brindisi
3-07	East Germany	D 1-1	Gelsenkirchen	WCr2	Houseman
12-10	Spain	D 1-1	Buenos Aires	Fr	Rogel
6-11	Chile	W 2-0	Santiago	CDC	Lopez.J, Ferrero
20-11	Chile	D 1-1	Buenos Aires	CDC	Galletti
27-06-1975	Bolivia *	W 2-1	Cochabamba	Fr	
18-07	Uruguay	W 3-2	Montevideo	NC	Alonso, Valdano 2
3-08	Venezuela	W 5-1	Caracus	SCr1	Luque 3, Kempes, Ardiles
6-08	Brazil	L 1-2	Belo Horizonte	SCr1	Asad
10-08	Venezuela	W 11-0	Rosario	SCr1	Killer 3, Kempes 2, Gallego, Ardiles,Zanabria 2, Bóveda, Luque
16-08	Brazil	L 0-1	Rosario	SCr1	
21-08	United States	W 6-0	Mexico City	Fr	Ardiles 2, Cardemas, Coscia 2, Valencia
24-08	Costa Rica	W 2-0	Mexico City	Fr	
31-08	Mexico	D 1-1	Mexico City	Fr	Coscia
25-02-1976	Paraguay	W 3-2	Asuncion	CA	Scotta.H 3
27-02	Brazil	L 1-2	Buenos Aires	CA	Kempes
20-03	Soviet Union	W 1-0	Kiev	Fr	Kempes
24-03	Poland	W 2-1	Chorzow	Fr	Scotta.H, Houseman
27-03	Hungary	L 0-2	Budapest	Fr	
8-04	Uruguay	W 4-1	Buenos Aires	CA	Kempes 2, Luque, Scotta.H
28-04	Paraguay	D 2-2	Buenos Aires	CA	Kempes 2
19-05	Brazil	L 0-2	Rio de Janeiro	CA	
9-06	Uruguay	W 3-0	Montevideo	CA	Luque, Kempes, Houseman
13-10	Chile	W 2-0	Buenos Aires	CDC	Ardiles, Bertoni
28-10	Peru	W 3-1	Lima	RCC	Houseman 2, Passarella
10-11	Peru	W 1-0	Buenos Aires	RCC	Passarella
28-11	Soviet Union	D 0-0	Buenos Aires	Fr	
27-02-1977	Hungary	W 5-1	Buenos Aires	Fr	Bertoni 3, Luque 2
22-03	Iran	D 1-1	Madrid	Fr	Bertoni
29-05	Poland	W 3-1	Buenos Aires	Fr	Bertoni 2, Luque
5-06	West Germany	L 1-3	Buenos Aires	Fr	Passarella
12-06	England	D 1-1	Buenos Aires	Fr	Bertoni
18-06	Scotland	D 1-1	Buenos Aires	Fr	Passarella
26-06	France	D 0-0	Buenos Aires	Fr	
3-07	Yugoslavia	W 1-0	Buenos Aires	Fr	Passarella
12-07	East Germany	W 2-0	Buenos Aires	Fr	Houseman, Carrascosa
24-08	Paraguay	W 2-1	Buenos Aires	Fr	Luque 2
31-08	Paraguay	L 0-2	Asuncion	Fr	
4-03-1978	Uruguay	D 0-0	Mar del Plata	Fr	
19-03	Peru	W 2-1	Buenos Aires	RCC	Houseman, Pagnanini
23-03	Peru	W 3-1	Lima	RCC	Luque, Passarella, Houseman
29-03	Bulgaria	W 3-1	Buenos Aires	Fr	Gallego, Ortiz, Ardiles
5-04	Rumania	W 2-0	Buenos Aires	Fr	Passarella 2
19-04	Rep. Ireland *	W 3-1	Buenos Aires	Fr	Luque, Ortiz, Villa
25-04	Uruguay	L 0-2	Montevideo	Fr	
3-05	Uruguay	W 3-0	Buenos Aires	Fr	Luque, Ardiles, Alonso
2-06	Hungary	W 2-1	Buenos Aires	WCr1	Luque, Bertoni
6-06	France	W 2-1	Buenos Aires	WCr1	Passarella, Luque

10-06	Italy	L 0-1	Buenos Aires	WCr1	
14-06	Poland	W 2-0	Rosario	WCr2	Kempes 2
18-06	Brazil	D 0-0	Rosario	WCr2	
21-06	Peru	W 6-0	Rosario	WCr2	Kempes 2, Luque 2, Tarantini, Houseman
25-06	Holland	W 3-1	Buenos Aires	WCf	Kempes 2, Bertoni
25-04-1979	Bulgaria	W 2-1	Buenos Aires	Fr	Houseman, Passarella
22-05	Holland	D 0-0	Berne	Fr	Won 8-7p
26-05	Italy	D 2-2	Rome	Fr	Valencia, Passarella
29-05 *	Rep. Ireland	D 0-0	Dublin	Fr	
2-06	Scotland	W 3-1	Glasgow	Fr	Luque 2, Maradona
18-07	Bolivia	L 1-2	La Paz	SCr1	Lopez.C
2-08	Brazil	L 1-2	Rio de Janeiro	SCr1	Coscia
8-08	Bolivia	W 3-0	Buenos Aires	SCr1	Passarella, Gaspari, Maradona
23-08	Brazil	D 2-2	Buenos Aires	SCr1	Passarella, Diaz.R
12-09	West Germany	L 1-2	Berlin	Fr	Castro
16-09	Yugoslavia	L 2-4	Belgrade	Fr	Passarella, Diaz.R
13-05-1980	England	L 1-3	London	Fr	Passarella
16-05	Rep. Ireland	W 1-0	Dublin	Fr	Valencia
21-05	Austria	W 5-1	Vienna	Fr	Maradona 3, Santamaria, Luque
18-09	Chile	D 2-2	Mendoza	Fr	Valencia, Diaz.R
9-10	Bulgaria	W 2-0	Buenos Aires	Fr	Maradona, Diaz.R
12-10	Poland	W 2-1	Buenos Aires	Fr	Passarella, Maradona
15-10	Czechoslovakia	W 1-0	Buenos Aires	Fr	Diaz.R
4-12	Soviet Union	D 1-1	Mar del Plata	Fr	Maradona
16-12	Switzerland	W 5-0	Cordoba	Fr	Diaz.R, Luque, Valencia, Maradona, Passarella
1-01-1981	West Germany	W 2-1	Montevideo	ML	Passarella, Diaz.R
4-01	Brazil	D 1-1	Montevideo	ML	Maradona
28-10	Poland	L 1-2	Buenos Aires	Fr	Passarella
11-11	Czechoslovakia	D 1-1	Buenos Aires	Fr	Gallego
9-03-1982	Czechoslovakia	D 0-0	Mar del Plata	Fr	
24-03	West Germany	D 1-1	Buenos Aires	Fr	Calderon
14-04	Soviet Union	D 1-1	Buenos Aires	Fr	Diaz.R
5-05	Bulgaria	W 2-1	Buenos Aires	Fr	Diaz.R, Passarella
12-05	Rumania	W 1-0	Rosario	Fr	Diaz.R
13-06	Belgium	L 0-1	Barcelona	WCr1	
18-06	Hungary	W 4-1	Alicante	WCr1	Maradona 2, Bertoni, Ardiles
23-06	El Salvador	W 2-0	Alicante	WCr1	Passarella, Bertoni
29-06	Italy	L 1-2	Barcelona	WCr2	Passarella
2-07	Brazil	L 1-3	Barcelona	WCr2	Diaz.R
12-05-1983	Chile	D 2-2	Santiago	Fr	Alonso, Gareca
23-06	Chile	W 1-0	Buenos Aires	Fr	Morete
14-07	Paraguay	L 0-1	Asuncion	Fr	
21-07	Paraguay	D 0-0	Buenos Aires	Fr	
10-08	Ecuador	D 2-2	Quito	SCr1	Burruchaga 2
24-08	Brazil	W 1-0	Buenos Aires	SCr1	Gareca
7-09	Ecuador	D 2-2	Buenos Aires	SCr1	Ramos.V, Burruchaga
14-09	Brazil	D 0-0	Rio de Janeiro	SCr1	
14-01-1984	India	W 1-0	Calcutta	Fr	Gareca
17-01	Poland	D 1-1	Calcutta	Fr	Ponce
20-01	China	L 0-1	Calcutta	Fr	
17-06	Brazil	D 0-0	Sao Paulo	Fr	
18-07	Uruguay	L 0-1	Montevideo	Fr	
2-08	Uruguay	D 0-0	Buenos Aires	Fr	
24-08	Colombia	L 0-1	Bogota	Fr	
1-09	Switzerland	W 2-0	Berne	Fr	Ponce, Dertycia
5-09	Belgium	W 2-0	Brussels	Fr	Trobbiani, Ruggeri
12-09	West Germany	W 3-1	Dusseldorf	Fr	Ponce 2, OG
18-09	Mexico	D 1-1	Monterrey	Fr	Burruchaga
25-10	Mexico	D 1-1	Buenos Aires	Fr	Gareca
28-04-1985	Paraguay	L 0-1	Asuncion	Fr	
5-05	Brazil	L 1-2	Salvador	Fr	Burruchaga
9-05	Paraguay	D 1-1	Buenos Aires	Fr	Maradona
15-05	Chile	W 2-0	Buenos Aires	Fr	Maradona, Burruchaga
26-05	Venezuela	W 3-2	San Cristobal	WCq	Maradona 2, Passarella
2-06	Colombia	W 3-1	Bogota	WCq	Pasculli 2, Burruchaga
9-06	Venezuela	W 3-0	Buenos Aires	WCq	Russo, Clausen, Maradona
16-06	Colombia	W 1-0	Buenos Aires	WCq	Valdano
23-06	Peru	L 0-1	Lima	WCq	
30-06	Peru	D 2-2	Buenos Aires	WCq	Pasculli, Gareca
14-11	Mexico	D 1-1	Los Angeles	Fr	Maradona
17-11	Mexico	D 1-1	Puebla	Fr	Ruggeri

Date	Opponent	Result	Venue	Comp	Scorers
26-03-1986	France	L 0-2	Paris	Fr	
30-04	Norway	L 0-1	Oslo	Fr	
4-05	Israel	W 7-2	Tel Aviv	Fr	Almiron 3, Maradona 2, Borghi, Tapia
2-06	South Korea	W 3-1	Irappuato	WCr1	Valdano 2, Ruggeri
5-06	Italy	D 1-1	Puebla	WCr1	Maradona
10-06	Bulgaria	W 2-0	Mexico City	WCr1	Valdano, Burruchaga
16-06	Uruguay	W 1-0	Puebla	WCr2	Pasculli
22-06	England	W 2-1	Mexico City	WCqf	Maradona 2
25-06	Belgium	W 2-0	Mexico City	WCsf	Maradona 2
29-06	West Germany	W 3-2	Mexico City	WCf	Brown, Valdano, Burruchaga
10-06-1987	Italy	L 1-3	Zurich	Fr	Maradona
20-06	Paraguay	L 0-1	Buenos Aires	Fr	
27-06	Peru	D 1-1	Buenos Aires	SCr1	Maradona
2-07	Ecuador	W 3-0	Buenos Aires	SCr1	Maradona 2, Caniggia
9-07	Uruguay	L 0-1	Buenos Aires	SCsf	
11-07	Colombia	L 1-2	Buenos Aires	SC3p	Caniggia
16-12	West Germany	W 1-0	Buenos Aires	Fr	Burruchaga
31-03-1988	Soviet Union	L 2-4	Berlin	Fr	Troglio, Maradona
2-04	West Germany	L 0-1	Berlin	Fr	
6-07	Saudi Arabia	D 2-2	Adelaide	Fr	Diaz.R 2
10-07	Brazil	D 0-0	Melbourne	Fr	
14-07	Australia	L 1-4	Sydney	Fr	Ruggeri
16-07	Saudi Arabia	W 2-0	Canbera	Fr	Simeone, Dertifcia
12-10	Spain	D 1-1	Seville	Fr	Caniggia
9-03-1989	Colombia	L 0-1	Barranquilla	Fr	
13-04	Ecuador	D 2-2	Guayaquil	Fr	Moreno 2
20-04	Chile	D 1-1	Santiago	Fr	Airez
2-07	Chile	W 1-0	Goiania	SCr1	Caniggia
4-07	Ecuador	D 0-0	Goiania	SCr1	
8-07	Uruguay	W 1-0	Goiania	SCr1	Caniggia
10-07	Bolivia	D 0-0	Goiania	SCr1	
12-07	Brazil	L 0-2	Rio de Janeiro	SCr2	
14-07	Uruguay	L 0-2	Rio de Janeiro	SCr2	
16-07	Paraguay	D 0-0	Rio de Janeiro	SCr2	
21-12	Italy	D 0-0	Cagliari	Fr	
14-01-1990	Guatemala *	D 0-0	Guatemala	Fr	
17-01	Mexico	L 0-2	Los Angeles	Fr	
28-03	Scotland	L 0-1	Glasgow	Fr	
3-05	Austria	D 1-1	Vienna	Fr	Burruchaga
8-05	Switzerland	D 1-1	Berne	Fr	Balbo
22-05	Israel	W 2-1	Tel Aviv	Fr	Maradona, Caniggia
8-06	Cameroon	L 0-1	Milan	WCr1	
13-06	Soviet Union	W 2-0	Naples	WCr1	Troglio, Burruchaga
18-06	Rumania	D 1-1	Naples	WCr1	Monzon
24-06	Brazil	W 1-0	Turin	WCr2	Caniggia
30-06	Yugoslavia	D 0-0	Florence	WCqf	Won 3-2 pens
3-07	Italy	D 1-1	Naples	WCsf	Caniggia Won 4-3 pens
8-07	West Germany	L 0-1	Rome	WCf	
19-02-1991	Hungary	W 2-0	Rosario	Fr	Franco, Mohamed
13-03	Mexico	D 0-0	Buenos Aires	Fr	
27-03	Brazil	D 3-3	Buenos Aires	Fr	Ferreyra, Franco, Bisconti
19-05	USA	W 1-0	Palo Alto	Fr	Franco
23-05	Soviet Union	D 1-1	Manchester	Fr	Ruggeri
25-05	England	D 2-2	London	Fr	Garcia, Franco
27-06	Brazil	D 1-1	Curitiba	Fr	Caniggia
8-07	Venezuela	W 3-0	Santiago	SCr1	Batistuta 2, Caniggia
10-07	Chile	W 1-0	Santiago	SCr1	Batistuta
12-07	Paraguay	W 4-1	Concepcion	SCr1	Batistuta, Simeone, Astrada, Caniggia
14-07	Peru	W 3-2	Santiago	SCr1	Latorre, Craviotto, Garcia
17-07	Brazil	W 3-2	Santiago	SCr2	Franco 2, Batistuta
19-07	Chile	D 0-0	Santiago	SCr2	
21-07	Colombia	W 2-1	Santiago	SCr2	Simeone, Batistuta
31-05-1992	Japan	W 1-0	Tokyo	Fr	Batistuta
3-06	Wales	W 1-0	Gifu	Fr	Batistuta
18-06	Australia	W 2-0	Buenos Aires	Fr	Batistuta
23-09	Uruguay	D 0-0	Montevideo	Fr	
16-10	Côte d'Ivoire	W 4-0	Riyadh	ICr1	Batistuta 2, Altamirano, Acosta
20-10	Saudi Arabia	W 3-1	Riyadh	ICf	Rodriguez, Caniggia, Simeone
26-11	Poland	W 2-0	Buenos Aires	Fr	Craviotto, Medina Bello
18-02-1993	Brazil	D 1-1	Buenos Aires	Fr	Mancuso
24-02	Denmark	D 1-1	Mar del Plata	AFT	Caniggia. Won 5-4 pens

17-06	Bolivia	W 1-0	Guayaquil	SCr1	Batistuta
20-06	Mexico	D 1-1	Guayaquil	SCr1	Ruggeri
23-06	Colombia	D 1-1	Guayaquil	SCr1	Simeone
27-06	Brazil	D 1-1	Guayaquil	SCqf	Rodriguez.L. Won 6-5p
1-07	Colombia	D 0-0	Guayaquil	SCsf	Won 6-5p
4-07	Mexico	W 2-1	Guayaquil	SCf	Batistuta 2
1-08	Peru	W 1-0	Lima	WCq	Batistuta
8-08	Paraguay	W 3-1	Asuncion	WCq	Medina Bello 2, Redondo
15-08	Colombia	L 1-2	Barranquilla	WCq	Medina Bello
22-08	Peru	W 2-1	Buenos Aires	WCq	Batistuta, Medina Bello
29-08	Paraguay	D 0-0	Buenos Aires	WCq	
5-09	Colombia	L 0-5	Buenos Aires	WCq	
31-10	Australia	W 1-0	Sydney	WCq	Balbo
17-11	Australia	W 1-0	Buenos Aires	WCq	OG
15-12	Germany	W 2-1	Miami	Fr	Diaz.H, Balbo
23-02-1994	Brazil	L 0-2	Recife	Fr	
20-04	Morocco	W 3-1	Salta	Fr	Balbo, Maradona, Perez.H
18-05	Chile	D 3-3	Santiago	Fr	Chamot, Balbo, Ruggeri
31-05	Israel	W 3-0	Tel Aviv	Fr	Batistuta 2, Caniggia
4-06	Croatia	D 0-0	Zagreb	Fr	
21-06	Greece	W 4-0	Boston	WCr1	Batistuta 3, Maradona
26-06	Nigeria	W 2-1	Boston	WCr1	Caniggia 2
30-06	Bulgaria	L 0-2	Dallas	WCr1	
3-07	Romania	L 2-3	Los Angeles	WCr2	Batistuta, Balbo
16-11	Chile	W 3-0	Santiago	Fr	Rambert, Espina, Escudero
21-12	Romania	W 1-0	Buenos Aires	Fr	Perez.H
27-12	Yugoslavia	W 1-0	Buenos Aires	Fr	Rambert
8-01-1995	Japan	W 5-1	Riyadh	ICr1	Rambert, Ortega.A, Batistuta 2, Chamot
10-01	Nigeria	D 0-0	Riyadh	ICr1	
13-01	Denmark	L 0-2	Riyadh	ICf	
15-02	Bulgaria	W 4-1	Mendoza	Fr	Gallardo 2, Rambert 2
13-05	South Africa	D 1-1	Johannesburg	Fr	Gallardo
31-05	Peru	W 1-0	Cordoba	Fr	Fabbri
14-06	Paraguay	W 2-1	Rosario	Fr	Berti, Acosta
22-06	Slovakia	W 6-0	Mendoza	Fr	Gallardo 2, Batistuta 2, Zanetti, Simeone
30-06	Australia	W 2-0	Buenos Aires	Fr	Balbo, Batistuta
8-07	Bolivia	W 2-1	Paysandu	SCr1	Batistuta, Balbo
11-07	Chile	W 4-0	Paysandu	SCr1	Batistuta 2, Simeone, Balbo
14-07	United States	L 0-3	Paysandu	SCr1	
17-07	Brazil	D 2-2 2-4p	Rivera	SCqf	Balbo, Batistuta

BOLIVIA

Bolivia are on the lowest rung of the South American ladder, but have the pleasure of knowing that they have at least taken part in three World Cup final tournaments and in 1963 were crowned South American champions, a feat that not even Chile or Colombia can boast of.

A Chilean, Leoncio Zuaznabar, founded the first club in Bolivia, Oruro Royal Club in 1896, but the game spread slowly throughout the rest of the country. The major cities are mostly located in the mountains of the Andes, so perhaps the slow growth is not surprising. The Federación Boliviana de Fútbol was formed in Cochabamba in 1925 and the following year it launched a national championship for representative sides, but the real power lay high up in the mountains in the capital La Paz.

In 1908 The Strongest were formed, and they remain the oldest senior club. Six years later the La Paz league was founded and it came to be regarded as the national league. Until clubs from outside La Paz were invited to take part in the league in the early 1950s, it was dominated by The Strongest and Bolivar. Since that time, however, clubs from Cochabamba and Santa Cruz have begun to make their mark, especially Jorge Wilsterman and Oriente Petrolero.

A major reorganisation took place in 1977 with the formation of a truly national league for the first time to replace the Campeonato Professional de Fútbol, as the La Paz league had become known. The standard has remained fairly low overall as the record in the Copa Libertadores shows: three semi-final appearances is equal to that of Venezuela, and together they stand at the bottom of overall standings in the competition.

The national side made its debut in the 1926 South American Championships but it was not an auspicious introduction to international football. Two goals were scored and 24 conceded in the four matches played. The experience the following year was not dissimilar, and the 19 goals against in three matches effectively put an end to their participation until 1945. The lure of the 1930 World Cup in Uruguay was too hard to resist, though, and surprisingly the games against Brazil and Yugoslavia were not the heavy defeats many expected them to be. Bolivia lost

4-0 on both occasions, results that were better than all bar one of their scores in the previous South American Championship excursions.

Entry into the Bolivarian Games in 1938, in which they finished an encouraging second to Peru, was followed by four successive appearances in the South American Championships in the 1940s. As expected the results were not good to start with but in the 1949 tournamment in Brazil, the Bolivians finished an astonishing fourth out of the eight entries. Victories over Chile, Uruguay, Ecuador and Colombia gave Bolivia real hope for the World Cup the following year in the same country. But any thoughts of a repeat victory over Uruguay, their only first round opponents, were quickly dashed by an 8-0 thrashing. Undeterred, Bolivia entered the 1953 South American Championships in Lima and spoilt the party by beating the hosts in the opening game, but it was downhill from then on and they finished next from bottom. Since then the national side has regularly taken part in the tournaments open to them.

ORDER OF MERIT

		Total			La P	Nat	Copa Lib		
		G	S	B	G	G	G	S	B
1	Bolivar	21	-	1	8	13	-	-	1
2	The Strongest	18	-	-	12	6	-	-	-
3	Jorge Wilsterman	8	-	1	-	8	-	-	1
4	Oriente Petrolero	3	-	-	-	3	-	-	-
5	Universitario	2	-	-	1	1	-	-	-
	Always Ready	2	-	-	1	1	-	-	-
	Deportivo Municipal	2	-	-	-	2	-	-	-
8	Blooming	1	-	1	-	1	-	-	1
9	Aurora	1	-	-	-	1	-	-	-
	Ayacucho	1	-	-	1	-	-	-	-
	Colegio Militar	1	-	-	1	-	-	-	-
	Chaco Petrolero	1	-	-	-	1	-	-	-
	Deportivo Militar	1	-	-	1	-	-	-	-
	Ferroviario	1	-	-	1	-	-	-	-
	Guabira	1	-	-	-	1	-	-	-
	Litoral	1	-	-	1	-	-	-	-
	Nimbles Sport	1	-	-	1	-	-	-	-
	Nimbles Rail	1	-	-	1	-	-	-	-
	San Jose Oruro	1	-	-	-	1	-	-	-

To the end of the 1994 season

The World Cup, in particular, has always been a favoured hunting ground. Bolivia's overall record is good because of one overwhelming advantage, the altitude of La Paz. Situated at over 12,000 feet above sea level, La Paz is the highest capital city in the world. The advantage to the Bolivian players, who are used to the thin air, is enormous, and they have used this to great effect in the World Cup. Argentina and Chile were beaten in 1957 and since then, had it not been for a poor away record, the world would have seen a lot more of the Bolivians than they have done. In 1993 they created history by beating Brazil in La Paz, the first time the Brazilians had ever lost a World Cup qualifier, and went on to win all of the qualifying matches in La Paz to reach the finals for only the third time. Outside of their fortress they were eventually brought down to earth, but not before gaining their first point and scoring their first goal in the finals.

The 1963 South American Championship, held in La Paz and Cochabamba, was another occasion on which Bolivia used the conditions to their advantage, as they won their only title to date. Although not as high as La Paz, at 8,000 feet altitude is still a significant factor in Cochabamba. Víctor Ugarte, captain of the side and the most famous Bolivian footballer of all time, utilised this as he led his team on an extraordinary run of results culminating in a 5-4 win over the Brazilians in Cochabamba.

Whenever a tournament involves the Bolivians playing at home, they are always in with a shout. They finished above Argentina in the 1970 World Cup qualifiers, won their group in 1978, finishing above Uruguay only to lose to Hungary in a play-off, and in 1979 beat both Brazil and Argentina at home in the South American Championship only to lose to both of them away and finish a point behind Brazil at the end. It is noticeable that their performances in this tournament improved when it was held on a home and away basis from 1975 until 1983 and have slumped again since it reverted back to single country location. If Bolivia are to win another tournament it is essential they persuade CONMEBOL that La Paz is just the place to spend two weeks in the South American winter!

Population: 7,322,000
Area, sq km: 1,098,581
% in urban areas: 50%
Capital city: La Paz

Federación Boliviana de Fútbol
Avda. 16 de Julio #782
Casilla Postal 484
Cochabamba
Bolivia
Tel: + 591 42 45889
Fax: + 591 42 82132

Year of formation	1925
Affiliation to FIFA	1926
Affiliation to CSF	1926
Registered clubs	305
Registered players	15 200
Professional players	300
Registered referees	322
National stadium	Estadio Nacional Olimpico de Hernándo Siles 55 000
National colours	Green/White/Green
Reserve colours	White/White/Green
Season	February - December (1st stage Feb - Sep, 2nd Sep - Dec)

THE RECORD

WORLD CUP

1930	QT Automatic - Final Tournament/1st round
1934	Did not enter
1938	Did not enter
1950	QT W-O in group 7 - Final Tournament/1st round
1954	Did not enter
1958	QT 2nd/3 in group 2
1962	QT 2nd/2 in group 2
1966	QT 3rd/3 in group 3
1970	QT 2nd/3 in group 1
1974	QT 3rd/3 in group 2
1978	QT 1st/3 in group 2
1982	QT 2nd/3 in group 1
1986	QT 3rd/3 in group 3
1990	QT 2nd/3 in group 1
1994	QT 2nd/5 in group 2 - Final Tournament/1st round

SOUTH AMERICAN CHAMPIONSHIP

1910-25	-

1926	5/5
1927	4/4
1929-42	-
1945	6/7
1946	6/6
1947	7/8
1949	4/8
1953	6/7
1955-57	-
1959	7/7
1959	-
1963	1/7 - Winners
1967	6/6
1975	8/10 - 1st round
1979	7/10 - 1st round
1983	8/10 - 1st round
1987	7/10 - 1st round
1989	9/10 - 1st round
1991	9/10 - 1st round
1993	11/12 - 1st round
1995	5=/12 - Quarter-finalists

SOUTH AMERICAN CLUB TOURNAMENTS

Copa Libertadores
Semi-finalists - Jorge Wilsterman 1981, Blooming 1985, Bolivar 1986
Super Copa
Ineligible to compete
CONMEBOL Cup
1st round - Oriente Petrolero 1992 1994

CLUB DIRECTORY

LA PAZ (Pop. - 992,000)

Bolivar Independiente Unificada (1925)
Estadio Nacional Olimpico de Hernándo Siles 55,000 – Sky blue, white trim

Club Deportivo Chaco Petrolero (1944)
Estadio Nacional Olimpico de Hernándo Siles 55,000 – Green & white stripes/White

Deportivo Municipal (1944)
Luis Lastra 10,000 – Maroon/White, green & white trim

The Strongest (1908)
'Achumani' Rafael Mendoza Castellon 40,000 – Yellow & black stripes/Black

Club Always Ready
'Achumani' Rafael Mendoza Castellon 40,000 – White with red sash/Black

Club Litoral
'Achumani' Rafael Mendoza Castellon 40,000 – Red, green & white stripes/White

Club 31 de Octubre
White with '31' on chest/White, green trim

Club Universitario
Estadio Nacional Olimpico de Hernándo Siles 55,000 – Blue, red & white trim

SANTA CRUZ DE LA SIERRA (Pop. - 441,000)

Club Blooming (1946)
Ramon 'Tahuichi' Aguilera Costas 40,000 – Sky blue/White

Club Destroyers (1948)
Ramon 'Tahuichi' Aguilera Costas 40,000 – Yellow/Blue

Club Guabira (1962)
Ramon 'Tahuichi' Aguilera Costas 40,000 – Red, blue trim

Club Oriente Petrolero (1955)
Ramon 'Tahuichi' Aguilera Costas 40,000 – Green/White

Club Real Santa Cruz (1962)
Ramon 'Tahuichi' Aguilera Costas 40,000 – White/White

COCHABAMBA (Pop. - 317,000)

Club Aurora (1935)
Félix Capriles 35,000 – Sky blue/White

Club Jorge Wilsterman (1949)
Félix Capriles 35,000 – Red/Blue

Club Petrolero (1950)
Félix Capriles 35,000 – Red & white stripes/Black

Club ORCOBOL
Félix Capriles 35,000 – Yellow & blue stripes/Blue

ORURO (Pop. - 187,000)

Club San José
Jesus Bermudez 'Monumental' 40,000 – White with sky blue 'V' /Sky blue

POTOSÍ (Pop. - 113,000)

Club Universitario
San Clemente – Blue with red sleeves/Blue

SUCRE (population - 86,000)

Club Independiente Petrolero
Estadio 'Patria del Morro' de Surapata – White, red trim

TARIJA (Pop. - 58,000)

Club Ciclon de la Pampa
Estadio IV Centenario – Sky blue & white stripes/Black

TRINIDAD (Pop. - 51,000)

Club Real Beni
Estadio Departmental – Green shirts with 2 white hoops/White

BOLIVIAN LEAGUE CHAMPIONS

LA PAZ LEAGUE

1914	The Strongest
1915	Colegio Militar
1916	The Strongest
1917	The Strongest
1918-21	-
1922	The Strongest
1923	The Strongest
1924	The Strongest
1925	The Strongest
1926	-
1927	Nimbles Sport
1928	Deportivo Militar
1929	Universitario La Paz
1930	The Strongest
1931	Nimbles Rail
1932	Bolivar
1933-34	-
1935	The Strongest
1936	Ayacucho
1937	Bolivar
1938	The Strongest
1939	Bolivar
1940	Bolivar
1941	Bolivar
1942	Bolivar
1943	The Strongest
1944	Ferroviario
1945-49	-
1950	Bolivar
1951	Always Ready
1952	The Strongest
1953	Bolivar

TORNEO INTEGRADA (La Paz, Cochabamba and Oruro)

1954	Litoral
1955	San José Oruro
1956	Bolivar
1957	Always Ready

TORNEO NACIONAL

1958	Jorge Wilsterman
1959	Jorge Wilsterman
1960	Jorge Wilsterman
1961	Deportivo Municipal
1962	-
1963	Aurora
1964	The Strongest
1965	Deportivo Municipal
1966	Bolivar
1967	Jorge Wilsterman
1968	Bolivar
1969	Universitario La Paz
1970	Chaco Petrolero
1971	Oriente Petrolero
1972	Jorge Wilsterman
1973	Jorge Wilsterman
1974	The Strongest
1975	Guabira
1976	Bolivar

LIGA PROFESIONAL

1977	The Strongest
1978	Bolivar
1979	Oriente Petrolero
1980	Jorge Wilsterman
1981	Jorge Wilsterman
1982	Bolivar
1983	Bolivar
1984	Blooming
1985	Bolivar
1986	The Strongest
1987	Bolivar
1988	Bolivar
1989	The Strongest
1990	Oriente Petrolero
1991	Bolivar
1992	Bolivar
1993	The Strongest
1994	Bolivar

INTERNATIONAL MATCHES PLAYED BY BOLIVIA

Date	Opponent	Result	Venue	Comp	Scorers
12-10-1926	Chile	L 1-7	Santiago	SC	Aguilar
16-10	Argentina	L 0-5	Santiago	SC	
23-10	Paraguay	L 1-6	Santiago	SC	Soto
28-10	Uruguay	L 0-6	Santiago	SC	
30-10-1927	Argentina	L 1-7	Lima	SC	Algorta
6-11	Uruguay	L 0-9	Lima	SC	
13-11	Peru	L 2-3	Lima	SC	Bustamente 2
17-07-1930	Yugoslavia	L 0-4	Montevideo	WCr1	
22-07	Brazil	L 0-4	Montevideo	WCr1	
8-08-1938	Ecuador	D 1-1	Bogota	BG	
11-08	Venezuela	W 3-1	Bogota	BG	
13-08	Peru	L 0-3	Bogota	BG	
16-08	Colombia	W 2-1	Bogota	BG	
22-08	Ecuador	W 2-1	Bogota	BG	
18-01-1945	Argentina	L 0-4	Santiago	SC	
24-01	Chile	L 0-5	Santiago	SC	
28-01	Brazil	L 0-2	Santiago	SC	
11-02	Ecuador	D 0-0	Santiago	SC	
15-02	Uruguay	L 0-2	Santiago	SC	
21-02	Colombia	D 3-3	Santiago	SC	Orozco, Romero, Fernandez
16-01-1946	Brazil	L 0-3	Buenos Aires	SC	
19-01	Argentina	L 1-7	Buenos Aires	SC	Peredo
26-01	Paraguay	L 2-4	Buenos Aires	SC	OG, Ortega
29-01	Uruguay	L 0-5	Buenos Aires	SC	
8-02	Chile	L 1-4	Buenos Aires	SC	OG
30-11-1947	Ecuador	D 2-2	Guayaquil	SC	Gutiérrez 2
4-12	Argentina	L 0-7	Guayaquil	SC	
9-12	Uruguay	L 0-3	Guayaquil	SC	
13-12	Colombia	D 0-0	Guayaquil	SC	
18-12	Paraguay	L 1-3	Guayaquil	SC	Tapia
27-12	Peru	L 0-2	Guayaquil	SC	
31-12	Chile	L 3-4	Guayaquil	SC	Tapia 2, Orgaz
5-01-1948	Venezuela	D 2-2	Lima	Fr	
6-04-1949	Chile	W 3-2	Sao Paulo	SC	Mena, Algañaraz, Godoy.B
10-04	Brazil	L 1-10	Sao Paulo	SC	Ugarte
17-04	Uruguay	W 3-2	Rio de Janeiro	SC	Ugarte, Algañarez, Gutiérrez
24-04	Ecuador	W 2-0	Sao Paulo	SC	Algañarez, Mena
27-04	Peru	L 0-3	Santos	SC	
30-04	Paraguay	L 0-7	Rio de Janeiro	SC	
6-05	Colombia	W 4-0	Rio de Janeiro	SC	Godoy 3, Ugarte
26-02-1950	Chile	W 2-0	La Paz	WCq	
12-03	Chile	L 0-5	Santiago	WCq	
2-07	Uruguay	L 0-8	Belo Horizonte	WCr1	
22-02-1953	Peru	W 1-0	Lima	SC	OG
25-02	Uruguay	L 0-2	Lima	SC	
1-03	Brazil	L 1-8	Lima	SC	Ugarte
8-03	Ecuador	D 1-1	Lima	SC	Alcón
16-03	Paraguay	L 1-2	Lima	SC	Ugarte
28-03	Chile	D 2-2	Lima	SC	Brown, Alcón
6-06-1957	Paraguay	L 2-5	Asuncion	PDC	
13-06	Paraguay	W 1-0	Asuncion	PDC	
18-08	Paraguay	D 3-3	La Paz	PDC	
21-08	Paraguay	W 2-1	La Paz	PDC	
22-09	Chile	L 1-2	Santiago	WCq	Brown
29-09	Chile	W 3-0	La Paz	WCq	Brown, Ugarte, Garcia
6-10	Argentina	W 2-0	La Paz	WCq	Alcócer, Ramirez
27-10	Argentina	L 0-4	Buenos Aires	WCq	
8-03-1959	Uruguay	L 0-7	Buenos Aires	SC	
11-03	Argentina	L 0-2	Buenos Aires	SC	
15-03	Paraguay	L 0-5	Buenos Aires	SC	
21-03	Brazil	L 2-4	Buenos Aires	SC	Garcia, Alcón
26-03	Chile	L 2-5	Buenos Aires	SC	Alcócer 2
29-03	Peru	D 0-0	Buenos Aires	SC	
15-07-1961	Uruguay	D 1-1	La Paz	WCq	Alcócer
30-07	Uruguay	L 1-2	Montevideo	WCq	Camacho
10-08-1962	Paraguay	W 3-1	Cochabamba	PDC	
12-08	Paraguay	W 3-2	La Paz	PDC	

Date	Opponent	Result	Venue	Comp	Scorers
17-02-1963	Paraguay	L 0-3	Asuncion	PDC	
19-02	Paraguay	L 1-5	Asuncion	PDC	
10-03	Ecuador	D 4-4	La Paz	SC	Lopez, Castillo, Camacho, Alcócer
17-03	Colombia	W 2-1	Cochabamba	SC	Alcócer, Castillo
21-03	Peru	W 3-2	La Paz	SC	Camacho, Alcócer, Garcia
24-03	Paraguay	W 2-0	Cochabamba	SC	Castillo, Garcia
28-03	Argentina	W 3-2	La Paz	SC	Castillo, Blacutt, Camacho
31-03	Brazil	W 5-4	Cochabamba	SC	Ugarte 2, Camacho, Garcia, Alcócer
25-07-1965	Paraguay	L 0-2	Asuncion	WCq	
17-08	Argentina	L 1-4	Buenos Aires	WCq	Vargas
22-08	Paraguay	W 2-1	La Paz	WCq	Ramirez, Castillo
29-08	Argentina	L 1-2	La Paz	WCq	OG
17-01-1967	Uruguay	L 0-4	Montevideo	SC	
22-01	Argentina	L 0-1	Montevideo	SC	
25-01	Paraguay	L 0-1	Montevideo	SC	
28-01	Venezuela	L 0-3	Montevideo	SC	
1-02	Chile	D 0-0	Montevideo	SC	
27-07-1969	Argentina	W 3-1	La Paz	WCq	Diaz, Blacutt, Alvarez
10-08	Peru	W 2-1	La Paz	WCq	Alvarez, OG
17-08	Peru	L 0-3	Lima	WCq	
24-08	Argentina	L 0-1	Buenos Aires	WCq	
15-08-1971	Chile *	L 3-4	La Paz	Fr	
11-06-1972	Peru	L 0-3	Curitiba	Clr1	
18-06	Yugoslavia	D 1-1	Campo Grande	Clr1	Pariente
21-06	Venezuela	D 2-2	Manaus	Clr1	
25-06	Paraguay	L 1-6	Manaus	Clr1	
24-03-1973	Peru	L 0-2	Lima	Fr	
31-03	Paraguay	D 1-1	La Paz	Fr	
29-04	Ecuador	D 3-3	La Paz	Fr	
6-05	Ecuador	D 0-0	Quito	Fr	
27-05	Brazil	L 0-5	Rio de Janeiro	Fr	
15-07	Peru	W 2-0	La Paz	Fr	
24-07	Chile	L 0-3	Santiago	Fr	
2-09	Paraguay	L 1-2	La Paz	WCq	Morales
9-09	Argentina	L 0-4	Buenos Aires	WCq	
23-09	Argentina	L 0-1	La Paz	WCq	
30-09	Paraguay	L 0-4	Asuncion	WCq	
27-06-1975	Argentina *	L 1-2	Cochabamba	Fr	
7-07	Paraguay	L 1-2	Cochabamba	Fr	
9-07	Ecuador	W 1-0	Cochabamba	Fr	
20-07	Chile	W 2-1	La Paz	SCr1	Mezza 2
27-07	Peru	L 0-1	Oruro	SCr1	
7-08	Peru	L 1-3	Lima	SCr1	Mezza
13-08	Chile	L 0-4	Santiago	SCr1	
6-02-1977	Paraguay	L 0-1	La Paz	PDC	
9-02	Paraguay	D 2-2	La Paz	PDC	
27-02	Uruguay	W 1-0	La Paz	WCq	Jiminez
6-03	Venezuela	W 3-1	Caracas	WCq	Mezza, Jiminez, Aguilar
13-03	Venezuela	W 2-0	La Paz	WCq	Jiminez, Aragones
27-03	Uruguay	D 2-2	Montevideo	WCq	Aguilar 2
12-06	Poland	L 1-2	La Paz	Fr	Jiminez
14-07	Brazil	L 0-8	Cali	WCq	
17-07	Peru	L 0-5	Cali	WCq	
29-10	Hungary	L 0-6	Budapest	WCq	
30-11	Hungary	L 2-3	La Paz	WCq	Aragones 2
10-07-1979	Paraguay	W 3-1	La Paz	PDC	
12-07	Paraguay	D 1-1	Cochabamba	Fr	
18-07	Argentina	W 2-1	La Paz	SCr1	Reynaldo 2
26-07	Brazil	W 2-1	La Paz	SCr1	Aragones 2
1-08	Paraguay	L 0-2	Asuncion	PDC	
8-08	Argentina	L 0-3	Buenos Aires	SCr1	
16-08	Brazil	L 0-2	Sao Paulo	SCr1	
2-07-1980	Poland	L 0-1	Santa Cruz	Fr	
26-08	Paraguay	D 1-1	La Paz	PDC	
28-08	Paraguay	L 1-3	Santa Cruz	Fr	
18-09	Paraguay	L 1-2	Asuncion	PDC	
9-11	Uruguay	L 1-3	Cochabamba	Fr	
30-11	Finland	W 3-0	La Paz	Fr	Aguilar, Paniagua, Del Llano
4-12	Finland	D 2-2	Santa Cruz	Fr	Paniagua, Aguilar
11-12	Uruguay	L 0-5	Montevideo	Fr	

25-01-1981	Czechoslovakia *	W 2-1	La Paz	Fr	
29-01	Czechoslovakia *	L 2-5	Santa Cruz	Fr	
1-02	Bulgaria	L 1-3	La Paz	Fr	Aragones
15-02	Venezuela	W 3-0	La Paz	WCq	Aguilar, Aragones, Reynaldo
22-02	Brazil	L 1-2	La Paz	WCq	Aragones
15-03	Venezuela	L 0-1	Caracas	WCq	
22-03	Brazil	L 1-3	Rio de Janeiro	WCq	Aragones
19-07-1983	Chile	L 1-2	La Paz	Fr	
3-08	Paraguay	W 2-1	La Paz	Fr	
5-08	Paraguay	L 1-3	Santa Cruz	Fr	
14-08	Colombia	L 0-1	La Paz	SCr1	
21-08	Peru	D 1-1	La Paz	SCr1	Romero
24-08	Chile	L 2-4	Arica	Fr	
31-08	Colombia	D 2-2	Bogota	SCr1	Melgar, Rojas
4-09	Peru	L 1-2	Lima	SCr1	Paniagua
3-02-1985	East Germany	W 2-1	La Paz	Fr	Antelo, Romero
6-02	Uruguay	L 0-1	Cochabamba	Fr	
17-02	Peru	L 0-3	Lima	Fr	
21-02	Ecuador	L 0-3	Quito	Fr	
24-02	Venezuela	L 0-5	Caracas	Fr	
21-04	Venezuela	W 4-0	Santa Cruz	Fr	
1-05	Peru	D 0-0	Santa Cruz	Fr	
26-05	Paraguay	D 1-1	Santa Cruz	WCq	Rojas
2-06	Brazil	L 0-2	Santa Cruz	WCq	
9-06	Paraguay	L 0-3	Asuncion	WCq	
30-06	Brazil	D 1-1	Sao Paulo	WCq	Sanchez
14-06-1987	Paraguay	L 0-2	Santa Cruz	Fr	
23-06	Uruguay	L 1-2	Montevideo	Fr	Rojas
28-06	Paraguay	D 0-0	Rosario	SCr1	
1-07	Colombia	L 0-2	Rosario	SCr1	
25-05-1989	Paraguay	W 3-2	Cochabamba	Fr	Pena, Garcia 2
1-06	Paraguay	L 0-2	Asuncion	Fr	
8-06	Uruguay	D 0-0	Santa Cruz	Fr	
14-06	Uruguay	L 0-1	Montevideo	Fr	
22-06	Chile	L 0-1	La Paz	Fr	
27-06	Chile	L 1-2	Santiago	Fr	Garcia
4-07	Uruguay	L 0-3	Goiania	SCr1	
6-07	Ecuador	D 0-0	Goiania	SCr1	
8-07	Chile	L 0-5	Goiania	SCr1	
10-07	Argentina	D 0-0	Goiania	SCr1	
20-08	Peru	W 2-1	La Paz	WCq	Melgar, Ramallo
3-09	Uruguay	W 2-1	La Paz	WCq	OG, Pena
10-09	Peru	W 2-1	Lima	WCq	Ramallo, Sanchez
17-09	Uruguay	L 0-2	Montevideo	WCq	
14-06-1991	Paraguay	L 0-1	Santa Cruz	PDC	
16-06	Paraguay	D 0-0	Asuncion	PDC	
7-07	Uruguay	D 1-1	Valparaiso	SCr1	Suarez
9-07	Brazil	L 1-2	Viña del Mar	SCr1	Sanchez
11-07	Colombia	D 0-0	Viña del Mar	SCr1	
13-07	Ecuador	L 0-4	Viña del Mar	SCr1	
29-01-1993	Honduras	W 3-1	Cochabamba	Fr	Quinteros 2, Villaroel
3-03	Paraguay	L 0-1	Asuncion	Fr	
6-03	Paraguay	W 2-1	Cochabamba	Fr	Moreno, Rios
12-03	El Salvador	D 2-2	San Salvador	Fr	Villaroel, Castillo
14-03	Honduras	D 0-0	San Pedro Sula	Fr	
16-03	Honduras	D 0-0	Tegucigalpa	Fr	
31-03	Chile	L 1-2	Arica	Fr	Rios
23-05	USA	D 0-0	Fullerton	Fr	
6-06	Peru	L 0-1	Lima	Fr	
13-06	Chile	L 1-3	La Paz	Fr	Sandy
17-06	Argentina	L 0-1	Guayaquil	SCr1	
20-06	Colombia	D 1-1	Machala	SCr1	Etcheverry
23-06	Mexico	D 0-0	Guayaquil	SCr1	
18-07	Venezuela	W 7-1	Caracas	WCq	Sanchez 3, Ramallo 3, Cristaldo
25-07	Brazil	W 2-0	La Paz	WCq	Etcheverry, Pena
8-08	Uruguay	W 3-1	La Paz	WCq	Sanchez, Etcheverry, Melgar
15-08	Ecuador	W 1-0	La Paz	WCq	Ramallo
22-08	Venezuela	W 7-0	La Paz	WCq	Ramallo, Melgar 2, Sanchez, Sandy, Etcheverry 2
29-08	Brazil	L 0-6	Recife	WCq	
12-09	Uruguay	L 1-2	Montevideo	WCq	Ramallo

19-09	Ecuador	D 1-1	Guayaquil	WCq	Ramallo
18-02-1994	USA	D 1-1	Miami	Fr	Moreno
20-02	Colombia	L 0-2	Miami	Fr	
26-03	USA	D 2-2	Dallas	Fr	Baldivieso, Pinedo
7-04	Colombia	W 1-0	Villavicencio	Fr	Pinedo
20-04	Romania	L 0-3	Bucharest	Fr	
4-05	Saudi Arabia	W 1-0	Cannes	Fr	Sanchez
11-05	Cameroon	D 1-1	Athens	Fr	Pena
13-05	Greece	D 0-0	Athens	Fr	
19-05	Iceland	L 0-1	Reykjavik	Fr	
24-05	Rep. Ireland	L 0-1	Dublin	Fr	
8-06	Peru	D 0-0	Santa Cruz	Fr	
11-06	Switzerland	D 0-0	Montreal	Fr	
17-06	Germany	L 0-1	Chicago	WCr1	
23-06	South Korea	D 0-0	Boston	WCr1	
27-06	Spain	L 1-3	Chicago	WCr1	Sanchez
21-09	Chile	W 2-1	Santiago	Fr	Ramallo, Pinedo
14-05-1995	Paraguay	D 1-1	Cochabamba	PDC	Melgar
9-06	Paraguay	D 0-0	Asuncion	PDC	Lost 3-4p
18-06	Venezuela	W 3-1	Valera	Fr	Cristaldo, Angola, Baldivieso
1-07	Peru	L 1-4	Lima	Fr	Sandy
8-07	Argentina	L 1-2	Paysandu	SCr1	Angola
11-07	United States	W 1-0	Paysandu	SCr1	Etcheverry
14-07	Chile	D 2-2	Paysandu	SCr1	Mercado, Ramos.M
16-07	Uruguay	L 1-2	Montevideo	SCqf	Sanchez

BRAZIL

After it dazzled the world for a generation, many felt that Brazilian football would be unable to recapture its past glories. In the 1950s and 1960s they were blessed with so many players of outstanding talent that in six World Cups Brazil reached the final on four occasions and won three of them, but after their 1970 triumph came failure after failure, even when they were the outstanding team, such as in 1982. The USA '94 tournament saw all that change, however, as the World Cup was won for a record fourth time.

Brazil has always been regarded as the spiritual home of football, primarily as a result of the teams produced in the fifties and sixties. They were so popular and successful because they combined supreme footballing skills with a carefree arrogance that left their opponents in awe of them, especially when those opponents came from outside of South America. To Europeans, players such as Pele and Garrincha attained an almost mystical quality because they never plied their trade in Europe as so many Argentines and Uruguayans did. Instead the only glimpses they caught of these players were at World Cups or when the Brazilian national team or teams like Santos came to Europe on tours.

Away from Europe, and beyond the gaze of those who admired them so much, the story of Brazilian football is a different matter altogether. Success has been limited for both the national side in the South American Championships and the club sides in the Copa Libertadores, so much so that the River Plate estuary, encompassing both Buenos Aires and Montevideo, is seen as the real home of football on the continent.

The structure of Brazilian football is certainly the reason why it has suffered in comparison to Uruguay and Argentina. The huge size of the country - it is the fifth biggest in the world and takes up more than half of the South American continent - has meant that only in recent years has there been any semblance of a national competition for club sides. Politically the country is divided into 27 states, many of which are larger in size and have bigger populations than an average size European country. Each state therefore has its own governing body for football and organises its own state league. The idea of a national league was just not feasible. Such a system, however, has left a legacy of chaos and infighting between the different organisations as they all vie for a say in how the game should be run.

Football is said to have been introduced into Brazil by Charles Miller, a worker with the Sao Paulo Railway Company at the end of the 19th century. As is the case with other South American countries, British residents in Brazil had formed sports clubs in which they spent much of their spare time playing cricket. Miller succeeded in persuading the Sao Paulo Athletic Club to start a football section, and soon other clubs followed suit.

Sao Paulo and Rio de Janeiro were the first cities to start playing football on a large scale and in 1901, the Campeonato Paulista de Futebol was founded in Sao Paulo, based on a strong British contingent. The first tournament was completed in 1902 and won by Charles Miller's Sao Paulo Athletic Club. Miller himself finished top scorer with 10 goals. It was not long before Rio got in on the act and formed the Liga Metropolitana de Football do Rio de Janeiro in 1905. Again the British presence was strong. Fluminense, another club founded by an Englishman, Oscar Cox, won the first tournament.

Brazilians of European descent other than the British very quickly took up the game. By 1914 all of the major clubs had been formed in Rio and Sao Paulo, and all in one way or another had links to one of the white European communities. Vasco da Gama were a Portuguese-based sailing club formed in 1898. Corinthians, though they were named after the famous English amateur side who made a tour of the country in 1910, were founded by five Brazilians of Portuguese descent. The Italians were not left out. Palestra Italia, later to become SE Palmeiras, was formed by Italian workers in the aftermath of an exhibition match played by Pro Vercelli and Torino in 1914, whilst Germania, as the name suggests, were the team of the German community.

Football also spread to other cities, most notably Belo Horizonte, Porto Alegre, Salvador, Recife, Curitiba and Fortaleza and by 1920 there were 15 state leagues in operation. Although under the jurisdiction of the Federacao Brasileira de Sports - later to become the Confederacao Brasileira de Desportes (CBD) - these leagues were run by state governing bodies who over the years built up a strong power base, which eventually led to much controversy in the 1970s as they began to flex their muscles.

Until the 1970s, however, the leagues in Rio de Janeiro and Sao Paulo were the most important competitions in the country. Although Rio select teams played Sao Paulo state selections every year in the Taca Correio da Manha from 1913 to 1923, and from 1923 to 1963 in the Campeonato Brasileiro de Selecoes, in which other state selections could enter, there was no national championship for clubs until 1950. Even then the Rio-Sao Paulo Championship, as the tournament was called, was not open to teams outside of the big two. Given that the Campeonato de Selecoes was won by either Rio or Sao Paulo every year bar 1934 when Bahia were the winners, this is perhaps not surprising.

Both the Rio and Sao Paulo leagues remained amateur and largely closed to the coloured population until the 1920s when a series of events changed the face of Brazilian football. Vasco da Gama emerged from the shadows of the more famous Rio clubs in 1923 when, playing a team containing coloured players, they ran away with the Rio title. Other clubs, realising the benefits of this untapped source of footballers, soon followed suit with the result that in terms of football at least, Brazil became the first racially-integrated country.

Administrative struggles also marked the early years of football in Rio but more especially in Sao Paulo where it was not uncommon to have two different leagues in operation. Professionalism was the cause that in the end united football in each of the cities, despite initially causing further splits. By the early 1940s, Brazil had emerged as a strong, racially-integrated, professional footballing nation capable of taking on the strongest of opponents. As the results of the national team show, before this time this had not been the case.

Brazil was rather slow in taking up international football. The difficulties in selecting a team from all of the different leagues were compounded by the huge distances involved in travelling to games. Therefore it was not until 1913 that any Brazilian representative side left the country to play a game. Surprisingly, Brazil's first registered representative match was played by a Bahia selection against a North American selection in August 1903 in Salvador. In 1906 a Sao Paulo selection lost heavily to the touring South African side, and in 1908 a touring Argentine combination played three matches against a Sao Paulo selection and one each against a Rio, Santos and a combined Brazilian selection. An Argentine combination toured again in 1912 whilst a Portuguese combination made the trip across the Atlantic in 1913.

With the formation of the Federacao Brasileira de Sports, a truly national team was picked for the first time on 21 July 1914 for a match against Exeter City, but the first full international was not played until two months later with a friendly match against Argentina in Buenos Aires, followed a week later by the first edition of the Roca Cup, an irregular competition played between the two countries. Brazil entered a team for the first South American Championship in 1916, but as in future editions, it did not prove to be a happy hunting ground. Over the next forty years the majority of the games played were in this competition and out of over twenty tournaments played, only three were won and in each case on Brazilian soil.

Despite the relative lack of success in the early years, Brazil produced many fine players, the most famous of whom were Artur Friedenreich, Leonidas da Silva, Domingos da Guia, Romeu, Tim and Fausto. Players like Leonidas would have won more caps for their country but for the chaos on the home front and disputes with neighbouring countries restricting the number of games played during the whole of the 1930s to just 22. Friedenreich, however, still found plenty of opportunities to score goals in domestic competitions and the 1329 goals he scored between 1909 and 1934 is a world record that will surely never be equalled.

Brazil entered the first World Cup in Montevideo, and in a result symptomatic of their fortunes at the time were knocked out by Yugoslavia in the first round. Since then the winning of the World Cup has become an obsession for everybody involved in Brazilian football. They have entered and qualified for every tournament held, the only country to do so. The 1934 tournament was no less disastrous than the first, as they lost to Spain in the first round. In 1938 Brazil showed their true potential for the first time, reaching the semi-finals, but overconfidence, not for the last time, lost them the semi-final against Italy. Inexplicably, Leonidas was rested for what the selectors assumed would be the final, but instead turned out to be the third place play-off!

The golden age of Brazilian football came between 1950 and 1970 and it is for this period that the Brazilians are best remembered. In 1949, in preparation for the 1950

World Cup which they had been given the responsibility of hosting, Brazil staged the South American Championship and won it despite being taken to a play-off by Paraguay. No less than 46 goals were scored in just 8 games as Ademir and Jair Pinto, to name just two, ran riot in their opponents' penalty area.

This form was repeated the following year in the World Cup, and perhaps there have never been more clear-cut favourites than Brazil that year. Twenty-one goals en route to the final game had many Brazilians celebrating before the game against Uruguay had begun. Brazil needed just a draw from the game to top the second round group and win the World Cup. When Friaca scored early in the second half they looked to be there, but in one of the greatest upsets in the history of the tournament, Uruguay scored twice to snatch the title from the hosts. Perhaps the result should not be considered that surprising. Consistently the masters of Brazil in the South American Championship, Uruguay knew the Brazilian style inside out and exploited that knowledge, even though they could not match them for skill or flair.

By 1954 the basis of a much more stable side was growing. In defence both Nilton and Djalma Santos were proving very effective whilst the midfield was being run effectively by Didi, but once again the World Cup was to prove elusive. In the famous quarter-final with Hungary, Brazil lost to the best team in the tournament, but not before violence flared on and off the field in a game that has become known as the 'Battle of Berne'.

Four years later the inevitable happened when Brazil finally won the tournament they had set their hearts on. The forward line of Garrincha, Vavá, Pelé and Zagalo was the clinching factor. Pelé was especially vital. His presence at only 17 caused a huge stir and he became an instant hero and a household name around the world after his performance against Sweden in the final. Most would class Pelé as the greatest footballer ever, above even Maradona, Di Stéfano or Cruyff, and for over a decade he came to epitomise Brazilian football. He appeared for Brazil in the 1958, 1962, 1966 and 1970 World Cup finals, though injury meant he did not appear in the final itself against Czechoslovakia in 1962. Instead it was Garrincha who was the driving force in a team that was almost identical to that of 1958.

The 1966 side that lost its crown in England was in a transitional stage and again Pelé did not have a happy time as he was continually fouled. He even threatened to give up football in the face of such treatment. Gone from the side were Didi, Nilton Santos, Vavá, Zito, Zózimo and Zagalo, whilst in had come Tostao, Gérson and Jairzinho. Portugal and Hungary qualified from the group and Brazil went home after the first round for only the third time in their history.

The 1970 side that won the World Cup in Mexico has been described as the best football team ever to take the field in a World Cup. At the back, Carlos Alberto marshalled a defence that liked to attack and so consequently relied on scoring more goals than they let in, but the mix worked. In attack, Pelé was back to his most masterful self and he, Jairzinho, Rivelino and Tostao were a potent force to match that of the 1958 forward line. No-one except England came close to matching the Brazilians in Mexico and their performance in the final against Italy was one of the best displays the World Cup has ever seen. A good Italian side were simply not in the same class, especially in the second half when the Brazilians seemed to toy with them as a cat would with a mouse. Their fourth goal, scored by the captain Carlos Alberto, typified the versatility of their game. The move involved nine passes both long and short, a mazy dribble and a lightning finish that had the Italian defence looking on in admiration.

From 1970 until 1994 the national side never reached the same heights and had to live in the shadow of the performances of the 1950-70 era. Only once, in 1982, did they come close, when the likes of Sócrates, Falcao, Junior and Zico played a brand of football reminiscent of 1970. Instead, the side tended to ape the rigid tactical approach of the Europeans and this did not stand them in good stead. This was especially true in the 1990 World Cup, and in a dreadful game against Argentina, the team lost in the second round to howls of derision back in Brazil.

The club scene in Brazil has also suffered since 1970. The big clubs from Rio and Sao Paulo had introduced an annual tournament in 1950 between the best teams from the two cities, the winners of which were regarded as national champions. Pressure from the other state leagues to be involved led to the Roberto Gomez Pedrosa tournament in 1967. Minas Gerais, Rio Grande do Sul and Parana were involved for the first time that year whilst the following year Bahia and Pernambuco were invited to send sides. The ball had started to roll and soon all the states in the country were anxious to take part, and as the Confederacao Brasileira de Futebol is in effect controlled by the various state governing bodies. Pressure from them led to the formation of a national championship in 1971. Throughout the 1970s the number of participants rose as even the smallest states demanded to take part, and by 1979 the national league consisted of 94 teams.

It has been the practice for the Brazilian season to be divided in half. The national championship now occupies the second half of the year, and the state leagues the first half. Football is thus played all year round with hardly a break. Increasingly the big clubs from Rio and Sao Paulo have become unhappy with the status quo, not just because of the number of games they play but also the long distances they have to travel to play the small teams in the national league. Threats of breakaways and the like have never materialised and club football continues on in its confused way. The mechanisms used for deciding the champions in either the national or the state leagues vary from year to year and from state to state, and have often been decided on after the tournament has started. The Brazilians are not keen on a European-style league and tend to have various stages to sustain interest, ultimately leading to a grand final.

ORDER OF MERIT

		All			Nat			Cup		State	Sth Am		
	Team	G	S	B	G	S	B	G	S	G	G	S	B
1	Santos	12	3	3	5	1	1	5	2	15	2	-	2
2	Palmeiras	10	5	4	8	3	3	2	-	18	-	2	1
3	Flamengo	8	4	5	6	2	2	1	1	22	1	1	3
4	São Paulo FC	7	9	3	3	7	1	-	-	18	4	2	2
5	Corinthians	6	4	5	5	4	4	1	-	20	-	-	1
6	Botafogo	5	5	4	3	4	2	1	1	15	1	-	2
	Cruzeiro	5	5	4	-	3	1	2	-	25	3	2	3
8	Vasco da Gama	4	7	3	4	6	3	-	1	17	-	-	-
9	Internacional	4	6	2	3	4	-	1	1	31	-	1	2
10	Grêmio	4	3	2	1	1	-	2	2	28	1	1	1
11	Fluminense	4	2	1	4	1	1	-	1	28	-	-	-
12	Atlético Mineiro	2	2	3	1	2	1	-	-	34	1	-	2
13	EC Bahia	2	2	-	1	-	-	1	2	40	-	-	-
14	Portuguesa	2	-	2	2	-	2	-	-	3	-	-	-
15	Guarani Campinas	1	1	1	1	1	-	-	-	-	-	-	1
16	Coritiba FC	1	-	-	1	-	-	-	-	29	-	-	-
	Criciúma	1	-	-	-	-	-	1	-	6	-	-	-
17	Fortaleza FC	-	2	-	-	-	-	-	2	30	-	-	-
18	Bangu	-	1	1	-	1	1	-	-	2	-	-	-
19	Goiâs AC	-	1	-	-	-	-	-	1	12	-	-	-
	Bragantino	-	1	-	-	1	-	-	-	1	-	-	-
	Sport Recife	-	1	-	-	-	-	-	1	27	-	-	-
	Nautico	-	1	-	-	-	-	-	1	18	-	-	-
	Vitória	-	1	-	-	1	-	-	-	13	-	-	-
	Ceara SC	-	1	-	-	-	-	-	1	27	-	-	-

To the end of the 1994 season and the 1995 Cup

Amid so much confusion it is perhaps not surprising that the Copa Libertadores has not been a favoured hunting ground for Brazilian clubs. The first difficulty in the 1960s was who should qualify, so a Brazilian Cup was introduced to find an entrant. From 1971 the national champions and runners-up qualified but in 1989 the Cup was re-introduced to qualify one team to join the national champions. Only two teams from either Rio or Sao Paulo have ever won the Copa Libertadores and only five Brazilian teams have won it at all. Pelé's Santos won it twice in the early 1960s, but since then only Flamengo, Sao Paulo FC, Gremio from Porto Alegre and Cruzeiro from Belo Horizonte have won it. This is all the more extraordinary considering the fact that until the 1980s, unlike the rest of South America, Brazilians did not tend to move abroad to play their football. Pelé, Tostao, Rivelino, Didi, Garrincha and Zico, for example, played almost all of their football at home. Didi spent one unsuccessful season at Real Madrid, whilst Zico returned home from Italy after two.

There is no doubt that Brazilian club football is in need of an urgent overhaul. If they do have anything to learn from Europe it is the benefit of a stable club structure. The case for abandoning the state leagues and implementing a streamlined national league is strong. The game in Brazil needs a focus and at present does not have one. Until it does and the clubs can woo back supporters that have almost disappeared except for the very big games, club football in Brazil will continue to struggle on.

Amidst all of this, however, in 1994 the national team finally won the World Cup again, after 24 years of waiting. Under Carlos Alberto Parreira, part of the coaching staff at the 1970 World Cup, Brazil played a disciplined game. Even with star players like Bebeto and Romario, the team was regarded as functional rather than brilliant, but it worked. The captain, Dunga, epitomised the new mood of relying on hard work and team spirit to see them through. Whether the World Cup win will have a positive impact on clubs in Brazil is less certain, but the possibilities are there. São Paulo FC have emerged to challenge the Argentine clubs while Cruzeiro, Atletico Mineiro and Botafogo have all won continental titles in the 1990s. There is no reason why the clubs should not take after the national team and succeed at the highest level.

Population: 150,368,000
Area, sq km: 8,511,965
% in urban areas: 75%
Capital city: Brasília

Confederação Brasileira de Futebol
Rua da Alfandega #70
PO Box 1078
20.070 Rio de Janeiro
Brazil
Tel: + 55 21 2215937
Fax: + 55 21 252 9294

Year of formation	1914
Affiliation to FIFA	1923
Affiliation to CSF	1916
Registered clubs	12 987
Registered players	551 300
Professional players	13 000
Registered coaches	4324
Registered referees	4950
National stadium	Maracaná, Rio de Janeiro 180 000
National colours	Yellow/Blue/White
Reserve colours	Blue/White/White
Season	February - June for either national or state leagues September - December for either national or state league

THE RECORD

WORLD CUP

1930	QT Automatic - Final Tournament/1st round
1934	QT W-O in group 2 - Final Tournament/1st round
1938	QT W-O in group 9 - Final Tournament/Semi-finalists/ 3rd place
1950	QT Automatic - Final Tournament/Runners-up
1954	QT 1st/3 in group 12 - Final Tournament/Quarter-finalists
1958	QT 1st/2 in group 1 - Final Tournament/Winners
1962	QT Automatic - Final Tournament/Winners
1966	QT Automatic - Final Tournament/1st round
1970	QT 1st/4 in group 2 - Final Tournament/Winners
1974	QT Automatic - Final Tournament/2nd round/ 4th place
1978	QT 1st/3 in group 1 - Final Tournament/2nd round/ 3rd place
1982	QT 1st/3 in group 1 - Final Tournament/2nd round
1986	QT 1st/3 in group 3 - Final Tournament/Quarter-finalists
1990	QT 1st/3 in group 3 - Final Tournament/2nd round
1994	QT 1st/5 in group 2 - Final Tournament/Winners

SOUTH AMERICAN CHAMPIONSHIP

1910	-

1916	3/4
1917	3/4
1919	1/4 - Winners
1920	3/4
1921	2/4
1922	1/5 - Winners
1923	4/4
1924	-
1925	2/3
1926-35	-
1937	2/6
1939	-
1941	-
1942	3/7
1945	2/7
1946	2/6
1947	-
1949	1/8 - Winners
1953	2/7
1955	-
1956	4/6
1957	2/7
1959	2/7
1959	3/5
1963	4/7
1967	-
1975	3/10 - Semi-finalists
1979	3/10 - Semi-finalists
1983	2/10 - Finalists
1987	5/10 - 1st round
1989	1/10 - Winners
1991	2/10 - 2nd round
1993	5=/12 - 2nd round
1995	2/12 - Finalists

SOUTH AMERICAN CLUB TOURNAMENTS

Copa Libertadores
Winners - Santos 1962, 1963, Cruzeiro 1976, Flamengo 1981, Gremio 1983, São Paulo FC 1992 1993
Finalists - Palmeiras 1961 1968, Sao Paulo FC 1974 1994, Cruzeiro 1977, Internacional 1980, Grêmio 1984
Supercopa
Winners - Cruzeiro 1991 1992, São Paulo FC 1993
Finalists - Cruzeiro 1988, Flamengo 1993
CONMEBOL Cup
Winners - Atlético Mineiro 1992, Botafogo 1993, São Paulo FC 1994

CLUB DIRECTORY

SÃO PAULO (Pop. 15,175,000)

São Paulo FC (1930)
Cicero Pompeu de Toledo 'Morumbi' 105,000 – White, red & black hoop/White
Previous names - Merger in 1930 of Paulistano & AA das Palmeiras. Reformed in 1935

Sport Club Corinthians Paulista (1910)
Alfredo Schuring 'Parque São Jorge' 15,000 – White/Black

Sociedade Esportiva Palmeiras (1914)
Estádio Palestra Italia 'Parque Antartica' 32,000 – Green/White
Previous name - Palestra Italia 1914-42

Associaçao Portuguesa de Deportes (1920)
Osvaldo Teixeira Duarte 'Canindé' 25,000 – Red & green hoops/White

The Estádio Paulo Machado de Carvalho 'Pacaembu' (75,000) is also used by the clubs occasionally.

RIO DE JANEIRO - (Pop. 10,150,000)

América FC (1904)
Wolney Braune 10,000 – Red/White

Atlético Clube Bangu (1904)
Moca Bonita 15,000 – Red & white stripes/White

Botafogo de Futebol e Regatas (1904)
Marechal Hermes 'Mané Garrincha' 18,000 – Black & white stripes/Black

Club de Regatas Flamengo (1895)
(Football team in 1911)
Estádio da Gávea 13,000 – Red & black hoops/White

Fluminense Football Club (1902)
Laranjeiras 10,000 – Maroon, green & thin white stripes/White

Clube de Regatas Vasco da Gama (1898)
São Januario 40,000 – White, black sash/White

All teams use the Maracaná (180,000) when necessary

BELO HORIZONTE (Pop. - 2,950,000) - Minas Gerais State

Clube Atlético Mineiro (1908)
Magalhaes Pinto 'Mineirao' 130,000 – Black & white stripes/Black

Esporte Clube Cruzeiro (1902)
Magalhaes Pinto 'Mineirao' 130,000 – Blue/White
Previous name - Società Sportiva Palestra Italia 1902-42

América FC (1912)
Parque Independencia 25,000 – Green & white stripes/White

RECIFE (Pop. - 2,625,000) - Pernambuco State

Sport Club Recife (1905)
Ilha do Retiro 40,000 – Red & black hoops/Black

Santa Cruz FC (1914)
José do Rego Maciel 'Colosso do Arruda' 114,000 – White with black, white & red hoop/Black

Nautico Clube Capibaribe (1901)
Estadio dos Aflitos 18,000 – Red & white stripes/White

América Clube de Futebol
Green/White

All the clubs use the Colosso do Arruda for big games

PORTO ALEGRE (Pop - 2,600,000) - Rio Grande do Sul State

Grêmio Foot-Ball Porto-Alegrense (1903)
Olimpico 70,000 – Black, blue & thin white stripes/Black

Sport Club Internacional Porto Alegre (1909)
José Pinheiro Borda 'Beira-Rio' 85,000 – Red/White

SALVADOR (Pop. - 2,050,000) - Bahia State

Esporte Clube Bahia (1931)
Otavio Mangabeira 'Fonte Nova' 80,000 – White/Blue, red trim
Previous names - Merger in 1931 of AA de Bahia & Baiano de Tênis

Esporte Clube Vitória (1899)
Manoel Barradas 32,000 – Red & black hoops/White

Ypiranga Esporte Clube
Otavio Mangabeira 'Fonte Nova' 80,000

FORTALEZA (Pop. - 1,825,000) - Ceara State

Ceara Sport Club (1914)
Black & white stripes/Black

Fortaleza FC (1918)
Thin blue, red & white hoops/Blue

Ferroviáro Atlético Clube (1933)
White with one red & one black hoop/White

América FC (1920)
Red/White

Calouros do Ar (1952)
Maroon, green & thin white stripes/White

All of these clubs use either the Estádio Governador Plácido Castelo 'Castelão' 130,000 or the Estádio Presidente Getúlio Vargas 40,000

CURITIBA (Pop. - 1,700,000) - Parana State

Coritiba FC (1909)
Antonio Couto Pereira 56,000 – White with two green hoops/Black

Clube Atlético Paranaense (1924)
Joaquim Américo 25,000 – Red & black hoops/White
Previous names - Merger in 1924 of Internacional & América

Paraná Clube (1990)
Durival de Brito or Erton Coelho – Red & blue halves/White

Previous names - Merger in 1990 of Colorado EC & Pinheiros. Colorado EC was a result of a merger in 1971 between Palestra Italia, Britânia & Ferroviária. Pinheiros were called Agua Verde until 1971

BRASILIA (Pop. - 1,567,000) - Distrito Federal

Brasilia Esporte Clube
Red/White

Taguatinga Esporte Clube
Estádio de Taguatina 35,000 – Blue/White

Sobradinho Esporte Clube
Black & white stripes/White

Associacão Desportiva Gama
Estádio da AA Cultural Mariano 30,000 – Green/White

All clubs use the Estádio Edson Arantes do Nascimento 'Pelézão' 45,000 or the Estádio Mané Garrincha 50,000

BELÉM (Pop. - 1,200,000) - Para State

Paysandu Sport Clube (1914)
Estádio da Curuzu 25,000 – Blue & white stripes/White

Clube do Remo
Evandro de Almeida 25,000 – White, blue trim

Tuna Luso Brasileira
White with green sash/Green

All clubs also use the Alacid Nunes 'Mangueirão' 120,000

CAMPINAS (Pop. - 1,125,000) - São Paulo State

Guarani FC (1911)
Brinco de Ouro da Princesa 49,000 – Green/White

Associacão Atlética Ponte Preta (1900)
Moises Lucarelli 30,000 – White with a black sash/White

SANTOS (Pop. - 1,065,000) - São Paulo State

Santos FC (1912)
Vila Belmiro 20,000 – White, black trim

GOIÂNIA (Pop. - 990,000) - Goiâs State

Goiânia
Leonido Caiado 'Serra Dourada' 76,000 – Black & white stripes/Black

Atlético Goiâniense
Antônio Acioly 5,000 or Serra Dourada – Red & black hoops/White

Goiâs Esporte Clube (1943)
Leonido Caiado 'Serra Dourada' 76,000 – Green/White

Villa Nova FC
Onézio Alvarenga 4,000 or Serra Dourada – Red/White

MANAUS (Pop. - 809,000) - Amazonia State

Nacional FC
Vivaldo Lima 75,000 – Blue/White

Atlético Rio Negro Clube
Vivaldo Lima 75,000 – Black & white hoops/Black

Nacional Fast Clube
Vivaldo Lima 75,000 – White with blue & red hoop/White

VITÓRIA (Pop. - 735,000) - Espirto Santo State

Rio Branco Atlético Clube
EstadioKleber Andrade 77,000 – Black/White

Desportiva Ferroviária
Engenheiro Alencar Araripe 'Gigante do Jardim' 35,000 – Maroon/White

Vitória FC
Salvador Venâncio da Costa 15,000 – Blue/White

SÃO LUIS (Pop. - 600,000) - Maranhão State

Moto Clube
Vila Passos 25,000 – Red & black hoops/Black

Sampaio Correa FC
Vila Passos 25,000 – Red, green & thin yellow stripes/White

Maranhão FC
Vila Passos 25,000 – Blue with red,white & black hoop/White

Vitória do Mar
Vila Passos 25,000

Clubs also use the Estádio Governador João Castelo 70,000

JOÃO PESSOA (Pop. - 550,000) - Paraiba State

Botafogo
José Américo de Almeida Filho 'Almeidão' 47,000 – White, black trim

Auto Esporte
José Américo de Almeida Filho 'Almeidão' 47,000 – Red & white stripes/White

SANTO ANDRÉ (Pop. - 549,000) - São Paulo State

Esporte Clube Santo André (1974)
Bruno José Daniel 22,000 – Blue/White

TERESINA (Pop. - 525,000) - Piaui State

Flamengo
Governador Alberto Silva 'Albertão' 60,000 – Red & black hoops/Black

River Atlético Clube
Governador Alberto Silva 'Albertão' 60,000 – White with red & black hoop/White

Piaui Esporte Clube
Governador Alberto Silva 'Albertão' 60,000 – Blue with a red hoop/Blue

Associacão Esportiva Tiradentes
Governador Alberto Silva 'Albertão' 60,000 – Yellow with blue sleeves/White

NATAL (Pop. - 510,000) - Rio Grande do Norte State

ABC
Marechal Humberto de Alencar 'Castelo Branco' 50,000 – Black & white stripes/Black

Alecrim FC
Marechal Humberto de Alencar 'Castelo Branco' 50,000 – Green/White

América FC
Marechal Humberto de Alencar 'Castelo Branco' 50,000 – Red, white trim

MACEIÓ (Pop. - 482,000) - Algoas State

CSA (Centro Sportivo Alagoana)
Gustavo Paiva 9,000 – Blue & white stripes/White

CRB (CR Brasil)
Severiano Gomes Filho 9,000 – Red/White

The main stadium in the city is the Estádio Estadual Lamenha Filho 'Pelezão' (75,000)

CAMPO GRANDE - Mato Grosso do Sul State

Operario FC
Pedro Pedrossian 55,000 – Black & white stripes/Black

Comercial EC
Pedro Pedrossian 55,000 – Red/White

CAMPO GRANDE (Pop. - 384,000) - Rio de Janeiro State

Campo Grande Atlético Clube
Italo de Cima 10,000 – Black & white stripes/White

VOLTA REDONDA (Pop. - 375,000) - Rio de Janeiro State

Volta Redonda FC (1976)
Silvio Paulinho de Oliveira 30,000 – Black, yellow & thin white stripes/Black

CAMPOS (Pop. - 366,000) - Rio de Janeiro State

Américano FC (1914)
Godofredo Cruz 25,000 – Black with central white stripe/Black

FLORIANÓPOLIS (Pop. - 365,000) - Santa Catarina State

Avai FC
Ressacada 120,000 – Blue & white stripes/White

Figueirense FC
Ressacada 120,000 – Black & white stripes/Black

ARACAJU (Pop. - 360,000) - Sergipe State
Club Sportivo Sergipe
João Hora 20,000 – Red/White

Associacão Desportiva Confiança
Dr. Lourival Baptista 'Batistão' 40,000 – Blue with white sleeves/White

FEIRA DE SANTANA (Pop. - 355,000) - Bahia State
Fluminense FC (1941)
Joia da Princesa 40,000 – White with a green & maroon V /White

JUIZ DE FORA (Pop. - 349,000) - Minas Gerais State
Tupi FC
José Procópio Teixeira 25,000 – Black & white stripes/White

LONDRINA (Pop. - 346,000) - Parana State
Londrina Esporte Clube
Estádio do Café – Sky blue & white stripes/White

JOINVILLE (Pop. - 302,000) - Santa Catarina State
Joinville Esporte Clube (1976)
Ernesto Schillen Sobrinho 25,000 – Black, red & thin white stripes/White
Previous names - Merger in 1976 of América & Caxias

RIBEIRÃO PRETO (Pop. - 300,000) - São Paulo State
Botafogo FC (1918)
Santa Cruz 60,000 – Red, black & thin white stripes/White

CAMPINA GRANDE (Pop. - 279,000) - Paraiba State
Campinense Clube
Plinio Lemos 7,000 – Red & black hoops/White

Treze FC
Presidente Vargas 10,000 – Black & white stripes/Black

Both clubs also use the Estádio Ernany Satiro 'Amigão' 40,000

CUIABÁ (Pop. - 279,000) - Mato Grosso State
Mixto Esporte Clube
Governador Jose Fragelli 'Verdao' 55,000 – Black with a white sash/Black

Clube Esportiva Dom Bosco
Governador Jose Fragelli 'Verdao' 55,000 – Sky blue & white stripes/Sky blue

PELOTAS (Pop. - 277,000) - Rio Grande do Sul State
GE Brasil (Grêmio Esportivo)
Bento Freitas 22,000 – Red/Black

Esporte Clube Pelotas (1908)
Boças de Lobo 18,000 – Yellow/Blue

SÃO JOSÉ DOS CAMPOS (Pop. - 268,000) - São Paulo State
São José Esporte Clube (1933)
Martins Pereira 18,000 – Blue/White

CAXIAS DO SUL (Pop. 266,000) - Rio Grande do Sul State
Esporte Clube Juventude (1913)
Alfredo Jaconi 40,000 – Green/White

Sociedade Esportiva e Recreativa Caxias (1935)
Estádio Centenario 30,000 – Maroon/White, blue & white trim

UBERLÂNDIA (Pop. - 230,000) - Minas Gerais State
Uberlândia Esporte Clube (1922)
Parque do Sabiá 75,000 – Green/White

ANÁPOLIS (Pop. - 225,000) - Goiâs State
Anápolis FC
Jonas Duarte 25,000 – Red, black & thin white stripes/Black

Associacão Atlética Anapolina
Jonas Duarte 25,000 – Red/White

GOVERNADOR VALADARES (Pop. - 216,000) - Minas Gerais State
Esporte Clube Democrata (1932)
Mamud Abbas 15,000 – Black & white stripes/White

CASCAVEL (Pop. - 200,000) - Parana State
Cascavel Esporte Clube
Olimpico Regional – Red, white & blue stripes/White

MARINGÁ (Pop. - 196,000) - Parana State
Grêmio Esportivo Maringá
Willie Davids 25,000 – Black & white stripes/Black

LIMEIRA (Pop. - 186,000) - São Paulo State
Associacão Atlética Internacional Limeira (1913)
Major José Levi Sobrinho 15,000 – Black & white stripes/Black

UBERABA (Pop. - 180,000) - Minas Gerais State
National FC (1944)
João Guido 30,000 – Black & white stripes/Black

Uberaba Sport Club (1917)
João Guido 30,000 – Red/White

RIO GRANDE (Pop. - 164,000) - Rio Grande do Sul State
Esporte Clube São Paulo (1908)
Aldo Dapuzzo 15,000 – Thin maroon, green & white stripes/White

PIRACICABA (Pop. - 179,000) - São Paulo State
Esporte Clube XV de Novembre (1913)
Barão de Sierra Negra 30,000 – Black & white stripes/Black

BAURU (Pop. - 178,000) - São Paulo State
Esporte Clube Noroeste (1910)
Alfredo de Castilho 18,000 – Red/White

SÃO JOSÉ DO RIO PRETO (Pop. - 172,000) - São Paulo State
América FC (1946)
Mário Alves de Mendonça 22,000 – Red/White

JUAZEIRO DO NORTE (Pop. - 159,000) - Ceara State
Guarani Esporte Clube (1941)
Romeirão 30,000 – Black & white stripes/Black

Icasa Esporte Clube (1963)
Romeirão 30,000 – Green/White

AMERICANA (Pop. - 156,000) - São Paulo State
Rio Branco Esporte Clube (1913)
Décio Vitta 16,000 – White/Black

ARARAQUARA (Pop. - 145,000) - São Paulo State
Associacão Ferroviária de Esportes (1950)
Adhemar de Barros 'Fonte Luminosa' 23,000 – Maroon/White

RIO BRANCO (Pop. - 145,000) - Acre State
Atlético Clube Juventos
Dom Giocondo Maria Grotti 4,000 – Maroon/Black

Atlético Acreano
Adauto Brito da Frota 4,000 – Blue/Blue

Rio Branco FC
Estádio Rio Branco 8,000

SÃO CARLOS (Pop. - 140,000) - São Paulo State
GE Sãocarlense (1976)
Luiz Augusto de Oliveira 'Luizão' 17,000 – Blue/Blue

CRICIÚMA (Pop. - 128,000) - Santa Catarina State
Criciúma Esporte Club (1947)
Heriberto Hulse 10,000 – Black, yellow & white hoops/Black
Previous name - Until 1978 known as Comerciario Esporte Clube

BRAGANÇA PAULISTA (Pop. - 105,000) - São Paulo State
Club Atlético Bragantino (1928)
Marcelo Stéfani 'Marcelão' – Black & white stripes/Black

ITAJAI (Pop. - 104,000) - Santa Catarina State
Club Nautico Marcilio Dias
Dr. Hercilio Luz 8,000 – Red & blue stripes/Blue

CHAPECO (Pop. - 100,000) - Santa Catarina State
Associacão Chapecoense de Futebol
Indio Conda 20,000 – White/White

TUBARÃO (Pop. - 82,000) - Santa Catarina State
Hercilio Luz FC
Vilas Oficinas 12,000 – Red/White

NOVA LIMA (Pop. - 35,000) - Minas Gerais State
Vila Nova AC (1908)
Nestadinho do Bonfim 25,000 – Red & white stripes/White

CRUZ DAS ALMAS - Bahia State
Galicia Esporte Clube
Barbosão – Blue/White

VARZEA GRANDE - Mato Grosso State
Club Esportiva Operario

ITABAIANA - Sergipe State
Associacão Olimpica Itabaiana
Etelvino Mendonça 8,000 – Thin blue, red & white stripes/White

SÃO PAULO TOURNAMENT

1937b Atlético Mineiro 9 Fluminense 6 Rio Branco 5
1950ad Corinthians 11 Vasco da Gama 10 Portuguesa 9
1951 Palmeiras 10 Corinthians 10 Bangu 7
1952ae Portuguesa 11 Vasco da Gama 11 Corinthians 10
1953 Corinthians 12 Vasco da Gama 11 São Paulo FC 10
1954 Corinthians 14 Fluminense 13 Palmeiras 12
1955 Portuguesa 13 Palmeiras 13 Botafogo 11
1956 -
1957 Fluminense 16 Flamengo 11 Vasco da Gama 11
1958 Vasco da Gama 15 Flamengo 13 Corinthians 11
1959 Santos 13 Vasco da Gama 12 Flamengo 11
1960 Fluminense 14 Botafogo 12 Flamengo 11
1961 Flamengo 6 Botafogo 5 Vasco da Gama 4
1962 Botafogo 6 São Paulo FC 3 Palmeiras 2
1963ae Santos 13 Corinthians 12 Fluminense 11
1964 Santos & Botafogo 14 Palmeiras 10
1965 Palmeiras 11 São Paulo FC 8 Portuguesa 8
1966 Corinthians,Santos,Vasco da Gama & Botafogo all 11

Play-offs
1951 Palmeiras..................3-2 3-1 ....Corinthians
1952 Portuguesa...............4-2 2-2 ....Vasco da Gama
1955 Portuguesa ....4-2..........................Palmeiras

ROBERTO GOMEZ PEDROSA TOURNAMENT

1967 Palmeiras 9 Internacional PA 7 Corinthians 5
1968 Santos 6 Internacional PA 2 Vasco da Gama 2
1969 Palmeiras 4 Cruzeiro 4 Corinthians 3
1970 Fluminense 5 Palmeiras 4 Atlético Mineiro 2

BRAZILIAN NATIONAL CHAMPIONSHIP

1971 Atlético Mineiro 4 São Paulo FC 2 Botafogo 0
1972 Palmeiras ....0-0..........................Botafogo
1973 Palmeiras 5 São Paulo FC 3 Cruzeiro 2
1974 Vasco Da Gama 4 Cruzeiro 4 Santos 2
1975 Internacional PA ....1-0..........................Cruzeiro
1976 Internacional PA ....2-0..........................Corinthians
1977 São Paulo FC..........0-0 3-2p........................Atlético Mineiro
1978 Guarani Campinas..1-0 1-0........................Palmeiras
1979 Internacional PA......2-0 2-1 ....Vasco da Gama
1980 Flamengo..................0-1 3-2........................Atlético Mineiro
1981 Grêmio.......................2-1 1-0........................São Paulo FC
1982 Flamengo..............1-1 0-0 1-0 ....Grêmio
1983 Flamengo....................1-2 3-0 ....Santos
1984 Fluminense ....1-0 0-0 ....Vasco da Gama
1985 Coritiba FC............1-1 6-5p........................Bangu
1986 São Paulo FC ......1-1 3-3 4-3p..................Guarani Campinas
1987 Flamengo.....................1-1 1-0 ....Internacional PA
1988 EC Bahia ....2-1 0-0 ....Internacional PA
1989 Vasco da Gama ....1-0.........................São Paulo FC
1990 Corinthians ....1-0 1-0 ....São Paulo FC
1991 São Paulo FC ....1-0 0-0 ....Bragantino
1992 Flamengo....................3-0 2-2 ....Botafogo
1993 Palmeiras....................1-0 2-0 ....Vitória
1994 Palmeiras....................3-1 1-1 ....Corinthians

In 1987 Sport Recife were declared champions after Flamengo refused to take part in a play-off. They are not regarded as such by any source.

BRAZILIAN CUP FINALS

1959 EC Bahia..............3-2 0-2 3-1 ....Santos
1960 Palmeiras....................3-1 8-2 ....Fortaleza
1961 Santos ....1-1 5-1 ....EC Bahia
1962 Santos ....4-3 1-3 5-0 ....Botafogo
1963 Santos ....6-0 2-0 ....EC Bahia
1964 Santos ....4-1 0-0 ....Flamengo
1965 Santos ....5-1 1-0 ....Vasco da Gama
1966 Cruzeiro ....6-2 3-2 ....Santos
1967 Palmeiras.............3-1 1-2 2-0 ....Nautico
1968 -
1969 Botafogo ....2-2 4-0 ....Fortaleza
1970-88 -
1989 Grêmio.......................0-0 2-1 ....Sport Recife
1990 Flamengo....................1-0 0-0 ....Goâis EC
1991 Criciúma ....1-1 0-0 ....Grêmio
1992 Internacional PA......1-2 1-0 ....Fluminense
1993 Cruzeiro ....0-0 2-1 ....Internacional PA
1994 Grêmio.......................0-0 1-0 ....Ceara SC
1995 Corinthians ....2-1 1-0 ....Grêmio

RIO DE JANEIRO STATE CHAMPIONSHIP

1906 Fluminense
1907 Fluminense / Botafogo
1908 Fluminense
1909 Fluminense
1910 Botafogo
1911 Fluminense
1912 Paissandu
1913 América FC
1914 Flamengo

		Rival Professional League
1915	Flamengo	
1916	América FC	
1917	Fluminense	
1918	Fluminense	
1919	Fluminense	
1920	Flamengo	
1921	Flamengo	
1922	América FC	***Rival Professional League***
1923	Vasco da Gama	
1924	Vasco da Gama	Fluminense
1925	Flamengo	
1926	Sao Cristovao	
1927	Flamengo	
1928	América FC	
1929	Vasco da Gama	
1930	Botafogo	
1931	América FC	
1932	Botafogo	
1933	Bangu	Botafogo
1934	Vasco da Gama	Botafogo
1935	América FC	Botafogo
1936	Fluminense	
1937	Fluminense	
1938	Fluminense	
1939	Flamengo	
1940	Fluminense	
1941	Fluminense	
1942	Flamengo	
1943	Flamengo	
1944	Flamengo	
1945	Vasco da Gama	
1946	Fluminense	
1947	Vasco da Gama	
1948	Botafogo	
1949	Vasco da Gama	
1950	Vasco da Gama	
1951	Fluminense	
1952	Vasco da Gama	
1953	Flamengo	
1954	Flamengo	
1955	Flamengo	
1956	Vasco da Gama	
1957	Botafogo	
1958	Vasco da Gama	
1959	Fluminense	

1960 América FC 37 Fluminense 36 Botafogo 35
1961 Botafogo 24 Flamengo 16 Fluminense 16
1962 Botafogo 40 Flamengo 38 Fluminense 36
1963 Flamengo 39 Fluminense 38 Bangu 36
1964 Fluminense 35 Bangu 35 Flamengo 34
1965 Flamengo 22 Bangu 20 Botafogo 17
1966 Bangu 32 Flamengo 29 Fluminense 26
1967 Botafogo 32 Bangu 30 Fluminense 24
1968 Botafogo 32 Vasco da Gama 29 Flamengo 26
1969 Fluminense 28 Flamengo 26 Botafogo 25
1970 Vasco da Gama 29 Fluminense 28 América 24
1971 Fluminense 30 Botafogo 29 Olaria 26
1972 Flamengo 4 Fluminense 2 Vasco da Gama 0
1973 Fluminense..................1-0............................Vasco da Gama
1974 Flamengo 3 Vasco da Gama 2 América 1
1975 Fluminense 2 Botafogo 2 Vasco da Gama 2
1976 Fluminense..................1-0............................Vasco da Gama
1977 Vasco da Gama......0-0 5-4p.......................Flamengo
1978 Flamengo*
1979 Flamengo*
1980 Fluminense..................1-0............................Vasco da Gama
1981 Flamengo..............0-2 0-1 2-1....................Vasco da Gama
1982 Vasco da Gama 4 Flamengo 2 América 0
1983 Fluminense 3 Flamengo 2 Bangu 1
1984 Fluminense 4 Flamengo 2 Vasco da Gama 0
1985 Fluminense 3 Bangu 2 Flamengo 1
1986 Flamengo..................0-0 2-0.........................Vasco da Gama
1987 Vasco da Gama 4 Flamengo 2 Bangu 0
1988 Vasco da Gama.......2-1 1-0.........................Flamengo
1989 Botafogo..................0-0 1-0.........................Flamengo
1990 Botafogo.......................1-0............................Vasco da Gama
1991 Flamengo..................1-1 4-2.........................Fluminense
1992 Vasco da Gama*
1993 Vasco da Gama..2-0 1-2 0-0**..................Fluminense
1994 Vasco da Gama 10 Flamengo 9 Fluminense 7
1995 Fluminense 33 Flamengo 32 Botafogo 30

* Teams won both league stages therefore no play-off
** Vasco won on more points scored in season

SÃO PAULO STATE CHAMPIONSHIP

		Rival League
1902	São Paulo Athletic	
1903	São Paulo Athletic	
1904	São Paulo Athletic	
1905	Paulistano	
1906	Germania	
1907	Internacional São Paulo	
1908	Paulistano	
1909	AA das Palmeiras	
1910	AA das Palmeiras	
1911	São Paulo Atletic	***Rival League***
1912	Américano	
1913	Américano	Paulistano
1914	Corinthians	São Bento
1915	Germania	AA das Palmeiras
1916	Corinthians	Paulistano
1917	Paulistano	
1918	Paulistano	
1919	Paulistano	
1920	Palestra Italia	
1921	Paulistano	
1922	Corinthians	
1923	Corinthians	
1924	Corinthians	
1925	São Bento	
1926	Palestra Italia	Paulistano
1927	Palestra Italia	Paulistano
1928	Corinthians	Internacional São Paulo
1929	Corinthians	Paulistano
1930	Corinthians	
1931	São Paulo FC	
1932	Palestra Italia	
1933	Palestra Italia	
1934	Palestra Italia	
1935	Santos	Portuguesa
1936	Palestra Italia	Portuguesa
1937	Corinthians	
1938	Corinthians	
1939	Corinthians	

1940 Palestra Italia 33 Portuguesa 30 Ipiranga 27
1941 Corinthians 35 São Paulo FC 31 Palestra Italia 30
1942 Palmeiras 36 Corinthians 33 São Paulo FC 32
1943 São Paulo FC 33 Corinthians 32 Palmeiras 29
1944 Palmeiras 32 São Paulo FC 29 Corinthians 28
1945 São Paulo FC 36 Corinthians 31 Palmeiras 29
1946 São Paulo FC 37 Corinthians 36 Portuguesa 28
1947 Palmeiras 36 Corinthians 32 Portuguesa 27
1948 São Paulo FC 34 Santos 32 Ipiranga 27
1949 São Paulo FC 36 Palmeiras 28 Portuguesa 27
1950 Palmeiras 32 São Paulo FC 31 Santos 31
1951 Corinthians 50 Palmeiras 43 Portuguesa 42
1952 Corinthians 52 São Paulo FC 46 Portuguesa 42
1953 São Paulo FC 49 Palmeiras 43 Corinthians 38
1954 Corinthians 42 Palmeiras 37 São Paulo FC 37
1955 Santos 40 Corinthians 39 São Paulo FC 38

1956 Santos 30 São Paulo FC 30 Corinthians 25
1957 São Paulo FC 30 Santos 29 Corinthians 28
1958 Santos 64 São Paulo FC 60 Corinthians 56
1959 Palmeiras 63 Santos 63 Ferroviaria 53
1960 Santos 50 Portuguesa 48 Corinthians 44
1961 Santos 53 Palmeiras 50 São Paulo FC 41
1962 Santos 51 São Paulo FC 43 Corinthians 42
1963 Palmeiras 50 São Paulo FC 43 Santos 36
1964 Santos 44 Palmeiras 41 Portuguesa 40
1965 Santos 53 Palmeiras 49 Corinthians 47
1966 Palmeiras 43 Corinthians 39 Santos 38
1967 Santos 41 São Paulo FC 41 Corinthians 37
1968 Santos 45 Corinthians 34 Ferroviaria 30
1969 Santos 5 Palmeiras 4 São Paulo FC 3
1970 São Paulo FC 27 Palmeiras 22 Ponte Preta 22
1971 São Paulo FC 36 Palmeiras 33 Portuguesa 28
1972 Palmeiras 37 São Paulo FC 36 Santos 29
1973 Santos..........0-0*..........Portuguesa
1974 Palmeiras..........1-1 1-0..........Corinthians
1975 São Paulo FC..........1-0 0-1 3-0p..........Portuguesa
1976 Palmeiras 19 XV de Novembro 14 Guarani 13
1977 Corinthians..........1-2 1-0 1-0..........Ponte Preta
1978 Santos..........1-1 2-1 0-2 **..........São Paulo FC
1979 Corinthians..........0-0 1-0 2-0..........Ponte Preta
1980 São Paulo FC..........1-0 1-0..........Santos
1981 São Paulo FC..........1-1 2-0..........Ponte Preta
1982 Corinthians..........1-0 3-1..........São Paulo FC
1983 Corinthians..........1-0 1-1..........São Paulo FC
1984 Santos 57 Corinthians 54 Palmeiras 52
1985 São Paulo FC..........3-1 2-1..........Portuguesa
1986 Internacional Limeira 1-1 2-1..........Palmeiras
1987 São Paulo FC..........2-1 0-0..........Corinthians
1988 Corinthians..........1-1 1-0..........Guarani
1989 São Paulo FC..........1-0 0-0..........São José
1990 Bragantino ***..........1-1 1-1..........Novorizontino
1991 São Paulo FC..........3-0 0-0..........Corinthians
1992 São Paulo FC..........4-2 2-1..........Palmeiras
1993 Palmeiras..........0-1 4-0..........Corinthians
1994 Palmeiras 47 São Paulo 41 Corinthians 41

Play-offs
1956 Santos..........4-2..........São Paulo FC
1959 Palmeiras..........2-2 1-1 2-1..........Santos
1967 Santos..........2-1..........São Paulo FC

* Both declared champions
** Santos awarded championship
*** Bragantino won on higher points scored during season

OTHER BRAZILIAN STATE CHAMPIONSHIPS

Acre State Champions
1989 Juventos
1990 Juventos
1991 Atlético Acreano
1992 Rio Branco
1993 Independencia
1994 Rio Branco

Algoas State Champions
1927 CRB
1928 CSA
1929 CSA
1930 CRB
1931-32 -
1933 CSA
1934 -
1935 CSA
1936 CSA
1937 CRB
1938 CRB
1939 CRB
1940 CRB
1941 CSA
1942 CSA
1943 -
1944 CSA
1945 Santa Cruz
1946 Barroso
1947 Alexandria
1948 Santa Cruz
1949 CSA
1950 CRB
1951 CRB
1952 CSA
1953 Ferroviario AC
1954 Ferroviario AC
1955 CSA
1956 CSA
1957 CSA
1958 CSA
1959 EC Capelense
1960 CSA
1961 CSA
1962 EC Capelense
1963 CSA
1964 CRB
1965 CSA
1966 CSA
1967 CSA
1968 CSA
1969 CRB
1970 CRB
1971 CSA
1972 CRB
1973 CRB
1974 CSA
1975 CSA
1976 CRB
1977 CRB
1978 CSA
1979 CRB
1980 CSA
1981 CSA
1982 CSA
1983 CRB
1984 CSA
1985 CSA
1986 CRB
1987 CRB
1988 CSA
1989 EC Capelense
1990 CSA
1991 CSA
1992 CRB
1993 CRB
1994 CSA

Most wins: CSA 34, CRB 21

Amazonia State Champions
1914 Manaus Atletic
1915 Manaus Atletic
1916 Nacional
1917 Nacional
1918 Nacional
1919 Nacional
1920 Nacional
1921 Rio Negro
1922 Nacional
1923 Nacional
1924-26 -
1927 Rio Negro
1928 Cruzeiro do Sul
1929 Manaus Sporting
1930 Cruzeiro do Sul
1931 Rio Negro
1932 Rio Negro
1933 Nacional
1934 Portuguesa
1935 Portuguesa
1936 Nacional
1937 Nacional
1938 Rio Negro
1939 Nacional
1940 Rio Negro
1941 Nacional
1942 Nacional
1943 Rio Negro
1944 Olimpico
1945 Nacional
1946 Nacional
1947 Olimpico
1948 Fast
1949 Fast
1950 Nacional
1951 América
1952 América
1953 América
1954 Fast
1955 Fast
1956 Auto Esporte
1957 Nacional
1958 Santos
1959 Auto Esporte
1960 Fast
1961 São Raimundo
1962 Rio Negro
1963 Nacional
1964 Nacional
1965 Rio Negro
1966 Olimpico
1967 Olimpico
1968 Nacional
1969 Nacional
1970 Fast
1971 Fast
1972 Nacional
1973 Rodoviaria
1974 Nacional
1975 Rio Negro
1976 Nacional
1977 Nacional
1978 Nacional
1979 Nacional
1980 Nacional
1981 Nacional
1982 Rio Negro
1983 Nacional
1984 Nacional
1985 Nacional
1986 Nacional
1987 Rio Negro
1988 Rio Negro
1989 Rio Negro
1990 Rio Negro
1991 Nacional
1992 Sul-América
1993 Sul-América
1994 América

Most wins: Nacional FC 34, Rio Negro 15

Bahia State Champions
1905 Internacional
1906 São Salvador
1907 São Salvador
1908 Vitória
1909 Vitória
1910 Santos Dumont
1911 SC Bahia

1912	Atlético
1913	Fluminense
1914	Internacional
1915	Fluminense
1916	Republica
1917	Ypiranga
1918	Ypiranga
1919	Botafogo
1920	Ypiranga
1921	Ypiranga
1922	Botafogo
1923	Botafogo
1924	AA de Bahia
1925	Ypiranga
1926	Botafogo
1927	Baiano de Tênis
1928	Ypiranga
1929	Ypiranga
1930	Botafogo
1931	EC Bahia
1932	Ypiranga
1933	EC Bahia
1934	EC Bahia
1935	Botafogo
1936	EC Bahia
1937	Galicia
1938	Botafogo / EC Bahia
1939	Ypiranga
1940	EC Bahia
1941	Galicia
1942	Galicia
1943	Galicia
1944	EC Bahia
1945	EC Bahia
1946	Guarani
1947	EC Bahia
1948	EC Bahia
1949	EC Bahia
1950	EC Bahia
1951	Ypiranga
1952	EC Bahia
1953	Vitória
1954	EC Bahia
1955	Vitória
1956	EC Bahia
1957	Vitória
1958	EC Bahia
1959	EC Bahia
1960	EC Bahia
1961	EC Bahia
1962	EC Bahia
1963	Fluminense
1964	Vitória
1965	Vitória
1966	Leonico
1967	EC Bahia
1968	Galicia
1969	Fluminense
1970	EC Bahia
1971	EC Bahia
1972	Vitória
1973	EC Bahia
1974	EC Bahia
1975	EC Bahia
1976	EC Bahia
1977	EC Bahia
1978	EC Bahia
1979	EC Bahia
1980	Vitória
1981	EC Bahia
1982	EC Bahia
1983	EC Bahia
1984	EC Bahia
1985	Vitória
1986	EC Bahia
1987	EC Bahia
1988	EC Bahia
1989	Vitória
1990	Vitória
1991	EC Bahia
1992	Vitória
1993	EC Bahia
1994	EC Bahia

Most wins: EC Bahia 42, Vitória 13, Ypiranga 10

Ceara State Champions

1920	Fortaleza FC
1921	Fortaleza FC
1922	Ceara SC
1923	Fortaleza FC
1924	Fortaleza FC
1925	Ceara SC
1926	Fortaleza FC
1927	Fortaleza FC
1928	Fortaleza FC
1929	Maguari
1930	Orion
1931	Ceara SC
1932	Ceara SC
1933	Fortaleza FC
1934	Fortaleza FC
1935	América
1936	Maguari
1937	Fortaleza FC
1938	Fortaleza FC
1939	Ceara SC
1940	Tramways
1941	Ceara SC
1942	Ceara SC
1943	Maguari
1944	Maguari
1945	Ferroviário AC
1946	Fortaleza FC
1947	Fortaleza FC
1948	Ceara SC
1949	Fortaleza FC
1950	Ferroviário AC
1951	Ceara SC
1952	Ferroviário AC
1953	Fortaleza FC
1954	Fortaleza FC
1955	Calouros do Ar
1956	Gentilândia
1957	Ceara SC
1958	Ceara SC
1959	Fortaleza FC
1960	Fortaleza FC
1961	Ceara SC
1962	Ceara SC
1963	Ceara SC
1964	Fortaleza FC
1965	Fortaleza FC
1966	América
1967	Fortaleza FC
1968	Ferroviário AC
1969	Fortaleza FC
1970	Ferroviário AC
1971	Ceara SC
1972	Ceara SC
1973	Fortaleza FC
1974	Fortaleza FC
1975	Ceara SC
1976	Ceara SC
1977	Ceara SC
1978	Ceara SC
1979	Ferroviário AC
1980	Ceara SC
1981	Ceara SC
1982	Fortaleza FC
1983	Fortaleza FC
1984	Ceara SC
1985	Fortaleza FC
1986	Ceara SC
1987	Fortaleza FC
1988	Ferroviário AC
1989	Ceara SC
1990	Ceara SC
1991	Fortaleza FC
1992	Fortaleza FC
1993	Ceara SC
1994	Ferroviário AC

Most wins: Fortaleza FC 30, Ceara SC 27

Distrito Federal de Brasilia Champions

1973	CEUB
1974	Pioneira
1975	-
1976	Brasilia EC
1977	Brasilia EC
1978	Brasilia EC
1979	Gama
1980	Brasilia EC
1981	Taguatinga
1982	Brasilia EC
1983	Brasilia EC
1984	Brasilia EC
1985	Sobradinho
1986	Sobradinho
1987	Brasilia EC
1988	Tiradentes
1989	Taguatinga
1990	Gama
1991	Taguatinga
1992	Taguatinga
1993	Taguatinga
1994	Gama

Most wins: Brasilia EC 8

Espirito Santo State Champions

1940	Américano
1941	Rio Branco AC
1942	Rio Branco AC
1943	Vitória
1944	Caxias
1945	Rio Branco AC
1946	Rio Branco AC
1947	Rio Branco AC
1948	Vale de Rio Doce
1949	Rio Branco AC
1950	Vitória
1951	Rio Branco AC
1952	Vitória
1953	Santo Antonio
1954	Santo Antonio
1955	Santo Antonio
1956	Vitória
1957	Rio Branco AC
1958	Rio Branco AC
1959	Rio Branco AC
1960	Santo Antonio
1961	Santo Antonio
1962	Santo Antonio
1963	Rio Branco AC
1964	Desportiva Ferroviária
1965	Desportiva Ferroviária
1966	Rio Branco AC
1967	Desportiva Ferroviária
1968	Rio Branco AC
1969	Rio Branco AC
1970	Rio Branco AC
1971	-
1972	Desportiva Ferroviária
1973	Rio Branco AC
1974	Desportiva Ferroviária
1975	Rio Branco AC
1976	Vitória
1977	Desportiva Ferroviária
1978	Rio Branco AC
1979	Desportiva Ferroviária
1980	Desportiva Ferroviária
1981	Desportiva Ferroviária
1982	Rio Branco AC
1983	Rio Branco AC
1984	Desportiva Ferroviária
1985	Rio Branco AC
1986	Desportiva Ferroviária
1987	Guarapari
1988	Ibiraçu
1989	Desportiva Ferroviária
1990	Colatina
1991	Muñiz Freire
1992	Desportiva Ferroviária
1993	Linhares
1994	Desportiva Ferroviária

Most wins: Rio Branco AC 21, Desportivo Ferroviária 14

Goiâs State Champions

1944	Atlético Goiâniense
1945	Goiânia
1946	Goiânia
1947	Atlético Goiâniense
1948	Goiânia
1949	Atlético Goiâniense
1950	Goiânia
1951	Goiânia
1952	Goiânia
1953	Goiânia
1954	Goiânia

1955	Atlético Goiâniense
1956	Goiânia
1957	Atlético Goiâniense
1958	Goiânia
1959	Goiânia
1960	Goiânia
1961	Vila Nova FC
1962	Vila Nova FC
1963	Vila Nova FC
1964	Atlético Goiâniense
1965	Anápolis
1966	Goiâs EC
1967	CRAC
1968	Goiânia
1969	Vila Nova FC
1970	Atlético Goiâniense
1971	Goiâs EC
1972	Goiâs EC
1973	Vila Nova FC
1974	Goiânia
1975	Goiâs EC
1976	Goiâs EC
1977	Vila Nova FC
1978	Vila Nova FC
1979	Vila Nova FC
1980	Vila Nova FC
1981	Goiâs EC
1982	Vila Nova FC
1983	Goiâs EC
1984	Vila Nova FC
1985	Atlético Goiâniense
1986	Goiâs EC
1987	Goiâs EC
1988	Atlético Goiâniense
1989	Goiâs EC
1990	Goiâs EC
1991	Goiâs EC
1992	Goiatuba
1993	Vila Nova FC
1994	Goiâs EC

Most wins: Goiânia 14, Goiâs EC 13, Vila Nova FC 12

Maranhão State Champions

1918	Fenix
1919	Luso
1920	Luso
1921	FAC
1922	Fenix
1923	FAC
1924	Luso
1925	Luso
1926	Luso
1927	Luso
1928	Vasco
1929	-
1930	Sampaio Correa
1931	Sirio
1932	Tupa
1933	Sampaio Correa
1934	Sampaio Correa
1935	Tupa
1936	-
1937	Maranhão AC
1938	Tupa
1939	Maranhão AC
1940	Sampaio Correa
1941	Maranhão AC
1942	Sampaio Correa
1943	Maranhão AC
1944	Moto
1945	Moto
1946	Moto
1947	Moto
1948	Moto
1949	Moto
1950	Moto
1951	Maranhão AC
1952	Vitória do Mar
1953	Sampaio Correa
1954	Sampaio Correa
1955	Moto
1956	Sampaio Correa
1957	Ferroviário
1958	Ferroviário
1959	Moto
1960	Moto
1961	Sampaio Correa
1962	Sampaio Correa
1963	Maranhão AC
1964	Sampaio Correa
1965	Sampaio Correa
1966	Moto
1967	Moto
1968	Moto
1969	Maranhão AC
1970	Maranhão AC
1971	Ferroviário
1972	Sampaio Correa
1973	Ferroviário
1974	Moto
1975	Sampaio Correa
1976	Sampaio Correa
1977	Moto
1978	Sampaio Correa
1979	Maranhão AC
1980	Sampaio Correa
1981	Moto
1982	Moto
1983	Moto
1984	Sampaio Correa
1985	Sampaio Correa
1986	Sampaio Correa
1987	Sampaio Correa
1988	Sampaio Correa
1989	Moto
1990	Moto
1991	Sampaio Correa
1992	Sampaio Correa
1993	Maranhão AC
1994	Maranhão AC

Most wins: Sampiao Correa 24, Moto 20, Maranhão AC 11

Mato Grosso State Champions

1974	Operario FC
1975	Comercial EC
1976	Operario FC
1977	Operario FC
1978	Operario FC
1979	Mixto
1980	Mixto
1981	Mixto
1982	Mixto
1983	CE Operario
1984	Mixto
1985	CE Operario
1986	CE Operario
1987	CE Operario
1988	Mixto
1989	Mixto
1990	Mixto
1991	Dom Bosco
1992	Sorriso
1993	Sorriso
1994	CE Operario

Most wins: Mixto 7

In 1979 the Federaçao Matogrossense do Sul was formed. Both Operario EC and Comercial EC joined this new body

Mato Grosso do Sul State Champions

1979	Operario FC
1980	Operario FC
1981	Operario FC
1982	Comercial EC
1983	Operario FC
1984	Corumbaense
1985	Comercial EC
1986	Operario FC
1987	Comercial EC
1988	Operario FC
1989	Operario FC
1990	Ubiratan
1991	Operario FC
1992	Nova Andradina
1993	Comercial EC
1994	Comercial EC

Most wins: Operario FC 11

Minas Gerais State Champions

1916	América FC
1917	América FC
1918	América FC
1919	América FC
1920	América FC
1921	América FC
1922	América FC
1923	América FC
1924	América FC
1925	América FC
1926	Atlético Mineiro
1927	Atlético Mineiro
1928	Palestra Italia
1929	Palestra Italia
1930	Palestra Italia
1931	Atlético Mineiro
1932	Atlético Mineiro/Vila Nova AC
1933	Vila Nova AC
1934	Vila Nova AC
1935	Vila Nova AC
1936	Atlético Mineiro
1937	Siderurgica
1938	Atlético Mineiro
1939	Atlético Mineiro
1940	Cruzeiro
1941	Atlético Mineiro
1942	Atlético Mineiro
1943	Cruzeiro
1944	Cruzeiro
1945	Cruzeiro
1946	Atlético Mineiro
1947	Atlético Mineiro
1948	América FC
1949	Atlético Mineiro
1950	Atlético Mineiro
1951	Vila Nova AC
1952	Atlético Mineiro
1953	Atlético Mineiro
1954	Atlético Mineiro
1955	Atlético Mineiro
1956	Atlético Mineiro/Cruzeiro
1957	América FC
1958	Atlético Mineiro
1959	Cruzeiro
1960	Cruzeiro
1961	Cruzeiro
1962	Atlético Mineiro
1963	Atlético Mineiro
1964	Siderurgica
1965	Cruzeiro
1966	Cruzeiro
1967	Cruzeiro
1968	Cruzeiro
1969	Cruzeiro
1970	Atlético Mineiro
1971	América FC
1972	Cruzeiro
1973	Cruzeiro
1974	Cruzeiro
1975	Cruzeiro
1976	Atlético Mineiro
1977	Cruzeiro
1978	Atlético Mineiro
1979	Atlético Mineiro
1980	Atlético Mineiro
1981	Atlético Mineiro
1982	Atlético Mineiro
1983	Atlético Mineiro
1984	Cruzeiro
1985	Atlético Mineiro
1986	Atlético Mineiro
1987	Cruzeiro
1988	Atlético Mineiro
1989	Atlético Mineiro
1990	Cruzeiro
1991	Atlético Mineiro
1992	Cruzeiro
1993	América FC
1994	Cruzeiro

Most wins: Atlético Mineiro 34, Cruzeiro 26, América 14

Para State Champions

1913	Remo
1914	Remo
1915	Remo
1916	Remo
1917	Remo
1918	Remo
1919	Remo
1920	Paysandu
1921	Paysandu
1922	Paysandu
1923	Paysandu

1924 Remo
1925 Remo
1926 Remo
1927 Paysandu
1928 Paysandu
1929 Paysandu
1930 Remo
1931 Paysandu
1932 Remo
1933 Remo
1934 Paysandu
1935 -
1936 Remo
1937 Tuna Luso
1938 Tuna Luso
1939 Tuna Luso
1940 Remo
1941 Tuna Luso
1942 Paysandu
1943 Paysandu
1944 Paysandu
1945 Paysandu
1946 -
1947 Paysandu
1948 Tuna Luso
1949 Remo
1950 Remo
1951 Tuna Luso
1952 Remo
1953 Remo
1954 Remo
1955 Tuna Luso
1956 Paysandu
1957 Paysandu
1958 Tuna Luso
1959 Paysandu
1960 Remo
1961 Paysandu
1962 Paysandu
1963 Paysandu
1964 Remo
1965 Paysandu
1966 Paysandu
1967 Paysandu
1968 Remo
1969 Paysandu
1970 Tuna Luso
1971 Remo
1972 Paysandu
1973 Remo
1974 Remo
1975 Remo
1976 Paysandu
1977 Remo
1978 Remo
1979 Remo
1980 Paysandu
1981 Paysandu
1982 Paysandu
1983 Tuna Luso
1984 Paysandu
1985 Paysandu
1986 Remo
1987 Paysandu
1988 -
1989 -
1990 Remo
1991 Remo
1992 Paysandu
1993 Remo
1994 Remo

Most wins: Remo 34, Paysandu 33, Tuna Luso 10

Paraiba State Champions

1917 Colegio Pio
1918 Cabo Branco
1919 Palmeiras
1920 Cabo Branco
1921 Palmeiras
1922 Pytaguares
1923 América
1924 Cabo Branco
1925 América
1926 Cabo Branco
1927 Cabo Branco
1928 Palmeiras
1929 Cabo Branco
1930 -
1931 Cabo Branco
1932 Cabo Branco
1933 Palmeiras
1934 Cabo Branco
1935 Palmeiras
1936 Botafogo
1937 Botafogo
1938 Botafogo
1939 Auto Esporte
1940 Treze
1941 Treze
1942 Astrea
1943 Astrea
1944 Botafogo
1945 Botafogo
1946 Filipeia
1947 Botafogo
1948 Botafogo
1949 Botafogo
1950 Treze
1951 -
1952 Red Cross
1953 Botafogo
1954 Botafogo
1955 Botafogo
1956 Auto Esporte
1957 Botafogo
1958 Auto Esporte
1959 Estrela do Mar
1960 Campinense
1961 Campinense
1962 Campinense
1963 Campinense
1964 Campinense
1965 Campinense
1966 Treze
1967 Campinense
1968 Botafogo
1969 Botafogo
1970 Botafogo
1971 Campinense
1972 Campinense
1973 Campinense
1974 Campinense
1975 Botafogo / Treze
1976 Botafogo
1977 Botafogo
1978 Botafogo
1979 Botafogo
1980 Campinense
1981 Treze
1982 Treze
1983 Treze
1984 Botafogo
1985 -
1986 Botafogo
1987 Auto Esporte
1988 Botafogo
1989 Treze
1990 Auto Esporte
1991 Campinense
1992 Auto Esporte
1993 Campinense
1994 Souza

Most wins: Botafogo 23, Campinense 14

Parana State Champions

1915 Internacional
1916 Coritiba FC
1917 América
1918 Britania
1919 Britania
1920 Britania
1921 Britania
1922 Britania
1923 Britania
1924 Palestra Italia
1925 Atlético Paranaense
1926 Palestra Italia
1927 Coritiba FC
1928 Britania
1929 Atlético Paranaense
1930 Atlético Paranaense
1931 Coritiba FC
1932 Palestra Italia
1933 Coritiba FC
1934 Atlético Paranaense
1935 Coritiba FC
1936 Atlético Paranaense
1937 Ferroviária
1938 Ferroviária
1939 Coritiba FC
1940 Atlético Paranaense
1941 Coritiba FC
1942 Coritiba FC
1943 Atlético Paranaense
1944 Ferroviária
1945 Atlético Paranaense
1946 Coritiba FC
1947 Coritiba FC
1948 Ferroviária
1949 Atlético Paranaense
1950 Ferroviária
1951 Coritiba FC
1952 Coritiba FC
1953 Ferroviária
1954 Coritiba FC
1955 Monte Alegre
1956 Coritiba FC
1957 Coritiba FC
1958 Atlético Paranaense
1959 Coritiba FC
1960 Coritiba FC
1961 Comercial
1962 Londrina
1963 Maringa
1964 Maringa
1965 Ferroviária
1966 Ferroviária
1967 Agua Verde
1968 Coritiba FC
1969 Coritiba FC
1970 Atlético Paranaense
1971 Coritiba FC
1972 Coritiba FC
1973 Coritiba FC
1974 Coritiba FC
1975 Coritiba FC
1976 Coritiba FC
1977 Maringa
1978 Coritiba FC
1979 Coritiba FC
1980 Cascavel
1981 Londrina
1982 Atlético Paranaense
1983 Atlético Paranaense
1984 Pinheiros
1985 Atlético Paranaense
1986 Coritiba FC
1987 Pinheiros
1988 Atlético Paranaense
1989 Coritiba FC
1990 Atlético Paranaense
1991 Paraná Clube
1992 Londrina
1993 Paraná Clube
1994 Paraná Clube

Most wins: Coritiba FC 29, Paraná Clube 24, Atlético Paranaense 18

Pernambuco State Champions

1915 Flamengo
1916 Sport Recife
1917 Sport Recife
1918 América CF
1919 América CF
1920 Sport Recife
1921 América CF
1922 América CF
1923 Sport Recife
1924 Sport Recife
1925 Sport Recife
1926 Torre
1927 América CF
1928 Sport Recife
1929 Torre
1930 Torre
1931 Santa Cruz
1932 Santa Cruz
1933 Santa Cruz
1934 Nautico
1935 Santa Cruz
1936 Tramways
1937 Tramways
1938 Sport Recife
1939 Nautico
1940 Santa Cruz
1941 Sport Recife
1942 Sport Recife
1943 Sport Recife
1944 América CF
1945 Nautico
1946 Santa Cruz
1947 Santa Cruz
1948 Sport Recife

1949 Sport Recife
1950 Nautico
1951 Nautico
1952 Nautico
1953 Sport Recife
1954 Nautico
1955 Sport Recife
1956 Sport Recife
1957 Santa Cruz
1958 Sport Recife
1959 Santa Cruz
1960 Nautico
1961 Sport Recife
1962 Sport Recife
1963 Nautico
1964 Nautico
1965 Nautico
1966 Nautico
1967 Nautico
1968 Nautico
1969 Santa Cruz
1970 Santa Cruz
1971 Santa Cruz
1972 Santa Cruz
1973 Santa Cruz
1974 Nautico
1975 Sport Recife
1976 Santa Cruz
1977 Sport Recife
1978 Santa Cruz
1979 Santa Cruz
1980 Sport Recife
1981 Sport Recife
1982 Sport Recife
1983 Santa Cruz
1984 Nautico
1985 Nautico
1986 Santa Cruz
1987 Santa Cruz
1988 Sport Recife
1989 Nautico
1990 Santa Cruz
1991 Sport Recife
1992 Sport Recife
1993 Santa Cruz
1994 Sport Recife

Most wins: Sport Recife 28, Santa Cruz 22, Nautico 18

Piaui State Champions

1918 Palmeiras
1919 Teresinense
1920 Artistico
1921 Militar
1922 Teresinense
1923 Artistico
1924 AE Tiradentes
1925 AE Tiradentes
1926 AE Tiradentes
1927 AE Tiradentes
1928 AE Tiradentes
1929 Artistico
1930 Artistico
1931 Militar
1932 Militar
1933 Artistico
1934 AE Tiradentes
1935 Militar
1936 Militar
1937 Militar
1938 Botafogo
1939 Flamengo
1940 Botafogo
1941 Botafogo
1942 Flamengo
1943 Botafogo
1944 Flamengo
1945 Flamengo
1946 Flamengo
1947 Botafogo
1948 River AC
1949 Botafogo
1950 River AC
1951 River AC
1952 River AC
1953 River AC
1954 River AC
1955 River AC
1956 River AC
1957 Botafogo
1958 River AC
1959 River AC
1960 River AC
1961 River AC
1962 River AC
1963 River AC
1964 Flamengo
1965 Flamengo
1966 Piaui EC
1967 Piaui EC
1968 Piaui EC
1969 Piaui EC
1970 Flamengo
1971 Flamengo
1972 AE Tiradentes
1973 River AC
1974 AE Tiradentes
1975 River AC / AE Tiradentes
1976 Flamengo
1977 River AC
1978 River AC
1979 Flamengo
1980 River AC
1981 River AC
1982 AE Tiradentes
1983 Auto Esporte
1984 Flamengo
1985 Piaui EC
1986 Flamengo
1987 Flamengo
1988 Flamengo
1989 River AC
1990 AE Tiradentes
1991 SE Picos
1992 4 de Julho
1993 4 de Julho
1994 SE Picos

Most wins: River AC 21, Flamengo 15, AE Tiradentes 11

Rio Grande do Norte State Champions

1920 ABC
1921 ABC
1922 América
1923 ABC
1924 América
1925 ABC
1926 ABC
1927 América
1928 ABC
1929 ABC
1930 América
1931 América
1932 ABC
1933 ABC
1934 ABC
1935 ABC
1936 ABC
1937 ABC
1938 ABC
1939 ABC
1940 ABC
1941 ABC
1942 -
1943 América
1944 ABC
1945 ABC
1946 Santa Cruz
1947 ABC
1948 América
1949 América
1950 ABC
1951 -
1952 América
1953 ABC
1954 ABC
1955 ABC
1956 América
1957 América
1958 ABC
1959 ABC
1960 ABC
1961 ABC
1962 ABC
1963 América
1964 Alecrim
1965 ABC
1966 ABC
1967 Alecrim
1968 Alecrim
1969 América
1970 ABC
1971 ABC
1972 ABC
1973 ABC
1974 América
1975 América
1976 ABC
1977 América
1978 ABC
1979 América
1980 América
1981 América
1982 América
1983 ABC
1984 ABC
1985 Alecrim
1986 Alecrim
1987 América
1988 América
1989 América
1990 ABC
1991 América
1992 América
1993 América
1994 ABC

Most wins: ABC 41, América 26

Rio Grande do Sul State Champions

1919 Brasil
1920 Guarani
1921 Grêmio
1922 Grêmio
1923-24 -
1925 Grêmio Bage
1926 Grêmio
1927 Internacional
1928 Américano
1929 Cruzeiro
1930 Pelotas
1931 Grêmio
1932 Grêmio
1933 São Paulo
1934 Internacional
1935 Farroupilha
1936 Rio Grande
1937 Grêmio Santanense
1938 Guarani
1939 Rio Grande
1940 Internacional
1941 Internacional
1942 Internacional
1943 Internacional
1944 Internacional
1945 Internacional
1946 Grêmio
1947 Internacional
1948 Internacional
1949 Grêmio
1950 Internacional
1951 Internacional
1952 Internacional
1953 Internacional
1954 Renner
1955 Internacional
1956 Grêmio
1957 Grêmio
1958 Grêmio
1959 Grêmio
1960 Grêmio
1961 Internacional
1962 Grêmio
1963 Grêmio
1964 Grêmio
1965 Grêmio
1966 Grêmio
1967 Grêmio
1968 Grêmio
1969 Internacional
1970 Internacional
1971 Internacional
1972 Internacional
1973 Internacional
1974 Internacional
1975 Internacional
1976 Internacional
1977 Grêmio
1978 Internacional
1979 Grêmio
1980 Grêmio
1981 Internacional
1982 Internacional
1983 Internacional
1984 Internacional

1985	Grêmio
1986	Grêmio
1987	Grêmio
1988	Grêmio
1989	Grêmio
1990	Grêmio
1991	Internacional
1992	Internacional
1993	Grêmio
1994	Internacional

Most wins: Internacional 32, Grêmio 29

Santa Catarina State Champions

1927	Avai
1928	Avai
1929	Caxias
1930	Avai
1931	Lauro Muller
1932	Figueirense
1933	-
1934	Atlético Florianopolis
1935	Figueirense
1936	Figueirense
1937	Figueirense
1938	CIP
1939	Figueirense
1940	Ipiranga
1941	Figueirense
1942	Avai
1943	Avai
1944	Avai
1945	Avai
1946	-
1947	América
1948	América
1949	Olimpico
1950	Carlos Renaux
1951	América
1952	América
1953	Carlos Renaux
1954	Caxias
1955	Caxias
1956	Operario
1957	Hercilio Luz
1958	Hercilio Luz
1959	Paulo Ramos
1960	Metropol
1961	Metropol
1962	Metropol
1963	Marcilio Diaz
1964	Olimpico
1965	Internacional
1966	Perdigao
1967	Metropol
1968	Comerciario
1969	Metropol
1970	Ferroviario
1971	América
1972	Figueirense
1973	Avai
1974	Figueirense
1975	Avai
1976	Joinville
1977	Chapecoense
1978	Joinville
1979	Joinville
1980	Joinville
1981	Joinville
1982	Joinville
1983	Joinville
1984	Joinville
1985	Joinville
1986	Criciuma
1987	Joinville
1988	Avai
1989	Criciuma
1990	Criciuma
1991	Criciúma
1992	Brusque
1993	Criciúma
1994	Figueirense

Most wins: Avai, Joinville 10

Sergipe State Champions

1918	Cotinguiba
1919	-
1920	Cotinguiba
1921	Industrial
1922	CS Sergipe
1923	Cotinguiba
1924	CS Sergipe
1925-26	-
1927	CS Sergipe
1928	CS Sergipe
1929	CS Sergipe
1930-31	-
1932	CS Sergipe
1933	CS Sergipe
1934	Palestra
1935	Palestra
1936	Cotinguiba
1937	CS Sergipe
1938	-
1939	Ipiranga
1940	CS Sergipe
1941	Riachuelo
1942	Cotinguiba
1943	CS Sergipe
1944	Vasco
1945	Ipiranga
1946	Olimpico
1947	Olimpico
1948	Vasco
1949	Palestra
1950	Passagem
1951	Confiança
1952	Cotinguiba
1953	Vasco
1954	Confiança
1955	CS Sergipe
1956	Santa Cruz
1957	Santa Cruz
1958	Santa Cruz
1959	Santa Cruz
1960	Santa Cruz
1961	CS Sergipe
1962	Confiança
1963	Confiança
1964	CS Sergipe
1965	Confiança
1966	América
1967	CS Sergipe
1968	Confiança
1969	Itabaiana
1970	CS Sergipe
1971	CS Sergipe
1972	CS Sergipe
1973	Itabaiana
1974	CS Sergipe
1975	CS Sergipe
1976	Confiança
1977	Confiança
1978	Itabaiana
1979	Itabaiana
1980	Itabaiana
1981	Itabaiana
1982	CS Sergipe / Itabaiana
1983	Confiança
1984	CS Sergipe
1985	CS Sergipe
1986	Confiança
1987	Vasco
1988	Confiança
1989	CS Sergipe
1990	Confiança
1991	CS Sergipe
1992	CS Sergipe
1993	-
1994	CS Sergipe

Most wins: CS Sergipe 26, Confiança 12

LEADING INTERNATIONAL GOALSCORERS

77	Pelé	(Santos,Cosmos)	1957-1971
54	Zico	(Flamengo,Udinese)	1971-1986
38	Jairzinho	(Botafogo)	1963-1982
36	Bebeto	(Flamengo,Vasco,La Coruña	1985-
32	Tostao	(Cruzeiro,Vasco)	1966-1972
31	Ademir Menezes	(Vasco,Fluminense)	1945-1953
30	Romario	(Vasco,PSV Eindhoven, Barcelona,Flamengo)	1987-
	Zizinho	(Flamengo,Bangu)	1942-1957
27	Careca I	(São Paulo,Napoli)	1982-1992
26	Rivelino	(Corinthians,Fluminense)	1965-1978

LEADING INTERNATIONAL APPEARANCES

100	Djalma Santos	(Portuguesa,Palmeiras, Atletico Parana)	1952-1968
95	Gilmar I	(Corinthians,Santos)	1953-1969
94	Rivelino	Corinthians,Fluminense)	1965-1978
92	Pelé	(Santos,Cosmos)	1957-1971
91	Claudio Taffarel	(Internacional,Parma,Reggiana)	1987-
90	Bebeto	(Flamengo,Vasco,La Coruña	1985-
88	Jorginho	(Flamengo,Bayer Leverkusen, Bayern München,Kashima Antlers)	1983-
87	Jairzinho	(Botafogo)	1963-1982
83	Gérson	(Flamengo,Botafogo,São Paulo)	1959-1972

INTERNATIONAL MATCHES PLAYED BY BRAZIL

20-09-1914	Argentina	L 0-3	Buenos Aires	Fr	
27-09	Argentina	W 1-0	Buenos Aires	RC	Rubens Salles
8-07-1916	Chile	D 1-1	Buenos Aires	SC	Demóstenes
10-07	Argentina	D 1-1	Buenos Aires	SC	Alencar
12-07	Uruguay	L 1-2	Buenos Aires	SC	Friedenreich
18-07	Uruguay	W 1-0	Montevideo	Fr	Mimi
3-10-1917	Argentina	L 2-4	Montevideo	SC	Lagreca, Neco
7-10	Uruguay	L 0-4	Montevideo	SC	

12-10	Chile	W 5-0	Montevideo	SC	Haroldo 2, Amilcar, Caetano, Neco
16-10	Uruguay	L 1-3	Montevideo	Fr	Neco
11-05-1919	Chile	W 6-0	Rio de Janeiro	SC	Neco 2, Friedenreich 3, Haroldo
18-05	Argentina	W 3-1	Rio de Janeiro	SC	Amilcar, Millon, Heitor Dominguez
25-05	Uruguay	D 2-2	Rio de Janeiro	SC	Neco 2
29-05	Uruguay	W 1-0	Rio de Janeiro	SCpo	Friedenreich
1-06	Argentina	D 3-3	Rio de Janeiro	Fr	Arlindo I, Haroldo
11-09-1920	Chile	W 1-0	Viña del Mar	SC	Alvariza
18-09	Uruguay	L 0-6	Viña del Mar	SC	
25-09	Argentina	L 0-2	Viña del Mar	SC	
12-10	Argentina	L 1-3	Buenos Aires	Fr	Osvaldo
2-10-1921	Argentina	L 0-1	Buenos Aires	SC	
12-10	Paraguay	W 3-0	Buenos Aires	SC	Machado 2, Candiotta
23-10	Uruguay	L 1-2	Buenos Aires	SC	Zezé I
17-09-1922	Chile	D 1-1	Rio de Janeiro	SC	Tatú
24-09	Paraguay	D 1-1	Rio de Janeiro	SC	Amilcar
1-10	Uruguay	D 0-0	Rio de Janeiro	SC	
15-10	Argentina	W 2-0	Rio de Janeiro	SC	Amilcar, Neco
22-10	Paraguay	W 3-1	Rio de Janeiro	SCpo	Formiga 2, Neco
22-10	Argentina	W 2-1	Sao Paulo	RC	Gamba 2
29-10	Paraguay	W 3-1	Sao Paulo	Fr	Imparatinho 2, Gamba
11-11-1923	Paraguay	L 0-1	Montevideo	SC	
18-11	Argentina	L 1-2	Montevideo	SC	Nilo
22-11	Paraguay	W 2-0	Montevideo	Fr	Zezé I, Nilo
25-11	Uruguay	L 1-2	Montevideo	SC	Nilo
2-12	Argentina	W 2-0	Buenos Aires	RC	Zezé I, Nilo
9-12	Argentina	L 0-2	Buenos Aires	RC	
6-12-1925	Paraguay	W 5-2	Buenos Aires	SC	Lagarto 2, Friedenreich, Filó, Nilo
13-12	Argentina	L 1-4	Buenos Aires	SC	Nilo
17-12	Paraguay	W 3-1	Buenos Aires	SC	Lagarto 2, Nilo
25-12	Argentina	D 2-2	Buenos Aires	SC	Nilo, Friedenreich
14-07-1930	Yugoslavia	L 1-2	Montevideo	WCr1	Preguinho
22-07	Bolivia	W 4-0	Montevideo	WCr1	Carvalho Leite, Preguinho 3
1-08	France	W 3-2	Rio de Janeiro	Fr	Heitor Dominguez 2, Friedenreich
10-08	Yugoslavia	W 4-1	Rio de Janeiro	Fr	Carvalho Leite 2, Benedicto II, Russinho
17-08	USA	W 4-3	Rio de Janeiro	Fr	Doca, Carvalho Leite, Preguinho, Teóphilo
6-09-1931	Uruguay	W 2-0	Rio de Janeiro	RBC	Nilo 2
4-12-1932	Uruguay	W 2-1	Montevideo	RBC	Leônidas da Silva 2
27-05-1934	Spain	L 1-3	Genoa	WCr1	Leônidas da Silva
3-06	Yugoslavia	L 4-8	Belgrade	Fr	Leônidas da Silva 2, Armandinho, Valdemar de Brito
27-12-1936	Peru	W 3-2	Buenos Aires	SC	Alfonsinho, Roberto I, Niginho
3-01-1937	Chile	W 6-4	Buenos Aires	SC	Patesko 2, Carvalho Leite, Luiz M.Oliveira 2, Roberto I
13-01	Paraguay	W 5-0	Buenos Aires	SC	Patesko 2, Luiz M.Oliveira 2, Carvalho Leite
19-01	Uruguay	W 3-2	Buenos Aires	SC	Bahia, Carvalho Leite, Niginho
30-01	Argentina	L 0-1	Buenos Aires	SC	
1-02	Argentina	L 0-2	Buenos Aires	SCpo	
5-06-1938	Poland	W 6-5	Strasbourg	WCr1	Leônidas da Silva 4, Perácio, Romeu Pelliciari
12-06	Czechoslovakia	D 1-1	Bordeaux	WCqf	Leônidas da Silva
14-06	Czechoslovakia	W 2-1	Bordeaux	WCqf	Leônidas da Silva, Roberto I
16-06	Italy	L 1-2	Marseille	WCsf	Romeu Pelliciari
19-06	Sweden	W 4-2	Bordeaux	WC3p	Leônidas da Silva 2, Romeu Pelliciari, Perácio
15-01-1939	Argentina	L 1-5	Rio de Janeiro	RC	Leônidas da Silva
22-01	Argentina	W 3-2	Rio de Janeiro	RC	Adilson, Leônidas da Silva, Perácio
18-02-1940	Argentina	D 2-2	Sao Paulo	RC	Leônidas da Silva 2
25-02	Argentina	L 0-3	Sao Paulo	RC	
5-03	Argentina	L 1-6	Buenos Aires	RC	Jair R.Pinto
10-03	Argentina	W 3-2	Buenos Aires	RC	Hércules 2, Leônidas da Silva
17-03	Argentina	L 1-5	Buenos Aires	RC	Leônidas da Silva
24-03	Uruguay	L 3-4	Rio de Janeiro	RBC	Pedro Amorim, Leônidas da Silva, Hércules
31-03	Uruguay	D 1-1	Rio de Janeiro	RBC	Leônidas da Silva
14-01-1942	Chile	W 6-1	Montevideo	SC	Pirilo 3, Patesko 2, Cláudio C.Pinho
17-01	Argentina	L 1-2	Montevideo	SC	Servílio I
21-01	Peru	W 2-1	Montevideo	SC	Pedro Amorim
24-01	Uruguay	L 0-1	Montevideo	SC	
1-02	Ecuador	W 5-1	Montevideo	SC	Pirilo 3, Tim, Zizinho
5-02	Paraguay	D 1-1	Montevideo	SC	Zizinho
14-05-1944	Uruguay	W 6-1	Rio de Janeiro	Fr	Eduardo Lima 2, Tesourinha, Isaías, Lelé, Rui
17-05	Uruguay	W 4-0	Sao Paulo	Fr	Jair R.Pinto 3, Heleno de Freitas
21-01-1945	Colombia	W 3-0	Santiago	SC	Heleno de Freitas, Jaime, Jorginho
28-01	Bolivia	W 2-0	Santiago	SC	Ademir Menezes, Tesourinha
7-02	Uruguay	W 3-0	Santiago	SC	Heleno de Freitas 2, Rui

Date	Opponent	Result	Venue	Comp	Scorers
15-02	Argentina	L 1-3	Santiago	SC	Ademir Menezes
21-02	Ecuador	W 9-2	Santiago	SC	Ademir Menezes 3, Jair R.Pinto 2, Heleno de Freitas 2, Zizinho 2
28-02	Chile	W 1-0	Santiago	SC	Heleno de Freitas
16-12	Argentina	L 3-4	Sao Paulo	RC	Zizinho, OG, Ademir Menezes
20-12	Argentina	W 6-2	Rio de Janeiro	RC	Ademir Menezes 2, Heleno de Freitas, Chico, Leônidas da Silva, Zizinho
23-12	Argentina	W 3-1	Rio de Janeiro	RC	OG, Heleno de Freitas, Eduardo Lima
5-01-1946	Uruguay	L 3-4	Montevideo	RBC	Jair R.Pinto 2, Zizinho
9-01	Uruguay	D 1-1	Montevideo	RBC	Heleno de Freitas
16-01	Bolivia	W 3-0	Buenos Aires	SC	Heleno de Freitas 2, Zizinho
23-01	Uruguay	W 4-3	Buenos Aires	SC	Jair R.Pinto, Heleno de Freitas, Chico
29-01	Paraguay	D 1-1	Buenos Aires	SC	Norival
3-02	Chile	W 5-1	Buenos Aires	SC	Zizinho 4, Chico
10-02	Argentina	L 0-2	Buenos Aires	SC	
29-03-1947	Uruguay	D 0-0	Sao Paulo	RBC	
1-04	Uruguay	W 3-2	Rio de Janeiro	RBC	Heleno de Freitas 2, Tesourinha
4-04	Uruguay	D 1-1	Montevideo	RBC	Danilo Alvim
11-04-1948	Uruguay	L 2-4	Montevideo	RBC	Canhotinho, Carlyle
3-04-1949	Ecuador	W 9-1	Rio de Janeiro	SC	Jair R.Pinto 2, Simao 2, Tesourinha 2, Ademir Menezes, Otávio, Zizinho
10-04	Bolivia	W 10-1	Sao Paulo	SC	Nininho 3, Cláudio C.Pinho 2, Zizinho2 Simao 2, Jair R.Pinto
13-04	Chile	W 2-1	Sao Paulo	SC	Cláudio C.Pinto, Zizinho
17-04	Colombia	W 5-0	Sao Paulo	SC	Ademir Menezes 2, Orlando de Ouro, Tesourinha, Canhotinho
24-04	Peru	W 7-1	Rio de Janeiro	SC	Jair R.Pinto 2, OG, Augusto, Orlando de Ouro, Ademir Menezes
30-04	Uruguay	W 5-1	Rio de Janeiro	SC	Jair R.Pinto 2, Danilo Alvim, Tesourinha, Zizinho
8-05	Paraguay	L 1-2	Rio de Janeiro	SC	Tesourinha
11-05	Paraguay	W 7-0	Rio de Janeiro	SC	Ademir Menezes 3, Jair R.Pinto, Tesourinha 2
6-05-1950	Uruguay	L 3-4	Sao Paulo	RBC	Ademir Menezes 2, Zizinho
7-05	Paraguay	W 2-0	Rio de Janeiro	OCC	Pinga I 2
13-05	Paraguay	D 3-3	Sao Paulo	OCC	Maneca, Baltazar I, Pinga I
14-05	Uruguay	W 3-2	Rio de Janeiro	RBC	Ademir Menezes 2, Chico
18-05	Uruguay	W 1-0	Rio de Janeiro	RBC	Ademir Menezes
24-06	Mexico	W 4-0	Rio de Janeiro	WCr1	Ademir Menezes 2, Jair R.Pinto, Baltazar I
28-06	Switzerland	D 2-2	Sao Paulo	WCr1	Alfredo II, Baltazar I
1-07	Yugoslavia	W 2-0	Rio de Janeiro	WCr1	Ademir Menezes, Zizinho
9-07	Sweden	W 7-1	Rio de Janeiro	WCr2	Ademir Menezes 4, Chico 2, Maneca
13-07	Spain	W 6-1	Rio de Janeiro	WCr2	Ademir Menezes 2, Chico 2, Zizinho, Jair R.Pinto
16-07	Uruguay	L 1-2	Rio de Janeiro	WCf	Friaca
6-04-1952	Mexico	W 2-0	Santiago	PAC	Baltazar I 2
10-04	Peru	D 0-0	Santiago	PAC	
13-04	Panama	W 5-0	Santiago	PAC	Rodrigues II 2, Pinga I, Baltazar I, Julinho I
16-04	Uruguay	W 4-2	Santiago	PAC	Baltazar I, Rodrigues II, Didi, Pinga I
20-04	Chile	W 3-0	Santiago	PAC	Ademir Menezes 2, Pinga I
1-03-1953	Bolivia	W 8-1	Lima	SC	Julinho I 4, Pinga I 2, Rodrigues II 2
12-03	Ecuador	W 2-0	Lima	SC	Ademir Menezes, Cláudio C.Pinho
15-03	Uruguay	W 1-0	Lima	SC	Ipojucan
19-03	Peru	L 0-1	Lima	SC	
23-03	Chile	W 3-2	Lima	SC	Baltazar I, Julinho I, Zizinho
27-03	Paraguay	L 1-2	Lima	SC	Nilton Santos
1-04	Paraguay	L 2-3	Lima	SCpo	Baltazar I 2
28-02-1954	Chile	W 2-0	Santiago	WCq	Baltazar I 2
7-03	Paraguay	W 1-0	Asuncion	WCq	Baltazar I
14-03	Chile	W 1-0	Rio de Janeiro	WCq	Baltazar I
21-03	Paraguay	W 4-1	Rio de Janeiro	WCq	Julinho I 2, Baltazar I, Maurinho
16-06	Mexico	W 5-0	Geneva	WCr1	Pinga I 2, Baltazar I, Didi, Julinho I
19-06	Yugoslavia	D 1-1	Lausanne	WCr1	Didi
27-06	Hungary	L 2-4	Berne	WCqf	Djalma Santos, Julinho I
18-09-1955	Chile	D 1-1	Rio de Janeiro	OHC	Pinheiro
20-09	Chile	W 2-1	Sao Paulo	OHC	Maurinho, Alvaro
13-11	Paraguay	W 3-0	Rio de Janeiro	OCC	Zizinho 2, Sabará
17-11	Paraguay	D 3-3	Sao Paulo	OCC	Maurinho, Canhoteiro, Humberto
24-01-1956	Chile	L 1-4	Montevideo	SC	Maurinho
29-01	Paraguay	D 0-0	Montevideo	SC	
1-02	Peru	W 2-1	Montevideo	SC	Alvaro, Zezinho
5-02	Argentina	W 1-0	Montevideo	SC	Luiz Trujilo
10-02	Uruguay	D 0-0	Montevideo	SC	
1-03	Chile	W 2-1	Mexico City	PAC	Luizinho RS, Raul

Date	Opponent	Result	Venue	Comp	Scorers
6-03	Peru	W 1-0	Mexico City	PAC	Larry
8-03	Mexico	W 2-1	Mexico City	PAC	Bodinho 2
13-03	Costa Rica	W 7-1	Mexico City	PAC	Chinezinho 3, Larry 3, Bodinho
18-03	Argentina	D 2-2	Mexico City	PAC	Enio Andrade, Chinezinho
8-04	Portugal	W 1-0	Lisbon	Fr	Gino
11-04	Switzerland	D 1-1	Zurich	Fr	Gino
15-04	Austria	W 3-2	Vienna	Fr	Didi, Gino, Zózimo
21-04	Czechoslovakia	D 0-0	Prague	Fr	
25-04	Italy	L 0-3	Milan	Fr	
1-05	Turkey	W 1-0	Istanbul	Fr	Djalma Santos
9-05	England	L 2-4	London	Fr	Paulinho V
12-06	Paraguay	W 2-0	Asuncion	OCC	Ferreira 2
17-06	Paraguay	W 5-2	Asuncion	OCC	Zizinho 2, Ferreira, Leônidas II, Ilton
24-06	Uruguay	W 2-0	Rio de Janeiro	CA	Canário, Zizinho
1-07	Italy	W 2-0	Rio de Janeiro	Fr	Ferreira, Canário
8-07	Argentina	D 0-0	Buenos Aires	CA	
5-08	Czechoslovakia	L 0-1	Rio de Janeiro	Fr	
8-08	Czechoslovakia	W 4-1	Sao Paulo	Fr	Pepe 2, Zizinho 2
13-03-1957	Chile	W 4-2	Lima	SC	Didi 3, Pepe
21-03	Ecuador	W 7-1	Lima	SC	Evaristo 2, Joel 2, Indio, Pepe, Zizinho
24-03	Colombia	W 9-0	Lima	SC	Evaristo 5, Didi 2, Zizinho, Pepe
28-03	Uruguay	L 2-3	Lima	SC	Evaristo, Didi
31-03	Peru	W 1-0	Lima	SC	Didi
3-04	Argentina	L 0-3	Lima	SC	
13-04	Peru	D 1-1	Lima	WCq	Indio
21-04	Peru	W 1-0	Rio de Janeiro	WCq	Didi
11-06	Portugal	W 2-1	Rio de Janeiro	Fr	Didi, Tite
16-06	Portugal	W 3-0	Sao Paulo	Fr	Zito, Altafini, Del Vecchio
7-07	Argentina	L 1-2	Rio de Janeiro	RC	Pelé
10-07	Argentina	W 2-0	Sao Paulo	RC	Pelé, Altafini
15-09	Chile	L 0-1	Santiago	OHC	
18-09	Chile	D 1-1	Santiago	OHC	Matos
4-05-1958	Paraguay	W 5-1	Rio de Janeiro	OCC	Zagalo 2, Dida, Vavá, Pelé
7-05	Paraguay	D 0-0	Sao Paulo	OCC	
14-05	Bulgaria	W 4-0	Rio de Janeiro	Fr	Moacir 2, Dida, Joel
18-05	Bulgaria	W 3-1	Sao Paulo	Fr	Pelé 2, Pepe
8-06	Austria	W 3-0	Uddevalla	WCr1	Altafini 2, Nilton Santos
11-06	England	D 0-0	Gothenberg	WCr1	
15-06	Soviet Union	W 2-0	Gothenberg	WCr1	Vavá 2
19-06	Wales	W 1-0	Gothenberg	WCqf	Pelé
24-06	France	W 5-2	Stockholm	WCsf	Pelé 3, Vavá, Didi
29-06	Sweden	W 5-2	Stockholm	WCf	Vavá 2, Pelé 2, Zagalo
10-03-1959	Peru	D 2-2	Buenos Aires	SC	Didi, Pelé
15-03	Chile	W 3-0	Buenos Aires	SC	Pelé 2, Didi
21-03	Bolivia	W 4-2	Buenos Aires	SC	Paulo Valentim 2, Pelé, Didi
26-03	Uruguay	W 3-1	Buenos Aires	SC	Paulo Valentim 3
29-03	Paraguay	W 4-1	Buenos Aires	SC	Pelé 3, Chinezinho
4-04	Argentina	D 1-1	Buenos Aires	SC	Pelé
13-05	England	W 2-0	Rio de Janeiro	Fr	Julinho I, Henrique
17-09	Chile	W 7-0	Rio de Janeiro	OHC	Pelé 3, Quarentinha 2, Dino Sani, Dorval
20-09	Chile	W 1-0	Sao Paulo	OHC	Quarentinha
5-12	Paraguay	W 3-2	Guayaquil	SC	Paulo PE 2, Zé de Mello
12-12	Uruguay	L 0-3	Guayaquil	SC	
19-12	Ecuador	W 3-1	Guayaquil	SC	Geraldo II, Paulo PE, Zé de Mello
22-12	Argentina	L 1-4	Guayaquil	SC	Geraldo II
27-12	Ecuador	W 2-1	Guayaquil	Fr	Traçaia, Zé de Mello
6-03-1960	Mexico	D 2-2	San Jose	PAC	Élton, Gilberto
10-03	Costa Rica	L 0-3	San Jose	PAC	
13-03	Argentina	L 1-2	San Jose	PAC	Juarez
15-03	Mexico	W 2-1	San Jose	PAC	Mengálvio, Alfeu
17-03	Costa Rica	W 4-0	San Jose	PAC	Juarez 2, Élton 2
20-03	Argentina	W 1-0	San Jose	PAC	Mílton I
29-04	Egypt	W 5-0	Cairo	Fr	Pepe 2, Quarentinha 2, Garrincha
1-05	Egypt	W 3-1	Alexandria	Fr	Pelé 3
6-05	Egypt	W 3-0	Cairo	Fr	Quarentinha 2, Garrincha
10-05	Denmark	W 4-3	Copenhagen	Fr	Quarentinha 2, Chinezinho, Pepe
26-05	Argentina	L 2-4	Buenos Aires	RC	Djalma Santos, Delem
29-05	Argentina	W 4-1	Buenos Aires	RC	Delem 2, Servílio II, Julinho I
29-06	Chile	W 4-0	Rio de Janeiro	Fr	Valdo I 2, Dida, Vavá
3-07	Paraguay	W 2-1	Asuncion	CA	Delem, Almir Albuquerque
9-07	Uruguay	L 0-1	Montevideo	CA	

Date	Opponent	Result	Venue	Comp	Scorers
12-07	Argentina	W 5-1	Rio de Janeiro	CA	Pepe 2, Pelé, Delem, Chinezinho
30-04-1961	Paraguay	W 2-0	Asuncion	OCC	Coutinho, Pepe
3-05	Paraguay	W 3-2	Asuncion	OCC	Coutinho 2, Quarentinha
7-05	Chile	W 2-1	Santiago	OHC	Garrincha, Didi
11-05	Chile	W 1-0	Santiago	OHC	Gérson
29-06	Paraguay	W 3-2	Rio de Janeiro	Fr	Joel, Dida, Henrique
21-04-1962	Paraguay	W 6-0	Rio de Janeiro	OCC	Didi, Pelé, Coutinho, Vavá, Garrincha, Nilton Santos
24-04	Paraguay	W 4-0	Sao Paulo	OCC	Pelé 2, Pepe, Vavá
6-05	Portugal	W 2-1	Sao Paulo	Fr	Zagalo, Zequinha
9-05	Portugal	W 1-0	Rio de Janeiro	Fr	Pelé
12-05	Wales	W 3-1	Rio de Janeiro	Fr	Garrincha, Coutinho, Pelé
16-05	Wales	W 3-1	Sao Paulo	Fr	Pelé 2, Vavá
30-05	Mexico	W 2-0	Viña del Mar	WCr1	Zagalo, Pelé
2-06	Czechoslovakia	D 0-0	Viña del Mar	WCr1	
6-06	Spain	W 2-1	Viña del Mar	WCr1	Amarildo 2
10-06	England	W 3-1	Viña del Mar	WCqf	Garrincha 2, Vavá
13-06	Chile	W 4-2	Santiago	WCsf	Garrincha 2, Vavá 2
17-06	Czechoslovakia	W 3-1	Santiago	WCf	Amarildo, Zito, Vavá
3-03-1963	Paraguay	D 2-2	Asuncion	Fr	Flávio, Hilton Chaves
10-03	Peru	W 1-0	Cochabamba	SC	Flávio
14-03	Colombia	W 5-1	La Paz	SC	Flávio 2, Marco Antônio, Oswaldo, Fernando
17-03	Paraguay	L 0-2	La Paz	SC	
24-03	Argentina	L 0-3	La Paz	SC	
27-03	Ecuador	D 2-2	Cochabamba	SC	Oswaldo 2
31-03	Bolivia	L 4-5	Cochabamba	SC	Flávio, Almir, Marco Antônio
13-04	Argentina	L 2-3	Sao Paulo	RC	Pepe 2
16-04	Argentina	W 5-2	Rio de Janeiro	RC	Pelé 3, Amarildo 2
21-04	Portugal	L 0-1	Lisbon	Fr	
24-04	Belgium	L 1-5	Brussels	Fr	Quarentinha
28-04	France	W 3-2	Paris	Fr	Pelé 3
2-05	Holland	L 0-1	Amsterdam	Fr	
5-05	West Germany	W 2-1	Hamburg	Fr	Coutinho, Pelé
8-05	England	D 1-1	London	Fr	Pepe
12-05	Italy	L 0-3	Milan	Fr	
17-05	Egypt	W 1-0	Cairo	Fr	Quarentinha
19-05	Israel	W 5-0	Tel Aviv	Fr	Quarentinha 2, Amarildo 2, Zequinha
30-05-1964	England	W 5-1	Rio de Janeiro	Fr	Rinaldo 2, Pelé, Julinho I, Roberto Dias
3-06	Argentina	L 0-3	Sao Paulo	Fr	
7-06	Portugal	W 4-1	Rio de Janeiro	Fr	Pelé, Jairzinho, Gérson 2
2-06-1965	Belgium	W 5-0	Rio de Janeiro	Fr	Pelé 3, Flávio, Rinaldo
6-06	West Germany	W 2-0	Rio de Janeiro	Fr	Flávio, Pelé
9-06	Argentina	D 0-0	Rio de Janeiro	Fr	
17-06	Algeria	W 3-0	Oran	Fr	Pelé, Dudu I, Gérson
24-06	Portugal	D 0-0	Oporto	Fr	
30-06	Sweden	W 2-1	Stockholm	Fr	Pelé, Gérson
4-07	Soviet Union	W 3-0	Moscow	Fr	Pelé 2, Flávio
7-09	Uruguay	W 3-0	Belo Horizonte	Fr	Rinaldo, Tupazinho, Germano
21-11	Soviet Union	D 2-2	Rio de Janeiro	Fr	Gérson, Pelé
17-04-1966	Chile	W 1-0	Santiago	OHC	Joao Carlos
20-04	Chile	L 1-2	Vina del Mar	OHC	Joao Carlos
14-05	Wales	W 3-1	Rio de Janeiro	Fr	Silva I, Servílio II, Garrincha
15-05	Chile	D 1-1	Sao Paulo	Fr	Rinaldo
18-05	Wales	W 1-0	Belo Horizonte	Fr	Lima
19-05	Chile	W 1-0	Rio de Janeiro	Fr	Gérson
4-06	Peru	W 4-0	Sao Paulo	Fr	Lima 2, Pelé, Paraná
5-06	Poland	W 4-1	Belo Horizonte	Fr	Tostao 2, Alcindo, Denilson
8-06	Poland	W 2-1	Rio de Janeiro	Fr	Silva I, Garrincha
8-06	Peru	W 3-1	Rio de Janeiro	Fr	Fidélis, Tostao, Edu
12-06	Czechoslovakia	W 2-1	Rio de Janeiro	Fr	Pelé 2
15-06	Czechoslovakia	D 2-2	Rio de Janeiro	Fr	Pelé, Zito
25-06	Scotland	D 1-1	Glasgow	Fr	Servílio II
30-06	Sweden	W 3-2	Gothenberg	Fr	Tostao 2, Gérson
12-07	Bulgaria	W 2-0	Liverpool	WCr1	Pelé, Garrincha
15-07	Hungary	L 1-3	Liverpool	WCr1	Tostao
19-07	Portugal	L 1-3	Liverpool	WCr1	Rildo
25-06-1967	Uruguay	D 0-0	Montevideo	RBC	
28-06	Uruguay	D 2-2	Montevideo	RBC	Paulo Borges 2
1-07	Uruguay	D 1-1	Montevideo	RBC	Dirceu Lopes
19-09	Chile	W 1-0	Santiago	Fr	Roberto Miranda
9-06-1968	Uruguay	W 2-0	Sao Paulo	Fr	Tostao, Sadí
12-06	Uruguay	W 4-0	Rio de Janeiro	Fr	Paulo Borges, Tostao, Gérson, Jairzinho

16-06	West Germany	L 1-2	Stuttgart	Fr	Tostao
20-06	Poland	W 6-3	Warsaw	Fr	Natal, Rivelino 2, Jairzinho 2, Tostao
23-06	Czechoslovakia	L 2-3	Bratislava	Fr	Natal, Carlos Alberto Torres
25-06	Yugoslavia	W 2-0	Belgrade	Fr	Carlos Alberto Torres, Tostao
30-06	Portugal	W 2-0	Lourenco Marq.	Fr	Rivelino, Tostao
7-07	Mexico	W 2-0	Mexico City	Fr	Jairzinho 2
10-07	Mexico	L 1-2	Mexico City	Fr	Rivelino
14-07	Peru	W 4-3	Lima	Fr	Natal, Roberto Miranda, Jairzinho, Carlos Alberto Torres
17-07	Peru	W 4-0	Lima	Fr	Rivelino, Gérson, Tostao, Jairzinho
25-07	Paraguay	W 4-0	Asuncion	OCC	Pelé 2, Toninho Guerreiro, Eduardo I
28-07	Paraguay	L 0-1	Asuncion	OCC	
7-08	Argentina	W 4-1	Rio de Janeiro	Fr	Valtencir, Roberto Miranda,Paulo César Lima, Jairzinho
11-08	Argentina	W 3-2	Belo Horizonte	Fr	Evaldo, Rodrigues III, Dirceu Lopes
31-10	Mexico	L 1-2	Rio de Janeiro	Fr	Carlos Alberto Torres
3-11	Mexico	W 2-1	Belo Horizonte	Fr	Pelé, Jairzinho
14-12	West Germany	D 2-2	Rio de Janeiro	Fr	Edu 2
17-12	Yugoslavia	D 3-3	Rio de Janeiro	Fr	Carlos Alberto Torres, Pelé, Babá II
19-12	Yugoslavia	W 3-2	Belo Horizonte	Fr	Vaguinho, Amauri, Ronaldo
7-04-1969	Peru	W 2-1	Porto Alegre	Fr	Jairzinho, Gérson
9-04	Peru	W 3-2	Rio de Janeiro	Fr	Pelé, Tostao, Edu
12-06	England	W 2-1	Rio de Janeiro	Fr	Tostao, Jairzinho
6-08	Colombia	W 2-0	Bogota	WCq	Tostao 2
10-08	Venezuela	W 5-0	Caracas	WCq	Tostao 3, Pelé 2
17-08	Paraguay	W 3-0	Asuncion	WCq	OG, Edu, Jairzinho
21-08	Colombia	W 6-2	Rio de Janeiro	WCq	Pelé, Tostao 2, Jairzinho, Edu, Rivelino
24-08	Venezuela	W 6-0	Rio de Janeiro	WCq	Tostao 3, Pelé 2, Jairzinho
31-08	Paraguay	W 1-0	Rio de Janeiro	WCq	Pelé
4-03-1970	Argentina	L 0-2	Porto Alegre	Fr	
8-03	Argentina	W 2-1	Rio de Janeiro	Fr	Jairzinho, Pelé
22-03	Chile	W 5-0	Sao Paulo	Fr	Gérson, Roberto Miranda 2, Pelé 2
26-03	Chile	W 2-1	Rio de Janeiro	Fr	Carlos Alberto Torres, Rivelino
12-04	Paraguay	D 0-0	Rio de Janeiro	Fr	
26-04	Bulgaria	D 0-0	Sao Paulo	Fr	
29-04	Austria	W 1-0	Rio de Janeiro	Fr	Rivelino
3-06	Czechoslovakia	W 4-1	Guadalajara	WCr1	Rivelino, Pelé, Jairzinho 2
7-06	England	W 1-0	Guadalajara	WCr1	Jairzinho
10-06	Romania	W 3-2	Guadalajara	WCr1	Jairzinho, Pelé 2
14-06	Peru	W 4-2	Guadalajara	WCqf	Rivelino, Tostao 2, Jairzinho
17-06	Uruguay	W 3-1	Guadalajara	WCsf	Clodoaldo, Jairzinho, Rivelino
21-06	Italy	W 4-1	Mexico City	WCf	Pelé, Gérson, Jairzinho, Carlos Alberto Torres
30-09	Mexico	W 2-1	Rio de Janeiro	Fr	Tostao, Jairzinho
4-10	Chile	W 5-1	Santiago	Fr	Roberto Miranda, Pelé, Jairzinho 2, Paulo César Lima
11-07-1971	Austria	D 1-1	Sao Paulo	Fr	Pelé
14-07	Czechoslovakia	W 1-0	Rio de Janeiro	Fr	Tostao
18-07	Yugoslavia	D 2-2	Rio de Janeiro	Fr	Rivelino, Gérson
21-07	Hungary	D 0-0	Rio de Janeiro	Fr	
24-07	Paraguay	W 1-0	Rio de Janeiro	Fr	Claudiomiro
28-07	Argentina	D 1-1	Buenos Aires	RC	Paulo César Lima
31-07	Argentina	D 2-2	Buenos Aires	RC	Tostao, Paulo César Lima
26-04-1972	Paraguay	W 3-2	Porto Alegre	Fr	Carlos Alberto Torres, Tostao, Dirceu Lopes
28-06	Czechoslovakia	D 0-0	Rio de Janeiro	Clr2	
2-07	Yugoslavia	W 3-0	Sao Paulo	Clr2	Leivinha 2, Jairzinho
5-07	Scotland	W 1-0	Rio de Janeiro	Clr2	Jairzinho
9-07	Portugal	W 1-0	Rio de Janeiro	Clf	Jairzinho
27-05-1973	Bolivia	W 5-0	Rio de Janeiro	Fr	Rivelino 2, Valdomiro, Leivinha 2
3-06	Algeria	W 2-0	Algiers	Fr	Rivelino, Paulo César Lima
6-06	Tunisia	W 4-1	Tunis	Fr	Paulo César Lima 2, Valdomiro, Leivinha
9-06	Italy	L 0-2	Rome	Fr	
13-06	Austria	D 1-1	Vienna	Fr	Jairzinho
16-06	West Germany	W 1-0	Berlin	Fr	Dirceu II
21-06	Soviet Union	W 1-0	Moscow	Fr	Jairzinho
25-06	Sweden	L 0-1	Stockholm	Fr	
30-06	Scotland	W 1-0	Glasgow	Fr	OG
31-03-1974	Mexico	D 1-1	Rio de Janeiro	Fr	Jairzinho
7-04	Czechoslovakia	W 1-0	Rio de Janeiro	Fr	Marinho Chagas
14-04	Bulgaria	W 1-0	Rio de Janeiro	Fr	Jairzinho
17-04	Rumania	W 2-0	Sao Paulo	Fr	Leivinha, Edu
21-04	Haiti	W 4-0	Brasilia	Fr	Paulo César Lima, Rivelino,Marinho Chagas, Edu
28-04	Greece	D 0-0	Rio de Janeiro	Fr	

Date	Opponent	Result	Venue	Comp	Scorers
1-05	Austria	D 0-0	Sao Paulo	Fr	
5-05	Rep. Ireland	W 2-1	Rio de Janeiro	Fr	Leivinha, Rivelino
12-05	Paraguay	W 2-0	Rio de Janeiro	Fr	Marinho Perez, Rivelino
13-06	Yugoslavia	D 0-0	Frankfurt	WCr1	
18-06	Scotland	D 0-0	Frankfurt	WCr1	
22-06	Zaire	W 3-0	Gelsenkirchen	WCr1	Jairzinho, Rivelino, Valdomiro
26-06	East Germany	W 1-0	Hanover	WCr2	Rivelino
30-06	Argentina	W 2-1	Hanover	WCr2	Rivelino, Jairzinho
3-07	Holland	L 0-2	Dortmund	WCr2	
6-07	Poland	L 0-1	Munich	WC3p	
30-07-1975	Venezuela	W 4-0	Caracas	SCr1	Romeu, Danival, Palhinha 2
6-08	Argentina	W 2-1	Belo Horizonte	SCr1	Nelhino 2
13-08	Venezuela	W 6-0	Belo Horizonte	SCr1	Roberto Batata 2, Nelhino, Danival, Campos, Palhinha
16-08	Argentina	W 1-0	Rosario	SCr1	Danival
30-09	Peru	L 1-3	Belo Horizonte	SCsf	Roberto Batata
4-10	Peru	W 2-0	Lima	SCsf	Zé Carlos, Campos
25-02-1976	Uruguay	W 2-1	Montevideo	CA	Nelinho, Rivelino
27-02	Argentina	W 2-1	Buenos Aires	CA	Lula, Zico
7-04	Paraguay	D 1-1	Asuncion	CA	Eneas
28-04	Uruguay	W 2-1	Rio de Janeiro	CA	Rivelino, Zico
19-05	Argentina	W 2-0	Rio de Janeiro	CA	Lula, Neca
23-05	England	W 1-0	Los Angeles	Fr	Roberto Dinamite
31-05	Italy	W 4-1	New Haven	Fr	Gil 2, Zico, Roberto Dinamite
4-06	Mexico	W 3-0	Guadalajara	Fr	Roberto Dinamite 2, Gil
9-06	Paraguay	W 3-1	Rio de Janeiro	CA	Roberto Dinamite 2, Zico
1-12	Soviet Union	W 2-0	Rio de Janeiro	Fr	Falcao, Zico
23-01-1977	Bulgaria	W 1-0	Sao Paulo	Fr	Roberto Dinamite
20-02	Colombia	D 0-0	Bogota	WCq	
9-03	Colombia	W 6-0	Rio de Janeiro	WCq	Roberto Dinamite 2, Zico, Marinho Chagas 2, Rivelino
13-03	Paraguay	W 1-0	Asuncion	WCq	OG
20-03	Paraguay	D 1-1	Rio de Janeiro	WCq	Roberto Dinamite
8-06	England	D 0-0	Rio de Janeiro	Fr	
12-06	West Germany	D 1-1	Rio de Janeiro	Fr	Rivelino
19-06	Poland	W 3-1	Sao Paulo	Fr	Paulo Isidoro, Reinaldo, Rivelino
23-06	Scotland	W 2-0	Rio de Janeiro	Fr	Zico, Toninho Cerezo
26-06	Yugoslavia	D 0-0	Belo Horizonte	Fr	
30-06	France	D 2-2	Rio de Janeiro	Fr	Edinho, Roberto Dinamite
10-07	Peru	W 1-0	Cali	WCq	Gil
14-07	Bolivia	W 8-0	Cali	WCq	Zico 4, Roberto Dinamite, Gil, Toninho Cerezo, Marcelo
1-04-1978	France	L 0-1	Paris	Fr	
5-04	West Germany	W 1-0	Hamburg	Fr	Nunes
19-04	England	D 1-1	London	Fr	Gil
1-05	Peru	W 3-0	Rio de Janeiro	Fr	Zico, Reinaldo 2
17-05	Czechoslovakia	W 2-0	Rio de Janeiro	Fr	Reinaldo, Zico
3-06	Sweden	D 1-1	Mar del Plata	WCr1	Reinaldo
7-06	Spain	D 0-0	Mar del Plata	WCr1	
11-06	Austria	W 1-0	Mar del Plata	WCr1	Roberto Dinamite
14-06	Peru	W 3-0	Mendoza	WCr2	Dirceu II 2, Zico
18-06	Argentina	D 0-0	Rosario	WCr2	
21-06	Poland	W 3-1	Mendoza	WCr2	Nelinho, Roberto Dinamite 2
24-06	Italy	W 2-1	Buenos Aires	WC3p	Nelinho, Dirceu II
17-05-1979	Paraguay	W 6-0	Rio de Janeiro	Fr	Éder, Zico 3, Nílton Batata
31-05	Uruguay	W 5-1	Rio de Janeiro	Fr	Edinho, Sócrates 2, Nílton Batata, Éder
26-07	Bolivia	L 1-2	La Paz	SCr1	Roberto Dinamite
2-08	Argentina	W 2-1	Rio de Janeiro	SCr1	Zico, Tita
16-08	Bolivia	W 2-0	Sao Paulo	SCr1	Tita, Zico
23-08	Argentina	D 2-2	Buenos Aires	SCr1	Sócrates 2
24-10	Paraguay	L 1-2	Asuncion	SCsf	Palhinha
31-10	Paraguay	D 2-2	Rio de Janeiro	SCsf	Falcao, Sócrates
8-06-1980	Mexico	W 2-0	Rio de Janeiro	Fr	Zé Sérgio, Serginho
15-06	Soviet Union	L 1-2	Rio de Janeiro	Fr	Nunes
24-06	Chile	W 2-1	Belo Horizonte	Fr	Zico, Toninho Cerezo
29-06	Poland	D 1-1	Sao Paulo	Fr	Zico
27-08	Uruguay	W 1-0	Fortaleza	Fr	Getúlio
25-09	Paraguay	W 2-1	Asuncion	Fr	Zé Sérgio, Reinaldo
30-10	Paraguay	W 6-0	Goiania	Fr	Zé Sérgio, Tita, Zico 2, Sócrates, Luizinho
21-12	Switzerland	W 2-0	Cuiaba	Fr	Sócrates, Zé Sérgio
4-01-1981	Argentina	D 1-1	Montevideo	ML	Edvaldo
7-01	West Germany	W 4-1	Montevideo	ML	Júnior, Toninho Cerezo, Serginho, Zé Sérgio

10-01	Uruguay	L 1-2	Montevideo	ML	Sócrates
1-02	Colombia	D 1-1	Bogota	Fr	Serginho
8-02	Venezuela	W 1-0	Caracas	WCq	Zico
14-02	Ecuador	W 6-0	Quito	Fr	Reinaldo 2, Sócrates 2, OG, Zico
22-02	Bolivia	W 2-1	La Paz	WCq	Sócrates, Reinaldo
14-03	Chile	W 2-1	Ribeirao Preto	Fr	Zico, Reinaldo
22-03	Bolivia	W 3-1	Rio de Janeiro	WCq	Zico 3
29-03	Venezuela	W 5-0	Goiania	WCq	Tita 2, Sócrates, Zico, Júnior
12-05	England	W 1-0	London	Fr	Zico
15-05	France	W 3-1	Paris	Fr	Zico, Reinaldo, Sócrates
19-05	West Germany	W 2-1	Stuttgart	Fr	Toninho Cerezo, Júnior
8-07	Spain	W 1-0	Salvador	Fr	Baltazar II
26-08	Chile	D 0-0	Santiago	Fr	
23-09	Rep. Ireland *	W 6-0	Maceio	Fr	Éder, Roberto.PE, Zico 4
28-10	Bulgaria	W 3-0	Porto Alegre	Fr	Roberto Dinamite, Zico, Leandro
26-01-1982	East Germany	W 3-1	Natal	Fr	Paulo Isidoro, Renato, Serginho
3-03	Czechoslovakia	D 1-1	Sao Paulo	Fr	Zico
21-03	West Germany	W 1-0	Rio de Janeiro	Fr	Júnior
5-05	Portugal	W 3-1	Sao Luiz	Fr	Júnior, Éder, Zico
19-05	Switzerland	D 1-1	Recife	Fr	Zico
27-05	Rep. Ireland	W 7-0	Uberlandia	Fr	Falcao, Sócrates 2, Serginho 2, Luizinho, Zico
14-06	Soviet Union	W 2-1	Seville	WCr1	Sócrates, Éder
18-06	Scotland	W 4-1	Seville	WCr1	Zico, Oscar, Éder, Falcao
23-06	New Zealand	W 4-0	Seville	WCr1	Zico 2, Falcao, Serginho
2-07	Argentina	W 3-1	Barcelona	WCr2	Zico, Serginho, Júnior
5-07	Italy	L 2-3	Barcelona	WCr2	Sócrates, Falcao
28-04-1983	Chile	W 3-2	Rio de Janeiro	Fr	Careca I, Éder, Renato
8-06	Portugal	W 4-0	Coimbra	Fr	Careca I 2, Sócrates, Pedrinho
12-06	Wales	D 1-1	Cardiff	Fr	Paulo Isidoro
17-06	Switzerland	W 2-1	Basle	Fr	Sócrates, Careca I
22-06	Sweden	D 3-3	Gothenburg	Fr	Marcio, Careca I, Jorginho II
28-07	Chile	D 0-0	Santiago	Fr	
17-08	Ecuador	W 1-0	Quito	SCr1	Roberto Dinamite
24-08	Argentina	L 0-1	Buenos Aires	SCr1	
1-09	Ecuador	W 5-0	Goiania	SCr1	Renato Gaúcho, Roberto Dinamite 2, Éder, Tita
14-09	Argentina	D 0-0	Rio de Janeiro	SCr1	
13-10	Paraguay	D 1-1	Asuncion	SCsf	Éder
20-10	Paraguay	D 0-0	Uberlandia	SCsf	
27-10	Uruguay	L 0-2	Montevideo	SCf	
4-11	Uruguay	D 1-1	Salvador	SCf	Jorginho II
10-06-1984	England	L 0-2	Rio de Janeiro	Fr	
17-06	Argentina	D 0-0	Sao Paulo	Fr	
21-06	Uruguay	W 1-0	Curitiba	Fr	Arturzinho
25-04-1985	Colombia	W 2-1	Belo Horizonte	Fr	Alemao, Casagrande
28-04	Peru	L 0-1	Brasilia	Fr	
2-05	Uruguay	W 2-0	Recife	Fr	Alemao, Careca I
5-05	Argentina	W 2-1	Salvador	Fr	Careca I, Alemao
15-05	Colombia	L 0-1	Bogota	Fr	
21-05	Chile	L 1-2	Santiago	Fr	Casagrande
2-06	Bolivia	W 2-0	Santa Cruz	WCq	Casagrande, OG
8-06	Chile	W 3-1	Porto Alegre	Fr	Zico 2, Leandro
16-06	Paraguay	W 2-0	Asuncion	WCq	Casagrande, Zico
23-06	Paraguay	D 1-1	Rio de Janeiro	WCq	Sócrates
30-06	Bolivia	D 1-1	Sao Paulo	WCq	Careca I
12-03-1986	West Germany	L 0-2	Frankfurt	Fr	
16-03	Hungary	L 0-3	Budapest	Fr	
1-04	Peru	W 4-0	Sao Luis	Fr	Casagrande 2, Alemao, Careca I
8-04	East Germany	W 3-0	Goiania	Fr	Müller, Alemao, Careca I
17-04	Finland	W 3-0	Brasilia	Fr	Marinho I, Oscar, Casagrande
30-04	Yugoslavia	W 4-2	Recife	Fr	Zico 3, Careca I
7-05	Chile	D 1-1	Curitiba	Fr	Casagrande
1-06	Spain	W 1-0	Guadalajara	WCr1	Sócrates
6-06	Algeria	W 1-0	Guadalajara	WCr1	Careca I
12-06	Nth. Ireland	W 3-0	Guadalajara	WCr1	Careca I 2, Josimar
16-06	Poland	W 4-0	Guadalajara	WCr2	Sócrates, Josimar, Edinho, Careca I
21-06	France	D 1-1	Guadalajara	WCqf	Careca I Lost 3-4 pens
19-05-1987	England	D 1-1	London	Fr	Mirandinha II
23-05	Rep. Ireland	L 0-1	Dublin	Fr	
26-05	Scotland	W 2-0	Glasgow	Fr	Raí, Valdo II
28-05	Finland	W 3-2	Helsinki	Fr	Romário, Valdo II, Müller
1-06	Israel	W 4-0	Tel Aviv	Fr	Romário 2, Dunga, Joao Paulo II

21-06	Ecuador	W 4-1	Florianopolis	Fr	Raí, Careca I, Müller, Jorginho
24-06	Paraguay	W 1-0	Porto Alegre	Fr	Valdo II
28-06	Venezuela	W 5-0	Cordoba	SCr1	Edu, OG, Careca I, Nelsinho, Romário
3-07	Chile	L 0-4	Cordoba	SCr1	
9-12	Chile	W 2-1	Uberlandia	Fr	Valdo II, Renato
12-12	West Germany	D 1-1	Brasilia	Fr	Batista
7-07-1988	Australia	W 1-0	Melbourne	Fr	Romário
10-07	Argentina	D 0-0	Melbourne	Fr	
13-07	Saudi Arabia	W 4-1	Melbourne	Fr	Geovani 2, Jorginho, Edmar
17-07	Australia	W 2-0	Sydney	Fr	Romário, Müller
28-07	Norway	D 1-1	Oslo	Fr	Edmar
31-07	Sweden	D 1-1	Stockholm	Fr	Jorginho
3-08	Austria	W 2-0	Vienna	Fr	Edmar, Andrade
12-10	Belgium	W 2-1	Antwerp	Fr	Geovani 2
15-03-1989	Ecuador	W 1-0	Cuiaba	Fr	Washington II
12-04	Paraguay	W 2-0	Teresina	Fr	Cristovao, Vivinho
10-05	Peru	W 4-1	Fortaleza	Fr	Zé do Carmo, Bebeto, Charles 2
24-05	Peru	D 1-1	Lima	Fr	Cristovao
8-06	Portugal	W 4-0	Rio de Janeiro	Fr	Bebeto, OG, Ricardo II, Charles
16-06	Sweden	L 1-2	Copenhagen	Fr	Cristovao
18-06	Denmark	L 0-4	Copenhagen	Fr	
21-06	Switzerland	L 0-1	Basle	Fr	
1-07	Venezuela	W 3-1	Salvador	SCr1	Bebeto, Geovani, Baltazar II
3-07	Peru	D 0-0	Salvador	SCr1	
7-07	Colombia	D 0-0	Salvador	SCr1	
9-07	Paraguay	W 2-0	Recife	SCr1	Bebeto 2
12-07	Argentina	W 2-0	Rio de Janeiro	SCr2	Bebeto, Romário
14-07	Paraguay	W 3-0	Rio de Janeiro	SCr2	Bebeto 2, Romário
16-07	Uruguay	W 1-0	Rio de Janeiro	SCf	Romário
23-07	Japan	W 1-0	Rio de Janeiro	Fr	Bismark
30-07	Venezuela	W 4-0	Caracas	WCq	Branco, Romário, Bebeto 2
13-08	Chile	D 1-1	Santiago	WCq	OG
20-08	Venezuela	W 6-0	Sao Paulo	WCq	Careca I 4, Silas, OG
3-09	Chile	W 1-0	Rio de Janeiro	WCq	Careca I. Abandoned after 65 mins
					Game awarded to Brazil by 2-0
14-10	Italy	W 1-0	Bologna	Fr	André Cruz
14-11	Yugoslavia	D 0-0	Joao Pessao	Fr	
20-12	Holland	W 1-0	Rotterdam	Fr	Careca I
28-03-1990	England	L 0-1	London	Fr	
5-05	Bulgaria	W 2-1	Campinas	Fr	Müller, Aldair
13-05	East Germany	D 3-3	Rio de Janeiro	Fr	Alemao, Careca I, Dunga
10-06	Sweden	W 2-1	Turin	WCr1	Careca I 2
16-06	Costa Rica	W 1-0	Turin	WCr1	Müller
20-06	Scotland	W 1-0	Turin	WCr1	Müller
24-06	Argentina	L 0-1	Turin	WCr2	
12-09	Spain	L 0-3	Gijon	Fr	
17-10	Chile	D 0-0	Santiago	Fr	
8-11	Chile	D 0-0	Belem	Fr	
13-12	Mexico	D 0-0	Los Angeles	Fr	
27-02-1991	Paraguay	D 1-1	Campo Grande	Fr	Neto
27-03	Argentina	D 3-3	Buenos Aires	Fr	Renato Gaúcho, Luis Henrique, Careca II
28-05	Bulgaria	W 3-0	Uberlandia	Fr	Neto 2, Joao Paulo II
27-06	Argentina	D 1-1	Curitiba	Fr	Neto
9-07	Bolivia	W 2-1	Viña del Mar	SCr1	Neto, Branco
11-07	Uruguay	D 1-1	Viña del Mar	SCr1	Joao Paulo II
13-07	Colombia	L 0-2	Viña del Mar	SCr1	
15-07	Ecuador	W 3-1	Viña del Mar	SCr1	Mazinho II, Santos, Luis Henrique
17-07	Argentina	L 2-3	Santiago	SCr2	Branco, Joao Paulo II
19-07	Colombia	W 2-0	Santiago	SCr2	Renato, Branco
21-07	Chile	W 2-0	Santiago	SCr2	Mazinho II, Luis Henrique
11-09	Wales	L 0-1	Cardiff	Fr	
30-10	Yugoslavia	W 3-1	Varginha	Fr	Luis Henrique, Rai, Müller
18-12	Czechoslovakia	W 2-1	Goiana	Fr	Elivelton, Rai
26-02-1992	United States	W 3-0	Fortaleza	Fr	Antonio Carlos, Rai 2
15-04	Finland	W 3-1	Cuiaba	Fr	Bebeto 2, Paulo Sergio
30-04	Uruguay	L 0-1	Montevideo	Fr	
17-05	England	D 1-1	London	Fr	Bebeto
31-07	Mexico	W 5-0	Los Angeles	Fr	Bebeto 2, Rai, Zinho, Paulo Sergio
26-08	France	W 2-0	Paris	Fr	OG, Luiz Henrique
24-09	Costa Rica	W 4-2	Paranavai	Fr	Rai 3, Renato Gaúcho
25-11	Uruguay	L 1-2	Campina Grande	Fr	Edmundo

16-12	Germany	W 3-1	Porto Alegre	Fr	Luiz Henrique, Bebeto, Jorginho
18-02-1993	Argentina	D 1-1	Buenos Aires	Fr	Luiz Henrique
17-03	Poland	D 2-2	Riberao Preto	Fr	OG, Muller
6-06	USA	W 2-0	New Haven	Fr	Careca II, Luis Carlos Winck
10-06	Germany	D 3-3	Washington	Fr	OG, Careca II, Luisinho
13-06	England	D 1-1	Washington	Fr	Marcio Santos
18-06	Peru	D 0-0	Cuenca	SCr1	
21-06	Chile	L 2-3	Cuenca	SCr1	Muller, Palinha
24-06	Paraguay	W 3-0	Cuenca	SCr1	Palinha 2, OG
27-06	Argentina	D 1-1	Guayaquil	Scqf	Muller. Lost 5-6p
8-07	Ecuador	D 0-0	Guayaquil	WCq	
14-07	Paraguay	W 2-0	Rio de Janeiro	Fr	Branco, Bebeto
25-07	Bolivia	L 0-2	La Paz	WCq	
1-08	Venezuela	W 5-1	Sao Cristobal	WCq	Rai, Bebeto 2, Branco, Palinha
8-08	Mexico	D 1-1	Maceio	Fr	Marcio Santos
15-08	Uruguay	D 1-1	Montevisdeo	WCq	Rai
22-08	Ecuador	W 2-0	Sao Paulo	WCq	Bebeto, Dunga
29-08	Bolivia	W 6-0	Recife	WCq	Rai, Muller, Bebeto 2, Branco, Ricardo Gomes
5-09	Venezuela	W 4-0	Belo Horizonte	WCq	Ricardo Gomes 2, Palinha, Evair
19-09	Uruguay	W 2-0	Rio de Janeiro	WCq	Romário 2
17-11	Germany	L 1-2	Cologne	Fr	Evair
16-12	Mexico	W 1-0	Guadalajara	Fr	Rivaldo
23-03-1994	Argentina	W 2-0	Recife	Fr	Bebeto 2
4-05	Iceland	W 3-0	Florianopolis	Fr	Ronaldo, Zinho, Viola
5-06	Canada	D 1-1	Edmonton	Fr	Romário
8-06	Honduras	W 8-2	San Diego	Fr	Romário 3, Bebeto 2, Cafú, Dunga, Rai
12-06	El Salvador	W 4-0	Fresno	Fr	Romário, Bebeto, Zinho, Rai
20-06	Russia	W 2-0	San Francisco	WCr1	Romário, Rai
24-06	Cameroon	W 3-0	San Francisco	WCr1	Romário, Marcio Santos, Bebeto
28-06	Sweden	D 1-1	Detroit	WCr1	Romário
4-07	USA	W 1-0	San Francisco	WCr2	Bebeto
9-07	Holland	W 3-2	Dallas	WCqf	Romário, Bebeto, Branco
13-07	Sweden	W 1-0	Los Angeles	WCsf	Romário
17-07	Italy	D 0-0	Los Angeles	WCf	Won 3-2p
23-12	Yugoslavia	W 2-0	Porto Alegre	Fr	Viola, Branco
22-02-1995	Slovakia	W 5-0	Fortaleza	Fr	Souza, Juninho, Tulio, Marcio Santos, Bebeto
29-03	Honduras	D 1-1	Goiana	Fr	Tulio
17-05	Israel	W 2-1	Tel Aviv	Fr	OG, Rivaldo
4-06	Sweden	W 1-0	Birmingham	Fr	Edmundo
6-06	Japan	W 3-0	Liverpool	Fr	Roberto Carlos, Zinho 2
11-06	England	W 3-1	London	Fr	Juninho, Ronaldo, Edmundo
29-06	Poland	W 2-1	Recife	Fr	Tulio 2
7-07	Ecuador	W 1-0	Rivera	SCr1	Ronaldo
10-07	Peru	W 2-0	Rivera	SCr1	Zinho, Edmundo
13-07	Colombia	W 3-0	Rivera	SCr1	Leonardo, Tulio, Juninho
17-07	Argentina	D 2-2	Rivera	SCqf	Edmundo, Tulio. Won 4-2p
20-07	United States	W 1-0	Maldonado	SCsf	Aldair
23-07	Uruguay	D 1-1	Montevideo	SCf	Tulio. Lost 3-5p

CHILE

After the 'big three', Chile is often regarded as the fourth strongest nation on the South American continent. It is somewhat surprising, therefore, that its first ever honour came in 1991 when Colo Colo won the Copa Libertadores. Until then Chile's history had been a tale of nearly but not quite.

The British in the port of Valparaiso and the neighbouring resort of Viña del Mar first introduced football to Chile, and the first club, Valparaiso FC, was formed in 1889. In 1895 nine clubs of mainly British origin formed the Football Association of Chile, the second oldest on the continent after Argentina.

Chile is a thin, elongated country and although roughly in the centre, the capital Santiago is a good distance from many of the major towns in the rest of Chile, so as football spread around the country regional associations were set up to administer the game. From 1910 until 1933 the Copa Arturo Allesandri was the main competition in the country. Played for by representative sides of the regional associations, all of which ran their own league, it was supplanted by the new professional national league in 1933.

Prime motivators for the new league were Colo Colo, formed in 1925 by dissident members of Magallanes. The Liga Metropolitana in Santiago formed the basis of the new national league, and from the start Colo Colo have been the dominant force. The area around Santiago has always been the most powerful, and only four teams from outside this region have ever won the championship.

Along with Colo Colo the most prominent sides have been the two university clubs, Universidad de Chile and Universidad Catolica, as well as Union Española.

Recently, however, provincial clubs have begun to challenge the supremacy of Santiago, none more so than Cobreloa from the small mining town of Calama in the north. Five times winners of the championship, they twice reached the final of the Copa Libertadores in the early 1980s.

The national side first took the field when they travelled to Buenos Aires for the unofficial South American Championship in 1910, although their first game was a friendly match against Argentina two days before the tournament got under way. Not until 1926, however, 23 matches later, did Chile win a game, despite the 1922 tournament being held in Viña del Mar. In 1926 Santiago staged the competition and, spurred on by David Arellano who had founded Colo Colo the previous year, Chile beat both Bolivia and Paraguay to finish third out of the five entrants, the first occasion on which they had not finished bottom. Also in good form was Guillermo Subiabre who finished the tournament as joint top scorer.

Chile made the trip to the Amsterdam Olympics in 1928 and luckily for them a consolation tournament for the first round losers had been arranged, so after losing to Portugal they did not have to go home after just one match. They fared much better in this tournament, beating Mexico and then drawing 2-2 with the hosts Holland. Entry into the 1930 World Cup nearly proved fruitful, but a 3-1 loss to Argentina in the final group match of the first round meant they were eliminated despite having beaten both France and Mexico. Once again their top player was Subiabre, but unfortunately for him there was a five-year gap before the next match.

The 1937 South American Championship in Buenos Aires produced another Chilean hero in Raul Toro, and he finished as the top scorer with 7 goals in 4 games. It did not do his side much good, however, as their poor showings in the tournament continued. They were generally weak in the tournaments played away from Chile but played well when they hosted the series, such as in 1945 and 1955.

Regular though not particularly successful competitors in the World Cup from 1950 onwards, Chile have taken part in five final tournaments out of the 11 held since that date. Only once have they progressed beyond the first round, and that was as hosts in 1962. Based in Santiago in the first round, Chile beat both Switzerland and Italy in their first two matches, though the latter has become known as the 'Battle of Santiago' as tempers flared between the two sides. Relations between Italy and the hosts were not good. A series of articles written by Italian journalists criticising Chile had not gone down well in Santiago and the hostility spilled over onto the pitch. Italy's Argentinian, Maschio, had his nose broken, two Italians were sent off and all hell broke loose in a match that was nearly abandoned.

The victory over Italy qualified Chile for a quarter-final tie against the Soviet Union in far away Arica. Leonel Sanchez, the top Chilean footballer of the time, gave his side the lead after 11 minutes, and a minute after Chislenko equalised Eladio Rojas scored the winner in what was without question the best result in the history of the country. The hosts were no match for the Brazilians in the semi-finals and bowed out of the tournament, although they had some consolation in winning the third place play-off against Yugoslavia. The 1962 World Cup was Chile's finest hour. Home advantage had played a large part in their third place and it is unlikely that the national side will ever reach the same heights again.

THE ORDER OF MERIT

		Total			Lge	Cup		Copa Lib		
		G	S	B	G	G	S	G	S	B
1	Colo Colo	28	5	2	19	8	4	1	1	2
2	Universidad de Chile	9	-	2	8	1	-	-	-	2
3	Universidad Catolica	8	7	4	6	2	6	-	1	4
4	Union Española	7	3	1	5	2	2	-	1	1
5	Cobreloa	6	4	1	5	1	2	-	2	1
6	Palestino	4	2	1	2	2	2	-	-	1
7	Wanderers Valparaiso	4	1	-	2	2	1	-	-	-
	Audax Italiano	4	1	-	4	-	1	-	-	-
9	Magallanes	4	-	-	4	-	-	-	-	-
	Everton	4	-	-	3	1	-	-	-	-
11	Cobresal	1	-	-	-	1	-	-	-	-
	Green Cross	1	-	-	1	-	-	-	-	-
	Huachipato	1	-	-	1	-	-	-	-	-
	Deportivo Iquique	1	-	-	-	1	-	-	-	-
	Santiago Morning	1	-	-	1	-	-	-	-	-
	Union San Felipe	1	-	-	1	-	-	-	-	-
17	Deportes La Serena	-	1	-	-	-	1	-	-	-
	Lota	-	1	-	-	-	1	-	-	-
	AF Vidal	-	1	-	-	-	1	-	-	-
20	O'Higgins	-	-	1	-	-	-	-	-	1

To the end of the 1994 season & 1993 cup

Further controversy erupted in the 1974 World Cup qualifying tournament. By beating Peru, Chile qualified to play the Soviet Union in a play-off for a place in West Germany. After drawing 0-0 in Moscow, the Soviet Union refused to play in the Estadio Nacional in Santiago. In 1973, Chile's left-wing government of President Allende had been overthrown by General Pinochet and the army, and when they rounded up all the left-wing and communist activists they were kept in the stadium. Few of them ever left. The Soviet Union did not feel able to play under such conditions, and after failing to turn up on the day they were disqualified. In one of the most bizarre sights ever seen at a football ground, the Chileans turned up for the game, kicked off and walked the ball into the Soviet goal.

Since then Chile have continued on their unremarkable way. In 1979 they reached the final of the South American Championships, but the route was not exactly perilous. Colombia and Venezuela were overcome in the first round and Peru in the semi-finals before they lost to Paraguay over three games in the final. They reached the final again in 1987, losing this time to Uruguay.

Two years later, Chile were involved in one of the most unsavoury incidents of recent years when during a crucial World Cup qualifier against Brazil, they tried to cheat their way into the finals when 1-0 down. A flare hit their goalkeeper Rojas, he was taken off injured, and the rest of the team also left the field, hoping that Brazil would be banned. It transpired, however, that the whole incident was planned and that Rojas' injuries were self-inflicted. It was Chile who were banned and prevented from taking part in USA '94; it was the third tournament in a row they had missed, their worst ever run.

In the aftermath of this episode, however, came Chile's finest moment with Colo Colo's victory in the 1991 Copa Libertadores. On the way to the final they beat both Nacional of Uruguay and Boca Juniors, and in the final they overcame defending champions Olimpia, winning the second leg 3-0 before a full house in the Estadio Nacional. The celebrations which followed are unlikely to be repeated in the near future, however, as since then Chile's 'nearly men' image has been reinforced. Universidad Catolica reached the final in 1993 but lost to São Paulo, whilst in the South American Championship the national side could no better then third in 1991, despite home advantage, and have subsequently found themselves upstaged by the emerging Colombians.

Population: 13,173,000
Area, sq km: 756,626
% in urban areas: 80%
Capital city: Santiago

Federación de Fútbol de Chile
Calle Erasmo Escala #1872
Casilla 3733
Santiago de Chile
Chile
Tel: + 56 2 2849000
Fax: + 56 2 2843510

Year of formation	1895
Affiliation to FIFA	1912
Affiliation to CSF	1916
Registered clubs	8071
Registered players	635 800
Professional players	770
Registered coaches	990
Registered referees	6435
National stadium	Estadio Nacional, Santiago 74,000
National colours	Red/Blue/White
Reserve colours	White/White/White
Season	February - December

THE RECORD

WORLD CUP

1930	QT Automatic - Final Tournament/1st round
1934	Did not enter
1938	Did not enter
1950	QT W-O in group 7 - Final Tournament/1st round
1954	Did not enter
1958	QT 3rd/3 in group 2
1962	QT Automatic - Final Tournament/Semi-finalists/ 3rd place
1966	QT 1st/3 in group 2 - Final Tournament/1st round
1970	QT 2nd/3 in group 3
1974	QT 1st/2 in group 3 - Final Tournament/1st round
1978	QT 2nd/3 in group 3
1982	QT 1st/3 in group 3 - Final Tournament/1st round
1986	QT 2nd/3 in group 2
1990	QT 2nd/3 in group 3
1994	Did not enter

SOUTH AMERICAN CHAMPIONSHIP

1910	3/3
1916	4/4
1917	4/4
1919	4/4
1920	4/4
1921	-
1922	5/5
1923	-
1924	4/4
1925	-
1926	3/5
1927	-
1929	-
1935	4/4
1937	5/6
1939	4/5
1941	3/5
1942	6/7
1945	3/7
1946	5/6
1947	4/8
1949	5/8
1953	4/7
1955	2/6
1956	2/6
1957	6/6
1959	4/7
1959	-
1963	-
1967	3/6
1975	6/10 - 1st round
1979	2/10 - Finalists
1983	5/10 - 1st round
1987	2/10 - Finalists
1989	5/10 - 1st round
1991	3/10 - 2nd round
1993	10/12 - 1st round
1995	11/12 - 1st round

SOUTH AMERICAN CLUB TOURNAMENTS

Copa Libertadores
Winners - Colo Colo 1991
Finalists - Colo Colo 1973, Union Espanola 1975, Cobreloa 1981 1982, Universidad Catolica 1993
Super Copa
Quarter-finals - Colo Colo 1994
CONMEBOL Cup
Semi-finals - Universidad de Chile 1994

CLUB DIRECTORY

SANTIAGO (Population - 4,100,000)

Audax Club Sportivo Italiano (1910)
Estadio Municipal de la Florida 5,000 – Green/White

Club Social y Deportivo Colo Colo (1925)
Estadio Monumental David Arellano 62,000 – White/Black

Club Deportivo Magallanes San Bernardo (1897)
Estadio Monumental David Arellano 62,000 – Sky blue & white stripes/Black

Club Palestino (1920)
La Cisterna 12,000 – Red, green & white stripes/Black

Club Deportivo Santiago Morning
Estadio Universidad de Santiago – White with a black 'V' /Black

Club Union Española (1909)
San Carlos 12,000 – Red/Blue, yellow trim

Club Deportivo Universidad Catolica (1937)
Santa Laura 35,000 – White with a blue hoop/Blue

Corporación de Fútbol de la Universidad de Chile (1911)
Santa Laura 35,000 – Blue, white trim with large 'U'

CONCEPCIÓN (Pop. - 675,000)

Club de Deportes Concepción (1966)
Estadio Regional de Concepción 33,000 – Violet/White

Club Deportivo Arturo Fernandezez Vial (1903)
Estadio Regional de Concepción 33,000 – Yellow & black stripes/Black

Club Deportivo Huachipato Talcahuano (1947)
Estadio Las Higueras 12,000 – Black & blue stripes/Blue

Deportivo Naval Talcahuano (1932)
El Morro de Talcahuano 15,000 – White/White

VALPARAISO (Pop. - 675,000)

Club de Deportes Everton Viña del Mar (1909)

Sausalito 20,000 – Blue with a yellow hoop/Blue

Santiago Wanderers de Valparaíso (1892)
Playa Ancha 18,000 – Green/White

ANTOFAGASTA (Pop. - 185,000)
Club de Deportes Antofagasta (1968)
Estadio regional de Antofagasta 26,000 – Sky blue & white halves/Sky blue

TEMUCO (Pop. - 157,000)
Club de Deportes Temuco (1916)
Estadio Municipal 28,000 – Green & white hoops/White
Previous name - Green Cross

RANCAGUA (Pop. - 139,000)
Club Deportivo O'Higgins (1955)
El Teniente 16,000 – Sky blue/Black

TALCA (Pop. - 128,000)
Club de Deportes Rangers Talca (1902)
Estadio Fiscal 10,000 – Red & black hoops/White

ARICA (Pop. - 126,000)
Club de Deportes Arica (1978)
Carlos Dittborn 17,000 – Sky blue/Black, black & white trim

IQUIQUE (Pop. - 110,000)
Club de Deportes Iquique (1978)
Municipal de Iquique 10,000 – Sky blue/White

VALDIVIA (Pop. - 100,000)
Club Deportes Valdívia
Parque Municipal 15,00 – Red & white stripes/Red

LA SERENA (Pop. - 83,000)
Club de Deportes La Serena (1955)
La Portada 15,000 – Red with white sleeves/Red

CALAMA (Pop. - 81,000)
Club de Deportes Cobreloa (1977)
Municipal de Calama 30,000 – Orange, white trim

COQUIMBO (Pop. - 62,000)
Club de Deportes Coquimbo Unido (1897)
Francisco Sánchez Rumoroso 10,000 – Yellow with black sleeves/Yellow

SAN FELIPE (Pop. - 31,000)
Club de Deportes Union San Felipe (1956)
Estadio Municipal 12,000 – White with a red sash/White

EL SALVADOR
Club de Deportes Cobresal (1979)
El Cobre 20,000 – White & orange stripes/Orange

CHILEAN LEAGUE CHAMPIONS

1933	Magallanes
1934	Magallanes
1935	Magallanes
1936	Audax Italiano
1937	Colo Colo
1938	Magallanes
1939	Colo Colo
1940	Universidad de Chile
1941	Colo Colo
1942	Santiago Morning
1943	Union Española
1944	Colo Colo
1945	Green Cross
1946	Audax Italiano
1947	Colo Colo
1948	Audax Italiano
1949	Universidad Catolica
1950	Everton
1951	Union Española
1952	Everton
1953	Colo Colo
1954	Universidad Catolica
1955	Palestino
1956	Colo Colo
1957	Audax Italiano
1958	Wanderers
1959	Universidad de Chile
1960	Colo Colo
1961	Universidad Catolica
1962	Universidad de Chile
1963	Colo Colo
1964	Universidad de Chile
1965	Universidad de Chile
1966	Universidad Catolica
1967	Universidad de Chile
1968	Wanderers
1969	Universidad de Chile
1970	Colo Colo
1971	Union San Felipe
1972	Colo Colo
1973	Union Española
1974	Huachipato
1975	Union Española
1976	Everton
1977	Union Española
1978	Palestino
1979	Colo Colo
1980	Cobreloa
1981	Colo Colo
1982	Cobreloa
1983	Colo Colo
1984	Universidad Catolica
1985	Cobreloa
1986	Colo Colo
1987	Universidad Catolica
1988	Cobreloa
1989	Colo Colo
1990	Colo Colo
1991	Colo Colo
1992	Cobreloa
1993	Colo Colo
1994	Universidad de Chile

CHILEAN CUP FINALS

1958	Colo Colo	2-2	Universidad Catolica
1959	Wanderers Valparaiso	5-1	Deportes La Serena
1960	-		
1961	Wanderers Valparaiso	2-0	Universidad Catolica
1962-73	-		
1974	Colo Colo	3-0	Wanderers Valparaiso
1975	Palestino	4-0	Lota
1976	-		
1977	Palestino	4-3	Union Española
1978	-		
1979	Universidad de Chile	2-1	Colo Colo
1980	Deportivo Iquique	2-1	Colo Colo
1981	Colo Colo	5-1	Audax Italiano
1982	Colo Colo	2-0	Universidad Catolica
1983	Universidad Catolica	2-1	Palestino
1984	Everton Viña del Mar	3-0	Universidad Catolica
1985	Colo Colo	1-0	Palestino
1986	Cobreloa	3-0	AF Vidal
1987	Cobresal	2-0	Colo Colo
1988	Colo Colo	1-0	Union Española
1989	Colo Colo	1-0	Universidad Catolica
1990	Colo Colo	3-2	Universidad Catolica
1991	Universidad Catolica	1-0	Cobreloa
1992	Union Española	3-1	Colo Colo
1993	Union Española	3-1	Cobreloa

LEADING INTERNATIONAL APPEARANCES

85 Leonel Sánchez	(Universidad de Chile)
70 Alberto Fouilloux	(Universidad Catolica)
58 Juan Carlos Letelier	(Cobreloa)
52 Pedro Araya	(Universidad de Chile)
52 Francisco Valdes	(Colo Colo)
52 Sergio Livingstone	(Universidad Catolica)

LEADING INTERNATIONAL GOALSCORERS

29 Carlos Caszely	(Colo Colo)
24 Leonel Sánchez	(Universidad de Chile)

INTERNATIONAL MATCHES PLAYED BY CHILE

Date	Opponent	Result	Venue	Comp	Scorers
27-05-1910	Argentina	L 1-3	Buenos Aires	Fr	Simmons
29-05	Uruguay	L 0-3	Buenos Aires	SC	
5-06	Argentina	L 1-5	Buenos Aires	SC	Campbell
11-09	Argentina	L 0-3	Viña del Mar	Fr	
21-09-1913	Argentina	L 0-2	Viña del Mar	Fr	
2-07-1916	Uruguay	L 0-4	Buenos Aires	SC	
6-07	Argentina	L 1-6	Buenos Aires	SC	Báez
8-07	Brazil	D 1-1	Buenos Aires	SC	Salazar
12-07	Argentina	L 0-1	Buenos Aires	Fr	
14-07	Uruguay	L 1-4	Montevideo	Fr	France
30-09-1917	Uruguay	L 0-4	Montevideo	SC	
6-10	Argentina	L 0-1	Montevideo	SC	
12-10	Brazil	L 0-5	Montevideo	SC	
22-10	Argentina	D 1-1	Buenos Aires	Fr	Muñoz.B
11-05-1919	Brazil	L 0-6	Rio de Janeiro	SC	
17-05	Uruguay	L 0-2	Rio de Janeiro	SC	
22-05	Argentina	L 1-4	Rio de Janeiro	SC	France
11-09-1920	Brazil	L 0-1	Viña del Mar	SC	
17-09	Argentina	D 1-1	Viña del Mar	SC	Dominguez.A
3-10	Uruguay	L 1-2	Viña del Mar	SC	Bolados
5-09-1921	Argentina	L 1-4	Viña del Mar	Fr	Saavedra
2-10	Argentina	D 1-1	Santiago	Fr	Fuentes
17-09-1922	Brazil	D 1-1	Rio de Janeiro	SC	Bravo
23-09	Uruguay	L 0-2	Rio de Janeiro	SC	
28-09	Argentina	L 0-4	Rio de Janeiro	SC	
5-10	Paraguay	L 0-3	Rio de Janeiro	SC	
22-10	Argentina	L 0-1	Buenos Aires	Fr	
25-11-1923	Uruguay	L 1-2	Montevideo	Fr	Leiva
3-12	Argentina	L 0-6	Buenos Aires	Fr	
12-10-1924	Uruguay	L 0-1	Santiago	Fr	
19-10	Uruguay	L 0-5	Montevideo	SC	
25-10	Argentina	L 0-2	Montevideo	SC	
1-11	Paraguay	L 1-3	Montevideo	SC	Dominguez
12-10-1926	Bolivia	W 7-1	Santiago	SC	Arellano 4, Subiabre, Ramirez.M, Moreno
17-10	Uruguay	L 1-3	Santiago	SC	Subiabre
31-10	Argentina	D 1-1	Santiago	SC	Saavedra
3-11	Paraguay	W 5-1	Santiago	SC	Subiabre 3, Ramirez.M 2
10-12-1927	Uruguay	L 2-3	Viña del Mar	Fr	Alfaro 2
27-05-1928	Portugal	L 2-4	Amsterdam	OGr1	Subiabre, Carbonell
5-06	Mexico	W 3-1	Arnhem	OGct	Subiabre 3
8-06	Holland	D 2-2	Rotterdam	OGct	Bravo, Alfaro
16-07-1930	Mexico	W 3-0	Montevideo	WCr1	Vidal, Subiabre 2
19-07	France	W 1-0	Montevideo	WCr1	Subiabre
22-07	Argentina	L 1-3	Montevideo	WCr1	Subiabre
6-01-1935	Argentina	L 1-4	Lima	SC	Carmona
18-01	Uruguay	L 1-2	Lima	SC	Giudici
26-01	Peru	L 0-1	Lima	SC	
30-12-1936	Argentina	L 1-2	Buenos Aires	SC	Toro
3-01-1937	Brazil	L 4-6	Buenos Aires	SC	Toro, Avendaño 2, Riveros
10-01	Uruguay	W 3-0	Buenos Aires	SC	Toro 2, Arancibia
17-01	Paraguay	L 2-3	Buenos Aires	SC	Toro 2
21-01	Peru	D 2-2	Buenos Aires	SC	Torres, Arancibia
15-01-1939	Paraguay	L 1-5	Lima	SC	Sorrel
22-01	Peru	L 1-3	Lima	SC	Dominguez.Al
29-01	Uruguay	L 2-3	Lima	SC	Muñoz, Luco
5-02	Ecuador	W 4-1	Lima	SC	Avendaño 2, Toro, Sorrel
26-02	Paraguay	W 4-1	Santiago	Fr	Toro 3, Sorrel
2-03-1940	Argentina *	L 1-4	Buenos Aires	Fr	Sorrel
9-03	Argentina *	L 2-3	Buenos Aires	Fr	Pizzaro, Muñoz
12-03	Uruguay	L 2-3	Montevideo	Fr	
5-01-1941	Argentina *	L 1-2	Santiago	Fr	Alonso
9-01	Argentina *	L 2-5	Santiago	Fr	Sorrel, Balbuena
2-02	Ecuador	W 5-0	Santiago	SC	Sorrel 2, Toro, Contreras, Arancibia
9-02	Peru	W 1-0	Santiago	SC	Pérez.R
16-02	Uruguay	L 0-2	Santiago	SC	
4-03	Argentina	L 0-1	Santiago	SC	
10-01-1942	Uruguay	L 1-6	Montevideo	SC	Contreras

Date	Opponent	Result	Venue	Competition	Scorers
14-01	Brazil	L 1-6	Montevideo	SC	Dominguez.Al
22-01	Paraguay	L 0-2	Montevideo	SC	
31-01	Argentina	D 0-0	Montevideo	SC	Abandoned 43 mins
5-02	Ecuador	W 2-1	Montevideo	SC	Dominguez.Al, Casanoya
7-02	Peru	D 0-0	Montevideo	SC	
14-01-1945	Ecuador	W 6-3	Santiago	SC	Alcantara 2, Hormazábal.F, Vera, Clavero 2
24-01	Bolivia	W 5-0	Santiago	SC	Clavero 3, Alcantára, Medina
31-01	Colombia	W 2-0	Santiago	SC	Medina, Piñero
11-02	Argentina	D 1-1	Santiago	SC	Medina
18-02	Uruguay	W 1-0	Santiago	SC	Medina
28-02	Brazil	L 0-1	Santiago	SC	
16-01-1946	Uruguay	L 0-1	Buenos Aires	SC	
19-01	Paraguay	W 2-1	Buenos Aires	SC	Araya, Cremaschi
26-01	Argentina	L 1-3	Buenos Aires	SC	Medina
3-02	Brazil	L 1-5	Buenos Aires	SC	Salfate
8-02	Bolivia	W 4-1	Buenos Aires	SC	Araya 2, Cremaschi 2
6-12-1947	Uruguay	L 0-6	Guayaquil	SC	
9-12	Peru	W 2-1	Guayaquil	SC	Varela.C, Saéz
11-12	Ecuador	W 3-0	Guayaquil	SC	López.PH 2, Peñaloza
16-12	Argentina	D 1-1	Guayaquil	SC	Riera
23-12	Paraguay	L 0-1	Guayaquil	SC	
29-12	Colombia	W 4-1	Guayaquil	SC	Sáez, Prieto, Infante, Riera
31-12	Bolivia	W 4-3	Guayaquil	SC	OG, López.PH, Sáez, Riera
6-04-1949	Bolivia	L 2-3	Sao Paulo	SC	Salamanca, Riera
13-04	Brazil	L 1-2	Sao Paulo	SC	López.PH
17-04	Ecuador	W 1-0	Rio de Janeiro	SC	Rojas.C
20-04	Colombia	D 1-1	Rio de Janeiro	SC	López.PH
27-04	Paraguay	L 2-4	Sao Paulo	SC	Cremaschi, Ramos
30-04	Peru	L 0-3	Sao Paulo	SC	
8-05	Uruguay	W 3-1	Belo Horizonte	SC	Infante 2, Cremaschi
26-02-1950	Bolivia	L 0-2	La Paz	WCq	
12-03	Bolivia	W 5-0	Santiago	WCq	Diaz.G 2, Campos, Prieto, Hormazábal
7-04	Uruguay	L 1-5	Santiago	Fr	Campos
9-04	Uruguay	W 2-1	Santiago	Fr	Campos, Diaz.G
25-06	England	L 0-2	Rio de Janeiro	WCr1	
29-06	Spain	L 0-2	Rio de Janeiro	WCr1	
2-07	United States	W 5-2	Recife	WCr1	Cremaschi 3, Robledo.G, Prieto
16-03-1952	Panama	W 6-1	Santiago	PAC	Prieto 3, Muñoz, Meléndez, Hormazábal
26-03	Mexico	W 4-0	Santiago	PAC	Diaz.G 2, Hormazábal, Prieto
2-04	Peru	W 3-2	Santiago	PAC	Meléndez, Prito, Cremaschi
13-04	Uruguay	W 2-0	Santiago	PAC	Cremaschi, Muñoz
20-04	Brazil	L 0-3	Santiago	PAC	
25-02-1953	Paraguay	L 0-3	Lima	SC	
1-03	Uruguay	W 3-2	Lima	SC	Molina 3
4-03	Peru	D 0-0	Lima	SC	
19-03	Ecuador	W 3-0	Lima	SC	Molina 2, Cremaschi
23-03	Brazil	L 2-3	Lima	SC	Molina 2
28-03	Bolivia	D 2-2	Lima	SC	Meléndez, Diaz.G
24-05	England	L 1-2	Santiago	Fr	OG
12-07	Spain	L 1-2	Santiago	Fr	Muñoz
26-07	Peru	W 2-1	Lima	PC	Hormazábal, Robledo.G
28-07	Peru	L 0-5	Lima	PC	
14-02-1954	Paraguay	L 0-4	Asuncion	WCq	
21-02	Paraguay	L 1-3	Santiago	WCq	Robledo.J
28-02	Brazil	L 0-2	Santiago	WCq	
14-03	Brazil	L 0-1	Rio de Janeiro	WCq	
17-09	Peru	W 2-1	Santiago	PC	Meléndez, Musso
19-09	Peru	L 2-4	Santiago	PC	Meléndez 2
27-02-1955	Ecuador	W 7-1	Santiago	SC	Hormazábal 3, Diaz.G 2, Robledo.J, Meléndez
6-03	Peru	W 5-4	Santiago	SC	Robledo.J 2, Hormazábal, Muñoz, Ramirez.J
13-03	Uruguay	D 2-2	Santiago	SC	Muñoz, Hormazábal
20-03	Paraguay	W 5-0	Santiago	SC	Meléndez 2, Muñoz 2, Hormazábal
30-03	Argentina	L 0-1	Santiago	SC	
18-09	Brazil	D 1-1	Rio de Janeiro	OHC	Ramirez
20-09	Brazil	L 1-2	Sao Paulo	OHC	Hormazábal
24-01-1956	Brazil	W 4-1	Montevideo	SC	Hormazábal 2, Meléndez, Sánchez.L
29-01	Argentina	L 0-2	Montevideo	SC	
6-02	Uruguay	L 1-2	Montevideo	SC	Ramirez.J
9-02	Peru	W 4-3	Montevideo	SC	Hormazábal, Muñoz, Fernandez.J, Sánchez.L
12-02	Paraguay	W 2-0	Montevideo	SC	Hormazábal, Ramirez.J

1-03	Brazil	L 1-2	Mexico City	PAC	Tello
8-03	Costa Rica	L 1-2	Mexico City	PAC	Hormazábal
11-03	Argentina	L 0-3	Mexico City	PAC	
15-03	Peru	D 2-2	Mexico City	PAC	Diaz.G, Cortés
18-03	Mexico	L 1-2	Mexico City	PAC	Tello
26-08	Czechoslovakia	W 3-0	Santiago	Fr	Robledo.J 2, Hormazábal
13-03-1957	Brazil	L 2-4	Lima	SC	Ramirez.J, Fernandez.J
16-03	Peru	L 0-1	Lima	SC	
21-03	Colombia	W 3-2	Lima	SC	Verdejo 2, Espinoza
24-03	Ecuador	D 2-2	Lima	SC	Ramirez.J 2
28-03	Argentina	L 2-6	Lima	SC	Fernandez.J 2
1-04	Uruguay	L 0-2	Lima	SC	
15-09	Brazil	W 1-0	Santiago	OHC	Meléndez
18-09	Brazil	D 1-1	Santiago	OHC	Fernandez
22-09	Bolivia	W 2-1	Santiago	WCq	Ramirez, Diaz.G
29-09	Bolivia	L 0-3	La Paz	WCq	
13-10	Argentina	L 0-2	Santiago	WCq	
20-10	Argentina	L 0-4	Buenos Aires	WCq	
7-03-1959	Argentina	L 1-6	Buenos Aires	SC	Alvarez
11-03	Paraguay	L 1-2	Buenos Aires	SC	Sánchez.L
15-03	Brazil	L 0-3	Buenos Aires	SC	
21-03	Peru	D 1-1	Buenos Aires	SC	Moreno
26-03	Bolivia	W 5-2	Buenos Aires	SC	Soto.J 2, Soto.M 2, Sánchez.L
2-04	Uruguay	W 1-0	Buenos Aires	SC	Moreno
17-09	Brazil	L 0-7	Rio de Janeiro	OHC	
20-09	Brazil	L 0-1	Sao Paulo	OHC	
18-11	Argentina	W 4-2	Santiago	Fr	Bello 2, Sánchez.L, Rios
16-03-1960	France	L 0-6	Paris	Fr	
23-03	West Germany	L 1-2	Stuttgart	Fr	Soto.J
30-03	Rep. Ireland	L 0-2	Dublin	Fr	
6-04	Switzerland	L 2-4	Basle	Fr	Soto.J, Tobar
13-04	Belgium	D 1-1	Brussels	Fr	Musso
1-06	Uruguay	L 2-3	Santiago	Fr	Moreno, Fouilloux
5-06	Uruguay	D 2-2	Montevideo	Fr	Sánchez.L 2
29-06	Brazil	L 0-4	Rio de Janeiro	Fr	
14-07	Spain	L 0-4	Santiago	Fr	
17-07	Spain	L 1-4	Santiago	Fr	Musso
18-12	Paraguay	W 4-1	Santiago	Fr	
21-12	Paraguay	W 3-1	Valparaiso	Fr	Cabrera 2, Moreno
19-03-1961	Peru	W 5-2	Santiago	Fr	Toro, Betta, Soto.M 2, Sánchez.L
26-03	West Germany	W 3-1	Santiago	Fr	Sanchez.L 2, Rojas.E
7-05	Brazil	L 1-2	Santiago	OHC	Soto.J
11-05	Brazil	L 0-1	Santiago	OHC	
12-10	Uruguay	L 2-3	Santiago	Fr	Fouilloux, Moreno
22-11	Soviet Union	L 0-1	Santiago	Fr	
9-12	Hungary	W 5-1	Santiago	Fr	Landa 2, Sánchez.L 2, Sepulveda
13-12	Hungary	D 0-0	Santiago	Fr	
30-05-1962	Switzerland	W 3-1	Santiago	WCr1	Sánchez.L 2, Ramirez.J
2-06	Italy	W 2-0	Santiago	WCr1	Ramirez.J, Toro
6-06	West Germany	L 0-2	Santiago	WCr1	
10-06	Soviet Union	W 2-1	Arica	WCqf	Sánchez.L, Rojas.E
13-06	Brazil	L 2-4	Santiago	WCsf	Toro, Sánchez.L
16-06	Yugoslavia	W 1-0	Santiago	WC3p	Rojas.E
7-11	Argentina	D 1-1	Santiago	CDC	Landa
21-11	Argentina	L 0-1	Buenos Aires	CDC	
23-03-1963	Uruguay	L 2-3	Montevideo	PDC	Ramirez.J 2
24-07	Uruguay	D 0-0	Santiago	PDC	
24-09-1964	Argentina	L 0-5	Buenos Aires	CDC	
14-10	Argentina	D 1-1	Santiago	CDC	Verdejo
15-04-1965	Peru	W 4-1	Santiago	PC	Lando 2, Araya 2
28-04	Peru	W 1-0	Lima	PC	Araya
9-05	Uruguay	D 0-0	Santiago	PDC	
16-05	Uruguay	D 1-1	Montevideo	PDC	Sánchez.L
14-07	Argentina	L 0-1	Buenos Aires	CDC	
21-07	Argentina	D 1-1	Santiago	CDC	Sánchez.L
1-08	Colombia	W 7-2	Santiago	WCq	Fouilloux 2, Mendez 2, Sánchez.L, Campos, Prieto
7-08	Colombia	L 0-2	Barranquilla	WCq	
15-08	Ecuador	D 2-2	Guayaquil	WCq	Campos, Prieto
22-08	Ecuador	W 3-1	Santiago	WCq	Sánchez.L, Marcos, Fouilloux
12-10	Ecuador	W 2-1	Lima	WCq	Sánchez.L, Marcos

Date	Opponent	Result	Venue	Comp	Scorers
23-02-1966	Soviet Union	L 0-2	Santiago	Fr	
17-04	Brazil	L 0-1	Santiago	OHC	
20-04	Brazil	W 2-1	Viña del Mar	OHC	Araya, Valdés
11-05	Mexico	L 0-1	Mexico City	Fr	
15-05	Brazil	D 1-1	Sao Paulo	Fr	Yávar
19-05	Brazil	L 0-1	Rio de Janeiro	Fr	
22-05	Wales	W 2-0	Santiago	Fr	Marcos, Tobar
29-05	Mexico	L 0-1	Santiago	Fr	
2-07	East Germany	L 2-5	Leipzig	Fr	Tobar, Fouilloux
13-07	Italy	L 0-2	Sunderland	WCr1	
15-07	North Korea	D 1-1	Middlesbrough	WCr1	Marcos
20-07	Soviet Union	L 1-2	Sunderland	WCr1	Marcos
30-11	Colombia	W 5-2	Santiago	SCq	Castro 2, Araya, Prieto, Saavedra
11-12	Colombia	D 0-0	Bogota	SCq	
18-01-1967	Venezuela	W 2-0	Montevideo	SC	Marcos 2
22-01	Paraguay	W 4-2	Montevideo	SC	Gallardo 2, Araya 2
26-01	Uruguay	D 2-2	Montevideo	SC	Gallardo, Marcos
28-01	Argentina	L 0-2	Montevideo	SC	
1-02	Bolivia	D 0-0	Montevideo	SC	
15-08	Argentina	W 1-0	Santiago	Fr	Araya
19-09	Brazil	L 0-1	Santiago	Fr	
8-11	Argentina	W 3-1	Santiago	Fr	Fouilloux 2, Reynoso
17-12	Soviet Union	L 1-4	Santiago	Fr	Reynoso
18-08-1968	Peru	W 2-1	Lima	PC	Valdés 2
21-08	Peru	D 0-0	Lima	PC	
28-08	Mexico	L 1-3	Mexico City	Fr	Sánchez.L
23-10	Mexico	W 3-1	Santiago	Fr	Reynoso, Olivares 2
27-11	Argentina	L 0-4	Rosario	CDC	
4-12	Argentina	W 2-1	Santiago	CDC	Fouilloux, Olivares
18-12	West Germany	W 2-1	Santiago	Fr	Araya, Fouilloux
28-05-1969	Argentina	D 1-1	Santiago	Fr	Velez
8-06	Paraguay	W 1-0	Asuncion	Fr	Araya
11-06	Argentina	L 1-2	La Plata	Fr	Olivares
15-06	Colombia	D 3-3	Bogota	Fr	Fouilloux, Reynoso, Laube
22-06	East Germany	W 1-0	Magdeburg	Fr	Yávar
6-07	Paraguay	D 0-0	Santiago	Fr	
13-07	Uruguay	D 0-0	Santiago	WCq	
15-07	Colombia	D 3-3	Bogota	Fr	Alube, Fouilloux, Reynoso
27-07	Ecuador	W 4-1	Santiago	WCq	Olivares 2, Valdés 2
3-08	Ecuador	D 1-1	Guayaquil	WCq	Olivares
10-08	Uruguay	L 0-2	Montevideo	WCq	
22-03-1970	Brazil	L 0-5	Sao Paulo	Fr	
26-03	Brazil	L 1-2	Rio de Janeiro	Fr	Castro
4-10	Brazil	L 1-5	Santiago	Fr	Messen
2-02-1971	East Germany	L 0-1	Santiago	Fr	
14-07	Paraguay	W 3-2	Santiago	Fr	Osorio, Castro 2
21-07	Argentina	D 2-2	Santiago	CDC	Viveros, Vásquez
4-08	Argentina	L 0-1	Buenos Aires	CDC	
8-08	Paraguay	L 0-2	Asuncion	Fr	
11-08	Peru	L 0-1	Lima	PC	
15-08	Bolivia	W 4-3	La Paz	Fr	Peralta 2, Messen, Osorio
18-08	Peru	W 1-0	Santiago	PC	Viveros
27-10	Uruguay	L 0-3	Montevideo	PDC	
3-11	Uruguay	W 5-0	Santiago	PDC	Osorio, Pacheco, Araya, Crisosto, Vásquez
27-01-1972	Mexico	L 0-2	Mexico City	Fr	
9-02	Haiti	L 0-1	Port au Prince	Fr	
31-05	Argentina	L 3-4	Santiago	CDC	Caszely, Valdés 2
14-06	Ecuador	W 2-1	Natal	Clr1	Crisosto, Caszely
18-06	Portugal	L 1-4	Recife	Clr1	Caszely
21-06	Rep. Ireland	W 2-1	Recife	Clr1	Caszely, Fouilloux
25-06	Iran	W 2-1	Recife	Clr1	Caszely 2
16-08	Mexico	L 0-2	Santiago	Fr	
25-09	Argentina	L 0-2	Buenos Aires	CDC	
14-04-1973	Haiti	D 1-1	Port-au-Prince	Fr	Galleguillos
21-04	Mexico	D 1-1	Mexico City	Fr	
24-04	Ecuador	D 1-1	Guayaquil	Fr	Caszely
29-04	Peru	L 0-2	Lima	WCq	
13-05	Peru	W 2-0	Santiago	WCq	Crisosto, Ahumada
13-07	Argentina	L 4-5	Buenos Aires	CDC	Ahumada 2, Crisosto, Caszely
18-07	Argentina	W 3-1	Santiago	CDC	Caszely 2, Crisosto

24-07	Bolivia	W 3-0	Santiago	Fr	Farias, Muñoz, Solis
5-08	Peru	W 2-1	Montevideo	WCq	Valdés, Farias
20-09	Mexico	W 2-1	Mexico City	Fr	Caszely 2
26-09	Soviet Union	D 0-0	Moscow	WCq	
21-11	Soviet Union	W *w-o*	Santiago	WCq	Soviet Union refused to play
24-04-1974	Haiti	W 1-0	Port au Prince	Fr	Garcia
26-04	Haiti	D 0-0	Port au Prince	Fr	
12-05	Rep. Ireland	L 1-2	Santiago	Fr	Valdés
14-06	West Germany	L 0-1	Berlin	WCr1	
18-06	East Germany	D 1-1	Berlin	WCr1	Ahumada
22-06	Australia	D 0-0	Berlin	WCr1	
6-11	Argentina	L 0-2	Santiago	CDC	
20-11	Argentina	D 1-1	Buenos Aires	CDC	Méndez
22-12	Paraguay	W 1-0	Santiago	Fr	Gamboa
4-06-1975	Uruguay	L 0-1	Montevideo	PDC	
25-06	Uruguay	L 1-3	Santiago	PDC	Pinto.H. Abandoned 78 mins
16-07	Peru	D 1-1	Santiago	SCr1	Crisosto
20-07	Bolivia	L 1-2	La Paz	SCr1	Gamboa
13-08	Bolivia	W 4-0	Santiago	SCr1	Araneda 2, Ahumada, Gamboa
20-08	Peru	L 1-3	Lima	SCr1	Reynoso
6-10-1976	Uruguay	D 0-0	Santiago	PDC	
13-10	Argentina	L 0-2	Buenos Aires	CDC	
26-01-1977	Paraguay	W 4-0	Santiago	Fr	Crisosto 3, Rojas
30-01	Uruguay	L 0-3	Montevideo	PDC	
2-02	Paraguay	L 0-2	Asuncion	Fr	
27-02	Ecuador	W 1-0	Guayaquil	WCq	Gamboa
6-03	Peru	D 1-1	Santiago	WCq	Ahumada
20-03	Ecuador	W 3-0	Santiago	WCq	Figueroa, Castro, OG
26-03	Peru	L 0-2	Lima	WCq	
15-06	Scotland	L 2-4	Santiago	Fr	Crisosto 2
13-06-1979	Ecuador	D 0-0	Santiago	Fr	
21-06	Ecuador	L 1-2	Guayaquil	Fr	Moscoso
11-07	Uruguay	W 1-0	Santiago	PDC	Figueroa
18-07	Uruguay	L 1-2	Montevideo	PDC	Quiroz
8-08	Venezuela	D 1-1	San Cristobal	SCr1	Peredo
15-08	Colombia	L 0-1	Bogota	SCr1	
29-08	Venezuela	W 7-0	Santiago	SCr1	Peredo 2, Rivas 2, Veliz, Soto.M, Yañez
5-09	Colombia	W 2-0	Santiago	SCr1	Caszely, Peredo
17-10	Peru	W 2-1	Lima	SCsf	Caszely 2
24-10	Peru	D 0-0	Santiago	SCsf	
28-11	Paraguay	L 0-3	Asuncion	SCf	
5-12	Paraguay	W 1-0	Santiago	SCf	Rivas
11-12	Paraguay	D 0-0	Buenos Aires	SCf	
24-06-1980	Brazil	L 1-2	Belo Horizonte	Fr	Yañez
21-08	Uruguay	D 0-0	Montevideo	PDC	
18-09	Argentina	D 2-2	Mendoza	Fr	Vargas, Castec
10-03-1981	Colombia	W 1-0	Santiago	Fr	Herrera
14-03	Brazil	L 1-2	Ribeirao Preto	Fr	Caszely
19-03	Colombia	W 2-1	Bogota	Fr	Caszely 2
19-04	Peru	W 3-0	Santiago	Fr	Moscoso 2, Caszely
29-04	Uruguay	L 1-2	Santiago	PDC	Rojas.M
24-05	Ecuador	D 0-0	Guayaquil	WCq	
7-06	Paraguay	W 1-0	Asuncion	WCq	Yañez
14-06	Ecuador	W 2-0	Santiago	WCq	Rivas, Caszely
21-06	Paraguay	W 3-0	Santiago	WCq	Caszely, Yañez, Neyra
5-07	Spain	D 1-1	Santiago	Fr	Caszely
15-07	Uruguay	D 0-0	Montevideo	PDC	
5-08	Peru	W 2-1	Lima	Fr	Caszely 2
26-08	Brazil	D 0-0	Santiago	Fr	
23-03-1982	Peru	W 2-1	Santiago	Fr	Letelier, Neyra
30-03	Peru	L 0-1	Lima	Fr	
19-05	Rumania	L 2-3	Santiago	Fr	Gamboa, Caszely
22-05	Rep. Ireland	W 1-0	Santiago	Fr	Gamboa
17-06	Austria	L 0-1	Oviedo	WCr1	
20-06	West Germany	L 1-4	Gijon	WCr1	Moscoso
24-06	Algeria	L 2-3	Oviedo	WCr1	Neyra, Letelier
28-04-1983	Brazil	L 2-3	Rio de Janeiro	Fr	Orellana 2
12-05	Argentina	D 2-2	Santiago	Fr	Orellana, Dubo
23-06	Argentina	L 0-1	Buenos Aires	Fr	
14-07	Colombia	D 2-2	Bogota	Fr	Aravena, Hurtado
19-07	Bolivia	W 2-1	La Paz	Fr	Aravena, Letelier

21-07	Peru	W 1-0	Lima	Fr	Soto.M
24-07	Paraguay	L 0-1	Asuncion	Fr	
28-07	Brazil	D 0-0	Santiago	Fr	
3-08	Peru	W 2-0	Arica	Fr	Letelier 2
17-08	Paraguay	W 3-2	Santiago	Fr	Aravena, Letelier, Hurtado
24-08	Bolivia	W 4-2	Santiago	Fr	Letelier, Aravena 3
1-09	Uruguay	L 1-2	Montevideo	SCr1	Orellana
8-09	Venezuela	W 5-0	Santiago	SCr1	Aravena 2, Arriza, Dubó, Espinoza
11-09	Uruguay	W 2-0	Santiago	SCr1	Dubo, Letelier
21-09	Venezuela	D 0-0	Caracas	SCr1	
17-06-1984	England	D 0-0	Santiago	Fr	
25-07	Canada	D 0-0	Edmonton	Fr	
28-10	Mexico	W 1-0	Santiago	Fr	Aravena
6-02-1985	Paraguay	W 1-0	Viña del Mar	Fr	Aravena
8-02	Finland	W 2-0	Viña del Mar	Fr	Letelier, Aravena
21-02	Colombia	D 1-1	Santiago	Fr	Letelier
24-02	Peru	L 1-2	Santiago	Fr	Rubio
3-03	Ecuador	D 1-1	Quito	WCq	Letelier
9-03	Peru	D 1-1	Lima	Fr	Aravena
17-03	Ecuador	W 6-2	Santiago	WCq	Puebla, Cazsely 2, Hisis, Aravena 2
24-03	Uruguay	W 2-0	Santiago	WCq	Rubio, Aravena
7-04	Uruguay	L 1-2	Montevideo	WCq	Aravena
15-05	Argentina	L 0-2	Buenos Aires	Fr	
21-05	Brazil	W 2-1	Santiago	Fr	Rubio, Caszely
8-06	Brazil	L 1-3	Porto Alegre	Fr	Nuñes
9-10	Paraguay	D 0-0	Asuncion	Fr	
17-10	Uruguay	W 1-0	Santiago	Fr	Neyra
27-10	Peru	W 4-2	Santiago	WCq	Aravena 2, Rubio, Hisis
29-10	Paraguay	D 0-0	Santiago	Fr	
3-11	Peru	W 1-0	Lima	WCq	Aravena
10-11	Paraguay	L 0-3	Asuncion	WCq	
17-11	Paraguay	D 2-2	Santiago	WCq	Rubio, Nunoz
7-05-1986	Brazil	D 1-1	Curitiba	Fr	Puyal
19-06-1987	Peru	W 3-1	Lima	Fr	Rodriguez, Basay, Zamorano
21-06	Peru	L 0-2	Lima	Fr	
24-06	Peru	W 1-0	Santiago	Fr	Hurtado
30-06	Venezuela	W 3-1	Cordoba	SCr1	Letelier, Contreras, Salgado
3-07	Brazil	W 4-0	Cordoba	SCr1	Basay 2, Letelier 2
8-07	Colombia	W 2-1	Cordoba	SCsf	Astengo, Vera
12-07	Uruguay	L 0-1	Buenos Aires	SCf	
9-12	Brazil	L 1-2	Uberlandia	Fr	Martinez
23-05-1988	Greece	L 0-1	Toronto	Fr	
25-05	Canada	L 0-1	Toronto	Fr	
1-06	United States	D 1-1	Santiago	Fr	
3-06	United States	W 3-1	San Diego	Fr	Hurtado, Salgado, Rojas.O
5-06	United States	W 3-0	Los Angeles	Fr	
13-09	Ecuador	W 3-1	La Serena	Fr	Salgado, Alvarez, Rodriguez
27-09	Paraguay	L 0-2	Asuncion	Fr	
29-09	Ecuador	D 0-0	Asuncion	Fr	
25-10	Peru	W 2-0	Arica	Fr	Espinoza, Gonzalez
1-11	Uruguay	D 1-1	Santiago	PDC	Espinoza
9-11	Uruguay	L 1-3	Montevideo	PDC	Espinoza
23-11	Peru	D 1-1	Lima	Fr	Mardones
29-01-1989	Ecuador	L 0-1	Guayaquil	Fr	
1-02	Peru	D 0-0	Armenia	Fr	
5-02	Colombia	L 0-1	Armenia	Fr	
20-04	Argentina	D 1-1	Santiago	Fr	Espinoza
5-05	Guatemala	W 1-0	Los Angeles	Fr	Martinez
7-05	El Salvador	W 1-0	Los Angeles	Fr	Cormeno
23-05	England	D 0-0	London	Fr	
26-05	Nth. Ireland	W 1-0	Belfast	Fr	Astengo
30-05	Scotland	L 0-2	Glasgow	Fr	
3-06	Egypt	L 0-2	Cairo	Fr	
19-06	Uruguay	D 2-2	Montevideo	Fr	Gonzalez, Pizarro
22-06	Bolivia	W 1-0	La Paz	Fr	Covarrubias
27-06	Bolivia	W 2-1	Santiago	Fr	Covarrubias, Pizarro
2-07	Argentina	L 0-1	Goiania	SCr1	
6-07	Uruguay	L 0-3	Goiania	SCr1	
8-07	Bolivia	W 5-0	Goiania	SCr1	Olmis, Ramirez, Astengo, Pizarro, Reyes
10-07	Ecuador	W 2-1	Goiania	SCr1	Olmis, Letelier
25-07	Peru	W 2-1	Arica	Fr	Tudor, Aravena
6-08	Venezuela	W 3-1	Caracas	WCq	Aravena 2, Zamorano

13-08	Brazil	D 1-1	Santiago	WCq	Basay
27-08	Venezuela	W 5-0	Mendoza	WCq	Letelier 3, Yañez, Vera
3-09	Brazil	L 0-1	Rio de Janeiro	WCq	Abandoned after 65 mins
					Game awarded to Brazil 2-0
17-10-1990	Brazil	D 0-0	Santiago	Fr	
8-11	Brazil	D 0-0	Belem	Fr	
9-04-1991	Mexico	L 0-1	Veracruz	Fr	
22-05	Rep. Ireland	D 1-1	Dublin	Fr	Estay
30-05	Uruguay	W 2-1	Santiago	Fr	Vega, Gonzalez
19-06	Ecuador	L 1-2	Quito	Fr	Vera
26-06	Uruguay	L 1-2	Montevideo	Fr	Rubio
30-06	Ecuador	W 3-1	Santiago	Fr	Rubio 2, Zamorano
6-07	Venezuela	W 2-0	Santiago	SCr1	Vilches, Zamorano
8-07	Peru	W 4-2	Concepcion	SCr1	Rubio, Contreras, Zamorano 2
10-07	Argentina	L 0-1	Santiago	SCr1	
14-07	Paraguay	W 4-0	Santiago	SCr1	Rubio, Zamorano, Estay, Vera
17-07	Colombia	D 1-1	Santiago	SCr2	Zamorano
19-07	Argentina	D 0-0	Santiago	SCr2	
21-07	Brazil	L 0-2	Santiago	SCr2	
31-03-1993	Bolivia	W 2-1	Arica	Fr	Estay, Sierra
30-05	Colombia	D 1-1	Santiago	Fr	Guevara
6-06	Colombia	L 0-1	Bogota	Fr	
9-06	Ecuador	W 2-1	Quito	Fr	Pizzarro, Barrera
18-06	Paraguay	L 0-1	Cuenca	SCr1	
21-06	Brazil	W 3-2	Cuenca	SCr1	Sierra, Zambrano 2
24-06	Peru	L 0-1	Cuenca	SCr1	
8-09	Spain	L 0-2	Alicante	Fr	
22-03-1994	France	L 1-3	Lyon	Fr	Zamorano
27-03	Saudi Arabia	W 2-0	Riyadh	Fr	Tudor, Marcilio
30-03	Saudi Arabia	D 2-2	Riyadh	Fr	Leppe, OG
30-04	USA	W 2-0	Albuquerque	Fr	Barrera, Gonzalez.P
18-05	Argentina	D 3-3	Santiago	Fr	Barrera 2, Salas
25-05	Peru	W 2-1	Santiago	Fr	Mendoza, Zamorano
22-09	Bolivia	L 1-2	Santiago	Fr	Tudor
16-11	Argentina	L 0-3	Santiago	Fr	
29-03-1995	Mexico	W 2-1	Los Angeles	Fr	Salas, Zamorano
19-04	Peru	L 0-6	Lima	Fr	
22-04	Iceland	D 1-1	Temuco	Fr	Salas
25-05	Northern Ireland	W 2-1	Edmonton	Fr	Valencia, Mardones
28-05	Canada	W 2-1	Edmonton	Fr	Valencia, Salas
16-06	New Zealand	W 3-1	Antofagasta	Fr	Ramirez, Fuentes, Ruiz
19-06	Paraguay	L 0-1	La Serena	Fr	
22-06	Turkey	D 0-0	Santiago	Fr	
8-07	United States	L 1-2	Paysandu	SCr1	Rozental
11-07	Argentina	L 0-4	Paysandu	SCr1	
14-07	Bolivia	D 2-2	Paysandu	SCr1	Basay.I 2

COLOMBIA

To find a country with a more turbulent football history than Colombia would be a difficult task. From shooting referees to paying players with money laundered from the drugs business, Colombia has it all. And who can forget the murder of Andres Escobar after his side's disappointing performance in USA '94? The Colombians have also enraged other nations by their flagrant disregard of the rules set down by FIFA, but despite all of this, after years of achieving little, Colombia is emerging as the biggest threat to the established powers of Argentina, Brazil and Uruguay.

As was common in South America, a port, Barranquilla, was the first place football really took a hold. Until the introduction of professionalism in 1948, Barranquilla was the centre of football in the country. The first ruling body of any kind in the country, the Liga de Football del Atlantico was founded there in 1924. Affiliation to FIFA occurred seven years later, but the fact that both these events happened some forty years after the first recorded game was played gives an indication as to how disjointed progress was.

Colombia is a very large country. Roughly half of the total area comprises the northern boundary of the Amazon basin, whilst much of the rest of the country is taken up by the northern reaches of the Andes. A majority of the cities are located in these mountains, so it is not surprising that communications were not good.

The first game adhering to the proper rules is said to have taken place in Bogota, the capital, in 1887, but for many years football was played on an ad hoc basis with no proper organisation. A national body was finally formed in 1938 and known as the Asociacion Colombiana de Futbol, but clubs in all the different provinces were under the control of various regional associations, not the ACF.

An annual tournament for representative teams from the various regional leagues was introduced, but the main role of the ACF was to put together a national side and in 1938, Colombia joined the Confederacion Centro-americano y del Caribe de Futbol and later that year made their international debut in the Central American and Caribbean Games. Bogota then hosted the Bolivar games at the end of the year, but neither tournament proved successful for the Colombians and it was five years before they played another game.

In 1940 the ACF decided to join the South American confederation in apparent contradiction to its membership of the CCCF, but from that time Colombia has stuck with South America and eventually gave up membership of the Central American body.

The early 1940s saw major developments at club level and they were ultimately to lead to notoriety for Colombia at the end of the decade. Professionalism was becoming a major issue and in 1939 the club that was to represent the new era in Colombian football was founded by two wealthy businessmen in Bogota. Known initially as Deportivo Municipal, in 1947 they officially adopted their nickname, 'Los Millonarios', a reference to the size of their bank balance.

Wealthy patrons became involved with other clubs also. The amateur era passed into history with the creation of a new professional league in 1948, but instead of making this a platform from which to build, Colombia hit the self-destruct button. Players were imported from all over South America and the league was an instant hit. In 1950 the DiMayor, as the league was known, broke away form the ACF, and there followed four years of turmoil that put Colombia on the world football map.

Known as the 'El Dorado' period, it saw Colombia assemble some of the world's best talent, much to the dismay of the rest of the world. After the breakaway, Colombia had been suspended from FIFA which meant that transfer fees did not have to be paid. At the same time a players' strike in both Argentina and Uruguay meant many of the continent's best players were available for transfer. Signing-on fees and wages higher than anywhere else meant that soon there were up to 70 Argentinians, 15 Uruguayans and six Britons, among others, playing in the DiMayor.

Among those tempted to Colombia were Alfredo Di Stefano, Nestor Rossi and Adolfo Pedernera, all major stars with River Plate before they came to Colombia. Even England was raided and Neil Franklin, the England centre-half at the time, was signed up by Millonarios' major cross-town rivals, Santa Fe.

El Dorado was not to last long, however. In 1954 FIFA accepted Colombia back into the fold, whilst most of the major stars had by then departed, in many cases to Europe. The bubble had well and truly burst, leaving many clubs in severe financial trouble. There had been 18 clubs in the DiMayor at its peak; by 1955 the number had shrunk to just 10. The reliance on foreign players, and the high standard they set, had left a dearth of home-grown talent. Spectator interest waned and Colombia slipped firmly into the international football backwaters from which it had briefly risen.

The national team proved a fairer indication of the standard of Colombian footballers. They had entered three editions of the South American Championship in the 1940s, and out of 20 games played only won one. Many of the defeats were substantial, and from 1949 until 1957 no further international matches were played. There was a brief flurry of international activity in 1957 which included a victory over Uruguay in the South American Championships, as well as a first attempt to qualify for the World Cup, but with a group containing Uruguay and Paraguay, Colombia placed comfortably last behind the other vastly more experienced sides.

It was a great surprise, therefore, when the Colombians did qualify for the 1962 finals, but with both Chile and Brazil qualifying automatically, all that involved was two games with Peru. A 1-0 win in Bogota was sufficient to see them through. Very much the unknown quantity, their 2-1 and 5-0 defeats by Uruguay and Yugoslavia respectively were redeemed by a superb display against the Soviet Union, their finest performance to that date. Losing 4-1 at one point, they fought back to draw 4-4. The experience was not built upon and the team faded back into obscurity until the mid-1970s.

At home, the DiMayor had struggled on after El Dorado. Millonarios briefly rose again in the late 1950s and early 1960s but the team did not have the same aura about it as before. In 1965, the self-destruct button was pushed once again with the creation of the Federacion del Futbol Colombiana as a direct challenge to the authority of the ACF. FIFA was called in to mediate in the dispute and ended up directly running the game until 1971 when a wholly new Federacion Colombiana de Futbol was formed. Meanwhile, 1968 saw a complete reorganisation of the league competition in response to the post El Dorado depression that had enveloped the game. A simple, European-style league was replaced by what can seem an unbelievably complicated structure.

Three phases were introduced, the Apertura, the Finalizacion and finally the Serie Definitiva. The precise system has varied from year to year since, but broadly speaking the first two phases are used to select a final group of clubs to play in the last stage, from which the champions emerge. Bonus points are awarded throughout the season which is why it was possible for America to win the 1983 championship with 19.75 points. The changes have largely been popular and since 1968 the league has been relatively stable and has improved in standard.

Much of this has been due to the progress made by the city of Cali. From 1968 until 1990 the city won the title on 12 occasions either through Deportivo Cali or

America Cali. Both were also the first Colombian clubs to make inroads in the Copa Libertadores. Deportivo were losing finalists in 1978, whilst America were losing finalists three years running in the mid-1980s. How much of this progress has been due to the Cali drug cartel helping to fund the game has never been proved, but more than one judge has been assassinated trying to find out!

Careful control on the number of foreigners in the league meant that in the 1970s local talent began to develop. Atletico Nacional of Medellin, another city with a large drugs cartel, even have a policy of only playing Colombian players, and this paid off in May 1989 when the event all Colombians had been waiting for occurred. Nacional won the Copa Libertadores, the first international trophy in the history of the country, amid scenes of unprecedented celebrations.

THE ORDER OF MERIT

		Total			League			Copa Lib		
		G	S	B	G	S	B	G	S	B
1	Millonarios Bogota	13	8	11	13	8	8	-	-	3
2	América Cali	8	7	9	8	4	5	-	3	4
3	At. Nacional Medellin	7	7	6	6	7	3	1	-	3
4	Independiente Santa Fe	6	2	5	6	2	4	-	-	1
5	Deportivo Cali	5	11	8	5	10	6	-	1	2
6	Atlético Junior	3	3	3	3	3	2	-	-	1
7	Independiente Medellin	2	4	3	2	4	3	-	-	-
8	Atlético Quindio	1	2	1	1	2	1	-	-	-
9	Deportes Caldas	1	-	1	1	-	1	-	-	-
10	Union Magdalena	1	-	1	1	-	1	-	-	-
11	Deportes Tolima	-	3	1	-	3	-	-	-	1
12	Boca Junior	-	2	2	-	2	2	-	-	-
13	Cúcuta	-	1	2	-	1	2	-	-	-
14	Pereira	-	-	4	-	-	4	-	-	-
15	Bucaramanga	-	-	3	-	-	3	-	-	-

To the end of the 1994 season

The fortunes of the national team have also risen in the corresponding period. In the 1975 South American Championship, Paraguay, Ecuador and Uruguay were beaten on the way to the final where the Colombians met Peru. Peru eventually won after a play-off in Caracas, but the signs were there that matters were improving. Players of the class of Willington Ortiz were starting to emerge, and by the 1980s the basis of a good national side was there. Under the leadership of Francisco Maturano, who also led Nacional to their Copa Libertadores success, Colombia finished third in the 1987 South American Championships in Argentina.

In 1990, with players like Carlos Valderrama, Alberto Iguaran, Bernardo Redin and the eccentric Rene Higuita in goal, Colombia qualified for the World Cup finals and when pressed, showed they were capable of living with the best. They certainly made their mark on the tournament, especially Higuita who showed goalkeepers how to win over the crowds, if not managers, with his interpretation of a goalkeeping sweeper.

Naturally the 1970s and 1980s have not been without their problems. Originally the 1986 World Cup was to be held in Colombia as recognition of the progress that was being made, but to the disappointment of all Colombians they had to pull out as the facilities and communications were not considered sufficient for a 24-team event.

The drugs problem has been a consistent source of worry, however, not just because of the money aspect. In November 1989, Daniel Ortega made a terrible mistake: he refereed a game honestly, and was assassinated outside the ground for his trouble, as one of the drug gangs had made a large bet on the game and had lost their money. This it seemed was just the tip of the iceberg - many strange refereeing decisions have been put down to bribery. The league was immediately suspended and a clean-up ordered, but it is difficult to do little more than scratch at the surface.

Colombia qualified for the 1994 World Cup, beating Argentina 5-0 in Buenos Aires in the process, but what should have been a national cause for celebration turned into a nightmare. With fears for the safety of the players, not one match was played in Colombia in the lead-up to the finals, yet nobody expected what happened to Andres Escobar. He scored an own goal against the USA as the team were eliminated in the first round, and on his return to Colombia he was gunned down outside a restaurant. First reports stated that his assassin shouted, 'That's for the own goal.' What is certain is that large amounts of betting took place on the game and it seems Escobar was the unwitting victim of another betting ring.

The irony is that before the tournament Colombia were many people's favourites to win the World Cup, such was the progress made by the game there. Whether or not the Colombians can remain at the top is doubtful: in 1993 Higuita was imprisoned for acting as a go-between in a kidnapping, whilst Faustino Asprilla, perhaps Colombia's greatest ever player, was arrested in 1995 for firing a gun in a crowded bar. It was all symptomatic of the chaos into which the game in Colombia is prone to descend.

Population: 32,978,000
Area, sq km: 1,141,748
% in urban areas: 67%
Capital city: Bogotá

Federación Colombiana de Fútbol
Avenida 32, #16-22
Apartado Aéreo 17.602
Bogotá
Colombia

Tel: + 57 1 2455370 / 2855220
Fax: + 57 1 2854340

Year of formation	1924
Affiliation to FIFA	1936
Affiliation to CONME	1940
Registered clubs	3805
Registered players	209 500
Professional players	460
Registered coaches	80
Registered referees	3098
National stadium	El Campin, Bogota 52 000
National colours	Red/Blue/Yellow
Reserve colours	Blue/White/Blue
Season	March - December (1st stage Mar-May, 2nd May-Jun, 3rd Jun-Oct, 4th Oct-Dec)

THE RECORD

WORLD CUP

1930-54	Did not enter
1958	QT 3rd/3 in group 3
1962	QT 1st/2 in group 3 - Final Tournament/1st round
1966	QT 3rd/3 in group 2
1970	QT 3rd/4 in group 2
1974	QT 2nd/3 in group 1
1978	QT 3rd/3 in group 1
1982	QT 3rd/3 in group 2
1986	QT 3rd/4 in group 1
1990	QT 1st/3 in group 2 - Final Tournament/2nd round
1994	QT 1st/4 in group 1 - Final Tournament/1st round

SOUTH AMERICAN CHAMPIONSHIP

1910-42	-
1945	5/7
1946	-
1947	8/8
1949	8/8
1953-56	-
1957	5/7
1959	-
1959	-
1963	7/7
1967	-
1975	2/10 - Finalists
1979	5/10 - 1st round
1983	7/10 - 1st round
1987	3/10 - Semi-finals
1989	6/10 - 1st round
1991	4/10 - 2nd round
1993	3/12 - Semi-finals
1995	3/12 - Semi-finals

SOUTH AMERICAN CLUB TOURNAMENTS

Copa Libertadores
Winners - Nacional Medellin 1989
Finalists - Deportivo Cali 1978. America de Cali 1985, 1986, 1987
Super Copa
Semi-finals - At. Nacional Medellin 1993
CONMEBOL Cup
Quarter-finals - Atlético Junior 1992

CLUB DIRECTORY

BOGOTA (Population - 4,260,000)

Club Deportivo Los Millonarios (1938)
El Campin 52,000 – Blue/White
Previous name - Deportivo Municipal 1938-46

Corporación Deportiva Independiente Santa Fé (1941)
El Campin 52,000 – Red, white sleeves/White

MEDELLIN (Pop. - 2,095,000)

Club Deportivo Independiente Medellín (1914)
Atanasio Girardot 36,000 – Red/Blue
Previous name - Medellin Fútbol Club 1914-51

Club Deportivo Atlético Nacional Medellín (1936)
Atanasio Girardot 36,000 – Green & white stripes/White
Previous names - Atlético Municipal 1936-49, Independiente Nacional 1958-60

Corporación Deportiva Envigado Fútbol Club (1989)
Polideportiva Sur 22,000 – Orange/Green

CALI (Pop. - 1,400,000)

Corporación Deportiva América Cali (1924)
Pascual Guerrero 61,000 – Red, white trim

Club Deportivo Cali (1908)
Pascual Guerrero 61,000 – Green/White
Previous name - Cali Futebol Club 1908-47

BARRANQUILA (Pop. - 1,140,000)

Corporación Popular Atlético Junior (1948)
Romelito Martinez 20,000 or Metropolitano 60,000 – Red & white stripes/Blue

BUCARAMANGA (Pop. - 550,000)

Club Atlético Bucaramanga (1949)
Alfonso Lopez 20,000 – Yellow/White, green trim

CARTAGENA (Pop. - 531,000)

Club Real Cartagena (1950)
Olimpico 'Pedro de Heredia' de la Cuidad Heroica 8,000 – Yellow with black & red hoop/Green
Previous name - Club Deportivo Sporting Barranquilla 1949-91

CUCUTA (Pop. - 445,000)

Corporacion Nuevo Cúcuta Deportivo (1949)
General Santander 10,000 – Black & red halves/White

PEREIRA (Pop. - 390,000)

Club Deportivo Pereira (1944)
Hernan Ramirez Villegas 25,000 – Red & yellow stripes/Black

MANIZALES (Pop. - 330,000)

Corporación Deportiva Once Philips (1947)
Fernando Londoño y Londoño 17,000 – White, red & green trim
Previous names - Deportes Caldas, Atlético Manizales, Once Caldas, Varta Caldas, Crystal Caldas

IBAGUE (Pop. - 292,000)

Corporación Club Deportes Tolima (1954)
Manuel Murillo Toro 25,000 – Yellow with white sleeves/Maroon

ARMENIA (Pop. - 187,000)

Corporación Centenario Deportes Quindio (1951)
Centenario 35,000 – Green with yellow 'V' /White

SANTA MARTA (Pop. - 177,000)

Asociación Deportiva Union Magdalena (1950)
Eduardo Santos 12,000 – Blue & red stripes/Blue

COLOMBIAN LEAGUE CHAMPIONSHIP

1948	Independiente Santa Fe 27 Atlético Junior 23 Deportes Caldas 20
1949	Millonarios 44 Deportivo Cali 44 Independiente Santa Fe 39
1950	Deportes Caldas 45 Millonarios 43 Deportivo Cali 41
1951	Millonarios 60 Boca Junior 49 Cúcuta 48
1952	Millonarios 46 Boca Junior 40 Pereira 37
1953	Millonarios 35 Atlético Quindio 33 Boca Junior 31
1954	At. Nacional Medellin 31 Atlético Quindio 25 Independiente Medellin 24
1955	Independiente Medellin 44 At. Nacional Medellin 39 Atlético Quindio 37
1956	Atlético Quindio 37 Millonarios 34 Boca Junior 33
1957	Independiente Medellin 54 Deportes Tolima 42 Cúcuta 41
1958	Independiente Santa Fe 48 Millonarios 47 Bucaramanga 44
1959	Millonarios 58 Independiente Medellin 52 Deportivo Cali 50
1960	Independiente Santa Fe 61 América Cali 55 Bucaramanga 54
1961	Millonarios 62 Independiente Medellin 54 Independiente Santa Fe 50
1962	Millonarios 62 Deportivo Cali 57 Pereira 53
1963	Millonarios 63 Independiente Santa Fe 61 Deportivo Cali 60
1964	Millonarios 57 Cúcuta 56 Independiente Medellin 54
1965	Deportivo Cali 62 At. Nacional Medellin 60 Millonarios 57
1966	Independiente Santa Fe 66 Independiente Medellin 63 Pereira 61
1967	Deportivo Cali 73 Millonarios 65 América Cali 61
1968	Union Magdalena....1-0 2-2........................Deportivo Cali
1969	Deportivo Cali 7 América Cali 3 Millonarios 2
1970	Deportivo Cali 7 Atlético Junior 7 Independiente Santa Fe 7

1971	Independiente Santa Fe 7 At. Nacional Medellin 7 Millonarios 6
1972	Millonarios 5 Deportivo Cali 4 Atlético Junior 3
1973	At. Nacional Medellin 6 Millonarios 3 Deportivo Cali 3
1974	Deportivo Cali 13 At. Nacional Medellin 11 Pereira 10
1975	Independiente Santa Fe 16 Millonarios 13 Deportivo Cali 13
1976	At. Nacional Medellin 14 Deportivo Cali 12 Millonarios 12
1977	Atlético Junior 15 Deportivo Cali 12 Millonarios 12
1978	Millonarios 9 Deportivo Cali 7 At. Nacional Medellin 5
1979	América Cali 8 Independiente Santa Fe 8 Union Magdalena 7
1980	Atlético Junior 9 Deportivo Cali 7 América Cali 4
1981	At. Nacional Medellin 8 Tolima 6 América Cali 5
1982	América Cali 20 Tolima 17 Millonarios 15
1983	América Cali 19.75 Atlético Junior 19 At. Nacional Medellin 19
1984	América Cali 20 Millonarios 18.25 Independiente Medellin 15
1985	América Cali 20.5 Deportivo Cali 20 Millonarios 18
1986	América Cali 22 Deportivo Cali 20.25 Millonarios 17.5
1987	Millonarios 22 América Cali 20.25 Independiente Santa Fe 18.25
1988	Millonarios 24.5 At. Nacional Medellin 24.5 América Cali 18.75
1989	-
1990	América Cali 9 At. Nacional Medellin 7 Bucaramanga 5
1991	At. Nacional Medellin 10.25 América Cali 7.5 Atlético Junior 6
1992	América Cali 9 At. Nacional Medellin 8 Deportivo Cali 7
1993	Atlético Junior 8.25 Independiente Medellin 8 At. Nacional Medellin 5.5
1994	At. Nacional Medellin 9 Millonarios 8.5 América Cali 7.5

INTERNATIONAL MATCHES PLAYED BY COLOMBIA

10-02-1938	Mexico	L 1-3	Panama City	CG	
12-02	Panama	W 4-0	Panama City	CG	
14-02	Costa Rica	L 1-3	Panama City	CG	
18-02	El Salvador	W 3-2	Panama City	CG	
22-02	Venezuela	L 1-2	Panama City	CG	
8-08	Peru	L 2-4	Bogota	BG	Botto 2
10-08	Ecuador	L 1-2	Bogota	BG	
13-08	Venezuela	W 2-0	Bogota	BG	Umana, Torres
16-08	Bolivia	L 1-2	Bogota	BG	Mejia
21-01-1945	Brazil	L 0-3	Santiago	SC	
28-01	Uruguay	L 0-7	Santiago	SC	
31-01	Chile	L 0-2	Santiago	SC	
7-02	Argentina	L 1-9	Santiago	SC	Mendoza
18-02	Ecuador	W 3-1	Santiago	SC	Mendoza, Berdugo, Granados
21-02	Bolivia	D 3-3	Santiago	SC	Berdugo, Granados, Gamez
9-12-1946	Curacao	W 4-2	Barranquilla	CG	Rubio, Granados 2, Berdugo
12-12	Venezuela	W 3-1	Barranquilla	CG	
14-12	Guatemala	W 4-2	Barranquilla	CG	
16-12	Puerto Rica	W 4-1	Barranquilla	CG	
18-12	Costa Rica	W 4-1	Barranquilla	CG	Rubio 2, Garcia, Granados
20-12	Panama	W 2-1	Barranquilla	CG	Rubio, Arango
2-12-1947	Uruguay	L 0-2	Guayaquil	SC	
4-12	Ecuador	D 0-0	Guayaquil	SC	
13-12	Bolivia	D 0-0	Guayaquil	SC	
18-12	Argentina	L 0-6	Guayaquil	SC	
20-12	Paraguay	L 0-2	Guayaquil	SC	
23-12	Peru	L 1-5	Guayaquil	SC	Arango
29-12	Chile	L 1-4	Guayaquil	SC	Granados
6-04-1949	Paraguay	L 0-3	Sao Paulo	SC	
10-04	Peru	L 0-4	Rio de Janeiro	SC	
17-04	Brazil	L 0-5	Sao Paulo	SC	
20-04	Chile	D 1-1	Rio de Janeiro	SC	Berdugo
24-04	Uruguay	D 2-2	Sao Paulo	SC	Castelbondo, Perez
3-05	Ecuador	L 2-3	Rio de Janeiro	SC	Garcia.R, Berdugo
6-05	Bolivia	L 0-4	Rio de Janeiro	SC	
13-03-1957	Argentina	L 2-8	Lima	SC	Gamboa, Valencia
17-03	Uruguay	W 1-0	Lima	SC	Arango
21-03	Chile	L 2-3	Lima	SC	Arango, Carrillo
24-03	Brazil	L 0-9	Lima	SC	
27-03	Peru	L 1-4	Lima	SC	Arango
1-04	Ecuador	W 4-1	Lima	SC	Alvarez, Gutierrez, Gamboa 2
16-06	Uruguay	D 1-1	Bogota	WCq	Arango
20-06	Paraguay	L 2-3	Bogota	WCq	Gutierrez, Diaz.R
23-06	Paraguay	L 1-2	Medellin	Fr	Panesso
30-06	Uruguay	L 0-1	Montevideo	WCq	
7-07	Paraguay	L 0-3	Asuncion	WCq	
30-04-1961	Peru	W 1-0	Bogota	WCq	Escobar
7-05	Peru	D 1-1	Lima	WCq	Gonzalez.H

1-04-1962	Mexico	L 0-1	Bogota	Fr	
4-04	Mexico	D 2-2	Cali	Fr	Klinger, Gamboa
25-04	Mexico	L 0-1	Mexico City	Fr	
30-05	Uruguay	L 1-2	Arica	WCr1	Zuluaga
3-06	Soviet Union	D 4-4	Arica	WCr1	Aceros, Coll, Rada, Klinger
7-06	Yugoslavia	L 0-5	Arica	WCr1	
10-03-1963	Argentina	L 2-4	Cochabamba	SC	Campillo, Aceros
14-03	Brazil	L 1-5	La Paz	SC	Gamboa
17-03	Bolivia	L 1-2	Cochabamba	SC	Botero
20-03	Paraguay	L 2-3	Cochabamba	SC	OG, Campillo
24-03	Peru	D 1-1	La Paz	SC	Salla
31-03	Ecuador	L 3-4	La Paz	SC	Salla 2, Gamboa
1-09	Costa Rica	L 4-5	Bogota	Fr	
4-09	Costa Rica	W 1-0	Cali	Fr	
20-07-1965	Ecuador	L 0-1	Barranquilla	WCq	
25-07	Ecuador	L 0-2	Guayaquil	WCq	
1-08	Chile	L 2-7	Santiago	WCq	Segrera 2
7-08	Chile	W 2-0	Barranquilla	WCq	Rada 2
30-11-1966	Chile	L 2-5	Santiago	SCq	Gamboa, Canon
11-12	Chile	D 0-0	Bogota	SCq	
11-08-1968	Argentina	L 0-1	Cali	Fr	
16-10	Mexico	L 0-1	Bogota	Fr	
4-02-1969	Mexico	L 0-1	Leon	Fr	
20-02	Soviet Union	L 1-3	Bogota	Fr	Santa
8-05	Peru	L 1-3	Bogota	Fr	Gonzalez.J
15-06	Chile	D 3-3	Bogota	Fr	Gonzalez.J 2, Gallego
18-06	Peru	D 1-1	Lima	Fr	Gallego
22-06	Ecuador	L 1-4	Guayaquil	Fr	Gonzalez.J
2-07	Uruguay	L 0-1	Cali	Fr	
15-07	Chile	D 3-3	Bogota	Fr	Gonzalez.J 2, Gallego
27-07	Venezuela	W 3-0	Bogota	WCq	Gonzalez.J 2, Segrera
2-08	Venezuela	D 1-1	Caracas	WCq	Tamayo
6-08	Brazil	L 0-2	Bogota	WCq	
10-08	Paraguay	L 0-1	Bogota	WCq	
21-08	Brazil	L 2-6	Rio de Janeiro	WCq	Mesa, Gallego
24-08	Paraguay	L 1-2	Asuncion	WCq	Segrera
20-05-1970	England	L 0-4	Bogota	Fr	
29-03-1972	Peru	D 1-1	Bogota	Fr	Moron
3-06	Venezuela	L 1-2	Caracas	Fr	Brand
6-06	Peru	D 0-0	Lima	Fr	
18-06	France	L 2-3	Salvador	Clr1	Pineros, Mesa
22-06	Argentina	L 1-4	Salvador	Clr1	Moron
15-02-1973	East Germany	L 0-2	Bogota	Fr	
27-05	Haiti	W 2-1	Port-au-Prince	Fr	Moron, Diaz.E
29-05	Haiti	L 1-2	Port-au-Prince	Fr	Moron
21-06	Ecuador	D 1-1	Bogota	WCq	Ortiz
24-06	Uruguay	D 0-0	Bogota	WCq	
28-06	Ecuador	D 1-1	Guayaquil	WCq	Ortiz
1-07	Peru	L 1-3	Lima	Fr	Moron
5-07	Uruguay	W 1-0	Montevideo	WCq	Ortiz
20-07-1975	Paraguay	W 1-0	Bogota	SCr1	Diaz.E
27-07	Ecuador	W 3-1	Quito	SCr1	Ortiz, Retat, Castro
30-07	Paraguay	W 1-0	Asuncion	SCr1	Diaz.E
7-08	Ecuador	W 2-0	Bogota	SCr1	Diaz.E, Calero
21-09	Uruguay	W 3-0	Bogota	SCsf	Angulo, Ortiz, Diaz.E
1-10	Uruguay	L 0-1	Montevideo	SCsf	
16-10	Peru	W 1-0	Bogota	SCf	Castro
22-10	Peru	L 0-2	Lima	SCf	
28-10	Peru	L 0-1	Caracas	SCf	
15-10-1976	Uruguay	L 1-2	Bogota	Fr	Rios
16-01-1977	Ecuador	L 0-1	Cali	Fr	
26-01	Ecuador	L 1-4	Quito	Fr	Retat
30-01	Yugoslavia	L 0-1	Bogota	Fr	
20-02	Brazil	D 0-0	Bogota	WCq	
24-02	Paraguay	L 0-1	Bogota	WCq	
6-03	Paraguay	D 1-1	Asuncion	WCq	Vilarete.E
9-03	Brazil	L 0-6	Rio de Janeiro	WCq	
18-07-1979	Peru	W 1-0	Lima	Fr	Ortiz
25-07	Peru	L 1-2	Bogota	Fr	Ortiz

1-08	Venezuela	D 0-0	San Cristobal	SCr1	
15-08	Chile	W 1-0	Bogota	SCr1	Diaz.E
22-08	Venezuela	W 4-0	Bogota	SCr1	Iguaran, Valverde, Chaparro, Moron
5-09	Chile	L 0-2	Santiago	SCr1	
5-01-1980	Venezuela	D 0-0	Caracas	Fr	
9-07	Poland	L 1-4	Bogota	Fr	Herrera
1-02-1981	Brazil	D 1-1	Bogota	Fr	Vilarete.E
10-03	Chile	L 0-1	Santiago	Fr	
15-03	Paraguay	W 2-0	Asuncion	Fr	Vilarete.E 2
19-03	Chile	L 1-2	Bogota	Fr	Ortiz
2-07	Spain	D 1-1	Bogota	Fr	Herrera
26-07	Peru	D 1-1	Bogota	WCq	Herrera
9-08	Uruguay	L 2-3	Montevideo	WCq	Sarmiento, Herrera
16-08	Peru	L 0-2	Lima	WCq	
13-09	Uruguay	D 1-1	Bogota	WCq	Herrera
14-07-1983	Chile	D 2-2	Bogota	Fr	Valderrama.D 2
26-07	Ecuador	D 0-0	Quito	Fr	
29-07	Ecuador	D 0-0	Bogota	Fr	
14-08	Bolivia	W 1-0	La Paz	SCr1	Valderrama.D
17-08	Peru	L 0-1	Lima	SCr1	
28-08	Peru	D 2-2	Bogota	SCr1	Prince, Fiorillo
31-08	Bolivia	D 2-2	Bogota	SCr1	Valderrama.D, Molina
23-01-1984	El Salvador	W 1-0	San Salvador	Fr	
2-08	Peru	D 1-1	Medellin	Fr	Prince
9-08	Peru	D 0-0	Lima	Fr	
24-08	Argentina	W 1-0	Bogota	Fr	Prince
9-10	Mexico	L 0-1	Los Angeles	Fr	
11-10	United States	L 0-1	Los Angeles	Fr	
1-02-1985	Switzerland	D 2-2	Bogota	Fr	Valderrama, Sarmiento
10-02	Poland	L 1-2	Bogota	Fr	Cordoba
14-02	Poland	W 1-0	Cali	Fr	Sarmiento
21-02	Chile	D 1-1	Santiago	Fr	Vilarete.E
24-02	Uruguay	L 0-3	Montevideo	Fr	
28-02	Paraguay	W 3-0	Asuncion	Fr	Cordoba, Iguaran, Vilarete.E
17-04	Paraguay	W 1-0	Pereira	Fr	Herrera
19-04	Paraguay	D 2-2	Bogota	Fr	Iguaran, Ortiz
25-04	Brazil	L 1-2	Belo Horizonte	Fr	Prince
28-04	Uruguay	W 2-1	Bogota	Fr	Ortiz, Iguaran
15-05	Brazil	W 1-0	Bogota	Fr	Lugo
26-05	Peru	W 1-0	Bogota	WCq	Prince
2-06	Argentina	L 1-3	Bogota	WCq	Prince
9-06	Peru	D 0-0	Lima	WCq	
16-06	Argentina	L 0-1	Buenos Aries	WCq	
23-06	Venezuela	D 2-2	San Cristobal	WCq	Ortiz, Herrera
30-06	Venezuela	W 2-0	Bogota	WCq	Cordoba, Herrera
27-10	Paraguay	L 0-3	Asuncion	WCq	
3-11	Paraguay	W 2-1	Cali	WCq	Angulo, Ortiz
11-06-1987	Ecuador	W 1-0	Medellin	Fr	Alvarez
14-06	Ecuador	L 0-3	Guayaquil	Fr	
1-07	Bolivia	W 2-0	Rosario	SCr1	Valderrama.C, Iguaran
5-07	Paraguay	W 3-0	Rosario	SCr1	Iguaran 3
8-07	Chile	L 1-2	Cordoba	SCsf	Redin
11-07	Argentina	W 2-1	Buenos Aries	SC3p	Gomez, Galleano
30-03-1988	Canada	W 3-0	Armenia	Fr	Perea, Valderrama.C, Trellez
14-05	United States	W 2-0	Miami	Fr	Iguaran 2
17-05	Scotland	D 0-0	Glasgow	Fr	
19-05	Finland	W 3-1	Helsinki	Fr	Arango, Higuita, Iguaran
24-05	England	D 1-1	London	Fr	Escobar
7-08	Uruguay	W 2-1	Bogota	Fr	Iguaran, Redin
3-02-1989	Peru	W 1-0	Pereira	Fr	Higuita
5-02	Chile	W 1-0	Armenia	Fr	Redin
9-03	Argentina	W 1-0	Barranquilla	Fr	Iguaran
24-06	United States	W 1-0	Miami	Fr	Valderrama.C
27-06	Haiti	W 4-0	Miami	Fr	Trellez, Iguaran, Valderrama.C, De Avila
3-07	Venezuela	W 4-2	Salvador	SCr1	Higuita, Iguaran 2, De Avila
5-07	Paraguay	L 0-1	Salvador	SCr1	
7-07	Brazil	D 0-0	Salvador	SCr1	
9-07	Peru	D 1-1	Recife	SCr1	Iguaran
6-08	Uruguay	D 0-0	Montevideo	Fr	

20-08	Ecuador	W 2-0	Barranquilla	WCq	Iguaran 2
27-08	Paraguay	L 1-2	Asuncion	WCq	Iguaran
3-09	Ecuador	D 0-0	Guayaquil	WCq	
17-09	Paraguay	W 2-1	Barranquilla	WCq	Iguaran, Hernandez
15-10	Israel	W 1-0	Barranquila	WCq	Usuriaga
30-10	Israel	D 0-0	Tel Aviv	WCq	
2-02-1990	Uruguay	L 0-2	Miami	Fr	
4-02	United States	D 1-1	Miami	Fr	Fajardo
20-02	Soviet Union	D 0-0	Los Angeles	Fr	
17-04	Mexico	L 0-2	Los Angeles	Fr	
22-04	United States	W 1-0	Miami	Fr	Guerrero
4-05	Poland	W 2-1	Chicago	Fr	Estrada, Iguaran
26-05	Egypt	D 1-1	Cairo	Fr	Rincon
2-06	Hungary	L 1-3	Budapest	Fr	Rincon
9-06	Arab Emirates	W 2-0	Bologna	WCr1	Redin, Valderrama
14-06	Yugoslavia	L 0-1	Bologna	WCr1	
[19-06	West Germany	D 1-1	Milan	WCr1	Rincon
23-06	Cameroon	L 1-2	Naples	WCr2	Redin
29-01-1991	Mexico	D 0-0	Leon	Fr	
3-02	Switzerland	L 2-3	Miami	Fr	De Avila, Rincon
5-06	Sweden	D 2-2	Stockholm	Fr	Rincon, Iguaran
25-06	Costa Rica	W 1-0	San Jose	Fr	De Avila
7-07	Ecuador	W 1-0	Valparaiso	SCr1	De Avila
11-07	Bolivia	D 0-0	Viña del Mar	SCr1	
13-07	Brazil	W 2-0	Viña del Mar	SCr1	De Avila, Iguaran
15-07	Uruguay	L 0-1	Viña del Mar	SCr1	
17-07	Chile	D 1-1	Santiago	SCr2	Iguaran
19-07	Brazil	L 0-2	Santiago	SCr2	
21-07	Argentina	L 1-2	Santiago	SCr2	De Avila
31-07-1992	USA	W 1-0	Los Angeles	Fr	Valencia
2-08	Mexico	D 0-0	Los Angeles	Fr	
24-02-1993	Venezuela	D 0-0	Sao Cristobal	Fr	
31-03	Costa Rica	W 4-1	Medellin	Fr	Valencia 2, De Avila, Pacheco
8-05	USA	W 2-1	Miami	Fr	Valencia, Garcia.A
21-05	Venezuela	D 1-1	Bogota	Fr	Garcia.A
30-05	Chile	D 1-1	Santiago	Fr	Arisitizabal
6-06	Chile	W 1-0	Bogota	Fr	Asprilla
16-06	Mexico	W 2-1	Machala	SCr1	Valencia, Aristizabal
20-06	Bolivia	D 1-1	Machala	SCr1	Maturana.O
23-06	Argentina	D 1-1	Guayaquil	SCr1	Rincon
26-06	Uruguay	D 1-1	Guayaquil	SCqf	Perea. Won 5-3p
1-07	Argentina	D 0-0	Guayaquil	SCsf	Lost 5-6p
3-07	Ecuador	W 1-0	Portoviejo	SC3p	Valencia
1-08	Paraguay	D 0-0	Barranquilla	WCq	
8-08	Peru	W 1-0	Lima	WCq	Rincon
15-08	Argentina	W 2-1	Barranquilla	WCq	Valenciano, Valencia
22-08	Paraguay	D 1-1	Asuncion	WCq	Rincon
29-08	Peru	W 4-0	Barranquilla	WCq	Valenciano, Rincon, Mendoza, Perez.W
5-09	Argentina	W 5-0	Buenos Aires	WCq	Rincon 2, Asprilla 2, Valencia
28-01-1994	Venezuela	W 2-1	Barinas	Fr	Trellez, Valenciano
6-02	Saudi Arabia	D 1-1	Jeddah	Fr	Valenciano
9-02	Saudi Arabia	W 1-0	Jeddah	Fr	Aristizabal
18-02	Sweden	D 0-0	Miami	Fr	
20-02	Bolivia	W 2-0	Miami	Fr	Asprilla, Perez.W
26-02	South Korea	D 2-2	Monterrey	Fr	Escobar, Aristizabal
3-03	Mexico	D 0-0	Mexico City	Fr	
7-04	Bolivia	L 0-1	Villavicencio	Fr	
17-04	Nigeria	W 1-0	Armenia	Fr	De Avila
3-05	Peru	D 1-1	Miami	Fr	Lozano
5-05	El Salvador	W 3-0	Miami	Fr	De Avila, Lozano, Valenciano
3-06	Northern Ireland	W 2-0	Boston	Fr	Perez.W, Valencia
5-06	Greece	W 2-0	New York	Fr	Gaviria, Rincon
18-06	Romania	L 1-3	Los Angeles	WCr1	Valencia
22-06	Colombia	L 1-2	Los Angeles	WCr1	Valencia
26-06	Switzerland	W 2-0	San Francisco	WCr1	Gaviria, Lozano
8-02-1995	Australia	D 0-0	Brisbane	Fr	
11-02	Australia	W 1-0	Sydney	Fr	Ricard
22-03	Uruguay	W 2-1	Medellin	Fr	Cabrera, Bermudez
17-06	Nigeria	W 1-0	Piscataway	Fr	Gomez.J

21-06	Mexico	D 0-0	Washington	Fr	
25-06	United States	D 0-0	Piscataway	Fr	
7-07	Peru	D 1-1	Rivera	SCr1	Asprilla
10-07	Ecuador	W 1-0	Rivera	SCr1	Rincon
13-07	Brazil	L 0-3	Rivera	SCr1	
16-07	Paraguay	D 1-1	Montevideo	SCqf	Rincon. Won 5-4p
19-07	Uruguay	L 0-2	Montevideo	SCsf	
2207	United States	W 4-1	Maldonado	SC3p	Quinonez, Valderrama, Asprilla, Rincon

ECUADOR

'Thank goodness for Colombia' would be a good motto for Ecuadoran football, for if it had not been for victories over their South American neighbours in the Bolivaran Games of 1938 and South American Championships of 1949, Ecuador would have been left without a win in their first twenty years of international football.

Guayaquil, the economic capital and chief port of Ecuador, unsurprisingly saw the first football, and in 1925 the Federación Deportiva Guayaquil was formed, a name later changed to the Federación Deportiva Nacional del Ecuador. This body controlled football as well as other sports, and it was not until 1957, with the creation of the Asociación Ecuatoriana de Fútbol, that football was governed by a separate body. Up until this time there was not much need for one. Regional associations oversaw competitions in all of the major cities, and outings for the international side were restricted to the South American Championships after their debut in the 1938 Bolivaran Games.

THE ORDER OF MERIT

		Total			Lge	Sth Am		
		G	S	B	G	G	S	B
1	Barcelona SC	11	1	4	11	-	1	4
2	CD Nacional	10	-	2	10	-	-	2
3	CS Emelec	8	-	-	8	-	-	-
4	LD Universitaria	4	-	2	4	-	-	2
5	Deportivo Quito	2	-	-	2	-	-	-
6	Everest	1	-	-	1	-	-	-

To the end of the 1994 season

The formation of the national championship in 1957 was an effort to bring the clubs of Guayaquil and Quito, the capital, into regular competition with each other. There is a fierce rivalry between the two cities, not just in sport, and between them they have won every championship played.

The major clubs from Guayaquil are Barcelona and Emelec, whilst in Quito, high up in the Andes, Deportivo Quito and Nacional Quito are joined by the last of the big five, Liga Deportivo Universitaria. They may dominate Ecuadoran football but their impact on South American football on the whole has been limited. Though semi-finalists in the Copa Libertadores on eight occasions, this has more to do with being grouped in the first round with clubs from either Venezuela or Bolivia than football prowess, with one notable exception.

In 1990, Barcelona made it right the way to the final after beating Progreso from Uruguay, Emelec and most impressively River Plate from Argentina on the way. The semi-final win over River Plate is perhaps the best performance to date by a team from Ecuador even if it did need penalties to separate the teams after the two legs had ended in 1-0 victories for the home sides.

In the final against Olimpia from Paraguay, Barcelona lost the tie in the second half of the first match in Asuncion. There was no way back from a two-goal deficit despite a capacity crowd in the home leg in Guayaquil and they went down 3-1 on aggregate.

Their final appearance does show that football in Ecuador is not stagnating and is showing signs of progress. From being the whipping boys at the South American Championships, though they are not seriously challenging for honours, they are no longer automatic walkovers and in 1989 and 1991 finished above Peru, Bolivia and Venezuela in the final championship rankings. They have come a long way since winning just eight games between 1938 and 1975. In 1993, as hosts of the event for only the third time, they had their best ever finish, reaching the semi-finals before losing to Mexico. They also lost the third place play-off to Colombia but prior to the semi-final defeat they had won six games in a row, a record-breaking feat they had never come close to before.

Ecuador's first entry into the World Cup was not at all successful as they lost heavily to Argentina in the two games played in 1962, but the attempt to qualify for England in 1966 proved to be the closest they have ever come to qualifying. Two of the eight wins they recorded between 1938 and 1975 came against Colombia within the space of five days, and a 2-2 draw with Chile at home meant a draw in Santiago would have seen them through. The 3-1 defeat still meant, however, that they would have to play off. Hopes were high for victory in neutral Lima, but it was not to be as they went down 2-1. Since then they have never seriously threatened to qualify, finishing last in their group on all but two occasions.

Playing that day for Ecuador was their most famous player of all time, Alberto Spencer. He, like most Ecuadorans of repute, ended up playing his football abroad. He made a great reputation for himself throughout South America and Europe with Peñarol, a team he helped to many honours. He also holds the distinctive record of being the record goalscorer in the Copa Libertadores with over 50 goals, a record, like Di Stéfano's in European competitions, that is unlikely to be beaten. Uruguay may have complained in the past of Italians poaching their players and then playing them in the national side, but they were quite capable of doing the same. Spencer ended up not only playing his club football in Uruguay, but he also appeared in the Uruguayan national team.

Population: 10,782,000
Area, sq km: 269,178
% in urban areas: 54%
Capital city: Quito

Asociación Ecuatoriana de Fútbol
Calle Jose Mascote #1.103
Castilla 7447
Guayaquil
Ecuador
Tel: + 593 4 371674
Fax: + 593 4 373320

Year of formation	1925
Affiliation to FIFA	1926
Affiliation to CONME	1930
Registered clubs	170
Registered players	31 000
Professional players	470
Registered coaches	87
Registered referees	170
National stadium	Modelo, Guayaquil 48 000
National colours	Yellow/Blue/Red
Season	March - December

THE RECORD

WORLD CUP

1930-58	Did not enter
1962	QT 2nd/2 in group 1
1966	QT 2nd/3 in group 2
1970	QT 3rd/3 in group 3
1974	QT 3rd/3 in group 1
1978	QT 3rd/3 in group 3
1982	QT 2nd/3 in group 3
1986	QT 3rd/3 in group 2
1990	QT 3rd/3 in group 2
1994	QT 4th/5 in group 2

SOUTH AMERICAN CHAMPIONSHIP

1910-37	-
1939	5/5
1941	5/5
1942	7/7
1945	7/7
1946	-
1947	6/8
1949	7/8
1953	7/7
1955	6/6
1956	-
1957	7/7
1959	-
1959	4/7
1963	6/7
1967	-
1975	9/10 - 1st round
1979	9/10 - 1st round
1983	9/10 - 1st round
1987	8/10 - 1st round
1989	7/10 - 1st round
1991	7/10 - 1st round
1993	4/12 - Semi-finals
1995	9/12 - 1st round

SOUTH AMERICAN CLUB COMPETITIONS

Copa Libertadores
Finalists - Barcelona 1990
Semi-finalists - Barcelona 1971 1972 1986 1987 1992, LDU Quito 1975 1976, Nacional Quito 1985
Super Copa
Ineligible to compete
CONMEBOL Cup
Semi-finalists - Nacional Quito 1992

CLUB DIRECTORY

QUITO (Population - 1,050,000)

Club Deportivo América (1939)
Olimpico de Batan 25,000 – Green/White

Sociedad Deportivo Aucas (1945)
Chillogallo 20,000 – Yellow/Red - Red trim

Sociedad Deportivo Quito (1955)
Atahualpa 40,000 – Blue & red stripes/White

Espoli Club (1986)
(**Es**cuela **Poli**cia)
Jorge Andrade – Maroon with blue sash/Blue

(LDU) Liga Deportivo Universitaria (1930)
Atahualpa 40,000 – White, red trim with 'U' on breast

Club Deportivo El Nacional (1963)
Atahualpa 40,000 – Grey with a red, blue & sky blue sash/Red
Previous name - Mariscal Sucre 1963-64

Club Universidad Catolica (1965)
Atahualpa 40,000 – Sky blue/Blue, white trim with 'U' on breast

GUAYAQUIL (Pop. - 1,255,000)

Barcelona Sporting Club (1925)
Monumental 'Isidro Romero Carbo' 55,000 – Yellow/Black, red & black trim

Club Sport Emelec (1929)
(**Em**presa **El**ectrica de **Ec**uador)
George Capwell 25,000 – Blue with grey sash/Grey

Club Everest (1925)
Modelo 40,000 – White/White

Valdez Sporting Club (1991)
Modelo 48,000 – Green, white trim
Previous name - Deportivo Filanbanco 1979-91

CUENCA (Pop. - 157,000)

Club Social y Cultural Deportivo Cuenca (1971)
Municipal 'Alejandro Serrano Aguilar' 22,000 – Red/Black, yellow trim

MACHALA (Pop. - 108,000)

Club Deportivo Audax Octubrino (1948)
Estadio 9 de Mayo 25,000 – White with green sash/White

MANTA (Pop. - 103,000)

Delfin Sporting Club (1988)
Jocay 8,000 – Blue, red & white trim

Club Social y Deportivo Green Cross (1961)
Jocay 8,000 – Green/White

PORTOVIEJO (Pop. - 102,000)

Liga Deportiva Universitaria Portoviejo (1969)
Reales Tamarindos 10,000 – White, green trim with 'U' on breast

AMBATO (Pop. - 100,000)

Club Macara Ambato (1939)
Bellavista 20,000 – Sky Blue/Blue

Club Tecnico Universitario (1971)
Bellavista 20,000 – Red & white stripes/White

ESMERALDAS (Pop. - 91,000)

Juventus (1979)
Teodoro Folke Anderson 25,000 – Red & white stripes/Red

Club Deportivo Esmeraldas Petrolero (1977)
Teodoro Folke Anderson 25,000 – White/Blue

RIOBAMBA (Pop. - 75,000)

River Plate (1950)
Olimpico 25,000 – White with red sash/Black

QUEVEDO (Pop. - 67,000)

Deportivo Quevedo (1950)
7 de Octubre 20,000 – Red, blue chest band/Blue

MILAGRO

Asociacion Deportivo Nueve De Octubre (1926)
Los Chirijos 10,000 – Red/White

LEAGUE CHAMPIONS OF ECUADOR

1957	Emelec
1958-59	-
1960	Barcelona
1961	Emelec
1962	Everest
1963	Barcelona
1964	Deportivo Quito
1965	Emelec
1966	Barcelona
1967	Nacional Quito
1968	Deportivo Quito
1969	Liga Deportiva Universitaria
1970	Barcelona
1971	Barcelona
1972	Emelec
1973	Nacional Quito
1974	Liga Deportivo Universitaria
1975	Liga Deportivo Universitaria
1976	Nacional Quito
1977	Nacional Quito
1978	Nacional Quito
1979	Emelec
1980	Barcelona
1981	Barcelona
1982	Nacional Quito
1983	Nacional Quito
1984	Nacional Quito
1985	Barcelona
1986	Nacional Quito
1987	Barcelona
1988	Emelec
1989	Barcelona
1990	Liga Deportivo Universitaria
1991	Barcelona
1992	Nacional Quito
1993	Emelec
1994	Emelec

INTERNATIONAL MATCHES PLAYED BY ECUADOR

Date	Opponent	Result	Venue	Comp	Scorers
8-08-1938	Bolivia	D 1-1	Bogota	BG	
10-08	Colombia	W 2-1	Bogota	BG	
11-08	Peru	L 1-9	Bogota	BG	
19-08	Venezuela	L 2-5	Bogota	BG	
22-08	Bolivia	L 1-2	Bogota	BG	
15-01-1939	Peru	L 2-5	Lima	SC	Herrera, Suarez
22-01	Uruguay	L 0-6	Lima	SC	
5-02	Chile	L 1-4	Lima	SC	Arenas
12-02	Paraguay	L 1-3	Lima	SC	Herrera
2-02-1941	Chile	L 0-5	Santiago	SC	
9-02	Uruguay	L 0-6	Santiago	SC	
16-02	Argentina	L 1-6	Santiago	SC	Freire
23-02	Peru	L 0-4	Santiago	SC	
18-01-1942	Uruguay	L 0-7	Montevideo	SC	
22-01	Argentina	L 0-12	Montevideo	SC	
25-01	Paraguay	L 1-3	Montevideo	SC	Herrera
28-01	Peru	L 1-2	Montevideo	SC	Jiminez
1-02	Brazil	L 1-5	Montevideo	SC	Alvarez
5-02	Chile	L 1-2	Montevideo	SC	Alcibar
14-01-1945	Chile	L 3-6	Santiago	SC	Raymondi 2, Mendoza
24-01	Uruguay	L 1-5	Santiago	SC	Aguayo
31-01	Argentina	L 2-4	Santiago	SC	Aguayo, Acevedo
11-02	Bolivia	D 0-0	Santiago	SC	
18-02	Colombia	L 1-3	Santiago	SC	Aguayo
21-02	Brazil	L 2-9	Santiago	SC	Aguayo, Albornoz
30-11-1947	Bolivia	D 2-2	Guayaquil	SC	Jiminez.J 2
4-12	Colombia	D 0-0	Guayaquil	SC	
11-12	Chile	L 0-3	Guayaquil	SC	
16-12	Uruguay	L 1-6	Guayaquil	SC	Garnica
20-12	Peru	D 0-0	Guayaquil	SC	
25-12	Argentina	L 0-2	Guayaquil	SC	
29-12	Paraguay	L 0-4	Guayaquil	SC	
3-04-1949	Brazil	L 1-9	Rio de Janeiro	SC	Chuchuca
10-04	Paraguay	L 0-1	Rio de Janeiro	SC	
13-04	Uruguay	L 2-3	Rio de Janeiro	SC	Arteaga, Vargas
17-04	Chile	L 0-1	Rio de Janeiro	SC	
20-04	Peru	L 0-4	Rio de Janeiro	SC	
24-04	Bolivia	L 0-2	Sao Paulo	SC	
3-05	Colombia	W 3-2	Rio de Janeiro	SC	Cantos, Vargas, Maldonado
28-02-1953	Peru	L 0-1	Lima	SC	
4-03	Paraguay	D 0-0	Lima	SC	
8-03	Bolivia	D 1-1	Lima	SC	Guzmán
12-03	Brazil	L 0-2	Lima	SC	
19-03	Chile	L 0-3	Lima	SC	
23-03	Uruguay	L 0-6	Lima	SC	
27-02-1955	Chile	L 1-7	Santiago	SC	Villacreces
9-03	Argentina	L 0-4	Santiago	SC	
13-03	Peru	L 2-4	Santiago	SC	Matute 2
16-03	Paraguay	L 0-2	Santiago	SC	
23-03	Uruguay	L 1-5	Santiago	SC	Matute

7-03-1957	Uruguay	L 2-5	Lima	SC	Cantos, Larraz
10-03	Peru	L 1-2	Lima	SC	Cantos
17-03	Argentina	L 0-3	Lima	SC	
21-03	Brazil	L 1-7	Lima	SC	Larraz
24-03	Chile	D 2-2	Lima	SC	Larraz, Cantos
1-04	Colombia	L 1-4	Lima	SC	Larraz
6-12-1959	Uruguay	L 0-4	Guayaquil	SC	
12-12	Argentina	D 1-1	Guayaquil	SC	Raffo
19-12	Brazil	L 1-3	Guayaquil	SC	Raffo
25-12	Paraguay	W 3-1	Guayaquil	SC	Spencer, Balseca, Cañarte
27-12	Brazil	L 1-2	Guayaquil	Fr	
4-12-1960	Argentina	L 3-6	Guayaquil	WCq	Spencer, Raffo 2
17-12	Argentina	L 0-5	Buenos Aires	WCq	
10-03-1963	Bolivia	D 4-4	La Paz	SC	Raymondi 2, Raffo, Bolaños
14-03	Paraguay	L 1-3	La Paz	SC	Raffo
17-03	Peru	L 1-2	La Paz	SC	Raffo
20-03	Argentina	L 2-4	Cochabamba	SC	Pineda, Palacios
27-03	Brazil	D 2-2	Cochabamba	SC	Gando, Raffo
31-03	Colombia	W 4-3	La Paz	SC	Raffo 2, Bolero, Gonzalez.F
20-07-1965	Colombia	W 1-0	Barranquilla	WCq	Muñoz
25-07	Colombia	W 2-0	Guayaquil	WCq	Raymondi 2
15-08	Chile	D 2-2	Guayaquil	WCq	Spencer, Raymondi
22-08	Chile	L 1-3	Santiago	WCq	Spencer
12-10	Chile	L 1-2	Lima	WCq	Gomez
21-12-1966	Paraguay	D 2-2	Guayaquil	SCq	
28-12	Paraguay	L 1-3	Asuncion	SCq	
22-06-1969	Colombia	W 4-1	Guayaquil	Fr	
6-07	Uruguay	L 0-2	Guayaquil	WCq	
20-07	Uruguay	L 0-1	Montevideo	WCq	
27-07	Chile	L 1-4	Santiago	WCq	Macias
3-08	Chile	D 1-1	Guayaquil	WCq	Rodriguez.T
29-04-1970	Mexico	L 2-4	Leon	Fr	
3-05	Mexico	L 2-3	Mexico City	Fr	
24-05	England	L 0-2	Quito	Fr	
11-06-1972	Portugal	L 0-3	Natal	Clr1	
14-06	Chile	L 1-2	Natal	Clr1	
18-06	Rep. Ireland	L 2-3	Natal	Clr1	
21-06	Iran	D 1-1	Recife	Clr1	
18-02-1973	East Germany	D 1-1	Quito	Fr	Tapia
24-04	Chile	D 1-1	Guayaquil	Fr	
29-04	Bolivia	D 3-3	La Paz	Fr	
6-05	Bolivia	D 0-0	Quito	Fr	
12-05	Haiti	W 2-1	Port au Prince	Fr	
15-05	Haiti	L 0-1	Port au Prince	Fr	
21-06	Colombia	D 1-1	Bogota	WCq	Muñoz
28-06	Colombia	D 1-1	Guayaquil	WCq	Muñoz
1-07	Uruguay	L 1-2	Quito	WCq	Estupinan
8-07	Uruguay	L 0-4	Montevideo	WCq	
22-06-1975	Peru	W 6-0	Quito	Fr	Paz 2, Castañeda, Lasso, Carrera 2
25-06	Peru	W 1-0	Guayaquil	Fr	OG
1-07	Peru	L 0-2	Lima	Fr	
9-07	Bolivia	L 0-1	Cochabamba	Fr	
24-07	Paraguay	D 2-2	Guayaquil	SCr1	Carrera, Lasso
27-07	Colombia	L 1-3	Quito	SCr1	Carrera
7-08	Colombia	L 0-2	Bogota	SCr1	
10-08	Paraguay	L 1-3	Asuncion	SCr1	Castañeda
20-10-1976	Uruguay	D 2-2	Quito	Fr	
4-01-1977	Uruguay	D 1-1	Montevideo	Fr	
9-01	Paraguay	L 0-2	Asuncion	Fr	
16-01	Colombia	W 1-0	Cali	Fr	
20-01	Venezuela	L 0-1	Caracus	Fr	
26-01	Colombia	W 4-1	Quito	Fr	
13-02	Paraguay	W 2-1	Quito	Fr	
20-02	Peru	D 1-1	Quito	WCq	Paz
27-02	Chile	L 0-1	Guayaquil	WCq	
12-03	Peru	L 0-4	Lima	WCq	
20-03	Chile	L 0-3	Santiago	WCq	
13-06-1979	Chile	D 0-0	Santiago	Fr	
21-06	Chile	W 2-1	Guayaquil	Fr	

11-07	Peru	L 1-2	Lima	Fr	
8-08	Peru	W 2-1	Quito	Fr	
29-08	Paraguay	L 1-2	Quito	SCr1	Torres Garcés
5-09	Uruguay	W 2-1	Guayaquil	SCr1	Tenorio, Alarcón
13-09	Paraguay	L 0-2	Asuncion	SCr1	
16-09	Uruguay	L 1-2	Montevideo	SCr1	Klinger
27-01-1981	Bulgaria	L 1-3	Quito	Fr	Mesias
14-02	Brazil	L 0-6	Quito	Fr	
17-05	Paraguay	W 1-0	Guayaquil	WCq	Klinger
24-05	Chile	D 0-0	Guayaquil	WCq	
31-05	Paraguay	L 1-3	Asuncion	WCq	Nieve
14-06	Chile	L 0-2	Santiago	WCq	
26-07-1983	Colombia	D 0-0	Quito	Fr	
29-07	Colombia	D 0-0	Bogota	Fr	
10-08	Argentina	D 2-2	Quito	SCr1	Vazquez, Vega
17-08	Brazil	L 0-1	Quito	SCr1	
1-09	Brazil	L 0-5	Goiania	SCr1	
7-09	Argentina	D 2-2	Buenos Aires	SCr1	Quiñones, Maldonado
22-01-1984	Romania	L 1-3	Guayaquil	Fr	Valencia
30-11	United States	D 0-0	New York	Fr	
2-12	United States	D 2-2	Miami	Fr	
4-12	Mexico	L 2-3	Los Angeles	Fr	
7-12	Honduras	D 0-0	Tegucigalpa	Fr	
9-12	Guatemala	L 0-1	Guatemala City	Fr	
12-12	El Salvador	D 0-0	San Salvador	Fr	
6-02-1985	East Germany	L 2-3	Guayaquil	Fr	Benitez, Cuvi
17-02	Finland	W 3-1	Ambato	Fr	Paz, Benitez 2
21-02	Bolivia	W 3-0	Quito	Fr	
3-03	Chile	D 1-1	Quito	WCq	Maldonado
10-03	Uruguay	L 1-2	Montevideo	WCq	Cuvi
17-03	Chile	L 2-6	Santiago	WCq	Baldeon
21-03	Peru	L 0-1	Lima	Fr	
31-03	Uruguay	L 0-2	Quito	WCq	
27-02-1987	Cuba	L 1-2	Havana	Fr	
2-03	Cuba	D 0-0	Havana	Fr	
11-06	Colombia	L 0-1	Medellin	Fr	
14-06	Colombia	W 3-0	Guayaquil	Fr	
19-06	Uruguay	L 1-2	Montevideo	Fr	
21-06	Brazil	L 1-4	Florianopolis	Fr	
2-07	Argentina	L 0-3	Buenos Aires	SCr1	
4-07	Peru	D 1-1	Buenos Aires	SCr1	Cuvi
2-06-1988	Canada	W 2-1	Guayaquil	Fr	
7-06	United States	W 1-0	Albuquerque	Fr	
10-06	United States	W 2-0	Houston	Fr	
12-06	United States	D 0-0	Fort Worth	Fr	
15-06	Honduras	D 1-1	Tegucigalpa	Fr	Machado
17-06	Honduras	W 1-0	Tegucigalpa	Fr	
19-06	Costa Rica	L 0-1	San Jose	Fr	
7-09	Paraguay	L 1-5	Guayaquil	Fr	Cuvi
13-09	Chile	L 1-3	La Serena	Fr	Cuvi
27-09	Uruguay	L 1-2	Asuncion	Fr	Izquierdo
29-09	Chile	D 0-0	Asuncion	Fr	
29-01-1989	Chile	W 1-0	Guayaquil	Fr	Aviles
15-03	Brazil	L 0-1	Cuiaba	Fr	
13-04	Argentina	D 2-2	Guayaquil	Fr	Aviles, Cuvi
3-05	Uruguay	L 1-3	Montevideo	Fr	Aviles
23-05	Uruguay	D 1-1	Quito	Fr	Aviles
18-06	Nth. Ireland	D 1-1	Port of Spain	Fr	Izquierdo
20-06	Peru	L 1-2	Port of Spain	Fr	Guerrero
2-07	Uruguay	W 1-0	Goiania	SCr1	Benitez
4-07	Argentina	D 0-0	Goiania	SCr1	
6-07	Bolivia	D 0-0	Goiania	SCr1	
10-07	Chile	L 1-2	Goiania	SCr1	Aviles
20-08	Colombia	L 0-2	Barranquilla	WCq	
3-09	Colombia	D 0-0	Guayaquil	WCq	
10-09	Paraguay	L 1-2	Asuncion	WCq	Aviles
24-09	Paraguay	W 3-1	Guayaquil	WCq	Aguinaga, Marsetti, Aviles
6-06-1991	Peru	W 1-0	Lima	Fr	Ron
19-06	Chile	W 2-1	Quito	Fr	Garay, Guerrero

25-06	Peru	D 2-2	Quito	Fr	Carcelen, Muñoz
30-06	Chile	L 1-3	Santiago	Fr	Aguinaga
7-07	Colombia	L 0-1	Valparaiso	SCr1	
9-07	Uruguay	D 1-1	Viña del Mar	SCr1	Aguinaga
13-07	Bolivia	W 4-0	Viña del Mar	SCr1	Aguinaga, Aviles 2, Ramirez
15-07	Brazil	L 1-3	Viña del Mar	SCr1	Muñoz
24-05-1992	Guatemala	D 1-1	Guatemala City	Fr	Hurtado
27-05	Costa Rica	L 1-2	San Jose	Fr	Caravalli
4-07	Uruguay	L 1-3	Montevideo	Fr	Fernandez
6-08	Costa Rica	D 1-1	Guayaquil	Fr	Tenorio
24-11	Peru	D 1-1	Lima	Fr	Zambrano
28-01-1993	Belarus	D 1-1	Guayaquil	Fr	Fernandez
31-01	Romania	W 3-0	Guayaquil	Fr	Hurtado, Gavica, Aviles
30-05	Peru	W 1-0	Quito	Fr	Fernandez
15-06	Venezuela	W 6-1	Quito	SCr1	Mouz, Noriega, Fernandez 2, Hurtado, Aguinaga
19-06	USA	W 2-0	Quito	SCr1	Aviles, Hurtado
22-06	Uruguay	W 2-1	Quito	SCr1	Aviles, Aguinaga
26-06	Paraguay	W 3-0	Quito	SCqf	Hurtado, OG, Aviles
30-06	Mexico	L 0-2	Guayaquil	SCsf	
3-07	Colombia	L 0-1	Portoviejo	SC3p	
18-07	Brazil	D 0-0	Guayaquil	WCq	
1-08	Uruguay	D 0-0	Montevideo	WCq	
8-08	Venezuela	W 5-0	Quito	WCq	Muñoz, Hurtado 3, Chala
15-08	Bolivia	L 0-1	La Paz	WCq	
22-08	Brazil	L 0-2	Sao Paulo	WCq	
5-09	Uruguay	L 0-1	Guayaquil	WCq	
12-09	Venezuela	L 1-2	Ciudad Guyana	WCq	Noriega
19-09	Bolivia	D 1-1	Guayaquil	WCq	Noriega
25-05-1994	Argentina	W 1-0	Guayaquil	Fr	Tenorio
17-08	Peru	L 0-2	Lima	Fr	
21-09	Peru	D 0-0	Machala	Fr	
24-05-1995	Scotland	L 1-2	Tokyo	KC	Hurtado.I
28-05	Japan	L 0-3	Tokyo	KC	
4-06	Zambia	W 4-0	Seoul	PC	Hurtado.E 4
10-06	Costa Rica	W 2-1	Seoul	PC	Hurtado.E, Diaz.E
12-06	Zambia	W 1-0	Seoul	PC	Diaz.E
7-07	Brazil	L 0-1	Rivera	SCr1	
10-07	Colombia	L 0-1	Rivera	SCr1	
13-07	Peru	W 2-1	Rivera	SCr1	Diaz.E, Mora.J

PARAGUAY

Traditional links with Argentina, Uruguay and Brazil meant that football developed relatively early in Paraguay despite its poverty and isolation, though strangely enough for South America, it is a Dutchman who is credited with first bringing the game to the country.

The Liga Paraguaya de Fútbol, the game's governing body, was formed in 1906 and as the name suggests it was founded to run the league from which it takes its name. Based in Asuncion, the league has been completely dominated by clubs from the capital. Foremost is Olimpia, formed in 1902, the oldest club in the country and by far the most successful. In them Paraguay can boast the fifth most successful club in the Copa Libertadores.

Cerro Porteño, Guarani, Libertad and Nacional are the only other clubs that have done well in a league that has seen a remarkably small shift in power over the years. Only Nacional and Libertad have fallen away, the former winning their last title in 1946. Like the leagues of other small South American countries, Paraguay has been susceptible to the advances of clubs from Brazil, Uruguay and Argentina as they seek to replace players lost to Europe.

Professionalism was introduced in 1935 but has not been a barrier to the flow of players abroad. Asuncion is simply not big enough to support a prosperous club structure. An indication of the uphill struggle clubs in Paraguay face is the fact that with grounds boasting a total capacity of nearly 300,000 within the city, almost half of the present-day population can be accommodated within them at any one time.

The Liga Paraguaya de Fútbol is also responsible for running the national team, though as it took 13 years for a Paraguayan side to take to the field, to begin with its priorities obviously lay with the league. In 1921 Paraguay was the fifth nation to take part in the South American Championships, but despite this long record of participation, along with Colombia and Venezuela they have never hosted the event. Their record in the tournament, though never outstanding, has been consistently good. Their initial match in the 1921 tournament saw a victory over Uruguay, whilst the following year they took Brazil to a play-off before finishing the tournament in second place. History repeated itself in 1949 when Paraguay again forced a play-off against Brazil by beating them on the last day of the tournament. Once again, however, the Brazilians were too strong for the normally resilient Paraguayans and they won 7-0 in convincing fashion.

Aside from the period when they were at war with Bolivia from 1932 until 1935, the national side regularly undertook international games outside the South American Championships. Their debut was made with four friendly games against Argentina in 1919 and that rivalry has continued down the years in the Rosa Chevalier Boutell Cup. Links with Brazil have been maintained through the Oswaldo Cruz Cup and with Uruguay in the Artigas Cup. Matches like these have helped keep the standard of the game up despite the relatively small population.

THE ORDER OF MERIT

		Total			Lge	Sth Am		
		G	S	B	G	G	S	B
1	Olimpia	37	4	7	34	3	4	7
2	Cerro Porteño	23	-	3	23	-	-	3
3	Guarani	8	-	1	8	-	-	1
4	Libertad	7	-	1	7	-	-	1
5	Nacional	6	-	-	6	-	-	-
6	Sportivo Luqueño	2	-	-	2	-	-	-
	Sol de América	2	-	-	2	-	-	-
8	Presidente Hayes	1	-	-	1	-	-	-

To the end of the 1994 season

Paraguay finally made their mark in the 1953 South American Championships, winning it for the first time, and were responsible for a tactical innovation that was to change world football. For the 1953 tournament the Paraguayan coach, Fleitas Solich, implemented a 4-2-4 system and they used it to good effect, winning the series after yet another play-off against the Brazilians. So impressed was Feola, the Brazilian coach, that he copied and perfected the system which eventually won the Brazilians the 1958 World Cup.

The irony of the situation was that Paraguay qualified for the tournament in Sweden as well but were knocked out in the first round despite beating Scotland and drawing with Yugoslavia. The late 1940s and 1950s were undoubtedly Paraguay's most successful era at international level and it was not until 1979 that the national side again caught the imagination.

That year turned out to be a memorable one for the country. As well as beating Chile to win the South American Championship for the second time, Olimpia won the Copa Libertadores, the first club from outside of the continent's big three to achieve such a feat. Boca Juniors, the reigning champions, were beaten 2-0 over two legs and to complete an amazing quadruple, Olimpia won the ensuing Inter-American club championship by beating Deportivo FAS of El Salvador as well as the World Club Championship against Malmö of Sweden, who were deputising for Nottingham Forest. Paraguay was therefore in possession of every continental trophy available.

Olimpia have continued to do well in the Copa Libertadores. Having been finalists in the first competition in 1960, they appeared in their third final in 1989, this time losing to Nacional Medellin of Colombia. They were back again in 1990 and won for the second time by beating Barcelona 3-1 on aggregate. That year also saw Olimpia win the South American Super Cup and as a result they were awarded the Recopa, a trophy for the winners of the annual game between the Copa Libertadores and Super Cup winners. There was a third consecutive final appearance in 1991 but once again it was to prove a disappointing experience as Colo Colo became the first Chilean club to win the tournament.

Should a South American Super League ever become a reality, Olimpia would undoubtedly be involved. Despite the national side's qualification for the 1986 World Cup in Mexico, their first appearance since 1958, it is Olimpia that all Paraguayans look to in the search for honours.

Population: 4,279,000
Area, sq km: 406,752
% in urban areas: 43%
Capital city: Asunción

Liga Paraguaya de Fútbol
Estadio de Sajonia
Calles Mayor Martínez y Alejo García
Asunción
Paraguay
Tel: + 595 21 81743
Fax: + 595 21 81743

Year of formation	1906
Affiliation to FIFA	1921
Affiliation to CONME	1921
Registered clubs	1500
Registered players	257 300
Registered coaches	150
Registered referees	302
National stadium	Defensores del Chaco, Asuncion 60 000
National colours	Red and white stripes/Blue/Blue
Season	March - November

THE RECORD

WORLD CUP

1930	QT Automatic - Final Tournament/1st round
1934	Did not enter
1938	Did not enter
1950	QT W-O in group 8 - Final Tournament/1st round
1954	Did not enter
1958	QT 1st/3 in group 3 - Final Tournament/1st round
1962	QT 2nd in CONCACAF
1966	QT 2nd/3 in group 3
1970	QT 2nd/4 in group 2
1974	QT 2nd/3 in group 2
1978	QT 2nd/3 in group 1
1982	QT 3rd/3 in group 3
1986	QT 2nd/3 in group 3 - Final Tournament/2nd round
1990	QT 2nd/3 in group 2
1994	QT 3rd/4 in group 1

SOUTH AMERICAN CHAMPIONSHIP

1910-20	-
1921	4/4
1922	2/5
1923	3/4
1924	3/4
1925	3/3
1926	4/5

1927	-
1929	2/4
1935	-
1937	3/6
1939	3/5
1941	-
1942	4/7
1945	-
1946	3/6
1947	2/8
1949	2/8
1953	1/7 - Winners
1955	5/6
1956	5/6
1957	-
1959	3/7
1959	5/5
1963	2/7
1967	4/6
1975	7/10 - 1st round
1979	1/10 - Winners
1983	3/10 - Semi-finalists
1987	9/10 - 1st round
1989	4/10 - 2nd round
1991	6/10 - 1st round
1993	5=/12 - Quarter-finals
1995	5=/12 - Quarter-finals

SOUTH AMERICAN CLUB COMPETITIONS

Copa Libertadores

Winners - Olimpia 1979, 1990

Finalists - Olimpia 1960, 1989, 1991

Super Copa

Winners - Olimpia 1990

CONMEBOL Cup

Finalists - Olimpia 1992

CLUB DIRECTORY

ASUNCION (Population - 700,000)

Club Cerro Cora (1925)
General Andres Rodriguez – Red & black stripes/Black

Club Cerro Porteño (1912)
Adriano Irala 30,000 – Blue & maroon stripes/White

Atlético Colegiales
Luciano Zacarias 20,000 – Red/Blue, white trim

Club Guarani (1903)
Rogelio Lorenzo Livieres 20,000 – Black & yellow stripes/Black

Club Libertad (1905)
Alfredo Stroessner 45,000 – Black & white stripes/Black

Club Nacional (1904)
Arsenio Erico 10,000 – White/Blue, red & blue trim

Club Olimpia (1902)
Manuel Ferreira 40,000 – White with a single black hoop/White

Club Presidente Hayes (1907)
Cancha 'Fortin' de Tacumbu 20,000 – Red & white stripes/Blue

Club Sol de América (1909)
Luis A. Giagni 8,000 – Blue/White

LUQUE (Pop. - 24,000)

Sportivo Luqueño (1921)
Feliciano Cáceres 38,000 – Blue & yellow stripes/Blue
Previous names - Merger in 1921 of Vencedor, Marte, Atlético & General Aquiño

PARAGUAYAN LEAGUE CHAMPIONS

1906	Guarani
1907	Guarani
1908	-
1909	Nacional Asuncion
1910	-
1911	Nacional Asuncion
1912	Olimpia
1913	Cerro Porteño
1914	Olimpia
1915	Cerro Porteño
1916	Olimpia
1917	Libertad
1918	Cerro Porteño
1919	Cerro Porteño
1920	Libertad
1921	Guarani
1922	-
1923	Guarani
1924	Nacional Asuncion
1925	Olimpia
1926	Nacional Asuncion
1927	Olimpia
1928	Olimpia
1929	Olimpia
1930	Libertad
1931	Olimpia
1932-34	-
1935	Cerro Porteño
1936	Olimpia
1937	Olimpia
1938	Olimpia
1939	Cerro Porteño
1940	Cerro Porteño
1941	Cerro Porteño
1942	Nacional Asuncion
1943	Libertad
1944	Cerro Porteño
1945	Libertad
1946	Nacional Asuncion
1947	Olimpia
1948	Olimpia
1949	Guarani
1950	Cerro Porteño
1951	Sportivo Luqueño
1952	Presidente Hayes
1953	Sportivo Luqueño
1954	Cerro Porteño
1955	Libertad
1956	Olimpia
1957	Olimpia
1958	Olimpia
1959	Olimpia
1960	Olimpia
1961	Cerro Porteño
1962	Olimpia
1963	Cerro Porteño
1964	Guarani
1965	Olimpia
1966	Cerro Porteño
1967	Guarani
1968	Olimpia
1969	Olimpia
1970	Cerro Porteño
1971	Olimpia
1972	Cerro Porteño
1973	Cerro Porteño
1974	Cerro Porteño
1975	Olimpia
1976	Libertad
1977	Cerro Porteño
1978	Olimpia
1979	Olimpia
1980	Olimpia
1981	Olimpia
1982	Olimpia
1983	Olimpia
1984	Guarani
1985	Olimpia
1986	Sol de América
1987	Cerro Porteño
1988	Olimpia
1989	Olimpia
1990	Cerro Porteño
1991	Sol de América
1992	Cerro Porteño
1993	Olimpia
1994	Cerro Porteño

LEADING INTERNATIONAL GOALSCORERS

13 Saturnino Arrúa	
13 Julio César Romero	(Sportivo Luqueño, NY Cosmos, Fluminense)
12 Gerardo Rivas	

LEADING INTERNATIONAL APPEARANCES

78 Roberto Fernandez	(Cerro Porteño, River Plate, Español, Deportivo Cali)
77 Juan Torales	(Libertad)
61 Rogelio Delgado	(Independiente,Universidad de Chile, Olimpia)

INTERNATIONAL MATCHES PLAYED BY PARAGUAY

Date	Opponent	Result	Venue	Comp	Scorers
11-05-1919	Argentina	L 1-5	Asuncion	Fr	
15-05	Argentina	L 0-3	Asuncion	Fr	
21-05	Argentina	L 1-2	Asuncion	Fr	Talavera
24-05	Argentina	L 1-2	Asuncion	Fr	Avilla
7-04-1921	Argentina *	W 3-1	Asuncion	Fr	Schaerer 2, Uriarte
14-04	Argentina *	D 2-2	Asuncion	Fr	Uriarte 2
9-10	Uruguay	W 2-1	Buenos Aires	SC	Rivas.G, López.E
12-10	Brazil	L 0-3	Buenos Aires	SC	
16-10	Argentina	L 0-3	Buenos Aires	SC	
2-11	Uruguay	L 2-4	Montevideo	Fr	Zelada, López.I
24-09-1922	Brazil	D 1-1	Rio de Janeiro	SC	Rivas.G
5-10	Chile	W 3-0	Rio de Janeiro	SC	Ramirez.C, López.I, Fretes.A
12-10	Uruguay	W 1-0	Rio de Janeiro	SC	Elizeche
18-10	Argentina	L 0-2	Rio de Janeiro	SC	
22-10	Brazil	L 1-3	Rio de Janeiro	SC	Rivas.G
29-10	Brazil	L 1-3	Sao Paulo	Fr	
20-05-1923	Argentina	W 2-0	Buenos Aires	RCB	OG, López.I
25-05	Argentina	L 0-1	Buenos Aires	RCB	
29-10	Argentina	L 3-4	Montevideo	SC	Rivas.G, Zelada, Fretes.A
4-11	Uruguay	L 0-2	Montevideo	SC	
11-11	Brazil	W 1-0	Montevideo	SC	López.I
22-11	Brazil	L 0-2	Montevideo	Fr	
15-05-1924	Argentina	L 1-3	Asuncion	RCB	Fleitas Solich
18-05	Argentina	W 2-1	Asuncion	RCB	Fleitas Solich, Rivas.G
12-10	Argentina	D 0-0	Montevideo	SC	
26-10	Uruguay	L 1-3	Montevideo	SC	Sosa.U
1-11	Chile	W 3-1	Montevideo	SC	López.I 2, Rivas.G
9-07-1925	Argentina	D 1-1	Buenos Aires	RCB	Fretes.A
12-07	Argentina	D 1-1	Buenos Aires	RCB	Fretes.A
14-07	Uruguay	W 1-0	Montevideo	Fr	López.I
18-07	Uruguay	W 1-0	Montevideo	Fr	Rivas.G
15-08	Uruguay	W 1-0	Asuncion	Fr	Rivas.G
19-08	Uruguay	L 0-1	Asuncion	Fr	
23-08	Uruguay	D 0-0	Asuncion	Fr	
29-11	Argentina	L 0-2	Buenos Aires	SC	
6-12	Brazil	L 2-5	Buenos Aires	SC	Rivas, Fretes.A
17-12	Brazil	L 1-3	Buenos Aires	SC	Fretes.A
20-12	Argentina	L 1-3	Buenos Aires	SC	Fleitas Solich
29-05-1926	Argentina	L 1-2	Asuncion	RCB	López.I
3-06	Argentina	L 1-2	Asuncion	RCB	Fretes.A
20-10	Argentina	L 0-8	Santiago	SC	
23-10	Bolivia	W 6-1	Santiago	SC	Ramirez.J 3, Ramirez.C 2, López.I
1-11	Uruguay	L 1-6	Santiago	SC	Fretes.L
3-11	Chile	L 1-5	Santiago	SC	Vargas
15-08-1928	Uruguay	W 3-1	Asuncion	Fr	Gonzalez.A, Ortega, Molinas
19-08	Uruguay	D 1-1	Asuncion	Fr	Ortega
1-11-1929	Uruguay	W 3-0	Buenos Aires	SC	Gonzalez.A 2, Lagos
10-11	Argentina	L 1-4	Buenos Aires	SC	Dominguez.D
16-11	Peru	W 5-0	Buenos Aires	SC	Gonzalez.A 3, Lino Nessi, Dominguez.D
17-07-1930	United States	L 0-3	Montevideo	WCr1	
20-07	Belgium	W 1-0	Montevideo	WCr1	Peña
19-04-1931	Argentina	L 0-1	Asuncion	Fr	
25-04	Argentina	D 1-1	Asuncion	Fr	Etcheverry
4-07	Argentina	D 1-1	Buenos Aires	RCB	Gonzalez.A
9-07	Argentina	L 1-3	Buenos Aires	RCB	Laterza
2-01-1937	Uruguay	W 4-2	Buenos Aires	SC	Gonzalez.A 2, Erico, Ortega
9-01	Argentina	L 1-6	Buenos Aires	SC	Gonzalez.A
13-01	Brazil	L 0-5	Buenos Aires	SC	
17-01	Chile	W 3-2	Buenos Aires	SC	Amarillo, Nuñez, Flor
24-01	Peru	L 0-1	Buenos Aires	SC	
15-01-1939	Chile	W 5-1	Lima	SC	Godoy 2, Barrios 2, Aquino
29-01	Peru	L 0-3	Lima	SC	
5-02	Uruguay	L 1-3	Lima	SC	Barrios
12-02	Ecuador	W 3-1	Lima	SC	Mingo, Bareiro, Godoy
26-02	Chile	L 1-4	Santiago	Fr	Ferreira
14-08	Argentina	L 0-1	Asuncion	RCB	

16-08	Argentina	D 2-2	Asuncion	RCB	Espinola, OG
18-02-1940	Argentina	L 1-3	Buenos Aires	RCB	Mingo
25-02	Argentina	L 0-4	Buenos Aires	RCB	
11-01-1942	Argentina	L 3-4	Montevideo	SC	Aveiro 2, Sanchez.V
18-01	Peru	D 1-1	Montevideo	SC	Barrios
22-01	Chile	W 2-0	Montevideo	SC	Barrios, Franco
25-01	Ecuador	W 3-1	Montevideo	SC	Franco, Mingo, Ibarrola
28-01	Uruguay	L 1-3	Montevideo	SC	Barrios
5-02	Brazil	D 1-1	Montevideo	SC	Franco
10-07-1943	Argentina	L 2-5	Asuncion	RCB	Ferreira, Mellone
11-07	Argentina	W 2-1	Asuncion	RCB	Marin, Alvarez
6-01-1945	Argentina	L 2-5	Buenos Aires	RCB	Fernandez, Benitez Cáceres
9-01	Argentina	L 3-5	Buenos Aires	RCB	Benitez Cáceres 2, Esquivel
7-07	Argentina	W 5-1	Asuncion	RCB	Sanchez.V, Fernandez, Benitez Cáceres, Villalba, Sosa
9-07	Argentina	L 1-3	Asuncion	RCB	Fernandez
12-01-1946	Argentina	L 0-2	Buenos Aires	SC	
19-01	Chile	L 1-2	Buenos Aires	SC	Rolón
26-01	Bolivia	W 4-2	Buenos Aires	SC	Villalba 2, Genes, Benitez Cáceres
29-01	Brazil	D 1-1	Buenos Aires	SC	Villalba
8-02	Uruguay	W 2-1	Buenos Aires	SC	Villalba, Rodriguez.A
2-12-1947	Argentina	L 0-6	Guayaquil	SC	
6-12	Peru	D 2-2	Guayaquil	SC	Villalba, Márin
13-12	Uruguay	W 4-2	Guayaquil	SC	Genes 2, Márin, Villalba
18-12	Bolivia	W 3-1	Guayaquil	SC	Márin, Avalos, Genes
20-12	Colombia	W 2-0	Guayaquil	SC	Villalba 2
23-12	Chile	W 1-0	Guayaquil	SC	Villalba
29-12	Ecuador	W 4-0	Guayaquil	SC	Márin 3, Genes
6-04-1949	Colombia	W 3-0	Sao Paulo	SC	López Fretes 2, Benitez.D
10-04	Ecuador	W 1-0	Rio de Janeiro	SC	Barrios.R
13-04	Peru	W 3-1	Rio de Janeiro	SC	Barrios.R, Arce, López Fretes
20-04	Uruguay	L 1-2	Sao Paulo	SC	Vazquez
27-04	Chile	W 4-2	Sao Paulo	SC	Arce 3, Benitez.D
30-04	Bolivia	W 7-0	Rio de Janeiro	SC	Benitez.D 4, Arce 2, Avalos
8-05	Brazil	W 2-1	Rio de Janeiro	SC	Avalos, Benitez.D
11-05	Brazil	L 0-7	Rio de Janeiro	SCpo	
25-03-1950	Argentina	D 2-2	Buenos Aires	RCB	OG, Sosa.F
29-03	Argentina	L 0-4	Buenos Aires	RCB	
30-04	Uruguay	W 3-2	Rio de Janeiro	Fr	Avalos, López.A, López Fretes
7-05	Brazil	L 0-2	Rio de Janeiro	OCC	
13-05	Brazil	D 3-3	Sao Paulo	OCC	Calonga, López Fretes, Sosa.F
29-06	Sweden	D 2-2	Curitiba	WCr1	López.A, López Fretes
2-07	Italy	L 0-2	Sao Paulo	WCr1	
25-02-1953	Chile	W 3-0	Lima	SC	Fernandez.R 2, Berni
4-03	Ecuador	D 0-0	Lima	SC	
8-03	Peru	D 2-2	Lima	SC	Fernandez.R, Berni
12-03	Uruguay	D 2-2	Lima	SC	López.A, Berni
16-03	Bolivia	W 2-1	Lima	SC	Romero.J, Berni
27-03	Brazil	W 2-1	Lima	SC	López.A, León
1-04	Brazil	W 3-2	Lima	SCpo	López.A, Gavilán, Fernandez.R
14-02-1954	Chile	W 4-0	Asuncion	WCq	Lugo, Parodi.S, Hermosilla, Parodi.J
21-02	Chile	W 3-1	Santiago	WCq	Lugo 2, Parodi.J
7-03	Brazil	L 0-1	Asuncion	WCq	
21-03	Brazil	L 1-4	Rio de Janeiro	WCq	Romerito
10-04	Uruguay	W 4-1	Montevideo	Fr	Martinez.E 2, Romero.J, Félix Vázquez
18-04	Uruguay	D 1-1	Asuncion	Fr	Martinez.E
2-03-1955	Argentina	L 3-5	Santiago	SC	Rólon, Villalba, Parodi
9-03	Uruguay	L 1-3	Santiago	SC	Rólon
16-03	Ecuador	W 2-0	Santiago	SC	Rólon 2
20-03	Chile	L 0-5	Santiago	SC	
23-03	Peru	D 1-1	Santiago	SC	Rólon
13-11	Brazil	L 0-3	Rio de Janeiro	OCC	
17-11	Brazil	D 3-3	Sao Paulo	OCC	Romero.J, Cañete, Rólon
21-01-1956	Uruguay	L 2-4	Montevideo	SC	Gómez.A 2
29-01	Brazil	D 0-0	Montevideo	SC	
1-02	Argentina	L 0-1	Montevideo	SC	
5-02	Peru	D 1-1	Montevideo	SC	Rólon
12-02	Chile	L 0-2	Montevideo	SC	
12-06	Brazil	L 0-2	Asuncion	OCC	
17-06	Brazil	L 2-5	Asuncion	OCC	Rólon, Jara Saguier

Date	Opponent	Result	Venue	Comp	Scorers
15-07	Uruguay	D 2-2	Asuncion	Fr	Gonzalez.H, Dominguez.V
15-08	Argentina	L 0-1	Asuncion	RCB	
6-06-1957	Bolivia	W 5-2	Asuncion	PDC	Aguero 2, Aguilera 2, Benitez.G
13-06	Bolivia	L 0-1	Asuncion	PDC	
20-06	Colombia	W 3-2	Bogota	WCq	Jara.A, Aguero, Aguilera
23-06	Colombia	W 2-1	Medellin	Fr	Amarilla, Aguero
7-07	Colombia	W 3-0	Asuncion	WCq	Jara.E, Jara.A, Aguilera
14-07	Uruguay	W 5-0	Asuncion	WCq	Amarilla 3, Aguero, Jara.A
28-07	Uruguay	L 0-2	Montevideo	WCq	
18-08	Bolivia	D 3-3	La Paz	PDC	Cayetano Ré 2, Dominguez
21-08	Bolivia	L 1-2	La Paz	PDC	Aguilera
20-04-1958	Argentina	W 1-0	Asuncion	Fr	Aveiro
26-04	Argentina	L 0-2	Buenos Aires	Fr	
4-05	Brazil	L 1-5	Rio de Janeiro	OCC	Aguero
7-05	Brazil	D 0-0	Sao Paulo	OCC	
8-06	France	L 3-7	Norrkoping	WCr1	Amarilla 2, Romero.J
11-06	Scotland	W 3-2	Norrkoping	WCr1	Aguero, Cayetano Ré, Parodi.J
15-06	Yugoslavia	D 3-3	Eskilstuna	WCr1	Parodi.J, Aguero, Romero.J
11-03-1959	Chile	W 2-1	Buenos Aires	SC	Aveiro 2
15-03	Bolivia	W 5-0	Buenos Aires	SC	Cayetano Ré 3, Sanabria.I, Aveiro
18-03	Uruguay	L 1-3	Buenos Aires	SC	Aveiro
22-03	Argentina	L 1-3	Buenos Aires	SC	Sanabria.C
29-03	Brazil	L 1-4	Buenos Aires	SC	Parodi.S
2-04	Peru	W 2-1	Buenos Aires	SC	Aveiro 2
1-05	Uruguay	W 3-1	Montevideo	Fr	Cayetano Ré, Nuñez.G
5-12	Brazil	L 2-3	Guayaquil	SC	Parodi.S, Benitez.G
9-12	Argentina	L 2-4	Guayaquil	SC	Lezcano, Cabral
22-12	Uruguay	D 1-1	Guayaquil	SC	Parodi.S
25-12	Ecuador	L 1-3	Guayaquil	SC	OG
3-07-1960	Brazil	L 1-2	Asuncion	CA	Cabrera
9-07	Argentina	L 0-1	Buenos Aires	CA	
13-07	Uruguay	L 1-2	Montevideo	CA	Cabral
18-12	Chile	L 1-4	Valparaiso	Fr	López.F
21-12	Chile	L 1-3	Santiago	Fr	Cabrera
30-04-1961	Brazil	L 0-2	Asuncion	OCC	
3-05	Brazil	L 2-3	Asuncion	OCC	Martinez.C 2
17-05	Argentina	D 0-0	Asuncion	Fr	
29-06	Brazil	L 2-3	Rio de Janeiro	Fr	Fretes, Parodi.S
12-10	Argentina	L 1-5	Buenos Aires	Fr	Gonzales.G
29-10	Mexico	L 0-1	Mexico City	WCq	
5-11	Mexico	D 0-0	Asuncion	WCq	
21-04-1962	Brazil	L 0-6	Rio de Janeiro	OCC	
24-04	Brazil	L 0-4	Sao Paulo	OCC	
10-08	Bolivia	L 1-3	Cochabamba	PDC	Insfran.E
12-08	Bolivia	L 2-3	La Paz	PDC	Samaniego, Nuñez.G
17-02-1963	Bolivia	W 3-0	Asuncion	PDC	Rodriguez, Valdez, Cabrera
19-02	Bolivia	W 5-1	Asuncion	PDC	Arambulo, Villamayor 2, Martinez.D, Cabrera
3-03	Brazil	D 2-2	Asuncion	Fr	Rodriguez, Insfran.E
14-03	Ecuador	W 3-1	La Paz	SC	Zárate 2, Quiñones
17-03	Brazil	W 2-0	La Paz	SC	Navarate, Ayala
20-03	Colombia	W 3-2	Cochabamba	SC	Cabrera 2, Valdez
24-03	Bolivia	L 0-2	Cochabamba	SC	
27-03	Peru	W 4-1	Cochabamba	SC	Martinez.D 2, Cabrera, Zárate
31-03	Argentina	D 1-1	La Paz	SC	Cabrera
15-10	Argentina	L 0-4	Asuncion	RCB	
29-10	Argentina	W 3-2	Buenos Aires	RCB	Ayala, Rojas.B 2
25-11-1964	Argentina	W 3-0	Asuncion	RCB	Candia, Ivaldi, Garcia
8-12	Argentina	L 1-8	Buenos Aires	RCB	Pavón
10-03-1965	Guatemala	W 4-1	Guatemala City	Fr	Riquelme, Cáceres 2, Ayala
14-03	Guatemala	W 3-0	Guatemala City	Fr	Riquelme, Rójas.J, Pavón
17-03	Costa Rica	L 0-1	San Jose	Fr	
19-03	Costa Rica	D 0-0	San Jose	Fr	
3-04	Peru	W 1-0	Lima	Fr	Riquelme
25-04	Uruguay	W 2-1	Asuncion	AC	Riquelme, Cáceres
1-05	Uruguay	L 0-4	Montevideo	AC	
25-07	Bolivia	W 2-0	Asuncion	WCq	Rodriguez, Rojas.J
1-08	Argentina	L 0-3	Buenos Aires	WCq	
8-08	Argentina	D 0-0	Asuncion	WCq	
22-08	Bolivia	L 1-2	La Paz	WCq	Mora.C

Date	Opponent	Result	Venue	Comp	Scorers
24-04-1966	Mexico	L 0-4	Mexico City	Fr	
15-05	Uruguay	D 2-2	Asuncion	AC	Gonzalez, Torres
18-05	Uruguay	L 1-3	Montevideo	AC	Torres
21-12	Ecuador	D 2-2	Guayaquil	SCq	Rójas.J, Apodaca
28-12	Ecuador	W 3-1	Asuncion	SCq	Mora.C 2, Del Puerto
18-01-1967	Argentina	L 1-4	Montevideo	SC	Mora.C
22-01	Chile	L 2-4	Montevideo	SC	Rivero, Apocada
25-01	Bolivia	W 1-0	Montevideo	SC	Del Puerto
29-01	Uruguay	L 0-2	Montevideo	SC	
1-02	Venezuela	W 5-3	Montevideo	SC	Rojas.J 2, Garay, Mora.C 2
13-10	Argentina	D 1-1	Asuncion	Fr	Fleitas
15-05-1968	Argentina	W 2-0	Asuncion	Fr	Mora.C, Garcia.A
2-06	Uruguay	D 0-0	Asuncion	AC	Abandoned after 70 mins
25-07	Brazil	L 0-4	Asuncion	OCC	
28-07	Brazil	W 1-0	Asuncion	OCC	Cabral
19-03-1969	Argentina	D 1-1	Rosario	Fr	Irala
9-04	Argentina	D 0-0	Asuncion	Fr	
8-06	Chile	L 0-1	Asuncion	Fr	
6-07	Chile	D 0-0	Santiago	Fr	
9-07	Peru	L 1-2	Lima	Fr	Mora.C
18-07	Peru	L 1-2	Lima	Fr	Sosa.A
7-08	Venezuela	W 2-0	Caracas	WCq	Rojas.P, Sosa.A
10-08	Colombia	W 1-0	Bogota	WCq	Martinez.A
17-08	Brazil	L 0-3	Asuncion	WCq	
21-08	Venezuela	W 1-0	Asuncion	WCq	Jimenez
24-08	Colombia	W 2-1	Asuncion	WCq	Arrúa 2
31-08	Brazil	L 0-1	Rio de Janeiro	WCq	
12-04-1970	Brazil	D 0-0	Rio de Janeiro	Fr	
22-10	Argentina	D 1-1	Asuncion	Fr	Irala
4-07-1971	Argentina	D 1-1	Asuncion	RCB	Arrúa
9-07	Argentina	L 0-1	Rosario	RCB	
14-07	Chile	L 2-3	Santiago	Fr	Arrúa 2
24-07	Brazil	L 0-1	Rio de Janeiro	Fr	
27-07	Peru	D 0-0	Lima	Fr	
8-08	Chile	W 2-0	Asuncion	Fr	Escobar, Arrúa
15-08	Peru	W 2-0	Asuncion	Fr	Arrúa 2
26-04-1972	Brazil	L 2-3	Porto Alegre	Fr	Escobar, Jiminez
25-05	Argentina	D 0-0	Salta	Fr	
11-06	Venezuela	W 4-1	Campo Grande	Clr1	Jiminez, Escobar, Maldonaldo 2
14-06	Peru	W 1-0	Campo Grande	Clr1	Godoy
21-06	Yugoslavia	L 1-2	Manaus	Clr1	Escobar
25-06	Bolivia	W 6-1	Manaus	Clr1	Arrúa 3, Maldonado 2, Dos Santos
28-03-1973	Peru	L 0-1	Lima	Fr	
31-03	Bolivia	D 1-1	La Paz	Fr	Jimenez
8-04	Peru	D 1-1	Asuncion	Fr	Maldonado
2-09	Bolivia	W 2-1	La Paz	WCq	Escobar, Insfran.J
16-09	Argentina	D 1-1	Asuncion	WCq	Arrúa
30-09	Bolivia	W 4-0	Asuncion	WCq	Insfran.J, Bareiro, Osorio, Arrúa
7-10	Argentina	L 1-3	Buenos Aires	WCq	Escobar
12-05-1974	Brazil	L 0-2	Rio de Janeiro	Fr	
22-12	Chile	L 0-1	Santiago	Fr	
12-06-1975	Uruguay	L 0-1	Asuncion	AC	
19-06	Uruguay	W 1-0	Montevideo	AC	Rolón
7-07	Bolivia	W 2-1	Cochabamba	Fr	Ocampo, Insfran.J
10-07	Peru	L 0-2	Lima	Fr	
20-07	Colombia	L 0-1	Bogota	SCr1	
24-07	Ecuador	D 2-2	Quito	SCr1	Kiese.H 2
30-07	Colombia	L 0-1	Asuncion	SCr1	Abandoned 45 mins
10-08	Ecuador	W 3-1	Asuncion	SCr1	Rolón 2, Báez.C
25-02-1976	Argentina	L 2-3	Asuncion	CA	Aquino, Báez.C
10-03	Uruguay	D 2-2	Montevideo	CA	Pesoa, Paniagua
7-04	Brazil	D 1-1	Asuncion	CA	Aquino
28-04	Argentina	D 2-2	Buenos Aires	CA	Rivera, Aquino
19-05	Uruguay	W 1-0	Asuncion	CA	Solalinde
9-06	Brazil	L 1-3	Rio de Janeiro	CA	Diaz.J
9-01-1977	Ecuador	W 2-0	Asuncion	Fr	Colmán, Aquino
12-01	Uruguay	D 1-1	Asuncion	AC	Solalinde
23-01	Uruguay	L 1-2	Montevideo	AC	Villalba
26-01	Chile	L 0-4	Santiago	Fr	

2-02	Chile	W 2-0	Asuncion	Fr	Baéz.C, Aifuch
6-02	Bolivia	W 1-0	La Paz	PDC	Bareiro
9-02	Bolivia	D 2-2	La Paz	PDC	Sosa.A, Aifuch
13-02	Ecuador	L 1-2	Quito	Fr	Espinola
24-02	Colombia	W 1-0	Bogota	WCq	Jara-Saguier
6-03	Colombia	D 1-1	Asuncion	WCq	Jara-Saguier
13-03	Brazil	L 0-1	Asuncion	WCq	
20-03	Brazil	D 1-1	Rio de Janeiro	WCq	Baéz.C
24-08	Argentina	L 1-2	Buenos Aires	Fr	Escobar
31-08	Argentina	W 2-0	Asuncion	Fr	OG, Espinola
17-05-1979	Brazil	L 0-6	Rio de Janeiro	Fr	
10-07	Bolivia	L 1-3	La Paz	PDC	Benitez.A
12-07	Bolivia	D 1-1	Cochabamba	Fr	Isasi
1-08	Bolivia	W 2-0	Asuncion	PDC	Solalinde, Meza
29-08	Ecuador	W 2-1	Quito	SCr1	Talavera, Solalinde
13-09	Ecuador	W 2-0	Asuncion	SCr1	Morel.E, Osorio
20-09	Uruguay	D 0-0	Asuncion	SCr1	
26-09	Uruguay	D 2-2	Montevideo	SCr1	Morel.E 2
10-10	Peru	W 3-2	Lima	Fr	Espinola, Morel.E, Acosta
24-10	Brazil	W 2-1	Asuncion	SCsf	Morel.E, Talavera
31-10	Brazil	D 2-2	Rio de Janeiro	SCsf	Morel.M, Romero.J (II)
28-11	Chile	W 3-0	Asuncion	SCf	Romero.J (II) 2, Morel.M
5-12	Chile	L 0-1	Santiago	SCf	
11-12	Chile	D 0-0	Buenos Aires	SCf	
26-08-1980	Bolivia	D 1-1	La Paz	PDC	
28-08	Bolivia	W 3-1	Santa Cruz	Fr	Florentin, Issasi, Michelagnoli
18-09	Bolivia	W 2-1	Asuncion	PDC	Mino, Lopez
25-09	Brazil	L 1-2	Asuncion	Fr	Benitez
30-10	Brazil	L 0-6	Goiania	Fr	
15-03-1981	Colombia	L 0-2	Asuncion	Fr	
17-05	Ecuador	L 0-1	Guayaquil	WCq	
31-05	Ecuador	W 3-1	Asuncion	WCq	Michelagnoli, Morel, Romero.J (II)
7-06	Chile	L 0-1	Asuncion	WCq	
21-06	Chile	L 0-3	Santiago	WCq	
2-06-1983	Uruguay	D 0-0	Asuncion	AC	
9-06	Uruguay	L 0-3	Montevideo	AC	
14-07	Argentina	W 1-0	Asuncion	Fr	Delgado
21-07	Argentina	D 0-0	Buenos Aires	Fr	
24-07	Chile	W 1-0	Asuncion	Fr	Hicks
3-08	Bolivia	L 1-2	La Paz	PDC	Florentin
5-08	Bolivia	W 3-1	Santa Cruz	PDC	Florentin 2, Delgado
17-08	Chile	L 2-3	Santiago	Fr	Olmedo, Delgado
25-08	Uruguay	D 0-0	Montevideo	Fr	
5-10	Peru	W 2-0	Lima	Fr	Romero.J (II), Torrales
7-10	Peru	W 4-1	Asuncion	Fr	Cabanas 2, Romero.J (II) 2
13-10	Brazil	D 1-1	Asuncion	SCsf	Morel.M
20-10	Brazil	D 0-0	Uberlandia	SCsf	
3-02-1985	Uruguay	L 0-1	Montevideo	AC	
6-02	Chile	L 0-1	Asuncion	Fr	
10-02	Uruguay	L 1-3	Asuncion	AC	Benitez
28-02	Colombia	L 0-3	Asuncion	Fr	
17-04	Colombia	L 0-1	Pereira	Fr	
19-04	Colombia	D 2-2	Bogota	Fr	Bobadilla, Ferreira
28-04	Argentina	W 1-0	Asuncion	Fr	
9-05	Argentina	D 1-1	Buenos Aires	Fr	Zabala
26-05	Bolivia	D 1-1	Santa Cruz	WCq	Nuñez
9-06	Bolivia	W 3-0	Asuncion	WCq	Mendoza, Jacquet, Romero.J (II)
16-06	Brazil	L 0-2	Asuncion	WCq	
23-06	Brazil	D 1-1	Rio de Janeiro	WCq	Romero.J (II)
9-10	Chile	D 0-0	Asuncion	Fr	
16-10	Peru	W 1-0	Lima	Fr	Ferreira
27-10	Colombia	W 3-0	Asuncion	WCq	Hicks, Romero, Cabanas
29-10	Chile	D 0-0	Santiago	Fr	
3-11	Colombia	L 1-2	Cali	WCq	Ferreira
10-11	Chile	W 3-0	Asuncion	WCq	Cabanas 2, Delgado
17-11	Chile	D 2-2	Santiago	WCq	Schettina, Romero.J (II)
29-01-1986	Canada	D 0-0	Vancouver	Fr	
11-02	Hong Kong	D 1-1	Hong Kong	Fr	Delgado
14-02	South Korea	W 3-1	Hong Kong	Fr	OG, Sandoval, Schetlina
16-02	Indonesia	W 3-2	Djakarta	Fr	Ramon, Zabala, Canete

26-02	Qatar	D 1-1	Doha	Fr	Delgado
1-03	Qatar	W 3-0	Doha	Fr	
8-03	Bahrain	W 2-1	Manama	Fr	Roman, Ordinario
12-03	Saudi Arabia	D 0-0	Dhahran	Fr	
20-05	Denmark	W 2-1	Bogota	Fr	Cabanas 2
4-06	Iraq	W 1-0	Toluca	WCr1	Romero.J (II)
7-06	Mexico	D 1-1	Mexico City	WCr1	Romero.J (II)
11-06	Belgium	D 2-2	Toluca	WCr1	Cabanas 2
18-06	England	L 0-3	Mexico City	WCr2	
14-06-1987	Bolivia	W 2-0	Santa Cruz	Fr	Palacios, Jacqet
20-06	Argentina	W 1-0	Buenos Aires	Fr	OG
24-06	Brazil	L 0-1	Porto Alegre	Fr	
28-06	Bolivia	D 0-0	Rosario	SCr1	
5-07	Colombia	L 0-3	Rosario	SCr1	
7-09-1988	Ecuador	W 5-1	Guayaquil	Fr	Roman.B, Almirom, Rivarola, Roman.A, Ferreira
12-09	Honduras	D 0-0	San Pedro Sula	Fr	
15-09	Honduras	W 2-0	Tegucigalpa	Fr	
17-09	El Salvador	W 1-0	San Salvador	Fr	Roman
21-09	Peru	W 1-0	Lima	Fr	Roman
27-09	Chile	W 2-0	Asuncion	Fr	Roman, OG
29-09	Uruguay	W 3-1	Asuncion	Fr	Palacios, Franco, Jacqet
12-10	Uruguay	L 0-2	Montevideo	Fr	
12-03-1989	Jamaica	W 3-0	Kingston	Fr	Jacqet, Palacios, Roman.G
15-03	Martinique *	W 2-0	Fort de France	Fr	
17-03	Guadeloupe *	W 2-0	Basse Terre	Fr	
19-03	Trinidad	D 2-2	Port of Spain	Fr	Caceres, Palacios
22-03	Trinidad	D 1-1	Arima	Fr	Franco
26-03	Venezuela	W 2-1	Caracas	Fr	Ferreira, Franco
30-03	Venezuela	D 0-0	Maturin	Fr	
12-04	Brazil	L 0-2	Teresina	Fr	
5-05	El Salvador	W 2-1	Los Angeles	Fr	
7-05	Guatemala	W 2-1	Los Angeles	Fr	Roman.B, Ferreyra
15-05	Peru	D 1-1	Asuncion	Fr	Roman.B
25-05	Bolivia	L 2-3	Cochabamba	Fr	Rojas, Franco
1-06	Bolivia	W 2-0	Asuncion	Fr	Ferreira 2
1-07	Peru	W 5-2	Salvador	SCr1	Canete 2, Neffa, Mendoza, OG
5-07	Colombia	W 1-0	Salvador	SCr1	Mendoza
7-07	Venezuela	W 3-0	Salvador	SCr1	Neffa, Ferreira 2
9-07	Brazil	L 0-2	Recife	SCr1	
12-07	Uruguay	L 0-3	Rio de Janeiro	SCr2	
14-07	Brazil	L 0-3	Rio de Janeiro	SCr2	
16-07	Argentina	D 0-0	Rio de Janeiro	SCr2	
27-08	Colombia	W 2-1	Asuncion	WCq	Ferreira, Chilavert
10-09	Ecuador	W 2-1	Asuncion	WCq	Cabanas, Ferreira
17-09	Colombia	L 1-2	Barranquilla	WCq	Mendoza
24-09	Ecuador	L 1-3	Guayaquil	WCq	Neffa
27-02-1991	Brazil	D 1-1	Campo Grande	Fr	Samaniego
14-06	Bolivia	W 1-0	Santa Cruz	PDC	Gonzalez
16-06	Bolivia	D 0-0	Asuncion	PDC	
6-07	Peru	W 1-0	Santiago	SCr1	Monzon
10-07	Venezuela	W 5-0	Santiago	SCr1	Neffa, Guirland, Monzon 2, Sanabria
12-07	Argentina	L 1-4	Santiago	SCr1	Cardozo
14-07	Chile	L 0-4	Santiago	SCr1	
3-03-1993	Bolivia	W 1-0	Asuncion	Fr	Franco
6-03	Bolivia	L 1-2	Cochabamba	Fr	Ferreira
10-06	Mexico	L 1-3	Mexico City	Fr	Struway
18-06	Chile	W 1-0	Cuenca	SCr1	Cabanas
21-06	Peru	D 1-1	Cuenca	SCr1	Monzon
24-06	Brazil	L 0-3	Cuenca	SCr1	
26-06	Ecuador	L 0-3	Quito	SCqf	
14-07	Brazil	L 0-2	Rio de Janeiro	Fr	
1-08	Colombia	D 0-0	Barranquilla	WCq	
8-08	Argentina	L 1-3	Asuncion	WCq	Struway
15-08	Peru	W 2-1	Asuncion	WCq	Mendoza, Chilavert
22-08	Colombia	D 1-1	Asuncion	WCq	Rivarola
29-08	Argentina	D 0-0	Buenos Aires	WCq	
5-09	Peru	D 2-2	Lima	WCq	Mendoza 2
14-05-1995	Bolivia	D 1-1	Cochabamba	PDC	Esteche
9-06	Bolivia	D 0-0	Asuncion	PDC	Won 4-3p
14-06	Argentina	L 1-2	Rosario	Fr	Baez

17-06	Turkey	D 0-0	Iquique	Fr	
19-06	Chile	W 1-0	Santiago	Fr	
22-06	New Zealand	W 3-2	Santiago	Fr	
7-07	Mexico	W 2-1	Maldonado	SCr1	Cardozo, Samaniego
9-07	Uruguay	L 0-1	Montevideo	SCr1	
12-07	Venezuela	W 3-2	Maldonado	SCr1	Cardozo, Villamayor, Gamarra
16-07	Colombia	D 1-1	Montevideo	SCqf	Villamayor. Lost 4-5p

PERU

Peru are a middle-ranking South American power noted most for the fine teams they fielded during the 1970s. The rest of their footballing history has been largely undistinguished, and as one of the poorest nations on the continent with bad political problems, the Peruvians have struggled in recent years.

Though football was played at the turn of the century by British residents and a league of sorts formed in Lima in 1912, it was not until 1922 that the Federación Peruana de Fútbol was founded in the same city. Four years later the Liga Nacional de Football was introduced, though it was not strictly a national league as only clubs from the Lima area were invited to take part.

Until the introduction of a proper national league in 1966, the league in Lima was the strongest and its winners were regarded as national champions. In 1972, further changes were introduced. A metropolitan league for the area around Lima was instituted and a complex network of regional leagues set up to qualify teams for a final decentralised tournament to find the national champions.

The strongest teams have traditionally been from Lima and include Alianza (the club of the poor), Universitario (the club of the rich), Sporting Cristal and from nearby Callao, Sport Boys, though since the league has opened up, teams from the regions have begun to make their presence felt more and more, even if as yet they do not constitute a great threat to the capital.

The national side made its debut in the 1927 South American Championships which the Peruvian federation had been given the privilege of organising. Home advantage counted for little although Bolivia, who had made their debut in the previous year's tournament, were beaten. Lima was often used as a venue for the tournament and in 1939 Peru made home advantage count.

Spurred on by their greatest player of these early years, Teodoro 'Lolo' Fernández, the Peruvians beat all four of their opponents to win the tournament, although of the big three only Uruguay were present. Entry into the initial World Cup did not result in any progress, but three years before their South American Championship success, and again with Fernandez at the helm, Peru had made an impact, though not of the right kind, at the 1936 Olympic Games in Berlin.

Professionalism had been introduced in 1931, but the Peru team that made the journey to Berlin was the strongest at their disposal. They comprehensively beat Finland in the first round but were then involved in an extraordinary game against Austria. With Peru winning 4-2 near the end of extra-time, the game was abandoned after a melee stemming from a misunderstanding over an Austrian substitution. The game was ordered to be replayed but the Peru team were told not to turn up to the game by their embassy who considered the decision unjust, and they returned home.

There was little progress made in the game and even the emergence of a number of great players in the late 1950s including Gomez Sanchez, Mosquera, Loyaza, Seminario and Joya did little to help the cause. A famous victory over England in 1959 only helped speed up the flow of players to Europe and other South American countries where the conditions for players were much better. Seminario and Mosquera made names for themselves in Spain and Portugal, whilst Joya, Gomez Sanchez and Loyaza were very successful in Argentina.

Peru will primarily be remembered for the great sides of the 1970s. Guided by the greatest Peruvian footballer of all time, Teofilo Cubillas, Peru were in great form in the 1970 World Cup, and if they had not met Brazil in the quarter-finals they might have progressed further. Surprisingly eliminated in the 1974 qualifiers after a play-off with Chile, they made up for that defeat by winning the 1975 South American Championships, beating Brazil in the semi-finals and Colombia in the final.

Qualification for the 1978 and 1982 World Cup finals did not see the team perform as well as they had done in the first half of the 1970s, especially in Spain in 1982. Cubillas was still in the team but it was his swansong in the international game. The 1978 tournament will be remembered for the Peru-Argentina game in the second round. The Peruvians had played some excellent football in the first round, but collapsed in the second, especially against Argentina against whom they lost 6-0. The result was greeted with cries of 'cheat' from Brazil who were eliminated as a result, though it seems unlikely that Peru actually threw the game. The result had more to do with inept organisation which saw Brazil's game with Poland and the Peru-Argentina game scheduled for different times, thereby allowing the Argentines the advantage of knowing exactly how many goals they needed to score to proceed to the final.

The 1980s and early 1990s have on the whole been a very poor time for the country as political violence has gone

THE ORDER OF MERIT

		Total			Lge	Copa Lib		
		G	S	B	G	G	S	B
1	Universitario	21	1	3	21	-	1	3
2	Alianza	15	-	2	15	-	-	2
3	Sporting Cristal	11	-	-	11	-	-	-
4	Sport Boys	6	-	-	6	-	-	-
5	Deportivo Municipal	4	-	-	4	-	-	-
6	Atlético Chalaco	2	-	-	2	-	-	-
	Mariscal Sucre	2	-	-	2	-	-	-
	Union Huaral	2	-	-	2	-	-	-
9	Defensor Lima	1	-	1	1	-	-	1
10	Centro Iqueno	1	-	-	1	-	-	-
	Deportivo San Agustin	1	-	-	1	-	-	-
	CS Progreso	1	-	-	1	-	-	-
	Melgar FC	1	-	-	1	-	-	-

To the end of the 1994 season

hand in hand with economic stagnation. Peru are in danger of losing their traditional standing in South America and joining the likes of Venezuela as also-rans. The 1990 World Cup qualifiers saw them finish bottom of their group, while since 1984 in the Copa Libertadores, never a happy hunting ground for their clubs, the Peruvian entrants have made the bottom two places in the first round their own.

Population: 22,332,000
Area, sq km: 1,285,216
% in urban areas: 69%
Capital city: Lima

Federación Peruana de Fútbol
Estadio Nacional, Puerta #4
Calle José Díaz
Lima
Perú
Tel: + 51 14 320517
Fax: + 51 14 320646

Year of formation	1922
Affiliation to FIFA	1924
Affiliation to CSF	1926
Registered clubs	10 000
Registered players	510 600
Professional players	650
Registered coaches	110
Registered referees	156
National stadium	Estadio Nacional, Lima 45 000
National colours	White with red sash/White/White
Reserve colours	Red/White/White
Season	Regional championships March - November National Championship November - February

THE RECORD

WORLD CUP

1930	QT Automatic - Final Tournament/1st round
1934-54	Did not enter
1958	QT 2nd/2 in group 1
1962	QT 2nd/2 in group 3
1966	QT 2nd/3 in group 1
1970	QT 1st/3 in group 1 - Final Tournament/Quarter-finalists
1974	QT 2nd/2 in group 3
1978	QT 1st/3 in group 3 - Final Tournament/2nd round
1982	QT 1st/3 in group 2 - Final Tournament/1st round
1986	QT 2nd/4 in group 1
1990	QT 3rd/3 in group 1
1994	QT 4th/4 in group 1

SOUTH AMERICAN CHAMPIONSHIP

1910-26	-
1927	3/4
1929	4/4
1935	3/4
1937	6/6
1939	1/5 - Winners
1941	4/5
1942	5/7
1945	-
1946	-
1947	5/8
1949	3/8
1953	5/7
1955	3/6
1956	6/6
1957	4/7
1959	5/7
1959	-
1963	5/7
1967	-
1975	1/10 - Winners
1979	4/10 - Semi-finalists
1983	4/10 - Semi-finalists
1987	6/10 - 1st round
1989	8/10 - 1st round
1991	8/10 - 1st round
1993	5=/12 - Quarter-finals
1995	11/12 - 1st round

SOUTH AMERICAN CLUB COMPETITIONS

Copa Libertadores
Finalists - Universitario 1972
Semi-finalists - Universitario 1967 1971 1975, Defensor Lima 1974, Alianza 1976 1978
Super Copa
Ineligible to compete
CONMEBOL Cup
Second Round - Deportivo Sipesa 1993, Sporting Cristal 1994

CLUB DIRECTORY

LIMA (Pop. - 4,608,000)

Club Alianza (1901)
Alejandro Villanueva 34,000 – Blue & white stripes/Blue

Atlético Chalaco Callao (1902)
Telmo Carbajo 15,000 – Red & white stripes/White

Club Defensor - Ciclista
(Merger in 1990 of Defensor & Ciclista)
Municipal de Chorillos – Black & white stripes/White

Club Deportivo San Agustin (1982)
Alianza or Universitario's – Yellow/Red
Previous names - Club Huracan San Isidro 1982-83. Merged with Club San Francisco (1970) to form Colegio San Augustin 1983-90

Club Atlético Defensor (1931)
Alianza or Universitario's – Maroon/White

Club Deportivo Municipal (1935)
Estadio Nacional 45,000 – White with a red sash/Black

Circolo Sportivo Internazionale (1986)
Municipal 10,000 – Blue/White
Previous name - Deportivo Cantolao until 1986

Sport Boys Callao (1927)
Telmo Carbajo 15,000 – Pink/Black

Club Sporting Cristal (1922)
Alejandro Villanueva 34,000 – Sky blue/White
Previous name - Sporting Tabaco 1922-55

Club Universitario de Deportes (1924)
Teodoro 'Lolo' Fernandez 15,000 – Cream, black trim
Previous name - Federación Universitaria 1924-33

AREQUIPA (Pop. - 446,000)

Melgar Fútbol Club (1915)
IV Centenario 10,000 – Red & black halves/Black
Previous name - Mariano Melgar

TRUJILLO (Pop. - 354,000)

Club Carlos Mannucci (1965)
Mansiche 10,000 – Blue/White

Club Sport Libertad (1887)
Mansiche 10,000 – Blue/Blue

CHIMBOTE (Pop. - 216,000)

Club Deportivo Sipesa
(**S**indicato de **Pes**cadores **S**ociedad **A**nonima)
Manuel Gomez Arellano – Blue/White

PIURA (Pop. - 207,000)
Club Atlético Grau (1919)
Miguel Grau 9,000 – White, black trim

Club Alianza Atlético Sullana (1920)
Estadio Campeones Olimpico's del '36 6,000 – White with a black sash/White

CUZCO (Pop. - 184,000)
Club Union Cienciano (1901)
Estadio Inca Garcilasco de la Vega 12,000 – Red/White
Previous name - Atlético Cienciano

IQUITOS (Pop. - 178,000)
Colegio Nacional de Iquitos (CNI)
Max Agustin 20,000 – White/White

Hungaritos Augustinos
Max Agustin 20,000 – Green/Green

HUANCAYO (Pop. - 164,000)
Club Deportivo Junin (1962)
IV Centenario 15,000 – Green & white stripes/White

ICA (Pop. - 114,000)
Octavio Espinoza Ica (1923)
Picasso Peralta 6,000 – Red/White

TACNA (Pop. - 97,000)
Club Deportivo Coronel Bolognesi (1929)
Guillermo Briceno 25,000 – Red, white trim

PUNO (Pop. - 67,000)
Club Alfonso Ugarte (1929)
Enrique Torres 25,000 – White with a red sash/Red

TALARA (Pop. - 57,000)
Atlético Torino (1952)
Campeonisimo 10,000 – Maroon with two white stripes/Maroon

CAJAMARCA (Pop. - 62,000)
(UTC) Universidad Tecnica de Cajamarca (1964)
Estadio Municipal 'Heroes de San Ramon' 30,000 – Cream/Black, maroon trim

HUANUCO (Pop. - 61,000)
Leon de Huánuco (1949)
Heráclito Tapia – Cream, maroon trim

HUACHO (Pop. - 43,000)
Juventud La Palma
Segundo Torres Aranado 15,000 – Sky blue/Black

MOQUEGUA (Pop. - 31,000)
Club Juvenil Los Angeles
25 de Noviembre 15,000 – Red/Red

Atlético Huracán
25 de Noviembre 15,000 – White/Blue

CHANCAY
La Joya-Iqueño (1987)
Victor Raul Haya 15,000 – White with a black sash/Black
Previous names - Formed when Centro Iqueño & Juventus La Joya merged

CHICLAYO
Club Juan Aurich (1922)
Elias Aguirre 20,000 – Red/White

HUARAL
Club Sport Union Huaral (1947)
Julio Lores Colán 10,000 – Red & white stripes/Black

TARMA
Asociacion Deportiva Tarma (1929)
Estadio Union 15,000 – Sky blue/White

PERUVIAN LEAGUE CHAMPIONSHIP

1926	CS Progreso
1927	Alianza
1928	Alianza
1929	Universitario
1930	Atlético Chalaco
1931	Alianza
1932	Alianza
1933	Alianza
1934	Universitario
1935	Sport Boys
1936	-
1937	Sport Boys
1938	Deportivo Municipal
1939	Universitario
1940	Deportivo Municipal
1941	Universitario
1942	Sport Boys
1943	Deportivo Municipal
1944	Mariscal Sucre
1945	Universitario
1946	Universitario
1947	Atlético Chalaco
1948	Alianza
1949	Universitario
1950	Deportivo Municipal
1951	Sport Boys
1952	Alianza
1953	Mariscal Sucre
1954	Alianza
1955	Alianza
1956	Sporting Cristal
1957	Centro Iqueño
1958	Sport Boys
1959	Universitario
1960	Universitario
1961	Sporting Cristal
1962	Alianza
1963	Alianza
1964	Universitario
1965	Alianza
1966	Universitario
1967	Universitario
1968	Sporting Cristal
1969	Universitario
1970	Sporting Cristal
1971	Universitario
1972	Sporting Cristal
1973	Defensor Lima
1974	Universitario
1975	Alianza
1976	Unión Huaral
1977	Alianza
1978	Alianza
1979	Sporting Cristal
1980	Sporting Cristal
1981	Mariano Melgar
1982	Universitario
1983	Sporting Cristal
1984	Sport Boys
1985	Universitario
1986	Colegio San Augustin
1987	Universitario
1988	Sporting Cristal
1989	Union Huaral
1990	Universitario
1991	Sporting Cristal
1992	Universitario
1993	Universitario
1994	Sporting Cristal

INTERNATIONAL MATCHES PLAYED BY PERU

1-11-1927	Uruguay	L 0-4	Lima	SC	
13-11	Bolivia	W 3-2	Lima	SC	Neira, Sarmiento, Montellanos
27-11	Argentina	L 1-5	Lima	SC	Villanueva
3-11-1929	Argentina	L 0-3	Buenos Aires	SC	
11-11	Uruguay	L 1-4	Buenos Aires	SC	Lizarbe
16-11	Paraguay	L 0-5	Buenos Aires	SC	
14-07-1930	Romania	L 1-3	Montevideo	WCr1	Ferreira
18-07	Uruguay	L 0-1	Montevideo	WCr1	
13-01-1935	Uruguay	L 0-1	Lima	SC	
20-01	Argentina	L 1-4	Lima	SC	Fernandez.T
26-01	Chile	W 1-0	Lima	SC	Montellanos
6-08-1936	Finland	W 7-3	Berlin	OGr1	Fernandez.T 5, Villanueva 2
9-08	Austria	W 4-2	Berlin	OGqf	Alcalde, Villanueva 2, Fernandez.T

27-12	Brazil	L 2-3	Buenos Aires	SC	Fernandez.T, Villanueva
6-01-1937	Uruguay	L 2-4	Buenos Aires	SC	Fernandez.T, Magallanes
16-01	Argentina	L 0-1	Buenos Aires	SC	
21-01	Chile	D 2-2	Buenos Aires	SC	Alcalde 2
24-01	Paraguay	W 1-0	Buenos Aires	SC	Magallanes
8-08-1938	Colombia	W 4-2	Bogota	BG	Ibanez 2, Fernandez.T, Alcalde
11-08	Ecuador	W 9-1	Bogota	BG	Espinar 3, Alcalde 4, Bielich 2
14-08	Bolivia	W 3-0	Bogota	BG	Fernandez.T 2, Alcalde
17-08	Venezuela	W 2-1	Bogota	BG	Bielich, Parades
15-01-1939	Ecuador	W 5-2	Lima	SC	Fernandez.T 2, Alcalde 2, Ibanez
22-01	Chile	W 3-1	Lima	SC	Fernandez.T 3
29-01	Paraguay	W 3-0	Lima	SC	Fernandez.T 2, Alcalde
12-02	Uruguay	W 2-1	Lima	SC	Alcalde, Bielich
19-01-1941	Argentina	D 1-1	Lima	RGP	Hurtado
26-01	Argentina	D 1-1	Lima	RGP	Magallanes
29-01	Argentina	L 0-3	Lima	RGP	
9-02	Chile	L 0-1	Santiago	SC	
12-02	Argentina	L 1-2	Santiago	SC	Socarraz
23-02	Ecuador	W 4-0	Santiago	SC	Fernandez.T 3, Vallejas
26-02	Uruguay	L 0-2	Santiago	SC	
18-01-1942	Paraguay	D 1-1	Montevideo	SC	Magallanes
21-01	Brazil	L 1-2	Montevideo	SC	Fernandez.T
25-01	Argentina	L 1-3	Montevideo	SC	Fernandez.T
28-01	Ecuador	W 2-1	Montevideo	SC	Quinonez, Guzman
1-02	Uruguay	L 0-3	Montevideo	SC	
7-02	Chile	D 0-0	Montevideo	SC	
6-12-1947	Paraguay	D 2-2	Guayaquil	SC	Castillo, Mosquera.M
9-12	Chile	L 1-2	Guayaquil	SC	Lopez.V
11-12	Argentina	L 2-3	Guayaquil	SC	Gomez.C, Lopez.V
20-12	Ecuador	D 0-0	Guayaquil	SC	
23-12	Colombia	W 5-1	Guayaquil	SC	Gomez.C 2, Mosquera.M, Guzman 2
25-12	Uruguay	L 0-1	Guayaquil	SC	
27-12	Bolivia	W 2-0	Guayaquil	SC	Guzman, Castillo
10-04-1949	Colombia	W 4-0	Rio de Janeiro	SC	Pedraza 2, Drago, Castillo
13-04	Paraguay	L 1-3	Rio de Janeiro	SC	Colunga
20-04	Ecuador	W 4-0	Rio de Janeiro	SC	Salinas, OG, Castillo, Pedraza
24-04	Brazil	L 1-7	Rio de Janeiro	SC	Salinas
27-04	Bolivia	W 3-0	Santos	SC	Drago 2, Heredia
30-04	Chile	W 3-0	Sao Paulo	SC	Mosquera.A 2, Castillo
4-05	Uruguay	W 4-3	Rio de Janeiro	SC	Mosquera.A, Castillo, Gomez.C 2
23-03-1952	Panama	W 7-1	Santiago	PAC	Lopez.V 5, Drago, Morales
30-03	Uruguay	L 2-5	Santiago	PAC	Barbadillo, Lopez.V
2-04	Chile	L 2-3	Santiago	PAC	Barbadillo, Lopez.V
10-04	Brazil	D 0-0	Santiago	PAC	
20-04	Mexico	W 3-0	Santiago	PAC	Rivera, Drago, Torres
22-02-1953	Bolivia	L 0-1	Lima	SC	
28-02	Ecuador	W 1-0	Lima	SC	Gomez.C
4-03	Chile	D 0-0	Lima	SC	
8-03	Paraguay	D 2-2	Lima	SC	Terry, Villamares
19-03	Brazil	W 1-0	Lima	SC	Navarrete
28-03	Uruguay	L 0-3	Lima	SC	
26-07	Chile	L 1-2	Lima	PC	Navarrete
28-07	Chile	W 5-0	Lima	PC	Terry 2, Heredia 2, Drago
17-09-1954	Chile	L 1-2	Santiago	PC	Gomez Sanchez
19-09	Chile	W 4-2	Santiago	PC	Terry, OG, Gomez Sanchez 2
6-03-1955	Chile	L 4-5	Santiago	SC	Castillo, Barbadillo, Heredia, Gomez Sanchez
13-03	Ecuador	W 4-2	Santiago	SC	Gomez Sanchez 2, OG, Mosquera.M
16-03	Argentina	D 2-2	Santiago	SC	Gomez Sanchez 2
23-03	Paraguay	D 1-1	Santiago	SC	Terry
30-03	Uruguay	W 2-1	Santiago	SC	Castillo, Gomez Sanchez
22-01-1956	Argentina	L 1-2	Montevideo	SC	Drago
28-01	Uruguay	L 0-2	Montevideo	SC	
1-02	Brazil	L 1-2	Montevideo	SC	Drago
5-02	Paraguay	D 1-1	Montevideo	SC	Lazon
9-02	Chile	L 3-4	Montevideo	SC	Castillo, Mosquera.M, Gomez Sanchez
28-02	Argentina	D 0-0	Mexico City	PAC	
4-03	Mexico	W 2-0	Mexico City	PAC	Drago, Gomez Sanchez
6-03	Brazil	L 0-1	Mexico City	PAC	
15-03	Chile	D 2-2	Mexico City	PAC	Lamas, Mosquera.M
17-03	Costa Rica	L 2-4	Mexico City	PAC	Salinas 2
10-03-1957	Ecuador	W 2-1	Lima	SC	Terry 2

16-03	Chile	W 1-0	Lima	SC	Mosquera.M
23-03	Uruguay	L 3-5	Lima	SC	Terry, Seminario, Mosquera.M
27-03	Colombia	W 4-1	Lima	SC	Terry, Rivera 2, Bassa
31-03	Brazil	L 0-1	Lima	SC	
6-04	Argentina	W 2-1	Lima	SC	Mosquera.M, Terry
9-04	Argentina	L 1-4	Lima	Fr	Minaya
13-04	Brazil	D 1-1	Lima	WCq	Terry
21-04	Brazil	L 0-1	Rio de Janeiro	WCq	
10-03-1959	Brazil	D 2-2	Buenos Aires	SC	Seminario 2
14-03	Uruguay	W 5-3	Buenos Aires	SC	Loayza 3, Gomez Sanchez, Joya
18-03	Argentina	L 1-3	Buenos Aires	SC	Terry
21-03	Chile	D 1-1	Buenos Aires	SC	Loayza
29-03	Bolivia	D 0-0	Buenos Aires	SC	
2-04	Paraguay	L 1-2	Buenos Aires	SC	Gomez Sanchez
17-05	England	W 4-1	Lima	Fr	Seminario 3, Joya
10-07-1960	Spain	L 1-3	Lima	Fr	Carrasco
19-03-1961	Chile	L 2-5	Santiago	Fr	Flores, Carrasco
30-04	Colombia	L 0-1	Bogota	WCq	
7-05	Colombia	D 1-1	Lima	WCq	Delgado
20-05-1962	England	L 0-4	Lima	Fr	
10-03-1963	Brazil	L 0-1	Cochabamba	SC	
13-03	Argentina	W 2-1	Cochabamba	SC	Tenemas, Zegarra
17-03	Ecuador	W 2-1	La Paz	SC	Leon, Mosquera.N
21-03	Bolivia	L 2-3	La Paz	SC	Gallardo, Leon
24-03	Colombia	D 1-1	La Paz	SC	Gallardo
27-03	Paraguay	L 1-4	Cochabamba	SC	Gallardo
3-04-1965	Paraguay	L 0-1	Lima	Fr	
15-04	Chile	L 1-4	Santiago	PC	Zegarra
28-04	Chile	L 0-1	Lima	PC	
16-05	Venezuela	W 1-0	Lima	WCq	Zegarra
2-06	Venezuela	W 6-3	Caracas	WCq	Mosquera.N, Zavalla 2, Leon 3
6-06	Uruguay	L 0-1	Lima	WCq	
13-06	Uruguay	L 1-2	Montevideo	WCq	Uribe.A
4-06-1966	Brazil	L 0-4	Sao Paulo	Fr	
8-06	Brazil	L 1-3	Belo Horizonte	Fr	Herera
28-07-1967	Uruguay	L 0-1	Lima	Fr	
30-07	Uruguay	L 1-2	Lima	Fr	Uribe.A
14-07-1968	Brazil	L 3-4	Lima	Fr	Leon 2, Zegarra
17-07	Brazil	L 0-4	Lima	Fr	
18-08	Chile	L 1-2	Lima	PC	Bailleti
21-08	Chile	D 0-0	Lima	PC	
29-08	Argentina	D 2-2	Lima	Fr	Casaretto 2
1-09	Argentina	D 1-1	Lima	Fr	Casaretto
20-10	Mexico	D 3-3	Lima	Fr	Casaretto 3
7-04-1969	Brazil	L 1-2	Porto Alegre	Fr	Gallardo
9-04	Brazil	L 2-3	Rio de Janeiro	Fr	Gallardo, Baylon
8-05	Colombia	W 3-1	Bogota	Fr	Ramirez.O, Cubillas, Leon
14-05	El Salvador	W 4-1	San Salvador	Fr	OG, Ramirez.O 2, Castaneda
20-05	Mexico	W 1-0	Mexico City	Fr	Leon
22-05	Mexico	L 0-3	Leon	Fr	
18-06	Colombia	D 1-1	Lima	Fr	Chumpitaz
27-06	Uruguay	W 1-0	Lima	Fr	Leon
9-07	Paraguay	W 2-1	Lima	Fr	Cubillas 2
18-07	Paraguay	W 2-1	Lima	Fr	OG, Leon
3-08	Argentina	W 1-0	Lima	WCq	Leon
10-08	Bolivia	L 1-2	La Paz	WCq	Challe
17-08	Bolivia	W 3-0	Lima	WCq	Cubillas, Cruzado, Gallardo
31-08	Argentina	D 2-2	Buenos Aires	WCq	Ramirez.O 2
9-02-1970	Romania	D 1-1	Lima	Fr	Cubillas
14-02	Soviet Union	D 0-0	Lima	Fr	
20-02	Soviet Union	L 0-2	Lima	Fr	
21-02	Bulgaria	L 1-3	Lima	Fr	Sotil
24-02	Bulgaria	W 5-3	Lima	Fr	Sotil 3, Challe, Cubillas
5-03	Mexico	L 0-1	Lima	Fr	
8-03	Mexico	W 1-0	Lima	Fr	Gallardo
15-03	Mexico	L 1-3	Mexico City	Fr	Challe
18-03	Mexico	D 3-3	Leon	Fr	Leon 2, Baylon
31-03	Uruguay	L 0-2	Montevideo	Fr	
18-04	Uruguay	W 4-2	Lima	Fr	Reyes 2, Leon, Gallardo
21-04	El Salvador	W 3-0	Lima	Fr	Gallardo, Sotil, Del Castillo
2-06	Bulgaria	W 3-2	Leon	WCr1	Gallardo, Chumpitaz, Cubillas

6-06	Morocco	W 3-0	Leon	WCr1	Cubillas 2, Challe
10-06	West Germany	L 1-3	Leon	WCr1	Cubillas
14-06	Brazil	L 2-4	Guadalajara	WCqf	Gallardo, Cubillas
27-07-1971	Paraguay	D 0-0	Lima	Fr	
11-08	Chile	W 1-0	Lima	PC	Sotil
15-08	Paraguay	L 0-2	Asuncion	Fr	
18-08	Chile	L 0-1	Santiago	PC	
29-03-1972	Colombia	D 1-1	Bogota	Fr	Munante
5-04	Mexico	L 1-2	Mexico City	Fr	Cubillas
19-04	Soviet Union	L 0-2	Kiev	Fr	
23-04	Romania	D 2-2	Bucharest	Fr	Rojas.P, Cubillas
26-04	Scotland	L 0-2	Glasgow	Fr	
3-05	Holland	L 0-3	Rotterdam	Fr	
6-06	Colombia	D 0-0	Lima	Fr	
11-06	Bolivia	W 3-0	Curitiba	Clr1	Gallardo, Castenada, Sotil
14-06	Paraguay	L 0-1	Campo Grande	Clr1	
18-06	Venezuela	W 1-0	Manaus	Clr1	Ramirez.O
25-06	Yugoslavia	L 1-2	Manaus	Clr1	Ramirez.O
9-08	Mexico	W 3-2	Lima	Fr	Munante, Fernandez.J 2
25-10	Argentina	L 0-2	Lima	RCC	
4-03-1973	Guatemala	W 5-1	Lima	Fr	Cubillas 2, Munante 2, Sotil
24-03	Bolivia	W 2-0	Lima	Fr	OG, Sotil
28-03	Paraguay	W 1-0	Lima	Fr	Sotil
8-04	Paraguay	D 1-1	Asuncion	Fr	Sotil
23-04	Panama	W 4-0	Lima	Fr	Cubillas, Munante, Ramirez.O, Mayorga
29-04	Chile	W 2-0	Lima	WCq	Sotil 2
13-05	Chile	L 0-2	Santiago	WCq	
1-07	Colombia	W 3-1	Lima	Fr	Bailetti 2, Ramirez.O
15-07	Bolivia	L 0-2	La Paz	Fr	
27-07	Argentina	L 1-3	Buenos Aires	RCC	Bailetti
5-08	Chile	L 1-2	Montevideo	WCq	Bailetti
22-06-1975	Ecuador	L 0-6	Quito	Fr	
25-06	Ecuador	L 0-1	Guayaquil	Fr	
1-07	Ecuador	W 2-0	Lima	Fr	Oblitas, Diaz.R
10-07	Paraguay	W 2-0	Lima	Fr	Ramirez.O 2
16-07	Chile	D 1-1	Santiago	SCr1	Rojas.P
27-07	Bolivia	W 1-0	Oruro	SCr1	Ramirez.O
7-08	Bolivia	W 3-1	Lima	SCr1	Ramirez.O, Cueto, Oblitas
20-08	Chile	W 3-1	Lima	SCr1	Rojas.P, Oblitas, Cubillas
30-09	Brazil	W 3-1	Belo Horizonte	SCsf	Casaretto 2, Cubillas
4-10	Brazil	L 0-2	Lima	SCsf	
16-10	Colombia	L 0-1	Bogota	SCf	
22-10	Colombia	W 2-0	Lima	SCf	Oblitas, Ramirez.O
28-10	Colombia	W 1-0	Caracas	SCf	Sotil
12-10-1976	Uruguay	D 0-0	Lima	Fr	
28-10	Argentina	L 1-3	Lima	RCC	Quesada
10-11	Argentina	L 0-1	Buenos Aires	RCC	
24-11	Uruguay	D 0-0	Montevideo	Fr	
9-02-1977	Hungary	W 3-2	Lima	Fr	Velasquez 2, Sotil
20-02	Ecuador	D 1-1	Quito	WCq	Oblitas
6-03	Chile	D 1-1	Santiago	WCq	Munante
12-03	Ecuador	W 4-0	Lima	WCq	Velasquez, Oblitas 2, Luces
26-03	Chile	W 2-0	Lima	WCq	Sotil, Oblitas
17-05	Mexico	D 1-1	Mexico City	Fr	Ramirez.O
24-05	Mexico	L 1-2	Monterrey	Fr	OG
26-05	Haiti	W 2-1	Port-au-Prince	Fr	Sotil, Luces
29-05	Haiti	D 2-2	Port-au-Prince	Fr	Velasquez, Ramirez.O
10-06	Poland	L 1-3	Lima	Fr	Luces
10-07	Brazil	L 0-1	Cali	WCq	
17-07	Bolivia	W 5-0	Cali	WCq	Cubillas 2, Velasquez 2, Rojas.P
19-03-1978	Argentina	L 1-2	Buenos Aires	RCC	Rojas.P
23-03	Argentina	L 1-3	Lima	RCC	Oblitas
1-04	Bulgaria	D 1-1	Lima	Fr	Ramirez.O
11-04	Mexico	W 1-0	Los Angeles	Fr	Goritti
22-04	China	W 2-1	Lima	Fr	Mosquera.R, Rojas.P
1-05	Brazil	L 0-3	Rio de Janeiro	Fr	
3-06	Scotland	W 3-1	Cordoba	WCr1	Cueto, Cubillas 2
7-06	Holland	D 0-0	Mendoza	WCr1	
11-06	Iran	W 4-1	Cordoba	WCr1	Velasquez, Cubillas 3
14-06	Brazil	L 0-3	Mendoza	WCr2	
18-06	Poland	L 0-1	Mendoza	WCr2	

21-06	Argentina	L 0-6	Rosario	WCr2	
11-07-1979	Ecuador	W 2-1	Lima	Fr	Ore, Mosquera.R
18-07	Colombia	L 0-1	Lima	Fr	
25-07	Colombia	W 2-1	Bogota	Fr	Duarte, Cueto
8-08	Ecuador	L 1-2	Quito	Fr	Ravello
30-08	Uruguay	W 2-0	Lima	Fr	Mosquera.R, Leguia
12-09	Scotland	D 1-1	Glasgow	Fr	Leguia
10-10	Paraguay	L 2-3	Lima	Fr	Chumpitaz, Lobaton
17-10	Chile	L 1-2	Lima	SCsf	Mosquera.R
24-10	Chile	D 0-0	Santiago	SCsf	
1-11	Mexico	L 0-1	Monterrey	Fr	
18-07-1980	Uruguay	D 0-0	Montevideo	Fr	
12-11	Uruguay	D 1-1	Lima	Fr	Uribe.J
4-02-1981	Czechoslovakia	L 1-3	Lima	Fr	Uribe.J
11-02	Bulgaria	L 1-2	Lima	Fr	Correa
19-04	Chile	L 0-3	Santiago	Fr	
26-07	Colombia	D 1-1	Bogota	WCq	La Rosa
5-08	Chile	L 1-2	Lima	Fr	Olaechea
16-08	Colombia	W 2-0	Lima	WCq	Barbadillo, Uribe.J
23-08	Uruguay	W 2-1	Montevideo	WCq	La Rosa, Uribe.J
6-09	Uruguay	D 0-0	Lima	WCq	
23-03-1982	Chile	L 1-2	Santiago	Fr	OG
30-03	Chile	W 1-0	Lima	Fr	Navarro
18-04	Hungary	W 2-1	Budapest	Fr	Uribe.J 2
25-04	Algeria	D 1-1	Algiers	Fr	Cueto
28-04	France	W 1-0	Paris	Fr	Oblitas
17-05	Rumania	W 2-0	Lima	Fr	Uribe.J, Velasquez
15-06	Cameroon	D 0-0	La Coruna	WCr1	
18-06	Italy	D 1-1	Vigo	WCr1	OG
22-06	Poland	L 1-5	La Coruna	WCr1	La Rosa
18-07-1983	Uruguay	D 1-1	Montevideo	Fr	Caballero
21-07	Chile	L 0-1	Lima	Fr	
3-08	Chile	L 0-2	Arica	Fr	
11-08	Uruguay	D 1-1	Lima	Fr	Navarro
17-08	Colombia	W 1-0	Lima	SCr1	Navarro
21-08	Bolivia	D 1-1	La Paz	SCr1	Navarro
28-08	Colombia	D 2-2	Bogota	SCr1	Malasquez 2
4-09	Bolivia	W 2-1	Lima	SCr1	Leguia, Caballero
5-10	Paraguay	L 0-2	Lima	Fr	
7-10	Paraguay	L 1-4	Asuncion	Fr	Caballero
13-10	Uruguay	L 0-1	Lima	SCsf	
20-10	Uruguay	D 1-1	Montevideo	SCsf	Malasquez
26-02-1984	Honduras	L 1-3	Lima	Fr	Hirano
2-08	Colombia	D 1-1	Medellin	Fr	Lobaton
9-08	Colombia	D 0-0	Lima	Fr	
19-09	Uruguay	L 0-2	Montevideo	Fr	
3-10	Uruguay	L 1-3	Lima	Fr	Lobaton
17-02-1985	Bolivia	W 3-0	Lima	Fr	Navarro 3
24-02	Chile	W 2-1	Santiago	Fr	Velasquez, Navarro
27-02	Uruguay	D 2-2	Montevideo	Fr	Navarro, Velasquez
9-03	Chile	D 1-1	Lima	Fr	Hirano
21-03	Ecuador	W 1-0	Lima	Fr	Hirano
23-04	Uruguay	W 2-1	Lima	Fr	Velasquez, Cueto
28-04	Brazil	W 1-0	Brasilia	Fr	Uribe.J
1-05	Bolivia	D 0-0	Santa Cruz	Fr	
26-05	Colombia	L 0-1	Bogota	WCq	
2-06	Venezuela	W 1-0	San Cristobal	WCq	Uribe.J
9-06	Colombia	D 0-0	Lima	WCq	
16-06	Venezuela	W 4-1	Lima	WCq	Navarro, Barbadillo, Hirano, Cueto
23-06	Argentina	W 1-0	Lima	WCq	Oblitas
30-06	Argentina	D 2-2	Buenos Aires	WCq	Velasquez, Barbadillo
20-09	Mexico	D 0-0	Los Angeles	Fr	
22-09	Mexico	L 0-1	San Jose	Fr	
16-10	Paraguay	L 0-1	Lima	Fr	
27-10	Chile	L 2-4	Santiago	WCq	Navarro 2
3-11	Chile	L 0-1	Lima	WCq	
23-01-1986	South Korea *	W 2-1	Trivandrum	JNC	
28-01	China *	L 1-3	Trivandrum	JNC	
30-01	India *	W 1-0	Trivandrum	JNC	
1-04	Brazil	L 0-4	Sao Luis	Fr	
19-06-1987	Chile	L 1-3	Lima	Fr	Navarro

Date	Opponent	Result	Venue	Comp	Scorers
21-06	Chile	W 2-0	Lima	Fr	Soto, Hirano
24-06	Chile	L 0-1	Santiago	Fr	
27-06	Argentina	D 1-1	Buenos Aires	SCr1	Reyna
4-07	Ecuador	D 1-1	Buenos Aires	SCr1	La Rosa
21-09-1988	Paraguay	L 0-1	Lima	Fr	
25-10	Chile	L 0-2	Arica	Fr	
23-11	Chile	D 1-1	Lima	Fr	Farfan
14-12	Uruguay	L 0-3	Montevideo	Fr	
1-02-1989	Chile	D 0-0	Armenia	Fr	
3-02	Colombia	L 0-1	Pereira	Fr	
10-05	Brazil	L 1-4	Fortaleza	Fr	Torres
15-05	Paraguay	D 1-1	Asuncion	Fr	Requena
18-05	Venezuela	W 2-1	Lima	Fr	Zegarra, Rey
24-05	Brazil	D 1-1	Lima	Fr	Dall'Orso
4-06	United States	L 0-3	New York	Fr	
16-06	Trinidad	L 1-2	Port of Spain	Fr	Manassero
20-06	Ecuador	W 2-1	Port of Spain	Fr	Olaechea, Navarro
25-06	Venezuela	L 1-3	San Cristobal	Fr	Rodriguez.C
1-07	Paraguay	L 2-5	Salvador	SCr1	Hirano, Manassero
3-07	Brazil	D 0-0	Salvador	SCr1	
5-07	Venezuela	D 1-1	Salvador	SCr1	Navarro
9-07	Colombia	D 1-1	Recife	SCr1	Hirano
25-07	Chile	L 1-2	Arica	Fr	Reynoso
20-08	Bolivia	L 1-2	La Paz	WCq	Del Solar
27-08	Uruguay	L 0-2	Lima	WCq	
10-09	Bolivia	L 1-2	Lima	WCq	Gonzalez
24-09	Uruguay	L 0-2	Montevideo	WCq	
6-06-1991	Ecuador	L 0-1	Lima	Fr	
12-06	Uruguay	W 1-0	Lima	Fr	Hirano
20-06	Uruguay	D 0-0	Montevideo	Fr	
25-06	Ecuador	D 2-2	Quito	Fr	Hirano, Rodriguez
6-07	Paraguay	L 0-1	Santiago	SCr1	
8-07	Chile	L 2-4	Concepcion	SCr1	Maestri, Del Solar
12-07	Venezuela	W 5-1	Santiago	SCr1	La Rosa 2, OG, Del Solar, Hirano
14-07	Argentina	L 2-3	Santiago	SCr1	Yanez, Hirano
24-11-1992	Ecuador	D 1-1	Lima	Fr	Ramirez
23-01-1993	Venezuela	D 0-0	Ciudad Guyana	Fr	
27-01	Honduras	D 1-1	Lima	Fr	Carranza
30-01	Belarus	D 1-1	Lima	Fr	Baroni
3-02	Romania	L 0-2	Lima	Fr	
26-05	USA	D 0-0	Mission Viejo	Fr	
30-05	Ecuador	L 0-1	Quito	Fr	
6-06	Bolivia	W 1-0	Lima	Fr	Gonzalez.A
11-06	Venezuela	W 3-1	Arequipa	Fr	Martinez.R, Maestri 2
18-06	Brazil	D 0-0	Cuenca	SCr1	
21-06	Paraguay	D 1-1	Cuenca	SCr1	Del Solar
24-06	Chile	W 1-0	Cuenca	SCr1	Del Solar
27-06	Mexico	L 2-4	Quito	SCqf	Del Solar, Reynoso
13-07	Uruguay	L 1-2	Lima	Fr	Saenz
17-07	Uruguay	L 0-3	Montevideo	Fr	
1-08	Argentina	L 0-1	Lima	WCq	
8-08	Colombia	L 0-1	Lima	WCq	
15-08	Paraguay	L 1-2	Asuncion	WCq	Del Solar
22-08	Argentina	L 1-2	Buenos Aires	WCq	Palacios
29-08	Colombia	L 0-4	Barranquilla	WCq	
5-09	Paraguay	D 2-2	Lima	WCq	Muchotrigo, Soto.J
3-05-1994	Colombia	L 0-1	Miami	Fr	
5-05	Honduras	L 1-2	Miami	Fr	Aguilar
25-05	Chile	L 1-2	Santiago	Fr	OG
8-06	Bolivia	D 0-0	Santa Cruz	Fr	
17-08	Ecuador	W 2-0	Lima	Fr	Palacios, Saenz
21-09	Ecuador	D 0-0	Machala	Fr	
19-10	Uruguay	L 0-1	Lima	Fr	
5-04-1995	Uruguay	L 0-1	Montevideo	Fr	
19-04	Chile	W 6-0	Lima	Fr	Maestri 3, Baroni 3
31-05	Argentina	L 0-1	Mendoza	Fr	
25-06	Slovakia	W 1-0	Lima	Fr	Solano
1-07	Bolivia	W 4-1	Lima	Fr	Ramirez.A 2, Pinillos, Solano
7-07	Colombia	D 1-1	Rivera	SCr1	Palacios
10-07	Brazil	L 0-2	Rivera	SCr1	
13-07	Ecuador	L 1-2	Rivera	SCr1	Tenorio

URUGUAY

Uruguay would seem to be in the dying throes of its status as a world power. Colombia looks set to replace it as one of the big three on the continent, and with a population that is ten times as large, perhaps this should not be too surprising. It would be wrong to write the Uruguayans off, however. Two World Cup titles, two Olympic titles - at a time that they were in effect the world championships - continuing success in the Copa America and eight South American club titles is not a record to be trifled with.

Football in Uruguay is really football in Montevideo, as all the major clubs are located within the city. Montevideo is just across the River Plate estuary from Buenos Aires, and these two cities formed the heartland of South American football at the beginning of the century. Like in Argentina, the English introduced the game to Uruguay. William Poole, an English professor at Montevideo University, formed Albion Football Club in 1886, whilst English workers on the Central Uruguayan Railway formed in 1891 a club that became known by the name of the district within which it was located, Peñarol. 1899 saw the merger of two clubs, Montevideo FC and Defensa, under the name of Nacional, and they along with Peñarol have dominated the game in a manner matched perhaps only by Rangers and Celtic in Scotland. Out of 88 league championships they have won all bar 16 and finished in second spot in all bar 20, a remarkable achievement. In the period from 1915 to 1977, only Rampla Juniors in 1927 and Wanderers in 1931 managed to wrest the title from them.

Given the predictability of much of the domestic fare, international football has always been of prime importance to the Uruguayans. The formation of a football association in 1900, at the behest of Peñarol and Nacional, saw not only the start of a league championship but also the formation of a national selection. On 16 May 1901 a representative side met an Argentine combination in Montevideo for the first ever international match played outside the British Isles.

Uruguay and Argentina have met more times than any other international pairing over the years due to their proximity and relative isolation. The Lipton and Newton Cups were an almost annual event and two trophies donated by each country's Ministry of Education were another source for friendly games. The most notable rivalry, however, has been in the South American Championships.

Though not an official championship, the tournament in 1910 set the standard for future events as both Argentina and Uruguay easily saw off the challenge of Chile to set up a deciding last game. The rivalry even then was huge and the original game had to be postponed until the following day as excited fans burnt down one of the grandstands!

Uruguay lost the match 4-1 to an in-form Argentine side, their goal scored by their most famous player in these early years, José Piendibene, the Peñarol centre-forward who played for the club from 1908 to 1930 and for the national side until 1921. Indeed he was the motivating force behind Uruguay's win in the next South American Championship, held in Buenos Aires again in 1916.

The golden age of Uruguayan football came just after Piendibene's retirement from international football when for over a decade Uruguay reigned supreme in the world. The 'Celeste', as they are known on account of their sky blue shirts, won the equivalent of three world championships with their victories in the 1924 and 1928 Olympic Games and their triumph in the first World Cup in 1930. The side that achieved these incredible feats was in essence the same throughout the whole period.

Captain and mentor was José Nasazzi and he was joined in defence by Pedro Arispe. In front of them they could rely on a midfield known as 'la costilla metalica', the iron curtain, consisting of José Andrade, Lorenzo Fernandez and Alvaro Gestido, whilst their attack was the most potent in the world with four of the most outstanding goalscorers of the time, Hector Castro, Pedro Petrone, Pedro Cea and most importantly Hector Scarone.

The Uruguayans took Europe by storm in 1924, delighting the Parisian crowds with their skill. They never looked in danger, beating Yugoslavia, America, France, Holland and then Switzerland in the final, scoring 20 goals in the process and conceding only two. In 1928 Europe knew what to expect but still could not cope, and just to emphasise the superiority of the River Plate Uruguay met their rivals Argentina in the final. Taken to a replay, the Celeste made no mistake in the second game and were crowned as Olympic Champions for the second time.

The 1930 World Cup triumph was the crowning glory of the side as they won the first edition on their own soil. Despite a poor European turn-out, it is generally agreed that Uruguay would have won whoever had made the trip. In the magnificent new Centenario stadium, built for the World Cup and to celebrate 100 years of independence, neither Peru or Romania were a match for the hosts in the first round. Neither were Yugoslavia in the semi-finals and they were brushed aside 6-1, setting the stage for a repeat of the 1928 Olympic final.

Once again the Uruguayans were triumphant, winning 4-2 after having been 2-1 down at half-time, and José Nasazzi became the first recipient of the Jules Rimet Cup. The victory signalled an extraordinary hiatus in the fixtures of the national side. Uruguay refused to make the journey to Italy to defend their title four years later and also declined to take part in 1938. There was not much action in the South American Championships either during the 1930s, and it was not until the early 1940s that the national side began playing regularly again.

This may have been due in part to the chaos at club level in the early 1930s caused by professionalism. As an issue, professionalism had been simmering since 1922 when Peñarol caused a split in the Association over payments to their players, and the situation was not resolved until 1932 when professionalism was legalised.

Professionalism has been a bitter-sweet pill for Uruguayan football. Without it they would have fallen behind their rivals, but it caused many disputes. All the clubs except Peñarol and Nacional could not afford it, and even the big two were hard pushed to pay the high wages expected by the players. A strike in 1949 lead to a large exodus, primarily to Colombia, whilst in the same year Peñarol would not release their players for the South American Championship, and the national team consequently finished a miserable sixth out of the eight teams taking part.

All was forgiven the following year as the national side, back at full strength, won the World Cup in neighbouring Brazil against all the odds. Bolivia were dispatched in the first round but in the final pool Uruguay were not expected to match the form of the Brazilians, who were scoring freely. The omens were not good after a draw with Spain in the first game, and despite a close win over Sweden, the Uruguayans had to beat Brazil in the Maracana to top the table and win the title.

THE ORDER OF MERIT

		Total			League			Sth Am		
		G	S	B	G	S	B	G	S	B
1	Peñarol	47	41	17	42	35	5	5	6	12
2	Nacional	38	39	20	35	35	12	3	4	8
3	Wanderers	4	4	14	4	4	14	-	-	-
4	River Plate (1902-20)	4	1	1	4	1	1	-	-	-
5	Defensor	3	3	8	3	3	8	-	-	-
6	Rampla Juniors	1	5	13	1	5	13	-	-	-
7	Danubio	1	2	5	1	2	4	-	-	1
8	Bella Vista	1	1	2	1	1	2	-	-	-
	River Plate	-	1	2	-	1	2	-	-	-
10	Central Español	1	-	4	1	-	4	-	-	-
11	Progreso	1	-	-	1	-	-	-	-	-
12	Cerro	-	1	6	-	1	6	-	-	-
13	Universal	-	1	4	-	1	4	-	-	-
14	Albion	-	1	1	-	1	1	-	-	-
15	Fénix	-	-	3	-	-	3	-	-	-
	Liverpool	-	-	3	-	-	3	-	-	-
17	Deutscher	-	-	2	-	-	2	-	-	-
18	Dublin	-	-	1	-	-	1	-	-	-
	Huracán	-	-	1	-	-	1	-	-	-
	Miramar	-	-	1	-	-	1	-	-	-
	Racing	-	-	1	-	-	1	-	-	-
	Uruguay	-	-	1	-	-	1	-	-	-

To the end of the 1994 season

When they fell behind to a Friaca goal early in the second half all looked lost, but in one of the most spirited comebacks of all time, first Schiaffino and then Ghiggia turned the Brazilians' world upside down to secure the victory. Uruguay were World Cup winners for a second time and had yet to lose a match in the tournament.

Four years later they travelled to Europe for the first time in the World Cup, and along with Hungary were regarded as the best team in the tournament. Indeed their semifinal defeat at the hands of the Magyars is often regarded as one of the best games of football ever played and would have made a perfect final. The stars of the early 1950s and the second great team that Uruguay had built were Juan Schiaffino, probably the most famous Uruguayan player ever, Victor Andrade, nephew of the great José Andrade of the 1930 team, Roque Maspoli in goal, Obdulio Varela, at centre-half the linchpin of the side, and Omar Miguez, the team's main goalscorer.

The sides of the 1920s and early 1950s have proved a heavy burden since as successive Uruguayan sides have failed to live up to this pedigree. The 1970 World Cup side containing Luis Cubilla, Ladislao Mazurkiewicz, Juan Mujica, Roberto Matosas and Pedro Rocha came close, but the reputation of that team lay more in the roots of club football than in the national side.

The year 1960 was a crucial one in Uruguayan football, for the new Copa Libertadores gave a new lease of life to both Peñarol and Nacional. All of a sudden they found themselves in the international spotlight. Peñarol have qualified for all but eight of the editions played, whilst Nacional have missed out on only 12, and between them they have appeared in 15 finals, winning eight of them. Peñarol were the inaugural winners and after Independiente are the second most successful club in the history of the tournament. Nacional, winners for the first time in 1971, rank third on the list.

Though often a shop window for the agents of the big European clubs, the Copa Libertadores has added spice to a somewhat predictable Uruguayan championship. All of the major clubs are located within Montevideo and until the 1970s clubs from outside did not take part in the the league. Since the reorganisation of the league the power of both Nacional and Peñarol has been slowly curtailed. Winners every season between 1932 and 1975, their stranglehold was first broken in 1976 by Defensor, but the decline has been most notable since the latter 1980s, including a run of five years when neither team won it.

With many of the best players moving abroad due to the perilous financial state of most Uruguayan clubs, the national team has struggled to retain its position at the top of the football hierarchy. Despite winning the 1983 and 1987 South American Championships thanks to players of the calibre of Enzo Francescoli and Carlos Aguilera, and repeating the feat on home territory in 1995 to give renewed hope for the future, the famous Celeste will have their work cut out not to be remembered only as the country that won a couple of world championships in the distant past.

Population: 3,033,000
Area, sq km: 176,215
% in urban areas: 86%
Capital city: Montevideo

Asociación Uruguaya de Fútbol
Guayabo 1531
Montevideo
Uruguay
Tel: + 598 2 407101 / 407106
Fax: + 598 2 407873

Year of formation	1900
Affiliation to FIFA	1923
Affiliation to CONME	1916
Registered clubs	1102
Registered players	163 600
Professional players	740
Registered coaches	378
Registered referees	132
National stadium	Estadio Centenario, Montevideo 75 000
National colours	Sky Blue/Black/Black
Reserve colours	White/White/White
Season	February - December

THE RECORD

WORLD CUP

1930	QT Automatic - Final Tournament/Winners
1934	Did not enter
1938	Did not enter
1950	QT W-O in group 8 - Final Tournament/Winners
1954	QT Automatic - Final Tournament/Semi-finalists/ 4th place
1958	QT 2nd/3 in group 3
1962	QT 1st/2 in group 2 - Final Tournament/1st round
1966	QT 1st/3 in group 1 - Final Tournament/Quarter-finalists
1970	QT 1st/3 in group 3 - Final Tournament/Semi-finalists/ 4th place
1974	QT 1st/3 in group 1 - Final Tournament/1st round
1978	QT 2nd/3 in group 2
1982	QT 2nd/3 in group 2
1986	QT 1st/3 in group 2 - Final Tournament/2nd round
1990	QT 1st/3 in group 1 - Final Tournament/2nd round
1994	QT 3rd/5 in group 2

SOUTH AMERICAN CHAMPIONSHIP

1910	2/3
1916	1/4 - Winners
1917	1/4 - Winners
1919	2/4
1920	1/4 - Winners
1921	3/4
1922	3/5
1923	1/4 - Winners
1924	1/4 - Winners
1925	-
1926	1/5 - Winners
1927	2/4
1929	3/4
1935	1/4 - Winners
1937	4/6
1939	2/5
1941	2/5
1942	1/7 - Winners
1945	4/7
1946	4/6
1947	3/8
1949	6/8
1953	3/7
1955	4/6
1956	1/6 - Winners
1957	3/7
1959	6/7
1959	1/5 - Winners
1963	-
1967	1/6 - Winners
1975	4/10 - Semi-finalists
1979	6/10 - 1st round
1983	1/10 - Winners
1987	1/10 - Winners
1989	2/10 - Second round
1991	5/10 - 1st round
1993	5=/12 - Quarter-finals
1995	1/12 - Winners

SOUTH AMERICAN CLUB TOURNAMENTS

Copa Libertadores
Winners - Penarol 1960 1961 1966 1982 1987, Nacional 1971 1980 1988
Finalists - Penarol 1962 1965 1970 1983, Nacional 1964 1967 1969

Super Copa
Finalists - Nacional 1990

CONMEBOL Cup
Finalists - Peñarol 1993 1994

CLUB DIRECTORY

MONTEVIDEO (Pop. - 1,550,000)

Club Atlético Bella Vista (1920)
Parque José Nasazzi 7,000 – Gold & white halves/Blue

Central Español FC (1905)
Parque Palermo 7,000 – Red & white stripes/Blue
Previous name - Central FC 1905-71

Club Atlético Cerro (1922)
Luis Troccoli 40,000 – Sky blue & white stripes/Blue

Danubio FC (1932)
Jardins del Hipodromo 18,000 – White with black sash/White

Club Atlético Defensor-Sporting (1913)
Luis Franzzini 15,000 – Violet/White
Previous names - Merged with Sporting Club de Montevideo in 1989

Liverpool FC (1915)
Belvedere 10,000 – Black & blue stripes/White

Club Nacional de Fútbol (1899)
Parque Central 15,000 – White/Blue, red & blue trim

Club Atlético Peñarol (1891)
Las Acacias, 'Pocitos' 10,000 – Black & yellow stripes/Black
Previous names - Central Uruguayan Railways Cricket Club 1891-1913

Club Atletico Progreso (1917)
Parque Abraham Paladino 7,000 – Yellow & red stripes/Black

Club Atletico River Plate (1932)
Parque Federico Saroldi 10,000 – Red & white stripes/White
A club also called River Plate existed from 1902-20, winning the championship in 1908 1910 1913 & 1914

Rampla Juniors FC (1914)
Olimpico 10,000 – Green & black stripes/Black

Montevideo Wanderers FC (1902)
Parque Alfredo Viera 12,000 – Black & white stripes/Black

All use Estadio Centenario when necessary

URUGUAYAN AMATEUR LEAGUE CHAMPIONSHIP

1900	Peñarol 12 Albion 8 Uruguay 2
1901	Peñarol 15 Nacional 12 Albion 8
1902	Nacional 20 Peñarol 16 Deutscher 9
1903	Nacional 24 Peñarol 22 Deutscher 10
1904	-
1905	Peñarol 16 Nacional 12 Wanderers 10
1906	Wanderers 18 Peñarol 14 Nacional 10
1907	Peñarol 17 Wanderers 13 Nacional 12
1908	River Plate 31 Nacional 26 Dublin 24
1909	Wanderers 35 Peñarol 34 River Plate 32
1910	River Plate 26 Peñarol 24 Nacional 22
1911	Peñarol 25 River Plate 17 Wanderers 17
1912	Nacional 25 Peñarol 19 Wanderers 18
1913	River Plate 22 Nacional 19 Central 14
1914	River Plate 26 Peñarol 24 Nacional 21
1915	Nacional 29 Peñarol 27 Universal 23
1916	Nacional 30 Peñarol 18 Wanderers 17
1917	Nacional 34 Peñarol 32 Universal 21
1918	Peñarol 32 Nacional 31 Universal 22
1919	Nacional 31 Universal 27 Peñarol 26
1920	Nacional 40 Peñarol 36 Central 25
1921	Peñarol 39 Nacional 37 Universal 31

1922	Nacional 36 Wanderers 35 Peñarol 28
1923	Nacional 37 Rampla Juniors 33 Bella Vista 30
1923	Wanderers
1924	Nacional 39 Bella Vista 33 Rampla Juniors 29
1924	Peñarol
1925	-
1926	Peñarol
1927	Rampla Juniors 57 Peñarol 54 Wanderers 50
1928	Peñarol 45 Rampla Juniors 37 Nacional 35
1929	Peñarol 47 Nacional 36 Rampla Juniors 29
1930	-
1931	Wanderers 39 Nacional 37 Rampla Juniors 31

URUGUAYAN PROFESSIONAL LEAGUE CHAMPIONSHIP

1932	Peñarol 40 Rampla Juniors 35 Nacional 32
1933	Nacional 46 Peñarol 46 Rampla Juniors 32
1934	Nacional 41 Peñarol 38 Wanderers 35
1935	Peñarol 31 Nacional 29 Wanderers 25
1936	Peñarol 30 Nacional 27 Rampla Juniors 24
1937	Peñarol 29 Nacional 28 Wanderers 21
1938	Peñarol 34 Nacional 31 Central 25
1939	Nacional 28 Peñarol 28 Wanderers 22
1940	Nacional 35 Rampla Juniors 25 Wanderers 24
1941	Nacional 40 Peñarol 31 Rampla Juniors 22
1942	Nacional 28 Peñarol 25 Wanderers 24
1943	Nacional 32 Peñarol 27 Miramar 17
1944	Peñarol 27 Nacional 27 Defensor 25
1945	Peñarol 31 Nacional 25 Defensor 22
1946	Nacional 32 Peñarol 28 River Plate 21
1947	Nacional 27 Peñarol 21 Rampla Juniors 21
1948	-
1949	Peñarol 34 Nacional 28 Rampla Juniors 23
1950	Nacional 30 Peñarol 28 Rampla Juniors 22
1951	Peñarol 29 Nacional 27 Rampla Juniors 22
1952	Nacional 31 Peñarol 31 Rampla Juniors 19
1953	Peñarol 32 Nacional 25 Rampla Juniors 22
1954	Peñarol 32 Danubio 24 Nacional 22
1955	Nacional 31 Peñarol 27 Danubio 18
1956	Nacional 32 Peñarol 29 Cerro 24
1957	Nacional 24 Peñarol 21 Defensor 20
1958	Peñarol 24 Nacional 23 Rampla Juniors 23
1959	Peñarol 26 Nacional 26 Racing 22
1960	Peñarol 28 Cerro 28 Nacional 24
1961	Peñarol 30 Nacional 27 Defensor 23
1962	Peñarol 33 Nacional 27 Fénix 18
1963	Nacional 31 Peñarol 30 Wanderers 21
1964	Peñarol 34 Rampla Juniors 22 Nacional 21
1965	Peñarol 32 Nacional 27 Cerro 25
1966	Nacional 28 Peñarol 26 Cerro 23
1967	Peñarol 33 Nacional 27 Cerro 21
1968	Peñarol 33 Nacional 27 Cerro 21
1969	Nacional 43 Peñarol 39 River Plate 28
1970	Nacional 45 Peñarol 38 Huracan 30
1971	Nacional 40 Peñarol 39 Liverpool 34
1972	Nacional 36 Peñarol 28 Defensor 26
1973	Peñarol 35 Nacional 29 Danubio 28
1974	Peñarol 36 Nacional 31 Liverpool 31
1975	Peñarol 38 Nacional 29 Liverpool 28
1976	Defensor 32 Peñarol 31 Nacional 28
1977	Nacional 36 Peñarol 35 Defensor 30
1978	Peñarol 39 Nacional 36 Fénix 24
1979	Peñarol 41 Nacional 38 Fénix 27
1980	Nacional 41 Wanderers 35 Peñarol 32
1981	Peñarol 44 Nacional 41 Wanderers 35
1982	Peñarol 39 Defensor 36 Nacional 32
1983	Nacional 38 Danubio 29 Defensor 29
1984	Central Español 35 Peñarol 34 Nacional 32
1985	Peñarol 32 Wanderers 28 Cerro 27
1986	Nacional * 35 Peñarol 34 Central Español 28
1987	Defensor 33 Nacional 30 Bella Vista 28
1988	Danubio 40 Peñarol 31 Defensor 31
1989	Progreso 20 Nacional 15 Peñarol 15
1990	Bella Vista 39 Nacional 32 Peñarol 31
1991	Defensor 34 Nacional 33 Wanderers 31
1992	Nacional 33 River Plate 28 Danubio 27
1993	Peñarol 36 Defensor 34 Danubio 32
1994	Peñarol..................1-1 1-1 2-1 ....Defensor

Play-offs

1933	Nacional	0-0 0-0 3-2	Peñarol
1939	Nacional	3-2	Peñarol
1944	Peñarol	0-0 3-2	Nacional
1952	Nacional	4-2	Peñarol
1959	Peñarol	2-0	Nacional
1960	Peñarol	3-1	Cerro
1986	Peñarol	0-0 4-3p	Nacional

* Nacional agreed to play-off if Peñarol finished less than two points behind them after Peñarol deducted two points

LIGUILLA PRE-LIBERTADORES

1974	Peñarol
1975	Peñarol
1976	Defensor
1977	Peñarol
1978	Peñarol
1979	Defensor
1980	Peñarol
1981	Defensor
1982	Nacional
1983	Danubio
1984	Peñarol
1985	Peñarol
1986	Peñarol
1987	Wanderers
1988	Peñarol
1989	Defensor
1990	Nacional
1991	Defensor
1992	Nacional
1993	Nacional
1994	Peñarol

LEADING INTERNATIONAL GOALSCORERS

29 Hector Scarone	(Nacional,Barcelona, Internazionale)	1917-1930
28 Angel Romano		1911-1927
26 Omar Miguez		1950-1958
24 Pedro Petrone	(Nacional, Fiorentina)	1923-1930
22 Carlos Aguilera	(Nacional, Racing, Peñarol, Genoa,Torino)	1983-
21 Fernando Morena	(Peñarol,Rayo Vallecano, Flamengo)	1971-1978
20 Hector Castro	(Nacional)	1926-1935

LEADING INTERNATIONAL APPEARANCES

78 Rodolfo Rodriguez		1976-1986
69 Angel Romano		1911-1927
65 Enzo Francescoli	(River Plate,Matra Racing, Marseille,Cagliari,River Plate)	1983-
60 Jorge Barrios		1980-
59 Carlos Aguilera	(Nacional, Racing, Peñarol, Genoa,Torino)	1983-
56 Nelson Gutierrez	(Peñarol,River Plate,Lazio, Verona)	1983-1990
55 William Martinez		1950-1965

INTERNATIONAL MATCHES PLAYED BY URUGUAY

Date	Opponent	Result	Venue	Comp	Scorers
16-05-1901	Argentina	L 2-3	Montevideo	Fr	Cespedes.B, Poole
20-07-1902	Argentina	L 0-6	Montevideo	Fr	
13-09-1903	Argentina	W 3-2	Buenos Aires	Fr	Cespedes.B 2, Cespedes.C
15-08-1905	Argentina	D 0-0	Buenos Aires	LC	
15-08-1906	Argentina	L 0-2	Montevideo	LC	
21-10	Argentina	L 1-2	Buenos Aires	NC	OG
15-08-1907	Argentina	L 1-2	Buenos Aires	LC	Zibecchi
6-10	Argentina	L 1-2	Montevideo	NC	Zumarin
15-08-1908	Argentina	D 2-2	Montevideo	LC	Bertone.J, Zumaran
13-09	Argentina	L 1-2	Buenos Aires	NC	Brachi
4-10	Argentina	W 1-0	Buenos Aires	MEA	Brachi
15-08-1909	Argentina	L 1-2	Buenos Aires	LC	Zumaran
19-09	Argentina	D 2-2	Montevideo	NC	Raymonda, Buck
10-10	Argentina	L 1-3	Buenos Aires	MEA	Raymonda
29-05-1910	Chile	W 3-0	Buenos Aires	SC	Piendibene, Brachi, Buck
12-06	Argentina	L 1-4	Buenos Aires	SC	Piendibene
15-08	Argentina	W 3-1	Montevideo	LC	Dacal, Scarone.C, Zibecchi
13-11	Argentina	D 1-1	Buenos Aires	MEA	Piendibene
27-11	Argentina	W 6-2	Buenos Aires	MEA	Seoanne 2, Scarone.C 2, Piendibene, Quaglia
30-04-1911	Argentina *	L 1-2	Montevideo	Fr	Canavessi
15-08	Argentina	W 2-0	Buenos Aires	LC	Piendibene, Dacal
17-09	Argentina	L 2-3	Montevideo	NC	Romano, Canavessi
8-10	Argentina	D 1-1	Montevideo	MEU	Piendibene
22-10	Argentina	L 0-2	Buenos Aires	MEA	
29-10	Argentina	W 3-0	Montevideo	MEU	Piendibene 2, Canavessi
25-02-1912	Argentina *	L 0-2	Buenos Aires	Fr	
15-08	Argentina	W 2-0	Montevideo	LC	Scarone.C, Dacal
25-08	Argentina	W 3-0	Montevideo	MEU	Scarone.C, Romano, Dacal
22-09	Argentina	W 1-0	Buenos Aires	MEA	Piendibene
6-10	Argentina	D 3-3	Buenos Aires	NC	Scarone.C, Romano, Dacal
1-12	Argentina	L 1-3	Montevideo	MC	Scarone.C
27-04-1913	Argentina *	D 0-0	Buenos Aires	Fr	
15-06	Argentina	D 1-1	Buenos Aires	SPC	Dacal
9-07	Argentina	L 1-2	Buenos Aires	SPC	Piendibene
13-07	Argentina *	W 5-4	Montevideo	Fr	
15-08	Argentina	L 0-4	Buenos Aires	LC	
31-08	Argentina	L 0-2	Buenos Aires	MEA	
28-09	Argentina *	L 0-4	Buenos Aires	Fr	
5-10	Argentina	W 1-0	Montevideo	MEU	Vallarino
26-10	Argentina	W 1-0	Montevideo	NC	Gorla
30-08-1914	Argentina	W 3-2	Montevideo	MEU	Vallarino, Dacal, OG
13-09	Argentina	L 1-2	Buenos Aires	MEA	Vallarino
18-07-1915	Argentina	L 2-3	Montevideo	MEU	Dacal, Lazaro
15-08	Argentina	L 1-2	Buenos Aires	LC	Piendibene
12-09	Argentina	W 2-0	Montevideo	NC	Piendibene 2
2-07-1916	Chile	W 4-0	Buenos Aires	SC	Piendibene 2, Gradin 2
12-07	Brazil	W 2-1	Buenos Aires	SC	Gradin, Tognola
14-07	Chile	W 4-1	Montevideo	Fr	
17-07	Argentina	D 0-0	Buenos Aires	SC	
18-07	Brazil	L 0-1	Montevideo	Fr	
15-08	Argentina	L 1-3	Buenos Aires	NC	Farinasso
15-08	Argentina	L 1-2	Montevideo	LC	Gradin
1-10	Argentina	L 0-1	Montevideo	MEU	
1-10	Argentina	L 2-7	Buenos Aires	MEA	Mongelar, Harley
29-10	Argentina	W 3-1	Montevideo	Fr	
18-07-1917	Argentina	L 0-2	Montevideo	MEU	
15-08	Argentina	L 0-1	Buenos Aires	LC	
2-09	Argentina	W 1-0	Montevideo	NC	Scarone.C
30-09	Chile	W 4-0	Montevideo	SC	Romano 2, Scarone.C 2
7-10	Brazil	W 4-0	Montevideo	SC	Romano 2, Scaorne.H, Scarone.C
14-10	Argentina	W 1-0	Montevideo	SC	Scarone.H
16-10	Brazil	W 3-1	Montevideo	Fr	
18-07-1918	Argentina	D 1-1	Montevideo	MEU	Gradin
28-07	Argentina	W 3-1	Montevideo	MEU	Romano 2, Gradin
15-08	Argentina	D 0-0	Buenos Aires	MEA	
25-08	Argentina	L 1-2	Buenos Aires	MEA	Somma
20-09	Argentina	D 1-1	Montevideo	LC	Perez.J
29-09	Argentina	L 0-2	Buenos Aires	NC	

Date	Opponent	Result	Venue	Comp	Scorers
13-05-1919	Argentina	W 3-2	Rio de Janeiro	SC	Scarone.C, Scarone.H, Gradin
17-05	Chile	W 2-0	Rio de Janeiro	SC	Scarone.C, Perez.J
25-05	Brazil	D 2-2	Rio de Janeiro	SC	Gradin, Scarone.C
29-05	Brazil	L 0-1	Rio de Janeiro	SCpo	
18-07	Argentina	W 4-1	Montevideo	MEU	Scarone.H 2, Perez.O, Romano
24-08	Argentina	W 2-1	Montevideo	NC	Romano, Villar
7-09	Argentina	W 2-1	Buenos Aires	LC	Scarone.H 2
19-10	Argentina	L 1-6	Buenos Aires	MEA	Fraga
7-12	Argentina	W 4-2	Montevideo	Fr	
18-07-1920	Argentina	W 2-0	Montevideo	MEU	Scarone.H, Romano
25-07	Argentina	W 3-1	Buenos Aires	NC	Piendibene, Romano, Somma
8-08	Argentina	L 0-1	Buenos Aires	MEA	
12-09	Argentina	D 1-1	Viña del Mar	SC	Piendebene
18-09	Brazil	W 6-0	Viña del Mar	SC	Romano, Somma, Perez.J, Campolo, Urdinarian
26-09	Chile	W 2-1	Viña del Mar	SC	Romano, Perez.J
9-10-1921	Paraguay	L 1-2	Buenos Aires	SC	Piendibene
23-10	Brazil	W 2-1	Buenos Aires	SC	Romano 2
30-10	Argentina	L 0-1	Buenos Aires	SC	
2-11	Paraguay	W 4-2	Montevideo	Fr	Buffoni 2, Campolo, Foglino
22-01-1922	Argentina	W 3-1	Buenos Aires	Fr	
22-07	Argentina	D 2-2	Montevideo	Fr	
27-08	Argentina	D 3-3	Buenos Aires	Fr	
23-09	Chile	W 2-0	Rio de Janeiro	SC	Urdinaran, Heguy
1-10	Brazil	D 0-0	Rio de Janeiro	SC	
8-10	Argentina	W 1-0	Rio de Janeiro	SC	Buffoni
12-10	Paraguay	L 0-1	Rio de Janeiro	SC	
22-10	Argentina	L 2-3	Buenos Aires	Fr	
11-11	Argentina	L 0-4	La Plata	Fr	
12-11	Argentina	W 1-0	Montevideo	LC	Romano
10-12	Argentina	W 1-0	Montevideo	MEU	Scarone.C
17-12	Argentina	D 2-2	Buenos Aires	NC	Scarone.C, Saldombide
25-05-1923	Argentina	W 2-0	Montevideo	Fr	
24-06	Argentina	D 0-0	Buenos Aires	LC	
15-07	Argentina	D 2-2	Buenos Aires	MEA	Romano, Oliveiri
22-07	Argentina	D 2-2	Montevideo	MEU	Romano, Saldombide
25-08	Argentina	D 1-1	Montevideo	Fr	
30-09	Argentina	L 0-2	Montevideo	MEU	
4-11	Paraguay	W 2-0	Montevideo	SC	Scarone.H, Petrone
25-11	Brazil	W 2-1	Montevideo	SC	Petrone, Cea
25-11	Chile	W 2-1	Montevideo	Fr	
2-12	Argentina	W 2-0	Montevideo	SC	Petrone, Somma
8-12	Argentina	W 3-2	Buenos Aires	Fr	
25-05-1924	Argentina	L 0-4	Buenos Aires	NC	
25-05	Argentina	W 2-0	Montevideo	Fr	
26-05	Yugoslavia	W 7-0	Paris	OGr1	Petrone 2, Cea 2, Scarone.H, Vidal
29-05	United States	W 3-0	Paris	OGr2	Petrone 3
1-06	France	W 5-1	Paris	OGqf	Petrone 2, Scarone.H 2, Romano
6-06	Holland	W 2-1	Paris	OGsf	Cea, Scarone.H
9-06	Switzerland	W 3-0	Paris	OGf	Petrone, Cea, Romano
10-08	Argentina	D 0-0	Buenos Aires	Fr	
31-08	Argentina	L 2-3	Montevideo	MEU	
21-09	Argentina	D 1-1	Montevideo	Fr	Petrone
2-10	Argentina	L 1-2	Buenos Aires	Fr	Cea
12-10	Chile	W 1-0	Santiago	Fr	
19-10	Chile	W 5-0	Montevideo	SC	Petrone 3, Romano, Zingone
26-10	Paraguay	W 3-1	Montevideo	SC	Petrone, Romano, Cea
2-11	Argentina	D 0-0	Montevideo	SC	
16-11	Argentina	W 1-0	Montevideo	Fr	
5-01-1925	Argentina	L 0-1	Buenos Aires	Fr	
14-07	Paraguay	L 0-1	Montevideo	Fr	
18-07	Paraguay	L 0-1	Montevideo	Fr	
15-08	Paraguay	L 0-1	Asuncion	Fr	
19-08	Paraguay	W 1-0	Asuncion	Fr	Fernandez.L
23-08	Paraguay	D 0-0	Asuncion	Fr	
17-10-1926	Chile	W 3-1	Santiago	SC	Borjas, Castro.H, Scarone.H
24-10	Argentina	W 2-0	Santiago	SC	Borjas, Scarone.H
28-10	Bolivia	W 6-0	Santiago	SC	Scarone.H 5, Romano
1-11	Paraguay	W 6-1	Santiago	SC	Castro.H 4, Saldombide 2
14-07-1927	Argentina	L 0-1	Montevideo	NC	
30-08	Argentina	W 1-0	Buenos Aires	LC	Scarone.H
1-11	Peru	W 4-0	Lima	SC	Sacco 2, Castro.H, OG

6-11	Bolivia	W 9-0	Lima	SC	Petrone 3, Figueroa 3, Arremon, Castro.H, Scarone.H
20-11	Argentina	L 2-3	Lima	SC	Scarone.H 2
10-12	Chile	W 3-2	Viña del Mar	Fr	Scarone.H, Castro.H, Petrone
30-05-1928	Holland	W 2-0	Amsterdam	OGr1	Scarone.H, Urdinaran
3-06	Germany	W 4-1	Amsterdam	OGqf	Petrone 3, Castro.H
7-06	Italy	W 3-2	Amsterdam	OGsf	Cea, Scarone.H, Campolo
10-06	Argentina	D 1-1	Amsterdam	OGf	Petrone
13-06	Argentina	W 2-1	Amsterdam	OGf	Figueroa, Scarone.H
15-08	Paraguay	L 1-3	Asuncion	Fr	
19-08	Paraguay	D 1-1	Asuncion	Fr	
30-08	Argentina	L 0-1	Buenos Aires	NC	
21-09	Argentina	D 2-2	Montevideo	LC	Petrone, Piriz
16-06-1929	Argentina	L 0-2	Buenos Aires	Fr	
16-06	Argentina	D 1-1	Montevideo	Fr	Carbone
20-09	Argentina	W 2-1	Montevideo	NC	Castro.H, Fernandez.L
28-09	Argentina	D 0-0	Buenos Aires	LC	
1-11	Paraguay	L 0-3	Buenos Aires	SC	
11-11	Peru	W 4-1	Buenos Aires	SC	Fernandez.E 3, Andrade.J
17-11	Argentina	L 0-2	Buenos Aires	SC	
25-05-1930	Argentina	D 1-1	Buenos Aires	NC	Petrone
18-07	Peru	W 1-0	Montevideo	WCr1	Castro.H
22-07	Romania	W 4-0	Montevideo	WCr1	Dorado, Scarone.H, Anselmo, Cea
27-07	Yugoslavia	W 6-1	Montevideo	WCsf	Cea 3, Anselmo 2, Iriarte
30-07	Argentina	W 4-2	Montevideo	WCf	Dorado, Cea, Iriarte, Castro
6-09-1931	Brazil	L 0-2	Rio de Janeiro	RBC	
15-05-1932	Argentina	L 0-2	Buenos Aires	Fr	
18-05	Argentina	W 1-0	Montevideo	Fr	Dorado
4-12	Brazil	L 1-2	Montevideo	RBC	Castro.H
21-01-1933	Argentina	W 2-1	Montevideo	Fr	Fernandez.E, Haebrili
5-02	Argentina	L 1-4	Buenos Aires	Fr	Matta
14-12	Argentina	L 0-1	Montevideo	Fr	
18-07-1934	Argentina	D 2-2	Montevideo	Fr	Garcia.J, Ciocca
15-08	Argentina	L 0-1	Buenos Aires	Fr	
13-01-1935	Peru	W 1-0	Lima	SC	Castro.H
18-01	Chile	W 2-1	Lima	SC	Ciocca 2
20-01	Argentina *	D 2-2	Buenos Aires	Fr	Amarillo, Castaldo
27-01	Argentina	W 3-0	Lima	SC	Castro.H, Taboada, Ciocca
18-07	Argentina	D 1-1	Montevideo	HGC	Piriz
15-08	Argentina	L 0-3	Buenos Aires	JMC	
9-08-1936	Argentina	L 0-1	Buenos Aires	JMC	
20-09	Argentina	W 2-1	Montevideo	HGC	Lago, Villdonica
2-01-1937	Paraguay	L 2-4	Buenos Aires	SC	Varela.S 2
6-01	Peru	W 4-2	Buenos Aires	SC	Varela.S 2, Camaiti 2
10-01	Chile	L 0-3	Buenos Aires	SC	
19-01	Brazil	L 2-3	Buenos Aires	SC	Piriz, Villadonica
23-01	Argentina	W 3-2	Buenos Aires	SC	Piriz, Varela.S, Ithurbide
10-10	Argentina	L 0-3	Montevideo	NC	
11-11	Argentina	L 1-5	Buenos Aires	LC	Muniz
18-06-1938	Argentina	L 0-1	Buenos Aires	JMC	
12-10	Argentina	L 2-3	Montevideo	HGC	Varela.S, Ciocca
22-01-1939	Ecuador	W 6-0	Lima	SC	Varela.S 3, Lago 2, Porta
29-01	Chile	W 3-2	Lima	SC	Lago, Chirmini, Camaiti
5-02	Paraguay	W 3-1	Lima	SC	Porta, Lago, Varela.S
12-02	Peru	L 1-2	Lima	SC	Porta
12-03-1940	Chile	W 3-2	Montevideo	Fr	Lago 2, Varela.S
24-03	Brazil	W 4-3	Rio de Janeiro	RBC	Varela.S 2, Perez.R, Rodriguez.R
31-03	Brazil	D 1-1	Rio de Janeiro	RBC	Varela.S
18-07	Argentina	W 3-0	Montevideo	HGC	Rivero 2, Porta
15-08	Argentina	L 0-5	Buenos Aires	JMC	
9-02-1941	Ecuador	W 6-0	Santiago	SC	Rivero 3, Gambetta, Porta, OG
16-02	Chile	W 2-0	Santiago	SC	Rivero, Magliano
23-02	Argentina	L 0-1	Santiago	SC	
26-02	Peru	W 2-0	Santiago	SC	Riephoff, Varela.O
10-01-1942	Chile	W 6-1	Montevideo	SC	Castro.L 2, Varela.O, Ciocca, Zapirain, Porta
18-01	Ecuador	W 7-0	Montevideo	SC	Varela.S 3, Porta 2, Zapirain, Gambetta
24-01	Brazil	W 1-0	Montevideo	SC	Varela.S
28-01	Paraguay	W 3-1	Montevideo	SC	Varela.S, Ciocca, Porta
1-02	Peru	W 3-0	Montevideo	SC	Castro.L, Chirmini, Porta
7-02	Argentina	W 1-0	Montevideo	SC	Zapirain
25-05	Argentina	L 1-4	Buenos Aires	NC	Zapirain
25-08	Argentina	D 1-1	Montevideo	LC	Alvarez

6-01-1943	Argentina *	L 0-1	Buenos Aires	Fr	
9-01	Argentina *	W 6-2	Montevideo	Fr	Garcia.A 2, Varela.O, Zapirain 2, Porta
28-03	Argentina	D 3-3	Buenos Aires	JMC	Medina 2, Castro.L
4-04	Argentina	L 0-1	Montevideo	HGC	
5-01-1944	Argentina *	L 1-3	Montevideo	Fr	Castro.L
8-01	Argentina *	D 3-3	Buenos Aires	Fr	Vazquez 2, Medina
29-01	Argentina *	W 2-1	Montevideo	Fr	Zapirain, Medina
29-01	Argentina *	L 2-6	Buenos Aires	Fr	Porta, Chirmini
14-05	Brazil	L 1-6	Rio de Janeiro	Fr	Tejera
17-05	Brazil	L 0-4	Sao Paulo	Fr	
24-01-1945	Ecuador	W 5-1	Santiago	SC	Garcia.A 3, Varela.O, Porta
28-01	Colombia	W 7-0	Santiago	SC	Garcia.A 2, Garcia.J 2, Ortiz, Porta, Riephoff
7-02	Brazil	L 0-3	Santiago	SC	
15-02	Bolivia	W 2-0	Santiago	SC	Porta, Falero
18-02	Chile	L 0-1	Santiago	SC	
25-02	Argentina	L 0-1	Santiago	SC	
18-07	Argentina	D 2-2	Montevideo	LC	Varela.O 2
15-08	Argentina	L 2-6	Buenos Aires	NC	Ortiz, Falero
29-12	Argentina *	D 1-1	Montevideo	Fr	Schiaffino
5-01-1946	Brazil	W 4-3	Montevideo	RBC	Riephoff 2, Medina, Volpi
9-01	Brazil	D 1-1	Montevideo	RBC	Medina
16-01	Chile	W 1-0	Buenos Aires	SC	Medina
23-01	Brazil	L 3-4	Buenos Aires	SC	Medina, Volpi, Vasquez
29-01	Bolivia	W 5-0	Buenos Aires	SC	Medina 4, Garcia.J
2-02	Argentina	L 1-3	Buenos Aires	SC	Riephoff
8-02	Paraguay	L 1-2	Buenos Aires	SC	OG
2-03-1947	Argentina *	L 1-2	Buenos Aires	Fr	Garcia.J
9-03	Argentina *	D 4-4	Montevideo	Fr	Godart 2, Claveres, Castro.E
29-03	Brazil	D 0-0	Sao Paulo	RBC	
1-04	Brazil	L 2-3	Rio de Janeiro	RBC	Medina, Pini
4-04	Brazil	D 1-1	Rio de Janeiro	Fr	Castro.L
2-12	Colombia	W 2-0	Guayaquil	SC	Falero, Britos
6-12	Chile	W 6-0	Guayaquil	SC	Garcia.J 2, Magliano 2, Britos, Sarro
9-12	Bolivia	W 3-0	Guayaquil	SC	Sarro, Falero, Riephoff
13-12	Paraguay	L 2-4	Guayaquil	SC	Magliano, Britos
16-12	Ecuador	W 6-1	Guayaquil	SC	Falero 2, Magliano, Puente, Sarro, Garcia.J
25-12	Peru	W 1-0	Guayaquil	SC	Falero
28-12	Argentina	L 1-3	Guayaquil	SC	Britos
4-04-1948	Brazil	D 1-1	Montevideo	RBC	Falero
11-04	Brazil	W 4-2	Montevideo	RBC	Magliano, Falero, Britos
18-05	Argentina *	L 0-1	Montevideo	Fr	
25-05	Argentina *	W 2-0	Buenos Aires	Fr	Gambetta, Magliano
13-04-1949	Ecuador	W 3-2	Rio de Janeiro	SC	Castro.R 2, Moreno.N
17-04	Bolivia	L 2-3	Rio de Janeiro	SC	Moll, Suarez.E
20-04	Paraguay	W 2-1	Sao Paulo	SC	Garcia.JM 2
24-04	Colombia	D 2-2	Sao Paulo	SC	Martinez.M, Ayala
30-04	Brazil	L 1-5	Rio de Janeiro	SC	Castro.R
4-05	Peru	L 3-4	Rio de Janeiro	SC	Castro.R, Ayala, Moll
8-05	Chile	L 1-3	Belo Horizonte	SC	Ayala
7-04-1950	Chile	W 5-1	Santiago	Fr	Carambula 2, Romero.C, Perez.J, OG
9-04	Chile	L 1-2	Santiago	Fr	Romero.C
30-04	Paraguay	L 2-3	Rio de Janeiro	Fr	Schiaffino, Miguez
6-05	Brazil	W 4-3	Sao Paulo	RBC	Schiaffino 2, Miguez 2
14-05	Brazil	L 2-3	Rio de Janeiro	RBC	Vilamide
18-05	Brazil	L 0-1	Rio de Janeiro	RBC	
2-07	Bolivia	W 8-0	Belo Horizonte	WCr1	Schiaffino 4, Miguez 2, Vidal, Ghiggia
9-07	Spain	D 2-2	Sao Paulo	WCr2	Ghiggia, Varela.O
13-07	Sweden	W 3-2	Sao Paulo	WCr2	Miguez 2, Ghiggia
16-07	Brazil	W 2-1	Rio de Janeiro	WCf	Schiaffino, Ghiggia
23-03-1952	Mexico	W 3-1	Santiago	PAC	Miguez, Perez.J
30-03	Peru	W 5-2	Santiago	PAC	Miguez 3, Perez.J, Vidal
6-04	Panama	W 6-1	Santiago	PAC	Abbadie 3, Santamaria, Miguez, Britos
13-04	Chile	L 0-2	Santiago	PAC	
16-04	Brazil	L 2-4	Santiago	PAC	Ghigggia, Loureiro
25-02-1953	Bolivia	W 2-0	Lima	SC	Romero.C, Puente
1-03	Chile	L 2-3	Lima	SC	Morel, Balseiro
12-03	Paraguay	D 2-2	Lima	SC	Romero.C, Pelaez
15-03	Brazil	L 0-1	Lima	SC	
23-03	Ecuador	W 6-0	Lima	SC	Mendez, Pelaez, Morel, Romero, Puente, Balseiro
28-03	Peru	W 3-0	Lima	SC	Pelaez 2, Romero.C
31-05	England	W 2-1	Montevideo	Fr	Miguez, Abaddie

Date	Opponent	Result	Venue	Comp	Scorers
10-04-1954	Paraguay	L 1-4	Montevideo	Fr	Miguez
18-04	Paraguay	D 1-1	Asuncion	Fr	Abbadie
23-05	Switzerland	D 3-3	Lausanne	Fr	Borges, Ambrois, Martinez.W
5-06	Saar	W 7-1	Saarbrucken	Fr	Ambrois 3, Schiaffino, Varela.O, OG 2
16-06	Czechoslovakia	W 2-0	Berne	WCr1	Miguez, Schiaffino
19-06	Scotland	W 7-0	Basle	WCr1	Borges 3, Miguez 2, Abbadie 2
26-06	England	W 4-2	Basle	WCqf	Borges, Varela.O, Schiaffino, Ambrois
30-06	Hungary	L 2-4	Lausanne	WCsf	Hohberg 2
3-07	Austria	L 1-3	Zurich	WC3p	Hohberg
9-03-1955	Paraguay	W 3-1	Santiago	SC	Borges, Miguez, Abbadie
13-03	Chile	D 2-2	Santiago	SC	Galvan 2
23-03	Ecuador	W 5-1	Santiago	SC	Abbadie 2, Perez.J, Galvan, Miguez
27-03	Argentina	L 1-6	Santiago	SC	Miguez
30-03	Peru	L 1-2	Santiago	SC	Morel
21-01-1956	Paraguay	W 4-2	Montevideo	SC	Escalada 2, Galvan, Roque
28-01	Peru	W 2-0	Montevideo	SC	Escalada, Miguez
6-02	Chile	W 2-1	Montevideo	SC	Borges, Miguez
10-02	Brazil	D 0-0	Montevideo	SC	
15-02	Argentina	W 1-0	Montevideo	SC	Ambrois
24-06	Brazil	L 0-2	Rio de Janeiro	CA	
1-07	Argentina	L 1-2	Montevideo	CA	Abbadie
15-07	Paraguay	D 2-2	Asuncion	Fr	Auscarriaga, OG
12-08	Czechoslovakia	W 2-1	Montevideo	Fr	Borges, Mendez
10-10	Argentina	L 1-2	Paysandu	Fr	Ambrois
14-11	Argentina	D 2-2	Buenos Aires	Fr	Ambrois, Miguez
7-03-1957	Ecuador	W 5-2	Lima	SC	Ambrois 4, Sasia.J
17-03	Colombia	L 0-1	Lima	SC	
20-03	Argentina	L 0-4	Lima	SC	
23-03	Peru	W 5-3	Lima	SC	Ambrois 4, Carranza
28-03	Brazil	W 3-2	Lima	SC	Campero 2, Ambrois
1-04	Chile	W 2-0	Lima	SC	Roque
23-05	Argentina	D 0-0	Montevideo	NC	
5-06	Argentina	D 1-1	Buenos Aires	LC	Correa
16-06	Colombia	D 1-1	Bogota	WCq	Ambrois
30-06	Colombia	W 1-0	Montevideo	WCq	Miguez
14-07	Paraguay	L 0-5	Asuncion	WCq	
28-07	Paraguay	W 2-0	Montevideo	WCq	Martinez.W, Benitez
6-04-1958	Argentina	W 1-0	Montevideo	Fr	Miguez
30-04	Argentina	L 0-2	Buenos Aires	Fr	
8-03-1959	Bolivia	W 7-0	Buenos Aires	SC	Sasia.J 2, Borges, Escalada, Guaglianone, Douksas, Perez.D
14-03	Peru	L 3-5	Buenos Aires	SC	De Marco, Sasia.J, Douksas
18-03	Paraguay	W 3-1	Buenos Aires	SC	De Marco, Sasia.J, Douksas
26-03	Brazil	L 1-3	Buenos Aires	SC	Escalada
30-03	Argentina	L 1-4	Buenos Aires	SC	De Marco
2-04	Chile	L 0-1	Buenos Aires	SC	
1-05	Paraguay	L 1-3	Montevideo	Fr	Escalada
6-12	Ecuador	W 4-0	Guayaquil	SC	Escalada, Perez.D, Silveira, Bergara
12-12	Brazil	W 3-0	Guayaquil	SC	Sasia.J 2, Escalada
16-12	Argentina	W 5-0	Guayaquil	SC	Bergara 2, Silveira 2, Sasia.J
22-12	Paraguay	D 1-1	Guayaquil	SC	Sasia.J
1-06-1960	Chile	W 3-2	Santiago	Fr	Bergara 2, Guaglianone
5-06	Chile	D 2-2	Montevideo	Fr	Guaglianone 2
9-07	Brazil	W 1-0	Montevideo	CA	Perez.D
13-07	Paraguay	W 2-1	Montevideo	CA	Rodriguez.H, Escalada
17-08	Argentina	L 0-4	Buenos Aires	CA	
15-07-1961	Bolivia	D 1-1	La Paz	WCq	Cubila.L
30-07	Bolivia	W 2-1	Montevideo	WCq	Cabrera, Escalada
12-10	Chile	W 3-2	Santiago	Fr	Pintos 2, Cubila
29-11	Soviet Union	L 1-2	Montevideo	Fr	Cubila
23-12	Hungary	D 1-1	Montevideo	Fr	Escalada
13-03-1962	Argentina	D 1-1	Montevideo	Fr	Alvarez
11-04	West Germany	L 0-3	Hamburg	Fr	
18-04	Hungary	D 1-1	Budapest	Fr	Silva
22-04	Czechoslovakia	L 1-3	Prague	Fr	Sasia.J
27-04	Soviet Union	L 0-5	Moscow	Fr	
2-05	Scotland	W 3-2	Glasgow	Fr	Sasia.J, Cubila 2
30-05	Colombia	W 2-1	Arica	WCr1	Cubila, Sacia.J
2-06	Yugoslavia	L 1-3	Arica	WCr1	Cabrera
6-06	Soviet Union	L 1-2	Arica	WCr1	Sacia.J
15-08	Argentina	L 1-3	Buenos Aires	LC	Mattera

23-03-1963	Chile	W 3-2	Montevideo	PDC	Pintos 2, Sasia.J
24-07	Chile	D 0-0	Santiago	PDC	
25-04-1964	Morocco	W 1-0	Casablanca	Fr	Castro.M
29-04	Nth. Ireland	L 0-3	Belfast	Fr	
6-05	England	L 1-2	London	Fr	Spencer
14-05	Austria	W 2-0	Vienna	Fr	Castro.M 2
20-05	Soviet Union	L 0-1	Moscow	Fr	
3-01-1965	East Germany	L 0-2	Montevideo	Fr	
25-04	Paraguay	L 1-2	Asuncion	AC	Toja
1-05	Paraguay	W 4-0	Montevideo	AC	Urrusmendi 2, Silva 2
9-05	Chile	D 0-0	Santiago	PDC	
16-05	Chile	D 1-1	Montevideo	PDC	Toja
23-05	Venezuela	W 5-0	Montevideo	WCq	Alvarez 3, Rocha, Meneses
30-05	Venezuela	W 3-1	Caracas	WCq	Rocha 2, Silva
6-06	Peru	W 1-0	Lima	WCq	Urruzmendi
13-06	Peru	W 2-1	Montevideo	WCq	Silva, Rocha
7-09	Brazil	L 0-3	Belo Horizonte	Fr	
4-12	Soviet Union	L 1-3	Montevideo	Fr	Rocha
15-05-1966	Paraguay	D 2-2	Asuncion	AC	Salva 2
18-05	Paraguay	W 3-1	Montevideo	AC	Morales, Perez.D
15-06	Israel	W 2-1	Tel Aviv	Fr	Abbadie 2
19-06	Rumania	L 0-1	Bucharest	Fr	
23-06	Spain	D 1-1	La Coruna	Fr	Perez.D
26-06	Portugal	L 0-3	Lisbon	Fr	
11-07	England	D 0-0	London	WCr1	
15-07	France	W 2-1	London	WCr1	Rocha, Cortes
19-07	Mexico	D 0-0	London	WCr1	
23-07	West Germany	L 0-4	Sheffield	WCqf	
4-01-1967	Romania	D 1-1	Montevideo	Fr	Urrusmendi
17-01	Bolivia	W 4-0	Montevideo	SC	Rocha, Castillo, OG, Oyarbide
21-01	Venezuela	W 4-0	Montevideo	SC	Urrusmendi 2, Oyarbide, OG
26-01	Chile	D 2-2	Montevideo	SC	Oyarbide, Rocha
29-01	Paraguay	W 2-0	Montevideo	SC	Perez.D, Urrusmendi
2-02	Argentina	W 1-0	Montevideo	SC	Rocha
25-06	Brazil	D 0-0	Montevideo	RBC	
28-06	Brazil	D 2-2	Montevideo	RBC	Rocha 2
1-07	Brazil	D 1-1	Montevideo	RBC	Urrusmendi
28-07	Peru	W 1-0	Lima	Fr	Rocha
30-07	Peru	W 2-1	Lima	Fr	Rocha, Bareno
21-05-1968	Mexico	D 3-3	Mexico City	Fr	Morales, Rocha, Mujica
28-05	Mexico	D 2-2	Mexico City	Fr	Mujica, Morales
2-06	Paraguay	D 0-0	Asuncion	AC	Abandoned after 70 mins
5-06	Argentina	L 0-2	Buenos Aires	NC	
9-06	Brazil	L 0-2	Sao Paulo	Fr	
12-06	Brazil	L 0-4	Rio de Janeiro	Fr	
20-06	Argentina	W 2-1	Montevideo	LC	Zubia, Morales
26-10	Mexico	L 0-2	Montevideo	Fr	
8-06-1969	England	L 1-2	Montevideo	Fr	Cubila.L
27-06	Peru	L 0-1	Lima	Fr	
2-07	Colombia	W 1-0	Cali	Fr	Bareno
6-07	Ecuador	W 2-0	Guayaquil	WCq	Bareno, Ancheta
13-07	Chile	D 0-0	Santiago	WCq	
20-07	Ecuador	W 1-0	Montevideo	WCq	Ancheta
10-08	Chile	W 2-0	Montevideo	WCq	Cortes, Rocha
31-03-1970	Peru	W 2-0	Montevideo	Fr	Maneiro, Cubila
8-04	Argentina	L 1-2	Buenos Aires	Fr	Zubia
15-04	Argentina	W 2-1	Montevideo	Fr	Rocha, Ubina
18-04	Peru	L 2-4	Lima	Fr	Barreno, Ancheta
2-06	Israel	W 2-0	Puebla	WCr1	Maneiro, Mujica
6-06	Italy	D 0-0	Puebla	WCr1	
10-06	Sweden	L 0-1	Puebla	WCr1	
14-06	Soviet Union	W 1-0	Mexico City	WCqf	Esparrago
17-06	Brazil	L 1-3	Guadalajara	WCsf	Cubila
20-06	West Germany	L 0-1	Mexico City	WC3p	
8-02-1971	East Germany	L 0-3	Montevideo	Fr	
10-02	East Germany	D 1-1	Montevideo	Fr	Zubia
14-07	Argentina	L 0-1	Buenos Aires	NC	
18-07	Argentina	D 1-1	Montevideo	LC	Bertocchi
27-10	Chile	W 3-0	Montevideo	PDC	Repetto, OG 2
3-11	Chile	L 0-5	Santiago	PDC	
23-05-1972	Spain	L 0-2	Madrid	Fr	

27-05	East Germany	L 0-1	Leipzig	Fr	
31-05	East Germany	D 0-0	Rostock	Fr	
14-06	Norway	W 1-0	Oslo	Fr	Lattuada
29-06	Soviet Union	L 0-1	Sao Paulo	Clr2	
2-07	Portugal	D 1-1	Sao Paulo	Clr2	Pavoni
6-07	Argentina	L 0-1	Porto Alegre	Clr2	
17-05-1973	Argentina	D 1-1	Buenos Aires	LC	Morena.F
23-05	Argentina	D 1-1	Montevideo	NC	Rey
6-06	Haiti	D 0-0	Port au Prince	Fr	
24-06	Colombia	D 0-0	Bogota	WCq	
1-07	Ecuador	W 2-1	Quito	WCq	Cubila, Morena.F
5-07	Colombia	L 0-1	Montevideo	WCq	
8-07	Ecuador	W 4-0	Montevideo	WCq	Morena.F 2, Cubila, Milar
19-07	Israel	W 2-1	Tel Aviv	Fr	Morena.F, Milar
23-03-1974	Haiti	W 1-0	Port au Prince	Fr	Morena.F
25-03	Haiti	D 0-0	Port au Prince	Fr	
28-03	Jamaica	W 3-0	Kingston	Fr	Morena.F 2, Mantegazza
21-04	Indonesia	W 3-2	Djakarta	Fr	Morena.F 2, Milar
26-04	Australia	D 0-0	Sydney	Fr	
28-04	Australia	L 0-2	Melbourne	Fr	
8-05	Rep. Ireland	W 2-0	Montevideo	Fr	Morena.F 2
15-06	Holland	L 0-2	Hanover	WCr1	
19-06	Bulgaria	D 1-1	Hanover	WCr1	Pavoni
23-06	Sweden	L 0-3	Dusseldorf	WCr1	
4-06-1975	Chile	W 1-0	Montevideo	PDC	Unanue
12-06	Paraguay	W 1-0	Asuncion	AC	Jimenez
19-06	Paraguay	L 0-1	Montevideo	AC	
25-06	Chile	W 3-1	Santiago	PDC	Revetria, Peruena, OG
18-07	Argentina	L 2-3	Montevideo	NC	Morena.F 2
21-09	Colombia	L 0-3	Bogota	SCsf	
1-10	Colombia	W 1-0	Montevideo	SCsf	Morena.F
25-02-1976	Brazil	L 1-2	Montevideo	CA	Ocampo
10-03	Paraguay	D 2-2	Montevideo	CA	Ocampo, Pereyra
8-04	Argentina	L 1-4	Buenos Aires	CA	Pereyra
28-04	Brazil	L 1-2	Rio de Janeiro	CA	Torres
19-05	Paraguay	L 0-1	Asuncion	CA	
9-06	Argentina	L 0-3	Montevideo	CA	
6-10	Chile	D 0-0	Santiago	PDC	
12-10	Peru	D 0-0	Lima	Fr	
15-10	Colombia	W 2-1	Bogota	Fr	
20-10	Ecuador	D 2-2	Quito	Fr	Victoriano 2
24-11	Peru	D 0-0	Montevideo	Fr	
4-01-1977	Ecuador	D 1-1	Montevideo	Fr	Rodriguez.R
12-01	Paraguay	D 1-1	Asuncion	AC	
23-01	Paraguay	W 2-1	Montevideo	AC	
30-01	Chile	W 3-0	Montevideo	PDC	
9-02	Venezuela	D 1-1	Caracas	WCq	Carrasco
27-02	Bolivia	L 0-1	La Paz	WCq	
17-03	Venezuela	W 2-0	Montevideo	WCq	Morena.F, Pereyra
27-03	Bolivia	D 2-2	Montevideo	WCq	Pereyra 2
8-06	West Germany	L 0-2	Montevideo	Fr	
15-06	England	D 0-0	Montevideo	Fr	
4-03-1978	Argentina	D 0-0	Mar del Plata	Fr	
25-04	Argentina	W 2-0	Montevideo	Fr	Maneiro, Morena.F
3-05	Argentina	L 0-3	Buenos Aires	Fr	
24-05	Spain	D 0-0	Montevideo	Fr	
31-05-1979	Brazil	L 1-5	Rio de Janeiro	Fr	Victorino
11-07	Chile	L 0-1	Santiago	PDC	
18-07	Chile	W 2-1	Montevideo	PDC	Victorino, Unanue
30-08	Peru	L 0-2	Lima	Fr	
5-09	Ecuador	L 1-2	Guayaquil	SCr1	Victorino
16-09	Ecuador	W 2-1	Montevideo	SCr1	Bica, Victorino
20-09	Paraguay	D 0-0	Asuncion	SCr1	
26-09	Paraguay	D 2-2	Montevideo	SCr1	Milar, Paz
15-03-1980	Italy	L 0-1	Milan	Fr	
18-03	Belgium	L 0-2	Brussels	Fr	
22-03	Yugoslavia	L 1-2	Sarajevo	Fr	OG
26-03	Luxembourg	W 1-0	Esch	Fr	Victorino
18-07	Peru	D 0-0	Montevideo	Fr	
21-08	Chile	D 0-0	Montevideo	PDC	
27-08	Brazil	L 0-1	Fortaleza	Fr	

Date	Opponent	Result	Venue	Comp	Scorers
9-11	Bolivia	W 3-1	Cochabamba	Fr	Victorino, Morales.J, De La Pena
12-11	Peru	D 1-1	Lima	Fr	Krasouski
8-12	Finland	W 6-0	Montevideo	Fr	Krasouski, Morales 2, Vargas, Siviero, Falero.M
11-12	Bolivia	W 5-0	Montevideo	Fr	Morales.J 2, Paz, Ramos, Victorino
18-12	Switzerland	W 4-0	Montevideo	Fr	Oliviera, Paz 3
30-12	Holland	W 2-0	Montevideo	ML	Ramos, Victorino
3-01-1981	Italy	W 2-0	Montevideo	ML	Morales.J, Victorino
10-01	Brazil	W 2-1	Montevideo	ML	Barrios, Victorino
29-04	Chile	W 2-1	Santiago	PDC	Nunez, Agresta
15-07	Chile	D 0-0	Montevideo	PDC	
9-08	Colombia	W 3-2	Montevideo	WCq	Paz, Morales.J 2
23-08	Peru	L 1-2	Montevideo	WCq	Victorino
6-09	Peru	D 0-0	Lima	WCq	
13-09	Colombia	D 1-1	Bogota	WCq	Victorino
20-02-1982	South Korea *	D 2-2	Calcutta	JNC	
22-02	China *	D 0-0	Calcutta	JNC	
25-02	India *	W 3-1	Calcutta	JNC	
28-02	China *	W 2-0	Calcutta	JNC	
2-06-1983	Paraguay	D 0-0	Asuncion	AC	
9-06	Paraguay	W 3-0	Montevideo	AC	Cabrera 2, Morena.F
18-07	Peru	D 1-1	Montevideo	Fr	Luzardo
11-08	Peru	D 1-1	Lima	Fr	Muhletaler
25-08	Paraguay	D 0-0	Montevideo	Fr	
1-09	Chile	W 2-1	Montevideo	SCr1	Acevedo, Morena.F
4-09	Venezuela	W 3-0	Montevideo	SCr1	Cabrera, Morena.F, Luzardo
11-09	Chile	L 0-2	Santiago	SCr1	
18-09	Venezuela	W 2-1	Caracas	SCr1	Santelli, Aguilera
21-09	Scotland	L 0-2	Glasgow	Fr	
26-09	Israel	D 2-2	Tel Aviv	Fr	Aguilera 2
13-10	Peru	W 1-0	Lima	SCsf	Aguilera
20-10	Peru	D 1-1	Montevideo	SCsf	Cabrera
27-10	Brazil	W 2-0	Montevideo	SCf	Francescoli, Diogo
4-11	Brazil	D 1-1	Salvador	SCf	Aguilera
13-06-1984	England	W 2-0	Montevideo	Fr	Acosta, Cabrera
21-06	Brazil	L 0-1	Curitiba	Fr	
18-07	Argentina	W 1-0	Montevideo	Fr	Barrios
2-08	Argentina	D 0-0	Buenos Aires	Fr	
19-09	Peru	W 2-0	Montevideo	Fr	Aguilera, Salazar
3-10	Peru	W 3-1	Lima	Fr	Barrios, Santin, Nadal
31-10	Mexico	D 1-1	Montevideo	Fr	Nadal
29-01-1985	East Germany	W 3-0	Montevideo	Fr	Aguilera, Da Silva, Francescoli
3-02	Paraguay	W 1-0	Montevideo	AC	Francescoli
6-02	Bolivia	W 1-0	Cochabamba	Fr	Pereyra
10-02	Paraguay	W 3-1	Asuncion	AC	Nadal 3
14-02	Finland	W 2-1	Montevideo	Fr	Aguilera, Nadal
24-02	Colombia	W 3-0	Montevideo	Fr	Aguilera, Francescoli, Nadal
27-02	Peru	D 2-2	Montevideo	Fr	Nadal, Cabrera
10-03	Ecuador	W 2-1	Montevideo	WCq	Aguilera, Ramos
24-03	Chile	L 0-2	Santiago	WCq	
31-03	Ecuador	W 2-0	Quito	WCq	Saralegui, Francescoli
7-04	Chile	W 2-1	Montevideo	WCq	Batista, Ramos
23-04	Peru	L 1-2	Lima	Fr	Carrasco
28-04	Colombia	L 1-2	Bogota	Fr	Aguilera
2-05	Brazil	L 0-2	Recife	Fr	
25-05	Japan	W 4-1	Tokyo	Fr	Aguilera 2, Da Silva 2
1-06	Malaysia	W 6-0	Kuala Lumpur	Fr	Carrasco, Alzugaray, Aguilera, Barrios, Pereyra, Cabrera
21-08	France	L 0-2	Paris	AFT	
17-10	Chile	L 0-1	Santiago	Fr	
2-02-1986	Canada	W 3-1	Miami	Fr	Aguilera, Ostolaza, Salazar
7-02	United States	D 1-1	Miami	Fr	Aguilera
16-02	Poland	D 2-2	Montevideo	Fr	Bossio, Salazar
13-04	Mexico	L 0-1	Los Angeles	Fr	
21-04	Wales	D 0-0	Wrexham	Fr	
23-04	Rep. Ireland	D 1-1	Dublin	Fr	OG
4-06	West Germany	D 1-1	Queretaro	WCr1	Alzamendi
8-06	Denmark	L 1-6	Nezahualcoyotl	WCr1	Francescoli
13-06	Scotland	D 0-0	Nezahualcoyotl	WCr1	
16-06	Argentina	L 0-1	Puebla	WCr2	
19-06-1987	Ecuador	W 2-1	Montevideo	Fr	Perdomo 2
23-06	Bolivia	W 2-1	Montevideo	Fr	Matosas, Alzamendi
9-07	Argentina	W 1-0	Buenos Aires	SCsf	Alzamendi

12-07	Chile	W 1-0	Buenos Aires	SCf	Bengoechea
7-08-1988	Colombia	L 1-2	Bogota	Fr	Herrera
27-09	Ecuador	W 2-1	Asuncion	Fr	Dalto, Herrera
29-09	Paraguay	L 1-3	Asuncion	Fr	Da Silva
12-10	Paraguay	W 2-0	Montevideo	Fr	Da Silva, Pereyra
1-11	Chile	D 1-1	Santiago	PDC	Vidal
9-11	Chile	W 3-1	Montevideo	PDC	Da Silva, Baez, Martinez.S
14-12	Peru	W 3-0	Montevideo	Fr	Francescoli 2, Sosa
22-04-1989	Italy	D 1-1	Verona	Fr	Aguilera
3-05	Ecuador	W 3-1	Montevideo	Fr	Martinez.S, Aguilera 2
23-05	Ecuador	D 1-1	Quito	Fr	Herrera
8-06	Bolivia	D 0-0	Santa Cruz	Fr	
14-06	Bolivia	W 1-0	Montevideo	Fr	Aguilera
19-06	Chile	D 2-2	Montevideo	Fr	Correa 2
2-07	Ecuador	L 0-1	Goiânia	SCr1	
4-07	Bolivia	W 3-0	Goiânia	SCr1	Ostolaza 2, Sosa
6-07	Chile	W 3-0	Goiânia	SCr1	Sosa, Alzamendi, Francescoli
8-07	Argentina	L 0-1	Goiânia	SCr1	
12-07	Paraguay	W 3-0	Rio de Janeiro	SCr2	Francescoli, Alzamendi, Paz
14-07	Argentina	W 2-0	Rio de Janeiro	SCr2	Sosa 2
16-07	Brazil	L 0-1	Rio de Janeiro	SCf	
6-08	Colombia	D 0-0	Montevideo	Fr	
27-08	Peru	W 2-0	Lima	WCq	Sosa, Alzamendi
3-09	Bolivia	L 1-2	La Paz	WCq	Sosa
17-09	Bolivia	W 2-0	Montevideo	WCq	Sosa, Francescoli
24-09	Peru	W 2-0	Montevideo	WCq	Sosa 2
2-02-1990	Colombia	W 2-0	Miami	Fr	Pedrucci, Castro
4-02	Costa Rica	W 2-0	Miami	Fr	Castro, Martinez.S
20-03	Mexico	L 1-2	Los Angeles	Fr	Suarez
25-04	West Germany	D 3-3	Stuttgart	Fr	Aguilera, Ostolaza, Revelez
18-05	Nth. Ireland	L 0-1	Belfast	Fr	
22-05	England	W 2-1	London	Fr	Ostolaza, Perdomo
13-06	Spain	D 0-0	Udine	WCr1	
17-06	Belgium	L 1-3	Verona	WCr1	Bengoechea
21-06	South Korea	W 1-0	Udine	WCr1	Fonseca
25-06	Italy	L 0-2	Rome	WCr2	
5-05-1991	United States	L 0-1	Denver	Fr	
7-05	Mexico	W 2-0	Los Angeles	Fr	Lopez.V, Ferreira
13-05	Costa Rica	W 1-0	San Jose	Fr	Cedres
30-05	Chile	L 1-2	Santiago	Fr	OG
12-06	Peru	L 0-1	Lima	Fr	
20-06	Peru	D 0-0	Montevideo	Fr	
26-06	Chile	W 2-1	Montevideo	Fr	Baez, Mendez
7-07	Bolivia	D 1-1	Valparaiso	SCr1	Castro
9-07	Ecuador	D 1-1	Viña del Mar	SCr1	Mendez
11-07	Brazil	D 1-1	Viña del Mar	SCr1	Mendez
15-07	Colombia	W 1-0	Viña del Mar	SCr1	Mendez
4-09	Spain	L 1-2	Oviedo	Fr	Guttierez
20-11	Mexico	D 1-1	Veracruz	Fr	Cedres
30-04-1992	Brazil	W 1-0	Montevideo	Fr	Paz
21-06	Australia	W 2-0	Montevideo	Fr	Martinez.S, Larrea
4-07	Ecuador	W 3-1	Montevideo	Fr	Kanapkis, Paz, Zalazar
25-07	Guatemala	W 2-1	Montevideo	Fr	Sanguinetti, Paz
2-08	Costa Rica	W 2-1	Montevideo	Fr	Sanguinetti
23-09	Argentina	D 0-0	Montevideo	Fr	
25-11	Brazil	W 2-1	Campina Grande	Fr	Cabrrera, Guerra
29-11	Poland	L 0-1	Montevideo	Fr	
20-12	Germany	L 1-4	Montevideo	Fr	OG
16-06-1993	USA	W 1-0	Ambato	SCr1	Ostolaza
19-06	Venezuela	D 2-2	Ambato	SCr1	Saralegui, Kanapkis
22-06	Ecuador	L 1-2	Quito	SCr1	Kanapkis
26-06	Colombia	D 1-1	Guayaquil	SCqf	Saralegui. Lost 3-5p
13-07	Peru	W 2-1	Lima	Fr	Sosa 2
17-07	Peru	W 3-0	Montevideo	Fr	Fonseca 2, Moran
25-07	Venezuela	W 1-0	San Cristobal	WCq	Herrera
1-08	Ecuador	D 0-0	Montevideo	WCq	
8-08	Bolivia	L 1-3	La Paz	WCq	Francescoli
15-08	Brazil	D 1-1	Montevideo	WCq	Fonseca
29-08	Venezuela	W 4-0	Montevideo	WCq	Kanapkis 2, Cedres, Sosa
5-09	Ecuador	W 1-0	Guayaquil	WCq	Sosa
12-09	Bolivia	W 2-1	Montevideo	WCq	Francescoli, Fonseca

19-09	Brazil	L 0-2	Rio de Janeiro	WCq	
13-10	Germany	L 0-5	Karlsruhe	Fr	
19-10-1994	Peru	W 1-0	Lima	Fr	Silva.D
18-01-1995	Spain	D 2-2	La Coruña	Fr	Fonseca, Bengoechea.P
1-02	Mexico	L 0-1	San Diego	Fr	
22-03	Colombia	L 1-2	Medellin	Fr	Canobbio
25-03	United States	D 2-2	Dallas	Fr	Otero, Poyet
29-03	England	D 0-0	London	Fr	
31-03	Yugoslavia	L 0-1	Belgrade	Fr	
5-04	Peru	W 1-0	Montevideo	Fr	Bengoechea.P
25-06	New Zealand	W 7-0	Paysandu	Fr	Fonseca 2, Sosa.R 2, Abeijon, Canobbio, Martinez.S
28-06	New Zealand	D 2-2	Rivera	Fr	Francescoli, Martinez.S
5-07	Venezuela	W 4-1	Montevideo	SCr1	Fonseca, Otero, Francescoli, Poyet
9-07	Paraguay	W 1-0	Montevideo	SCr1	Francescoli
13-07	Mexico	D 1-1	Montevideo	SCr1	Saralegui
16-07	Bolivia	W 2-1	Montevideo	SCqf	Otero, Fonseca
19-07	Colombia	W 2-0	Montevideo	SCsf	Adinolfi, Otero
23-07	Brazil	D 1-1	Montevideo	SCf	Bengoechea.P. Won 5-3 on pens

VENEZUELA

Venezuela is the weakest of all the ten South American countries and the only one in which football is not the national sport, that accolade falling to baseball. Oil resources mean that Venezuela is a relatively prosperous country, but although there is now a professional league, progress has been slow and the standard does not look like matching that of either Ecuador or Bolivia in the near future.

Historically Venezuela has more in common with football in Central America than in South America and it was to the Confederacion Centroamericano y del Caribe de Futbol that they affiliated in 1938. The Federación Venezolana de Fútbol had been founded 12 years previously in Caracas, although the first organised competition stretches back five years prior to that.

In 1921 a group of Caracas-based clubs set up their own league which was taken over by the new federation in 1926, and despite a break-away in 1929 when two leagues were in operation, the national amateur league continued to operate until the major reorganisation of 1956, the date when professionalism was legalised.

The national side made its debut in the 1938 Central American and Caribbean Games and later in the same year took part in the Bolivaran Games in Barranquilla but did not play regularly until the mid-1960s, reflecting the low priority attached to the game by the population as a whole.

The professional league gave rise to a whole new breed of clubs, which as their names suggest - Portugues, Deportivo Italia - are run loosely along ethnic lines, a factor that further alienates the sport from the general public. There are a surprising number of foreign players in the league, but attendances remain low. Success in the Copa Libertadores has been restricted to three semi-final appearances between 1977 and 1984, but on each occasion the Venezuelan team has finished bottom of their semi-final group.

Honours have been spread evenly among the clubs and, surprisingly, among the cities in Venezuela. Caracas has found its dominant position challenged in particular by San Cristobal and Mérida, especially since the beginning of the 1980s as teams like Deportivo Tachira and Estudiantes Mérida have forced the Caracas teams like Deportivo Italia, Galicia and Portugues into the background.

THE ORDER OF MERIT

		Total			Lge	Copa Lib		
		G	S	B	G	G	S	B
1	Portuguesa	5	-	1	5	-	-	1
2	Galicia FC	4	-	-	4	-	-	-
	Deportivo Italia	4	-	-	4	-	-	-
	Deportivo Portugues	4	-	-	4	-	-	-
	Sport Maritimo	4	-	-	4	-	-	-
	Unión Atlético Táchira	4	-	-	4	-	-	-
7	Caracas FC	3	-	-	3	-	-	-
8	ULA Mérida	2	-	1	2	-	-	1
9	Estudiantes Mérida	2	-	-	2	-	-	-
10	Atlético San Cristobal	1	-	1	1	-	-	1
11	Banco Obrero	1	-	-	1	-	-	-
	Deportivo Espanol	1	-	-	1	-	-	-
	Deportiva Lara	1	-	-	1	-	-	-
	Mineros de Guyana	1	-	-	1	-	-	-
	Union Deportiva Canarias	1	-	-	1	-	-	-
	Universidad Central	1	-	-	1	-	-	-
	Valencia	1	-	-	1	-	-	-

Entry into the 1966 World Cup was the country's first real taste of international competition, and was followed the year after by their first appearance in the South American Championships. They surprisingly finished above Bolivia in that tournament but have been last in every tournament since. Fixtures are almost exclusively in both of these competitions, for which Venezuela are now regular entrants.

If Venezuela are to make any strides in world football they will have to improve on a record that shows just one win in the South American Championships, against Bolivia in 1967, and two in the World Cup qualifiers, against Bolivia in 1981 and Ecuador in 1993.

Population: 19,735,00
Area, sq km: 912,000
% in urban areas: 84%
Capital city: Caracas

Federación Venezolana de Fútbol
Ave. Este Estadio Nacional
Quinta Claret #28
El Paraíso, Apartado Postal 14160
Candelaria, Caracus
Venezuela
Tel: + 58 2 4618010
Fax: + 58 2 4618010

Year of formation	1926
Affiliation to FIFA	1952
Affiliation to CONME	1952
Registered clubs	1483
Registered players	80 300
Professional players	570
Registered coaches	475
Registered referees	391
National stadium	Estadio Olimpico, Caracas 30 000
National colours	Dark red/White/White
Reserve colours	White/White/White
Season	September - June

THE RECORD

WORLD CUP

1930-62	Did not enter
1966	QT 3rd/3 in group 1
1970	QT 4th/4 in group 2
1974	Did not enter
1978	QT 3rd/3 in group 2
1982	QT 3rd/3 in group 1
1986	QT 4th/4 in group 1
1990	QT 3rd/3 in group 3
1994	QT 5th/5 in group 2

SOUTH AMERICAN CHAMPIONSHIP

1910-63	Did not enter
1967	5/6
1975	10/10 - 1st round
1979	10/10 - 1st round
1983	10/10 - 1st round
1987	10/10 - 1st round
1989	10/10 - 1st round
1991	10/10 - 1st round
1993	9/12 - 1st round
1995	12/12 - 1st round

SOUTH AMERICAN CLUB COMPETITIONS

Copa Libertadores
Semi-finalists - Portuguesa Acarigua 1977. Deportivo San Cristobal 1983, ULA Merida 1984
Super Copa
Ineligible to compete
COMNEBOL Cup
Quarter-finals - Caracas FC 1993, Minerven 1994

CLUB DIRECTORY

CARACAS (Pop. - 3,600,000)

Caracas FC (1967)
Estadio Nacional 'Brigido Iriarte' 12,000 – White, sky blue trim

Deportivo Italia (1952)
Estadio Nacional 'Brigido Iriarte' 12,000 – Blue/White

Galicia Futbol Club (1960)
Estadio Nacional 'Brigido Iriarte' 12,000 – White with sky blue sash/White

Club Sport Maritimo de Venezuela (1959)
Estadio Olimpico 30,000 – Red & green stripes/White

Club Deportivo Portugues (1950)
Estadio Olimpico 30,000 – Red & green stripes/White

Universidad Central Venezoelana
Estadio Olimpico 30,000 – Green & white stripes/White

BARQUISIMENTO (Pop. - 497,000)

Unión Deportiva de Lara FC (1951)
Estadio Farid Richa 15,000 – Red/Blue

CIUDAD GUAYANA (Pop. - 314,000)

FC Deportivo Mineros de Guyana (1981)
Estadio Olimpico 10,000 – Sky blue & white stripes/Black

SAN CRISTÓBAL (Pop. - 198,000)

Unión Atlético Táchira (1974)
Pueblo Nuevo 30,000 – Yellow & black stripes/Black
Previous name - Deportivo Tachira

Atlético San Cristobal (1981)
Estadio San Cristobal 20,000 – Green & white stripes/White
Previous names - Deportivo San Cristobal

MÉRIDA (Pop. - 143,000)

Estudiantes de Mérida FC (1952)
Guillermo Soto Rosas 15,000 – Red & white stripes/Blue

ULA Mérida (1977)
(Universidad de Los Andes FC)
Guillermo Soto Rosas 15,000 – Blue & white stripes/Blue

ACARIGUA (Pop. - 126,000)

Portuguesa FC (1926)
José Antonio Páez 20,000 – White with a red & black hoop/White

Valencia FC (1960)
José Antonio Paez 10,000 – Green/White

BARINAS (Pop. - 110,000)

Atlético Zamora (1976)
La Carolina 10,000 – Black & white stripes/White

CORO (Pop. - 96,000)

Atlético Universitario Falco
Universitario 10,000 – Violet/White

PUERTO LA CRUZ (Pop. - 53,000)

Anzoategui FC (1969)
Félix Velázquez 15,000 – Yellow/Red

PORLAMAR (Isl de Margarita) (Pop. - 51,000)

Atlético Pepeganda (1987)
Guatemare 15,000 – White/White

EL CALLAO (Pop. - 6,000)

Minerven FC (1985)
El Callao 3,000 – Blue, white trim

VENEZUELAN AMATEUR LEAGUE CHAMPIONS

1921	America
1922	Centro Atlético
1923	America
1924	Centro Atlético
1925	Loyola SC
1926	Centro Atlético
1927	Venzoleo FC
1928	Deportivo Venezuela
1929	Deportivo Venezuela & Centro Atlético
1930	Centro Atlético
1931	Deportivo Venezuela
1932	Union SC
1933	Deportivo Venezuela
1934	Union SC
1935	Union SC
1936	Dos Caminos SC
1937	Dos Caminos SC
1938	Dos Caminos SC
1939	Union SC
1940	Union SC
1941	Litoral FC
1942	Dos Caminos SC
1943	Loyola SC
1944	Loyola SC
1945	Dos Caminos SC
1946	Deportivo Espanol
1947	Union SC
1948	Loyola SC
1949	Dos Caminos SC
1950	Union SC
1951	Universidad Central
1952	Le Salle
1953	Universidad Central
1954	Deportivo Vasco
1955	Le Salle

VENEZUELAN PROFESSIONAL LEAGUE CHAMPIONS

1956	Banco Obrero
1957	Universidad Central
1958	Deportivo Portugues
1959	Deportivo Espanol
1960	Deportivo Portugues
1961	Deportivo Italia
1962	Deportivo Portugues

1963	Deportivo Italia	1974	Galicia FC	1985	Estudiantes Merida
1964	Galicia FC	1975	Portuguesa	1986	Tachira
1965	Deportivo Lara	1976	Portuguesa	1987	Maritimo
1966	Deportivo Italia	1977	Portuguesa	1988	Maritimo
1967	Deportivo Portugues	1978	Portuguesa	1989	Mineros de Guyana
1968	Union Dep. Canarias	1979	Tachira	1990	Maritimo
1969	Galicia FC	1980	Estudiantes Merida	1991	ULA Merida
1970	Galicia FC	1981	Tachira	1992	Caracas FC
1971	Valencia	1982	Atletico San Cristobal	1993	Sport Maritimo
1972	Deportivo Italia	1983	ULA Merida	1994	Caracas FC
1973	Portuguesa	1984	Tachira	1995	Caracas FC

INTERNATIONAL MATCHES PLAYED BY VENEZUELA

10-02-1938	Panama	L 1-2	Panama City	CG	
14-02	Mexico	L 0-1	Panama City	CG	
17-02	Costa Rica	L 0-5	Panama City	CG	
20-02	El Salvador	L 2-3	Panama City	CG	
22-02	Colombia	W 2-1	Panama City	CG	
11-08	Bolivia	L 1-3	Bogota	BG	
13-08	Colombia	L 0-2	Bogota	BG	
17-08	Peru	L 1-2	Bogota	BG	
19-08	Ecuador	W 5-2	Bogota	BG	
12-12-1946	Colombia	L 1-3	Barranquilla	CG	
14-12	Curacao	L 0-1	Barranquilla	CG	
17-12	Panama	L 1-2	Barranquilla	CG	
20-12	Costa Rica	L 2-4	Barranquilla	CG	
23-12	Guatemala	W 3-2	Barranquilla	CG	
26-12	Puerto Rico	W 6-0	Barranquilla	CG	
5-01-1948	Bolivia	D 2-2	Lima	BG	
8-03-1956	Panama	W 1-0	Port-au-Prince	Fr	
10-03	Haiti	D 1-1	Port-au-Prince	Fr	
14-03	Panama	W 4-2	Port-au-Prince	Fr	
16-03	Haiti	L 0-3	Port-au-Prince	Fr	
16-05-1965	Peru	L 0-1	Lima	WCq	
23-05	Uruguay	L 0-5	Montevideo	WCq	
30-05	Uruguay	L 1-3	Caracas	WCq	Tortolero
2-06	Peru	L 3-6	Caracas	WCq	Motta, Scovino, Ellie
18-01-1967	Chile	L 0-2	Montevideo	SC	
21-01	Uruguay	L 0-4	Montevideo	SC	
25-01	Argentina	L 1-5	Montevideo	SC	Santana
28-01	Bolivia	W 3-0	Montevideo	SC	Scovino, Santana, Gonzalez.P
1-02	Paraguay	L 3-5	Montevideo	SC	Mendoza, Santana, Scovino
27-07-1969	Colombia	L 0-3	Bogota	WCq	
2-08	Colombia	D 1-1	Caracas	WCq	Mendoza
7-08	Paraguay	L 0-2	Caracas	WCq	
10-08	Brazil	L 0-5	Caracas	WCq	
21-08	Paraguay	L 0-1	Asuncion	WCq	
24-08	Brazil	L 0-6	Rio de Janeiro	WCq	
13-11-1971	Trinidad	W 1-0	Caracas	Fr	
3-06-1972	Colombia	W 2-1	Caracas	Fr	
11-06	Paraguay	L 1-4	Campo Grande	Clr1	
14-06	Yugoslavia	L 0-10	Curitiba	Clr1	
18-06	Peru	L 0-1	Manaus	Clr1	
21-06	Bolivia	D 2-2	Manaus	Clr1	
16-12-1973	Dominican Rep.	W 1-0	Caracas	Fr	
30-07-1975	Brazil	L 0-4	Caracas	SCr1	
3-08	Argentina	L 1-5	Caracas	SCr1	Iriarte
10-08	Argentina	L 0-11	Rosario	SCr1	
13-08	Brazil	L 0-6	Belo Horizonte	SCr1	
20-01-1977	Ecuador	W 1-0	Caracas	Fr	
9-02	Uruguay	D 1-1	Caracas	WCq	Flores
6-03	Bolivia	L 1-3	Caracas	WCq	Iriarte
13-03	Bolivia	L 0-2	La Paz	WCq	
17-03	Uruguay	L 0-2	Montevideo	WCq	
31-03-1978	China	L 0-1	Caracas	Fr	
1-08-1979	Colombia	D 0-0	San Cristobal	SCr1	
8-08	Chile	D 1-1	San Cristobal	SCr1	Carbajal
22-08	Colombia	L 0-4	Bogota	SCr1	

29-08	Chile	L 0-7	Santiago	SCr1	
5-01-1980	Colombia	D 0-0	Caracas	Fr	
5-07	Costa Rica	D 1-1	Valera	Fr	
11-01-1981	Neth. Antilles	L 1-2	Willemstad	Fr	
18-01	Neth. Antilles	W 1-0	Caracas	Fr	
8-02	Brazil	L 0-1	Caracas	WCq	
15-02	Bolivia	L 0-3	La Paz	WCq	
15-03	Bolivia	W 1-0	Caracas	WCq	Acosta
29-03	Brazil	L 0-5	Goiania	WCq	
28-06	Spain	L 0-2	Caracas	Fr	
4-09-1983	Uruguay	L 0-3	Montevideo	SCr1	
8-09	Chile	L 0-5	Santiago	SCr1	
18-09	Uruguay	L 1-2	Caracas	SCr1	Febles
21-09	Chile	D 0-0	Caracas	SCr1	
24-01-1984	Mexico	L 0-3	Iraputo	Fr	
24-02-1985	Bolivia	W 5-0	Caracas	Fr	
21-04	Bolivia	L 0-4	Santa Cruz	Fr	
26-05	Argentina	L 2-3	San Cristobal	WCq	Torres, Marquez
2-06	Peru	L 0-1	San Cristobal	WCq	
9-06	Argentina	L 0-3	Buenos Aires	WCq	
16-06	Peru	L 1-4	Lima	WCq	Febles
23-06	Colombia	D 2-2	San Cristobal	WCq	Cadeño, Amor
30-06	Colombia	L 0-2	Bogota	WCq	
28-06-1987	Brazil	L 0-5	Cordoba	SCr1	
30-06	Chile	L 1-3	Cordoba	SCr1	Acosta
26-03-1989	Paraguay	L 1-2	Caracas	Fr	
30-03	Paraguay	D 0-0	Maturin	Fr	
18-05	Peru	L 1-2	Lima	Fr	Dominguez
25-06	Peru	W 3-1	San Cristobal	Fr	Rivas.H, Febles, Rivas.S
1-07	Brazil	L 1-3	Salvador	SCr1	Maldonado
3-07	Colombia	L 2-4	Salvador	SCr1	Maldonado 2
5-07	Peru	D 1-1	Salvador	SCr1	Maldonado
7-07	Paraguay	L 0-3	Salvador	SCr1	
30-07	Brazil	L 0-4	Caracas	WCq	
6-08	Chile	L 1-3	Caracas	WCq	Fernandez
20-08	Brazil	L 0-6	Sao Paulo	WCq	
27-08	Chile	L 0-5	Mendoza	WCq	
6-07-1991	Chile	L 0-2	Santiago	SCr1	
8-07	Argentina	L 0-3	Santiago	SCr1	
10-07	Paraguay	L 0-5	Santiago	SCr1	
12-07	Peru	L 1-5	Santiago	SCr1	OG
23-01-1993	Peru	D 0-0	Ciudad Guyana	Fr	
24-02	Colombia	D 0-0	San Cristobal	Fr	
21-05	Colombia	D 1-1	Bogota	Fr	Rivas.S
11-06	Peru	L 1-3	Arequipa	Fr	Palencia
15-06	Ecuador	L 1-6	Quito	SCr1	Dolguetta
19-06	Uruguay	D 2-2	Ambato	SCr1	Dolguetta, Rivas.S
22-06	USA	D 3-3	Quito	SCr1	Dolguetta 2, Echenaussi
18-07	Bolivia	L 1-7	Puerto Ordaz	WCq	Palencia
25-07	Uruguay	L 0-1	San Cristobal	WCq	
1-08	Brazil	L 1-5	San Cristobal	WCq	Garcia.J
8-08	Ecuador	L 0-5	Quito	WCq	
22-08	Bolivia	L 0-7	La Paz	WCq	
29-08	Uruguay	L 0-4	Montevideo	WCq	
5-09	Brazil	L 0-4	Belo Horizonte	WCq	
12-09	Ecuador	W 2-1	Ciudad Guyana	WCq	Garcia.J, Morales
29-01-1994	Colombia	L 1-2	Barinas	Fr	Rodriguez
18-06-1995	Bolivia	L 1-3	Valera	Fr	Garcia.J
5-07	Uruguay	L 1-4	Montevideo	SCr1	Dolguetta
9-07	Mexico	L 1-3	Maldonado	SCr1	OG
12-07	Paraguay	L 2-3	Maldonado	SCr1	Miranda, Dolguetta

AFRICA

Africa can safely be regarded as the 'New Continent' of world football, and if the 20th century was a tale of Europe and South America, the 21st could see Africa rise to the top of the pile. In the early 1960s it was predicted that an African country would win the World Cup by the end of the century. One still might, but the likelihood would have been greatly increased had a fairer number of places been allotted to the continent in the final tournament. The allocation has increased from one to two in 1982, three for 1994, and will be five in 1998, but with 51 members, the one in ten chance of qualifying afforded to African countries still compares unfavourably with the one in two chance the South Americans have.

Football in Africa is really a tale of the second half of the century, for not until the shackles of colonialism had been thrown off in the 1960s was there any serious movement to organise the game. Until that point, football in sub-Saharan Africa, especially, was organised from the Football Association in London or the French Federation in Paris, Britain and France being the two major colonial powers on the continent.

African football has traditionally been strongest in the area north of the Sahara desert. The Egyptians, for instance, have had a football association since 1921 and qualified for the World Cup finals as long ago as 1934. Six years previously they even reached the semi-finals of the football tournament of the Olympic Games. Morocco, Algeria and Tunisia also have leagues dating from the 1920s. Only Ghana, Nigeria and Zaire, formerly the Belgian Congo, can claim the same for 'Black Africa'.

The year 1957 was a key one for Africa. Not only was the Confédération Africaine de Football formed, but Ghana, under Kwame Nkrumah, lit the torch of African awareness by gaining independence from Britain. As nation after nation broke away from their European rulers, a football revolution was triggered, the ramifications of which are just beginning to be felt.

The highlight to date remains the performance of Cameroon in the 1990 World Cup in Italy when they reached the quarter-finals, although their performance was not the first outstanding one by an African country in a World Cup, nor the last. Algeria were good enough to beat the eventual finalists, West Germany, in 1982 in Spain, whilst Morocco four years later won their first round group ahead of England, Portugal and Poland, before going out to a last-minute goal against the West Germans in the second round. There was similar misfortune for the Nigerians in 1994 when they were denied a place in the quarter-finals by a last-minute goal from Italy's Roberto Baggio.

The population in Africa is growing fast. Nigeria, for example, currently has a population of just under 120 million, but by the year 2010 it will have grown to an estimated 220 million. The population of the continent as a whole is expected to rise from the present 600 million to over 1600 million by the year 2025. This, coupled with the fact that football is unrivalled in the affections of the majority of Africans, makes for an exciting scenario.

Perhaps more than any other regional body, the African Football Confederation has been crucial to the development of football in the countries under its wing. The concept of forming the CAF was first realised at the 1954 World Cup and it came to fruition in 1957 at the Grand Hotel in Khartoum. The Charter members were the four African countries who by that stage had independent football associations: Egypt, Ethiopia, South Africa and Sudan.

At the same time as this meeting, the first African Cup of Nations was held at the new stadium in Khartoum and one of the three pillars of CAF policy was established. The African Cup of Champion Clubs followed seven years later, and the African Cup Winners Cup 11 years after that. These three competitions have been vital in helping the spread of football in Africa, and in overcoming the barriers that both poverty and the great distances involved in travelling to matches present. In 1992 a third club tournament was launched, the CAF Cup, similar to the UEFA and CONMEBOL Cups in that it is for the best of the rest. The CAF also presides over two youth tournaments and the football tournament of the All-African Games.

Poverty is an ever-increasing factor, as Africa is now the only continent which is poorer than it was twenty years ago. Famine has swept through areas of the north-east, as well as other parts of the continent, and bloody civil wars have erupted. This makes for an often harsh environment for football to operate in, but they are factors which African football will have to overcome. Perhaps the biggest obstacle that Africa has to face, though, is that of improving facilities. Too much of the money made by football is lost to corrupt officials, and little gets spent on proper pitches, training facilities or decent stadia. Clubs are too often reliant on the whims of a rich sponsor or the goodwill of the government to pay wages and travelling expenses. Until clubs become self-sufficient, little will change.

Club football is crucial to the development of the game. Already there is a comprehensive club structure in most countries that can accommodate the large number of excellent players being produced. The next challenge is to keep these players from being tempted abroad in vast numbers by creating the wealth in the game to reward them. Far too many go to France and Belgium and end up playing for second-rate clubs just to earn a living. For every Abedi Pele and George Weah at the top of the ladder there are scores of other Africans wasting away in the mediocrity of the French second division.

The exodus does have two positive effects, however. First, it brings more tactical awareness to the national sides when the exiles return for competitions like the Cup of Nations, and second, it also provides the basis of a future generation of African coaches with international experience. Of the 12 teams taking part in the 1992 Cup of Nations, half were coached by foreigners. If a proportion of the 250 Africans currently employed by European clubs can return at some stage and help develop the game in their homeland, Africa will eventually see the benefits.

No-one is expecting every African country to produce teams capable of winning the World Cup, but in Algeria, Cameroon, Egypt, Ghana, Ivory Coast, Kenya, Morocco, Nigeria, Senegal, Zaire, Zambia, Zimbabwe and now South Africa, Africa already has a very strong frontline of states ready to challenge for honours worldwide.

THE AFRICAN GOVERNING BODY

Confédération Africaine de Football
5 Shareh Gabalaya
Guezira, Cairo
Egypt
Tel: + 20 2 3412497
Fax: + 20 2 3420114

Year of formation: 1957

MEMBERS - 51
Algeria – Angola – Benin – Botswana – Burkina Faso – Burundi – Cameroon – Cape Verde Islands – Central African Republic – Chad – Congo – Côte d'Ivoire – Djibouti – Egypt – Equatorial Guinea – Ethiopia – Gabon – Gambia – Ghana – Guinea – Guinea-Bissau – Kenya – Lesotho – Liberia – Libya – Madagascar – Malawi – Mali – Mauritania – Mauritius – Morocco – Mozambique – Namibia – Niger – Nigeria – Rwanda – Sao Tomé e Principe – Senegal – Seychelles – Sierra Leone – Somalia – South Africa – Sudan – Swaziland – Tanzania – Togo – Tunisia – Uganda – Zaire – Zambia – Zimbabwe

NON-MEMBERS - 4
Comoros – Eritrea – Mayotte – Réunion

Presidents

Abdelaziz Abdallah Salem	Egypt	1957-58
Abdelaziz Mostafa	Egypt	1958-68
Abdel Halim Mohamed	Sudan	1968-72
Ydnekatchew Tessema	Ethiopia	1972-88
Issa Hayatou	Cameroon	1988-

General Secretaries

Youssef Mohamed	Egypt	1957-58
Mostafa Kamel Mansour	Egypt	1958-61
Mourad Fahmy	Egypt	1961-82
Mustapha Fahmy	Egypt	1982

AFRICAN FOOTBALLER OF THE YEAR

From 'France Football'

1970

1	Salif Keita	Saint-Étienne	MLI	54
2	Laurent Pokou	ASEC Abidjan	CIV	28
	Ubugreisha	Al Ismaili	EGY	28
4	Kalala	TP Englebert	ZAI	19
5	Lalmas	CR Belcourt	ALG	15
6	Petit Sory	Hafia FC Conakry	GUI	9
7	Allal	FAR Rabat	MOR	5
	Robert Mensah	Asante Kotoko	GHA	5
	Ossey Coffie	Asante Kotoko	GHA	5
10	4 players on 4 points			

1971

1	Ibrahim Sunday	Asante Kotoko	GHA	29
2	Robert Mensah	Asante Kotoko	GHA	15
3	Lea	Canon Yaoundé	CMR	13
4	Laurent Pokou	ASEC Abidjan	CIV	8
	Attouga	Club Africain	TUN	8
6	Kibonge	Victoria Club	ZAI	6
	Francois M'Pele	AC Ajaccio	COG	6
	Koum	AS Monaco	CMR	6
	Lalmas	CR Belcourt	ALG	6
	Kallet	Africa Sports	CIV	6

1972

1	Cherif Souleymane	Hafia FC Conakry	GUI	21
2	Tshimen Bwanga	TP Mazembe	ZAI	16
3	Petit Sory	Hafia FC Conakry	GUI	14
4	Hanni	Al Ahly	EGY	12
5	Ahmed Farras	Mohammedia	MOR	11
	Hadfi		ALG	11
7	Malik		GHA	10
8	Abougreisha		EGY	8
	Minga		COG	8
	N'Tumba		ZAI	8

1973

1	Tshimen Bwanga	TP Mazembe	ZAI	49
2	Mwamba Kazadi	TP Mazembe	ZAI	44
3	Laurent Pokou	ASEC Abidjan	CIV	41
4	Kakoko		ZAI	29
5	Ahmed Faras		MOR	18
6	Yaw Sam		GHA	16
7	Kembo		ZAI	15
8	Cherif Souleymane		GUI	9
9	Moheddine		TUN	8
	Kibonge		ZAI	8
	Attouga		TUN	8

1974

1	Paul Moukila	CARA Brazzaville	COG	57
2	Lobilo	AS Vita Kinshasa	ZAI	32
3	Chehata		EGY	28
4	Chama		ZAM	16
5	Ahmed Faras		MOR	14
6	N'Daye		ZAI	10
7	Kakoko		ZAI	8
8	Yanghat		COG	6
	Mwamba Kazadi		ZAI	6
	Mana		ZAI	6
	Amasha		EGY	6
	Mambo Sasa		TAN	6

1975

1	Ahmed Faras	Mohammedia	MOR	28
2	N'Jolea	Hafia FC Conakry	GUI	24
	Roger Milla	Canon Yaoundé	CMR	24
4	Tarak Dhiab		TUN	16
5	Sagna		SEN	15
6	Petit Sory		GUI	10
7	Larbi		MOR	9
8	Gaafar		EGY	7
	Attouga		TUN	7
10	3 players on 5 points			

1976

1	Roger Milla	Canon Yaoundé	CMR	33
2	Papa Camara	Hafia FC Conakry	GUI	32
3	Ali Bencheikh	Mouloudia d'Algiers	ALG	27
4	Bengally Sylla	Hafia FC Conakry	GUI	26
5	Ahmed Faras	Mohammedia	MOR	12
	Betroumi		ALG	12
7	Lalbi		MOR	11
	Attouga		TUN	11
9	Tarak Dhiab		TUN	10
	Petit Sory		GUI	10

1977

1	Tarak Dhiab	Esperance Tunis	TUN	45
2	Papa Camara	Hafia FC Conakry	GUI	33
3	Odegbami	IICC Shooting Stars	NGA	29
4	Mohamed Polo		GHA	15
5	Bwalya		ZAM	6
6	Ali Bencheikh		ALG	5
7	Attouga		TUN	4
8	Gaafar		EGY	3
	Bahamboula		COG	3
	Cherif Souleymane		GUI	3

1978

1	Karim Abdoul Razak	Asante Kotoko	GHA	58
2	Ali Bencheikh	Mouloudia d'Algiers	ALG	33
3	Thomas N'Kono	Canon Yaoundé	CMR	29
4	Christian Chukwu	Enugu Rangers	NGA	25
5	Bengally Sylla	Hafia FC Conakry	GUI	20
6	Tarak Dhiab	Al Ahly Jeddah	TUN	18
7	Temime Lahzani		TUN	12
8	Manga Onguene	Canon Yaoundé	CMR	10
9	Philip Omondi		UGA	9
10	4 players on 4 points			

1979

1	Thomas N'Kono	Canon Yaoundé	CMR	55
2	Adolf Armah	Hearts of Oak	GHA	23
3	Kerfalla Bangoura	Horoya AC Conakry	GUI	15
4	Abdoulaye Campaore	Bobo Dioulasso	VOL	13
5	Nahashion Oluoch	Gor Mahia	KEN	9
6	Kiyika		ZAI	8
7	Felix Agbonifo		NGA	7
8	Pascal Miezan	ASEC Abidjan	CIV	6
9	Muda Lawal	IICC Shooting Stars	NGA	5
10	4 players on 4 points			

1980

1	Manga Onguene	Canon Yaoundé	CMR	64
2	Segun Odegbami	IICC Shooting Stars	NGA	41
3	Théophile Abega	Canon Yaoundé	CMR	18
4	Lakhdar Belloumi	GCR Mascara	ALG	13
5	Ayel Mayele	AS Bilima	ZAI	12
	Thomas N'Kono	Canon Yaoundé	CMR	12
7	Mustapha Kouici	CR Belcourt	MOR	11
8	Elunga Massengo	TP Mazembe	ZAI	7
9	Tadj Bensaoula	Mouloudia Oran	ALG	6
	Mwamba Kazadi	TP Mazembe	ZAI	6

1981

1	Lakhdar Belloumi	GCR Mascara	ALG	78
2	Thomas N'Kono	Canon Yaoundé	CMR	54
3	Ali Fergani	JE Tizi-Ouzou	ALG	26
4	Eugène Ekoule	Union Douala	CMR	18
5	Théophile Abega	Canon Yaoundé	CMR	16
	Aziz Bouderbala	WAC Casablanca	MOR	16
7	Segun Odegbami	IICC Shooting Stars	NGA	8
8	Cheik Keita	AS Kaloum Stars	GUI	6
9	Koffi Kouadio	ASEC Abidjan	CIV	4
10	Badou Zaki	WAC Casablanca	MOR	4

1982

1	Thomas N'Kono	Español	CMR	83
2	Salah Assad	FC Mulhouse	ALG	54
3	Lakhdar Belloumi	GCR Mascara	ALG	36
4	Mahmoud Al Khatib	Al Ahly Cairo	EGY	28
5	Théophile Abega	Canon Yaoundé	CMR	23
	Peter Kaumba	Power Dynamos	ZAM	23
7	Albert Asase	Asante Kotoko	GHA	22
8	Opoku Afriyie	Asante Kotoko	GHA	13
9	Rabah Madjer	MA Hussein Dey	ALG	9
10	Chaabane Merzekane	MA Hussein Dey	ALG	8

1983

1	Mahmoud Al Khatib	Al Ahly Cairo	EGY	98
2	Opoku N'Ti	Asante Kotoko	GHA	89
3	Rafiou Moutairou	Agaza Lomé	TGO	19
4	Théophile Abega	Canon Yaoundé	CMR	18
	Antoine Bell	Al Mokaouloum	CMR	18
	Karim Abdul Razak	Al Mokaouloum	GHA	18
7	Cheikh Seck	ASC Diaraf Dakar	SEN	11
8	Mohamed Ali Nasser	Al Ahly Cairo	EGY	7
	Mustapha Haddaoui	Raja Casablanca	MOR	7
	Rabah Madjer	Racing Club Paris	ALG	7

1984

1	Théophile Abega	FC Toulouse	CMR	124
2	Ibrahim Youssef	Zamalek	EGY	65
	Antoine Bell	Al Mokaouloum	CMR	65
4	Henry Nwosu	New Nigerian Bank	NGA	47
5	Taher Abou Zeid	Al Ahly Cairo	EGY	28
	Youssouf Fofana	AS Cannes	CIV	28
	Mahmoud Al Khatib	Al Ahly Cairo	EGY	28
8	Stephen Keshi	New Nigerian Bank	NGA	16
9	Lakhdar Belloumi	GCR Mascara	ALG	12
10	Clifton Msiya	Berrick Power	MWI	12

1985

1	Mohamed Timoumi	FAR Rabat	MOR	113
2	Rabah Madjer	FC Porto	ALG	45
3	Djamel Menad	JE Tizi-Ouzou	ALG	39
	Ibrahim Youssef	Zamalek	EGY	39
5	Badou Zaki	WAC Casablanca	MOR	33
6	Youssouf Fofana	AS Monaco	CIV	31
7	Lakhdar Belloumi	GCR Mascara	ALG	20
8	Abedi Pelé	Dragons de l'Ouème	GHA	19
9	Francois Bocande	FC Metz	SEN	17
10	Roger Milla	Saint-Étienne	CMR	16
	Wa Mbati Mobati	AS Bilima	ZAI	16

1986

1	Badou Zaki	Real Mallorca	MOR	125
2	Aziz Bouderbala	FC Sion	MOR	88
3	Roger Milla	Montpellier	CMR	80
4	Taher Abou Zeid	Al Ahly Cairo	EGY	47
5	Mohamed Timoumi	Real Murcia	MOR	35
6	Francois Bocande	Paris Saint-Germain	SEN	13
	Abdelmajid Dolmy	Raja Casablanca	MOR	13
	Abedi Pelé	Chamois Niortais	GHA	13
9	Efford Chabala	Nkana Red Devils	ZAM	11
	Nacer Drid	Mouloudia Oran	ALG	11

1987

1	Rabah Madjer	FC Porto	ALG	130
2	Youssouf Fofana	AS Monaco	CIV	63
3	Francois Oman-Biyik	Stade Lavallois	CMR	52
4	Magdi Abdelghani	Al Ahly Cairo	EGY	37
5	Taher Abou Zeid	Al Ahly Cairo	EGY	25
6	Kennedy Malunga	Club Brugge	MWI	24
7	Peter Dawo	Gor Mahia	KEN	21
8	Abedi Pelé	Olympique Mareseille	GHA	17
9	Ambrose Ayoyi	AFC Leopards	KEN	15
10	Roger Milla	Montpellier	CMR	14

1988

1	Kalusha Bwalya	Cercle Brugge	ZAM	111
2	Roger Milla	Montpellier	CMR	68
3	Youssouf Fofana	AS Monaco	CIV	40
4	George Weah	AS Monaco	LBR	32
5	Aziz Bouderbala	Matra Racing Paris	MOR	27
	Peter Rufai	SC Lokeren	NGA	27
7	Stephen Keshi	RSC Anderlecht	NGA	14
	Emmanuel Kunde	Stade de Reims	CMR	14
9	Jacques Kingambo	St. Truidense	ZAI	13
10	Antoine Bell	SC Toulon	CMR	12

1989

1	George Weah	AS Monaco	LBR	133
2	Antoine Bell	Girondins Bordeaux	CMR	105
3	Kalusha Bwalya	PSV Eindhoven	ZAM	49
4	Abedi Pelé	Lille OSC	GHA	40
5	Francois Oman-Biyik	Stade Lavallois	CMR	31
6	Magdi Abdelghani	Beira Mar	EGY	30
7	Ahmed Shoubeir	Al Ahly Cairo	EGY	28
8	Stephen Tataw	Tonnerre Yaoundé	CMR	19
9	Stephen Keshi	RSC Anderlecht	NGA	18
10	Hossam Hassan	Al Ahly Cairo	EGY	17

1990

1	Roger Milla	St Denis	CMR	209
2	Cherif El Ouazani	Aydinspor	ALG	64
3	Rabah Madjer	FC Porto	ALG	60
	Francois Oman-Biyik	Stade Rennais	CMR	60
5	Ahmed Shoubeir	Al Ahly Cairo	EGY	49
6	Hany Ramzy	Neuchâtel Xamax	EGY	41
7	Cyrille Makanaky	Málaga	CMR	34
8	George Weah	AS Monaco	LBR	26
9	Abedi Pelé	Olympique Marseille	GHA	23
10	Hossam Hassan	PAOK Salonika	EGY	22

1991

1	Abedi Pelé	Olympique Marseile	GHA	159
2	George Weah	AS Monaco	LBR	106
3	Francois Oman-Biyik	AS Cannes	CMR	52
4	Kalusha Bwalya	PSV Eindhoven	ZAM	30
5	Nii Lamptey	RSC Anderlecht	GHA	29
6	Antony Yeboah	Eintracht Frankfurt	GHA	20
7	Roger Mendy	AS Monaco	SEN	18
8	Abdoulaye Traoré	ASEC Abidjan	CIV	16
9	Youssouf Fofana	AS Monaco	CIV	14
10	Aziz Bouderbala	Olympique Lyonnais	EGY	13

1992

1	Abedi Pelé	Olympique Marseille	GHA	198
2	George Weah	Paris Saint-Germain	LBR	161
3	Anthony Yeboah	Eintracht Frankfurt	GHA	64
4	Abdoulaye Traoré	ASEC Abidjan	CIV	36
5	Alain Gouamene	Raja Casablanca	CIV	33
6	Japhet N'Doram	FC Nantes	CHD	30
7	Peter Ndlovu	Coventry City	ZIM	24
8	Rashidi Yekini	Vitoria Setubal	NGA	20
9	Kalusha Bwalya	PSV Eindhoven	ZAM	15
10	Rachid Daoudi	WAC Casablanca	MOR	14

1993

1	Abedi Pelé	Olympique Lyonnais	GHA	119
2	Anthony Yeboah	Eintracht Frankfurt	GHA	117
3	Rashidi Yekini	Vitoria Setubal	NGA	104
4	Victor Ikpeba	AS Monaco	NGA	57
5	George Weah	Paris Saint-Germain	LBR	56
6	Kalusha Bwalya	PSV Eindhoven	ZAM	48
7	François Oman-Biyik	RC Lens	CMR	28
8	Rachid Daoudi	WAC Casablanca	MOR	20
9	Peter Ndlovu	Coventry City	ZAM	19
10	Abdoulaye Traore	ASEC Abidjan	CIV	16

1994

1	George Weah	Paris Saint-Germain	LBR	148
2	Emmanuel Amunike	Sporting CL	NGA	133
3	Daniel Amokachi	Everton	NGA	99
4	Rashidi Yekini	Olympiakos	NGA	87
5	Kalusha Bwalya	América, Mexico	ZAM	37
6	Anthony Yeboah	Eintracht Frankfurt	GHA	32
7	Finidi George	Ajax	NGA	31
8	Joël Tiéhi	Le Havre AC	CIV	22
9	Japhet N'Doram	FC Nantes	TCH	18
	Augustine Okocha	Eintracht Frankfurt	NGA	18

AFRICAN FOOTBALLER OF THE YEAR

From 'Afrique Football'

1991

1	Abedi Pele	Olympique Marseille	GHA	206
2	George Weah	AS Monaco	LBR	146
3	Nii Lamptey	RSC Anderlecht	GHA	68
4	Kalusha Bwalya	PSV Eindhoven	ZAM	35
5	Roger Mendy	AS Monaco	SEN	31
6	Faouzi Rouissi	Club Africain	TUN	27
7	Francois Oman-Biyik	AS Cannes	CMR	21
8	Abdoulaye Traoré	ASEC Abidjan	CIV	19
9	Majid Musisi	Nakivubo Villa	UGA	17
10	Peter Ndlovu	Coventry City	ZIM	14

1992

1	Abedi Pele	Olympique Marseille	GHA	192
2	George Weah	Paris Saint-Germain	LBR	167
3	Alain Gouaméné	Raja Casablanca	CIV	60
4	Abdoulaye Traoré	ASEC Abidjan	CIV	53
5	Anthony Yeboah	Eintracht Frankfurt	GHA	52
6	Rashidi Yekini	Vitoria Setubal	NGA	30
7	Richard Owubokiri	Boavista	NGA	22
8	Nii Lamptey	RSC Anderlecht	GHA	19
9	Japhet N'Doram	FC Nantes	CHD	18
10	Kalasha Bwalya	PSV Eindhoven	ZAM	16

1993

1	Rashidi Yekini	Vitoria Setubal	NGA	152
2	Abedi Pele	Olympique Lyonnais	GHA	118
3	Anthony Yeboah	Eintracht Frankfurt	GHA	98
4	Kalusha Bwalya	PSV Eindhoven	ZAM	76
5	George Weah	Paris Saint-Germain	LBR	61
6	Francois Oman-Biyik	RC Lens	CMR	45
7	Rachid Daoudi	WAC Casablanca	MOR	42
8	Serge-Alain Maguy	Africa Sports	CIV	22
9	Peter Ndlovu	Coventry City	ZAM	19
10	Thomson Oliha	Africa Sports		13
	Abdelhafid Tasfaout	Mouloudia Oran	ALG	13
	Abdoulaye Traoré	ASEC Abidjan	CIV	13

1994

1	Emmanuel Amunike	Sporting CL	NGA	178
2	George Weah	Paris Saint-Germain	LBR	114
3	Daniel Amokachi	Everton	NGA	97
4	Rashidi Yekini	Olympiakos	NGA	74
5	Joel Tiéhi	Le Havre AC	CIV	43
6	Kalusha Bwalya	América, Mexico	ZAM	38
7	Abedi Pele	Torino	GHA	24
8	Finidi George	Ajax	NGA	23
9	Kenneth Malitoli	Esperance Tunis	ZAM	21
	Japhet N'Doram	FC Nantes	CHD	21

THE AFRICAN CUP OF NATIONS

The African Cup of Nations is the showpiece of African football and is held every two years in a designated country. For many years a simple knock-out qualifying tournament was used to reduce the number of entrants to just eight finalists, but for the 1992 tournament in Senegal it was decided to increase the number of finalists to twelve. For the 1996 event that has been increased further to sixteen. The hosts and previous winners have always received a bye into the final tournament. Since 1992 the qualifying competition has been organised on a group basis rather than a knock-out formula.

The first finals took place in Khartoum at the same time as the formation of the Confédération Africaine de Football. South Africa were initially involved and were drawn against Ethiopia in the semi-finals, but only agreed to send either an all-black or all-white team. CAF insisted on a multi-racial one and so the South Africans withdrew and until they were readmitted to the confederation in 1992 they played no part in African football.

The first five editions were confined to only ten different entrants and did not involve any qualifying rounds. Egypt won the first two tournaments and reached the final of the third having played only six matches, so small was the number of entries at the time. Ghana won the fourth tournament in 1963 and were the dominant power for the rest of the decade, winning again in 1965 and reaching the final in 1968 and 1970. In 1965 a regulation was passed allowing each nation to play only two overseas-based players. This rule remained in force until 1982 when, due to the increasing numbers of players earning their living abroad, it was felt that the value of the tournament was being undermined.

In 1968 the formula for the tournament was changed to cope with the increasing number of countries wishing to take part. A qualifying round was introduced and the number of finalists increased to eight. The countries surrounding the river Congo were the first to make their mark in the new-style tournament. Congo Kinshasa, as Zaire was previously known, won in 1968; their smaller neighbours, the Congo, were victorious in 1972, and in 1974, having qualified for the World Cup, Zaire went to West Germany as African champions after winning their second title in Egypt.

The biggest surprise of the 1970s was the failure of Guinea's national side to add to the many honours won by their clubs. They came close in 1976, finishing second behind Morocco, who themselves have never really shone despite qualifying for the World Cup on two occasions. That 1976 win remains their only triumph, and is in line with a poor showing generally by the North African countries, the real powers in club football. Egypt in 1986 and Algeria in 1990 both won on home ground, but neither they, Morocco nor Tunisia seem to travel well.

Since the late 1970s, West Africa has been the dominant force. Ghana regained some of their previous form by winning two further titles, which leaves them, with four titles, as clear overall leaders, whilst Cameroon and Nigeria have been especially powerful since 1980. The Nigerians have won twice and lost in the final three times, twice against Cameroon, who, had they not lost to Egypt on penalties in 1986, would have been the first team to claim a hat-trick of titles.

Release of players from European clubs has often been a problem, but by moving the tournament to January, when much of Europe is in a mid-season break, the problem has been alleviated. Television companies around the world have begun to take the Cup of Nations seriously, the presence of famous names from European football undoubtedly being the spur, and the future of the competition looks brighter than ever.

1957	Egypt	4-0	Ethiopia
1959	Egypt	2-1	Sudan
1962	Ethiopia	4-2	Egypt
1963	Ghana	3-0	Sudan
1965	Ghana	3-2	Tunisia
1968	Congo Kinshasa	1-0	Ghana
1970	Sudan	1-0	Ghana
1972	Congo	3-2	Mali
1974	Zaire	2-2 2-0	Zambia
1976	Morocco	1-1	Guinea
1978	Ghana	2-0	Uganda
1980	Nigeria	3-0	Algeria
1982	Ghana	1-1 7-6p	Libya
1984	Cameroon	3-1	Nigeria
1986	Egypt	0-0 5-4p	Cameroon
1988	Cameroon	1-0	Nigeria
1990	Algeria	1-0	Nigeria
1992	Côte d'Ivoire	0-0 11-10p	Ghana
1994	Nigeria	2-1	Zambia

	Country	G	S	B	Finals	S-Finals
1	Ghana	4	3	-	7	5
2	Egypt	3	1	3	3	7
3	Nigeria	2	3	3	5	7
4	Cameroon	2	1	1	3	5
5	Zaire	2	-	-	2	3
6	Sudan	1	2	1	3	2
7	Algeria	1	1	2	2	5
8	Côte d'Ivoire	1	-	4	1	5
9	Ethiopia	1	1	1	1	3
10	Morocco	1	-	1	-	3
11	Congo	1	-	-	1	2
12	Zambia	-	2	2	2	4
13	Tunisia	-	1	1	1	2
14	Uganda	-	1	-	1	2
15	Guinea	-	1	-	-	-
	Libya	-	1	-	1	1
	Mali	-	1	-	1	2
18	Senegal	-	-	-	-	1

1957

I. EDITION, SUDAN

FIRST ROUND/SEMI-FINALS

Ethiopia received a walkover, after South Africa were forced to withdraw

Khartoum Stadium, Khartoum, 10-02-1957

Egypt	2 (Raafat 21, El Diba 72)
Sudan	1 (Manzul 58)

FINAL

Khartoum Stadium, Khartoum, 16-02-1957. Referee: Youssef, Sudan

EGYPT 4 (El Diba 4)
ETHIOPIA 0

Egypt - Brascos - Mossaad, Dali - Fanaguili, Hanafi, Kotb - Tewfik, El Diba, Attia, Alaa, Hamdi

Ethiopia - Gila - Ayele, Adale - Adamu, Asefaw, Berthe - Kebede, Zewode, Abreha, Netsere, Berhane

Top scorer El Diba, Egypt 5

1959

II. EDITION, EGYPT

Al Ahli Stadium, Cairo, 22-05-1959

Egypt 4 (Gohri 29 42 73, Cherbini 64)
Ethiopia 0

Al Ahli Stadium, Cairo, 25-05-1959

Sudan 1 (Drissa 40)
Ethiopia 0

Al Ahli Stadium, Cairo, 29-05-1959. Referee: Guisebatic, Yugoslavia

EGYPT 2 (Issam 12 89)
SUDAN 1 (Manzul 65)

Egypt - Heykal - Yakin, Tarek Selim - Fanaguili, Al-Hamouli, Ismail - Bahig, Cherif El-Far, Salah Selim, Gohri, Cherbini

Sudan - Samir - Mutawakil, Bashir - Syam, Hassan Abd, Mahina - Kabir, Zoubeir, Drissa, Seddik Manzul, Wahaga

	Eg	Su	Et	Pl	W	D	L	F	A	Pts
EGYPT	-	2-1	4-0	2	2	0	0	6	1	4
SUDAN	-	-	1-0	2	1	0	1	2	2	2
ETHIOPIA	-	-	-	2	0	0	2	0	5	0

Top scorer Gohri, Egypt 3

III. EDITION, ETHIOPIA

FIRST ROUND/SEMI-FINALS

Haile Selassie Stadium, Addis Ababa, 14-01-1962

Ethiopia 4 (Luciano 2, Girma, Menguistou)
Tunisia 2 (Marrichko, Moncef Cherif)

Haile Selassie Stadium, Addis Ababa, 18-01-1962

Egypt 2 (Abdelfattah Badawi 50, Salah Selim)
Uganda 1 (Jonathan 16)

3RD PLACE

Haile Selassie Stadium, Addis Ababa, 20-01-1962

Tunisia 3 (Djedidi, Moncef Cherif, Meddeb)
Uganda 0

FINAL

Haile Selassie Stadium, Addis Ababa, 21-01-1962. Referee: Brooks, Uganda

ETHIOPIA 4 (Girma 74, Menguistou 84 117, Italo 101)
EGYPT 2 (Abdelfattah Badawi 35 75)

Ethiopia - Gila - Kiflom, Asmelash, Berhe, Awade - Tesfaye, Luciano - Girma, Menguistou, Italo, Guetacheou

Egypt - Heykal - Ahmed Mostafa, Raafat, Tarak - Fanaguili, Badawi.M - Salah Selim, Taha, Cherbini, Chehta, Abdelfattah Badawi

Top scorers Badawi, Egypt 3
Menguistou, Ethiopia 3

1963

IV. EDITION, GHANA

FIRST ROUND

Group 1

Accra Stadium, Accra, 24-11-1963

Ghana 1 (Mfum 9)
Tunisia 1 (Djedidi 36)

Accra Stadium, Accra, 26-11-1963

Ghana 2 (Acquah 2)
Ethiopia 0

Accra Stadium, Accra, 28-11-1963

Ethiopia 4
Tunisia 2

	Gh	Et	Tu	Pl	W	D	L	F	A	Pts
GHANA	-	2-0	1-1	2	1	1	0	3	1	3
ETHIOPIA	-	-	4-2	2	1	0	1	4	4	2
TUNISIA	-	-	-	2	0	1	1	3	5	1

Group 2

Kumasi Stadium, Kumasi, 24-11-1963

Egypt 6 (Chazli 42 44 81 87, Riza 30 32)
Nigeria 3 (Okepe 78, Bassey 82, Onya 89)

Kumasi Stadium, Kumasi, 26-11-1963

Sudan 2 (Djaksa 60 75)
Egypt 2 (Chazli 5, Riza 7)

Kumasi Stadium, Kumasi, 28-11-1963

Sudan 4
Nigeria 0

	Su	Eg	Ni	Pl	W	D	L	F	A	Pts
SUDAN	-	2-2	4-0	2	1	1	0	6	2	3
EGYPT	-	-	6-3	2	1	1	0	8	5	3
NIGERIA	-	-	-	2	0	0	2	3	10	0

3RD PLACE

Accra Stadium, Accra, 30-01-1963

Egypt 3 (Riadh, Taha, Chazli)
Ethiopia 0

FINAL

Accra Stadium, Accra, 1-12-1963. Referee: Abdelkader, Tunisia

GHANA 3 (Aggrey-Fynn 62, Mfum 72 82)
SUDAN 0

Ghana - Ankrah - Crentsil, Aggrey-Fynn, Odametey, Simmons - Obiley, Adarkwa Ofei Dodo, Mfum, Acquah, Salisu

Sudan - Sabbit - Samir, Kabir, Amin, Omar - Zarzour, Magid - Ibrahima, Djaksa, Nagy, Jagdoul

Top scorer Chazli, Egypt 6

1965

V. EDITION, TUNISIA

FIRST ROUND

Group 1

Zouiten, Tunis, 12-11-1965

Tunisia 4 (Chaibi 32, Djedidi 62, Delhoum 80, Lahmar 84)
Ethiopia 0

Zouiten, Tunis, 14-11-1965

Senegal 0
Tunisia 0

Zouiten, Tunis, 19-11-1965

Senegal	5	(Louis Camara 3 52, Gueye 37, Matar Niang 48 53)
Ethiopia	1	(Luciano 12)

	Tu	Se	Et	Pl	W	D	L	F	A	Pts
Tunisia	-	0-0	4-0	2	1	1	0	4	0	3
Senegal	-	-	5-1	2	1	1	0	5	1	3
Ethiopia	-	-	-	2	0	0	2	1	9	0

Group 2

Maarouf, Sousse, 12-11-1965

Ghana	5	(Osei Kofi 13, Ben Acheampong 18 59, Jones 84 89)
Congo Kinshasa	2	(Kalala 43 45)

Maarouf, Sousse, 14-11-1965

Côte d'Ivoire	3	(Mangle 14 59 80)
Congo Kinshasa	0	

Maarouf, Sousse, 19-11-1965

Ghana	4	(Ben Acheampong 20, Kwamenti 43, Lutdrot 52, Osei Kofi 70)
Côte d'Ivoire	1	(Bleziri 66)

	Gh	IC	CK	Pl	W	D	L	F	A	Pts
Ghana	-	4-1	5-2	2	2	0	0	9	3	4
Côte d'Ivoire	-	-	3-0	2	1	0	1	4	4	2
Congo Kinshasa	-	-	-	2	0	0	2	2	8	0

3RD PLACE

Zouiten, Tunis, 21-11-1965

Côte d'Ivoire	1	(Yoboue 35)
Senegal	0	

FINAL

Zouiten, Tunis, 21-11-1965. Referee: Chekaimi, Algeria

GHANA	3	(Odoi 37 96, Kofi 79)
TUNISIA	2	(Chetali 47, Chaibi 67)

Ghana - Naawu - Ben Kusi, Acquah, Odametey, Evans - Kwamenti, Mensah - Osei Kofi, Jones, Kofi Pare, Odoi

Tunisia - Attouga - Benzerti, Douiri, Habacha, Lamine - Chetali, Chaibi Sassi, Gribaa, Delhoum, Djedidi

Top scorers Kofi, Ghana 3
Ben Acheampong, Ghana 3
Mangle, Côte d'Ivoire 3

1968

VI. EDITION

QUALIFYING TOURNAMENT

Group 1

	Se	Gu	Lb	Pl	W	D	L	F	A	Pts
SENEGAL	-	4-1	4-1	4	2	1	1	9	6	5
Guinea	3-0	-	3-0	4	2	1	1	9	6	5
Liberia	1-1	2-2	-	4	0	2	2	4	10	2

Play-off

Senegal ....2-1 ....Guinea

Group 2

	Al	Ml	BF	Pl	W	D	L	F	A	Pts
ALGERIA	-	1-0	3-1	4	4	0	0	9	2	8
Mali	0-3	-	4-0	4	2	0	2	5	4	4
Upper Volta	1-2	0-1	-	4	0	0	4	2	10	0

Group 3

	IC	Ng	To	Pl	W	D	L	F	A	Pts
COTE D'IVOIRE	-	2-0	3-0	4	3	1	0	7	0	7
Nigeria	0-0	-	4-2	4	1	1	2	4	5	3
Togo	0-2	1-0	-	4	1	0	3	3	9	2

Group 4

Egypt ....3-2 2-2 ....Libya
Uganda ....2-1 3-3 ....Kenya

Uganda ....0-1 ....**EGYPT**

Uganda qualified after Egypt withdrew

Group 5

	CB	Tu	Ca	Pl	W	D	L	F	A	Pts
CONGO BRAZZAVILLE	-	W-O	2-1	3	2	1	0	3	2	5
Tunisia	1-1	-	4-0	4	1	1	2	5	3	3
Cameroon	-	2-0	-	3	1	0	2	3	6	2

Group 6

Congo Kinshasa. ....3-2 0-1 2-1 ....Sudan
Tanzania ....1-0 1-1 ....Mauritius

CONGO KINSHASA ....W-O ....Tanzania

Ethiopia qualified as hosts, Ghana as holders

FINAL TOURNAMENT
ETHIOPIA, 12TH - 21ST JANUARY 1968

FIRST ROUND

Group 1

Haile Selassie Stadium, Addis Ababa, 12-01-1968

Ethiopia	2	(Girma, Luciano)
Uganda	1	(Ouma)

Haile Selassie Stadium, Addis Ababa, 12-01-1968

Côte d'ivoire	3	(Pokou 25 65, Bozon 15)
Algeria	0	

Haile Selassie Stadium, Addis Ababa, 14-01-1968

Ethiopia	1	(Bekouresion 86)
Côte d'Ivoire	0	

Haile Selassie Stadium, Addis Ababa, 14-01-1968

Algeria	4	(Lalmas 15 25 70, Khalem 60)
Uganda	0	

Haile Selassie Stadium, Addis Ababa, 16-01-1968

Côte d'Ivoire	2	(Pokou, Mangle)
Uganda	1	(Obua)

Haile Selassie Stadium, Addis Ababa, 16-01-1968

Ethiopia	3	(Menguistou 16, Shewangezaw 19, Luciano 27)
Algeria	1	(Amirouche 68)

	Et	IC	Al	Ug	Pl	W	D	L	F	A	Pts
Ethiopia	-	1-0	3-1	2-1	3	3	0	0	6	2	6
Côte d'Ivoire	-	-	3-0	2-1	3	2	0	1	5	2	4
Algeria	-	-	-	4-0	3	1	0	2	5	6	2
Uganda	-	-	-	-	3	0	0	3	2	8	0

Group 2

Saba, Asmara, 12-01-1968

Ghana	2	(Osei Kofi 63, Mfum 87)
Senegal	2	(Diongue 10, Diop 65)

Saba, Asmara, 12-01-1968

Congo Kinshasa	3	(Muwawia 19, Kabamba 27)
Congo Brazzaville	0	

Saba, Asmara, 14-01-1968
Senegal 2 (Diop 27, Diock 86)
Congo Brazzaville 1 (Foutika 31)

Saba, Asmara, 14-01-1968
Ghana 2 (Osei Kofi 17, Mfum 84)
Congo Kinshasa 1 (Mokili 42)

Saba, Asmara, 16-01-1968
Congo Kinshasa 2 (Kidumu, Tshimanga)
Senegal 1 (Diouck)

Saba, Asmara, 16-01-1968
Ghana 3
Congo Brazzaville 1

	Gh	CK	Se	CB	Pl	W	D	L	F	A	Pts
GHANA	-	2-1	2-2	3-1	3	2	1	0	7	4	5
ZAIRE	-	-	2-1	3-0	3	2	0	1	6	3	4
SENEGAL	-	-	-	2-1	3	1	1	1	5	5	3
CONGO BRAZZAVILLE	-	-	-	-	3	0	0	3	2	8	0

SEMI-FINALS

Haile Selassie Stadium, Addis Ababa, 19-01-1968
Congo Kinshasa 3 (Kidumu 3, Mungamuni 16 100)
Ethiopia 2 (Luciano 25, Menguistou 65)

Saba, Asmara, 19-01-1968
Ghana 4 (Mfum 2, Sunday, Odoi)
Côte d'Ivoire 3 (Pokou 2, Konan Henri)

3RD PLACE

Haile Selassie Stadium, Addis Ababa, 21-01-1968
Côte d'Ivoire 1 (Pokou 28)
Ethiopia 0

FINAL

Haile Selassie Stadium, Addis Ababa, 21-01-1968. Referee: El Diba, Egypt
CONGO KINSHASA 1 (Kalala 66)
GHANA 0

Congo Kinshasa - Kazadi - Mange, Katumba, Tshimanga, Mukombo - Kibonge, Kassongo - Kalala, Kidumu, Kembo, Mungamuni

Ghana - Naawu - Crentsil, Eshun, Odametey, Kusi - Sunday, Odoi - Kofi, Attuquayefio, Mfum, Malik

Top scorer Pokou, Côte d'Ivoire 6

1970

VII. EDITION

QUALIFYING TOURNAMENT
FIRST ROUND

Algeria .... 2-0 0-1 .... Morocco
Egypt .... W-O .... Somalia
Guinea .... 4-0 1-1 .... Togo
Kenya .... 0-1 1-1 .... **Tanzania**
Mali .... W-O .... Upper Volta
Mauritius .... 2-3 2-2 .... **Zambia**
Niger .... W-O .... Nigeria
Senegal .... W-O .... Sierra Leone
Uganda .... 1-1 0-2 .... **Cameroon**

SECOND ROUND

EGYPT .... 1-0 1-1 .... Algeria
ETHIOPIA .... 7-0 2-1 .... Tanzania
GHANA .... 6-0 9-1 .... Niger
Mali .... 0-0 0-4 .... **COTE D'IVOIRE**
Senegal .... 1-1 3-4 .... **GUINEA**
Zambia .... 2-2 1-2 .... **CAMEROON**

Sudan qualified as hosts, Congo-Kinshasa as holders

FINAL TOURNAMENT
SUDAN, 6TH - 16TH FEBRUARY 1970

FIRST ROUND

Group 1

Municipal Stadium, Khartoum, 6-02-1970, 14,000
Cameroon 3 (Koum 57 66, Ndoga 60)
Côte d'Ivoire 2 (Pokou 25 45)

Municipal Stadium, Khartoum, 6-02-1970, 14,000
Sudan 3 (Gagarine 43, Hasabu 47, Djaksa 85)
Ethiopia 0

Municipal Stadium, Khartoum, 8-02-1970, 9,000
Cameroon 3 (Tsebo 21, Manga 43, Ndoga 70)
Ethiopia 2 (Menguistou 12 75)

Municipal Stadium, Khartoum, 8-02-1970, 9,000
Côte d'Ivoire 1 (Tahi 89)
Sudan 0

Municipal Stadium, Khartoum, 10-02-1970, 9,000
Côte d'Ivoire 6 (Losseni 16, Pokou 21 60 71 80 87)
Ethiopia 1 (Menguistou 33)

Municipal Stadium, Khartoum, 10-02-1970, 9,000
Sudan 2 (Djaksa 20, Hasabu 60)
Cameroon 1 (Tsebo 34)

	IC	Su	Ca	Et	Pl	W	D	L	F	A	Pts
CÔTE D'IVOIRE	-	1-0	2-3	6-1	3	2	0	1	9	4	4
SUDAN	-	-	2-1	3-0	3	2	0	1	5	2	4
CAMEROON	-	-	-	3-2	3	2	0	1	7	6	4
ETHIOPIA	-	-	-	-	3	0	0	3	3	12	0

Group 2

Municipal Stadium, Wad Madani, 7-02-1970, 7,000
Ghana 2 (Owusu 29 32)
Congo Kinshasa 0

Municipal Stadium, Wad Madani, 7-02-1970, 7,000
Egypt 4 (Abugreisha 5 10, Chazli 73, Taha Bisri 65)
Guinea 1 (Edente 25)

Municipal Stadium, Wad Madani, 9-02-1970, 3,000
Congo Kinshasa 2 (Kalonzo 70, Mungamuni 72)
Guinea 2 (Petit Sory 5, Edente 55)

Municipal Stadium, Wad Madani, 9-02-1970, 3,000
Egypt 1 (Abdelrazak 70)
Ghana 1 (Sunday 60)

Municipal Stadium, Wad Madani, 11-02-1970, 3,000
Ghana 1 (Owusu 50)
Guinea 1 (Tolo 10)

Municipal Stadium, Wad Madani, 11-02-1970, 3,000
Egypt 1 (Abugreisha 71)
Congo Kinshasa 0

	Eg	Gh	Gu	CK	Pl	W	D	L	F	A	Pts
EGYPT	-	1-1	4-2	1-0	3	2	1	0	6	3	5
GHANA	-	-	1-1	2-0	3	1	2	0	4	2	4

GUINEA	-	-	-	2-2	3	0	2	1	5	7	2
CONGO KINSHASA	-	-	-	-	3	0	1	2	2	5	1

SEMI-FINALS

Municipal Stadium, Khartoum, 14-02-1970, 12,000
Sudan 2 (El Issed 83 102)
Egypt 1 (Chazli 84)

Municipal Stadium, Khartoum, 14-02-1970, 12,000
Ghana 2 (Sunday 21, Malik 100)
Côte d'Ivoire 1 (Losseni 78)

3RD PLACE

Municipal Stadium, Khartoum, 16-02-1970, 12,000
Egypt 3 (Chazli 3 14 50)
Côte d'Ivoire 1 (Pokou 72)

FINAL

Municipal Stadium, Khartoum, 16-02-1970, 12,000. Referee: Tesfaye, Ethiopia
SUDAN 1 (El Issed 12)
GHANA 0
Sudan - Aziz - Kaunda, Suliman, Amin, Samir - Bushara, Bushra - El Issed, Djaksa, Dahish, Hasabu
Ghana - Mensah - Boye, Mingle, Eshun, Acquah - Ghartey, Attuquayafio, Sunday Folley, Owusu, Malik

Top scorer Pokou, Côte d'Ivoire 8

VIII. EDITION

QUALIFYING TOURNAMENT
FIRST ROUND

Algeria	3-1 0-3	**Morocco**
Gabon	1-2 0-1	**Côte d'Ivoire**
Ghana	W-O	Upper Volta
Guinea	1-0 0-0	Senegal
Libya	0-1 1-2	**Egypt**
Kenya	2-0 1-0	Ethiopia
Madagascar	2-1 1-4	**Mauritius**
Niger	0-1 1-3	**Mali**
Nigeria	0-0 1-2	**Congo**
Tanzania	1-1 1-5	**Zambia**
Togo	2-1 0-0	Dahomey
Uganda	1-4 0-1	**Zaire**

SECOND ROUND

Guinea	0-0 1-3	**MALI**
Côte d'Ivoire	3-2 0-2	**CONGO**
KENYA	2-1 0-0	Mauritius
MOROCCO	3-0 2-3	Egypt
TOGO	0-0 1-0	Ghana
Zambia	2-1 0-3	**ZAIRE**

Cameroon qualified as hosts, Sudan as holders

FINAL TOURNAMENT
CAMEROON, 23RD FEBRUARY - 5TH MARCH 1972

FIRST ROUND

Group 1

Omnisports, Yaoundé, 23-02-1972
Cameroon 2 (Ndoga 7, Ndongo 20)
Kenya 1 (Niva 44)

Omnisports, Yaoundé, 24-02-1972
Mali 3 (Bakary Traoré 10, Keita.F 46, Bako Traoré 49)
Togo 3 (Kaolo 45 60 81)

Omnisports, Yaoundé, 26-02-1972, 45,000
Mali 1 (Touré)
Kenya 1 (Ouma 60)

Omnisports, Yaoundé, 26-02-1972, 45,000
Cameroon 2 (Joseph 64, Mve 79)
Togo 0

Omnisports, Yaoundé, 28-02-1972, 45,000
Togo 1 (Kaolo 60)
Kenya 1 (Makunda 30)

Omnisports, Yaoundé, 28-02-1972, 45,000
Cameroon 1 (Lea 67)
Mali 1 (Keita.F 43)

	Ca	Ml	Ke	To	Pl	W	D	L	F	A	Pts
CAMEROON	-	1-1	2-1	2-0	3	2	1	0	5	2	5
MALI	-	-	1-1	3-3	3	0	3	0	5	5	3
KENYA	-	-	-	1-1	3	0	2	1	3	4	2
TOGO	-	-	-	-	3	0	2	1	4	6	2

Group 2

Omnisports, Douala, 25-02-1972, 40,000
Congo 1 (Moukila 45)
Morocco 1 (Maaroufi 34)

Omnisports, Douala, 25-02-1972, 40,000
Zaire 1 (Mayanga 53)
Sudan 1 (Hasabu 55)

Omnisports, Douala, 27-02-1972
Morocco 1 (Faras 32)
Sudan 1 (Bushara 49)

Omnisports, Douala, 27-02-1972
Zaire 2 (Ntumba 15 61)
Congo 0

Omnisports, Douala, 29-02-1972, 20,000
Zaire 1 (Mayanga 36)
Morocco 1 (Faras)

Omnisports, Douala, 29-02-1972, 20,000
Congo 4 (Mbono 8 55, M'Pele 32, Banamboula 46)
Sudan 2 (Kamal 37 44)

	Zr	Co	Mr	Su	Pl	W	D	L	F	A	Pts
ZAIRE	-	2-0	1-1	1-1	3	1	2	0	4	2	4
CONGO	-	-	1-1	4-2	3	1	1	1	5	5	3
MOROCCO	-	-	-	1-1	3	0	3	0	3	3	3
SUDAN	-	-	-	-	3	0	2	1	4	6	2

SEMI-FINALS

Omnisports, Douala, 2-03-1972
Congo 1 (Minga 31)
Cameroon 0

Omnisports, Douala, 2-03-1972
Mali 4 (Traoré.A 17, Touré 68, Keita.F 48 92)
Zaire 3 (Ntumba 6, Kakoko 61, Ngassebe 78)

3RD PLACE

Omnisports, Yaoundé, 4-03-1972
Cameroon 5 (Akono 4, Ndongo 31, Owona 32, Mouthe 34, Ndoga 42)
Zaire 2 (Kakoko 13, Mayanga 17)

FINAL

Omnisports, Yaoundé, 5-03-1972. Referee: Aouissi, Algeria

CONGO 3 (M'Bono 57 59, M'Pele 63)
MALI 2 (Diakhite 42, Traoré.M 75)

Congo - Matsima - Dengaky, Ngassaki, Ndolou, Niangou - Minga, Balekita, M'Pele - Bahamboula, Matongo (Ongania), M'Bono (Moukila)

Mali - Keita.M - Moctar, Sangare, Kidian, Cheikna - Bakary Traoré, Traoré.O Touré (Traoré.M), Keita.S (Traoré.A), Keita.F, Diakhité

Top scorer Keita.F, Mali 5

IX. EDITION

QUALIFYING TOURNAMENT
PRELIMINARY ROUND

Central African Republic .... W-O .... Gabon
Sierra Leone .... W-O .... Benin
Somalia .... 2-0 0-5 .... Uganda

FIRST ROUND

Algeria .... W-O .... Libya
Cameroon .... W-O .... Niger
Central African Republic .... 4-2 1-2* .... **Côte d'Ivoire**
Ethiopia .... 2-1 0-3 .... **Tanzania**
Ghana .... 3-2 0-1 5-3p .... Senegal
Guinea .... W-O .... Togo
Lesotho .... 0-0 1-5 .... **Mauritius**
Sierra Leone .... 1-1 2-4 .... **Mali**
Sudan .... 1-1 1-2 .... **Nigeria**
Uganda .... 1-0 2-1 .... Kenya
Upper Volta .... 0-5 1-4 .... **Zaire**
Zambia .... 3-1 1-2 .... Madagascar
* Central African Republic disqualified

SECOND ROUND

Cameroon .... 2-1 0-2 .... **ZAIRE**
Ghana .... 0-3 0-1 .... **COTE D'IVOIRE**
Mali .... 2-2 1-1 * .... **GUINEA**
Tanzania .... 1-1 0-0 * .... **MAURITIUS**
UGANDA .... 2-1 1-1 .... Algeria
ZAMBIA .... 5-1 2-3 .... Nigeria
* Won on penalties

Egypt qualified as hosts, Congo as holders

FINAL TOURNAMENT
EGYPT, 1ST - 14TH MARCH 1974

FIRST ROUND

Group 1

International Stadium, Cairo, 1-03-1974

Egypt 2 (Abugreisha 6, Khalil 52)
Uganda 1 (Mubiru 28)

Mehalla Stadium, Mehalla, 2-03-1974, 4,000

Zambia 1 (Kaushi 2)
Côte d'Ivoire 0

International Stadium, Cairo, 4-03-1974, 40,000

Egypt 3 (Abdel Azim 4, Taha Basri 18, Abugreisha 53)
Zambia 1 (Chitalu 10)

Mehalla Stadium, Mehalla, 3,000, 4-03-1974, 3,000

Côte d'Ivoire 2 (Kobinan 2)
Uganda 2 (Mubiru 2)

International Stadium, Cairo, 6-03-1974, 10,000

Egypt 2 (Chazli 1, Khalil 44)
Côte d'Ivoire 0

Mehalla Stadium, Mehalla, 6-03-1974, 2,000

Zambia 1 (Kapita)
Uganda 0

	Eg	Zm	Ug	IC	Pl	W	D	L	F	A	Pts
EGYPT	-	3-1	2-1	2-0	3	3	0	0	7	2	6
ZAMBIA	-	-	1-0	1-0	3	2	0	1	3	3	4
UGANDA	-	-	-	2-2	3	0	1	2	3	5	1
CÔTE D'IVOIRE	-	-	-	-	3	0	1	2	2	5	1

Group 2

Damanhour Stadium, Damanhour, 3-03-1974

Zaire 2 (Ndaye 18 65)
Guinea 1 (Sylla.B 25)

Municipal Stadium, Alexandria, 3-03-1974, 5,000

Congo 2 (Moukila, Lakou)
Mauritius 0

Municipal Stadium, Alexandria, 5-03-1974, 8,000

Congo 2 (M'Bono 70, Minga 81)
Zaire 1 (Mayanga 25)

Damanhour Stadium, Damanhour, 5-03-1974, 1,000

Guinea 2 (Morcire 2)
Mauritius 1 (Imbert)

Municipal Stadium, Alexandria, 7-03-1974, 7,000

Guinea 1 (Edente 60)
Congo 1 (Ndomba 65)

Damanhour Stadium, Damanhour, 7-03-1974

Zaire 4 (Mayanga 2, Ndaye, Kakoko)
Mauritius 1 (Imbert)

	Co	Zr	Gu	Mr	Pl	W	D	L	F	A	Pts
CONGO	-	2-1	1-1	2-0	3	2	1	0	5	2	5
ZAIRE	-	-	2-1	4-1	3	2	0	1	7	4	4
GUINEA	-	-	-	2-1	3	1	1	1	4	4	3
MAURITIUS	-	-	-	-	3	0	0	3	2	8	0

SEMI-FINALS

International Stadium, Cairo, 9-03-1974, 50,000

Zaire 3 (Ndaye 55 72, Kidumu 61)
Egypt 2 (OG 41, Abugreisha 54)

Municipal Stadium, Alexandria, 9-03-1974, 2,000

Zambia 4 (Chanda 3, Mapulanga)
Congo 2 (Ndomba, M'Pele)

3RD PLACE

International Stadium, Cairo, 11-03-1974, 5,000

Egypt 4 (Mostafa Abdou 5, Chehata 18 80, Abugreisha 62)
Congo 0

FINAL

International Stadium, Cairo, 12-03-1974. Referee: Gamar, Libya

ZAIRE 2 (Ndaye 65 117)
ZAMBIA 2 (Kaushi 40, Sinyangwe 120)

Zaire - Kazadi - Mwepu, Bwanga, Lobilo, Ngoie - Mavuba, Mana - Mayanga, Ndaye, Kidumu, Kakoko

Zambia - Mwape - Musenge, Chama, Makwaza, Mbaso - Simutowe, Simulambo Mapulanga, Chanda, Kaushi, Sinyangwe

Replay. International Stadium, Cairo, 14-03-1974, 1,000. Referee: Gamar, Libya
ZAIRE 2 (Ndaye 30 76)
ZAMBIA 0
Zaire - Kazadi - Mwepu, Mukombo, Bwanga, Lobilo - Mavuba, Mana, Mayanga Ndaye, Kidumu, Kakoko
Zambia - Mwape - Musenge, Chama, Makwaza, Mbaso - Simutowe, Simulambo, Mapulanga - Chanda, Kaushi, Sinyangwe

Top scorer Ndaye, Zaire 9

X. EDITION

QUALIFYING TOURNAMENT
PRELIMINARY ROUND

Mali ....W-O .... Lesotho
Morocco ....3-0 3-0 .... Gambia
Niger ....W-O .... Benin
Somali ....0-2 1-0 .... **Burundi**
Togo ....1-0 2-0 .... Liberia
Tunisia * ....1-0 0-1 .... Libya
* Won on penalties

FIRST ROUND

Burundi ....0-3 0-2 .... **Egypt**
Cameroon ....3-0 0-4 .... **Togo**
Congo ....1-0 1-2 .... Côte d'Ivoire
Mali ....3-1 0-4 .... **Ghana**
Morocco ....4-0 1-2 .... Senegal
Niger ....2-4 0-3 .... **Guinea**
Nigeria ....W-O .... Central African Republic
Sudan ....1-0 2-0 .... Kenya
Tanzania ....W-O .... Madagascar
Tunisia ....1-1 2-1 .... Algeria
Uganda ....4-0 1-1 .... Mauritius
Zambia ....3-3 6-1 .... Malawi

SECOND ROUND

Congo ....0-1 1-2 .... **NIGERIA**
Ghana ....2-0 0-2 * .... **MOROCCO**
Tanzania ....1-1 2-5 .... **EGYPT**
Togo ....2-2 0-2 .... **GUINEA**
Tunisia ....3-2 1-2 .... **SUDAN**
Zambia ....2-1 0-3 .... **UGANDA**
* Won on penalties

Ethiopia qualified as hosts, Zaire as holders

FINAL TOURNAMENT
ETHIOPIA, 29TH FEBRUARY - 14TH MARCH 1976

FIRST ROUND

Group 1

Addis Ababa Stadium, Addis Ababa, 29-02-1976
Ethiopia 2 (Sheferaw 2, Tesfaye 83)
Uganda 0

Addis Ababa Stadium, Addis Ababa, 29-02-1976
Egypt 1 (Taha Basri 43)
Guinea 1 (Sylla.B 44)

Addis Ababa Stadium, Addis Ababa, 3-03-1976
Egypt 2 (Abdou 26, Taha Basri 32)
Uguanda 1 (Obua 21)

Addis Ababa Stadium, Addis Ababa, 3-03-1976
Guinea 2 (N'Jo Léa 15, Petit Sory 85)
Ethiopia 1 (Sheferaw 40)

Addis Ababa Stadium, Addis Ababa, 5-03-1976
Guinea 2 (N'Jo Léa 2, Sylla.B 20)
Uganda 1 (Muguwa 85)

Addis Ababa Stadium, Addis Ababa, 5-03-1976
Egypt 1 (Chehata 28)
Ethiopia 1 (Mohamed Ali 46)

	Gu	Eg	Et	Ug	Pl	W	D	L	F	A	Pts
GUINEA	-	1-1	2-1	2-1	3	2	1	0	5	3	5
EGYPT	-	-	1-1	2-1	3	1	2	0	4	3	4
ETHIOPIA	-	-	-	2-0	3	1	1	1	4	3	3
UGANDA	-	-	-	-	3	0	0	3	2	6	0

Group 2

Dire Dawa Stadium, Dire Dawa, 1-03-1976
Nigeria 4 (Baba Otu 28 44, Ojebode 37, Usiyan 90)
Zaire 2 (Kabasu 51,)

Dire Dawa Stadium, Dire Dawa, 1-03-1976
Morocco 2 (Cherif 1, Abouali 58)
Sudan 2 (Gagrine 9 79)

Dire Dawa Stadium, Dire Dawa, 4-03-1976
Nigeria 1 (Usiyan 8)
Sudan 0

Dire Dawa Stadium, Dire Dawa, 4-03-1976
Morocco 1 (Zahraoui 80)
Zaire 0

Dire Dawa Stadium, Dire Dawa, 6-03-1976
Morocco 3 (Faras 8, Tazi 19, Larbi 81)
Nigeria 1 (Ojebode 5)

Dire Dawa Stadium, Dire Dawa, 6-03-1976
Zaire 1 (Ndaye 41)
Sudan 1 (Gagarine 14)

	Mr	Ng	Su	Zr	Pl	W	D	L	F	A	Pts
MOROCCO	-	3-1	2-2	1-0	3	2	1	0	6	3	5
NIGERIA	-	-	1-0	4-2	3	2	0	1	6	5	4
SUDAN	-	-	-	1-1	3	0	2	1	3	4	2
ZAIRE	-	-	-	-	3	0	1	2	3	6	1

FINAL ROUND

Addis Ababa Stadium, Addis Ababa, 9-03-1976
Guinea 1 (Papa Camara 88)
Nigeria 1 (Lawal 52)

Addis Ababa Stadium, Addis Ababa, 9-03-1976
Morocco 2 (Faras 23, Zahraoui 88)
Egypt 1 (Abu Rehab 34)

Addis Ababa Stadium, Addis Ababa, 11-03-1976
Morocco 2 (Faras 82, Guezzar 87)
Nigeria 1 (Baba Otu 50)

Addis Ababa Stadium, Addis Ababa, 11-03-1976
Guinea 4 (N'Jo Léa 24 65, OG 53, Morcire 62)
Egypt 2 (Abdou 33, Siaguy 86)

Addis Ababa Stadium, Addis Ababa, 14-03-1976
Nigeria 3 (Llerika 35, 62, Lawal 82)
Egypt 2 (Khatib 7, Ussama 41)

Addis Ababa Stadium, Addis Ababa, 14-03-1976. Referee: Chayu, Zambia
MOROCCO 1 (Baba 86)
GUINEA 1 (Cherif 33)

Morocco - Hazzaz - Cherif, Baba, Claoua, Mehdi (Guezzar), Larbi - Semmat, Zahraoui - Tazi, Faras, Abouali (Dolmy)
Guinea - Sylla - Bangoura, Morcire, Cherif, Diarra - Sylla.I, Papa Camara - Jansky, Petit Sory, N'Jo Léa, Sylla.B (Mory Kone)

	Mr	Gu	Ng	Eg	Pl	W	D	L	F	A	Pts
Morocco	-	1-1	2-1	2-1	3	2	1	0	5	3	5
Guinea	-	-	1-1	4-2	3	1	2	0	6	4	4
Nigeria	-	-	-	3-2	3	1	1	1	5	5	3
Egypt	-	-	-	-	3	0	0	3	5	9	0

Top scorer N'Jo Léa, Guinea 4

1978

XI. EDITION

QUALIFYING TOURNAMENT PRELIMINARY ROUND

Malawi ....1-1 2-3 .... **Mauritius**

FIRST ROUND

Algeria ....4-1 1-2 .... Kenya
Upper Volta ....0-1 1-4 .... **Côte d'Ivoire**
Cameroon ....2-0 0-4 .... **Congo**
Egypt ....2-2 2-3 .... **Tunisia**
Gabon ....Bye
Guinea ....3-0 2-0 .... Libya
Mali ....W-O .... Niger
Mauritius ....2-3 0-1 .... **Ethiopia**
Senegal ....2-1 1-0 .... Togo
Sierra Leone ....1-1 0-2 .... **Nigeria**
Uganda ....W-O .... Tanzania
Zambia ....W-O .... Sudan

SECOND ROUND

Algeria ....2-0 0-2 * .... **ZAMBIA**
CONGO ....3-2 3-3 .... Gabon
Ethiopia ....0-0 1-2 .... **UGANDA**
Senegal ....3-1 0-3 .... **NIGERIA**
TUNISIA ....3-0 2-3 .... Guinea
Côte d'Ivoire .... ** .... Mali

* Won on penalties
** Both teams were disqualified. Upper Volta were given a place in the finals, having been beaten by Côte d'Ivoire in the second round.

Ghana qualified as hosts, Morocco as holders

FINAL TOURNAMENT
GHANA, 5TH - 18TH MARCH 1978

FIRST ROUND

Group 1

Accra Stadium, Accra, 5-03-1978, 50,000
Ghana 2 (Afriye 21, Abdul Razak 55)
Zambia 1 (Kapita 8)

Accra Stadium, Accra, 5-03-1978, 50,000
Nigeria 4 (Chukwu 17, Adekiye 31, Odegbami 44 82)
Upper Volta 2 (Hien 50, Koita 52)

Accra Stadium, Accra, 8-03-1978, 60,000
Zambia 2 (Phiri.P 20, Phiri.B)
Upper Volta 0

Accra Stadium, Accra, 8-03-1978, 60,000
Ghana 1 (Kluste 76)
Nigeria 1 (Odegbami 33)

Accra Stadium, Accra, 10-03-1978, 25,000
Zambia 0
Nigeria 0

Accra Stadium, Accra, 10-03-1978, 25,000
Ghana 3 (Al Hassan 3 59, Mohamed)
Upper Volta 0

	Gh	Ng	Zm	BF	Pl	W	D	L	F	A	Pts
Ghana	-	1-1	2-1	3-0	3	2	1	0	6	2	5
Nigeria	-	-	0-0	4-2	3	1	2	0	5	3	4
Zambia	-	-	-	2-0	3	1	1	1	3	2	3
Upper Volta	-	-	-	-	3	0	0	3	2	9	0

Group 2

Kumasi Stadium, Kumasi, 6-03-1978
Morocco 1 (Amcharrat 29)
Tunisia 1 (Kaabi 63)

Kumasi Stadium, Kumasi, 6-03-1978
Uganda 3 (Omondi 1, Semwanga 31, Kisitu 81)
Congo 1 (Mamounoubala 80)

Kumasi Stadium, Kumasi, 9-03-1978, 50,000
Tunisia 3 (Kamates 36, Ben Aziza 38 83)
Uganda 1 (Musenze 71)

Kumasi Stadium, Kumasi, 9-03-1978, 50,000
Morocco 1 (Amcharrat 28)
Congo 0

Kumasi Stadium, Kumasi, 11-03-1978, 20,000
Congo 0
Tunisia 0

Kumasi Stadium, Kumasi, 11-03-1978, 20,000
Uganda 3 (Kisitu 13, Msereko 32, Omondi 36)
Morocco 0

	Ug	Tu	Mr	Co	Pl	W	D	L	F	A	Pts
Uganda	-	1-3	3-0	3-1	3	2	0	1	7	4	4
Tunisia	-	-	1-1	0-0	3	1	2	0	4	2	4
Morocco	-	-	-	1-0	3	1	1	1	2	4	3
Congo	-	-	-	-	3	0	1	2	1	4	1

SEMI-FINALS

Accra Stadium, Accra, 14-03-1978, 10,000
Ghana 1 (Razak 57)
Tunisia 0

Kumasi Stadium, Kumasi, 14-03-1978
Uganda 2 (Nasur 11, Omondi 58)
Nigeria 1 (Eyo 54)

3RD PLACE

Nigeria v Tunisia. Match abandoned after 30 minutes with the score at 1-1. Nigeria were awarded the match 2-0

FINAL

Accra Stadium, Accra, 18-03-1978, 40,000. Referee: El Ghoul, Egypt
GHANA 2 (Afriye 38 64)
UGANDA 0
Ghana - Carr - Paha, Quaye, Acquaye, Dadzie - Kyenkyehen, Yawson, Seidi, Afriye, Razak, Ahmed
Uganda - Ssali - Semwanga, Musenze, Lwanga, Kirundu - Kiganda, Nasur, Nsereko - Omondi, Kisitu, Isabirye (Lubega)

Top scorer Omondi, Uganda 4

XII. EDITION

QUALIFYING TOURNAMENT
PRELIMINARY ROUND

Madagascar	2-1 1-5	**Malawi**
Mauritius	0-1 2-1	Lesotho
Benin	W-O	Niger

FIRST ROUND

Benin	1-0 1-4	**Côte d'Ivoire**
Congo	4-2 1-4	**Zaire**
Guinea	3-0 0-3 *	Cameroon
Libya	2-1 1-1	Ethiopia
Malawi	0-2 0-2	**Zambia**
Mauritania	2-2 1-4	**Morocco**
Mauritius	3-2 0-4	**Tanzania**
Togo	2-0 0-1	Gambia
Algeria	W-O	Burundi
Egypt	W-O	Somalia
Kenya	W-O	Tunisia
Sudan	W-O	Uganda

* Guinea won on penalties

SECOND ROUND

ALGERIA	3-1 0-1	Libya
Kenya	3-1 0-3	**EGYPT**
MOROCCO	7-0 1-2	Togo
Sudan	2-0 0-4	**CÔTE D'IVOIRE**
TANZANIA	1-0 1-1	Zambia
Zaire	3-2 1-3	**GUINEA**

Nigeria qualified as hosts, Ghana as holders

FINAL TOURNAMENT
NIGERIA, 8TH - 22ND MARCH 1980

FIRST ROUND

Group 1

Surulere, Lagos, 8-03-1980, 80,000
Nigeria 3 (Lawal 11, Onyedika 35, Odegbami 85)
Tanzania 1 (Mkambi 54)

Surulere, Lagos, 8-03-1980, 80,000
Egypt 2 (Hammam 8, Mokhtar 20)
Côte d'Ivoire 1 (Ani Gome 7)

Surulere, Lagos, 12-03-1980, 55,000
Egypt 2 (Chehata 32, Nour 38)
Tanzania 1 (Wazir 86)

Surulere, Lagos, 12-03-1980, 55,000
Nigeria 0
Côte d'Ivoire 0

Surulere, Lagos, 15-03-1980, 70,000
Tanzania 1 (Wazir 59)
Côte d'Ivoire 1 (Kobenan 7)

Surulere, Lagos, 15-03-1980, 70,000
Nigeria 1 (Isima 15)
Egypt 0

	Ng	Eg	IC	Ta	Pl	W	D	L	F	A	Pts
NIGERIA	-	1-0	0-0	3-1	3	2	1	0	4	1	5
EGYPT	-	-	2-1	2-1	3	2	0	1	4	3	4
CÔTE D'IVOIRE	-	-	-	1-1	3	0	2	1	2	3	2
TANZANIA	-	-	-	-	3	0	1	2	3	6	1

Group 2

Liberty Stadium, Ibadan, 9-03-1980, 40,000
Ghana 0
Algeria 0

Liberty Stadium, Ibadan, 9-03-1980, 40,000
Guinea 1 (Moussa Camara 8)
Morocco 1 (Tahir Mustapha 7)

Liberty Stadium, Ibadan, 13-03-1980, 20,000
Algeria 1 (Belloumi 90)
Morocco 0

Liberty Stadium, Ibadan, 13-03-1980, 20,000
Ghana 1 (Klutse 69)
Guinea 0

Liberty Stadium, Ibadan, 16-03-1980, 20,000
Algeria 3 (Bensaoula 12 49, Benmiloudi 37)
Guinea 2 (Diawara 82, Bangoura 90)

Liberty Stadium, Ibadan, 16-03-1980, 20,000
Morocco 1 (Labied 44)
Ghana 0

	Al	Mr	Gh	Gu	Pl	W	D	L	F	A	Pts
ALGERIA	-	1-0	0-0	3-2	3	2	1	0	4	2	5
MOROCCO	-	-	1-0	1-1	3	1	1	1	2	2	3
GHANA	-	-	-	1-0	3	1	1	1	1	1	3
GUINEA	-	-	-	-	3	0	1	2	3	5	1

SEMI-FINALS

Surulere, Lagos, 19-03-1980, 70,000
Nigeria 1 (Owolabi 9)
Morocco 0

Liberty Stadium, Ibadan, 19-03-1980, 5,000
Algeria 2 (Assad 55, Benmiloudi 62)
Egypt 2 (Khatib 32, Sayed 47)
Algeria won 4-2 on penalties

3RD PLACE

Surulere, Lagos, 21-03-1980, 5,000
Morocco 2 (Labied 9 78)
Egypt 0

FINAL

Surulere, Lagos, 22-03-1980, 80,000. Referee: Tesfaye, Ethiopia
NIGERIA 3 (Odegbami 2 42, Lawal 50)
ALGERIA 0

Nigeria - Best - Adiele, Chukwu, Tunde, Isima - Atuegbu, Odiye, Owolabi, Odegbami, Lawal, Amiesemaka

Algeria - Cerbah - Merzekane, Horr, Khedis, Kouici - Mahyouz, Fergani, Belloumi - Bensaoula (Madjer), Benmiloudi (Guemri), Assad

Top scorers Odegbami, Nigeria 3
Labied, Morocco 3

1982

XIII. EDITION

QUALIFYING TOURNAMENT
PRELIMINARY ROUND

Angola	1-1 0-0	**Congo**
Liberia	0-0 1-1	Gambia
Madagascar	0-0 1-1	Mauritius
Malawi	0-1 1-1	**Zimbabwe**
Mali	2-0 1-2	Mauritania

Mozambique..........6-1 1-2 ....Lesotho
Senegal..........2-0 2-1 ....Sierra Leone
Upper Volta..........W-O..........Gabon
Guinea Equatorial..........W-O..........Benin
Rwanda..........W-O..........Uganda

FIRST ROUND

Algeria..........5-1 0-3 ....Mali
Cameroon..........4-0 2-2 ....Togo
Ethiopia..........1-0 0-1 4-3p ....Rwanda
Ghana..........1-1 1-0..........Congo
Morocco..........3-1 5-0..........Liberia
Tunisia..........1-0 0-0 ....Senegal
Zaire..........2-1 3-3 ....Mozambique
Zimbabwe..........0-1 0-2..........**Zambia**
Kenya..........3-5 0-2..........**Egypt**
Guinea..........W-O ....Guinea Equatorial
Madagascar..........W-O ....Tanzania
Upper Volta..........Bye

SECOND ROUND

ALGERIA..........7-0 1-1..........Upper Volta
CAMEROON..........5-1 1-2 ....Madagascar
GHANA..........2-2 2-1 ....Zaire
Guinea..........2-2 1-1 ....**ETHIOPIA**
Morocco..........2-1 0-2 ....**ZAMBIA**
TUNISIA..........W-O..........Egypt

Libya qualified as hosts, Nigeria as holders

FINAL TOURNAMENT
LIBYA, 5TH - 19TH MARCH 1982

FIRST ROUND

Group 1

11th June Stadium, Tripoli, 5-03-1982, 40,000
Libya 2 (Garana 58, Issawi 76)
Ghana 0 (Al Hassan 28, Opoku Nti 89)

11th June Stadium, Tripoli, 5-03-1982, 40,000
Cameroon 1 (Mbida 50)
Tunisia 1 (Gabsi 49)

11th June Stadium, Tripoli, 9-03-1982, 40,000
Cameroon 0
Ghana 0

11th June Stadium, Tripoli, 9-03-1982, 40,000
Libya 2 (OG 42, El Borosi 83)
Tunisia 0

11th June Stadium, Tripoli, 12-03-1982, 40,000
Ghana 1 (Essien 28)
Tunisia 0

11th June Stadium, Tripoli, 12-03-1982, 40,000
Libya 0
Cameroon 0

	Ly	Gh	Ca	Tu	Pl	W	D	L	F	A	Pts
LIBYA	-	2-2	0-0	2-0	3	1	2	0	4	2	4
GHANA	-	-	0-0	1-0	3	1	2	0	3	2	4
CAMEROON	-	-	-	1-1	3	0	3	0	1	1	3
TUNISIA	-	-	-	-	3	0	1	2	1	4	1

Group 2

28th March Stadium, Benghazi, 7-03-1982, 5,000
Nigeria 3 (Keshi 27 84, Ademola 40)
Ethiopia 0

28th March Stadium, Benghazi, 7-03-1982, 5,000
Algeria 1 (Merzekane 85)
Zambia 0

28th March Stadium, Benghazi, 10-03-1982, 5,000
Zambia 1 (Munshya 68)
Ethiopia 0

28th March Stadium, Benghazi, 10-03-1982, 5,000
Algeria 2 (OG 44, Assad 65)
Nigeria 1 (Osigwe 40)

28th March Stadium, Benghazi, 13-03-1982, 5,000
Algeria 0
Ethiopia 0

28th March Stadium, Benghazi, 13-03-1982, 5,000
Zambia 3 (Kaumba 25, Njovu 80, OG 81)
Nigeria 0

	Al	Zm	Ng	Et	Pl	W	D	L	F	A	Pts
ALGERIA	-	1-0	2-1	0-0	3	2	1	0	3	1	5
ZAMBIA	-	-	3-0	1-0	3	2	0	1	4	1	4
NIGERIA	-	-	-	3-0	3	1	0	2	4	5	2
ETHIOPIA	-	-	-	-	3	0	1	2	0	4	1

SEMI-FINALS

28th March Stadium, Benghazi, 16-03-1982, 5,000
Ghana 3 (Al Hassan 4 103, Opoku Nti 90)
Algeria 2 (Zidane 29, Assad 62)

11th June Stadium, Tripoli, 16-03-1982, 50,000
Libya 2 (Beshari 38 84)
Zambia 1 (Kaumba 29)

3RD PLACE

11th June Stadium, Tripoli, 18-03-1982, 2,000
Zambia 2 (Kaumba 2, Munshya 25)
Algeria 0

FINAL

11th June Stadium, Tripoli, 19-03-1982, 50,000. Referee: Ramlochun, Mauritius
GHANA 1 (Al Hassan 35)
LIBYA 1 (Beshari 70)
Ghana won 7-6 on penalties

Ghana - Owusu - Haruna Yusif, Sampson.L, Paha, Sampson.K - Asase, Quarshie, Kofi Badu (Abedi Pele) - Essein (Opoku Nti), Al Hassan, Abbrey Kofi

Libya - Kouafi - El Ageli, Zeiw, Sola, Beshari - Majdoub (El Borosi), Garana, El Fergami (Abubaker), Ferjani - Issawi, Gonaim

Top scorer Al Hassan, Ghana 4

1984

XIV. EDITION

QUALIFYING TOURNAMENT
PRELIMINARY ROUND

Gabon..........2-2 0-4 ....**Angola**
Malawi..........2-0 2-0..........Zimbabwe
Mali..........3-1 0-1 ....Gambia
Niger..........0-0 0-1..........**Senegal**
Somalia..........0-1..........Rwanda
Tanzania..........1-1 2-3..........**Uganda**
Togo..........3-0 1-0 ....Sierra Leone
Benin..........W-O..........Liberia
Mauritius..........W-O ....Lesotho
Mozambique..........W-O ....Swaziland

FIRST ROUND

Algeria 6-2 1-1 Benin
Congo 2-0 0-2 * **Egypt**
Ethiopia 1-0 0-1 * Mauritius
Guinea 0-1 0-2 **Togo**
Libya 2-1 0-1 **Senegal**
Madagascar 1-0 1-2 Uganda
Morocco 4-0 0-2 Mali
Mozambique 3-0 0-4 **Cameroon**
Nigeria 2-0 0-1 Angola
Sudan 2-1 0-0 Zambia
Tunisia 5-0 1-0 Rwanda
Malawi W-O Zaire
* Egypt and Ethiopia qualified on penalties

SECOND ROUND

CAMEROON 5-0 0-2 Sudan
EGYPT 1-0 0-0 Tunisia
Ethiopia 2-1 0-3 **TOGO**
Madagascar 0-1 1-1 **MALAWI**
NIGERIA 0-0 0-0 4-3p Morocco
Senegal 1-1 0-2 **ALGERIA**

Côte d'Ivoire qualified as hosts, Ghana as holders

FINAL TOURNAMENT
CÔTE D'IVOIRE, 4TH - 18TH MARCH 1984

FIRST ROUND

Group 1

Houphouet Boigny, Abidjan, 4-03-1984, 50,000
Côte d'Ivoire 3 (Koffi.T 27, Fofana 62, Goba 75)
Togo 0

Houphouet Boigny, Abidjan, 4-03-1984, 50,000
Egypt 1 (Abou Zeid 75)
Cameroon 0

Houphouet Boigny, Abidjan, 7-03-1984, 40,000
Cameroon 4 (Djonkep 6, Abega 21 60, Aoudou 45)
Togo 1 (Moutairou 54)

Houphouet Boigny, Abidjan, 7-03-1984, 40,000
Egypt 2 (Abou Zeid 66 72)
Côte d'Ivoire 1 (Miezan 53)

Houphouet Boigny, Abidjan, 10-03-1984, 40,000
Egypt 0
Togo 0

Houphouet Boigny, Abidjan, 10-03-1984, 40,000
Cameroon 2 (Milla 42, Djonkep 61)
Côte d'Ivoire 0

	Eg	Ca	IC	To	Pl	W	D	L	F	A	Pts
EGYPT	-	1-0	2-1	0-0	3	2	1	0	3	1	5
CAMEROON	-	-	2-0	4-1	3	2	0	1	6	2	4
CÔTE D'IVOIRE	-	-	-	3-0	3	1	0	2	4	4	2
TOGO	-	-	-	-	3	0	1	2	1	7	1

Group 2

Municipal Stadium, Bouaké, 5-03-1984, 10,000
Nigeria 2 (Nwosu 13, Ehilegbu 31)
Ghana 1 (Opoku Nti 19)

Municipal Stadium, Bouaké, 5-03-1984, 10,000
Algeria 3 (Bouiche 29, Belloumi 36, Fergani 38)
Malawi 0

Municipal Stadium, Bouaké, 8-03-1984, 15,000
Malawi 2 (Waya 7, Msiya 35)
Nigeria 2 (Temile 39 41)

Municipal Stadium, Bouaké, 8-03-1984, 15,000
Algeria 2 (Menad 75, Bensaoula 85)
Ghana 0

Municipal Stadium, Bouaké, 11-03-1984, 3,000
Algeria 0
Nigeria 0

Municipal Stadium, Bouaké, 11-03-1984, 3,000
Ghana 1 (Ampadu 32)
Malawi 0

	Al	Ng	Gh	Mw	Pl	W	D	L	F	A	Pts
ALGERIA	-	0-0	2-0	3-0	3	2	1	0	5	0	5
NIGERIA	-	-	2-1	2-2	3	1	2	0	4	3	4
GHANA	-	-	-	1-0	3	1	0	2	2	4	2
MALAWI	-	-	-	-	3	0	1	2	2	6	1

SEMI-FINALS

Houphouet Boigny, Abidjan, 14-03-1984, 15,000
Nigeria 2 (Keshi 43, Ali Bala 75)
Egypt 2 (Soliman 25, Abou Zeid 38)
Nigeria won 8-7 on penaties

Municipal Stadium, Bouaké, 14-03-1984, 15,000
Cameroon 0
Algeria 0
Cameroon won 5-4 on penalties

3RD PLACE

Houphouet Boigny, Abidjan, 17-03-1984, 1,000
Algeria 3 (Madjer 67, Belloumi 70, Yahi 88)
Egypt 1 (Abdelghani 74)

FINAL

Houphouet Boigny, Abidjan, 18-03-1984, 50,000. Referee: Bennaceur, Tunisia
CAMEROON 3 (Ndjeya 32, Abega 79, Ebongué 84)
NIGERIA 1 (Lawal 10)
Cameroon - Bell - Toubé, Ndjeya, Doumbé Léa, Sinkot - Abega, Mbida, Aoudou Ebongué, Milla, Djonkep (Kundé)
Nigeria - Okala - Kingsley, Keshi, Eboigbe, Shofoluwe - Lawal, Adesina (Okoku), Edobor - Ali Bala (Temile), Nwosu, Etokebe

Top scorer Abou Zeid, Egypt 4

1986
XV. EDITION

QUALIFYING TOURNAMENT
PRELIMINARY ROUND

Gambia 3-2 0-2 **Sierra Leone**
Liberia 3-1 0-3 **Mauritania**
Mali 1-0 2-2 Benin
Mauritius 0-0 0-3 **Mozambique**
Somalia 1-0 0-1 3-4p **Kenya**
Tanzania 0-1 3-1 Uganda
Zaire 2-0 1-1 Gabon
Zimbabwe 3-0 5-1 Swaziland

FIRST ROUND

Algeria 4-0 1-1 Mauritania
Congo 2-5 0-0 **Zaire**
Ghana 1-1 4-1 Guinea
Côte d'Ivoire 6-0 1-1 Mali

Libya 2-0 0-1 Tunisia
Madagascar 0-1 2-5 **Zimbabwe**
Malawi 1-1 1-1 5-6p **Mozambique**
Togo 0-1 1-1 **Senegal**
Kenya W-O Sudan
Morocco W-O Sierra Leone
Nigeria W-O Tanzania
Zambia W-O Ethiopia

SECOND ROUND

CÔTE D'IVOIRE 2-0 0-0 Ghana
Kenya 0-0 0-3 **ALGERIA**
Libya 2-1 1-2 3-4p **MOZAMBIQUE**
MOROCCO 1-0 0-0 Zaire
Nigeria 0-0 0-1 **ZAMBIA**
Zimbabwe 1-0 0-3 **SENEGAL**

Egypt qualified as hosts, Cameroon as holders

FINAL TOURNAMENT
EGYPT, 7TH - 21TH MARCH 1986

FIRST ROUND

Group 1

International Stadium, Cairo, 7-03-1986, 45,000
Senegal 1 (Youm 66)
Egypt 0

International Stadium, Cairo, 7-03-1986, 45,000
Côte d'Ivoire 3 (Traoré.A 24 52, Pascal 85)
Mozambique 0

International Stadium, Cairo, 10-03-1986, 50,000
Senegal 2 (Pape Fall 27, Bocande 83)
Mozambique 0

International Stadium, Cairo, 10-03-1986, 50,000
Egypt 2 (Shawky 72, Abdel Hamid 83)
Côte d'Ivoire 0

International Stadium, Cairo, 13-03-1986, 55,000
Côte d'Ivoire 1 (Traoré.A 71)
Senegal 0

International Stadium, Cairo, 13-03-1986, 55,000
Egypt 2 (Abou Zeid 13 15)
Mozambique 0

	Eg	IC	Se	Mz	Pl	W	D	L	F	A	Pts
EGYPT	-	2-0	0-1	2-0	3	2	0	1	4	1	4
CÔTE D'IVOIRE	-	-	1-0	3-0	3	2	0	1	4	2	4
SENEGAL	-	-	-	2-0	3	2	0	1	3	1	4
MOZAMBIQUE	-	-	-	-	3	0	0	3	0	7	0

Group 2

Alexandria Stadium, Alexandria, 8-03-1986, 20,000
Cameroon 3 (Milla 48, Mfédé 81 88)
Zambia 2 (Chabala 68, Kalusha Bwalya 85)

Alexandria Stadium, Alexandria, 8-03-1986, 20,000
Algeria 0
Morocco 0

Alexandria Stadium, Alexandria, 11-03-1986, 10,000
Zambia 0
Algeria 0

Alexandria Stadium, Alexandria, 11-03-1986, 10,000
Cameroon 1 (Milla 89)
Morocco 1 (Karim 72)

Alexandria Stadium, Alexandria, 14-03-1986, 15,000
Morocco 1 (Karim 20)
Zambia 0

Alexandria Stadium, Alexandria, 14-03-1986, 15,000
Cameroon 3 (Kana 65 70, Milla 72)
Algeria 2 (Madjer 61, Maroc 74)

	Ca	Mr	Al	Zm	Pl	W	D	L	F	A	Pts
CAMEROON	-	1-1	3-2	3-2	3	2	1	0	7	5	5
MOROCCO	-	-	0-0	1-0	3	1	2	0	2	1	4
ALGERIA	-	-	-	0-0	3	0	2	1	2	3	2
ZAMBIA	-	-	-	-	3	0	1	2	2	4	1

SEMI-FINALS

International Stadium, Cairo, 17-03-1986, 90,000
Egypt 1 (Abou Zeid 80)
Morocco 0

Alexandria Stadium, Alexandria, 17-03-1986, 10,000
Cameroon 1 (Milla 46)
Côte d'Ivoire 0

3RD PLACE

International Stadium, Cairo, 20-03-1986, 1,000
Côte d'Ivoire 3 (Ben Salah 8, Kouadiou 38 66)
Morocco 2 (Rhiati 44, Sahil 85)

FINAL

International Stadium, Cairo, 21-03-1986, 100,000. Referee: Bennaceur, Tunisia
EGYPT 0
CAMEROON 0
Egypt won 5-4 on penalties
Egypt - Batal - Yassine, Chehata, Omar (Mayhoub), Sedki - Kassem, Abdelghani, Abou Zeid (Yehia), Abdelhamid - Abdou, Khatib
Cameroon - N'Kono - N'Dip, Aoudou, Kundé, Sinkot - Mbouh, Kana, Mbida Ebongue (Oumarou), Milla, Mfédé

Top scorers Milla, Cameroon 4
Traoré.A, Côte d'Ivoire 4

1988

XVI. EDITION

QUALIFYING TOURNAMENT
PRELIMINARY ROUND

Angola 1-0 0-1 5-3p Gabon
Central African Republic 1-2 1-5 **Congo**
Ethiopia 4-2* **Tanzania**
Guinea 2-1 1-0 Gambia
Sierra Leone 2-1 1-1 Liberia
Uganda 5-0 0-0 Somalia
Madagascar W-O Mauritius
Rwanda W-O Lesotho
Togo W-O Guinea Equatorial
Tunisia W-O Mali
* Ethiopia withdrew

FIRST ROUND

Algeria 1-0 1-1 Tunisia
Cameroon 5-1 1-3 Uganda
Ghana 1-2 0-0 **Sierra Leone**
Côte d'Ivoire 2-0 2-1 Congo
Kenya 2-0 1-2 Madagascar
Mozambique 1-1 2-3 **Zimbabwe**
Nigeria 2-0 1-1 Togo
Senegal 4-0 0-0 Guinea
Sudan 1-0 1-1 Tanzania

Zaire 3-0 0-1 Angola
Libya W-O Zambia
Malawi W-O Rwanda

SECOND ROUND

ALGERIA W-O Libya
CAMEROON 2-0 0-1 Sudan
Malawi 1-2 0-2 **CÔTE D'IVOIRE**
NIGERIA 3-0 0-2 Sierra Leone
Senegal 0-0 0-0 2-4p **ZAIRE**
Zimbabwe 1-1 0-0 ^ **KENYA**

Morocco qualified as hosts, Egypt as holders

FINAL TOURNAMENT
MOROCCO, 13TH - 27TH MARCH 1988

FIRST ROUND

Group 1

Mohammed V, Casablanca, 13-03-1988, 70,000
Morocco 1 (Krimau 43)
Zaire 1 (Lutonadio 88)

Mohammed V, Casablanca, 13-03-1988, 70,000
Algeria 1 (Belloumi 16)
Côte d'Ivoire 1 (Traoré.A 48)

Mohammed V, Casablanca, 16-03-1988, 10,000
Côte d'Ivoire 1 (Traoré.A 74)
Zaire 1 (Kabongo 37)

Mohammed V, Casablanca, 16-03-1988, 40,000
Morocco 1 (Haddaoui 52)
Algeria 0

Mohammed V, Casablanca, 19-03-1988, 80,000
Algeria 1 (Ferhaoui 36)
Zaire 0

Mohammed V, Casablanca, 19-03-1988, 90,000
Morocco 0
Côte d'Ivoire 0

	Mr	Al	IC	Zr	Pl	W	D	L	F	A	Pts
Morocco	-	1-0	0-0	1-1	3	1	2	0	2	1	4
Algeria	-	-	1-1	1-0	3	1	1	1	2	2	3
Côte d'Ivoire	-	-	-	1-1	3	0	3	0	2	2	3
Zaire	-	-	-	-	3	0	2	1	2	3	2

Algeria qualified on drawing of lots.

Group 2

Moulay Abdallah Stadium, Rabat, 14-03-1988, 7,000
Cameroon 1 (Milla 5)
Egypt 0

Moulay Abdallah Stadium, Rabat, 14-03-1988, 7,000
Nigeria 3 (Yekini 6, Edobor 13, Okosieme 33)
Kenya 0

Moulay Abdallah Stadium, Rabat, 17-03-1988, 15,000
Cameroon 1 (Milla 21)
Nigeria 1 (Okwaraji 2)

Moulay Abdallah Stadium, Rabat, 17-03-1988, 15,000
Egypt 3 (Abdelhamid 2 65, Younis 58)
Kenya 0

Moulay Abdallah Stadium, Rabat, 20-03-1988, 25,000
Cameroon 0
Kenya 0

Moulay Abdallah Stadium, Rabat, 20-03-1988, 25,000
Egypt 0
Nigeria 0

	Ng	Ca	Eg	Ke	Pl	W	D	L	F	A	Pts
Nigeria	-	1-1	0-0	3-0	3	1	2	0	4	1	4
Cameroon	-	-	1-0	0-0	3	1	2	0	2	1	4
Egypt	-	-	-	3-0	3	1	1	1	3	1	3
Kenya	-	-	-	-	3	0	1	2	0	6	1

SEMI-FINALS

Mohammed V, Casablanca, 23-03-1988, 45,000
Cameroon 1 (Makanaky 78)
Morocco 0

Moulay Abdallah Stadium, Rabat, 23-03-1988, 35,000
Nigeria 1 (OG 39)
Algeria 1 (Maatar 86)
Nigeria won 9-8 on penalties

3RD PLACE

Mohammed V, Casablanca, 26-03-1988, 40,000
Morocco 1 (Nader 67)
Algeria 1 (Belloumi 87)
Algeria won 4-3 on penalties

FINAL

Mohammed V, Casablanca, 27-03-1988, 50,000. Referee: Idrissa, Senegal
CAMEROON 1 (Kundé 55)
NIGERIA 0
Cameroon - Bell - Massing, Kundé, Ntamark - Tataw, Mbouh, M'fédé, Biyik.K Makanaky, Milla, Olleolle (Abena)
Nigeria - Rufai - Sofoluwe, Keshi, Eboigbe, Omokaro - Nwosu, Okosieme, Eguavon - Folorunso (Edobor), Okwaraji, Yekini

Top scorers
Abdelhamid, Egypt 2
Belloumi, Algeria 2
Milla, Cameroon 2
Traoré.A, Côte d'Ivoire 2

1990

XVII. EDITION

QUALIFYING TOURNAMENT

PRELIMINARY ROUND

Angola 4-1 0-0 Guinea Equatorial
Gabon 3-0 0-1 Burkina Faso
Liberia 0-1 0-3 **Mali**
Mauritius 3-0 0-1 Seychelles
Tanzania 1-1 1-1 1-3p **Swaziland**
Ethiopia W-O Uganda
Guinea W-O Gambia
Libya W-O Mauritania
Mozambique W-O Madagascar

FIRST ROUND

Angola 0-2 1-4 **Côte d'Ivoire**
Ethiopia 1-0 1-6 **Egypt**
Gabon 1-0 0-1 5-3p Ghana
Guinea 1-1 0-3 **Nigeria**
Mali 0-0 1-1 Morocco
Mauritius 1-4 0-1 **Zimbabwe**
Mozambique 0-1 0-3 **Zambia**
Sudan 1-0 0-1 5-6p **Kenya**
Swaziland 0-2 1-1 **Malawi**
Senegal W-O Togo
Tunisia W-O Libya
Zaire W-O Sierra Leone

SECOND ROUND

EGYPT 2-0 0-0 Zaire
NIGERIA 3-0 1-1 Zimbabwe
Malawi 2-3 0-0 **KENYA**
Mali 2-2 1-3 **CÔTE D'IVOIRE**
SENEGAL 3-0 1-0 Tunisia
ZAMBIA 3-0 1-2 Gabon

Algeria qualified as hosts, Cameroon as holders

FINAL TOURNAMENT
ALGERIA, 2ND - 16TH MARCH 1990

FIRST ROUND

Group 1

Stade Olympique, Algiers, 2-03-1990, 65,000
Algeria 5 (Madjer 36 58, Menad 69 72, Amani 88)
Nigeria 1 (Okocha 82)

Stade Olympique, Algiers, 3-03-1990
Côte d'Ivoire 3 (Traoré.A 53 60, Kagui 73)
Egypt 1 (Abdel 75)

Stade Olympique, Algiers, 5-03-1990, 45,000
Nigeria 1 (Yekini 8)
Egypt 0

Stade Olympique, Algiers, 5-03-1990, 45,000
Algeria 3 (Menad 23, El Ouazani 81, Oudjani 82)
Côte d'Ivoire 0

Stade Olympique, Algiers, 8-03-1990, 80,000
Nigeria 1 (Yekini 3)
Côte d'Ivoire 0

Stade Olympique, Algiers, 8-03-1990, 80,000
Algeria 2 (Amani 39, Saib 43)
Egypt 0

	Al	Ng	IC	Eg	Pl	W	D	L	F	A	Pts
ALGERIA	-	5-1	3-0	2-0	3	3	0	0	10	1	6
NIGERIA	-	-	1-0	1-0	3	2	0	1	3	5	4
CÔTE D'IVOIRE	-	-	-	3-1	3	1	0	2	3	5	2
EGYPT	-	-	-	-	3	0	0	3	1	6	0

Group 2

Annaba, 3-03-1990
Zambia 1 (Chikabala 58)
Cameroon 0

Annaba, 3-03-1990
Senegal 0
Kenya 0

Annaba, 6-03-1990
Zambia 1 (Makwaza 40)
Kenya 0

Annaba, 6-03-1990
Senegal 2 (Diallo 45, Ndao 56)
Cameroon 0

Annaba, 9-03-1990
Zambia 0
Senegal 0

Annaba, 9-03-1990
Cameroon 2 (Maboang 28 69)
Kenya 0

	Zm	Se	Ca	Ke	Pl	W	D	L	F	A	Pts
ZAMBIA	-	0-0	1-0	1-0	3	2	1	0	2	0	5
SENEGAL	-	-	2-0	0-0	3	1	2	0	2	0	4
CAMEROON	-	-	-	2-0	3	1	0	2	2	3	2
KENYA	-	-	-	-	3	0	1	2	0	3	1

SEMI-FINALS

Stade Olympique, Algiers, 12-03-1990, 80,000
Algeria 2 (Menad 4, Amani 62)
Senegal 1 (OG 20)

Annaba, 12-03-1990, 35,000
Nigeria 2 (Okechukwu 18, Yekini 77)
Zambia 0

3RD PLACE

Stade Olympique, Algiers, 15-03-1990, 8,000
Zambia 1 (Chikabala 73)
Senegal 0

FINAL

Stade Olympique, Algiers, 16-03-1990, 80,000
ALGERIA 1 (Oudjani 38)
NIGERIA 0

Algeria - Demani - Benhalima, Kegharia, Serrar, Ait-Abderrahmane - El Ouazani (Neftah), Amani, Saib - Madjer, Oudjani (Rahim), Menad
Nigeria - Agui - Okechukwu, Anijekwu, Semitoje - Uwe (Aminu), Adesina, Kpakor, Oliha, Ogunlana (Omokachi) - Yekini, Elahor

Top scorer - Menad, Algeria 4

XVIII. EDITION

QUALIFYING TOURNAMENT

Group 1

	Cm	SL	Gu	Ma	Pl	W	D	L	F	A	Pts
CAMEROON	-	1-0	1-0	0-0	6	3	3	0	5	1	9
SIERRA LEONE	1-1	-	0-1	2-0	6	2	2	2	5	4	6
GUINEA	0-0	1-2	-	2-1	6	2	2	2	5	5	6
MALI	0-2	0-0	1-1	-	6	0	3	3	2	7	3

Group 2

	Eg	Tu	Ch	Et	Pl	W	D	L	F	A	Pts
EGYPT	-	2-2	5-1	2-0	4	3	3	0	13	5	9
TUNISIA	2-2	-	2-1	2-0*	4	3	3	0	10	5	9
CHAD	0-0	0-0	-	2-0*	4	2	2	2	6	7	6
ETHIOPIA	0-2*	0-2	0-2*	-	4	0	0	6	0	12	0

* Ethiopia withdrew after 2 games. The unplayed games were all awarded to their opponents 2-0

Group 3

	CI	Mo	Ni	Ma	Pl	W	D	L	F	A	Pts
CÔTE D'IVOIRE	-	2-0	1-0	2-0	6	5	0	1	9	3	10
MOROCCO	3-1	-	2-0	4-0	6	4	0	2	11	4	8
NIGER	0-1	1-0	-	7-1	5	2	0	3	8	5	4
MAURITANIA	0-2*	0-2	-	-	5	0	0	5	1	17	0

Liberia withdrew

* Côte d'Ivoire awarded the match 2-0

Group 4

	Gh	Ng	BF	To	Be	Pl	W	D	L	F	A	Pts
GHANA	-	1-0	2-0	2-0	4-0	8	5	2	1	11	2	12
NIGERIA	0-0	-	7-1	3-0	3-0	8	4	3	1	15	3	11
BURKINA FASO	2-1	1-1	-	2-0	2-0	8	4	1	3	10	13	9
TOGO	0-1	0-0	1-0	-	2-0	8	2	2	4	4	9	6
BENIN	0-0	0-1	1-2	1-1	-	8	0	2	6	2	15	2

Group 5

	Zm	Md	Sw	An	Pl	W	D	L	F	A	Pts
ZAMBIA	-	2-1	5-0	1-0	6	4	1	1	11	4	9
MADAGASCAR	0-0	-	-	0-0	5	2	2	1	3	2	6
SWAZILAND	2-1	0-1	-	1-1	5	1	2	2	4	9	4
ANGOLA	1-2	0-1	1-1	-	6	0	3	3	3	6	3

Group 6

	Ke	Mz	Su	Pl	W	D	L	F	A	Pts
KENYA	-	1-0	2-1	4	2	0	2	4	4	4
MOZAMBIQUE	2-1	-	1-0	4	2	0	2	3	3	4
SUDAN	1-0	1-0	-	4	2	0	2	3	3	4

Mauritius withdrew

Group 7

	Co	Zi	Ml	Pl	W	D	L	F	A	Pts
CONGO	-	2-0	2-1	4	3	1	0	7	3	7
ZIMBABWE	2-2	-	4-0	4	1	2	1	8	6	4
MALAWI	0-1	2-2	-	4	0	1	3	3	9	1

Seychelles withdrew

Group 8

	Zr	Ga	Ug	Ta	Pl	W	D	L	F	A	Pts
ZAIRE	-	2-1	1-0	2-0	6	3	1	2	6	4	7
GABON	0-0	-	1-0	1-0	6	2	3	1	3	2	7
UGANDA	2-1	0-0	-	3-2	6	2	2	2	6	6	6
TANZANIA	1-0	0-0	1-1	-	6	1	2	3	4	7	4

Senegal qualified as hosts, Algeria as holders

FINAL TOURNAMENT
SENEGAL, 12TH - 26TH JANUARY 1992

FIRST ROUND

Group 1

Stade de l'Amitie, Dakar, 12-01-1992, 75,000

Nigeria 2 (Siasia 13, Keshi 88)
Senegal 1 (Bocande 38)

Stade de l'Amitie, Dakar, 14-01-1992, 8,000

Nigeria 2 (Yekini 7 15)
Kenya 1 (Weche 89)

Stade de l'Amitie, Dakar, 16-01-1992, 45,000

Senegal 3 (Sane 46, Bocande 68, Diagre 89)
Kenya 0

	Ng	Se	Ke	Pl	W	D	L	F	A	Pts
NIGERIA	-	2-1	2-1	2	2	0	0	4	2	4
SENEGAL	-	-	3-0	2	1	0	1	4	2	2
KENYA	-	-	-	2	0	0	2	1	5	0

Group 2

Stade de l'Amitie, Dakar, 12-01-1992, 70,000

Cameroon 1 (Kana Biyik 22)
Morocco 0

Stade de l'Amitie, Dakar, 14-01-1992, 11,000

Zaire 1 (Kana 90)
Morocco 1 (Rokbi 89)

Stade de l'Amitie, Dakar, 16-01-1992, 18,000

Cameroon 1 (Oman Biyik 16)
Zaire 1 (Tueba 2)

	Cm	Za	Ma	Pl	W	D	L	F	A	Pts
CAMEROON	-	1-1	1-0	2	1	1	0	2	1	3
ZAIRE	-	-	1-1	2	0	2	0	2	2	2
MOROCCO	-	-	-	2	0	1	2	1	2	1

Group 3

Stade Aline Sitoe Diatta, Ziguinchor, 13-01-1992, 7,000

Côte d'Ivoire 3 (Traoré.A 14, Fofana 37, Tiehi 90)
Algeria 0

Stade Aline Sitoe Diatta, Ziguinchor, 15-01-1992, 6,000

Côte d'Ivoire 0
Congo 0

Stade Aline Sitoe Diatta, Ziguinchor, 17-01-1992, 7,000

Congo 1 (Tchibota 7)
Algeria 1 (Bouiche 44)

	CI	Co	Al	Pl	W	D	L	F	A	Pts
CÔTE D'IVOIRE	-	0-0	3-0	2	1	1	0	3	0	3
CONGO	-	-	1-1	2	0	2	0	1	1	2
ALGERIA	-	-	-	2	0	1	1	1	4	1

Group 4

Stade Aline Sitoe Diatta, Ziguinchor, 13-01-1992, 7,000

Zambia 1 (Bwalya 60)
Egypt 0

Stade Aline Sitoe Diatta, Ziguinchor, 15-01-1992, 6,000

Ghana 1 (Pelé 64)
Zambia 0

Stade Aline Sitoe Diatta, Ziguinchor, 17-01-1992, 7,000

Ghana 1 (Yeboah 90)
Egypt 0

	Gh	Zm	Eg	Pl	W	D	L	F	A	Pts
GHANA	-	1-0	1-0	2	2	0	0	2	0	4
ZAMBIA	-	-	1-0	2	1	0	1	1	1	2
EGYPT	-	-	-	2	0	0	2	0	2	0

QUARTER-FINALS

Stade de l'Amitie, Dakar, 20-01-1992, 6,000

Côte d'Ivoire 1 (OG 90)
Zambia 0

Stade de l'Amitie, Dakar, 19-01-1992, 45,000

Cameroon 1 (Ebongue 86)
Senegal 0

Stade de l'Amitie, Dakar, 19-01-1992, 30,000

Nigeria 1 (Yekini 22)
Zaire 0

Stade de l'Amitie, Dakar, 20-01-1992, 7,000

Ghana 2 (Yeboah 26, Pelé 51)
Congo 1 (Tchibota 55)

SEMI-FINALS

Stade de l'Amitie, Dakar, 23-01-1992, 25,000

Côte d'Ivoire 0
Cameroon 0
Côte d'Ivoire won 3-1 on penalties

Stade de l'Amitie, Dakar, 23-01-1992, 30,000

Ghana 2 (Pelé 44 Opoku 53)
Nigeria 1 (Adepoju 11)

3RD PLACE

Stade de l'Amitie, Dakar, 25-01-1992, 2,000

Nigeria 2 (Ekpo 76, Yekini 89)
Cameroon 1 (Maboang 81)

FINAL

Stade de l'Amitie, Dakar, 26-01-1992, 60,000. Referee: Séné, Senegal

CÔTE D'IVOIRE 0
GHANA 0

Côte d'Ivoire - Gouaméné - Aka, Sam, Sekana, Hobou - Gadji-Celi, Magui, Otokoré (Traoré.M), Sié - Traoré.A (Kassy-Kouadio), Tiéni
Ghana - Ansah - Armah, Ampeah, Baffoe, Asare - Abroah, Gyamfi (Naawu), Lamptey, Mensah - Opoku, Yeboah
Côte d'Ivoire won 11-10 on penalties

Top Scorer - Rashidi Yekini, Nigeria 4

1994

XIX. EDITION

QUALIFYING TOURNAMENT PRELIMINARY ROUND

Lesotho .... 0-0 4-0 .... Botswana
Guinea Bissau .... 3-1 1-0 .... Cape Verde

Group 1

	Ga	Ca	Ni	Be	Pl	W	D	L	F	A	Pts
GABON	-	0-0	3-0	2-0	6	4	2	0	10	2	10
CAMEROON	0-0	-	2-0	2-0	6	3	3	0	7	0	9
NIGER	1-3	0-0	-	4-1	6	2	1	3	7	10	5
BENIN	1-2	0-3	1-2	-	6	0	0	6	3	15	0

Group 2

	Ni	Ug	Et	Su	Pl	W	D	L	F	A	Pts
NIGERIA	-	2-0	6-0	4-0	6	3	2	1	12	1	8
UGANDA	0-0	-	3-1	1-0	6	2	3	1	7	6	7
ETHIOPIA	1-0	2-2	-	3-0	6	2	1	3	7	12	5
SUDAN	0-0	1-1	1-0	-	6	1	2	3	2	9	4

Group 3

	SL	Al	Se	GB	Pl	W	D	L	F	A	Pts
SIERRA LEONE	-	1-0	2-0	2-0	6	4	2	0	9	1	10
ALGERIA	0-0	-	4-0	3-1	6	4	1	1	13	4	9
SENEGAL	1-1	1-2	-	3-0	6	2	1	3	8	9	5
GUINEA-BISSAU	0-3	1-4	0-3	-	6	0	0	6	2	18	0

Algeria were disqualified after fielding an ineligible player. Togo were also disqualified from the group midway through. Their results had been as follows
Senegal .... 2-0 1-1 .... Togo
Togo .... 0-0 0-4 .... Algeria
Togo .... 0-0 .... Guinea-Bissau
Sierra Leone .... 0-0 .... Togo

Group 4

	Za	Ke	Mo	Le	Pl	W	D	L	F	A	Pts
ZAIRE	-	0-1	2-0	7-0	6	3	2	1	13	3	8
KENYA	1-3	-	4-1	3-0	6	3	2	1	11	6	8
MOZAMBIQUE	0-0	0-0	-	3-0	6	1	3	2	5	7	5
LESOTHO	1-1	2-2	1-1	-	6	0	3	3	4	17	3

Group 5

	Za	Zi	SA	Ma	Pl	W	D	L	F	A	Pts
ZAMBIA	-	0-0	3-0	2-1	6	4	2	0	10	2	10
ZIMBABWE	1-1	-	4-1	2-0	6	3	3	0	9	3	9
SOUTH AFRICA	0-1	1-1	-	0-0	6	1	2	3	5	10	4
MAURITIUS	0-3	0-1	1-3	-	6	0	1	5	2	11	1

Group 6

	Gu	Bu	Co	Pl	W	D	L	F	A	Pts
GUINEA	-	2-2	1-0	4	1	3	0	5	4	5
BURUNDI	2-2	-	1-0	4	1	3	0	5	4	5
CONGO	0-0	0-0	-	4	0	2	2	0	2	2

Play-off
Guinea .... 0-0 5-4p .... Burundi

Chad were disqualified midway through. Their results had been as follows
Chad .... 0-3 .... Guinea
Congo .... 2-0 .... Chad

Group 7
GHANA .... 1-0 2-0 .... Liberia

Both Tanzania and Burkina Faso withdrew midway through. Their results had been as follows
Tanzania .... 2-2 .... Ghana
Burkina Faso .... 1-1 .... Liberia
Liberia .... 1-1 .... Tanzania
Ghana .... 3-0 .... Burkina Faso

Group 8

	Ma	Eg	Mo	Mw	Pl	W	D	L	F	A	Pts
MALI	-	2-1	2-1	2-1	6	3	1	2	8	7	7
EGYPT	2-1	-	1-1	2-0	6	2	2	2	6	5	6
MOROCCO	1-0	0-0	-	0-1	6	2	2	2	5	4	6
MALAWI	1-1	1-0	0-2	-	6	2	1	3	4	7	5

Libya withdrew

Tunisia qualified as hosts, Côte d'Ivoire as holders

FINAL TOURNAMENT TUNISIA
26TH MARCH - 10TH APRIL 1994

FIRST ROUND

Group 1

Stade Olympique, El Menzah, Tunis, 26-03-1994, 45,000
Mali 2 (Coulibaly 26, Sidibé 34)
Tunisia 0

Zouiten, Tunis, 28-03-1994, 8,000
Zaire 1 (Basaula 48)
Mali 0

Stade Olympique, El Menzah, Tunis, 30-03-1994, 45,000
Zaire 1 (Nsumbu 56)
Tunisia 1 (Nouissi 41p)

	Za	Ma	Tu	Pl	W	D	L	F	A	Pts
ZAIRE	-	1-0	1-1	2	1	1	0	2	1	3
MALI	-	-	2-0	2	1	0	1	2	1	2
TUNISIA	-	-	-	2	0	1	1	1	3	1

Group 2

Stade Olympique, El Menzah, Tunis, 26-03-1994, 30,000
Nigeria 3 (Yekini 18 88, Adepoju 72)
Gabon 0

Zouiten, Tunis, 28-03-1994, 6,000
Egypt 4 (Mansour 1, El Gamal 22, Samad 55 59)
Gabon 0

Stade Olympique, El Menzah, Tunis, 30-03-1994, 30,000
Nigeria 0
Egypt 0

	Eg	Ni	Ga	Pl	W	D	L	F	A	Pts
EGYPT	-	0-0	4-0	2	1	1	0	4	0	3
NIGERIA	-	-	3-0	2	1	1	0	3	0	3
GABON	-	-	-	2	0	0	2	0	7	0

Group 3

Stade Olympique, Sousse, 27-03-1994, 10,000
Côte d'Ivoire 4 (Tiéhi 9 67 75, Guel 34)
Sierra Leone 0

Stade Olympique, Sousse, 29-03-1994, 6,000
Zambia 0
Sierra Leone 0

Stade Olympique, Sousse, 31-03-1994, 6,000
Zambia 1 (Malitoli.K 80)
Côte d'Ivoire 0

	Za	CI	SL	Pl	W	D	L	F	A	Pts
Zambia	-	1-0	0-0	2	1	1	0	1	0	3
Côte d'Ivoire	-	-	4-0	2	1	0	1	4	1	2
Sierra Leone	-	-	-	2	0	1	1	0	4	1

Group 4
Stade Olympique, Sousse, 27-03-1994, 10,000
Ghana 1 (Akunor 87)
Guinea 0

Stade Olympique, Sousse, 29-03-1994, 6,000
Senegal 2 (Gueye 46p, Tendeng 50)
Guinea 1 (Camara.A 44)

Stade Olympique, Sousse, 31-03-1994, 6,000
Ghana 1 (Polley 88)
Senegal 0

	Gh	Se	Gu	Pl	W	D	L	F	A	Pts
Ghana	-	1-0	1-0	2	2	0	0	2	0	4
Senegal	-	-	2-1	2	1	0	1	2	2	2
Guinea	-	-	-	2	0	0	2	1	3	0

QUARTER-FINALS
Stade Olympique, El Menzah, Tunis, 2-04-1994, 2,000
Nigeria 2 (Yekini 51 71p)
Zaire 0

Stade Olympique, El Menzah, Tunis, 2-04-1994, 3,000
Mali 1 (Traoré.S 64)
Egypt 0

Stade Olympique, Sousse, 3-04-1994, 8,000
Zambia 1 (Sakala 39)
Senegal 0

Stade Olympique, Sousse, 3-04-1994, 8,000
Côte d'Ivoire 2 (Tiehi 30, Traoré.A 82)
Ghana 1

SEMI-FINALS
Stade Olympique, El Menzah, Tunis, 6-04-1994, 2,000
Nigeria 2 (Iroha 26, Yekini 40)
Côte d'Ivoire 2 (Bassolé 19 31)
Nigeria won 4-2 on penalties

Stade Olympique, El Menzah, Tunis, 6-04-1994, 2,000
Zambia 4 (Litana 8, Saileti 31, Kalusha Bwalya 47, Malitoli.K 71)
Mali 0

3RD PLACE
Stade Olympique, El Menzah, Tunis, 10-04-1994, 15,000
Côte d'Ivoire 2 (Koné 2, Ouattara 68, Sié 70)
Mali 1 (Diallo 46)

FINAL
Stade Olympique, El Menzah, Tunis, 10-04-1994, 25,000.
Referee: Lim Kee Chong, Mauritius
NIGERIA 2 (Amunike 5 46)
ZAMBIA 1 (Litana 3)

Nigeria - Rufai - Eguavoen, Okafor, Okechukwu, Iroha - George (Siasia), Oliseh, Okocha (Ugbade) - Amunike, Yekini, Amokachi. Tr: Westerhof
Zambia - Phiri - Malitoli.M, Chongo, Litana, Chiyangi - Joel Bwalya (Johnson Bwalya), Sakala, Mulenga (Makwaza) - Malitoli.K, Saileti, Kalusha Bwalya. Tr: Porterfield

Top scorer Rashidi Yekini, Nigeria 5

OTHER TOURNAMENTS

CAF also organises two youth championships which act as qualifying competitions for the world events. The youth cup is the longest running of the two, dating from 1979. For the 1991 edition, its format was changed from being purely a knock-out event to include qualifying rounds and a final tournament. It is now known as the Junior Nations Cup.

The 1995 Under-17 championship was the first to be organised at that age-level. Previously teams had taken part in a qualifying tournament for the World Championship, but it was nothing more than that and no overall winner emerged.

AFRICAN UNDER-17 CHAMPIONSHIP

1995	Ghana	3-1	Nigeria

AFRICAN YOUTH CUP

1979	Algeria	2-1 2-3	Guinea
1981	Egypt	1-1 2-0	Cameroon
1983	Nigeria	2-2 2-1	Côte d'Ivoire
1985	Nigeria	1-1 2-1	Tunisia
1987	Nigeria	2-1 2-0	Mali
1989	Nigeria	2-1 2-0	Mali
1991	Egypt	2-1	Côte d'Ivoire
1993	Ghana	2-0	Cameroon
1995	Cameroon	4-0	Burundi

AFRICAN CLUB COMPETITIONS

African club competitions centre around three CAF-organised tournaments, the African Cup of Champion Clubs, the African Cup Winners Cup and the CAF Cup. The Champions Cup is open to the league champions of each country, the Cup Winners Cup to the winners of the main knockout tournament in each country, and the CAF Cup to the best of the rest. In each case the previous year's winners are entitled to defend their title.

The African Cup of Champion Clubs is now a major feature on the calendar of world football. It had always been the intention of the African Football Confederation to promote club football, but in 1957 not many clubs were in a position to play teams from other cities, let alone other countries. Not until 1964 did a Champions Cup seem remotely feasible. Leagues were springing up in every country following independence, and representatives of 14 of them played off for the right to be represented in the first edition, to be staged in Ghana. In that historic three-day tournament in Accra, Oryx Douala from Cameroon beat not only the hosts Real Republicans, who were in effect the Ghanaian national side, but also Stade Malien to win the first title.

Very much influenced by the organisation of the European Cup, the format was changed for the second edition two years later. Each tie was to be contested on a home and away basis with the highest aggregate scorers qualifying for the next round. In the event of these being tied, the number of away goals would be the deciding factor, and in the final resort, penalties. Unlike the European Cup, however, the final was to be staged over two legs, as a neutral venue was thought unlikely to attract a big enough crowd.

The tournament has gone through two very distinct phases. Until the early 1980s sub-Saharan clubs were pre-eminent. Since then, however, North African teams have been totally dominant, a pattern that has also been reflected in the Cup Winners Cup. The early years of the Champions Cup had been dominated by the clubs of West and Central Africa. TP Englebert, later renamed TP Mazembe, appeared in four of the first six finals and another club from Zaire, Vita Kinshasa, won the tournament in 1973. Ghana was also well represented, particularly by the great Asante Kotoko club who, like TP Englebert, appeared in four finals, although they only emerged victorious once.

The competition really came to life in the early 1970s, with Cameroon and Guinea the major forces of the time. Canon Yaoundé, Union Douala and Tonnerre Yaoundé (from Cameroon) and Hafia and Horoya Conakry (Guinea) all made their names in this period. Hafia Conakry were especially dominant, appearing in five Champions Cup finals between 1972 and 1978 with a team that was feared throughout the continent. The attacking line-up of Petit Sory, Papa Camara, Bangaly Sylla, Cherif Soulayeman, N'Jolea, Tollo and Jansky has perhaps yet to be equalled in African club football.

Before the 1980s, sides from North Africa had shown little interest in the club competitions. Al Ismaili won the Champions Cup in 1969 but were not regarded as the best Egyptian team, whilst Mouloudia Algiers won the cup for Algeria in 1976. The eighties saw the North Africans begin to realise what they were missing out on, and fairly soon they made their mark. Asante Kotoko's win in the 1983 Champions Cup marks the last occasion on which the trophy was held by a sub-Saharan nation.

The Cup Winners Cup too has been the domain of the North Africans since the early 1980s. Al Ahly from Cairo, who have emerged as one of the finest clubs Africa has produced, won the competition three years on the trot, the only club to have achieved such a feat. On the third occasion they actually gave up their place in the Champions Cup to take part, but they returned to the champions' event the following year and promptly won that as well. This was all on top of a victory and a final appearance in the Champions Cup in 1981 and 1982: six years, six final appearances and five victories!

They were not the only North Africans at it. Zamalek, their great Cairo rivals, have won the Champions Cup three times, whilst their compatriots Al Makoaloum have won the Cup Winners Cup twice. Clubs from Tunisia, Algeria and Morocco too, have all contributed to this phenomenal success. It is up to the sub-Saharan Africans to match the very professional club structure of their rivals in the north, and there are signs that this is indeed occurring. The Nigerians are beginning to make their presence felt, and as the largest country on the continent they have definitely been the major underachievers to date at club level, with only five titles to their name.

The hope is that the African champions will soon be invited to take part in the World Club Championship with the winners of the European Cup and Copa Libertadores. Certainly, there is little reason for their continued exclusion.

THE AFRICAN CUP OF CHAMPION CLUBS

Year	Winner	Score	Runner-up
1964	Oryx Douala	2-1	Stade Malien
1965	-		
1966	Stade Abidjan	1-3 4-1	AS Real Bamako
1967	TP Englebert	1-1 2-2	Asante Kotoko
1968	TP Englebert	5-0 1-4	Etoile Filante
1969	Al Ismaili	2-2 3-1	TP Englebert
1970	Asante Kotoko	1-1 2-1	TP Englebert
1971	Canon Yaoundé	0-3 2-0 1-0	Asante Kotoko
1972	Hafia FC Conakry	4-2 3-2	Simba FC
1973	AS Vita Kinshasa	2-4 3-0	Asante Kotoko
1974	CARA Brazzaville	4-2 2-1	Mehalla Al Kubra
1975	Hafia FC Conakry	1-0 2-1	Enugu Rangers
1976	Mouloudia d'Algiers	3-0 0-3 4-1p	Hafia FC Conakry
1977	Hafia FC Conakry	1-0 3-2	Hearts of Oak
1978	Canon Yaoundé	0-0 2-0	Hafia FC Conakry
1979	Union Douala	0-1 1-0 5-3p	Hearts of Oak
1980	Canon Yaoundé	2-2 3-0	AS Bilima
1981	JE Tizi-Ouzou	4-0 1-0	AS Vita Kinshasa
1982	Al Ahly Cairo	3-0 1-1	Asante Kotoko
1983	Asante Kotoko	0-0 1-0	Al Ahly Cairo
1984	Zamalek	2-0 0-0	Shooting Stars
1985	FAR Rabat	5-2 1-1	AS Bilima
1986	Zamalek	2-0 0-2 4-2p	Africa Sports
1987	Al Ahly Cairo	0-0 2-0	Al Hilal
1988	Entente Setif	0-1 4-0	Iwuanyanwu Owerri
1989	Raja Casablanca	1-0 0-1 4-2p	Mouloudia d'Oran
1990	JS Kabylie	1-0 0-1 5-3p	Nkana Red Devils
1991	Club Africain	5-1 1-1	Nakivubo Villa
1992	WAC Casablanca	2-0 0-0	Al Hilal
1993	Zamalek	0-0 0-0 7-6p	Asante Kotoko
1994	Esperance Tunis	0-0 3-1	Zamalek

THE AFRICAN CUP WINNERS CUP

1975	Tonnerre Yaoundé	1-0 4-1	Stella Abidjan
1976	Shooting Stars	4-1 0-1	Tonnerre Yaoundé
1977	Enugu Rangers	4-1 1-1	Canon Yaoundé
1978	Horoya AC Conakry	3-1 2-1	MA Hussein-Dey
1979	Canon Yaoundé	2-0 6-0	Gor Mahia
1980	TP Mazembe	3-1 1-0	Africa Sports
1981	Union Douala	2-1 0-0	Stationery Stores
1982	Al Mokaouloum	2-0 2-0	Power Dynamos
1983	Al Mokaouloum	1-0 0-0	Agaza Lomé
1984	Al Ahly Cairo	1-0 0-1 4-2p	Canon Yaoundé
1985	Al Ahly Cairo	2-0 0-1	Leventis United
1986	Al Ahly Cairo	3-0 0-2	AS Sogara
1987	Gor Mahia	2-2 1-1	Esperance Tunis
1988	CA Bizerte	0-0 1-0	Ranchers Bees
1989	Al Merreikh	1-0 0-0	Bendel United
1990	BCC Lions	3-0 1-1	Club Africain
1991	Power Dynamos	2-3 3-1	BCC Lions
1992	Africa Sports	1-1 4-0	Vital'O
1993	Al Ahly Cairo	1-1 1-0	Africa Sports
1994	DC Motema Pembe	2-2 3-0	Kenya Breweries

CAF CUP

1992	Shooting Stars	0-0 3-0	Nakivubo Villa
1993	Stella Club Abidjan	0-0 2-0	Simba SC
1994	Bendel Insurance	0-1 3-0	Primeiro de Maio

RESULTS

1964

CHAMPIONS CUP

SEMI-FINALS

Oryx Douala (CMR) ... 2-1 ... Real Republicans (GHA)
Stade Malien (MLI) ... 3-1 ... Cotton Club (ETH)

FINAL

Accra Stadium, Accra, 7-02-1964
ORYX DOUALA 2
STADE MALIEN 1

1966

CHAMPIONS CUP

FIRST ROUND

Etoile Filante (VOL) ... 2-0 1-4 ... **Stade Abidjan** (CIV)
Etoile Filante (TGO) ... 0-3 0-3 ... **Asante Kotoko** (GHA)
Diables Noirs (COG) ... 1-2 2-0 ... Dragons (ZAI)
Ethio-Cement (ETH) ... 1-4 0-6 ... **Al Hilal** (SDN)
Oryx Douala (CMR) ... Bye
Conakry I (GUI) ... W-O ... US Goree (SEN)
Invincible Eleven (LBR) ... 2-3 0-6 ... **AS Real Bamako** (MLI)

QUARTER-FINALS

Asante Kotoko ... 0-1 2-2 ... **Stade Abidjan**
Al Hilal ... 6-1 4-1 ... Diables Noirs
Oryx Douala ... Bye
AS Real Bamako ... 2-1 3-2 ... Conakry I

SEMI-FINALS

Al Hilal ... 1-0 2-4 ... **Stade Abidjan**
Oryx Douala ... 2-4 2-3 ... **AS Real Bamako**

FINAL

1st leg. Omnisport, Bamako, 11-12-1966
AS REAL BAMAKO 3
STADE ABIDJAN 1

2nd leg. Houphouet Boigny, Abidjan, 25-12-1966
STADE ABIDJAN 4
AS REAL BAMAKO 1

1967

CHAMPIONS CUP

PRELIMINARY ROUND

Secteur 6 (NIG) ... 3-2 1-3 ... **Al Ittihad** (LBY)
AS Fonctionnaires (VOL) ... W-O ... Augustinians (GMB)

FIRST ROUND

TP Englebert (ZAI) ... 2-0 1-3 ... Abeilles FC (COG)
Al Ittihad (LBY) ... W-O ... Diamant Yaoundé (CMR)
Al Hilal (SDN) ... 0-1 1-3 ... **Olympic Alexandria** (EGY)
St. Georges (ETH) ... W-O ... Bitumastic (UGA)
Djoliba AC (MLI) ... W-O ... Invincible Eleven (LBR)
AS Fonctionnaires (VOL) ... 0-2 1-1 ... **Conakry II** (GUI)
Stade Abidjan (CIV) ... 2-1 0-0 ... Modela Lomé (TGO)
AS St. Louisienne (SEN) ... 2-3 0-3 ... **Asante Kotoko** (GHA)

QUARTER-FINALS

TP Englebert ... W-O ... Al Ittihad
St. Georges ... 3-2 ... Olympic Alexandria
Djoliba AC ... 2-1 0-0 ... Conakry II
Stade Abidjan ... 1-3 2-5 ... **Asante Kotoko**

SEMI-FINALS

TP Englebert ... 3-1 1-2 ... St. Georges
Asante Kotoko ... 1-1 2-1 ... Djoliba AC

FINAL

1st leg. Kumasi Stadium, Kumasi, 19-11-1967
ASANTE KOTOKO 1
TOUT PUISSANT ENGLEBERT 1

2nd leg. 20th May stadium, Kinshasa, 26-11-1967
TOUT PUISSANT ENGLEBERT 2
ASANTE KOTOKO 2
TP Englebert were awarded the cup after Asante Kotoko refused to take part in a play-off

1968

CHAMPIONS CUP

PRELIMINARY ROUND

Secteur 6 (NIG) ... 1-1 1-3 ... **US Ouagadougou** (VOL)
Police Mogadishu (SOM) ... W-O ... Cosmopolitans (TAN)
FAR Rabat (MOR) ... W-O ... Augustinians (GMB)
Etoile du Congo (COG) ... W-O ... Mighty Blackpool (SLE)

FIRST ROUND

Africa Sports (CIV) ... 2-0 4-4 * ... TP Englebert (ZAI)
Etoile du Congo (COG) ... 1-2 3-4 ... **Oryx Douala** (CMR)
Stationery Stores (NGA) 3-2 1-2 ** Cape Coast Dwarfs (GHA)
FAR Rabat (MOR) ... 2-0 1-0 ... Foyer France (SEN)
Police Mogadishu (SOM) ... 1-1 1-3 ... **Al Mourada** (SDN)

Abaluhya FC (KEN)..............1-1 3-1...................St. Georges (ETH)
Mighty Barolle (LBR)..................1-2 ....**Conakry II** (GUI)
US Ouagadougou (VOL).........1-4 0-2...........**Etoile Filante** (TGO)

* Africa Sports disqualified
** Stationery Stores won on lots

QUARTER-FINALS

TP Englebert..........................3-0 2-0............................Oryx Douala
FAR Rabat..........................1-0 1-2 2-2 * ....Stationery Stores
Abaluhya FC..........................3-0 1-3 ....Al Mourada
Etoile Filante..............................3-0 ....Conakry II

* FAR Rabat won on penalties

SEMI-FINALS

TP Englebert..........................1-1 3-1 ....FAR Rabat
Abaluhya FC..............................2-0 0-4.........................**Etoile Filante**

FINAL

1st leg. 20th May Stadium, Kinshasa, 16-03-1969
TOUT PUISSANT ENGLEBERT 5
ETOILE FILANTE 0

2nd leg. Eyadema Stadium, Lome, 30-03-1969
ETOILE FILANTE 4
TOUT PUISSANT ENGLEBERT 1

1969

CHAMPIONS CUP

PRELIMINARY ROUND

Africa Sports (CIV)...............5-1 2-0 ......Olympique Sportif (GAB)
Hoga Mogadishu (SOM)...........2-0 1-4..........................**Burri** (SDN)
Young Africans (TAN).........4-1 0-2 ....Fitarikandro (MDG)
St. Eloi (ZAI)...............................W-O ....US Cattin (CTA)

FIRST ROUND

TP Englebert (ZAI) ....2-1 2-2 ....Africa Sports (CIV)
Secteur 6 (NIG) ....1-5 0-3...........**Etoile Filante** (TGO)
Caiman Douala (CMR)............0-0 1-3..........................**St. Eloi** (ZAI)
USFRAN (VOL) ....2-7 ....**Conakry II** (GUI)
St. Georges (ETH)....................0-0 0-5 ....**Young Africans** (TAN)
Asante Kotoko (GHA)..........5-1 1-1 ....Patronage St. Anne (COG)
Burri (SDN)..................................2-4 1-0 ....**Gor Mahia** (KEN)
Al Tahadi (LBY) ....0-5 0-3......................**Al Ismaili** (EGY)

QUARTER-FINALS

TP Englebert..........................4-1 0-1 ....Etoile Filante
Conakry II................................7-2 3-1...St. Eloi
Asante Kotoko ....1-1 1-1 * ....Young Africans
Al Ismaili ....3-1 1-1 ....Gor Mahia
* Asante won on lots

SEMI-FINALS

TP Englebert..........................4-0 3-5 ....Conakry II
Asante Kotoko..........................2-2 2-3 ....**Al Ismaili**

FINAL

1st leg. 20th May Stadium, Kinshasa, 22-12-1969
TOUT PUISSANT ENGLEBERT 2
AL ISMAILI 2

2nd leg. International Stadium, Cairo, 9-01-1970
AL ISMAILI 3
TOUT PUISSANT ENGLEBERT 1

1970

CHAMPIONS CUP

FIRST ROUND

Asante Kotoko (GHA) ....Bye
Stationery Stores (NGA)....3-1 3-2 ....Forces Armees (DAH)
Nakuru All Stars (KEN).........Bye
Young Africans (TAN) ....4-0 2-4......US Fonctionnaires (MDG)
Lavori Publici (SOM) ....2-1 2-4 ....**Prisons FC** (UGA)
Tele SC Asmara (ETH)...........Bye
Al Hilal (SDN) ....Bye
Al Ismaili (EGY)..........................Bye
AS Kaloum Star (GUI)...........Bye
CR Belcourt (ALG) ....5-3 ** ....**ASC Jeanne d'Arc** (SEN)
AS Real Bamako (MLI) ....3-0 2-2........AS Fonctionnaires (VOL)
Stade Abidjan (CIV) ....Bye
Modele Lomé (TGO) ....Bye
Secteur 6 (NIG) ....0-2 2-1 ....**Union Douala** (CMR)
Aigle Royal (GAB) ....0-3 5-2...............**CARA Brazzaville** ....(COG)
TP Englebert (ZAI)..................Bye
** CR Belcourt withdrew, Jeanne d'Arc qualified

SECOND ROUND

Stationery Stores....................3-2 0-1 ** ....**Asante Kotoko**
Nakuru All Stars ....1-0 1-3 ....**Young Africans**
Prisons FC...............................3-2 1-2 * ....Tele SC Asmara
Al Ismaili ....1-0 0-0 ....Al Hilal
AS Kaloum Star......................3-1 1-2 ....ASC Jeanne d'Arc
AS Real Bamako ....2-3 2-6 ....**Stade Abidjan**
Union Douala..............................0-0 1-1 * ....**Modele Lomé**
TP Englebert...........................3-0 2-2 ....CARA Brazzaville
* Prisons and Modele won on lots
** 2nd match abandoned. Stationery Stores disqualified

QUARTER-FINALS

Young Africans...........................1-1 0-2 ....**Asante Kotoko**
Al Ismaili ....4-1 2-1 ....Prisons FC
Stade Abidjan ....1-1 3-4..................**AS Kaloum Star**
Modele Lomé...............................0-0 1-3........................**TP Englebert**

SEMI-FINALS

Al Ismaili.....................................0-0 0-2 ....**Asante Kotoko**
AS Kaloum Star..........................1-2 1-3.........................**TP Englebert**

FINAL

1st leg. Kumasi Stadium, Kumasi, 10-01-1971
ASANTE KOTOKO 1
TOUT PUISSANT ENGLEBERT 1

2nd leg. 20th May Stadium, Kinshasa, 24-01-1971
TOUT PUISSANT ENGLEBERT 1
ASANTE KOTOKO 2

1971

CHAMPIONS CUP

FIRST ROUND

Canon Yaoundé (CMR)........7-3 2-1 ....AS Solidarite (GAB)
AS Vita Club (ZAI) ....Bye
AS Porto Novo (DAH)............0-1 0-2..**Victoria Mokanda** (COG)
Dynamic Togolais (TGO) ......Bye
Secteur 6 (NIG) ....1-1 0-1 ....**Enugu Rangers** (NGA)
AS Kaloum Star (GUI)...........Bye
ASC Diaraf (SEN) ....3-0 0-4 ....**Stade Malien** (MLI)
ASEC Abidjan (CIV)................Bye
Abaluhya FC (KEN)...................0-0 1-3 ......**Great Olympics** (GHA)

Maseru United (LSO) 1-2 2-3 **MMM Tamatave** (MDG)
Young Africans (TAN) 2-0 0-0 Lavori Publici (SOM)
Coffee FC (UGA) Bye
Al Ismaili (EGY) Bye
Esperance Tunis (TUN) 0-0 1-0 Al Ahly Benghazi (LBY)
Al Merreikh (SDN) 2-1 0-1 5-4p Tele SC Asmara (ETH)
Asante Kotoko (GHA) Bye

SECOND ROUND

AS Vita Club 2-0 1-3 3-4p **Canon Yaoundé**
Victoria Mokanda 1-2 0-2 **Dynamic Togolaise**
AS Kaloum Star 3-3 1-2 **Enugu Rangers**
Stade Malien 2-2 1-2 **ASEC Abidjan**
MMM Tamatave 2-1 0-4 **Great Olympics**
Coffee FC W-O Young Africans
Al Ismaili W-O Esperance Tunis
Al Merreikh 2-1 0-1 4-5p **Asante Kotoko**

QUARTER-FINALS

Dynamic Togolaise 1-2 3-4 **Canon Yaoundé**
Enugu Rangers 0-1 0-2 **ASEC Abidjan**
Coffee FC 0-0 0-2 **Great Olympics**
Al Ismaili 0-0 0-3 **Asante Kotoko**

SEMI-FINALS

ASEC Abidjan 2-1 1-4 **Canon Yaoundé**
Great Olympics 1-1 0-1 **Asante Kotoko**

FINAL

1st leg. Kumasi Stadium, Kumasi, 5-12-1971
ASANTE KOTOKO 3
CANON YAOUNDÉ 0

2nd leg. Militaire Garoua, Yaoundé, 19-12-1971
CANON YAOUNDÉ 2
ASANTE KOTOKO 0

Play-off. Militaire Garoua, Yaoundé, 21-12-1971
CANON YAOUNDÉ 1
ASANTE KOTOKO 0
Match abandoned but the result stood

1972

CHAMPIONS CUP

FIRST ROUND

Hafia FC (GUI) 4-1 1-1 ASFAN Niamey (NIG)
Canon Yaoundé (CMR) Bye
ASFA Dakar (SEN) 3-0 3-2 AS Cotonou (DAH)
ASFA Ouagadougou (VOL) 1-3 0-1 **Djoliba AC** (MLI)
Aigle Nkongsamba (CMR) 3-1 0-1 Olympique Real (CTA)
Dynamic Togolaise (TGO) Bye
Africa Sports (CIV) Bye
TP Mazembe (ZAI) 2-0 1-1 AS Police (GAB)
Hearts of Oak (GHA) W-O Abaluhya FC (KEN)
WNDC Ibadan (NGA) Bye
AS St. Michael (MDG) 2-0 0-1 Young Africans (TAN)
Majantja Maseru (LSO) 2-2 0-9 **Kabwe Warriors** (ZAM)
Al Ahly Tripoli (LBY) W-O Al Merreikh (SDN)
Al Ismaili (EGY) Bye
St. Georges (ETH) 3-1 1-1 Lavori Publici (SOM)
Simba FC (UGA) Bye

SECOND ROUND

Canon Yaoundé 3-2 1-4 **Hafia FC**
ASFA Dakar 2-0 0-2 * **Djoliba AC**
Dynamic Togolaise 1-1 3-4 **Aigle Nkongsamba**
Africa Sports 1-2 2-5 **TP Mazembe**
WNDC Ibadan 1-0 0-3 **Hearts of Oak**
Kabwe Warriors 2-1 3-0 AS St. Michael
Al Ismaili 0-1 2-1 3-4p **Al Ahly Tripoli**
Simba FC 4-0 1-1 St. Georges
* Forces Armees withdrew

QUARTER-FINALS

Hafia FC 3-0 1-2 Djoliba AC
TP Mazembe 4-1 2-1 Aigle Nkongsamba
Hearts of Oak 7-2 1-2 Kabwe Warriors
Al Ahly Tripoli 1-1 0-3 **Simba FC**

SEMI-FINALS

TP Mazembe 3-2 * **Hafia FC**
Hearts of Oak 1-1 0-1 **Simba FC**
* TP Mazembe withdrew

FINAL

1st leg. 28th September Stadium, Conakry, 10-12-1972
HAFIA CONAKRY 4
SIMBA FOOTBALL CLUB 2

2nd leg. Nakivubo, Kampala, 22-12-1972
SIMBA FOOTBALL CLUB 2
HAFIA CONAKRY 3

1973

CHAMPIONS CUP

FIRST ROUND

AS Vita Club (ZAI) Bye
Mighty Jets (NGA) 2-1 0-1 * Jeanne d'Arc (VOL)
ASFA Dakar (SEN) 2-2 2-4 **Modele Lomé** (TGO)
Stade Malien (MLI) Bye
Hafia FC (GUI) Bye
ASEC Abidjan (CIV) 2-1 3-1 Mighty Barolle (LBR)
CARA Brazzaville (COG) 1-0 2-2 Sports Dynamic (BDI)
Leopards Douala (CMR) Bye
FC Horsed (SOM) 3-1 0-5 **Al Ismaili** (EGY)
Al Ahly Benghazi (LBY) Bye
Simba FC (UGA) Bye
Kenya Breweries (KEN) 1-1 1-1 5-4p Tele SC Asmara (ETH)
Kabwe Warriors (ZAM) Bye
Fortior Mahajanga (MDG) 5-1 1-2 Maseru Police (LSO)
Young Africans (TAN) 1-2 1-1 **Al Merreikh** (SDN)
Asante Kotoko (GHA) Bye
* Jeanne d'Arc withdrew, Mighty Jets qualified

SECOND ROUND

AS Vita Club W-O Mighty Jets
Stade Malien 2-1 0-0 Modele Lomé
Hafia FC 2-1 3-4 3-2p ASEC Abidjan
Leopards Douala 2-0 0-1 CARA Brazzaville
Al Ismaili 4-1 1-0 Al Ahly Benghazi
Kenya Breweries 3-1 1-2 Simba FC
Kabwe Warriors 4-0 3-0 Fortior Mahajanga
Al Merreikh 1-1 0-3 **Asante Kotoko**

QUARTER-FINALS

Stade Malien 0-3 1-4 **AS Vita Club**
Hafia FC 2-4 3-2 **Leopards Douala**
Kenya Breweries 0-0 1-2 * Al Ismaili
Kabwe Warriors 2-1 0-2 **Asante Kotoko**
* Ismaili withdrew, Breweries qualified

SEMI-FINALS

AS Vita Club 3-0 1-3 Leopards Douala
Kenya Breweries 0-2 1-2 **Asante Kotoko**

FINAL

1st leg. Kumasi Stadium, Kumasi, 25-11-1973

ASANTE KOTOKO 4
AS VITA CLUB 2

2nd leg. 20th May Stadium, Kinshasa, 16-12-1973

AS VITA CLUB 3
ASANTE KOTOKO 0

1974

CHAMPIONS CUP

FIRST ROUND

CARA Brazzaville (COG)..3-1 4-0 ....Zalang (GAB)
AS Vita Club (ZAI) ....Bye
Bendel Insurance (NGA) ....7-0 0-1 ....Secteur 7 (NIG)
Djoliba AC (MLI) ....Bye
Mighty Barolle (LBR) ....0-0 0-2 ....**ASEC Abidjan** (CIV)
Modele Lomé (TGO) ....3-0 0-1 ....AS Porto Novo (DAH)
Hafia FC (GUI) ....Bye
Ports Authority (SLE) ....3-2 1-3....**ASC Jeanne d'Arc** (SEN)
Linare FC (LSO) ....1-3 1-2 ....**SC Simba** (TAN)
Green Buffaloes (ZAM) ....4-1 2-1 ....JS Antalaha (MDG)
Olympique Real (CTA) ....4-0 0-1 ....Simba FC (UGA)
Hearts of Oak (GHA) ....Bye
Abaluhya FC (KEN) ....Bye
Tele SC Asmara (ETH) ....W-O ....FC Horsed (SOM)
Al Ahly Tripoli (LBY) ....2-2 0-3 ....**Al Hilal** (SDN)
Mehalla Al Kubra (EGY) ....Bye

SECOND ROUND

CARA Brazzaville ....4-0 0-3 ....AS Vita Club
Djoliba AC ....2-0 0-1 ....Bendel Insurance
ASEC Abidjan ....3-0 ....Modele Lomé
ASC Jeanne d'Arc ....W-O ....Hafia FC
Green Buffaloes ....1-2 0-1 ....**SC Simba**
Hearts of Oak ....6-1 3-3 ....Olympique Real
Abaluhya FC ....2-0 0-1 ....Tele SC Asmara
Mehalla Al Kubra ....4-1 1-4 4-2p ....Al Hilal

QUARTER-FINALS

Djoliba AC ....0-0 0-3 ....**CARA Brazzaville**
ASEC Abidjan ....2-1 0-1 ....**ASC Jeanne d'Arc**
Hearts of Oak ....1-2 0-0 ....**SC Simba**
Mehalla Al Kubra ....3-0 1-1 ....Abaluhya FC

SEMI-FINALS

CARA Brazzaville ....2-0 4-1 ....ASC Jeanne d'Arc
SC Simba ....1-0 0-1 0-3p ....**Mehalla Al Kubra**

FINAL

1st leg. Revolution Stadium, Brazzaville, 29-11-1974

CARA BRAZZAVILLE 4
MEHALLA AL KUBRA 2

2nd leg. Mehalla Stadium, Mehalla, 13-12-1974

MEHALLA AL KUBRA 1
CARA BRAZZAVILLE 2

1975

CHAMPIONS CUP

FIRST ROUND

Hafia FC (GUI) ....W-O ....Real Banjul (GMB)
AS Vita Club (ZAI) ....4-0 1-1 ....Petrosport FC (GAB)
Silures (VOL) ....3-2 2-0......Etoile Porto Novo (DAH)
CARA Brazzaville (COG)......Bye
Olympic Niamey (NIG) ....0-2 1-4 ....**ASEC Abidjan** (CIV)
ASFA Dakar (SEN) ....Bye
Djoliba AC (MLI) ....2-0 1-0 ....Mighty Blackpool (SLE)
Bame Monrovia (LBR) ....0-1 1-3 ....**Lome I** (TGO)
Mehalla Al Kubra (EGY) ....Bye
Uganda Express FC (UGA)1-0 0-0 ....FC Horsed (SOM)
Embassoria (ETH) ....1-1 0-2 ....**Inter Star** (BDI)
ASDR Fatima (CTA) ....3-0 0-2 * ....**Al Merreikh** (SDN)
Green Buffaloes (ZAM) ....W-O ....Corps Enseignant (MDG)
Bata Bullets (MWI) ....W-O ....Matlama FC (LSO)
Young Africans (TAN) ....Bye
Great Olympics (GHA) ....0-2 1-2 ....**Enugu Rangers** (NGA)
* Fatima withdrew during the second match

SECOND ROUND

AS Vita Club ....2-0 0-3 ....**Hafia FC**
CARA Brazzaville ....4-0 5-4 ....Silures
ASEC Abidjan ....1-1 1-1 6-5p ....ASFA Dakar
Djoliba AC ....1-1 2-3 ....**Lome I**
Uganda Express FC ....1-1 0-1 ....**Mehalla Al Kubra**
Inter Star ....0-0 2-4 ....**Al Merreikh**
Bata Bullets ....0-2 2-3 ....**Green Buffaloes**
Enugu Rangers ....0-0 1-1 ....Young Africans

QUARTER-FINALS

CARA Brazzaville ....2-0 0-2 3-4p ....**Hafia FC**
ASEC Abidjan ....1-0 1-3 ....**Lome I**
Mehalla Al Kubra ....2-1 0-0 ....Al Merreikh
Green Buffaloes ....2-2 1-2 ....**Enugu Rangers**

SEMI-FINALS

Hafia FC ....1-0 1-1 ....Lome I
Mehalla Al Kubra ....3-1 0-3 ....**Enugu Rangers**

FINAL

1st leg. 28th September Stadium, Conakry, 7-12-1975

HAFIA CONAKRY 1
ENUGU RANGERS 0

2nd leg. Surulere, Lagos, 20-12-1975

ENUGU RANGERS 1
HAFIA CONAKRY 2

CUP WINNERS CUP

FIRST ROUND

Mighty Jets (NGA) ....2-2 0-0 **Tonnerre Yaoundé** (CMR)
Al Ittihad (EGY) ....2-0 0-0 ....St. Georges (ETH)
Fortior Mahajanga (MDG).....Bye
Mufulira Wanderers (ZAM)3-0 3-1 ....Jeshi Zanzibar (TAN)
Wallidan (GMB) ....0-0 0-2....**ASC Jeanne d'Arc** (SEN)
Postel Sport (DAH) ....1-0 0-3 **AS Tempete Mocaf** (CTA)
Ifodje Atakpame (TGO)......1-0 2-2 ....Sahel SC (NIG)
Stella Abidjan (CIV) ....1-0 1-0 ....Mighty Barolle (LBR)

QUARTER-FINALS

Al Ittihad ....4-0 0-3 * ....**Tonnerre Yaoundé**
Mufulira Wanderers ....W-O ....Fortior Mahajanga
ASC Jeanne d'Arc ....1-1 3-1 ....AS Tempete Mocaf
Ifodje Atakpame ....0-1 0-4 ....**Stella Abidjan**
* Al Ittihad withdrew during the second match

SEMI-FINALS

Tonnerre Yaoundé ....1-0 2-2 ....Mufulira Wanderers
ASC Jeanne d'Arc ....2-2 1-2 ....**Stella Abidjan**

FINAL

1st leg. Houphouet Boigny, Abidjan, 30-11-1975

STELLA ABIDJAN 0
TONNERRE YAOUNDÉ 1

2nd leg. Omnisport, Yaoundé, 14-12-1975
TONNERRE YAOUNDÉ 4
STELLA ABIDJAN 1

1976

CHAMPIONS CUP

FIRST ROUND
Al Ahly Benghazi (LBY) 3-2 1-3 **Mouloudia d'Algiers** (ALG)
Al Ahly Cairo (EGY) Bye
Al Merreikh (SDN) Bye
Luo Union (KEN) 3-1 2-0 St. Georges (ETH)
Green Buffaloes (ZAM) Bye
Corps Enseignant (MDG) 4-2 1-4 **SC Simba** (TAN)
Uganda Express FC (UGA) 1-0 0-1 4-3p Caiman Douala (CMR)
Enugu Rangers (NGA) Bye
ASEC Abidjan (CIV) Bye
Silures (VOL) W-O ASFAN Niamey (NIG)
CARA Brazzaville (COG) 4-0 0-2 CS Imana (ZAI)
Asante Kotoko (GHA) W-O Okoume (GAB)
ASC Diaraf (SEN) 6-1 4-1 Balantas Mansoa (GNB)
Lome I (TGO) Bye
Real Banjul (GMB) 0-2 0-2 **Djoliba AC** (MLI)
Hafia FC (GUI) Bye

SECOND ROUND
Mouloudia d'Algiers 3-0 0-1 Al Ahly Cairo
Luo Union W-O Al Merreikh
Green Buffaloes 3-2 1-0 SC Simba
Enugu Rangers 0-0 2-2 Uganda Express FC
ASEC Abidjan 2-0 2-0 Silures
Asante Kotoko 1-0 1-2 CARA Brazzaville
Lome I 1-1 0-1 **ASC Diaraf**
Djoliba AC 2-1 0-2 **Hafia FC**

QUARTER-FINALS
Mouloudia d'Algiers 6-3 1-0 Luo Union
Green Buffaloes 3-1 0-3 **Enugu Rangers**
Asante Kotoko 2-1 0-1 **ASEC Abidjan**
ASC Diaraf 2-2 0-4 **Hafia FC**

SEMI-FINALS
Enugu Rangers 2-0 0-3 **Mouloudia d'Algiers**
ASEC Abidjan 3-0 0-5 **Hafia FC**

FINAL
1st leg. 28th September Stadium, Conakry, 5-12-1976
HAFIA CONAKRY 3
MOULOUDIA CHALLIA ALGIERS 0

2nd leg. 5th July Stadium, Algiers, 18-12-1976
MOULOUDIA CHALLIA ALGIERS 3
HAFIA CONAKRY 0
Mouloudia d'Algiers won 4-1 on penalties

CUP WINNERS CUP

PRELIMINARY ROUND
Bata Bullets (MWI) 2-4 4-0 Fortior Mahajanga (MDG)
Liberté FC (NIG) 0-5 1-4 **Al Ahly Tripoli** (LBY)
Canon Yaoundé (CMR) 3-0 3-1 Petrosport FC (GAB)
Ports Authority (GMB) 1-4 1-2 **Kadiogo** (VOL)

FIRST ROUND
Shooting Stars (NGA) 3-0 2-0 Kenya Breweries (KEN)
Bata Bullets (MWI) 1-0 0-4 **Rokana United** (ZAM)
Mechal Army (ETH) 5-2 1-2 Youth League (TAN)
Zamalek (EGY) 3-0 1-2 Al Ahly Tripoli (LBY)
Canon Yaoundé (CMR) 2-1 0-1 **AS Vita Club** (ZAI)
US Goree (SEN) 1-0 2-6 Stella Abidjan (CIV)
Kadiogo (VOL) 1-0 0-7 **AS Kaloum Star** (GUI)
CS Lama Kara (TGO) 1-2 0-3 **Tonnerre Yaoundé** (CMR)

QUARTER-FINALS
Shooting Stars 3-2 1-1 Rokana Utd
Mechal Army 2-0 0-6 **Zamalek**
AS Vita Club 2-0 3-3 US Goree
Tonnerre Yaoundé 0-0 2-1 AS Kaloum Star

SEMI-FINALS
Zamalek 2-0 0-2 3-5p **Shooting Stars**
AS Vita Club 1-1 1-3 **Tonnerre Yaoundé**

FINAL
1st leg. Surulere, Lagos, 27-11-1976
SHOOTING STARS 4
TONNERRE YAOUNDÉ 1

2nd leg. Omnisport, Yaoundé, 12-12-1976
TONNERRE YAOUNDÉ 1
SHOOTING STARS 0

1977

CHAMPIONS CUP

FIRST ROUND
Hafia FC (GUI) Bye
Vautour Club M'gou (GAB) 2-4 2-4 **Diables Noirs** (COG)
SC Simba (TAN) W-O Highlanders (SWZ)
Water Corporation (NGA) Bye
UDIB Bissau (GNB) 0-1 0-5 **Djoliba AC** (MLI)
SC Gagnoa (CIV) W-O AS Tempete Mocaf (CTA)
Union Douala (CMR) 2-0 1-0 Silures (VOL)
TP Mazembe (ZAI) 1-1 0-3 **Lome I** (TGO)
Mufulira Wanderers (ZAM) 1-1 2-2 Maseru United (LSO)
Gor Mahia (KEN) 1-2 2-1 5-3p Yamaha Wanderers (MWI)
Kampala CC (UGA) 1-0 3-0 Mechal Army (ETH)
Mouloudia d'Algiers (ALG) Bye
FC Horsed (SOM) 1-1 0-3 **Al Ahly Cairo** (EGY)
Olympic Niamey (NIG) 2-4 2-2 **Al Medina** (LBY)
ASC Diaraf (SEN) 3-0 2-0 ASC Garde National (MTN)
St. Joseph (LBR) 1-3 1-2 **Hearts of Oak** (GHA)

SECOND ROUND
Diables Noirs 0-1 1-1 **Hafia FC**
Water Corporation 0-0 1-0 SC Simba
SC Gagnoa 1-3 1-1 **Djoliba AC**
Union Douala 1-1 1-1 3-4p **Lome I**
Gor Mahia 2-1 2-4 **Mufulira Wanderers**
Kampala CC 1-1 2-3 **Mouloudia d'Algiers**
Al Ahly Cairo 7-2 0-1 Al Medina
ASC Diaraf 1-1 1-2 **Hearts of Oak**

QUARTER-FINALS
Water Corporation 4-2 0-3 **Hafia FC**
Djoliba AC 2-0 0-1 * **Lome I**
Mouloudia d'Algiers 2-1 0-2 **Mufulira Wanderers**
Al Ahly Cairo 1-0 0-3 **Hearts of Oak**
* Djoliba suspended, Lome I qualified

SEMI-FINALS
Lome I 2-1 0-2 **Hafia FC**
Mufulira Wanderers 5-2 0-3 **Hearts of Oak**

FINAL
1st leg. Accra Stadium, Accra, 4-12-1977

HEARTS OF OAK 0
HAFIA CONAKRY 1

2nd leg. 28th September Stadium, Conakry, 18-12-1977
HAFIA CONAKRY 3
HEARTS OF OAK 2

CUP WINNERS CUP

FIRST ROUND

Enugu Rangers (NGA) ....0-0 1-1 ....Al Ahly Tripoli (LBY)
Electric Sports (ETH) ....Bye
CS Lama Kara (TGO)..............1-0 1-3 ....**Anges ABC** (GAB)
ASF Police (SEN)........................Bye
Stade Abidjan (CIV) ....Bye
Wallidan (GMB)........................1-1 0-0...........**Espoirs Nouakchott** (MTN)
Bata Bullets (MWI)...............4-1 1-2.........Gangama United (UGA)
Shooting Stars (NGA) ....Bye
Al Ittihad (EGY)........................Bye
Luo Union (KEN)........................1-0 * ....**MP Constantine** (ALG)
Ndola United (ZAM) ....Bye
Matlama FC (LSO)....................2-5 2-6 ....**Rangers Intern'al** (TAN)
Liberté FC (NIG) ....1-1 1-6...................**Kadiogo** (VOL)
AS Kaloum Star (GUI)...........Bye
Cedar United (LBR) ....1-1 0-1 ....**Sporting Clube** (GNB)
Canon Yaoundé (CMR).........W-O ....Red Star Bangui (CTA)

* Luo Union withdrew before the second game. MP Constantine qualified

SECOND ROUND

Enugu Rangers......................4-0 2-0 ....Electric Sports
ASF Police ....8-1 0-0 ....Anges ABC
Stade Abidjan ....3-0 1-3 ....Espoirs Nouakchott
Shooting Stars........................4-1 0-1 ....Bata Bullets
MP Constantine.........................1-0 1-3.................................**Al Ittihad**
Ndola United ....1-2 1-1 ....**Rangers International**
Kadiogo ....2-1 1-1 ....AS Kaloum Star
Sporting Clube Bissau..............0-4 1-7 ....**Canon Yaoundé**

QUARTER-FINALS

Enugu Rangers........................0-0 2-1 ....ASF Police
Stade Abidjan ....2-0 0-3 ....**Shooting Stars**
Al Ittihad ....2-0 0-0 ....Rangers International
Kadiogo ....2-1 1-4 ....**Canon Yaoundé**

SEMI-FINALS

Shooting Stars.........................0-0 0-0 2-4p...............**Enugu Rangers**
Al Ittihad ....1-0 0-2 ....**Canon Yaoundé**

FINAL

1st leg. Surulere, Lagos, 26-11-1977
ENUGU RANGERS 4
CANON YAOUNDÉ 1

2nd leg. Omnisports, Yaoundé, 14-12-1977
CANON YAOUNDÉ 1
ENUGU RANGERS 1

1978

CHAMPIONS CUP

FIRST ROUND

Canon Yaoundé (CMR) ....Bye
Hardware Stars (MWI)............1-1 0-4 ....**Al Merreikh** (SDN)
Corps Enseignant (MDG)...........1-2 ....**Matlama FC** (LSO)
Green Buffaloes (ZAM)..........Bye
Kampala CC (UGA) ....1-1 2-0....................FC Horsed (SOM)
Al Ahly Cairo (EGY)................Bye
SCAF Tocages (CTA)...............1-3 1-1......**Olympic Niamey** (NIG)
Enugu Rangers (NGA)............Bye
AS Vita Club (ZAI) ....Bye
SC Simba (TAN) ....2-0 0-1 ......Vautour Club M'gou GAB
Al Tahadi (LBY) ....3-1 2-3..................Medr Babur (ETH)
JE Tizi-Ouzou (ALG) ....Bye
Silures (VOL) ....7-0 3-2 ....Benfica (GNB)
Africa Sports (CIV) ....Bye
ASC Garde National (MTN)3-1 2-2 ....Wallidan (GMB)
Hafia FC (GUI) ....Bye

SECOND ROUND

Canon Yaoundé....................2-0 1-2 ....Al Merreikh
Green Buffaloes ....1-0 0-0 ....Matlama FC
Kampala CC ....W-O ....Al Ahly Cairo
Enugu Rangers..........................W-O ....Olympic Niamey
AS Vita Club.............................1-0 1-0 ....SC Simba
JE Tizi-Ouzou...........................1-0 2-0 ....Al Tahadi
Africa Sports ....2-1 1-3 ....**Silures**
Hafia FC.....................................5-0 1-0...............ASC Garde National

QUARTER-FINALS

Canon Yaoundé......................2-0 1-1 ....Green Buffaloes
Enugu Rangers........................3-1 1-0 ....Kampala CC
JE Tizi-Ouzou..............................3-2 0-1 ....**AS Vita Club**
Silures ....0-4 1-4.....................................**Hafia FC**

SEMI-FINALS

Canon Yaoundé...............0-0 0-0 6-5p ....Enugu Rangers
Hafia FC.....................................2-0 1-3 ....AS Vita Club

FINAL

1st leg. 28th September Stadium, Conakry, 3-12-1978, 35,000
HAFIA CONAKRY 0
CANON YAOUNDÉ 0

2nd leg. Omnisport, Yaoundé, 17-12-1978, 80,000
CANON YAOUNDÉ 2
HAFIA CONAKRY 0

CUP WINNERS CUP

PRELIMINARY ROUND

Zumunta AC (NIG)..................0-3 0-5 ....**Horoya AC** (GUI)
Lavori Publici (SOM) ....0-1 0-1 ....**Al Hilal** (SDN)
UDIB Bissau (GNB)...................3-1 0-2...........**Espoirs Nouakchott** (MTN)
Sucoma Chikwawa (MWI).......1-1 0-1 **Fortior Mahajanga** (MDG)
Simba FC (UGA)...............1-1 1-1 5-4p ....St. Georges (ETH)
Al Medina (LBY).......................W-O ....Sodiam Bangui (CTA)

FIRST ROUND

Shooting Stars (NGA)..............3-1 0-3 ....**Horoya AC** (GUI)
Caiman Douala (CMR) ....2-0 1-3.........FC 105 Libreville (GAB)
Zamalek (EGY) ....1-1 2-1 ....Al Hilal (SDN)
Kadiogo (VOL) ....2-0 0-0 ..Espoirs Nouakchott (MTN)
Mufulira Wanderers (ZAM)3-1 1-1 ....Fortior Mahajanga (MDG)
KMKM Zanzibar (TAN) ....2-0 1-1 ....Simba FC (UGA)
Inter Club (COG)..................0-0 4-1 ....SC Alliance (CIV)
MA Hussein-Dey (ALG).......2-1 1-1 ....Al Medina (LBY)

QUARTER-FINALS

Horoya AC...............................4-1 3-3 ....Caiman Douala
Zamalek...2-1 0-1 ....**Kadiogo**
Mufulira Wanderers..............W-O.........................KMKM Zanzibar
MA Hussein-Dey......................3-0 2-1 ....Inter Club

SEMI-FINALS

Kadiogo ....3-2 0-1 ....**Horoya AC**

Mufulira Wanderers ....2-1 0-1 ....**MA Hussein-Dey**

FINAL

1st leg. 5th July Stadium, Algiers, 24-11-1978

MILAHA ATHLETIC HUSSEIN-DEY 1
HOROYA ATHLETIC CLUB CONAKRY 3

2nd leg. 28th September Stadium, Conakry, 10-12-1978

HOROYA ATHLETIC CLUB CONAKRY 2
MILAHA ATHLETIC HUSSEIN-DEY 1

1979

CHAMPIONS CUP

FIRST ROUND

Union Douala (CMR) ....Bye
Al Ahly Tripoli (LBY)..........1-2 0-2**Mouloudia d'Algiers** (ALG)
Kenya Breweries (KEN) ....* ....Al Merreikh (SDN)
Desportivo Maputo (MOZ) ....3-2 0-1..........**Matlama FC** (LSO)
Zamalek (EGY)..........2-1 ....Simba FC (UGA)
Ogaden Anbassa (ETH) ....W-O ....Bata Bullets (MWI)
Dragons de l'Ouème (BEN)....0-2 1-3 ....**Africa Sports** (CIV)
CS Imana (ZAI) ....Bye
US Goree (SEN)..........2-0 1-1..ASC Garde National (MTN)
Etoile du Congo (COG) ......2-0 1-1..........FC 105 Libreville (GAB)
SC Simba (TAN) ....0-4 5-0 ..Mufulira Wanderers (ZAM)
Raccah Rovers (NGA)..........Bye
Hafia FC (GUI)..........Bye
ASDR Fatima (CTA)..........1-1 1-1 4-5p ....**Silures** (VOL)
St. Joseph (LBR)..........0-0 0-1 ....**Real Banjul** (GMB)
Mighty Blackpool (SLE)........2-0 0-2 2-4p ...**Hearts of Oak** (GHA)
* Both clubs withdrew

SECOND ROUND

Mouloudia d'Algiers..........2-0 0-2 1-2p..........**Union Douala**
Matlama FC ....Bye
Zamalek..........W-O..........Ogaden Anbassa
Africa Sports..........1-0 0-2 ....**CS Imana**
Etoile du Congo ....2-3 0-1 ....**US Goree**
SC Simba..........0-0 0-2..........**Raccah Rovers**
Hafia FC..........1-0 0-1 1-0p..........Silures
Hearts of Oak..........2-0 1-1..........Real Banjul

QUARTER-FINALS

Matlama FC ....1-3 0-2 ....**Union Douala**
Zamalek..........3-1 0-1 *..........**CS Imana**
US Goree ....2-0 0-1 ....Raccah Rovers
Hafia FC ....2-0 0-3..........**Hearts of Oak**
* 2nd match abandoned. CS Imana qualified

SEMI-FINALS

CS Imana..........1-2 0-1 ....**Union Douala**
US Goree..........1-2 1-4..........**Hearts of Oak**

FINAL

1st leg. Accra Stadium, Accra, 2-12-1979

HEARTS OF OAK 1
UNION DOUALA 0

2nd leg. Omnisports, Yaoundé, 16-12-1979

UNION DOUALA 1
HEARTS OF OAK 0
Union Douala won 5-3 on penalties

CUP WINNERS CUP

FIRST ROUND

Sportive Mongomo (EQG)......1-3 1-5 ....Canon Yaoundé (CMR)
Espoirs Nouakchott (MTN)1-0 0-1 4-5p ....**Wallidan** (GMB)
Pan African (TAN) ....0-1 1-0 5-4p..........Omedla (ETH)
AS Vita Club (ZAI)..........Bye
Maxaquene Maputo (MOZ) ....0-3 0-1 ....**AC Sotema** (MDG)
Maseru United (LSO) ....2-1 4-5..........FC Notwane (BWA)
SC Gagnoa (CIV)..........3-1 1-0 ....Cedar United (LBR)
Bendel Insurance (NGA) ....1-0 5-1 ....Petrosport FC (GAB)
Horoya AC (GUI)..........Bye
UDIB Bissau (GNB)..........1-1 1-2 **Bai-Bureh Warriors** (SLE)
Al Nasr (LBY)..........W-O ....USCA Bangui (CTA)
CM Belcourt (ALG) ....Bye
Kadiogo (VOL) ....0-1 1-0 4-2p........Asante Kotoko (GHA)
Requins de l'At'q (BEN)..........Bye
Nsambya FC (UGA)..........W-O ....Al Nil Khartum (SDN)
Gor Mahia (KEN)..........W-O ....Al Ittihad (EGY)

SECOND ROUND

Wallidan..........1-2 0-1 ....**Canon Yaoundé**
Pan African ....2-1 0-1 ....**AS Vita Club**
Maseru United ....0-1 1-4..........**AC Sotema**
Bendel Insurance..........1-0 1-0..........SC Gagnoa
Bai-Bureh Warriors ....0-1 0-3 ....**Horoya AC**
CM Belcourt..........4-2 1-0..........Al Nasr
Kadiogo ....3-1 1-1..........Requins de l'Atlantique
Gor Mahia..........0-0 1-1 ....Nsambya FC

QUARTER-FINALS

AS Vita Club..........3-1 1-6 ....**Canon Yaoundé**
AC Sotema ....0-2 2-0 3-5p ....**Bendel Insurance**
CM Belcourt ....0-3 1-3 ....**Horoya AC**
Kadiogo ....1-2 1-2..........**Gor Mahia**

SEMI-FINALS

Canon Yaoundé..........1-0 0-0 ....Bendel Insurance
Gor Mahia..........1-0 2-0 ....Horoya AC

FINAL

1st leg. Nyayo, Nairobi, 25-11-1979

GOR MAHIA 0
CANON YAOUNDÉ 2

2nd leg. Omnisport, Yaoundé, 9-12-1979

CANON YAOUNDÉ 6
GOR MAHIA 0

1980

CHAMPIONS CUP

FIRST ROUND

Canon Yaoundé (CMR) ....3-0 4-3....Primeiro de Agosto (ANG)
Wallidan (GMB)..........1-1 0-1 ....**Silures** (VOL)
Benfica (GNB)..........0-4 2-3 ....**Stella Abidjan** (CIV)
Dragons de l'Ouème (BEN)....0-0 0-3**Mouloudia d'Algiers** (ALG)
Olympique Real (CTA) ....0-1 1-3 ....**Etoile du Congo** (COG)
ASC Garde National (MTN)...1-1 0-2 ....**Hafia FC** (GUI)
FC Horsed (SOM) ....0-0 0-2 ....**Gor Mahia** (KEN)
Bendel Insurance (NGA) ......W-O ....Commercial Bank (UGA)
Union Douala (CMR) ....Bye
Linare FC (LSO)..........2-1 0-3 ....**SC Simba** (TAN)
Ela Nguema (EQG)..........1-0 0-4......**Semassi Sokodé** (TGO)
Mighty Blackpool (SLE) ....1-2 0-2 ....**ASF Police** (SEN)
AS Niamey (NIG) ....0-1 0-2..........**Djoliba AC** (MLI)
Anges ABC (GAB)..........2-3 2-2..........**Hearts of Oak** (GHA)
Fortior Mahajanga (MDG) ...W-O ....Limbe Leaf Wand. (MWI)
Costa do Sol (MOZ)..........0-0 1-3..........**AS Bilima** (ZAI)

SECOND ROUND

Silures ....0-1 0-3 ....**Canon Yaoundé**
Stella Abidjan ....4-2 1-3..........**Mouloudia d'Algiers**
Etoile du Congo ....0-1 1-0 3-1p ....Hafia FC

Bendel Insurance 1-2 3-2 Gor Mahia
SC Simba 2-4 0-1 **Union Douala**
Semassi Sokodé 1-1 0-1 **ASF Police**
Djoliba AC 1-1 0-1 **Hearts of Oak**
AS Bilima 3-0 1-1 Fortior Mahajanga

QUARTER-FINALS

Canon Yaoundé 2-0 1-3 Mouloudia d'Algiers
Etoile du Congo 3-2 0-1 **Bendel Insurance**
ASF Police 0-3 3-2 **Union Douala**
Hearts of Oak 1-3 0-1 **AS Bilima**

SEMI-FINALS

Canon Yaoundé 0-0 4-2 Bendel Insurance
Union Douala 1-0 1-5 **AS Bilima**

FINAL

1st leg. Militare Garoua, Yaoundé, 30-11-1980
CANON YAOUNDÉ 2
AS BILIMA 2

2nd leg. 20th May Stadium, Kinshasa, 14-12-1980
AS BILIMA 0
CANON YAOUNDÉ 3

CUP WINNERS CUP

FIRST ROUND

Township Rollers (BWA) 2-2 1-4 **TP Mazembe** (ZAI)
Kampala CC (UGA) 3-1 2-1 Marine Club (SOM)
Pan African (TAN) 4-3 1-1 AC Sotema (MDG)
Shooting Stars (NGA) Bye
Ramogi Mombassa (KEN) Bye
Matlama FC (LSO) 2-0 3-2 Palmeiras Beira (MOZ)
Esperance Tunis (TUN) W-O Ader Club (NIG)
Kadiogo (VOL) 4-1 1-4 4-2p Wulum Stars (SLE)
MA Hussein-Dey (ALG) 7-0 0-1 ASC Ksar (MTN)
Casa Sports (SEN) 5-1 1-0 Bula FC (GNB)
Dynamo Douala (CMR) Bye
Eleven Wise FC (GHA) 3-0 1-0 Sodiam Bangui (CTA)
Buffles de Borgou (BEN) 1-2 3-5 **Agaza Lomé** (TGO)
Horoya AC (GUI) Bye
Atletico Malabo (EQG) 2-2 1-3 **US Mbila-Nzambi** (GAB)
Africa Sports (CIV) W-O Dingareh (GMB)

SECOND ROUND

TP Mazembe 1-0 2-2 Kampala CC
Pan African 0-1 1-1 **Shooting Stars**
Matlama FC 1-1 0-0 **Ramogi Mombassa**
Kadiogo W-O Esperance Tunis
Casa Sports 1-1 0-2 **MA Hussein-Dey**
Eleven Wise FC 2-1 1-1 Dynamo Douala
Agaza Lomé 0-0 0-0 2-1p Horoya AC
Africa Sports 3-2 1-1 * US Mbila-Nzambi
* 2nd match abandoned. Africa Sports qualified

QUARTER-FINALS

TP Mazembe 2-1 1-2 3-0p Shooting Stars
Ramogi Mombassa 0-3 0-1 **Kadiogo**
Eleven Wise FC 1-1 1-4 **MA Hussein-Day**
Agaza Lomé 1-1 0-1 **Africa Sports**

SEMI-FINALS

TP Mazembe 2-0 1-1 Kadiogo
Africa Sports 1-0 2-2 MA Hussein-Dey

FINAL

1st leg. Houphouet Boigny, Abidjan, 25-11-1980
AFRICA SPORTS 1
TOUT PUISSANT MAZEMBE 3

2nd leg. 20th May Stadium, Kinshasa, 7-12-1980
TOUT PUISSANT MAZEMBE 1
AFRICA SPORTS 0

1981

CHAMPIONS CUP

FIRST ROUND

Al Ahly Tripoli (LBY) 0-0 1-2 **JE Tizi-Ouzou** (ALG)
FC Horsed (SOM) W-O SC Simba (TAN)
Shooting Stars (NGA) 7-1 0-2 Township Rollers (BWA)
Dynamos Harare (ZIM) 5-0 1-1 Linare FC (LSO)
Agaza Lomé (TGO) W-O Benfica (GNB)
US Mbila-Nzambi (GAB) 1-0 0-1 4-2p AS Real Bamako (MLI)
Nile Breweries FC (UGA) 2-1 USCA Bangui (CTA)
Al Ahly Cairo (EGY) 3-1 1-1 Abaluhya FC (KEN)
AS Kaloum Star (GUI) 2-1 1-0 Starlight (GMB)
Asante Kotoko (GHA) 3-0 1-1 Invincible Eleven (LBR)
Canon Yaoundé (CMR) Bye
SEIB Diourbel (SEN) 2-1 1-2 3-4p **ASEC Abidjan** (CIV)
Nchanga Rangers (ZAM) 1-0 4-0 Highlanders (SWZ)
MMM Tamatave (MDG) 2-4 0-2 **Costa do Sol** (MOZ)
East End Lions (SLE) 1-1 0-1 **Silures** (VOL)
Primeiro de Agosto (ANG) 1-1 1-2 **AS Vita Club** (ZAI)

SECOND ROUND

FC Horsed 1-2 **JE Tizi-Ouzou**
Shooting Stars 1-2 0-3 **Dynamos Harare**
US Mbila-Nzambi 2-0 0-1 Agaza Lomé
Nile Breweries FC 2-0 0-5 **Al Ahly Cairo**
Asante Kotoko 1-0 1-3 **AS Kaloum Star**
Canon Yaoundé 0-0 1-3 **ASEC Abidjan**
Costa do Sol 1-3 1-3 **Nchanga Rangers**
Silures 0-1 3-3 **AS Vita Club**

QUARTER-FINALS

JE Tizi-Ouzou 3-0 2-2 Dynamos Harare
US Mbila-Nzambi 1-1 0-3 **Al Ahly Cairo**
AS Kaloum Star 2-1 2-1 ASEC Abidjan
AS Vita Club 4-1 0-2 Nchanga Rangers

SEMI-FINALS

JE Tizi-Ouzou W-O Al Ahly Cairo
AS Vita Club 1-0 0-0 AS Kaloum Star

FINAL

1st leg. Omnisport, Tizi-Ouzou, 27-11-1981
JEUNESSE ELECTRONIQUE TIZI-OUZOU 4
AS VITA CLUB KINSHASA 0

2nd leg. 20th May Stadium, Kinshasa, 13-12-1981
AS VITA CLUB KINSHASA 0
JEUNESSE ELECTRONIQUE TIZI-OUZOU 1

CUP WINNERS CUP

FIRST ROUND

Nacional Benguela (ANG) 1-7 0-6 **Union Douala** (CMR)
Lubumbashi Sport (ZAI) 4-3 0-1 **FC 105 Libreville** (GAB)
Zindourma (NIG) * Esperance Tunis (TUN)
Kampala CC (UGA) 1-0 0-2 **Entente Setif** (ALG)
Palmeiras Beira (MOZ) W-O Highlanders (SWZ)
Matlama FC (LSO) 1-1 0-2 **Power Dynamos** (ZAM)
TP Mazembe (ZAI) 5-0 2-0 ASDR Fatima (CTA)
Sekondi Hasaacas (GHA) W-O CS Nere (EQG)
Reveil Daloa (CIV) 2-1 0-1 **Djoliba AC** (MLI)
Kadiogo (VOL) 3-2 1-2 **Semassi Sokodé** (TGO)
Gor Mahia (KEN) W-O Coastal Union (TAN)

Lavori Publici (SOM) W-O Zamalek (EGY)
Real Republicans (SLE) 2-0 1-2 ASC Jeanne d'Arc (SEN)
Gbessia AC (GUI) W-O Estrela Negra (GNB)
CAPS United (ZIM) 8-1 AS St. Michael (MDG)
Stationery Stores (NGA) 1-0 0-1 5-4p Al Ahly Benghazi (LBY)
* Both clubs withdrew

SECOND ROUND

FC 105 Libreville 1-3 0-1 **Union Douala**
Entente Setif Bye
Palmeiras Beira 1-1 0-5 **Power Dynamos**
Sekondi Hasaacas 2-1 1-0 TP Mazembe
Djoliba AC 3-0 1-0 Semassi Sokodé
Gor Mahia 3-0 0-1 Lavori Publici
Real Republicans 1-2 0-2 **Gbessia AC**
CAPS United 1-0 0-1 1-3p **Stationery Stores**

QUARTER-FINALS

Union Douala 5-0 1-1 Entente Setif
Power Dynamos 1-0 1-3 **Sekondi Hasaacas**
Djoliba AC 2-0 0-1 Gor Mahia
Gbessia AC 0-1 1-3 **Stationery Stores**

SEMI-FINALS

Union Douala 2-1 2-3 Sekondi Hasaacas
Stationery Stores 0-0 1-0 Djoliba AC

FINAL

1st leg. Omnisport Yaoundé, 22-11-1981
UNION DOUALA 0
STATIONERY STORES 0

2nd leg. Surulere, Lagos, 5-12-1981
STATIONERY STORES 1
UNION DOUALA 2

1982

CHAMPIONS CUP

PRELIMINARY ROUND

AS Police (MTN) 0-2 1-1 **Adjidjas FAP** (BEN)
Atletico Malabo (EQG) 0-1 1-3 **Sporting Moura** (CTA)
Mhlume Peacemakers (SWZ) 1-0 2-2 Maseru Brothers (LSO)
Vital'O (BDI) 3-1 0-1 Rayon Sports (RWA)

FIRST ROUND

Lavori Publici (SOM) 0-0 0-1 **Al Ahly Cairo** (EGY)
Textile Pungue (MOZ) 1-2 0-2 **Young Africans** (TAN)
Green Buffaloes (ZAM) 0-0 2-0 Vital'O (BDI)
AS Somasud (MDG) 4-0 0-2 Mhlume Peacemakers (SWZ)
Adjidjas FAP (BEN) 1-3 1-3 **Stella Abidjan** (CIV)
RS Kouba (ALG) 1-1 3-1 KAC Kenitra (MOR)
AS Kaloum Star (GUI) 3-0 0-1 Real Republicans (SLE)
Primeiro de Agosto (ANG) 1-1 0-3 **Enugu Rangers** (NGA)
FC Lupopo (ZAI) 4-2 3-0 Sporting Moura (CTA)
Dynamos Harare (ZIM) 2-2 2-1 Defence Force (BWA)
US Mbila-Nzambi (GAB) W-O US Goree (SEN)
Etoile du Congo (COG) 1-1 0-1 **AS Real Bamako** (MLI)
Al Hilal (SDN) 1-0 0-1 4-1p JE Tizi-Ouzou (ALG)
Kampala CC (UGA) 3-0 1-4 AFC Leopards (KEN)
Invincible Eleven (LBR) 1-0 1-1 Tonnerre Yaoundé (CMR)
Semassi Sokodé (TGO) 3-2 0-2 **Asante Kotoko** (GHA)

SECOND ROUND

Al Ahly Cairo 5-0 1-1 Young Africans
Green Buffaloes 3-0 3-1 AS Somasud
Stella Abidjan 1-0 0-1 3-4p **RS Kouba**
Enugu Rangers 0-0 1-0 AS Kaloum Star
FC Lupopo 0-0 1-1 Dynamos Harare
US Mbila-Nzambi 1-0 0-2 **AS Real Bamako**
Al Hilal 0-2 1-3 **Kampala CC**
Invincible Eleven 0-0 0-3 **Asante Kotoko**

QUARTER-FINALS

Al Ahly Cairo 3-1 0-1 Green Buffaloes
Enugu Rangers 5-0 2-1 RS Kouba
FC Lupopo 2-0 2-3 AS Real Bamako
Asante Kotoko 6-0 1-1 Kampala CC

SEMI-FINALS

Enugu Rangers 1-0 0-4 **Al Ahly Cairo**
FC Lupopo 1-2 0-2 **Asante Kotoko**

FINAL

1st leg. International Stadium, Cairo, 28-11-1982
AL AHLY CAIRO 3
ASANTE KOTOKO 0

2nd leg. Kumasi Stadium, Kumasi, 12-12-1982
ASANTE KOTOKO 1
AL AHLY CAIRO 1

CUP WINNERS CUP

PRELIMINARY ROUND

Zindourma (NIG) 3-0 0-4 **ASC Garde National** (MTN)

FIRST ROUND

Hay el Arab (SDN) 1-1 1-3 **Al Mokaouloum** (EGY)
Desportivo Maputo (MOZ) W-O Printing Agency (SOM)
ASC Garde National (MTN) 0-1 0-2 **Dynamo Douala** (CMR)
Kamboi Eagles (SLE) 0-4 0-6 **Africa Sports** (CIV)
CARA Brazzaville (COG) 1-0 0-2 **USK Algiers** (ALG)
Bendel Insurance (NGA) 2-0 1-0 Agaza Lomé (TGO)
Mighty Barolle (LBR) 0-0 0-1 **ASF Police** (SEN)
Wallidan (GMB) 1-0 1-4 **Hearts of Oak** (GHA)
Requins de l'Atl'q (BEN) 0-1 0-0 **Djoliba AC** (MLI)
Ela Nguema (EQG) 0-2 1-6 **Union Douala** (CMR)
FC 105 Libreville (GAB) 1-1 2-2 Gbessia AC (GUI)
TAAG Luanda (AGO) 0-0 0-0 4-5p **AS Vita Club** (ZAI)
Maseru Rovers (LSO) 0-1 0-1 **CAPS United** (ZIM)
Gor Mahia (KEN) 2-3 **Dynamo Fima** (MDG)
Mukura VS (RWA) 0-4 0-4 **Pan African** (TAN)
Coffee FC (UGA) 0-0 0-2 **Power Dynamos** (ZAM)

SECOND ROUND

Al Mokaouloum 3-2 2-0 Desportivo Maputo
Dynamo Douala 1-2 0-1 **Africa Sports**
Bendel Insurance 3-1 0-2 **USK Algiers**
ASF Police 1-0 0-1 3-4p **Hearts of Oak**
Union Douala 0-1 0-3 **Djoliba AC**
AS Vita Club 4-0 0-0 FC 105 Libreville
CAPS United 1-1 3-2 Dynamo Fima
Pan African 1-0 0-1 3-5p **Power Dynamos**

QUARTER-FINALS

Africa Sports 2-0 0-3 **Al Mokaouloum**
USK Algiers 2-1 0-2 **Hearts of Oak**
AS Vita Club 0-0 0-1 **Djoliba AC**
CAPS United 1-2 0-3 **Power Dynamos**

SEMI-FINALS

Al Mokaouloum 1-1 2-1 Hearts of Oak
Power Dynamos 2-1 0-0 Djoliba AC

FINAL

1st leg. Independence Stadium, Lusaka, 21-11-1982
POWER DYNAMOS 0
AL MOKAOULOUM 2

2nd leg. International Stadium, Cairo, 3-12-1982
AL MOKAOULOUM 2
POWER DYNAMOS 0

1983

CHAMPIONS CUP

PRELIMINARY ROUND
AS Police (MTN)........................1-3 0-1 ....Sierra Fisheries (SLE)
ASC Diaraf (SEN)...................4-0 2-0 ....Ports Authority (GMB)
Fantastique (BDI).......................2-1 0-1 ......**Olympique Real** (CTA)
Highlanders (SWZ)................2-1 1-0........Township Rollers (BWA)

FIRST ROUND
FC 105 Libreville (GAB)...........1-2 0-2 ....**Asante Kotoko** (GHA)
CARA Brazzaville (COG) ..6-1 2-0.................Dragons FC (EQG)
AS Bilima (ZAI).......................5-1 3-4 ....Semassi Sokodé (TGO)
Enugu Rangers (NGA) ....0-1 0-1 ....**Sierra Fisheries** (SLE)
KAC Kenitra (MOR)...............W-O ....Benfica (GNB)
Djoliba AC (MLI).......................0-0 0-1 ....**Hafia FC** (GUI)
Al Ahly Tripoli (LBY).................0-1 0-2..........**JE Tizi-Ouzou** (ALG)
Africa Sports (CIV).............0-0 0-0 0-3p ....**ASC Diaraf** (SEN)
Nkana Red Devils (ZAM)....2-2 1-0.................Highlanders (SWZ)
Wagad Mogadishu (SOM) ....1-2 0-0...............**Pan African** (TAN)
Matlama FC (LSO).....................1-2 1-3**Ferrovario Maputo** (MOZ)
Nakivubu Villa (UGA) ....4-2 1-1 ....Dynamo Fima (MDG)
Petro Atletico (AGO)...........3-1 3-2...........Olympique Real (CTA)
Canon Yaoundé (CMR)........2-0 0-1 ..Dragons de l'Ouème (BEN)
Dynamos Harare (ZIM).......5-1 0-3 ....AFC Leopards (KEN)
Al Ahly Cairo (EGY)..............1-0 0-0 ....Al Merreikh (SDN)

SECOND ROUND
CARA Brazzaville.......................3-2 0-2 ....**Asante Kotoko**
AS Bilima ....1-0 1-1 ....Sierra Fisheries
KAC Kenitra ....4-0 0-0 ....Hafia FC
JE Tizi-Ouzou ....0-1 0-0....................................**ASC Diaraf**
Nkana Red Devils............0-0 0-0 4-2p ....Pan African
Ferrovario Maputo.......................1-2 0-3 ....**Nakivubu Villa**
Petro Atletico ....0-0 3-4 ....**Canon Yaoundé**
Al Ahly Cairo ....4-1 2-1 ....Dynamos Harare

QUARTER-FINALS
Asante Kotoko.........................3-0 0-2 ....AS Bilima
KAC Kenitra...................................1-1 1-2...................................**ASC Diaraf**
Nkana Red Devils....................4-0 1-2.............................Nakivubu Villa
Al Ahly Cairo ....5-0 0-1 ....Canon Yaoundé

SEMI-FINALS
ASC Diaraf.......................................2-1 0-2 ....**Asante Kotoko**
Nkana Red Devils ....0-0 0-2 ....**Al Ahly Cairo**

FINAL
1st leg. International Stadium, Cairo, 27-11-1983
AL AHLY CAIRO 0
ASANTE KOTOKO 0

2nd leg. Kumasi Stadium, Kumasi, 11-12-1983
ASANTE KOTOKO 1
AL AHLY CAIRO 0

CUP WINNERS CUP

PRELIMINARY ROUND
Maseru Rovers (LSO)...........2-1 1-1 ....Young Aces (SWZ)
Vital'O (BDI)............................1-2 3-0 ....Gor Mahia (KEN)

FIRST ROUND
Vital'O (BDI) ....0-0 1-6 ......**Al Mokaouloum** (EGY)
Kampala CC (UGA) ....2-0 0-1 ....FC Horsed (SOM)
UBAC Bangui (CTA)..................0-0 0-2 ....**Al Ahly Wa Medani** ....(SDN)
KMKM Zanzibar (TAN)..............2-3 0-4.............**CAPS United** (ZIM)
Green Buffaloes (ZAM) ....5-1 1-1 ..Maxaquene Maputo (MOZ)
Maseru Rovers (LSO) ....3-2 0-2 ....**AC Sotema** (MDG)
ASF Police (SEN) ....1-0 0-0 ....Raja Casablanca (MOR)
Bai-Bureh Warriors (SLE).........0-1 2-3 ....**Horoya AC** (GUI)
ASEC Abidjan (CIV) ....4-1 1-2 ....Buffles du Borgou (BEN)
CAP Owendo (GAB)...................0-1 0-0 ..**Stationery Stores** (NGA)
Trarza Rosso (MTN)..................0-0 1-8.............**DNC Algiers** (ALG)
Stade Malien (MLI) ....W-O ....Ajuda Sports (GNB)
Ela Nguema (EQG).....................0-1 0-4 ....**AS Vita Club** (ZAI)
Primeiro de Maio (AGO).........3-2 0-2 ....**AS Cheminots** (COG)
Al Nasr (LBY) ....1-1 0-4 ..**Sekondi Hasaacas** (GHA)
Dragons Yaoundé (CMR).........0-3 1-4 ....**Agaza Lomé** (TGO)

SECOND ROUND
Al Mokaouloum ....2-2 2-2 3-1p..........................Kampala CC
Al Ahly Wad Medani ....0-2 0-5.......................**CAPS United**
Green Buffaloes ....2-0 0-0 ....AC Sotema
Horoya AC...............................2-1 1-0 ....ASF Police
ASEC Abidjan ....W-O ....Stationery Stores
DNC Algiers.............................2-0 1-2 ....Stade Malien
AS Cheminots...............................1-2 0-2 ....**AS Vita Club**
Sekondi Hasaacas ....0-0 1-4 ....**Agaza Lomé**

QUARTER-FINALS
CAPS United...................................2-1 0-2 ....**Al Mokaouloum**
Green Buffaloes.............................1-0 0-2 ....**Horoya AC**
DNC Algiers ....1-2 0-1 ....**ASEC Abidjan**
Agaza Lomé...........................2-0 0-2 4-2p...............................AS Vita Club

SEMI-FINALS
Horoya AC ....0-1 0-3 ....**Al Mokaouloum**
ASEC Abidjan.................................2-2 0-0 ....**Agaza Lomé**

FINAL
1st leg. Eyadema, Lome, 20-11-1983
AGAZA LOMÉ 0
AL MOKAOULOUM 1

2nd leg. International Stadium, Cairo, 2-12-1983
AL MOKAOULOUM 0
AGAZA LOMÉ 0

1984

CHAMPIONS CUP

PRELIMINARY ROUND
Township Rollers (BWA) ....0-2 1-1 ....**LPF Maseru** (LSO)
Desportivo Maputo (MOZ)1-1 1-0....Manzini Wanderers (SWZ)
Real Banjul (GMB) ....0-0 0-2.........**Sporting Clube** (GNB)
Real Republicans (SLE).........1-0 0-0 ....Invincible Eleven (LBR)
Atletico Malabo (EQG) ....2-0 1-6 ..**Primeiro de Maio** (AGO)
Kiyovu Sports (RWA).............W-O ....ADMARC Tigers (MWI)
US Ouagadougou (VOL) ....0-2 1-3.........**Dragons de l'Ouème** ....(BEN)

FIRST ROUND
Zamalek (EGY) ....3-0 1-1 ....CS Sfax (TUN)
Young Africans (TAN)..................1-1 0-1 ....**Gor Mahia** (KEN)
Al Hilal (SDN) ....1-1 0-1 ......**Printing Agency** (SOM)
Nkana Red Devils (ZAM).....5-0 1-0 ....LPF Maseru (LSO)
Kampala CC (UGA) ....6-1 3-2 ..Desportivo Maputo (MOZ)
HTMF Mahajanga (MDG) ....0-3.........**Dynamos Harare** (ZIM)
Sporting Clube (GNB) ....W-O...........................Hafia FC (GUI)
JE Tizi-Ouzou (ALG)..............1-0 2-1 ....Real Republicans (SLE)

Africa Sports (CIV)....2-1 2-4....**Semassi Sokodé** (TGO)
Asante Kotoko (GHA)....1-1 1-2..**Primeiro de Maio** (AGO)
Sanga Balende (ZAI)....2-1 4-1....Kiyovu Sports (RWA)
FC 105 Libreville (GAB)....3-1 5-1....ASDR Fatima (CTA)
Al Medina (LBY)....0-0 1-2....**MAS Fès** (MOR)
AS Real Bamako (MLI)....2-2 0-2....**Dragons de l'Ouème** (BEN)
Vital'O (BDI)....1-0 0-3 **Tonnerre Yaoundé** (CMR)
Shooting Stars (NGA)....2-0 0-1....SEIB Diourbel (SEN)

SECOND ROUND
Zamalek....1-0 *....Gor Mahia
Printing Agency....2-1 0-3....**Nkana Red Devils**
Kampala CC....0-0 1-2....**Dynamos Harare**
JE Tizi-Ouzou....W-O....Sporting Clube Bissau
Primeiro de Maio....2-0 0-2 3-4p....**Semassi Sokodé**
Sanga Balende....2-0 0-2 **....**FC 105 Libreville**
MAS Fès....3-0 0-1....Dragons de l'Ouème
Shooting Stars....4-0 0-4 5-4p....Tonnerre Yaoundé
* Match abandoned after 38 minutes. Tie awarded to Zamalek
** 2nd match abandoned after 55 minutes. FC 105 qualify

QUARTER-FINALS
Nkana Red Devils....1-1 1-5....**Zamalek**
Dynamos Harare....2-0 0-2 2-3p....**JE Tizi-Ouzou**
Semassi Sokodé....W-O....FC 105 Libreville
MAS Fès....1-1 1-4....**Shooting Stars**

SEMI-FINALS
JE Tizi-Ouzou....3-1 0-3....**Zamalek**
Shooting Stars....5-1 1-2....Semassi Sokodé

FINAL
1st leg. International Stadium, Cairo, 23-11-1984
ZAMALEK 2
SHOOTING STARS 0

2nd leg. Surulere, Lagos, 8-12-1984
SHOOTING STARS 0
ZAMALEK 0

CUP WINNERS CUP

PRELIMINARY ROUND
Avia Sports (CTA)....0-0 0-1 *....GD Lage (EQG)
Mighty Barolle (LBR)....3-0 0-0....Hawks (GMB)
Pantheres Noires (RWA)....0-0 1-1....Inter Star (BDI)
* 2nd match abandoned after 80 minutes. Tie awarded to Avia

FIRST ROUND
Al Ahly Cairo (EGY)....3-1 2-0....CLAS Casablanca (MOR)
Mouloudia d'Algiers (ALG)4-0 0-2....Racing Club (VOL)
Pantheres Noires (RWA)....0-3 1-3....**Scarlets Nakuru** (KEN)
Costa do Sol (MOZ)....0-2 1-0....**Nakivubu Villa** (UGA)
Requins de l'Atl'q (BEN)....2-1 0-3....**ASEC Abidjan** (CIV)
Great Olympics (GHA)....0-0 4-0....Djoliba AC (MLI)
Al Merreikh (SDN)....1-0 1-0....KMKM Zanzibar (TAN)
Al Mokaouloum (EGY)....7-0 0-2....FC Horsed (SOM)
ES du Sahel (TUN)....1-1 0-1....**Al Ahly Tripoli** (LBY)
ASC Diaraf (SEN)....2-0 1-2....Mighty Blackpool (SLE)
Red Arrows (ZAM)....9-1 3-1....Linare FC (LSO)
Mighty Barolle (LBR)....2-1 1-3....**AS Vita Club** (ZAI)
Agaza Lomé (TGO)....W-O....CAP Owendo (GAB)
Enugu Rangers (NGA)....W-O....Horoya AC (GUI)
Dynamo Fima (MDG)....6-1 0-1....Highlanders (SWZ)
Canon Yaoundé (CMR)....3-0 1-1....Avia Sports (CTA)

SECOND ROUND
Mouloudia d'Algiers....1-0 1-3....**Al Ahly Cairo**
Scarlets Nakuru....0-3 1-2....**Nakivubu Villa**
Great Olympics....2-1 0-2....**ASEC Abidjan**
Al Merreikh....0-0 0-2....**Al Mokaouloum**
ASC Diaraf....2-1 0-3....**Al Ahly Tripoli**
AS Vita Club....2-1 0-1....**Red Arrows**
Enugu Rangers....1-0 1-0....Agaza Lomé
Dynamo Fima....0-1 0-1....**Canon Yaoundé**

QUARTER-FINALS
Al Ahly Cairo....1-0 1-2....Nakivubu Villa
ASEC Abidjan....2-1 1-3....**Al Mokaouloum**
Red Arrows....2-0 0-3....**Al Ahly Tripoli**
Canon Yaoundé....5-0 0-3....Enugu Rangers

SEMI-FINALS
Al Ahly Cairo....0-0 1-1....Al Mokaouloum
Canon Yaoundé....1-0 0-1 4-5p *....Al Ahly Tripoli
* Al Ahly Tripoli withdrew before the final and were replaced by Canon

FINAL
1st leg. International Stadium, Cairo, 30-11-1984
AL AHLY CAIRO 1
CANON YAOUNDÉ 0

2nd leg. Omnisport, Yaoundé, 30-12-1984
CANON YAOUNDÉ 1
AL AHLY CAIRO 0
Al Ahly Cairo won 4-2 on penalties

1985

CHAMPIONS CUP

PRELIMINARY ROUND
ASC Garde National (MTN)1-0 2-1....Sporting Clube (GNB)
Ground Force (ETH)....1-2 0-2....**Vital'O** (BDI)
Highlanders (SWZ)....4-1 0-2....LFP Maseru (LSO)
Petro Atletico (AGO)....4-1 1-1....AS Tempete Mocaf (CTA)
Ports Authority (GMB)....W-O....ASFA Ouagadougou (BFA)

FIRST ROUND
FAR Rabat (MOR)....8-0....Ports Authority (GMB)
CA Bizerte (TUN)....1-0 1-1..ASC Garde National (MTN)
Enugu Rangers (NGA)....2-0 2-1....Petro Atletico (AGO)
AS Kaloum Star (GUI)....1-0 2-2....Real Republicans (SLE)
Scarlets Nakuru (KEN)....2-1 0-1....**Vital'O** (BDI)
Tonnerre Yaoundé (CMR)....2-1 0-1....**AS Sogara** (GAB)
Nakivubu Villa (UGA)....4-2 0-2....**Al Hilal** (SDN)
Zamalek (EGY)....W-O....Marine Club (SOM)
Stella Abidjan (CIV)....1-1 0-3....**US Goree** (SEN)
Lions de l'Atakory (BEN)....0-1 0-3....**Hearts of Oak** (GHA)
Power Dynamos (ZAM)....4-0 2-1....KMKM Zanzibar (TAN)
Black Rhinos (ZIM)....1-0 3-1....Highlanders (SWZ)
GCR Mascara (ALG)....4-0 0-3....Al Ittihad (LBY)
Invincible Eleven (LBR)....3-0 1-1 *....**Stade Malien** (MLI)
Agaza Lomé (TGO)....0-1 1-2 **CARA Brazzaville** (COG)
AS Bilima (ZAI)....3-0 1-0....Township Rollers (BWA)
* Invincible Eleven disqualified. Tie awarded to Stade Malien

SECOND ROUND
CA Bizerte....1-4 1-0....**FAR Rabat**
AS Kaloum Star....2-0 1-3....Enugu Rangers
Vital'O....3-1 1-1....AS Sogara
Zamalek....4-0 1-1....Al Hilal
US Goree....3-0 0-1....Hearts of Oak
Power Dynamos....0-2 1-1....**Black Rhinos**
Stade Malien....2-0 0-3....**GCR Mascara**
AS Bilima....1-1 1-0....CARA Brazzaville

QUARTER-FINALS
FAR Rabat....3-0 0-3 3-1p....AS Kaloum Star

Vital'O .... 1-0 2-5 .... **Zamalek**
Black Rhinos .... 2-0 0-3 .... **US Goree**
GCR Mascara .... 0-0 0-3 .... **AS Bilima**

SEMI-FINALS

Zamalek .... 1-0 0-1 3-4p .... **FAR Rabat**
AS Bilima .... 2-0 0-1 .... US Goree

FINAL

1st leg. Moulay Abdallah Stadium, Rabat, 30-11-1985
FORCES ARMEES ROYAL RABAT 5
AS BILIMA 2

2nd leg. Mobuto Stadium, Lubumbashi, 22-12-1985
AS BILIMA 1
FORCES ARMEES ROYAL RABAT 1

CUP WINNERS CUP

PRELIMINARY ROUND

Dragons de l'Ouème (BEN) 8-0 2-1 .... Atletico Malabo (EQG)
Inter Star (BDI) .... 3-1 0-2 * .... Waxool (SOM)
Trarza Rosso (MTN) .... W-O .... Racing Club (BFA)
* Waxool disqualified. Tie awarded to Inter Star

FIRST ROUND

AS Marsa (TUN) .... 0-0 0-4 .... **Al Ahly Cairo** (EGY)
SC Simba (TAN) .... 5-0 0-1 .... Shoe Factory (ETH)
Primeiro de Agosto (AGO) .... 1-0 0-3 .... **Dihep di Nkam** (CMR)
Dragons de l'Ouème (BEN) 3-1 0-1 .... CS Imana (ZAI)
Inter Star (BDI) .... 1-2 0-3 .... **Kampala CC** (UGA)
Lioli FC (LSO) .... 1-1 1-2 .... **Gweru United** (ZIM)
Stade Abidjan (CIV) .... 3-1 1-5 .... **FC 105 Libreville** (GAB)
Trarza Rosso (MTN) .... 1-1 0-2 .... **Al Nasr** (LBY)
AFC Leopards (KEN) .... 2-0 1-2 .... Al Merreikh (SDN)
Manzini Wanderers (SWZ) .... 0-0 0-2 .... **Mufulira Wanderers** (ZAM)
Mighty Barolle (LBR) .... 1-0 0-3 .... **Asante Kotoko** (GHA)
SCAF Tocages (CTA) .... 3-2 0-2 .... **ASFOSA Lomé** (TGO)
ASC Jeanne d'Arc (SEN) .... 1-0 1-0 .... RS Kenitra (MOR)
Djoliba AC (MLI) .... 0-0 0-2 .... **Mouloudia d'Oran** (ALG)
Horoya AC (GUI) .... 2-0 0-1 .... Wallidan (GMB)
Old Edwardians (SLE) .... 0-0 1-4 .... **Leventis United** (NGA)

SECOND ROUND

SC Simba .... 2-1 0-2 .... **Al Ahly Cairo**
Dragons de l'Ouème .... 1-0 1-2 .... Dihep di Nkam
Kampala CC .... 3-1 1-1 .... Gweru United
FC 105 Libreville .... 2-1 1-3 .... **Al Nasr**
Mufulira Wanderers .... 1-1 1-1 3-5p .... **AFC Leopards**
ASFOSA Lomé .... 1-1 0-0 .... **Asante Kotoko**
ASC Jeanne d'Arc .... 0-0 1-1 .... Mouloudia d'Oran
Leventis United .... 0-0 1-1 .... Horoya AC

QUARTER-FINALS

Dragons de l'Ouème .... 1-1 0-4 .... **Al Ahly Cairo**
Kampala CC .... 1-0 0-1 2-4p .... **Al Nasr**
Asante Kotoko .... 2-0 0-2 4-5p .... **AFC Leopards**
ASC Jeanne d'Arc .... 0-1 0-1 .... **Leventis United**

SEMI-FINALS

Al Ahly Cairo .... W-O .... Al Nasr
Leventis United .... 2-0 0-1 .... AFC Leopards

FINAL

1st leg. International Stadium, Cairo, 22-11-1985
AL AHLY CAIRO 2
LEVENTIS UNITED 0

2nd leg. Surulere, Lagos, 7-12-1985
LEVENTIS UNITED 1
AL AHLY CAIRO 0

1986

CHAMPIONS CUP

PRELIMINARY ROUND

UDIB Bissau (GNB) .... W-O .... East End Lions (SLE)
Etoile Filante (BFA) .... W-O .... ASC Ksar (MTN)
Lioli FC (LSO) .... 2-3 0-4 .... **Maji Maji** (TAN)
Manzini Wanderers (SWZ) .... 1-3 2-3 .... **AC Sotema** (MDG)
Pantheres Noires (RWA) .... 3-0 2-1 .... Wagad Mogadishu (SOM)
SCAF Tocages (CTA) .... 4-1 2-1 .... Juvenil Reyes (EQG)

FIRST ROUND

Zamalek (EGY) .... 5-1 1-1 .... Pantheres Noires (RWA)
Dynamos Harare (ZIM) .... 5-1 .... Maji Maji (TAN)
FC Darnah (LBY) .... 2-1 0-2 .... **Kampala CC** (UGA)
Inter Star (BDI) .... 2-1 1-1 .... US Tshinkunku (ZAI)
FAR Rabat (MOR) .... W-O .... UDIB Bissau (GNB)
FC 105 Libreville (GAB) .... 1-0 0-2 .... **SCAF Tocages** (CTA)
ASC Jeanne d'Arc (SEN) .... 0-0 0-2 .... **MAS Fès** (MOR)
Canon Yaoundé (CMR) .... 3-0 0-2 .... Primeiro de Maio (AGO)
Nkana Red Devils (ZAM) .... 4-1 1-2 .... AC Sotema (MDG)
Kenya Breweries (KEN) .... 0-0 1-2 .... **Brewery Jimma** (ETH)
Horoya AC (GUI) .... 4-0 1-3 .... Invincible Eleven (LBR)
Hearts of Oak (GHA) .... 2-0 0-1 .... Wallidan (GMB)
Al Merreikh (SDN) .... 2-1 0-1 .... **Esperance Tunis** (TUN)
JE Tizi-Ouzou (ALG) .... 5-0 1-1 .... Etoile Filante (BFA)
ASFOSA Lomé (TGO) .... 0-2 0-2 **New Nigeria Bank** (NGA)
Africa Sports (CIV) .... 1-0 0-1 4-3p .... Requins de l'Atl'q (BEN)

SECOND ROUND

Zamalek .... 2-1 2-0 .... Dynamos Harare
Kampala CC .... 1-1 1-2 .... **Inter Star**
SCAF Tocages .... 0-1 1-6 .... **FAR Rabat**
MAS Fès .... 1-0 0-3 .... **Canon Yaoundé**
Brewery Jimma .... 0-0 0-0 3-4p .... **Nkana Red Devils**
Horoya AC .... 1-2 0-2 .... **Hearts of Oak**
JE Tizi-Ouzou .... 2-1 0-1 .... **Esperance Tunis**
Africa Sports .... 5-0 0-2 .... New Nigeria Bank

QUARTER-FINALS

Inter Star .... 1-0 0-3 .... **Zamalek**
Canon Yaoundé .... 2-0 0-1 .... FAR Rabat
Nkana Red Devils .... 2-0 1-1 .... Hearts of Oak
Africa Sports .... 1-0 1-2 .... Esperance Tunis

SEMI-FINALS

Canon Yaoundé .... 2-1 0-2 .... **Zamalek**
Nkana Red Devils .... 1-1 0-0 .... **Africa Sports**

FINAL

1st leg. International Stadium, Cairo, 28-11-1986
ZAMALEK 2
AFRICA SPORTS 0

2nd leg. Houphouet Boigny, Abidjan, 21-12-1986
AFRICA SPORTS 2
ZAMALEK 0
Zamalek won 4-2 on penalties

CUP WINNERS CUP

PRELIMINARY ROUND

Kamboi Eagles (SLE) .... W-O .... AS Police (MTN)
Ela Nguema (EQG) .... 0-0 1-3 .... **AS Fonct. Bobo-D** (BFA)
Al Merreikh (SDN) .... 1-1 0-1 **AS Tempete Mocaf** (CTA)
LPF Maseru (LSO) .... 0-0 2-3 **Fortior Mahajanga** (MDG)
Highlanders (SWZ) .... 4-2 1-2 .... Kiyovu Sports (RWA)
Starlight (GMB) .... 3-1 1-1 .... Benfica (GNB)

Vital'O (BDI) 1-0 1-2 Petrolium (SOM)

FIRST ROUND

Al Ahly Cairo (EGY) 2-0 0-1 Uganda Express FC (UGA)
Highlanders (SWZ) 1-1 2-2 Shoe Factory (ETH)
Fortior Mahajanga (MDG) 2-2 0-1 **Miembeni** (TAN)
Highlanders (ZIM) 1-3 0-2 **Power Dynamos** (ZAM)
Ferroviaro Huila (AGO) 1-3 0-0 **FC Kalamu** (ZAI)
Vital'O (BDI) 1-1 0-1 **AFC Leopards** (KEN)
Mouloudia d'Oran (ALG) W-O Kamboi Eagles (SLE)
AS Tempete Mocaf (CTA) 2-0 0-3 **Al Ismaili** (EGY)
CS Hammam-Lif (TUN) Bye
Starlight (GMB) 1-1 1-1 3-4p **ASC Diaraf** (SEN)
AS Kaloum Star (GUI) 1-0 0-2 **DHJ Jadida** (MOR)
AS Fonct. Bobo-D (BFA) 1-0 1-5 **Al Ahly Tripoli** (LBY)
Foadan Dapaong (TGO) 3-0 1-2 SC Gagnoa (CIV)
Mighty Barolle (LBR) 2-1 0-0 Union Douala (CMR)
Dragons de l'Ouème (BEN) 2-0 * Abiola Babes (NGA)
AS Sogara (GAB) 3-0 0-1 Sekondi Hasaacas (GHA)
* Match abandoned. Both teams disqualified

SECOND ROUND

Highlanders 0-5 0-3 **Al Ahly Cairo**
Miembeni 1-1 0-5 **Power Dynamos**
AFC Leopards 1-1 1-3 **FC Kalamu**
Al Ismaili 1-0 0-0 Mouloudia d'Oran
ASC Diaraf 2-1 0-1 **CS Hammam-Lif**
DHJ Jadida W-O Al Ahly Tripoli
Mighty Barolle 3-2 0-2 **Foadan Dapaong**
AS Sogara Bye

QUARTER-FINALS

Al Ahly Cairo 2-0 0-1 Power Dynamos
FC Kalamu 2-0 0-3 **Al Ismaili**
DHJ Jadida 0-0 0-0 3-4p **CS Hammam-Lif**
AS Sogara 3-1 2-1 Foadan Dapaong

SEMI-FINALS

Al Ahly Cairo 0-0 1-1 Al Ismaili
CS Hammam-Lif 0-0 0-3 **AS Sogara**

FINAL

1st leg. International Stadium, Cairo, 21-11-1986
AL AHLY CAIRO 3
AS SOGARA 0

2nd leg. Omar Bongo, Libreville, 7-12-86
AS SOGARA 2
AL AHLY CAIRO 0

1987

CHAMPIONS CUP

PRELIMINARY ROUND

BTM Antananarivo (MDG) 1-1 1-2 **Maji Maji** (TAN)
Juvenil Reyes (EQG) W-O Sporting Moura (CTA)
Matlama FC (LSO) 1-0 2-0 Gaborone United (BOT)
Municipality (SOM) 1-0 0-2 **Pantheres Noires** (RWA)
Sporting Clube (GNB) W-O Old Edwardians (SLE)
Petro Atletico (AGO) 3-1 1-0 Maxaquene Maputo (MOZ)
Tamil Cadets SC (MRI) 3-2 1-2 **Highlanders** (SWZ)

FIRST ROUND

Al Ahly Cairo (EGY) 4-0 1-1 Pantheres Noires (RWA)
AFC Leopards (KEN) 1-0 1-0 Maji Maji (TAN)
Mighty Barolle (LBR) 2-1 0-0 Horoya AC (GUI)
Africa Sports (CIV) 2-1 1-0 ASFOSA Lome (TGO)
Nkana Red Devils (ZAM) 1-1 1-0 Petro Atletico (AGO)
Zamalek (EGY) W-O Juvenil Reyes (EQG)
WAC Casablanca (MOR) 3-1 * AS Police (MTN)
Asante Kotoko (GHA) W-O Sporting Clube (GNB)
Requins de l'Atl'q (BEN) 0-0 0-7 **Canon Yaoundé** (CMR)
ASC Jeanne d'Arc (SEN) 2-1 0-2 **Entente Setif** (ALG)
Dynamos Harare (ZIM) 6-1 2-1 Highlanders (SWZ)
FC Lupopo (ZAI) 1-0 0-0 FC 105 Libreville (GAB)
ES Hammam-Sousse (TUN) W-O Al Ittihad (LBY)
AS Real Bamako (MLI) 0-0 0-4 **Leventis United** (NGA)
Nakivubu Villa (UGA) 4-0 1-0 Matlama FC (LSO)
Al Hilal (SDN) 2-0 1-0 Inter Star (BDI)
* AS Police disqualified. Tie awarded to WAC

SECOND ROUND

Al Ahly Cairo 6-0 1-2 AFC Leopards
Africa Sports 2-1 1-1 Mighty Barolle
Nkana Red Devils 1-0 0-2 **Zamalek**
WAC Casablanca 1-1 0-2 **Asante Kotoko**
Entente Setif 0-0 1-2 **Canon Yaoundé**
Dynamos Harare 3-1 1-1 FC Lupopo
ES Hammam-Sousse 2-1 0-1 **Leventis United**
Nakivubu Villa 2-1 0-1 **Al Hilal**

QUARTER-FINALS

Africa Sports 2-0 0-2 2-4p **Al Ahly Cairo**
Zamalek 2-0 1-5 **Asante Kotoko**
Canon Yaoundé 2-1 1-1 Dynamos Harare
Al Hilal 2-1 0-0 Leventis United

SEMI-FINALS

Al Ahly Cairo 2-0 0-1 Asante Kotoko
Al Hilal 1-0 0-1 4-1p Canon Yaoundé

FINAL

1st leg. The Stadium, Khartum, 29-11-1987
AL HILAL 0
AL AHLY CAIRO 0

2nd leg. International Stadium, Cairo, 18-12-1987
AL AHLY CAIRO 2
AL HILAL 0

CUP WINNERS CUP

PRELIMINARY ROUND

Stade Malien (MLI) W-O Real Republicans (SLE)
RLDF Maseru (LSO) 1-1 1-1 5-3p Swallows FC (SWZ)

FIRST ROUND

Marine Club (SOM) 0-2 0-3 **Gor Mahia** (KEN)
Al Merreikh (SDN) 2-0 1-0 Blue Bats (UGA)
Okwahu United (GHA) 2-0 1-1 FC Kalamu (ZAI)
LPRC Oilers (LBR) 1-1 0-0 **Entente II Lomé** (TGO)
Inter Club Luanda (AGO) 1-1 0-2 **Vital'O** (BDI)
Highlanders (ZIM) 1-0 0-1 2-5p **Miembeni** (TAN)
Rail Douala (CMR) 1-0 0-2 **US Mbila-Nzambi** (GAB)
CO Kakande Boke (GUI) 0-3 1-4 **Dragons de l'Ouème** (BEN)
Abiola Babes (NGA) W-O Ela Nguema (EQG)
ASF Douanes (SEN) 2-0 1-4 **ASEC Abidjan** (CIV)
RLDF Maseru (LSO) 3-2 0-2 **HTMF Mahajanga** (MDG)
Estrela Vemelha (MOZ) 0-1 0-3 **Nchanga Rangers** (ZAM)
WKF Collo (ALG) W-O FC Batafa (GNB)
Stade Malien (MLI) 0-1 0-4 **FAR Rabat** (MOR)
Mukura VS (RWA) 1-1 0-5 **Al Tersana** (EGY)
ASC Garde National (MTN) 1-3 0-4 **Esperance Tunis** (TUN)

SECOND ROUND

Al Merreikh 1-1 0-0 **Gor Mahia**
Entente II Lomé 2-0 0-0 Okwahu United
Miembeni 0-1 1-3 **Vital'O**
Dragons de l'Ouème 1-0 0-1 4-2p US Mbila-Nzambi

Abiola Babes 2-0 0-2 4-2p ASEC Abidjan
HTMF Mahajanga 2-2 1-2 **Nchanga Rangers**
WKF Collo 3-2 1-5 **FAR Rabat**
Al Tersana 0-0 0-2 **Esperance Tunis**

QUARTER-FINALS

Gor Mahia 4-1 0-0 Entente II Lomé
Dragons de l'Ouème 2-0 0-1 Vital'O
Nchanga Rangers 1-1 1-2 **Abiola Babes**
FAR Rabat 1-0 1-3 **Esperance Tunis**

SEMI-FINALS

Dragons de l'Ouème 0-0 2-3 **Gor Mahia**
Abiola Babes 1-0 0-2 **Esperance Tunis**

FINAL

1st leg. El Mensah, Tunis, 21-11-1987
ESPERANCE SPORTIVE TUNIS 2
GOR MAHIA 2

2nd leg. Kasarani, Nairobi, 5-12-1987
GOR MAHIA 1
ESPERANCE SPORTIVE TUNIS 1
Gor Mahia won on away goals

1988

CHAMPIONS CUP

PRELIMINARY ROUND

Ela Nguema (EQG) 0-1 0-4 **Etoile du Congo** (COG)
Manzini Wanderers (SWZ) 2-0 4-1 Township Rollers (BWA)
Pantheres Noires (RWA) 2-2 0-1 **Wagad Mogadishu** (SOM)
RLDF Maseru (LSO) 2-0 0-3 **Sunrise FC** (MUS)
Sierra Fisheries (SLE) 0-1 0-0 **AS Police** (MTN)

FIRST ROUND

Stade Malien (MLI) 1-1 0-4 **Entente Setif** (ALG)
ES Hammam-Sousse (TUN) W-O Al Nasr (LBY)
Etoile de Congo (COG) 0-0 0-2 **Inter Star** (BDI)
Asante Kotoko (GHA) 2-0 0-2 2-4p **FC 105 Libreville** (GAB)
Sunrise FC (MUS) 2-1 2-2 Black Rhinos (ZIM)
Matchedje Maputo (MOZ) 3-1 1-2 Jos Nosy Be (MDG)
Manzini Wanderers (SWZ) 1-4 1-1 **Nakivubu Villa** (UGA)
Young Africans (TAN) 0-0 0-4 **Al Ahly Cairo** (EGY)
Invincible Eleven (LBR) 0-1 0-0 **FAR Rabat** (MOR)
AS Police (MTN) 2-0 0-2 10-9p SEIB Diourbel (SEN)
Shabana Kisii (KEN) 1-0 1-4 **Kabwe Warriors** (ZAM)
Wagad Mogadishu (SOM) 1-1 0-6 **Al Hilal** (SDN)
AS Kaloum Star (GUI) 0-2 1-3 **Africa Sports** (CIV)
Petro Atletico (AGO) 2-1 1-0 TP Mazembe (ZAI)
Doumbe Sans' Mango (TGO) 0-1 0-1 **Tonnerre Yaoundé** (CMR)
Iwuanyanwu Owerri (NGA) 2-0 1-0 Requins de l'Atl'q (BEN)

SECOND ROUND

ES Hammam-Sousse 2-1 0-2 **Entente Setif**
FC 105 Libreville 2-1 1-1 Inter Star
Sunrise FC 2-0 1-5 **Matchedje Maputo**
Nakivubu Villa 2-3 1-3 **Al Ahly Cairo**
FAR Rabat 5-0 1-2 AS Police
Kabwe Warriors 0-0 1-3 **Al Hilal**
Africa Sports 3-0 1-2 Petro Atletico
Iwuanyanwu Owerri 2-0 2-3 Tonnerre Yaoundé

QUARTER-FINALS

FC 105 Libreville 3-1 0-3 **Entente Setif**
Al Ahly Cairo 2-0 0-1 Matchedje Maputo
Al Hilal 1-0 0-3 **FAR Rabat**
Iwuanyanwu Owerri 2-0 1-2 Africa Sports

SEMI-FINALS

Entente Setif 2-0 0-2 4-2p Al Ahly Cairo
Iwuanyanwu Owerri 4-1 1-4 5-3p FAR Rabat

FINAL

1st leg. Liberty Stadium, Ibadan, 26-11-1988, 25,000
IWUANYANWU OWERRI 1
ENTENTE PLASTICIENS SETIF 0

2nd leg. Constantine, 9-12-1988, 40,000
ENTENTE PLASTICIENS SETIF 4
IWUANYANWU OWERRI 0

CUP WINNERS CUP

PRELIMINARY ROUND

Matlama FC (LSO) 2-1 0-4 **Maxaquene Maputo** (MOZ)
Mukura VS (RWA) 5-1 0-3 Highlanders (SWZ)
AS Sigui Kayes (MLI) 0-0 0-0 3-4p **Real Republicans** (SLE)
Wallidan (GMB) 3-0 * AS Douanes (MTN)
* Match abandoned. Tie awarded to Wallidan

FIRST ROUND

CA Bizerte (TUN) 0-1 1-0 6-5p USM El Harrach (ALG)
FC Horsed (SOM) 0-0 1-1 Al Mourada (SDN)
Real Republicans (SLE) W-O Al Medina (LBY)
Wallidan (GMB) W-O KAC Marrakech (MOR)
AFC Leopards (KEN) 1-1 4-0 CAPS United (ZIM)
Kampala CC (UGA) 0-1 0-1 **FC Kalamu** (ZAI)
ASC Jeanne d'Arc (SEN) 3-0 2-1 ASKO Kara (TGO)
Atletico Malabo (EQG) 3-1 0-5 **Diamant Yaoundé** (CMR)
US Mbila-Nzambi (GAB) 1-1 0-0 * **Inter Club** (COG)
ASC Bouaké (CIV) W-O Dragons de l'Ouéme (BEN)
Mukura VS (RWA) 0-1 0-1 **Gor Mahia** (KEN)
BTM Antananarivo (MDG) 3-1 0-0 Miembeni (TAN)
Muzinga (BDI) 0-1 1-1 **Ferroviaro Lubango** (AGO)
Maxaquene Maputo (MOZ) 1-3 0-1 **Power Dynamos** (ZAM)
ASFAG Conakry (GUI) W-O Hearts of Oak (GHA)
Ranchers Bees (NGA) 4-1 1-1 Mighty Barolle (LBR)
* 2nd match abandoned. Tie awarded to Inter Club

SECOND ROUND

FC Horsed 0-2 0-7 **CA Bizerte**
Real Republicans 0-0 0-1 **Wallidan**
AFC Leopards 4-1 0-2 FC Kalamu
ASC Jeanne d'Arc 1-2 1-2 **Diamant Yaoundé**
Inter Club 1-0 1-1 ASC Bouaké
Gor Mahia 2-1 1-0 BTM Antananarivo
Power Dynamos 1-0 2-5 **Ferroviaro Lubango**
Ranchers Bees 1-0 1-1 ASFAG Conakry

QUARTER-FINALS

CA Bizerte W-O Wallidan
AFC Leopards 1-0 0-1 4-5p **Diamant Yaoundé**
Gor Mahia 2-1 1-4 **Inter Club**
Ferroviaro Lubango 1-1 2-4 **Ranchers Bees**

SEMI-FINALS

Diamant Yaoundé 1-0 0-3 **CA Bizerte**
Inter Club 1-0 0-2 **Ranchers Bees**

FINAL

1st leg. Liberty Stadium, Ibadan, 19-11-1988, 20,000
RANCHERS BEES 0
CLUB ATHLETIQUE BIZERTE 0

2nd leg. El Menzah, Tunis, 3-12-1988, 40,000
CLUB ATHLETIQUE BIZERTE 1
RANCHERS BEES 0

1989

CHAMPIONS CUP

PRELIMINARY ROUND

Ela Nguema (EQG)....1-0 0-4....**ASDR Fatima** (CTA)
Highlanders (SWZ)....2-0....Pan African (TAN)
Matlama FC (LSO)....0-1 1-4....**Defence Force** (BWA)
Mighty Blackpool (SLE)....W-O....Benfica (GNB)
St. Louis (SYC)....0-0 1-0....COSFAP Ant'arivo (MDG)
Zumunta AC (NIG)....0-2 1-1....**Etoile Filante** (BFA)

FIRST ROUND

Raja Casablanca (MOR)....2-0 0-1....ASC Jeanne d'Arc (SEN)
JAC Port-Gentil (GAB)....1-0 0-1 5-3p....Africa Sports (CIV)
Iwuanyanwu Owerri (NGA)4-1 0-0....Mighty Barolle (LBR)
Inter Club (COG)....2-1 2-2....Petro Atletico (AGO)
Entente Setif (ALG)....1-0 0-1 3-5p..**Mighty Blackpool** (SLE)
Djoliba AC (MLI)....1-0 0-0....Horoya AC (GUI)
AS Vita Club (ZAI)....4-0 2-1....Mukungwa (RWA)
Tonnerre Yaoundé (CMR)..2-0 3-0....ASDR Fatima (CTA)
Nkana Red Devils (ZAM)....4-1 1-1....Defence Force (BWA)
Fire Brigade SC (MUS)....1-0 1-0....St. Louis (SYC)
Uganda Express FC (UGA)4-0 1-2....Highlanders (SWZ)
Desportivo Maputo (MOZ)....2-2 1-1....**Zimbabwe Saints** (ZIM)
Zamalek (EGY)....2-1 0-1....**Al Mourada** (SDN)
AFC Leopards (KEN)....0-0 1-1....Inter Star (BDI)
Esperance Tunis (TUN)....2-1 0-0....Etoile Filante (BFA)
Mouloudia d'Oran (ALG)....W-O....Al Ittihad (LBY)

SECOND ROUND

Raja Casablanca....0-0 1-1....JAC Port-Gentil
Iwuanyanwu Owerri....2-1 1-2 4-5p....**Inter Club**
Mighty Blackpool....2-1 0-0....Djoliba AC
AS Vita Club....1-1 1-3....**Tonnerre Yaoundé**
Nkana Red Devils....5-1 3-2....Fire Brigade SC
Zimbabwe Saints....0-1 1-0 4-3p....Uganda Express FC
AFC Leopards....1-0 0-3....**Al Mourada**
Mouloudia d'Oran....2-3 3-1....Esperance Tunis

QUARTER-FINALS

Raja Casablanca....2-0 0-1....Inter Club
Mighty Blackpool....0-1 1-3....**Tonnerre Yaoundé**
Zimbabwe Saints....0-0 1-2....**Nkana Red Devils**
Al Mourada....1-0 0-4....**Mouloudia d'Oran**

SEMI-FINALS

Raja Casablanca....2-0 2-2....Tonnerre Yaoundé
Nkana Red Devils....1-0 2-5....**Mouloudia d'Oran**

FINAL

1st leg. Mohammed V, Casablanca, 3-12-1989, 40,000
RAJA CLUB ATHLETIQUE CASABLANCA 1
MOULOUDIA PETROLIERS ORAN 0

2nd leg. Oran, 15-12-1989, 25,000
MOULOUDIA PETROLIERS ORAN 1
RAJA CLUB ATHLETIQUE CASABLANCA 0
Raja won 4-2 on penalties

CUP WINNERS CUP

PRELIMINARY ROUND

Moneni Pirates (SWZ)....2-0 0-1....RLDF Maseru (LSO)

FIRST ROUND

Al Merreikh (SDN)....W-O....Al Ahly Tripoli (LBY)
CO Kakande Boke (GUI)....0-0 0-1....**CA Bizerte** (TUN)
Vautour Club M'gou (GAB)....1-0 1-3..**Sagrada Esperanca** (AGO)
Union Vesper (EQG)....0-1 0-2 **Patronage St Anne** (COG)
Panthère Bangangte (CMR)....0-0 1-2....**LPRC Oilers** (LBR)
ASI Abengourou (CIV)....W-O....UDIB Bissau (GNB)
Coastal Union (TAN)....2-3 0-2....**Costa do Sol** (MOZ)
Gor Mahia (KEN)....W-O....Nakivubu Villa (UGA)
Dynamos Harare (ZIM)....0-1 1-1....**BFV FC** (MDG)
Moneni Pirates (SWZ)....1-1 0-5....**Power Dynamos** (ZAM)
Stade Malien (MLI)....3-0 0-0....COT Tunis (TUN)
Liberté FC (NIG)....1-0 0-4....**USK Algiers** (ALG)
USCA Bangui (CTA)....3-3 0-2....**FC Kalamu** (ZAI)
Etincelles (RWA)....1-0 1-1....Vital'O (BDI)
AS Fonctionnaires (BFA)....1-0 1-2....ASC Linguère (SEN)
Diamond Stars (SLE)....0-0 0-2....**Bendel United** (NGA)

SECOND ROUND

CA Bizerte....1-0 0-2....**Al Merreikh**
Patronage Saint Anne....2-1 0-0....Sagrada Esperanca
ASI Abengourou....3-2 0-2....**LPRC Oilers**
Costa do Sol....1-2 0-0....**Gor Mahia**
BFV FC....1-2 3-1....Power Dynamos
Stade Malien....1-0 0-1 3-4p....**USK Algiers**
Etincelles....0-0 0-1....**FC Kalamu**
AS Fonctionnaires....1-3 0-2....**Bendel United**

QUARTER-FINALS

Al Merreikh....2-0 1-1....Patronage Saint Anne
Gor Mahia....0-0 3-1....LPRC Oilers
USK Algiers....1-3....**BFV FC**
Bendel United....2-0 1-0....FC Kalamu

SEMI-FINALS

Gor Mahia....1-0 0-2....**Al Merreikh**
Bendel United....4-1 0-0....BFV FC

FINAL

1st leg. Khartoum Stadium, Khartoum, 25-11-1989, 40,000
AL MERREIKH 1
BENDEL UNITED 0

2nd leg. Benin, 9-12-1989, 30,000
BENDEL UNITED 0
AL MERREIKH 0

1990

CHAMPIONS CUP

PRELIMINARY ROUND

ASKO Kara (TGO)....1-0 2-0....ASFA Yennega (BFA)
AC Sotema (MDG)....1-0 1-2....Defence Force (BWA)
MBC (SOM)....1-0 2-4....**St. Louis** (SYC)
Malindi (TAN)....0-0 1-2....**Mukungwa** (RWA)
Inter Star (BDI)....2-0 0-3....**Petro Atletico** (AGO)
AS Kaloum Star (GUI)....2-0 1-0....Benfica (GNB)
Al Ittihad (LBY)....6-1 0-2....Olympic Niamey (NIG)
Renaissance (CHD)....2-2 0-1....**SCAF Tocages** (CTA)
Dragons de l'Ouème (BEN)....0-0 0-3....**Mighty Barolle** (LBR)
Arsenals (LSO)....1-0 3-0....Denver Sundowns (SWZ)

FIRST ROUND

JS Kabylie (ALG)....6-0 4-0....ASKO Kara (TGO)
AS Sogara (GAB)....0-2 0-1....**Etoile du Congo** (COG)
Sunrise FC (MUS)....4-1 0-2....AC Sotema (MDG)
AFC Leopards (KEN)....4-2 3-3....St. Louis (SYC)
Al Hilal (SDN)....4-0 2-0....Mukungwa (RWA)
Dynamos Harare (ZIM)..1-1 1-1 5-4p....Petro Atletico (AGO)
FAR Rabat (MOR)....4-0 1-1....AS Kaloum Star (GUI)
Asante Kotoko (GHA)....4-0 1-1....Freetown United (SLE)
ASC Diaraf (SEN)....1-0 0-3....**Iwuanyanwu Owerri** (NGA)

CS Imana (ZAI) 1-0 0-3 **Africa Sports** (CIV)
Al Ahly Cairo (EGY) 5-0 3-0 Al Ittihad (LBY)
Esperance Tunis (TUN) 2-0 1-0 Stade Malien (MLI)
Racing Bafoussam (CMR) 2-1 0-0 SCAF Tocages (CTA)
Raja Casablanca (MOR) 2-0 1-2 Mighty Barolle (LBR)
Ferroviario Maputo (MOZ) 1-0 0-2 **Arsenals** (LSO)
Nkana Red Devils (ZAM) 3-1 1-0 Uganda Express FC (UGA)

SECOND ROUND

Etoile du Congo 2-2 0-2 **JS Kabylie**
Sunrise FC 1-1 0-3 **AFC Leopards**
Dynamos Harare 2-1 0-1 **Al Hilal**
FAR Rabat 3-3 0-1 **Asante Kotoko**
Africa Sports 1-1 2-3 **Iwuanyanwu Owerri**
Al Ahly Cairo 0-0 0-0 2-4p **Esperance Tunis**
Racing Bafoussam W-O Raja Casablanca
Arsenals 0-3 1-5 **Nkana Red Devils**

QUARTER-FINALS

AFC Leopards 2-1 0-3 **JS Kabylie**
Al Hilal 2-2 1-2 **Asante Kotoko**
Iwuanyanwu Owerri 2-1 1-1 Esperance Tunis
Racing Bafoussam 0-1 1-2 **Nkana Red Devils**

SEMI-FINALS

Asante Kotoko 1-0 0-2 **JS Kabylie**
Nkana Red Devils 1-0 1-0 Iwuanyanwu Owerri

FINAL

1st leg. Stade Olympique, Algiers, 30-11-1990

JEUNESSE SPORTIVE KABYLIE 1
NKANA RED DEVILS 0

2nd leg. Independence Stadium, Lusaka, 22-12-1990

NKANA RED DEVILS 1
JEUNESSE SPORTIVE KABYLIE 0
JS Kabylie won 5-3 on penalties

CUP WINNERS CUP

PRELIMINARY ROUND

Anse Boileau (SYC) 0-5 1-12 **Pamba SC** (TAN)
Desportivo Maputo (MOZ) 2-0 2-0 RLDF Maseru (LSO)
Liberté FC (NIG) 0-0 1-2 **FC Tourbillon** (CHD)
Moneni Pirates (SWZ) 0-0 1-6 **Vital'O** (BDI)

FIRST ROUND

BCC Lions (NGA) 1-0 1-1 Entente II Lome (TGO)
Rayon Sports (RWA) 1-0 0-3 **Diables Noirs** (COG)
Olympique Real (CTA) 1-0 0-1 3-4p **Requins de l'Atl'q** (BEN)
US Ouakam (SEN) 2-0 1-0 Tonnerre Yaoundé (CMR)
Vital'O (BDI) 1-1 1-1 5-3p FC Kalamu (ZAI)
LPRC Oilers (LBR) 0-0 0-1 **East End Lions** (SLE)
Darryn Textiles (ZIM) 1-4 0-1 **Red Arrows** (ZAM)
Desportivo Maputo (MOZ) 0-1 1-0 5-3p Ferroviaro Lubango (AGO)
Al Merreikh (SDN) 3-0 Al Suguar (LBY)
FC Tourbillon (CHD) 0-0 0-2 **Petrosport FC** (GAB)
Kenya Breweries (KEN) 0-0 2-1 Nakivubu Villa (UGA)
Pamba SC (TAN) 0-0 1-2 **BTM Antananarivo** (MDG)
AS Real Bamako (MLI) 1-2 0-2 **Hearts of Oak** (GHA)
Mankona Guedeckou (GUI) 0-2 0-2 **AS Sotra** (CIV)
AS Fonctionnaires (BFA) 0-1 0-2 **MAS Fès** (MOR)
Relizane (ALG) 1-4 0-2 **Club Africain** (TUN)

SECOND ROUND

Diables Noirs 2-0 0-3 **BCC Lions**
Requins de l'Atlantique 0-0 0-1 **US Ouakam**
East End Lions 0-0 0-2 **Vital'O**
Desportivo Maputo 3-2 0-0 Red Arrows
Petrosport FC 2-0 0-2 3-4p **Al Merreikh**
Kenya Breweries 1-1 0-0 **BTM Antananarivo**
AS Sotra 1-1 1-2 **Hearts of Oak**
MAS Fès 1-0 0-4 **Club Africain**

QUARTER-FINALS

US Ouakam 0-1 1-3 **BCC Lions**
Desportivo Maputo 1-0 1-2 Vital'O
BTM Antananarivo 0-0 0-1 **Al Merreikh**
Hearts of Oak 2-0 0-2 5-6p **Club Africain**

SEMI-FINALS

Desportivo Maputo 2-1 1-6 **BCC Lions**
Al Merreikh 1-0 0-1 3-4p **Club Africain**

FINAL

1st leg. Surulere, Lagos, 24-11-1990

BCC LIONS 3
CLUB AFRICAIN 0

2nd leg. El Menzah, Tunis, 8-12-1990

CLUB AFRICAIN 1
BCC LIONS 1

1991

CHAMPIONS CUP

PRELIMINARY ROUND

ASF Fianarantsoa (MDG) 4-1 0-0 St. Louis (SYC)
Brewery Addis (ETH) W-0 Jadidka (SOM)
RLDF Maseru (LSO) 0-3 0-0 **Pamba SC** (TAN)
Denver Sundowns (SWZ) 0-1 1-0 4-2p Gaborone United (BWA)
Ifodje Atakpeme (TGO) 0-0 1-3 **FC Sahel Niamey** (NIG)
AS Tempete Mocafe (CTA) 2-4 0-4 **Petro Atletico** (AGO)

FIRST ROUND

Club Africain (TUN) 5-1 2-1 Requins de l'Atl'q (BEN)
Port Autonome (SEN) 0-0 0-1 **Djoliba AC** (MLI)
JS Kabylie (ALG) 6-0 0-1 TPES (CHD)
FC Sahel Niamey (NIG) 0-0 1-3 **WAC Casablanca** (MOR)
Union Douala (CMR) 3-0 2-1 Etoile Filante (BFA)
Inter Club (COG) 2-1 0-1 **Vital'O** (BDI)
Sunrise FC (MUS) 6-0 1-2 Denver Sundowns (SWZ)
Nkana Red Devils (ZAM) 6-0 ASF Fianarantsoa (MDG)
Iwuanyanwu Owerri (NGA) 3-0 0-2 Old Edwardians (SLE)
FC Lupopo (ZAI) 1-1 0-0 **JAC Port-Gentil** (GAB)
Hearts of Oak (GHA) 4-2 1-3 **Petro Atletico** (AGO)
Al Ittihad (LBY) 0-2 0-0 **ASEC Abidjan** (CIV)
Al Ahly Cairo (EGY) W-O Brewery Addis (ETH)
Gor Mahia (KEN) 1-0 0-4 **Highlanders** (ZIM)
Matchedje Maputo (MOZ) 1-1 0-1 **Pamba SC** (TAN)
Al Merreikh (SDN) 1-0 0-1 7-8p **Nakivubo Villa** (UGA)

SECOND ROUND

Club Africain 2-0 0-0 Djoliba AC
JS Kabylie 1-0 0-3 **WAC Casablanca**
Union Douala 2-0 0-0 Vital'O
Nkana Red Devils 4-1 0-2 Sunrise FC
Iwuanyanwu Owerri 5-0 2-1 JAC Port-Gentil
Petro Atletico 1-0 0-1 1-3p **ASEC Abidjan**
Al Ahly Cairo 3-1 1-0 Highlanders
Nakivubo Villa 4-1 1-2 Pamba SC

QUARTER-FINALS

Club Africain 2-0 0-1 WAC Casablanca
Union Douala 2-1 0-1 **Nkana Red Devils**
Iwuanyanwu Owerri 3-0 0-3 6-5p AESC Abidjan
Al Ahly Cairo 2-0 0-2 2-4p **Nakivubo Villa**

SEMI-FINALS

Club Africain 3-0 1-4 Nkana Red Devils
Nakivubo Villa 3-2 1-1 Iwuanyanwu Owerri

FINAL

1st leg. El Menzah, Tunis, 23-11-1991, 40,000

CLUB AFRICAIN 5
NAKIVUBO VILLA 1

2nd leg. Nakivubo Stadium, Kampala, 14-12-1991, 25,000

NAKIVUBO VILLA 1
CLUB AFRICAIN 1

CUP WINNERS CUP

PRELIMINARY ROUND

Primeiro de Agosto (AGO) 7-0 2-1 Nashua Black Af'ns (NAM)
Small Simba (TAN) 1-0 1-3 **Highlanders** (SWZ)
Olympic Niamey (NIG) 5-1 3-1 Faca FC (CTA)
Plaisance (SYC) 1-3 0-3 Rivatex (KEN)

FIRST ROUND

Rivatex (KEN) 1-0 2-4 **Power Dynamos** (ZAM)
Highlanders (SWZ) 1-1 0-0 **Al Ittihad** (SDN)
AS Marsa (TUN) 5-0 Ports Authority (SLE)
ASFA Yennega (BFA) 1-0 0-1 3-2p Asante Kotoko (GHA)
Renaissance (CHD) 0-1 0-3 **Al Mokaouloum** (EGY)
BFV FC (MDG) 1-0 1-3 **Kampala CC** (UGA)
Shell FC (GAB) 2-0 1-1 Stationery Stores (NGA)
Arsenals (LSO) 2-0* **Inter Star** (BDI)
ASC Linguère (SEN) 1-0 1-7 **Entente Setif** (ALG)
SC Gagnoa (CIV) 2-0 0-2 5-4p Stade Malien (MLI)
Olympic Niamey (NIG) 2-0 1-3 Prevoyance FC (CMR)
Semassi Sokodé (TGO) 0-0 1-2 **DC Motema Pembe** (ZAI)
Dynamos Harare (ZIM) 5-1 2-0 Maxaquene Maputo (MOZ)
Primeiro de Agosto (AGO) 0-0 1-2 **Diables Noirs** (COG)
Al Medina (LBY) W-O Ground Force (ETH)
Dragons de l'Ouème (BEN) 2-0 0-3 **BCC Lions** (NGA)
* Inter qualified

SECOND ROUND

Power Dynamos 2-1 2-0 Al Ittihad
ASFA Yennega 3-1 0-2 AS Marsa
Al Mokaouloum 2-0 0-1 Kampala CC
Shell FC 1-0 1-3 **Inter Star**
Entente Setif 4-0 1-2 SC Gagnoa
DC Motema Pembe 2-1 1-2 4-3p Olympic Niamey
Diables Noirs 0-2 1-1 **Dynamos Harare**
BCC Lions 2-0 0-0 Al Medina

QUARTER-FINALS

ASFA Yennega 1-1 0-0 **Power Dynamos**
Inter Star 0-0 0-0 5-4p Al Mokaouloum
DC Motema Pembe 2-1 0-2 **Entente Setif**
Dynamos Harare 1-1 0-3 **BCC Lions**

SEMI-FINALS

Power Dynamos 2-1 2-2 Inter Star
BCC Lions 1-0 1-1 Entente Setif

FINAL

1st leg. Surelere, Lagos, 17-12-1991, 40,000

BCC LIONS 3
POWER DYNAMOS 2

2nd leg. Independence Stadium, Lusaka, 1-12-1991, 20,000

POWER DYNAMOS 3
BCC LIONS 1

1992

CHAMPIONS CUP

PRELIMINARY ROUND

St. Louis (SYC) 1-3 1-4 **Young Africans** (TAN)
Defence Force (BWA) 1-1 0-1 **Mbabane Highlanders** (SWZ)
Arsenal (LSO) 3-0 1-0 Eleven Arrows (NAM)
Port Autonome (SEN) 0-0 0-0 1-3p **SC Praia** (CPV)
Tourbillon (CHD) 0-0 1-1 FACA FC (CTA)
LPRC Oilers (LBR) 1-0 1-3 **Mighty Blackpool** (SLE)
El Nguema (EQG) * 2-3 **Primeiro de Agosto** (EQG)
Sahel FC (NIG) 2-1 2-1 Postel Sport (BEN)
St. Georges (ETH) 2-1 0-3 **Al Ittihad** (LBY)
AS Police (MTN) 1-1 1-1 4-5p **AS Real Bamoko** (MLI)
* El Nguema withdrew before the second leg

FIRST ROUND

AS Real Bamoko (MLI) 2-1 0-2 **WAC Casabalnca** (MOR)
Diables Noirs (COG) 2-1 0-4 **Julius Berger** (NGA)
Arsenal (LSO) 2-1 0-1 **Kampala CC** (UGA)
Mbabane Highlanders (SWZ) 0-2 1-7 **Nkana Red Devils** (ZAM)
Mikishi (ZAI) 1-1 0-2 **Asante Kotoko** (GHA)
Inter Star (BDI) 2-0 0-3 **Costa do Sol** (MOZ)
Horoya Conakry (GUI) 2-0 0-2 5-4p Esperance Tunis (TUN)
Etoile Filante (BFA) 1-2 0-2 **ASEC Abidjan** (CIV)
Young Africans (TAN) 0-2 1-1 **Al Ismaili** (EGY)
Sahel SC (NIG) 2-1 0-2 **MO Constantine** (ALG)
Primeiro de Agosto (AGO) 1-0 2-0 AS Sogara (GAB)
SC Praia (CPV) 0-0 1-3 **Club Africain** (TUN)
Al Ittihad (LBY) 1-0 0-2 **Gor Mahia** (KEN)
Mighty Blackpool (SLE) 2-1 1-2 3-4p **Canon Yaoundé** (CMR)
Sunrise FC (MUS) 2-3 1-0 **AS Sotema** (MDG)
Tourbillon (CHD) 2-1 0-1 **El Hilal** (SDN)

SECOND ROUND

Julius Berger 0-0 1-2 **WAC Casablanca**
Kampala CC 0-4 0-2 **Nkana Red Devils**
Costa do Sol 1-2 1-2 **Asante Kotoko**
Horoya Conakry 1-2 0-4 **ASEC Abidjan**
MO Constantine 1-0 0-1 2-3p **Al Ismaili**
Primeiro de Agosto 2-0 0-3 **Club Africain**
Gor Mahia 0-0 1-1 Canon Yaoundé
AS Sotema 2-1 * **El Hilal**
* AS Sotema withdrew

QUARTER-FINALS

Nkana Red Devils 2-1 1-3 **WAC Casablanca**
ASEC Abidjan 1-2 3-2 Asante Kotoko
Club Africain 3-3 1-3 **Al Ismaili**
Gor Mahia 2-0 0-2 2-4p **El Hilal**

SEMI-FINALS

ASEC Abidjan 3-1 0-2 **WAC Casablanca**
Al Ismaili 0-1 0-0 **El Hilal**

FINAL

1st leg. Casablanca, 29-11-1992, 80,000

WYDAD AC CASABLANCA 2
EL HILAL 0

2nd leg. Khartoum, 13-12-1992

EL HILAL 0
WYDAD AC CASABLANCA 0

CAF CUP

FIRST ROUND

Shooting Stars (NGA) Bye
Djoliba (MLI) 2-1 0-1 **USCB** (BFA)
Diamant Yaoundé (CMR) 2-0 1-1 ASCOT (CHD)
Mbongo Sports (ZAI) 3-0 2-0 Pep. African Stars (NAM)
ASM Oran (ALG) 4-0 1-2 Air Mauritanie (MTN)
Al Wahda (LBY) 1-0 2-2 Al Mourada (SDN)
Ndiambour (SEN) 0-0 0-0 5-4p East End Lions (SLE)

CA Bizerte (TUN) 3-0 1-1 Zumunta (NIG)
Linare (LSO) 0-0 0-4 **Ferroviario Maputo** (MOZ)
Esperança Sagrada (AGO) W-O Mufulira Wanderers (ZAM)
Etoile du Congo (COG) 5-0 0-1 Desportivo Mongomo (EQG)
AS Gagnoa (CIV) 3-0 0-1 Petroca
AS Kaloum Stars (GUI) 3-0 1-5 **ASMO** (GAB)
Real Tamale (GHA) 1-0 0-1 5-6p **Dragons de l'Oueme** (BEN)
Kisumu Postal (KEN) 2-1 2-0 Small Simba (TAN)
Nakivubo Villa (UGA) 3-1 2-1 Moneni Pirates (SWZ)

SECOND ROUND

USCB 1-1 0-3 **Shooting Stars**
Mbongo Sports 0-0 1-1 Diamant Yaoundé
ASM Oran 3-0 1-3 El Wahda
Ndiambour 1-0 1-4 **CA Bizerte**
Ferroviario Maputo 3-2 2-3 5-4p Esperança Sagrada
AS Gagnoa 2-0 1-0 Etoile du Congo
Dragons de l'Oueme 0-0 0-3 **ASMO**
Nakivubo Villa 1-0 1-0 Kusumu Postal

QUARTER-FINALS

Shooting Stars 1-0 0-1 4-3p Mbongo Sports
ASM Oran 0-0 0-2 **CA Bizerte**
AS Gagnoa 0-2 1-3 **Ferroviario Maputo**
Nakivubo Villa 3-1 0-1 ASMO

SEMI-FINALS

CA Bizerte 2-0 0-3 **Shooting Stars**
Ferroviario Maputo 1-1 1-1 2-4p **Nakivubo Villa**

FINAL

1st leg. Nakivubo Stadium, Kampala, 14-11-1992
NAKIVUBO VILLA 0
SHOOTING STARS 0

2nd leg. Ibadan, 28-11-1992, 50,000
SHOOTING STARS 3
NAKIVUBO VILLA 0

CUP WINNERS CUP

PRELIMINARY ROUND

Mogas 90 (BEN) 3-0 0-2 Postel 2000 (CHD)
Denver Sundowns (SWZ) 5-3 1-1 Club de Gaza (MOZ)
DR Fatima (CTA) 3-0 1-1 Atletico Malabo (EQG)
Ports Authority (SLE) 3-0 0-1 Douanes (MTN)
Center Chiefs (BWA) W-O Chief Santos (NAM)
Railways SC (TAN) 1-0 0-1 3-2p Matlama (LSO)

FIRST ROUND

Ports Authority (SLE) 2-2 0-4 **Africa Sports** (CIV)
AS Mande (MLI) 2-0 0-5 **USM Bel Abbes** (ALG)
Denver Sundowns (SWZ) 1-3 1-3 **Kabwe Warriors** (ZAM)
AFC Leopards (KEN) 2-1 0-2 **Al Ahly** (EGY)
Mogas 90 (BEN) 0-0 1-1 ES Sahel (TUN)
Diaraf Dakar (SEN) 0-1 2-2 **ASFAG** (GUI)
Invincible Eleven (LBR) 0-2 1-0 **Great Olympics** (GHA)
Petro Atletico (AGO) 1-0 0-1 3-4p **DC Motema Pembe** (ZAI)
Al Merreikh (SDN) 1-0 1-1 Express FC (UGA)
Railways SC (TAN) W-O Highlanders (ZIM)
USM (GAB) 2-0 0-0 ASFA Yennega (BFA)
Olympic FC (NIG) 1-0 0-0 Al Ahly Benghazi (LBY)
DR Fatima (CTA) 1-0 0-0 Tonnerre Yaoundé (CMR)
Elecsport (COG) 2-0 0-1 El Kanemi Warriors (NGA)
Centre Chiefs (BWA) 0-2 0-4 **Power Dynamos** (ZAM)
Vital'O (BDI) 2-0 0-2 4-3p BTM (MDG)

SECOND ROUND

Africa Sports 5-1 1-1 USM Bel Abbes
Kabwe Warriors 1-0 0-1 3-4p **Al Ahly**
Mogas 90 3-1 0-1 ASFAG
DC Motema Pembe 4-2 0-1 Great Olympics
Railways SC 2-1 1-3 **Al Merreikh**
Olympic FC 3-2 0-1 **USM**
Elecsport 1-0 1-4 **DR Fatima**
Vital'O W-O Power Dynamos

QUARTER-FINALS

Al Ahly 2-0 0-3 **Africa Sports**
Mogas 90 0-0 0-3 **DC Motema Pembe**
Al Merreikh 3-0 1-2 USM
DR Fatima 0-0 1-2 **Vital'O**

SEMI-FINALS

Africa Sports 4-2 1-1 DC Motema Pembe
Al Merreikh 1-0 2-4 **Vital'O**

FINAL

1st leg. Bujumbura, 22-11-1992
VITAL'O 1
AFRICA SPORTS 1

2nd leg. Houphet-Boigny, Abidjan, 6-12-1992
AFRICA SPORTS 4
VITAL'O 0

SUPER CUP

Houphet-Boigny, Abidjan, 10-01-1993, 40,000
AFRICA SPORTS 2
WAC CASABLANCA 2
Africa Sports won 5-3 on penalties

1993

CHAMPIONS CUP

PRELIMINARY ROUND

St. George (ETH) 1-1 0-1 **Malindi** (TAN)
LCS Gunners (BWA) 0-1 0-5 **Kaiser Chiefs** (RSA)
Kiyovu Sport (RWA) W-O Bata Bullets (MWI)
Matlama (LSO) 2-1 1-3 **Sunrise SC** (MUS)
Costa do Sol (MOZ) 2-1 0-0 Ramblers (NAM)
Mbabane Highlanders (SWZ) 0-1 0-2 **AC Sotema** (MDG)
Etoile Filante (BFA) W-O Sporting Clube Bissau (GNB)
Djoliba (MLI) 1-0 1-1 ASC Sonader (MTN)
LPRC Oilers (LBR) W-O Etoile Filante (TGO)
Akonangui (EQG) 1-2 0-2 **TP USCA** (CTA)
Primeiro de Agosto (AGO) W-O Buffles de Borgou (BEN)
ASC Ndiambour (SEN) 1-1 2-1? Mindelense (CPV)
Sahel SC (NIG) 2-0 2-0 Elect Sport (CHD)

FIRST ROUND

Malindi (TAN) 0-1 0-4 **Zamalek** (EGY)
Kiyovu Sports (RWA) 2-5 1-4 **Kaizer Chiefs** (RSA)
Primeiro de Agosto (AGO) 2-2 0-2 **Racing Bafoussam** (CMR)
Etoile Filante (BFA) 1-0 0-2 **Mouloudia d'Oran** (ALG)
AS Sogara (GAB) 2-0 0-0 Etoile du Congo (COG)
Club Africain (TUN) W-O LPRC Oilers (LBR)
ASC Ndiamdour (SEN) 2-1 1-3 **WAC Casablanca** (MOR)
TP USCA (CTA) 1-3 2-2 **Stationery Stores** (NGA)
Djoliba (MLI) 1-1 0-2 **ASEC Abidjan** (CIV)
Costa do Sol (MOZ) W-O Union Bilombe (ZAI)
AC Sotema (MDG) W-O Black Aces (ZIM)
Nakivubo Villa (UGA) 1-0 1-2 Vital'O (BDI)
AFC Leopards (KEN) 1-1 0-1 **Nkana Red Devils** (ZAM)
Sunrise SC (MUS) 2-0 1-0 Al Hilal (SDN)

KAC Marrakech (MOR) 5-0 0-1 Horoya AC (GUI)
Sahel SC (NIG) 0-0 0-2 **Asante Kotoko** (GHA)

SECOND ROUND

Kaizer Chiefs 2-1 0-1 **Zamalek**
Racing Bafoussam 1-0 0-2 **Mouloudia d'Oran**
AS Sogara 1-0 2-2 Club Africain
WAC Casablanca 3-1 1-4 **Stationery Stores**
ASEC Abidjan 2-0 1-1 Costa do Sol
AC Sotema 0-2 2-6 **Nakivubo Villa**
Nkana Red Devils 0-0 1-1 Sunrise SC
Asante Kotoko 3-0 0-1 KAC Marrakesh

QUARTER-FINALS

Zamalek 4-0 1-1 Mouloudia d'Oran
AS Sogara 3-2 0-1 **Stationery Stores**
Nakivubo Villa 1-1 * **ASEC Abidjan**
Nkana Red Devils 1-0 0-3 **Asante Kotoko**
*Nakivubo withdrew

SEMI-FINALS

Zamalek 3-1 0-1 Stationery Stores
ASEC Abidjan 3-1 0-2 **Asante Kotoko**

FINAL

1st leg. Kumasi Stadium, Kumasi
ASANTE KOTOKO 0
ZAMALEK 0

2nd leg. International Stadium, Cairo, 10-12-1993
ZAMALEK 0
ASANTE KOTOKO 0
Zamalek won 7-6 on penalties

CAF CUP

PRELIMINARY ROUND

Insurance FC (ETH) 2-1 1-1 Rayon Sports (RWA)
Desportes Travadores (CPV) 0-0 0-0 5-6p **ASC Air Mauritanie** (MTN)
Entente II (TGO) W-O UDIB (GNB)
Tourbillon (CHD) 1-1 3-2 Fatima (CTA)
Linare (LSO) 1-1 2-4 **Young Ones** (NAM)

FIRST ROUND

Stella Club (CIV) W-O Kambui Eagles (SLE)
Shooting Stars (NGA) 2-1 0-1 **Segui de Kayes** (MLI)
Petrosport (COG) 3-0 0-1 Requins de l'Atlantique (BEN)
Entente II (TGO) 0-3 2-2 **Mbilinga** (GAB)
Zumunta (NIG) 1-1 2-0 ASFA Yennega (BFA)
ASC Air Mauritanie (MTN) 0-1 3-1 ASFAG (GUI)
Young Ones (NAM) W-O Profund Warriors (ZAM)
Insurance FC (ETH) 0-0 1-1 El Merreikh El Obayed (SDN)
FC Scribe (ZAI) 0-0 0-2 **Atletico Sport Aviacao** (AGO)
Tourbillon (CHD) 0-0 0-3 **Canon Yaoundé** (CMR)
MDC United (MWI) 1-1 0-6 **Hellenic** (RSA)
Coffee SC (UGA) 0-1 1-0 4-5p **Gor Mahia** (KEN)
Jeanne d'Arc (SEN) 0-0 1-6 **USM Harrach** (ALG)
FDA Forester (LBR) 0-2 1-5 **Hearts of Oak** (GHA)
Manzini Warriors (SWZ) W-O CAPS United (ZIM)
SC Simba (TAN) 0-0 1-1 Ferroviario Maputo (MOZ)

SECOND ROUND

Segui de Kayes 0-2 0-3 **Stella Club**
Mbilinga 3-0 2-0 Petrosport
Zumunta 2-0 2-1 ASC Air Mauritanie
Young Ones 2-1 0-7 **Insurance FC**
Atletico Sport Aviacao 0-0 2-0 Canon Yaoundé
Hellenic 3-1 0-2 **Gor Mahia**
Hearts of Oak 3-2 2-3 5-6p **USM Harrach**
SC Simba 1-0 1-0 Manzini Warriors

QUARTER-FINALS

Stella Club 1-1 2-2 Mbilinga
Insurance FC 2-0 0-1 Zumunta
Atletico Sport Aviacao 0-0 0-0 4-2p Gor Mahia
SC Simba 3-0 0-2 USM Harrach

SEMI-FINALS

Stella Club 3-0 0-1 Insurance FC
SC Simba 3-1 0-0 Atletico Sport Aviacao

FINAL

1st leg. Stade Houphet Boigny, Abidjan
STELLA CLUB ABIDJAN 0
SC SIMBA 0

2nd leg. Dar es Salaam
SC SIMBA 0
STELLA CLUB ABIDJAN 2

CUP WINNERS CUP

PRELIMINARY ROUND

Liverpool (NAM) 1-1 1-0 GF Tafic FC (BWA)
Jomo Cosmos (RSA) 1-0 6-0 Denver Sundowns (SWZ)
Silver Strikers (MWI) 0-2 1-2 **Arsenal** (LSO)
Pamba SC (TAN) 0-1 2-1 Mukura Victory (RWA)
Tempete Mocaf (CTA) 1-2 1-1 **Petro Atletico** (AGO)
ASC SNIM-SEM (MTN) W-O Benfica (GNB)
Semassi Sokode (TGO) W-O Diamond Stars (SLE)
Gazelle (CHD) 1-0 0-2 **El Nguema** (EQG)
Hafia FC Conakry (GUI) 2-0 0-1 Stade Malien (MLI)

FIRST ROUND

Al Ahly (EGY) 5-0 0-0 Pamba SC (TAN)
Clube de Gaza (MOZ) 2-2 1-1 **Arsenal** (LSO)
Wankie FC (ZIM) 0-2 1-1 **Kenya Breweries** (KEN)
El Merreikh (SDN) 3-0 0-2 Express FC (UGA)
Stade Tunisien (TUN) 1-0 0-0 Hafia FC Conakry (GUI)
Voradep FC (GHA) 0-0 0-1 **US Goree** (SEN)
Olympic Mvolyé (CMR) 1-0 0-0 RC Kadiogo (BFA)
El Kanemi Warriors (NGA) 4-0 0-0 El Nguema (EQG)
COSFAP (MDG) 0-2 2-3 **Jomo Cosmos** (RSA)
Kabwe Warriors (ZAM) 2-1 1-1* **Prince Louis** (BDI)
CARA Brazzaville (COG) 1-0 1-3 **Petro Atletico** (AGO)
DC Motema Pembe (ZAI) 6-1 ** Liverpool (NAM)
JS Kabylie (ALG) 8-1 3-1 ASC SNIM-SEM (MTN)
Dragons de l'Ouème (BEN) 4-0 2-2 Olympic FC (NIG)
Delta (GAB) 1-0 0-2 **Semassi Sokodé** (TGO)
Africa Sports (CIV) W-O NPA Anchors (LBR)
*Second game abandoned. Kabwe disqualified
**Liverpool disqualified

SECOND ROUND

Arsenal 0-1 0-1 **Al Ahly**
Kenya Breweries 1-1 0-1 **El Merreikh**
Stade Tunisien 2-0 0-1 US Goree
El Kanemi Warriors 4-0 0-3 Olympic Mvolyé
Prince Louis 3-3 0-4 **Jomo Cosmos**
DC Motema Pembe 0-0 2-2 Petro Atletico
JS Kabylie 4-0 0-3 Dragons de l'Ouème
Africa Sports 4-0 3-0 Semassi Sokodé

QUARTER-FINALS

El Merreikh 1-2 1-5 **Al Ahly**
El Kanemi Warriors 1-0 1-1 Stade Tunisien
DC Motema Pembe 2-1 0-1 **Jomo Cosmos**
Africa Sports 4-0 0-1 JS Kabylie

SEMI-FINALS

Al Ahly 3-0 0-0 El Kanemi Warriors
Jomo Cosmos 1-1 0-4 **Africa Sports**

FINAL

1st leg. Stade Houphet Boigny, Abidjan

AFRICA SPORTS 1
AL AHLY 1

2nd leg. International Stadium, Cairo, 3-12-1993

AL AHLY 1
AFRICA SPORTS 0

SUPER CUP

FNB Stadium, Johannesburg, 16-01-1994, 28,000

ZAMALEK 1
AL AHLY 0

1994

CHAMPIONS CUP

PRELIMINARY ROUND

Saint Pierroise (REU)...........4-0 2-2 ....Mbabene Swallows (SWZ)
Lobatse Gunners (BWA)....2-0 3-3 ....Chief Santos (NAM)
Electric (ETH) ....3-2 2-2.............Kiyovu Sports (RWA)
ASC Sonader (MTN) ....2-0 0-0 ....Academia do Sol (CPV)
Postel 2000 (CHD) ....0-1 0-2 **AS Tempete Mocaf** (CTA)
Mighty Barolle (LBR) ....W-O ....Semassi Sokode (TGO)

FIRST ROUND

Esperance Tunis (TUN) ....3-2 5-0 ....Etoile Filante (BFA)
East End Lions (SLE).............0-2 2-0 2-3p ....**Stade Malien** (MLI)
Racing Bafoussam (CMR) ......Bye
Iwuanyanwu Nationale.......3-1 3-0 ....Zumunta (NIG) (NGA)
AS Vita Club (ZAI)................1-1 5-0.......Lobatse Gunners (BWA)
Arsenal (LSO)............................0-1 1-4 ....**Mamelodi Sundowns** (RSA)
Kaloum Stars (GUI)...................0-3 1-0 **AS Tempete Mocaf** (CTA)
Mouloudia d'Oran (ALG)....0-2 4-0 ....ASC Sonader (MTN)
Nkana Red Devils (ZAM) ....Bye
Costa do Sol (MOZ).............2-3 2-0 ....Saint Pierroise (REU)
Fire Brigade (MUS) ....1-2 1-1 ....**BTM** (MDG)
Al Merreikh (SDN)....................0-1 0-1 ....**Simba** (TAN)
Petro Atletico (AGO)................1-2 0-0 ....**AS Sogara** (GAB)
Wydad AC Casablanca (MOR) ....0-2 6-1 Semassi Sokode (TGO)
Gor Mahia (KEN)...................1-3 2-0............................Electric (ETH)
Zamalek (EGY) ....W-O ....Express FC (UGA)

SECOND ROUND

Stade Malien ....0-1 0-3...................**Esperance Tunis**
Iwuanyanwu Nationale.......1-2 3-2.....................Racing Bafoussam
AS Vita Club............................2-1 2-3..............Mamelodi Sundowns
Mouloudia d'Oran.................7-4 3-0..........................Tempete Mocaf
Costa do Sol ....1-0 0-2 ....**Nkana Red Devils**
Simba ....1-0 0-0................................BTM
AS Sogara................................W-O ....WAC Casablanca
Gor Mahia...................................1-1 1-2.................................**Zamalek**

QUARTER-FINALS

Esperance Tunis.....................3-0 1-1 ....Iwuanyanwu Nationale
Mouloudia d'Oran...................W-O ....AS Vita Club
Nkana Red Devils..................4-1 0-2...Simba
Zamalek...................................1-0 2-2...................................AS Sogara

SEMI-FINALS

Esperance Tunis.....................3-1 2-2 ....Mouloudia d'Oran
Zamalek...................................2-0 0-1 ....Nkana Red Devils

FINAL

1st leg. International Stadium, Cairo, 4-12-1994, 90,000

ZAMALEK 0
ESPERANCE SPORTIVE TUNIS 0

2nd leg. El Menzah, Tunis, 17-12-1994, 45,000

ESPERANCE SPORTIVE TUNIS 3
ZAMALEK 1

CAF CUP

PRELIMINARY ROUND

Linare (LSO)...............................0-1 0-2 ....**Saint Denis** (REU)
Boavista FC (CPV)....................3-1 1-4 ....**Diamond Stars** (SLE)

FIRST ROUND

Stade Centrafricain (CTA).......1-4 1-2 ..**Bendel Insurance** (NGA)
Fulani (LBR)................................W-O ....Mogas 90 (BEN)
Olympic Niamey (NIG).........W-O ....Elect Sport (CHD)
Racing Club (BFA).....................1-3 2-1 ....**US Chaouia** (ALG)
AS Garde Nationale (MTN)....1-3 1-1...............**JS Kairouan** (TUN)
AS Nianan de Koulikoro ...2-0 1-1 ....Delta FC (GAB) (MLI)
Gaborone United (BWA) ....0-2 1-0**Ferroviaro Maputo** (MOZ)
Saint Denis (REU).......................Bye
Coffee Marketing (ETH)...........0-4 2-1 ....**Al Mourada** (SDN)
Young Africans (TAN)...............0-2 1-0 ....**Moroka Swallows** (RSA)
Diamond Stars (SLE)........0-1 1-0 4-3p.......................Kamsar (GUI)
Gomido (TGO) ....0-3 0-0......**Unisport Bafang** (CMR)
AFC Leopards (KEN) ....W-O...............Nakivubo Villa (UGA)
Moneni Pirates (SWZ)............Bye
AS Bantous (ZAI)...................2-1 1-0 ....Mukura Victory (RWA)
Primeiro de Maio (AGO)......W-O ....Young Ones (NAM)

SECOND ROUND

Bendel Insurance.....................W-O ....Fulani
US Chaouia ....6-0 * ....Olympic Niamey
JS Kairouan ....3-1 1-3 6-5p ....AS Nianan de Koulikoro
Saint Denis ....1-0 2-2..........................Ferroviaro Maputo
Moroka Swallows.......................0-0 1-2...............................**El Mourada**
Diamond Stars ....2-1 2-0 ....Unisport Bafang
AFC Leopards.........................2-0 1-0 ....Moneni Pirates
Primeiro de Maio ....5-1 2-4 ....AS Bantous
*Olympic withdrew after first leg

QUARTER-FINALS

Bendel Insurance.............1-0 0-1 4-2p............................US Chaouia
Saint Denis ....5-3 0-1 ....JS Kairouan
El Mourada ....W-O ....Diamond Stars
AFC Leopards..............................2-1 0-1 ....**Primeiro de Maio**

SEMI-FINALS

Saint Denis...................................1-0 1-4.................**Bendel Insurance**
El Mourada ....0-0 3-5 ....**Primeiro de Maio**

FINAL

1st leg. Citadela, Luanda, 20-11-1995

PRIMEIRO DE MAIO 1
BENDEL INSURANCE 0

2nd leg. National Stadium, Benin City, 4-12-1994, 40,000

BENDEL INSURANCE 3
PRIMEIRO DE MAIO 0

CUP WINNERS CUP

PRELIMINARY ROUND

US Tamponnaise (REU).........W-O ....AS Cimelta (MDG)

Eleven Men in Flight (SWZ)	3-1	Township Rollers (BWA)

FIRST ROUND

DC Motema Pembe (ZAI)	0-2 2-0 5-4p	Anges de Fatima (CTA)
Mighty Blackpool (SLE)	W-O	Postel (BEN)
Djoliba AC (MLI)	0-2 0-0	**MA Hussein Dey** (ALG)
BCC Lions (NGA)	0-0 2-1	ASFB (BFA)
Olympic de Beja (TUN)	0-1 3-0	Sahel SC (NIG)
St. George (ETH)	W-O	Al Ahly Cairo (EGY)
Canon Yaoundé (CMR)	0-1 2-0	ASA (AGO)
Hafia Conakry (GUI)	0-3 1-3	**Agaza Lomé** (TGO)
Mbilinga (GAB)	13-0	Renaissance (CHD)
LPRC Oilers (LBR)	W-O	AS Snim-Sem (MTN)
Eleven Men in Flight (SWZ)	Bye	
Malindi (TAN)	W-O	Kamapala CC (UGA)
US Tamponnaise (REU)	Bye	
Total Aces (RSA)	2-1 6-1	Bantu (LSO)
Al Hilal (SDN)	1-4 1-0	**Rayon Sports** (RWA)
Kenya Breweries (KEN)	3-1 2-0	Ferroviaro de Beira (MOZ)

SECOND ROUND

DC Motema Pembe	3-0 0-2	Mighty Blackpool
BCC Lions	2-0 2-0	MA Hussein Dey
St. George	2-0 0-3	**Olympic de Beja**
Agaza Lomé	W-O	Canon Yaoundé
Mbilinga	W-O	LPRC Oilers
Malindi	1-0 1-0	Eleven Men in Flight
Total Aces	1-0 2-4	**US Tamponnaise**
Kenya Breweries	W-O	Rayon Sports

QUARTER-FINALS

BCC Lions	2-1 2-4	**DC Motema Pembe**
Agaza Lomé	6-1 1-4	Olympic de Beja
Mbilinga	4-0 0-1	Malindi
Kenya Breweries	1-0 1-1	US Tamponnaise

SEMI-FINALS

DC Motema Pembe	3-1 1-1	Agaza Lomé
Mbilinga	1-1 3-5	**Kenya Breweries**

FINAL

1st leg. Stade 20 Mai, Kinshasa, 27-11-1994

DARING CLUB MOTEMA PEMBE	2
KENYA BREWERIES	2

2nd leg. Nyayo Stadium, Nairobi, 10-12-1994, 28,000

KENYA BREWERIES	0
DARING CLUB MOTEMA PEMBE	3

SUPER CUP

Alexandria, 20-01-1995

ESPERANCE SPORTIVE TUNIS	3
DARING CLUB MOTEMA PEMBE	0

COMBINED AFRICAN CLUB COMPETITIONS

	Team	Country	G	S	B
1	Al Ahly Cairo	EGY	6	1	2
2	Canon Yaoundé	CMR	4	2	2
3	TP Mazembe	ZAI	3	2	1
4	Hafia FC Conakry	GUI	3	2	-
5	Zamalek	EGY	3	1	2
6	Asante Kotoko	GHA	2	5	3
7	Shooting Stars	NGA	2	1	1
8	Al Mokaouloum	EGY	2	-	1
	JS Kabylie	ALG	2	-	1
	Union Douala	CMR	2	-	1
11	Africa Sports	CIV	1	3	-
12	Enugu Rangers	NGA	1	1	3
13	Bendel Insurance	NGA	1	1	2
	AS Vita Club Kinshasa	ZAI	1	1	2
15	Gor Mahia	KEN	1	1	1
	Tonnerre Yaoundé	CMR	1	1	1
17	BCC Lions	NGA	1	1	-
	Club Africain	TUN	1	1	-
	Esperance Tunis	TUN	1	1	-
	Power Dynamos	ZAM	1	1	-
	Stella Abidjan	CIV	1	1	-
22	Al Ismaili	EGY	1	-	3
23	FAR Rabat	MOR	1	-	2
	Horoya AC Conakry	GUI	1	-	2
	Al Merreikh	SDN	1	-	2
26	Oryx Douala	CMR	1	-	1
	Entente Setif	ALG	1	-	1
	CA Bizerte	TUN	1	-	1
	Daring Club Motema Pembe	ZAI	1	-	1
31	CARA Brazzaville	COG	1	-	-
	Mouloudia d'Algiers	ALG	1	-	-
	Raja Casablanca	MOR	1	-	-
	Stade Abidjan	CIV	1	-	-
	WAC Casablanca	MOR	1	-	-
36	Hearts of Oak	GHA	-	2	2
37	Al Hilal	SDN	-	2	1
38	AS Bilima	ZAI	-	2	-
	Nakivubo Villa	UGA	-	2	-
40	Nkana Red Devils	ZAM	-	1	5
41	Iwuanyanwu Owerri	NGA	-	1	2
42	Kenya Breweries	KEN	-	1	1
	NA Hussein-Dey	ALG	-	1	1
	Mehalla Al Kubra	EGY	-	1	1
	Agaza Lomé	TGO	-	1	1
	Moulodia d'Oran	ALG	-	1	1
	SC Simba	TAN	-	1	1
	Stationery Stores	NGA	-	1	1
49	Etoile Filante	TGO	-	1	-
	Leventis United	NGA	-	1	-
	Primeiro de Maio	AGO	-	1	-
	Ranchers Bees	NGA	-	1	-
	AS Real Bamako	MLI	-	1	-
	Simba FC	UGA	-	1	-
	AS Sogara	GAB	-	1	-
	Stade Malien	MLI	-	1	-
	Vital'O	BDI	-	1	-
58	ASEC Abidjan	CIV	-	-	5
59	Djoliba AC	MLI	-	-	3
	Mufulira Wanderers	ZAM	-	-	3
	US Goree	SEN	-	-	2
	ASC Jeanne d'Arc	SEN	-	-	2
	Kadiogo	BFA	-	-	2
	AS Kaloum Star	GUI	-	-	2
	AFC Leopards	KEN	-	-	2
	Lomé I	TGO	-	-	2
67	Abiola Babes	NGA	-	-	1
	Atletico Sport Aviacao	AGO	-	-	1
	BFV FC	MDG	-	-	1
	Cotton Club	ETH	-	-	1
	Diamant Yaoundé	CMR	-	-	1
	ASC Diaraf	SEN	-	-	1
	Dragons de l'Ouème	BEN	-	-	1
	Al Ahly Tripoli	LBY	-	-	1
	Al Ittihad	EGY	-	-	1
	Al Nasr	LBY	-	-	1
	Ferroviarrio Maputo	MOZ	-	-	1
	Great Olympics	GHA	-	-	1
	CS Hammam-Lif	TUN	-	-	1
	CS Imana	ZAI	-	-	1
	Insurance	ETH	-	-	1
	Inter Club	COG	-	-	1

	Team	Country	G	S	B
	Inter Star	BDI	-	-	1
	Jomo Cosmos	RSA	-	-	1
	Kakimbo FC	GUI	-	-	1
	El Kanemi Warriors	NGA	-	-	1
	Leopard Douala	CMR	-	-	1
	FC Lupopo	ZAI	-	-	1
	Desportivo Maputo	MOZ	-	-	1
	Mbilinga	GAB	-	-	1
	El Mourada	SDN	-	-	1
	Real Republicans	GHA	-	-	1
	Saint Denis	REU	-	-	1
	St. Georges	ETH	-	-	1
	Sekondi Hasaacas	GHA	-	-	1
	Semassi Sokode	TGO	-	-	1

COUNTRY RECORDS IN THE COMBINED AFRICAN CLUB COMPETITIONS

	Country	G	S	B	Finals	S-Finals
1	Egypt	12	3	10	15	25
2	Cameroon	8	3	9	11	20
3	Nigeria	5	8	9	13	22
4	Zaire	5	5	6	10	16
5	Guinea	4	2	5	6	11
6	Algeria	4	2	4	6	10
7	Côte d'Ivoire	3	4	5	7	12
8	Morocco	3	-	2	3	5
9	Tunisia	3	2	2	5	7
10	Ghana	2	7	8	9	17
11	Zambia	1	2	8	3	11
12	Sudan	1	2	4	3	7
	Kenya	1	2	4	3	7
14	Congo	1	-	1	1	2
15	Uganda	-	3	-	3	3
16	Togo	-	2	4	2	6
17	Mali	-	2	3	2	5
18	Angola	-	1	1	1	2
	Burundi	-	1	1	1	2
	Tanzania	-	1	1	1	2
	Gabon	-	1	1	1	2
22	Senegal	-	-	5	-	5
23	Ethiopia	-	-	3	-	3
24	Burkina Faso	-	-	2	-	2
	Libya	-	-	2	-	2
	Mozambique	-	-	2	-	2
	Benin	-	-	1	-	1
	Madagascar	-	-	1	-	1
	Reunion	-	-	1	-	1
	South Africa	-	-	1	-	1

CHAMPIONS CUP MEDALS TABLE

	Team	Country	G	S	B
1	Hafia FC Conakry	GUI	3	2	-
2	Canon Yaoundé	CMR	3	-	2
3	Zamalek	EGY	3	1	1
4	Asante Kotoko	GHA	2	5	3
5	TP Mazembe	ZAI	2	2	1
6	Al Ahly Cairo	EGY	2	1	2
7	JS Kabylie	ALG	2	-	1
8	AS Vita Club Kinshasa	ZAI	1	1	1
9	FAR Rabat	MOR	1	-	2
	Al Ismaili	EGY	1	-	2
11	Oryx Douala	CMR	1	-	1
	Union Douala	CMR	1	-	1
13	CARA Brazzaville	COG	1	-	-
	Mouloudia d'Algiers	ALG	1	-	-
	Raja Casablanca	MOR	1	-	-
	Club Africain	TUN	1	-	-
	Esperance Tunis	TUN	1	-	-
	Entente Setif	ALG	1	-	-
	Stade Abidjan	CIV	1	-	-
	WAC Casablanca	MOR	1	-	-
21	Hearts of Oak	GHA	-	2	1
	Al Hilal	SDN	-	2	1
23	AS Bilima	ZAI	-	2	-
24	Nkana Red Devils	ZAM	-	1	5
25	Enugu Rangers	NGA	-	1	3
26	Iwuanyanwu Owerri	NGA	-	1	2
27	Mehalla Al Kubra	EGY	-	1	1
	Mouloudia d'Oran	ALG	-	1	1
29	Africa Sports	CIV	-	1	-
	Etoile Filante	TGO	-	1	-
	Nakivubo Villa	UGA	-	1	-
	AS Real Bamako	MLI	-	1	-
	Shooting Stars	NGA	-	1	-
	Simba FC	UGA	-	1	-
	Stade Malien	MLI	-	1	-
36	ASEC Abidjan	CIV	-	-	4
37	US Goree	SEN	-	-	2
	AS Kaloum Star	GUI	-	-	2
	Lomé I	TGO	-	-	2
40	Bendel Insurance	NGA	-	-	1
	Kenya Breweries	KEN	-	-	1
	Cotton Club	ETH	-	-	1
	ASC Diaraf	SEN	-	-	1
	Djoliba AC	MLI	-	-	1
	Great Olympics	GHA	-	-	1
	CS Imana	ZAI	-	-	1
	ASC Jeanne d'Arc	SEN	-	-	1
	Kakimbo FC	GUI	-	-	1
	AFC Leopards	KEN	-	-	1
	Leopard Douala	CMR	-	-	1
	FC Lupopo	ZAI	-	-	1
	Mufulira Wanderers	ZAM	-	-	1
	Real Republicans	GHA	-	-	1
	St. Georges	ETH	-	-	1
	Semassi Sokode	TGO	-	-	1
	SC Simba	TAN	-	-	1
	Stationery Stores	NGA	-	-	1
	Tonnerre Yaoundé	CMR	-	-	1

CHAMPIONS CUP BY COUNTRY

	Country	G	S	B	Finals	S-Finals
1	Egypt	6	3	6	9	15
2	Cameroon	5	-	6	5	11
3	Algeria	4	1	2	5	7
4	Zaire	3	5	4	8	12
5	Guinea	3	2	3	5	8
6	Morocco	3	-	2	3	5
7	Ghana	2	7	6	9	15
8	Tunisia	2	-	-	2	2
9	Côte d'Ivoire	1	1	4	2	6
10	Congo	1	-	-	1	1
11	Nigeria	-	3	7	3	10
12	Mali	-	2	1	2	3
	Sudan	-	2	1	2	3
14	Uganda	-	2	-	2	2
15	Zambia	-	1	6	1	7
16	Togo	-	1	3	1	4
17	Senegal	-	-	4	-	4
18	Ethiopia	-	-	2	-	2
	Kenya	-	-	2	-	2
20	Tanzania	-	-	1	-	1

CUP WINNERS CUP MEDALS TABLE

	Team	Country	G	S	B
1	Al Ahly Cairo	EGY	4	-	-
2	Al Mokaoulum	EGY	2	-	1
3	Africa Sports	CIV	1	2	-
	Canon Yaoundé	CMR	1	2	-
5	Gor Mahia	KEN	1	1	1
	BCC Lions	NGA	1	1	-
	Power Dynamos	ZAM	1	1	-
	Tonnerre Yaoundé	CMR	1	1	-
9	Horoya AC Conakry	GUI	1	-	2
	Al Merreikh	SDN	1	-	2
11	Daring Club				
	Motema Pembe	ZAI	1	-	1
	Shooting Stars	NGA	1	-	1
13	CA Bizerte	TUN	1	-	-
	Enugu Rangers	NGA	1	-	-
	TP Mazembe	ZAI	1	-	-
	Union Douala	CMR	1	-	-
17	NA Hussein-Dey	ALG	-	1	1
	Agaza Lomé	TGO	-	1	1
	Bendel Insurance	NGA	-	1	1
20	Club Africain	TUN	-	1	-
	Kenya Breweries	KEN	-	1	-
	Leventis United	NGA	-	1	-
	Ranchers Bees	NGA-	1	-	
	AS Sogara	GAB	-	1	-
	Stationery Stores	NGA	-	1	-
	Stella Abidjan	CIV	-	1	-
	Esperance Tunis	TUN	-	1	-
	Vital'O	BDI	-	1	-
29	Djoliba AC	MLI	-	-	2
	Kadiogo	BFA	-	-	2
	Mufulira Wanderers	ZAM	-	-	2
32	Abiola Babes	NGA	-	-	1
	ASEC Abidjan	CIV	-	-	1
	BFV FC	MDG	-	-	1
	Diamant Yaoundé	CMR	-	-	1
	Dragons de l'Ouème	BEN	-	-	1
	Al Ahly Tripoli	LBY	-	-	1
	Al Ittihad	EGY	-	-	1
	Al Nasr	LBY	-	-	1
	CS Hammam-Lif	TUN	-	-	1
	Hearts of Oak	GHA	-	-	1
	Inter Club	COG	-	-	1
	Inter Star	BDI	-	-	1
	Al Ismaili	EGY	-	-	1
	ASC Jeanne d'Arc	SEN	-	-	1
	Jomos Cosmos	RSA	-	-	1
	El Kanemi Warriors	NGA	-	-	1
	AFC Leopards	KEN	-	-	1
	Desportivo Maputo	MOZ	-	-	1
	Mbilinga	GAB	-	-	1
	Sekondi Hasaacas	GHA	-	-	1
	Entente Setif	ALG	-	-	1
	AS Vita Club				
	Kinshasa	ZAI	-	-	1
	Zamalek	EGY	-	-	1

CUP WINNERS CUP BY COUNTRY

	Country	G	S	B	Finals	S-Finals
1	Egypt	6	-	4	6	10
2	Nigeria	3	5	4	8	12
3	Cameroon	3	3	1	6	7
4	Zaire	2	-	2	2	4
5	Côte d'Ivoire	1	3	1	4	5
6	Kenya	1	2	2	3	5
7	Tunisia	1	2	1	3	4
8	Zambia	1	1	2	2	4
9	Guinea	1	-	2	1	3
	Sudan	1	-	2	1	3
11	Algeria	-	1	2	1	3
12	Burundi	-	1	1	1	2
	Gabon	-	1	1	1	2
	Togo	-	1	1	1	2
15	Burkina Faso	-	-	2	-	2
	Ghana	-	-	2	-	2
	Libya	-	-	2	-	2
	Mali	-	-	2	-	2
19	Benin	-	-	1	-	1
	Congo	-	-	1	-	1
	Madagascar	-	-	1	-	1
	Mozambique	-	-	1	-	1
	Senegal	-	-	1	-	1
	South Africa	-	-	1	-	1

CAF CUP MEDALS TABLE

	Team	Country	G	S	B
1	Bendel Insurance	NGA	1	-	-
	Shooting Stars	NGA	1	-	-
	Stella Club Abidjan	CIV	1	-	-
4	Nakivubo Villa	UGA	-	1	-
	Primeiro de Maio	AGO	-	1	-
	Simba SC	TAN	-	1	-
7	CA Bizerte	TUN	-	-	1
	Ferroviarrio	MOZ	-	-	1
	Insurance	ETH	-	-	1
	Atletico Sport				
	Aviacao	AGO	-	-	1
	Saint Denis	REU	-	-	1
	El Mourada	SDN	-	-	1

CAF CUP BY COUNTRY

	Country	G	S	B	Finals	S-Finals
1	Nigeria	2	-	-	2	2
2	Côte d'Ivoire	1	-	-	1	1
3	Angola	-	1	1	1	2
4	Tanzania	-	1	-	1	1
	Uganda	-	1	-	1	1
6	Ethiopia	-	-	1	-	1
	Mozambique	-	-	1	-	1
	Reunion	-	-	1	-	1
	Sudan	-	-	1	-	1
	Tunisia	-	-	1	-	1

To the end of the 1994 tournaments

REGIONAL TOURNAMENTS IN AFRICA

Because of the huge size of the continent, regional tournaments have always been popular in Africa. The African Football Confederation divides its members up into five groupings based on geographical and historical links, and the five controlling bodies organise the tournaments under their jurisdiction. The only exception to this is North Africa, where links with the Middle East are strong and the Arab Football Union organises a Champions Cup, a Cup Winners Cup and a tournament for the national teams in which North African sides are invited to compete.

The area with the most established tournaments is East Africa, where the Gossage Cup dates back to 1927. It was there, too, that the first regional club competitions took place outside of North Africa, with the introduction of the East and Central African Club Championship in 1974. Given their lack of success at pan-African level, this tournament has proved to be a mainstay of club football in East Africa. The same could be said for the tournament for national sides; under its present format the East and Central African Senior Challenge Cup has been played since 1973, though its predecessor dates back a further eight years.

An area that is just developing is Southern Africa. Due to the political difficulties in the region, Malawi, Zambia and Zimbabwe have historically been part of the East African body. With the new regime in South Africa, however the trio have joined the potentially powerful Southern African Football Confederation, though they have yet to play anything other than youth tournaments.

The weakest of the regional bodies is the Central African Association, with the UDEAC tournament for national sides being the only regular competition it organises. The West African Football Union has perhaps the biggest task of them all, with more members than any other and a large area under its control. Tournaments for the national sides are sub-divided into even smaller regions, although the West African Club Championship is open to everyone. It is a very prestigious tournament and has been held every year since 1977.

THE REGIONAL FEDERATIONS

Confederation of Southern African Football Associations
PO Box 1396
Gaborone
Botswana
Founded: 1982

Union of Football Associations of Central Africa
BP 1363
Yaoundé
Cameroon
Founded: 1979

Confederation of East and Central African Football Associations
PO Box 49295
Nairobi
Kenya
Founded: 1970

West African Football Union
BP V 307
Abidjan
Côte d'Ivoire
Founded: 1975

Arab Football Union
PO Box 5844
Riyadh
Saudi Arabia
Year of formation: 1974

NORTH AFRICA

North Africa has for many years been the closest link the rest of the world has had with African football. Their leagues are among the oldest on the continent, their national teams have been playing longer, and in players like Larbi Ben Barek, Just Fontaine and Rachid Mekhloufi, North Africa provided Europe with some fine players even before the flood gates opened in the 1970s. Proximity to Europe has also been a telling factor in the organisation of football in Egypt, Libya, Algeria, Morocco and Tunisia, the countries which make up the region. Egypt entered the 1920 Olympic Games and featured regularly in competitions before the Second World War, whilst French North Africa, though excluded from international competition, had a lively domestic scene.

Egypt was the first African country to join FIFA, two years after the founding of its football association in 1921, and as the only independent nation on the continent, apart from the remote Liberia, continued to be the sole African representative until Sudan joined in 1948. Few would dispute that club football in Egypt is the strongest in Africa. A year after the Egyptian Football Association was formed, the Farouk Cup was introduced and until 1949, when the national league was formed, this was the main competition. After that date it became known simply as the Cup of Egypt, and like the league it has been dominated by the clubs from Cairo, in particular Al Ahly and Zamalek.

Zamalek and Al Ahly regularly attract crowds of 100,000 to the International Stadium for matches against each other, and it is because of support like this that they have been able to prosper. On only seven occasions in its entire history has the Egyptian league been won by another team. To emphasise their superiority, between them they have won nine African club titles. Only Al Makoualoum have risen to challenge this hegemony, and they too have won an African club title.

Algeria has a good league set-up although, unlike in Egypt, the composition of clubs now differs greatly from when the league started. Algeria was the largest state in French North Africa and had three leagues operational on its territory, one based in each of Algiers, Oran and Constantine. The winners of these league and cup competitions used to take part in the North African Club Championship and the North African Cup respectively, along with their counterparts in Morocco and Tunisia, the other two states under French rule. Since independence there has only been one league in Algeria and it has produced the top team in Africa on four occasions. JS Kabylie twice, Entente Setif and Mouloudia Challia from Algiers have all won the African Cup of Champion Clubs.

Club names are prone to change in Algeria depending on the political mood. JS Kabylie for instance were known as JE Tizi-Ouzou for many years in an attempt to curb regional sentiments - Kabylie is the area of the Berbers and they were using the club to vent their feelings. Politics in Algerian football is not new; at the time of the struggle for independence, many of the great Algerian footballers of the time joined up with the FLN team which acted as a focus for anti-French feeling by touring Africa and playing matches. In 1977 a massive reorganisation was undertaken whereby all clubs were attached to a major industrial concern. Mouloudia Challia thereby became known as Mouloudia Petrioliers, as they were attached to the national oil company, though all the clubs have recently reverted to their pre-1977 names.

Nowhere in Africa can match the political interference that has taken place in Libyan football, however, as two examples serve to show. In the 1984 Cup Winners Cup, Al Ahly of Tripoli, against the odds, reached the final where they were due to meet their namesakes from Cairo. But at that time Egypt and Libya were not on good terms politically and so the Libyans refused to turn up in Cairo, forfeiting their place to Canon Yaounde. On the other hand, in a case perhaps unique in football, Libya withdrew from a qualifying tie in the 1990 World Cup against Algeria as a token of gratitude for Algerian support after the bombing of Tripoli by the United States. Quite what the capacity crowd waiting for the game to start in the Tripoli Stadium thought about such a magnanimous gesture is not known.

Both Morocco and Tunisia, the other North African countries, can lay claim to excellent club sides. Tunisia, despite its small size, won the Champions Cup with Club Africain in 1991 and Esperance in 1994, and the Cup Winners Cup in 1988 with CA Bizerte. In Morocco the network of clubs is extremely well distributed geographically, unlike most of Africa where all the big clubs tend to be located in the capital, and perhaps the second largest city. There are major clubs in all of the big Moroccan cities: Marrakech, Rabat, Casablanca, Kenitra, Oujda, Fes and Mohammedia can all boast championship-winning sides. Only three clubs, however, have gone on to win the African Cup of Champion Clubs, FAR Rabat in 1985, Raja Casablanca in 1989 and Wydad Casablanca in 1992.

It is not only with its club sides that North Africa has won renown in recent years. Morocco in 1970, 1986 and 1994, Tunisia in 1978, Algeria in 1982 and 1986, and Egypt in 1990 have all qualified for the World Cup finals. Only Cameroon, Nigeria and Zaire have managed to do the same in the whole of the rest of Africa. Once there, North Africa's representatives have invariably made their mark on the tournament. In 1970 Morocco gave the West Germans a shock in the first round before losing 2-1, and managed to hold Bulgaria to a draw. Sixteen years later in Mexico they qualified for the second round, topping their group ahead of England, Poland and Portugal before West Germany once again denied them, this time with a last-minute winner.

Tunisia had kept up the good work in 1978, beating Mexico convincingly - the first ever win by an African side in the World Cup finals - and holding West Germany to a draw, but Algeria gave perhaps the best performance of the lot in 1982 and again West Germany were involved. In a thrilling match in Gijón the Algerians, inspired by Lakdar Belloumi and Rabah Madjer, two of the finest African footballers of all time, beat the West Germans 2-1. A further victory over Chile almost assured them of a second round place, which they were denied only by a wicked piece of gamesmanship by Austria and Germany, who contrived to see all three teams finish on four points. Algeria, with the worst goal difference, lost out and went home justifiably crying 'cheat'.

Given this success in the World Cup, it is surprising that the North Africans have not done better in the Cup of Nations. Egypt have won on three occasions, but two of these were in the first two tournaments when there were only three participants. Their other victory was on home soil in 1986. Algeria did likewise in 1990, their only win to date, whilst Morocco's sole triumph came in Ethiopia in 1976.

For so long the major force in African football, there can be no doubt that the region's dominance is being eroded, with West Africa and South Africa set to challenge its position. At the 1992 Cup of Nations all three North African representatives finished bottom of their first round groups and were eliminated, leaving all eight quarter-finalists hailing from south of the Sahara, and in 1994 seven of the eight quarter-finalists were black African, even though the tournament was held in Tunisia. It may be some while, however, before North Africa can be similarly matched at club level. Unlike the rest of the continent, their best players tend to stay at home and this gives them a huge advantage.

THE NORTH AFRICAN CLUB CHAMPIONSHIP

1919	Racing Club Tunis	TUN
1920	AS Maritime Oran	ALG
1921	SC Bel Abbes Oran	ALG
1922	FC Blideen Alger	ALG
1923	SC Bel Abbes Oran	ALG
1924	SC Bel Abbes Oran	ALG
1925	SC Bel Abbes Oran	ALG
1926	SC Bel Abbes Oran	ALG
1927	Gallia Sports Alger	ALG
1928	FC Blideen Alger	ALG
1929	AS Saint Eugene Alger	ALG
1930	Club des Joyeusetes Oran	ALG
1931	US Marocaine	MOR
1932	US Marocaine	MOR
1933	US Marocaine	MOR
1934	Racing Universitaire Alger	ALG
1935	Gallia Club Oran	ALG
1936	Gallia Sports Alger	ALG
1937	Jeunesse Bône AC	ALG
1938	Racing Universitaire Constantine	ALG
1939-40	-	
1941	US Marocaine	MOR
1942-45	-	
1946	Gallia Sports Alger	ALG
1947	WAC Casablanca	MOR
1948	WAC Casablanca	MOR

1949	WAC Casablanca	MOR
1950	WAC Casablanca	MOR

THE NORTH AFRICAN CUP

1930	Club des Joyeusetes Oran	ALG
1931	Racing Universitaire Alger	ALG
1932	Club des Joyeusetes Oran	ALG
1933	Club des Joyeusetes Oran	ALG
1934	Club des Joyeusetes Oran	ALG
1935	Italia de Tunis	TUN
1936	Racing Universitaire Alger	ALG
1937	Olympique Marocaine	MOR
1938	Stade AM Casablanca	MOR
1939-45	-	
1946	US Marocaine	MOR
1947	US Athletique Casablanca	MOR
1948	WAC Casablanca	MOR
1949	AS Saint Eugene Alger	ALG

MAGHREB CHAMPIONS CUP

1970	CR Belcourt	ALG
1971	CR Belcourt	ALG
1972	CR Belcourt	ALG
1973	Etoile du Sahel	TUN
1974	Club Africain	TUN
1975	Club Africain	TUN

MAGHREB CUP WINNERS CUP

1969	RS Settat	MOR
1970	Club Africain	TUN
1971	MA Algiers	ALG
1972	SCC Mohammedia	MOR
1973	Mouloudia d'Algiers	ALG
1974	-	
1975	Etoile du Sahel	TUN

WEST AFRICA

West Africa is a patchwork of large and small nations consisting of 16 countries, although CAF sub-divides the area into a Zone A and Zone B. There are five powerful football states among these nations: Côte d'Ivoire, Guinea, Ghana, Nigeria and Senegal. The rest are by no means football outcasts, but as of yet have not proved themselves in the club tournaments or the Cup of Nations. Ghana and Nigeria are the most renowned and remain the only African countries to have won world titles at any level. Nigeria were World Under-17 champions in 1985 and 1993, whilst Ghana won the same title in 1991 and the World Youth Cup in 1993. Football came with British rule and was quick to spread through both countries. By the 1920s football was popular enough amongst the locals for leagues to be formed in many of the towns, helped along by British organisation.

In Ghana, the most famous of the teams formed around this time were Hearts of Oak (1911) of Accra, Asante Kotoko (1926) based in Kumasi and Eleven Wise (1919) in Sekondi. Due to poor communications, competitions did not take on a nationwide character until the late 1950s when a national league and cup were introduced for the first time. Instead tournaments were organised for teams in a town or region. Asante Kotoko, for instance, made their name in the Asanthene Cup where they had a great rivalry with Cornerstones of Kumasi. In Accra, the City Championship Cup was the domain of both Hearts of Oak and Steadfast.

Independence saw the creation of the Ghana Football Association, taking over from the Gold Coast Football Association which had been formed in 1922. It was responsible for the implementation of the new league and cup and for fielding a national side. Because of the head start Ghana had, they were the most successful nation in Africa in the 1960s. In an age of footballing innocence, Ghanaian footballers such as Baba Yara, Ibrahim Sunday, Robert Mensah and Wilberforce Mfum were the toast of African football, but it is a legacy that has been hard to live up to. The 'Black Stars', as the national side is known, have managed to do reasonably well, and despite some lapses and the surprising failure to qualify for a World Cup, they have remained at the forefront of the game in Africa. Nations Cup wins in 1978 and 1982 are testament to this.

Nigeria, on the other hand, have not found the task so easy. With a vast population and huge oil resources, the Nigerians were expected to be leading the pack by a long way. Unlike Ghana, however, Nigeria did not have a well-founded club structure from the beginning, and clubs are still prone to fade away. There have been no Asante Kotokos blazing a trail for the rest to follow. Another factor was the late formation, in 1945, of the Nigeria Football Association, which came 23 years after its counterpart in Ghana. The Challenge Cup was introduced in that year and until the national league was formed in 1972 it remained the only nationwide competition. It is still regarded by some as the top competition in the country. This may perhaps help explain the greater success of Nigerian teams in the Cup Winners Cup compared to the Champions Cup.

Only since the 1970s has Nigerian football begun to progress rapidly, and the focus for its development was club football. Outside of Lagos, representative teams had always entered the Challenge Cup but in 1970, due to the huge increase in the number of clubs being formed throughout the country, it became a clubs-only competition. In 1972 the next important step was taken when the national league was formed and it has always been well represented by clubs from most of the major towns. Both the national side and the club sides have profited from this new-found stability. After not qualifying for the final tournament of the Cup of Nations until 1976, Nigeria have since reached the final on five occasions, winning twice, in 1980 on home territory and in 1994 in Tunisia, having just qualified for the World Cup in the USA.

The most famous Nigerian footballer in the 1950s was

Tesilimi Balogun and he did much to spread the gospel of the game. The late 1970s provided Nigeria with its first generation of great players including the likes of Segun Odegbami, Muda Lawal and Christian Chukwu, but it was the 1990s which first saw players become really well known outside Nigeria. Stephen Keshi, Rashidi Yekini, Daniel Amokachi, Emmnuel Amunike, Finidi George and Augustine Okacha have all made a big impact with European clubs. In America the Nigerians were just two minutes away from the World Cup quarter-finals and are favourites to be the first African team to lift the trophy.

The other successful West African nations were all French colonies and they include Guinea, the Ivory Coast - or Côte d'Ivoire as they prefer to be called - and Senegal. Guinea, though very strong in the 1970s at both club and national level, have faded alarmingly. At the height of their power they possessed the best team Africa had seen: Petit Sory, Papa Camara, Bangaly Sylla, Cherif Soulayeman, N'Jolea, Tollo and Jansky will not be forgotten in a hurry, but they have not been replaced by players of equal quality.

The Ivory Coast have inherited their mantle as the top Francophile nation in the region. Blessed with a sound club structure based around the Abidjan quartet of ASEC, Africa Sports, Stella and Stade Abidjan, they have a healthy if not startling record. Until their victory in the 1992 Cup of Nations, they were often likened to Yugoslavia; always there displaying great skill, but never quite consistent enough to actually win titles. Though the league in the Ivory Coast is one of the most stable on the continent, French club football has been a great temptation for many of their top footballers, such as Youssouf Fofana and Abdoulaye Traoré in recent years and Laurent Pokou in the past. The league has been dominated by Abidjan clubs, but teams like SC Ganoa, Reveil Doloa and ASC Bouaké are starting to make more of an impact.

Senegal are not as strong as the other four West African powers, never having won a title at club or national level. The country does produce good footballers such as Francoise Bocande and Souleyman Sane, the majority of whom end up in France, and it is from this base that the national team is built. The 1992 Cup of Nations was a good pointer as to how far they have still to go: on home territory, they could do no better than the quarter-finals.

One or two of the region's other nations have made their presence felt now and again. Mali reached the final of the All-Africa Games in 1965, a year after Stade Malien had reached the final of the initial African Cup of Champion Clubs, whilst two years later Real Bamoko lost to Stade Abidjan in the second Champions Cup. Since 1972, when the national side were runners-up to Congo in the Cup of Nations, their only performance of note has been reaching the semi-finals in 1994. The other nation to have made its mark briefly is Togo. In 1968 Etoile Filante lost in the final of the Champions Cup to TP Englebert and in 1983 Agaza Lomé reached the final of the Cup Winners Cup before losing to Al Mokaouloum.

There are four regional tournaments. At club level the West African Club Championship is disputed between the runners-up of the national leagues of the region, not the champions. For the national sides, the CEDEAO tournament, named after the economic trade grouping, was supposed to be a regional championship but there has never been much enthusiasm for it, nor for the Zone 3 tournament for which Ghana, Nigeria, Benin, Burkina Faso (formerly Upper Volta), Côte d'Ivoire, Liberia, Niger and Togo qualify. Only the Zone 2 tournament has proved popular, and mostly because of the intense rivalry between Senegal and Guinea. Other nations entitled to take part are Cape Verde, Gambia, Guinea-Bissau, Mali, Mauritania and Sierra Leone. Along with the WAFU Club Cup it is the only tournament currently played.

ZONE 2: THE AMILCAR CABRAL CUP

Year	Winner	Score	Runner-up
1979	Senegal	1-0	Mali
1980	Senegal	1-0	Gambia
1981	Guinea	0-0 6-5p	Mali
1982	Guinea	3-0	Senegal
1983	Senegal	3-0	Guinea-Bissau
1984	Senegal	0-0 5-4p	Sierra Leone
1985	Senegal	1-0	Gambia
1986	Senegal	3-1	Sierra Leone
1987	Guinea	1-0	Mali
1988	Guinea	0-0 4-2p	Mali
1989	Mali	3-0	Guinea
1990	-		
1991	Senegal	1-0	Cape Verde
1993	Sierra Leone	2-0	Senegal

ZONE 3

Year	Winner	Score	Runner-up
1982	Ghana	2-1	Togo
1983	Ghana	3-1	Togo
1984	Ghana	1-1*	Togo
1986	Ghana	1-0	Togo
1987	Ghana	2-1	Liberia

*Ghana won on penalties

CEDEAO TOURNAMENT

Year	Winner	Score	Runner-up
1983	Ivory Coast	1-0	Togo
1985	Senegal	2-0	Ivory Coast
1987	Ivory Coast	2-1	Liberia
1989	Nigeria	0-0 *	Senegal
1991	Côte d'Ivoire	1-0	Senegal

* Nigeria won on penalties

THE WEST AFRICAN CLUB CHAMPIONSHIP

1977	Stade Abidjan (CIV) bt Kalum Star (GUI)
1978	AS Forces Armees (SEN) bt Entente II (TGO)
1979	ASF Police (SEN) bt Enugu Rangers (NGA)
1980	ASF Police (SEN) bt Sharks Port Harcourt (NGA)
1981	Stella Abidjan (CIV) 1-3 4-0 ASF Police (SEN)
1982	Sekondi Hassacas (GHA) 1-0 0-0 Spartans Owerri (NGA)
1983	New Nigeria Bank (NGA) 2-0 0-0 Sekondi Hassacas (GHA)
1984	New Nigeria Bank (NGA) 3-2 1-0 Stade Malien (MLI)
1985	Africa Sports (CIV) 3-0 2-0 New Nigeria Bank (NGA)
1986	Africa Sports (CIV) 2-0 0-2 6-5p Asante Kotoko (GHA)

1987	Cornerstone (GHA) 1-1 1-1 4-2p Stella Abidjan (CIV)
1988	ASFAG Conakry (GUI) 1-2 1-0 New Nigeria Bank (NGA)
1989	Ranchers Bees (NGA) 3-1 1-2 ASEC Abidjan (CIV)
1990	ASEC Abidjan (CIV) 1-0 1-1 Djoliba AC (MLI)
1991	Africa Sports (CIV) 1-1 2-1 Lobi Bank (NGA)
1992	Stade Malien (MLI) 1-0 3-0 Hafia Conakry (GUI)
1993	Bendel Insurance (NGA) 1-1 2-0 Mogas 90 (BEN)
1994	Bendel Insurance (NGA) 1-0 1-1 Plateau United (NGA)

EAST AFRICA

East Africa produces some of the finest athletes in the world and was the main area of British control during the first half of the century, so it is surprising that in football terms it should be the weakest of all the regions in Africa. Perhaps one factor in this lack of success is the importance of its regional tournaments, which are often more keenly contested than the continental cups. Another is the lack of experience of football outside the region; very few players from Burundi, Ethiopia, Kenya, Rwanda, Somalia, the Sudan, Tanzania or Uganda, the nations which make up East Africa, ever ply their trade elsewhere. Though this benefits the local leagues in that there is no player-drain, it does mean that new ideas and tactics are missing.

Ethiopia and Sudan were among the early shakers and movers in African football but have both seen their role steadily diminish over the years, due in no small part to the disastrous effects of famine and civil war that have plagued both countries. Both have won the Cup of Nations, Ethiopia in 1962 when it was held in Addis Ababa, and Sudan in 1970 when Khartoum hosted the event for the second time. They were founder members of CAF along with Egypt and South Africa; Sudan has had a football association since 1936, Ethiopia since 1943.

In the period of occupation by Italy from 1936-41, Ethiopia had a 'Sports Office for the Indigenous' which strictly forbade any inter-racial matches and designated certain sports fields as out of bounds for the locals. It was as well for Ethiopian football, therefore, that Italian rule was brief; it was not a helpful attitude for the world champions of the time to take, when they were in an excellent position to assist in the spread of the game. Club football has never been strong in Ethiopia, but in Sudan two clubs, Al Hilal and Al Merreikh, stand well above the rest and both have known success in the African club competitions. Against all the odds, Sudanese football found its feet again in the late 1980s as Merreikh won the Cup Winners Cup in 1989, following on from Hilal's Champions Cup final appearance of two years earlier.

Kenya, Uganda and Tanzania have a long football rivalry dating back to the 1920s in the form of the Gossage Cup, a tournament named after a Governor of the time and played by representative sides of each country. In the 1970s it took on a new form as the East and Central African Challenge Cup, and the entry has expanded over the years to include Malawi, Zambia, Zimbabwe, Sudan, Ethiopia and Somalia, although the first three have recently withdrawn. Uganda's football association dates back to 1924, Kenya's to 1932 and Tanzania's to 1930. Zanzibar, which remained an independent nation from Tanzania until 1964, still fields a side in the East and Central African Challenge Cup. Neither the national nor the club sides from these three nations have been very successful. There is an intense rivalry in Kenya between Gor Mahia and AFC Leopards (formerly Abaluhya), and the former remain Kenya's only African title holders after winning the Cup Winners Cup in 1987. Simba FC from Uganda managed to reach the Champions Cup final in 1972, as did their compatriots Nakivubo Villa in 1991, but such achievements are few. In the Cup of Nations, the story is no different. Uganda's appearance in the 1978 final, in which they lost to Ghana in Accra, marks the only significant impact the three countries have made on the tournament. Tanzania is the weakest of the trio, having made the finals on only one occasion.

The other two nations, Burundi and Rwanda, are keen competitors but little more. Both are among the most remote countries in the world and this will always hold them back, as will the bloody conflict which erupted there in 1994. In the region as a whole, however, there is tremendous potential for football. It is a popular sport and there are many fine athletes about. Perhaps for once a strong case could be made for encouraging players to play in Europe. The experience could be the impetus the area needs to start challenging the rest of Africa for honours.

THE GOSSAGE CUP 1927-1972

26 wins	Uganda
12	Kenya
4	Tanzania
1	Zanzibar

THE FRIENDSHIP CUP OF THE EAST AFRICAN ZONE

1966	Ethiopia		
1967	Sudan	1-1 5-3	Ethiopia
1969	Sudan	1-0	Ethiopia

THE EAST AFRICAN CHALLENGE CUP

1965	Tanzania
1966	Tanzania
1967	Kenya
1968	Uganda
1969	Uganda
1970	Uganda
1971	Kenya

EAST AND CENTRAL AFRICAN SENIOR CHALLENGE CUP

1973	Uganda	2-1	Tanzania
1974	Tanzania	1-1 5-3p	Uganda
1975	Kenya	0-0 4-3p	Malawi
1976	Uganda	2-0	Zambia

1977	Uganda	0-0 5-3p	Zambia
1978	Malawi	3-2	Zambia
1979	Malawi	3-2	Kenya
1980	Sudan	1-0	Tanzania
1981	Kenya	1-0	Tanzania
1982	Kenya	1-1 5-3p	Uganda
1983	Kenya	1-0	Zimbabwe
1984	Zambia	0-0 3-0	Malawi
1985	Zimbabwe	2-0	Kenya
1986	-		
1987	Ethiopia	1-1 5-4p	Zimbabwe
1988	Malawi	3-1	Zambia
1989	Uganda	3-3 2-1p	Malawi
1990	Uganda	2-0	Sudan
1991	Zambia	2-0	Kenya
1992	Uganda	1-0	Tanzania
1993	-		
1994	Tanzania	2-2 4-3p	Uganda

THE EAST AND CENTRAL AFRICAN CLUB CHAMPIONSHIP

1974	SC Simba (TAN)	Lge	Abaluhya FC (KEN)
1975	Young Africans (TAN)	2-0	SC Simba (TAN)
1976	Luo Union (KEN)	2-1	Young Africans (TAN)
1977	Luo Union (KEN)	1-0	FC Horsed (SDN)
1978	Kampala CC (UGA)	0-0 (p)	SC Simba (TAN)
1979	Abaluhya FC (KEN)	1-0	Kampala CC (UGA)
1980	Gor Mahia (KEN)	3-2	Abaluhya FC (KEN)
1981	Gor Mahia (KEN)	1-0	SC Simba (TAN)
1982	AFC Leopards (KEN)	1-0	Rio Tinto (ZIM)
1983	AFC Leopards (KEN)	2-1	ADMARC Tigers (MAW)
1984	AFC Leopards (KEN)	2-1	Gor Mahia (KEN)
1985	Gor Mahia (KEN)	2-0	AFC Leopards (KEN)
1986	El Merreikh (SDN)	2-2 4-2p	Young Africans (TAN)
1987	Nakivubo Villa (UGA)	1-0	El Merreikh (SDN)
1988	Kenya Breweries (KEN)	2-0	El Merreikh (SDN)
1989	Kenya Breweries (KEN)	3-0	Coastal Union (TAN)
1990	Nakivubo Villa		
1991	SC Simba (TAN)	3-0	Nakivubo Villa (UGA)
1992	SC Simba (TAN)	1-1 5-4p	Yanga (TAN)
1993	Yanga (TAN)	2-1	Nakivubo Villa (UGA)
1994	El Merreikh (SDN)	1-0	SC Simba (TAN)
1995	SC Simba (TAN)	1-1 5-3p	Express FC (UGA)

CENTRAL AFRICA

Central Africa is made up of eight countries, though in the Central African games Angola, Burundi and Rwanda, not classified in the region by CAF, are also invited to take part. The big three are Cameroon, Congo and Zaire, though the latter two have seen their influence decline in recent years. In Cameroon, the region has the most famous of all Africa's teams. In the 1990 World Cup they were ten minutes away from reaching the semi-finals before two penalties given away carelessly let England off the hook in what was undoubtedly the best match of the tournament. That performance earned Africa a third slot in the 1994 finals. Cameroon had already impressed in the 1982 World Cup in Spain when Italy, the eventual winners, qualified for the second round at their expense only by virtue of having scored more goals. Cameroon's star player in both tournaments was Roger Milla.

A relatively late developer in football, Cameroon was the only country under French rule which was not affiliated to the French Football Federation, and the situation was made even more complicated by the division of the country into British and French Protectorates. This was only resolved in 1961 when the northern part of the British-controlled territory voted to join Nigeria and the south Cameroon. Oryx Douala, one of the famous pre-independence clubs, were quick to take up the challenge of the new African Cup of Champion Clubs, and they hold a special place in African football folklore as its first winners. Since then, however, other clubs from Yaounde and Douala have emerged, most notably Canon and Tonnerre from the former and Union from the latter. These three have dominated both the league and cup since the 1970s.

In African club competitions in the seventies Canon, Tonnerre and Union were unstoppable, winning eight titles and appearing in a further three finals. Since Union's win in the 1981 Cup Winners Cup, however, the titles have dried up and the focus has switched to the national side as the Indomitable Lions, as they are known, have swept all before them. On three consecutive occasions from 1984-88 they appeared in the final of the Cup of Nations, and were only denied a trio of titles when Egypt won the 1986 competition on penalties.

Although Milla has stolen much of the limelight with his displays for the national team, especially in the 1990 World Cup, Cameroon have been represented by many fine players. Thomas N'Kono and Antoine Bell are two of the most celebrated goalkeepers not only in Africa but also in Europe, the destination of most of the top Cameroon players. Players like Emmanuel Kunde, Paul M'Fede, Cyril Makanaky and Emile M'Bouh have all helped put Cameroon on the map. Such is their reputation now that despite a relatively small population, it will take some knocking to get them off the perch on which they currently stand, even if performances since 1990 have not been quite so impressive, with matters not helped by a series of bitter disputes within the federation.

Zaire is the biggest country of the region both in terms of population and size, so it was no surprise when they became the first black African country to reach the World Cup finals in 1974. Humiliated by a 9-0 defeat against Yugoslavia, they have suffered deeply since that outing and have only recently emerged from the shadows again. Yet football has a long history in the country. Zaire was Belgium's largest colony and under their guidance the Association Royale Sportive Congolaise was founded in Leopoldville (later Kinshasa) in 1919, making it the second oldest association on the continent after South Africa. There was a thriving league, started three years earlier, confined at first to Leopoldville. A league was also started in Elizabethville (later Lumbumbashi) but for many years the main focus was the Pool Championship. Stanley Pool, the lake which separated the Belgian Congo from the French Congo and its capital Brazzaville, gave its name to a championship played between sides from the two countries which lasted from 1923 until independence.

From the late 1960s until 1974, Zaire was the most powerful country in Africa. Twice winners of the Cup of Nations, their main clubs, AS Vita from Kinshasa and TP Englebert from Lubumbashi, also collected three continental club honours between them. Although TP Mazembe, as Englebert are now known, won the Cup Winners Cup in 1980 and Daring Club Motema Pembe did so in 1994, teams from Zaire have not been as predominant as they were before. The contrast is even more marked for the national side. Since winning the Cup of Nations in 1974 they have only managed to qualify for the final tournament on four occasions since.

The French Congo, known for a while as Congo Brazzaville but now simply as Congo, have suffered much the same fate. As winners of the 1972 Cup of Nations thanks in no small measure to Francois M'Pele, Congo's most famous player, and of the Champions Cup in 1974 with CARA Brazzaville, the country's most famous club, the future looked rosy. Since then, however, very little of substance has been achieved. With a population of only two million it is perhaps not surprising that this should be the case. One would expect a country like Gabon, with a similar population but vast oil resources, to be in a much better position to succeed, and in the UDEAC tournament this has indeed been the case. Of the remaining countries, the Central African Republic has been too racked with poverty to pay much attention to football, whilst the football authorities in Chad do not take too kindly to paying their dues to FIFA or CAF and have spent many years in the wilderness.

UDEAC TOURNAMENT

1984	Cameroon	2-2 5-4p	Congo
1985	Gabon	3-0	Congo
1986	Cameroon	4-1	Chad
1987	Cameroon	1-0	Chad
1988	Gabon	1-0	Cameroon
1989	Cameroon	2-1	Central African Republic
1990	Congo	2-1	Cameroon

CENTRAL AFRICAN GAMES FOOTBALL TOURNAMENT

1976	Cameroon	3-2	Congo
1981	Zaire	Lge	Congo
1987	Cameroon	2-0	Angola

SOUTHERN AFRICA

Few doubt that southern Africa could well become one of the growth regions of world football. Now that apartheid has all but crumbled away in South Africa, more and more attention will be focused on the region, which has for many years been a backwater of the game. South Africa may have been a founder member of CAF but it has never played a part in African football, only recently has its northern neighbour Zimbabwe been able to join in, both Angola and Mozambique have been fighting fierce civil wars, and as a puppet state of the South Africans Namibia was also an international outcast until its independence in 1990.

The rump of active football nations left consisted of Zambia, Malawi, Botswana, Lesotho, Swaziland, Madagascar, the Comores Islands and Mauritius, hardly a task force to take on the world. In the new order that is likely to emerge, South Africa, Zimbabwe, Zambia, Angola and Mozambique look set to be the strongest. Most attention will unavoidably fall on South Africa. As a nation the South Africans have a sporting history to match even the best in the world. Before their international exile because of apartheid, their rugby and cricket teams were world-beaters. The Springboks, as the rugby side is called, were especially feared, but like everything in South Africa rugby was run along racial lines and remained a sport that was largely a preserve of the white minority population. The exciting aspect about the future of South African football will be that for the first time the black majority will be able to make their mark on international sport, for it is football, not rugby or cricket, that is the passion of the people, a factor commonly ignored by supporters of the other sports.

Football did not escape the horrors of apartheid and its roots are deeply entrenched in the country's colonial past. In 1882 the British province of Natal founded an association for the game, three years after South Africa's first club, Pietermaritzburg County, was formed. Along with the association in New South Wales in Australia, this body was the first of its kind outside Britain. Cape Province, the other British territory, soon followed suit and in 1892 the two were the prime movers behind the new Football Association of South Africa, the oldest national body in Africa.

The Dutch areas of Transvaal and Orange Free State quickly took to the game as well. In 1892 the Currie Cup was introduced for representative teams of the four provinces; it has been dominated by Transvaal and Natal. In 1959 professionalism was introduced and the National Professional Football League (NPFL) started. Until this point there had been a variety of local leagues and tournaments, but the NPFL, later known simply as the NFL, was the first to be open to the whole country, although at first only clubs from Johannesburg and Pretoria were represented. An all-white league from the start, the NFL suffered greatly when in 1972 the non-white National Professional Soccer League was founded. It was an instant hit among the black population. Faced with this stiff competition, the NFL agreed to merge with the NPSL in 1978 and later became known as the National Soccer League.

From that time, on the playing field at least, football was one of the few racially-integrated activities in the country. There have been problems of who actually controls the game, but in January 1992 the CAF were sufficiently confident that a single governing body was in place that they welcomed South Africa back into the fold. The following June the South Africans celebrated their return with three matches against Cameroon, thereby ending almost 30 years of international exile.

For many years Zimbabwe was in a similar position to South Africa. As Rhodesia, and before that as Southern Rhodesia, they too became outcasts as a result of the racial policies of their government. Rhodesia became an independent country after UDI in 1965 and immediately joined FIFA, but CAF would have nothing to do with them until the advent of black majority rule in 1980. After a brief flirtation with the World Cup in 1970, the Rhodesians were suspended from FIFA and did not take part again until 1982, as Zimbabwe, but their form since has not been particularly impressive either at international or club level. They have yet to qualify for the Cup of Nations, while the club sides have found it impossible to progress beyond the quarter-finals of the African championships.

Zimbabwe's neighbours Zambia, known before independence as Northern Rhodesia, have fared better and in 1991 took their first continental honour when Power Dynamos won the Cup Winners Cup. The Northern Rhodesia Football Association was formed in 1929 and affiliated to the Nyasaland Football Association in present-day Malawi. After independence in 1964, the Zambians lacked any neighbours to the south to play against and so concentrated their efforts on the tournaments played by the East and Central confederation. In 1974 they lost to Zaire in the final of the Cup of Nations and since then they have reached the semi-finals twice and the final again in 1994. In 1988 at the Seoul Olympics the Zambians caused a sensation by defeating the professional Italian side 4-0 to reach the quarter-finals before losing to West Germany. But in 1993 Zambia made world headlines when the plane carrying the national team to a World Cup qualifier crashed off the coast of Gabon, killing everyone on board including 18 players. Even then, under the leadership of Kalusha Bwalya, Zambia's most famous player, they almost made it to the finals in America and, in a remarkable rebuilding process, reached the final of the Nations Cup in Tunis where they lost 2-1 to Nigeria.

Zambia and later Zimbabwe's lack of nearby quality opposition was not helped by the unstable situations in many of the neighbouring countries. Mozambique may have produced two of the greatest ever footballers in Eusebio and Mario Coluña, but since the Portuguese upped and left Mozambique and Angola in 1975, both countries have produced nothing but bloody conflict. Namibia, another neighbour, had been involved in yet another South African-sponsored civil war, although since independence in 1990 Namibians have taken part in African football for the first time.

None of the other nations of the region have contributed much to the game. The vast, under-populated Botswana, the tiny kingdoms of Lesotho and Swaziland, Mauritius and Madagascar are all keen competitors but have achieved little of note. Only Malawi, in the East and Central African competitions, make their presence felt occasionally. The region may not have much of a history, but it is a time of change and only Angola still remains at war. It is possible that a regional championship of sorts could emerge to help get all of the countries on their feet, but in the future southern Africans will have their eyes very much on the African and world titles at stake; who would bet against South Africa being the first African country to host the World Cup?

ALGERIA

Population: 25,337,000
Area, sq km: 2,381,741
% in urban areas: 49%
Capital city: Algiers

Fédération Algérienne de Football
Route Ahmed Ouaked
BP 39
Algiers-Dely-Ibrahim
Algeria
Tel: + 213 2 365938
Fax: + 213 2 366181
Telex: 61378

Year of formation	1962
Affiliation to FIFA	1963
Affiliation to CAF	1964
Registered clubs	320
Registered players	123 000
Registered coaches	2800
Registered referees	2100
National stadium	Stade Olympique, Algiers 80 000
National colours	Green/White/Red
Reserve colours	White/White/White
Season	September - June

THE RECORD

WORLD CUP

1930-66	Did not enter
1970	QT 1st round
1974	QT 1st round
1978	QT 2nd round
1982	QT Qualified - Final tournament/1st round
1986	QT Qualified - Final tournament/1st round
1990	QT 3rd round
1994	QT 1st round - 1st/3 in group 1 2nd round - 3rd/3 in group A

AFRICAN CUP OF NATIONS

1957-65	Did not enter
1968	QT Qualified - Final tournament/1st round
1970	QT 2nd round
1972	QT 1st round
1974	QT 2nd round
1976	QT 1st round
1978	QT 2nd round
1980	QT Qualified - Final tournament/Finalists
1982	QT Qualified - Final tournament/Semi-finalists/4th place
1984	QT Qualified - Final tournament/Semi-finalists/3rd place
1986	QT Qualified - Final tournament/1st round
1988	QT Qualified - Final tournament/Semi-finalists/3rd place
1990	QT Automatic - Final tournament/Winners
1992	QT Automatic - Final tournament/1st round
1994	QT 2nd/4 in group 3 - Disqualified

AFRICAN GAMES

Winners 1978

AFRICAN CLUB COMPETITIONS

African Champions Cup
Winners - Mouloudia d'Algiers 1976, JS Kabylie 1981 1990, ES Setif 1988
Finalists - Mouloudia d'Oran 1989
Cup Winners Cup
Finalists - NA Hussein-Dey 1978
CAF Cup
Quarter-finalists - ASM Oran 1992, USM El Harrach 1993, US Chaouia 1994

ALGIERS LEAGUE CHAMPIONS

1920	FC Blideen
1921	FC Blideen
1922	FC Blideen
1923	FC Blidden
1924	AS Boufarik
1925	US Blideenne
1926	GS d'Orleansville
1927	Gallia Sports
1928	FC Blideen
1929	AS Saint Eugene
1930	AS Boufarik
1931	Gallia Sports
1932	AS Boufarik
1933	Racing Universitaire
1934	Racing Universitaire
1935	AS Saint Eugene
1936	Gallia Sports
1937	AS Boufarik
1938	AS Boufarik
1939-40	-
1941	AS Boufarik
1942	AS Saint Eugene
1943	AS Saint Eugene
1944	AS Saint Eugene & Mouloudia Algiers
1945	Racing Universitaire
1946	Galiia Sports
1947	Olympique Hussein-Dey
1948	Olympique Hussein-Dey
1949	Olympique Hussein-Dey

CONSTANTINE LEAGUE CHAMPIONS

1922	AS Bonoise
1923	US Constantine
1924	US Constantine
1925	US Constantine
1926	JS Philippeville
1927	Racing Philippeville
1928	Stade Olympique Setif
1929	AS Bônoise
1930	Stade Olympique Setif
1931	Racing Philippeville
1932	JS Guelmoise
1933	JS Guelmoise
1934	JS Guelmoise
1935	Jeunesse Bône AC
1936	-
1937	Jeunesse Bône AC
1938	Jeunesse Bône AC
1939	MO Constantine
1940-44	-
1945	USM Setif
1946	USM Bône
1947	JS Jijelli
1948	MO Constantine
1949	AS Bône
1950	USM Setif

ORAN LEAGUE CHAMPIONS

1920	AS Maritime
1921	SC Bel Abbés
1922	SC Bel Abbés
1923	SC Bel Abbés
1924	SC Bel Abbés
1925	SC Bel Abbés
1926	SC Bel Abbés
1927	SC Bel Abbés
1928	AS Maritime
1929	Club Joyeusetes
1930	Gallia Club Oran
1931	Club Joyeusetes
1932	USM Oran
1933	Club Joyeusetes
1934	-
1935	Gallia Club Oran
1936	Club Joyeusetes
1937	Club Joyeusetes
1938	Club Joyeusetes
1939	-
1940	AS Maritime
1941	Club Joyeusetes
1942	USM Oran
1943	USM Oran
1944	USM Oran
1945	USM Oran
1946	SC Bel Abbés
1947	FC Oran
1948	USM Oran
1949	USM Oran
1950	GC Mascara

ALGERIAN NATIONAL LEAGUE CHAMPIONS

1963	USM Algiers
1964	USM Annaba
1965	CR Belcourt
1966	CR Belcourt
1967	NA Hussein-Dey
1968	Entente Setif
1969	CR Belcourt
1970	CR Belcourt
1971	Mouloudia d'Oran
1972	Mouloudia d'Algiers
1973	JS Kabylie
1974	JS Kabylie
1975	Mouloudia d'Algiers
1976	Mouloudia d'Algiers
1977	JS Kawkabi
1978	Mouloudia d'Algiers
1979	Mouloudia d'Algiers
1980	JE Tizi-Ouzou
1981	RS Kouba
1982	JE Tizi-Ouzou
1983	JE Tizi-Ouzou
1984	GCR Mascara
1985	JE Tizi-Ouzou
1986	JE Tizi-Ouzou
1987	Entente Setif
1988	Mouloudia d'Oran
1989	JE Tizi-Ouzou
1990	JS Kabylie
1991	MO Constantine
1992	Mouloudia d'Oran
1993	Mouloudia d'Oran
1994	US Chaouia
1995	JS Kabylie

ALGERIAN CUP WINNERS

1963	Entente Setif
1964	Entente Setif
1965	MC Saida
1966	CR Belcourt
1967	Entente Setif
1968	Entente Setif
1969	CR Belcourt
1970	CR Belcourt
1971	Mouloudia d'Algiers
1972	Hamra-Annaba
1973	Mouloudia d'Algiers
1974	USM Maison Carrée
1975	MMouloudia d'Oran
1976	Mouloudia d'Algiers
1977	JS Kawkabi
1978	CM Belcourt
1979	MA Hussein Dey
1980	Entente Setif
1981	USK Algiers
1982	DNC Algiers
1983	Mouloudia d'Algiers
1984	Mouloudia d'Oran
1985	Mouloudia d'Oran
1986	JE Tizi-Ouzou
1987	USM El-Harrach
1988	USK Algiers
1989	-
1990	Entente Setif
1991	USM Bel Abbés
1992	JS Kabylie
1993	-
1994	JS Kabylie
1995	CR Belouizdad

CLUB DIRECTORY

ALGIERS (Pop. - 1,507,000)

Mouloudia Challia Algiers
Previous names: MP Algiers

CR Belouizdad
Previous names: CR Belcourt 1962-80, CM Belcourt 1980-93

NA Hussein Dey
Previous names: NA Hussein Dey 1946-76, NAHD/CNAN 1976-78, MA Hussein Dey 1978-8?

USM Algiers
Previous names: USK Algiers, U Algiers

JHD Algiers
Previous names: DNC Algiers

USM El Harrach
Previous names: US Maison Carrée

RC Kouba
Stadium: Belhaddad 8,000
Previous name: RS Kouba

ORAN (Pop. - 628,000)

Mouloudia Challia Oran
Previous names: MP Oran

ASM Oran
Previous names: ASC Oran

CONSTANTINE (Pop. - 440,000)

MO Constantine
Previous names: MP Constantine

CS Constantine

ANNABA (Pop. - 305,000)
USM Annaba
Previous name: Hamra Annaba

SETIF (Pop. - 117,000)
Entente Setif
Previous names: EP Setif

SIDI BEL ABBÉS (Pop. - 102,000)
USM Bel Abbés

RELIZANE (Pop. - 86,000)
RC Relizane

MASCARA (Pop. - 64,000)
GCR Mascara

TIZI-OUZOU (Pop. 61,000)
JS Kabylie
Previous names: JS Kabylie 1946-75, JS Kawkabi 1975-77, JE Tizi-Ouzou 1977-89

OUM EL BOUAGHI
US Chaouia

ANGOLA

Population: 10,002,000
Area, sq km: 1,246,000
% in urban areas: 26%
Capital city: Luanda

Federacão Angolana de Futebol
BP 3449
Luanda
Angola
Tel: + 244 2 338635
Fax: + 244 2 321945
Telex: 2580 palanca an

Year of formation	1979
Affiliation to FIFA	1980
Affiliation to CAF	1980
Registered clubs	278
Registered players	13000
Registered coaches	15
Registered referees	297
National stadium	Citadela, Luanda 35 000
National colours	Red/Black/Red
Reserve colours	White/White/White
Season	April - January

THE RECORD

WORLD CUP

1930-82	Did not enter
1986	QT 2nd round
1990	QT 2nd round
1994	QT 3rd/4 in group 3

AFRICAN CUP OF NATIONS

1957-80	Did not enter
1982	QT pr round
1984	QT 1st round
1986	Did not enter
1988	QT 1st round
1990	QT 1st round
1992	QT 4th/4 in group 5
1994	Did not enter

AFRICAN CLUB COMPETITIONS

African Champions Cup
2nd round - Petro Atletico 1983 1988 1991. Primeiro de Maio 1984. Primeiro de Agosto 1992
Cup Winners Cup
Quarter-finals - Ferroviario Lubango 1988
CAF Cup
Finalists - Primeiro de Maio 1994
Semi-finals - AS Aviacao 1993

ANGOLAN LEAGUE CHAMPIONS

1979	Primeiro de Agosto
1980	Primeiro de Agosto
1981	Primeiro de Agosto
1982	Petro Atletico
1983	Primeiro de Maio
1984	Petro Atletico
1985	Primeiro de Maio
1986	Petro Atletico
1987	Petro Atletico
1988	Petro Atletico
1989	Petro Atletico
1990	Petro Atletico
1991	Primeiro de Agosto
1992	Primeiro de Agosto
1993	Petro Atletico
1994	Petro Atletico

ANGOLAN CUP WINNERS

1980	Nacional Benguela
1981	TAAG Luanda
1982	Primeiro de Maio
1983	Primeiro de Maio
1984	Primeiro de Agosto
1985	Ferroviaro Huila
1986	Inter Club Luanda
1987	Ferroviario Lubango
1988	Sagrada Esperanca
1989	Ferroviario Lubango
1990	Primeiro de Agosto
1991	Primeiro de Agosto
1992	Petro Atletico
1993	-
1994	Petro Atletico

CLUB DIRECTORY

LUANDA (Pop. - 1,458,000)
Petro Atletico
Primeiro de Agosto
Atletico Aviacao (formerly Desportivo TAAG)
Inter Club
Sagrada Esperanca

BENGUELA (Pop. - 155,000)
FC Nacional
Primeiro de Maio
Academica Lobito

LUBANGO (Pop. - 95,000)
Ferroviario Lubango
Sporting Lubango

BENIN

(Formerly Dahomey, until 1975)

Population: 4,741,000
Area, sq km: 112,600
% in urban areas: 19%
Capital city: Porto Novo

Fédération Béninoise de Football
BP 965
Cotonou
Benin
Tel: + 229 330537
Fax: + 229 312485
Telex: 5245 sonacop cotonou

Year of formation	1968
Affiliation to FIFA	1969
Affiliation to CAF	1969
Registered clubs	117
Registered players	17 000
Registered referees	61
National stadium	Stade de l'Amitie 35,000
National colours	Green/Green/Green
Reserve colours	Red/Green/Green
Season	November - June

THE RECORD

WORLD CUP

1930-70	Did not enter
1974	QT 1st round
1978	Did not enter
1982	Did not enter
1986	QT 1st round
1990	Did not enter
1994	QT 1st round - 4th/4 in group 6

AFRICAN CUP OF NATIONS

1957-70	Did not enter
1972	QT 1st round
1974-78	Did not enter
1980	QT 1st round
1982	Did not enter
1984	QT 1st round
1986	QT 1st round
1988	Did not enter
1990	Did not enter
1992	QT 5th/5 in group 4
1994	QT 4th/4 in group 1

AFRICAN CLUB COMPETITIONS

African Cup
2nd round - Dragons de l'Ouème 1984
Cup Winners Cup
Semi-finalists - Dragons de l'Ouème 1987
CAF Cup
2nd round - Dragons de l'Ouème 1992

BENIN LEAGUE CHAMPIONS

1969	FAD
1970	AS Porto Novo
1971	AS Cotonou
1972	AS Porto Novo
1973	AS Porto Novo
1974	Etoile Sportive Porto Novo
1975-77	-
1978	Dragons de l'Ouème
1979	Dragons de l'Ouème
1980	Buffles de Borgou
1981	Adjidjas FAP
1982	Dragons de l'Ouème
1983	Dragons de l'Ouème
1984	Lions de l'Atakory
1985	Requins de l'Atlantique
1986	Dragons de l'Ouème
1987	Requins de l'Atlantique
1988	-
1989	Dragons de l'Ouème
1990	Requins de l'Atlantique
1991	Postel Sport
1992	Buffles de Borgou
1993	-
1994	Dragons de l'Ouème

BENIN CUP WINNERS

1978	Requins de l'Atlantique
1979	Buffles de Borgou
1980	-
1981	Requins de l'Atlantique
1982	Buffles de Borgou
1983	Requins de l'Atlantique
1984	Dragons de l'Ouème
1985	Dragons de l'Ouème
1986	Dragons de l'Ouème
1987	-
1988	Requins de l'Atlantique
1989	Requins de l'Atlantique
1990	Dragons de l'Ouème
1991	-
1992	Dragons de l'Ouème

CLUB DIRECTORY

COTONOU (Pop. - 478,000)
Requins de l'Atlantique
Association Sportive Cotonou
Adjidjas FAP

PORT NOVO (Pop. - 164,000)
Dragons de l'Ouème
Postel Sport
Etoile Sportive
AS Porto Novo

PARAKOU (Pop. - 92,000)
Buffles de Borgou

BOTSWANA

Population: 1,295,000
Area, sq km: 581,730
% in urban areas: 21%
Capital city: Gaborone

Botswana Football Association
PO Box 1396
Gaborone
Botswana
Tel: + 267 300279
Fax: + 267 300280
Telex: 2977 bd

Year of formation	1970
Affiliation to FIFA	1976
Affiliation to CAF	1976
Registered clubs	168
Registered players	11000
Registered coaches	8
Registered referees	23
National stadium	National Stadium, Gaborone 20 000
National colours	Sky blue/White/Sky blue
Reserve colours	White/White/White
Season	February - October

THE RECORD

WORLD CUP

1930-90	Did not enter
1994	QT 3rd/3 in group 5

AFRICAN CUP OF NATIONS

1957-92	Did not enter
1994	QT preliminary round

AFRICAN CLUB COMPETITIONS
African Champions Cup
Never past the 1st round
Cup Winners Cup
Never past the 1st round
CAF Cup
Never past the 1st round

BOTSWANAN LEAGUE CHAMPIONS

1978	FC Notwane
1979	Township Rollers
1980	Township Rollers
1981	Defence Force (BDF XI)
1982	Township Rollers
1983	Township Rollers
1984	Township Rollers
1985	Township Rollers
1986	Gaborone United
1987	Township Rollers
1988	Defence Force
1989	Defence Force
1990	Gaborone United
1991	Defence Force (BDF XI)
1992	Extension Gunners
1993	Extension Gunners
1994	Extension Gunners

CLUB DIRECTORY

GABORONE (Pop. - 95,000)
Botswana Defence Force
Gaborone United
FC Notwane
Township Rollers

LOBATSE
Extension Gunners

BURKINA FASO

(Formerly Upper Volta until 1984)

Population: 9,012,000
Area, sq km: 274,200
% in urban areas: 8%
Capital city: Ouagadougou

Fédération Burkinabè de Football
BP 57
Ouagadougou
Burkina Faso
Tel: + 226 340488
Fax: + 226 340489

Year of formation	1960
Affiliation to FIFA	1964
Affiliation to CAF	1964
Registered clubs	57
Registered players	27 000
Registered referees	71
National stadium	Stade du 4 Aout Ouagadougou 4000
National colours	Red/Green/Red
Reserve colours	White/White/White
Season	October - July

THE RECORD

WORLD CUP

1930-74	Did not enter
1978	QT 1st round
1982	Did not enter
1986	Did not enter
1990	QT 1st round
1994	QT 1st round - Group 8 with drew

AFRICAN CUP OF NATIONS

1957-65	Did not enter
1968	QT 3rd in group
1970	Did not enter
1972	Did not enter
1974	QT 1st round
1976	QT 1st round
1978	QT Qualified - Final tournament/1st round
1980	Did not enter
1982	QT 2nd round
1984-88	Did not enter
1990	QT pr round
1992	QT 3rd/5 in group 4
1994	QT group 7 - withdrew

AFRICAN CLUB COMPETITIONS
African Cup
Quarter-finalists - Silures 1978
Cup Winners Cup
Semi-finalists - Kadiogo 1978 1980
CAF Cup
2nd round - USCB 1992

BURKINA FASO LEAGUE CHAMPIONS

1965	Etoile Filante
1966	AS Fonctionnaires Ouagadougou
1967	US Ouagadougou
1968	USFERAN
1969	AS Fonctionnaires Ouagadougou
1970	ASFA Ouagadougou
1971	ASFA Ouagadougou
1972	Jeanne d'Arc
1973	Jeanne d'Arc
1974	Silures
1975	Silures
1976	Silures
1977	Silures
1978	Silures
1979	Silures
1980	Silures
1981	Silures
1982	-
1983	US Ouagadougou
1984	ASFA Ouagadougou
1985	Etoile Filante
1986	-
1987	-
1988	Etoile Filante
1989	ASFA Yennega
1990	Etoile Filante
1991	Etoile Filante
1992	Etoile Filante
1993	Etoile Filante
1994	Etoile Filante

CLUB DIRECTORY

OUAGADOUGOU (Pop. - 441,000)
ASFA Ouagadougou
Etoile Filante
Jeanne d'Arc
Union Sportive Ouagadougou
Association Sportive Fonctionnaires
ASFA Yennega
Silures - Folded 1982

BOBO DIOULASSO (Pop. - 228,000)
Union Sportive Foyer Rails National (USFRAN)
Racing Club
Association Sportive Bobo-Dioulasso
Kadiogo - Folded 1982

BURUNDI

Population: 5,451,000
Area, sq km: 27,834
% in urban areas: 7%
Capital city: Bujumbura

Fédération de Football du Burundi
BP 3426
Bujumbura
Burundi
Tel: + 257 212891
Fax: +257 212891

Year of formation	1948
Affiliation to FIFA	1972
Affiliation to CAF	1972
Registered clubs	132
Registered players	2600
Registered referees	125
National stadium	Stade Prince Louis, Bujumbura 20,000
National colours	Red/White/Green
Season	October - July

THE RECORD

WORLD CUP

1930-90	Did not enter
1994	QT 3rd/3 in group 1

AFRICAN CUP OF NATIONS

1957-74	Did not enter
1976	QT 1st round
1978-92	Did not enter
1994	QT 2nd/3 in group 6

AFRICAN CLUB COMPETITIONS

African Cup
Quarter-finalists - Vital'O 1985, Inter Star 1986
Cup Winners Cup
Semi-finalists - Inter Star 1991
CAF Cup
Have never entered

BURUNDI LEAGUE CHAMPIONS

1972	Sports Dynamic
1973	Sports Dynamic
1974	Inter FC
1975-78	-
1979	Vital'O
1980	-
1981	Prince Louis
1982	Fantastique
1983	Vital'O
1984	Vital'O
1985	Inter FC
1986	Inter FC
1987	Inter FC
1988	Inter FC
1989	Inter FC
1990	Vital'O
1991	Inter Star
1992	Vital'O
1993	Vital'O
1994	Fantastique

CLUB DIRECTORY

BUJUMBURA (Pop. - 273,000)
Inter Star
Vital'O
Burundi Sports Dynamic
Fantastique
Prince Louis FC
Muzinga

CAMEROON

Population: 11,900,000
Area, sq km: 465,458
% in urban areas: 42%
Capital city: Yaoundé

Fédération Camérounaise de Football
BP 1116
Yaoundé
Cameroon
Tel: + 237 202538
Fax: + 237 202538
Telex: 8568 jeunspo kn

Year of formation	1960
Affiliation to FIFA	1962
Affiliation to CAF	1963
Registered clubs	267
Registered players	119 000
Registered coaches	15
Registered referees	381
National stadium	Omnisport, Yaoundé 70 000
National colours	Green/Red/Yellow
Reserve colours	Yellow/Green/Red
Season	November - July

THE RECORD

WORLD CUP

1930-66	Did not enter
1970	QT 1st round
1974	QT 2nd round
1978	QT 1st round
1982	QT Qualified - Final tournament/1st round
1986	QT 2nd round
1990	QT Qualified - Final Tournament/Quarter-finalists
1994	QT 1st round - 1st/3 in group 2 - Final Tournament/1st round

AFRICAN CUP OF NATIONS

1957-65	Did not enter
1968	QT 3rd/3 in group 5
1970	QT Qualified - Final tournament/1st round
1972	QT Automatic - Final tournament/Semi-finalists/3rd place
1974	QT 2nd round
1976	QT 1st round
1978	QT 1st round
1980	QT 1st round
1982	QT Qualified - Final tournament/1st round
1984	QT Qualified - Final tournament/Winners
1986	QT Automatic - Final tournament/Finalists
1988	QT Qualified - Final tournament/Winners
1990	QT Automatic - Final tournament/1st round
1992	QT 1st/4 in group 1 - Final tournament/Semi-finalists/4th place
1994	QT 2nd/4 in group 1

AFRICAN CLUB COMPETITIONS

African Cup

Winners - Oryx Douala 1964, Canon Yaoundé 1971 1978 1980 Union Douala 1979

Cup Winners Cup

Winners - Tonnerre Yaoundé 1975, Canon Yaoundé 1979, Union Douala 1981

Finalists - Tonnerre Yaoundé 1976, Canon Yaoundé 1977 1984

CAF Cup

Never past 1st round

CAMEROON LEAGUE CHAMPIONS

1961	Oryx Douala
1962	Caiman Douala
1963	Oryx Douala
1964	Oryx Douala
1965	Oryx Douala
1966	Diamant Yaoundé
1967	Oryx Douala
1968	Caiman Douala
1969	Union Douala
1970	Canon Yaoundé
1971	Aigle Nkongsamba
1972	Leopards Douala
1973	Leopards Douala
1974	Canon Yaoundé
1975	Caiman Douala
1976	Union Douala
1977	Canon Yaoundé
1978	Union Douala
1979	Canon Yaoundé
1980	Canon Yaoundé
1981	Tonnerre Yaoundé
1982	Canon Yaoundé
1983	Tonnerre Yoaunde
1984	Tonnerre Yaoundé
1985	Canon Yaoundé
1986	Canon Yaoundé
1987	Tonnerre Yaoundé
1988	Tonnerre Yaoundé
1989	Racing Bafoussam
1990	Union Douala
1991	Canon Yaoundé
1992	Racing Bafoussam
1993	Racing Bafoussam
1994	Aigle NKongsamba

CAMEROON CUP WINNERS

1956	Oryx Douala
1957	Canon Yaoundé
1958	Tonnerre Yaoundé
1959	-
1960	Lions Yaoundé
1961	Union Douala
1962	Lions Yaoundé
1963	Oryx Douala
1964	Diamant Yaoundé
1965	Lions Yaoundé
1966	Lions Yaoundé
1967	Canon Yaoundé
1968	Oryx Yaoundé
1969	Union Douala
1970	-
1971	Diamant Yaoundé
1972	Diamant Yaoundé
1973	Canon Yaoundé
1974	Tonnerre Yaoundé
1975	Canon Yaoundé
1976	Canon Yaoundé
1977	Canon Yaoundé
1978	Canon Yaoundé
1979	Dynamo Douala
1980	Union Douala
1981	Dynamo Douala
1982	Dragons Yaoundé
1983	Canon Yaoundé
1984	Dihep de Nkam
1985	Union Douala
1986	Canon Yaoundé
1987	Tonnerre Yaoundé
1988	Panthère Bangangte
1989	Tonnerre Yaoundé
1990	Prevoyance FC Yaoundé
1991	Tonnerre Yaoundé
1992	L'Olympic Mvolyé
1993	Canon Yaoundé
1994	L'Olympic Mvolyé

CLUB DIRECTORY

DOUALA (Pop. - 1,029,000)

Caiman
Oryx
Leopard
Union
Rail
Dynamo

YAOUNDÉ (Pop. - 653,000)

Tonnerre
Dragons
Lions
Canon
Diamant
Prevoyance FC

BAFOUSSAM (Pop. - 89,000)

Racing Club

YABASSI

Dihep di Nkam

N'KONGSAMBA

Aigle

BANGANGTE

Panthère

CAPE VERDE

Population: 339,000
Area, sq km: 4,033
% in urban areas: 33%
Capital city: Praia

Federacao Cabo-Verdiana de Futebol
CP 234
Praia
Cape Verde Islands
Tel: + 238 611362
Fax: + 238 612964
Telex: 6005 areas cv

Year of formation	1982
Affiliation to FIFA	1986
Affiliation to CAF	1986
Registered clubs	60
Registered players	4 400
Registered coaches	10
Registered referees	66
National stadium	Estadio da Varzea, Praia 8000
National colours	Green/Green/Green
Reserve colours	White/White/White
Season	October - July

THE RECORD

WORLD CUP

1930-90 Did not enter

AFRICAN CUP OF NATIONS

1957-92 Did not enter
1994 QT preliminary round

AFRICAN CLUB COMPETITIONS

African Cup

First round - Sporting Praia 1992

Cup Winners Cup

Have never entered

CAF Cup

Never past preliminary round

CLUB DIRECTORY

PRAIA (Pop. - 37,000)

Sporting Praia
Desportivo Praia
Boavista Praia
Santacruz Praia
Vitoria Praia

MINDELO (Pop. - 36,000)

Academica Mindelo
Derby Mindelo

CENTRAL AFRICAN REPUBLIC

Population: 2,875,000
Area, sq km: 622,436
%in urban areas: 33%
Capital city: Bangui

Fédération Centrafricaine de Football
BP 886
Bangui
Central African Republic
Tel: + 236 61 2141
Fax: None

Year of formation	1937
Affiliation to FIFA	1963
Affiliation to CAF	1965
Registered clubs	256
Registered players	9400
Registered Coaches	12
Registered referees	92
National stadium	Barthèlemy Boganda, Bangui 35 000
National colours	Sky blue/White/Red
Reserve colours	Red/Red/Red
Season	October - July

THE RECORD

WORLD CUP

1930-94 Did not enter

AFRICAN CUP OF NATIONS

1957-72	Did not enter
1974	QT 1st round
1976-86	Did not enter
1988	QT pr round
1990-94	Did not enter

AFRICAN CLUB COMPETITIONS

African Cup

2nd round - Olympique Real 1974, SCAF Tocages 1985

Cup Winners Cup

Quarter-finalists - AS Tempete Mocaf 1975

CAF Cup

Never past 1st round

CENTRAL AFRICAN REPUBLIC LEAGUE CHAMPIONS

1973	Olympique Real
1974	ASDR Fatima
1975	Olympique Real
1976	AS Tempete Mocaf
1977	SCAF Tocages
1978	ASDR Fatima
1979	Olympique Real
1980	USCA Bangui
1981	Sporting Moura
1982	Olympique Real
1983	ASDR Fatima
1984	AS Tempete Mocaf
1985	SCAF Tocages
1986	Sporting Moura
1987	-
1988	ASDR Fatima
1989	SCAF Tocages
1990	AS Tempete Mocaf
1991	FACA FC
1992	USCA Bangui
1993	AS Tempete Mocaf

CLUB DIRECTORY

BANGUI (Population - 473,000)

SCAF Tocages (Stade Central Africaine)
USCA Bangui (Union Sportive Central Africaine)
Association Sportive Tempete Mocaf
Sporting Moura
Sodiam
ASDR Fatima (Association Sportive Diables Rouges Fatima)
Olympique Real
Avia Sports

CHAD

Population: 4,944,000
Area, sq km: 1,284,000
% in urban areas: 23%
Capital city: N'Djamena

Fédération Tchadienne de Football
BP 886
N'Djamena
Tel: + 235 514038
Fax: +235 514397

Year of formation	1962
Affiliation to FIFA	1988
Affiliation to CAF	1988
National stadium	Stade de N'Djamena
National colours	White/White/White

THE CONGO

Population: 2,326,000
Area, sq km: 342,000
% in urban areas: 51%
Capital city: Brazzaville

Fédération Congolaise de Football
BP 4041
Brazzaville
Congo
Tel: + 242 815101
Fax: None
Telex: 5210 kg

Year of formation	1962
Affiliation to FIFA	1962
Affiliation to CAF	1966
Registered clubs	250
Registered players	14 800
Registered coaches	43
Registered referees	136
National stadium	Stade de la Révolution, Brazzaville 50 000
National colours	Red/Red/Red
Reserve colours	White/Red/White
Season	November - August

THE RECORD

WORLD CUP

1930-70	Did not enter
1974	QT 1st round
1978	QT 2nd round
1982-90	Did not enter
1994	3rd/3 in group 4

AFRICAN CUP OF NATIONS

1957-65	Did not enter
1968	QT 1st/4 in group 6 - Final tournament/1st round
1970	Did not enter
1972	QT Qualified - Final tournament/Winners
1974	QT Automatic - Final tournament/Semi-finalists/4th place
1976	QT 2nd round
1978	QT Qualified - Final tournament/1st round
1980	QT 1st round
1982	QT 1st round
1984	QT 1st round
1986	QT 1st round
1988	QT 1st round
1990	Did not enter
1992	QT 1st/3 in group 7 - Final tournament/Quarter-finalists
1994	QT 3rd/3 in group 6

AFRICAN GAMES

Winners 1965

AFRICAN CLUB COMPETITIONS

African Cup

Winners - CARA Brazzaville 1974

Cup Winners Cup

Semi-finalists - Inter Club 1988

CAF Cup

Never past 2nd round

CONGO LEAGUE CHAMPIONS

1965	Diables Noirs
1966	Abeilles FC
1967	Etoile du Congo
1968	Patronage
1969	CARA Brazzaville
1970	Victoria Club Mokanda
1971	CARA Brazzaville
1972	CARA Brazzaville
1973	CARA Brazzaville
1974	CARA Brazzaville
1975	CARA Brazzaville
1976	Diables Noirs
1977	Inter Club
1978	Etoile du Congo
1979	Etoile du Congo
1980	Etoile du Congo
1981	Etoile du Congo
1982	CARA Brazzaville
1983	Kotoko Mfoa
1984	CARA Brazzaville
1985	Etoile du Congo
1986	Patronage
1987	Etoile du Congo
1988	Inter Club
1989	Etoile du Congo
1990	Inter Club
1991	Diables Noirs
1992	Etoile du Congo
1993	-
1994	Etoile du Congo

CONGO CUP WINNERS

1982	AS Cheminots
1983	Etoile du Congo
1984	AS Cheminots
1985	Inter Club
1986	CARA Brazzaville
1987	Inter Club
1988	Patronage
1989	Diables Noirs
1990	Diables Noirs
1991	Elecsport
1992	CARA Brazzaville
1993	-
1994	EPB

CLUB DIRECTORY

BRAZZAVILLE (Pop. - 585,000)
CARA Brazzaville (Club Athletique Renaissance Aiglons)
Etoile du Congo
Diables Noirs
Inter Club
Kotoko Mfoa

POINTE-NOIR (Pop. - 294,000)
Abeilles FC
Patronage Sainte Anne
EPB (Enterprise de Peinture et des Batiments)

LUBOMO
AS Cheminots

KOUILOU
Victoria Club Mokanda

COTE D'IVOIRE

Population: 12,657,000
Area, sq km: 320,763
% in urban areas: 43%
Capital city: Abidjan and Yamoussoukro

Fédération Ivoirienne de Football
Av 1 Treichville
BP 1201
Abidjan 01
Côte d'Ivoire
Tel: + 225 240027
Fax: + 225 244308
Telex: 22722 fif ci

Year of formation	1960
Affiliation to FIFA	1960
Affiliation to CAF	1960
Registered clubs	120
Registered players	12 800
Registered coaches	16
Registered referees	250
National stadium	Felix Houphouet-Boigny, Abidjan 36,000
National colours	White/Orange/Green
Reserve colours	Orange/White/Orange
Season	December - August

THE RECORD

WORLD CUP

1930-70	Did not enter
1974	QT 3rd round
1978	QT 3rd round
1982	Did not enter
1986	QT 2nd round
1990	QT 2nd round
1994	QT 1st round - 1st/3 in group 5 2nd round - 2nd/3 in group 1

AFRICAN CUP OF NATIONS

1957-63	Did not enter
1965	3rd place
1968	QT 1st/3 in group 3 - Final tournament/Semi-finalists/3rd place
1970	QT Qualified - Final tournament/Semi-finalists/4th place
1972	QT 2nd round
1974	QT Qualified - Final tournament/1st round
1976	QT 1st round
1978	QT 2nd round
1980	QT Qualified - Final tournament/1st round
1982	Did not enter
1984	QT Automatic - Final tournament/1st round
1986	QT Qualified - Final tournament/Semi-finalists/3rd place
1988	QT Qualified - Final tournament/1st round
1990	QT Qualified - Final tournament/1st round
1992	QT 1st/4 in group 3 - Final tournament/Winners
1994	QT Automatic - Final Tournament/Semi-finalists/3rd place

AFRICAN CLUB COMPETITIONS

African Cup
Winners - Stade Abidjan 1966
Finalists - Africa Sports 1986

Cup Winners Cup
Finalists - Stella Abidjan 1975, Africa Sports 1980

CAF Cup
Winners - Stella Abidjan 1993

CÔTE D'IVOIRE LEAGUE CHAMPIONS

1960	Onze Freres
1961	-
1962	Stade Abidjan
1963	Stade Abidjan
1964	ASEC Abidjan
1965	Stade Abidjan
1966	Stade Abidjan
1967	Africa Sports
1968	Africa Sports
1969	Stade Abidjan
1970	ASEC Abidjan
1971	Africa Sports
1972	ASEC Abidjan
1973	ASEC Abidjan
1974	ASEC Abidjan
1975	ASEC Abidjan
1976	SC Gagnoa
1977	Africa Sports
1978	Africa Sports
1979	Stella Club
1980	ASEC Abidjan
1981	Stella Club
1982	Africa Sports
1983	Africa Sports
1984	Stella Club
1985	Africa Sports
1986	Africa Sports
1987	Africa Sports
1988	Africa Sports
1989	Africa Sports
1990	ASEC Abidjan
1991	ASEC Abidjan
1992	ASEC Abidjan
1993	ASEC Abidjan
1994	ASEC Abidjan

CÔTE D'IVOIRE CUP WINNERS

1960	Espoir de Man
1961	Africa Sports
1962	ASEC Abidjan
1963	Jeunesse
1964	Africa Sports
1965	-
1966	-
1967	ASEC Abidjan
1968	ASEC Abidjan
1969	ASEC Abidjan
1970	ASEC Abidjan
1971	Stade Abidjan
1972	ASEC Abidjan
1973	ASEC Abidjan
1974	Stella Club
1975	Stella Club
1976	Stade Abidjan
1977	Africa Sports
1978	Africa Sports
1979	Africa Sports
1980	Reveil Daloa
1981	Africa Sports
1982	Africa Sports
1983	ASEC Abidjan
1984	Stade Abidjan
1985	Africa Sports
1986	Africa Sports
1987	ASC Bouake
1988	ASI Abengouron
1989	Africa Sports
1990	SC Gagnoa
1991	Africa Sports
1992	ASEC Abidjan
1993	Africa Sports
1994	Stade Abidjan

CLUB DIRECTORY

ABIDJAN (Pop. - 1,950,000)
ASEC Abidjan (Association Sportive Employeés Commercial)

Stade Abidjan
Africa Sports
Association Sportive Sotra
Stella Club

BOUAKE (Pop. - 275,000)
ASC Bouaké (Association Sportive Culturelle)
Sporting Club Alliance

DALOA (Pop. - 85,000)
Reveil Club

GAGNOA (Pop. - 42,000)
Sporting Club Gagnoa
Onze Freres

DJIBOUTI

Population: 470,000
Area, sq km: 23,000
% in urban areas: 75%
Capital city: Djibouti 220,000

Federatio Djiboutienne de Football
BP 1916
Djibouti
Fax: + 253 340950

Year of formation	1977
Affiliation to FIFA	1994
Affiliation to CAF	1994
Registered players	2000
National Stadium	Hassan Gouled Djibouti 10,000
Season	October - June

THE RECORD

WORLD CUP

1930-94 Did not enter

AFRICAN CUP OF NATIONS

1957-94 Did not enter

AFRICAN CLUB COMPETITIONS

Have never entered

EGYPT

Population: 53,170,000
Area, sq km: 997,739
% in urban areas: 43%
Capital city: Cairo

All Ettihad el Masri li Korat el Kadam
Egyptian Football Association
5 Shareh Gabalaya, Guezira
Al Borg Post Office
Cairo
Egypt

Tel: + 20 2 3401793
Fax: + 20 2 3417817
Telex: 23504 KORA

Year of formation	1921
Affiliation to FIFA	1923
Affiliation to CAF	1957
Registered clubs	2370
Registered players	23 000
Registered coaches	841
Registered referees	843
National stadium	International Stadium, Cairo 100 000
National colours	Red/White/Black
Reserve colours	Green/Green/Green
Season	September - June

THE RECORD

WORLD CUP

1930	Did not enter
1934	QT 1st/4 in group 4 - Final tournament/1st round
1938	Did not enter
1950	Did not enter
1954	QT 2nd/2 in group 9
1958-70	Did not enter
1974	QT 1st round
1978	QT 4th round
1982	QT 3rd round
1986	QT 3rd round
1990	QT Qualified - Final tournament/1st round
1994	QT 1st round 2nd/4 in group 3

AFRICAN CUP OF NATIONS

1957	Winners
1959	Winners
1962	Finalists
1963	3rd place
1965	Did not enter
1968	QT 1st/4 in group 4 - withdrew
1970	QT Qualified - Final tournament/Semi-finalists/3rd place
1972	QT 2nd round
1974	QT Automatic - Final tournament/Semi-finalists/3rd place
1976	QT Qualified - Final tournament/2nd round/4th place
1978	QT 1st round
1980	QT Qualified - Final tournament/Semi-finalists/4th place
1982	QT 2nd round
1984	QT Qualified - Final tournament/Semi-finalists/4th place
1986	QT Automatic - Final tournament/Winners
1988	QT Automatic - Final tournament/1st round
1990	QT Qualified - Final tournament/1st round
1992	QT 1st/4 in group 2 - Final tournament/1st round
1994	QT2nd/4 in group 8 - Final tournament/Quarter-finals

AFRICAN GAMES

Winners 1987

AFRICAN CLUB COMPETITIONS

African Champions Cup
Winners - Ismaili 1969, Al Ahly 1982 1987, Zamalek 1984 1986 1993
Finalists - Mehalla 1974, Al Ahly 1983, Zamalek 1994
Cup Winners Cup
Winners - Arab Contractors 1982 1983, Al Ahly 1984 1985 1986 1993
CAF Cup
Have never entered

EGYPTIAN LEAGUE CHAMPIONS

1949	Al Ahly
1950	Al Ahly
1951	Al Ahly
1952	-
1953	Al Ahly
1954	Al Ahly
1955	-
1956	Al Ahly
1957	Al Ahly
1958	Al Ahly
1959	Al Ahly
1960	Zamalek
1961	Al Ahly
1962	Al Ahly
1963	Al Tersana
1964	Zamalek
1965	Zamalek
1966	Olympic
1967	Ismaili
1968-72	-
1973	Mehalla Al Kubra
1974	-
1975	Al Ahly
1976	Al Ahly
1977	Al Ahly
1978	Zamalek
1979	Al Ahly
1980	Al Ahly
1981	Al Ahly
1982	Al Ahly
1983	Al Mokaouloum
1984	Zamalek
1985	Al Ahly
1986	Al Ahly
1987	Al Ahly
1988	Zamalek
1989	Al Ahly
1990	Al Ahly
1991	Ismaili
1992	Zamalek
1993	Zamalek
1994	Zamalek
1995	Al Ahly

FAROUK CUP

1922	Cairo International SC
1923	Cairo International SC
1924	Al Ahly
1925	Al Ahly
1926	Al Ittihad
1927	Al Ahly
1928	Al Ahly
1929	Al Tersana
1930	Al Ahly
1931	Al Ahly
1932	Zamalek

1933	Olympic
1934	Olympic
1935	Zamalek
1936	Al Ittihad
1937	Al Ahly
1938	Zamalek
1939	Al Teram SC
1940	Al Ahly
1941	Zamalek
1942	Al Ahly
1943	Al Ahly & Zamalek
1944	Zamalek
1945	Al Ahly
1946	Al Ahly
1947	Al Ahly
1948	Al Ittihad

CUP OF EGYPT

1949	Al Ahly
1950	Al Ahly
1951	Al Ahly
1952	Zamalek
1953	Al Ahly
1954	Al Tersana
1955	Zamalek
1956	Al Ahly
1957	Zamalek
1958	Zamalek & Al Ahly
1959	Zamalek
1960	Zamalek
1961	Al Ahly
1962	Zamalek
1963	Al Ittihad
1964	Suez Canal
1965	Al Tersana
1966	Al Ahly
1967	Al Tersana
1968-72	-
1973	Al Ittihad
1974	-
1975	Zamalek
1976	Al Ittihad
1977	Zamalek
1978	Al Ahly
1979	Zamalek
1980	-
1981	Al Ahly
1982	-
1983	Al Ahly
1984	Al Ahly
1985	Al Ahly
1986	Al Tersana
1987	Zamalek
1988	Zamalek
1989	Zamalek
1990	Al Mokaouloum
1991	Al Ahly
1992	Al Ahly
1993	Al Ahly
1994	-
1995	Al Mokaouloum

CLUB DIRECTORY

CAIRO (Pop. - 6,052,000)
Al Ahly Sporting Club
Zamalek Sporting Club
Al Mokaouloum (Also known as Arab Contractors)
Al Tersana (Also known as Arsenal)

ALEXANDRIA (Pop. - 2,917,000)
Olympic Sporting Club
Al Ittihad (Also known as Union Recreation)

PORT SAID (Pop. - 399,000)
Al Mesri Sporting Club

MAHALLAH AL KUBRA (Pop. - 385,000)
Mehalla Sporting Club

MANSURAH (Pop. - 375,000)
Al Mansurah Sporting Club

TANTA (Pop. - 334,000)
Tanta Sporting Club

ISMAILI (Pop. - 235,000)
Al Ismaili Sporting Club

EQUATORIAL GUINEA

Population: 350,000
Area, sq km: 28,051
% in urban areas: 60%
Capital city: Malabo

Federacion Equatoguineana de Futbol
BP 471
Malabo
Equatorial Guinea
Tel: + 240 9 2392
Fax: + 240 9 3353
Telex: 999 1111 eg

Year of formation	1976
Affiliation to FIFA	1986
Affiliation to CAF	1986
Registered clubs	42
Registered players	2400
Registered coaches	27
Registered referees	67
National stadium	Estadio La Paz, Malabo 15 000
National colours	Red/Red/Red
Reserve colours	Green/Green/Green

THE RECORD

WORLD CUP

1930-94	Did not enter

AFRICAN CUP OF NATIONS

1957-80	Did not enter
1982	QT 1st round
1984-88	Did not enter
1990	QT pr round
1992	Did not enter
1994	Did not enter

AFRICAN CLUB COMPETITIONS

African Cup
Never past the first round

Cup Winners Cup
Never past the first round

CAF Cup
Never past the first round

GUINEA EQUATORIAL LEAGUE CHAMPIONS

1979	Real Rebola
1980	FC Mongomo
1981	Atletico Malabo
1982	Atletico Malabo
1983	FC Dragons
1984	CD Ela Nguema
1985	CD Ela Nguema
1986	CD Ela Nguema
1987	CD Ela Nguema
1988	CD Ela Nguema
1989	CD Ela Nguema
1990	CD Ela Nguema
1991	CD Ela Nguema
1992	Akonangui FC

CLUB DIRECTORY

MALABO (Pop. - 30,000)
Atletico Malabo
GD Lage

ELA NGUEMA
Clube Deportivo Ela Nguema
Atletico Ela Nguema

BATA
Dragons FC
Union Vesper

ETHIOPIA

Population: 50,341,000
Area, sq km: 1,223,500
% in urban areas: 10%
Capital city: Addis Ababa

Yeitiopia Football Federechin
Addis Ababa Stadium
PO Box 1080
Addis Ababa
Ethiopia
Tel: + 251 1 514453
Fax: + 251 1 513345
Telex: 21377 nesco et

Year of formation	1943
Affiliation to FIFA	1953
Affiliation to CAF	1957
Registered clubs	767
Registered players	74 900
Registered coaches	1016
Registered referees	5484
National stadium	Addis Ababa Stadium 30 000
National colours	Green/Yellow/Red
Reserve colours	Red/Green/Yellow
Season	September - June

THE RECORD

WORLD CUP

1930-58	Did not enter
1962	QT 2nd round
1966	Did not enter
1970	QT 2nd round
1974	QT 2nd round
1978	QT 1st round
1982	QT 1st round
1986	QT 1st round
1990	Did not enter
1994	QT 3rd/4 in group 6

AFRICAN CUP OF NATIONS

1957	Finalists
1959	3rd place
1962	Winners
1963	4th place
1965	1st round
1968	QT Automatic - Final tournament/Semi-finalists/4th place
1970	QT Qualified - Final tournament/1st round
1972	QT 1st round
1974	QT 1st round
1976	QT Automatic - Final tournament/1st round
1978	QT 2nd round
1980	QT 1st round
1982	QT Qualified - Final tournament/1st round
1984	QT 2nd round
1986	Did not enter
1988	QT 1st round
1990	QT 1st round
1992	QT 4th/4 in group 2
1994	QT 3rd/4 in group 2

AFRICAN CLUB COMPETITIONS

African Cup

Semi-finalists - Cotton Club 1964, St. Georges 1967

Cup Winners Cup

Quarter-finalists - Mechal Army 1976

CAF Cup

Semi-finalists - Insurance FC 1993

ETHIOPIAN LEAGUE CHAMPIONS

1943-64	-
1965	Ethio-cement
1966	St. Georges
1967	St. Georges
1968	St. Georges
1969	Tele Asmara
1970	Tele Asmara
1971	St. Georges
1972	Tele Asmara
1973	Tele Asmara
1974	Embassoria
1975	St. Georges
1976	Mechal Army
1977	Medr Babur
1978	Ogaden Anbassa
1979-83	-
1984	Ground Force
1985	Brewery Jimma
1986	Brewery Jimma
1987-89	-
1990	Brewery Addis
1991	St Georges
1992	St Georges
1993	Electric Sports

CLUB DIRECTORY

ADDIS ABABA (Pop. - 1,500,000)

Saint Georges Sports Association
Cotton Club
Mechal Army
Ground Force
Electric Sports

ASMARA (Pop. - 275,000)

Eritrea Shoe Factory
Tele Sporting Club

DIRE DAWA (Pop. - 98,000)

Ogaden Anbassa
Ethio-Cement

GABON

Population: 1,171,000
Area, sq km: 267,667
% in urban areas: 40%
Capital city: Libreville

Fédération Gabonaise de Football
BP 181
Libreville
Gabon
Tel: + 241 744747
Fax: None
Telex: 5526 go

Year of formation	1962
Affiliation to FIFA	1963
Affiliation to CAF	1967
Registered clubs	300
Registered players	10 000
Registered referees	90
National stadium	Omnisport, Libreville 30,000
National colours	White/White/White
Reserve colours	Blue/Yellow/Green
Season	October - July

THE RECORD

WORLD CUP

1930-86	Did not enter
1990	QT 2nd round
1994	QT 2nd/3 in group 7

AFRICAN CUP OF NATIONS

1957-70	Did not enter
1972	QT 1st round
1974	Did not enter
1976	Did not enter
1978	QT 2nd round
1980	Did not enter
1982	Did not enter
1984	QT pr round
1986	QT pr round
1988	QT pr round
1990	QT 2nd round
1992	QT 2nd/4 in group 8
1994	QT1st/4 in group 1 - Final Tournament/1st round

AFRICAN CLUB COMPETITIONS

African Cup

Quarter-finalists - US Mbila Nzambi 1981. FC 105 1984 1988

Cup Winners Cup

Finalists - AS Sogara 1986

CAF Cup

Quarter-finalists - ASMO 1992, Mbilinga 1993

GABON LEAGUE CHAMPIONS

1968	Olympique Sportif
1969	Aigle Royal
1970	Aigle Royal
1971	AS Solidarite
1972	Olympique Sportif
1973	AS Police
1974	Zalang COC
1975	Petrosports FC
1976	Vautour Club Mangoungou
1977	Vautour Club Mangoungou
1978	FC 105
1979	Anges ABC
1980	US Mbila Nzambi
1981	US Mbila Nzambi
1982	FC 105
1983	FC 105
1984	AS Sogara
1985	FC 105
1986	FC 105
1987	FC 105
1988	US Mbila Nzambi
1989	AS Sogara
1990	JAC Port Gentil
1991	AS Sogara
1992	AS Sogara
1993	AS Sogara
1994	AS Sogara

CLUB DIRECTORY

Libreville (Pop. - 235,000)

FC 105 (Football Canon)
US Mbila Nziami - Previously Mbila Nzambi
Olympique Sportif
Aigle Royal
Vautour Club Mangounou
AS Solidarite
Anges ABC
Zalang

PORT GENTILE (Pop. - 124,000)

AS Sogara
Petrosport FC
Shell FC
JAC Port Gentile
Delta FC

GAMBIA

Population: 860,000
Area, sq km: 10,689
% in urban areas: 20%
Capital city: Banjul (Previously Bathurst)

Gambia Football Association
PO Box 523
Banjul
The Gambia
Tel: + 220 496980
Fax: + 220 394962
Telex: 2262 fisco gv

Year of formation	1952
Affiliation to FIFA	1966
Affiliation to CAF	1962
Registered clubs	30
Registered players	1800
Registered referees	27
National stadium	Box Bar Stadium, Banjul 10 000
National colours	White/White/White
Reserve colours	Blue/Blue/White
Season	November - July

THE RECORD

WORLD CUP

1930-78	Did not enter
1982	QT 1st round
1986	QT 1st round
1990	Did not enter
1994	Did not enter

AFRICAN CUP OF NATIONS

1957-74	Did not enter
1976	QT pr round
1978	Did not enter
1980	QT 1st round
1982	QT pr round
1984	QT pr round
1986	QT pr round
1988	QT pr round
1990-94	Did not enter

AFRICAN CLUB COMPETITIONS

African Cup
2nd round - Real Banjul 1979
Cup Winners Cup
2nd round - Wallidan 1979
CAF Cup
Have never entered

GAMBIAN LEAGUE CHAMPIONS

1973	Ports Authority
1974	Wallidan
1975	Real Banjul
1976	-
1977	Wallidan
1978	Real Banjul
1979	Wallidan
1980	Starlight
1981	Starlight
1982	Ports Authority
1983	Real Banjul
1984	Ports Authority
1985	Wallidan
1986	Wallidan
1987	Wallidan
1988	Wallidan
1989	Wallidan
1990	Wallidan
1991	Wallidan
1992	Wallidan
1993	Hawks

CLUB DIRECTORY

BANJUL (Population - 95,000)
Real Banjul
Wallidan
Ports Authority
Starlight
Augustinians
Hawks

GHANA

Population: 15,020,000
Area, sq km: 238,533
% in urban areas: 31%
Capital city: Accra

Ghana Football Association
PO Box 1272
Accra
Ghana
Tel: + 233 21 666697
Fax: +233 21 668590
Telex: 2519 sports gh

Year of formation	1957
Affiliation to FIFA	1958
Affiliation to CAF	1958
Registered clubs	185
Registered players	11 200
Registered referees	376
National stadium	Accra Sports Stadium 34 000
National colours	White/White/White
Reserve colours	Yellow/Yellow/ Yellow
Season	January - November

THE RECORD

WORLD CUP

1930-58	Did not enter
1962	QT 2nd round
1966	Did not enter
1970	QT 2nd round
1974	QT 3rd round
1978	QT 1st round
1982	Did not enter
1986	QT 3rd round
1990	QT 1st round

AFRICAN CUP OF NATIONS

1957-62	Did not enter
1963	Winners
1965	Winners
1968	QT Automatic - Final tournament/Finalists
1970	QT Qualified - Final tournament/Finalists
1972	QT 2nd round
1974	QT 2nd round
1976	QT 2nd round
1978	QT Automatic - Final tournament/Winners
1980	QT Automatic - Final tournament/1st round
1982	QT Qualified - Final tournament/Winners
1984	QT Automatic - Final tournament/1st round
1986	QT 2nd round
1988	QT 1st round
1990	QT 1st round
1992	QT 1st/5 in group 4 - Final tournament/Finalists
1994	QT 1st/2 in group 7 - Final Tournament/Quater-finalists

AFRICAN CLUB COMPETITIONS

African Cup
Winners - Asante Kotoko 1970 1983
Finalists - Asante Kotoko 1967 1971 1973 1982, Hearts of Oak 1977 1979
Cup Winners Cup
Semi-finalists - Sekondi Hasaacas 1981, Hearts of Oak 1982
CAF Cup
2nd round - Hearts of Oak 1993

GHANAIAN LEAGUE CHAMPIONS

1957	Hearts of Oak
1958	Hearts of Oak
1959	Asante Kotoko
1960	Eleven Wise FC
1961	-
1962	Hearts of Oak
1963	Asante Kotoko
1964	Asante Kotoko
1965	Asante Kotoko
1966	Real Republicans
1967	Asante Kotoko
1968	Cape Coast Dwarfs
1969	Asante Kotoko
1970	Asante Kotoko
1970	Great Olympics
1971	Hearts of Oak
1972	Asante Kotoko
1973	Hearts of Oak
1974	Great Olympics
1975	Asante Kotoko
1976	Hearts of Oak
1977	Hearts of Oak
1978	Hearts of Oak
1979	Hearts of Oak
1980	Asante Kotoko
1981	Asante Kotoko
1982	Asante Kotoko
1983	Asante Kotoko
1984	Hearts of Oak
1985	Hearts of Oak
1986	Asante Kotoko
1987	Asante Kotoko
1988	-
1989	Asante Kotoko
1990	Hearts of Oak
1991	Asante Kotoko

1992	Asante Kotoko
1993	Asante Kotoko
1994	Goldfields
1995	Goldfields

GHANAIAN CUP WINNERS

1958	Asante Kotoko
1959	Cornerstones
1960	Asante Kotoko
1961	-
1962	Real Republicans
1963	Real Republicans
1964	Real Republicans
1965	Real Republicans
1966-68	-
1969	Cape Coast Dwarfs
1970-72	-
1973	Hearts of Oak
1974	Hearts of Oak
1975	Great Olympics
1976	Asante Kotoko
1977	-
1978	Asante Kotoko
1979	Hearts of Oak
1980	-
1981	Hearts of Oak
1982	Eleven Wise FC
1983	Great Olympics
1984	Asante Kotoko
1985	Sekondi Hasaacas
1986	Okwahu United
1987	Hearts of Oak
1988	-
1989	Hearts of Oak
1990	Hearts of Oak
1991	-
1992	Voradep
1993	Goldfields
1994	Hearts of Oak

CLUB DIRECTORY

ACCRA (Pop. - 1,250,000)
Hearts of Oak
Great Olympics
Real Republicans (Folded 1966)

KUMASI (Pop. - 600,000)
Asante Kotoko
Cornerstones

SEKONDI (Pop. - 175,000)
Sekondi Hasaacas
Eleven Wise FC

TAMALE (Pop. - 168,000)
Real Tamale United

CAPE COAST (Pop. - 86,000)
Cape Coast Dwarfs

OBUASSI (Pop. - 60,000)
Obuassi Goldfields

NKAWKAW
Okwahu United

GUINEA-BISSAU

Population: 973,000
Area, sq km: 36,125
% in urban areas: 28%
Capital city: Bissau

Federacao de Football da Guinea-Bissau
Apartado 75
1035 Bissau - Codex
Guinea-Bissau
Tel: + 245 201918
Fax: + 245 201918
Telex: 250 publico bi

Year of formation	1974
Affiliation to FIFA	1986
Affiliation to CAF	1986
Registered clubs	16
Registered players	1300
Registered coaches	29
Registered referees	31
National stadium	Lino Correia 12 000
National colours	Green/Green/Green
Reserve colours:	Yellow/Yellow/ Yellow
Season	October - July

THE RECORD

WORLD CUP

1930-94	Did not enter

AFRICAN CUP OF NATIONS

1957-92	Did not enter
1994	QT 4th/4 in group 3

AFRICAN CLUB COMPETITIONS

African Cup
2nd round - Sporting Clube Bissau 1984
Cup Winners Cup
2nd round - Sporting Club Bissau 1977
CAF Cup
Never past preliminary round

GUINEA-BISSAU LEAGUE CHAMPIONS

1975	Balantes
1976	UDIB Bissau
1977	Benfica
1978	-
1979	Benfica
1980	Benfica
1981	-
1982	Benfica
1983	Sporting Clube Bissau
1984	Sporting Clube Bissau
1985	UDIB Bissau
1986	Sporting Clube Bissau
1987	Sporting Clube Batafa
1988	Benfica
1989	Benfica
1990	Sporting Clube Bissau
1991	-
1992	Sporting Clube Bissau
1993	-
1994	Porto FC

CLUB DIRECTORY

BISSAU (Pop. - 109,000)
Benfica
Uniao Deportiva Internacional Bissau (UDIB)
Sporting Clube
Ajuda Sport

BATAFA
Sporting Clube

MANSOA
Balantas

GUINEA

Population: 6,876,000
Area, sq km: 245,857
% in urban areas: 23%
Capital city: Conakry

Fédération Guinéenne de Football
PO Box 262
Conakry
Guinea
Tel: + 224 443204
Fax: + 224 413673
Telex: 22302 mj ge

Year of formation	1959
Affiliation to FIFA	1961
Affiliation to CAF	1962
Registered clubs	351
Registered players	14 200
Registered coaches	48
Registered referees	136
National stadium	Stade du 28 Septembre, Conakry 40 000
National colours	Red/Yellow/Green
Reserve colours	White/White/White
Season	November - July

THE RECORD

WORLD CUP

1930-70	Did not enter
1974	QT 2nd round
1978	QT 3rd round
1982	QT 3rd round
1986	QT 2nd round
1990	QT 1st round
1994	QT 1st round - 1st/2 in group 9 2nd round - 3rd/3 in group 3

AFRICAN CUP OF NATIONS

1957-65	Did not enter
1968	QT 2nd in group

1970	QT Qualified - Final tournament/1st round
1972	QT 2nd round
1974	QT Qualified - Final tournament/1st round
1976	QT Qualified - Final tournament/2nd round/2nd place
1978	QT 2nd round
1980	QT Qualified - Final tournament/1st round
1982	QT 2nd round
1984	QT 1st round
1986	QT 1st round
1988	QT 1st round
1990	QT 1st round
1992	QT 3rd/4 in group 1
1994	QT 1st/3 in group 6 - Final Tournament/1st round

AFRICAN CLUB COMPETITIONS

African Cup

Winners - Hafia FC Conakry 1972 1975 1977

Finalists - Hafia FC Conakry 1976 1978

Cup Winners Cup

Winners - Horoya AC Conakry 1978

CAF Cup

Never past 1st round

GUINEA LEAGUE CHAMPIONS

1965	Conakry I
1966	Conakry II
1967	Conakry II
1968	Conakry II
1969	Conakry I
1970	Conakry I
1971	Hafia FC
1972	Hafia FC
1973	Hafia FC
1974	Hafia FC
1975	Hafia FC
1976	Hafia FC
1977	Hafia FC
1978	Hafia FC
1979	Hafia FC
1980	Kaloum Star
1981	Kaloum Star
1982	Hafia FC
1983	Hafia FC
1984	Kaloum Star
1985	Hafia FC
1986	Horoya AC
1987	Kaloum Star
1988	Horoya AC
1989	Horoya AC
1990	Horoya AC
1991	Horoya AC
1992	Horoya AC
1993	Kaloum Star
1994	Horoya AC

CLUB DIRECTORY

CONAKRY (Pop. - 800,000)

Hafia FC - Previously Conakry II
Horoya AC
Kaloum Star - Previously Conakry I
Gbessia AC
Kakimbo FC
ASFAG Conakry

KENYA

Population: 24,872,000
Area, sq km: 582,646
% in urban areas: 19%
Capital city: Nairobi

Kenya Football Federation
Nyayo National Stadium
PO Box 40234
Nairobi
Kenya
Tel: + 254 2 501825
Fax: + 254 2 501120
Telex: 24069 spicers ke

Year of formation	1932
Affiliation to FIFA	1960
Affiliation to CAF	1968
Registered clubs	351
Registered players	32 000
Registered referees	1300
National stadium	Nyayo, Nairobi 35 000
National colours	Red/Red/Red
Reserve colours	Green/Green/Green
Season	February - November

THE RECORD

WORLD CUP

1930-70	Did not enter
1974	QT 3rd round
1978	QT 2nd round
1982	QT 1st round
1986	QT 2nd round
1990	QT 2nd round
1994	QT 2nd/2 in group 9

AFRICAN CUP OF NATIONS

1957-65	Did not enter
1968	QT 1st round
1970	QT 1st round
1972	QT Qualified - Final tournament/1st round
1974	QT 1st round
1976	QT 1st round
1978	QT 1st round
1980	QT 2nd round
1982	QT 1st round
1984	Did not enter
1986	QT 2nd round
1988	QT Qualified - Final tournament/1st round
1990	QT Qualified - Final tournament/1st round
1992	QT 1st/3 in group 6 - Final tournament/1st round
1994	QT Automatic - Withdrew

AFRICAN CLUB COMPETITIONS

African Cup

Semi-finalists - AFC Leopards 1968, Kenya Breweries 1973

Cup Winners Cup

Winners - Gor Mahia 1987

Finalists - Gor Mahia 1979, Kenya Breweries 1994

CAF Cup

Quarter-finalists - Gor Mahia 1993 AFC Leopards 1994

KENYAN LEAGUE CHAMPIONS

1963	Nakuru All Stars
1964	Luo Union
1965	Liverpool
1966	Abaluhya United
1967	Abaluhya United
1968	-
1969	Gor Mahia
1970	Abaluhya United
1971	-
1972	Kenya Breweries
1973	Abaluhya
1974	Gor Mahia
1975	Luo Union
1976	Gor Mahia
1977	Kenya Breweries
1978	Kenya Breweries
1979	Gor Mahia
1980	Abaluhya
1981	AFC Leopards
1982	AFC Leopards
1983	Gor Mahia
1984	Gor Mahia
1985	Gor Mahia
1986	AFC Leopards
1987	Shabana Kissi
1988	AFC Leopards
1989	AFC Leopards
1990	Gor Mahia
1991	Gor Mahia
1992	AFC Leopards
1993	Gor Mahia
1994	Kenya Breweries

KENYAN CUP WINNERS

1986	Gor Mahia
1987	Gor Mahia
1988	Gor Mahia
1989	Kenya Breweries
1990	Rivatex
1991	AFC Leopards
1992	Kenya Breweries
1993	Kenya Breweries
1994	AFC Leopards

CLUB DIRECTORY

NAIROBI (Pop. - 1,286,000)

Gor Mahia
AFC Leopards - Formerly Abaluhya United and Abaluhya
Kenya Breweries Nairobi

MOMBASSA (Pop. - 442,000)
Luo Union
Ramogi

NAKURU (Pop. - 101,000)
Nakuru All Stars
Scarlets

KISII
Shabana Kisii

LESOTHO

Population: 1,760,000
Area, sq km: 30,355
% in urban areas: 16%
Capital city: Maseru

Lesotho Football Association
PO Box 1879
Maseru 100
Lesotho
Tel: + 266 311291
Fax: + 266 310194
Telex: 4493 sports lo

Year of formation	1932
Affiliation to FIFA	1964
Affiliation to CAF	1964
Registered clubs	88
Registered players	16 800
Registered referees	21
National stadium	Setsotho Stadium, Maseru 20 000
National colours	Blue/Green/White
Reserve colours	White/Blue/Blue
Season	February - October

THE RECORD

WORLD CUP

1930-70	Did not enter
1974	QT 1st round
1978	Did not enter
1982	QT 1st round
1986-94	Did not enter

AFRICAN CUP OF NATIONS

1957-72	Did not enter
1974	QT 1st round
1976	Did not enter
1978	Did not enter
1980	QT pr round
1982	QT pr round
1984-92	Did not enter
1994	QT 4th/4 in group 4

AFRICAN CLUB COMPETITIONS
African Champions Cup
Quarter-finalists - Matlama FC 1979
Cup Winners Cup
2nd round - Maseru United 1979, Matlama FC 1980, Arsenal 1993
CAF Cup
Never past the 1st round

LESOTHO LEAGUE CHAMPIONS

1970	Maseru United
1971	Majantja
1972	Police
1973	Linare
1974	Matlama
1975	FC Maseru
1976	Maseru United
1977	Matlama
1978	Matlama
1979	Linare
1980	Linare
1981	Maseru Brothers
1982	Matlama
1983	LPF Maseru
1984	LPF Maseru
1985	Lioli Teyateyaneng
1986	Matlama
1987	RLDF Maseru
1988	Matlama
1989	Arsenal
1990	RLDF Maseru
1991	Arsenal
1992	Matlama
1993	Arsenal
1994	RLDF Maseru

CLUB DIRECTORY

MASERU (Pop. - 109,000)
Arsenal
Matlama FC
Maseru Brothers
Maseru United
Maseru Rovers
Royal Lesotho Defence Force (RLDF Maseru)

LERIBE
Linare FC

LIBERIA

Population: 2,595,000
Area, sq km: 99,067
% in urban areas: 39%
Capital city: Monrovia

The Liberia Football Association
PO Box 1066
Monrovia
Liberia
Tel: + 231 222177
Fax: + 231 735003
Telex: 44220 exm li

Year of formation	1936
Affiliation to FIFA	1962
Affiliation to CAF	1962
Registered clubs	40
Registered players	4600
Registered coaches	48
Registered referees	50
National stadium	National Sports Complex, Monrovia 35 000
National colours	Red/White/Blue
Reserve colours	Blue/White/Red
Season	January - October

THE RECORD

WORLD CUP

1930-78	Did not enter
1982	QT 2nd round
1986	QT 1st round
1990	QT 2nd round
1994	QT 1st round - group 2 withdrew

AFRICAN CUP OF NATIONS

1957-65	Did not enter
1968	QT 3rd in group
1970-74	Did not enter
1976	QT pr round
1978	Did not enter
1980	Did not enter
1982	QT 1st round
1984	Did not enter
1986	QT pr round
1988	QT pr round
1990	QT pr round
1992	Did not enter
1994	QT 2nd/2 in group 7

AFRICAN CLUB COMPETITIONS
African Cup
2nd round - Invincible Eleven 1982, Mighty Barolle 1987
Cup Winners Cup
Quarter-finalists - LPRC Oilers 1989
CAF Cup
Never past first round

LIBERIAN LEAGUE CHAMPIONS

1965	Invincible Eleven
1966	Invincible Eleven
1967	Mighty Barolle
1968-71	-
1972	Mighty Barolle
1973	Mighty Barolle
1974	Mighty Barolle
1975	-
1976	St. Joseph
1977	-
1978	St. Joseph
1979	St. Joseph
1980	Invincible Eleven
1981	Invincible Eleven
1982	-
1983	Invincible Eleven
1984	Invincible Eleven
1985	Invincible Eleven
1986	Mighty Barolle
1987	Invincible Eleven
1988	Mighty Barolle
1989	Mighty Barolle
1990	-
1991	LPRC Oilers
1992	LPRC Oilers
1993	Mighty Barolle
1994	NPA Anchors

CLUB DIRECTORY

MONROVIA (Pop. - 465,000)
Mighty Barolle
St. Joseph Warriors
Invincible Eleven
Cedar United
LPRC Oilers
Bame Monrovia

LIBYA

Population: 4,206,000
Area, sq km: 1,757,000
% in urban areas: 75%
Capital city: Tripoli

Libyan Arab Jamahiriya Football Federation
PO Box 5137
Tripoli
Libya
Tel: + 218 21 4442646
Fax: +218 21 444610
Telex: 20896 KURATP LY

Year of formation	1962
Affiliation to FIFA	1963
Affiliation to CAF	1965
Registered clubs	89
Registered players	58 300
Registered coaches	1578
Registered referees	721
National stadium	11 June Stadium, Tripoli 70 000
National colours	Green/White/Green
Reserve colours	White/Green/White
Season	September - April

THE RECORD

WORLD CUP

1930-66	Did not enter
1970	QT 1st round
1974	Did not enter
1978	QT 1st round
1982	QT 2nd round
1986	QT 4th round
1990	QT 2nd round
1994	Did not enter

AFRICAN CUP OF NATIONS

1957-65	Did not enter
1968	QT 1st round
1970	Did not enter
1972	QT 1st round
1974	Did not enter
1976	QT pr round
1978	QT 1st round
1980	QT 2nd round
1982	QT Automatic - Final tournament/Finalists
1984	QT 1st round
1986	QT 2nd round
1988	QT 2nd round
1990	QT 1st round
1992	Did not enter
1994	Did not enter

AFRICAN CLUB COMPETITIONS

African Cup
Q-finals - Al Ittihad 1967. Al Ahly Tripoli 1972
Cup Winners Cup
Semis - Al Ahly Tripoli 1984, Al Nasr 1985
CAF Cup
2nd round - Al Wahda 1992

LIBYAN LEAGUE CHAMPIONS

1964	Al Ahly Tripoli
1965	Al Ittihad
1966	-
1967	Al Tahaddy
1968	-
1969	Al Ittihad
1970	Al Ahly Benghazi
1971	Al Ahly Tripoli
1972	Al Ahly Benghazi
1973	Al Ahly Tripoli
1974	Al Ahly Tripoli
1975	Al Ahly Benghazi
1976	Al Medina
1977	Al Tahaddy
1978	Al Ahly Tripoli
1979	-
1980	Al Ahly Tripoli
1981	-
1982	Al Ahly Tripoli
1983	Al Medina
1984	Al Ahly Tripoli
1985	Al Adhara
1986	Al Ahly Tripoli
1987	Al Nasr
1988	Al Ittihad
1989	Al Ittihad
1990	Al Ittihad
1991	Al Ittihad
1992	Al Ahly Benghazi
1993	Al Ahly Tripoli
1994	Al Ahly Tripoli

CLUB DIRECTORY

TRIPOLI (Pop. - 990,000)
Al Ahly (National)
Al Ittihad
Al Medina
Municipal

BENGHAZI (Pop. - 435,000)
Al Ahly (National)
Al Tahaddy
Al Nasr
Municipal

MADAGASCAR

Population: 11,980,000
Area, sq km: 587,041
% in urban areas: 21%
Capital city: Antananarivo

Fédération Malagasy de Football
C/O Comite National de Coordination du Football
BP 4409
Antananarivo 101
Madagascar
Tel: + 261 2 28051
Fax: None
Telex: 22393 motel mg

Year of formation	1961
Affiliation to FIFA	1962
Affiliation to CAF	1963
Registered clubs	775
Registered players	9200
Registered coaches	15
Registered referees	477
National stadium	Municipal de Mahamasina, Antananarivo 15 000
National colours	Red/White/Green
Reserve colours	White/Red/Green
Season	February - November

THE RECORD

WORLD CUP

1930-78	Did not enter
1982	QT 2nd round
1986	QT 2nd round
1990	Did not enter
1994	QT 2nd/3 in group 8

AFRICAN CUP OF NATIONS

1957-70	Did not enter
1972	QT 1st round
1974	QT 1st round
1976	Did not enter
1978	Did not enter
1980	QT pr round
1982	QT 2nd round
1984	QT 2nd round
1986	QT 1st round
1988	QT 1st round
1990	Did not enter
1992	QT 2nd/4 in group 5
1994	Did not enter

AFRICAN CLUB COMPETITIONs

African Champions Cup
2nd round - MMM Tamatave 1971, Fortior 1973, AS Somasud 1982, AC Sotema 1992

1993, BTM 1994

Cup Winners Cup

Semi-finalists - BFV FC 1989

CAF Cup

Have never entered

MADAGASCAR LEAGUE CHAMPIONS

1968	Fitarikandro
1969	US Fonctionnaries
1970	MMM Tamatave
1971	AS St. Michael
1972	Fortior Mahajanga
1973	Antalaha
1974	Corps Enseignant
1975	Corps Enseignant
1976	-
1977	Corps Enseignant
1978	AS St. Michael
1979	Fortior Mahajunga
1980	MMM Tamatave
1981	AS Somasud
1982	Dinamo Fima
1983	Dinamo Fima
1984	-
1985	AC Sotema
1986	BTM Antananarivo
1987	Jos Nosy Be
1988	COSFAP Antananarivo
1989	AC Sotema
1990	ASF Fianarantsoa
1991	AC Sotema
1992	AC Sotema
1993	BTM

CLUB DIRECTORY

ANTANANARIVO (Pop. - 663,000)

COSFAP Antananarivo

BTM Antananarivo

BFV FC

FIANARANTSOA (Pop. - 130,000)

ASF Fianarantsoa

TOAMASINA (Pop. - 100,000)

MMM Tamatave

MAHAJUNGA (Pop. - 85,000)

Athletic Club Sotema

Fortior Cote Ouest

HTMF Mahajunga

TOLARIA (Pop. - 55,000)

Association Sportive Somasud

Association Sportive Corps Enseignant

HELL-VILLE

Jos Nosy Be

MALAWI

Population: 8,831,000

Area, sq km: 118,484

% in urban areas: 11%

Capital city: Lilongwe

Football Association of Malawi
PO Box 865
Blantyre
Malawi
Tel: + 265 636686
Fax: + 265 636941
Telex: 4526 sports mi

Year of formation	1966
Affiliation to FIFA	1967
Affiliation to CAF	1968
Registered clubs	280
Registered players	7400
Registered coaches	150
Registered referees	290
National stadium	Kamuzu, Blantyre 50 000
National colours	Red/White/Red
Reserve colours	White/White/White
Season	March - December

THE RECORD

WORLD CUP

1930-74	Did not enter
1978	QT 1st round
1982	QT 1st round
1986	QT 2nd round
1990	QT 2nd round
1994	Did not enter

AFRICAN CUP OF NATIONS

1957-74	Did not enter
1976	QT 1st round
1978	QT Pr round
1980	QT 1st round
1982	QT pr round
1984	QT Qualified - Final tournament/1st round
1986	QT 1st round
1988	QT 2nd round
1990	QT 2nd round
1992	QT 3rd/3 in group 7
1994	QT 4th/4 in group 8

AFRICAN CLUB COMPETITIONS

African Cup

2nd round - Bata Bullets 1975

Cup Winners Cup

2nd round - Bata Bullets 1977

CAF Cup

Never past 1st round

CLUB DIRECTORY

BLANTYRE (Pop. - 331,000)

Bata Bullets

ADMARC Tigers

Hardware Stars

Limbe Leaf Wanderers (formerly Yamaha Wanderers)

LILONGWE (Pop. - 233,000)

Civics

Silver Strikers

MALI

Population: 8,151,000

Area, sq km: 1,240,192

% in urban areas: 22%

Capital city: Bamako

Fédération Malienne de Football
Stade Mamadou Konate
BP 1020
Bamako
Mali
Tel: + 223 224254
Fax: + 223 230322
Telex: 0985 1200 mj

Year of formation	1960
Affiliation to FIFA	1962
Affiliation to CAF	1963
Registered clubs	76
Registered players	12 000
Registered coaches	65
Registered referees	145
National stadium	Omnisports, Bamako 25 000
National colours	Green/Yellow/Red
Reserve colours	White/Red/White
Season	October - June

THE RECORD

WORLD CUP

1930-94	Did not enter

AFRICAN CUP OF NATIONS

1957-65	Did not enter
1968	QT 2nd in group
1970	QT 2nd round
1972	QT Qualified - Final tournament/Finalists
1974	QT 2nd round
1976	QT 1st round
1978	QT 2nd round
1980	Did not enter
1982	QT 1st round
1984	QT 1st round
1986	QT 1st round
1988	Did not enter
1990	QT 2nd round
1992	QT 4th/4 in group 1
1994	QT 1st/4 in group 8 - Final Tournament/Semi-finalists/4th place

AFRICAN CLUB COMPETITIONS

African Cup

Finalists - Stade Malien 1964, AS Real Bamako 1966

Cup Winners Cup

Semi-finalists - Djoliba AC 1981 1982

CAF Cup

Never past 2nd round

MALI LEAGUE CHAMPIONS

1980	AS Real Bamako

1981	AS Real Bamako
1982	Djoliba
1983	AS Real Bamako
1984	Stade Malien
1985	Djoliba
1986	AS Real Bamako
1987	Stade Malien
1988	Djoliba
1989	Stade Malien
1990	Djoliba
1991	Real Bamako
1992	Djoliba
1993	Stade Malien
1994	-

MALI CUP WINNERS

1961	Stade Malien
1962	Real Bamako
1963	Stade Malien
1964	Real Bamako
1965	Djoliba
1966	Real Bamako
1967	Real Bamako
1968	Real Bamako
1969	Real Bamako
1970	Stade Malien
1971	Djoliba
1972	Stade Malien
1973	Djoliba
1974	Djoliba
1975	Djoliba
1976	Djoliba
1977	Djoliba
1978	Djoliba
1979	Djoliba
1980	Real Bamako
1981	Djoliba
1982	Stade Malien
1983	Djoliba
1984	Stade Malien
1985	Stade Malien
1986	Stade Malien
1987	Sigui Kayes
1988	Stade Malien
1989	Real Bamako
1990	Stade Malien
1991	Real Bamako
1992	Stade Malien
1993	Djoliba
1994	Stade Malien

CLUB DIRECTORY

BAMAKO (Pop. - 646,000)
Djoliba Athletic Club
Association Sportive Real Bamako
Stade Malien

MAURITANIA

Population: 1,999,000
Area, sq km: 1,030,700
% in urban areas: 34%
Capital city: Nouakchott

Fédération de Football de la République de Mauritanie
BP 566
Nouakchott
Mauritania
Tel: + 222 2 59057
Fax: + 222 2 59057
Telex: 577 mtn nktt rim

Year of formation	1961
Affiliation to FIFA	1964
Affiliation to CAF	1968
Registered clubs	59
Registered players	1500
Registered coaches	44
Registered referees	97
National stadium	Fode Capi Camara Nouakchott 6 000
National colours	Yellow/Blue/Green
Reserve colours	Green/Yellow/Yellow
Season	November - July

THE RECORD

WORLD CUP

1930-74	Did not enter
1978	QT pr round
1982-94	Did not enter

AFRICAN CUP OF NATIONS

1957-78	Did not enter
1980	QT 1st round
1982	QT pr round
1984	Did not enter
1986	QT 1st round
1988	Did not enter
1990	Did not enter
1992	QT 4th/4 in group 3
1994	Did not enter

AFRICAN CLUB COMPETITIONS

African Cup
2nd round - Espoirs Nouakchott 1977
Cup Winners Cup
2nd round - ASC Garde Nationale 1978
CAF Cup
2nd round - ASC Air Mauritanie 1993

MAURITANIAN LEAGUE CHAMPIONS

1976	ASC Garde Nationale
1977	ASC Garde Nationale
1978	ASC Garde Nationale
1979	ASC Garde Nationale
1980	-
1981	AS Police
1982	AS Police
1983	AS Ksar
1984	ASC Garde Nationale
1985	AS Ksar
1986	AS Police
1987	AS Police
1988	AS Police
1989	-
1990	AS Police
1991	AS Police
1992	AS Sonader Ksar
1993	AS Sonader Ksar
1994	ASC Garde Nationale

CLUB DIRECTORY

NOUAKCHOTT (Pop. - 285,000)
Association Sportive Culturelle Garde Nationale
Association Sportive Police
Association Sportive Culturelle Sonader Ksar
Association Sportive Forces Armees
Espoirs Nouakchott

MAURITIUS

Population: 1,080,000
Area, sq km: 2,040
% in urban areas: 40%
Capital city: Port Louis

Mauritius Football Association
2nd Floor #303-305, Chancery House
14 Lislet Geoffroy Street
Port Louis
Mauritius
Tel: + 230 2121418
Fax: + 230 2084100
Telex: 4427 msa iw

Year of formation	1952
Affiliation to FIFA	1962
Affiliation to CAF	1963
Registered clubs	397
Registered players	14 800
Registered coaches	130
Registered referees	57
National stadium	Sir Anerood Ruganath, Pamplemousse 40 000
National colours	Red/White/Red
Reserve colours	White/White/Red
Season	September - June

THE RECORD

WORLD CUP

1930-70	Did not enter
1974	QT 2nd round
1978	Did not enter
1982	Did not enter
1986	QT 1st round
1990	Did not enter

AFRICAN CUP OF NATIONS

1957-65	Did not enter
1968	QT 4th/4 in group 6
1970	QT 1st round
1972	QT 2nd round
1974	QT Qualified - Final tournament/1st round
1976	QT 1st round
1978	QT 1st round
1980	QT 1st round
1982	QT pr round
1984	QT 1st round
1986	QT pr round
1988	Did not enter
1990	QT 1st round
1992	Did not enter
1994	QT 4th/4 in group 5

AFRICAN CLUB COMPETITIONS

African Champions Cup
2nd round - Sunrise FC 1988 1990 1991 1993. Fire Brigade 1989
Cup Winners Cup
Have never entered
CAF Cup
Have never entered

MAURITIUS LEAGUE CHAMPIONS

1970	FC Dodo
1971	Police Club
1972	Police Club
1973	Fire Brigade
1974	Fire Brigade
1975	Hindu Cadets
1976	Muslim Scouts
1977	Hindu Cadets
1978	Racing Club
1979	Hindu Cadets
1980	Fire Brigade
1981	Police Club
1982	Police Club
1983	Fire Brigade
1984	Fire Brigade
1985	Fire Brigade
1986	Tamil Cadets
1987	Sunrise SC
1988	Fire Brigade
1989	Sunrise SC
1990	Sunrise SC
1991	Sunrise SC
1992	Sunrise SC
1993	Fire Brigade
1994	Fire Brigade

CLUB DIRECTORY

PORT LOUIS (Pop. - 139,000)
Fire Brigade Sports Club
Police Club
Cadets Sports Club
Scouts Sports Club
Cadets United

CUREPIPE (Pop. - 64,000)
Sunrise FC
Curepipe Cosmos

MOROCCO

Population: 25,113,000
Area, sq km: 458,730
% in urban areas: 45%
Capital city: Rabat

Fédération Royale Marocaine de Football
Av Ibn Sina, CNS Bellevue
BP 51
Rabat
Morocco
Tel: + 212 7 672706
Fax: +212 7 671070
Telex: 32940 FERMFOOT M

Year of formation	1955
Affiliation to FIFA	1956
Affiliation to CAF	1966
Registered clubs	1080
Registered players	27 600
Registered coaches	272
Registered referees	897
National stadium	Mohamed V, Casablanca 80,000
National colours	Red/Red/Red
Reserve colours	Green/Green/Green
Season	September - June

THE RECORD

WORLD CUP

1930-58	Did not enter
1962	QT 3rd round
1966	Did not enter
1970	QT Qualified - Final tournament/1st round
1974	QT 4th round
1978	QT 1st round
1982	QT 4th round
1986	QT Qualified - Final tournament/2nd round
1990	QT 2nd round
1994	QT 1st round - 1st/4 in group 6, 2nd round - 1st/3 in group 2 - Final Tournament/1st round

AFRICAN CUP OF NATIONS

1957-68	Did not enter
1970	QT 1st round
1972	QT qualified - Final tournament/1st round
1974	Did not enter
1976	QT Qualified - Final tournament/Winners
1978	QT Automatic - Final tournament/1st round
1980	QT Qualified - Final tournament/Semi-finalists/3rd place
1982	QT 2nd round
1984	QT 2nd round
1986	QT Qualified - Final tournament/Semi-finalists/4th place
1988	QT Automatic - Final tournament/Semi-finalists/4th place
1990	QT 1st round
1992	QT 2nd/4 in group 3 - Final tournament/1st round
1994	QT 3rd/4 in group 8

AFRICAN CLUB COMPETITIONS

African Cup
Winners - FAR Rabat 1985, Raja Casablanca 1989
Cup Winners Cup
Quarter-finalists - DHJ Jadida 1986, FAR Rabat 1987
CAF Cup
Have never entered

MOROCCAN LEAGUE CHAMPIONS

1916	CA Casablanca
1917	US Marocaine
1918	US Marocaine
1919	US Marocaine
1920	Olympique Marocaine
1921	Olympique Marocaine
1922	Olympique Marocaine
1923	US Fes
1924	Olympique Marocaine
1925	US Fes
1926	US Athletique
1927	Stade Marocaine
1928	-
1929	US Athletique
1930	Olympique Marocaine
1931	Stade Marocaine
1932	US Marocaine
1933	US Marocaine
1934	US Marocaine
1935	US Marocaine
1936	Olympique Marocaine
1937	Olympique Marocaine
1938	US Marocaine
1939	US Marocaine
1940	US Marocaine
1941	US Marocaine
1942	US Marocaine
1943	US Marocaine
1944	Stade Marocaine
1945	Racing Avant-Garde
1946	US Marocaine
1947	US Athletique
1948	WAC Casablanca
1949	WAC Casablanca
1950	WAC Casablanca
1951	WAC Casablanca
1952-56	-
1957	WAC Casablanca
1958	KAC Marrakech
1959	EJS Casablanca
1960	KAC Kenitra
1961	FAR Rabat
1962	FAR Rabat
1963	FAR Rabat
1964	FAR Rabat
1965	MAS Fès
1966	WAC Casablanca
1967	FAR Rabat
1968	FAR Rabat
1969	WAC Casablanca
1970	FAR Rabat
1971	RS Settat
1972	ADM Casablanca
1973	KAC Kenitra
1974	RBM Beni Mellal
1975	MC Oujda
1976	WAC Casablanca
1977	WAC Casablanca
1978	WAC Casablanca
1979	MAS Fès
1980	Chebab Mohammedia
1981	KAC Kenitra
1982	KAC Kenitra
1983	MAS Fès
1984	FAR Rabat
1985	MAS Fès
1986	WAC Casablanca
1987	FAR Rabat
1988	Raja Casablanca
1989	FAR Rabat
1990	WAC Casablanca
1991	WAC Casablanca
1992	KAC Marrakech
1993	WAC Casablanca
1994	Olympic Casablanca
1995	COD Meknes

MOROCCAN CUP WINNERS

1957	MC Oujda
1958	MC Oujda
1959	FAR Rabat
1960	MC Oujda
1961	KAC Kenitra
1962	MC Oujda
1963	KAC Marrakech
1964	KAC Marrakech
1965	KAC Marrakech
1966	COD Meknes
1967	FUS Rabat
1968	Raja Casablanca
1969	RS Settat
1970	WAC Casablanca
1971	FAR Rabat
1972	Chabab Mohammedia
1973	FUS Rabat
1974	Raja Casablanca
1975	Chabab Mohammedia
1976	FUS Rabat
1977	Raja Casablanca
1978	WAC Casablanca
1979	WAC Casablanca
1980	MAS Fès
1981	WAC Casablanca
1982	Raja Casablanca
1983	CLAS Casablanca
1984	FAR Rabat
1985	FAR Rabat
1986	FAR Rabat
1987	KAC Marrakech
1988	-
1989	WAC Casablanca
1990-1	-
1992	Olympic Casablanca
1993	WAC Casablanca

CLUB DIRECTORY

RABAT (Pop. - 980,000)
Forces Armees Royales (FAR Rabat)
Fatah Union Sportive (FUS Rabat)
Stade Marocaine

CASABLANCA (Pop. - 2,475,000)
Wydad Athletique Club (WAC Casablanca)
Raja Club Athletique
Centrale Laitiere Association Sportive (CLAS)
Olympic Casablanca

FES (Pop. 535,000)
Maghreb Athletique Sport (MAS Fès)

MARRAKECH (Pop. - 535,000)
Kawkab Athletique Club (KAC Marrakech)

TANGIERS (Pop. - 370,000)
Ittihad Tanger

OUJDA (Pop. - 260,000)
Molodiat Club Oujda (MC Oujda)

KENITRA (Pop. - 188,000)
Kenitra Athletique Club

MOHAMMEDIA (Pop. - 105,000)
Chabab Mohemmedia

EL JADIDA (Pop. - 81,000)
Diffaa Hassani El Jadida (DHJ El Jadida)

MOZAMBIQUE

Population: 15,696,000
Area, sq km: 812,379
% in urban areas: 13%
Capital city: Maputo

Federacao Mocambicana de Futebol
Avenue Samora Machel 11-2
Caixa Postal 1467
Maputo
Mozambique
Tel: + 258 1 426475
Fax: + 258 1 422968
Telex: 6-222 perco mo

Year of formation	1978
Affiliation to FIFA	1978
Affiliation to CAF	1978
Registered clubs	144
Registered players	3600
Registered coaches	264
Registered referees	73
National stadium	Estadio de Machava, Maputo 60 000
National colours	Red/Red/Black
Reserve colours	Yellow/Black/Yellow
Season	February - November

THE RECORD

WORLD CUP

1930-78	Did not enter
1982	QT 1st round
1986	Did not enter
1990	Did not enter
1994	QT 3rd/3 in group 7

AFRICAN CUP OF NATIONS

1957-80	Did not enter
1982	QT 1st round
1984	QT 1st round
1986	QT Qualified - Final tournament/1st round
1988	QT 1st round
1990	QT 1st round
1992	QT 2nd/3 in group 6
1994	QT 3rd/4 in group 4

AFRICAN CLUB COMPETITIONS

African Champions Cup
Quarter-finals - Matchadje 1988
Cup Winners Cup
Semi-finals - Desportivo Maputo 1990
CAF Cup
Semi-finals - Ferroviario Maputo 1992

MOZAMBIQUE LEAGUE CHAMPIONS

1976	Textafrica
1977	Grupo Desportivo Maputo
1978	Grupo Desportivo Maputo
1979	Costa do Sol
1980	Costa do Sol
1981	Textil Pungue Beira
1982	Ferroviario Maputo
1983	Grupo Desportivo Maputo
1984	Maxaquene
1985	Maxaquene
1986	Maxaquene
1987	Matchedje
1988	Grupo Desportivo Maputo
1989	Ferroviario Maputo
1990	Matchadje
1991	Costa do Sol
1992	Costa do Sol
1993	Costa do Sol
1994	Costa do Sol

CLUB DIRECTORY

MAPUTO (1,069,000)
Matchedje
Desportos da Costa do Sol
Club Desportos Maxaquene
Clube Ferroviario
Grupo Desportivo Maputo

BEIRA (Population - 291,000)
Ferroviario Beira
Palmeiras Beira

NAMIBIA

Population: 1,302,000
Area, sq km: 823,144
% in urban areas: 26%
Capital city: Windhoek

Namibian Football Federation
18 Curt von Francois
PO Box 1345
2000 Windhoek
Namibia
Tel: + 264 61 220066
Fax: + 265 61 221304

Year of formation	1990
Affiliation to FIFA	1992
Affiliation to CAF	1990
Registered clubs	244
Registered players	7320
National stadium	Independence, Windhoek 40 000
National colours	Blue/White/Red
Reserve colours	Red/White/Blue
Season	February - November

THE RECORD

WORLD CUP

1930-90	Did not enter
1994	QT 3rd/3 in group 8

AFRICAN CUP OF NATIONS

1957-94	Did not enter

AFRICAN CLUB COMPETITIONS

African Cup
Never past 1st round

Cup Winners Cup
Never past 1st round
CAF Cup
Never past 1st round

CHAMPIONS - 1994 Black Africa
CUP WINNERS - Blue Waters

NIGER

Population: 7,779,000
Area, sq km: 1,186,408
% in urban areas: 21%
Capital city: Niamey

Fédération Nigerienne de Football
Stade National Niamey
BP 10299
Niamey
Niger
Tel: + 227 734705
Fax: + 227 735512
Telex: 5527

Year of formation	1967
Affiliation to FIFA	1967
Affiliation to CAF	1967
Registered clubs	106
Registered players	5000
Registered referees	74
National stadium	Stade 29 Juillet 7000
National colours	Orange/White/Green
Reserve colours	Green/White/Orange
Season	October - July

THE RECORD

WORLD CUP

1930-74	Did not enter
1978	QT pr round
1982	QT 3rd round
1986	Did not enter
1990	Did not enter
1994	QT 2nd/3 in group 5

AFRICAN CUP OF NATIONS

1957-68	Did not enter
1970	QT 2nd round
1972	QT 1st round
1974	Did not enter
1976	QT 1st round
1978-82	Did not enter
1984	QT pr round
1986-90	Did not enter
1992	QT 3rd/4 in group 3
1994	QT 3rd/4 in group 1

AFRICAN CLUB COMPETITIONS

African Cup
2nd round - Olympic Niamey 1978
Cup Winners Cup
2nd round - Olympic Niamey 1991
CAF Cup
Quarter-finalists - Zumunta 1993

NIGER LEAGUE CHAMPIONS

1966	Secteur 6
1967	Secteur 6
1968	Secteur 6
1969	Secteur 6
1970	Secteur 6
1971	ASFAN Niamey
1972	-
1973	Secteur 7
1974	Olympic FC
1975	ASFAN Niamey
1976	Olympic FC
1977	Olympic FC
1978	Olympic FC
1979	-
1980	AS Niamey
1981	AS Niamey
1982	AS Niamey
1983	Djan-Gorzo Maradi
1984	Espoir FC Zinder
1985	Zumunta AC
1986	-
1987	Sahel SC
1988	Zumunta AC
1989	Olympic FC
1990	Olympic FC
1991	Sahel SC
1992	Sahel SC
1993	Zumunta AC
1994	Sahel SC

CLUB DIRECTORY

NIAMEY (Pop. - 398,000)
Liberté FC
Secteur 6
Association Sportive Niamey
Association Sportive Forces Armees (ASFAN Niamey)
Sahel Sporting Club
Olympic Niamey FC
Zumunta Athletic Club

ZINDER (Pop. - 120,000)
Espoir FC Zinder
Zindourma

MARADI (Pop. - 112,000)
Djan-Gorzo FC

NIGERIA

Population: 119,812,000
Area, sq km: 923,768
% in urban areas: 31%
Capital city: Lagos

Nigeria Football Association
National Stadium
PO Box 466
Lagos
Nigeria
Tel: + 234 1 5450310
Fax: + 234 1 5450282
Telex: 26570 NFA NG

Year of formation	1945
Affiliation to FIFA	1959
Affiliation to CAF	1959
Registered clubs	530
Registered players	60 400
Registered referees	1384
National stadium	Surulere, Lagos 50 000
National colours	Green/Green/Green
Reserve colours	White/White/White
Season	February - November

THE RECORD

WORLD CUP

1930-58	Did not enter
1962	QT 1st round
1966	Did not enter
1970	QT 3rd round
1974	QT 2nd round
1978	QT 4th round
1982	QT 4th round
1986	QT 3rd round
1990	QT 2nd round
1994	QT 1st round - 1st/3 in group 4, 2nd round - 1st/3 in group 1 - Final Tournament - 2nd round

AFRICAN CUP OF NATIONS

1957-62	Did not enter
1963	1st round
1965	Did not enter
1968	QT 2nd/3 in group 3
1970	Did not enter
1972	QT 1st round
1974	QT 2nd round
1976	QT Qualified - Final tournament/2nd round/3rd place
1978	QT Qualified - Final tournament/Semi-finalists/3rd place
1980	QT Automatic - Final tournament/Winners
1982	QT Automatic - Final tournament/1st round
1984	QT Qualified - Final tournament/Finalists
1986	QT 2nd round
1988	QT Qualified - Final tournament/Finalists
1990	QT Qualified - Final tournament/Finalists
1992	QT 2nd/5 in group 4 - Final tournament/Semi-finalists/3rd place
1994	QT 1st/4 in group 2 - Final Tournament/Winners

AFRICAN GAMES
Winners 1973

AFRICAN CLUB COMPETITIONS

African Cup
Finalists - Enugu Rangers 1975, IICC Shootng Stars 1984, Iwuanyanwu Owerri 1988
Cup Winners Cup
Winners - IICC Shooting Stars 1976, Enugu Rangers 1977, BCC Lions 1990
Finalists - Stationery Stores 1981, Leventis United 1985, Ranchers Bees 1988, Bendel United 1989, BCC Lions 1991
CAF Cup
Winners - Shooting Stars 1992, Bendel Insurance 1994

NIGERIAN LEAGUE CHAMPIONS

1972	Mighty Jets
1973	Bendel Insurance
1974	Enugu Rangers
1975	Enugu Rangers
1976	IICC Shooting Stars
1977	Enugu Rangers
1978	Racca Rovers
1979	Bendel Insurance
1980	IICC Shooting Stars
1981	Enugu Rangers
1982	Enugu Rangers
1983	IICC Shooting Stars
1984	Enugu Rangers
1985	New Nigeria Bank
1986	Leventis United
1987	Iwuanyanwu Owerri
1988	Iwuanyanwu Owerri
1989	Iwuanyanwu Owerri
1990	Iwuanyanwu Owerri
1991	Julius Berger
1992	Stationery Stores
1993	Iwuanyanwu Owerri
1994	BCC Lions

NIGERIAN FA CHALLENGE CUP WINNERS

1945	Marine
1946	Lagos Railways
1947	Marine
1948	Lagos Railways
1949	Lagos Railways
1950	GO Urion
1951	Lagos Railways
1952	Lagos Pan Bank
1953	Kano
1954	Calabar
1955	Port Harcourt
1956	Lagos Railways
1957	Lagos Railways
1958	Port Harcourt
1959	Ibadan Lions
1960	Lagos EDN
1961	Ibadan Lions
1962	Police
1963	Port Harcourt
1964	Lagos Railways
1965	Lagos EDN
1966	Ibadan Lions
1967	Stationery Stores
1968	Stationery Stores
1969	Ibadan Lions
1970	Lagos EDN
1971	IICC Shooting Stars
1972	Bendel Insurance
1973	-
1974	Enugu Rangers
1975	Enugu Rangers
1976	Enugu Rangers
1977	IICC Shooting Stars
1978	Bendel Insurance
1979	IICC Shooting Stars
1980	Bendel Insurance
1981	Enugu Rangers
1982	Stationery Stores
1983	Enugu Rangers
1984	Leventis United
1985	Abiola Babes
1986	Leventis United
1987	Abiola Babes
1988	Iwuanyanwu Owerri
1989	BCC Lions
1990	Stationery Stores
1991	El Kanemi Warriors
1992	El Kanemi Warriors
1993	BCC Lions
1994	BCC Lions

CLUB DIRECTORY

LAGOS (Pop. - 1,213,000)
Julius Berger
Stationery Stores FC
Water Corporation FC

IBADAN (Pop. - 1,144,000)
Leventis United
IICC Shooting Stars

KANO (Pop. - 538,000)
Raccah Rovers
Kano Pillars

PORT HARCOURT (Pop. 327,000)
Sharks Port Harcourt
Nigerian Ports Authority

KADUNA (Pop. - 273,000)
Ranchers Bees

ENUGU (Pop. - 252,000)
Enugu Rangers International
Udoji United

BENIN CITY (Pop. - 183,000)
Bendel Insurance FC
New Nigerian Bank FC

JOS (Pop. - 164,000)
Mighty Jets
Plateau United

GBOKO (Pop. - 49,000)
BCC Lions

OWERRI (Pop. - 32,000)
Iwuanyanwu Nationale

RWANDA

Population: 7,232,000
Area, sq km: 26,338
% in urban areas: 6%
Capital city: Kigali

Fédération Rwandaise de Football Amateur
BP 2000
Kigali
Rwanda
Tel: + 250 82605
Fax: + 250 76574
Telex: 22504 public rw

Year of formation	1972
Affiliation to FIFA	1976
Affiliation to CAF	1976
Registered clubs	167
Registered players	7500
Registered coaches	191
Registered referees	321
National stadium	Stade Amahoro, Kigali 25 000
National colours	Red/Green/Yellow
Reserve colours	Green/Red/Yellow
Season	August - March

THE RECORD

WORLD CUP

1930-94	Did not enter

AFRICAN CUP OF NATIONS

1957-80	Did not enter
1982	QT 1st round
1984	QT 1st round
1986	Did not enter
1988	QT 1st round
1990-94	Did not enter

AFRICAN CLUB COMPETITIONS

African Cup
Never past the first round
Cup Winners Cup
2nd round - Etincelles 1989
CAF Cup
Never past the first round

RWANDAN LEAGUE CHAMPIONS

1981	Rayon Sports
1982	-
1983	Kiyovou Sports
1984	Pantheres Noires
1985	Pantheres Noires
1986	Pantheres Noires
1987	Pantheres Noires
1988	Mukungwa Ruhengeri
1989	Mukungwa Ruhengeri
1990	-
1991	-
1992	Kiyovou Sports
1993	Kiyovou Sports

CLUB DIRECTORY

KIGALI (Pop. - 181,000)
Pantheres Noires
Kiyovou Sports

BUTARE
Rayon Sports
Mukura Victory Sports

RUHENGERI
Mukungwa

GISENYI
Etincelles

SAO TOME & PRINCIPE

Population: 121,000
Population: 121,000
Area, sq km: 1,001
% in urban areas: 39%
Capital city: Sao Tomé

Federacion Santomense de Futebol
PO Box 42
Sao Tomé
Sao Tomé and Príncipe
Tel: + 239 12 22311
Fax: + 239 12 21365
Telex: 213 publico stp

Year of formation	1975
Affiliation to FIFA	1986
Affiliation to CAF	1986
Registered clubs	40
Registered players	880
Registered coaches	15
Registered referees	30
National stadium	Estadio 12 de Julho, Sao Tomé 5000
National colours	Green/Green/Green
Reserve colours	Yellow/Yellow/ Yellow
Season	April - March

THE RECORD

WORLD CUP
1930-94 Did not enter

AFRICAN CUP OF NATIONS
1957-92 Did not enter

AFRICAN CLUB COMPETITIONS
African Champions Cup
Have never entered
Cup Winners Cup
Have never entered
CAF Cup
Have never entered

SAO TOMÉ LEAGUE CHAMPIONS

1977	Vitoria Riboque
1978	Vitoria Riboque
1979	Vitoria Riboque
1980	Desportivo Guadelupe
1981	Desportivo Guadelupe
1982	Praia Cruz
1983	-
1984	Andorinhas
1985	Praia Cruz
1986	Vitoria Riboque
1987	-
1988	6 de Setembro
1989	Vitoria Riboque
1990	OS Operacios
1991	Santana
1992	OS Operacios

CLUB DIRECTORY

SAO TOME (Pop. - 17,000)
Vitoria Riboque
Praia Cruz
6 de Setembro
Desportivo Guadelupe

SENEGAL

Population: 7,277,000
Area, sq km: 196,722
% in urban areas: 38%
Capital city: Dakar

Fédération Sénégalaise de Football
Stade de l'Amite
Route de l'Aeroport de Yoff
BP 7021
Dakar
Senegal
Tel:+ 221 243524
Fax: + 221 243524
Telex: 13048 publidk sg

Year of formation	1960
Affiliation to FIFA	1962
Affiliation to CAF	1963
Registered clubs	75
Registered players	15 800
Registered referees	179
National stadium	Stade de l'Amitè, Dakar 60 000
National colours	Green/Yellow/Red
Reserve colours	Red/Yellow/Green
Season	October - July

THE RECORD

WORLD CUP

1930-66	Did not enter
1970	QT 1st round
1974	QT 1st round
1978	QT 1st round
1982	QT 1st round
1986	QT 1st round
1990	Did not enter
1994	QT 1st round - 1st/3 in group 7 2nd round - 3rd/3 in group 2

AFRICAN CUP OF NATIONS

1957-62	Did not enter
1965	4th place
1968	QT 1st/3 in group 1 - Final tournament/1st round
1970	QT 2nd round
1972	QT 1st round
1974	QT 1st round
1976	QT 1st round
1978	QT 2nd round
1980	Did not enter
1982	QT 1st round
1984	QT 2nd round
1986	QT Qualified - Final tournament/1st round
1988	QT 2nd round
1990	QT Qualified - Final tournament/Semi-finalists/4th place
1992	QT Automatic - Final tournament/Quarter-finalists
1994	QT 3rd/4 in group 3 - Final Tournament/Quarter-finalists

AFRICAN CLUB COMPETITIONS
African Cup
Semi-finalists - ASC Jeanne d'Arc 1974, US Goreé 1979 1985, ASC Diaraf 1983
Cup Winners Cup
Semi-finalists - ASC Jeanne d'Arc 1975
CAF Cup
Never past second round

SENEGAL LEAGUE CHAMPIONS

1970	ASC Diaraf
1971	ASFA Dakar
1972	ASFA Dakar
1973	ASC Jeanne d'Arc
1974	ASFA Dakar
1975	ASC Diaraf
1976	ASC Diaraf
1977	ASC Diaraf
1978	US Goreé
1979	AS Police
1980	SEIB Diourbel
1981	US Goreé
1982	ASC Diaraf
1983	SEIB Diourbel
1984	US Goreé
1985	ASC Jeanne d'Arc
1986	ASC Jeanne d'Arc
1987	SEIB Diourbel
1988	ASC Jeanne d'Arc
1989	ASC Diaraf
1990	Port Autonome
1991	Port Autonome
1992	Ndiambour
1993	AS Douanes
1994	Ndiambour

SENEGAL CUP WINNERS

1961	Espoir St. Louis
1962	ASC Jeanne d'Arc
1963	US Rail
1964	US Ouakam
1965	US Goreé
1966	AS St. Louisienne
1967	Foyer France-Senegal
1968	Foyer France-Senegal
1969	ASC Jeanne d'Arc
1970	ASC Diaraf
1971	ASC Linguère
1972	US Goreé
1973	ASC Diaraf
1974	ASC Jeanne d'Arc
1975	ASC Diaraf

1976	ASF Police
1977	Saltigué
1978	ASF Police
1979	Casa Sport
1980	ASC Jeanne d'Arc
1981	ASF Police
1982	ASC Diaraf
1983	ASC Diaraf
1984	ASC Jeanne d'Arc
1985	ASC Diaraf
1986	AS Douanes
1987	ASC Jeanne d'Arc
1988	ASC Linguère
1989	US Ouakam
1990	ASC Linguère
1991	ASC Diaraf
1992	US Goreé
1993	ASC Diaraf
1994	ASC Diaraf

CLUB DIRECTORY

DAKAR (Pop. - 1,248,00)
ASC Jeanne d'Arc Dakar
ASC Diaraf Dakar
ASF Police Dakar
AS Douanes Dakar
US Goree Dakar
ASFA Dakar
US Ouakam
Port Autonome

THIES (Pop. - 156,000)
US Rail

SAINT LOUIS (Pop. - 91,000)
AS St. Louisienne
ASC Linguère

ZINGUINCHOR (Pop. - 106,000)
Casa Sports

DIOURBEL (Pop. - 76,000)
SEIB Diourbel (Societe Electrique Industrial de Baol)
ASC - Association Sportive Culturelle
AS - Association Sportive
US - Union Sportive
USFA -Association Sportive Forces Armees

SEYCHELLES

Population: 68,000
Area, sq km: 453
% in urban areas: 47%
Capital city: Victoria

Seychelles Football Federation
PO Box 580
Mont Fleuri
Victoria
Seychelles
Tel: + 248 24126
Fax: + 248 23518
Telex: 2240 culspt sz

Year of formation	1976
Affiliation to FIFA	1986
Affiliation to CAF	1986
Registered clubs	28
Registered players	1700
Registered referees	44
National stadium	People's Stadium, Victoria 7,000
National colours	Red/White/Red
Reserve colours	White/Red/White
Season	July - May

THE RECORD

WORLD CUP

1930-94	Did not enter

AFRICAN CUP OF NATIONS

1957-88	Did not enter
1990	QT pr round
1992	Did not enter
1994	Did not enter

AFRICAN CLUB COMPETITIONS
African Champions Cup
Never past the first round
Cup Winners Cup
Never past the first round
CAF Cup
Have never entered

SEYCHELLES LEAGUE CHAMPIONS

1986	St. Louis
1987	St. Louis
1988	St. Louis
1989	St. Louis
1990	St. Louis
1991	St Louis

CLUB DIRECTORY

VICTORIA (Pop. - 23,000)
St. Louis

ANSE BOILEAU
Anse Boileau FC

PLAISANCE
Plaisance FC

SIERRA LEONE

Population: 4,151,000
Area, sq km: 71,740
% in urban areas: 28%
Capital city: Freetown

Sierra Leone Amateur Football Assn.
Siaka Stevens Stadium
Brookfields
PO Box 672
Freetown
Sierra Leone
Tel: + 232 22 241872
Fax: + 232 22 240562
Telex: 3210 booth sl

Year of formation	1923
Affiliation to FIFA	1967
Affiliation to CAF	1967
Registered clubs	104
Registered players	2300
Registered coaches	51
Registered referees	109
National stadium	Siaka Stevens, Freetown 30 000
National colours	Green/White/Blue
Reserve colours	Blue/White/Blue
Season	February - December

THE RECORD

WORLD CUP

1930-70	Did not enter
1974	QT 1st round
1978	QT 1st round
1982	QT 1st round
1986	QT 1st round
1990	Did not enter
1994	Did not enter

AFRICAN CUP OF NATIONS

1957-72	Did not enter
1974	QT 1st round
1976	Did not enter
1978	QT 1st round
1980	Did not enter
1982	QT pr round
1984	QT pr round
1986	QT 1st round
1988	QT 2nd round
1990	Did not enter
1992	QT 2nd/4 in group 1
1994	QT 1st/4 in group 3 - Final Tournament/1st round

AFRICAN CLUB COMPETITIONS
African Cup
Quater-finalists - Mighty Blackpool 1989
Cup Winners Cup
2nd round - Bai-Bureh Warriors 1979, Real Republicans 1981 1988, East End Lions 1990
CAF Cup
Quarter-finalists - Diamond Stars 1994

SIERRA LEONE LEAGUE CHAMPIONS

1978	Mighty Blackpool
1979	Mighty Blackpool
1980	East End Lions
1981	Real Republicans
1982	Sierra Fisheries
1983	Real Republicans
1984	Real Republicans
1985	East End Lions
1986	Sierra Fisheries
1987	Sierra Fisheries
1988	Mighty Blackpool

1989	Freetown United
1990	Old Edwardians
1991	Mighty Blackpool
1992	-
1993	East End Lions

CLUB DIRECTORY

FREETOWN (Pop. - 525,000)
Real Republicans
Mighty Blackpool Sports Club
Sierra Fisheries
Ports Authority
Freetown United
Old Edwardians St. Edwards
East End Lions

KENEMA (Pop. - 52,000)
Kamboi Eagles

BONBALI
Walum Stars

PORT LOKO
Bai-Bureh Warriors

SOMALIA

Population: 7,555,000
Area, sq km: 637,000
% in urban areas: 35%
Capital city: Mogadishu

Somali Football Federation
Ministry of Sports
CP 247
Mogadishu
Somalia

Year of formation	1951
Affiliation to FIFA	1961
Affiliation to CAF	1968
Registered clubs	46
Registered players	2300
Registered coaches	122
Registered referees	251
National stadium	Mogadishu Stadium, Mogadishu 40 000
National colours	Sky blue/White/ White
Reserve colours	White/White/White
Season	November - July

THE RECORD

WORLD CUP

1930-78	Did not enter
1982	QT 1st round
1986-94	Did not enter

AFRICAN CUP OF NATIONS

1957-72	Did not enter
1974	QT pr round
1976	QT pr round
1978-82	Did not enter
1984	QT pr round
1986	QT pr round
1988	QT pr round
1990-94	Did not enter

AFRICAN CLUB COMPETITIONS

African Cup
2nd round - FC Horsed 1981. Printing Agency 1984
Cup Winners Cup
2nd round - Lavori Publici 1981. FC Horsed 1988
CAF Cup
Have never entered

SOMALIAN LEAGUE CHAMPIONS

1967	Somali Police
1968	Hoga Mogadishu
1969	Lavori Publici
1970	Lavori Publici
1971	Lavori Publici
1972	Horsed
1973	Horsed
1974	Horsed
1975	Mogadishu Municipality
1976	Horsed
1977	Horsed
1978	Horsed
1979	Horsed
1980	Horsed
1981	Lavori Publici
1982	Wagad
1983	Printing Agency
1984	Marine Club
1985	Wagad
1986	Mogadishu Municipality
1987	Wagad

CLUB DIRECTORY

MOGADISHU (Pop. - 600,000)
Horsed
Printing Acency
Marine Club
Somali Police
Wagad

SOUTH AFRICA

Population: 30,797,000
Area, sq km: 1,123,226
% in urban areas: 56%
Capital city: Pretoria

South African Football Association
First National Bank Stadium
PO Box 910
Johannesburg 2000
South Africa
Tel: + 27 11 4943522
Fax: + 27 11 4943447

Year of formation	1892
Affiliation to FIFA	1952-1976 (Suspended 1964-76) 1992
Affiliation to CAF	1957 and 1992
Registered clubs	51 900
Registered players	1 039 000
National stadium	Soccer City, Johannesburg 75 000
National colours	Gold/Black/White
Season	January - November

THE RECORD

WORLD CUP

1930-90	Did not enter
1994	QT 2nd/3 in group 4

AFRICAN CUP OF NATIONS

1957-92	Did not enter
1994	QT 3rd/4 in group 5

AFRICAN CLUB COMPETITIONS

African Cup & CAF Cup
Never past second round
Cup Winners Cup
Semi-finalists - Jomo Cosmos 1993

SOUTH AFRICAN LEAGUE CHAMPIONS

(NPSL 1971-84, NSL 1985-present)

1971	Orlando Pirates
1972	AmaZulu
1973	Orlando Pirates
1974	Kaizer Chiefs
1975	Orlando Pirates
1976	Kaizer Chiefs
1977	Kaizer Chiefs
1978	Lusitano
1979	Kaizer Chiefs
1980	Highlands Park
1981	Kaizer Chiefs
1982	Durban City
1983	Durban City
1984	Kaizer Chiefs
1985	Bush Bucks
1986	Rangers
1987	Jomo Cosmos
1988	Mamelodi Sundowns
1989	Kaizer Chiefs
1990	Mamelodi Sundowns
1991	Kaizer Chiefs
1992	Kaizer Chiefs
1993	Mamelodi Sundowns
1994	Orlando Pirates

SOUTH AFRICAN CUP (SUPER BOWL)

Known as Mainstay Cup 1978-88

1978	Wits University
1979	Kaizer Chiefs
1980	Orlando Pirates
1981	Kaizer Chiefs
1982	Kaizer Chiefs
1983	Moroka Swallows
1984	Kaizer Chiefs
1985	Bloemfontein Celtic
1986	Mamelodi Sundowns
1987	Kaizer Chiefs
1988	Orlando Pirates
1989	Moroka Swallows
1990	Jomo Cosmos

1991	Moroka Swallows
1992	Kaizer Chiefs
1993	Witbank Aces
1994	Vaal Professionals

COCA-COLA (LEAGUE) CUP

1984	Kaizer Chiefs
1985	Wits University
1986	Kaizer Chiefs
1987	Bush Bucks
1988	Kaizer Chiefs
1989	Kaizer Chiefs
1990	Mamelodi Sundowns
1991	Dynamos
1992	AmaZulu
1993	Umtata Bucks
1994	Qwa Qwa Stars
1995	Wits University

TOP EIGHT CUP

1972	Orlando Pirates
1973	Orlando Pirates
1974	Kaizer Chiefs
1975	Moroka Swallows
1976	Kaizer Chiefs
1977	Kaizer Chiefs
1978	Orlando Pirates
1979	Moroka Swallows
1980	Witbank Black Aces/Kaizer Chiefs
1981	Kaizer Chiefs
1982	Kaizer Chiefs
1983	Orlando Pirates
1984	Wits University
1985	Kaizer Chiefs
1986	Arcadia
1987	Kaizer Chiefs
1988	Mamelodi Sundowns
1989	Kaizer Chiefs
1990	Mamelodi Sundowns
1991	Kaizer Chiefs
1992	Kaizer Chiefs
1993	Orlando Pirates
1994	Kaizer Chiefs
1995	Wits University

NATIONAL FOOTBALL LEAGUE

1959	Durban City
1960	Highlands Park
1961	Durban City
1962	Highlands Park
1963	Addington
1964	Highlands Park
1965	Highlands Park
1966	Highlands Park
1967	Port Elizabeth City
1968	Highlands Park
1969	Durban Spurs
1970	Durban City
1971	Hellenic
1972	Durban City
1973	Cape Town City
1974	Arcadia Shepherds
1975	Highlands Park
1976	Cape Town City
1977	Highlands Park

NFL (CASTLE) CUP

1959	Rangers
1960	Durban City
1961	Highlands Park
1962	Durban City
1963	Addington
1964	Durban City
1965	Highlands Park
1966	Highlands Park
1967	Highlands Park
1968	Durban City
1969	Maritzburg
1970	Cape Town City
1971	Cape Town City
1972	Durban United
1973	Highlands Park
1974	Arcadia Shepherds
1975	Highlands Park
1976	Cape Town City
1977	Highlands Park

CLUB DIRECTORY

JOHANNESBURG (3,650,000)

Jomo Cosmos (1983)
Rustenberg – Navy blue
Previous names: Highlands Park, Highlands Powerlines. Jomo Sono (ex-NY Cosmos) bought franchise of Highlands Park, previously all-white club.

Kaizer Chiefs (1970)
Rand Stadium – Gold/Black
Previous names: Kaizer XI

Moroka Swallows (1947)
Ellis Park – Maroon/White
Previous names: Corrugated FC, Moroka Swallows, Big XV and Real Moroka

Orlando Pirates (1937)
Orlando – Black/White
Previous names: Orlando Boys Club

Wits University (1922)
Milpark – Blue/White

CAPE TOWN (Pop. - 1,790,000)

Cape Town Spurs (1969)
Athlone – Red/White

Hellenic (1958)
Green Point – Blue/White

Santos (1982)
Athlone – Red/White

DURBAN (Pop. - 1,550,000)

AmaZulu (1939)
King's Park – Green/White
Previous names: Zulu Royals

Manning Rangers (1928)
Chatsworth

PRETORIA (Pop. - 960,000)

Mamelodi Sundowns (1970)
Green/Yellow

Pretoria City (1985)
Berea Park – Red/White

BLOEMFONTEIN (Pop. - 235,000)

Bloemfontein Celtic (1967)
Seisa Ramabodu – Green/White

SUDAN

Population: 28,311,000
Area, sq km: 2,503,890
% in urban areas: 29%
Capital city: Khartoum

Sudan Football Association
PO Box 437
Khartoum
Sudan
Tel: +249 11 76633
Fax: + 249 11 81160
Telex: 23007 kora sd

Year of formation	1936
Affiliation to FIFA	1948
Affiliation to CAF	1956
Registered clubs	750
Registered players	81 000
Registered coaches	85
Registered referees	1412
National stadium	Municipal, Khartoum 45 000
National colours	White/White/White
Reserve colours	Green/White/White
Season	July - June

THE RECORD

WORLD CUP

1930-54	Did not enter
1958	QT 3rd round
1962	Did not enter
1966	Did not enter
1970	QT 3rd round
1974	QT 1st round
1978	Did not enter
1982	QT 2nd round
1986	QT 2nd round
1990	QT 1st round
1994	Did not enter

AFRICAN CUP OF NATIONS

1957	3rd place
1959	2nd place
1962	Did not enter
1963	Finalists
1965	Did not enter
1968	QT 1st round
1970	QT Qualified - Final tournament/Winners
1972	QT Automatic - Final tournament/1st round
1974	QT 1st round
1976	QT Qualified - Final tournament/1st round

1978	Did not enter
1980	QT 2nd round
1982	Did not enter
1984	QT 2nd round
1986	Did not enter
1988	QT 2nd round
1990	QT 1st round
1992	QT 3rd/3 in group 6
1994	QT4th/4 in group 2

AFRICAN CLUB COMPETITIONS
African Cup
Finalists - Al Hilal 1987
Cup Winners Cup
Winners - Al Merreikh 1989
CAF Cup
Semi-finalists - Al Mourada 1994

SUDANESE LEAGUE CHAMPIONS

1964	Al Hilal
1965	Al Hilal
1966	Al Hilal
1967	Al Hilal
1968	Al Mourada
1969	Burri
1970	Al Merreikh
1971	Al Merreikh
1972	Al Merreikh
1973	Al Merreikh
1974	Al Hilal
1974	Al Merreikh
1975	Al Merreikh
1976	-
1977	Al Merreikh
1978	Al Merreikh
1979	-
1980	-
1981	Al Hilal
1982	Al Merreikh
1983	Al Hilal
1984	Al Hilal
1985	Al Merreikh
1986	Al Hilal
1987	Al Hilal
1988	Al Hilal
1989	Al Hilal
1990	Al Merreikh
1991	Al Hilal
1992	Al Hilal Port Sudan
1993	Al Merreikh
1994	Al Hilal

CLUB DIRECTORY

KHARTUM (Pop. - 924,000)
Al Hilal
Al Nil
Al Mourada
Burri

UMM DURMAN (Pop. - 526,000)
Al Merreikh

PORT SUDAN (Pop. - 206,000)
Hay el Arab

WAD MADANI (Pop. - 141,000)
Al Ahly Wad Madani

SWAZILAND

Population: 770,000
Area, sq km: 17,364
% in urban areas: 22%
Capital city: Mbabane

National Football Association of Swaziland
PO Box 641
Mbabane
Swaziland
Tel: + 268 46852
Fax: + 268 46206
Telex: 2245 EXP WD

Year of formation	1964
Affiliation to FIFA	1976
Affiliation to CAF	1976
Registered clubs	136
Registered players	16 400
Registered coaches	6
Registered referees	41
National stadium	Somholo, Manzini 20 000
National colours:	Blue/White/Blue
Reserve colours	White/White/White

THE RECORD

WORLD CUP

1930-90	Did not enter
1994	QT 2nd/3 in group 2

AFRICAN CUP OF NATIONS

1957-84	Did not enter
1986	QT pr round
1988	Did not enter
1990	QT 1st round
1992	QT 3rd/4 in group 5
1994	Did not enter

AFRICAN CLUB COMPETITIONS
African Champions Cup
Never past the first round
Cup Winners Cup
2nd round - Highlanders 1986, Eleven Men in Flight 1994
CAF Cup
2nd round - Manzini Wanderers 1993, Moneni Pirates 1994

SWAZILAND LEAGUE CHAMPIONS

1980	Mbabane Highlanders
1981	Peacemakers
1982	Mbabane Highlanders
1983	Manzini Wanderers
1984	Mbabane Highlanders
1985	Manzini Wanderers
1986	Mbabane Highlanders
1987	Manzini Wanderers
1988	Mbabane Highlanders
1989	Denver Sundowns
1990	Denver Sundowns
1991	Mbabane Highlanders
1992	Mbabane Highlanders
1993	Mbabane Swallows
1994	Eleven Men in Flight

CLUB DIRECTORY

MBABANE (Pop. - 38,000)
Mbabane Highlanders
Mbabane Swallows
Royal Leopards

MANZINI (Pop. - 30,000)
Denver Sundowns
Manzini Wanderers
Moneni Pirates

MHLUME
Peacemakers

TANZANIA

Population: 24,403,000
Area, sq km: 942,799
% in urban areas: 17%
Capital city: Dodoma

Football Association of Tanzania
PO Box 1574
Dar es Salaam
Tanzania
Tel: + 255 51 32334
Fax: None
Telex: 41873 tz

Year of formation	1930
Affiliation to FIFA	1964
Affiliation to CAF	1960
Registered clubs	351
Registered players	49 200
Registered coaches	50
Registered referees	320
National stadium	National Stadium, Dar es Salaam 25,000
National colours	Yellow/Yellow/ Yellow
Reserve colours	Green/Black/Green
Season	September - August

THE RECORD

WORLD CUP

1930-70	Did not enter
1974	QT 1st round
1978	Did not enter
1982	QT 2nd round
1986	QT 1st round
1990	Did not enter

AFRICAN CUP OF NATIONS

1957-65	Did not enter
1968	QT 2nd/4 in group 6
1970	QT 2nd round
1972	QT 1st round

1974	QT 2nd round
1976	QT 2nd round
1978	Did not enter
1980	QT Qualified - Final tournament/1st round
1982	Did not enter
1984	QT pr round
1986	QT 1st round
1988	QT 1st round
1990	QT pr round
1992	QT 4th/4 in group 8
1994	Did not enter

AFRICAN CLUB COMPETITIONS

African Champions Cup

Semi-finalists - SC Simba 1974

Cup Winners Cup

Quarter-finalists - Rangers International 1977, KMKM Zanzibar 1977

CAF Cup

Finalists - SC Simba 1993

TANZANIAN LEAGUE CHAMPIONS

1965	Dar Sunderland
1966	Dar Sunderland
1967	Cosmopolitans
1968	Young Africans
1969	Young Africans
1970	Young Africans
1971	Young Africans
1972	SC Simba
1973	SC Simba
1974	Young Africans
1975	Mseto
1976	SC Simba
1977	SC Simba
1978	SC Simba
1979	SC Simba
1980	SC Simba
1981	Young Africans
1982	Pan African
1983	Young Africans
1984	KMKM Zanzibar
1985	Maji Maji
1986	Maji Maji
1987	Young Africans
1988	Pan African
1989	Malindi
1990	Pamba SC
1991	Young Africans
1992	Malindi
1993	SC Simba

CLUB DIRECTORY

DAR ES SALAAM (Pop. - 1,300,000)

Young Africans (Yanga)
Pan African Sports Club
Sports Club Simba - Previously Dar Sunderland
Rangers International
Youth League

ZANZIBAR (Pop. - 119,000)

Small Simba
KMKM Zanzibar (Zanzibar Navy)
Miembeni

TANGA (Pop. - 121,000)

Coastal Union

SONGEA

Maji Maji

SHINYANGA

Pamba Sports Club

TOGO

Population: 3,764,000
Area, sq km: 56,785
% in urban areas: 23%
Capital city: Lomé

Fédération Togolaise de Football
CP 5
Lomé
Togo
Tel: + 228 212698
Fax: + 228 221696
Telex: 5015 cnot tg

Year of formation	1960
Affiliation to FIFA	1962
Affiliation to CAF	1963
Registered clubs	144
Registered players	18 400
Registered referees	147
National stadium	Stade Général Eyadema, Lomé 20 000
National colours	Red/White/Red
Reserve colours	White/White/White
Season	October - July

THE RECORD

WORLD CUP

1930-70	Did not enter
1974	QT 1st round
1978	QT 2nd round
1982	QT 2nd round
1986	Did not enter
1990	Did not enter
1994	QT 4th/4 in group 3

AFRICAN CUP OF NATIONS

1957-65	Did not enter
1968	QT 3rd/3 in group 3
1970	QT 1st round
1972	QT Qualified - Final tournament/1st round
1974	Did not enter
1976	QT 2nd round
1978	QT 1st round
1980	QT 2nd round
1982	QT 1st round
1984	QT Qualified - Final tournament/1st round
1986	QT 1st round
1988	QT 1st round
1990	Did not enter
1992	QT 4th/5 in group 4
1994	QT Group 3 - Withdrew

AFRICAN CLUB COMPETITIONS

African Cup

Finalists - Etoile Filante 1968

Cup Winners Cup

Finalists - Agaza Lomé 1983

CAF Cup

Never past first round

TOGOLESE LEAGUE CHAMPIONS

1965	Etoile Filante
1966	Modele Lomé
1967	Etoile Filante
1968	Etoile Filante
1969	Modele Lomé
1970	Dynamic Lomé
1971	Dynamic Lomé
1972	Modele Lomé
1973	Modele Lomé
1974	Lomé I
1975	Lomé I
1976	Lomé I
1977	-
1978	-
1979	Semassi Sokodé
1980	Agaza Lomé
1981	Semassi Sokodé
1982	Semassi Sokodé
1983	Semassi Sokodé
1984	Agaza Lomé
1985	ASFOSA
1986	ASFOSA
1987	Doumbe Sausanné-Mango
1988	ASKO Kara
1989	ASKO Kara
1990	Ifodje Atakpame
1991	-
1992	Etoile Filante
1993	Semassi Sokode
1994	Semassi Sokode

CLUB DIRECTORY

LOME (Pop. - 400,000)

Agaza Omnisports Club
Aiglons de Lomé
Association Sportive de la Foret Sacree (ASFOSA Lomé)
Entente II
AC Modele (Folded 1974)
Etoile Filante (Folded 1974)
Dynamic Togolais (Folded 1974)

SOKODE (Pop. - 48,000)

Semassi de Sokode

LAMA KARA

Association Sportive de Kozah (ASKO Kara)
Club Sportive Lama Kara

SANSANNE MANGO
Doumbe

ATAKPAME
Ifodje

TUNISIA

Population: 8,182,000
Area, sq km: 154,530
% in urban areas: 53%
Capital city: Tunis

Fédération Tunisienne de Football
2 Rue Hamza Abdelmottaleb
El Menzah VI
Tunis
Tunisia
Tel: + 216 1 233303
Fax: + 216 1 767929
Telex: 14783 FTFOOT TN

Year of formation	1956
Affiliation to FIFA	1960
Affiliation to CAF	1960
Registered clubs	1100
Registered players	29 400
Registered referees	590
National stadium	Stade Olympique El Menzah, Tunis 50,000
National colours	Red/White/Red
Reserve colours	White/White/White
Season	September - June

THE RECORD

WORLD CUP

1930-58	Did not enter
1962	QT 1st round
1966	Did not enter
1970	QT 2nd round
1974	QT 2nd round
1978	QT Qualified - Final tournament/1st round
1982	QT 1st round
1986	QT 4th round
1990	QT 3rd round
1994	QT 1st round - 2nd/4 in group 6

AFRICAN CUP OF NATIONS

1957	Did not enter
1959	Did not enter
1962	3rd place
1963	1st round
1965	Finalists
1968	QT 2nd/3 in group 5
1970-74	Did not enter
1976	QT 2nd round
1978	QT Qualified - Final tournament/Semi-finalists/4th place
1980	Did not enter
1982	QT Qualified - Final tournament/1st round
1984	QT 2nd round
1986	QT 1st round
1988	QT 1st round
1990	QT 2nd round
1992	QT 2nd/4 in group 2
1994	QT Automatic - Final Tournament/First round

AFRICAN CLUB COMPETITIONS

African Cup
Winners - Club Africain 1991, Esperance 1994
Cup Winners Cup
Winners - CA Bizerte 1988
Finalists - ES Tunis 1987, Club Africain 1990
CAF Cup
Semi-finalists - CA Bizerte 1992

TUNISIAN LEAGUE CHAMPIONS

1921	Racing Club
1922	Stade Gauloise
1923	Stade Gauloise
1924	Racing Club
1925	Sporting Club
1926	Stade Gauloise
1927	Sporting Club
1928	Avant Garde
1929	US Tunisienne
1930	US Tunisienne
1931	Italia de Tunis
1932	US Tunisienne
1933	Sfax Railway
1934	Italia de Tunis
1935	Italia de Tunis
1936	Italia de Tunis
1937	Savoia de la Goulette
1938	CS Gabesien
1939-40	-
1941	Esperance Tunis
1942-43	-
1944	CA Bizerte
1945	CA Bizerte
1946	Club Africain
1947	Club Africain
1948	CA Bizerte
1949	Etoile du Sahel
1950	CS Hammam-Lif
1951-55	-
1956	CS Hammam-Lif
1957	Stade Tunisien
1958	Etoile du Sahel
1959	Esperance Tunis
1960	Esperance Tunis
1961	Stade Tunisien
1962	Stade Tunisien
1963	Etoile du Sahel
1964	Club Africain
1965	Stade Tunisien
1966	Etoile du Sahel
1967	Club Africain
1968	Sfax Railway
1969	CS Sfax
1970	Esperance Tunis
1971	CS Sfax
1972	Etoile du Sahel
1973	Club Africain
1974	Club Africain
1975	Esperance Tunis
1976	Esperance Tunis
1977	JS Kairouan
1978	CS Sfax
1979	Club Africain
1980	Club Africain
1981	CS Sfax
1982	Esperance Tunis
1983	CS Sfax
1984	CA Bizerte
1985	Esperance Tunis
1986	Etoile du Sahel
1987	Etoile du Sahel
1988	Esperance Tunis
1989	Esperance Tunis
1990	Club Africain
1991	Esperance Tunis
1992	Club Africain
1993	Esperance Tunis
1994	Esperance Tunis
1995	CS Sfax

CUP OF TUNIS

1922	Avant Garde
1923	Racing Club
1924	Stade Gauloise
1925	Sporting Club
1926	Stade Gauloise
1927-28	-
1929	US Tunisiene
1930	US Tunisiene
1931	Racing Club
1932	US Tunisiene
1933	US Tunisiene
1934	US Tunisiene
1935	Italia de Tunis
1936	Stade Gauloise
1937	Sporting Club
1938	Esperance Tunis
1939-40	-
1941	US Ferryville
1942-43	-
1944	Olympique Tunis
1945	Patrie FC Bizerte
1946	CS Hammam-Lif
1947	CS Hammam-Lif
1948	CS Hammam-Lif
1949	CS Hammam-Lif
1950	CS Hammam-Lif
1951-55	-
1956	Stade Tunisien
1957	Etoile du Tunis
1958	Stade Tunisien
1959	Etoile du Sahel
1960	Stade Tunisien
1961	AS Marsa
1962	Stade Tunisien
1963	Etoile du Sahel
1964	Esperance Tunis
1965	Club Africain
1966	Stade Tunisien
1967	Club Africain
1968	Club Africain
1969	Club Africain
1970	Club Africain
1971	CS Sfax
1972	Club Africain
1973	Club Africain
1974	Etoile du Sahel
1975	Etoile du Sahel
1976	Club Africain

1977	AS Marsa
1978	-
1979	Esperance Tunis
1980	Esperance Tunis
1981	Etoile du Sahel
1982	CA Bizerte
1983	Etoile du Sahel
1984	AS Marsa
1985	CS Hammam-Lif
1986	Esperance Tunis
1987	CA Bizerte
1988	COT Tunis
1989	Club Africain
1990	AS Marsa
1991	Etoile du Sahel
1992	Club Africain
1993	Olympique Béja
1994	AS Marsa

CLUB DIRECTORY

TUNIS (Pop. - 1,225,000)
Club Africain
Esperance Sportive (ES Tunis)
Stade Tunisien
Club Sportif Cheminots
Club Olympique des Transports (COT Tunis)

SFAX (Pop. - 310,000)
Club Sportif (CS Sfax)
Sfax Railway Sports

SOUSSE (Pop. - 160,000)
Etoile Sportive du Sahel (ES Sahel)

BIZERTE (Pop. - 94,000)
Club Athletique (CA Bizerte)

KAIROUAN (Pop. - 72,000)
JS Kairouan

HAMMAM-LIF (Pop. - 47,000)
Club Sportif Hammam-Lif

BÉJA (Pop. - 46,000)
Olympique Béja
AS Marsa

UGANDA

Population: 16,928,000
Area, sq km: 241,040
% in urban areas: 9%
Capital city: Kampala

Federation of Uganda Football Associations
PO Box 20077
Kampala
Uganda
Tel: + 256 41 254477
Fax: + 256 41 245580
Telex: 61272 public

Year of formation	1924
Affiliation to FIFA	1959
Affiliation to CAF	1959
Registered clubs	400
Registered players	47 000
Registered referees	910
National stadium	Nakivubo, Kampala 35 000
National colours	Yellow/Black/Yellow
Reserve colours	Red/Red/Black
Season	January - November

THE RECORD

WORLD CUP

1930-74	Did not enter
1978	QT 2nd round
1982	Did not enter
1986	QT 1st round
1990	QT 1st round
1994	Did not enter

AFRICAN CUP OF NATIONS

1957	Did not enter
1959	Did not enter
1962	4th place
1963	Did not enter
1965	Did not enter
1968	QT 2nd/4 in group 4 - Final tournament/1st round
1970	QT 1st round
1972	QT 1st round
1974	QT Qualified - Final tournament/1st round
1976	QT Qualified - Final tournament/1st round
1978	QT Qualified - Final tournament/Finalists
1980	Did not enter
1982	Did not enter
1984	QT 1st round
1986	QT pr round
1988	QT 1st round
1990	Did not enter
1992	QT 3rd/4 in group 8
1994	QT 2nd/4 in group 2

AFRICAN CLUB COMPETITIONS

African Cup
Finalists - Simba FC 1972, Nakivubu Villa 1991
Cup Winners Cup
Quarter-finalists - Nakivubo Villa 1984, Kampala CC 1985
CAF Cup
Finalists - Nakivubo Villa 1992

UGANDAN LEAGUE CHAMPIONS

1966	Express FC
1967	Bitumastic
1968	-
1969	Prisons FC
1970	Coffee FC
1971	Simba FC
1972	Simba FC
1973	Simba FC
1974	Express FC
1975	Express FC
1976	Kampala CC
1977	Kampala CC
1978	Kampala CC
1979	Commercial Bank
1980	Nile FC
1981	Kampala CC
1982	Nakivubo Villa
1983	Kampala CC
1984	Nakivubo Villa
1985	Kampala CC
1986	Kampala CC
1987	Nakivubo Villa
1988	Express FC
1989	Express FC
1990	Nakivubo Villa
1991	Kampala CC
1992	Nakivubo Villa
1993	Express FC
1994	Nakivubo Villa

CLUB DIRECTORY

KAMPALA (Pop. - 460,000)
Kampala City Council Sports Club
Uganda Express FC
Nakivubo Villa Sports Club
Prisons Football Club
Coffee Football Club
Gangama United
Nsambya Football Club

JINJA (Pop. - 55,000)
Nile Breweries Football Club

ZAIRE

Population: 34,138,000
Area, sq km: 2,345,095
% in urban areas: 44%
Capital city: Kinshasa

Fédération Zaireoise de Football-Association
BP 1284
Rue Dima #10
Kinshasa 1
Zaire
Tel: None
Fax: + 87 11 506555

Year of formation	1919
Affiliation to FIFA	1964
Affiliation to CAF	1963
Registered clubs	3800
Registered players	37 800
Registered coaches	600
Registered referees	2850
National stadium	Stade 20 Mai, Kinshasa 60 000
National colours	Green/Yellow/Yellow
Reserve colours	Yellow/Green/Green
Season	August - May

THE RECORD

WORLD CUP

1930-70	Did not enter

1974	QT Qualified - Final tournament/1st round
1978	QT 2nd round
1982	QT 3rd round
1986	Did not enter
1990	QT 2nd round
1994	QT 3rd/3 in group 2

AFRICAN CUP OF NATIONS

1957-63	Did not enter
1965	1st round
1968	QT 1st/4 in group 6 - Final tournament/Winners
1970	QT Qualified - Final tournament/1st round
1972	QT Qualified - Final tournament/Semi-finalists/4th place
1974	QT Qualified - Final tournament/Winners
1976	QT Automatic - Final tournament/1st round
1978	Did not enter
1980	QT 2nd round
1982	QT 2nd round
1984	Did not enter
1986	QT 2nd round
1988	QT Qualified - Final tournament/1st round
1990	QT 2nd round
1992	QT 1st/4 in group 8 - Final tournament/Quarter-finalists
1994	QT 1st/4 in group 4 - Final tournamentQuarter-finalists

AFRICAN CLUB COMPETITIONS

African Cup

Winners - TP Mazembe 1967 1968, Vita Club Kinshasa 1973

Finalists - TP Mazembe 1969 1970, AS Bilima 1980 1985, Vita Club Kinshasa 1981

Cup Winners Cup

Winners - TP Mazembe 1980

CAF Cup

Quarter-finalists - Mbongo Sports 1992

THE POOL CHAMPIONSHIP

1923	CO Kinshasa
1924	CO Kinshasa
1925	CO Kinshasa
1926	CO Kinshasa
1927	AS Kinshasa
1928	AS Kinshasa
1929	ES Congolaise
1930	CO les Nomades Kinshasa
1931	CA Brazzavillois
1932	AS Kinshasa
1933	AS Portuguesa
1934	AS Portuguesa
1935	AS Portuguesa
1936	CS Belge Leopoldville
1937	CA Brazzavillois
1938	CS Belge Leopoldville
1939	AS Portuguesa
1940	AS Portuguesa
1941	CA Brazzavillois
1942	Nomades FC
1943	Nomades FC
1944	AS Portuguesa
1945	CA Brazzavillois
1946	Nomades FC
1947	CS Belge Leopoldville
1948	CS Belge Leopoldville
1949	CA Brazzavillois
1950	CS Belge Leopoldville

CUP DE LEOPOLDVILLE

1928	ES Congolaise
1929	CO les Nomades Kinshasa
1930	ES Congolaise
1931	AS Kinshasa
1932	Diables Rouge
1933	-
1934	AS Portuguesa
1935	AS Portuguesa
1936	CS Belge Leopoldville
1937	CA Brazzavillois
1938	CS Belge Leopoldville

CHAMPIONS OF ZAIRE

1990	FC Lupopo
1991	Mikishi
1992	US Bilombe
1993	AS Vita Club
1994	AS Vita Club

CUP WINNERS OF ZAIRE

1964	Daring Club Motema Pembe
1965	Dragond Kinshasa
1966	Toute Puissant Englebert
1967	Toute Puissant Englebert
1968	St. Eloi
1969-70	-
1971	AS Vita Club
1972	AS Vita Club
1973	AS Vita Club
1974	CS Imana
1975	AS Vita Club
1976	Toute Puissant Mazembe
1977	AS Vita Club
1978	CS Imana
1979	AS Bilima
1980	AS Vita Club
1981	FC Lupopo
1982	AS Bilima
1983	Sanga Balende
1984	AS Bilima
1985	US Tshinkunku Kalamu
1986	FC Lupopo
1987	Daring Club Motema Pembe
1988	AS Vita Club
1989	Daring Club Motema Pembe

CHALLENGE PAPA KALALA

1982	AS Vita Club
1983	AS Vita Club
1984	Daring Club Motema Pembe
1985	Daring Club Motema Pembe
1986	Kalamu Kinshasa
1987	Kalamu Kinshasa
1988	Kalamu Kinshasa
1989	Kalamu Kinshasa

CLUB DIRECTORY

KINSHASA (Pop. - 3,000,000)

Daring Club Motema Pemba - Previously Club Sportive Imana

Amicale Sportive Bilima - Previously Dragons

Association Sportive Vita Club

FC Kalamu

LUBUMBASHI (Pop. - 543,000)

Toute Puissant Mazembe (TP Mazembe) - Formerly TP Englebert

FC Lubumbashi Sport

Mikishi

MBUJI-MAYI (Pop. - 423,000)

Sanga Balende

KANANGA (Pop. - 290,000)

FC Lupopo - Previously St. Eloi

Union Sportive Tshinkunku

MBANDAKA (Pop. - 125,000)

Club Sportif Mokanda

ZAMBIA

Population: 8,456,000
Area, sq km: 752,614
% in urban areas: 44%
Capital city: Lusaka

Football Association of Zambia
PO Box 34751
Lusaka
Zambia
Tel: + 260 1 221145
Fax: + 260 1 225046 za faz
Telex: 40204

Year of formation	1929
Affiliation to FIFA	1964
Affiliation to CAF	1964
Registered clubs	240
Registered players	19 900
Professional players	350
Registered referees	290
National stadium	Independence Stadium, Lusaka 25,000
National colours	Green/Copper/Copper
Reserve colours	Copper/Copper/Green
Season	March - November

THE RECORD

WORLD CUP

1930-66	Did not enter
1970	QT 1st round

1974	QT 4th round
1978	QT 3rd round
1982	QT 2nd round
1986	QT 3rd round
1990	QT 2nd round
1994	QT 1st round - 1st/3 in group 8, 2nd round - 2nd/3 in group 2

AFRICAN CUP OF NATIONS

1957-68	Did not enter
1970	QT 2nd round
1972	QT 2nd round
1974	QT Qualified - Final tournament/Finalists
1976	QT 2nd round
1978	QT Qualified - Final tournament/1st round
1980	QT 2nd round
1982	QT Qualified - Final tournament/Semi-finalists/3rd place
1984	QT 1st round
1986	QT Qualified - Final tournament/1st round
1988	Did not enter
1990	QT Qualified - Final tournament/Semi-finalists/3rd place
1992	QT 1st/4 in group 5 - Final tournament/Quarter-finalists
1994	QT 1st/4 in group 5 - Final Tournament/Finalists

AFRICAN CLUB COMPETITIONS

African Champions Cup

Finalists - Nkana Red Devils 1990

Cup Winners Cup

Winners - Power Dynamos 1991

Finalists - Power Dynamos 1982

CAF Cup

Have never entered

ZAMBIAN LEAGUE CHAMPIONS

1962	Roan United
1963	Mufulira Wanderers
1964	City of Lusaka
1965	Mufulira Wanderers
1966	Mufulira Wanderers
1967	Mufulira Wanderers
1968	Kabwe Warriors
1969	Mufulira Wanderers
1970	Kabwe Warriors
1971	Kabwe Warriors
1972	Kabwe Warriors
1973	Zambia Army
1974	Zambia Army
1975	Green Buffaloes
1976	Mufulira Wanderers
1977	Green Buffaloes
1978	Mufulira Wanderers
1979	Green Buffaloes
1980	Nchanga Rangers
1981	Green Buffaloes
1982	Nkana Red Devils
1983	Nkana Red Devils
1984	Power Dynamos
1985	Nkana Red Devils
1986	Nkana Red Devils
1987	Kabwe Warriors
1988	Nkana Red Devils
1989	Nkana Red Devils
1990	Nkana Red Devils
1991	Power Dynamos
1992	Nkana Red Devils
1993	Nkana FC
1994	Power Dynamos

CLUB DIRECTORY

LUSAKA (Pop. - 535,000)
City of Lusaka
Red Arrows
Green Buffaloes - Previously Zambia Army
Zamsure
Zanaco

KITWE (Pop. - 283,000)
Power Dynamos
Nkana FC (previously Rokana United, Nkana Red Devils)

NDOLA (Pop. - 250,000)
Ndola United

MUFULIRA (Pop. 138,000)
Mufulira Wanderers

KABWE (Pop. - 127,000)
Kabwe Warriors

ZIMBABWE

Population: 9,369,000
Area, sq km: 390,759
% in urban areas: 25%
Capital city: Harare

Zimbabwe Football Association
PO Box CY 114
Causeway
Harare
Zimbabwe
Tel: + 263 4 23942
Fax: + 263 4 24076
Telex: 22299 soccer zw

Year of formation	1950
Affiliation to FIFA	1965
Affiliation to CAF	1980
Registered clubs	610
Registered players	42 700
National stadium	National Stadium, Harare 60 000
National colours	Green/White/Red
Reserve colours	White/Red/Green
Season	February - November

THE RECORD

WORLD CUP

1930-66	Did not enter
1970	QT 2nd round (As Rhodesia)
1974	Did not enter
1978	Did not enter
1982	QT 2nd round
1986	QT 1st round
1990	QT 2nd round
1994	QT 2nd round - 2nd/3 in group 3

AFRICAN CUP OF NATIONS

1957-80	Did not enter
1982	QT 1st round
1984	QT pr round
1986	QT 2nd round
1988	QT 2nd round
1990	QT 2nd round
1992	QT 2nd/4 in group 7
1994	QT 2nd/4 in group 5

AFRICAN CLUB COMPETITIONS

African Champions Cup

Quarter-finalists - Dynamos 1981 1984 1987, Black Rhinos 1985, Zimbabwe Saints 1989

Cup Winners Cup

Quarter-finalists - CAPS United 1982 1983, Dynamos 1991

CAF Cup

Have never entered

ZIMBABWE LEAGUE CHAMPIONS

1962	Bulawayo Rovers
1963	Dynamos
1964	St. Pauls
1965	Dynamos
1966	St. Pauls
1967	Tornados
1968	Sables
1969	Sables
1970	Dynamos
1971	Arcadia United
1972	Sables
1973	Metal Box
1974	Sables
1975	Chibuku
1976	Dynamos
1977	Zimbabwe Saints
1978	Dynamos
1979	CAPS United
1980	Dynamos
1981	Dynamos
1982	Dynamos
1983	Dynamos
1984	Black Rhinos
1985	Dynamos
1986	Dynamos
1987	Black Rhinos
1988	Zimbabwe Saints
1989	Dynamos
1990	Highlanders
1991	Dynamos
1992	Black Aces
1993	Bulawayo Highlanders
1994	Dynamos

ZIMBABWE CUP WINNERS

1962	Bulawayo Rovers
1963	Salisbury Callies
1964	-

1965	Salisbury City Wanderers
1966	Mangula
1967	Salisbury Callies
1968	Arcadia United
1969	Arcadia United
1970	Wankie
1971	Chibuku
1972	Mangula
1973	Wankie
1974	Chibuku
1975	Salisbury Callies
1976	Dynamos
1977	Zimbabwe Saints
1978	Zisco Steel
1979	Zimbabwe Saints
1980	CAPS United
1981	CAPS United
1982	CAPS United
1983	CAPS United
1984	Black Rhinos
1985	Dynamos
1986	Highlanders
1987	CAPS United
1988	Dynamos
1989	Dynamos
1990	Highlanders
1991	Dynamos
1992	Wankie
1993	Tanganda Mutare
1994	Blackpool

CLUB DIRECTORY

HARARE (Pop. - 890,000)
Black Aces
CAPS United
Dynamos
Blackpool

BULAWAYO (Pop. - 413,000)
Zimbabwe Saints
Bulawayo Highlanders
Bulawayo Wanderers

GWERU (Pop. - 78,000)
Gweru United

MUTARE (Pop. - 69,000)
Black Rhinos
Tanganda

CONCACAF

The Confederación Norte-Centroamericana y del Caribe de Fútbol, or CONCACAF for short, is with the exception of Oceania the weakest of the continental confederations, and for many years seemed to exist in order that Mexico could be guaranteed a place at the World Cup. The present body dates only from 1961; before that there had been a confusion of bodies claiming responsibility over the game in the region, or various parts of it. Part of the problem is that CONCACAF is not a recognisable geographical entity. By rights there should be a confederation for all the countries of the Americas, as existed in the 1950s, but this body never had any jurisdictional power as the South American confederation was unwilling to see its own control weakened. Nowadays the countries that make up CONCACAF would similarly be unwilling to relinquish their three automatic World Cup berths.

In 1924 the Congreso Deportivo Centroamericano was founded and this became the Organizacion Deportiva Centroamericano y del Caribe. Its primary function was to organise the Central American and Caribbean Games which started in 1930, and in which there was a football tournament. Before the 1938 edition of those Games it was decided to found a football-only governing body and so the Confederación Centroamericana y del Caribe de Fútbol, or the CCCF, came into being. Its charter members included Colombia and Venezuela from South America, most of the Central American nations, as well as Haiti, Puerto Rico and Jamaica from the Caribbean. It organised a new tournament, the Championship of the CCCF, which was open to amateurs and professionals.

In 1939 a short-lived North American Football Confederation, containing the United States, Cuba and Mexico, was founded and two championships played, but by 1961 the Mexicans in particular were keen to revitalise the international game in the region, which the CCCF had never really got to grips with, and that year they became one of the founding members of CONCACAF along with Cuba, Guatemala, Honduras and the Netherland Antilles. Other members soon followed and by 1970 there were 14 in all. Since then the number has risen to 30 as the tiny islands of the Caribbean have made the effort to join. CONCACAF's major role has been to organise championships both for the clubs and the national sides, but two concerns have always dominated its activities.

First, Mexico is by far and away the strongest of all the nations affiliated. When their sides take the club championship seriously, teams from other nations do not really stand a chance. Even worse for CONCACAF has been Mexico's total indifference to the championship for national sides, so much so that it was abandoned as a separate event in the 1970s and the winners of the World Cup qualifying competition were regarded as champions. The other problem has been the attitude of the United States, whose national and club sides have shunned both CONCACAF competitions. The New York Cosmos et al had more important matters on their mind than playing in some backwater tournament, or so it seemed.

CONCACAF could, however, be one of the growth regions of the future because finally the United States is beginning to take football seriously, spurred by its hosting of the 1994 World Cup. In 1992 CONCACAF moved their offices from Guatemala City to New York in a bid to attract more finance, whilst the previous year they had launched the CONCACAF Gold Cup, the first edition of which contained, for the first time, the majority of countries in the region, including all the big names. The club competition is also undergoing a transformation, albeit more slowly, and recently it became the American Airlines Cup. Although Costa Rican sides won in 1993 and 1994, generally Mexican clubs still dominate.

Confederación Norte-Centroamericana y del Caribe de Fútbol
717 Fifth Avenue, 13th Floor
New York
NY 10022
USA
Tel: + 1 212 3080044
Fax: + 1 212 3081851

Year of formation - 1961

MEMBERS - 30
Antigua and Barbuda – Aruba – Bahamas – Barbados – Belize – Bermuda – Canada – Cayman Islands – Costa Rica – Cuba – Dominica – Dominican Republic – El Salvador – Grenada – Guatemala – Guyana – Haiti – Honduras – Jamaica – Mexico – Netherlands Antilles – Nicaragua – Panama – Puerto Rico – Saint Lucia – Saint Kitts and Nevis – Saint Vincent and the Grenadines – Suriname – Trinidad and Tobago – United States of America

ASSOCIATE MEMBERS - 1
Virgin Islands of the US

NON MEMBERS - 8
Anguilla – British Virgin Islands – French Guiana – Guadeloupe – Martinique – Montserrat – St Pierre and Miquelon – Turks and Caicos Islands

THE NORTH CENTRAL AMERICAN AND CARIBBEAN CHAMPIONSHIPS

1941	Costa Rica
1943	El Salvador
1946	Costa Rica
1948	Costa Rica
1951	Panama
1953	Costa Rica
1955	Costa Rica
1957	Haiti
1960	Costa Rica
1961	Costa Rica
1963	Costa Rica

1965	Mexico
1967	Guatemala
1969	Costa Rica
1971	Mexico
1973	Haiti
1977	Mexico
1981	Honduras
1985	Canada
1989	Costa Rica
1991	United States
1993	Mexico

1941

1ST CHAMPIONSHIP OF THE CCCF

SAN JOSE, COSTA RICA, 8TH - 18TH MAY 1941

	CR	ES	Cu	Pa	Ni	Pl	W	D	L	F	A	Pts
COSTA RICA	-	3-1	6-2	7-0	7-2	4	4	0	0	23	5	8
El Salvador	-	-	2-2	4-3	8-0	4	2	1	1	15	8	5
Curacao	-	-	-	3-3	9-1	4	1	2	1	16	12	4
Panama	-	-	-	-	5-2	4	1	1	2	11	16	3
Nicaragua	-	-	-	-	-	4	0	0	4	5	29	0

1943

2ND CHAMPIONSHIP OF THE CCCF

SAN SALVADOR, 5TH - 19TH DECEMBER 1943

	ES	CR	Gu	Ni	Pl	W	D	L	F	A	Pts
EL SALVADOR	-	4-3	2-2	10-1	6	4	1	1	28	12	9
Costa Rica	4-2	-	2-3	7-0	6	3	0	3	21	15	6
Guatemala	1-2	4-2	-	-	4	2	1	1	10	8	5
Nicaragua	1-8	2-3	-	-	4	0	0	4	4	28	0

1946

3RD CHAMPIONSHIP OF THE CCCF

SAN JOSE, COSTA RICA, 23RD FEB - 13TH MARCH 1946

	CR	Gu	ES	Ho	Pa	Ni	Pl	W	D	L	F	A	Pts
COSTA RICA	-	1-4	4-0	5-0	7-0	7-1	5	4	0	1	24	5	8
Guatemala	-	-	w	l	d	w	5	3	1	1			7
El Salvador	-	-	-	3-1	w	w	5	3	0	2			6
Honduras	-	-	-	-	l	w	5	2	0	3			4
Panama	-	-	-	-	-	l	5	1	1	3			3
Nicaragua	-	-	-	-	-	-	5	1	0	4			2

1948

4TH CHAMPIONSHIP OF THE CCCF

HELD IN GUATEMALA CITY

	CR	Gu	Cu	ES	Pa	Pl	W	D	L	F	A	Pts
COSTA RICA	-	1-1	2-1	3-1	3-1	8	5	1	2	25	11	11
Guatemala	3-2	-	-	-	-	2	1	1	0	4	3	3
Curacao	4-1	-	-	-	-	2	1	0	1	5	3	2
El Salvador	0-6	-	-	-	-	2	0	0	2	1	9	0
Panama	0-7	-	-	-	-	2	0	0	2	1	10	0

1951

5TH CHAMPIONSHIP OF THE CCCF

Winners - PANAMA

1953

6TH CHAMPIONSHIP OF THE CCCF

Winners - COSTA RICA

1955

7TH CHAMPIONSHIP OF THE CCCF

Winners - COSTA RICA

1957

8TH CHAMPIONSHIP OF THE CCCF

HELD IN CURACAO, 11TH - 25TH AUG 1957

	Ha	Cu	Ho	Pa	Cu	Pl	W	D	L	F	A	Pts
HAITI	-	3-1	2-1	3-1	6-1	4	4	0	0	14	4	8
Curacao	-	-	1-1	3-0	2-0	4	2	1	1	7	4	5
Honduras	-	-	-	2-1	2-0	4	2	1	1	6	4	5
Panama	-	-	-	-	1-0	4	1	0	3	3	8	2
Cuba	-	-	-	-	-	4	0	0	4	1	11	0

1960

9TH CHAMPIONSHIP OF THE CCCF

HELD IN HAVANA, CUBA 14TH - 28TH FEB 1960

	CR	NA	Ho	Su	Cu	Pl	W	D	L	F	A	Pts
COSTA RICA	-	1-1	1-1	3-1	5-0	4	2	2	0	10	3	6
Netherland Antilles	-	-	3-3	1-0	4-3	4	2	2	0	9	7	6
Honduras	-	-	-	1-1	1-2	4	0	3	1	6	7	3
Suriname	-	-	-	-	2-0	4	1	1	2	4	5	3
Cuba	-	-	-	-	-	4	0	0	4	5	12	0

1961

10TH CHAMPIONSHIP OF THE CCCF

HELD IN SAN JOSE, COSTA RICA, MARCH 1961

FIRST ROUND

Group 1

	CR	Ha	Gu	Pa	Cu	Pl	W	D	L	F	A	Pts
Costa Rica	-	3-0	4-2	6-1	-	4	4	0	0	17	4	8
Haiti	-	-	-	3-1	2-1	4	3	0	1	8	6	6
Guatemala	-	1-3	-	-	2-0	4	2	0	2	7	7	4
Panama	-	-	0-2	-	1-0	4	1	0	3	3	11	2
Cuba	1-4	-	-	-	-	4	0	0	4	2	9	0

Group 2

	ES	Ho	NA	Ni	Pl	W	D	L	F	A	Pts
El Salvador	-	1-0	-	10-2	3	2	1	0	11	2	5
Honduras	-	-	4-2	-	3	2	0	1	10	3	4
Netherland Antilles	0-0	-	-	2-1	3	1	1	1	4	5	3
Nicaragua	-	0-6	-	-	3	0	0	3	3	18	0

FINAL ROUND

	CR	ES	Ho	Ha	Pl	W	D	L	F	A	Pts
COSTA RICA	-	4-0	3-0	8-0	3	3	0	0	15	0	6
El Salvador	-	-	5-1	2-0	3	2	0	1	7	5	4
Honduras	-	-	-	2-0	3	1	0	2	3	8	2
Haiti	-	-	-	-	3	0	0	3	0	12	0

1963

1ST CHAMPIONSHIP OF CONCACAF

SAN SALVADOR, 23RD - 7TH APRIL 1963
FIRST ROUND

Group 1

	Ho	ES	Pa	Gu	Ni	Pl	W	D	L	F	A	Pts
Honduras	-	2-2	1-0	2-1	1-0	4	3	1	0	6	3	7
El Salvador	-	-	1-1	1-1	6-1	4	1	3	0	10	5	5
Panama	-	-	-	2-2	5-0	4	1	2	1	8	4	4
Guatemala	-	-	-	-	3-1	4	1	2	1	7	6	4
Nicaragua	-	-	-	-	-	4	0	0	4	2	15	0

Group 2

	CR	NA	Me	Ja	Pl	W	D	L	F	A	Pts
Costa Rica	-	1-0	0-0	6-0	3	2	1	0	7	0	5
Neth. Antilles	-	-	2-1	2-1	3	2	0	1	4	3	4
Mexico	-	-	-	8-0	3	1	1	1	9	2	3
Jamaica	-	-	-	-	3	0	0	3	1	16	0

FINAL ROUND

	CR	ES	NA	Ho	Pl	W	D	L	F	A	Pts
COSTA RICA	-	4-1	1-0	2-1	3	3	0	0	7	2	6
El Salvador	-	-	3-2	3-0	3	2	0	1	7	6	4
Netherland Antilles	-	-	-	4-1	3	1	0	2	6	5	2
Honduras	-	-	-	-	3	0	0	3	2	9	0

1965

2ND CHAMPIONSHIP OF CONCACAF

HELD IN GUATEMALA CITY, 28TH MARCH - 11TH APRIL 1965

	Me	Gu	CR	ES	NA	Ha	Pl	W	D	L	F	A	Pts
MEXICO	-	2-1	1-1	2-0	5-0	3-0	5	4	1	0	13	2	9
Guatemala	-	-	0-0	4-1	3-2	3-0	5	3	1	1	11	5	7
Costa Rica	-	-	-	1-2	6-0	3-1	5	2	2	1	11	4	6
El Salvador	-	-	-	-	1-1	3-1	5	2	1	2	7	9	5
Netherland Antilles	-	-	-	-	-	1-1	5	0	2	3	4	16	2
Haiti	-	-	-	-	-	-	5	0	1	4	3	13	1

1967

3RD CHAMPIONSHIP OF CONCACAF

HELD IN TEGUCIGALPA, HONDURAS 5TH - 19TH MARCH 1967

	Gu	Me	Ho	Tr	Ha	Ni	Pl	W	D	L	F	A	Pts
GUATEMALA	-	1-0	0-0	2-0	2-1	2-0	5	4	1	0	7	1	9
Mexico	-	-	1-0	4-0	1-0	4-0	5	4	0	1	10	1	8
Honduras	-	-	-	1-0	2-0	1-1	5	2	2	1	4	2	6
Trinidad	-	-	-	-	3-2	3-1	5	2	0	3	6	10	4
Haiti	-	-	-	-	-	2-1	5	1	0	4	5	9	2
Nicaragua	-	-	-	-	-	-	5	0	1	4	3	12	1

1969

4TH CHAMPIONSHIP OF CONCACAF

HELD IN SAN JOSE, COSTA RICA FROM 23RD NOV - 8TH DEC 1969

	CR	Gu	NA	Me	Tr	Ja	Pl	W	D	L	F	A	Pts
COSTA RICA	-	1-1	2-1	2-0	5-0	3-0	5	4	1	0	13	2	9
Guatemala	-	-	6-1	1-0	2-0	0-0	5	3	2	0	10	2	8
Neth. Antilles	-	-	-	2-2	3-1	2-1	5	2	1	2	9	12	5
Mexico	-	-	-	-	0-0	2-0	5	1	2	2	4	5	4
Trinidad	-	-	-	-	-	3-2	5	1	1	3	4	12	3
Jamaica	-	-	-	-	-	-	5	0	1	4	3	10	1

1971

5TH CHAMPIONSHIP OF CONCACAF

HELD IN PORT OF SPAIN, TRINIDAD FROM 20TH NOVEMBER 5TH DECEMBER 1971

	Me	Ha	CR	Cu	Tr	Ho	Pl	W	D	L	F	A	Pts
MEXICO	-	0-0	1-0	1-0	2-0	2-1	5	4	1	0	6	1	9
Haiti	-	-	0-0	0-0	6-0	3-1	5	2	3	0	9	1	7
Costa Rica	-	-	-	3-0	1-3	2-1	5	2	1	2	6	5	5
Cuba	-	-	-	-	2-2	3-1	5	1	2	2	5	7	4
Trinidad	-	-	-	-	-	1-1	5	1	2	2	6	12	4
Honduras	-	-	-	-	-	-	5	0	1	4	5	11	1

1973

6TH CHAMPIONSHIP OF CONCACAF

Winners - HAITI

1977

7TH CHAMPIONSHIP OF CONCACAF

Winners - MEXICO

1981

8TH CHAMPIONSHIP OF CONCACAF

Winners - HONDURAS

1985

9TH CHAMPIONSHIP OF CONCACAF

Winners - CANADA

1989

10TH CHAMPIONSHIP OF CONCACAF

Winners - COSTA RICA

CONCACAF GOLD CUP

Perhaps the most significant development in CONCACAF in recent years has been the rekindled interest in the United States' national side. In an effort to boost the level of competition in the region, America was a major backer for the CONCACAF Gold Cup introduced in 1991. A separate CONCACAF championship had not been held since the 1971 tournament in Trinidad, won by Mexico.

The aim of the Gold Cup was to rekindle that idea and exploit the growing interest in the game. In 1991 Costa

Rica won the first Central American UNCAF Cup and qualified with Honduras and Guatemala for the first Gold Cup finals later that year. They were joined by Jamaica and Trinidad, winners and runners-up of the 1991 Shell Caribbean Cup, and the three North American countries, Canada, the USA and Mexico. The tournament, played in America, gave the hosts their first international honour at senior level when they beat Honduras on penalties after a goalless final in Los Angeles.

Two years later the organisers decided to stage the tournament jointly in Mexico and America. It was no surprise that both 'home' teams reached the final, which was held this time in Mexico City. The Mexicans, who had been beaten by the USA in the semi-finals in 1991, gained revenge with a 4-0 win and were in scintillating form throughout the tournament, scoring 28 goals in five games with Canada, Martinique and Jamaica bearing the brunt.

1ST CONCACAF GOLD CUP

QUALIFYING ROUNDS
Jamaica and Trinidad qualify from the Caribbean
Costa Rica, Honduras and Guatemala qualify from Central America

NORTH AMERICA
For the North American Championship

	Me	US	Ca	Pl	W	D	L	F	A	Pts
Mexico	-	2-2	3-0	2	1	1	0	5	2	3
United States	-	-	2-0	2	1	1	0	4	2	3
Canada	-	-	-	2	0	0	2	0	5	0

All three qualify

FINAL TOURNAMENT
Held in Los Angeles 28th June - 7th July 1991

FIRST ROUND

Group 1

	Ho	Me	Ca	Ja	Pl	W	D	L	F	A	Pts
Honduras	-	1-1	4-2	5-0	3	2	1	0	10	3	5
Mexico	-	-	3-1	4-1	3	2	1	0	8	3	5
Canada	-	-	-	3-2	3	1	0	2	6	9	2
Jamaica	-	-	-	-	3	0	0	3	3	12	0

Group 2

	US	CR	Tr	Gu	Pl	W	D	L	F	A	Pts
United States	-	3-2	2-1	3-0	3	3	0	0	8	3	6
Costa Rica	-	-	1-2	2-0	3	1	0	2	5	5	2
Trinidad	-	-	-	0-1	3	1	0	2	3	4	2
Guatemala	-	-	-	-	3	1	0	2	1	5	2

SEMI-FINALS
United States .... 2-0 .... Mexico
Honduras .... 2-0 .... Costa Rica

3RD PLACE
Mexico .... 2-0 .... Costa Rica

FINAL
Coliseum, Los Angeles, 7-07-1991, 39,000

UNITED STATES 0
HONDURAS 0
USA won 4-3 on penalties

USA - Meola - Caligiuri, Balboa, Doyle, Clavijo - Quinn, Henderson, Murray (Kinnear), Perez - Vermes, Wynalda (Eck)

Honduras - Rivera (Cruz) - Castro, Martinez, Flores, Zapata - Anariba, Yearwood, Funez, Espinoza - Calix, Bennett (Vallejo)

1993

2ND CONCACAF GOLD CUP

QUALIFYING ROUNDS
Jamaica and Martinique qualify from the Caribbean
Costa Rica, Honduras and Panama qualify from Central America
The United States, Canada and Mexico qualify from North America

FINAL TOURNAMENT
Held in Dallas and Mexico City, 10th - 26th July 1993

FIRST ROUND

Group 1

	US	Ja	Ho	Pa	Pl	W	D	L	F	A	Pts
United States	-	1-0	1-0	2-1	3	3	0	0	4	1	6
Jamaica	-	-	3-1	1-1	3	1	1	1	4	3	3
Honduras	-	-	-	5-1	3	1	0	2	6	5	2
Panama	-	-	-	-	3	0	1	2	3	8	1

Group 2

	Me	CR	Ca	Ma	Pl	W	D	L	F	A	Pts
Mexico	-	1-1	8-0	9-0	3	2	1	0	18	1	5
Costa Rica	-	-	1-1	3-1	3	1	2	0	5	3	4
Canada	-	-	-	2-2	3	0	2	1	3	11	2
Martinique	-	-	-	-	3	0	1	2	3	14	1

SEMI-FINALS
Mexico .... 6-1 .... Jamaica
United States .... 1-0 .... Costa Rica

3RD PLACE
Costa Rica .... 1-1 .... Jamaica

FINAL
Azteca, Mexico City, 26-07-1993, 120,000

MEXICO 4 (Ambriz, OG, Zaguinho, Cantu)
UNITED STATES 0

Mexico - Campos - Suarez, Ambriz, Ramirez Perales, Ramon Ramirez - Hernandez, Salvador (Noriega), Mora (Cantu), Del Olmo - Rodriguez, Alves Zaguinho. Tr: Baron

USA - Meola - Doyle, Kooiman, Dooley, Harkes - Wynalda, Jones (Kinnear), Armstrong, Wegerle (Moore) - Henderson, Lalas. Tr: Milutinovic

CONCACAF YOUTH CHAMPIONSHIP FOR UNDER-20S

1962 Mexico
1964 El Salvador
1970 Mexico
1973 Mexico
1974 Mexico
1976 Mexico
1978 Mexico
1980 Mexico
1982 United States
1984 Mexico
1986 Canada
1988 Costa Rica
1990 Mexico
1992 Mexico
1994 Honduras

CONCACAF UNDER-17 CHAMPIONSHIP

1983 United States
1985 Mexico

1987	Mexico
1988	Cuba
1990	Mexico
1992	United States
1994	Costa Rica

THE FOOTBALL TOURNAMENT OF THE CENTRAL AMERICAN AND CARIBBEAN GAMES

1926	Mexico
1930	Cuba
1935	Mexico
1938	Mexico
1946	Colombia
1950	Neth. Antilles
1954	El Salvador
1959	Mexico
1962	Neth. Antilles
1966	Mexico
1970	Cuba
1974	Cuba
1978	Cuba
1982	Venezuela
1986	Cuba
1990	Mexico

CONCACAF CLUB TOURNAMENTS

Although the overall standard of its club football lags behind Europe, South America and Africa, the CONCACAF region does contain one of the world's strongest leagues: in Mexico, club football has a huge following and generates large amounts of revenue, some of which is used to entice players from all over South America to play in the Mexican league. It is not unknown for the 110,000-capacity Azteca stadium to sell out for big games, and large crowds are common in most of the major cities. It is a standard which the Central American and Caribbean countries cannot hope to match, so when Mexican clubs take the CONCACAF Champion Clubs Cup seriously it is something of an unequal struggle.

The first tournament kicked off on 25 March 1962 with five Central American countries represented and two from the Caribbean. Mexico made the total entry eight and Guadalajara duly emerged as the first champions, beating Comunicaciones of Guatemala in a two-legged final just under five months later. After this promising start the tournament then fell prey to lack of interest, logistical problems and disputes. The entry for 1963 rose by one to nine and Racing Club of Haiti qualified to meet Guadalajara in the final, but a trip to the Caribbean did not seem a worthwhile undertaking and the holders pulled out, leaving Racing as unlikely champions. It was to be the first of many unplayed final ties.

The next two tournaments did not even get that far, both being abandoned in the early stages, and delays built up to such an extent that the 1966 event did not get started at all. On 6 August 1967 the sixth tournament got underway with eight clubs but crucially no Mexican entry, leaving the way free for El Salvador's Alianza to beat Jong Colombia from the Netherlands Antilles in a three-legged final played in March 1968.

It has usually been the practice to divide the entrants into zones, of North America, Central America and the Caribbean. In 1968 Toluca won the North zone, Aurora the Central and Transvaal the Caribbean, but CONCACAF expelled the latter two sides leaving Toluca as champions in yet another controversy-dogged event. There were no such problems the following year but in 1970 the three regional winners again did not contest the final when Deportivo Saprissa and Transvaal withdrew. Cruz Azul were declared champions, their second successive triumph, and in 1971 they made it three in a row when they beat Liga Deportiva Alajuelense 5-1 in Mexico City: both clubs had finished level on points in a six-team final tournament in Guatemala.

The number of entries for that edition had been a record 18 and the tournament's prospects had never looked better, but for the rest of the decade the Mexican clubs lost interest and, perhaps more damagingly, none of the NASL clubs from North America ever entered. The event became something of a sideshow in which the likes of Transvaal, Municipal and Aguila could flourish. Mexican support for the tournament has been sporadic since, although more consistent from the early 1980s. América, in particular, have always found a place for it in their fixture list, and with four victories are the most successful side in the history of the event, followed by Cruz Azul and UNAM with three apiece. In recent years new sponsorship has brought fresh hope and a Cup Winners Cup has been introduced. Mexico, the only country with a strong, established domestic cup competition, not surprisingly won two of the first three editions.

CONCACAF CHAMPIONS CUP

1962	Guadalajara CD (MEX)	1-0 5-0	Comunicaciones (GUA)
1963	Racing Club (HAI)	W-O	Guadalajara CD (MEX)
1964	Not completed		
1965	Not completed		
1966	-		
1967	Alianza (SLV)	1-2 3-0 5-3	Jong Colombia (ANT)
1968	Toluca (MEX)	Walk-over	
1969	Cruz Azul (MEX)	0-0 1-0	Comunicaciones (GUA)
1970	Cruz Azul (MEX)	Walk-over	
1971	Cruz Azul (MEX)	5-1	LD Alajuelense (CRC)
1972	Olimpia (HND)	0-0 2-0	Robin Hood (SUR)
1973	Transvaal (SUR)	W-O	
1974	Municipal (GUA)	2-1 2-1	Transvaal (SUR)
1975	Atletico Español (MEX)	3-0 2-1	Transvaal (SUR)
1976	Aguila (SLV)	W-O	Robin Hood (SUR)
1977	América (MEX)	1-0 0-0	Robin Hood (SUR)

1978	Univ. Guadalajara (MEX) North winners		
	Comunicaciones (GUA) Central winners		
	Defence Force (TTO) Caribbean winners		
1979	Deportivo FAS (SLV)	1-0 8-0	Jong Colombia (ANT)
1980	UNAM (MEX)	2-0	Univ. de Honduras (HND)
1981	Transvaal (SUR)	1-0 1-1	Atlético Marte (SLV)
1982	UNAM (MEX)	2-2 3-0	Robin Hood (SUR)
1983	Atlante (MEX)	1-1 5-0	Robin Hood (SUR)
1984	Violette (HAI)	W-O	
1985	Defence Force (TTO)	2-0 0-1	Olimpia (HND)
1986	LD Alajuelense (CRC)	4-1 1-1	Transvaal (SUR)
1987	América (MEX)	2-0 1-1	Defence Force (TTO)
1988	Olimpia (HND)	2-0 2-0	Defence Force (TTO)
1989	UNAM (MEX)	1-1 3-1	Piñar del Rio (CUB)
1990	América (MEX)	2-2 6-0	Piñar del Rio (CUB)
1991	Puebla (MEX)	3-1 1-1	Police FC (TTO)
1992	América (MEX)	1-0	LD Alajuelense (CRC)
1993	Deportivo Saprissa (CRC)	2-2 *	Leon (MEX)
1994	CS Cartagines (CRC)	3-2	Atlante (MEX)

* Played on a league system

ORDER OF MERIT

	Team	Country	G	S
1	América	MEX	4	-
2	Cruz Azul	MEX	3	-
	UNAM	MEX	3	-
4	Transvaal	SUR	2	3
5	Defence Force	TTO	2	2
6	Olimpia	HND	2	1
7	Comunicaciones	GUA	1	2
	LD Alajuelense	CRC	1	2
9	Guadalajara CD	MEX	1	1
10	Atlante	MEX	1	1
11	Aguila	SLV	1	-
	Alianza	SLV	1	-
	Atlético Español	MEX	1	-
	Cartagines	CRC	1	-
	Deportivo FAS	SLV	1	-
	Deportivo Saprissa	CRC	1	-
	Municipal	GUA	1	-
	Peubla	MEX	1	-
	Racing Club	HAI	1	-
	Toluca	MEX	1	-
	Univ. Guadalajara	MEX	1	-
	Violette	HAI	1	-
23	Robin Hood	SUR	-	5
24	Jong Colombia	ANT	-	2
	Piñar del Rio	CUB	-	2
26	Atlético Marte	SLV	-	1
	Leon	MEX	-	1
	Police FC	TTO	-	1
	Univ. de Honduras	HND	-	1

	Country	G	S
1	Mexico	16	3
2	Costa Rica	3	2
3	El Salvador	3	1
4	Suriname	2	8
5	Trinidad	2	3
6	Guatamala	2	2
	Honduras	2	2
8	Haiti	2	-
9	Cuba	-	2
	Neth. Antilles	-	2

To the end of the 1994 tournament

1962

NORTH - Guadalajara DC MEX
CENTRAL - Comunicaciones GUA, Aguila SLV, Liga Deportiva Alajuelense CRC, CS Herediano CRC, Olimpia HND
CARIBBEAN - Estrella Haitiana HTI, Sithoc ANT

FINAL

1st leg. Guatamala City, 29-07-1962

Comunicaciones 0
Guadalajara CD 1

2nd leg. Guadalajara, 21-08-1962

Guadalajara CD 5
Comunicaciones 0

1963

NORTH - Guadalajara CD MEX, New York Hungarians USA, Oro MEX
CENTRAL - Xelaju MC GUA, Deportivo Saprissa CRC, Deportivo FAS SLV, VIDA HND
CARIBBEAN - Racing Club HTI, Sithoc ANT

FINAL

Racing Club won after Guadalajara withdrew from the final

1964–66

Tournaments abandoned

1967

NORTH - Philadelphia Ukranians USA, Young Men's BER
CENTRAL - Alianza SLV, Aurora FC GUA, Flor de Caña NIC, Olimpia HND
CARIBBEAN - Jong Colombia ANT, Regiment TTO

FINAL

1st leg. San Salvador, 17-03-1968

Alianza 1
Jong Colombia 2

2nd leg. Willemstad, 19-03-1968

Jong Colombia 0
Alianza 3

Play-off. 24-03-1968

Alianza 5
Jong Colombia 3

1968

NORTH - Toluca MEX, Greek-Americans USA, Somerset Cricket BER
CENTRAL - Aurora FC GUA, Alianza SLV, Liga Deportiva Alajuelense CRC, Olimpia HND
CARIBBEAN - Transvaal SUR, Scherpenheuvel ANT

FINAL

Toluca were declared champions after Transvaal and Aurora FC were suspended.

1969

NORTH - Cruz Azul MEX, Toluca MEX, Somerset Cricket BER
CENTRAL - Comunicaciones GUA, Aguila SLV, Motagua HND, Deportivo Saprissa CRC, Univ. Catolica NIC
CARIBBEAN - Jong Colombia ANT, Violette HTI

FINAL

1st leg. Guatemala City, 18-09-1969

Comunicaciones 0
Cruz Azul 0

2nd leg. Mexico City, 30-09-1969
Cruz Azul 1
Comunicaciones 0

1970

NORTH - Cruz Azul MEX, Greek-Americans USA
CENTRAL - Deportivo Saprissa CRC, Atlético Marte SLV, Diriangen NIC, Municipal GUA, Olimpia HND
CARIBBEAN - Transvaal SUR, Mapple TTO, Racing Club HTI, Santos JAM, SUBT ANT

FINAL

Cruz Azul were declared winners after Deportivo Saprissa and Transvaal withdrew

1971

NORTH - Cruz Azul MEX, Rochester Lancers USA, Elizabeth SC USA, Guadalajara CD MEX, Pembroke BER
CENTRAL - Comunicaciones GUA, Liga Deportiva Alajuelense CRC, Aurora FC GUA, Diriangen NIC, Deportivo FAS SLV, Motagua HND, Atlético Marte SLV, Olimpia HND, Deportivo Saprissa CRC
CARIBBEAN - Transvaal SUR, Estrella Roja ANT, Aguila Negra HTI, Thomas United GUY

FINAL TOURNAMENT

Held in Guatemala City, 12th - 26th March 1972

	CA	LD	Co	RL	Tr	ER	Pl	W	D	L	F	A	Pts
Cruz Azul	-	3-1	3-1	1-1	1-1	9-0	5	3	2	0	17	4	8
Liga Deportiva Alajuelense	-	-	2-0	1-0	2-0	2-1	5	4	0	1	8	4	8
Comunicaciones	-	-	-	3-1	1-1	7-0	5	2	1	2	12	7	5
Rochester Lancers	-	-	-	-	2-0	2-0	5	2	1	2	6	5	5
Transvaal	-	-	-	-	-	1-0	5	1	2	2	3	6	4
Estrella Roja	-	-	-	-	-	-	5	0	0	5	1	21	0

Play-off. Mexico City, 19-04-1972
Cruz Azul 5
Liga Deportiva Alajuelense 1

1972

NORTH - América MEX, Toluca MEX
CENTRAL - Olimpia HND, Santa Cecilia NIC, Union Española PAN, VIDA HND
CARIBBEAN - Robin Hood SUR, Aguila Negra HTI, Don Bosco HTI, Transvaal SUR

FINAL

1st leg. Paramaribo, 28-01-1973
Robin Hood 0
Olimpia 0

2nd leg. Tegucigalpa, 31-01-1973
Olimpia 2
Robin Hood 0

1973

NORTH - Devonshire Colts BER, North Village BER
CENTRAL - Aguila SLV, Liga Deportiva Alajuelense CRC, Comunicaciones GUA, Juventud Olimpica SLV, Municipal GUA, Olimpia HND, Santa Cecilia NIC, Deportivo Saprissa CRC, VIDA HND
CARIBBEAN - Transvaal SUR, Jong Colombia ANT, Robin Hood SUR, SUBT ANT, Univ. Catolica DOM

FINAL

Transvaal were declared winners after the teams from the north and central section withdrew

1974

NORTH - Devonshire Colts BER, Maccabee Los Angeles USA, North Village BER
CENTRAL - Municipal GUA, Alianza SLV, Aurora FC GUA, CS Cartagines CRC, Marathon HND, Motagua HND, Negocios Internacional SLV, Santa Cecilia NIC
CARIBBEAN - Transvaal SUR, Robin Hood SUR, Jong Colombia ANT, Real Rincon ANT

FINAL

1st leg. Guatemala City, 24-10-1974
Municipal 2
Transvaal 1

2nd leg. Paramaribo, 27-10-1974
Transvaal 1
Municipal 2

1975

NORTH - Atlético Español MEX, Aguilas Blancas CAN, Monterrey MEX
CENTRAL - Aurora FC GUA, Real España HND, CS Herediano CRC, Motagua HND, Municipal GUA, Negocios Internacional SLV, Deportivo Saprissa CRC
CARIBBEAN - Transvaal SUR, Montecarlo DOM, Racing Club HTI, Robin Hood SUR, Santos JAM, Univ. Catolica DOM, Violette HTI

FINAL

1st leg. Paramaribo, 7-03-1976
Transvaal 0
Atlético Español 3

2nd leg. Mexico City, 9-03-1976
Atlético Español 2
Transvaal 1

1976

NORTH - Inter-Giuliana USA, Italia CAN, León MEX
CENTRAL - Aguila SLV, Alianza SLV, Aurora FC GUA, Diriangen NIC, Real España HND, Olimpia HND
CARIBBEAN - Robin Hood SUR, Christianburg ANT, Jong Colombia ANT, Malvern TTO, Palo Seco TTO, Thomas United GUY, Voorward SUR

FINAL

Aguila were declared champions after Robin Hood withdrew from the final

1977

NORTH - América MEX
CENTRAL - Aguila SLV, Diriangen NIC, México CRC, Municipal GUA, Deportivo Saprissa CRC
CARIBBEAN - Robin Hood SUR, Defence Force TTO, Pelé GUY, TECSA TTO, Victory HTI, Violette HTI, Voorward SUR, YMCA GUY

FINAL

1st leg. Paramaribo, 15-01-1978
Robin Hood 0
América 1

2nd leg. Mexico City, 18-01-1978
América 0
Robin Hood 0

1978

NORTH - Univ. Guadalajara MEX, Maccabee Los Angeles USA, UNAM MEX
CENTRAL - Comunicaciones GUA, CS Cartigines CRC,

Diriangen NIC, Deportivo FAS SLV, Municipal SLV, Municipal GUA, Deportivo Saprissa CRC, Univ. Catolica NIC
CARIBBEAN - Defence Force TTO, Jong Holland ANT, Pelé GUY, Racing Club HTI, TECSA TTO, Thomas United GUY, Transvaal SUR, Voorward SUR

FINAL
Universidad Guadalajara, Comunicaciones and Defence Force were declared joint champions

1979

NORTH - Soccer Universidad USA, Univ. Nuevo León MEX
CENTRAL - Deportivo FAS SLV, Alianza SLV, CS Herediano CRC
CARIBBEAN - Jong Colombia ANT, Defence Force TTO, Don Bosco DOM, Jong Holland ANT, Leo Victor SUR, Palo Seco TTO, Robin Hood SUR, Santos JAM

FINAL
1st leg. Willemstad, 22-12-1979
Jong Colombia 0
Deportivo FAS 1

2nd leg. San Salvador, 29-12-1979
Deportivo FAS 8
Jong Colombia 0

1980

NORTH - UNAM MEX, Brooklyn Dodgers USA, Cruz Azul MEX, Hotel International BER, Sacramento Gold USA
CENTRAL - Univ. de Honduras HND, Aguila SLV, CS Cartagines CRC, Coban Imperial GUA, Comunicaciones GUA, CS Herediano CRC, Marathón HND, Santiagueño SLV
CARIBBEAN - Robin Hood SUR, Defence Force TTO, Jong Colombia ANT, Police Force TTO, SUBT ANT

FINAL TOURNAMENT
In Tegucigalpa. 8th - 12th February 1981

	UN	UH	RH	Pl	W	D	L	F	A	Pts
UNAM	-	2-0	3-0	2	2	0	0	5	0	4
Univ. de Honduras	-	-	1-1	2	0	1	1	1	3	1
Robin Hood	-	-	-	2	0	1	1	1	4	1

1981

NORTH & CENTRAL - Atlético Marte SLV, Cruz Azul MEX, Juventud Retalteca GUA, Marathón HND, Real España HND, Santiagueño SLV, Univ. Neuvo León MEX
CARIBBEAN - Transvaal SUR, Defence Force TTO, Kentucky Memphis TTO, Robin Hood SUR, St Thomas College, SUBT ANT, Yama Sun Oil

FINAL
1st leg. Paramaribo, 30-01-1982
Transvaal 1
Atlético Marte 0

2nd leg. Paramaribo, 2-02-1982
Transvaal 1
Atlético Marte 1

1982

NORTH & CENTRAL - UNAM MEX, Brooklyn Dodgers USA, Cruz Azul MEX, New York Freedoms USA, Deportivo FAS SLV, VIDA HND, Comunicaciones GUA, Independiente SLV, Xelaju MC GUA
CARIBBEAN - Robin Hood SUR, Defence Force TTO, Palo Seco TTO, Don Bosco DOM, Transvaal SUR

FINAL
1st leg.
Robin Hood 0
UNAM 0

2nd leg.
UNAM 2
Robin Hood 1

1983

NORTH & CENTRAL - Atlante MEX, Atlético Marte SLV, Comunicaciones GUA, Independiente SLV, Motagua HND, New York Freedoms USA, Olimpia HND, Deportivo Saprissa CRC, Suchitepéquez GUA, Univ. Nuevo León MEX
CARIBBEAN - Robin Hood SUR, Dakota de Aruba ANT, Defence Force TTO, Kentucky Memphis TTO, Leo Victor SUR, SUBT ANT

FINAL
1st leg. Paramaribo, 22-01-1984
Robin Hood 1
Atlante 1

2nd leg. Mexico City, 1-02-1984
Atlante 5
Robin Hood 0

1984

NORTH & CENTRAL - Aguila SLV, Comunicaciones GUA, Deportivo FAS SLV, Guadalajara CD MEX, Hotel International BER, Jacksonville USA, New York Freedoms USA, Puebla MEX, Sagrada Familia CRC, Suchitepéquez GUA, Univ. de Honduras HND, VIDA HND
CARIBBEAN - Violette HTI, Aigle Noir ANT, ASL Sports TTO, Cygne Noir GDP, Defence Force TTO, Guayama Cruz Azul PUR, Riviere Pilotte MTQ, St Georges CAY, Sportif Moulien GDP, SUBT ANT, Victory HTI

FINAL
Violette were declared champions as the Central and Northern group was not completed

1985

NORTH & CENTRAL - Olimpia HND, Aguila SLV, América MEX, Aurora FC GUA, Croatians Chicago USA, Deportivo FAS SLV, Guadalajara CD MEX, Hotel International BER, Suchitepéquez GUA, VIDA HND
CARIBBEAN - Defence Force TTO, Aiglon MTQ, Boys Town JAM, Golden Star MTQ, Gonaives HTI, Jong Holland ANT, JSC GDP, Mont Joly CAY, Robin Hood SUR, St Francois TTO, SUBT ANT, Tivoli Gardens JAM, Transvaal SUR, Violette HTI, Weymouth Wales BAR

FINAL
1st leg. Port of Spain, 19-01-1986
Defence Force 2
Olimpia 0

2nd leg. Tegucigalpa, 26-01-1986
Olimpia 1
Defence Force 0

1986

FINAL
1st leg. Alajuela
LD Alajuelense 4
Transvaal 1

2nd leg. Paramaribo
Transvaal 1
LD Alajuelense 1

1987

FINAL
1st leg. Port of Spain, 21-10-1987
Defence Force 1
América 1

2nd leg. Mexico City, 29-10-1987
América 2
Defence Force 0

1988

FINAL

1st leg. Teguagalpa
Olimpia 2
Defence Force 0

2nd leg. Port of Spain
Defence Force 0
Olimpia 2

1989

FINAL

1st leg. Piñar del Rio
Piñar del Rio 1
UNAM 1

2nd leg. Mexico City, 6-02-1990
UNAM 3
Piñar del Rio 1

1990

FINAL

1st leg. Piñar del Rio, 19-02-1991
Piñar del Rio 2
América 2

2nd leg. Mexico City, 12-03-1991
América 6
Piñar del Rio 0

1991

NORTH - Dandy Town BER, Pembrook H.D. BER, Brooklyn Italians USA, Eagles USA, Puebla MEX, Universidad Guadalajara MEX
CENTRAL - Tauro PAN, América NIC, Deportivo Saprissa CRC, Deportivo Esteli NIC, Liga Deportivo Alajuelense CRC, Amador PAN, Duurly's BLZ, Luis Angel Firpo SLV, Real España HND, Verdes BLZ, Municipal GUA, Alianza SLV, Motagua HND, Comunicaciones GUA
CARIBBEAN - Scolaire GDP, US Marinoise MTQ, Striker CYM, Racing Club HTI, AS Capoise HTI, Sithoc, ANT, Black Lions JAM, International CYM, SUBT ANT, Transvaal SUR, Olympique Marin MTQ, Geldar Kourou GFR, Police FC TTO, Reno JAM, Robin Hood SUR, Defence Force TTO, L'Etoile du Morne GDP

FINAL

1st leg. Puebla, 18-09-1991
Puebla 3
Police FC 1

2nd leg. San Fernando, 24-09-1991
Police FC 1
Puebla 1

1992

NORTH - San Francisco Blackhawks USA, Dallas Rockets USA, UNAM MEX, América MEX, Vancouver CAN, Hamilton International BER
CENTRAL - Eurokickers PAN, La Victoria BLZ, Diriangen NIC, Cemcol Crown BLZ, Tauro PAN, Deportivo Esteli NIC, Luis Angel Firpo SLV, Comunicaciones GUA, Motagua HND, Municipal GUA, LD Alajuelense CRC, Deportivo Saprissa CRC, Real España HND, Aguila SLV
CARIBBEAN - San Cristobal DOM, Unique ISV, Guayama PUR, Rockmaster ISV, US Robert MTQ, Strikers CYM, L'Aiglon Lamentin MTQ, Solidarit GDP, Scholars CYM, Etoile du Morne GDP, Racing Club ARU, Sithoc ANT, Transvaal SUR, Trintoc TTO, Geldar Kourou GFR, Robin Hood SUR, Jong Colombia ANT, Mayaro United TTO

FINAL

Santa Ana, 5-01-1993
América 1
Liga Deportivo Alajuelense 0

1993

NORTH - Leon MEX, Puebla MEX, Hercules USA
CENTRAL - Acroz BLZ, Real España HND, Colon PAN, Communicacion GUA, LD Alajuelense CRC, Juventus BLZ, Diriangen NIC, Alianza SLV, Motagua HND, Municipal GUA, Plaza Amador PAN, Juventus NIC, Deportivo Saprissa CRC, Luis Angel Firpo SLV
CARIBBEAN - La Juventa GDP, Tempete HTI, Club Francis MTQ, Coca Cola ISV, Racing HTI, L'Aiglon du Lamentin MTQ, Sithoc ANT, T & T Hawks TTO, Club Colonial GUY, Robin Hood SUR, Trintoc FC TTO, Juventus ANT, Leo Victor SUR, ASL Sport GUY, L'Etoile du Morne GDP

FINAL TOURNAMENT

Held in Guatemala City 1st - 6th December 1993

	DS	Le	Mu	RH	Pl	W	D	L	F	A	Pts
Deportivo Saprissa CRC	-	2-2	0-0	9-1	3	1	2	0	11	3	4
Leon MEX	-	-	0-0	4-0	3	1	2	0	6	2	4
Municipal GUA	-	-	-	3-0	3	1	2	0	3	0	4
Robin Hood SUR	-	-	-	-	3	0	0	3	1	16	0

1994

NORTH - Atlante MEX, Los Angeles Salsa USA, Monterrey MEX,
CENTRAL - Alcroz BLZ, Alianza SLV, Aurora GUA, CS Cartagines CRC, Comunicaciones GUA, Diriangen NIC, Herediano CRC, Juventus NIC, La Victoria BLZ, Luis Angel Firpo SLV, Olimpia HND, Petrotela HND
CARIBBEAN - Club Franciscain MTQ, FC AK Regina GFR, J & J Construction ATG, Jong Colombia ANT, Leo Victor SUR, Racing Club HTI, Red Star de PAP GDP, Robin Hood SUR, Sithoc ANT, Scolaire GDP, Suzuki Newtown United KNA, Racing Club ARU, River Plate ARU, US Robert MTQ, US Sinnamary GFR, Villa Lions ATG, Violette HTI

FINAL

San Jose California, 5-02-1995
CS Cartagines 3
Atlante 2

CONCACAF CUP WINNERS CUP

1991 Atlético Marte (SLV)
1992 -
1993 Monterrey (MEX) ....Lge.................Real España (HND)
1994 Necaxa (MEX) ....3-0.................Aurora (GUA)

1993

FINAL TOURNAMENT

2nd - 6th June 1993

	Mo	RE	LA	Su	Pl	W	D	L	F	A	Pts
Monterrey MEX	-	1-1	4-3	2-0	3	2	1	0	7	4	5
Real España HDN	-	-	0-0	8-0	3	1	2	0	9	1	4
LA Firpo SLV	-	-	-	6-1	3	1	1	1	9	5	3
Suchitepéquez GUA	-	-	-	-	3	0	0	3	1	16	0

1994

Necaxa MEX	5-1	CD Mexico MEX
Aurora GUA	2-0 1-2	Atletico Marte SLV
Diriangen NIC	0-1 0-2	Real Maya HON
Lambada BAR	1-0 1-1	Racing Club MTQ
Malta Caribs TRI	1-1 1-2	Lambada
SNL SUR	0-0 0-0	Olympique de Morne GUA
Lambada	3-0 1-0	Olympique de Morne

FINAL TOURNAMENT

Held in Miami 2nd- 4th December 1994

SEMI-FINALS

Real Maya	1-2	Aurora
Lambada	1-4	Necaxa

3RD PLACE

Real Maya	1-0	Lambada

FINAL

Aurora	0-3	Necaxa

CANADA

Curiously, Canada's football headquarters can be found in James Naismith Drive, a street named after the inventor of basketball, which neatly symbolises the way the indigenous North American sports have overshadowed football. Only once have Canada made a mark in football and that was when they qualified for the finals of the World Cup in 1986. Football is not high on the Canadian list of priorities. Ice hockey is the national pastime, a distinctive brand of gridiron called Canadian football is played, and Canadian baseball teams take part in North America's Major League. Following the pattern of baseball and ice hockey in which the United States and Canada share the same league, Canadian soccer teams took part in the great NASL experiment of the 1970s through the Vancouver Whitecaps, Olympique de Montreal, Edmonton Drillers and Toronto Metros, and in the process won two Soccer Bowl finals.

A club called Montreal Football Club was founded in 1868 and in these early years the Association code was played in a number of universities in the country. McGill University in Montreal, however, were ultimately to determine the destiny of the game and unfortunately for football they favoured rugby. In a famous match with Harvard University in 1874, McGill won over their American counterparts to the oval ball code and the North American continent has not looked back since. The game eventually developed into the present-day American and Canadian gridiron football, and soccer, as it is known there, has not stood a chance.

The Association code did not die altogether and in 1886 a team representing Canada travelled to Newark to play the United States in a challenge match, a journey they repeated the following year. Though some have doubted the validity of the matches as full internationals, they do represent a landmark in world football history. If treated as full internationals they are the first such games to be played anywhere outside the British Isles. In 1888 a Canadian team travelled to Scotland, while three years later another made the same journey and played games against representative sides from England, Scotland and Wales, in what marked the first visit to Britain by a foreign team. In 1904 Galt Football Club from Ontario, a major centre of football at the time, played the United States in the St Louis Olympic Games. Although football was only an exhibition sport, the Canadian side beat two representative sides from America to win the title and this remains the country's only honour to date.

In 1912 the Dominion of Canada Football Association was formed, the predecessor of the current Canadian Soccer Association. They introduced a cup competition for the champion team of each province and a trophy was donated by the Duke of Connaught. Until the late 1980s this remained the only national tournament for clubs in the country. Though football had made encouraging progress, it continued to fall behind the indigenous sports in popularity. A tour was made to Australia in 1924 and a second to New Zealand three years later but this was the only international activity until 1957, apart from three games against the United States in between the two tours. Various provinces attempted to introduce professionalism at one time or another during this period, aided by the European immigrant communities that were swelling the population of Canada, but none was lastingly successful. Due to the enormous size of the country there was no cohesive structure to the game, and it was only played with any great enthusiasm in British Colombia, Ontario and Quebec.

A national eleven was put together to enter the 1958 World Cup and in June 1957 Canada eventually played their first game on home soil with a 5-1 victory over the United States. Though the Americans were beaten in both qualifying matches, Mexico won twice in Mexico City to end Canada's first venture into the World Cup. The 1960s saw a reappraisal of the game in Canada. In 1961 the Eastern Canada Professional Soccer League was formed and this lasted until 1966. The following year Canadian clubs joined the fledgling North American Soccer League, and until 1984 when the NASL collapsed, football in Canada was represented by teams from Montreal, Toronto, Edmonton and Vancouver at various times, the highlights being the victories in the Soccer Bowl by the Toronto Metros in 1976 and the Vancouver Whitecaps in 1979, both coming when the NASL was at its peak. The demise of the NASL was a serious blow to football in the country.

The World Cup qualification in 1986 may well be seen as a knock-on effect from the 18 years of professional football, as the majority of the team had played for NASL clubs. The fact that Mexico, the hosts, qualified automatically for the finals undoubtedly had much to do with Canada's achievement, but they still managed to see off

Costa Rica and Honduras in the final qualifying round. The Canadians failed to score in the finals but were by no means disgraced, suffering only narrow defeats against France, the Soviet Union and Hungary.

Success has otherwise not been easy to come by. Even when the Olympic Games were held in Montreal in 1976 the national side could not get past the North Koreans in the first round, and since 1986, despite the introduction of the Canadian Soccer League in 1987, the national side have struggled to make an impact. In the 1991 North American Championship they placed a poor third behind Mexico and the United States, and could not get past the first round of the CONCACAF Gold Cup in Los Angeles later in the year. In 1993 they even suffered an 8-0 thrashing at the hands of Mexico.

Population: 26,620,000
Area, sq km: 9,970,610
% in urban areas: 75%
Capital city: Ottawa 819,000
Major Cities: Toronto 3,427,000, Montreal 2,921,000, Vancouver 1,380,000

The Canadian Soccer Association
1600 James Naismith Drive
Gloucester
Ontario, ONT. K1B
Canada
Tel: + 1 613 7485667
Fax: + 1 613 7451938

Year of formation	1912
Affiliation to FIFA	1912
Affiliation to CONC	1978
Registered clubs	1600
Registered players	509 300
Professional players	200
Registered Coaches	25 300
Registered Referees	3057
National stadium	Olympic Stadium, Montreal 64 000
National colours	Red/Red/Red
Reserve Colours -	White/White/White
Season	May - November

THE RECORD

WORLD CUP

1930-54	Did not enter
1958	QT 1st round
1962	Did not enter
1966	Did not enter
1970	QT 1st round
1974	QT 1st round
1978	QT 2nd round
1982	QT 2nd round
1986	QT Qualified - Final tournament/1st round
1990	QT 2nd round
1994	QT 3rd round - Lost in Oceania play-off

CANADIAN SOCCER LEAGUE

1987	Calgary Kickers	2-1	Hamilton Steelers
1988	Vancouver 86ers	4-1	Hamilton Steelers
1989	Vancouver 86ers	3-2	Hamilton Steelers
1990	Vancouver 86ers	6-1	Hamilton Steelers
1991	Vancouver 86ers	5-3	Toronto Blizzard
1992	Winnipeg Fury	2-0 1-1	Vancouver 86ers

League disbanded. Vancouver 86ers, Toronto Blizzard and Montreal Impact all joined the American Professional Soccer League

CHALLENGE CUP WINNERS

1913	Norwood Wanderers
1914	Norwood Wanderers
1915	Winnipeg Scots
1916-18	-
1919	Grand Trunk Quebec
1920	Westinghouse Ontario
1921	Toronto Scots
1922	Hillhurst Calgary
1923	Nanaimo
1924	Weston University
1925	Toronto Ulsters
1926	Weston University
1927	Nanaimo
1928	New Westminster Royals
1929	CNR Montreal
1930	New Westminster Royals
1931	New Westminster Royals
1932	Toronto Scots
1933	Toronto Scots
1934	Verduns Montreal
1935	Aldreds Montreal
1936	New Westminster Royals
1937	Johnston Nationals
1938	North Shore Vancouver
1939	Radials Vancouver
1940-45	-
1946	Toronto Ulsters
1947	St Andrews Vancouver
1948	Carsteel Montreal
1949	North Shore Vancouver
1950	Vancouver City
1951	Ulster United Toronto
1952	Steelco Montreal
1953	New Westminster Royals
1954	Scottish Winnipeg
1955	New Westminster Royals
1956	Halecos Vancouver
1957	Ukrainia SC Montreal
1958	New Westminster Royals
1959	Alouetts Montreal
1960	New Westminster Royals
1961	Concordia Montreal
1962	Scottish Winnipeg
1963	-
1964	Columbus Vancouver
1965	Vancouver Firefighters
1966	Vancouver Firefighters
1967	Toronto
1968	Toronto Royals
1969	Columbus Vancouver
1970	Manitoba Selects
1971	Eintracht Vancouver
1972	New Westminster Blues
1973	Vancouver Firefighters
1974	Calgary Springer Kickers
1975	London Boxing Club Victoria
1976	Victoria West SC
1977	Columbus Vancouver
1978	Columbus Vancouver
1979	Victoria West SC
1980	St John Dry Dock
1981	Toronto Ciociario
1982	Victoria West SC
1983	Vancouver Firefighters
1984	Victoria West SC
1985	Vancouver Croatia
1986	Hamilton Steelers
1987	Lucania SC
1988	Holy Cross
1989	Scarborough Azzurri
1990	Vancouver Firefighters
1991	Norvan SC
1992	Norvan SC
1993	West Side Rino
1994	Edmonton Ital-Canadians

INTERNATIONAL MATCHES PLAYED BY CANADA

28-11-1885	United States	W 1-0	Newark	Fr	Gibson
25-11-1886	United States	L 2-3	Newark	Fr	Doll 2

Date	Opponent	Result	Venue	Comp	Scorers
16-11-1904	United States	W 7-0	St. Louis	OGf	Hall 3, Steep, McDonald 2, Taylor
17-11	United States	W 4-0	St. Louis	OGf	Taylor 2, OG
7-06-1924	Australia	L 2-3	Brisbane	Fr	Linning, Forrest
14-06	Australia	W 1-0	Sydney	Fr	Stobbart
23-06	Australia	L 1-4	Sydney	Fr	Forrest
28-06	Australia	D 0-0	Newcastle	Fr	
12-07	Australia	W 4-1	Adelaide	Fr	Wilson 2, Linning, Stobbart
26-07	Australia	L 0-1	Sydney	Fr	
5-08	New Zealand	D 1-1	Auckland	Fr	
27-06-1925	United States	W 1-0	Montreal	Fr	McLaine
8-11	United States	L 1-6	Brooklyn	Fr	Burness
6-11-1926	United States	L 2-6	Brooklyn	Fr	Faulkner, Graham
25-06-1927	New Zealand	D 2-2	Dunedin	Fr	OG, Williams
2-07	New Zealand	W 2-1	Christchurch	Fr	Archibald, Turner
9-07	New Zealand	L 0-1	Wellington	Fr	
23-07	New Zealand	W 4-1	Auckland	Fr	Davidson, Archibald 2, Gibson
22-06-1957	United States	W 5-1	Toronto	WCq	Philley.B, Hughes 2, Stewart, McLeod.N
30-06	Mexico	L 0-3	Mexico City	WCq	
4-07	Mexico	L 0-2	Mexico City	WCq	
6-07	United States	W 3-2	St. Louis	WCq	Philley.B, Stewart, Steckiw
21-06-1967	Cuba	D 1-1	Edmonton	OGq	Hansen
24-06	Cuba	L 1-2	Edmonton	OGq	Hansen
6-10-1968	Bermuda	W 4-0	Toronto	WCq	Vigh, Zanatta, Papadakis 2
17-10	United States	W 4-2	Toronto	WCq	McPate 2, Patterson, Vigh
20-10	Bermuda	D 0-0	Hamilton	WCq	
26-10	United States	L 0-1	Atlanta	WCq	
30-05-1971	Bermuda	W 3-0	Hamilton	OGq	Zanatta, Parsons, Schepers
13-06	Bermuda	D 1-1	Toronto	OGq	Schepers
20-08-1972	United States	W 3-2	St. John's	WCq	Parsons, Twamley, Johnson
24-08	Mexico	L 0-1	Toronto	WCq	
29-08	United States	D 2-2	Baltimore	WCq	MacKay, Douglas
2-09	Guatemala	D 2-2	Guatemala City	Fr	Young, Schiraldi
5-09	Mexico	L 1-2	Mexico City	WCq	Robinson
1-08-1973	Poland	L 1-3	Toronto	Fr	Aubert
5-08	United States	L 0-2	Windsor	Fr	
28-09	Malta	L 0-2	Gzira	Fr	
7-10	Luxembourg	W 2-0	Luxembourg	Fr	Parsons, Schiraldi
10-11	Haiti	L 1-5	Port au Prince	Fr	Parsons
12-11	Haiti	W 1-0	Port au Prince	Fr	Bennett
12-04-1974	Bermuda	D 0-0	Hamilton	Fr	
9-10	East Germany	L 0-2	Frankfurt	Fr	
31-10	Poland	L 0-2	Warsaw	Fr	
5-01-1975	Cuba	L 0-4	Havana	Fr	
6-07	Poland	L 1-8	Montreal	Fr	Douglas
9-07	Poland	L 1-4	Toronto	Fr	Bennett
29-07	East Germany	L 0-3	Toronto	Fr	
31-07	East Germany	L 1-7	Ottawa	Fr	Rose
19-07-1976	Soviet Union *	L 1-2	Montreal	OGr1	Douglas
21-07	North Korea	L 1-3	Toronto	OGr1	Douglas
24-09	United States	D 1-1	Vancouver	WCq	Bolitho
10-10	Mexico	W 1-0	Vancouver	WCq	Parsons
20-10	United States	L 0-2	Seattle	WCq	
27-10	Mexico	D 0-0	Toluca	WCq	
22-12	United States	W 3-0	Port au Prince	WCq	Budd, Lenarduzzi, Bolitho
11-09-1977	Trinidad	D 1-1	Port of Spain	Fr	Roe
8-10	El Salvador	L 1-2	Monterrey	WCq	Roe
12-10	Surinam	W 2-1	Mexico City	WCq	Parsons, Bakic
16-10	Guatemala	W 2-1	Mexico City	WCq	Parsons, Lenarduzzi
20-10	Haiti	D 1-1	Monterrey	WCq	Bakic
22-10	Mexico	L 1-3	Monterrey	WCq	Parsons
1-04-1979	Bermuda	L 0-3	Hamilton	OGq	
27-05	Bermuda	L 2-5	Ottawa	OGq	Burke, Sweeney
15-09-1980	New Zealand	W 4-0	Vancouver	Fr	Mitchell 2, Stojanovic, Lenarduzzi
17-09	New Zealand	W 3-0	Edmonton	Fr	Miller 2, Lenarduzzi
18-10	Mexico	D 1-1	Toronto	WCq	Stojanovic
25-10	United States	D 0-0	Fort Lauderdale	WCq	
1-11	United States	W 2-1	Vancouver	WCq	Iarusci, Segota
9-11	Honduras	L 0-2	Tegucigalpa	Fr	
11-11	Guatemala	W 1-0	Guatemala City	Fr	Mitchell
16-11	Mexico	D 1-1	Mexico City	WCq	Gray
12-10-1981	Trinidad	W 4-2	Port of Spain	Fr	Mitchell 2, Stojanovic, Segota

2-11	El Salvador	W 1-0	Tegucigalpa	WCq	Stojanovic
6-11	Haiti	D 1-1	Tegucigalpa	WCq	Stojanovic
12-11	Honduras	L 1-2	Tegucigalpa	WCq	Bridge
15-11	Mexico	D 1-1	Tegucigalpa	WCq	Bridge
21-11	Cuba	D 2-2	Tegucigalpa	WCq	McLeod, Iarusci
8-05-1983	Bermuda	W 6-0	Burnaby	OGq	Felix 2, Sudeyko, Pakos, Connor, McNally
15-05	Bermuda	D 1-1	Hamilton	OGq	Pakos
12-06	Scotland	L 0-2	Vancouver	Fr	
16-06	Scotland	L 0-3	Edmonton	Fr	
19-06	Scotland	L 0-2	Toronto	Fr	
6-12	Mexico	L 0-5	Iraputo	Fr	
11-12	Honduras	L 1-3	San Pedro Sula	Fr	Pakos
14-12	Honduras	L 0-1	Tegucigalpa	Fr	
28-03-1984	Haiti	W 1-0	Port au Prince	Fr	Bridge
26-05	Italy	L 0-2	Toronto	Fr	
25-07	Chile	D 0-0	Edmonton	Fr	
30-07	Iraq	D 1-1	Cambridge	OGr1	Gray
1-08	Yugoslavia *	L 0-1	Annapolis	OGr1	
3-08	Cameroon	W 3-1	Cambridge	OGr1	Mitchell 2, Vrablic
6-08	Brazil *	D 1-1	Palo Alto	OGqf	Mitchel. Lost on pens
16-10	Algeria	L 0-1	Algiers	Fr	
21-10	Tunisia	L 0-2	Tunis	Fr	
24-10	Morocco	L 2-3	Rabat	Fr	James, Miller
30-10	Cyprus	D 0-0	Nicosia	Fr	
2-11	Egypt	L 0-1	Cairo	Fr	
10-03-1985	Trinidad	W 2-1	Port of Spain	Fr	Vrablic, DeLuca
13-03	Jamaica	D 1-1	Montego Bay	Fr	Vrablic
17-03	Jamaica	D 0-0	Kingston	Fr	
21-03	Costa Rica	L 0-1	San Jose	Fr	
24-03	Costa Rica	D 0-0	San Jose	Fr	
2-04	United States	W 2-0	Vancouver	Fr	Vrablic 2
4-04	United States	D 1-1	Portland	Fr	Pakos
13-04	Haiti	W 2-0	Victoria	WCq	Vrablic, Sweeney
20-04	Guatemala	W 2-1	Victoria	WCq	Mitchell 2
5-05	Guatemala	D 1-1	Guatemala City	WCq	Mitchell
8-05	Haiti	W 2-0	Port au Prince	WCq	Mitchell, Vrablic
2-06	Ghana	W 2-1	Seoul	PC	Mitchell, Norman
9-06	Iraq	L 1-6	Kwangju	PC	Catliff
17-08	Costa Rica	D 1-1	Toronto	WCq	James
25-08	Honduras	W 1-0	Tegucigalpa	WCq	Pakos
1-09	Costa Rica	D 0-0	San Jose	WCq	
14-09	Honduras	W 2-1	St. John's	WCq	Pakos, Vrablic
29-01-1986	Paraguay	D 0-0	Vancouver	Fr	
2-02	Uruguay	L 1-3	Miami	MC	Pakos
5-02	United States	D 0-0	Miami	MC	
27-04	Mexico	L 0-3	Mexico City	Fr	
10-05	Wales	W 2-0	Toronto	Fr	Vrablic, Gray
19-05	Wales	L 0-3	Vancouver	Fr	
24-05	England	L 0-1	Burnaby	Fr	
1-06	France	L 0-1	Leon	WCr1	
6-06	Hungary	L 0-2	Iraputo	WCr1	
9-06	Soviet Union	L 0-2	Iraputo	WCr1	
24-08	Singapore	W 1-0	Singapore	MLC	Vrablic
25-08	Malaysia	W 5-0	Singapore	MLC	Hooper, Vrablic 2, Ianiero, Cubellis
27-08	North Korea	D 0-0	Singapore	MLC	
30-08	Indonesia	W 4-0	Singapore	MLC	Vrablic, Chueden, Bunbury, Ianiero
31-08	China	L 0-1	Singapore	MLC	
4-09	North Korea	L 0-2	Singapore	MLC	
6-09	Singapore	W 1-0	Singapore	MLC	Bunbury
30-09-1987	El Salvador	L 1-2	San Salvador	Fr	Bunbury
2-10	Honduras	D 1-1	Tegucigalpa	Fr	Catliff
6-10	Mexico	L 0-4	Toluca	Fr	
18-02-1988	Bermuda	D 0-0	Hamilton	Fr	
26-03	Peru	W 3-1	Lima	Fr	Hooper, DeSantis, Catliff
30-03	Colombia	L 0-3	Armenia	Fr	
5-04	Jamaica	W 4-0	Kingston	Fr	Catliff 3
7-04	Jamaica	D 0-0	Montego Bay	Fr	
19-05	Greece	L 0-1	Montreal	Fr	
21-05	Greece	L 0-3	Toronto	Fr	
25-05	Chile	W 1-0	Toronto	Fr	Bridge
28-05	Greece	D 0-0	Toronto	Fr	

17-06	Costa Rica	L 0-1	Montreal	Fr	
15-07	Poland	L 1-2	Toronto	Fr	Sweeney
1-10	Trinidad	W 2-1	Port of Spain	Fr	Catliff, Mitchell
9-10	Guatemala	L 0-1	Guatemala City	WCq	
15-10	Guatemala	W 3-2	Burnaby	WCq	Bridge, Mitchell 2
12-04-1989	Denmark	L 0-2	Aalborg	Fr	
8-06	Belgium	L 0-2	Ottawa	Fr	
6-05-1990	United States	W 1-0	Vancouver	Fr	Catliff
13-05	Mexico	W 2-1	Burnaby	Fr	Catliff 2
14-03-1991	Mexico	L 0-3	Los Angeles	NAC	
16-03	United States	L 0-2	Torrance	NAC	
28-06	Honduras	L 2-4	Los Angeles	CCr1	Mitchell 2
30-06	Mexico	L 1-3	Los Angeles	CCr1	Lowery
3-07	Jamaica	W 3-2	Los Angeles	CCr1	Mitchell, Miller, Limniatis
2-04-1992	China	W 5-2	Victoria	Fr	Catliff 2, Odinga, Gilbert, Muirhead
20-05	Scotland	L 1-3	Toronto	Fr	Catliff
13-06	Hong Kong	W 3-1	Toronto	Fr	Peschisolido, Valentine, Berdusco
3-09	United States	L 0-2	St John's	Fr	
9-10	United States	D 0-0	Greensboro	Fr	
18-10	Jamaica	D 1-1	Kingston	WCq	Mitchell
25-10	El Salvador	D 1-1	San Salvador	WCq	Miller
1-11	Jamaica	W 1-0	Toronto	WCq	Mitchell
8-11	El Salvador	L 2-3	Toronto	WCq	Miller, Mitchell
15-11	Bermuda	W 4-2	Burnaby	WCq	Bunbury 3, Aunger
6-12	Bermuda	D 0-0	Hamilton	WCq	
4-03-1993	United States	D 2-2	Costa Mesa	Fr	MacDonald, Catliff
9-03	South Korea	L 0-2	Vancouver	Fr	
11-03	South Korea	W 2-0	Victoria	Fr	Catliff, Berdusco
24-03	Costa Rica	W 1-0	San Jose	Fr	Miller
4-04	Honduras	D 2-2	Tegucigalpa	WCq	Mitchell, Bunbury
11-04	El Salvador	W 2-0	Vancouver	WCq	Bunbury, Catliff
18-04	Honduras	W 3-1	Vancouver	WCq	Mobilio, OG, Catliff
25-04	Mexico	L 0-4	Mexico City	WCq	
2-05	El Salvador	W 2-1	San Salvador	WCq	Catliff, Mobilio
9-05	Mexico	L 1-2	Toronto	WCq	Bunbury
11-07	Costa Rica	D 1-1	Mexico City	CCr1	Dasovic
15-07	Martinique	D 2-2	Mexico City	CCr1	Aunger, Bunbury
18-07	Mexico	L 0-8	Mexico City	CCr1	
31-07	Australia	W 2-1	Edmonton	WCq	Watson, Mobilio
15-08	Australia	L 1-2	Sydney	WCq	Hooper
1-06-1994	Morocco	D 1-1	Montreal	Fr	Doliscat
5-06	Brazil	D 1-1	Edmonton	Fr	Berdusco
8-06	Germany	L 0-2	Toronto	Fr	
10-06	Spain	L 0-2	Montreal	Fr	
12-06	Holland	L 0-3	Toronto	Fr	
24-01-1995	Denmark	L 0-1	Toronto	Fr	
26-01	Portugal	D 1-1	Toronto	Fr	Bunbury
22-05	Northern Ireland	W 2-0	Edmonton	Fr	Peschisolido 2
28-05	Chile	L 1-2	Edmonton	Fr	Peschisolido
4-06	Turkey	L 1-3	Toronto	Fr	Thomson
7-06	Turkey	L 0-3	Montreal	Fr	

MEXICO

Unfortunately for Mexican football, the country is situated in a footballing no-man's land. To the north is the largely uninterested United States, to the south the small states of Central America and to the east the islands of the Caribbean. With a strong tradition in football that has seen it stage two World Cups, Mexico appears out on a limb, never maximising the potential that undoubtedly exists there.

Football came to Mexico at the end of the 19th century and in particular to Mexico City, already at that time one of the world's largest cities. (Now, with its population conservatively estimated at 14 million, it is *the* largest.) It was not long before a league was founded and in 1903 Mexico saw its first championship played. Based as it was in the capital, it remained the domain of clubs from Mexico City until the 1940s.

The most famous of these clubs were España, Reforma and América. España were the most successful and they remain the leading championship winners with 14 titles despite the fact that none of them have come after 1945. They and Reforma flourished in an age of amateurism, but like South America, Mexico was not exempt from the rise of professionalism and the organisational squabbles that went with it. In 1927, some 24 years after the league had started and primarily to organise a national team and gain recognition from FIFA, the Federación Mexicana de Fútbol Asociación was formed. It immediately ran into trouble over professionalism and in 1931 was replaced by another governing body which was prepared to sanction payment.

The composition of the league has changed greatly since its introduction as clubs from the other large cities have entered the fray, most notably from Guadalajara, but also from Monterrey, Puebla, Leon and the small city of Toluca. Mexico has over a million registered players, one of the largest figures in the world, so its club base is very strong. Clubs like Leon and Deportivo Guadalajara tapped into these resources and built teams capable of taking on those from the capital. Leon's triumph in 1948 marked a watershed in Mexican club football and was followed by the complete domination of the late 1950s and 1960s by Deportivo Guadalajara. Although América remain a powerful force in the capital, Cruz Azul and UNAM, formed after the introduction of professionalism, have joined them as the major focus of attention.

In one concession to their northern neighbours, the Mexican league, after being run on a straight league basis for many years, has adopted the system so favoured of the major American sports. Four divisions of five teams, the members of which play all the teams from the other leagues, qualify two teams each for the end of season playoffs, ending with a grand final. It is a system that seems to work and is popular with the fans, and compared to some of the complicated systems used in the South American countries it has a lot to recommend it.

The formation of the federation in 1927 saw the national side take the field for the first time in the 1928 Olympic Games, but Mexico's Olympic adventure lasted just one game as Spain, their first opponents, defeated them heavily. So as not to return home after just one game, the side entered the consolation tournament, but here too they were handed a first round defeat, this time at the hands of Chile. Two years later Mexico entered the first World Cup in Montevideo, and over the years the tournament has been the focus of their fixture list, given the lack of competitive games elsewhere. Ten appearances in the finals certainly shows the strength of Mexico vis-a-vis their Central American neighbours, but their performances once there give a fairer indication of their world status: not until 1962 did they manage to win a game. Taking part in five successive tournaments at this time was Antonio Carbajal, one of Mexico's most celebrated players. The famous goalkeeper played in every World Cup from 1950 to 1966, a feat not yet equalled.

It is easy to decry Mexico's record in the World Cup finals - five of their seven victories have come in their 'home' tournaments - but in friendly matches against European and South American touring sides, or whilst on tour themselves, victories have been scored against all of the top nations. Prior to the late 1960s, apart from the World Cup, international games were organised on a very haphazard basis. The Mexicans threw a lot of support behind the Panamerican Confederation in the 1950s as it sought to end its isolation, but the organisation faded away in the early 1960s and Mexico has had to be content with being a part of CONCACAF.

Many believe Mexico's future lies with CONMEBOL and in the past there have been attempts to join, which have always been blocked on geographical grounds, although since 1993 they have been invited to take part in the South American Championships, actually reaching the final in their debut year. Mexican clubs would certainly benefit from a similar invitation to enter the Copa Libertadores; at present they take part in the CONCACAF Club Championship. Club football is not strong in CONCACAF and the Mexican league stand way above the rest of the region. It is a league which can even tempt foreigners into its ranks, most notably from Argentina and Brazil, though it is still prone to lose its best players, most notably Hugo Sanchez, the star of the 1980s Real Madrid side. Its relative isolation does keep the flow at a minimum, however.

Mexico has twice been at the centre of world football by staging the World Cup in 1970 and 1986, both of which proved to be excellent tournaments. Indeed, the 1970 edition is often regarded as the best ever staged. The country as a result has some of the finest stadia in the world, none more so than the magnificent Azteca in Mexico City. With its 110,000 capacity fitted tightly around the pitch, for spectators at least there is probably no better football arena.

Their quarter-final placings in 1970 and 1986 represent Mexico's best achievements in international football to date. The 1986 side was especially good. Led by Sanchez, they almost reached the semi-finals but lost out to West Germany on penalties. The Mexicans were not allowed to enter the 1990 World Cup as they were suspended by FIFA for fielding an over-age player in a youth tournament, but in 1994 they were back, only to go out on penalties again, this time in the second round to Bulgaria. On the strength of their victory in the 1993 Gold Cup Mexico appeared in the 1995 Intercontinental Cup and were a couple of minutes away from reaching the final before conceding a late equaliser to Denmark and then suffering the inevitable defeat in the penalty shoot-out!

Population: 81,883,000
Area, sq km: 1,958,201
% in urban areas: 72%
Capital city: Mexico City

Federación Mexicana de Fútbol Asociacion A.C.
Abraham Gonzalez #74
CP 06600, Col. Juarez
Mexico 6 D.F
Mexico
Tel: + 52 5 5662155
Fax: + 52 5 5667580
Telex: 1771678 msutme
Year of formation 1927
Affiliation to FIFA 1929

Affiliation to CONC	1961
Registered clubs	117
Registered players	1,402,000
Professional Players	2800
Registered referees	25 170
National stadium	Azteca, Mexico City 110 000
National colours	Green/White/Red
Reserve colours	Red/Blue/Blue
Season	September - June

THE RECORD

WORLD CUP

1930	QT Automatic - Final tournament/1st round
1934	QT 3rd round
1938	Did not enter
1950	QT 1st/3 in group 9 - Final tournament/1st round
1954	QT 1st/3 in group 11 - Final tournament/1st round
1958	QT Qualified - Final tournament/1st round
1962	QT Qualified - Final tournament/1st round
1966	QT Qualified - Final tournament/1st round
1970	QT Automatic - Final tournament/Quarter-finalists
1974	QT 2nd round
1978	QT Qualified - Final tournament/1st round
1982	QT 2nd round
1986	QT Automatic - Final tournament/Quarter-finalists
1990	Did not enter
1994	QT Qualified - Final tournament/2nd round

SOUTH AMERICAN CHAMPIONSHIP

1993	Runners-up
1995	Quarter-finalists

CONCACAF CHAMPIONSHIP

Winners - 1965 1991 1977 1993

CONCACAF CLUB TOURNAMENTS CHAMPIONS CUP

Winners - Guadalajara CD 1962, Toluca 1968, Cruz Azul 1969 1970 1971, Atletico Español 1975, América 1977 1987 1990 1992, Universidad Guadalajara 1978, UNAM 1980 1982 1989, Atlante 1983, Puebla 1991

Runners-up - Guadalajara CD 1963, Leon 1993, Atlante 1994

CUP WINNERS CUP

Winners - Monterrey 1993, Necaxa 1994

CLUB DIRECTORY

MEXICO CITY (Pop. - 14,100,000)

Club de Fútbol de América (1916)
Azteca 110,000 – Yellow/Yellow
Previous names - Merger in 1916 of Record FC & Colón FC

Club de Fútbol Atlante (1916)
Azulgrana 52,000 – Red & blue stripes/Blue
Previous names - Sinaloa 1916-17, Lusitania 1917-18, U-53 1918-20

Club Deportivo Social y Cultural Cruz Azul (1927)
Azteca 110,000 – White/White
Previous name - Cruz Azul Jasso. Moved to Mexico City in 1971

Club Impulsora del Deportivo Necaxa (1923)
Azteca 110,000 – Red & white stripes/White
Previous names - Merger in 1923 of Luz y Fuerza & Tranvias. Known as Atlético Español 1971-82

Club Universidad Nacional Autónoma de Mexico (UNAM) (1954)
Olimpico 65,000 – Blue with Puma on chest/Blue

GUADALAJARA (Pop. - 2,325,000)

Atlas Guadalajara (1916)
Jalisco 70,000 – Black & red halves/Black

Club Deportivo Guadalajara (1906)
Jalisco 70,000 – Red & white stripes/Blue
Previous name - Unión Guadalajara 1906-08

Club Universidad Autonoma de Guadalajara 'Los Tecos' (1971)
3 de Marzo 30,000 – White with owl on chest/White

Club Universidad de Guadalajara 'Los Leones Negros' (1970)
Jalisco 70,000 – Black, red & yellow stripes/Black

MONTERREY (Pop. - 2,015,000)

Club de Fútbol Monterrey (1945)
Estadio Tecnologico 33,000 – Blue & white stripes/Blue

Club Deportivo Universidad de Nuevo León (1967)
Universitario 43,000 – Yellow with blue hoop/Yellow

PUEBLA (Pop. - 1,055,000)

Club Puebla de la Franja (1943)
Cuauhtemoc 40,000 – White with a sky blue sash/White

LEÓN (Pop. - 593,000)

Club Social y Deportivo León (1920)
Nou Camp 39,000 – Green/White
Previous name - León Atlético 1920-44

VERACRUZ (Pop. - 330,000)

Club Deportivo Veracruz (1943)
Nuevo de Veracruz 37,000 – Red with a blue V/Blue

TORREON (Pop. - 328,000)

Club Santos Laguna (1982)
Corona 18,000 – Green & white hoops/Green

MORELIA (Pop. - 238,000)

Club Atlético Morelia (1947)
José Maria Morelos 42,000 – Yellow with red sash/Blue

TOLUCA (Pop. - 199,000)

Club Deportivo Toluca (1917)
La Bombonera 30,000 – Red/Red

QUERÉTARO (Pop. - 178,000)

Club de Fútbol Querétaro (1990)
Corregidora 40,000 – Black & blue stripes/Black

MEXICAN LEAGUE CHAMPIONS

1903	Orizaba Athletic Club
1904	Mexico Cricket Club
1905	Pachuca Athletic Club
1906	Reforma Athletic Club
1907	Reforma Athletic Club
1908	British Club
1909	Reforma Athletic Club
1910	Reforma Athletic Club
1911	Reforma Athletic Club
1912	Reforma Athletic Club
1913	Club Mexico
1914	España Club
1915	España Club
1916	España Club
1917	España Club
1918	Pachuca Athletic Club
1919	España Real Club
1920	España Real Club
1921	España Real Club
1922	España Real Club
1923	Asturias
1924	España Real Club
1925	América
1926	América
1927	América
1928	América
1929	Marte
1930	España Real Club
1931	-
1932	Atlante
1933	Necaxa
1934	España Real Club
1935	Necaxa
1936	España Real Club
1937	Necaxa
1938	Necaxa
1939	Asturias
1940	España Real Club
1941	Atlante
1942	España Real Club
1943	Marte

Professional League

1944	Asturias
1945	España Real Club
1946	Veracruz
1947	Atlante
1948	León

1949	León
1950	Veracruz
1951	Atlas
1952	León
1953	Tampico
1954	Marte
1955	Zacatepec
1956	León
1957	Guadalajara CD
1958	Zacatepec
1959	Guadalajara CD
1960	Guadalajara CD
1961	Guadalajara CD
1962	Guadalajara CD
1963	Oro Jalisco
1964	Guadalajara CD
1965	Guadalajara CD
1966	América
1967	Toluca
1968	Toluca
1969	Cruz Azul
1970	Guadalajara CD
1970	Cruz Azul *
1971	América
1972	Cruz Azul
1973	Cruz Azul
1974	Cruz Azul
1975	Toluca
1976	América
1977	UNAM
1978	Universidad Nuevo León
1979	Cruz Azul
1980	Cruz Azul
1981	UNAM
1982	Universidad Neuvo León
1983	Puebla
1984	América
1985	América
1985	América *
1986	Monterrey *
1987	Guadalajara CD
1988	América
1989	América
1990	Puebla
1991	UNAM
1992	León
1993	Atlante
1994	Univ. Autonoma Guadalajara
1995	Necaxa

* Shortened editions due to the World Cup

COPA TOWER

1908	Pachuca Athletic Club
1909	Reforma Athletic Club
1910	Reforma Athletic Club
1911	British Club
1912	Pachuca Athletic Club
1913	-
1914	Club Mexico
1915	España Club
1916	Rovers
1917	España Club
1918	España Club
1919	España Club
1920	-
1921	Club Mexico

COPA ELIMINATORIA

1922	Asturias
1923	Asturias
1924	Asturias
1925	Necaxa
1926	Necaxa
1927-32	-

COPA MEXICO

1933	Necaxa
1934	Asturias
1935	-
1936	Necaxa
1937	Asturias
1938	América
1939	Asturias
1940	Asturias
1941	Asturias
1942	Atlante
1943	Moctezuma
1944	España Real Club
1945	Puebla
1946	Atlas
1947	Moctezuma
1948	Veracruz
1949	León
1950	Atlas
1951	Atlante
1952	Atlante
1953	Puebla
1954	América
1955	América
1956	Toluca
1957	Zacatepec
1958	León
1959	Zacatepec
1960	Necaxa
1961	Tampico
1962	Atlas
1963	Guadalajara CD
1964	América
1965	América
1966	Necaxa
1967	León
1968	Atlas
1969	Cruz Azul
1970	Guadalajara CD
1971	-
1972	León
1973	León
1974	América
1975	UNAM
1976	Universidad Nuevo León
1977-87	-
1988	Puebla
1989	Toluca
1990	Puebla
1991	Monterrey
1992	Universidad Nuevo León
1993	-
1994	-
1995	Necaxa

INTERNATIONAL MATCHES PLAYED BY MEXICO

1-01-1923	Guatemala	W 3-2	Guatemala City	Fr	Izquierdo, Ortiz, Lopez.A
4-01	Guatemala	L 1-3	Guatemala City	Fr	Ortiz
7-01	Guatemala	W 4-1	Guatemala City	Fr	Izquierdo, Ortiz, Lopez.A 2
9-12	Guatemala	W 2-1	Mexico City	Fr	Lopez.A, Guadarrama
12-12	Guatemala	W 2-0	Mexico City	Fr	Garces, Ortiz
16-12	Guatemala	D 3-3	Mexico City	Fr	Garces, Lopez.A 2
30-05-1928	Spain	L 1-7	Amsterdam	OGr1	Carreño
5-06	Chile	L 1-3	Arnhem	OGct	Sota.E
13-07-1930	France	L 1-4	Montevideo	WCr1	Carreño
16-07	Chile	L 0-3	Montevideo	WCr1	
19-07	Argentina	L 3-6	Montevideo	WCr1	Rosas.F 2, Gayon
4-03-1934	Cuba	W 3-2	Mexico City	WCq	Mejia 3
11-03	Cuba	W 5-0	Mexico City	WCq	Rosas.F, Sota.J, Mejia 3
18-03	Cuba	W 4-1	Mexico City	WCq	Marcos, Alonso.M, Ruvalcaba
24-05	United States	L 2-4	Rome	WCq	Alonso.M, Meija
27-03-1935	El Salvador	W 8-2	San Salvador	CAG	Garcia.V 2, Lozano.T 2, Lopez.H 2, Lores, Garcia Cortina
28-03	Guatemala	W 5-1	San Salvador	CAG	Garcia.V, Lozano.T, Lopez.H 2, Lores
30-03	Cuba	W 6-1	San Salvador	CAG	Rosas.F, Lopez.H 2, Lores, Perez.L
1-04	Honduras	W 8-2	San Salvador	CAG	Lozano, Lopez.H 3, Lores 3, Perez.L
2-04	Costa Rica	W 2-0	San Salvador	CAG	Lozano, Perez.L
12-09-1937	United States	W 7-2	Mexico City	WCq	Lopez.A 2, Alonso.M 2, Arguelles 2, Casarin

17-09	United States	W 7-3	Mexico City	WCq	Casarin 2, Alonso.M 3, Garcia, Arguelles
26-09	United States	W 5-1	Mexico City	WCq	Garcia 2, Ruiz 2, Arguelles
10-02-1938	Colombia	W 3-1	Panama	CAG	Arguelles, De La Fuente, Casarin
14-02	Venezuela	W 1-0	Panama	CAG	Alonso.M
18-02	El Salvador	W 6-0	Panama	CAG	De La Fuente, Arguelles, Garcia.L 2, Casarin 2
20-02	Panama	D 2-2	Panama	CAG	De La Fuente, Casarin
22-02	Costa Rica	W 2-1	Panama	CAG	Casarin 2
13-07-1947	United States	W 5-0	Havana	NAC	Lopez.A 3, Segura, Ruiz.R
17-07	Cuba	W 3-1	Havana	NAC	Septien, Segura, Lopez.A
2-08-1948	Korea	L 3-5	London	OGr1	
4-09-1949	United States	W 6-0	Mexico City	NAC/WCq	De La Fuente 3, Flores.N, Luna, Septien
11-09	Cuba	W 2-0	Mexico City	NAC/WCq	Luna, Casarin
18-09	United States	W 6-2	Mexico City	NAC/WCq	Ortiz, Casarin 3, Ochoa, De La Fuente
25-09	Cuba	W 3-0	Mexico City	NAC/WCq	Naranjo 2, Flores.N
24-06-1950	Brazil	L 0-4	Rio de Janeiro	WCr1	
29-06	Yugoslavia	L 1-4	Porto Alegre	WCr1	Ortiz
2-07	Switzerland	L 1-2	Porto Alegre	WCr1	Casarin
23-03-1952	Uruguay	L 1-3	Santiago	PAC	Septien
26-03	Chile	L 0-4	Santiago	PAC	
6-04	Brazil	L 0-2	Santiago	PAC	
10-04	Panama	W 4-2	Santiago	PAC	Septien 3, Martinez
20-04	Peru	L 0-3	Santiago	PAC	
19-07-1953	Haiti	W 8-0	Mexico City	WCq	Aranauda 3, Balcázar 3, Télez, Gómez
27-12	Haiti	W 4-0	Port au Prince	WCq	Lamadrid 2, Balcázar, Avalos
10-01-1954	United States	W 4-0	Mexico City	WCq	Naranjo, Lamadrid, OG, Balcázar
14-01	United States	W 3-1	Mexico City	WCq	Torres.A 2, Lamadrid
16-06	Brazil	L 0-5	Geneva	WCr1	
19-06	France	L 2-3	Geneva	WCr1	Lamadrid, Balcázar
26-02-1956	Costa Rica	D 1-1	Mexico City	PAC	Calderon
4-03	Peru	L 0-2	Mexico City	PAC	
8-03	Brazil	L 1-2	Mexico City	PAC	Del Aguila
13-03	Argentina	D 0-0	Mexico City	PAC	
18-03	Chile	W 2-1	Mexico City	PAC	Calderon 2
7-04-1957	United States	W 6-0	Mexico City	WCq	Gutierrez.C, Reyes 3, Hernández.A 2
28-04	United States	W 7-2	Long Beach	WCq	Hernández.A 3, Gutierrez.C, Hernández.H 2, Sesma
30-06	Canada	W 3-0	Mexico City	WCq	González.C 2, Gutierrez.C
4-07	Canada	W 2-0	Mexico City	WCq	Gutierrez.C, Sesma
20-10	Costa Rica	W 2-0	Mexico City	WCq	Belmonte, Lopez
27-10	Costa Rica	D 1-1	San Jose	WCq	Lopez.L
8-06-1958	Sweden	L 0-3	Stockholm	WCr1	
11-06	Wales	D 1-1	Stockholm	WCr1	Belmonte
15-06	Hungary	L 0-4	Sandviken	WCr1	
1-03-1959	Costa Rica	W 3-1	Mexico City	Fr	Hernandez.H 3
8-03	Costa Rica	W 2-1	San Jose	Fr	Hernandez.H 2 *Abandoned*
24-05	England	W 2-1	Mexico City	Fr	Cardenas.R, Reyes
7-03-1960	Brazil	D 2-2	San Jose	PAC	Mercado, Reyes
10-03	Argentina	L 2-3	San Jose	PAC	Hernandez.H, Gonzalez
12-03	Costa Rica	D 1-1	San Jose	PAC	Ventre
15-03	Brazil	L 1-2	San Jose	PAC	Mercado
17-03	Argentina	L 0-2	San Jose	PAC	
20-03	Costa Rica	W 3-0	San Jose	PAC	Gonzalez, Del Aguila, Mercado
26-06	Holland	W 3-1	Mexico City	Fr	Hernández.H, González.C, Diaz.I
6-11	United States	D 3-3	Los Angeles	WCq	Reyes 2, Mercado
13-11	United States	W 3-0	Mexico City	WCq	Diaz.I, Reyes, Mercado
22-03-1961	Costa Rica	L 0-1	San Jose	WCq	
5-04	Neth Antilles	W 7-0	Mexico City	WCq	Flores.F 3, Reyes 2, Gonzales.E 2
12-04	Costa Rica	W 4-1	Mexico City	WCq	Cardenas.R, Gutierrez.C, Flores.F, Mercado
19-04	Holland	W 2-1	Amsterdam	Fr	Gonzales, Flores.P
30-04	Czechoslovakia	L 1-2	Ostrava	Fr	Reyes
10-05	England	L 0-8	London	Fr	
16-05	Norway	D 1-1	Bergen	Fr	Gutierrez.C
21-05	Neth Antilles	D 0-0	Willemstad	WCq	
29-10	Paraguay	W 1-0	Mexico City	WCq	Reyes
5-11	Paraguay	D 0-0	Asuncion	WCq	
28-03-1962	Argentina	L 0-1	Buenos Aires	Fr	
1-04	Colombia	W 1-0	Bogota	Fr	Ortiz
4-04	Colombia	D 2-2	Cali	Fr	Hernández.H, Ortiz
26-04	Colombia	W 1-0	Mexico City	Fr	Reyes
22-05	Wales	L 1-2	Mexico City	Fr	Jasso 2
30-05	Brazil	L 0-2	Vina del Mar	WCr1	
3-06	Spain	L 0-1	Vina del Mar	WCr1	
7-06	Czechoslovakia	W 3-1	Vina del Mar	WCr1	Diaz.I, Del Aguila, Hernández.H

Date	Opponent	Result	Venue	Comp	Scorers
24-03-1963	Neth Antilles	L 1-2	San Salvador	CCr1	Ortiz
28-03	Jamaica	W 8-0	San Salvador	CCr1	Pereda 2, Garrido, Ortiz 2, Diaz.I 2, Morales
30-03	Costa Rica	D 0-0	San Salvador	CCr1	
28-02-1965	Honduras	W 1-0	San Pedro	WCq	Diaz.I
4-03	Honduras	W 3-0	Mexico City	WCq	González, Reyes, Aussin
7-03	United States	D 2-2	Los Angeles	WCq	González, Reyes
12-03	United States	W 2-0	Mexico City	WCq	Diaz.I, Navarro
28-03	El Salvador	W 2-0	Guatemala City	CC	Diaz.I, Valdivia
1-04	Neth Antilles	W 5-0	Guatemala City	CC	Fragoso 3, Cisneros 2
4-04	Haiti	W 3-0	Guatemala City	CC	Cisneros, Fragoso
7-04	Costa Rica	D 1-1	Guatemala City	CC	Ruvalcaba
11-04	Guatemala	W 2-1	Guatemala City	CC	Cisneros, Fragoso
25-04	Costa Rica	D 0-0	San Jose	WCq	
3-05	Jamaica	W 3-2	Kingston	WCq	Jáuregui, Cisneros, Padilla
7-05	Jamaica	W 8-0	Mexico City	WCq	Diaz.I 3, Fragoso 2, Cisneros 2, Padilla
16-05	Costa Rica	W 1-0	Mexico City	WCq	Fragoso
24-04-1966	Paraguay	W 7-0	Mexico City	Fr	Fragoso 3, Padilla 2, Cisneros 2
3-05	Chile	W 1-0	Mexico City	Fr	Borja
30-05	Chile	W 1-0	Santiago	Fr	Fragoso
19-06	Switzerland	D 1-1	Lausanne	Fr	Padilla
22-06	Nth. Ireland	L 1-4	Belfast	Fr	Pena.G
29-06	Italy	L 0-5	Florence	Fr	
13-07	France	D 1-1	London	WCr1	Borja
16-07	England	L 0-2	London	WCr1	
19-07	Uruguay	D 0-0	London	WCr1	
5-01-1967	Switzerland	W 3-0	Mexico City	Fr	Pereda, Borja 2
6-03	Nicaragua	W 4-0	Tegucigalpa	CC	Arellano 3, Lapuente
10-03	Guatemala	L 0-1	Tegucigalpa	CC	
12-03	Trinidad	W 4-0	Tegucigalpa	CC	Estrada 2, Cerda, Bustos
14-03	Haiti	W 1-0	Tegucigalpa	CC	Pereda
19-03	Honduras	W 1-0	Tegucigalpa	CC	Prado
28-05	Soviet Union	L 0-2	Leningrad	Fr	
22-08	Argentina	W 2-1	Mexico City	Fr	Fragoso 2
3-03-1968	Soviet Union	D 0-0	Mexico City	Fr	
7-03	Soviet Union	D 1-1	Leon	Fr	Hernández.G
10-03	Soviet Union	D 0-0	Mexico City	Fr	
21-05	Uruguay	D 3-3	Mexico City	Fr	Bustos, Hernandez.G
28-05	Uruguay	D 2-2	Mexico City	Fr	Bustos 2
7-07	Brazil	L 0-2	Mexico City	Fr	
10-07	Brazil	W 2-1	Mexico City	Fr	Borja 2
18-10	Colombia	W 1-0	Bogota	Fr	Borja
20-10	Peru	D 3-3	Lima	Fr	Borja, Pena, Cisneros
23-10	Chile	L 1-3	Santiago	Fr	Borja
26-10	Uruguay	W 2-0	Montevideo	Fr	Borja, Cisneros
31-10	Brazil	W 2-1	Rio de Janeiro	Fr	Diaz, Fragoso
3-11	Brazil	L 1-2	Belo Horizonte	Fr	Borja
22-12	West Germany	D 0-0	Mexico City	Fr	
1-01-1969	Italy	L 2-3	Mexico City	Fr	Borja, González.J
5-01	Italy	D 1-1	Mexico City	Fr	Padilla
22-01	Denmark	W 3-0	Mexico City	Fr	OG, Gonzalez.J, Borja
4-02	Colombia	W 1-0	Leon	Fr	Fragoso
6-04	Portugal	D 0-0	Lisbon	Fr	
10-04	Luxembourg	L 1-2	Luxembourg	Fr	Borja
16-04	Belgium	L 0-2	Brussels	Fr	
23-04	Spain	D 0-0	Seville	Fr	
1-05	Sweden	L 0-1	Malmo	Fr	
6-05	Denmark	L 1-3	Copenhagen	Fr	Fragoso
8-05	Norway	W 2-0	Oslo	Fr	Fragoso 2
20-05	Peru	L 0-1	Mexico City	Fr	
22-05	Peru	W 3-0	Leon	Fr	Borja 2, Bustos
1-06	England	D 0-0	Mexico City	Fr	
5-11	Belgium	W 1-0	Mexico City	Fr	Velarde
11-11	Norway	W 4-0	Mexico City	Fr	Onofre, Padilla, Ponce, Velarde
28-11	Jamaica	W 3-0	San Jose	CC	
2-12	Costa Rica	L 0-2	San Jose	CC	
4-12	Guatemala	L 0-1	San Jose	CC	
6-12	Neth Antilles	D 2-2	San Jose	CC	
8-12	Trinidad	D 0-0	San Jose	CC	
15-02-1970	Bulgaria	D 1-1	Mexico City	Fr	Diaz.I
18-02	Bulgaria	W 2-0	Leon	Fr	Rivas.M, Basaguren
22-02	Sweden	D 0-0	Mexico City	Fr	
26-02	Soviet Union	D 0-0	Mexico City	Fr	
1-03	Sweden	L 0-1	Puebla	Fr	

Date	Opponent	Result	Venue	Comp	Scorers
5-03	Peru	W 1-0	Lima	Fr	Basaguren
8-03	Peru	L 0-1	Lima	Fr	
15-03	Peru	W 3-1	Mexico City	Fr	Padilla, Onofre, Lopez
18-03	Peru	D 3-3	Leon	Fr	Borja, Lopez, Hernández
29-04	Ecuador	W 4-2	Leon	Fr	
3-05	Ecuador	W 3-2	Mexico City	Fr	
31-05	Soviet Union	D 0-0	Mexico City	WCr1	
7-06	El Salvador	W 4-0	Mexico City	WCr1	Valdivia 2, Fragoso, Basaguren
11-06	Belgium	W 1-0	Mexico City	WCr1	Pena
14-06	Italy	L 1-4	Toluca	WCqf	Gonzalez
30-09	Brazil	L 1-2	Rio de Janeiro	Fr	Lopez
2-12	Australia	W 3-0	Mexico City	Fr	Valdivia 2, Gomez
17-02-1971	Soviet Union	D 0-0	Guadalajara	Fr	
19-02	Soviet Union	D 0-0	Mexico City	Fr	
7-07	Greece	D 1-1	Mexico City	Fr	Estrada.L
16-08	East Germany	L 0-1	Guadalajara	Fr	
8-09	West Germany	L 0-5	Hannover	Fr	
12-09	Morocco	L 1-2	Casablanca	Fr	Rodriguez
18-09	East Germany	D 1-1	Leipzig	Fr	Borja
22-09	Yugoslavia	L 0-4	Sarajevo	Fr	
25-09	Italy	L 0-2	Genoa	Fr	
3-10	Greece	L 0-1	Salonica	Fr	
13-10	Bermuda	W 2-0	Hamilton	CCq	Borja, Lopez
16-10	Bermuda	W 4-0	Mexico City	CCq	Borja, Velarde 2, Lopez
21-11	Haiti	D 0-0	St Ferdinand	CC	
26-11	Trinidad	W 2-0	Port of Spain	CC	Jiminez, Rodriguez
28-11	Cuba	W 1-0	St Ferdinand	CC	Rodriguez
2-12	Costa Rica	W 1-0	Port of Spain	CC	Rodriguez
4-12	Honduras	W 2-1	Port of Spain	CC	Mucino 2
27-01-1972	Chile	W 2-0	Mexico City	Fr	Lopez 2
5-04	Peru	W 2-1	Mexico City	Fr	Mucino, Borja
6-08	Costa Rica	L 0-1	San Jose	Fr	
9-08	Peru	L 2-3	Lima	Fr	Borja, Pulido
16-08	Chile	W 2-0	Santiago	Fr	Victorino, Borja
24-08	Canada	W 1-0	Toronto	WCq	Borbolla
3-09	United States	W 3-1	Mexico City	WCq	Victorino, Bustos, Borja
5-09	Canada	W 2-1	Mexico City	WCq	Victorino, Bustos
10-09	United States	W 2-1	Los Angeles	WCq	Ceballos, Borbolla
12-10	Costa Rica	W 3-1	Mexico City	Fr	Borja 3
7-02-1973	Argentina	W 2-0	Mexico City	Fr	Borja, Bustos
21-04	Chile	D 1-1	Mexico City	Fr	
5-08	Poland	L 0-1	Los Angeles	Fr	
8-08	Poland	L 1-2	Monterrey	Fr	Guzman.J
20-09	Chile	L 1-2	Mexico City	Fr	Pulido
16-10	United States	W 2-0	Puebla	Fr	Victorino, Bustos
30-11	Guatemala	D 0-0	Port au Prince	WCq	
3-12	Honduras	D 1-1	Port au Prince	WCq	Lopez.H
8-12	Neth Antilles	W 8-0	Port au Prince	WCq	Mucino 4, Lopez.H 2, Pulido, Lapuente
14-12	Trinidad	L 0-4	Port au Prince	WCq	
18-12	Haiti	W 1-0	Port au Prince	WCq	Borja
31-03-1974	Brazil	D 1-1	Rio de Janeiro	Fr	Manzo
5-09	United States	W 3-1	Monterrey	Fr	Gonzalez, Lopez 2
8-09	United States	W 1-0	Dallas	Fr	Trujillo
17-08-1975	Costa Rica	W 7-0	Mexico City	Fr	Alvarado, Damian, Delgado 2, Cuellar, Vargas 2
24-08	United States	W 2-0	Mexico City	Fr	Delgado, Borja
31-08	Argentina	D 1-1	Mexico City	Fr	Vargas
20-10	Israel	L 0-1	Tel Aviv	Fr	
4-06-1976	Brazil	L 0-3	Guadalajara	Fr	
3-10	United States	D 0-0	Los Angeles	WCq	
10-10	Canada	L 0-1	Vancouver	WCq	
15-10	United States	W 3-0	Puebla	WCq	Dávila, Solis, Damian
27-10	Canada	D 0-0	Toluca	WCq	
1-02-1977	Yugoslavia	W 5-1	Leon	Fr	Chaves, OG, Isiordia, Jiminez, Vasquez Ayala
8-02	Yugoslavia	L 0-1	Monterrey	Fr	
22-02	Hungary	D 1-1	Mexico City	Fr	Solis
17-05	Peru	D 1-1	Mexico City	Fr	Real
24-05	Peru	W 2-1	Monterrey	Fr	Vasquez Ayala, Acevedo
14-06	West Germany	D 2-2	Mexico City	Fr	Isiordia, OG
27-09	United States	W 3-0	Monterrey	Fr	Jiminez, Ortega
9-10	Haiti	W 4-1	Mexico City	WCq	Rangel 3, Sanchez.H
12-10	El Salvador	W 3-1	Mexico City	WCq	Rangel 2, Cardenas.J
15-10	Surinam	W 8-1	Monterrey	WCq	Isiordia 2, Sanchez.H 2, Jiminez 2, Rangel, Chavez
19-10	Guatemala	W 2-1	Mexico City	WCq	Cardenas.J, Vasquez Ayala

22-10	Canada	W 3-1	Monterrey	WCq	Guzman 2, Sanchez.H
15-02-1978	El Salvador	W 5-1	San Salvador	Fr	Vasquez, Ayala, Sanchez.H 3, Lugo
5-04	Bulgaria	W 3-0	Mexico City	Fr	Mendizabal, Ortega, Lugo
11-04	Peru	L 0-1	Los Angeles	Fr	
26-04	Spain	L 0-2	Granada	Fr	
3-05	Finland	W 1-0	Helsinki	Fr	Sanchez.H
2-06	Tunisia	L 1-3	Rosario	WCr1	Vasquez Ayala
6-06	West Germany	L 0-6	Cordoba	WCr1	
10-06	Poland	L 1-3	Rosario	WCr1	Rangel
1-11-1979	Peru	W 1-0	Monterrey	Fr	Medina
21-11	Finland	D 1-1	Mexico City	Fr	Medina
4-12	El Salvador	W 2-0	San Salvador	Fr	Sanchez.H 2
18-12	El Salvador	D 1-1	Texcoco	Fr	Sanchez.H
23-01-1980	Czechoslovakia	W 1-0	Leon	Fr	Cisneros
26-02	South Korea	L 0-1	Los Angeles	Fr	
18-03	Honduras	W 1-0	Tegucigalpa	Fr	González
8-04	Honduras	W 5-0	Toluca	Fr	Sanchez.H 2, Manzo.Ag 2, González
15-04	Guatemala	W 4-2	Guatemala City	Fr	Manzo.Ag 2, Mendizabal, Sanchez.H
29-04	Guatemala	D 2-2	Toluca	Fr	Sanchez,H, Castro
8-06	Brazil	L 0-2	Rio de Janeiro	Fr	
20-08	New Zealand	L 0-4	Auckland	Fr	
24-08	Australia	D 2-2	Sydney	Fr	Castro, González
26-08	Australia	D 1-1	Melbourne	Fr	Castro
30-08	Fiji	W 2-0	Suva	Fr	Ortega, González
2-09	Tahiti	W 1-0	Papetu	Fr	Castro
18-10	Canada	D 1-1	Toronto	WCq	Sanchez.H
9-11	United States	W 5-1	Mexico City	WCq	Sanchez.H, Camacho 2, Mendizabal, González
16-11	Canada	D 1-1	Mexico City	WCq	Sanchez.H
23-11	United States	L 1-2	Lauderdale	WCq	Sanchez.H
20-01-1981	Bulgaria	D 1-1	Mexico City	Fr	Sanchez.H
10-02	South Korea	W 4-0	Mexico City	Fr	Rodriguez, Castro, Lira, Ordura
24-06	Spain	L 1-3	Mexico City	Fr	Sanchez.H
1-11	Cuba	W 4-0	Tegucigalpa	WCq	Sanchez.H 2, Castro, Manzo
6-11	El Salvador	L 0-1	Tegucigalpa	WCq	
11-11	Haiti	D 1-1	Tegucigalpa	WCq	Sanchez.H
15-11	Canada	D 1-1	Tegucigalpa	WCq	Castro
22-11	Honduras	D 0-0	Tegucigalpa	WCq	
15-03-1983	Costa Rica	W 1-0	San José	Fr	Aguirre
22-03	Costa Rica	W 1-0	Mexico City	Fr	Marquez
5-04	Guatemala	W 2-0	Los Angeles	Fr	Diaz, Padilla
25-10	El Salvador	W 5-0	Los Angeles	Fr	Aguirre, Padilla, Manzo.Ag, Diaz 2
22-11	Sweden	W 2-0	Morelia	Fr	Diaz.M, Chaves
6-12	Canada	W 5-0	Iraputo	Fr	
24-01-1984	Venezuela	W 3-0	Irapuato	Fr	Diaz, OG, Aguirre
4-02	Italy	L 0-5	Rome	Fr	
8-08	Rep. Ireland	D 0-0	Dublin	Fr	
11-08	East Germany	D 1-1	Berlin	Fr	Quirate
16-08	Finland	W 3-0	Helsinki	Fr	Aguirre, Hernández.J, Negrete
19-08	Soviet Union	L 0-3	Leningrad	Fr	
22-08	Sweden	D 1-1	Malmo	Fr	Aguirre
25-08	Hungary	W 2-0	Budapest	Fr	Negrete, Boy
18-09	Argentina	D 1-1	Monterrey	Fr	Negrete
9-10	Colombia	W 1-0	Los Angeles	Fr	Boy
11-10	El Salvador	W 1-0	Los Angeles	Fr	Jiminez
17-10	United States	W 2-1	Mexico City	Fr	
25-10	Argentina	D 1-1	Buenos Aires	Fr	Flores
28-10	Chile	L 0-1	Santiago	Fr	
31-10	Uruguay	D 1-1	Montevideo	Fr	Muñoz
11-11	Trinidad	W 2-0	Port of Spain	Fr	Negrete, España
4-12	Ecuador	W 3-2	Los Angeles	Fr	Aguirre, Trejo, Flores
5-02-1985	Poland	W 5-0	Queretaro	Fr	Boy, Negrete 2, Barbosa, Flores.L
6-02	Switzerland	L 1-2	Queretaro	Fr	Farfan
26-02	Finland	W 2-1	Acapulco	Fr	Hermosillo, Farfan
2-06	Italy	D 1-1	Mexico City	Fr	Aguirre
9-06	England	W 1-0	Mexico City	Fr	Flores.L
15-06	West Germany	W 2-0	Mexico City	Fr	Negrete, Flores.L
27-08	Bulgaria	D 1-1	Los Angeles	Fr	Boy
20-09	Peru	D 0-0	Los Angeles	Fr	
22-09	Peru	W 1-0	San Jose	Fr	Hermosillo
11-10	Libya	L 1-3	Benghazi	Fr	Negrete
15-10	North Yemen	W 2-0	Sana'a	Fr	Flores, Dominguez
16-10	Jordan	D 0-0	Amman	Fr	
20-10	Egypt	L 1-2	Cairo	Fr	

25-10	Kuwait	D 0-0	Kuwait City	Fr	
14-11	Argentina	D 1-1	Los Angeles	Fr	Boy
17-11	Argentina	D 1-1	Puebla	Fr	Aguirre
3-12	South Korea	W 2-1	Los Angeles	Fr	Flores 2
7-12	Algeria	W 2-0	Mexico City	Fr	Negrete, Boy
10-12	South Korea	W 2-1	Guadalajara	Fr	Boy, Hermosillo
14-12	Hungary	W 2-0	Mexico City	Fr	Hermosillo, Boy
15-02-1986	East Germany	L 1-2	San Jose	Fr	Flores.L
19-02	Soviet Union	W 1-0	Mexico City	Fr	Aguirre
13-04	Uruguay	W 1-0	Los Angeles	Fr	Aguirre
27-04	Canada	W 3-0	Mexico City	Fr	Aguirre, Flores.L, Negrete
17-05	England	L 0-3	Los Angeles	Fr	
3-06	Belgium	W 2-1	Mexico City	WCr1	Quirarte, Sanchez.H
7-06	Paraguay	D 1-1	Mexico City	WCr1	Flores.L
11-06	Iraq	W 1-0	Mexico City	WCr1	Quirarte
15-06	Bulgaria	W 2-0	Mexico City	WCr2	Negrete, Servin
21-06	West Germany	D 0-0	Monterrey	WCqf	Lost 1-4 pens
13-01-1987	El Salvador	W 3-1	Los Angeles	Fr	Hernandez, Lira, Galindo
7-03	China	W 3-2	Leon	Fr	Luna, Hernandez.J, Galindo
6-10	Canada	W 4-0	Toluca	Fr	Hernandez.J, España, Moreno, Hermosillo
13-01-1988	Honduras	W 1-0	San Pedro Sula	Fr	Flores.L
14-02-1989	Poland	W 3-1	Los Angeles	Fr	Zague, OG, Moreno.P
21-02	Guatemala	W 2-1	Los Angeles	Fr	Negrete, Hermosillo
23-02	El Salvador	W 2-0	Los Angeles	Fr	Guzman, Farfan
8-08	South Korea	W 4-2	Los Angeles	Fr	Pelaez
17-01-1990	Argentina	W 2-0	Los Angeles	Fr	Munoz.C, Zague
20-03	Uruguay	W 2-1	Los Angeles	Fr	Davalos, Pelaez
17-04	Colombia	W 2-0	Los Angeles	Fr	OG, Pelaez
10-05	United States	W 1-0	Vancouver	Fr	Flores.L
13-05	Canada	L 1-2	Burnaby	Fr	Flores.L
2-06	Belgium	L 0-3	Brussels	Fr	
13-12	Brazil	D 0-0	Los Angeles	Fr	
29-01-1991	Colombia	D 0-0	Leon	Fr	
12-03	United States	D 2-2	Los Angeles	NAC	Valdez, Espinoza
13-03	Argentina	D 0-0	Buenos Aires	Fr	
14-03	Canada	W 3-0	Los Angeles	NAC	Zague 2, Duana
9-04	Chile	W 1-0	Veracruz	Fr	Espinoza
7-05	Uruguay	L 0-2	Los Angeles	Fr	
28-06	Jamaica	W 4-1	Los Angeles	CCr1	Galindo 2, Zague, Hermosillo
30-06	Canada	W 3-1	Los Angeles	CCr1	Hermosillo, De la Torre, Galindo
3-07	Honduras	D 1-1	Los Angeles	CCr1	Hermosillo
5-07	United States	L 0-2	Los Angeles	CCsf	
7-07	Costa Rica	W 2-0	Los Angeles	CC3p	Farfan, Galindo
20-11	Uruguay	D 1-1	Veracruz	Fr	Jimenez
27-11	Costa Rica	D 1-1	Los Angeles	Fr	Garcia Aspe
4-12	Hungary	W 3-0	Leon	Fr	Garcia.L, Gutierrez, De la Torre
8-03-1992	CIS	W 4-0	Mexico City	Fr	Aguirre, Valdez, De la Torre, Bernal
11-03	CIS	D 1-1	Tampico	Fr	Garcia.L
26-07	El Salvador	W 2-1	San Salvador	Fr	Uribe 2
31-07	Brazil	L 0-5	Los Angeles	Fr	
2-08	Colombia	D 0-0	Los Angeles	Fr	
17-08	Russia	L 0-2	Moscow	Fr	
19-08	Bulgaria	D 1-1	Sofia	Fr	Espinoza
26-08	Romania	L 0-2	Bucharest	Fr	
7-10	El Salvador	W 2-0	Los Angeles	Fr	De la Torre, Hermosillo
14-10	Germany	D 1-1	Dresden	Fr	Hermosillo
22-10	Croatia	L 0-3	Zagreb	Fr	
8-11	St. Vincent	W 4-0	Kingstown	WCq	Zague, Suarez, Uribe 2
15-11	Honduras	W 2-0	Mexico City	WCq	De la Torre, Uribe
22-11	Costa Rica	W 4-0	Mexico City	WCq	Garcia.L 2, Suarez, De la Torre
29-11	Costa Rica	L 0-2	San Jose	WCq	
6-12	St. Vincent	W 11-0	Mexico City	WCq	Uribe 3, Hermosillo 4, Bernal 3, Zague
13-12	Honduras	D 1-1	Tegucigalpa	WCq	Uribe
20-01-1993	Italy	L 0-2	Florence	Fr	
27-01	Spain	D 1-1	Las Palmas	Fr	Suarez
10-02	Romania	W 2-0	Monterrey	Fr	Galindo, Cruz
4-04	El Salvador	L 1-2	San Salvador	WCq	Garcia Aspe
11-04	Honduras	W 3-0	Mexico City	WCq	Flores.L, Sanchez.H, Ambriz
18-04	El Salvador	W 3-1	Mexico City	WCq	Ambriz, Garcia.L, Ramirez.R
25-04	Canada	W 4-0	Mexico City	WCq	Ramirez.R 2, Flores.L, Garcia Aspe
2-05	Honduras	W 4-1	Tegucigalpa	WCq	Garcia Aspe, Flores.L, Garcia.L, OG
9-05	Canada	W 2-1	Toronto	WCq	Sanchez.H, Cruz

10-06	Paraguay	W 3-1	Mexico City	Fr	Flores.L, Garcia Aspe, Zague
16-06	Colombia	L 1-2	Machala	SCr1	Zague
20-06	Argentina	D 1-1	Guayaquil	SCr1	Patino
23-06	Bolivia	D 0-0	Portoviejo	SCr1	
27-06	Peru	W 4-2	Quito	SCqf	Garcia Aspe 2, Zague, Galindo
30-06	Ecuador	W 2-0	Guayaquil	SCsf	Sanchez.H, Ramirez.R
4-07	Argentina	L 1-2	Guayaquil	SCf	Galindo
11-07	Martinique	W 9-0	Mexico City	CCr1	Zague 7, Ramirez.R, Hernández.J
15-07	Costa Rica	D 1-1	Mexico City	CCr1	OG
18-07	Canada	W 8-0	Mexico City	CCr1	Rodriguez 2, Mora 2, Zague 2, Salvador 2
22-07	Jamaica	W 6-1	Mexico City	CCsf	Salvador 3, Mora, Zague, Ambriz
25-07	United States	W 4-0	Mexico City	CCf	Ambriz, OG, Zague, Cantu
8-08	Brazil	D 1-1	Maceio	Fr	Garcia Aspe
22-09	Cameroon	W 1-0	Los Angeles	Fr	Guzman
6-10	South Africa	W 4-0	Los Angeles	Fr	Patino, OG, Galindo 2
13-10	United States	D 1-1	Washington	Fr	Del Olmo
20-10	Ukraine	W 2-1	San Diego	Fr	Salvador, Galindo
3-11	China	W 3-0	San Diego	Fr	Ambriz, Salvador, Hermosillo
16-12	Brazil	L 0-1	Guadalajara	Fr	
22-12	Germany	D 0-0	Mexico City	Fr	
19-01-1994	Bulgaria	D 1-1	San Diego	Fr	Hermosillo
26-01	Switzerland	L 1-5	Oakland	Fr	Duran
2-02	Russia	L 1-4	Oakland	Fr	Garcia Aspe
25-02	Sweden	W 2-1	Fresno	Fr	Hernández, Rodriguez
3-03	Colombia	D 0-0	Mexico City	Fr	
4-06	United States	L 0-1	Los Angeles	Fr	
11-06	Nth. Ireland	W 3-0	Miami	Fr	Garcia.L 2, Hermosillo
19-06	Norway	L 0-1	Washington	WCr1	
24-06	Rep. Ireland	W 2-1	Orlando	WCr1	Garcia.L 2
28-06	Italy	D 1-1	New York	WCr1	Bernal
5-07	Bulgaria	D 1-1	New York	WCr2	Garcia Aspe
15-12	Hungary	W 5-1	Los Angeles	Fr	Hermosillo 2, Suarez, Ramirez.R, Galindo
6-01-1995	Saudi Arabia	W 2-0	Riyadh	ICr1	Garcia.L 2
10-01	Denmark	D 1-1	Riyadh	ICr1	Garcia.L. Lost 2-4p
13-01	Nigeria	D 1-1	Riyadh	IC3p	Ramirez.R. Won 5-4p
1-02	Uruguay	W 1-0	San Diego	Fr	Rizo
29-03	Chile	L 1-2	Los Angeles	Fr	Garcia.L
18-06	United States	L 0-4	Washington	Fr	
21-06	Colombia	D 0-0	Washington	Fr	
24-06	Nigeria	W 2-1	Dallas	Fr	Garcia Aspe, Ambriz
7-07	Paraguay	L 1-2	Maldonado	SCr1	Garcia.L
9-07	Venezuela	W 3-1	Maldonado	SCr1	Garcia.L 2, Espinoza
13-07	Uruguay	D 1-1	Montevideo	SCr1	Garcia.L
17-07	United States	D 0-0	Paysandu	SCqf	Lost 1-4p

UNITED STATES OF AMERICA

Had it not been for two games played in 1874 between Harvard University and McGill University of Montreal, football today might be the national sport in the United States. In the second of these two matches, Harvard were persuaded to use an oval ball instead of the usual round one, and immediately took to it. From that they developed the handling code, and what Harvard do, others usually follow. If the US had stuck with the Association rules, who knows, they might well have become the strongest football nation in the world, indeed it would have been surprising if they had not. Instead they have the barest rump of the game, very popular at school level, we are always reminded, but with no infrastructure for developing the talent once it has left school. Efforts have continually been made to popularise the game, most notably through the North American Soccer League in the 1970s and the 1994 World Cup, but football does not have 'Made in the USA' stamped on it and so is likely to remain on the periphery of American sporting life.

The first club in America was Oneida Football Club, which was formed in 1862 in Boston by Gerritt Smith Miller, but unfortunately no longer exists. It is interesting to note that its foundation predates any club outside England - no club in Scotland had been formed by that time. All of its members came from the substantial English community located in Boston. Prior to the Harvard-McGill games, the round ball had found favour with most of the major universities on the East coast of the country. The Princeton rules, based on the 1863 Football Association rules, were drawn up in 1873 by Yale, Colombia, Rutgers and Princeton universities, but they were superseded in 1876 when Harvard, Yale and Colombia met to form the Intercollegiate Football Association and the rugby code was adopted as the basis for the rules of the game.

Once it was no longer played in the universities, football became the pastime of the numerous ethnic communities and was often centred around the factories which sponsored the teams and provided the grounds on which they played. Despite the formation in 1884 of the American Football Association by a group of Britons, the organisation of the game on a country-wide basis was haphazard. Numerous regional associations appeared, some adhering to amateurism, others allowing semi-professionalism. Particular hotspots of the game at this time included St Louis, New York, Philadelphia, New Jersey and Fall River.

Four international games were organised in these early years, two matches against Canada in Newark in 1885 and 1886 and the two exhibition matches at the St Louis Olympic Games in 1904, also against Canada. The validity of these matches as full internationals is open to some debate, but they do represent the first games played outside the British Isles which could be considered as such. The 1904 sides were actually two separate teams from St Louis called the St Rose Kickers and the Christian Brothers College, but they went under the banner of the United States.

The American Football Association, which had affiliated to the association in London, was eventually superseded in 1913 by the rival American Amateur Football Association under the aegis of the United States Football Association, later known as the United States Soccer Federation, and it was admitted to FIFA the same year. Its first task involved the organising of the first nationwide competition for all of the clubs that were now under its control. The National Open Challenge Cup, introduced the following year, is the yardstick by which football in America can be measured until the formation of the North American Soccer League in the late 1960s. It was joined in 1924 by the National Amateur Cup and both these competitions still run today.

Football's association with ethnic communities, part of its problem in America, is clear from the list of winners of both competitions. From the New York Greek Americans to the Philadelphia Ukrainians, and the Los Angeles Armenians to the German-Hungarian Soccer Club from Brooklyn, one is left in little doubt as to the composition of the teams. This has tended to alienate Americans even further from what they already consider a foreign sport.

The 1920s also saw the first attempt by the US to establish a proper league. The American Soccer League (ASL), in many ways the forerunner of the NASL, kicked off in 1921 and lasted until 1932. In its history the 12-strong league boasted 55 European internationals from nine different countries among its ranks and in 1926 a match between the New York Giants and Indiana Flooring drew a crowd of 46,000 to the New York Polo Grounds, a record until the 1970s. Efforts were also made to enter the US team in international competitions. They took part in the 1924 and 1928 Olympic Games and in the first World Cup in 1930, beating both Belgium and Paraguay in the first round in Montevideo to qualify for the semi-finals. There they faced Argentina, who had bundled them out of the Olympics two years previously with an 11-2 thrashing, so it was no surprise when they lost 6-1. Five of the team were former Scottish professionals.

Four years later the team was represented again in the final tournament, but had the misfortune to meet the hosts Italy in the first round and lost 1-0. There then followed a 13-year hiatus. As members of the North American Confederation, two series with Mexico and Cuba were played in the late 1940s for the North American Championship, neither of which proved successful. They did, however, prepare the American side for one of the biggest upsets the world has ever seen, in the 1950 World Cup. Unlike the 1930 side, the team representing the United States in Brazil that year was made up almost entirely of American born-and-bred players. In the first match, despite leading 1-0 with only 10 minutes remaining, the team contrived to lose 3-1 against Spain, but their second match against England in Belo Horizonte is indelibly etched into history. One of their few 'foreigners', Larry Gaetjens from Haiti, scored a goal that saw the mighty English humbled. So surprising was the result to those back in England that one newspaper thought there had been a mistake in the telegram and printed the result as 10-1 rather than 0-1! Defeat against Chile in the final match meant that the team returned home after the first round, but once again the World Cup had passed the country by. Not until the late 1960s did the population of America stand up and take note of what was by then far and away the most popular sport in the world.

Talk of football in the United States and the things that first come to mind are the 1950 defeat of England, the 1994 World Cup and the NASL. For nearly 20 years the United States conducted an experiment in winning over the American public to football, and the only conclusion that could be reached at the end was that Americans simply did not like the game and probably never would. Aside from the two national cup competitions, there were numerous local leagues spread around the country, one even calling itself the ASL, which had full-time professionalism. In 1960 the International Soccer League was set up, consisting of 11 foreign teams and the New York Americans, and was won in the first year by Bangu from Brazil in the final against Kilmarnock from Scotland. Unfortunately not many teams took it seriously and in 1965 the league folded.

Two years later, however, big business began looking at football: if successful in winning over Americans, they stood to make a lot of money. The United States Soccer Federation, realising the growing interest, sanctioned the United Soccer Association as the controlling body of the new national league and in 1967 it got off the ground. Ten franchises were sold and teams imported wholesale to represent these cities. The first winners were the Los Angeles Wolves with a team composed entirely of players from Wolverhampton Wanderers in England. A rival league was also set up at the same time but in 1968 the two leagues were persuaded to merge, and at last the United States had a truly national league, which included Canada as well.

The NASL, as it was known from 1968, was modelled on those that existed in American football and baseball, from the system of franchising down to the cheerleaders. New clubs were created in an attempt to get away from the ethnic image of the game and to spread it around the country to cities like Miami, Atlanta and Kansas, to whom it was new. Although the number of Americans taking part in the league grew over the years, it was always dominated by foreigners, even if they were relatively well known. The best known of these were Pelé and Franz Beckenbauer, both of whom played for the best known and most popular of the clubs created, the New York Cosmos, backed by Warner Communications. For a while it seemed as if the experiment was working. The money was there, gates were high, especially in New York, and the level of play was to a good standard. It was not to last, however.

One by one clubs folded as the owners, disappointed by profit levels, pulled the plug on their teams, and in 1984 the NASL itself folded. The major problem was that the game had been built up on an artificial basis. Clubs will only survive and even thrive if they have a history that players, supporters and owners can identify with. None of the NASL clubs had that, and so from the very start the idea was doomed to failure. Football was simply not allowed to grow naturally, and no matter how much money was thrown at it, the conditions were not right. All the ethnic leagues still survive in the United States and as these represent the only areas where there is any tradition in the American game, perhaps the NASL should have paid more attention to them, as should administrators in the future.

FIFA, despite the failure of the NASL, still regarded the United States as unconquered virgin territory full of dollars that could make their way into its coffers, and so in a decision roundly condemned at the time, they awarded the 1994 World Cup to America, in an attempt to give the game another boost. One of the conditions of the award was that a professional league should be introduced there, but by the time the World Cup was staged this had not happened, the start date having been delayed several times. The tournament itself passed off extremely well, although whether the World Cup would have a lasting influence and enable Major League Soccer (MLS) to grab the attention of the American public was always doubtful. There is at least sufficient interest for soccer not to revert to the absolute obscurity of former years, and the USA women's team were world champions in 1991. Perhaps it is with them that the country's best hope in soccer lies.

Population: 251,394,000
Area, sq km: 9,529,063
% in urban areas: 76%
Capital city: Washington D.C.

United States Soccer Federation
US Soccer House
1801-1811 S. Prairie Ave
Chicago IL 60616
United States of America
Tel: + 1 312 8081300
Fax: + 1 312 8081301
Telex: 450024 us soccer fed

Year of formation	1913
Affiliation to FIFA	1913
Affiliation to CONC	1961
Registered clubs	5375
Registered players	3 189 100
Professional players	700
Registered coaches	12 000
Registered referees	30 449
National stadium	Rose Bowl, Los Angeles 104 000
National colours	White/Blue/White
Reserve colours	Red/White/Blue
Season	April - September

THE RECORD

WORLD CUP

1930	QT Automatic - Final tournament/Semi-finalists
1934	QT 1st/4 in group 1 - Final tournament/1st round
1938	Did not enter
1950	QT 2nd/3 in group 9 - Final tournament/1st round
1954	QT 2nd/3 in group 11
1958	QT 1st round
1962	QT 1st round
1966	QT 1st round
1970	QT 2nd round
1974	QT 1st round
1978	QT 1st round
1982	QT 2nd round
1986	QT 2nd round
1990	QT Qualified - Final tournament/1st round
1994	QT Automatic - Final tournament/2nd round

SOUTH AMERICAN CHAMPIONSHIP

1993	12/12 1st round
1995	4/12 Semi-finalists/4th place

CONCACAF CHAMPIONSHIP

Winners - 1991

MAJOR LEAGUE SOCCER

Begins April 1996. Ten franchises have been awarded and the cities will contest the league as follows:

Western Conference
Dallas
Denver
Kansas City
Los Angeles
San Jose

Eastern Conference
Boston
Columbus
New York
Tampa
Washington

THE A-LEAGUE

Formerly the American Professional Soccer League (see opposite):

Atlanta Ruckus
Colorado Foxes
Montreal Impact
New York Centaurs
Seattle Sounders
Toronto Rockets
Vancouver 86ers

NASL SOCCER BOWL FINALS

1967	Los Angeles Wolves	6-5	Washington Whips
1967	Oakland Clippers	0-1 4-1	Baltimore Bays
1968	Atlanta Chiefs	0-0 3-0	San Diego Toros
1969	Kansas City Spurs	*	Atlanta Chiefs
1970	Rochester Lancers	3-0 1-3	Washington Darts
1971	Dallas Tornado	1-2 4-1 2-0	Atlanta Chiefs
1972	New York Cosmos	2-1	St. Louis Stars

1973	Philadelphia Atoms	2-0	Dallas Tornado
1974	Los Angeles Aztecs	4-3	Miami Toros
1975	Tampa Bay Rowdies	2-0	Portland Timbers
1976	Toronto Metros	3-0	Minnesota Kicks
1977	New York Cosmos	2-1	Seattle Sounders
1978	New York Cosmos	3-1	Tampa Bay Rowdies
1979	Vancouver Whitecaps	2-1	Tampa Bay Rowdies
1980	New York Cosmos	3-0	Fort Lauderdale Strikers
1981	Chicago Sting	1-0	New York Cosmos
1982	New York Cosmos	1-0	Seattle Sounders
1983	Tulsa Roughnecks	2-0	Toronto Blizzard
1984	Chicago Sting	2-1 3-2	Toronto Blizzard

* Run solely on a league basis

WESTERN SOCCER LEAGUE

1985	San Jose Earthquakes
1986	Hollywood Kickers
1987	San Diego Nomads
1988	Seattle Storm
1989	San Diego Nomads
1990	San Francisco Bayhawks

AMERICAN SOCCER LEAGUE

1988	Washington Diplomats
1989	Fort Lauderdale Strikers
1990	Maryland Bays

AMERICAN PROFESSIONAL SOCCER LEAGUE

1989	Fort Lauderdale Strikers	3-2	San Diego Nomods
1990	Maryland Bays	1-1 4-3p	San Francisco Blackhawks
1991	San Francisco Blackhawks	1-3 2-0 4-2p	Albany Capitals
1992	Colorado Foxes	1-0	Tampa Bay Rowdies
1993	Colorado Foxes	3-1	Los Angeles Salsa
1994	Montreal Impact	1-0	Colorado Foxes

UNITED STATES NATIONAL OPEN CHALLENGE CUP

1914	Brooklyn Field Club, NY	2-1	Brooklyn Celtic
1915	Bethlehem Steel, Pa	3-1	Brooklyn Celtic
1916	Bethlehem Steel, Pa	1-0	Fall River Rovers, Mass
1917	Fall River Rovers, Mass	1-0	Betlehem Steel, Pa
1918	Bethlehem Steel, Pa	2-2 3-0	Fall River Rovers, Mass
1919	Bethlehem Steel, Pa	2-0	Paterson, NJ
1920	Ben Millers, Mo	2-1	Fore River, Mass
1921	Robins Dry Dock, NY	4-2	Scullin Steel, Mo
1922	Scullin Steel, Mo	3-2	Todd Shipyard, NY
1923	Paterson, NJ	2-2 W-O	Scullin Steel, NY
1924	Fall River, Mass	4-2	Vesper Buick, NJ
1925	Shawsheen, Mass	3-0	Canadian Club Chicago
1926	Bethlehem Steel, Pa	7-2	Ben Millers, Mo
1927	Fall River, Mass	7-0	Holley Carburetor, Mich
1928	New York Nationals	2-2 3-0	Bricklayers, Ill
1929	Hakoah All Stars, NY	2-0 3-0	Madison Kennels, Mo
1930	Fall River, Mass	7-2 2-7	Bruell Insurance
1931	Fall River, Mass	6-2 1-1	Bricklayers, Ill
1932	New Bedford, Mass	3-3 5-2	Stix, Baer & Fuller, Mo
1933	Stix, Baer & Fuller, Mo	1-0 2-1	New York Americans
1934	Stix, Baer & Fuller, Mo	4-2 2-3 5-0	Pawtucket Rangers, RI
1935	Central Breweries, Mo	5-0 1-1 1-3	Pawtucket Rangers, RI
1936	German-American, Pa	2-2 3-1	St. Louis Shamrocks, Mo
1937	New York Americans	0-2 4-2	St. Louis Shamrocks, Mo
1938	Sparta ABA Chicago	4-0 4-2	St. Mary's Celtic, NY
1939	St. Mary's Celtic, NY	1-0 4-1	Manhatten Beer, Ill
1940	Sparta ABA Chicago	0-0 2-2 *	Baltimore DC
1941	Pawtucket, RI	4-2 4-3	Chrysler Detroit
1942	Gallatin Pittsburgh	2-1 4-2	Pawtucket, RI
1943	Brooklyn Hispano	2-2 4-2	Morgan-Strasser, Pa
1944	Brooklyn Hispano	4-0	Morgan-Strasser, Pa
1945	Brookhattan, NY	4-1 2-1	Cleveland Americans
1946	Chicago Vikings	1-1 2-1	Ponta Delgada, Mass
1947	Ponta Delgada, Mass	6-2 3-2	Sparta ABA Chicago
1948	Simpkins-Ford, Mo	3-1	Brookhattan, NY
1949	Morgan Pittsburgh	2-0 4-0	Philadelphia Nats
1950	Simpkins-Ford, Mo	2-1 1-4	Ponta Delgada, Mass
1951	German-Hungarian, NY	2-2 6-2	Heidelberg, Pa
1952	Harmarville, Pa	3-1 4-1	Philadelphia Nats
1953	Chicago Falcons	2-0 1-1	Harmarville, Pa
1954	New York Americans	1-0 2-0	Kutis SC, Mo
1955	Eintracht SC, NY	2-1	Danish Americans, Ca
1956	Harmarville, Pa	0-1 3-1	Chicago Schwaben
1957	Kutis SC, Mo	3-0 3-1	Hakoah New York
1958	Los Angeles Kickers	2-1	Pompei Baltimore
1959	Canvasbacks, Ca	4-3	Fall River, Mass
1960	Ukrainian Nationals, Pa	5-3	Los Angeles Kickers
1961	Ukrainian Nationals, Pa	2-2 5-2	Los Angeles Scots
1962	New York Hungaria	3-2	San Francisco Scots
1963	Ukrainian Nationals, Pa	1-0	Los Angeles Armenians
1964	Los Angeles Kickers	2-2 2-0	Ukranian Nationals, Pa
1965	New York Ukranians	1-1 3-0	Hansa Chicago
1966	Ukrainian Nationals, Pa	1-0 3-0	Orange County, Ca
1967	Greek-Americans, NY	4-2	Orange County, Ca
1968	Greek-Americans, NY	1-1 1-0	Chicago Olympic
1969	Greek-Americans, NY	1-0	Montebello Armenians
1970	Elizabeth, NJ	2-1	Los Angeles Croatia
1971	New York Hota	6-4	San Pedro Yugoslavs
1972	Elizabeth, NJ	1-0	San Pedro Yugoslavs
1973	Maccabee Los Angeles	5-3	Cleveland Inter
1974	Greek-Americans, NY	2-0	Chicago Croatians
1975	Maccabee Los Angeles	1-0	Inter-Giuliana, NY
1976	San Francisco AC	1-0	Inter-Giuliana, NY
1977	Maccabee Los Angeles	5-0	German-Hungarian, Pa
1978	Maccabee Los Angeles	2-0	Vasco da Gama, Conn
1979	Brooklyn Dodgers	2-1	Chicago Croatians
1980	New York Freedoms	3-2	Maccabee Los Angeles
1981	Maccabee Los Angeles	5-1	Brooklyn Dodgers
1982	New York Freedoms	4-3	Maccabee Los Angeles
1983	New York Freedoms	4-3	Kutis SC, Mo

1984	AO Krete, NY	4-2	Chicago Croatians
1985	Greek-Americans, Ca	2-0	Kutis SC, Mo
1986	Kutis SC, Mo	1-0	San Pedro Yugoslavs
1987	España Washington	1-0	Mitre Eagles, WA
1988	Busch SC, Mo	2-1	Greek-Americans, Ca
1989	Kickers St Petersburg	2-1	Greek-Americans/ Atlas, NY
1990	Chicago Eagles	2-1	Brooklyn Italians
1991	Brooklyn Italians	1-0	Richardson Rockets, Tx
1992	San Jose Oaks	2-1	Vasco da Gama, Conn
1993	CD Mexico, Ca	5-0	German-Hungarian, Pa
1994	Greek-Americans, Ca	3-0	Bavarian Leinenkugel

UNITED STATES NATIONAL AMATEUR CHALLENGE CUP

1924	Fleisher Yarn, Pa.	3-0	Swedeish-American, Mich
1925	Toledo, Ohio	3-1	McLeod Council, NJ
1926	Defenders, Mass	1-0	Heidelberg, Pa
1927	Heidelburg, Pa	3-0	La Flamme Cobblers, Mass
1928	-		
1929	Heidelburg, Pa	9-0	1st German, NJ
1930	Rafterys, Mass	3-3 *	Gallatin SC Pittsburgh
1931	Goodyear, Ohio	1-1 2-0	Black Cats, Mass
1932	Cleveland Shamrocks	2-1	Santo Christo, Mass
1933	German-American, Pa	5-1	McKnight Beverage, Pa
1934	German-American, Pa	1-1	Heidelburg, Pa
1935	Riehl SC, Pa	3-0	All American Cafe, Mo
1936	Brooklyn-German	2-1	Castle Shannon, Pa
1937	Trenton Highlander, NJ	1-0	Castle Shannon, Pa
1938	Ponta Delgada, Mass	2-0	Heidelburg, Pa
1939	St. Michael's, Mass	3-1	Gallatin, Pa
1940	Morgan-Strasser, Pa	1-0	Firestone, Mass
1941	Fall River, Mass	2-1	Chrysler, Mich
1942	Fall River, Mass	4-3	Morgan USCO, Pa
1943	Morgan-Strasser, Pa	4-1	Santa Maria, Md
1944	Eintracht SC, NY	5-2	Morgan Strasser, Pa
1945	Eintracht SC, NY	1-0	Rafterys, Mass
1946	Ponta Delgada, Mass	5-0	Castle Shannon, Pa
1947	Ponta Delgada, Mass	4-1	Curry Vets, Pa
1948	Ponta Delgada, Mass	4-1	Curry Vets, Pa
1949	Elizabeth, NJ	6-1	Zenthoefer Furs, Mo
1950	Ponta Delgada, Mass	0-1 4-1	Harmarville, Pa
1951	German-Hungarian, NY	4-3	Harmarville, Pa
1952	St. Louis Raiders	3-1	Lusitano, Mass
1953	Ponta Delgada, Mass	2-0	Chicago Slovaks
1954	Beadling SC Pittsburgh	2-5 5-1	Simpkins, Mo
1955	Heidelberg Tornadoes, Pa	2-2 5-0	Chicago Eagles
1956	Kutis SC, Mo	1-0	Philadelphia Ukrainians
1957	Kutis SC, Mo	1-1	Rochester Ukrainians
1958	Kutis SC, Mo	2-1	Beadling, Pa
1959	Kutis SC, Mo	5-0 2-2	St. Andrew Scots, Mich
1960	Kutis SC, Mo	4-0	Patchogue New York
1961	Kutis SC, Mo	1-0 3-3	Italian-American, Conn
1962	Carpathia Kickers Detroit	4-0	American-Hungarian, NJ
1963	Italian-Americans, NY	1-0	St. Ambrose, Mo
1964	Schwaben Chicago	4-0	German-Hungarians, NY
1965	German-Hungarians, Pa	6-0	St. Ambrose, Mo
1966	Chicago Kickers	5-2	Italian-Americans, NY
1967	Italian-Americans Hartford	2-0	Kutis SC, Mo
1968	Chicago Kickers	2-1	Carpathia Kickers, Mich
1969	British Lions Washington	4-1	Kutis SC, Mo
1970	Chicago Kickers	6-5	German-Hungarians, Pa
1971	Kutis SC, Mo	4-1	Inter-Italian, Ohio
1972	Busch SC, Mo	1-0	New Bedford Portuguese
1973	Inter Philadelphia	3-2	San Jose Grenadiers
1974	Inter Philadelphia	4-3	Big 4 Chevrolet, Mo
1975	Chicago Kickers	1-0	Scotland SC, NJ
1976	Milwaukee Bavarian	3-2	Trenton, NJ
1977	Denver Kickers	3-1	German-Hungarians, Pa
1978	Denver Kickers	8-3	Inter-Italia, Ohio
1979	Atlanta Datagraphic	1-0	San Francisco Glens
1980	Busch SC, Mo	3-2	Atlanta Datagraphic
1981	Busch SC, Mo	3-2	Philadelphia Bayern
1982	Seattle Croatia	1-0	Virginia Kicks
1983	Denver Kickers	2-1	Bavarian/Pabst, Wis
1984	Mean Green, Tx	5-0	Ukrainian, Mich
1985	España Washington	2-1	Mitre Eagles, WA
1986	Fairfax Spartans	3-0	Busch SC, Mo
1987	Polish-American, NY	3-1	Atlanta Datagraphic
1988	Mean Green, Tx	1-0	Philadelphia-Inter
1989	Chicago Eagles	2-1	Philadelphia Inter
1990	Kickers St Petersburg	1-0	San Francisco Glens
1991	Scott Gallagher Missouri	3-1	El Farolito, Ca
1992	Madison 56ers	2-1	IFC Greensboro, NC
1993	Murphy's Pub, WA	2-1	Scott Gallagher, Mo
1994	Denver Kickers	1-0	Chicago Eagles
1995	Denver Kickers	1-0	Team Lapine, NY

INTERNATIONAL MATCHES PLAYED BY THE UNITED STATES OF AMERICA

28-11-1885	Canada	L 0-1	Newark	Fr	
25-11-1886	Canada	W 3-2	Newark	Fr	Swarbuck, Gray, McGurck
16-11-1904	Canada	L 0-7	St. Louis	OGf	
17-11	Canada	L 0-4	St. Louis	OGf	
20-08-1916	Sweden	W 3-2	Stockholm	Fr	Spalding, Ellis, Cooper
3-09	Norway	D 1-1	Oslo	Fr	Ellis
26-05-1924	Estonia	W 1-0	Paris	OGpr	Straden
29-05	Uruguay	L 0-3	Paris	OGr1	

10-06	Poland	W 3-2	Warsaw	Fr	Straden 2, OG
16-06	Rep. Ireland	L 1-3	Dublin	Fr	Rhody
27-06-1925	Canada	L 0-1	Montreal	Fr	
8-11	Canada	W 6-1	Brooklyn	Fr	Brown 3, Stark 3
6-11-1926	Canada	W 6-2	Brooklyn	Fr	Brown 2, Auld 2, Marshall, Florrie
30-05-1928	Argentina	L 2-11	Amsterdam	OGr1	Findley 2
10-06	Poland	D 3-3	Warsaw	Fr	Ryan, Gallacher, Hunter
13-07-1930	Belgium	W 3-0	Montevideo	WCr1	McGhee 2, Patenaude
17-07	Paraguay	W 3-0	Montevideo	WCr1	Patenaude 2, Florie
26-07	Argentina	L 1-6	Montevideo	WCsf	Brown
17-08	Brazil	L 3-4	Rio de Janeiro	Fr	Patenaude 2
24-05-1934	Mexico	W 4-2	Rome	WCq	Donelli 4
27-05	Italy	L 1-7	Rome	WCr1	Donelli
13-07-1947	Mexico	L 0-5	Havana	NAC	
20-07	Cuba	L 2-5	Havana	NAC	
6-08-1948	Norway	L 0-1	Oslo	Fr	
11-08	N.Ireland	L 0-5	Belfast	Fr	
4-09-1949	Mexico	L 0-6	Mexico City	NAC	
14-09	Cuba	D 1-1	Mexico City	NAC	Wallace
18-09	Mexico	L 2-6	Mexico City	NAC	Wattman, Souza
21-09	Cuba	W 5-2	Mexico City	NAC	Matevich 2, Souza, Wallace, Bahr
25-06-1950	Spain	L 1-3	Curtiba	WCr1	Souza
29-06	England	W 1-0	Belo Horizonte	WCr1	Gaetjens
2-07	Chile	L 2-5	Recife	WCr1	Pariani, Souza
30-04-1952	Scotland	L 0-6	Glasgow	Fr	
8-06-1953	England	L 3-6	New York	Fr	Decker 2, Atheneos
10-01-1954	Mexico	L 0-4	Mexico City	WCq	
14-01	Mexico	L 1-3	Mexico City	WCq	Looby
3-04	Haiti	W 3-2	Port au Prince	WCq	Looby, Casey, Chachurian
4-04	Haiti	W 3-0	Port au Prince	WCq	Looby, Mendoza
25-08-1955	Iceland	L 2-3	Reykjavik	Fr	Looby
7-04-1957	Mexico	L 0-6	Mexico City	WCq	
28-04	Mexico	L 2-7	Long Beach	WCq	Murphy.E
22-06	Canada	L 1-5	Toronto	WCq	Keough
6-07	Canada	L 2-3	St. Louis	WCq	Murphy.J, Mendoza
28-05-1959	England	L 1-8	Los Angeles	Fr	Murphy.E
6-11-1960	Mexico	D 3-3	Los Angeles	WCq	Bicek, Zerhusen, Fister
13-11	Mexico	L 0-3	Mexico City	WCq	
27-05-1964	England	L 0-10	New York	Fr	
7-03-1965	Mexico	D 2-2	Los Angeles	WCq	Bicek, Shmotoolocha
12-03	Mexico	L 0-2	Mexico City	WCq	
17-03	Honduras	W 1-0	San Pedro	WCq	Murphy.E
21-03	Honduras	D 1-1	Tegucigalpa	WCq	Murphy.E
15-09-1968	Israel	D 3-3	New York	Fr	Millar, Roy
25-09	Israel	L 0-4	Philadelphia	Fr	
17-10	Canada	L 2-4	Toronto	WCq	Roy, Stritzl
20-10	Haiti	W 6-3	Port au Prince	Fr	
21-10	Haiti	L 2-5	Port au Prince	Fr	
23-10	Haiti	W 1-0	Port au Prince	Fr	
27-10	Canada	W 1-0	Atlanta	WCq	Albrecht
2-11	Bermuda	W 6-2	Kansas City	WCq	Millar 3, Baker 2, Roy
10-11	Bermuda	W 2-0	Hamilton	WCq	Roy, OG
20-04-1969	Haiti	L 0-2	Port au Prince	WCq	
11-05	Haiti	L 0-1	San Diego	WCq	
20-08-1972	Canada	L 2-3	St. John's	WCq	Roy, Getzinger
29-08	Canada	D 2-2	Baltimore	WCq	Roy, Geimer
3-09	Mexico	L 1-3	Mexico City	WCq	Roy
10-09	Mexico	L 1-2	Los Angeles	WCq	Geimer
17-03-1973	Bermuda	L 0-4	Hamilton	Fr	
20-03	Poland	L 0-4	Lodz	Fr	
3-08	Poland	L 0-1	Chicago	Fr	
5-08	Canada	W 2-0	Windsor	Fr	Grgurev, Liveric
10-08	Poland	L 0-4	San Francisco	Fr	
12-08	Poland	W 1-0	New Britain	Fr	Trost
9-09	Bermuda	W 1-0	Hartford	Fr	Brewster
16-10	Mexico	L 0-2	Puebla	Fr	
3-11	Haiti	L 0-1	Port au Prince	Fr	
5-11	Haiti	L 0-1	Port au Prince	Fr	
13-11	Israel	L 1-3	Tel Aviv	Fr	Roy
15-11	Israel	L 0-2	Beersheba	Fr	
5-09-1974	Mexico	L 1-3	Monterrey	Fr	Vaninger

Date	Opponent	Result	Venue	Comp	Scorers
8-09	Mexico	L 0-1	Dallas	Fr	
26-03-1975	Poland	L 0-7	Poznan	Fr	
4-04	Italy	L 0-10	Rome	Fr	
24-06	Poland	L 0-4	Seattle	Fr	
19-08	Costa Rica	L 1-3	Mexico City	Fr	McCully
21-08	Argentina	L 0-6	Mexico City	Fr	
24-08	Mexico	L 0-2	Mexico City	Fr	
24-09-1976	Canada	D 1-1	Vancouver	WCq	Bandov
3-10	Mexico	D 0-0	Los Angeles	WCq	
15-10	Mexico	L 0-3	Puebla	WCq	
20-10	Canada	W 2-0	Seattle	WCq	Rys, Veee
10-11	Haiti	D 0-0	Port au Prince	Fr	
12-11	Haiti	D 0-0	Port au Prince	Fr	
14-11	Haiti	D 0-0	Port au Prince	Fr	
22-12	Canada	L 0-3	Port au Prince	WCq	
15-09-1977	El Salvador	W 2-1	San Salvador	Fr	Davis, Villa
18-09	Guatemala	L 1-3	Guatemala City	Fr	Bellinger
22-09	El Salvador	W 1-0	San Salvador	Fr	Davis
25-09	Guatemala	L 0-2	Guatemala City	Fr	
27-09	Mexico	L 0-3	Monterrey	Fr	
30-09	El Salvador	D 0-0	Los Angeles	Fr	
6-10	China	D 1-1	Washington	Fr	Villa
10-10	China	W 1-0	Atlanta	Fr	
16-10	China	W 2-1	San Francisco	Fr	Villa, Nanchoff.G
3-09-1978	Iceland	D 0-0	Reykjavik	Fr	
6-09	Switzerland	L 0-2	Lucerne	Fr	
20-09	Portugal	L 0-1	Lisbon	Fr	
3-02-1979	Soviet Union	L 1-3	Seattle	Fr	Davis
11-02	Soviet Union	L 1-4	San Francisco	Fr	Liveric
2-05	France	L 0-6	East Rutherford	Fr	
7-10	Bermuda	W 3-1	Hamilton	Fr	Liveric, Bandov, Makowski
10-10	France	L 0-3	Paris	Fr	
26-10	Hungary	W 2-0	Budapest	Fr	Nanchoff.L, Di Bernardo
29-10	Rep Ireland	L 2-3	Dublin	Fr	Villa, Di Bernardo
4-10-1980	Luxembourg	W 2-0	Luxembourg	Fr	Davis, Hulcer
7-10	Portugal	D 1-1	Lisbon	Fr	Davis
25-10	Canada	D 0-0	Lauderdale	WCq	
1-11	Canada	L 1-2	Vancouver	WCq	Villa
9-11	Mexico	L 1-5	Mexico City	WCq	Davis
23-11	Mexico	W 2-1	Lauderdale	WCq	Moyers 2
21-03-1982	Trinidad	W 2-1	Port of Spain	Fr	Davis, Veee
8-04-1983	Haiti	W 2-0	Port au Prince	Fr	Borja, Durgan
30-05-1984	Italy	D 0-0	New Jersey	Fr	
29-09	Neth Antilles	D 0-0	Curacao	WCq	
6-10	Neth Antilles	W 4-0	St. Louis	WCq	Coker 2, Di Bernardo, Kapp
9-10	El Salvador	W 3-1	Los Angeles	Fr	Davis, Ladouceur, Hooker
11-10	Colombia	W 1-0	Los Angeles	Fr	Coker
14-10	Guatemala	L 0-4	Guatemala City	Fr	
17-10	Mexico	L 1-2	Mexico City	Fr	Van der Beck
30-11	Ecuador	D 0-0	New York	Fr	
2-12	Ecuador	D 2-2	Miami	Fr	Ladouceur, Sharp
8-02-1985	Switzerland	D 1-1	Tampa	Fr	Van der Beck
2-04	Canada	L 0-2	Vancouver	Fr	
4-04	Canada	D 1-1	Portland	Fr	Perez
15-05	Trinidad	W 2-1	St Louis	WCq	Borja, Peterson
19-05	Trinidad	W 1-0	Torrance	WCq	Caligiuri
26-05	Costa Rica	D 1-1	San Jose	WCq	Kerr
31-05	Costa Rica	L 0-1	Torrance	WCq	
16-06	England	L 0-5	Los Angeles	Fr	
5-02-1986	Canada	D 0-0	Miami	Fr	
7-02	Uruguay	D 1-1	Miami	Fr	Murray
23-05-1987	Canada	L 0-2	St. John's	OGq	
30-05	Canada	W 3-0	St. Louis	OGq	Krumpe 2, Gabarra
8-06	Egypt	L 1-3	Seoul	Fr	Hantak
12-06	South Korea	L 0-1	Pusan	Fr	
16-06	Thailand	W 1-0	Chongju	Fr	Hantak
10-08	Trinidad	W 3-1	Indianapolis	Fr	Hantak 2, Klopas
12-08	El Salvador	D 0-0	Indianapolis	Fr	
5-09	Trinidad	W 4-1	St. Louis	Fr	Goulet 3, Stollmeyer
20-09	Trinidad	W 1-0	Port of Spain	Fr	Perez
18-10	El Salvador	W 4-2	San Salvador	Fr	Perez 2, Goulet, Klopas
10-01-1988	Guatemala	L 0-1	Guatemala City	Fr	

13-01	Guatemala	W 1-0	Guatemala City	Fr	Agoos
14-05	Colombia	L 0-2	Maimi	Fr	
25-05	El Salvador	W 4-1	Indianapolis	Fr	Goulet 2, Davis, OG
1-06	Chile	D 1-1	Stockton	Fr	Eichmann
3-06	Chile	L 1-3	San Diego	Fr	Borja
5-06	Chile	L 0-3	Fresno	Fr	
7-06	Ecuador	L 0-1	Alburquerque	Fr	
10-06	Ecuador	L 0-2	Houston	Fr	
12-06	Ecuador	D 0-0	Fort Worth	Fr	
14-06	Costa Rica	W 1-0	San Antonio	Fr	Ryerson
13-07	Poland	L 0-2	New Britan	Fr	
24-07	Jamaica	D 0-0	Kingston	WCq	
13-08	Jamaica	W 5-1	St. Louis	WCq	Klopas 2, Bliss, Krumpe, Perez
16-04-1989	Costa Rica	L 0-1	San Jose	WCq	
30-04	Costa Rica	W 1-0	St. Louis	WCq	Ramos
13-05	Trinidad	D 1-1	Torrance	WCq	Trittschuh
4-06	Peru	W 3-0	New Jersey	Fr	Murray, Ramos, Bliss
17-06	Guatemala	W 2-1	Connecticut	WCq	Murray, Eichmann
24-06	Colombia	L 0-1	Miami	Fr	
13-08	South Korea	L 1-2	Los Angeles	Fr	Harkes
17-09	El Salvador	W 1-0	Tegucigalpa	WCq	Perez
8-10	Guatemala	D 0-0	Guatemala City	WCq	
5-11	El Salvador	D 0-0	St. Louis	WCq	
14-11	Bermuda	W 2-1	Cocoa Beach	Fr	Eichmann, Doyle
19-11	Trinidad	W 1-0	Port of Spain	WCq	Caligiuri
2-02-1990	Costa Rica	L 0-2	Miami	Fr	
4-02	Colombia	L 1-2	Miami	Fr	Wynalda
13-02	Bermuda	W 1-0	Hamilton	Fr	Sullivan
24-02	Soviet Union	L 1-3	Palo Alto	Fr	Harkes
10-03	Finland	W 2-1	Tampa	Fr	Murray, Caligiuri
20-03	Hungary	L 0-2	Budapest	Fr	
28-03	East Germany	L 2-3	Berlin	Fr	Murray, Vermes
8-04	Iceland	W 4-1	St. Louis	Fr	Wynalda, Murray, Trittschuh
22-04	Colombia	L 0-1	Miami	Fr	
5-05	Malta	W 1-0	Piscataway	Fr	Wynalda
9-05	Poland	W 3-1	Hershey	Fr	Murray, Vermes, Sullivan
30-05	Liechtenstein	W 4-1	Eschen	Fr	Vermes, Balboa, Wynalda, Henderson
2-06	Switzerland	L 1-2	St. Gallen	Fr	Murray
10-06	Czechoslovakia	L 1-5	Florence	WCr1	Caligiuri
14-06	Italy	L 0-1	Rome	WCr1	
19-06	Austria	L 1-2	Florence	WCr1	Murray
28-07	East Germany	L 1-2	Milwaukee	Fr	Eck
15-09	Trinidad	W 3-0	Charlotte	Fr	Vermes, Murray, Eichmann
10-10	Poland	W 3-2	Warsaw	Fr	Murray, Vermes 2
18-11	Trinidad	D 0-0	Port of Spain	Fr	
21-11	Soviet Union	D 0-0	Port of Spain	Fr	
19-12	Portugal	L 0-1	Oporto	Fr	
2-03-1991	Switzerland	L 0-1	Miami	Fr	
21-02	Bermuda	L 0-1	Hamilton	Fr	
12-03	Mexico	D 2-2	Los Angeles	NAC	Washington, Murray
16-03	Canada	W 2-0	Torrance	NAC	Washington, Murray
5-05	Uruguay	W 1-0	Denver	Fr	Vermes
19-05	Argentina	L 0-1	Palo Alto	Fr	
1-06	Rep. Ireland	D 1-1	Foxboro	Fr	Wynalda
29-06	Trinidad	W 2-1	Los Angeles	CCr1	Murray, Balboa
1-07	Guatemala	W 3-0	Los Angeles	CCr1	Murray, Quinn, Wynalda
3-07	Costa Rica	W 3-2	Los Angeles	CCr1	Vermes, Perez, OG
5-07	Mexico	W 2-0	Los Angeles	CCsf	Doyle, Vermes
7-07	Honduras	D 0-0	Los Angeles	CCf	Won 4-3 pens
28-08	Romania	W 2-0	Brasov	Fr	Balboa, Murray
4-09	Turkey	D 1-1	Istanbul	Fr	Klopas
14-09	Jamaica	W 1-0	High Point	Fr	Gjonbalaj
19-10	North Korea	L 1-2	Washington	Fr	Murray
24-11	Costa Rica	D 1-1	Dallas	Fr	Kinnear
25-01-1992	CIS	L 0-1	Miami	Fr	
2-02	CIS	W 2-1	Detroit	Fr	Wynalda, Balboa
12-02	Costa Rica	D 0-0	San Jose	Fr	
18-02	El Salvador	L 0-2	San Salvador	Fr	
26-02	Brazil	L 0-3	Fortaleza	Fr	
11-03	Spain	L 0-2	Valladolid	Fr	
18-03	Morocco	L 1-3	Casablanca	Fr	Perez

Date	Opponent	Result	Venue	Comp	Scorers
4-04	China	W 5-0	San Francisco	Fr	Perez 2, Wynalda 2, Kinnear
29-04	Rep. Ireland	L 1-4	Dublin	Fr	Wynalda
17-05	Scotland	L 0-1	Denver	Fr	
30-05	Rep. Ireland	W 3-1	Washington	Fr	Balboa, Ramos, Harkes
3-06	Portugal	W 1-0	Chicago	Fr	Wegerle
6-06	Italy	D 1-1	Chicago	Fr	Harkes
14-06	Australia	L 0-1	Orlando	Fr	
27-06	Ukraine	D 0-0	Piscataway	Fr	
31-07	Colombia	L 0-1	Los Angeles	Fr	
2-08	Brazil	L 0-1	Los Angeles	Fr	
3-10	Canada	W 2-0	St. John's	Fr	Sorber, Vermes
9-10	Canada	D 0-0	Greensboro	Fr	
15-10	Saudi Arabia	L 0-3	Riyadh	ICr1	
19-10	Côte d'Ivoire	W 5-2	Riyadh	ICr1	Murray 2, Balboa, Jones, Wynalda
30-01-1993	Denmark	D 2-2	Tampa	Fr	Murray, Moore
7-02	Romania	D 1-1	Santa Barbara	Fr	Kinnear
13-02	Russia	L 0-1	Orlando	Fr	
21-02	Russia	D 0-0	San Francisco	Fr	
3-03	Canada	D 2-2	Costa Mesa	Fr	Kinnear, Murray
10-03	Hungary	D 0-0	Nagoya	Fr	
14-03	Japan	L 1-3	Tokyo	Fr	Perez
23-03	El Salvador	D 2-2	San Salvador	Fr	Allnutt, Jones
25-03	Honduras	L 1-4	Tegucigalpa	Fr	Allnutt
9-04	Saudi Arabia	W 2-0	Riyadh	Fr	Moore, Michallik
17-04	Iceland	D 1-1	Costa Mesa	Fr	Vermes
8-05	Colombia	L 1-2	Miami	Fr	Lalas
23-05	Bolivia	D 0-0	Fullerton	Fr	
27-05	Peru	D 0-0	Mission Viejo	Fr	
6-06	Brazil	L 0-2	New Haven	Fr	
9-06	England	W 2-0	Boston	Fr	Dooley, Lalas
13-06	Germany	L 3-4	Chicago	Fr	Dooley 2, Stewart
16-06	Uruguay	L 0-1	Ambato	SCr1	
19-06	Ecuador	L 0-2	Quito	SCr1	
22-06	Venezuela	D 3-3	Quito	SCr1	Henderson, Lalas, Kinnear
10-07	Jamaica	W 1-0	Dallas	CCr1	Wynalda
14-07	Panama	W 2-1	Dallas	CCr1	Wynalda, Dooley
17-07	Honduras	W 1-0	Dallas	CCr1	Lalas
21-07	Costa Rica	W 1-0	Dallas	CCsf	Kooiman
25-07	Mexico	L 0-4	Mexico City	CCf	
31-08	Iceland	W 1-0	Reykjavik	Fr	Stewart
8-09	Norway	L 0-1	Oslo	Fr	
13-10	Mexico	D 1-1	Washington	Fr	Jones
16-10	Ukraine	L 1-2	High Point	Fr	Dooley
23-10	Ukraine	L 0-1	Bethlehem	Fr	
7-11	Jamaica	W 1-0	Fullerton	Fr	Lalas
14-11	Cayman Islands	W 8-1	Mission Viejo	Fr	Kinnear 2, Moore 2, Agoos, Chung 2, Santel
5-12	El Salvador	W 7-0	Los Angeles	Fr	Kinnear 2, Moore 4, Perez
18-12	Germany	L 0-3	San Francisco	Fr	
15-01-1994	Norway	W 2-1	Tampa	Fr	Balboa, Jones
22-01	Switzerland	D 1-1	Fullerton	Fr	OG
29-01	Russia	D 1-1	Seattle	Fr	Lalas
10-02	Denmark	D 0-0	Hong Kong	Fr	
13-02	Romania	L 1-2	Hong Kong	Fr	Balboa
18-02	Bolivia	D 1-1	Miami	Fr	Burns
20-02	Sweden	L 1-3	Miami	Fr	Perez
12-03	South Korea	D 1-1	Fullerton	Fr	Balboa
26-03	Bolivia	D 2-2	Dallas	Fr	Perez 2
16-04	Moldova	D 1-1	Jacksonville	Fr	Sorber
20-04	Moldova	W 3-0	Davidson	Fr	Klopas, Lapper, Reyna
24-04	Iceland	L 1-2	San Diego	Fr	Klopas
30-04	Chile	L 0-1	Alburquerque	Fr	
7-05	Estonia	W 4-0	Fullerton	Fr	Klopas, Reyna, Balboa, Moore
15-05	Armenia	W 1-0	Fullerton	Fr	Klopas
25-05	Saudi Arabia	D 0-0	Piscataway	Fr	
28-05	Greece	D 1-1	New Haven	Fr	Klopas
4-06	Mexico	W 1-0	Los Angeles	Fr	Wegerle
18-06	Switzerland	D 1-1	Detroit	WCr1	Wynalda
22-06	Colombia	W 2-1	Los Angeles	WCr1	OG, Stewart
26-06	Romania	L 0-1	Los Angeles	WCr1	
4-07	Brazil	L 0-1	San Francisco	WCr2	
7-09	England	L 0-2	London	Fr	

19-10	Saudi Arabia	L 1-2	Dhahran	Fr	Klopas
19-11	Trinidad	L 0-1	Port of Spain	Fr	
22-11	Jamaica	W 3-0	Kingston	Fr	Kirovski, Klopas 2
11-12	Honduras	D 1-1	Fullerton	Fr	Kirovski
25-03-1995	Uruguay	D 2-2	Dallas	Fr	Kerr, Stewart
22-04	Belgium	L 0-1	Brussels	Fr	
28-05	Costa Rica	L 1-2	Tampa	Fr	Caligiuri
11-06	Nigeria	W 3-2	Boston	Fr	Harkes, Balboa, Jones.C
18-06	Mexico	W 4-0	Washington	Fr	Wegerle, Dooley, Harkes, Reyna
25-06	Colombia	D 0-0	Piscataway	Fr	
8-07	Chile	W 2-1	Paysandu	SCr1	Wynalda 2
11-07	Bolivia	L 0-1	Paysandu	SCr1	
14-07	Argentina	W 3-0	Paysandu	SCr1	Klopas, Lalas, Wynalda
17-07	Mexico	D 0-0	Paysandu	SCqf	Won 4-1p
20-07	Brazil	L 0-1	Maldonado	SCsf	
22-07	Colombia	L 1-4	Maldonado	SC3p	Moore

CENTRAL AMERICA

Central America has traditionally been the stronghold of CONCACAF. Costa Rica, Guatemala, Honduras and El Salvador are the strongest of the seven nations, although all are very much in the shadow of Mexico. The political turmoil that has characterised the area has not helped either. Civil war has been waged in El Salvador and Nicaragua, but the most famous incident relating to football remains the Fútbol War between El Salvador and Honduras in 1969.

The countries faced each other in the semi-finals of the CONCACAF World Cup qualifying group in June 1969 and rioting followed each of the matches, particularly the second game which El Salvador won to force a play-off. Salvadorean migrant workers were at the centre of the dispute and after their team defeated the Hondurans in the play-off, the tension reached boiling point and the El Salvador armed forces invaded Honduras to protect their nationals from persecution.

Costa Rica is perhaps the best of the Central American nations so it was surprising that 1990 was the first time they had made it to the World Cup finals. During the 1940s, 50s and 60s, they won nine continental titles against one for El Salvador, Guatemala and Panama, and none for Honduras, but somehow never made it to the World Cup. Instead both Honduras and El Salvador qualified before they did, though neither matched Costa Rica's success once there. In Italy the Costa Ricans defeated both Scotland and Sweden to qualify for the second round before going down to Czechoslovakia. El Salvador, on the other hand, lost all three of their games in 1970 and 1982, the latter adventure including a 10-1 thrashing at the hands of Hungary, whilst Honduras' only final appearance in 1982 resulted in two draws, with Spain and Northern Ireland, and a loss to Yugoslavia.

Costa Rica also has a good club structure. A championship was started in 1921, before any of their rivals, in which the top clubs have been Herediano, Liga Deportivo Alajuelense and, since the war, Deportivo Saprissa. The other major clubs in the region are Alianza, Deportivo FAS and Atletico Marte from El Salvador, Comunicaciones in Guatemala and Olimpia in Honduras. Until the CONCACAF Club Championship can develop into an internationally recognised tournament in place of the rather shabby event at present, progress is likely to be limited in all of these countries. Political stability would also be a useful asset, but in an area where football has caused one war already, don't count on it.

UNCAF CUP

1991

PRELIMINARY ROUND

Panama	2-0	0-3	Honduras
Nicaragua	2-3	0-2	El Salvador

FINAL TOURNAMENT

Held in San Jose, Costa Rica, 26th May - 29th 1991

	CR	Ho	Gu	ES	Pl	W	D	L	F	A	Pts
Costa Rica	-	2-0	1-0	7-1	3	3	0	0	10	1	6
Honduras	-	-	0-0	2-1	3	1	1	1	2	3	3
Guatemala	-	-	-	0-0	3	0	2	1	0	1	2
El Salvador	-	-	-	-	3	0	1	2	2	9	1

1992

PRELIMINARY ROUND

Costa Rica	6-0	2-0	Nicaragua

FINAL TOURNAMENT

Held in Tegucigalpa, Honduras from 5th - 9th March 1993

	Ho	CR	Pa	ES	Pl	W	D	L	F	A	Pts
Honduras	-	2-0	2-0	3-0	3	3	0	0	7	0	6
Costa Rica	-	-	2-0	1-0	3	2	0	1	3	2	4
Panama	-	-	-	1-1	3	0	1	2	1	5	1
El Salvador	-	-	-	-	3	0	1	2	1	5	1

Panama qualified for the 1993 Gold Cup on the toss of a coin

BELIZE

Population: 189,000
Area, sq km: 22,965
% in urban areas: 51%
Capital city: Belmopan 3,000
Major Cities: Belize City 49,000, Orange Walk 10,000

Belize National Football Association
PO Box 20
Belmopan
Belize
Tel: + 501 2 30461
Fax: + 501 2 31367

Year of formation	1980
Affiliation to FIFA	1986
Affiliation to CONC	1986
Registered Clubs	80
Registered players	5500
Registered Coaches	20
Registered Referees	55
National Stadium	People's Stadium, Orange Walk 10 000
National colours	Blue/White/Blue

THE RECORD

WORLD CUP

1930-94 Did not enter

COSTA RICA

Population: 3,015,000
Area, sq km: 51,100
% in urban areas: 51%
Capital city: San José 1,040,000

Federación Costarricense de Fútbol
Apartado 670-1000
Calle 40-Ave.Ctl 1
San José
Costa Rica
Tel: + 506 2 221544
Fax: + 506 2 552674
Telex: 3394 dider cr

Year of formation	1921
Affiliation to FIFA	1921
Affiliation to CONC	1962
Registered clubs	431
Registered players	6900
Professional players	500
Registered coaches	28
Registered referees	85
National stadium	Estadio Nacional, San José 30 000
National colours	Red/Blue/White
Reserve colours	White/White/White
Season	March - October

THE RECORD

WORLD CUP

1930-54	Did not enter
1958	QT 2nd round
1962	QT 2nd round
1966	QT 2nd round
1970	QT 1st round
1974	QT 1st round
1978	QT 1st round
1982	QT 1st round
1986	QT 3rd round
1990	QT Qualified - Final tournament/2nd round
1994	QT 2nd round

CCCF AND CONCACAF CHAMPIONSHIP

Winners - 1941, 1946, 1948, 1953, 1955, 1960, 1961, 1963, 1969, 1989

CONCACAF CLUB TOURNAMENTS CHAMPIONS CUP

Winners - Deportivo Saprissa 1993, Liga Deportiva Alajeulense 1986, CS Cartagines 1994

Finalists - Deportivo Saprissa 1978, Liga Deportiva Alajuelense 1992

COSTA RICAN LEAGUE CHAMPIONS

1921	CS Herediano
1922	CS Herediano
1923	CS Cartagines
1924	CS Herediano
1925	CS La Libertad
1926	CS La Libertad
1927	CS Herediano
1928	LD Alajuelense
1929	CS LA Libertad
1930	CS Herediano
1931	CS Herediano
1932	CS Herediano
1933	CS Herediano
1934	CS La Libertad
1935	CS Herediano
1936	CS Cartagines
1937	CS Herediano
1938	Orion FC
1939	LD Alajeulense
1940	CS Cartagines
1941	LD Alajeulense
1942	CS La Libertad
1943	Universidad Nacional
1944	Orion FC
1945	LD Alajeulense
1946	CS La Libertad
1947	CS Herediano
1948	CS Herediano
1949	LD Alajeulense
1950	LD Alajeulense
1951	CS Herediano
1952	Deportivo Saprissa
1953	Deportivo Saprissa
1954	-
1955	CS Herediano
1956	-
1957	CS Herediano
1958	LD Alajeulense
1959	LD Alajeulense
1960	LD Alajeulense
1961	CS Herediano
1962	Deportivo Saprissa
1963	CS Uruguay
1964	Deportivo Saprissa
1965	Deportivo Saprissa
1966	LD Alajeulense
1967	Deportivo Saprissa
1968	Deportivo Saprissa
1969	Deportivo Saprissa
1970	LD Alajeulense
1971	LD Alajeulense
1972	Deportivo Saprissa
1973	Deportivo Saprissa
1974	Deportivo Saprissa
1975	Deportivo Saprissa
1976	Deportivo Saprissa
1977	Deportivo Saprissa
1978	CS Herediano
1979	CS Herediano
1980	LD Alajeulense
1981	CS Herediano
1982	Deportivo Saprissa
1983	LD Alajeulense
1984	LD Alajeulense
1985	CS Herediano
1986	ML Puntarenas
1987	CS Herediano
1988	Deportivo Saprissa
1989	Deportivo Saprissa
1990	-
1991	LD Alajeulense
1992	LD Alajeulense
1993	CS Herediano
1994	Deportivo Saprissa

CLUB DIRECTORY

San José (Pop. - 670,000)

Deportivo Saprissa (1935)
Ricardo Saprissa 40,000 – Maroon/Maroon

LIMÓN (Pop. - 52,000)

Asociación Deportiva Limonense (1961)
Juan Gobán 5,000 – Green with white sash/White

ALAJUELA (Pop. - 34,000)

Liga Deportiva Alajuelense (1919)
Alejandro Morera Soto 15,000 – Black and red stripes/Black

PUNTARENAS (Pop. - 29,000)

Club Municipal Puntarenas (1952)
Lito Pérez 6,000 – Orange/Orange

CARTAGO (Pop. - 28,000)

Asociación Deportiva Cartagines (1906)
Fello Meza 10,000 – Blue with white sleeves/White

HEREDIA (Pop. - 21,000)

Club Sport Herediano (1921)
Eladio Rosabel Cordero 12,000 – Yellow with red sash/Black

SAN ISIDRO DE CORONADO

Club Deportivo Uruguay (1936)
Estadio Labrador – Black with white sash/White

EL SALVADOR

Population: 5,221,000
Area, sq km: 21,041

% in urban areas: 48%
Capital city: San Salvador 459,000

Federación Salvadoreña de Fútbol
Av J.M. Delgado, Col. Escalon
Centro Español, Apartado 1029
San Salvador
El Salvador
Tel: + 503 2237362
Fax: + 503 2986426

Year of formation	1935
Affiliation to FIFA	1938
Affiliation to CONC	1962
Registered clubs	944
Registered players	67 700
Professional players	3000
Registered coaches	14
Registered referees	60
National stadium	Estadio Nacional de Flor Blanca, San Salvador 60 000
National colours	Blue/White/Blue
Reserve colours	White/White/White
Season	January - November

THE RECORD

WORLD CUP

1930-66	Did not enter
1970	QT Qualified - Final tournament/1st round 1974 QT 1st round
1978	QT 2nd round
1982	QT Qualified - Final tournament/1st round
1986	QT 2nd round
1990	QT 3rd round
1994	QT 3rd round

CCCF CHAMPIONSHIP

Winners - 1943

CONCACAF CLUB TOURNAMENTS CHAMPIONS CUP

Winners - Alianza 1967, Aguila 1976 Deportivo FAS 1979
Finalists - Atlético Marte 1981

CUP WINNERS CUP

Winners - Atlético Marte 1991

EL SALVADOR LEAGUE CHAMPIONS

1926	Chinameca SC
1927	Hercules
1928	Hercules
1929	Hercules
1930	Hercules
1931	Hercules
1932	Hercules
1933	Hercules
1934	CD Maya
1935	CD Maya
1936	CD 33
1937	CD 33
1938	CD 33
1939	España
1940	Quequeisque
1940	Quequeisque
1942	Quequeisque
1943	Quequeisque
1944	Quequeisque
1945	Quequeisque
1946	Libertad
1947	Libertad
1948	-
1949	Once Municipal
1950	Dragón
1951	Deportivo FAS
1952	Dragón
1953	Deportivo FAS
1954	Atlético Marte
1955	Atlético Marte
1956	Atlético Marte
1957	Aguila
1958	Aguila
1959	Deportivo FAS
1960	-
1961	Aguila
1962	Deportivo FAS
1963	Deportivo FAS
1964	Aguila
1965	Aguila
1966	Alianza
1967	Alianza
1968	Aguila
1969	Atlético Marte
1970	Atlético Marte
1971	Juventud Olímpica
1972	Aguila
1973	Juventud Olímpica
1974	Platense
1975	Aguila
1976	Aguila
1977	Deportivo FAS
1978	Deportivo FAS
1979	Santìagueño
1980	Atlético Marte
1981	Deportivo FAS
1982	Atlético Marte
1983	Aguila
1984	Deportivo FAS
1985	Atlético Marte
1986	Alianza
1987	Aguila
1988	LA Firpo
1989	Alianza
1990	LA Firpo
1991	LA Firpo
1992	LA Firpo
1993	Alianza

CLUB DIRECTORY

SAN SALVADOR (Pop. - 459,000)

Alianza Fútbol Club (1959)
Estadio Cuscatlán 47,000 – White/White
Previous names - Alianza Intercontinental. Prior to 1959 known as Atlético Constancia

Club Deportivo Atlético Marte (1950)
Flor Blanca 60,000 – Blue/Blue
Previous names - Merger in 1950 of CD Libertad and CD Alacranes

SANTA ANA (Pop. - 212,000)

Club Deportivo FAS (1947)
(Fútbolistas Asociados Santecos)
Oscar Alberto Quiteño – Blue and red halves/Blue
Previous names - Merger in 1947 of Fuerte 22, Olimpic, Mecca and Excelsior

SAN MIGUEL (Pop. - 164,000)

Club Deportivo Aguila (1926)
Juan Francisco 'Cariota' Barraza – Orange with a black hoop/Black

USULUTÁN (Pop. - 32,000)

Club Deportivo Luis Angel Firpo (1923)
Estadio Municipal – White with a red and blue hoop/White

GUATEMALA

Population: 9,197,000
Area, sq km: 108,889
% in urban areas: 38%
Capital: Guatemala City 1,057,000

Federación Nacional de Fútbol de Guatemala C.A.
Palacio de los Deportes
Segundo Nivel, Zona 4
Guatemala Ciudad
Guatemala
Tel: + 502 2 326211
Fax: + 502 2 315745
Telex: 3195 petrogu

Year of formation	1926
Affiliation to FIFA	1933
Affiliation to CONC	1961
Registered clubs	1600
Registered players	78 300
Professional players	220
Registered coaches	77
Registered referees	250
National stadium	Mateo Flores, Guatemala City 50 000
National colours	White and Blue stripes/Blue/White
Reserve colours	White/Blue/White
Season	January - December

THE RECORD

WORLD CUP

1930-54	Did not enter
1958	QT 1st round
1962	QT 1st round
1966	Did not enter
1970	QT 1st round
1974	QT 2nd round
1978	QT 2nd round
1982	QT 1st round
1986	QT 2nd round
1990	QT 3rd round
1994	QT 1st round

CONCACAF CHAMPIONSHIP
Winners - 1967

CONCACAF CLUB TOURNAMENTS CHAMPIONS CUP
Winners - Municipal 1974, Comunicaciones 1978
Finalists - Comunicaciones 1962 1969

CUP WINNERS CUP
Finalists - Aurora 1994

CLUB DIRECTORY

GUATEMALA CITY (Pop. - 1,700,000)

Club Deportivo Municipal (1936)
Mateo Flores 50,000 – Red/Blue

Comunicaciones Fútbol Club (1950)
Mateo Flores 50,000 – Cream/White

Aurora Fútbol Club (1945)
Estadio de Ejercito – Yellow & black stripes/Black

QUETZALTENANGO (Pop. - 88,000)
Club Xelaju Mario Camposeco
Mario Camposeco – Yellow with two black hoops/Black

ESCUINTLA (Pop. - 73,000)
Club Escuintla
Green/White

MAZATENANGO (Pop. - 20,000)
Club Deportivo Suchitepequez
Carlos Salazar – Blue and white diagonal halves/White

RETALHULEU (Pop. - 45,000)
Club Juventud Retalteca
Oscar Monterrosa Izaguirre – Blue & white stripes/White

PUERTO BARRIOS (Pop. - 24,000)
Club Izabal JC
Roy Fearon – White/White

GUATEMALAN LEAGUE CHAMPIONS

1955	Municipal
1956	Comunicaciones
1957	-
1958	Comunicaciones
1959	Aurora
1960	Comunicaciones
1961	-
1962	Xelaju
1963	-
1964	Municipal
1965	Aurora
1966	Municipal
1967	Aurora
1968	Aurora
1969	Comunicaciones
1970	Municipal
1971	Comunicaciones
1972	Comunicaciones
1973	Municipal
1974	-
1975	-
1976	Municipal
1977	-
1978	Comunicaciones
1979	-
1980	Comunicaciones
1981	Comunicaciones
1982	Comunicaciones
1983	Suchitepequez
1984	-
1985	Comunicaciones
1986	Aurora
1987	Comunicaciones
1988	Comunicaciones
1989	Suchitepequez
1990	-
1991	Comunicaciones
1992	Municipal
1993	Aurora
1994	Comunicaciones

HONDURAS

Population: 4,674,000
Area, sq km: 112,088
% in urban areas: 40%
Capital city: Tegucigalpa 551,000

Federación Nacional Autonoma de Fútbol de Honduras
Apartado Postal 827
Costa Oeste del Estadio Nacional
Tegucigalpa D.C.
Honduras
Tel: + 504 311432
Fax: + 504 311428

Year of formation	1935
Affiliation to FIFA	1946
Affiliation to CONC	1961
Registered clubs	1050
Registered players	25 100
Professional players	900
National stadium	Norte e Sur, Tegucigalpa 50 000
National colours	Blue/Blue/Blue
Reserve Colours -	White/White/White
Season	February - December

THE RECORD

WORLD CUP

1930-58	Did not enter
1962	QT 1st round
1966	QT 1st round
1970	QT 2nd round
1974	QT 2nd round
1978	Did not enter
1982	QT Qualified - Final tournament/1st round
1986	QT 3rd round
1990	QT 1st round
1994	QT 3rd round

CONCACAF CLUB TOURNAMENTS CHAMPIONS CUP
Winners - Olimpia 1972 1988
Finalists - Univ. de Honduras 1980, Olimpia 1985

CLUB DIRECTORY

TEGUCIGALPA (Pop. - 604,000)
Club Deportivo Olimpia
Norte e Sur 50,000 – White/White

Club Deportivo Motagua
Norte e Sur 50,000 – Blue/Blue

SAN PEDRO SULA (Pop. - 362,000)
Club Deportivo Marathón
Francisco Morazán 22,000 – Green/White

Real España
Francisco Morazán 22,000 – Yellow/Black

LA CEIBA (Pop. - 68,000)
Club Deportivo VIDA
Las Tapias or Nilmo Edwards – Red/Blue

Club Deportivo Victoria
Las Tapias or Nilmo Edwards – Blue/White

PUERTO CORTÉS (Pop. - 42,000)
Club Platénse
Excelsior – White/White

HONDURAS LEAGUE CHAMPIONS

1965	Platense
1966	Olimpia
1967	Olimpia
1968	Motagua
1969	Olimpia
1970	Motagua
1971	Olimpia
1972	-
1973	Motagua
1974	Real España
1975	Real España
1976	Real España
1977	Olimpia
1978	Motagua
1979	Marathon
1980	Real España
1981	Vida
1982	Olimpia
1983	Vida
1984	Olimpia
1985	Marathon

1986	Olimpia
1987	Olimpia
1988	Real España
1989	Olimpia
1990	Real España
1991	-
1992	Motagua
1993	Olimpia
1994	Real España

NICARAGUA

Population: 3,871,000
Area, sq km: 130,700
% in urban areas: 60%
Capital city: Managua 682,000

Federación Nicaraguense de Fútbol
Instituto Nicaraguense de Deportes
Apartado Postal 976 0 383
Managua
Nicaragua
Tel: + 505 2 664134
Fax: + 505 2 664134

Year of formation	1931
Affiliation to FIFA	1950
Affiliation to CONC	1968
Registered clubs	31
Registered players	1600
Registered referees	14
National stadium	Estadio Nacional, Managua 30 000
National colours	Blue/Blue/Blue
Reserve colours	White/White/White
Season	September - June

THE RECORD

WORLD CUP

1930-90	Did not enter
1994	QT 1st round

CLUB DIRECTORY

MANAGUA (Pop. - 682,000)
America FC - Red/Red

Batista - Blue with yellow hoop/Blue

Juventus FC - Red and white stripes/White

Mint PS - Yellow/Green

MASAYA (Pop. -75,000)
Deportivo Masaya - Green/Green

CHINANDEGA (Pop. - 75,000)
Chinandega FC - White with red sash/Red

DIRIAMBA (Pop. - 19,000)
Diriangen FC - Black and white stripes/White

PANAMA

Population: 2,418,000
Area, sq km: 75,517
% in urban areas: 52%
Capital city: Panama City 411,000
Federación Nacional de Fútbol de Panama
Apartado Postal 6-1811
El Dorado
Panama City
Panama
Tel: + 507 270454
Fax: + 507 270460

Year of formation	1937
Affiliation to FIFA	1938
Affiliation to CONC	1960
Registered clubs	65
Registered players	24 000
Registered coaches	36
Registered referees	73
National stadium	Estadio Revolución, Panama City 22 000
National colours	Red and white Stripes/Blue/Red
Reserve colours	Blue and white Stripes/White/White
Season	September - June

THE RECORD

WORLD CUP

1930-90	Did not enter
1994	QT 1st round

CCCF CHAMPIONSHIP
Winners - 1951

CLUB DIRECTORY

PANAMA CITY (Pop. - 1,116,000)
Alianza Fútbol Club
Artes y Oficios 3,000 – Green with white hoop/White

Independiente Santa Fe
Agustin Sánchez – White with green sash/White

Panama Viejo
Estadio Revolución 22,000 – Yellow with green hoop/Green

Plaza Amador Fútbol Club
Estadio Revolución 22,000 – Blue/Red

Deportivo Seguros La Previsora
Estadio Revolución 22,000 – Red with white sleeves/White

Tauro Fútbol Club
Estadio Pedregal – Black and white stripes/Black

THE CARIBBEAN

The Caribbean is the birthplace of some of the best sportsmen in the world and has a rich tradition in sporting circles. The reason? Cricket. The West Indies cricket team has for decades been the best in the world and even an island as small as Antigua has produced the finest cricketer of recent years in Vivian Richards, whilst Barbados, only marginally bigger, produced perhaps the greatest cricketer of all time, Sir Gary Sobers.

The result is that football is almost non-existent as a sport, especially in the islands that were former British colonies. Jamaica, Barbados, Antigua, Guyana and Trinidad are all major Test cricket locations and so the base is just not there to support anything like a proper football structure capable of making an impact. Cricket is not the only distraction. American influence in the area is marked and so it is not surprising to learn that sports such as baseball are popular in Cuba and Puerto Rico, while other sports such as American football are also popular with television viewers in the region as a whole.

Haiti remain the only Caribbean side to have qualified for the World Cup finals since the war, although Trinidad have come close on two occasions, in 1974 when a dubious refereeing decision cost them the game against Haiti, and in 1990 when a defeat by the United States at home in their final game saw them miss out on the trip to Italy. Cuba qualified in 1938 but did not have to play any games to get there, although they did beat Romania once in France. At national level the only other achievement of note was Haiti's victory in the 1957 championship of the CCCF, but this was in a dreadfully weak field in a tournament held in Curacao.

At club level, Transvaal from Curacao, Defence Force

from Trinidad and Violette and Racing Club from Haiti have all won the CONCACAF Club Championship, but this is not symptomatic of any great strength in the respective leagues, but is more a reflection on the weakness of the tournament as a whole.

The introduction in 1989 of the Shell Caribbean Cup hopefully marked the start of a new era for football in the region. For the first time the major countries got together to play a tournament, and it has been contested annually ever since, except in 1990 when the Musilmeen insurrection in Trinidad halted proceedings. Trinidad and Jamaica have done well, but so too have Martinique, the French dominion which is not even a part of CONCACAF. With the introduction of the planned Caribbean League, football can only get stronger.

SHELL CARIBBEAN CUP

Contested by the national teams of football associations affiliated with the Caribbean Union. In odd-numbered years it also serves as a qualifying competition for the CONCACAF Gold Cup, with both finalists qualifying.

1989

FINAL
Held in Bridgetown, Barbados

Trinidad & Tobago .... 2-1 .... Grenada

1990

Tournament abandoned

1991

FINAL TOURNAMENT
Held in Jamaica from 23rd May - 2nd June 1991

FIRST ROUND
Group 1

	Tr	SL	Ma	DR	Pl	W	D	L	F	A	Pts
Trinidad & Tobago	-	1-2	1-0	7-0	3	2	0	1	9	2	4
St. Lucia	-	-	0-0	0-0	3	1	2	0	2	1	4
Martinique	-	-	-	4-1	3	1	1	1	4	2	3
Dominican Rep	-	-	-	-	3	0	1	2	1	11	1

Group 2

	Ja	Gu	CI	Pl	W	D	L	F	A	Pts
Jamaica	-	6-0	3-2	2	2	0	0	9	2	4
Guyana	-	-	2-1	2	1	0	1	2	7	2
Cayman Islands	-	-	-	2	0	0	2	3	5	0

Cuba withdrew

SEMI-FINALS
Jamaica .... 2-0 .... St. Lucia
Trinidad & Tobago .... 3-1 .... Guyana

3RD PLACE
St. Lucia .... 4-1 .... Guyana

FINAL
Jamaica .... 2-0 .... Trinidad & Tobago

1992

FINAL TOURNAMENT
Held in Trinidad, 17th - 26th June 1992

FIRST ROUND
Group A

	TT	Ma	Su	An	P	W	D	L	F	A	Pts
Trinidad & Tobago	-	2-1	1-0	7-0	3	3	0	0	10	1	6
Martinique	-	-	4-1	4-1	3	2	0	1	9	4	4
Surinam	-	-	-	1-1	3	0	1	2	2	6	1
Antigua	-	-	-	-	3	0	1	2	2	12	1

Group B

	Ja	Cu	Gu	SV	P	W	D	L	F	A	Pts
Jamaica	-	0-0	1-0	2-0	3	2	1	0	3	0	5
Cuba	-	-	2-0	1-0	3	2	1	0	3	0	5
Guadeloupe	-	-	-	1-0	3	1	0	2	1	3	2
St Vincent & the Grenadines	-	-	-	-	3	0	0	3	0	4	0

SEMI-FINALS
Jamaica .... 1-0 .... Martinique
Trinidad & Tobago .... 1-0 .... Cuba

3RD PLACE
Martinique .... 1-1 5-3p .... Cuba

FINAL
Trinidad & Tobago .... 3-1 .... Jamaica

1993

FINAL TOURNAMENT
Held in Jamaica from 21st - 30th May 1993

FIRST ROUND
Group 1

	Ja	SK	PR	SM	Pl	W	D	L	F	A	Pts
Jamaica	-	4-1	1-0	2-0	3	3	0	0	7	1	6
St. Kitts & Nevis	-	-	1-0	2-2	3	1	1	1	4	6	3
Puerto Rico	-	-	-	3-0	3	1	0	2	3	2	2
St. Maarten	-	-	-	-	3	0	1	2	2	7	1

Group 2

	Ma	TT	SV	SL	Pl	W	D	L	F	A	Pts
Martinique	-	3-2	3-0	2-0	3	3	0	0	8	2	6
Trinidad & Tobago	-	-	4-1	1-1	3	1	1	1	7	5	3
St. Vincent	-	-	-	4-1	3	1	0	2	5	8	2
St. Lucia	-	-	-	-	3	0	1	2	2	7	1

SEMI-FINALS
Martinique .... 1-1 4-3p .... St. Kitts & Nevis
Jamaica .... 3-0 .... Trinidad & Tobago

3RD PLACE PLAY-OFF
Trinidad & Tobago .... 3-2 .... St. Kitts & Nevis

FINAL
Martinique .... 0-0 6-5p .... Jamaica

1994

FINAL TOURNAMENT
Held in Trinidad. 7th - 17th April 1994

FIRST ROUND
Group 1

	TT	Gu	Ba	Do	Pl	W	D	L	F	A	Pts
TRINIDAD & TOBAGO	-	0-0	2-0	5-0	3	2	1	0	7	0	7
GUADALOUPE	-	-	2-2	5-0	3	1	2	0	7	2	5
BARBADOS	-	-	-	1-1	3	0	2	1	3	5	2
DOMINICA	-	-	-	-	3	0	1	2	1	11	1

Group 2

	Ma	Su	Ha	Cl	Pl	W	D	L	F	A	Pts
MARTINIQUE	-	2-0	3-0	1-1	3	2	1	0	6	1	7
SURINAM	-	-	1-1	2-0	3	1	1	1	3	3	4
HAITI	-	-	-	3-2	3	1	1	1	4	6	4
CAYMAN ISLANDS	-	-	-	-	3	0	1	2	3	6	1

SEMI-FINALS
Trinidad & Tobago ....3-2 ....Surinam
Martinique ....4-2....................Guadeloupe

3RD PLACE
Guadeloupe....................2-0 ....Surinam

FINAL
Trinidad & Tobago ....7-2....................Martinique

1995

FINAL TOURNAMENT.
Held in Cayman Islands and Jamaica. 19th - 30th July 1995

FIRST ROUND
Group 1

	CI	SV	FG	An	Pl	W	D	L	F	A	Pts
CAYMAN ISLANDS	-	2-2	1-0	2-0	3	2	1	0	5	2	7
ST. VINCENT	-	-	1-3	5-1	3	1	1	1	8	6	4
FRENCH GUIANA	-	-	-	1-2	3	1	0	2	4	4	3
ANTIGUA	-	-	-	-	3	1	0	2	3	8	3

Group 2

	TT	Cu	Ja	SL	Pl	W	D	L	F	A	Pts
TRINIDAD & TOBAGO	-	2-0	0-1	5-0	3	2	0	1	7	1	6
CUBA	-	-	2-1	2-0	3	2	0	1	4	3	6
JAMAICA	-	-	-	2-1	3	2	0	1	4	3	6
ST. LUCIA	-	-	-	-	3	0	0	3	1	9	0

SEMI-FINALS
Trinidad ....9-2 ....Cayman Islands
St Vincent ....3-2 ....Cuba

3RD PLACE
Cuba ....3-0 ....Cayman

FINAL
Trinidad ....5-0 ....St Vincent

ANTIGUA & BARBUDA

Population: 80,600
Area, sq km: 441
% in urban areas: 32%
Capital city: Saint John's 36,000

The Antigua Football Association
PO Box 773
St. John's
Antigua
Tel: + 1 809 4623945
Fax: + 1 809 4622649

Year of formation	1928
Affiliation to FIFA	1970
Affiliation to CONC	1980
Registered clubs	60
Registered players	1200
Registered referees	61
National stadium	Recreation Ground 12 000
National colours	Gold/Black/Black
Reserve colours	White/Gold/Red
Season	August - December

THE RECORD

WORLD CUP

1930-70	Did not enter
1974	QT 1st round
1978	Did not enter
1982	Did not enter
1986	QT 1st round
1990	QT 1st round
1994	QT 1st round

ARUBA

Population: 62,000
Area, sq km: 193
Capital city: Oranjestad 19,000

Arubaanse Voetbal Bond
PO Box 376
Oranjestad
Aruba
Tel: + 297 8 28016
Fax: + 297 8 20624

Year of formation	1932
Affiliation to FIFA	1988
Affiliation to CONC	1988
Registered clubs	50
Registered players	1000
National stadium	Guillermo Trinidad, Oranjestad 10 000
National colours	Yellow/Blue/Yellow
Season	May - November

THE RECORD

WORLD CUP
1930-94 Did not enter

THE BAHAMAS

Population: 253,000
Area, sq km: 13,939
% in urban areas: 59%
Capital city: Nassau 168,000

The Bahamas Football Association
PO Box N 8434
Nassau NP
The Bahamas
Tel: + 1 809 3266895
Fax: + 1 809 3226017

Year of formation	1967
Affiliation to FIFA	1968
Affiliation to CONC	1981
Registered clubs	14
Registered players	950
Registered coaches	6
Registered referees	8
National stadium	Thomas Robinson, Nassau 15,000
National colours	Yellow/Black/Yellow
Reserve colours	Red/White/Red
Season	October - May

THE RECORD

WORLD CUP
1930-94 Did not enter

BARBADOS

Population: 257,000
Area, sq km: 430
% in urban areas: 44%
Capital city: Bridgetown 102,000

Barbados Football Association
PO Box 1362
Bridgetown
Barbados
Tel: + 1 809 4261170
Fax: + 1 809 4380363

Year of formation	1910
Affiliation to FIFA	1968
Affiliation to CONC	1968
Registered clubs	92
Registered players	2200
Registered referees	63
National stadium	National Stadium, Bridgetown 12 000
National colours	Blue/Gold/Blue
Reserve colours	Gold/Blue/Gold
Season	January - May

THE RECORD

WORLD CUP

1930-74	Did not enter
1978	QT 1st round
1982-90	Did not enter
1994	QT pr round

BERMUDA

Population: 59,000
Area, sq km: 54
% in urban areas: 100%
Capital city: Hamilton 1,000

The Bermuda Football Association
PO Box HM 745
Hamilton 5 HM CX
Bermuda
Tel: + 1 809 2952199
Fax: + 1 809 2950773
Telex: 3441 bfa ba

Year of formation	1928
Affiliation to FIFA	1962
Affiliation to CONC	1966
Registered clubs	30
Registered players	2200
Registered coaches	9
Registered referees	39
National stadium	National Stadium, Hamilton 10,000
National colours	Blue/White/White
Reserve colours	Red/White/White
Season	September - April

THE RECORD

WORLD CUP

1930-66	Did not enter
1970	QT 1st round
1974-90	Did not enter
1994	QT 2nd round

CAYMAN ISLANDS

Population: 25,000
Area, sq km: 264
Capital city: George Town 12,000

Cayman Islands Football Association
PO Box 178
George Town - Grand Cayman
Tel: + 1 809 9494733
Fax: + 1 809 9498738

Year of formation	1966
Affiliation to FIFA	1992
Affiliation to CONC	1992
Registered clubs	25
Registered players	875
National stadium	National Stadium, Georgetown 8000
National colours	Red/Blue/White

THE RECORD

WORLD CUP

1930-94	Did not enter

CUBA

Population: 10,603,000
Area, sq km: 110,861
% in urban areas: 72%
Capital city: Havana 2,077,938

Asociacion de Fútbol de Cuba
C/O Comite Olimpico Cubano
Calle 13, #601, Esq C. Vedado
La Habana, ZP 4
Cuba
Tel: + 537 403581
Fax: + 537 409037
Telex: 511332 inder cu

Year of formation	1924
Affiliation to FIFA	1932
Affiliation to CONC	1961
Registered clubs	70
Registered players	15 900
Registered referees	160
National stadium	Juan Abrantes, Havana 18 000
National colours	White/Blue/White
Reserve colours	Red/White/White
Season	July - November

THE RECORD

WORLD CUP

1930	Did not enter
1934	QT 2nd round
1938	QT W-O in group 9 - Final tournament/Quarter-finalists
1950	QT 3rd/3 in group 9
1954-62	Did not enter
1966	QT 1st round
1970	Did not enter
1974	Did not enter
1978	QT 1st round
1982	QT 1st round
1986	Did not enter
1990	QT 1st round
1994	Did not enter

CONCACAF CLUB TOURNAMENTS
CHAMPIONS CUP
Finalists - Piñar del Rio 1989 1990

CLUB DIRECTORY

HAVANA
Ciudad Havana
Red/White

Deportivo Central FAR
Blue & black stripes/Black

Province

PINAR DEL RIO
Pinar del Rio
Green/Black

DOMINICA

Population: 85,000
Area, sq km: 751
Capital city: Roseau 22,000

Dominica Football Association
PO Box 372
Roseau
Dominica
Tel: + 1 809 4492173
Fax: + 1 809 4481111

Year of formation	1970
Affiliation to FIFA	1994
Affiliation to CONC	1994
Registered clubs	30
Registered players	500
National colours	Green/Green/Yellow

THE RECORD

WORLD CUP

1930-94	Did not ente

DOMINICAN REPUBLIC

Population: 7,170,000
Area, sq km: 48,443
% in urban areas: 60%
Capital city: Santo Domingo 1,600,000

Federación Dominicana de Fútbol
Apartado de Correos #1953
Santo Domingo
Dominican Republic
Tel: + 1 809 5426923
Fax: + 1 809 5426923
Telex: 817240

Year of formation	1953

Affiliation to FIFA	1958
Affiliation to CONC	1964
Registered clubs	128
Registered players	12 600
Registered referees	64
National stadium	Olimpico Juan Pablo Duarte, Santo Domingo 30 000
National colours	Blue/White/Red
Reserve colours	White/White/Red
Season	March - December

THE RECORD

WORLD CUP

1930-74	Did not enter
1978	QT 1st round
1982-90	Did not enter
1994	QT pr round

GRENADA

Population: 101,000
Area, sq km: 345
Capital city: St. George's 7,000

Grenada Football Association
2 Hillsborough Street
PO Box 326
St. George's
Grenada
Tel: + 1 809 4401986
Fax: + 1 809 4401986
Telex: 3431 cw bur

Year of formation	1924
Affiliation to FIFA	1976
Affiliation to CONC	1976
Registered clubs	15
Registered players	1700
Registered coaches	9
Registered referees	16
National stadium	Queen's Park, St. George's 8,000
National colours	Green and Yellow Stripes/Red/Green
Reserve colours	Green/Yellow/Red
Season	July - December

THE RECORD

WORLD CUP

1930-78	Did not enter
1982	QT 1st round
1986-94	Did not enter

GUADELOUPE

Population: 410,000
Area, sq km: 230
Capital city: Basse-Terre

Ligue de Football Guadeloupe
Rue de la Ville D'Orly
Guadeloupe
Tel: + 590 829 886
Fax: + 590 830 141

Guadeloupe is not affiliated to FIFA or CONCACAF, but only to the French Federation

National colours	Green/White/Green

THE RECORD

WORLD CUP

1930-94	Did not enter

CLUB DIRECTORY

BASSE-TERRE

Cygne Noir
Green & black stripes/Black

Racing Club
Yellow/Black

MORNE-A-L'EAU

Olympique
Sky blue/Sky blue

Etoile Filante
Red/White

POINT-A-PITRE

Red Star
Green/White

Solidarité Scolaires
Blue/Red

GUYANA

Population: 756,000
Area, sq km: 215,083
% in urban areas: 28%
Capital city: Georgetown 150,000

Guyana Football Association
PO Box 10727
Georgetown
Guyana
Tel: + 592 2 71146
Fax: + 592 2 56676

Year of formation	1902
Affiliation to FIFA	1968
Affiliation to CONC	1969
Registered clubs	34
Registered players	2400
Registered coaches	6
Registered referees	40
National stadium	Cricket Club, Georgetown 15 000
National colours	Green/Green/Yellow
Reserve colours	Yellow/Green/Yellow
Season	March - December

THE RECORD

WORLD CUP

1930-74	Did not enter
1978	QT 1st round
1982	QT 1st round
1986	QT 1st round
1990	QT 1st round
1994	QT pr round

HAITI

Population: 5,862,000
Area, sq km: 27,400
% in urban areas: 27%
Capital city: Port-au-Prince 514,000

Fédération Haitienne de Football
Stade Sylvio Cator
Port-au-Prince
Haiti
Tel: + 509 1 223237
Fax: None

Year of formation	1904
Affiliation to FIFA	1933
Affiliation to CONC	1957
Registered clubs	40
Registered players	8600
Registered referees	41
National stadium	Sylvio Cator 25 000
National colours	Red/Black/Red
Reserve colours	White/Black/Red
Season	November - May

THE RECORD

WORLD CUP

1930	Did not enter
1934	QT 1st round
1938	Did not enter
1950	Did not enter
1954	QT 3rd/3 in group 11
1958-66	Did not enter
1970	QT 3rd round
1974	QT Qualified - Final tournament/1st round
1978	QT 2nd round
1982	QT 2nd round
1986	QT 2nd round
1990	Did not enter
1994	QT pr round

CCCF CHAMPIONSHIP
Winners - 1957

CONCACAF CLUB TOURNAMENTS
CHAMPIONS CUP
Winners - Racing Club 1966, Violette 1984

CLUB DIRECTORY

PORT-AU-PRINCE

Racing Club (1923)
Yellow/Blue

Violette AC (1918)
Green/White

Aigle Noir (1951)
Green/Black

PETION VILLE
Don Bosco (1949)
Yellow/Black

CAP HATIEN
AS Capoise (1930)
Red/White

ST MARC
Tempete (1970)
Blue/White

JAMAICA

Population: 2,391,000
Area, sq km: 10,991
% in urban areas: 51%
Capital city: Kingston 524,000

Jamaica Football Federation
2 Coolwater Avenue
Kingston 19
Jamaica
Tel: + 1 809 9290484
Fax: + 1 809 9290483
Telex: 2224 fedlasco ja

Year of formation	1910
Affiliation to FIFA	1962
Affiliation to CONC	1963
Registered clubs	266
Registered players	9000
Registered referees	122
National stadium	National Stadium, Kingston 40,000
National colours	Green/Black/Green
Reserve colours	Gold/Black/Gold
Season	August - April

THE RECORD

WORLD CUP

1930-62	Did not enter
1966	QT 2nd round
1970	QT 1st round
1974	Did not enter
1978	QT 1st round
1982	Did not enter
1986	Did not enter
1990	QT 2nd round
1994	QT 2nd round

JAMAICAN LEAGUE CHAMPIONS

1974	Santos
1975	Santos
1976	Santos
1977	Santos
1978	Arnett Gardens
1979	-
1980	Santos
1981	Cavalier FC
1982	-
1983	Tivoli Gardens
1984	Boys' Town
1985	JDF
1986	Boys' Town
1987	Seba United
1988	Wadadah
1989	Boys' Town
1990	Reno
1991	Reno
1992	Wadadah
1993	Hazard United
1994	Violet Kickers

JAMAICAN CUP WINNERS

1992	Seba United
1993	Olympic Gardens
1994	Harbour View FC
1995	Seba United

CLUB DIRECTORY

KINGSTON
Cavalier FC
White/Black

Santos
Green & yellow stripes/White

Tivoli Gardens
Orange/Black

Boys Town
Red/Red

MONTEGO BAY
Whadadah
Green/Yellow

Seba United
Red & green stripes/Green

SAVANNAH DEL MAR
Reno
Blue/White

MAY PEN
Hazard United
Blue/Yellow

ST JAMES' COUNTY
Violet Kickers
Blue/Blue

MARTINIQUE

Population: 370,000
Area, sq km: 336
Capital city: Fort de France

Ligue Martiniquaise de Football
2 Avenue St John Perse
BP 365
97204 Fort de France
Martinique

Martinique is not affiliated to FIFA or CONCACAF, but only to the French Federation

THE RECORD

WORLD CUP

1930-94	Did not enter

CLUB DIRECTORY

FORT DE FRANCE
Golden Star
Yellow/Blue

Olympique
Red/White

LE ROBERT
US Robert
Green/White

LE LAMENTIN
Aiglons
Red/Red

LE FRANCOIS
Club Franciscain
Green/Black

NETHERLANDS ANTILLES

Population: 196,000
Area, sq km: 800
% in urban areas: 92%
Capital city: Willemstad 125,000

Nederlands Antiliaanse Voetbal Unie
PO Box 341
Curacao
Netherlands Antilles
Tel: + 599 9 688748
Fax: + 599 9 616740
Telex: 1046 ennia na

Year of formation	1921
Affiliation to FIFA	1932
Affiliation to CONC	1961
Registered clubs	85
Registered players	3900
Professional players	300
Registered coaches	17
Registered referees	35
National stadium	Korsou, Curacao 12 000
National colours	White/White/Red
Reserve colours	Blue/Blue/Red
Season	August - February

THE RECORD

WORLD CUP

1930-54	Did not enter
1958	QT 1st round
1962	QT 2nd round
1966	QT 1st round
1970	QT 1st round
1974	QT 2nd round
1978	QT 1st round
1982	QT 1st round
1986	QT 1st round
1990	QT 2nd round
1994	QT pr round

CONCACAF CLUB CHAMPIONSHIP

Finalists - Jong Colombia 1967 1979

CLUB DIRECTORY

CURACAO

Jong Colombia
Yellow, blue sleeves/Blue

SUBT (Sport Unie Brion Trappers)
Yellow/Yellow

Sithoc
Blue/Blue

Scherpenheuvel
Green/Green

PUERTO RICO

Population: 3,336,000
Area, sq km: 9,104
% in urban areas: 70%
Capital city: San Juan 431,000

Federación Puertorriquena de Fútbol
Coliseo Roberto Clemente
PO Box 4355
Hato Rey, 00919-4355
Puerto Rica
Tel: + 1 809 7642025
Fax: + 1 809 7642025
Telex: 0206 3450296

Year of formation	1940
Affiliation to FIFA	1960
Affiliation to CONC	1962
Registered clubs	175
Registered players	9000
Registered referees	135
National stadium	Sixto Escobar, San Juan 12 000
National colours	Red and White stripes/Blue/Blue
Reserve colours	White/Blue/Red
Season	March - June

THE RECORD

WORLD CUP

1930-70	Did not enter
1974	QT 1st round
1978	Did not enter
1982	Did not enter
1986	QT 1st round
1990	QT 1st round
1994	QT pr round

SAINT LUCIA

Population: 151,000
Area, sq km: 617
% in urban areas: 46%
Capital city: Castries 55,000

St. Lucia National Football Union
PO Box 255
Castries
St. Lucia
Tel: + 1 809 31519
Fax: + 1 809 4524127
Telex: 6394 for aff lc

Year of formation	Unknown
Affiliation to FIFA	1988
Affiliation to CONC	1988
Registered clubs	100
Registered players	880
National stadium	Mindo Philip Park, Castries 5000
National colours	Blue/Black/Blue

THE RECORD

WORLD CUP

1930-94 Did not enter

ST KITTS & NEVIS

Population: 44,000
Area, sq km: 269
Capital city: Basseterre 18,000

St. Kitts & Nevis Amateur Football Association
PO Box 465
Basseterre
St. Kitts
Tel: + 1 809 4652521
Fax: + 1 809 4651042
Telex: 6822 horsfdskb kc

Year of formation	1932
Affiliation to FIFA	1992
Affiliation to CONC	1992
Registered clubs	36
Registered players	600
National stadium	Warner Park 8000
National colours	Black/Black/Gold

THE RECORD

WORLD CUP

1930-94 Did not enter

ST VINCENT & THE GRENADINES

Population: 115,000
Area, sq km: 389
% in urban areas: 25%
Capital city: Kingstown 19,000

St. Vincent and the Grenadines Football Federation
PO Box 1278
Kingstown
St. Vincent
Tel: + 1 809 4571971
Fax: + 1 809 4572970

Founded	
Affiliation to FIFA	1988
Affiliation to CONC	1988
Registered clubs	100
Registered players	700
National colours	Green/Blue/Yellow

THE RECORD

WORLD CUP

1930-90	Did not enter
1994	QT 2nd round

SURINAM

Population: 411,000
Area, sq km: 163,820
% in urban areas: 65%
Capital city: Paramaribo 67,000

Surinaamse Voetbal Bond
Cultuuruinlaan 7
PO Box 1223
Paramaribo
Surinam
Tel: + 597 473112
Fax: + 597 479718

Year of formation	1920
Affiliation to FIFA	1929
Affiliation to CONC	1961
Registered clubs	460
Registered players	9900
Registered coaches	56

Registered referees	218
National stadium	Surinam Stadion, Paramaribo 21 000
National colours	Red/White/White
Reserve colours	Green/Green/Green
Season	March - December

THE RECORD

WORLD CUP

1930-58	Did not enter
1962	QT 1st round
1966	QT 1st round
1970	QT 1st round
1974	QT 1st round
1978	QT 2nd round
1982	QT 1st round
1986	QT 2nd round
1990	Did not enter
1994	QT 1st round

CONCACAF CLUB TOURNAMENTS
CHAMPIONS CUP

Winners - Transvaal 1973 1981
Finalists - Transvaal 1974 1975 1986, Robin Hood 1972 1976 1977 1982 1983

SURINAM LEAGUE CHAMPIONS

1950	Transvaal
1951	Transvaal
1952	Voorwaarts
1953	Robin Hood
1954	Robin Hood
1955	Robin Hood
1956	Robin Hood
1957	Voorwaarts
1958	-
1959	Robin Hood
1960	-
1961	Robin Hood
1962	Transvaal
1963	Leo Victor
1964	Robin Hood
1965	Transvaal
1966	Transvaal
1967	Transvaal
1968	Transvaal
1969	Transvaal
1970	Transvaal
1971	Robin Hood
1972	-
1973	Transvaal
1974	Transvaal
1975	Robin Hood
1976	Robin Hood
1977	Voorwaarts
1978	Leo Victor
1979	Robin Hood
1980	Robin Hood
1981	Robin Hood
1982	Leo Victor
1983	Robin Hood
1984	Robin Hood
1985	Robin Hood
1986	Robin Hood
1987	Robin Hood
1988	Robin Hood
1989	Robin Hood
1990	Transvaal
1991	Transvaal
1992	Robin Hood
1993	Robin Hood
1994	Robin Hood

CLUB DIRECTORY

PARAMARIBO (Pop. - 67,000)
Robin Hood (1945)
Green/Red

Leo Victor SV (1934)
Orange/Orange

SV Transvaal (1921)
Green and white stripes/Green

TRINIDAD AND TOBAGO

Population: 1,233,000
Area, sq km: 5,128
% in urban areas: 51%
Capital city: Port of Spain 58,000

Trinidad and Tobago Football Association
Cor. Duke & Scott - Bushe Street
PO Box 400
Port of Spain
Trinidad
Tel: + 1 809 6252880
Fax: + 1 809 6277661

Year of formation	1906
Affiliation to FIFA	1963
Affiliation to CONC	1964
Registered clubs	124
Registered players	5600
Registered coaches	114
Registered referees	296
National stadium	Queen's Park Oval, Port of Spain 25 000
National colours	Red/Black/Red
Reserve colours	Black/Red/Black
Season	January - December

THE RECORD

WORLD CUP

1930-62	Did not enter
1966	QT 1st round
1970	QT 1st round
1974	QT 2nd round
1978	QT 1st round
1982	QT 1st round
1986	QT 2nd round
1990	QT 3rd round
1994	QT 1st round

CONCACAF CLUB TOURNAMENTS
CHAMPIONS CUP

Winners - Defence Force 1978 1985
Finalists - Defence Force 1987 1988, Police FC 1991

CLUB DIRECTORY

PORT OF SPAIN
Trintoc
Red & white stripes/Black

Superstar Rangers
Red/Red

ECM Motown
Yellow & blue halves/Blue

Malvern United
White/Maroon

CHAGUARAMAS
Defence Force
Gold/Blue

ST JAMES
Police FC
Blue/Blue

MAYARO
Mayaro United
Blue/White

SAN FRANCOIS
San Francois National
Maroon/White

ASIA

Considering that Asia contains over half of the world's population, it has made a surprisingly feeble impact on football at the world level. Within Asia itself, however, the game thrives, with a multitude of tournaments and events. Some countries are more keen than others; China and India, the biggest two, who between them account for 2 billion of the world's 5 billion people, have shown little interest, whilst the Middle East, sustained by its large oil revenues, has taken to the game in a big way.

Football is largely a post-war phenomenon and has had to fight off competition from other sports. Cricket and hockey remain the passions of the Indian sub-continent, whilst American influence post-1945, especially in the Far East, has resulted in the widespread popularity of baseball, most notably in Japan, Korea, Taiwan and the Philippines.

Due to the weakness of club football in all but a few countries, the national sides are often the focus of the game, and there are plenty of tournaments to occupy their time. The two main ones are the Asian Cup, started in 1956, and the football tournament of the Asian Games, first played in 1951. There is also a vast array of non-AFC sponsored events, the most notable of which are the Merdeka Cup, organised by the FA of Malaysia since 1957, and the President's Cup, held in South Korea since 1971.

The first international match on Asian soil took place in February 1913 in Manila. As part of the Far Eastern Games, the Philippines challenged China to a match which they won 2-1. Two years later in Shanghai a second game was played, which China this time won. Japan then joined in for the third Games in Tokyo but were beaten so heavily by both China and the Philippines that they did not enter the fourth tournament. From the 1921 Games in Shanghai to the final edition in 1934, all three countries entered, but on only one occasion, in 1930 when Japan shared the title with them, did China not emerge as outright winners.

Football was played elsewhere in Asia at this time as both English and French colonists introduced the game. India, for example, has a national football federation dating from 1937, and a league in Calcutta dating from 1898, before even most Europeans had organised one. Others too had some semblance of organised football and by 1940 seventeen countries had a national football association. The game, however, remained marginalised and small-scale throughout the continent, and was mainly played by the numerous foreigners resident.

In 1951 the first real progress was made when India organised the first Asian Games. The football tournament was a big hit and at the next Games three years later the Asian Football Confederation was formed. Delegates travelling with Afghanistan, Burma, Hong Kong, India, Indonesia, Japan, the Republic of Korea, Malaysia, Pakistan, the Philippines, Singapore, Taiwan and the Republic of Vietnam put in place an organisation that was to play a key role in the development of the game on the continent.

The first task the AFC undertook was to organise a championship of their own. Unlike the football tournament of the Asian Games, the Asian Cup, as it was called, was open to both amateurs and professionals, though in reality this has never been an issue given the tiny number of professional Asian footballers. Also unlike the Asian Games, qualifying groups were organised, on a geographical basis, to produce finalists who would play in a designated country. The pattern was set for future years. With both the Asian Cup and the football tournament of the Asian Games occurring every four years, Asia in effect had a continental championship every two years.

The overall level of the game in Asia does continue to lag behind the rest of the world, however, a fact recognised by FIFA when it awarded two extra places to Africa for the 1998 World Cup but only only definite extra place to Asia. According to one commentator, the problems can be attributed to 'finance, diet, religious customs, political infighting, corruption and administrative incompetence' - but then many of these problems exist elsewhere in the world.

Apart from the Asian Cup and the football tournament of the Asian Games, there are many tournaments catering for the national sides of the region. The dubious 'A' grade status given to internationals in some of these minor events has led to much debate as to the true number of 'international' matches played by Asian countries, and especially the number of caps won by some of the leading players. It is common practice for countries to play an Olympic team or an under-21 team without making this clear, and furthermore, many European opponents are listed as representing their country when in fact they are simply club sides on tour!

The Merdeka Cup is the longest running of all these tournaments. First played in 1957, for many years it was an annual event in the fixture lists of countries from south-east Asia. Held in the Malaysian capital Kuala Lumpur, and occasionally in Ipoh, as part of the country's independence celebrations, it was instrumental in the development of football in Asia as it provided an ideal, annual opportunity for courses on coaching, refereeing and so on. Its importance has been diminished since the 1980s due to the proliferation of other tournaments, and many of the contestants are no more than average European club sides. In terms of prestige it now lags behind the President's (now Korea) Cup held in South Korea. As one of the major football and economic powers in the region, Korea has been able to maintain a high standard of entry in its competition.

The late 1960s and early 1970s saw the initial burst of new tournaments following in the footsteps of the Merdeka. In 1968 the King's Cup, held annually in Thailand, was introduced, followed in 1970 by the Jakarta

Anniversary Tournament. South Vietnam also held an annual competition, but the real growth occurred in the 1980s. The Jawaharal Nehru Gold Cup in India made its first appearance in 1982; in the first few years it fielded the best sides any Asian tournament has managed to assemble to date. But China, Pakistan, Bangladesh, Singapore and even Brunei and Nepal have all got in on the act, and the idea of staging international events became so devalued that in 1988 the AFC decreed that they could be staged only every two years. Unfortunately this has done little to revive a flagging concept.

In addition to all these events there are three regional competitions of some import, the Arabian Gulf Tournament, whose entrants include Bahrain, Iraq, Kuwait, Oman, Qatar, Saudi Arabia and the United Arab Emirates, and the football tournaments of the South Asian Federation Games and the South East Asian Games. The first involves Bangladesh, Bhutan, India, Maldives, Nepal, Pakistan and Sri Lanka, and is held every second year as part of a bigger tournament. The same is also true for the South East Asian Games whose participants include Brunei, Indonesia, Malaysia, Myanmar, Philippines, Singapore, Vietnam, Laos, Kampuchea and Thailand.

Economically, Asia is a growth region, and the countries on the Pacific Rim are developing into one of the world's major economic power blocs. Money is starting to filter down to the game, and in 2002 either Japan or South Korea will host the World Cup. Both now have strong professional leagues, and the growth of the game in Japan has been particularly impressive, with a host of South American and European stars appearing in the J-League. It is somewhat reminiscent of the NASL in the United States in the 1970s, but the J-League looks on much firmer ground.

Other countries look set to follow the lead set by the Japanese and the Koreans. There is huge potential for football in both China and India, whilst the addition of five ex-Soviet republics to the AFC in 1994 will inevitably strengthen the Asian game. Indeed, Uzbekistan won the 1994 Asian Games football tournament, and Neftchi Fergana, the Uzbek champions, were only a penalty shoot-out away from the 1994 Asian Champions Cup final.

THE ASIAN GOVERNING BODY

Asian Football Confederation
Wisma Olympic Council of Malaysia
1st Jalan Hang Jebat
50150 Kuala Lumpur
Malaysia
Tel: + 60 3 2384860
Fax: + 60 3 2384862

Year of formation - 1954

MEMBERS - 41
Afghanistan – Bahrain – Bangladesh – Brunei – China – Chinese Taipei – Hong Kong – India – Indonesia – Iran – Iraq – Japan – Jordan – North Korea – South Korea – Kampuchea – Kazakhstan – Kuwait – Kyrgyzstan – Laos – Lebanon – Macao – Malaysia – Maldives – Myanmar – Nepal – Oman – Pakistan – Philippines – Qatar – Saudi Arabia – Singapore – Sri Lanka – Syria – Tajikstan – Thailand – Turkmenistan – United Arab Emirates – Uzbekistan – Vietnam – Yemen

ASSOCIATE MEMBERS - 2
Bhutan – Guam

NON MEMBERS - 1
Mongolia

Presidents of the AFC

Man Kam-Lo, Hong Kong	1954
Kwok Chan, Hong Kong	1954-56
S.T. Loney, Hong Kong	1956-57
N.C. Chan, Hong Kong	1957-58
Tunku Abdul Rahman Putra Al-Haj, Malaysia	1958-77
Kamiz Atabi, Iran	1977-78
Tan Sri Haji Hamzah, Malaysia	1977-94
Sultan Haji Ahmad Shah	1994-

General Secretaries of the AFC

Lee Wai-Tong, Hong Kong	1954-65
Koe Ewe-Teik, Malaysia	1965-74
Dato Teoh Chye Hin, Malaysia	1974-78
Peter Velappan, Malaysia	1978-

ASIAN CUP

1956	South Korea	2-1 *	Israel
1960	South Korea	3-0 *	Israel
1964	Israel	2-0 *	India
1968	Iran	3-1 *	Burma
1972	Iran	2-1	South Korea
1976	Iran	1-0	Kuwait
1980	Kuwait	3-0	South Korea
1984	Saudi Arabia	2-0	China
1988	Saudi Arabia	0-0 4-3p	South Korea
1992	Japan	1-0	Saudi Arabia

* As the tournament was decided on a league basis, technically there was no final tie. The matches listed are those between the first and second placed teams

	Country	G	S	B	Finals	S-Finals
1	Iran	3	-	2	2	5
2	South Korea	2	3	1	3	3
3	Saudi Arabia	2	1	-	3	3
4	Israel	1	2	1	-	-
5	Kuwait	1	1	1	2	3
6	Japan	1	-	-	1	1
7	China	-	1	2	1	4
8	Myanmar (Burma)	-	1	-	-	-
	India	-	1	-	-	-
10	Hong Kong	-	-	1	-	-
	Taiwan	-	-	1	-	-
	Thailand	-	-	1	-	1
13	North Korea	-	-	-	-	1
	Iraq	-	-	-	-	1
	Cambodia	-	-	-	-	1
	United Arab Emirates	-	-	-	-	1

The Asian Cup was introduced by the Asian Football Confederation in 1956 as a championship for its national sides. Hong Kong was awarded the staging of the first tournament, given its pioneering role in founding the AFC. The hosts were given a bye and so, effectively, were the Israelis as both Pakistan and Afghanistan refused to play them; the situation of Israel, along with that of Taiwan, would become the AFC's most pressing problem.

The finals were contested on a league basis and the six matches in the Government Stadium were very well attended by an enthusiastic Hong Kong public. The home side opened the tournament with a game against Israel which they were unlucky to lose, but Israel were generally disappointing and much more was expected of them. In the crucial game against South Korea they were 2-0 down before they started to test the Koreans, but by then it was too late.

The South Koreans have always been the strongest team in Asia along with Iran, and until the 1980 edition these two countries dominated the Asian Cup. The Koreans won the first two tournaments, the second of which was at home in 1960. The number of entrants increased from seven to eleven, but the final tournament remained in the same format until 1972. Then, as the number of entrants continued to grow, the league system was replaced with a combination of league and knock-out, and it now consists of eight teams divided into two groups of four, from which four teams qualify for the semi-finals.

The crucial game of the 1960 tournament was again the South Korea-Israel encounter. In an example of how popular the game was becoming, the match, played at Seoul's Hyochang Park Stadium, witnessed chaotic scenes. Boisterous fans broke down gates and overran the police to gain access to the stadium, which was overlooked by a hill that effectively doubled its capacity to 40,000. The Korean Prime Minister, attending the game as guest of honour, was even forced to leave during the first half because he could not see! Israel, who were still regarded as the strongest side in Asia, could not resist the Koreans who ran out 3-0 winners.

The third Asian Cup was the poorest tournament of the first three. Though played in front of big crowds in Haifa, Jerusalem, Jaffa and Ramat Gan, the standard of football was certainly not as high as it had been in Seoul four years previously. Sir Stanley Rous, attending the tournament on FIFA's behalf, also commented on the relatively poor level of sportsmanship shown by the teams. In purely practical terms, the choice of Israel as the venue was not a wise one, coming hard on the heels of the political furore at the Asian Games in Djakarta.

That the Israelis won was partly due to the fact that the defending champions, South Korea, did not send their strongest team, instead keeping it at home for an Olympic qualifying match against South Vietnam in Seoul. The decisive game of the tournament was played early on between India and Israel, but if the Koreans had beaten Israel by three clear goals in the final match before 40,000 spectators in Ramat Gan, they would have won the title for the third time in succession. Instead, Israel won 2-1 to take the title and the Koreans had to settle for third place.

The 1960s saw the rise of Iran, who succeeded in achieving what the South Koreans had failed to do as they won three Asian Cups in a row, in 1968, 1972 and 1976. In addition to this, the Iranians appeared in the final of the 1966 Asian Games and won the gold medal in 1974. To crown over a decade of success they made the journey to Argentina for the 1978 World Cup, before the fall of the Shah the following year brought to a temporary end their period of dominance. Their Asian Cup success was remarkable in that from 1968 to 1976 they won every single match they played in the competition. Even since then their record has been good, and in the three tournaments played they have reached the semi-finals on each occasion. In the late 1960s Burma (now Myanmar) were on the verge of challenging the supremacy of Iran and Korea, winning the Asian Games twice and finishing runners-up to Iran in the 1968 Asian Cup. However, the military regime then clamped down on contacts with the outside world, and the country has been in isolation ever since.

The 1970s saw a major shift begin to take place in the balance of power in Asia, as petro-dollars prompted the emergence of the Arab nations of the Middle East. The Gulf states were soon spending massive amounts of money on football facilities and coaches, and by the end of the decade the results were beginning to show. Kuwait reached the 1976 Asian Cup final and in 1980 they won the title. Two years later in the Asian Games, they reached their third final before losing to neighbours Iraq.

Saudi Arabia were also becoming a force and in both 1984 and 1988 they confirmed their supremacy by winning the Asian Cup. Oil revenues were the telling factor - of the five Asian countries who have qualified for the World Cup since 1982, four have been oil-rich Gulf states: Saudi, Kuwait, Iraq and the United Arab Emirates. Only South Korea, who have continued to be a strong force throughout the years, have managed to break that monopoly.

In the future, China will undoubtedly emerge as one of the strongest forces on the continent, if not the world; sheer weight of numbers indicates that this is likely to be the case. After years of isolation due to the presence of Taiwan in the AFC, the Chinese joined that body in 1974 and then FIFA in 1979. Those who expected them to make an immediate impact were disappointed. In three attempts China have failed to qualify for the World Cup, and although they have reached three semi-finals in the Asian Cup, the title still eludes them. As coaching methods become more widespread and more experience is gained, however, they are sure to pose a threat in the future.

1956

I. EDITION

QUALIFYING COMPETITION

Group I

Israel qualified after Afghanistan and Pakistan withdrew

Group 2

	SK	Ta	Ph	Pl	W	D	L	F	A	Pts
South Korea	-	2-0	3-0	4	4	0	0	9	1	8
Taiwan	1-2			4						
Philippines	0-2			4						

Group 3

	SV	Ma	Ca	Pl	W	D	L	F	A	Pts
South Vietnam	-	3-3		2						
Malaysia	-	-	9-2	2	1	1	0	12	5	3
Cambodia	-	-	-	2						

Hong Kong qualified as hosts

FINAL TOURNAMENT. HONG KONG. 1ST - 15TH SEPTEMBER 1956

	SK	Is	HK	SV	Pl	W	D	L	F	A	Pts
South Korea	-	2-1	2-2	5-3	3	2	1	0	9	6	5
Israel	-	-	3-2	2-1	3	2	0	1	6	5	4
Hong Kong	-	-	-	2-2	3	0	2	1	6	7	2
South Vietnam	-	-	-	-	3	0	1	2	6	9	1

Deciding game.Government Stadium, Hong Kong, 8-09-1956, 25,000

SOUTH KOREA 2 (Woo Sang-Koon 53, Soung Rak-woon 65)

ISRAEL 1 (Stelmach 71)

South Korea - Ham Hung-chul - Chai Tai-sung, Park Jai-sung - Son Myong-sup, Kim Jin-woo, Kim Chi-sung - Choi Chung-min, Soung Rak-woon, Kim Yung-Jin, Woo Sang-koon, Kim Dong-Keun

Israel - Hodorov - Zliberstein, Kramer - Chaldi, Schneur, Rabinovitz - Glazer, Stelmach, Kaufman, Rosenbaum, Mirimovitz

II. EDITION

QUALIFYING COMPETITION

Group 1

Tournament in Calcutta and Cochin

	Is	Ir	Pa	In	Pl	W	D	L	F	A	Pts
Israel	-	0-3	2-0	3-1	6	3	2	1	10	8	8
Iran	1-1		4-1	2-1	6						
Pakistan	2-2		1-0		6						
India	1-2				6						

Group 2

Tournament in Singapore

	SV	Ma	Si	Pl	W	D	L	F	A	Pts
South Vietnam	-	1-0	4-1	2	2	0	0	5	1	4
Malaysia	-	-	5-2	2	1	0	1	5	3	2
Singapore	-	-	-	2	0	0	2	3	9	0

Group 3

Tournament in Manilla

Taiwan qualified

South Korea qualified as hosts

FINAL TOURNAMENT. SOUTH KOREA. 14TH - 23RD OCTOBER 1960

	SK	Is	Ta	SV	Pl	W	D	L	F	A	Pts
South Korea	-	3-0	1-0	5-1	3	3	0	0	9	1	6
Israel	-	-	1-0	5-1	3	2	0	1	6	4	4
Taiwan	-	-	-	3-1	3	1	0	2	3	3	2
South Vietnam	-	-	-	-	3	0	0	3	3	13	0

Deciding game. Hyochang Park, Seoul, 17-10-1960, 20,000

SOUTH KOREA 3

ISRAEL 0

Israel - Chodorov - Benvenisti, Mosseisko - Amor, Lefkovitch, Tisch - Nahari, Stelmach, Rafi Levy, Menczell, Glazer

1964

III. EDITION

QUALIFYING COMPETITION

Group 1

India

Group 2

Hong Kong

Group 3

South Korea

Israel qualified as hosts

FINAL TOURNAMENT. ISRAEL. 26TH MAY - 3RD JUNE 1964

	Is	In	SK	HK	Pl	W	D	L	F	A	Pts
Israel	-	2-0	2-1	1-0	3	3	0	0	5	1	6
India	-	-	2-0	3-1	3	2	0	1	5	3	4
South Korea	-	-	-	1-0	3	1	0	2	2	4	2
Hong Kong	-	-	-	-	3	0	0	3	1	5	0

Deciding game. Bloomfield Jaffa, 29-05-64, 20,000

ISRAEL 2 (Spiegler 27, Aharoni 77)

INDIA 0

Israel - Visoker - Primo, Leon - Tisch, Katzav, Bacher - Aharoni, Stelmach, Levi.S, Spiegler, Kalish

India - Thangaraj - Sekhar, Ghosh - Franco, Singh.J, Sinha - Singh.I, Kahn, Appalaraju, Goswami, Arumainaygam

1968

IV. EDITION

QUALIFYING COMPETITION

Group 1

Tourament in Burma

	Bu	Ca	Pa	In	Pl	W	D	L	F	A	Pts
Burma	-	1-0	2-0	2-0	3	3	0	0	5	0	6
Cambodia	-	-	1-0	3-1	3	2	0	1	4	2	4
Pakistan	-	-	-	1-1	3	0	1	2	1	4	1
India	-	-	-	-	3	0	1	2	2	6	1

Group 2

Tournament in Hong Kong

	HK	Th	SV	Ma	Si	Pl	W	D	L	F	A	Pts
Hong Kong	-	2-0	2-0	3-1	2-0	4	4	0	0	9	1	8
Thailand	-	-	0-1	1-0	4-1	4	2	0	2	5	4	4
South Vietnam	-	-	-	0-2	3-0	4	2	0	2	4	4	4
Malaysia	-	-	-	-	1-1	4	1	1	2	4	5	3
Singapore	-	-	-	-	-	4	0	1	3	2	10	1

Group 3

Tournament in Taipei

	Ta	Ja	SK	In	Ph	Pl	W	D	L	F	A	Pts
Taiwan	-	2-2	1-0	3-2	9-0	4	3	1	0	15	4	7
Japan	-	-	2-1	2-1	2-0	4	3	1	0	8	4	7
South Korea	-	-	-	1-1	7-0	4	1	1	2	9	4	3
Indonesia	-	-	-	-	6-0	4	1	1	2	10	6	3
Philippines	-	-	-	-	-	4	0	0	4	0	24	0

Iran qualified as hosts, **Israel** as holders

FINAL TOURNAMENT. IRAN. 10TH - 19TH MAY 1968

	Ir	Bu	Is	Ta	HK	Pl	W	D	L	F	A	Pts
Iran	-	3-1	2-1	4-0	2-0	4	4	0	0	11	2	8
Burma	-	-	1-0	1-1	2-0	4	2	1	1	5	4	5
Israel	-	-	-	4-1	6-1	4	2	0	2	11	5	4
Taiwan	-	-	-	-	1-1	4	0	2	2	3	10	2
Hong Kong	-	-	-	-	-	4	0	1	3	2	11	1

Deciding game. Amjadieh, Tehran, 16-05-1968, 30,000
IRAN 3 (Kalani 2, Bahzadi)
BURMA 1 (Aung Khin)

1972

V. EDITION

QUALIFYING COMPETITION

Group 1
Iraq

Group 2
Kuwait

Group 3
Cambodia

Group 4
South Korea

Thailand qualified as hosts, **Iran** as holders

FINAL TOURNAMENT. THAILAND. 7TH - 19TH MAY 1972

PRELIMINARY GAMES
South Korea .... 0-0 .... Iraq
Iran .... 2-0 .... Cambodia
Kuwait .... 2-0 .... Thailand

FIRST ROUND

Group 1

	Ir	Th	Iq	Pl	W	D	L	F	A	Pts
Iran	-	3-2	3-0	2	2	0	0	6	2	4
Thailand	-	-	1-1	2	0	1	1	3	4	1
Iraq	-	-	-	2	0	1	1	1	4	1

Group 2

	SK	Ca	Ku	Pl	W	D	L	F	A	Pts
South Korea	-	4-1	1-2	2	1	0	1	5	3	2
Cambodia	-	-	4-0	2	1	0	1	5	4	2
Kuwait	-	-	-	2	1	0	1	2	5	2

SEMI-FINALS
Iran .... 2-1 .... Cambodia
South Korea .... 1-1 2-1p .... Thailand

3RD PLACE
Thailand .... 2-2 5-3p .... Cambodia

FINAL
Suphachalasai, Bangkok, 19-05-1972, 8,000
IRAN 2 (Jabary 48, Khalani 107)
SOUTH KOREA 1 (Lee Whae-taek 65)

1976

VI. EDITION

QUALIFYING COMPETITION

Group 1
Kuwait and **South Yemen**. Bahrain, Lebanon, Pakistan and Syria withdrew

Group 2
Tournament in Baghdad

	Iq	SA	Qa	Af	Pl	W	D	L	F	A	Pts
Iraq	-	1-1	1-0	3-1	6	5	1	0	14	3	11
Saudi Arabia	1-2	-	2-1	2-0	6	3	1	2	12	5	7
Qatar	0-3	1-0	-	2-1	6	2	1	3	5	8	5
Afghanistan	0-4	0-6	1-1	-	6	0	1	5	3	18	1

Group 3
Tournament in Bangkok

	Ma	Th	SK	In	SV	Pl	W	D	L	F	A	Pts
Malaysia	-	1-0	2-1	0-0	3-0	4	3	1	0	6	1	7
Thailand	-	-	1-0	3-1	4-0	4	3	0	1	8	2	6
South Korea	-	-	-	1-0	1-0	4	2	0	2	3	3	4
Indonesia	-	-	-	-	2-1	4	1	1	2	3	5	3
South Vietnam	-	-	-	-	-	4	0	0	4	1	10	0

Group 4
Tournament in Hong Kong
First round

	Ch	HK	NK	Ja	Si	Br	Pl	W	D	L	F	A	Pts
China	-	1-0	1-0	-	-	10-1	3	3	0	0	12	1	6
Hong Kong	-	-	-	0-0*	-	3-0	3	2	0	1	3	1	4
North Korea	-	-	-	1-0	1-0	-	3	2	0	1	2	1	4
Japan	-	-	-	-	2-1	-	3	1	0	2	2	2	2
Singapore	-	-	-	-	-	6-0	3	1	0	2	7	3	2
Brunei	-	-	-	-	-	-	3	0	0	3	1	19	0

* Hong Kong won 4-3 on penalties

Semi-finals
China .... 2-1 .... Japan
North Korea .... 3-3 11-10p .... Hong Kong

FINAL
North Korea .... 2-0 .... **China**

Iran qualified as hosts and holders

FINAL TOURNAMENT. IRAN. 3RD - 13TH JUNE 1976

North Korea, Saudi Arabia and Thailand withdrew

FIRST ROUND

Group 1

	Ku	Ch	Ma	Pl	W	D	L	F	A	Pts
Kuwait	-	1-0	2-0	2	2	0	0	3	0	4
China	-	-	1-1	2	0	1	1	1	2	1
Malaysia	-	-	-	2	0	1	1	1	3	1

Group 2

	Ir	Iq	SY	Pl	W	D	L	F	A	Pts
Iran	-	2-0	8-0	2	2	0	0	10	0	4
Iraq	-	-	1-0	2	1	0	1	1	2	2
South Yemen	-	-	-	2	0	0	2	0	9	0

SEMI-FINAL
Iran .... 2-0 .... China
Kuwait .... 3-2 .... Iraq

3RD PLACE
China .... 1-0 .... Iraq

FINAL

Azadi, Tehran, 13-06-1976

IRAN 1

KUWAIT 0

1980

VII. EDITION

QUALIFYING COMPETITION

Group 1

Tournament in Abu Dhabi

Final placings:

ARAB EMIRATES

SYRIA

BAHRAIN

LEBANON

Group 2

Tournament in Dacca

	Qa	Ba	Af	Pl	W	D	L	F	A	Pts
QATAR	-	3-1	3-0	4	3	1	0	10	2	7
BANGLADESH	1-1	-	3-2	4	1	2	1	7	8	4
Afghanistan	0-3	2-2	-	4	0	3	1	4	11	1

Group 3

Tournament in Bangkok

Preliminary Games

Thailand .... 3-1 .... Indonesia

Malaysia .... 3-1 .... Sri Lanka

North Korea .... 3-0 .... Hong Kong

Group 1

	Ma	NK	In	Pl	W	D	L	F	A	Pts
MALAYSIA	-	1-1	4-1	2	1	1	0	5	2	3
NORTH KOREA	-	-	3-1	2	1	1	0	4	2	3
INDONESIA	-	-	-	2	0	0	2	2	7	0

Group 2

	Th	HK	SL	Si	Pl	W	D	L	F	A	Pts
THAILAND	-	1-0	4-0	4-0	3	3	0	0	9	0	6
HONG KONG	-	-	5-0	3-1	3	2	0	1	8	2	4
SRI LANKA	-	-	-	4-0	3	1	0	2	4	9	2
SINGAPORE	-	-	-	-	3	0	0	3	1	11	0

SEMI-FINALS

Malaysia .... 0-0 5-4p .... Hong Kong

North Korea .... 1-0 .... Thailand

3RD PLACE

Hong Kong .... 2-1 .... Thailand

FINAL

NORTH KOREA .... 1-0 .... **MALAYSIA**

Group 4

Tournament in Manila

	SK	Ch	Ma	Ph	Pl	W	D	L	F	A	Pts
SOUTH KOREA	-	1-0	4-1	5-0	3	3	0	0	10	1	6
CHINA	-	-	2-1	5-0	3	2	0	1	7	2	4
MACAO	-	-	-	2-1	3	1	0	2	4	7	2
PHILIPPINES	-	-	-	-	3	0	0	3	1	12	0

KUWAIT qualified as hosts, **IRAN** as holders

FINAL TOURNAMENT. KUWAIT. 15TH - 30TH SEPTEMBER 1980

FIRST ROUND

Group 1

	Ir	NK	Sy	Ch	Ba	Pl	W	D	L	F	A	Pts
IRAN	-	3-2	0-0	2-2	7-0	4	2	2	0	12	4	6
NORTH KOREA	-	-	2-1	2-1	3-2	4	3	0	1	9	7	6
SYRIA	-	-	-	1-0	1-0	4	2	1	0	3	2	5
CHINA	-	-	-	-	6-0	4	1	1	2	9	5	3
BANGLADESH	-	-	-	-	-	4	0	0	4	2	17	0

Group 2

	SK	Ku	Ma	Qa	Em	Pl	W	D	L	F	A	Pts
SOUTH KOREA	-	3-0	1-1	2-0	4-1	4	3	1	0	10	2	7
KUWAIT	-	-	3-1	4-0	1-1	4	2	1	1	8	5	5
MALAYSIA	-	-	-	1-1	2-0	4	1	2	1	5	5	4
QATAR	-	-	-	-	2-1	4	1	1	2	3	8	3
ARAB EMIRATES	-	-	-	-	-	4	0	1	3	3	9	1

SEMI-FINALS

Kuwait .... 2-1 .... Iran

South Korea .... 2-1 .... North Korea

3RD PLACE

Iran .... 3-0 .... North Korea

FINAL

Kuwait City, 28-09-1980

KUWAIT 3

SOUTH KOREA 0

1984

VII. EDITION

QUALIFYING COMPETITION

Group 1

Tournament in Jakarta

	Ir	Sy	Id	Th	Ba	Ph	Pl	W	D	L	F	A	Pts
IRAN	-	3-1	1-0	15-0	5-0	7-1	5	5	0	0	21	2	10
SYRIA	-	-	2-1	2-3	2-2	2-0	5	3	0	2	9	8	6
INDONESIA	-	-	-	2-1	2-1	1-0	5	3	0	2	6	5	6
THAILAND	-	-	-	-	2-1	3-0	5	3	0	2	9	10	6
BANGLADESH	-	-	-	-	-	3-2	5	1	0	4	6	13	2
PHILIPPINES	-	-	-	-	-	-	5	0	0	5	3	16	0

Group 2

Tournament in Jeddah

Final placings:

SAUDI ARABIA

ARAB EMIRATES

OMAN

SRI LANKA

NEPAL

Group 3

Tournament in Calcutta

	SK	In	Ma	Pa	NY	Pl	W	D	L	F	A	Pts
SOUTH KOREA	-	1-0	0-0	6-0	6-0	4	3	1	0	13	0	7
INDIA	-	-	2-1	2-0	4-0	4	3	0	1	8	2	6
MALAYSIA	-	-	-	5-0	4-1	4	2	1	1	10	3	5
PAKISTAN	-	-	-	-	4-1	4	1	0	3	4	14	2
NORTH YEMEN	-	-	-	-	-	4	0	0	4	2	18	0

Group 4

Tournament in Guangzhou

	Ch	Qa	Jo	HK	Af	Pl	W	D	L	F	A	Pts
CHINA	-	1-0	6-0	2-0	6-0	4	4	0	0	15	0	8
QATAR	-	-	2-0	1-0	8-0	4	3	0	1	11	1	6
JORDAN	-	-	-	1-1	6-1	4	1	1	2	7	10	3
HONG KONG	-	-	-	-	0-0	4	0	2	2	1	4	2
AFGHANISTAN	-	-	-	-	-	4	0	1	3	1	20	1

Singapore qualified as hosts, **Kuwait** as holders

FINAL TOURNAMENT. SINGAPORE. 1ST - 16TH DECEMBER 1984

FIRST ROUND

Group 1

	SA	Ku	Qa	Sy	SK	Pl	W	D	L	F	A	Pts
Saudi Arabia	-	1-0	1-1	1-0	1-1	4	2	2	0	4	2	6
Kuwait	-	-	1-0	3-1	0-0	4	2	1	1	4	2	5
Qatar	-	-	-	1-1	1-0	4	1	2	1	3	3	4
Syria	-	-	-	-	1-0	4	1	1	2	3	5	3
South Korea	-	-	-	-	-	4	0	2	2	1	3	2

Group 2

	Ch	Ir	Em	Si	In	Pl	W	D	L	F	A	Pts
China	-	0-2	5-0	2-0	3-0	4	3	0	1	10	2	6
Iran	-	-	3-0	1-1	0-0	4	2	2	0	6	1	6
Arab Emirates	-	-	-	1-0	2-0	4	2	0	2	3	8	4
Singapore	-	-	-	-	2-0	4	1	1	2	3	4	3
India	-	-	-	-	-	4	0	1	3	0	7	1

SEMI-FINALS

Saudi Arabia .... 1-1 5-4p .... Iran
China .... 1-0 .... Kuwait

3RD PLACE

Kuwait .... 1-1 5-3p .... Iran

FINAL

National Stadium, Singapore, 16-12-1984, 40,000
SAUDI ARABIA 2 (Shaye Nafisah 10, Majed Abdullah 47)
CHINA 0

IX. EDITION

QUALIFYING COMPETITION

Group 1
Tournament in Abu Dhabi

	Em	Ch	NY	Th	Ba	In	Pl	W	D	L	F	A	Pts
Arab Emirates	-	0-0	2-1	3-0	4-0	3-0	5	4	1	0	12	1	9
China	-	-	0-0	5-0	4-0	1-1	5	2	3	0	10	1	7
North Yemen	-	-	-	3-3	0-0	1-0	5	1	3	1	5	5	5
Thailand	-	-	-	-	1-1	1-0	5	1	2	2	5	12	4
Bangladesh	-	-	-	-	-	0-0	5	0	3	2	1	9	3
India	-	-	-	-	-	-	5	0	2	3	1	6	2

Group 2
Tournament in Kuala Lumpur

	Ku	Ja	Jo	Ma	Pa	Pl	W	D	L	F	A	Pts
Kuwait	-	1-0	0-0	5-0	3-0	4	3	1	0	9	0	7
Japan	-	-	1-1	1-0	4-1	4	2	1	1	6	3	5
Jordan	-	-	-	0-0	1-0	4	1	3	0	2	1	5
Malaysia	-	-	-	-	4-0	4	1	1	2	4	6	3
Pakistan	-	-	-	-	-	4	0	0	4	1	12	0

Group 3
Tournament in Katmandu

	Sy	Ir	NK	HK	Ne	Pl	W	D	L	F	A	Pts
Syria	-	1-1	2-1	2-0	3-0	4	3	1	0	8	2	7
Iran	-	-	0-0	2-0	3-0	4	2	2	0	6	1	6
North Korea	-	-	-	1-0	1-0	4	2	1	1	3	2	5
Hong Kong	-	-	-	-	0-0	4	0	1	3	0	5	1
Nepal	-	-	-	-	-	4	0	1	3	0	7	1

Group 4
Tournament in Jakarta

	Ba	SK	In	SY	Pl	W	D	L	F	A	Pts
Bahrain	-	2-0	0-0	2-0	3	2	1	0	4	0	5
South Korea	-	-	4-0	1-1	3	1	1	1	5	3	3
Indonesia	-	-	-	1-0	3	1	1	1	1	4	3
South Yemen	-	-	-	-	3	0	1	2	1	4	1

Qatar qualified as hosts, **Saudi Arabia** as holders

FINAL TOURNAMENT. QATAR 2ND - 18TH DECEMBER 1988

FIRST ROUND

Group 1

	SK	Ir	Qa	Em	Ja	Pl	W	D	L	F	A	Pts
South Korea	-	3-0	3-2	1-0	2-0	4	4	0	0	9	2	8
Iran	-	-	2-0	1-0	0-0	4	2	1	1	3	3	5
Qatar	-	-	-	2-1	3-0	4	2	0	2	7	6	4
Arab Emirates	-	-	-	-	1-0	4	1	0	3	2	4	2
Japan	-	-	-	-	-	4	0	1	3	0	6	1

Group 2

	SA	Ch	Sy	Ku	Ba	Pl	W	D	L	F	A	Pts
Saudi Arabia	-	1-0	2-0	0-0	1-1	4	2	2	0	4	1	6
China	-	-	3-0	2-2	1-0	4	2	1	1	6	3	5
Syria	-	-	-	1-0	1-0	4	2	0	2	2	5	4
Kuwait	-	-	-	-	0-0	4	0	3	1	2	3	3
Bahrain	-	-	-	-	-	4	0	2	2	1	3	2

SEMI-FINALS

Saudi Arabia .... 1-0 .... Iran
South Korea .... 2-1 .... China

3RD PLACE

Iran .... 0-0 3-0p .... China

FINAL

Khalifa, Doha, 18-12-1988
SAUDI ARABIA 0
SOUTH KOREA 0
Saudi Arabia won 4-3 on penalties

1992

X. EDITION

QUALIFYING COMPETITION

Group 1
Tournament in Qatar

	Qa	Sy	Om	Pl	W	D	L	F	A	Pts
Qatar	-	4-2	4-0	2	2	0	0	8	2	4
Syria	-	-	1-0	2	1	0	1	3	4	2
Oman	-	-	-	2	0	0	2	0	5	0

Group 2
Tournament in Dubai

	UA	Ku	Ba	Pl	W	D	L	F	A	Pts
Arab Emirates	-	3-2	3-1	2	2	0	0	6	3	4
Kuwait	-	-	2-0	2	1	0	1	4	3	2
Bahrain	-	-	-	2	0	0	2	1	5	0

Group 3
Tournament in Calcutta

	Ir	In	Pa	Pl	W	D	L	F	A	Pts
Iran	-	3-0	7-0	2	2	0	0	10	0	4
India	-	-	2-0	2	1	0	1	2	3	2
Pakistan	-	-	-	2	0	0	2	0	9	0

Group 4
Tournament in Singapore

	Ch	In	Ma	Si	Pl	W	D	L	F	A	Pts
China	-	2-0	4-0	1-0	3	3	0	0	7	0	6

					Pl	W	D	L	F	A	Pts
Indonesia	-	-	1-1	2-1	3	1	1	1	3	4	3
Malaysia	-	-	-	1-1	3	0	2	1	2	6	2
Singapore	-	-	-	-	3	0	1	2	2	4	1

Group 5
Tournament in Bangkok

	Th	SK	Ba	Pl	W	D	L	F	A	Pts
Thailand	-	2-1	1-0	2	2	0	0	3	1	4
South Korea	-	-	6-0	2	1	0	1	7	2	2
Bangladesh	-	-	-	2	0	0	2	0	7	0

Group 6
Tournament in Pyongyang

	NK	Ma	HK	Ta	Pl	W	D	L	F	A	Pts
North Korea	-	2-0	0-0	6-0	3	2	1	0	8	0	5
Macau	-	-	2-2	2-0	3	1	1	1	4	4	3
Hong Kong	-	-	-	0-0	3	0	3	0	2	2	3
Taiwan	-	-	-	-	3	0	1	2	0	8	1

Japan qualified as hosts, **Saudi Arabia** as holders

FINAL TOURNAMENT. HIROSHIMA. 29TH OCTOBER - 8TH NOVEMBER 1992

FIRST ROUND

Group A

	Ja	UA	Ir	NK	Pl	W	D	L	F	A	Pts
Japan	-	0-0	1-0	1-1	3	1	2	0	2	1	4
Arab Emirates	-	-	0-0	2-1	3	1	2	0	2	1	4
Iran	-	-	-	2-0	3	1	1	1	2	1	3
North Korea	-	-	-	-	3	0	1	2	2	5	1

Group B

	SA	Ch	Qa	Th	Pl	W	D	L	F	A	Pts
Saudi Arabia	-	1-1	1-1	4-0	3	1	2	0	6	2	4
China	-	-	2-1	0-0	3	1	2	0	3	2	4
Qatar	-	-	-	1-1	3	0	2	1	3	4	2
Thailand	-	-	-	-	3	0	2	1	1	5	2

SEMI-FINALS

Japan....................3-2 ....China
Saudi Arabia....................2-0....................United Arab Emirates

3RD PLACE

China....................1-1 4-3p ....United Arab Emirates

FINAL

Hiroshima Park Main Stadium, Hiroshima, 8-11-1992, 40,000. Referee: Al-Sharif, Syria

JAPAN 1 (Takagi 36)
SAUDI ARABIA 0

Japan - Maekawa - Horiike, Hasiratani, Ihara, Tsunami - Ramos, Kitazawa, Yoshida (Katsuya), Fukuda - Miura, Takagi. Tr: Ooft

Saudi - Al-Shujaa - Al-Dosari, Al-Khlawi, Al-Roomi, Al-Alwi - Amin, Al-Bishi, Al-Muwallid, Al-Thunyan - Falatah (Mehalel), Owairan. Tr: Nelson

THE FOOTBALL TOURNAMENT OF THE ASIAN GAMES

1951	India	1-0	Iran
1954	Taiwan	5-2	South Korea
1958	Taiwan	3-2	South Korea
1962	India	2-1	South Korea
1966	Burma	1-0	Iran
1970	Burma	0-0 *	South Korea
1974	Iran	1-0	Israel
1978	North Korea	0-0 *	South Korea
1982	Iraq	1-0	Kuwait
1986	South Korea	2-0	Saudi Arabia
1990	Iran	0-0 4-1p	North Korea
1994	Uzbekistan	4-2	China

* In 1970 and 1978 the gold medal was shared between the two finalists

	Country	G	S	B	Finals	S-Finals
1	South Korea	3	3	1	6	8
2	Iran	2	2	-	4	4
3	India	2	-	1	2	4
4	Myanmar (Burma)	2	-	1	2	3
5	Taiwan	2	-	-	2	2
6	North Korea	1	1	-	2	4
7	Iraq	1	-	-	1	2
8	Uzbekistan	1	-	-	1	1
9	Kuwait	-	1	2	1	3
10	China	-	1	1	1	2
	Saudi Arabia	-	1	1	1	2
12	Israel	-	1	-	1	1
13	Japan	-	-	2	-	3
14	Malaysia	-	-	2	-	2
15	Indonesia	-	-	1	-	3
16	Afghanistan	-	-	1	-	1
17	Singapore	-	-	-	-	1
	Thailand	-	-	-	-	1
	South Vietnam	-	-	-	-	1

India organised the first Asian Games and eleven nations gathered in the newly constructed New Delhi National Stadium on 4 March 1951. Six of these countries had brought teams for the football tournament, but it was no surprise that the standard of football played was not of the highest quality. With home advantage India were obvious favourites; of all the nations taking part they had the most organised football set-up. They dispatched Indonesia in the opening round and Afghanistan in the semi-final with some ease, but in the final they met Iran and were extremely lucky to win, relying on a fine defensive display and an opportunist goal by Mewalal four minutes into the second half. It is interesting to note that in these early years of Asian football, most games were played over 80 and not 90 minutes.

The second Asian Games in Manila built upon the success of the first and the football tournament doubled in size. It opened in spectacular style with a 3-3 draw in the newly built Rizal Memorial stadium between South Korea and Hong Kong, two of the strongest sides, who had unfortunately been drawn together in the first round. South Korea won the group and reached the final at their first attempt. In later years the Koreans would be a familiar sight contesting the final and losing, as they did on this occasion. Taiwan won the tournament but that did not reflect the standard of the football in their country - the side consisted exclusively of players from Hong Kong, who chose to represent a team that was simply called 'China'. At that time the association in Taipei claimed responsibility for the game on mainland China, and this theoretically included Hong Kong. The Taiwan issue was to be a major focus of attention over the years in Asia, but in Manila the team, at least, were worthy winners.

In Tokyo in 1958 the Asian Games began to lose their innocence. In all the sports there was acrimony with complaints about biased refereeing or incompetent officials. Football did not escape, but despite the referees the standard of the play continued to improve. For the second successive Games Taiwan and Korea contested the final and again it was won by Taiwan, represented, as in 1954, by footballers based in Hong Kong.

The fourth Games, staged in the Indonesian capital Djakarta in 1962, were again the scene of bitter confrontations, not on the pitch this time but among the administrators. Indonesia's decision to rescind the invitations of Taiwan and Israel outraged the Indian delegation who even tried to have the name changed from the Asian Games, arguing that they were now nothing of the sort. Taiwan's absence meant that the football tournament was without the reigning champions, but still South Korea could not take advantage of their absence. After again playing the best football of the tournament, they lost their third final in a row, this time to the champions of the first tournament, India.

The situation of Taiwan and Israel continued to pose problems for the authorities and nowhere was this more evident than at the 1974 Asian Games in Tehran when Israel reached the final thanks to both North Korea and Kuwait refusing to play them in the semi-final group. As the Arab nations joined the AFC, sheer force of numbers weighed against Israel, and they and Taiwan were both expelled from the AFC in 1975. The Israelis have since wandered the world in search of a footballing home; Taiwan, on the other hand, were recently accepted back into the Asian fold.

1951

1ST ASIAN GAME
NEW DELHI, 4TH - 11TH MARCH

FIRST ROUND

India .... 3-0 .... Indonesia
Afghanistan .... Bye
Japan .... Bye
Iran .... 2-0 .... Burma

SEMI-FINALS

India .... 3-0 .... Afghanistan
Iran .... 3-2 .... Japan

FINAL

New Delhi. 11-05-1951

INDIA 1 (Mewalal 44)
IRAN 0

India - Anthony - Papan, Manna - Lateef, Singh.C, Noor Mohammed - Venkatesh, Guha Thakurta, Mewalal, Ahmed Khan, Nandy
Iran - Agha Hosseini - Hadjian, Aroumy - Azad, Amir Araghy, Souroudi - Nadar Afshar, Ansari, George, Barounmand, Shakibi

1954

2ND ASIAN GAMES
MANILA, 1ST - 8TH MAY

FIRST ROUND

Group 1

	Ta	SV	Ph	Pl	W	D	L	F	A	Pts
Taiwan	-	3-2	4-0	2	2	0	0	7	2	4
South Vietnam	-	-	3-2	2	1	0	1	5	5	2
Philippines	-	-	-	2	0	0	2	2	7	0

Group 2

	Bu	Pa	Si	Pl	W	D	L	F	A	Pts
Burma	-	2-1	1-1	2	1	1	0	3	2	3
Pakistan	-	-	6-2	2	1	0	1	7	4	2
Singapore	-	-	-	2	0	1	1	3	7	1

Group 3

	In	In	Ja	Pl	W	D	L	F	A	Pts
Indonesia	-	4-0	5-3	2	2	0	0	9	3	4
India	-	-	3-2	2	1	0	1	3	6	2
Japan	-	-	-	2	0	0	2	5	8	0

Group 4

	SK	HK	Af	Pl	W	D	L	F	A	Pts
South Korea	-	3-3	8-2	2	1	1	0	11	5	3
Hong Kong	-	-	4-2	2	1	1	0	7	5	3
Afghanistan	-	-	-	2	0	0	2	4	12	0

SEMI-FINALS

Taiwan .... 4-2 .... Indonesia
South Korea .... 2-2 * .... Burma
* Won on drawing of lots

3rd PLACE

Burma .... 5-4 .... Indonesia

FINAL

Manila. 8-05-1954

TAIWAN 5 (Yiu Cheuk-yin 8, Chu Wing-keung 20 62, Szeto Man 43, Ho Ying-fun 77)
SOUTH KOREA 2 (Choi Tur-min 33, Pakil Kap 66)

Taiwan - Hau Yung-sang - Lau Yee, Chan Fai-lung - Ng Kee-cheung, Tong Sheung, Ho Ying-fun - Lee Tai-fai, Chu Wing-Keung, Yiu Cheuk-yin, Mok Chun-wah, Szeto Man

1958

3RD ASIAN GAMES
TOKYO, 25TH MAY - 1ST JUNE

FIRST ROUND

Group 1

	Ta	SV	Pa	Ma	Pl	W	D	L	F	A	Pts
Taiwan	-	-	3-1	2-1	2	2	0	0	5	2	4
South Vietnam	-	-	1-1	6-1	2	1	1	0	7	2	3
Pakistan	-	-	-	-	2	0	1	1	2	4	1
Malaysia	-	-	-	-	2	0	0	2	2	8	0

Group 2

	In	In	Bu	Pl	W	D	L	F	A	Pts
Indonesia	-	2-1	4-2	2	2	0	0	6	3	4
India	-	-	3-2	2	1	0	1	4	4	2
Burma	-	-	-	2	0	0	2	4	7	0

Group 3

	HK	Ph	Ja	Pl	W	D	L	F	A	Pts
Hong Kong	-	4-1	2-0	2	2	0	0	6	1	4

					Pl	W	D	L	F	A	Pts
Philippines	-	-	1-0		2	1	0	1	2	4	2
Japan	-	-	-		2	0	0	2	0	3	0

Group 4

	SK	Is	Si	Ir	Pl	W	D	L	F	A	Pts
South Korea	-	-	2-1	5-0	2	2	0	0	7	1	4
Israel	-	-	2-1	4-0	2	2	0	0	6	1	4
Singapore	-	-	-	-	2	0	0	2	2	4	0
Iran	-	-	-	-	2	0	0	2	0	9	0

QUARTER-FINALS

Taiwan 2-0 Israel
Indonesia 5-2 Philippines
India 5-2 Hong Kong
South Korea 3-1 South Vietnam

SEMI-FINALS

Taiwan 1-0 Indonesia
South Korea 3-1 India

3RD PLACE

Indonesia 4-1 India

FINAL

Tokyo. 1-06-1958

TAIWAN 3 (Mok Chun-wah 55, Lau Yee 75, Chan Fai-hung 98)
SOUTH KOREA 2 (Lee 16, Choi 76)

1962

4TH ASIAN GAMES
DJAKARTA, 25TH AUG - 4TH SEPT

FIRST ROUND

Group 1

	SK	In	Ja	Th	Pl	W	D	L	F	A	Pts
South Korea	-	2-0	1-0	3-2	3	3	0	0	6	2	6
India	-	-	2-0	4-1	3	2	0	1	6	3	4
Japan	-	-	-	3-1	3	1	0	2	3	4	2
Thailand	-	-	-	-	3	0	0	3	4	10	0

Group 2

	Ma	SV	In	Ph	Pl	W	D	L	F	A	Pts
Malaysia	-	0-3	3-2	15-1	3	2	0	1	18	6	4
South Vietnam	-	-	0-1	6-0	3	2	0	1	9	1	4
Indonesia	-	-	-	6-0	3	2	0	1	9	3	4
Philippines	-	-	-	-	3	0	0	3	1	27	0

SEMI-FINALS

India 3-2 South Vietnam
South Korea 2-1 Malaysia

3RD PLACE

Malaysia 4-1 South Vietnam

FINAL

Djakarta, 4-09-1962

INDIA 2
SOUTH KOREA 1

1966

5TH ASIAN GAMES
BANGKOK, 10TH - 20TH DECEMBER

FIRST ROUND

Group 1

	Th	Bu	SK	Pl	W	D	L	F	A	Pts
Thailand	-	1-1	3-0	2	1	1	0	4	1	3
Burma	-	-	1-0	2	1	1	0	2	1	3
South Korea	-	-	-	2	0	0	2	0	4	0

Group 2

	Ja	Ir	In	Ma	Pl	W	D	L	F	A	Pts
Japan	-	3-1	2-1	1-0	3	3	0	0	6	2	6
Iran	-	-	4-1	2-0	3	2	0	1	7	4	4
India	-	-	-	2-1	3	1	0	2	4	7	2
Malaysia	-	-	-	-	3	0	0	3	1	5	0

Group 3

	In	Si	SV	Ta	Pl	W	D	L	F	A	Pts
Indonesia	-	3-0	0-0	3-1	3	2	1	0	6	1	5
Singapore	-	-	5-0	3-3	3	1	1	1	8	6	3
South Vietnam	-	-	-	2-1	3	1	1	1	2	6	3
Taiwan	-	-	-	-	3	0	1	2	5	8	1

QUARTER-FINALS

Group A

	Ja	Si	Th	Pl	W	D	L	F	A	Pts
Japan	-	5-1	5-1	2	2	0	0	10	2	4
Singapore	-	-	2-0	2	1	0	1	3	5	2
Thailand	-	-	-	2	0	0	2	1	7	0

Group B

	Bu	Ir	In	Pl	W	D	L	F	A	Pts
Burma	-	1-0	2-2	2	1	1	0	3	2	3
Iran	-	-	1-0	2	1	0	1	1	1	2
Indonesia	-	-	-	2	0	1	1	2	3	1

SEMI-FINALS

Iran 1-0 Japan
Burma 2-0 Singapore

3RD PLACE

Japan 2-0 Singapore

FINAL

Suphachalasai, Bangkok, 20-12-1966

BURMA 1 (Aung Khin 66)
IRAN 0

1970

6TH ASIAN GAME
BANGKOK, 10TH - 20TH DECEMBER

FIRST ROUND

Group 1

	SK	In	Ir	Pl	W	D	L	F	A	Pts
South Korea	-	0-0	1-0	2	1	1	0	1	0	3
Indonesia	-	-	2-2	2	0	2	0	2	2	2
Iran	-	-	-	2	0	1	1	2	3	1

Group 2

	Ja	Bu	Ca	Ma	Pl	W	D	L	F	A	Pts
Japan	-	2-1	1-0	1-0	3	3	0	0	4	1	6
Burma	-	-	2-1	1-0	3	2	0	1	4	3	4
Cambodia	-	-	-	2-0	3	1	0	2	3	3	2
Malaysia	-	-	-	-	3	0	0	3	0	4	0

Group 3

	In	Th	SV	Pl	W	D	L	F	A	Pts
India	-	2-2	2-0	2	1	1	0	4	2	3
Thailand	-	-	1-0	2	1	1	0	3	2	3
South Vietnam	-	-	-	2	0	0	2	0	3	0

QUARTER-FINALS

Group A

	Ja	In	In	Pl	W	D	L	F	A	Pts
Japan	-	1-0	2-1	2	2	0	0	3	1	4

				Pl	W	D	L	F	A	Pts
India	-	-	3-0	2	1	0	1	3	1	2
Indonesia	-	-	-	2	0	0	2	1	5	0

Group B

	Bu	SK	TH	Pl	W	D	L	F	A	Pts
Burma	-	1-0	2-2	2	1	1	0	3	2	3
South Korea	-	-	2-1	2	1	0	1	2	2	2
Thailand	-	-	-	2	0	1	1	3	4	1

SEMI-FINALS

Burma .... 2-0 .... India
South Korea .... 2-1 .... Japan

3RD PLACE

India .... 1-0 .... Japan

FINAL

Suphachalasai, Bangkok, 20-12-1970, 35,000
BURMA 0
SOUTH KOREA 0
Gold medal shared

1974

7TH ASIAN GAMES
TEHRAN, 2ND - 15TH SEPTEMBER

FIRST ROUND

Group 1

	Ku	SK	Th	Pl	W	D	L	F	A	Pts
Kuwait	-	4-0	3-2	2	2	0	0	7	2	4
South Korea	-	-	1-0	2	1	0	1	1	4	2
Thailand	-	-	-	2	0	0	2	2	4	0

Group 2

	Ir	NK	Ch	In	Pl	W	D	L	F	A	Pts
Iraq	-	1-0	1-0	3-0	3	3	0	0	5	0	6
North Korea	-	-	2-0	4-1	3	2	0	1	6	2	4
Taiwan	-	-	-	7-1	3	1	0	2	7	4	2
India	-	-	-	-	3	0	0	3	2	14	0

Group 3

	Is	Ma	Ja	Ph	Pl	W	D	L	F	A	Pts
Israel	-	8-3	3-0	6-0	3	3	0	0	17	3	6
Malaysia	-	-	1-1	11-0	3	1	1	1	15	9	3
Japan	-	-	-	4-0	3	1	1	1	5	4	3
Philippines	-	-	-	-	3	0	0	3	0	21	0

Group 4

	Ir	Bu	Pa	Ba	Pl	W	D	L	F	A	Pts
Iran	-	2-1	7-0	6-0	3	3	0	0	15	1	6
Burma	-	-	5-1	4-0	3	2	0	1	10	3	4
Pakistan	-	-	-	5-1	3	1	0	2	6	13	2
Bahrain	-	-	-	-	3	0	0	3	1	15	0

SEMI-FINALS

Group A

	Ir	Ma	Iq	SK	Pl	W	D	L	F	A	Pts
Iran	-	1-0	1-0	2-0	3	3	0	0	4	0	6
Malaysia	-	-	0-0	3-2	3	1	1	1	3	3	3
Iraq	-	-	-	1-1	3	0	2	1	1	2	2
South Korea	-	-	-	-	3	0	1	2	3	6	1

Group B

	Is	NK	Ku	Bu	Pl	W	D	L	F	A	Pts
Israel	-	2-0*	2-0*	3-0	3	3	0	0	7	0	6
North Korea	-	-	2-0	2-2	3	1	1	1	4	4	3
Kuwait	-	-	-	5-2	3	1	0	2	5	6	2
Burma	-	-	-	-	3	0	1	2	4	10	1

* Games awarded to Israel after opponents refused to play

3RD PLACE

Malaysia .... 2-1 .... North Korea

FINAL

Aryamehr Stadium, Tehran, 15-09-1974, 100,000
IRAN 1 (OG 23)
ISRAEL 0

1978

8TH ASIAN GAMES
BANGKOK, 9TH - 20TH DECEMBER

FIRST ROUND

Group 1

	Ir	Ch	SA	Qa	Pl	W	D	L	F	A	Pts
Iraq	-	2-0	1-1	2-1	3	2	1	0	5	2	5
China	-	-	1-0	3-0	3	2	0	1	4	2	4
Saudi Arabia	-	-	-	2-2	3	0	2	1	3	4	2
Qatar	-	-	-	-	3	0	1	2	3	7	1

Group 2

	Ma	In	Ba	Pl	W	D	L	F	A	Pts
Malaysia	-	1-0	1-0	2	2	0	0	2	0	4
India	-	-	3-0	2	1	0	1	3	1	2
Bangladesh	-	-	-	2	0	0	2	0	4	0

Group 3

	SK	Ku	Ja	Ba	Pl	W	D	L	F	A	Pts
South Korea	-	2-0	3-1	5-1	3	3	0	0	10	2	6
Kuwait	-	-	2-0	3-0	3	2	0	1	5	2	4
Japan	-	-	-	4-0	3	1	0	2	5	5	2
Bahrain	-	-	-	-	3	0	0	3	1	12	0

Group 4

	NK	Th	Bu	Pl	W	D	L	F	A	Pts
North Korea	-	3-0	3-0	2	2	0	0	6	0	4
Thailand	-	-	2-1	2	1	0	1	2	4	2
Burma	-	-	-	2	0	0	2	1	5	0

SEMI-FINALS

Group A

	SK	Ch	Th	Ma	Pl	W	D	L	F	A	Pts
South Korea	-	1-0	3-1	1-0	3	3	0	0	5	1	6
China	-	-	4-1	7-1	3	2	0	1	11	3	4
Thailand	-	-	-	2-1	3	1	0	2	4	8	2
Malaysia	-	-	-	-	3	0	0	3	2	10	0

Group B

	NK	Ir	Ku	In	Pl	W	D	L	F	A	Pts
North Korea	-	1-0	2-2	3-1	3	2	1	0	6	3	5
Iraq	-	-	3-0	3-0	3	2	0	1	6	1	4
Kuwait	-	-	-	6-1	3	1	1	1	8	6	3
India	-	-	-	-	3	0	0	3	2	12	0

3RD PLACE

China .... 1-0 .... Iraq

FINAL

Suphachalasai, Bangkok, 20-12-1978
SOUTH KOREA 0
NORTH KOREA 0
Gold medal shared

1982

9TH ASIAN GAMES
NEW DELHI, 19TH NOV - 4TH DEC

FIRST ROUND

Group 1

	In	Ch	Ba	Ma	Pl	W	D	L	F	A	Pts
India	-	2-2	2-0	1-0	3	2	1	0	5	2	5

					Pl	W	D	L	F	A	Pts
China	-	-	1-0	1-0	3	2	0	1	4	2	4
Bangladesh	-	-	-	2-1	3	1	0	2	2	4	2
Malaysia	-	-	-	-	3	0	0	3	1	4	0

Group 2

	NK	SA	Th	Sy	Pl	W	D	L	F	A	Pts
North Korea	-	2-2	3-0	1-1	3	1	2	0	6	3	4
Saudi Arabia	-	-	1-0	1-1	3	1	2	0	4	3	4
Thailand	-	-	-	3-1	3	1	0	2	3	5	2
Syria	-	-	-	-	3	0	2	1	3	5	2

Group 3

	Ja	Ir	SK	SY	Pl	W	D	L	F	A	Pts
Japan	-	1-0	2-1	3-1	3	3	0	0	6	2	6
Iran	-	-	1-0	2-0	3	2	0	1	3	1	4
South Korea	-	-	-	3-0	3	1	0	2	4	3	2
South Yemen	-	-	-	-	3	0	0	3	1	8	0

Group 4

	Ku	Ir	Bu	Ne	Pl	W	D	L	F	A	Pts
Kuwait	-	2-1	4-0	3-0	3	3	0	0	9	1	6
Iraq	-	-	4-0	3-0	3	2	0	1	8	2	4
Burma	-	-	-	3-0	3	1	0	2	3	8	2
Nepal	-	-	-	-	3	0	0	3	0	9	0

QUARTER-FINALS

Iraq .... 1-0 .... Japan
Saudi Arabia .... 1-0 .... India
North Korea .... 1-0 .... China
Kuwait .... 1-0 .... Iran

SEMI-FINALS

Iraq .... 1-0 .... Saudi Arabia
Kuwait .... 3-2 .... North Korea

FINAL

National Stadium, New Delhi, 4-12-1982

IRAQ 1
KUWAIT 0

1986

10TH ASIAN GAMES
SEOUL, 20TH SEPTEMBER - 5TH OCTOBER

FIRST ROUND

Group 1

	Em	Ir	Om	Th	Pa	Pl	W	D	L	F	A	Pts
Arab Emirates	-	2-1	0-0	2-1	1-0	4	3	1	0	5	2	7
Iraq	-	-	4-0	2-1	5-1	4	3	0	1	12	4	6
Oman	-	-	-	0-0	3-1	4	1	2	1	3	5	4
Thailand	-	-	-	-	6-0	4	1	1	2	8	4	3
Pakistan	-	-	-	-	-	4	0	0	4	2	15	0

Group 2

	SK	Ch	Ba	In	Pl	W	D	L	F	A	Pts
South Korea	-	4-2	0-0	3-0	3	2	1	0	7	2	5
China	-	-	5-1	2-1	3	2	0	1	9	6	4
Bahrain	-	-	-	3-0	3	1	1	1	4	5	3
India	-	-	-	-	3	0	0	3	1	8	0

Group 3

	SA	In	Qa	Ma	Pl	W	D	L	F	A	Pts
Saudi Arabia	-	2-0	1-0	3-1	3	3	0	0	6	1	6
Indonesia	-	-	1-1	1-0	3	1	1	1	2	3	3
Qatar	-	-	-	1-1	3	0	2	1	2	3	2
Malaysia	-	-	-	-	3	0	1	2	2	5	1

Group 4

	Ku	Ir	Ja	Ba	Ne	Pl	W	D	L	F	A	Pts
Kuwait	-	1-0	2-0	4-0	5-0	4	4	0	0	12	0	8
Iran	-	-	2-0	4-0	6-0	4	3	0	1	12	1	6
Japan	-	-	-	4-0	5-0	4	2	0	2	9	4	4
Bangladesh	-	-	-	-	1-0	4	1	0	3	1	12	2
Nepal	-	-	-	-	-	4	0	0	4	0	17	0

QUARTER-FINALS

South Korea .... 1-1 5-4p .... Iran
Indonesia .... 2-2 4-3p .... Arab Emirates
Kuwait .... 1-1 5-4p .... China
Saudi Arabia .... 1-1 9-8p .... Iraq

SEMI-FINALS

South Korea .... 4-0 .... Indonesia
Saudi Arabia .... 2-2 5-4p .... Kuwait

3RD PLACE

Kuwait .... 5-0 .... Indonesia

FINAL

Olympic Stadium, Seoul, 5-10-1986, 75,000

SOUTH KOREA 2 (Cho Kwang-rae 8, Byun Byung-joo 85)
SAUDI ARABIA 0

1990

11TH ASIAN GAMES
BEIJING, 22ND SEPTEMBER - 6TH OCTOBER

FIRST ROUND

Group 1

	SK	Ch	Si	Pa	Pl	W	D	L	F	A	Pts
South Korea	-	2-0	7-0	7-0	3	3	0	0	16	0	6
China	-	-	5-1	3-0	3	2	0	1	8	3	4
Singapore	-	-	-	6-1	3	1	0	2	7	13	2
Pakistan	-	-	-	-	3	0	0	3	1	16	0

Group 2

	Ir	NK	Ma	Pl	W	D	L	F	A	Pts
Iran	-	2-1	3-0	2	2	0	0	5	1	4
North Korea	-	-	0-0	2	0	1	1	1	2	1
Malaysia	-	-	-	2	0	1	1	0	3	1

Group 3

	Th	Ku	HK	Ye	Pl	W	D	L	F	A	Pts
Thailand	-	2-1	2-0	0-0	3	2	1	0	4	1	5
Kuwait	-	-	2-1	0-0	3	1	1	1	3	3	3
Hong Kong	-	-	-	2-0	3	1	0	2	3	4	2
Yemen	-	-	-	-	3	0	2	1	0	2	2

Group 4

	SA	Ja	Ba	Pl	W	D	L	F	A	Pts
Saudi Arabia	-	2-0	4-0	2	2	0	0	6	0	4
Japan	-	-	3-0	2	1	0	1	3	2	2
Bangladesh	-	-	-	2	0	0	2	0	7	0

QUARTER-FINALS

Iran .... 1-0 .... Japan
South Korea .... 1-0 .... Kuwait
Thailand .... 1-0 .... China
North Korea .... 0-0 4-3p .... Saudi Arabia

SEMI-FINALS

Iran .... 1-0 .... South Korea
North Korea .... 1-0 .... Thailand

3RD PLACE

South Korea .... 1-0 .... Thailand

FINAL

Workers Stadium, Beijing, 6-10-1990, 70,000

IRAN 0
NORTH KOREA 0
Iran won 4-1 on penalties

1994

12TH ASIAN GAMES
HIROSHIMA, 2ND - 16TH OCTOBER

FIRST ROUND

Group 1
TURKMENISTAN
CHINA

Group 2

	Uz	SA	Ma	HK	Th	Pl	W	D	L	F	A	Pts
UZBEKISTAN	-	4-1	5-0	1-0	5-4	4	4	0	0	15	5	8
SAUDI ARABIA	-	-	2-1	2-1	4-2	4	3	0	1	9	8	6
MALAYSIA	-	-	-	4-3	1-1	4	1	1	2	6	11	3
HONG KONG	-	-	-	-	2-1	4	1	0	3	6	8	2
THAILAND	-	-	-	-	-	4	0	1	3	8	12	1

Group 3

	SK	Ku	Om	Ne	Pl	W	D	L	F	A	Pts
SOUTH KOREA	-	0-0	2-0	11-0	3	2	1	0	13	0	5
KUWAIT	-	-	2-2	8-0	3	1	2	0	10	2	4
OMAN	-	-	-	1-0	3	1	1	1	3	4	3
NEPAL	-	-	-	-	3	0	0	3	0	20	0

Group 4

	Jp	AE	Qa	My	Pl	W	D	L	F	A	Pts
JAPAN	-	1-1	1-1	5-0	3	1	2	0	7	2	4
ARAB EMIRATES	-	-	2-2	2-0	3	1	2	0	5	3	4
QATAR	-	-	-	2-2	3	0	3	0	5	5	3
MYANMAR	-	-	-	-	3	0	1	2	2	9	1

QUARTER-FINALS

Uzbekistan .... 3-0 .... Turkmenistan
South Korea .... 3-2 .... Japan
Kuwait .... 2-1 .... Arab Emirates
China .... 2-0 .... Saudi Arabia

SEMI-FINALS

Uzbekistan .... 1-0 .... South Korea
China .... 2-0 .... Kuwait

3RD PLACE

Kuwait .... 2-1 .... South Korea

FINAL

Hiroshima, 16-10-1994

UZBEKISTAN 4
CHINA 2

THE ASIAN YOUTH CUP

1959 South Korea
1960 South Korea
1961 Indonesia & Burma
1962 Thailand
1963 South Korea & Burma
1964 Burma & Israel
1965 Israel
1966 Israel & Thailand
1967 Israel
1968 Burma
1969 Burma & Thailand
1970 Burma
1971 Israel
1972 Israel
1973 Iran
1974 Iran & India
1975 Iran & Iraq
1976 Iran & North Korea
1977 Iraq
1978 Iraq & South Korea
1980 South Korea
1982 South Korea
1984 China
1986 Saudi Arabia
1988 Iraq
1990 South Korea
1992 Saudi Arabia
1994 Syria

THE ASIAN UNDER-17 TOURNAMENT

1984 Saudi Arabia
1986 South Korea
1988 Saudi Arabia
1990 Qatar
1992 China
1994 Japan

THE SOUTH EAST ASIAN GAMES

1959 South Vietnam
1961 Malaysia
1965 Burma & Thailand
1967 Burma
1969 Burma
1971 Burma
1973 Burma
1975 Thailand
1977 Malaysia
1979 Malaysia
1981 Thailand
1983 Thailand
1985 Thailand
1987 Indonesia
1989 Malaysia
1991 Indonesia

THE SOUTH ASIAN ASSOCIATION OF REGIONAL CO-OPERATION TOURNAMENT

1993 India
1995 Sri Lanka

THE ARABIAN GULF TOURNAMENT

1970 Kuwait
1972 Kuwait
1974 Kuwait
1976 Kuwait
1979 Iraq
1982 Kuwait
1984 Iraq
1986 Kuwait
1988 Iraq
1990 Kuwait
1992 Qatar
1994 Saudi Arabia

THE FAR EASTERN GAMES

1913 Philippines .... 2-1 .... China
1915 China .... 1-0 .... Philippines
1917 China 4 Philippines 2 Japan 0
1919 China .... 2-1 1-2 3-2 .... Philippines
1921 China 4 Philippines 2 Japan 0
1923 China 4 Philippines 2 Japan 0
1925 China 4 Philippines 2 Japan 0
1927 China 4 Japan 2 Philippines 0
1930 China & Japan 3 Philippines 0
1934 China 6 Dutch East Indies 2 Philippines 2 Japan 2

ASIAN CLUB COMPETITIONS

League football is not strong in Asia and indeed many put the continent's poor impact on world football down to the lack of a well-founded club structure in the majority of countries. However, efforts are being made to rectify this situation through the reintroduction of the Asian Champion Teams' Cup; it is hoped that the tournament will stimulate increased awareness of club football.

First contested in the late 1960s for four editions, the tournament was resumed again in 1985 and has been held each year since. It does, however, face enormous logistical problems, the most basic being the enormous size of 'Asia'. After all, Riyadh and Seoul are as far apart as Madrid and Rio de Janeiro. A second problem is just who qualifies to take part, as some countries cannot admit to having a national league, and in some which do, representative rather than club sides take part.

That is not to decry Asian club football totally. South Korea, Japan, Bangladesh, Calcutta, Hong Kong and the majority of the Gulf states do have well established leagues that, given the right circumstances, do capture the attention of the public, but it is a hard battle, as a glance at the television screens of the continent will tell you. Wherever you look there is Italian, English, German and Spanish football being screened, but little of the local variety.

In the early editions of the competition, an Israeli club appeared in all of the four finals and won it three times. The monopoly was broken once, by the Taj club from Iran. As Israel does not take part anymore and none of the Iranian clubs of the time exist any longer, the links between the old event and the new are patchy. The victorious team in the 1991 edition, Esteghlal, are the team of the Iranian army, as were Taj, but there the similarity ends.

Japan and Saudi Arabia have been the dominant countries since the reintroduction, with three final appearances each, and their two leagues are among the strongest in Asia, as both can afford the facilities and the coaches. Others included would be South Korea, who in 1983 introduced a professional super league of teams attached to some of the country's biggest industrial concerns. It proved succesful enough for Japan to follow suit in 1992, although in Japan's case most of the franchises taken up were by clubs that already existed.

Above all the others, however, stands Hong Kong, whose league for many years was the only professional one in Asia. It not only attracted most of the best Asian players but also a good number of Europeans and South Americans, who were seeking to make some money at the end of their careers. Given that it is - just - still a colony of Great Britain, the link with players from the English and Scottish leagues has been strong.

There is a long way to go before Asian club football catches up even with that of Africa. The ultimate goal would be for the Asian champions to take part in a four way club championship of the world with the European Cup, Copa Libertadores and African Champions Cup winners - but it could be a good many years before that happens.

THE ASIAN CHAMPION TEAMS' CUP

1967 Hapoel Tel Aviv (ISR) ...... 2-1 .... FA Selangor (MYS)
1968 Maccabi Tel Aviv (ISR) ..... 1-0 .... Yangzee (KOR)
1969 -
1970 Taj Club (IRN) .... 2-1 .... Hapoel Tel Aviv (ISR)
1971 Maccabi Tel Aviv (ISR) ... W-O .... Police Club (IRQ)
1972-84 -
1985 Daewoo Royals (KOR) ... 3-1 .... Al Ahly (KSA)
1986 Furukawa (JPN) .... 4-3 .... Al Hilal (KSA)
1987 Yomiuri (JPN) .... W-O .... Al Hilal (KSA)
1988 Al Saad (QAT) .... 2-3 1-0 .... Al Rasheed (IRQ)
1989 Liaoning (CHN) .... 2-1 1-1 .... Nissan (JPN)
1990 Esteghlal SC (IRN) .... 2-1 .... Liaoning CHN
1991 Al Hilal (KSA) .... 1-1 4-3p .... Esteghlal SC (IRN)
1992 Pass (IRN) .... 1-0 .... Al Shabab (KSA)
1993 Thai Farmers Bank (THA) 2-1 .... Omani Club (OMN)
1994 Thai Farmers Bank (THA) 1-0 .... Al Arabi (QAT)

THE ASIAN CUP WINNERS CUP

1990 Pirouzi (IRN) .... 0-0 1-0 .... Al Muharraq (BHR)
1991 Nissan (JPN) .... 1-1 5-0 .... Al Nasr (KSA)
1992 Nissan (JPN) .... 1-1 1-0 .... Pirouzi (IRN)
1993 Al-Qadisiyah (KSA) ...... 4-2 2-0 .... South China (HKG)
1994 Yokohama Flugels (JPN) .. 2-1 .... Al Shaab (UAE)

1967

CHAMPION TEAMS' CUP

TOURNAMENT IN BANGKOK
FIRST ROUND

Hapoel Tel-Aviv (ISR) .... Bye
Tungsten Mining (KOR) .... Bye
South China (HKG) .... 1-0 0-2 .... **Bangkok Bank** (THA)
FA Selangor (MYS) .... 0-0 2-1 .... Vietnam Customs (SVM)

SECOND ROUND

Hapoel Tel-Aviv .... Bye
Tungsten Mining .... Bye
FA Selangor .... 1-0 0-0 .... Bangkok Bank

SEMI-FINALS

Hapoel Tel-Aviv .... Bye
Tungsten Mining .... 0-0 0-1 .... **FA Selangor**

FINAL

HAPOEL TEL-AVIV 2
FA SELANGOR 1

1968

CHAMPION TEAMS' CUP

TOURNAMENT IN BANGKOK
FIRST ROUND

Group A

	Ya	My	BB	VP	ML	Pl	W	D	L	F	A	Pts
Yangzee (KOR)	-	5-0	1-0	4-1	7-0	4	4	0	0	17	1	8
Mysore State (IND)	-	-	1-1	2-1	2-1	4	2	1	1	5	8	5
Bangkok Bank (THA)	-	-	-	1-1	4-0	4	1	2	1	6	3	4
Vietnam Police (SVT)	-	-	-	-	7-0	4	1	1	2	10	7	3
Manila Lions (PHI)	-	-	-	-	-	4	0	0	4	1	20	0

Group B

	Ma	TK	TC	Pe	Ko	Pl	W	D	L	F	A	Pts
Maccabi Tel-Aviv (ISR)	-	3-2	0-0	1-1	5-0	4	2	2	0	9	3	6
Toyo Kogyo (JPN)	-	-	1-0	2-0	1-0	4	3	0	1	6	3	6
Tehran Club (IRN)	-	-	-	4-2	4-0	4	2	1	1	8	3	5
Perak AFA (MYS)	-	-	-	-	6-2	4	1	1	2	9	9	3
Kowloon Motor Bus (HKG)	-	-	-	-	-	4	0	0	4	2	16	0

SEMI-FINALS

Maccabi Tel-Aviv .... 6-1 .... Mysore State
Yangzee .... 2-0 .... Toyo Kogyo

THIRD PLACE

Toyo Kogyo .... 2-0 .... Mysore State

FINAL

MACCABI TEL-AVIV 1
YANGZEE 0

1970

CHAMPION TEAMS' CUP

TOURNAMENT IN TEHRAN. 1ST - 10TH APRIL

FIRST ROUND

Group A

	TC	CH	FA	Pl	W	D	L	F	A	Pts
Taj Club (IRN)	-	3-0	3-0	2	2	0	0	6	0	4
Club Homenetmen (LIB)	-	-	4-2	2	1	0	1	4	5	2
FA Selangor (MYS)	-	-	-	2	0	0	2	2	7	0

Group B

	Ha	PS	WB	Po	Pl	W	D	L	F	A	Pts
Hapoel Tel-Aviv (ISR)	-	3-1	3-1	5-0	3	3	0	0	11	2	6
PSMS (IDN)	-	-	1-0	4-0	3	2	0	1	6	3	4
West Bengal (IND)	-	-	-	2-1	3	1	0	2	3	5	2
Police (THA)	-	-	-	-	3	0	0	3	1	11	0

SEMI-FINALS

Hapoel Tel-Aviv .... W-O .... Club Homenetmen
Taj Club .... 2-0 .... PSMS

THIRD PLACE

Club Homenetmen .... 1-0 .... PSMS

FINAL

TAJ CLUB 2
HAPOEL TEL-AVIV 1

1971

CHAMPION TEAMS' CUP

TOURNAMENT IN BANGKOK. 21ST MARCH - 2ND APRIL

FIRST ROUND

Inter group games

ROK Army .... 2-1 .... Bangkok Bank
Al Schurta .... 3-2 .... Taj Club
Al Arabi .... 8-1 .... Punjab FA
Maccabi Tel-Aviv .... 1-0 .... Perak AFA
Al Arabi .... 3-0 .... Perak AFA
Taj Club .... 2-1 .... ROK Army
Bangkok Bank .... 2-0 .... Punjab FA
Maccabi Tel-Aviv .... W-O .... Al Schurta
ROK Army .... 3-0 .... Perak AFA
Taj Club .... 0-0 .... Al Arabi
Maccabi Tel-Aviv .... 4-1 .... Punjab FA
Al Schurta .... 2-0 .... Bangkok Bank
Taj Club .... 3-0 .... Perak AFA
ROK Army .... 1-0 .... Al Arabi
Al Schurta .... 6-1 .... Punjab FA
Maccabi Tel-Aviv .... 4-1 .... Bangkok Bank

Group A

	Pl	W	D	L	F	A	Pts
ROK Army (KOR)	4	3	0	1	7	3	6
Taj Club (IRN)	4	2	1	1	7	4	5
Al Arabi (KUW)	4	2	1	1	11	2	5
Perak AFA (MYS)	4	0	0	4	0	10	0

Group B

	Pl	W	D	L	F	A	Pts
Maccabi Tel-Aviv (ISR)	4	4	0	0	9	2	8
Al Schurta (IRQ)	4	3	0	1	11	3	6
Bangkok Bank (THA)	4	1	0	3	4	8	2
Punjab FA (IND)	4	0	0	4	3	20	0

SEMI-FINALS

Maccabi Tel-Aviv .... 2-0 .... ROK Army
Al Schurta .... 2-0 .... Taj Club

THIRD PLACE

Taj Club .... 3-2 .... ROK Army

FINAL

Maccabi Tel-Aviv were declared the winners after the Al Schurta from Iraq refused to play Maccabi

1972–1984

No competition

1985

CHAMPION TEAMS' CUP

QUALIFYING COMPETITION

Group 1

FIRST ROUND

Al Ittihad (SYR) .... W-O
Al Rasheed (IRQ) .... 4-0 .... Amman Club (JOR)

SECOND ROUND

Ittihad Club beat Al Rasheed to qualify

Group 2

Tournament in Dubai with Al Ahly KSA, Al Arabi KUW, Al Fanja OMN, Muharraq BHR, Al Rayyan QAT and Al Ain UAE

FINAL

Al Ahly .... 2-1 .... **Al Arabi**

Both clubs qualified, but Al Arabi withdrew from the final tournament

Group 3

Tournament in Colombo

	EB	AK	Sa	Pl	NR	Va	Pl	W	D	L	F	A	Pts
East Bengal (IND)	-	1-0	1-0	2-0	7-0	9-0	5	5	0	0	20	0	10
Abahani Krira Ch. (BGD)	-	-	4-1	3-0	2-1	8-1	5	4	0	1	17	4	8
Saunders SC (SRI)	-	-	-	2-2	2-1	7-0	5	2	1	2	12	8	5
Pakistan Int. Air. (PAK)	-	-	-	-	0-0	6-1	5	1	2	2	8	8	4
New Road Team (NPL)	-	-	-	-	-	6-0	5	1	1	3	8	11	3
Valencia (MDV)	-	-	-	-	-	-	5	0	0	5	2	36	0

Group 4
Tournament in Jakarta

	TB	BB	TB	MA	AP	Pl	W	D	L	F	A	Pts
Tiga Berlian (IDN)	-	1-1	5-0	2-0	7-0	4	3	1	0	15	1	7
Bangkok Bank (THA)	-	-	2-0	5-1	1-0	4	3	1	0	9	2	7
Tiong Bahru (SIN)	-	-	-	0-0	2-0	4	1	1	2	2	7	3
Malacca AFA (MYS)	-	-	-	-	1-0	4	1	1	2	2	7	3
Angkata Persenjata (BRU)	-	-	-	-	-	4	0	0	4	0	11	0

Play-off
Bankok Bank .... 1-0 .... Tiga Berlian
Both clubs qualified

Group 5

	Se	Ap	Li	Pl	W	D	L	F	A	Pts
Seiko (HKG)	-	2-1	2-1	4	3	0	1	6	6	6
April 25 (PRK)	4-1	-	3-1	4	2	1	1	8	4	5
Liaoning (CHN)	0-1	0-0	-	4	0	1	3	2	6	1

Seiko qualified, but withdrew from the final tournament

Group 6
Daewoo Royals (KOR) .... 9-0 5-1 * .... Wa Seng (MAC)
* Both games in Seoul

FINAL TOURNAMENT. JEDDAH. 19TH - 29TH OCTOBER 1985

FIRST ROUND

Group A

	AA	TB	EB	Pl	W	D	L	F	A	Pts
Al Ahly (KSA)	-	1-0	2-1	2	2	0	0	3	1	4
Tiga Berlian (IDN)	-	-	2-0	2	1	0	1	2	1	2
East Bengal (IND)	-	-	-	2	0	0	2	1	4	0

Group B

	DR	IC	BB	Pl	W	D	L	F	A	Pts
Daewoo Royals (KOR)	-	1-0	3-1	2	2	0	0	4	1	4
Ittihad Club (SYR)	-	-	3-0	2	1	0	1	3	1	2
Bangkok Bank (THA)	-	-	-	2	0	0	2	1	6	0

SEMI-FINALS

Daewoo Royals .... 3-0 .... Tiga Berlian
Al Ahly .... 1-0 .... Ittihad Club

3RD PLACE

Tiga Berlian .... 1-0 .... Ittihad Club

FINAL

Al Ahly stadium, Jeddah, 24-01-1986

DAEWOO ROYALS 3 (Byung-joo, Yang-ha, Sin-woo)
AL AHLY 1 (Dabu)

1986

CHAMPION TEAMS' CUP

QUALIFYING TOURNAMENT FIRST ROUND

Group 1
Police FC (SYM) .... W-O

Group 2
Al Talabah (IRQ) .... 2-1 * .... Al Wahda (NYM)
* Played in Saan'a

Group 3
Tournament in Bahrain
Al Hilal, KSA and **Al Arabi**, QAT, qualified at the expense of teams from the United Arab Emirates, Oman and Kuwait

Group 4
Tournament in Colombo
Malavan SC, IRN and **Saunders**, SRI, qualified at the expense of Habib Bank, PAK and Victory SC, MDV

Group 5
Selangor FA (MYS) .... 1-0 1-0 * .... Port Authority (THA)
* Both games in Kuala Lumpur

Group 6
Tournament in Brunei
Tiga Berlian, IDN qualified for the second round at the expense of Air Force, PHI and Daerah Brunei, BRU

Group 7
April 25 (PRK) .... 0-0 0-1 .... **Liaoning** (CHN)
Furukawa (JPN) .... Bye

Group 8
Tournament in Hong Kong
South China (HKG) .... 1-0 .... Hap Kuan (MAC)
Hap Kuan (MAC) .... W-O .... Lucky Goldstar (KOR)

SECOND ROUND

Group A
Tournament in Baghdad

	AT	AA	Sa	Pl	W	D	L	F	A	Pts
Al Talabah (IRQ)	-	2-0	4-0	2	2	0	0	6	0	4
Al Arabi (QAT)	-	-	9-0	2	1	0	1	9	2	2
Saunders (SRI)	-	-	-	2	0	0	2	0	13	0

Group B
Tournament in Saudi Arabia

	AH	Po	Pl	W	D	L	F	A	Pts
Al Hilal (KSA)	-	5-0	2	2	0	0	7	0	4
Police FC (SYM)	0-2	-	2	0	0	2	0	7	0

Malavan withdrew

Group C
Tournament in Hong Kong

	Li	TB	SC	Pl	W	D	L	F	A	Pts
Liaoning (CHN)	-	0-0	1-0	2	1	1	0	1	0	3
Tiga Berlian (IDN)	-	-	1-1	2	0	2	0	1	1	2
South China (HKG)	-	-	-	2	0	1	1	1	2	1

Group D
Tournament in Kuala Lumpur

	Fu	Se	HK	Pl	W	D	L	F	A	Pts
Furukawa (JPN)	-	2-1	3-1	2	2	0	0	5	2	4
Selangor FA (MYS)	-	-	5-0	2	1	0	1	6	2	2
Hap Kuan (MAC)	-	-	-	2	0	0	2	1	8	0

FINAL TOURNAMENT. RIYADH, 26TH - 30TH DECEMBER 1986

	Fu	AH	Li	AT	Pl	W	D	L	F	A	Pts
Furukawa (JPN)	-	4-3	1-0	2-0	3	3	0	0	7	3	6
Al Hilal (KSA)	-	-	2-1	2-1	3	2	0	1	7	6	4
Liaoning (CHN)	-	-	-	2-2	3	0	1	2	3	5	1
Al Talaba (IRQ)	-	-	-	-	3	0	1	2	3	6	1

Decisive game. Riyadh, 26-12-1986

FURUKAWA 4
AL HILAL 3

1987

CHAMPION TEAMS' CUP

FIRST ROUND

Group 1
Tournament in Kuwait

	AK	AH	AM	AN	AF	Pl	W	D	L	F	A	Pts
Al Kazma (KUW)	-	0-1	3-0	1-0	2-0	4	3	0	0	6	1	6

						Pl	W	D	L	F	A	Pts
Al Hilal (KSA)	-	-	2-3	0-0	3-0	4	2	1	1	6	3	5
Al Muharraq (BHR)	-	-	-	0-1	2-1	4	2	0	2	5	7	4
Al Nasr (UAE)	-	-	-	-	2-3	4	1	1	2	3	4	3
Al Fanja (OMN)	-	-	-	-	-	4	1	0	3	4	9	2

Group 2
Tournament in Bangladesh

	AR	MB	Mo	MM	AF	Pl	W	D	L	F	A	Pts
Al Rasheed (IRQ)	-	2-0	5-1	6-1	10-0	4	4	0	0	23	2	8
Mohun Bagan (IND)	-	-	2-2	6-1	4-1	4	2	1	1	12	6	5
Mohammedan (BGD)	-	-	-	6-2	3-1	4	2	1	1	12	10	5
Manang Marsyangdi (NPL)	-	-	-	-	4-1	4	1	0	3	8	19	2
Air Force (PAK)	-	-	-	-	-	4	0	0	4	3	21	0

Group 3
Tournament in Male, Maldives

	BB	AF	Vi	Pl	W	D	L	F	A	Pts
Bangkok Bank (THA)	-	0-0	7-0	2	1	1	0	7	0	3
Air Force (SRI)	-	-	1-1	2	0	2	0	1	1	2
Victory SC (MDV)	-	-	-	2	0	1	1	1	8	1

Group 4
Tournament in Bandung, Indonesia

	FT	TB	TB	KR	Pl	W	D	L	F	A	Pts
Federal Territory (MYS)	-	2-0	0-0	8-1	3	2	1	0	10	1	5
Tiga Berlian (IDN)	-	-	3-0	5-1	3	2	0	1	8	3	4
Tiong Baru (SIN)	-	-	-	3-2	3	1	1	1	3	5	3
Kota Rangers (BRU)	-	-	-	-	3	0	0	3	4	16	0

Group 5
Tournament in Dalian, China

	Au	Ap	HK	Pl	W	D	L	F	A	Pts
August 1st (CHN)	-	2-0	3-0	2	2	0	0	5	0	4
April 25th (PRK)	-	-	2-1	2	1	0	1	2	3	2
Hap Kuan (MAC)	-	-	-	2	0	0	2	1	5	0

Group 6
South China (HKG)..................1-0 0-2..........................**Yomiuri** (JPN)

Yomiuri qualified for the semi-finals

SEMI-FINALS

Group A
Tournament in Riyadh

	AH	AR	BB	Pl	W	D	L	F	A	Pts
Al Hilal	-	2-1	4-0	2	2	0	0	6	1	4
Al Rasheed	-	-	6-1	2	1	0	1	7	3	2
Bangkok Bank	-	-	-	2	0	0	2	1	10	0

Group B
Tournament in Kuala Lumpur

	Yo	FT	AK	Au	Pl	W	D	L	F	A	Pts
Yomiuri	-	0-1	2-1	2-0	3	2	0	1	4	2	4
Federal Territory	-	-	1-1	1-1	3	1	2	0	3	2	4
Al Kazma	-	-	-	1-0	3	1	1	1	3	3	3
August 1st	-	-	-	-	3	0	1	2	1	4	1

FINAL

Yomiuri declared champions after Al Hilal withdrew

1988

CHAMPION TEAMS' CUP

FIRST ROUND

Group 1
Tournament in Doha

	AR	AS	AF	AA	Pl	W	D	L	F	A	Pts
Al Rasheed (IRQ)	-	0-0	3-0	6-0	3	2	1	0	9	0	5
Al Saad (QAT)	-	-	4-1	1-0	3	2	1	0	5	1	5
Al Futuwa (SYR)	-	-	-	1-0	3	1	0	2	2	7	2
Al Ansar (LIB)	-	-	-	-	3	0	0	3	0	8	0

Group 2
Tournament in Sharjah, United Arab Emirates

	AI	AK	AS	AF	AR	Pl	W	D	L	F	A	Pts
Al Ittifaq (KSA)	-	1-1	1-0	1-0	3-1	4	3	1	0	6	2	7
Al Kazma (KUW)	-	-	3-0	3-1	2-0	4	3	1	0	9	2	7
Al Sharjah (UAE)	-	-	-	4-1	2-0	4	2	0	2	6	5	4
Al Fanja (OMN)	-	-	-	-	1-0	4	1	0	3	3	8	2
Al Rifaa (BHR)	-	-	-	-	-	4	0	0	4	1	8	0

Group 3
Tournament in Calcutta

	MB	AF	CT	Ka	Pl	W	D	L	F	A	Pts
Mohun Bagan (IND)	-	1-0	8-0	4-2	4	3	0	0	13	2	6
Al Fanja (OMN)	-	-	8-1	5-1	4	2	0	1	13	3	4
Cresent Textile (PAK)	-	-	-	2-1	4	1	0	2	3	17	2
Kathmandu SC (NPL)	-	-	-	-	4	0	0	2	4	11	0

Group 4
Tournament in Dacca, Bangladesh

	Mo	Pi	Sa	Pl	W	D	L	F	A	Pts
Mohammedan (BGD)	-	2-1	0-0	2	1	1	0	2	1	3
Piroozi (IRN)	-	-	5-0	2	1	0	1	6	2	2
Saunders SC (SRI)	-	-	-	2	0	1	1	0	5	1

Group 5
Tournament in Bangkok

	AF	Pa	NM	Ge	Be	Pl	W	D	L	F	A	Pts
Air Force (THA)	-	2-1	2-1	9-0	9-0	4	4	0	0	22	2	8
Pahang FA (MYS)	-	-	0-0	2-1	5-1	4	2	1	1	8	4	5
Niac Mitra (IDN)	-	-	-	1-1	3-1	4	1	2	1	5	4	4
Geylang International (SIN)	-	-	-	-	3-1	4	1	1	2	5	13	3
Belait (BRU)	-	-	-	-	-	4	0	0	4	3	20	0

Group 6
Tournament in Guangzhou

	Ap	Gz	Ya	SC	WS	Pl	W	D	L	F	A	Pts
April 25th (PRK)	-	1-0	3-1	3-0	4-0	4	4	0	0	11	1	8
Guangdong (CHN)	-	-	3-1	1-0	7-1	4	3	0	1	11	3	6
Yamaha (JPN)	-	-	-	1-1	9-2	4	1	1	2	12	9	3
South China (HKG)	-	-	-	-	3-0	4	1	1	2	4	5	3
Wa Seng (MAC)	-	-	-	-	-	4	0	0	4	3	23	0

SEMI-FINALS

Group A
Tournament in Guangzhou

	AR	Gz	AK	MB	Pl	W	D	L	F	A	Pts
Al Rasheed	-	1-1	2-0	4-0	3	2	1	0	7	1	5
Guangdong	-	-	1-1	6-0	3	1	2	0	8	2	4
Al Kazma	-	-	-	1-0	3	1	1	1	2	3	3
Mohun Bagan	-	-	-	-	3	0	0	3	0	11	0

Air Force withdrew

Group B
Tournament in Kuantan, Malaysia

	AS	AI	Ap	Mo	Pa	Pl	W	D	L	F	A	Pts
Al Saad	-	2-1	2-1	2-2	2-0	4	3	1	0	8	4	7
Al Itifaq	-	-	1-1	3-1	4-1	4	2	1	1	9	5	5
April 25th	-	-	-	0-1	2-0	4	1	1	2	4	4	3
Mohammedan	-	-	-	-	1-2	4	1	1	2	5	7	3
Pahang FA	-	-	-	-	-	4	1	0	3	3	9	2

FINAL

1st Leg. Baghdad, 31-03-1989, 10,000

AL RASHEED 3 (Radhi, Kadhum 2)
AL SAAD 2 (Salman.K, Ghanim)

2nd Leg. Doha, 6-04-1989, 5,000

AL SAAD 1 (Salman.K)
AL RASHEED 0
Al Saad won on away goals

1989

CHAMPION TEAMS' CUP

FIRST ROUND

Group 1
Tournament in Amman, Jordan

	AD	AR	AA	AS	AA	Pl	W	D	L	F	A	Pts
Al Deffatain (JOR)	-	2-1	0-0	3-0	2-0	4	3	1	0	7	1	7
Al Rasheed (IRQ)	-	-	0-0	3-0	1-0	4	2	1	1	5	2	5
Al Ansar (LIB)	-	-	-	0-2	2-1	4	1	2	1	2	3	4
Al Saad (QAT)	-	-	-	-	0-0	4	1	1	2	2	6	3
Al Ahly (NYM)	-	-	-	-	-	4	0	1	3	1	5	1

Group 2
Tournament in Bahrain

	AA	AM	AF	AW	AH	Pl	W	D	L	F	A	Pts
Al Arabi (KUW)	-	1-2	1-1	2-1	4-2	4	2	1	1	8	6	5
Al Muharraq (BHR)	-	-	2-0	1-2	1-1	4	2	1	1	6	4	5
Al Fanja (OMN)	-	-	-	3-0	2-1	4	2	1	1	6	4	5
Al Wasl (UAE)	-	-	-	-	1-0	4	2	0	2	4	6	4
Al Hilal (KSA)	-	-	-	-	-	4	0	1	3	4	8	1

Group 3
Tournament in Muscat, Oman

	AF	Sa	Pu	Ka	Pl	W	D	L	F	A	Pts
Al Fanja (OMN)	-	3-1	2-0	5-0	3	3	0	0	10	1	6
Salgaocar SC (IND)	-	-	0-0	3-0	3	1	1	1	4	3	3
Punjab FC (PAK)	-	-	-	1-1	3	0	2	1	1	3	2
Kathmandu SC (NPL)	-	-	-	-	3	0	1	2	1	9	1

Group 4
Tournament in Ahwaz, Iran

	Sh	Mo	OB	Vi	Pl	W	D	L	F	A	Pts
Shahin FC (IRN)	-	1-0	5-0	5-0	3	3	0	0	11	0	6
Mohammedan (BGD)	-	-	3-1	7-2	3	2	0	1	10	4	4
Old Bens SC (SRI)	-	-	-	3-1	3	1	0	2	4	9	2
Victory SC (MDV)	-	-	-	-	3	0	0	3	3	15	0

Group 5
Tournament in Kuala Lumpur, Malaysia

	KL	PJ	Ge	AF	Mu	Pl	W	D	L	F	A	Pts
Kuala Lumpur FA (MYS)	-	2-1	4-2	6-0	7-1	4	4	0	0	19	4	8
Pelita Jaya FC (IDN)	-	-	4-1	3-0	2-1	4	3	0	1	10	4	6
Geylang International (SIN)	-	-	-	3-0	5-1	4	2	0	2	11	9	4
Air Force (PHI)	-	-	-	-	1-0	4	1	0	3	1	12	2
Muara FC (BRU)	-	-	-	-	-	4	0	0	4	3	15	0

Group 6
Tournament in Shenyang, China

	Li	Ni	Ch	HK	Pl	W	D	L	F	A	Pts
Liaoning (CHN)	-	1-0	1-1	5-1	3	2	1	0	7	2	5
Nissan (JPN)	-	-	2-0	9-0	3	2	0	1	11	1	4
Chadongcha FC (PRK)	-	-	-	2-0	3	1	1	1	3	3	3
Hap Kuan (MAC)	-	-	-	-	3	0	0	3	1	16	0

SEMI-FINALS

Al Deffatain, Al Muharraq and Al Arabi all withdrew

Group A
Tournament in Kuala Lumpur

	Ni	KL	AF	Pl	W	D	L	F	A	Pts
Nissan	-	2-1	1-0	2	2	0	0	3	1	4
Kuala Lumpur FA	-	-	2-0	2	1	0	1	3	2	2
Al Fanja	-	-	-	2	0	0	2	0	3	0

Group B
Tournament in Jakarta, Indonesia

	Li	AR	Sh	PJ	Pl	W	D	L	F	A	Pts
Liaoning	-	0-0	2-0	1-0	3	2	1	0	3	0	5
Al Rasheed	-	-	5-0	1-1	3	1	2	0	6	1	4
Shahin FC	-	-	-	2-0	3	1	0	2	2	7	2
Pelita Jaya FC	-	-	-	-	3	0	1	2	1	4	1

FINAL

1st leg. Yokohama, 22-04-1990

NISSAN 1 (Sandoro)
LIAONING 2 (Fu Bo, Sandoro og)

2nd leg. Shenyang, 29-04-1990

LIAONING 1 (Xu Hui)
NISSAN 1 (Kazushi Kimura)

1990

CHAMPION TEAMS' CUP

QUALIFYING TOURNAMENT

Group 1
Tournament in Baghdad

	AR	AR	AY	Pl	W	D	L	F	A	Pts
Al Rasheed (IRQ)	-	2-1	1-0	2	2	0	0	3	1	4
Al Ramtha (JOR)	-	-	3-1	2	1	0	1	4	3	2
Al Yarmouk (YEM)	-	-	-	2	0	0	2	1	4	0

Group 2
Al Saad (QAT) ....1-1 0-1............**Esteghlal SC** (IRN)
Esteghlal qualified for the final tournament

Group 3
The Gulf Cooperation Council Club Tournament was cancelled due to the political crisis in the region

Group 4
Tournament in Quetta, Pakistan

	AN	PA	Ra	Pl	W	D	L	F	A	Pts
Al Nasr (OMN)	-	0-0	2-0	2	1	1	0	2	0	3
Pakistan Airlines (PAK)	-	-	1-0	2	1	1	0	1	0	3
Ranipokhari (NPL)	-	-	-	2	0	0	2	0	3	0

Group 5
Tournament in Dhaka, Bangladesh

	Mo	Sa	CL	Pl	W	D	L	F	A	Pts
Mohammedan (BGD)	-	2-1	5-0	2	2	0	0	7	1	4
Salgaocar SC (IND)	-	-	3-1	2	1	0	1	4	3	2
Club Lagoons (MDV)	-	-	-	2	0	0	2	1	8	0

Group 6
Tournament in Singapore

	PJ	BB	Ge	Pl	W	D	L	F	A	Pts
Pelita Jaya FC (IDN)	-	2-1	0-0	2	1	1	0	2	1	3
Bangkok Bank (THA)	-	-	2-1	2	1	0	1	3	3	2
Geylang International (SIN)	-	-	-	2	0	1	1	1	2	1

Group 7
Tournament in Pyongyang, North Korea

	Ap	Li	Ni	Pl	W	D	L	F	A	Pts
April 25th (PRK)	-	1-0	1-0	2	2	0	0	2	0	4
Liaoning (CHN)	-	-	3-2	2	1	0	1	3	3	2
Nissan (JPN)	-	-	-	2	0	0	2	2	4	0

FINAL TOURNAMENT. DHAKA, BANGLADESH, 19TH - 29TH JULY 1991

FIRST ROUND

Group 1

	Li	PJ	AN	Pl	W	D	L	F	A	Pts
Liaoning	-	1-0	1-1	2	1	1	0	2	1	3
Pelita Jaya	-	-	3-0	2	1	0	1	3	1	2
Al Nasr	-	-	-	2	0	1	1	1	4	1

Al Rasheed withdrew

Group 2

	Es	Ap	Mo	BB	Pl	W	D	L	F	A	Pts
Esteghlal	-	2-1	1-1	2-0	3	2	1	0	5	2	5
April 25th	-	-	0-0	4-3	3	1	1	1	5	5	3
Mohammedan	-	-	-	1-1	3	0	3	0	2	2	3
Bangkok Bank	-	-	-	-	3	0	1	2	4	7	1

SEMI-FINALS

Esteghlal .... 2-0 .... Pelita Jaya
Liaoning .... 3-0 .... April 25th

3RD PLACE

April 25th .... 2-2 7-6p .... Pelita Jaya

FINAL

Dhaka Stadium, Dhaka, 29-07-1991
ESTEGHLAL SPORTS CLUB 2 (Barvagh, Marfavy)
LIAONING 1 (Xu Hui)

CUP WINNERS CUP

FIRST ROUND

Punjab (PAK) .... 2-4 0-9 .... **Pirouzi** (IRN)
Daewoo Royals (KOR) .... Bye
Al Faisaly (JOR) .... W-O .... Al Qadisiyah (KUW)
Al Shabab (UAE) .... Bye
Al Hilal (KSA) .... Bye
Mohammedan (BGD) .... W-O .... Renown (SRI)
Tiga Berlian (IDN) .... 1-1 2-2 .... Geylang International (SIN)
Mohan Bagan (IND) .... 0-1 0-4 .... **Dalian** (CHN)
Al Fanja (OMN) .... 1-3 0-0 .... **Al Arabi** (QAT)
Al Muharraq (BHR) .... 5-1 3-0 .... Al Nijmeh (LIB)

SECOND ROUND

Pirouzi .... W-O .... Daewoo Royals
Al Hilal .... 7-0 2-1 .... Mohammedan
Tiga Berlian .... * .... Dalian
Al Faisaly .... 0-1 0-1 .... **Al Shabab**
Al Arabi .... 1-0 0-4 .... **Al Muharraq**

* both clubs withdrew

SEMI-FINALS

Al Hilal .... 0-0 0-1 .... **Pirouzi**
Al Muharraq .... 1-0 2-2 .... Al Shabab

FINAL

Pirouzi .... 0-0 1-0 .... Al Muharraq

1991

CHAMPION TEAMS' CUP

FINAL TOURNAMENT. DOHA, QATAR, 12TH - 22ND DECEMBER 1991

FIRST ROUND

Group A

	AR	AS	PA	Mo	Pl	W	D	L	F	A	Pts
Al Rayyan (QAT)	-	2-1	3-1	3-1	3	3	0	0	8	3	6
Al Shabab (UAE)	-	-	3-1	2-1	3	2	0	1	6	4	4
Port Authority (THA)	-	-	-	4-1	3	1	0	2	6	7	2
Mohammedan (BGD)	-	-	-	-	3	0	0	3	3	9	0

Group B

	AH	Es	Py	Pl	W	D	L	F	A	Pts
Al Hilal (KSA)	-	1-0	2-0	2	2	0	0	3	0	4
Esteghlal SC (IRN)	-	-	1-1	2	0	1	1	1	2	1
Pyongyang (PRK)	-	-	-	2	0	1	1	1	3	1

SEMI-FINALS

Al Hilal .... 1-0 .... Al Shabab
Esteghlal .... 2-1 .... Al Rayyan

3RD PLACE

Al Rayyan .... 4-1 .... Al Shabab

FINAL

Doha, 22-12-1991
AL HILAL 1
ESTEGHLAL SC 1
Al-Hilal won 4-3 on pens

CUP WINNERS CUP

FIRST ROUND

Nissan (JPN) .... 6-0 0-0 .... Geylang (SIN)
Abahani Krira Cha. (BGD) .... 0-0 0-1 .... **East Bengal** (IND)
Sinugba (PHI) .... Bye
Port Trust (PAK) .... 0-6 0-3 .... **Pupuk Kaltim** (IDN)
Al Ramtha (JOR) .... 0-1 2-0 .... Al Ahly (BHR)
Al Sharjah (UAE) .... 2-1 0-1 .... **Dofar** (QAT)
Malavan (IRN) .... Bye
Al Saad (KUW) .... 1-1 1-1 2-4p .... **Al Kazma** (KUW)
Al Nasr (KSA) .... 2-1 2-1 .... Al Ansar (LIB)

SECOND ROUND

East Bengal .... 1-3 0-4 .... **Nissan**
Pupuk Kaltim .... W-O .... Sinugba
Al Ramtha .... 1-0 1-1 .... Dofar
Malavan .... Bye
Al Kazma .... 0-1 1-2 .... **Al Nasr**

EXTRA ROUND

Malavan .... 1-1 0-0 .... **Al Ramtha**

SEMI-FINALS

Nissan .... 2-0 0-0 .... Pupuk Kaltim
Al Ramtha .... 0-1 1-2 .... **Al Nasr**

FINAL

Nissan .... 1-1 5-0 .... Al Nasr

1992

CHAMPION TEAMS' CUP

FINAL TOURNAMENT. BAHRAIN, 12TH - 22ND JANUARY 1993

FIRST ROUND

Group A

	Yo	AS	AM	Ar	Pl	W	D	L	F	A	Pts
Yomiuri (JPN)	-	0-0	2-0	3-0	3	2	1	0	5	0	5
Al Shabab (KSA)	-	-	1-1	3-0	3	1	2	0	4	1	4
Al Muharraq (BHR)	-	-	-	3-0	3	1	1	1	4	3	3
Arseto (IDN)	-	-	-	-	3	0	0	3	0	9	0

Group B

	AW	Pa	Wo	Pl	W	D	L	F	A	Pts
Al Wasl (UAE)	-	1-0	10-0	2	2	0	0	11	0	4

Pass (IRN)	-	-	1-1	2	0	1	1	1	2	1
Wohaib (PAK)	-	-	-	2	0	1	1	1	11	1

SEMI-FINALS

Pass ... 2-1 ... Yomiuri
Al Shabab ... 2-2 4-3p ... Al Wasl

3RD PLACE

Al Wasl ... 4-3 ... Yomiuri

FINAL

Bahrain, 22-01-1993

PASS 1
AL SHABAB 0

CUP WINNERS CUP

FIRST ROUND

Nissan (JPN) ... Bye
Pupuk Kaltin (IDN) ... W-O ... Sing Tao (HKG)
Pakistan Int. Airways (PAK) ... * ... York (SRI)
Mohamedan (BGD) ... Bye
Quang Nam Danang (VIE) ... W-O ... Balestier (SIN)
Al Ittihad (KSA) ... Bye
Al Arabi (KUW) ... 0-0 1-0 ... Al Ahly (QAT)
Al Ramtha (JOR) ... 3-2 1-5 ... **Baniyas** (UAE)
Al Fanja (OMN) ... W-O ... Mohamedan (IND)
Pirouzi (IRN) ... W-O ... SAFA (LIB)
* Both clubs withdrew

SECOND ROUND

Pupuk Kaltin ... 1-1 1-3 ... **Nissan**
Quang Nam Danang ... W-O ... Mohamedan
Al Arabi ... 0-1 1-2 ... **Al Ittihad**
Baniyas ... Bye
Pirouzi ... 0-0 2-0 ... Fanja

EXTRA ROUND

Pirouzi ... 2-1 1-1 ... Baniyas

SEMI-FINALS

Quang Nam Danang ... 1-1 0-3 ... **Nissan**
Pirouzi ... 1-0 1-1 ... Al Ittihad

FINAL

Nissan ... 1-1 1-0 ... Pirouzi

1993

CHAMPION TEAMS' CUP

WEST ASIA

PRELIMINARY ROUND

Pass (IRN) ... 2-0 2-1 ... Al-Ahly (YEM)
Al Ansar (LEB) ... 0-0 3-1 ... Al-Ittihad (QAT)

FIRST ROUND

Paas (IRN) ... 0-0 ?-? 4-5p ... **Al Ansar** (LEB)
Al-Shabab (KSA) ... 5-2 7-1 ... Al-Arabi (KUW)
Muharraq (BHR) ... 2-1 1-1 ... Sharjah (UAE)
Al Ansar, Al-Shabab and Muharraq qualified for the final tournament. Al Shabab later withdrew

CENTRAL ASIA

Omani Club (OMN) ... 5-0 ... Defence Lahore (PAK)

Omani Club and Victory from the Maldives qualified for the finals. Jawniya and Abahani Krira Chadra withdrew. Victory withdrew before the finals

SOUTH EAST ASIA

FIRST ROUND

Arema (IDN) ... 1-0 2-1 ... Quang Nam-Dang (VIE)
Thai Farmers Bank (THA) ... W-O ... Pahang (MYS)

FINAL

Arema ... 2-2 1-4 ... **Thai Farmers Bank**

EAST ASIA

PRELIMINARY ROUND

Leng Ngan (MAC) ... 3-0 0-1 ... Pa Team (PHI)

FINAL ROUND

Liaoning (CHI) ... 9-0 6-3 ... Leng Ngan (MAC)
Eastern (HKG) ... 1-0 1-3 ... **Verdy Kawasaki** (JPN)
Liaoning and Verdy qualified for the finals

FINAL TOURNAMENT. BANGKOK, THAILAND, 28TH JANUARY - 7TH FEBRUARY 1994

Group 1

	VK	Om	AA	Pl	W	D	L	F	A	Pts
Verdy Kawasaki (JPN)	-	1-0	2-0	2	2	0	0	3	0	4
Omani Club (OMN)	-	-	1-0	2	1	0	1	1	1	2
Al Ansar (LEB)	-	-	-	2	0	0	2	0	3	0

Group 2

	Li	TF	AM	Pl	W	D	L	F	A	Pts
Liaoning (CHN)	-	1-1	1-0	2	1	1	0	2	1	3
Thai Farmers Bank (THA)	-	-	2-2	2	0	2	0	3	3	2
Al Muharraq (BHR)	-	-	-	2	0	1	1	2	3	1

SEMI-FINALS

Thai Farmers ... 1-1 3-1p ... Verdy Kawasaki
Omani Club ... 4-1 ... Liaoning

3RD PLACE

Verdy Kawasaki ... 4-1 ... Liaoning

FINAL

National Stadium, Bangkok, 7-02-1994

THAI FARMERS 2 (Phamobal, Totavee)
OMANI CLUB 1 (Salim)

CUP WINNERS CUP

FIRST ROUND

Al Wehda (BHR) ... 1-0 1-4 ... **Al Qadisiyah** (KSA)
Mohamedan (BGD) ... Bye
New Radiant (MDV) ... 3-0 2-0 ... Youth League (PAK)
Pirouzi (IRN) ... 0-1 2-1 ... Al Salmiya (KUW)
Al Arabi (QAT) ... W-O ... Al Nasr (UAE)
Nissan (JPN) ... 5-0 1-0 ... AFP (PHI)
Saigon Port (VIE) ... W-O ... Sarawak (MAS?
Semen Padang (IDN) ... Bye
East Bengal (IND) ... 6-2 0-2 ... Zawra'a (IRQ)
South China (HKG) ... 2-0 0-1 ... Dalian (CHN)

SECOND ROUND

Al Qadisiyah ... Bye
Mohamedan ... 8-0 ... **New Radiant**
Pirouzi ... Bye
Al Arabi ... Bye
Nissan ... Bye
Semen Padang ... 1-0 1-1 ... Saigon Port
East Bengal ... 0-1 1-4 ... **South China**

QUARTER-FINALS

Al Qadisiyah W-O New Radiant
Pirouzi 1-1 1-2 **Al Arabi**
Semen Padang 2-1 0-11 **Nissan**
South China Bye

SEMI-FINALS

Al Arabi 1-1 0-1 **Al Qadisiyah**
South China W-O Nissan

FINAL

South China 2-4 0-2 **Al Qadisiyah**

1994

CHAMPION TEAMS' CUP

FINAL TOURNAMENT

Held in Bangkok, 27th - 29th January 1995

SEMI-FINALS

Al Arabi (QAT) 2-0 Ilwha Chunma (KOR)
Thai Farmers Bank (THA) 2-2 3-0p Neftchi Fergana (UZB)

3RD PLACE

Neftchi Fergana 1-0 Ilwha Chunma

FINAL

Bangkok, 29-01-1995, 8,000

THAI FARMERS BANK 1 (Natipong Sritong-in 82)
AL ARABI 0

CUP WINNERS CUP

FINAL TOURNAMENT

Held in Sharjah, UAE, 20th - 22nd January 1995

SEMI-FINALS

Yokohama Flugels (JAP) 4-2 TOT Thailand (THA)
Al Shaab (UAE) 1-1 4-3p Al Ittihad (KSA)

3RD PLACE

Al Ittihad 1-1 3-0p TOT Thailand

FINAL

Sharjah, 22-01-1995

YOKOHAMA FLUGELS 2 (Watanabe 37 95)
AL SHAAB 1 (Keita 74)

ARAB CHAMPIONS CUP

1981	Al Schurta	IRQ
1984	Al Ittifaq	KSA
1985	Al Rasheed	IRQ
1986	Al Rasheed	IRQ
1987	Al Rasheed	IRQ
1988	Al Ittifaq	KSA
1992	WAC Casablanca	MOR
1993	Al Shabab	KSA
1994	Esperance Tunis	TUN
1995	Al Halal	KSA

ARAB CUP WINNERS CUP

1989	Stade Tunisien	TUN
1991	Olympic Casablanca	MOR
1993	Olympic Casablanca	MOR
1994	Olympic Casablanca	MOR
1995	Al Ahly	KSA

AFGHANISTAN

Population: 15,592,000
Area, sq km: 652,225
% in urban areas: 18%
Capital city: Kabul 1,424,000

The Football Federation of the National Olympic Committee
PO Box 756
Kabul
Afghanistan
Tel: + 114 20579

Year of formation	1922
Affiliation to FIFA	1948
Affiliation to AFC	1954
Registered clubs	30
Registered players	4800
Registered coaches	20
Registered referees	18
National stadium	National Stadium, Kabul 25,000
National colours	All White
Reserve colours	Green/White/Green
Season	September - January

THE RECORD

WORLD CUP

1930-94	Did not enter

ASIAN CHAMPIONSHIP

1956-68	Did not enter
1972	
1976	QT 4th/4 in group 2
1980	QT 3rd/3 in group 2
1984	QT 5th/5 in group 4
1988	Did not enter
1992	Did not enter

ASIAN GAMES

1951	Semi-finalists
1954	1st round
1958-94	Did not enter

ASIAN CLUB COMPETITIONS

Have never entered

BAHRAIN

Population: 503,000
Area, sq km: 692
% in urban areas: 82%
Capital city: Manama 151,000

Bahrain Football Association
PO Box 5464
Bahrain
Tel: + 973 728218
Fax: + 973 729361
Telex: 9040 fab bn

Year of formation	1951
Affiliation to FIFA	1966
Affiliation to AFC	1970
Registered clubs	25
Registered players	3200
Registered coaches	180
Registered referees	55
National stadium	Isa Town Stadium, Manama 16,000
National colours	White/Red/Red
Reserve colours	All Blue
Season	September - May

THE RECORD

WORLD CUP

1930-74	Did not enter
1978	QT R1 2nd/3 in group 4
1982	QT R1 4th/5 in group 2
1986	QT R1 1st/2 in group 4, R2 2nd/2
1990	Did not enter
1994	QT R1 2nd/5 in group 4

ASIAN CHAMPIONSHIP

1956-68	Did not enter
1972	
1976	Did not enter
1980	QT 3rd/4 in group 1
1984	Did not enter
1988	QT 1st/4 in group 4 - Final tournament/1st round
1992	QT 3rd/3 in group 2

ASIAN GAMES

1951-70	Did not enter
1974	1st round
1978	1st round
1982	Did not enter
1986	1st round
1990	Did not enter
1994	1st round

ASIAN CLUB COMPETITIONS

Asian Champion Teams' Cup
Final tournament - Muharraq 1993 1994
Asian Cup Winners Cup
Finalists - Muharraq 1990

LEAGUE CHAMPIONS OF BAHRAIN

1957	Muharraq
1958	Muharraq
1959	Al Nasr
1960	Muharraq
1961	Muharraq
1962	Muharraq
1963	Muharraq
1964	Muharraq
1965	Muharraq
1966	Muharraq
1967	Muharraq
1968	Bahrain Club
1969	Al Ahly
1970	Muharraq
1971	Muharraq
1972	Al Ahly
1973	Muharraq
1974	Muharraq
1975	Al Arabi
1976	Muharraq
1977	Al Ahly
1978	Bahrain Club
1979	Al Hala
1980	Muharraq
1981	Bahrain Club
1982	West Riffa
1983	Muharraq
1984	Muharraq
1985	Bahrain Club
1986	Muharraq
1987	West Riffa
1988	Muharraq
1989	Bahrain Club
1990	West Riffa
1991	Muharraq
1992	Muharraq
1993	West Riffa
1994	East Riffa
1995	Muharraq

BANGLADESH

Population: 113,005,000
Area, sq km: 143,998
% in urban areas: 24%
Capital city: Dhaka 5,300,000

Bangladesh Football Federation
Stadium
Dhaka-1000
Bangladesh
Tel: + 880 2 236072
Fax: + 880 2 864769

Year of formation	1972
Affiliation to FIFA	1974
Affiliation to AFC	1974
Registered clubs	1,265
Registered players	44 500
Registered coaches	20
Registered referees	996
National stadium	Dhaka Stadium 55 000
National colours	Orange/White/Green
Reserve colours	White/White/Green
Season	January - June

THE RECORD

WORLD CUP

1930-82	Did not enter
1986	QT R1 4th/4 in group 6
1990	QT R1 3rd/4 in group 5
1994	QT R1 4th/5 in group 6

ASIAN CHAMPIONSHIP

1956-76	Did not enter
1980	QT 2nd/3 in group 2 - Final tournament/1st round
1984	QT th/6 in group 1
1988	QT 5th/6 in group 1
1992	QT 3rd/3 in group 5

ASIAN GAMES

1951-74	Did not enter
1978	1st round
1982	1st round
1986	1st round
1990	1st round
1994	Did not enter

ASIAN CLUB COMPETITIONS

Asian Champion Teams' Cup
Semi-finalists - Mohammedan Sporting 1988
Asian Cup Winners Cup
Quarter-finalists - Mohammedan Sporting 1990 1992

DHAKA LEAGUE CHAMPIONSHIP

1948	Victoria Sporting
1949	East Pakistan Gymkhana
1950	Dhaka Wanderers
1951	Dhaka Wanderers
1952	Bengal Government Press
1953	Dhaka Wanderers
1954	Dhaka Wanderers
1955	Dhaka Wanderers
1956	Dhaka Wanderers
1957	Mohammedan Sporting
1958	Azad Sporting
1959	Mohammedan Sporting
1960	Dhaka Wanderers
1961	Mohammedan Sporting
1962	Victoria Sporting
1963	Mohammedan Sporting
1964	Victoria Sporting
1965	Mohammedan Sporting
1966	Mohammedan Sporting
1967	East Pakistan IDC
1968	East Pakistan IDC
1969	Mohammedan Sporting
1970	East Pakistan IDC
1971-72	-
1973	Bangladesh IDC
1974	Abahani Krira Chakra
1975	Mohammedan Sporting
1976	Mohammedan Sporting
1977	Abahani Krira Chakra
1978	Mohammedan Sporting
1979	Bangladesh Jute Mill Corp.
1980	Mohammedan Sporting
1981	Abahani Krira Chakra
1982	Mohammedan Sporting
1983	Abahani Krira Chakra
1984	Abahani Krira Chakra
1985	Abahani Krira Chakra
1986	Mohammedan Sporting
1987	Mohammedan Sporting
1988	Mohammedan Sporting
1989	Mohammedan Sporting
1990	Abahani Krira Chakra
1991	-
1992	Abahani Krira Chakra
1993	Abahani Krira Chakra

BRUNEI DARUSSALAM

Population: 259,000
Area, sq km: 5,765
% in urban areas: 63%
Capital city: Bandar Seri Begawan 52,000

Brunei Amateur Football Association
PO Box 2010
Bandar Seri Begawan
Brunei
Tel: + 673 2 242033
Fax: + 673 2 242267
Telex: bu 2575

Year of formation	1959
Affiliation to FIFA	1969
Affiliation to AFC	1970
Registered clubs	22
Registered players	2500
Registered coaches	21
Registered referees	50

National stadium	Hassanal Bolkiah, Bandar Seri Begawan 40 000
National colours	Gold/Black/Gold
Reserve colours	Red/White/Red
Season	September - March

THE RECORD

WORLD CUP

1930-82	Did not enter
1986	QT R1 4th/4 in group 7
1990	Did not enter
1994	Did not enter

ASIAN CHAMPIONSHIP

1956-72	Did not enter
1976	QT 6th/6 in group 4
1980-92	Did not enter

ASIAN GAMES

1951-94	Did not enter

PEOPLE'S REPUBLIC OF CHINA

Population: 1,133,683,000
Area, sq km: 9,572,900
% in urban areas: 51%
Capital city: Beijing 6,800,000

Football Association of the People's Republic of China
9 Tiyuguan Road
Beijing
China
Tel: + 86 1 7017018
Fax: + 86 1 5112533
Telex: 22034 acsf cn

Year of formation	1924
Affiliation to FIFA	1931-58 & 1979
Affiliation to AFC	1974
Registered clubs	1045
Registered players	4 300 000
Registered coaches	950
Registered referees	2584
National stadium	Workers Stadium, Beijing 63 000
National colours	Red/White/Red
Reserve colours	White/White/White
Season	February - September

THE RECORD

WORLD CUP

1930-78	Did not enter
1982	QT R1 1st/6 in group 4, R2 3rd/4
1986	QT R1 2nd/4 in group 7
1990	QT R1 1st/4 in group 5, R2 4th/6
1994	QT R1 2nd/5 in round 1

ASIAN CHAMPIONSHIP

1956-72	Did not enter
1976	QT 2nd/6 in group 4 - Final tournament/Semi-finalists/ 3rd place
1980	QT 2nd/4 in group 4 - Final tournament/1st round
1984	QT 1st/5 in group 4 - Final tournament/Finalists
1988	QT 2nd/6 in group 1 - Final tournament/Semi-finalists/ 4th place
1992	QT 1st/4 in group 4 - Final tournament/Semi-finalists/ 3rd place

ASIAN GAMES

1951-74	Did not enter
1978	Semi-finalists/3rd place
1982	Quarter-finalists
1986	Quarter-finalists
1990	Quarter-finalists
1994	Finalists

ASIAN CLUB COMPETITIONS

Asian Champion Teams' Cup
Winners - Liaoning 1989
Finalists - Liaoning 1990
Semi-finalists - Liaoning 1986 1993, August 1st 1987, Guangzhou 1988
Asian Cup Winners Cup
Quarter-finalists - Dalian 1990

CHINESE NATIONAL CHAMPIONSHIP

1926	South China
1927	South China
1928	East China
1929	East China
1930	South China
1931	East China
1932	-
1933	East China
1934-46	-
1946	Tsing Peh
1947	Tung Hwa & East China
1948	East China & Tsing Peh
1949	Tsing Peh
1950	-
1951	North East China
1952	-
1953	Army
1954	North East China
1955	Central Institute of Physical Culture
1956	-
1957	Tianjin
1958	Beijing
1959	Army
1960	Tianjin
1961	Shanghai
1962	Shanghai
1963	Beijing Youth
1964	Beijing Physical Culture Institute
1965	Jilin
1966-72	-
1973	Beijing
1974	Army
1975	Guangxi
1976	Beijing
1977	Army
1978	Liaoning
1979	Guangdong
1980	Tianjin
1981	Army
1982	Beijing
1983	Shanghai
1984	Beijing
1985	Liaoning
1986	Army
1987	Guangdong
1988	Liaoning
1989	Liaoning
1990	Liaoning
1991	Liaoning
1992	Liaoning
1993	Liaoning
1994	Dalian

CLUB DIRECTORY

SHANGHAI (Pop. - 9,300,000)
Shanghai Football Club

BEIJING (Pop. - 6,450,000)
Beijing Football Club

TIANJIN (Pop. - 5,460,000)
Tianjin Football Club

SHENYANG (Pop. - 4,290,000)
Liaoning Football Club

GUANGZHOU (Pop. - 3,050,000)
Guangzhou Football Club
Guangdong Football Club

CHENGDU (Pop. - 2,470,000)
Sichuan Football Club

XI'AN (Pop. - 1,686,000)
August 1st Football Club (Army)

DALIAN (Pop. - 1,680,000)
Dalian Football Club

KUNMING (Pop. - 1,520,000)
Kunming Army Unit

HONG KONG

Population: 5,841,000
Area, sq km: 1,074
% in urban areas: 100%
Capital city: Victoria

The Hong Kong Football Association Ltd
55 Fat Kwong Street, Homantin
Kowloon
Hong Kong
Tel: + 852 27129122
Fax: + 852 27604303
Telex: 40518 fahkg hx

Year of formation	1914

Affiliation to FIFA	1954
Affiliation to AFC	1954
Registered clubs	69
Registered players	6400
Professional players	300
Registered coaches	142
Registered referees	161
National stadium	Hong Kong Stadium 40 000
National colours	Red/White/Red
Reserve colours	White/White/White
Season	September - May

THE RECORD

WORLD CUP

1930-70 Did not enter
1974 QT R1 4th/7 in group A
1978 QT R1 1st/5 in group 1, R2 5th/5
1982 QT R1 3rd/6 in group 4
1986 QT R1 1st/4 in group 7, R2 2nd/2
1990 QT R1 4th/4 in group 6
1994 QT R1 4th/5 in group 4

ASIAN CHAMPIONSHIP

1956 QT Automatic - Final tournament/3rd place
1960
1964 QT 1st/ in group 2 - Final tournament/4th place
1968 QT 1st/5 in group 2 - Final tournament/5th place
1972
1976 QT 3rd/6 in group 4
1980 QT 3rd/7 in group 3
1984 QT 4th/5 in group 4
1988 QT 4th/5 in group 3
1992 QT 3rd/4 in group 6

ASIAN GAMES

1951 Did not enter
1954 1st round
1958 Quarter-finalists
1962-86 Did not enter
1990 1st round
1994 1st round

ASIAN CLUB COMPETITIONS

Asian Cup Winners Cup

Finalists - South China 1993

HONG KONG LEAGUE CHAMPIONS

1946 Royal Air Force
1947 Sing Tao
1948 Kitchee
1949 South China
1950 Kitchee
1951 South China
1952 South China
1953 South China
1954 Kowloon Motor Bus Co.
1955 South China
1956 Eastern
1957 South China
1958 South China
1959 South China
1960 South China
1961 South China
1962 South China
1963 Yuen Long
1964 Kitchee
1965 Happy Valley
1966 South China
1967 Kowloon Motor Bus Co.
1968 South China
1969 South China
1970 Jardines
1971 Rangers
1972 South China
1973 Seiko
1974 South China
1975 Seiko
1976 South China
1977 South China
1978 South China
1979 Seiko
1980 Seiko
1981 Seiko
1982 Seiko
1983 Seiko
1984 Seiko
1985 Seiko
1986 South China
1987 South China
1988 South China
1989 Happy Valley
1990 South China
1991 South China
1992 South China
1993 Eastern
1994 Eastern
1995 Eastern

HONG KONG CUP WINNERS

1975 Seiko
1976 Seiko
1977 Rangers
1978 Seiko
1979 Yuen Long
1980 Seiko
1981 Seiko
1982 Bulova
1983 Bulova
1984 Eastern
1985 South China
1986 Seiko
1987 South China
1988 South China
1989 Lei Sun
1990 South China
1991 South China
1992 Ernest Borel
1993 Eastern
1994 Eastern
1995 Rangers

HONG KONG SENIOR SHIELD WINNERS

1946 Navy 'B
1947 Sing Tao
1948 Sing Tao
1949 South China
1950 Kitchee
1951 Kowloon Motor Bus Co.
1952 Sing Tao
1953 Eastern
1954 Kitchee
1955 South China
1956 Eastern
1957 South China
1958 South China
1959 South China
1960 Kitchee
1961 South China
1962 South China
1963 Kwong Wah
1964 Kitchee
1965 South China
1966 Rangers
1967 Sing Tao
1968 Yuen Long
1969 Jardines
1970 Sing Tao
1971 Rangers
1972 South China
1973 Seiko
1974 Seiko
1975 Rangers
1976 Seiko
1977 Seiko
1978 Happy Valley
1979 Seiko
1980 Seiko
1981 Seiko
1982 Eastern
1983 Happy Valley
1984 Bulova
1985 Seiko
1986 South China
1987 Eastern
1988 South China
1989 South China
1990 Happy Valley
1991 South China
1992 Sing Tao
1993 Eastern
1994 Eastern
1995 Rangers

HONG KONG VICEROY CUP WINNERS

1970 Jardines
1971 Eastern
1972 South China
1973 Seiko
1974 Rangers
1975 Rangers
1976 Happy Valley
1977 Caroline Hill
1978 Seiko
1979 Seiko
1980 South China
1981 Eastern
1982 Bulova
1983 Bulova
1984 Seiko
1985 Seiko
1986 Seiko
1987 South China
1988 South China

1989	Lei Sun
1990	Lei Sun
1991	South China
1992	Ernest Borel
1993	South China
1994	South China
1995	Sing Tao

INDIA

Population: 853,373,000
Area, sq km: 3,166,414
% in urban areas: 27%
Capital city: New Delhi 8,156,000

All India Football Federation
Green Lawns
Talap, PO Box 429
Cannanore 670 002
Kerala
India
Tel: + 91 497 500199
Fax: + 91 497 500923
Telex: 805 286

Year of formation	1937
Affiliation to FIFA	1948
Affiliation to AFC	1954
Registered clubs	2000
Registered players	1 280 000
Registered referees	4300
National stadium	Salt Lake, Calcutta 120 000
National colours	Sky blue/White/Blue
Reserve colours	White/Blue/White
Season	March - November

THE RECORD

WORLD CUP

1930-82	Did not enter
1986	QT R1 2nd/4 in group 6
1990	Did not enter
1994	QT R1 5th/5 in group 4

ASIAN CHAMPIONSHIP

1956	Did not enter
1960	QT 4th/4 in group 1
1964	QT 1st/ in group 1 - Final tournament/2nd place
1968	QT 4th/4 in group 1
1972-80	Did not enter
1984	QT 2nd/5 in group 3 - Final tournament/1st round
1988	QT 6th/6 in group 1
1992	QT 2nd/3 in group 3

ASIAN GAMES

1951	Winners
1954	1st round
1958	Semi-finalists/4th place
1962	Winners
1966	1st round
1970	Semi-finalists/3rd place
1974	1st round
1978	Semi-finalists/4th in group
1982	Quarter-finalists
1986	1st round
1990	Did not enter
1994	Did not enter

ASIAN CLUB COMPETITIONS

Asian Champion Teams' Cup
Semi-finalists - Mysore State 1968, Mohun Bagan 1988
Asian Cup Winners Cup
Quarter-finalists - East Bengal 1991

CALCUTTA LEAGUE CHAMPIONS

1898	Gloucestershire Regiment
1899	Calcutta Football Club
1900	Royal Irish Rifles
1901	Royal Irish Rifles
1902	King's Own Scottish Borderers
1903	93rd Highlanders
1904	King's Own Regiment
1905	King's Own Regiment
1906	Highland Light Infantry
1907	Calcutta Football Club
1908	Gordon Light Infantry
1909	Gordon Light Infantry
1910	Dalhousi
1911	70th Company RGA
1912	Black Watch
1913	Black Watch
1914	91st Highlanders
1915	10th Middlesex Regiment
1916	Calcutta Football Club
1917	Lincolnshire Regiment
1918	Calcutta Football Club
1919	12th Special Service Battalion
1920	Calcutta Football Club
1921	Dalhousi
1922	Calcutta Football Club
1923	Calcutta Football Club
1924	Cameron Highlanders
1925	Calcutta Football Club
1926	North Staffordshire Regiment
1927	North Staffordshire Regiment
1928	Dalhousi
1929	Dalhousi
1930	-
1931	Durham Light Infantry
1932	Durham Light Infantry
1933	Durham Light Infantry
1934	Mohammedan Sporting
1935	Mohammedan Sporting
1936	Mohammedan Sporting
1937	Mohammedan Sporting
1938	Mohammedan Sporting
1939	Mohun Bagan
1940	Mohammedan Sporting
1941	Mohammedan Sporting
1942	East Bengal
1943	Mohun Bagan
1944	Mohun Bagan
1945	East Bengal
1946	East Bengal
1947	-
1948	Mohammedan Sporting
1949	East Bengal
1950	East Bengal
1951	Mohun Bagan
1952	East Bengal
1953	-
1954	Mohun Bagan
1955	Mohun Bagan
1956	Mohun Bagan
1957	Mohammedan Sporting
1958	Eastern Railway
1959	Mohun Bagan
1960	Mohun Bagan
1961	East Bengal
1962	Mohun Bagan
1963	Mohun Bagan
1964	Mohun Bagan
1965	Mohun Bagan
1966	East Bengal
1967	Mohammedan Sporting
1968	-
1969	Mohun Bagan
1970	East Bengal
1971	East Bengal
1972	East Bengal
1973	East Bengal
1974	East Bengal
1975	East Bengal
1976	Mohun Bagan
1977	East Bengal
1978	Mohun Bagan
1979	Mohun Bagan
1980	-
1981	Mohammedan Sporting
1982	East Bengal
1983	Mohun Bagan
1984	Mohun Bagan
1985	East Bengal
1986	Mohun Bagan
1987	East Bengal
1988	East Bengal
1989	East Bengal
1990	Mohun Bagan
1991	East Bengal
1992	Mohun Bagan
1993	East Bengal
1994	Mohun Bagan

SANTOSH TROPHY WINNERS

1941	Bengal
1942	-
1943	-
1944	Delhi
1945	Bengal
1946	Mysore
1947	Bengal
1948	-
1949	Bengal
1950	Bengal
1951	Bengal
1952	Mysore
1953	Bengal
1954	Bombay
1955	Bengal
1956	Andrha Pradesh
1957	Andrha Pradesh
1958	Bengal
1959	Bengal
1960	Services
1961	Railways
1962	Bengal
1963	Maharashtra
1964	Railways
1965	Andrha Pradesh

1966	Railways
1967	Mysore
1968	Mysore
1969	Bengal
1970	Punjab
1971	Bengal
1972	Bengal
1973	Kerala
1974	Punjab
1975	Bengal
1976	Bengal
1977	Bengal
1978	Bengal
1979	Bengal
1980	Punjab
1981	Bengal
1982	-
1983	Bengal & Goa
1984	Goa
1985	Punjab
1986	Punjab
1987	Bengal
1988	Punjab
1989	Bengal
1990	Bengal
1991	Maharashtra
1992	Kerala
1993	Bengal
1994	Bengal

FEDERATION CUP

1977	ITI Bangalore
1978	East Bengal/Mohun Bagan
1979	BSF Jullundur
1980	Mohun Bagan/East Bengal
1981	Mohun Bagan
1982	Mohun Bagan
1983	Mohammedan Sporting
1984	Mohammedan Sporting
1985	East Bengal
1986	Mohun Bagan
1987	Mohun Bagan
1988	Salgacor
1989	Salgacor
1990	Kerala Police
1992	Mohun Bagan
1993	Mohun Bagan
1994	Mohun Bagan
1995	Jagatif Cotton & Textile (JCT)

CLUB DIRECTORY

CALCUTTA
Mohun Bagan
East Bengal
Mohasmmedan Sporting

All use Salt Lake Stadium 120,000

BOMBAY
Mahindra
Air India

Both use Cooperage Stadium 16,000

MADRAS
Indian Bank
Railway

Both use Nehru Stadium 38,000

GOA
Dempo Sporting
Churchill Bros
Salgascar

All use Nehru Stadium 35,000

DELHI
JCT
BSF

Both use Nehru Stadium 25,000

BANGALORE
Indian Telephone

CALICUTT
Titanium
Kerala Police

Both use Newer Stadium 25,000

INDONESIA

Population: 180,763,000
Area, sq km: 1,948,732
% in urban areas: 26%
Capital city: Jakarta 7,829,000

Persatuan Sepakbola Seluruh Indonesia
All Indonesia Football Federation
Main Stadium Senayan, Gate VII
PO Box 2305
Jakarta 10001
Indonesia
Tel: + 62 21 5731541
Fax: + 62 21 5734386
Telex: 65739 pssi ia

Year of formation	1930
Affiliation to FIFA	1952
Affiliation to AFC	1954
Registered clubs	2880
Registered players	1 200 000
Registered coaches	1019
Registered referees	337
National stadium	Senayan, Jakarta 110 000
National colours	Red/White/Red
Reserve colours	White/White/Red
Season	June - June

THE RECORD

WORLD CUP

1930	Did not enter
1934	Did not enter
1938	QT W-O in group 10 - Final tournament/1st round
1950	Did not enter
1954	Did not enter
1958	QT R1 1st/2 in group 1, R2 withdrew
1962-70	Did not enter
1974	QT R1 6th/8 in group B
1978	QT R1 4th/5 in group 1
1982	QT R1 3rd/5 in group 1
1986	QT R1 1st/4 in group 6, R2 2nd/2
1990	QT R1 3rd/4 in group 6
1994	QT R1 4th/5 in group 3

ASIAN CHAMPIONSHIP

1956	Did not enter
1960	-
1964	-
1968	QT 4th/5 in group 3
1972	-
1976	QT 4th/5 in group 3
1980	QT 6th/7 in group 3
1984	QT /6 in group 1
1988	QT 3rd/4 in group 4
1992	QT 2nd/4 in group 4

ASIAN GAMES

1951	1st round
1954	Semi-finalists/4th place
1958	Semi-finalists/3rd place
1962	1st round
1966	Quarter-finalists
1970	Quarter-finalists
1974-82	Did not enter
1986	Semi-finalists/4th place
1990	Did not enter
1994	Did not enter

ASIAN CLUB COMPETITIONS

Asian Champion Teams' Cup
Semi-finalists - PSMS 1970, Tiga Berlian 1985, Pelita Jaya 1989 1990
Asian Cup Winners Cup
Semi-finalists - Pupuk Kaltin 1991

INDONESIAN NATIONAL CHAMPIONS

1980	Warna Agung
1981	-
1982	NIAC Mitra
1983	NIAC Mitra
1984	Yanita Utama Bogor
1984	Yanita Utama Bogor
1985	Tiga Berlian
1986	Tiga Berlian
1987	-
1988	NIAC Mitra
1989	Pelita Jaya
1990	Pelita Jaya
1991	-
1992	Arseto
1993	Arema
1994	Pelita Jaya

INDONESIAN CUP WINNERS

1985	Arseto
1986	Makassar Utama
1987	Tiga Berlian
1988	Tiga Berlian
1989	Tiga Berlian
1990	-
1991	-
1992	Semen Padang
1993	-
1994	Gelora Dewata

IRAN

Population: 56,293,000
Area, sq km: 1,948,732
% in urban areas: 26%
Capital city: Tehran 6,042,000

Football Federation of the Islamic Republic of Iran
Shahid Shirody Stadium
PO Box 15815 / 1881
Tehran
Iran
Tel: + 98 21 8825534
Fax: + 98 21 8835672
Telex: 212691 nocir

Year of formation	1920
Affiliation to FIFA	1948
Affiliation to AFC	1958
Registered clubs	6326
Registered players	1 200 000
Registered coaches	1200
Registered referees	2000
National stadium	Azadi, Tehran 100 000
National colours	Green/White/Red
Reserve colours	White/White/White
Season	June - February

THE RECORD

WORLD CUP

1930-70	Did not enter
1974	QT R1 2nd/8 in group B
1978	QT R1 1st/3 in group 3, R2 1st/5 - Final tournament/1st round
1982	Did not enter
1986	Did not enter
1990	QT R1 2nd/4 in group 5
1994	QT R1 1st/4 in group 2, R2 5th/6

ASIAN CHAMPIONSHIP

1956	Did not enter
1960	QT 2nd/4 in group 1
1964	
1968	QT Automatic - Final tournament/Winners
1972	QT Automatic - Final tournament/Winners
1976	QT Automatic - Final tournament/Winners
1980	QT Automatic - Final tournament/Semi-finalists/3rd place
1984	QT 1st/6 in group 1 - Final tournament/Semi-finalists/3rd place
1988	QT 2nd/5 in group 3 - Final tournament/Semi-finalists/3rd place
1992	QT 1st/3 in group 3 - Final tournament/1st round

ASIAN GAMES

1951	Finalists
1954	Did not enter
1958	1st round
1962	Did not enter
1966	Finalists
1970	1st round
1974	Winners
1978	Did not enter
1982	Quarter-finalists
1986	Quarter-finalists
1990	Winners
1994	1st round

ASIAN CLUB COMPETITIONS

Asian Champion Teams' Cup
Winners - Taj Club 1970, Esteghlal SC 1990, Pass Club 1992
Finalists - Esteghlal SC 1991
Semi-finalists - Taj Club 1971, Shahin 1989

Asian Cup Winners Cup
Winners - Pirouzi 1990
Finalists - Pirouzi 1992

IRANIAN LEAGUE CHAMPIONS

1974	Persepolis
1975	Taj
1976	Persepolis
1977	Persepolis
1978	Pas
1979	Shahbaz
1980	Persepolis
1981-85	-
1986	Malavan SC
1987	-
1988	Pirouzi
1989	Shanin FC
1990	Esteghlal SC
1991	-
1992	Pas
1993	Pas
1994	Saipa

IRAQ

Population: 17,754,000
Area, sq km: 435,052
% in urban areas: 70%
Capital city: Baghdad 5,348,000

Iraqi Football Association
Olympic Committee Building
Palestine Street
Baghdad
Iraq
Tel: + 964 1 7729990
Fax: + 964 1 7728424
Telex: 214074 irfa ik

Year of formation	1948
Affiliation to FIFA	1951
Affiliation to AFC	1971
Registered clubs	155
Registered players	1900
Registered coaches	120
Registered referees	190
National stadium	Sha'ab, Baghdad 50 000
National colours	White/Green/White
Reserve colours	Green/White/White
Season	October - May

THE RECORD

WORLD CUP

1930-70	Did not enter
1974	QT R1 3rd/8 in group B
1978	Did not enter
1982	QT R1 2nd/5 in group 2
1986	QT R1 1st/3 in group 6, R2 1st/2, R3 1st/2 - Final tournament/1st round
1990	QT R1 2nd/4 in group 1
1994	QT R1 1st/5 in group 1, R2 4th/6

ASIAN CHAMPIONSHIP

1956-68	Did not enter
1972	QT 1st/ in group 1 - Final tournament/1st round
1976	QT 1st/4 in group 2 - Final tournament/Semi-finalists/4th place
1980-92	Did not enter

ASIAN GAMES

1951-70	Did not enter
1974	Semi-finalists/3rd in group
1978	Semi-finalists/4th place
1982	Winners
1986	Quarter-finalists
1990	Did not enter
1994	Did not enter

ASIAN CLUB COMPETITIONS

Asian Champion Teams' Cup
Finalists - Police Club 1971, Al Rasheed 1988
Semi-finalists - Al Talaba 1986, Al Rasheed 1987 1989
Asian Cup Winners Cup
Never past the first round

IRAQI LEAGUE CHAMPIONS

1974	Al Tayeran
1975	Al Tayeran
1976	Al Zewra
1977	Al Zewra
1978	Al Mena
1979	Al Zewra
1980	Al Schurta
1981	Al Talaba
1982	Al Talaba
1983	Sal-el-Deen
1984	Al Jaische
1985	Al Rasheed
1986	Al Talaba
1987	Al Rasheed
1988	Al Rasheed
1989	Al Rasheed
1990	Al Rasheed
1991	Al Zewra
1992	-
1993	-
1994	-
1995	Al Zewra

JAPAN

Population: 123,692,000
Area, sq km: 377,835
% in urban areas: 76%
Capital city: Tokyo 8,278,000

The Football Association of Japan
Kishi Memorial Hall
1-1-1 Jinnan, Shibuya-Ku
Tokyo
Japan
Tel: + 81 3 34762011
Fax: + 81 3 34762291
Telex: 2422975 fotjpn j

Year of formation	1921
Affiliation to FIFA	1929-45 & 1950
Affiliation to AFC	1954
Registered clubs	4523
Registered players	2 232 000
Registered coaches	394
Registered referees	6100
National stadium	National Stadium, Tokyo 62 000
National colours	Blue/White/Blue
Reserve colours	White/Blue/White
Season	May - November

THE RECORD

WORLD CUP

1930-50	Did not enter
1954	QT 2nd/2 in group 13
1958	Did not enter
1962	QT 3rd/4 in group 10
1966	Did not enter
1970	QT R1 3rd/3 in group 1
1974	QT R1 4th/4 in group A
1978	QT R1 3rd/3 in group 2
1982	QT R1 4th/7 in group 4
1986	QT R1 1st/3 in group 8, R2 1st/2, R3 2nd/2
1990	QT R1 2nd/4 in group 6
1994	QT R1 1st/5 in group 6, R2 3rd/6

ASIAN CHAMPIONSHIP

1956	Did not enter
1960	-
1964	-
1968	QT 2nd/5 in group 3
1972	
1976	QT 4th/6 in group 4
1980	QT Did not enter
1984	QT Did not enter
1988	QT 2nd/5 in group 2 - Final tournament/1st round
1992	QT Automatic - Final tournament/Winners

ASIAN GAMES

1951	Semi-finalists
1954	1st round
1958	1st round
1962	1st round
1966	Semi-finalists/3rd place
1970	Semi-finalists/4th place
1974	1st round
1978	1st round
1982	Quarter-finalists
1986	1st round
1990	Quarter-finalists
1994	Quarter-finalists

ASIAN CLUB COMPETITIONS

Asian Champion Teams' Cup
Winners - Furukawa 1986, Yomiuri 1987
Finalists - Nissan 1989
Semi-finalists - Toyo Kogyo 1968, Yomiuri 1992, Verdy Kawasaki 1993
Asian Cup Winners Cup
Winners - Nissan 1991 1992, Yokohama Flugels 1994
Semi-finalists - Nissan 1993

JAPANESE NATIONAL CHAMPIONS

1965	Toyo Kogyo
1966	Toyo Kogyo
1967	Toyo Kogyo
1968	Toyo Kogyo
1969	Mitsubishi
1970	Toyo Kogyo
1971	Yanmar Diesel
1972	Hitachi
1973	Mitsubishi
1974	Yanmar Diesel
1975	Yanmar Diesel
1976	Furukawa
1977	Fujita
1978	Mitsubishi
1979	Fujita
1980	Yanmar Diesel
1981	Fujita
1982	Mitsubishi
1983	Yomiuri
1984	Yomiuri
1985	Furukawa
1986	Furukawa
1987	Yomiuri
1988	Yamaha
1989	Nissan
1990	Nissan
1991	Yomiuri
1992	Yomiuri

THE J-LEAGUE

1993	Verdy Kawasaki
1994	Verdy Kawasaki

ENGLISH FA CUP

1921	Tokyo FC
1922	Nagoya FC
1923	Astra
1924	Rijyo Club
1925	Rijyo Club
1926	-
1927	Kobe High School
1928	Waseda University
1929	Kansei Gakuin University
1930	Kansei Gakuin University
1931	Tokyo Imperial University
1932	Keio Club
1933	Tokyo OB
1934	-
1935	All Keijyo FC
1936	Keio BRB
1937	Keio University
1938	Waseda University
1939	Keio BRB
1940	Keio BRB
1941-45	-

EMPEROR'S CUP

1946	Tokyo University
1947-48	-
1949	Tokyo University
1950	All Kansei Gakuin
1951	Keio BRB
1952	All Keio
1953	All Kansei Gakuin
1954	Keio BRB
1955	All Kansei Gakuin
1956	Keio BRB
1957	Chuo University
1958	Kansei Gakuin Club
1959	Kansei Gakuin Club
1960	Furukawa Electric
1961	Furukawa Electric
1962	Chuo University
1963	-
1964	Waseda University
1965	Yawata Steel
1966	Toyo Kogyo
1967	Waseda University
1968	Toyo Kogyo
1969	Yanmar Diesel
1970	Toyo Kogyo
1971	Yanmar Diesel
1972	Mitsubishi
1973	Hitachi
1974	Mitsubishi
1975	Yanmar Diesel
1976	Hitachi
1977	Furukawa
1978	Fujita
1979	Mitsubishi
1980	Fujita
1981	Mitsubishi
1982	Nippon Kokan
1983	Yamaha
1984	Nissan
1985	Yomiuri
1986	Nissan
1987	Yomiuri
1988	Yomiuri
1989	Nissan
1990	Nissan
1991	Matsushita
1992	Nissan
1993	Nissan
1994	Yokohama Flugels
1995	Bellmare Hiratsuka

JAPAN SOCCER LEAGUE CUP

1976	Hitachi
1977	Furukawa
1978	Mitsubishi

1979	Yomiuri
1980	Nippon Kokan
1981	Mitsubishi & Toshiba
1982	Furukawa
1983	Yanmar Diesel
1984	Yanmar Diesel
1985	Yomiuri
1986	Furukawa
1987	Nippon Kokan
1988	Nissan
1989	Nissan
1990	Nissan
1991	Yomiuri
1992	Verdy Kawasaki
1993	Verdy Kawasaki
1994	Verdy Kawasaki

CLUB DIRECTORY

TOKYO (Pop. - 27,700,000)
Bellmare Hiratsuka (1968)
Komazawa 20,000 – Yellow/Green
Previous name: Fujita Football Club

JEF United (1946)
Ichihara 15,000 – Yellow/Green
Previous name: JR East Furukawa Football Club

Kashiwa Reysol
Previous name: Hitachi

Verdy Kawasaki (1969)
Todoroki 15,000 – Green/White
Previous name: Yomiuri Nippon

Urawa Red Diamonds (1951)
Urawa 15,000 – Red/White
Previous name: Mitsubishi Motors FC

Yokohama Marinos (1972)
Mitsuzawa 15,000 – Blue/White
Previous name: Nissan Football Club

Yokohama Flugels
Yokohama Stadium
Previous name: All Nippon Airways

OSAKA (Pop. - 2,648,000)
Cerezo Osaka (1991)
Suita 23,000 – Blue/Black

Dnev Yanmar Diesel (1957)
Kobe 20,000 – Red/Red

Gamba Osaka (1991)
Suita 23,000 – Blue/Black
Previous name: Matsushita

NAGOYA (Pop. - 2,142,000)
Nagoya Grampus Eight (1991)
Nagoya 15,000 – Red/Red
Previous name: Toyota FC

HIROSHIMA (Pop. - 1,575,000)
Sanfrecce Hiroshoma FC (1992)
Hiroshoma 15,000 – Purple/White
Previous name: Toyo Kogyo 1938-81, Mazda FC 1981-92

SHIZUOKA (Pop. - 470,000)
Shimizu S-Pulse (1991)
Shimizu 15,000 – Orange/Orange

IWATA (Pop. - 80,000)
Jubilo Iwata (1972)
Yamaha 8,000 – Blue/Blue
Previous name: Yamaha Motors Football Club

KASHIMA (Pop. - 40,000)
Kashima Antlers
Kashima 15,000
Previous name: Sumitomo

JORDAN

Population: 3,169,000
Area, sq km: 88,946
% in urban areas: 69%
Capital city: Amman 936,000

Jordan Football Association
PO Box 1054
Amman
Jordan
Tel: + 962 6 624481
Fax: + 962 6 624454
Telex: 22415 foball jo

Year of formation	1949
Affiliation to FIFA	1958
Affiliation to AFC	1970
Registered clubs	98
Registered players	41 000
Registered coaches	133
Registered referees	114
National stadium	International Stadium, Amman 30 000
National colours	All White
Reserve colours	All Sky blue
Season	June - December

THE RECORD

WORLD CUP

1930-82	Did not enter
1986	QT R1 3rd/3 in group 2
1990	QT R1 3rd/4 in group 1
1994	QT R1 4th/5 in group 1

ASIAN CHAMPIONSHIP

1956-80	Did not enter
1984	QT 3rd/5 in group 4
1988	QT 3rd/5 in group 2
1992	Did not enter

ASIAN GAMES

1951-94	Did not enter

ASIAN CLUB COMPETITIONS
Asian Champion Teams' Cup

Asian Cup Winners Cup
Semi-finalists - Al Ramtha 1991

JORDANIAN LEAGUE CHAMPIONS

1959	Al Faisaly
1960	Al Faisaly
1961	Al Faisaly
1962	Al Faisaly
1963	Al Faisaly
1964	Al Faisaly
1965	Al Faisaly
1966	Al Faisaly
1967	-
1968	Al Faisaly
1969	Al Faisaly
1970	Al Faisaly
1971	Al Faisaly
1972	Al Faisaly
1973	Al Faisaly
1974	Al Faisaly
1975	Al Ahly
1976	Al Faisaly
1977	Al Faisaly
1978	Al Ahly
1979	Al Ahly
1980	Al Wehdat
1981	Al Ramta
1982	Al Ramta
1983	Al Faisaly
1984	Amman Club
1985	Al Faisaly
1986	Al Faisaly
1987	Al Deffatain
1988	Al Wehdat
1989	Al Ramta
1990	Al Faisaly
1991	Al Faisaly
1992	Al Wehdat
1993	Al Faisaly
1994	Al Faisaly
1995	Al Wehdat

JORDANIAN CUP WINNERS

1981	Al Faisaly
1982	Al Faisaly
1983	Al Wehdat
1984	Al Faisaly
1985	Al Jazira
1986	Al Wehdat
1987	Al Arabi
1988	Al Faisaly
1989	Al Wehdat
1990	Al Faisaly
1991	Al Ramta
1992	Al Ramta
1993	Al Faisaly
1994	Al Faisaly
1995	Al Faisaly

KAMPUCHEA

Population: 8,592,000
Area, sq km: 181,916
% in urban areas: 12%,
Capital city: Phnom Penh 564,000

Fédération Khmère de Football Association
CP 101
Complex Sportif National
Phnom Penh
Kampuchea
Tel: + 855 15 915494
Fax: + 855 23 26501

Year of formation	1933
Affiliation to FIFA	1953
Affiliation to AFC	1957
Registered clubs	30
Registered players	2400
Registered coaches	50
Registered referees	93
National stadium	CSN (Complex Sportif National), Phnom Penh 60 000
National colours	Red/White/Red
Reserve colours	Blue/White/Blue
Season	November - October

THE RECORD

WORLD CUP

1930-94	Did not enter

ASIAN CHAMPIONSHIP

1956	QT 3rd/3 in group 3
1960	-
1964	-
1968	QT 2nd/4 in group 1
1972	QT 1st/ in group 3 - Final tournament/Semi-finalists/4th place
1976-92	Did not enter

ASIAN GAMES

1951-66	Did not enter
1970	1st round
1974-94	Did not enter

KAZAKHSTAN

Population: 16,536,000
Area, sq km: 2,717,300
Capital city: Almaty

The Football Association of the Republic of Kazakstan
44 Abai Street
480072 Almaty
Kazakhstan
Tel: + 327 2 674472
Fax: + 327 2 671885
Telex: 251347 trek su

Year of formation	1914
Affiliation to FIFA	1994
Affiliation to AFC	1994
Registered clubs	5700
Registered players	260 000
National stadium	Central, Almaty 30 000
National colours	All Yellow
Season	April - November

THE RECORD

WORLD CUP

1930-94	Did not enter

ASIAN CHAMPIONSHIP

1956-92	Did not enter

ASIAN GAMES

1951-94	Did not enter

ASIAN CLUB COMPETITIONS

Asian Champion Teams' Cup
Never past the first round
Asian Cup Winners Cup
Never past the first round

CLUB DIRECTORY

ALMATY (Pop. - 1,190,000)
CSKA Almaty
Dynamo Almaty

Kairat Almaty (1954)
Kazakstan Stadion - Red/White
Previous names: Lokomotiv 1954-55, Uriozai 1955-56, Kairat Alma-Ata 1956-92

QARAGHANDY (Pop. - 614,000)
Shakhtyor Qaraghandy
Previous name: Shakhtyor Karaganda

SHYMKENT (Pop. - 393,000)
SKIF Ordabasy

SEMEY (Pop. - 334,000)
Spartak Semey
Previous name: Spartak Semipalatinsk

PAVLODAR (Pop. - 331,000)
Ansat Pavlodar
Previous name: Traktor Pavlodar

ÖSKEMEN (Pop. - 324,000)
Vostok Öskemen
Previous name: Vostok Ust' Kamenogorsk

ZHAMBYL (Pop. - 307,000)
Taraz Zhambyl

AQMOLA (Pop. - 277,000)
Tselinnik Aqmola

AQTÖBE (Pop. - 253,000)
Aktyubinets Aqtöbe

PETROPAVL (Pop. - 241,000)
Yenbek Petropavlosk

QOSTANAY (Pop. - 224,000)
Khimik Qostanay

QYZLORDA (Pop. - 153,000)
Kaisar Qyzlorda

KAZAKHSTAN LEAGUE CHAMPIONS

1992	Kairat Alma-Ata
1993	Ansat Pavlodar

KAZAKHSTAN CUP WINNERS

1992	Kairat Almaty
1993	Dostyk Almaty

NORTH KOREA

Population: 22,937,000
Area, sq km: 122,400
% in urban areas: 64%
Capital city: Pyongyang 2,000,000

Football Association of the Democratic People's Republic of Korea
Munsin-Dong 2
Dongdaewon District
Pyongyang
North Korea
Tel: + 850 2 814164
Fax: + 850 2 814403
Telex: 5472 kp

Year of formation	1945
Affiliation to FIFA	1958
Affiliation to AFC	1974
Registered clubs	90
Registered players	286 000
Registered referees	720
National stadium	Moranbong, Pyongyang 90 000
National colours	Red/White/Red
Reserve colours	White/Green/White
Season	March - November

THE RECORD

WORLD CUP

1930-62	Did not enter
1966	QT 1st/2 - Final tournament/ Quarter-finalists
1970	Did not enter
1974	QT R1 5th/8 in group B
1978	Did not enter
1982	QT R1 2nd/6 in group 4
1986	QT R1 2nd/3 in group 8
1990	QT R1 1st/4 in group 6, R2 6th/6
1994	QT R1 1st/5 in group 3, R2 6th/6

ASIAN CHAMPIONSHIP

1956-68	Did not enter
1972	-
1976	QT 1st/6 in group 2 - Withdrew
1980	QT 1st/7 in group 3 - Final tournament/Semi-finalists/ 4th place

1984	Did not enter
1988	QT 3rd/5 in group 3
1992	QT 1st/4 in group 6 - Final tournament/1st round

ASIAN GAMES

1951-70	Did not enter
1974	Semi-finalists/4th place
1978	Winners
1982	Semi-finalists/4th place
1986	Did not enter
1990	Finalists
1994	Did not enter

ASIAN CLUB COMPETITIONS

Asian Champion Teams' Cup

Semi-finalists - April 25th 1988 1990

Asian Cup Winners Cup

Have never entered

SOUTH KOREA

Population: 42,793,000
Area, sq km: 99,237
% in urban areas: 69%
Capital city: Seoul 10,726,000

Korea Football Association
110-39 Kyeonji-Dong
Chongro-Ku
Seoul
South Korea
Tel: + 82 2 7336764
Fax: + 82 2 7352755
Telex: kfasel k 25373

Year of formation	1928
Affiliation to FIFA	1948
Affiliation to AFC	1954
Registered clubs	90
Registered players	1 300 000
Registered coaches	526
Registered referees	485
National stadium	Olympic Stadium, Seoul 100 000
National colours	Red/Red/Red
Reserve colours	Blue/Blue/Blue
Season	March - November

THE RECORD

WORLD CUP

1930-50	Did not enter
1954	QT 1st/2 in group 13 - Final tournament/1st round
1958	Did not enter
1962	QT 2nd/4 in group 10
1966	Did not enter
1970	QT 2nd/3 in group 1
1974	QT R1 1st/7 in group 1, R2 2nd/2
1978	QT R1 1st/3 in group 2, R2 2nd/5
1982	QT R1 2nd/4 in group 3
1986	QT R1 1st/3 in group 5, R2 1st/2, R3 1st/2 - Final tournament/1st round
1990	QT R1 1st/4 in group 4, R2 1st/6 - Final tournament/1st round
1994	QT R1 1st/5 in group 4, R2 2nd/6 - Final tournament/1st round

ASIAN CHAMPIONSHIP

1956	QT 1st/3 in group 2 - Final tournament/Winners
1960	QT Automatic - Final tournament/Winners
1964	QT Automatic - Final tournament/3rd place
1968	QT 3rd/5 in group 3
1972	QT 1st/ in group 4 - Final tournament/Finalists
1976	QT 3rd/5 in group 3
1980	QT 1st/4 in group 4 - Final tournament/Finalists
1984	QT 1st/5 in group 3 - Final tournament/1st round
1988	QT 2nd/4 in group 4 - Final tournament/Finalists
1992	QT 2nd/3 in group 5

ASIAN GAMES

1951	Did not enter
1954	Finalists
1958	Finalists
1962	Finalists
1966	1st round
1970	Winners
1974	Semi-finalists/4th in group
1978	Winners
1982	1st round
1986	Winners
1990	Semi-finalists/3rd place
1994	Semi-finalists/3rd place

ASIAN CLUB COMPETITIONS

Asian Champion Teams' Cup

Winners - Daewoo Royals 1985
Finalists - Yangzee 1968
Semi-finalists - Tungsten Mining 1967, ROK Army 1971, Ilwha Chunma 1994

Asian Cup Winners Cup

Quarter-finalists - Daewoo Royals 1990

SOUTH KOREAN PRO-FOOTBALL LEAGUE

1983	Halleluyah Eagles 20 Daewoo Royals 19 Yukong Elephants 17
1984	Daewoo Royals1-0 1-1 Yukong Elephants
1985	Lucky Goldstar 27 POSCO Atoms 25 Daewoo Royals 25
1986	Hyundai Tigers 23 Daewoo Royals 16 Yukong Elephants 15
1987	Daewoo Royals 46 POSCO Atoms 40 Yukong Elephants 27
1988	POSCO Atoms 27 Hyundai Tigers 25 Yukong Elephants 24
1989	Yukong Elephants 49 Lucky Goldstar 47 Daewoo Royals 42
1990	Lucky Goldstar 39 Daewoo Royals 35 Posco Atoms 28
1991	Daewoo Royals
1992	POSCO Atoms 35 Ilhwa Chunma 34 Hyundai Tigers 32
1993	Ilhwa Chunma
1994	Ilhwa Chunma 54 Yukong Elephants 51 POSCO Atoms 50

KUWAIT

Population: 2,143,000
Area, sq km: 17,818
% in urban areas: 95%
Capital city: Kuwait City

Kuwait Football Association
Udailiyya, Bl 4
Al-Ittihad Street
PO Box 2029
13021 Safat
Kuwait
Tel: + 965 2555851
Fax: + 965 2555935
Telex: 22600 kt

Year of formation	1952
Affiliation to FIFA	1962
Affiliation to AFC	1964
Registered clubs	14
Registered players	2500
Registered coaches	42
Registered referees	49
National stadium	Al Qadesseyah 25 000
National colours	All Blue
Reserve colours	Red/White/Red
Season	October - May

THE RECORD

WORLD CUP

1930-70	Did not enter
1974	QT R1 7th/8 in group B
1978	QT R1 1st/3 in group 4, R2 3rd/5
1982	QT R1 1st/4 in group 3, R2 1st/4 - Final tournament/1st round
1986	QT R1 2nd/3 in group 3
1990	QT R1 2nd/3 in group 3
1994	QT R1 2nd/4 in group 5

ASIAN CHAMPIONSHIP

1956-68	Did not enter
1972	QT 1st/ in group 2 - Final tournament/1st round
1976	QT W-O in group 1 - Final tournament/Finalists
1980	QT Automatic - Final tournament/Winners
1984	QT Automatic - Final tournament/Semi-finalists/3rd place
1988	QT 1st/5 in group 2 - Final tournament/1st round
1992	QT 2nd/3 in group 2

ASIAN GAMES

1951-70	Did not enter
1974	Semi-finalists/3rd in group
1978	Semi-finalists/3rd in group
1982	Finalists
1986	Semi-finalists/3rd place

1990	Quarter-finalists
1994	Semi-finalists/3rd place

ASIAN CLUB COMPETITIONS

Asian Champion Teams' Cup

Semi-finalists - Al Kazma 1987 1988

Asian Cup Winners Cup

Quarter-finalists - Al Kazma 1991, Al Arabi 1992

KUWAITI LEAGUE CHAMPIONS

1962	Al Arabi
1963	Al Arabi
1964	Al Arabi
1965	Al Kuwait
1966	Al Arabi
1967	Al Arabi
1968	Al Kuwait
1969	Al Qadisiyah
1970	Al Arabi
1971	Al Qadisiyah
1972	Al Kuwait
1973	Al Qadisiyah
1974	Al Kuwait
1975	Al Qadisiyah
1976	Al Qadisiyah
1977	Al Kuwait
1978	Al Qadisiyah
1979	Al Kuwait
1980	Al Arabi
1981	Al Salmiyah
1982	Al Arabi
1983	Al Arabi
1984	Al Arabi
1985	Al Arabi
1986	Al Kazmah
1987	Al Kazmah
1988	Al Arabi
1989	Al Arabi
1990	Al Jabaa
1991	-
1992	Al Qadisiyah
1993	Al Arabi
1994	Al Kazmah
1995	Al Salmiyah

KUWAITI CUP WINNERS

1962	Al Arabi
1963	Al Arabi
1964	Al Arabi
1965	Al Qadisiyah
1966	Al Arabi
1967	Al Qadisiyah
1968	Al Qadisiyah
1969	Al Arabi
1970	Al Yarmouk
1971	Al Arabi
1972	Al Qadisiyah
1973	-
1974	Al Qadisiyah
1975	Al Qadisiyah
1976	Al Kuwait
1977	Al Kuwait
1978	Al Kuwait
1979	Al Qadisiyah
1980	Al Kuwait
1981	Al Arabi
1982	Al Kazmah
1983	Al Arabi
1984	Al Kazmah
1985	Al Kuwait
1986	Al Fheyheel
1987	Al Kuwait
1988	Al Kuwait
1989	Al Qadisiyah
1990	Al Kazmah
1991	-
1992	Al Arabi
1993	Al Salmiyah
1994	Al Qadisiyah

KYRGYZSTAN

Population: 4,290,000
Area, sq km: 198,500
Capital city: Frunze

Tel: + 331 2 225492
Fax: + 331 2 267004
Telex: 251239 salam su

Year of formation	1992
Affiliation to FIFA	1994
Affiliation to AFC	1994
Registered players	20 000
National stadium	Spartak, Bishek 20 000
National colours	All Red
Season	April - November

THE RECORD

WORLD CUP

1930-94 Did not enter

ASIAN CHAMPIONSHIP

1956-92 Did not enter

ASIAN GAMES

1951-94 Did not enter

KYRGYZSTAN LEAGUE CHAMPIONS

1992	Alga Bishkek
1993	Alga-RIIF Bishkek
1994	Kant Oil

KYRGYZSTAN CUP WINNERS

1992	Alga Bishkek
1993	Alga-RIIF Bishkek

CLUB DIRECTORY

BISHKEK (Pop. - 616,000)

Alga-RIIF Bishkek
Pevious names: Alga Frunze, Alga Bishkek
Instrumentalishnik Bishkek
Selmashevets Bishkek
Shumkar-SKIF Bishkek

OSH (Pop. - 213,000)

Alai Osh

SOKULUK

SKA Dostuk

TOKMAK

Spartak Tokmak

KANT

Kant Oil

LAOS

Population: 4,024,000
Area, sq km: 236,800
% in urban areas: 16%
Capital city: Vientiane 377,000

Fédération de Foot-Ball Lao
C/O Direction des Sports-Education Physique et artistique
BP 268
Vientiane
Laos
Tel: + 856 21 6008
Fax: + 856 21 6008

Year of formation	1951
Affiliation to FIFA	1952
Affiliation to AFC	1968
Registered clubs	76
Registered players	2000
Registered referees	64
National stadium	Stade National, Vientaine 11 000
National colours	Red/White/Blue
Reserve colours	Blue/White/Red
Season	October - May

THE RECORD

WORLD CUP

1930-94 Did not enter

ASIAN CHAMPIONSHIP

1956-88 Did not enter

ASIAN GAMES

1951-94 Did not enter

LEBANON

Population: 2,965,000
Area, sq km: 10,230
% in urban areas: 80%
Capital city: Beirut 200,000

Fédération Libanaise de Football Association

PO Box 4732
Omar Ibn Khattab Street
Beirut
Lebanon
Tel: + 961 1 868099
Fax: + 961 1 349529
Telex: 21404 liball

Year of formation	1933
Affiliation to FIFA	1935
Affiliation to AFC	1964
Registered clubs	105
Registered players	23 600
Registered referees	87
National stadium	Camille Champum, Beirut 60 000
National colours	Red/White/Red
Reserve colours	White/White/Red
Season	October - June

THE RECORD

WORLD CUP

1930-90	Did not enter
1994	QT R1 3rd/5 in group 4

ASIAN CHAMPIONSHIP

1956-76	Did not enter
1980	QT 4th/4 in group 1
1984-92	Did not enter

ASIAN GAMES

1951-94	Did not enter

ASIAN CLUB COMPETITIONS

Asian Champion Teams' Cup
Semi-finalists - Homentmen 1970
Asian Cup Winners Cup
Never past the first round

LEBANESE LEAGUE CHAMPIONS

1934	Al Nahda
1935	American University
1936	Sika
1937	American University
1938	American University
1939	Sika
1940	-
1941	Sika
1942	Al Nahda
1943	Al Nahda
1944	Homentmen
1945	Homentmen
1946	Homentmen
1947	Al Nahda
1948	Homentmen
1949	Al Nahda
1950	-
1951	Homentmen
1952	-
1953	-
1954	Homentmen
1955	Homentmen
1956	Racing
1957	Homentmen
1958-60	-
1961	Homentmen
1962	-
1963	Homentmen
1964	-
1965	Racing
1966	-
1967	Chabiba Mazraa
1968	-
1969	Homentmen
1970	Racing
1971	-
1972	-
1973	Al Nejmeh
1974	-
1975	Al Nejmeh
1976-87	-
1988	Al Ansar
1989	Al Ansar
1990	Al Ansar
1991	Al Ansar
1992	Al Ansar
1993	Al Ansar
1994	Al Ansar
1995	Al Ansar

MACAU

Population: 461,000
Area, sq km: 17
Capital city: Macau 416,000

Associacao de Futebol de Macau
PO Box 920
Macau
Tel: + 853 71996
Fax: + 853 260148

Year of formation	1939
Affiliation to FIFA	1976
Affiliation to AFC	1976
Registered clubs	52
Registered players	1100
Registered coaches	6
Registered referees	27
National stadium	Campo Desportivo, Macau 12 000
National colours	Green/White/Green
Reserve colours	White/White/Red
Season	September - June

THE RECORD

WORLD CUP

1930-78	Did not enter
1982	QT R1 6th/6 in group 4
1986	QT R1 3rd/4 in group 7
1990	Did not enter
1994	QT R1 4th/4 in group 5

ASIAN CHAMPIONSHIP

1956-76	Did not enter
1980	QT 3rd/4 in group 4
1984-88	Did not enter
1992	QT 2nd/4 in group 6

ASIAN GAMES

1951-94	Did not enter

MALAYSIA

Population: 17,886,000
Area, sq km: 330,442
% in urban areas: 38%
Capital city: Kuala Lumpur 1,103,000

Persatuan Bolasepak Malaysia
Wisma Fam, Tingkat 3
Jalan SS5A/9, Kelana Jaya
47301 Petaling Jaya
Selangor
Malaysia
Tel: + 60 3 7763766
Fax: + 60 3 7757984
Telex: fam pj ma 36701

Year of formation	1933
Affiliation to FIFA	1956
Affiliation to AFC	1954
Registered clubs	450
Registered players	176 000
Registered coaches	480
Registered referees	1223
National stadium	Shah Alam, Kuala Lumpur 81 000
National colours	Yellow/Black/Yellow
Reserve colours	White/White/White
Season	February - September

THE RECORD

WORLD CUP

1930-70	Did not enter
1974	QT R1 5th/7 in group A
1978	QT R1 3rd/5 in group 1
1982	QT R1 3rd/4 in group 3
1986	QT R1 2nd/3 in group 5
1990	QT R1 2nd/4 in group 4
1994	QT R1 3rd/4 in group 5

ASIAN CHAMPIONSHIP

1956	QT 2nd/3 in group 3
1960	QT 2nd/3 in group 2
1964	-
1968	QT 4th/5 in group 2
1972	-
1976	QT 1st/5 in group 3 - Final tournament/1st round
1980	QT 2nd/7 in group 3 - Final tournament/1st round
1984	QT 3rd/5 in group 3
1988	QT 4th/5 in group 2
1992	QT 3rd/4 in group 4

ASIAN GAMES

1951	Did not enter
1954	Did not enter
1958	1st round
1962	Semi-finalists/3rd place
1966	1st round
1970	1st round
1974	Semi-finalists/3rd place
1978	Semi-finalists/4th in group
1982	1st round
1986	1st round
1990	1st round
1994	1st round

ASIAN CLUB COMPETITIONS

Asian Champion Teams' Cup

Finalists - Selangor 1967

Semi-finalists - Federal Territory 1987, Pahang 1988, Kuala Lumpur 1989

Asian Cup Winners Cup

Have never entered

MALAYSIA CUP WINNERS

1921	Singapore
1922	Selangor
1923	Singapore
1924	Singapore
1925	Singapore
1926	Perak
1927	Selangor
1928	Singapore & Selangor
1929	Singapore & Selangor
1930	Singapore
1931	Perak
1932	Singapore
1933	Singapore
1934	Singapore
1935	Selangor
1936	Selangor
1937	Singapore
1938	Selangor
1939	Singapore
1940	Singapore
1941-47	-
1948	Negri Sembilan
1949	Selangor
1950	Singapore
1951	Singapore
1952	Singapore
1953	Penang
1954	Penang
1955	Singapore
1956	Selangor
1957	Perak
1958	Penang
1959	Selangor
1960	Singapore
1961	Selangor
1962	Selangor
1963	Selangor
1964	Singapore
1965	Singapore
1966	Selangor
1967	Perak
1968	Selangor
1969	Selangor
1970	Perak
1971	Selangor
1972	Selangor
1973	Selangor
1974	Penang
1975	Selangor
1976	Selangor
1977	Singapore
1978	Selangor
1979	Selangor
1980	Singapore
1981	Selangor
1982	Selangor
1983	Pahang
1984	Selangor
1985	Johore
1986	Selangor
1987	Kuala Lumpur
1988	Kuala Lumpur
1989	Kuala Lumpur
1990	Kedah
1991	Johore
1992	Pahang
1993	Kedah
1994	Singapore

MALDIVES

Population: 214,000
Area, sq km: 298
% in urban areas: 25%
Capital city: Male 46,000

Football Association of Maldives
Sports Division
Male 20-04
Maldives
Tel: + 960 317006
Fax: + 960 317005
Telex: 77039 minhom mf

Year of formation	1983
Affiliation to FIFA	1986
Affiliation to AFC	1983
Registered clubs	62
Registered players	5000
Registered coaches	2
Registered referees	30
National stadium	National Stadium, Male
National colours	Green/Red/White
Season	November - February

THE RECORD

WORLD CUP

1930-94 Did not enter

ASIAN CHAMPIONSHIP

1956-92 Did not enter

ASIAN GAMES

1951-94 Did not enter

MALDIVES LEAGUE CHAMPIONS

1983	Valencia
1984	Valencia
1985	Valencia
1986	Victory SC
1987	Victory SC
1988	Victory SC
1989	Club Lagoons

MYANMAR

Population: 41,675,000
Area, sq km: 676,577
% in urban areas: 23%
Capital city: Yangon 2,513,000

Myanmar Football Federation
Aung San Memorial Stadium
Kandawgalay Post Office
Yangon
Tel: + 95 1 75249
Fax: + 95 1 72716
Telex: 21253 sped bm

Year of formation	1947
Affiliation to FIFA	1947
Affiliation to AFC	1958
Registered clubs	600
Registered players	21 000
Registered coaches	60
Registered referees	1840
National stadium	Aung San Memorial Stadium, Rangoon 45 000
National colours	Red/White/Red
Reserve colours	White/White/White
Season	May - February

THE RECORD

WORLD CUP

1930-94 Did not enter

ASIAN CHAMPIONSHIP

1956	Did not enter
1960	-
1964	-
1968	QT 1st/4 in group 1 - Final tournament/2nd place
1972	-
1976-92	Did not enter

ASIAN GAMES

1951	1st round
1954	Semi-finalists/3rd place
1958	1st round
1962	Did not enter
1966	Winners
1970	Winners
1974	Semi-finalists/4th in group
1978	1st round
1982	1st round
1986	Did not enter
1990	Did not enter
1994	1st round

NEPAL

Population: 18,910,000
Area, sq km: 147,181
% in urban areas: 8%
Capital city: Kathmandu 235,000

All Nepal Football Association
Desareth Rangashala
Tripureshwor
PO Box 2090
Kathmandu
Nepal
Tel: + 977 1 215703
Fax: + 977 1 223246
Telex: 2390 NSC NP

Year of formation	1951
Affiliation to FIFA	1970
Affiliation to AFC	1971
Registered clubs	82
Registered players	1300
Registered coaches	43
Registered referees	77
National stadium	Dasarath Rangashala, Kathmandu 35 000
National colours	Red/Blue/White
Season	June - August

THE RECORD

WORLD CUP

1930-82	Did not enter
1986	QT R1 3rd/3 in group 5
1990	QT R1 4th/4 in group 4
1994	Did not enter

ASIAN CHAMPIONSHIP

1956-80	Did not enter
1984	QT 5th/5 in group 2
1988	QT 5th/5 in group 3
1992	Did not enter

ASIAN GAMES

1951-78	Did not enter
1982	1st round
1986	1st round
1990	Did not enter
1994	1st round

NEPALESE LEAGUE CHAMPIONS

1985	New Road Team
1986	Manang Marsyangdi
1987	Kathmandu SC
1988	Kathmandu SC
1989	Ranipokhari

OMAN

Population: 1,468,000
Area, sq km: 300,000
% in urban areas: 9%
Capital city: Muscat 85,000

Oman Football Association
PO Box 6462
Ruwi, Muscat
Oman
Tel: + 968 787638
Fax: + 968 787632
Telex: 5320 football on

Year of formation	1978
Affiliation to FIFA	1980
Affiliation to AFC	1979
Registered clubs	51
Registered players	21 900
Registered referees	95
National stadium	El Shorta, Muscat 45 000
National colours	White/Red/White
Reserve colours	Red/White/Red
Season	October - May

THE RECORD

WORLD CUP

1930-86	Did not enter
1990	QT R1 4th/4 in group 1
1994	QT R1 3rd/4 in group 2

ASIAN CHAMPIONSHIP

1956-80	Did not enter
1984	QT 3rd/5 in group 2
1988	Did not enter
1992	QT 3rd/3 in group 1

ASIAN GAMES

1951-82	Did not enter
1986	1st round
1990	Did not enter
1994	1st round

ASIAN CLUB COMPETITIONS

Asian Champion Teams' Cup
Finalists - Omani Club 1993
Semi-finalists - Al Fanja 1989
Asian Cup Winners Cup
Quarter-finalists - Al Fanja 1992

PAKISTAN

Population: 122,666,000
Area, sq km: 796,095
% in urban areas: 32%
Capital city: Islamabad 204,000
Major city: Karachi 5,208,000

Pakistan Football Federation
183 Abu Bakar Block
New Garden Town
Lahore
Pakistan
Tel: + 92 42 5832786
Fax: + 92 42 7281541
Telex: 47643 pff pk

Year of formation	1948
Affiliation to FIFA	1948
Affiliation to AFC	1960
Registered clubs	2700
Registered players	97 000
Registered coaches	23
Registered referees	204
National stadium	Karachi Stadium 86 000
National colours	Green/White/Green
Reserve colours	White/White/White
Season	March - October

THE RECORD

WORLD CUP

1930-86	Did not enter
1990	QT R1 3rd/3 in group 3
1994	QT R1 5th/5 in group 1

ASIAN CHAMPIONSHIP

1956	Did not enter
1960	QT 3rd/4 in group 1
1964	QT 3rd in group 1
1968	QT 3rd/4 in group 1
1972-80	Did not enter
1984	QT 4th/5 in group 3
1988	QT 5th/5 in group 2
1992	QT 3rd/3 in group 3

ASIAN GAMES

1951	Did not enter
1954	1st round
1958	1st round
1962-70	Did not enter
1974	1st round
1978	Did not enter
1982	Did not enter
1986	1st round
1990	1st round
1994	Did not enter

PAKISTAN NATIONAL CHAMPIONS

1948	Karachi Red
1949	-
1950	Baluchistan
1951	-
1952	Punjab
1953	Punjab
1954	Punjab
1955	Punjab
1956	Baluchistan
1957	Punjab
1958	Punjab Blue
1959	Baluchistan
1960	Dacca
1961	Dacca
1962	Dacca
1963	Karachi
1964	Karachi
1965	-
1966	Karachi
1967	-
1968	Peshawar
1969	Pakistan Railways
1970	Chittagong
1971	Pakistan International Airlines
1972	Pakistan International Airlines
1973	Karachi Yellow
1974	Pakistan International Airlines
1975	Sind Red
1976	Pakistan International Airlines
1977	-
1978	Pakistan International Airlines
1979	Karachi Red
1980	Karachi Red
1981	Pakistan International Airlines
1982	Habib Bank
1983	WAPDA
1984	Pakistan Railways
1985	Quetta
1986	Pakistan Air Force
1987	-
1988	-
1989	Punjab Red
1990	Punjab Red
1991	WAPDA
1992	WAPDA

1993	Defence Lahore
1994	Pakistan Army

THE PHILIPPINES

Population: 64,480,000
Area, sq km: 300,000
% in urban areas: 42%
Capital city: Manila 1,876,000

Philippine Football Federation
Room 207, Administration Building
Rizal Memorial Sports Complex
Vito Cruz
Metro Manilla
Philippines
Tel: + 63 2 594655
Fax: + 63 2 587724
Telex: 65014 poc paca pn

Year of formation	1907
Affiliation to FIFA	1928
Affiliation to AFC	1954
Registered clubs	650
Registered players	145 000
Registered coaches	600
Registered referees	1230
National stadium	Jose Rizal Memorial, Manila 30 000
National colours	Blue/White/Blue
Reserve colours	White/Blue/Red
Season	July - April

THE RECORD

WORLD CUP

1930-94	Did not enter

ASIAN CHAMPIONSHIP

1956	QT 3rd/3 in group 2
1960	-
1964	-
1968	QT 5th/5 in group 3
1972	-
1976	Did not enter
1980	QT 4th/4 in group 4
1984	QT 6th/6 in group 1
1988	Did not enter
1992	Did not enter

ASIAN GAMES

1951	Did not enter
1954	1st round
1958	Quarter-finalists
1962	1st round
1966	Did not enter
1970	Did not enter
1974	1st round
1978-94	Did not enter

QATAR

Population: 444,000
Area, sq km: 11,427
% in urban areas: 88%
Capital city: Doha 217,000

Qatar Football Association
PO Box 5333
Doha
Qatar
Tel: + 974 351641
Fax: + 974 411660
Telex: 4749 qatfot dh

Year of formation	1960
Affiliation to FIFA	1970
Affiliation to AFC	1972
Registered clubs	12
Registered players	2000
Registered coaches	54
Registered referees	40
National stadium	Khalifa, Doha 40 000
National colours	White/Maroon/ White
Reserve colours	Maroon/White/ Maroon
Season	October - May

THE RECORD

WORLD CUP

1930-74	Did not enter
1978	QT R1 3rd/3 in group 4
1982	QT R1 3rd/5 in group 2
1986	QT R1 2nd/3 in group 2
1990	QT R1 1st/4 in group 1, R2 3rd/6
1994	QT R1 2nd/5 in group 3

ASIAN CHAMPIONSHIP

1956-72	Did not enter
1976	QT 3rd/4 in group 2
1980	QT 1st/3 in group 2 - Final tournament/1st round
1984	QT 2nd/5 in group 4 - Final tournament/1st round
1988	QT Automatic - Final tournament/1st round
1992	QT 1st/3 in group 1 - Final tournament/1st round

ASIAN GAMES

1951-74	Did not enter
1978	1st round
1982	Did not enter
1986	1st round
1990	Did not enter
1994	1st round

ASIAN CLUB COMPETITIONS

Asian Champion Teams' Cup
Winners - Al Saad 1988
Finalists - Al Arabi 1994
Semi-finalists - Al Rayyan 1991
Asian Cup Winners Cup
Semi-finalists - Al Arabi 1993

QATARI LEAGUE CHAMPIONS

1973	Al Esteklal
1974	Al Saad
1975	-
1976	Al Rayyan
1977	Al Esteklal
1978	Al Rayyan
1979	Al Saad
1980	Al Saad
1981	Al Saad
1982	Al Rayyan
1983	Al Arabi
1984	Al Rayyan
1985	Al Arabi
1986	Al Rayyan
1987	Al Saad
1988	Al Saad
1989	Al Saad
1990	Al Rayyan
1991	Al Arabi
1992	Al Itihad
1993	Al Arabi
1994	Al Arabi
1995	Al Rayyan

EMIR'S CUP

1973	Al Ahly
1974	Al Esteklal
1975	Al Saad
1976	Al Esteklal
1977	Al Saad
1978	Al Arabi
1979	Al Arabi
1980	Al Arabi
1981	Al Ahly
1982	Al Saad
1983	Al Arabi
1984	Al Arabi
1985	Al Saad
1986	Al Saad
1987	Al Ahly
1988	Al Saad
1989	Al Arabi
1990	Al Arabi
1991	Al Ahly
1992	Al Ahly
1993	Al Arabi
1994	Al Saad

SAUDI ARABIA

Population: 14,131,000
Area, sq km: 2,240,000
% in urban areas: 73%
Capital city: Riyadh 1,308,000

Saudi Arabian Football Federation
North Al-Morabbaa Quarter
PO Box 5844
Riyadh 11432
Saudi Arabia

Tel: + 966 1 4822240
Fax: + 966 1 4821215
Telex: 404300 safotb sj

Year of formation	1959
Affiliation to FIFA	1959
Affiliation to AFC	1972
Registered clubs	173
Registered players	128 000
Registered coaches	309
Registered referees	504
National stadium	Malaz, Riyadh 30 000
National colours	Green/White/Green
Reserve colours	All White
Season	September - March

THE RECORD

WORLD CUP

1930-74	Did not enter
1978	QT R1 2nd/3 in group 3
1982	QT R1 1st/5 in group 2, R2 4th/4
1986	QT R1 2nd/2 in group 1
1990	QT R1 1st/3 in group 2, R2 5th/6
1994	QT R1 1st/4 in group 5, R2 1st/6 - Final tournament/ 2nd round

ASIAN CHAMPIONSHIP

1956-72	Did not enter
1976	QT 2nd/4 in group 1 - Withdrew
1980	Did not enter
1984	QT 1st/5 in group 2 - Final tournament/Winners
1988	QT Automatic - Final tournament/Winners
1992	QT Automatic - Final tournament/Finalists

ASIAN GAMES

1951-74	Did not enter
1978	1st round
1982	Semi-finalists/3rd place
1986	Finalists
1990	Quarter-finalists
1994	Quarter-finalists

ASIAN CLUB COMPETITIONS

Asian Champion Teams' Cup

Winners - Al Hilal 1991
Finalists - Al Ahly 1985, Al Hilal 1986 1987, Al Shabab 1992
Semi-finalists - Al Ittifaq 1988

Asian Cup Winners Cup

Winners - Al Qadisiyah 1993
Finalists - Al Nasr 1991
Semi-finalists - Al Hilal 1990, Al Ittihad 1992

SAUDI ARABIAN LEAGUE CHAMPIONS

1977	Al Hilal
1978	Al Ahly
1979	Al Hilal
1980	Al Nasr
1981	Al Nasr
1982	Al Ittihad
1983	Al Ittifaq
1984	Al Ahly
1985	Al Hilal
1986	Al Hilal
1987	Al Ittifaq
1988	Al Hilal
1989	Al Nasr
1990	Al Hilal
1991	Al Shabab
1992	Al Shabab
1993	Al Shabab
1994	Al Nasr

SAUDI CUP WINNERS

1958	Al Wehda
1959	Al Ittihad
1960	Al Ittihad
1961	-
1962	-
1963	Al Ahly
1964	Al Ittihad
1965	-
1966	Al Ahly
1967	Al Wehda
1968	Al Ittihad
1969	Al Ittifaq
1970	Al Ahly
1971	Al Ahly
1972	Al Ahly
1973	Al Ahly
1974	Al Ahly
1975	-
1976	Al Nasr
1977	Al Nasr
1978	Al Ahly
1979	Al Ahly
1980	-
1981	Al Nasr
1982	-
1983	Al Ahly
1984	-
1985	Al Ittifaq
1986	Al Nasr
1987	Al Ittifaq
1988	Al Ittihad
1989	Al Hilal
1990	Al Nasr
1991	Al Ittihad
1992	Al Qadisiyah
1993	Al Shabab
1994	Al Riyadh

CLUB DIRECTORY

RIYADH (Pop. - 1,308,000)
Al Hilal
Al Nasr
Al Shabab
Al Riyadh

JEDDAH (Pop. - 1,500,000)
Al Ahly
Al Ittihad

DAMMAM (Pop. - 200,000)
Al Qadisiyah
Al Ittifaq

SINGAPORE

Population: 2,718,000
Area, sq km: 622
% in urban areas: 100%
Capital city: Singapore City State 2,718,000

Football Association of Singapore
Jalan Besar Stadium
Tyrwhitt Road
Singapore 0820
Tel: + 65 2931477
Fax: + 65 2933728
Telex: sinfa rs 37683

Year of formation	1892
Affiliation to FIFA	1952
Affiliation to AFC	1954
Registered clubs	250
Registered players	158 000
Registered coaches	359
Registered referees	125
National stadium	National Stadium 65 000
National colours	Sky blue/Sky blue/ Sky blue
Reserve colours	White/White/White
Season	April - August

THE RECORD

WORLD CUP

1930-74	Did not enter
1978	QT R1 2nd/5 in group 1
1982	QT R1 5th/6 in group 4
1986	QT R1 3rd/3 in group 8
1990	QT R1 3rd/4 in group 4
1994	QT R1 3rd/3 in group 3

ASIAN CHAMPIONSHIP

1956	Did not enter
1960	QT 3rd/3 in group 2
1964	-
1968	QT 5th/5 in group 2
1972	-
1976	QT 5th/6 in group 4
1980	QT 7th/7 in group 7
1984	QT Automatic - Final tournament/1st round
1988	Did not enter
1992	QT 4th/4 in group 4

ASIAN GAMES

1951	Did not enter
1954	1st round
1958	1st round
1962	Did not enter
1966	Semi-finalists/4th place
1970-86	Did not enter
1990	1st round
1994	Did not enter

SINGAPORE LEAGUE CHAMPIONS

1975	Geylang International
1976	Geylang International

1977	Geylang International
1978	Singapore Armed Forces
1979	Tampines Rovers
1980	Tampines Rovers
1981	Singapore Armed Forces
1982	Farrer Park United
1983	Tiong Bahru
1984	Tampines Rovers
1985	Police SA
1986	Singapore Armed Forces
1987	Tiong Bahru
1988	Geylang International
1989	Geylang International
1990	Geylang International
1991	Geylang International
1992	Geylang International
1993	Geylang International
1994	Perth Kangaroos

SRI LANKA

Population: 17,103,000
Area, sq km: 65,610
% in urban areas: 21%
Capital city: Colombo 609,000

Football Federation of Sri Lanka
2 Old Grandstand
Race Course, Reid Avenue
Colombo 7
Sri Lanka
Tel: + 94 1 696179
Fax: + 94 1 580721
Telex: 21537 metalix ce

Year of formation	1939
Affiliation to FIFA	1950
Affiliation to AFC	1958
Registered clubs	600
Registered players	21 000
Registered referees	347
National stadium	Sugathadasa, Colombo 25 000
National colours	Maroon/White/ White
Reserve colours	White/White/ Maroon
Season	September - March

THE RECORD

WORLD CUP

1930-90	Did not enter
1994	QT R1 5th/5 in group 6

ASIAN CHAMPIONSHIP

1956-76	Did not enter
1980	QT 5th/7 in group 3
1984	QT 4th/5 in group 2
1988	Did not enter
1992	Did not enter

ASIAN GAMES

1951-94	Did not enter

SYRIA

Population: 12,116,000
Area, sq km: 185,180
% in urban areas: 50%
Capital city: Damascus 1,361,000

Association Arabe Syrienne de Football
General Sport Federation Building
October Stadium
Baremke
Damascus
Syria
Tel: + 963 11 3335866
Fax: + 963 11 215346
Telex: spotfed 411578

Year of formation	1936
Affiliation to FIFA	1937
Affiliation to AFC	1970
Registered clubs	102
Registered players	16 600
Registered coaches	532
Registered referees	490
National stadium	Al Abbassiyne, Damascus 45 000
National colours	All White
Reserve colours	All Red
Season	September - June

THE RECORD

WORLD CUP

1930-38	Did not enter
1950	QT 2nd/2 in group 2
1954	Did not enter
1958	QT R1 2nd/2 in group 4
1962-70	Did not enter
1974	QT R1 4th/8 in group B
1978	QT R1 3rd/3 in group 3
1982	QT R1 5th/5 in group 2
1986	QT R1 1st/3 in group 3, R2 1st/2, R3 2nd/2
1990	QT R1 2nd/3 in group 2
1994	QT R1 2nd/4 in group 2

ASIAN CHAMPIONSHIP

1956-76	Did not enter
1980	QT 2nd/4 in group 1 - Final tournament/1st round
1984	QT 2nd/6 in group 1 - Final tournament/1st round
1988	QT 1st/5 in group 3 - Final tournament/1st round
1992	QT 2nd/3 in group 1

ASIAN GAMES

1951-78	Did not enter
1982	1st round
1986-94	Did not enter

ASIAN CLUB COMPETITIONS

Asian Champion Teams' Cup
Semi-finalists - Ittihad 1985
Asian Cup Winners Cup
Have never entered

SYRIAN LEAGUE CHAMPIONS

1967	Al Ittihad
1968	Al Ittihad
1969	Al Majd
1970	Al Majd
1971	-
1972	-
1973	Al Jaish
1974	-
1975	Al Karama
1976	Al Jaish
1977	Al Ittihad
1978	-
1979	Al Jaish
1980	Al Shourta
1981	-
1982	Teshrin
1983	Al Karama
1984	Al Karama
1985	Al Jaish
1986	Al Jaish
1987	Jabala
1988	Jabala
1989	Jabala
1990	Al Foutoua
1991	Al Foutoua
1992	Al Foutoua
1993	Al Ittihad
1994	Al Horria

SYRIAN CUP WINNERS

1966	Al Ittihad
1967	Al Shourta
1968	Al Shourta
1969	Al Shourta
1970	Al Maghazel
1971-2	-
1973	Al Ittihad
1974-77	-
1978	Al Majd
1979	-
1980	Al Shourta
1981	Al Shourta
1982	Al Ittihad
1983	Al Karama
1984	Al Ittihad
1985	Al Ittihad
1986	Al Jaish
1987	Al Karama
1988	Al Foutoua
1989	Al Foutoua
1990	Al Foutoua
1991	Al Foutoua
1992	Al Horria
1993	Al Wahda
1994	Al Ittihad

TAIWAN

Population: 20,221,000
Area, sq km: 36,000

% in urban areas: 73%
Capital city: Taipei 2,702,000

Chinese Taipei Football Association
100 Kuang-Fu South Road
Taipei
Taiwan
Tel: + 886 2 7117710
Fax: + 886 2 7117713
Telex: 24195 educa taipei

Year of formation	1936
Affiliation to FIFA	1954
Affiliation to AFC	1955-76 & 1990
Registered clubs	55
Registered players	18 300
Registered coaches	423
Registered referees	447
National stadium	Chung-Shan, Taipei 30 000
National colours	Blue/White/Red
Reserve colours	White/White/White
Season	August - March

THE RECORD

WORLD CUP

1930-54	Did not enter
1958	QT R1 2nd/2 in group 1
1962-74	Did not enter
1978	QT R1 3rd/3 in Oceania group
1982	QT R1 4th/5 in group 1
1986	QT R1 4th/4 in Oceania group
1990	QT R1 2nd/2 in Oceania group
1994	QT R1 4th/4 in group 2

ASIAN CHAMPIONSHIP

1956	QT 2nd/3 in group 2
1960	QT 1st/ in group 3 - Final tournament/3rd place
1964	-
1968	QT 1st/5 in group 3 - Final tournament/4th place
1972	-
1976-88	Did not enter
1992	QT 4th/4 in group 6

ASIAN GAMES

1951	Did not enter
1954	Winners
1958	Winners
1962	Did not enter
1966	1st round
1970	Did not enter
1974	1st round
1978-94	Did not enter

TAJIKISTAN

Population: 5,109,000
Area, sq km: 143,100
Capital city: Dushanbe

Tajikistan Football Federation
44 Rudaki Avenue
PO Box 26
734025 Dushanbe
Tajikistan
Tel: + 377 2 212363
Fax: + 377 2 21 2447
Telex: 116286 shakh

Year of formation	1991
Affiliation to FIFA	1994
Affiliation to AFC	1994
Registered clubs	1800
Registered players	71 000
National stadium	Central, Dushanbe 22 000
National colours	White/Red/White
Season	April - November

THE RECORD

WORLD CUP

1930-94	Did not enter

ASIAN CHAMPIONSHIP

1956-92	Did not enter

ASIAN GAMES

1951-94	Did not enter

TAJIKISTAN LEAGUE CHAMPIONS

1992	Pamir Dushanbe
1993	Sitora Dushanbe

TAJIKISTAN CUP WINNERS

1992	Pamir Dushanbe
1993	Sitora Dushanbe

CLUB DIRECTORY

DUSHANBE (Pop. - 595,000)

Pamir Dushanbe (1947)
Central 22,000 – Blue/Blue

Sitora Dushanbe
Sokhibkor Dushanbe

KHUJANO (Pop. - 160,000)

Khodhzent Klaujand
Previous names: Khodzhent Leninabad

Saikhun Chkalovsk

QURGHONTEPPA (Pop. - 55,000)

Stroitel Qurghonteppa
Previous names: Vakhsk Kurgan-Tyube

THAILAND

Population: 56,217,000
Area, sq km: 513,115
% in urban areas: 19%
Capital city: Bangkok 5,716,000

The Football Association of Thailand
C/O National Stadium
Rama I Road
Bangkok
Thailand
Tel: + 66 2 2141058
Fax: + 66 2 2154494
Telex: 20211 fat th

Year of formation	1916
Affiliation to FIFA	1925
Affiliation to AFC	1957
Registered clubs	168
Registered players	216 000
Registered referees	150
National stadium	Suphachalasai, Bangkok 45 000
National colours	Crimson/White/Crimson
Reserve colours	White/White/White
Season	November - April

THE RECORD

WORLD CUP

1930-70	Did not enter
1974	QT R1 7th/7 in group A
1978	QT R1 5th/5 in group 1
1982	QT R1 4th/5 in group 1
1986	QT R1 3rd/4 in group 6
1990	QT R1 4th/4 in group 5
1994	QT R1 3rd/5 in group 6

ASIAN CHAMPIONSHIP

1956	Did not enter
1960	-
1964	-
1968	QT 2nd/5 in group 2
1972	QT Automatic - Final tournament/Semi-finalists/3rd place
1976	QT 2nd/5 in group 3 - Withdrew
1980	QT 4th/7 in group 3
1984	QT 4th/6 in group 1
1988	QT 4th/6 in group 1
1992	QT 1st/3 in group 5 - Final tournament/1st round

ASIAN GAMES

1951-58	Did not enter
1962	1st round
1966	Quarter-finalists
1970	Quarter-finalists
1974	1st round
1978	Semi-finalists/3rd in group
1982	1st round
1986	1st round
1990	Semi-finalists/3rd place
1994	1st round

ASIAN CLUB COMPETITIONS

Asian Champion Teams' Cup
Winners - Thai Farmers Bank 1993 1994
Semi-finalists - Bangkok Bank 1987
Asian Cup Winners Cup
Have never entered

TURKMENISTAN

Population: 3,534,000
Area, sq km: 488,100
Capital city: Ashkhabad

Turkmenistan Football Federation
44 Engels Street
744000 Ashkhabad
Turkmenistan
Tel: + 3632 253844
Fax: + 3632 290646
Telex: 116175 tinto su

Year of formation	1992
Affiliation to FIFA	1994
Affiliation to AFC	1994
Registered players	75 000
National stadium	Central, Ashkhabad 12 000
National colours	Green/White/Green
Season	April - November

THE RECORD

WORLD CUP
1930-94 Did not enter

ASIAN CHAMPIONSHIP
1956-92 Did not enter

ASIAN GAMES
1951-90 Did not enter
1994 Quarter-finalists

TURKMENISTAN CHAMPIONS

1992	Kopet-Dag Ashkhabad
1993	Kopet-Dag Ashkhabad
1994	Kopet-Dag Ashkhabad

TURKMENISTAN CUP WINNERS

1993 Kopet-Dag Ashkhabad

CLUB DIRECTORY

ASHKHABAD (Pop. - 398,000)
Kopet-Dag Ashkhabad
TSKT Ashkhabad

NEBIT-DAG
Nebitchi Nebit-Dag

MARY
Merv Mary

TURKMENBASHI
Khazar Turkmenbashi
Previous name: Khazar Krasnovodsk

UNITED ARAB EMIRATES

Population: 1,903,000
Area, sq km: 77,700
% in urban areas: 86%
Capital city: Abu Dhabi 243,000

United Arab Emirates Football Association
PO Box 5458
Dubai
United Arab Emirates
Tel: + 971 4 823444
Fax: + 971 4 823700
Telex: 47623 uaefa em

Year of formation	1971
Affiliation to FIFA	1972
Affiliation to AFC	1974
Registered clubs	25
Registered players	4500
Registered coaches	57
Registered referees	109
National stadium	Zayed Sports City, Abu Dhabi 60 000
National colours	All White
Reserve colours	All Red
Season	October - May

THE RECORD

WORLD CUP
1930-82 Did not enter
1986 QT R1 1st/2 in group 1, R2 2nd/2
1990 QT R1 1st/3 in group 3, R2 2nd/6 - Final tournament/ 1st round
1994 QT R1 2nd/5 in group 6

ASIAN CHAMPIONSHIP
1956-76 Did not enter
1980 QT 1st/4 in group 1 - Final tournament/1st round
1984 QT 2nd/5 in group 2 - Final tournament/1st round
1988 QT 1st/6 in group 1 - Final tournament/1st round
1992 QT 1st/3 in group 2 - Final tournament/Semi-finalists/ 4th place

ASIAN GAMES
1951-82 Did not enter
1986 Quarter-finalists
1990 Did not enter
1994 Quarter-finalists

ASIAN CLUB COMPETITIONS
Asian Champion Teams' Cup
Semi-finalists - Al Shabab 1991, Al Wasl 1992
Asian Cup Winners Cup
Semi-finalists - Al Shabab 1990

UNITED ARAB EMIRATES LEAGUE CHAMPIONS

1975	Al Ahly
1976	Al Ahly
1977	Al Ain
1978	Al Nasr
1979	Al Nasr
1980	Al Ahly
1981	Al Ain
1982	Al Wasl
1983	Al Wasl
1984	Al Ain
1985	Al Wasl
1986	Al Nasr
1987	Al Sharjah
1988	Al Wasl
1989	Al Sharjah
1990	Al Shabab
1991	-
1992	Al Wasl
1993	Al Ain
1994	Al Sharjah
1995	Al Shabab

UZBEKISTAN

Population: 19,905,000
Area, sq km: 447,400
Capital city: Tashkent

Uzbekistan Football Federation
Massiv Almazar
Furkat Street 15/1
700003 Tashkent
Uzbekistan
Tel: + 3712 454948
Fax: + 3712 443183
Telex: 116108 ptb su

Year of formation	1946
Affiliation to FIFA	1994
Affiliation to AFC	1994
Registered clubs	15 000
Registered players	217 000
National stadium	Pachtakor, Tashkent 54,000
National colours	Blue/White/Blue
Season	April - November

THE RECORD

WORLD CUP
1930-94 Did not enter

ASIAN CHAMPIONSHIP
1956-92 Did not enter

ASIAN GAMES
1951-90 Did not enter
1994 Winners

ASIAN CLUB COMPETITIONS
Asian Champion Teams' Cup
Semi-finalists - Neftchi Fergana 1994

UZBEKISTAN LEAGUE CHAMPIONS

1992	Neftchi Fergana & Pachtakor Tashkent
1993	Neftchi Fergana
1994	Neftchi Fergana

UZBEKISTAN CUP WINNERS

1993	Pachtakor Tashkent

CLUB DIRECTORY

TASHKENT (Pop. - 2,325,000)
CSKA Tashkent (1979)
Previous name: FKA Pachtakor 1979-92

Pachtakor Tashkent (1956)
Pachtakor 60,000 – Red/Black

Politotdel-RUOR Tashkent
Traktor Tashkent

SAMARKAND (Pop. - 366,000)
Dynamo Samarkand
Previous name: Marakanda Samarkand

NAMANGAN (Pop. - 308,000)
Nobakhor Namangan

ANDIZHAN (Pop. - 293,000)
Navruz Andizhan

FERGANA (Pop. - 200,000)
Neftchi Fergana

KOKAND (Pop. - 182,000)
Temirsulchi Kokand

ALMALYK (Pop. - 114,000)
Kimyogar Almalyk

DZHIZAK (Pop. - 102,000)
Sogdiana Dzhizak

TERMEZ (Pop. - 72,000)
Surkhan Termez

VIETNAM

Population: 66,128,000
Area, sq km: 329,566
% in urban areas: 20%
Capital city: Hanoi 1,088,000
Major city: Ho Chi Minh City (Prev. Saigon) 3,169,000

Association de Football de la Republique du Vietnam
36 Boulevard Tran-phu
Hanoi
Vietnam
Tel: + 84 2 52480
Fax: + 84 42 32455

Year of formation	1962
Affiliation to FIFA	1964
Affiliation to AFC	1954
Registered clubs	55
Registered players	30 500
Registered referees	181
National stadium	Stade Hang Day, Hanoi 40 000
National colours	Red/White/Red
Reserve colours	White/White/Red
Season	November - May

THE RECORD

WORLD CUP

1930-70	Did not enter
1974	QT R1 6th/7 in group A
1978-90	Did not enter
1994	QT R1 5th/5 in group 3

ASIAN CHAMPIONSHIP

1956	QT 1st/3 in group 3 - Final tournament/4th place
1960	QT 1st/3 in group 2 - Final tournament/4th place
1964	
1968	QT 3rd/5 in group 2
1972	-
1976	QT 5th/5 in group 3
1980-92	Did not enter

ASIAN GAMES

1951	Did not enter
1954	1st round
1958	Quarter-finalists
1962	Semi-finalists/4th place
1966	1st round
1970	1st round
1974-94	Did not enter

ASIAN CLUB COMPETITIONS
Asian Champion Teams' Cup

Asian Cup Winners Cup
Semi-finalists - Quang Nam Danang 1992

VIETNAMESE NATIONAL CHAMPIONS

1981	Tong Cuc Duong Sat
1982	Cau Lac Bo Quan Doi
1983	Cau Lac Bo Quan Doi
1984	Cong An Hanoi
1985	Cong Nghiep Ham Nam Ninh
1986	Cang Siagon
1987	Cau Lac Bo Quan Doi
1988	Cong An Hanoi
1989	Dong Thap
1990	-
1991	-
1992	Quang Nam Danang
1993	Quang Nam Danang
1994	Port Saigon
1995	Ho Chi Minh City Police

YEMEN

Population: 11,546,000
Area, sq km: 472,099
% in urban areas: 24%
Capital city: Sana'a and Aden

Yemen Football Association
PO Box 908
Sana'a
Yemen
Tel: + 967 1 215720
Fax: + 967 1 263182
Telex: 2710 youth ye

Year of formation	1940 (South) 1976 (North)
Affiliation to FIFA	1967 (South) 1980 (North)
Affiliation to AFC	1967 (South) 1980 (North)
Registered clubs	26
Registered players	101 000
Registered coaches	27
Registered referees	120
National stadium	National Stadium, Sana'a 50 000
National colours	All Green
Season	October - April

THE RECORD

WORLD CUP

1930-82	Did not enter
1986	QT R1 3rd/3 in group 3 (North) & 2nd/2 in group 4 (South)
1990	QT R1 3rd/3 in group 2 (North)
1994	QT R1 3rd/5 in group 1

ASIAN CHAMPIONSHIP

1956-72	Did not enter
1976	QT W-O in group 1 - Final tournament/1st round (South)
1980	Did not enter
1984	QT 5th/5 in group 3 (North)
1988	QT 3rd/6 in group 1 (North) & 4th/4 in group 4 (South)
1992	Did not enter

ASIAN GAMES

1951-78	Did not enter
1982	1st round (South)
1986	Did not enter
1990	1st round
1994	1st round

OCEANIA

Although the Oceania Football Confederation governs football in more than one sixth of the area of the world, it is not considered important enough by FIFA to grant it voting rights on its executive committee. The two major countries in the Oceania confederation are Australia and New Zealand, and they are joined by six of the larger nations among the many Pacific islands. The problem is that few of them can claim football to be the major sport in their respective countries.

New Zealand won the first rugby World Cup in 1987 and Australia followed them as winners four years later, but rugby is even more deeply ingrained in the culture of the rest of the region. Both Fiji and Western Samoa have reached the quarter-finals of that event, whilst Papua New Guinea, the Solomon Islands and Tonga are all regarded as strong opponents on their day. Only in the former French territories of Tahiti, New Caledonia and Vanuatu is football the main pastime, and their small populations severely limit their prospects. Not to be underestimated either is the American influence in the region which has ensured the spread of baseball and American football, especially in Guam and American Samoa.

Due to the enormous distances involved international activity is extremely restricted, even for New Zealand and Australia. An Oceania tournament has been played on two occasions, but neither was a conspicuous success and since 1980 it has not been thought worthwhile to organise a third. A similar tournament for clubs is simply out of the question. The only other regional tournament of any import is the football tournament of the South Pacific Games and this has been dominated by Tahiti and New Caledonia.

Oceania's future was put in jeopardy in the early 1970s when Australia sought affiliation with the Asian Football Confederation in an attempt to increase the level of competition, but their approaches were rejected. Instead both Australia and New Zealand have had to be content with entries into both the World Cup and Olympic Games, as well as friendly matches against touring European sides.

The World Cup is now a major feature but only Australia, Fiji and New Zealand entered before 1994, Tahiti, the Solomon Islands, Vanuatu and Western Samoa making their first appearance in the qualifiers for USA '94. Australia and New Zealand have qualified for the finals once each, but on each occasion they did so through the Asian qualifying tournament. In 1974 Australia beat Iran and South Korea in crucial matches, whilst in 1982 New Zealand defeated China in a play-off in Singapore. Neither team was particularly remarkable and they relied on their larger physique, as well as their greater experience, to overcome their opponents.

Since then a separate qualifying group has been set aside for Oceania, although crucially the region is not guaranteed a place in the finals. In 1986 the winners were forced to play-off against a European side, in 1990 against a South American opponent, and in 1994 against first Canada from CONCACAF and then Argentina. That there was no Oceania representative at the 1994 finals was therefore hardly surprising.

Australia has the best football set-up in the region thanks mainly to the large number of ethnic communities present in the country. Team names like St George Budapest, Sydney Croatia and Brunswick Juventus left no doubt as to their origin, but this has hampered the growth of the game amongst native Australians who see it largely as an alien sport. So worried have the authorities and the clubs been that many attempts have been made to drop the ethnic tags, but such moves never prove popular, or lasting.

Football faces stiff competition from a host of other sports in Australia. The national game is Australian Rules football, a hybrid of rugby, football and Gaelic football played on a pitch that often doubles as a cricket field, hence its enormous size. In typical Australian fashion however, 'Aussie Rules' is not played throughout the country but largely in the south, particularly in Victoria, as well as Western Australia; while in Queensland and New South Wales, rugby league is the number one code. Also competing for the attention of the public are cricket, rugby union and individual sports like athletics and swimming. Football has therefore taken a back seat, and until the 1960s played very little part in national life at all.

Between 1946 and 1960, 1.6 million immigrants made their way to Australia, mainly from Europe, and this was the initial boost the game needed. An association had been in existence since 1882, but it was replaced in 1961 by the current federation, in order to run the game at home in a more organised fashion and revive the national side, which had lain dormant for many years. From the late 1950s until 1976 each state ran its own league, the best being in New South Wales, Victoria and South Australia. In 1977 Australia finally got a national league, beneath which the state leagues continue to operate. The national league has never had an easy path. Gates are invariably low, except for the play-offs at the end of the season, and travel expenses are high, because of the vast size of the country. Although it is called the 'national' league, no teams from either Tasmania or Western Australia are included. In the latter's case, travel expenses would simply be prohibitive. In recent years the league has seen the rise of a number of Australian players who continue their careers in Europe, the most famous being Craig Johnston who won many honours with Liverpool.

In New Zealand, the second power in the region, football at least faces much more clear-cut opposition than in Australia. Rugby Union dominates the national sporting life to the almost complete exclusion of football. Only amongst the British community is it played with any great vigour. Formed in 1891, the New Zealand Football Association initially supervised a competition called the Brown Shield, but the most important development came in 1923 when a cup presented by the English naval ship HMS Chatham was introduced as an annual knockout competition for club sides. This remains a major feature on the fixture list and was joined in 1970 by a national championship. Despite very poor attendances, the national league has given a boost to the clubs in New Zealand, who up until that point, had played in poorly organised local leagues. It undoubtedly also helped the 'All Whites', as the national side is known in order to distinguish it from rugby's All Blacks, to qualify for the 1982 World Cup where they helped make their group one of the most entertaining in the tournament.

The future does not look very bright, however, for New Zealand or the rest of the Oceania members. The region was not granted an automatic berth in the expanded World Cup in 1998, although the winners this time might fancy their chances of winning the play-off against the fourth-placed Asian nation. At youth level, by contrast, the region has always had an automatic place in the two junior World Cups and the game at this level is flourishing, Australia, being particularly strong. At all levels, however, the Pacific island states will continue to flounder, for the incentive is simply not there without a real chance of qualification for the World Cup finals. Until then the oval ball, with its World Cup, will continue to increase in popularity at the expense of the round one.

Oceania Football Confederation
PO Box 62-586
Central Park
Auckland 6
New Zealand
Tel: + 64 9 5258161
Fax: + 64 9 5258164

MEMBERS - 10
Australia – Cook Islands – Fiji – French Polynesia - Tahiti – New Zealand – Papua New Guinea – Solomon Islands – Tonga – Vanuatu – Western Samoa

ASSOCIATE MEMBERS - 4
American Samoa – New Caledonia – Niue Island – Northern Marianas

NON MEMBERS - 12
Christmas Island – Cocos Islands – Kiribati – Marshall Islands – Micronesia – Nauru – Norfolk Island – Palau – Pitcairn Island – Tokelau – Tuvalu – Wallis and Fotuna

1973

1ST OCEANIA CUP

HELD IN NEW ZEALAND, 17TH - 24TH FEBRUARY

	NZ	Ta	NC	NH	Fi	Pl	W	D	L	F	A	Pts
New Zealand	-	1-1	2-1	3-1	5-1	4	3	1	0	11	4	7
Tahiti	-	-	2-1	0-0	4-0	4	2	2	0	7	2	6
New Caledonia	-	-	-	4-1	2-0	4	2	0	2	8	5	4
New Hebrides	-	-	-	-	2-1	4	1	1	0	4	8	3
Fiji	-	-	-	-	-	4	0	0	4	2	13	0

THIRD PLACE
New Caledonia ....2-1 ....New Hebrides

FINAL
New Zealand ....2-0 ....Tahiti

1980

2ND OCEANIA CUP

HELD IN NOUMEA, NEW CALEDONIA, 22ND FEB - 3RD MARCH 1980

Group 1

	Ta	Fi	NZ	SI	Pl	W	D	L	F	A	Pts
Tahiti	-	6-3	3-1	12-1	3	3	0	0	21	5	6
Fiji	-	-	4-0	3-1	3	2	0	1	10	7	4
New Zealand	-	-	-	6-1	3	1	0	2	7	8	2
Soloman Islands	-	-	-	-	3	0	0	3	3	21	0

Group 2

	Au	NC	PN	NH	Pl	W	D	L	F	A	Pts
Australia	-	8-0	11-2	1-0	3	3	0	0	20	2	6
New Caledonia	-	-	8-0	4-3	3	2	0	1	12	11	4
Papua N. Guinea	-	-	-	4-3	3	1	0	2	6	22	2
New Hebrides	-	-	-	-	3	0	0	3	6	9	0

3RD PLACE
New Caledonia ....2-1 ....Fiji

FINAL
Australia...4-2 ....Tahiti

AUSTRALIA

Population: 17,073,000
Area, sq km: 7,682,300
% in urban areas: 85%
Capital city: Canberra

Australia Soccer Federation
1st Floor
23-25 Frederick Street
Rockdale
NSW 2216
Australia
Tel: + 61 2 380699
Fax: + 61 2 3806155
Telex: aa 170512

Year of formation	1961
Affiliation to FIFA	1963
Affiliation to OFC	1966
Registered clubs	1860
Registered players	512 200
Registered referees	3020
National stadium	National Stadium, Canberra 30 000
National colours	Gold/Green/White
Reserve colours	GreenWhiteGreen
Season	March - October

THE RECORD

WORLD CUP

1930-62	Did not enter
1966	QT 2nd/2
1970	QT R1 1st/3 in group 1, R2 2nd/2
1974	QT R1 1st/8 in group B, R2 1st/2 - Final tournament/1st round
1978	QT R1 1st/3 in Oceania group, R2 4th/5
1982	QT R1 2nd/5 in group 1
1986	QT 1st/4 in Oceania group. Lost European - Oceania play-off
1990	QT 2nd/5 in Oceania group
1994	QT R1 1st/3 in group 1, R2 bt New Zealand, Won Oceania - CONCACAF play-off, Lost Oceania - South America play-off

AUSTRALIAN NATIONAL CHAMPIONS

1977	Sydney City Hakoah
1978	West Adelaide Hellas
1979	Marconi

1980	Sydney City Hakoah
1981	Sydney City Hakoah
1982	Sydney City Hakoah
1983	St. George Budapest
1984	South Melbourne Hellas
1985	Brunswick Juventus
1986	Adelaide City Juventus
1987	APIA-Leichhardt
1988	Marconi
1989	Marconi
1990	Sydney Olympic
1991	South Melbourne Hellas
1992	Adelaide City Juventus
1993	Marconi
1994	Adelaide City
1995	Melbourne Knights

AUSTRALIAN CUP WINNERS

1977	Brisbane City
1978	Brisbane City
1979	Adelaide City Juventus
1980	Marconi
1981	Brisbane Lions
1982	APIA Leichhardt
1983	Sydney Olympic
1984	Newcastle Rosebud
1985	Sydney Olympic
1986	Sydney City Hakoah
1987	Sydney Croatia
1988	APIA Leichhardt
1989	Adelaide City Juventus
1990	South Melbourne Hellas
1991	Parramatta Melita
1992	Adelaide City Juventus
1993	Heidelberg United
1994	Parramatta Eagles
1995	Melbourne Knights

CLUB DIRECTORY

SYDNEY (Pop. - 3,364,000)

Sydney City Hakoah
Folded 1987

Sydney Olympic
St. George Stadium – White/Blue

Sydney United
Croatian Sports Centre – Red/White
Previous name: Sydney Croatia

APIA Leichhardt
Folded 1992

St. George Budapest

Marconi - Fairfield
Marconi Stadium – Green/White

Parramatta Eagles
Melita Stadium - White/White
Previous name: Melita Eagles

MELBOURNE (Pop. - 2,832,000)

South Melbourne
Middle Park – Blue/Blue
Previous name: South Melbourne Hellas

Melbourne Knights
Croatian Sports Centre – Red/White
Previous name: Melbourne Croatia

Heidelberg United
Olympic Village – Yellow/Black
Previous name: Heidelberg Alexander

Melbourne Brunswick United
Western Oval – Black & white stripes/White
Previous name: Brunswick Juventus

BRISBANE (Pop. - 1,149,000)

Brisbane Strikers
Perry Park – White/White

Brisbane City
Brisbane Lions

ADELAIDE (Pop. - 977,000)

Adelaide City
Hindmarsh Stadium – Black& white stripes/Black
Previous name: Adelaide City Juventus

West Adelaide Sharks
Hindmarsh Stadium – White/White
Previous name: West Adelaide Hellas

NEWCASTLE (Pop. - 405,000)

Newcastle BHP Breakers
Mitre 10 Stadium – Maroon/Blue
Previous name - Newcastle United

WOLLONGONG

Wollongong Wolves

COOK ISLANDS

Population: 19,000
Area, sq km: 293
Capital city: Rarotonga

Cook Islands Football Federation
PO Box 473
Rarotonga
Cook Islands
Tel: + 682 20335
Fax: + 682 20335

Year of formation	1971
Affiliation to FIFA	1994
Registered clubs	9
National colours	Green/Green/Gold
Season	October - December

THE RECORD

WORLD CUP

1930-94	Did not enter

FIJI

Population: 740,000
Area, sq km: 18,274
% in urban areas: 38%
Capital city: Suva 69,000

Fiji Football Association
PO Box 2514
Suva
Fiji
Tel: + 679 300453
Fax: + 679 304642

Year of formation	1938
Affiliation to FIFA	1963
Affiliation to OFC	1963
Registered clubs	200
Registered players	3200
National stadium	National Sports Stadium, Suva 25 000
National colours	White/Black/Black
Reserve colours	Black & white hoops/Black/Black
Season	February - October

THE RECORD

WORLD CUP

1930-78	Did not enter
1982	QT R1 5th/5 in Asia group 1
1986	Did not enter
1990	QT R1 4th/5 in Oceania group
1994	QT R1 2nd/3 in Oceania group 2

NEW ZEALAND

Population: 3,389,000
Area, sq km: 270,534
% in urban areas: 83%
Capital city: Wellington

New Zealand Football Association
PO Box 18 296
Glen Innes
Auckland
New Zealand
Tel: + 64 9 5256120
Fax: + 64 9 5256123

Year of formation	1891
Affiliation to FIFA	1948
Affiliation to OFC	1966
Registered clubs	350
Registered players	89 200
Registered coaches	91
Registered referees	872
National stadium	Mt. Smart, Auckland 45 000
National colours	All White
Reserve colours	Black/White/White
Season	October - May

THE RECORD

WORLD CUP

1930-66	Did not enter
1970	QT R1 2nd/2 in group 2
1974	QT R1 8th/8 in group B
1978	QT R1 2nd/3 in Oceania group
1982	QT R1 1st/5 in group 1, R2 2nd/4 - Final tournament/1st round
1986	QT R1 3rd/4 in Oceania group
1990	QT R1 3rd/5 in Oceania group
1994	QT R1 1st/3 in Oceania group 2

NEW ZEALAND NATIONAL CHAMPIONS

1970	Blockhouse Bay
1971	Eastern Suburbs
1972	Mount Wellington
1973	Christchurch United
1974	Mount Wellington
1975	Christchurch United
1976	Wellington Diamond United
1977	North Shore United
1978	Christchurch United
1979	Mount Wellington
1980	Mount Wellington
1981	Wellington Diamond United
1982	Mount Wellington
1983	Manurewa
1984	Gisbourne City
1985	Wellington Diamond United
1986	Mount Wellington
1987	Christchurch United
1988	Christchurch United
1989	Napier City Rovers
1990	Waitakere City
1991	Christchurch United
1992	Napier City Rovers
1993	Waitakere City
1994	North Shore United

CHATHAM CUP WINNERS

1923	Seacliff
1924	Auckland Harbour Board
1925	Wellington YMCA
1926	Sunnyside
1927	Ponsonby
1928	Petone
1929	Tramways
1930	Petone
1931	Tramurewa
1932	Wellington Marist
1933	Ponsonby
1934	Auckland Thistle
1935	Wellington Hospital
1936	Western
1937	-
1938	Waterside
1939	Waterside
1940	Waterside
1941-44	-
1945	Western
1946	Wellington Marist
1947	Waterside
1948	Christchurch Technical
1949	Petone
1950	Eden
1951	Eastern Suburbs
1952	North Shore United & Western
1953	Eastern Suburbs
1954	Onehunga
1955	Western
1956	Stop Out
1957	Seatoun
1958	Seatoun
1959	Northern
1960	North Shore United
1961	Northern
1962	Hamilton Technical
1963	North Shore United
1964	Mount Roskill
1965	Eastern Suburbs
1966	Miramar Rangers
1967	North Shore United
1968	Eastern Suburbs
1969	Eastern Suburbs
1970	Blockhouse Bay
1971	Western Suburbs
1972	Christchurch United
1973	Mount Wellington
1974	Christchurch United
1975	Christchurch United
1976	Christchurch United
1977	Nelson United
1978	Manurewa
1979	North Shore United
1980	Mount Wellington
1981	Dunedin City
1982	Mount Wellington
1983	Mount Wellington
1984	Manurewa
1985	Napier City Rovers
1986	North Shore United
1987	Gisbourne City
1988	Waikato United
1989	Christchurch United
1990	Mount Wellington
1991	Christchurch United
1992	Miramar
1993	Napier City Rovers
1994	Waitakere City

PAPUA NEW GUINEA

Population: 3,671,000
Area, sq km: 462,840
% in urban areas: 14%
Capital city: Port Moresby 152,000

Papua New Guinea Football Association
PO Box 1716
Boroko
Papua New Guinea
Tel: + 675 722391
Fax: + 675 721941
Telex: tototra ne 23436

Year of formation	1962
Affiliation to FIFA	1963
Affiliation to OFC	1963
Registered clubs	1200
Registered players	13400
Registered referees	20
National stadium	Sir Hubert Murray, Stadium, Port Moresby 20 000
National colours	Red/Black/Red
Reserve colours	All White
Season	February - November

THE RECORD

WORLD CUP

1930-94	Did not enter

SOLOMON ISLANDS

Population: 319,000
Area, sq km: 28,370
% in urban areas: 15%
Capital city: Honiara 30,000

Solomon Islands Football Federation
PO Box 140
Honaria
Solomon Islands
Tel: + 677 23553
Fax: + 677 23715

Affiliation to FIFA	1988
Affiliation to OFC	1988
Registered players	2600
National stadium	Lawson Tawa, Honaria 12 000
National colours	Blue, yellow & green thirds/Green/White
Season	May - December

THE RECORD

WORLD CUP

1930-90	Did not enter
1994	R1 3rd/3 in Oceania group 1

TAHITI

Population: 197,000
Area, sq km: 4,000
% in urban areas: 55%
Capital city: Papeete 103,000

Lique de Football de Polynesie
BP 650
Papeete
Tahiti
French Polynesia
Tel: + 689 420410
Fax: + 689 421679

Year of formation	1938
Affiliation to FIFA	1990
Registered clubs	205
Registered players	15 500
National stadium	Stade Olympique, Papeete 15 000
National colours	Red/White/White
Season	February - October

THE RECORD

WORLD CUP

1930-90	Did not enter
1994	R1 2nd/3 in Oceania group 1

TONGA

Population: 105,000
Area, sq Km: 671
% in urban areas: 30%
Capital city: Nuku'alofa 21,000

Tonga Football Association
PO Box 36
Nuku'alofa
Kingdom of Tonga
Tel: + 676 21366
Fax: + 676 24260

Year of formation	1965
Affiliation to FIFA	1994
Registered clubs	23
Registered players	350
National colours	Red/White/Red

THE RECORD

WORLD CUP

1930-94	Did not enter

VANUATU

Population: 147,000
Area, sq km: 12,190
% in urban areas: 18%
Capital city: Port Vila 19,000

Vanuatu Football Federation
PO Box 226
Port Vila
Vanuatu
Tel: + 678 22009
Fax: + 678 23579

Year of formation	1934
Affiliation to FIFA	1988
Affiliation to OFC	1988
National colours	Gold/Black/Gold
Season	March - September

THE RECORD

WORLD CUP

1930-90	Did not enter
1994	R1 3rd/3 in Oceania group 2

WESTERN SAMOA

Population: 165,000
Area, sq km: 2,831
% in urban areas: 21%
Capital city: Apia 33,000

Western Samoa Football Association
Ministry of Youth, Sports and Culture
Private bag
Apia
Western Samoa
Tel: + 685 22822
Fax: + 685 21312
Telex: 233 treasury sx

Year of formation	1968
Affiliation to FIFA	1986
Affiliation to OFC	1986
Registered clubs	33
Registered players	1750
Registered coaches	2
Registered referres	28
National stadium	Apia Park 12 000
National colours	Blue/White/Blue
Season	June - September

THE RECORD

WORLD CUP

1930-94	Did not enter

BIBLIOGRAPHY

Auf der Heyde P. (1994), **Soccer Yearbook '94.** (Impact Africa).

Bacorevic A. (1986), **Tempo Specijalno.** (Tempo).

Baker B. (1992), **South African Soccer.**

Barrett N. (1973), **World Soccer from A to Z.** (Rainbird).

Barrett N. (1980), **Purnell's New Encyclopedia of Association Football.** (Purnell).

Barrett N. (1994), **The Daily Telegraph Football Chronicle.** (Carlton).

Bestard M, (1991), **Football in South America.** (BPPC Wheatons).

Camkin J. (1958), **World Cup 1958.** (Rupert Hart-Davis).

Cazal J. & Oreggia M. (1989), **Israel 1948-1989.** (AFSF).

Clayton D. & Buitenga J. (1991), **The International Matches of Czechoslovakia, East Germany, Greece, Lithuania, Latvia, Estonia, Iceland, Romania and Portugal**

Confédération Africaine de Football (1987), **1957-1987.** (CAF).

C.S.F. (1989), **Copa Libertadores de America. 30 Años.** (CSF).

C.S.F. (1991), **Confederacion Sudamericana de Futbol. 75 Años. 1916-1991.** (CSF).

Cullen D. (1993), **Ireland on the Ball.** (ELO).

Derksen J. et al (1989), **Het Nederlands Elftal. De Historie van Oranje 1905-1989.** (Voetbal International).

Evans P. (1990), **World Cup 90.** (Hodder & Stoughton).

Fabian A.H. & Green G. (eds) (1961), **Association Football.** (Four volumes). (Caxton).

Faroe FA (1991), **Skipan.** (FFA).

Finn R. (1970), **World Cup 1970.** (Robert Hale).

Freddi C. (1991), **England Football Fact Book.** (Guinness).

Gibson A. & Pickford W. (1906), **Association Football and the Men Who Made It.** (Four volumes). (Caxton. Reprint 1988).

Glanville B. (1980), **The History of the World Cup.** (Faber & Faber).

Glanville.B. (1964), **The World Football Handbook.** (Hodder & Stoughton).

Glanville B. (1991), **Champions of Europe.** (Guinness).

Golesworthy M. (1957), **The Encyclopaedia of Association Football.** (Robert Hale).

Gomez Anguas J. (1995), **A History of Football in Mexico.** (Heart Books).

Gowarzewski A. (1992), **Mistrzostwa Europy.** 3 (GIA).

Gowarzewski A. (1992), **Od Realu do Barcelony.** 4 (GIA).

Gowarzewski A. (1993), **Puchar Zdobywcow.** 6 (GIA).

Gowarzewski A. (1993), **Rocznik 1993-94.** 7 (GIA).

Gowarzewski A. (1993), **Herosi Mundiali.** 8 (GIA).

Gowarzewski A. (1994), **Mistrzostwa Swiata.** 9 (GIA).

Gowarzewski A. (1994), **World Cup USA '94.** 10 (GIA).

Gowarzewski A. (1994), **Rocznik 1994-95.** 11 (GIA).

Graham A. (1994), **Ex Soviet Republics. Part 1 & Part 2.** (Skye Soccer Books).

Grüne.H (1992), **Enzyklopädie de Europäischen Fussballvereine.** (Agon).

Hammond M. (1988), **The European Football Yearbook.** (Facer).

Hammond M. (1991), **The European Football Handbook.** (Sports Projects Ltd)

Hammond M. (1991), **Eurosoccer Statistics.** (Sports Projects Ltd).

Hammond M. (1991), **The European Football Yearbook 1991/92.** (Sports Projects Ltd).

Hammond M. (1992), **The European Football Yearbook 1992/93.** (Sports Projects Ltd).

Hammond M. (1993), **The European Football Yearbook 1993/94.** (Sports Projects Ltd).

Hammond M. (1994), **The European Football Yearbook 1994/95.** (Sports Projects Ltd).

Hammond M. (1992), **Playing in Europe 1992-93.** (Sports Projects).

Hammond M. (1993), **Playing in Europe 1993-94.** (Sports Projects).

Heimann K. & Jens K. (1992), **Kicker Almanach.** (Copress).

Henshaw R. (1979), **The Encyclopedia of World Soccer.** (New Republic Books).

Henshaw R. & LaBlanc M. (1994), **The World Encyclopedia of Soccer.** (Visible Ink).

Hereng J. (1990), **Annuaire Footbal 1989-1990.** (Vumpress: Groot-Bijgaarden).

Hockings R. (1993), **Nations of Europe Volume One.** (Articulate).

Hockings R. (1993), **Nations of Europe Volume Two.** (Articulate).

Inarsa T. (1989), **Anuario de Futbol 1989-1990.** (Todosport).

Inglis S. (1990), **The Football Grounds of Europe.** (Willow Books).

Ionescu R. & Riley G. (1992), **Romania.** (EFRB).

Jeffrey G. (1963), **European International Football.** (Nicholas Kaye).

Jose C. (1989), **NASL.** (Breedon).

Kit A. & JL & Belaid A. (1993), **Atlas Mondial du Football. 1994.** (AMF).

Kit A. & JL & Belaid A. (1994), **Atlas Mondial du Football. 1995.** (AMF).

Kuper S. (1994), **Football Against the Enemy.** (Orion).

Lahtinen E et al. (1994), **Jalkapallokirja 1994.** (SPJ).

Lanzarini A. (1992), **Calcio Mondo 1992-93.** (Conti).

Lanzarini A. (1993), **Calcio Mondo 1993-94.** (Conti).

Laszlo M. (1987), **Futball-adattar II.** (Sportpropaganda).

Lever J. (1983), **Soccer Madness.** (University of Chicago).

Libotte A. (1985), **Almanacco Calcistico Svizzero.** (GDP Sport).

Lo Presti S. (1988), **Annuario del Calcio Mondiale. 1988-89** (SET).

Lo Presti S. (1989), **Annuario del Calcio Mondiale. 1989-90** (SET).

Lo Presti S. (1990), **Annuario del Calcio Mondiale. 1990-91** (SET).

Lo Presti S. (1991), **Annuario del Calcio Mondiale. 1991-92** (SET).

BIBLIOGRAPHY Continued

Lo Presti S. (1992), **Annuario del Calcio Mondiale. 1992-93** (SET).

Lo Presti S. (1993), **Annuario del Calcio Mondiale. 1993-94** (SET).

Lo Presti S. (1994), **Annuario del Calcio Mondiale. 1994-95** (SET).

McIlvanney H. (1966), **World Cup 1966.** (Eyre and Spottiswoode).

McIlvanney H. & Hopcraft A. (1970), **World Cup 1970.** (Eyre and Spottiswoode).

Mason T. (1995), **Passion of the People? Football in South America.** (Verso).

Matthews P. (1993), **The Guinness Who's Who of Sport.** (Guinness).

Meisl W. (1956), **Soccer Revolution.** (Phoenix).

Meyer S. (1986), **Europa. 1889-1986.** (Desktop publication).

Morgan J & Emery D, (1978), **World Cup '78.** (Woodhead-Faulkner).

Morrison I. (1990), **The World Cup.** (Breedon).

Mraz I. et al. (1980), **Svet Devadesati minut. 2 vols.** (Olimpia).

Muller-Mohring M. (1993), **1000 Tips.** (Klartext).

Murray B. (1994), **Football. A History of the World Game.** (Scholar Press).

O'Neill T. (1991), **European Football Line-ups 1872-1919.** (Desktop publication).

Parr M. (1992), **Latin American Soccer Review 1992.** (Desktop publication).

Portelli L. (1994), **The Football Year Book. Malta 1993-94.** (Progress Press).

Radnedge K. (1994), **The Ultimate Encyclopedia of Soccer.** (Hodder & Stoughton).

Ramirez G. (1991), **Football in Ecuador.** (Soccer Book Publishing).

Rethacker J. (1989), **Football 1989.** (L'Equipe).

Robinson J. (1988), **The European Championship. 1958-1988.** (Marksman).

Robinson P. (1995), **Canada 1885-1995.** (Soccer Book Publishing).

Robinson P. (1995), **Israel 1934-1995.** (Soccer Book Publishing).

Rohr B & Simon G (1988), **Lexikon Fussball.** (VEB).

Rollin J. (1993), **Soccer Who's Who.** (Guinness).

Rostkowski D. (1988), **Short History of Polish Football.** (Desktop publication).

Rothmans (1970-95), **Football Yearbook.** (Queen Anne Press).

Saunders D. (1963), **World Cup 1962.** (Heinemann).

Sbornoi I. (1989), **International Matches of the Soviet Union. 1952-88.** (Soviet Sport).

Sigurdsson V. (1989), **Islensk Knattspyrna 1989.** (Bokautgafan Skjaldborg).

Soar P. (eds). (1984), **The Hamlyn World Encyclopedia of Football.** (Hamlyn).

Stramare R. (1989), **Sud America I.** (Desktop publication).

Thomas M. (1988), **African Football Handbook.** (Desktop publication).

Trifari E. et al. (1994), **Soccer the Game, and the World Cup.** (Rizzoli).

Twydell D. (1994), **The Little Red Book of Chinese Football.** (Yore).

United States Soccer Federation (1994), **United States Soccer.** (USSF).

Van Dijk F. (1988), **100 Years of League Football in Europe.** (Desktop publication).

Van Hoof S. & Guerra T. (1989), **Encyclopedia of Peruvian Football.** (Desktop publication).

Van Hoof S. & Villareal J. (1991), **Colombia. 1938-1991.** (Desktop publication).

Van Hoof S. & Sandoval J. (1991), **La Celeste Uruguay 1901-91.** (Desktop publication).

Van Hoof S & Parr M. (1994), **The North and Latin American Football Guide 1993-94.** (Heart Books).

Van Hoof S & Parr M. (1995), **The North and Latin American Football Guide 1994-95.** (Heart Books).

Versi A. (1986), **Football in Africa.** (Collins).

Wangerin D. (1993), **The Fussball Book.**

Yametti C. (1991), **Historia de la Seleccion de Futbol Argentina 1893-1991.** (CIHF).

Yametti C. (1994), **Futbol en Argentina 1891-1994.**

Constant use has also been made of the following magazines

African Soccer (London)

World Soccer (London)

France Football (Paris)

Guerin Sportivo (Turin)

Onze Mondial (Paris)

Afrique Football (Paris)

Asian Football Confederation News (Hong Kong)

APPENDIX

A-Z of sides from Europe and South America who have taken part in international club competitions, showing their country of origin.

EUROPE

Club	*Country*
ÅAB Ålborg	DEN
Aarau	SUI
Aberdeen	SCO
Åbo IFK	FIN
Académica de Coimbra	POR
Adanaspor	TUR
Admira-Wacker	AUT
AEK Athens	GRE
AEK Larnaca	CYP
AEL Limassol	CYP
ÅGF Åarhus	DEN
AIK Stockholm	SWE
Airdrieonians	SCO
Ajax	HOL
Akademik Sofia	BGR
Akademisk København	DEN
Albpetrol Patosi	ALB
Alliance Dudelange	LUX
Altay Izmir	TUR
Anderlecht	BEL
Angers	FRA
Angoulême	FRA
Ankaragücü	TUR
Anorthosis Famagusta	CYP
Apoel Nicosia	CYP
Apollon Limassol	CYP
Apolonia Fier	ALB
Ararat Yerevan	ARM
Ards	NIR
Arges Pitesti	ROM
Aris Bonnevoie	LUX
Aris Limassol	CYP
Aris Salonica	GRE
Arka Gdynia	POL
Arsenal	ENG
Aston Villa	ENG
Atalanta	ITA
Athinaikos	GRE
Athletic Bilbao	ESP
Athlone Town	IRL
Atlético Madrid	ESP
Åtvidabergs	SWE
Auxerre	FRA
Avenir Beggen	LUX
AZ Alkmaar	HOL
B 1901 Nykobing	DEN
B 1903 København	DEN
B 1909 Odense	DEN
B 1913 Odense	DEN
B 93 København	DEN
B'36 Tórshavn	FRO
B'68 Toftir	FRO
B'71 Sandur	FRO
Bacau	ROM
Baia Mare	ROM
Ballymena United	NIR
Bangor	NIR
Bangor City	WAL
Baník Ostrava	CZE
Barcelona	ESP
Barreirense	POR
Barry Town	WAL
Basel	SUI
Bastia	FRA
Bayer 04 Leverkusen	FRG/GER
Bayer 05 Uerdingen	FRG/GER
Bayern München	FRG/GER
Beerschot	BEL
Beitar Jerusalem	ISR
Békéscsabai	HUN
Belenenses	POR
Belvedur Isola	YUG/SVN
Benfica	POR
Beroe Stara Zagora	BGR
Besa Kavajë	ALB
Besiktas	TUR
Beveren	BEL
Birmingham City	ENG
Blackburn Rovers	ENG
Boavista	POR
Boby Brno	CZE
Bodö-Glimt	NOR
Bohemians Dublin	IRL
Bohemians Praha	CZE
Bologna	ITA
Boluspor	TUR
Bor	YUG
Borac Banja Luka	BOS/YUG
Borussia Dortmund	FRG/GER
Borussia Mönchengladbach	FRG/GER
Botev Plovdiv	BGR
Botev Vratsa	BGR
Braga	POR
Brage	SWE
Brann Bergen	NOR
Brasov	ROM
Bray Wanderers	IRL
Brøndbyernes	DEN
Bryne Stavanger	NOR
Burnley	ENG
Bursaspor	TUR
Caen	FRA
Cagliari	ITA
Cannes	FRA
Cardiff City	WAL
Carl Zeiss Jena	GDR/GER
Carrick Rangers	NIR
Casino Salzburg	AUT
CDNA Sofia	BGR
Celta Vigo	ESP
Celtic	SCO
Cercle Brugge	BEL
Cesena	ITA
Charleroi	BEL
Chaves	POR
Chelsea	ENG
Chemie	GDR/GER
Chemie Leipzig	GDR/GER
Chemnitzer Fussball Club	GDR/GER
Chernomorets Burgas	BGR
Chernomorets Odessa	UKR/URS
Chîmea Rimnicu Vîlcea	ROM
Cliftonville	NIR
Club Brugge	BEL
Coleraine	NIR
Cork Celtic	IRL
Cork City	IRL
Cork Hibernians	IRL
Corvinul Hunedoara	ROM
Coventry City	ENG
Crisana Oradea	ROM
Croatia Zagreb	CRO/YUG
Crusaders	NIR
Crvena Zvezda	YUG
Csepel SC	HUN
CSKA Moskva	RUS/URS
Cwmbran Town	WAL
DAC Dunajská Streda	CZE/SVK
Degerfors	SWE
Deportiva Las Palmas	ESP
Deportivo La Coruña	ESP
Derby County	ENG
Derry City	NIR/IRL
Dinamo Bucuresti	ROM
Dinamo Tiranë	ALB
Dinamo Zagreb	CRO/YUG
Diósgyöri	HUN
Distillery	NIR
Djurgårdens	SWE
Dnepr Dnepropetrovsk	UKR/URS
Drogheda United	IRL
Drumcondra	IRL
Dukla Banská Bystrica	CZE/SVK
Dukla Praha	CZE
Dunav Ruse	BGR
Dundalk	IRL
Dundee	SCO
Dundee United	SCO
Dunfermline Athletic	SCO
Dynamo Berlin	GDR/GER
Dynamo Dresden	GDR/GER
Dynamo Kiev	UKR/URS
Dynamo Minsk	BLR
Dynamo Moskva	RUS/URS
Dynamo Tbilisi	GEO/URS
Dynamo Zilina	CZE/SVK
Eintracht Frankfurt	FRG/GER
Eintracht Braunschweig	FRG/GER
Ekranas Panevezys	LTU
Elbasani	ALB
Electroputere Craiova	ROM
Elfsborg	SWE
EPA Larnaca	CYP
Esbjerg	DEN
Eskisehirspor	TUR
Español	ESP
Estrela da Amadora	POR
Etar Veliko Tarnovo	BGR
Everton	ENG
F'91 Dudelange	LUX
Fandok Bobrujsk	BLR
FC Amsterdam	HOL
FC Den Haag	HOL
FC Groningen	HOL
FC København	DEN
FC Linz	AUT
FC Tirol Innsbruck	AUT
FC Utrecht	HOL
Fenerbahçe	TUR
Ferencváros	HUN
Feyenoord	HOL
FH Hafnarfjördur	ISL
Finn Harps	IRL
Fiorentina	ITA
First Vienna FC	AUT
FK Austria	AUT
FK Sarajevo	BOS/YUG
Flamurtari Vlorë	ALB
Flora Tallinn	EST
Floriana	MLT
FOLA Esch	LUX
Fortuna Düsseldorf	FRG/GER
Fortuna Sittard	HOL
Fram Reykjavík	ISL
Fredrikstad	NOR
Frem København	DEN
Fremad Amager	DEN
Frigg Oslo	NOR
Fyllingen	NOR
GAIS Göteborg	SWE
Galatasaray	TUR
Galway United	IRL
Genclerbirligi	TUR
Genoa 1893	ITA
Gent	BEL
Germinal Ekeren	BEL
GI Gotu	FRO
Girondins Bordeaux	FRA
Gjövik Lyn	NOR
GKS Katowice	POL
GKS Tichy	POL
Glenavon	NIR
Glentoran	NIR
Gloria Bistrita	ROM
Go Ahead Deventer	HOL
Górnik Zabrze	POL
Gottwaldov	CZE
Göztepe Izmir	TUR
Grasshopper-Club	SUI
Grazer AK	AUT
Grevenmacher	LUX
Gwardia Warszawa	POL
Györi Rába ETO	HUN
Gzira United	MLT
Haarlem	HOL
Hajduk Split	CRO/YUG
Haka	FIN

APPENDIX Continued

Haladás ... HUN
Hallescher Fussball Club ... GDR/GER
Halmstads ... SWE
Hamburger SV ... FRG/GER
Hammarby ... SWE
Hamrun Spartans ... MLT
Hannover '96 ... FRG/GER
Hansa Rostock ... GDR/GER
Hapoel Beer Sheva ... ISR
Hapoel Petah Tikva ... ISR
Haugar ... NOR
HB Tórshavn ... FRO
Heart of Midlothian ... SCO
Hertha BSC ... FRG/GER
Hibernian Edinburgh ... SCO
Hibernians ... MLT
HIFK Helsinki ... FIN
HJK Helsinki ... FIN
Holbaek ... DEN
Home Farm ... IRL
Honvéd ... HUN
HPS Helsinki ... FIN
Hvidovre ... DEN
IA Akranes ... ISL
IBA Akureyri ... ISL
IBK Keflavík ... ISL
IBV Vestmannaeyjar ... ISL
IFK Göteborg ... SWE
IFK Malmö ... SWE
IFK Norrköping ... SWE
Ikast ... DEN
Ilves Tampere ... FIN
Inter Cardiff ... WAL
Internacionál Bratislava ... CZE/SVK
Internazionale ... ITA
Ipswich Town ... ENG
Iraklis Salonica ... GRE
Jazz Pori ... FIN
Jeunesse d'Esch ... LUX
Jeunesse Hautcharage ... LUX
Jiul Petrosani ... ROM
Juventus ... ITA
KA Akureyri ... ISL
1.FC Kaiserslautern ... FRG/GER
Kalmar ... SWE
Karabakh Agdam ... AZE
Karl-Marx-Stadt ... GDR/GER
Karlsruher ... FRG/GER
Kastoria ... GRE
KB København ... DEN
KI Klaksvik ... FRO
Kickers Offenbach ... FRG/GER
Kilmarnock ... SCO
Kispest-Honvéd ... HUN
Klubi Sportiv Tiranë ... ALB
Kocaelispor ... TUR
Koge ... DEN
1.FC Köln ... FRG/GER
Komló ... HUN
Kongsvinger ... NOR
Koparit Kuopio ... FIN
1.FC Kosice ... CZE/SVK
KPV Kokkola ... FIN
KR Reykjavík ... ISL
Kremser SC ... AUT
KTP Kotka ... FIN
KuPS Kuopio ... FIN
Kuusysi Lahti ... FIN
La Chaux-de-Fonds ... SUI
Landskrona BoIS ... SWE
Lanerossi-Vicenza ... ITA
Larissa ... GRE
Lausanne-Sports ... SUI
Lazio ... ITA
Le Havre ... FRA
Lech Poznan ... POL
Lechia Gdansk ... POL
Leeds United ... ENG
Legia Warszawa ... POL
Leicester City ... ENG
Leixoes ... POR
Levski Sofia ... BGR
Levski-Spartak ... BGR
Liègeois ... BEL
Lierse SK ... BEL
Lille OSC ... FRA
Lilleström ... NOR
Limerick ... IRL
Linfield ... NIR
Linzer ASK ... AUT
Liverpool ... ENG
LKS Lódz ... POL
Lokeren ... BEL
Lokomotiv Moskva ... RUS/URS
Lokomotiv Plovdiv ... BGR
Lokomotiv Sofia ... BGR
Lokomotiva Kosice ... CZE/SVK
Lokomotive Leipzig ... GDR/GER
Lugano ... SUI
Luzern ... SUI
Lyngby ... DEN
Maccabi Haifa ... ISR
Maccabi Tel Aviv ... ISR
1.FC Magdeburg ... GDR/GER
Malmö FF ... SWE
Manchester City ... ENG
Manchester United ... ENG
Maribor Branik ... YUG/SVN
Marítimo ... POR
Marsa ... MLT
Mechelen ... BEL
Mersin Idmanyurdu ... TUR
Merthyr Tydfil ... WAL
Metalist Kharkov ... UKR/URS
Metz ... FRA
Miedz Legnica ... POL
Milan ... ITA
Mjöndalen ... NOR
Molde ... NOR
Molenbeek ... BEL
Monaco ... FRA
Montpellier ... FRA
Morton ... SCO
Moss ... NOR
Motherwell ... SCO
Motor Zwickau ... GDR/GER
MP Mikkeli ... FIN
MSV Duisburg ... FRG/GER
MTK Budapest ... HUN
Mura Murska Sobota ... YUG/SVN
MyPa ... FIN
NAC Breda ... HOL
Naestved ... DEN
Nancy-Lorraine ... FRA
Nantes ... FRA
Napoli ... ITA
Napredak Krusevak ... YUG
NEA Salamina ... CYP
NEC Nijmegan ... HOL
Neftchi Baku ... AZE
Neman Grodno ... BLR
Neuchâtel Xamax ... SUI
Newcastle United ... ENG
Nice ... FRA
Nikol Tallinn ... EST
Nîmes Olympique ... FRA
NK Zagreb ... CRO/YUG
Norma Tallinn ... EST
Norwich City ... ENG
Nottingham Forest ... ENG
1.FC Nürnberg ... FRG/GER
OB Odense ... DEN
Odense Select XI ... DEN
Odra Opole ... POL
OFI Crete ... GRE
OFK Beograd ... YUG
Olimpija Ljubljana ... YUG/SVN
Olimpija Riga ... LVA
Olympiakos Nicosia ... CYP
Olympiakos Pireaus ... GRE
Olympique Lyonnais ... FRA
Olympique Marseille ... FRA
Omonia Nicosia ... CYP
OPS Oulu ... FIN
Orduspor ... TUR
Örebro ... SWE
Örgryte ... SWE
Osasuna ... ESP
Östers ... SWE
Otelul Galati ... ROM
Panahaiki Patras ... GRE
Panathinaikos ... GRE
Panionios Athens ... GRE
PAOK Salonica ... GRE
Paris Saint-Germain ... FRA
Parma ... ITA
Partick Thistle ... SCO
Partizan Beograd ... YUG
Partizani Tiranë ... ALB
Pécsi MSC ... HUN
Perugia ... ITA
Petrolul Ploiesti ... ROM
Pirin Blagoevgrad ... BGR
Plastika Nitra ... CZE/SVK
Pogon Szczecin ... POL
Poletehnica Timisoara ... ROM
Polonia Bytom ... POL
Portadown ... NIR
Portimonense ... POR
Porto ... POR
Progrés Niedercorn ... LUX
PSV Eindhoven ... HOL
Publicum Celje ... YUG/SVN
Queens Park Rangers ... ENG
Quimigal ... POR
Rabat Ajax ... MLT
Racing Club de Paris ... FRA
Racing Club Lens ... FRA
Racing Club Strasbourg ... FRA
Rad Beograd ... YUG
Radnicki Nis ... YUG
RAF Jelgava ... LVA
Randers Freja ... DEN
Rangers ... SCO
Rapid Bucuresti ... ROM
Rapid Wien ... AUT
Real Betis ... ESP
Real Madrid ... ESP
Real Oviedo ... ESP
Real Sociedad ... ESP
Real Valladolid ... ESP
Real Zaragoza ... ESP
Red Boys Differdange ... LUX
Reipas Lahti ... FIN
Rijeka ... CRO/YUG
Roda JC Kerkrade ... HOL
Roma ... ITA
ROMAR Mazeikiai ... LTU
RoPS Rovaniemi ... FIN
Rosenborg ... NOR
Rot-Weiss Erfurt ... GDR/GER
Rot-Weiss Essen ... FRG/GER
Rotor Volgograd ... RUS/URS
Rouen ... FRA
Royal Antwerp FC ... BEL
Ruch Chorzów ... POL
1.FC Saarbrücken ... FRG/GER
Sabadell ... ESP
Sachsenring Zwickau ... GDR/GER
Saint-Étienne ... FRA
Sakaryaspor ... TUR
Salgótárjan ... HUN
Salgueiros ... POR
Sampdoria ... ITA
Sarpsborg ... NOR
Schalke 04 ... FRG/GER
Sedan ... FRA
Seraing ... BEL
Servette ... SUI
Sevilla ... ESP
Shachter Donetsk ... UKR/URS
Shamrock Rovers ... IRL
Sheffield Wednesday ... ENG
Shelbourne ... IRL
Shirak Gyumri ... ARM
Shumen ... BGR
Sigma Olomouc ... CZE
Silkeborg ... DEN
Siófoki ... HUN

APPENDIX Continued

Club	Country
Sion	SUI
SKA Karpati Lvov	UKR/URS
SKA Rostov-Na-Donu	RUS/URS
Skeid Oslo	NOR
Skonto Riga	LVA
Slask Wroclaw	POL
Slavia Praha	CZE
Slavia Sofia	BGR
Sliema Wanderers	MLT
Sligo Rovers	IRL
Sliven	BGR
Sloboda Tuzla	BOS/YUG
Slovan Bratislava	CZE/SVK
Sochaux	FRA
SOFK Lyn	NOR
Southampton	ENG
Sparta Praha	CZE
Sparta Rotterdam	HOL
Spartak Hradec Králové	CZE
Spartak Moskva	RUS/URS
Spartak Plovdiv	BGR
Spartak Trnava	CZE/SVK
Spartak Varna	BGR
Spartak Vladikavkaz	RUS/URS
Spora Luxembourg	LUX
Sporting CP	POR
Sporting Gijón	ESP
Sredets	BGR
St. Gallen	SUI
St. Johnstone	SCO
St. Mirren	SCO
St. Patrick's Athletic	IRL
Stade de Reims	FRA
Stade Dudelange	LUX
Stade Français	FRA
Stade Lavallois	FRA
Stade Rennais	FRA
Staevnet	DEN
Stahl Brandenburg	GDR/GER
Stal Mielec	POL
Stal Rzeszów	POL
Standard Club Liège	BEL
Start Kristiansand	NOR
Steaua Bucuresti	ROM
Stoke City	ENG
Strömgodset	NOR
Studentesc Bucuresti	ROM
Sturm Graz	AUT
Sunderland	ENG
SV Stockerau	AUT
Swansea City	WAL
Swift Hesperange	LUX
Szombierki Bytom	POL
Tasmania 1900 Berlin	FRG/GER
Tatabányai	HUN
Tatran Presov	CZE/SVK
Tavria Simferopol	UKR/URS
Tekstilschik Kamyshin	RUS/URS
Teuta Durrës	ALB
Tiligul Tiraspol	MOL
Tîrgu Mures	ROM
Torino	ITA
Torpedo Moskva	RUS/URS
Tottenham Hotspur	ENG
Toulouse	FRA
TPS Turku	FIN
TPV Tampere	FIN
Trabzonspor	TUR
Trakia Plovdiv	BGR
Trelleborgs	SWE
Tresnjevka Zagreb	CRO/YUG
Tromsö	NOR
TSV München 1860	FRG/GER
Turan Tauz	AUT
Twente Enschede	HOL
Újpesti	HUN
Union Luxembourg	LUX
Union Paralimni	CYP
Union Sportive Rumelange	LUX
Union St. Gilloise	BEL
Union Teplice	CZE
Universitatea Cluj-Napoca	ROM
Universitatea Craiova	ROM
University College Dublin	IRL
UTA Arad	ROM
Vác FC	HUN
Valencia	ESP
Vålerengens	NOR
Valletta	MLT
Valur Reykjavík	ISL
Vanlose	DEN
Vardar Skoplje	MKD/YUG
Vasas	HUN
Vasas ETO Györ	HUN
Vejle	DEN
Velez Mostar	BOS/YUG
Verona	ITA
VfB Stuttgart	FRG/GER
Victoria Bucuresti	ROM
Videoton	HUN
Viking Stavanger	NOR
Víkingur Reykjavík	ISL
Viktoria Plzen	CZE
Viktoria Zizkov	CZE
Vitesse Arnhem	HOL
Vitkovice	CZE
Vitória Guimarães	POR
Vitória Setúbal	POR
Vllaznia Shkodër	ALB
Vojvodina Novi Sad	YUG
Vorwärts Berlin	GDR/GER
VSS Kosice	CZE/SVK
Waregem	BEL
Waterford United	IRL
Watford	ENG
Werder Bremen	FRG/GER
West Bromwich Albion	ENG
West Ham United	ENG
Wettingen	SUI
Widzew Lódz	POL
Wiener Neustadt	AUT
Wiener Sport-Club	AUT
Willem II Tilburg	HOL
Wisla Kraków	POL
Wismut Aue	GDR/GER
Wismut Karl-Marx-Stadt	GDR/GER
Wolverhampton Wanderers	ENG
Wrexham	WAL
Wuppertaler	FRG/GER
Young Boys	SUI
Zaglebie Lubin	POL
Zaglebie Sosnowiec	POL
Zaglebie Walbrzych	POL
Zalgiris Vilnius	LTU
Zarja Lugansk	UKR/URS
Zeljeznicar Sarajevo	BOS/YUG
Zenit Leningrad	RUS/URS
Zimbru Chisinau	MOL
Zürich	SUI
Zurrieq	MLT

SOUTH AMERICA

Club	*Country*
31 de Octubre	BOL
Alfonso Ugarte	PER
Alianza	PER
Always Ready	BOL
América Cali	COL
América Quito	ECU
Argentinos Juniors	ARG
Atlético Chalaco	PER
Atlético Colegiales	PAR
Atlético Junior	COL
Atlético Mineiro	BRA
Atlético San Cristobal	VEN
Atlético Torino	PER
Aurora	BOL
Bahia	BRA
Bangu	BRA
Barcelona	ECU
Bella Vista	URU
Blooming	BOL
Boca Juniors	ARG
Bolivar	BOL
Botafogo	BRA
Bragantino	BRA
Caracas FC	VEN
Cerro Cora	PAR
Cerro Porteño	PAR
Chaco Petrolero	BOL
Cobreloa	CHI
Cobresal	CHI
Colegio San Augustin	PER
Colo Colo	CHI
Concepción	CHI
Coquimbo	CHI
Corinthians	BRA
Coritiba	BRA
Criciúma	BRA
Cruzeiro	BRA
Cuenca	ECU
Danubio	URU
Defensor	PER
Defensor	URU
Deportivo Cali	COL
Deportivo Espanol	ARG
Deportivo Italia	VEN
Deportivo Municipal	BOL
Deportivo Municipal	PER
Deportivo Quito	ECU
Emelec	ECU
Estudiantes de Mérida	VEN
Estudiantes La Plata	ARG
Everest	ECU
Everton	CHI
Ferrocarril Oeste	ARG
Filanbanco	ECU
Flamengo	BRA
Fluminense	BRA
Galicia	VEN
Gimnasia y Esgrima La Plata	ARG
Grêmio	BRA
Guabira	BOL
Guarani	BRA
Guarani	PAR
Huachipato Talcahuano	CHI
Huracán	ARG
Independiente	ARG
Independiente Medellín	COL
Internacional	BRA
Jorge Wilsterman	BOL
Juan Aurich	PER
Lanús	ARG
Lara	VEN
LDU Quito	ECU
Libertad	PAR
Litoral	BOL
Magallanes	CHI
Maritimo	VEN
Melgar	PER
Millonarios	COL
Mineros de Guyana	VEN
Minerven	VEN
Montevideo Wanderers	URU
Nacional Asuncion	PAR
Nacional Medellín	COL
Nacional Montevideo	URU
Nacional Quito	ECU
Nautico	BRA
Newell's Old Boys	ARG
Nueve De Octubre	ECU
O'Higgins	CHI
Olimpia	PAR
Oriente Petrolero	BOL
Palestino	CHI
Palmeiras	BRA
Peñarol	URU
Pepeganda	VEN
Portugues	VEN
Portuguesa	VEN
Progreso	URU

APPENDIX Continued

Quilmes ARG
Racing Club ARG
Rangers Talca CHI
River Plate ARG
Rosario Central ARG
San José BOL
San Lorenzo ARG
Santa Fé COL
Santiago Wanderers CHI
Santos BRA
São Paulo FC BRA
Sipesa PER
Sol de América PAR
Sport Boys PER
Sport Club Recife BRA
Sporting Cristal PER
Sportivo Luqueño PAR
Táchira VEN
Tecnico Universitario ECU
The Strongest BOL
Tolima COL
ULA Mérida VEN
Union Española CHI
Union Huaral PER
Union Magdalena COL
Union San Felipe CHI
Universidad Catolica CHI
Universidad Catolica Quto ECU
Universidad de Chile CHI
Universitario BOL
Universitario PER
UTC Cajamarca PER
Valdez ECU
Valencia VEN
Vasco da Gama BRA
Velez Sarsfield ARG